P9-CCS-453

Encyclopedia of American Religions

ISSN 1066-1212

Encyclopedia of American Religions

SIXTH EDITION

J. Gordon Melton

GALE

DETROIT • LONDON

J. Gordon Melton

Gale Research Staff:

Jolen Marya Gedridge, *Editor*
Michael Reade and Stephanie Samulski, *Contributing Associate Editors*
Talitha Jean, *Contributing Assistant Editor*
Rita Runchock, *Managing Editor*

Theresa Rocklin, *Manager, Technical Support Services*
Charles Beaumont, *Programmer/Analyst*

Mary Beth Trimper, *Production Director*
Evi Seoud, *Assistant Production Manager*
Deborah Milliken, *Production Assistant*

Cynthia Baldwin, *Product Design Manager*
Barbara J. Yarrow, *Graphic Services Manager*
Gary Leach, *Desktop Publisher*

Eleanor Allison, *Manager, Data Entry*
Janine Whitney, *Coordinator, Data Entry*
Beverly Jendrowski, *Senior, Data Entry Associate*
Nikkita Bankston, Maleka Imrana,
Arlene A. Kevonian, and Shanitta L. Watkins, *Data Entry Associates*

ISBN 0-8103-8417-5
ISSN 1066-1212

Printed in the United States of America

10 9 8 7 6 5 4 3 2 1

Contents

Part I—Introductory Essays

Part II—Historical Essay Chapters

97666

Part III—Directory Listings Sections

Indexes

Preface

Professionally, I have been looking at the religious life of North America for the past quarter of a century and for most of that time, in one form or another, I have been involved with the *Encyclopedia of American Religions*. During my years in graduate school, in what now seems like the ancient past, the problem of deciphering the shape of the overall structures of organized religion in America came to dominate my research. Since then the ongoing dynamics of the religious community have provided more than enough new data to keep me interested, and to keep the pages of this volume alive with new information.

For both historical and sentimental reasons, we continue to carry in this new edition the Preface to the first edition originally published twenty years ago. It serves as a reminder of my perception of what I define as "primary religious groups" (replacing the older term denominations), as well as what are the main long-term building blocks of the religious community in a free society. Even though various kinds of movements, trends, fads, and religious phenomena emerge on the forefront, the denominational groupings remain consistent. They remain decade after decade (in some cases century after century) and while the number of denominations grows as the population grows, the denominations persist in providing the stable substructure for religious expression.

During the last three decades, various renewal movements have come and gone. Prominent among them were the Ecumenical movement, with its hope of widespread denominational mergers; the Charismatic movement, which hoped to unite the churches around the experience of the gifts of the Spirit; the Jesus People movement, which reached out to the street people of the hippie counter-culture; the New Age movement, which announced the coming of a new era of peace and light, and most recently, the Promise Keepers. Each of these movements emphasized a new idea (or reaffirmed an old idea), called attention to a fresh appropriation of spiritual reality, and/or offered a new hope of changing the social order for the better. As these different renewal movements emerged, they brought a new level of excitement to the previously existing churches and groups, which had tended to fall into a routinized existence, and activated people for whom religion had been at best a nominal reality. Then as movements ran their course and died out, they often gave birth to new denominations hoping to perpetuate the insights and gains of the movement. Many new denominations drew members, initially, from older groups most affected by the new movement.

One continuing ideal that has permeated each renewal movement has been that of unity, the overcoming of the various fractures in the social order, especially those which divide people of differing religious commitments. In fact, the unifying ideals are rarely manifested beyond the attendance of members of different groups at the meetings sponsored by the renewal movement. Those who promote unifying hopes and goals almost never confront the very important issues that have produced the different religious communities in all of their variety, nor do they concern themselves with the continuing concerns that keep the groups separated. They are rarely prepared to engage in the most difficult task of negotiating the dissolution of traditional boundaries, nor equipped to offer sufficient rationale for groups to put aside their traditional differences. Any particular religious group offers a range of real benefits to their adherents. Renewal movements offer a new treat, but cannot substitute for all that occurs at the average local religious center (congregation). While religious homogeneity sounds good; in practice it is difficult for any single organization to hold the many ways of being religious preferred and adopted by people.

In the meantime, the churches and religious groups provide leadership, education, facilities, and other resources for the week-by-week expression of religious commitments of individuals. While various movements come and go, the congregational centers of the various denominational groups remain. It is into them that individuals have poured their religious commitments and resources. They may be altered more or less permanently by various renewal movements, but before the movement emerged, the denominations were there creating a context out of which a renewal effort was generated and from which an alternative agenda could be produced.

While there is still no visible effective trend toward the uniting of the different religious groups, these groups have found a wide variety of means of cooperating in matters of vital importance to them. Thus over the years, religious groups have founded different councils, associations, and agencies that, most importantly, allow for the overcoming of any latent feelings of hostility and/or fear that might exist between differing groups and, then facilitate joint action around various issues that do not threaten the sovereignty or existence of the affiliated churches and religious groups. Such cooperative organizations now exist on all levels, from interfaith groups that bring leaders from the wide spectrum of religious life into dialogue, to groups that operate across the spectrum of the larger religious groupings (Christianity, Judaism, Islam, Buddhism, Hinduism), to those that bring together groups in a single denominational family.

In this sixth edition of the *Encyclopedia of American Religions* we continue the effort to update the organizations that exist. An Historical Essay Chapter (and corresponding Directory Listing Section), entitled Anglicanism, details the story of the emergence of the Church of England and its independence from the Roman Catholic Church. Then in each of the Directory Listing Sections, the appropriate organizations working within each family group of religious bodies are listed and described.

While providing new material on Anglican organizations, this new edition of the *Encyclopedia* also continues to serve its prime directive of providing basic information (updated as much as possible) on each of the hundreds of religious communities operating in North America. As the population grows and as we become more urbanized, the number of new groups continues to grow. I have also continued to add entries on those groups that have existed in the past but have since died out. This new edition also includes over 200 new entries detailing churches, sects, and new religions not mentioned in previous editions.

The *Encyclopedia* has come to serve a unique role in providing information about American religion. While we expect the government to gather information on almost every other area of life, it cannot, by law, gather information on religion and religious preferences. Thus we must rely on a small number of private organizations to assemble and process the relevant data. It pleases me that this project, which has dominated my scholarly life, has met a real need for information on the religious dimensions of this most religious of countries. It is my hope that this new edition will continue to be as valuable in providing authoritative information on the ever increasing pluralistic context of our life together.

J. Gordon Melton
October 1998

Introduction to the Sixth Edition

The *Encyclopedia of American Religions (EAR),* now in its sixth edition, provides a comprehensive survey of religious and spiritual groups in North America. The *Encyclopedia* continues in its role as "an indispensable guide to the confused landscape of American Religion" *(Choice)* by providing both an historical perspective and current information on the many groups that constitute America's religious life.

EAR covers currently functioning religious groups and groups that are no longer active. Most group covered meet the following criteria:

➤ seeks the chief religious loyalty of its members
➤ promotes its particular view
➤ satisfies one of the following conditions of size:

— if the group is organized into congregations, has two or more congregations, or has one congregation with more than 2,000 members who make a measurable impact on the country through mass media

— if not organized into congregations, membership is drawn from more than one state and from beyond a single metropolitan area

Several groups not meeting the size requirements outlined above have been included. These groups, such as Satanists, espouse beliefs that are at odds with those of most people in the United States and Canada. Despite their limited numbers, these groups have been included to illustrate the religious complexity and diversity of America.

New in This Edition

The sixth edition of the *Encyclopedia* contains over 2,100 descriptive entries on religious bodies, including over 200 new to this edition, and represents a complete revision and expansion of the previous edition. This edition also features:

A new Historical Essay Chapter and corresponding Directory Listing Section on **Anglicanism.**

A consolidated **Master Name and Keyword Index.** The former Educational Institutions, Periodicals, Personal Name, and Religious Organizations and Institutions indexes have been merged to form the Master Name and Keyword Index, providing a one-stop listing of all key details mentioned in this edition.

Enhanced **Subject Index** citations. The full name for each organization is now listed under a given subject term with the book entry number to enable a user to quickly target a search.

Catchwords have been added to the top outer corners of each index page to enable users to quickly identify the contents of that page.

Content and Arrangement

The *Encyclopedia* consists of three parts, which are followed by three indexes:

➤ Part I—Two **Introductory Essays** trace the development of religion in America and Canada.

➤ Part II—24 **Historical Essays** discuss the growth and development of the 20 major religious families and traditions.

► Part III—The **Directory Listings** are organized into 23 sections and provide contact and descriptive information on the various groups that comprise the 20 families and traditions. Two remaining directory sections—Unclassified Christian Churches and Unclassified Religious Groups—include those groups that cannot be classified within any of the distinct religious families.

The **Geographic, Subject,** and **Master Name and Keyword Indexes** facilitate access to information provided in this edition.

For additional details on the content, arrangement, and indexing of *EAR,* consult the **User's Guide,** following the introductions.

Compilation Methods

The information contained in the entries has been assembled from material obtained directly from the religious bodies listed. Each group was asked to update and return a revision form containing information on their organization, and the majority of organizations graciously complied. In some cases, follow-up telephone conversations were held. In addition, the resources of the American Religions Collection at the University of California Santa Barbara were also used. The collection contains a variety of both primary and secondary materials on the religious traditions and leaders of North America.

Author Brings Unique Perspective

Dr. J. Gordon Melton has been studying America's religious landscape for more than twenty years. A graduate of Garrett Theological Seminary in Evanston, Illinois, with a Ph.D. from Northwestern University, Dr. Melton is nationally recognized as a leading authority on religion, particularly the newer, small groups. Melton's current undertakings include teaching responsibilities at the University of California Santa Barbara, heading the Institute for the Study of American Religion, and authoring articles and reference works on American religion. Among the many Gale titles authored by Melton are the *New Age Encyclopedia, Religious Leaders of America,* and *The Churches Speak Series.*

For additional details on the author and the impetus for undertaking the *Encyclopedia,* see the "Selections from the Introduction to the First Edition" following this introduction.

Companion Volumes Complement EAR's Coverage of Religion in North America

The *Encyclopedia of American Religions: Religious Creeds* contains the full text of more than 450 religious creeds, confessions, statements of faith, summaries of belief, and articles of religion currently acknowledged by many of the religious groups described in this edition of the *Encyclopedia.* It also includes extensive notes on the history and textual variations of the creeds.

The *Directory of Religious Organizations in the United States* provides contact and descriptive information on some 2,500 for-profit and nonprofit organizations that provide services for, information on, or support for, the primary religious bodies described in *EAR,* as well as those organizations that seek to influence these bodies.

EAR Also Available in Electronic Formats

The *Encyclopedia of American Religions* is also available for licensing on magnetic tape or diskette in a fielded format. The database is for internal data processing and nonpublishing purposes only. Either the complete database or a custom selection of entries may be ordered. For more information, contact the Electronic Services Department at 800-877-GALE.

Comments and Suggestions Welcomed

Comments, suggestions, and information on new organizations or organizations not currently listed are welcomed. Please contact:

Dr. J. Gordon Melton
Institute for the Study of American Religion
Box 90709
Santa Barbara, CA 93190-0709

or

Gale Research
27500 Drake Rd.
Farmington Hills, MI 48331-3535
Telephone (248) 699-GALE
Toll-Free (800) 347-GALE
Fax (248) 699-8062

Selections from the Introduction to the First Edition

The *Encyclopedia of American Religions* explores the broad sweep of American religions and describes over 1,200 [now 2,100] churches. Some churches in the *Encyclopedia,* such as certain Hindu and Jewish bodies, follow a tradition several thousand years old. Others were born yesterday, like Garner Ted Armstrong's Church of God International, formed in the summer of 1978. With few exceptions, if a church existed in the United States in 1976 [now 1996], it is discussed in the *Encyclopedia.*

In my years of study of American religion I discovered three kinds of religious institutions: primary religious bodies (i.e., churches), secondary organizations that serve the primary bodies, and tertiary organizations that strive to change the primary bodies. The *Encyclopedia* treats only the primary religious bodies, but it does refer to the two other kinds of institutions, so some comment on all three types is necessary here.

In defining primary religious bodies (a church, denomination, sect, or cult), I established certain criteria. First, a church seeks the chief religious loyalty of its members. Second, it meets requirements of size. If it is organized into congregations, it has at least two congregations, or it has one congregation of more than 2,000 members who make a measurable impact on the country through the mass media. If a church is not organized into congregations, it meets the size requirement when its members come from more than one state and from beyond a single metropolitan area. The third criterion concerns faith: a primary religious body tends to promote its particular views. For instance, it may encourage belief or disbelief in the Trinity. Or it may try to discourage the wearing of neckties; some holiness churches consider wearing neckties ostentatious.

I waived the size requirement for primary religious bodies whose beliefs are at odds with those of most people in our culture. For example, some Satanic groups are discussed in the *Encyclopedia* although they do not have enough members to meet my size criterion for primary religious bodies. The vast majority of churches in the *Encyclopedia* do, however, meet my three criteria.

Most primary religious bodies share other traits. Their leaders "marry and bury," as the saying goes. The churches usually hope to expand: they plan to make converts and form additional congregations. Finally, a number of primary religious bodies, though under-represented in America, have large foreign branches.

Much of the money and time given to religious enterprises in the United States is channeled not into the primary religious bodies, but into secondary and tertiary religious institutions. Secondary religious organizations, service agencies, perform tasks for one or more primary body. The tasks include missionary work, the education of seminarians, the publication of church materials, the sale of religious articles, and care for orphans and the aged.

Tertiary organizations try to change a number of primary religious bodies by promoting one special issue. For example, ecumenical organizations seek the unity of churches. However, few churches supporting the ecumenical organizations have specific plans to merge with other churches; so ecumenists try to change the attitudes of the churches. Among the country's ecumenical groups are several that draw members from various religious families (e.g., the National Council of Churches and the National Association of Evangelicals) and many more whose members are limited to one family (e.g., the Christian Holiness Association, the Pentecostal Fellowship of North America, the World Baptist Alliance, the International New Thought Alliance, the American Council of Witches, the Midwest Pagan Council, and the Buddhist Council of Hawaii).

Tertiary organizations have been formed to promote peace (the Fellowship of Reconciliation), a belief in creation instead of evolution (the Bible Science Association, Inc.), the psychic (the Spiritual Frontiers Fellowship), spiritual healing (the International Order of St. Luke, the Physician), Pentecostalism (the Full Gospel Businessmen's Fellowship, International), and Sabbatarianism (the Bible Sabbath Association).

Because the country is virtually flooded with secondary and tertiary organizations the primary religious bodies form only a small percentage of American religious institutions. It is to the primary bodies, though, that the secondary and tertiary organizations look for members and support.

In describing America's 1,200 [2,100] primary religious bodies, I am departing from the church-sect-cult categories of Ernst Troeltsch. He pioneered in describing various Christian bodies, not in doctrinal, but in social terms, treating churches as far more than defenders of certain beliefs. In the latter part of his work, *The Social Teachings of the Christian Churches* (New York: Macmillian, 1931), Troeltsch examined the Christian churches of post-Reformation Europe. He discovered three types of groups: the dominant state churches, the sect groups (schismatic groups that broke away from the state churches), and the mystical groups (the latter came to be called cults). Unfortunately, American sociologists applied Troeltsch's categories to American religions. With time, the popular media attached pejorative connotations to the words "sect" and "cult," connotations Troeltsch never intended. To understand Troeltsch properly, one must remember that he described only Christian religions. Furthermore, he studied countries with Christian state churches, to which all citizens were expected to belong. The United States has no state church and has far more non-Christian churches than Europe had before 1800, the terminal point of Troeltsch's study.

American religions do not yield to so simplistic a set of categories as the church-sect-cult triad. Instead of using those three classifications, I examined religions family by family and have found 17 [now 20] distinct families. This approach, I hope, does justice to the amazing variety found within the American religious experience. Ten [11] of the 17 [20] religious families in the United States basically follow Christian beliefs and practices; seven [9] do not.

Within the 17 [20] families of American religions, the member bodies of each family share a common heritage, thought world (theology in its broadest sense), and lifestyle. These three features define each individual religious body and illuminate its relationship to other churches in the family.

It has become fashionable to use other characteristics in classifying religious bodies, characteristics such as ethnicity, class, racial composition, type of leadership (priest? guru? pastor?), and the degree of acceptance of or hostility to the world. While these characteristics provide useful information, they are entirely inadequate in explaining the formation, development, relationships, and continuing life of the broad spectrum of America's religious bodies. Elements of ethnicity are, for example, most helpful in identifying sub-groups within the older European church traditions brought to America in the eighteenth and nineteenth centuries. Lutheran, Reformed, and Pietist churches split along ethnic lines, each sub-group using its own language. But as language barriers disappeared, the ethnic orientation of the churches diminished. Thus Swedish Baptists in America are more likely to develop joint programs, to merge, or to share missionary concerns with German or English or even black Baptists than with Swedish Lutherans or Swedish Pentecostals. The strength of family relationships overrides ethnic considerations.

In order to understand any family or its members, it is necessary to understand the family's heritage, thought world, and lifestyle. In many families, one of the three features—heritage, thought world, and lifestyle—is dominant. For the Lutheran family and those churches within the liturgical family, heritage is the feature setting them apart from other churches. Lifestyle is the key feature for four families in particular: the Communal, Holiness, Pentecostal, and Psychic families. Group ownership of property and certain self-imposed disciplines put communes into a class of their own. A day-to-day striving for perfect love dominates holiness preaching and teaching, with worldly activities prohibited. Pentecostals seek certain gifts of spirit, such as speaking in tongues, prophesying, and healing, so Pentecostals have a distinctive lifestyle in both their worship and their daily lives. Finally, the psychics are set apart from other religious groups because of their interest in extrasensory perception, psychokinesis, and communication with spirits through seances and visions.

If heritage and lifestyles distinguish certain families so does the thought world for other families. For fundamentalists and for the Protestant churches, especially those that follow John Calvin's Reformed theology, the features distinguishing them from each other is their thought world. They hold divergent views on these topics in particular: sacrament, ecclesiology, the sovereignty of God, perfection, and the nature of the end of time. But even where there is agreement, sharing a thought world does not necessarily mean holding identical views. Rather, it means sharing some beliefs that set the context for constant debate over specifics. Adventists, for example, expect Christ to return soon, but violently argue among themselves about the nature of his return, the possibility of pinpointing the date of his return, and the significance of certain world events as signs of his return.

Of particular interest to me are the families of "hidden religions" outside the country's religious mainstream. The spiritualists who hold seances are within the hidden families; so are the Buddhists, the Sufis, and the witches in their covens. Such groups are invisible to many Americans, but often they have large national followings. Several congregations that belong to these sizable but hidden families meet within a few blocks of my home in Evanston, Illinois. But had I not searched hard for these congregations, I would never have found them.

Many years of searching have gone into my study of America's religions. I might be better qualified to study the country's religions if I were a detective instead of a Methodist minister. I have examined endless printed material and interviewed countless church founders and leaders—all with the aim of understanding the heritage, lifestyle, and thought world of the religions. To say the least, the task has had its challenges. Some churches exaggerate or deny aspects of their lifestyle or history. Many Pentecostals say their church was founded at Pentecost, in 33 A.D., and hide their recent origins. Other churches try to gloss over the career their founder led before establishing their church. Among such founders, David Berg (of the Children of God), L. Ron Hubbard (of the Church of Scientology), A. A. Allen (of the Miracle Revival Fellowship), and Sun Myung Moon (of the Unification Church), have followed or still follow vocations quite different from that of a spiritual leader. For example, Hubbard was an undercover agent for the Los Angeles Police Department, a fiction writer, and an explorer before founding his church.

Some religious bodies function as such but deny their religious nature. One such organization is the World Plan Executive Council, popularly called Transcendental Meditation. Others dislike denominational labels and refuse to list themselves in the phone book or give brochures to non-members. The Cooneyites, also called the Two-by-Two's, have developed the shunning of publicity into a fine art.

To paint a picture of America's religious bodies in 1978 is not to describe them as they will be in 1988 [or 1998]. Families dwindle and expand. The major church in a family (one that claims more than half the family's members) may divide in half in a decade, torn by schism. Smaller churches in a family may consolidate—e.g., through merging all-black and all-white churches. Lutherans, once divided according to European ethnic origins and language, have consolidated in this century and then redivided over doctrinal issues. The Eastern religious bodies in this country—originally composed of Hindu and Buddhist immigrants—have attracted young American devotees, thereby blending the West with the East. Despite changes within families, however, the identity of the families remains the same. An intense conservatism governs religious bodies; they would rather lose dissident members than change. Further, churches rarely jump from one family to another. Theological and organizational patterns tend to perpetuate themselves. True, institutions adjust to the changing society, but only begrudgingly. The division of religions into families (denominationalism) is fundamental to religious life in the United States. We do not live in a post-denominational age. The ideals of ecumenism have swept through American Christianity, firing imaginations, creating cooperation structures, and breaking down walls of intolerance and hostility between religions. But if ecumenism has illustrated anything, it has been this: the religious family is strong. It will endure.

J. Gordon Melton

User's Guide

The *Encyclopedia of American Religions* consists of three parts:

- Introductory Essays
- Historical Essay Chapters
- Directory Listings Sections

and three indexes. Each part is fully described below.

Part I—Introductory Essays

"The Development of American Religion: An Interpretive View" and "Religion in Canada: An Historical Survey, 1500 to the Present" provide an overview of American and Canadian religion. Each essay concludes with a select list of bibliographic source materials.

Together these introductory essays present a comprehensive picture of the evolution of North American religion and project some trends for the immediate future. These essays also place the essays covering each denominational family history, comprising Part II of the *Encyclopedia,* into a larger context.

Part II—Historical Essay Chapters

This portion of the *Encyclopedia* contains 24 general essays that trace historically the rise of the 20 major religious families and traditions, as outlined on the "Contents" pages, into which most U.S. and Canadian bodies can be classified. A select list of bibliographic source materials appears at the end of each chapter.

Part III—Directory Listings Sections

The directory listings are organized into 26 sections. The first 24 sections correspond to the Historical Essay Chapters in Part II and contain contact and descriptive information on the individual churches, religious bodies, and spiritual groups that constitute each major religious family. The remaining two directory sections—Unclassified Christian Churches and Unclassified Religious Groups—include those groups that cannot be classified within any of the distinct religious families.

Whenever available or appropriate, a directory listing typically contains the following categories of information in the order listed.

1. Entry Number. A sequential entry number precedes each entry and is used in the indexes to refer to it.

2. Organization Name and Acronym. The official name of the organization and, if available, acronym.

3. Address. The street location and/or mailing address of the organization appears directly under its name. If the organization is defunct or no current address could be located for the current edition, it is noted here.

4. Alternate Address. Provides, if applicable, the address of an organization's Canadian or international headquarters, or an address at which the organization may be contacted.

5. Description. A discussion of the organization's history, beliefs, organization, and leaders, generally paraphrased from information obtained from the organization itself. This data preserves, as closely as possible, the original wording from a questionnaire response, website, etc., in order to avoid any misinterpretation of the organization's beliefs, etc.

6. Membership. Most recent statistics as reported by the group, including, as appropriate, number of members, centers, congregations, churches, and ministers. The geographic location of the various congregations, churches, or other groups may also be provided. If no membership statistics are provided, the phrase "not reported" appears.

7. Educational Facilities. An alphabetical listing of post-secondary educational institutions sponsored and/or supported by the group. Each listing includes the city and state/province in which the institution is located.

8. Periodicals. Periodicals and newsletters issued by the group. Unless otherwise noted, publications are available from the address provided at the beginning of the entry.

9. Remarks. Includes additional information not applicable to the basic headings listed above. It could include comments or interpretation by those outside the organization.

10. Sources. Provides complete bibliographic citations, arranged alphabetically, of selected source materials used to develop the entry as well as sources for further reading. With this edition, Web sites have been added for some of the new listees.

Indexes

Access to information appearing in Parts I, II, and III is facilitated through the following indexes:

Geographic Index
Arranges organizations included in Part III, the Directory Listings Sections, according to the countries in which they are located. The United States appears first, with entries arranged alphabetically by state and subarranged by city. Canadian entries are listed next, with entries arranged alphabetically by province and subarranged by city. International entries follow alphabetically by country, with entries subarranged by city within country. Entries include organization name and address, followed by the entry number in parentheses.

Subject Index
Provides access to the material in Part III through a selected list of subject terms. References include the full organization name and book entry number. The index also includes *see* and *see also* references.

Because of the difference between the essays and directory listings sections, citations referring to pages in the Introductory Essays and Historical Essay Chapters are designated with *"p."* References to directory listings include the full organization name and book entry number.

Master Name and Keyword Index
Provides a single alphabetic arrangement of all religious organizations, acronyms, individuals, educational facilities, periodicals, and other significant details mentioned in Parts I, II, and III. (Publications cited within the "Sources" rubric of the directory listings or at the end of the essays are not included in the index.) The index also includes inversions on significant keywords appearing in the names of organizations, periodicals, and other entities. (Due to their prevalence, keyword inversions are not provided for "Church," "Religion," and similar terms.)

Periodical titles are rendered in *italic* type.

The leading articles "A," "An," and "The" are disregarded for filing purposes within the index. Thus, "The Prayer of Peace" will be found filed under "P" and not "T."

Because of the difference between the essays and directory listings sections, citations referring to pages in the introductory and historical essays are designated with *"p."* and are separated from the directory listings sections citations with a semicolon. A **boldface** number following an organization name indicates that organization's main entry in the directory sections.

Key to Abbreviations

&	And	D.D.	Doctor of Divinity
A.B.	Bachelor of Arts	D.Th.	Doctor of Theology
AB	Alberta	DC	District of Columbia
A.M.	Master of Arts	DDS	Doctor of Dental Science
Abp.	Archbishop	DE	Delaware
Admin.	Administrative, Administrator	Dir.	Dirs. Director, Directors
AK	Alaska	Div.	Division
AL	Alabama	Dom.	Domestic
Apt.	Apartment	Dr.	Doctor, Drive
AR	Arkansas	E.	East
Assoc.	Associate	Ed.D.	Doctor of Education
Asst.	Assistant	Exec.	Executive
Ave.	Avenue	Expy.	Expressway
AZ	Arizona	FL	Florida
b.	born	Fl.	Floor
B.A.	Bachelor of Arts	For.	Foreign
B.D.	Bachelor of Divinity	Fr.	Father
B.L.	Bachelor of Laws, Bachelor of Literature, Bachelor of Letters	FSC	Fratres Scholarum Christianarum
		FSE	Brothers of the Holy Eucharist
B.S.	Bachelor of Science	FSP	Pious Society of the Daughters of St. Paul
B.Theo.	Bachelor of Theology	Ft.	Fort
BC	British Columbia	Fwy.	Freeway
Bd.	Board	GA	Georgia
Bldg.	Building	Gen.	General
Blvd.	Boulevard	GU	Guam
Bp.	Bishop	HI	Hawaii
Brig.	Brigadier	Hon.	Honorary
Bro.	Brother	Hwy.	Highway
Bus.	Business	IA	Iowa
c.	circa	ID	Idaho
c/o	Care of	IHM	Sisters of the Immaculate Heart of Mary
CA	California	IL	Illinois
CAE	Certified Association Executive	IN	Indiana
Card.	Cardinal	Inc.	Incorporated
CEO	Chief Executive Officer	Intl.	International
Chm.	Chairman	J.C.B.	Bachelor of Canon Law, Bachelor of Civil Law
Chwn.	Chairwoman	J.C.D.	Doctor of Canon Law, Doctor of Civil Law
CM	Congregatio Missioni Sancti Vicentiia Paulo, Congregatio Mariae	J.D.	Doctor of Jurisprudence, Doctor of Law
		J.U.D.	Doctor of Both Laws (i.e. Canon and Civil)
Cmdr.	Commander	Jr.	Junior
CMF	Congregation of Missionary Sons of the Immaculate Heart of the Blessed Virgin Mary	KS	Kansas
		KY	Kentucky
		L.Th.	Licentiate in Theology
CO	Colorado	LA	Louisiana
Co.	Company	LL.B.	Bachelor of Laws
Col.	Colonel	Ln.	Lane
Coord.	Coordinator	Ltd.	Limited
Corp.	Corporation	M.A.	Master of Arts
Corr.	Corresponding	M.Div.	Master of Divinity
CSA	Sisters of the Congregation of St. Agnes	M.R.E.	Master of Religious Education
CSC	Congregation of the Holy Cross	M.Re.	Master of Religion
CSJ	Congregation of St. Joseph	M.S.	Master of Science
CSP	Paulists	M.Th.	Master of Theology
CT	Connecticut	MA	Massachusetts
Ct.	Court	Maj.	Major
Cust.	Customer	MB	Manitoba
CZ	Canal Zone	MD	Doctor of Medicine, Maryland
d.	died	ME	Maine

Mgr.	Manager	Rep.	Representative
MI	Michigan	Rev.	Reverend
MIC	Missionary Sisters of the Immaculate Conception	RFD	Rural Free Delivery
		RI	Rhode Island
Min.	Minister	Rm.	Room
Mktg.	Marketing	RR	Rural Route
MN	Minnesota	RSCJ	Society of the Sacred Heart
MO	Missouri	RSM	Sisters of Mercy
MS	Mississippi	Rte.	Route
Msgr.	Monsignor	S.	South
MSW	Master of Social Work	S.S.L.	Licentiate of Sacred Scripture
MT	Montana	S.T.B.	Bachelor of Sacred Theology
Mt.	Mount	S.T.D.	Doctor of the Science of Theology, Doctor of Sacred Theology
Mus.B.	Bachelor of Music		
Mus.D.	Doctor of Music	S.T.L.	Reader in Sacred Theology, Licentiate in Sacred Theology
N.	North		
Natl.	National	S.T.M.	Master of Arts in Theology
NB	New Brunswick	SC	South Carolina
NC	North Carolina	SD	South Dakota
ND	North Dakota	SE	Southeast
NE	Nebraska, Northeast	Sec.	Secretary
NF	Newfoundland	Serv.	Service
NH	New Hampshire	SJ	Societas Jesu
NJ	New Jersey	SHCJ	Society of the Holy Child Jesus
NM	New Mexico	SK	Saskatchewan
No.	Number	SL	Sisters of Loretto at the Foot of the Cross
NS	Nova Scotia	SM	Sisters of Mercy
NT	Northwest Territories	SND	Sisters of Notre Dame
NV	Nevada	Sq.	Square
NW	Northwest	Sr.	Senior, Sister
NY	New York	SSCC	Congregation of the Sacred Hearts of Jesus and Mary
OAR	Order of the Augustinian Recollects		
OCD	Order of Discalced	SSE	Sisters of St. Carmelites Elizabeth
Ofc.	Officer	SSJ	Sisters of St. Joseph
OFM	Order of Friars Minor	St.	Saint, Street
OH	Ohio	Sta.	Station
OK	Oklahoma	STD	Doctor of the Science of Theology
OMI	Oblats de Marie Immaculee	Ste.	Sainte, Suite
ON	Ontario	SW	Southwest
OP	Ordo Praedicatorum	Ter(r)	Terrace, Territory
OR	Oregon	Th.B.	Bachelor of Theology
OSA	Order of St. Augustine	Th. D.	Doctor of Theology
OSB	Ordo Sancti Benedicti	Th.M.	Master of Theology
OSC	Order of St. Clare	TN	Tennessee
OSF	Order of St. Francis	Tpke.	Turnpike
OSU	Order of St. Ursula	Treas.	Treasurer
PA	Pennsylvania	TX	Texas
PE	Prince Edward Island	U.S.	United States
Ph.B.	Bachelor of Philosophy	U.S.A.	United States of America
Ph.D.	Doctor of Philosophy	UT	Utah
Pkwy.	Parkway	V.P.	Vice President
Pl.	Place	VA	Virginia
PO Box	Post Office Box	ven.	Venerable
PQ	Quebec	VI	Virgin Islands
PR	Puerto Rico	VPM	Voix du Peuple Murundi
Pres.	President	VT	Vermont
Prod.	Producer	W.	West
Prof.	Professor	WA	Washington
Prog.	Program	WI	Wisconsin
Prop.	Proprietor	WV	West Virginia
Rd.	Road	WY	Wyoming
RD	Rural Delivery	YT	Yukon Territory
Reg.	Regional		

Essay 1

The Development of American Religion: An Interpretive View

INTRODUCTION. The United States is currently home to more than 1,500 different primary religious organizations—churches, sects, cults, temples, societies, missions—each seeking to be the place of expression of the primary religious allegiances and sentiments of its members and adherents. The majority of these organizations are Christian churches, and the overwhelming majority of Americans who engage in any outward religious activity are members of one of the more than 900 Christian denominations. Prior to the 1880s, the Christian churches had little competition, except for the Native American religions, which they saw at best as dying faiths soon to be replaced by Christianity. The churches enjoyed the favor of the influential elite of society. They had the support of the government, the approbation of the press, and the control of education at all levels. At the same time, however, the churches also faced a public, the majority of which regarded religion with attitudes that varied from indifference to open hostility. Simply expressed, the church existed as an instrument of the state, another element in the overall system of social control.

In the United States, that situation began to change dramatically at the time of the American Revolution. With the exception of several New England states, formal ties between church and state were cut, and each succeeding decade brought an end to more and more of the numerous informal ones. For many congregations, the Revolution included the loss either temporarily or completely of their buildings. The Anglican church lost the most, and its situation was made all the more severe by the sudden departure of the majority of its ministers to England and the loss of its legal status.

After the war, groups that had assumed the controlling positions in American religious life began to take second place to groups that had played little or no prior role in the nation's life. The changes became evident during the Second Great Awakening, the popular term usually applied to the period of the rise of the Methodists, Baptists, Disciples of Christ, and Cumberland Presbyterians and the evangelistic endeavor that led to their churching of the then western frontier. From the beginning of the nineteenth century, the church has moved from a position of disestablishment in the midst of an indifferent public to the creation of what amounts to a powerful new religious establishment through its ownership of ever-increasing sums of real estate and stock and its steady penetration of the indifferent public, the majority of which it has finally won to its membership. The last two centuries have seen Christian church membership increase in both number and percentage of the population every decade. Since 1900, while the nation's population increased three and a half times, church membership increased sevenfold. At the same time, the church has step-by-step relinquished control of education, lost its favored status in the press, and must fight for its right to criticize the government or lobby for what it considers just laws. The church has also been rent with schism (from 20 denominations in 1800 to more than 900 in 1988), while at the same time having to face competition from the literally hundreds of different varie-

ties of the great world religions and an imposing assortment of new innovative American faiths, including a revived and assertive Native American spirituality.

This *Encyclopedia* covers the story of American religion from the entrance in the sixteenth century of the Europeans determined to convert the Native Americans through the pluralistic religious situation of the late twentieth century. It is a story of religious conquests and losses, the search for simply a place to be alone, the rise and fall of utopian dreams, and the attempts by different religions to find ways to exist in close proximity with constant war and rumor of war.

THE NATIVE AMERICANS IN 1500: THE FIRST SETTLERS. 10,000 years ago, 40,000 years ago, or even more than 100,000 years ago, depending upon which source is consulted, the first human settlers in what today is called North America arrived. They may have walked, or they may have built a crude boat, but they crossed the Bering Strait (periodically in the past a land bridge) and moved across the continent to establish their residences, learn the arts of survival and culture, and generally claim the land for their people. Over the years they differentiated themselves as separate peoples (tribes, nations, etc.) emphasizing hunting, agriculture, trading and/or fishing in their conquests of the very different environments, climates, and resources the land provided. They also developed religion, which took at least as many forms as there were tribes.

Possibly 30 million Indians inhabited North America in 1500. They were divided into groups that spoke over 200 languages. They also showed such immense variation in religion as to make it improper to speak of an Indian *religion*, rather a number of Indian *religions*.

However, the white people who began their conquest of North America in the sixteenth century paid little attention to the Native Americans' religions. Beyond writing up accounts of them with varying levels of sophistication, the European program was to totally replace Indian religions with the observance of Christianity. For this reason, the religions of the Indians and the faiths of European origins, until recently, rarely interacted. Once the Europeans took control, Indian religions were offered no role in the conquering culture and to a large extent were eradicated, either by the deaths of their adherents or their conversion to some form of Christianity.

MAJOR THEMES IN THE DEVELOPMENT OF AMERICAN RELIGION. In the movement from the religious situation in 1500 to that of the late nineteenth century, four factors arise as dominant elements in the shaping of American religious patterns: *immigration, religious freedom, proselytism,* and *denominationalism.* Of the more than 1,500 religious groups that presently exist in the United States, the overwhelming majority originated by the direct immigration of their members/practitioners to the United States, and their establishing centers for worship and for the recruitment of new members among the general population. The largest number of the remaining groups are schisms of those immigrant groups. The actual number of new religions that have developed in America, apart from Native American faiths, is relatively small, and such indigenous American religions are all the more noteworthy for that fact: Adventism (which includes both Seventh-Day Adventism and the Jehovah's Witnesses), Christian Science, New Thought, Theosophy, Pentecostalism, and Scientology.

Understanding *immigration* as the first of the four factors shaping American religious life also underscores the role of ethnic–national settlements in setting the initial patterns of American religious life during the colonial period. Spanish Catholics came to Florida, New Mexico, and California. French Catholics settled the Gulf Coast from Mobile to New Orleans and the Mississippi River Valley north to St. Louis and St. Paul. The British settled New England and the southern colonies. The Dutch came into New York (formerly New Netherlands), the Swedes colonized Delaware, and the Germans made up a substantial portion of William Penn's colony. In the nineteenth century, the patterns of immigration would again change the face of American religion as, for example, Germans and Scandinavians moved into the area north and west of Chicago to create the still dominant Lutheran belt from Milwaukee to Butte. The influx of Italians and Irish would take control of New England from British Congregationalists and place it in the hands of Roman Catholics. The influx of Hispanics into the area north of the Rio Grande River would return that area lost to Protestants at the time of the gold rush to Roman Catholic hegemony.

The overall consideration of immigration must not neglect the role of immigration laws, especially after 1882, in shaping religious patterns in America. For example, the normal growth of Asian religions, which were being established among immigrants in the last half of the nineteenth century, was thwarted by the imposition of a series of laws from 1882 to 1924. But the 1924 law, which all but stopped immigration from Asia, also stopped the flow from Southern and Eastern Europe. Thus while the law slowed the growth of Eastern religions, it also strongly affected Judaism, Eastern Orthodoxy, and Islam. In like measure, the lifting of the 1924 restrictions in 1965 contributed directly to the massive expansion of these religions during the last two decades and is even now completely altering the overall shape and structure of the American religious community.

Religious freedom, both in concept and practice, has expanded in America. Credit for the first accomplishments in that direction must go to the early colonists in New York, Rhode Island, Pennsylvania, and Maryland. An early symbol of that expanded freedom was the colonists' reception of Jewish settlers. Generations before most Europeans were thinking about religious toleration, the Dutch had become the most religiously tolerant nation on the continent. In their American colonies that tolerance was demonstrated by the welcome given to fleeing Brazilian Jews, who established the first synagogue in North America in New York. Rhode Island, which had been founded by Roger Williams while fleeing the intolerance of the Massachusetts Puritans, welcomed the second congregation of Jews. It is not surprising to find one of the other colonial congregations in Philadelphia.

Religious liberty was, of course, greatly advanced by the American Revolution and the Bill of Rights to the Constitution. That the constitutional convention refused to grant any group, in this case any Christian church, the power, prestige, and privilege of being the nation's established religious body was both an important experiment and a significant act of infidelity. As an experiment, it tested a major axiom of European thought, that a nation needed one religious body (i.e., a state church) as a necessary force in uniting the nation and assisting in social control. In America's post-Revolutionary success, the experiment proved the untruth of the assumption. At the same time, the experiment would not have been possible had not the convention also recognized both that no religious group served more than a small fraction of the popula-

tion, and that the great majority of the public were not supporters of any religious organization. This twofold observation was amply verified in the decades after the Revolution when, in total, the churches could only claim on their roles less than 20 percent of the now free people.

The freedom guaranteed by the First Amendment has been steadily broadened during the last 200 years. Within a few decades all of the states dropped the last remnants of their formal religious establishments. The implications of the First Amendment for unpopular religions have gained increasing attention and clarity. And the society itself tolerates an ever-increasing variety of religious belief and practice. The heightened toleration experienced during this century has been disseminated from the large impersonal urban complexes, which both permit divergent religious groups to develop apart from the watchful and critical eyes of small-town society and provide a concentrated pool of the potential recruits needed by any new religion in its critical first years of existence.

The freedom to practice a new religion includes the freedom to *proselytize* (or, to induce someone to convert to one's faith). From 1800 to the present, no activity apart from immigration has so altered the pattern of American religion as the evangelical efforts of religious groups. Following the American Revolution, the older colonial churches dominated the religious life. However, they were prepared neither in theology nor organization to respond to the irreligious public that confronted them at the end of the eighteenth century. The Methodists and Baptists, both of whom were evangelically oriented, were prepared, and by the middle of the nineteenth century, they replaced the Congregationalists, Presbyterians, and Episcopalians as the largest dominant church bodies, a position they have never relinquished.

At the same time, in the religiously free situation, innovative religious movements, movements which would have been suppressed by the government under a state-church regime, were permitted to grow and proselytize as well. Thus early in the nineteenth century, new Christian churches such as the Cumberland Presbyterian Church and the Disciples of Christ broke from older bodies, and completely new ways of doing religion appeared, from Swedenborgians to Latter-Day Saints (Mormons), from Spiritualists to Transcendentalists. The number of new religious gestalts multiplied decade by decade. Soon after each new religious movement organized, it further divided thus producing an array of similar organizations and eventually new religious denominational families. Throughout the nineteenth century, almost all of the major new divergent religious thrusts were Christian. However, during the last two decades of the nineteenth century, Hinduism, Buddhism, and Islam were introduced into American life and looked for converts among a public only 35 percent of whom had joined a church.

During the twentieth century, the role of proselytizing activity has been spectacular. As the nation's population multiplied three and a half times (from 75 million to 250 million), Christian church membership multiplied seven times, and the percentage of church members doubled from slightly over 30 percent to more than 65 percent. Religious affiliation climbed even higher as the Jewish, Muslim, Buddhist, Hindu, and occult-metaphysical communities, minuscule at the turn of the century, each developed constituencies numbering in the millions.

The dual effect of freedom of religion and proselytizing activity leads directly to the consideration of *denominationalism*. In a religiously free society, denominations, voluntary religious associations of like-minded (and like-spirited) people, are the basic form of the religious life. In spite of the various predictions of the fading of denominations (through the ecumenical movement) or the decline of their importance (through increasing individualized religion), they remain, and for the foreseeable future will remain, the bedrock of American religion. Denominations are the stable primary religious associations formed in those societies that do not impose a single dominant religious structure. In a state-church society, for example, there is one "religion" and may be a number of dissenting "sects." In a free society there are a number of more or less competing religious organizations, no one of which has a majority of the population in its membership. Some organizations, because of such factors as their many years in existence, their inherent appeal, and/or their aggressive programs for conversion, have many members. Others, primarily because they are new, lack substantial appeal, and/or limit proselytizing efforts, remain small.

Denominations, whatever their size, provide the primary religious identification for most religious people. They offer regular times and facilities for the affirmation of beliefs in group activity, worship, study, and service. Often associated with and supported by the denominations are a variety of what might be termed secondary or paradenominational religious organizations. These organizations usually specialize in one limited task in relation to one or a small group of similar primary religious organizations. Included among the paradenominational organizations are independent publishers, religious leadership training schools (seminaries, Bible colleges, etc.), missionary organizations, evangelical ministries, and social service agencies. On occasion a secondary or paradenominational structure (especially evangelical ministries engaged in the conversion of individuals) will transform into a new primary group and enlarge its services to include all of those normally provided by a primary religious group. Within an evangelical group, such a transformation can be noted when the group stops sending its recruits to the supporting denominational structures and begins forming congregations of its converts. Such a transformation occurred in the 1970s among some Jewish-Christian evangelical groups, which began to form ethnic Jewish-Christian synagogues.

Within the pluralistic environment of the late twentieth century, the formation of so many new competing religious groups has eroded the exclusive and dominant positions of some of the older and more established religious organizations. This erosion of position has been most evident in the major defeats suffered by conservative Christian groups on such issues as abortion legislation, prayer in public schools, the display of religious symbols in government-owned facilities, and the elimination of the Christian facade that had been placed over many facets of public and social life. Interpreted by many as signs of secularization, the defeats are more adequately understood when seen as manifestations of (1) the growing seriousness with which dissenting religious positions are treated and (2) an increasing sensitivity toward religious concerns that has developed within the public sphere. Coupled with this new sensitivity is the loss of ability by even the most powerful religious bodies to enforce their own ideas on the populace at large, especially at the national level. What power that remains is largely a veto power.

With these forces in mind, we can now turn to a brief consideration of the movement of religion from the arrival of the Spanish conquistadors and padres to the complex pluralistic religious environment of today. That development will be considered in six overlapping periods. The Native American period begins in prehistory and extends to the nineteenth century. The Catholic Era began around 1500 and continued in part of the country until the nineteenth century. The period of Western European (primarily British) conquest begins around 1600, with the arrival of the settlers in Virginia. The Revolutionary Era begins with the disruptions of the 1770s and carries through the transitions into the new religious environment established by the Constitution. The period of the churching of the nation can be said to begin in 1801 and to continue to this day. The period of transition from Christian dominance into a pluralistic society of shared religious hegemony began in the 1880s and has also continued to this day.

THE NATIVE AMERICANS TO 1800. The first settlers came into North America in the prehistoric past and moved across the continent, eventually settling almost every niche. By the time of the coming of the Europeans, the differing peoples manifested a wide variety of governmental structures, economic systems, and family forms. The structure of their religious life was equally varied, and there are few threads that run through all the Indian religions. As is true of most religion prior to the segregation of life into the modern distinction between secular and sacred, Indian religions tended to be at one with the whole life of the people among whom they existed. Religion was intimately tied to the problems of tribal survival, the self-identity of individuals as tribal members, and the organization of tribal routine.

Just as the religious aspect of life was integrated into other aspects of tribal life, so tribal life was integrated into the natural environment chosen by the tribe for its home, including the climate, terrain, and the animal and plant life. Indians took the land seriously and lived by its seasonal changes. Survival demanded an intense and intimate relationship with nature, and that nature was seen to be permeated with life power, sometimes viewed as one force, but often differentiated into many particular powers.

Some Europeans thought of the Indians as being without religion, an opinion that highlights some essential truths about Native American spirituality. There was, for example, no word or term in any Indian language that could be translated "religion." There was also, generally speaking, a lack of what might be considered worship, since in most Indian religions, ceremonies and actions were not a matter of supplication of a deity so much as the development of a working relationship with the sacred realm. Ceremonies and action created a matrix within which life moved, and that movement tended to be circular, following the coming, going, and return of the seasons. The sacred realm was the realm of the pervasive powers.

Living with the powers that existed in and sustained the world led many tribes to develop forms of magic, the art and practice of manipulating the spirit powers. Most tribes had functionaries who practiced the arts of magic and used them for good or ill. These "religious" leaders were among those most threatened by the arrival of Christianity and its priests.

The particular life and beliefs of the different tribes were articulated in a variety of *myths* that described in story format the underlying structure of reality. These verbal expressions of life, which ranged from the sacred to the mundane, embodied the Indians' rather sophisticated understandings of both the immediate environment and the larger world, gave a rationale for the accepted behavioral standards for the tribe, and supplied the answers to the basic religious questions.

The coming of the Europeans had little immediate impact for the great majority of Indian tribes who encountered white people only with the push to settle the interior of the continent in the nineteenth century. However, those tribes located on the lands first colonized frequently faced disastrous results. Not an insignificant amount of damage was done by the spread of new diseases in defense of which the Native American had no weapons of immunity nor medicine. Measles and small pox were especially deadly. At the very least, those Indians residing in close proximity to the new settlements became the targets of missionary efforts. Almost every church group, soon after its arrival in the New World and its establishment of a stable presence among the white settlers, turned its attention to missionary activity among the Indians. The most extensive missions were established by Roman Catholics in the St. Lawrence River Valley, Florida, the Gulf Coast, and across the Southwest from Texas to California. John Eliot is remembered as the primary missionary supported by the New England Puritans. The desire to support his work inspired the formation in England in 1649 of one of the first of the voluntary missionary societies, soon to become so popular in evangelical circles. Anglican missions to the Indians were promoted by one of these societies, the Society for the Propagation of the Gospel (SPG) in Foreign Parts.

Despite the dedication of the missionaries, their efforts often fell victim to seemingly unrelated forces that tended not only to destroy the missions but the Native American's entire culture. For example, King Philip's War (1675–76) led to the destruction of the towns of the ''Praying Indians'' established so successfully by Eliot's converts. Other missions were destroyed when the land upon which they were established changed hands from one nation to another, usually after a war. In such a manner many of the Catholic missions were lost to the British.

However, the missions themselves tended to intrude in most destructive ways into the Indians' culture. Typical of the disruption of Indian life caused by the Europeans was the Spanish movement into the land of the Chumash Indians who inhabited the California coast from present-day Malibu to San Luis Obispo. The Spanish found the Chumash organized into numerous villages each ruled by a chief, termed a *wots*, who provided moral authority and general guidance. The wots was assisted by a *paha*, who presided at the principal festivals and ceremonies. The Chumash had established a hunting–fishing–gathering–trading economy, which had in turn produced an artistic culture of high standards. When the Spanish first arrived in 1769, the Chumash welcomed the new settlers and provided them needed items from their abundant supply.

The missionaries who accompanied the Spanish explorers discovered that the Chumash lived in a larger universe permeated with power that had been scattered through the world at the point of creation. Individuals were allowed to use the power, if they possessed the proper knowledge. They could also gain access to the powers through a dream helper, a personified form of a natural reality, such as a bear, an eagle, or even a plant such as *datura*. Important to Chumash ''religion'' was the balancing of all the powers that existed. Special people, *antaps*, knew the secret knowledge to keep the powers balanced.

However, with the arrival of the Spanish, the village organization, the economy, and the religious tradition were attacked at the core. The Indians were invited to convert to the Roman Catholic faith and to abandon the villages for the mission. At the mission an alternative economy was established that included candle making, agriculture, iron working, and masonry. The missions and pueblos provided a new economy that soon involved enough Indians that it undercut the older economy still maintained by those who refused to accept mission life. But those Indians who did move to the pueblo were often blocked in their participation in the new economy. They were trapped between the long-term goals of the missionaries and the immediate objectives of the colonial government. In the sixty-plus years of their existence, the missions completely obliterated the old village life of the Chumash. The mission period ended in 1833 with secularization, the removal of the missions from the control of the Franciscans and the redistribution of their lands to Mexican settlers. The Chumash were thus left with neither the villages of their ancestors nor the new life forced upon them by the missions. Those who survived retained but a remnant of their original beliefs and practices.

Other Indian tribes in those lands first invaded by Europeans in the seventeenth century reacted in a variety of ways toward their new neighbors. Most at first accepted the Europeans and allowed Christian priests to move among them. Others, some following an initial acceptance, found themselves at war with both the white settlers and their ministers. The settlers increasingly wanted the Indians' territory and resources, and the ministers wanted to change their religious perspective. As the Indians fought the encroachments of Christianity, the churches counted the victims of such fighting as martyrs.

In the end, however, the Indians were forced to seek some means of accommodating to the reality of a permanent European presence. Some accepted the settlers, even to the point of taking sides in the periodic wars, while at the same time resisting the missionaries' pressure to change their thoughts and ways. They signed treaties and gave concessions. But the trends were against them, and gradually they were forced into designated parcels of land and targeted for conversion by the various churches. As the dust of the

American Revolution settled, there was still hope that the Indians' life and religions could survive to some extent, but the new nation on the East Coast of the continent had caught a vision of the West and eagerly rushed to claim it as its own. In the process it was quite willing to push the Indian out of the way.

THE CATHOLIC ERA: THE COMING OF THE SPANISH. The largest religious body in the United States today and throughout the twentieth century has been the Roman Catholic Church. Its members were also the first to arrive, conquer, and colonize parts of the land now making up the United States. Shortly after the discovery of the New World by Christopher Columbus, the rulers of Spain appealed to Pope Alexander VI to settle the dispute between Spain and Portugal over their claims to the new lands. In 1493, the pope drew a line in the middle of the Atlantic, east of which Portugal would have hegemony and west of which Spain would operate. The line would have left Portugal with Africa and the islands off the Atlantic coast, but without any access to the new world. In 1494 the line was moved farther west and as a result Portugal received Brazil. From Cuba and then Mexico, Spain began a program of conquest and settlement that included North America. The governmental drive to develop the Spanish empire and the church's desire to convert and Christianize the native populations often came into conflict. While the church won many smaller victories in its attempts to champion the cause of humane treatment, in the end, the government usually dominated the situation.

The actual movement of Spain into what is now the United States was occasioned by the settlement in Florida of a group of French Huguenots (Protestants) along the St. Johns River (near present-day Jacksonville) in 1564. Having previously claimed Florida as its own, the offended Spanish established a settlement at St. Augustine and quickly moved to destroy the St. Johns River colony. From there, Spanish missionaries established missions that at one point reached as far north as South Carolina and briefly the Chesapeake Bay area. The missions in Florida, in spite of their ups and downs, were most successful through several generations.

The second movement of Spain into what is now the United States was from Mexico in the Southwest. In 1540 Francisco Vasquez de Coronado began his famous trek which took him from New Mexico to central Kansas. In his easternmost exploration, he came upon the village of Quivera. Returning to his advance base in New Mexico, Coronado ordered his expedition members home. The Franciscans, however, decided to stay. Two of their number, Brother John of the Cross and Brother Luis Descalona, settled in the Bernalillo-Pecos area of New Mexico. Father Juan de Padilla journeyed back to Quivera. Brother John and Brother Luis were successful to the point of angering the Indians' own religious functionaries. They eventually disappeared, believed to have been killed. Father de Padilla was successful at Quivera, but was killed when he tried to extend his work to other tribes.

Further movement into the southwest was to wait a generation. In 1598, an expedition headed by Juan de Onate moved into New Mexico and established a settlement along the Rio Grande River. The church built at this settlement, called San Juan and later San Gabriel, was the second oldest church in America. The site now is in ruins, for in 1609 a new capital for the territory was established at Santa Fe, and San Gabriel abandoned. Missionary work led to the founding of some 11 missions by 1617 and 43 by 1625. The work of the missions was not without its problems. There was much resistance by many of the New Mexico tribes to the missionary efforts and a number of priests were killed. The Indians' resentment of both the efforts to destroy their culture and the cruelty of the Spanish rulers boiled over in 1680. Led by a medicine man, Pope, the Indians revolted and drove the Spanish south of El Paso. It was 12 years before the Spanish moved back into New Mexico and established a permanent presence. About this same time, a Jesuit priest, Father Eusebio Kin (d. 1711), was traveling through northern Mexico and Arizona. In 1697 he founded San

Xavier del Bac, the beginning of a small but continuous Roman Catholic presence in the territory.

The Spanish government and the Franciscan missionaries moved into Texas in 1691 but abandoned the work in 1693, after an Indian revolt. A permanent presence was established in 1703 at a mission along the Rio Grande. In 1715, following the development of a plan to both conquer the land and convert the Indians, the original missions were again occupied, and under the capable leadership of Father Antonio Margil de Jesus, the missionary work extended throughout the territory.

THE ARRIVAL OF THE FRENCH. While Spain and Spanish Roman Catholicism were occupying Florida and establishing their hegemony from Texas to California in the Southwest, France was moving from its original settlements in the St. Lawrence River Valley of Canada to claim territory along the Atlantic coast, in the Great Lakes region, through the Mississippi Valley, and along the Gulf Coast west of Florida. Actually, the first Roman Catholic chapel in the New World was erected on an island off the coast of Maine in 1604, though the colony on the island soon failed. The French initiated their more permanent settlement in 1608 at Quebec, which they used as a base for Jesuit missionaries who fanned out to work among the tribes in the land along what is now the Canada-United States border, primarily the Mohawk, Iroquois, Algonquin, and Huron. The Indian mission became famous more for the martyrs it produced than the numbers it converted. In the 1640s, a number of priests including Isaac Joques and Jean de Brebeuf were tortured and killed. The work was lost in the 1700s as the British took over the territory from the French.

In 1669, a Jesuit priest, Jacques Marquette (1637–1675), began the French push into the Great Lakes region. His initial exploratory trip was followed by a career working among the Indians of Illinois and Wisconsin, the first mission being established in 1684. He was followed by others. The work initiated by Marquette was balanced by exploration and settlement along the Gulf Coast as early as 1685 when Robert LaSalle, who had followed Marquette's explorations by some of his own in the Great Lakes in 1678 and in the Mississippi Valley in 1682, sailed into the Gulf in 1685 and founded Fort St. Louis on the coast of what is now Texas. His actions also established Spain and France as competitors in east Texas. Following LaSalle's short-lived experiment, others established Biloxi (1697), Mobile (1702), and New Orleans (1718). New Orleans would become the major dissemination point for Catholicism northward along the Mississippi River. In New Orleans, the first religious institute for women, the Ursuline Convent, was built, and from there the missionary work among the southern Indians was launched.

The progress of the Roman Catholic work in North America, indeed of religion in general, was greatly altered in 1769 by events on the other side of the world. The Seven Years War, which involved the three major powers in North America, was concluded and on February 10th the Treaty of Paris signed. Britain received most of the territory claimed by France, including Canada and all their American territory east of the Mississippi River (except New Orleans). From Spain Britain received Florida, in partial exchange for Cuba. Except for Quebec, Catholic influence was radically curtailed for several generations in the colonies ceded to Britain. The ceding of Louisiana to Spain in 1769 did little to assist the spread of Catholicism there, which continued with a predominantly French constituency. Spanish Catholicism was expanding in only one place—California. While the first Spanish expedition led by Juan Rodriguez Cabrillo had sailed along the California coast in 1542, it was not until 1769, the year of the Treaty of Paris, that settlement and the opening of a mission in California began at San Diego. Following the establishment of Spanish towns, Father Junipero Serra (1713–1784) founded nine missions along the coast of California, the first of 21 such missions opened as far north as Sonoma. Unfortunately, the push into California came just as

Spain was weakening at home, hence it was unable to properly exploit the new colony.

The Catholic work west of the Mississippi grew slowly through the arrival of new settlers and the conversion of the Indians, but was increasingly thwarted by the westward push of the new American nation. First, in 1800 France again took control of Louisiana, but sold it to the United States three years later. Further westward expansion of the United States climaxed in the Treaty of Guadalupe Hildago in which Mexico ceded Texas, New Mexico, most of Arizona, and California to the United States. With quick and massive movement of predominantly non-Catholic settlers into the formerly Catholic southwest after the treaty, the Catholic era can be said to have come to an end.

THE BRITISH ERA: ANGLICANS AND CONGREGATIONALISTS. The movement of Western and Northern Europeans and their religions into the North American continent, apart from the Viking explorations, began in the late fifteenth century with the arrival of John Cabot. On his first voyage (1497) he probably reached as far south as Maine and on his second (1499–1501) he seems to have sailed along the coast from Maine to Maryland. However, it would not be until 1584 that exploitation of the American coast began with the attempted settlement of a colony on Roanoke Island, and the more important and subsequently successful colony at Jamestown in 1606. With the establishment of Jamestown, the Church of England came to North America (though previously services had been held by chaplains assigned to the explorers' ships). To a largely unknown priest of the Church of England, Robert Hunt, goes the honor of having been the first non-Catholic Christian minister to reside and pastor in North America. He came to Jamestown in the spring of 1607. His career was short and the date of his death never recorded. He died along with the majority of the early Jamestown settlers. The more substantial career of Alexander Whitaker (1585–1616), who arrived in 1611 to serve the church at the new settlement of Henrico, is also more illustrative of the progress of the Church of England. Whitaker served the colony for many years and actively promoted increased migration by Britons.

Virginia became but the first of the British settlements along the Atlantic coast. In 1620, a group of Puritan Separatists, popularly called the Pilgrims, landed at Plymouth, Massachusetts. They were followed a decade later by a second group, this time non-Separatist Puritans, called simply the Puritans, who founded the Massachusetts Bay Colony and began to spread out across Massachusetts, Connecticut, and most of New England. The range of opinion represented by the Pilgrims, the Puritans, and the Church of England is the product of a whole era of post-Reformation church life in Great Britain.

England had gone through the Protestant Reformation of the sixteenth century in a much different manner from most of the countries on the continental mainland. It had emerged during the reign of Elizabeth I with a church that drew major components from both Roman Catholicism and Protestantism. The Church of England, Anglicanism, was the inheritor of Elizabeth's *via media*. However, there were Protestants who were not content with anything less than a fully Protestant church. Their cause was strengthened by the union of Scotland and England in 1607 with the advent of James I to the throne. Scotland had gone through a reformation and established Presbyterianism.

Puritanism is the name given to the movements whose goal was to purge the Church of England of its unwanted Romanish elements. The different Puritan sects disagreed as to the priorities for a purification of the church. One group looked for some minor changes, mostly of a pietistic and worshipful nature within the Church of England, but sought no basic changes in its government. Others looked to the Presbyterians of Scotland for their model. They sought the establishment of Presbyterianism as the state church of England. The most radical of all, the Separatists, wished to separate from any state church, and call only committed disciples of Christ into a visible and voluntary fellowship. Alexander Whitaker was a mild Puritan, loyal to the established church, but with definite Presbyterian tendencies. The Pilgrims of Plymouth were Separatists. The Puritans of Massachusetts and Connecticut were neither Presbyterians nor Separatists. In their new setting they developed a new form of Puritanism, Congregationalism. Like the Separatists, these Puritans wanted a congregation of converted believers and wanted to place authority for the governance of the church in the local congregation. Unlike the Separatists, however, they wished to remain in close association with the state, to be the established church for their colonies, to identify as much as possible church membership with membership in the political community. Only church members could vote or hold government office. They sought to possess all of the prerogatives of the Church of England since they were but its purified branch, not a separate schismatic body. And the Puritans in at least one important aspect copied the church of the homeland, in that they were as little tolerant of those who deviated from the Puritan path as the Elizabethan bishops in England had been of the Puritans.

THE OTHER COLONIES. While Anglicanism was spreading from its base in Virginia and Congregationalism was spreading through New England, other colonies were being formed with quite different religious bases. Early in the seventeenth century the Dutch had begun to explore the coast of America. In 1609 Henry Hudson sailed up the river that now bears his name as far as the present city of Albany, New York, and staked a Dutch claim for the area. The Dutch established the colony of New Netherlands in 1624 and two years later founded New Amsterdam on Manhattan Island. As tolerant as the Dutch were, they still retained a state church which, since the overthrow of the Spanish, had been reformed. Thus, at the beginning of the colony's life, two lay officers, called in the Dutch Reformed structure "comforters of the sick," were among the earliest settlers. Peter Minuit (1580–1658), Director General of the colony, famous for his purchase of Manhattan, was a French Reformed lay elder who led services until 1628 when Jonas Michaelius (1577–?), the first ordained Reformed minister, arrived in the New World to begin a three-year pastorate. He immediately organized a congregation, still in existence today and known as the Marble Collegiate Church, the oldest continuously existing Protestant church in North America. The term "collegiate" referred to the collegial relationship that developed among the early Reformed congregations formed in New Netherlands. Reformed congregations spread on Long Island and northward along the Hudson River. In 1642, the church at Fort Orange (now Albany) was organized by Johannes Megapolensis (1603–1670).

The colony enjoyed its most prosperous period during the governorship of Peter Stuyvesant (1646–64). Stuyvesant administered the company's religious policies, which included both discouraging the establishment of competing worship centers and encouraging very diverse groups to migrate to the colony. Thus, Stuyvesant recognized the chaos created by the adherents of so many different churches in his colony, but continually refused to let them organize. For example, in 1649, when a group of Lutherans called a minister from Holland, Stuyvesant forbade him to preach and eventually forced him to return to Europe. Interestingly, the company took a quite different perspective on Jews, who, over Stuyvesant's protests, were welcomed as refugees in 1654 from the former Dutch colonies in Brazil. In New Netherlands, they organized the first Jewish congregation and built the first synagogue.

In 1638, Swedes founded Ft. Christiana (now Wilmington, Delaware), and the following year Reorus Torkillus, the first Lutheran minister in America, arrived to establish true and befitting worship in the Lutheran mode. Lutheranism spread among the Swedish and Finnish settlers until 1655 when the Dutch overran the colony and took control. They permitted one Lutheran pastor to remain and Lutheran worship to continue.

Conditions changed considerably in 1664 when the British took New Netherlands and changed it to New York. While open-

ing an Anglican chapel, the government was forced to adopt a policy of liberal toleration of a variety of worship among its new predominantly non-Anglican subjects. A generation later the government imposed an Anglican establishment on the colony, although the Dutch were allowed to continue their distinctive worship and survive today as the Reformed Church in America.

A new life for Roman Catholicism began in Maryland. Two Jesuits arrived in 1634 with the first colonists that included both Catholics and Protestants. Struggling with the problems of continued actions against the Catholic community (the Jesuits were expelled in the early 1640s), the colony passed a Toleration Act in 1649 that granted freedom of worship to all Christian sects. That act stayed in effect until 1692 when the Church of England was officially established. However, by that time the presence of so many dissenters kept the establishment weak and allowed the strong Catholic presence to remain largely unmolested.

Rhode Island originated in the dissenting views of Roger Williams, a teacher in the Congregational Church in Massachusetts. Unhappy with Williams' Separatist tendencies, in 1635 the authorities banished him from the colony. Finding temporary shelter among the Pilgrims at Plymouth, he moved on in 1636 to found Rhode Island. Drawing upon his experience with Puritan intolerance and his Separatist opinions, he established a colony and society far ahead of its time. Government and religion were separated and the persecuted sects, such as the Quakers, welcomed. Like many who adopted a Separatist perspective, Williams became a Baptist and is generally credited with founding the first Baptist congregation in America, though he soon withdrew from the Baptists and thereafter labeled himself a mere "Seeker."

As important as Williams is to Rhode Island and Baptist history, his real import is in the development of the sectarian tradition of church-state relations. Williams is the ultimate source and Rhode Island the ultimate example for the perspective on religious freedom that would eventually come to the fore in America. In 1644, he authored one of the great classics of religious liberty, *The Bloody Tenant of Persecution*, that would voice in full the ideals of religious freedom, far earlier than those Puritan voices in the next century who would begin to grapple with the breakdown of Congregationalist authority among New Englanders. In 1663 his ideals would be written into the Rhode Island charter.

Following the example of Williams, William Penn created Pennsylvania as a haven for Quakers and other religious minorities. The first settlers into Penn's colony were Welshmen who arrived in 1682, but they were soon followed by the Quakers and representatives of numerous German groups, Penn having recruited heavily among Germany's persecuted sects. As a result Pennsylvania not only became the originating point for groups such as the Mennonites, Amish, German Rosicrucians, and the Church of the Brethren, but also for the German Lutheran and Reformed churches.

Thus by the last decades of the seventeenth century, the southern and middle colonies (except for Pennsylvania) had an Anglican establishment, and the New England colonies (except for Rhode Island) were still dominated by Congregationalism. Throughout the 1600s, the Congregational establishment remained strong enough to deal with (banish, imprison, or execute) most dissidents. To the contrary, the Church of England's establishment was weak in most areas, there being no bishop in the colonies and many parishes lacking priests. This weakness was due primarily to the presence in significant numbers of both the irreligious and the dissenting sects, especially the Presbyterians and the Baptists, and in Maryland, the Roman Catholics, none of which had anything to gain from a strong Church of England presence.

THE EIGHTEENTH CENTURY. Toward the end of the seventeenth century, changes in England were causing people to look more positively at the church in what was emerging as the British Empire and to promote means to strengthen it. Initial efforts were made to extend the church into areas where it had little or no presence. King's Chapel was forced upon Boston in 1692. The next year, New York passed an establishment act even though there had been no call for Anglican worship. The minuscule Anglican community of Philadelphia organized Christ Church in 1694.

The most important step in the revival and extension of the Church of England in the colonies followed the appointment of Thomas Bray (1656–1730) as commissary for Maryland in 1696. Bray, unable to travel to America immediately, devoted his time to the organizing of the Society for the Promotion of Christian Knowledge, which began sending libraries to the New World. After a brief sojourn in the colonies in 1699, Bray returned to England and organized the Society for the Propagation of the Gospel (SPG) in 1701. With backing at the highest levels of the church, the society recruited priests for America and sent over 300 men to staff the churches during the next three-quarters of a century. The SPG put the Church of England in a position to compete with the other churches, but much of its gains were countered by the growth of Presbyterians, Baptists, and, later in the century, the influx of Pietism.

Presbyterians had been coming into the colonies throughout the seventeenth century but had been overwhelmed and in many cases, especially in New England, absorbed by the Congregationalists. Scattered Presbyterian churches were formed in New Jersey as early as 1667, but it was not until the arrival of Francis Makemie (1658–1708) in 1683 that the church began to assume a significant presence. Makemie traveled through the middle colonies organizing churches among the Scottish, Irish, and British settlers. The first presbytery was organized in Philadelphia in 1706 and included churches in Virginia, Maryland, and Delaware. It soon reached out to congregations in New York and New Jersey, and by 1716 was able to divide into four presbyteries and form a synod. The continued immigration from Scotland and Ireland promoted the rapid increase of the church's membership during the first half of the century and its spread throughout the colonies.

The development of Presbyterianism in the American colonies coincided with the emergence of a new movement in Germany. Philip J. Spener (1635–1705), a Lutheran minister at Frankfurt, began to appeal for a deeper Christian life through prayer, Bible study, loving service, and the informal gatherings of Christians. These issues were addressed in his 1675 dissertation, *Pia Desideria*, out of which the Pietist Movement was born. Forced out of Frankfurt he found his way to Berlin where he received the support in 1694 to found the University at Halle, which became the institutional center of the movement. The movement received a considerable boost in the early 1700s when Moravian refugees, Czechoslovakian Protestants, settled on the estate of Count Zinzendorf, which they renamed Herrnhut.

Pietism was spread to America primarily by the correspondence of American ministers with the Pietist leaders and became visible through the development of an evangelistic thrust among Presbyterians. The beginnings of this "revival" party is usually attributed to German-born Theodore J. Frelinghuysen, (c. 1691–1748), who came to America as a Dutch Reformed minister, and William Tennent (1673–1746), founder of the "log cabin" college in Bucks County, near Philadelphia. Among his most capable students were his three sons, Gilbert, John, and William Jr. The development of the Presbyterian revivalists began to split the Presbyterians over the acceptance and rejection of the new emphases.

Moravian Pietism was brought to the United States in 1735 by a group under the direction of Bishop August G. Spangenberg (1704–1792). On the voyage across the Atlantic, Spangenberg had a most important encounter with a young Anglican minister, John Wesley. The event led Wesley to worship with the Moravians upon his return to London and became integral to the series of events leading to his spiritual awakening in 1738. Wesley would go on to lead the most important phase of the Pietist Movement in England, Methodism. Among Wesley's close friends and asso-

ciates from college days was George Whitefield (1714–1770). In 1739, Whitefield called Wesley to Bristol, England, to take charge of his ministry among the miners. The move was, for Wesley, an important step in the development of Methodism. Whitefield's trip to America became a major event in the development of American religion.

George Whitefield began his evangelistic tour of the American colonies in Georgia. As he moved northward he rallied his support and each stop involved more people in what became a national revival of religion. It would later be called the Great Awakening. By the time he reached New England in the fall of 1740, the revival had drawn many unconverted into the churches; it sparked the Presbyterian and Baptist membership, which soared at a spectacular rate between 1740 and 1780. But the Awakening would also lead directly to major splits among the Presbyterians, Congregationalists, and even the Baptists, many of whom rejected what they saw as the emotional excesses of the meetings led by Whitefield and his imitators. People would often react in seemingly uncontrolled fits in the process of responding to the preacher's call to turn from sin. There is every evidence that rejection of the revivalism was strongest among the wealthier and educated classes in the cities and most acceptance found among the poorer and less educated peoples in the countryside.

In 1741 the Presbyterians divided into New School (accepting of revivalism) and Old School. The Congregationalists of New England experienced measurable losses as a new wave of Separatist congregations were formed by those persons most affected by the revival. The Separatists insisted upon a converted regenerate membership and tended to accept adult baptism as a sign of the regeneration. While some would eventually return to the Congregationalist fold, most of these congregations would become Baptist. Meanwhile, the Regular Baptists also split, as new Separate Baptists demanded that church members give clear evidence of a conversion experience. In their enthusiasm for the revival, they developed what seemed to the older Baptists to be an informal and noisy worship style, led by preachers who spoke in a distinctive, shrill, sing-song manner.

As the revival progressed among the English-speaking colonists, at least one new group that was to take on some importance in the next century appeared. German Lutherans began to filter into New Jersey, Pennsylvania, and New York in the first half of the century. The first congregation was organized at Hackensack, New Jersey, around 1704. By 1750, there was a string of congregations along the Hudson River through New Jersey into southeast Pennsylvania.

Attempts to organize were stifled in New York by the Dutch regime (which favored the Reformed church) and slowed in New Jersey and Pennsylvania where German settlers were slow to adapt to a government that would supply tax money for neither the building of churches nor the support of the ministry. The most prominent minister among the Lutherans was Henry Muhlenberg (1711–1787). Muhlenberg arrived in 1742 from the Pietist center at Halle, and brought some of that spirit with him. In 1748 he organized the Evangelical Lutheran Ministerium of Pennsylvania, regarded as the first Lutheran synodical organization in America. The second synod, the New York Ministerium, was not created until after the Revolutionary War, in 1786.

All churches were assisted by the attention given religion by the Great Awakening, and those who most readily adopted the revivalistic techniques began a generation of growth. By the beginning of the American Revolution, though almost totally confined to New England, the Congregationalists retained their status as the largest church in the colonies, with approximately 675 congregations. They were followed by the Presbyterians with 450, the Anglicans and Baptists with approximately 400, and lesser numbers of Lutherans (more than 200), Quakers (190), Reformed (180), and Roman Catholic (50). Had it not been for the American Revolution, there is every reason to believe that the churches in the American colonies might have developed much as they did in Canada. Because of the Revolution, a different course would be taken.

And because of the Revolution, it is important to make note of Methodism, the main organization in the British phase of the eighteenth century Evangelical Awakening. In the 1750s Methodism spread through England and reached Wales, Ireland, and Scotland. At about the same time, Methodists began to migrate to the American colonies, and by 1766 the first Methodist chapel was established by Robert Strawbridge (d. 1781) at Leesburg, Virginia. In 1769 Methodist founder John Wesley sent the first two preachers to oversee and promote the work in America. While centers were being established in the cities and at a few plantations along the coast, Methodism had barely begun when its work was interrupted by the Revolution. No one was aware of the difference in American religion it was to make once peace returned.

REVOLUTION AND TRANSITION. The churches in the colonies had gone through wars before. After each they had merely resumed their work and returned to normal. But the Revolution was different. It was not just another war. It destroyed a whole way of life and produced a new society. Religiously considered, the new nation that arose out of the success of the Revolution provided a distinct way of structuring religion, voluntary associations cut off both from official state support and public revenues. Each church would have to adjust to the new ways, and as might be expected, some would do it with far greater acumen than others. Necessary to the coming of this new world was a new religious-philosophical element that began to intrude upon the thinking of America's social and literary elites in the decades prior to the fight with the British homeland.

THE DEVELOPMENT OF DEISM. Nurtured within the bosom of Anglicanism as the Revolution approached was a new philosophy that denied the major affirmations of orthodox Christianity and set itself against the churches' leadership role. The new perspective was called Deism, and its importance lay not so much in the number of its adherents (which seems to have been quite small), but in 1) its acceptance by many of the men who were to provide the theoretical framework for the Revolution and the Constitution of the new nation, 2) the compatibility of its major affirmations with the irreligious elements of the American public, and 3) the role it played in further diluting the strength of the Church of England.

Such leading figures as Thomas Jefferson, Benjamin Franklin, George Washington, and James Madison, while retaining their formal affiliation with the established church, had left it in their hearts and begun to speak against it. Striking at the heart of Anglican control in the colonies, they opposed the designation of the Church of England (or any church) as the established church in the new nation.

Deists undergirded their attack on established religion with a general attack upon traditional Christianity. They derided theologians for creating complicated and speculative cosmologies beyond the comprehension of the people. They focused especially upon the concept of particular revelation, that God revealed certain truths to one person and not everyone, and the dogmas (such as the Trinity) that were derived from those claims of revelation. They argued that real religion was centered upon issues of reason and morality. They elevated reason above all religious speculation and demanded a rational Christianity.

The passing of the First Amendment with its clauses on religious freedom, though hammered through by the Deists, represents the coming together of the sectarian Protestant arguments for religious liberty that had developed out of persecution, and the Deist arguments that had developed out of their theological speculations and general anticlericalism. While Roger Williams had argued for freedom from persecution and the creation of a free environment for proselytization of unbelievers, the Deists bemoaned the evils of speculative systems imposed by clerics on an unwilling public. They had despaired of finding theological truth around

which to unify amid the variety of opinions everywhere espoused. Such religious speculation was of little consequence. All religions agreed upon the need for moral behavior, and a rational moral code included most everything that was important religiously. Given the Deist stance, no reason remained for persecuting people or even for demanding conformity on matters of mere religious opinion and speculation.

THE EFFECT OF DISESTABLISHMENT. The Revolution, or more directly, the resulting Constitution of the new nation, served to free religion within the republic. While apologists for state-established religion have argued for its role in promoting religion in general and have cited disestablishment as a sign of societal secularization, religious establishments have done as much to suppress religious expression as they have to support it. Established religions, such as colonial Congregationalism in New England, were organized in accord with the wishes of the social elite. Through the state religion, the government controlled, regulated, and limited religious expression. It discouraged the formation and expression of religion, especially among those most alienated from the ruling class. It thus kept and/or drove many otherwise potentially religious people into a state of irreligion, by limiting their choice to a religion in which they do not believe or no religion at all.

In situations dominated by a state religion, only the most committed (in New England's case, the Quakers) persist in their religious alternative as the state attempts to bring them into conformity. The volumes on religious persecution are filled with accounts of those who did resist, and American colonial history has its chapters in such volumes.

In freeing those formerly persecuted for their religious impulses, the First Amendment also created a situation in which new innovative religious gestalts could emerge, And as new varieties of religion became available, greater numbers became involved with the religious life. In the United States, the long term result of religious freedom has been the steady growth of the percentage of the population who claim membership in a religious group (beginning with little more than 15 percent in 1790) and, in the last half of the twentieth century, the voluntary movement of the overwhelming majority of the American public into religious organizations (currently above 75 percent). The destruction of government-backed religious controls has produced the most religious nation on earth.

AFTERMATH OF THE REVOLUTION. The American Revolution, significant battles of which occurred in every part of the colonies, thoroughly disrupted the entire country. For the churches, it meant disruption of services, confiscation and even destruction of church buildings, and loss of members. Congregations were divided by conflicting loyalties, though interestingly enough, no new church bodies appeared as a result of the war.

In one sense the Congregationalists were least affected by the war. A number of ministers were identified with the Patriots' cause, and in spite of the church's identification with the state prior to the Revolution, its conflicts with the British government (such as its resistance to the planting of a Church of England congregation in Boston) left it in good standing when peace returned. Congregationalism did not, however, remain unscathed. First, it suffered an immediate loss of membership and a membership drain through the remainder of the century as British Loyalists left New England to resettle in Canada. Also, even though Congregationalism was the country's largest church body and had its membership concentrated in New England, it had to recognize that the majority of New Englanders were not church members. Out of that recognition, Connecticut passed a Toleration Act in 1784, a prelude to complete disestablishment in 1818. Massachusetts, the last to separate church and state, disestablished the church in 1833.

In the long run, Congregationalism suffered more severely from the spread of the deistic religious spirit in New England. Harvard had already become infected with anti-Trinitarian thought, and by the time Massachusetts disestablished, the church was in the midst of the Unitarian controversy that would result in the loss of many of its most prominent parishes. In spite of the losses to Canada and to the Unitarians, Congregationalism continued to grow at a very slow pace, but it steadily fell in the ranking of Protestant churches. It continued to exert a significant influence for another century primarily through its educational leadership and the allegiance of New England's elite to its ranks.

As the war closed, there was some doubt as to whether Anglicanism could ever find a place in American life. Identified as the church of the enemy, it existed in an extremely hostile atmosphere. The SPG missionaries deserted it. Of the few who remained, many were not allowed to serve their parishes because of their Loyalist sympathies. The rector at Boston's King's Chapel defected to the Unitarian cause and took the church with him.

Disestablishment also came swiftly and harshly to the Church of England in the colonies. The church had been so intricately tied into secular structures, disestablishment destroyed both its financial base and legal status. Formerly somewhat dependent on the leadership of bishops, of which it now had none, it lost almost a decade in the search of episcopal authority. The need for a bishop led the Connecticut parishes to reorganize and select one of their number, Samuel Seabury (1729–1796), as their bishop-elect. He was able to obtain apostolic orders from the nonjuring Scottish bishops (bishops whose church rejected the established Presbyterian church of Scotland), but the ministers and parishes in the southern and middle colonies did not want Scottish orders. They reorganized and elected William White (1748–1836), Samuel Provoost (1742–1815), William Smith, and David Griffith as their bishops-elect and waited for an opening in England. White and Provoost were finally able to obtain orders in London in 1787. They proceeded to organize the Protestant Episcopal Church in the U.S.A. and rebuild its work among the still loyal members located primarily in southeastern Pennsylvania, Delaware, Maryland, and Virginia. They also were able to bring the work under Seabury in New York and Connecticut into the larger fellowship. Like the Congregationalists, the new church was able to keep the allegiance of many of the new nation's more wealthy citizens.

Entering the country in the 1760s, the Methodists were almost too small to count as the Revolution began. However, they were solidly identified with the Church of England, having constituted themselves as a religious society within that church. Because of Wesley's political tracts, they were also identified with the Tory cause. Like the Anglican priests, the Methodist preachers, except for Francis Asbury (1745–1816), returned to England as a result of the Revolution. Methodism was largely shut down and Asbury forced to live in retirement during the war years. After the war, the Methodists were the first to greet Washington with protestations of loyalty, and then quickly turned to the task of reorganizing in the light of the changed situation. In 1784 the American preachers met at Barrett's Chapel in rural Maryland to organize the Methodist Episcopal Church. They elected Asbury their first bishop and began to develop their life now free of the Church of England. They were, along with the Baptists, to receive the greatest benefits from the changes that occurred.

Presbyterians, primarily identified with the Revolution, lost little, considering that their churches, concentrated in New Jersey, Pennsylvania, and Delaware, were in close proximity to much of the fighting. They benefited greatly from the continued influx of Scottish and Scottish-Irish immigrants, and membership grew substantially from 1770 through the end of the century.

Few groups so benefited from the Revolution as did the Baptists. They had been the most vocal of the two major dissident churches in colonial America, especially upon the issues of religious freedom and disestablishment, and had become as a whole strong supporters of the Revolution. After the war, they led the fight in New England for disestablishment and when it occurred were quick to claim the spoils.

Like the Baptists, the Quakers held their own during the war years. As a group the pacifist Friends did not participate, a perenni-

al source of community hostility during wartime, but the war did not seem to stop their growth. They began the nineteenth century as one of the larger colonial bodies.

The Dutch Reformed and the German groups (Lutheran, Reformed, Mennonite, etc.) of Pennsylvania were basically dependent upon immigration for growth. The war seemed but a momentary pause in the slow growth of the Dutch and the rapid growth of the German groups, with the Reformed and Lutherans receiving the most increase. The German Lutherans had begun to arrive in the colonies early in the eighteenth century. They came from all sections of the still divided nation-to-be and were only beginning to be organized as the war began. Leading spokespersons represented a wide spectrum of opinion on the Revolution, from those opposed to the colonists' cause to those who defended the German king who sat on the British throne. When the war ended the Lutherans resumed their very basic task of learning to build churches, print religious literature, and provide pastoral leadership in a land that refused to support their church in ways they had been taught to expect.

THE CHURCHING OF THE WEST: CHANGE THROUGH IMMIGRATION AND PROSELYTISM. By the turn of the century, all of the churches had recovered from the war and reorganized for work in the new United States. The new country presented them with a monumental task. Within the first generation the geographical area of the United States greatly expanded, first to the Mississippi River and then by the Louisiana Purchase to the Rockies and beyond. Along with the geographical expansion, the population exploded due to immigration. Beginning with almost four million in 1790 (when the first census was taken), the population tripled by 1830 and almost doubled again by the time of the Civil War. After the war, the numbers increased even more dramatically, with over 12 million coming in each of the last two decades of the century.

Throughout the century, no religious group was able to adequately cope with the massive population growth. Few, other than the Roman Catholics, could cross the language barrier from English majority to the German minority (the only significant minority through the early nineteenth century). In the attempts, however, religious groups could essentially adopt one of three programs: First, some religious groups sought out those immigrants who shared their Old World country of origin and defined their basic task as providing them with the American version of the same familiar church that they had left at home. Many groups, mostly the non-English- speaking ones such as the Lutherans, received most of their growth in this manner, the Roman Catholic Church being most successful.

Second, many immigrant groups, both English-speaking and not, brought their religion with them and established a new branch of the church of their homeland in America. Thus the number of new denominations increased steadily as most of the European sects were transplanted to America. In the establishment and growth of the predominantly immigrant/ethnic churches and religions lies half the story of American religion in the next century.

Third, the majority of the population had left behind a situation in which church membership and citizenship were largely synonymous, and in their new free situation they chose to support no religion, profess no religious affiliation, and/or join no church. Churches could begin massive efforts to bring the population into the religious life they offered. Most churches engaged in evangelism, some limited to one language or ethnic group. In the relative success of their evangelistic endeavors lies the other half of the story of the next phase in American religion.

THE SECOND GREAT AWAKENING. Symbolic of the changes that were to occur in the new nation was a conference of Methodist ministers in Lexington, Kentucky, April 15–16, 1790. Though still establishing itself along the eastern seaboard, Methodism was already reaching out to the new settlers on the other side of the mountains. Under Bishop Asbury's direction, 12 preachers departed the conference to ride their circuits throughout Kentucky and into Tennessee. Six years later the church had recruited enough members and preachers to justify formally designating the area as a new conference, and in so doing, the general conference further enlarged the new conference to include all of the as yet un-churched territory to the west and north.

While Methodists were directing their circuit riders into the newly settled land, the lay-oriented Baptists were migrating in large numbers, setting up worship in private homes, and establishing chapels led by part-time farmer preachers. By 1800 they had no less than ten associations (of congregations) west of the mountains.

No less than the Methodists and the Baptists, the Presbyterians and Congregationalists felt the responsibility to plant Christian churches in the West. To some extent they had been influenced by the revivalistic fervor that had been present throughout the eighteenth century. Very soon after the war they began to form missionary societies and recruit ministers to pastor among their members who had migrated westward, to gather new converts, and to establish missions among the Indians. At least theoretically realizing the scope of the daily growing task, in 1801 the two theologically similar groups laid aside their organizational differences to unite efforts to convert the West. Missionaries were recruited and sent west to establish congregations, build colleges, and civilize the wilderness.

In the expanding frontier, measures as dramatic as the expanding country were needed. Some means of attracting the attention of the scattered and irreligious populous was needed. The program of the Plan of Union led to the establishment of some churches among groups of transplanted Easterners. These new congregations called the available seminary-trained pastors, and developed the familiar forms of parish life. Following such a plan, both Congregational and Presbyterian churches began to appear in the new population centers in the West. Because of their more efficient organizational structure, the Presbyterians were better equipped to plant congregations systematically, and soon turned the earlier situation around and received many of the scattered Congregational churches into their membership.

The program of the Presbyterians and the Congregationalists was simply inadequate for the West. They could not train ministers fast enough to serve the growing population. They could not move fast enough to keep up with the expanding frontier. Most importantly, they could not adapt fast enough to the new society being created in the West. The two churches, especially the Congregationalists, began to be left behind.

In contrast, the Methodists and the Baptists seemed perfectly suited to the new land. They were extremely mobile. Since they emphasized their preachers' willingness and ability to preach far above any educational demands, they could train and deploy new circuit riders with great speed. They gave revivalistic and evangelistic activity their highest priority. They stood ready to exploit any means to winning the unsaved.

The first new means for churching the frontier was the camp meeting. The idea grew out of a sacramental conference among Presbyterian churches under the leadership of James McGready (1758?–1817) in the Red River area of Kentucky. McGready was a graduate of the "Log Cabin" college and an enthusiastic preacher. At a four-day sacramental meeting held for the Red River church he served in 1800, emotions flowed freely and many were converted, especially by the unplanned exhortations of a visiting Methodist, John McGee. McGready, noting the excitement, publicized the next meeting and news of the events at Red River spread across the region. The next summer, over 10,000, including preachers of a variety of denominations, attended the gathering at Cane Ridge, Kentucky. The event became a turning point. The camp meeting combined entertainment, a break in the loneliness of farm life, and religion.

The Methodists and Baptists, and those Presbyterians associated with McGready, lost no time in integrating the camp meeting

into their regular program. In 1801 alone, the Methodists organized over 400 of them. But the Presbyterians in the East were not as enthusiastic. They condemned its excesses in 1805 and rejected McGready's work in the newly formed Cumberland Presbytery. In no small part, the church simply could not supply ministers fast enough to keep up with the new churches created out of the evangelistic efforts of McGready. Unable to reconcile his differences with the church, McGready and his colleagues formed the Cumberland Presbyterian Church.

The Cane Ridge meeting also changed the thinking of Presbyterian minister Barton Stone (1772–1844) who came away not only with a revivalistic mission but a conviction that the different churches who gathered at Cane Ridge should put away their differences and unite in the task of converting the frontier. Stone and his followers left the Presbyterian church and assumed the simple designation of Christian. In a similar action Thomas and Alexander Campbell withdrew from the Baptists in western Pennsylvania and took the name Disciples of Christ. Finally discovering each other, the two groups united in 1832.

Thus present on the frontier were four groups ready to evangelize the land, and evangelize they did. The Baptists, already among the larger church bodies due to their revivalistic efforts in the previous century, quickly moved to become the largest church body in America during the decades immediately after the Revolution. However, the Methodists moved even quicker. From a few thousand members in 1784, they jumped ahead of the Baptists in the 1820s and during the rest of the century never looked back. The Cumberland Presbyterians were able to keep pace for most of the time, and after the 1832 merger of the Stone and Campbell movements, the Disciples of Christ enjoyed spectacular growth.

About the same time that Methodist membership surpassed the other churches, a new phase of revivalism began with the introduction of the "new measures." Developed by Congregationalist evangelist Charles G. Finney (1792–1875), the new measures were designed to create a climate for revival and promote the crisis of decision, and in the hands of Finney and those who learned his techniques they brought literally millions into the churches. The techniques included the use of protracted meetings, community-wide evangelistic campaigns with no announced ending date; testimony meetings in which people told of their conversion experience (even females talked); the anxious bench, a place designated for those wrestling with decision; and cottage prayer meetings. The new measures, rejected by Finney's church, but adopted with great success by Baptists and Methodists, institutionalized revivalism.

IMMIGRATION IN THE NINETEENTH CENTURY. While the evangelistic endeavors of the Methodists and Baptists were altering the shape of the religious community, immigration was having an equal effect. Of the millions that immigrated prior to the Civil War, the single largest group was Irish, followed by the Germans. The Irish were predominantly Roman Catholic and while most Germans were Lutheran, many were also Roman Catholic. In addition, with the purchase of Louisiana, the French Roman Catholics of the territory were brought into the American Church. By mid-century, Roman Catholic membership rivaled that of the Methodists and Baptists. By the end of the century, with additional immigration from Poland and Italy, the church had jumped out ahead of both and emerged as the largest religious group in America.

The growth of the church is easily traced through the development of its hierarchy. Following the Revolution, John Carroll (1735–1815) was first appointed in 1784 superior of the American mission and in 1790 consecrated as the first bishop for the United States with his see in Baltimore. In 1808 Baltimore was made an archdiocese and New York City, Philadelphia, Boston, and Bardstown, Kentucky, received bishops. In 1846, 1847 and 1853 respectively, archdioceses were named in Oregon City (later Portland) for the American Northwest, St. Louis, and San Francisco.

During the second half of the century, the sites of the early bishops on the East Coast would be elevated to metropolitan (archdiocese) status, as would Chicago, Dubuque, St. Paul, and Milwaukee.

Second only to Roman Catholicism in receiving positive results from immigration were the Lutherans. First from massive German immigration in the first half of the century and then from Scandinavian immigration in the last half, the Lutherans grew in spite of their overall rejection of revivalism. The impact of Lutheranism on the country was, however, severely limited by the splintered condition of the church. As groups of Lutherans flocked into the country and settled in the frontier, they retained their linguistic and national boundaries, tended to organize separate synods in each region of the country, and were further split by internal doctrinal discord. Of major concern for the German community were issues of Pan-Germanism (i.e., union with the German Reformed Church) and the confessional-doctrinal emphasis championed by Charles P. Krauth (1823–1882) opposed to the pietist-experiential emphasis championed by Samuel S. Schmucker (1799–1873). By mid century, the Lutherans were divided into over 100 separate autonomous bodies. Since the end of the Civil War, they have pursued a process of union that has seen that number reduced to fewer than 20, with the overwhelming majority now in one denomination, The Evangelical Lutheran Church in America (1988).

The Presbyterians, apart from the Cumberlands, were able to hold their own in the growing nation because of significant immigration from Scotland and Northern Ireland. Like the Lutherans, the Scots brought with them the problems of the homeland, and in America the Presbyterians split into a number of bodies reflective of the Scottish divisions.

During the nineteenth century, the Quakers received no significant immigrant support, faced a major schism just as the western movement grew in significance, and abandoned growth in the South over the slavery issue. Most importantly, Quakers quickly discovered that aggressive revivalism conflicted with their emphasis upon the inner light. Early in the century, they simply ceased to grow in significant numbers. They remain as a small body whose significance lies in its idealistic dissent on a number of issues such as peace and social justice, which has placed it outside the mainstream of American life but given it a remarkable role as an agent for change in that society.

SLAVERY AND THE DEVELOPMENT OF THE BLACK CHURCHES. In the nineteenth century, one issue seriously split the American religious community: slavery and its accompanying racial attitudes. The slavery issue, considered in its broadest aspect, had two overarching influences on the development of religious life in America. First, it split several of the older predominantly white denominations so deeply that the divisions have yet to be healed. Second, it led to the development of a number of separate predominantly black denominations.

As the division between the white people of the North and South widened over the institution of slavery, the churches that included those people felt the same tension as the nation. The largest of the Protestant groups, the Methodist Episcopal Church, divided first. It had originally tried to keep the peace in the family by pushing the abolitionists out into the Wesleyan Methodist Church in 1843. But the next year it opened the general conference with the scandal of a bishop from Georgia who had inherited some slaves. Bishop Andrew refused to move from his home state, was unable by Georgia law to free his slaves, and planned to continue as an active raveling bishop. The church, unable to resolve the issue, voted to divide itself into two jurisdictions. The outcome was a division of the church into the Methodist Episcopal Church and the Methodist Episcopal Church, South.

The Baptists faced a similar problem precipitated by the refusal of the American Baptist Foreign Missionary Convention to accept slaveholders for positions as missionaries. In 1844 the Alabama and Georgia state conventions had forced the issue. After their rebuff in 1845, the Southerners formed the Southern Baptist Convention. The Presbyterians waited until the war began, but in 1861, they too split into two bodies.

The issues raised by the slavery debates in the middle of the nineteenth century had been argued by the Methodists in the northern states soon after the formation of the Methodist Episcopal Church. Staunchly abolitionist at its beginning, it stepped back from its position as it grew in the South. Northern congregations that had been integrated began to institute segregationist policies. Blacks were relegated to balconies, were the last to be served communion, and were generally treated as second class citizens. Some walked out and formed all black congregations. Finally, in the early nineteenth century, the majority of free black people in the North left the Methodist Episcopal Church to found three black denominations: the African Methodist Episcopal Church, the African Methodist Episcopal Zion Church, and the Union Church of Africans. The first black Baptist churches in the North were organized in Boston (1804), New York (1808), and Philadelphia (1809). It was not until the 1830s that the first associations were formed, the Providence Baptist Association in Ohio and the Wood River Association in Illinois. Missionary work by blacks led to the formation of the most substantial organizations. The American Baptist Missionary Convention formed by blacks in 1840 not only sent foreign missionaries, but directed the organization of Baptist freedman after the Civil War.

In the South, black Baptists appeared as the church spread among slave owners. The first congregations of Baptists were not organized until just before the American Revolution, however, as most slave owners were reluctant to allow independent organizations, including religious ones, among the slaves. Methodist slaves were known from almost the time of Methodism's arrival in the colonies in the 1760s. Quite early they were organized into classes and at least two black local preachers, Harry Hoosier and Richard Allen, traveled and preached with Francis Asbury.

After the Civil War, the black Baptist and Methodist churches enjoyed a period of growth as they expanded their work among the freedmen. Churches such as the African Methodist Episcopal Church, under the control of northern freed blacks, had not been allowed to recruit in the South, and quickly made up for lost time. The Methodists also added a new major organization, the Colored (now Christian) Methodist Episcopal Church, originally composed of the former slave members of the Methodist Episcopal Church, South, segregated during the Reconstruction era. Black Baptists formed a number of regional and national organizations that merged in the 1890s to become the National Baptist Convention. Most black people in the United States are Baptists, approximately 60 percent if we can believe the figures. The several million Methodists form the second greatest block.

In lesser numbers, black people have been proselytized by and have responded to most religious traditions found in America, and have formed religious organizations representative of those different religious families. After the Civil War, most of the larger denominations established missions among the freedman. Unfortunately, apart from slavery, Northerners showed the same racial attitudes concerning blacks that were prevalent in the South. Even so, some blacks became (Northern) Methodists, Presbyterians, Congregationalists, Episcopalians, and Roman Catholics. While welcoming black members as a whole, these churches instituted a pattern of racial segregation at the congregational and regional levels. On the other hand, in joining the predominantly white denominations, black church members brought into the black community all of the diverse religious commitments, theological tensions, and variation in worship of white society. As in the white community, the black denominational structures became the stable organizational units that shaped the larger religious community and set the pattern of belief and action at the congregational level. The varying response to issues facing the black community—the ethiopianism of the 1930s, the Civil Rights movement in the 1960s (which split the Baptists), and the attempt to identify a common black religious experience in the 1970s—has largely followed denominational biases.

THE INDIAN RESPONSE TO THE WESTERN SPREAD OF CHRISTIANITY.

Early Indian policy of the newly formed United States focused upon the "civilization" of the Indian and envisioned the Christian churches as the main agent in that process. In 1819 the government passed a measure creating a "Civilization Fund" through which it subsidized church missions that aimed not only at conversion but Americanization of the Native Americans. Even prior to the 1819 action, pressures were mounting for the removal of the Indians to the far west. A major step in that program followed the discovery of gold in Georgia, and the subsequent passing of the Removal Act of 1830 that pushed most of the members of Five Tribes out of the Southeast.

Following the Civil War, as serious settlement west of Independence, Missouri, expanded, the settlers' demands for Indian lands led to a series of Indian wars and the confinement of the Indians to designated reservations. The pressures on the Indians in the face of the overrun of the land by whites and the development of the dependency of the Indians on the government and the churches, had two significant religious consequences. First, many Indians responded to the evangelical efforts of the hundreds of missions established by Christian churches and converted to Christianity.

Almost all of the larger church bodies have Indian members, the result of missions established in the nineteenth or early twentieth century. In recent years, the majority of the older Christian churches have also moved to remove the Native American congregations from any stigma as a mission and to integrate them into the total life of the denomination. However, many smaller churches and independent missionary agencies continue to support "missions" on or near the reservations and have, since World War II, developed additional missions in the urban centers where many Indians migrated.

As the Indian life was disrupted by the westward rush of white society, some Indians who did not accept Christianity developed alternatives that attempted to go beyond the tradition of any particular tribe and reach all Native Americans with a combination of religious fervor and political protest. Of the several movements that developed, the Ghost Dance movement was by far the most important. Born among the Paiute in the 1870s, the movement found its great prophet in Wovoka (1858–1932), a Paiute who lived most of his life in Nevada. Near his thirtieth birthday, he had a revelation during a solar eclipse. To those who practiced the distinctive circular dance already a part of the movement, the revelation promised a return of the Indian dead, the eradication of sickness, and a time of prosperity. A date during 1891 was set for the change. In the meantime, he urged followers to drop any overt hostility to the whites and become "civilized." The prophecy found immediate support among the Plains tribes, especially among the Oglala Sioux. They introduced the holy shirt, the design of which had been received in a vision, which would protect the wearer from any harm, even the bullets of the U. S. Army.

The Ghost Dance movement climaxed at Wounded Knee (1890) where 300 Ghost Dance participants were killed; a clear demonstration of the inability of the shirts to provide the promised protection. While the dance survived into the middle of the twentieth century, it had lost its mass appeal and left a vacuum soon to be replaced with another movement developed in Mexico. The peyote religion spread as the ghost dance receded, and offered a mystical alternative to the earlier apocalyptic movement. Drawing upon both Christian and Native American themes, it added the strong psychological impact of the peyote's ability to alter consciousness. While preaching many of the values that the white culture wished to spread among the Indians, it, in addition, offered a note of defiance in its use of the peyote. After the formal incorporation of the movement as the Native American Church in 1918, it spread among numerous Indian tribes and became a powerful force in building the Native Americans' identity as one people. It also enjoyed an interesting history in the courts as it established its right to use the sacred cactus.

THE POST-WAR SCHISM OF AMERICAN PROTESTANTS.

In the last half of the nineteenth century, the major North American Protestant groups were rent with controversy. Tensions became evident as a new set of issues that demanded a response confronted the churches. The challenges of the new issues were qualitatively different from those at the beginning of the century that had demanded an increase in activity and endeavor. These issues appeared as new ideas that carried the force of scientific and academic backing. They also demanded acceptance of a totally new world view.

From Germany came a new way of looking at the Bible. Critical scholars had begun to question the accuracy of the biblical texts in several ways. Some challenged the legitimacy of the miracle stories in the name of science. What could not happen within the boundaries of the known laws of the universe, probably did not happen. Others challenged the integrity of the texts, especially the first five books of the Bible. They denied the Mosaic authorship and suggested that these books were a complex edited narrative created by combining into a single text several older texts that had been written by different people in different circumstances. The new scholarship was seen by many as defying the authority of the Bible, which most Christians understood rather literally.

For many the challenge to biblical authority by the German critics seemed to resonate with the new claims in the sciences of geology and biology. Geologists studying the nature of various earth-building processes, such as volcanos, concluded that the Earth was not a few thousand years old, but hundreds of thousands, even millions of years old. Charles Darwin and his colleagues concluded that not only had life forms evolved from one species to another but that even humanity was a product of evolution from other primates. The new sciences presented a complete alternative to the literal biblical account of God creating the species and separately creating the first man and woman.

Also, as the overseas mission programs of the churches expanded, interest in and information about religions in foreign lands grew. To some, it became evident that Buddhism, Hinduism, Islam, and the other great world religions offered a sophisticated spirituality and would not simply capitulate in the face of the presentation of the Christian message. Some voices arose to suggest that Eastern religions could possibly teach the West something vital and important. The impact of the other religions was brought home at the 1893 World's Parliament of Religions where Hindu Swami Vivekananda, theosophist Annie Besant, and Buddhist Anagarika Dharmapala drew huge audiences.

While new ideas challenged church leaders' thoughts, immigration was producing unprecedented growth in American urban centers ill equipped to deal with sudden heavy population increases. Industrialists looking for cheap labor exploited the new urbanites. Slums appeared as many immigrants were crowded into inadequate housing. Drunkenness was common. Churches could not (or would not) expand fast enough to serve the immigrants (many of whom spoke no English and/or came from Roman Catholic countries). Scholars and activists began to suggest that older solutions to social problems, usually directed towards reforming individuals through hygiene, education, and hard work, were inadequate. What America needed was a change in the system that allowed slums and exploited workers to exist. Answers were suggested by the new science of sociology, which suggested that social problems could be solved by human manipulation of social structures. Among the most popular solutions was some form of socialism.

Church leaders responded to these intellectual and social challenges in basically two ways. A growing number of them suggested a positive response to the new ideas and began to seek ways of reconciling Christianity to biblical criticism, evolution, the existence of sophisticated world religions, and the crises in the cities.

Those who took such a positive stance, yielding to the demands of the modern age, came to be called Modernists. Other church leaders saw in the Modernist revisions of the faith not just adapting to a new situation but the destruction of Christianity and its replacement by a different gospel. They responded by calling their ministerial colleagues and the churches of the land to once again affirm the nonnegotiable fundamentals of the faith, and in so doing they became known as Fundamentalists.

Modernism, the progenitor of contemporary liberal Protestantism, came to be identified with a variety of specific opinions. Modernists accepted biblical criticism and redefined the nature of biblical authority. In the process they discarded the literal interpretation of the early chapters of Genesis and the biblical miracle stories and emphasized instead the eternal lessons to be drawn from them. Modernists accepted the opinions of geologists and biologists about the age of the universe and the evolutionary origin of humanity. However, they suggested that evolution was not a process without obvious purpose; that it did not follow natural selection, but derived from the constant action of God, drawing life and humanity to higher levels of attainment. This perspective was called theistic evolution.

In their encounter with world religions, Modernists such as James Freeman Clarke, a Unitarian professor teaching at the University of Chicago, attempted to make the case for the superiority of Christianity, not as true religion over against the falsehood of all other religions, but as the most true religion in a world of religions of partial truths. Each religion contains elements recognized as good and noble, but only Christianity contains goodness and truth in their fullness. As a major expression of this approach, the League of Liberal Clergymen in Chicago organized the World's Parliament of Religions in 1893.

In their response to the cities, Modernists borrowed well known biblical symbols that they identified with the socialist program of radical changes in late nineteenth century society. They spoke of building the kingdom of God and ushering in a millennium of peace and justice through the reorganization of social patterns. They called their message the social gospel.

Modernist theology was optimistic in the extreme and based upon a positive view of human nature. Humanity, in its opinion, had evolved beyond its animal nature over many thousands of years. The human condition was not so much due to sin and human depravity. It was an effect of the continued presence of the animal past. Humans had evolved out of the animal world, and they could now evolve mentally and spiritually; they inevitably must evolve into the life of the kingdom of God. Progress became the watchword of Modernism, and a utopian hope for humanity's future undergirded every action.

Fundamentalists claimed that Modernism undercut biblical authority in the name of science and replaced Christian commitments with a different religion, hardly recognizable as Christian. As the nineteenth century moved to its close, they began to see seminary professors spreading Modernism in their class rooms and ministers voicing it from prominent pulpits. The most visible erosion appeared in the Baptist, Presbyterian, and Congregationalist churches, those older churches with a strong Calvinist confessional heritage. In the first stage of the battle, the conservatives charged individuals with deviating from confessional standards. Beginning in the 1870s, the public was treated to a series of heresy trials, the most famous being the Presbyterian actions against David Swing, Charles Briggs, and Henry Perserved Smith. A variety of denominations took official action (from censoring to dismissal) against instructors in their schools who voiced Modernist opinions.

At first, the conservatives showed their strength, but by the turn of the century sentiment turned against them. The denominations became reluctant to condemn Modernists who were filling more and more denominational posts. Sensing a loss of control, the conservatives began to organize. Interdenominational conferences, the most famous being the annual gatherings at Niagara Falls, provided places for conservatives to find strength, strategize, and organize. Out of the Niagara conferences came a series of statements of faith affirming "fundamental" beliefs. The conservatives also began to establish independent schools where fundamental doctrines would be upheld and taught. Among the first were Moody Bible Institute in Chicago and the Philadelphia College of the Bible.

The conservative cause received a significant boost in the first decade of the twentieth century when Presbyterian California oilman Lyman Stewart began to divert money to the conservative cause. In 1906 he helped establish the Bible Institute of Los Angeles, which became the nexus for West Coast Fundamentalists. He brought R. A. Torrey from Moody to be the dean of the college. Withdrawing from Immanuel Presbyterian Church, he gave the initial endowment for the independent Church of the Open Door, the pulpit of which Torrey also assumed. He gave money toward the production of the Scofield Reference Bible (published in 1909), whose notes, written by lawyer turned pastor C. I. Scofield, systematically presented the Fundamentalist position. In 1909 he gave the money to produce a series of booklets, *The Fundamentals*, which were mailed to pastors across the country. These booklets, which gave the conservatives their name, launched a new assertive phase of the conservative movement. That new phase took organizational form immediately after World War I, with the formation of the World Christian Fundamental Association.

Fundamentalism and Modernism represent two distinctly different ways of viewing the world and Christianity. The battles of the nineteenth century set the issues and created two camps within each of the affected denominations. In the decades between the World Wars the growing hostility between the camps would lead to showdown battles that finally divided the Presbyterians and Baptists, and left the Modernists firmly in control of the older denominations. The Fundamentalists were pushed out into new denominations, the formation of which permanently institutionalized the Fundamentalist-Modernist controversy and has kept it alive to this day. The cleavage within the Protestant camp in North America between conservative evangelical Protestants and liberal Protestants shows no sign of being resolved, as both sides have strong support from large denominational bodies.

METHODISTS DIVIDE. While Presbyterians and Baptists launched their fights over doctrinal issues, the Methodists had little time for the debate. They believed that heartfelt religion and the living of the Christian life were more important than doctrinal purity. Then when the early Niagara conferences began to produce doctrinal statements, the Methodists had little sympathy for the emphasis placed upon the depravity of man. They championed the possibility of human perfection and the need for sanctified holy living.

After the Civil War the church had been swept by a revival as evangelists promised the born again Methodists the possibility of a second encounter with the Holy Spirit as dramatic and almost as important as the first born again experience. This encounter, this second blessing, as it was termed, would go beyond justifying the sinner and guaranteeing a place in heaven; it would actually make the Christian blessed in perfect love. This theme of Holiness and perfection had been present, with varying emphases, throughout Methodist history. But as it reached a new peak in its acceptance, numerous Holiness camp meeting associations were established throughout the several Methodist denominations.

In the 1880s, Methodists began to back away from the Holiness emphasis. Prominent leaders championed the cause of gradual growth in grace over against a single critical event such as the second blessing. Critics also charged that the associations were placing too much emphasis upon the minutiae of the personal habits of Christians. District superintendents struggled to control the otherwise independent Holiness associations. The tension reached a climax in Illinois where Holiness leaders began to call for members to "come out" of the indifferent and often hostile Methodist church and form independent Holiness congregations. While never leaving in large enough numbers to slow the steadily climbing Methodist membership figures, many Holiness people did separate to found congregations that would soon band together in small regional Holiness denominations. A few of these remain today, but most merged into the older schismatic Methodist churches that had retained a Holiness emphasis (the Wesleyans and the Free Methodist Church) or combined with other regional bodies to form national denominations, such as the Church of the Nazarene.

Even before the independent Holiness groups had consolidated their gains, the movement was swept with a new teaching that originated in a Holiness Bible school in Topeka, Kansas, under the leadership of Charles Fox Parham. The teaching promised that not only was there a second blessing available to Christians, there was a third: the baptism of the Holy Spirit. While the second blessing cleansed the heart, the third filled the believer with power. Accompanying Spirit baptism and confirming its truth, proponents asserted, were supernatural manifestations, the gifts of the Spirit, the first and most important being the individual's miraculously speaking in a foreign language which, under normal circumstances, he or she did not understand. They saw speaking in tongues as a new revival of the events of Pentecost described in the biblical Book of Acts.

Pentecostalism was taken from Topeka to Houston by Parham and from Houston to Los Angeles by Parham's student, William J. Seymour, a black Holiness preacher. In Los Angeles Pentecostal manifestations created a sensation, and for over three years Seymour led daily meetings held in the building on Azusa Street to which visitors flocked from around the continent. Within those three years the Pentecostal movement spawned congregations across North America.

The Holiness and Pentecostal movements attracted the most conservative Methodists just as Fundamentalism would later attract the most conservative Baptists and Presbyterians. By the time of the major schisms in the 1920s, Methodism had already lost many of those who would possibly have aligned themselves with the Fundamentalists, especially in their affirmations of biblical authority and creation. Methodism passed through the heat of the Fundamentalist battles with only minor skirmishes. But just as Fundamentalism created a major schism in Protestantism, so too did the Holiness and Pentecostal movements, both now claiming millions of adherents in America and still growing.

HOMEGROWN RELIGION. In the midst of the expansion of religion as the nation was being churched in the nineteenth century, new religious impulses appeared among the New Englanders who were being subjected to the efforts of the revivalists. Though often beginning with issues raised by the older religious groups, they provided new solutions and in the process created genuinely new gestalts of the religious life. Among the first was the Latter-Day Saints, popularly called the Mormons. Sharing many common roots with the equally indigenous Disciples of Christ, the church sought a unity of religions of the frontier, and found that unity in a new revelation given to Joseph Smith Jr. Spiritualism grew up in reaction to scientific critiques of religious hopes for an afterlife. Accepting the critique, it then utilized scientific models to claim that spiritualist phenomena provided "proof" that life after death is real. New England Transcendentalism, centered upon the community at Brook Farm, was among the first American religions to draw upon Asian wisdom themes.

While Mormonism and Spiritualism emerged in the countryside, the important late nineteenth century groups, Theosophy, Christian Science, and New Thought, started their work in the cities—New York, Boston, and Chicago. Over the years each movement produced numerous splinter groups (over 100, for example, can be traced to Theosophy) that would result in the formation of a new family of religions. Each would also build its own agenda without particular reference to the continuing life of the Christian churches and the ideas deemed important in their centers of learning.

The same impulse that produced the nineteenth century sectarian movements was similar to impulses that had sought expression in previous centuries. Only in the nineteenth century, the promise of religious freedom allowed these groups to emerge, proselytize, and to a relative degree prosper. In previous centuries, their founders would possibly have been outlawed and the groups hounded out of existence. In this century they had only to withstand the press of popular opinion.

IMMIGRATION 1880–1924. By 1880 the population of the United States had reached above 50 million. During the next 25 years, before the brakes were applied to immigration, it would double. People from many nationalities, previously represented by only scattered individuals, now came in large numbers. In colonial times, immigration had brought those religious groups that still dominate the patterns of American religious life. After the American Revolution and through most of the nineteenth century, immigration would continually add members to the older groups and steadily bring new ones, most of which were variations of the older groups. The spurt of immigration between 1880 and 1924 would substantially alter America's religious landscape (already bulging with the indigenous innovative religions) by markedly increasing the variety of religious expression. Greeks, Romanians, Bulgarians, and Serbians brought all the variations of Eastern Orthodoxy. Russian and Polish Jews overwhelmed and recreated the small German Jewish community. The Japanese added their expressions of Buddhism to the Chinese forms. Indians brought Sikhism and Hinduism.

Eastern Orthodoxy had been introduced into California in the early nineteenth century and into Alaska even earlier. However, it remained small and the few parishes of the Russian Orthodox Church housed believers of every national-ethnic group. In the late nineteenth century, immigration brought people from predominantly Orthodox lands in such numbers that each was in turn able to organize separate parishes and eventually form separate dioceses. Some groups, such as the Ukrainians, were able to create autonomous jurisdictions for the first time in the free climate of North America. After the Russian Revolution, and again after World War II, the Orthodox churches would further divide along political lines creating even more new church groups.

Jews had come to America in three waves. In the seventeenth century, a small number of Sephardic Jews (Jews with a Spanish background) emigrated to the colonies. The first synagogue, Congregational Shearith Israel was organized in New York in 1728. The second synagogue, in Newport, Rhode Island, still stands, but its members were driven out by the British capture of the city during the Revolution. There were approximately 3,000 Jews in America as the colonial era ended.

During the nineteenth century enough German Jews came into the United States to overwhelm the small colonial community. By 1840 there were approximately 15,000 Jews. Most importantly, the new immigrants were heirs of a liberalizing influence that had grown among German synagogues. They wanted revision of the traditional forms of Jewish life and worship, stripping away nonessential items that tended to alienate the non-Jewish community. By the middle of the century, in religiously free America, they created a new way of doing Judaism: Reform Judaism. In response the more traditional Jews organized to defend their old ways; they became known as Orthodox Jews.

The wave of Eastern European Jews that began in the 1880s overwhelmed the German Jewish community as completely as it had overwhelmed the colonial community. Over three million came, and both Orthodox and Reform communities vied for the immigrants' allegiance. In the midst of this tension, a new form of Judaism that attempted to mediate between the two camps appeared. Conservative Jews respected the tradition, but made some mild reforms of what were considered less essential items. Over several decades, each group attained approximately the same number of adherents, and each organized both rabbinical and congregational associations on a national level.

Religiously, the Jewish community is built around the three ways of doing Judaism: Reform, Conservative, and Orthodox. Equally important, standing outside of these three groups, were the large number of Jews who adhered to none of the three. As with the settled Gentile community, approximately one-half of the Jewish immigrants acknowledged no religious affiliation. Over the years, in the pluralistic climate of the United States, many of those unattached Jews found their way into the wide variety of non-Jewish religions, especially non-Christian forms, and some became prominent leaders. Others created Jewish versions of non-Jewish religions such as Christian Science and Humanism.

No groups were so affected by the immigration laws as were the Asians. In the 1850s the Chinese began to arrive in America in large numbers. While many were Christians, a large number followed the several Chinese faiths, especially Buddhism. Anti-Chinese feeling led to the passage of an exclusion act in 1882. Japanese and Filipinos began to move into the West Coast to replace the Chinese as cheap labor. They brought their Buddhism and Catholicism respectively. However, public opinion began to turn against the Japanese and in 1908 a "gentleman's agreement" was reached with Japan to limit further immigration. During the first decade of the twentieth century, East Indians, mostly Punjabi, also came into Washington, Oregon, and California. As with the Japanese, they found themselves the object of public hostility. In 1917 Congress passed an Asian Exclusion Act that stopped immigration from all of Asia, except Japan. Prior to the 1917 act, several forms of both Hinduism and Buddhism had been introduced into America and had attracted non-Asian converts. After the 1917 act, that growth, now slowed considerably, continued through the development of non-Asian Hindu and Buddhist groups, most of which were small, with membership limited to a single urban center. They often existed quietly for years, relatively unknown even by their immediate neighbors.

However, in 1924 an omnibus immigration quota act, which assigned strict limits to the number of immigrants from each country that could enter the United States, stopped significant immigration not only from Asia, including Japan, but also from Southern and Eastern Europe. Thus not only was the spread of Buddhism and Hinduism stifled, but the growth of the Eastern Orthodox and Jewish communities measurably slowed. Since each of these communities possessed strong ethnic bondings that prevented evangelism outside of the ethnic group, further growth depended upon the community's birth rate.

TWENTIETH CENTURY PLURALISM: NEW PATTERN FOR THE TWENTIETH CENTURY. At the beginning of the twentieth century, between thirty and forty percent of the American populous were affiliated with a church or religious group. The majority of America remained unchurched, but a tremendous growth had been experienced by religion in general and the Christian churches in particular. They had doubled the percentage of the population religious affiliated. While the population had grown by 3-1/2 times, church membership had more than doubled that rate. In the process the number of different religious denominations also expanded greatly. There were fewer than 40 denominations in 1800. By the beginning of the twentieth century, some 200 different religious bodies representing 16 different denominational families could be found. Now there are more than 1,500.

Most religious people were in the major Christian bodies, the largest of which had become the Roman Catholic church. Over against Catholicism, the major Protestant churches found some unity and saw themselves collectively as the majority party in the land. In 1908 they gave expression to that unity by creating the Federal Council of Churches. The creation of the Federal Council occurred as the churches were facing the great conservative-liberal split between Fundamentalists and Modernists and be-

tween Methodism and the Holiness and Pentecostal churches. The council became the forum of liberal Protestantism. Among its first acts was the adoption of a slightly altered version of the Methodist Social Creed, an early statement of social concerns that incorporated important elements of the social gospel.

The council became the first successful expression of the ecumenical movement. Holding aloft the ideal of the unity of Christianity, in stark contrast to the numerous denominational divisions of the church, especially in America, ecumenists expressed the desire for the organic unity of Protestantism. The movement generated periodic waves of enthusiasm throughout the twentieth century, and can claim major accomplishments in the uniting of churches within the several Protestant families highlighted by the formation of the Evangelical Lutheran Church in America from mergers in 1918, 1930, 1960, and 1988; the United Methodist Church from mergers in 1939 and 1968; the Presbyterian Church (USA) from mergers in 1906, 1958, and 1983; and the United Church of Christ from mergers in 1931, and 1948.

Rejection of the council and the liberal ecumenical movement became an additional affirmation for the Fundamentalists as they pulled out of the larger denominations. In its place they organized two councils, the American Council of Christian Churches (1941) and the National Association of Evangelicals (1942), the former being the more conservative of the two. They limited their ecumenical activity to those with whom they were in essential doctrinal agreement. Pentecostals gave outward expression both to their growth and their distinctive presence in the American community by the organization of the Pentecostal Fellowship of North America. Years earlier, at the beginning of the Holiness revival, a National Holiness Campmeeting Association had been created. During the twentieth century it went through a process of reorganization to emerge as a council of Holiness churches, and in 1970 took the name, Christian Holiness Association.

The first half of the twentieth century continued the pattern of growth for the various religious groups, in the midst of which, liberal Protestants extended the ecumenical ideal to open contacts and build bridges of understanding with the Roman Catholic and Jewish communities. Those contacts were fruitful enough in the public sphere that by the middle of the century, sociologist Will Herberg could rightfully speak of America's three faiths—Protestant, Catholic, and Jew.

But other groups were also growing. The nineteenth century foreign language groups went through a process of Americanization and were ready to interact with the larger community. The Eastern Orthodox leaders formed the Standing Council of Orthodox bishops in 1960. The International New Thought Alliance formed earlier in the century had grown up with the metaphysical churches.

SINCE 1965. The gradual restructuring that had been occurring throughout the twentieth century was given a new impetus in 1965. That year Congress rescinded the Asian Exclusion Act and redistributed immigration quotas, allowing Asian, Eastern European, and Middle Eastern countries to send immigrants as never before. In the decades since its passing, this single act has done more to readjust the religious community in America than any other force. This action once again allowed the flow of immigrants from those countries that had been excluded in 1917 and 1924. The result has been twofold.

First, those communities that have their roots in Eastern and Southern Europe have been strengthened. Second, immigration from Islamic countries has for the first time occurred in significant numbers, with believers from throughout the diverse Muslim world settling in America. Eastern religions have extended their presence in America through both first-generation immigrant organizations and the unexpected conversion of thousands of young adult Americans to both Buddhism and guru-led Hindu religions. Over 100 different Hindu denominations have been planted in America since 1965 and over 75 forms of Buddhism currently exist. Each community now claims from three to five million adherents. Their rate of growth continues to be among the highest in the country.

During the twentieth century, the New Thought metaphysical churches (Religious Science, Divine Science, and the Unity School of Christianity) have become a familiar sight on American street corners. Now numbering adherents in the hundreds of thousands, their influence has permeated the mainstream of American culture through the spread of their literature. Unity material, especially its devotional monthly *Daily Unity*, now enters millions of homes. Even more noticeable was the spread of metaphysical thought through the extensive ministry of ministers such as the late Norman Vincent Peale, and more recently Robert Schuller and Oral Roberts, all of whom have been heavily influenced by New Thought ideas.

Occult religions, among the least understood religious options, have broken out of the small esoteric groupings that were so typical at the beginning of the twentieth century. Spiritualism, often thought of as merely a nineteenth century fad, experienced noticeable periods of revival after every war, and perpetuated itself in all of the major urban complexes. Theosophy, based upon teachings delivered to Helena Petrovna Blavatsky by what she claimed were ascended masters of wisdom, while never claiming more than a few tens of thousands of members, has spawned over 100 like organizations. Thus while occultism has yet to claim the number of, for example, Buddhism or Hinduism, it can truthfully claim this century as the time of an occult revival. Astrology reaches a steadily growing segment of the public. One needs no better indicator of the penetration of public consciousness by occult (as well as related Easter) ideas than the recent surveys that revealed that almost one-fourth of Americans believe in the concept of reincarnation, the idea that human souls inhabit a series of physical bodies over several lifetimes.

While the number of people attracted to metaphysics and the occult has increased with each generation, the distrust of organization that permeates both movements has stymied the growth of metaphysical groups to the extent that the spread of metaphysical ideas would seem to warrant. To perpetuate itself, the community must rely upon periods of the revival of its major concerns within the larger secular community, as it has yet to develop structures that can pass its teachings to the next generation through more traditional family structures. The New Age Movement of the 1980s, was the latest period of revival. It raised public awareness of metaphysical and occult ideas, brought thousands into the previously established occult-metaphysical fellowships, led to the formation of many new ones, and has seen the emergence of a network of metaphysical bookstores across North America.

AMERICAN RELIGIOUS GROUPS IN THE NEW MILLENNIUM. As of the 1990s, American religion can be seen as divided into 10 recognizable groups of denominations, each of which claims a substantial number of adherents through the membership of its member denominations. Each group is united by some common beliefs and commitments and separated from other groups by adherence to a distinct way of doing religion. Six of these groups are Christian and together can claim both a majority of American citizens and the bulk of America's religious adherents. The Christian community is divided into Roman Catholic, Eastern Orthodox, Liberal Protestant, Conservative Evangelical, Holiness, and Pentecostal-Charismatic.

There are over 50 million Roman Catholics in America making it three times larger than its closest competitor, the Southern Baptist Convention. It exists both as a single organization, and as a very inclusive mixture of ethnic parishes, religious orders, and diverse theologies. The church assumed an important role in the nineteenth century. It grew to become the nation's largest religious body and in many cities claimed the allegiance of the majority of citizens. Its earlier attempts to integrate its life into the American fabric and become an active participant in shaping social policy were thwarted by strong anti-Catholic sentiments, one of the few concerns around which competing Protestant sects could unite. Also, at the end of the nineteenth century, some prominent Catholic leaders proposed a program for realigning the church in America with some important American values. They called the church to emphasize its similarities with Protestantism rather than the differences. Unfortunately, this program, which became known in Europe as "Americanism," was denounced in a papal encyclical in 1899, and the American church pulled back from what appeared to be a new era of broad cultural engagement in favor of concentration upon more internal concerns. Only since World War II, with the generation of new leadership, the changes wrought at Vatican II, and the election of John F. Kennedy as president, has the church enjoyed a more positive image and been accepted as a stable and legitimate part of the American religious landscape. Its new and acknowledged role in American society is manifest in the thoughtful attention now given the regular pronouncements on public policy made by the National Conference of Catholic Bishops.

Similar, but in may ways essentially distinct from Roman Catholicism, is Eastern Orthodoxy. Emerging to prominence in America in the early twentieth century, the Orthodox groups have been committed to the preservation of both the Orthodox faith and the ethnic heritage of their constituencies. After the Russian Revolution, and with the spread of Communism following World War II, they were united by the problems resulting from the emergence of governments hostile to religion in many of their ethnic homelands. In the wake of World War II they have emerged as vocal participants, as well as a force with which to be reckoned, in the wider debates and ecumenical discussions. Many of the Orthodox groups, besides uniting in the Standing Conference of Orthodox Bishops, have extended their influence through affiliation with the National Council of Churches.

In the late nineteenth and early twentieth century, Protestantism split into at least four major camps, each distinct enough from the other and united enough to be considered a separate religious grouping. Aligned within the National Council of Churches (which superseded the Federal Council of Churches) are the major liberal Protestant denominations. They include the Protestant Episcopal Church, the Evangelical Lutheran Church in America, the Presbyterian Church (USA), the United Church of Christ, the United Methodist Church, the American Baptist Churches in the U.S.A., and the six major black Protestant groups (three Methodist churches and three Baptist conventions). As a whole, these are the older and larger Protestant bodies, the most socially oriented, the most accepting of contemporary scholarship (both secular and sacred), the most visible religious bodies in America.

One measure of the relative prominence of religious groups in a society is the role given particular religious groups in a public setting, and during most of American history, Protestantism's leadership in shaping America was religiously unchallenged. Liberal Protestantism, as it took control of the older, larger church organizations, assumed possession of that leadership position. Through the National Council and its constitutive bodies, liberal Protestantism continues that tradition of leadership and guidance to the nation on the important national and international social issues. Slowly it has acknowledged that it now shares that leadership position with at least the Roman Catholic Church and the Jewish community. But as the twentieth century draws to a close, that primal leadership role is actively challenged at every turn, especially by the three conservative dissenting Protestant groups: the evangelical conservatives (whose most conservative element is Fundamentalism), the Holiness churches, and the Pentecostals (or charismatics). These groups have rejected the leadership of the older Protestant groups. Counting the 16-million member Southern Baptist Convention as a part of the evangelical conservative grouping (as its most liberal wing), it has claimed a constituency of some 40 million, equal in size to the combined membership of the affiliates of the National Council of Churches. Based upon that assessment of support, evangelical conservatives emerged in the public sphere in the 1980s as a group claiming the Protestant heritage of leadership over against that of the National Council of Churches and their member organizations. They have claimed additional support from the membership of the liberal Protestant churches, which has been repeatedly shown to be out of step with their church's public pronouncements. Liberal Protestantism has also been unique in its steady loss of members since the 1960s. Evangelicals claim, with some justification, that those members have been lost to evangelical churches, which in fact adhere more closely to the American Protestant tradition.

The Holiness and Pentecostal churches have been identified with the conservative evangelical camp on some basic issues such as the mutual affirmation of the authority of the Bible, and on important public positions such as opposition to abortion, support of prayer and the teaching of creationism in the public schools, and support for the state of Israel. They have remained distinct bodies within the evangelical consensus due to intense doctrinal differences, such as their support for a female ministry. Both Holiness and Pentecostal groups have grown throughout the twentieth century, but during the last two decades Pentecostalism has made spectacular strides. It has, for example, come to dominate the air time given religion on radio and television. The Church of God in Christ with over three million members has led Pentecostalism in overtaking Methodism in the number of black adherents. The Assemblies of God now claims over two million and both the United Pentecostal Church and the Church of God (Cleveland, Tennessee) have over a half million members.

The various major groups of Christians follow what are described in the chapters of this *Encyclopedia* as denominational families. But among Anglicans, Lutherans, Presbyterians, Congregationalists, Methodists, and Baptists the split between liberal and conservative groupings seems to rival the denominational families structures in importance. That split between conservatives and liberals, however, relates to a limited (though important) number of theological and social issues, which together constitute only a small percentage of the churches' religious life. Conservative and liberal Lutherans, for example, still agree on the majority of issues that make them Lutheran. The same could be said for the other denominational families. And while they align themselves on certain issues along liberal and conservative lines, they also participate in family traditions that have both national and international organizational expression. In that regard, liberals and conservatives will join together to support fellowship groups such as the Lambeth Conference of Bishops of the Anglican Communion, the Lutheran World Federation, the World Alliance of Reformed Churches (Presbyterian and Congregational), The World Methodist Council, and the Baptist World Fellowship.

The larger denominational communities still have responsibility for congregational life, worship, the production of educational materials, pastoral care, and continuing the family traditions. Those family traditions remain very much alive, and attempts to unite groups across those family lines in either liberal or conservative Protestant churches have failed time and again because of strongly-held denominational differences. The Consultation on Church Union, so promoted in the 1970s, is merely the most recent prominent example of such failure. The commitments to denominational distinctions provides stability amid shifting perspectives on various social issues and ephemeral ecumenical enthusiasms.

The American Jewish community is the most prominent religious community in America apart from the several Christian groups and the only one with a continuous presence since the colonial period. In the public sphere, George Washington acknowledged their presence after the Revolution, Jewish chaplains served on both sides during the Civil War, and during the twentieth century, Jewish rabbis have been invited to preside equally with Protestant and Catholic leaders in public religious celebrations, such as Thanksgiving.

New openness toward the Jewish community has come in the wake of the Holocaust (a reference to the six million Jews killed during the Nazi regime), the establishment of the state of Israel, and the new position toward the Jewish community articulated by the Roman Catholic Church during the Second Vatican Council. The Vatican statement, promulgated in 1965, refuted a once popular Christian position that blamed the Jews for Christ's death and has created a new basis for Jewish-Christian dialogue. That dialogue has tended to focus upon two issues: the Middle East and the evangelization of Jews by Christians. In the last generation, Roman Catholics and liberal Protestants have largely withdrawn support for missionary activities toward the Jewish community, but have been most supportive of Palestinians in the Middle East. Evangelical Christians, on the other hand, have continued to increase support for Jewish missionary endeavors while at the same time supporting the complete backing for Israel by the American government.

In the new dialogue, the major spokespersons for the Jewish community are the American Jewish Committee and the Synagogue Council of America. The former provides a meeting ground for both secular and religious Jews, and the latter represents the different Jewish congregational and rabbinical associations in a manner similar to the National Council of Churches.

Arising to challenge the Jewish position in America, the Islamic community has, since World War II, paralleled the spectacular growth of Methodism after the American Revolution. It now virtually equals the Jewish community in size and has emerged as a potent political force balancing the Jewish-allied support for Israel in the public debates on the Middle East. Awareness of the size of the Islamic community was quite low until recently because of public images that identified it solely with the Arab world. In fact the Islamic world stretches from Indonesia through China and India, through the Arab world, and across the African continent. In America it has received the additional support of a significant number of black people (who now constitute more than 20 percent of its total). Only in the 1970s did impressive mosques (the Islamic houses for prayer and worship) become visible in most American cities.

The Islamic community will not in the foreseeable future challenge in size any of the Christian families. But with religious pluralism growing, as the largest non-Christian religious group, its agenda will be taken with increasing seriousness and will, in all likelihood, lead to significant shifts in public positions taken by the Christian community.

The presence of Buddhists and Hindus in significant numbers in America is leading to a second significant shift in American religion. Accommodation to the presence of Jews in an otherwise Christian-dominated society was made from an appeal the a shared heritage as the children of Abraham and Moses. Islam is also a product of that same heritage. However, Hinduism and Buddhism provide the most complete alternative to the most basic perspective of Christianity. Dismissed for many decades as cults, Hindu and Buddhist groups began their rise above that negative label as large Asian immigrant communities have emerged in the last generation. Asian can now be found at every level and in every power center in American culture. And are forcing the encounter of Asian and non-Asian Americans at every level of society.

The Buddhist community matured the quickest. Two visible signs of that maturity appeared in 1987 with the naming of the first Buddhist chaplain in the armed forces and the formation of the American Buddhist Congress. Operating much like the National Council of Churches, the Congress provides a vehicle for Buddhism's engagement with American society, actively works for a more adequate understanding of Buddhists and Buddhism in American life, and gives voice to the Buddhist community's opinions on matters of public policy. Less organized nationally, Hindus are represented by the Hindu Vishwa Parishad, a national ecumenical agency.

Not to be forgotten in the massive pluralism so evident in contemporary American life is the continuance and the revival of Native American religions and religious traditions. While most Native Americans are now members of Christian churches, the traditional religions were never totally stamped out, and in many tribes a core of people who practiced the old religions continued and survived into the present. Then in the 1970s, along with the spread of numerous young-adult-oriented new religions, a variety of new Native American religions drawing heavily on traditional themes and traditionalist movements within particular tribes appeared. These new movements have a double importance. Not only have they given new life to traditional faiths, they have produced the first visible influx of traditional Native American religion into the white culture. During the 1980s, non-Native Americans who identified with environmental concerns, the occult, and/or transpersonal psychology found parallel concerns in Native American themes of oneness with the sacred land, shamanism, and the transformative power of Native American rituals.

Besides the large families of religious groups described above, America is the home to a number of other diverse religious groups from the 4.5-million-member Church of Jesus Christ of Latter-day Saints to the very small Wicca/Pagan covens of 10 to 15 members. There is a small but vocal atheist-humanist community, the religiously irreligious, so to speak, important far beyond its size because of its strong support within the academic world. While the relative sizes of the individual communities vary, America, and to a lesser extent Canada, have become a microcosm of world religion. Every major world religious community is now present in strength. While a majority of Americans have become Christian (and the community as a whole shows no evidence of declining), the climate of mutual respect and honor demanded by pluralism in a free religious society has given the world religions and interfaith issues the highest priority on the agenda of the older Christian bodies, which had until a generation ago largely limited interfaith contact to Jewish-Christian dialogue. The results of this new pluralism are only beginning to be discerned.

Selected Sources on American Religious History

[Note: Further listings related to each religious family group are given at the end of each chapter. Besides including some of the latest and best general works on American religion, the sources listed below include some of the more prevalent books produced during the past the sixty years.]

Albanese, Catherine L. *America: Religions and Religion*. Belmont, CA: Wadsworth Publishing Company, 1992. 548 pp.

Carmody, John. *Exploring American Religion*. Mountain View, CA: Mayfield Publishing, 1990. 376 pp.

Corbett, Julia Mitchell. *Religion in America*. Upper Saddle River, NJ: Prentice-Hall, 1997.

Corrigan, John. *Religion in America*. New York: Macmillan, 1992. 450 pp.

Gaustad, Edwin Scott. *Dissent in American Religion*. Chicago: University of Chicago Press, 1973. 184 pp.

———. *A Documentary History of Religion in America*. Grand Rapids, MI: William B. Eerdmans Publishing House, 1982. 2 Vols.

———. *Historical Atlas of Religion in America*. New York: Harper & Row, 1976. 189 pp.

———. *A Religious History of America*. New York: Harper & Row, 1966. 421 pp.

Handy, Robert T. *A Christian America*. New York: Oxford University Press, 1981. 269 pp.

Hudson, Winthrop S. *Religion in America*. 5th ed. New York: Charles Scribner's Sons, 1992. 486 pp.

Hutchinson, William R. *The Modernist Impulse in American Protestantism*. Oxford: Oxford University Press, 1976. 347 pp.

Johnson, Douglas W., Paul R. Packard, and Bernard Quinn. *Churches and Church Membership in the United States, 1971*. Washington, DC: Glenmary Research Center, 1971. 237 pp.

Johnson, Paul E., ed. *African American Christianity: Essays in History*. Berkeley, CA: University of California Press, 1994. 189 pp.

Marsden, George M. *Fundamentalism and American Culture*. Oxford: Oxford University Press, 1980. 307 pp.

Marty, Martin E., ed. *Out Faiths*. Royal Oak, MI: Cathedral Publishers, 1975. 236 pp.

———. *Pilgrims in Their Own Land*. Boston, MA: Little, Brown and Company, 1984. 500 pp.

———. *Protestantism in the United States*. New York: Charles Scribner's Sons, 1986. 290 pp.

Mead, Sidney E. *The Lively Experiment*. New York: Harper & Row, 1963. 220 pp.

———. *The Nation with the Soul of a Church*. New York: Harper & Row, 1975. 158 pp.

Melton, J. Gordon. *Biographical Dictionary of Cult and Sect Leaders*. New York: Garland Publishing Company, 1986. 354 pp.

———. *Religious Bodies in the United States: A Directory*. New York: Garland Publishing Company, 1992. 312 pp.

———. *Religious Leaders of America*. Detroit: Gale Research, 1991. 604 pp.

Morris, Richard R. *Encyclopedia of American History*. New York: Harper & Brothers, 1953. 776 pp.

Moyer, Elgin S. with Earle Cairns. *The Wycliffe Biographical Dictionary of the Church*. Chicago: Moody Press, 1982. 449 pp.

Murphy, Larry G., Jr., J. Gordon Melton, Gary L. Ward, eds. *Encyclopedia of African American Religions*. New York: Garland Publishing, 1993. 926 pp.

Myers, Gustavus. *History of Bigotry in the United States*. New York: Capricorn, 1960. 474 pp.

Noll, Mark, et al, eds. *Eerdman's Handbook to Christianity in America*. Grand Rapids, MI: William B. Eerdmans Publishing Company, 1983. 507 pp.

Piepkorn, Arthur C. *Profiles in Belief*. New York: Harper & Row, 1977–79. 3 Vols.

Quinn, Bernard, et al. *Churches and Church Membership in the United States, 1980*. Atlanta, GA: Glenmary Research Center, 1980. 321 pp.

Smith, H. Shelton, Robert T. Handy, and Lefferts A. Loetscher. *American Christianity*. New York: Charles Scribner's Sons, 1960. 2 Vols.

Sweet, William Warren. *Religion in Colonial America*. New York: Charles Scribner's Sons, 1951. 367 pp.

———. *The Story of Religion in America*. New York: Harper & Brothers, 1939. 656 pp.

Wentz, Richard E. *Religion in the New World*. Minneapolis, MN: Fortress Press, 1990. 370 pp.

Williams, Peter. *America's Religious Traditions and Culture*. New York: Macmillan, 1990. 478 pp.

Essay 2

Religion in Canada: An Historical Survey, 1500 to the Present

THE INITIAL CONQUEST OF CANADA: NATIVE AMERICANS IN CANADA. During the centuries before the invasion and conquest of what is today known as Canada, as with the United States, the vast territory was inhabited by the many Native American tribes. The density of population was not great, there being an estimated 220,000 persons in 1500. Most affected by the first European settlements were tribes such as the Hurons, which inhabited the shores of the St. Lawrence River, but eventually almost every tribe felt the impact of the spreading out of European culture and governmental rule. The establishment of the dominance of the European settlers effectively did away with the self sufficient cultures of the Indians and eventually made them dependent upon the larger resources developed by the new arrivals.

While much of the religious life of the tribes was either destroyed or transformed as tribal members responded to Christian missionary efforts, the story of North American Indian religion, especially as it continues in its contemporary forms, is integral to the story of Canadian religion.

As with the Native Indian tribes in what is now the United States, the Indians of Canada had a significant variation of religious belief and practice from the Huron and Algonquin in the east, to the Blackfoot of the plains, to the Eskimo of the Arctic reaches, to the Kwakiutl and the other tribes of British Columbia known so widely for their totem poles. They also shared with the Native Americans the characteristic of integrating religion into their tribal self identity and survival. Because of the harsher climate, the religion of the Canadian Indians reflected their tie to the land and the needs of survival even more than was the case with the tribes further south.

The initial settlement of the Europeans in the 1600s had its impact primarily upon the tribes of the St. Lawrence Valley. Both the Hurons and the Iroquois became entangled in the wars of the British and French for control of Canada and the subject of various missionary activities. The first Jesuits arrived in 1611, and it is among the Hurons and Iroquois that many of them worked. It is also among these tribes, quite apart from the missionaries, that the most destructive influence of the European intrusion became manifest. The Jesuits became trapped in the war that developed between the two tribes over the supply of beaver fur that was being rapidly exhausted through the early decades of the seventeenth century. The Indians had become dependent upon the European goods that they purchased with fur. In the resultant hostilities the Hurons were annihilated.

With the exception of the few traders that began to penetrate the interior of Canada, the majority of Canadian Indians did not have to deal with the whites until the nineteenth or even the twentieth century. The British initiated the penetration of the west through fur trading companies that established settlements along the coast of Hudson Bay. During the 1700s, the traders began the serious push inland that led to the company's control of the western half of Canada that persisted until it gave way to the new Dominion of Canada in the last half of the nineteenth century.

After the French era, as Canadians moved into Indian lands and gradually took possession of most of them, the level of hostilities proved to be far lower than in the United States. Canada established a pattern of making treaties with the Indians that included land grants and with few exceptions honoring those treaties. It also pursued a policy of punishing violations of the treaties by non-Indians.

The relatively peaceful nature of the long-term relationship between the Canadian government and the Indian tribes has allowed for the development of Christian missions and the conversion of the majority of Indians to Christianity. Roman Catholics, the Anglican Church, and the churches now composing the United Church of Canada all developed strong missions, especially in western Canada. On the other hand, traditional Indian religions have been able to survive and may be found among tribes in all sections of the country.

Especially notable among the surviving tribal religions of Canada are the Eskimo religions, which had been dominated by the shamans, the ubiquitous leaders in Eskimo religious matters. The shamans, much like a modern medium, entered a trance state during which they allowed various spirits to take possession of their consciousness and use their body to speak and dance. Integral to the shaman's work, and almost definitive of shamanism as opposed to common mediumship, was "soul flight," in which the shaman was believed to send his/her soul to the spirit realm on some errand such as the obtaining of advice on an important question that had arisen in the tribe.

The practice of shamanism was also seen as integral to the survival of Eskimo tribes in which starvation was frequently an immediate problem. They would predict (and even try to control) the weather and the supply of game. They would send their soul to placate a goddess such as Sedna, believed to control the sea mammals, or to locate the caribou and entice its appearance for the hunters. It was their job to spot violations of taboos that were believed to inhibit the luck of the hunt. They also attempted to improve fertility in the tribe using their special powers to aid barren females. The extent of the practice of shamanism has been significantly limited by the inroads of not only Christianity but of secular education and the modern technological world in general. Its future is unclear, given the current rebirth of shamanism in other areas of the culture.

THE ARRIVAL OF EUROPEANS IN CANADA. It is currently assumed that the first sighting of North America by a European occurred around the year 986 C.E. when Bjarni Herjulfson and his crew of Norse sailors were blown off course while sailing in the waters off Greenland. Some 15 years later, Leif Ericson explored the coast of North America, though scholars disagree as to the exact area described in the early accounts of his trips. Several other trips followed, however, the full extent of Norse exploration has been greatly hindered by the production of a number of fraudulent artifacts purporting to be relics of the Norse explorers.

For the purposes of later history, however, the exploration of Canada really began with the arrival of John Cabot off Newfoundland in the summer of 1497. Cabot's voyage was followed by other explorers looking for the Northwest Passage, as well as French ships that began exploitation of the fishing grounds off Newfoundland. Both the British and French established their early claim to Canadian territory. Then in 1534 Jacques Cartier arrived at the mouth of the St. Lawrence River to confirm the claim on New France made by Giovanni de Verranzano in 1523. Further British claims to present day Canada would be delayed until the 1570s and the three voyages of Martin Frobisher followed by John Davis, George Weymouth, and John Knight.

During the sixteenth century, the economic pursuits of the explorers and their financial backers overrode any religious goals that might have been expressed for the new world that was being discovered. The first settlers were not particularly religious people. Nevertheless, both Roman Catholicism and Anglicanism were introduced, though no permanent structures were created. Cartier included among his crew a priest who celebrated the first mass in Canada when the ship docked at Gaspe Peninsula. Anglican services were first held by a Master Wolfall, chaplain on Frobisher's third voyage. The first communion service, according to the rite of the Church of England, was held in 1578 in Baffinland. During the century, French efforts were concentrated upon the St. Lawrence Valley, to be joined by the British settlement of Newfoundland after Frobisher's voyages.

In the late 1500s the French settled and began seriously to develop the trading business in the St. Lawrence. Though the companies were responsible for supplying and supporting Roman Catholic priests in their Canadian centers, they did little to further the cause of religion during the remaining years of the sixteenth century. One must look to England for the emergence of the religious impulse in any public manner. In 1583, Sir Humphrey Gilbert was sent to claim Newfoundland for England, and in the establishment of the colony he proclaimed that worship according to the Church of England should prevail. However, he was lost at sea on his return voyage home, and the colony soon dissolved.

Finally, early in the seventeenth century, a permanent religious structure was created with the founding first of Arcadie (1603–1613) in Nova Scotia and subsequently of Quebec (1608) by Samuel de Champlain (ca.1570–1635). Champlain not only introduced Roman Catholic worship into his settlements, but seems to have been the first to articulate forcefully the desire to convert the indigenous residents of the surrounding lands. To that end, in 1615 he introduced the Roman Catholic Order of Recollects (one of several Franciscan orders), and when they proved ineffective, in 1625 he invited the Jesuits to begin work. Arriving with the first wave of Jesuits was Father Jean Brebeuf, who authored a number of reports that provide some of the best observations on French Canada during the 15 years between the first report and 1649, the year of Brebeuf's death by torture at the hands of those he was attempting to convert. During Brebeuf's Canadian career, the French territory expanded, new towns such as Montreal (1642) were founded, and more priests arrived (the Sulpicians joined the first two orders in the 1640s).

The success of the Catholic missionaries was demonstrated clearly in 1659 when Francois de Montmorency Laval (1623–1708) was appointed Vicar Apostolic for Canada. That appointment was not disconnected from the increased interest in New France by the king who designated it an official colony by a royal decree just four years later. Further growth of the church led to Laval being named the first bishop of Quebec in 1674.

The unfruitful Protestant efforts to colonize Canada continued in the 1600s, when a group of Danish Lutherans established a short-lived settlement on Hudson Bay. Their minister was among the first to die of scurvy, which ravaged the colony shortly after it was settled. Meanwhile, under James I the British renewed their interest in Canada. In 1610 he issued a charter for a colony in Newfoundland. John Gay of Bristol responded by establishing a "plantation" on Conception Bay and in 1612 brought Erasmus Stourton, an Anglican priest, to the colony. Stourton thus became the first resident non-Roman Catholic clergyman to reside in Canada. Stourton remained in Canada for 15 years during which time a charter for a Scottish (Presbyterian) settlement was issued by James I (1622) on the lands formerly settled by the ill-fated colony in Arcadie. The new colony, however, was no sooner established on a permanent basis than war broke out between France and England. In the treaty settling the conflict in 1632, Nova Scotia was returned to France and the settlers moved to Newfoundland. In 1633 Charles I chartered the colony of Newfoundland and decreed in the document that the worship according to the prayer book of the Church of England should be conducted (by ship's officers in the absence of clergymen) each Sunday.

THE BRITISH ERA IN CANADA: THE END OF FRENCH DOMINANCE. During the rest of the century, both British and French colonization of Canada continued, though the French expansion into the upper reaches of the St. Lawrence and Great Lakes region far outstripped any British efforts. As colonization proceeded, British and French Canadians also found themselves in ongoing conflict as the worldwide interests of their home countries continually overlapped. The intermittent hostile actions periodically disrupted their lives and altered the development of Canada. During the seventeenth century the French were able to continue their expansion in spite of the conflict, but after 1698 the trend of world events began to favor the British in Canada. In that year the Anglican Society for the Promotion of Christian Knowledge began to actively support the Reverend John Jackson, the minister resident in St. John's, Newfoundland (and the only Church of England priest in the territory). Three years later they turned their commitment over to the newly created missionary organization, the Society for the Propagation of the Gospel (SPG), which began to send missionaries into Canada. The British position and that of the Church of England was greatly improved in 1713 when the Treaty of Utrecht ended French–British hostilities for a generation. The British moved to build and consolidate their strength in Canada.

The beginning of the end of French power can be more clearly seen with the reopening of war in 1744. Their successful action against the French stronghold of Louisburg in Nova Scotia, and its subsequent return with the peace treaty signed in 1748, forced the British to further strengthen their position in Nova Scotia. In 1749, they founded the city of Halifax as a military stronghold to counter Louisburg. The establishment of Halifax became a signal event in Canadian religious history, for it was here that the religious patterns that have dominated subsequent Canadian history initially became visible. Immediately after the founding of the community, non-Roman Catholic Christianity in all of its variety appeared in Eastern Canada.

Responding to government action, the SPG promised six ministers and six school masters to the new city, and shortly after their arrival, on June 13, 1750, the foundation stone of St. Paul's Church was laid. (Today's St. Paul's congregation worships in the oldest church building in Canada.) And, since King George of England was also king of Hanover, he encouraged his German subjects to emigrate. German Lutherans became a significant percentage of the early population of the new town and moved to erect St. George's Lutheran Church the following year. A German Reformed congregation also appeared, and St. Matthew's Church (which served both Congregationalists and Presbyterians and was filled by British subjects from Ireland, Scotland, and New England) rounded out the religious life of the community.

The stabilization of life in Halifax was accomplished just as war returned. In 1755 the British moved against Arcadie and removed the French settlers (later to be immortalized in Longfellow's poem "Evangeline"). In 1758 Louisburg fell and the following year Quebec fell. With the capture of Quebec, the British effectively ended French control of Canada, though further action continued into the next year. Following the fall of Quebec, the first Anglican service in the city was conducted in the chapel of the Ursuline Convent by a former Roman Catholic priest, Michel Houdin, chaplain for the British forces.

UNDER BRITISH RULE. The Treaty of Paris of 1763, which made official the accomplishments of the war, also necessitated the altering of relations between the French Canadians and the now hostile government. While guaranteed religious freedom by the treaty, the British government moved to replace the Roman bishop with an Anglican one and to subvert the stability of the Catholic community by sending all the children to Anglican schools. When a new bishop was selected, the government refused to permit his consecration. The property of the Recollects and the Jesuits was confiscated, and both orders, as well as the Sulpicians, were forbidden to receive new members from abroad. This trend was reversed in 1774 when the Act of Quebec granted a high degree of tolerance. The local suspicion toward the Catholic community was appreciably lessened when the French not only refused to support the Americans' attempt to gain them as allies in the American Revolution but actively joined efforts to turn back the attempted invasion by the rebels.

Meanwhile, as soon as the war had ended, more Protestant groups made their way to Canada, though they came not so much to the newly conquered territory but to the Maritime Provinces, where so many Protestant firsts occurred. The first truly Presbyterian church in Canada was founded at Londonderry, Nova Scotia, in 1761 by a group of Irish Presbyterian immigrants. The growth of both Congregationalism and Presbyterianism throughout the decade led in 1770 to a somewhat unique occurrence brought about by the inability of the German Reformed congregation in Halifax to obtain a minister from Pennsylvania. They decided to have one of their own members, Bruin Romcas, ordained. In response to their situation, two Congregationalist ministers joined with two Presbyterian ministers to constitute a presbytery for purposes of the ordination.

Around 1760 the first Baptists arrived to take possession of the land abandoned by the Arcadians. The arrival of the small Baptist community in Nova Scotia coincided with the expansion of the Congregationalists, both groups migrating from New England. Many of the Congregationalists were partial to the New Light position, which accepted the theology and practices of the Great Awakening. Many New Lights found themselves more at home with the Baptists than with their more staid Old Light Congregationalists. The issue was forcefully raised by one Henry Alline, a talented New Light preacher who forced a division of the Congregationalists. Alline's followers soon drifted into the Baptist camp and provided the initial substance out of which a significant Canadian Baptist church would emerge.

Finally, around 1775, as Alline's influence was reaching its peak, there appeared from among a group of Cornish immigrants in Nova Scotia the first Methodists. William Black Jr. emerged as their leader and traveled the communities of the province both establishing Methodism and opposing Alline. After the American Revolution, Black looked to the Methodists in the United States for assistance. He traveled to Maryland in 1784 to attend the organizational session of the Methodist Episcopal Church. For a number of years he attached himself to the American church, by which he was eventually ordained, and from which he was assigned assistants to extend his missionary endeavors. Eventually, however, the Canadians grew to resent American leadership and Black turned to the Wesleyan Methodists in England who accepted responsibility for the now growing work.

Of more than passing interest was the development in Nova Scotia of both Methodist and Baptist work among blacks. During the American Revolution, many blacks, most former slaves, were promised freedom and a stake if they remained loyal to Britain. After losing the war, the British transported many of these black people to Nova Scotia, particularly to some towns along the southeastern coast. Among them were both Baptist and Methodist preachers, who led the congregations formed in the several black communities. Black regularly visited the Methodists. Over the next few years the blacks waited on the British government, which never gave the promised stake. Finally, the British abolitionists raised the money to transport them to Freetown, Sierra Leone, where they became the seed from which the Baptist and Methodist churches of that country were to grow.

In the generation after the founding of the city of Halifax, the major religious pattern to be developed in the next centuries of Canadian history was established. The Church of England (or Anglican church) and those Protestant churches introduced into Nova Scotia during the 1750s and 1760s joined the Roman Catholic Church in creating a dominant consensus in Canadian religious life and thus initiated the major factor in the emerging Canadian religious story. Any account of Canadian religion must center upon the movement of the Roman Catholics, Anglicans, Presbyterians, Congregationalists, Methodists, Lutherans, and Baptists in their efforts to church the sprawling nation, their successes and failures in relating to one another, and their ability to adjust to the growing ethnic and religious pluralism of twentieth century Canadian life. The focus upon these groups certainly does not deny or diminish the important contributions of the hundreds of other Canadian religious groups. It merely recognizes that due to the simple appeal of these groups to the masses of Canadian citizens, they set the pace to which the others must relate.

At least two other groups found their way into Canada during this initial period and opened their own niches in the religious community. For example, as early as 1762, American Quakers arrived in Nova Scotia from Nantucket, Rhode Island. Though their original effort to settle did not last many years, it heralded a more permanent Quaker thrust into Canadian life a few years later. Second, the missionary-minded Moravian Church, directing their attention farther north, arrived in 1771 when missionary Jens Haven established work at Nain, Labrador. The Moravians pioneered both Christian missionary and educational work among the Eskimo population. While never large, it was the forerunner of other like efforts.

THE SETTLEMENT OF LOWER AND UPPER CANADA (QUEBEC AND ONTARIO). Even as the settlement and development of the church in Nova Scotia and the Maritime Provinces proceeded, the new British administration had to deal with the 70,000 French-speaking residents living in Canada proper, over which they now had governmental control. The British showed every intent of replacing Roman Catholic authority with the complete establishment of the Church of England. They confiscated the properties of the Jesuits and Recollects and forbade all orders to accept novices. They initiated plans to educate all Catholic children in Anglican schools. Loyal Catholics in both Canada and France registered their opposition in every way possible. Assisted by the unrest in the colonies to the south, a decade of protest met with measurable success. Not needing a second revolt on their hands, the British moved to pacify the French by passing the Quebec Act of 1774. Although it returned some measure of religious toleration to the Catholic community, antagonism continued for many years while the Church of England continued to pursue other means of cutting into Catholic support. However, the Roman Catholic community continued to grow and by 1784 numbered 130,000, aided substantially by the immigration of Catholics from the Highlands of Scotland during this period.

Though the British took control of eastern Canada and the St. Lawrence River Valley in 1763, growth of the Church of England was slow, at least for several decades. Primarily the colonies to the south attracted more immigrants from Europe due to the warmer climate. Thus a population favorable to Anglicanism did not arrive in great numbers until after the American Revolution sent waves of Loyalists north to escape rebel rule. Most of these were Loyalist Protestants and many were Anglicans. The growth provided by the Loyalists justified the establishment of the first see for British North America, and Charles Inglis (1734–1816) was consecrated as the first bishop in 1787 with his seat in Halifax, Nova Scotia. Six years later Jacob Mountain (1749–1825) was concentrated as the first bishop of Canada with his seat in Quebec City.

Faced with the continued resistance of the French Canadians to proselytizing actions and to ensure that they remained peaceful and loyal British subjects, the Parliament in England passed the Constitutional Act of 1791. It divided Canada by setting off Lower Canada (Quebec), where most of the French lived, from Upper Canada (Ontario), where most of the British lived. Ontario was just beginning to receive the first waves of Loyalists. Each province had a separate parliament but was administratively under a single governor-in-chief. Important for the churches, the act also set aside land for the support of the clergy of the Church of England and made specific provision for the support of Anglican clergy and the erection of rectories. The provisions of the 1791 act greatly assisted the Anglican church in its spread and development across Canada. Parishes were established, churches and schools erected, and new ministries initiated. While not leading to success in Quebec, the expansion of the church in Ontario was demonstrated by the necessity of placing a bishop in Toronto in 1839. Government support undoubtedly gave the Anglicans immense advantage for several decades, but also seriously hindered the church's long-term development. The bishop's attempt to administer the Canadian church's affairs from England discouraged local development of active lay commitment. Thus when the government withdrew financial support several generations later, the church had to quickly create a new ecclesiastical structure equipped to mobilize member loyalty and voluntary financial support.

Upper Canada, now known as Ontario, was soon to become the most densely populated section of Canada, and religiously the most diverse. The Loyalists brought with them the great variety of religions previously established in the American colonies. And, as Upper Canada was opened, new settlers directly from the British Isles brought with them the profusion of sects that arose as Protestant dissenters proliferated both in number and in number of factions.

Presbyterians were among the most numerous of the new settlers. As early as 1791 Presbyterian congregations started by American ministers appeared on the Niagara Peninsula and by 1833 founded the Niagara Presbytery. Growth was assisted by the movement into the church of many former Congregationalists. They were soon joined by immigrants directly from Scotland who established congregational outposts of the Church of Scotland and of the several dissenting groups that had been created through protests over the taking of a loyalty oath and complaints over the church's patronage system. Each group established its own synod, leaving the Presbyterians with the task of reconciling their differences, most of which were nondoctrinal and irrelevant to the Canadian environment.

Methodism, having gotten its Canadian start in Nova Scotia, found a second unrelated beginning in Upper Canada in the settlements of the war veterans in the 1780s. In 1791, Methodist Bishop Francis Asbury directed the Reverend William Losee from New York into Upper Canada where he oversaw the construction of the first Methodist chapel in the region, which was built on Paul Huff's farm near the Bay of Quinte. Most influential in the development of the church were the Ryersons, originally an Anglican family who settled near Lake Erie in 1799. The sons all became Methodists, and Egerton Ryerson (1803–1882), in particular, manifested a marked ability as an educator and apologist for the family's new faith, who were frequent targets of Anglican critics. Originally trained for the legal profession, Ryerson joined the ministry in the 1820s and rose to prominence as the first editor of the Methodist periodical *The Christian Guardian*. Among his many accomplishments, he fought to break the hold of the Anglicans on university education, and eventually became the first principal of Victoria College.

The original work of the Methodists in Upper Canada was under the care of the Methodist Episcopal church, which had been organized in the United States in 1784. During the early nineteenth century, Methodists from the several factions in England—the Wesleyans, the Primitive Methodists, the Bible Christians—established competitive work and taunted those who were still attached to the disloyal former colonies. The War of 1812 clearly demonstrated the problem of any church organization attempting to hold a membership across the American–Canadian border. After the war, Canadian Methodists initiated a staged break with their American comrades and merged with the British Wesleyan Connection in 1833.

Because of the very visible support of prominent Congregationalist ministers in the American Revolution, the equally important existence of many Congregationalist Loyalists is frequently overlooked. While most of these Loyalists left the United States by the short and easy sea route from New England to Nova Scotia, by the first decade of the 1800s Congregationalist congregations appeared in Quebec among settlers who simply stepped across the border from Vermont. The period of the greatest Congregationalist expansion was during the ministry of Henry Wilkes, for more than fifty years pastor of a church in Montreal. He established Canadian ties with British Congregationalists and received funds from the London Missionary Society for the establishment of congregations in both Canadas. Wilkes did much to change the bad image of Congregationalists, whose identification with the Revolution had caused many of their number to become Presbyterians.

Lutherans led a migration of people of German background into the Canadas in the late eighteenth century. They were accompanied in their migrations by members of other German groups, with whom they had to compete to gain and even hold members. While many of these settlers were dedicated to keeping the German language alive, the inevitable process of Americanization took its toll. They also lost members to the English-speaking Anglicans and the evangelistically-oriented Methodists. The first wave of Lutherans, war veterans, received grants of land in Dundas, Lennox, and Addington counties in the 1780s. A decade later, responding to an invitation for Germans to settle in Ontario, a group of unhappy New York residents managed to receive a grant of 64,000 acres upon which the town of Markham was built.

In spite of the early and continued establishment of new congregations throughout the first half of the nineteenth century, the Lutherans suffered from a dire lack of clergy leadership and a resultant isolation of one organization from another. Only in the middle of the century, as Lutherans in the Synod of Pittsburgh learned of the state of the Ontario Lutherans, were qualified ministers sent to their aid. A Canadian Conference was finally created in 1853.

Baptists entered Upper and Lower Canada in three waves, the first coming into the Niagara area just as the Revolution commenced. Baptists filtered into Quebec in the 1790s and were joined in 1815 by a group migrating from Scotland. Once settled, the Baptists spread quickly. An association formed in 1816 became the precursor of many more. However, the Baptists were very hesitant to unite in larger efforts above the associational level. Inherently independent, they were further divided over the question of the admission of non-Baptists to communion. Only in 1851, when the issue of the disposal of the government's clergy reserves (in which the Baptists by principle never participated) became a significant issue, did the Baptists finally form The Regular Baptist Missionary Convention of Canada West.

FURTHER NEW CHURCHES. During the period of the initial settlement of Upper Canada, a number of new church groups were introduced into the country. The encouragement of German immigration, for example, brought not only Lutherans but Mennonites and United Brethren as well. The first Mennonites came into the Niagara Peninsula in 1786 and during the next three decades approximately 2,000 migrated into Ontario. Many were a part of the predominantly Lutheran settlement at Markham. Others founded Ebytown, now the city of Kitchener. In 1824 the first congregation of Amish settled in Waterloo County.

Early in the nineteenth century, Germans from two groups heavily influenced by the Methodists—the United Brethren in Christ and the Evangelical Association—began to preach and build churches among the German-speaking settlements. In 1816 John Dreisbach of the Evangelical Association traveled in Ontario, but did not establish any congregations. However, four years earlier, United Brethren had been among German immigrants who moved from Pennsylvania into the Waterloo area. By 1825 a circuit had been established, and the Ontario Conference was created in 1856. Permanent Evangelical Association work had an unusual beginning. Several Waterloo families who had returned to the United States encountered association members in Ohio. Informed of the Canadian situation, ministers began to travel to Chippewa and the Waterloo area, and subsequently the other German-speaking communities. The first German-language Sunday school in Canada was founded by the Evangelical Association ministers at what is now Kitchener.

Before diverting attention from German-speaking groups, it should be noted that among the migrants into Upper Canada after the Revolution were members of the Church of the Brethren, a pacifist group. Their church did not assume any permanent presence, however, as some of the families soon returned to the United States.

The great movement to church the western United States (then the area from the Appalachians to the Mississippi River), usually termed the Second Great Awakening, spawned several new denominations, among them the Christian Church (Disciples of Christ). Very soon after its formation, this highly evangelical group, loosely organized and, except for its few peculiar emphases, doctrinally close to the Baptists, moved into Canada almost immediately. In 1807 Thomas Campbell had formed the first rudimentary organization, the Christian Association, and by 1810 work had spread to the Maritime Provinces. A few years later centers could be found at Poplar Hill and Norval in Upper Canada.

During the first half of the nineteenth century, Ontario also became the home of a number of groups that had broken from the mainstream of the Western Christian tradition. Most of these groups were imported from the United States where they had originally emerged. As early as 1832 Unitarians under the leadership of Benjamin Workman began to gather in Montreal. His efforts would become the basis for a strong congregation, but not before he had moved on to Toronto, where in 1845 he formed the first Unitarian congregation in Canada. While the Church of Jesus Christ of Latter-day Saints did not move into Canada in a substantial fashion until late in the century, it did make an important incursion in 1842. Missionaries in Toronto that year converted John Taylor. Taylor left Toronto for Nauvoo, Illinois, and became a close associate of Mormon leader Joseph Smith, Jr. He was one of the two men to survive the attack in which Smith was murdered; he eventually became president of the church. He is remembered today as one of the last leaders of the church to vigorously defend the practice of polygamy.

JEWISH PRESENCE IN CANADA TO 1850. Though an occasional Jew will make a brief appearance at odd moments in Canadian history, the French ban on Jewish presence in New France served to keep them out of Canada until the middle of the eighteenth century. In 1749 some Sephardic Jews (of Spanish-Portuguese origin) organized in Halifax and bought a cemetery. However, the small, short-lived community soon disappeared. A decade later the first of a number of prominent Jewish merchants in Upper and Lower Canada appeared in the person of Samuel Jacobs who settled near Montreal. He was joined the next year by Samuel Hart who established his headquarters in Three Rivers. As other Jews arrived, several of whom prospered in their businesses, Congregation Shearith Israel, modeled on the congregation of the same name in New York City, was formed. Though most of the

members were of English background (and thus would seem to favor the Ashkenazic worship forms), they adopted the Sephardic ritual of their New York brethren, and in 1777 they erected a building. Congregation Shearith Israel seems to be but one of the two Canadian synagogues during the next several generations. Records also speak of the "Hart synagogue" in Three Rivers. By 1825 there were still fewer than 100 Jews in Canada. This lack of numbers did not keep them in 1828 from petitioning for full recognition as a religious community (which would allow them to keep their own records of births, marriages, and deaths), which was granted the next year. Then in 1832 Canadian Jews were granted their equal rights as British subjects (which removed any barriers to their holding public office or serving as officers in the military), a privilege not granted British Jews until 1858.

Though still small in comparison to the total population, the Jewish population in Upper Canada grew perceptively during the middle nineteenth century. A Jewish community emerged in Toronto in the 1840s. Following a general pattern in new Jewish communities, first, in 1849 a cemetery was purchased, and then a congregation, the Sons of Israel, was organized in 1856. In 1859 a second congregation, following the Ashkenazic ritual, was opened in Montreal. By 1860 there were approximately 1,200 Jews in Canada.

THE CANADIAN ERA BEGINS: MID-CENTURY CHANGES. During the middle of the nineteenth century, the major issue affecting all of the Christian churches in Canada was the changing relationship between the Canadian government and the Anglican church. By the action of the British government in the decades after the fall of Quebec, the Church of England in Canada became the established church of Canada. By law and with the backing of public funds, the worship and education of the people in the tradition of the Church of England was to be developed, encouraged, and maintained. Ministers were directly responsible to the Lord Bishop of London. In 1787 the Crown appointed the first bishop for British North America, and the governors of Nova Scotia and Quebec were given specific orders to assist him in the exercise of his jurisdictional duties. The church, in spite of local episcopal authority, remained in a missionary situation and developed no synodical structures.

In 1791, integral to the action that separated the two Canadas (Upper and Lower), the government set aside lands specifically for the support of the clergy and the church. As the church expanded, the government provided revenue to create new dioceses and appoint bishops. Decade by decade, however, forces grew in favor of unifying the separated Canadian provinces into a single governmental entity under a form of home rule that would be largely autonomous of England without breaking completely with the empire. The growing autonomy in the Canadian government forced significant shifts in the relations between the Anglican Church in Canada, the Church of England, and the governments. The crux of the changes centered upon the disposition of the clergy reserves.

Vocal opposition to the 1791 provisions for clergy land grants had arisen from the beginning. Secular interests demanded the use of the revenues from the lands (which consisted of some 2.5 million acres) for other purposes, such as nonsectarian public education. The churches joined the battle from their varying perspectives. Some opposed the unfair advantage given the Anglicans (especially the Presbyterians who wanted their share in light of their establishment in Scotland), while some, such as the Canadian branch of the Free Church of Scotland, opposed government support of churches on principle. The Anglicans were heavily dependent on these lands, which directly supplemented the financial support from the church in England and the Society for the Propagation of the Gospel, the foreign missionary structure of the Church of England. The loss to the church would be significant. By mid-century, however, it was a foregone conclusion that the loss would occur, and in 1853 all of the clergy land reserves were secularized. The drawn-out battle over the clergy reserves had also created an unwanted side effect for the Anglicans. By focusing the shared opposition to the Anglican's favored-child status, the issue united the Protestant churches against the Church of England in Canada.

The financial concerns thrust a second issue upon the Canadian Anglicans: the development of self-government. Because of its status as a missionary arm of the Church of England, it had not been free to develop internally. Each diocese worked as a separate unit directly responsible to authorities in England. In 1851, as the land reserves issue was reaching a climax, five of the seven Canadian bishops met and called for the creation of a province of Canada under a metropolitan (archbishop) and the creation of diocesan synods that would include lay participation. These new structures would facilitate the transformation of the church into a voluntary association that relied upon its own membership for its major financial support. The first synod, that of the Diocese of Toronto, met in 1857. Four years later the bishop of Montreal was appointed metropolitan of the Canadian province and an initial provincial synod for what was to be termed the "Church of England in Canada" held. The province did not include Manitoba and the territories to the west, which developed as a separate province, as did British Columbia. Eventually, in 1893 the several provinces were united into an autonomous General Synod under a Primate of All Canada. Thus by the end of the century the Anglicans in Canada had emerged as another independent member of the developing worldwide Anglican Communion.

RELIGION MOVES INTO THE CANADIAN WEST: WHERE IS RUPERT'S LAND? Chartered in 1670, the Hudson Bay Company had been given exclusive rights to the land north and west of Ontario. During the last half of the nineteenth century their monopoly collided with the needs of Canada for expanded territory. Land was becoming scarce, immigration was increasing, and population was exploding. At the same time a new sense of Canadian nationalism emerged with some degree of support from the British homeland. The completion of the transcontinental railroad across the United States (1869) merely highlighted the advantages of such a railroad across Canada.

Thus in 1867, when the four Canadian provinces (Ontario, Quebec, Newfoundland, and the Maritime) united in a confederation, they immediately looked west. In 1870 the confederation took in Rupert's Land, today known as Manitoba, and in 1871, on the condition that a transcontinental railroad be built, it added British Columbia. Railroad construction began soon afterward, and the line to Winnipeg was finished in 1881. It took only four more years to complete the track to the Pacific Coast. Though Alberta and Saskatchewan would not become provinces until 1905, the completion of the railroad effectively opened them to massive immigration. The older churches, which had already established initial centers, quickly moved in with the new immigrants, and just as importantly, numerous new religious groups found a home in the newly opened territory.

In 1812 Thomas Douglas, the fifth Earl of Selkirk (1771–1820), with the cooperation of the Hudson Bay Company, founded Kildonan, a community of Scottish immigrants, on the Red River near present-day Winnipeg. In order to protect the settlers from the rival North West Company, he hired some German mercenaries. Concerned for the religious life of the soldiers, many of whom were Roman Catholic, he requested a priest, and in 1818 the Diocese of Quebec sent Father Joseph Norbert Abbe Provencher. Besides serving the immediate community, he began to expand work to neighboring sites and to Indian and Eskimo missions. He soon received the aid of the Oblates of Mary, who took special responsibility for the missionary work. The growth of the work initiated by Provencher led in 1844 to his being named Vicar Apostolic, and in 1847 he became the first bishop of St. Boniface (Manitoba). During the first half of the nineteenth century, Provencher provided the foundation for Roman Catholic expansion in western Canada through the conversion of the native population, the immigration of Catholics from around the world, and the recruitment of members from among the new (but previously non-Catholic) settlers.

Anglican work in the West was initiated by the Reverend John West, who served at Kildonan in the absence of a Presbyterian minister, which the colonists really wanted. With Anglican funds he built two schools, one for the colonists' children and one for the Indians. His missionary endeavors produced one priest, Henry Budd, from the Indian parishioners. His efforts were bolstered in 1822 when the Church Missionary Society decided to take responsibility for Indian missions and began to send clergymen from England. By 1849, two years after the naming of a Roman Catholic bishop, David Anderson was consecrated the first Anglican bishop of Rupert's Land. In 1865 Robert Machray became bishop of Rupert's Land, a post he held for the rest of the century. During this period, operating independently of the province (limited to the dioceses to the east until the creation of the General Synod in 1893), he developed Rupert's Land into a separate province that included nine dioceses between Manitoba and the Rocky Mountains.

THE OTHER CHURCHES COME TO MANITOBA. The Methodists' movement into the Northwest followed a series of unusual events in England. The Canadian Methodist preacher Egerton Ryerson had an Indian friend, Peter Jones, who traveled to England. His speeches before a variety of Methodist audiences excited them over the possibilities of missionary work among the Indians of Upper Canada. Learning of Jones' work, Hudson Bay company officials, possibly looking for a way to gain some social control (through religion) over the Indians, invited the Methodists into their territory. To the company, Jones seemed a living demonstration that the Methodists could deal with the native population. Within a few years the Wesleyan Methodist Connection, bypassing the Canadian Methodists, sent James Evans, Thomas Hurlburt, and Peter Jacobs to establish work on Manitoulin Island. Evans soon broke with the Hudson Bay Company and established Norway House in northern Manitoba. Among his major contributions was the development of a syllabic system for printing the Cree Indian language, a system that was easily adapted to other languages. Evans career overlapped that of Robert Rundel, who moved among the tribes farther west from his base in Edmonton, Alberta.

The Wesleyans supported the missions around Norway House and Edmonton for several decades but in 1853 turned the work over to the Canadian Methodists. The following year John Ryerson made a trip through the territory and in his report made note that he uncovered 18 Protestant missionaries, of which 13 were Anglican, four Methodist, and one Presbyterian.

That one Presbyterian was John Black, a recent graduate of Knox College (Toronto), who had settled in Kildonan to serve the Scots who had waited 20 years for a Presbyterian minister. Black stayed in Kildonan for over 30 years. The Presbyterian work expanded in the 1860s through James Nisbet, who went out from Kildonan to found the town of Prince Albert, Saskatchewan, and initiate Presbyterian work in that future province.

By mid-century settlers began to trickle into western Canada in increasing numbers, and the other churches came soon to provide their spiritual nurture. In 1873 the first Baptist missionary arrived in Winnipeg, and throughout the decade churches were started in Saskatchewan and Alberta. The Baptists turned their attention to the various non-English-speaking immigrants who began to pour into the area and soon raised up a number of ethnic churches. Early churches tended to be located along the railroad route, which brought the immigrants to their new homes.

ACROSS THE ROCKIES: EVEN FARTHER WEST. British Columbia developed somewhat independently of the steady western movement of Canadian life. In like measure, the stream of both Roman Catholic and Anglican development flowed along an independent course only to be merged at the end of the nineteenth century. In British Columbia two paths to the farthest reaches of Canada converged. Many of the earliest settlers trekked northward from California along the Pacific Coast. Then in 1792 Alexander MacKenzie made it over the mountains to the coast and initiated the rich fur trade that was started by the North West Company in 1806. The West Coast remained company territory (the North West Company and then, after 1821, Hudson Bay Company) until British Columbia joined the confederation in 1871. Also, during much of this time (until the settlement of the boundary between Canada and the United States in 1846), the entire Pacific Coast north of California was disputed territory. As a result, the progress of the Roman Catholic missionary work, begun in 1838, in the area was delayed almost a decade when the Bishop of Quebec who had initiated work in the Oregon Territory questioned his prerogative in sponsoring the mission. The territory seemed to also belong to the Bishop of St. Louis, in the United States.

That Oregon Mission included not only Oregon and Washington, but Fort Vancouver and all of British Columbia. Soon after the arrival, the first priests, Francis Norbet Blanchet and Modeste Demers, began to envision the possibilities of bringing the Indian population into the church. They saw a bright future if only a bishop, with authority to recruit a cadre of priests and religious workers, could be sent to the Northwest. Within a year they began to request a bishop. In 1843 Rome responded by appointing Blanchet as vicar apostolic for the territory. Blanchet, somewhat overwhelmed, requested that the vast territory under his authority be further divided. Then, immediately after the border between the United States and Canada was established by treaty in 1846, the Holy See named Blanchet bishop of Oregon and the same day (July 24) appointed him archbishop of a new province of Oregon City. Four day later his brother, Augustine Magloire Blanchet, was named bishop of Walla Walla (Washington), and the next year Modeste Demers became bishop of Vancouver, as part of the Oregon City province.

From 1847 the work prospered for several years, only to be ravaged by the California gold rush. By 1855 only seven priests were left in the province, the rest having followed their flocks south. Three years later, the diocese' fortunes reversed with the discovery of gold on the Fraser River in British Columbia, and the town of New Westminster emerged quickly as a new population center. With the completion of the railroad in the 1880s the number of residents of British Columbia steadily increased and the work of the church stabilized into a pattern of growth that has continued to follow the population trends.

The Church of England in Canada was much slower to respond to the needs on the Canadian Pacific Coast than was the Roman Catholic Church. In part it was distracted by its mid-century problems of building a new financial base and redefining itself independently of the bishops in England. Also, being a national church, the settlement of the boundary dispute with the United States had much more severe implications for the extension of the ministry.

Following the 1846 treaty, the Hudson Bay Company abandoned its major post on the Columbia River and in 1849 founded Fort Victoria on Vancouver Island. An Anglican priest, R. J. Staines, was appointed priest and schoolmaster of the new settlement. He worked alone for a decade, there finally being the addition of a lay teacher in 1857 and a missionary to the Indians in 1858. Then in the wake of the discovery of gold and the influx of thousands into the area, an urgent request for assistance in British Columbia fell into the hands of a wealthy and devout heiress in London. She endowed a bishopric for British Columbia, and in 1859 the Reverend George Hills was consecrated for the new diocese. Hills recruited men and raised funds before his arrival in Victoria in 1860. With this initial financial backing from the Church of England, he was able to organize the work without financial support from the Canadian government, and he put it on a firm and stable foundation from the beginning. The new Dioceses of New Westminster (at the mouth of the Fraser River) and Caledonia (centered on the headwaters of the Fraser) created in 1879, become the backbone of the province of British Columbia in the next century.

The initiation of Congregationalist work in British Columbia grew out of concern in Great Britain for slaves who had escaped their life in the United States and found their way to the Vancouver area. In 1859 the Colonial Missionary Society sent a minister to Victoria both to create a church and serve the black residents. His interracial efforts met strong opposition from the larger community of white residents and the work collapsed when the Society withdrew the missionary. A decade later a second missionary was sent, and he organized two congregations, one each in 1879 and 1881. But little progress could be cited for Congregationalism in western Canada as a whole. It had trouble competing with the more aggressive Presbyterians and Methodists.

The other Protestant churches lagged behind in their movement to the coast. A Presbyterian minister arrived at Fort Camosun on Vancouver Island in 1861. Beginning in the courthouse, he established what was the only Presbyterian congregation west of Kildonan. A Baptist, John Morton, arrived in 1862 to homestead some 600 acres of what is now downtown Vancouver. A generation later, enough Baptist churches had been formed to justify the formation of the Baptist Convention of British Columbia in 1897.

With the formation of the Roman Catholic and Anglican dioceses in western Canada and the movement of the older churches into the territory, especially after the completion of the railroad, the initial churching of Canada could be said to have been completed. All of the churches were to continue to grow and spread as the population grew, but that growth consisted of the spreading of the already dominant structure. In the process of that further growth, a number of issues were to come to the fore to which the churches would have to give their time and energy. As their sister churches south of the border, all of the Canadian churches were forced to respond to those same new ideas and realities that emerged so forcefully as factors of late nineteenth century life—biblical criticism, the biological and geological sciences, urbanization, and historical consciousness—out of which was to grow an embittered phase of the Fundamentalist-Modernist controversy. By the end of the century, the Protestants were focused upon the possibilities of building a united church from the multitude of sectarian and regional church bodies.

OTHER GROUPS IN WESTERN CANADA. Dating largely from the opening of the West by the railroad, Canada became home to a wide variety of ethnic groups and an even wider variety of new (at least for Canada) religions. Among the first new groups to arrive in the West, Mennonites from Russia settled along the Red River south of Winnipeg in 1874. A second wave after World War II settled on farms in Alberta, Saskatchewan, and Manitoba. In the United States these Mennonites split into several factions, the largest being the General Conference Mennonite Church.

After the Mennonites, other churches also representative of the European Free Church tradition have found western Canada a suitable place for settlement. Possibly the most controversial of these groups is the Doukhobors, which began to arrive in 1899. Controversy followed their attempts to keep their religious practices intact in the face of Canadian laws (such as those dictating educational standards). One group has been accused of violent (at least against property) protest, and some fame has come to the groups for the practice of shedding their clothes in public situations as a means of additional protest.

Following their inability to reach a suitable accord with the United States government after its entry into the war, the pacifist communally-organized Hutterite Brethren systematically sold their American farms and relocated in western Canada. Though many later returned to the United States, the Hutterites retain a strong Canadian presence.

Eastern Europeans also began to move into western Canada prior to the turn of the century and continued after immigration restrictions were lifted in the United States in 1924. For example, over 8,000 Romanians, mostly farmers, came to Alberta, Saskatchewan, and Manitoba prior to World War I. The first church, St. Nicholas, was built in Regina, Saskatchewan, in 1902. Canadian Ukrainians, now headquartered in Winnipeg, were present in numbers when the struggle for Ukrainian independence led them to organize separately from the Russian Orthodox Church. The first congregation was formed in Saskatoon, Saskatchewan.

Scandinavian ministers came into Manitoba as early as the 1870s to begin work among the Swedes. An Evangelical Covenant Church was organized at Winnipeg in 1904, about which time ministers of the Evangelical Free Church arrived to initiate work among the Norwegians and Danes. The first Evangelical Free Church was organized in 1913.

Mormons, members of the Church of Jesus Christ of Latter-Day Saints, also made their entry into Canada during this period. In 1887 a group of 41 led by Charles Ora Card migrated north from Salt Lake City to what is today the province of Alberta. At that time Canada had no laws against polygamy. They founded the town of Cardston, about 40 miles from Lethbridge, where a temple was built and from which the church has spread throughout Canada. At a later date, members of the Reorganized Church of Jesus Christ of Latter-Day Saints would also begin to colonize Canada.

As with the United States, Asian immigration into Canada commenced on the West Coast following the gold rush. Of the Chinese who flocked to the gold fields, many stayed to introduce Buddhism to Canada. By the end of the nineteenth century, Indians, primarily Punjabis, migrated to British Columbia and brought their Sikh faith with them. The construction of the first house of worship, a *Gurdwara*, was initiated in 1906 in Vancouver.

These churches mentioned represent only a few of the many ethnic church groups that were established in western Canada, only to be joined by new indigenous churches that split from the older church bodies. Together they have given western Canada the same pluralistic flavor so evident in the large urban centers in the eastern half of the nation.

A NEW CONSCIOUSNESS FOR A NEW CENTURY: THE GROWTH OF MODERNISM AND FUNDAMENTALISM. Modernism, a theological perspective that accepted and even celebrated the changing world of the late nineteenth and early twentieth century, blossomed in Canada as it did throughout the West. Responding to the scholarly community, the Modernists embraced the new "scientific" approach to history (as exemplified in critical methodologies) and society (through the new discipline of sociology), and the radical new assertions of biology and geology. British scholars exposed Canadian churchmen to the historical-critical methods of Bible study as early as 1860 through the publication of the book *Essays and Reviews*, which attempted to inform the British public about the new German scientific critique of scripture. In Canada the book initiated a continuing debate over the authority of the Bible, the integrity of the biblical text, and the nature of miracles, that led to the adoption of both historical and textual criticism in Bible classes in most Canadian seminaries. In like measure, Charles Darwin's *Origin of the Species* (1859) and *The Descent of Man* (1871) provoked extended and heated debate over the supernatural origins of humanity, a debate that still divides. The issues raised by Darwin were given added weight by the new discoveries in geological sciences, which called for pushing back the age of the Earth by hundreds of thousands of years. Modernists accepted the new discoveries and developed a theology that placed humanity within the unfolding process of evolution.

Canadians also responded to the social displacements of urbanization, especially as Toronto and Montreal grew with the late nineteenth century influx. By the 1890s Canadian voices had arisen to address the social implications of Christianity and build new urban ministries. In 1890, for example, Presbyterian D. J. McDonnell opened mission houses near the slums in Toronto and began night classes for the education of working women. Closely tied to

the social gospel was a new belief in the goodness and perfectibility of humans that saw the race progressing into the kingdom of God. Given a new view of their long history on Earth, thinkers began to project a future in almost utopian terms.

Among the leading Canadian Modernists was Presbyterian George Monro Grant (1835–1902), author of the best selling book *Ocean to Ocean*, an optimistic look at the Canadian future first published in 1873. First at Dalhousie University and then at Queen's Theological College he championed the Modernist cause, demanding that all religious teaching become intellectually respectable. He was joined by Professors John Watson and George Paxton Young.

The progress of Modernist thought was not always smooth. Methodist George Workman was forced to resign his post at Victoria University in 1899 after his public denial of the "dictation theory" of biblical inspiration, a frequent step in the acceptance of biblical critical methodology. Finding a post at another school, he was again forced out in 1907. D. J. McDonnell, pastor of St. Andrew's Church in Toronto, though acquitted, was forced to stand trial by the General Assembly of the Canadian Presbyterian Church for a comment denying the doctrine of everlasting hell.

Possibly the most disturbed by the growth of the new theological perspectives were the Baptists. Shortly after the turn of the century charges were leveled at McMaster University, the Baptist's university in Toronto, with the primary target being one professor, H. T. Matthews. Matthews was accused of attacking the integrity of the Book of Genesis. Arising to lead the attack on McMaster was Thomas T. Shields, the pastor of Jarvis Avenue Baptist Church in Toronto, soon to become an internationally known spokesperson for Fundamentalism, the conservative theological perspective that based its perspective on a defense of the unique Divine authority of the Bible and the traditional Christian affirmations (the fundamentals). Fundamentalists vigorously fought the growing acceptance of critical methods of Bible study, the social gospel, and evolution. After an examination, the Baptist Convention of Ontario and Quebec exonerated Matthews, which led Shields and his supporters to break with the conventions. Several new Baptist groups emerged from that break.

By World War II the issues raised by the controversy had been settled in the Modernists' favor, and the majority of the churches had gone on to other matters. In Canada, Fundamentalism remained strong only in a few smaller conservative churches.

THE MOVE TO UNIFY. At the same time that Modernism grew within the larger churches, a drive to unite the scattered sects of Protestantism gathered strength. While there had been no schisms among Canadian Protestants, such as those that rent the churches in the United States at the time of the Civil War, the churches in the late nineteenth century existed in a disunited state because of sectional divisions over the vast Canadian territory, as well as the establishment of many similar but organizationally separate churches by each new wave of immigrants. Efforts to unify led to the formation of the United Church of Canada in 1925 and the Canadian Council of Churches in 1944.

The work of uniting the churches began as individual denominations found similar groups of like mind and began a process of denominational family cooperation. For example, in the early nineteenth century the Methodists searched out means to bring together the nonepiscopal British Wesleyans with those who were episcopally led. The process of a merger culminated in 1864 when the Canadian branches of all the various British Methodists merged into a single Methodist body for the country. The even larger number of Presbyterian bodies followed a similar pattern between 1817 and 1879. The Congregationalists had two major unions in 1906 and 1907.

While the Methodists, Presbyterians, and Congregationalists were merging their denominational families, as early as the 1860s serious proposals for unions across denominational lines were entertained by Methodists and Presbyterians. Similar proposals were considered in the 1870s by Congregationalists and Presbyterians and a decade later by Anglicans with all three denominations. However, nothing came of these discussions prior to the turn of the century.

Then in 1902, an idea originally suggested by George M. Grant in 1874 of a united "Church of Canada," began to bear fruit. That year the Methodist general conference issued an overture to its sister denominations to appoint committees to plan for union. The overture was received favorably by the Presbyterians and Congregationalists at their gatherings during the next two years, and the three initiated work on a "basis of union" document in December 1904. After four years an agreement was reached and passed on to the three churches. Main topics of discussion included doctrine (which led the Baptists to decline participation) and polity (over which the Anglicans ultimately withdrew). A variety of names were proposed and discussed. Once submitted to the denominations, a lengthy struggle to gain commitment to the plan and the proper enabling legislation to have the plan adopted and implemented ensued. Finally, in 1925 the Methodist, Presbyterian, and Congregationalist Churches merged to form the United Church of Canada, which immediately assumed its place as the third major church body in the country.

By the time of the formation of the United Church of Canada, the spirit of Christian cooperation and unity, at least on the councilor level, was growing. In the United States the Federal Council of Christian Churches was fruitfully functioning. On the international level the conferences that were to lead to the formation of the World Council of Churches were underway. The idea of a council to facilitate communication, prevent duplication of efforts, coordinate ministries, and provide fellowship seemed both useful and a practical step toward unity. Thus in 1944, 12 denominations came together to form the Canadian Council of Churches. It included both Protestant and Eastern Orthodox bodies. Over the years the Lutherans, one of the few major Christian bodies not among the charter members, joined, while the Baptist Federation of Canada withdrew (even though its major component, the Baptist Convention of Ontario and Quebec, immediately joined). In more recent years the Canadian Conference of (Roman) Catholic Bishops has become an associate member. The council now includes the overwhelming majority of Canadian Christians in its member organizations.

JUDAISM FROM 1850 TO THE PRESENT. Though always a small minority, the Jewish community of Canada spread as the country grew. They were among the first settlers in the west. A synagogue appeared in Victoria, British Columbia, in the 1860s. The first informal congregational service was held in Winnipeg in 1882 and Congregation Beth El was organized two years later. A congregation is noted in Regina, Saskatchewan, in 1913.

Beginning in the late nineteenth century, Jews migrated to Canada in large numbers. Over 80,000 arrived between 1900 and the beginning of World War I. Most of the new arrivals were Orthodox, and even though Reform Judaism had appeared among Canadians quite early, it never gained the support it had in the United States. During the period between the wars, the religious segment of the community did align itself with the three main Jewish groups, Conservative, Reform, and Orthodox, with both Sephardic and Ashkenazic Orthodox congregations in existence. Most of the congregations also aligned with one of the several congregational associations headquartered in New York City.

Immediately after World War II, Canadian Jewry experienced a second major wave of immigration, as survivors of the war and the Holocaust poured into the country. During the last generation, the community has grown from 200,000 to approximately 300,000. Again, the new arrivals tended to be Orthodox, and included members of several Hassidic groups (such as the Lubavitchers) and have kept the community predominantly Orthodox, though the growth of Conservative congregations has been noticeable and a few Reconstruction synagogues have appeared.

THE OTHER RELIGIONS. Throughout Canada since the middle of the nineteenth century, the larger church bodies have been

faced with the organizational splintering of Christendom. While finding some unity in the formation of the United Church of Canada and the Canadian Council of Churches described above, their efforts have always been countered by the schisms in Canadian church bodies. For example, a large minority of the Presbyterian Church refused to join the United Church of Canada, and remains today as a separate organization though a member of the Canadian Council of Churches. Added to the schisms are the arrival of new churches from Europe and, most importantly, the constant importation of the hundreds of sectarian bodies that have formed in the United States and view Canada as a mission field.

During the 1850s, for example, Spiritualism, which had started in New York, had spread across Canada from Ontario to the Maritimes, and letters attesting to the power of the spiritualistic phenomena regularly filled the pages of the early spiritualist periodicals. During the twentieth century, Canadians formed several national associations.

The Holiness movement came to Canada in the 1800s and produced some new churches, the most prominent being that led by Ralph Cecil Horner (1854–1921), a former Methodist. He organized and led the Holiness Movement Church, but when asked to retire as its bishop in 1919, he left to found the Standard Church of America.

Pentecostalism spread quickly to Canada from the 1906 revival on Azusa Street in Los Angeles. Canadians then were to initiate two of the important teachings in Pentecostalism, which were to lead to the development of two new subgroupings producing a score of new denominational organizations. Possibly the first Canadian Pentecostal was R. E. McAleister. At a camp meeting in Los Angeles in 1913, he preached on water baptism in the name of "Jesus only," thus initiating what was to become the Apostolic or non-Trinitarian Pentecostalism. Then in 1948 in western Canada, at an independent Bible school, the Sharon Orphanage and School at North Battleford, Saskatchewan, a Pentecostal revival began and swept across North America. The Latter Rain Revival brought a new emphasis on prophecy and the laying-on-of-hands to Pentecostalism and, though considering itself a nondenominational movement, it produced more than 20 new denominations in North America.

The Church of Christ, Scientist came to Canada during the life of its founder, Mary Baker Eddy, and in 1906–1907 became the location of two important court cases involving Christian Scientists. In both cases, parents who had used Christian Science treatment in the place of standard medical assistance were convicted of manslaughter in the death of their children.

While a growing number of Christian sects found their way to Canada prior to World War II, in more recent decades, Canada has faced the same rapid proliferation of new and diverse groups, especially in its major cities, as has the United States. Many of these groups have been imported from the United States, but many have also come directly from Asia and the Middle East (usually by way of Europe or Australia). For example, the Baha'i Faith was brought to Canada in 1903 when Canadian architect William Sutherland Maxwell married an American. However, it was not until 1949 that the work grew to a point that it could be set apart under its own National Spiritual Assembly. Included among the recently arrived are not only teachers seeking to convert Canadians, but also a new wave of Asian immigrants who are building Buddhist and Hindu temples. Besides the more well known, such as the Unification Church and the International Society for Krishna Consciousness, Canada is the headquarters of the Zen Lotus Society, Yasodhara Ashram Society, the Sivananda Vedanta Yoga Centers, and the Kabalarian Philosophy.

Thus Canada is currently at one with the whole of Western society. While showing no sign of giving up Christianity, which shows every sign of continuing as the faith of the majority of Canadians in the foreseeable future, Canada is now home to an ever-increasing number of the world's faiths which are arising to take their place in building the future of the nation.

CANADIAN RELIGION: A CONTEMPORARY OVERVIEW.
Looking at Canadian religion over the last two decades one can see two very contradictory trends. On the one hand, as sketched out above, Canada has become home to the same kind of diverse religious life that characterizes the contemporary West. Thus to leave one of the older churches is not necessarily to drop out of the religious life, and the decline of the dominant liberal Protestant faiths should not be taken as a sign of the secularization of society as much as a readjustment in the face of an increasingly diverse religious economy.

Reginald Bibby, however, has tracked the more negative side of the Canadian religion story, both the decline of church membership over the last generation and the more startling decline in church attendance. All of the major denominations, including the Roman Catholics, showed a membership increase in the decades immediately following World War II, but peaked in the late 1960s and began to decline in the 1970s. The decline has not been reversed. All during this period the population increased, and thus the percentage of people affiliated with a faith declined decade by decade. Equally important, the percentage of church members attending church regularly dropped off dramatically, by almost 50 percent for Roman Catholics and over 50 percent for Protestants.

The interpretation of these different trends varies considerably, but suggests that Canada offers a very open and fluid religious situation as it prepares for the twenty-first century. At the same time, due to the very spread-out nature of the country, a reversal of the increasingly entrenched direction that religion is taking may be difficult to achieve.

Selected Sources on Canadian Religious History

GENERAL SOURCES

Bibby, Reginald W. *Fragmented Gods: The Poverty and Potential of Religion in Canada*. Toronto: Irwin Publishing, 1987. 319 pp.

Grant, John Webster. *The Canadian Experience of Church Union*. Richmond, VA: John Knox Press, 1967. 106 pp.

———. *The Church in the Canadian Era*. Toronto: McGraw-Hill Ryerson, 1972. 241 pp.

Kilbourn, William. *Religion in Canada*. Toronto: McClelland and Stewart, 1868. 128 pp.

Masters, Donald C. *A Short History of Canada*. Princeton, NJ: Van Nostrand Company, 1958. 191 pp.

McInnis, Edgar. *Canada, A Political and Social History*. Toronto: Rinehart & Company, 1959. 619 pp.

Moir, John S. *The Church in the British Era*. Toronto: McGraw-Hill Ryerson, 1972. 230 pp.

Silcox, Claris Edwin. *Church Union in Canada*. New York: Institute of Social and Religious Research, 1933. 493 pp.

Wilson, Douglas J. *The Church Grows in Canada*. Toronto: Canadian Council of Churches, 1966. 224 pp.

MAJOR RELIGIOUS BODIES IN CANADA

Carrington, Philip. *The Anglican Church in Canada*. Toronto: Collins, 1963. 320 pp.

Centennial of Canadian Methodism. Toronto: William Briggs, 1891. 339 pp.

Cronmiller, Carl R. *A History of the Lutheran Church in Canada*. Toronto: Evangelical Lutheran Synod of Canada, 1961. 288 pp.

Epp, Frank H. *Mennonites in Canada, 1920–1940*. Toronto: Macmillan of Canada, 1982. 640 pp.

Guenter, Jacob G. *Men of Steele*. Saskatoon, SK: The Author, 1981. 261 pp.

Quiring, Walter, and Helen Bartel. *Mennonites in Canada: A Pictorial Review*. Altona, MB: D. W. Friesen & Sons, 1961. 208 pp.

Rosenberg, Stuart E. *The Jewish Community in Canada*. Toronto: McClelland and Stewart, 1970. 231 pp.

Sanderson, J. E. *The First Century of Methodism in Canada*. Toronto: William Briggs, 1908–10. 2 Vols.

Walker, J. U. *History of Wesleyan Methodism in Halifax*. Halifax: Hartley and Walker, 1834. 279 pp.

Chapter 1
Interfaith and Ecumenical Family of Organizations

Consult the "Contents" pages to locate the entries in Part III,
the Directory Listings Sections, that comprise this family.

Amid the variety of long-term trends noticeable in the religious life of Western culture since the sixteenth century Reformation, the move toward religious diversity has been most evident. With the break up of the Roman Catholic dominance of religious expression and the assumption of control in large areas of Europe by Anglican, Lutheran, and Calvinist churches, not only was Roman Catholic hegemony limited, but the loose control at the boundaries of the newly established communities invited further diversity and disruption of what unity remained. At the same time Europe was expanding across the Atlantic into a new world, ideas supportive of broad freedoms of religious expression were circulating among settlers who had already cut major social ties to the homeland.

Through the nineteenth century, Europe continued its expansionist ways. The leading nations established colonies in Africa, the South Seas, the mainland of Asia, and the Middle East. The United States and Canada pushed their ambitions for territorial expansion across North America. Everywhere the Europeans and Americans went, they found new and different religions, radically diverse from the beliefs and practices of the Christianity and Judaism with which they were most familiar. A few scholars began to study these new faiths, and to share their findings first with colleagues back home, and then as the century came to an end, with the public at large. A small but significant minority of these early students of the world's religions found in these newly discovered faiths what had been lacking in their own religious upbringing and became the first modern Western converts to Islam, Buddhism, and Hinduism.

By the second half of the nineteenth century, the major Protestant churches of Europe and North America were gearing up for a worldwide missionary endeavor which would literally carry them to every country of the world, to many areas which had yet to be mapped. Through the last decades of the century, books, from superficial travelogues to scholarly texts, would document what the missionaries found. From this time forward, the theological task would include the incorporation of knowledge of the presence of so many different religions outside of the Abrahamic lineage (i.e., neither Judaism, Christianity, nor Islam). Eastern intellectual leaders would confront the learned centers of the West with the subtleties of Indian philosophy, the Buddhist parallels to Christianity, and the Imperial power behind Shintoism.

While there were many shades of opinion, two essential approaches emerged which would dominate the Western religious community's response to the ever-increasing levels of religious pluralism through the twentieth century. One group of leaders saw in the existence of the world's different religions an opportunity, if not a real moral imperative, to learn and understand. Each of these leaders possessed an appreciation for the accomplishments, ethical integrity, and spiritual life of at least one of the world's religious communities and could by analogy extend that appreciation to the other communities. In the beginning of the twentieth century, almost all Westerners saw Christianity as superior to the other religions, they also could not deny the many likenesses each of the different faiths shared with one another and with Christianity. Such an approach undergirded the organization and furtherance of interfaith activities.

A second group of leaders saw in the existence of the world's different religions as a challenge to their Christian faith. Foreign lands dominated by Buddhists, Hindus, Muslims and other smaller (in number of adherents) faiths called them first to create and then back the international missionary enterprise. However, the reaffirmation of Christianity's superiority and uniqueness accompanying the missionary enterprise also highlighted the scandal of Christianity's many divisions, especially when a heated debate from home was carried to the mission field and became focused in the rival recruitment activities of two mission stations in the same community. Christian leaders were spurred to cooperative and coordinated activity by the necessity of presenting a united front on the mission field (which in the nineteenth century included the American West) and making the most of the missionary dollars.

Those who saw the world primarily as a target for evangelism tended to move toward Christian ecumenical endeavors. While many arguments based in abstract theological ideals could and would be made for Christians to put aside their sectarian differences, to find their oneness in their common affirmation of the same Christ, and to cooperate in what all saw as important endeavors, the argument from the missionary field would remain dominant for many decades.

INTERFAITH BEGINNINGS—THE WORLD'S PARLIAMENT OF RELIGIONS. Unitarian James Freeman Clarke, while a professor at Harvard Divinity School, pioneered the study of what he termed "comparative theology." As defined by him, the field's first problem was "analytical, being to distinguish each religion from the rest." He compared different religions to see wherein they agreed and wherein they differed. But the next problem, he added, "is synthetical, and considers the adaptation of each system to every other, to determine its place, use, and value, in reference to universal or absolute religion," (*Ten Great Religions*, 1868, 1895). As information about different religions filtered back into the West, the early academic students of world religion began the task of sketching out the upward evolutionary trend they discerned in religious life and thought. This trend led directly to the crown and pinnacle of Christianity in its liberal Protestant form. Tieing all of the religions together was an ideal and absolute religion to which any particular faith more or less conformed and by which it could be measured.

Such a perspective fit in quite nicely with the positive evolutionary thought of the day with its intense faith in human progress. As Clarke further noted of his intellectual discipline, the study of comparative religion "shows the relation of each particular religion to human civilization and observes how each religion of the world is a step in the progress of humanity. It shows that both the positive and negative side of a religion make it a preparation for a higher religion, and that the universal religion must root itself in the decaying soil of partial religions. Christianity was superior to the other religions as it was a post-tribal faith capable of serving all humankind and an ever-evolving faith as shown by the appearance of Protestantism out of Catholicism (or Papal religion)."

While one would be hard pressed to defend Clarke's position today, it was shared by his scholarly colleagues and by many liberal religious leaders. It also supported the first great interfaith effort, the World's Parliament of Religions, held in Chicago in the fall of 1893. The Parliament actually grew out of another event, the Columbian Exposition, a massive celebration of the four-hundredth anniversary of Columbus' discovery of America. As Congresses were created to give expression to each area of human knowledge, the question of religion arose, and in 1891 Presbyterian minister J. H. Barrows was chosen to chair a committee to consider the question of the appropriateness of a congress of religion.

Barrows' committee quickly reached a consensus that such a congress was a worthy enterprise and that it should consist of representatives of all of the world's major religions. In reaching that decision they set off a debate over the form that such a meeting could have and the relationship of different religions to each other implicit in such a gathering. It was the hope of the committee in issuing a call for cooperation in the holding of such a congress that it would be an expression of mutual respect and not sow any additional seeds of discord (as many who opposed the idea feared).

Once the conference was set, representatives of many different Christian churches and all of the major non-Christian religious groups chose to participate, but for a variety of very different reasons. The more idealistic groups believed that in their coming together, to talk about the overriding concerns of the era, that the great truths which they believed permeated all religions would come to the fore and point a direction for the uplifting of humankind and the solving of its major problems. Many of the smaller groups saw the Parliament as a platform from which they could state their case to a large audience. Some of the Eastern religions seized the opportunity to refute what they considered to be misrepresentations of them in Christian literature. In the end, some joined in simply so as not to be left out.

The Parliament was a magnificently staged production; the building presently housing the Art Institute of Chicago having been constructed especially for its sessions. It opened to a full house of 4,000 in the main hall on September 11, 1893, and continued for 17 days. While each of the represented religions had ample opportunity to sing its own praises (and a number of groups held special sessions for its adherents), the program of the Parliament centered upon the discussion of various social issues from the status and role of women to the imperative for religions to assist the rise of African Americans. Crime, labor relations, international arbitration, and general social reform received the attention of a cadre of presenters.

Interestingly enough, the stars of the Parliament were not the famous preacher/orators of the day, but two virtual unknowns: British Theosophical leader Annie Besant and Indian teacher Swami Vivekananda. Besant, well-known in England for her oratorical skills, received an enthusiastic response for her talk to the Theosophists denominational congress. Whenever Swami Vivekananda spoke, the large hall had to be used to accommodate the crowd who flocked to hear the charismatic young teacher who so articulately and vigorously defended his homeland and his Hindu faith.

The Parliament's planners were unable to predict the major consequences of their establishing the series of meetings. The gathering became an unprecedented opportunity for representatives of Buddhism, Hinduism and Islam to present their teachings to a virgin audience. Capable speakers from each community, to the surprise of their audience, demonstrated that their religion was sophisticated enough to stand beside anything the West had to offer and a few members of the audience decided that these new foreign faiths offered a valid alternative to the Christianity or Juda-

ism in which they had been raised. Plans emerged to follow up on what they had heard at the Parliament. Swami Vivekananda stayed in the United States to teach and eventually organize the first Hindu center in the country, the Vedanta Society of New York. Muslim leader Alexander Russell Webb also moved to New York City where he opened the first mosque in the country and midwifed the emergence of the Muslim community. Buddhists had already established a presence in the United States, though generally confined to ethnic communities in California during the gold rush, but now made arrangements not only to accept Western converts, but to actively offer their faith to Westerners.

The primary motivating force behind the World's Parliament of Religions, the Liberal Protestant leaders, like James Freeman Clarke, believed in the moral and ideological superiority of Christianity as the particular religious expression that most closely approached their ideal of a universal and absolute religion. They did not fare as well at the Congress as compared to other perspectives, but following the Congress, they were able to institutionalize their program of promoting Liberal Protestantism when Caroline E. Haskell endowed the Barrows Lectures through the University of Chicago. The lectures were named in honor of John Henry Barrows, the university's professor who served as president of the Parliament. The endowment called for a set of lectures to be given annually in Calcutta, India, (and other cities of India as appropriate) on the relationship of Christianity to other religions. In this manner, the case for Christianity could be regularly presented before an audience of educated Hindus with the hope that they would come to see the convincing claims of Christian faith. Barrows himself delivered the first set of lectures, collectively titled "Christianity the World Religion." The series continued for several years, but there was no report of any converts, especially among Indian influentials, from the presentations.

Possibly the most substantial fruit of the Parliament was the more formal organization of the most liberal wing of American religion into a cooperative organization, the American Congress of Liberal Religious Societies. Even before the Congress, Unitarian and Universalist Church leaders, primarily in the Midwest, had been cooperating in the production of a Chicago-based periodical, *Unity*. The Parliament inspired them to take the additional step of creating a national organization that would bring together not only liberal Christians but Reform Jews, Ethical Culturists, and other liberal religious voices for cooperative endeavors. Some 200 people attended the organizational meeting in 1894 at Chicago's prominent Sinai Temple, the Reform Jewish synagogue on the shores of Lake Michigan.

The new Congress of Religion emerged around the ideal of what it termed "undogmatic" religion and looked for the organization of nonsectarian churches and societies based upon absolute religious liberty. Members included not only churches and synagogues also belonging to older denominations (including one Quaker congregation) but several new independent churches such as Jenken Lloyd Jones' All Souls Church in Chicago. The Congress went through several name changes, emerging in 1900 as simply the Congress of Religion.

Changes in the religious alignment of the major supporters of the Congress of Religion made it increasingly obsolete after the turn of the century. But in the meantime Unitarian leaders in New England (where liberal religion actually enjoyed its greatest strength) founded a cooperative organization with the ponderous name of the International Congress of Unitarian and other Liberal Religious Thinkers and Workers. This Congress drew support from the center of both the Unitarian and Universalist movements as opposed to the older Congress of Religion that had claimed the most liberal and radical religionists among its key supporters. At its meeting in Boston in 1907, the International Congress proposed the formation of a national federation of religious liberals, somewhat like the newly formed Federal Council of Churches (see below) then in process of formation, and among the major Protestant organizations. Thus as the Congress of Religion faded, the new Federation of Religious Liberals of America arose to take its place.

The Federation was unburdened by the "nonsectarian" language of the older Congress and did not threaten established denominational interests. Using the Federal Council of Churches model, leaders avoided the anti-denominational activity of calling for the formation of independent unaligned congregations. Approximately 1,000 attended the first gathering in Philadelphia in 1909. Its establishment orientation was clearly demonstrated in 1913 when the entire social program of the Federal Council of Churches was adopted as its own. The National Council would meet regularly until the early 1930s when it fell victim to the Depression.

In the meantime, the international body (which, following a series of name changes, finally emerged as the International Congress of Religious Liberals) had its ups and downs especially through the period following World War I. In 1930 the weakening organization was superseded by the International Association for the Promotion of Liberal Christianity and Religious Freedom with a secretariat located in Amsterdam. World War II again disrupted the organization and headquarters returned to the United States. More recently it revived as the International Association for Religious Freedom and reestablished its European presence with a secretariat in Frankfort, Germany. It is currently the oldest international interfaith organization in existence, and in the last generation has built a vital program focused in its Triennial congresses.

The devastation of World War I gave birth to visionaries who saw the role that a unified world religious community could play in the post-war recovery. Among them were such very different people as Charles Frederick Weller and Jane Addams in Chicago, Sir Francis Younghusband in England and His Highness, the Maharaja Geakwar of Baroda, Gujurat, India. Their vision merged with the aspirations of others and in 1924 led three American groups—the League of Neighbors, the Union of East and West, and the Fellowship of Faiths—to unite their efforts in the formation of what would become the World Fellowship of Faiths. Beginning in 1925 the new Fellowship held an initial meeting in New York City, followed by additional gatherings across the United States, in London, and in India. Affiliated meetings soon spread across Europe and into the West Indies.

As news was received that a World's Fair would be held in Chicago in 1933, suggestions for a meeting analogous to the 1893 World's Parliament of Religions began circulating and plans for a gathering of a World Fellowship of Faiths got underway. Two important steps beyond the Parliament of 1893 were suggested for the 1933 event: First, greater emphasis would be placed upon religious communities applying their faith to solving human problems with a resulting deemphasis upon their simply restating their position on various issues. Second, the term "faiths," rather than "religions," would be used so that fellowship leaders would understood that their conversation was not limited to members of formally organized religions; all types of spiritual consciousness and conviction would be included in the dialogue established by the Fellowship.

In the end, the Fellowship moved faster than the World's Fair, and thus, in the summer of 1933, 83 sessions of the World Fellowship of Faiths were convened in an effort that surpassed the original Parliament in both size and scope. More than 250 key religious and secular leaders from around the world participated, from Methodist bishop Francis McConnell, who served as National Chairman of the 1933 gathering, to Professor John Dewey, a Humanist, to Duke Kwei Nyamikye Kuntu of the Gold Coast, a leader of the Ashanti African religion. Following the meeting, Charles Frederick Weller collected the papers and published them in a massive volume.

Out of the 1933 meetings, Sir Francis Younghusband took the lead and a second congress was held in London in 1936. Earlier in his life, while in Tibet in 1903, Younghusband had a mystical experience of what he described as "a mighty joy-giving power" that was at work in the world. His religious experience also led him to a belief in the mystical sense of the unity of all people. He saw in his interfaith work the task of making religious leaders aware of the mystical unity which transcended their religious differences. Among his early attempts at spreading his message, apart from his several books, was an address he gave to the Religions of the Empire Conference, a more scholarly informational meeting held in London in 1924.

Younghusband used his aristocratic connections to bring a set of speakers to the 1936 congress that were equally eminent to those assembled by Francis McConnell three years previously. He also did some innovative programming by setting up dialogues and discussions between the participants as part of the program. Previously, such events had simply consisted of paper presentations without the public interaction that held the possibility of open conflict. In Younghusband's presence, such potentially disastrous discussions were carried out in an atmosphere of respect and even good humor.

The contacts leading up to the 1936 meeting nurtured the new consensus reached by the interfaith leadership in the mid thirties of the insufficiency of religious *tolerance* as an ideal. Tolerance carried the notion of condescension, with the more powerful, established Western religions acting graciously toward their inferior religious counterparts in the rest of the world; while better than religious persecution and suppression, it was inadequate for reaching the goals of the Fellowship. Thus leaders began to give vocal support to ideals of mutual appreciation, of each participant in the dialogue being able to honor the faith of others. As the implications of this position were slowly understood, people engaged in dialogue with the adoption of an attitude of listening and openness to others as they spoke out of their faith commitments. This view would come to dominate interfaith dialogue, and on occasion involved a radical and personal shift in perspective by people of deep religious commitment who also engaged in such dialogue over a period of time

Immediately after the 1936 meeting, a continuation committee with Younghusband as chairman was established. Annual congresses were held for the next three years, but were cut short due to the outbreak of World War II and then Younghusband's subsequent death in 1942. The Fellowship continued in the decades after the war and has done a monumental job in the United Kingdom of keeping alive the interfaith vision. After the war, the Fellowship responded to the full resistance of a Christian movement responding to war-torn Europe and unwilling to consider interfaith concerns in the midst of its own intrafaith enthusiasms. However, slowly, its work has born fruit as England's own religious diversity has been recognized.

INTERFAITH ACTIVITY SINCE WORLD WAR II. World War II significantly disrupted most of the fragile interfaith ties that had been built during the 1920s and 1930s. By the time the world recovered, many of the leaders active in the pre-war interfaith movement had retired from the scene, and the war itself released forces that were to reorder political and social relationships internationally. Colonialism's days were numbered. Beginning with the loss of colonies by the losing countries in the war, and the move to Indian independence, the entire colonial system began to be dismantled. For religions, this change meant a significant shift in power relationships between the religious leaders of the colonial powers and the religious leaders of once conquered nations. Buddhists, Hindus, and Muslims around the world tolerated no implications of second-class participation in dialogues that were to take place with their European and North American counterparts.

Along with the political shifts came the formation of the United Nations and the adoption in 1948 of the Universal Declaration of Human Rights. The very existence of such a body gave status to the different religions that dominated the member nations of the

UN. The declaration specifically empowered those religions in its statement that read, "Every one has the right to freedom of thought, conscience and religion; this right includes freedom to change his religion or belief, and freedom, either alone or in community with others and in public or private to manifest his religion or belief in teaching, practice, worship and observance." The Universal Declaration largely embodied the understanding of the secular state inherent in Western thought, which suggested that in the eyes of the state, all religions are equal and that the state is not to choose among them so much as to protect the right of each to exist in the larger social community. In such a situation, religion relinquishes its use of the state's coercive power in spreading its message.

Increasingly, with the independence of India, the changes wrought by the Chinese Revolution, the travel privileges afforded residents of the British Commonwealth, and the new openness to immigration expressed by the United States after 1965, representatives of and adherents to the world's religions moved to the West and established worshipping communities. And, like the Christian missionaries of the nineteenth century, they moved to gather converts from among those who had been born and raised in Europe and the Americas. As those communities have grown, related institutions such as colleges, seminaries, monasteries, and publishing houses have slowly emerged. Building interfaith relationships was no longer necessarily tied to international travel and global gatherings. Any of the world's urban centers was now home to the spectrum of the world's religions.

At least in the West, interfaith activity and contact dipped to its lowest since before 1893 in the decade immediately after the World War II. Amid other pressing recovery needs, it tended to be pushed aside. When it did reemerge in strength, it did so in the service of a vital human interest—world peace. Occasioned by the Cuban missile crisis, which brought the United States and the Soviet Union to the brink of war, Dr. Dana McLean Greeley, Methodist Bishop John Wesley Lord, Rabbi Maurice N. Eisenfrath, and Bishop (later Cardinal) John Wright gathered together to discuss the possibility of creating an international structure involving religious leaders working for peace. An initial conference to this end was held in New York City in 1964 and a National Inter-Religious Conference on Peace was held two year later in Washington, D.C. Early in 1967, Dr. Homer Jack and an associate made a world tour to test the waters on convening an international conference. The positive reception they encountered led to the formation of the first International Inter-Religious Symposium on Peace in New Delhi, India, in 1968, by which time many of the American delegates were deeply involved in the anti-Vietnam War protest movement.

The work of the conference in New Delhi would be continued two years later by the international conference on peace held in Kyoto, Japan, in 1970 at which the more than 300 delegates from some 40 countries established the World Conference on Religion and Peace. Since that time the WCRP has held its World Assemblies every five years, spawned numerous national and local affiliate groups to advocate the organization's peace concerns, and developed a variety of social programs, especially some responding to the needs of refugees of war.

The WCRP has had a vital international program with concern focused on a single issue: peace. The other type of successful interfaith organization has been built around a very different kind of focus: the dialogue between two (or on occasion, three) religions aimed at resolving problems between the two communities or responding to the mutual threats faced by both communities. During the twentieth century, the most fruitful of such dialogues has been carried out between Jewish and Christian leaders. While wandering broadly through religious, social, and political issues common to the two groups, the bedrock of the conversation has been the elimination of anti-Semitism and, by extension, the eradication of all forms of ethnic, racial, and religious prejudice.

No interfaith activity has commanded the time and energy as has Jewish-Christian dialogue, and efforts were only increased as the severe damage done to the Jewish community during the Nazi Holocaust became more generally known. The statement on the Jews by the Roman Catholic Church's Vatican II Council, followed by similar statements from various Protestant church bodies, created new openings around which dialogue could proceed.

Beginning with initial organizations in the 1920s, today the cause of Christian-Jewish understanding is served by a set of organizations which function from the international and national levels to local congregations. Through the last half of the twentieth century, the Middle Eastern situation has continued to boil even as Muslims have developed a significant presence in North America and the United Kingdom. In the shifting context, three party dialogues between Christians, Jews, and Muslims have emerged though they have yet to have the measurable impact on public consciousness as have the Christian-Jewish dialogues.

1993: A SECOND WORLD'S PARLIAMENT. The approaching centennial of the original World's Parliament of Religions occasioned reflection by the leaders of the religious community in Chicago, some of whom began early in the 1980s to suggest that an appropriate moment was approaching to consider what had occurred as a result of the forces released at the first parliament, and initiate a new effort at interfaith dialogue and activity. Twenty years of immigration had transformed the religious outlines of the Chicago Metropolitan Area, by then home to substantial communities of Buddhists, Hindus, and Muslims, with smaller assemblies of Zoroastrians, Sikhs, Ismaili, and Shintoists. It was the North American headquarters of the Baha'is, and had congregations of most of the world's new religions.

In spite of a slow start and at times doubts as to whether the meeting would actually be held, the Centennial Parliament of the World's Religions was finally convened with over 6,000 in attendance. The Parliament drew speakers as establishment-oriented as a Roman Catholic Cardinal, as questionable as a Neo-Pagan priestess, and as controversial as African American leader Louis Farrakhan. The attendees adopted a lengthy ethical statement and various continuing efforts have been initiated.

It is yet to be seen what may grow out of the 1993 Parliament but initially, even in the planning (led by the Hindu, Buddhist, and Muslim communities) and later in observing the participants, a distinct difference between 1893 and 1993 was evident. Non-Christian groups not present at the 1893 gathering saw the Parliament as a time to assert their presence in the West and the newer religions seized the opportunity to inform the older religious community of their desire to be recognized and to participate as partners in any ongoing dialogue.

Paralleling the efforts of the new Parliament, a second continuing effort at interfaith dialogue emerged as part of the global efforts of Korean evangelist Sun Myung Moon to united the world's people. Moon, founder and leader of the controversial Unification Church, encouraged the formation of the Global Congress of the World's Religions—originally suggested by a professor at the Unification Seminary—and poured a considerable amount of the church's resources into bringing religious leaders from around the world into both regional meetings and occasional large international gatherings. In 1985 the Global Congress was superseded by the Assembly of the World's Religions. The Assembly has provided the most stable continuing international interreligious dialogue from the 1960s to the 1990s, but has been hampered by the boycotting of its meeting by many key religious figures who have rejected any association with Moon.

Both the 1993 Parliament of the World's Religions and the activities of the Assembly of the World's Religions point to the overwhelming problem faced by those who would engage in interfaith dialogue. Such activity is usually done without the backing of the community of faith of the participants and often by people who do not have the ear of the decision making leadership of their own faith community. Such interfaith gatherings have no direct impact upon the larger religious community and accomplishments must be measured otherwise—in the insights, discoveries, and agreements reached by participants who then return to the larger religious community to exercise leadership informed by their interfaith experience. Slowly, a community of people deeply committed to their own faith and traditions, and also committed to the "appreciation" of the faith and spiritual wisdom of people of other faiths, has emerged and a global context, at least in principle, in which dialogue can be nurtured has been set in place.

INTRAFAITH ECUMENISM. In the West, the splitting of the Christian movement into warring factions had become a constant element of the church's life to which accommodation had to be made. The churches in the easternmost nations, Syria and beyond, followed what, from the standpoint of the western churches, were heretical paths. Eastern Orthodoxy and Roman Catholicism went their separate ways at the end of the first Christian millennium. Then the West was traumatized in the sixteenth century by the splitting of Christian Europe into Roman, Anglican, Lutheran, and Reformed territories with bothersome Anabaptists popping up in various unexpected locations. Still, depending upon where one stood to look around, the number of factions immediately available was rather limited. Even the threat of Lutheranism and Anglicanism seemed to pale for Papal authorities in light of the incursions of Muslim Turkish forces up the Danube valley beyond Budapest to the very gates of Vienna.

The number of actual religious competitors (i.e., different churches) remained relatively small until the seventeenth century when Pietism and Puritanism sent shock waves through Protestantism and the rise of Deism and Freethought challenged the whole Christian enterprise as then constituted. Numerous new movements began to appear, some harshly suppressed, but most finding havens of tolerance, even it they had to flee across the Atlantic to the new world.

As Christendom splintered, counter voices calling for the unity of the Christian movement arose along with theologies that affirmed the unity of the church even in the face of the obvious administrative factionalism. These voice, however, expressed the minority point of view. Even into the twentieth century, it was often difficult for Protestants and Catholics to put aside the bitter events of the Reformation era and to forgive each other for the excesses and deaths in the religious wars and persecutions; open hostilities ceased only to be replaced with the harshest of polemics. And even among the various Protestant groups harsh rhetoric could be heard as each proclaimed its superiority to rivals and championed its peculiar insight onto the gospel message.

Only in the nineteenth century, with the major Reformation and Puritan Protestant groups having gained some solid organizational power and having stabilized their position in the larger society, could Protestant leaders begin to think in terms of some kind of understanding that might lead to their engagement in cooperative endeavors in the face of common goals and tasks. Much of that commonality came from the opportunity for global expansion as Europeans began their explorations of the rest of the world and as North Americans moved across the continent to claim it and settle it for the United States and Canada.

The churches' responses to the forces operating on them at the beginning of the nineteenth century can be seen in the Plan of Union of 1801 and the emergence of the Disciples of Christ Movement. By the beginning of the nineteenth century, westward migration was seen as a major theme in American life, and it was obvious to the leaders of the two largest Protestant churches of New England that they were expending much energy in taking their quarrel over church polity into the newly opened territories west of the Appalachian Mountains. Hence, in 1801, they worked out an agreement by which they cut their competition in the American West and divided the rest of the world into exclusive missionary areas. The plan worked for a generation, until the Congregationalists perceived that it gave the Presbyterians a distinct advantage in the west and pulled out in 1852.

The Disciples of Christ was a new denomination that arose in the American West partially in response to the sectarian bickering

between the various Presbyterian, Baptist, and Methodist churches. It refused to accept a "denominational" name (though its doctrine was largely a Baptist Calvinist theology including the Baptist free church perspective that eschewed any sacraments (in favor of the ordinances of baptism and the Lord's supper) and radically limited any organization above the congregational level. While opposing sectarianism, the founders failed to perceive that sectarianism or denominationalism was the form of religious life in a free secular society. Where the physical coercion of the state did not operate, religious debate never resolved issues, only made each party more resolute in their position. In such a setting, their own nonsectarian ideal became simply another sectarian perspective held by the group denominated as the Disciples of Christ.

Thus it was that a more realistic attempt to unite Christians across denominational lines, to present a common front, to work on mutual tasks that could be done most effectively by cooperation, and to avoid denominational bickering, emerged in the early nineteenth century with the suggestion of the formation of an international alliance of Protestant (or Evangelical) churches. The original suggestion seems to have come from several European church leaders, but four Americans quickly emerged as champions of the cause: Leonard Bacon, Robert Baird, William Patton, and Samuel Schumacher. Their initial efforts culminated in the formation in 1839 of the Society for the Promotion of Christian Unity, one of a variety of voluntary societies supported primarily by the Congregationalists and the older Lutheran and Reformed churches in nineteenth century America. The effectiveness of the organization, however, was hampered by the divisions that were then occurring in the larger Protestant bodies due to the slavery crisis.

In the midst of the conflicting tensions of organization breakups and calls for union, British leaders issued a call for a conference in London in August 1846 for the purpose of forming an international Evangelical Alliance. Given the participation of leaders from the Church of England, the new alliance had to handle the question of denominationalism very carefully and structured itself as a coalition of individual Christians, not denominations, and made clear that no intentions of creating a new super church or world church administratively existed.

The conference was able to reach some agreement on essential beliefs and affirmed common Christian doctrines of the authority of the Bible, the Trinity, the deity of Christ, the sanctifying work of the Holy Spirit, and future life in heaven and hell. In distinction from Roman Catholicism, general assent was given to the doctrine of justification by faith alone. It was also obvious that Roman Catholicism was seen as the major presence to which some response was necessary. The conference struggled with the issue of making defining affirmations but in such a way as to not override the equally important belief in the right of private judgment on the reading and interpretation of scripture. Issues of predestination, election, and free will (the issues that divided Anglicans and Methodists from Presbyterians and Congregationalists) were avoided entirely. Unitarians and Universalists (nontrinitarians) were defined as outside the Evangelical camp.

The conference considered two plans for its governance. One plan would have had the British firmly in control with various national affiliates. However, a more acceptable plan for governing the proposed alliance offered a confederation model established around six national units. Each national unit would be the equal of the others and would carry out its program and send delegates to an international conference that would gather periodically. The adoption of this plan, however, floundered on the subsequent controversy that arose over American slavery and the unwillingness of the Europeans to enter into any union with slaveholders. While some progress toward an international alliance was reached, in the end it fell apart as the Americans withdrew.

As a result of the London meeting, an international Evangelical Alliance continued to exist in the weakest sense, and meetings were held regularly in Europe through the remainder of the century. Britain dominated the movement and on a more practical level took the lead in spreading the Evangelical gospel worldwide. Meanwhile, the American delegates returned home and in 1846 formed an Evangelical Alliance for the United States, but it soon floundered as the Civil War approached. It was reorganized after the war in 1867, though strength was initially concentrated in the northern urban centers. The life of the alliance in America was placed in the hands of theologian Philip Schaff, businessman William E. Dodge, and general secretary Josiah Strong. Emphasis was placed on social work, organization at the community level, and evangelism toward the unchurched.

The alliance era, both nationally and internationally, forms the first chapter in the modern ecumenical movement. The work of the prospering alliance was continually undercut, however, in the face of denominational growth programs that led to increasing competition for members by denominations, and in the regular emergence of new denominations that were often bitter foes of the group from which they had just departed. The alliance's most noticeable continuing contribution to American religious culture was the annual Week of Prayer for Christian Unity. During the late nineteenth century, however, the alliance had significant success in promoting religious liberty and protecting Protestant missionaries from oppressive governments around the world.

Also competing with the World Evangelical movement was the movement by various denominational families to pull together and reaffirm their common roots. The first were the Anglicans who in 1865 called the initial Lambeth Conference to gather at the Church of England's headquarters, Lambeth Palace, London. While initially dealing with internal issues of the national bodies in communion with the Church of England, it expanded its program to provide a focus for defining relationships with like churches around the world and set policy on the nature of such relationships.

Reformed and Presbyterian churches held an initial gathering of what was called the Alliance of Reformed Churches throughout the World holding the Presbyterian System in 1873. Three years later the General Conference of the Methodist Episcopal Church issued the call for what eventually evolved into the first Methodist Ecumenical Conference in London in 1881. That conference met every decade for more than half a century until it was superseded by the present World Methodist Council. In 1889 the Old Catholic Churches of Europe formed the Union of Utrecht. Following the suggestion of Canadian Congregationalists in 1885, an International Congregational Council assembled in London in 1891. The Baptist World Alliance grew out of the gathering of Baptists from 23 countries in London in 1905.

These denominational family structures outwardly cooperated fully with the pandenominational organizations and generally saw themselves as an extension and expression of such ecumenical work. However, at the practical level, these family groups supplied additional competition for the time and resources of individuals' and churches' financial resources for ecumenical endeavors. As calls for church union arose in the pandenominational organizations, the practical effect was the union of members of the denominational families. Unions across denominational lines were the rarest of occurrences in American Christianity, and in fact were only effective in countries where Protestant Christians were a distinct and somewhat beleaguered minority.

THE FEDERAL COUNCIL ERA. Astute observers of the Protestant Christian Community at the beginning of the twentieth century could see looming signs of radical change and the prospect of trouble ahead. Intense debates were moving forward on issues that had embedded themselves into the religious community—the new sciences of biology and geology were challenging biblical authority just as the new insights of the historical (higher or destructive) criticism of the Bible were coming out of Germany. The social gospel was suggesting a marked redirection of church life away from evangelism toward social planning and a building of a more just society. Immigration was beginning to reshape city life. Ever-increasing knowledge of world religions on the one hand and a growing atheist movement on the other were challenging the theological framework of traditional Christianity.

However, few were prepared at the turn of the century to see in these forces the rationale for radically altering church life. In fact, the larger Protestant denominations were enjoying an era of growth and had just clearly come to see themselves as functionally constituting America's established religions in a country with no official establishment. Over against the religions of the world, over against a Roman Catholic Church (by this time by far the largest single church body in the United States) and over against the still significant number of unchurched citizens, the Protestant churches reigned supreme in the religious community.

Through the decade following the Civil War, the Evangelical Alliance had been the primary organizational expression of that Protestant establishment, but with the passing of its initial core of powerful leadership in the 1890s, the alliance was left a shell of its former self. In its stead a new prophet arose in the person of Elias B. Sanford (1843–1932). A Congregationalist with Methodist roots, Sanford proposed the formation of a delegated Federal Council of Churches. It would go beyond the Evangelical Alliance, an organization of individual members, but would stay away from ideas aimed at creating a single super church or amalgamation with the Roman Catholics.

The Federal Council would allow the Protestant churches to speak with a united voice on those many issues in which they in fact had agreement and to exert greater influence on the moral climate and social conditions of the day. Without initially adopting the social gospel perspective, the council did represent a positive response to the demands for more attention to the social context than had previously been given by the churches. At the time of the Council's formation, it adopted a revised form of the social statement adopted a few years earlier by the Methodist Episcopal Church, South. Rather than develop the full program that some might expect, the Council chose instead to nurture a variety of other independent ecumenical groups which had already established hegemony over particular areas of concern.

The formation of the Federal Council in the United States coincided with the need felt by Christians internationally to provide for more coordinated activity on the mission field. Working in areas where Christianity was a new religion and where the Christian community was small and represented an intrusion into a traditional culture, missionaries felt drawn to fellowship with their colleagues from other churches. In such settings, denominational particularities inherited by them from another century faded in importance and a more common witness to the faith emerged. Missionaries became the new champions of the notion that the division of Christianity into warring factions was the great hindrance to their work. These divisions were of even less concern to recent converts who saw the European and American churches importing a foreign history into their countries which not only did not help them become better Christians but actively slowed their progress.

The problems over church divisions were continually raised and discussed at the great mission conferences held in London (1854, 1878, 1888), New York (1854, 1900), and Edinburgh, Scotland, (1910). The Edinburgh conference was distinctive in much the same way as the Federal Council. It had a new leader, John R. Mott, a Methodist layman with a strong sense of Christian unity and missionary zeal, and it was a delegated conference with official representatives from the different missionary societies, both independent and denominationally affiliated. Out of this conference came a new organization, the International Missionary Council, which provided a continuing opportunity for ecumenical relationships to grow.

The Edinburgh Missionary Conference supplied some impetus for the formation of a sister movement to begin the discussion of the relationships of Christians to fellow Christians of other denominations. In the years following Edinburgh, proposals were generated to begin conferences discussing issues of what was then termed "Faith and Order." Though slowed by the outbreak of World War I, the first international Conference on Faith and Order convened in Lasagna, Switzerland, in 1927. It too established a body to insure that deliberations were pursued on an ongoing basis, a Continuation Committee, and agreed to meet again a decade later. The International Missionary Council, and the Continuation Committee on Faith and Order, spawned an international ecumenical discussion of immense importance both for the consensus it slowly built, at least among liberal Protestants, and the relationships it created among the leaders of various denominations. Their work would be carried on through World War II and the new era signaled by the formation of the World Council of Churches.

Back in the United States, the major churches were slowly becoming battlegrounds as fundamentalists, the more conservative branch of the church, and the modernists, the more liberal branch, slowly divided into two camps. The modernists were defined by their embracing of many of the new elements of twentieth-century society: the critical approach to the biblical text, the progressive view of human society undergirded by the belief in evolution, a desire to reorganize society into a more just social order, and the understanding that other religions had some truth in them. Each of these ideas carried immense potential for affecting the life of the Christian Church from the highest international office to the local congregation. Collectively, modernists tended to undermine biblical authority, challenge traditional understandings of sin and grace, and to focus upon social and political issues rather than membership recruitment and evangelism. They carried great intellectual appeal and slowly came to dominate many of the leading seminaries.

As World War I, a decidedly uniting factor in churches, came to an end, fundamentalist and conservative voices were raised against the growing visible presence of modernists in key denominational positions, especially the denominational staff, mission boards, and seminary faculties. The debate heated to a boiling point through the 1920s, especially in the northern Presbyterian and Baptist churches. By the early 1930s, it was evident to the fundamentalists that they had delayed too long and had lost control of the denominational apparatus and the seminaries (where the great majority of future leaders would be trained). Thus a series of schisms began to occur in which many of the conservative leaders resigned and formed a series of new denominations with such names as the Orthodox Presbyterian Church, the Bible Presbyterian Church, the Conservative Baptist Association, and the General Association of Regular Baptist Churches.

As the schisms occurred, fundamentalists were divided into three distinct camps. Many of the fundamentalists refused to participate in the schisms and remained in the older denominations. They became the core of continuing conservative caucuses in most of the large liberal Protestant bodies. Those who did split divided primarily over the issue of separatism. Some fundamentalists argued for complete separation from modernists and from those who associate with modernists (i.e., the fundamentalists who remained in the larger denominations). Others simply withdrew from what they felt had become an apostate denomination but kept ties to individuals inside those denominations whom they knew otherwise to be sound doctrinally. As World War II began, the separatist fundamentalists became a group unto themselves, while the nonseparatists and those still within the denominations made common cause and became the core of a new movement, Evangelicalism.

ECUMENISM SINCE WORLD WAR II. Through the 1940s, forces unleashed through the first half of the century would coalesce, organize, and reorganize to produce the essential ecumenical establishment as it exists at present. The United States would exert tremendous leverage on the world scene as the nation who came out of the war not only victorious, but among the least damaged. It would lead in the postwar reconstruction efforts and its churches would play a prominent role. There would also be the attempt to carry the issues that split the American church in the 1930s to the rest of the world and in effect impose the divisions on Christians.

In 1941, the separationists among the fundamentalists, now largely confined to several relatively small denominations, organized the American Council of Christian Churches. It had as its standard of membership the agreement on a very conservative Protestant theological position and opposition to all forms of liberalism as represented in the Federal Council of Churches. As the relations with the Soviet Union soured, and the Cold War began, it was articulate in the cause of anti-Communism.

The American Council found capable leadership in the person of Carl McIntire, a Presbyterian leader who had aligned himself with the conservative J. Gresham Machen at Princeton, but then split with Machen over premillennialism and separatism. A talented speaker, McIntire pastored a large congregation in Collinswood, New Jersey, and for many decades hosted a national radio show, *The Twentieth Century Reformation Hour.*

Having built a viable American organization, as news of the impending organization of the World Council of Churches spread, McIntire organized what international support he could and formed the International Council of Christian Churches. The International Council chose Amsterdam in 1948 as their place and time of organization, the exact spot chosen by the World Council of Churches. The confusion that ensued among reporters who little understood, in many cases, the difference between the two organizations, gave the International Council an immediate boost, and it would frequently be accused of attempting to disrupt the World Council by deliberately creating confusion and spreading the false image that it represented a much larger constituency than it actually did.

Eventually, at the end of the 1960s, McIntire had a falling out with a number of his colleagues in the United States and was removed from his position with the American Council of Christian Churches. McIntire, and those that supported him, regrouped as the American Christian Action Council. The split in what was already a relatively small group largely silenced the American Council's voice as a viable alternative on the national religious scene. In the meantime, the International Council continued though without the bulk of its American support. It found some strength among older missionary churches that had consistently been more conservative than their European and American parent bodies. Out of the International Council also came a set of denominational family intra-faith groups that parallel the larger liberal Protestant denominational family structures.

Spurred along by the formation of the American Council, nonseparatist conservative leaders primarily among Presbyterian, Congregationalist, and Baptist Churches also sought a means of uniting their voices and of creating a structure that would speak to their unique situation. First, they wanted to speak as conservative Protestants over against liberal Protestantism, but distinguish themselves from the separatist fundamentalists. While some were in new denominations such as the Orthodox Presbyterians and Conservative Baptists, many, if not the majority of conservative leaders were still in the larger denominations. They needed a name to distinguish themselves and found it in the term "Evangelical," at times using the designation of "Neo-Evangelical." They needed an organization that would unite both those Evangelicals still in the older denominations and those in the newer Evangelical denominations. They found the solution in the National Association of Evangelicals, founded in 1942, which provided for membership by denominations, organizations, local congregations, and/or individuals. Thus a conservative pastor and his congregation, though officially a member of a liberal Protestant denomination, could also affiliate with the NAE.

Conservative leaders who remained within the older denominations had the problem of access to a seminary. As most of the seminaries had been captured by the liberals, they had nowhere to send ministerial candidates who could form a continuing source of conservative leadership for the next generation. They saw the possibility of the Evangelical perspective simply dying out in the older churches. That problem was partially solved by the formation of Fuller Theological Seminary, an independent seminary firmly rooted in the traditional Calvinist theology shared by Baptists, Congregationalists, and Presbyterians. The formation of Fuller, located in Pasadena, California, also served as an announcement that Evangelicals were prepared to continue to confront their liberal counterparts on the academic level.

As the National Association of Evangelicals grew, it had to come to grips with the new alignments within conservative Protestantism as a whole, arguably the most important factor in that reordering being the spectacular success of Pentecostalism in the wake of the charismatic movement of the 1970s. Frequently derided through the first half of the twentieth century, Pentecostals grew to strength by mid-century, founded their own family intra-faith organization, the Pentecostal Fellowship of North America and began holding the World Pentecostal Conferences. They came out of World War II with a distinctly ecumenical stance that found embodiment in the ministry of David DuPlessis, a South African who wandered the world introducing the Pentecostal movement to any and all Christians who would listen. Equally important were organizations like the Full Gospel Businessman's Fellowship International that brought lay people of all denominations together in their common experience of the Pentecostal gifts of the Holy Spirit. Pentecostals soon found a national hero in Oral Roberts, the first successful televangelist.

As Pentecostals gained a new level of success in the 1970s, and as they sought entrance into the National Association of Evangelicals, all of whose formal entrance and fellowship requirements they fully met, slowly the barriers between Evangelicals from a Calvinist theological background and those from Methodist backgrounds (i.e., Holiness and Pentecostal) began to crumble. The NAE emerged as the voice of this much larger reordered Evangelical movement and its influence in making public policy (an arena once left entirely to the Federal and National Councils of Churches) had steadily grown.

FROM FEDERAL TO NATIONAL COUNCIL. Some of the most important changes to come out of World War II were the cooperative efforts of the American and European churches in the rebuilding of Europe. These efforts provided an agenda by which the interfaith trends that had been projected so strongly prior to the war could be revived and reach some culmination. Ecumenical ideals, left on hold during the war, were revived and took on visible form in the creation of the World Council of Churches. The essential outlines of a plan to bring the various ecumenical groups together into a single international organization had been put together as early as 1937 and a specific proposal for a World Council of Churches was developed over the next year. Only the war stood between the promulgation of that plan and its implementation.

The World Council of Churches was formed in Amsterdam in 1948 and brought together many of the larger churches of North America and Europe. While a modest number of churches from Africa, Asia, and South America were included from the beginning, much of the subsequent history of the Council has been built around its expanding perspective on world Christianity and its gradual incorporation of, especially, Asian and African churches in its membership and leadership.

Through the Council, a series of national and regional ecumenical councils have been organized. In the United States, the immediate effect of the Council's formation was the added impetus it gave to the creation of a more effective ecumenical body serving the larger denominations. While the Federal Council of Churches had worked for half a century, by the 1940s its manifold limitations were quite visible to all. In name it was a council of churches, but in fact the logical work load of such an organization was parceled out to more than a dozen specialized agencies. This segregation of concern had hindered American participation in the various discussions that had led to the formation of the World Council.

Not the least of the factors underlying the cry for a more effective council, however, was the vision projected by a few for a united Protestant church for America. Such a church had come into existence in Canada in 1925. Also, in the years prior to World War II, a number of intra-family mergers among the Methodist, Lutheran, and Reformed churches seemed a possible preliminary stage for the merger of churches across denominational family lines. The existence of a more effective council of churches would facilitate such mergers.

Thus it came about that a massive reorganization of American ecumenical structures occurred in 1950. The new National Council of the Churches of Christ in the U.S.A. brought together the older Federal Council with a number of specialized agencies such as the United Council of Church Women and the International Council of Religious Education, many of which survived as divisions of the National Council. New offices were opened on Riverside Drive in Manhattan.

The National Council of Churches has, for almost a half century, been the most important cooperative religious organization functioning in the United States. Representing more that 40,000,000 Christians, it has been effective in providing a united voice for the liberal Christian community. It has been especially effective in providing consultation to legislators in Washington, D.C. relative to action on a host of social concerns such as support for the poor and needy and separation of church and state, to more organizational matters such as chaplains for the armed services and federal prison system.

During the years of its existence, the National Council, like the Federal Council before it, was the center of controversy especially as it involved itself in controversial social issues such as the Civil Rights Movement and the Middle East Conflict. It took leading role in reintegrating Eastern Orthodox leadership into the Ecumenical scene in the post-Stalinist era and was deeply involved in the peace efforts during the Vietnam War.

The vision of a united Protestant church, however, has not been realized. During the 1960s and 1970s, interest in the possibility of such a united church rose to new heights, especially in the wake of Vatican II. One promising plan popularly called COCU (for Church of Christ Uniting) would have brought together nine churches including the United Methodist Church, several of the African American Methodists, the Episcopal Church, and the United Presbyterian Church. While it gained some initial support, it soon floundered both on sacramental issues (about which the Episcopalians were the least compromising) and from a general lack of broad support of the lay constituencies of the several denominations. Those most interested in the proposed united church were unable to communicate any real benefits it would bring.

The failure of COCU vividly demonstrated the trend against religious groups merging across denominational family lines. During the last century of ecumenical endeavor in the United States, only one such merger has occurred, the 1931 merger of the Christian and Congregational Churches (though in fact many of the Christian Church congregations were later lost as they one-by-one pulled out of the merged body).

By the 1980s, few were left to rally liberal Protestants around a vision of a united Protestant church, though officially the COCU plan is still alive. Most members of the National Council see the future as one of cooperative endeavor but not organizational unity. In the meantime, they and their member churches face the problem of eroding support. All of the leading liberal Protestant churches have been steadily losing members since the 1960s and, given the growth of population, even more rapidly losing their relative position in the society. However, given the lack of any other religious coalition with a similarly large constituency, the Council remains a most significant organization in American religious life.

THE ROMAN CATHOLIC CHURCH. The Roman Catholic Church is the largest single religious organization in the world. It is also the largest church body in both the United States and Canada. While twice as many people in America identify themselves as Protestant, they are scattered in hundreds of denominations, the largest being the Southern Baptist Convention, less than half the size of the Roman Catholic Church. Traditionally, the Roman Catholic Church has called for the reunion of Christendom but has seen as the norm for that reunion the return of all other churches to a state of communion with the Bishop of Rome.

Even the largest of non-Roman Christian churches appear minuscule when compared to the Roman Catholic Church, and until the twentieth century, no church or related groups of churches provided what could be thought of as international competition to the Roman Catholic Church. The formation of the World Council of Churches changed that situation. The subsequent making of common cause between many divergent elements of non-Roman Christianity also provided a symbolic point of dialogue between Rome and the thousands of "other" churches scattered around the globe. As negotiations proceeded between the members of the World Council, dialogue could open between the World Council and Rome. Individuals on both sides of that dialogue proposed a variety of means by which agreement on many issues, acknowledgment of each other's legitimacy, and even some degree of eventual union could be reached.

The first step in that dialogue was greatly influenced by what some see as the fruition of the work of many, and what others see as a happenstance (or in theological terms, a miracle, the work of providential grace). It came in the form of a new bishop in Rome, Pope John XXIII, a man many said was elected because no compromise could be reached between the supporters of the "real" candidates for the office. He was initially thought of as an interim pope.

But Pope John XXIII caught the imagination of a whole generation with his spirituality, sense of humor, and graciousness. He was loved by Protestants as much as Roman Catholics and it was he who called the first church council in almost a century, a council that would bring numerous changes to the church internally, among them being the rewriting of the rules for Catholic/non-Catholic relationships. By far the most significant statement affecting interreligious relationships would be the one denying the guilt of the Jews collectively for the death of Jesus. That statement came to symbolize a new era for all Christians (not just Roman Catholics) assuming responsibility for the persecution of the Jews through the centuries, culminating with the Holocaust. It has been the starting point and a large percentage of the substance of all Jewish-Christian dialogue ever since.

The World Council of Churches sent official observers to Vatican II, and their presence undoubtedly affected the final wording of the document that opened a new era in Protestant and Orthodox contact. Harsh language was gone and Roman Catholics everywhere were encouraged to build relationships with the "separated brethren." Through the 1970s and into the 1980s, ecumenical contacts flourished, an era of good feeling was launched, and a new base of familiarity and trust was erected between Christians and Jews that now provides the foundation for ongoing discussions on a myriad of issues.

POST-VATICAN CHANGES IN AMERICA. During the euphoria that accompanied the flurry of ecumenical contacts during the post-Vatican era, few noticed that even as the Christian community was drawing together, the shape of the religious landscape was changing dramatically. Beginning in 1965, large numbers of Muslims, Buddhists and Hindus began flowing into the United States. While all three communities had been present in the United States for many decades, the new immigrants turned these once isolated ethnic enclaves into significant participants in the larger religious

community. With annual growth in the tens of thousands from both immigration and converts, the Hindu, Buddhist, and Muslim presence will play an increasing role in the creation of public policy. Each is now served by organizations analogous to the National Council of Churches.

One cannot fully understand the shifting story of contemporary interfaith and ecumenical relationships without returning to some consideration of the Jewish community. Jews had been in America from the beginning, but their numbers grew many times from massive immigration between 1880 and 1924, when the same highly restrictive immigration laws that blocked Asians from entering the country were passed. In the American context, like the Christian community, the Jewish community experienced both the freedoms of a modern secular society and the pressures from contemporary intellectual concerns; and also like the Christian churches, the synagogues divided along linguistic lines and by the extent of their Americanization. By the mid-twentieth century, three major communities were discernible—Orthodox, Conservative, and Reform—and a number of additional divisions were on the horizon.

Thus, internal pressures such as the need to speak with some united voice on issues not related to those which divided religious Jews, and external pressures such as the continuing pressure of anti-Semitism and, more recently, the desire to support the state of Israel, led Jewish leaders to develop cooperative structures between congregational and rabbinical associations. Of these associations the most important one is Synagogue Council of America founded in 1926 as the coordinating body between Orthodox, Conservative, and Reform rabbinical and congregational organizations.

Over all, the trend in Western religion is toward greater organizational splintering and theological diversity. Ecumenical and interfaith organizations will not reverse that trend, but do provide a vital function in reducing the social tension created by the loss of religious consensus. They create a forum in which different religions can gain some knowledge and understanding of each other; a vehicle by which the religious concerns of a select community can be communicated to the society as a whole; an organization in which people with very different religious perspectives can discover their common aspirations and learn to work together for the common good; and a social setting in which people, having been introduced to their neighbors of a different religious background, can discover their common humanity.

Sources—Interfaith and Ecumenical Family of Organizations

INTERFAITH ACTIVITIES

Beversluis, Joe, ed. *A Sourcebook for the Community of Religions*. Chicago: The Council for a Parliament of the World's Religions, 1994. 240 pp.

Braybrooke, Marcus. *Inter-Faith Organizations, 1893–1979*. New York: Edwin Mellen Press, 1980. 213 pp.

Bryant, M. Darrol, and Frank Flinn, eds. *Interreligious Dialogue: Voices from a New Frontier*. New York: Paragon House, 1989. 234 pp.

Clark, Francis, ed. *Interfaith Directory*. New York: International Religious Foundation, 1987. 178 pp.

Clarke, James Freeman. *Ten Great Religions*. Boston: Houghton, Mifflin, 1895.

Miller, John W. *Interfaith Dialogue: Four Approaches*. Waterloo, ON: University of Waterloo Press, 1986. 99 pp.

Miller, Russell E. *The Larger Hope: The Second Century of the Universalist Church in America, 1870–1970*. Boston: Unitarian Universalist Association, 1985. 766 pp.

Weller, Charles Frederick, ed. *World Fellowship*. New York: Liveright Publishing Corporation, 1935. 986 pp.

CHRISTIAN ECUMENISM

Bilheimer, Robert S. *Breakthrough: The Emergence of the Ecumenical Tradition*. Grand Rapids, MI: William B. Eerdmans Publishing Company, 1989. 238 pp.

Burgess, Joseph A., ed. *In Search of Christian Unity: Basic Consensus, Basic Differences*. Minneapolis: Fortress Press, 1991. 259 pp.

Carpenter, Joel A. ed. *A New Coalition: Early Documents of the National Association of Evangelicals*. New York: Garland Publishing, 1988. 63 pp.

Cavert, Samuel McCrea. *The American Churches in the Ecumenical Movement, 1900–1968*. New York: Association Press, 1968. 288 pp.

———. *Church Cooperation and Unity in America: A Historical Review, 1900–1970*. New York: Association Press, 1970. 400 pp.

Desseaux, Jacques. *Twenty Centuries of Ecumenism*. New York: Paulist Press, 1984. 103 pp.

Fey, Harold, ed. *A History of the Ecumenical Movement, 1948–1968*. Vol. II. Philadelphia: Westminster Press, 1970. 524 pp.

Jordan, Philip D. *The Evangelical Alliance for the United States of America, 1847–1900: Ecumenism, Identity and the Religion of the Republic*. New York: Edwin Mellen Press, 1982. 277 pp.

Kinnamon, Michael. *Truth and Community: Diversity and Its Limits in the Ecumenical Movement*. Grand Rapids, MI: William B. Eerdmans Publishing Company, 1988. 118 pp.

McDonnel, John J. *The World Council of Churches and the Catholic Church*. New York: Edwin Mellen Press, 1985. 467 pp.

Rouse, Ruth, and Stephen Charles Neill. *A History of the Ecumenical Movement, 1517–1948*. Vol. I. Philadelphia: Westminster Press, 1967. 838 pp.

Chapter 2

Western Liturgical Family
Part I: Catholicism

Consult the "Contents" pages to locate the entries in Part III,
the Directory Listings Sections, that comprise this family.

During the last generation, on both the scholarly and popular levels, a debate has raged over the nature of the Christian presence in the United States. Is the United States a Christian nation? Quite apart from the political debate that has attempted to define the United States as a Christian nation, a step in the argument for the adoption of specific laws by the government in support of Christian theological and moral positions, scholars have reached vastly different conclusions concerning America's Christian past. Some have argued that the United States is a product of Western Christian civilization. Others have just as eloquently argued that the formation of the United States was a primary action in the move toward a secular post-Christian society and that the unique ideas that made the revolution possible were the anti-clerical Enlightenment notions that critiqued traditional Christian notions in its elevation of the legitimacy of revolution, the rights of the individual, and a rational democratic government.

That argument aside, both sides would admit that Christianity, through its various denominational expressions, was the primary religious community at the time of the American Revolution, though only a small minority of the populous were church members, and that Christianity has never given up its hegemony. Second, in observing contemporary religions, it is noted that a vast majority of the people are members of the more than 900 Christian denominations currently functioning in the United States. A slightly lower percentage is found in Canada. Interestingly, the movement of a majority of the population into formal church affiliation, which seems to have occurred in the 1940s, occurred contemporaneously with the spread of a remarkable pluralism and the development for the first time of a significant Muslim, Hindu, and Buddhist presence joining what had always been a small but significant Jewish presence. This pluralism has taken on additional importance due to its concentration in the major cities (New York, Chicago, and especially Los Angeles). This interfaith pluralism, coupled with the hundreds of divisions within Christianity, has led to the development of a secular public civil language that often masks the continuing Christian role in the development of the cultural life of the public. In this regard Canada is only slightly different from the United States.

Thus to understand the shape and structure of North American religion, one must come to grips with the Christian tradition. The largest single grouping of North American religions are those groups that claim to have direct organizational continuity with the apostolic church of the first century. These churches hammered out the doctrinal position through the doctrinal controversies from the fourth to the eighth centuries. They include the Roman Catholic Church, the Church of England, and the various Eastern Orthodox churches. A second major group of churches emerged at the time of the Protestant Reformation in the sixteenth century (Lutheran, Reformed-Presbyterian, and European Free Church traditions). Determinative for North American religion, a century after the Reformation, in Great Britain, the Puritan movement gave birth to the independent churches, which began to argue for a separation of religion and government. Independence found its major expression in the Baptist churches, whose influence was extended through the Adventist and Fundamentalist movements of the nineteenth and twentieth centuries. Finally, in the eighteenth century, the Pietist movement, which placed great emphasis on personal religion, swept across Europe. The major product of the Pietist awakening for North American religion, Methodism, emerged as a major Christian expression in North America in the 1800s and extended its influence through the Holiness and Pentecostal movements, both of which are based on Methodism.

Christianity came to North America with the European explorers beginning in the sixteenth century. Arriving and establishing a permanent presence very early in what is now the United States and Canada was Roman Catholicism (currently the largest single denomination of Christians in both countries). Through it, and the Church of England (now represented by the Episcopal Church and Anglican Church of Canada), the oldest surviving Christian traditions in the West became firmly established in North America. Together with the various denominations that offer slight variations of Catholic and Anglican church life, they constitute the Western Liturgical Family.

In Eastern Europe and the Eastern Mediterranean basin, a form of Christianity similar to Roman Catholicism and Anglicanism developed but had Greek, rather than Latin, as a basic working language. These two traditions (the Western Latin and Eastern Greek) began to diverge even during the definitive era as their doctrinal consensus was being affirmed (fourth through eighth centuries). The Eastern Orthodox and non-Chalcedonian churches, discussed in chapter two, share all of the structural distinctions of the Western Churches, differing only on some relatively minor points of doctrine: preference for a Greek-based liturgy, and a distinct national heritage. Together the Eastern and Western churches logically form one Liturgical family, but for purposes of this *Encyclopedia*, they are considered as two families—Western and Eastern.

THE DEVELOPMENT OF THE LITURGICAL FAMILY. A strong liturgical life is the most distinguishing feature of the oldest Christian churches that have continued to present day. Of course, these churches have other distinguishing characteristics—creeds, orders, sacraments, language, and culture. Liturgy, however, is the place where these other characteristics find their expression, so it seems appropriate to group these churches together as the liturgical family. In this family are the many church bodies of four major traditions: the Eastern Orthodox tradition, the non-Chalcedonian Orthodox tradition, the Western Roman tradition, and the Anglican tradition.

Most of the liturgical churches celebrate seven sacraments: baptism, the eucharist, holy orders, unction, marriage, confirmation, and penance. Few topics exist among Christians on which there is such a variety of thinking as on the number and nature of the sacraments. Some nonliturgical groups, such as the Methodists, celebrate only two sacraments—baptism and holy communion—while other nonliturgical groups, such as the Baptists, have no sacraments. Some churches consider baptism and holy communion not as sacraments but as ordinances, and add a third ordinance, footwashing. A fully developed sacramental system, however, characterizes the members of the liturgical family.

Other characteristics of the liturgical churches are allegiance to creeds and belief in Apostolic succession. Each creed, a statement of doctrines, originated in the early centuries of the church or is a variation on an early creed. Each church professes that it inherits an unbroken line of authority from the Apostles who founded the Christian church at Pentecost.

Speaking of this unbroken line, Bishop Sion Manoogian says of the Armenian church, "The Armenian Church was founded by two of the Apostles of Our Lord, St. Thaddeus and St. Bartholomew, in the first century. This is the reason for its sometimes being called the Armenian Apostolic Church" (Sion Manoogian, *The Armenian Church* n.p., n.d. 2, 15). Dean Timothy Andrews says of the Greek Orthodox Church, "It is the church founded by Christ, received its mission on Pentecost, propagated throughout the world by the Holy Apostles" (Timothy Andrews, *What Is the Orthodox Church?* [pamphlet, 1964], 7). The Church of the East traces its conversion, establishment, and Apostolic succession to the 70 disciples (Luke 10:1) and the 12 Apostles, but more particularly to Mar Shimun Koopa (St. Simon Peter), Mar Tooma (St. Thomas), Mar Addai (St. Thaddeus), Mar Mari (St. Mari, one of the 70 disciples), and Mar Bar Thulmay (St. Bartholomew). The Roman Catholic Church traces its origins to St. Peter, the first bishop of Rome.

People hold conflicting views concerning the relationship of the four traditions of the liturgical family to the Apostles and to the first century church. Most agree, however, that the peculiar traits of the traditions evolved as Christianity spread to various cultures and as church councils formulated doctrines. The Counciliar Era, a time of debate and discussion, lasted from 325 C.E. to 787 C.E. Seven councils were held during that time.

The First Ecumenical Council was called in 325 C.E. at Nicea, near Constantinople (Istanbul), in present-day Turkey. The Council turned its attention to the relationship of God the Father and God the Son in Christian thinking. Controversy had been raised by the teachings of a man named Arius about the nature of Christ. Arius said the Son is not of the same "substance" as the Father, thus denying the essential full divinity of Jesus Christ. Rather, Arius contended, the Son, was created by the Father as an agent for creating the world. The council condemned Arius and declared his teaching heretical. This action caused an immediate defection in the church in Egypt, where Arius resided. In various places Arian Christians remained in some force for several centuries. The "barbarians" who sacked Rome in 401 C.E. were in fact Arian Christians, and since the sixth century a beautiful Arian baptistry has stood near the Orthodox one in Ravenna, Italy, a symbol of the town standing in the boundary between the orthodox and Arian communities.

The Council at Nicea also promulgated a creedal statement that presented a summary of the basic affirmations of Christianity: a transcendent deity who related to humanity as their parental creator, of salvation through the atoning work of Jesus Christ, the sustaining work of the Holy Spirit, the church as the organizational expression of the faith, and continued existence for Christians in a heavenly state. The Nicene Creed not only set the basic perspective of the faith accepted by almost all Christians since, but also set the stage for the theological discussions that worked out the positions on various open questions not covered by the creedal statement. The Nicene statement, more than any other document, defines orthodox Christianity, and its basic position would provide the consensus that was never questioned when the various schisms occurred over the centuries. Even most of the modern "non-creedal" churches basically accept the decisions of the Council of Nicea in their definition of Christian belief.

The Second Council met at Constantinople in 381 C.E. and continued the development of the doctrine of the Trinity. Christianity affirms the existence of One God who is manifest as a Trinity of Father, Son, and Holy Spirit. Those who gathered at Constantinople affirmed that the Three—Father, Son, and Holy Spirit—are co-eternal and consubstantial.

The Third Council met at Ephesus in 431 C.E. This council met to discuss the opinions of Nestorius, who had been made patriarch of Constantinople in 428 C.E., concerning the relationship of the divine and human in Jesus Christ. Nestorius believed that Christ was not the Son of God, but that God was living in Christ. The two natures, said Nestorius, were separable. The debate centered upon the use of the phrase "Theotokos" (Greek for "Mother of God"). The Nestorians rejected the term, saying that Mary bore Christ, not God. The council ruled against Nestorius and deposed him as patriarch. A Nestorian Council was organized a few days later and deposed its opposition. Although Nestorius was imprisoned and eventually banished to Egypt, his followers formed a strong church in Syria and Persia. Later missionary activity carried the Nestorian church into India and China. It is represented today by the Church of the East, one of the churches of the non-Chalcedonian Orthodox tradition (meaning they did not participate and/or accept the rulings of the next council).

The Fourth Council met at Chalcedon in 451 C.E. It drafted what came to be known as the Chalcedonian Creed:

"Therefore, following the holy Fathers we all with one accord teach men to acknowledge one and the same Son, our Lord Jesus Christ, at once complete in Godhead and complete in manhood, truly God and truly man, consisting also of a reasonable soul and body; of one substance with the Father as regards his Godhead, and at the same time of one substance with us as regards his manhood; like us in all respects, apart from sin; as regards his Godhead, begotten of the Father before the ages, but yet as regards his manhood begotten, for us men and for our salvation, of Mary the Virgin, the God-bearer; one and the same Christ, Son, Lord, Only-begotten, recognized IN TWO NATURES, WITHOUT CONFUSION, WITHOUT CHANGE, WITHOUT DIVISION, WITHOUT SEPARATION; the distinction of natures being in no way annulled by the union, but rather the characteristics of each nature being preserved and coming together to form one person and subsistence, not as parted or separated into two persons, but one and the same Son and Only-begotten God the Word, Lord Jesus Christ; even as the prophets from earliest times spoke of him, and our Lord Jesus Christ himself taught us, and the creed of the Fathers has handed down to us."

This creed is considered the "orthodox" solution to the various theological (primarily Christological) problems considered by the early church and now agreed upon by the Roman Catholic, Anglican and Eastern Orthodox Churches as well as most Protestant churches. However, some Eastern and Egyptian Christians rejected the creed's emphasis on the two natures of Christ. The non-Chalcedonian Orthodox tradition is one of the four main traditions of the liturgical family. They use the creedal statement promulgated by the Council of Nicea in 325 C.E., but not the Chalcedonian statement. Many non-Chalcedonians were called Monophysites because they felt the human and divine in Christ constituted only one nature. Today the Armenian church and the Coptic church represent part of the non-Chalcedonian Orthodox tradition.

The first four councils—at Nicea, Constantinople, Ephesus, and Chalcedon—served to isolate the non-Chalcedonian Orthodox tradition from the Eastern Orthodox and Western Roman traditions. The Eastern Orthodox tradition developed centers of authority in Antioch, Alexandria, and Constantinople. The Western branch's center of authority was in Rome. This East-West division was more a cultural than a doctrinal separation. The churches allowed culture and politics to lead them toward an eventual break. When the official division came in 1054 with mutual excommunications, the churches were declaring to the world what had already been a reality for some time. This explanation is not to say that there are no important differences of doctrine, rites, or ecclesiastical practices between the two churches, or to deny that these differences have grown stronger since 1054. It is merely to show how even these pale into insignificance when set against the glaring differences caused by rival cultures, conflicting empires, and 800 years of lack of meaningful communication.

Of the three oldest traditions of the liturgical family—the Eastern Orthodox tradition, the non-Chalcedonian Orthodox tradition, and the Western Roman tradition—only the third failed to remain fairly stable throughout the nineteenth century. In the first tradition, the Eastern Orthodox Church split jurisdictions along national and cultural lines. It was able to preserve unity by granting local autonomy to the various national groups. In the non-Chalcedonian Orthodox tradition, the Coptic Church and the Armenian Church fell under the rule of rising Islam after the sixth century. The force of an overpowering enemy served to keep them both small and united. In the Western Roman tradition, however, the Roman Catholic Church attempted an imperial stance, trying to provide a religious blanket to cover all of Western culture. Consequently, it was to suffer when secular power deserted it. Not only did the various Protestant and post-Protestant groups break off from it, but the fourth major liturgical tradition emerged from it: the Anglican.

The Church in England had been at odds with the see of Rome as early as Thomas A'Becket, the twelfth-century Archbishop of Canterbury. In the sixteenth century, the marriage problems of Henry VIII caused the break with Rome. With few immediate changes in the church beyond confiscation of church property by Henry, the Church of England had to wait for the Protestantizing of King Edward VII and the mediating of Queen Elizabeth I for a genuinely new orientation. The development and spread of the Elizabethan prayerbook alone is reason to look upon the Anglicans as a separate liturgical tradition.

Each of the four major liturgical traditions was brought to the United States by immigration of its Old World disciples. The traditions came as structures to preserve the Old World customs and cultures in the secular environment of the United States. Churches were founded wherever a significant group of immigrants or their descendants resided. These churches remained under the supervision of ancient sees and kept much closer contact with the sees than with neighboring American churches. There was little attempt to evangelize beyond the boundaries of the immigrants' particular ethnic groups. Schism would wait until the twentieth century for most groups, when Americanization and the desire for native American bishops would become major issues.

ROMAN CATHOLICISM. Out of the conciliar era, the Roman Catholic Church emerged as the single ecclesiastical body dominating the life of Western Europe for Italy and Spain to Ireland and Scandinavia. As such it came to have a special and unique role in shaping Western European history. It held sway, with only minor competition from relatively small dissenting groups, until the sixteenth century. Taking an inclusive view of its role in society, it was able to absorb and provide space for a variety of religious enthusiasts and divergences through the development and sponsoring of religious orders, and the allowances for a wide variety of local practices peculiar to a particular region. It also had considerable room for those who broke its rules to reconcile themselves and come back into the good graces of the ecclesiastical authorities.

While many of the peculiarities of Roman Catholicism will be discussed in its entry in the Directory Listings section, it is fruitful at this point to note some aspects of the medieval church that characterized it in its relationship to Western society. For example, in the chaos that followed the collapse of the Roman Empire, as the Ancient world made the transition to the Medieval period, the Roman Catholic Church emerged as an integrating element in Western Europe and came to provide a variety of services that allowed some semblance of order to return as the transition to the synthesis of the Middle Ages was developed.

Most importantly for later theological development, the Church developed through its sacramental system a theological worldview that encompassed all of the stages of human life. Across Europe, the land was laid out in parishes, and a church building placed in that parish for the gathering of the community. Ideally church membership and community membership overlapped completely, and the church frequently kept the vital records of the surrounding territory. Thus the operation of the sacramental world of the Church would begin even before someone was born as the individual's parents would live in the community and participate in the church. A short time after birth the baby would be presented for baptism, a ritual that welcomed the child into membership in the church. As the child grew, it would be taught Christian doctrine and practice, and at some point intensively so, through the memorizing of the catechism. The catechism presented the Church's doctrine in the form of an ordered series of questions and answers. When the child was deemed of age, s/he would be passed through the sacrament of confirmation and immediately afterward, for the first time, receive the sacrament of the Eucharist, the ritually offered body and blood of Christ. The Eucharist is the most holy of Christian sacraments.

From the time of confirmation, the individual was considered an adult by the church. Regularly, usually once a week, but minimally once a year, the individual went through the sacrament of penance in which sins were verbally confessed to a priest who, as a representative of the church and of God, pronounced forgiveness and set some actions that were to be done by the individual as recompense for the wrong. After the priest pronounced forgiveness of sin and the individual participated in the rite of penance, s/he was ready to receive the Eucharist. In general the Eucharist was only to be received after a period of hours during which food had not been consumed and, as such, the Eucharistic service was usually held the first thing in the morning after which a meal breaking the fast (i.e., breakfast) would be eaten.

The Eucharist provided a week-by-week and even day-by-day means of both building a moral society and of continually reintegrating individuals as they deviated, broke the moral rules, and sought to right themselves in the eyes of the community and the divine order. It became the means of reconciling neighborly quarrels and restoring those guilty of gross crimes. One's eternal destiny depended upon being in fellowship with God and the church. The right to receive the Eucharist was a primal sign of the existence of that fellowship. To break fellowship, by unrepentant sin or heresy (espousing incorrect belief on an essential issue of doctrine), was a serious matter, and could lead to a formal act of a denial of the sacraments, i.e., ex-communication. Ex-communication was not a denial of membership in the church so much as a public statement that someone was out of communion with God and the church and hence not fit to receive its primary sacrament.

After one became an adult (and in the Middle Ages one was recognized as an adult at a much younger age than at present), a set of special sacraments would become available. One could for example choose a mate and find the church's sanction through the sacrament of marriage. For most, that was a one-time occurrence (unless of course a spouse died, at which time one was free to marry a second time or to pursue other options). One could also choose to enter the priesthood or a monastic life, and thus become one of the people set aside to keep the sacramental system and perform the sacramental acts. In the priesthood, one would pass through the sacrament of ordination to holy orders. Within the Roman Catholic Church there were a variety of levels to holy orders, but three became important—deacon, priest, and bishop. By the Middle Ages, the priesthood was celibate and, hence, holy orders and marriage did not mix (a characteristic that would come to distinguish Roman Catholicism from Eastern Orthodoxy). Those who entered holy orders were in effect married to the church. Females who entered a convent were seen as married to Christ.

The church was also present to oversee the last hours of life and to ease the movement into the afterlife. The goal of the Christian was heaven, the place where God resided. Those who died outside of the state of grace, with a serious sin that had not been repented and forgiven, were destined for eternal separation from God, i.e., hell. Hell became the object of numerous speculations and many employed their imaginations vividly to describe the horrors of separation from God, often in the most excruciating language.

The average Christian who died in a state of grace was destined for heaven, but usually had yet to make amends for all of the sins they had committed; to enter heaven one had not only to be forgiven but holy. Thus purgatory was posited as a place where one could finish the process of paying back (in suffering) for one's sins and thus reach a state of holiness to enter heaven.

A very few persons were seen to have become so holy in this life as to be ready to enter heaven directly at the moment of their death. They were also possessed of an abundance of sanctity that could be supernaturally applied to assist the average sinful Christian. It was an act of piety to pray for the abundance of the saints to be applied to lessen the suffering of someone, possibly a beloved parent or family member, in purgatory.

It might be obvious how the teachings on purgatory, designed to account for the need to satisfy justice, could become corrupted. In general, one affected their stay or another's stay in purgatory by acts of prayer and piety. Among the acts of piety would be giving of one's income or possessions to aid the poor or to assist the church in its mission. It did not take long for some church authorities to see the financial possibilities of manipulating the fear of purgatory to raise money. In fact, it was the charge of the reformers of the sixteenth century that the Roman Catholic Church was selling guarantees of freedom from purgatory to people who contributed to the building of Saint Peter's, the headquarter's church now located in Vatican City.

To insure that one was in a state of grace at the moment of death, as it approached, ideally, a priest would be present to anoint the body with oil and pronounce forgiveness, the sacrament of extreme unction. The church then oversaw the funeral services and the burying of the body in ground especially consecrated for that purpose.

The church had by the Middle Ages developed a holistic theology and practice that was totally integrated into the secular order. As that powerful system became corrupt, and through the fifteenth century, many people agreed that a Reformation was necessary. However, it is difficult to reform without significantly tampering with such a system. Thus cleaning at the corruption became identified with questioning doctrines, such as purgatory, and questioning the very basis of the church's authority, which emanated from Rome, and the close relationship of that authority with the coercive powers of the state.

The questioning of the authority of the Roman Catholic Church would, in the sixteenth century, lead to the splitting of the Roman church and the emergence of the Anglican (chapter 3), Lutheran (chapter 5), and the Reformed-Presbyterian (chapter 6) Churches, each with a territory over which they had hegemony. Also emerging was the European Free Church (chapter 10) bodies, which renounced any tie to the state governmental system. The sixteenth-century churches would then become the parents of new traditions. Most important for North America, a second reforming tradition, the Puritans (who attempted various programs to "purify" the Church in Great Britain) gave birth to the Baptists (chapter 11) and the Congregationalists (chapter 6). Later calls for reformation and renewal would call forth the Methodist (chapter 7), Holiness (chapter 8), Pentecostal (chapter 9), Fundamentalist (chapter 12), and Adventist (chapter 13) churches.

Emerging within the Western Liturgical tradition but remaining basically liturgical churches, were the Church of England, the parent church of the worldwide Anglican Communion, and the Old Catholic Church. Both have major representative bodies in North America, and both have, in the last half of the twentieth century, given birth to numerous smaller schismatic bodies.

THE OLD CATHOLIC MOVEMENT. The Western Roman liturgical tradition suffered other divisions beside that of the Anglicans.

The most important, because of its generation of so many new church bodies, was the Old Catholic movement, which dates from the 1870s but has its roots in a disturbance in the seventeenth century in Port Royal, France. At Port Royal, Jansenists—members of a mystical movement that carried on the work of Dutch theologian Cornelius Jansen (1585–1638)—found themselves in opposition to the Jesuits, priests of a religious order obedient to the pope. Jansenists believed that the human will was not free and that redemption was limited to only some of humankind. Thus Jansenists were condemned by the pope and opposed by the Jesuits. The Jesuits accused the Jansenists of being Protestants, hence heretics; the Jansenists accused the Jesuits of despotism and laxity in doctrine and discipline. In alliance with the French monarchy, the Jesuits began a persecution that eventually broke the power of the Jansenists, many of whom fled to Holland in the territory of the see of Utrecht.

As the Jansenists moved into Holland from Port Royal, Utrecht's newly consecrated bishop, Peter Codde, entered into relations with them. When the pope demanded that Codde subscribe to the condemnation of the Jansenists, he refused and accused of Jansenism. Rival parties developed—one behind Codde and another behind Theodore de Cock. De Cock, for various reasons, was banished from Holland by the government. Codde was deposed by the pope and ceased exercising his functions.

Without episcopal functionaries, the see soon began to wither, as no ordinations or confirmations could occur. This problem was somewhat alleviated by the unexpected stop in Amsterdam of Dominique Marie Varlet, newly consecrated bishop of Babylon, on his way to Persia in 1719. In Amsterdam, he confirmed more than 600 children, the first confirmed in 17 years. For this act he was suspended from office. He returned to Europe and settled in Amsterdam. In 1724 Varlet consented to consecrate a new archbishop of Utrecht, Cornelius van Steenoven. When van Steenoven died shortly thereafter, Varlet consecrated Cornelius Wuytiers. Several other consecrations for neighboring dioceses such as Harlem and Deventer followed, insuring that the apostolic succession would not be lost. For approximately 150 years the Church of Utrecht, commonly called the Old Catholic Church, continued with only episcopal supervision as the dividing line between it and Rome.

Though the Old Catholic movement traces its history back to the see of Utrecht in Holland in 1702, it dates officially from the 1870s and the reaction to the declaration of papal infallibility at the First Vatican Council. In 1870 the First Vatican Council declared the pope infallible when speaking on matters of faith and morals. A number of Roman Catholics saw this position as a new doctrine, a deviation from the tradition, and many Roman Catholics left their church and sought communion with the Church of Utrecht. Even before the council, opposition in anticipation of the declaration arose, particularly in Germany. In 1871 in Munich a congress of opponents, led by Von Schulte, a professor of canon law, was held. Three hundred delegates, including representatives from the churches of Utrecht and England, came. These representatives organized the Old Catholic Church along national lines. In 1873 Joseph Hubert Reinkens, a professor of church history at Breslau, was elected bishop and was consecrated by the bishop of the church at Deventer. A constitution was adopted in 1874 that recognized national autonomy and established an international Synod of Bishops. The archbishop of Utrecht now presides over the episcopal conference.

The Old Catholic Church retained most of the doctrines of Rome but rejected ecclesiastical unity under the pope. In 1874 the Old Catholic Church dropped the compulsory fasting and auricular confession of the Roman Catholic Church, and feast days were reduced. By 1880 vernacular mass began to replace the Latin. The seven sacraments were continued, but baptism and the Eucharist were elevated to prime importance. The Roman Catholic Church has recognized the validity of Old Catholic (Utrecht) orders though it considers the exercise of the episcopal powers illegal.

THE OLD CATHOLIC CHURCH IN ENGLAND AND THE UNITED STATES. Because the Church of England (the Anglican Church) was so similar to the Old Catholic Church on the European continent, no attempt was made to introduce the latter church into England. However, during the nineteenth century there arose men who wished to function as bishops outside of either the Roman or Anglican communions. In some cases these were former priests in older communions. Some were representatives of ethnic communities expressing nationalistic enthusiasms. The Old Catholic movement developed an anti-authoritarian character. Most of its bishops have been self-appointed and have small followings. They have pressed for recognition of orders while keeping independence of jurisdiction. As an attempt at legitimization, they have sought recognition or reconsecration by bishops of the Eastern Orthodox Church (often after rebuff by the archbishop of Utrecht, the head of the Old Catholic Church). What began as a specific protest against the pope's authority turned into a drive by independent bishops to set up schismatic dioceses. With the growth of independent dioceses and recognition by various Eastern and Western churches, the variation in ritual and doctrine has increased tremendously.

As the Old Catholic movement developed in America, a chaotic episcopal scene emerged. Many bishops claim dioceses that exist only on paper and ordinations by bishops whose existence cannot be verified. A few churches seem to be oriented to serve the homosexual community. A few have been confidence schemes.

In the United States, most of the Old Catholic churches derive their orders through two lines of succession, that of Joseph Rene Vilatte or Arnold Harris Mathew. A third faction traces its lineage to miscellaneous Eastern and Western orders through Hugh George de Willmott Newman. Neither Vilatte's nor Mathew's churches remained in communion with the European Old Catholic churches, which entered into full communion with the Church of England in 1932 and with most of the churches of the Anglican communion by 1936.

Arnold Harris Mathew. Arnold Harris Mathew (1852–1919) began his professional career as a Roman Catholic priest. After serving several parishes, he became a Unitarian. He flirted with the Church of England for a while, changed his name, and married. Eventually he made peace with Rome and settled down as a layman and author. He penned a number of items, including a collaboration in editing the third edition of H. C. Lea's *History of Sacerdotal Celibacy in the Christian Church* early in this century. Then in September 1907 he began corresponding with Bishop Eduard Herzog, an Old Catholic bishop in Switzerland. In these letters, and later ones to Bishop J. J. Van Theil of Harlem, he suggested the formation of an Old Catholic church in England.

Mathew had in the years previous to his correspondence become associated with a group of disgruntled ex-Catholics, led by Father Richard O'Halloran. Under O'Halloran's guidance, Mathew was elected bishop of the Old Catholics in England. The problem was how to get valid orders. The church at Utrecht, the central see of the Old Catholic Church, was very hesitant, but finally on April 22, 1908, Mathew was consecrated in Utrecht by the archbishop, under protest from the Anglicans.

Mathew returned to England to find that O'Halloran had lied to him and there was no following waiting to accept him as their bishop. Mathew immediately wrote the archbishop of Utrecht informing him of the deceit and offering to resign. When his resignation was refused, Mathew accepted his circumstances as a mission. The Reverend W. Noel Lambert turned over his independent chapel to become Mathew's headquarters, renamed St. Willibrord's Procathedral.

In 1910 Mathew secretly consecrated two ex-Roman Catholic priests as bishops without informing Utrecht and without the assistance of other validly consecrated bishops. Mathew declared his independence from Utrecht and succeeded in building a small church. He died in lonely poverty, but before his death, Mathew set the stage for Old Catholicism in America.

Among Bishop Mathew's significant consecrations were those of Prince de Landas Berghes et de Rache, Duc de St. Winock, who established Mathew's succession in the United States, and Frederick Samuel Willoughby, who founded the Liberal Catholic Church. Mathew's consecrations also included that of John Kowalski of the Polish Mariavite Church.

The Duc de Landas Berghes was an Austrian nobleman consecrated by Bishop Mathew of the Old Catholic Church on June 28, 1913, probably with the idea of setting up an independent church in Austria. De Landas Berghes was prevented from returning to Austria from England because of World War I, however, and fled to the United States to escape arrest as an enemy alien. During his short career, before his submission to Rome in 1919, he consecrated as bishops Fathers W. H. Francis Brothers and Henry Carfora, the direct sources of most Old Catholic bodies in America to date because of the many men that they consecrated as bishops.

Joseph Rene Vilatte. The man who first brought the Old Catholic Church to America was Joseph Rene Vilatte. French-born, Vilatte appeared in Wisconsin in the 1880s preaching Old Roman Catholic doctrines among French and Belgian immigrants. He had a checkered religious education under an ex-Roman Catholic priest, Father Charles Chiniquy, and had come to believe both Roman Catholic and Protestant positions invalid. After marked success in Wisconsin, Vilatte went to Berne and obtained ordination from Bishop Herzog, but a protest from the Anglicans prevented his obtaining consecration from Utrecht, the central see of the Old Catholic Church. After a long search, he finally obtained consecration as archbishop of the archdiocese of America on May 29, 1892, from Archbishop Alvarez of Ceylon, who had received his orders from the Syro-Jacobite Church of Malabar.

Vilatte briefly returned to Roman Catholicism in 1899–1900, but soon became frustrated, resumed his independent work, and for the next 20 years operated as an archbishop for the American Catholic Church. Given his Roman background and his Orthodox orders, it is not surprising that both Old Catholic and independent Eastern Orthodox jurisdictions sprang from his activity. Also, because the Syro-Jacobite Church of Malabar refused to recognize the various consecrations he performed, even for leaders in his own church, he became further removed from the mainstream of American church life. Finally, in 1925, he again returned to the Roman Catholic Church and, renouncing his separatist and independent course of action, died in the arms of *Mater Ecclesia*. His own American Catholic Church, after the death of Archbishop Frederick E. J. Lloyd, Vilatte's successor, was taken over by bishops with Theosophical leanings and moved totally into the Liberal Catholic Church community.

Hugh George de Willmott Newman. Among the most colorful bishops in the independent Catholic community, Hugh George de Willmott Newman (1905–79) can be credited with introducing an increasingly common practice among the autonomous bishops, that of seeking numerous reconsecrations in order to legitimize an otherwise minuscule ecclesiastical jurisdiction by having its bishop embody a wide variety of lines of apostolic succession, both East and West. Such jurisdictions would symbolize the ecumenical church.

Newman was originally consecrated in 1944 by Dr. William Bernard Crow, whose orders derived from Luis Mariano Soares (Mar Basilius) of the small Syro-Chaldean church in India, Ceylon, Socotra, and Messina. However, within the next decade Newman received no less than nine additional consecrations, usually in ceremonies in which he in turn reconsecrated the other bishop (thus passing along the apostolic lineages he had already received). Of the several consecrations swapped by Newman, that with W. D. de Ortega Maxey of the Apostolic Episcopal Church was most important for the American scene, as Maxey not only established an American branch of Newman's Catholicate of the West, but became the prime source for American bishops to receive Newman's lineages.

Episcopally led churches have traditionally based their legitimacy on their ability to trace their line of succession from the original 12 Apostles. That is, for a bishop to be validly consecrated, and thus able to validly ordain priests, that bishop must himself be consecrated by a validly consecrated bishop. Thus, the story of the independent Old Catholic jurisdictions in America is the story of the search for legitimacy through ever more valid consecrations. It has become common for independent bishops to receive multiple consecrations, especially after changing allegiance to a different jurisdiction.

The importing of Eastern orders for a Western church, and the intermingling of Eastern and Western lineages in bishops such as Newman, also initiated a complex mixing of liturgies. The independent jurisdictions have felt free to adopt, regardless of the practices of the body from which they received their apostolic succession, any number of liturgies—Roman, Anglican, Eastern, or even Theosophical—while some have written their own. Since many of the American jurisdictions are quite small, with an unpaid clergy and congregationally owned property, one of the few real decisions the bishop can make is in regard to the liturgies that the congregations may use.

Adopting the practice introduced by Bishop Mathew of having an unpaid clergy, the Old Catholic (and independent Orthodox) church has splintered into more than 100 jurisdictions. Priests and bishops, since they have no financial tie to any given jurisdiction, can leave at will, and frequently do. The constant flux within the jurisdictions has made the problem of straightening out the line of succession extremely complex; however, the work begun in this area by H. R. T. Brandweth, Peter Anson, and Arthur C. Piepkorn has been expanded in recent years by Karl Pruter, Bertil Persson, and Alan Bain.

TRADITIONAL ROMAN CATHOLICISM. In the 1960s, the Second Vatican Council made a number of sweeping changes in the life of the Roman Catholic Church; changes that were implemented over the next decades. Many of the more conservative leaders opposed the changes, especially the dropping of the Latin liturgy in favor of the spoken languages of the local worshipping community. Two archbishops, Ngo-Dinh-Thuc of Vietnam, and Marcel LeFebvre of Switzerland, became vocal critics. Both sought a conservative alternative within the Post Vatican II Church and eventually both, without Papal approval, consecrated bishops to lead the communities that had been excommunicated by the Roman Catholic Church. The Thuc bishops have in turn consecrated other bishops, and reconsecrated bishops who had received Old Catholic orders, and from their hands several independent jurisdictions have flowed.

Archbishop LeFebvre resisted consecrating any new bishops and through the 1980s made repeated attempts to negotiate a means by which traditionalists could remain and function openly within the present church authority, but was rebuffed by the highest church authorities in the Vatican. In 1987, in the realization that he was growing old and reaching the end of his life, he asked that a commission for traditionalist Catholics be established and that he be allowed to consecrate three bishops to carry on his work. These negotiations fell through in the spring of 1988. On June 30, 1988, he, assisted by Brazilian bishop de Castro Meyer, consecrated four bishops. As a result all participants were excommunicated; the Roman Catholic Church branded them as schismatics.

Traditionalists associated with the Society of St. Pius X, the organization founded by LeFebvre, as do members of some of the other traditionalist groups, consider themselves good Roman Catholics, even though they have their own bishops and worship in separate local congregations headed by priests assigned by

these bishops. They pray for the Pope by name at every mass as well as the Roman Catholic bishop in whose diocese the services of the society are held. They adhere to all the Roman Catholic dogma. The society's seminaries adhere to all of the provisions for seminaries as found in the documents of the Second Vatican Council. They have refused to associate with the Old Catholics, who deny Papal authority, and with the mass of heterodox independent episcopal jurisdictions now found in Europe and North America.

Sources—Western Liturgical Family

The study of Roman Catholicism in America is focused in the American Catholic Historical Association, c/o Mullen Library, Catholic University of America, Washington, DC 20064. It publishes the *Catholic Historical Review*. In addition to CUA, significant archives of Roman Catholic materials can also be found at St. Charles Boromeo Seminary (Philadelphia), Notre Dame University (Notre Dame, Indiana), St. Mary's Seminary and University (Roland Park, Maryland), Georgetown University (Washington, DC), and St. Louis University (St. Louis, Missouri).

On Canadian Roman Catholic history, contact the Research Center in Religious History in Canada, c/o St. Paul University, 223 Main Street, Ottawa, Ontario K1S 1C4.

Anglican historical studies are brought together by the Historical Society of the Episcopal Church, P. O. Box 2247, Austin, TX 78768. In addition to the Society's archives in Austin, other significant archival deposits are found at the Berkeley Divinity School at Yale (New Haven, Connecticut), General Theological Seminary (New York City), and the Episcopal Church headquarters in New York City. The Historical Society publishes the quarterly journal *Anglican and Episcopal History*.

THE WESTERN LITURGICAL TRADITION

Aland, Kurt. *A History of Christianity.* Philadelphia: Fortress Press, 1985. 474 pp.

Algermissen, Konrad. *Christian Denominations.* St. Louis: B. Herder Book Co., 1946. 1051 pp.

Frankforter, A. Daniel. *A History of the Christian Movement.* Chicago: Nelson-Hall, 1978. 317 pp.

Johnson, Paul. *A History of Christianity.* London: Weidenfeld and Nicolson, 1976. 556 pp.

McGonicle, Thomas D. *A History of the Christian Church: From its Jewish Origins to the Reformation.* New York: Paulist Press, 1988. 218 pp.

Mirgeler, Albert. *Mutations of Western Christianity.* New York: Herder and Herder, 1965. 158 pp.

The Oxford Illustrated History of Christianity. New York: Oxford University Press, 1990. 724 pp.

Sheldon, Henry C. *Sacerdotalism in the Nineteenth Century.* New York: Abingdon, 1909. 461 pp.

Thompson, Baird. *Liturgies of the Western Church.* Cleveland: The World Publishing Company, 1962. 434 pp.

ROMAN CATHOLICISM

Bokenkotter, Thomas. *A Concise History of the Catholic Church.* Garden City, NY: Doubleday, 1977. 431 pp.

Brantl, George, ed. *Catholicism.* New York: Washington Square Press, 1962. 277 pp.

Foy, Felician A. *Catholic Almanac.* Huntington, IN: Our Sunday Visitor, issued annually.

———. *A Concise Guide to the Catholic Church.* Huntington, IN: Our Sunday Visitor, 1984. 158 pp.

Frederic, Catherine. *The Handbook of Catholic Practices.* New York: Hawthorn Books, 1964. 320 pp.

McKenzie, John L. *The Roman Catholic Church.* New York: Holt, Rinehart and Winston, 1969. 288 pp.

THE ROMAN CATHOLIC CHURCH IN NORTH AMERICA

Catholicism in America. New York: Harcourt, Brace and Company, 1954. 242 pp.

Carey, Patrick W. *The Roman Catholics.* Westport, CT: Greenwood Press, 1993. 375 pp.

Dolan, Jay P. *The American Catholic Experience: A History from Colonial Times to the Present.* Garden City, NY: Doubleday & Company, 1985. 504 pp.

Ellis, John Tracy. *American Catholicism.* Garden City, NY: Doubleday, 1965. 196 pp.

————. *Documents of American Catholic History.* Chicago: Henry Regnery Company, 1967. 2 Vols.

Gallup, George. *The American Catholic People: Their Beliefs, Practices and Values.* Garden City, NY: Doubleday & Company, 1987. 206 pp.

Hennesey, James. *American Catholics.* Oxford: Oxford University Press, 1981. 397 pp.

Kelly, George A. *The Battle for the American Church.* Garden City, NY: Doubleday, 1979. 513 pp.

Maynard, Theodore. *The Story of American Catholicism.* Garden City, NY: Doubleday, 1960. 694 pp.

ROMAN CATHOLIC THOUGHT

Abbott, Walter, ed. *The Documents of Vatican II.* New York: Guild Press, 1966. 793 pp.

Abell, Aaron I. *American Catholic Thought on Social Questions.* Indianapolis: Bobbs-Merrill, 1968. 571 pp.

Berkouwer, G. C. *Recent Developments in Roman Catholic Thought.* Grand Rapids, MI: Wm. B. Eerdmans Publishing Company, 1958. 81 pp.

Bokenkotter, Thomas. *Essential Catholicism.* Garden City, NY: Doubleday, 1985. 437 pp.

Burghardt, Walter J., and William F. Lynch. *The Idea of Catholicism.* New York: Meridian Books, 1960. 479 pp.

A Catholic Catechism. New York: Herder and Herder, 1958. 448 pp.

Fremantle, Anne. *The Papal Encyclicals.* New York: New American Library, 1956. 317 pp.

O'Brien, John A. *Understanding the Catholic Faith.* Notre Dame, IN: Ave Maria Press, 1955. 281 pp.

Trese, Leo J. *The Creed—Summary of the Faith.* Notre Dame, IN: Fides Publishers, 1963. 155 pp.

ROMAN CATHOLIC LITURGY

Dalmais, Irene Henri. *Principles of the Liturgy.* Collegeville, MN: Liturgical Press, 1987. 301 pp.

Lefebvre, Gaspar. *The Spirit of Worship.* New York: Hawthorn Books, 1959. 127 pp.

Martimort, Aime Georges. *The Church at Prayer: An Introduction to the Liturgy.* 4 Vols. Collegeville, MN: Liturgical Press, 1986–88.

Segundo, Juan Luis. *The Sacraments Today.* New York: Maryknoll, 1974. 154 pp.

The Treasures of the Mass. Clyde, MO: Benedictine Convent of Perpetual Adoration, 1957. 128 pp.

ROMAN CATHOLIC POLITY

McKnight, John P. *The Papacy.* London: McGraw-Hill Publishing Company, 1953. 400 pp.

Scharp, Heinrich. *How the Catholic Church Is Governed.* New York: Paulist Press, 1960. 128 pp.

Tillard, J. M. R. *The Bishop of Rome.* Wilmington, DE: Michael Glazier, 1983. 242 pp.

EASTERN RITE ROMAN CATHOLICISM

Attwater, Donald. *The Christian Churches of the East.* Milwaukee: Bruce Publishing Company, 1961. 232 pp.

————. *Eastern Catholic Worship.* New York: Devin-Adair Company, 1945. 224 pp.

Liesel, N. *The Eastern Catholic Liturgies.* Westminster, MD: Newman Press, 1960. 168 pp.

ANTI-CATHOLICISM

Billington, Ray Allen. *The Protestant Crusade.* New York: Macmillan, 1938. 514 pp.

Chiniquy, Charles. *Fifty Years in the Church of Rome.* Grand Rapids, MI: Baker Book House, 1960. 597 pp.

de la Bedoyere, Michael. *Objections to Roman Catholicism.* Philadelphia: J. B. Lippencott Company, 1965. 185 pp.

McLoughlin, Emmett. *Famous Ex-Priests.* New York: Lyle Stuart, 1968. 224 pp.

OLD CATHOLICISM

Anson, Peter F. *Bishops at Large.* London: Faber and Faber, 1964. 593 pp.

Bain, Alan. *Bishops Irregular.* Bristol, Eng.: The Author, 1985. 256 pp.

Brandreth, H. R. T. *Episcopi Vagantes and the Anglican Church.* London: S.P.C.K., 1961. 140 pp. Rept.: [Highlandsville, MO]: St. Willibrord Press, 1987.

Clarke, Boden. *Lords Temporal & Lords Spiritual.* San Bernardino, CA: Borgo Press, 1985. 136 pp.

Conger, Yves. *Challenge to the Church.* Huntington, IN: Our Sunday Visitor. 1976. 96 pp.

Davies, Michael. *Pope Paul's New Mass.* Dickinson, TX: Angelus Press, 1980. 673 pp.

Ford, James Ismael. *Episcopi Vagantes and the Challenge to Catholic Ministry.* Berkeley, CA: Pacific School of Religion, M.A. thesis, 1992.

Groman, E. Owen, and Jonathan E. Trela. *Three Studies in Old Catholicism.* Scranton, PA: Savonarola Theological Seminary Alumni Association, 1978. 37 pp.

Huelin, Gordon, ed. *Old Catholics and Anglicans, 1931–1981.* Oxford: Oxford University Press, 1983. 177 pp.

Moss, C. B. *The Old Catholic Movement.* Eureka Springs, AK: Episcopal Book Club, 1977. 368 pp.

Piepkorn, Arthur Carl. *Profiles in Belief.* Vol. I. New York: Harper & Row, 1977. pp. 29–56, 73–80.

Pruter, Karl, ed. *A Directory of Autocephalous Bishops of the Apostolic Succession.* San Bernadino, MO: St. Willibrord Press, 1996.

Pruter, Karl, and J. Gordon Melton. *The Old Catholic Sourcebook.* New York: Garland, 1983. 254 pp.

Ward, Gary L. *Independent Bishops: An International Directory.* Detroit, MI: Apogee Books, 1990. 524 pp.

Chapter 3

Western Liturgical Family
Part II: Anglicanism

Consult the "Contents" pages to locate the entries in Part III,
the Directory Listings Sections, that comprise this family.

Christianity probably entered the British Isles in the second century, as there was an organized church among the Celtic tribes by the third century. In the fifth century, the Romans withdrew and the southern half of what became England was invaded by a Germanic people (Angles, Saxons, and Jutes) who pushed the Celts westward. Though initially resistant, the Anglo-Saxon tribes were evangelized both by Celts under St. Aidan (Ireland and Wales had been Christianized in the fifth century) and Roman Catholics under St. Augustine. In the seventh century the British formalized its incorporation into Roman Catholicism.

The eastern shore was subject to Danish invasions through the eighth and ninth centuries, adding a new element into the churchs membership. In the eleventh century a singularly new element was added to the mix with the conquest of England by the Norman forces under William the Conqueror. The coming of the Normans also strengthened British ties to the church in Rome. Over the next centuries, the British Church served as a unifying force among the various tribal strains significantly present in the emerging nation. However, there were also repeated controversies over the extent of papal authority and its intrusion into British affairs both secular and ecclesiastical.

Had the Continental Reformation under Martin Luther not occurred, there is reason to believe England would have continued as a branch of the Roman Church which, like the French, German, or American church, has its own characteristics. However, the challenges to church authority across northern Europe provided an environment in which England could challenge Rome's hegemony, though it moved in a very different direction from that articulated by the continental reformers.

England, of course, had its own prophets of reform. John Wycliffe challenged the church's abuse of wealth and power and he attacked the church's doctrine of transubstantiation, the idea that the elements in the Mass actually change substantively into the body and blood of Christ. He believed this kind of magical notion merely assisted the clergy in holding onto unscriptural authority. To back his arguments he translated, published, and preached from a new edition of the Scripture in the vernacular.

THE EMERGENCE OF INDEPENDENT ANGLICANISM. Under King Henry VIII (1509–1547), the Church of England came into open conflict with papal authority. They were not doctrinal problems, however. The pope had allowed Henry to marry his brother's widow, Catherine of Aragon, and in 1521 Henry had taken the time to author a refutation of one of Luther's writings. As a result of his volume, *Assertion of the Seven Sacraments Against Luther,* the pope awarded him the title "Defender of the Faith." But two issues of central importance to him as the king of England would undo his cordial relationship with Rome: his desire for a male heir and his financial needs.

Henry first moved against Catherine. She had born six children, only one of which, Mary, had survived. He asked for a divorce, an act that would call the papacy's relationships with Catherine's powerful relatives into question, and the pope refused. Eventually,

the Church of England renounced allegiance to the pope and accepted Henry's supremacy over ecclesiastical law. They backed their position by withholding money that was traditionally paid annually to Rome. In 1533 he forced the selection of Thomas Cranmer as the new Archbishop of Canterbury (the most powerful office in the Church of England), and Cranmer in turn declared the marriage with Catherine null and void. Anne Boleyn became his new wife.

Though the pope threatened excommunication, the British Parliament passed a series of acts that finalized the independence of the Church of England. The initial measure forbade payment to Rome, denied appeals to Rome, and placed powers heretofore exercised by the pope into the hands of the Archbishops of Canterbury and York. The Act of Succession (1534) declared Mary illegitimate and named Elizabeth (Anne Boleyn's daughter) as heir. Later that year, the Act of Supremacy made it a crime punishable by death to not accept the Act of Succession or to fail to acknowledge the supremacy of the king.

Having already taken steps to separate from Rome, Henry also saw in the church, which possessed great wealth through its extensive land holdings, a means of supplementing his always tenuous treasury. Henry ordered the new Archbishop of Canterbury to survey the many monasteries across the countries. Cranmer reported that extensive corruption was founded, and in 1536 Henry closed most of them and pocketed the income from the sale of their lands.

Through the 1540s Henry married several more times, finally had a son, Edward, and ended his reign by moving against the Protestants who had begun to surface. While breaking with Rome under Henry, the Church of England retained its structure, with bishops, clergy, church buildings, and congregations, but it continued under the Archbishop of Canterbury rather than the pope. The church was also still completely Roman in doctrine, liturgy, and organization.

Under Edward VII, who ascended the throne at the age if ten, England began to align outwardly with the reformers. The Council of Regency, appointed to administer the country until Edward came of age, was dominated by people with Protestant leanings. Cranmer published a *Protestant Prayer Book* for use in all the churches, and Parliament passed a series of decrees that changed the face of the church over the next three years. Exponents of the Reformed Church were brought to England to teach and Cranmer authored a doctrinal statement, the "Forty-two Articles," that embodied the reformed position.

England might have come into the reformed camp at that point had it not been for the sickliness of Edward, who passed away before reaching adulthood. He was succeeded by his older sister Mary, a devout Roman Catholic with a memory of the indignities showed her mother. She married a Spaniard, abolished Cranmer's prayer book, and moved against the Protestant church leaders. The extensive nature of her persecutions earned her the label "Bloody Mary." The country was on the verge of revolution when Mary died after only five years on the throne.

Mary's death brought Elizabeth I to the throne. Her half-century of rule is remembered as one of the great eras in England's history.

It was during this time that the distinctions of the Anglican tradition were developed. Seeking to create strong and peaceful land, she compromised the demands of the two warring factions. A new Prayer Book was issued and a set of Thirty-nine Articles, derived from the Forty-two Articles, promulgated. Some of the articles, which continued to embody the reformed theological perspective, condemned specific Roman Catholic practices. Purgatory, indulgences, venerating saints' relics, and celebrating the liturgy in any tongue other than the vernacular were among the Roman elements condemned. However, Elizabeth retained the traditional episcopal structure.

Elizabeth I, aware that Edward and Mary had strong support for their choices of religions, adopted a *via media* (middle way), blending Roman Catholic and Protestant elements.

Opposition to the compromises came from both sides, but Elizabeth was affected most by the objections of the Roman Catholics. In 1570 she was excommunicated by the pope. She uncovered several plots to have her assassinated and replaced with Mary Queen of Scots. She gradually gave up any hope of reconciling with the pope, who, in 1588 supported the building and launching of the Spanish Armada against England. The defeat of the Armada remains one of the crucial turning points of European history. In one of the final acts against Elizabeth, in 1596 the pope declared that Anglican episcopal orders were not valid.

Early in Elizabeths reign, a number of Roman Catholic bishops had resigned. In response, Archbishop Matthew Parker moved to fill the vacant seats, which caused Rome to conclude that the Apostolic Succession had been lost. This action soured Anglican/Roman Catholic relations into the twentieth century and has yet to be fully resolved. Steps at healing the Roman Anglican split have been taken in atmosphere of good will generated by Vatican II.

The Book of Common Prayer, the Anglican liturgical book that replaced the Roman missal, has gone through several editions. The edition published during Elizabeth's reign is crucial: it makes concrete the distinctive character of Anglicanism that has continued to this day. That edition includes the Thirty-nine Articles of Religion, creeds, a church calendar, and texts of liturgical services. Material on the sacraments in that edition is intentionally vague, to allow various interpretations of the Eucharist. Anglicans recognize only two sacraments—baptism and the Lord's Supper. Anglican doctrine on the church shifted from the Roman emphasis on the bishop to the Calvinist emphasis on the congregation. *The Book of Common Prayer* asserts that the church exists where the Word of God is preached, the sacraments are duly administered, and the faithful are gathered.

A certain Anglophilia characterizes the Church of England. When Rome commissioned St. Augustine to be a missionary in England in 597 C.E., he found Christians already in England. Over the centuries since the final break with Rome, many Anglicans have insisted that their church was not formed by Rome and that the Anglican Church in England predates the arrival of the Roman Catholic Church to the British Isles. Anglicanism is thus a tradition separated from Roman Catholicism by its liturgical differences, its condemnation of some Roman beliefs and practices, and its alignment with British tradition. With the expansion of England in the seventeenth century, the Anglican tradition spread throughout the world.

ENGLAND AFTER ELIZABETH. The development of the Church of England did not cease with the imposition of the *via media,* and Elizabeth's long reign and ability to triumph over her enemies did much to set it firmly in place. Elizabeth never married, and hence had no children to succeed her. She was succeeded by James I, the son of Mary Queen of Scots. During his two decades on the throne (1603–1625), his Catholic tendencies were stymied by the discovery of plots to assassinate him. Instead of giving in to the demands of his Roman Catholic subjects, he supported the new Puritan translation of the Bible, and a series of laws restricting Roman Catholic participation in various activities. He then tested the Puritan strength with a refusal to allow further revisions of the Prayer Book.

The reign of James' successor, Charles I, saw the rise to power of Archbishop William Laud. He was a champion of Anglicanism and initiated policies that infuriated the Puritans who were Protestants in the reformed tradition who wished to further purify the Church of England of its Romanish remnants and who controlled Parliament. Charles found himself in a contest of will with Parliament. Matters came to a head when the Scots revolted. Parliament used the situation to assert its control. In the end, Parliament called for an assembly of Puritan clergy to meet at Westminster and advise the Parliament. They proceeded to write what were to become the defining documents of British Presbyterianism, the Westminster Confession of Faith, the Directory of Worship, and the Catechism. In 1645 Parliament forbade the continued use of the Prayer Book and outlawed Anglicanism with its Catholic remnants.

The civil war that followed brought Oliver Cromwell to power. He articulated a policy of religious toleration (Roman Catholics and Anglicans excepted), and then through a Commission of Triers he began to systematically move the British church toward the austere reformed faith demanded by the Puritan leaders. But a number of his reforms went against the very heart of popular exercise of faith. For example, he outlawed dancing and Christmas and other festivals. He also saw to the dismantling of numerous ornate church altar areas. Each act cost him valuable support. He was able to hold the country together while alive, but his son was driven from power and Charles II (1660–1685), a Roman Catholic ascended the throne.

Under Charles II, the Anglican Church resumed its place as the national Church of England, a position it has not since relinquished, and the real struggle among the Christians of the British Isles shifted to finding some means of accommodating the many dissenting groups which were present in the culture. A major landmark was the Toleration Act of 1689 which granted liberty of worship to all except Roman Catholics and Unitarians (who did not affirm the Christian doctrine of the Trinity).

THE WORLDWIDE ANGLICAN COMMUNION. While Britons were trying to decide who would rule and what kind of government would direct the country, they were also pursuing an expansionist policy in regards to the New World across the Atlantic. Beginning in the eighteenth century, the British actively settled the east coast of the North American continent. Some Anglicans responded in 1649 by founding the Society for the Propagation of the Gospel in New England. The society picked up the support of John Eliot, already in Massachusetts working among the Native Americans. Its efforts were supplemented by the Society for Promoting Christian Knowledge (SPCK) founded in 1698 and the Society for the Propagation of the Gospel in Foreign Parts (SPG) founded in 1701. Most of the Anglican clergy operating in North America prior to the American Revolution were sent through the SPG.

The American Revolution had a marked effect on the spread of Anglicanism. The missionary societies withdrew from the new United States, and redirected their efforts elsewhere. By that time, England was establishing the first centers of what would become their vast colonial empire of the nineteenth century. Joined by the Church Missionary Society and the London Missionary Society, both founded in 1795, the SPG set to the tasks of providing church life for British colonists (and expatriates around the world in non-colonial settings) and evangelizing non-Christian populations that came under the hegemony of the British government.

The nineteenth century was the era of massive expansion of Christianity in all parts of the world, carried in large part by the European colonial enterprise. Anglicanism became a worldwide faith centered upon the colonists that responded to the efforts of the missionaries in setting up the Church of England everywhere the British erected settlements. Given the extensive nature of the British Empire, it is not surprising that by the beginning of the twentieth century Anglicanism had established itself throughout the Orient, across India and Africa, and to a lesser extent in South America.

Just as the previous two centuries had seen the vast expansion of the British colonial empire, the twentieth century has seen a major change in Englands relationships with colonial states, signaled in 1931 by the formation of the British Community (or Commonwealth) of Nations. Among the first acts of the Commonwealth was the reordering of relations through the granting of independence to Canada, New Zealand, Australia, and South Africa. India and Pakistan gained independence in 1947, and during the next decade most of the former colonies also either gained independence through armed conflict or were granted it. Most recently changing status was Hong Kong, which in 1997 again became part of China. Many former colonies chose to remain part of the Commonwealth, but others went their own ways.

The dismantling of the empire was in some cases anticipated by the reordering of the relationships within the Church of England internationally. Beginning in the middle of the nineteenth century, church names began to change, for example the Church of England in Canada changed to the Anglican Church in Canada, which was later granted independent status and joined the worldwide Anglican Communion as a sister church. Such changes were most frequently accompanied by the development of an indigenous leadership, the organization of dioceses and archdioceses, and the naming of a primate (leading bishop) from among the country's citizens.

The Protestant Episcopal Church (now known simply as the Episcopal Church) in the Unites States was the first church granted recognition as an independent body, a decision made after and in light of the success of the American Revolution. The first Anglican bishop outside of the British Isles was named for Canada in 1787, Charles Inglis, Bishop of Halifax, Nova Scotia. Through the next century, missions were established and grew into dioceses, but each diocese operated autonomously and reported directly to England. Finally in 1861 the first provincial synod for the Church of England in Canada met. That church continued to transform, and emerged in 1897 as an autonomous body.

Around the world the story of the emergence of the various independent jurisdictions which now compose worldwide Anglicanism is distinct for each nation or region. The first to attain independent status was New Zealand (1957), but the overwhelming majority of the autonomous provinces were created after World War II. Many arose not only in the rush to end colonialism, but in the euphoria of the mid-twentieth century ecumenical movement. In a variety of countries where Christianity was a minority movement, Anglicans joined Congregationalists, Methodists, and Presbyterians to create national Protestant churches, the most prominent being the Church of North India, the Church of South India, the Church of Pakistan, and the Church of Bangladesh.

Of particular interest because of its intrusion into Anglican affairs in the last generation is the church in the Philippines. The Philippine Independent Church (PIC) emerged out of the Spanish American War in which the United States took over the island nation and the indigenous PIC established, creating a schism between it and the Roman Catholic Church. The PIC founder led the church into unitarianism, a trend that was checked by his successor and in 1947 the church officially accepted a Trinitarian creed and was accepted by the Episcopal Church (in the United States) as a sister church. In the meantime, a Philippine Episcopal Church had been established in the common pattern to service British expatriates and missionize the indigenous population. Both churches continue to the present.

ANGLICANISM IN AMERICA. The Anglican tradition entered North America with the coming of the British explorers in the sixteenth century. Worship according to the Church of England was established at St. John's, Newfoundland, in 1583, where the Reverend Erasmus Stourton became the first Anglican minister to reside in North America. Anglican services were held for the first time in what is now the United States on August 13, 1587, at the ill-fated Roanoke colony in Virginia. They were permanently established in 1607 in Jamestown. The first minister at Jamestown was Robert Hunt, who died soon after his arrival in America. His efforts were followed by the more substantive career of Alexander Whitaker, who served the colony as pastor of Henrico, the second church in Virginia.

Throughout the 1600s, the Church of England spread through British North America, finally entering Puritan Boston in 1692. It was given a significant boost in 1701 by the establishment of the SPG as a foreign missionary arm for the Church of England, and by the arrival of society founder Thomas Bray. Appointed commissioner, with some of the powers of a bishop, Bray settled in Maryland and directed the missionary endeavor. The work in Canada expanded immensely in the late eighteenth century, following a series of events beginning with the British seizure of Quebec (1759) and the subsequent Treaty of Paris in 1763, which gave Canada to the British. The American Revolution then sent large numbers of British loyalists northward. The growth is no better symbolized than by the placing of Charles Inglis, a former parish priest from New York, in Halifax as the first bishop of the Church of England in Canada in 1787.

While aiding church growth in Canada, the American Revolution almost destroyed Anglicanism in the American colonies. Identified as antipatriotic by the public, the Church of England in America also lost its legal status, most of its priests (who returned to England), and its financial base. The church was virtually cut off from the homeland because the bishops in England initially refused to pass along episcopal orders. Samuel Seabury, elected bishop by the remaining priests in Connecticut, was consecrated by Scottish bishops in 1784. It was not until 1787, the same year a bishop was placed in Nova Scotia, that William White and Samuel Provoost were consecrated in London and a working accord was reached between the new Protestant Episcopal Church in the United States and the Church of England.

While the church in America grew as an independent body, the church in Canada prospered as a missionary branch of the Church of England and was officially designated as the Church of England in Canada; it changed its name to the Anglican Church in Canada in 1955.

TRADITIONALIST ANGLICANISM. The Protestant Episcopal Church, the Anglican Church in Canada, the Reformed Episcopal Church (a nineteenth-century evangelical splinter group), and a few congregations of the Philippine Independent Church provided the main substance of the Anglican tradition for North America until the mid-1960s. There had been several smaller schisms, but not until the 1960s did the Episcopal Church suffer its first widespread losses from members withdrawing in protest over modernist changes in the church, primarily related to a shifting moral code (manifest in new attitudes toward sexuality), revisions of the Prayer Book, and the acceptance of females into the priesthood. The initial schism of 1964 and the subsequent formation of the Anglican Orthodox Church brought widespread unrest that heightened in 1976 after females had been ordained in both Canada and the United States.

The (Anglican Catholic Church (ACC) and the Anglican Catholic Church in Canada (ACCC) are the two largest bodies of the 20 or more churches formed among dissenting Anglicans. As they were formed, each of the new jurisdictions faced the problem of apostolic succession. The Anglican Orthodox Church had accepted old Catholic and independent Orthodox orders. In the 1970s, ACC and ACCC leaders turned to the international Anglican Communion for support, and found it initially in the Philippine Independent Church.

Bishop Francisco Pagtakhan, the PIC missionary bishop whose jurisdiction covered North America, performed the initial consecrations. As additional new Anglican jurisdictions were established, Pagtakhan was joined by two colleagues, Bishops Sergio Mondala and Lupe Rosete, and together performed a series of consecrations during the early 1980s. As a result of these and other actions, Pagtakhan had severe disagreements with the church in the Philippines in the mid-1980s, and eventually left to form the Philippine Independent Catholic Church, which has now established parishes in North America.

The independent Anglicans who emerged in the 1970s have been the most conservative wing of Anglicanism. While most are concentrated in the few larger churches that grew out of the 1976 meeting in St. Louis (especially the Anglican Catholic Church and the Anglican Catholic Church in Canada), the number of new jurisdictions has continued to increase.

Sources—Anglicanism

Anglican historical studies are brought together by the Historical Society of the Episcopal Church, PO Box 2247, Austin, TX 78768. In addition to the societys archives in Austin, other significant archival deposits are found at the Berkeley Divinity School at Yale (New Haven, Connecticut), General Theological Seminary (New York City), and the Episcopal Church headquarters in New York City. The Historical Society publishes the quarterly journal *Anglican and Episcopal History*.

CHURCH OF ENGLAND AND THE WORLDWIDE ANGLICAN COMMUNION

Dart, J. L. C. *The Old Religion*. London: S.P.C.K., 1956. 210 pp.

Flindall, R. P., ed. *The Church of England, 1815–1948*. London: S.P.C.K., 1972. 497 pp.

Hardy, E. R., Jr., ed. *Orthodox Statements on Anglican Orders*. New York: Morehouse-Gorham Co., 1946. 72 pp.

Holloway, Richard, ed. *The Anglican Tradition*. Wilton, CT: Morehouse-Barlow Co., 1984.

Neill, Stephen. *Anglicanism*. London: A. R. Mowbrays, 1977. 421 pp.

Wand, J. W. C. *What the Church of England Stands For*. London: A. R. Mowbray, 1951. 131 pp.

Whale, John. *The Anglican Church Today: The Future of Anglicanism*. London: Mowbray, 1988. 102 pp.

ANGLICANISM IN NORTH AMERICA

Addison, James Thayer. *The Episcopal Church in the United States, 1789–1931*. New York: Charles Scribner's Sons, 1951. 400 pp.

DeMille, George E. *The Episcopal Church Since 1900*. New York: Morehouse-Gorham Co., 1955. 223 pp.

Herklots, H. G. G. *The Church of England and the American Episcopal Church*. London: A. R. Mowbray & Co., 1966. 183 pp.

Konolige, Kit and Frederica Konolige. *The Power of Their Glory*. N.p.: Wyden Books, 1978. 408 pp.

Lewis, Harold T. *Yet with a Steady Beat: the African American Struggle in the Episcopal Church*. Valley Forge, PA: Trinity Press International, 1996. 253 pp.

Manross, William W. *A History of the American Episcopal Church*. New York: Morehouse-Gorham Co., 1950. 415 pp.

Sydnor, William. *Looking at the Episcopal Church*. Wilton, CT: Morehouse-Barlow Co., 1980. 142 pp.

Woolverton, John Frederick. *Colonial Anglicanism in North America*. Detroit: Wayne State University Press, 1984. 331 pp.

THE NEW ANGLICANS

Armentrout, Donald S. *Episcopal Splinter Groups*. Sawanee, TN: The School of Theology, The University of the South, 1985.

Dibbert, Roderic B. *The Roots of Traditional Anglicanism*. Akron, OH: DeKoven Foundation of Ohio, 1984. 13 pp.

A Directory of Churches of the Continuing Anglican Tradition. Eureka Springs, AK: Fellowship of Concerned Churchmen, 1983–84.

Joseph, Murray. *Priests Forever*. Valley Forge, PA: The Brotherhood of the Servants of the Lord, 1975. 16 pp.

Opening Addresses of the Church Congress at St. Louis, Missouri, 14–16 September 1977. Amherst, VA: Fellowship of Concerned Churchmen, 1977.

A Retired Priest. *The Broken Body*. N.p.: The Author, 1980. 38 pp.

Chapter 4
Eastern Liturgical Family

Consult the "Contents" pages to locate the entries in Part III,
the Directory Listings Sections, that comprise this family.

THE EASTERN ORTHODOX TRADITION. The Eastern Orthodox church continues the church established in the Apostolic era, the first generation of Christianity, in the Eastern Mediterranean Basin. The Eastern church and the Western Roman church formally coexisted as two branches of the same church for centuries. However, cultural differences, politics, and doctrinal disagreements finally led to official division and mutual excommunication in 1054. By that time the Eastern church dominated the eastern Mediterranean basin, spreading through Greece, Egypt, Asia Minor, some of the Arab countries, and the Balkans. It would later spread northward through Eastern Europe and become the dominant faith in Romania, the Ukraine, and Russia. Then in the early Middle Ages, its dominance would be weakened by the loss of the "heretical" churches (the non-Chalcedonian Orthodox churches) and most thoroughly by the Moslem conquests.

In each area it came to dominate, the Eastern church developed an episcopal structure of national autonomous sees. Certain older sees were more prominent and had been designated patriarchates. They included Alexandria, Antioch, Jerusalem, and Constantinople. In more recent years, patriarchates have been designated in Bulgaria, Serbia, Russia, and Romania. Autocephalous churches, headed by a bishop but without a patriarchate, exist in the Ukraine, Cypress, Albania, Greece, Poland, and Georgia. Autonomous churches, headed by a bishop, self-governing on internal matters, but dependent on a patriarchate for the appointment of its primate (head bishop) and relations with other churches, exist in Finland, Estonia, Czechoslovakia, Latvia, and Lithuania, and at the monastic community at Mt. Sinai.

The Eastern church finds its spiritual unity in the office of the Ecumenical Patriarchate headquartered at Istanbul (formerly known as Constantinople and the lead city of the Eastern Byzantine Empire), though his position of primacy is one of honor, not power. All of the patriarchs are of equal authority and none has the right to interfere with the work in another's territory. The patriarchates and leaders of various national churches have expanded their authority into the West as parishioners have moved into Europe and the Americas. Jurisdiction for the Greek-speaking Orthodox in the West has been placed under the authority of the Ecumenical Patriarchates, though the Church of Greece now has a small number of parishes in North America. The various Orthodox churches are "in communion" with each other and in the United States the bishops of the churches who directly relate to the ecumenical patriarch work together as the Standing Conference of Canonical Orthodox Bishops in the Americas. Most Orthodox Christians in America are members of these churches.

THE SPREAD OF ORTHODOXY. During the first century C.E., the Christian movement established centers around the Mediterranean Basin. As the movement grew, Jerusalem, Alexandria, Antioch, and Constantinople became the leading centers from which the movement emanated through the Eastern half of the Roman Empire. Jerusalem was the ancient biblical center. Antioch was the place mentioned in the book of Acts where the followers of Jesus were first called Christians. Alexandria, the Egyptian city, was the center of orthodoxy in the face of the majority of Egyptian Christians refusal to accept the promulgations of the Council of Chalcedon in 451 C.E. Constantinople was, of course, the capital of the Empire established by Constantine. In 451 it was named second only to Rome in importance.

During the years of the Byzantine Empire, the Christian movement had already begun its thrust into the East which would see the establishment of Christian movements as far east as India and strong Christian nations in such places as Armenia. Most of the work to the East would, like Egypt, be lost during the conciliar era as different national churches refused to accept the latest promulgation of one council or another. Also, contact with these churches would be additionally hindered by the rise of Islam, which decimated their ranks in many areas.

The loss of the Eastern churches would be replaced by the movement of Christianity northward into the Balkans, Romania, and Russia. These lands, which today we think of as traditionally Orthodox, only began to be reached by missionaries in the ninth century. Christianity was introduced into Bulgaria around 845 C.E. when Boris, the ruler, accepted the new faith and imposed it upon the people. A short time later Christians from Moravia came into the country and introduced the Old Slavonic liturgy which had been developed by the missionaries Cyril and Methodius. The church adhered to Constantinople when the Christian movement split in 1054. A bishop resided in Okhrida (or Akrida) in western Bulgaria and in Tirnova in the East. The Bulgarian bishops existed autonomously until the Turkish conquest of the land in 1393 when Tirnova was absorbed into Okhrida.

Christianity was introduced among the Serbian people as early as the seventh century, but effective evangelization efforts did not occur until the end of the ninth century. It was not until the last half of the twelfth century that the Serbians were united into a single state, and finally in the year 1219 a bishopric was established. A synod in 1346 declared the church autonomous. While leaning toward Rome for many years, the Serbian church gradually shifted allegiance to the East.

Romanians, a Latin people living in a land surrounded largely by Slavic peoples, received Latin/Western Christianity as early as the third century. In the ninth century the Bulgarians conquered the area and imposed their Eastern Slavonic ways on the Christian community. Their Orthodoxy became an issue in their continuing conflict with their Hungarian neighbors (Roman Catholics) to the north and Orthodoxy became integral to the emerging national identity. The Romanian church made some gain after the land was overrun by the Turks and was able to gain some degree of independence from the Bulgarian authorities.

Crucial for the future of the church in the southern Balkans was the fall of Constantinople in 1453. The fall of the capital of the old Eastern Roman Empire ended any hope of its comeback. It also brought the "headquarters" of Eastern Christianity under the thumb of a Muslim government. In the eighteenth century, the

Turkish Empire would attempt to organize all the Christians in its empire under the authority of the Patriarch in Constantinople, an action that would be greatly resented by many.

A most notable gain for Orthodoxy occurred toward the end of the tenth century when Prince Vladimir of Kiev (Ukraine) invited missionaries from Constantinople into his land. In 988 he "gave" Christianity to his people and it is from that date later generations would date the conversion of the land to Christianity. Entirely dependent upon Constantinople, when the church in Russia adhered to Eastern Orthodoxy during the schism of 1054. Several centuries later, after Kiev fell to the Mongol invasion, the center of Russian orthodoxy moved to Moscow and the Moscow Patriarchate ruled over the lands controlled by the Russian government. Included in these lands were the Ukrainians and the Byelorussians, both people with a separate language and culture, who have periodically attempted to exist as an autonomous church body.

The Turkish invasion of the lands of the southern Balkans had a telling effect upon the churches under its control. In the eighteenth century, the Turks imposed the idea that all Christians were under Constantinople. In 1767 the government suppressed the independent, bishoprics and the Greek church, headquartered at Constantinople, followed with a period of Hellenization. The most important effect was the imposition of the Greek language in the worship of all monasteries and the larger churches. Old Slavonic, which had existed as primarily a liturgical language, was slowly forgotten. The Turkish government reversed its policy in 1856 and declared the freedom and equality of the Christians residing in the Empire. That new policy, and the accompanying gradual disintegration of the Ottoman Empire through the nineteenth century, allowed autonomous national churches to reemerge.

Romania emerged as an independent nation by several steps in the nineteenth century. Under the reign of Alexander Kuza, which began in 1864, a fully independent country allowed the emergence of a Romanian church independent of Constantinople. Constantinople formally recognized the new situation in 1885.

The Serbian church also lost its autonomy in 1767 and went through a period of Hellenization. Like Romania, Serbia gained its independence in stages through the nineteenth century. It was declared an autonomous state in 1879 and the independent status of the church immediately followed. The Serbian church gained from the establishment of Yugoslavia following World War I, suffered by the rise of a secular Marxist government after World War II, and has yet to rebound from the war that followed the recent break-up of the country.

The Bulgarian church began to lobby for independence from Constantinople as part of an overall effort by Bulgarians to free themselves from Turkish control. This finally occurred in 1878. Ecclesiastical independence, however, was gained in 1870. The patriarch in Constantinople excommunicated the Bulgarian bishops two years later and considered the Bulgarian church schismatic until 1945, when it was finally recognized as an autonomous body.

The Orthodox churches of the southern Balkans have experienced great ups and downs through the twentieth century as various boundaries changed, often radically, and successive governments adopted different policies toward Christianity. Some formerly independent jurisdictions have disappeared altogether. Through the twentieth century, they have seen the disappearance of the Ottoman Empire, the emergence of Communism and its dominance for many decades in Russia, Romania, Serbia, and Bulgaria, and the recent overthrow of Communist governments. Since World War II, those Eastern Orthodox churches in countries under Communist control experienced schisms among members outside of the country. Many members argued that the leadership had departed from the faith by becoming puppets of the Communist governments.

Throughout this whole period, Greece has a unique and interesting history. It was on the border between East and West with a background of orientation toward Rome but was later assigned to the territory of the Eastern Roman Empire. It eventually leaned toward the Eastern church and its ecclesiastical life directly under Constantinople. It was conquered by the Turks in the fifteenth century, but as it was already part of the land under the Patriarchate in Constantinople, little change in church structure occurred. Then in the nineteenth century a successful civil war freed much of the land from Turkish control. In 1831, the Greek church declared itself free of the control of the Patriarchate, who still resided in territory controlled by the hated Turks. The territory of the Church of Greece grew in stages, but has suffered periodically due to government instability.

One particularly grievous event was the adoption of the Western calendar early in this century. The abandonment of the old Julian calendar became a symbol of unwanted change, and the Old Calendar conservatives have been a small but vocal group continually causing problems for the church ever since.

Since World War II the Eastern churches have become involved in the worldwide ecumenical movement and have developed friendly relationships with Western Protestant churches through structures such as the World Council of Churches. This new openness to non-Orthodox Christians brought many charges that the church was changing and adopting un-Orthodox practices.

THE DOCTRINAL POSITION OF EASTERN ORTHODOXY. To most Americans, familiar with only the Roman and Anglican traditions, the Eastern Orthodox tradition presents several distinctive features. The celibate priesthood of the Roman Catholic church is not demanded. In the East priests marry (though they must do so before ordination). Monks do not. Bishops are drawn from the ranks of the monks. Priests who are not monks are not eligible for the episcopacy. The Eastern church does not recognize the authority of the bishop of Rome over the various patriarchs of the Eastern church.

The Eastern churches recognize only the seven ecumenical councils held between 325 C.E. and 787 C.E. because no further councils occurred at which the bishops of Rome and the Eastern patriarchs worked together. In their acceptance of these councils, the Eastern church is doctrinally at one with Roman Catholicism and the churches of the Western tradition. This doctrinal consensus has been illustrated in the latter twentieth century by the meetings of the Ecumenical Patriarch and the pope, and their membership along with Protestant and Free churches in the World Council of Churches and other regional and national ecumenical bodies.

After the formal split between the Roman Catholic church and the Eastern churches, The Roman church continued to hold councils at which new doctrinal positions were promulgated. Several of these remain as unacceptable doctrines to the Eastern Church which, for example, rejects the *filioque* doctrine as popularized in the western church beginning in the fifth century. *Filioque* is the Latin word for "and the Son," added to the Western version of the creed to assert the equality of the Father and the Son by suggesting that the Holy Spirit proceeds from both the Father and the Son. Some theologians of the Eastern church insisted the Holy Spirit proceeds from the Father through the Son. The Eastern church rejected the *filioque* doctrine partly on biblical grounds, in that John 15:26 makes no mention of the Son and instead speaks of "the Spirit of truth who proceeds from the Father."

The Greek *Liturgy of St. Chrysostom* is used throughout the Eastern church. The various national bodies have translated it into their native tongues, and in America, English translations are being increasingly used.

Those areas where Orthodoxy exists only as a small minority religion, geographically removed from the ancient centers, are designated Orthodoxy in Diaspora. The single largest diaspora community is the more than three million Orthodox Christians in the United States.

ORTHODOXY IN NORTH AMERICA. Orthodoxy entered the United States in the eighteenth century following the discovery of

Alaska by Russians in 1741. In 1743 an Aleutian by the name of Andreu Islands was baptized. The Russian Orthodox Church was firmly established in 1794 when seven monks came to Paul's Harbor and consecrated the first church. By 1841 a seminary was in operation in the Aleutian Islands. The first diocese, created after Alaska was purchased by the United States, was moved to San Francisco in 1872.

Spotty movement of Orthodox Christians into North America began in the first part of the nineteenth century, but did not become significant until the 1890s. Prior to 1891, the only parishes were those in Alaska and the single church in San Francisco. At this time, the Russian Orthodox Church included members from all ethnic backgrounds and had all of North America under its hegemony. Then, the movement of people from the Middle East and from Eastern and Southern Europe increased significantly because of growing tension in Russia, Turkish and Russian expansion, and the general suffering occasioned by World War I, until it was all but stopped by the immigration quota limitations imposed in 1924. Immigrants settled in the northern and eastern urban centers but found their way to the prairies of western Canada and the farmland of California. As significant numbers of each national group arrived, they began efforts to form their own unique parishes and then to organize separate dioceses. By the early twentieth century, the Russian church began to lose its ethnic parishes and the various ethnic branches of the Orthodox church formed.

As these new branches were formed, one by one, most were severely tested by two outside forces. First, the inevitable process of Americanization—the demands of conformity, especially in language—divided the generations, and on occasion led to schism. Of more concern, however, was the Russian Revolution and the spread of atheist regimes in predominantly Orthodox countries. As the Orthodox churches have tended to be aligned with the state, the loss of state support was devastating. The actual hostility of a government that appeared ready to either destroy or subvert the church to its own purposes called into question the relationship of American and Canadian churches to the patriarchal headquarters caught in the revolutionary situations. Some Americans demanded loyalty to the patriarchs and accommodation to the new regimes, while others with equal strength demanded autonomy from the homeland. Beginning in the 1920s with the Russians and accelerating after World War II, schism rent almost every branch of Eastern Orthodoxy in North America.

The structure of American Orthodoxy was dramatically changed in 1970 with the creation of the Orthodox church in America by the merger of several of the Russian churches. Russian Orthodoxy, by reason of its early arrival date, has always had a primacy in America. Many of the currently existing independent Orthodox bodies were formed under its care. In recent years, the growth of the Greek Orthodox Church in America has led to challenges to Russian primacy, challenges based on the claims of the ecumenical patriarch in Istanbul as the first among equals in world Orthodoxy. The argument was somewhat academic since each American church was directly related to a different overseas see. The Orthodox Church in America, unattached to a foreign see, was authorized by Patriarch Alexis in Moscow, whose right to grant such status has been questioned by the Greek Orthodox church.

The new body, the Orthodox Church in America, aims at uniting Orthodox of all ethnic groups into a single American Orthodox body. This is the natural result of a growing demand for American autonomy. Archbishop Philip of the Antiochean Church has been among the new church's most vocal advocates. The new body is the only Orthodox church which has all of the structures necessary to continue without outside help. These structures include seminaries, monasteries, and charitable institutions.

THE EMERGENCE OF INDEPENDENT ORTHODOXY IN THE TWENTIETH CENTURY. During the nineteenth century, Orthodox believers from many of the European national churches mi-

grated to America. A few, such as the Greeks, remained autonomous and eventually formed their own ethnic church. Others, such as the Syrians, began as an ethnic group under the care of the Russian church, which, because it was the first Orthodox church to establish work, had a special hegemony within the United States. Once in the United States with its multiethnic atmosphere, geographically removed from its homeland, the Orthodox church became subject to a variety of forces that split its community into a number of ecclesiastical factions. The first major splinter began as a movement to unite American Orthodoxy.

Aftimios Ofiesh (1890–1971) came to America in 1905 to work among Syrians, then a part of the Russian Orthodox church. In 1917 he was consecrated bishop for the Syrian work, succeeding Bishop Raphael Hawaweeny. On February 2, 1927, the Russian bishops gave him the duty of caring for the American-born Orthodox, especially the English-speaking parishes, not otherwise being given proper care. By their action they created a new jurisdiction, the American Orthodox church, as an autonomous body with a filial relationship to the Russian church.

The project met immediate opposition. The non-Russian bishops were not supportive of a united American Orthodoxy as proposed and the ecumenical patriarch, the nominal head of all Orthodox churches, denounced the project as schismatic. The Greeks were angered by Ofiesh's publication of a magazine, *Orthodox Catholic Reporter*. Especially offended were the Episcopalians, who considered themselves the American form of Orthodoxy and who were providing the Russians with large amounts of financial support. They applied pressure on Metropolitan Platon to abandon Ofiesh. Even though soon abandoned by the Russians, Ofiesh continued in his project and, beginning with Emmanuel Ato-Hotab (1927) and Sophonius Bashira (1928), he consecrated four bishops to head his independent work.

The problem with Ofiesh was not the only trouble to disturb the Russian church during the 1920s. As a result of the Russian Revolution and the coming to power of an antireligious regime, the close allegiance of the church to the Russian government was called into question, especially after the imprisonment of the patriarch of Moscow in 1922. Soviet supporters within the Russian church in 1924 organized a sobor (convention) of what came to be called the Living Church faction. They voiced support of the Soviet government and elected the only American at the sobor, John Kedrowsky, bishop of America. He came to America and with his sons, Nicholas (later his successor as bishop of America) and John, and through court action took control of St. Nicholas Cathedral in New York City. However, he was rejected by a synod of the American Russian church in 1924 that declared its autonomy in administrative matters from the church in Russia.

While the Russians were splintering into several factions, the Greeks, never under Russian control, were having their own problems. In 1908, the Greek parishes in America were transferred from the direct authority of the ecumenical patriarch to the holy synod of the church in Greece. That arrangement did not provide the necessary leadership for the burgeoning American church, so in 1918, the ecumenical patriarch began the process of establishing the American church as an archdiocese, a task finally accomplished in 1922. However, that arrangement also did not resolve the leadership question, and in 1930 the ecumenical patriarch reasserted his hegemony in America by appointing a representative to come to the United States and take over leadership of the archdiocese.

Meanwhile, as organizational trouble plagued the church, it was further divided by internal problems in Greece. A faction of the American membership opposed the transfer of the allegiance of the American church from the church in Greece to the ecumenical patriarch. In the 1930s they removed themselves from the archdiocese and sought consecration of a new bishop by the church in Greece. Thus in 1934, Christopher Contogeorge, with the blessing of the church in Greece, was consecrated the archbishop of Philadelphia by Albanian Bishop Fan Stylin Noli, assisted by Bishop Sophonius Bashira. Archbishop Christopher was the consecrator of Bishop John Kedrowsky's successor, Nicholas Kedrowsky.

By the mid-1930s Archbishop Christopher and Bishops Sophonius, Nicholas (Kedrowsky), and Fan constituted a group of independent Orthodox bishops both organizationally and emotionally separated from the larger body of Orthodox bishops and faithful. These four participated in a number of consecrations of new bishops, both in their several jurisdictions and in other independent Orthodox churches. From their lineage came Bishops Joseph Klimowicz, Walter A. Propheta, and Peter A. Zurawetzky, who in turn consecrated most of the men who head the presently existing independent Orthodox churches.

There is one strain of independent Orthodoxy that has a history independent of the bishops discussed above, that which derives from Archbishop Joseph Rene Vilatte of the American Catholic church (discussed in the previous chapter as one of the founders of Old Catholicism in America). Vilatte's episcopal orders came from a small Orthodox body in India and during the later years of his life he consecrated individuals who adopted an Orthodox stance, most notably George A. McGuire, founder of the African Orthodox Church. Also, at least one person from the Vilatte lineage participated in the consecration of Propheta.

Finally, it should be noted that just as both Orthodox and Catholic jurisdictions derived from the work of Vilatte, so too have they both derived from the independent Orthodox bishops. Most notably, Christ Catholic church derived as an Old Catholic body from the previous jurisdiction of Peter Zurawetzky.

THE NON-CHALCEDONIAN ORTHODOX CHURCHES. Separating during the years of the great Ecumenical Councils, the Christian churches of Egypt, Armenia, and the Middle East, for a variety of reasons, refused to ratify one or more of the creeds, primarily the Chalcedonian Creed of 451 C.E., which most of the Eastern Orthodox world accepted as a standard of orthodox Christian faith. Both the Roman Catholic church and the Eastern Orthodox churches have branded these churches as heretical in faith, though the Armenian church has vigorously protested such labeling as a misunderstanding of its position both theologically and relationally to the Council of Chalcedon.

The Nestorians. The monk Nestorius, who became patriarch of Constantinople in 428 C.E., believed that Christ was not the Son of God, but that God was living in Christ. The two natures of Christ—divine and human—were separable, said Nestorius. Further, he said Mary bore the human Christ, not God. Thus she was not "Theotokos," the God-bearer. And it was not God who suffered and died. Nestorius preached his doctrines throughout the Eastern church. In 431 C.E., the Third Council of the early church met at Ephesus to treat the teachings of Nestorius. The council ruled that Mary was "Theotokos," and that the human and divine natures are inseparably bound together in the one person of Christ. The council condemned Nestorius, declared his teachings heretical, and deposed him as patriarch of Constantinople. These actions began a four-year battle of ecclesiastical and imperial politics. The result was Nestorius' banishment and the burning of his books.

The Nestorians continued to spread Nestorius' beliefs. They conducted missionary work in Persia, India, and China and won followers in Arabia and Egypt. Under the Mohammedans they were essentially free from persecution until the modern era. They survive to this day as the Church of the East. Their largest losses have been to proselytizing efforts by Roman Catholics, Jacobites (to whom they lost much of the church in India), and more recently Protestants.

The Church of the East belongs to the non-Chalcedonian Orthodox tradition in the sense that it opposes the statement of the Council at Chalcedon, 451 C.E., that Christ was "begotten...of Mary the Virgin, the God bearer."

When the Nestorians were rediscovered in the 1830s by Protestant missionaries, their preservation of an old Aramaic dialect also became news. They have since made this dialect the language of their Scripture translation. The seven sacraments they observe are baptism, ordination, the holy eucharist, anointing, remission of sins, holy leaven, and the sign of the cross. The holy leaven refers to the belief that a portion of the bread used at the Last Supper was brought to the East by the Apostle Thaddeus and every eucharist in the Church of the East is made from bread continuous with that meal. The sign of the cross is considered a sacrament and a very specific formula is prescribed for its rubric.

As with all of the Eastern churches, relation with a particular Apostle is assumed. The Church of the East claims a special relationship with the Apostle Thaddeus, who visited the kingdom of Oshroene soon after Pentecost, and with Mari (one of the 70 disciples). Supposedly there was correspondence between Abgar, the ruler of Oshroene, and Christ, in which the former invited Jesus to settle at Edessa, the capital city.

The liturgy of the Church of the East is that of the "Holy Apostles Addai and Mari" (Saints Thaddeus and Mari), who brought it from Jerusalem. The leadership of the church is found in the patriarchate, which has since 1350 been hereditary in the family of Mar Shimun. Since the patriarch is celibate, the office passes from uncle to nephew. Under the patriarch are the metropolitans and bishops. The priests are allowed to marry at any time, even after their ordination.

The Monophysites. The Monophysite churches, like the Eastern Orthodox and Roman Catholic, emphasize liturgy in their church life; they believe strongly in an Apostolic succession, and they derive their doctrinal position from the ancient creeds. Their distinctiveness comes from the content of their creed, which differs more from both Constantinople and Rome than the latter two differ from each other. The Monophysite churches are united on doctrine, but have lines of succession and liturgy with a national flavor.

The distinct Monophysite doctrines derive from the fifth century discussions on the nature of Christ. It was the Monophysite position that Christ was one person of one (mono) nature (physis), the divine nature absorbing the human nature. In the context of the debate, Monophysitism was opposed to Nestorianism, which said that Christ had two natures but that they were separable.

Monophysitism was condemned by the Fourth Council of the early church, held at Chalcedon in 451 C.E. The council formulated what came to be called the Chalcedonian Creed, which says Christ is "of one substance with the Father as regards his Godhead, and at the same time of one substance with us as regards his manhood." Rejecting this creed, most of the Armenian, northern Egyptian, and Syrian churches broke away from the main body of the Christian church. In general, the Monophysite churches accept only the first three councils of the early Christian church (those at Nicea, Constantinople, and Ephesus) as valid and binding.

Theologians continue to debate Monophysite Christology. Some writers contend that the Monophysite churches are Eutychean; i.e., that they follow the teaching of Archimandrite Eutyches, a monk of Constantinople, who asserted the unity of nature in Christ in such a way that the human nature was completely fused and absorbed in the divine. Others, however, assert that the Monophysite churches (at least some of them) are not Eutychean, but Orthodox with a very "undeveloped terminology." The Armenian, Syrian, and Coptic churches represent the Monophysite tradition, but they deny the label "Monophysite" and deny that they teach any submergence of Christ's human nature.

The Armenian Churches. According to tradition, Christianity was brought to Armenia by Thaddeus and Bartholomew, two of the original 12 apostles. By 260 C.E., a bishopric had been established in Armenia and was referred to in Eusebius's *Ecclesiastical History*. In 301 C.E. Tiridates II, the King of Armenia, became the first Christian monarch. St. Gregory the Illuminator, who converted Tiridates, worked with the King's blessing to organize the Armenian church. Through the church a written language was developed and a literate Armenian culture emerged. As is common with Monophysite churches, the Armenian church accepted only the first three ecumenical councils (those at Nicea, Constantinople, and Ephesus), and uses the Nicene Creed. Members of the Armenian church did not attend the Council of Chalcedon in 451 C.E. and rejected its decisions.

Ecclesiastical authority in the Armenian church was invested in the catholikos who originally resided at Vagharshabat in central Armenia. There, close to the palace, Gregory built Etchmiadzin, the great cathedral. Because of changing political fortunes, the catholikos was frequently forced to move, first to Dovin (484), then among other places to Argina (944), Tauplour (1054), Domnplov (1065), and finally to Sis, in the Kingdom of Lesser Armenia or Cilicia (1293). In 1441 an assembly was held at Etchmiadzin and a catholikos was installed. The catholikos at Sis at that time took the title catholikos of Cilicia. Both sees—Etchmiadzin and Cilicia—have functioned until the present.

There are several minor peculiarities in the Armenian church's sacraments, distinguishing it from other churches in the liturgical family. Holy communion is customarily celebrated only on Sunday and on special occasions and cannot be celebrated twice in the same day. Pure wine (without water) and unleavened bread are used and the laity receive the eucharist by intinction. The eucharist is served to infants immediately after baptism by touching the lips with the elements.

Armenians in America. During the last 1500 years Armenia has suffered foreign domination and persecution by Moslems and Russians. The most terrible of these persecutions were the ones begun by the Turks in 1890 and carried on intermittently for the next 30 years. The effect was practically to destroy and scatter the Armenian nation. The arrival of Armenians in America really dates from the immigration begun as a result of the massacres. The antireligious persecution by the Russians after World War I followed the Turkish onslaughts.

Armenians in America began to form churches in the early twentieth century. The first was organized in 1891 in Worcester, Massachusetts. After 1921 American Armenians began to divide politically into two factions. One group remained intense nationalists, loyal to an independent Armenia and its symbols. The other group, often described as Pro-Soviet, accommodated themselves to and then supported the inevitable Russian dominance of Armenia. The political division was deeply felt throughout the entire American Armenian community, including the church.

Though practically autonomous, the Armenian church in America recognized the authority of the catholikos of Etchmiadzin. Archbishop Levon Tourian was designated by the see of Etchmiadzin as the supreme prelate of the Armenian Apostolic Church in America. Shortly after his arrival he managed to offend both political parties in contradictory statements concerning the nationalist flag. The continued polarization of the two factions led in 1933 to a split in the church itself.

The split occurred during the annual meeting of the national church council. Pro-Soviet lay delegates began to hold rump sessions and from their meeting a second church was, in effect, begun. While there was little doubt of the legal continuance through the church council, Archbishop Tourian recognized the Pro-Soviet group and declared some of the nationalist priests "unfrocked." A few months later Bishop Tourian was assassinated during High Mass in New York City. So deep was the split in the Armenian community that, as one writer observed, "Armenians have come to hate one another with a passion that has exceeded at times even a hatred for the Turks" (Sarkis Atamian, *The Armenian Community* [New York: Philosophical Library, 1955], 358).

The Syrian Churches. Antioch, an ancient city of Syria, is the place where the followers of Jesus were first called Christians (Acts 11:26). In the early centuries, Antioch was the center of a large Christian movement rent by the Monophysite controversy concerning whether Christ had two natures, human and divine, or one

(mono) nature (physis). Jacob Baradeus, a resident of Antioch though bishop of Edessa, was both a favorite of Empress Theodora and a fervent Monophysite. After his consecration in 542 C.E., he toured all of the area from Turkey to Egypt organizing churches. Those churches under his authority were to take his name in later years.

The evangelical zeal of the Jacobites was hindered and many of their gains destroyed in the conquests of Islam. In 1665 the Jacobites gained strength in India and Ceylon when the Nestorian Malabar Christians came under the Antiochean patriarch. This action more than doubled the size of the church and today makes up more than 60 percent of its worldwide membership of 100,000.

The Jacobites have several distinctive practices. Baptism is by triune infusion (pouring). Auricular confession to the priest is not used. During the eucharist the priest waves his hand over the elements to symbolize the operation of the Holy Spirit. The action is also used in ordination ceremonies.

The Coptic Churches of Egypt and Ethiopia. At one time the church in Egypt, the Coptic church, was among the largest in Christendom. But in 451 C.E., Dioscurus, the patriarch of Alexandria, was deposed by the Council of Chalcedon, the fourth of the general councils in the early centuries of Christianity. There began an era of persecution of the Copts, first by their fellow Christians and then after 640 C.E. by the Arab conquerors. Beginning with heavy taxes, the persecutions became bloody toward the end of the first millennium C.E. By the end of the Middle Ages, the Coptic church had shrunk from six million to 15,000 members. Growth since that time has been slow, but religious toleration in the nineteenth century helped, and by the middle of the twentieth century, there were three to five million members.

The Coptic church developed its own traditions. Its members are proud of Egypt as the childhood home of Jesus and the location of the ministry of St. Mark, who traditionally is credited with Egypt's initial evangelization. Several liturgies are used, but the most popular is the Liturgy of St. Basil, written by St. Basil the Great (b. 330 C.E.). There is particular veneration of the Virgin, manifest in the 32 feasts in her honor during the ecclesiastical year. In 1971 she is said to have appeared over the Coptic Cathedral in Cairo.

The head of the Coptic church is the patriarch of Alexandria with his see at Cairo. In 1971 this office was assumed by Pope Shenouda III. On May 6, 1973, Pope Shenouda greeted Pope Paul VI with a kiss of peace on a visit to St. Peter's Basilica in Rome.

Ethiopia accepted Christianity in the fourth century and the first bishop, Frumentius, was consecrated by Athanasius, who was the patriarch of Alexandria. The Ethiopian church came under the jurisdiction of the Coptic church in Egypt and followed its theological lead. Isolated by its mountains, Ethiopia withstood the advances of Islam but was cut off from the rest of Christendom. It reached its heights of glory in the thirteenth century under King Lalibela, who gave his name to a city of churches, 10 of which were hewn from solid rock. Modern history for this church began when Catholic missionaries sought to bring the Abyssinians under the Roman pontiff. They almost succeeded in the seventeenth century when for a few years Roman Catholicism was accepted by the ruler.

The Ethiopian church differs from the Coptic church in that it has absorbed strong Jewish traits. It accepts the Apocrypha as scripture, venerates the Sabbath along with Sunday, recognizes Old Testament figures as saints, and observes many Old Testament regulations on food and purification.

Sources—Eastern Orthodox Family

Prominent archives of the Eastern Orthodox tradition in North America are located at the Department of Archives and History (Orthodox Church in America), Syosset, New York; Logos Mission Center (Greek), PO Box 4319, St. Augustine, FL 32085; and the headquarters of the Ukrainian Orthodox Church of the U.S.A., Box 495, South Bound

Brook, New Jersey. The Standing Conference of Canonical Orthodox Bishops in America has sponsored the Orthodox Theological Society in America that provides for both theological and historical inquiry.

Ecumenism Among the Nonchacedonians. While the issue dividing the Nonchacedonian church from Eastern Orthodoxy have in nowise been put aside, some mutual recognition has occurred in the decades since World War II. Armenian, Coptic, Indian, and Syrian churches have been admitted to the World Council of Churches, and its several cooperating regional an national organizations such as the National Council of Churches of Christ in the U.S.A.

EASTERN ORTHODOXY

Adeney, Walter F. *The Greek and Eastern Churches.* New York: Charles Scribner's Sons, 1908. 634 pp.

Attwater, Donald. *The Dissident Eastern Churches.* Milwaukee: The Bruce Publishing Company, 1937. 349 pp.

Benz, Ernst. *The Eastern Orthodox Church.* Garden City, NY: Doubleday, 1963. 230 pp.

Bulgakov, Sergius. *The Orthodox Church.* London: Centenary Press, 1935. 224 pp.

Fitzgerald, Thomas E. *The Orthodox Church.* Westport. CT: Greenwood Press, 1995.

Handbook of American Orthodoxy. Cincinnati: Forward Movement Publications, 1972. 191 pp.

Kuzmission, Joe. *Eastern Orthodox World Directory.* Boston: Braden Press, 1968. 305 pp.

Lau, Emhardt Burgess. *The Eastern Church in the Western World.* Milwaukee: Morehead Publishing Co., 1928. 149 pp.

Le Guillou, M. J. *The Spirit of Eastern Orthodoxy.* Glen Rock, NJ: Paulist Press, 1964. 121 pp.

Orthodoxy, A Faith and Order Dialogue. Geneva: World Council of Churches, 1960. 80 pp.

Parishes and Clergy of the Orthodox, and Other Eastern Churches in North and South America. New York: Joint Commission on Cooperation with the Eastern and Old Catholic Churches of the General Convention of the Protestant Episcopal Church, 1964-65. 187 pp. Rev. ed., 1967-68. 184 pp. Rev. ed., 1970-71. 208 pp.

Roberson, Ronald G. *The Eastern Christian Churches.* Rome, Italy: Pont. Institutum Studiorum Orientalium, 1988. 43 pp.

Schmemann, Alexander. *The Historic Road of Eastern Orthodoxy.* New York: Holt, Rinehart and Winston, 1963. 343 pp.

Taft, Robert F. *The Oriental Orthodox Churches in the United States.* Washington, DC: Secretariat, Bishops Committee on Ecumenical and Interreligious Affairs, National Conference of Catholic Bishops, 1986. 28 pp.

Zernov, Nicolas. *The Church of Eastern Christians.* London: Society for Promoting Christian Knowledge, 1942. 114 pp.

ORTHODOX LITURGY

Dalmais, Irenee-Henri. *Eastern Liturgies.* New York: Hawthorn Books, 1960. 144 pp.

The Orthodox Liturgy. London: Society for Promoting Christian Knowledge, 1964. 110 pp.

Sokolof, D., comp. *A Manual of the Orthodox Church's Divine Service.* Jordanville, NY: Holy Trinity Russian Orthodox Monastery, 1968. 166 pp.

Wybrew, Hugh. *The Orthodox Liturgy: the Development of the Eucharistic Liturgy in the Byzantine Rite.* London: SPCK, 1989. 189 pp.

ORTHODOX THEOLOGY

Allen, Joseph J. *Orthodox Synthesis.* Crestwood, NY: St. Vladimir's Seminary Press, 1981. 231 pp.

Lossky, Vladimir. *The Mystical Theology of the Eastern Church.* London: James Clarke & Co., 1957. 252 pp.

Maloney, George A. *A History of Orthodox Theology Since 1453.* Belmont, MA: Nordland Publishing Co., 1976. 388 pp.

Platon, Metropolitan. *The Orthodox Doctrine of the Apostolic Eastern Church.* London, 1857. Reprint. New York: AMS Press, 1969. 239 pp.

INDEPENDENT ORTHODOXY

Anson, Peter F. *Bishops at Large.* London: Faber and Faber, 1964. 593 pp.

Bain, Alan. *"Bishops Irregular."* Bristol, England: The Author, 1985. 256 pp.

Brandreth, H. R. T. *Episcopi Vagantes and the Anglican Church.* London: SPCK, 1961. 140 pp. Reprint.: Highlandsville, MO: St. Willibord Press, 1985.

Clark, Boden. *Lords Temporal & Lords Spiritual.* San Bernardino, CA: Borgo Press, 1987.

Morris, John W. *"The Episcopate of Aftimios Ofiesh."* *The Word* Part One: 25, 2 (February 1981) 5-9; Part Two: 25, 3 (March 1981) 5-9.

Pruter, Karl, and J. Gordon Melton. *The Old Catholic Sourcebook.* New York: Garland Publishing, Inc., 1983. 254 pp.

Tillett, Gregory. *Joseph Rene Vilatte: A Bibliography.* Sydney, Australia: The Vilatte Guild, 1980. 23 pp.

Ward, Gary I. *Independents Bishops: An International Directory.* Detroit, MI: Apogee Books, 1990. 524 pp.

NON-CHALCEDONEAN ORTHODOXY

Butler, Alfred J. *The Ancient Coptic Churches of Egypt.* Oxford: Clarendon Press, 1884. 2 Vols.

Elmhardt, William Chauncey, and George M. Lamsa. *The Oldest Christian People.* New York: AMS Press, 1970. 141 pp.

Fortescue, Adrian. *The Lesser Eastern Churches.* London: Catholic Truth Society, 1913. 468 pp.

Issac, Ephraim. *The Ethiopian Church.* Boston: Henry N. Sawyer Company, 1968. 59 pp.

McCullough, W. Stewart. *A Short History of Syriac Christianity to the Rise of Islam.* Chico, CA: Scholars Press, 1982. 197 pp.

Meinardus, Otto, F. A. *Christian Egypt Faith and Life.* Cairo: The American University in Cairo Press, 1970. 513 pp.

Ramban, Kadavil Paul. *The Orthodox Syrian Church, Its Religion and Philosophy.* Puthencruz, Syria: K. V. Pathrose, 1973. 167 pp.

St. Mark and the Coptic Church. Cairo: Coptic Orthodox Patriarchate, 1968. 164 pp.

Sarkissian, Karekin. *The Council of Chalcedon and the Armenian Church.* New York: The Armenian Church Prelacy, 1965. 264 pp.

———. *The Witness of the Oriental Orthodox Churches.* Artelias, Lebanon: The Author, 1970. 91 pp.

Chapter 5

Lutheran Family

Consult the "Contents" pages to locate the entries in Part III,
the Directory Listings Sections, that comprise this family.

During the Middle Ages the Roman Catholic Church was able to create a religious community that, however fragile, was able to unify most of Europe, from Italy and Spain in the South to Norway and Sweden in the North. After a number of centuries of control of religious life in the West, the reform movement begun by Martin Luther (1483–1546) not only challenged but broke the hegemony of the church in most of northern and western Europe. Luther's teachings, coupled with the power of the German princes who supported him, precipitated a dramatic break with Roman authority not only in Germany and Scandinavia (which embraced Lutheran ideas) but in Switzerland, Great Britain, and Holland, which followed Luther's lead away from the Roman Catholic Church, but in differing directions.

Lutheranism embraces the two basic precepts of Luther's writings: first, that salvation is by grace through faith alone; and second, that the Bible is the sole rule of faith and the sole authority for doctrine. Lutheranism is distinct from other Reformation churches because of its continued emphasis on a sacramental liturgy and because of Luther's understanding of the eucharist.

LUTHERAN DOCTRINE. Word and sacrament are the keystones of Lutheran church life. "Word" refers to the appeal to the Bible instead of to both the Bible and tradition. "Sacrament" refers to the high regard Lutherans have for the two sacraments they observe—baptism and the eucharist—and Luther's theology of the eucharist. Luther's belief that salvation is by grace through faith alone finds expression in Lutherans' interpretation of the Bible and reliance on it, and in their celebration of the sacraments.

A discussion of the importance of the Word to Lutherans must start with Luther's background. He was a Bible scholar and a professor at the University of Wittenburg in Germany. He translated the Bible into German and based his theology on the Bible. Before he broke with the Roman Catholic Church, he was an Augustinian monk who strove to merit salvation through ascetic practices. In studying the Bible, however, he found that salvation does not come by man's action but only by God's free gift. Thus comes the emphasis on man's sinfulness in Lutheranism: a person who breaks one law is as guilty as a person whose whole life is the breaking of laws. Luther saw that the whole point of Christ's coming was to bring salvation; human beings could not earn it by themselves.

It remains for each person to welcome grace by faith in Christ. This emphasis contrasts with the traditional Roman Catholic emphasis on both faith and good works. Further, this emphasis contradicts a practice popular in Luther's time—the selling of indulgences (by which people paid to cancel the punishment they would receive in purgatory for their sins). Proceeds from the sale of indulgences in Germany were being used, among their causes, to finance the building of St. Peter's Basilica in Rome.

Luther's discovery that the righteousness (goodness) of God is man's only reason for hope came during the winter of 1513–14, in what is called his "tower experience," so named because it occurred while he was in the monastery tower. Among biblical passages supporting his doctrines are Romans 1:17: "For in it (the gospel of Jesus) the righteousness of God is revealed through faith, for faith. He who through faith is righteous shall live," and Ephesians 2:8: "For by grace you have been saved through faith. This is not your own doing, but the gift of God, not because of works, lest anyone should boast."

Because of Gutenberg's invention of the printing press in the fifteenth century, Luther's translation of the Bible was made widely available. His translation of the New Testament was published in 1522, and the Old Testament in 1534, and they quickly became best-sellers in Germany. Lutherans then and now have used the Bible as their only standard for faith and doctrine. Further, Luther used it to counter a range of traditional Catholic elements. First, Luther found that only two sacraments, baptism and the eucharist, had a biblical basis. Hence Lutherans do not consider the following to be sacraments: penance, confession, holy orders, unction, and marriage. Second, Luther argued against a number of practices that Roman Catholics consider sanctioned by tradition if not by the Bible. For example, he argued that the celibate priesthood has no biblical basis, and he soon left the Augustinian order, in which he functioned as a priest and married a former nun. Among pious practices Lutherans abandoned were monastic life, the veneration of relics, radical fasting, pilgrimages, hair-shirts, scourges, and the rosary. Lutheran piety instead developed around hearing the Word in the liturgy, receiving the eucharist, and reading the Bible. Third, Luther cited the Bible to counter the authority of the pope, and claimed the Bible as the source of his own authority to reform the church.

To discuss the importance of "sacrament" for Lutherans involves treating both Luther's understanding of the eucharist, and other elements discussed in the next section that make Lutheran liturgy distinctive.

Luther's doctrine of the eucharist is called consubstantiation, a departure from the Roman Catholic doctrine called transubstantiation. Luther suggested that Christ is present everywhere, but his presence is especially focused in the eucharist. The bread and wine still exist, but under the guise of bread and wine is Christ, who is received by the believer physically. This reception occurs, said Luther, because of Christ's promise at the Last Supper that it would occur. The doctrine of transubstantiation, on the other hand, suggests that the essence of bread and wine are replaced by the essence of Christ, who thus becomes present physically.

The doctrine of consubstantiation allowed Lutherans to preserve their liturgical worship instead of denying the sacraments altogether. So Lutheran liturgy is distinct from that of, for example, the Anabaptists, who do not have any sacraments, although they do observe a memorial meal as an ordinance. The consubstantiation doctrine also kept Lutherans from following the Reformed tradition, which replaces belief in Christ's physical presence in the sacramental elements with belief only in his spiritual presence in the eucharist.

LUTHERAN LITURGY. Lutheranism vies with the historic Catholic and Orthodox traditions for its emphasis on liturgy. In the early 1520s Luther began revising the Sunday service and found himself in conflict with those reformers, such as Andreas von Carlstadt, who looked for radical changes in the worship. Luther developed a form of worship in Wittenburg which followed the form of the Roman liturgy but which emphasized the use of the vernacular in preaching, in the liturgy, and in hymns. Vestments, candles, and pictures became optional. The church calendar remained in use.

Luther did change the format of the service by bringing the sermon into the worship, and on days when the eucharist was not served, a sermon substituted for it. Gregorian music was continued but gradually was replaced. The medieval outline that was standard for each liturgical service continued and remains basic in Lutheran liturgy. This outline is reflected in the *Agenda,* forms of worship adopted by the Lutheran churches in the United States in 1958.

No discussion of Lutheran liturgy would be complete without mention of Lutheran hymnology. All Protestants are familiar with Luther's "A Mighty Fortress Is Our God," a popular anthem which became known as the battle hymn of the Reformation. In 1524 Luther published his first hymn book and a second was published before the year was out. The popular hymns not only spread Luther's ideas on man's sinfulness and God's righteousness, but became integral to the worship and distinguish Lutheran liturgy from most other liturgical services.

POLITY. Polity is largely a low-priority subject among Lutherans. Bishops, though rare, have not been entirely unknown. The tendency generally, however, is for churches to operate somewhere between a congregational polity and a form of presbyterianism in which power is vested in the synod or body of ministers.

Luther advocated cooperation between church and state. He said a Christian ruler, acting in a Christian manner, should govern the secular sphere, and the church should govern the religious sphere. Thus the Christian ruler and the church, each in their respective spheres, would oversee the activities of all the people in the state.

THE "CONFESSING" CHURCH. Luther's doctrinal insights and his criticisms of Roman Catholicism were first publicly presented in the Ninety-five Theses he nailed to the church door in Wittenburg in 1517, and then in the three treatises of 1521. His position did not find confessional status until 1530, with the Augsburg Confession. Princes who were following Luther and breaking the unity of the Roman Catholic Church had to account for that to the Holy Roman Emperor. So they presented the Augsburg Confession to him to explain their position. As written by Philip Melanchthon (1497–1560), a professor of Greek and a New Testament scholar at Wittenburg, it has remained the central statement of Lutheran essentials. It includes traditional Christian beliefs, those articulated during the conciliar era from the fourth to eighth centuries, such as belief in the Trinity and the resurrection of the body. But it goes further to elaborate on statements concerning humanity, specifically, on man's sinfulness, forgiveness of sin, and justification by grace through faith alone. Lutherans rallied around the Augsburg Confession, and Roman Catholics united against it. It became the standard under which Lutherans later entered the Thirty Years' War.

The Augsburg Confession began the practice of the "confessing" church. Typically, when pressed by a contemporary situation, Lutheran (and Reformed) churches will summarize a stance in the form of a "confession of faith" which says to the world, "Here we stand; we can do no other." In the twentieth century, for example, such statements were issued to counter Nazism.

To the Augsburg Confession were added other confessions and documents which further clarified a Lutheran position as opposed to other religions. These documents include the Larger and Small Catechism (1529), written by Luther, the Smalcald Articles (1537), and the Formula of Concord (1577). These, along with the three ecumenical creeds (the Apostles' Creed, the Nicene Creed, and the Chalcedonian Creed), were collected in 1580 into the *Book of Concord.* This collection constitutes the basic body of Lutheran doctrinal writings, a clear statement of the truths Lutherans feel are taught in Scripture and the starting point for other theological endeavors.

ORIGINS. At least three dates vie with each other for the beginning of Lutheranism. The most widely accepted date is October 31, 1517, the day Luther nailed his Ninety-five Theses for debate to the door of the Castle Church in Wittenburg. Outside the scholarly circles of Lutheran seminaries, this date goes virtually unrivaled as the beginning date not only of Lutheranism but also of the entire Reformation. Lutheran scholars have pointed out, however, that other dates are worthy of consideration. Some cite Luther's discovery of the meaning of the righteousness of God during the winter of 1513–14. This was the so-called "tower experience," which supplied the theological insights inherent in the Ninety-five Theses.

The third and most valid year for the origin of Lutheranism is 1530. The years 1514 and 1517 cannot really qualify as dates of origin because no Lutheran church existed then. The year 1530 brought the publishing of the Augsburg Confession. What had been an almost chaotic movement had a symbolic document around which to rally. The congregations which wished to identify with Luther could be said to have become a public entity.

LUTHERANS IN AMERICA. After 1530, Lutheranism spread in Germany, Sweden, Denmark, Finland, and Norway. An independent church was established in each country. But when the Lutherans came to the U.S., they entered a vast country as compared to the smaller European states. Lutherans from any one European country were scattered throughout America, seeking good farm land especially in the Midwest and along the Southern seaboard. Everywhere they spread, each linguistic group established a synod, an autonomous Lutheran church. Each group was independent of the churches of other linguistic groups, and typically was independent of the churches in other American states. The rapid immigration in the nineteenth century led to the creation by 1850 of more than 150 separate independent Lutheran church bodies. Since that time, the major trend in the history of American Lutheranism has been the story of the merger of these 150 synods into the relatively few Lutheran churches today.

For no other family of American religions does national origin make such a difference. For example, the Roman Catholics, who came to the United States from all over Europe, remained one ecclesiastical entity when they arrived here. Roman Catholic immigrants from various national and linguistic groups did not create diverse denominational bodies. To give another example, most Methodists came to the U.S. from the British Isles and did not create churches divergent from the European Methodist churches (with two minor exceptions). For neither Catholics nor Methodists did national origin matter as much as for Lutherans.

Lutheranism did not enter North America by the establishment of the usual center on the Atlantic coast. It made its appearance, if briefly, in Manitoba, on Hudson's Bay. In 1619, the year before the Puritans landed in Massachusetts, Jens Munck, a Danish explorer, founded a colony at what is today known as Fort Churchill. Among the colonists was Rasmus Jensen (1579–1620), a Lutheran pastor. The colony prospered for several months until in the dead of winter scurvy began to kill its residents. Only three men remained to sail back to Denmark in the spring. It would be more than 100 years before a second group of Lutherans would arrive in what today is Canada, this time to a more hospitable climate in Nova Scotia.

During the 1740s Lutherans descended upon Nova Scotia from two directions. The first group arrived from Maine where a German colony had been created in 1740 by Samuel Waldo. They were part of an expedition to capture Louisburg from the French. After the battle, a few of the Germans remained and settled in the new English city of Halifax. There they were joined in 1749 by some Germans who came with the original 4,000 settlers and in 1750 by a group of about 300 German colonists. A church, St. George's, was organized and a building erected. The congregation, however, was continually beset by pastors who converted to Anglicanism. Eventually the church was lost, but not before a permanent Lutheran congregation was established at Lunenburg, a congregation still in place when the loyalist German subjects of King George who had been in America began to arrive in Canada after the American Revolution.

Lutheranism was first brought to the United States by Swedes who established a colony, Fort Christina, on the Delaware River in 1638. The Reverend Reorus Torkillus, the first Lutheran pastor in the New World, accompanied them. The Swedes were bolstered by the arrival of German Lutherans who began to settle in Pennsylvania in the last half of the century. By the middle of the eighteenth century, they were firmly entrenched in Pennsylvania and the surrounding territory. In March 1734 the Salzburgers created a third Lutheran center in Georgia.

In 1742 Henry Melchior Muhlenberg came to the colonies, and from his work and ministry, organized Lutheranism in America is dated. Installed as pastor of three congregations in Pennsylvania, he began to reach out to other parishes and to write Germany for continued help. In 1748 he led in the organization of the Ministerium of Pennsylvania, the first Lutheran synod in the colonies. He also opened his home to ministerial candidates. In 1792 a new constitution was adopted. Lay persons were first allowed to come to meetings of ministers in 1796, and the organizational tie to Germany was effected in that year.

The decades following the war were ones of expansion and the addition of new synods—New York (1786), North Carolina (1803), Ohio (1818), Maryland (1820), and Tennessee (1820). The General Synod (1820) was a cooperating body for the various state synods. Accompanying the growth was the emergence of tension over the issue of Americanization. Theologian Samuel S. Schmucker became a leading "liberal" who advocated the use of English in worship and a strong "pietistic" emphasis (a stress on piety and religious experience instead of on rigid doctrinal conformity). Schmucker was opposed by the newly arriving immigrants, who came in great numbers in the second quarter of the century; they were orthodox and conservative.

Emerging as the leader of the "conservatives" was Carl Ferdinand Wilhelm Walther, who had migrated from Saxony in 1839. He published *Der Lutheraner* to argue his position and was influential in setting the form of Lutheranism for such synods as Missouri (1846), Buffalo (1845), and Iowa (1854).

During the middle of the century, the Scandinavian Lutherans began to arrive in great numbers and to form their own synods. The first Norwegian Synod was formed in 1846. The Swedes in the General Synod joined with recent immigrants to form the Augustana Synod in 1860. Lars Paul Esbjorn led the Swedish schism. Other synods were formed by the Finns (1890) and Danes (1872), Icelanders (1885,). Finns (1890), and Slovaks (1902).

The great strength of Lutheranism shifted away from the East Coast in the nineteenth century and became dominant in the states north and west of Chicago. Centers were established along the Mississippi River at St. Louis, Rock Island, and Minneapolis.

The large influx of immigrants who took control away from the older, liberal eastern leaders like Schmucker delayed but could not avoid the problems created by Americanization. The use of English and adaptation to "American" mores increasingly plagued the church and reached its culmination during World War I. There is little doubt that English-speaking churches were able to fan the flames of prohibition by attacking their German brethren who supported German brewers such as Schlitz and Anheuser-Busch.

From the last quarter of the nineteenth century until the present time, the major thrust in the Lutheran family has been intrafamily ecumenism. Although Lutherans have entered ecumenical discussions with those of other faiths, these discussions have never reached the stage of definite plans for a merger. Within Lutheranism, however, there has been a century of merger by the multitude of independent synodical bodies established in the nineteenth century. Merger was usually preceded by the formation of cooperative councils. The more conservative Lutheran churches formed the Lutheran Synodical Conference in 1872. The conference included such synods as the Missouri Synod, the Synod of Evangelical Lutheran Churches, the Evangelical Lutheran Synod, and, until 1892, the three synods of Wisconsin, Michigan, and Minnesota. Only the Missouri Synod and the Synod of Evangelical Lutheran Churches remained in the Lutheran Synodical Conference. For all practical purposes, the conference fell apart, due to the Missouri Synod's negotiations through the 1960s with more liberal Lutheran bodies. The National Lutheran Council (1918–66) and the American Lutheran Conference became the arena for the largest number of mergers by various linguistic traditions as they became Americanized. Major mergers in the 1960s made these obsolete and they were replaced by the Lutheran Council in the U.S.A., in which the three larger churches participated: the Lutheran Church in America, the American Lutheran Church, and the Lutheran Church-Missouri Synod. In 1977 the Missouri Synod withdrew from the council.

The withdrawal of the Missouri Synod from the Lutheran Council in the U.S.A. occurred during an internal controversy which was to bring conservative forces to the forefront of the synod's life. It also led to the withdrawal of many of the synod's more liberal members, those generally associated with Concordia Theological Seminary. Those who left the synod in 1976 formed the Association of Evangelical Lutheran Churches. They almost immediately joined into ongoing merger talks with the two larger Lutheran bodies, the Lutheran Church in America and the American Lutheran Church. That three-way merger was completed in 1987 and the new church, the Evangelical Lutheran Church in America (1988) was officially inaugurated on January 1, 1988. The new church currently counts over half of all Lutherans in the United States in its membership, though more than 2.5 million remain in the Missouri Synod. In the years immediately prior to the merger, a number of conservative theological and renewal movements had appeared in the two larger Lutheran churches. At the time of the merger, several of these became the nucleus around which emerged schismatic churches which rejected the merger.

In 1997, the Evangelical Lutheran Church in America (1988) took a major step in reconciling itself to the churches which grew out of the Reformation, namely the major churches of the Reformed tradition in America. It voted to share Communion and extend pulpit fellowship to the Presbyterian Church (USA), the Reformed Church in America, and the United Church of Christ. All four churches have had a longstanding mutual relationship through the National Council of Churches. The ELCA is also moving to create a similar relationship with the Episcopal Church. In taking these actions, the ELCA has further strained its relationship with the Lutheran Church-Missouri Synod, with whom it does not share either Communion or pulpit fellowhip.

THE APOSTOLIC LUTHERANS. One group, the Finnish Apostolic Lutherans, has developed to a large extent outside of the main thrust of Lutheran history in America. The product of an intense pietistic movement originating in a geographically isolated part of northern Scandinavia, and centered in a relatively isolated part of the United States, the Apostolics have moved along a distinct pathway, though still very Lutheran in faith and life. Their small numbers have, due to their splintering, accounted for a relatively large number of Lutheran church bodies.

In the 1840s, in northern Sweden in the area generally called Lapland, a young pastor, Lars Levi Laestadius, led a revival in the state church, the Swedish Lutheran church. The movement was based on Laestadius' powerful preaching of repentance. The revival spread from Kaaresuvanto to all of northern Scandinavia. Characteristic of the revival were deep sorrow for sin, public confession of sin before the whole congregation, and the experience of deliverance. Among the leaders of the emerging revival was Juhani Raattamaa, a lay preacher. Raattamaa discovered the Power of the Keys, the practice of absolution by which a representative of the church laid hands on the penitent and pronounced forgiveness. The penitent was to believe these words as if Christ had pronounced them. The Laestadians believed that God sent times of visitation on all peoples and that there were Christians in all churches, but they laid emphasis on the need to follow the Bible to attain salvation.

Finns (Laplanders) and other Scandinavians from near the Arctic area began to migrate to America in the 1860s due to economic problems in Scandinavia. They settled in Minnesota and the Upper Peninsula of Michigan. Antti Vitikka began to preach among the Finns and in 1870 gathered a Laestadian group at Calumet, Michigan. The congregation called Solomon Korteniemi as their pastor and in 1872–73 organized the Solomon Korteniemi Lutheran Society. Korteniemi proved a poor leader and was succeeded by John Takkinen, sent from Sweden. Under his leadership in 1879 the name "Apostolic" Lutheran was chosen.

The Apostolic Lutherans grew and prospered in their American home but quickly became rent with controversy, which splintered them into five separate churches. Each faction goes under the name of Apostolic Lutheran and is distinguished by its nickname and its doctrine and practice. Only one group has organized formally as a church body.

The first schism in the Apostolic Lutheran movement occurred in the Calumet congregation in 1888. Members opposed to the "harsh rule" of Takkinen elected John Roanpaa and seized the church property. In 1890 Arthur Leopold Heideman arrived from Lapland to serve this new congregation.

In Europe in 1897, the Laestadians split into the Church of the First Born and the Old Laestadians. In America, the Takkinen congregation aligned with the Church of the First Born and the followers of Arthur Heideman aligned with the Old Laestadians.

Another schism occurred in Europe when a Pietist party, called the New Awakening, left its Pietist church in Finland. In 1910 the New Awakening sent Mikko Saarenpaa and Juho Pyorre to America.

These three prime groups, the Old Laestadians, the Church of the First Born, and the New Awakening, share the common Laestadian Lutheran doctrinal heritage as transmitted through Raattamaa. Raattamaa had taught that justification and conversion came by hearing the Gospel preached by the church of Christ. The New Awakening, however, believed that conversion could occur without hearing the Word. The New Awakening accused the Laestadians of moral laxity and emphasized a strict moral life. The New Awakening also departed from the other Laestadians on their belief in the "third use of the law," i.e., that the Ten Commandments were in force for Christians. For the Old Laestadians the only law was the law of Christ, the commandments of love. The Old Laestadians tended to believe that the church must be outwardly one. Hence they tended to be ultra-exclusivist.

A fourth schism occurred among the Old Laestadians when an emphasis on evangelism—redemption, forgiveness, and the righteousness of Christ—was opposed to an emphasis on Christian life and conduct and the repentance from sin. The evangelicals were inspired by the fervent preaching of Heideman and felt that the preaching of free grace would produce good fruit of itself.

The Apostolic Lutherans have always had a congregational government, in part a reaction to Scandinavian Lutheran episcopacy. Like other extreme congregationalists, they have resisted organization but can be distinguished by doctrinal position, periodicals, and foreign alignments.

Sources—The Lutheran Family

The study of American Lutheranism is focused through the Lutheran Historical Conference, 801 DeMun Ave., St. Louis, MO 63105, which publishes *Lutheran Historical Conference Essays and Reports.* Major archival depositories are at the headquarters of the Evangelical Lutheran Church in America, 8765 W. Higgins Rd., Chicago, IL 60631, and at Concordia Historical Institute, on the campus of Concordia Theological Seminary (a seminary of the Lutheran Church-Missouri Synod) in St. Louis. Other significant archives are located at the Evangelical Lutheran Church in America.

MARTIN LUTHER

Bainton, Roland. *Here I Stand.* New York: Abingdon-Cokesbury, 1950.

Booth, Edwin. *Martin Luther, Oak of Saxony.* Nashville: Abingdon-Press, 1966. 271 pp.

Lehman, Hartmut. *Martin Luther in the American Imagination.* Munich, German: W. Fink, 1988. 349 pp.

Luther, Martin. *Three Treatises.* Philadelphia: Fortress Press, 1960. Frequently reprinted.

———. *Works.* Edited by Jaroslav Pelikan and Helmut T. Lehman. 55 Vols. St. Louis: Concordia Publishing House and Philadelphia: Fortress Press, 1958–67.

Ritter, Gerhard. *Luther, His Life and Works.* New York: Harper & Row, 1963. 256 pp.

What Luther Says, An Anthology. St. Louis: Concordia Publishing House, 1959.

THE LUTHERAN CHURCH WORLDWIDE

Bergendoff, Conrad. *The Church of the Lutheran Reformation.* St. Louis: Concordia Publishing House, 1967. 339 pp.

Bodensieck, Julius, ed. *The Encyclopedia of the Lutheran Church.* Minneapolis: Augsburg Publishing House, 1965. 3 Vols.

Lucker, Edwin L., ed. *Lutheran Cyclopedia.* St. Louis: Concordia Publishing House, 1975. 845 pp.

Lutheran Churches of the World. Minneapolis: Augsburg Publishing House, 1972. 333 pp.

Nelson, E. Clifford. *The Rise of World Lutheranism.* Philadelphia: Fortress Press, 1982. 421 pp.

Vajta, Vilmos, ed. *The Lutheran Church, Past and Present.* Minneapolis: Augsburg Publishing House, 1977. 392 pp.

LUTHERANS IN NORTH AMERICA: HISTORICAL

Cronmiller, Carl R. *A History of the Lutheran Church in Canada.* Toronto: Evangelical Lutheran Synod of Canada, 1961. 288 pp.

Nelson, E. Clifford, ed. *The Lutherans in North America.* Philadelphia: Fortress Press, 1980. 564 pp.

Nichol, Todd W. *All These Lutherans.* Minneapolis: Augsburg Publishing House, 1986. 126 pp.

Thorkelson, Wilmar. *Lutherans in the U.S.A.* Minneapolis: Augsburg Publishing House, 1969.

Wallace, Paul A. W. *The Muhlenbergs of Pennsylvania.* Philadelphia: University of Pennsylvania, 1950. 358 pp.

Weideraenders, Robert C., and Walter G. Tillmanns. *The Synods of American Lutheranism.* N.p.: Lutheran Historical Conference, 1968. 209 pp.

Wentz, Abdel Ross. *A Basic History of Lutheranism in America.* Philadelphia: Muhlenburg Press, 1964. 439 pp.

Wolf, R. C. *Documents of Lutheran Unity in America.* Philadelphia: Fortress Press, 1966. 672 pp.

DOCTRINAL

Allbeck, Willard Dow. *Studies in the Lutheran Confessions.* Philadelphia: Fortress Press, 1968. 306 pp.

Arnold, Duane W. H. and C. George Fry. *The Way, the Truth, and the Life.* Grand Rapids, Mich: Baker Book House, 1982. 300 pp.

Gritsch, Eric W., and Robert W. Jenson. *Lutheranism.* Philadelphia: Fortress Press, 1976. 214 pp.

Hamsher, Paul O. *This I Believe, My Lutheran Handbook.* Lima, Ohio: The C.S.S. Publishing Co., n.d. 86 pp.

Mildenberger, Friedrich. *Theology of the Lutheran Confessions.* Philadelphia: Fortress press, 1986. 257 pp.

Schink, Edmund. *Theology of Lutheran Confessions.* Philadelphia: Muhlenberg Press, 1961.

Schramm, W. E. *What Lutherans Believe.* Columbus, Ohio: Wartburg Press, 1946. 156 pp.

LITURGY

Reed, Luther D. *The Lutheran Liturgy.* Philadelphia: Muhlenberg Press, 1947. 824 pp.

Stauffer, S. Anita, Gilbert A. Doan, and Michael B. Aune. *Lutherans at Worship.* Minneapolis: Augsburg Publishing House, 1978. 96 pp.

POLITY

Asheim, Ivar, and Victor R. Gold, eds. *Episcopacy in the Lutheran Church.* Philadelphia: Fortress Press, 1970. 261 pp.

Chapter 6
Reformed-Presbyterian Family

Consult the "Contents" pages to locate the entries in Part III,
the Directory Listings Sections, that comprise this family.

The Lutheran Reformation centered in Germany provided a climate in which further efforts to reform the Western Roman Church could proceed. In Switzerland that reforming activity led to the establishment of the Reformed Church based on the work of John Calvin (1509–1564), who established himself in Geneva, Switzerland, in the 1540s. Subsequently, his thought would come to dominate Holland, Scotland, and parts of Germany, and to be received by significant minorities in France and Hungary. The various churches that trace their origins to Calvin are set apart from other Christian churches by their theology (Reformed) and church government (Presbyterian).

Calvin's theological system was shaped by his belief in God's sovereignty in creation and salvation. The other major theological tenets of Calvinism—predestination and limited atonement—are built on this belief in God's sovereignty. Strictly interpreted, predestination means that the number and identity of "the elect" (those who are saved) were ordained by the sovereign God before the beginning of the world. Christ's atonement for sin was thus limited to the elect; salvation is not possible for all humanity, but only for those predestined to be saved. The issue of a strict or lenient interpretation of predestination has divided both European and American Calvinists.

Churches in the Reformed-Presbyterian tradition have a presbyterial form of church government. The presbytery is a legislative and/or judicial body composed of clergy and laity in equal numbers from the churches of a given region. The laity are elected by the members of the church. The word "presbytery" is also sometimes used to refer to the ruling body of the local church, but the name "Presbyterian" derives from the regional governing body.

Thus the name of this family has been designated "Reformed" for Calvin's theology (an attempt to reform the Roman Catholic church) and "Presbyterian" for the form of church government based on the presbytery. The name for this tradition also reflects history. On the continent, Calvinists established Reformed churches. In the British Isles, predominantly in Scotland, Calvinists established Presbyterian churches. In America, both the Reformed churches and the Presbyterian churches belong to the same Reformed-Presbyterian tradition, along with the Congregational churches. In this chapter, the word "Reformed" applies to Calvinist theology, worship, and churches using Calvinist theology. The word "Reformed" is not used to refer to the whole Reformation, a movement much broader than Calvinism, although Calvin played a major role in that movement.

Reformed theology involves many beliefs in addition to the distinguishing tenets mentioned above—beliefs in God's sovereignty, in predestination, and in limited atonement. Reformed churches join the Roman Catholics, Anglicans, the Eastern Orthodox, and the Lutherans in accepting the theological decisions reached during the conciliar era (fourth to eighth centuries). These are expressed in the creeds of the early centuries of Christianity: beliefs in the parental creator God, Christ and his atoning and salvic work, the Holy Spirit, the resurrection of the Body, and the Christian's life with God after the experience of death.

Beyond these beliefs come those shared by Reformed theology with Lutherans and other Protestant theologies: the belief in salvation by grace through faith, and the reliance on the Bible as the sole authority for faith and doctrine. With the followers of Martin Luther and Ulrich Zwingli, the leader of the Reformation in Zürich and German-speaking Switzerland, Calvinists were Protestants in that they both spoke forth their faith, and that they disagreed with various doctrines and practices of the Roman Catholic Church during the sixteenth century movement called the Reformation. The Protestant emphasis on salvation by grace through faith stands opposed to the Roman Catholic understanding of salvation which is worked out through a life of faith and good works. Further, when Protestants claim the Bible as their sole authority for faith and doctrine, they negate the Roman Catholic reliance on both the Bible and tradition. Reformed churchmen were generally hostile toward practices sanctioned by tradition unless the practices could be substantiated by Scripture.

Within Reformed theology, the definition of the church makes no reference to bishops or apostolic succession (the line of succession by ordination from the Apostles to modern times), two elements that are crucial to churches in the liturgical tradition. Instead, Reformed theology defines the church as the place where the "pure doctrine of the gospel is preached" and the "pure administration of the sacraments" is maintained. By the "pure doctrine of the gospel" is meant the gospel preached by ordained ministers according to Calvinist emphases (e.g., the authority of the Bible, the sovereignty of God, and predestination). By the "pure administration of the sacraments" is meant the administration only of baptism and the Lord's Supper as sacraments. This practice contrasts with Roman Catholicism's celebration of seven sacraments and some churches' rejection of all sacraments. (The Zwinglians and the Anabaptists serve as two examples of those rejecting all the sacraments. Zwinglians considered the eucharist a memorial meal, not a sacrament. The Anabaptists had no sacraments but did have ordinances, including foot washing and adult baptism.)

Though not without some differences, Lutherans and Roman Catholics accepted the doctrine of the real physical presence of Christ in the sacraments. The followers of Calvin supplanted this idea with the belief in the spiritual presence apprehended by faith. Calvins perspective changes in the sacrament as a special focus of Christ's presence in the world moves away from the sacramental world of the liturgical churches. The Reformed world is a secular world. God is present and can be apprehended by one of faith.

Worship in a Reformed church is centered on the preaching of the sermon, which ideally combines the exposition of Scripture with the ordered presentation of a great truth of the faith. While having been influenced by the emotive appeal of the Methodists in modern times, the Reformed sermon still serves primarily a teaching function. Prayers and hymns rehearse the basic tenets of the Reformed faith—confession, forgiveness, and the acknowledgement of the sovereignty of God. Hymns for many years were limited to the Psalms set to music, and the church produced many editions of Psalters. Most now use hymn books, though the Psalms remain important.

As spelled out in the Second Helvetic Confession (1566), the characteristics of Reformed worship are the Word of God properly preached to the people, decent meeting spaces purged of anything offensive to the church, and services conducted in order, modesty, discipline, and in the language of the people. Gone are the aesthetic/theological/sacramental appeals of worship. Gone are "offensive" elements such as statues, vestments, saints' festivals, indulgences, pilgrimages, and relics. Reformed worship is directed on a cognitive level—preaching, worship understandable to the layman, logical thoughts and ordered behavior, and a disciplined atmosphere.

The Reformed theological position was codified in confessions in the sixteenth and seventeenth centuries. The main Reformed confessions are the First Helvetic Confession (1536), the Belgic Confession (1561), the Second Helvetic Confession (1566), the Canons of the Synod of Dort (1619), and the Westminster Confession of Faith (1647). Also necessary to understanding the Reformed faith is the Heidelberg Catechism (1693). The above description of Reformed theology aligns with these confessions, all of which agree on a basic doctrinal position and in addition address whatever current crisis and/or local debate prompted the confessions. Along with other documents written by the Westminster Assembly of Divines in the 1640s, the Westminster Confession is the confession that has had the greatest impact on English-speaking church bodies in the Reformed-Presbyterian tradition. Most Baptists, which are Reformed in theology while rejecting the Presbyterian organization, have written or accepted confessions of faith derived from the Westminster documents.

Calvin developed the doctrine of two spheres of action, the secular and religious. Although his Reformed church in Geneva was a state church, he ended any interference of the state in church affairs such as the celebration of church festivals or the appointment of church officials. Calvin set up a theocracy, a form of government designed to have God as its head. The church defined the magistrates' authority as coming from God and the church had power over the magistrates in that magistrates were church members. Thus religion had considerable power over all social activities; for some years Calvin was the most powerful man in Geneva. The theocracy was patterned on church life described in Calvin's monumental theological treatise, *Institutes of the Christian Religion.*

The presbyterial system is a state church system and was designed for intimate communion with the secular authority. It was based on a parish system in which the country would be divided into geographic areas with one church to a parish. All people who had been baptized would be members. The church and state together, each in its proper area, would keep order. The most notable example of the interworking of church and state in Geneva concerned a heretic, Michael Servetus. Above the technical objections to his denial of orthodox Christian doctrines, Servetus had brought great offense to Roman Catholics and Protestants alike by his comparing the Trinity to the three-headed hound of hell. Calvin condemned Servetus as a heretic, and subsequently the secular authorities in Geneva tried and executed him.

Within the presbyterial system of the Reformed-Presbyterian tradition, clergy and lay people together rule the church. The preaching elders (ministers) are the pastors and teachers. The ruling elders (lay people) are to assist the teaching elders in discipline and in the governance and administration of the church. Deacons collect the offering and see to its distribution. In the local congregation, the ministers and elders together make up the consistory or session, occasionally called the presbytery. In some cases the deacons also belong to the consistory. All ministers and elders are called and elected by the other elders.

The ministers and elders form a series of judicial and legislative bodies. The local consistories (or sessions) are organized into what is variously termed a presbytery, classis or coetus. From this body of all the ministers in a given region, plus an equal number of elected elders, comes the name for the presbyterial form of government. The presbyters, those in the presbytery, have the power within the church. Several presbyteries (usually a minimum of three) may come together to form a synod (or classis) and synods may form an even larger body such as the General Assembly of the Presbyterian Church (U.S.A.). Each body has specific functions and usually a protest of a decision at one level can be appealed to a higher level. (In actual practice among some Presbyterian churches, a congregational form of government prevails and the presbytery functions as an advisory forum to facilitate cooperative endeavor.)

Both Luther and Calvin established state churches, as did Ulrich Zwingli. Zwingli died in 1531; his church in Zurich, Switzerland, was soon absorbed into Calvin's Reformed church. The Anabaptists (discussed in Chapter Eight) opposed all state churches, whether Lutheran, Calvinist, or Roman Catholic, and they were persecuted by the state churches. The Reformation brought its share of bloodshed.

Calvin's doctrine, more than the doctrine of any other religion, moved with the rising mercantile society and justified secular activity in the world. By contrast, Anabaptism was a world-denying view that sheltered the elect against a hostile, sinful, secular society. The Anabaptist tradition continues in the Mennonites, the Amish, the Quakers, and the Church of the Brethren. Lutheranism retained a more sacred character than Calvinism; Lutheranism spread by refurbishing Catholic forms. Calvinism, however, rose on the emerging middle class of Western Europe.

Calvin, who lived from 1509 to 1564, wrote the single most influential Protestant theological text, the *Institutes of the Christian Religion,* and was the first Protestant systematic theologian. He gained a reputation for intellectual brilliance while a student in Paris. After a 1533 sermon in which he pleaded for the reform of the Roman Catholic Church, he was forced to leave Paris. In Geneva, he introduced reforms, but in 1538 he was forced to leave Geneva because of the severity of the reforms. (Later his church would be characterized by stern morality, austerity, and insistence on attending church.) A noted preacher, Calvin went to Strassburg for several years and from there he maintained communication with those in Geneva. In 1541 the people of Geneva recalled him. From then on Geneva was the headquarters for Calvin and the Reformed Church.

There the future leaders of Calvin's reform found a haven from non-Calvinist magistrates of other areas. William Tyndale, Miles Cloverdale, and John Knox exported Calvin's ideas from Geneva to the British Isles. By 1600 representatives of the Reformed faith were making themselves heard throughout all of Central Europe.

THE SPREAD OF CALVINISM. As early as 1555 a Protestant congregation was organized in France by a disciple of Calvin. In 1559 the first synod of the French Reformed Church met. The next centuries for the French Reformed Church, or the Huguenots as they were popularly called, were years of persecution. In 1598 Henry IV issued the Edict of Nantes and began a brief period of toleration. But Louis XIV revoked the edict in 1685, and periods of persecution followed until the Constitution of 1795 granted religious freedom.

Reformed church advocates entered the Netherlands very soon after Calvin's reign in Geneva began. The religious wars which followed led to revolution by the Protestants and the formation of two countries, predominantly Reformed Holland and predominantly Catholic Belgium. This separation was completed in 1579 under the Protestant leader, William of Orange. In Holland in 1618 a major controversy which had troubled Calvinism for several decades reached a climax with the Synod of Dort. The synod was called to refute what was considered the theological heresies of Jacob Arminius (1560–1609), former professor of theology at the University of Leyden. In 1610, the year after Arminius' death, his followers summarized his theories in a five point remonstrance, which led to his followers becoming known as the Remonstrants.

Arminius' revision of Calvin's thought affirmed: (1) a general atonement, i.e., that Christ died for every person; (2) that God's foreknowledge of who would accept Christ's saving grace came before his predestination and election of them; (3) that God's grace could be resisted; (4) that humans were fallen and in need of God's grace, but were capable of responding to it; (5) that while with God's grace victory over sin was possible, it was also possible for individuals to fall away from grace. The Synod of Dort responded by affirming that: (1) Christ died only for those elected to salvation; (2) predestination and election to salvation constituted an act of God's sovereign will (rather than being the natural result of his foreknowledge); (3) God's grace given to an individual is irresistible; (4) humans were so depraved that they could do nothing for their own salvation; (5) God's elect will persevere to the end.

The canons of the Synod of Dort became the official doctrine of the Dutch church and of many Reformed church bodies. Armenian ideas found their way to England and became the hallmark of John Wesley and the Methodists. Among those in attendance at Dort were several of the British Separatists then residing in Holland who later to come to America as the Pilgrims. In contrast, Armenian ideas found their way to England and became the theological starting point for John Wesley and the Methodists of the eighteenth century.

No other centers of Reformed faith on the continent grew as did Switzerland, France, and Holland. However, the faith did seep into the surrounding countries, and synods were formed in what is today the Czech Republic and Hungary. Also, in northern Italy the Reformed faith began to dominate the Waldensians, a group which had separated from the Roman Catholic Church in the previous century. Because of its affinity with Lutheranism, the Reformed church moved north into Germany and, while never challenging Lutherans for control, became a large minority religion. It is from this body that the 1693 Heidelberg Catechism emerged; its teaching was to have a profound influence on the interpretation of Calvin in Reformed history.

The leading center of Reformed faith in the British Isles was Scotland. John Knox, a devout follower of Calvin, returned to Scotland in 1559 after a year and a half on a French galley and 12 years' exile in Europe. He found the country ripe for Protestantism. He quickly became the leader of the cause which in another year saw the Scottish parliament abolish Catholicism and begin to set up Presbyterianism, the name given the Reformed Church in Scotland. Despite recurrent battles with then Episcopal England, Presbyterianism was firmly settled in Scotland and became the seedbed from which the Reformed movement could spread to Ireland and England.

In 1603 James I of England invited the Scots to settle the rebels' land in Ulster (Northern Ireland) which had been forfeited to the crown. So many came to Ireland that soon Ulster was dominantly Protestant and, in spite of James' Catholic preferences, he reasoned that Presbyterians were better than people with no religion at all. Irish Catholics were not so quick to give in to the Protestant intruders and religious wars ensued. By 1642 things had quieted to a point that the first presbytery in Ireland could be formed, but a stable accord has never been reached between Irish Catholics and Presbyterians.

PURITANISM. In England, Reformed-Presbyterian thinking was labeled Puritanism. This name came as a result of the different Reformed thinkers' uniting around the issue of "further purifying the church," as the latter stages of the Reformation brought Elizabeth I to the throne in 1558 with her *via media* solution to religious strife. (For a discussion of Elizabeth's blending of both Roman Catholic and Protestant elements, see the section in Chapter Three on the Anglican tradition.) The two major groups within Puritanism were the Independents and the Presbyterians. Most Puritans were Reformed in their thinking, but beyond that they varied from those who merely wished to simplify church vestments and worship, to the Independents who wished to set up a congregationally-organized church, one in which the highest authority lay within the local church instead of in a regional or national governing body. The years 1558 to 1649 were years of struggle, persecutions, war, and on-again, off-again toleration among proponents of the various churches in England. In 1649 Puritan Oliver Cromwell succeeded in his revolt against the monarchy and established the Puritan Commonwealth. Although Cromwell was an Independent, the Presbyterians were dominant in Parliament, so when Cromwell's reign began, Presbyterianism became the dominant church in England. Up to that time the Presbyterians and Independents had sustained a united front against the Episcopalian state church of the monarchy. However, once Puritanism gained the position of state church, the factions within Puritanism— Presbyterians and Independents—no longer needed to be united against Episcopalianism and their differences with each other intensified. The Congregationalists, a group within the Independents, began to press for a state church based on a congregational system instead of on a presbyterial system. The Congregationalists wanted to remain attached to the Church of England in the sense that the Congregationalists would preach the doctrines of the Church of England but they would choose their own ministers, own their own property, and would not come under the authority of the bishops of the Church of England. The Congregationalists were opposed by another party within the Independents, the Separatists. This latter party wished to become separate from any episcopal entanglements.

In 1660 Presbyterianism lost its state church position because the monarchy was restored to power, and the Anglican Church returned as the state church. Presbyterians became another small English sect among other sects. The Restoration therefore meant the end of Presbyterian ecclesiastical power, but Reformed theology remained equally dominant in most of England's Puritan bodies—Presbyterians, Congregationalists, and Separatists.

Years before Cromwell came to power, Parliament paved the way for the establishment of Presbyterianism by abolishing the system of bishops in 1642–43. Parliament also convoked the Westminster Assembly of Divines to reorder the Church of England. This assembly, meeting for a number of years, produced the three most important works in Reformed history (apart from Calvin's *Institutes* from which they derived): *The Larger and Shorter Catechisms, the Westminster Confession of Faith,* and the *Directory of Public Worship.* Even though only four Scots were in the Westminster Assembly, the Church of Scotland quickly adopted the Westminster documents. These documents remain to this day the basic works in doctrine and standards for most Presbyterian churches around the world.

With time, the Separatists, a group within the Independents, divided into Brownists and Baptists. Robert Browne was among the first to move toward the idea of a "sect" church of pure Christians as opposed to a universal or state church of all baptized citizens. The Baptists were even more radical than the Brownists. The Baptists were anti-liturgical, not having any sacraments. For them baptism is an ordinance and is reserved for adults instead of being available also to children.

The various groups mentioned above existed as parties within the Puritan movement in England from the late 1500s until the 1689 Act of Toleration, which allowed them freedom to develop fully as distinct sects. The Brownists, however, gradually faded from existence as a separate group.

IN NORTH AMERICA. Among the very first European Christians in the New World were members of the Reformed church. As early as 1564, Huguenots (French Protestants), fleeing persecution, settled along the St. John's River near present-day Jacksonville, Florida. The colony was destroyed the next year by the Spanish who had already claimed the territory. During the last half of the century, others began to flee to the towns of New France along the St. Lawrence River. They continued to arrive until forbidden to migrate by Cardinal Richelieu in 1628. Huguenots did not prosper, but a few did survive in Canada until the fall of Quebec in 1749. They were soon absorbed into other Protestant churches.

With the establishment of Halifax in 1749, German and Dutch members of the Reformed church, as well as Congregationalists and Presbyterians (primarily from Scotland), became residents of the new city. At first they shared the same building. As years passed they spread through Nova Scotia founding churches. Growth of the Reformed faith was greatly augmented by the arrival of the Loyalists, many from New England, after the American Revolution. The first synods were formed in 1795 and 1796 by two factions of the Scottish Presbyterians.

Dissension, already high among the Scots, increased with the arrival of the New Englanders, among whom was Henry Alline, a fervent disciple of Newlightism, the revival-oriented separatist Congregationalism which had been inaugurated by the First Great Awakening (1740s), prior to the American Revolution. Alline drew away many Congregationalists into independent congregations which eventually became the birthing place of the Baptists of the province.

The story of the Reformed-Presbyterian tradition in colonial America is the story of the establishment of American branches of the various European Reformed churches. As early as 1611 the Reverend Alexander Whitaker arrived in Virginia with his Presbyterian views. The Pilgrims and Puritans arrived in the 1620s to establish American Congregationalism. Dutch Calvinists were in New York as early as 1623. French Huguenots, who settled along the coast in a number of different communities, quickly Americanized and joined the Presbyterian Church. The backbone of American Presbyterianism was the vast migration of the Scottish-Irish Ulsterites. Between 1705 and 1775 more than 500,000 Ulsterites reached America and settled in its middle section, particularly the Carolinas. Germans began to arrive in the late 1600s and settled in Pennsylvania where the Calvinists among them organized the German Reformed Church.

Francis Makemie, recognized as the father of American Presbyterianism, landed in the colonies in 1683 to begin organizing the scattered Presbyterians. About 1705 (the date is not clear), he organized the first presbytery (of Philadelphia). Makemie died in 1708 as the great Scottish-Irish immigration was beginning. In 1717 the Synod of Philadelphia was organized with 19 ministers, 40 churches, and 3,000 members.

The Reformed traditions have displayed several interesting patterns of growth in America. The churches of the Reformed tradition (with the possible exception of Presbyterianism) are regional churches. Largely continental in their background, they are concentrated in those areas in the Northeast and Midwest where large-scale German migration occurred. The Congregationalists were located largely in the Northeast but gained strength in the Midwest through mergers in 1931 and 1958.

Significant in the spread of the Reformed churches were the anti-evangelical, anti-revivalistic policies of church leaders in the eighteenth and nineteenth centuries. The Reformed churches gained new members largely through groups of laymen who migrated West, formed congregations, and called a pastor.

Education has been a major contribution of the Reformed tradition to Protestantism. The churches always insisted on a college-trained clergy, and they created numerous colleges for that purpose. They have based their program on a theologically sound-teaching ministry. A large number of the outstanding theologians in American history were out of this tradition—Cotton Mather, Jonathan Edwards, John Williamson Nevin, Horace Bushnell, Benjamin Warfield, and Reinhold and H. Richard Niebuhr.

The Plan of Union of 1801 was an agreement between Presbyterians and Congregationalists concerning their frontier congregations. (The "frontier" of the early 1800s was the area west of the Allegheny Mountains.) The Plan of Union stipulated that in those

areas where small groups of Presbyterians and Congregationalists resided, the two groups would unite and be served by a minister from either church. Because more Presbyterian ministers went to the frontier than Congregationalist ministers, most of those united churches became Presbyterian.

Splintered into a number of separate denominational bodies in the nineteenth century, Presbyterians made significant strides in bringing members together into one organization during the twentieth century. The most important step in the merging process was accomplished in 1983 when the two largest Presbyterian bodies, split since before the Civil War, merged to form the Presbyterian Church (U.S.A.). The story of this church and its antecedents constitutes the majority of Presbyterian history in the United States.

CONGREGATIONALISM—A VARIATION OF THE REFORMED TRADITION. Congregationalism, a form of Puritanism that lies between Presbyterianism and Separatism, is somewhat unique in that it developed in America within the Massachusetts Bay Colony and was then taken back to England. In contrast to the Presbyterians, who looked for the development of a state church modeled on the theocracy which Calvin established in Geneva and headed by a synod of elders (presbyters), the Congregationalists looked for a state church that was congregationally oriented. While agreeing with the Separatists on the issue of the local church, Congregationalists disagreed with them in that they wished to keep their supportive ties to the state. In colonial America, Separatism was first represented by the Pilgrims at Plymouth, Massachusetts. All three groups were Reformed in their theology and acknowledged the Westminster documents, but differed fundamentally on their desires for church organization and its relation to the state. Eventually, Congregationalism would absorb the Separatists of Plymouth (those not lost to Unitarianism), but a new separatist movement would emerge in the 1700s and survive as Baptists.

Congregational organization had four distinctive features. First, the church was built on the covenant of people together. A church was not formed until the people constituted it. Second, the church was tied to a place. It was the covenanted people in a specific location. Ideally, the whole countryside would be divided into parishes, geographic areas each with one congregation. The importance of place is reflected in the fact that the Mayflower Compact (a civil version of the church covenant) was not drawn up until the Pilgrims reached the New World. Third, the church was to be an established church. In New England it had intimate ties with the government, and ministers drew their salaries from the civil authority. Finally, the church was to be the sacred institute for the society. The clergy spoke directly to issues of public morals, expected to be consulted on matters of importance to public life, and often represented the colony as political figures.

The early Congregationalists have often been confused with those Independents who desired a church totally cut off from state affiliation, control, and finance. While it is true that Congregationalism later became independent of state authority, it is well to keep in mind the movement's original aim to be a state church.

Meeting at Cambridge, Massachusetts, in 1648, representatives of the four Puritan colonies issued what came to be called *The Cambridge Platform*. It became the basic document of Congregational policy in New England. As stated in the Platform, "The Government of the Church is a mixed Government . . . in respect of Christ the Head and King of the Church, and the sovereign power residing in Him, it is a Monarchy; in respect of the Body of Brotherhood of the Church, and Power from Christ granted unto them, it resembles a Democracy; in respect of the Presbytery, and Power committed unto them, it is an Aristocracy." The basic unit was the visible congregation united into one body by a covenant. The care of the church was left to elders (pastors, teachers, and ruling elders) and deacons, all elected by the congregation.

Churches, though equal, were to maintain communion with one another by means of synods. Synods, though not of the essence of the church, were deemed necessary to the times, to establish truth and peace. Composed of elders and other messengers, synods were to "debate and determine controversies of Faith and Cases of Conscience; to clear from the Word holy directions for the Holy Worship of God, and good Government of the Church; to hear witness against maladministration and corruption of manners in any particular church; and to give Directions for the Reformation thereof." Churches were enjoined not to remove themselves from the communion of the other churches. In its developed form, Congregationalism was very close to Presbyterianism rather than to the independent congregational policy which later became typical of the Baptists. Developed Congregationalism was also far removed from the free church structure of the Plymouth Brethren.

A key element in Congregationalism was the power granted by the church to the secular magistrate. The magistery was encouraged to restrain and punish idolatry, blasphemy, heresy, schism, and like actions. When the power of the magistery was removed from Congregationalism by the American Revolution, the churches adopted an independent congregationalism, but always with a tendency to presbyterial forms.

Some have asserted that Congregationalism was a noncreedal church. However, when asked to prepare a creed, the same body that drew up the Cambridge Platform adopted the Westminster Confession of Faith, which placed Congregationalism doctrinally within British Calvinism (Puritanism).

The first branch of the Reformed tradition in America was Congregationalism, the church of the Massachusetts Puritans. They landed in 1620 and 1630 and established their theocracy. Their church operated as a state church until disestablished after the American Revolution. It adopted the Westminster Confession shortly after promulgation by the English believers. It was the church of the New England patriots, Harvard and Yale universities, and of famous ministers, including Jonathan Edwards, Timothy Dwight, Cotton Mather, Thomas Hooker, and Charles Chauncy. It also became the seedbed upon which Unitarianism, Universalism, and Christian Science were to grow. Only in the twentieth century, as it became a major force in Reformed family ecumenism, did it produce schismatic churches.

Sources—Reformed-Presbyterian Family

Historical work on the reformed Church tradition is given focus through the Commission on History of the Reformed Church in America, c/o New Brunswick Theological Seminary, New Brunswick, NJ 08901. The Christian Reformed Church archives are at Calvin College, Grand rapids, MI 49056.

Presbyterian history is coordinated by the Presbyterian Historical Association and Department of History of the Presbyterian Church (USA), 425 Leonard St., Philadelphia, PA 28757. A second center, which served the former southern Presbyterian Church in the U.S., is to be found at the Historical Foundation, Montreat, NC 28757.

Congregational history is parceled out among the surviving structures of the churches that merged to form the United Church of Christ. Both the Evangelical and Reformed Historical Society and the Archives of the United Church of Christ are at the Lancaster Theological Seminary, Lancaster, PA 17603. The archives of the former Evangelical and Reformed Church are at Eden Theological Seminary in St. Louis, Missouri. The Congregational Christian Historical Society and the Congregational Library are at 14 Beacon Street, Boston, MA 02108.

The central archives of the United Church of Canada is at Victoria University in Toronto.

HISTORY, EUROPEAN

Grimm, Harold J. *The Reformation Era*. New York: Macmillan, 1954. 675 pp.

Leith, John H. *An Introduction to the Reformed Tradition*. Atlanta: John Knox Press, 1977. 253 pp.

Loetscher, Lefferts A. *A Brief History of the Presbyterians*. 4th ed. Philadelphia: Westminister Press, 1983.

McGrath, Alister E. *Life of John Calvin: A Study in the Shaping of Western Culture*. Oxford: Basil Blackwell, 1990.

McNeill, John T. *The History and Character of Calvinism*. New York: Oxford University Press, 1954. 466 pp.

Reaman, G. Elmore. *The Trail of the Huguenots*. London: Frederick Muller, 1964. 318 pp.

Reed, R. C. *History of the Presbyterian Churches of the World*. Philadelphia: Westminister Press, 1912. 408 pp.

Thompson, Ernest Trice, and Elton M. Eenigenburg. *Through the Ages*. Richmond, Va: The CLC Press, 1965. 480 pp.

HISTORY, NORTH AMERICAN

Armstrong, Maurice, Lefferts A. Loetscher, and Charles A. Anderson. *The Presbyterian Enterprise*. Philadelphia: The Westminster Press, 1956. 336 pp.

Bratt, James D. *Dutch Calvinism in Modern America*. Grand Rapids, MI. William B. Eerdmans Publishing Co., 1984. 329 pp.

Jamison, Wallace N. *The United Presbyterian Story*. Pittsburgh: The Geneva Press, 1958. 253 pp.

Lingle, Walter L. *Presbyterians, Their History and Beliefs*. Richmond, VA: John Knox Press, 1944. 127 pp.

Slosser, Gaius Jackson, ed. *They Seek a Country*. New York: Macmillan, 1955. 330 pp.

Trinterud, Leonard J. *The Forming of an American Tradition*. Philadelphia: Westminister Press, 1949. 352 pp.

Watts, George B. *The Waldenses in the New World*. Durham, NC: Duke University Press, 1941. 309 pp.

THEOLOGY

Beardslee, John W., III, ed. *Reformed Dogmatics*. New York: Oxford University Press, 1965. 471 pp.

Bratt, John H., ed. *The Heritage of John Calvin*. Grand Rapids, MI: William B. Eerdmans Publishing Company, 1973. 222 pp.

Calvin, John. *The Institutes of the Christian Religion*. 2 Vols. Philadelphia: Westminster Press, 1960.

Cochrane, Arthur C., ed. *The Reformed Confessions of the Sixteenth Century*. Philadelphia: Westminster Press, 1966. 336 pp.

Geer, Felix B. *Basic Beliefs of the Reformed Faith*. Richmond, VA: John Knox Press, 1960. 80 pp.

Gettys, Joseph M. *What Presbyterians Believe*. Clinton, SC: The Author, 1953. 128 pp.

Osterhaven, M. Eugene. *The Spirit of the Reformed Tradition*. Grand Rapids, MI: William B. Eerdmans Publishing Company, 1971. 190 pp.

Schaff, Philip. *Creed Revision in the Presbyterian Churches*. New York: Charles Scribner's Sons, 1890. 67 pp.

LIFE AND WORSHIP

Mackay, John A. *The Presbyterian Way of Life*. Englewood Cliffs, NJ: Prentice-Hall, 1960. 238 pp.

Melton, Julius. *Presbyterian Worship in America*. Richmond, VA: John Knox Press, 1967. 173 pp.

Nichols, James Hastings. *Corporate Worship in the Reformed Tradition*. Philadelphia: Westminster Press, 1968. 190 pp.

CONGREGATIONALISM

Hiemert, Alan, and Andrew Delbanco, eds. *The Puritans in America*. Cambridge: Harvard University Press, 1985. 438 pp.

Jenkins, Daniel. *Congregationalism: A Restatement*. London: Faber and Faber, 1954. 152 pp.

Starkey, Marion L. *The Congregational Way*. Garden City, NY: Doubleday, 1966. 342 pp.

Walker, Williston. *The Creed and Platforms of Congregationalism*. Philadelphia: Pilgrim Press, 1960. 604 pp.

Wells, Donald F. *Reformed Theology in America*. Grand Rapids, MI: William F. Eerdmans Publishing Co., 1985.

Youngs, J. William T. *The Congregationalists*. New York: Greenwood Press, 1990. 376 pp.

Chapter 7
Pietist-Methodist Family

Consult the "Contents" pages to locate the entries in Part III,
the Directory Listings Sections, that comprise this family.

By the end of the seventeenth century, the Anglican, Lutheran, and Reformed churches of Europe were seen by many as having become rigid, lifeless, and rather impersonal. Some of their members yearned for a more intimate, personal, lively and spontaneous expression of their religious feelings. This desire led to the movement called Pietism and in turn gave rise to three new groups of churches—the Moravian churches, the Swedish Evangelical churches, and the Methodist (Wesleyan) churches—all of which will be treated in this chapter. Piety, a term that refers directly to the following of religious "duties," came to mean the adoption of spiritual disciplines that promote the individual's personal religious life.

From its beginning, Pietism, by its very existence, challenged the Anglican, Lutheran, and Calvinist churches. While the movement was seen by supporters as an alternative to scholastic theology and a dry worship experience, many church leaders viewed any such informal alternative as primarily challenging the church's hegemony over religious matters in society, and they tended to treat the Pietists with hostility and in some cases initiated actual persecutions. To accomplish their goals, the Pietists emphasized (1) a Bible-centered faith, (2) the experienced Christian life (guilt, forgiveness, conversion, holiness, and love within community), and (3) free expression of faith in hymns, testimony, and evangelical zeal. The earliest representatives of the movement include Philipp Jacob Spener (1635–1705) and August Hermann Francke (1663–1727).

Spener is credited with originating a basic form taken by Pietists—the *collegia pietatis* (association of piety). In despair over the impossibility of reforming Lutheranism, he began to organize small groups which met in homes for Bible study, prayer, and discussions, leading to a deeper spiritual life. These groups spread throughout Europe and were known in England as religious societies.

Francke was Spener's most famous disciple. Forced out of the University of Leipzig and later dismissed from the University of Erfurt, he became a teacher at the newly formed University of Halle and turned it into a Pietist center. During the three decades Francke taught there, Halle graduated more than 200 ministers a year. Besides the deeply experienced faith taught at Halle, Francke encouraged missionary endeavors. He began an orphan house in 1698. Knowledge of his work brought financial help and allowed the work to include a pauper school, a Bible institute, a Latin school, and other facilities to aid destitute children. Most early missionaries came from among Halle's graduates.

From Halle, Pietism spread throughout the world. Correspondence between Francke and Cotton Mather led to the establishment of religious societies in the Boston churches, and Pietistic literature lay directly behind the American revival movement of the 1730s and 1740s called the Great Awakening. In Germany, Pietism renewed the Moravian Church, which then began to spread its own version of Pietism. The Moravian Church carried the Pietist faith to England where Pietism became a strong influence on John Wesley, the founder of the Methodist movement. Moravians working in Sweden helped establish the Swedish Evangelical Church. Thus three groups of churches emerged from the Pietist movement: the Moravian churches, the Swedish Evangelical churches, and the Methodist churches.

However, most of Pietism's influence was absorbed by the Lutheran Church and the Calvinist groups (the Reformed Church, the Presbyterian Church, and the Congregational Church). Although Pietism did lead to schism in some of the American churches, most of the schismatic churches eventually reunited with their parent bodies.

A note of contrast: the Pietist churches are very different from the European Free churches. The latter, discussed in Chapter Eight, include the Mennonites, the Amish, the Quakers, and the Brethren. The Pietists were distinct from the European Free churches because the Pietists were open to traditional Christian practices and beliefs, and lacked hostility to their parent bodies. Instead of rejecting the forms of the past, as the European Free churches did, the Pietists worked with the forms of the past and sought the life of the spirit within them. In general, the free churches of the past and the present have opposed infant baptism, opposed traditional ideas of church and sacrament, and opposed many liturgical practices. In contrast, Pietists have accepted Reformation ideas of church and sacrament, have baptized infants, and have used simplified versions of liturgical forms. Whereas the European free churches sprang up as a protest to state churches (whether those were Roman Catholic, Anglican, Lutheran, or Calvinist), Pietist groups began as societies within Protestant state churches and only later removed themselves from their parent churches and became independent entities.

THE MORAVIANS. The Moravian churches of today exist only because the Pietist movement gave life to an almost extinguished Moravian Church. Thus the Moravians are distinct among Pietists: the Moravians represent not so much a new church created by Pietism as a renewed church recreated by Pietism. That recreation occurred in 1727. The story of the Moravian churches, however, starts in the ninth century with the founding of the early Moravian Church.

Cyril and Methodius, missionaries of the Greek Orthodox Church, arrived in the ninth century in Moravia, an area in what is now the Czech Republic. There they established a Greek-based Slavic church. At first the Moravians were encouraged by the Roman Catholic Church, but in later centuries Rome forced a Latin rite upon them. The Moravians considered this a repressive move. They became discontented with Catholicism, and their discontent was heightened by a young priest named John Hus (1369–1415). From his pulpit in Prague, he began to throw challenges in the face of the Roman Church. He questioned the practice of selling indulgences, which were promises of the remission of punishment due for sins. Hus also questioned the denial of the cup to the laity in holy communion, and the moral corruption of the papacy. Hus's career coincided with the time when three men were claiming to be the pope, each having a segment of Europe behind him. In 1414, when the Council of Constance was called primarily to heal an internal schism within the Roman church, church authorities also invited Hus, with a safe conduct promise, to state his case. Instead, after hearing and rejecting him, the church had him arrested and burned at the stake. The Hussite Wars followed and eventually Hus's followers, concluding that Hus's ideas would never positively affect the Roman church, formed their own church—the Unitas Fratrum or "Unity of the Brethren."

During its early years, the church existed as a Reformed Roman church, turning to Bishop Stephen of the Italian Waldensian Church for apostolic ordination. It published the Bible in the Czech vernacular—the Kralitz Bible, which affected the Czech-speaking people as strongly as Luther's Bible affected Germany. A second round of religious wars in the late sixteenth and early seventeenth centuries all but destroyed the once prosperous Unitas Fratrum. On June 21, 1621, 15 Brethren leaders were beheaded in Prague. The persecutions brought an end to all visible manifestation of the Unitas Fratrum and re-established Roman hegemony in Bohemia and Moravia.

In 1722 a few families from the former Unitas Fratrum made their way from Moravia to Saxony, a region in East Germany. Soon more than 300 exiles had settled in Saxony at Herrnhut, the estate of Count Zinzendorf. The exiles conferred and drew up a "Brotherly Agreement." Their bickering, though, led the fatherly Zinzendorf to invite as many as would come to a communion service at his manor church on August 13, 1727. This date is considered to be the birth of the Renewed Unitas Fratrum (or Moravian Church) as there occurred an amazing "outpouring of the power of God," which Moravians compared to Pentecost. The wranglings and strife were over. Zinzendorf received a copy of the "discipline" of the old Unitas Fratrum and began to set the church in order. Ordination in the apostolic succession was secured from Daniel Ernest Jablonsky. Jablonsky, a court preacher in Berlin, was one of the ordained bishops in the line of the old Unitas Fratrum. He ordained David Nitschman as the first bishop of the restored church.

The arrival of the Moravians on the estate of Zinzendorf largely determined the Moravian future. Zinzendorf was a Pietist and he led the Moravians into placing great stress upon religious experience and the relation of the individual with God. Numerous forms were developed to foster this deep faith. Among them was the love feast, an informal service centering on holy communion but also including a light meal, singing, and a talk by the officiating minister. The litany, a lengthy prayer form for corporate and private devotions, was added to the Herrnhut services in 1731. Its present form is a modified Lutheran litany. The idea of small groups of dedicated Christians meeting together regularly for worship and exhortation and service was taken from the German Pietists and used extensively, especially in the mission field. Moravian meetings were the model of early Methodist societies developed by John Wesley.

The *Daily Texts* was a book that grew from a need of the early Herrnhut settlers, the need for a "watchword" from the Scripture for daily use. They at first copied scriptural passages by hand on bits of paper to be drawn from a container each day. This practice evolved into an annual volume of texts. For each day there was a text from both the Old and New Testaments and a hymn stanza to amplify the text. This book has had an influence far beyond the membership of the church, as it circulates widely to nonmembers.

The most characteristic aspect of Moravian piety was its mission program. Zinzendorf, early in his life, became convinced that he was destined to do something about the neglected peoples of the world. In 1731 he traveled to Copenhagen, where he met Anthony Ulrich, an African slave from the Danish West Indies. Ulrich told Zinzendorf of his people's plight. Back at Herrnhut, Zinzendorf related Ulrich's story, preparing the way for the slave to arrive and tell it himself. The response was immediate, and David Nitschmann and Leonhard Dober were chosen as the first mis-

sionaries to the oldest Moravian mission—St. Thomas. The Moravians then proceeded to initiate missions all over Europe. Zinzendorf, a Lutheran himself, gave strict orders for the Moravians not to encroach upon state church prerogatives. They arrived in their mission territories as merely preachers of the Word and were thus welcomed in many Protestant lands. In England they moved into an established Anglican church structure and set up "religious societies" for Bible study and prayer, never encouraging anyone to leave the state church. John Wesley was a member of one of these societies for a while.

In 1872 re-entrance into Czechoslovakia was permitted with the Edict of Toleration, and the first congregation in Bohemia was established in 1872. Other mission work included British Guiana, Surinam, Southern Africa, Java, Nicaragua, Jordan, Alaska, and Labrador, all established before 1900. In 1735 the Moravians came to the American colonies.

Moravians in America. The settling of Moravians in America in 1735 had a two-fold purpose: the securing of a settlement in the New World in case Germany again became intolerant, and a mission to the Indians. The first group of settlers in the New World was led by Bishop August Gottlieb Spangenberg. He traveled to Georgia on the same ship that brought John Wesley, the founder of Methodism, to the colony of George Oglethorpe. Wesley was impressed with Spangenberg and the Moravians and records a number of conversations with Spangenberg. Soon after settling in Savannah, the Moravians opened an Indian school. The Moravians were, however, caught in the war between the British (Georgia) and the Spanish (Florida). Their refusal to bear arms led to their being looked down upon by their neighbors. By 1740 the Moravians left Georgia for Pennsylvania. They established the town of Nazareth and the following year Bishop Nitschmann arrived and began to settle Bethlehem. In December of 1741, Zinzendorf arrived, and on Christmas day he organized the Moravian Congregation in Bethlehem, the first in America.

Under Spangenberg's leadership a semi-communal arrangement was worked out in Bethlehem which soon made it a self-sufficient settlement, able to bear its own mission program to the Indians. Churches were soon organized at Nazareth and Lilitz in Pennsylvania, and Hope, New Jersey.

In 1749 the British Parliament acknowledged the Moravian Church as "an Ancient Protestant Episcopal Church," thus in effect giving an invitation to settle in other British colonies. The Moravians took advantage of Parliament's recognition of their church and settled in North Carolina on property owned by Lord Granville. Rising persecution in Germany encouraged other Moravians to come to America.

Spangenberg and five others went to North Carolina in 1752 and had surveyors lay out what is now Forsyth County. The first settlers, 15 in all, arrived in 1753 and settled in Bethabara. In 1766 the permanent settlement of Salem was laid out. From this beginning other churches and settlements developed.

Moravian settlements in Canada originated as an extension of their continued missions to convert the Indians. After an unsuccessful attempt in 1752 to establish a mission to the Indians along the Labrador coast, Moravian missionaries were able to find work in 1771 in Nain. By the early nineteenth century four stations were activated along the rugged terrain across the Labrador Basin from New Herrnhut, the Moravian settlement in Greenland. A second thrust into Canada occurred in 1792 when, in an effort to escape a possible Indian war, missionaries moved into Canada along the Thames River and established Fairfield, Ontario. Though destroyed in the war of 1812, the center was rebuilt and became a stop along the underground railroad for slaves fleeing to Canada. A third field in Canada opened in 1894 when some German families who had moved to Alberta from Russia contacted the church headquarters in Pennsylvania and asked for affiliation. By encouraging the development of this colony and adding members who moved into the area from the eastern United States, the church grew and now has its own Canadian District to serve the congregations of Western Canada.

METHODISM. Among Methodist historians there is a wide disagreement about when Methodism began; however, organizational continuity in the Wesleyan movement dates to late 1739 when the first society was formed by John Wesley and 18 other persons "desiring to flee from the wrath to come. . .and be saved from their sins." The number of societies grew and in 1744 the first Methodist conference was held as Wesley called his lay ministers together to confer with him. After discussions, Wesley made all the decisions and then assigned the preachers to their tasks.

Methodism's founder, John Wesley (1703-91), the son of an Anglican clergyman, attended Oxford to study for the ministry. While at Oxford he formed a religious society called the Holy Club by other students. To this group was first applied the derisive title "Methodists" partly because of their strict daily schedules.

Wesley left Oxford and became a missionary to the Indians in Georgia. This adventure ended in failure. However, while on the voyage to America he encountered the Moravians and was very impressed with their simple piety and their leader Bishop August Gottlieb Spangenberg. In Georgia, he also encountered the writings of Scottish Pietist Thomas Halyburton, whose personal religious experience closely paralleled his own. Arriving back in London, Wesley affiliated with the Moravians and in particular with Peter Bohler, who would soon be on his way to America as a missionary to the slaves. Activity with Bohler led Wesley to his own crisis experience which occurred at the religious society at Aldersgate on May 24, 1738. Wesley described what happened in his *Journal*:

"In the evening, I went very unwillingly to a Society in Aldersgate Street, where one was reading Luther's Preface to the Epistle to the Romans. About a quarter before nine, while he was describing the change which God works in the heart through faith in Christ, I felt my heart strangely warmed. I felt I did trust in Christ; Christ alone, for salvation; and an assurance was given me, that he had taken away my sins, even mine, and saved me from the law of sin and death."

This experience became the turning point in Wesley's life. During the next year he visited Germany and lived among the Moravians but then broke with the Moravians over several points of practice, and began the United Societies. Innovations by Wesley included field preaching, the use of lay preachers (Wesley's assistants), and the discipline of the societies.

The United Societies were originally groups of dedicated Christians within the Church of England. As with continental Pietism, doctrine was not at issue as much as the application of doctrine to life. Some doctrinal innovations did occur concerning the Christian life—Wesley's emphasis on the witness of the Spirit and Christian perfection. These doctrines often led to excesses and accusations of "enthusiasm," the eighteenth century euphemism for "fanaticism."

Those who experienced this evangelical awakening were organized into societies, the basic document of which was the General Rules. Those in the society were expected to evidence their desire for salvation:

First: by doing no harm, avoiding evil of every kind, especially that which is most generally practiced.

Second: by doing good of every possible sort, and as far as possible to all men.

Third: by attending upon the ordinances of God.

Wesley wrote that following the third rule involved the public worship of God, the ministry of the Word (either read or expounded), the Supper of the Lord, family and private prayer, searching the Scriptures, and fasting and abstinence.

The society was to be thought of as a gathering of people, not as a place. Wherever the society met was where it held its regular worship services and most importantly the quarterly meeting. Once each quarter Wesley visited each society. He inquired into the lives of the members relative to the General Rules and issued quarterly tickets. The tickets admitted members to the society for the next three months. Wesley served communion and usually a love feast was held, an informal service centering on holy communion but also including a light meal, singing, and a talk.

Wesley lived almost the entire century and the issue of doctrinal standards for Methodism came to the fore late in his life. Early doctrinal concerns had been set in the *Minutes of the Conference* but additional doctrinal questions were raised in 1777 by the predestinarian Calvinists and in the 1780s by the establishment of the Methodist Episcopal Church in America. The Calvinist controversy set Methodism firmly against predestinarian doctrines. Wesley opposed the Calvinist idea of irresistible grace: if grace comes, you cannot refuse it; if it does not come, you cannot obtain it. Wesley said grace is freely given to each person and each person can freely respond to the gospel. The formation of American Methodism caused Wesley to set doctrinal standards in his letter to the preachers in America: "Let all of you be determined to abide by the Methodist doctrine and discipline published in the four volumes of *Sermons* and the *Notes on the New Testament*, together with the *Large Minutes of the Conference*."

To Wesley's *Sermons*, the *Notes on the New Testament*, and the *Large Minutes of the Conference*, the Twenty-five Articles of Religion were added as a fourth source for determining the Methodist perspective on doctrine. The articles were derived from the Thirty-nine Articles of Religion of the Church of England, of which they are an abridgment. Wesley specifically excluded the Anglican articles on hell, creeds, predestination, bishops, excommunication, and the authority of the church, and he shortened others.

The remaining articles cover the major affirmation of traditional Christianity—the Trinity, Christ (including His virgin birth and physical resurrection), the sufficiency of the Bible, sin, and the salvation of humanity. The church is viewed as the place where the Word of God is preached and the sacraments duly administered. There are two sacraments—baptism (usually by sprinkling) and the Lord's Supper.

A number of the items specifically refute Roman Catholic doctrines concerning the existence of voluntary works above and beyond the commandments of God, purgatory, other sacraments, mass as a sacrificial ceremony, celibate priests, and the uniformity of worship services. Methodists receive both elements (bread and wine) in the Lord's Supper rather than just the bread.

Methodists are set apart from the free church position of the Mennonites by their acknowledgment of the legitimacy of taking oaths in legal situations.

The Articles of Religion grounded Methodism in the traditional Christian doctrines as established during the conciliar ear of united Christianity (fourth to eighth century) and the creeds promulgated by those councils, especially the Nicene and Chacedonian creeds are used in Methodist worship. The *Sermons*, *Notes*, and *Minutes* stated Methodist opinion on current issues.

The Articles of Religion are also derivative of continental Reformed confessions and place Methodism in a Reformed theological tradition. The Reformed tradition, based on the work of John Calvin, shows up most clearly in articles v, ix, xii, xiii, xvi, and in the anti-Roman Catholic articles x, xi, xiv, xv, xix, xx, and xxii. Methodists have always identified with Reformed theologian Jacob Arminius, whom they interpreted as rejecting the Calvinist emphasis on predestination. Wesley named the first Methodist periodical *The Arminian Magazine*. The Twenty-five Articles of Religion are a common core of doctrinal agreement for all Methodists and are included in doctrinal statements by almost all Methodist bodies.

In England, Methodism remained as a society within the Anglican church and as such, was spread throughout the British Commonwealth by the missionary vision and activity of the Reverend Thomas Coke. The British Wesleyans became independent of the Anglican church in 1795.

Wesleyanism in America. Methodist history in the colonies began in the 1760s with the migration of Methodist laypeople and preachers. The first society on record was in Leesburg, Virginia, in 1766, and the second in New York City. Methodism spread in the middle colonies and developed early centers in Baltimore, Philadelphia, and Wilmington.

The first crisis for American Methodists was the Revolutionary War. Because of their attachment to the Church of England and Wesley's antirevolutionary traits, their loyalty was suspect. After the war, because of the independence of the colonies from England, Wesley decided to allow the American Methodists to set up an independent church. In September 1784, he ordained Thomas Coke as a superintendent and sent him to America with instructions to set up the church and to ordain Francis Asbury. This organization was accomplished at the Christmas Conference held at Lovely Lane Chapel in Baltimore, Maryland.

Francis Asbury (1745–1816) was second only to Wesley in molding American Methodism. He came to America in 1771 and during his first 13 years of service emerged as the unquestioned leader of the American brethren. He was ordained bishop in December 1784 (the American preachers preferred the term bishop to superintendent) and formed the Methodist Episcopal Church. At the time neither the Roman Catholics nor the Anglicans had a bishop present in the former American colonies. His appointments of ministers to their congregations covered the United States, Nova Scotia, and Antigua.

As the Methodists grew in number, their organization became more sophisticated, but several features important for understanding Methodists and their schisms have remained constant. These features are the conference and itineracy. The basic structure of Methodism is the conference, a name derived from Wesley's practice of having regular meetings with his preachers to confer with them before deciding on issues. The local church charge conference, district conference, annual conference, and general conference form a hierarchy of authority. The local church charge conference is the annual business meeting of the local congregation. There the congregation elects officers and sets the budget. The district conference is primarily a funnel; it lets local congregations know the messages of bishops and annual conferences. The annual conference is a regional conference chaired by the bishop, whose duty it is to assign ministers to their churches (charges) each year, and to publish those assignments at the annual conference. The annual conference is the most important structure for developing the program mandated by the general conference. The general conference is made up of representatives of all the annual conferences in the country. The general conference meets quadrennially, is the church's highest legislative and policy-making body, and writes the *Discipline*, the book of church order and organization.

The phrase "annual conference" has a meaning in addition to that described above. For a minister to belong to an annual conference means that he or she has contractual relationships with the church in that area. The minister gives up membership in any local church and is a "member" of the annual conference. S/he also agrees to be available for assignment, and the church guarantees that he or she will receive an assignment, termed an "appointment" to a congregation (or other ministry task) and also receive a salary. The phrase "annual conference" thus connotes an association of ministers, a fellowship, a sense of belonging.

Itineracy is the second important structural feature of Methodism. Ministers itinerate; that is, they travel to various congregations within their own region (usually part of a state) as they are assigned by the bishop and annual conference of that region. The assignments were traditionally for one year, but the length of the minister's stay has steadily expanded. In addition to itinerant ministers, Methodists have both ordained and unordained local preachers who do not travel but belong to only one congregation. They are licensed by the church and they preach, assist the minister, and occasionally act as interim pastors.

During the nineteenth century the itinerant, the circuit rider of folklore, would often be assigned to a charge with 20 or 30 preaching points on it. The circuit rider would travel his entire circuit every two, three, or four weeks. The effect of this type of organization was to cover the land, but it also put the ministers in many places on weekdays—not on Sundays. This became an issue in the nineteenth century as Methodism grew and stable congregations emerged which wanted to meet on Sundays instead of on weekdays.

GERMAN METHODISTS. During the first generation, Methodism in America spread among German-speaking people in the middle Colonies, and independent German congregations and leaders emerged. Attempts to merge the English-speaking and German-speaking Methodist and Pietist groups in the early 1800s failed. A major factor in the failure was Bishop Asbury's belief that there should be no perpetuation of German work since English would quickly be the only language in America. Asbury was essentially correct, but he failed to foresee the large German migrations through the 1800s. Eventually the Methodist Episcopal Church had to organize its own German-speaking mission to cope with the demand for ministry.

Two separate Wesleyan churches developed among America's German-speaking population: the United Brethren in Christ, and the Evangelical Association. These two churches merged with each other and then with the United Methodist Church. Prior to these mergers, various schismatic churches formed from the two German-speaking churches.

One of the most interesting schismatic churches is now defunct: the Republican United Brethren Church. It was formed by members of the White River Conference of the United Brethren in Christ during the Mexican War. The church's origin can be traced to an informal meeting of ministers and members of the White River Conference at Dowell Meeting House, Franklin Circuit, Indiana, on March 12, 1848. At the meeting, a resolution was passed protesting conference action concerning the Reverend P. C. Parker. (Parker had been expelled from the ministry for "immorality" because of his participation in the war.) This resolution was refused publication; therefore, an appeal was made to the general conference. The 1853 general conference, however, sustained Parker's expulsion and passed a strong anti-war resolution. The convention also acted in support of a belief in "the doctrine of the natural, hereditary, and total depravity of man." That doctrine refers to the sinfulness of man after the fall, by which sinfulness the will is in bondage and is unable to turn to God. The protest of the three actions of the general conference became the formal basis for withdrawal. At a meeting at Union Chapel, Decatur County, Indiana, on September 8–12, 1853, the new church was organized. The church was small (the first conference listed only two charges) and existed for only a short time. In the 1860s, the church became part of the Christian Union.

AFRICAN AMERICAN METHODISM. Of the religiously affiliated African Americans, the second largest number belong to Methodist churches. (The largest number belong to Baptist churches.) African Americans were a part of Methodism almost from the beginning; first mentioned by John Wesley, the founder of Methodism, in his *Journal* were servants of Nathaniel Gilbert, the pioneer of Methodism in the West Indies. In America they were members of the earliest societies, a few being named in the records. At least two, Richard Allen and Harry Hoosier, were present at the Christmas Conference in Baltimore in 1784, when the American Methodist Church was established as a separate church from English Methodism. Harry Hoosier traveled often with Bishop Francis Asbury, the first Methodist bishop, and Richard Allen emerged as the leader of the Philadelphia black Methodist group. By 1800 a large free black constituency was present in Baltimore, New York, Wilmington, North Carolina, and Philadelphia, quite apart from the large membership among the slaves.

Forms in keeping with the master-slave relationship were adopted as more and more African Americans became church members. These included segregated services, church galleries, and later separate congregations. Dislike of practices derogatory of African Americans became apparent first among the free black members in the Northern urban centers and led to the formation of several independent denominations. After the Civil War, criticism of the past led to most former slaves leaving the Methodist Episcopal Church, South, the dominant Methodist group in the southern United States, and the great majority of former slaves affiliating with one of the independent African Methodist churches. A lesser number formed independent African conferences within the northern Methodist Episcopal Church. Today African Methodism is primarily carried by the African Methodist Episcopal Church, the African Methodist Episcopal Zion Church, and the Christian Methodist Episcopal Church.

NON-EPISCOPAL METHODISM. No concern—except for the race issue—has led to the number of schisms within Methodism as has the periodic protest against the episcopal polity of the Methodist Episcopal Church and its successor bodies. The first group to depart over polity questions and to subsequently form a non-episcopal church was the Republican Methodists led by James O'Kelley. His small church eventually became a part of the Christian Church (a constituent part of the present-day United Church of Christ). More significant, however, was the Methodist Protestant schism in the 1920s. This created the first major alternative to the Methodist Episcopal Church and finally merged with the two large episcopal branches in 1939. The merger of the Methodist Protestant Church left many of its pastors and members dissatisfied and led to no less than six schisms. Members refused to move from the relatively small denomination into the 10 million-member Methodist Church (1939–1968), now the United Methodist Church. They also rejected the episcopal system and, in the South, feared the possibility of racial integration, which finally occurred in United Methodism in the 1960s. Such churches as the Methodist Protestant Church (1939–), headquartered in Mississippi, and the Bible Protestant Church (now known as the Fellowship of Fundamental Bible Churches) centered in New Jersey, originated from the merger of the Methodist Protestant Church in 1939.

Besides the schisms growing out of the Methodist Protestant Church, there have been other protests that included rejection of episcopal authority and led to the formation of new church bodies. Most notable was the Congregational Methodist movement in Georgia in the 1880s. More recently the Southern Methodists and the Evangelical Methodists have followed that pattern. One could also see the holiness movement (generally regarded as the only doctrinal schism in Methodism) as a polity schism caused by the inability of the bishops and district superintendents to control the numerous holiness associations that had emerged to focus holiness doctrinal concerns. In fact, most holiness churches adopted a nonepiscopal form of government.

METHODISM IN BRITISH AMERICA: Methodism developed in Canada and the West Indies quite apart from its development in the United States. The first Methodist work in Canada began in 1765 under the direction of Lawrence Coughlan, an Irishman. However Coughlan was ordained as an Anglican priest in 1867 and took his work into the Church of England in Canada with him. A more permanent Methodist presence occurred in 1772 when a group of settlers from Yorkshire in Southwest Great Britain found their way to Nova Scotia. Among them were some Methodists, and among the Methodists was William Black (1760–1834). Converted in 1779, he began almost immediately to preach in the scattered settlements, especially spurred by the anti-Methodist remarks of Newlight (later Baptist) preacher, Henry Alline. He sought assistance from England and Methodist founder John Wesley placed him in contact with the Methodists in the American colonies.

As the arrival of numerous Loyalists in Nova Scotia swelled Black's responsibilities, in 1783 he finally journeyed to the United States to seek help from the Methodist Episcopal Church. The work developed quickly, and as it grew he was appointed presiding elder for the Nova Scotia District. The relationship with the American church continued until 1800 when it was shifted to the British Wesleyan Conference, by which time it had spread through the Maritime Provinces.

As the work was spreading through the Maritimes, a second thrust into Canada developed when William Losee (1757–1832) was sent by Bishop Francis Asbury to check upon the Methodists among the Loyalists (people who moved to Canada during and after the American Revolution) who had settled in the neighborhood of Kingston, Ontario. The new mission was initially placed under the care of the New York Conference, but the need for separating it from American control became evident, especially following the War of 1812. Unfortunately, a misunderstanding occurred in early negotiations with the British Wesleyans that prevented their being allowed to assume responsibility for the Ontario congregations as they had in Nova Scotia. Thus in 1824 the Canadian work was set apart as the independent Methodist Episcopal Church in Canada.

Still a third beginning for Methodism in Canada followed the formation of a Wesleyan Methodist mission in Western Canada in 1840 when James Evans (1801–1846) was appointed as a missionary in Rupert's Land (Manitoba). From his settlement at Norway House, north of present-day Winnipeg, he began a mission to the Indians, which led to his development of a new script for use with the Indian languages. His accomplishments opened the west to a vital Methodist presence.

During the nineteenth century, a variety of forms of Methodism, representatives of the different British splinter groups, entered Canada. Prior to 1884, the Canadian Methodists went through a process of merger that brought almost all of them into a single body, the Methodist Church, Canada. That body merged into the United Church of Canada in 1925 and now continues as a constituent part of that church.

Methodism in the West Indies started with the return of Nathaniel Greene to his plantation on Antigua in 1760. During his just completed trip to England, he had encountered John Wesley, founder of Methodism, and been converted. He organized a class of more than 200, mostly African slaves who lived on the plantation, and it is from this class that Methodism spread throughout the islands. Work in the islands was given a significant boost by the visits of Thomas Coke, Wesley's assistant, beginning in the winter of 1786-87, and picked up by the Wesleyan Methodist Missionary Society (in England) after Coke's death in 1814. The work became independent as the autonomous Methodist Church in the Caribbean and the Americas in 1967.

At the beginning of the twentieth century, West Indian Methodists migrated to the United States. Rather than affiliate with any of the Methodist churches they found, all of which had an episcopal polity, they organized to carry on the work much as they had been used to in the island. Thus the United Wesleyan Methodist Church of America came into existence. In more recent years, the United Methodist Church has developed a close working relationship with the West Indian Methodist Conference and has accepted some oversight of the United Wesleyans in the United States.

UNITED METHODISM. The Methodist tradition in America is presently carried largely by the United Methodist Church. Founded in 1968, it is the successor to the Methodist Episcopal Church, the larger major bodies that broke from it in the nineteenth century, and the several independent German Methodist organizations. At the beginning of the twentieth century, Methodism was initially embodied in eight denominational organizations. In 1939, three of these, the Methodist Episcopal Church, the Methodist Episcopal Church, South, and the Methodist Protestant Church merged to form the Methodist Church. Then in 1946 the United Brethren in Christ and the Evangelical Association, the two primary German Methodist associations merged to form the Evangelical United Brethren. The Methodist Church and the Evangelical United Brethren merged in 1968 to form the United Methodist

Church. The United Methodist Church is the third largest church in America (behind the Roman Catholic Church and the Southern Baptist Convention) and is the home to the majority of people who called themselves Methodists. The largest group of Methodists outside of United Methodism are in the three African churches.

Sources—Pietist-Methodist Family

Historical studies of the Moravian Church in America are focused at the archives of the two American provinces: Northern Province, 214 E. Center St., Nazareth, PA 18064; and Drawer M., Salem Station, Winston-Salem, NC 27108. *The Moravian Historian* (semi-annual) comes from the Pennsylvania center.

Methodist studies are focused at the Historical Society of the United Methodist Church, the World Methodist Historical Society, and the General Commission on Archives and History of the United Methodist Church, all of which are located on the campus of Drew University, Box 127, Madison, NJ 07940. The Commission publishes the quarterly journal *Methodist History*.

PIETISM

Gerdes, Egon W. "Pietism Classical and Modern." *Concordia Theological Journal*, April 1968, pp. 257–68.

Stoeffler, F. Ernest. *German Pietism During the Eighteenth Century.* Leiden: E. J. Brill, 1973. 282 pp.

SCANDINAVIAN PIETISTS

Covenant Memories, 1885–1935. Chicago: Covenant Book Concern, 1935. 495 pp.

Norton, H. Wilbert, et al. *The Diamond Jubilee Story of the Evangelical Free Church of America.* Minneapolis: Free Church Publications, 1959. 335 pp.

Olsson, Karl A. *By One Spirit.* Chicago: Covenant Press, 1962. 811 pp.

———. *A Family of Faith.* Chicago: Covenant Press, 1975. 157 pp.

———. *Into One Body—by the Cross.* 2 Vols. Chicago: Covenant Press, 1985–86.

MORAVIANS

Hamilton, J. Taylor, and Kenneth G. Hamilton. *History of the Moravian Church.* Bethlehem, PA: Interprovincial Board of Christian Education, Moravian Church in America, 1983. 723 pp.

Schattschneider, Allen W. *Through Five Hundred Years.* Bethlehem, PA: Comenius Press, 1956. 148 pp. Rev. ed.: 1982. 146 pp.

Weinlick, John Rudolf. *Count Zinzendorf.* New York: Abingdon Press, 1956. 240 pp.

THE WESLEYAN TRADITION

Bishop, John. *Methodist Worship.* London: Epworth Press, 1950. 165 pp.

Bucke, Emory Stevens, ed. *The History of American Methodism.* 3 vols. New York: Abingdon, 1965.

Davies, Rupert, and Gordon Rupp, eds. *A History of the Methodist Church in Great Britain.* 3 vols. London: Epworth Press, 1965–83.

Green, Vivian H. H. *John Wesley.* London: Nelson, 1964. 168 pp.

Nagler, Arthur Wilford. *Pietism and Methodist.* Nashville: Publishing House of the M. E. Church, South, 1918. 200 pp.

Rack, Harry D. *Reasonable Enthusiast: John Wesley and the Rise of Methodism.* London: Epworth Press, 1989. 656 pp.

Schmidt, Martin. *John Wesley, A Theological Biography.* 2 vols. New York: Abingdon, 1963–73.

UNITED METHODISM

Albright, Raymond W. *A History of the Evangelical Church.* Harrisburg, PA: The Evangelical Press, 1956. 501 pp.

Andersen, Arlow W. *The Salt of the Earth.* Nashville: Norwegian-Danish Methodist Historical Society, 1962. 338 pp.

Davis, Lyman E. *Democratic Methodism in America.* New York: Fleming H. Revell, 1921. 267 pp.

Douglas, Paul F. *The Story of German Methodism.* New York: The Methodist Book Concern, 1939. 361 pp.

Eller, Paul Himmel. *These Evangelical United Brethren.* Dayton, OH: The Otterbein Press, 1950. 128 pp.

Godbold, Albea, ed. *Forever Beginning, 1766–1966.* Lake Junaluska, NC: Association of Methodist Historical Societies, 1967. 254 pp.

Graham, J. H. *Black United Methodists.* New York: Vantage Press, 1979. 162 pp.

Harmon, Nolan B. *Encyclopedia of World Methodism.* N.p., n.d.

———. *Understanding the United Methodist Church.* Nashville: Abingdon, 1977. 176 pp.

Norwood, Frederick A. *Sourcebook of American Methodism.* Nashville: Abingdon, 1982. 683 pp.

———. *The Story of American Methodism.* Nashville: Abingdon, 1974. 448 pp.

Stokes, Mack B. *Major United Methodist Beliefs.* Nashville: Abingdon, 1971. 128 pp.

Tuell, Jack M. *The Organization of the United Methodist Church.* Nashville: Abingdon, 1977. 174 pp.

Wallenius, C. G., and E. D. Olson. *A Short Story of the Swedish Methodism in America.* Chicago, 1931. 55 pp.

Washburn, Paul. *An Unfinished Church: A Brief History of the Evangelical United Brethren and the Methodist Church.* Nashville: Abingdon Press, 1984.

Wunderlich, Friedrich. *Methodist Linking Two Continents.* Nashville: The Methodist Publishing House, 1960. 143 pp.

OTHER METHODISTS

Richardson, Harry V. *Dark Salvation.* Garden City, NY: Doubleday, 1976. 324 pp.

Chapter 8

Holiness Family

Consult the "Contents" pages to locate the entries in Part III,
the Directory Listings Sections, that comprise this family.

The desire to follow in a somewhat literal sense Christ's admonition, "Be ye perfect as my father in heaven is perfect" (Matt. 5:48), has resulted in Holiness churches. These churches take the drive for perfection or Holiness as their primary focus and are distinguished from most other Christian churches by the unique doctrinal framework within which Holiness or sanctification is understood. The corollary to this drive has been separation from Christians who do not in their opinion reach high enough toward the goal of perfection. Thus Holiness churches are also distinct from other churches because of this focus on perfection and the resultant separatist practices.

John Wesley, the founder of Methodism, gave impetus to the formation of Holiness churches. Though the Wesleyan movement of the eighteenth century was only in part a perfectionist movement, Wesley did encourage the ethical life and a goal of perfection, and numerous churches now strive for what they call Wesleyan Holiness.

Wesley's understanding of perfection developed through two phases: first, an emphasis on sinlessness, and second, on love. While at Oxford as a college student, Wesley formed the holy club, a group of students in search of the holy life. In his early sermon "Christian Perfection," Wesley defined perfection as Holiness, saying Christians are perfect in that they are free from outward sin. Wesley felt mature Christians are free from evil tempers and thoughts, and such perfection is possible in this life.

Wesley was immediately challenged for his doctrine of perfection. In answer to his accusers he had to emphasize that perfection did not apply to mistakes, infirmity, knowledge, or freedom from temptation. Also, he said there was no perfection that did not admit of further progress. Wesley himself began to see the harmful consequences of defining perfection as absence of sin, and he redefined perfectionism in terms of love. His ideas on perfection are gathered together in his *Plain Account of Christian Perfection.* The line between the Pietist-Methodist family and the Holiness family is difficult to draw. There have always been individual Methodists who stressed Holiness and sanctification. Further, many Holiness churches are schismatic bodies that broke away from various Methodist churches, and some Holiness churches use the word Methodist in their titles. However, Holiness churches place greater stress than Methodist churches on the second blessing and on a lifestyle reflecting sanctification.

THE UNDERSTANDING OF HOLINESS. The distinctive elements of the Holiness way of being Christian are their teachings concerning sanctification and perfection, and the lifestyle they believe should naturally flow from such teachings. The sanctification experience, also called the second blessing or second work of grace in the life of the believer, culminates a process of becoming holy that begins when the believer accepts Jesus Christ as his/her personal Savior. The first step in the process, justification, the first work of grace, is also called the born again experience. That event is followed by a period of growth in grace, in becoming actually holy in one's life. Both justification and the growing process are

seen as involving the activity of the Holy Spirit within the individual. The process should culminate in the second work of grace, in which the Holy Spirit cleanses the heart from sin and imparts his indwelling presence, giving power for living the Christian life. A consensus opinion on sanctification is found in the statement of the Wesleyan Church.

Inward sanctification begins the moment one is justified. From that moment until a believer is entirely sanctified, he grows daily in grace and gradually dies to sin. Entire sanctification is effected by the baptism of the Holy Spirit, which cleanses the heart of the child of God from all inbred sin through faith in Jesus Christ. It is subsequent to regeneration and is wrought instantaneously when the believer presents himself a living sacrifice, holy and acceptable to God, and is thus enabled through His grace to love God with all the heart and to walk in all His holy commandments blameless. The crisis of cleansing is preceded and followed by growth in grace and the knowledge of our Lord and Savior, Jesus Christ. When man is fully cleansed from all sin, he is endued with the power of the Holy Spirit for the accomplishment of all to which he is called. The ensuing life of Holiness is maintained by a continuing faith in the sanctifying blood of Christ, and is evidenced by an obedient life.

In John Wesley's thought, the process of sanctification was to be seen as the goal toward which the Christian's life led. The arrival at the state of sanctification in which one was freed from sin and made perfect in life generally occurred only at the end of one's days on earth. However, in the mid-nineteenth century, deriving in large part from the ministry of evangelist Phoebe Palmer, coeditor of *The Path of Holiness,* a prominent Methodist and Holiness magazine, a subtle but important divergence with Wesley crept into Holiness thought. In her writing and speaking, Palmer began to picture sanctification as more the beginning of the Christian life rather than the goal. As Charles Edward White has cogently pointed out in his study *The Beauty of Holiness,* Palmer advocated sanctification as the immediate possibility of any believer, and she encouraged all, no matter how new in the faith, to seek it as the instantaneous gift of the Holy Spirit. This subtle change of emphasis led both to a renewed concentration upon the search for Holiness among Methodists, but also created a reaction from many Methodists who saw in Wesley's understanding of the gradual process of the development of the life of Holiness a reason to reject the renewed emphasis upon sanctification.

In the last half of the nineteenth century, personal Holiness, symbolized by a rigid code of behavior, became the distinguishing theme in the Holiness movement. John Wesley, who wrote the *General Rules* for the Methodists, is the source of this trend. He disapproved of flashy clothes, costly apparel, and expensive jewelry, and in the early nineteenth century Holiness schisms from Methodism, a consistent voice was one deploring the departure of the Methodists from the *General Rules.* The strictest personal codes came in the late nineteenth century. They were in part a reaction to the social gospel emphasis in the larger denominations.

There is also strong evidence that such codes were and are tied to the frustrations of people left behind by urbanization, mechanization, and population growth. Without status in mass society, people reject it and find virtue in the necessity of their condition. Holiness was and is to be found in asceticism and rejection of worldliness.

The rejection of worldliness has led to typical Holiness disagreements over exactly what constitutes worldliness. Churches have split over the acceptance of television or a style of clothing, such as neckties. Other issues include the attitude toward divorced people, cosmetics, swimming with the opposite sex, dress in high school gym classes, and the cutting of females' hair (I Cor. 11: 1–16).

At one time the Holiness movement concentrated much of its attention on social issues and public morality. The Wesleyan and Free Methodists both were abolitionist and at different times the Holiness movement was tied to the great crusades for temperance and women's rights. Beginning with the co-mingling of Wesleyan and Quaker ideas during the era of John Gurney, pacifism has had a strong hold on the Holiness movement and is the major remnant of the social imperative. Many Pentecostal churches have inherited this pacifist emphasis.

Among the Holiness groups, sacraments have not been an important part of church life. Some churches have two sacraments—baptism and the Lord's Supper—as the Wesleyan Church does. Some consider baptism and the Lord's Supper to be ordinances, not sacraments. Churches such as the General Eldership of the Churches of God add footwashing as a third ordinance. Finally, other churches, most notably the Salvation Army, have neither ordinances nor sacraments.

HOLINESS MOVEMENT IN AMERICA. The strain of perfectionism in Wesleyan teaching was not the most emphasized doctrine in early nineteenth century Methodism. On the heels of the great American revival of 1837–38, however, centers of interest in the Wesleyan doctrine of perfection or Holiness, as it was termed, emerged. One phase of this interest came in 1839 with the sanctification experienced by Charles G. Finney. Sanctification, in this context, means Holiness; it means becoming perfect in love. Finney, a Congregationalist and the most famous evangelist of his day, had learned of sanctification from the Methodists and from his own reading of Wesley's *Plain Account of Christian Perfection.* At the same time, Finney became involved in a search for social Holiness, making society perfect in love, understanding justice to be the social form of love. Finney defended women's rights, participated in the antislavery crusade, and as a pacifist protested the Mexican War (1846–48). After experiencing sanctification in 1839, Finney began to write on it and preach it. In 1844 his colleague at Oberlin College, Asa Mahan, published his book *Scripture Doctrine of Christian Perfection,* which became the major statement of the Oberlin position. Because of his non-Methodist background, Finney had a great effect on other soon-to-be Holiness greats—T. C. Upham, William Boardman, and A. B. Earle. Thus, the first wave of Holiness in the United States began outside of Methodism, by Methodized Presbyterians, Baptists, and Congregationalists. Prior to 1855 the only Methodist who had gained any reputation for perfectionist thinking was Timothy Merritt, editor of the *Guide to Christian Perfection* (later called the *Guide to Holiness*), but Finney had raised the issue for the whole Methodist Episcopal Church, and Methodists could no longer ignore their heritage.

Without any weakening or demise of the Oberlin Holiness crusade, the Holiness movement began a new phase after the revival of 1857–58. The new center of interest was the "Tuesday Meeting for the Promotion of Holiness" led by Phoebe Palmer from her base as a member of Allen Street Methodist Church in New York City. Palmer's efforts were aided by the publication of two books, *Christian Purity* by Randolph S. Foster and *The Central Idea of Christianity* by Jesse T. Peck. Both men were soon to be Methodist

bishops. The revival that was spreading from Allen Street to the whole of Methodism was interrupted by the Civil War, but picked up momentum as soon as the hostilities ceased. During the war, the Palmers, Phoebe and her husband, Walter, bought Merritt's *Guide to Holiness* and in 1866 they toured the country, establishing centers of the sanctified wherever they preached.

It was not long until ministers rallied to the cause. The camp meeting proved to be the prime structure to carry on the work and in 1867 William Osborn of the South New Jersey Conference of Methodists and John S. Inskip of New York set up a national camp meeting at Vineland, New Jersey. During this camp meeting the "National Camp Meeting Association for the Promotion of Holiness" was formed, and Inskip became its first president. Bishop Matthew Simpson personally aided the work, which prospered under episcopal approval.

The Holiness movement grew tremendously among Methodists in the first decade after the Civil War. In 1872 Jesse T. Peck, Randolph S. Foster, Stephen Merrill, and Gilbert Haven, all promoters of the Holiness revival, were elected Methodist bishops; with their encouragement, the movement was given vocal support through the church press. In 1870 a second national press organ was begun by William McDonald of the New England Conference. *The Advocate of Holiness* became the organ of the Camp Meeting Association. The revival reached some of the most influential members of the church: Daniel Steele, first president of Syracuse University and then professor of systematic theology at Boston University; William Nast, father of German Methodism; Bishop William Taylor; wealthy layman Washington C. DePauw; and women's rights leader Frances Willard. A new generation of preachers came along ready to make their mark as ministers of the Holiness gospel: Beverly Carradine, J. A. Wood, Alfred Cookman, John L. Brasher, and Milton L. Haney. The movement grew and developed, and, like the Finney revival, there was little or no fear of schism.

While this new work spread quickly among the Methodists, that begun by Finney did not die but continued to bear fruit. While the Oberlin position never really caught on with non-Methodists, leaders from the Quakers, Presbyterians, and Baptists preached the second blessing. William Boardman carried the message to England, where, in conjunction with R. Pearsall Smith, a Presbyterian, he began the "Oxford Union Meeting for the Promotion of Scriptural Holiness." The Oxford meetings then formed the base for the Keswick Movement, which became the main carrier of the Holiness movement in the Church of England. Smith's wife, Hannah, wrote one of the great classics of the Keswick era, *The Christian's Secret of a Happy Life.* The Keswick brand of Holiness, which emphasized the giving of power instead of the cleansing from sin, gained its adherents in the United States: Dwight L. Moody, R. A. Torrey, Adroniram J. Gordon, A. B. Simpson, and evangelist Wilbur Chapman.

At the height of this wave of success something went wrong. Schisms began to dominate the movement, and a third phase began: the establishment of independent Holiness churches. The voice for schism began to be heard in the 1880s, became dominant in the 1890s, and by 1910 had almost totally removed the Holiness movement from the main denominations into independent Holiness churches. The movement out of Methodism was a response to at least three forces antagonistic to the Holiness movement. First, a theological critique began to be heard. Men such as J. M. Boland, author of *The Problem of Methodism,* attacked the second blessing doctrine and maintained that sanctification was accomplished at the moment of conversion. James Mudge in his *Growth in Holiness Toward Perfection or Progressive Sanctification* argued for progressive rather than instantaneous sanctification. Borden Parker Bowne, representing a growing army of German-trained theologians, simply dismissed the whole issue of sanctification as irrelevant. (In the Lutheran and Presbyterian theologies, sanctification and justification were not separated as they were in Wesleyan and Methodist perspectives.)

The second force of growing concern to Methodist leaders was the mass of uncontrollable literature and organizations the Holiness movement was producing. By 1890 the number of books, tracts, pamphlets, and periodicals coming off the press to serve the Holiness movement was enormous. Independent camp meeting associations covered the country and in many places competed with local churches for the allegiance of members. Since camp meetings were independent, bishops and district superintendents had only the power of moral suasion to control what happened at the meetings or what was read throughout the movement. For some, this state of affairs was felt as a direct threat to their power. Others were genuinely concerned with excesses, fanaticism, and heterodox teaching. In either case, the loss of control led to an anti-Holiness polemic.

The third cause for the Holiness schism is found in the genuine shift of power that occurred between 1870 and 1890 in the Methodist Episcopal Church and the Holiness movement itself. By 1890 the bishops who promoted the Holiness movement and gave it official sanction had been replaced largely by others who were cool to the Holiness heat. Within the Holiness movement itself were regional and national leaders who were unhappy under the yoke of an unsympathetic hierarchy that was moving further away from their position each day. Not wishing to be confined in their ministry, they left the church. Among the first to leave were Daniel S. Warner, who founded the Church of God at Anderson, Indiana, and John P. Brooks. Brooks, a leader in the Western Holiness Association, in 1887 published *The Divine Church,* which called for all true Holiness Christians to come out of Methodism's church of mammon. *The Divine Church* became the theological guide to lead the way to the formation of independent churches.

The "come-out" movement created pressure on those who chose to stay in to justify their position. Thus, the 1890s saw loyalists publishing books against "come-outism," and calling for strengthening of the camp meetings. Beverly Carradine called for remaining in the church, but favored the establishment of independent Holiness colleges. Asbury College in Wilmore, Kentucky, and Taylor University in Indiana, represent the partial success of Carradine's view. These efforts by the loyalists were significantly unsuccessful, however, and by 1910 only minor pockets of Holiness teaching (such as the Brasher Campgrounds in Alabama) remained in the larger Methodist churches. As the twentieth century comes to a close, these churches are dying out.

CONTEMPORARY DEVELOPMENTS. Possibly because of the intense controversy during the formative years of the older Holiness churches, there is a strong sense of identity within the Holiness family among the various members. This image is focused not only in the doctrinal unity and similarity of lifestyle, but in the several ecumenical structures. These structures are home to a wide range of groups, from those who still keep ties with the United Methodist Church (Wesleyans, Free Methodists), all the way over to groups like the Church of God of the Mountain Assembly, which has Baptist origins.

The oldest ecumenical structure is the Christian Holiness Association. This body, which includes most of the larger Holiness churches in its membership, is a continuation of the National Holiness Camp Meeting Association, which guided the movement from the 1870s. After the establishment of the various denominational structures it remained as a meeting ground for these new organizations and those who remained in their original churches, primarily Methodists. Increasingly, it served the denominational bodies and in 1970 assumed its present name to recognize that fact.

One longstanding, if minor, theme in the Holiness movement was that perpetuated by the Keswick Conventions. Growing up primarily among the Holiness supporters of the Church of England, it supported the idea of suppression of the evil tendencies

in man, as opposed to the eradication taught by the Wesleyans. Keswick ideas did not produce many new groups but did find a home among one large body, the Christian and Missionary Alliance.

THE GLENN GRIFFITH MOVEMENT. Through the mid-twentieth century, the Holiness churches found themselves more and more accommodating to the world, especially in decisions concerning new realities (such as television and other contemporary forms of "worldly" entertainment) which were not an issue in previous generations. Some of its members protested this accommodation. They say they wish to preserve the "old-fashioned Scriptural Holiness" in which they were raised. The leader of this movement was the Reverend Glenn Griffith, a former minister from the Church of the Nazarene. The revival services he held in 1955 at a location between Nampa and Caldwell, Idaho, attracted many people to him. His movement spread, finding advocates in all of the larger Holiness churches. Adopting many of Griffith's ideas, ministers and members left those churches and formed a number of new denominations through the 1960s.

Even before Griffith gave focus to the protest movement, Rev. H. E. Schmul had facilitated fellowship among conservative Holiness churches and ministers through the Interdenominational Holiness Convention. It was begun by Schmul, a Wesleyan Methodist minister, in 1947. Its magazine, *Convention Herald,* served as a placement service for evangelists seeking appointments for revival meetings. Leaders of the various splinter movements within Holiness churches had participated in the Interdenominational Holiness convention. After the new churches were formed, these leaders moved into key positions in the Convention. The Interdenominational Holiness Convention continues to operate informally with membership open to individuals, congregations, and churches.

Sources—Holiness Family

Studies in the Holiness tradition are focused by the Christian Holiness Association, 225 S. Walnut St., P.O. Box 100, Wilmore, KY 40390, which publishes the semi-annual *Holiness Digest.* Nearby is the B. L. Fisher Library at Absurd Theological Seminary, which houses a large Holiness collection. Primary denominational archives are at the Church of the Nazarene headquarters in Kansas City, Missouri, and the Marston Memorial Historical Center at the Free Methodist Church world headquarters in Indianapolis, Indiana.

GENERAL SOURCES ON SANCTIFICATION AND HOLINESS

Dieter, Melvin E., et al. *Five Views of Sanctification.* Grand Rapids, MI: Academic Books, 1987.

Fenelon, Francois de Salignac de La Mothe. *Christian Perfection.* New York: Harper & Row, 1947.

Finney, Charles G. *An Autobiography.* Westwood, NJ: Fleming H. Revell, 1876.

———. *Sanctification.* Fort Washington, PA: Christian Literature Crusade, n.d.

Law, William. *A Serious Call to a Devout and Holy Life.* New York: E. P. Dutton, 1906.

Lindstrom, Harold. *Wesley and Sanctification.* New York: Abingdon, 1946.

THE HOLINESS MOVEMENT IN AMERICA

Bundy, David D. *Keswick: A Bibliographical Introduction to the Higher Life Movements.* Wilmore, KY: B. L. Fisher Library, Asbury Theological Seminary, 1975.

Dayton, Donald W. *The American Holiness Movement, A Bibliographic Introduction.* Wilmore, KY: B. L. Fisher Library, Asbury Theological Seminary, 1971.

Dayton, Donald W., David W. Faupel, and David d. Bundy, eds. *The Higher Christian Life: A Bibliographical Overview.* New York: Garland Press, 1985.

Dieter, Melvin Easterday. *The Holiness Revival of the Nineteenth Century.* Metuchen, NJ: Scarecrow Press, 1980.

A Guide to the Study of the Holiness Movement. Metuchen, NJ: Scarecrow Press, 1974.

Jones, Charles Edwin. *Black Holiness: A Guide to the Study of Black Participation in Wesleyan Perfectionist and Glossolalic Pentecostal Movements.* Metuchen, NJ: American Library Association/Scarecrow Press, 1987.

Lambert, D. W. *Heralds of Holiness.* Stoke-on-Trent: M.O.V.E. Press, 1975.

Miller, William Charles. *Holiness Works: A Bibliography.* Kansas City, MO: Nazarene Publishing House, 1986.

Nazarene Theological Seminary. *Master Bibliography of Holiness Works.* Kansas City, MO: Beacon Hill Press, 1965.

Peters, John Leland. *Christian Perfectionism and American Methodism.* New York: Abingdon, 1956.

Pollock, J. C. *The Keswick Story.* London: Hodder & Stoughton, 1964.

Smith, Timothy L. ''The Holiness Crusade.'' In vol. II of *The History of American Methodism.* Ed. Emory Stevens Buck. Nashville: Abingdon, 1965, pp. 608–59.

———. *Revivalism and Social Reform.* Nashville: Abingdon, 1957.

White, Charles Edward. *The Beauty of Holiness.* Grand Rapids: Francis Asbury Press, 1986.

HOLINESS THOUGHT

Arthur, William. *The Tongue of Fire.* Winona Lake, IN: Light and Life Press, n.d.

Boyd, Myron F., and Merne A. Harris, comps. *Projecting Our Heritage.* Kansas City: Beacon Hill Press of Kansas City, 1969.

Carradine, Beverly. *The Sanctified Life.* Cincinnati: The Revivalist, 1897.

Foster, Randolph S. *Christian Purity.* New York: Nelson & Phillips, 1869.

Kuhn, Harold B., ed. *The Doctrinal Distinctives of Asbury Theological Seminary.* Wilmore, KY: Asbury Theological Seminary, n.d.

Palmer, Phoebe. *Faith and Its Effects.* New York: Walter C. Palmer, 1854.

Rose, Delbert E. *A Theology of Christian Experience.* Minneapolis: Bethany Fellowship, 1965.

CRITICAL APPRAISALS

Boland, J. M. *The Problem of Methodism.* Nashville: The Author, 1889.

Ironside, Harold A. *Holiness, the False and the True.* New York: Loizeaux Brothers, 1947.

Mudge, James B. *Growth in Holiness Toward Perfection, or Progressive Sanctification.* New York: Hunt and Eaton, 1895.

Nevins, John W. *The Anxious Bench.* Chambersburg, PA: German Ref. Church, 1844.

Warfield, Benjamin B. *Perfectionism.* Philadelphia: The Presbyterian and Reformed Publishing Co., 1958.

Chapter 9

Pentecostal Family

Consult the "Contents" pages to locate the entries in Part III,
the Directory Listings Sections, that comprise this family.

The Pentecostal movement is one of the more spectacular religious phenomena of the twentieth century. Born as the century began, it now claims several million Americans and millions more overseas. As Pentecostals have taken their place in the world Christian community, they have emphasized their orthodoxy. Theologically, with the exception of the Apostolic Pentecostals discussed below, Pentecostals are situated firmly within the conciliar tradition (fourth to eighth century) during which time the major consensus on the beliefs of Christian orthodoxy was reached. They also have no disagreement with the major affirmations of the Protestant Reformation concerning the authority of the Bible, salvation by faith alone, and the priesthood of believers. In fact, the statements of belief of the various Pentecostal churches reflect their heritage, be that heritage Methodist (chapter 7) or Holiness (chapter 8) or Baptist (chapter 11). The dividing line between Pentecostal churches and the mainline Protestant churches has been clear, though, from the beginning of modern Pentecostalism in 1901. What makes Pentecostals distinct?—their new form of religious experience, which is grounded in what is termed glossolalia, i.e., speaking in tongues.

The unique Pentecostal experience begins in the conscious search for the gift of speaking in tongues as a sign of having been blessed with the baptism of the Holy Spirit. That baptism may be defined as the dwelling of the Holy Spirit in the individual believer. From the initial experience of the baptism of the Holy Spirit and speaking in tongues, the believer may expect to also manifest other gifts of the Holy Spirit as originally manifested in the New Testament church (I Cor. 12:4–11). Those gifts include healing, prophecy, wisdom (knowledge unattainable by natural means), and discernment of spirits (seeing nonphysical beings such as angels and demons).

SPEAKING IN TONGUES. Glossolalia, speaking in tongues, was a part of the experience of Jesus' disciples at Pentecost (Acts 2) and reappeared at several important points in the growing church. In Paul's *Epistle to the Corinthians*, "tongues" are mentioned as one gift or "charisma" among others such as healing, working miracles, and prophecy. "Tongues" usually appear in connection with other "gifts of the Spirit" although, historically, the other gifts have often appeared without the accompanying verbal gift. The experience of "tongues," if not common, was well known in the ancient world. The phenomenon is manifest today in a number of tribal religions, as well as among Pentecostals.

What are "tongues"? To the outsider, hearing someone speak in "tongues" is like hearing gibberish. To the Pentecostal, it is speaking under the control of the Holy Spirit. Pentecostal lore is full of tales of people who have been able to speak in a foreign language at a moment of crisis, although they did not know the language. Believers regard such instances as supernatural occurrences.

Social scientists generally look to a different explanation. Linguist William Samarin would separate glossolalia from xenoglossia. Glossolalia, says Samarin, is not truly a language. It is a verbal-

ized religious experience. Only a few vowels and consonants are used, not enough to make a language as we know it. Glossolalia is the common prayer speech heard at Pentecostal churches. Xenoglossia is the utterance of an existent foreign language by one who has no knowledge of it. A rare occurrence, it nevertheless has been noted and recorded in the literature of psychical research. Outside of Pentecostal circles, both telepathy and spirit contact have been hypothesized as the source of the xenoglossia. Possibly more important as an explanation is cryptonesia, forgotten memory. It is possible for a young person, for example, to learn much of a language from simply hearing others speak it, apart from any formal training. In later years, any conscious memory of that language can be lost to memory, but reappear in an altered state of consciousness.

LIFESTYLE AND WORSHIP. Along with the new form of religious experience centered upon speaking in tongues comes the second distinguishing mark of the Pentecostal: a lifestyle reordered around that religious experience. The Pentecostal convert lets his or her religious experience dominate daily life. The Pentecostal encourages others to have the baptism of the Holy Spirit; Pentecostals talk about that experience often; when they pray, they pray in tongues; they see healings as signs of God's immediate presence; they pay attention to other gifts of the Holy Spirit; and finally, they tend to look down on those who do not speak in tongues.

Through the first half of the twentieth century, Pentecostals were frequently and pejoratively called "holy rollers" a reference to their free, loud, participatory style of worship and their constant attention to the gifts of the Spirit, especially tongues. In contrast to the more orderly services in the Methodist, Baptist, and Presbyterian churches, Pentecostals seem to have a very free, spontaneous service that includes hymns that emphasize rhythm, extemporaneous prayers, and frequent interruption of the service with "amen's" and "tongues." Those who visit Pentecostal services for the first time are startled by the seeming lack of order. The freedom and spontaneity are limited, however. Even the most free congregation falls into a narrow pattern, repeated week after week with little variation.

It is the worship and the lifestyle keyed to religious experience—the constant search for the experience and the endless talk about it—that really separate Pentecostalism from the older Protestant denominations. Such distinctions are more felt than rationalized and are rarely articulated.

When conservative Christians such as Baptists and the Reformed discuss the doctrinal differences between themselves and the Pentecostal movement, they focus upon disagreements about the baptism of the Holy Spirit and the gifts of the Spirit. Theologians out of the Reformed tradition tend to believe that the gifts of the Spirit were given to the early church and disappeared after the Apostles died. Other critics, however, observe the likeness between the religious expressions of Pentecostals and those of non-Christians, including the Spiritualist and occult movements. A few have charged the Pentecostals with a form of demon possession. By contrast, the Pentecostals insist the end of time is near, and the words of the prophet Joel (Joel 3:1) are being fulfilled:

"It shall come to pass in the last days, says God, that I will pour out my Spirit on all mankind: Your sons and daughters shall prophesy, your young men shall see visions and your old men shall dream dreams."

According to Acts 2:17, Peter referred to this passage on the original Day of Pentecost as being fulfilled in the foundation of the Christian church.

HEALING. If speaking in tongues makes Pentecostals controversial, so does healing. Objections to healing center not as much on the reality of healing as on the form that healing ministries have assumed. Mainline Christians are offended by the seeming over-familiarity with God assumed in praying for God to heal, as well as the loud, demanding style of many evangelists. The critics also object to the emotional, crowd-psychology-oriented healing services that seem to manipulate those in attendance. Typical of the criticisms was the controversy that erupted in the 1970s on the former child-evangelist, Marjoe Gortner. Gortner had conducted healing services as a child, but came to the decision that what he was doing was not valid. So he invited filmmakers to follow him in a year's work of Pentecostal healing, filming what he did. The resultant movie and book were released as an exposé of Pentecostal healing. Gortner's critique appeared on the heels of critiques of healing that had emerged anew in the post-World War II healing movement that grew out of the work of William M. Branham, which produced superstar Oral Roberts and were followed by similar negative judgments leveled against Katheryn Kuhlman.

In the mid-1980s, skeptical stage magician James Randi did a survey of Pentecostal healers, among whom he found two, Peter Popoff and W. V. Grant, Jr., who were carrying on plainly fraudulent activity to create the appearance of miracles in their healing services. Using tricks well known to stage magicians, they claimed to receive information supernaturally. But in fact, the information was being transmitted to them by accomplices. In exposing the two questionable healers, Randi actually did the movement a great service. He believed that most of the healers he investigated were self-deluded, but were nevertheless sincere in what they were doing.

In spite of such criticisms, however, the Pentecostals raised an important issue for contemporary Christians: the question of healing as a sign of God's work among his people. Pentecostals join both Christian Scientists, who refrain from using medicine and doctors, and Episcopalians in raising this issue. An Episcopalian physician, Charles Cullis, held healing services at the turn of this century in his summer camp at Old Orchard, Maine. Many of the spiritual healing ministries in this country can be traced from Cullis to the Emmanuel Movement (emanating from the Emmanuel Episcopal Church in Boston early in this century) to healing evangelists such as Aimee Semple McPherson to more recent organizations such as the ecumenical Order of St. Luke the Physician, the spiritual heir of the Emmanuel Movement. Thus Pentecostal healing activity fit into a much larger interest in healing as a gift of the Spirit within Christianity.

"TONGUES" IN HISTORY. The first manifestation of "tongues" in the modern era occurred in the late seventeenth century in France. The times were a blend of persecution and miraculous events. After the revocation of the Edict of Nantes (1685), state suppression of Protestants began in southern France, among other places. In the mountainous region of Languedoc in the 1680s more than 10,000 people were victims of the stake, galley, and wheel. Partially in reaction to this persecution, strange paranormal phenomena began to occur. At Vivaris, in southern France, a man had a vision and heard a voice say, "Go and console my people." At Berne, people saw apparitions and heard voices. There arose prophets who were viewed as miraculous be-

cause, although young and untutored, they spoke fluently and with wisdom.

Among the French mountain villages was a poor unlettered girl, Isabella Vincent. The daughter of a weaver, Isabella left home after her father accepted a bribe to become a Catholic and after she witnessed a massacre of Huguenots (French Calvinists). She was a Huguenot, and she fled to her Huguenot godfather. On February 12, 1688, she had her first ecstatic experience. She entered a trance in which she spoke in tongues and prophesied. She called for repentance, especially from those who had forsaken their faith for gold. Her fame spread. People marveled at her perfect Parisian French and her ability to quote the mass *verbatim* and refute it. She was finally arrested, but others rose to take her place. In 1700, a movement began among the youth, and children as young as three entered ecstatic states and prophesied. Continued persecution was followed by war and eventual migration to other parts of Europe, where these people became known as the French Prophets.

A few manifestations of "tongues" were noted in the eighteenth century among the Quakers in England and the Methodists in America. In the 1830s, however, two groups emerged who spoke in tongues with some frequency: in England, the Catholic Apostolic Church, and in America, the Church of Jesus Christ of Latter-day Saints. Both accepted the experience as part of a gifted, charismatic church life. Then, after the Civil War, "tongues" began to manifest themselves within the holiness churches and thus came into historical continuity with the present-day Pentecostal movement. In 1875, the Reverend R. B. Swan, a holiness minister, was one of five people in Providence, Rhode Island, who spoke in tongues. This group grew and soon became known as the "Gift People." Jethro Walthall reported speaking in tongues as early as 1879. This evangelist from Arkansas at first accepted tongues as part of a total experience of "being carried outside of himself," but later identified it with Pentecost and became a superintendent of the Assemblies of God, discussed in this chapter. In 1890, Daniel Awrey, an evangelist from Ohio, experienced "tongues." In the 1890s, members attending the meetings of R. G. Spurling in Tennessee and North Carolina, and W. F. Bryant of Camp Creek, North Carolina, spoke in tongues. The experience was later identified with Pentecost and these two men became leaders in the Church of God (Cleveland, Tennessee) also discussed in this chapter. Besides these and other isolated incidents of "tongues," in the 1890s, there appeared a new movement in the holiness church that was to be a direct precursor of Pentecostalism as it exists today—the fire baptism.

As a movement, fire baptism was an "experience" preached by some holiness ministers looking for something more than their holiness experience had given them. The first such minister was the Reverend B. H. Irwin who had derived the experience from the writings of John Fletcher, an early Methodist. Fletcher, in his works, had spoken of a "baptism of burning love," but it is doubtful if he was implying any of what Irwin was seeking. Fire baptism, a personal religious experience of being filled with and empowered by the Holy Spirit, took its name from the Holy Spirit's descent upon the Apostles in the form of tongues of flame—the first Pentecost. In 1895, the first fire-baptized congregation (the first church to seek and receive fire baptism) was organized at Olmitz, Iowa. From there fire baptism was spread by itinerant evangelists. Holiness leaders labeled this new experience, which they termed "The Fire," heresy and fanaticism. Opposition did not keep the teaching from spreading and, within three years, there were nine state associations organized and six more waiting to form, including two in Canada. Formal organization of the Fire-Baptized Holiness Association took place in 1898 at Anderson, South Carolina, and a periodical, *Live Coals of Fire*, was started in 1899. Later, the Fire-Baptized Holiness Association was to accept as a body the Pentecostal emphasis on speaking in tongues as a sure sign of the Spirit's presence within the believer. The early experience of tongues and the development of the Fire-Baptized Holiness Association set the nineteenth century stage for the twentieth century Pentecostal movement. Three years would be significant in its development—1901, 1906, and 1914.

Tongues have periodically appeared in the christian tradition, and cases have been noted in a variety of non-Christian religion. However, it is to be noted that the experience of tongues by itself is not Pentecostalism. Pentecostalism was not built around a mere outbreak of spontaneous experiences of tongues. Rather, it consists of the conscious focus upon the experience of tongues as a sign of the reception of the Holy Spirit, and of activity (primarily prayer) directed toward the reception of the gift, and subsequent to receiving it, the conscious search for other gifts of the Spirit. Thus the history of Pentecostalism ultimately leads not to incidents of tongues in history, but to a Bible school in the American Midwest in the first year of the twentieth century.

1901—Topeka, Kansas. The beginnings of the modern Pentecostal movement originated in the ministry of the Reverend Charles Parham. Having left the Methodist Episcopal Church, Parham eventually opened the Bethel Healing Home in 1898 in Topeka. He had been inspired by the healing ministry of John Alexander Dowie of Zion, Illinois. In 1900, he began an extended tour of holiness and healing ministries from Chicago to New York to Georgia. Returning to Topeka, Parham found his work undermined and usurped. Undaunted, he purchased a building just outside of town and began the Bethel Bible College in the fall of 1900. Over the Christmas holidays, before leaving to speak in Kansas City, he assigned his students the task of investigating the "baptism of the Spirit," sometimes called the Pentecostal blessing. Upon returning, Parham got a report: "To my astonishment, they all had the same story, that while different things occurred when the Pentecostal blessing fell, the indisputable proof on each occasion was that they spoke with other tongues" (Sarah E. Parham, *The Life of Charles F. Parham* [Rept: Joplin, MO: Press of the Hunter Printing Co., 1969], 52).

Immediately they turned to seek a baptism with an indication given by utterance in "tongues." On January 1, 1901, the Spirit fell, first on Agnes Ozman, and a few days later on many others, and then on Parham himself.

Thus Agnes Ozman became the first person in modern times self-consciously first to seek and then to receive the experience of speaking in tongues (glossolalia) as a sign of being "baptized with the Holy Spirit." At that moment was inaugurated the Pentecostal Movement.

This small beginning, of fewer than 40 people, did not portend the growth that was to come. Parham closed the school and with his students set out to spread the message of the new Pentecost. He traveled and preached through Missouri and Kansas, and climaxed his tour with a revival in Galena, Kansas, which lasted for four months in the winter of 1903–4. In 1905, he began work in Texas for the first time. He made Houston his headquarters and in December 1905 opened a Bible school. Parham at this point let the mantle of leadership pass to William J. Seymour, who studied under Parham in Houston.

1906—Azusa Street, Los Angeles, California. The Pentecostal scene shifts to the West, to California, where in 1906 William J. Seymour, an African American holiness minister, arrived to preach at a small Baptist church. The church refused to hear him after his first sermon, but he was invited to preach at a member's home on Bonnie Brae Street. After three days of his preaching, the Spirit fell and "tongues" were heard on the West Coast. The meeting quickly outgrew the small home and a former Methodist church building was rented on Azusa Street. From here was to develop the revival that was to send the Pentecostal experience around the world.

The Pentecostal outpouring in Los Angeles did not occur in a vacuum, but was the culmination of earlier events. From the spring of 1905, Frank Bartlemen and Joseph Smale had been giving wide publicity to the 1904 Wales revival under Evans Roberts.

From Armenia, a number of Pentecostals who spoke in tongues had arrived to begin a new life in America. All quickly lent support to the Bonnie Brae phenomena.

After the initial speaking in tongues on April 9, the meeting grew and spread. Significant in this growth was the occurrence on April 18, just nine days after the initial experience, of the great San Francisco earthquake. More than 125,000 tracts relating the earthquake to the Azusa Street happenings and the "endtime" were promptly distributed. News of the revival was also widely circulated in holiness and other religious periodicals. Attracted by the excitement, people came to Los Angeles from across the country. As they received the baptism, they went home to spread the word. Pentecostal centers appeared in Illinois, New York, North Carolina, Sweden, England, India, and Chile.

Prior to the present generation, Pentecostals have had a peculiar problem in dealing forthrightly with their history. Leadership of the movement he founded was lost to Charles Parham who, like B. H. Urwin before him, was ostracized because of a personal scandal. Parham was accused of homosexuality, a particularly horrible sin in the eyes of conservative Christians. Then, the new leadership provided by Seymour was gradually rejected because of his race and by the beginning of World War I his ministry was largely limited to African peoples around the country. National leadership passed to white ministers who went to Azuza Street and returned home to found the various Pentecostal denominations.

1914—Hot Springs, Arkansas. From 1901 until 1914, the Pentecostals existed primarily within the holiness movement. The holiness movement was oriented toward an experience that ratified the believer's sanctity, the experience of the "second blessing," after which the believer would be holy forever. As the Pentecostal movement spread, many holiness churches accepted speaking in tongues as a final guarantee of holiness, a more sure sign than the "second blessing," and they called the Pentecostal "baptism of the Holy Spirit" the third experience. (The first, preceding the second blessing, was justification—the discovery of Christ as the personal savior.)

The holiness movement thus had supplied the basic problem (sanctification, life in the Spirit) that had caused concern for the "baptism of the Holy Spirit." The early Pentecostal leaders and members came from holiness churches, and holiness periodicals spread the word of the revival. Most important, the holiness churches, like the synagogues for Paul, became the first centers for Pentecostal evangelism. Out of the Holiness movement came such churches as the Pentecostal Holiness Church and the Church of God (Cleveland, Tennessee). However, growth of Pentecostalism caused many holiness churches and leaders to express strong disapproval of it. Resistance varied from the relatively mild policy of the Christian and Missionary Alliance to radical rejection by the Pentecostal Nazarene Church, which even dropped the word "Pentecostal" from its title to manifest its firm opposition.

Growing hostility, factionalism within the movement, and the need for coordination of activities led in December 1913 to a call for a 1914 meeting at the Grand Opera House, Hot Springs, Arkansas, of all who desired fuller cooperation. Out of this meeting grew the Assemblies of God. More important, from this organization came the impetus for the eventual organization of additional independent churches. Pentecostal denominationalism had begun in earnest.

With time, three Pentecostal churches took a special place in the American Pentecostal movement: the Assemblies of God, the Church of God (Cleveland, Tennessee), and the Church of Our Lord Jesus Christ of the Apostolic Faith. Many other Pentecostal churches are offshoots of these three or are modeled on them and deviate from them on only a few points.

For practical purposes, a parenthetical subtitle is given to some churches in this encyclopedia. Thus the Church of God (Cleveland, Tennessee) calls itself simply the Church of God, but its headquarters are in Cleveland, Tennessee, so that is added to its title to distinguish it from the more than a hundred other denominations who call themselves the Church of God.

As various Pentecostal churches came into existence, they adopted different forms of church government. Some are congregational, some connectional. The congregational churches share four characteristics: the local churches operate autonomously; they choose their own ministers; they own their property themselves; and they allow their regional and national church bodies to have only advisory authority over the local churches. In connectional churches, the regional and national church bodies have varying levels of power to legislate on doctrinal and organizational matters. Some Pentecostal churches with a connectional polity are close to a presbyterial system; some are close to an episcopal system with bishops (and superintendents).

CONTEMPORARY DEVELOPMENTS. Two very noticeable trends have been evident in Pentecostalism in the last half of the twentieth century. First, among the second and third generation Pentecostal denominations, a marked tendency to lessen the overtly emotional, loud, and spontaneous lifestyle has been quite noticeable, particularly in urban centers. Symbolic is the regular use of printed weekly church bulletins that specify an order of worship for the Sunday morning service.

Also these same Pentecostal bodies have pursued the development of ecumenical structures both among themselves and with non-Pentecostal churches. Ecumenical efforts within Pentecostalism began with the World Conference of Pentecostals held at Zurich, Switzerland, in May 1947. This conference inspired the formation of the Pentecostal Fellowship of North America, constituted at Des Moines, Iowa, October 26–28, 1948. This body has among its members all the larger trinitarian Pentecostal denominations (17 Canadian and United States bodies representing more than one million members in 1970).

Meetings of Pentecostals around the world have continued (Paris, 1949; London, 1952; Stockholm, 1955; Toronto, 1958; Jerusalem, 1961; Helsinki, 1964; Rio de Janeiro, 1967; and Dallas, 1970). Along with these conferences have been attempts, increasingly successful, to engage the older ecumenical bodies in dialogue. Emerging as the central figure in the effort was David J. DuPlessis, a South African Assemblies of God minister (1905–87). DuPlessis was a key organizer of the early world Pentecostal conferences, worked on the staff of the Second Assembly of the World Council of Churches in Evanston, Illinois, in 1954, and generally served as Pentecostalism's roving ambassador to non-Pentecostal Christians.

The second trend within Pentecostalism has been the regular outbreaks of international Pentecostal revivals that have been seen both as recapitulating the revival at Azusa Street in the face of a movement that many feel has lost much of the Pentecostal spirit and signaling the hoped for culmination of this age. The first such revival in the years following World War II began in 1948 in Western Canada and was known as the Latter Rain revival. It was followed by the healing revival in the 1960s led by William M. Branham. In the late 1960s the charismatic movement brought pentecostalism into the Roman Catholic Church and all of the major Protestant denominations. Each of these revivals became the source of doctrinal and behavioral disagreements and each soon led to the formation of new Pentecostal denominations. Most recently, a new wave of revivalism, some have termed it the "Third Wave," has swept the charismatic churches which are entering their second generation, and it in turn has created further new denominations.

SUBFAMILIES. Doctrinal, racial, and linguistic differences have led Pentecostals to divide into seven subfamilies. Additional small groups may be discerned, such as the snake handlers, but the far-reaching divisions have resulted in only seven subfamilies. In general, Pentecostals fall into three doctrinal groups, all of which split along racial lines. After a period of racial harmony in the first generation whites either withdrew or pushed black mem-

bers out of interracial denominations and only a few groups, such as the Pentecostal Assemblies of the World, are able to hold a significant minority membership across racial lines. Until the 1980s, for example, Africans were still largely excluded from the Pentecostal ecumenical bodies. Differences over the doctrines of holiness and the Trinity divided Pentecostals into three main groupings, while race further divided them into six.

In the meantime, Pentecostalism was carried by some Spanish-speaking people who attended the revival at Azusa Street to Mexico and then to South America. There it developed a life of its own and numerous indigenous Pentecostal denominations have arisen. As immigration from Latin American began to speed up in the last half of the twentieth century, members of these groups have begun to establish branches of primarily Puerto Rican and Mexican churches in Spanish-speaking neighborhoods in the cities of the United States. These have been integrated into the move to acknowledge Hispanic peoples' rights in the country and have emerged in such strength as to now constitute a separate subfamily of Pentecostal churches.

The earliest doctrinal disagreement occurred between those Pentecostals who came out of the holiness movement, primarily former Methodists, and those who came directly into the Pentecostal experience, primarily former Baptists. The holiness people saw the Pentecostal experience (receiving the baptism of the Holy Spirit and speaking in tongues) as a third experience following justification and sanctification. The Baptists insisted that any believer was capable of receiving the Pentecostal experience, without the intermediate "second blessing" assuring sanctification, the key experience of the holiness movement. Many Pentecostals split over the issue of two experiences (justification and the baptism of the Holy Spirit) or three experiences (justification, sanctification, and the baptism of the Holy Spirit).

No sooner had these two positions become evident than another serious theological issue arose. A group of ministers began to preach a "Jesus only" doctrine that amounted to a monotheism of the second person of the Trinity. This denial of the Trinity by what are generally termed "Apostolic" Pentecostals, reaches back to the centuries-old consensus of Christianity and resulted in the most serious family split, and the "Jesus only" people generally do not participate in the family ecumenical structures. Blacks have formed especially large denominations of the "Jesus only" type.

This discussion of Pentecostal subfamilies would be incomplete without a mention of neo-Pentecostalism. That is the movement of the 1960s and 1970s to form Pentecostal fellowships within the mainline Christian denominations. Neo-Pentecostalism also goes by the name of charismatic renewal. Its leaders were never a part of the older Pentecostal bodies, and formed charismatic fellowships within the Roman Catholic, Lutheran, United Methodist, Presbyterian, and Episcopal churches.

Since the 1970s these fellowships have served two functions. First, they have kept many Pentecostals within their mainline Christian churches, making unnecessary their move to the older Pentecostal churches. At the same time, however, they became the borning ground of new denominations, separate from both the older Pentecostal churches and the mainline Christian churches could form. These new charismatic denominations largely follow the doctrinal lead of the Assemblies of God and differs from it primarily by their unwillingness to own the name "Pentecostal," which is still a derogatory term in some circles, as opposed to "Charismatic."

THE APOSTOLIC, ONENESS, OR "JESUS ONLY" MOVEMENT. In 1913 at the Los Angeles Pentecostal camp meeting, the fledgling Pentecostal movement, barely beginning its second decade of existence, came face to face with a new issue. R. E. McAlister, a popular preacher, speaking before a baptismal service, shared his thoughts that, in the apostolic church, baptism was not done with a Trinitarian formula but in the name of Jesus Christ. While raising much opposition, McAlister's message found favor with a few such as Frank J. Ewart and John C. Scheppe. Scheppe's emotional acceptance of the "new" idea had a powerful impact on the camp. Ewart afterwards joined McAlister in a revival meeting in Los Angeles and began to note results whenever he called upon the name of Jesus.

The movement spread under the leadership of Ewart and evangelist Glenn A. Cook. They were able to bring in such key leaders as Garfield Thomas Haywood of Indianapolis, E. N. Bell, and H. A. Goss, all prominent leaders in the Assemblies of God. Ewart soon became editor of *Meat in Due Season*, the first oneness periodical.

The advocacy of oneness ideas, mostly by church who in 1914 came together to form the Assemblies of God, culminated in a discussion and decision in 1916 at the Assemblies of God General Council meeting in St. Louis. A strong Trinitarian stance was placed within the Statement of Beliefs. One hundred and sixty-six ministers were expelled by that act and many Assemblies were lost; the era of formation of "oneness" churches began.

The oneness Pentecostals deny the traditional Christian doctrine of the Trinity in favor of an affirmation of the "oneness" of God. Jesus is identified with God the Father (Isaiah 9:6, John 10:30) and God the creator (John 1:1) as the bodily presence of God. The Holy Spirit is not considered a third person within the Trinity but the spirit and power of God and Christ. Salvation is by repentance, and water baptism is considered an essential part of salvation. Baptism is by immersion in the name of Jesus only (Acts 2:38). Oneness people avoid the common trinitarian formula taken from Matthew 28:19.

Apart from the Trinitarian and baptismal questions, oneness people are typical Pentecostals. The oneness message has had particular appeal among African Americans, and the largest bodies are primarily black in membership. Of the several Apostolic Churches, the United Pentecostal Church is the largest predominantly white church.

AFRICAN AMERICAN PENTECOSTAL CHURCHES. There has been vigorous discussion in both popular and scholarly literature of the tie-in between black religion and Pentecostalism. Much of this discussion has been plainly derogatory and borders on racism. Pentecostalism, distinguished by its emotionalism and escapism, has been seen as an example of "primitive" religious forms. Fortunately, the growth of neo-Pentecostalism has led to a complete re-evaluation of the authenticity of the Pentecostal forms as basic religious expressions. With the new appreciation comes the opportunity to see, with new perspective, the key role that African Americans played in the early development of Pentecostalism, and more importantly, the manner in which they have taken the form far beyond its development by their white brothers and sisters.

Modern Pentecostalism began in the short-lived Topeka Bible School founded by Charles Parham. Among those students who received the baptism of the Holy Spirit was an African American woman, Sister Lucy Farrow. It was Sister Farrow who took Pentecostalism to Houston and opened the door for Parham to begin his Bible school there. Among his pupils was one W. J. Seymour, a black minister with the Church of God (Anderson, Indiana).

After Seymour received Parham's message, he traveled to Los Angeles where in 1906 he gathered a group of black believers into meetings that were eventually held at the Azusa Street Mission. As the gifts of the Spirit became manifest, whites began to attend the meetings and receive the baptism from Seymour who led the services.

Racism was overcome for only a short time; almost immediately white leaders began to develop their own movements. Although most Pentecostal churches remained integrated for one or two decades, eventually almost all of the groups split along racial lines. There is little doubt that the early splintering among Pentecostals throughout the country was because the black leadership at Azusa was unacceptable to whites.

The preaching of "Jesus only" by Garfield Thomas Haywood, a black minister in Indianapolis, forced the Assemblies of God to

deal with the "oneness" doctrine that denied the Trinity. Haywood's congregation became a nucleus for the first "oneness" denomination, the Pentecostal Assemblies of the world.

Pentecostalism swept through the black community and created some large, if relatively hidden, denominations. They compiled impressive figures for foreign mission work in Africa and the West Indies, where Pentecostalism has become a significant element in the larger Christian community. The Church of God in Christ now claims upwards of five million members worldwide.

DELIVERANCE (HEALING) MOVEMENT. Almost from the beginning, healing has been a major emphasis of the Pentecostal movement. It represents the culmination of a healing movement begun in evangelical churches by Charles Cullis, an Episcopal physician in Boston who held healing services at the turn of this century at his summer camp at Old Orchard, Maine. Albert Benjamin Simpson was healed at this camp and later made healing part of his four-fold gospel that presented Christ as savior, sanctifier, *healer,* and coming king. In the early years of this century F. F. Bosworth, Paul Rader, John D. Lake, and Smith Wigglesworth were popular healing evangelists and, of course, Aimee Semple McPherson became the most popular of all. The years between the wars saw the emergence of numerous independent healing evangelists, popular targets of exposé writers.

After the Second World War a group consciousness developed among some of the Pentecostal evangelists. In 1946 the Reverend William Marrion Branham, then a Baptist minister, claimed a visit by an angel and was told to start a healing ministry. That visit was the beginning of a remarkable "supernatural" ministry of healings, prophecies, and other paranormal phenomena. Branham began to tour the country in revival meetings. In 1947, Gordon Lindsay began *The Voice of Healing Magazine*. Gradually, without giving up their independence, other evangelists became associated with Branham and their activities included in *The Voice of Healing*. Branham died in 1965. In the years since his passing, deliverance ministers have emerged as a significant force within Pentecostalism.

In many cases, the deliverance evangelists have remained independent and travel at the request of churches or groups such as the Full Gospel Businessman's Fellowship. Others led large evangelistic missionary organizations. Evelyn Wyatt, T. L. Osborn, and Morris Cerullo head such organizations. Others became heads of church-forming bodies (both in the United States and abroad) that constitute new primary religious groups. These included W. V. Grant, William Branham, Gordon Lindsay, Kathryn Kuhlman, and A. A. Allen. For most of the above, evangelistic endeavors among members of Pentecostal and mainline Christian churches were the primary activity, with their deliverance churches forming relatively small bases of operation.

SNAKE HANDLING. One group of Pentecostals are sharply distinguished from the rest by their peculiar practice of "preaching the signs." In the Gospel of Mark 16: 17–18, Jesus promised his followers that certain signs would follow them: speaking in tongues, the ability to heal the sick, and the casting out of demons. Most Pentecostals accept these three. Those who "preach the signs," however, go beyond these to accept Jesus' further promise that they may take up venomous serpents and drink poisons without experiencing any harm. This promise has led to the practice popularly called snake handling. The original group that practiced the signs, that is, that handled snakes and drank poison (usually strychnine) in worship services, arose very soon after the Pentecostal movement spread to the Appalachian Mountain region.

In 1909 George Went Hensley, a preacher with the Church of God (Cleveland, Tennessee) in rural Grasshopper Valley, became convinced that the references in Mark 16: 17–19 to taking up poisonous snakes and drinking poison were, in fact, commands. He captured a rattlesnake and brought it to an open air revival meeting for participants to handle as a test of their faith. In 1914 Ambrose J. Tomlinson, head of the Church of God, asked Hensley to demonstrate snake handling to the church's annual assembly, and, with his tacit approval, the practice soon spread throughout the mountainous and rural South.

Those who engage in snake handling are Pentecostals who accept the basic theology by which people seek and receive the baptism of the Holy Spirit, evidenced by speaking in tongues. Snake handlers also accept the rigid ethical code of most holiness and Pentecostal bodies: dress is plain; the Bible is consulted on all questions in an attempt to discern worldly behavior; the kiss of peace is prominent. The snake handlers, however, go beyond the Pentecostals in their belief that holding venomous reptiles and drinking poison are signs of an individual's faith and possession of the Holy Spirit. The handling of snakes and drinking of poison are done while in an ecstatic state, referred to by members as "being in the Spirit."

The first and crucial test of the practice of snake handling was the near-fatal bite received by Garland Defries, which led to much unfavorable publicity and caused many snake handlers, who thought themselves immune to bites, to reevaluate the practice. Snake handling came under considerable attack within the Church of God, whose leaders denounced it as fanaticism. In 1928 the church formally forbade its continuation, thus forcing the snake handlers into separate congregations and small churches, primarily in rural areas.

A second test of snake handling came in 1945 when Lewis Ford, a member of the Dolly Pond Church of God with Signs Following (Dolly Pond, Tennessee), was fatally bitten. His death brought the first widespread public attention to the dangers of snake handling and led the State of Tennessee to legislate against it. Despite this legislation the practice continues in clandestine meetings in Tennessee and throughout the South.

Periodically, a person will be bitten and die at a snake handling meeting. Such rare occurrences usually become the subject of media attention with accompanying outcries against the practice. However, given their infrequency, these deaths have usually led to little more than a few ephemeral attempts to regulate the behavior of church members. The churches soon resume their normal routine. In 1975, some meaningful action was taken following the death of two church members from drinking poison. The Tennessee Supreme Court moved to strengthen that state's prohibitions on both snake handling and the ingestion of poison at religious services.

Snake handlers were back in the news in 1991 when Glenn Summerford, a snakehandling preacher in Alabama, went on trial for forcing his wife Darlene to thrust her hand in a box of rattlesnakes. She survived but Summerford was arrested and convicted of attempted murder. Over this century, in spite of the regular participation of poisonous snakes in religious services through the eastern half of the United States and the regular ingestion of poison in seemingly lethal doses, relatively few have died, less than 100.

THE LATTER RAIN MOVEMENT. During the mid-twentieth century, one new movement has deeply affected the development of Pentecostalism. Beginning in a small Bible college in western Canada in 1948, the Latter Rain Movement found enough initial support among leaders in the two largest Pentecostal groups in the United States and Canada respectively, the Assemblies of God and the Pentecostal Assemblies of Canada, that each moved quickly to suppress its influence among their ministers and churches.

The movement began as a revival at Sharon Orphanage and Schools in North Battleford, Saskatchewan, among students assembled by former Pentecostal Assemblies ministers George Hawtin and P. G. Hunt and Four-Square Gospel minister Herrick Holt. The revival was accompanied by a visible manifestation of the gifts of the Spirit, especially healing. As word of the events were spread, visitors came to North Battleford and invitations were issued for the leaders to come to different parts of the continent.

As it developed, the movement was characterized by an emphasis upon the gifts of healing and prophecy, the practice of the laying-on-of-hands to impart gifts to different people, and allegiance to the five-fold ministry of Ephesians 4:11. As the movement spread, it was accused of fanaticism and the leadership of the Assemblies of God moved against it. In 1949 the general council passed a six-part resolution, denouncing the movement because, among other practices, (1) it relied too heavily upon present-day apostles and prophets (i.e., a self-appointed charismatic leadership); (2) it practiced the confessing and pronouncing of forgiveness by one member upon another; (3) it advocated the practice of bestowing spiritual gifts by the laying-on-of-hands; and (4) it distorted Scripture so as to arrive at conclusions not generally accepted by members of the Assemblies.

Though neither experienced any major wholesale defections, both the Pentecostal Assemblies of Canada and the Assemblies of God began to lose pastors and their churches. Possibly the most prominent defection was Stanley Frodsham, longtime editor of the *Pentecostal Evangel*, who withdrew from the Assemblies of God after its 1949 resolution. Within a short time the movement was firmly entrenched in Vancouver, British Columbia; Portland, Oregon; Detroit, Michigan; Memphis, Tennessee; Los Angeles, California; and Philadelphia, Pennsylvania, from which it decimated across the United States. During the 1950s, especially as the healing revival led by William Marrion Branham and Oral Roberts grew, the Latter Rain spread.

Many of the early centers grew into large congregations, and a few emerged as seeds for new denominations (or more precisely, congregational associations). Some of these were distinguished by the peculiar teachings and emphases of the founder/leader. Such groups as the Church of the Living Word, the Body of Christ Movement, and the International Evangelical Church and Missionary Association are prominent examples.

Sources—Pentecostal Family

Study of the twentieth century Pentecostal tradition is focused by the Society for Pentecostal Studies, P. O. Box 2671, Gaithersburg, MD 20886, which publishes the semi-annual journal *Pneuma*. Significant archives are found at Oral Roberts University, Tulsa, OK 74105; the Pentecostal Research Center of the Church of God, P. O. Box 3448, Cleveland, TN 37320; and the Assemblies of God Archives, 1445 Boonville Ave., Springfield, MO 65892. The Assemblies of God Archives publishes the quarterly *Assemblies of God Heritage*.

GENERAL SOURCES

Burgess, Stanley M., and Gary B. McGee, eds. *Dictionary of Pentecostal and Charismatic Movements*. Grand Rapids, MI: Regency Reference Library, 1988.

Hunter, Harold D. *Spirit Baptism, A Pentecostal Alternative*. Washington, DC: University Press of America, 1983.

Kelsey, Morton T. *Tongue Speaking*. Garden City, NY: Doubleday, 1968.

Kydd, Ronald A. N. *Charismatic Gifts in the Early Church*. Peabody, MA: Hendrickson Publishers, 1984.

Poewe, Karla O., ed. *Charismatic Christianity as a Global Culture*. Columbia, SC: University of South Carolina Press, 1994.

Roebling, Karl. *Pentecostals Around the World*. Hicksville, NY: Exposition Press, 1978.

Sherrill, John L. *They Speak with Other Tongues*. Westwood, NJ: Fleming H. Revell Company, 1965.

Synan, Vinson. ed. *Aspects of Pentecostal-Charismatic Origins*. Plainfield, NJ: Logos International, 1975.

———. *The Holiness-Pentecostal Movement in the United States*. Grand Rapids: William B. Eerdmans Publishing Company, 1971.

———. *The Twentieth Century Pentecostal Explosion*. Altemonte Springs, FL: Creation House, 1987.

BIBLIOGRAPHICAL SOURCES

Faupel, David W. *The American Pentecostal Movement, A Bibliographical Essay.* Wilmore, KY: B. L. Fisher Library, Asbury Theological Seminary, 1972.

A Guide to the Study of the Pentecostal Movement. 2 Vols. Metuchen, NJ: Scarecrow Press, 1983.

Jones, Charles Edwin. *Black Holiness; A Guide to the Study of Black Participation in Wesleyan Perfectionist and Glossolalic Pentecostal Movements.* Netuchen, NJ: American Theological Library Association/Scarecrow Press, 1987.

Martin, Ira J. *Glossolalia, The Gift of Tongues, A Bibliography.* Cleveland, TN: Pathway Press, 1970.

HISTORICAL SOURCES

Bartleman, Frank. *How Pentecost Came to Los Angeles.* Los Angeles: Privately Printed, 1928.

Davis, Clars. *Azusa Street Till Now: Eyewitness Accounts of the Move of God.* Tulsa, OK: Harrison House, 1989.

Davis, George T. B. *When the Fire Fell.* Philadelphia: The Million Testaments Campaign, 1945.

Dayton, Donald. *"From Christian Perfection to the Baptism of the Holy Ghost": A Study in the Origin of Pentecostalism.* Chicago: The Author, 1973.

Ewart, Frank J. *The Phenomenon of Pentecost.* Hazelwood, MO: World Aflame Press, 1975.

Frodsham, Stanley H. *With Signs Following.* Springfield, MO: Gospel Publishing House, 1946.

Gaver, Jessyca Russel. *Pentecostalism.* New York: Award Books, 1971.

Hollenweger, Walter J. *The Pentecostals: The Charismatic Movement in the Church.* Minneapolis: Augsburg, 1972.

Kendrick, Klaude. *The Promise Fulfilled.* Springfield, MO: Gospel Publishing House, 1961.

McClug, L. Grant, Jr. *Azusa Street and Beyond.* South Plainfield NJ; Bridge Publishing, 1986.

Nichols, Thomas R. *Azusa Street Outpouring.* Hanford, CT: Great Commission International, 1979.

Riss, Richard Michael. *The Latter Rain Movement of 1948 and the Mid-twentieth Century Evangelical Awakening.* Vancouver, BC: Regent College, 1979.

Strachey, Ray. *Group Movements of the Past.* London: Faber & Faber Ltd., 1934.

Valdez, A. C., and James F. Scheer. *Fire on Azusa Street.* Costa Mesa, CA: Gift Publications, 1980.

Wallace, Mary H. *Profiles of Pentecostal Preachers.* Hazelwood, MO: World Aflame Press, 1983.

Wagner, Wayne, ed. *Touched by the Fire.* Plainfield, NJ: Logos International, 1978.

Whittaker, Colin C. *Pentecostal Pioneers.* Springfield, MO: Gospel Publishing House, 1983.

GLOSSOLALIA AND THE SPIRITUAL GIFTS

Goodman, Felicitas D. *Speaking in Tongues, A Cross-Cultural Study of Glossolalia.* Chicago: University of Chicago Press, 1972.

Kildahl, John P. *The Psychology of Speaking in Tongues.* New York: Harper & Row, 1972.

Samarin, William. *Tongues of Men and Angels.* New York: Macmillan Company, 1972.

Sneck, William Joseph. *Charismatic Spiritual Gifts.* Washington, DC: University Press of America, 1981.

APOSTOLIC OR ONENESS PENTECOSTALS

Clanton, Arthur J. *United We Stand.* Hazelwood, MO: The Pentecostal Publishing House, 1970.

Foster, Fred J. *Their Story: Twentieth Century Pentecostals.* Hazelwood, NJ: World Aflame Press, 1981.

Richardson, James C., Jr. *With Water and Spirit.* Martinsville, VA: The Author, n.d.

Symposium on Oneness Pentecostalism, 1988 and 1990. Hazelwood, MO: World Aflame Press, 1990.

BLACK PENTECOSTALS

Hollenweger, Walter J. *Black Pentecostal Concept.* Special issue of *Concept 30* (1970).

Nelson, Douglas J. *For Such a Time as This, The Story of Bishop William J. Seymour and the Azusa Street Revival.* Birmingham, England: University of Birmingham, Ph.D. Dissertation, 1981.

Tinney, James S. "William J. Seymour: Father of Modern Day Pentecostalism." In *Black Apostles.* Ed. Randall K. Burkett and Richard Newman. Boston: 1978.

DELIVERANCE MOVEMENT

Harrell, David Edwin, Jr. *All Things Are Possible.* Bloomington: Indiana University Press, 1975.

Melton, J. Gordon. *A Reader's Guide to the Church's Ministry of Healing.* Independence, MO: The Academy of Religion and Psychical Research, 1977.

SIGNS MOVEMENT

Carden, Karen W., and Robert W. Pelton. *The Persecuted Prophets.* New York: A. S. Barns & Co., 1976.

Covington, Dennis. *Salvation on Sand Mountain: Snake Handling and Redemption in Southern Appalachia.* Reading, MA: Addison-Wesley, 1994.

Holliday, Robert K. *Tests of Faith.* Oak Hill, WV: The Fayette Tribune, 1968.

Kimbrough, David L. *Taking Up Serpents:Snake Handlers of Eastern Kentucky* Chapel Hill, NC: University of North Carolina, 1995. 232 pp.

La Barre, Weston. *They Shall Take Up Serpents.* New York: Schocken, 1969.

NEOCHARISMATIC MOVEMENT

Bradfield, Cecil David. *Neo-Pentecostalism, A Sociological Assessment.* Washington, DC: University Press of America, 1979.

A Charismatic Reader. New York: Evangelical Book Club, 1974.

Culpepper, Robert H. *Evaluating the Charismatic Movement.* Valley Forge, PA: Judson Press, 1977.

O'Connor, Edward D. *The Pentecostal Movement in the Catholic Church.* Notre Dame, IN: Ave Maria Press, 1971.

Quebedeaux, Richard. *The New Charismatics.* Garden City, NY: Doubleday, 1976.

Shakarian, Demos. *The Happiest People in the World.* Old Tappen, NJ: Chosen Books, 1975.

Synan, Vinson. *In the Latter Days.* Ann Arbor, MI: Servant Books, 1984.

NON-PENTECOSTAL EVALUATIONS OF PENTECOSTALISM

Bauman, Louis S. *The Tongues Movement.* Winona Lake, IN: Brethren Missionary Herald Co., 1963.

Charismatic Countdown. Washington, DC: Review and Herald Publishing Association, 1974.

Dollar, George W. *The New Testament and New Pentecostalsim.* Minneapolis: Central Baptist Theological Seminary, 1978.

Gustafson, Robert R. *Authors of Confusion*. Tampa, FL: Grace Publishing Company, 1971.

Kinghorn, Kenneth Cain. *Gifts of the Spirit*. Nashville, TN: Abingdon, 1976.

Noorbergen, Rene. *Charisma of the Spirit*. Mountian View, CA: Pacific Press Publishing Association, 1973.

Robinson, Wayne A. *I Once Spoke in Tongues*. Old Tappen, NJ: Spire Books, 1975.

Stolee, H. J. *Pentecostalism*. Minneapolis: Augsburg Publishing House, 1936.

The Latter Rain Movement

Hoekstra, Raymond G. *The Latter Rain*. Portland, OR: Wings of Healing, 1950.

Riss, Richard Michael. *The Latter Rain Movement of 1948 and the Mid-Twentieth Century Evangelical Awakening*. Vancouver, BC: Regent College M.A. Thesis, 1979.

Chapter 10
European Free-Church Family

Consult the "Contents" pages to locate the entries in Part III,
the Directory Listings Sections, that comprise this family.

Over the past generation, histories of the Reformation, the sixteenth-century protest movement that began in the Roman Catholic Church and eventually split that organization into a number of national fragments, have begun to reflect the recognition that a vital part of the Protestant Reformation story was written by the radical reformers. The radicals were independent groups and people who protested Luther's and Calvin's continued tie to the state. Considered by such Lutherans and Calvinists as revolutionaries, mystics, anarchists, and heretics, they were the object of scorn for all. However, as George H. Williams noted in his groundbreaking study of the radicals, "They have the same significance for the interpretation of the whole of modern church history as the discoveries in the Dead Sea caves and in upper Egypt are having for New Testament studies and early church history" (*The Radical Reformation* [Philadelphia: The Westminster Press, 1962], xix).

Who were the radical reformers? They were men who, like Luther and Calvin, were interested in the reform of the church but who, because of a variety of backgrounds, outlooks, and theologies, placed their emphases on much different points as the crux of needed reform. For most, faith, sacrament, and liturgy were not as significant as the doctrine of the church in its relation to the state. The radicals frowned upon involvement in secular activity and were typically persecuted by the state. Most radicals came from the lower class, so they built upon the traditional adversary relationship between the lower class and the ruling class. The radicals took the ideas of the Reformation (ideas such as the priesthood of believers and the freedom of the Christian man) to such an extreme that Luther and Calvin were horrified.

Most of the radicals came to a bloody end in war or persecution, and many saw their movements entirely destroyed. Because of this destruction, men such as Thomas Müntzer, Hans Denck, and Michael Sattler did not leave even a surviving remnant to carry on their work. Others, such as Caspar Schwenckfeld, Jacob Hutter, and Melchior Hofmann, were able to leave movements which survived and exist today. Among the churches that trace their roots to the radical reformers are the Mennonites, the Amish, the Brethren, the Quakers, and the Free Church Brethren. All of these churches belong to the free church family, meaning that they are not only not state churches but ideologically opposed to state churches. They exist as free associations of adult believers, people old enough to make a free decision to join their fellowship. The free churches emphasize free will, contrasting sharply with strict Calvinists who believe in predestination—that the number and identity of the elect was ordained before the beginning of the world.

The radical Reformation can be dated from Christmas Day 1521, more than four years after Luther's Ninety-five Theses were nailed to the church door in Wittenburg. On this day, Andreas Bodenstein of Carlstadt—a man simply referred to as Carlstadt by historians—celebrated the first "Protestant" communion. (Protestant services today follow the trend set by that service.) He preached, and without having donned liturgical vestments, read the "Mass.

He omitted all references to sacrifice, did not elevate the host, and gave both bread and wine. Each act was a significant repudiation of a belief or practice of the Roman Catholic Church. Behind this communion service was the strong contention of the supremacy of spirit over letter, the supremacy of grace over works, and the common priesthood of all believers. From these events were to flow others initiated by men who were already thinking as Carlstadt.

The career of Thomas Müntzer (1490?–1525) was one of the results of the activity of Carlstadt. In 1520, Müntzer appeared at Zwickau, a town in Saxony, where, as minister to one of the churches, his radicalism began to emerge. He urged people to respond spontaneously and immediately to the leadings of the Holy Spirit. He defined the church as spirit-filled saints gathered together in a community. His definition avoided any mention of bishops or sacraments and thus was at odds with a traditional understanding of the church. He aroused the laity in support of him against his more conservative colleagues. After being removed from his pastorate, Müntzer spent several years as a wandering preacher, becoming more and more radical and embittered. In a famous sermon in 1524 before the German princes, he called upon them to take up the sword to defeat the forces of anti-Christ (the pope) and bring in the kingdom.

A number of events, including an astrological conjunction, converged in 1524 and occasioned an uprising of the peasants of Germany. Not the least of these events was the preaching of Müntzer and his radical colleagues. As the Peasants' War began, Müntzer, having given up on the immovable princes, joined the peasants' forces at Mühlhausen. He was ready to wield his sword for the kingdom. He saw the Peasants' War as his instrument. When the revolt was put down, Müntzer was captured. His career ended on the executioner's block and his flock was scattered.

Contemporaneous with Müntzer's short career in the north, other radical reformists appeared in southern Germany and Austria. Their first spokesman was Hans Denck. While at Nuremberg as rector of a parish school, Denck had come under the influence of Carlstadt and Müntzer. Denck was expelled from Nuremberg by Lutherans who feared him as a competitor. In the fall of 1525, Denck became the spiritual leader of a group at Augsburg. In the spring of 1526 (under the influence of Swiss refugee Balthasar Hubmaier), he led in the reconstitution of his group as a truly reformed church by the adoption of the apostolic practice of believer's baptism. By that practice, only adult believers in Christ were baptized, the procedure believed to have been used by the Apostles. Thus anabaptism, or rebaptism of those who were baptized as infants, emerged as a central factor in the radical reformation. Denck saw the church as an adult, self-disciplined fellowship. His criteria for understanding the church naturally excluded infants, thus *antipedobaptism* (literally against the baptism of infants) became a central teaching of the movement. From this belief and this practice was to come the fully developed Anabaptist understanding of the church as an association of adults (not children) acting freely.

Denck was forced out of several cities as his reputation caught up with him. In 1527, he arrived in Augsburg to participate in a synod of Anabaptist leaders. After the meeting, many were arrested and died martyrs' deaths, so the meeting is called the Martyrs' Synod.

The main item of concern for the synod was the eschatalogical program of John Hut, an Austrian Anabaptist leader who had been rebaptized by Denck. Hut repudiated the peasants for taking up arms and interpreted current events as symbols of the nearness of the end of time. God would do his work. The saints, while suffering at present, would live to see the new kingdom appear. Hut proceeded to build an underground movement throughout Bavaria and Austria.

When the synod met, three issues concerning the coming kingdom were under discussion: the manner and time of its approach, the role of Anabaptists to prepare for it, and the role of the magistery in the present time. No clear-cut decisions were reached on these points. After the synod, Hut was arrested and died in a fire in his cell. The inability of the synod to bring the radicals into one mind, the attacks of the Lutherans on some radical excesses in doctrine, and disillusionment with his role in God's reformation led Denck to recant. He died of the plague a few years later.

Contemporaneous with the rise of South German and Austrian Anabaptists was the rise of Swiss Anabaptists, popularly known as the Swiss Brethren, under the leadership of Michael Sattler. Within the Swiss Brethren a mature, articulate Anabaptist stance would be formed, and from them would come the most important statement of the Anabaptist position.

Swiss Anabaptism arose in the 1520s to protest a state church. The church in question was that of Ulrich Zwingli (1484–1530), the leader of the Reformation in Switzerland. Zwingli took religious control of the canton of Zurich, with the power structures of Zurich establishing the Zwinglian Church for all in the area. The Swiss Brethren insisted that only the righteous should belong to the church, not every person who happened to reside in the territory controlled by the state. After the vote to establish the Zwinglian Church, the Swiss Brethren withdrew from Zurich.

They determined to continue their efforts to restore the true Church. Two leaders of the Swiss Anabaptists, Conrad Grebel and George Blaurock, became the center of controversy. On January 21, 1525, layman Grebel rebaptized Blaurock, a priest, and that action led to months of disputation. The brethren grew, even though they were persecuted. Doctrinally, they had a double problem. First, they had to counter Zwingli's ideas, which were very popular. Second, they had to clarify for people their differences with Müntzer and Hut. Müntzer and Hut had poor reputations, and people mistakenly associated the Swiss Brethren with them. It was in the attempt to refute Müntzer and Hut that Michael Sattler came forward as a leader of refugees in Strassburg. Upon his return to Switzerland, Sattler found himself leader of the Schleitheim Synod. There the mature Anabaptist position was hammered out in a document originally called "The Brotherly Union of a Number of Children of God Concerning Seven Articles," now called the Schleitheim Confession.

Schleitheim Confession. The Schleitheim Confession set the distinctives of the Anabaptist position. Rejecting the state church in which citizenship and church membership were almost the same, the Anabaptists were looking for a church of true believers. Hence they acknowledged baptism for converted adult believers only and limited the taking of communion to those who had been rightfully baptized. Having given up the disciplinary machinery of the state, they were left with the ban, a form of excommunication of fallen and as yet unrepentant members, as their only tool of discipline. They admonished Anabaptists to withdraw from the world and its wickedness. In that light, church members were to make no use of the sword, for either secular or sacred purposes. That po-

sition extended to an avoidance of serving as a magistrate. Finally, the Anabaptists refused to take oaths. All of these positions were based upon their study of the Bible. (A complete copy of the Schleitheim Confession is to be found in the accompanying volume, *The Encyclopedia of American Religions: Religious Creeds*.)

From the Schleitheim Confession emerges the distinctive doctrinal and ethical position of the Anabaptist churches. This stance would be accepted, with minor modifications, by the various bodies that survived the era of persecution. The church is composed of those united to Christ by believer's baptism and who have separated themselves from the evil world. The church is a minority group of pilgrims in a hostile world trying to isolate themselves from its influence and forces. Specifically, certain items—war, the use of violent force against one's neighbor, civic affairs, courts, oaths, worldly amusements, and serving as a magistrate—are to be studiously avoided as things of the world.

Pacifism, in particular, has arisen as the essential point in the avoidance ethic and these churches have been characterized as the historical peace churches. Christians obey the laws of the land, as is possible for pacifists (and any attempting to live withdrawn), but their essential authority is to be found in the church.

The church is the disciplined fellowship. It appoints its own leadership and accepts its authority as the leadership administers it. Its prime force is the ban, a practice based on Matthew 18:15–17, which is similar to excommunication. Menno Simons is credited with emphasizing a modified form of banning termed shunning, in which the church stops all dealing with an erring brother, including eating with him, with the intent of winning him back to the straight and narrow. This practice is based on I Corinthians 5:11.

The church was opposed to both popish and anti-popish works and church services. From this position comes a lay-oriented, non-liturgical, non-creedal, Bible-oriented church. Their opposition to the state church, a position that was articulated as well as manifested by their very existence, led to the appellation, "free church." Non-liturgical worship in its extreme form can be seen in the classic Quaker service.

The Bible is the prime document from which the Anabaptists derive their belief and practice. Their method of Biblical interpretation, which will not utilize tradition and philosophy, becomes literalistic. Sacraments become ordinances, symbolic acts: baptism is an initiatory ceremony and the Lord's Supper a memorial act. Foot washing, for which there is not a more unequivocal command than either baptism or the Lord's Supper, is also practiced, especially in those churches of Swiss origin.

Though all the European free churches believe in adult baptism, they have a wide variety of modes. The Mennonites pour water on the person being baptized, while the Church of the Brethren has triune immersion, the practice of entering the water once for each person of the Trinity.

LATER HISTORY. After the Schleitheim Confession, three events were to remold the Anabaptists—the fall of the town of Münster; the death of the martyrs; and the rise of Menno Simons.

The Radical Reformation had continually been punctuated by apocalyptic thinking, including a few instances of militancy. These tendencies came to a climax in the town of Münster. Radicalization there began with the pastor, Bernard Rothmann. His popular sermons led to the Protestantization of the community in 1531. Rothmann's Lutheran views became more and more radical, and he began to defend believer's baptism. Other Anabaptists heard of Rothmann and began to flock to Münster as the new Jerusalem. Among the immigrants were Jan Mathijs and his major supporter, Jan of Leiden. The immigrants adopted the apocalyptic theory that the end of time was imminent and would be caused by God's direct intervention in human affairs.

By the beginning of 1534, the radicalization of the city was complete and Mathijs was quickly rising to power. All Catholics and Lutherans were expelled, and the city armed itself for the siege that would follow that expulsion. Mathijs imposed his religious beliefs. The town adopted a communist lifestyle while it made military preparations for the siege. In the midst of these reforms Mathijs was killed. Jan of Leiden took over and began to set up a theocracy with himself as God's vicar. The strict discipline worked effectively during the siege. After a particularly heavy battle, Jan introduced polygamy.

The beleaguered city finally was betrayed and captured. Jan had imposed ruthless authority on the people. After his capture, he was tortured to death. With only a few minor exceptions, the Münster episode ended any apocalypticism in the Anabaptism movement.

That episode, however, did not bring to a close the killings of Anabaptists. *The Martyrs Mirror,* a book which functions for Anabaptists much as John Foxe's *Book of Martyrs* functions for English Protestants, records the trail of blood of Anabaptists killed for their faith. The book was first published in 1554. Persecution left a stamp upon the members of the free churches, who came to see themselves literally as wandering pilgrims in a hostile world.

Anabaptists flocked to Menno Simons in the Netherlands. Emerging in 1537 as a leader, Menno began a series of books that set down a moderate free church position and rallied the disintegrating Anabaptist forces. It is to Menno's credit that the forces were held together and survived until 1577 when toleration was granted in Holland. The followers of Menno became, with few exceptions, the surviving Anabaptist community.

In addition to the apocalyptic Anabaptism of Münster and the moderate Anabaptism of the Swiss Brethren was a third form of Anabaptism. It turned inward in what has been termed a spiritualist or mystical movement. Among the first to espouse the spiritualist perspective was Hans Denck. An early leader in the Anabaptist movement, Denck recanted in his despair at its divisions and began to turn inward. He had long been a student of the mystic John Tauler, and to Tauler he turned. He began to preach of the God who meets us as a light, a word, and a presence. He was followed by others such as Sebastian Franck, Johann Bünderlin, and Christian Entfelder.

As a whole, the spiritual Anabaptists collected no following and left no following. One exception was Caspar Schwenckfeld, a Silesian courtier turned prophet. In successive steps, he became a disciple of Luther, a critic of the Reformation as outward and shallow, an Anabaptist theologian with some peculiar views on the sacraments and Christ, and a mystic leader with a large following that still exists. But Schwenckfeld was the exception.

What the spiritual reformers did primarily was to create a literature with Anabaptist devotional and mystic leanings that became the basis of a mystical movement within the free churches much like the one in medieval Catholicism and the inspiration for later mystical, devotional movements, primarily Quakerism and to a certain extent Pietism. Each of these strains was to find a home in colonial Pennsylvania.

SWISS AND DUTCH MENNONITES. The central surviving Anabaptist tradition owes its name to one of its major leaders, Menno Simons (1496?–1561). Simons, a Dutchman, was born in Witmarsum in the Netherlands. While a Roman Catholic priest, Simons was led to believe that the bread and wine were *not* the real body and blood of Christ. A 1531 execution of an Anabaptist led him to investigate infant baptism. Continued investigation of Anabaptist views convinced him they were right. Finally, in 1536, a year after his own brother's death as an Anabaptist, Menno Simons left his Catholic heritage. Because of his abilities, he immediately became a leader in the Anabaptist community. His main tasks became keeping the community protected from authorities and free from militarism (which had led Anabaptists to take complete control of Münster and wage a long battle to defend it) and from heresies such as apocalyptic beliefs that the world would soon end through God's direct intervention. Some of Menno's followers found toleration in East Friesland in the Netherlands under the

Countess Anne. It was she, in recognizing the peaceful followers of Menno in contradistinction to the militarists and apocalyptics, who first dubbed them "Menists." The main part of Simon's active life was spent writing in defense of his new-found faith and hiding from the authorities, who had put a price on his head.

Menno's views were similar to those outlined by the Swiss Brethren at Schleitheim. It can be argued, and has been, that the Mennonites are the legitimate inheritors of the Swiss-German Anabaptist tradition, as most of the other Anabaptists have disappeared from the contemporary world. In essentials, the Mennonites certainly share the Swiss and German Anabaptists' views on rebaptism, pacifism, religious toleration, separation of church and state, opposition to capital punishment, opposition to holding office, and opposition to taking oaths. On two points only did Menno Simons differ—his use of the ban and his doctrine of incarnation.

Menno joined in the argument with the Brethren on the strict versus the liberal use of the ban. Menno advocated the strict use as the only means to keep the church free of corrupt sects. He also advocated "avoidance" or shunning all who were banned. Shunning was centered upon the idea of not eating with the person under the ban; this practice created a significant ingroup problem when one member of a family was under the ban. The practice of avoidance was liberalized over the years by the main body of Mennonites, but originally it was their distinguishing feature.

Menno has also been accused of compromising the humanity of Christ by minimizing the human properties said to have been received from Mary. This slight difference in Christology, which led many to accuse him of antitrinitarianism, has not been a major factor in recent Mennonite history.

The unique doctrinal position of the Mennonites was systematized in 1632 in the Dordrecht Confession, named for the town in the Netherlands at which it was written. It is consistent with the Schleitheim Confession, but deals more systematically with basic Christian affirmations. It affirms God as Father, Son, and Holy Ghost (the Trinity); the restoration of all humanity though Christ, who was foreordained to his saving work before the foundation of the world; and the incarnation of Christ as the Son of God. Those who are obedient through faith and follow the precepts of the New Testament are considered Christ's children. Baptism is for repentant adult believers. The visible church consists of those who have been baptized and incorporated into the communion of saints on earth. Within that church, the Lord's Supper is observed as an ordinance, as is the washing of the feet.

The state is seen as the gift of God and Mennonites are admonished to pray for it and support it in all manners not directly opposed to the commandments of God. Two ways in which God's will and the state are seen to conflict are in the state's demand for oaths and in its drafting of young men for military service. The Mennonites generally refuse to take oaths (for example, in a court of law) or to bear arms.

In one respect the Dordrecht Confession goes beyond the Schleitheim Confession. Not only does it advocate the use of the ban (excommunication) but also of shunning (avoidance of eating, drinking or socializing with a fallen and unrepentant church member). This practice, still used in some of the more conservative Mennonite bodies, has been a source of considerable controversy especially when it has become an issue between a church member and a spouse who is being shunned. On such cases the church is not allowed to eat dinner with the spouse.

The Mennonite movement spread slowly, and the late 1500s was a period in which many names were added to the roll of martyrs. The movement spread into Germany and Switzerland, building on small groups of Anabaptists already there. Mennonites settled and migrated as rulers first allowed toleration and then rescinded the privilege. In 1763, Catherine the Great of Russia offered religious toleration to German settlers who would populate the southern Steppes. Moravians, Mennonites, and Hutterites flocked to Russia; the Mennonites, mostly Prussians, settled in Crimea and Taurie. The Mennonites developed in southern Russia a unique history because of the special status granted them by the Russian government. A self-governing Mennonite community arose, the government approaching that of a theocracy. The end of Russian paradise came in the 1870s when the Czar introduced universal military service as a policy among the German colonists. This policy was part of a general Russification program in face of the growing military power of Prussia. The Mennonites, pacifists, refused to join the military. So in 1874, a six-year mass immigration to the United States and Canada began. Those that remained in Russia prospered until 1917 when they became victims of the Bolsheviks. They still survive, however, in small scattered communities.

MENNONITES IN AMERICA. Reference to Mennonites in America occurs as early as 1643 in the records of New Netherlands. In 1633, a communal experiment led by Cornelius Pieter Plockhoy appeared on Delaware Bay, then a part of New Netherlands. The first permanent Mennonite colony was established in 1683 at Germantown, Pennsylvania; this date is usually accepted by Mennonites as their date of origin in America. Several factors encouraged Mennonites to come to the U.S. First, religious persecution in Europe caused many to immigrate. Second, William Penn and George Fox were seeking German converts and appealed to members of Mennonite communities to come to America. Finally, the German Quakers (former Anabaptists) already in America wrote their friends and relatives asking them to move to Pennsylvania.

This growing Mennonite element is credited with American history's first public protest against slavery and was very influential in the later Quaker antislavery position. The Mennonites were an agricultural people and began to spread north and west of Germantown. The group's size was bolstered by immigration from the Palatine in the early eighteenth century.

The Revolutionary War became the first major crisis in the American Mennonite community, leading to their first schism. The issue was support of the Continental Congress. The majority argued that they could not support the Congress because such support would involve them in the war.

One leader, Christian Funk, argued in favor of support, including the special war tax, drawing support from Jesus' words on taxation (Matt. 22:21). Funk was excommunicated and with his followers formed the Mennonite Church (Funkite), which existed until the mid-nineteenth century. It died as all the participants in the original dispute died.

Continued immigration and the natural expansion of the Mennonites, who are prone to have large families, forced them west looking for new land. The early nineteenth century found Mennonites making settlements in Ontario and the Old Northwest Territory, and after the Civil War, the prairie states. This growing migration and wide separation geographically set the stage for formation of schismatic churches that would reach major proportions in the 1880s.

While no distinct and sharp lines can be drawn, there are rough ethnological distinctions within the Mennonite community. Some of the American splintering of churches can be traced to the Swiss, Dutch, or German background of the colonies. The largest distinction among the Mennonites as a whole is between the Western European and Russian settlers. Most of the Western European Mennonites came in the initial wave of settlers into Pennsylvania in the eighteenth century and pushed west into Canada and Indiana. The Russian immigrants are those Mennonites who migrated in the nineteenth century and settled in the western United States, primarily Kansas, and Canada.

Mennonites have been proud of a heritage of biblical theology and avoidance of hairsplitting, unproductive attempts at philosophical sophistries. Nevertheless, they have a definite theological heritage in Swiss and Dutch Anabaptist ideas. Except for the distinctive themes illustrated in the Schleitheim Confession, Mennonites would have little problem with the major affirmations of mainline Christian churches. These have never been a point of conflict.

Crucial for Mennonites are ecclesiology and separation from the world. Mennonites share a doctrine of the church based on the concept of ecclesia, the called-out fellowship of believers in mission. The tendency is to emphasize the local congregation and to build wider fellowships based on a commonality of belief. Ministers (bishops) arise out of the fellowship as do deacons; the exact methods for choosing them varies. Casting lots was a favorite method. The Dordrecht Confession of 1632 was adopted by the American church and is still a doctrinal standard for most Mennonites. According to the Dordrecht confession, the Bible is the source of belief, and emphasis is placed upon the believer's direct encounter with the living Christ and the work of the Spirit within. The pietism, emphasis on the practical life in the Spirit, is worked out in the mutual, shared existence of the church. The church, not the state, is the basic society for the true Christian, according to the Dordrecht Confession.

THE AMISH. Among the more liberal Swiss Mennonites of the late seventeenth century there arose a party led by Jacob Amman, a minister in the Emmenthal congregation. Because his family records have not been found, little can be said of him except for the practices he promoted among both the Swiss Mennonites and the Swiss Brethren. Amman insisted upon a strict interpretation of discipline. For his practices he appealed to Menno Simons's writings and to the Dordrecht Confession of Faith of 1632, which has become the recognized statement of doctrine for both Amish and Old Mennonites in America.

In his preaching, Amman stressed the practice of avoidance. A member whose spouse was under the ban was neither to eat nor sleep with him or her until the ban was lifted. Amman also reintroduced foot washing. Non-religious customs of the period—hooks and eyes instead of buttons, shoestrings instead of buttons, bonnets and aprons, broad brimmed hats, and beards and long hair—became identifying characteristics of church members.

All of the Mennonites during Amman's time were in a loose federation and strove to remain of one mind. Amman's strict interpretation of the "avoidance" clause in the ban led to a division among the Mennonites, with some following Amman and separating themselves from the others. Amman placed under the ban all who disagreed with him. After a few years of separation, Amman and his associates tried to reconcile with the other Mennonites, but the reconciliation efforts failed. Since then, the Amish have been independent of the Mennonites.

In the early 1700s, the Amish began to appear in America, the earliest congregation on record being the one along North Kill Creek in Berks County, Pennsylvania. Colonies were later planted in eastern Pennsylvania, Ohio, Indiana, Illinois, and Iowa. Until recently, their strength had been in Lancaster County, Pennsylvania.

The Amish represent a reactionary faction in the Mennonite movement. They have gone far beyond a practice common to Western Christianity of seeking to actualize an apostolic church. The Amish have attempted to freeze a culture, that of the late seventeenth century. As time has passed and the surrounding culture has discarded more and more elements of Jacob Amman's time, greater and greater pressure has been placed on the Amish to conform with the modern world. Each generation has brought new issues to Amish leaders. Decisions must constantly be made on accommodating to the prevailing culture on different points. Public school laws, consolidated farming (and the shortage of available farm lands), automobile-oriented road systems, and tourists are just a few of the issues that have joined perennial Amish problems such as in-breeding. A lack of consensus on these issues has produced the several schisms they have experienced.

In order to deal with the various "liberal" trends and local schisms, a general conference was held in Wayne County, Ohio, in 1862, followed by others annually for several years. The conferences only accentuated the various trends. Before the conferences were discontinued, the more conservative "Old Order" Amish withdrew and organized separately. Others formed more liberal bodies that have moved toward the Mennonites in practice.

THE RUSSIAN MENNONITES. Some Anabaptist brethren, instead of coming to America, chose instead to go to Russia at the invitation of Catherine the Great in the 1760s. Catherine wanted colonists to develop newly acquired territory and promised religious freedom and local autonomy. Colonies were settled mainly in southern Russia and the Crimean area. Yet there arose in Russia a "pharaoh who knew not Joseph," Czar Alexander II.

In 1870, a program of Russification was begun by the Czar. Its thrust was directed at German colonists, including the Mennonites, whose presence seemed threatening to the rising Russian military power. Local autonomy was ended, the Russian language was to replace German, schools were to come under Russian tutelage, and exemption from universal military service was dropped. Immigration seemed the only recourse for the Mennonites. Among those who came to America, many belonged to the Mennonite Church, the first church described in this chapter. Other Russian immigrants belonged to churches that, in Russia had broken off from the Mennonite church there. The settlers brought these previously formed schismatic churches to America: the Evangelical Mennonite Church (Kleine Gemeinde), the Evangelical Mennonite Brethren Conference, the Mennonite Brethren Church, and the Crimean Brethren, whose members in this country joined the Mennonite Brethren Church in 1960. These churches are described below, as is the General Conference Mennonite Church, which was formed in this country instead of in Russia.

The first immigrants to North America included Bernard Warkentin, Cornelius Jansen, and David Goerz, who were prominent in the resettlement program. New communities were established in open lands from Oklahoma to Manitoba, with the largest settlements in Kansas.

THE BRETHREN. Among those awakened by the Pietist movement of the late seventeenth century, a movement that stressed personal piety over rigid doctrinal conformity, was a group of citizens of the Palatinate, an area now in West Germany. Influenced by the Mennonites in the vicinity, they decided to separate themselves from the state church. Their leader, Alexander Mack, recorded the event: "In the year 1708 eight persons agreed to establish a covenant of a good conscience with God, to accept all ordinances of Jesus Christ as an easy yoke, and thus to follow after their Lord Jesus—their good and loyal shepherd—as true sheep in joy or sorrow until the blessed end. . . . These eight persons united with one another as brethren and sisters in the covenant of the cross of Jesus Christ as a church of Christian believers" (Donald F. Durnbaugh, *European Origins of the Brethren*. [Elgin, IL: The Brethren Press, 1958], 121). As a part of the act of forming the new church, they rebaptized themselves, thus placing themselves in the Anabaptist tradition, a tradition reinforced by their German language upon their arrival in America.

While the Palatinate had changed state churches after the religious wars, neither Catholics, Lutherans, nor Reformed were happy with separatists, i.e., those who wanted to separate from the state church. People like the Brethren were subject to persecution, and rather than give up their faith, the Brethren migrated, first to Wittgenstein and then the Netherlands. Toleration diminished even more as they began to receive members from the state church.

During this time, the Brethren became influenced by Gottfried Arnold, a historian. Arnold had written several books on the early life of the church that he believed normative for all Christians. He introduced through his writings the idea of triune immersion as the proper mode of baptism. The believer, on his knees in the water, is immersed three times in the name of the Father, Son, and Holy Spirit. The Brethren also continued a close contact with the Mennonites.

By 1719, little more than a decade after their formation, the Brethren began to think about the New World as a home. Having become familiar with William Penn's experiment in Pennsylvania from his continental visits and those of his Quaker followers, they began to migrate to Germantown. The migration was completed by 1735 and the few remaining Brethren in Europe became Mennonites.

The first Brethren Church in America was established in 1723 after the Brethren had corresponded with their European counterparts. They chose Peter Becker (1687–1758) as their pastor. He proceeded to baptize the first American converts and preside over the first love feast, a service that included footwashing, a group meal, and the Lord's Supper. This church is the mother congregation of the present-day Church of the Brethren.

THE FRIENDS (QUAKERS). The middle 1600s in England was a time in which the early stages of the Reformation were beginning to be felt in a practical way. Dissidents whose perspective reflected the religious ferment of the continent began to appear. One of the men whose perspective was in line with that of the continental radical reformers was George Fox (1624–1691)—mystic, psychic, social activist, and founder of the Quakers.

Fox had begun to preach in 1647 after experiencing an inner illumination and hearing a voice that said, "There is One, even Christ Jesus, that can speak to thy condition." The experiences of the inner light came as a psychic-spiritual awakening, and Fox developed a reputation as "a young man with a discerning spirit." Fox was a powerful preacher and a charismatic personality. A wide variety of the gifts of the Spirit (I Cor. 12:4–11) appeared regularly throughout his ministry.

Fox was an intense activist on the social scene. He was an early prohibitionist and a preacher against holidays, entertainments and sports, saying that such activities directed man's thoughts to vanity and looseness. During the wars waged when Oliver Cromwell ruled England, Fox emerged as a peace advocate, a position held by many radical reformers. Thrown into prison for his activities, he converted the jailer and became a pioneer prison reformer.

A group of followers soon gathered around Fox and, in 1667, they were organized into a system of monthly, quarterly, and yearly meetings. Their one doctrinal peculiarity was their belief in the inner light. The Quakers believed that God's revelation was not limited to the Bible but continued in a living daily contact between the believer and the divine Spirit. The light would lead to the road to perfection. Fox's followers, always on the edge of mere subjectivism, escaped it by constantly testing their light by the teachings and example of Jesus.

The Bible is the source book of the Quaker faith and from it Fox drew many ideas which became part of the peculiar ethos of Quaker life and an offense to non-Quakers. For example, Fox believed that much of the activity of the world was vanity. He exhorted Quakers to lead simple lives which were not wasted in frivolity. Dress was to be simple. No wigs were to be worn, nor were gold or vain decorations on clothing. A Quaker costume developed from these injunctions. The biblical use of the familiar tense (thy and thou) became standard for Quakers, although most have now deserted this practice.

The Quaker organization was built around "meetings" for friends in a certain area. These meetings—monthly, quarterly, and yearly—handled business on an increasingly geographical basis. For many years, the monthly and quarterly meetings handled organization and discipline. They developed as needs manifested themselves. As early as 1668, a "General Meeting of Ministers" was held. This meeting, repeated in 1672, evolved into the yearly meeting as a general organizational body. Thus the word "meeting" can mean "church."

Quaker worship also took on a particular form, in negative reaction to Anglican formality and liturgy and in positive reaction to the inner light doctrine. Without clergy, the Quakers would sit in silence and wait for the Spirit to move. Often, no word would be spoken, but as Francis Howgill noted: "The Lord of heaven and earth we found to be near at hand, and we waited on him in pure silence, our minds out of all things, His heavenly presence appeared in our assemblies, when there was no language, tongue or speech from any creature."

Through the years under the influence of other Protestants, particularly the holiness churches that take John Wesley as their founder, free church worship patterns began to replace the Quaker meeting. For example, the Quakers adopted such practices of the holiness churches as a more programmed worship service, with a minister who would preach. Contemporary Quakers can be divided into the unprogrammed, who follow the old Quaker meeting format, and the programmed, who have an ordered worship that includes hymns, vocal prayer, Bible reading, and a sermon.

QUAKERS IN THE UNITED STATES. Quakers found their way to America within a decade of the beginning of George Fox's public ministry in England; individuals arrived as early as 1655. They found at first no more favorable home in the colonies than they had left in England. However, soon Rhode Island became their sanctuary and the first meeting was established there in 1661. George Fox's visit in 1671–73 spurred the growth of the infant group.

In the 1660s, the man destined to become the most important figure in the early life of the Quakers in the colonies—William Penn (1644–1718)—joined the British Friends. Penn was the son of a British admiral, and becoming a Quaker after meeting George Fox, he became deeply impressed by the problem of persecution that they faced. Heir to a small fortune from the king, Penn accepted a tract of land (the state of Pennsylvania) instead of the money. Here he established a Quaker colony and began the great experiment of trying to mold a colony on a biblical model. To the everlasting credit of Penn, religious freedom was the order of the day, even for Jews and Turks.

In the next century, American Quakers would begin to make social history. Believing as they did in social justice, especially as it expressed itself in the equality of man, Quakers would begin a campaign against slavery. One of their number, John Woolman, would be a widely traveled leader in early Christian anti-slavery efforts. A mission was begun among the Indians, in line with the same belief in the equality of man. Friends controlled the Pennsylvania government until 1756, when they gave up their seats rather than vote for war measures during the French and Indian War.

The first General Meeting of Friends was held in 1681 at Burlington, New Jersey, and for several years one was held each year at both Burlington and Philadelphia. In 1685, these two meetings assumed the name The General Yearly Meeting for Friends of Pennsylvania, East Jersey, and of the Adjacent Provinces. This became the Philadelphia Yearly Meeting, the oldest Quaker group still in existence in the United States.

Quakers, induced by the promise of freedom of conscience, migrated into tracts of land in the southern United States and established large settlements. Slavery soon became an issue and in the decades before, and after 1800, most Quakers left the South as a protest and moved to Indiana and Ohio. To this day, Quaker strength lies across the Midwest and is virtually non-existent south of the Ohio River.

As Quakerism expanded westward, regionally based yearly meetings were formed as autonomous units but in harmony with eastern counterparts. As time passed and issues came and went, these yearly meetings became the basis for denominational units and late nineteenth century ecumenical endeavors.

The general unity of American Friends remained until the 1820s, when schism began to rend the Friends and produced the various denominational bodies that exist today. Philadelphia remains as a home of broadly based, if more conservative, Quakerism.

Quakers, while fitting clearly within the free church tradition and following the European spiritual Anabaptist faith, deviate from other groups at several points. The baptism issue, a matter of intense Anabaptist interest, was solved by dropping water baptism entirely. As a natural outgrowth of Schwenckfelder belief in the primacy of the spiritual, Quakers hold that the one baptism of Ephesians 4:4–5 is the inward baptism of the Holy Spirit. (See the article on the Schwenckfelder Church in America.) Women also have had an unusual status, their right to full participation having been accepted at an early date. They were accepted into the ministry earlier than in most other churches.

Doctrinally, Quakers have followed a Protestant lead and profess a belief in the fatherhood of God, Jesus Christ as Lord and Savior, the Holy Spirit, salvation by faith, and the priesthood of believers. Quakers do, however, take a free church anti-creedal stance, and while most Quaker bodies have a statement of belief, they usually preface it with a disclaimer against a static orthodoxy, and a wide range of beliefs are present. Evangelical practices became a dominant element in the nineteenth century and, as the century closed, Wesleyan holiness became a force. In the early twentieth century, a liberal-conservative split began to emerge, leading to several schisms. The conservative elements tended to identify with holiness ideals and withdrew from the larger Friends' Meetings to form most of the smaller bodies. The Evangelical Friends Alliance formed in 1847 serves as an ecumenical body for the conservatives.

While divided into several denominations, Quakers have been able to keep an intense social activism witness in some intra-family structures. The American Friends Service Committee founded during World War I emerged as an expression of national loyalty seeking to serve in war-alternative activities. It has gained wide respect for its refugee work. The Friends Committee for National Legislation is a non-partisan lobby group.

OTHER EUROPEAN FREE CHURCHES. Besides the churches in the four main free church traditions that have been discussed above, Europe has been the birthing place of numerous free church groups over the centuries. Some of these are the product of the particular ministry of one person, the church forming around his/her teachings. Some have followed the emergence of a revival movement in a given limited area. Still others represent a renewal of piety among a particular ethnic group within a larger society or the protest of what is felt to be a repressive action by a state church. In each case, however, they represent a new religious impulse separate from a country's dominant religious establishment. The great majority of the European free churches have never been transplanted to North America.

Among the groups that have come, one set arrived from Russia. Beginning with what was termed the Great Schism in the seventeenth century, the Russian Orthodox Church watched a series of dissenting sects emerge to disturb the unity of the religious landscape. In the 1650s, the somewhat natural division between the better educated urban hierarchy of the Russian church and the poorer and less educated clergy and laity in the scattered rural communities was accentuated by a controversy over ritual. The controversy centered around Nikon (1605–1681), a young monk who, having attained the favor of the czar, rose from obscurity to become the church's patriarch. Nikon tried to introduce a greater degree of uniformity into Orthodox worship, using the Greek church as his standard. He placed very high on his program the correcting of the numerous corrupt service books then in use. Most of his changes were received as simply new innovations. Gradually, as unrest with changes led to the burning of new ritual books, the Czar abandoned him, and Nikon was banished. However, at the same council of the church in 1666 at which Nikon was deposed, his reforms were adopted. Those who opposed the reforms, the Raskol, were excommunicated. The Raskol, or Old Believers, developed as a separate body after the council. They would later divide into two main groups, the *Popovtsy,* or priestists and the *Bezpopovtsy,* or priestless.

The immediate problem of the Popovtsy was the establishment of episcopal leadership, as no bishops chose to join with them.

Bishops were most necessary for the ordination of priests. For almost two centuries, they gained their priests from among those who left the state church. It was not until the nineteenth century that they were able to develop a hierarchy. In 1844 some Old Believers residing in the territory controlled by the Austro-Hungarian Empire were able to persuade the government to designate an Old Believers' episcopal see at Bela Krynica (or Belokrinitsa). In 1846, Ambrose, the former bishop of Sarajevo, assumed the new position. Before the Russian government could react, Ambrose consecrated a number of bishops for the Popovtsy Old Believers. Bishops in this "Belokrinitskaya" line of succession continue to the present with archbishops in Moscow and in Galati, Romania (where the see of Bela Krynica moved after being overrun by the Russians during World War II).

In 1918, in the wake of the Russian Revolution, Patriarch Tikhon consecrated a bishop for the "Yedinovertsy," a group of Old Believers that had made a partial peace with the established church at the beginning of the nineteenth century. The established church had agreed to ordain their priests and allow them to follow the old rites. Their first bishop was killed in 1921 by the Communists, and it is believed that his successor met a similar fate. A third line of Popovtsy, the *Beglopopovtsy,* or Wandering Priestists, gained their own episcopal authority in the Soviet Union following World War II. The archbishop resides at Kuibyshev (Samara).

The second group of Old Believers, the Bezpopovtsy, originated as people began to argue against the legitimacy of an episcopally ordained priesthood who alone could dispense the sacraments. As the basic argument was accepted, disagreements as to its implications multiplied. Some argued that they possessed a presbyterial succession of priestly authority and that their priests, ordained by a presbytery (a group of priests rather than a bishop), were able to administer the sacraments. Others argued that the Russian Church had gone into apostasy and hence lost the sacramental office altogether. As differing opinions appeared, so did numerous divisions of the Bezpopovtsy. Without a hierarchy to provide a point of visible unity, differing parties turned into new sects with great ease. Eventually, most groups moved to limit their sacraments to those which laymen could administer—baptism and absolution. Communion was either dropped (some claiming that every meal eaten in the right spirit constituted a communion with Christ) or served with elements believed to have been consecrated in the days of true priests, that is, before Nikon.

Marriage became the most crucial problem for the Priestless, as such unions can only be consecrated by a valid priest. Some tried celibacy, while others did away with marriage but allowed sexual relations as a concession to the flesh. Eventually, most adopted a form of marriage that was simply blessed by the community elder.

Somewhat different in their origin are the various groups that arose around new mystical impulses in the decades after the Great Schism. Leaders of these new groups emphasized the role of inner illumination, the place of morality over ritual, and the need for simple biblical faith uncorrupted by the teachings of the Greek fathers. Among the most important of these new groups were the Khlysty, the Doukhobors, and the Molokans.

The Khlysty originated in 1631 in Kostroma Province when a peasant, Daniel Filippov, proclaimed himself God Sabaoth, who had come to give new commandments to the people. He selected another peasant to be his main prophet whom he designated as the Christ. The mystical and ascetic doctrine of the Khlysty found many supporters throughout Russia, and a series of Christs appeared to lead the group from generation to generation. The periodic attempts by the government to suppress them usually spurred their further spread.

Among people in the Ukraine attracted to the mystical emphases, but repulsed by some of their more radical notions, there arose a sect called the Doukhobors (literally, Spirit Wrestlers), originally a derisive name given to them by the Russian archbishop at Ekate-

rinoslav. During the leadership of Sabellius Kapustin over the group, they were deported to the Molochnye Valley. Kapustin took the opportunity to reorganize the Doukhobors into a communal society. Leadership continued in Kapustin's family after his death until 1886. At that time a split occurred and Peter Verigin emerged as the leader of the larger faction. It was he who arranged for most of his followers to leave Russia for Canada at the end of the nineteenth century. With the assistance of Leo Tolstoy, approximately 7,400 settled in western Canada beginning in 1899.

The Molokans were started by Simeon Uklein (1733–?), the son-in-law of a Doukhobor leader in the late eighteenth century. He rejected his father-in-laws disdain for the Bible and his claims to be "Christ." Taking approximately 70 followers, he formed a rival group. He proclaimed the Bible the sole authority for the faithful and rejected the allegorical methods so favored by the more mystical sects. He emphasized moral content more than concerns for inner illumination. Among their moral precepts was pacifism.

The Molokans' problems in Russia began with the introduction of compulsory military service by the Czar, but became crucial after their refusal to bear arms in the Russo-Japanese War. Approximately 2,000 came to the United States between 1904 and the beginning of World War I.

Besides the Russian groups, free churches from various parts of Europe such as Norway and Switzerland have been transplanted to America. In all likelihood, others, as yet operating quietly out of members' homes, have arrived, and more will come in the future.

ECUMENISM. European Free-Churches provide a church home to people who have left the more established and state churches of Europe. They do not share a common theological heritage, except for sharing some basic affirmation with all of Christendom. Thus, there are no ecumenical structures which unite these churches in a common organization. The free churches have a common heritage of persecution by the older churches. They have disassociated themselves from such ecumenical organization as the World Council of Churches and National Council of Churches, which traditionally have been dominated by the older Reformation churches.

The free churches should not be seen as unresponsive to twentieth century ecumenical imperative. They generally favor structures that demand less commitment than the council of churches. They have formed family ecumenical structures for those churches which share either a Mennonite (World Mennonite Conference) or Friends (Friends World Committee for Consultation) heritage.

Sources—European Free Church

Mennonites, among the most historically conscious of religious communities, have established a number of historical libraries. The Archives of the Mennonite Church is at 1700 S. Main, Goshen, IN 46526, and issues the *Mennonite Historical Bulletin.* Canadian history and archives are focused at the Mennonite Heritage Centre supported by the General Conference of Mennonites in Canada, 600 Shaftsbury Blvd., Winnipeg, Manitoba R3P 0M4.

The primary archives of the Church of the Brethren is at 1451 Dundee Ave., Elgin, IL 60521. The nearby Bethany Theological Seminary publishes the quarterly *Brethren Life and Thought.*

The Friends support the Friends Historical Library at Swathmore College, Swathmore, PA 19081 and the Friends Historical Association, headquartered at the Haverford College Library, Haverford, PA 19041. The association publishes the semi-annual *Quaker History.*

General Sources

Durnbaugh, Donald F. *The Believer's Church.* New York: The Macmillan Co., 1968. 315 pp.

Grimm, Harold J. *The Reformation Era.* New York: Macmillan Co., 1973. 594 pp.

Jones, Rufus M. *Spiritual Reformers of the Sixteenth and Seventeenth Centuries.* Boston: Beacon Press, 1914. 362 pp.

Littell, Franklin H. *The Anabaptist View of the Church.* New York: The Macmillan Co., 1952. 231 pp.

Spotts, Charles D. *Denominations Originating in Lancaster County, Pennsylvania.* Lancaster, PA: Franklin and Marshall College Library, 1963. 41 pp.

Williams, George H. *The Radical Reformation.* Philadelphia: The Westminster Press, 1962. 924 pp.

THE MENNONITES

Bender, Harold S. *Two Centuries of American Mennonite Literature, 1727–1928.* Goshen, IN: The Mennonite Historical Society, 1929.

The Complete Writings of Menno Simons, 1491–1561. Scottsdale, PA: Herald Press, 1956. 1092 pp.

Epp, Frank H. *Mennonites in Canada, 1786–1920.* Toronto: Macmillan of Canada, 1974. 480 pp.

Mennonites of Canada, 1920–1940. Toronto: Macmillan of Canada, 1982. 640 pp.

Hostetler, Beulah Stauffer. *American Mennonites and Protestant Movements.* Scottdale, PA: Herald Press, 1987. 366 pp.

Hostetler, John A. *Mennonite Life.* Scottsdale, PA: Herald Press, 1959. 39 pp.

Loewen, Harry, ed. *Mennonite Images: Historical, Cultural, and Literary Images Dealing With Mennonite Issues.* Winnipeg, MB: Hyperion Press, 1980. 279 pp.

MacMaster, Richard K. *Land, Piety, Peoplehood.* Scottdale, PA: Herald Press, 1985. 340 pp.

The Mennonite Encyclopedia. 4 Vols. Scottsdale, PA: Mennonite Publishing House, 1955–59.

Quiring, Walter and Helen Bartel *Mennonites in Canada, A Pictorial Review.* Altona, MN: D. W. Friesen & Sons, 1961. 208 pp.

Redekop, Calvin W. *Mennonite Society.* Baltimore, MD: Johns Hopkins University Press, 1989. 397 pp.

Smith, C. Henry. *The Mennonites.* Berne, IN: Mennonite Book Concern, 1920. 340 pp.

Smith, Elmer L. *Meet the Mennonites.* Witmer, PA: Allied Arts, 1961. 42 pp.

Springer, Nelson P., and A. J. Klassen. *Mennonite Bibliography, 1631–1961.* 2 vols. Scottsdale, PA: Herald Press, 1977.

Waltner, James H. *This We Believe.* Newton, KS: Faith and Life Press, 1968. 230 pp.

Wenger, John Christian. *The Doctrines of the Mennonites.* Scottsdale, PA: Mennonite Publishing House, 1950. 160 pp.

THE AMISH

Hostetler, John A. *Amish Life.* Scottsdale, PA: Herald Press, 1959. 39 pp. Rev. ed.: 1983. 48 pp.

———. *Amish Society.* Baltimore: The Johns Hopkins Press, 1963. Rev. ed.: 1993. 435 pp.

———. *An Annotated Bibliography on the Amish.* Scottsdale, PA: Mennonite House, 1951. 100 pp.

Kraybill, Donald B. *The Riddle of Amish Society.* Baltimore: Johns Hopkins University Press, 1989. 304 pp.

Rice, Charles S., and Rollin C. Stinmetz. *The Amish Year.* New Brunswick, NJ: Rutgers University Press, 1956. 224 pp.

Schreiber, William. *Our Amish Neighbors.* Chicago: University of Chicago Press, 1962. 227 pp.

Smith, Elmer Lewis. *The Amish.* Witmer, PA: Applied Arts, 1966. 34 pp.

———. *The Amish People.* New York: Exposition Press, 1958. 258 pp.

THE RUSSIAN MENNONITES

Smith, C. Henry. *The Coming of the Russian Mennonites.* Berne, IN: Mennonite Book Concern, 1927. 296 pp.

Stucky, Harley J. *A Century of Russian Mennonite History in America.* North Newton, KS: Mennonite Press, Inc., 1974. 119 pp.

THE BRETHREN

The Brethren Encyclopedia. 2 Vols. Philadelphia, PA: The Brethren Encyclopedia, Inc., 1983.

Durnbaugh, Donald F. "A Brethren Bibliography, 1713–1963." *Brethren Life and Thought* 9, 1–2 (Winter and Summer, 1964): 3–177.

———. *The Brethren in Colonial America.* Elgin, IL: The Brethren Press, 1967. 659 pp.

———. *The European Origins of the Brethren.* Elgin, IL: Brethren Press, 1958. 463 pp.

———. "Guide to Research in Brethren History." Elgin, IL: Church of the Brethren General Board, 1977. 16 pp.

Holsinger, H. R. *History of the Tunkers and the Brethren Church.* Lathrop, CA: The Author, 1901. 827 pp.

Mallot, Floyd E. *Studies in Brethren History.* Elgin, IL: Brethren Publishing House, 1954. 382 pp.

Sappington, Roger E. *The Brethren in the New Nation.* Elgin, IL: Brethren Press, 1976. 496 pp.

Willoughby, William G. *Counting the Cost.* Elgin, IL: Brethren Press, 1979. 176 pp.

THE FRIENDS (QUAKERS)

Baltzell, E. Digby. *Puritan Boston and Quaker Philadelphia.* Boston: Beacon Press, 1979. 585 pp.

Barbour, Hugh. *The Quakers.* New York: Greenwood Press, 1988. 407 pp.

Barbour, Hugh, and Arthur O. Roberts. *Early Quaker Writings, 1650–1700.* Grand Rapids, MI: William B. Eerdmans Publishing Co., 1973. 622 pp.

Benjamin, Philip S. *The Philadelphia Quakers in the Industrial Age.* Philadelphia: Temple University Press, 1976. 301 pp.

Brinton, Howard H. *Children of Light.* New York: Macmillan Co., 1938. 416 pp.

Comfort, William Wistar. *The Quaker Way of Life.* Philadelphia: The Blakiston Co., 1945. 178 pp.

Elliott, Errol T. *Quakers on the American Frontier.* Richmond, IN: Friends United Press, 1969. 434 pp.

Evans, Thomas. *A Concise Account of the Religious Society of Friends.* Philadelphia: Friends Books Store, n.d. 161 pp.

Friends Directory of Meeting, Churches, and Worship Groups in the Section of the Americas & Resource Guide. Philadelphia, PA: Friends World Committee for Consultation, Section of the Americas, 1996. 256 pp.

Holder, Charles Frederick. *The Quakers in Great Britain and America.* Los Angeles: Neuner Co., 1913. 669 pp.

Jones, Rufus. *The Quakers in the American Colonies.* New York: W. W. Norton & Co., 1966. 606 pp.

Kenworthy, Leonard S. *Quakerism.* Durbin, IN: Prinit Press, 1981. 215 pp.

Peck, George T. *What Is Quakerism?: A Primer.* Wallingford, PA: Pendle Hill Publications, 1988. 47 pp.

Quakers Around the World. London: Friends World Committee for Consultation, 1994. 157 pp.

Van Etten, Henry. *George Fox and the Quakers.* New York: Harper, 1959. 191 pp.

Other European Free Church Traditions

Bolshakoff, Serge. *Russian Nonconformity*. Philadelphia: Westminster Press, 1921. 192 pp.

Conybeare, Frederick C. *Russian Dissenters*. Cambridge, MA: Harvard University Press, 1921. 370 pp.

Struve, Nikita. *Christians in Contemporary Russia*. New York: Charles Scribner's Sons, 1967. 464 pp.

Chapter 11

Baptist Family

Consult the "Contents" pages to locate the entries in Part III,
the Directory Listings Sections, that comprise this family.

The Baptist churches are free churches, called "free" to show that they are free associations of adult believers. Other free-churches include those in the European free-church family, discussed in the previous chapter, and those in the independent Fundamentalist family, discussed in the next chapter. A cursory examination might suggest that the Baptists are a subgroup of the European free-church family, which includes the Mennonites, the Amish, the Brethren, and the Quakers. The Baptists, like that family, are anti-authoritarian, lay-oriented, and nonliturgical; they oppose state churches, and they baptize adult believers, not infants.

But the size of the Baptist churches and their continued growth suggest significant differences between the Baptists and the relatively small European free-church family, and such is the case. The Baptists make up the second largest family on the American religious scene, second only to Roman Catholics. One difference between the Baptists and the smaller European free churches is historical. The Baptists emerged out of British Puritanism, whereas the European free churches developed from the initial efforts of the continental radical reformers. Second, Baptists are free from some significant hindrances to growth that characterize the European free churches. These hindrances include pacifism, the ban (a form of excommunication), and prohibitions against participation in public life such as voting, holding public office, and serving in the armed forces. Finally, the Baptists' evangelistic revivalistic lifestyle has attracted many followers. All of these factors help explain why great numbers of people find the Baptist churches appealing.

HISTORY. History is a problem for the Baptists. When and where did the Baptists originate? Baptist scholars give widely divergent answers to that question.

One school, the earliest to appear in Baptist circles, holds to what has popularly been called the "Jerusalem-Jordan-John theory." These scholars believe that the Baptists can be dated to John the Baptist and his baptism of Jesus in the Jordan River. David Benedict, writing in the second decade of the nineteenth century, expresses this view:

"All sects trace their origin to the Apostles, or at least to the early ages of Christianity. But men, and especially the powerful ones, have labored hard to cut off the Baptists from this common retreat. They have often asserted and taken much pains to prove that the people now called Baptists originated with the mad men of Mumnster, about 1522. We have only to say to this statement, that it is not true. And not withstanding all that has been said to the contrary, we still date the origin of our sentiments, and the beginning of our denomination, about the year of our Lord twenty-nine or thirty; for at that period John the Baptist began to immerse professed believers in Jordan and Enon, and to prepare the way for the coming of the Lord's Annointed, and for the setting up of his kingdom." (David Benedict, *A General History of the Baptist Denomination in America and Other Parts of the World* [Boston: Lincoln and Edmunds, 1813], 1:92).

Followers of this school generally deny that the term Protestant has any reference to them because, they assert, they predate Lu-

ther. They are also concerned with what might be thought of as an "apostolic succession" of Baptist congregations and take great pains to define and locate it.

A second group of scholars criticized the first group for seeking a continuity of organization and called upon them to seek rather a continuity of doctrine. The second group tended to locate Baptist organizational origins in the Anabaptist wing of the Reformation. (Anabaptists called for an adult believer's baptism, which necessitated the rebaptism of those baptized as infants.) This second view was theologically, if not historically, attractive for a church that sought to recreate the first century church. As Thomas Armitage put it:

"If it can be shown that their churches are the most like the Apostolic that now exist, and that the elements which make them so have passed successfully through the long struggle, succession from the times of their blessed Lord gives them the noblest history that any people can crave. To procure a servile imitation of merely primitive things has never been the mission of Baptists. Their work has been to promote the living reproduction of New Testament Christians, and so to make the Christlike old, the ever delightfully new. Their perpetually fresh appeal to the Scriptures as the only warrant for their existence at all must not be cut off, in a foolish attempt to turn the weapons of the hierarchy against itself. The sword of the Spirit must still be their only arm of service, offensive and defensive. An appeal to false credentials now would only cut them off from the use of all that now remains undiscovered and unapplied in the word of God. The distinctive attribute in the Kingdom of Christ is life; not an historic life, but a life supernatural, flowing eternally from Christ alone by his living truth." (Thomas Armitage, *A History of the Baptists* [New York: Bryan, Taylor and Co., 1887], 11–12).

The final school of thought on Baptist origins, which gained ascendancy in the twentieth century, looks to seventeenth-century England for the beginnings of the Baptist movement. Robert Torbet, a twentieth-century exponent of this view, pointed out in relation to the first school:

"To say, however, that any single one of these early segments of the Christian church may be identified definitively with the communion we now know as Baptists is to make an assertion which lacks convincing historical support. That there are similarities of teaching between each of these groups and the Baptists is not to be denied. Yet, although it is not possible to trace a clear lineage of Baptists as an historical entity back to the early church, Baptist history may certainly be traced from the stirring days of the Protestant Reformation." (Robert G. Torbet, *A History of Baptists* [Chicago: The Judson Press, 1950], 15).

Torbet also refuted the Anabaptist theory by holding up the difference between Baptist and Anabaptist theology:

"Baptists have not shared with Anabaptists the latter's aversion to oath-taking and holding public office. Neither have they adopted the Anabaptists' doctrine of pacifism, or their theological views concerning the incarnation, soul sleeping, and the necessity of observing an apostolic succession in the administration of baptism." (Torbet, 62).

One could also note the lack of vital intercourse and familial attachment between the contemporary Baptist churches and the contemporary Anabaptist churches (i.e., the Mennonites, Hutterites, and Amish) and the lack of Anabaptists in Baptist ecumenical bodies.

Henry C. Vedder is cited by Torbet as an able exponent of the third school. Vedder believed that "after 1610 we have an unbroken succession of Baptist Churches" (Torbet, 201). Further support for this third school is found in the theology of the early Baptists: they continued to operate out of their basic Calvinist theology, deviating at two points—the sacraments and the church—rather than adopt a Mennonite theology which was adjusted for their use. While they differ with their Presbyterian and Congregationalist forefathers on two issues, they disagree with the Anabaptists on a number of issues.

English Baptists can trace their history to Holland where Separatists had located after the execution of some of their leaders in 1593. John Smyth's congregation and another led by John Robinson arrived in Holland in the first decade of the seventeenth century. In a short time Smyth issued a tract, *The Differences of the Churches of the Separation* (1608), in which he explained why the two congregations could not fellowship. Baptism was not an issue; extemporaneous preaching was. Smyth's congregation became heavily influenced by the Dutch Mennonites and in the winter of 1608–09, Smyth and about 40 people were rebaptized. Continued Anabaptist influence led to schism, however, and Smyth, whose congregation was absorbed by the Mennonites, returned to England. The schism resulted from the collision of the Calvinists' belief in predestination and the Mennonites' belief in free will. Thomas Helwys, the leader of the schismatic group, tried to reject both by adopting an Armenian theology. He also rejected any attempt at tracing the Apostolic succession of the true church.

John Smyth founded the first Baptist Church on English soil in 1611. In England and later in America, the first Baptists were Armenian in their theology instead of Calvinist. That means the first Baptists believed in a "general" atonement—salvation is possible for all—not in the "particular" atonement or limited atonement— predestination—of the Calvinist Baptists. Thus the first Baptists were called General Baptists; the Calvinist Baptists were called Particular Baptists. The growth of Smyth's church and local squabbles among Baptists led to the founding of five more churches in England by 1630 and 41 more by 1644.

The founding of the second main grouping of Baptists, the Particular Baptists, came about through the Puritans' move toward a Baptist position in the 1630s. In 1638, a group in the church at Southwark pastored by Henry Jacob rejected Congregational Church baptism because it was of the Church of England. Anabaptism began to emerge; dismissals led to the formation of a Calvinistic Baptist church pastored by John Spilsbury.

Among these Particular Baptists (or Calvinistic Baptists), the issue of immersion as the correct mode of baptism was raised. In 1644, they promulgated the London Confession of Faith, which provided for immersion and incorporated Calvinist theology with a call for religious freedom. This confession outlined the major issues which were to separate Baptists from other Christian bodies. Baptists would be congregationally governed but completely separated from the state. While being orthodox Christians, they would hold to adult baptism by immersion as the Apostolic, hence correct, mode of baptism. They would divide among themselves on Calvinist and Armenian lines.

A third Baptist group believed that Saturday was the true Sabbath. This belief arose as early as 1617. Overall, Seventh-day Baptists have never made up a large percentage of Baptists, but have persisted as one of the oldest continually existing Baptist bodies, and have been the ultimate source of almost all Sabbatarian teaching in the United States.

In rejecting affiliation with the state and asserting the sovereignty of the local congregation, Baptists took the major step toward their typical form of congregational government. The next step came in the 1600s when various issues led local congregations to associate together in order to present a united front on an issue. As early as 1624, General Baptists issued a common document against the Mennonites. In 1644, Particular Baptists issued the London Confession. These united-front gatherings eventuated into associations—regular structures for affiliation of congregations. As a rule, General Baptists began to move toward strong associations with more centralized authority, while Particular Baptists tended toward a very loose organization.

BELIEFS. Baptists have generally been among those churches which professed a "noncreedal" theology. This position does not imply an absence of either doctrinal standards or creedal statements. Rather, it suggests that Baptists assign a secondary role to creeds in the life of the church, that they recognize their subordination to the Bible, and that they attempt (by no means always successfully) to refrain from calling individuals to account for their dissent from any particular creedal formulation. In that tone, the Baptists have continually produced confessions of faith with the purpose of acknowledging consensus internally and of informing the world of their stance in relation to other churches.

Among the first of the Baptist confessions were the London Confessions of 1644 and 1677, the latter a revision of the Presbyterian's Westminster Confession, a second edition of which appeared in 1688. In the United States the Philadelphia Confession of 1742, based upon the English Baptists' confessions, circulated widely until the middle of the nineteenth century. Then it began to be superseded by the New Hampshire Confession, which would subsequently assume importance as the most used and revised statement of belief for American Baptists. The confession was approved in 1833 by the Baptist Convention of New Hampshire and represented a modification of the strict Calvinism of the older British confessions whose authors were trying to affirm their close theological ties to the Presbyterians and Congregationalists.

The New Hampshire Confession might have become a mere relic had not J. Newton Brown inserted it in the 1853 edition of *The Baptist Church Manual*, issued by the American Baptist Publication Society. From there it passed into other church manuals used by National (i.e., black), Southern, and Landmark Baptists. It was also found acceptable by some of the fundamentalist Baptists. (For a copy of the text of the New Hampshire Confession (and other Baptist confessions) see the *Encyclopedia of American Religions: Religious Creeds.*)

Briefly, the confession summarized the traditional Christian affirmations of the much longer and more detailed London and Philadelphia confessions. Following the practice of the Westminster Confessions, it begins with an affirmation of the authority of Scripture, followed by paragraphs on the Trinity, the role of grace in the salvation of sinful humanity, and the nature of Christ as the mediator between God and humanity. The major emphasis of the confession is salvation and the Christian life, in which the confession reflects a middle ground between the two major groupings [Calvinist (predestination) and Armenian (free will)] within the larger Baptist community. The confession affirms both Calvinist emphases such as the depravity of humans, the absolute need of God's grace, and the perseverance of the saints, as well as Armenian emphases such as the free gift of salvation to all and the role of human free agency.

The Baptist Confessions place the Baptist clearly in the theological center of Christianity. They affirm the major conclusions of the ecumenical councils of the Christian movement which occurred from the fourth to the eighth century and were embodied in the Nicene and Chalcedonian creeds. They also affirm the principle doctrines of the Protestant Reformation on such issues as the authority of the Bible, salvation by faith alone, and the priesthood of believers.

The confession's very brief statement on the relation of Christians to civil government is similar to the position of both Presbyterians (Westminster Confession) and Mennonites (Dordrecht Confession) in affirming a proper role of civil government and the duty of the Christian to obey it in all matters not opposed to the will of God. Not mentioned, but assumed from earlier statements, the confession denies the Mennonite positions on bearing arms, oaths, and holding government office.

The sacraments are central to the differences between Baptists and the other groups of the Puritan milieu out of which the Baptists emerged. Baptists have generally rejected the notion of sacrament in their consideration of the common Christian rites of baptism and the Lord's Supper. They have termed these rites ordinances, by which they affirm that they are followed out of obedience to God's command (in Scripture). Baptists deny that they have in and of themselves any supernatural effects. The Lord's Supper is considered a memorial meal. Baptism by immersion is seen as an emblem of the believer's faith. It is limited to adults, those old enough to make a profession of faith.

Also at issue between the Baptists and other Puritans was the doctrine of the church and its relation to the state. The Baptist rejected both episcopal (leadership by bishops) and presbyterian (leadership by elders) forms of polity in which a leadership beyond the local church is in authority. To Baptists, the local church is the main focus of church life and authority. Each local church is autonomous and affiliated with other churches for fellowship, common endeavors, and advice. Neither another local church nor a judicatory higher than the local church should be given the power to dictate to any local congregation (though, of course, a group of churches may judge a minister or congregation so different in belief and practice as to be out of fellowship with them). While Congregationalists also favored the power of the local church, Baptists rejected the Congregationalists' attempts to tie themselves to the state. The Congregational Church, when given the opportunity in the Massachusetts colony, tried to establish itself as the one true church, with the state's backing. Under Congregationalist rule, Baptists suffered greatly from the associated intolerance.

IN AMERICA. Some Baptists came to America from England; some emerged from the established British churches in the colonies. The earliest Baptist churches were founded by Roger Williams and John Clarke in Rhode Island. First Church in Providence, founded by Williams, dates to 1639, and Clarke's Newport congregation to 1648. Apart from the Rhode Island churches, the early Baptists were persecuted for not allowing their infants to be baptized. This persecution was all but ended in 1691 with the Americanization of the British government's 1689 Act of Toleration.

In the 1680s, Baptists began to enter the middle colonies. A short-lived congregation was founded in 1684, and, in 1688, the Pennepack Church in Philadelphia opened. Because of the lack of established churches in the middle colonies, the Baptists were to thrive here in a way not possible in the Northeast or South until after the Revolutionary War.

In 1707, the first Baptist association in the colonies was formed. The Philadelphia Association was patterned on an English model. It was a very loose association acting only as an advisory body. To it was left the task of disciplining the ministers and of acting as a council of ordination. In 1742, the association adopted the London Confession of Particular Baptists of 1689, thus identifying American Baptists with Calvinist doctrine. Benjamin Griffith and Jenkin Jones added a statement on the relation of churches and the association "based on theological agreement."

In the South, Baptists arrived in the late 1600s and formed the first Baptist church in 1714. The earliest Baptists were Armenians, which means they opposed strict Calvinist views on predestination and instead believed people were given free will so they could choose whether or not to follow the gospel. From the Armenian Baptists would come the Free-Will Baptist associations.

In the early 1700s the Great Awakening, a revival movement which spread through the colonies in the 1740s, began to affect the Baptists. Their number increased tremendously, but they also found themselves involved in new controversy. Among the Particular Baptists arose the Separatist Baptists, whose membership requirement was the personal experience of regeneration (in modern terms, the "born again" experience, involving an awareness of Jesus as personal savior). The Separatist Baptists separated themselves from those who practiced anything less. Among both the Particularists (now called Regulars) and the Separatists, divisions arose on the emotional appeal of revivalism. The New Lights were for it and the Old Lights against it. A final union of the various Particular groups was effected in 1801. The 1700s also saw the rise of Particular Baptists to predominance over the General Baptists in most areas.

The 1800s were a time of significant growth for Baptists, who were beginning to structure themselves and develop the adjuncts of a successful church—a publishing concern, a missionary arm, and institutions of higher education. In 1824, the Triennial Convention was formed. This meeting was, at its inception, a convention of associations called together for missionary concerns. "The General Missionary Convention of the Baptist Denomination in America" was the official designation, but the meeting every three years was popularly called the Triennial Convention. While missionary in its base, it became the forum in which many issues would be argued and out of which most schisms would come. Most Calvinistic Baptists, in the beginning, related themselves to the convention.

IN CANADA. Baptists in Canada had three separate starts, each essentially unrelated to the others, which are currently reflected in the three large regional conventions which make up the Canadian Baptist Federation. The first Baptists in Canada came from New England to Nova Scotia around 1760 to move onto land vacated because of the government's expulsion of the Arcadians. Ebenezer Moulton arrived from Massachusetts in 1761 and founded the first Baptist church at Horton (now Wolfville). Though Moulton left the ministry and Canada two years later, his congregation survives and is the oldest Baptist church in the country.

Coming with the Baptists were a number of Congregationalists and Presbyterians, among whom were some who had accepted revivalism and its associated phenomena. They were called Newlights. A break began between the Newlights and the more staid traditional Congregationalists and Presbyterians, with the Newlights moving to form independent Separatist congregations. Into this situation stepped Henry Alline (1748–1784), devoted Newlight preacher. His efforts throughout the New England settlements brought many Presbyterians and almost all of the Congregationalists into the Newlight Separatist camp. As in the United States, these Separatist congregations eventually identified themselves as Baptists, and, by the time of the merger between the Newlights and the older Baptists, the former actually constituted the bulk of the Baptist movement in the Maritimes.

There were enough Baptists in Nova Scotia and New Brunswick by 1798 to form an initial association. As the work extended, the other associations formed. These associations came together in 1846 to constitute what is known to today as the Baptist Convention of the Maritime Provinces.

A decade after the first Baptists arrived in Nova Scotia, other Baptists slipped across the American Border into Ontario and Quebec. The migration increased with the influx of Loyalists after the American Revolution. However, the first congregation was not formed until 1788, at Beamsville on the western tip of the peninsula in southern Ontario. From this early church established by Jacob Beam, Sr., the Baptist movement spread through Ontario. The first congregation formed in Quebec was a rural church established in 1794. Baptist growth was small in the province. The first association was formed in 1836 in the Bay of Quinte area. Other associations including a missionary association, were formed over the century. Finally in 1888, the Baptist work came together as the Baptist Convention of Ontario and Quebec.

Further west, Baptist settlement began in 1862 when John Morton began to farm some 600 acres of what is now downtown Vancouver. The Reverend McDonald, a home missionary, initiated work in 1873 in the prairie provinces from his residence in Winnipeg. As the railroad was laid, congregations were formed in the communities along the rail line. Many of the churches were built around converts from the various ethnic groups which moved onto the new farm land. Consolidation of the western work led to the formation of the Baptist Union of Western Canada in 1909.

The three Baptist conventions, joined by a small group of French-speaking Baptists in Quebec, came together in 1946 to form the Canadian Baptist Federation. The federation is a loosely organized body and much of the work of the denomination was retained by the several member conventions.

THE GROWTH OF THE LARGER BAPTIST BODIES IN THE UNITED STATES. The founding of the Triennial Convention was a signal for other cooperative efforts to form. The American Baptist Publication Society began in 1824, the American Baptist Home Mission Society in 1832, and the American Foreign Bible Society in 1837. A number of state societies and conventions were also organized. These were the building blocks out of which a national group consciousness could grow and from which a national convention or the equivalent of a national denomination eventually could emerge. It is difficult to say just when that national consciousness emerged, but it was certainly before 1907, when the American Baptist Convention was formed. That convention represents a gradual move toward centralization.

Proceedings in the Triennial Convention moved in the 1830s from missions to educational leadership and publications. In the 1840s, however, a new issue emerged—slavery. In April 1840, an "American Baptist Anti-Slavery Convention" was organized to press the issue which had been resisted earlier as a topic for consideration.

At the 1841 Triennial Convention, the Southerners, led by Richard Fuller, protested the abolitionist agitation and argued that, while slavery was a calamity and a great evil, it was not a sin according to the Bible. The Savannah River Association threatened to withdraw cooperation unless the abolitionists were dismissed from the board of managers. The debate began a controversy that would result in the gradual withdrawal of the Southern Baptists from participation in convention activities and from support of the *Missionary Magazine* and missions.

The 1844 session proved decisive; the Southern delegates showed up in force with several test cases. The Alabama Convention sent a query to the Board of Foreign Missions asking "whether or not slaveholders are eligible and entitled equally with nonslaveholders to all the privileges and immunities of the several Unions." The Georgia Baptists chose a slave-owner as a missionary and forwarded his appointment to the Home Mission Society as a test case. The convention dodged the issues by referring them to the respective subsidiary boards.

Because the issue of slavery was raised in the nomination from Georgia, the board ruled that it was not at liberty to consider it. The Alabama query was answered in the negative. Appointment of a slaveholder would make the Northern brethren responsible for an institution they could not conscientiously sanction. The situation of the mission board was further complicated by the formation of a Free Mission Society, which refused "tainted" Southern money. In the face of these two issues, the Southern members decided to withdraw, and in 1845, they formed the Southern Baptist Convention.

The split brought to the forefront a second issue between Southern and Northern Baptists, organizational centralization. The Southern Baptist Convention became a single organization overseeing all the activities which were separated in the Northern boards and conventions. Some 300 churches entered the new church convention, which met every two years.

The Northern and Southern churches are similar in church government, both being congregationally oriented, and in doctrine, both accepting the New Hampshire Confession of Faith. The Southern church, in fact, is more centralized in its aggressive mission activity, and has expanded northward in the twentieth century. The Northern church has been much more open to modern theological trends, the ecumenical movement, and social activism, and it tends to be more "liberal" in its outlook.

As a rule, ecumenical participation by Baptists has been hindered by both the extreme congregational polity and the demand for doctrinal unity with those with whom they fellowship. Many of the missions established in the nineteenth and twentieth centuries outgrew their mission status as they became autonomous indigenous churches. They now fellowship through the Baptist World Alliance. The larger Baptist bodies, however, have tended to refrain from the affiliation with non-Baptists in such organizations as the National and World Council of Churches or even the National Association of Evangelicals. In Canada the Canadian Baptist Federation joined, then withdrew, from the Canadian Council of Churches.

CONSERVATIVE BAPTIST MOVEMENT. In the early decades of the twentieth century, the Northern Baptist Convention, like its presbyterian counterpart, was rent asunder by the fundamentalist-modernist controversy. Among the Baptists, the Fundamentalist movement focused on the issues of social action and the deviation from doctrine by missionaries. The Fundamentalists opposed the post-World War I policies which seemed to involve unsuitable social activism, and they opposed the sending of missionaries who did not hold a strong conservative Baptist position. When the convention turned away from their demands, the members of the Fundamentalist Fellowship organized, in 1920, the Conservative Baptist Fellowship (CBF) to continue their understanding of the gospel.

For many years, the CBF continued within the Northern Baptist Convention, but during World War II, plans for separation were pursued. Over the years, at least five new Baptist denominations have resulted from splintering associated with the CBF.

The Conservative Baptist Movement must also be seen as a reaction to the centralization signaled by the formation of the Northern Baptist Convention, itself, in 1907. An extreme congregational polity exists in churches belonging to the Conservative Baptist Fellowship. Congregations associate freely. Mission work is carried on by separate but approved mission agencies; schools tend to operate similarly.

PRIMITIVE BAPTISTS. In the years following the American Revolution, a great wave of enthusiasm for missions swept across the American church. Among the Baptists, this enthusiasm was occasioned by the acceptance of the Baptist view on immersion by two Congregationalist missionaries on their voyage to the mission field in India. Having lost the support of the American Board of Commissioners for Foreign Missions, Adoniram Judson and Luther Rice turned to the Baptists to support their work.

In response to Rice's appeal, a new structure, "the General Missionary Convention of the Baptist Denomination in the United States for Foreign Missions," was created in 1814. In 1815, Elder Martin Ross presented to the Kehukee Association meeting at Fishing Creek, North Carolina, a report on the new mission board. Elder Ross had already built up a reputation for missionary zeal. In 1803, he had placed his concern before the association in the form of a query:

"Is not the Kehukee Association, with her numerous and respectable friends, called on in Providence, in some way, to step forward in support of that missionary spirit which the great God is so wonderfully reviving amongst the different denominations of good men in various parts of the world?" (Cushing Biggs Hassell and Sylvester Hassell, *History of the Church of God from Creation to A.D. 1885, Including Especially the History of the Kehukee Primitive Baptist Association* [Atlanta, GA: Turner Lassetter, 1962; reprint of original edition, Middletown, NY: Gilbert Beebe's Sons, 1886], 721).

In both 1803 and 1815, Ross met with a favorable response. Similar actions were occurring across the country. Nevertheless, there remained a minority who viewed the missionary movement as an innovation and who, a decade later, were able to unite in opposition to a number of "new" causes. An effective voice arose in the Kehukee to confront the eloquent Martin Ross. Joshua Lawrence, of no formal education but great native ability, authored a "Declaration of Principles" for the churches of the Kehukee Association. At the 1827 association meeting, a lengthy debate on the declaration was followed by a resolution to "discard all Missionary Societies, Bible Societies and Theological Seminaries, and the practices heretofore resorted to for their support, in begging money from the public." The Kehukee Association further resolved:

"If any persons should be among us, as agents of any of said societies, we hereafter discountenance them in those practices; and if under a character of a minister of the gospel, we will not invite them into our pulpits; believing these societies and institutions to be the inventions of men, and not warranted from the Word of God."

Masonry was one of the issues combined with opposition to the new missionary groups, and the Kehukee reacted against members who joined the lodge. We "declare non-fellowship with them and such practices altogether" (Hassell and Hassell, 736–37). The lengthy action was finally adopted in complete consensus. There were no dissenting votes.

This action did not go unopposed by those who had for years supported the missionary cause, both within and outside of the Kehukee Association. Within the association, churches began to withdraw and to continue their support of mission societies. Other associations withdrew their letter of correspondence (doctrinal and ethical similarity) with Kehukee. One of these, the Neuse Association (North Carolina), split in 1830–31, and the Contentea Association was formed around the Kehukee position against missionary groups. The Little River and the Nauhunty associations adopted the Kehukee position at the same time.

In August 1832, the County Line Association came out in opposition to missionary societies. The following month a similar action was taken at an "unofficial" meeting of some churches of the Baltimore Association who gathered at the Black Rock church in Baltimore County in Maryland. The action at Black Rock was significant, as it was bringing the issue close to Philadelphia, home of the mission board. In the North, those opposed to mission societies were called "Blackrockers."

No segment of the Baptist church, particularly in the South, was unaffected by the debates, and, as associations were divided, a unitive consciousness of being the "true," "primitive," or "old school" Baptist church developed among those who refused to support what they termed "innovations." A national body of like-minded believers who registered their consciousness of one another through "letters of correspondence" began to emerge. By 1840, Primitive Baptist associations covered what was then the United States, reaching north into Pennsylvania and west to Missouri and Texas.

Primitive Baptist beliefs were hammered out in debates with the growing Missionary Baptist movement on the one hand and the Arminianism of the United and the Free Will Baptists on the other hand. (Arminians believe salvation is possible for all through free will, a belief opposed to the predestination believed in by the strict Calvinists.) The heritage of the Primitive Baptists was the New Hampshire Confession and British Puritan Calvinism. Primitive Baptists' response was to affirm their traditional Calvinism and independency. Primitive Baptists are not, as a whole, theologically trained, and their differences have arisen over acceptance or rejection of traditional statements.

The Statement of Faith is included in most copies of annual association minutes. Typically, the statement will include articles on the Trinity, the Scriptures as the only rule of faith and practice, original sin, human depravity, election, perseverance of the saints, baptism by immersion, closed communion, the resurrection, and

ordination. Differences among Primitive Baptists will be manifest primarily on the doctrine of election and/or predestination. All hold to a belief in election, that God elected the saved before the foundation of the world. Some go beyond, and hold that God predestined everything that comes to pass. Upon that doctrine, associations have split. Foot washing is practiced by many Primitive Baptists, but very few make it a test for fellowship. Some consider it an ordinance. The King James Version of the Bible is preferred. Secret societies are frowned upon.

Primitive Baptists have an extreme congregational form of government, and many assert in their articles of faith that an association has no right to assume any authority over local churches. For the overwhelming number of Primitive Baptists, there is no organization above the loose associations which typically cover several counties. Associations consist of representative member churches and can sit in advisory capacities only.

Except for the few Primitive Baptist groups which have organized more formally, there are no headquarters, institutions, or official publications. As with the Plymouth Brethren, periodicals become a major means of communication and are identified with various divisions. Generally speaking, each periodical will serve a specific geographic area for a particular doctrinally definable group.

The local church consists of members, deacons, and elders. Members must be adult baptized believers. Deacons oversee the temporal affairs. Ministers have little or no theological training and, typically, no salary. They are expected to study the Scriptures. No musical instruments are used in worship. Sermons are delivered extemporaneously, in a distinctive sing-song voice. Also associated with the Primitives is Sacred Harp singing, a cappella singing in four-part harmony which sounds much like eighteenth century folk music.

While not organized in an hierarchical fashion, there is a definite organizational structure to the Primitive Baptist movement which can be defined by doctrine and by letters of correspondence. Each association has a sister association to which it sends annual letters of greeting. Such letters are recognition of being in communion and professing similar doctrines. Doctrinal differences among associations in correspondence manifest the generally low level of doctrinal freedom allowed. With rare exceptions, associations in correspondence will not overlap geographically. Several groups have taken steps to organize more formally and to form supra-associational structures. Finally, race has also become a means of distinguishing a set of corresponding associations.

If one defines a primary religious body among the Primitive Baptists as an association and those associations with which it is in correspondence and has doctrinal unity, no fewer than 13 distinct Primitive Baptist groups emerge. Each one of these bodies meets the criteria of a primary religious group as outlined in the introduction. Each asks for the primary allegiance of its members, has two or more centers of operation, and has at least one item of doctrine or organizational principle that will be distinctive from its closest neighbor.

AFRICAN AMERICAN BAPTISTS. Baptist missions among the African slaves date to the beginning of Baptist history and the efforts made among the African members of Roger Williams' Providence Church. But in the 1700s as Baptists moved into the South, slaves grew to be a large percentage of the membership. The first black Baptist church was formed at Silver Bluff, South Carolina, between 1773 and 1775, and was made up of residents of the plantation of John Galphin. Leadership was provided by a Brother Palmer, the church's founder, the Reverend David George, and the Reverend George Lisle. The late date of this formation is symbolic more of the hesitancy of slave owners to allow separate churches (which could become independent centers for subversive activities) than of any lack of success preaching the gospel among the slaves. Within a few years, a second church was formed at Williamsburg, Virginia, at the initiation of the white

Baptists. A third church was formed in Savannah in 1779. From these three, others sprang up across the South.

Northern blacks established Baptist churches after the turn of the century. The Jay Street Church of Boston was founded in 1804, with New York (1808) and Philadelphia (1809) following in quick succession. The Boston and New York churches were formed by the Reverend Thomas Paul. The Abyssinian Baptist Church in New York would later be pastored by the flamboyant Congressman Adam Clayton Powell (1908–1972).

Like their white brethren, the blacks were active in foreign mission work, sending a missionary to Haiti in 1824. In 1821, the Reverends Lott Carey and Collins Teague were sent by the Triennial Convention to work in Liberia. They traveled to their new home with a group of blacks sponsored by the African Colonization Society.

As the reaction of slave owners to slave revolts cut into the freedom of slaves to spread their religion, and as many slaves fled north and west, Baptist churches spread in the Midwest. In 1836, the Providence Baptist Association in Ohio became the first Black Baptist Association in the country. Two years later in Illinois, the Wood River Association was formed. In 1840, the American Baptist Missionary Convention was formed by black Baptists in the Northeast and mid-Atlantic states. It was active in freedman's aid as the Civil War drew to a close.

After the Civil War, several organizational attempts met with varying success until, in 1879, the Reverend W. W. Colley returned from Africa with a vision of the role of black Baptist churches. At a meeting in Montgomery, Alabama, in 1880, the Foreign Mission Baptist Convention of the U.S.A. was formed. This convention became the rallying point of black Baptists, and its organization is usually accepted as the founding date of the National Baptist Convention, U.S.A., Inc., the largest African American Baptist organization. Within the Foreign Mission Baptist Convention, machinery was provided for the calling of a meeting at which the American National Baptist Convention was formed in 1886. In 1893, a third body, the Baptist National Educational Convention, was formed. Other regional bodies joined in these national efforts, and the stage was set for the formation of the National Baptist Convention in 1895.

GENERAL BAPTISTS. The first Baptists in both England and America were Arminian in their theology, meaning they adhered to the reformed theology articulated by Dutchman Jacob Arminius and held that salvation was possible for all. They believed in a "general" atonement (thus the name "General Baptists") in opposition to the "particular" atonement or strict predestination of the Calvinist Baptists, who said the number and identity of the elect were predetermined before the world began. John Smyth founded the first Baptist church in England in 1611; many General Baptists in America trace their seventeenth-century roots to Smyth. The English Baptists faced persecution, but were able to set up a central organization, "the General Assembly," in the 1660s. By 1699, this assembly included some 10 local associations.

In America, the General Baptist history begins in 1639 with Roger Williams' church at Providence, Rhode Island. Other churches spread in the East over the next century. In the first decade of the eighteenth century, General Baptist centers were established in the South. A group settled in Virginia and, in 1709, applied to England for a minister. The minister died soon after his arrival, and the church moved to North Carolina under the leadership of William Sojourner. In the same year, Paul Palmer baptized nine persons and formed the Chestnut Ridge Church in Maryland. He, too, moved to North Carolina. Through his labors, William Parker was converted; under Palmer, Parker, and Sojourner, a thriving General Baptist movement was organized.

Much of the General Baptist work was lost to the militant Calvinists in the late 1700s. The Philadelphia Association absorbed the Northern Baptists and their missionaries, and organized the Kehukee Association from members in North Carolina. Those not absorbed by the Kehukee became known as "Free-Willers," a name that stuck.

SEVENTH-DAY BAPTISTS. Seventh-Day or Saturday worship has been a recurring issue raised by serious students of the Bible. For the Baptists who were in search of ways to recover the primitive church, it was an early theme. Modern Sabbatarians find it practiced throughout Christian history, but its modern history begins in the 1550s with scattered reports of Sabbatarians among the British reformers. As early as 1595, a book was published on the question by Nicholas Bownd.

The first congregation of Seventh-Day Baptists seems to have arisen in 1617 under the leadership of John Trask in London. The church met at Millyard and it had a checkered existence as a result of continued persecution. A second congregation was added in 1640 at Nutton, Gloucestershire. The congregation included both Sunday and Saturday worship at first, but by the end of the century, the Sabbatarians were in control. In all, some 15 congregations seem to have existed by 1700.

In 1664, a member of the Bell Lane Seventh-Day Baptist Church of London, the Reverend Stephen Mumford, came to America and affiliated with the Newport, Rhode Island, Baptists. He began to raise the Sabbath issue, encountering both support and opposition, the latter from the church elders. On December 23, 1671, he formed the Newport congregation, the first Seventh-Day Baptist church in America.

Other individuals migrated to America from various Sabbatarian Baptist churches in England. In most cases, they existed as Baptists until driven out as heretics. Churches were formed at Philadelphia (1680s) and Piscutaway, New Jersey (1705). Over the century, growth was slow but steady. The Sabbatarians spread throughout the colonies, south to Georgia.

Among the pietists of Germany, a second strain of Sabbatarianism developed in the wake of the Bible study promoted by Francke and Spener. Among these Sabbatarians was the famous Woman in the Wilderness Commune that settled along Wissahickon Creek near Germantown, Pennsylvania, in 1694. They were among a number of German dissenters who settled in Pennsylvania at the invitation of William Penn. They were early in communication with both Abel Noble, founder of the Philadelphia Church, and the Newport Brethren. The community dissolved in the early 1700s.

In 1720, Conrad Beissel arrived in Philadelphia ready to join the Wissahickon brethren; only then did he learn of the community's demise. However, he was able to meet with a few of its former members. The following year Beissel went west to Lancaster County and founded a settlement. In 1724, he made a tour of the coastal settlements, visiting the Labadist Community at Bohemia Manor and the Rhode Island Sabbatarian Baptists. Shortly after that visit, he became a Sabbatarian himself. Through the influence of the German Baptist Brethren, he became a Baptist in 1725 and later the leader of the newly organized Conestoga Church near his home. Under Beissel and a Brother Lamech, who kept the diary of the congregation, the sabbatarian issue was raised to prominence.

In 1728, the split in the congregation became effective, and Beissel formed an independent sabbatarian church. Beissel immediately published an apology, *Mystyrion Anomias,* on the seventh-day Sabbath. Further activities led to the formation in 1732 of the famous Ephrata Cloister, a communal Seventh-Day Baptist group, from which others would grow.

CHRISTIAN CHURCH (DISCIPLES OF CHRIST) AND RELATED CHURCHES. Many members of the Christian Church (Disciples of Christ) and its sister bodies would be offended by being thought of as "Baptists," but they would also, upon reflection, find many reasons for being considered in a chapter with the Baptist family. The Christian Church began with three ex-Presbyterian ministers in the early 1800s, two of whom belonged to a Baptist association from 1813 to 1830. The Christian Church holds some beliefs and practices in common with Baptists; for example, believers' baptism by immersion, the celebration of the Lord's Supper as a memorial meal, and the effort to restore New Testament Christianity.

The Christian Church had its origin in the work of three ex-Presbyterian ministers—Thomas and Alexander Campbell and Barton Stone. The Campbells were Scots-educated Irishmen who had, during their years of training, become heavily influenced by some Presbyterian leaders who had adopted a free-church position. (Free churches oppose state churches and are anti-authoritarian, lay-oriented, nonliturgical, and noncreedal. They practice adult baptism, not infant baptism.) Presbyterian leaders John Glas, Robert Sandeman, and the Haldane brothers had left their respective churches to establish independent congregations. In America, other anti-authoritarian movements were begun by Methodist James O'Kelly and Baptists Abner Jones and Elias Smith.

Thomas Campbell came to America in 1807 and joined the Philadelphia Synod of the Presbyterian Church, but his name was removed from the rolls in May 1807 under charges of heresy. Thomas founded the Christian Association of Washington (Pennsylvania) to give form to the anti-authoritarian protest. At about the same time, Alexander Campbell broke with the Scotch Presbyterians and sailed for America.

The Campbells, repulsed by the Presbyterians, began to form congregations, the first of which was the Brush Run Church. In 1813, the Campbells and their followers united with the Red Stone Baptist Association, a union which lasted until 1830. During those 17 years, the central ideas of the Campbells crystallized. Some of those ideas were in direct conflict with Baptist precepts, a development which led to the dissolution of fellowship in 1830.

The ideas which eventually caused the schism were clustered around the notion of "Restoration"—the striving to restore New Testament Christianity. While restoration, in itself, would not be objectionable to Bible-oriented Christians, the implementation of restoration with specific programs and notions was not so acceptable. For example, in direct contradiction to Baptist teaching, Alexander Campbell began to teach a distinction between grace and law, and the New Testament versus the Old Testament. He wanted to establish the New. Organizationally, the Campbells were also becoming involved in the same struggle that produced the Primitive Baptist church in the East and South—the rejection of associations and other supracongregational structures with power to legislate for the member churches. Associations, said the Campbells, were for fellowship and edification only. Alexander Campbell, in the pages of the *Christian Baptist,* which he published, also began to speak against the mission boards.

A major thrust of Campbellite thinking concerned the unity of the church, a common problem in early nineteenth-century Protestantism. The Campbellites felt that a restoration of the New Testament would include a union of all Christians as an essential aspect of the primitive order. Of course, other church bodies did not agree on what constituted primitive Christianity. For example, churches with strong supracongregational structures gave many reasons for their system as opposed to a congregational system, while the restoration movement became known for its defense of the congregational system.

While he was among the Baptists, the sacraments or ordinances became a major issue for Alexander Campbell, and believers' baptism by immersion replaced the common presbyterial form (pouring). The Lord's Supper was viewed as a memorial meal; although as it came to be practiced, it has been a point of distinction between the Christian Church and other churches. The Lord's Supper was commemorated each Sunday and was open to all Christians, even those who had not been immersed.

Barton Stone was the third person chiefly credited for the formation of the Christian Church. In the early 1800s, he began to have doubts about both the doctrine and polity of his Presbyterian Church. After his ministering at the camp meeting at Cane Ridge,

he and four other ministers were censured by the Synod of Kentucky. They withdrew and formed the Springfield Presbytery. The Presbytery was dissolved on June 28, 1809, and in a celebrated document—"The Last Will and Testament of the Springfield Presbytery"—founders set out their protest of Presbyterian polity. Emphasis was on the independence of the local church, the Scriptures as the only authority, and conferences of churches for fellowship and edification only. The group took the name "Christian Church."

In 1830, the Campbells finally departed from the Baptists, and correspondence with Barton Stone, already initiated, continued. The two groups following the Campbells and Stone consummated a merger in 1832. No sectarian designation was wanted, so several "non-sectarian" names began to be used—Christian Church and Disciples of Christ being the most common.

At the heart of the Disciples' organization was a protest of certain structures which they saw present in Christendom. They protested the division of Christianity, which they called a result of sectarian ideas (as expressed in creeds) and church polity not based on the Bible. They took the "Bible only" as their uniting creed and an ultracongregational polity as the New Testament form. They did not like any structures which either usurped the duties of the local church (as mission societies did) or which exerted power over the church, as some Baptist associations, presbyteries, or bishops did. They at first saw themselves as independent societies functioning as a leaven for the lump of sectarian Christianity.

Between 1830 and 1849, the Disciples experienced rapid growth. Fellowship was expressed in quarterly and annual meetings of regional gatherings. Independent colleges and publishing interests were founded and continued. Then in 1849, the first general convention was held. Its purpose was to further the work of the societies and to represent them. The convention adopted the name "American Christian Missionary Society," and its task centered on church extension, foreign missions, and evangelism. Over the next 60 years, other agencies were formed to handle specific tasks. They reported to the annual convention.

By the turn of the century, the creation of a number of boards and agencies led to a demand for centralization and coordination. A debate was precipitated when the 1910 convention adopted a resolution to form one general convention of the Disciples, which would unify all organizations, coordinate the collection of money, and make more efficient the administration. Finally in 1917, the International Convention was organized.

In the twentieth century, the Restoration movement divided into three major divisions. The Disciples of Christ began with the formation of the International Convention in 1917. It took periodic steps which brought it into denominational Christianity and associated with other liberal Protestant churches in the major ecumenical councils. Three groups that rejected the abandonment of the non-denominational stance of the movement's founders are the non-instrumental Churches of Christ (whose membership is largely centered in the South), the Christian Churches, and Churches of Christ. All three groups are about the same strength. The theologically conservative Churches of Christ has experienced a number of schisms, the most important one being the formation of the International Churches of Christ (ICC) in the 1980s. The ICC, also known as the Boston movement, emerged out of a revival movement within the main body of the Churches of Christ, but eventually departed on a number of important points, especially on the matter of more centralized church authority, the discipling of members, and the use of instrumental music in worship.

Since 1849, there have been several schisms within the restoration movement. These groups retain a large doctrinal consensus and vary only on a few points at issue in their founding and on polity.

CHRISTADELPHIANS. The Christadelphians date to 1844 when Dr. John Thomas, a physician in Richmond, Virginia, began a monthly magazine, *The Herald of the Future Age.* Dr. Thomas, who had immigrated from England in 1832, became associated with Alexander Campbell and the Christian Church, which Campbell and his brother helped form. Over the years, however, Thomas found himself in disagreement on a number of points of doctrine. He came to feel that knowledge and belief of the gospel must precede baptism, and he was rebaptized. A polemic began which led to a complete break in 1844. Groups began to form and were termed *ecclesias* (the Greek word for assembly from which the word ecclesiastical is derived).

The Christadelphians hold views similar to those of the Campbells, but are non-Trinitarians and resemble the early Unitarians in Christology. The Holy Spirit is God's power which executes his will. Thomas also denied man's natural immortality and believed that man was unconscious from death to the resurrection. At the end time, Christ will appear visibly; all believers will be resurrected and judged, and the kingdom will be established. The kingdom will be the kingdom of Israel restored in the Holy Land. The wicked will be annihilated. Most important, Thomas taught that baptism by immersion after receiving knowledge of the gospel was essential for salvation. Closed communion is practiced. The Christadelphians do not participate in politics, voting, war; nor do they hold civil office.

The organization of the ecclesias is congregational. Each ecclesia elects local officers, serving brethren. The serving brethren include managing brethren and presiding brethren. The former conduct the temporal affairs and the latter the speaking, teaching, and pastoral work. Groups of ecclesias meet in fraternal gatherings which have no legislative powers.

In the 1890s, a controversy which developed between Robert Roberts and J. J. Andrew, two leading brothers in England, spread among the Christadelphians. The controversy involved the issue of what was termed ''resurrectional responsibility'' and split the Christadelphians into two factions generally termed the Amended and Unamended.

Sources—The Baptist Family

The study of the Baptist movement is supported by the American Baptist Historical Society, 1106 S. Goodman St., Rochester, NY 14620, which maintains the official depository library for the American Baptist Churches of America and the World Baptist Alliance, operates the American Baptist Center at Valley Forge, Pennsylvania, and publishes the *American Baptist Quarterly*; and the Historical Commission of the Southern Baptist Convention, 901 Commerce St., Ste. 400, Nashville, TN 37203, which operates the convention's archives and publishes *Baptist History and Heritage*. The Seventh-day Baptist Historical Society is located at the headquarters in Janesville, Wisconsin, and the most complete Primitive Baptist archives is at Elon College, North Carolina. The Canadian Baptist Archives is located at McMaster Divinity College in Hamilton, Ontario.

The Disciples of Christ Historical Society (and archives collection) is at 1101 Nineteenth Ave., S., Nashville, TN 37212. It publishes the quarterly *Discipliana*.

BAPTIST ORIGINS AND HISTORY

Armitage, Thomas. *A History of the Baptists*. New York: Bryan Taylor & Co., 1887. 978 pp.

Baptist Advance. Forest Park, IL: Roger Williams Press, 1964. 512 pp.

Benedict, David E. *A General History of the Baptist Denomination in America and Other Parts of the World*. Boston: Lincoln & Edmunds, 1819. 470 pp.

Brackney, William H., ed. *Baptist Life and Thought: 1600–1980.*. Valley Forge, PA: Judson Press, 1983. 448 pp.

———. *The Baptists*. New York: Greenwood Press, 11988. 327 pp.

Collinsworth, J. R. *The Pseudo Church Doctrines of Anti-Pedo-Baptists Defined and Refuted*. Kansas City, MO: Hudson-Kimberly Publishing Company, 1892. 496 pp.

The Encyclopedia of Southern Baptists. 3 Vols. Nashville: Broadman Press, 1958.

Newman, Albert Henry. *A History of Anti-Pedobaptism*. Philadelphia: American Baptist Publication Society, 1897. 414 pp.

Torbet, Robert G. *A History of the Baptists*. Philadelphia: Judson Press, 1963. 585 pp.

THE BAPTISTS IN NORTH AMERICA

Armstrong, O. K., and Marjorie Moore Armstrong. *The Indomitable Baptists*. Garden City, NY: Doubleday, 1967. 392 pp.

Baker, Robert A. *A Baptist Source Book*. Nashville: Broadman Press, 1966. 216 pp.

Boney, William Jerry, and Glenn A. Iglehart. *Baptists & Ecumenism*. Valley Forge, PA: Judson Press, 1980. 177 pp.

Boyd, Jesse L. *A History of Baptists in America 1845*. New York: The American Press, 1957. 205 pp.

Brackney, William H., ed. *Baptist Life and Thought: 1600–1980, A Source Book*. Valley Forge, PA: Judson Press, 1983. 448 pp.

Gaver, Jessyca Russell. *''You Shall Know the Truth.''* New York: Lancer Books, 1973. 368 pp.

McBeth, H. Leon. *The Baptist Heritage*. Nashville, TN: Broadman Press, 1987. 850 pp.

Stiansen, P. *History of the Norwegian Baptists in America*. Chicago: The Norwegian Baptist Conference of America and the American Baptist Publication Society, 1939. 344 pp.

Wood, James E., Jr. *Baptists and the American Experience*. Valley Forge, PA: Judson Press, 1976. 384 pp.

BAPTIST THOUGHT

Bush, L. Russ, and Tom J. Nettles. *Baptists and the Bible*. Chicago: Moody Press, 1980. 456 pp.

Carson, Alexander. *Baptism, Its Mode and Its Subjects*. Evansville, IN: The Sovereign Grace Book Club, n.d. 237 pp.

Lumpkin, W. L. *Baptist Confessions of Faith*. Chicago: Judson Press, 1959. 430 pp.

Robinson, H. Wheeler. *Baptist Principles*. London: The Carey Kingsgate Press, 1925. 74 pp.

Wallace, O. C. S. *What Baptists Believe*. Nashville: Broadman Press, 1934.

PRIMITIVE BAPTISTS

Hassell, Sylvester. *History of the Church of God*. Middletown, NY: Gilbert Beebe's Sons, 1886. 1008 pp.

Piepkorn, Arthur Carl. ''The Primitive Baptists of North America.'' *Baptist History and Heritage*, 7, No. 1 (January 1972), pp. 33–51.

Rushton, William. *A Defence of Particular Redemption*. Elon College, NC: W. J. Berry, 1971. 48 pp.

BLACK BAPTISTS

Brawley, Edward M., ed. *The Black Baptist Pulpit*. Freeport, NY: Books for Libraries Press, 1971. 300 pp.

Fitts, Leroy. *A History of Black Baptists*. Nashville, TN: Broadman Press, 1985. 368 pp.

McCall, Emmanuel L., comp.*The Black Christian Experience*. Nashville, TN: Broadman Press, 1972. 126 pp.

Washington, James Melvin.*Frustrated Fellowship*. Macon, GA: Mercer University Press, 1986. 226 pp.

GENERAL BAPTISTS

Latch, Ollie. *General Baptists in Church History*. Poplar Bluff, MO: General Baptist Press, 1968. 130 pp.

SEVENTH-DAY BAPTISTS

Seventh Day Baptists in Europe and America. 2 vols. Plainfield, NJ: American Sabbath Tract Society for the Seventh Day Baptist General Conference, 1910.

THE RESTORATION MOVEMENT

Dowling, Enos E. *The Restoration Movement.* Cincinnati Standard Publishing, 1964. 128 pp.

Ford, Harold W. *A History of the Restoration Plea.* Oklahoma City, OK: Semco Color Press, 1952. 217 pp.

Gates, Errett. *The Early Relation and Separation of the Baptists and Disciples.* Chicago: The Christian Century Company, 1904. 124 pp.

Harrell, David Edwin. *The Social Sources of Division in the Disciples of Christ.* Athens, GA: Publishing Systems, Inc., 1973. 458 pp.

Humbert, Royal. *Compend of Alexander Campbell's Theology.* St. Louis: Bethany Press, 1961. 295 pp.

McAleister, Lester G. and William E. Tucker. *Journey of Faith.* St. Louis, MO: Bethany Press, 1975. 506 pp.

Murch, James DeForest. *Christians Only.* Cincinnati: Standard Publishing, 1962. 392 pp.

CHRISTADELPHIANS

A Declaration of the Truth Revealed in the Bible. London: "The Dawn" Book Supply, 1970. 30 pp.

Roberts, Robert. *Christendom Astray.* London: "The Dawn" Book Supply, n.d. 462 pp.

Thomas, John. *A Brief Exposition of the Prophecy of Daniel.* Birmingham, England: "The Christadelphian," 1947. 122 pp.

———. *The Last Days of Judah's Commonwealth and Its Latter Day Restoration.* West Beach Post Office, South Australia: Logos Publications, 1969. 99 pp.

Chapter 12
Independent Fundamentalist Family

Consult the "Contents" pages to locate the entries in Part III,
the Directory Listings Sections, that comprise this family.

Fundamentalism is the name given to a conservative movement within Protestantism in the early twentieth century. It was characterized by an intense affirmation of biblical authority and allegiance to a modest number of essential Christian doctrines, most of which had been called into question by the so-called modernists who had absorbed a variety of new currents of intellectual thought from sociology to evolution. What became known as Fundamentalism, however, derives from the thought of British teacher/theologian John Nelson Darby (1800–1882). The movement he began in England in the 1820s attempted a more thoroughgoing revival of primitive Christianity than either the earlier Puritan or Wesleyan movements. Unlike its Puritan and Wesleyan predecessors, the new movement was not content merely to purify or revive the existing church, but sought to recreate the Apostolic church. The prime methods used to recover Apostolic life were intense concentration on the Bible, and the adoption of a biblical lifestyle, theology, and ecclesiology.

JOHN NELSON DARBY. Probably no Christian thinker in the last 200 years has so affected the way in which English-speaking Christians view the faith, and yet has received so little recognition of his contribution as John Nelson Darby. Why this anonymity? One can only guess. It might be that the theological movement he began was so historical that it was programmed to forget its roots, its originator. It might be that its disestablishment orientation worked for a breakdown of communication which left the second generation without a knowledge of its heritage. In any case, the thinking of a large number of Christians finds its source in the unique biblical theology that Darby evolved in the nineteenth century. From his ideas have sprung modern-day fundamentalism, the later work of Dwight L. Moody and the Moody Bible Institute in Chicago, the *Scofield Reference Bible*, the *Companion Bible*, and a number of churches that bear names such as Bible Church, Bereans, Grace Gospel, Brethren, Independent Fundamentalist, and Gospel Assembly. Moreover, as a result of Darby's work, a number of Christians in the larger denominations would one day read with relish the works of such men as I. M. Haldeman, William Graham Scroggie, Clarence Larkin, G. Campbell Morgan, James H. Brooks, and William E. Blackstone, to name a few.

Who was Darby? John Nelson Darby was an Anglican priest ordained in 1826, who, through the study of the Scripture, came to reject the idea of a state church. Darby's dissent led him to withdraw from the Anglican Church in 1827 and begin the pursuit of a non-denominational approach to church life, establishing fellowship groups of Christians who had also come out of the existing denominational structure. It was Darby's view that the true church is a temporary structure, set up by God between the cross and the second coming, and composed of a number of individual believers. This concept dominates Darby's thinking.

In 1827, the famous Albury Conferences on prophetic studies—conferences held at Albury Park, an estate near London—caused Darby to think about eschatology. The term "eschatology" refers to the end time and includes consideration of death,

heaven and hell, judgment, the second coming of Christ, and the millennium (Christ's reign on earth for a thousand years). Darby created a new system of thought called dispensationalism. Dispensationalism is a view of the Bible as a history of God's dealing with man in terms of various periods (dispensations) of history. The church had often seen history, on a theological or numerological basis, as divided into three or seven periods. But it was Darby who began a division of the biblical story based on God's method of dealing with his people. Darby's system had seven basic dispensations; one period, Israel's, was divided into three subperiods. The system was roughly as follows:

1. (Paradisaical state) to the flood
2. Noah—government
3. Abraham—calling and election
4. Israel
-a. Under the law—Moses
-b. Under the priesthood
-c. Under the kings—Saul
5. Gentiles (begins with Nebuchadnezzar)
6. The Spirit (the present?)
7. The fullness of time

While Darby was fairly clear about the early dispensations, his discussion of the present and future is vague and at times seemingly contradictory. To ease the confusion, Darby's theological successors (particularly C. I. Scofield and Harry A. Ironside) refined his system into what has become the basis for most modern discussion of dispensational schemes. Scofield's seven dispensations are:

1. Innocence—from creation to the fall of Adam
2. Conscience—from the fall to the flood
3. Government—from Noah to Abraham
4. Promise—from Abraham to Moses
5. Law—from Moses to Jesus
6. Grace—from the cross to the second coming
7. Personal reign of Christ—from the second coming to and including eternity

Dispensational schemes solve several basic biblical problems. They clear up some of the baffling biblical contradictions by shifting contradictory passages to different dispensations. For example, when one reads all of the passages concerning the end of time and the events surrounding the second coming of Christ, one is left confused as to what will happen. Passages in Thessalonians, the Book of Revelation, and Matthew offer seemingly contradictory pictures of the future which the dispensationalists were able to reconcile by their rather complex outline of future events. The dispensationalists were also able to reconcile the obvious difference between the small New Testament church and the large ecclesiastical organizations by which they were surrounded. The true church (i.e., the church of the dispensationalists) was ever the small body of the faithful called out from Babylon (i.e., large religious organizations). Finally, the dispensationalists offered a rationale for change. Each dispensation was initiated by a renewed action of God toward his people, by which God tries to reach his chosen ones. The failure of each successive action leads inevitably to the cross, said the dispensationalists. And the failure of the New Testament church to realize the promises given to it must lead inevitably to a final dispensation in which Christ is acknowledged as the universal ruler.

Second only to dispensationalism as a key idea of Darby is his ecclesiology. Darby had early come to reject denominated, primarily state-church, Christianity, and he tackled the problem of the "Nature and Unity of the Church of Christ" in his first pamphlet in 1828. He attacked as the enemy of the work of the Holy Spirit anyone "who seeks the interests of any particular denomination." No formal union of outward-professing bodies is desirable. Unity is to be found in "the Unity of the Spirit and can only be in the things of the Spirit, and therefore can only be perfected in spiritual persons. . .Believers know that all who are born of the Spirit have substantial unity of mind, so as to know each other, and love each other as brethren." Churches influenced by Darby's ecclesiology generally have a statement of belief in the spiritual unity of believers in Jesus Christ.

Darby established assemblies of like-minded believers tied together by their consensus and their fellowship. They accepted no authority except the "charismatic" leadership of Darby and other talented teachers who soon arose in their midst. There were no bishops or overseers.

The gospel assembly became the central building block among Darby's followers and imitators. The assembly was a local gathering of like-minded Christians. Each person was both layman and minister, and each assembly was independent and tied to the other assemblies only by the bonds of doctrinal consensus and fellowship.

No name for the group was accepted, although biblical designations such as Church of God and, most popularly, Brethren, were often used. The lack of designation has been a characteristic that has persisted and has often made the Brethren an invisible part of the on-going religious life of any community in which they reside. Few groups of Brethren publish their membership statistics.

While they had no formal ministry, the Brethren did display an intense evangelical zeal and began to develop structures that could be used without infringing on the autonomy of the assembly. First, there emerged in the assemblies gifted teachers and evangelists who, by the consent of the assembly, taught the Bible and preached the gospel. The majority of the assembly, of course, had responsibilities in reaching the lost with the gospel. The more talented of the teachers and evangelists began to travel and speak at neighboring assemblies, and, by such informal means, a professional ministry developed.

A major new form that evolved as an expression of the biblical priority in the life of the Brethren was the Bible reading. This sermon-like presentation usually involved the tracing of a key word or idea, such as "creation" or "church," through a series of otherwise disconnected passages, with the speaker briefly commenting on each passage. The Bible reading evolved out of the Reading Meeting of the British Brethren, where students would gather in a home and together search the Scripture.

A very active publishing ministry was initiated by the voluminous writings of Darby. Pamphlets and tracts were soon joined by books and periodicals. Last to arise were Brethren-owned printing and publishing houses, which were owned by some prominent Brethren who published as a service to the brotherhood, but, in matters of business, functioned as entrepreneurs. As the movement grew and schisms developed, the publishers became the spokesmen for different factions that could be distinguished, primarily, by the literature they accepted as orthodox. Publishers, in the absence of ministerial associations and national conventions, have become the major molders of opinion in the otherwise informally organized assemblies.

The assemblies, as a rule, reject any doctrinal formulation or creed, though Darby emphasized that unity of mind was an essential feature of the Church of God. There was, and is, informally, however, a very rigid orthodoxy and doctrinal stand, particularly about the nature of the church. Almost all of the schisms within the Darbyite movement were articulated as doctrinal disputes and appeared as a breakdown of doctrinal consensus. Of course, a major disagreement concerns the amount of latitude in belief that is possible without destroying the unity of mind.

Darby accepted the orthodox Protestantism of the Reformation on the central issues of belief in God, the Trinity, the divinity of Christ, the person and work of the Holy Spirit, the Bible as the Word of God, and the necessity of man's repentance, forgiveness, and salvation. Where Darby differed from the Protestants of the Reformation was in the issues of ecclesiology and eschatology.

While never developing an expectancy of Christ's imminent return to the degree that the Adventists did, the Brethren were in the forefront of nineteenth-century emphasis on the approaching end of the age, and they promoted speculative interpretation of Scriptural statements on the nature and order of eschatological events. Their speculations took the form of prophecy. Prominent in the dispensational scheme is a particular form of eschatology, usually termed premillennialism.

It was Darby's belief that people could be divided, for eschatological purposes, into three groups—the Jews, the Church of God (Christians), and the Gentiles (all non-Christians who were not Jews). The first event in the eschatological framework is the invisible coming of Christ to gather his saints, both living and dead, and take them away as described in Paul's First Epistle to the Thessalonians (4:13–18). This event is called the "secret rapture" of the saints. The rapture is the signal of God's rejection of the Gentiles, particularly nominal Christians; but after the rapture, his work is begun among the Jews, who convert and become preachers of Christianity to the lost world for seven years during which Satan is unleashing his most terrible woes. This seven-year period is called the tribulation (Rev. 7:14). At the end of the tribulation period, Christ and his army will come to do battle with Satan and his allies. After Christ's victory, a thousand years (the millennium) of peace will ensue. The remnant who come to Christ during the tribulation shall live on earth while the raptured saints reign with God in heavenly glory.

At the end of the millennium occurs the judgment of the Great White Throne. Satan, bound for the millennium, is loosed for a last bit of activity before his destruction. Finally, the wicked dead (non-Christians) are resurrected and judged, and the saints are given their eternal reward. This was a relatively new eschatological schema, but as it grew in popularity along with the corollary dispensational view of history, it set the issues of debate for other Bible students and conservative Christians. The rapture itself was the main point of attack by Darby's opponents. It involved an "invisible return," or secret rapture, by Christ seven years before the visible second coming.

THE DEVELOPING MOVEMENT. Darby's theology began to influence a large number of Bible students. First, such men as Charles H. Mackintosh (usually designated as C.H.M.), William Trotter, and William Kelly joined Darby's movement, and began to write and expound Darby's system. As early as 1859, Darby visited Canada, with other visits in 1864 and 1866. In 1870, 1872–73, and 1874, he visited most of the major United States cities. In 1872, Moody discovered the Brethren, who spent several days introducing Moody to dispensational thought. As Darby and his associates toured America, such leading clergy as Adroniram J. Gordon and James H. Brooks opened both their minds and their pulpits to the new truth. As a result of the massive body of literature this movement created, along with its nondenominational character and association with Moody, a large segment of conservative Christianity accepted it. In the 1880s and 1890s, the thought became institutionalized in many Bible colleges, the most famous of which was Moody Bible Institute in Chicago. It should be noted that while Darby's theology became popular, many people who accepted it never accepted the ecclesiology nor became Brethren, a fact that often gave Darby and his followers moments of consternation.

Two books appeared which greatly increased the popularity of Darbyism. The first was *Jesus Is Coming* by William E. Blackstone. This eschatologically oriented book appeared in 1878 and was an immediate success. Though its topic was the second coming, its treatment was thoroughly dispensational. The book after a century is still in print. The second book was the *Scofield Reference Bible*. C. I. Scofield was a St. Louis lawyer converted under Moody's preaching. Later, he moved to Dallas and became a Congregational minister. His first dispensational work appeared in 1888, *Rightly Dividing the Word of Truth*, which is also still in print. In the 1890s Scofield set up a Bible study course used at many of the Bible colleges, including Moody. In 1902, he commenced work on the reference Bible which appeared in 1909. It immediately became the cardinal work in the movement and has become the standard by which to judge the dispensational movement. In 1967, a new *Scofield Reference Bible*, edited by a committee of prominent dispensationalists and with minor additions to Scofield's notes in the light of later research, appeared.

Widespread use of the *Scofield Reference Bible* has led to growth in orthodox dispensationalism, and the book has become the source from which leaders in the movement have deviated to launch new teaching. For instance, Moody Bible Institute graduate J. C. O'Hair developed the Grace Gospel movement, which rejects water baptism.

Following Scofield's pattern have been a large number of conservative ministers, both denominational and independent. For many years, I. M. Haldeman, pastor of the First Baptist Church of New York City, wrote on dispensationalism. His most significant book in this vein is *A Dispensational Key to the Holy Scriptures*, which was published in 1915. Manifesting the way dispensational teaching readily adapts itself to pictorial presentations, two authors had great success specializing in publishing diagramic texts of dispensationalism. Clarence Larkin's *Dispensational Truth* and Ray O. Brown's *Truth on Canvas* became very popular.

Darby's movement grew out of the traditional theology of the Church of England. While noncreedal, it, in fact, accepted all of the affirmations of the more notable creeds promulgated by the ecumenical councils of the Christian movement during the conciliar era (fourth to eighth centuries), most notably the Nicene and Chalcedonian Creeds. Darby also affirmed the major ideas of the Protestant Reformation such as the authority of the Bible, salvation by faith alone, and the priesthood of believers. However, in his new emphases he also set up the possibility of endless deviations from that tradition.

Eschewing the developments and experience of the church over the centuries, Darby emphasized Bible Study and placed great authority in the hands of people knowledgeable of the Bible in great detail. He also placed great stress on a resolution of Bible passages to emphasize the full and complete revelation of God. Finally, he placed a great emphasis upon prophecy and eschatology, the most speculative aspect of Christian belief. It seems inevitable in such a situation that variant understandings of biblical passages and differences on Christian theology would come to the fore. Such was the case, and it led to the splitting of the Brethren movement into a hist of fragments. It also led to a major new doctrinal perspective among British Bible students.

In England, two scholars, Ethelbert W. Bullinger and Charles Welch, contemporaries of C. I. Scofield, produced a major deviation in the Darbyite manner of thinking. What Scofield called the dispensation of grace begins with the cross, the resurrection, and Pentecost, and goes to the second coming of Christ. Bullinger divided this period into two dispensations, so that one dispensation covers the era of the Apostolic church. This added dispensation begins with Pentecost and closes with the end of the ministry of the apostles and Paul. In the Bible, this era traces the church from

Acts 2 to Acts 28:25–28, and was to be considered separate from the body of Christ mentioned in Colossians and Ephesians. Also, Bullinger identified the bride of Christ in Revelation as being entirely a Jewish remnant church to be built at the end, and not at all the body of Christ. Bullinger, through his popular writings, and Welch, in his continuance of Bullinger's thought, have occasioned discussion and some acceptance of their teachings. A major debate among dispensationalists, producing the Grace Gospel movement discussed below, concerns one's views toward Bullinger's thought. In America, Bullinger's teachings have taken hold and produced several groups. A spin-off of Bullingerism is the work of A. E. Knoch, discussed below.

During the twentieth century, followers of Darby's teaching in the Scofield vein remained a conservative wing in the major churches. However, during the 1920s, as a result of the heated fundamentalist-modernist controversy, groups which were dispensational in their stance began to form. This new emergence of dispensational-thinking, independent bodies, along with the continued splintering of the older bodies, has left no fewer than thirty-nine groups growing out of Darby's teaching.

PLYMOUTH BRETHREN. The Plymouth Brethren is the group given to the movement originally founded by John Nelson Darby and his associates. The meeting at Plymouth, England, became the most prominent assembly in the otherwise unnamed movement and, as the group refused to be denominated, others began to informally refer to the group as the Brethren from Plymouth. Within the growing movement, a separation appeared in the 1840s. One leader, Benjamin W. Newton, differed with Darby on both eschatology and ecclesiology. Newton denied Darby's idea of the saints' rapture, and emphasized the autonomy of the local assembly as opposed to the unity of the whole movement. Darby's attack on Newton was characterized as violent and vindictive. Division at Plymouth was followed by accusations against Newton for holding a heretical Christology. The assembly at Bethesda, formerly a Baptist congregation, had been received into the Brethren as a group. In 1848, the Bethesda congregation received some of the Newton people at the Lord's Supper. The ensuing controversy led to the permanent division of the movement into the "Open" Brethren and the "Exclusive" Brethren.

The basic division concerns the doctrine of separation. The Exclusive Brethren believe in receiving no one at the Lord's table who is not a true Christian in the fullest sense, including being a member of a fully separated assembly (an assembly of Brethren who associate only with Brethren and not with persons from other churches). The Open Brethren, on the other hand, receive all believers to be true Christians (Brethren), even if other members of their church might hold allegedly false doctrine. The Exclusive Brethren have established several "circles of fellowship", that is, groups of mutually approved assemblies in which the decision of one assembly is binding on all.

Because the Brethren refuse to accept denominational labels, early in the twentieth century the United States Bureau of the Census chose to designate them with Roman numerals. This mode of reference was followed by Elmer T. Clark in *The Small Sects in America* and by Frank S. Mead in various editions of *The Handbook of Denominations in the United States*. (This numerical system of reference is noted for the entries in the directory section of this encyclopedia.)

FUNDAMENTALISM. The arrival of fundamentalism as a movement within American Christianity is usually dated from 1910 and the publication of a series of booklets entitled *The Fundamentals: A Testimony of Truth*. The booklets, printed by two wealthy Presbyterians, Los Angeles oilmen Lyman and Milton Stewart, were distributed freely and were the textbooks for what in the 1920s became the fundamentalist-modernist controversy. Fundamentalism so defined is usually viewed as a reaction to modernism, asserting traditional standards against the new theology and its search for scientific compatibility. While there is much truth in that definition, it is limited. It misses the essentially affirmative nature of fundamentalism and the century-old movement, of which early twentieth century fundamentalism is but one passing phase.

Fundamentalism was, in its best form, an affirmative assertion of certain ideas concerning Bible truth. At its beginning, it was a discovery by clergy and laymen of American Protestant churches of the dispensational theology of John Nelson Darby, discussed early in this chapter. Conservative and evangelical, fundamentalism became a rallying point for church leaders and, during the late nineteenth century, was one of the major thrusts of Christianity in America.

In the mid-nineteenth century, the ideas of William Miller brought to public consciousness the doctrine of the second coming of Christ and the dispensational theology of Darby, with its emphasis upon the premillennial literal return of Jesus. In America, Darby found that people accepted his ideas without leaving their own church to join the Brethren. Outstanding Christian leaders became vocal exponents of dispensational theology. Possibly none was as effective as evangelist Dwight L. Moody, who had been deeply affected by Brethren evangelist Harry Moorhouse. Leading ministers—Adoniram J. Gordon, Arthur T. Pierson, William G. Moorehead, and James H. Brooks—were all changed by Brethren thinking.

In 1869, a group of ministers associated with a millennial periodical, *Waymarks in the Wilderness*, held the first of what became the Believers Meeting for Bible Study. The ministers met to promote belief in the "doctrine of the verbal inspiration of the Bible, the personality of the Holy Spirit, the atonement of (Christ's) sacrifice, the priesthood of Christ, the two natures in the believer, and the personal imminent return of our Lord from heaven." In 1883, the annual meetings were moved to Niagara-on-the-Lake, Ontario, and thus became known as the "Niagara Conference on Prophecy."

Part of the aim of the Niagara Conference was to manifest the primitive idea of the ecclesia, the church. Thus the conference was the ministers' means of forming what Darby called the church, a gathering of believers free of denominational systems. However, the ministers did not leave their mainline denominations. They gathered for the informal closeness and doctrinal purity that Darby said should characterize the church. They used the Bible reading as developed by the Brethren, and they accepted Darby's ideas on dispensationalism and his eschatology.

In 1890, a definitive step for the whole course of fundamentalism occurred. The Niagara Conference adopted a "creedal statement." The 14-point statement was highly determinative of the movement's future course and set its priorities. The premillennial return of Christ is asserted as the answer to the impossibility of converting the world in this dispensation. The conference accepted the premillennialist's idea that the world is becoming less Christian, with evolution not bringing real human progress, thus necessitating Christ's direct intervention before the millennium. The conference was dominated by a mixture of Darby's ideas (especially on eschatology) and what is termed Princeton theology, a conservative Reformed developed at Princeton Theological Seminary. Princeton theology had developed new language to assert the authority of the Bible in the face of challenges by Darwinism and liberal theology. It affirmed that the Bible (in its original text) was inerrant, the Scriptures are Christ-centered, and all of the books of the Bible are equally inspired.

The Niagara statement also included the Reformed theological emphasis on human depravity and salvation by the blood of Christ which were assertively detailed in six articles. Almost all of the attendees at the Niagara Conference were from churches of the reformed heritage, and it is not surprising that support for the Niagara statement drew the majority of its response from churches of the Reformed heritage (Baptist, Presbyterian, Reformed, and Congregational). In the 1920s, Fundamentalism had its major battle ground in the Baptist and Presbyterian churches.

Fundamentalists also cut off other conservative Christians who might have offered some support. For example, they denied the second blessing (a major idea of the Holiness movement—the second blessing is a personal religious experience after which the believer is believed perfected for life), and two ideas of the Adventists—soul-sleep and annihilationism. Soul-sleep is the idea that the soul exists in an unconscious state from death until the resurrection of the body. Annihilationism means the belief that the wicked are destroyed instead of existing in eternal torment. While some Methodists and some Adventists would, in the 1920s, agree on the "five fundamentals," the Methodists and Adventists were not prominent in the fundamentalist movement.

From the 14-point Niagara statement, five were lifted up as the most essential, the very fundamental beliefs of anyone who could be considered a Christian. The five fundamentals, as they came to be known, are the inspiration and infallibility of the Bible, the deity of Christ (including his virgin birth), the substitutionary atonement of Christ's death, the literal resurrection of Christ from the dead, and the literal return of Christ in the Second Advent. These points assume the truth of the ecumenical creeds, the Nicene and Chadedonian. At the height of the modernist-fundamentalist controversy in the 1920s, the fundamentals would become the crucial points at issue.

The group consciousness of the leaders of the Niagara Conference was solidified in the several Bible institutes which were founded in the late nineteenth century. The most influential of these was the Moody Bible Institute in Chicago, but others, including the Bible Institute of Los Angeles (BIOLA), Philadelphia Bible Institute, the Toronto Bible Training School, and the Northwestern Bible Training School in Minneapolis, contributed to the cause. These schools institutionalized fundamentalism and, more important, helped train its future leaders.

In the early years of the twentieth century, the most prominent of the fundamentalist leaders was Arno E. Gaebelein, a former Methodist who left that church after accepting the dispensational theology. He began a magazine, *Our Hope*, in 1899. He also helped finance the work on the *Scofield Reference Bible*, the single most influential source of Darby's theology in the modern era.

New life flowed into the movement with the publication of *The Fundamentals* in 1910, and Darbyite fundamentalism came into direct conflict with emerging liberalism in the decade before World War I. *The Fundamentals* followed the lead of the Niagara Creed in asserting the verbal inerrancy of Scripture, the Calvinist doctrine of human depravity, and the imminent second coming. As modernist thinking grew, polemic led to polarization within American Protestantism, and polarization was followed by the formation of new denominations. The modernist thinking was highlighted by a theology that accepted the theory of evolution and by higher biblical criticism, the study of the Bible in the light of the findings of secular historians and archeologists.

The new denominations occasioned by the fundamentalist controversy were of two kinds. First, from the several large Protestant bodies arose fundamentalist churches that differed only from their parent bodies by acceptance of a fundamentalist mind-set with which to interpret the parent bodies' own doctrinal statements. Second, there emerged new religious bodies that encompassed the total fundamentalist thrust and were the truly American form of the Plymouth Brethren tradition discussed earlier in this chapter. These have been referred to as the undenominated churches, since they were organized in loose fellowships. They had a dispensational theology with the Reformed emphasis of Niagara, and became the ecclesiastical products of the Bible Institutes.

Fundamentalism of both kinds split into essentially two parties. One group emphasizes separation from all apostasy and from particular forms of evil such as communism, the National Council of

Churches, and organizations that compromise the faith. A second group, a later development, is more positive and emphasizes its conservative theology. Neo-evangelicalism is the name generally associated with this new movement, which has tried to be honest with natural science, conversant on philosophy and theology, and socially concerned.

The separatists have been associated with the American Council of Christian Churches (ACCC) and the ministry of Dr. Carl McIntire, whose organ of expression has been the *Christian Beacon*. McIntire is the head of the Bible Presbyterian Church. Membership in the ACCC is made up largely of small separatist bodies. The more inclusive approach is advocated by the National Association of Evangelicals (NAE). It includes a wide range of bodies which accept its minimal statement of faith. The NAE accepts not only church bodies, but also conferences and local churches, or groups not otherwise affiliated. The independent magazine, *Christianity Today*, is the most important periodical of neo-evangelicalism, though the NAE has its own organ, *United Evangelical Action*.

THE GRACE GOSPEL MOVEMENT. As John Nelson Darby's dispensational theology gained acceptance in evangelical circles, it was inevitable that variations would arise. One such variation is attributed to Anglican Ethelbert William Bullinger, who published a new outline of dispensational history in his book *How to Enjoy the Bible*. His seven dispensations are outlined in a symmetrical manner:

A. The Edenic State (Innocence)
–B. Mankind as a whole (Patriarchal)
—C. Israel (under Law)
——D. The Church of God. The Secret.
———The Dispensation of Grace
—C. Israel (Judicial)
–B. Mankind as a whole (Millennial)
A. The Eternal State (Glory)

Evident in much of Bullinger's writings is a desire for symmetry and mathematical order, which influenced greatly his interpretation of the Scriptures. For Bullinger, the Edenic State went from creation to the fall; the patriarchal dispensation went from the fall to Moses; the dispensation of Israel under the law went from Moses through Pentecost to the beginning of Paul's ministry and therefore included the Apostolic church. The fourth dispensation is the present. It is the time of the church of God, the Christian church as influenced by the ministry of Paul and therefore directed not to the Jews but to the Gentiles. Bullinger called this period "the secret" because to Paul was revealed the secret hidden from the ages, the secret of God's grace replacing the law and reaching beyond the Jews to the Gentiles (Ephesians 3:1–6). For Bullinger, the next dispensation is a judgment period for the Jews in which the Jews will be judged according to their own law, not according to the grace of Christianity. The judgment period occurs before the tribulation, a conclusion based on Jeremiah 30. The sixth dispensation includes the tribulation and millennium, as discussed early in this chapter with the material on John Nelson Darby, who originated dispensationalism. Bullinger's seventh dispensation is eternity.

The crucial item in Bullinger's work had to do with his interpretation of the transition from the third to the fourth dispensation. Bullinger sees in the Gospels, Acts, and New Testament Epistles a development in several stages. The Gospels belong to the third dispensation and have one baptism, John's water baptism. In Acts and the early Pauline epistles, there are two baptisms—John's and the baptism of the Spirit. In the later Pauline epistles, representing the start of the fourth dispensation, there is again only one baptism—the Spirit baptism (Ephesians 4:5—"There is one Lord, one faith, one baptism"). The immediate significance of so dividing Scripture is to say that, in the church age, water baptism has no place. Its long-term significance is to assert Paul's latter letters as

the principle documents for the Christian and the one's through which the others should be interpreted.

Strongly influenced by Bullinger was Charles H. Welch, who, in 1929, began *The Berean Expositor* in London and authored several books. As "ultradispensationalism" developed, a strict differentiation was made between the church of Acts and the body of Christ which had its beginning with Paul's pronouncements in Acts 28:25–28, telling the church to direct its efforts to the Gentiles instead of to the Jews. The Gospels are purely Israelitish. With Pentecost, the church was inaugurated; its distinctives were the sign-gifts (miracles), water baptism, and the Lord's Supper. However, these ceased with the beginning of the body of Christ with its one baptism. Bullinger and Welch also taught that the body of Christ was distinct from the bride of Christ, which was identified with a remnant of Israel. The Churches of Asia in Revelation 2:3 are seen as future Jewish churches that will become Christian.

Among the additional beliefs of Bullinger and Welch, for which they were most criticized by fundamentalists, were *annihilationism*, or the belief that the wicked are destroyed instead of existing in eternal torment; *soul-sleep*, or the idea that the soul exists in an unconscious state from death to the resurrection of the body; and the belief that the Lord's Supper is not to be observed in the post-Acts church. There is some dispute concerning whether or not Bullinger actually taught annihilation for the wicked, but Welch certainly did.

In the 1920s, the views of Bullinger began to spread in America. The first advocates were Pastor J. C. O'Hair, a graduate of Moody Bible Institute in Chicago and minister of the North Shore Church in Chicago, and Dr. Harry Bultema of the Berean Church in Muskegon, Michigan. O'Hair, a member of the Independent Fundamental Churches of America and a prolific writer on dispensationalism, published many pamphlets and Bible studies and was active in conferences and a radio ministry. He frequently wrote and spoke of the "blunder of the church," by which he meant the confusion of the hope, calling, and program of Israel with the hope, calling, and program of the church. O'Hair's discussion of Israel includes the early Apostolic church, which existed within the Jewish community. O'Hair did not want Christians to confuse that church with the church as influenced by Paul's later epistles and therefore directed to the Gentiles in a much broader program than the Apostolic church which was directed to Jews. The church influenced by Paul's later epistles is the church of the present, the church existing in the dispensation of grace. Thus O'Hair's teaching came to be called the Grace Gospel position.

During the 1930s there was an increase in the number of ministers and Bible churches that held the Grace Gospel position. Early centers developed in Milwaukee, Wisconsin; Paterson, New Jersey; St. Louis, Missouri; Grand Rapids and Holland, Michigan; and Indianapolis and Evansville, Indiana.

Welch made his first visit to Canada in 1927 and, in 1955, made a trip both to Canada and the United States. After World War II, a following which accepted annihilationism and did not practice the Lord's Supper (as did O'Hair) developed around Welch.

Sources—The Independent Fundamentalist Family

DISPENSATIONALISM

Bass, Clarence B. *Backgrounds to Dispensationalism*. Grand Rapids, MI: Baker Book House, 1960. 184 pp.

Bowman, John Wick. "Dispensationalism." *Interpretation*, 10, No. 2 (April 1956), pp. 170–87.

Brown, Roy L. *Truth on Canvas*. Waterloo, IA: The Cedar Book Fund, 1939. 240 pp.

Ehlert, Arnold D., comp. *A Bibliographic History of Dispensationalism*. Grand Rapids, MI: Baker Book House, 1965. 110 pp.

Huebner, R. A. *The Truth of the Pre-Tribulation Rapture Recovered.* Morganville, NJ: Present Truth Publishers, 1973. 81 pp.

Humberd, R. I. *The Dispensations.* Flora, IN: Christian Book Depot, n.d. 116 pp.

Kraus, C. Norman. *Dispensationalism in America: Its Rise and Development.* Richmond: John Knox Press, 1958. 156 pp.

Larkin, Clarence. *Dispensational Truth.* Philadelphia: Rev. Clarence Larkin Est., 1920. 176 pp.

MacPherson, Dave. *The Unbelievable Pre-Trib Origin.* Kansas City, MO: Heart of America Bible Society, 1973. 123 pp.

Scofield, C. I. *Rightly Dividing the Word of Truth.* Westwood, NJ: Fleming H. Revell, 1896. 64 pp.

———. *Scofield Bible Correspondence Course.* 4 Vols. Chicago: Moody Bible Institute, 1960.

Sisco, Paul E. *Scofield or the Scriptures.* Alden, NY: The Author, n.d. 65 pp.

Zens, Jon. *Dispensationalism: A Reformed Inquiry into Its Leading Figures and Features.* Phillipsburg, NJ: Presbyterian and Reformed Publishing Co., 1980. 57 pp.

The Plymouth Brethren and John Nelson Darby

Coad, Roy. *A History of the Brethren Movement.* Exeter: The Paternoster Press, 1968. 336 pp.

Darby, John Nelson. *The Collected Writings.* 35 vols. Oak Park, IL: Bible Truth Publishers, 1971.

Ehlert, Arnold D. *Brethren Writers.* Grand Rapids, MI: Baker Book House, 1965. 83 pp.

Miller, Andrew. *"The Brethren" (Commonly So-called).* Kowloon, Hong Kong: Christian Book Room, n.d. 213 pp.

Neatby, William Blair. *A History of the Plymouth Brethren.* London: Hodder and Stoughton, 1901. 357 pp.

Noel, Napoleon. *The History of the Brethren.* 2 Vols. Denver: W. F. Knapp, 1934.

Pickering, Hy. *Chief Men Among the Brethren.* London: Pickering & Inglis, 1918. 223 pp.

Turner, W. G. *John Nelson Darby.* London: C. A. Hammond, 1944. 88 pp.

Weremchuk, Max S. *John Nelson Darby: A Biography.* Neptune, NJ: Loizeaux Brothers, 1992. 256 pp.

Fundamentalism

Barr, James. *Fundamentalism.* Philadelphia: Westminster Press, 1978. 379 pp.

Beale, David O. *In Pursuit of Purity: American Fundamentalism Since 1850.* Greenville, SC: Unusual Publications, 1986. 457 pp.

Blackstone, William E. *Jesus Is Coming.* New York: Fleming H. Revell, 1908. 252 pp.

Cole, Stewart G. *The History of Fundamentalism.* New York: Richard R. Smith, 1931. 360 pp.

Cook, David C. *Memoirs.* Elgin, IL: David C. Cook Publishing Company, 1929. 188 pp.

Curtis, Richard C. *They Called Him Mister Moody.* Garden City, NY: Doubleday, 1962. 378 pp.

Deremer, Bernard. *Moody Biblical Institute, A Pictorial History.* Chicago: Moody Press, 1960. 128 pp.

Dollar, George W. *A History of Fundamentalism in America.* Greenville, SC: Bob Jones University Press, 1973. 411 pp.

English, E. Schuyler. *H. A. Ironside, Ordained of the Lord.* Oakland, CA: Western Book and Tract Company, 1946. 276 pp.

Falwell, Jerry. *The Fundamentalist Phenomenon.* Garden City, NY: Doubleday, 1981. 269 pp.

Furniss, Norman F. *The Fundamentalist Controversy, 1918–1931.* New Haven: Yale University Press, 1954. 199 pp.

Gaebelein, Arno Clemens. *The Conflict of the Ages.* New York: Publication Office "Our Hope," 1933. 171 pp.

Haldeman, I. M. *The Coming of Christ Both Pre-millennial and Imminent.* New York: Charles C. Cook, 1906. 325 pp.

Lawrence, Bruce B. *Defenders of God; the Fundamentalist Revolt Against the Modern Age.* San Francisco, CA: Harper & Row, 1989. 306 pp.

Magnuson, Norris A. *American Evangelicalism: An Annotated Bibliography.* West Cornwall, CT: Locust Hill Press, 1990. 495 pp.

Pruter, Karl. *Jewish Christians in the United States, A Bibliography.* New York: Garland Publishing, 1987. 192 pp

Russell, C. Allyn. *Voices of American Fundamentalism.* Philadelphia: Westminster Press, 1976. 304 pp.

Sandeen, Ernest R. *The Roots of Fundamentalism.* Chicago: University of Chicago Press, 1970. 328 pp.

Two Christian Laymen. *The Fundamentals.* 8 vols. Chicago: Testimony Publishing Co., n.d.

Weber, Timothy P. *Living in the Shadow of the Second Coming.* New York: Oxford University Press, 1979. 232 pp.

Grace Gospel Movement

Bullinger, E. W. *The Foundations of Dispensational Truth.* London: Lamp Press, 1959. 287 pp.

———. *Selected Writings.* London: Lamp Press, 1960. 296 pp.

Hoste, William. *Bullingerism or Ultra-Dispensationalism Exposed.* Fort Dodge, IA: n.d. 32 pp.

Ironside, Harold A. *Wrongly Dividing the Word of Truth.* Neptune, NJ: Loizeaux Brothers, n.d. 66 pp.

O'Hair, J.C. *Bible Messages of Grace and Glory.* Chicago: The Author, n.d. 17 pp.

———. *The Great Blunder of the Church.* Chicago: The Author, n.d. 70 pp.

Stewart, Alex. H. *Bullingerism Exposed.* New York: Loizeaux Brothers, n.d. 15 pp.

Chapter 13

Adventist Family

Consult the "Contents" pages to locate the entries in Part III,
the Directory Listings Sections, that comprise this family.

During its first generation, Christians believed that the Risen Christ would soon return to finish the changes begun during his public ministry. When his return was delayed, many stopped looking, but some in each generation believed they were living in the last days and expected Christ to return in their lifetime. Increasingly over the last two centuries, since the rise of Napoleon and the secularization of church-state relations he heralded, each generation has produced a variety of groups who preach a type of faith that has been called apocalyptic, chiliastic, or millennial. The movements have been characterized by the expectation of the immediate return of Christ to bring a final end to "this evil order" and replace it with a new world of supreme happiness and goodness. At every turning point in the history of Christianity, people supporting such movements appeared, sometimes within the mainstream of church activities as disturbers of accepted patterns of life and sometimes at the outer edge of church activities as critics and reformers. Always their presence is felt because they promote an idea that orthodox Christians have said to be integral to the faith.

Adventists and millenialists have however usually gone beyond the mere affirmation that Christ will return in the future to actually predict the time of his imminent appearance, either by setting a definite date or suggesting that it will occur in this present generation. Such a definite projection of the climax of history thus becomes a great motivation for members to both reform their lives and act in appropriate ways in light of that event. If history is to end in a few years, life decisions must be made in light of that event from the large decisions about career or marriage to lesser decisions about the use of resources, choice of friends, and activity during leisure time.

APOCALYPTICISM IN HISTORY. Christianity inherited its bent toward apocalypticism from its Jewish forefathers. Both the book of Daniel in the Old Testament and the apocryphal works of Jewish apocalypticism, such as the Assumption of Moses and the Books of Enoch, were part of the thought-world in which early Christians lived. For later generations, however, the book of Daniel was to be the important text. Penned in the second century B.C.E., Daniel purports to be a product of the sixth century B.C.E. The first half of the book tells the story of Daniel and some friends of his who were faithful to God while living under foreign political control. The last half details some visions of future history, stretching from sixth century Babylon to the reign of Antiochus Epiphanes in the second century. These visions, in and of themselves apocalyptic, provided the material from which future apocalyptics would draw.

Apocalypticism was integrated into the lifestyle of the early church. Many expected the imminent return of Jesus to finish what was begun on Calvary. Such a belief sustained them in times of persecution and gave hope for the improvement of their lot in life in the near future. The signposts of this belief are found in such biblical passages as Mark 13, Matthew 24, I Thessalonians 4:13–18, and, preeminently, in the vision of John the Revelator. Just as Daniel emerged as the central piece of Jewish apocalypticism, so Revelation soon pushed aside other Christian apocalypses and became the one book of the vast literature to be canonized (included in the Bible).

Revelation purports to be the ecstatic vision of John, an official in the Church of Asia Minor (now Turkey). His vision has a special message for each of seven churches and contains a lengthy scenario of the future course of history, which centers on the church. The vision culminates with a picture of the end of time and the establishment of the kingdom of God in its totality.

A vast amount of work has been done by scholars describing the nature of apocalyptic literature, with a surprising amount of unanimity in their understanding. The apocalyptist has a particular view of time and history, evil, God's relation to the world, the groups of which he is a part, and the worth of man's activity in the world. The apocalyptist sees history and time as lineal. History, begun at some point in the distant past, has continued on a more or less steady course to the present. The present is just short of the climax of the whole scheme of time. The climax will be a great supernatural happening that will destroy the present system and replace it with a new and better divine system.

The cosmic struggle of good and evil, of God and the devil, determines the course of history, and good is losing. The believer feels this loss on a quite personal level as persecution, deprivation, or moral indignation. But while evil seems to be progressing to an ultimate victory, it will be stopped short by the intervention of God, who will completely eliminate its power in the world.

God has a very close and personal relationship to the world. He began the course of history and has never ceased to intervene at various points. He caused the formation of a remnant of his people to witness to him. And he will step in to crush the evil forces before they completely conquer the good.

The course of history is personalized and internalized by the apocalyptist. He sees history as made for and centering upon himself and his ingroup. His group has been chosen; although they are on the bottom of the social ladder now, they will be on top as soon as God acts. This reversal of position will take place in the very near future.

The nearness of the end of this age puts a new perspective on man's activity in the world. As the date for the end closes in upon man, the value of normal activity decreases. Attention might be given to such Biblical admonitions as, "For the future, men who have wives should live as though they had none, and those that mourn as though they did not, and those who are glad as though they were not glad, and those who buy as though they did not own a thing,. . . For the outward order of things is passing away." (I Cor. 7:29–31). Normal activity is now replaced with a stepped-up campaign to spread the message of the coming cataclysm, for "the gospel must first be published among all nations." Not always, but quite often, an intense moral imperative is associated with the end-time. This phenomenon is seen as apocalyptists combine with the reformers who look to moral and social reform as a means to hold back an impending doom.

This type of moral apocalypticism is seen most pointedly in men such as Jeremiah, Thomas Müntzer, and George Storrs.

The apostle Paul, himself, had to deal with Christians who fell away from the apocalyptic stance of the early church. In his letter to the Thessalonians he had to answer those who were questioning why so many had died before Christ returned. But as the church grew, what for Paul was a minor incident became for the church a major problem leading it to redefine its faith. As the distance between the believers and Calvary grew, the sensibleness of an apocalyptic lifestyle diminished. So during the second, third, and fourth centuries, a battle raged—a theological battle, but much more, a battle over the whole approach and stance of the church toward the world.

Symbolic of this fight is the issue of the canonization of the book of Revelation. During the second century, this visionary masterpiece circulated from Asia Minor to Antioch and Rome. It found its earliest exponent in Justin Martyr, and about the year 200, the Muratonian Canon lists Revelation as Scripture. Irenaeus in Gaul and Tertullian in North Africa accepted and reflected Revelation in their writings.

One of the first millennial sects, the Montanists, picked up the apocalyptic stance and made it a central part of its message. Montanus tried to gather in his movement some of the spiritual, prophetic, and visionary attributes of the early church, in what was considered by many an heretical stance. The movement spread from Phrygia and eventually claimed Tertullian as an adherent in North Africa.

The first works rejecting Revelation as scriptural and of Apostolic authorship were produced by the anti-Montanists. So effective were these writings that, about 215 C.E., Hippolytus wrote a carefully worded defense of the controversial book. Then in the middle of the third century, the great scholar Origen put the Alexandrians behind the canonicity. Origen's allegorizing and spiritualizing of the text gave the church a means of accepting the work while strongly rejecting its literal millennialism (belief that Christ would literally reign on earth with his saints for 1,000 years). Even though the place of Revelation was somewhat open until the fifth century, Origen's acceptance of it, followed a century later by that of Athanasius, assured Revelation a place in the Bible.

By the early fifth century, with few exceptions, the canon was set. There needed only to be stated an authoritative position that the church would accept that would reconcile its four hundred years of waiting for Christ to return, the existence of Revelation in the canon, and the refutation of millennialism. Such a position was stated by Augustine in his magnum opus, *The City of God*. He pointed out that some had misunderstood John's Revelation and had construed it so as to produce "ridiculous fancies." Augustine reworked the literal eschatology of John in such a way that the church, while still remaining in God's history, did not live in the imminent expectation of the climax of history. God still operates in history with his chosen ones, and He is holding back evil even now. In effect, Augustine was saying that John was not painting a picture so much of the end of time as the manner in which the church progresses as it moves through both time and space. Thus, Augustine was able to keep the hope of Christ's coming to the faithful, but was able to push it effectively into the distant future. That Augustine's view could become acceptable to the church as a whole reflects not only Augustine's scholarship but also the change of position the church had undergone from a persecuted sect to the state religion of the Roman Empire. In any case, from Augustine's time to the present, any group which projected an immediate second coming was to find itself on the fringe of the church and, while the church was closely tied to the state, a persecuted minority.

But millennialists continued to arise, and while their leaders were usually of the educated, hence upper classes, the members were usually of the disinherited classes who combined their millennialism with a social protest movement. For example, in seventh century Syria, the early Christian form of the *Sibylline Oracles* appeared to bring consolation to Syrian Christians living under Moslem oppression. According to these oracles, an emperor, Methodius, is to arise and begin the final battle with the Antichrist. This battle results in an Antichrist victory, but the victory is short-lived because of the return of Christ for the final judgment. In the Middle Ages, millennial movements arose and then disappeared on numerous occasions, reflecting the high degree of social turmoil that was to result in the social revolutions of the sixteenth century. The eleventh century saw several mass millennial movements, particularly the First Crusade in 1095. Led by popular leaders such as Peter the Hermit, large armies were formed to christianize Jerusalem. One army stopped in the Rhine Valley and performed the first massacre of European Jews. The movement, itself, died, partly in exhaustion after a few miles of travel, partly on the battlefields near Constantinople.

In the twelfth century, a Cistercian monk, Joachim of Fiore, produced, between 1190 and 1195, an eschatological scheme that was to be the most influential apocalyptic understanding for the Middle Ages. He identified his new vision of history as the everlasting gospel that according to Revelation was to be preached in the last days. Joachim's scheme pictured history as an ascent in three stages, the Father's law, Christ's gospel, and the Spirit's culmination of history. Taking Matthew 1 as his starting point, Joachim counted 42 generations from Abraham to Christ and saw this as a type of the gospel age. Assuming a generation is 30 years, Joachim reasoned that the movement from the gospel to the Spirit must take place between 1200 and 1260. A new order of monks must arise to preach this message and thus prepare the way. He believed 12 patriarchs would arise to convert the Jews. Antichrist would reign for three and one-half years, after which he would be overthrown, and the age of the Spirit would begin.

Popular leaders grasped Joachim's ideas and tied them to the popular fallen hero, Frederick I, who was killed on the third crusade in 1190. A new Frederick was to arise, and he was seen as the "emperor of the last days." This movement grew when Frederick I's grandson became Frederick II. This brilliant figure did much to foster the growing messianism about himself. In 1229, he went on a crusade and crowned himself king of Jerusalem, which he had temporarily recaptured. When Pope Innocent IV put Frederick and Germany under the interdict, Frederick retorted by expanding his role to include chastisement of the church. Because Innocent was so immoral himself, his interdict had no effect. In 1240, the writings of Joachim's disciples inflamed the masses, which were heading for a major break with papal power in Europe. The movement was ended suddenly by Frederick's death in 1250. The ideas that started with Joachim were reinterpreted, and for several hundred years the dream of a resurrected Frederick was the vision that supported protest in central Europe.

One of the more famous of the chiliastic sects were the Taborites, the radical wing of the Hussite movement in fifteenth-century Czechoslovakia. These followers of the martyred John Hus united a political and economic revolt with their millennial aspirations soon after Hus's death in 1514. They went beyond Hus in their adherence to literal Biblical authority. The bitter struggle for control of Czechoslovakia helped precipitate doomsday worries. In 1519, a group of ex-Catholic priests began to preach openly the coming of the last days and the destruction in February 1520 of every town by fire (like Sodom). Everyone was called upon to flee to five towns, Taborite strongholds, destined to be saved. When the destruction did not occur, the Taborite leaders called upon their followers to take up the sword in a holy war. It was not until 1534 that the Taborites were finally defeated and, with them, their millennial hopes.

It seems more than coincidence that in Frederick's Germany the Reformation was to occur, and that out of the social upheaval caused by the Reformation, the next great movement of popular millennialism was to arise. Its leader was Thomas Müntzer. He was only one of many who saw the social and religious turmoil of the Reformation era as the sign of the end of an age, but he was the most famous. Others holding up the vision of the millennium were John Hut, Melchior Hofmann, and Augustine Bader.

Müntzer came by his view in study with Nicholas Storch, a weaver in Zwickau, and a former resident of the old Taborite lands. Müntzer believed that the Turks (Antichrist) would soon rule the world, but that the elect would then rise up and annihilate all the godless, and the millennium would begin. In his famous 1524 sermon, he called upon the princes of Germany to join him in this righteous war. Rejected by the princes, he turned to the poor. His League of the Elect became a power base from which was built a proletarian army at Mühlhausen and Frankenhausen. In two battles, the princes defeated Müntzer's army and captured and executed Müntzer, thus ending another phase of millennialism.

England had its share in millennial hopes. Anti-Cromwellian forces found an ally in the Fifth Monarchy Men, a movement that crystallized in the 1650s. This group looked to Jesus to establish a fifth world monarchy. The previous four, following the image in Daniel 2, were Assyria, Persia, Greece, and Rome (which still existed as the Roman Catholic Church). After spending time in evangelical work, the Monarchy Men concluded it was time for them to take up the sword of the Lord. In 1657 and 1661, they attempted two uprisings, both unsuccessful. Their military defeats eventually led to their annihilation.

Various millennial, chiliastic, and messianic movements continued to arise, and date-setting for Christ's second coming continued to be a popular activity. With the arrival of religious pluralism, toleration, and freedom, few millennialists fell victim to the sword, gradually replaced with public ridicule. The early nineteenth century saw a renewal of the imminent expectation of the second coming of Jesus. Edward Irving, founder of the Catholic Apostolic Church in the 1830s, proclaimed the second coming in England, setting the date as 1864. Dr. Joseph Wolff, a converted Jew, toured England and the U.S. lecturing on the second coming. Both men had been spurred into action by the French Revolution and Napoleon. Until his martyrdom, Joseph Smith, Jr., founder of the Mormons, established locale after locale as the headquarters of the kingdom of God. It was, however, a poor farmer in upper New York State who founded the movement that still exists as America's main Adventist movement, and thereby originated the uniquely American brand of the millennial hope.

MILLENNIALISM IN AMERICA. The American millennial movement that today is known as Adventism had its beginnings in New York, started there by William Miller, a Baptist layman. Miller had settled in New York after the War of 1812. For a period Miller was a Deist, denying that God interferes with the laws of the universe and stressing morality and reason rather than religious belief. Then Miller began to study the Bible. This study, which lasted about two years, seemed to satisfy his major doubts, but also convinced him that he was living near the end of his age. Further study over several more years convinced him not only that the end was near, but also that he had to go and tell the world about it. His first labors were at Dresden, New York, where a revival followed his speaking in 1831.

He continued to speak in the area as pulpits opened to him. Within a year, he was able to accept no more than half of his speaking invitations. In 1832, the *Vermont Telegraph* published a series of 16 articles written by Miller, the first of many works he was to write. The next year, a 64-page pamphlet was widely circulated.

In September 1833, Miller was given a license to preach by the Baptists. For the next 10 years, Miller lived the life of an itinerant evangelist, preaching and teaching his message of the imminent return of Jesus. The Methodists, Baptists, and Congregationalists were eager to hear Miller's words. In 1836, Miller published his lecture in his first book, *Evidences from Scripture and History of the Second Coming of Christ about the Year 1843: Exhibited in a Course of Lectures.* This book, plus a new edition of the earlier pamphlet, gave great impetus to the movement. Others began to join Miller and preach his doctrine. Most notably, in 1839, Joshua Himes invited Miller to preach in his Boston church. Himes was the man with promotional and organizational talent to lift the movement out of local interest into national prominence. In March of 1840, Himes began publication of the movement's first periodical, *Signs of the Times.* By autumn, the movement had grown to the extent that a decision was made to hold a conference on the second coming of the Lord Jesus Christ. This conference opened October 13, 1840, at Chardon Street Church in Boston. Early leaders were among those in attendance—Josiah Litch, Joseph Bates, and Henry Dana Ward. The conference spent its time discussing the views that Miller had expounded in his pamphlets and book.

Miller believed that "God has set bounds, determined times, and revealed unto his prophets the events long before they were accomplished." These times were revealed by both plain declaration and by figurative language. From his study of Daniel and Revelation, Miller believed that he had deciphered the chronology concerning the end of the age. He began with the principle that a prophetic day is equal to a year (see Ezekiel 4:6). The key passages were Daniel 8:14, "unto 2,300 days, then shall the sanctuary be cleansed, or justified," and Daniel 9:24, "Seventy weeks are determined upon thy people. . . to make an end of sins." Miller saw the end of the 70 weeks (490 days or 490 years) as C.E. 33, at the cross of Jesus. From this date, he pushed backward to 457 B.C.E. ("the going forth of the commandment to Ezra to restore the law and the people of Jerusalem") as the beginning. Since, as Miller argued, the 70 weeks were part of the 2,300 days, the 2,300 days could be seen to begin also in 457 B.C. Thus, the cleansing of the sanctuary would be in 1843. Though Miller bolstered this chronology with several other figures which also ended in 1843, this set of figures was the basic one.

From these figures, Miller and his associates could build a history based on the events described in Revelation and Daniel, and this chronology of prophetic history worked out mathematically. Miller published such a work covering the Old Testament period and showing that 1843 was the end of the sixth millennium since creation. In his books, he also pointed the way for his followers to fill in the history from C.E. 33 to the present.

The Boston conference was so successful that in ensuing weeks other conferences in other cities were held to explain and discuss Miller's message, which Himes had now renamed "the midnight cry." As the movement grew, opposition increased, and the established denominations began to take action to counteract Miller's influence. Formerly cooperative churches closed their doors to Miller and his associates. Numerous accounts appeared of ministers and laymen being expelled from their churches. In one famous case, L. S. Stockman was tried for heresy before his presiding elders in the Maine Conference of the Methodist Episcopal Church and was later expelled. In 1843, the *New York Christian Advocate*, the principle organ of the Methodists, carried a series of articles against Millerism, which vied for space with the anti-Romanist articles attacking the Roman Catholic Church.

Miller's movement was taking on a more definite shape in this period. Before the end in 1843, the first camp meeting was held at East Kingston, New Hampshire. In November, the second periodical, *The Midnight Cry*, was begun. Miller was also sharpening his views. Until 1843, Miller had been vague about the second coming as being "about the year 1843." But on January 1, he committed himself to a more definite stance: "I am fully convinced that somewhere between March 21st, 1843 and March 21st, 1844, according to the Jewish mode of computation of time, Christ will come."

With tension running high as March approached, there appeared in the late February sky a large comet. Its appearance was a complete surprise, without a warning from the astronomers. And this was just one of a number of spectacular events of the night sky that found its way into print. March 14, 1843, came and went. Now, new issues began to emerge. The increased opposition of the churches made meeting houses hard to secure. Also, large numbers of Adventists had no prior religious connection from which they could gain nourishment. These two factors, plus the growing size of the movement, led Charles Fitch to start the inevitable "come out" movement, urging those who believed in Christ's imminent return to come out of their denominational churches and form their own churches. Fitch was opposed by Miller, but the pressure to "come out" only increased.

In 1844, as the March 14 deadline passed without the second coming, Miller had approximately 50,000 followers across the East and Midwest. Miller had earlier written of his views, "If this chronology is not correct, I shall despair of ever getting from the Bible and history a true account of the age of the world." In May 1844, Miller wrote to his followers, "I confess my error and acknowledge my disappointment."

But 50,000 enthusiastic followers could not just be turned away. While a few dropped out, most would not. In a short time, adjustments in Miller's chronology were made. In August, Samuel S. Snow put forth the "seventh month" scheme that looked to October 22, 1844, as the real date of return. Tension reached a new high. On October 22, the Adventists gathered to await the Lord. However, as one author put it, "But the day came. And Christ did not."

The Great Disappointment, as the Adventists have termed the reaction to the non-happening of October 22, 1844, left the movement in chaos. Miller again acknowledged the error but remained confident in the imminent return of Jesus. Other leaders also found themselves in the same boat. Miller refuted any further attempts to set dates and gradually retired from active leadership in the movement. But forces already in operation were now prepared to weld these organized believers into a number of denominational bodies. These are treated below.

Adventist theology at any time is usually built upon and accepts the theological perspectives of its parent bodies, making the necessary apocalyptic adjustments. Since almost all American Adventist bodies can be traced directly to Miller, the Baptist lay preacher, it is not surprising to find that popular Baptist theology has had a great influence on Adventism. There is general agreement on the doctrines concerning the Bible, God, Christ, and the sacraments. The idea of ordinances (instead of sacraments), baptism by immersion, and the practice of foot washing, particularly, further manifest Baptist origins. Sabbatarianism was transmitted directly by the Seventh-Day Baptists.

Eschatology took up two articles in the Baptists' 1833 New Hampshire Confession of Faith and provided a base from which Miller could speculate that "the end of this world is approaching." The Adventists, however, went far beyond the Baptists in speculations. The Adventists also raised the issue of man's innate immortality by denying it and have, in the twentieth century, been in the forefront of groups proposing a view that has been accepted by many biblical scholars.

Ethical positions among Adventists have shown two seemingly divergent trends. An emphasis on the Old Testament and on the law as mandatory for Christians has developed out of the acceptance of the Sabbath. Some groups have gone so far as to celebrate Jewish holidays and dietary laws. The celebration of the Sabbath has been promoted by the ecumenical Bible Sabbath Association, which was formed as a counterpart of the Lord's Day Alliance of the United States. Formed in 1945, the Bible Sabbath Association promotes the observance of the Sabbath and publishes a directory of Sabbath-keeping organizations. A second ethical trend emerged as the Adventists became involved in the great social crusades of the two decades preceding the Civil War. Many Adventists were vocal abolitionists and ardent supporters of the peace movements. Pacifism remains a common Adventist position; the well-publicized refusal of the Jehovah's Witnesses to be drafted is derived from their Millerite heritage.

THE SACRED NAME MOVEMENT. No one knows exactly who first raised the issue of God's name as being an important doctrinal consideration. Certainly, in the 1920s the International Bible Students on their way to becoming the Jehovah's Witnesses raised the issue forcefully. Twentieth-century scholarship had, however, begun to emphasize belief that "Yahweh" was the correct pronunciation of the "YHWH," the spelling of God's name in Hebrew. There were slight variations in spelling and pronunciation, as will be noted. By the mid-1930s there were members and ministers, primarily of the Church of God (Seventh-Day), who were beginning to use the "sacred name" and to promote the cause actively. One person associated with these efforts was Elder J. D. Bagwell of Warrior, Alabama. By the end of 1938, the Faith Bible and Tract Society had been organized. In July 1939, the Assembly of YHWH was chartered in the state of Michigan. About the same time, the Assembly of Yahweh Beth Israel was also formed.

No single force in spreading the Sacred Name movement was as important as *The Faith* magazine. This magazine was formed to support the Old Testament festivals as being contemporarily valid. Gradually the editor, Elder C. O. Dodd, began to use "Jehovah," then "Jahoveh," "Yahovah," "Yahavah," and "Yahweh." Dodd edited *The Faith* from its founding in 1937 until his death in 1955.

During the 1940s, several assemblies were formed and new periodicals begun. Some of these became substantial movements and continue today as primary religious bodies. Having come primarily out of the Church of God (Seventh-Day), the assemblies follow the Adventist and Old Testament emphases, including the observance of the Jewish festivals. The main divergence is over the name issue and exactly what spelling and pronunciation the name has. The common designation for local gatherings is "assembly," a literal translation of the Greek "ecclesia."

The Sacred Name movement is often thought of as the "Elijah Message," a reference to Elijah's words in I Kings 18:36 that extol Yahweh as the Elohim of Israel.

CHARLES TAZE RUSSELL'S BIBLE STUDENTS. Following any apocalyptic failure, such as the Millerite disappointment of 1844, there are several options open to the followers. The disbanding of the group and a return to pre-excitement existence is a minority option. Spiritualization—the process of claiming that the prophecy was in error to the extent of its being seen as a visible historical event, and the attempt to reinterpret it as a cosmic, inner, invisible, or heavenly event—is most popular. A final trend for disappointed apocalyptics is to return to the source of revelation (the Bible, psychic-prophet, or analysis of contemporary events) and seek a new date. (An obvious, less committed form is to set a vague date, usually verbalized as "the near future.")

After the 1844 disappointment, leaders and periodicals rose and fell as they projected new dates and had to live with their failures. Few spawned groups that lasted beyond the projected dates. Speculations on the winter of 1853–54 lay behind the formation of the Advent Christian Church. A small group led by Jonas Wendell projected an 1874 date. Disappointed followers spiritualized the 1874 date and projected a new date, 1914. In 1876, Charles Taze Russell came across an issue of *The Herald of the Morning*, Nelson H. Barbour's magazine, which extolled the views of Jonas Wendell, and a whole new era in Adventist thought began.

Russell (1852-1916) was born in Pittsburgh, Pennsylvania, of Scotch-Irish Presbyterians, and was reared in his father's clothing store chain. Shaken by "infidel claims," he began a religious quest that led, in 1870, to Jonas Wendell. He joined Wendell's group, but soon disagreed on the manner of Christ's return. Then, in 1876, he met Barbour and united with him in beginning anew the suspended *Herald of the Morning* and co-authoring *Three Worlds or Plan of Redemption*.

By the time of his association with Barbour, Russell had come to accept three ideas which are thoroughly ingrained in the movement he began and characteristic of it. First, he rejected a belief in hell as a place of eternal torment. Second, he left the Wendell Adventists because he had discovered the true meaning of *parousia* (the Greek word usually translated "return"). Russell believed that it meant *presence* and he arrived at the conclusion that, in 1874, the Lord's presence had begun. Finally, Russell began to arrive at a new doctrine of the atonement, or ransom. Adam, he believed, received death as a just sentence, but his offspring received death by inheritance. Jesus' act of sacrifice counteracted the death penalty. Because of Adam, all were born without the right to live. Because of Jesus, all had inherited sin canceled. Thus, all people were guaranteed a second chance, a trial in which enlightenment and experience would be followed by a choice either to belong to God or be a rebel deserving of death. This "second chance" would be offered during the millennium, Christ's reign on earth with his saints for one thousand years.

Russell's doctrine of the ransom also included a role for the church as an atoning force. Derived in part from Paul's Epistle to the Colossians 1:24 and from an allegorical interpretation of the Hebrew sacrifice of the bull (i.e., Christ) and the goat (i.e., the church) on the day of atonement described in Leviticus 16, Russell taught that the church as the body of Christ is by its present suffering offering a spiritual sacrifice to God.

Inherent in Russell's beliefs was a denial of certain orthodox ideas such as the Trinity. He outlined a personal lineage that began with Arius (fourth century C.E.) whose atonement idea was close to Russell's and included the ecclesiastical rebels—Luther, Peter Waldo, and John Wycliff.

After meeting Barbour, Russell drew support from other Adventists such as J. H. Paton, A. P. Adams, and A. D. Jones. This coalition lasted until 1878, when Barbour, who had set April as the month when the church would go to heaven, suffered a loss of support by the disconfirmation of his prophecy. (He further deviated with some speculations on the atonement.) Russell, Paton, and Jones withdrew their support of Barbour, and Russell began, with their assistance, *Zion's Watch Tower and Herald of Christ's Presence*, which was sent free to all of Barbour's subscribers. Paton soon was to join the ranks of dissenters, and he left Russell to expound his own speculations in his periodical, *Zion's Day Star*.

The first issue of the *Watch Tower* in 1879 is a convenient date to begin the history of Russell's movement. To the *Watch Tower* was soon added abundant literature to help a growing number of Bible students who were popularly called "Millennial Dawn Bible Students." They came together to study the Scriptures with the help of Russell's writings. Russell began to publish tracts, a number of which were combined into *Food for Thinking Christians*. He also called for a thousand preachers to spread the gospel by distributing the *Watch Tower* and his tracts.

In 1881, Zion's Watch Tower Tract Society was set up. In 1886, the first of six volumes of *Studies in the Scripture* appeared. The publishing of Volume I, *The Plan of the Ages*, marked an upward turning point in the development of the movement, as it provided the substantial ideological base to *Watch Tower* readers. By 1889, more than 100,000 copies of *The Plan of the Ages* were in print.

The pattern of the Bible Student movement's growth was typical of the growth of a number of loosely affiliated religious groups. Local congregations were formed by people impressed with Russell's views and writings. They were related directly to Russell primarily through the *Watch Tower*. The work was spread mostly by volunteers. Gradually, there arose colporteurs, who spent from half to all of their time in the work and who earned their living by selling Russell's books (with a 64 percent discount).

In 1894, pilgrims were added to the structure as traveling preachers and teachers to local congregations. Pilgrims were paid by the central office. A plan for local elders or leaders to sell their ideas to new areas was begun in 1911.

Extension of the work also occurred through a number of events that generated a great deal of publicity. In particular, Rus-

sell enjoyed debates, at which he was a master. His 1903 debate with E. L. Eaton, a Methodist minister, and with Elder L. S. White of the Disciples of Christ did much to spread the movement.

As the movement emerged, certain ideas came to the fore; none were so prominent as chronology and the 1914 date. *The Plan of the Ages* was God's calendar for dealing with men. Reminiscent of John Nelson Darby's teachings was Russell's division of history into a number of eras. According to Russell's chart in *The Plan of the Ages*, the first dispensation from Adam to the flood demonstrated the inability of angels to improve the world. The patriarchal age (from the flood to Jacob's death) was followed by the Jewish age, which lasted until Christ's death. The gospel age of 1845 years ended in 1874. That year marked the dawning of the millennial age, which would begin with a "harvest period" or millennial dawn period of 40 years.

The millennial dawn period (1874–1914) would be marked by a return of the Jews to Palestine and the gradual overthrow of the Gentile nations. All would be climaxed in 1914 with the glorification of the saints, the establishment of God's direct rule on earth, and the restoration of man to perfection on earth. The coincidence of the apocalyptic date with World War I was viewed by Russell's followers as a cause for great hope, sharply contrasting the disappointments that had followed other predictions. The war was interpreted as God's direct intervention in the affairs of humanity and a signal of the beginning of the world's end. (Russell revised the date to 1918 later and died in 1916, before the second disconfirmation.)

A final significant idea was the doctrine of the future church. Russell believed from his reading of Revelation 7:4–9 that the church consisted of 144,000 saints from the time of Christ to 1914, who would receive the ultimate reward of becoming "priests and kings in heaven." Others would make up a class of heavenly servants termed "the great company." The idea of two classes of believers was illustrated by numerous biblical characters (most notably Elijah, taken to heaven, and Elisha, his servant), who were seen as types of the classes.

Russell and his ideas would become the subject of much controversy after his death. Some leaders would ascribe to him a cosmic role and identify him with the good and faithful servant of Matthew 25:21. Others would argue over the significance of the harvest, which supposedly ended in 1914. Some would feel that the harvest closed in 1914 and that the 144,000 were all chosen by then. Others would consider the harvest open and continue to gather the 144,000. Similar to the differences on the harvest would be differences on the identification of the Elijah and Elisha classes.

When Russell died, he left behind him a charismatically run organization in the hands of a board of directors and editorial committee. The next decade was marked by controversy, schism, the rise to power of Judge J. F. Rutherford, and the emergence of Jehovah's Witnesses.

THE SOUTHCOTTITES. Before William Miller created an Adventist movement in the United States in the 1830s and 1840s, an Adventist movement flowered in England. The focus of the English movement was Joanna Southcott (1750–1814). In the 1790s, she began to profess visions, to write them down in both prose and verse, and to gather a following. She was convinced that she was a prophetess. Several predictions, including France's conquest of Italy under the unknown general Bonaparte, created some attention.

The thrust of her message was placed within an orthodox Christian framework and centered upon the imminent return of Christ. What made the prophecy distinctive was the peculiar "doctrine of the bride." A feminist, Joanna began to speculate on the crucial role of women in the Bible and the role of the "woman clothed with the sun" (Rev. 12:1), who would bring forth the male child who would rule the nations with a rod of iron. She identified the woman with the bride of the Lamb (Rev. 19:7), and then identified both of them with herself.

She began a movement to mobilize England. Joanna's real impact dates from 1801, when she first published her prophecies abroad in several booklets. These booklets brought her first disciples, among whom she began a practice of sealing. Accepting the apocalyptic vision of a world delivered into the hands of Satan, she believed that the key to the devil's overthrow was to have a sufficient number of people renounce him and be sealed as of the Lord. She distributed the seals to all who would sign up for them. They were written on square sheets of paper upon which a circle was drawn. Inside the circle Joanna wrote "The sealed of the Lord, the Elect and Precious, Man's Redemption to Inherit the Tree of Life, to be made Heirs of God and Joint Heirs with Jesus Christ." The paper would be folded and sealed with wax and with the monogram I. C. and two stars. Critics accused Joanna of selling the seals, but she denied it.

In 1814, at 64 years of age, she had a climactic revelation. Having identified herself with the woman in Revelation 12, she was always concerned with the child the woman was to bear. Joanna's voice told her to prepare for the birth of a son. This child was identified in Joanna's thinking with Shiloh (Gen. 49:10). She began to show signs of pregnancy and was declared pregnant by several doctors. The followers prepared for a new virgin birth. As the time of the delivery approached, she took an earthly husband. When the baby failed to arrive and the symptoms of the hysteric pregnancy left, Joanna's strength ebbed and she died in December 1814.

Followers and leaders alike were thrown into chaos. Among those who did not leave, there were attempts to regroup the forces, and a number of separate churches resulted. Most were confined to England, but a few found their way to America.

BRITISH ISRAELISM. Growing up largely with Adventist circles, and picking ideas from them at random—nontrinitarian theology, Sabbatarianism, sacred name emphases, and dispensationalism—the British Israelite Bible students emerged as a separate distinct group in American religion during the decade after World War I. They experienced a steady growth into the 1940s but seemed to wane in the 1950s and 1960s. During the 1970s, however, the movement experienced a new wave of revival in its most militant wing, popularly called the Identity Movement.

Though only visible in the United States since World War I, British Israelism, the Identity Movement, traces its history to ancient Israel. In actual fact, its history begins in the late eighteenth century in England, where one of the more popular avocations of Bible students was the attempt to discover the present-day identity of the so-called 10 lost tribes of Israel—the 10 tribes carried away into captivity by Shalmaneser, the king of Assyria in 721 B.C. (II Kings 17). Since 1800, numerous speculations have appeared, but only two opinions, apart from the generally accepted one that the tribes were assimilated into the peoples of the Middle East, ever gained a wide following. The first of these speculations identified the American Indians as the tribes. That speculation was promulgated by Joseph Smith, the founder of the Church of Jesus Christ of Latter-Day Saints. The second speculation was the identification of the tribes with Anglo-Saxon peoples by the British Israelites.

Scotsman John Wilson, who in 1840 published his theories in *Our Israelitish Origins*, is generally looked upon as the founder of the British Israelites. His appearance of scholarship and his oratorical abilities were enough to sell his notion to the public.

Wilson was by no means the first to make the British-Israelite identification. As early as 1649, John Sadler (b. 1615) speculated on the idea in his *Rights to the Kingdom* and seemed to have advised Oliver Cromwell on readmitting the Jews to England. In the eighteenth century, Dr. Abade of Amsterdam, a Protestant theologian, is reported to have said: "Unless the ten tribes have flown into the air, or have been plunged into the center of the earth, they must be sought for in the north and west, and in the British Isles" (Anton Darms, *The Delusion of British Israel* [New York: Loizeaux Brothers, Bible Truth Depot, n.d.], 15).

The real originator of the idea, however, was Canadian Richard Brothers (b. 1757), a psychic visionary who settled in London in the 1780s. He began to publish the content of revelations that identified himself as a descendant of King David and demanded the crown of England. He was found guilty of treason, but insane, and sent to an asylum. Brothers' ideas caught on with some influential men such as Orientalist Nathaniel Brassey Halhed, Quaker psychic William Bryan, and Scottish lawyer John Finleyson. The defeat of Napoleon was the marked confirmation of their ideas.

The basics of British Israelite theology are quite simple, although a working knowledge of the Old Testament is required to trace the intricacies of the logic. The basic premise is that Israel and Judah were two entities, the former comprising the northern 10 tribes, and the latter the two southern ones after 922 B.C. Members of the northern kingdom, after being freed from captivity, wandered into Europe and settled in northwest Europe, Scandinavia, and the British Isles. Jeremiah, the prophet, is believed to have transported Tea-Tephi, the daughter of King Zedekiah, to Ireland to marry Prince Herremon, thus continuing Israel's royal lineage. James I was the first descendant of this union to reign in London.

Different countries of Europe are to be identified with the different tribes; Britain and the United States are descendants of Joseph's two sons Ephraim and Manasseh, and, as such, are particularly blessed (Genesis 48). The tribe of Dan has, in fulfillment of prophecy (Genesis 49:17), left numerous signposts of its tribal meanderings—Dan River, Denmark, Danube River, and others.

From this basic theology, other observations are made in correlating biblical quotes with isolated facts of archaeology, legendary materials, history, and philology. Wilson was the first to note the correlation between the Hebrew word for covenant, "brith," and "Britain." The Stone of Scone is believed to have been from the throne in Jerusalem, brought to Ireland by Jeremiah. (Actually, it was quarried in Scotland.)

British Israelism has attracted much attention because of its racist tendencies, especially in the United States. Implicit in the theory is the superiority of the Anglo-Saxon, which is seen as a religious superiority, much as with any chosen people doctrine. The Jews were seen as "kin" to the Anglo-Saxons. In a famous quote, J. H. Allen said: "Understand us: we do not say that the Jews are not Israelites; they belong to the posterity of Jacob, who was called Israel; hence they are all Israelites. But the great bulk of Israelites are not the Jews, just as the great bulk of Americans are not Californians, and yet all Californians are Americans; also, as in writing the history of America we must of necessity write the history of California, because California is a part of America; but we could write a history of California without writing a history of America" (J. H. Allen, *Judah's Sceptre and Joseph's Birthright* [Boston: A. A. Beauchamp, 1930], 71).

Numerous refutations of British Israelism have been written from a perspective of orthodox history and theology. These have, in spite of their often vitriolic nature, conclusively refuted the bulk of British Israelite speculations. They, however, have missed the point: whatever success British Israelism has had has been as a religious and emotional expression of British imperialism and American manifest destiny. There is a definite correlation between the rise and fall of those ideas and the popularity of British Israelism. The dismantling of the British Empire has had a devastating effect upon the movement.

John Wilson's book was published in America in 1850 and found isolated disciples but no real following until after World War I. In 1886, M. M. Eshelman was introduced to British Israelism by an 80-year-old immigrant to Illinois, William Montgomery. In the pages of *The Gospel Messenger*, published at Mt. Morris, Illinois, Eshelman began to write of his ideas, and in 1887, he published a book, *Two Sticks*. Then in 1902, the Reverend J. H. Allen published *Judah's Sceptre and Joseph's Birthright*. These two books became the major items selling British Israelism to an American audience.

The British Israel movement was at its height in the 1930s and 1940s. It never reached the development or popularity in America that it had in England, but in the late 1940s, it could boast a national audience among both congregational members and radio respondents. Two seminaries were functioning in 1950. The British Israel hypothesis—that Anglo-Saxons are descendants of the ten lost tribes of Israel—was finding support among people who would by no means identify themselves with the movement itself. What remain today are the remnants of that once healthy national movement.

One of the early important structures created by the movement was Dayton Theological Seminary, which functioned from 1947 into the early 1950s. It was founded by Millard J. Flenner, an ex-Congregational minister and pastor of the Church of the Covenants in Dayton. Among the teachers was Conrad Gaard, who was pastor for many years of the Christian Chapel Church in Tacoma. As head of the Destiny of America Foundation, he was a significant writer and radio minister until his death in 1969. Gaard helped Dayton graduates keep in touch through his travels and tours.

Quite apart from the mainline of the British Israel movement, one Church of God adventist radio minister, Herbert W. Armstrong, integrated British Israelism into his thought and wrote a paraphrase of Allen's *Judah's Sceptre and Joseph's Birthright*. His miniscule ministry, began in Eugene, Oregon, in the 1930s, began to blossom after his move to Pasadena, California, in 1947. Under its present name, the Worldwide Church of God, it introduced literally millions of people to British Israelism and now claims approximately 100,000 members, the single most successful such group to ever exist. In the 1990s, however, under Armstrong's successor, the church not only dropped its British-Israel ideology, but most of the ideas that made it distinctive; it has adopted an orthodox Evangelical Christian theological perspective.

THE MODERN IDENTITY MOVEMENT. British Israel is implicitly anti-Semitic and antiblack. However, in the middle of the twentieth century British Israelism became associated with several groups that actively and explicitly anti-Semitic and antiblack such as the Ku Klux Klan, and, after World War II, the neo-Nazi movement. Among those generally credited with bringing these two forces together is the Reverend Gerald L. K. Smith (1898-1976), founder of the Christian Nationalist Crusade. Besides publishing pro-Anglo Saxon material, Smith published and freely circulated a large amount of defamatory material on blacks and Jews. The work of Smith and of his former lieutenant Wesley Swift, gave rise in the 1970s to a quite recognizable group within the larger British Israel community.

The Identity Movement, a name taken from their "identifying" modern white people as the literal ancestors of the ancient Israelites, has become increasingly controversial because of its identification with violent and illegal actions and the growing opposition it has provoked among the more established religious community, both Christians and Jews, of America. While various watchdog organizations had developed a concern for the emerging movement in previous decades, in the early 1980s, public attention began to focus on one center, called the Church, the Sword, and the Arm of the Lord (C.S.A.), located on the Arkansas-Missouri border. In 1983, Gordon Kahl, a leader with the Posse Comitatus, an anti-tax group associated with the large Identity Movement, killed two U. S. marshals in South Dakota. Fleeing the scene of the crime, he was arrested in Arkansas not far from C.S.A. A year later, an Arkansas state trooper was killed by a man identified as a former resident of C.S.A. Then in 1985, the leader of C.S.A. was arrested for racketeering and sentenced to 20 years in jail, an event that led to the dissolution of the group.

As events at C.S.A. were unfolding, authorities were also moving against one Identity group known as the Order. The group was composed primarily of former members of the Church of Jesus Christ Christian, Aryan Nations headquartered in Hayden Lake, Idaho, which had grown out of the church founded by Wesley Swift in Southern California. Members of the group were believed responsible for a series of robberies in 1983 and 1984 as well as the death of David Berg, an outspoken Jewish radio talk show host in Denver, who was shot in 1984. One leader of the order, Robert Jay Matthews, was killed in a shootout as law officers attempted to arrest him. Ten others were convicted in 1985 of racketeering.

In 1987, 15 leaders of the Identity Movement were indicted on a series of charges from conspiracy to kill government officials to violating David Berg's civil rights. However, the 15 were found not guilty in a trial the following year.

Sources—The Adventist Family

The Seventh-day Adventists have archives at several of their schools, but the most prominent collections are at the church's headquarters, 6840 Eastern Ave., NW, Washington, DC, and at Andrews University, Berrien Springs, MI. The Advent Christian Church supports the Adventists Archives at Aurora College, Aurora, Illinois.

ADVENTISM, MILLENNIALISM, AND APOCALYTICISM

Case, Shirley Jackson. *The Millennial Hope*. Chicago: University of Chicago Press, 1918. 253 pp.

Chamberlin, E. R. *Antichrist and the Millennium*. New York: E. P. Dutton, 1975. 244 pp.

Froom, Edwin Leroy. *The Conditionalist Faith of Our Fathers*. 2 Vols. Washington, DC: Review and Herald Publishing Association, 1966.

———. *The Prophetic Faith of Our Fathers*. 4 vols. Washington, DC: Review and Herald Publishing Association, 1950–54.

Grosso, Michael. *Millennium Myth: Love and Death at the End of Time*. Wheaton, IL: Quest Books, 1995.

Harrison, J. F. C. *The Second Coming, Popular Millenarianism, 1780–1850*. London: Routledge & Kegan Paul, 1979. 277 pp.

Hunter, Anthony. *The Last Days*. London: Anthony Blond, 1958. 232 pp.

O'Leary, Stephen. *Arguing the Apocalypse: A Theory of Millennial Rhetoric*. New York: Oxford University Press, 1994. 314 pp.

Rist, Martin. "Introduction to the Revelation of St. John the Divine." In *The Interpreters Bible*. Vol. XII. New York: Abingdon, 1974, pp. 617–27.

St. Clair, Michael. *Millennial Movements in Historical Context*. New York: Garland Publishing, 1992. 373 pp.

Schmithals, Walter. *The Apocalyptic Movement*. Nashville: Abingdon, 1975. 255 pp.

ADVENTISM IN AMERICA

Directory of Sabbath-Observing Groups. Fairview, OK: The Bible Sabbath Association, 1980. 147 pp.

Gaustad, Edwin Scott. *The Rise of Adventism*. New York: Harper & Row, 1974.

Nichol, Francis D. *The Midnight Cry*. Washington, DC: Review and Herald Publishing Association, 1944. 576 pp.

Sears, Clara Endicott. *Days of Delusion*. Boston: Houghton Mifflin Co., 1924. 264 pp.

Seventh-Day Adventist Encyclopedia. Washington, DC: Review and Herald Publishing Association, 1966. 1454 pp.

WILLIAM MILLER

Bliss, Sylvester. *Memoirs of William Miller*. Boston: Joshua V. Himes, 1853. 426 pp.

A Brief History of William Miller, the Great Pioneer in Adventist Faith. Washington, DC: Review and Herald Publishing Association, 1915.

Gale, Robert. *The Urgent Call*. Washington, DC: Review and Herald Publishing Association, 1975. 158 pp.

White, James. *Sketches of the Christian Life and Public Labors of William Miller*. Battle Creek, MI: Steam Press, 1875. 413 pp.

ELLEN G. WHITE AND THE SEVENTH-DAY ADVENTISTS

Bull, Malcolm. *Seeking a Sanctuary: Seventh-day Adventism and the American Dream.* San Francisco: Harper & Row, 1989. 319 pp.

A Critique of Prophetess of Health. Washington, DC: The Ellen G. White Estate, General Conference of S.D.A., 1976. 127 pp.

Damsteegt, P. Gerard. *Foundation of the Seventh-Day Adventist Message and Mission.* Grand Rapids, MI: William B. Eerdmans Publishing Co., 1977. 348 pp.

Delafield, D. A. *Ellen G. White and the Seventh-Day Adventist Church.* Mountain View, CA: Pacific Press Publishing Association, 1963. 90 pp.

Noobergen, Rene. *Ellen G. White, Prophet of Destiny.* New Canaan, CT: Keats Publishing, 1972. 241 pp.

Numbers, Ronald L. *Prophetess of Health, A Study of Ellen G. White.* New York: Harper & Row, 1976. 271 pp.

CHURCHES OF GOD (SEVENTH DAY)

Bjorling, Joel. *The Churches of God, Seventh Day, A Bibliography.* New York: Garland Publishing, 1987. 296 pp.

Hopkins, Joseph. *The Armstrong Empire.* Grand Rapids: William B. Eerdmans Publishing Co., 1974. 304 pp.

Nickels, Richard C. *A History of the Seventh Day Church of God.* Vol. I. Sheridan, WY: The Author, 1977. 397 pp.

———. *Six Papers on the History of the Church of God.* Sheridan, WY: Giving & Sharing, 1977.

SABBATARIANISM

Armstrong, Herbert W. *The Resurrection Was Not on Sunday.* Pasadena, CA: Ambassador College, 1972. 14 pp.

———. *Which Day Is the Sabbath of the New Testament?* Pasadena, CA: Worldwide Church of God, 1971. 23 pp.

Dellinger, George. *A History of the Sabbath Resurrection Doctrine.* Westfield, IN: Sabbath Research Center, 1982. 33 pp.

Haynes, Carlyle B. *From Sabbath to Sunday.* Washington, DC: Review and Herald Publishing Association, 1928. 128 pp.

Love, William Deloss. *Sabbath and Sunday.* Chicago: Fleming H. Revell, 1896. 325 pp.

SACRED NAME MOVEMENT

Dugger, A. N., and C.O. Dodd. *A History of the True Church.* Jerusalem: n.p., 1968. 318 pp.

"Let Your Name Be Sanctified." Brooklyn: Watchtower Bible and Tract Society of New York, 1961. 382 pp.

Meyer, Jacob O. *The Memorial Name—Yahweh.* Bethel, PA: The Assemblies of Yahweh, 1978. 76 pp.

Rutherford, J. F. *Vindication.* Vol. I. Brooklyn: Watchtower Bible and Tract Association, 1931. 346 pp.

Snow, L. D. "A Brief History of the Name Movement in America." *The Eliyah Messenger and Field Reporter*, May 1966, pp. 1, 4, 7, 12.

Traina, A. B. *The Holy Name Bible.* Brandywine, MD: Scripture Research Association, 1980. 346 pp.

CHARLES TAZE RUSSELL AND THE BIBLE STUDENTS

Beckford, James A. *The Trumpet of Prophecy.* Oxford: Basil Blackwell, 1975. 244 pp.

Bergman, Jerry. *Jehovah's Witnesses and Kindred Groups: An Historical Compendium and Bibliography.* New York: Garland Publishing, 1984. 370 pp.

Cole, Marley. *Triumphant Kingdom.* New York: Criterion Books, 1957. 256 pp.

Gruss, Edmond Charles. *Apostles of Denial.* N.p.: Presbyterian and Reformed Publishing Co., 1970. 324 pp.

Penton, M. James. *Apocalypse Delayed.* Toronto: University of Toronto Press, 1985. 400 pp.

Rogerson, Alan. *Millions Now Living Will Never Die.* London: Constable, 1969. 216 pp.

White, Timothy. *A People for His Name.* New York: Vantage Press, 1967. 418 pp.

JOANNA SOUTHCOTT

Balleiene, G. R. *Past Finding Out.* New York: Macmillan Co., 1956. 151 pp.

The Life and Journal of John Wroe. Ashton-under-Lyne: Trustees of the Society of Christian Israelites, 1900. 639 pp.

Matthews, Ronald. *English Messiahs.* London: Methuen & Co., 1936. 230 pp.

BRITISH ISRAELISM

Allen, J. H. *Judah's Sceptre and Joseph's Birthright.* Boston: A. A. Beauchamp, 1930. 377 pp.

Armstrong, Herbert W. *The United States and Britain in Prophecy.* Pasadena, CA: Worldwide Church of God, 1980. 163 pp.

Barkun, Michael. *Religion and the Racist Right: the Origins of the Christian Identity Movement.* Chapel Hill, NC: University of North Carolina Press, 1994. 290 pp.

Coates, James. *Armed and Dangerous.* New York: Hill and Wang, 1987. 294 pp.

Darms, Anton. *The Delusion of British-Israel.* New York: Loizeaux Brothers, Bible Truth Depot, n.d. 224 pp.

Haberman, Frederick. *The Climax of the Ages Is Near.* St. Petersburg, FL: The Kingdom Press, 1940. 94 pp.

Hate Groups in America. New York: Anti-Defamation League of B'nai B'rith, 1982. 107 pp.

Kaplan, Jeffrey. *Radical Religion in America.* Syracuse, NY: Syracuse University Press, 1997. 245 pp.

Mackendrick, W. G. *The Roadbuilder. The Destiny of the British Empire and the U.S.A.* London: Covenant Publishing Co., 1931. 213 pp.

Roy, Ralph Lord. *Apostles of Discord.* Boston: Beacon Press, 1953. 437 pp.

Schwartz, Alan M., et al. "The 'Identity Churches': A Theology of Hate." *ADL Facts* 28, No. 1 (Spring 1983), p. 116.

Swift, Wesley A. *Testimony of Tradition and the Origin of Races.* Hollywood, CA: New Christian Crusade Church, n.d. 34 pp.

Wilson, J. *Our Israelitish Origins.* Philadelphia: Daniels & Smith, 1850. 237 pp.

Identity Movement. Chapel Hill, NC: University of North Carolina Press, 1994. 290 pp.

Coates, James. *Armed and Dangerous.* New York: Hill and Wang, 1987. 294 pp.

Darms, Anton. *The Delusion of British-Israel.* New York: Loizeaux Brothers, Bible Truth Depot, n.d. 224 pp.

Haberman, Frederick. *The Climax of the Ages Is Near.* St. Petersburg, FL: The Kingdom Press, 1940. 94 pp.

Hate Groups in America. New York: Anti-Defamation League of B'nai B'rith, 1982. 107 pp.

Mackendrick, W. G. *The Roadbuilder. The Destiny of the British Empire and the U.S.A.* London: Covenant Publishing Co., 1931. 213 pp.

Roy, Ralph Lord. *Apostles of Discord.* Boston: Beacon Press, 1953. 437 pp.

Schwartz, Alan M., et al. "The 'Identity Churches': A Theology of Hate." *ADL Facts* 28, No. 1 (Spring 1983), p. 116.

Swift, Wesley A. *Testimony of Tradition and the Origin of Races.* Hollywood, CA: New Christian Crusade Church, n.d. 34 pp.

Wilson, J. *Our Israelitish Origins.* Philadelphia: Daniels & Smith, 1850. 237 pp.

Chapter 14

Liberal Family

Consult the "Contents" pages to locate the entries in Part III,
the Directory Listings Sections, that comprise this family.

The modern world has, along with its pluralism, been characterized by the rise of religious skepticism. Skepticism had two major thrusts. It first challenged the hegemony of orthodox forms of religion that dominated cultures through powerful inclusive religious organizations backed by the state's power. The separation of church and state thus became a standard element in the skeptic's program. In the Christian West, the skeptics also challenged ideas at the very heart of Christian thinking. Brought together in this chapter as the "liberal" family of churches and "religious" organizations are those groups that have challenged the orthodox Christian dominance of Western religious life: unitarianism, universalism, and infidelism. Unitarianism championed the idea of a unitary God over the Christian's trinitarian God. Unitarianism necessarily involved the additional denial of the divinity of Jesus. Closely related to Unitarianism, Universalism affirmed that God will save all humanity and thus denied the Christian belief in Hell.

The several forms of infidelism—deism, rationalism, humanism, atheism, etc.—moved in an even more radical direction, away from the religious life (and any need for piety, prayer, worship, or devotion) toward human-centered philosophies that tended to denounce all religion or at best paid lip service to a few abstract religious ideas. What are in this chapter termed liberals thus fit on a continuum between Unitarians, who still acknowledge the viability of the religious life, and the more radical atheist infidels.

The origin and much of the continuing life of liberalism lie in its attack upon the dictates of Christian orthodoxy. (Orthodoxy may be described as the mainline Christian faith that adheres to the authority of the Scriptures and the three ancients summaries of Christian truth—the Nicene, Chalcedonian, and Apostles' creeds.) Thus, the liberal tradition has a secondary nature, protesting existent churches. The differences within the tradition can be gauged by how far various liberal groups deviate from orthodox beliefs.

Most liberals defend the individual's right to believe as s/he wishes, and the privilege to not believe at all if reason leads to disbelief. Liberals therefore have been in the forefront of fights for religious liberty and have joined with persecuted minorities in the debates on religious freedom as those of the late eighteenth century in France and the United States.

In America, beginning in the eighteenth century, liberals dissented from the established orthodoxy primarily of New England Calvinism and to a lesser extent Protestantism in general. Before the Civil War, American liberals were judged by themselves and others only in relation to the creed from which they deviated. Therefore, they were called, by themselves and others, by such negative names as anti-trinitarian, atheist and infidel. After the Civil War, though, liberals began to see themselves in a new light and described themselves in such positive terms as secularists, humanists, and liberals.

As an intellectual movement, liberalism stresses the power of man's reason to perfect the world. This emphasis on reason is coupled with a high regard for the worth of each human being. Liberals hold the self-image of being on the progressive cutting edge of human history, striving for the freedom of the individual. Although never very numerous, liberals have had tremendous influence on society as the public accepted their ideals. The Bill of Rights in the United States Constitution, for example, stands as a landmark of the liberal tradition.

What is liberal for one generation may become conservative for another generation. For example, in the 1920s, to be a liberal meant to be in the labor movement. Today, though, to be a liberal often means to be against the labor movement because labor is seen as part of the establishment. Thus, liberalism takes on new meanings with time. Also, at any given moment in history, liberals tend to be more united by their opposition to the current orthodoxy than by any positive idea they might promote. They have lacked the positive thrust that builds such movements as Methodism or Calvinism. Their common history of protesting orthodoxy, however, does tie them together, so both Unitarians and atheists (infidels) can be seen as belonging to the liberal tradition, although both might be unhappy at being lumped together.

The Enlightenment of the eighteenth century identified liberals with the high regard for reason. As religion shifted away from God and supernaturalism, only two bases for religion were left: man's feelings and man's mind. An arational mysticism became the hallmark of the liberals who chose feelings as the base for their religion. The transcendentalists followed the arational path, developing an idealistic movement that emphasized the union of the individual with the spiritual reality underlying all life. Most liberals, however, opted for the rational. They said man was the product of a law-abiding nature and reasonable thinking could reveal the universal laws that permeated everything.

Science was the product of rationalism. Science discovered the tangible world of indestructible particles. What was real was what could be seen, felt, and, most importantly, measured. The law-abiding world could be observed and documented. From observation came knowledge, and, by extension, liberals concluded the only knowledge worth having was that produced by scientific observation. Scientific method, said liberals, could be applied to the study of religion and from it a scientific religion, acceptable to all, could emerge. Beneath the diversity of ideas and practices could be found the great religious values, some reasoned. Others reasoned that if those values were not found, religion could be destroyed altogether.

The scientist's emphasis on the visible world gave way to secularism as a worldview. The search for values in this world and this life became part of the lifestyle of the liberal tradition.

As comparative religion became a major study, its findings became a major factor in the development of liberalism. The study of the world's religions revealed that all of the major religions of the world were undergirded with a sophisticated theology and an educated intelligentsia. As more solid information on the major faiths filtered out of the scholarly enclaves, a search for a universal religion began. Liberals hoped such a religion, laying aside each religion's peculiarities and distinctive ideas and practices, and built upon "essentials" or common factors all shared (seen as the natural religious particles), could command the respect of all. Books such as *The World's Sixteen Crucified Saviors* provided ample material to attack Christianity's distinctiveness.

In the nineteenth century, many liberals adopted the four-fold creed of evolution, reason, science, and materialism. From Darwin and Herbert Spencer, liberals learned to think in terms of progress. Not only nature, but also human culture was progressing. For liberalism, the great stumbling block to progress was ignorance, and the great tool to aid progress was education. Thus the alliance of liberalism and the university was a natural one.

ETHICS. The anti-mystical intellectualism within the main body of the liberal tradition led to a dominance of ethical concerns. Liberals followed their triumphs in the Bill of Rights with active involvement in the great crusades of the pre-Civil War era. Always the liberals could be found standing with those issues that aimed at great freedom for the individual. They swelled the ranks of the abolition, peace, prison reform, and women's rights movements. In the liberal religion camp were Julia Ward Howe, Lucy Stone, Robert Dale Owen, and Lucretia Mott. In the twentieth century, liberals were prominent in the labor, sexual freedom, and civil rights movements.

Interestingly enough, ethics has also been a major point of Christianity's attack upon liberals, especially atheists. Christians have argued that in giving up a belief in revelation, God and the Bible, that a belief in absolute values and moral law has also been given away and that the attack upon traditional religion leads to amorality and immorality. Liberals have countered such assertions with the fact that atheism has in fact no track record of unethical activity; to the contrary, liberal leaders have been in the forefront of the advocacy of moral concerns, especially in the public sphere.

THE FORMS OF FAITH. The active revolt against specific religious forms, which eventuated in the atheists' attack upon religion itself, does not lead to worship, piety, and prayer. These occur only on the extreme right wing of the liberal movement. The dominant activity of liberalism has been the communication of information, at first in the sermon and, more frequently as time passed, in the lecture. Great emphasis has been placed upon the education of members and the public, particularly their sensitization on moral issues.

The efforts at education and sensitization have been carried on by the liberal press. Liberal periodicals, most of which were independently published, have been the backbone of the movement from the early nineteenth century. The liberals' oldest periodical still in existence is *The Truth Seeker*, founded in 1873. Books attacking orthodoxy and religion are subsidized and circulated. Some have become popular items.

HISTORICAL DEVELOPMENT. The liberals look to an amazing number of radicals in Christian history as precursors of their movements. Various liberals claim as precursors such figures as Origen, Pelagius, and Leonardo da Vinci. The real beginning of the line of descent, however, is generally conceded to be Michael Servetus, whose *On the Errors of the Trinity* (1532) challenged traditional notions of the triune god, which he compared to the three-headed hound of hell of ancient mythology. Fleeing from Spain, he arrived in Geneva expecting a welcome from the Protestants, only to discover that they were as vehemently opposed to his theological position as were the Roman Catholics. Martyred by John Calvin, Servetus has become a symbol of free religion fighting orthodox intolerance. However, other reformers of similar anti-trinitarian opinions led parts of Europe into a unitarian perspective. Socinius converted Poland, and Francis David converted a large segment of Transylvania. In 1568, the only Unitarian king in history, John Sigismund, issued the Western world's first edict of religious toleration.

In seventeenth century Europe, the Enlightenment offered liberal alternatives to traditional Christian beliefs. In particular, the De-

ists of England preached a religion stripped of orthodox accretions. Deists argued that the Creator does not interfere with the laws of the universe. Deists pictured God somewhat like a watchmaker who makes a watch, winds it up, and leaves it to run on its own. God, they said, leaves the world to follow its own course. The Deists advocated a natural religion based on human reason and morality rather than revelation. Deism found a ready audience among the educated and upper classes of both England and America. Many of the leaders of the American Revolution identified themselves with the Deist idea world, particularly Washington, Jefferson, Franklin, and Madison. By the time of the American Revolution, the three key ideas of the liberals—unitarianism, universalism, and infidelism—had matured and had come to dominate the liberals' dissenting orientation. With each of these three ideas was carried a fight for religious freedom and a battle against the abuses of clericalism.

Universalism had been preached in America as early as the 1740s by Dr. George de Bonneville in Pennsylvania. In 1770, major impetus was given to the movement by the arrival of John Murray from England. Murray had been raised a Methodist and had become a class leader. Impressed with George Whitefield, he left Methodism and associated himself with Whitefield's independent London tabernacle. While in London he became a universalist and was expelled from the tabernacle membership when he refused to "confine his sentiments to his own bosom." After his arrival in the new world, Murray itinerated and preached his universalism, which had by 1775 created such an impact that pamphlets were written against him. About this time universalist congregations began to appear. Murray's followers in Gloucester, Massachusetts, who had belonged to the Congregational Church, had their membership suspended. So, in 1779, they formed the Independent Church of Gloucester. The movement to form churches grew, and in 1786 the Articles of Association for Universalist Churches were promulgated, although the association itself was short-lived. In the 1790s Hosea Ballou appeared on the scene to continue the leadership of the aging John Murray. His newspaper, the *Winchester Profession*, became the standard for Universalist views. In 1790, at a convention in Philadelphia, Articles of Faith and a Plan of Government were adopted. Thus, universalism became the first of the liberal views to solidify into an organizational structure.

In the eighteenth century unitarianism was preached in England and America. Theophilus Lindsey founded the British Unitarian movement in 1774 after his resignation from the Anglican priesthood. In New England, unitarianism originated in the Congregational Church, but it was not until 1794, when Joseph Priestley migrated to America, that churches were founded that took the name Unitarian.

During the pre-Civil War nineteenth century, three men—William Ellery Channing, Ralph Waldo Emerson, and Theodore Parker—in succession dominated unitarian thought. The liberal debate in America centered around them.

In the second decade of the nineteenth century William Ellery Channing, a congressional minister, was the leading intellectual among unitarians, which originally existed as a liberal wing in the Congregational Church. His 1819 sermon at the funeral of Jered Sparks became the unitarians' manifesto. In 1825 Channing led in founding the American Unitarian Association, a missionary group. Most members of Unitarian churches date their beginnings from one of these two events. Channing is credited with emphasizing ethics instead of theology, an emphasis that has become a hallmark of Unitarian churches.

In the 1830s, Ralph Waldo Emerson and the transcendentalists were at their intellectual apex. Emerson's efforts to sell his monist position, most notably through his famous speech to Harvard Divinity School in 1838, were rebuffed for the time. But Emerson, his colleagues at Brook Farm (an experimental, communitarian venture of the transcendentalists), and the raft of romantic literature flooding America from England could not long be denied.

Theodore Parker stands as the symbol of the union of unitarian thinking with transcendentalism. While unitarianism could not contain Emerson, it was forced to accept Parker. He combined three elements: the philosophical, which appealed to unitarians because of their emphasis on the mind; the mystical, which appealed to the transcendentalists; and the practical, which appealed to the liberals because of their desire to improve society. Parker, applying transcendental ideals in concrete situations, was an abolitionist and a spokesman against the fugitive slave law. His sermon at the ordination of Charles Shackford in 1841, entitled "The Transient and Permanent in Christianity," set the tone for liberal Christianity for his generation and served further to drive a wedge between the orthodox and liberal Congregationalists that was to result in the formal break between them after the Civil War.

For the origins of what in the nineteenth century was called infidelity (the complete rejection of theism, the church, and piety), one immediately turns to France and the works of Voltaire and his contemporaries. These perspectives reached their culmination in the radically anti-clerical, anti-religious aspect of the French Revolution. In its early days in America, the adjective French was often used to modify infidelity. The first exponent on the American scene was Ethan Allen, the revolutionary war hero, who published his *Reason the Only Oracle of Man* in 1784. This publication was essentially a restatement of deism, emphasizing man and his reason. For various reasons the work made little impact. But in 1794 Thomas Paine published his *Age of Reason*, which was an immediate success. The *Age of Reason* became the Bible of the free thought movement, and Paine quickly moved from being hero of the revolution to becoming the symbol of evil infidelity to the orthodox.

The free thought tradition gradually replaced the deist tradition of the eighteenth century. The transition can be marked in the 1790s by the leadership of Elihu Palmer and the beginnings of local free thought societies. The free thought movement stressed the importance of the inquiring mind, scientific methodology, and philosophical thinking. The movement opposed orthodoxy in religion, orthodoxy being the mainline Christian tradition based on Scripture and the creeds. Palmer, from 1791 until his death in 1806, was instrumental in the founding and leadership of at least three different radical societies, the most important being the Deistical Society of New York City. This society published the *Temple of Reason*, one of the first periodicals in America supporting an infidel tradition. After Palmer's death in 1806, there were about 20 years of silence from the free thought camp. Then in the 1820s Robert Owen founded his New Harmony experiment in Indiana, which gave the U.S. many of its firsts in education and community service.

In 1827, the free thought voice was heard again with the establishment of the Free Press Association in New York City. Before the end of the decade, societies were founded in Philadelphia, Pennsylvania; Woodstock, Vermont; Patterson, New Jersey; Schuylkill, Pennsylvania; Wilmington, Delaware; and St. Louis, Missouri. In the 1830s and 1840s societies were also founded in a number of other northern and Midwestern communities. Many adopted the name of Free Inquirers. Moral Philanthropists and Rationalists were also popular names. Attempts at national organization in 1828 and 1835 failed. A short-lived attempt to form The Infidel Society for the Promotion of Mental Liberty began in 1845 but died in 1848.

Other attempts waited until after the Civil War. Meanwhile, the liberals, both Christian and free thought, found themselves caught in circumstances that worked against organization. First, due to the Congregational Church's polity of local independency and the local nature of the infidel societies, leaders had no one but their local constituency to please. National organization tended to work against the very freedom that was so highly prized. Second,

the decades before the Civil War were a period of intense social change; and involvement in the antislavery crusade, women's rights, and other social causes took much of the energy that could have gone into organizational building. The close of the war ended the era of social activism and two generations of existence had caused a shift of emphasis in liberal thought. It began to turn from its primary emphasis on a critique of its religious origins toward the development of a positive position, setting the stage for the solidification of the liberal forces.

The last four decades of the nineteenth century were a time of organization of liberal churchmen. On April 7, 1865, just five days before the surrender of Lee at Appomattox, a National Convention of Unitarian Churches met in New York City to organize a National Conference of Unitarian Churches. Transcendentalists, not happy with the overly orthodox position of the National Conference, organized the Free Religious Association (FRA) in 1867. Among the leaders of the FRA were John Weiss, Samuel Johnson, Octavius Brooks Frothingham, Thomas Wentworth Higginson, and David Wasson. The radicals who formed the FRA in turn found themselves divided between the mystical transcendentalists and the scientifically oriented members. The latter organized as the National Liberal League in 1875. The issue around which they organized was a movement in the 1860s by evangelicals for a constitutional amendment that would wed church and state. Specifically, the amendment would tie the Protestant churches closely to national political institutions, from the president and Congress on down. The Liberal League countered with a program to achieve complete separation of church and state. The Liberal League itself divided over support of obscenity laws, and the group favoring a complete lifting of censorship formed the National Liberal League of America.

The thrust of most of these organizations lasted only one generation. As the issues that gave them birth died, they passed from the scene and were often absorbed by more stable bodies such as the Unitarian churches. This absorption liberalized the stable groups. Replacing the organizations that died were new associations that gathered to respond to new issues. One such association was the Union of Liberal Clergymen, formed following the Parliament of Religions in 1893. The Union of Liberal Clergymen promoted progress, reverence for law, science, and an openness to new knowledge, and contended that the church should be a school of the humanities.

ATHEISM. Increasingly, since the Renaissance, some people have denied the very existence of a God. Many atheists were intellectuals—scholars and university professors—giants in their own particular disciplines. Included are such figures as Thomas Hariot, Christopher Marlowe, and Pierre Bayle. It was not, however, until the nineteenth century that atheism became a force with significant support.

Many Deists walked a tightrope between belief in a God who did not act upon his world and outright denial of his existence. In the nineteenth century the university provided a haven for those who wished to declare themselves as atheists. Like its deistic predecessor, atheism was built upon an attack of the Christian churches in the nineteenth century. Primarily, however, it was an intellectual movement that launched an attack on theology and natural religion. The movement's perspective was that of scientific materialism, the theory that the basic reality of the universe is material and is therefore observable and scientifically measurable.

Among the major atheists in the nineteenth century are Karl Marx, Ludwig Feuerbach, Auguste Comte, Annie Besant, and Charles Bradlaugh. Often forgotten, but important in any history of atheism, is poet Percy Bysshe Shelley. Shelley was expelled from Oxford in 1811 for writing *The Necessity of Atheism*. His lengthy poem *Queen Mab* became a poetic reinforcement to his earlier essay. Reflecting on the death of an atheist, he cries:

There is no God!
Nature confirms the faith this death-groan sealed:

Let heaven and earth, let man's revolving race,
His ceaseless generations tell the tale.
The Spirit of Nature was posed as an alternative to God.

In the twentieth century Bertrand Russell, A. J. Ayer, and Julian Huxley were among the outspoken atheists. As a whole, however, the atheists mentioned above were isolated individuals who served as background for the organized movements that began to emerge in the years after the Civil War. *The Truth Seeker*, a liberal periodical, while not atheist oriented to begin with, allowed atheist notices to be printed and served as a means of communication. Only after World War I were efforts to affiliate atheist bodies in larger organizations successful. As they have emerged in the twentieth century, atheists insist that first and foremost they are people with a positive approach to life that find no need to assert the existence of a deity. Their popular designation as people who deny the existence of God is an image created by their necessary attempts to explain their position in the face of a more dominant theistic population.

Sources—The Liberal Family

The study of the unitarian and universalist traditions is carried forth by the Unitarian Universalist Historical Society, 25 Beacon St., Boston, MA 02108. The society published the *UUHS Proceedings* biennially. There is no comparable structure for the study of the more radical humanist, atheist, and rationalist traditions.

GENERAL SOURCES

Baumer, Franklin L. *Religion and the Rise of Skepticism*. New York: Harcourt Brace and World, 1960. 308 pp.

Bratton, Fred Gladstone. *The Legacy of the Liberal Spirit*. Boston: Beacon Press, 1943. 319 pp.

Brown, Marshall G., and Gordon Stein. *Freethought in the United States, A Descriptive Bibliography*. Westport, CT: Greenwood Press, 1978. 146 pp.

Sheldon, Henry C. *Unbelief in the Nineteenth Century*. New York: Eaton & Mains, 1907. 399 pp.

Stein, Gordon. *Robert G. Ingersoll, A Checklist*. Kent, OH: Kent State University Press, 1969. 128 pp.

UNITARIANISM AND UNIVERSALISM

Albee, Ernest. *A History of English Unitarianism*. New York: Collier Books, 1962. 383 pp.

Miller, Russell E. *The Larger Hope*. 2 Vols. Boston: Unitarian Universalist Association, 1979, 1985.

Parke, David B. *The Epic of Unitarianism*. Boston: Beacon Press, 1957. 164 pp.

Scott, Clinton Lee. *The Universalist Church of America, A Short History*. Boston: Universalist Historical Society, 1957. 124 pp.

Three Prophets of Religious Liberalism: Channing, Emerson, Parker. Boston: Beacon Press, 1961. 152 pp.

Wilbur, Earl Morse. *A History of Unitarianism*. Cambridge, MA: Harvard University Press, 1946. 617 pp.

Williams, George Huntston. *American Universalism*. Boston: Beacon Press, 1971. 94 pp.

DEISM AND FREETHOUGHT

Darrow, Clarence, and Wallace Rice. *Infidels and Heretics*. Boston: Stratford Co., 1929. 293 pp.

Hawke, David Freeman. *Paine*. New York: Harper & Row. 1974. 500 pp.

Ingersoll, Robert G. *Ingersoll's Greatest Lectures*. New York: The Freethought Press Association, 1944. 419 pp.

Koch, G. Adolf. *Republican Religion*. New York: Henry Holt and Co., 1933. 334 pp.

May, Henry F. *The Enlightenment in America*. New York: Oxford University Press, 1976. 419 pp.

Morais, Herbert M. *Deism in Eighteenth Century America*. New York: Russell & Russell, 1960. 203 pp.

Persons, Stow. *Free Religion*. Boston: Beacon Press, 1947. 162 pp.

Tribe, David. *100 Years of Freethought*. London: Elek, 1967. 259 pp.

HUMANISM

Hawton, Hector. *The Humanist Revolution*. London: Barrie and Rockliff, 1963. 247 pp.

Lamont, Corliss. *The Philosophy of Humanism*. New York: F. Ungar Pub. Co., 7th rev. ed., 1990. 326 pp.

Walker, Joseph. *Humanism as a Way of Life*. New York: Macmillan, 1932. 83 pp.

ATHEISM

Brooks, David M. *The Necessity of Atheism*. New York: The Freethought Press Association, 1933. 322 pp.

Buckley, Michael L. *At the Origins of Modern Atheism*. New Haven, CT: Yale University Press, 1987. 445 pp.

Stein, Gordon. *The Encyclopedia of Unbelief*. Buffalo, NY: Prometheus Books, 1985. 2 Vols.

———, ed. *An Anthology of Atheism and Rationalism*. Buffalo, NY: Prometheus Books, 1980. 354 pp.

CHRISTIAN-ATHEIST CONTROVERSY

Blackie, John Stuart. *The Natural History of Atheism*. New York: Scribner, Armstrong & Co., 1878. 253 pp.

Graham, Lloyd M. *Deceptions and Myths of the Bible*. New York: Bell, 1979. 484 pp.

Lewis, Joseph. *The Bible Unmasked*. New York: The Freethought Press Association, 1926. 236 pp.

McCabe, Joseph. *The Sources of the Morality of the Gospels*. London: Watts, 1914. 315 pp.

Marty, Martin E. *The Infidel: Freethought and American Religion*. Cleveland: World Publishing Co., 1961. 224 pp.

Micelli, Vincent P. *The Gods of Atheism*. New Rochelle, NY: Arlington House, 1973. 490 pp.

Wheless, Joseph. *Forgery in Christianity*. Moscow, ID: Psychiana, 1930. 428 pp.

Chapter 15
Latter-day Saints Family

Consult the "Contents" pages to locate the entries in Part III,
the Directory Listings Sections, that comprise this family.

"After I had retired to the place where I had previously designed to go, having looked around me, and finding myself alone, I kneeled down and began to offer up the desires of my heart to God. I had scarcely done so, when immediately I was seized upon by some power which entirely overcame me, and had such an astonishing influence over me as to bind my tongue so that I could not speak. Thick darkness gathered around me, and it seemed to me for a time as if I were doomed to sudden destruction. But, exerting all of my powers to call upon God to deliver me out of the power of this enemy which had seized upon me, and at the very moment when I was ready to sink into despair and abandon myself to destruction—not to an imaginary ruin, but to the power of some actual being from the unseen world, who had such marvelous power as I had never before felt in any being—just at this moment of great alarm, I saw a pillar of light exactly over my head, above the brightness of the sun, which descended gradually until it fell upon me.

"It no sooner appeared than I found myself delivered from the enemy which held me bound. When the light rested upon me I saw two personages, whose brightness and glory defy all description, standing above me in the air. One of them spake unto me, calling me by name, and said, pointing to the other—'This is my beloved son, hear him!'

"My object in going to inquire of the Lord was to know which of all the sects was right, that I might know which to join. No sooner, therefore, did I get possession of myself, so as to be able to speak, than I asked the personages who stood above me in the light, which of all the sects was right—and which I should join. I was answered that I must join none of them, for they were all wrong, and the personage who addressed me said that all their creeds were an abomination in His sight: that those professors were all corrupt; that 'they draw near to me with their lips, but their hearts are far from me; they teach for doctrines the commandments of men: having a form of godliness, but they deny the power thereof.' He again forbade me to join with any of them: and many other things did he say unto me, which I cannot write at this time. When I came to myself again, I found myself lying on my back, looking up into heaven. When the light had departed, I had no strength; but soon recovering in some degree, I went home" (Joseph Smith, *History of the Church*. Salt Lake City: Deseret Book Co., 1902–1912, 1:5–6).

Thus is described by the man to whom it occurred the first event that led to the founding in 1830 of the Church of Jesus Christ of Latter-day Saints; the man—Joseph Smith, Jr.

Vermont-born Joseph Smith had moved to western New York in 1815 at the age of 10, along with many others who flooded the area following the War of 1812. With the immigrants came the revival-oriented church to stoke the fires of their emotions and burn the Word of God into their pioneer hearts. So successful had the evangelists been that observers would look upon western New York and label it "the burned-over district," the product of wave after wave of evangelical fervor and spiritual fire. It was in this

same area that Charles Finney, discussed in the chapter on the holiness movement, made his triumphant tours of the late 1820s and early 1830s.

In this context Joseph Smith began to be moved by religious concerns and, like so many before him, to be confused by the plethora of churches, each claiming to speak God's truth. And in this context Smith began to see the visions (including the one related above) that resulted in his founding a new church to be the embodiment of God's true revelation. The two personages in the first vision (later identified as Jesus and God the Father) were followed by John the Baptist and various angelic beings in other visions. One of the angels gave to Smith in 1827 the plates of gold upon which was engraved what is now known as the *Book of Mormon*. The engraving was in what Smith called a reformed Egyptian language. Also given were two divining stones, the "Urim and Thummim" (*Exodus* 28:30), used to translate the tablets of reformed Egyptian text. The stones could be compared to crystal balls.

The story related in the *Book of Mormon* purported to be the history of two groups of people: the Jeredites, who came to America directly after the attempt to build the Tower of Babel, and the Israelites, who came following the destruction of Jerusalem in the sixth century B.C.E. The former group had been destroyed shortly before the arrival of the second group. The second group was essentially destroyed in the fourth century C.E., and Native Americans remained as its only remnant. The last of the prophets among the second group was commanded to write a history, which was buried in New York.

In 1830, the *Book of Mormon* was published and the church organized. Both events had an immediate impact on the religious community and began a debate that has grown in intensity to this very day. The *Book of Mormon* was attacked, and the Mormons became outcasts.

But the *Book of Mormon* was not the only new revelation of Joseph Smith. His other major works were the *Book of Moses*, the *Book of Abraham*, and an inspired translation of the Bible. At regular intervals new revelations were given for specific purposes. These were gathered in a collection in 1833 as the *Book of Commandments*, now called the *Doctrine and Covenants* (D.C.). Also, there were fragmentary works and mention of other major works which were never undertaken because of Smith's untimely death. References to the *Doctrine and Covenants* are given with the initials D.C. and the number of the section under consideration. The *Book of Mormon* contains books within it, as does the Bible. References to the *Book of Mormon* resemble biblical references (e.g., *II Nephi* 2:46–47).

THE IMPETUS TO SCHISM. Smith's many revelations created a number of problems for Mormon theology. They also built into the system a ready-made impetus to schism. It did not take long for others to get the idea, "If Joseph Smith can, then I can also." So that, quite apart from the issue of the truth or falsity of the *Book of Mormon* or other writings produced by Smith, his example continually excited would-be prophets to action. Common to almost every Mormon group is one or more leaders who receive revelations. These leaders originated as disturbers of the peace in each new church center as the Saints migrated from Kirkland, Ohio, to Independence, Missouri, to Nauvoo, Illinois, and finally, after Smith's murder, to Salt Lake City, Utah.

The church was hardly organized before Brother Hiram Page began to obtain revelations concerning the church through "a certain stone." Smith soon learned that his confidant, Oliver Crowley, and David Whitmer had been taken in by Page, but Smith was able to handle this situation in a church conference. Page recanted, and he and Crowley were sent on a mission to preach to the Indians.

After the movement of Smith's followers to Kirkland, Ohio, genuine schism began to occur. Wycam Clark led a group of former Saints who established the short-lived Pure Church of Christ. A Mr. Hawley walked barefoot 600 miles from New York to tell Smith that he was no longer the prophet. In 1831, Smith was able to reconcile a group called "the family" to full status in the church. This communal group had joined the Mormons as a body and had to be persuaded to follow "the more perfect law." In 1832, a Mr. Hoton and a Mr. Montague organized a body of which the former was president and the latter bishop. The group fell apart when the bishop accused the president of visiting the "pork barrel" (stored supplies), and the president accused the bishop of visiting his wife.

The years 1837–38 were difficult for Smith, as two major movements took sheep from his flock. Warren Parrish, treasurer of the Kirkland Safety Society, became disillusioned with Smith's prophetic ability and withdrew. He and a number of prominent Latter-day Saints who joined him founded the Church of Christ. Also, there appeared in Kirkland an unnamed woman called the Kirkland seeress. She had a black stone and she prophesied that either David Whitmer or Martin Harris would succeed Smith, who had fallen into transgression. The movement in support of the anti-Josephite revelations was strong enough to spread to Missouri. No record of the eventual fate of the girl is known. *The History of the Church* by Smith has only a proclamation issued in the fall of 1837 expressing hope for the reclamation of David Whitmer and others. In 1838 the Saints moved to Missouri to a town called Far West. In 1839 they were forced to leave Far West, so they settled in Nauvoo, Illinois, and stayed there until Joseph Smith's death in 1844. In 1840 George M. Hinkle, a colonel in the militia that defended the Mormons at Far West, Missouri, founded the Church of Jesus Christ, the Bride the Lamb's Wife, at Moscow, Iowa. Hinkle, a trusted confidant of Smith, had a significant role in turning Joseph, his brother, Hiram, and others over to General Lucas of the Missouri militia. "Hinkle" has since been synonymous in Mormon circles with traitor. In 1845 Hinkle's church merged with Sidney Rigdon's Church of Christ.

In the 1840s during the Nauvoo era, Smith reached the height of his power. Nauvoo, in Hancock County, became the largest city in Illinois and, because of the evenly divided makeup of Illinois politics, it held the balance of power between Democrats and Republicans. Because Smith kept switching sides, the Mormons became a hated people. Added to the political situation was the jealousy of the people of Hancock County at the success of the whole Nauvoo enterprise. During the entire stay of the Mormons at Nauvoo, tensions were on the rise and schism could always find its support among gentile haters of the Saints.

At least three major schisms occurred here, each contributing to the downfall of the Mormon establishment. In 1842, the High Council excommunicated Oliver Olney, would-be prophet, who moved to nearby Squaw Grove, Illinois, to establish headquarters and to publish his anti-Smith literature. He was still publishing as late as 1845 but his full history is not known. Also in 1842, Gladden Bishop was for a second time excommunicated, this time for "having received, written and published or taught certain revelations not consistent with the Doctrine and Covenants of the

Church." Bishop began setting up splinter churches and then rejoining the Saints. He is known to have had followings at various times at Little Sioux, Iowa; in California, Wisconsin, Ohio, and Salt Lake City. After being in and out of the church several times, he was excommunicated permanently.

But the major trouble for Smith at Nauvoo came from a schism caused by William Law and his associates—Wilson Law, Robert and Charles Foster, and C. L. Higbee. They and a large following left the church and set up a rival organization in Nauvoo with William Law at the head of it. This schism meant more than just the loss of some members. In May 1844, Law announced a newspaper to support his views. He then obtained an indictment against Smith for adultery and polygamy. Robert Foster obtained an indictment against Smith for false swearing. Francis Higbee sued for slander, demanding $5,000. On June 7, 1844, the first and only issue of the *Nauvoo Expositer* appeared. The Nauvoo Legion, after Smith declared the paper a public nuisance, destroyed it. This proved to be a political blunder and as news spread across the state, public pressure mounted against the Saints and Joseph Smith. He was forced to flee from Nauvoo to Iowa. He soon returned to Illinois.

The Law affair was significant in the series of episodes that led in 1844 to the arrest of Joseph Smith, his brother, Hiram, John Taylor, and Willard Richards. On June 27, 1844, a mob broke into the jail at Carthage, Illinois, and killed Joseph and Hiram and wounded Taylor. The sudden and violent death of its leader left the church he founded in chaos. Smith had left no undeniable successor, only a martyr's image and a history of prophecy. The Saints were essentially united, but there began a power struggle that split the movement into at least four groups that, over the years, spawned more than 50 additional bodies.

Following the death of Joseph Smith, Jr., and the haste with which Nauvoo had to be abandoned, the church divided into several factions. Sidney Rigdon was among the first to claim to be Smith's successor, and a few followed him back to Pennsylvania. James Jesse Strang also claimed to be Smith's successor and some followed him to Wisconsin and eventually to Beaver Island, Michigan. The largest group took their guidance from Brigham Young and migrated to Utah. This group survives today as the Church of Jesus Christ of Latter-day Saints.

Many church members had not "gathered" at Nauvoo, but remained scattered around the Midwest. In the decade after Smith's death, attempts were made to reorganize these groups under Joseph Smith III, the prophet's son. He at first refused his father's mantle, but in 1859 accepted. The New Organization was formed, which in 1860 became known as the Reorganized Church of Jesus Christ of Latter-day Saints. It drew some of its early strength from the followers of Strang who defected after his death in 1856. Still others who did not make the trek to Utah quietly moved back to Independence, Missouri, and bought the tract of land that had been cited in the *Doctrine and Covenants* as the site of the temple in the coming kingdom of Zion predicted by Smith.

BELIEFS. The key idea in Smith's theology was restorationism, the restoring of the Apostolic church that had been lost. Restorationism had been a major concept of the Disciples of Christ movement founded by Alexander Campbell from which Smith's early confidant, Sidney Rigdon, came. Smith believed that the true church died with the first generation of apostles and was restored only with his ordination. The ordination at the hands of John the Baptist occurred on May 15, 1829, when Smith and Oliver Cowdery were given the Priesthood of Aaron. Subsequently, the Priesthood of Melchizedek was conferred and the church was formally established (April 6, 1830). Along with this restoration of the Apostolic church came a set of doctrines and a church order.

The "Articles of Faith," written shortly before Joseph Smith's death, are still used by the Church of Jesus Christ of Latter-day Saints and most of the groups that have derived from it. The average non-Mormon needs some interpretation of the Articles, as they are worded to present Mormon doctrine in a format and with words quite familiar to members in most older traditional Christian denominations. However, the meaning of the affirmations is often quite distinct. For example, the first article affirms a belief in God, the Eternal Father, and in His Son, Jesus Christ, and in the Holy Spirit. What might seem a statement of belief in the traditional Christian doctrine of the Trinity is in fact an affirmation of belief in three separate divine personages, i.e., what is generally termed tritheism.

The articles deny original sin, affirming that humans are not punished for Adam's sin, just their own. Christ's atonement establishes a condition by which individuals may be saved if they are obedient to the laws and ordinances of God. There are four ordinances—faith, repentance, baptism by immersion, and the laying on of hands for the gift of the Holy Ghost.

Part of what was revealed to Joseph Smith was the proper organization of the restored church. Derived according to biblical texts, the true church is headed by apostles, prophets, pastors, teachers, evangelists, and others.

The church recognizes both the Bible and the *Book of Mormon* to be the Word of God. Not mentioned in the articles are the supplementary writing to which authority is given, the *Pearl of Great Price*, which contains the *Book of Moses* and the *Book of Abraham*, and the *Doctrine and Covenants*. Smith also began work on an inspired translation of the Bible. It is not used by the Utah-based Church of Jesus Christ of Latter-day Saints, which prefers the King James Version, but is used by the Reorganized Church of Jesus Christ of Latter-day Saints headquarter in Independence, Missouri. Revelation is believed to be open, and new revelations are added to the *Doctrine and Covenants* as they are received by the church president. New revelations are quite rare, but now form a distinct body of material by which the Utah-based church and Missouri-based reorganized church differ.

The statement also affirms that the future kingdom of Zion will be built, not at Jerusalem in the Holy Land, but on the American continent. According to the *Doctrine and Covenants,* Zion will be centered on present-day Independence, Missouri. Others believe it will be centered on Salt Lake City. Prior to the establishment of Zion, there will be a "gathering" of the Saints in the immediate area.

ORGANIZATION. The restoration determined the nature of the church, which was to be organized after a revealed pattern. Two orders of priesthood were set up. The Aaronic Priesthood is the lesser order; all adult males are members, and from it are drawn deacons, teachers, and priests. The Melchizedek Priesthood is the higher order, and from it come the church's leadership—elders, seventies, high priests, and the presidency.

Organizationally, the church is ruled by a series of councils. Leading the church is the first presidency, composed of three people—the president and two other high priests elected by the 12 apostles. When the office of the first presidency is filled, the council of 12 apostles officiates under its direction as a traveling presiding council. Unanimous decisions by the council of 12 have authority equal to the decisions of the first presidency. Thus the first presidency and council of the 12 function very much like the pope and college of cardinals in the Roman Catholic Church.

The presiding quorum of 70 and the presiding bishopric comprise the other two ruling councils. The presiding bishopric holds jurisdiction over the duties of other bishops in the church and over the organization of the Aaronic Priesthood.

CURRENT MORMON DIVISIONS. Most Mormons may be divided into Utah Mormons and Missouri Mormons, names that often refer to their history more than to their current headquarters. The churches known as "Utah Mormons" either have their headquarters in Salt Lake City, Utah, or were established by a former member of the Church of Jesus Christ of Latter-day Saints. The great majority of present-day Mormons are members of the Utah-based church. The churches known as "Missouri Mormons" re-

jected the direction of Brigham Young, who led a large group, but by no means all, of the Saints to Salt Lake City. The early leaders of this church gathered the Saints who had dwelt across the Midwest into a new reorganized church body with headquarters eventually established in Missouri. The Missouri Mormons have strongly emphasized Joseph Smith, Jr.'s prophecy (D.C. 51) that the temple was to be built in Independence, Missouri.

No turmoil has so affected the Restoration movement founded by Joseph Smith, Jr., as did the controversy over the practice of polygamy in the post-Civil War era. Polygamy seems to have been introduced into the church in Nauvoo by Smith and to have contributed to Smith's assassination. Emma Smith, Joseph Smith's first wife, seems to have never accepted the idea though she acquiesced during his life time. She remained in Nauvoo and did not travel to Salt lake City even though enticed by Brigham Young. She emerged as an anti-polygamy champion and affiliated with the Reorganized church, which strongly denounced polygamy, especially as it emerged as a public doctrine in Utah in the 1850s.

In Utah, polygamy was practiced and then openly proclaimed. Its practice was ingrained in the social structure (though only a minority of males were wealthy enough to participate) and it was a keystone of the Utah church's doctrine of salvation and the after life. It was also an irritant to the larger non-Mormon religious community that made it the object of a fervent crusade to rid the land of what was perceived by many a blatant immorality. After the Civil War the federal government moved against the church with a series of actions asserting its hegemony in Utah and its hostility to the continuance of polygamy.

Twenty years of practice had made polygamy an essential part of the Mormon social system and theology, and it was only after a lengthy battle against overwhelming odds that the church slowly capitulated. This capitulation began in the form of a manifesto in 1890 by President Wilford Woodruff abolishing the practice of plural marriage. The manifesto was unanimously adopted by the vote of the Latter-day Saints Church conference. Quietly, however, the practice was continued, and only a series of actions through the first quarter of the twentieth century—excommunicating those who either conducted plural marriage ceremonies or entered into a polygamous relationship—finally eradicated the practice from the Church.

Reaction to the threats of excommunication soon became manifest. Several polygamy-practicing groups formed but were broken up during World War I. After the war new groups were formed, which have continued to this day. Most of the groups of polygamy-practicing Mormons accept a common history that dates to an incident they claim occurred in 1886, four years prior to the manifesto. They argue that on September 26, 1886, at a meeting of church leaders to consider a document prepared by George Q. Cannon, the first counselor, on the polygamy question, President John Taylor is supposed to have spent a night in conversation with Joseph Smith, Jr., and the Lord. The next morning President Taylor denounced the document and asked each to pledge himself to the principle of plural marriage. After the meeting, five copies were made of the revelation of the Lord on plural marriage; and five men—Samuel Bateman, Charles H. Wilkins, George Q. Cannon, John W. Woolley, and Lorin C. Woolley—were given authority to administer the covenant (i.e., plural marriage) and to see that no year passed without some children being born in the covenant. Taylor also prophesied that during the time of the seventh president (who turned out to be Heber J. Grant), the church was to go into spiritual and temporal bondage, and "one strong and mighty" would appear (D.C. 85). The Latter-day Saints Church claims this meeting never occurred and was a later fiction created by Lorin Woolley.

Among the polygamists are Mormons called fundamentalists. They are distinguished from other polygamy-practicing groups in that they claim only to possess the presidency of the high priesthood. Other polygamy-practicing groups claim to possess both the presidency of the high priesthood and the presidency of the church.

In 1929 Joseph White Musser, the leader and most prolific writer among the fundamentalists, claimed he had received authority from Taylor's five disciples. He further claimed that after the manifesto was issued, the office of the president of the church and the president of the high priesthood were separated and the latter given to the fundamentalists. Hence the priesthood has authority apart from the church leadership. Musser felt that the movement away from polygamy was but one of several changes and departures from the faith made by the church. The fundamentalists believe in what is termed the Adam-God theory (as originally taught by Brigham Young) that "Adam is Our Father and Our God and is the literal Father of Jesus." Almost all fundamentalists claim authority through Musser and read his voluminous writings in his several books and the magazine *The Star of Truth,* which he published for many years.

The polygamists are living outside the laws of both the Latter-day Saints Church and the United States, and most have retreated into the desert and mountainous regions to escape legal and social pressure. They are somewhat of an embarrassment to the Latter-day Saints Church, which wishes to ignore them.

Sources—Latter-day Saints Family

The study of Latter-day Saints history, life, and thought is nurtured by the Mormon History Association, P. O. Box 7010, Univ. Sta., Provo, UT 84602. It publishes the *Journal of Mormon History.*

GENERAL SOURCES

Arbaugh, George Bartholomew. *Revelation in Mormonism.* Chicago: University of Chicago Press, 1932. 252 pp.

Carter, Kate B. *Denominations That Base Their Beliefs on the Teachings of Joseph Smith.* Salt Lake City: Daughters of the Utah Pioneers. 1969. 68 pp.

Cory, Delbert J. *A Comparison Study of the Basic Thought of the Major "Latter Day Saint" Groups.* Oberlin, OH: The Author, 1963. 42 pp.

Goodliffe, Wilford Leroy. *America Frontier Religion: Mormons and Their Dissenters, 1830—1900.* University of Idaho, Ph.D. Dissertation, 1976. 287 pp.

Rich, Russell B. *Little Known Schisms of the Restoration.* Provo, UT: Brigham Young University, 1967. 76 pp.

———. *Those Who Would Be Leaders.* Provo, UT: Brigham Young University, 1967. 89 pp.

Shields, Steven L. *Divergent Paths of the Restoration.* Bountiful, UT: Restoration Research, 1982. 282 pp.

———. *The Latter Day Saints Churches, An Annotated Bibliography.* New York: Garland, Publishing, 1987. 281 pp.

Tullis, F. LaMond, ed. *Mormonism, A Faith for All Cultures.* Provo, UT: Brigham Young University Press, 1978. 365 pp.

Van Nest, Albert J. *A Directory of the "Restored Gospel" Churches.* Evanston, IL: Institute for the Study of American Religion, 1984. 32 pp.

JOSEPH SMITH, JR.

Anderson, Richard Lloyd. *Joseph Smith's New England Heritage.* Salt Lake City: Deseret Book Co., 1971. 230 pp.

———. "The Reliability of the Early History of Lucy and Joseph Smith." *Dialogue,* 4, No. 2 (Summer 1969), pp. 12–28.

Brodie, Fawn M. *No Man Knows My History.* New York: Alfred A. Knopf, 1945. 495 pp.

Huntress, Keith. *Murder of an American Prophet.* San Francisco: Chandler Publishing Co., 1960. 232 pp.

Nibley, Hugh. *No Ma'am That's Not History.* Salt Lake City: Bookcraft, 1946. 62 pp.

Smith, Lucy Mack. *Joseph Smith and His Progenitors.* Lamoni, IA: Reorganized Church of Jesus Christ of Latter Day Saints, 1912. 371 pp.

Taves, Ernest H. *Trouble Enough, Joseph Smith and the Book of Mormon.* Buffalo, NY: Prometheus Books, 1984. 280 pp.

MORMON HISTORY

Allen, James B. *The Story of the Latter-day Saints.* Salt Lake City, UT: Deseret Book Co., 1976. 722 pp.

Arrington, Leonard J. *Brigham Young: American Moses.* New York: 1985.

———. *Great Basin Kingdom.* Lincoln: University of Nebraska Press, 1966. 538 pp.

Arrington, Lenord J., and Davis Bitton. *The Mormon Experience.* New York: Alfred A. Knopf, 1979. 404 pp.

Backman, Milton V., Jr. *Eyewitness Accounts of the Restoration.* Orem, Ut: Grandin Book Co., 1983. 239 pp.

Bitton, Davis, and Maureen Ursenbach Beecher, eds. *New Views of Mormon History: Essays in Honor of Leonard J. Arrington.* Salt Lake City, UT: University of Utah Press, 1987. 480 pp.

Mullen, Robert. *The Latter-day Saints: The Mormons of Yesterday and Today.* Garden City, NY: Doubleday, 1966. 316 pp.

O'Dea, Thomas F. *The Mormons.* Chicago: University of Chicago Press, 1957. 289 pp.

Rich, Russell R. *Ensign to the Nations.* Provo, UT: Brigham Young University Publications, 1972. 663 pp.

Shipps, Jan. *Mormonism, the Story of a New Religious Tradition.* Urbana: University of Illinois Press, 1985. 211 pp.

Stegner, Wallace. *The Gathering of Zion.* New York: McGraw-Hill, 1971. 331 pp.

LATTER-DAY SAINTS BELIEFS

McConkey, Bruce R. *Mormon Doctrine.* Salt Lake City: Bookcraft, 1966. 856 pp.

Living Truths from the Book of Mormon. Salt Lake City: The Sunday School of the Church of Jesus Christ of Latter-day Saints, 1972. 330 pp.

Richards, LeGrand. *A Marvelous Work and a Wonder.* Salt Lake City: Deseret Book Co., 1968. 452 pp.

Smith, Joseph F. *Gospel Doctrine.* Salt Lake City, Deseret Book Co., 1969. 553 pp.

CHRISTIAN REFUTATIONS OF THE LATTER-DAY SAINTS

Ahmanson, John. *Secret History.* Chicago: Moody Press, 1984. 179 pp.

Anderson, Einar. *Inside Story of Mormonism.* Grand Rapids: Kregal Publications, 1973. 162 pp.

Fraser, Gordon H. *Is Mormonism Christian?* Chicago: Moody Press, 1977. 192 pp.

McElveen, Floyd. *Will the "Saints" Go Marching In?* Glendale, CA: G/L Publications, 1977. 175 pp.

Ropp, Harry L. *The Mormon Papers.* Downers Grove, IL: InterVarsity Press, 1977. 118 pp.

Sackett, Chuck. *What's Going On There?* Thousand Oaks, CA: Ex-Mormons for Jesus, 1982. 64 pp.

Smith, John L. *I Visited the Temple.* Clearfield, UT: The Utah Evangel Press, 1966. 104 pp.

Tanner, Jerald, and Sandra Tanner. *Mormonism—Shadow or Reality?* Salt Lake City: Modern Microfilm Co., 1972. 587 pp.

MORMON SCRIPTURES

Campbell, Alexander. *An Analysis of the Book of Mormon.* Boston: Benjamin H. Greene, 1832. 16 pp.

Kirkham, Francis W. *A New Witness for Christ in America.* Independence, MO: Press of Zion's Printing and Publishing Co., 1951. 429 pp.

Nelson, Dee Jay. *Joseph Smith's "Eye of Ra."* Salt Lake City: Modern Microfilm Co., 1968. 32 pp.

———. *A Translation of Facsimile No. 3 in the Book of Abraham.* Salt Lake City: Modern Microfilm, 1989. 32 pp.

Nibley, Hugh. *Abraham in Egypt.* Salt Lake City: Deseret Book Co., 1981. 288 pp.

Prince, Walter Franklin. "Psychological Tests for the Authorship of the Book of Mormon." *American Journal of Psychology,* 28, No. 3 (July 1917), pp. 373–89.

Tanner, Jerald, and Sandra Tanner. *Did Spalding Write the Book of Mormon?* Salt Lake City: Modern Microfilm Co., 1977. 105 pp.

POLYGAMY

Anderson, J. Max. *The Polygamy Story: Fiction and Fact.* Salt Lake City: Publishers Press, 1979. 166 pp.

Bailey, Paul. *Grandpa Was a Polygamist.* Los Angeles: Western Lore Press, 1960. 181 pp. Rev. ed. as: *Polygamy Was Better Than Monotony.* New York: Ballantine Books, 1972. 180 pp.

Ballard, Melvin J., et al. *Marriage.* Salt Lake City: Truth Publishing Co., n.d. 107 pp.

Beadle, J. H. *Polygamy.* The Author, 1904. 604 pp.

Bradley, Martha S. *Kidnapped from that Land.* Salt Lake City, UT: University of Utah Press, 1993.

Collier, Fred C. "Re-Examining the Lorin Woolley Story." *Doctrine of the Priesthood,* 1, No. 2 (February 1981), pp. 1–17.

Foster, Lawrence. *Religion and Sexuality.* Urbana: University of Illinois Press, 1984. 363 pp.

The Most Holy Principle. 4 Vols. Murray, UT: Gems Publishing Co., 1970–75.

Merrill, Melissa. *Polygamist's Wife.* New York: Paperback Books, 1977. 176 pp.

Musser, Joseph White. *Celestial or Plural Marriage.* Salt Lake City: Truth Publishing Co., 1970. 154 pp.

Openshaw, Robert R. *The Notes.* Pinesdale, MT: Bitterroot Publishing Co., 1980. 616 pp.

Shook, Charles A. *The True Origins of Mormon Polygamy.* Cincinnati: Standard Publishing Co., 1914. 213 pp.

Taylor, Samuel Woollwy. *Family Kingdom.* New York: New American Library, 1951. 254 pp.

Tullidge, Edward W. *The Women of Mormondom.* New York: The Author, 1877. 552 pp.

VanWagner, Richard S. *Mormon Polygamy: A History.* Salt Lake City, UT: Signature Books, 1986. 313 pp.

Wallace, Irving. *The Twenty-seventh Wife.* New York: New American Library, 1962. 400 pp.

Whitney, Helen Mar. *Plural Marriage as Taught by the Prophet Joseph.* Salt Lake City: Juvenile Instructor Office, 1882. 52 pp.

Young, Kimball. *Isn't One Wife Enough.* New York: Henry Holt and Co., 1954. 476 pp.

Chapter 16
Communal Family

Consult the "Contents" pages to locate the entries in Part III,
the Directory Listings Sections, that comprise this family.

"The group of believers was one in mind and heart. No one said that any of his belongings were his own, but they all shared with one another everything they had." These verses from the Book of Acts 4:32 (along with statements in Acts 2) have inspired countless generations of Christians to forsake secular society and attempt to find a new style of living in communalism and the common life. Sources in pre-Christian society may have influenced early Christian practice. The ancient Cretes and Greeks adopted certain aspects of the communalist life style. The Essene community at Qumran represents an attempt in the Jewish community at a communal alternative.

It is not until the fourth century, however, that communalism becomes a real force in Western society, and interestingly enough, its form is the same as in the East—monasticism. Like the Christians, Buddhists, particularly in China, developed monastic communities as an attempt at authentic religious living in the face of a culture that was only nominally religious. For Western Christianity, the monastic ideal was a reaction to the establishment of Christianity as the state church, with mass conversions and baptisms which the monks said brought everybody into the church instead of making the church an assembly of true believers. Unlike the early church, which merely pooled its resources, monasticism presented a thorough-going communalism.

Inherent in the monk's life was the acceptance of an equality of life with the other brothers in the community. *Poverty* and the renunciation of the world were the prime means to this end. In the *chastity* rule an alternative to family life, a main distraction to community allegiance, was offered. In *obedience* to the abbot and in acceptance of the rules came the strong social system to replace the one ingrained from youth, as well as a discipline to enforce the new order.

The result was, of course, the success of the movement to which the church responded by accepting some monastic goals for its clergy, principally chastity. However, the very success of the movement had consequences that threatened the existence of the monastic communities. They became wealthy and their wealth became a part of the problem of the Middle Ages as they became an adjunct to the power structures instead of an alternative.

Francis of Assisi was the one who raised the issue of poverty in monastic circles. Sophistry had undermined the poverty ideal, thought Francis. While individually giving up all property, collectively the monasteries were rich and the monks (without individually owning anything) could nevertheless *use* all the order's wealth. Francis advocated a poverty of *use*, and this real poverty ideal raised an issue that threatened the medieval church. In the face of this threat, the church hierarchy rejected Francis, burned his books, and rewrote his rules for the order. After Francis, various attempts were made to reform the monasteries, but few, if any, understood the heart of the issue. The inability to reform the monasteries was a factor leading to Henry VIII's plundering of them during the Reformation Era.

In the pre-Reformation and Reformation eras, various communal experiments were tried, mostly as part of the radically militant wing of various reformist movements. Typical were the Taborites and Munsterites. The Taborites arose after the execution in 1415 of John Hus, the Czech reformer. Taborite communities developed on Bohemian hillsides and a conscious imitation of early Christian communalism was practiced. The most important of these communities, on a hill near Bechyne Castle, was named Mount Tabor. Tabor was to be the site of the second coming of Christ (Mark 14), and the group derived its own name from the new Mount Tabor. Anti-German, intensely nationalistic, anti-Roman Catholic, and biblicist, the Taborites were attempting a new social order outside that of Bohemia or even Western Europe. For this reason, they were themselves subject to persecution by both Roman Catholics and Hussites. In 1420, Martinek Hauska appeared, preaching the end-time and calling for all to flee to the mountaintops for safety. The mountaintops to which he referred were, of course, the five Taborite communities. The success led to a call for a holy war to exterminate sin and sinners and thus purify the land and bring in the millennium.

The millennium was to be characterized as an anarcho-communism. There would be no authority figures, taxes, rents, or private property. Since it was a classless society, it would begin by a massacre of the rich. Communal coffers were established. When these ran low, the Taborites "took from the enemies of God what God has given for his children" (i.e., they stole what they needed from any nearby non-Taborite). The Taborites, well supplied militarily, continued to exist for a generation, but were broken and splintered by war, messianic figures claiming to be Christ, doctrinal divergences and, primarily, an inability to produce the goods needed to survive. They eventually died out as a social experiment.

During the Reformation, communalism emerged among the radical reformers. In 1534, the New Jerusalem was established at Munster by Bernard Rothmann, Jan of Leiden, and Jan Mathijs. The leaders imposed communalism on an essentially reluctant community. They began by collecting all the financial resources into the community treasure, effecting the change by making the surrender of money the test of true Christianity. Demands on food and shelter followed as the ideal became a disappearance of the distinction between thine and mine. Mathijs emerged as the ruling authority, but was killed in a scouting raid against the Catholic forces now besieging the city. Jan of Leiden took over and began the imposition of an exacting moral code. Artisans were commandeered and made community employees. The sexual mores were changed. Jan took advantage of the three-to-one ratio of women to men and declared polygamy the order of the day. Jan, himself, took fifteen wives, and the polygamy soon disintegrated into promiscuity.

After an early victory over the Catholic forces, Jan of Leiden proclaimed himself king of the world and instituted a wave of terror against community dissidents. The early victory of the reformers only led to greater efforts by the Catholic forces, who laid an even stronger siege to Munster. Eventually, they starved the community to death, and Jan of Leiden was executed.

The experiences at Munster and Tabor were typical in many ways of medieval communal groups. Though Munster was an extreme case, communalists associated with the Reformation tended to be militant in their approach to authority structures other than their own. Possibly related to their militancy was their own experience of having been persecuted, and a resulting short life span. When they gained power, they became the persecutor. The Taborite practice of the appropriation of property of noncommunalists was also widespread. The sexual reforms, mostly advocating polygamy, were common. With such models, it is no wonder that communalism did not experience another revival for several centuries. A few isolated attempts appeared, but only in the early 1800s did a new wave of communalism arise.

THE NINETEENTH CENTURY COMMUNAL SURGE. American communal history is generally focused upon the early nineteenth century, the era of some of the most important communal experiments. However, the significance of the communes founded after 1960 have been recognized, and communal history is now generally seen as having progressed through three phases: (1) prior to 1860; (2) from 1860 to 1960; and (3) since 1960. The first phase begins in the seventeenth century with the establishment of such groups as Plockhoy's Commonwealth in Delaware (1663), the Labadist Community in Maryland (1683), and the Society of the Woman in the Wilderness outside of Philadelphia (1694). Others were founded through the 1700s, and the rate of community formation increased dramatically in the late eighteenth century with the coming of the Shakers. The numerous attempts by the followers of Robert Owen (1820s) and Charles Fourier (1840s) to found communities crowned the first phase of communal life in America and their relatively quick demise ended it.

The nineteenth century burst of communalism grew out of the Enlightenment of the eighteenth century and the rise of intellectual concern with social order. The followers of Claude Henri Saint-Simon are usually accredited with the beginning of egalitarian reformist ideas, but roots to Saint-Simon's thought are deep in the trends of eighteenth century philosophy. In the 1820s, followers of Saint-Simon began a community, which, after Saint-Simon's death, was moved to Menilmontant by its leader, Enfantin. In 1832, Enfantin was condemned for teaching free love, and communalism suffered a setback from which it never recovered in France.

Among the French socialist writers was Etienne Cabet, who put his communalist ideals in an 1840 book, *Voyage en Icarie*. In 1848, he and some followers settled in Fanin County, Texas, but health problems forced them to Illinois, where they settled at Nauvoo, which had recently been abandoned by the Mormons. Branch colonies were established in Iowa and Missouri, but Cabet's death in 1856 was a nearly fatal blow. One colony in Iowa did survive until the end of the century.

More important for the eventual rise of communal groups were the ideas of Charles Fourier (1772–1837). Fourier saw the world organized in phalanxes (his name for a single community) in which communism would be practiced in both labor and production. A strong order would exist for discipline, and loyalty to the phalanx (a central idea) would replace national and family ties. Marriage would be regulated on a polyandric system, with women having many husbands. The vision of Fourier gripped the imagination of the Western world.

One of the people who adopted Fourier's vision was George Ripley. His concerns were laid down in a lengthy letter to Ralph Emerson on November 9, 1840. Ripley looked for a place where a natural union between intellectual pursuits and labor could be achieved by combining the two. He proposed to do this on a tract of land that would be a farm, garden, and college, all in one. This adventure, thought Ripley, would yield industry without drudgery

and equality without vulgarity. It would do away with the evils of capitalism and competition. Each family would retain some private property, thus allowing individuality to continue. About ten to twelve families would start the experiment, which would grow slowly. The adults would be paid interest on their investment and wages for their labor. There would be no great wealth but a comfortable living.

Government would be by consensus expressed in open meetings. On September 29, 1841, the Articles of Association for Brook Farm were drawn up after the members spent a summer near West Roxbury, Massachusetts. The Articles called for full support of children to age ten and their education until age twenty. The youth would work for half wages and, at twenty, would decide to stay as a full member or leave without obligation to the community. Income would come to the community through a boarding school and a farm. Later, printing and manufacturing would be added.

Problems arose in the community, however; an internal critique identified several sources of the friction. There was a lack of well planned operating procedures. The only real community experience was eating together when there should have been more sharing on other levels. No common religious life existed. No confrontation with the basic problem of divided love had been made.

After making this critique, the members revived their interest in Fourier's ideas. Albert Brisbane, an ardent disciple of Fourier, joined Brook Farm, and it was on its way to becoming a successful phalange. Population increased and a house (phalanstery) was begun. But before it could become self-sufficient, a smallpox epidemic took a heavy toll on its members, some of whom died, and some of whom fled. A fire destroyed the phalanstery. In November 1846, Brook Farm was declared a failure and the project ended.

More successful was the phalanx at Hopedale, Massachusetts. Begun in 1841, it prospered for 11 years under the able guidance of Adin Ballou, a Unitarian and Spiritualist. Altogether, 175 people lived at Hopedale. Its success was built upon Ballou's strong leadership and a strict moral and behavioral code. Religious freedom was allowed. The project failed, however, after Ballou withdrew as leader.

Communities drawing on the enthusiasm of the French philosophers, but based more directly on religious, mainly New Testament, ideals also flourished in the nineteenth century. Of significance were the Rappites, German separatists who migrated to Pennsylvania in the early 1800s. In 1803–04, they settled in Butler County, Pennsylvania, and in 1805, promulgated their Articles of Agreement. They were German pietists and millennialists. They were led by George Rapp, who was given almost complete control over the community. Regulation of sexual life began in 1807 when the community became celibate. Equality was a high ideal and a uniform dress was adopted. A community graveyard without markers was also used. In 1814, the group migrated en masse up the Wabash River from Evansville to New Harmony, Indiana.

Here they established one of the most successful communities in American history. In 1818, the final break with the past was made when all property records, hence all claims by individuals on the community's property, were destroyed by vote of the community. The Rappites became known for their innovations. They were the first to develop prefabricated houses, many of which still stand. They diversified their economy and became, in a short time, entirely self-sufficient. They made wagons, distilled whiskey, cultivated silk, and had an early printing center for the Wabash Valley. Success threatened their faith, so in 1824, they sold the property and returned to Pennsylvania. They built a new town, Economy, near Pittsburgh.

The beginning of the end came in the late 1820s when Father Rapp, without consulting the community, published a second set of Articles of Agreement. While these articles merely stated in writing what was happening in practice, discontent at Rapp's impertinence arose. To counter the dissatisfaction, Rapp began to emphasize the nearness of the second coming of Christ in his sermons and to propose a group journey to meet him in the Holy Land. The apocalypticism was rewarded in 1832 by the appearance in Economy of "Count Leon," a professed returned Christ and the anointed of God. He took approximately 250 of the Rappites with him when he left. The "Count Leon" incident was followed by disagreement on celibacy and Rapp's paternal control. Rapp was subsequently forced to modify his articles.

In 1834, Father Rapp's adopted son, who had been the financial genius of the community, died. With his passing much of the community's financial success passed also. In 1847, Father Rapp died, and without his unitive personality, the community disintegrated. Both New Harmony and Economy are only tourist spots today.

COMMUNALISM IN AMERICA: THE SECOND PHASE. There was a noticeable decline in the formation of new communal societies from the mid 1840s to the beginning of the Civil War. The hiatus in community formation, which continued for almost a decade after the war, was broken by the migration of the Hutterites, a people who share a religious background (including a commitment to pacifism) with the Russian Mennonites. In 1874, reacting to the introduction of compulsory military service in Russia, they migrated to the United States. The first three colonies, containing approximately 400 people, were founded in South Dakota. The colonies multiplied until again faced with military service during World War I. In a relatively short time they moved to Canada and spread across the prairie. In 1934, they began a second and this time successful attempt to colonize South Dakota. As of the mid-1980s, they had more than 300 colonies across the western part of Canada and in the western U.S. states bordering Canada. The Hutterites alone have founded more communities than all of the communal groups before them combined. They remain today as the single most successful communal group past or present.

As the Hutterite communal thrust was gaining strength, a second more secular communal push emerged which was rooted in the utopian visions of Edward Bellamy. In 1887, Bellamy's novel *Looking Backward, 1000–1887* projected a vision of economic equality to be reached in the foreseeable future. It sold 200,000 copies by 1890 and led to the formation of Nationalist Clubs in 28 states. During the 1890s Bellamy's novel, at times combined with various degrees of Marxist thought, inspired a variety of new communal experiments, including a group of colonies in the Puget Sound area of Washington. Endorsed by Helena P. Blavatsky, the founder of the Theosophical Society, the book also led to the formation of several explicitly Theosophical communities during the early twentieth century.

After World War I the number of new communities continued to grow out of most diverse theoretical constructions. They included: Jewish Socialists, occultists, Mormons, orthodox Christians, anarchists, and radical Marxists. Even without counting the Hutterites, more communities were begun in the second phase of American communal life (1860–1960) than in the two centuries of the first phase.

COMMUNALISM IN AMERICA: THE THIRD PHASE. The third phase of communal growth in America started in the 1960s as part of the larger counter culture, or hippie, movement. Beginning in the summer of 1967, a number of young adults flocked to California in search of a cultural alternative to the middle class life in which they had been raised. Labeled "flower children" because of their habit of giving flowers to people they encountered on the street, they soon became distinguished by their use of psychedelic drugs. In both Los Angeles and San Francisco, economic necessity led them to adopt communalism, and as communalism grew, they made the discovery of the new quality it added to their lives. After the media, time, and drugs destroyed the hippie communities in the urban areas, many of the former hippies headed for rural America and launched a back-to-the-land movement. Others scattered through the cities and formed various kinds of urban cooperatives. The impulse remained strong through the 1970s but began

to wane in the 1980s. Of the hundreds of communities formed, however, a number (mostly religious) have survived to take their place in communal history.

One new set of the recent communities shared the common roots of the hippie and the Jesus People, the Christian evangelical movement that emerged among the hippies. Numerous Christian communes, Jesus People U.S.A. of Chicago being possibly the most successful, sprang up. They were joined by occult New Age communities that combined hippie values with New Age visions of communes as transforming agents in society. A most successful secular communal experiment is Twin Oaks, a Virginia community built on the principles of behaviorist psychologist B. F. Skinner. The scholarly interest in communalism also spawned the National Historical Communal Societies Association headquartered at the Communal Studies Center at the University of Southern Indiana in Evansville.

THE MARKS OF A SUCCESSFUL COMMUNITY. Of the many communities begun in America since 1800, only a few have survived any length of time. That is, only a few have survived long enough for a child born in the commune to become an adult member. From those that have survived and from a study of the demises of those that failed, some characteristics of successful and unsuccessful communities emerge. As a beginning, it might be noted that sex and close interpersonal relations are rarely the cause of a community's failure. These two items often bring discontent and a change of membership, but in only the rarest of cases do they lead to a total breakup of the community. Even Plato, in the *Republic*, recognized the necessity of a strong order in sexual relations. He proposed a community of wives. It is characteristic of communities either at the beginning or very soon thereafter (sex is a question that does not wait long to be asked) to organize personal relationships in a social pattern. The human organism has proved adaptable to a seemingly infinite variety of patterns, from monogamy, to polygamy and polyandry, to free love of both traditional and Oneida varieties, to group marriage (which might include homosexual attachments), and to chastity, the most popular regulation. The particular form is not important; that sex be regulated is important.

Among the most influential of the patterns of sexual conduct in American religious groups is the complex marriage system developed by the Oneida community. The group was formed in Putney, Vermont, in the early 1840s, and moved to Oneida, New York, in the mid-1840s. The community endured for a generation, dissolving in 1880. The Oneida community's sexual mores were established by John Humphrey Noyes, the founder of the community. Early in his career Noyes began to preach against monogamy as an exclusive attachment that limited love. As a first step in developing his new system Noyes discovered what he called male continence, the practice of intercourse without the male reaching climax. (This practice was widespread among Tibetan Buddhists, and was called karezza.) By using this technique, numerous pregnancies could be avoided. Thus men of the Oneida community could cohabit with a number of women without giving the community the burden of many new members. As finally worked out, cohabitation within the Oneida community was regulated by a system of ascending fellowship. In this system, those seen as more perfect (the older members) tended to have sexual encounters with the younger members. All encounters were arranged by a third party, and records were kept to prevent any exclusive relationships from developing.

A study of the history of many communes that have died out indicates five main reasons for their failure. First, communities *founded for shallow reasons* (for example, by persons merely wanting to escape their former lives) do not survive. *Poor planning* by those inexperienced in meeting the total needs of people is a prime cause of failure, particularly now, when so many communalists were raised in the city in complete ignorance of rural life. Anarchy, *a lack of order*, is another cause. Production of items (food, money, shelter, restrooms, etc.) necessary to survival becomes everyone's job but no one's responsibility. A common time for communes to dissolve is immediately following the first snow. *Hostility from the surrounding community* has been a strong force in disrupting communal existence. This hostility comes as a reaction to the different styles of life and the often deviant (from the local surrounding community) moral standards of communalists. Refusal to allow Oneida's sexual mores to prevail was a significant factor in its eventual demise. Hostility in New Mexico has all but destroyed many communes there. The final factor in communal disruption is *success*. Communes, if successful in reaching their original goals, financial or otherwise, will pose new goals often drawn from the surrounding world. Thus, keeping the communal ideal before the group is a continuing function. Communities in Zion, Illinois; Amana, Iowa; and New Harmony, Indiana; all suffered from success.

The successful commune (i.e., one that survives) will have several of the following characteristics, no one of which is sufficient in itself. The presence of a *strong leader* has been noted in many surviving communes. She/he supplies the unity and authority, and functions somewhat as a patriarchal figure. His/her power may be drawn from psychic, oratorical, or intellectual abilities, or just from personality. Such present-day communes as the Ananda Cooperative Community of Kriyananda, the One World Family of Allen Noonan, and the Farm of Stephen are good examples. In the absence of a strong leader, a *strong system of social control and behavior* can function in his/her stead. This system, which may be formal or informal, must regulate enough of the life of the community for the necessities of life to be provided and a quality of life sustained. Many communes survive the death of their founders by adopting such a system based on the founders' teachings. *Economic self-sufficiency* is vital to a community's existence. Parasites can exist only for a couple of years. *Removal* from the outside world, in its most effective form geographically, is an early necessity. The establishment of a commune means changing habits and mores ingrained since childhood. It is best accomplished in a period of isolation, without old distractions. It can be done by a careful regulation of the possessions and material resources used by the community. After establishment, a careful check on new ideas must be made, and those destructive to the community's life countered.

The basic problem for communal groups is always, then, living as a subculture in a dominant culture which is often hostile and which always aims at assimilation and uniformity. Just as eternal vigilance is the price of freedom, eternal confrontation is the price of continued communal life.

THE DEMISE OF THE SOVIET UNION. The fall of Marxism in the former U.S.S.R. has spurred the re-examination of communalism by the growing number of scholars of communal life. This new look has coincided with a de-emphasis on questions of measuring the "success" of communes and a refocus of attention on the role of communalism as a stage in the ongoing development of communities, and of communal living as a choice for one phase of an individual's life. In this light communes can be seen as *temporary* structures that cease to exist as they succeed in reaching the particular goal or goals of their founders. They serve their purpose for the people involved, who then move on to another social organization. Frequently, at the economic level, communal structures provide a bridge for people to enter mainstream society. On the social level, communities teach people to live with others with a new degree of intimacy, which prepares them to participate in a nuclear family. A developmental approach to understanding communalism allows new standards by which to judge communal experiments.

Sources—The Communal Family

The study of communal groups and life in North America is focused and nurtured by the Communal Studies Association, which may be reached c/o Center for Communal Studies, University of Southern Indiana, Evansville, IN 47712. The Association publishes the annual journal, *Communal Studies*.

GENERAL SOURCES

Communities Directory: A Guide to Cooperative Living. Rutledge, MO: Fellowship for Intentional Community, 1996. 440 pp.

Dare, Philip, ed. *American Communes to 1860: A Bibliography*. New York: Garland Publishing, 1990.

Fogarty, Robert S. *American Utopianism*. Itaska, IL: F. E. Peacock Publishers, 1972. 175 pp.

Kanter, Rosebeth Moss. *Commitment and Community*. Cambridge: Harvard University Press, 1972. 303 pp.

Melton, J. Gordon, and Robin Martin. *A Bibliography of American Communalism*. Evanston, IL: Institute for the Study of American Religion, n.d. 23 pp.

Mercer, John. *Communes*. Dorchester, Dorset: Prism Press, 1984. 152 pp.

Miller, Timothy. *American Communes, 1860–1960: A Bibliography*. New York: Garland Publishing, 1990. 583 pp.

Muncy, Raymond Lee. *Sex and Marriage in Utopian Communities*. Bloomington: Indiana University Press, 1973. 275 pp.

The 1990/91 Directory of Intentional Communities: A Guide to Cooperative Living. Evansville, IN: Fellowship for Intentional Community/ Stelle, IL: Communities Publications, Cooperative, 1990. 312 pp. With periodic updates and new editions.

Oved, Yaacov. *Two Hundred Years of American Communes*. New Brunswick, NJ: Transaction Publishers, 1993. 500 pp.

Pitzer, Donald E. *America's Communal Utopias*. Chapel Hill: University of North Carolina Press, 1997. 537 pp.

Rexroth, Kenneth. *Communalism: From Its Origins to the Twentieth Century*. New York: Seabury Press, 1974. 316 pp.

Richter, Peyton E. *Utopias, Social Ideals and Communal Experiments*. Boston: Holbrook Press, 1971. 321 pp.

COMMUNES IN AMERICA PRIOR TO 1860

Bester, Arthur. *Backwoods Utopias*. Philadelphia: University of Pennsylvania Press, 1970. 330 pp.

Lockwood, George B. *The Harmony Movement*. New York: Dover Publications, 1971. 404 pp.

Mandelker, Ira L. *Religion, Society and Utopia in Nineteenth-Century America*. Amherst, MA: University of Massachusetts Press, 1984. 181 pp.

Sachse, Julius F. *The German Pietists of Provincial Pennsylvania*. Philadelphia: The Author, 1895. 504 pp.

Wisby, Herbert A., Jr. *Pioneer Prophetess*. Ithaca, NY: Cornell University, 1964. 232 pp.

COMMUNES IN AMERICA 1860–1960

Hine, Robert. *California's Utopian Communities*. New Haven: Yale University Press, 1966. 209 pp.

Kagan, Paul. *New World Utopias*. New York: Penguin Books, 1975. 191 pp.

Veysey, Laurence. *The Communal Experience*. Chicago: University of Chicago Press, 1978. 495 pp.

COMMUNES IN AMERICA AFTER 1960

Berger, Bennett M. *The Survival of a Counterculture*. Berkeley; University of California Press, 1981. 264 pp.

Fitzgerald, George R. *Communes, Their Goals, Hopes, Problems*. New York: Paulist Press, 1971. 214 pp.

Fracchia, Charles A. *Living Together Alone*. San Francisco: Harper & Row, 1979. 186 pp.

Gardner, Hugh. *The Children of Prosperity*. New York: St. Martin's Press, 1978. 281 pp.

Hedgepath, William, and Dennis Stock. *The Alternative Life in New America*. New York: Collier-Macmillan, 1970. 191 pp.

Houriet, Robert. *Getting Back Together*. New York: Avon, 1971. 408 pp.

McLaughlin, Corrine, and Gordon Davidson. *Builders of the Dawn: Community Lifestyle in a Changing World*. Shutesbuty, MA: Sirius Publishing, 1986. 372 pp.

Mellis, Charles J. *Committed Communities*. Pasadena, CA; William Carey Library, 1976. 138 pp.

Chapter 17
Christian Science-Metaphysical Family

Consult the "Contents" pages to locate the entries in Part III,
the Directory Listings Sections, that comprise this family.

Christian Science and New Thought are two movements that generally do not like to speak of each other. They are now two very distinct movements with a number of obvious differences. Yet while distinct, they also are related. They both emerged within a few years of each other in the United States and then internationally. They shared historical roots both in the idealistic philosophy of the nineteenth century and in the search for alternative means for healing at a time when the healing arts were still in a very primitive state. In combining these two roots, they found some agreement concerning the role of "Mind" as the agent in healing. As a matter of fact, it is the confusion between the movements, and the intense polemics concerning their separation, that led in large part to the mutual denial of their common roots.

The first movement to appear was Christian Science. It took its main embodiment in the Church of Christ, Scientist, founded by Mary Baker Eddy. However, within a few years of its launching, teacher-practitioners of Christian Science appeared claiming to be true to the memory and teachings of Eddy, but not affiliated with the church she headed. While bearing little continuity from generation to generation, there has always existed a group of such independent Christian Scientists.

Also, from the first years of Christian Science, there appeared a growing number of practitioners-teachers who had started their careers with the Church of Christ, Scientist, and/or the writings of Eddy, but who differed with her on one or more important issues. The most important of these people was Emma Curtis Hopkins, a former student of Eddy's. Around her, originally under the label of Christian Science, grew a movement that soon departed on an increasing number of points from Eddy. By the end of the century it had left the world of Christian Science and had become known as New Thought. Freed from its attachment to Eddy, New Thought quickly developed as a national movement in its own right.

THE FORERUNNERS. Christian Science and New Thought brought together insights from several traditions in nineteenth century America that had sought an alternative to the growing materialism that dominated both public discourse and religious thought. Although it frequently tried to appropriate the dominant Christianity of its culture, it also deviated at a number of important points, especially (in its New England context) from the larger Puritan worldview embodied in the Westminster Confession of Faith and the Cambridge Platform. The alternatives asserted the reality of a spiritual world, the importance of mystical experience, and the healing value of invisible forces operating on the mind and body. This tradition is often called the metaphysical tradition and is defined best by the ideas of the several writer-thinkers who dominated the tradition as it developed through the early nineteenth century: Franz Anton Mesmer, Emanuel Swedenborg, Phineas Parkhurst Quimby, Ralph Waldo Emerson, and Warren Felt Evans.

Franz Anton Mesmer (1734–1815), an Austrian physician, discovered what he claimed was an amazing healing force. Astrology and the forces that made it work, an important element in eighteenth century medical training and the subject of his doctoral dissertation, became the launching point of his discovery. Asked to summarize his teachings for the French Academy of Science in the 1780s, he produced the "21 Propositions." In this brief statement, he described a subtle fluid universally diffused through nature. This fluid had the property of receiving and communicating impulses between material bodies. The fluid could be used for the cure of all diseases (those of the nerves immediately and others over a period of time) and to produce a somnambulistic state or mesmeric trance.

Though rebuffed in his attempt to find acceptance with the Academy, Mesmer's ideas found many disciples during the next decades. Scientists tried to refine his theory and discover convincing ways of demonstrating the existence of the magnetic force. Disciples of mesmerism appeared in America throughout the 1830s. Popular lecturers toured the country speaking about and demonstrating the unusual properties of animal magnetism. Eventually, the mesomeric sleep was separated from the rest of the phenomena and the theories about fluids discarded. The magnetic state survives today as the hypnotic state, an altered state of consciousness brought about primarily by suggestion. Spiritualism perpetuated the theories of mesomeric healing fluid or force. The theories still exist, though slightly altered by reference to more recent science. The fluid has been transformed into electromagnetic energy, part of the invisible light spectrum.

An early contemporary of Mesmer's, Swedish scientist Emanuel Swedenborg (1688–1772), is most noted for his communications with angelic beings, the results of which filled many volumes of theological treatises and biblical commentaries. Systematized, his thought became the basis of the Church of the New Jerusalem. The church, founded in England shortly after Swedenborg's death, was brought to the United States just after the American Revolution and spread throughout the Northeast. By the middle of the nineteenth century, it has reached the Midwest and one church had even been planted in San Francisco.

It is frequently hard to understand Swedenborg's popularity in the last century in light of his being so ignored in the late twentieth century. However, one cannot understand Spiritualism without reference to his thought and his metaphysical assumptions, which would become major building blocks taken over by Mary Baker Eddy and her students. First, he championed the notion of the priority of the world of Spirit over that of matter. Spirit was the ultimately real, matter only a frail shadow of secondary existence. Matter assumed its reality only in its possession of a correspondence to the spiritual. Second, based upon the priority of Spirit and the "law of correspondence" between the spiritual and the material, Swedenborg offered a true spiritual interpretation of scripture to enhance the more mundane literal (i.e., materialistic) interpretation. Often adding lengthy glossaries to his books, Swedenborg proposed a spiritual meaning to various individual concepts, people, and events in the Bible. Although differing in content, both Eddy and Hopkins would follow a similar method in interpreting scripture. Within New Thought, the method of metaphysical interpretation would lead to the monumental *Metaphysical Bible Dictionary* (1932) compiled by Charles S. Fillmore of the Unity School of Christianity.

Among the people most affected by the mesmerist movement was Phineas P. Quimby (1802–1866). As a young clockmaker in Belfast, Maine, Quimby attended a mesmerist lecture-demonstration by Dr. Robert Collyer in 1838. Fascinated, he began to experiment with mesmerism and found a suitable subject in Lucius Burkmer, a person who easily slipped into a trance state. While entranced, Burkmer would frequently diagnose and prescribe for illnesses of people brought before him. Quimby noted on several occasions that people were healed by taking a prescribed medicine that had no real medicinal value. Gradually, Quimby discarded any hypotheses about magnetic fluid and attributed the healing agency to what he termed "mind."

Quimby equated God with Wisdom, Science, or First Cause. Wisdom contains all truth, ideas, and knowledge. Wisdom, his favorite term, gives forth an essence that fills all of space, much as perfume fills a room with its odor. This essence is not Wisdom, but has the character of Wisdom. Matter is created out of this essence, and matter then condenses into the various forms and elements. Out of the most gross matter, man was created and breathed with the essence of God, or mind. Quimby compares the individual with a locomotive. The body is the locomotive itself. Mind is the steam that drives it forward. Wisdom is the engineer.

Quimby saw mind as a separate independent reality apart from matter. It is invisible and intelligent. Disease is a malfunction of mind caused by error (a false idea) condensing into the material. The major sources of error, in Quimby's opinion, were religion, reason, and medicine, and he frequently denounced clergy, teachers, and doctors who perpetuated the wisdom (or more correctly, the opinions) of the world and taught people they were sick and going to die. Such diseased ideas led to illness and eventual death. Through the use of the mind, however, Quimby could convince people of the error of false opinion and replace it with the Truth of Wisdom or Science. Once the Truth was implanted in the mind of the patient, it could operate directly upon the body to heal. This Science was the same as that taught by Christ and could properly be called the Science of the Christ.

Toward the end of his life, though Quimby took a few students, he could by no means be said to have started a movement. One of his students, Warren Felt Evans, to be discussed below, began a healing practice but did not take students of his own. Two of Quimby's students, Annetta and Julius Dresser, did little with what they had learned from him until some years later, after the fourth student, Mary Baker Eddy, had begun a movement developing ideas concerning health and healing.

Though living as contemporaries of each other, there is no evidence that Quimby and Ralph Waldo Emerson (1803–1882) took particular note of each other. Their life's work moved in different arenas. Emerson had left the ministry to develop a kind of nature mysticism and to work as a writer/ lecturer. In the process he became the most noted spokesperson for the Transcendentalist Movement. During the 1830s, having been inspired by Swedenborg (from whom he frequently drew his concepts), having absorbed some of the basics of Hinduism through the Bhagavad Gita, and having adopted the new Romanticism from Europe, he argued for a united world view based upon the priority of mind. To Emerson, the world was the product of one mind (God) that is everywhere active (i.e., immanent in nature). Whatever opposes that one mind eventually comes to nought. Good is positive, is real. Evil does not really exist, it is merely the privation of good, not an opposing reality in itself. All things proceed out of the same spirit-mind-good, and our alignment with that good brings strength. The realization of this truth, concluded Emerson, awakens within humanity the religious sentiment.

Most people, even that vast majority who disagreed with his conclusions, read Emerson. In him, the metaphysical tradition found its most significant nineteenth century propagandist, and through him and his colleagues reached a vast audience.

Warren Felt Evans (1817–1887) had been a student of Quimby, but before that he had become a devotee of Emanuel Swedenborg, so much so that he forsook his Methodist training and became a minister in the Church of the New Jerusalem. But Evans was a sickly man, and along the way he turned to Quimby, under whom he was returned to a degree of health. After Quimby's death, Evans moved to a Boston suburb and opened a healing practice. However, while acknowledging a certain debt to Quimby, he quietly discarded Quimby's ideas and methods. Instead, he found in the broader Swedenborgian world view a more adequate framework to conduct his therapeutic work. In developing a Swedenborgian interpretation of healing and health, he expanded the tradition in a direction that Swedenborg had never explored. In the end, Evans returned to a mesomeric model, identifying Swedenborg's concept of the divine "influx" with the healing power.

The issue of the extent to which the major figures in the metaphysical tradition referred to or even knew about each other is a matter of intense scholarly debate. It is known, for example, that Emerson read Swedenborg, and Quimby absorbed the magnetist tradition. The well-read Evans seems to have taken ideas from numerous sources, including Hinduism. But there is little to link Mesmer and his contemporary Swedenborg, or Emerson and his contemporary Quimby. Together, however, Mesmer, Swedenborg, Quimby, Emerson, and Evans created a common language, a concern for healing, and an emphasis upon the reality and immanence of the spiritual, which undergirded the work of Mary Baker Eddy and the students who would come after her.

CHRISTIAN SCIENCE. "At the commencement of the study of Metaphysical science, we must acquaint ourselves with its Principle whereby to gain the demonstration of this Principle in healing the sick. For the sake of brevity, these first lessons are arranged in questions and answers.

"Question—What is God?

"Answer—Jehovah is not a person. God is Principle.

"Question—What is Principle?

"Answer—Principle is Life, Truth and Love, Substance and Intelligence.

"Question—Is there more than one Principle?

"Answer—There is not. The varied manifestations of science have but one Principle, for there is but one God. All science expresses God, and is governed by Principle" (Mary Baker Eddy, *The Science of Man by Which the Sick Are Healed* [Lynn, MA: Luther C. Parker, 1879]).

Mary Baker Eddy (1821–1910), the discoverer of Christian Science and founder of the Church of Christ, Scientist, grew up in a devout New England Congregationalist home. Her early formal education had been limited by her poor health, but she recovered enough in her teen years to attend Holmes Academy. She married in 1843, but her husband died just months before the birth of their child, an event that signaled another period of poor health for the still youthful Mary.

She married again in 1853. Her husband, George Patterson, joined the Union Army during the Civil War, during which he was captured. Meanwhile, Mary had heard of Phineas P. Quimby and in 1862 she traveled to Portland, Maine, to receive treatment. Within a month she was seemingly cured and wrote in praise of Quimby to the newspaper in Portland. Her first stay in Portland, which lasted for three months, began the most crucial and controversial period of her career. It is evident that Quimby had opened up a new direction for her and that she initially gave him enthusiastic credit for an improvement of health. In later years Eddy's critics would quote her words of appreciation as a means of discrediting her own unique contributions. Hence her relation to Quimby bears close scrutiny.

Her years as a student-associate of Quimby were ones of fluctuating health. After an initial improvement, her health would fail, only to improve when she returned to Maine. Also, while obviously engaged in the study of Quimby's ideas, and enthusiastically using his methods on others, she was not an uncritical student. Like Evans, she had trouble accepting his concept of mind as spiritual matter (as did Evans), and she could not reconcile Quimby's hostility to religion with her own continuing Christian faith. In spite of these differences, Quimby helped her, and she continued her association with him until his death on January 16, 1866. A few days later she wrote her oft-quoted poem in his memory, "Lines in the Death of P. P. Quimby, who healed with the truth that Christ taught, in contradistinction to all isms."

The death of Quimby, however, was to be immediately followed by the events that were to move her into a distinct realm of thought and practice and separate her forever from Quimby's ideas and ways. On February 1, 1866, while visiting in Lynn, Massachusetts, Eddy fell on the ice. The next day she was found to be suffering from severe internal spasms. Taken back to her home in Swampscott, she was confined to her bed. Those in attendance varied in their opinion about her recovery, some even doubting its possibility. Then on February 4, given a Bible to read and left to meditate alone, she was overwhelmed with the conviction that her life was in God and that God was the only Life, the sole reality of existence. In that discovery came her healing. She got out of bed, dressed, and walked into the next room to the astonishment of all present.

The next months and years would be ones of personal turmoil, punctuated by her divorcing her husband for desertion, and her growing comprehension of the implication of the insight received at the time of her healing. During the next decade she would engage in intensive Bible study, struggling to understand the implications of God as healer versus Quimby's notion of mind as healer. In 1870 she formed a partnership with Richard Kennedy as a practitioner and teacher, and in August held her first class. She also began the writing that would eventually become *Science and Health with Key to the Scripture*, the first edition of which was published in 1875 (as simply *Science and Health*).

In 1876 the Christian Scientist Association was formed as a fellowship of Eddy's personal students, among whom was Asa Gilbert Eddy, whom she married in 1877. In 1879 the Church of Christ, Scientist was organized, and two years later Eddy was ordained by her students as its pastor. In 1882 she moved from Lynn to Boston and opened the Massachusetts Metaphysical College. At the college, she taught the basic classes, the successful completion of which allowed students to become Christian Science practitioners. As the classes proceeded, students opened Christian Science offices in Boston, in the nearby cities, and gradually in urban centers around the United States and Canada. Chicago quickly arose as the strongest center for Christian Science outside of New England.

As a result of the circulation of *Science and Health* and the work of Eddy's students, Christian Science began to blossom. Before it could establish itself, however, Eddy had to deal with a situation that has distorted the entire history of the Church of Christ, Scientist, and those movements derived from it. The events began with the resignation in 1880 of Edward J. Arens, a former student of Eddy's, from the Christian Scientist Association. Before the year was out he published a pamphlet entitled, *The Science of the Relation Between God and Man and the Distinction Between Spirit and Matter*. It seemed to rely heavily upon *The Science of Man*, a booklet originally used as her textbook, and *Science and Health*. Eddy considered filing suit, but at first rejected the notion.

Then in 1882, another former student of Phineas P. Quimby's, Julius Dresser, returned to Boston after having spent several years in California. He took a Christian Science class from Arens, and in February of 1883 launched an attack upon Eddy in the *Boston Globe* in which he accused her of stealing the thought of Quimby, and presenting his ideas as her own under a new label of Christian Science. Eddy answered him. Dresser wrote a second article,

which Eddy again answered. In the wake of the series, Eddy filed suit against Arens for plagiarism. Arens tried to refute the charge with a counter charge. Since Eddy had plagiarized from Quimby, he could not be held accountable for any copying from Eddy. He lost the case, and the court ordered the destruction of 3,000 copies of his pamphlet.

Though Eddy won the case, she did so in the absence of Quimby's unpublished papers, as Quimby's son refused to release them for the trial. As a result, Eddy's critics claimed that Arens lost only because he was unable to produce the crucial Quimby manuscripts. The lack of the manuscripts allowed Julius Dresser (1838–1893) and his wife, Annetta Dresser, to continue the attack upon Eddy for the rest of their lives. And their son Horatio Dresser (1866–1954) perpetuated the controversy for decades to come. He would in later years be called upon to write the history of New Thought, the movement that grew out of Christian Science, and in his 1919 work he would enshrine Quimby and largely bypass Eddy. Then a few years later, when the *Quimby Manuscripts* finally became available, Dresser was chosen to edit the published version.

By the time that the *Quimby Manuscripts* were published, the controversy that began in 1883 had taken on proportions equal to the two parties involved. Christian Scientists frequently tried to argue that Eddy's connection to Quimby was inconsequential, while advocates of New Thought argued that she was totally Quimby's student who merely presented his ideas in a distorted version. Both positions have become untenable in the light of the publication of the Quimby papers and the subsequent historical work. On the one hand, it is impossible to dismiss the role of Quimby in giving direction to Eddy's thought and in providing her a language not otherwise available. At the same time, to equate Quimby's and Eddy's thought is to distort both. They had a profound disagreement on most issues vital to each, such as the existence of matter and the role of religion. More definitively, there is a basic distinction between the thorough-going idealism of Eddy as contrasted with the mind-material dualism of Quimby.

THE DEVELOPMENT OF THE CHURCH OF CHRIST, SCIENTIST. Surviving in spite of the Quimby controversy, Eddy built a national and international church. In so doing she tried to create a body that adhered as far as possible to the Congregationalism of her childhood. Its tenets affirmed the inspired Bible as the sufficient rule leading to eternal life, the one supreme and infinite God, salvation through Christ, and the crucifixion and resurrection of Jesus. One oft-quoted summary of the basic perspective is called the Statement of Being:

"There is no life, truth, intelligence, nor substance in matter. All is infinite Mind and its infinite manifestations, for God is All-in-all. Spirit is immortal Truth; matter is mortal error. Spirit is the real and the eternal; matter is the unreal and temporal. Spirit is God, and man is His image and likeness. Therefore man is not material; he is spiritual."

Ministers from more traditional Christian churches rejected her formulation of doctrine arguing that she had poured such new meaning into the affirmations and placed them in such a foreign context as to make them say something completely different from traditional Christianity.

Christian Science progressed through the 1880s. The sale of *Science and Health* necessitated new printings that allowed for its constant revision. In 1883 the first issue of the *Journal of Christian Science* appeared. In 1884 Eddy added an advanced class to the Metaphysical College's curriculum. Graduates of these "normal" classes were certified not only to be practitioners, but to hold their own classes and train new practitioners. Many formed Christian Science institutes in cities across the United States. By 1886 these institutes had produced enough new practitioners to create the National Christian Scientist Association (the Christian Scientist Association being limited to personal students of Eddy's).

Then, almost as soon as the organization was established, Eddy had second thoughts about attempts to organize the movement at all. In the fall of 1889 she took action by successively disbanding the Christian Scientist Association, the Massachusetts Metaphysical College, and the Church of Christ, Scientist. Earlier in the year she had turned the journal over to the National Christian Scientist Association, but after its 1890 meeting its members did not gather. Around the country, however, Christian Science churches were being organized and buildings erected. While she reconsidered the structure of the movement, she worked on a major revision of *Science and Health*.

In 1892 the manifestation of the new direction for the organization of the movement began to appear. In 1892, in Boston, she formed The First Church of Christ, Scientist, generally known as The Mother Church. Twenty students became the first members. Tenets, rules, and by-laws were adopted. The Mother Church then assumed the central organizational role in the Christian Science movement. Around it the older remnants (branch churches, for example) of the movement would be reoriented, and from it new elements (the Board of Lectureship, for example) would grow. Membership in The Mother Church became essential for anyone wishing to be active in the movement, as it was a requirement for anyone wishing to take the basic Christian Science class. Local churches continued to exist as autonomously governed bodies, but followed the organizational rules and procedures as laid down in the *Church Manual* of The Mother Church. After 1892, The Mother Church and those in communion with it constituted the center of the Christian Science movement. However, there were always those who were attracted to the teachings and practice of the church but who rejected its organizational formation.

INDEPENDENT CHRISTIAN SCIENCE. Almost from the beginning of her work, Eddy was faced with students who defected but who wished to continue practicing what she had taught them. In some cases these were students who disagreed on one or two points of belief, but appreciated Eddy's teachings as a whole. More often, students rejected the demands of the organization and/or the lack of variance in belief it allowed. In any case, as early as 1880 former students of Eddy's established offices and retained their previous designation as Christian Science practitioners.

The first significant former student to establish offices was Edward J. Arens, slowed but not stopped by the loss to Eddy in court. He founded the University of the Science of Spirit and authored his own textbook, *The Old Theology*. Even before the 1883 trial, Arens had been making Christian Science history in Chicago. One of his students, George B. Charles, was the first Christian Science practitioner active in Chicago. In 1882 Charles introduced Christian Science to the Sherman family. After their study with him, Bradford Sherman, his wife, Martha Sherman, and their son, Roger Sherman, traveled to Boston and in 1883 took the basic class in Christian Science directly from Eddy. After their return to Chicago they operated for many years as her authorized representatives.

On October 23, 1881, eight students of the early Lynn group resigned from the Christian Scientist Association, among them Amanda Rice and Elizabeth Stuart. Both continued to practice what they had been taught. Rice introduced Christian Science on the West Coast, while Stuart taught throughout New England and is most remembered as the teacher of some of the most prominent of the New Thought leaders—Leander Whipple and Charles Brodie Patterson.

Throughout the 1880s, as the Church of Christ, Scientist was spreading across the country and becoming a national church body, an increasing number of individual students defected. Possibly the greatest loss was Emma Curtis Hopkins, editor of the *Christian Science Journal*, who moved to Chicago and founded the Hopkins Metaphysical Association and the Christian Science Theological Seminary, the seed organizations from which New Thought emerged. Even before Hopkins arrived, both A. J. Swartz and Joseph Adams had established rival offices and begun publishing periodicals, *The Mind Cure Journal* and the *Chicago Chris-

tian Scientist*. Luther M. Marston, a graduate of Eddy's first normal class, remained in Boston as head of the Boston College of Metaphysical Science and editor of the *Mental Healing Monthly*. Mary Plunkett, who had left for Chicago with Hopkins in 1885, moved to New York City several years later to form the International Christian Science Association and another rival journal.

Looking out to see all these independent organizations flourishing, Eddy turned in 1888 to face another mass defection of students in Boston. The occasion for the disruption was the case of Abby H. Corner, a practitioner who was working with her pregnant daughter. At the time of the delivery, both the daughter and the baby died. Corner was indicted for manslaughter. The Christian Scientist Association defeated a motion to contribute to the defense (Eddy preferred contributions come from individual Christian Scientists). In response, Sarah Crosse, a member of the association's Committee on Publication and a relative of Corner's, attacked Eddy and the association's leadership. She gained some support but not enough to take over the association, so with her supporters she withdrew. Crosse founded the *Boston Christian Scientist*. Crosse's defection was all the more devastating as it came on the heels of the loss of one of the most prominent Chicago practitioners, Ursula Gestefeld (1845–1921), who would later associate with the New Thought Movement.

Among the last breaks between the church and a prominent student prior to Eddy's death was the case of Augusta Stetson (1842–1928). In 1886 Eddy had sent Stetson to New York to lead the work. The work grew under her able care, and around the turn of the century the members built a large Christian Science Institute (teaching facility) on Central Park West with an adjacent home for Stetson. Then in 1902 Eddy limited the terms of first readers, the position Stetson formally held in New York, to three years. She resigned but remained the popular leader. Then in 1909 she was accused of both deviating in her teachings and of building a personal following. She was dismissed from the church on Eddy's orders.

When Eddy died without reinstating her, Stetson turned the institute, of which she had remained in charge, into the headquarters of what was termed the "Church Triumphant." She continued to preach, teach, and write for the rest of her life.

INDEPENDENTS IN THE TWENTIETH CENTURY. Eddy's death in 1910 created a new series of problems for the church and led to even more independent Christian Science organizations. This second set of groups grew out of the organizational crisis created by the *Church Manual*. The *Church Manual*, which set the rules for the Mother Church and those individuals and organizations related to it, left many actions (such as filling vacancies in church offices) dependent upon the approval of the pastor (Eddy) who died without naming a successor. Eddy also left two separately created corporations that seemed to have overlapping jurisdictions.

Among the first publicly to discuss the problem of trying to operate the church according to the *Manual* was a British Christian Scientist, Annie C. Bill. She suggested a novel solution. The church must be dissolved and reorganized under a new manual (or constitution). She declared herself to be Eddy's successor, based in part upon her articulation of both the problem and the solution. At this time Bill had been an ex-member of the church for several years, having resigned in 1909. Unsuccessful in having the board of directors of The Mother Church recognize her (though one former member of the board, John V. Dittemore, did join her), she formed the Christian Science Parent Church. Interestingly enough, after Bill's death, her church underwent a change of leadership similar to the one she had advocated for the Church of Christ, Scientist, and emerged as the Church of Integration, which survived into the 1950s.

Quite apart from Bill, in 1918 the organizational crisis in the church resulted in a legal case between the board of publication and the board of directors of the Mother Church. This period, known as the time of the Great Litigation, finally resulted in the court declaring the board of directors to be the ultimate authority in the church. The litigation also led to the dismissal of Herbert W. Eustace (d. 1957), a member of the board of publication, who went on to become a popular writer and practitioner among independents.

During the twentieth century any number of practitioners left the church to develop their own work independently. Unlike Bill, they have generally refrained from attempting to organize anything resembling a church. Rather they have adopted a notion suggested by Geoffrey Hamlin in his 1922 booklet Notes on the Manual and Trust Deed. Hamlin argued that since the organization of the Mother Church depended so heavily on Mary Baker Eddy, possibly she intended that the church should dissolve after her death. Henceforth, Christian Science should continue without the centralized structure, through the many autonomous churches and practitioners, tied together only by their mutual loyalty to Eddy. For many of the practitioners who became independent, that idea, coupled with a bad experience with the board of directors, served to prevent their creating large church-like organizations. Most independents merely continued quietly as practitioners. Some privately published and circulated their own writings. A few formed small informal organizations that facilitated their personal (and necessarily limited) healing work and/or published and distributed independent Christian Scientist writings. Few of these organizations had any continuity from generation to generation, but as they died (with the retirement or death of the individual head) new ones arose.

Among the prominent practitioners asked to leave the Church of Christ, Scientist, have been Peter V. Ross (d. 1947), Alice L. Orgain, Glenn A. Kratzer, William W. Walter, and Lillian de Waters. Others who left, often in the midst of controversy, include Margaret Laird, Hugh A. Studdert-Kennedy, Edward A. Kimball, Bicknell Young, Arthur Corey, Frederick Dixon, John Doorly, and possibly the most famous outside of Christian Science circles, Joel Goldsmith (1892–1964). Goldsmith's work continues under the name Infinite Way. In 1955 the International Metaphysical Association was founded as an umbrella organization for many of the former Christian Scientists. It circulated the works of Ethel Schroeder, Peggy Brooks, Max Kappeler, and Gordon Brown. Closely related to the association was the Rare Book Company of Freehold, New Jersey, which continues to publish and distribute the books and writings of the independents.

After several decades with few new prominent independent centers being created, a new wave of independence began on October 11, 1975, when Reginald G. Kerry, a worker at the church center in Boston, sent a lengthy open letter to all the practitioners and branch churches listed in the Christian Science Journal. He noted with alarm the decline in membership during the previous two decades and a financial crisis because of overspending on the new center building. He charged gross mismanagement of funds in the treasurer's office, abuse of authority in the Department of Branches and Practitioners, immorality among all levels of the church's staff at the center, and negligence on the part of the board of directors. He demanded membership action. Responses included further accusations of problems within the church and its center in Boston.

Practitioners who left the church came forward, and a court case ensued. In 1977 the Plainfield, New Jersey, congregation had its name removed from the listing in the Christian Science Journal. The Mother Church asked it to discontinue use of the name "Christian Science." It went to court and won the right to continue as an independent Christian Science church. Another group of independents organized as the United Christian Scientists and filed suit to have the textbook, long past its normal 56-year copyright allotment, declared in the public domain. They won the case. As the Kerry letters continued to arrive, Ann Beals, a practitioner from Pasadena, California, opened The Bookmark, a publishing and mail order distributing company with a branch in England, to as-

sist in the circulation of the materials in the cause of the independent movement.

Kerry, The Bookmark, and the recent independents represent a new generation of independent Christian Science, many of whom have only a passing acquaintance with the earlier independent literature. The Bookmark largely distributes a distinct set of literature from that offered through the Rare Book Company. While lacking association with the earlier independents, the new wave has accepted their thesis concerning Eddy's desire to have The Mother Church dissolve and turn Christian Science into a decentralized movement.

NEW THOUGHT. By the mid-1880s, an array of healers, most of them in some manner related to Christian Science, were functioning in America, especially in the immediate vicinity of Boston, the other northern urban centers, and a few places in the Midwest, most notably Chicago. Itinerant healers reached almost every American community of any size at some point during the year. Among the large number of Christian Science practitioners radiating from the centers in Boston and Chicago, the independents ranged from those who tried to stick firmly to what they had been taught as members of the Church of Christ, Scientist to those who merely used Eddy as a point of departure. Among the causes of their deviation was their interaction with other nonconventional religious healers, most notably Spiritualists (such as W. J. Colville), theosophists (such as M. J. Barnett), and even a few Christian healers such as A. B. Simpson and Charles Cullis. Quimby student Warren Felt Evans practiced in a Boston suburb and authored a number of books, while the Dressers, making common cause with the independents, continued their attack on Eddy. Into this chaotic situation stepped Emma Curtis Hopkins (1853–1925).

Hopkins first encountered Christian Science in 1881 and two years later moved to Boston to study with Eddy. After taking Eddy's primary class, she was invited to assume editorial duties for the Christian Science Journal in early 1884 as Eddy was preparing for an extended trip to Chicago. Her work on the journal continued until November 1885 when she had a sudden break with Eddy, the church, and the Christian Scientist Association. She moved to Chicago and the next summer opened the Emma Hopkins College of Metaphysical Science (modeled on the Massachusetts Metaphysical College) and offered her first classes. Her work was an immediate success, and during the fall enough students had gathered around to form the Hopkins Metaphysical Association.

As word spread about her work, students began to travel to Chicago to study with her, and she began to travel to other places—Milwaukee, San Francisco, New York City. By the end of 1887, she was bringing order out of the chaos by bringing the scientists and students into a string of associated centers that stretched from Maine to California. Not yet content, in 1888 she transformed the college into the Christian Science Theological Seminary and offered advanced training for students planning to enter the Christian Science ministry. (At that time Eddy was the only person ordained within Christian Science, and since her death the movement has continued to be led by lay people.) In January 1889 she held the first graduation ceremonies from the seminary, and assuming the office of bishop, she became the first woman to ordain others to the ministry in modern times.

The ordination service highlighted the unique innovation that Hopkins was making in the whole Christian Science milieu. First, Hopkins attracted primarily women to her school. Among the 22 graduates ordained in that first service in 1889 only two were men, both husbands of women who were ordained. Second, the service highlighted Hopkin's innovative approach to Christian Science itself. Her theology now assigned women a key position in God's activity in history, especially notable in her consideration of the doctrine of the Trinity. She adopted a form of Trinitarian thought first articulated by Joachim of Fiore (1145–1202) in the twelfth century. Joachim pictured God's distinct manifestation through the different periods of history. God the Father, the first aspect, exemplified the ancient patriarchal ideal. The second era, which began around the time of the birth of the Nazarene (i.e., Jesus), was a time for the masses to free themselves from oppression. The third period, that of the Spirit, the Truth-Principle, or the Mother-Principle, was the time for the rise of women. While Eddy has been cited as a woman who assumed a role usually denied women, and is credited with creating a new public role for women, Hopkins now articulated a thorough-going feminist theology and opened the Christian ministry to her female students. After ordaining her students, she sent them to create new churches and ministries around the country.

Thus Hopkins, somewhat reluctantly, created the very thing most independents eschewed, a growing organized movement. Then, having trained more than 100 ministers, in 1895 Hopkins retired, closed the seminary, and moved to New York City. She spent the rest of her years taking students on a one-on-one basis. Her former students scattered across the United States and Canada to establish their own variations on Hopkins' thought, just as she had made numerous alterations on Eddy's.

THE DEVELOPING MOVEMENT. As Hopkins' students established their own centers they began to differentiate themselves from the Christian Science with which they had begun. The search for other names began. Myrtle and Charles Fillmore in Kansas City adopted the name Unity, possibly inspired by the Unity Publishing Company, the publishing arm of the International Christian Science Association. Melinda Cramer, one of Hopkins' students in San Francisco, renamed her work Divine Science. Faculty member Helen Van Anderson moved to Boston after the seminary closed to form the Church of the Higher Life. Faculty member Annie Rix Militz established the Homes of Truth on the West Coast. George and Mary Burnell formed the Burnell Foundation in Los Angeles. Clara Stocker introduced Albert C. Grier to Hopkins, and he in turn founded the Church of the Truth. One of Hopkins' last students, Ernest S. Holmes, founded the Institute (later, the Church) of Religious Science. In the early twentieth century, these students passed their lineage to the next generation of students. Each ultimately derived their authority for ministry from Hopkins and Eddy, and they eventually found a modest degree of unity in the name of New Thought. First suggested in the 1890s, by the beginning of World War I it was the generally accepted designation.

New Thought distinguished itself from Christian Science in a variety of ways. First, it came under the leadership of an ordained ministry, though many lay teacher-writers (such as Clara Stocker and Harriet Emilie Cady) did yeoman service. Second, it developed a decentralized movement that celebrated its diversity of opinion. Third, almost from the beginning it developed an emphasis upon prosperity. Without losing the healing emphasis of Christian Science, New Thought leaders reasoned that poverty was as unreal as disease and taught students to live out of the abundance of God. Fourth, while some of the groups, such as the Unity School of Christianity, retained a specifically Christian emphasis, the movement as a whole moved to what it saw as a more universal position that acknowledged all religious traditions as having value.

Significant in the developing presentation of New Thought was Thomas Troward. A retired judge who had served many years in India, Troward developed what amounted to a second career as a New Thought lecturer. His importance came in the introduction of new psychological concepts into the movement in the early twentieth century. Specifically, he argued for the differentiation of the mind into its objective (waking consciousness) and its subjective (unconscious) aspect. In so doing he opened the movement to the new concept of the dynamic subconscious, a concept missing in both Eddy and Hopkins. Holmes would take Troward's main insights and use them in creating Religious Science.

After several abortive attempts to unite the various New Thought groups, the International New Thought Alliance was finally formed in 1914. It quickly moved to produce a statement of agreement that became its first Declaration of Principles. A revised statement was adopted in 1957. While showing some similarity to the idealistic thought of Eddy, it had moved considerably away from some of her ideas and made no specifically Christian affirmations. It affirmed the belief in God as Universal Wisdom, Love, Life, Truth, Power, Peace, Beauty, and Joy; that the universe is the body of God and that human beings are invisible spiritual dwellers inhabiting bodies and that human beings continue, grow, and change after death. This statement highlights what is often thought of as the main difference between Christian Science and New Thought. While not leaving the common idealism, New Thought has assigned a more positive role to the body and the material world. Matter is not mortal error; while the material is secondary, it is also the manifestation of spiritual reality. One can begin to see the distinctions by comparing the Christian Science Statement of Being, (quoted above) and that of Divine Science:

–God is all, both invisible and visible.

–One Presence, One Mind, One Power is all.

–This One that is all perfect life, perfect love, and perfect substance.

–Man is an individualized expression of God and is ever one with this perfect life, perfect love, and perfect substance.

Both Christian Science and New Thought look to a manifestation of the Truth they teach in the individual's life. That manifestation is usually referred to as "demonstration." To move from sickness to health is to demonstrate healing. To move from poverty to wealth is to demonstrate abundance.

To aid in demonstration is the role of the practitioner, a professional who has been trained in the arts of healing prayer. While each church trains its practitioners in slightly different ways, and advocates slightly different techniques by which they are to work, all of the churches discussed in this chapter provide their membership with the assistance of healing prayer specialists. To pray for healing or some other concern is frequently spoken of as "treating" for health or the improvement of relationships or prosperity. In New Thought churches some practitioners specialize in assisting the manifestation of abundance. (The Unity School of Christianity is a major exception. It has no practitioners, though it does have licensed Unity teachers, which are somewhat analogous.)

Sources—Christian Science-Metaphysical Family

The study of the metaphysical groups is given focus by the Society for the Study of Metaphysical Religion, c/o the Unity-Progressive Theological Seminary, P. O. Box 7753, Clearwater, FL 3418-7753. It publishes *JSSMR, The Journal of the Society for the Study of Metaphysical Religion.*

Archives for Christian Science and related movements are located at the Church of Christ Scientist headquarters in Boston, Massachusetts. A significant collection of Christian Science material has been donated by William Braden to the Perkins School of Theology Library in Dallas, Texas. There are several archives of New Thought material, among the most significant are those included in the American Religions Collection at the Davidson Library of the University of California-Santa Barbara, Santa Barbara, California; the library of the Unity of School of Christianity, Unity Village, Missouri; the library at the headquarters of United Church of Religious Science, Los Angeles, California; and the archive of the New Thought movement at the International New Thought Alliance, Mesa, Arizona.

GENERAL SOURCES

Fuller, Robert C. *Mesmerism and the American Cure of Souls.* Philadelphia: University of Pennsylvania Press, 1982. 227 pp.

Judah, J. Stillson. *The History and Philosophy of the Metaphysical Movements in America.* Philadelphia: Westminster Press, 1967. 317 pp.

Melton, J. Gordon. *A Reader's Guide to the Church's Ministry of Healing*. Independence, MO: The Academy of Religion and Psychical Research, 1977. 102 pp.

Meyer, Donald. *The Positive Thinkers*. New York: Pantheon Books, 1980. 396 pp.

Parker, Gail Thain. *Mind Cure in New England*. Hanover, NH: University Press of New England, 1973. 197 pp.

Podmore, Frank. *Mesmerism and Christian Science*. London: Methuen, 1909. 299 pp.

Zweig, Stefan. *Mental Healers*. New York: Frederick Ungar Publishing Co., 1962. 363 pp.

THE FORERUNNERS—QUIMBY AND EVANS

Clark, Mason Alonzo, ed. *The Healing Wisdom of Dr. P. P. Quimby*. Los Altos, CA: Frontal Lobe, 1982. 127 pp.

Dresser, Annetta Gertrude. *The Philosophy of P. P. Quimby*. Boston: George H. Ellis, 1895. 114 pp.

Dresser, H. W. *The Quimby Manuscripts*. New York: Thomas Y. Crowell, 1921. 474 pp.

Evans, Warren Felt. *The Divine Law of Cure*. Boston: H. H. Carter & Co., 1884. 302 pp.

———. *Esoteric Christianity and Mental Therapeutics*. Boston: H. H. Carter & Karrick, 1886. 174 pp.

———. *The Mental Cure*. Boston: Colby & Rich, 1869.

———. *Mental Medicine*. Boston: 1873. 15th ed.: Boston: H. H. Carter & Co., 1885. 216 pp.

———. *The Primitive Mind Cure*. Boston: H. H. Carter & Karrick, 1885. 215 pp.

———. *Soul and Body*. Boston: H. H. Carter & Co., 1876. 147 pp.

Hawkins, Ann Ballew. *Phineas Parkhurst Quimby*. Los Angeles: DeVorss & Co., 1951. 56 pp.

Quimby, Phineas Parkhurst. *Immanuel*. Mokelumne Hill, CA: Health Research, 1960. 109 pp.

MARY BAKER EDDY AND CHRISTIAN SCIENCE

Beasley, Norman. *The Continuing Spirit*. New York: Duell, Sloan and Pearce, 1956. 403 pp.

———. *The Cross and the Crown*. New York: Duell, Sloan and Pearce, 1952. 664 pp.

Braden, Charles S. *Christian Science Today*. London: George Allen & Unwin, 1959. 432 pp.

Christian Science: A Sourcebook of Contemporary Materials. Boston: Christian Science Publishing Society, 1990. 345 pp.

Eddy, Mary Baker. *Science and Health*. Boston: Christian Scientist Publishing Company, 1875. 456 pp. Authorized edition: *Science and Health with Key to the Scripture*. Boston: Trustees Under the Will of Mary Baker G. Eddy, 1906. 700 pp.

———. *The Science of Man by Which the Sick Are Healed*. Lynn, MA: Luther C. Parker, 1879. 22 pp.

Gottschalk, Stephen. *The Emergence of Christian Science in American Religious Life*. Berkeley: University of California Press, 1973. 305 pp.

Knee, Stuart E. *Christian Science in the Age of Mary Baker Eddy*. Westport, CT: Greenwood Press, 1994. 158 pp.

Leishman, Thomas Linton. *Why I Am a Christian Scientist*. Boston: Beacon Press, 1966. 245 pp.

Peel, Robert. *Christian Science, Its Encounter with American Culture*. Garden City, NY: Doubleday, 1965. 224 pp.

———. *Mary Baker Eddy*. 3 Vols. New York: Holt, Rinehart and Winston, 1966, 1971, 1977.

Studdert-Kennedy, Hugh A. *Christian Science and Organized Religion*. Los Gatos, CA: The Farallon Foundation, 1961. 170 pp.

Swihart, Altman K. *Since Mrs. Eddy*. New York: Henry Holt and Company, 1931. 402 pp.

What Makes Christian Science Christian. Boston: The Christian Science Publishing Society, 1982. 30 pp.

NEW THOUGHT

Anderson, Alan. *Horatio W. Dresser and the Philosophy of New Thought*. Boston: Boston University, Ph.D. dissertation, 1963. 356 pp.

Beebe, Tom. *Who's Who in New Thought*. Lakemont, GA: CSA Press, 1977. 318 pp.

Braden, Charles S. *Spirits in Rebellion*. Dallas: Southern Methodist University Press, 1963. 571 pp.

Dresser, Horatio. *A History of the New Thought Movement*. London: George G. Harrap & Co., n.d. 352 pp.

———. *Spiritual Health and Healing*. New York: Thomas Y. Crowell, 1922. 314 pp.

Larson, Martin A. *New Thought: A Modern Religious Approach*. New York: Philosophical Library, 1939. 458 pp.

Chapter 18
Spiritualist, Psychic, and New Age Family

Consult the "Contents" pages to locate the entries in Part III,
the Directory Listings Sections, that comprise this family.

From the beginning of recorded history, men have claimed powers of mind and spirit far surpassing those commonly recognized by twentieth-century science. Men have claimed knowledge from beyond the capabilities of the five senses: the power to move objects by thought and the ability to talk to beings whose permanent home is not our world. In ancient Greece, the temple at Delphi was a center of this psychic world. There lived Pythia, a psychic who prophesied for visiting dignitaries. Given in hexametric verse, these prophecies were often of a cryptic nature. Possibly the most famous story of Delphi comes from Herodotus. Croesus, king of Lydia in the time of Cyrus of Persia, was feeling the pressure of Cyrus and decided to do battle with him. Beforehand, he consulted the oracle of Delphi, who told him, "Croesus, having crossed the Halys (River), will destroy a great empire." Confident of victory, Croesus crossed the river and was thoroughly defeated. Croesus demanded an explanation. The Oracle replied bluntly that a great empire, Lydia, had fallen as predicted.

Socrates is often cited in ancient literature as a psychic of note. While a child, he became aware of a voice that spoke to him. The voice never commanded particular acts, but forbade wrong action.

Through the twentieth century, parapsychologists, those scientists who investigate the psychic, developed a vocabulary by which the psychic can be understood. Dr. J. B. Rhine of Duke University spearheaded this effort. Extrasensory perception (ESP) is the term Rhine coined to describe man's ability to perceive information and encounter a world beyond the commonly recognized senses. ESP is of several basic kinds. Telepathy is mind-to-mind (subconscious-to-subconscious) communication. Clairvoyance is perception of the world beyond the senses without any other mind's help. Precognition is a perception of events in the future. Psychokinesis (PK) is mind over matter; Rhine saw spiritual healing as one prominent example of psychokinesis. In years of exacting experiments, Rhine and his colleagues attempted to document the existence of these four phenomena. As the work has progressed, an additional technical vocabulary has been developed.

Beyond these four basic forms of psychic perception, psychic people also describe many other experiences, which parapsychologists also attempted to explore. Some are plainly particular varieties of one of these four inclusive terms, as, for example, spiritual healing, a special case of psychokinesis. Others are not so clearly of these four. Astral travel, for example, is the experience of the conscious self being outside the body. Mediumship/channeling involves clairvoyance and/or telepathic communication with entities (the dead, ascended masters, angels, etc.) claimed to have an existence in a different realm, a realm other than the world of our normal waking consciousness.

In the 1960s, investigation of the healing power so long claimed by sensitive people and members of different religious groups was begun in earnest. Such people as Bernard Grad of McGill University in Montreal and Justa Smith of Rosary College in Buffalo, New York, began to demonstrate, under carefully controlled laboratory conditions, the reality of a power that could heal mice, stimulate the growth and yield of plants, and change the growth rate of enzymes. From such work as this, a new science, paraphysics, emerged.

Beyond the realm of the purely psychical is the realm of the *occult*. Occult is a word that originally meant "hidden," the opposite of "apocalypse," that which is revealed. In contemporary science, however, it has come to be applied generally to practices that were once part of the "hidden wisdom." These practices include various arts of divination—astrology, numerology, tarot cards, palmistry, and tea leaves—to mention a few.

THE BIBLICAL PSYCHIC TRADITION TO 1800. Although aware of the ancient world in general, contemporary psychics are most aware of one aspect of the ancient world—the biblical tradition. They hold that, from cover to cover, the Bible is a psychic book, replete with incidents that in today's terminology are properly called psychic. These include incidents of spirit communication (Matthew 17:1–9, I Samuel 28), clairvoyance (John 4:16–29), healing (I Kings 5:1–27, Acts 3:3–11), prophecy (Acts 11:28; 21:1–13), and divination (Matthew 2:1–2, Acts 1:15–26).

Among characters in the Old Testament, Samuel is the pristine example of what in the modern world would be called a psychic. According to the account of his life, as a young child, Samuel was taken to Eli, Israel's corrupt psychic, to be dedicated to God. Shortly afterwards, he had his psychic awakening in the famous incident when a voice called out his name (I Samuel 3). Clearly descriptive of the major activity in Samuel's day-to-day life was the incident that initially brought him into contact with the future King Saul (I Samuel 9). The young Saul, the son of Kish, woke one morning to discover that his father's donkeys had disappeared. He looked in vain for the lost herd. His servant suggested that Samuel, the prophet, might be able to help, for as the writer of I Samuel noted:

"Before time in Israel when a man went to inquire of God, thus he said, 'Come let us go to the seer; for he that is now called a Prophet was before time called a Seer'" (v. 9).

Samuel received a clairvoyant vision of Saul long before Saul's arrival and went out to meet him. Instead of speaking to Saul of donkeys, Samuel began to give Saul a precognitive vision of his future as king of Israel. He then anointed him. Only after the anointing did Samuel talk of the lost donkeys, revealing that they had returned home. When Saul became king, Samuel became his chief psychic advisor, a popular office in the ancient world. After Samuel's death, Saul went to a medium, a woman at Endor, to try to contact Samuel's spirit (I Samuel 28).

Psychics studying the New Testament look to Jesus as the paradigm of a psychic, one upon whom they can model their own lives. Jesus' miracles are interpreted in psychic categories. The transfiguration, in which Jesus talks to the visible spirits of several long-dead personages, Moses and Elijah, is seen as a materialization. There are also incidents of psychic healing (Mark 7:31–37, Matthew 20:29–34), psychokinesis (Mark 11:12–14, 20–21, Acts

13:6), clairvoyance (Matthew 2:13, Acts 10:1–33), and precognition (Mark 10:32–34, Acts 27:9–44). Psychic talents are given the name "gifts of the Spirit" by Paul (I Corinthians 12:4–11).

Irenaeus and other writers in the Christian movement noted the continuation of these gifts in the second-century church. Through the following centuries, different writers noted the steady appearance of psychic events until modern times.

The modern psychic community really dates from the new psychical research that began to appear in the late seventeenth century. In the face of Deism, which denied the possibility of miracles or communication with spirits, researchers began to publish accounts of supernatural incidents that "proved" the existence of the invisible world. These included incidents of simple clairvoyance and precognition (often in dreams), astral travel, witchcraft and possession, ghosts, and spirit communication. Among the many writers who contributed to this research are Joseph Glanvill, Cotton Mather, Increase Mather, Richard Baxter, and John Wesley (founder of Methodism).

A contemporary of Wesley, Emanuel Swedenborg, became the first psychic-medium of import in modern times. In the late 1700s, he published many books that he claimed to be accounts of his contacts and visits to another world—the astral world of spirits. A later contemporary of Wesley and Swedenborg was Franz Anton Mesmer, who developed magnetic (or psychic) healing, giving it a scientific frame of reference.

THE PSYCHIC IN AMERICA. The psychic history of America is as old as the settlement by Europeans. From the beginning, witchcraft and occultism reared their heads in New England in patterns not unlike those of their English homeland. Among the first occultists was Tituba, the slave of the Reverend Samuel Parris of Salem, who taught the Parris children occult practices brought from her West Indian homeland. Voudou dolls were found in the house of Goodwife Glover during the witchcraft trials of 1692, an indication that occult arts were more widespread than many thought.

Healing, psychic readings, and even black magic were rife among the Pennsylvania Dutch, whose Powwow men were both feared and venerated.

In the 1830s and 1840s, a number of healers, hypnotists, and phrenologists toured America, writing and lecturing. The disciples of healer Franz Anton Mesmer (1734–1815), most notably Charles Poyen, created a movement of magnetists before the Civil War. They defined animal magnetism as the energy flowing from healer to patient during psychic healing and from hypnotist to client in hypnotism. Their ranks included radical Methodist preacher LeRoy Sunderland. They were followed by the spiritualists, who gave us the first American psychic tradition. Their goal was proof of survival (the person's survival beyond bodily death) through evidence of spirit contact (contact with the dead).

The growth of Spiritualism, coupled with flamboyant press coverage and charges of fraud, caused many scientists and intellectuals to become interested in psychic phenomena. This interest led to the formation of the Society for Psychical Research in England in 1882 and to the establishment of the American Society of Psychical Research (ASPR) in 1884. Among the leading members of the ASPR were William James and Josiah Royce. Much of the energy of members of ASPR in the nineteenth century was dedicated to research on mediumistic phenomena. In this endeavor, William James who spent a number of years observing medium Leonora Piper, believed he had found sufficient proof of survival beyond death.

A new day in psychical research arrived when J. B. Rhine began his work at Duke University in the 1930s. Rhine completely revamped psychical research, giving it a new name, parapsychology, and a new method. Rhine took the psychic event into the laboratory, demonstrating it in repeatable experiments. In 1968, new impetus was given to psychical research as the West became aware that extensive parapsychological endeavors were occurring in the U.S.S.R. and Eastern Europe. Among the sources of knowledge about that research was a best selling book by two young reporters, Sheila Ostrander and Lynn Schroeder. Their *Psychic Discoveries Behind the Iron Curtain* gave the majority of Americans their first look at Russian research in the psychic and gave parapsychologists additional motivation for expanding their efforts.

After the Civil War, psychic alternatives to Spiritualism began to appear. Former Spiritualists Pascal Beverly Randolph and Helena Petrovna Blavatsky initiated Rosicrucianism and the Theosophical Society. After the turn of the century, a host of nonspiritualist psychic groups appeared. Some of these were oriented to Eastern philosophy; others, to parapsychology. The last to arrive in any number were the revived occultists.

A NOTE ON LIFESTYLE. The contemporary psychic community is oriented on psychic experience. In this regard, they resemble the Pentecostal community who are also oriented on religious experiences, and when viewed objectively the type of experiences are very similar, though they are described in quite different terms. For both, experience is itself important. Psychic people differ slightly from New Thought metaphysicians, who are oriented more to results and a meaning context. In being oriented to religious experience, psychics share a lifestyle with mystics and pietists of all ages.

Psychics have also leaned toward a "scientific" demonstration of the truth of their faith. Psychics see their religious beliefs proved in the everyday repetition of verifiable psychic events. Spiritualists believe that the truth of survival comes in data received through mediums. For some, the truth is in the deep philosophy that comes through an otherwise shallow person who operates as a channel. For others, the truth is found in the very existence of an invisible world of psychic perception, continually demonstrated by clairvoyance.

This *desire for scientific verification* gives the psychic community a peculiar relation to scientists, to whom they are continually looking for verification. To date, there has been at least a relative degree of correlation, and the growth of data from parapsychology has had a profound effect on the religious psychic community. Such data provide content for continual discussion and make the psychic community almost impervious to religious traditions that lack such contemporary scientific verification.

SWEDENBORG AND THE NEW JERUSALEM. The life and experience of Emanuel Swedenborg (1688–1772), the son of a Swedish Lutheran bishop, were to make him one of the great religious lights of the eighteenth century. That he is not as well remembered as some of his contemporaries, such as John Wesley and Jonathan Edwards, does not so much belie his significance as illustrate the psychic movement's tendency to belittle history.

Swedenborg was reared a pious Lutheran. As a young man, he took up the study of science; mathematics and astronomy were his favorite subjects. After a period abroad gaining an education, he settled in Sweden to begin a scientific career and was appointed to a position on the Board of Mines in 1724. His publication of several volumes a decade later led to his recognition by the scientific community and an invitation to become a corresponding member of the Royal Academy of Sciences in St. Petersburg, Russia.

His work with the Bureau of Mines led him to concentrate his scientific study in the field of geology. His practical suggestions spurred the improvement of mining procedures throughout Sweden and actually laid the foundation for a science of geology in that country. He published one of the first exhaustive works on metallurgy, and his efforts led to the founding of the science of crystallography. His published works might seem overly philosophical by contemporary standards, but they indicate an ecumenicity of mind, not any lack of scientific acumen.

As early as 1736, however, a different side of Swedenborg began to emerge. He started to take account of unusual dreams and bodily states that he did not fully understand. The crisis in his thinking came in 1744, when he began to realize that intellectual pursuits were ultimately unsatisfying and that he must submit his life to divine guidance. Three years later, he made public his changed perspective, resigned his position with the Bureau of Mines, and devoted the remainder of his life to developing his ideas and publishing them abroad.

At this point, Swedenborg became what today would be called a medium, one who has contact with disincarnate spirit entities. He claimed that, in his visions, he traveled to spirit realms and from spirit entities (primarily angels) gained revelatory knowledge of the nature of life, life after death, and God. The crux of his philosophy is set forth in five long treatises and a commentary on the Bible.

The central theme in Swedenborg's system is the "law of correspondences." He believed that there were two realms of created existence, the physical (phenomenal) and the spiritual (real). Between the two, there is everywhere an exact correspondence. As a seer/visionary, Swedenborg was able to discern these correspondences. He turned especially to the Scripture; his commentaries were aimed at elucidating its spiritual meaning.

The revelatory data upon which Swedenborg spent so much of his time concerned the nature of life after death. He claimed to have gained this knowledge by traveling (astral travel) to the spirit world. From these experiences, he came to believe that man and woman were immortal. He denied the resurrection of the body, and believed that man's soul immediately passes to conscious spirit existence. Souls find themselves moving toward the prime of adult life; that is, the souls of people who died as children will progress to maturity and the souls of those who died in old age will return to the vigor they had in younger adulthood.

As one dies, the soul goes to an intermediate spirit abode between heaven and hell, where preparation for the final state is made. Periodic visits of the soul after reaching heaven or hell are made to this intermediate state, so that appreciation or understanding of the final abode can be heightened by contrast.

Swedenborg deviated from orthodox Lutheranism on several other points. For example, he denied the orthodox doctrine of the Trinity (one God in three persons), avowing instead that God is one in three principles, each of which is manifest in Jesus Christ. Swedenborg believed the Father is the principle of love, "ineffable and exhaustless"; the Son is the principle of divine wisdom; and the Holy Spirit is the energy of divinity that operates in humans to inspire, console, and sanctify them.

Between 1749 and 1756, the multi-volume commentary on Genesis and Exodus, *Arcana Coelestia*, was published. Other works followed. The books had little response in Sweden, and Swedenborg did little to proselytize, aside from making his ideas available. For example, he wrote his books in Latin, not Swedish. A few persons were impressed with his clairvoyance, demonstrated in his famous vision of the Stockholm Fire of 1759 at a time when he was three hundred miles away from that city.

It was in England that his teachings found greatest acceptance. Shortly after Swedenborg's death in 1774, several men—the Reverend John Cowles, the Reverend Thomas Hartley, and Thomas Cookworthy—began to translate the material into English. In 1783, Robert Hindmarsh began to search for other interested parties. As a result of his efforts, a weekly meeting, originally called the Theosophical Society, was established in London. This body was constituted the New Jerusalem Church in 1787. Today it is often called simply the New Church.

The translation, publication, and dissemination of Swedenborg's religious writings was a major thrust of New Church activity from the outset. Under Cowles' leadership, the Society for Printing and Publishing the Writing of Emmanuel Swedenborg was established in 1810.

Members of the New Church migrated to the colonies and formed a society in Baltimore in 1792. Other societies were soon formed along the coast as far south as Charleston, South Carolina, and as far west as Madison Town, Indiana.

SPIRITUALISM. In the First Book of Samuel, Chapter 28, according to Spiritualists, there occurs one of the most famous single incidents of mediumship in the history of the West. As the story goes, Saul, King of Israel, was to face the Philistines and became afraid of their might. After consulting his dreams, his royal psychics, and the Urim and Thummim (an ancient divination device), he visited a medium at Endor, asking that she call up Samuel, Saul's departed psychic counselor. To everyone's surprise, Samuel appeared and condemned Saul.

In Matthew 17, the other famous mediumistic event, popularly known as the transfiguration, is recorded. Jesus and three Apostles were present when two long-dead figures, Moses and Elijah, appeared and conversed with Jesus. In modern Spiritualist terminology, this event would be called a materialization seance, a gathering at which a spirit or something immaterial takes visible form.

Mediumistic phenomena are as old as mankind. Archeological, anthropological, and historical literature is full of references to professed intercourse with the spirit world. In the so-called primitive culture, the shaman was a combination of medium, psychic, and magician, as were psychics operating under various labels in the ancient Mediterranean world. However, in spite of the ancient phenomena and practices to which Spiritualism is an heir, Spiritualism is itself a relatively new phenomenon, related to the peculiar thrust of Western religion since the late 1600s. The true ancestors of Spiritualism are not so much the ancient mediums, but the Puritan and Wesleyan theologians who cited examples of psychic phenomena to prove the existence of the unseen world to their skeptical readers. In the late 1600s, as the polemic against the existence of witchcraft grew, and as Deism, which denied the validity of any intercourse with spirit entities, emerged, several Puritan theologians began to issue numerous accounts of the spirit world.

The National Spiritualist Association of Churches defines Spiritualism as: "the Science, Philosophy and Religion of a continuous life, based upon the demonstrable fact of communication by means of mediumship, with those who live in the Spirit World" (*Constitution and Bylaws* [Washington, DC: National Spiritualist Association, 1930], 7). The demonstration of survival was not a necessity, nor even a major theme of psychic-mediumistic phenomena, until the modern age began to doubt survival. In this respect, Spiritualism is the direct inheritor of Puritan Wesleyan concerns.

In 1681, Joseph Glanvill published his *Saducismus Triumphatus*, which was followed by like books written by Increase Mather, Richard Baxter, and Cotton Mather. John Wesley, the founder of Methodism, states the issue of the British evangelicals succinctly in an introduction to his lengthy discussion of the mediumship of Elizabeth Hobson:

"I take knowledge these are at the bottom of the outcry which has been raised, and with such insolence spread through the nation, in direct opposition not only to the Bible, but the suffrage of the wisest and best of men in all ages and nations. They well know (whether Christians know it or not), that the giving up of witchcraft is, in effect, giving up the Bible; and they know, on the other hand, that if but one account of the intercourse of men with separate spirits be admitted, their whole castle in the air (Deism, Atheism, Materialism) falls to the ground. I know no reason, therefore, why we should suffer even this weapon to be wrested out of our hands. Indeed there are numerous arguments besides, which abundantly confute their vain imaginations. But we need not be hooted out of one; neither reason nor religion require this" (John Wesley, *The Journal* [London: The Epworth Press, 1914], V:265).

That these men, not the many psychics of every age, are the immediate ancestors of the Spiritualists is amply documented in the literature of Spiritualism as well as in the creedal statements, where continual reference is made to the central emphasis of Spiritualism—*the belief in personal survival of death, which can be demonstrated by mediumship.* This belief and emphasis on survival and mediumship distinguishes Spiritualism from other psychic groups.

Spiritualism is secondarily the child of the psychic activity of the eighteenth century. This activity was centered in the work of two men—Swedenborg (discussed in an earlier section of this chapter) and Franz Anton Mesmer. Mesmer had, in the 1770s and 1780s, discovered and articulated a form of psychic healing that included both magnetic healing and hypnotism. Denounced by the French Academy in 1784, Mesmer died in disgrace, but many of his students took his magnetic philosophy and hypnotism to England and the United States. As the result of the publication of the *Progress of Animal Magnetism in New England* by Charles Poyen in 1837 and widespread lecturing by him and other magnetic students, the issue of man's psychic nature was raised across the country in the early 1840s. In 1843, one of these roving mesmerists spurred interest in a young shoemaker-apprentice, Andrew Jackson Davis. With this encounter, modern Spiritualism can be said to have begun.

Davis was born in Blooming Grove, New York, in 1826. After hearing the lectures on mesmerism, Davis sought out a local hypnotist, William Levington, and was placed in a trance. He immediately showed clairvoyance; claims were made that he could duplicate the practices of the magnetists. The following year he had a vision of Galen, the famous Greek physician, and soon after, of Emanuel Swedenborg. These visions changed his life, and he began a career as healer and seer. He claimed abilities to diagnose and heal, converse with spirits, and channel knowledge from the omnipotent mind. Davis published a number of books over the next thirty years. Although not widely read today, these books were most influential in the formative years of Spiritualism.

Davis, like Swedenborg, pictured six spheres of existence in the afterlife. At death, man gravitates to that sphere most akin to his state of being at death. From this sphere, he continues to progress toward God through the higher spheres or "summerland." Thus mankind is in a state of continual progression upward. The progression scheme was common in early Spiritualism.

The event to which most American Spiritualists look more than to Davis as the birth of their faith occurred on March 31, 1848. Then Kate Fox, a young woman, began to get a rational response from some mysterious rapping noises in her home in Hydesville, New York. Kate and her two sisters discovered that the rapping sounds would respond to their hand clapping. With a little practice, they were able to work out a code by which they were able to communicate with Mr. Splitfoot, as they called him, supposedly a disincarnate entity. Mr. Splitfoot rapped out his name as Charles B. Roena, and told them he had been murdered in that house some years previously. Neighbors came to witness the rapping. No less famous a person than Horace Greeley supported the veracity of the Fox sisters against charges of fraud. News of the Fox sisters' mediumship spread, and soon other psychics who could communicate began to appear. Some were slate mediums: the spirits wrote their messages with chalk on slates. Other mediums tipped tables. Still others went into trances and allowed spirits to use their voice boxes. Physical mediums, who could produce materialized images of the spirits, appeared. Within a decade of the Civil War, what was to become a spiritualist movement was developing.

Spiritualism, once publicized, spread quickly across the continent. Spiritualism was almost immediately taken to California as people responded both to the spirits and to the gold rush, and by 1855, an unnamed medium, who was also a prominent lawyer, was holding regular seances in his parlor in San Francisco. Even before it went west, Spiritualism traveled northward to Canada where early centers developed in Toronto, London, Ottawa, and St. Catherines. A Mrs. Swaim is remembered as the chief medium in Toronto, while John Spetique was the organizer of activities in London. In 1858, a British medium who had moved to Boston,

Emma Hardinge, toured Quebec and the Maritime Provinces speaking and demonstrating spirit contact. From these early endeavors Spiritualism grew slowly throughout the country.

The years between 1880 and 1920 were the era of the great mediums. During this time, numerous books purporting to be revelations from the spirit world were produced. These provided alternate material to both Swedenborg and Davis. They included *Oahspe* by John B. Newbrough and the *Aquarian Gospel of Jesus Christ* by Levi H. Dowling. Both are still in print and are heavily read in the spiritualist movement. Among the mediums to be tested with outstanding results in this era were Gladys Osborne Leonard, Leonora Piper, and Winifred Coombe-Tennant.

THE ORGANIZATION. Spiritualism has developed several forms that carry its teachings. These include the camp, the church, the seance, and the development class. The camp developed in the Chautauqua era and was modeled on that famous camp, which was located in New York and began operating in the mid-nineteenth century. Scattered around the country, the various Spiritualist camps provide a leisurely setting for lectures, mediumistic readings, and general propaganda efforts. These assume major effort in the summer for both churched and unchurched mediums who experience a summer slack.

The local Spiritualist groups are organized into churches, organized on a Protestant model. The head medium is usually listed as pastor with the other mediums being listed as assistants. The Sunday morning service is similar in form to the average Protestant church service except (1) the content will be Spiritualist in content, (2) at times, the pastor may go into a trance before delivering the sermon/lecture, and (3) at the close of the service members of the congregation may receive psychic readings (usually called spirit greetings).

The real heart of Spiritualism is the seance. This meeting is conducted by a medium for as many as 50 people. It is usually in the dark, and the people are seated in a circle. From an entranced state, the medium may provide spirit phenomena of a wide variety, including the levitation of objects and materialization. Usually a spirit control speaks through the medium—the spirit control is the person from the spirit realm who regularly speaks through the medium and is thought of as the medium's constant companion. The word "control" is used because the medium's vocal chords are said to be controlled by the person from the spirit realms while the medium is in a trance. The spirit control often gives those at the seance information about their loved ones who have died.

The development class is the final major form of Spiritualism. As the name implies, the class is for the development and training of psychic abilities, especially mediumistic ones. Meditation is basic to development, but other techniques and practices vary, depending on the medium.

Mediums themselves are largely supported by individual readings (the conveying of greetings from the spirit world) for church members. Building on the experiences of contact with the departed, the Sunday worship services take second place to actual experiences of phenomena. Events in which psychic readings occur are always the best attended.

The Spiritualist camp remains a vital force within the movement. A mixture of leisure, lectures, and a number of mediums attract believers during the summer (or local tourist season) and are a vital source of revenue for many mediums serving small churches. Some camps serve as schools for mediums-in-training, providing exposure and a working-learning situation.

The great problem that has hampered the development of Spiritualism is fraud. As soon as Spiritualism emerged, fraudulent practices by various mediums were uncovered. Mediums claimed to demonstrate a variety of phenomena for which they claimed spirit agency. As psychical researchers became more and more sophisticated in their ability to perceive conjuring tricks, the number of exposures increased. Henry Slade, a famous slate medium, for example, was continually exposed. The movement was deeply affected in 1888, when Margaretta and Kate Fox confessed and then demonstrated how they had supposedly made the original rappings. Margaretta retracted her confession the next year and was accepted back into the ranks of Spiritualism, but the confessions still are not forgotten.

In the early years of this century, Harry Houdini, the famous magician, turned his attention to mediums, becoming one of the most famous exposers of fraud in the history of American Spiritualism. A master magician himself, Houdini knew all the devices used to fool the naive sitter at the seance. As a result of the efforts of psychical researchers and several magicians concerned about conjuring being passed off as the result of paranormal effects, much of the physical phenomena so prominent in Spiritualism in the early twentieth century has largely disappeared from the movement.

Many people assumed that fraudulent mediumship had been driven out of Spiritualism by the likes of Houdini, but as recently as 1960, a major exposé of fraudulent mediums was reported, complete with pictures, in the important Spiritualist tabloid, the *Psychic Observer*. A youthful psychical researcher, Dr. Andrija Puharich, and editor Thomas O'Neill discovered Mabel Riffle, one of the most famous mediums in the country and the secretary of Camp Chesterfield (Indiana), fraudulently giving materialization seances. Besides the removal of some of the mediums from the camp (at least one was still there in 1972), the main result of the exposé was the withdrawal of financial support for the *Psychic Observer*, forcing O'Neill to sell out.

Those within the psychic community note that, overall, fraud is not common and is, in the main, confined to a few independent mediums and several of the Spiritualist camps. The major practice is the attempt by mediums and psychics to pad a little psychic ability with many bland generalities. Apologists insist that the constant demand for psychic readings is responsible. The mediums have to perform on demand, but the nature of psychic power is such that it does not always function on demand. Still, there is no doubt that fraud has been the one single force keeping Spiritualism from becoming the powerful element in the North American religious community that it is, for example, in Brazil and Great Britain.

CHANNELING. Simultaneously with the emergence of Spiritualism, there was an impulse not only to prove the existence of life after death, but also to gain some detailed information from the unique sources of the spirit world concerning the nature of spirit existence and the structure of the universe. In other words, there was the desire to understand the Spiritualist metaphysical system derived from spirit communication. Although the primary emphasis in Spiritualism has been to prove survival and the continuance of life after bodily death, the secondary emphasis to understand the spirit world and the real nature of life on earth has been a determining force in the history of spiritualist groups. Some schisms in early Spiritualism grew out of this secondary emphasis.

Channeling is like most spiritualist activity in that it retained the centrality of mediumship, however, the medium, usually termed a "channel," tended to be in contact with evolved spirit entities, spirits that were once human and now in the spirit world have evolved and have access to higher levels of wisdom and knowledge. These entities are viewed as wise and spiritual masters, who function very much as the bodhisattvas in Buddhism who return from their elevated state to teach humankind.

Channeling was important to some early mediums such as Andrew Jackson Davis and Thomas Lake Harris, both of whom published long works derived from channeling sessions. John B. Newbrough's *Oahspe* and Levi H. Dowling's *Aquarian Gospel of Jesus Christ* were both channeled volumes produced near the turn of the century. The early work of Davis and Harris did much to define Spiritualism as a separate movement. As the century progressed, however, a variety of different influences, especially Theosophy, made their presence known. Through the twentieth century, nu-

merous channels have appeared offering a wide variety of Spiritualist world views.

During the nineteenth century, Spiritualism in the United States was quite hostile to ideas of reincarnation. However, through the twentieth century, channeled works have been a major influence introducing reincarnation and the usually associated idea of karma into Spiritualist thinking. Today channels are almost totally agreed on the ideas of evolution and reincarnation. Humans are usually seen as fallen or entrapped spirit-beings, evolving through many lifetimes toward a pure spiritual existence. Karma, interpreted by Spiritualists as "the Spiritual law of cause and effect," is operative. Humans must overcome their bad karma, the consequences of bad actions, usually those of an earlier incarnation, and try to create good karma, leading to evolvement to a higher spiritual existence through good deeds.

Spiritualist channeling groups, groups which have little or no activity at contact of the recently deceased relatives and friends of group members, but center on discourses by evolved spirits speaking through the medium, have emerged periodically through the twentieth century. However, in recent decades the number of such groups has grown markedly. In such groups, the spirit entity speaking through the channel is the teaching authority for the group. Actual teachings tend to make reference to all the major world religions, and much is drawn from Hinduism via theosophy. Hindu elements include beliefs in reincarnation; a view of all existence as forming a mystic whole; and the communication with spiritual masters who are similar to the bodhisattvas.

During the 1980s, as the New Age movement became a dominant force in the American psychic community, channeling received a startling new life. This new burst began with a set of books written by Jane Roberts (pseudonym of Jane Butts) that she claimed were dictated by a spirit entity known as Seth. Roberts, somewhat of a recluse, rarely made public appearances, but the books of Seth's teachings sold quite well. On the heels of Seth's success, several new talented mediums (channels) emerged and attracted attention. Possibly the most famous was JZ Knight, a full trance medium, who channels an entity named Ramtha. Others mediums, all of whom are still active as of the mid-1990s, include Robert Purcell (Lazaris), Penny Torres (Mafu), Pat Rodegast (Emmanuel), and Kevin Ryerson (John). Common to the new group of mediums is their general lack of contact with older Spiritualist leaders (Ryerson being a prominent exception) and their adherence to Eastern/theosophical teachings. Generally, the newer channels agree on the identification of the self with the divine and the individual's power to create a world of happiness, health, and success.

Usually channels work out of a single center, surrounded by a relatively small group dedicated to the transcription and dissemination of the communications from the entities being channeled. These transcriptions, and/or video and audio tape recordings, are then distributed around the country and the world to supporters. For some, the one center may also include a place for worship (or meditation), at which regular gatherings are held. For most, gatherings are held in rented spaces. Many of the channels would not think of themselves as religious; however, they often function as the main religious teacher for their supporters.

Channeled material shows evidence of being drawn from a diversity of sources. Some comes out of the UFO contactee community, while most comes from theosophy, the "I AM" Religious Activity, and other occult teachings. Groups such as the Agasha Temple of Wisdom and the University of Life Church, somewhat traditional Spiritualist churches with a strong emphasis upon channeling, serve as a transition between classical Spiritualism and the new channeling groups.

DRUG-ORIENTED GROUPS. Since ancient times religious bodies have made use of various substances that altered consciousness and aided in the production of ecstatic states. According to some scholars, the Hindu god of sacrifice and the rituals associated with him are tied to the *Amanita muscaria*, a mushroom widely used because of its hallucinogenic powers. Most famous of the ancient drug-oriented bodies was the Dionysian religion, based on Dionysius, the god of the vine. Other Greek-based religions became famous for their use of alcohol. In pre-Colombian America, the Aztecs, Huichol, and various Mexican Indians ate peyote and related plants ceremonially.

Throughout Western history, various persons have discovered drugs with differing consciousness-altering properties and have then incorporated these into religious practices. At the beginning of the twentieth century, William James mentioned the use of nitrous oxide to stimulate the mystical consciousness. Most famous of the early twentieth-century drug users was Aleister Crowley, who used hashish and opium in his magical work for many years.

A new era in consciousness-expansion by the use of drugs began in 1938 when Dr. Albert Hofmann, a Swiss biochemist, synthesized d-lysergic acid diethylamide (LSD) tartrate from the rye fungus called ergot. In 1943, he accidentally absorbed some of the new drug, thus discovering its unusual properties. It caused a distortion of space and time and produced hallucinations. It also produced a state of consciousness in which the objective world took on a new meaning. The effects have been termed "psychedelic." In the wake of Hofmann's discovery, other psychedelic drugs were catalogued and became known in medical and academic circles. They began to be used in hospitals for the treatment of neuroses and psychoses.

In the 1950s, widespread experiments with LSD began to occur, some secretly sponsored by the government. Aldous Huxley wrote a popular account of his use of mescaline, another psychedelic drug, comparing his experiences with those described in the *Tibetan Book of the Dead*. In the early 1960s, reports began to appear of the experiences of those who took LSD. Many reported mystic and religious awakenings. The experiments eventuated in the watershed event of the era, the 1963 firing at Harvard of Professors Timothy Leary and Richard Alpert for involving students in reckless experiments with LSD.

Timothy Leary had been introduced in 1960 to tioanactyle, the psychedelic mushroom, by a Mexican anthropologist. His first "trip" was life-shaking and described as the "deepest religious experience" of his life. He proceeded to begin experiments with psychedelic drugs at Harvard. He introduced them to his colleague, Richard Alpert. After their firing, Leary became the psychological center of a drug-oriented generation, while Alpert soon felt he had exhausted the drug experience and traveled to India only to emerge as a Hindu guru, Baba Ram Dass. The story of the religious drug movement from this point becomes one of legal battles to establish open practice of psychedelic groups under the Constitution. In 1966, the use of LSD, except for very limited research purposes, was declared illegal. Several of these cases will be discussed below under individual groups. The loss of some of these cases has decimated the ranks of the once-powerful movement.

An early confrontation of the drug groups and the law came in Dutchess County, New York, where Leary and his group (which he founded in 1966 as the League for Spiritual Discovery) along with Art Kleps' Neo-American Church and the non-drug-using Sri Rama Ashrama had taken refuge on the estate of William Mellon Hitchcock, in Millbrook. In December 1966, the Dutchess County police raided Millbrook and arrested Leary, Kleps, Hitchcock, and others. As a result of the raid and the publicity and pressure, Hitchcock evicted the psychedelic groups. Leary's career in the next decades became one of fleeing the law and brief jail sentences, before he was finally able to work out his settlement of personal issues emerging form his drug-oriented prophethood.

While at Millbrook, Leary began to publish the first of the numerous books he has since written. *Psychedelic Prayers After the Tao Te Ching* became the handbook of the League. Leary describes the psychedelic experience as being on three levels—

neural, cellular, and molecular. In the first level, one tunes into patterns of neurological signals that are usually censored from mental life. The cellular consciousness transcends the symbolic game and the sensory apparatus, and people experience raw sensory bombardment and cellular hallucination. The molecular consciousness transcends even further and contacts elemental energies that crackle and vibrate within the cellular structure. The content of molecular consciousness is what, in mystic terminology, is called the "white light," "the ovid," or "the inner light."

Continued legal pressures and unanimous court decisions against psychedelic drug use have largely driven supporters from the ranks or into an underground existence. The League for Spiritual Discovery no longer exists, and most of the other drug oriented groups have also been abandoned. Only one or two drug-oriented churches remain, living in the fading hope of a court reversal or a change in the laws governing the use of psychedelic drugs.

A major result of the drug culture was to spur work in parapsychology (the study of ESP, psychokinesis, etc.), particularly in the area of altered states of consciousness. The particular experiences of psychedelically-induced states also resemble many visionary, mystical, and psychic experiences. Drug users have found more openness to their concerns in areas of the psychic community than in any other religious family.

FLYING SAUCER GROUPS. On June 24, 1947, history was made in the skies of the state of Washington near Mount Rainier when Kenneth Arnold saw a series of nine bright disks flying across the heavens in front of his plane. He described the objects as "saucers," and, when the media repeated his quote, flying saucers became a new reality with which Americans had to contend. Arnold's sighting was followed by others. In July, a picture of a flying saucer, or UFO (unidentified flying object), was given wide coverage in the press before it proved to be a weather balloon. Toward the end of July, the Maury Island (Washington) sighting was followed by the death of two investigators from the Air Force. Only later was the hoax element of the Maury Island incident revealed.

Time and *Life* devoted space to the saucers. The next major incident in the history of UFOs was the death of Captain Thomas Mantell on January 7, 1948. Mantell died in a plane crash as he was chasing a UFO over Louisville, Kentucky. Other major sightings included those by two Eastern Airlines pilots, Clarence S. Chiles and John B. Whitted, and by Lt. George F. Gorman of the North Dakota National Guard.

Already, in 1947, Project Sign had been established by the newly created United States Air Force to investigate reports of UFOs. In July 1949, a Project Sign report concluded that UFOs really were "interplanetary vehicles." The investigations were upgraded in 1949, and were called Project Grudge. Investigation proceeded normally until 1952, in spite of charges of coverup made by UFO buffs such as Major Donald Keyhoe. In 1952, however, there were major sightings for several evenings over Washington, D.C. That same year APRO (Aerial Phenomena Research Organization) was founded in Tucson, Arizona, as the first national UFO study organization. The founding of APRO marked the beginning of a movement that was to grow significantly during the next 15 years.

A major segment of the UFO movement consisted of the growing number of people who claimed to have met and talked with the occupants of the UFOs. Emanuel Swedenborg claimed to have conversed with beings of the solar system in the eighteenth century. During the nineteenth and early twentieth centuries, a number of people, mostly psychics, claimed to have had visits with inhabitants of other planets and wrote about these visits and circulated their writings within the psychic community. These instances of claimed contact with extra-terrestrial beings form a background for modern claims of contact as much as do the UFO phenomena.

After the UFO sightings drew national attention, the first to say he met and talked with UFO occupants was George Adamski. In his first book he detailed 1952 contact with the space brothers and displayed pictures of their craft. Later books actually included silhouette pictures of Venusians. Adamski's books drew freely from Theosophic literature, including quotations from the *Book of Dazan*, written by Madame Helena Petrovna Blavatsky, founder of Theosophy, and containing her comments on Venusians. Adamski was quickly followed by others, such as George Williamson, Truman Bethurum, Cedric Allingham, Orfeo M. Angelucci, Carl Anderson, and Buck Nelson. These later contacts varied greatly in their accounts; each contacted visitors from different planets and lived in different parts of the United States. For some, the objects were, plainly, advanced space craft. For others like Angelucci, they were objects from another dimension. In psychic jargon, they were creatures of a high vibratory rate who lowered their vibration in order to contact earth. Both Bethurum and Anderson claimed to have ridden in the spaceships.

The emergence of those who said they had contacted the UFO occupants in the early 1950s led to a split among those concerned with the strange objects in the sky. One group, the investigators of unidentified flying objects, continued to seek answers about their nature. The second group, having made contact with what it claimed to be extra-terrestrial entities, knew what the "UFOs" were, and concentrated their efforts upon telling others the message of the space brothers. The term flying saucer has come to refer to extra-terrestrial craft.

Through these early contacts, the space brothers began to articulate a message. While it varied at many specific points, its central ideas were common. The space brothers were more highly evolved (either culturally or psychically) beings who were coming to aid their younger brothers. They brought a message of concern about the course of man, whose materialistic nature (or some other evil) is leading him to destruction. Through the mediation of the beautiful space people, however, this destruction can be averted by following the message of love they bring. The space brothers are said to be constantly around, in a guiding paternity.

The continued appearance of UFOs and, especially, the messages of contactees (those contacted by UFO occupants), led many to begin a search for UFOs in history. Newly discovered accounts became a standard part of UFO literature. The Fortean Society aided in the explication of these. These followers of Charles Fort had been collecting UFO data for many years. Other students discovered accounts of UFOs in the Bible.

Certain events were quickly seen as cryptic accounts of UFO visitors from the skies. The most quoted account is of Ezekiel and the wheels in the air. More sophisticated study pointed to possible UFO involvement in the movement of the Israelites out of Egypt, as described in the Biblical book of Exodus. One author, Presbyterian minister Barry H. Downing, postulated that the word "cloud" was a code word for Biblical UFOs and "angels" a word for extra-terrestrial visitors. He cited several incidents where UFO action occurred: Genesis 32:24–25, Exodus 14:19–20, Exodus 40:33–38, Joshua 10:12–14, II Kings 2:1, Matthew 17:1–8, Luke 2, and Acts 1. Of interest is his understanding of Miriam's leprosy as skin irritation from a UFO contact.

Several later visionary experiences have also come to be seen as UFO landings. For example, ufologist Jacques Vallee noted that the last visit of the Virgin at Fatima, Portugal, early in this century was accompanied by a bright sun-like object dancing in the sky and the dropping of angel hair, a fluffy substance often associated with UFOs. More recent writers, such as Erich von Däniken, have even speculated that the human race is descended from space beings, not from lower mammalian forms.

Early Contactee Groups. Besides the rather personal effort being made by individuals to spread the space brother gospel through speaking and writing, several people who were in telepathic contact with UFOs began to gather a group around them, channel regular messages daily or weekly, and publish these messages abroad. These groups were modeled upon the Theosophic/I

AM groups, and many of the hierarchical orders of Theosophy began to appear as space brothers. The Heralds of the New Age began in the 1950s to send out messages from the saucer world. Even though located in New Zealand, it was the single most influential group even in North America. It formed a network, through the mail, of others interested in UFO material. In the United States, a young psychic, Gloria Lee, joined in these efforts. The Cosmos Research Foundation rallied to her support in the late 1950s. Gloria Lee's guide was an entity from Jupiter, identified only as J.W. Besides the regular mailings from the Foundation, J.W. wrote two books through Gloria Lee entitled, *Why We Are Here* and *The Changing Condition of Your World*. Highly Theosophical in nature, they include much material reminiscent of both Madame Blavatsky and Alice Bailey.

In 1962, the 37 year old Lee went to Washington with the model and plans of a space ship, given her by J. W. Following his instructions Lee secured herself in a hotel room to await word from government officials on her model. Once in her room, she began a Gandhi-like fast. On November 28, 1962, she lapsed into a coma, ending her 66-day fast in death on December 2. The Cosmos Research Foundation soon died with the loss of its leader, but Lee became a martyr figure for the cause. Within two months, the Heralds of the New Age began to channel messages from her and soon produced a book, *The Going and the Glory*, purporting to be from her. Other groups followed suit, and, in the wake of Lee's death, a number of other space brothers began to emerge from oblivion.

Another early UFO group was Christ Brotherhood, Inc., founded in 1956 by Wallace C. Halsey, a World War II veteran and engineer-turned-minister. Both psychic and engineering interests led Halsey to the study of UFOs. In 1962, the space brothers instructed Tarna, his wife, to set up a tape recorder near his bed and to put the microphone on his chest. While asleep in bed, Halsey began audibly to channel the message of coming destruction and the gathering of a remnant who would be saved.

In 1963, on a flight from Utah to Nevada in a light plane, Halsey disappeared. No trace of either him or the plane had been found. However, within a short time, Michael X. Barton, a metaphysical lecturer and writer in Los Angeles who had known Halsey, began to receive messages from him. The messages detailed the location of the missing plane. Though the plane was not found, several UFOs were sighted during the course of the search, and through messages Dr. Halsey described his departure in a UFO to Boston. The story of Barton's search was published, and Halsey joined the list of martyrs. Not until 1977 was Halsey's plane finally located.

During the 1970s and 1980s, the contactee community has continued to grow slowly. While few of the original 1950s contactees remain (Ruth Norman of Unarius being a prominent exception), new contactees have emerged and the number of books describing their encounters and detailing the teachings channeled from the space brothers has grown impressively. As the New Age Movement emerged in the 1980s, and channeling took on a new life, contactees shared in a the new period of high interest. Among the New Age channels, Ken Carey (Raphael) and Thelma B. Terrell, publicly known as Tuella (who channels a variety of space entities), are representative of those who claim to be in contact with extraterrestrials.

Not a small portion of the credit for the continued growth of the contactee movement through the 1980s must go to the ufological community, which during the decade, for the first time, gave serious systematic consideration to the stories of direct contact with extraterrestrials. Ufologists initially turned their attention to what were termed encounters of the third kind and then to the accounts of abductions of individuals by entities in UFOs, the subject of several best-selling books. Though ufologists denounce many of the contactees, their research on close encounters and abductions has served to make their claims more believable to the general public.

THE NEW AGE MOVEMENT. Many psychic/occult bodies in the United States do not readily fit among either the Spiritualists or the Ancient Wisdom [discussed in the following chapter] occult groups. Given the constant ferment of the occult community, new impulses are constantly appearing. In the 1970s, however, a new generation of psychic/occult/spiritual seekers arose, who on the one hand rejected the Spiritualist emphasis upon spirits and mediums and refused the more negative designation "occult," while on the other hand identified strongly with the new wave of Eastern teachers that became visible in the late 1960s. In the fervor of their discovery of the psychic/spiritual dimensions of life, they began to see themselves as the harbingers of a new age for humanity. By the mid-1970s a loosely organized New Age Movement could be clearly discerned. The New Age ideal swept through the psychic, occult, and metaphysical communities and the hope for a coming age of love and peace affected people of many backgrounds.

The New Age Movement originated in the 1960s in Great Britain, but its beginnings in North America could be discerned in 1971–72, the period of the appearance of the first popular book representative of the movement (*Be Here Now* by Baba Ram Dass, 1971), the first national periodical (*East-West Journal*, 1971), and the first national network directories (*Year One Catalog* by Ira Friedlander and the *Spiritual Community Guide*, 1972).

As it emerged, the movement was very loosely organized, though it included within it some highly structured and even authoritarian groups. The movement is centered upon a vision of radical transformation of society and the individual, though the means for accomplishing that transformation vary widely from group to group and individual to individual. On the individual level the transformation is very personal and mystical. The accomplished personal transformation provides the model for eventual social transformation. New Age theorist Marilyn Ferguson described it as an open conspiracy by transformed people to complete a process of transformation in their neighbor and in society as a whole.

In the New Age, it was hoped that a new universal religion, based not upon creeds and the division of social groups into denominations and religions, but one having as its goal the development of a mystical consciousness or awareness, would arise. God would be seen as the unifying principle that binds nature and humanity together in a whole. Loyalty to humanity would transcend personal loyalties to more limited social groups, such as nations and clans.

New Agers basically differed among themselves in their opinions on the exact path that would provide the surest way into the New Age, in part related to their alignment with a particular religious tradition. A wide variety of occult-spiritual techniques were proposed, taught, and adopted by various segments of the movement. These techniques vary from vegetarianism and communalism to different forms of meditation, yoga, and magic.

The New Age Movement peaked in the 1980s and the hope of an imminent change in the social order has largely disappeared as the 1990s progressed. However, the movement not only revived many of the older occult groups but spawned a number of new movements, some more of a spiritualist nature and some theosophical. Included in the directory section of this encyclopedia are a number of groups that originated in the New Age Movement and have also adopted a complete religious worldview and lifestyle. Such groups will provide the basis for a full religious life for those associated with them, including regular worship, religious literature, learning experiences, and a program oriented around a spiritual practice and/or discipline.

Sources—The Spiritualist, Psychic, New Age Family

General Sources

Judah, J. Stillson. *The History and Philosophy of the Metaphysical Movements in America*. Philadelphia: Westminster Press, 1967. 317 pp.

Kerr, Howard, and Charles L. Crow, eds. *The Occult in America*. Urbana: University of Illinois Press, 1983. 246 pp.

Melton, J. Gordon. *Encyclopedia of Occultism and Parapsychology*. 2 Vols. Detroit: Gale Research Company, 1996.

Swedenborg and the New Jerusalem

Block, Marguerite Beck. *The New Church in the New World*. New York: Henry Holt and Company, 1932. 464 pp.

Pendleton, William Frederic. *Topics from the Writings*. Bryn Athyn, PA: The Academy Book Room, 1928. 249 pp.

Sigstedt, Cyriel Odhner. *The Swedenborg Epic*. New York: Bookman Associates, 1952. 517 pp.

Silver, Ednah C. *Sketches of the New Church in America*. Boston: Massachusetts New Church Union, 1920. 314 pp.

Spalding, John Howard. *Introduction to Swedenborg's Religious Thought*. New York: Swedenborg Publishing Association, 1977. 235 pp.

Toksvig, Signe. *Emanuel Swedenborg, Scientist and Mystic*. New Haven: Yale University Press, 1948. 389 pp.

Trobridge, George. *Swedenborg, Life and Teachings*. New York: Swedenborg Foundation, 1907. 298 pp.

Woofenden, William Ross. *Swedenborg Researcher's Manual*. Bryn Athyn, PA: Swedenborg Scientific Association, 1988. 366 pp.

Spiritualism—General Sources

Barbanell, Maurice. *This Is Spiritualism*. London: Herbert Jenkins, 1959. 223 pp.

Carter, Huntley, ed. *Spiritualism, Its Present-Day Meaning*. Philadelphia: J. B. Lippincott, 1920. 287 pp.

Davis, Andrew Jackson. *The Harmonial Philosophy*. Chicago: Advanced Thought Publishing Co., n.d. 428 pp.

Keene, M. Lamar. *The Psychic Mafia*. New York: St. Martin's Press, 1976. 177 pp.

Lawton, George. *The Drama of Life After Death*. London: Constable & Company, 1933. 668 pp.

Nelson, Geoffrey K. *Spiritualism and Society*. New York: Shocken Books, 1969. 307 pp.

Pearsall, Ronald. *The Table-Rappers*. New York: St. Martin's Press, 1972. 258 pp.

Skultans, Vieda. *Intimacy and Ritual*. London: Routledge & Kegan Paul, 1974. 106 pp.

Psychical Research and Spiritualism

Ashby, Robert T. *A Guide Book for the Study of Psychical Research*. New York: Samuel Weiser, 1972. 190 pp.

Douglas, Alfred. *Extra-Sensory Powers*. Woodstock, NY: Overbrook Press, 1977. 392 pp.

Gauld, Alan. *The Founders of Psychical Research*. New York: Schocken Books, 1968. 389 pp.

Moore, R. Laurence. *In Search of White Crows*. New York: Oxford University Press, 1977. 310 pp.

Spiritualism—History

Baer, Hans A. *The Black Spiritual Movement: A Religious Response to Racism*. Knoxville: University of Tennessee Press, 1984. 221 pp.

Brandon, Ruth. *The Spiritualists*. New York: Alfred A. Knopf, 1983. 315 pp.

Brown, Slater. *The Heyday of Spiritualism*. New York: Hawthorne Books, 1970. 264 pp.

Centennial Book of Modern Spiritualism in America. Chicago: The National Spiritualist Association of United States of America, 1948. 253 pp.

Grand Souvenir Book. World Centennial Celebration of Modern Spiritualism. San Antonio: Federation of Spiritual Churches and Associations, 1948. 200 pp.

Pond, Mariam Buckner. *Time Is Kind.* New York: Centennial Press, 1947. 334 pp.

Todorovich, Thomas E., ed. *The Centennial Memorial of Modern Spiritualism Records, 1848–1948.* St. Louis: National Spiritualist Association of U.S.A., 1948. 157 pp.

FLYING SAUCERS AND UFOS

Eberhart, George M. *UFOs and the Extraterrestrial Contact Movement: A Bibliography.* Metuchen, MD: Scarecrow Press, 1986. 2 Vols.

Flamonde, Paris. *The Age of Flying Saucers.* New York: Hawthorn Books, 1971. 288 pp.

Fuller, Curtis G., ed. *Proceedings of the First International UFO Congress.* New York: Warner Books, 1980. 440 pp.

Jacobs, David Michael. *The UFO Controversy.* Bloomington: Indiana University Press, 1975. 362 pp.

Steiger, Brad. *The Aquarian Revelations.* New York: Dell, 1971. 158 pp.

Zinsstag, Lou, and Timothy Good. *George Adamski, the Untold Story.* Kent, England: Ceti Publications, 1983. 208 pp.

PSYCHEDELICS

Castenada, Carlos. *The Teachings of Don Juan.* New York: Ballantine Books, 1969. 276 pp.

DeMille, Richard. *Castaneda's Journey: The Power and the Allegory.* Santa Barbara, CA: Capra Press, 1976. 205 pp.

———. *The Don Juan Papers.* Santa Barbara, CA: Ross-Erikson, 1980. 518 pp.

Kleps, Art. *Millbrook.* Oakland, CA: Bench Press, 1977. 354 pp.

La Barre, Weston. *The Peyote Cult.* New York: Schocken Books, 1969. 260 pp.

Leary, Timothy. *Flashbacks.* Los Angeles: J. B. Tarcher, 1983. 397 pp.

Masters, R. E. L., and Jean Houston. *The Varieties of Psychedelic Experience.* New York: Delta, 1967. 326 pp.

Weil, Gunther M., Ralph Metzner, and Timothy Leary, eds. *The Psychedelic Reader.* New York: Citadel Press, 1971. 260 pp.

THE NEW AGE MOVEMENT

Allen, Mark. *Chrysalis.* Berkeley, CA: Pan Publishing, 1978. 179 pp.

Ferguson, Marilyn. *The Aquarian Conspiracy.* Los Angeles, CA: J. B. Tarcher, 1980. 448 pp.

Joshua. *Journeys of an Aquarian Age Networker.* Palo Alto, CA: New Life Printing Co., 1982. 333 pp.

Lewis, James R., and J. Gordon Melton, eds. *Perspective on the New Age.* Albany, NY: State University of New York Press, 1992. 369 pp.

Melton, J. Gordon, Jerome Clark, and Aidan A. Kelly. *New Age Religion.* Detroit, MI: Gale Research, 1990. 586 pp.

Raschke, Carl A. *The Interruption of Eternity.* Chicago: Nelson—Hall, 1980. 271 pp.

Satin, Mark. *New Age Politics.* New York: Delta, 1979. 349 pp.

Spangler, David. *Towards a Planetary Vision.* Forres, Scot.: Findhorn Foundation, 1977.

Wilber, Ken. *The Spectrum of Consciousness.* Wheaton, IL: Theosophical Publishing House, 1977. 374 pp.

Chapter 19

Ancient Wisdom Family

Consult the "Contents" pages to locate the entries in Part III,
the Directory Listings Sections, that comprise this family.

The idea of the existence of an ancient hidden (occult) wisdom, an alternative to the dominant Christian orthodoxy, perpetuated by a lineage of secret adepts until such time as the wisdom could again be given to humanity, has a long history in the West. It was clearly stated, however, in the early seventeenth century in the primary documents announcing the existence of the Rosicrucian Order and a central part of the myth of the revived Freemasonry of the eighteenth century. Perpetuated through Freemasonry and Rosicrucianism, the idea experienced a marked revival in the nineteenth century with the formation of several public Rosicrucian bodies, the Theosophical Society, and some new occult orders. By the end of the nineteenth century, these new occult organizations formed a distinct alternative to Spiritualism, the main form of occultism through the century, and could be found in both the United States and England. Rather than contact with spirits of the deceased and a desire to demonstrate the proof of life after death, these occultists claimed to be the bearers of a hidden (i.e., occult) wisdom that had been passed to them from contemporary representatives of a lineage of teachers whose beginning was in the remote past. Now available for the first time in centuries, it could be given to those individuals prepared to receive it.

The accounts of the emergence of an ancient wisdom follow usually one of three basic formats. First, a person claims to have made direct contact with the present bearers of the lineage usually in some remote corner of the earth (for example, Tibet, Egypt, Arabia). From the teachers of the lineage that person returns to civilization to disclose its essential truths. Second, the wisdom may be revived through the rediscovery of texts, long hidden away, which contain its teachings. Most frequently, however, rediscovery of the ancient wisdom comes through a special person who is able to enter into the occult realms, not accessible to ordinary persons, and be taught the secret wisdom directly by various occult masters. The Great White Brotherhood is a common designation for those who have kept the ancient wisdom through the centuries. The term may be applied to a group of noncorporeal beings (some of who may occasionally take a human body) or to a group entirely or partially composed of individuals currently living on earth.

Two main ancient wisdom schools have appeared in the English-speaking West—the Rosicrucians and the Theosophists. The former claimed to have obtained the ancient wisdom from Christian Rosencreutz who discovered it during travels in the Near East. Helena Petrovna Blavatsky, the first Theosophist to discourse with the masters extensively, claimed to have recovered an ancient document of which no copies had survived in the mundane world, the *Stanzas of Dyzan*, which summarized occult truth.

Besides the Theosophists and Rosicrucians, and those groups that have derived from them (Arcane School of Alice A. Bailey and the "I AM" Religious Activity of Guy W. and Edna W. Ballard), there are few that have found an alternative source for acquiring the ancient wisdom. Also, several groups, drawing upon the theosophical model, have developed variations on it within other religious traditions. Thus Paul Twitchell, founder of ECKANKAR,

while drawing the content of his teaching primarily from the literature of the Sant Mat Sikh tradition, claimed to have traveled to what he termed "soul realms" to translate and bring humanity various ancient documents. Similarly, flying saucer contactees, most of whom came out of a spiritualist tradition, identified the extraterrestrial entities with whom they claimed contact as the Great White Brotherhood.

Typically, ancient wisdom groups are modeled upon the ancient gnostic schools rather than contemporary churches. They offer instruction in occult truth through classes and correspondence courses. Upon manifesting their accomplishment of a body of teachings and mastery of certain occult techniques, the student is awarded a degree and admitted to instruction in the next level. Groups vary in the number of levels of work offered, the nature of the oversight given to students, and the strictness in applying any standards by which they judge the completion of a degree by a student. Thus one group may have ten degrees, limit contact with students to correspondence, and be very lax in advancing the student through the degrees. Another group may have only four degrees, do all their work in small groups, and advance students only after the student demonstrates the proper competence level in both occult theory and practice (clairvoyance, psychokinesis).

The Rosicrucians, growing out of a story published in the seventeenth century in Germany, is the oldest of the several ancient wisdom groups with any following in the United States.

ROSICRUCIANS. "The Rosicrucian Order had its traditional conception and birth in Egypt in the activities of the Great White Lodge" (H. Spencer Lewis, *Rosicrucian Questions and Answers*, 9th edition [San Jose, CA: Supreme Grand Lodge of AMORC, 1969], 33). So begins one account of the history of the Rosicrucians. Actually, if there were historical continuity between any Egyptian secret occult order (or any other ancient group) and modern Rosicrucians, documents attesting to this connection have never been made public. Twentieth-century American Rosicrucian groups appear to be highly eclectic bodies drawing on the Western magical tradition, Theosophy, Freemasonry, and modern parapsychology in varying degrees. The interaction with Theosophy has been extensive and there are many likenesses. But, while Theosophy was founded in 1875, the Rosicrucians attempt to document their organizational continuity with the mystery-schools of the ancient Mediterranean Basin.

The first actual mention of a possible Rosicrucian group was the appearance in the second decade of the seventeenth century of a pamphlet, the *Fama Fraternitatis*, in Germany, written by someone under the pseudonym of Christian Rosencreutz (C.R.). The *Fama Fraternitatis*, translated, is the *Discovery of the Most Laudable Order of the Rosy Cross*. The book detailed the travels of C.R. to the Mediterranean Basin in the early 1400's, where he acquired all wisdom about the microcosm and macrocosm, attunement with the All, the nature of health and disease, and other occult wisdom.

Returning to Germany, C.R. saw the world was not ready for him, so he lived quietly, affiliating with three followers and then four more. These eight were the original Rosicrucians in Germany. They agreed on the following points:

They would not profess anything but curing the sick without reward,

They would wear no special habit,

They would meet every year in the House *Sancti Spiritus*,

The brothers would choose their successors,

The letters "R.C." would be their only seal and character, and

The fraternity would remain secret for one hundred years.

C.R. died in 1484, at age 106. Knowledge of the location of his secret tomb was lost and its rediscovering by a brother created a great stir. The tomb's inscription said that after 120 years he would return. The meaning was that the Rosicrucian Order would surface again in 1604 and take all initiates who were worthy.

There was great response to the pamphlet *Fama Fraternitatis* from doctors, the altruistic, and those who just wanted to live 106 years. In 1615, a second pamphlet, promised by the first, was issued. It attacked the present worldly situation and boasted of the wisdom of C.R. (i.e., the magical world) and the importance of the secrecy of the order.

Many commentators have suggested that a Lutheran pastor, Valentin Andreae (1586–1654), was the author of the pamphlet, since he was admitted author of the 1616 novel, *The Hermetic Romance or the Chemical Wedding; written in High Dutch by Christian Rosencreutz*. From this time forward, sporadic works claiming to be products of a secret fraternity of Rosicrucians appeared. Evidences of other secret fraternities of an occult nature also are in the record. One such group is the Illuminati, founded in 1676 by Adam Weishaupt. In 1670, the Abbé de Villars published *The Count of Gabalis or Extravagant Mysteries of the Cabalists and Rosicrucians*. It was outwardly an attack on the Rosicrucians (thus good evidence of their existence), but many have seen it as an attempt to spread occultism by making public its ideas. De Villars was murdered a few years later, by the Rosicrucians, it was rumored.

English Rosicrucianism was given its direction by Robert Fludd, alchemist and author of the *Apologia Compendiaria Fraternitatem de Rosea Cruce* in 1616. He is the probable source of the rumor that Francis Bacon was a Rosicrucian. Among the founders of the English Rosicrucians was William Lilly, the famous astrologer. British Rosicrucians were pro-alchemy, as opposed to those on the continent at that time. Rosicrucian lodges proliferated in the eighteenth century. Many were fraudulent, but many were legitimate attempts at forming societies attuned to Rosicrucian ideals. It was also at this time that the free intercourse between the Rosicrucians and Freemasons occurred and Freemasons added a Rosicrucian degree to their initiations.

FREEMASONRY. The dominant role of Freemasonry as a fraternal organization has often obscured its very crucial role in the building of modern occult tradition and many histories of the modern occult movement make only passing mention of them. What is today known as Freemasonry emerged in the seventeenth century out of the older craft guilds of stone workers. The guilds included a secret wisdom, the knowledge of architecture used in the building of many churches and public structures, which was carefully guarded. By the seventeenth century, many nonmasons had been "accepted" into membership in guilds as friendly associates. The number of such "accepted" members grew steadily and by the middle of the century some lodges were dominated, if not entirely composed of, "accepted masons, rather than nay who claimed knowledge of the builder's art." The fellowships of accepted masons served as covers for occult speculation and activity.

In 1771, four lodges of accepted masons came together to form the Grand Lodge of England. The third grand master, Rev. John Theophilus Dasaguliers, used his social and professional status (he was chaplain to the prince of Wales) to spread the movement and the authority of the Grand Lodge not only across Great Britain but

to France. However, the Scottish and Irish lodges organized separately in the 1850s as the Ancient Grand Lodge and only merged with their English brethren in 1813 to become the United Grand Lodge.

The Accepted Masons built a speculative gnostic occult cosmology with borrowed symbols from the stone workers as religious symbols. God became known as the Great Architect of the Universe. The Great Pyramid of Egypt, an exemplary achievement of the stoneworkers' skill, was portrayed in masonic symbolism as a building constructed of 72 stones, one each for the possible combinations of the Tetregrammaton, the name of God in Hebrew that consisted of four letters. This symbolic pyramid was capped by the all-seeing eye of God. The masonic pyramid can be seen on the American one-dollar bill, which pictures the Great Seal of the United States strongly influenced by several masons among the country's founders.

The different Lodges in the eighteenth century developed an elaborate degree system loosely tied to an understanding of a universe emanated in layers from the realm of the Divine. The rituals associated with each rite (or set of degrees) were filled with occult content and seemingly in a constant state of flux and development. Eventually, the 33 degree system still used in British and American Masonic came to dominate the lodges of the United Grand Lodge.

Masonry came to the United States from England in 1730 when Daniel Coxe was appointed Provincial Grand Master of New York, New Jersey, and Pennsylvania. Among the members soon welcomed into membership was a youthful Benjamin Franklin whose task it became to publish the first American edition of *The Constitution of the Free-masons* by James Anderson in 1734. The lodges, especially in the middle colonies, became meeting grounds for revolutionaries and welcomed among their members George Washington, James Monroe, Paul Revere, Benedict Arnold, and Patrick Henry.

That so many revolutionaries were Masons gave early American masonry some connection with its Continental counterparts. Masonic and Rosicrucian lodges also became the focus of efforts at democratic reform and became the object of both Church and government hostility. As early as 1738, the Roman Catholic Church issued a pronouncement condemning Masonry and in Europe Masons were identified with various efforts to overthrow monarchial regimes. In England and the United States masonry developed in a nonpolitical manner and became the birthing place for much of modern Rosicrucianism.

In 1865, a Masonic-based Rosicrucian body was founded in London by Robert Wentworth Little. The Societas Rosicruciana in Anglia was modeled on the German "Fratres of the Golden and Rosy Cross" of the previous century, and membership was confined to master masons. This group became the breeding ground of the Hermetic Order of the Golden Dawn.

Like those of Theosophy and Freemasonry, Rosicrucian teachings are a form of gnosticism and mysticism. Transmutation, psychic development, and meditative/yogic disciplines are stressed. Teachings are differentiated into outer or public teachings (which include most of the philosophic material) and inner, for-member-only, teachings (which include most of the instruction on ritual and development exercises). It is difficult for nonmembers to obtain the secret materials, especially from the smaller bodies.

As in Masonic rituals, a system of initiation through a number of degrees is used, each initiation admitting members into deeper and more secret knowledge. Most Rosicrucian groups have published books covering their general orientation, which they sell to the general public and place in libraries. Some of these have become widely used, quite apart from any involvement in the group that published it.

ROSICRUCIANISM IN AMERICA. The history of Rosicrucians in the United States dates to 1694 with the arrival of the Chapter of Perfection in Germantown, Pennsylvania. The Chapter, composed of Rosicrucians who derived their teachings from mystic Jacob Boehme, the Kabbalah, and several German psychic visionaries, built an observatory and Temple and thrived for a generation, but slowly died away after the death of its leader, Kelpius. The Chapter left no group to carry on its work, but the first pow-wow magicians, the Pennsylvania Dutch practitioners of folk magic, once belonged to the Chapter of Perfection. No further reference to Rosicrucians in America occurs until the nineteenth century, when Pascal Beverly Randolph, the founder of the first of the present Rosicrucian bodies, appeared.

While largely forgotten in North America, Paschal Beverly Randolph (1825–1875) was the premier occult theorist of the nineteenth century. Growing up as Spiritualism was making its impact upon the West, he would author more than 20 books that would offer Americans the first major alternative system of occult thought. Four years before Robert Wentworth Little founded the first viable European Rosicrucian group, Randolph launched the Rosicrucian Fraternity in America. He advocated the idea of reincarnation and was the first to write extensively on themes of occult sexuality. Randolph continually had to fight racial prejudice (his mother was black) and misunderstandings of his sexual ideas, but his works survived him to provide the foundation upon which the likes of Helena Petrovna Blavatsky were to later build.

THEOSOPHY. The reputation of Helena Petrovna Blavatsky (1831–1891) has largely outlived the scandal that surrounded her for the last twenty-five years of her life, and she is now recognized as one of the most influential writers in the whole psychic/occult world. Through her two major books, *Isis Unveiled* (1877) and especially *The Secret Doctrine* (1888), she has taught several generations about occult lore, and the Theosophical Society she founded has become a major force in the occult community.

Blavatsky was born in Russia in 1831 of an aristocratic family. She became an early student of the occult and showed mediumistic tendencies. In 1851, she began a life of wandering that took her to India. She claimed contact with the mahatmas, persons who had evolved to a point from which they have become conscious co-workers with the divine plan of the ages and are thus beings of great authority, attainment, and responsibility. Their wisdom guides all movements for growth, particularly the Theosophical Society. During her life, Blavatsky claimed constant contact with them.

Blavatsky went to England and the United States and became deeply involved in Spiritualism (she was later to become a major antagonist). In 1873, she met Henry Steele Olcott, and together they founded the Theosophical Society in New York in 1875. *Isis Unveiled* became the society's central document. As the first president, Olcott became the chief administrator in the movement and Blavatsky's right arm.

The Theosophical Society set three objectives for itself:

1. To form a nucleus of the Universal Brotherhood of Humanity without distinction of race, creed, sex, caste, or color.

2. To encourage the study of Comparative Religion, Philosophy, and Science.

3. To investigate the unexplained laws of nature and the powers latent in man.

The original society was an outgrowth of Spiritualism, and, in her early writings, Blavatsky still rejected reincarnation. She claimed that Spiritualist phenomena were genuine but were the work of lower astral entities rather than disincarnates.

In 1879, Olcott and Blavatsky sailed for India and established permanent headquarters in Adyar. Blavatsky discovered Hinduism and Buddhism and became fascinated with them as continuations of the ancient wisdom of Egypt and the Mediterranean. Also, at this time, the concept of the mahatmas or masters came to the fore. From a special altar in her home at Adyar and a few other places, letters from the masters in the spirit world began to arrive.

Madame Blavatsky's cosmology is the basis of theosophical thought. To the novice, the cosmology is a highly complicated

Pleroma of Gods and lesser entities, organized in a divine hierarchy and controlling the overall evolution of the earth. Aiding the hierarchy are the mahatmas or masters, men who have evolved to an almost semi-divine status and who directly represent the hierarchy to the human race. The masters are the key to the theosophical system. As in most Gnostic systems, numerical symmetry is a feature; the numbers three, seven, and ten continually arise.

At the top of the occult hierarchy is God, usually referred to as the Cosmic Logos. He expresses himself as a Trinity, usually thought of in Hindu categories as Creator, Preserver, and Destroyer. (Brahma, Vishnu, and Shiva are the Hindu deities.) There are also seven Planetary Logoi; every star in the universe is assigned to one of these logoi. Our sun and solar system are assigned to the Solar Logos, the Lord of this system and God for mankind. The Solar Logos emanates a Trinity (Father, Son, and Holy Ghost) and seven logoi. Along with these logoi, there are a number of lesser angelic entities called Devas.

Mankind is the product of a lengthy evolutionary process. The earth (and universe) is in the midst of a seven-stage cycle. The first three stages are steps toward materialization; the fourth is crystallization, and the last three will be characterized by spiritualization and a return to spirit. We live in the fourth stage now. Mankind appeared at the beginning of the fourth round and has furthered his physical evolvement from lower life forms through the merger of his spirit with the body, welded together with the mind. Thus, physical evolvement of more complicated material animal forms met Spirit being thrust into matter, and, because spirit and matter could not be joined in themselves, Mind became the intermediate principle.

Man's evolvement takes him through seven root races, each of which has seven subraces. The first three root races perfected the union of matter and spirit; the fourth expresses the union; the last three will represent the struggle of the spirit to be free of matter. We now live in the Fifth Root Race. The third race was the Lemurian, so named for the mythical submerged continent in the Pacific Ocean, and the fourth was the Atlantean, so named for Atlantis, the supposed paradisiacal origin of man. The Fifth Root Race, the Aryan, finds its culmination in the Anglo-Saxon subrace. From this point, mankind will evolve into spiritual adepts.

Man, himself, is a complicated being composed of seven bodies ranking from his pure spirit true self to the gross material body. These planes of existence are outlined thus:

1. Divine — Adi
2. Monadic — Anupadaka
3. Spiritual — Nirvanic
4. Intuitional — Buddhic
5. Mental — Mental
6. Astral — Astral
7. Physical — Physical

In this list, the terms on the right are the proper terms, several of them being the Eastern words for the planes of existence. The terms on the left are explanatory of the proper terms. Level six, the astral, is a low-grade immaterial plane that is not very highly regarded; it is occupied by such lesser figures as ghosts. Level two, the monadic, is the level of union with all that exists.

Man is a spark of divinity that manifests itself as a trinity of spirit, intuition, and mentality. Man assumes a body appropriate to each level of functioning. As he moves downward, each body he assumes is composed of denser substance. The astral and the physical are the densest, and these are discarded at death. It is the Theosophist belief that most Spiritualist phenomena are centered on contact with the astral plane and "discarded astral shells"; Theosophists often complain that Spiritualists are engaged in lower psychism.

In the present evolutionary struggle to become free from matter, humanity is hindered because its consciousness is stuck in the gutter of the physical plane. The goal of this life is to raise the consciousness to higher levels. Humankind is hindered in this goal by each body's inability to apprehend the higher vibration rate of the less dense substance above it, but man is helped by various occult practices, reincarnation, and the masters from the spirit world.

Theosophy offers a number of occult practices, such as meditation and yoga, as techniques to help the self to reach life on higher planes. These techniques, common to most religious traditions, overcome the tendency to place attention purely on the physical plane.

Reincarnation is the educative process by which the self is given repeated opportunities to rediscover its true life. Humans take on successive bodies until they overcome attachments to the lower planes. Each life is a representation of the state of evolvement of the soul in previous lives.

By far the greatest help to human evolvement are the masters. These are spiritual giants, men and women who have progressed far beyond the human race, who no longer need to incarnate, but who do so in order to aid the struggling race. They form an intermediate hierarchy between man and the Solar rulers. The hierarchy of masters is given a name by position. Each position is currently filled by entities who were once incarnated on this physical plane and who are known, in many cases, as great spiritual giants. The masters are organized in a complicated system, much as the Solar Hierarchy is organized.

At the top is the Lord of the World, the agent of the Solar Logos. Under him is the Trinity of Buddhas. These four are often referred to as Sanat Kumara and the Three Kumaras. The three department heads in the hierarchy are Will, Love/Wisdom, and Intelligence. Each of these has a representative: Manu Vaivasvata, Bodhisattva Maitreya, and the Maha Chohan. The hierarchical assistants, who manifest Will, Love/Wisdom, and Intelligence to humans, are the Seven Rays. The first three of these Rays (Master Morya, Master Koot Hoomi, and the Venetian Master) are called the Three Aspects or Major Rays. The other four are called the Four Attributes or Minor Rays (Master Serapis, Master Hilarion, Master Jesus, and Master Prince Rakoczi). Morya manifests Will to humans; Koot Hoomi manifests Love/Wisdom; and the other five masters manifest Intelligence. [Various Theosophical groups spell Koot Hoomi's name differently—sometimes Kuthumi, sometimes Kut Hoomi.] Master Jupiter is an assistant to Morya with a special relationship to India. Master Djual Khool is an assistant to Koot Hoomi with a special relationship to the Theosophical Society. The following chart shows the hierarchical arrangement. Those numbered are the Seven Rays.

Sanat Kumara

Three Buddhas

Will	Love Wisdom	Intelligence
Manu Vaivasvata	Bodhisattva Maitreya	The Maha Chohan
Master Morya	2 Master Koot Hoomi	3 Venetian Master
Master Jupiter	Master Djual Khool	4 Master Serapis
		5 Master Hilarion
		6 Master Jesus
		7 Master Prince Rakoczi

These masters are very confusing at first until one realizes that their names designate their positions, not their name in this earthly life. The entities who presently hold those positions have reappeared in physical form throughout history, but not always as the individual one might expect from a casual perusal of the chart. For example, the position in the hierarchy called Master Jesus is now filled by the person who was known on earth as the Greek figure, Apollonius. The masters, their characteristics, and their most famous incarnations are charted below:

1. Morya	Power and Strength	A Tibetan
2. Koot Hoomi	Wisdom	Pythagoras
3. The Venetian	Adaptability	Plotinus
4. Serapis	Harmony and Beauty	
5. Hilarion	Science	Iambichus
6. Jesus	Purity and Devotion	Apollonius
7. Prince Rakoczi	Ordered Service (Ceremonial Magic)	Rosencreutz and Roger Bacon

The one known on earth as Jesus in this life was a reincarnation of Shri Krishna and is now filling the position of Bodhisattva Maitreya. Master Jupiter is the special guardian of India, and Djual Khool is especially attached to the leaders of the Theosophical Society. The masters work through the leadership of the Theosophical Society and thus become the teachers of the human race. They possess the wisdom that mankind needs to escape the repetition of incarnations and rise to the spiritual home. The Seven Rays use the seven colors of the rainbow in aiding people.

While the masters speak in cognitive language, the wisdom of which they speak is occult (hidden) and, in the long run, available only by the apprehension of the higher self. Like the knowledge that comes out of the relationship of loving another person, it cannot be reduced to statements or adequately conveyed by words.

Theosophy, as a movement, developed centers of work in the United States, England, and India, but the major issues were being decided in India. In Adyar, Madame Blavatsky had set up headquarters. From there, her continued contact with the masters grew at an increasing rate. Quite apart from the Theosophical system, the question of the existence of the masters became the issue for the last years of Blavatsky's leadership.

In 1884, while both Olcott and Blavatsky were in England, Emma Coulomb and her husband, who were in charge in Madame Blavatsky's home, passed some materials to Christian missionaries, who published them and attacked what they considered fraud in the production of the messages from the masters. The messages, which appeared in the specially designed cabinet with secret openings to Madame Blavatsky's bedroom and to another room in her house, were credited to Madame Blavatsky herself.

The newly founded Society of Psychical Research (SPR) sent Richard Hodson, a young British scholar, to investigate the whole matter. He quickly found the opening from Blavatsky's bedroom into the place where the master's letters were delivered. In a lengthy report, he concluded that Blavatsky's phenomena were fraudulent and described at great length how various seemingly miraculous incidents had occurred. The SPR report was a major blow and signaled a period of eclipse for the Theosophical Society.

In 1888, Blavatsky formally constituted and for the rest of her life headed what was known as the Esoteric Section (ES). The ES became an inner group of trusted students to whom she taught an advanced course of occultism. While not an official part of the society, it tended to include the most dedicated theosophists who, in effect, became an elite controlling group.

Madame Blavatsky settled in London in 1887, where she was visited by Annie Besant, a young radical activist and orator who had made quite a name for herself as a colleague of atheist Charles Bradlaugh. Besant, having read The Secret Doctrine, was ready to leave her liberal background and become a theosophist. Madame Blavatsky recognized her talent and encouraged her. As a result of their effort during the last five years of Blavatsky's life, the Society recovered and expanded in Europe. Some outstanding workers, such as George R.S. Mead and Mabel Collins, were attracted to the Society. Colonel Olcott continued to offer his administrative ability.

Upon Madame Blavatsky's death in 1891, Annie Besant's star began to rise. She succeeded Blavatsky as head of the Esoteric Section. During the next decade, with Olcott's help, the Society became a world-wide organization. Shortly before his death in 1907, Olcott received a message from the masters "appointing" Besant the new president. With her strong leadership, a new era began, and the Society started a process of slow and steady growth that has resulted in its spread to all parts of the globe. Its literature now is distributed to the entire occult/psychic community. Only three things marred Besant's career—the Leadbeater affair, the Krishnamurti affair, and the loss of strong leaders in America and Germany who disagreed with her on points of administration and doctrine.

Charles W. Leadbeater, a priest in the Church of England, joined the Theosophical Society in 1883. Soon afterward, he went to India, at the insistence of Master K, to aid in its defense. A talented occultist, he became a popular lecturer and writer. In 1895, he became assistant secretary of the European Section and a close friend of Besant, with whom he co-authored several books. The primary content of these books was the clairvoyant exploration of the cosmology of Madame Blavatsky. Gradually, these books became the dominant literature of the movement.

The crisis with Leadbeater came in 1906. Charges were preferred against Leadbeater for giving immoral sexual advice to some youths who had been left in his charge. He had taught the boys the practice of masturbation as a means of dealing with their own physical problems (sexual urges). Annie tried to defend her friend, who was being attacked from all quarters. The scandal was eventually overcome, and Leadbeater remained active in the Theosophical Society, but the blot on Besant continued to be used by her adversaries.

During the early years of the century, Besant, also with input from Leadbeater, began to talk of the coming to visibility again in the flesh of an Avatar, a world teacher, to lead the world into a new stage of evolution. In a series of lectures in 1909 on "The Changing World," she declared that a new race was coming and a new Christ was to appear. Then in the winter of 1908–09, a Theosophical Society member in Adyar named Narayaniah asked the Society to care for his motherless boys, among them, Jiddu Krishnamurti.

Leadbeater, now living in Adyar, immediately became attached to Krishnamurti, whom he called Alcyone, meaning the calmer of storms. Convinced that Krishnamurti was destined to be a great spiritual leader, Leadbeater became his teacher. During the next two years, Leadbeater worked with him psychically, and the product was a now-famous little book, *At the Feet of the Master.* Besant soon became convinced that Krishnamurti was the body to be used by the Bodhisattva (Avatar) for his new appearance. In January 1912, a new periodical, *Herald of the Star,* was begun, to announce his appearance. Already formed as a preparatory organization was the Order of the Star of the East. The material advocating his cause began to roll off the Adyar presses.

But obstacles asserted themselves before the new Christ could begin his mission. Krishnamurti's father demanded the return of his son; the sexual charges against Leadbeater were revived, and a series of court cases initiated. The court finally ruled in the favor of the Theosophical Society. The Order of the Star of the East progressed until Krishnamurti, himself, began to reject his assigned role in 1929. The Order of the Star of the East then died for lack of a messiah.

Over the period of the various scandals from the 1880s until the 1930s, schisms were rending the Theosophical Society. As various leaders and groups jockeyed for power, they found themselves disgusted with Leadbeater and opposed to many of Besant's new ideas. Alternate messages from the masters began to appear through different channels, challenging Besant's authority. The story of these schisms is the story of the development of the Theosophical subfamily of religious groups.

Theosophy in America. The Theosophical Society had been founded in New York City in 1875, at which time co-founder William Q. Judge became the group's counsel. After Olcott and Madame Blavatsky moved to India, the activity level of the American organization fell measurably. Judge gradually revived it, and it was

reconstituted in 1886. Judge also became head of the American branch of the Esoteric Section (ES), authored a number of books, including the classic *Ocean of Theosophy*, and edited the Society's two periodicals, *The Path* and *The Theosophical Forum.*

From the first there had been resentment at the control of American Theosophy from India. Judge also hoped eventually to become the international president of the Theosophical Society and hence did not favor the rise of Annie Besant. Her triumphant American tour, which included speaking to overflow crowds at the World's Parliament of Religions in Chicago in 1893, did not help the situation.

Besant was able, however, to work out a temporary arrangement to share power in the Esoteric Section—Judge in America and she in Europe and India. This arrangement came about partly as a result of Judge's proposal of the plan, and the subsequent appearance of a message from Master Morya with the words, "Judge's plan is right." As other messages appeared, remarks that they were emanating from Judge rather than the masters became formal charges. Unfortunately, there was no mechanism for handling such charges, so the supposedly bogus messages were given to the newspapers, which attacked Judge viciously. Judge retorted by declaring that Annie Besant was no longer head of the Theosophical Society and was under the control of dark forces.

In 1895, at the American Theosophists' Convention in Boston, the Americans declared themselves independent of the British and Indian headquarters and formed the Theosophical Society in America. Seventy-five American branches went with Judge. Fourteen remained loyal to Adyar and were rechartered as the American Theosophical Society (now called the Theosophical Society of America), with Alexander Fullerton as president. During the twentieth century, these two rival Theosophical societies have become the source for a number of new groups, most especially those growing out of the work of Alice Bailey and Guy W. Ballard.

LIBERAL CATHOLIC CHURCH. During the second decade of the twentieth century, theosophical ideas became established among the priests of the independent Old Roman Catholic Church in Great Britain, which had been established by Bishop Arnold Harris Matthew in 1908. In 1914, little realizing the implications of his act, Matthew consecrated Frederick Samuel Willoughby, an active theosophist, as a bishop in his church. Over the next year, however, he realized that theosophy was threatening to overwhelm his jurisdiction. In August 1915 he condemned Theosophy and ordered all of his clergy to sever their ties with the Society. Still unaware of the extent of theosophical penetration of the church's priesthood, he saw the majority of his priests resign.

The disruption took most of the strength from the Old Roman Catholic Church, which never recovered from the loss and today remains a small inconsequential organization. The resigned priests reorganized and elected James Ingall Wedgewood as their bishop. Willoughby consecrated him in 1916 and Wedgewood sailed soon afterward around the world on tour. In Australia he met with Charles Leadbeater, who was living there in a kind of self-imposed exile, and consecrated him regionary bishop for the subcontinent. Leadbeater would later write the major theological books reworking the Christian tradition in a theosophical/gnostic mode.

At a synod in 1918, the new organization adopted the name Liberal Catholic Church. The following year, Wedgewood went to the United States and there consecrated Irving Steiger Cooper as the regionary bishop for the United States. Cooper, who had earlier worked with Leadbeater, assumed major duties in developing a liturgy for the new church. In 1934 he published a first edition of a complete book of worship as the *Ceremonies of the Liberal Catholic Rite.* The Liberal Catholic Church spread into most countries where the Theosophical Society was established and has continued as a small body for people attracted to the Society who also wish to participate in a liturgical worship program. Other branches of the theosophical movement generally saw the Church in negative terms.

THE ALICE BAILEY MOVEMENT. Alice La Trobe Bateman (1880–1949), a teenage church school teacher in the Church of England, was stunned one Sunday morning to see the door to her home open and a tall stranger with a turban walk in and speak to her. He told her of important work already mapped out for her future. This event was but one of a number of psychical/mystical happenings that, coupled with world travel for the Young Men's Christian Association (YMCA) and an unsuccessful marriage, brought her to the Theosophical Society in Pacific Groves, California.

Theosophical teachings of a divine plan for humanity, a hierarchy of masters, and reincarnation and karma appealed to her. Also, it was at the Theosophical Society that she saw a picture of the man in the turban, who was identified as the Master Koot Hoomi. He figures in the cosmology of the Theosophical Society, discussed in the preceding section of this chapter. She became active in the Society and there met Foster Bailey, whom she married. He became national secretary of the Society, and Alice, editor of the *Messenger*, the sectional magazine.

In 1919, Alice was approached by a Master Djwhal Khul (D.K.), who requested that he become her control in the transmission by clairvoyant telepathy of a series of books. After first objecting, Alice began to receive (channel) *Initiation, Human and Solar*, her first book. Nineteen books in all were dictated between 1919 and 1960; still other books were written by Alice and/or Foster.

At first, the chapters of *Initiation, Human and Solar* were received with some enthusiasm and were serialized in *The Theosophist*, but then publication abruptly stopped. Concurrently, trouble developed within the Esoteric Section of the Theosophical Society over the dictations. Alice complained that Annie Besant, the head of the Society, acted autocratically, demanded that members cut outside ties and swear loyalty to her, and allowed contact with the masters from the spirit world only with her consent. The trouble came to a head at the 1920 convention, when Mrs. Besant's supporters were placed in all the key offices, and both Foster and Alice were dismissed from their positions. They thus became free to pursue their own work of transmitting the material from D.K. (Theosophists spell his name Djual Khool.)

Alice Bailey's teachings resemble Theosophy closely, with the description of the divine hierarchy, the seven rays, and the evolution of humans to higher levels. Humans had evolved by 1920 to the point where one could look toward the new age when groups could form advanced training schools to prepare for the real esoteric schools. In the 1930s, this observation took on an eschatological emphasis when it was revealed that, because of the spiritual yearnings of humanity, the new age was coming closer. According to the followers of Alice Bailey, this reappearance of the Christ is being accomplished by the power of the divine hierarchy being brought into this world and by service based on the love of humanity. A two-pronged program is being implemented to carry through the double emphasis.

To encourage the advent of the Christ, meditation groups are set up to help channel the energy from the hierarchy. Each group or person is seen as a point of light radiating the power of the world. A particularly effective way of channeling makes use of what Bailey promulgated as the Great Invocation. It is repeated slowly and with solemnity while one visualizes the funneling down of power from the hierarchy. Various Bailey groups reprint and distribute this prayer, and it is often used by other people with little comprehension of Bailey's understanding of its intent:

From the point of Light within the Mind of God
Let light stream forth into the minds of men.
Let Light descend on Earth.
From the Point of Love within the Heart of God
Let love stream forth into the hearts of men.
May Christ return to Earth.
From the centre where the Will of God is known
Let purpose guide the little wills of men—
The purpose which the Masters know and serve.
From the centre which we call the race of men
Let the Plan of Love and Light work out.
And may it seal the door where evil dwells.
Let Light and Love and Power restore the Plan on Earth.

Particular times of the month and year are periods when special spiritual energies are available from the hierarchy. The period of the full moon is such a time; meditation groups always gather on the evening of the full moon to celebrate and meditate. On three of these full moon dates occur the great spiritual festivals. Eventually, all men will celebrate these three festivals as focal points of the hierarchical year. The festival of Easter occurs with the full moon in April and is the time of active forces of restoration of the Christ. The festival of Wesak occurs in May, the time of Buddha's forces of enlightenment. The festival of Goodwill is in June when the forces of reconstruction are active. The festivals also illustrate Alice Bailey's belief in the synthesis of East and West into a new unity of mankind.

The program of service has found expression in the New Group of World Servers. Within this nebulous body are those who, desiring to be disciples of the masters from the spirit world, work as intermediaries between the hierarchy and the mass of humanity. The second group is composed of people of goodwill who, knowing nothing of the hierarchy, nevertheless strive for goodwill under the guidance of the masters' disciples. From this ideal of service have come a number of practical programs in education and political realignment.

In 1923, the Baileys founded the Arcane School. After Alice's death in 1949, the movement splintered, and a number of full-moon meditation groups emerged. All of the Alice Bailey groups agree on the content of teachings, though few individuals can master the voluminous writings. All gather for the full moon and celebrate the festivals. In southern California, most of the groups cooperate in publicizing and holding the celebrations. The main differences among the groups concern non-acceptance of the Bailey family leadership and local autonomy in spreading the teaching. Among members of the psychic community, the Bailey disciples have the reputation for evangelical fervor and proselyting activity. This proselyting zeal is often based on the Theosophical notion of the astral versus the higher spiritual planes. Nonbelievers are often seen as enmeshed in lower psychism.

THE "I AM" RELIGIOUS MOVEMENT. Among the most colorful of the several divergences within the larger Theosophical Movement is the "I AM" Religious Activity founded by Guy W. Ballard (1878–1939) and his wife, Edna W. Ballard (1886–1971). Guy Ballard, a mining engineer during his early life, had decided, in 1929 upon completion of a job in the West, to visit Mt. Shasta, California. As early as the 1880s, the mountain had been seen as the home of a lost race of mystic adepts from Atlantis who lived inside the massive volcanic structure. Throughout the next half-century, the occult legends had grown, and Ballard, a student of occult metaphysics, was intrigued.

One day during his visit while hiking up the side of the mountain, Ballard knelt to dip water from a mountain stream. A young man appeared and offered him "a much more refreshing drink than spring water." The cup was filled with a vivifying white liquid that the stranger identified as Omnipotent Life itself. The young man continued to talk of abundant supply, reincarnation, and the laws of cause and effect. As he did, he changed into the mystical figure of Saint Germain, the seventeenth-century occultist, now an Ascended Master.

Saint Germain described his task as that of initiating the Seventh Golden Age, the permanent "I AM" Age of Eternal Perfection on Earth. During the previous six centuries he had searched Europe for someone in human embodiment strong enough and pure enough that the Instruction of the Great Law of Life could be released through them. Having failed to find such a person, he turned to America and eventually located Ballard. He designated Ballard, his wife Edna, and son Donald, the only Accredited Messengers of the Ascended Masters.

During the ensuing months, Ballard had numerous experiences with Saint Germain and other Ascended Masters about which he regularly informed his wife through a series of letters. Upon his return to Chicago, where the family dwelt, Edna's position as a Messenger was confirmed and she began regular contact. Using the pen name Godfre Ray King, Guy Ballard recorded his initial experiences with Saint Germain, which were published as two volumes in 1934, *Unveiled Mysteries* and *The Magic Presence*. These were followed by additional volumes, including *The "I AM" Discourses* (1936), a series of lectures by Saint Germain, which summarize the basic teachings; *"I AM" Adorations and Affirmations* (1935), which give the text for the decrees (the peculiar "I AM" form of prayer); and a hymn book, *"I AM" Songs* (1938). A periodical, *The Voice of the I AM*, appeared in the spring 1936.

In 1932 the Ballards began to release the message of the Ascended Masters to the public. They formed the Saint Germain Foundation to administer the work and the Saint Germain Press to publish their materials. In 1934 they held the first public 10-day class in Chicago at the Civic Opera House. During the next few years similar classes were held in New York, Philadelphia, Boston, Miami, and Los Angeles. More than 7,000 attended the Los Angeles classes. By the time of Guy Ballard's death in 1939, the movement claimed more than one million students (though the actual number seems much smaller).

According to the "I AM" teaching, in 1929 the Ascended Masters instituted a new thrust of activity. There had, of course, been previous thrusts, such as that initiated through Madame Blavatsky and the Theosophical Society. This new thrust was begun by Saint Germain, the Lord of the Seventh Ray, who in previous incarnations claimed to be the Old Testament prophet Samuel, the British Saint Alban, and Sir Francis Bacon. As Bacon, he claimed to have authored the Shakespearean plays. In 1684 he "illumined and raised His body" and spent a period of time in the Himalayas only to return to Europe at the time of the French Revolution. During the past centuries, he has worked in America, the seat of the new civilization, which is to be the permanent condition on the planet in the future.

Saint Germain taught the nature and importance of the "I AM" Presence, the Mighty Presence of Light, God in Action. The "I AM" Presence emanates from the Mighty Creative Fire, the Great Central Sun, the impersonal Source of reality in our world. Out of its abundance, the Great Central Sun pours forth the Primal Light. That primal light is the basis for all manifested form, both the visible and invisible world. Through the individualization of the light, everything comes into existence.

The term, "I AM," refers to that Primal Light, the Opulence and Energy of God. Individualized, it is the essence of each person. It is to be constantly invoked and activated. The individual's "I AM Presence" is the real point of contact with divine reality, and hence properly referred to as the Presence of God within each person. It is visualized in a chart used by "I AM" students that shows an individual surrounded in a column of purple flame. Above him, connected by a shaft of white light is the "I AM" Presence, pictured as a person clothed in golden light surrounded by a circular rainbow of light, a color radiance indicative of the accumulated good of previous lives.

The "I AM" Presence is invoked by the use of decrees, affirmative commands for the "I AM" Presence to initiate action. In calling upon the "I AM" Presence, the violet flame pictured around each person is activated as a purifying fire to burn undesirable personal conditions away. A wide variety of decrees for handling both personal and social situations are used by "I AM" students. Most controversial are the several negative decrees that target specific conditions for annihilation, to be blasted from existence.

These come, it should be noted, with instructions that such decrees can be used only for the dissipation of discord and imperfection. They can have no effect upon that which is good, and are certainly not to be directed against any individual, though they may be directed to a negative condition surrounding a person.

Assisting and guiding humanity, both individuals in their personal conditions as well as the human race in its process of evolving, are the Ascended Masters. A Master is an individual who has passed through several human incarnations but, by his own effort, has generated the conditions necessary to rise above human limitations (ascend) and escape the necessity of continued reembodiment. Such Ascended Masters radiate love and power, which can be called upon to correct the various destructive currents that retard humanity. Each master, a visible tangible Being, has a particular quality or talent that is invoked for particular situations.

The steady progress of the "I AM" movement was interrupted by a series of events that began shortly after the sudden death of Guy Ballard in 1939. Several former students became vocal critics of the Activity. One, Gerald B. Bryan, wrote a series of books against the Foundation. Finally in 1941, Edna and Donald Ballard and several members of the staff of the Foundation were indicted for mail fraud, in reference to their promotion of the "I AM" movement through the mail. In a trial, which began in December 1941, the Ballards were charged with making a variety of fraudulent misrepresentations and false promises to some ex-members who testified that the Ballards were not only advocating a false religion but that they knew it to be false. They were convicted. Subsequently, the postal department denied both the Foundation and the Press their privilege to use the mail.

The conviction was appealed, and in 1944 a landmark decision in religious liberty was granted in the Supreme Court's ruling that reversed the judgment. Justice Douglas, in stating the opinion of the Court, asserted, "Men may believe what they cannot prove. They may not be put to the proof of their religious doctrines or beliefs." The case, sent down for review, was finally dismissed in 1946.

During the period of the initial trial and the subsequent appeals, the "I AM" Religious Activity became the victim of a hostile press, and many students left the movement. The ending of criminal litigation set the stage for the rebuilding of the movement, even though additional legal action over the next decade was required to handle the problems created by the original conviction. For example, eight years of further action were needed to reverse the effects of 1943 decision of the Post Office Department and return full use of the mail system. (During the intervening years, the Foundation and Press had distributed materials through American Express.) The period of rebuilding also set the stage for the formation of new organizations by individuals who agreed with the essentials of the Ascended Masters' teachings, but who also claimed subsequent direct contact with additional teachings.

Sources—The Ancient Wisdom Family

Research on occult history is given focus by the Theosophical History Foundation, which may be contacted at the Department of Religious Studies, California State University, Fullerton, 1800 North State College Blvd., Fullerton, CA 92634-9480. It publishes the quarterly journal, *Theosophical History*. Significant collections of theosophical literature are available at the headquarters of the Theosophical Society in Pasadena, California; at the headquarters of the Theosophical Society in Wheaton, Illinois; and at the Krotona Institute (affiliated with the Theosophical Society in America) in Ojai, California. The largest academic collection is found in the American Religions Collection at Davidson Library at the University of California-Santa Barbara, Santa Barbara, California.

GENERAL SOURCES

Braden, Charles S. *These Also Believe.* New York: Macmillan, 1949. 491 pp.

Ellwood, Robert S., Jr. *Religious and Spiritual Groups in Modern America*. Englewood Cliffs, NJ: Prentice-Hall, 1973. 334 pp.

Godwin, Joscelyn. *The Theosophical Enlightenment*. Albany, NY: State University of New York Press, 1994. 448 pp.

Hall, Manly Palmer. *Great Books on Religion and Eastern Philosophy*. Los Angeles: Philosophical Research Society, 1966. 85 pp.

Judah, J. Stillson. *The History and Philosophy of the Metaphysical Movements in America*. Philadelphia: Westminster Press, 1967. 317 pp.

Kies, Cossete N. *The Occult in the Western World, An Annotated Bibliography*. Hamden, CT: Library Professional Publications, 1986. 233 pp.

ROSICRUCIANISM

Allen, Paul M., ed. *A Christian Rosenkreutz Anthology*. Blauvelt, NY: Rudolph Steiner Publications, 1968. 702 pp.

Clymer, R. Swinburne. *The Rosicrucian Fraternity in America*. 2 Vols. Quakertown, PA: Rosicrucian Foundation, 1935.

Deveney, John Patrick. *Paschal Beverly Randolph: A Nineteenth Century Black American Spiritualist, Rosicrucian, and Sex Magician*. Albany: State University of New York Press, 1997. 607 pp.

McIntosh, Christopher. *The Rosy Cross Unveiled*. Wellingborough: Aquarian Press, 1980. 160 pp.

Voorhis, Harold V. B. *Masonic Rosicrucian Societies*. New York: Press of Henry Emmerson, 1958. 146 pp.

Waite, Arthur Edward. *The Brotherhood of the Rosy Cross*. London: Rider, 1924. 249 pp.

———. *The Real History of the Rosicrucians*. London: n.p., 1887. 446 pp.

Yates, Frances A. *The Rosicrucian Enlightenment*. London: Routledge & Kegan Paul, 1972. 269 pp.

THEOSOPHY

Campbell, Bruce F. *A History of the Theosophical Movement*. Berkeley: University of California Press, 1980. 249 pp.

Cranston, S. C. *HPB: the Extraordinary Life and Influence of Helena Blavatsky, Founder of the Modern Theosophical Movement*. New York: G. P. Putnam's Sons, 1993. 648 pp.

Ellwood, Robert. *Theosophy*. Wheaton, IL: Theosophical Publishing House, 1986. 226 pp.

Johnson, K. Paul. *The Masters Revealed: Madam Blavatsky and the Myth of the Great White Brotherhood*. Albany, NY: State University of New York Press, 1994. 288 pp.

Meade, Marion. *Madame Blavatsky*. New York: G. P. Putnam's Sons, 1980. 528 pp.

Mills, Joy. *100 Years of Theosophy*. Wheaton, IL: Theosophical Publishing House, 1987. 215 pp.

Murphet, Howard. *Hammer on the Mountain*. Wheaton, IL: Theosophical Publishing House, 1972. 339 pp.

Nethercot, Arthur H. *The First Five Lives of Annie Besant*. Chicago: University of Chicago Press, 1960. 419 pp.

———. *The Last Four Lives of Annie Besant*. Chicago: University of Chicago Press, 1963. 483 pp.

Rogers, L. W. *Elementary Theosophy*. Wheaton, IL: Theosophical Press, 1956. 269 pp.

Ryan, Charles J. *H. P. Blavatsky and the Theosophical Movement*. Pasadena, CA: Theosophical University Press, 1975. 358 pp.

Washington, Peter. *Madame Blavatsky's Baboon: A History of the Mystics, Mediums, and Misfits Who Brought Spiritualism to America*. New York: Schrocken Books, 1993. 470 pp.

Winner, Anna Kennedy. *The Basic Ideas of Occult Wisdom*. Wheaton, IL: Theosophical Publishing House, 1970. 113 pp.

ALICE BAILEY

Bailey, Alice A. *The Unfinished Autobiography*. New York: Lucas Publishing Company, 1951. 305 pp.

Sapat, Peter. *The Return of the Christ and Prophecy*. Philadelphia: Dorrance & Company, 1978. 293 pp.

Sinclair, John R. *The Alice Bailey Inheritance*. Wellingborough, Northamptonshire, UK: Turnstone Press, 1984. 208 pp.

Thirty Years Work. New York: Lucis Publishing Company, n.d. 32 pp.

LIBERAL CATHOLIC CHURCH

Cooper, Irving S. *Ceremonies of the Liberal Catholic Rite*. Ojai, CA: St. Alban Press, 1964. 380 pp.

Hodson, Geoffrey. *The Inner Side of Church Worship*. Wheaton, IL: Theosophical Press, 1948. 82 pp.

———. *The Priestly Ideal*. London: St. Alban Press, 1971. 76 pp.

Leadbeater, Charles Webster. *The Hidden Side of Christian Festivals*. Los Angeles: St. Alban Press, 1920. 508 pp.

———. *The Science of the Sacraments*. Los Angeles: St. Alban Press, 1920. 560 pp.

The Liturgy According to the Use of the Liberal Catholic Church. London: St. Alban Press, 1983. 469 pp.

Norton, Robert. *The Willow in the Tempest: a Brief History of the Liberal Catholic Church in the United States of America from 1917 to 1942*. London: St. Alban Press, 1990. 318 pp.

Tillett, Gregory. *The Elder Brother*. London: Routledge & Kegan Paul, 1982. 337 pp.

"I AM" RELIGIOUS ACTIVITY

King, Godfre Ray [Guy W. Ballard]. *The Magic Presence*. Chicago: Saint Germain Press, 1935. 393 pp.

———. *The Unveiled Mysteries*. Chicago: Saint Germain Press, 1935. 260 pp.

Prophet, Elizabeth Clare. *The Great White Brotherhood*. Malibu, CA: Summit University Press, 1983. 356 pp.

OTHER OCCULT ORDERS

Hall, Manly Palmer. *Man, The Grand Symbol of the Mysteries*. Los Angeles: Philosophical Research Society, 1947. 420 pp.

———. *Self-Unfoldment by Disciplines of Realization*. Los Angeles: Philosophical Research Society, 1946. 221 pp.

———. *What the Ancient Wisdom Expects of Its Disciples*. Los Angeles: Philosophical Research Society, 1945. 79 pp.

Jones, Marc Edmund. *Occult Philosophy*. Stanwood, WA: Sabian Publishing Society, 1971. 436 pp.

Perkins, Lynn F. *The Masters as New Age Mentors*. Lakemont, GA: CSA Press, 1976. 228 pp.

Schure, Edward. *From Sphinx to Christ*. San Francisco: Harper & Row, 1970. 284 pp.

Shepherd, A. P. *A Scientist of the Invisible*. New York: British Book Centre, 1959. 222 pp.

William, Sir. *The Occults in Council or the Great Learning*. Denver: The Smith-Brooks Printing Co., 1901. 408 pp.

Chapter 20

Magick Family

Consult the "Contents" pages to locate the entries in Part III,
the Directory Listings Sections, that comprise this family.

Magick, as its most prominent twentieth-century theoretician defined it, is "the science and art of causing change to occur in conformity to the will" (Aleister Crowley, *Magic Without Tears* [St. Paul, Minn: Llewellyn Publications, 1973], 27). Another described it as "an effect without an observable cause" and owing "nothing to the physical laws of our everyday world" (David Conway, *Magick/An Occult Primer* [New York: E. P. Dutton, 1972], 19). Neither definition is, in fact, complete. The latter, for example, could apply as well apply to almost any incident of PK (psychokinesis) or mind over matter. Father Richard Woods supplements these definitions by describing magick as the "art of employing the mysterious supernatural forces believed to underpin the universe in order to produce desired effects at will" (Richard Woods, *The Occult Revolution/A Christian Meditation* [New York: Herder and Herder, 1971], 30). Father Woods's definition is weakened by its use of the word supernatural, but does make the point that a particular view of the world is implicit in magick. That is, the world is made up of forces which impinge upon man; the object of magick is to come to terms with the world by coming to terms with these forces. Inherent in each of these definitions is the belief in a power of which most people are unaware and to which most of those who believe in it lack access. In spite of the alienation of the majority of people from the magical worldview, magick has become the life-orientation of a growing number of persons in contemporary America.

Inherent in the magical world-view is the notion of control and manipulation. These are forces that manipulate man, victimizing him until he becomes the controlling agent. One witch defines magick as "the art of producing a desired effect or result through the use of various techniques such as incantations and presumably assuring human control of supernatural agencies or the forces of nature" (Sybil Leek, *Diary of a Witch* [Englewood Cliffs, N.J.: Prentice-Hall, 1968], 4). In its demonic aspect such control can lead to the manipulation of people by curses (i.e., black magick), but fortunately, such black magick is by no means a major practice among magicians.

Magicians vary widely in their beliefs and are intensely individualistic. Nevertheless, there are a few characteristics (beyond magick) common to the groups herein classified as members of the magick family. These characteristics include ritual, secret ancient wisdom, and a tradition which has its roots in the pre-Christian world.

Ritual, for magicians, is much more than the ordering principle in worship. It is seen as a very useful tool in focusing the power of the individual and in concentrating the thoughts of members of a group on a common object of concern. Beyond these functions, the ritual effects a merging of reality and the mysterious. The climax of the ritual is the evocation or invocation of a deity for some specific purpose. Well performed ritual affects a person on all levels, thus achieving the coordination of outside effects (color, music, meditative practices, chants, and words) with the inner dimensions of the self. The successful ritual brings about a change in the state of consciousness. To help produce this state, some groups even use various psychedelic drugs.

Those groups for which ritual is the apex of magical activity wear ritual garb and use elaborate facilities. Such facilities may be anything from the temple of a magical lodge to the circle of a witch's coven (a small group of witches). Garb ranges from full-length robes to nudity (Gardnerian witches). Implements of worship include various kinds of sacred objects: the athame (ritual knife) of the witch, the rod of hazelwood, the sword, the incense burner. These objects are for ritual use only and are carefully protected from profane eyes. Most magicians also take a ritual name, to be used with other initiated brethren. This name may be that of a great magician of the past, like John Dee, or it may even be a motto. (William Butler Yeats's name was "Daemon est Deus Inversus," which in translation means "the Devil is the reverse side of God.")

Secrecy is a vital part of the magician's life style. It provides protection from a hostile world that does not understand magick and thrill seekers who are attracted to magick for shallow reasons, such as the chance to participate in an orgy. For most, however, secrecy is an element of the faith, which they believe is for the few. (The masses, being neither prepared nor intelligent enough, would misuse, degrade, and be unable to understand the teachings. Such vulgarization of the faith would destroy the power of the ritual.)

Secrecy is bolstered by a system of initiations and degrees. New members, after a probationary period, are given a basic initiation. Some groups have only one initiation, others may have three, ten, twenty-three, or even more. Initiation to each higher degree gives one access to a greater amount of secret material and presupposes an added proficiency in the magical arts.

The material which is kept secret is the magical knowledge of the group. This knowledge may consist of rituals, various incantations, metaphysical teachings, and the more powerful magical formulas. There are also the particular group's secrets, such as the magical names of members.

Most magical world views include a belief in reincarnation, alchemy, the Atlantis myth, and astrology and the other divining arts. Many groups would argue that their tenets constitute not a religion but a philosophy with possible religious overtones. Most groups adopt a new calendar and practice their ceremonies according to an astrological or Egyptian year. Some have begun to articulate their practices in Jungian archetypical terms.

Possibly as important as any characteristic, which the magical groups share, is their common history. The works of the ancient mystery schools, the Gnostics, and more recently, Francis Barrett, Eliphas Levi, Louis Claude de Saint-Martin, MacGregor Mathers, and Aleister Crowley appear in the histories of all the various magical subdivisions. This common history manifests not only a common effort, but also a consensus as to which issues are important enough to generate polemics, a consensus which is most important to the creation of a family group.

The differences between magical groups reflect those issues around which debate centers. Groups vary in particulars of ritual, in organization, in attitudes toward drugs and in the specific calendar used. The major groups vary on the particular aspect of ancient wisdom with which they identify. Related to the particular ancient wisdom (Egyptian, Druidic, Hebrew, etc.) are varying ideas about deity. Some groups are close to Unitarian Christianity; others are unashamedly polytheistic.

A SHORT HISTORY OF MAGICK. Magick that was a common practice of the ancient and even prehistoric world is a truism today. The magical world of the shaman, the alchemist, the magi, the voodoo cult, and the medieval witchcraft trials have been given ample treatment in historical, archaeological, anthropological, and psychological literature. Most modern magical groups take much inspiration from two magical groups which developed in the Middle Ages—the Knights Templar and the Kabbalists.

KNIGHTS TEMPLAR. The Knights Templar was formed in 1118 by Hugh de Payens and Geoffrey de Saint-Omer. The group was sanctioned in its primal mission to protect Jerusalem for Christian pilgrims by the king of Jerusalem and by the pope. The order developed into a monastic and then a magical group, and much Gnostic-like theology was taught by Hugh and his followers. The group learned the "mysteries of true Christianity" from the Johannites, a magical sect operating in Jerusalem in the twelfth century. Caught in a power play with the king of France two hundred years after its founding, the wealthy and powerful organization was destroyed almost overnight, and Jacques de Molay, the leader, was burned at the stake. The charges of black magick leveled against them were never really proved, but that they were a magical fraternity is little doubted.

The role of the Templars in occult history received new life in the years immediately after the French revolution. Masonry arrived in France from Great Britain with a message that it was the product of knights who survived the fourteenth century holocaust by quietly settling in England. Out of the Masonic discussions of the templars there arose one Bernard-Raymond Fabre-Palaprat (1773–1838). In 1804 he announced that he had discovered documents proving that the old Templar Order had continued led by a succession of Grand Masters, the last of whom, Duke Louis Hercule Timoleon de Cross, was killed in 1792. Fabre-Palaprat thus was free to reconstitute the order and proclaim himself the new Grand Master. He also founded an associated esoteric Catholic "Johannine" church and consecrated its first bishop, Ferdinand-Francois Chatel (1795–1857).

The activity of Fabre-Palaprat and his successors infused Templar terminology into the European occult community and provided a foundation in both French- and German-speaking lands upon which various "templar" organizations could be created. Among the groups which have roots in the neo-Templar worldview, if not direct organizational ties, are the German-based groups, the Ordo Templi Orientis (later made famous by Aleister Crowley) and the Ordo Nvi Templi founded by Jorg Lanz von Liebenfels.

KABBALAH. Development of the Kabbalah from older Hebrew sources had begun in Babylon in the early Middle Ages. The most important book, the *Book of Zolar*, was a thirteenth century product of Moses de Leon (1250–1305). Kabbalists believe the world can be grasped through numbers and letters, and that their job is to discover the meaning hidden in the numbers and letters through traditional methods. The number "ten" is the basic organizing principle of the universe. Through the ten numbers (sephirot), the basic working principles of life are organized and are pictured in the Sephirotic tree. The Sephirot are emanations of God, who is at the top of the tree and man climbs the tree, by means of magick, to the divine.

Each Sephirot represents an aspect of life as well as a realm of attainment for the Kabbalistic student. Above the first Sephirot is the Ein Soph, the ineffable ground of all being, i.e., God. The Ein Soph emanates the ten Sephirot. Each Sephirot has a name and quality ascribed to it. They are as follows:

1. Kether—being or existence;
2. Chochmah—wisdom;
3. Binah—intelligence or understanding;
4. Chesed—mercy or love;
5. Geburah—strength and/or severity;
6. Tiphareth—beauty;
7. Netzach—firmness;
8. Hod—glory;
9. Yesod—foundation;
10. Malkuth—kingdom

An eleventh Sephirot, not pictured, lies concealed behind and between Chochmah and Binah. It is Daath—knowledge (of the sexual kind, as spoken of in the opening chapters of Genesis). Daath often takes prominence in the systems of Kabbalistic groups which practice sex magick.

THE NINETEENTH CENTURY. Also developed in the Middle Ages (the fourteenth century) was the Tarot, though its present form is a nineteenth century refinement of the work of such men as Eliphas Levi, Aleister Crowley, and A. E. Waite. Each of the seventy-eight cards carries a complicated picture full of occult symbolism, much of it Kabbalistic. Today the Tarot is one of the most popular forms of divination.

The modern history of magick begins in the late eighteenth century when magical groups, no longer fearful of persecution, began to emerge into the public eye concurrently with the rise of a dilettante interest in occultism in Western Europe. In 1784, Ebenezer Sibley published his *Celestial Sciences,* which contained a lengthy section on magick and necromancy. That same year, Count de Gebelin published a book which connected the Tarot with the Egyptian Book of Thoth. At the turn of the century, Francis Barrett gathered a magical group around him, and in 1801 he published *The Magus,* which became that group's textbook on magic and alchemy.

The real impetus to the spread of magick came in the early 1800s when an ex-Catholic seminarian, Alphonse-Louis Constant, rediscovered the Kabbalah, the Tarot, and the whole magical tradition. He became familiar with Barrett's work and joined a group called the Saviours of Louis XVII. The group's leader, Ganneau, believed that he was the reincarnation of Louis XVII and preached a form of revolutionary royalism. Toward the mid-century, Constant left the group and in the 1850s published his *Dogma and Ritual of High Magic* followed by the *History of Magic* and *Key of the Great Mysteries.* In his writings, he claimed for magick both antiquity and potency and said it was the only universally valid religion. Constant, in publishing these books, took the Kabbalistic pen name Eliphas Levi. Levi was to become over the next decades the teacher of the many magical traditions that began to flourish. Rosicrucians, ritual magicians, and witches all would look to Levi for direction, even as they formed highly differentiated groups.

RITUAL MAGICK. The rise of ritual magick is understandable only in light of the blending of several traditions which emerged forcefully in mid-nineteenth century England. On the one hand, Spiritualism and what was to become Theosophy were having a major cultural impact. (Spiritualists they received messages from the world of the spirits while Theosophist claimed contact with a groups of advanced occult Masters. By 1855, the *Yorkshire Spiritual Telegraph,* England's first Spiritualist newspaper, was existed.) This helped to stir popular interest in things supernatural. On the other hand, the magical writings of Levi, the existence of the Societas Rosicruciana in Anglia (SRIA) and the continuing impact of speculative Freemasonry provided fertile soil in which new magical orders could grow. In the 1850s and 1860s, a group using Barrett's *Magus* gathered around the psychic, Fred Hockley, trying to make use of magick formulas. In 1888, the two traditions merged to produce the Isis-Urania Temple of the Golden Dawn.

The founders of the Temple and the Hermetic Order of the Golden Dawn (OGD) which it represented included the Rev. A. F. A. Woodford, Kenneth R. H. Mackenzie, Dr. Wynn Westcott, and S.

L. MacGregor Mathers. All except Woodford had been members of the SRIA, but Woodford had been the one to inherit, in 1885, the magical manuscripts owned by Fred Hockley, upon which the ritual of OGD would be built. Westcott decoded the manuscripts, and Mathers systematized them into a useful form. The material also contained the Nuremberg mailing address of Anna Sprengel, who seemed to be a Rosicrucian of high degree. Mathers reportedly corresponded with her, receiving voluminous materials and the charter for the Isis-Urania Temple. Other temples were soon founded in Edinburgh, Weston-super-Mare, Bradford, and Paris.

In 1897, Westcott left the Order of the Golden Dawn, and Mathers took complete control. Mathers had already gained a wide reputation for his occult scholarship. He had reworked Barrett's texts and produced a grimore, or magical text, of superior quality. He also published a book on the Kabbalah. By 1892, he had moved to Paris. From there, he conducted the OGD.

Under Mathers' leadership the order developed a ritual and world view from which other groups would create variations. This system is generally termed Western magick. The basic idea was the Hermetic principle of the correspondence of the microcosm (the human being) and the macrocosm (the whole, the universe). Any principle that exists in the universe also exists in man. The trained occultist can become attuned to these cosmic forces. In the process, invocation and evocation become standard practices. *Invocation* is the "calling down" into the self of a cosmic force, with a purely psychological result. *Evocation* is the "calling up" of that same force from the depths of the self, and it may result in objective physical phenomena. The correspondences also include relationships between colors, shapes, Kabbalah, etc., and the universe. A second belief is in the will's power. The trained will can do anything. Central to magick is the will, its training and activity.

The ritual magician also looks to other planes of existence, usually referred to as astral planes. These planes are inhabited by entities other than human beings, to which names such as secret chiefs, Oliponthic forces, and the gods are given. Much magical work is in the astral. Finally, most ritual magicians have adopted a Kabbalistic initiation system wherein each grade is given a numerical symbol related to the Tree of Life. The numerical symbol uses two numbers, the number on the right being identical to the number of the Sephirot, and the number on the left being the opposite of that Sephirotic number. The names Zelator Adeptus Minor and Theoricus Adeptus Minor are simply two names for the same grade. The chart of the grades and their numerical symbols comes from *Ritual Magic in England* by Francis King.

FIRST ORDER

Grade	Numerical Symbol
Neophyte	0° = 0°
Zelator	1° = 10°
Theoricus	2° = 9°
Practicus	3° = 8°
Philosophus	4° = 7°

(The Link-Lord of the Paths of the Portal in the Vault of the Adepti.)

SECOND ORDER

Grade	Numerical Symbol
Zelator Adeptus Minor	5° = 6°
Theoricus Adeptus Minor	
Adeptus Major	6° = 5°
Adeptus Exemptus	7° = 4°

THIRD ORDER
(The Secret Chiefs)

Grade	Numerical Symbol
Magister Templi	8° = 3°
Magus	9° = 2°
Ipsissimus	10° = 1°

All the founders of the OGD began as 7 degrees = 4 degrees, a degree conferred by Sprengel. (Mathers himself claimed to have contacted the secret chiefs in 1892.)

The most prominent member of the OGD was Aleister Crowley, whose magical thought has come to dominate modern magical practice. Reared in an Exclusive Plymouth Brethren home, Crowley had been introduced to magick in a book by Arthur E. Waite. His Kabbalistic studies led him in 1898 to the OGD. Crowley rose quickly in the order, but was refused initiation to Adeptus Minor because of his moral turpitude (in this case, homosexuality). However, Crowley went to Paris and was initiated (5° = 6°) by Mathers. His initiation led to a split in the order in London.

In 1904 Crowley received a communication in Cairo from the astral with instruction for the establishment of a new order, which he set up in 1907. It was called the Astrum Argentinum (silver star). In 1909, he began publishing the *Equinox* to spread his ideas.

Crucial to understanding Crowley and his followers is Crowley's Cairo revelation. At this time an entity called Aiwass communicated a prose poem entitled *Liber al Vel Legis*, i.e., *The Book of Law*. The Egyptian magick favored by Crowley is manifested in this cryptic work, which divides history into the aeon of Isis (or matriarchy) until 500 B.C., the aeon of Osiris (or patriarchy) until 1904, and the aeon of Horus (beginning in 1904). The aeon of Horus, the son, is one of the dominance of Thelema or Will. From the book came Crowley's themes: "'Do what thou wilt' shall be the whole of the Law;" "Every man and every woman is a star," and "Love is the Law, Love under Will." These three phrases constantly reappear in Crowley's writing. By them, Crowley meant that each person is to move in his true course through the cosmos as marked out by the nature of his position, the law of his growth, and the impulse of his past. One's duty is to be determined to experience the suitable event at each moment. Love is an art of uniting with a part of Nuit, the total possibilities of every kind. Each act must be willed so as to fulfill, not thwart, one's true nature.

Around the turn of the century, Karl Keller founded the Ordo Templi Orientis (OTO), a ritual magick group which taught sex magick. Crowley joined the OTO and was made the head of its British affiliate. OTO sexual magick seems to have arisen from the discussions of occult perspectives on sexuality which had be held in a number of different occult groups. Given the circulation of the oriental sex manuals discovered, translated and published by Sir Richard Burton, it is not surprising that in the late nineteenth and early twentieth century individuals began to explore the possibilities of sex magic. Aleister Crowley discovered sex magic in the process of working on some rituals and was aware of its potential prior to his encounter with the OTO.

Crowley immediate jumped into a leadership position in the OTO and led it during the last quarter century of his life. Upon his death in 1947, Karl Johannes Germer succeeded to the outer headship of the order. Germer had been with Crowley in England, but returned to Germany in the 1930s. He was arrested in Hitler's purges of occult groups and spent some time in a concentration camp.

He was deported in 1941 and came to the United States. He died in 1962 without designating a successor. In continental Europe, Karl Metzger, a Swiss disciple, assumed leadership, in England, Kenneth Grant filled the vacuum. No leader was present in America for several years until the end of the 1960s. Grady McMurtry emerged claiming authority from several letters he had been sent by Crowley in the 1940s which authorized him to act in the event of a lack of leadership.

RITUAL MAGICK IN AMERICA. Ritual magick was brought to America from Britain by Americans who had joined the OGD. However, the real beginning was Crowley's several visits in 1905 and 1915. Shortly before World War I, Charles Stansfeld Jones (Frater Achad) opened OTO branches in Vancouver, Los Angeles and (possibly) Washington, D.C. C. S. Jones was Crowley's magical child, but the two soon split. Crowley visited the Vancouver lodge in 1915. He met Winifred T. Smith (Frater 132) while there and gave permission to open an OTO lodge, which he did. Smith moved to Pasadena, California, and, upon Achad's fall from favor with Crowley, became head of the American OTO. Smith's move to Pasadena begins one of the most bizarre episodes in American religious history.

Once in Pasadena, Smith seduced Helen Parsons, the wife of Frater 210, known in public life as John W. (Jack) Parsons, an explosives expert and key man at the California Institute of Technology, who had joined Smith's OTO lodge in Pasadena. After Helen had a child by Smith, Parsons took Betty, Helen's younger sister, as his mistress and magical partner. At this point, probably in 1945, a new Frater in the person of L. Ron Hubbard appeared on the scene, and two distinct accounts exist as to what happened between Parsons and his new "assistant."

According to recent accounts published by the OTO, Parsons developed an immediate liking for Hubbard and took him into the OTO work, though Hubbard never formally became a member, nor was he properly initiated. The two worked together on several magical operations, including an attempt to produce a moonchild. In this process, while Parsons engaged in ritual intercourse, Hubbard acted as a seer to describe the concurrent events on the astral plane. The act was supposed to induce a spirit into the child produced by the intercourse.

Early in 1946, Parsons and Hubbard had a parting of the ways. Parsons claimed that Hubbard had persuaded him to sell the property of the Agape Lodge, after which Hubbard, along with Parsons' sister-in-law Betty, absconded with the money. Hubbard's wife filed for divorce. He reappeared on a newly purchased yacht off the Florida coast. Parsons pursued him, and on July 5, 1946, a confrontation occurred. Hubbard had sailed at 5 p.m. At 8 p.m., Parsons performed a full invocation to "Bartzabel." At that same moment a squall struck the yacht and ripped the sails, thus forcing Hubbard to port. Parsons was able to recover only a small percentage of the money, however.

Hubbard's account (and that of the present day Church of Scientology that he founded), denies any attachment of Hubbard to the OTO. Rather, the church claims that Hubbard was sent to investigate Parsons because the Pasadena headquarters of the Lodge also housed a number of nuclear physicists who lived there while working at Cal Tech. These physicists were among 64 later dismissed from government service as insecure. Hubbard asserts that due to his efforts the headquarters were torn down, a girl rescued from the group, and the group ultimately destroyed.

Both stories stand and in fact may be genuine perceptions of the events since Hubbard obviously did not make his "investigative" function known until some years later. Hubbard's story is consistent with the observation that the present Church of Scientology shows no direct OTO influence.

Though weakened by Hubbard's actions, the Agape Lodge was not destroyed by him. Parsons did that himself. In 1949, he took the oath of AntiChrist and adopted the magical name "Belarion Armiluss Al Dajjal AntiChrist." Then in 1952, in a still unexplained occurrence, he was killed when his home laboratory exploded. According to the late Louis Culling, Parsons had been making bootleg nitroglycerine to sell to earn money to keep the work going after the loss of the Lodge's treasury.

Besides the Agape Lodge, several other lodges were formed in the years after World War I. One of these was the Choronzon Club, or Great Brotherhood of God (GBG), formed in Chicago in 1931. The head of the GBG was C. F. Russell, who had been with Crowley in Sicily; Russell later split with Crowley. Among the Choronzon Club's members was Louis T. Culling, who in 1969, published its ritual as the *Complete Magical Curriculum of the GBG.* Its three degrees were preceded by some basic occult training. The sexual magick began with Alphaism, a discipline of complete chastity in thought, word and deed; moved to Dianism, or Karezza, prolonged sexual congress without orgasm, and finished with Quodosch, similar to the completed heterosexual activity of the OTO ninth degree. Culling, head of the San Diego Lodge of the Great Brotherhood of God, left in 1938 to join the OTO.

Another derivative of the Order of the Golden Dawn was the Order of the Portal, a lodge headquartered in Boston in the late 1920's and early 1930's. It was headed by Aleta Baker and was the most overtly Christian of the various OGD offshoots, though it emphasized belief in the bisexuality of God and the equality of woman.

Little information is available on the present practices of ritual magick groups. They are secret material, given in written form to only a few leaders and carefully guarded by the members. However, rituals used by a number of defunct lodges have become available. The publication of the OGD rituals resulted in the dissolution of two groups that were using them. The published rituals show a remarkable similarity; present rituals are most certainly derivatives of these, with changes suitable to particular needs and uses. Also, in recent years, almost all of the rituals of the OTO have been published.

WITCHCRAFT. The current growth of witchcraft (the craft of the *wicca* or wise ones) can be dated to 1951, when the last of the British witchcraft laws was repealed, and to the subsequent publication in 1954 of *Witchcraft Today* by Gerald B. Gardner, a self-proclaimed witch from the Isle of Man in Britain. Gardner's book signaled to the world that witches still existed. His work was based upon the thesis of Margaret Murray that witchcraft had existed since pre-Christian times in small, scattered, occult groups practicing the old pagan religion and hidden in fear of persecution. Many contemporary witches accepted Murray's historical thesis, but the legitimacy of her conclusions is now a matter of intense debate in the occult community.

There can be little doubt that various, mostly agricultural religions existed in Europe at the time that the Christian Church was in the process of becoming the dominant religious form of Europe. There is also little doubt that in the 1500s, the church turned its inquisitional powers on something called witchcraft. What was described as witchcraft was a mixture of the local religions, a number of things the church wished to suppress, and many things which existed solely in the imaginations of the early inquisitors. It was during this era that various new images of witchcraft, particularly the one connecting it with Satan worship, were published.

Many men, women, and even children died in the witch scare that gripped Europe in the sixteenth and seventeenth centuries. In the face of the myth of satanic witchcraft, some genuine Satanists and even genuine witches arose. The most famous incident was the Black Mass scandal which rocked the court of Louis XIV and led to the arrest of more than 300 persons. In the 1670s, Madame LaVoisin, one of Louis XIV's mistresses, suspected she was losing Louis' affection and hired a priest to say Black Masses, hoping thereby to win back the king. Some of the masses included the killing of babies; some of the masses were offered on Madame LaVoisin's nude body. Louis imprisoned or banished the participants in the heinous affairs.

Contemporary witchcraft bears little resemblance to the witchcraft described in the literature of the witchcraft trials. Going beyond the medieval image, modern witches try to separate themselves from any connection with Satanism. Rather than reacting to Christianity (i.e., being anti-Christians), they see themselves as an alternative faith (like Buddhism or Islam). As magicians, they have selected the old faiths of Europe with which to identify.

Just what are the elements of wiccan faith? This question is not an easy one to answer, there being a wide variety of definitions in the literature. First, witchcraft is a religion. There is much more to the adherents' faith than just magick. Witchcraft offers a world-view, a relationship to deity, a community for worship, and an ethical code. Of course, magick and psychic development are a part of the religion; much of the ritual and energy of witches is spent in their practice. "Witchcraft is the raising and manipulation of psychic power," says one witch.

Wicca is polytheistic, finding its pantheon in various European pre-Christian nature religions. The prime deities are the Goddess and God, usually represented as the Triple Goddess and Horned God. The triple aspects of the Goddess are maiden, mother, and crone. There are different explanations of the origin of these gods, although most agree that the Goddess is ascendent in modern cultic expressions. Psychic development, besides being training for magick, is also for communion with the deity. (The Horned God was connected with Satan by medieval witch-hunters, and Satan has been pictured since with a goatee and cloven hoofs.)

The two essential books of the witch are the grimoire and the book of shadows. The grimoire is the book of spells and magical procedures. The best known grimoires are medieval: the *Greater Key of Solomon the King* and *The Book of the Sacred Magic of Abra-Melin the Mage,* both translated and published in the late 1800s. The book of shadows is the traditional book of rituals. According to custom, it is copied by hand by each individual witch, and thus no two copies are alike.

The basic organization of witches is the coven, though there is also an associational tie between covens of like belief and practice, especially where one coven has broken off from another and owes its initiation to the other. Such a relationship exists in the Gardnerian covens; it consists of 13 people (an optimum number which may vary from four to 20) who meet regularly to practice witchcraft. The regular meeting of the coven is called an *esbat;* but eight times a year there are seasonal festivals, the sabbats. The most famous festival is October 31, Halloween or Samhaim. Others include Candlemas or Oimelc (February 2), May Eve or Beltane (April 30), August Eve or Lammas (August 1), and the lesser sabbats—the two solstices (June 22 and December 22) and the equinoxes (March 21 and September 21). The eight festivals are reflected in the common practice of publishing witch-oriented periodicals eight times a year.

Most covens have both a basic initiation and higher initiations which are reserved for potential and actual priests and priestesses, who are the coven leaders. There are usually three degrees which require a year and a day between each initiation. Work within the coven is done with a magick circle of nine feet in diameter drawn on the floor or ground. Magick is done within the circle, which functions both for protection and concentration. Within the circle are placed the various magical items. They include: the *athame* (a ritual knife); the *pentacle* (a disc-shaped talisman); a chalice; and a sword. These items vary from coven to coven. The *athame* is most ubiquitous.

Many covens worship in the nude (i.e., skyclad); but in most, street clothes or ritual robes are worn. When the robe is worn it is bound with a cord, the color of which designates the degree of initiation. The work of the coven covers all religious practices (psychic healing and problem-solving playing a big part) and includes hand fasting (marriage).

Witches share with all magicians a belief in reincarnation and the manipulative world-view. They also place belief in the power of spells. They cast spells for the healing of themselves and others, for their own betterment (financially, sexually) and, on rare occasions, against someone else. For most witches, the magical world-view is tempered by a poetic-mystical appreciation of nature. In their writings are numerous references to ecology, to living naturally and, in a few cases, to vegetarianism. For most, acceptance of the gods is a poetic expression of attunement with the forces of life.

AFRICAN WITCHCRAFT. Voodoo, the major folk religion of Haiti, is an African form of magick and witchcraft mixed with New World elements, complete with the ruling mother goddess, a pantheon of lesser deities (correlated to specific human needs), a psychic ritual and a manipulative world-view. Voodoo has a significant history in the eighteenth and nineteenth centuries, particularly in the Creole country. In the nineteenth century, Dr. John and, later, Marie Laveau, the voodoo queen of New Orleans, openly flaunted their magical powers in public. They were followed by Dr. Alexander and Lou Johnson.

For a number of reasons, modern witchcraft practice has had little input from voodooism, apart from the romantic aura of the word. This lack of intercourse can be traced to a number of elements, the same that have prevented many books on voodoo from appearing. Voodoo is not a literary religion; this source material must be gathered directly from practitioners. Practitioners are few in number and hard to find. They are mostly members of the black community or recent immigrants from the Caribbean. The latter often have a language barrier to overcome.

As the term "voodoo" is found in popular American usage, it refers to at least four distinct phenomena. The first, *voodoo* proper, is the magical religion brought from Haiti in the late 1700's. It is a mixture of French Catholicism and the religion of the Ibos, Magos and Dahomeans. Its leading god is Damballah, the serpent. The second, *Santeria,* is a mixture of Iberian Catholicism and Yoruba religion. Its main god is Chango, god of fire and stone. It is found throughout most of Latin America, and in Brazil is called Macumba. The third, the *Conjure Man* (or *Root Doctor*) in the Southern United States, is an adoption by blacks of European magick but is associated with voodoo because of the mystique of New Orleans. This phenomenon does not seem to produce groups, as such. The fourth, the *Bruja* (or Latin American witch), is often placed under the voodoo label, but is more closely related to the folk witchcraft traditions. Besides the widespread practice of voodoo and Santeria, as evidenced by the numerous botanicas (stores which sell magical ingredients) in most urban centers, there are at least three public voodoo-like groups.

Voodoo and its relatives exist in America today; its outward manifestations can be found in the black, Puerto Rican, and Cuban communities of major cities of the United States and in the occult supply shops which sell magical items. Such items include yerbabuena and perejil, herbs which, when used properly, are assumed to have powers to keep away evil. Other items, such as bat's blood and graveyard dust, are also available.

WITCHCRAFT IN AMERICA. The history of witchcraft in America begins with the first settlers. As early as 1636, New England colonists felt a need to pass a law against witchcraft. In 1648, the first execution under this law occurred. (Note: There is little similarity between witches as defined by seventeenth century Puritans and contemporary practitioners of the craft.) New England persecution of witches reached a climax at Salem in 1692. Spurred by confessions of occult practices by a Jamaican servant and the finding of voodoo dolls at the home of Goodwife Nurse, the community launched a massive witch-hunt which led to the death of a number of persons. In the wake of the killings, realization by the community of what it had done led to reaction against any belief whatsoever in the existence of witches. The history of American witchcraft then switches to Pennsylvania.

Among the Pennsylvania Dutch there is the survival of what seems to be a genuine "witchcraft-like" practice, locally termed *powwowing.* One must call it witchcraft-like because, while it involves magick and the psychic, it is theologically a Christian derivative with Kabbalistic elements. The practitioners are Bible believers, who feel themselves to be supernaturally endowed with their powers. The most obvious manifestations of the powwow power are the many colorful hex signs on the farmhouses in Eastern Pennsylvania. Each sign is a circle; within the circle are birds, hexagonal stars, etc.

Powwowers are, in essence, Christianized witches working in the agricultural society of the Pennsylvania Dutch. They have a grimoire (a book of spells and magical procedures), *The Long Lost Friend,* by John Hohman, and they are as feared for their ability to hex as they are liked and sought after for their ability to heal. *The Long Lost Friend,* first published in 1819, is an eclectic compilation from the Kabbalah, Albertus Magus (a magician), German folklore, folk medicine, etc.

No group of what could be called a powwow cult exists, but the power of powwow belief is demonstrated by the sporadic trials of people for murder and various lesser offenses because of "victims' " beliefs that they were hexed.

The magical folklore which produced the powwow practices can be traced to medieval Germany and was brought to America by the Rosicrucians who settled in Germantown, Pennsylvania, in the 1690s. When their group, known as the Woman in the Wilderness, dissolved, its members passed its teaching on as a popular magical lore. The lore included a belief in astrology, amulets and charms, herbal medicine, and the psychic powers of gifted people.

Prior to the 1960s, there were only a few manifestations of witchcraft in America apart from the powwow men. There were isolated areas that had the equivalent of the powwower, but not in such strength or prominence. Such an area was the Shenandoah Valley in Virginia and Pennsylvania, where practitioners had a German heritage. Occasionally, there was a witchcraft trial such as the one which occurred in Omaha, Nebraska, in 1939. A woman accused a local "witch" of casting spells against her. The "witch" was found guilty and expelled from the community.

THE GARDNERIAN REVIVAL. Many contemporary witches claim associations with witches, covens, and/or a faith which they can trace backward for many generations. However, little evidence to substantiate those claims has been brought forward and several have proved to be without any basis in fact. Most witches are converts who have come into the movement since 1960. While a few can trace their ancestry to individuals accused of witchcraft in the sixteenth and seventeenth centuries, there is no evidence of any survival of the practice within the families during the intervening centuries.

During the 1970s, a very few active covens with a history predating 1960 were located, but overwhelmingly, modern witchcraft can be traced to the work of Gerald B. Gardner (1884–1964), a retired British civil servant. Gardner had only a minimal amount of education and in his teen years moved to Ceylon (now Sri Lanka) where he worked on a plantation. During the next thirtynine years he worked at various government and private jobs throughout India and Southeast Asia. He became an accomplished amateur anthropologist and authored the standard work on the *kris,* the Indonesian ceremonial weapon. In Palestine, he participated in the excavation of a site centered upon the worship of the goddess Astaroth.

Upon his return to England just before World War II, Gardner associated himself with the Corona Fellowship of Rosicrucians, founded by Mabel Besant-Scott, daughter of theosophist Annie Besant. Through the group, he met some witches who introduced him to one Dorothy Clutterbuck. According to Gardner, She initiated him into witchcraft. After the death of the priestess of the coven to which he belonged, he was allowed to describe some of the life of the group in a novel, *High Magic's Aid* (1949), published under his magical name, "Scire." Then in 1954, following the repeal of the Witchcraft Laws in England in 1951, he published *Witchcraft Today,* which gave a more detailed picture of what Gardner described as a dying religion. The book, however, initiated a revival of interest, and led to a new generation of witches who turned to Gardner for initiation.

Recent research has done much to discredit Gardner's account of the rise of modern witchcraft. Examination of his papers sold to

"Ripley's Believe It or Not" by his daughter and the publication of several sets of rituals which he and his associates gave to various initiates, have disclosed a radically different account of the origin of Gardnerian witchcraft. Rather than being initiated into a pre-existing Wiccan religion, it appears Gardner created the new religion out of bits and pieces of Eastern religions and Western occult and magical material.

Basic rituals were adapted from ritual magic texts such as the *Greater Key of Solomon,* the writings of Aleister Crowley, and Freemasonry (into which Gardner had been initiated in Ceylon). Beginning with the eight ancient Pagan *Sabbats* (agricultural festivals) as major holy days, he added regular biweekly gatherings at the *esbats* full and new moon. From the Malayan *kris,* he developed the *athame,* (the witch's ritual knife). Having become a practitioner of nudism as a result of sunbaths taken while recovering from an illness, he ordained that rituals were to be done in the nude, or *skyclad* (a term used to describe the nude sadhus of India). He also incorporated several Eastern religious practices (ritual scourging) and beliefs (karma and reincarnation). In 1948 he published a novel, *A Goddess Arrives,* which described a Goddess-worshipping faith.

By 1954 Gardner and the small group he had gathered around him had created Wicca (or Wica), a religion more accommodating to a popular audience than ritual magic could ever be. During the late 1950s and early 1960s, Wiccan initiates took Gardner's rituals and formed separate covens, and slowly the movement began to spread. One initiate, Alexander Sanders (d. 1988), revised the rituals slightly and began a new "Alexanderian" lineage of witchcraft. Though beginning entirely from Gardnerian rituals, Sanders created a fictionalized story of his having begun his career in witchcraft after being initiated as a child by his grandmother. Sybil Leek, another witch who began her practice with Gardnerian rituals, came to America in the late 1960's. Before becoming famous as a professional occultist, she formed several covens in different locations around the United States.

The Gardnerian origin of contemporary covens is often obscured by the adoption of designations such as "traditional" and "hereditary" to indicate their allegiance to a non-Gardnerian form of witchcraft and by implication their derivation from a pre-Gardnerian lineage of Witchcraft. However, while covens deviate at particular points, they all adhere to Gardner's original belief system, retain the unique elements of Gardnerian ritual, and perpetuate the overall pattern of practice that he originated. Certainly, numerous variations of his original rituals have been developed and a few entirely new sets of rituals composed, but all have proved to be products of the post-Gardnerian era, and follow the ritual pattern he established in the 1950s.

Witches may practice alone, but most are organized into covens, which meet biweekly at the new and full moon and eight times a year for the major holidays. Most covens have abandoned nudity and do their rituals in robes, though strict Gardnerians and Alexanderians retain the practice.

GARDNERIAN WICCA IN THE UNITED STATES. Gardnerian Wicca or Witchcraft was brought to the United States in the mid-1960s by Raymond and Rosemary Buckland. Longtime students of the occult, they heard of Gardner and traveled to the Isle of Man, where he operated a witchcraft and magic museum. There they went through a intensive program in Gardner's witchcraft and were initiated into both the first and second degrees (which is contrary to standard practice that requires a year and a day between initiations). Upon their return, they formed a coven on Long Island and became the center of a burgeoning movement. Much of the spread of the movement was due to the Bucklands' availability to the media whose interest was sparked both by the witchcraft museum they owned and their willingness to be interviewed and photographed as witches.

Soon after witchcraft spread across America, other people attracted to the Goddess faith began to create variations on it. One set of variations became known as neopaganism. Donna Cole, a Chicago witch who had received her initiation in England in the late 1960s, composed a set of rituals, similar to Gardner's, but much more worshipful and celebrative and less focused upon magic. These rituals circulated through the witchcraft community in the United States and became the basis of a set of Pagan Way temples, several of which served as outer courts for the more secret and exclusive witchcraft groups. The term "neopaganism" was actually coined by Tim Zell (now known as Otter Zell) who also composed a set of alternative rituals and founded a new group, the Church of All Worlds.

Neopagan groups differ primarily from witchcraft groups by their rejection of the designation witch. They will also occasionally vary by their use of a term other than coven to designate groups (nest, grove, etc.) or by their adoption of a particular pre-Christian tradition (Druidic, Norse, Egyptian) from which to draw the inspiration and symbology of their ritual life. For purposes of this encyclopedia, all witchcraft and neopagan groups will be treated as products of the Gardnerian revival, from which they are believed to have originated.

SATANISM. Often confused with witchcraft is the worship of Satan; witches, however, are quick to protest such identification and to assert the strong distinction between the two. The basic distinction is the relation to Christianity. Witchcraft logically (if not chronologically) pre-dates Christianity. That is, it exists in its own right, much as other non-Christian religions. (There is some doubt that any religion can grow up in Western culture without direct reaction to Christianity, but the witches are certainly articulating the possibility.) Witchcraft exists as an alternative to the Christian faith, much as do Buddhism and Hinduism.

Satanism, on the other hand, is logically subsequent to Christianity and draws on it in representing an overthrow of the Christian deity in favor of its adversary. It stands in polemical relation to Christianity and, in both belief and ritual, uses Christian elements, which are changed and given new meaning. The most famous element used by Satanists is the Black Mass, an obvious corruption of Christian liturgies.

Apart from their allegiance to Satan and resultant dislike for the Christian church, Satanists do share in common the magical world-view of witches. Many Satanists openly claim witchcraft as their own. Their most vocal exponent, Anton LaVey, has entitled one of his books, *The Compleat Witch.* Satanists have as an unwitting ally the conservative Christian press, which would like to brand witches as Satanists (and lump all psychics in with them). They are also aided by a tradition stemming from the era of the great witch trials, when witchcraft was defined as the worship of Satan. One could easily make the case that contemporary Satanism is a product of Christian polemics. Paranoid perceptions of "the enemy" have led to irrational accusations concerning beliefs, obscenities, profanities, rituals and behavior patterns. These accusations merely gave people new ideas; the anti-witch books became the textbooks for Satanic practices.

Contemporary Satanism seems to have little connection organizationally with earlier Satanism. Books on black magick, Satanism, and the psychic in general seem to provide the source, and the contemporary psychic scene, the setting, from which Satanic practices could emerge. The magical writings of Aleister Crowley have been influential in many areas.

Satanists do share a number of symbols (and ritual practices) with all magical religions, but several are unique and distinctive. The inverted pentagram, the five-pointed star with the single point down, is the most frequently used. The Horned God in the form of the goat of Mendes is common. The pentagram is often stamped upon the goat's forehead. Not seen as often as some might think is the black inverted cross. With the decline in power of the Roman Catholic Church (since the days of the Holy Roman Empire), from which most Satanists come, the Black Mass is not practiced much.

As one studies the contemporary Satanist scene, two distinct realities emerge. On the one hand are what are frequently termed the "sickies." These are disconnected groups of occultists who employ Satan worship to cover a variety of sexual, sado-masochistic, clandestine, psychopathic, and illegal activities. These groups typically engage in grave-robberies, sexual assaults and bloodletting (both animal and human). These groups are characterized by a lack of theology, an informality of gatherings, ephemeral life, and disconnectedness from other similar group. Usually they are discovered only in the incident that breaks up the group.

On the other hand are the public groups which take Satanism as a religion seriously and have developed articulate theologies which do not resemble in many ways what one might expect. Their systems closely resemble liberal Christian theologies with the addition of a powerful cultural symbol (Satan), radically redefined. There is a wide gulf between the second type of Satanist and its "sick" cousin. While, theologically, the Christian might find both reprehensible, their behavior is drastically different and the groups should not be confused.

During the mid-1970s, Satanism experienced a significant decline. Several new Satanist groups did appear, the most notable being the Temple of Set, which developed a rather unique Satanic theology based upon Egyptian motifs. By the mid-1980s, while Satanism itself showed little sign of a revival, a new wave of anti-Satanism began to emerge around charges that Satanist groups were actually present in large numbers and that proof of their existence was in process of coming forth. Some saw the emergence of Satanic symbols in the youth culture as a sign that a heavy recruitment of teenagers was occurring. Evidence cited for Satanic activity, though they were virtually invisible, included the overt Satanic themes that had begun to appear in rock music, the popular fantasy game *Dungeons and Dragons,* and the testimony of former Satanists converted to evangelical Christianity.

More sinister Satanist groups were reportedly centered upon the ritual abuse of children. Some law enforcement officials claimed to see an increase in ritually slaughtered animals. However, in spite of attempts to locate Satanist groups by law enforcement officials and widespread attention focused by anti-Satanist groups, direct evidence of any significant new growth of Satanism has yet to be produced and much counter evidence has surfaced. Many of the claims of ritual abuse of children and even the stories of some evangelical Christian converts have proved unfounded and/or based on a hoax. In the mid-1970s an extensive study of more than 12,000 reports of Satanic activity failed to produce a single Satanist or Satanic group.

Sources—The Magick Family

A large collection of materials on the revival of magical religion in the last half of the twentieth century can be found in the American Religions Collection at Davidson Library at the University of California-Santa Barbara, Santa Barbara, California.

GENERAL SOURCES

Bonewits, P. E. I. *Real Magic.* Berkeley, Calif.: Creative Arts Book Co., 1979.

Green, Marian. *Magic for the Aquarian Age.* Wellingborough: Aquarian Press, 1983.

Mauss, Marcel. *A General Theory of Magic.* New York: W. W. Norton & Company, 1972.

Melton, J. Gordon, and Isotta Poggi. *Magic, Witchcraft and Paganism in America, A Bibliography.* New York: Garland Publishing, 1992.

HISTORY OF MAGIC

Cavendish, Richard. *A History of Magic.* New York: Taplinger Publishing, 1977.

Gilbert, R. A. *The Golden Dawn, Twilight of the Magicians.* Wellingborough: Aquarian Press, 1983.

Howe, Ellic. *The Alchemist of the Golden Dawn*. Wellingborough: Aquarian Press, 1985.

———. *The Magicians of the Golden Dawn*. London: Routledge and Kegan Paul, 1972.

King, Francis. *Ritual Magic in England*. London: Neville Spearman, 1970.

McIntosh, Christopher. *Eliphas Levi and the French Occult Revival*. New York: Samuel Weiser, 1974.

Thomas, Keith. *Religion and the Decline of Magic*. New York: Charles Scribner's Sons, 1971.

Webb, James. *The Occult Establishment*. LaSalle, Ill.: Open Court Publishing, 1976.

———. *The Occult Underground*. LaSalle, Ill.: Open Court Publishing, 1974.

RITUAL MAGICK

Ashcroft-Nowicki, Dolores. *First Steps in Ritual*. Wellingborough: Aquarian Press, 1982.

Conway, David. *Magic, An Occult Primer*. New York: E. P. Dutton, 1972.

Crowley, Aleister. *Magick in Theory and Practice*. New York: Castle Books, n.d.

Gilbert, R. A. *The Golden Dawn, Twilight of the Magicians*. Wellingborough, Northamptonshire, England: Aquarian Press, 1983.

Greer, Mary K. *Woman of the Golden Dawn*. Rochester, VT: Park Street Press, 1995. 489 pp.

King, Francis. *Techniques of High Magic*. New York: Warner Destiny Books, 1976.

Levi, Eliphas. *The History of Magic*. London: W. Rider & Sons, 1913.

McIntosh, Christopher. *The Devil's Book Bookshelf*. Wellingborough, Northamptionshire, England: Aquarian Press 1985.

Smith, Timothy D'arch. *The Books of the Beast*. Wellingborough, Northamptonshire, England: Crucible, 1987.

———. *Transcendental Magic*. London: G. Redway, 1896.

Regardie, Israel. *Ceremonial Magic*. Wellingborough: Aquarian Press, 1980.

WITCHCRAFT

Baroja, Julio Caro. *The World of the Witches*. Chicago: University of Chicago Press, 1965.

Boyer, Paul, and Stephen Nissenbaum. *Salem Possessed*. Cambridge: Harvard University Press, 1974.

Clifton, Chas. S., ed. *Witchcraft Today*. Book One: The Modern Craft Movement. St. Paul, Minn.: Llewellyn Publications, 1992.

Hansen, Chadwick. *Witchcraft at Salem*. New York: New American Library, 1969.

Kieckhefer, Richard. *European Witch Trials*. Berkeley: University of California Press, 1976.

Monter, E. William. *European Witchcraft*. New York: John Wiley & Sons, 1969,

Russell, Jeffery Burton. *A History of Witchcraft*. London: Thames and Hudson, 1980.

AFRO-CARIBBEAN RELIGION

Gonzalez-Wippler, Migene. *Santeria*. New York: Julian Press, 1973.

Haskins, James. *Witchcraft, Mysticism and Magic in the Black World*. Garden City, N.Y.; Doubleday, 1974.

Langguth, A. J. *Macumba*. New York: Harper & Row, 1975.

Pelton, Robert W. *The Complete Book of Voodoo*. New York: G. P. Putnam's Sons, 1972.

MODERN WITCHCRAFT AND PAGANISM

Adler, Margot. *Drawing Down the Moon*. Boston, Mass.: Beacon Press, 1987.

A Book of Pagan Rituals. New York: Samuel Weiser, 1978.

Bracelin, J. L. *Gerald Gardner: Witch*. London: Octagon Press, 1960.

Farrar, Janet, and Stewart Farrar. *Eight Sabbats for Witches*. London: Robert Hale, 1081.

———. *The Witches' Way*. London: Robert Hale, 1984.

Farrar, Janet, and Stewart Farrar. *Eight Sabbats for Witches.*. London: Robert Hale, 1981.

———. *The Witches' Way*. London: Robert Hale, 1984.

Farrar, Stewart. *What Witches Do*. New York: Coward, McCann & Geohegan, 1971.

Gardner, Gerald. *Witchcraft Today*. London: Jarrolds, 1968.

Kelly, Aidan A. *Crafting the Art of Magic*. St. Paul, Minn.: Llewellyn Publications, 1991.

Miller, David L. *The New Polytheism*. New York: Harper & Row, 1974.

Starhawk. *Dreaming in the Dark*. Boston: Beacon Press, 1982.

———. *The Spiral Dance*. San Francisco: Harper & Row, 1979.

Valiente, Doreen. *An ABC of Witchcraft*. New York: St. Martin's Press, 1973.

———. *The Rebirth of Witchcraft*. Custer, WA: Phoenix Publishing Inc., 1989.

SATANISM

Ashton, John. *The Devil in Britain and America*. Ann Arbor, Mich.: Gryphon Books, 1971.

Laver, James. *The First Decadent*. New York: Citadel Press, 1955.

Lyons, Arthur. *Satan Wants You*. New York: The Mysterious Press, 1988.

Richardson, James T., Joel Best, and David G. Bromley. *The Satanism Scare*. New York: Aldine de Gruyter, 1991.

Wolfe, Burton H. *The Devil's Avenger*. New York: Pyramid Books, 1974.

Chapter 21

Middle Eastern Family
Part I: Judaism

Consult the "Contents" pages to locate the entries in Part III,
the Directory Listings Sections, that comprise this family.

"O give thanks to the Lord of lords,
for his steadfast love endures forever;
to him who alone does great wonders,
to him who by understanding made the heavens,
for his steadfast love endures forever;
to him who spread out the earth upon the waters,
to him who made the great lights,
the sun to rule over the day,
the moon and stars to rule over the night,
to him who smote the first-born of Egypt,
and brought Israel out from among them,
with a strong hand and an outstretched arm,
to him who divided the Red Sea in sunder,
and made Israel pass through the midst of it,
but overthrew Pharaoh and his host in the Red Sea,
to him who led his people through the wilderness,
to him who smote great kings,
and slew famous kings,
Sihon, king of the Amorites,
and Og, king of Bashan,
and gave their land as a heritage,
a heritage to Israel his servant,
for his steadfast love endures forever."
(Psalm 136)

In this song to the steadfast love of Yahweh written in a later era, the story of the origin of the Jewish community is told. Recounted are the events during the life of Moses, a Hebrew and the adopted son of a pharaoh of Egypt. Reared a prince, Moses forsook his palace to lead his enslaved people out of Egypt, into the wilderness and to the very edge of their new home in Canaan, where he mediated to them the Covenant Law (Torah). These events and the subsequent movement into Canaan welded the nomadic tribes into a nation and made Moses the founder of one of the world's great faiths. While there is a history before Moses, it was the Exodus-Sinai event that made the people. The history of the Jewish people is found in the *Torah, Prophets,* and *Writings,* which together comprise what Christians call the Old Testament. A second great body of writings, the *Talmud,* begun as an exegetical commentary on Scripture, and including other religious wisdom, was written over the period of a millennium following the time of exile.

The next major event that changed the course of Israel's history was the Diaspora, the scattering of the Jews beyond Jerusalem. Never a happy people under outside rulers or occupation armies, the Jews had continuously made trouble for Rome. In A.D. 70, in an attempt to solve the problem, a Roman army destroyed Jerusalem and the Temple. With the destruction of the Temple, Jewish worship and religious life was changed. It had to be refocused upon the synagogue (congregation), and the Jews were scattered abroad as never before. There had, of course, been Jewish communities throughout the Mediterranean basin before this time, but now the center of Jewish life shifted to these dispersed communities.

During the Middle Ages, Jews established communities throughout Europe. Times of tolerant acceptance were inter-spersed with persecution, attempts at forced conversion, and the emergence of a few Jews as prominent money lenders. Lending money for profit, an almost necessary practice in modern states, was denied Christians at this time.

Throughout modern history, Jews have settled in Europe, looking for a home in the midst of exile. They rose to positions of power. Always committed to education, they produced many of the molders of Western culture—Sigmund Freud, Karl Marx, Martin Buber, Ludwig Wittenstein. Nonetheless, they periodically suffered intense persecution.

One cannot understand contemporary American Jews without grasping their reaction to the most brutal episode of the Diaspora: the Holocaust. In Germany during World War II the Nazis exterminated more than six million Jews—men, women, and children—in an almost successful attempt to eliminate them from the continent.

As a result of the Holocaust, an independent Jewish state was finally established in Palestine. The establishment of Israel was both the aftermath of the Holocaust and the culmination of a Zionist movement that had begun in the late nineteenth century. Among the Jews, the overwhelming majority is now at least nominally Zionist; there are only a few small anti-Zionist organizations in the United States.

Jewish beliefs begin and end in the Exodus. It was this event that called the community together and it is from this event that the community draws its life. Beliefs and morals, ritual and custom, all are all ultimately derived from or inspired by the covenant made at Sinai. Central to these beliefs is the Shema, which is repeated in the morning and evening synagogue service: "Hear O Israel, the Lord Our God is One Lord" (Deut. 6:4).

Also basic are the beginning sentences in the Covenant document of Sinai, popularly known as the Ten Commandments (Exodus 20:1–7):

"And God spoke all these words, saying,

"I am the Lord your God, who brought you out of the land of Egypt, out of the house of bondage.

"You shall have no other gods before me.

"You shall not make yourself a graven image, or any likeness of anything that is in heaven above, or that is in the earth beneath, or that is in the water under the earth; you shall not bow down to them or serve them, for I the Lord your God am a jealous God, visiting the iniquity of the fathers upon the children to the third and the fourth generation of those who hate me, but showing steadfast love to thousands of those who love me and keep my commandments.

"You shall not take the name of the Lord your God in vain, for the Lord will not hold him guiltless who takes his name in vain.

"Remember the sabbath day, to keep it holy. Six days you shall labor, and do all your work, but the seventh day is a sabbath to the Lord your God, in it you shall not do any work, you, or your son, or your daughter, your manservant, or the sojourner who is within your gates; for in six days the Lord made heaven and earth, the sea, and all that is in them and rested the seventh day; therefore, the Lord blessed the sabbath day and hallowed it.

"Honor your father and your mother, that your days may be long in the land which the Lord your God gives you.

"You shall not kill.

"You shall not commit adultery.

"You shall not steal.

"You shall not bear false witness against your neighbor.

"You shall not covet your neighbor's house; you shall not covet your neighbor's wife, or his manservant, or his maidservant, or his ox, or his ass, or anything that is your neighbor's."

While making creeds has never been a Jewish preoccupation, on a number of occasions in the nineteenth and twentieth centuries, attempts to summarize Jewish belief have been made. Many of these began with the twelfth century creed authored by Moses Maimonides, the most acceptable traditional summary of Jewish belief. In 13 statements, Maimonides affirmed belief in one God who is incorporeal and eternal, the only object of true prayer. The biblical Moses is cited as the greatest prophet due to his reception of God's law, which will never be changed or superceded. God acts in history to punish evildoers and reward the just. At some point in the future a Messiah will come. Also, there will be a resurrection from the dead.

As the Reform, Conservative, and Reconstructionist branches of Judaism have arisen, they each have produced statements summarizing their disagreements with traditional orthodoxy and setting forth their distinctive teachings. For example, the Columbus Platform of 1937, the most definitive statement of Reform Judaism, speaks to the issue of law (Torah) in which it differs from Orthodoxy, but then goes on to speak to issues of ethics, social justice, peace, and the nature of the religious life, not mentioned by Maimonides. [The text of these various statements have been compiled in *The Encyclopedia of American Religions: Religious Creeds.*]

Basic to Judaism is the concept of Torah. Narrowly, Torah is the Book of Moses, the five books in the Christian Old Testament known as Genesis, Exodus, Leviticus, Numbers, and Deuteronomy. It is the story of God's calling a nation. More broadly, however, Torah is a teaching, a way of life based on the dictates of Israel's God given in the written Torah. More broadly still, Torah is the covenant of Israel by which Yahweh became their God and Israel became Yahweh's people.

No description of Jewish life would be complete without mention of the notion of the chosen people. Always undergirding Jewish actions has been the belief, more or less articulated, that Yahweh had chosen the Jews for a special role. This choosing occurred at the time of Abraham and was reaffirmed at the Exodus—Sinai event and, while the exact significance of this new status has been widely debated, it remains a controlling concept. The effect on Jewish life of this idea has been tremendous, both in keeping the Jews from too ready an assimilation in their many surrounding cultures and in making them easy targets for persecution.

Also important to Judaism are the five great feasts. Passover, in early spring, is a commemoration of the Exodus—Sinai event with specific reference to the Lord's passing over Jewish homes when he slew the first-born in each household in Egypt (Exodus 12). Pentecost, in late May or early June, commemorates the giving of the Ten Commandments to Moses. The Feast of Tabernacles marks the Jewish wanderings in the desert (Exodus 23:14, 34:23). The Feast of Lights or Hanukkah celebrates the purification of the Temple in 164 B.C. by the Maccabees after its defilement by Antiochus Epiphanes, a Syrian ruler. Purim honors the rescue of the Jewish people by Mordecai and the heroine, Esther.

The important days in the Jewish calendar begin with Rosh Hashana, New Year's Day, which is followed by 10 days of penitence. This period culminates in the single most important day of the Jewish year, Yom Kippur, the Day of Atonement.

The basic organization of Judaism is the congregation or synagogue, which may be constituted wherever there are 10 males.

This is the basic governing body in Judaism, which is congregationally structured. The synagogue has as its pastor a rabbi (teacher). The congregation usually sponsors a school for its children. The school may be conducted only one day a week for several hours to give minimum preparation for Bar Mitzvah, the coming of age ceremony for Jewish youth, but ideally, the synagogue would have a total educational system to meet both secular and religious needs.

JEWS IN AMERICA. The story of Jews in America began in the fifteenth century with the arrival of Columbus. Several of the members of the crew were converted Jews, victims of the Spanish persecution. There are even some who have attempted to make a case that Columbus was a Jew, though the evidence is far from convincing at present. The Spanish and Portuguese Jews helped finance Columbus' voyages, and many early Jews in America were Marranos, secret Jews who had accepted Christian baptism but still practiced their Jewish faith in the privacy of their homes, a practice kept alive in the face of the Inquisition in Spain. Others were refugees, Jews who were exiled for not converting to Christianity.

Many refugees fled to Holland, became prosperous and produced many great scholars and thinkers, such as Baruch Spinoza. When the Dutch made war in Brazil and South America in the early 1600s, many Marranos there sided with them as a fifth column. The first openly Jewish community in the Americas—Kahal Kodesh, the Holy Congregation—was founded in Recife, Brazil, in the 1630s. Recife fell to the Portuguese in 1654 and the Jews had to immigrate. Many returned to Holland; others moved to new Dutch settlements in America. Curacao, a Dutch island off Venezuela, became the location of a congregation in 1656, the oldest still in existence in the New World.

Some of the fleeing Jews came to New York City, then New Amsterdam, where they joined the few Jews who had migrated directly from Holland to continue their trading. Peter Stuyvesant, the governor, was not happy to have Jewish refugees; it was only over a period of time that a cemetery, a congregation, and a synagogue were allowed. A corner of the old cemetery can still be visited in Manhattan.

In 1682, after New York had become English property, toleration was granted and a building was rented for use as a synagogue. In 1728, the group organized as Congregation Shearith Israel, the Remnant of Israel, and built the first synagogue. The second settlement of Jews in an area now part of the United States, often claiming precedence over the New York settlement, was in Newport, Rhode Island. Religious toleration and the opportunity to trade were the two attractions for Jewish settlers. The cemetery, founded in 1677, is older than New York's. The synagogue, built in 1763, still stands, but the congregation was dispersed during the Revolution when the British captured Newport. The Jews were rebels and only a few returned after the war. At present, the old synagogue is being used by a new group of Eastern European immigrants who are completely unrelated to the original settlers.

Other Jewish communities in the United States began to appear after the Revolution, composed of immigrants and the few Jews scattered throughout the colonies. Evidence of Jews in New England before 1780 is sparse, though one Judah Morris got a master's of arts degree at Harvard in 1820. In 1822, he became a Christian and taught Hebrew at the Cambridge School. Other early centers of Judaism were Philadelphia and Lancaster, Pennsylvania; Richmond, Virginia; Charleston, South Carolina; and Savannah, Georgia. The Jews thus were here at the founding of the nation and the group has grown with the nation as an integral part of its history. In this respect, the Jews differ radically from other non-Christian religious communities that established their first organizations in America in the nineteenth century.

All the early Jews in America were Sephardim; that is, they came from Spain and Portugal or were descendants of Jews from these countries. All six pre-nineteenth century congregations (New York, Newport, Philadelphia, Savannah, Charleston and

Richmond) were Sephardic in ritual. The Sephardim were soon joined by Ashkenazim, Jews from Germany and central Europe, mostly Poland. There were differences of rite between the two, and there was also a feeling among the Sephardim that they were the elite of the Jewish community. Thus, in 1802 in Philadelphia and in 1825 in New York City, the Ashkenazim withdrew to form their own organization.

Before 1836, immigration of Jews had been an individual matter. After 1836, immigrations of entire groups of Jews from single locations in Europe, primarily Germany and the German-speaking areas in Central Europe, began. These poor immigrants, mostly retail merchants, formed most of the Jewish communities in inland American cities.

Eastern European Jews had arrived in small numbers in the eighteenth century and, in 1848, the first Eastern European synagogue was formed in Buffalo, New York. But motivated by pogroms and Russia's anti-Jewish decrees, mass immigrations began in 1881. To the 250,000 Jews in the United States in 1880 were added almost two million from Eastern Europe. In 1880, there were 270 synagogues; in 1916, before World War I halted the immigration, there were 1,902.

With the arrival of the Eastern European Jews, a new issue arose within the American Jewish community—Zionism. In contradistinction to German Jews who saw Judaism as primarily a religion, Eastern European Jews saw it as a religious culture and nationality. Following the lead in 1896 of Viennese journalist Theodor Herzl, they began to clamor for a Jewish homeland. The first American Zionist Congress was held in 1897. The Central Conference of American Rabbis (Reform) reacted by unanimously condemning Zionism. The early recognition of the growth of Zionism came with the 1917 Balfour Declaration that committed England to the Zionist cause. The United States endorsed the declaration in 1922 along with its acceptance of the British protectorate of Palestine. These actions, and the dedication to the cause by outstanding Jewish leaders such as Louis D. Brandeis, finally swung the support of American Jews behind Zionism. By 1945, 80 percent of American Jews favored a Jewish commonwealth in Palestine. The founding of Israel has turned Zionism mainly into a program of support for Israel, a program of fund-raising and political lobbying.

During the twentieth century, the Jewish community became a settled and stable feature of American life and began to build synagogues and schools in urban centers throughout the land. Various national fellowships of rabbis and congregations formed as divisions on ritual law and the nature of Judaism developed. The main organizations were formed around the well-known distinctions of Orthodox, Conservative, Reform and, more recently, Reconstructionist Judaism. Less well known was the development of the Hasidic community in Brooklyn after World War I. This community was small until 1946, when large migrations of survivors of the Holocaust began. The Hasidim, at one time nearly half of European Jewry, now appear to be remaking the Jewish community as it grows, through both evangelistic efforts and a high birth rate.

JEWS IN CANADA. Though the first Jews in what is Canada today came there during the French era, they were officially banned by the French government from settlement in New France. Hence it was not until the British founding of Halifax in 1749 that a Jewish community became visible. A small Sephardic community organized very early in Halifax, and is first known from its purchase of a cemetery in 1750. It was short-lived, however, and a more permanent settlement of primarily British Jews, most of whom were merchants, emerged at the end of the decade in Lower Canada (Quebec). Congregation Shearith Israel, modeled on the Sephardic congregation in London and on the one with the same name in New York City, opened as the first such synagogue in Canada. A building was erected in 1777. A second synagogue was founded at Three Rivers at the end of the century. The community grew slowly, and 50 years after the congregation was founded, there were still less than 100 Jews in the Canadian colonies.

The 1840s saw the emergence of a Jewish community in Toronto, Upper Canada (now Ontario). In 1849 the Toronto Hebrew Congregation was founded. It was followed in 1856 by the Sons of Israel congregation, organized by English Jews. These congregations were merged in 1858 to become the Toronto Hebrew Congregation-Holy Blossom Temple. Other early congregations were founded in Hamilton and Kingston. Most of the Jews came to Canada from England, and few German Jews ventured that far north. As a result, a Reform Jewish community never really developed there.

In 1881, Czar Alexander II was assassinated, and a pogrom against the Jews began the next year. Russian Jews began a mass exodus to North America. During the 1880s, a string of congregations were established across Canada. Many of the newcomers went west into the newly opened territories, especially Winnipeg which developed Canada's third largest Jewish community. In 1881 there were only 2,393 Jews in Canada (more than 2,000 of which were in Quebec and Ontario). By the end of the century that number had grown to 16,000. By 1920 it had grown to more than 125,000. As the community grew, it continued to concentrate in the three cities of Montreal, Toronto, and Winnipeg.

The absence of the wave of German Jewish immigration that so altered American Jewry has given Canadian Jewry a distinctively Orthodox cast. By 1953 there were but three Reform congregations, though 10 more were added by 1970. The majority of the nineteenth century congregations have become Conservative in orientation and by 1960 there were more than 20 such centers affiliated with the United Synagogues of America. In contrast, by 1970 there were approximately 175 Orthodox congregations, some affiliated with the congregational associations in the United States and some unaffiliated.

By 1981, there had been some shift in the community, including a consolidation of synagogues and the emergence of a stronger Conservative element, though the community remained decidedly Orthodox. Of 112 synagogues reported that year, 53 were Orthodox, 43 Conservative, 14 Reform, and 2 Reconstructionist.

As early as 1919 there was an attempt to organize a Canadian Jewish Congress, but it soon dissolved. It was revived in 1934, in the face of the Nazi threat, and is noteworthy in facilitating the immigration of over 40,000 Jews to Canada after World War II. Today it is headquartered in Montreal.

HASIDISM. The phenomenon of the mystic, reacting to formal religion by seeking a closer direct experience of the divine, is common in religious history. Judaism has had its share of mysticism. In the late Middle Ages, the Messianic claimant, Shabbetai Zevi (b. 1676), offered such a direction. In the following century, a more stable form would appear in Hasidism, a Kabbalistic Judaism attributable to the efforts of Israel Baal Shem Tov (1700–1760), a rabbi in Ukraine.

Hasidic teachings are plainly Orthodox but also mystical. Baal Shem Tov taught that all men were equal before God and that piety, devotion, purity, prayer, and the Torah were more important than study, learning, or ascetic practices. The Kabbalah provided a framework for mystic integration of the Bible. [The Kabbalah is discussed as a Jewish magical system in the preceding chapter.] The virtues of *Shiflut* (humility), *Simcha* (joy), and *Hillahavut* (enthusiasm) were emphasized. The movement spread rapidly and, at its height, attracted about half the Jews in Europe, particularly those in Poland and the Slavic countries.

Organizationally, the movement began to focus on local charismatic leaders called the zaddikim, or righteous ones. Unlike the rabbi, or teacher, known for his scholarship and wisdom, the zaddik, who might also be a rabbi, was honored for his mystic powers—miracle working, shamanism, and personal magnetism. Organizationally, zaddikim came to lead segments of the movement and created dynasties by passing on the charisma to sons or followers. Thus schools or sub-sects, as in Sufism, were formed.

The Hasidic movement aroused the indignation of non-Hasidic Jews, and a lengthy, bitter era of polemic followed. Eventually, Hasidism was forced to retreat. The twentieth century brought new problems as pogroms began in Russia. Many Hasidim migrated. The Holocaust, of course, all but wiped out European Hasidism. Fortunately, many of the rebbes, a common title for the zaddikim, escaped and sought to make new homes for their followers in Israel and America.

The first Hasidim in America were members of that initial wave of Eastern European immigrants to America that began in the 1880s. For lack of an Hasidic synagogue or zaddik (all of whom were still in Europe), they often became indistinguishable from other Orthodox Jews. Separated from their zaddik, they became discouraged in the attempt to perpetuate Hasidism. After World War I, several zaddikim came to the United States, including the Ukrainian Twersky Zaddik. They gathered followers, but did not begin to reach outward to seek new believers. The real era of Hasidic growth in the United States began after World War II. Led by the Lubavicher Rebbe, Hasidic zaddikim, especially from Poland and Hungary, came to the United States after escaping from Hitler.

The Hasidim, as a whole, settled in Brooklyn in that section designated as Williamsburg. There they have created a unique social structure—an isolated urban religious culture. Williamsburg is a haven of "true" Judaism. They have been able not only to survive but even prosper, in spite of an economic system that seeks to assimilate them. The vitality of Hasidism is shown in the emergence of new Hasidic groups among younger Jews. A strong emphasis on tradition, social service, celebration, communal life, and experiment with radical ideas is characteristic of their lifestyle. Though largely ignored by most writers on American Judaism, the Hasidim are currently the fastest growing segment of American Judaism. This growth comes from both proselytization within the wider Jewish community and a high birth rate.

BLACK JEWS. Among the black population of the early nineteenth century were some individuals who became legends as regular worshipers at the local synagogues. Possibly the most famous was Old Billy, who in the first half of the nineteenth century was a faithful attendant at the Charleston, South Carolina, synagogue. He described himself as a Rachabite (Jeremiah 35:2ff) and, accordingly, abstained from all wines and liquor. Other black members have been noted by various authors. To this day, and in growing numbers since the 1950s, there are black members of white Jewish congregations.

A real spur to African Americans to elect Judaism as an alternative to Christianity was the discovery in the late nineteenth century by French explorer Joseph Halevy of the Falashas, the Black Jews of Ethiopia. For centuries a legend had circulated in Europe that Black Jews, descendants of the Queen of Sheba, had lived in Ethiopia, but most believed that if they ever existed they had long ago disappeared. Knowledge in the West of their present existence increased in the 1920s, when Jacques Faitlovitch of the University of Geneva followed up previous pro-Falasha committee activities with a passionate revival of efforts to aid them. While African American Jews like to identify with them, the Falashas have no direct connection with Judaism in the African American community. As a matter of fact, much recent scholarship has concluded that the Falashas are probably not Negroid, though in addition to the Falashas, isolated pockets of African Black Jews, products of interracial marriages, have been discovered.

While the African Jews supplied much inspiration for the American Black Jewish movement, the biblical faith of rural America supplied the content. Black people, Bible students, were quick to identify with the Ethiopians and, in their search for identity and status in the white culture, began to see a special place for themselves as Jews. Proponents cite all the references to the Ethiopians (such as I Kings 10, Isaiah 18:1–2, Amos 9:7 and Acts 8:26–40);

attempts are also made to prove that the true Jews were black. Psalm 119:83, in which the author sees himself as becoming like a bottle (King James Version) in the smoke, is a passage popularly quoted as proof of the existence of black Jews in biblical times.

The Christian biblical origin of the movement is made by the early leaders who articulated its postulates. Warren Roberson, one of the first prophets of Black Jewishness, spoke of himself as a second Jesus Christ. Another called his group the Church of God and Saints of Christ. It would be hard to find a more Christian designation.

Along with Rabbi Richileiu's Moorist Zionist Temple, the contemporary Black Jewish movement is generally traced to three men who appeared in Northern urban black centers at the turn of the century. Two of these, F. S. Cherry and William S. Crowdy, founded movements that still exist and are discussed in entries below. The third, the first of several New York City-based leaders, was Elder Warren Roberson. Roberson was a notorious charismatic leader who alternated between being Messianic and being a sex cult priest. He spent several terms in jail, which only added to his aura as a persecuted black savior.

Roberson's group and its several spin-offs, such as Rabbi Ishi Kaufman's Gospel of the Kingdom Temple, were swept up into the Garveyite movement. Coming from the West Indies, Marcus Garvey instilled within his followers and admirers a dream of a black nation where black men would rule. Since white Christianity had enslaved and tamed black people, an alternative had to be found. Judaism provided one such alternative. With the encouragement of Arnold Josiah Ford, Garvey's choirmaster and self-proclaimed Ethiopian Jew, a new phase of history began.

Ford tried to get Garvey to accept Judaism, but he refused, whereupon Ford organized the Moorish Zionist Church, in which he taught that all Africans were Hebrews. He followed Garvey's nationalistic program. He united his efforts with another self-professed Jew, Mordecai Herman, but they soon parted ways. Ford then organized, in 1924, the Beth B'nai Abraham congregation (BBA). Both groups were able to obtain funds from white Jews, which allowed them to survive through the next decade. Additionally, elements of Islamic lore (possibly also from the Garvey movement) crept into Ford's theology.

The BBA came to an abrupt end in 1931 when Ford decided to sail for Europe. He gave his blessing to a new leader, Wentworth Arthur Matthew, whose career initiated the present phase of Black Judaism. Ford disappeared to Africa (he later died in Ethiopia), but had laid the groundwork for a widespread Black Judaism. Today, a number of independent synagogues are located in black urban areas around the country.

Sources—The Middle Eastern Family, Part I

GENERAL SOURCES

For its size, the Jewish community is one of the most scholarly in North America. Study of Judaism is integral to the various institutions of higher learning and the history and culture of American Jews is particularly the domain of the American Jewish Historical Society headquartered at 2 Thornton Rd., Waltham, MA 02154. The Society publishes *American Jewish History* (quarterly) and has established a network of local Jewish historical groups across North America.

Bamberger, Bernard J. *The Story of Judaism.* New York: Schocken Books, 1964. 484 pp.

Rosenthal, Gilbert S. *The Many Faces of Judaism.* New York: Behrman House, 1978. 159 pp.

Seldin, Ruth. *Image of the Jews, Teachers' Guide to Jews and Their Religion.* New York: KTAV Publishing House, 1970. 151 pp.

Werblowsky, R. J. Zwi, and Geoffrey Wigoder. *The Encyclopedia of the Jewish Religion.* New York: Holt, Rinehart and Winston, 1965. 415 pp.

JUDAISM IN AMERICA

Feldstein, Stanley. *The Land That I Show You*. Garden City, NY: Doubleday, 1979. 606 pp.

Glazer, Nathan. *American Judaism*. Chicago: University of Chicago Press, 1957. 176 pp.

Hardon, John A. *American Judaism*. Chicago: Loyola University Press, 1971. 372 pp.

Learsi, Rufus. *The Jew in America: A History*. Cleveland: World Publishing Company, 1954. 382 pp.

Lebeson, Anita Libman. *Pilgrim People*. New York: Minerva Press, 1975. 651 pp.

Marcus, Jacob Rader. *United States Jewry, 1776–1985*. 4 Vols. Detroit, MI: Wayne State University Press, 1993.

Neusner, Jacob. *Understanding American Judaism*. 2 vols. New York: KTAV Publishing House, 1975.

Ruderman, Jerome. *Jews in American History, A Teacher's Guide*. New York: KTAV Publishing House, 1974. 224 pp.

Shapiro, Edward S. *A Time for Healing: American Jewry Since World War II*. Baltimore, MD: Johns Hopkins University Press, 1992. 313 pp.

JEWISH THOUGHT

Barish, Louis, and Rebecca Barish. *Basic Jewish Beliefs*. New York: Jonathan David, 1961. 222 pp.

Eisenstein, Ira. *Varieties of Jewish Belief*. New York: Reconstructionist Press, 1966. 270 pp.

Fackenheim, Emil L. *God's Presence in History*. New York: Harper & Row, 1970. 104 pp.

Gordis, Robert. *Judaism for the Modern Age*. New York: Farrar, Straus and Cudahy, 1955. 368 pp.

Heschel, Abraham Joshua. *God in Search of Man*. New York: Meridian Books, 1959. 437 pp.

Neuser, Jacob. *Understanding Jewish Theology*. KTAV Publishing House, 1973. 280 pp.

JEWISH LIFE AND CUSTOMS

Maslin, Simeon J., ed. *Gates of Mitzvah*. New York: Central Conference of American Rabbis, 1979. 165 pp.

Posner, Raphael, Uri Kaploun, and Shalom Cohon, eds. *Jewish Liturgy*. New York: Leon Ameil Publisher, 1975. 278 pp.

Trepp, Leo. *The Complete Book of Jewish Observance*. New York: Behrman House, 1980. 370 pp.

HASSIDISM

Abelson, J. *Jewish Mysticism*. New York: Hermon Press, 1969. 182 pp.

Aron, Milton. *Ideas and Ideals of the Hassidim*. New York: Citadel Press, 1969. 350 pp.

Bokser, Ben Zion. *The Jewish Mystical Tradition*. New York: Pilgrim Press, 1981. 277 pp.

Buber, Martin. *The Origin and Meaning of Hassidism*. New York: Horizon Press, 1960. 254 pp.

Dresner, Samuel H. *The Zaddik*. New York: Schocken Books, 1974. 312 pp.

Mintz, Jeome R. *Hasidic People: A Place in the New World*. Cambridge, MA: Harvard University Press, 1992. 433 pp.

Rabinowitz, H. *A Guide to Hassidism*. New York: Thomas Yoseloff, 1960. 163 pp.

Rubenstein, Aryeh. *Hassidism*. Jerusalem: Ketter Books, 1975. 120 pp.

ANTI-SEMITISM AND THE HOLOCAUST

Cohn, Norman. *Warrant for Genocide*. Baltimore: Penguin Books, 1970. 336 pp.

Levin, Nora. *The Holocaust*. New York: Schocken Books, 1973. 768 pp.

Littell, Franklin H. *The Crucifixion of the Jews*. New York: Harper & Row, 1975. 153 pp.

Poliakov, Leon. *The History of Anti-Semitism*. New York: Schocken Books, 1974. 340 pp.

Singerman, Robert. *Antisemitic Propaganda*. New York: Garland Publishing, 1982. 448 pp.

Tumin, Melvin M. *An Inventory and Appraisal of Research on American Anti-Semitism*. New York: Freedom Books, 1961. 185 pp.

BLACK JUDAISM

ben-Jochanman, Josef. *We: The Black Jews*. New York: Alkebu-lan Books and Educational Materials Associates, 1983. 408 pp.

Goitein, S. D. *From the Land of Sheba*. New York: Schocken Books, 1973. 142 pp.

Rapoport, Louis. *The Lost Jews*. New York: Stein and Day, 1980. 252 pp.

Winsor, Rudolph R. *From Babylon to Timbuktu*. New York: Exposition Press, 1969. 151 pp.

Chapter 22

Middle Eastern Family
Part II: Islam, Zoroastrianism, Baha'i

Consult the "Contents" pages to locate the entries in Part III,
the Directory Listings Sections, that comprise this family.

ISLAM. With only a few hundred thousand adherents in 1965 when the emigration barriers from predominantly Islamic countries were liberalized, Islam has grown to the point that it is challenging Judaism's position as the second largest religious community (Christianity being the largest) in America. Its growth has also propelled it from being the faith of a few ethnic enclaves to a powerful presence in national political debates and in every segment of urban society, due in no small measure to its association with oil and the turmoil of the Middle East. While not yet as well organized as the Jewish community, the Muslim community is rapidly gaining a high level of political sophistication.

ORIGINS. "There is but one God and Muhammed is His Apostle" is the great standard under which Islam has become the religion of one-seventh of the world's population. Islam means submission, in this case submission to Allah, the creator-ruler God of Muslim faith.

Islam was founded out of the experiences of Muhammed (570–632), an Arabian, born and raised in Mecca. He married a widow named Khadijah, with whom he fathered a daughter Fatima, and settled down to a rather mundane life. Part of his custom, however, was to spend part of each year in the mountains meditating and fasting. Around the year 611 C.E. he began to have a series of encounters with the angel Gabriel. The angel spoke to him of the oneness of God and of God's distaste of idolatry. The message of the angel would later be written down in a book, the Qur'an, sometimes translated as Koran. He began to teach in Mecca, but found few converts and a great deal of hostility from leaders of the older religions. Therefore, in 622 Muhammad and his followers moved to a neighboring village, Medina, where they were offered refuge. This migration is known as the Hijra, or migration, and Muslims date their calendars from this time.

Muhammed himself is seen as the last of a series of apostles who have preached the unity of God and warned of the end-time judgment. The 28 earlier prophets include Adam, Noah, Moses, John the Baptist, and Jesus. The judgment they described is a cataclysmic event when the trumpet will sound for men to stand and be called to account. Paradise and hell wait to receive the just and the damned.

Belief in Allah, the supreme God, is the essential component of Islamic faith. He is seen as the transcendent Being, creator and sustainer of the universe. He is the law-giver, the arbiter of good and evil, and the judge at the end-time. The affirmation concerning Allah is amply captured in the opening lines of the Qur'an:

"In the name of Allah, the Beneficent, the Merciful Praise be to Allah, Lords of the Worlds. The Beneficent, the Merciful. Owner of the Day of Judgment. Thee (alone) we worship; Thee (alone) we ask for help. Show us the straight path. The Path of those whom Thou has favored; who go astray". (Pickthall translation)

Existing with God are his angelic messengers. Chief among these is Gabriel, who communicated the Qur'an to Muhammed. (Opposing the angels are the *satans* or devils.) The Qur'an is the written revelation of God, accepted as transcribed by Muhammed.

It is to be distinguished from Muhammed's teachings, which are based on the Qur'an and are the prime tool for understanding it. The Qur'an, a book of some 300 pages, is divided into 114 suras or chapters, which are arranged (with the exception of Sura I) in order of length, the longest first. These suras were given at various periods throughout Muhammed's life.

The Qur'an and writings about Muhammed have yielded to codification and this law has become a basic unifying force in the Muslim world. Outward manifestation of the law is most readily seen in the five central observances of Muslim life: 1) the observance of ritual prayer five times daily; 2) the giving of alms to the poor; 3) fasting during the month of Ramadan; 4) a pilgrimage to Mecca, holy city of the Muslims, at least once during a person's lifetime; and 5) striving in the way of God. Beyond these, are a number of ritual and legal requirements, such as refraining from eating pork and from usury.

From Medina, Islam spread steadily in what today are Saudi Arabia, Syria, Iraq, Jordan and Egypt. The rise of the new faith released a tremendous amount of cultural and intellectual energy that produced a new Arab religious culture. The spread of Islam in the Middle Ages carried it west across North Africa into Spain, north into Turkey, south along the African coast, and east into Persia. Further expansion carried the faith into what are today the southern provinces of the former Soviet Union. The movement into Europe was turned back at Vienna in the sixteenth century.

Within orthodox Islam, various schools of thought developed, but in the seventh century, a major schism occurred among the followers of Ali, the fourth caliph of Islam and the husband of Fatima, hence the son-in-law of Muhammed. Ali assumed the role of caliph, the spiritual and temporal ruler of Islam, in 656 C.E. He moved his capital to Kufa in present-day Iraq. While he was in Kufa, leadership in the Muslim community was focused there. But upon his death in 661, only five years later, the political power shifted back to Syria, a move disliked by the Iraqis. Their political goals found religious expression in a new doctrine—the exclusive right of the house of Ali to the caliphate. In forming this doctrine, the House of Ali had to repudiate the first three caliphs: Abu Bakr, Omar, and Othman, three reverend companions of Muhammed. The Arabs who held this doctrine are called Shi'a and are distinguished from the main body of orthodox or Sunni Muslims.

Shi'a Muslims recognize the leadership of twelve Imams who descended from Ali through his two sons, al-Husayn and al-Hasan. These twelve leaders did not have an easy time and few died a natural death. In 878 C.E. the twelfth Imam disappeared before his death. Rather than naming a new caliph, he became remembered as the hidden Imam destined to return at the end of the age to usher in an era of true Islam. Thus the Shi'as also have been referred to as the Twelvers. Shi'a Muslims are especially strong in Iran, Iraq, and Pakistan.

MUSLIMS IN AMERICA. There is probably no group whose presence in American history has been as well hidden as that of the Muslims. Like many minority groups, the Muslims appeared

177

in the New World in the days of the Colonies. Istfan the Arab was a guide to Franciscan explorer Marcos de Niya in Arizona in 1539. Nosereddine, an Egyptian, settled in the Catskills of New York in the 1500s and was burned at the stake for murdering an Indian princess.

In the seventeenth century the possibility of Muslims settling in America was noted by Roger Williams, founder of Rhode Island, who sought to create a colony that welcomed "even the Turks" and their unconventional (by Christian standards) worship. A number of Muslims did arrive in America in the eighteenth and early nineteenth century, but did not come of their own accord. They were slaves captured from among the West African tribes that had converted to Islam. Once in America, however, their religion was as little welcomed as that of other Africans, and suffered the same destruction. The first Arab Muslims to arrive in America as the beginnings of the present day Arab Muslim community came in the nineteenth century. One of the first of these Arab emigrants became a folk hero. His name was Haj Ali and he assisted the U.S. Army with their experiments with breeding camels in the Arizona desert in 1850s. He is remembered today under his corrupted name, Hi Jolly:

"Hi Jolly was a camel driver, long time ago.
He followed Mr. Blaine a way out West.
He didn't mind the burning sand,
In that God forsaken land,
But he didn't mind the pretty girls the best.
"Hi Jolly! Hey Jolly!
Twenty miles today, by golly.
Twenty more before the morning light.
Hi Jolly, Hey, I
Gotta be on my way
I told my gal I'd be home Sunday night."

As early as the 1860s, Syrians and Lebanese, fleeing the invading Turks, came to the United States. But the first serious attempts to establish Islam in America followed the conversion of Muhammed Alexander Russell Webb in 1888. Webb was the American Consul in Manila at the time of his conversion, but returned to New York in 1892. The following year, he opened the Oriental Publishing Company and began a periodical, *The Moslem World*, of which he was editor. He also wrote a number of booklets. In the same year, he was the only defender of Islamic faith presented at the World's Parliament of Religions at Chicago. He died in 1916.

Contemporaneous to Muhammed Alexander Russell Webb's activities was the beginning of large scale immigration from the Eastern Mediterranean—Syria, Lebanon, Iran, India, Turkey and other predominantly Muslim countries. They fanned out across the United States and into the Upper Midwest. Three thousand Polish Muslims and a small community of Circassian (Russian) Muslims also settled in New York. The American Muslim community was distinguished by two characteristics: it was heavily male in population and extremely clannish. National and subnational communities formed in Northern urban centers, particularly Detroit. Little effort either to keep records or to reach out toward non-Muslim neighbors was made.

Early organization attempts were made wherever large Muslim population centers developed, though the first mosque (after the one opened by Webb in New York City) was built in rural Ross, North Dakota. A second mosque appeared in Highland Park, Michigan (a Detroit suburb), in 1919 and within a few years centers were operating in Michigan City (Indiana), Chicago, Toledo, Cedar Rapids, Milwaukee, Akron, Philadelphia, and Baltimore. Within communities, divisions developed along national lines. About this time, with the arrival of Shakh Duoad from Bermuda in 1920, the story of African American Muslims became intertwined with that of the Middle Eastern immigrants.

A major event in the American Muslim community was the dedication in 1957 of the Islamic Center in Washington, D.C. Built in part with money from fifteen sponsoring countries with the idea of serving the diplomatic community, it also has served as a symbolic point of unity for the diverse Islamic community.

Through the 1970s and 1980s, the Muslim community, long confined to a few ethnic pockets, underwent a dramatic expansion. Spearheading the faith's rapidly expanding presence in the United States was large scale immigration from predominantly Islamic countries (from Pakistan and Iran to Egypt and Turkey). Seemingly overnight, mosques have sprung up in every major urban area, with a strong concentration in the Midwest, Southern California, and the New York metropolitan area. Assisting in this spectacular growth has been the discovery of Islam by many African Americans. While the primary attraction to Islam came in what the mainstream of the community considers a heretical form of the faith, that preached by the old Nation of Islam, with its intense racial teachings, as the Nation moved toward adoption of orthodox Islamic teachings, most of the members moved into the orthodox Muslim camp.

Estimates of the size of the Islamic community in America vary widely. On the low end of the scale, some suggest less than a million. They argue that even though many have moved to America from Muslim countries, a large percentage of emigrants were Christians seeking a more hospitable religious climate. On the other end some argue that Islam is already the size of the Jewish community, five to seven million, and ready to outnumber them in the very near future. As of the early 1990s, some figure in the scale of one to three million seems a reasonable estimate.

AFRICAN AMERICAN MUSLIMS. No one knows when the first Black Muslim came to America, but it is well known that Africans south of the Sahara had developed Islamic centers prior to the time of the slave trade, and that Muslims were among the first slaves in the United States. Morroe Berger notes that such slaves tended to be viewed as superior by both themselves and other slaves; they were often educated, and they resisted acculturation and assimilation, thus retaining their faith longer.

Timothy Dwight, while in New York, recorded a visit with a slave from the South who told him stories of other Muslims. William B. Hodgson, an ethnologist, mentions five Muslim slaves in an 1852 work. One, Bul-Ali, was a slave-driver on a Sapelo Island, Georgia, plantation. C. C. Jones, a missionary who authored *The Religious Instruction of the Negroes in the United States*, noted that Muslim slaves, under pressure from Christianizing forces, would try accommodations to the new faith by equating God with Allah and Jesus with Muhammed. Berger concluded that, while no definite connection can be made between twentieth century Black Muslims and those who might have survived the slave era, nevertheless, "It is quite possible that some of the various American Muslim groups of the past half century or so had their roots in these vestiges, that the tradition was handed down in a weak chain from generation to generation" (Morroe Berger, "The Black Muslims," *Horizon* 6 [January 1964]: 49–64).

A new era for Islam within the African American community began in 1913 when Noble Drew Ali (born Timothy Drew) initiated the Moorish Science Temple of America. Ali's thought was, to say the least, a very different version of what orthodox Muslims might consider Islam. He, for example, published a Koran that he had put together from American occult literature, rather than issuing either a translated or edited version of the Muslims' Qur'an. Ali died in 1929 and while his movement continued, the thrust into the black community he began was picked up by a new group, the Nation of Islam. Also in the 1920s, the Amadiyya Muslims, a movement that originated in India, began a mission to proselytize Americans in 1921. As it turned out, their major successes were also in the African American community, and the North American branch of the movement, through no prior intention, became largely a black movement.

Black Muslims are to be partly understood in terms of black nationalism, a movement to locate liberation from white oppression in the ownership and control of land, specifically a land that black people could call their own. Sometimes that aspiration was focused upon Africa, as expressed, for example, in the Universal Negro Improvement Association, the organization founded by Marcus Garvey early in the century. It advocated a turn toward Ethiopia (symbolic of all of Africa) as a national homeland through which African Americans could shape their identity. The Nation of Islam took the idea even further and called for the establishment of a Black nation in North America to be carved out of several Southern states.

By 1960, Islam had spread through the black community, primarily because of the development of the Nation of Islam. During the 1960s and 1970s, the African American Muslim community went through a disruptive and even violent era, punctuated by the assassination of Malcolm X, a leading Muslim spokesperson who had left the Nation of Islam, and the attempted assassination of Hamaas Addul Khaalis, another former leader in the nation who had founded a rival movement. Following the death of Elijah Muhammad, longtime leader of the Nation of Islam in 1975, things began to change. Wallace D. Muhammad, Elijah Muhammad's son and successor, began to lead the movement into the orthodox Muslim camp. While losing some support, such as that of Louis Farrakhan, he was able to take most of the movement with him and today many centers have been welcomed and integrated into the larger Islamic community.

SUFISM. The word "Sufism" is used to describe a wide variety of mystical and disciplined orders found throughout the Islamic world. No one knows the origin of the term, and several explanations vie for acceptance. Some relate the term to *suf*, or wool, denotative of the wool garments worn by some Sufis. Others see a connection to the Hebrew *en sof*, the name for the infinite Divine in Jewish mysticism. Still others derive it from *safa*, the Arabic word for purity, or from *sophia*, the Greek word for wisdom. These several explanations do not exhaust the options.

Whatever the origin of their name, the Sufis appear to have developed from the ascetic pietism evident from the very first generation of the followers of Muhammed. From these early ascetics arose the *gussas* or storytellers, popular preachers of the Koran, and from the storytellers came the idea of the Madhi, the divinely guided one who will help bring the ultimate victory of Islam by means of a cosmic event. In the eighth century, the ascetic movement began to take on a mystical aspect, and true Sufism emerged.

Once launched, Sufism became a popular religious movement that developed its own forms and peculiarities. The *dhikr* and *sama*, the recitation of and meditation upon the Qur'an by the congregations, began to rival the mosque. The ecstatic experience offered the immediate knowledge of God, as compared to the second-hand knowledge of the theologians, who were replaced by the Sufi leaders, the *shaikhs*. These official teachers gained their position through charismatic authority. Outstanding shaikhs became founders of new schools of Sufism and were often regarded as saints after they died. Also, in contradistinction to the Qur'an, which looks down upon the unmarried state, many Sufi leaders practiced celibacy.

Sufism was an eclectic movement drawing on Christian and Gnostic elements. A pantheistic theology began to emerge, a possibility in any mystical system. More popular was a non-theological approach that accepted orthodoxy but included mysticism. One major innovation was the development of a gnostic spiritual hierarchy, populated with the saints and headed by the *Qutb*, the Pole of the World. The Qutb, who superintends the world through his hosts, resembles closely the platonic "demiurge," a subordinate deity who is the creator of the material world.

Love and fear vie in Sufi mysticism as the primary motivating force. Fear was the early focus of Sufi pietism, and the horror of hell was held up to men. Later, love assumed a dominant position. Rabi'a al-Adawiya (b. 801), a female saint and mystic, summed up the emphasis in a poem:

"I love Thee with two loves, love of my happiness,
And perfect love, to love Thee as is Thy due.
My selfish love is that I do naught
But think on Thee, excluding all beside,
But that purest love, which is Thy due,
Is that the veils which hide Thee fall, and I gaze on Thee.
No praise to me either this or that,
Nay, Thine the praise for both that love and this."

Sufism was in a constant battle for existence with the ruling orthodox religious leaders until the twelfth century. The change from persecution to acceptance is possibly attributable to the career of al-Ghazali (b. 1111), a man of marked intellectual acumen and religious insight. Beginning with a search for ultimate reality, he pursued a course through theology and philosophy and ended with the personal experience of God and Sufi mysticism. Al-Ghazali's greatest contribution seems to have been the creation of a religious synthesis through which Sufism could be accepted in an orthodox system and orthodoxy could become an acceptable framework for the Sufis.

The changes that came with al-Ghazali allowed the development of the Sufi schools. He promoted the idea that disciples should move in close association to their shaikh, who then began to assume a status like that of a Hindu guru. Brotherhoods built around a shaikh grew, and initiation ceremonies were adopted. Initiates would often leave to found affiliated groups. A popular school thus could spread (and on occasion did) throughout the Islamic world. When the leader died, an initiate would inherit the former leader's role and prayer rug.

According to Sufi tradition, 12 orders were founded prior to the establishment of the Ottoman Empire. The first was the Uwaisi, founded by Uwais following a vision of the Angel Gabriel in 659 C.E., less than forty years after the Hegira. Uwais pulled all of his teeth out in memory of Muhammed, who lost two teeth in a battle. His imposition of that same sacrifice for members insured that the Uwaisi remained small in size. The remaining 11 schools or orders, most of which have taken the name of their founder, are: Ill-wani, Adhani, Sustami, Saqati, Qadiri, Rifai, Nurbakhshi, Suharwardi, Qubrawi, Shazili, Mavlana, and Badawi. (Spelling of the names of the various Sufi orders varies from author to author as each tries to render the sound of the name into English. No standard spelling has yet been developed.)

Since the establishment of the Ottoman Empire and the subsequent spread of Islam from Indonesia to Albania, the number of orders has grown immensely and no catalog exists (though detailed lists for some countries do exist). The main orders in India at present are the Chishti, the Qadiri, the Suharwardi, and the Naqshbandi, two of which are of later origin. Other orders are prominent in other countries. Orders also have split into suborders. For example, both the Nizami and Sabiri suborders of the Chishti Order have a following in the United States, in the Chishti Order in America and the Sufi Order (headed by Pir Vilayat Khan) respectively.

In their homeland, members of orders can frequently be distinguished by the peculiar clothes they wear. Apparel will vary in color and style, especially the headgear. Several of the orders have become famous for their peculiar ritual formats, which include the whirling dances of the Jerrahi and the howling of the Rifai.

The first Sufi group to become visible in America was the Sufi Order, founded in the early twentieth century by Hazrat Khan. He was followed by Georgei Gurdjieff, the spiritual teacher so influenced by Sufism, who created a unique modern variation on the Sufi orders. During the 1970s representatives of many Sufi groups migrated to the United States and organized groups. Also, since the end of World War II, the Middle East, like India, has become the site for pilgrimages by spiritual seekers looking for mystic teachers. Several who found their gurus in a Sufi shaikh returned to the United States to found American branches of their shaikh's orders.

ZOROASTRIANISM. Zoroaster (or Zarathustra) was a Persian prophet and religious teacher of the seventh century B.C.E. who worked a monotheistic revolution in his native land. According to tradition, Zoroaster, when he was about 30 years of age, was admitted into the presence of Ahura Mazda, the supreme being, and was personally instructed in the doctrines of the new faith. Over the next few years, he received visions of the six archangels, the chief attendants and agents of Mazda. After 11 years of frustrating work, he was able to convert Vishtapa (Hystaspes), one of the rulers of Iran, who aided Zoroaster in spreading the new faith with two holy wars.

Zoroaster's faith was monotheistic. Mazda is the all-wise creator and absolute sovereign. Mazda demands righteousness and promises to help to men who follow truthfulness and justice and foster agriculture. The righteous will attain heaven. In the oldest Zoroastrian texts, Angra Mainyu appears as an evil spirit, but only in later years was he to arise as the evil counterpart of Mazda and to transform Zoroastrianism into a thorough-going dualism. The main representatives of this dualistic Zoroastrianism are the Parsees, many of whom have migrated to North America in recent decades.

BAHA'I WORLD FAITH. Among the newest of the several religious traditions to grow beyond the country of its founding into an international movement, the Baha'i World Faith originated in Persia (now Iran) in the mid-nineteenth century. Baha'is generally date their founding to the work of Siyyad Ali Muhammad of Shiraz (1819–1850), a prophet who declared himself the Bab, i.e., the Gate, through whom people would know about the advent of another messenger of God. His proclamations were made within the context of Islamic expectation of the Madhi, the successor of the previous messenger, Muhammed, the founder of Islam. The Bab began his prophetic work in 1844, but after gaining a large following he encountered the opposition of the country's Muslim leaders. He was eventually imprisoned by the Shah and, in 1850, executed.

Among the Bab's followers was Mirza Husayn-Ali (1817–92). During the time of the Bab's imprisonment, at a conference of his followers, he assumed the title "Baha," and emerged as one of the principal figures in the Babi community. In 1852, Jinab-i-Baha, as he was then called, was imprisoned in another wave of anti-Babi persecution. While languishing in a Tehran jail, he received the first intimations that he was, in fact, the one of whom the Bab spoke, "Him Whom God shall make manifest." Soon released from prison, he gradually assumed the prime leadership role among the Babis. Finally, in 1863, to a small group of family and friends, he announced his conviction that he was the Promised One foretold by the Bab.

Jinab-i-Baha's initial proclamation came just as a large segment of the Babi community was beginning an exile, first in Constantinople and then in Adrianople (now Edirne, Turkey). In Adrianople, he openly proclaimed his new role and new name, Baha'u'llah, "the Glory of God," through a series of letters, called tablets, sent to many world rulers and political leaders.

In 1868, Baha'u'llah and his family were further banished to Akka (now Acre) in Palestine, where he lived the remainder of his life, first at a penal colony and from 1879 in a residence in the city. During this period he wrote his most important book, the *Kitab-i-Agdas* (the Most Holy Book), the book of laws for Baha'is, as well as numerous shorter works, all now considered to have the authority of scripture.

Baha'u'llah was succeeded by his son, Abbas Effendi (1844–1921), who took the name Abdu'l-Baha, "the Slave of Baha." A devoted follower of his father even before the initial proclamation of his role in 1866, he followed Baha'u'llah into exile and wrote the first history of the movement in 1886. He assumed control of the movement under the authority of his father's will.

As the Center of the Covenant, Abdu'l-Baha directed the international spread of the movement. Following his confinement from 1901 to 1908 and the discontinuance of travel restrictions in 1911, he made the first of several foreign tours. A world tour the following year brought him to the United States, where he dedicated the grounds for the Baha'i temple in Wilmette, Illinois. Returning to Palestine just before World War I, he settled in Haifa, where Turkish authorities again confined him until the British took control.

As the interpreter of Baha'u'llah, Abdu'l-Baha summarized the major themes of the new faith revealed by his father. He emphasized its universal character: that all religions were essentially one and that all the prophets of God, the Great Manifestations, taught the same religion. He expounded the eleven principles of the Baha'i Faith: (1) the independent investigation of truth; (2) the oneness of the human race; (3) that religion should be the cause of love and affection (not hate); (4) the conformity of religion to science and reason; (5) the abolition of religious, racial, political, and patriotic prejudice; (6) the equal opportunity to the means of existence; (7) the equality of persons before the law; (8) universal peace; (9) the noninterference of religion in politics; (10) the equality of the sexes; and (11) the power of the Holy Spirit as the means of spiritual development. He also advocated a universal language and universal compulsory education.

Abdu'l-Baha was succeeded by his nephew Shoghi Effendi, who did much to develop the international organization and administration of the faith. Under Shoghi Effendi, the Baha'is established a following on every continent. Since his death, a more collective form of leadership has emerged.

BAHA'IS IN AMERICA. The Baha'i faith was brought to America in 1892 by a Lebanese convert, Ibrahim Kheiralla. A former businessman, Kheiralla proved to be an energetic teacher and soon gathered groups of eager students. The first Baha'i groups were formed in Chicago, New York, Boston, and Kenosha, Wisconsin.

During the 1890s, there were almost no copies of English translations of the writings of Baha'u'llah in print. In the absence of published volumes, Kheiralla taught a full course on the Baha'i faith, but presented what Baha'is soon discerned was a highly distorted version influenced by Kheiralla's occult speculations. Eventually Kheiralla published his peculiar teachings in several books. Kheiralla's deviations from Baha'i teachings reached a crisis during a pilgrimage by American Baha'is to meet Abdu'l-Baha during the winter of 1898–99. Abdu'l-Baha's discovery of the content of Kheiralla teachings led to a heated argument and to Andu'l-Baha's rejection of Kheiralla's speculative presentation of the faith. Kheiralla in turn rejected Abdu'l-Baha and, continuing in his own presentation of the faith, took supporters from the Chicago and Kenosha Baha'i groups and established a rival organization. The Behaists, as Kheiralla termed his followers, existed for several decades, but then disbanded. Kheiralla is now remembered as a covenant breaker, a term applied to individuals who attempt to establish rival Baha'i organizations, and American Baha'is generally remember their history as beginning with Thornton Chase, the first American convert.

BAHA'IS IN CANADA. Baha'ism in Canada began in 1898 when Gus Magee, a Chicago newspaperman who had interviewed an early Baha'i believer, passed on what he had learned to a niece who lived in London, Ontario. The niece told her mother, who traveled to Chicago with her two daughters for lessons in faith. The faith began in Quebec in 1902 when May Bolles, who had married Canadian architect William Sutherland Maxwell, moved to Montreal. The Maxwell home became the center of Baha'i activities, which received a boost in 1912 when Baha'u'llah came to Montreal. Later, Shoghi Effendi, the guardian of the faith, married Mary Maxwell, their daughter.

Originally, the Baha'i work in Canada was incorporated under the care of the Spiritual Assembly, which was headquartered in the United States. It grew slowly until the 1930s, but in 1937 a seven year plan was inaugurated that led to the formation of at least one Baha'i local assembly in every state and province of the country. In 1949, the work in Canada had grown to the point that it was set apart from the United States and its own Spiritual Assembly was incorporated.

Sources—Middle Eastern Family, Part II

ISLAM—GENERAL SOURCES

Study of Islam in America has grown primarily in the religious studies departments of various universities but has been given some focus in *The Muslim World*, a quarterly journal published by the Duncan Black Macdonald Center for the Study of Islam and Christian/Muslim Relations, c/o Hartford Seminary, 77 Sherman St., Hartford, CT 06105. Those seeking information on the American Muslim community may contact the American Muslim Council, 121 New York Ave., N.W., Ste 525, Washington, DC 20005.

The Baha'i center in Illinois houses the American Baha'i Faith Archives and Library, which can be contacted for further information on the Baha'i faith. It is located at 535 Sheridan Road, Willmette, IL 60091.

Abdalati, Hummudah. *Islam in Focus.* N.p.: The Author, n.d. 211 pp.

Ede, David. *Guide to Islam.* Boston: G. K. Hall & Co., 1983. 261 pp.

Farah, Ceasar E. *Islam.* Woodbury, NY: Barron's Educational Series, 1968. 306 pp.

Galwash, Ahmad A. *The Religion of Islam.* 2 Vols. Doha, Qatar: Educational and Cultural Ministry, 1973.

Geddes, C. L. *An Analytical Guide to the Bibliographies on Islam, Muhammad, and the Qur'an.* Denver: American Institute of Islamic Studies, 1973. 102 pp.

———. *Books in English on Islam, Muhammad, and the Qur'an: A Selected and Annotated Bibliography.* Denver: American Institute of Islamic Studies, 1976. 68 pp.

Haneef, Suzanne. *What Everyone Should Know About Islam and Muslims.* Chicago: Kazi Brothers, 1979. 202 pp.

Hussain, Asaf. *Islamic Movements in Egypt, Pakistan and Iran.* London: Mansell Publishing, 1983. 168 pp.

Islam in Paperback. Denver: American Institute of Islamic Studies, 1969. 70 pp.

Maududi, Sayyid Abul Ala. *Towards Understanding Islam.* Lahore, Pakistan: Idara Tarjuman-Ul-Quran, 1974. 179 pp.

Nomani, M. Manzoor. *Islamic Faith and Practice.* Lucknow, India: Academy of Islamic Research and Publications, 1973. 168 pp.

Rahman, Fazlur. *Islam.* Garden City, NY: Doubleday, 1968. 331 pp.

MUSLIMS IN AMERICA

Elkholy, Abdo A. *The Arab Moslems in the United States.* New Haven, CT: College and University Press, 1966. 176 pp.

Haddad, Yvonne Yazbeck. *Islamic Values in the United States.* New York: Oxford University Press, 1987. 196 pp.

Haddad, Yvonne Yazbeck, ed. *The Muslims of America.* New York: Oxford University Press, 1991. 249 pp.

Khalidi, Omar, ed. *Indian Muslims in North America.* Watertown, MA: South Asia Press, 1989. 99 pp.

Koszegi, Michael A., and J. Gordon Melton. *Islam in North America: A Sourcebook.* New York: Garland Publishing, 1992. 414 pp.

Metcalf, Barbara Daly. *Making Muslim Space in the North American and Europe.* Berkeley: University of California Press, 1996. 264 pp.

Richardson, E. Allen. *Islamic Cultures in North America.* New York: Pilgrim Press, 1981. 64 pp.

Waugh, Earle H., Baha Abu-Laban, and Regula B. Qureshi, eds. *The Muslim Community in North America.* Edmonton, AB: University of Alberta Press, 1983. 316 pp.

Williams, Raymond Brady. *Religions of Immigrants from India and Pakistan: New Threads in the American Tapestry.* Cambridge: Cambridge University Press, 1988. 326 pp.

SHI'ITE MUSLIMS

Fischer, Michael M. S. *Debating Muslims: Cultural Dialogues in Postmodernity and Tradition.* Madison, WI: University of Wisconsin Press, 1990. 564 pp.

Haddad, Yvonne. *Islamic Values in the United States.* New York: Oxford University Press, 1987. 196 pp.

Khomeini, Ruhollah. *Islamic Government.* New York: Manor Books, 1979. 154 pp.

Lalljee, Iman. *Know Your Islam.* Elmhurst, NY: Tahrike Tarsile Qur'an, 1986. 255 pp.

Tabatabai, Allamah Sayyid Muhammad Husayn. *Shi'ite Islam.* Houston, TX: Free Islamic Literature, 1979. 253 pp.

ul-Amine, Hasan. *Shorter Islamic Shi'ite Encyclopedia.* Beirut: n.p., 1969. 355 pp.

SUFISM

Arberry, A. J. *Sufism.* New York: Harper & Row, 1950. 141 pp.

Baldick, Julian. *Mystical Islam: An Introduction to Sufism.* London: B. Tauris & Co., 1989. 208 pp.

Driscoll, J. Walter, and the Gurdjieff Foundation of California. *Gurdjieff, An Annotated Bibliography.* New York: Garland Publishing, 1985. 363 pp.

Grisell, Ronald. *Sufism.* Berkeley, CA: Rose Books, 1983. 112 pp.

Nicholson, Reynold A. *The Mystics of Islam.* New York: Schocken Books, 1975. 178 pp.

Rastogi, T. C. *Islamic Mysticism Sufism.* London: East-West Publications, 1982. 126 pp.

Shah, Indries. *The Diffusion of Sufi Ideas in the West.* Boulder, CO: Keysign Press, 1972. 212 pp.

———. *The Sufis.* Garden City, NY: Doubleday, 1971. 451 pp.

Shah, Sirdar Ikbal Ali. *Islamic Sufism.* New York: Samuel Weiser, 1971. 299 pp.

Subhan, John A. *Sufism, Its Saints and Shrines.* New York: Samuel Weiser, 1970. 412 pp.

Trimingham, J. Spencer. *The Sufi Orders of Islam.* London: Oxford University Press, 1971. 333 pp.

Williams, L. F. Rushbrook. *Sufi Studies: East and West.* New York: E. P. Dutton, 1974. 260 pp.

BLACK MUSLIMS

Austin, Allan D. *African Muslims in Antebellum America, A Sourcebook.* New York: Garland Publishers, 1984. 759 pp.

Barboza, Steven. *American Jihad: Islam After Malcolm X.* New York: Doubleday, 1994. 370 pp.

Craig, H. A. L. *Bilal.* London: Quartet Books, 1977. 158 pp.

Essien-Udom, E. U. *Black Nationalism.* New York: Dell, 1962. 448 pp.

Lee, Martha F. *The Nation of Islam, an American Millinarian Movement.* Studies in Religion and Society 21. Lewiston, NY: The Edwin Mellen Press, 1988. 163 pp.

Lincoln, C. Eric. *The Black Muslims in America.* Boston: Beacon Press, 1961. 276 pp.

Mansour, Khalid Abdullah Taria Al, and Faissal Fahd Al Talal. *The Challenges of Spreading Islam in America.* San Francisco: The Authors, 1980. 213 pp.

AHMADIYYA

Ahmad, Mirza Bashiruddin Mahmud. *Ahmadiyyat or True Islam.* Washington, DC: The American Fazl Mosque, 1951. 246 pp.

Dard, A. R. *Life of Ahmad.* Lahore: Tabshir Publication, 1948. 629 pp.

Hammann, Louis J. *Ahmadiyyat: An Introduction.* Washington, DC: Ahmadiyya Movement in Islam, 1985. 13 pp.

Khan, Muhammad Zafrulla. *Ahmadiyyat, The Renaissance of Islam*. Lahore: Tabshir Publications, 1978. 360 pp.

Nafwi, S. Abul Hasan Ali. *Oadianism, A Critical Study*. Lucknow, India: Academy of Islamic Research and Publications, 1974. 167 pp.

ZOROASTRIANISM

Bode, Dastur Framroze Ardeshir, and Piloo Nanavutty. *Songs of Zarathushtra*. London: George Allen & Unwin, 1952. 127 pp.

Dawson, Miles Menander. *The Ethical Religion of Zoroaster*. New York: AMS Press, 1969. 271 pp.

Hinnells, John R. *Zoroastrians in Britain*. Oxford: Claredon Press, 1996. 336 pp.

Masani, Rustom P. *The Religion of the Good Life, Zoroastrianism*. London: George Allen & Unwin, 1938. 189 pp.

Modi, Jivanji J. *The Religious Ceremonies and Customs of the Parsees*. New York: Garland Publishing, 1979. 536 pp.

BAHA'I FAITH

Balyuzi, H. M. *'Abdu'l-Baha*. London: George Ronald, 1971. 560 pp.

Bjorling, Joel. *The Baha'i Faith, A Historical Bibliography*. New York: Garland Publishing, 1985. 168 pp.

Baha'u'llah, The King of Glory. London: George Ronald, 1980. 539 pp.

Collins, William P. *Bibliography of English-Language Works on the Babi and Baha'i Faith, 1845–1985*. Willmette, IL: Baha'i Publishing Trust, 1991. 550 pp.

Edward Granville Browne and the Baha'i Faith. London: George Ronald, 1970. 142 pp.

Gayer, Jessyca Russell. *Baha'i Faith*. New York: Award Books, 1967. 222 pp.

Hatcher, William S., and J. Douglas Martin. *The Baha'i Faith*. San Francisco: Harper & Row, 1984. 226 pp.

Miller, William McElwee. *The Baha'i Faith: Its History and Teachings*. South Pasadena, CA: William Carey Press, 1974.

Perkins, Mary, and Philip Hainsworth. *The Baha'i Faith*. London: Ward Lock Educational, 1980. 96 pp.

Release the Sun. Wilmette, IL: Baha'i Publishing Trust, 1971. 250 pp.

Sears, William. *The Prisoner of Kings*. Toronto: General Publishing Company, 1971. 240 pp.

Stockman, Robert S. *The Baha'i Faith in America*. Wilmette, IL: Baha'i Publishing Trust, 1985. 277 pp.

Chapter 23

Eastern Family
Part I: Hinduism, Jainism, Sikhism

Consult the "Contents" pages to locate the entries in Part III,
the Directory Listings Sections, that comprise this family.

HINDUISM. What is Hinduism? Of no major religious community is this type of question more difficult to answer. It is without an individual founder, has only a vaguely defined relation to an authoritative scripture, and has no single set of issues around which it can orient itself. Some writers, in the face of this frustration, have tried to turn these problems into a positive polemic for Hinduism by seeing its systematic anarchy as a sign of Hinduism's universal character. "Hinduism is absolutely indefinite...It rejects nothing. It is all-comprehensive, all-absorbing, all-complacent," says one Hindu writer.

Yet on a second look, Hinduism is not so vague as might first appear. While there is a great diversity of opinion among Hindus, it is no greater than among Christians. While Hinduism has no founders, it does have some mythological figures to which it relates. Despite a variety of ideas and emphases, Hindus do possess certain ideas in common, such as a belief in reincarnation and karma, and they do practice certain disciplines, the most common of which is yoga. Hindus also relate to a common history, that of India. Certain writings have a great value for them although the Vedas and Upanishads have only rarely functioned as has the Bible or Qur'an. Hinduism might thus be defined as a set of religions that positively relate to several mythological figures (Krishna, Rama), some metaphysical ideas and practices (reincarnation, karma, yoga), two sets of writings (the Vedas and Upanishads), and a people's history. That definition seems to describe justly the Hindus while distinguishing them from other religious groupings, particularly the Jains and Sikhs (also discussed in this chapter).

Indian and Hindu history can be divided roughly into four periods. The first is defined as pre-Vedic. Prior to the invasion of India by the Aryans, or Indo-Europeans, a culture on a par with that of the ancient Mediterranean basin existed, the artifacts of which have only recently and partially been uncovered. While religious articles have been found, no picture of this people's religious faith has emerged.

The second or Vedic period begins with the invasion of India by the Indo-Europeans. The waves of Aryan migration have been variously dated from 5000 B.C.E. to 1500 B.C.E. The primary document of this period is the *Rig Veda*, the oldest of India's existing sacred books. The *Rig Veda* is actually 10 books of hymns and prayers to the gods, collected probably about 1000 B.C.E. The Vedas present a very vigorous, worldly religion oriented to nature and a pastoral, agricultural life. These people of the Vedic period had a positive view of the world and saw their survival of death as a continuation of the good life. Along with the various gods, particular attention was paid to Soma, the deified intoxicant of the soma plant.

The third period of India's history begins in the several centuries following 1000 B.C.E. and represents a significant shift in religious outlook, which the Aryan invasion must have brought to the previous Indian culture. The change in outlook is from a positive view of life to a pessimistic world-fleeing one. The two ideas that symbolized this change are transmigration or reincarnation and

karma. Transmigration is the idea that a person may go through a succession of earthly lives, in some of which he may be an animal (and in more extreme forms of Hinduism, a plant). All of life is on the wheel of rebirth, and the goal of life is to escape physical rebirth by reaching spiritual perfection. Part of the rationale for the rebirth theory is karma. Karma is the principle of retribution, an inexorable law of justice that brings upon the individual the consequences of his actions—whether the actions were performed in his current life or in an earlier life. The goal in life is to escape karma, good or bad.

Escape from karma is by absorption in the world-soul, Brahman. How can absorption be accomplished? Some groups advocate attention to ceremonies at the local temple, others emphasize the moral life. Among the more common answers among those Hindu groups that have a presence in North America is *yoga,* a spiritual discipline designed to lead man to self-integration and then to integration with Brahman. The best known of the several forms of yoga in the West (though not as widely practiced in India or among Indian Americans) is *hatha yoga,* which includes a series of body postures (*asanas*) designed to bring the body into a state of harmony. Hatha yoga is a discipline used in the East for body integration and control and as a preliminary to the four higher forms of yoga. In the West, hatha yoga has been put to a variety of uses in physical culture quite apart from Hindu notions.

The four paths to God by yoga are *bhakti yoga* (to God through devotion and/or love), *jnana yoga* (to God through knowledge), *karma yoga* (to God through work), and *raja* (royal) *yoga* (to God through meditative exercises). These four, more advanced yogas are designed for the various types of people, according to Hindu analysis. Some people, being basically reflective, find the ideas and the philosophical, logical demonstrations of jnana yoga suited to their innate patterns. By taking thought, the jnana yoga student can come to a realization that many levels of self are finite, and the student can discern his eternal self beyond the finite qualities of size, shape, emotions, etc. For the basically emotional person, bhakti yoga gives direction to man's most powerful emotion, love. Man tends to become like that which he loves; thus, bhakti yoga directs man's amazing potentials of love toward God. A major feature of bhakti yoga is *japa,* the practice of repeating the name of God. (A Christian form of this practice is the Jesus prayer in classical Russian Orthodoxy.) The active person can be guided on a path to God through work. The smallest activity of life can be done wisely as a Godward practice—karma yoga. The highest path to God is through raja yoga, the royal road to reintegration. By meditation, the self penetrates the layers of the merely human until it reaches the beyond that is within. While bhakti yoga is most popular in India, raja tends to be the most popular in North America.

Associated with the Upanishads were several subsidiary developments. The most important was the rise of the Brahmins, the priestly class, as the highest level of the caste system in India. The rule of the Brahmins would dominate Indian life and lead to reactions by later movements. The idea of *maya* or illusion developed at this period. Common to most Hinduism is the belief that outward life and suffering are mere illusion and that realization of this fact will lead to release from suffering. *Ahimsa* is the highest of ethical precepts for Hinduism (it is also popular in several other religions) and is the vow of non-injury to life, non-killing. Ahimsa is the foundation of vegetarianism.

Later Developments. The collecting of the Upanishads became a watershed in Hindu history as it completed the writings to which Hindus would give a more or less universal authority. From these writings the various schools of interpretation would arise, and to these writings later movements would react. Development proceeded at a normal pace until the early 1800s when a disjunctive event, the invasion and conquest of India by England, changed the whole course of Indian history. The coming of the British marked the arrival of an alien culture and an alien religion, backed by political power. In the face of the development of a vigorous Christian mission, an initial defensive reaction was followed by a creative Hindu Renaissance, which produced a number of outstanding leaders (such as Ram Mohan Roy and Sri Ramakrishna) and movements. These movements, in many cases, were important in the nationalist drives of the twentieth century and in Hinduism's movement into North America.

Within Hindu circles, four figures are particularly important—*guru, swami, avatar,* and *chela*. A guru is a religious teacher who instructs the chela (or pupil) basically out of the knowledge s/he has received either by inspired realization or years of practice of a spiritual discipline. The ideal of the guru is to become a *satguru*, or perfect master. The knowledge to be imparted by the guru to the chela is both technique and the mystic reality (Brahman), which is the goal of the religious life. The guru may also be a swami (or monk) who also functions as a teacher and religious leader. Some gurus are also recognized as an avatar, i.e., an incarnation of God, and thus properly an object of veneration and worship.

Increasingly, since the British made Christianity a force in India, the guru and swami have taken on a new function. In pre-Christian India, there was little or no congregational worship apart from the large seasonal festivals. The guru arose as a leader of an isolated ashram (retreat center) inhabited by only a few close disciples. Increasingly, the guru has become a resident of a population center and the leader of mass movements. Influenced by Christian worship, the urban ashram with regular gatherings of the guru's followers is becoming a significant mode of religious expression.

THE HINDU SAMPRADAYAS. Like American Christianity, Indian Hinduism is divided into a number of denominational-like groups, called *sampradayas*. Basic to Hinduism is the division of those groups in the northern half of the nation from those in the southern half. They work on different ritual calendars, which causes them to celebrate major festivals at different times. A second major division, roughly analogous to the Christian divisions of Catholic, Protestant, and Orthodox, separates Hindu groups into the Vaishnava, Shaiva, and Shakta. The Vaishnava groups worship Vishnu as the primary deity in the Hindu pantheon and emerged as a recognizable group around the fifth century B.C.E. In India, the majority of temples seen throughout the countryside are Vaishnava centers, and Vaishnava holymen, both monks and individual renounciates, can be seen in their typical white robes and the vertical markings (*tilaks*) on their foreheads. Over the centuries, Vaishnavas have focused their attention upon a variety of Vishnu's incarnations; however, that of Krishna has been the most popular. The merger of Vishnu, the hero of the Hindu classic the *Mahabharata*, with Vasudeva-Krishna occurred over the period of the writing of the *Mahabharata* and becomes complete in the *Bhagavad Gita*, a late insertion into the text.

The Gita also introduces a prime emphasis of Vaishnava Hinduism, bhakti yoga or devotional service. The volume, a dialogue between the god Krishna and his human devotee Arjuna, discusses the more traditional approach to the deity through gifts, sacrifices, and austerities (i.e., jnana and raja yoga), and then points the reader to the truer path of devoted service as the means to really approach Vishnu-Krishna.

Over the centuries, four main Vaishnava sampradayas (denominations) have arisen. The Sri Vaishnavas, traditionally considered the oldest of the four, is said to have started with Vishnu and his wife Shri Lakshmi (hence the popular name of the group), but emerged as a distinct path under Ramanuja in the early twelfth century. Ramanuja most clearly established both the position of theistic worship as opposed to the allegiance to an impersonal divine reality of the Saivites and the legitimacy of devotional service as the way of salvation.

The Nimbarki (or Namawat) Sampradaya was founded by Nimbarkiacharya who taught a theology that might be termed dualistic monism. Human souls (and the world in general) are seen as both different from God, being endowed with their own qualities and limitations, but at the same time not different since God is omnipresent and souls depend upon Him.

The Madhwaguariya Sampradaya was founded by the famous Bengali fifteenth century saint Chaitanya Mahaprabhu. Centering his activity upon the Gita and the *Srimad Bhagavatam*, a voluminous devotional work on Krishna, Chaitanya taught the practice of *sankirtan*, the multiple recitation of the God's name, as the most acceptable form of devotional activity in the present age. His perspective became well known in America in the 1970s through the high visibility of the Hare Krishna Movement, one of several representatives of the Madhwaguariya in the West.

The Brahma Sampradaya, generally traced to Madhwacharya in the thirteenth century, centers its worship on Vayu, the air god. According to Madhwacharya, regarded as an incarnation of Vayu, Vishnu communicated his truths to Brahma who in turn spread them to humanity through the aid of Vayu. Present day salvation comes by worship of Vayu.

Competing with the Vaishnavas for the loyalties of Hindus are the Shaivas, those who worship Shiva (or Siva) as the one great God. Shiva appears very early in the Vedas and Upanishads as a principle deity, but the *Mahabharata* contains a full description of the popular Shiva. He is seen as both the great yogi who practices jnana and raja yoga in his mountain home and the creative deity symbolized by his lingam (phallus), a symbol centrally located in many Shaiva temples and worn (as is the yoni of his wife) by many devotees.

Two figures stand out in Shaiva history, Patanjali and Shankaracharya. Patanjali, about whom almost nothing is known (including the century in which he lived), brought together the scattered teachings on yoga and organized them into a system of practice, the following of which constituted the major method by which an individual could become united or yoked to God. Within the Shaiva community, yoga is given varying degrees of emphasis from those who practice it as the major avenue of spiritual enlightenment, to those who integrate it into a larger slavic scheme, to those who discount its significance. The practice of hatha yoga (asanas) is much more prominent in the American Hindu community than in India.

The goal of Patanjali's system was *samadhi*, a state of cosmic awareness reached through the control of body and mind. Practice begins with the negative discipline of *yama* (abstention from violence, falsehood, theft, incontinence, and acquisitiveness) and the positive observance of *niyama* (purity, contentment, austerities, study, and dedicated activity). Accompanying these overall disciplines was the practice of *asanas* (postures) of hatha yoga, *pranayama* (disciplined breathing), and *pratyahara* (detachment of the mind from senses by which it is connected to the outside world). Once the mind and body are suppressed, the yogi can progress to the ultimate three stages, *dharana* (contemplation), *dhayna* (meditation), and *samadhi*.

A major reorganization of Shaiva thought and worship occurred in the eighth century under Shankaracharya (788–820 C.E.).

Shankaracharya became the major exponent of *advaita* (nondualistic or monistic) philosophy centered upon the sole reality of the impersonal Brahman. Brahman, the really real, is devoid of qualities. The phenomenal world with its qualities, designations, and forms is *maya*, illusion, believed to be real because of *avidya* (ignorance). If the world is illusion, so are most religious practices and beliefs, such as that in a personal god. The avenue beyond ignorance is jnana (knowledge) resulting from withdrawal from maya and contemplation on Brahman.

Shankaracharya's perspective led in two directions. First and foremost, he had little concern for lay Hindus and believed that jnana could only truly be practiced by one living a renounced life. He thus gave a great impetus to the orders of renounciates, the sanyasis. On a practical level, he reorganized the sanyasin around four monastic centers (one in each part of India) and 10 orders, two or three of which were attached to each math (or monastery). The leaders of the four Sankara maths are among the most respected leaders in all of Hinduism, though their ultimate power is more informal that organizational. The four centers and the orders attached to each are as follows:

Jyotir Math (North)
  –Giri
  –Parwat
  –Sagar
Shringeri (South)
  –Saraswati
  –Bharati
  –Puri
Govardhan (East)
  –Arayna
  –Van
Sharda (West)
  –Tirtha
  –Ashram

A sanyasi renounces any connection with the world, including his family and any means of worldly occupation and support, and dons an orange (ochre) robe. He may be nomadic for part or all of his life. He may also engage in religious teachings, and many of the twentieth century Hindu sampradayas have been formed by a sanyasi (or his Vaishnava counterpart) who gathers a personal following.

While Shankaracharya discounted most religious practice, he did recognize its possible value as a preparation for jnana and the renounced life. Thus, Sankara's philosophy mixed with the popular temple worship of Shiva and the associated deities in what is termed the Smarta tradition. Smartas follow the sutras or aphorisms of the Smriti, or memorized tradition. These detail the practices accompanying proper worship of the Vedic deities. The Smartas emphasize the *dharmma* (duties) of *puja* (worship).

Typical of Smarta ritual is the *puja* of the five shrines, centered upon the worship of five deities: Shiva; Vishnu; Ganesh (Ganesa), the elephant-headed god who removes obstacles; Surya, the sun god; and Durga, the consort of Shiva. The Smarta tradition has been brought to the United States by Hindu immigrants during the last two decades.

The third major group of Hindus, present in the United States in much greater proportion than in India, the Shaktas worship Shakti, one name of the female consort of Shiva. The practices of the Shaktas dramatize within the human the reunion of the passive Shiva with the dynamic Shakti, thus bringing enlightenment. This tradition emerged out of the Shaiva tradition around the fifth century B.C.E. with the production of a new set of ritual books called Agamas or Tantras.

The Shaktas or Tantrics, as they are popularly called, emphasize the presence of the Shakti or female power within the human body. Commonly referred to as kundalini, a coil of power resting in potential at the base of the spine, it can be activated by specific practices and ritual procedures. Like a snake, kundalini awakens and springs upward.

Tantrics have also developed a unique view of the human body as possessing, in addition to the physical body, a subtle anatomy consisting of seven *chakras* (cosmic energy centers) located along the spine from its lower tip to the crown of the head, tied together by *nadas* (energy pathways). The practice of kundalini yoga releases the Shakti to rise through the chakras to the crown chakra. By thus bringing the dynamic Shakti back into union with the more passive Shiva, enlightenment is produced.

The Shaktas are also to be distinguished from the Shaivas by their acceptance of the world. Enlightenment is to be received by using the world, not by denying it. The most controversial practice of the Shaktas has been the ritual use of the very items Shaivas avoid as most harmful to the person seeking spiritual progression since they excite the outward senses. The so-called *pancamakara* (five m's) ritual involves the partaking of wine, meat, fish, grain (considered an aphrodisiac), and sexual intercourse (in Sanskrit each word begins with "m"). In the West, the word tantra has become (though quite incorrectly) synonymous with any form of sexual magic.

HINDUISM IN AMERICA. The history of Hinduism in America begins long before any guru came to the United States to expound his tenets. During the seventeenth century, colonists and missionaries began an active relationship with India that led to the translation into English of many of the Hindu sacred writings. Some of these, particularly the *Bhagavad Gita*, had a direct and powerful influence upon New Englanders, particularly Ralph Waldo Emerson and the other leaders of the Transcendentalist movement.

As the Transcendentalists absorbed the insights of Hindu literature, Hindus were responding to the impact of Christianity. Among the reformist movements that developed both as a positive response to Christianity and a new presentation of Hinduism was The Brahmo Samaj, led by Ram Mohan Roy. The Brahmo Samaj was based upon the monotheism of the Upanishads and advocated the abandonment of all image worship. Roy's first book, *The Precepts of Jesus* (1820), reprinted in America in 1825, aroused a great deal of controversy but found some acceptance among early Unitarians. In the 1850s, Unitarian Charles Dall and Brahmo Samaj leader Keschub Chunder Sen developed a friendship that led to a relationship between the two organizations that is still active.

The first Hindu guru to come to America was a representative of the Brahmo Samaj. Protap Chunder Mozoomdar delivered his first American address on September 2, 1883, in the parlor of the widow of Ralph Waldo Emerson in Concord, Massachusetts. His brief tour was the only appearance by a Hindu teacher until the monumental events of 1893.

In 1893, Mozoomdar was one of several Hindus who came to America for the World's Parliament of Religions. His addresses at this first international conclave between representatives of the major Eastern and Western faiths was eclipsed, however, by the appearance of Swami Vivekananda, the young flamboyant disciple of the late Sri Ramakrishna. His impact was so great that he left the Parliament to tour the country for two years and eventually founded the first Hindu movement in America, the Vedanta Society. Returning to India in 1895, he organized the scattered disciples of Ramakrishna and found two, Swamis Abhedananda and Turiyananda, to head the Vedanta groups already formed in New York and San Francisco, respectively.

A small wave of immigration from India beginning in the 1890s brought other teachers. Swami Rama Tirtha, a young sanyasi, arrived in 1902 and lectured throughout America for the next two years. That same year, Baba Premanand Bharati, a Bengali disciple of Sri Chaitanya, began a five year stay during which time he organized the Krishna Samaj. He left behind disciples who carried his memory into the 1980s.

These early teachers from India were joined by Westerners who adopted Hindu teachings and expounded them through writings and the formation of groups. No writer surpassed the popularity of William Walker Atkinson, who began to write books on Hindu teachings under the pseudonym of Swami Ramacharacka in 1903. His thirteen books have remained in print since their initial appearance. Pierre Bernard, known to his followers by his religious name, Oom the Omnipotent, founded the first tantric organization, the Tantrick Order of America. In spite of the several scandals which hit it, Bernard's group lasted for several decades, and his nephew Theos Bernard wrote several classical texts in hatha yoga.

The growth of Hinduism was stymied in the decades during and after World War I. A growing anti-Asian sentiment, primarily directed against Chinese and Japanese Americans, included the Indians in its attack that led to the passing of the Asian Exclusion Act of 1917. This action effectively cut off Asian immigration for several generations and stymied what would have become, in all likelihood, the steady growth of Hinduism in the United States. Several years later, as the result of a lawsuit brought by Bhagat Singh Thind, an Indian Sikh, the Supreme Court ruled Indians ineligible for citizenship, an act that also revoked the citizenship to some who had already received it. Then, in 1927, Hinduism was viciously attacked in a best-selling volume, *Mother India,* by Katherine Mayo, a book credited with affecting Indian-American relations for a generation.

The Hindu community grew very slowly in the half century after the passing of the Asian Exclusion Act, but it did grow. A number of teachers were able to emigrate just prior to the passing of the law, and several stayed to found movements. For example, Besudeb Bhattacharya, a young playwright, came to New York, where he assumed the religious name Pundit Acharya and founded the Temple of Yoga, the Yoga Research Institute, and Prana Press. The most successful of the several gurus was Paramahansa Yogananada, who arrived in 1922 to attend an interfaith conference, but stayed to found the Yogoda-Satsang, known today as the Self-Realization Fellowship. His *Autobiography of a Yogi* (1946) was immensely popular and assisted the spread of Hinduism far beyond the fellowship.

Besides those mentioned above, other teachers who founded movements upon which modern American Hinduism is built were A. K. Mozumdar (Messianic World Message); Swami Omkar (Shanti Ashrama); Sri Deva Ram Sukul (Dharma Mandal); Rishi Krishnananda (Para-Vidya Center; Sant Ram Mandal [Universal Brotherhood Temple and School of Eastern Philosophy]); and Swami A. P. Mukerji (Transcendent Science Society). Joining them were a number of teachers who did not found their own groups but wrote a number of books that enjoyed a circulation among those interested in Eastern and esoteric philosophies, such as Bhagwan Singh Gyanee and Rishi Singh Grewal. Theosophy also contributed greatly to the growth of Hinduism through its continued dissemination of Indian books through the American occult community and its promotion of Jiddu Krishnamurti as the vehicle for the coming world savior.

Krishnamurti, a young Indian boy, had been picked out in the early twentieth century to be the cosmic figure predicted in Theosophical literature. He lectured through the 1920s on behalf of the Theosophical cause, while for health reasons he settled in Ojai, California. Then, in 1927, he renounced his messianic role and began a career as an independent teacher. Beginning with the remnants of his Theosophical following, he gradually attracted both an international audience and a following among academics. He became a forceful element in the build up of interest in Hinduism noticeable after World War II, whose most visible component, the spread of hatha yoga, was a far cry from Krishnamurti's emphases.

Just as 1893 and 1917 had become years of dramatic junctures in the history of American Hinduism, so was 1965. In the fall of that year, the Asian Exclusion Act was repealed and the immigration quotas from Asia were placed on a par with those of Europe.

The number of Indian immigrants jumped dramatically. Also, during the years that the Exclusion Act was in force, Indian teachers who were not opposed to teaching Hinduism to Westerners emerged in significant numbers. As quotas allowed, they came to America and began to build movements, primarily among young adults. Though Shaiva yoga teachers and Shakta tantric teachers were most successful, Vaishnavas were also represented.

The greatest number of Indian immigrants have not been teachers motivated by goals of building an American following; rather, they have been Hindu lay people faced with the task of reestablishing traditional and familiar temple structures in the West. As their numbers have increased, they have banded together to erect both Shaiva and Vaishnava temples and have brought priests from India to lead the ritual activities. The emergence of these traditional temples has completed the spectrum of Indian religion in North America. At present, the only significant element of Indian religious practice not evident in the larger Western Hindu community are the bands of holy men that roam the Indian countryside, many without clothes, living off the alms of the working people.

Also serving the Indian-American community is the Vishwa Hindu Parishad, an ecumenical group that has provided contact for Hindus across the boundaries created both by sectarian differences and the several Indian languages.

SIKHISM. The early sixteenth century was a time of bitter conflict in North India. A series of invasions that culminated in 1526 established Muslim supremacy. The Punjab area was one of the most hotly contested regions and it was here that Guru Nanak (1469–1539), the founder of Sikhism, was born. One day while bathing in a river, he had a vision of God's presence in which he was told to go into the world and teach the repetition of the name of God, the practice of charity, meditation and worship, and the keeping of ritual purity through absolution.

According to tradition, after a full day of silence, he uttered the pronouncement, "There is no Hindu (follower of the native faith of India) and no Musselman (Muslim)." He adopted a unique garb, which combined both Hindu and Muslim features, and developed an eclectic faith that took elements from many religions, mainly from Hindus and Muslims. From Islam he taught of One Creator God, called the True Name to avoid such designations as Allah or Vishnu. From Hinduism he taught the ideas of karma, reincarnation, and the ultimate unreality of the world. Nanak also emphasized the unique role of the guru (teacher) as necessary to lead people to God. After Nanak's death, nine gurus followed him in succession.

The fourth guru, Baba Ram Dass, began the Golden Temple of Amritsar, the present headquarters of the world Sikh community. The fifth guru, Arjan, completed the temple and installed the *Siri Guru Granth Sahib*, or *Adi Granth*, the collected writings of Nanak and the other gurus, within it.

The tenth guru, Gobind Singh (1666–1708), had the second most significant role in molding the Sikh community—second only to Nanak. Gobind Singh completed the *Adi Granth* and militarized the Sikhs by forming the Khalsa, the Community of the Pure. Members were initiated by baptism in which they drank and were sprinkled with sweetened water stirred with a sword. They changed their name to Singh (Lion) and adopted the five K's: (1) Kesh, or long hair, a sign of saintliness; (2) Kangh, a comb for keeping the hair neat; (3) Kach, short pants for quick movement in battle; (4) Kara, a steel bracelet signifying sternness and restraint; and (5) Kirpan, a sword of defense.

After Gobind Singh's death, the *Adi Granth* became the guru and no further human guru's were allowed. The military emphasis continued, however, and Sikhs served with distinction in British army units.

Sikhism in North America. As early as 1790, some unnamed East Indian visitors, possibly Sikhs, were said to have landed in Salem, Massachusetts. They were very much the exceptions, as Sikhs, mostly from Northern and Eastern India (the Punjab region), rarely traveled to the New World prior to the twentieth century. They were among the major religious groups not represented at the 1893 World's Parliament of Religions.

At the end of the nineteenth century, some Punjabis did develop a wander lust, seemingly occasioned by the 1897 diamond-jubilee celebration in London for Queen Victoria. On their return journey, the Sikh regiment that played at the event was taken across Canada. Members of the troop were impressed with the potential for farming in the prairie provinces. Traveling by way of Hong Kong, a few Sikhs reached Canada as early as 1903. In 1904 there were a reported 204 Sikhs in British Columbia. Most would arrive during the next four years. Of the several thousand who came into Canada, some settled in British Columbia, others headed immediately for the United States. Measures restricting Indian immigration into British Columbia and discriminatory legislation against the Indians by the government caused a shift of movement from Canada to the United States. Many Canadian Sikhs migrated southward. By 1915, there were approximately 7,000 Indians in America, the overwhelming majority being Sikhs and residents of California.

The first gurdwara, the Sikh's house of worship, where the copy of the scripture, the *Sri Guru Granth Sahib*, is enshrined and housing for the needy is provided, was begun in Vancouver in the summer of 1906 and opened in January 1908. It was modeled on the gurdwara in Hong Kong. Four years later a gurdwara was opened in Stockton, California. During the early twentieth century others were constructed in California and western Canada.

In 1917, the United States stopped almost all immigration from Asia and the Sikh community then numbering only in the thousands, stopped growing. The mostly male population found wives among their non-Indian neighbors, many of whom were Mexican. Immigration began to flow again after the 1965 change in immigration laws and the Sikh community has grown considerably. It is no longer bound to the West Coast and has established gurdwaras across the continent. In the 1970s, the Punjabi Sikh community was joined by a new organization, the Sikh Dharma, headed by Shri Singh Sahib Bhai Harbhajan Singh Khalsa Yogiji, popularly known simply as Yogi Bhajan. Bhajan concentrated his efforts on converting non-Indian Americans to the Sikh faith and has succeeded in building a national organization during his two decades of activity.

JAINISM. Jainism developed in the sixth century B.C.E. out of the teachings of Vardhamana Mahavira (599–527 B.C.E.) who, like his contemporary, Buddha, was born of a wealthy family that he rejected to become an ascetic. After some 20 years of meditation and mortification, he discovered enlightenment and became a *jina*, a conqueror, from which the name of the community he founded took its name. By the time of Mahavira's death, his followers numbered about ten thousand.

Jain theology is atheistic. It poses the existence of two realities—*jivas*, eternal souls, and *ajivas*, eternal, non-living, material elements. Humans are forced into cycles of reincarnation because their jiva has attached itself to ajiva. Attachment is by *karma*, the energy of the soul. Liberation is by directing one's life to reducing karma. Among the practices that aid liberation are: ahimsa, the non-hurting of life; preservation; proper control over the mind, speech, and body; carefulness, proper care in walking, speaking, eating, lifting, and lying; ascetic observances; meditation; and right conduct.

The austere practices required of Jains have led to some extremes. For example, the Digambara Jains reject the ownership of all property, including clothes, and encourage the practice of going naked. One recent visitor to the United States, Muni Sushil Kumarji, a Jain monk, made news because of the mask he wore (to prevent inhaling flies) and the brush he used (to gently sweep insects from his path so he would not step on them).

In 1893, Virchand A. Gandhi traveled to Chicago to address the World Parliament of Religions, a most impressive task. Like

Jains to follow, Gandhi was opposed by many co-religionists who felt that any travel, other than by foot, was morally wrong. From that time to 1972, only a few Jains, such as Champat Rai Jain, who ventured to England in the 1930s, found their way to the West. By 1975, a community of some 200 was reported in Chicago, with others scattered in various urban centers.

Sources—The Eastern Family, Part I

GENERAL SOURCES

Dasgupta, Shashibhusan. *Obscure Religious Cults.* Calcutta: Firma K. L. Mukhopadhyay, 1969. 436 pp.

Farquhar, J. N. *An Outline of the Religious Literature of India.* Dehli: Mitilal Banarsidass, 1967. 451 pp.

Ghurye, G. S. *Indian Sadhus.* Bombay: Popular Prakashan, 1964. 260 pp.

Griswold, Henry DeWitt. *Insights into Modern Hinduism.* New York: Henry Holt and Company, 1934. 288 pp.

Hopkins, Thomas J. *The Hindu Religious Tradition.* North Scituate, MA: Duxbury Press, 1971. 156 pp.

Johnson, Linda. *Daughters of the Goddess: The Women Saints of India.* St. Paul, MN: Yes International Publishers, 1994. 128 pp.

Pararignanar, Saiva Ilakkia. *The Development of Saiviam in South India.* Dharmapuram Adhinam, 1964. 359 pp.

Pereira, Jose. *Hindu Theology.* Garden City, NY: Doubleday, 1976. 558 pp.

Renou, Louis. *The Nature of Hinduism.* New York: Walker and Company, 1962. 155 pp.

Santucci, James A. *An Outline of Vedic Literature.* Missoula, MT: Scholars Press, 1976. 69 pp.

Tripathi, B. D. *Sadhus of India.* Bombay: Popular Prakashan, 1978. 258 pp.

Uban, Sujan Singh. *The Gurus of India.* London: Fine Books, 1977. 175 pp.

Wilson, H. H. *Religious Sects of the Hindus.* Calcutta: Susil Gupta, 1958. 221 pp.

HINDUISM IN AMERICA

Fisher, Maxine P. *The Indians of New York.* Columbia, MO: South Asia Books, 1980. 165 pp.

Jackson, Carl T. *The Oriental Religions and American Thought.* Westport, CT: Greenwood Press, 1981. 302 pp.

Kamath, M. V. *The United States and India, 1776–1976.* Washington, DC: The Embassy of India, 1976. 222 pp.

Riepe, Dale. *The Philosophy of India and Its Impact on American Thought.* Springfield, IL: Charles C. Thomas Publisher, 1970. 339 pp.

Thomas, Wendell. *Hinduism Invades America.* Boston: Beacon Press, 1930. 300 pp.

SIKHISM

Cole, W. Owen, and Piara Singh Sambhi. *The Sikhs.* London: Routledge & Kegan Paul, 1978. 210 pp.

Dhillon, Mahinder Singh. *A History Book of the Sikhs in Canada and California.* Vancouver, BC: Shromani Akali Dal Association of Canada 1981. 519 pp.

Juergensmeyer, Mark, and N. Gerald Barrier, eds. *Sikh Studies.* Berkeley, CA: Graduate Theological Union, 1979. 230 pp.

Kaur, Sardarni Premka. *Guru for the Aquarian Age.* Albuquerque, NM: Brotherhood of Life Books, 1972. 131 pp.

Macauliffe, Max Arthur. *The Sikh Religion.* New Delhi: S. Chand & Company, 1978. 6 Vols.

Mathur, L. P. *Indian Revolutionary Movement in the United States of America*. Delhi, India: S. Chand & Co., 1970. 169 pp.

Singh, Gopal. *The Religion of the Sikhs*. Bombay: Asia Publishing House, 1971. 191 pp.

SANT MAT

Fripp, Peter. *The Mystic Philosophy of Sant Mat*. London: Neville Spearman, 1964. 174 pp.

Johnson, Julian. *The Path of the Masters*. Punjab, India: Radha Soami Satsang Beas, 1972. 572 pp.

———. *With a Great Master in India*. Beas, India: Radha Swami Sat Sang, 1953. 200 pp.

Lane, David Christopher. *Radhasoami Parampara in Definition and Classification*. Berkeley, CA: M.A. thesis, Graduate Theological Union, 1981. 132 pp.

———. *The Radhasoami Tradition: A Critical History of Guru Successorship*. New York: Garland Publishing, 1992. 351 pp.

JAINISM

Gopalan, Subramania. *Outlines of Jainism*. New York: Halsted Press, 1973. 205 pp.

Jain, Muni Uttam Kamal. *Jaina Sects and Schools*. Delhi: Concept Publishing Company, 1975. 162 pp.

Roy, Ahim Kumar. *A History of the Jainas*. New Delhi: Gitanjali Press, 1984. 179 pp.

Stevenson, Mrs. Sinclair (Margaret). *The Heart of Jainism*. New Dehli: Munshiram Manoharlal, 1970. 336 pp.

Chapter 24

Eastern Family
Part II: Buddhism, Shintoism, Japanese New Religions

Consult the "Contents" pages to locate the entries in Part III,
the Directory Listings Sections, that comprise this family.

BUDDHISM. Buddhism can be traced to the experiences of Siddhartha Gautama, born a prince around 560 B.C.E. at Lumbini near the capital of the Kingdom of Shakya, India. Gautama is often called Shakyamuni or Sakyamuni, after his birthplace. According to early accounts of his life, Gautama grew up in the court and was shielded from contact with the real mundane world of the people he would someday rule. He married at 17 and fathered a child. However, his life changed dramatically in 529 B.C.E. when he departed from the palace, abandoned his worldly existence, and began a career as a wandering seeker for the meaning of life. Gautama spent the next six years visiting various Indian religious groups, sitting with several teachers of renown, and experimenting with many religious practices, such as asceticism and meditation. His search ended in 523 B.C.E., while he was in meditation and contemplation at the foot of a tree, a "Bodhi tree," located at Sarnath, a site still considered a hallowed Buddhist shrine. As this period of meditation began, Gautama is said to have made the following vow:

"Let my body be dried up on this seat,
Let my skin and bones and flesh be destroyed
So long as Bodhi is not attained...
My body and thought will not be removed from
this seat."

He attained the "Bodhi," or enlightenment, in 523 B.C.E., and as a result became known as Gautama the Buddha or the Enlightened One. After this enlightenment, Buddha began to preach and teach, and a group of disciples gathered around him. A movement began to grow, particularly in northwest India. Buddha died of dysentery about 480 B.C.E.

Much of the essence of Buddhism is found in the teachings of the Buddha, which outline the Dharma, the true way of life. The Dharma is remarkably simple, for all its profundity, and lends itself easily to a brief summary. All Buddhists share a belief in the Buddha's Dharma, which centers upon the four basic truths and the "noble eightfold path." The four basic truths are: 1) all existence entails suffering; 2) the cause of suffering is desire, i.e., the thirst for pleasure, prosperity, and continued life (it is this thirst for continued life that begets rebirth); 3) the way to escape suffering, existence, and rebirth is to rid one's self of desire; and 4) to be emancipated from desire, one must follow the eightfold path.

The noble eightfold path is pictured in the eight-spoked wheel, a symbol second only to the seated Buddha as a sign of Buddhist faith. The path consists of: 1) right understanding, 2) right resolve, 3) right speech, 4) right conduct, 5) right livelihood, 6) right effort, 7) right attention, and 8) right concentration. Various Buddhist groups would accept the eightfold path but disagree on their interpretation of it and the emphasis on, and priority of, certain aspects of it. This difference will often be manifest in the words that English Buddhist groups use to translate the language of the eightfold path in their literature.

For example, some groups, leaning toward a more intellectualized Buddhism, will translate the first step of the path as right belief

or knowledge. Zen Buddhists, pointing to the mystic and indescribable nature of Buddhist experience, will often translate it as right vision. Interpretations of right concentration, or the goal of nirvana, range from the present-mindedness of mystic Buddhism, which finds nirvana in the mystical experience, to the otherworldliness of various groups of Buddhists. Some of the variations will become evident below.

The basic scriptures of Buddhism, the *Tripitaka* or *Three Baskets*, are divided into the Vinaya, the Sutras, and the Abhidhamma. The Vinaya consists basically of rules for the monks and information on Buddha's life. The Sutras are a collection of material attributed to the Buddha and his close disciples. How much is actually Buddha's words is a matter of debate. The Abhidhamma is composed of discourses of Gautama. Other scriptures have been added to the *Tripitaka* by various national Buddhist bodies, and each particular group has its own interpretive material.

SPREAD OF BUDDHISM. Buddhism arose as a reformist sect of Hinduism and included many elements of Hindu thought within it, although it modified greatly certain ideas, such as the transmigration of the soul. After the crisis of Buddha's death, a council, which has become known in Buddhist history as the First Council, was held under the leadership of Kashyapa, a disciple of Buddha. Some basic decisions about doctrine and discipline were made that enabled the Buddhist movement to be organized and to spread. The Second Council was held in 377 B.C.E. after a group of monks revolted against the strict rules of the order and decided to reinterpret them. The Vaishali Council decided in favor of the strict interpretation and the lax monks seceded from the order. They represent the first major schismatic school.

The next significant date in Buddhist history is 270 B.C.E. This year saw the emergence of the Indian Empire with its ruler Asoka, the man who did more for the spread of Buddhism than anyone since its founder. In remorse and regret produced by his wars of conquest, Asoka was led to become a Buddhist monk (while still the emperor). Until Asoka, Buddhism was a local Indian sect, but with Asoka's help it was spread throughout his kingdom, to all of India, and into Ceylon, Nepal, and central Asia. Asoka had inherited an intensely missionary understanding of his faith from Buddhist scripture and implanted it within the movement. This missionary zeal has distinguished Buddhism from almost all other indigenous faiths of Southern Asia.

By the time of Asoka, Buddhism had begun to develop an extensive literature. First steps toward the development of a canon were probably made during Asoka's time at the so-called Third Council. This council was called to deal with the problems created by the large increase in nominal members, a result of the extensive growth following Asoka's missionary endeavors.

After Asoka's death, the center of Buddhism shifted to the Northwest (Kashmir, Kabul, Bactria, etc.), where a Greek friendly to Buddhism had established himself in power. The role of the Greek king, Menander, was doubly important. He provided a haven for Buddhists from Asoka's successors who were less than

189

devoted admirers of the growing faith. He also provided the influence that led to Buddhist art, particularly statues of Gautama. No representations of the Buddha survive prior to this period.

In the centuries before and after Asoka, the two main schools of Buddhism began to take a more pronounced form. The first of the schools to emerge was called Hinayana, or the Lesser Vehicle. Hinayana looked to the writings of Sariputra, an early disciple of Buddha whose method of interpreting Buddha's teachings was very conservative and emphasized the role of the monk and the monastic life as the way to nirvana. In reaction to the monk-oriented faith of Hinayana, there arose Mahayana Buddhism, the Greater Vehicle, which dates itself to Ananda and other early disciples of Buddha who did not accept the interpretations of Sariputra. Mahayana was much more open to the role of non-monks in the faith and held as a goal the ultimate salvation of all living beings. This universalist tendency made it a more efficient vehicle in which to carry the faith across Southeast Asia to Japan. As Buddhism spread, it not only took upon itself the national characteristics of each country but also generally related itself to one of the two major schools.

A term often used interchangeably with Hinayana is Theravada. The term applies to the *Tripitaka* or *Pali Canon* of Buddha's writing. The *Tripitaka* was finally put into writing during the first century B.C.E. The Hinayanists accepted it but the Mahayanists accepted only part of it and developed their own canon, which included various sutras that have become the basis of the widely differing Mahayana groups. Included would be such writings as the Lotus Sutra (used by Nichiren), the Diamond Sutra (used by some Zen groups) and the Sukhavati-Vyuha (used by the Pure Land groups).

Southeast Asian (Theravada) Buddhism. Asoka's son, Prince Mahinda, took Buddhism to Ceylon. Although the exact details of the conversion process are buried in legendary material, there is no doubt that Mahinda's activity established Buddhism in Anuradhapura, the capital, and among the royal family. Asoka sent to the new converts a scion of the sacred Bohdi tree, which is still preserved and venerated to the new converts, and the monastery Mahinda established became a center from which the stricter Hinayana could be spread.

Burma, like Ceylon, probably first heard of Buddhism as a result of Asoka's missionaries. For a period, a small Buddhist community established by Mahayanists vied for the allegiance of the people, but Hinayana became firmly established as the dominant faith in the sixth century C.E. following the spread of a Hinayanist revival emanating from Madras in India.

Thailand, formerly Siam, represents the other main center of the Hinayanist school. The origin of Buddhism in Thailand has been lost, but early in the Christian era Mahayana forms of Buddhism were co-existing with Brahmanism (Hinduism). Mahayana could possibly have entered from Cambodia during the era that the Cambodians ruled most of Indochina. (The Cambodians had received Buddhism from Indian merchants and settlers just as they had received Brahmanism.) The Siamese began their rise to power in the eleventh century C.E. and controlled the country by the end of the thirteenth century. In the complexity of war and its resulting chaos, Hinayana entered the country and in a relatively short time had supplanted both Mahayana and Brahmanism. As Hinayana grew in Thailand, it spread also to neighboring Cambodia. Hinduism was already yielding to Mahayana there, and both then gave way to Hinayana.

By the modern era, Hinayana Buddhism had a firm control from Ceylon along the southern coast of Asia, to Indochina. This growth, while impressive, was eclipsed by that accomplished by Mahayana with its more universal appeal. Several cases have been noted in which Hinayana came into a country only after Mahayana had been present for some time.

Chinese Buddhism. China received Buddhist missionaries possibly as early as 200 B.C.E. and quickly became the great center of Mahayana Buddhism. The importance of China was heightened as Hinduism reasserted itself in India in the face of a growing Buddhism and all but drove Buddhism from its Indian homeland. As Buddhism interacted with the religions of China, numerous variations of it (including what was to become Zen) sprang up. But over the centuries, the various Buddhist groups have evolved into what is usually the eclectic mixture of Buddhism, Confucianism, and Taoism that had been popularized throughout mainland China. The faith is a form of Buddhism centered on bodhisattvas, who function somewhat like saints in Roman Catholicism. Religious structures, temples, are dedicated to a particular bodhisattva; Kwan Yin, the goddess of mercy, is a popular one. Other bodhisattvas have lesser positions, and a temple thus gives the appearance of having a pantheon represented in the statuary. The most popular form of Buddhism in China (as in Japan) centers on Amida Buddha with his promise of a Pure Land, or the Lotus Heaven, to which men are brought by faith in the Buddha. In China, Amida is known as Omito Fu.

Confucius, the Latinized name given Master K'ung, born in China in 551 B.C.E., was the great teacher of morals, practical religion, and philosophy. During his early twenties, he entered a time of seclusion to mourn his mother's death and found it a time of deep thought. By the age of thirty he was a teacher and later became chief judge of his own district of Lu. After a life of success and failures, he died in 479 B.C.E. His teachings—emphasizing family (including ancestor worship), morality, and respect for authority—became part of the Chinese way of life.

Lao-Tzu, the reputed founder of Taoism, was an early contemporary of Confucius. His name, which means "little old child," derives from a legend that he was born an old man. We know little about him beyond his retirement from public life and his composition of the *Tao Te Ching*, the chief religious book of the Taoists. A disciple, Chuang-tse, wrote a commentary on his master's work, which is also a part of the sacred writing. The teachings center on the nature of the Tao or Way. The Way is mystical, natural, and highly ethical, but vague and open to wide interpretation. The influence of Taoism has largely survived through the sacred writings, which are widely read, and a folk religion that merged the mystical faith of Taoism with the ancient polytheistic, magical religion of pre-Taoist China.

The common form of presenting Chinese religion as a separate topic in itself is legitimate. Yet, in its American manifestations, Chinese religion should be considered within a Buddhist context. John F. Mulholland, in his survey of *Hawaii's Religions*, reflects upon the Buddhist affiliation of many members of America's Asian community:

"When the Chinese immigrants prospered, the children went to private schools. If the school was Catholic or Episcopal and required or expected all students to be baptized, the children were baptized. The second and third generations found that in Hawaii they were expected to have a religion, and since the lack of religious designation in China was confusing, many Chinese simply said they were Buddhist. There were no organized Buddhist groups and no membership requirements as Christian churches had. The temples were privately owned or existed in connection with Chinese societies. As the Japanese Buddhists built temples which related them to Japan, so the Chinese began to emphasize the Buddhist part of their multiple religion."

Korean Buddhism. From China, Buddhism spread to Korea. Buddhism in Korea differs markedly from Buddhism in other Asian societies in that, during the modern era, the various schools of Buddhist thought began to emphasize their commonality over their differences. As a result, the several organizations were able not only to reverse the process of splintering but finally, in 1935, to unite into a single organization, the Chogye sect, from which most contemporary groups derive.

Buddhism entered what is today called Korea in 372 C.E., when it was brought from China to the Kingdom of Koguryo, a state covering the northern portion of the peninsula. From there it spread southward to the kingdoms of Paekche and Silla. It flourished in the United Kingdom created by Silla in 668 C.E. during which time Zen was introduced along with the original Mahayana (called Chiao in Korea) forms. Nine schools of Zen developed around nine outstanding masters and six schools of Chiao emerged.

Through the next centuries, Buddhism waxed and waned, always remaining in competition with Confucius' thought and popular folk religion. Zen experienced a revival in the twelfth century when Master Pojo (1158–1210) advocated a union of thought that found favor with the varying Zen schools. A century and a half later, in 1356, under Master T'aego (1301–1382), a merger of all the Zen schools into the Chogyejong was accomplished. Master T'aego was one of several priests who had risen to prominence in the land and had been given the title "national teacher" by the king.

The Yi Dynasty (1392–1910) became a time of great suffering for Korean Buddhism, as the ruling powers generally assumed a hostile posture toward it. Buddhism was suppressed and Zen almost died out, though in the face of opposition Buddhism became more united. In 1424 two of the Chiao sects united with the Chogyejong to form the Sonjong while the remaining Chiao sects united into the Kyojong. Only in the late eighteenth century did government policies toward Buddhism relax. King Chongyo began to lift negative government regulations, and in the nineteenth century Buddhism began a revival, further spurred in the 1890s by the arrival of many Japanese Buddhist priests. In 1904, for the first time, the government ended its control of Buddhist temples. The revival of Buddhism, the cooperation with the Japanese priests, and the new freedom, however, came to an abrupt halt in the second decade of the twentieth century after Japan occupied Korea in 1910. The occupation government reclaimed control of the temples. Nationalistic feelings led to a new sense of unity by Korean Buddhists over against the Japanese. The growth of those sentiments led in 1935 to the merger of the Sonjong and Kyojong into the single Chogye sect, which dominates Korean Buddhism to this day.

Japanese Buddhism. From China, Buddhism spread to Korea and then to Japan. Japanese Buddhism is critical to an understanding of North American Buddhism as the overwhelming majority of North American Buddhists were, at least prior to the 1970s, followers of one of the Japanese Buddhist traditions. When it first entered Japan, Buddhism was not attractive enough to win many converts from Shinto, the national religion of Japan, but Buddhism was granted toleration from the emperor. The building of the new capital at Nara in 710 C.E. marked the turning point in Japanese Buddhist history. During the Nara period, the emperor accepted Buddhism and made it the state religion. A number of the Chinese Buddhist sects, including Jojitsu, Sanron, Hosso, Kusha, Ritsu, and Kegon, were introduced (most of these are now represented in North America). In 807, the Tendai sect was brought to Japan. It was more open to the laity than the Nara sects, which tended to be rather exclusive. Esoteric (tantric) Buddhism was introduced the following century.

In the twelfth century, Honen and his disciple Shinran brought the Pure Land Sect from China to Japan. Long before Honen (1133–1212) organized the Jodo, or Pure Land Sect, there had been a belief in the Amitabha (Amida), a benevolent deity who dwells in a Western paradise to which men may gain access by calling upon his name. But it was Honen who gave the idea an independent form, thereby establishing a new school of thought. Various groups whose beliefs derive from Honen and Shinran are called the Shin groups.

Honen's basic disagreement with most Buddhists of his day was over whether one gained salvation by *jiriki*, one's own strength, or by *tariki*, another's strength. He believed firmly in tariki, in this case the power of the bodhisattva Amida acquired by calling upon his name. The practice of calling upon Amida is

named *nembutsu*. Those who repeat the nembutsu are promised rebirth into the Western paradise. In the Pure Land, all enjoy powers and bliss. It is a step toward nirvana. The nembutsu, according to Honen, should be repeated often and with sincerity, deep belief, and longing.

The most important of Honen's students was Shinran (1173–1262), a monk and friend of Honen. The innovative Shinran abolished monasticism, permitted priests to marry, and promoted the worship of Amida and, to a lesser extent, Shakya (Shakyamuni—Gautama Buddha). Only the relics and images of Amida are allowed. Salvation is attained through faith alone, as a gift of Amida. Honen believed that man is saved by faith, but that ritual and working for others help.

The central act of all Shin groups is the repetition of the nembutsu. "Namu Amida Butsu" (to bow or submit to the one who is enlightened) is repeated often and is said before the statue of Amida Buddha. To repeat the nembutsu is to be one with Amida.

After Shinran's death, the Shin group gradually split into the Jodo (or Jodo-shu) and Shinshu groups. The Jodo look more to Honen and the Shinshu more to Shinran. The Shinshu grew slowly and in the medieval period fell victim to the various political upheavals and wars. Shinran's daughter supervised construction of the Hongwanji, or Temple of the Original View, in Kyoto, which became the headquarters of the True Pure Land Sect. In 1496, a temple, which became the new Shinshu center, was founded at Yamashina. Yamashina was destroyed in 1532 and the headquarters were moved to Ishiyama. In 1570, Oda Nobunaga, a feudal lord who was spreading Christianity to counteract Buddhism's power, attacked Ishiyama and eventually (after 10 years) destroyed it. Oda Nobunaga (1532–1582) defended Christianity in conjunction with the missionary work of Francis Xavier, but Nobunaga's aim was less to spread Christianity than to destroy Buddhism. He considered the Buddhists a threat to his power. As a result of the evacuation by the chief abbot from Ishiyama, a disagreement arose among his sons as to how long the Shinshu should have fought Nobunaga, and a split developed. Ieyasu, the shogun of Japan, fearing the growth of the Shinshu among the people, took advantage of the split to divide the group. He sided with the elder son and gave him a tract of land upon which to build an Hongwanji. The supporters of the younger son are now known as the Honpa Hongwanji, and the supporters of the elder as the Higashi Hongwanji. Their differences were largely administrative, but, as time has passed, the Honpa groups have been the more progressive and adaptive to change.

The thirteenth century saw the appearance of Nichiren, another outstanding Buddhist teacher who began as a reformer and Buddhist ecumenist but became the founder of the Nichiren-shu. (*Shu* means religion.) Nichiren believed that in the teachings known as the Lotus Sutra he had found the primitive, true Buddhism that could unite the many sects. He attacked the other sects' beliefs and won many followers as he traveled around Japan.

One of the central ideas in Japanese Buddhism, usually associated with Nichiren, is *mappo*, or end of the law. Nichiren divided history into three millennia, the first of which began with Buddha's death. The last phase or mappo, began in 1050 C.E. In this last period, salvation is to be obtained through belief in the Lotus Sutra.

Zen Buddhism. Zen was also introduced into Japan about this time. Zen is the mystical school of Buddhism. It stands in relation to Buddhism much as Sufism does to Islam and contemplative Catholicism does to Christianity. It arose in the interaction of Buddhist philosophy with Taoist meditative techniques. The actual founder was Tao-sheng (360–434), who added to Buddhist meditative techniques the doctrine of instantaneous enlightenment—the attainment in one single act of illumination of the goal of mystical truth in both its objective and subjective aspects.

Recognized by many Zen students as the founder of Zen is Bodhidharma (d. 534), who came from his native India to teach Zen in China during most of his mature life. He is termed the first patriarch and is credited with the addition of "wall-contemplation" to Zen practice. He was followed by five other patriarchs—Hui-k'o, Seng-ts'an, Tao-hsin, Hung-jen, and Hui-neng. Hui-neng is ranked next to Bodhidharma as the second (and actual) founder of Zen.

As Zen continued to develop in China, it went through the familiar process of schism and adoption of new ideas and practices. Among the new practices developed was the use of the *koan*. The koan is an anecdotal event or utterance of the masters given to disciples as problems. It is used as a means to enlightenment. The koan led to the development of the two major schools of Zen which still exist. One school, Lin-chi, accepted the koan and used it extensively. In reaction, a second school, Ts'ao-tung, emerged and was characterized by its doctrine of silent illumination. Ts'ao-tung saw the koan as "gazing on the word." Transported to Japan, the Lin-chi sect became Rinzai Zen, and Ts'ao-tung became Soto Zen. These two schools were both transferred to the United States. In pure Rinzai Zen, people use the koan; in pure Soto Zen, people do not. Most groups are neither pure Rinzai or Soto, but lie between those two extremes.

One popular koan often used as the first exercise for Rinzai students is the *mu* koan. Mu, meaning no or nothing in Sino-Japanese, is understood as the nothing that contains everything. Mu is to be experienced, not intellectualized.

Dogen (1200–1253), the founder of Japanese Soto, is the originator of the typical Zen method of meditation, *zazen*. As described by Dogan, zazen proceeds thus:

"If you wish to attain enlightenment, begin at once to practice *zazen*. For this meditation a quiet chamber is necessary, while food and drink must be taken in moderation. Free yourself from all attachments, and bring to rest the ten thousand things. Think of neither good nor evil and judge not right nor wrong. Maintain the flow of mind, of will, and of consciousness; bring to an end all desires, all concepts and judgments. Do not think about how to become a Buddha.

"In terms of procedure, first put down a thick pillow and on top of this a second (round) one. One may chose either a full or half cross-legged position. In the full position one places the right foot on the left thigh and the left foot is placed on the right thigh. In the half position only the left foot is placed upon the right thigh. Robe and belt should be worn loosely, but in order. The right hand rests on the left foot, while the back of the left hand rests in the palm of the right. The two thumbs are placed in juxtaposition.

"The body must be maintained upright, without inclining to the left or to the right, forward or backward. Ears and shoulders, nose and navel must be kept in alignment respectively. The tongue is to be kept against the palate, lips and teeth are kept firmly closed, while the eyes are to be kept always open.

"Now that the bodily position is in order, regulate your breathing. If a wish arises, take note of it and then dismiss it. In practicing thus persistently you will forget all attachments and concentration will come of itself. That is the art of *zazen*. Zazen is the Dharma gate of great rest and joy." (Heinrich Dumoulin, *A History of Zen Buddhism* [Boston: Beacon Press, 1969], 161).

The essence of zazen is to achieve the full and perfect equilibrium of the organism.

Next to Dogen, Hakuin (1685–1768) was the greatest Zen master and was the one who revived Rinzai Zen in Japan. Hakuin described the tension of the disciple when confronted with the koan. This tension is the "great doubt." Hakuin also described *satori*, the great enlightenment, which is a central concern of Zen. In the various reports of satori, one again finds the range of reflections on mystical experience, this time described in Buddhist categories.

The *roshi* is the prime official in Zen. The roshi is the master, the one who has attained the goals of Zen meditation and has the knowledge and maturity to aid others in attaining them. There is a tendency toward a Buddhist version of apostolic succession in Zen, the roshis tending to see themselves in a lineage of Zen mas-

ters and to be in a school formed by a succession of patriarchs. In America, most Zen is derived from Jito Gasan, a Japanese Zen master and head of Engaku Temple. He passed on the Rinzai tradition to Imakita Kosen (1816–1892), a Japanese master who was fascinated with Western culture and among whose students was Soyen Shaku, the first Zen teacher to visit the United States.

Tibetan Buddhism. The last place that Buddhism invaded as a conquering missionary faith was Tibet. The date traditionally given is 747 C.E., when Padmasambhava brought tantric Buddhism to Tibet. In the mountainous terrain, Buddhism mixed with Bon, the native religion, the aim of which was the magical control of evil spirits and the use of cosmic powers. Tibetan Buddhism thus emerged as a somewhat magical faith, distinct from either Chinese or Indian Buddhism.

The older sects still emphasize the magic tantra and make wide use of the mantra and the mandala. The mantra is a phonetic form (the most popular being "om" and "om mani padme hum"—meaning the jewel in the heart of the lotus, the center of truth). The very sound of the mantra has a psychological effect and is aimed at producing deep mystical experience. A mandala is a circular drawing representative of the universe, a cosmogram whose center is thought to be the metaphysical center of the universe. It is used as an aid in worship.

Tantric Buddhism is based on the belief that everything is permeated by a single power (Shakti) emanating from God. This force manifests itself in three ways: positive masculine, negative feminine, and most important, the union of the two. What is true on a cosmic level is considered true on a human, individual level. The union of opposites, a major goal in tantric practice, is accomplished by the disciplines of yoga, the most controversial aspect of which includes ritual sexual intercourse.

Tantric sexual ritual involves the male practitioner's partaking of the 5 M's (True Things)—*madya* (wine), *mamsha* (meat), *matsya* (fish), *mudra* (parched grain), and *maithuna* (coitus). Tantric rituals can be practiced in three modes. The Sattvio Sadhana, or symbolic school, has spiritualized tantra. The Rajasic Sadhana uses material substitutes for the 5 M's. The Kaula Sadhana practices a literal partaking of the 5 M's. The symbolic and substitutionary partaking of the 5 M's are usually termed "right-hand" tantra. Such practice is typical of the Japanese Shingon sect. The literal school, which performs ritual sexual intercourse, is generally said to practice "left-hand" tantra. The object of tantra is twofold: the union of the individual with the divine, and the gaining of magical power which can be used to do miraculous works.

After the initial establishment of Buddhism in Tibet, a period began in 838 C.E. In which rulers inimical to Buddhism halted its progress. Also, during the period toward the end of the tenth century, government instability created opportunities for the development of Buddhism. Atisha (982-1054), who arrived from India in western Tibet in 1042, was in the forefront of the religions resurgence. His efforts were bolstered by a new generation of Buddhist leaders that included Marpa (1012-1096) and Naropa (1016-1100). Out of their work a new wave of Buddhist schools was created and over the next few centuries, Tibet became a Buddhist country.

Tibetan Buddhism is divided into several major schools which are split into subsects. The Nyingma or Old Ones are constituted by those who trace their lineage to the first transmission of Buddhism under Guru Rinpoche (Padmasambhava), who the Nyingma see as the manifestation of the god Avalokiteshvara and even the equal of Buddha. They also claim Guru Rinpoche hid his teachings in texts to await times when people would be ready for them. These Nyingma texts are considered treasures and prominent lamas (priests) who possess such texts are honored.

The Kadam or Bound to Command School, traces its existence to Atisha and emphasizes the building of monasteries noteworthy for their disciplined life and guru devotion. This group has been absorbed into the Gelugpa as a subsect.

The Sakya School derives from the work of Konchog Gyalpo (1034-1102), a disciple of Drogmi (992-1072), a later contemporary of Atisha. Their integration of sutra (written text) and tantra is designed to produce liberation in a single lifetime.

The Kagyu or Transmitted Command School traces its lineage to Naropa, Marpa, and Marpas chief disciple, Milarepa (1052-1135). It places great emphasis on practical mysticism and the speedy attainment of Enlightenment. The Kagyu has been among the least monastic of the schools and requires neither celibacy nor association with a monastery from its members.

A reform, led by Tsong-kha-pa at the turn of the fifteenth century, created an additional major Buddhist school in Tibet. It attempted to tighten the monastic discipline, insisted on celibacy, reduced the emphasis on magic, and effected strong organization. Tsong-kha-pa also founded a monastery, Ganden, east of Llasa, which grew into a large monastic university. In 1416 and 1419, two similar monasteries were created. These became the leading centers of learning for Buddhism and assisted the Gelugpa School in becoming the dominant Buddhist school in the land.

Tsong-kha-pas reforms were accomplished at the time when the newer schools were teaching that the head of the chief monasteries were bodhisattvas. When a *lama*, or monastery ruler, died, a search was made for a new incarnation of him born at the time of his death. As the Gelugpa School became a dominant force, its leader became the chief lama of Tibet. The Dalai Lama is still the the nominal head of Tibet's Buddhists. Second only to the Dalai Lama is the Panchen Lama, head of the monastic complex of Tashihunpo.

Tibetan Buddhism was thoroughly disrupted by the Chinese invasion of Tibet in 1959. Many of the leading teachers, including the Dalai Lama, fled the country in order to preserve Tibetan traditions and practice in the face of what they feared would be hostile and destructive new rulers. Their fears were to a large extent realized. Most of the great monasteries were leveled, many monks killed and those who survived were forced into secular labor, and many texts (some irreplaceable) were torched. In the wake of the institution of Chinese control in Tibet, the center of Tibetan Buddhism moved to northern India in the kingdoms of Nepal and Bhutan, and the West. Here, an attempt to keep pre-1950s Tibetan culture and religion alive has been launched, including the preservation and translation of all text smuggled out of Tibet into Western languages. Integral to the survival of Tibetan Buddhism has been the contact with the western world. Many teachers have come to the West and established teaching centers attracting a new generation of believers among non-Tibetans. The growth of their Western community has been crowned by the recognition of several Westerners as the reincarnation of prominent lamas.

BUDDHISM IN NORTH AMERICA. Buddhism came to America in several waves beginning with the Chinese immigrants attracted by the discovery of gold in California. A second wave came with the Japanese entry into Hawaii and California in the last two decades of the nineteenth century. Buddhist growth in the U.S. was blocked in the first half of the twentieth century by anti-Asian immigration laws. A third wave of immigration began in 1965 following the passing of a new immigration law favorable to Asians. This last wave revitalized Buddhism in America.

Buddhism in North America is best understood in the context of its international spread. In spite of valiant attempts to create an American Buddhism, most Buddhist bodies in the United States still represent transplanted forms of the many varied schools of thought and practice. The community is still structured by its immigration patterns. Overwhelmingly, Buddhists have come to the United States from Asia and entered the country through one of the West Coast ports, usually Los Angeles. As the twentieth century comes to a close, forty percent of all Buddhists in America reside in Southern California. The Los Angeles Metropolitan Area has become unique in the Buddhist world as the single place where representative organizations of every major school of Buddhism can be found in a single urban center.

Southeastern Asian (Theravada) Buddhism in North America. Prior to 1965, the story of Buddhism in America was largely the story of the emigration of Japanese Buddhists to Hawaii and the West coast and the spread of Japanese forms of Buddhism in the Caucasian population. The presence of Theravada Buddhism was limited to a few intellectuals and the diplomatic mission personnel from the several Southeast Asian countries in New York City and Washington, D.C. The situation changed dramatically after the beginning of and the spread of the Vietnam War to surrounding countries and the replacing of the Asian Exclusion Act by the new immigration regulations of 1965. During the 1970s, a great wave of immigrants from Vietnam (increased by special legislation passed after the withdrawal of United States forces from the country), Cambodia, Laos, and Thailand moved to the West Coast and the northern American urban centers. Slowly, they have organized congregations, established temples, and developed national associations. The Theravada centers consist almost entirely of first generation, non-English-speaking, Asian Americans. As of the 1980s, language remained a barrier to the spread of Theravada Buddhism to the Caucasian population, though initial signs of its spreading began to emerge around the followers of the few English-speaking Theravada teachers.

Chinese Buddhism in North America. The Chinese came to the United States before the Japanese, their major immigration occurring between 1854 and 1883, when a law stopping further Chinese migration was passed. By 1880, more than 100,000 Chinese had settled in America, primarily on the West Coast.

The 1850s saw the arrival of the first large groups of Chinese to labor in the United States. Although the majority were Christians, having been recruited from the mission stations in China, many were not. Those who remained loyal to traditional religious patterns set up family altars and shrines. They soon became the source of numerous complaints about "heathen Mongolians," and were targeted by a reinforced Christian missionary movement.

As early as 1878, a Chinese monk brought both a Kwan Yin and a Kwan Tai statue to Honolulu and built a temple, or joss house, to Kwan Yin. (Kwan Tai was a military hero of the third century B.C.E. who was later canonized.) In 1887, three joss houses were reported. During World War II, one observer reported seven temples on Oahu and another on Kauai. Chinese joss houses appeared on the West Coast before 1900. Much of the Chinese faith is centered on these joss houses, particularly the small family shrines still found throughout Chinese American communities in California and Hawaii.

A modern revival of Buddhism in a Chinese mode has resulted in the establishment of a number of centers across the country, many of which have been formed by expatriates from the Maoist revolution and immigrants from Taiwan. Some of these serve Chinese Americans; others were formed by American converts or by Americans who found themselves in China as missionaries or soldiers and were converted abroad. Independent Chinese Buddhist associations have formed to serve each of these groups.

Most Chinese Buddhist centers are located in the metropolitan areas of Honolulu, San Francisco, Los Angeles, Vancouver, and New York City. The existence of these centers, often only blocks apart but administratively independent, manifest the variety within Chinese Buddhism, as well as the distinctions formed by migration at different times and from different sections of China.

Chinese began to arrive in Canada at the time of the gold rush on the Fraser River in 1868. Approximately 2,000 came during the first two years. Several thousand more seemed to have arrived during the 1870s. In 1881 there were an estimated 4,300 Chinese in Canada (almost all in British Columbia). Three years later the number had grown to 10,000, most recruited to build the Canadian Pacific Railroad. After the railroad was constructed, they found jobs in the fishing industry. Lesser numbers continued to enter Canada until immigration was blocked in 1923. At the same time, Chinese were encouraged and assisted in living in the country.

Only a minority of the Chinese in British Columbia were Buddhist, a large percentage being either Confucians or Christians. For

Buddhists, joss houses were established similar to the pattern in California, and over the years temples have been erected to serve the Buddhist community.

Korean Buddhism in North America. Korean migration since 1965 has been proportional to that of other Asian countries, but most of the new Korean Americans are Christians. However, a few Korean Buddhist priests have come to the United States and at least one Zen priest, Master Seung Sahn Sunim, has been able to create a national organization.

Japanese Buddhism in North America. Japanese immigration began with the arrival of large numbers of laborers in Hawaii on June 19, 1868. Further Japanese immigration was encouraged until 1907, when limits were placed upon it. At present, approximately one-third of the Hawaiian population is Japanese. Because the early Japanese came to Hawaii as plantation laborers, the work of establishing Buddhism began in the countryside, usually on a plantation, and then moved to Honolulu as plantation life soured for the Japanese. Buddhist settlements in California came only a short time after those in Hawaii, as Japanese immigrants also settled on the West Coast. In many cases, the Buddhist missionary from Japan would stop in Hawaii on his way to California. The growth of the community, however, was stymied by the 1907 law.

The name of the first Buddhist in America is lost to history, but in 1889 Soryu Kagahi of the Honpa Hongwanji arrived in Honolulu to minister to Buddhists on the plantations. Under his leadership a temple, the first in America, was built in April 1889, in Hilo, where he had found many former Buddhists ready to reactivate their faith. In the fall, he returned to Japan and soon disappeared from history. For the next 10 years, things did not go well for Hawaiian Buddhists. They were frequently visited by renegade Buddhist priests who took their hard-earned wages and then skipped town. Such practices left the Japanese open to the very active Christian mission.

Pleas for help were finally heard by the Buddhists in Japan, who sent their official representatives. To Hawaii came Jotei Matsuo, a Jodo-shu priest (1894), and Ejun Miyamoto of the Honpa Hongwanji (1897). Within a decade, four more of the Buddhist sects—the Higashi Hongwanji, the Shingon, the Nichiren, and the Soto Zen—arrived. In 1899, Yemyo Imamura, the bishop who was to dominate Buddhism in Hawaii until his death in 1932, took up residence in Honolulu.

As early as 1898, the Honpa Hongwanji sent two priests to survey possibilities for an American mission. A mission in San Francisco was established after the arrival of the Reverends Shuyei Sonoda and Kakuryo Nishijimi in September 1899. These two men organized the Young Men's Buddhist Association and, by 1905, had consecrated a church, which became the mainland headquarters of the Jodo Shin Buddhists.

Japanese migration to Canada began in 1877 and proceeded slowly until the mid-1890s. Between 1895 and the beginning of World War I, almost 30,000 Japanese came into Canada, though over half of these soon moved on to the United States. Migration dropped after the war and did not pick up again until the mid-1960s, though it has never reached the level of the first decade of this century.

The Honpa Honwanji, or Shin Buddhists, were the primary group to take responsibility for the Japanese-Canadians and, answering a request from the community, the Reverend Senju Sasaki arrived in Vancouver in 1904. The first church was constructed in 1911. During the initial phase of organization and growth, the Canadian work was placed under the American Buddhist Mission headquarters in San Francisco. It became independent in 1933, but both the American and Canadian work retained the same bishop. Like the Buddhist work in the United States, the work in Canada was totally disrupted by World War II. After the war, the work was reorganized and prospered with renewed immigration. In 1968, the Honpa Honwanji work in Canada was fully separated from that in the continental United States.

In the years since the renewal of immigration, other Japanese Buddhist groups have also colonized in Canada and a diverse religious community is emerging.

Zen Buddhism in North America. Zen came to America in 1893 when a Renzai monk, Soyen Shaku (1859–1919), addressed the World's Parliament of Religions in Chicago. A graduate of the Western-oriented Keio University, he, despite strong opposition, traveled to the land of the "barbarians" to speak on "The Law of Cause and Effect, as Taught by the Buddha." After his brief visit, during which he did not make the impact of either the Hindu Swami Vivekananda or theosophist Annie Besant, he returned to Kamakura. In 1905, he again came to the United States as the guest of the Alexander Russells in San Francisco. After a year of hospitality, he ended his stay with a national and then a world tour. The remainder of his life was spent as a leader in Japanese Zen.

Soyen had been a student of Imakita Kosen, renowned in nineteenth century Buddhism as one who took Western thought and culture seriously. After Kosen's death, his students came to the West and became the real founders of American Zen. One of these students was Daisetz Teitaro Suzuki, a lay scholar, who, through his books, has done more to enlighten American audiences about Zen than any other single person. Another of Kosen's students, Sokatsu Shaku (1869–1954), became a teacher in Tokyo. In 1906, he came to America with six disciples. The group settled in Berkeley but soon moved to a farm in Hayward, California. After discovering their inability to farm profitably, they moved to San Francisco. Gradually, each returned to Japan, leaving no visible organization behind. The last of the group to return was Shigetsu Sasaki, who completed his Zen training in Japan and came again to the United States as a roshi with the new name of Sokei-an. His settlement in New York in 1928 marked the beginning of a continuous Rinzai history in America.

Soto Zen came to the United States in 1903. It began in Hawaii when the Reverend Senyei Kawahara came to Honolulu and erected a temple on the West Loch side of Pearl Harbor. Within a few years Ryuki Hirai, another Soto priest, joined him and built a temple at Waialua to the north of Oahu. Other temples were added on Maui and Kauai as later priests arrived. Then, in 1913, Bishop Hosen Isobe was sent to Honolulu, where a temple was built under his direction the following year. The mission spread to Kona on the Big Island, Hawaii, in 1916. (Soto Buddhists look upon the arrival of Bishop Isobe as the real beginning of Soto Zen in America.)

After beginning the work in Hawaii, Bishop Isobe brought Soto to California. He organized Zenshuji Mission (now called the Soto Mission) in the home of Toyokichi Nagasaki in Los Angeles in 1922. The history of Soto Zen in America is continuous from that time.

The history of Zen in America, like the history of Buddhism, would be incomplete without mention of those non-Asian Americans who played a significant role in its spread and influence. Notable is Ruth Fuller Everett Sasaki, possibly the first American student of Zen in Japan. She came to New York in 1938 after work in a Japanese monastery and became a prime supporter of the First Zen Institute and editor of *Cat's Yawn*, its first magazine. In 1944 after four years of widowhood, she married Sokei-an Sasaki Roshi, a move that stabilized the institute during the final year of the war. Widowed a second time, she moved to Japan where she became the first non-Asian priest and abbess of a temple, the Ryosen-an, and spent her life translating her late husband's work.

Chester F. Carlson, who discovered the process of xerography, was typical of several wealthy benefactors of Zen Buddhism. He was the first founder of the Zen Mountain Center of Tassajara Springs, California, but kept his support of Buddhist causes quiet during his lifetime.

Tibetan Buddhism in North America. Since the Chinese occupation of Tibet in 1959, each of the major Tibetan Buddhist sects and subsects have arrived in the United States, and their several representatives have established a number of separate organizations. Unlike Southeast Asian Buddhism, language has not been as significant a factor in slowing the spread of Tibetan Buddhism in the Caucasian population, and by the mid-1980s, Caucasian disciples far outnumbered Tibetan American Buddhists.

Much support for Tibetan Buddhism was generated by American sympathy for their plight in the face of the Chinese. Organizations such as the Tibetan Friendship Group, headquartered in Ojai, California, have combined efforts with the Dalai Lama's Office of Tibet in New York City to focus attention upon the political and humanitarian side of the Tibetans' situation.

During the 1990s, Tibetan Buddhism has been one of the significant growing edges of the North American Buddhist community. Numerous new centers covering the spectrum of Tibetan Buddhist thought have been opened. Buddhists have also been among the most organized and ecumenical of religious communities and are noteworthy for their networking and as the century comes to a close, their presence on the Internet. In the United States, Buddhists have formed the American Buddhist Congress, modeled somewhat on the National Council of Churches.

Western Buddhists. The growth of Buddhism in America as a result of Japanese emigration coupled with the increase of world religious studies in American universities set the stage for a number of Americans to become Buddhists. They were largely attracted by Buddhist philosophy and ethics, but followed their studies with full identification with the faith. Often gaining their understanding from books, instead of Buddhist religious teachers, they found like-minded believers and formed Buddhist study societies. Typical of the Western-led Buddhist societies, such as the English language groups founded by Ernest Hunt after World War I in Hawaii, has been a desire to transcend the sectarian rivalries within Buddhism.

Among the first Westerners attracted to Buddhism, though never a professing Buddhist, was Paul Carus of the Open Court Publishing Company in LaSalle, Illinois. Attracted to Zen Master Soyen Shaku at the World's Parliament of Religions in 1893, he saw Buddhism as a worthy nontheistic alternative to the Christianity he had already rejected. In 1894 he published his compilation of Buddhist texts, *The Gospel of the Buddha*, and sent it to Soyen Shaku in Japan, who gave it to Daisetz Teitaro Suzuki to translate into Japanese. Carus later brought Suzuki to Illinois, and from their collaboration came one of the first major thrusts of American Buddhist history.

Central to the rise of Buddhism in America has been the work of a number of non-Asian who were attracted to the philosophy of Buddhism and became articulate spokespeople to an audience never reached by the Asian priests. Such a person was Dwight Goddard, who formed the Fellowship Following Buddha, which operated out of his home in Thetford, Vermont. Ernest Hunt (1876–1967), who became a Buddhist on the eve of taking his orders as an Anglican priest, settled in Hawaii in 1915 and became head of the English Department of the Honpa Hongwanji in 1927. He was the main interpreter to the English-speaking Hawaiians for the next 40 years. Mrs. Thomas Foster, a wealthy Honolulu heiress, was typical of several wealthy converted Buddhists who contributed financially to its promulgation. The Fosters had become interested in Buddhism through Dr. Wilhelm Hillebrand of Germany, and they became heavy investors in the Banaras excavations in India at the place where Buddha was enlightened. (The Soto Temple in Honolulu is built on an Indian model.) The botanical gardens in Honolulu are named for Mrs. Foster.

Like many non-Christian religions, Buddhism profited greatly from participation in the 1893 World's Parliament of Religions in connection with the Columbian Exposition in Chicago, Illinois. In all, seven papers were given, two by Anagarika Dharmapala of Sri Lanka. They covered the basics of Buddha's life, the Hinayana (of Siam), the Mahayana (of Japan), and Buddha's teaching. Dharma-

pala particularly tried to show Buddhism's superiority, and the several Japanese speakers tried to counter what they believed to have been unjust criticism of Buddhism by non-Japanese. "There are very few countries in the world so misunderstood as Japan," began Kinza Riuge Hirai ("What Buddhism Teaches of Man's Relation to God, and Its Influence on Those Who Have Received It," in *The World's Congress of Religions*, ed. J. W. Hanson [Chicago: The Monarch Book Company, 1894], 395). The special program on Buddhism to the whole congress on the evening of September 26 featured addresses by Soyen Shaku, Jitsuzen Ashitzu, K. R. Hirai, and Swami Vivekananda, a Hindu who offered his own appreciation of Buddha. Of significance was the absence of any representative of Buddhism from China.

Buddhist groups in America are of three kinds. Most are transplanted Chinese, Japanese, and other Asian sects that keep more or less close contact with a parent body. This contact may be formal and organizational, or may be merely by the continuation of a teaching. The second kind are the schismatic groups of the first kind. Schisms have occurred over differences of practice and emphasis, beliefs, and race. A common pattern in Buddhist groups is for a basically Asian body to grow by additions of Caucasians, only to find itself splintering along racial lines as soon as the Caucasian members are a large enough group. The third type of body is the philosophical Buddhist center formed usually around one or more leaders who have settled in the United States after study in Japan.

SHINTO. Shinto, "The Way of the Gods," is the indigenous religion of Japan. Its polytheistic *kami* were, by and large, essentially the patronal deities of the *uji*, or clans, of ancient Japan. They were also associated with nature since their worship was often conducted in beautiful locations that engendered a great sense of natural awe, such as waterfalls.

Shinto holds to a strong sense of purity, as against ritual pollution. Hence, its shrines are often located outside the human community or on its fringes, away from the pollutions of blood, sickness, and death, and amid the natural purity of nature. Even those shrines now located in the midst of modern cities are situated, if possible, in a park-like setting amid a few stately trees. Shintoists ritually purify themselves before worship.

Most Shinto kami are of mythological background and are rooted in local communities. Some Shinto myths, especially those important to the imperial house, are contained in two of Japan's oldest books, the *Kohiki* (712 C.E.) and the *Nihonshoki* (720 C.E.). They tell of the generation of the Japanese Islands and the kami by the primal parents Izanagi and Izanami, and of the goddess Amaterasu, associated with the Sun and the ancestress of the imperial family. Some figures in historical times have been enshrined as kami after their deaths, down to the Emperor Meiji (1852–1912), whose shrine is the most prominent in Tokyo.

Shinto *jinja*, or shrines, are typically modest buildings of simple but graceful lines, demarcated by the distinctive *torii*, or Shinto gate. A few, influenced by Chinese styles of architecture, are ornate and colorful. A shrine is essentially the symbolic home of its kami. The kami-presence is indicated by such signs as a mirror and *gohei*, or zigzag pieces of paper on a stick. Worshippers often approach shrines individually for brief moments of worship, clapping their hands twice before praying.

Shinto public worship centers around *matsuri*, or festivals. They are generally scheduled in accordance with the agricultural cycle, at seed time in the spring, midsummer, or harvest. On these occasions, and more often at larger shrines, priests present offerings, most often vegetables, fruit, rice, rice-wine, and seafood, in a solemn and decorous manner, placing them on a table before the shrine's main sanctuary. Then a *norito*, or solemn prayer, is read. After the offerings are removed, other activities involving the participation of the community may occur: *kagura*, or sacred dance, processions, carnival-like fairs, even sacred horse races or boat races. These will depend upon the traditions of the community; matsuri are often occasions of local distinctiveness and pride.

Shinto, as the way of the kami, was not thought of as a distinct religion until after the introduction of Buddhism in the sixth century C.E. made it necessary to distinguish it from the import faith. During the medieval and early modern periods Shinto shrines were frequently in close association with Buddhist temples, the kami being often thought of as guardians, students, or even alternative expressions of Japan's rich pantheon of Mahayana buddhas and bodisattvas. After the Meiji Restoration of 1868 commenced Japan's modernization, however, the government forced a draconic separation of shrines and temples, the situation that still generally greets the visitor today.

The increasingly nationalistic regime of 1868–1945 also put Shinto under direct state control and used it as a symbol and vehicle of its ideology, emphasizing its legitimation of the divine authority of the sovereign in whose name its wars were fought and sacrifices demanded. After 1945 Shinto was separated from the state and generally reverted to its local bases, though the Emperor still performs certain Shinto rituals in his personal capacity, and the Daijosiai, or Shinto accession rite, was celebrated by the Emperor Akihito in 1990. Most shrines are owned and administered by local organizations. There are also some "sectarian" Shinto groups, registered as such by the prewar government, promoting particular doctrines, practices, or places of pilgrimage. Some of the "new religions" such as Tenrikyo, Konkokyo, and Omoto, have some Shinto roots and employ some typically Shinto forms of worship, though they intend worship to be for a monotheistic rather than a polytheistic deity.

Most Japanese maintain a relationship to both Shinto and Buddhism, having traditional ties to both a shrine and a temple. Characteristically, funerals are conducted in temples and weddings in shrines, since the religion of kami is popularly felt to deal especially with the joyous family and community occasion of this life.

Shinto came to America with the Japanese immigration of the late nineteenth century. A shrine was constructed in Hilo, Hawaii, in 1898, and others followed on both the Big Island and Oahu. Shinto prospered there until the 1930s, when growing concern over Japanese imperialism led to criticism of Shinto priests as agents of a foreign power. After Pearl Harbor, the shrines were confiscated and their priests interned. However, most of the shrines were either recovered, or rebuilt, after the war. There have been few if any Shinto shrines in the mainland U.S. apart from tiny altars in homes or places of business. (This section on Shinto prepared with the cooperation of Robert S. Ellwood.)

JAPANESE NEW RELIGIONS. Recently there has been a significant amount of literature devoted to studying what have come to be called the Japanese new religions. These are religions that have been founded since 1800, but which have made their impact in the twentieth century, particularly since religious freedom was declared in Japan after World War II. These religions do share a number of characteristics, the most important being their inroads into the membership of the older Buddhist and Shinto faiths.

However, the new religions do not share a common heritage, thought-world, or lifestyle. Groups such as Nichiren Shoshu and Rissho Kosei Kai are clearly variations on a theme by Buddha. A second set of groups, such as Tenrikyo and Konko Kyo, is clearly Shinto in basic faith. Seicho-No-Ie is an example of a third grouping, which are psychic and metaphysical (New Thought). This third group has shown in America a movement toward psychic and New Thought advocates; therefore, Seicho-No-Ie is discussed in the chapter on New Thought. A fourth grouping is made up of the few miscellaneous bodies, of which only one, Perfect Liberty Kyodan, has found its way to America.

Characteristic of many of the new groups is the influence of Christianity, though different groups have picked up different elements. Church, the idea of group worship, has been picked up by many Buddhists. As in India, with the ashram, "church" has

shown itself to be a powerful concept. The Konkokyo seems to have been influenced by the Roman Catholic confession in its *toritsugi*, a form of group confession and meditation. In no case, at least in those that have come to America, has Christianity become the dominant element.

In the fifty years since the end of World War II, there has been a steady growth of independent religious life signaled by the continuous appearance of several new religions annually. The most recent of these religions have drawn their converts primarily from people born and raised to adulthood after the war; observers of Japanese religion have dubbed them the "new new" religions. A few have had remarkable success in inserting themselves into Japanese life. One such group, the AUM Shinri Kyo, a separatist Buddhist group, became the object of intense news coverage following its being accused of having released a poisonous gas in Tokyo's subway system in 1995.

Sources—The Eastern Family, Part II

GENERAL SOURCES

Buddhist studies have proliferated in American universities in recent decades. The work of Buddhist scholars is given focus through the International Association of Buddhist Studies, 1900 Addison Street, Berkeley, CA 94704, and the American Society of Buddhist Studies, 214 Centre St., New York, NY 10013.

Ch'en, Kenneth K. S. *Buddhism*. Woodbury, NY: Barron's Educational Series, 1968. 297 pp.

Conze, Edward. *Buddhism: Its Essence and Development*. New York: Harper & Row, 1959. 223 pp.

———, trans. *Buddhist Scriptures*. Baltimore: Penguin Books, 1959. 250 pp.

Dutt, Nalinaksha. *Buddhist Sects in India*. Delhi: Motilal Banarsidass, 1978. 297 pp.

Haga, Hideo. *Japanese Folk Festivals Illustrated*. Tokyo: Miura Printing Co., 1970. 223 pp.

Harvey, B. Peter. *An Introduction to Buddhism: Teachings, History, and Practices*. New York: Cambridge University Press, 1990. 374 pp.

International Buddhist Directory. London: Wisdom Publications, 1985. 120 pp.

Jayatilleke, K. N. *The Message of the Buddha*. New York: The Free Press, 1974. 262 pp.

Kalupahana, David J. *Buddhist Philosophy*. Honolulu: University Press of Hawaii, 1976. 189 pp.

March, Arthur C. *A Buddhist Bibliography*. London: The Buddhist Lodge, 1935. 257 pp.

Robinson, Richard H. *The Buddhist Religion*. Belmont, CA: Dickenson Publishing Company, 1970. 136 pp.

Saunders, E. Dale. *Buddhism in Japan*. Philadelphia: University of Pennsylvania Press, 1964. 328 pp.

Schuman, Hans Wolfgang. *Buddhism*. Wheaton, IL: Theosophical Publishing House, 1973. 200 pp.

Shojun, Bando, et al., eds. *A Bibliography of Japanese Buddhism*. Tokyo: CIIB Press, 1958. 180 pp.

Snelling, John. *The Buddhist Handbook: A Complete Guide to Buddhist Schools, Teaching, Practice, and History*. Rochester, VT: Inner Traditions, 1991. 337 pp.

The Teaching of Buddha. Tokyo: Bukkyo Dendo Kyokai, 1966. 300 pp.

Yoo, Yushin. *Books on Buddhism*. Metuchen, NJ: Scarecrow Press, 1976. 251 pp.

BUDDHISM IN NORTH AMERICA

Fields, Rick. *How the Swans Came to the Lake*. Boulder, CO: Shambhala, 1986. 445 pp.

Friedman, Lenore. *Meetings with Remarkable Women.* Boston, MA: Shambhala, 1987.

Hunter, Louise H. *Buddhism in Hawaii.* Honolulu: University of Hawaii Press, 1971. 266 pp.

Kalbacker, Catherine Elmes. *Zen in America.* Lansing: Ph.D. dissertation, University of Michigan, 1972. 213 pp.

Keshima, Tetsuden. *Buddhism in America.* Westport, CT: Greenwood Press, 1977. 272 pp.

Layman, Emma McCoy. *Buddhism in America.* Chicago: Nelson-Hall, 1976. 342 pp.

Lorie, Peter and Julie Fookes, comp. *The Buddhist Directory: The Total Resource Guide.* Rutland, VT: Charles E. Tuttle, 1997. 424 pp.

Melton, J. Gordon. *A Bibliography of Buddhism in America, 1880–1940.* Santa Barbara, CA: Institute for the Study of American Religion, 1985. 13 pp.

Morreale, Don, Ed. *The Complete Guide to Buddhist America.* Boston: Shambhala, 1973. 403 pp.

Peiris, William. *The Western Contribution to Buddhism.* Delhi: Motilal Bonarsidass, 1973. 287 pp.

Prebish, Charles S. *American Buddhism.* North Scituate, MA: Duxbury Press, 1979. 220 pp.

Tamney, Joseph B. *American Society in the Buddhist Mirror.* New York: Garland Publishing, 1992. 191 pp.

THERAVADA BUDDHISM

Dhiravamsa, V. R. *The Way of Non-Attachment.* New York: Schocken Books, 1975. 160 pp.

Dutt, Sukumar. *Buddhism in East Asia.* New Delhi: Indian Council for Cultural Relations, 1966. 225 pp.

Hamilton-Merritt, Jane. *A Meditator's Diary.* New York: Harper & Row, 1976. 155 pp.

Jumsai, M. L. Manich. *Understanding Thai Buddhism.* Bangkok: Chalermnit Press, 1973. 124 pp.

JAPANESE MAYAHANA BUDDHISM

Anesaki, Masaharu. *Nichiren, The Buddhist Prophet.* Cambridge: Harvard University Press, 1949. 160 pp.

Nakai, Gendo. *Shinran and His Religion of Pure Faith.* Kyoto: Shinshu Research Institute, 1937. 260 pp.

Suzuki, Beatrice Lane. *Mahayana Buddhism.* New York: Macmillan, 1969. 158 pp.

ZEN BUDDHISM

Becker, Ernest. *Zen: A Rational Critique.* New York: W.W. Norton, 1961. 192 pp.

Dumoulin, Heinrich. *A History of Zen Buddhism.* Boston: Beacon Press, 1963. 335 pp.

Humphreys, Christmas. *A Western Approach to Zen.* Wheaton, IL: Theosophical Publishing House, 1972. 212 pp.

Suzuki, D. T. *Zen Buddhism.* Garden City, NY: Doubleday, 1956. 294 pp.

Tworkov, Helen. *Zen in America: Five Teachers and the Search for an American Buddhism.* New York: Kodansha International, 1994. 271 pp.

Watts, Alan. *The Way of Zen.* New York: Pantheon Books, 1968. 236 pp.

CHINESE BUDDHISM

Pachow, W. *Chinese Buddhism.* Washington, DC: University Press of America, 1980. 260 pp.

Thompson, Laurence G. *Chinese Religion: An Introduction.* Belmont, CA: Dickenson Publishing Company, 1969. 119 pp.

Yu, Lu K'uan (Charles Luk). *Practical Buddhism.* Wheaton, IL: Theosophical Publishing House, 1973. 167 pp.

KOREAN BUDDHISM

Brief Introduction to Korean Buddhism. Los Angeles: Korean Buddhist Sangha Association of Western Territory of the U.S.A., 1984. 38 pp.

Seo, Kyung-Bo. *A Study of Korean Buddhism Approached through the Chidangjip.* Walnut Creek, CA: Walnut Creek Zendo, 1960(?). 411 pp.

Shin-yong, Chun, ed. *Buddhist Culture in Korea.* Seoul, Korea: Si-sa-yong-o-sa Publishers Inc., 1982. 134 pp.

TIBETAN BUDDHISM

Anderson, Walt. *Open Secrets.* New York: Viking Press, 1979. 230 pp.

Blofeld, John. *The Tantric Mysticism of Tibet.* New York: Causeway Books, 1974. 257 pp.

Dasgupta, Shashi Bhushan. *An Introduction to Tantric Buddhism.* Boulder, CO: Shambhala, 1974. 211 pp.

Hoffman, Helmut. *The Religions of Tibet.* New York: Macmillan, 1961. 199 pp.

Sopa, Lhundup, and Jeffery Hopkins. *Practice and Theory of Tibetan Buddhism.* New York: Grove Press, 1976. 164 pp.

SHINTO

Aston, W. G. *Shinto, The Way of the Gods.* London: Longmans Green & Co., 1905. 390 pp.

Ballou, Robert O. *Shinto, The Unconquered Enemy.* New York: Viking Press, 1945. 239 pp.

Ross, Floyd Hiatt. *Shinto, The Way of the Gods.* Boston: Beacon Press, 1965. 187 pp.

Sectarian Shinto (The Way of the Gods). Tokyo: The Japan Times & Mail, 1939. 62 pp.

TAOISM

Blofeld, John. *Taoism, The Road to Immortality.* Boulder: Shambhala, 1978. 195 pp.

Cleary, Thomas S. *Vitality, Energy, Spirit: A Taoist Source Book.* Boston: Shambhala, 1991. 281 pp.

Legge, James, trans. *I Ching Book of Changes.* New Hyde Park, NY: University Books, 1964. 448 pp.

Waley, Arthur. *The Way and Its Power.* New York: Grove Press, 1968. 262 pp.

Welch, Holmes. *Taoism, The Parting of the Way.* Boston: Beacon Press, 1965. 194 pp.

CONFUCIANISM

Chai, Ch'u, and Winberg Chai. *Confucianism.* Woodbury, NY: Barron's Educational Series, 1973. 202 pp.

Taylor, Rodney L. *The Way of Heaven: An Introduction to the Confucian Religious Life.* Boston: Shambhala, 1986. 37 pp.

The Wisdom of Confucius. New York: Books, Inc., 1960. 236 pp.

NEW RELIGIONS OF JAPAN

Ellwood, Robert S., Jr. *The Eagle and the Rising Sun.* Philadelphia: Westminster Press, 1974. 224 pp.

McFarland, H. Neill. *The Rush Hour of the Gods.* New York: Macmillan, 1967. 267 pp.

Offner, Clark B. *Modern Japanese Religions.* New York: Twayne Publishers, 1963. 296 pp.

Thomsen, Harry. *The New Religions of Japan.* Rutland, VT: Charles E. Tuttle Company, 1963. 268 pp.

Section 1

Interfaith and Ecumenical Family of Organizations

Consult the Contents pages to locate the essay in Part II, Historical Essay Chapters,
that provides an historical discussion of this family

Interfaith Groups

★1★

Berkeley Area Interfaith Council
2340 Durant Ave.
Berkeley, CA 94704-1607

While the Berkeley Area Interfaith Council is a local organization designed to serve the needs of the Berkeley/Oakland area of the San Francisco Bay community in California, the wide publicity given to its very active program has conferred it an unusual status and recognition in interfaith work in North America. It grew out of the former Berkeley Council of Churches, which had become known in the years immediately following World War II for its political activism but which began to dwindle by the beginning of the 1970s. In 1971 the idea was placed before the council to become more inclusive.

The idea of a new council became a reality in 1973 with the hiring of a full-time director, the Rev. William Shive, whose desire to live a simple life coincided with the minuscule salary the council could afford. He began the task of visiting all of the different churches and religious groups of the community. The council met each month in a different center, the host taking the lead in explaining what their group was all about as part of a program that would include a discussion on some topic of widespread interest. By the end of the 1970s the council had become involved in religious freedom controversies, advocacy of gay rights, and various local issues.

In spite of ups and downs, the council has survived, and most recently it has worked on the follow-up to the World's Parliament of Religions meeting held in Chicago in 1993. The Council has become a part of the San Francisco Bay Area Interfaith Coalition.

Sources:

Magalis, Elaine. "Methodists, Moonies, and Mormons." *New World Outlook* (May 1979): 1620.

★2★

Canadian Ecumenical Action
Current address not obtained for this edition.

Canadian Ecumenical Action is described as a multi-faith community services society. It was founded in 1973 as the People's Opportunity in Ecumenical Mission by a group of Christians under the leadership of the Rev. Val Anderson. In 1975 the group began the *Canadian Ecumenical News.* Gradually people of other faiths were included and the group emerged as an interfaith work. The group operates primarily in western Canada.

Canadian Ecumenical Action seeks to promote interfaith understanding; provide information and resources on world religions to the community and encourage interfaith dialogue on community issues; and promote community service programs. *Canadian Ecumenical News* carries announcements of interfaith activities across Canada. The organization is headed by a planning board of 15 people. Board members serve as interested individuals rather than official representatives of their religious community.

Membership: Participants in Canadian Ecumenical Action come from the many different religious communities represented in Canada.

Periodicals: *Canadian Ecumenical News.*

★3★

Inter-Religions Federation for World Peace
% Frank Kaufmann
4 West 43rd St.
New York, NY 10036

The Inter-Religions Federation for World Peace grew out of an older organization, the Global Congress of the World's Religions. The Global Congress developed from an initial proposal for a centennial celebration of the World's Parliament of Religions, originally held in 1893 in Chicago, Illinois. The proposal was made by Dr. Warren Lewis, then a professor of church history at the Unification Theological Seminary. It received the backing of the seminary, which sponsored several exploratory meetings in the late 1970s. The Global Congress was formally organized in 1980 and during the next few years sponsored a regular series of consultations around the world.

In the mid-1980s, the Global Congress acquired the sponsorship of the International Religious Foundation, one of the arms of the Unification Church which had supplied it with financial and personnel resources. Its activity was then divided between two structures: the Council for the World's Religions, which promoted worldwide interfaith meetings, and the Assembly of the World's Religions, which met every few years. The assembly, which involves the leadership of the council, also draws upon the resources of the larger International Religious Foundation. Assembly meetings have been held in 1985 (McAfee, New Jersey) and 1990 (San Francisco, California). At the 1990 assembly meeting, Rev. Sun Myung Moon announced the formation of the Inter-Religious Federation for World Peace.

The federation, formally established in 1991, has as its goal peace, which includes: peace within one's self and one's family peace within societies and among nations; peace within religions and among religious traditions; peace within and among cultures; and peace between the human and natural worlds. It is the belief of the leadership that inter-religious peace is essential for world peace and that a respect for religious pluralism is a key element of modern life. The federation is headed by an interfaith presiding council assisted by a board of advisors composed of a large number of religious leaders and scholars. An executive staff administers the day-to-day work of the federation.

Membership: In 1997 there were 11 regional councils located in key cities around the world.

Periodicals: *IRFWP Newsletter.*

Sources:

Bryant, M. Darrol, John Maniatus, and Tyler Hendricks, eds. *Assembly of the World's Religions, 1985: Spiritual Unity and the Future of the Earth*. New York: International Religious Foundation, 1985.

Lewis, Warren, ed. *Towards a Global Congress of the World's Religions*. Barrytown, NY: Unification Theological Seminary, 1978.

Thompson, Henry O. *The Global Congress of the World's Religions: Proceedings, 1980–82*. Barrytown, NY: Unification Theological Seminary, 1982.

Walsh, Thomas G., ed. *Assembly of the World's Religions, 1990: Transmitting Our Heritage to Youth and Society*. New York: Interreligious Foundation, 1992.

★4★

The National Conference for Community and Justice
71 First Ave., 11th Floor
New York, NY 10003

Alternate Address: International Council of Christians and Jews, Martin Buber House, Werlestrasse 2, D-64646, Heppenheim, Germany; Canadian Council of Christians and Jews, 2 Carlton St., Ste 820, Toronto, ON M5B 1J3.

The National Conference for Community and Justice was founded in 1927 as the National Conference of Jews and Christians for the Advancement of Justice, Amity and Peace, but had been known through most of its long history as the National Conference of Christians and Jews. Founded primarily to promote goodwill and understanding between Protestants, Roman Catholics, and Jews, in large part to deal with the problem of anti-Semitism, in the last several decades it has seen the need to push its work into ever-larger arenas of inter-group conflict and to use its expertise in the promotion of interreligious, interracial, and intercultural understanding. The organization was founded by Charles Evans Hughes, Newton D. Baker, S. Parkes Cadman, Roger W. Straus, and Carlton J. H. Hayes. The work extended to Canada in 1940 with the formation of the Canadian Council of Christians and Jews and to Europe in 1950 with the organization of the World Brotherhood (now embodied in the International Council of Christians and Jews).

Through the years, The National Conference has promoted interreligious dialogue, especially between Jewish and Christian leaders, and in the 1980s moved into the very needful area of Jewish/Christian/Muslim dialogue. It has also begun fruitful dialogues between African Americans, the Jewish community, and the larger non-Jewish white population.

The National Conference operates through regional offices located in most major U. S. cities. Its policies are set by the 200-member national board of trustees and administered by the 22-member executive board.

Membership: The National Conference is not directly sponsored by religious organizations, though individuals from many different churches and synagogues are members.

Sources:

Braybrooke, Marcus. *Inter-Faith Organizations, 1893–1979: An Historical Directory*. New York: Edwin Mellen Press, 1980.

★5★

Temple of Understanding
% Cathedral Church of St. John the Divine
1047 Amsterdam Ave. (at 112th St.)
New York, NY 10025

The Temple of Understanding grew out of the vision of Judith Hollister for a center for the promotion of understanding between the world's religions, a recognition of the oneness of the human family, and ultimately the organization of a spiritual United Nations. The ideas as put forth in the 1950s were warmly received by a number of prominent leaders around the globe, from Eleanor

Roosevelt to Albert Schweitzer, who in 1960 became "founding friends" of the temple.

The temple is headed by a president, a board of directors, an advisory board, and an international committee. Over the years the temple has held a number of Spiritual Summit Conferences. Plans have existed for many years to create a permanent home of the temple on land near Washington, D.C., but financial resources to construct the facility have not been forthcoming as yet.

Periodicals: The temple cooperates with the World Congress of Faiths in the production of *World Faiths Insight*.

Sources:

Braybrooke, Marcus. *Inter-Faith Organizations, 1893–1979: An Historical Directory*. New York: Edwin Mellen Press, 1980.

★6★

World Conference on Religion and Peace
% Secretary-General
777 United Nations Plaza, 12th Floor
New York, NY 10017

Alternate Address: International headquarters: 14 chemin Auguste-Vilbert, 1218 Grand Saconnex, Geneva, Switzerland.

The World Conference on Religion and Peace (WCRP) grew out of an initiative to bring religious resources to bear on the world situation threatening to lead to war. It calls people of different faiths to unite in a common effort for world peace.

The work that led to the founding of WCRP can be traced to 1962 and to Unitarian-Universalist leader Dr. Dana McLean Greeley, who brought together Rabbi Maurice N. Eisendrath, Bp. John Wesley Lord (Methodist), and Bp. John Wright (Roman Catholic). The occasion for their first gathering was the Cuban missile crisis. Their informal gatherings led to an initial conference in New York in 1964 and a National Inter-Religious Conference on World Peace in Washington, D.C., in 1966. The next year, two representatives of the National Conference made a round-the-world tour to ascertain support for an international meeting.

An initial International Inter-Religious Symposium on Peace in 1968 led directly to the first World Conference on Peace held in Kyoto, Japan, in 1970, at which time the WCRP was formally established. The founding of WCRP occurred in the wake of the heightened war effort in Vietnam. Since that time, WCRP has been given status as a United Nations Non-Governmental Agency. It has carried on a regular program of relief to the victims of war and speaking to nations either at war or threatening to go to war.

Periodicals: *Religion for Peace*, 14 chemin Auguste-Vilbert, 1218 Grand Saconnex, Geneva, Switzerland.

Sources:

Braybrooke, Marcus. *Inter-Faith Organizations, 1893–1979: An Historical Directory*. New York: Edwin Mellen Press, 1980.

★7★

World Fellowship of Religions
% Siddhachalam
RD 4, Box 374, Mud Pond Rd.
Blairstown, NJ 07825

Alternate Address: International headquarters: c-599, Chetna Marg, New Delhi, India.

The World Fellowship of Religions was founded in the 1950s in India but now has branches in more than 30 countries. It was founded by Jain master H.H. Acharya Sushil Kumarji Maharaj, who presented an initial proposal for the fellowship in 1955. This led to the World Conference of All Religions held in Delhi in 1957, following which the World Fellowship of Religions was formally inaugurated. It has held regular world conferences, primarily in India, ever since.

WFR has as its goals the promotion of peace, the establishment of right human relationships, and the building of right human relationships through love, equality, compassion, and friendship. It has created a number of projects to directly help suffering people, such as the setting up of medical facilities and development of nutrition programs. WFR works on the basis that nonviolence is essential to its cooperative program.

Periodicals: *Siddhachalam Newsletter.*

Sources:

Clark, Francis, ed. *Interfaith Directory.* New York: International Religious Foundation, 1987.

Christian Ecumenical Organizations

★8★
American Council of Christian Churches
625 E. 4th St.
PO Box 5455
Bethlehem, PA 18015

The American Council of Christian Churches was founded in 1941 as an expression of not only the fundamentalist-modernist split in American Protestantism, but also the growing split among conservative Christians into fundamentalist separatists and evangelicals. The American Council represented the most conservative wing of Protestant thought, generally characterized by an affirmation of both the infallibility and inerrancy of the Bible and a desire to separate fully from the heresy and apostasy which it saw gaining control of liberal Protestantism, then embodied in the Federal Council of Churches of Christ in America. The American Council has also rejected as unacceptable the willingness of some conservative Christians, with whom it agrees theologically, to cooperate on programs or be a part of otherwise liberal Protestant projects and groups.

The leading figure in the formation of the council was Carl McIntire, founder of the Bible Presbyterian Church. McIntire had left the Presbyterian Church in 1936 during the fundamentalist controversy, but because of his acceptance of premillennial eschatology McIntire was at odds with other conservative fundamentalists such as J. Gresham Machen and the Orthodox Presbyterian Church. Thus in 1941 McIntire became the first president of the American Council of Christian Churches (ACCC), dominated it for a quarter of a century, and led it through a series of controversies.

In 1948, McIntire led in the founding of the International Council of Christian Churches, which held its first meeting in Amsterdam, the Netherlands, shortly before the inaugural meeting of the World Council of Churches in that same city. McIntire was accused of deliberately trying to interfere with the World Council and mislead the public. In 1950 he sponsored a project to send Christian literature into Eastern Europe and the Soviet Union via balloons. Such actions began to cost him the allegiance of many leading conservative Christians who had originally given the ACCC its support. Then in 1956 the Bible Presbyterian Church split after a majority repudiated McIntire. Three years later the ACCC itself acted to remove McIntire from its board, and it moved on to a new phase of its existence.

The ACCC remains in opposition to the ecumenical movement as embodied in the World Council of Churches and the National Council of the Churches of Christ in the U.S.A. and regularly assumes a position in opposition to those bodies it feels are contrary to biblical doctrine. In like measure, the ACCC is opposed to the National Association of Evangelicals and prohibits members from holding joint membership. In 1987 the ACCC supported the formation of the Council of Bible Believing Churches now the World Council of Biblical Churches, International, a worldwide fellowship association of fundamentalist churches.

Membership: The ACCC includes among its members the following: Evangelical Methodist Church of America; Fellowship of Fundamental Bible Churches; Fellowship of Independent Method-

ists; Free Presbyterian Church of North America; Fundamental Methodist Church; General Association of Regular Baptist Churches; Independent Churches Affiliated; and Tioga River Christian Conference. In addition, an unreported number of independent congregations are also affiliated with the ACCC.

Periodicals: *Fundamental News Service.*

Sources:

Mayer, F. E. *The Religious Bodies of America.* St. Louis, MO: Concordia Publishing House, 1956.

Roy, Ralph Lord. *Apostles of Discord.* Boston: Beacon Press, 1953.

★9★
Canadian Council of Churches
40 St. Clair St.
Toronto, ON, Canada M4T 1M9

The Canadian Council of Churches (also known as the Council canadian des Eglises) was founded in 1944, a product of the ecumenical movement which would soon lead to the formation of the World Council of Churches and the immediate necessity for coordinated action by churches both during and after World War II. Member churches are required to confess Jesus Christ as Lord and Savior according to the Bible and seek to fulfill their common calling to the glory of God. The council seeks to give visible expression to the unity of its member bodies in Jesus Christ.

The council attempts to further ecumenism, to speak to social problems of the day, to facilitate the encounter of Christians of different denominations, and to respond creatively to social change. It operates through the leadership of a president, a general board, a general secretary, and commissions on world concerns and Canadian concerns. Its assembly meets triennially. The council cooperates with the World Council of Churches and nurtures the development of regional and local church councils throughout Canada.

Membership: Member denominations include the following: Anglican Church of Canada; Armenian Church of America-Diocese of Canada; Baptist Convention of Ontario and Quebec; Christian Church (Disciples of Christ); Coptic Orthodox Church of Canada; Ethiopian Orthodox Church in Canada; Evangelical Lutheran Church in Canada; Greek Orthodox Diocese of Toronto; Orthodox Church in America, Diocese of Canada; Polish National Catholic Church; Presbyterian Church in Canada; Reformed Church in America-Classis of Ontario; Religious Society of Friends-Canada Yearly Meeting; Salvation Army-Canada and Bermuda; and United Church of Canada. In addition, the Canadian Conference of Catholic Bishops (the Roman Catholic Church) is an associate member.

Sources:

Directory of Christian Councils. Geneva: World Council of Churches, 1985.

★10★
Council of Bible Believing Churches International
625 E. 4th St.
PO Box 5455
Bethlehem, PA 18015

The World Council of Bible Believing Churches International was founded in 1987 as the Council of Bible Believing Churches International as an association of Fundamentalist Christian churches at the instigation of the American Council of Christian Churches (ACCC). From 1948 to 1969, the American Council had an international affiliate, the International Council of Christian Churches (ICCC). However, in 1969, the ACCC removed Carl McIntire from its board, and the International Council of Christian Churches, which McIntire had been instrumental in founding, had sided with him. The ICCC and the ACCC discontinued their relationship. The council sees itself as an issue-oriented body whose members have come together to speak to the major concerns of Fundamentalist Christians worldwide.

Along with the ACCC, with whom it shares its headquarters facilities, the council is a conservative Protestant body affirming the infallibility and inerrancy of the Bible and the need for complete separation from heresy and apostasy such as the council believes is manifest in the World Council of Churches and the National Council of the Churches of Christ in the U.S.A. To council members, separation includes militant opposition to Romanism, Ecumenism, Materialism, Communism, and every other thing that is contrary to sound doctrine. Members of the council cannot be affiliated with, or represented in any manner by, the World Council of Churches or any of its affiliates, the World Evangelical Fellowship (WEF) or any of its affiliates, the International Council of Christian Churches (ICCC) or any of its affiliates, the modern Charismatic Movement, or the Ecumenical Movement.

The council is governed by an executive committee which includes representatives from each member body.

Membership: North American members of the council are the same as those in the American Council of Christian Churches: Evangelical Methodist Church of America; Fellowship of Fundamental Bible Churches; Fellowship of Independent Methodists; Free Presbyterian Church of North America; Fundamental Methodist Church; General Association of Regular Baptist Churches; Independent Churches Affiliated; and Tioga River Christian Conference.

★11★
Evangelical Fellowship of Canada
175 Riviera Dr.
Markham, ON, Canada L3R 5J6

Alternate Address: Mailing Address: Box 8800, Sta. B, Willowdale, ON M2K 2R6, Canada.

The Evangelical Fellowship of Canada was founded in 1964 and serves conservative Protestant denominations, organizations, congregations, and individuals. It has a doctrinal stance like that of the National Association of Evangelicals (NAE), which emphasizes the Bible as the infallible Word of God and the necessity of salvation by faith in Jesus Christ. Like the NAE, it is a member of the World Evangelical Fellowship. It provides Protestant Christians with an alternative to the Canadian Council of Churches.

Membership: In the early 1990s, the fellowship had 27 denominations in its membership and in addition had 88 affiliated organizations and 756 local congregations.

★12★
Federal Council of the Churches of Christ in America
(Defunct)

The Federal Council of the Churches of Christ in America was the dominant ecumenical structure in American Christianity during the first half of the twentieth century. Prior to its formation there had been much cooperative work by various Protestant church groups, but none had moved on to the national level to organize an official cooperative body that would have the official backing of the respective denominations. The need for such a cooperative body grew out of the desire to have a more influential voice in solving the new state of urban problems that had arisen with the dramatic expansion of the cities in the 1880s and 1890s.

In 1898 the National Council of the Congregational Churches called for a gathering to consider such a structure. Then in 1900 an unofficial National Federation of Churches and Christian Workers formed with the purpose of planning a conference of church representatives to strategize about building a closer working relationship. Elias B. Sanford, corresponding secretary of the Open and Institutional Church League, took the lead in advocacy of the new federation. In 1901 Sanford gained the signatures of 25

prominent church leaders to issue a call for a national federation. In 1902 plans for a national conference of official delegates were initiated, and a conference date set in 1905. Later in 1902, the Methodist Episcopal Church, South, became the first to offer a positive response.

In 1905, 29 denominations sent delegates to a planning conference in New York City, where a "Plan of Federation" was developed looking toward the creation of the Federal Council. It had been assumed that the denominations were in substantial agreement theologically, and little mention was made of doctrinal divergences (the most acrimonious phase of the fundamentalist-modernist controversy being yet two decades in the future). The American Unitarian Association, a nontrinitarian group, did not attend. The conference submitted its proposed plan to the various denominations.

The council was designed as a delegated body centered upon the common witness of its denominational members. Each denomination was apportioned members according to size, but each group had a minimum of four delegates. It was to be an advisory body to facilitate communication among the different churches and allow them to speak with a common voice on important issues. Committees were appointed to work in the various phases of church life such as evangelism, Sunday observance, temperance, etc., though they had little financial support or power to act. The Federal Council also sought to build regional and local ecumenical councils around the country to implement the National Council's work.

Thirty-three denominations were represented in 1908 at the gathering in Philadelphia to inaugurate the Federal Council of Churches. It immediately had to face the competition it posed for older cooperative organizations that specialized in a single area of church life—Sunday schools, foreign missions, youthwork, etc. Thus the council moved first into an as-yet poorly addressed area, social concerns. From the Methodists it borrowed a social statement which it reworked as "The Social Ideals of the Churches." This statement set the Federal Council on a course that would, in the next decades, clearly identify it with the more liberal and "social gospel" theological perspectives which became such an important part of what was being termed "modernist" theology. Several of the smaller, more conservative denominations soon dropped out of membership because of what they perceived as too much emphasis on social issues.

Since the ecumenical movement owed much of its inspiration to concerns in the mission field between competing missionary programs, the council attempted to address that issue and spoke to the need for spreading to foreign lands the spirit of cooperation expressed by the existence of the council in America. This perspective would lead to a later shift of emphasis by American churches, who moved funds away from the sending of missionaries to the undergirding of indigenous churches in former mission fields.

The Federal Council survived the era of World War I and joined in rebuilding efforts after the war. It survived the fundamentalist-modernist controversy and saw the organization of two competing groups during World War II, the American Council of Christian Churches representing separatist fundamentalists, and the National Association of Evangelicals representing more mainline conservative Protestants.

After the war, the growing ecumenical movement, signaled by the efforts to organize the World Council of Churches, also gave voice to those who wished that a more centralized agency, bringing together all of the concerns now spread out among a number of ecumenical structures, could be created. While the Federal Council was that in name, in fact it did not operate effectively in areas such as foreign missions, religious education, and women's concerns. Therefore a plan was drawn up to unite the Federal Council with a number of other agencies, and on January 1, 1951, the Federal Council was superseded by the National Council of the Churches of Christ in the U.S.A.

Sources:

Cavert, Samuel McCrea. *The American Churches in the Ecumenical Movement, 1900–1968.* New York: Association Press, 1968.

★13★
International Council of Christian Churches (ICCC)
% Suzanne L. Deacon, Sec.
756 Haddon Ave.
Collingswood, NJ 08108

The International Council of Christian Churches (ICCC) was founded in 1948 by a number of conservative Protestant Christians, the most prominent being Dr. Carl McIntire, also the founder of the Bible Presbyterian Church in Collinwood, New Jersey. It was the international counterpart of the American Council of Christian Churches (ACCC), founded in 1941, also very much inspired by the efforts of McIntire. However, in 1969, McIntire and the ACCC went their separate ways and McIntire founded the American Christian Action Council (ACCC). At that time, the ICCC recognized the ACAC, now known as the ICCC in America.

The ICCC has grown out of the split within twentieth-century Protestantism between fundamentalists and modernists and represents the continuing allegiance to fundamentalist positions. Also, in the 1940s, as fundamentalists split into two factions, the ICCC was aligned with the more conservative faction. It upholds the inerrancy and infallibility of the Bible and calls Christians to separate themselves from all evil, especially heresy and apostasy.

The major target of the ICCC has been the modern ecumenical movement as represented in the World Council of Churches and the National Council of the Churches of Christ in the U.S.A. The ICCC has often been criticized for holding its meetings in the same city and at relatively close times to the World Council's meetings.

Membership: At its fiftieth anniversary in Amsterdam in 1998, the ICCC reported 700 denominations from over 100 countries in its membership.

Sources:

Harden, Margaret C., comp. *A Brief History of the Bible Presbyterian Church and Its Agencies.* Privately published, 1968.

Mayer, F. E. *The Religious Bodies of America.* St. Louis, MO: Concordia Publishing House, 1956.

★14★
National Association of Evangelicals
Box 28
Wheaton, IL 60187

The National Association of Evangelicals (NAE) grew out of the reorganization of conservative Protestants following the most eventful phase of the fundamentalist-modernist controversy of the 1920s and 1930s. Through the first decades of the twentieth century, conservative Protestants had seen many of the major denominations, especially the Methodists, Baptists, and Presbyterians in the northern states, become dominated by what they considered approaches to Christianity that abandoned essential beliefs and placed an undue emphasis on social reform, with a resulting deemphasis on missions and evangelism.

The battle between conservatives (the fundamentalists) and the liberals (the modernists) led to the liberals taking control of most of the denominational leadership, and increasingly in the 1930s, to many conservatives leaving to form new schools, mission-sending agencies, and denominations. By the end of the 1930s, fundamentalists seemed to have divided into two mutually exclusive camps. In this context many conservatives began a reevaluation of their situation. They were in agreement with the conservative theological emphasis of the fundamentalists of the 1920s but were upset at what appeared an unwarranted separatism and fear of the modern world. These conservatives wanted to embrace modern learning, which they felt could be accommodated to their

theological commitments. Also, many did not want to separate from the denominational heritage in which they had grown up and wanted to be able to work with their modernist colleagues in areas not relating directly to their doctrinal conflicts. This position became known as Neo-evangelicalism.

The National Association of Evangelicals emerged as one of the organizational expressions of Neoevangelicalism. It included among its leaders representatives from those churches which had resisted the pull of modernism, new churches formed out of the fundamentalist controversy, and conservative pockets that remained in most of the older liberal Protestant denominations. Liberal Protestant denominations had previously organized into the Federal Council of the Churches of Christ in America. In 1941, separatist fundamentalists had organized the American Council of Christian Churches in opposition to the Federal Council at every point.

Thus in 1942, evangelicals effected a national organization. Direct inspiration for the National Association was given by the successes of the regional New England Evangelical Fellowship which had formed in the late 1930s. Not limited to denominational membership, it allowed denominations, individual congregations, and various organizations and schools to become members. Members are united by a seven-point confession of faith that affirms belief in the Bible as the authoritative and infallible Word of God, the Trinity, the divinity of Christ, the human need of salvation, the ministry of the Holy Spirit, the resurrection of humans, and the spiritual unity of believers.

The NAE has developed a broad program to serve its members, the most important being to provide a united witness for Evangelical Christians. It assists mission agencies in their interaction with foreign governments, has developed a relief arm to assist the needy around the world, and interacts with the armed forces on the matter of chaplaincies for member organizations. It also reaches out through National Religious Broadcasters, the National Sunday School Association, and its Evangelism and Spiritual Life Commission. As the NAE has matured, it has also spoken on a variety of social issues and has established an Office of Public Affairs in Washington, D.C.

The National Association is a member of the World Evangelical Fellowship, whose North American headquarters are located in the NAE headquarters building in Wheaton, Illinois.

Membership: Membership in the NAE is held by a number of denominations, who provide the bulk of its support, and several hundred evangelical organizations. Denominational members include the following: Advent Christian Church; Assemblies of God; Baptist General Conference; Brethren Church (Ashland, Ohio); Brethren in Christ Church; Christian and Missionary Alliance; Christian Catholic Church (Evangelical Protestant); Christian Church of North America; Christian Reformed Church of North America; Christian Union; Church of Christ in Christian Union; Church of God (Cleveland, Tennessee); Church of God of the Mountain Assembly; Church of the Nazarene; Church of the United Brethren in Christ; Congregation Holiness Church; Conservative Baptist Association of America; Conservative Congregational Christian Conference; Elim Fellowship; Evangelical Christian Church; Evangelical Church of North America; Evangelical Congregational Church; Evangelical Free Church of America; Evangelical Friends International/North America; Evangelical Mennonite Church; Evangelical Methodist Church; Evangelical Presbyterian Church Evangelistic Missionary Fellowship; Fire-Baptized Holiness Church of God of the Americas; Free Methodist Church of North America; General Association of General Baptists; International Church of the Foursquare Gospel; International Pentecostal Church of Christ; International Pentecostal Holiness Church; Mennonite Brethren Churches, USA; Midwest Congregational Christian Fellowship; Missionary Church; Open Bible Standard Churches; Pentecostal Church of Christ; Pentecostal Free Will Baptist Church; Presbyterian Church in America; Primitive Methodist Church, USA; Reformed Episcopal Church; Reformed Presbyterian Church of North America; Salvation Army; Wesleyan Church; and World Confessional Lutheran Association. In addition, members and congregations of many other denominations are also related to the NAE.

Periodicals: *United Evangelical Action.* • *NAE Washington Insight.*

Sources:

Carpenter, Joel A., ed. *A New Evangelical Coalition: Early Documents of the National Association of Evangelicals.* New York: Garland Publishing, 1988.

NAE Resolutions. Wheaton, IL: National Association of Evangelicals, 1985.

Shelley, Bruce L. *Evangelism in America.* Grand Rapids, MI: Eerdmans Publishing House, 1967.

★15★

National Black Evangelistic Association
5736 N. Albina Ave.
Portland, OR 97217

The National Black Evangelistic Association was founded in 1963 as the National Negro Evangelical Association as a cooperative organization for conservative African-American ministers and churches. Most of the founding members were Baptist. In 1970 the association attracted 1,500 delegates to the first African-American conference on evangelism, which met at St. Stephen Baptist Church in Kansas City, Missouri. The building of lines of communication among African-American evangelicals and the development of local evangelistic programs have provided a focus for the association. In 1988 the association founded the Institute of Black Evangelical Thought and Action.

Membership: Not reported.

Periodicals: *NBEA Outreach.* •*Journal.*

★16★

National Council of the Churches of Christ in the U.S.A.
475 Riverside Dr.
New York, NY 10027

The National Council of Churches of Christ in the U.S.A. is the largest of the several Christian ecumenical councils operating in the United States. It includes among its member organizations most of the older liberal Protestant churches and many of the American branches of the Eastern Orthodox churches.

The National Council was founded in 1950 by representatives of 29 Protestant, Anglican, and Orthodox bodies who met at Cleveland, Ohio. The council represented the merger of 12 previously existing national ecumenical organizations, the most important being the Federal Council of the Churches of Christ in America, which it superseded. The 11 remaining bodies included the Foreign Missions Conference of North America, Home Missions Council of North America, International Council of Religious Education, Missionary Education Movement of the United States and Canada, National Protestant Council on Higher Education, United Council of Church Women, United Stewardship Council, Church World Service, Interseminary Committee, Protestant Film Commission, and the Protestant Radio Commission. Three years later, the Student Volunteer Movement merged into the council. In its formation, the National Council followed the example previously set by the World Council of Churches (founded in 1948), and many of its leaders also served as American representatives in World Council work.

The council was established, among other purposes, to manifest the churches' oneness in Christ, to continue the work of the predecessor agencies, to renew the life of the church, to foster cooperation, and to speak as a single voice on important public and social issues. In this last function, like the former Federal Council of Churches, the National Council has remained involved in con-

troversy which peaked during the Civil Rights Movement of the 1960s, to which it gave its full support. In recent years the council has had to delineate its membership criteria more carefully, as various groups such as the Holy Spirit Association for the Unification of World Christianity (or Unification Church) and the Metropolitan Community Churches (based in the homosexual community) have applied for membership and been rejected.

The council is headed by its president, a general board (representative of the member churches), and a general secretary. It is organized into four working units: Education, Communication and Discipleship; Church World Services and Witness; Prophetic Justice; and Unity and Relationships. There is also a department of Finance and Administration. Through its various units and subunits, the council speaks to its constituency and the general public. Policy statements are issued by the general board. The general board meets annually and its membership is drawn from the members of the General Assembly, which meets triennially.

Membership: Most members of the National Council are also members of the World Council of Churches, though some are represented through their international headquarters, which may be in another country: African Methodist Episcopal Church; African Methodist Episcopal Zion Church; American Baptist Churches in the U.S.A.; Antiochian Orthodox Christian Archdiocese of North America; Apostolic Catholic Assyrian Church of the East; Christian Church (Disciples of Christ); Christian Methodist Episcopal Church; Church of the Brethren; Coptic Orthodox Church; Diocese of the Armenian Church in America; Episcopal Church; Evangelical Lutheran Church in America; Friends United Meeting; General Convention of the Swedenborgian Church; Greek Orthodox Archdiocese of North and South America; Hungarian Reformed Church in America; International Council of Community Churches; General Assembly of the Korean Presbyterian Church in America; Moravian Church in America; National Baptist Convention of America; National Baptist Convention, U.S.A.; Orthodox Church in America; Philadelphia Yearly Meeting of the Religious Society of Friends; Polish National Catholic Church of America; Presbyterian Church (U.S.A.); Progressive National Baptist Convention; Reformed Church in America; Patriarchal Parishes of the Russian Orthodox Church in the U.S.A.; Serbian Orthodox Church in the U.S.A. and Canada; Syrian Orthodox Church of Antioch; Ukrainian Orthodox Church in America; United Church of Canada; United Church of Christ; and United Methodist Church. Membership has remained fairly stable over the years, though a few churches have left and others have joined.

Periodicals: The council and its program units issue a number of periodicals and newsletters, not the least of which is the annual *Yearbook of American Churches.*

Sources:

Cavert, Samuel McCrea. *The American Churches in the Ecumenical Movement, 1900–1968.* New York: Association Press, 1968.

★17★

National Fraternal Council of Negro Churches
(Defunct)

The National Fraternal Council of Negro Churches was a pioneering African-American ecumenical organization founded in Chicago, Illinois, in 1934 as the Negro Fraternal Council of Churches. Bishop Reverdy C. Ransom of the African Methodist Episcopal Church was the first president of the council. From the original seven-member organization, the council grew to 12 organizations which were to dominate its life. The council was somewhat modeled on the Federal Council of Churches and represented the most liberal Protestant denominations. It divided its work into 12 working areas which paralleled those of the Federal Council, though with some specialized work areas such as race relations, Africa, and peace. The Fraternal Council had a Washington,

D.C., office to monitor legislation of special interest to the African-American community.

The council functioned well for a generation. Among its accomplishments was the founding of the Interdenominational Theological Center in Atlanta, Georgia. However, as the civil rights movement gained center stage, the council's leadership role fell to other, newer organizations, and it gradually faded in importance.

Membership: Members of the council included the following: African Methodist Episcopal Church; African Methodist Episcopal Zion Church; African Orthodox Church; Bible Way Church of Our Lord Jesus Christ World Wide; Central Jurisdiction of the Methodist Episcopal Church; Christian Methodist Episcopal Church; Church of God in Christ; Church of God and Saints of Christ; Metropolitan Community Church of Christ; National Baptist Convention, U.S.A.; National Baptist Convention of America; and United American Free Will Baptist Church.

Sources:

Guzman, Jessie Parkhurst. *Negro Yearbook.* Tuskegee, AL: Department of Records and Research, Tuskegee Institute, 1947.

★18★
World Council of Churches
425 Riverside Dr.
New York, NY 10115

Alternate Address: International Headquarters: Box 66, 150 route de Ferney, 1211 Geneva 20, Switzerland.

The World Council of Churches, the primary organization representing the Christian community outside of the Roman Catholic Church, grew out of and is the major expression of the ecumenical movement of the twentieth century. International cooperation of Anglican and Protestant churches had been carried on through the first half of the century by three distinct bodies, each concerned with a special area of Christian church life: the Universal Christian Council for Life and Work, the Continuation Committee of the World Conference of Faith and Order, and the International Missionary Council. In 1933, William Adams Brown suggested to Anglican Abp. William Temple that representatives of these organizations, along with the World Alliance for International Friendship and the Student Christian Movement, begin conversations about their common future.

Archbishop Temple initiated informal discussions, which led in 1937 to a proposal to form a World Council of Churches. Work began on a constitution in 1938. The council was to include those churches which accepted Jesus Christ as God and Savior. Deliberations were slowed by the advent of World War II; however, the American members of the provisional committee opened an office in New York City and created an American Committee for the World Council of Churches. The provisional committee resumed its work in 1946.

The inaugural Assembly of the World Council was held in Amsterdam, the Netherlands, in 1948. The desire for the council was spurred by the formation of the United Nations and the perceived need for a means of staying in contact with it. The council seeks to be a visible symbol of the unity of the individual Christian churches, to encourage their common witness for Christ, and to support their worldwide missional thrusts. The council assigned itself the tasks of facilitating common action by its member bodies, promoting cooperation among various churches, and promoting the growth of ecumenical conferences.

The council carries out its program through regular meetings of its General Assembly and a continuing program centered upon its headquarters in Geneva, Switzerland. There is a full-time general staff that operates under the guidance of the general secretary. Along with the general secretariat, there are three Program Units: Faith and Witness, Justice and Service, and Education and Renewal.

Integral to the carrying out of the council's work are the many regional and national councils, which in North America include the National Council of the Churches of Christ in the U.S.A. and the Canadian Council of Churches. Individual churches may be members of the World Council of Churches irrespective of their membership in one of the national councils.

Membership: The World Council of Churches currently consists of more than 300 member churches, including from North America the following: African Methodist Episcopal Church; African Methodist Episcopal Zion Church; American Baptist Churches in the U.S.A.; Anglican Church of Canada; Apostolic Catholic Assyrian Church of the East; Canadian Yearly Meeting of the Society of Friends; Christian Church (Disciples of Christ); Christian Methodist Episcopal Church; Church of the Brethren; Evangelical Lutheran Church in America; Evangelical Lutheran Church of Canada; Friends General Conference; Friends United Meeting; Hungarian Reformed Church in America; International Council of Community Churches; International Evangelical Church; Moravian Church in America; National Baptist Convention of America; National Baptist Convention, U.S.A.; Orthodox Church in America; Polish National Catholic Church of America; Presbyterian Church of Canada; Presbyterian Church (U.S.A.); Progressive National Baptist Convention; Reformed Church in America; United Church of Canada; United Church of Christ; and United Methodist Church. In addition, many international churches with members in North America, including the various Orthodox bodies, are represented through their international headquarters.

Periodicals: *The Ecumenical Courier.* • *The Ecumenical Review.* • *One World.* • *International Review of Missions.*

Sources:

Cavert, Samuel McCrea. *The American Churches in the Ecumenical Movement, 1900–1968.* New York: Association Press, 1968.

Directory of Christian Councils. Geneva: World Council of Churches, 1985.

van der Bent, Ans J., ed. *Handbook of Member Churches: World Council of Churches.* Geneva: World Council of Churches, 1982.

★19★
World Evangelical Fellowship
Box WEF
Wheaton, IL 60189

Alternate Address: International Headquarters: 141 Middle Rd., 05-05 GSM Bldg., Singapore 0718.

The World Evangelical Fellowship (WEF) was founded in 1951 but sees itself as the continuation of the Evangelical Alliance, which was founded in England in 1846 and had a vital life through the rest of the nineteenth century. The alliance suffered greatly from the rise of liberal Protestantism and its capture of most of the leading Protestant denominations in the early twentieth century.

WEF serves as a coordinating and fellowship agency for all Evangelical groups, which have attained a growing presence around the world. It has a representative national organization in more than 110 countries. Regional organizations serve Asia, Europe, Africa, Latin America, and the Caribbean.

Membership: In North America the World Evangelical Fellowship operates through the Evangelical Fellowship of Canada and the National Association of Evangelicals (with whom it shares headquarters space). Worldwide, in 1997 WEF reported its 110 national and regional fellowship represented some 150 million believers in 60,000 congregations.

Periodicals: *Evangelical World.* • *Evangelical Review of Theology*, Box 1943, Birmingham, AL 35201.

Sources:

Fuller, W. Harold. *People of the Mandate-the Story of World Evangelical Fellowship.* Grand Rapids, MI. Baker Book House, 1996. 214pp.

Section 2
Western Liturgical Family

Consult the Contents pages to locate the essay in Part II, Historical Essay Chapters,
that provides an historical discussion of this family

Intrafaith Organizations

★20★
Ecumenical Communion of Catholic and Apostolic Churches
℅ Rt. Rev. Michael D. Owen
6825 W. Wilshire Blvd.
Oklahoma City, OK 74137

As its name implies, the Ecumenical Communion of Catholic and Apostolic Churches (ECCAC) is an ecumenical fellowship of churches of the Christian tradition. It was founded in the mid-1990s to bear witness through worship, ministry, and life to the essential unity that already spiritually exists among all the branches of the historic Catholic faith. It recognizes that the one true Holy Catholic Church includes equally the Roman Catholic communion and all those in communion with her, all of the autocephalous communions and jurisdictions of the Eastern Orthodox Church, those provinces of the worldwide Anglican Communion which hold to orthodox, historic apostolic faith and order (including the "Continuing Church" movements within Anglicanism), and the orthodox, valid communions of the Old Catholic Church and other valid and orthodox branches or autocephalous communions with true apostolic succession, faith and worship. It considers all ecclesial communions who can clearly trace their lines of apostolic succession and who hold to historic, apostolic, and Catholic order and practice in their faith and worship (as defined by the ancient and undivided Church and reflected in the teaching of the first seven Ecumenical Councils of the early Christian Church) as valid and orthodox.

In practical terms, the unity that is sought will be worked out whileembracing a diversity of historic, orthodox Catholic liturgies, as used by the major branches of Catholic and Orthodox Christianity from the beginning. These would include the Divine Liturgy of St. John Chrysostom, the Novus Ordo of the Roman Catholic Church, Anglican liturgies, Western Rite Orthodox liturgies, and others recognized as expressions of rites used historically within the broad scope of orthodox, Catholic Christianity worldwide.

The ECCAC believes that Christian unity can best be restored by the return of all Christian communions to the principles of unity exemplified by the undivided Catholic Church during the first stages of its existence that includes as an inherent component the affirmation of:

1. The Holy Scriptures of the Old and New Testaments as the revealed Word of God, "containing all things necessary to salvation" and as being the rule and ultimate standard of faith

2. the creeds, i.e., the Apostles' Creed, as the baptismal symbol the Nicene Creed, as the sufficient statement of the Christian faith; and the Athanasian Creed, or Quicunque Vult, as of great value in articulating the essentials of true Catholic and orthodox Christian faith

3. the sacraments as outward signs which confer the very grace they signify. These sacraments were ordained by Christ and are at least seven in number: baptism, anointing the sick, confirmation, matrimony, the Holy Eucharist, holy orders, and reconciliation.

4. the Historic Episcopate, locally adopted in the methods of its administration to the varying needs of the people.

5. The Seven General or Ecumenical Councils only, which are recognized by the whole of Catholic Christendom, held respectively in Nicea (325 A.D.), Constantinople (381), Ephesus (430), Chalcedon (451), Constantinople (553), Constantinople (680), and Nicea (787).

At a meeting in Brooklyn, New York, in 1995, all of the bishops of the Ecumenical Communion consecrated each other subconditious, and subsequent newly affiliating bishops are free to mingle lines of apostolic succession with all members of the communion. At a meeting in San Antonio, Texas, in 1996, ECCAC members accepted a set of protocols or agreements by which the communion is governed. All members of the communion are considered to be in communion with all the other members. Intercommunion does not require members of the communion to accept all doctrinal opinions, sacramental devotions, or liturgical practices of the other, but each accepts the others as holding to all the essentials of the Christian faith.

Membership: Members of the ECCAC in 1998 were the American Old Catholic Church, the American Catholic Orthodox Church, Saint Matthew American Catholic Church, the Anglican Church of the United States, the Communion of Evangelical Episcopal Churches, the Ecumenical Catholic Church, the Free Catholic Communion, and the Diocese of St. Paul the Apostle.

Sources:

Barrett, David B. *World Christian Encyclopedia.* New York: Oxford, 1982.

★21★
Independent Catholic Clergy Association
Box 6903
Glendale, CA 91205

The Independent Catholic Clergy Association is a fellowship of clergy from various Independent and Old Catholic jurisdictions. It was founded in 1986 to promote the spread of Christianity, to provide fellowship, to establish a forum for discussion of present issues, and to advance the cause of the Independent Orthodox and Old Catholic tradition. Among its first accomplishments was the attainment of television air time for one of its members during Pope John Paul II's visit to Los Angeles, California, in 1987.

The association holds monthly meetings in Southern California and promotes the formation of similar gatherings in other parts of the United States.

Periodicals: *The Independent.*

★22★
Old Catholic Churches
1307 Bethany Ln.
Gloucester, ON, Canada K1J 8P3

Formerly known as the Old Roman Catholic Church, tThe Old Catholic Churches was originated with Earl Anglin James who had been consecrated as bishop of Toronto by Abp. Carmel Henry Carfora of the North American Old Roman Catholic Church in 1945. The following year, however, he associated himself with Hugh George de Willmott Newman (Mar Georgius) of the Catholicate of the West. During the summer of 1946, Mar Georgius had extended the territory of the Catholicate to the United States through Wallace David de Ortega Maxey. In November, by proxy, he enthroned James as exarch of the Catholicate of the West in Canada. James was given the title Mar Laurentius and became archbishop and metropolitan of Acadia.

Mar Laurentius led a colorful career as an archbishop of the Old Roman Catholic Church. He claimed a vast following, at times in the millions. He collected degrees, titles and awards, and as freely gave them out to those associated with him. He became affiliated with a wide variety of international associations. In 1965, he consecrated Guy F. Hamel and named him his coadjutor with right of succession. After James' retirement in 1966, Hamel was enthroned as the Universal Patriarch and assumed the title of H. H. Claudius I.

Hamel became one of the most controversial figures in Old Catholic circles. He was ordained in 1964 by Bp. William Pavlik of the Ontario Old Roman Catholic Church. However, before the year was over, he went under Mar Laurentius. After becoming head of the Old Roman Catholic Church, Hamel began to appoint an international hierarchy, a list of which was published in the April 1968 issue of *C. P. S. News*, the church's periodical. The list included not only most of the Old Catholic bishops in the United States and Canada (many of whom have taken pains to denounce Hamel) but also many people who were never associated with him—the Rev. Arthur C. Piepkorn (Lutheran theologian), Archbishop Irene (Orthodox Church in America), and Bp. Arthur Litchtenberger (Protestant Episcopal Church). The publication of this list, which enraged many whose names were listed and amused others who recognized the names of many long-dead prelates, Hamel continued to lead the Old Roman Catholic Church more recently renamed Old Catholic Churches.

The Old Catholic Churches follow the creeds of the early Christian Church and the Pre-Vatican II rituals. All seven sacraments are administered, and devotion to the Virgin Mary, as well as the veneration of images and relics of the saints is espoused.

Membership: Not reported.

Periodicals: *C. S. P. World News.*

Sources:

Disciplinary Canons and Constitutions of the Old Roman Catholic Church (Orthodox Orders). Havelock, ON: C.S.P. News, 1967.

Hamel, Guy F. Claude. *Broken Wings.* Cornwall, ON: Vesta Publications, 1980.

___. *The Lord Jesus and the True Mystic.* Toronto: Congregation of St. Paul, [1968].

★23★

Union of Independent Catholic Churches of the North American Old Catholic Church

% The Rt. Rev. Bill Peckenpaugh, OSFL
135 Fiske St.
Silverton, OR 97381-2012

Alternate Address: Most Rev. Diana Dale, Presiding Bishop, ACOC, 2311 Fountainview, No. 64, Houston, TX 77057.

The Union of Independent Catholic Churches of the North American Old Catholic Church (UICC) is a cooperative fellowship established in the fall of 1993. Its existence was formalized by a Concordat of Intercommunion between the Apostolic Catholic Orthodox Church, the Agape of Jesus Independent Catholic Church (now the Independent Catholic Church of America (ICCA)), and the Apostolic Independent Catholic Church. The union attempts to strengthen its members in their unity of service

to Christ, while allowing each to keep its separate identity. It promotes the sharing of resources (such as liturgical, educational, and pastoral materials and opportunities) and responsibilities for some projects (such as chaplaincy training and clinical pastoral education training) among members.

Each of the bishops, representing their own jurisdictions, have also affirmed mutual intercommunion among their churches. The specifics of this affirmation follow the form published by the Old Catholic Church of the Netherlands, as follows:

1.Each Communion (jurisdiction) recognizes the catholicity and independence of the others and maintains its own.

2.Each jurisdiction agrees to admit members of the other signing jurisdictions to participate in the sacraments.

3.Intercommunion does not require from the jurisdictions the acceptance of all doctrinal, sacramental devotion, or liturgical practices characteristic of the others, but implies that each believes the others to hold all the essentials of the apostolic Christian faith.

Membership: In 1997 the union included the Apostolic Catholic Orthodox Church, the Independent Catholic Church of America, the Apostolic Independent Catholic Church, the United Catholic Church (UCC), and several independent Catholic and Orthodox bishops as members.

Sources:

http://www.wp.com/wdpeck/uicc.htm/.

Roman Catholic Church

★24★

Roman Catholic Church
National Conference of Catholic Bishops
1312 Massachusetts Ave. NW
Washington, DC 20005

[Introductory note: The Roman Catholic Church is by far the largest ecclesiastical community in the United States, more than three times as large as the Southern Baptist Convention, its closest rival. That fact, coupled with its position as the largest Christian body in the world and as such the bearer of much of the Christian tradition, gives it a special position in any survey of religious bodies. Overwhelmingly Western Christian churches can trace their origins to dissent from Roman Catholicism, on one or more points. Even within a predominantly Protestant country such as the United States, the Roman Catholic Church provides a measuring rod by which other Christian groups (approximately two-thirds of those treated in this *Encyclopedia*) can locate themselves. Understanding the lives of these groups presupposes some knowledge of their variation from Catholicism. The Roman Catholic Church was also one of the first churches to come to America, bringing with it the long history of Western Christianity. The matter of the origin of the Roman tradition and of the emergence of the See of Rome as the dominant body in the West is a matter of intense debate among ancient-church historians. Most agree, however, that by the fifth century Rome was the ecclesiastical power in the West, and Rome's bishop was the leading episcopal authority. Further, for the next millennium, the story of Christianity in the West is largely the story of Rome. The detailing of this story and the elaboration of this developing tradition is far beyond the scope of this volume. Interested readers are referred to the volumes cited at the end of this entry for a sample of books which treat those topics. This volume will merely provide a summary of basic material about the Church and its historical development in the West, the emergence of religious orders, its history in the United States, its basic beliefs and practices, and its organization. The long history of the Church and some of its sanctioned but less than universal practices (Eastern rite liturgies, localized forms of piety, etc.) will be treated primarily as background for understanding those groups that have dissented with the Church.]

History. The Roman Catholic Church is that Christian religious community whose members are "baptized and incorporated in Christ, profess the same faith, partake of the same sacraments and are in communion with and under the government of the successor of St. Peter, the pope, and the bishops in union with him." (quoted from *A Concise Guide to the Catholic Church* by Felician A. Foy). The rise of the Roman Catholic Church to a position of dominance within the Christian community can be traced through a series of steps beginning with the geographical spread of the Church throughout the Roman Empire and beyond and the emergence of an authority structure built around bishops (mentioned in the New Testament, but hardly the figures of authority as exist today). Then the conversion of the Emperor Constantine pulled the Church out of its role as just another religion competing in the Roman forum.

In 303 C.E. Diocletian initiated a plan designed to stabilize the vast empire he ruled. He divided it into Eastern and Western sections. Over each section he placed a senior emperor assisted by a junior emperor with the right of succession. Diocletian then voluntarily resigned and the four appointees took his place: the senior emperor Constantius Chlorus and his junior partner, Severus in the West, and Galerius and his junior partner, Maximinus, in the East. However, upon the death of the emperor in the West, his son Constantine usurped the power and Severus, the rightful successor, was killed.

In the midst of his rise to power Constantine identified himself with (only much later was he baptized) what was at the time a very small Christian community. According to Christian historian Eusebius, he saw a vision over the Milvian bridge where he was to meet his rival. The vision was of a cross in the sky with words around it saying, "In this sign you will conquer." Constantine ordered this sign painted on the shields of his soldiers; defeated his rival, and emerged as sole ruling power in the West. One of his first acts was to give Christianity freedom by granting it an equal legal status with paganism. In the East, Galerius followed Constantine's lead. Under Constantine, the idea that Christianity best flourished under the protection of the empire began its ascendancy along with its corollary that the empire and the emperor were not only capable but were in fact divinely appointed to rule and to render that protection. Both the centuries of intimate union between the "Christian" state and the Christian Church and the church-state theory based upon that union were initiated at this time, even before the Church became the dominant religious power in the empire.

Then in 330 C. E., Constantine transferred his capital from Rome to Byzantium (now Istanbul) in the East. He renamed it Constantinople and over the next decades initiated a whole new thrust in culture. But in so doing, he abandoned Rome and created a severe power vacuum throughout the West. The Church and the bishop of Rome, the Pope, emerged as the organization with both the will and the ability to accomodate to the new situation. Christian bishops took up temporal authority and, given the emperors' acceptance of their role, became an elite ruling class. The bishops in the more important towns of the empire came to be known as archbishops and those in the major cities, such as Antioch, Alexandria, Constantinople, Rome, were known as patriarchs. The Roman patriarch assumed some preeminence both as successor to Peter, who died in Rome, and patriarch of the significant urban center in the West.

But while the bishop of Rome claimed a primacy of honor and privilege, the Eastern patriarchs, claimed a similiar prestige as well. The emperor resided in the East. The ecumenical councils were held there. Most Christians lived there, where Christianity had begun and had its longest history. However, the Western Church had an opportunity for growth and development that it would not miss.

Pope Gregory the Great, elected in 590, in a very real sense the founder of the modern papal structure, began the process of centralizing the entire Western Church, then loosely organized into a set of dioceses, upon Rome. He brought to the office a vision, discipline, missionary instinct, and sense of order and rule to the church. If the pope's power of jurisdiction and supremacy had been ill defined previously, it was Gregory who sharpened the definition. A high civil official before becoming a monk, he used his organizational ability to reorganize church finances, thus making it financially independent. He consolidated and expanded the Church's power. He exercised hegemony for the Church throughout the West and sent forth missionaries (usually monks) to claim lands for the faith. He took major steps to convert the Germanic tribes, end Arianism in Spain, and gain the loyalty of the Irish church. Gregory sent Saint Augustine to England where he converted the king and established the see at Canterbury. The papacy emerged as the international center of the Western Church in power as well as prestige. The church that emerged under Gregory's successors looked to Rome, not to the Emperor in Constantinople nor his representative at Ravenna.

Two centuries after Gregory, the emperor Charlemagne (742-814) consolidated secular political rule in almost all of Europe and reestablished an empire to match the spiritual realm delineated by the Church. A bond was forged, and the marriage between the Western Church and the Western empire took place. The Eastern emperor became a mere figurehead to the West.

The dissipation of Charlemagne's empire into the hands of numerous local monarchs set the stage for Pope Gregory VII, elected in 1073, the founder of the papal monarchy. By Gregory's time, Western Christendom had grown "larger" than the territory of any empire. Gregory, monarch of his own country, but more importantly, the representative of a religion that transcended the boundaries of both his country and the empire as it then existed, began to assume more universal powers, full political and spiritual supremacy. He encouraged remote territories such as Spain, Denmark, and Hungary to accept the protection of the Holy See, implying that he, the pope, was the real universal center of things rather than any emperor. He insisted that the pope could be judged by none; that the pope alone could depose, move and/or restore bishops. He took authority to depose rulers or to absolve subjects from their allegiance to their rulers. Under Gregory and his successor, the Papacy exercised its greatest temporal authority in the West. The extensive corruption of that power, felt throughout the church at every level, created the need for reform and set the stage for Martin Luther, John Calvin, and the Protestant and Radical Reformers.

The Reformation can best be seen as the convergence of numerous factors upon Northern and Western Europe in the sixteenth century. The Church was beset with internal problems and was also filled with voices calling for its reform and a new emphasis upon spirituality in place of its preoccupation with political involvement. Several centuries of reform efforts had also coincided with the rise of strong national states which further stripped the Holy Roman Emperor of real power to hold structures together in the West. Once Luther's cause gained support, other independent reform efforts proceeded, ranging from those of Calvin in Switzerland and Henry VIII in England to the more radical Swiss Brethren (Mennonites) and Unitarians. Once the political power supporting the Roman Catholic Church was broken, the establishment of various independent and locally controlled churches became possible.

The Reformation divided the West among five Christian traditions (Roman, Lutheran, Reformed, Anglican, and Free Church) and fostered the further division of the non-Roman traditions into the many individual organizations with linguistic, political, nationalistic, and doctrinal divergences, leading, of course, to the numerous churches seen in this century (and described in various sections of the *Encyclopedia*). While Rome remained in control of the largest block of territory, it had to devise new ways of relating to religiously divided societies, especially in those countries which had both a Roman Catholic presence and a hostile Protestant ruler.

The Reformation also occurred at the same time as the discovery, exploration, and settlement of the Americas. Roman Catholicism settled in most of South and Central America and became the dominant religious force. In North America, with the early settlers, the Church found a much different situation, i.e., a predominantly Protestant society moving quickly toward a religious freedom and pluralism not hinted at since the days of the Roman Empire.

A note about religious orders: the forces of reform that disrupted the Church in the sixteenth century were not new to Western Christianity. Reform had been expressed and acted upon by numerous movements throughout its history. Some of these reformers became rival movements, largely remembered today as the great heretical movements (Gnosticism, Montanism, etc.). When the Church gained access to political power, it turned upon those movements and left a record of persecution that came back to haunt it in later centuries. However, with reformist, mystical, and enthusiastic movements not defined as heretical (but nevertheless potentially schismatic) the Church had a more creative solution in the formation of ordered religious communities. The schismatic tendencies of, for example, Protestantism and the Free Church families, constantly led to the formation of new sects. In Roman Catholicism, however (and to a lesser extent in Eastern Orthodoxy), these tendencies resulted in the various orders of monks, nuns, and lay brothers and sisters. Many such orders show all of the characteristics of sectarian bodies, including liturgical and theological peculiarities, distinctive dress, and special missional emphases. The only difference is that these groups remain in allegiance to the bishop of Rome. Many orders operate effectively outside of local diocesan control and report directly to the orders' officials, who in turn report directly to the Pope or curia. Of course, by accepting new religious movements as ordered communities, the Church is able both to nurture geniune religious enthusiasms and control their excesses.

From the fifth to the twelfth centuries, there was practically only one religious order in the church: the Benedictines. Then, in the twelfth century, a variety of new types of religious communities appeared on the scene with many derivative branches. Not only was the Benedictine Order no longer held to be the only safe road to heaven but, by the twelfth century, a noticeable decline had set in. Some monasteries had become socially exclusive and had become fossilized into great symbols of stability from which no innovations could be expected. New orders were needed. First, there were the Augustinians (Luther's order), an informal group compared to the structured Benedictines, dedicated to practical service to others (in contrast to self perfection of the former monks) and to survival in a world of change. The Cistercians, on the other hand, wanted to flee change, flux, and the world and return to pristine Benedictine rigor and purity. They moved into the some of the uninhabited lands of Europe, first growing rapidly, then like the Benedictines before them, succumbing to success.

The new town culture of the late Middle Ages brought into existence the two most influential orders of the time, the Franciscans and Dominicans. Founded by middle class men (Francis of Assisi was the son of a merchant) as an order of brothers (fratello in Italian) or friars, they were not, as older orders, to withdraw from the world but to penetrate it. They gave to the age the common spectacle of the traveling friar and itinerant preacher.

Roman Catholicism in America. The Roman Catholic Church came to America with the early Spanish and French explorers. Priests accompanied Hernando de Soto and Francisco Coronado, and some, like Jacques Marquette and Junipero Serra, became explorers in their own right. The first missions were begun in Florida after the founding of St. Augustine in 1565. Spanish priests and (after 1573) Franciscans developed the missions. The settlement of large segments of America by European Catholic countries largely determined the earliest religious development of America. Florida, the Gulf Coast of present-day Alabama and Mississippi, California, and the Southwest were Spanish territory. The French settled Canada, Louisiana, and the Mississippi Valley. The early

Catholic hegemony is reflected in the many towns named for the saints they revered.

Under the leadership of an English Catholic convert, George Calvert (who became the first Baron of Baltimore) a small band of British Catholics settled on the East Coast and, in 1634, founded the colony of Maryland. In stark contrast to their neighbors in Pennsylvania, many of whom had come to America fleeing Roman Catholic persecution, these Catholics had come fleeing Protestant attacks. In 1649 Calvert issued the famous Act of Toleration offering the "free exercise" of religion to residents. Unfortunately, Catholic control of the colony was soon lost, and in 1654 the Act was repealed and Catholicism prohibited. Four Catholics were executed and the Jesuits driven out. Not until 1781 were Catholics allowed to participate in public life.

Catholicism existed in America for over two centuries without a bishop. There had been no confirmations and all clergy were ordained abroad. Since 1757, the colonies had been nominally under the bishop in London, but after the American Revolution a resident bishop was needed. The person chosen for the task was John Carroll, a member of the most prominent Catholic family in the colonies and a cousin to Charles Carroll, one of the signers of the Declaration of Independence. By the end of the century Carroll would have approximately 50,000 Catholics under his care.

During the nineteenth century, several factors shaped the life of the Church. First, the dominance of people of British and German ancestry, both with a strong anti-Catholic bias from the days of the Reformation, meant that Catholics would frequently have to exist in a hostile environnment. (This reached its height in the mid-nineteenth century during the so-called Know Nothing era.) Secondly, the Church grew massively as literally millions of immigrants from predominantly Roman Catholic countries poured into the United States. At the same time, the Church became divided internally into many ethnic groupings, as Catholics from different countries and speaking different languages settled into homogeneous communities. They tended to locate in pockets in the cities and recreated (as much as possible) life in the old country. To this day many of the nation's leading cities retain a large Catholic element and many neighborhoods retain remants of these immigrant communities. The many ethnic groups also contrasted strongly with the predominantly Irish clergy and hierarchy. Attempts to play down ethnicity and "Americanize" parishes (in part by assigning priests from outside the predominant ethnic group in a parish) caused considerable friction. It was also the cause of the only major schism from within the Church in the United States, the Polish National Catholic Church. The parochial school system, mandated in 1884, was originally established to assist Catholic immigrants as they adjusted to life in non-Catholic America.

Growth of the Church during the nineteenth century (which lasted until immigration from mostly Catholic countries was curtailed in 1921) was spectacular. By 1822 Baltimore had been designated an archepiscopal see and bishops resided in Boston; New York; Philadelphia; Norfolk, Virginia; New Orleans; and Bardstown, Kentucky. By 1900 there were over 12,000,000 Catholics in the United States (eclipsing by far the largest Protestant church), and by 1930 there were over 20,000,000. During the next half-century, Church membership would more than double in size.

Beliefs. The Roman Catholic Church bases its beliefs on the revelation of God as given through the Bible, and on tradition handed down from the Apostles through the Church. The essential beliefs have come to be summarized in several creedal statements, especially those developed by the early ecumenical councils: the Apostles Creed, Nicene Creed, and Athanasian Creed. Until recently, new converts to the Church were asked to sign a "Profession of Faith," which included a rejection of a number of false doctrines, a promise of obedience to the Church, and a statement of belief. Though no longer required, the statement of belief, printed below, remains an authoritative guide to the Church's essential belief:

"One only God, in three divine Persons, distinct from and equal to each other, that is to say, the Father, the Son, and the Holy Ghost; the Catholic doctrine of the Incarnation, Passion, Death, and Resurrection of our Lord Jesus Christ; the personal union of the two natures, the divine and the human; the divine maternity of the most holy Mary, together with her spotless virginity; the true real and substantial presence of the Body and Blood, together with the Soul in the Eucharist; the seven Sacraments instituted by Jesus Christ for the salvation of mankind, that is to say, Baptism, Confirmation, Eucharist, Penance, Extreme Unction, Orders, and Matrimony; Purgatory, the Resurrection of the Dead, Everlasting Life; the primacy, not only of honor, but also of jurisdiction, of the Roman Pontiff, successor of St. Peter, prince of the apostles, Vicar of Jesus Christ, the veneration of the saints and their images; the authority of the Apostolic and Ecclesiastical traditions, and of the Holy Scriptures, which we must interpret and understand, only in the sense which our holy mother, the Catholic Church, has held, and does hold; and everything else that has been defined, and declared by the Sacred Canons, and by the General Councils, and particularly by the holy Council of Trent and delivered, defined and declared by the General Council of the Vatican, especially concerning the primacy of the Roman Pontiff and his infallible teaching authority."

Defined by the first Vatican Council, the doctrine of papal infallibility remains the most controversial of Roman Catholic beliefs. It grows out of and is an expression of the Church's long held belief in its being kept from error by the power of the Holy Spirit. The Pope's words are considered infallible only when speaking *ex cathedra*, i.e., in his office as pastor and doctor of all Christians, and when defining doctrine on matters of faith or morals to be held by all Christians. More often than not, Papal statements do not fall into this category. However, Catholics are enjoined to give heed to Papal messages as part of their obedience to the Church's teaching authority.

Two relatively recent papal statements in which the Pope has been deemed to have spoken *ex cathedra* concerned what is possibly the second most controversial area of Roman Catholic doctrine (at least to most Protestant Christians), the understanding of the Virgin Mary. During the nineteenth century the veneration of the Virgin Mary took on a new importance within Roman Catholicism, and it found expression in numerous new pietistic forms and practices, many built around the several apparitions, such as those at Lourdes (France) and Fatima (Portugal). In the last century the doctrine of the Immaculate Conception (the sinless birth of Mary) was declared. In 1950 her bodily assumption into heaven was defined.

Supplementing the beliefs of the Church are the moral precepts which are considered binding upon each Church member. They are required to do the following: 1. Participate in Mass on Sundays and specified holy days and to abstain from work and business concerns that impede worship; 2. Fast and abstain on appointed days (primarily during the Lenten season); 3. Confess their sins at least annually; 4. Receive the Eucharist during the Easter season (for American Catholics between the first Sunday of Lent and Trinity Sunday); 5. Contribute to the support of the Church; and 6. Observe the laws of the Church concerning marriage.

Worship in the Catholic Church is centered upon the liturgy, the major components being the following: the Eucharist (the Mass) and the other six sacraments; sacramentals (sacramental-like signs such as holy water, rosaries, holy medals, etc.); sacred art; sacred music; the prayer cycle of the Liturgy of the Hours (the Divine Office); and the designation of the liturgical year and calendar.

Individuals are brought into the Church through baptism, through which original sin is washed away. The Mass, instituted by Christ at the Last Supper, is a real sacrifice of Christ using the elements of bread and wine. During the liturgy of the Mass, the Church teaches that the bread and wine change (the change is termed "transubstantiation") into the body and blood of Christ.

The Eucharist is the major sacramental expression encountered by Church members on a regular basis. Confirmation, usually given to youth or adult converts immediately after finishing a period of instruction in the faith, is generally conferred by the bishop, and it empowers individuals with the force of the Holy Spirit. Penance is the means by which the faithful confess and receive forgiveness for present sin. Holy Orders sets aside Catholic males (unmarried and celibate) for specified priestly functions. The annointing of the sick (unction) is performed when the individual is in danger of death, in hope of an improvement in the state of health, as well as for forgiveness of sins at the time of death. Finally, matrimony binds two people together in God's eyes.

Over the years, supplementing the sacramental life, the Church has broadly defined the life and structure of faith through the liturgical calendar. The calendar focuses attention on the essentials of the faith and commemorates the life of the Virgin Mary and the saints. The liturgical year begins with Advent and includes as its high points Christmas, Lent, Easter, and Pentecost. Worship is further enhanced by the promotion of a variety of devotional practices, inluding prayers said using the rosary, novenas, and meditation on the stations of the cross (picturing Christ's passion and death).

Organization. The Roman Catholic Church derives its authority as the Church founded by Christ through the Apostles. The signs of Christ's Church are its oneness in doctrine, worship, and practice; its holiness by the indwelling of the Holy Spirit; its apostolic nature; and its catholicity or universal aspect. The Apostolic authority has been passed, generation by generation, through the bishops of the Church, especially the Pope, the successor to Peter, the first bishop of Rome. The Pope resides in Vatican City, a small sovereign state outside of Rome, Italy. The curia is located there, where the college of cardinals meets.

The Pope, the Supreme Pastor of Christians, is elected by the College of Cardinals. The College, which evolved out of the synod of the clergy of the diocese of Rome, includes the principal advisors and assistants to the Pope, who help administer the affairs of the Church. It was officially constituted in 1150, and 29 years later the selection of its members was left to the reigning Pope. Members of the College are of three types: cardinal bishops, the bishops of dioceses geographically neighboring the diocese of Rome; cardinal priests, bishops of dioceses away from Rome who have been assigned to a church in Rome; and cardinal deacons, bishops assigned to administrative offices in the Roman curia. Generally, the archbishops of the most important sees in the United States are appointed cardinal priests.

The offices of the Roman Catholic Church that administer its affairs worldwide are called the curia. It includes the Secretariat of State, the Council for the Public Affairs of the Church, and numerous other departments, congregations, tribunals, and secretariats. Worldwide, the Church is divided into a number of dioceses. The largest and most important are designated archdioceses, with an archbishop who generally has some supervisory rights over the neighboring dioceses. Dioceses are grouped into provinces, provinces into regions, and regions into conferences. In 1966, bishops in the United States were formed into the National Catholic Conference in the United States. The Church as a whole is governed according to canon law, the rules of the Church. A revised edition of that law, written during the Second Vatican Council, was issued in 1981. The 1,752 canons cover all aspects of Church life, from the nature and structure of the Church to the rights and obligations of the faithful.

In the years after the split between the Roman Catholic Church and the Eastern Orthodox Churches in the eleventh century, communities that had a history as Eastern Orthodox were converted to Catholicism, and they came under the jurisdiction of the Pope. In many cases these churches were allowed to keep their Eastern liturgical life. There are six patriarchs who preside over nongeographical dioceses of all of the faithful of their respective rite, wherever in the world they might be found. These churches retain a married priesthood. Eastern rite Catholics began to emigrate to the United States in the late 1700s, and parishes were founded in the nineteenth century. The presence of Eastern Catholic and Eastern Orthodox parishes so close together in the relatively free environment of the United States facilitated the movement of members (and sometimes even whole parishes) from one church to another.

Membership: In 1989 there were 57,019,948 members, 53,111 priests, and 23,500 parishes in the United States. In Canada there were 11,375,914 members, 11,302 priests, and 5,922 parishes. There are over 851 million Roman Catholics worldwide.

Educational Facilities: For a complete list of institutions of higher learning supported by the Roman Catholic Church see the latest edition of either *The Official Roman Catholic Directory* (New York: P. J. Kenedy & Sons) or *Catholic Almanac* (Huntington, IN: Our Sunday Visitor). Each is regularly revised and updated.

Periodicals: There are over 500 church-related newspapers and 300 magazines published in the United States. For a complete list see the latest edition of either the *Catholic Almanac* or *The Official Roman Catholic Directory*.

Sources:

Burggraff, Aloysius J. *Handbook for New Catholics.* Glen Rock, NJ: Paulist Press, 1960.

Burghardt, Walter J., and William F. Lynch. *The Idea of Catholicism.* New York: Meridian, 1960.

Daughters of St. Paul. *Basic Catechism with Scripture Quotations.* Boston: St. Paul Editions, 1984.

Ellis, John Tracy. *American Catholicism.* Garden City, NY: Doubleday, 1965.

_____, ed. *Documents of American Catholic History.* 2 vols. Chicago: Henry Regnery, 1967.

Foy, Felician A. *A Concise Guide to the Catholic Church.* Huntington, IN: Our Sunday Visitor, 1984.

Frederic, Sister M. Catherine. *The Handbook of Catholic Practices.* New York: Hawthorn Publishers, 1964.

Hennesey, James. *American Catholics.* Oxford: Oxford University Press, 1981.

Kohmescher, Matthew F. *Catholicism Today.* New York: Paulist Press, 1980.

Maynard, Theodore. *The Story of American Catholicism.* Garden City, NY: Doubleday, 1960.

McKenzie, John L. *The Roman Catholic Church.* New York: Holt, Rinehart and Winston, 1969.

Tillard, J. M. R. *The Bishop of Rome.* Wilmington, DE: Michael Glazier, 1983.

Scharp, Heinrich. *How the Catholic Church is Governed.* New York: Paulist Press, 1960.

Independent and Old Catholic Churches

★25★
African-American Catholic Congregation
1015 I St. NE
Washington, DC 20002

The African-American Catholic Congregation was founded in 1989 by George A. Stallings, Jr. (b. 1948), a former priest of the Roman Catholic Church. Raised a Roman Catholic, Stallings began his education for the priesthood at the age of 16. He completed his education in Rome and was ordained in 1974. In 1976 he was assigned to the parish church of St. Teresa of Avila, a predominantly black congregation in Washington, D.C. He served as a lecturer at both St. Mary's Seminary in Emmitsburg, Maryland,

and the Washington Theological Union. He also emerged as an activist within the black community in Washington.

While successful as a parish priest, Stallings became increasingly critical of the Roman Catholic Church and charged it with a deep-seated racism. In 1988 Abp. James Hickey removed Stallings from St. Teresa and made him Archdiocesan Evangelist with the special task of evangelizing within the black community. However, relations between Stallings and Hickey grew increasingly worse. Stallings withdrew and Hickey moved to excommunicate him and those who supported the new congregation he formed, Imani Temple. Imani is a Swahili word for "faith." He subsequently opened churches in Philadelphia, Pennsylvania; Norfolk, Virginia; Baltimore, Maryland; and a second congregation in Washington, D.C.

Following his break with the Roman Catholic Church, Stallings turned to the independent Catholic movement, and on May 12, 1990, was consecrated by Abp. Richard W. Bridges of the American National Catholic Church (formerly the American Independent Catholic Church). Stallings also adopted some of the distinctive perspectives of the Old Catholic Church: allowing priests to marry, accepting divorced and remarried individuals into full membership, and allowing artificial birth control. The church also allows women to make decisions about abortion and has organized a variety of social outreach ministries.

Membership: Not reported. There are five congregations.

Sources:

Grogan, David. "A Black Catholic Priest's Renegade Church Stirs Up an Unholy Furor." *People* 32, 5 (July 31, 1989): 26-28.

Historical and Doctrinal Digest of the African-American Catholic Congregation. Washington, DC: African-American Catholic Congregation, 1990.

★26★
American Apostolic Catholic Church
℅ Mt. Rev. Richard Cardarelli
547C Hilliard St.
Manchester, CT 06040

The American Apostolic Catholic Church is a small independent Old Catholic jurisdiction founded in the 1980s.

Membership: Not reported.

Sources:

Pruter, Karl. *The Directory of Autocephalous Bishops of the Apostolic Sucession.* San Bernadino, CA: Brogo Press, 1906. 104 pp.

Ward, Gary. *Independent Bishops: An International Directory.* Detroit: Apogee Books, 1990. 524 pp.

★27★
American Catholic Church—Old Catholic
Church of the Good Shepherd
5420 Clark Ave.
Lakewood, CA 90712

The American Catholic Church—Old Catholic was established in 1986 by the Most Rev. E. Paul Raible. Raible was consecrated on April 24, 1988, by Bp. Forest Barber of the Brazilian Catholic Apostolic Church and Bp. Joseph H. Palumbo. He was consecrated *sub conditione* two months later by Abp. Francisco Pagtakhan of the Philippine Independent Catholic Church, assisted by Abp. Emilio Federico Rodriguez y Fairfield of the Mexican National Catholic Church, Bp. Forest Barber, Abp. Bertil Persson of the Apostolic Episcopal Church, and Bp. Paul G. W. Schultz of the Philippine Independent Catholic Church.

The American Catholic Church—Old Catholic is Catholic in faith and practice. It follows conventional Roman Catholicism, with a full sacramental ministry, but does not believe that infallibility can exist exclusively within the papal ministry. It allows priests and bishops to marry, welcomes remarried Catholics into membership, and allows the use of artificial contraceptives. Women are encouraged to take a more active role in the church's lay ministry. The church is opposed to the ordination of women.

Membership: Eight priests serve 150 parishoners in the single parish in Lakewood, California. Several parishes recently withdrew from the jurisdiction.

Sources:

Hackman, Peter. *A Way of Being Catholic in Today's World.* Orange, CA: Saint Matthew Old Catholic Church, [1990].

★28★
American Catholic Church (Syro-Antiochean)
Current address not obtained for this edition.

In the late 1930s, Abp. Daniel C. Hinton, the third primate of the American Catholic Church, resigned in favor of Bp. Percy Wise Clarkson. Clarkson was the founder-pastor of the jurisdiction's most successful parishes in Laguna Beach, California. However, he had strong theosophical leanings, and strengthened the tendency to move the American Catholic Church into theological alignment with the Liberal Catholic Church. Among those who strongly opposed the direction in which Clarkson was leading was Ernest Leopold Peterson (d. 1959), a black man who had been consecrated in 1927 by the former primate, Abp. Frederick E. J. Lloyd. Peterson authored the liturgy used by the church prior to Clarkson's leadership.

Peterson withdrew from Clarkson's jurisdiction and formed the American Catholic Church (Syro-Antiochean), which continued in the faith and practice of the American Catholic Church. In 1950, Peterson consecrated Herbert F. Wilkie, who succeeded as primate in 1959.

Membership: The church reported 40 churches, 4,663 members, and 66 clergy in 1961, but as of the last report in 1979, three churches, 501 members, and eight clergy remained.

★29★
American Old Catholic Church
Current address not obtained for this edition.

The American Old Catholic Church is an independent Old Catholic body founded in the 1990s and closely identifies with other Catholic communities that have become independent of the Roman Catholic Church. It considers itself to be an authentic Catholic community in that it possesses a leadership with apostolic succession back to the original apostles; maintains a faithful adherence to the apostolic tradition; and actively participates in the sacramental ministry of the historic Catholic Church.

The church believes that Jesus commissioned His apostles to be the first leaders of His church. Before they died, they appointed others to lead the church. These leaders were called bishops. This appointment was a sacrament called ordination. The Holy Apostles ordained the first bishops to be their successors. These bishops in turn ordained others to succeed them. This sacred line of leadership is called apostolic succession. The American Old Catholic Church derives its apostolic succession through the independent Catholic Archbishop of Utrecht. The Archbishop of Utrecht traces his apostolic succession back to the Holy Apostles.

The apostolic tradition begins with the apostles who proclaimed and taught the message of Jesus. The tradition was passed on in the written letters of the apostles, which were collected into what we now call the New Testament and in an "oral tradition" that is to be found in the community. The Liturgy (the Mass and the sacraments) embody both the written and oral traditions of the apostles.

The American Old Catholic Church practices the seven sacraments of the historic Catholic Church, including: baptism, confirmation, the Holy Eucharist, reconciliation, the sacrament of the

sick, marriage, and holy orders. The American Old Catholic Church does not accept papal infallibility and exists independently of papal jurisdiction. Both priests and bishops are permitted to marry. Women are encouraged to be more fully involved in the ministry of the church. Divorced people who remarry are able to be reconciled to the church through the grace of God and, therefore, are not excluded from the sacraments. A divorced person may remarry with the blessing of the church. Artificial contraception is considered an issue of conscience between husband, wife, and God. Since each Catholic is seen as an equal part of the church, lay people are encouraged to play a prominent role in the church. No Christian is excluded from the sacramental ministry. All baptized Christians are invited to participate in the worship and sacraments of the church.

The church is a member of the Ecumenical Communion of Evangelical Episcopal Churches.

Membership: Not reported.

Sources:

Pruter, Karl. *The Directory of Autocephalous Bishops of the Apostolic Succession.* San Bernadino, CA: Brogo Press, 1906. 104 pp.

★30★
American Orthodox Catholic Church, Archdiocese of Ohio
(Defunct)

The American Orthodox Catholic Church, Archdiocese of Ohio was a short-lived religious organization established by the M. Rev. Charles T. Sutter. He had been pastor of St. Jude's parish, now a part of the Orthodox Catholic Church of North and South America, but was consecrated in 1979 by Abp. Richard B. Morrill (Mar Apriam) of the Holy Orthodox Catholic Church, Eastern and Apostolic. Sutter established his see in Zanesville, Ohio and by early 1982 had established parishes in Miami and Pompano Beach, Florida; a religious order in Coconut Creek, Florida (the Missionary Order of Saint Jude the Apostle); and a school in Rogers, Arkansas (the University of the Holy Transfiguration). However, in the summer of 1982, Sutter dissolved the corporation and retired from his priestly and episcopal offices. Information on the subsequent fate of the several parishes is not available.

★31★
American Orthodox Catholic Church—Western Rite Mission, Diocese of New York
% Most Rev. Joseph J. Raffaele
318 Expressway Dr. S.
Medford, NY 11763

Joseph J. Raffaele, a Roman Catholic layperson, founded St. Gregory's Church, an independent traditionalist Latin-rite parish, in Sayville, New York, on August 28, 1973. Three months later, he was ordained by Bp. Robert R. Zaborowski of the Archdiocese of the American Orthodox Catholic Church in the U.S. and Canada (now called the Mariavite Old Catholic Church). Raffaele developed a congregation among traditionalists who felt spiritually alienated from the post-Vatican II Roman Catholic Church. The parish grew slowly, and Raffaele and his assistants continued to work in secular jobs, devoting evenings and weekends to the church. The parish moved from Sayville to Shirley to Ronkonkoma, New York. During the mid-1970s Bishop Zaborowski insisted upon the acceptance of Mariavite (i.e. Polish) liturgical patterns by the congregations under his jurisdiction. Both St. Gregory's and Father Raffaele left the Mariavite Old Catholic Church. Shortly after, Archbishop Zaborowski issued an excommunication decree.

Raffaele joined the Mount Athos Synod under Bp. Charles R. McCarthy (a bishop in the American Orthodox Catholic Church under Abp. Patrick J. Healy). On July 18, 1976, McCarthy consecrated Raffaele and raised his associate priest, Gerard J. Kessler, to the rank of monsignor. Six months later, in December 1976, St.

Gregory's and Raffaele, due to some personal disagreements with McCarthy, left the Mt. Athos Synod and became an independent jurisdiction, the American Orthodox Catholic Church-Western Rite Mission, Diocese of New York.

The new jurisdiction continues as a traditionalist Latin Rite Catholic Church, though Eastern Rite usage is allowed. The jurisdiction accepts the Baltimore Catechism (minus the papal references) as a doctrinal authority and uses the 1917 Code of Canon Law (again minus the papal references). Clerical celibacy is not demanded, but female priesthood is rejected. No collection is taken on Sunday at worship services. Communion is open to all.

In 1978 St. Matthias Church, in Yonkers, New York, was begun as the first mission parish. In 1979 St. Gregory's moved into a newly purchased building in Medford, New York. That same year, Raffaele consecrated Elrick Gonyo as an independent Uniate bishop in Stuyvesant, New York. In 1979, Raffaele and Gonyo consecrated Kessler as the auxiliary bishop for the jurisdiction.

The church sponsors three religious orders, the Society of St. Gregory the Great (for priests, brothers and nuns); the Benedictine Order of St. Michael the Archangel, a community for Benedictine nuns in Colorado; and the Oblates of the Blessed Sacrament, a community of priests headquartered in Trenton, New Jersey.

In 1986, the church reported a significant spiritual renewal within the jurisdiction that led to the production of a new contemporary liturgy. The new mass was first used at the parish at Medford on Pentecost Sunday 1986 and now coexists with the Tridentine Rite. The renewal also launched an exploration of new nonparochial forms of ministry to extend the missionary outreach, including an intercessory prayer circuit, a healing ministry, and the use of lay ministers. Glad Tidings Ministries, a multimedia spiritual outreach also arose out of the renewal.

Membership: In 1997 there were 987 members (including clergy). Besides the main parish in Medford, New York, there were ministry centers in Florida, New Jersey, Arizona, and Colorado.

Periodicals: *Glad Tidings.*

Sources:

"Milestones," *American Orthodox Catholic Church.* Medford, NY: St. Gregory's Church, 1983.

The Inquirers Handbook, Medford, NY: American Orthodox Cahtolic Church—Western Rite Diocese of New York, n.d. 18 pp.

★32★
American Traditional Catholic Church (ATCC)
Valencia, CA

The American Traditional Catholic Church is an independent Old Catholic/Anglican jurisdiction. The church follows the teachings and traditions of Holy Scripture as expressed in the Seven Ecumenical Councils, and the teachings and traditions of the Old Catholic Movement as presented in the Treaty of Utrecht, the Treaty of Bonn, the 14 Theses of the Old Catholic Union, and the Lambeth Quadrilateral. The Statement of Faith and Belief of the ATCC is expressed confessionally through the three ancient creeds: The Athanasian Creed (c. 296–373 A.D.), the Nicene Creed (c. 325 A.D.), and the Apostles' Creed (second century C.E.).

The ATCC is not in communion with Rome; it is subject neither to the jurisdiction of the pope nor the Roman Catholic Magesterium. However, it recognizes that the pope is "primus et patris", that is "first among equals" among all bishops of all Catholic traditions. Pronouncements from the Vatican and the Holy Father are only binding on members of the ATCC provided that those pronouncements do not contradict the teachings and traditions of Holy Scripture and the Ecumenical Councils of the undivided church. The ATCC follows Old Catholic tradition in promoting the exercise of individual conscience. However, the exercise of conscience must be in accord with the teachings and traditions referenced above and must not bring scandal to either the church or

its membership. This church, with a few exceptions, follows the canons of the Roman Rite of 1917, those exceptions being addressed in the documents of the Old Catholic Movement.

The ATCC is headed by the presiding bishop although no directive is issued without the concurrence of the church's board of directors. The presiding bishop may, with board concurrence, appoint or entertain the nomination of a candidate as suffragan (auxiliary) bishop or vicar to oversee new missional enterprises. The ATCC follows the traditional practice of ordination of an eligible candidate to the four minor orders (Porter, Lector, Exorcist, and Acolyte) and the three major orders (Subdeaconate, Deacon, and Priest). The American Traditional Catholic Church does not provide for the ordination of women to Holy Orders, although recognizing that women have a viable role in the life of the church. The ATCC does not discriminate based on race, creed, color, lifestyle orientation, marital status, age, or national origin, and with exception of the ordination of women, does not discriminate based on sex/gender.

The church administers the seven sacraments of baptism, confession, Holy Communion, confirmation, holy matrimony, holy orders, and extreme unction. Of those seven, the administration of holy orders and confirmation is reserved to the bishop.

The ATCC sponsors an ordered community, the Discalced Carmelite Servants of Mercy-Disciples of the Blessed Sacrament, which exists as an episcopal institute (i.e., accountable to the presiding bishop rather than a suffragan bishop or vicar forraine).

Membership: Not reported.

Sources:

http://www.atcc.com/.

★33★
Apostolic Catholic Church in America
5311 13th Ave. S.
Seattle, WA 98108

The Apostolic Catholic Church in America was founded as the African Orthodox Church of the Moors in 1984 by Frs. Paul David Strong, Robert Neuman, and Christopher Reynolds. It was originally designed to meet the particular needs of African Americans. Fr. Strong was elected bishop and consecrated in November 1994 by Bp. Tedi Weber, operating under the authority of Abp. Joseph Vredenburgh of the Mar Thoma Orthodox Church. The church was renamed the Orthodox Catholic Church of the Moor in 1995, and then adopted its present name in 1996, a reflection of its emergence as a multiethnic and multicultural body.

The Apostolic Catholic Church in America is an inclusive, multicultural, and gay-friendly church. It welcomes the divorced and remarried, and assumes that all baptized Christians are entitled to the sacraments of Christ's church. The church accepts the teachings of the Seven Ecumenical Councils and the ancient creeds. It adheres to the Bible and Tradition. The church is organized with deacons, priests, and bishops. It practices the seven sacraments and allows both Eastern and Western rites, though recently the archbishop has published the church's own liturgy, which is widely utilized throughout the church. The church also practices foot washing.

The church supports several ordered communities including the Servants of Saint Benedict the Moor, the Franciscan Order of Saint Benedict the Moor, and the Order of Saint John the Divine.

Membership: In 1997 the church reported six congregations worldwide with 70 members. There was one congregation in Milan, Italy, and one in Canada.

Periodicals: *Quarterly Newsletter.*

Sources:

Strong, Paul David, with Anthony P. Begonja. *The Order of Mass.* Seattle, WA: Apostolic Catholic Church in America, 1996. 33 pp.

★34★
Apostolic Catholic Orthodox Church
% Most Rev. Diana C. Dale
2650 Fountainview, Ste. 444
Houston, TX 77057

The Apostolic Catholic Orthodox Church is a small independent jurisdiction founded in the mid-1990s by its presiding bishop, Diana C. Dale. It sponsors the St. Francis of Assisi Worship Community and the Institute of Worklife Ministry Center for Industrial Chaplaincy, both in Houston. It is a member of the Union of Independent Catholic Churches of the North American Old Catholic Church.

Membership: Not reported.

★35★
Apostolic Episcopal Church
80-46 234th St.
Queens, NY 11427

The Apostolic Episcopal Church was founded in 1925 by Arthur Wolfort Brooks (1898-1948), a former Episcopal Church clergyman. Brooks was succeeded as presiding bishop by Wallace David de Ortega Maxey, Harold F. Jarvis, John More-Moreno, Robert Ramm, and, most recently, Abp. Bertil Persson, who resides in Sweden. Archbishop Ramm also served as Archbishop of the Province of the West. Upon his retirement, he was succeeded by Abp. Paul G. W. Schultz, who passed away in 1995.

In the meantime, in 1992, Fr. Francis Cajetan Spataro (b. 1936) was consecrated as a bishop by Archbishop Persson and designated as the Episcopal leader of the Western Rite Vicariate of New York City and the Hudson Valley, New York. The following year he became the rector of the New York chapter of the Order of Corporate Reunion, an organization formed in 1874 dedicated to the reunion of the many jurisdictions of the Anglican and Eastern Orthodox Churches.

Following the death of Archbishop Schultz, Abp. Donald E. Hugh was named to succeed him. Together, Archbishop Hugh and Bishop. Spataro decided to withdraw from Archbishop Persson's jurisdiction, the Apostolic Episcopal Church International, and to that end merged the Apostolic Episcopal Church and the Order of Corporate Reunion and created a new corporation, the Apostolic Episcopal Church—Order of Corporate Reunion. However, in 1997, Bishop Spataro decided to return to the Apostolic Episcopal Church International and reinstituted the incorporation of both the Apostolic Episcopal Church and the Order of Corporate Reunion in New York.

Membership: Not reported.

Periodicals: *The Tower of St. Cassian.*

★36★
Apostolic Episcopal Church, Diocese of California/Nevada
1933 73rd Ave.
Oakland, CA 94621

The Apostolic Episcopal Church, Diocese of California/Nevada, traces its history to the founding of the United Catholic Conference in 1973 by Bp. Donald Pierce Weeks, then the vicar general of the Old Roman Catholic Church (then led by Abp. Richard A. Marchenna). Bishop Weeks served an Anglo-Catholic parish that wanted to withdraw from the Old Roman Catholic Church, which primarily used a Tridentine Roman liturgy. In 1976 Weeks was consecrated by Abp. Wallace David de Ortega Maxey, assisted by Abp. Ramon Verostek and Bp. Dwayne Houser, and established the Diocese of California/Nevada. The United Catholic Conference merged into the Ancient Christian Fellowship.

In 1993, Weeks established Holy Angels Christian Community of the Ancient Christian Fellowship to reach out to people affected by AIDS/HIV and those addicted to drugs and alcohol. In 1995 the work under Weeks came under the jurisdiction of the Apostolic Episcopal Church International headed by Swedish Abp. Bertil Persson. The Diocese of California/Nevada was designated the church's Western Province with authority over all work in the western United States. Included in the diocese are the Oratory of Saint Ambrose, Holy Angels Catholic Church; the Sanctuary of East Oakland, the Sanctuary of West Contra Costa County; the Daniel Brockman House for Men, the Bishop Maxey House, and the Doris Powell Home for Women, all in the Greater San Francisco Bay Area. Plans have been made for expansion into Nevada and Southern California.

The Apostolic Episcopal Church was founded in 1925 in New York by Bp. Arthur Wolfort Brooks, formerly an Episcopal church clergyman. Over the years leadership of the church moved to England and eventually to Sweden when Archbishop Persson became the presiding bishop following the retirement of Abp. Robert Ramm.

The Diocese of California/Nevada has adopted a set of Thirty-nine Articles of Religion derived from those of the Church of England.

Membership: Not reported.

★37★
Apostolic Episcopal Church—Order of Corporate Reunion
PO Box 2401
Apple Valley, CA 92307

The Apostolic Episcopal Church grew out of a missionary movement by a group of American churchmen in the state of New York to provide spiritual ministrations for the scattered adherents of the Near Eastern churches. The movement began in 1922, but it was not until 1924 that a group succeeded in forming the Anglican Universal Church of Christ in the United States of America (Chaldean). In 1925, through canonical authority, Mar Antoine Lefberne, as a special commissariat of the patriarch of the Chaldean Catholic Church, consecrated Arthur Wolfort Brooks (1888-1948), who took the ecclesiastical name Mar John Emmanuel. Brooks, a clergyman of the Episcopal Church, who at his own request had resigned in 1926, left the Anglican Universal Church in 1927 and formed his own jurisdiction, the Apostolic Episcopal Church (Holy Eastern Catholic and Apostolic Orthodox Church).

The new church initially spread by absorbing other independent missionary congregations such as the African American parish in Manhattan headed by Fr. John More-Moreno. As the church grew, other bishops were added. In 1934, Brooks consecrated Harold F. Jarvis and Charles W. Keller. In 1946, he elevated Wallace D. de Ortega Maxey the superintendent of the Caribbean Episcopal Church of the British Isles; chaplain of Scandinavia for the Patriarchal Order of the Holy Cross of Jerusalem of the Melkite-Greek Catholic Church under Patriarch Maximos V. Hakim; Metropolitan Bishop of Scandinavia of the Western Orthodox Catholic Church in America; and bishop of Ordo Supremus Militaris Templi Hierosolymiteni.

Following Brooks' death in 1948, he was succeeded by Maxey who resigned in 1951. His successor, Lowel Paul Wadle served for two years and following his resignation was succeeded by Metropolitan-Archbishop Hugh George de Willmott Newman, the Patriarch of Glastonbury. Newman, commonly known as Mar Geogius, headed the church until his death in 1979. He was succeeded by William Henry Hugo Newman-Norman (Mar Seraphim) who served as Patriarch of Glastonbury from 1979 to 1994. In 1994 he was consecrated as a bishop of the Coptic Orthodox Church and resigned all affiliation with the Apostolic Episcopal Church. In the interim following his death the Most Rev. Paul G. W. Schultz, also at the time the apostolic administrator of the American Archdiocese of the Philippine Independent Catholic Church assumed leadership. He passed away on September 13, 1995, and was succeeded by Archbishop Donald E. Hugh, who has moved to reorganize and revive the American work.

The church is also intimately associated with the Order of Corporate Reunion originally founded in 1874 in London, England, to confer valid Apostolic Orders on individuals it considered qualified with a particular emphasis on the union of Anglican and Eastern Orthodoxy. Today the O.C.R. emphasizes the reunion of the various independent orthodox catholic groups. Rt. Rev. Francis C. Spataro is the current Rector Pro-Provincial of the O.C.R.

The Apostolic Episcopal Church considers itself a conservative body in the Chaldean Orthodox tradition. It is guided by the Holy Scripture, the Apostolic Constitution, Teachings and Creed. It accepts the rulings of the initial three Ecumenical Councils and recognizes the spirit of the remaining four. It accepts the seven sacraments and possesses an apostolic succession through the order of Corporate Reunion.

At the time Archbishop Hugh succeeded to the leadership of the AEC, it was the American branch of the Apostolic Episcopal Church International headed by Swedish Abp. Bertil Persson. However, Hugh soon rejected the archbishop's leadership and in 1995 reincorporated both the Apostolic Episcopal Church and the Order of Corporate Reunion as a single entity, the Apostolic Episcopal Church—Order of Corporate Reunion. At that time, the church severed its relationship with Archbishop Persson and Bp. Donald Pierce Weeks, whom Persson had consecrated as Archbishop of California-Nevada.

In 1997, Bp. Francis Spataro, who headed the church's Western Vicariate in New York, decided to return to Archbishop Persson's jurisdiction. The Apostolic Episcopal Church—Order of Corporate Reunion now exists as a small jurisdiction under Hugh's leadership. It has also established a concordat with its sister church, the Holy Celtic Church, also headed by Hugh.

Membership: Not reported.

Remarks: Almost immediately after his consecration, Abbinga returned to his native Holland and established the Apostolic Episcopal Church in that country. However, On October 28, 1946, little more than a month after his original consecration, he accepted consecration from Hugh George de Willmott Newman (Mar Georgius), who had consecrated Mar David I. Over the next six years, his tendencies toward theosophy and the Liberal Catholic Church (in which he had been a priest) reasserted themselves, and he gradually drifted from the Apostolic Episcopal Church. In 1952, following his excommunication by Mar Georgius, he founded an independent jurisdiction, the Oosters Apostolisch Episcopale Kerk.

Sources:

The Divine Liturgy, Holy Eucharist. Queens, NY: Apostolic Episcopal Church, 1943.

Persson, Bertil. *An Apostolic Episcopal Ministry. Archbishop Arthur W. Brooks and Christ's Church By-the-Sea. In Memory and Inspiration*. Phoenix, AZ: St. Michael's Press, 1992.

___. *A Collection of Documentation on the Apostolic Succession of Joseph Rene Vilatte with Brief Annotations*. Solna, Sweden: The Author, 1974.

Persson, Bertil, and Shmouel Warda. *Aramaic Idioms of Eshoo (Jesus) Explained*. Solna, Sweden: St. Ephrem's Institute, 1978.

★38★

Apostolic Old Catholic Church
% Rt. Rev. Hans B. Kroneberg
1157 N. Bronson Ave.
Los Angeles, CA 90038

The Apostolic Old Catholic Church is a small jurisdiction founded in the 1980s in Los Angeles, California, by Bp. Hans Kroneberg, formerly of the American Hebrew Eastern Orthodox Greek Catholic Church. He was ordained by Ronald I. Bessler and then in 1979 consecrated by Bp. David Voris. Kroneberg, though consecrated in an Eastern Orthodox tradition, follows a Western

Roman rite. The jurisdiction is centered upon a congregation in Los Angeles.

Membership: Not reported.

Sources:

Ward, Gary L. *Independent Bishops: An International Directory*. Detroit, MI: Apogee Books, 1990.

★39★

Apostolic Orthodox Old Catholic Church
PO Box 879
Chicago, IL 60690

The Apostolic Orthodox Old Catholic Church is a Spanish-speaking Old Catholic Church founded in 1985 in Chicago, Illinois, by Rt. Rev. Jorge Rodriguez. Rodriguez was born in Colombia. He subsequently moved to Chicago where he was raised a Roman Catholic and decided to go into the priesthood. He also came to oppose what he saw as a common problem in Latin America, the dominance of much of the Roman Catholic Church by repressive right-wing bishops.

Rodriguez was consecrated in 1985 by Most Rev. Victor Herard of the Haitian Eglese Apostoloque, assisted by archbishops Roberto Toca of the Catholic Church of the Antiochine Rite, and Carl St. Clair. Since its founding, the Apostolic Orthodox Old Catholic Church has established a ministry to the elderly in Chicago and a mission to Latin America where the church, known as the Ecclesia Catholica Apostolica Orthodoxa, is establishing congregations as alternatives to the less progressive dioceses of the Roman Catholic Church. There are a reported five bishops and 150 priests in Colombia, Ecuador, Panama, and Venezuela.

Membership: In 1990 there was only one center in the United States, located in Chicago, with three priests and 100 members. There were a reported 10,000 members in Latin America.

Educational Facilities: The Association has no college, but students are urged to attend Union Bible College, Westfield, Indiana, and God's Bible College, Cincinnati, Ohio.

★40★

Archdiocese of the Antiochean Catholic Church in America
% Most. Rev. Gordon Mar Peter
PO Box 1061
Campton, KY 41301

The Archdiocese of the Antiochean Catholic Church in America was founded in 1991 when the former Diocese of Lexington (covering the States of Kentucky, Tennessee, and Ohio) of the Church of Antioch separated as an independent jurisdiction. The Diocese of Lexington had been created in 1986 when Antiochean Bishop H. Gordon Hurlburt had moved to Compton, Kentucky, from Wichita, Kansas. Hurlburt, who assumed the ecclesiastical name Gordon Mar Peter, had been consecrated in 1981 by Archbishop Herman Adrian Spruit, Primate of the Church of Antioch. Originally consisting of the states of Tennessee and Kentucky, the diocese was expanded to include Ohio in 1987. In 1990 Hurlburt consecrated Victor C. Herron as his coadjutor.

Over the years, Gordon Mar Peter and the clergy of the diocese moved away from the theosophical perspective which has dominated the Church of Antioch toward a traditional Orthodox position best described as monophysite, similar to that of the Coptic and Ethiopian churches. The church affirms that "The Son . . . of one essence with the Father, took the nature of humanity . . . so that two whole and perfect natures, that is to say, the Godhead and Mankind, were joined together in One Person, Jesus, whom we call the Christ, never to be divided." It accepts as dogma the first three ecumenical councils and endorses the last four councils and the Declaration of the Old Catholics at Utrecht (1889) in so far as they agree with the first three councils. There are seven sacraments.

The church is headed by Gordon Mar Peter as Metropolitan and Most Rev. Victor as coadjutor. Women are admitted into the priesthood. Bishop Victor conducts a weekly television program in Knoxville, Tennessee.

Membership: Not reported. There are congregations in Campton, Kentucky; Knoxville and Kodiak, Tennessee; and Cleveland, Ohio.

Periodicals: *Chrism.*

★41★
Archepiscopate Ordinariate of Healing Arts Missionaries and Chaplains in America

Current address not obtained for this edition.

The Archepiscopate Ordinariate of Healing Arts Missionaries and Chaplains in America is a small Catholic jurisdiction founded by Dr. Arthur J. Garrow, who is a chiropractor and founder of the Southern California College of Chiropractic. After many years as a chiropractor, Garrow was ordained to the priesthood in 1985 by Bp. Paul G. W. Schultz and consecrated as a bishop the following year. The jurisdiction serves as a home for priests who wish to work as chaplains or to bring a spiritual element into healing activity.

Membership: Not reported.

★42★
Catholic Charismatic Church of Canada
La Cite de Marie
11,141 Rte. 148, RR 1
Ste. Scholastique
Mirabel, PQ, Canada J0N 1S0

The Catholic Charismatic Church of Canada was founded in 1957 by the M. Rev. Andre Barbeau, the church's archbishop, also known as Patriarch Andre the First, a former Roman Catholic priest in the Diocese of Montreal. In 1968, he was consecrated by Bp. Charles Brearly of the Old Holy Catholic Church, a small British Old Catholic jurisdiction. The purpose of founding the church was "to assist the Roman Catholic Church in its mission as a supplemental rite." Since his consecration, Patriarch Andre has responded to statements in the reports of Vatican II inviting new rites and the formation of new patriachates as they are needed. The Catholic Charismatic Church is conceived as such a new venture, "a new stem, spouting out of the Church, a progressive-conservative sort of Patriarchate." Immediately after its establishment, Archbishop Barbeau petitioned the pope concerning the status of the rite.

The church follows the teachings and practices of Roman Catholicism. It observes the seven sacraments and supports the papacy in all matters. It has offered the Roman Catholic Church its new rite, one written by the patriarch, which obligates itself only to the essentials of the Catholic faith. It seeks to preserve a proper freedom. Also, limiting itself to the essentials, the church sees itself as being a ready avenue for reconciling former Catholics to the church. The rite is also charismatic, meaning that it is a mystical liturgy.

The church is headed by its archbishop. There are other bishops and a number of priests. Though there are several parishes, such as the Holy Wisdom Community in San Diego, California, most priests are worker priests and are encouraged to create household sanctuaries. As mysticism and religious experience is emphasized over scholastic endeavors, priests are not required to have the seminary education usually expected of a Roman Catholic priest. Priests are not committed to celibacy, and may marry. Individuals not wishing to assume priestly duties are invited to become part of the permanent deaconate. While the church has not accepted women priests as yet, neither has it closed the door on the possibility. The church's headquarters, La Cite de Marie (the

City of Mary), established in rural Quebec, was in part inspired by *The City of God*, a mystical classic written by Mary of Agreda.

Membership: Not reported.

Remarks: Over the years, for purposes of establishing ecumenical relations, Archbishop Barbeau has received a number of reconsecrations, a common practice among independent Catholic jurisdictions. In 1973, he was consecrated by G. R. Armstrong (of unknown affiliation). In 1976, he was consecrated by Robert S. Zeiger, then of the Apostolic Catholic Church of the Americas, assisted by Gordon I. DaCosta. That same year he was consecrated by German Bishop Joseph Maria Thiesen of L'Eglise Catholique Apostolique Primitive D'Antioche et le Tradition Syro-Byzantine. In 1980 he was consecrated by Patrick McReynolds of the American Orthodox Catholic Church, assisted by Andre Letellier and J. Letellier.

Sources:

Barbeau, Archbishop Andre. *Liturgie des Saints Mysteres*. Montreal, PQ: La Cite de Marie, 1971.

★43★
Catholic Christian Church

Current address not obtained for this edition.

Wallace David de Ortega Maxey began his episcopal career on January 2, 1927, when he was consecrated by William Montgomery Brown, a bishop in the Old Catholic Church in America, at that time headed by Abp. W. H. Francis Brothers. Maxey functioned in various capacities during the next two decades, including a period as general secretary of the Temple of the People, an international theosophical body headquartered in Halcyon, California. During the 1940s he became associated with the Apostolic Episcopal Church founded by Arthur Wolfort Brooks. He traveled to England at the close of World War II and was consecrated again by Hugh George de Willmott Newman and named Supreme Hierarch of the Catholicate of the Americas. Upon Maxey's return to New York, Brooks, who had previously accepted the title of hierarch of the Catholicate of the United States, reconsecrated Maxey and placed him in charge of the Apostolic Episcopal Church on the West Coast. Maxey served the two intertwined bodies and, for a period following Brooks death in 1948, he headed them. However, in 1951, he resigned his episcopal positions and joined the Universalist Church.

In 1977 Archbishop Maxey again assumed authority as an archbishop and founded the Christian Catholic Church. With the assistance of Archbishop Joachim of the Western Orthodox Church in America, he consecrated Alan S. Stanford as his coadjutor. Stanford now heads ministries in San Francisco, California, through the church's chapel, the Holy Order of the Society of St. Jude Thaddeus, and the National Catholic Street Ministry Project. In addition to the work in San Francisco, the church reports three mission stations. There are two bishops and three priests.

Membership: Not reported.

★44★
Catholic Church of the Apostles of the Latter Times
% Monastery of the Magnificat
Box 308
St. Jovite, PQ, Canada J0T 2H0

The Catholic Church of the Apostles of the Latter Times is comprised of the Apostles of Infinite Love, Order of the Mother of God, as requested by the Blessed Virgin Mary in her apparition at La Salette, France, in 1846. The Apostles of Infinite Love was founded in France in 1935 with ecclesiastical approval by Fr. Michael Collin (d. 1974), a French priest ordained in 1933 who claimed a mystical consecration which made him a bishop. In 1950 he declared he had received full apostolic authority directly from Christ, in a manner like that received by St. Paul; he claimed universal jurisdiction, on the same level as the Bishop of Rome. His headquarters were in Clemery, Lorraine, France. In 1951 it was widely reported that Fr. Collin had been defrocked by the church, but his alleged condemnation never occurred and has never been found in any official acts of the Holy See. In 1960 he took a more public stance, claiming to be Pope Clement XV, the Mystical Pope named in the Third Secret of Fatima (the final part of the message received by the children who claimed to communicate with the Blessed Virgin at Fatima, Portugal in 1917, which was never made public). His followers, and those of Fr. John of the Trinity after him, have been frequently referred to as the Renewed Church of Jesus Christ.

Fr. Collin named Fr. John of the Trinity superior general of the order in 1962. In the 1940s Fr. John, then a young religious brother with the Hospitaler Brothers of St. John of God in Montreal, had several visions in which he was told to establish a community of new Apostles that would provide leadership in the age to come; he also saw the future Clement XV. Thus the Brothers of Jesus Mary came into being in 1953 near Montreal, with a decree of foundation signed by Pope Pius XII . The Brothers merged with the Apostles of Infinite Love in 1962, when Fr. John was ordained and consecrated a bishop by Clement, and the motherhouse of the Order of the Mother of God was transferred to St. Jovite, Quebec; the Rule given by the Virgin at La Salette was adopted. Since then, the community has founded mission houses throughout Canada, in the United States, Europe, the West Indies, and Latin America. Members from all these regions have joined the order, including religious brothers and sisters, and lay disciples.

A crisis came in 1967 when Fr. John was attacked by Canadian Roman Catholic priests because of his association with Clement. In 1968 he claimed he received visions in which he was chosen as Universal Shepherd of the Holy Church with the name Gregory XVII. Several mystics in Canada and elsewhere are said to have had confirmatory revelations in this regard. On May 9, 1969, Clement confirmed in writing that Fr. John was his successor with the name of Gregory XVII. Gregory concurred with Clement in saying that the official Church of Rome had fallen into apostasy but differed over his hostility to the person of Pope Paul VI, not wishing to attack any individual with degrading accusations. Many of Clements French followers did not recognize Gregory's authority; but their number dwindled, Clement passed away in 1974, and the group at Clemery ceased to exist. Meanwhile, the order in Canada announced that Peter was no longer in Rome and that papal authority had passed to Gregory.

The Catholic Church of the Apostles of the Latter Times, as well as the Order of the Mother of God, exists as a non-profit corporation. The faith, doctrine, tradition and practices of this church are Christian Catholic: while wanting to return to the evangelical simplicity and purity of early Christianity, it maintains a doctrinal unity with the traditional Catholic Church. It has effected certain changes in discipline, the most noteworthy one being the ordination of women to the priesthood. It is staunch in its devotion to the Virgin Mary, practices perpetual adoration of the Blessed Sacrament, and has a distinct eschatology built around the person of its papal leader, Gregory XVII. His followers claim that many prophecies, both ancient and modern, point to him as the "Great Pontiff" chosen by God to renew the Church and bring about Christian unity.

Membership: In 1997, the Order of the Mother of God included over 250 religious brothers and sisters and several hundred followers in North Amrica, Latin America, the Caribbean, Africa, and Europe. There are four congregations in the United States, 15 in Canada, and nine in other countries.

Periodicals: *Magnificat.*

Remarks: There is one other movement which derives from Clement XV, the Church of St. Joseph, in Cicero, Illinois, which is not connected to the church led by Pope Greogry XVII.

Sources:

Barette, Jean-Marie. *The Prophecy of the Apostles of the Latter Times.* St. Jovite, PQ: Manificat, 1988.

Cote, Jean. *Prophet without Permit—Father John of the Trinity.* N.p.: Pro Manscripto, 1988.

de la Trinite, Fr. Jean-Gregory. *Escaping the Shipwreck.* St. Jovite, PQ: Editions Magnificat, 1976.

The Eclipse of the Church. St. Jovite, PQ: Editions Magnificat, 1971.

Gregory XVII. *Peter Speaks to the World: Universal Encyclical for Christian Unity.* St. Jovite, PQ: Magnificat, 1989.

Gregory XVII. *Universal Encyclical for Christian Unity.* St. Jovite, PQ: Editions Magnificat, 1975.

John Gregory of the Trinity, Fr. *Escaping the Shipwreck.* St. Jovite, PQ: editions Magnificat, 1976.

___. *Questions and Answers on the Apostles of Infinite Love.* St. Jovite, PQ: Monastery of the Magnificat of the Mother of God, 1989.

___. *When Bad Faith Hides Behind the Law.* St. Jovite, PQ: Magnificat, 1968.

St. Pierre, Catherine. *Thou Art Peter.* St. Jovite, PQ: Magnificat, 1994.

When Prophecy Comes True. St. Jovite PQ: Editions Magnificat, 1972.

★45★
Catholic Church (Pope Michael I)
4137 102nd Rd.
Delia, KS 66418

Pope Michael I is the leader of a small group of former Roman Catholics who feel that the church has moved into a state of apostasy as a result of which the present Pope John Paul II and the bishops have lost their authority. Pope Michael I was born in 1959 as David Bawden. As a young aspirant to the priesthood, he became dissatisfied with the changes in the church following Vatican II and came to the conclusion, as had other Catholic Traditionalists, that the church was seriously committed to errors of doctrine and practice. He affiliated with the Society of St. Pius X, one of the leading organizations of the larger Traditionalist movement, and moved to Switzerland, where the society had a seminary. He transferred to the society's seminary then in Armada, Michigan. However, he was dismissed without cause from the seminary. He then moved to St. Mary's College where he worked in various positions through 1980 until his resignation from the society in March 1981. He had concluded that the society and the whole traditionalist movement was heretical.

On December 26, 1983, he issued a letter asserting that Traditionalist priests had no right to operate chapels or to confer the Sacraments. He expanded upon this letter in a 16-page treatise, "Jurisdiction During the Great Apostasy," in 1985. He teamed up with Teresa Stanfill Benns from Denver, Colorado, to produce a book, *Will the Catholic Church Survive the Twentieth Century?*, published in 1900. It included the 1985 treatise and additional material written in response to that treatise. The book argued that the majority of masses, baptisms, and confessions within the Roman Catholic Church are invalid due to the reform of Vatican II and the leadership of an invalid pope, and true Catholics should cease attendance at English-language masses. He also argued that the present day was the time of the anti-Christ whom he identified as Pope Paul VI. Paul died, but his authority was passed to John Paul I and John Paul II, thus giving the appearance of being slain, recovering, and living anew. He suggested that in 1958 Cardinal Alfredo Ottavani was in fact elected pope, but his place was usurped by Pope John XXIII.

Bawden further suggested that a precedent had been established for the election of a pope apart from the action of the College of Cardinals. Thus on July 16, 1990, six people, including Bawden's parents, gathered in Belvue, Kansas, and elected Bawden as the new pope. A chapel and papal headquarters was initially established in their resale shop, The Question Mark, in Belvue. On November 1, 1993, Pope Michael I moved his papal office to its present location in Delia, Kansas.

Michael I is not ordained to the priesthood and thus does not say mass. He is awaiting the emergence of a bishop unaffected by the post-Vatican changes to ordain him and believes that some have survived either in Russia or China. Meanwhile, he conducts Sunday services of prayer and preaching to those who have accepted his authority.

Membership: In 1997, there were 52 members in four congregations, all in the United States.

Sources:

Benns, Teresa Stanfill, and David Bawden. *Will the Catholic Church Survive the Twentieth Century?* Privately published, 1987.

Crumbo, Christine. "The Thrift Store Pope." *The Wichita Eagle* (July 19, 1990).

★46★
Catholic Life Church
Current address not obtained for this edition.

The Catholic Life Church was founded in 1971 by the Rev. A. L. Mark Harding and the Rev. Peter A. Tonella, a former Roman Catholic priest who had married in the 1950s. Tonella first joined the Protestant Episcopal Church but soon left it to become bishop of St. Petersburg, Florida, under Bp. Peter A. Zurawetzky of the Christ Orthodox Catholic Patriarchate. The church grew quickly, ministering to Latinos in Denver, Colorado, where the church had gathered several congregations. Mark Harding, who was consecrated bishop by Tonella and Walter X. Brown of the Archdiocese of the Old Catholic Church, supported the small denomination with funds he earned as the owner and operator of four pornographic bookstores in Denver. The church virtually disappeared when Harding, who had become its patriarch, was arrested and sentenced to prison. After his confinement ended in the fall of 1981, Harding resumed his ministry as patriarch and presiding bishop.

Membership: Not reported.

★47★
Charismatic Catholic Church: Independent Rite of America
% Mt. Rev. Daniel C. Braun
102 Freay Rd.
Rocky Point, NY 11128

The Charismatic Catholic Church: Independent Rite of America is a small jurisdiction founded in 1981 by Bp. Daniel C. Braun. It is a Western Rite church which is open to and encourages the charismatic gifts of the Spirit, including speaking in tongues, healing, and prophecy. The jurisdiction is based in the St. Francis of Assisi Church in Rocky Point, New York.

Membership: Not reported.

Sources:

Ward, Gary L. *Independent Bishops: An International Directory.* Detroit, MI: Apogee Books, 1990.

★48★
Christ Catholic Church
% Most Rev. Karl Pruter
Box 98
Highlandsville, MO 65669

Christ Catholic Church was founded in 1965 by the Rev. Karl Pruter, a Congregationalist minister deeply involved in the liturgically-oriented Free Catholic Movement, a fellowship among ministers and lay people of the Congregational and Christian Churches. The movement did not fare well after the 1957 merger of the Congregational-Christian Churches with the Evangelical and Re-

formed Church to form the United Church of Christ. The subsequent splintering found leaders of the movement in different denominations. In despair, Pruter made a pilgrimage to Europe in 1965, where he met with many Old Catholic leaders. Returning to the United States, he settled in Boston, Massachusetts, and searched for a free catholic church and/or bishop. Finding neither, he turned to independent Orthodox Archbishop Peter A. Zurawetzky, and under his authority began a church in Bostons Back bay area. He emphasized the contemplative life, mysticism, and an experiential faith. The growing congregation soon opened a mission in Deering, New Hampshire.

In 1967 Archbishop Peter, assisted by Archbishop Uladyslau Ryzy-Ryski of the American World patriarchs, consecrated Father Pruter to the episcopacy as bishop of the Diocese of Boston. The next year, he designated the diocese as an independent communion. The two jurisdictions met in synod and accepted the constitutions and Canons given to the new body by Archbishop Peter.

The church's headquarters moved from Boston to New Hampshire to Scottsdale, Arizona, to Chicago, and finally to Highlandsville, Missouri in the early 1980s. There Bishop Pruter served as pastor of the Cathedral Church of the Prince of Peace, a small chapel described as the smallest cathedral in the world. In 1989 Christ Catholic Church received into membership the Ontario Old Catholic Church consisting of a single parish in Toronto, Ontario. The churchs pastor, Bishop Frederick P. Dunleavy, had been consecrated by Archbishop Pruter in 1988. In 1991 Dunleavy was elected to succeed Pruter, as the new presiding bishop of Christ Catholic Church.

Under Archbishop Dunleavy, the church adopted an expansionist policy. The immediate fruit of that policy was the merger, approved in December 1992, with the Liberal Catholic Church of Ontario (LCCO). The merged body became known as Christ Catholic Church International (CCCI), and the presiding bishop of the former Liberal Catholic Church of Ontario became the new presiding bishop of the merged church. CCCI continued to grow in both Canada and the United States. However, Archbishop Pruter and the priests of the Christ Catholic Church began to question some of the actions of their new Canadian members. Included in these actions was their joining the Fellowship of Independent Orthodox Churches led by Matriarch Meri Louise Spruit of the Church of Antioch. This affiliation, though short-lived, was most disturbing as it seemed to indicate both a tolerance of heterodox theosophical ideas and an openness to females in the priesthood. The now retired Archbishop Pruter also objected to the use by many of the Canadian parishes of the St. Francis Liturgy which contained objectionable selections from the post-Vatican II Roman Catholic liturgy.

As complaints mounted, in 1995 Archbishop Pruter called for a dissolution of the merger between Christ Catholic Church and the former Liberal Catholic Church of Ontario. He came out of retirement and reorganized the former parishes under his leadership as Christ Catholic Church. Those who did not agree with Pruter continued as Christ Catholic Church International.

Christ Catholic Church is headed by Archbishop Pruter who has over the decades of his career been a most aggressive publisher for the several interests that have dominated his life. St. Willibrords Press, which he founded, has become the major publisher of Old Catholic literature in North America. Pruter is the author of many tracts and pamphlets as well as more substantive books such as *The Teachings of the Great Mystics* and *A History of the Old Catholic Church.* He also operates Tsali Bookstore, which specializes in Native American literature, and Cathedral Books, which specializes in peace literature.

Christ Catholic Church is Old Catholic in faith. It adheres to the Holy Scriptures, the ecumenical creeds, the seven ecumenical councils, and the Confession of Utrecht. The church uses the vernacular liturgy, "The Christ Catholic Mass," which follows the Old Catholic pattern.

Membership: In 1997 the church reported 10 parishes in the United States (with approximately 1,000 members).

Educational Facilities: Bishop Varlet School of Theology, Highlandsville, Missouri.

St. George Theologate, Highlandsville, Missouri.

Periodicals: *St. Willibrord Journal.*

Remarks: As this volume goes to press, word was received that on April 17, 1988, Bishop Pruter consecrated Frederick P. Dunleavy of the Ontario Old Roman Catholic Church to the episcopacy and that the two jurisdictions have been united.

Sources:

Pruter, Karl. *A History of the Old Catholic Church.* Scottsdale, AZ: St. Willibrord's Press, 1973.

___. *The Story of Christ Catholic Church.* Chicago: St. Willibrord's Press, 1981.

___. *The Teachings of the Great Mystics.* Goffstown, NH: St. Willibrord's Press, 1969.

Pruter, Karl, and J. Gordon Melton. *The Old Catholic Sourcebook.* New York: Garland, 1983.

★49★
Christ Catholic Church International
% St. Lukes Cathedral
5165 Palmer Ave.
Niagara Falls, ON, Canada L2G 1Y4

Christ Catholic Church International (CCCI) was formed in 1993 by the merger of several Old Catholic jurisdictions and has subsequently grown through further mergers and individual evangelistic outreach.

Among the constituent bodies of CCCI was the Liberal Catholic Church of Ontario (LCCO), which began in the 1930s with an independent Old Catholic parish, the Church of St. Francis of Assisi, in Hamilton, Ontario, organized by a former Anglican priest, William H. Daw. Daw was consecrated in 1955 by Edward M. Matthew and installed as the presiding bishop of the autonomous LCCO. Bp. John Henry Vincent Russell succeeded Daw in 1974. Russell had been consecrated in 1960, and along with several priests had founded and established Blessed Trinity parish in Hamilton. During Russell's term, oratories were established in Brantford, Ontario, and North Hero, Vermont, and a parish opened in Niagara Falls, Ontario. Bp. Thomas D. J. McCourt succeeded Russell in 1985, and was succeeded the following year by Bp. Donald William Mullen.

A second constituent body of CCCI was Christ Catholic Church, in 1993 headquartered in Toronto. Christ Catholic Church came into Canada in 1989 when the Ontario Old Catholic Church merged into the Christ Catholic Church based in the United States. The Ontario Old Catholic Church dates to 1962 with the consecration of William Pavlik by Abp. Richard A. Marchenna of the Old Roman Catholic Church. In 1963 Pavlik created a separate jurisdiction and consecrated his successor, Nelson D. Hillyer. Hillyer was eventually succeeded by Frederick P. Dunleavy. Dunleavy was consecrated in 1988 by Bp. Karl Pruter of the Christ Catholic Church and in 1991 succeeded him.

In 1992, negotiation between the Liberal Catholic Church of Ontario and Christ Catholic Church began and resulted in Dunleavy's bringing his jurisdiction into what became Christ Catholic Church International. An election for bishop of the new church resulted in the selection of Most Rev. Donald W. Mullen.

The period immediately following the merger included further expansion. Rt. Rev. Gerard La Plante and the Old Catholic Church of British Columbia Society joined the CCCI and four former priest of the Mercian Orthodox Catholic Church were granted "episcopal protection" by the CCCI.

The Old Catholic Church of British Columbia Society dates to the mid-1920s and the establishment of an independent Catholic parish in Vancouver under the leadership of Fr. J. P. Kirk. Kirk was succeeded by Fr. H. J. Barney, who served the parish for over 30 years. He was succeeded by Fr. Gerard LaPlante in 1975. In 1978 the church, finding itself no longer in full agreement, became independent, and Fr. LaPlante was consecrated as bishop. While autonomous, the church remained in full communion with the LCCO.

Issues that came to the fore in the early years of Christ Catholic Church International included some objections to the church's St. Francis liturgy which contained selections from the post-Vatican II Roman Catholic liturgy. The actions of the College of Bishops were questioned by several clergy who felt that the consecration of three of the Mercian priests had been made prematurely.

The new church also affiliated with the ecumenical Fellowship of Independent Orthodox Churches. Bishop Pruter led the opposition to membership, which he saw as a major mistake by the church's leadership. Pruter came out of retirement and reorganized Christ Catholic Church. CCC and CCCI have continued in dialogue, and hope for eventual reconciliation is high.

CCCI is both Old Catholic and Orthodox Catholic in faith and practice. CCCI holds to the teachings of the first seven Ecumenical Councils, the Declaration of the Old Catholic Union of Utrecht, and the creeds of the undivided church. As part of the mystical Body of Christ, CCCI affirms and teaches an apostolic succession vested in the bishops of the Catholic Church and passes that succession through Holy Orders. The holding of such Holy Orders is a prerequisite for the valid celebration of the sacraments. THE CCCI further believes that each bishop has the teaching/administrative authority granted to the apostles by Jesus Christ, and that this authority is not limited to a single bishop regardless of office or position, but is equally and jointly held by all bishops.

Matters of faith and morals may be defined for the church only but the College of Bishops in light of Sacred Scripture and Apostolic Tradition.

CCCI is a founding member of the Federation of Orthodox Catholic Churches United Sacramentally (FOCUS), and during the period of its membership has been led to emphasize the Orthodox element of its faith and practice.

Membership: In 1997 the church reported more than 7,800 members worldwide of which 2,960 were in the United States, 3,880 in Canada, and 1,000 in Europe and Australia.

Educational Facilities: St. Mary's Seminary, Niagara Falls, Ontario.

Periodicals: *St. Luke Magazine.*

★50★
Christ Catholic Orthodox Church
PO Box 17600
Euclid, OH 44117-0006

Christ Catholic Orthodox Church, an American Orthodox Christian church, originally the Western Orthodox Church in America, was founded by then Rev. James F. Mondok, who was given a mandate to build the church. It was granted a charter in January 1984 by the state of Ohio. Reverend Mondok was consecrated in June 1984 in Pittsburgh, Pennsylvania, by Abp. Charles David Luther, assisted by Bps. Alan Bain and Paul Brennan. He established his seat in Euclid, Ohio. The church traces its lineage through Carlos Duarte Costa and Stephen Meyer Corradi-Scarella, as well as the African Orthodox Church, among other lines of episcopal succession. The church's name change occurred in 1988.

Christ Catholic Orthodox Church uses a modern Orthodox Divine Liturgy. Seminarians are trained at St. Seraphim's Center for Theological Studies. Associated with the church is an Orthodox branch of the Secular Order of St. Francis and the Minor Order of Paduans, an order devoted to St. Anthony of Padua. The church sees itself as following the intention of Abp. Aftimios Ofiesh in building a broad American Orthodox church (as opposed to an ethnically based Orthodox church operating in the United States).

The church teaches that in extreme cases, women may become ordained on priests. Clergy are to remain celibate.

The church is headed by a council of bishops that includes Presiding Bp. James Mondok and Abps. Frank Vandeventer and Anthony Claret. They lead the church in participation in a variety of ecumenical outreach programs, worldwide including work in hospitals and in chaplancies throughout the world and the veterans.

Membership: In 1994, the church reported some 6,584 people involved in their congregations and ministry programs worldwide. There were nine bishops, twenty-five priests, fourteen deacons, one subdeacon, and a number of lay ministers.

Educational Facilities: St. Seraphim's Center for Theological Studies, Cleveland, Ohio.

Periodicals: *The Voice of the Fisherman.*

★51★
Christian Catholic Church (Old Catholic) in the United States of America
1205 Thomas Blvd.
Springdale, AR 72762

The Christian Catholic Church (Old Catholic) in the United States of America is an independent Old Catholic jurisdiction founded on July 9, 1988, by its present presiding bishop, Mt. Rev. Raymond E. Sawyer (b. 1946), assisted by Mt. Rev. Albert W. Smith, who serves as the church's suffragan bishop. On May 10, 1988, the Synod of the Old Catholic Diocese of Salt Lake City and Dependencies (now part of the Christian Catholic Church) named Sawyer bishop-elect, and he was consecrated in the Cathedral Church of Saint Luke the Evangelist on July 9, 1988, with immediate canonical release, by Abps. Andre Barbeau and Andre Letellier of the Catholic Charismatic Church of Canada. In 1990 he received consecration, sub conditione, from Bp. Karl Pruter of Christ Catholic Church. Bishop Smith (b. 1951) was consecrated by Bishop Sawyer on July 3, 1989.

The Christian Catholic Church accepts the authority of the first Seven Ecumenical Councils of the undivided Church; the ancient creeds, and the traditional mysteries or sacraments (seven) of the Church. It also accepts the Orthodox proscription against modification to the Nicene Creed (and hence does not include the filioque clause) in the text of the creed as repeated in the Mass. Western Rite liturgies are utilized, though with special permission; Anglican or Episcopal parishes that are admitted into the jurisdiction may use the Liturgy of St. Tikkhon (an amended liturgy of the *Book of Common Prayer* used by canonical Orthodoxy for that same purpose). Women may not be admitted to the priesthood.

The church is a member of the Federation of Independent Catholic and Orthodox Bishops.

Membership: Not reported.

★52★
Christian Orthodox Catholic Church
United States Chancery Office
795 La Playa St., No. 1
San Francisco, CA 94121-3258

The Christian Catholic Church was founded in 1988 by Most Rev. Richard P. Lane, its presiding bishop. Lane had previously served for 16 years as a priest in the North American Old Roman Catholic Church-Utrecht Succession and two years as episcopal vicar to Abp. E. R. Verostek, the church's presiding bishop. Verostek consecrated Lane in 1987. The Christian Orthodox Catholic Church was formed the same year that Verostek retired. It was Lane's opinion that the more traditional approaches of the Church did not meet the needs of the people and he has taken the lead in developing an updated liturgy and offering contemporary forms of spirituality while remaining in the basic orthodox Old Catholic theological structure of the North American Old Roman Catholic Church.

The church adheres to the Apostles' and Nicene Creeds and the doctrines promulgated by seven Ecumenical Councils. It practices an open communion to which all baptized Christians, of any denomination, may participate. Seven sacraments are celebrated. Married men are admitted to the priesthood.

The church is headed by Bishop Lane. There is one diocese (California), two districts (Illinois and Arizona), and a protectorate (Florida).

Membership: In 1991, the church reported five mission parishes and nine clergy.

Educational Facilities: St. Ignatius School of Theology, San Francisco, California.

★53★
Church of St. Joseph
2307 S. Laramie
Cicero, IL 60650

The Church of Saint Joseph began as an independent traditionalist Catholic parish in the 1960s by Fr. Henry Lovett, a former associate of Fr. Gommar A. DePauw, head of the Catholic Traditionalist Movement. Lovett moved to Illinois from New Jersey with the intention of creating a parish to be aligned to DePauw's efforts, but disagreements with him led to the founding of St. Joseph's as a completely independent effort. Lovett looked at several other traditionalist groups (i.e., those opposed to the innovations of Vatican II), but rejected affiliation with any. In 1970 he met John Higgins, who had recently been consecrated as a bishop by Pope Clement XV, the traditionalist French priest who claimed to be the true pope. Higgins was consecrated soon after Bp. Jean de la Trinite, head of the Order of the Mother of God and Clement's major North American supporter, had broken away from Clement's jurisdiction. Lovett invited Higgins to come to Cicero as the episcopal leader for the parish.

Higgins first heard of Michael Collin, the French papal claimant, while studying in Rome. Higgins traveled to Clemery, Lorraine, where he concluded he had discovered the secret of Fatima. In 1917 at Fatima, Portugal, three children claimed to have seen the Blessed Virgin. Among the several messages she gave was one "secret," which was supposed to be revealed in 1960. As of 1986, that secret, written down by one of the three children who saw the Virgin, is the private possession of the Vatican and has never been revealed. Speculation on its content has been a major object of speculation by Marian devotees. Higgins believed that the content of the message was that beginning in 1960, "There shall be no more conclaves for the election of the Pope." Instead, each pope will choose his successor. Pope John XXIII, it is claimed, chose Clement XV.

Higgins saw Clement as the instrument by which the Roman Catholic Church could be returned to its pre-Vatican II state. However, following Clement's death in 1974, Higgins broke with the French followers and refused to accept any of the several claimants to his position. The parish follows pre-Vatican belief and practice, except for its belief in Clement's authority.

Membership: There is but a single congregation affiliated with Bishop Higgins, with several hundred members.

Sources:

Blei, Norbert. "Catholics Reborn." *Chicago Sunday Sun-Times, Midwest Magazine* (November 30, 1975).

★54★
Church of Utrecht in America
℅ Mt. Rev. Derek Lang
2103 S. Portland St.
Los Angeles, CA 90007

History. The American Prelature continues the ministry begun by Abp. Richard A. Marchenna (1932-1982) as the Old Roman

Catholic Church. Marchenna's consecration to the bishopric in 1941 by Abp. Carmel Henry Carfora (1916-1958) began a tumultuous career in Carfora's North American Old Roman Catholic Church culminated in his deposition and excommunicated in 1952. With several clergy and four parishes, he organized the Old Roman Catholic Church and entered into communion with Gerard George Shelley, originally consecrated by Marchenna. Shelley, while serving as bishop in England, had received the lineage of B. M. Williams, and claimed the direct succession of Abp. Arnold Harris Mathew, who had founded the Old Catholic Church in England.

Following Carfora's death, Marchenna laid claim to Carfora's succession through Cyrus A. Starkey. Starkey, Carfora's coadjutor, who left the North American Old Roman Catholic Church after Carfora's death, had asked Marchenna to become the supreme primate of the Old Roman Catholic Church.

Marchenna slowly put together one of the larger of the Old Catholic jurisdictions. Then, in 1974, he consecrated an openly homosexual priest, Fr. Robert Clement, head of the Eucharistic Catholic Church. That action led to his break with Shelley and the loss of many of his priests. Following Marchenna's death, Derek Lang, formerly episcopal vicar for Nicaragua and regionary bishop for North America at the time of Marchenna's death, assumed the leadership of the now decimated jurisdiction. Among other offices, Marchenna had appointed Lang Titular Bishop of Middleburg (a sixteenth-century diocese that had ceased to exist). He began to reorganize it into the American Prelature, thus "replacing the less modest titles and structures used by his predecessors." He also moved the headquarters to the West Coast. More recently, the American Prelature became the Church of Utrecht in America.

Beliefs. The Church of Utrecht in America follows the belief and practices of pre-Vatican I Roman Catholicism and the North American Old Roman Catholic Church, differing only in matters of administration. It accepts the decrees promulgated by the Council of Trent (1565) but does not accept the infallibility of the pope or other documents related to the excessive powers inherent in the pope's teaching office.

Organization. The Church of Utrecht in America is headed by its archbishop. He oversees work in Los Angeles, California; and a hospital, seminary, and mission in Nicaragua.

Membership: In 1988, the church reported approximately 2,000 members (and some 20,000 constituents), mostly in Nicaragua. There were two centers in Los Angeles.

Educational Facilities: St. Martin's Seminary, La Esperanza, Zelaya, Nicaragua.

Sources:

Old Catholic Church (Utrecht Succession). Chicago: Old Catholic Press of Chicago, [1980].

★55★
Community of Catholic Churches
℅ Thomas Sargent
3 Columbia St.
Hartford, CT 06106

The Community of Catholic Churches is a small jurisdiction formed in 1971 as a result of a group of Old Catholic priests and bishops deciding to abandon the traditional Catholic hierarchical structure. They removed the purely administrative functions from their ecclesiastical offices and formed a fellowship of clergy and parishes. Priests kept their sacredotal functions and provided priestly leadership for the parishes, most of which are house churches. The group is led by Senior Bishop Thomas Sargent and Convenor, the Most Rev. Lorraine Morgenson.

The Community generally follows Catholic doctrine and practice, but sets no particular doctrinal standard for members. It also allows the option of dual membership in other churches. It differs from other Old Catholic groups in tha t it had been willing to ordain both females and homosexuals to the priesthood.

Membership: In 1984 the Community of Catholic Churches claimed five churches, nine clergy, and 60 confirmed members.

★56★
Ecclesia Catholica Traditionalis "Conservare et Praedicare"
Box 26414
San Francisco, CA 94126-6414

The Ecclesia Catholica Traditionalis "Conservare et Praedicare" is an independent Catholic church community, whose mission is "to preserve and to proclaim" the traditional Catholic faith. It holds all the truths, doctrines, and dogmata of the Catholic Church since its Apostolic beginnings and subscribes to all seven Ecumenical Councils of the Church, as well as subsequent councils in accord with the tradition of the church, the early fathers, and sacred Scripture.

The community is jurisdictionally independent of the Holy See, although it acknowledges the Bishop of Rome (the Pope) as the successor of St. Peter and spiritual head of the Church. The community received an Apostolic Blessing from Pope John Paul II on July 13, 1985.

The community undertakes as its special vocation to preserve and practice the traditional liturgy of the church as a living liturgy. The western rite of the community preserves in full the traditional Latin ("Tridentine") rite, in addition to the Dominican rite. The eastern rite of the community preserves the East Syriac rite. The community preserves and administers the seven sacraments and sacramentals in their traditional form.

Originally founded on May 22, 1983, by the Most Rev. Thaddeus B. J. Alioto as the Ancient Tridentine Catholic Church, the community changed its legally registered name on May 29, 1990, to Ecclesia Catholic Traditionalis "Conservare et Praedicare." The community's Archbishop Primate Thaddeus was consecrated on May 22, 1983, by His Beatitude Mar David I (Wallace David de Ortega Maxey), whose apostolic succession descends through His Eminence Antonio Cardinal Barerini, nephew of Pope Urban VII, and through additional Eastern lines.

Membership: In January 1992 the overall community consisted of five activity centers: the secular western-rite community of Sts. Dominic and Francis (San Francisco) and four religious communities: The Franciscan Mariavite Monastery of St. Mary of the Angels of the Little Portion (Kelseyville, California), the eastern-rite Mt. Izla Monastery (Curlew, Washington), the eastern-rite Valley Mission of St. Thomas (Fall City, Washington), and the western-rite third Order of St. Dominic (Glendale, Oregon). The community is served by a total of nine priests and eight other clergy and religious.

Remarks: Mar David I's career has carried him through a variety of ecclesiastical organizations and positions. In 1951 he resigned his position with the Catholicate of the West and joined the Universalist Church. In 1970 (at a time when the Catholicate had no American parishes or priests in the United States) he resumed his episcopal role and consecrated Alan S. Stanford, with whom he founded the Catholic Christian Church. A few years later, however, he disassociated himself from Stanford.

★57★
Ecumenical Catholic Diocese of America
151 Regent Pl.
West Hemstead, NY 11552

In 1984 a number of former priests of the Roman Catholic Church formulated a plan for responding to the unresolved problems of Vatican II. Growing out of a number of renewal groups, the priests sought a means to implement a practical ecumenism which would bring Christians together across denominational lines; equal rights for females; a more pastoral approach to divorce and remarriage; and a role for married priests. Many of the leaders of the new movement were themselves married. The priests called for an alternative church-like organization characterized by all of the features of institutionalized catholicism, but flexible enough to respond to the major unresolved problems. Such an organization would provide a place for those not served by the Roman Catholic Church, such as married priests, former nuns, and dissatisfied Catholics who were having difficulty forming their spiritual lives.

Plans for the new diocese were implemented at a gathering in Chicago in August 1984 by representatives of four Catholic renewal groups: The Federation of Christian Ministries, Women Church Speaks, CORPUS, and Maryknoll-in-Dispersion. Prior to the gathering, Fr. Peter Brennan of West Hempstead, New York, received Old Catholic episcopal orders and was chosen the diocese's first bishop. He is assisted by Patrick Callahan of Yorba Linda, California.

The Ecumenical Catholic Diocese of America considers itself a progressive Roman Catholic Church attempting to move the church in a forward, rather than conservative, direction. Except for those issues which brought it into existence, the Ecunemical Catholic Diocese of America is in basic agreement with the Roman Catholic Church. It considers itself under the wider pastoral care of the pope and views the papacy as the center of Christian unity. While respecting the pope, the Ecumenical Catholic Diocese of America is jurisdictionally independent.

Membership: Not reported.

★58★

Evangelical Catholic Church
PO Box 6821
Phoenix, AZ 85005-6821

The Evangelical Catholic Church began as a movement to promote liturgical piety within the Lutheran Church-Missouri Synod in Michigan and Indiana. In 1965 a small group founded the Order of the Servants of the Holy Cross. That society withdrew from the Missouri Synod in the early 1970s and in 1977 affiliated as a monastic order with the newly formed Evangelical Catholic Church under the leadership of Rev. Karl Julius Barwin. Barwin was consecrated in 1989 by bishops Bertil Persson, Emilio Federico Rodriguez y Fairfield, Arthur J. Garrow, Carroll Lowery, and Howard Van Orden. Barwin's apostolic lineage is Orthodox and, through Perrson, can be traced to Patriarch Alexy of Moscow.

Barwin affirms roots within the Lutheran community and the Evangelical Catholic Church is seen as representative of those Lutherans who most closely affirm their place within the larger Catholic world. The church's emblem incorporates Martin Luther's coat of arms within it, and the *Book of Concord* is accepted as a doctrinal standard. The church has a high Lutheran understanding of the Eucharist. It is unique in its belief that the Eucharist should be given to infants and children who are confirmed at the time of baptism.

During the 1980s, the Order of the Servants of the Holy Cross disbanded. The Confraternity of the Holy Sacrament of the Sacred Body and Most Precious Blood of Our Lord Jesus Christ is currently associated with the church. The confraternity is a devotional society which advocates a return to Catholic piety and the adoration of Christ in the Eucharist. It is headed by its secretary-general Ronald A. Cross. In 1993 the Center for Christian Arts and Iconography in Republic, Missouri, affiliated with the E.C.C.

Membership: In 1995 the church reported three congregations serving 18 families.

Periodicals: *The Intercession Paper.*

Sources:

The Church. Phoenix, AZ: Evangelical Catholic Church, n.d. Brochure.

Infant Communion. Phoenix, AZ: Evangelical Catholic Church, n.d. Brochure.

★59★

Evangelical Catholic Communion
Current address not obtained for this edition.

The Evangelical Catholic Communion was formed in 1960 by Michael A. Itkin and other members of the Eucharistic Catholic Church. The new organization took its name from the group formed by Ulric Vernon Herford in England in 1902 following his consecration by Mar Basilius of the Syro-Chaldean Church in India, Ceylon, Socotra, and Messina, a small Orthodox Church headquartered in southern India. Itkin's second consecration by Christopher Maria Stanley carried the apostolic lineage from Herford through British Abp. Hugh George de Willmott Newman. In 1968 the Itkin-led group split. Itkin founded the Community of the Love of Christ, while the remaining members reorganized under Marlin P. B. Ballard.

The communion describes itself as an independent body of believers, Catholic in faith, standing for social justice, peace, and goodwill among men. It emphasizes the love of God and neighbor; the communion of man with man; the living of a sacramental life; and the uniting of humanity into one sacramental faith. It is governed by a Holy Synod.

The several bishops and their dioceses tend to follow an independent course. Most congregations are small and led by ordained worker/priests who earn their livelihood in secular pursuits. Occupations within the helping professions are preferred. Bishop Ballard died in 1994 and the present status of the communion is unknown.

Membership: Not reported. As a policy, the Communion does not give out statistics of membership. The Universal Christian Church has centers in Baltimore, Maryland; Newberry, Vermont; Hartford, Connecticut; Lake Worth, Florida; and Houston, Texas.

★60★

Evangelical Orthodox (Catholic) Church in America (Non-Papal Catholic)
Current address not obtained for this edition.

The Evangelical Orthodox (Catholic) Church in America (Non-Papal Catholic) was originally founded as the Protestant Orthodox Western Church in 1938 by Bp. Wilhelm Waterstraat in Santa Monica, California. When he retired in 1940 he chose as his successor Fr. Frederick Littler Pyman. In 1943 Pyman was consecrated bishop by Abp. Carmel Henry Carfora, of the North American Old Roman Catholic Church (Rogers). Under Bishop Pyman the Protestant Orthodox Western Church remained an integral part of Archbishop Carfora's jurisdiction until 1948, when Pyman withdrew and changed the name of the Church to The Evangelical Orthodox (Catholic) Church in America (Non-Papal Catholic).

Bishop Pyman had hoped to create a "bridge church," and he led his small denomination in adopting the Leipsic Interim of 1548, a document drawn up as part of a sixteenth-century process to create reconciliation of Protestant and Catholic differences. But the twentieth century promulgation under Bp. Wilhelm Waterstraat and Bishop Pyman drew no reaction from either Protestants or Catholics.

In most respects the church adheres closely to the Old Catholic position. The church recognizes the office and authority of the Supreme Pontiff, but only Christ is considered infallible. Clerical celibacy is optional. Oral confession is not required. Both the Latin and vernacular mass is said.

Upon Bishop Pyman's retirement in the 1970s, the leadership of the church passed to Abp. Perry R. Sills, who had been enthroned as Bishop Pyman's successor and Second Regionary Bishop on June 30, 1974. On the previous day he had been consecrated by Archbishop Pyman, and Bishops Larry L. Shaver, William Elliot Littlewood and Basil. In 1984 Sills affiliated with the Patriarchal Synod of the Orthodox Catholic Church of America, an association of independent bishops.

Membership: In the early 1980s the church reported six parishes and 10 clergy, but gave no membership figures.

Sources:

The Evangelical Orthodox (Catholic) Church. Santa Monica, CA: Committee on Education, Regionary Diocese of the West, 1949.

★61★
For My God and My Country
W5703 Shrine Rd.
Neceda, WI 54646-7916

For My God and Country is an organization which developed as a result of the visions of the Blessed Virgin Mary by Mary Ann Van Hoff (d. 1984) and the subsequent establishment of the Queen of the Holy Rosary Mediatrix of Peace Shrine, an independent Catholic shrine at Necedah, Wisconsin. Van Hoof had her first apparition of the Virgin on November 12, 1949, one year after a reported apparition in Lipa City, Philippines. Then on April 7, 1950 (Good Friday), a series of apparitions were announced by the Virgin and as promised occurred on May 28 (Pentecost), May 29, May 30, June 4 (Trinity Sunday), June 16 (Feast of the Sacred Heart), and August 15 (Feast of the Assumption). As word of the apparitions spread, crowds gathered. More than 100,000 people attended the events of August 15, 1950.

On June 24, 1950, the chancery office of the Diocese of LaCrosse (Wisconsin) released information that a study of the apparitions had been initiated. In August, Bp. John Treacy announced that preliminary reports had questioned the validity of the apparitions, and he placed a temporary ban on special religious services at Necedah. He temporarily lifted the ban for the announced event on August 15. An estimated 30,000 people attended a final apparition on October 7, at which it was claimed that the sun whirled in the sky just as at the more famous site of Marian apparitions at Fatima, Portugal in 1917. On October 18, the group that had grown around Van Hoof published an account of the visions and announced that a shrine was to be built and completed by May 28, 1951, the anniversary of the first public apparition.

In spite of the negative appraisal by Bishop Treacy and an editorial in the Vatican's newspaper in 1951 condemning the visions, the activity at Necedah continued, and people attended the public events at which Van Hoof claimed to be conversing with the Virgin Mary. Finally, in June, 1955, Treacy issued a public statement declaring the revelations at Necedah false and prohibiting all public and private worship at the shrine. Approximately 650 pilgrims attended the August 15, 1955 (Feast of the Assumption), apparition in defiance of Treacy's ban. In September, details of the exhaustive study of the shrine (by then operating under the corporate name For My God and My Country, Inc.) were released. The report attacked Van Hoof as a former spiritualist who had never been a practicing Roman Catholic. While the report of the diocese lessened support, worship at the shrine continued, and efforts were made to have a second study conducted. Finally, in 1969, Bp. F. W. Freking, Treacy's successor as bishop of LaCrosse, agreed to reexamine the case. For a time during the study, the shrine was closed to visitors. In 1970 the commission again produced a negative report, and in June 1972, Freking warned the corporation officers to cease activities or face church sanctions. Such sanctions were invoked in May 1975, when seven people were put under an interdict. In spite of the interdict, the work at the shrine has continued although there were several problems in the intervening years. In 1979, leaders of the shrine affiliated it with the small independent North American Old Catholic Church, Ultrajectine Tradition. In the wake of the resignation of the bishops and priests of that church, it dissolved (see Remarks). Then on May 18, 1984, Mary Ann Van Hoof died. In spite of these setbacks, the group that has developed around the shrine, many of whose members had moved into the immediate area, have continued to pursue the program initiated under the direction of the visions. In line with a strong anti-abortion polemic, the Seven Sorrows of Our Sorrowful Mother Infant's Home has been opened to assist unwed mothers and unwanted children. The construction of the St. Francis Home for Unfortunate Men has also continued, and work on the House of Prayer constructed at the Sacred Spot of the Apparitions has been initiated.

Membership: As of 1988 there were more than 300 people affiliated with For My God and Country residing in the Necedah area, with several thousand supporters scattered around North America.

Periodicals: *Shrine Newsletter.*

Remarks: For several years the shrine was affiliated with the now defunct North American Old Roman Catholic Church, Ultrajectine Tradition. That affiliation was formally acknowledged in May 1979, with the presentation to the shrine's supporters of Old Catholic Bishop Edward Michael Stehlik as archbishop and metropolitan of the church. On May 28, 1979, Stehlik dedicated the shrine, 29 years after the first public apparition. The church was at one in doctrine with the Roman Catholic Church, except in its rejection of the authority of the papal office. Stehlik has been consecrated by Bishop Julius Massey of Plainfield, Illinois, pastor of an independent Episcopal Church. Massey had been consecrated by Denver Scott Swain of the American Episcopal Church.

The North American Old Catholic Church, Ultrajectine Tradition faced one crisis after another. During 1980 Stehlik and the priests he brought around him came under heavy attack in the press for falsifying their credentials. Stehlik's assistant, Bishop David E. Shotts, formerly of the Independent Ecumenical Catholic Church, was arrested for violation of parole from an earlier conviction of child molestation. Then in January 1981, Stehlik quit the church, denounced the apparitions as a hoax, and returned to the Roman Catholic Church. He was succeeded by Francis diBenedetto, whom he had consecrated. However, on May 29, 1983, diBenedetto, in the midst of a service at the shrine, announced his resignation, further labeled the shrine a hoax, and returned to the Roman Catholic Church. In the wake of diBenedetto's leaving, a large number of adherents also quit and returned to communion with the Roman Catholic Church.

Sources:

Swan, Henry H. *My Work at Necedah.* 4 vols. Necedah, WI: For My God and My Country, 1959.

Van Hoof, Mary Ann. *The Passion and Death of Our Lord Jesus Christ.* Necedah, WI: For My God and My Country, 1975.

___. *Revelations and Messages.* 2 vols. Necedah, WI: For My God and My Country, 1971-78.

★62★
Free Catholic Church
% St. Thomas the Doubter Free Catholic Church
1010 University Ave., No. 158
San Diego, CA 92103

The Free Catholic Church was founded in the early 1980s by Most Rev. Thomas Charles Clary (b. 1927). In the early 1990s Clary had joined the Free Catholic Church International, an independent jurisdiction founded by Most Rev. Michael Sherwood Daigneault, formerly of the Church of Antioch. Clary founded and pastored the Free Catholic Church of SS. Mary Magdalene & Thomas, Apostles, in Washington, D.C. Then, on April 30, 1994, he was consecrated by Bps. Brian Turkingham, Martha Teresa Schultz, and Judy Carolyn Adams. He subsequently moved to San Diego, California, and founded the Free Catholic Church.

The church is similar in faith and practice to the Church of Antioch. It keeps fraternal relationships with other Free Catholic jurisdictions, many of whom also have their roots in the Church of Antioch, and is affiliated with the International Council of Community Churches.

Membership: In 1997, the Church reported 105 congregations and 20,000 members in the United States and an additional 5000 members overseas in congregations in Germany, Southeast Asia, and Latin America.

Educational Facilities: Free Catholic Seminary.

Periodicals: *The Free Catholic.*

Sources:

Constitution, By-Laws, and Statues. San Diego. CA: Free Catholic Church, 1995. 52pp.

★63★
Hispanic-Brasilian Confraternity of Christian Doctrine, Saint Pius X

% Most Rev. Msgr. Hector Gonzales
10 Stagg St.
Brooklyn, NY 11206

The Hispanic-Brasilian Confraternity of Christian Doctrine, Saint Pius X, can be traced to December 8, 1958, when Fr. Hector Gonzalez formed the Puerto Rican National Catholic Church as a Spanish-speaking Old Catholic body for the Commonwealth. The original intentions and hope were to affiliate with the Polish National Catholic Church, and the new church adhered strictly to the Declaration of Utrecht of September 24, 1889, one of the definitive documents of Old Catholicism. Gonzales opened negotiations with the primate of the Polish National Catholic Church in 1959.

The PNCC withdrew from the negotiations in 1960, in part due to the presence of the Protestant Episcopal Church (with whom, at that time, it was in full communion) on the island. Gonzales then turned to Eastern Orthodoxy, and in 1961 was received into the Patriarchial Exarchate of the Russian Orthodox Church in the Americas. The next year his church was registered as La Santa Iglesia Catolica Apostolica Orthodoxa de Puerto Rico, Inc., i.e.. The Holy Catholic Apostolic Church of Puerto Rico. The church for a time kept its revised tridentine ritual, with a few necessary Orthodox alterations. However, within a short time, the Orthodox liturgy was translated into Spanish and introduced into the Puerto Rican parishes. Gradually, other changes were introduced, and some members began to feel that the church had lost its identity and was being totally absorbed into Russian Orthodoxy, as its Spanish Western Rite Vicariate.

Gonzales led the fight against the Russification of the vicariate, but after the replacement of Abp. John Wendland as head of the Exarchate, he found that he had lost his major support within the jurisdiction. In 1968, with his followers, Gonzales withdrew and reestablished the Western Rite Vicariate. Parishes and missions were organized in the Dominican Republic, the United States, and Brazil. In 1977, for the sake of the future of the movement, the clergy and laity together decided to seek the episcopacy for Gonzalez. As a bishop, however, strict restrictions were imposed upon him. He is allowed to perform the minor episcopal functions, especially the rite of confirmation, and in some extreme cases the ordination of men to the diaconate and priesthood. However, he is not allowed to consecrate or assist in the consecration of anyone to the episcopal office.

Gonzales received epicopal consecration from the hands of the Portuguese bishop Dom Luis Silva y Vieria. Bishop Vieria's apostolic succession comes from a dissident Roman Catholic group in Brazil (the Independent Catholic Church in Brazil) formerly headed by Monsignor Salomao Ferraz. Ferraz was received as a bishop in the Archdiocese of Sao Paulo by order of Pope Pius XII. Pope John XXIII appointed him Auxiliary of Sao Paulo. Later Pope Paul VI appointed him to one of the commissions working on Vatican II. Before his reception into the Roman Catholic Church, however, he had been consecrated a bishop by Dom Carlos Duarte Costa, leader of the Catholic Apostolic Church in Brazil and former Roman Catholic Bishop of Bocatu. In 1979, in recognition of the

geographical spread of the movement, its name changed to the United Hispanic Old Catholic Episcopate. The term "Old Catholic" created enormous confusion for the movement. The term was chosen to indicate its adherence to pre-Vatican II doctrine and practice, and in no way implied the group's association with the Old Catholicism that had appeared in protest of papal infallibility after Vatican I. Therefore, Msgr. Gonzalez and the jurisdiction's clergy, with the approval of the laity, moved to change the offical name to more accurately reflect its position. The episcopate became the Confraternity of Christian Doctrine with the name of its patron saint, Pope Pius X, added as a means of honoring the virtues of the late pope, known as a true defender of the faith and a champion against modernism.

The confraternity continued to use the Roman Tridentine Rite Liturgy of Pope Pius V and the revised liturgy of Pope John XXIII. It accepts the seven traditional sacraments of the Roman Catholic Church, all the councils of the church including Vatican II. It recognizes the pope as the Vicar of Christ and bishop of Rome and acknowledges the See of Rome as the center of Catholic Christianity. Since the total separation from Eastern Orthodoxy, the church demands clerical celibacy. Many of the currently active clergy were ordained in the Roman Catholic Church in the years prior to Vatican II.

Membership: In 1992 the Confraternity reported 32,432 members in the Western hemisphere. In the United States the confraternity was served by one bishop and 14 priests. There were 27 priests and members of religious orders serving overseas in Argentina, Brazil, Chile, Colombia, Costa Rica, Puerto Rico, and Spain.

Sources:

Actual Facts about the Russian Orthodox Church. Brooklyn, NY: Hispanic-Brasilian Confraternity of Christian Doctrine, Saint Pius X, 1988.

The Hispanic-Brasilian Confraternity of Christian Doctrine. Brooklyn, NY: Confraternity Publications, 1989.

Welcome to Our Chapel. Brooklyn, NY: Confraternity Publications, n.d.

★64★
Holy Palmarian Church
Current address not obtained for this edition.

The Holy Palmarian Church began when apparitions of the Blessed Virgin Mary were claimed to have been experienced by Clemente Dominguez Gomez (b. 1946) of Palmar de Troya, Spain. Gomez began seeing the Virgin and having accompanying prophetic visions in 1968. The content of these visions, which included predictions of a number of cataclismic events (schism in the Catholic Church following the death of Pope Paul VI and a Communist revolution in Spain after the death of General Francisco Franco), were circulated internationally soon after they began. In 1970 the Roman Catholic Archbishop of Seville denounced them as lacking any validity. During the 1970s, the messages were circulated in the United States and trips to America were sponsored by St. Paul's Guild in Orwell, Vermont, and the Mount Carmel Center in Santa Rosa, California, though neither center was ever given formal status in the Holy Palmarian Church.

Other claims of Marian apparitions contemporaneous to those at Palmar de Troya took a decided traditionalist stance against the innovations introduced by Vatican II. In the face of continued rebuff by the Catholic hierarchy, Gomez's followers formed the Carmelite Order of the Holy Face. Gomez came into contact with retired Vietnamese Abp. Pierre Martin Ngo-Dinh-Thuc, formerly archbishop of Hue. Thuc was also a traditionalist, then living in Italy. On December 31, 1975, Thuc traveled to Spain and ordained Gomez and four of his associates. On January 11, 1976, he consecrated Gomez, one of the other recently ordained priests, and three additional priests from other dioceses to the episcopacy. During 1976 Gomez and his associated bishops ordained and consecrated other priests and bishops. In September 1976, Thuc, Gomez, and all the affiliated priests and bishops were formally suspended from performing their priestly offices and excommunicated. Almost immediately Thuc repented his action, and the excommunication (though not the suspension) was lifted.

After the death of Pope Paul VI in 1978, Gomez was declared the new pope by his supporters and took the name Pope Gregory XVII. By this time the Palmarian Church had spread throughout the Roman Catholic world, particularly in the Spanish-speaking part.

Membership: Not reported.

★65★
Independent African American Catholic Rite
Church of Martin de Porres
PO Box 41449
Washington, DC 20018

The Independent African American Catholic Rite grew out of the movement led by Rev. George A. Stallings who, in January 1990, established the African-American Catholic Congregation in Washington, D.C. During the years immediately prior to his excommunication by the Roman Catholic Church and his organizing his following in an independent jurisdiction, Stallings had developed a network of support which included Fr. Bruce E. Greening. Greening formed the second congregation of the African-American Catholic Congregation, the Umoja Temple, also in Washington, D.C.

In February 1990, Greening and the Umoja Temple left Stallings' jurisdiction and attempted to reconcile with the Roman Catholic Church. They asked only that they be allowed a five-year period to experiment with the liturgy and that their pastor, Father Greening, be reinstated in the church's priesthood. They were unable to obtain a response to their overtures.

The Umoja Temple then changed its name to the Church of St. Martin de Porres, the Black saint from Peru canonized in 1963. On June 15, 1990, it declared its independence from Rome and elected Father Greening its bishop. He was consecrated on September 28, 1990, by Archbishop Stafford Sweeting, the present Patriarch of the African Orthodox Church. The church is committed to the empowerment of African Americans through the development of institutional ownership, the nurturance of an indigenous clergy and lay leadership, and the encouragement of Black-owned businesses. The church sees itself redressing the inability of the Roman Catholic Church to be inclusive by ministering to those who have been neglected.

Membership: Not reported.

Sources:

Payne, Wardell J., ed. *Directory of African American Religious Bodies: A Compendium by the Howard University School of Divinity.* Washington, DC: Howard University Press, 1991.

★66★
Independent Catholic Church of America
% Bp. Maurice McCormick
8701 Brittany Dr.
Louisville, KY 40220

The Independent Catholic Church of America (ICCA) is an independent, sacramental church continuing the teaching and fellowship of the Apostles through the particular tradition of the Old Catholic Church of Utrecht. The ICCA respects the Roman Catholic Church, and also the pope as the Bishop of Rome and the first among equals, but does not adhere to a belief in the infallibility of the pope nor his universal authority. Although papal infallibility and jurisdiction were the two primary doctrinal reasons for the separation of the Old Catholic churches, since then, several other doctrinal differences have arisen (such as the ordination of women).

The ICCA adheres to the essentials of faith and doctrine as expressed in the traditional creeds of the church (viz., Nicene, Apostles'), in various declarations, and in the doctrinal formulations of the ecumenical councils held prior to the Great Schism (between Rome and the Orthodox church) of 1054.

While no one person is the "head" of the ICCA, Bp. Maurice McCormick serves as the coordinating bishop (i.e., in addition to his duties as a bishop, he also acts as an executive secretary). Every bishop in the ICCA is considered an equal among equals. The ICCA recognizes that those who are married may receive a call to sacerdotal ministry, and that those who received a call to ministry while single may also be called to a life of marriage. There are no restrictions (such as married being allowed to serve only as permanent deacons, or bishops being chosen only from unmarried celibate priests). The ICCA also ordains qualified women to all ranks of the clergy.

The ICCA does not consider divorce, or remarriage after divorce, a legitimate barrier to the reception of any sacraments. It does not prohibit using contraceptive devices. The ICCA abhors abortion, which it sees as the ending of a potential human life. It strongly encourages women with unwanted pregnancies to consider options to abortion, but will not turn a woman who has had an abortion away from the church. The ICCA also accepts gays and lesbians as children of God and welcomes them into full participation in church life and worship.

The ICCA is a member of the Union of Independent Catholic Churches of the North American Old Catholic Church.

Membership: Not reported.

Educational Facilities: Agape of Jesus Seminary, Fort Myers, Florida, and Ottawa, Ontario.

Heed University School of Theology, Hollywood, Florida.

Sources:

http://www.wp.com/wdpeck/.

★67★
Independent Catholic Church of America (Cronin)
Current address not obtained for this edition.

Alternate Address: The Independent Catholic Church of America is a small Old Catholic jurisdiction founded by Mt. Rev. Patrick M. Cronin. Cronoin was consecrated as a bishop of the Western Orthodox Church in America on June 4, 1988, by Luis Fernando Castillo-Mendez of the Igreja Catolica Apostolica Brasileira assisted by Richard J. Ingram of the Western Orthodox Church in America and Walbert Rommel Coelho of the Igreja Catolica Apostolica Brasileira. Cronin withdrew from the Western Orthodox Church five months after his consecration and subsequently formed the Independent Catholic Church in America. It is similar in belief and practice to its parent body, the issues leading to its formation being administrative, not doctrinal.

Membership: Not reported.

★68★
Independent Catholic Churches
3460 Powerline Rd.
Fort Lauderdale, FL 33309

The Independent Catholic Churches is a small independent Old Catholic jurisdiction founded by Mt. Rev. Richard E. Drews. Drews had been consecrated in 1969 by William Andrew Prazsky of the Autocephalous Slavonic Orthodox Catholic Church (in Exile) and soon afterwards formed the Reformed Orthodox Church in America. The Independent Catholic Churches (also known as the Independent Catholic Archdiocese of Florida) superseded the Reformed Orthodox Church. Most recently, Abp. Drews has been succeeded by Abp. Robert Caudill.

The church is Old Catholic in faith and practice and independent in administration. Included is an outreach to the Hispanic community of Florida where most of its congregations are located.

Membership: In 1997 the jurisdiction reported 600 members.

Sources:

Barrett, David B. *World Christian Encyclopedia*. New York: Oxford, 1982.

★69★
Independent Ecumenical Catholic Church (Shotts)
(Defunct)

The Independent Ecumenical Catholic Church was formed in 1976 by Rev. John Michael Becket, a former Universalist minister, and Bp. David E. Shotts. Father Becket was placed in charge of Saint Jude Abbey and the Brothers of the Sacred Rosary. However, the year after its founding, Father Becket left the church and placed himself under the Ecumenical Catholic Communion headed by M. P. B. Ballard.

The church followed the Tridentine Roman Catholic liturgy, but used the English translation of 1951. Its doctrine was Catholic, all seven sacraments were served. No excommunication was recognized. Flowing from its commitment to ecumenicity, members of a variety of Christian groups, including some Protestant churches, were allowed to take communion.

Membership: In 1977 the church reported four churches, 200 members, and eight ordained clergy. However, in 1979 Shotts, who had been charged in a child molestation case, also abandoned the church and placed himself under Archbishop Edward Stelik of the North American Old Catholic Church, Ultrajectine Tradition, headquartered in Necedah, Wisconsin. The Independent Ecumenical Catholic Church is presumed to have dissolved.

★70★
Independent Old Roman Catholic Hungarian Orthodox Church of America
% Edward C. Payne, Catholicos-Metropolitan
Box 290261
Weatherfield, CT 06129-0261

The Independent Old Roman Catholic Hungarian Orthodox Church of America was founded in 1970 as the Independent Catholic Church by Bp. Edward C. Payne. Payne was consecrated in 1969 by Abp. Hubert A. Rogers of the North American Old Roman Catholic Church (Rogers). Originally, he rejected the liturgy used by the N.A.O.R.C.C. and decreed that the Anglican Rite be used by his congregations as it most nearly corresponded to the Scriptural norm of St. Paul's First Letter to the Corinthians.

Soon after the establishment of the Independent Catholic Church, Payne was attracted to Eastern Orthodoxy. He met Abp. Peter A. Zurawetzky, who was in communion with Payne's consecrator, and through Zurawetsky he met Abp. Uladyslau Ryzy-Ryski, who was consecrated by Zurawetsky and who had been constructing the American World Patriarchs. It was Ryzy-Ryski's goal to establish an international association of ethnic Orthodox jurisdictions by appointing archbishops over each national group. In 1972, he elevated Payne to be archbishop of New England, in an archdiocese affiliated with the American World Patriarchs. Three years later he elevated Payne to be metropolitan of Ugro-Finnic Peoples and patriarch of the Orthodox Catholic Autocephalous Church of Hungary in Dispersion.

At that time, Payne, who was Hungarian by birth, had about 20 Hungarian families in his Connecticut congregation, and other families in his archdiocese in Pennsylvania and Florida. During the intervening years, Payne has asserted the Hungarian roots of the church, both through the orders that can be traced through the N.A.O.R.C.C. to the Austro-Hungarian Archbishop, the Duc de Landas Berghes, and the role assigned by Ryzy-Ryski. This heritage led to adoption of the jurisdiction's present name in 1984.

The church is Old Catholic in doctrine and practice and accepts the Declaration of Utrecht. It rejects papal infallibility as well as the universal pastorship of the pope. It also rejects the recent doctrinal statements on the Immaculate Conception and Bodily Assumption of the Virgin Mary. Open communion is practiced. No ordination of homosexuals or women is allowed.

Membership: In 1992 the church reported seven congregations, 18 clergy, and approximately 250 members in the United States, and one congregation, and approximately 100 members in Canada.

Educational Facilities: Independent Catholic Seminarium, Hartford, Connecticut.

Periodicals: *The Independent Catholic*. Send orders to 171 Colby, Hartford, CT 06106.

★71★
Infant Jesus of Prague Catholic Church
3442 W. Woodlawn St.
San Antonio, TX 78228

The Infant Jesus of Prague Catholic Church was founded in 1977 in San Antonio, Texas, by Msgr. John Gabriel (b. 1948). Following his ordination in 1979 by Bp. Paul Gilbert Russell of the Holy Orthodox Catholic Church, he founded the Society of the Archangel Gabriel of the Incarnate Word (Gabrielite Fathers). He was consecrated in 1983 by Russell.

Membership: In 1997 the church reported 400 members in two churches.

Sources:

Pruter, Karl. *The Directory of Autocephalous Bishops of the Apostolic Succession*. San Bernadino, CA: Brogo Press, 1906. 104 pp.

Ward, Gary. *Independent Bishops: An International Directory*. Detroit: Apogee Books, 1990. 524 pp.

★72★
Latin-Rite Catholic Church
Box 16194
Rochester, NY 14616

The Latin-Rite Catholic Church is the American branch of the church aligned to Abp. Pierre Martin Ngo-Dinh-Thuc, the traditionalist leader of an international Roman Catholic movement which rejects the authority of the current pope, Pope John Paul II. Thuc was formerly archbishop of Hue, Viet Nam, who retired to Italy during the papacy of Pope Paul VI and the sessions of Vatican II. He was strongly opposed to the innovations introduced by the church council and in December 1975 ordained a group of men associated with the claimed apparitions of the Blessed Virgin Mary at Palmar de Troya, Spain. The following month he consecrated five priests to the episcopacy. Thuc, and all those whom he consecrated, were suspended from exercising their office and excommunicated by the papacy. Thuc repented, and his excommunication was lifted. However, Thuc's suspension from his bishop's office was not lifted. The other bishops and priests did not recant their actions but went on to form the Holy Palmarian Church.

Thuc remained in retirement until April 1981, when he again exercised his office of bishop by consecrating George J. Musey, head of the Servants of the Sacred Heart of Jesus and Mary, Friendwood, Texas. In October 1981, Thuc secretly consecrated two traditionalist priests from Mexico, Moises Carmona and Adolfo Zamora. Formerly supporters of traditionalist Abp. Marcel Lefebvre, they rejected his leadership when reports surfaced of negotiations with the Vatican. After their consecration, Carmona and Zamora established the Union Catolica Trento (Tridentine Catholic Union), referring to the allegiance to the canons of the Council of Trent prior to Vatican II. In May 1982, he consecrated Fr. Gerard des Lauriers (d. 1988), a former supporter of traditionalist Archbishop Lefevre, who in turn consecrated Gunther Storch of Munich, Germany (1985); Robert McKenna of Connecticut (1986); and Franco Munari of Italy (1987).

Soon after the establishment of the church in Mexico, Thuc's lineage was further extended in the United States with the consecration of Louis Vezelis, head of the Order of St. Francis of Assisi in Rochester, New York. Vezelis was consecrated in 1982 by Carmona, assisted by Zamora and Musey.

Soon after Vezelis' consecration, the Latin-Rite Church was founded at Coeur d'Alene, Idaho, by Abp. Francis K. Schuckardt who had been consecrated in 1971 by traditionalist Bp. Daniel Q. Brown. Schuckardt believed and taught that Pope John XXIII was neither a true nor false pope, but an interim pope, but he believed John XXIII's successors (Paul VI, John Paul I, John Paul II) to be false popes. This position was based on an underlying premise that the Vatican had been taken over by Freemasons who had murdered Pope Pius XII in order to complete their infiltration of the Curia. John Paul II was seen to be an instrument of the Freemasons. By introducing the New Mass and the false pope, the Roman Catholic church had moved into apostasy. Schuckardt and seven people broke with the Roman Catholic church in 1968 and began a new organization promoting traditionalist life and values. Within a short time the Tridentine Latin-Rite Church had grown to more than 800 members, and by 1980 there were approximatly 3,000. Schuckardt established the Congregation of the Mary Immaculate Queen, "and through it the Our Lady of Fatima Cell Movement," the prime structure through which it reached out to traditionalist Roman Catholics around the United States. In 1978 the congregation bought Mount Saint Michael, a former Jesuit center in Spokane, which became its main headquarters. The 350-acre tract now houses the congregation, a seminary, the cell movement, two parochial schools, and several related organizations. The movement encountered stiff opposition from the Roman Catholic church in the Northwest, which officially condemned the group. Former members accused it of cult-like practices and filed lawsuits, one of which resulted in a substantial judgment against the group. However, in 1984, Schuckardt split with the remaining leadership of the Tridentine Latin-Rite Catholic Church and he, with a small number of followers, left. The Tridentine Latin-Rite Church then came under the episcopal authority of Bishop Musey.

Meanwhile, the Orthodox Roman Catholic Church Movement, founded by Fr. Francis E. Fenton and led through the early 1980s by Fr. Robert McKenna, had developed some irreconcilable differences with McKenna who was moving into the influence of the movement developing around Thuc. After his consecration in 1986, the ORCM dissolved and McKenna took those who were willing into the Latin Rite Catholic church. In 1987, McKenna consecrated two other bishops, J. Vida Elmer of New York and Richard Bedingfeld, British-born leader of a traditionalist movement among the Zulus of South Africa. Musey consecrated Conrad Altenbach (d. 1986) of Milwaukee, Wisconsin, in 1984 and in 1987 consecrated a French priest, Michael Main, head of an Augustinian order in Thiviers, France.

Membership: Not reported. In 1986 centers were to be found in most states of the union, Canada, and New Zealand.

Educational Facilities: Mount St. Michael Seminary, Spokane, Washington.

Periodicals: *The Seraph.* Available from the Order of St. Francis of Assisi, Box 16194, Rochester, NY 14616. • *The Reign of Mary.* Send orders to North 8500 St. Michael's Road, Spokane, WA 99207. • *Salve Regina.* Send orders to Box 40025, Spokane, WA 99202.

★73★

Mariavite Old Catholic Church, Province of North America
℅ Robert R. Zaborowski
2803 10th St.
Wyandotte, MI 48192-4994

The Mariavite Old Catholic Church was incorporated in 1972 as the American Orthodox Catholic Church (changed in 1973 to the Archdiocese of the Old Catholic Church in America and Canada). It assumed its present name in 1974. The founder of the church is the Robert R. J. M. Zaborowski who claims apostolic lin-

eage from the Mariavite Old Catholic Church headquartered at Plock, Poland.

The Mariavite Movement can be traced to the mid-nineteenth century in Poland and the founding of a variety of new monastic communities within the Roman Catholic Church which stressed the inner life and spirituality. Among these was a sister house opened in 1886 at Plock, by Feliksa Magdalena Kozlowska (1862-1921), known more popularly by her religious name, Mother Maria Francis. The new community followed the second rule of the Franciscians (originally written for the Sisters of St. Clare) to which was added a particular devotion to the Most Blessed Sacrament exposed to view in the monstrance and a form of life modeled after that of the Virgin Mary during her life at Nazareth. The name Mariavite derives from the Latin words meaning "Mary's life."

Mother Maria Francis was also a visionary, and her visions received a considerable amount of publicity. As a result the community at Plock grew into a movement throughout Poland which included both men and women and attracted a number of priests. It's spread also attracted the attention of church authorities who began to attack both the visions of Mother Maria Francis and the appropriateness of such a movement being led by a female. The appointment of Fr. John Kowalski to the position of Minister General of the Congregation of Mariavite Priests in 1903 did little to ease the tension. In 1904 the church demanded the disbanding of the order which was followed in 1906 by the excommunication of Kowalski and Mother Maria Francis. While most of their former following disavowed their relationship with Roman Catholicism, they decided to continue their movement. They formed the independent Mariavite Congregation. Kowalski traveled to Holland and in 1909 was consecrated to the episcopate by Abp. Gerard Gul of the Old Catholic Church. The church was renamed the Mariavite Old Catholic Church. Following the death of Mother Maria Francis, Bishop Kowalski assumed full leadership of the church. During his reign a number of controversial practices were introduced including a married priesthood and the ordination of females to the priesthood. Also the Latin mass was rendered into Polish. The new practices were largely opposed by both the church's membership and leadership, and several schisms occurred. In 1923 one group led by four priests left the church and founded the Old Catholic Church in Poland. A few years later a second group founded the Old Catholic Church of Poland. Finally, in 1935, the general chapter of the Mariavite order and several bishops under Kowalski deposed Kowalski from office and took control of the Mariavite Old Catholic Church. (Kowalski then moved with his following to the town of Felicianow and reorganized as the Mariavite Catholic Church.)

As a former Roman Catholic who had affiliated with the Old Catholic movement, Zaborowski became acquainted with the Old Catholic Church of Poland and was ordained by one one of its episcopal leaders, Abp. Joseph Anthony Mazur. At the time of his ordination, he also became acquainted with Abp. Francis Ignatius Boryszewski of the Polish Catholic Church, an independent jurisdiction headquartered in Jersey City, New Jersey. In 1972, assisted by some French bishops with Mariavite orders, Boryszewski (who also possessed Mariavite orders) consecrated Zaborowski. Upon the death of Archbishop Boryszewski later that year, Zaborowski succeeded to the role of archbishop and the following year changed the name of the jurisdiction to reflect its Mariavite heritage.

The Mariavite Old Catholic Church follows the orthodox theological heritage of the Mariavite Old Catholic Church of Plock. It accepts the early creeds of the undivided Catholic Church, but considers the statement of papal infallibility erroneous and the recent pronouncement of the dogmas of the Immaculate Conception and the Assumption of the Virgin Mary as invalid. It recognizes the seven sacraments. Auricular confession is optional. Special devotion is paid to the Lord Jesus Christ as present in the Blessed Sacrament and members are obliged to render such devotion a minimum of one hour per week plus an hour per month in a congregational gathering. Special devotion to Mary as Our Lady of Perpetual Help is also practiced. The church is headed by its prime bishop (Archbishop Zaborowski) and the council. The council is selected by the General Chapter of the Church (composed of all bishops and clergy). All clergy belong to the Religious Order of St. Francis of Assisi. However, they do not live together in a monastery. Rather they serve as parish priests and missionaries. Clergy, who follow the first and third Rule of St. Francis, are assisted by lay brothers and sisters who adhere to only the third Rule and nuns who follow the Rule of St. Clare.

Membership: The Mariavite Old Catholic Church has reported a spectacular rate of growth. From its modest beginnings (it reported only 487 members, in eight centers and 32 clergy in 1972), it claimed, by 1980, to have 301,009 members in 117 churches served by 25 clergy in the United States. An additional 48,990 members were claimed for the 58 churches in Canada and several hundred members were claimed for churches in France and West Germany. By 1990, the church claimed 357,608 members and affiliates, 48 clergy, and 159 parishes in the United States as well as an additional 31,104 members in several congregations in Paris, France and Germany. In 1995 the Church reported 356,034 members and affiliate, 48 clergy and 157 parishes in the United States and Canada as well as 1 bishop, 6 clergy, and 29, 105 members in France and Germany.

Educational Facilities: The Mariavite Academy of Theological Studies, Wyandotte, Michigan.

Periodicals: *The Mariavita Monthly.* • *The Mariavite Bulletin.* • The Mariavita Newsletter.

Remarks: A number of factors have raised doubt about the accuracy of the facts and figures reported by the Mariavite Old Catholic Church. In spite of its reported growth from 1972 to 1980, observers have been unable to locate any of the congregations affiliated with the church except the small chapel in Archbishop Zaborowski's residence in Wyandotte, Michigan. Zaborowski has consistently refused to share with inquirers the names and address of any of the claimed parishes or their priests. Doubts have also been raised about Archbishop Zaborowski's ordination and consecration. During the early 1970s he circulated copies of his ordination (1968) and consecration (1972) certificates. They bore the names of Bishop Francis Mazur and Ambrose as prime officiants, and they were on forms bearing the title "Antiqua Ecclesia Romanae Catholicae" (i.e. "Old Roman Catholic Church"). It was supposed by observers (and claimed by Zaborowski) that he had been ordained by the same Bishop Francis Mazur who had been consecrated by Archbishop Carmel Henry Carfora of the North American Old Roman Catholic Church. More recently, Zaborowski has circulated a different set of certificates bearing the title of the Mariavite Old Catholic Church, Province of North America (a name not used until two years after his consecration) and bearing signatures of Archbishop (not bishop) Francis A. Mazur and Archbishop Francis Ignatius Boryszewski as prime officiants. The signatures on the two ordination certificates do not resemble each other in the least. (Archbishop Zaborowski had claimed that he himself had confused the Bishop Mazur consecrated by Carfora and Archbishop Mazur of the Old Catholic Church of Poland.) The earlier ordination certificate also carries no signatures of any other bishops who might have assisted in the ordination. In like measure, Zaborowski claims that Archbishop Boryszewski wished his role in the consecration service suppressed until his death, and hence it was not revealed until 1975. However, the signatures of those bishops whose names appear on both consecration certificates vary in great detail. It should also be noted that even a third ordination certificate exists which claims that Zaborowski was ordained in 1965 by a Roman Catholic bishop, the Most Rev. G. Krajenski (living in exile) and signed by the Most Rev. Cardinal Wojtyla, Ordinary of the Diocese of Kracow. Neither exist on any registry of Roman Catholic bishops.

Sources:

Peterkiewicz, Jerzy. *The Third Adam.* London: Oxford University Press, 1975.

Zaborowski, Robert R. *Catechism.* Wyandotte, MI: Ostensoria Publications, 1975.

___. *The Sacred Liturgy.* Wyandotte, MI: Ostensoria Publications, 1975.

____. *What Is Mariavitism?* Wyandotte, MI: Ostensoria Publications, 1977.

★74★
Mexican National Catholic Church
4011 E. Brooklyn Ave.
East Los Angeles, CA 90022

During the presidency of General Plutarco E. Callas (1924-28), Mexico put into effect provisions of the 1917 Constitution aimed at curbing the political power of the Roman Catholic Church. With Callas' tacit consent, a rival Mexican-controlled Catholic body free from any connection to foreign interests was formed. The leaders turned to Abp. Carmel Henry Carfora of the North American Old Roman Catholic Church (Rogers) for episcopal orders. On October 17, 1926, Carfora consecrated successively Jose Joaquin Perez y Budar, Antonio Benicio Lopez Sierra, and Macario Lopez y Valdez. Perez y Budar became primate and patriarch.

Before returning to Mexico, Bp. Lopez y Valdez visited his family in Los Angeles, California, and contacted a Bp. Roberto T. Gonzalez, pastor of El Hogar de la Verdad, an independent spiritualist church operating within the Mexican community in East Los Angeles. Lopez developed a friendly relationship with Gonzalez. Gonzalez died in 1928, and two years later, Lopez consecrated Gonzalez's successor, Alberto Luis Rodriguez y Durand. By this act the Mexican National Catholic church was able to extend its territory into Southern California. El Hogar de la Verdad gradually became known as the Old Catholic Orthodox Church of St. Augustine of the Mystical Body of Christ.

Over the next decades, as church-state relations improved in Mexico, the National Church, which by 1928 had claimed 120 priests and parishes in 14 Mexican states, began to dissolve. The largest remnant united with the Orthodox Church in America and became its Mexican Exarchate in 1972. Its bishop, Jose Cortes y Olmas was named exarch. The Los Angeles parish survived as the single American outpost of the church. In 1955, Bishop Rodriguez, being in poor health, consecrated Emilio Federico Rodriguez y Fairfield as his successor.

In 1962, Fairfield decided to affiliate with the Canonical Old Roman Catholic Church, the American branch of the Old Roman Catholic Church headed by British Abp. Gerard George Shelley. Following Shelley's death, Fairfield joined Bp. John Humphreys in consecrating a new archbishop in 1982. When Shelley's successor, Michael Farrell, resigned a month after his consecration, Fairfield emerged as the senior bishop of the church. Then in 1983, with the death of Jose Cortes y Olmas, Fairfield became the sole possessor of episcopal orders from the Mexican National Catholic Church. On September 13, 1983, he was installed as archbishop-primate of the Iglesia Ortodoxa Catolica Apostolica Mexicana.

Membership: Only one parish, in East Los Angeles, California, of the Mexican National Catholic Church remains. It has less than 100 members.

Sources:

Schultz, Paul. *A History of the Apostolic Succession of Archbishop Emile F. Rodriguez-Fairfield from the Mexican National Catholic Church, Iglesia Ortodoxa Catolica Apostolica Mexicana.* Glendale, CA: The Author, 1983.

★75★

New Catholic Communion (NCC)
1750 Kalakaua Ave., No. 3-183
Honolulu, HI 96826-3785

The New Catholic Communion (NCC) is an independent Catholic jurisdiction established in Hawaii in December 1994 by Most Rev. Daniel J. Dahl (b. 1944) and a group of five individuals with the idea of becoming a new unique form of committed spiritual expression for clergy and lay people operating as equals outside parish structures, coordinated and staffed by the NCC Secular Institute, whose members live both in community or as lay persons. Bp. Dahl had moved to Hawaii in 1963 and became a businessman. In 1976 he was ordained to the priesthood and the following year consecrated as a bishop by Abp. Joseph MacCormick of the Old Catholic Church in America. His apostolic lineage can be traced to Most Rev. Dom Carlos Duarte Costa of Brazil. Following the decision to form the NCC, he was elected its bishop and apostolic president. He also serves as pastor of Archangel Sanctuary, a ministry on Waikiki Beach.

The New Catholic Communion recognizes the primacy of honor held by the Bishop of Rome as Patriarch of the West, but also honors as equals all of the other historic apostolic Patriarchates, including the Patriarch of Moscow. It accepts the essential directives of the church's first Seven Ecumenical Councils and acknowledges that eminent definition of the central truths of the Christian faith are found in the original Nicene Creed. It practices the seven traditional sacraments, and the sacramental system is held as a primary means by which believers receive divine grace and share, united together, a unique spiritual life.

NCC clergy and members come from a mixed background of Roman Catholic, Eastern Orthodox, and Episcopalian heritage. NCC liturgy incorporates many of the Western Church's rituals along with ancient Eastern Orthodox Christian rites.

NCC seeks to offer a pastoral approach that assists each member to develop a practical and relevant spirituality. It is a belief that many sincere Christians have become alienated from their churches and are not receiving Christian ministry. Among them are divorced persons, those who use birth control, people with alternative lifestlyes, dedicated single parents, those whose families have abandoned them, young adults, the elderly, gays, and lesbians, all of whom need a ministry that fosters unity by expressing the encompassing love of God. To such is the NCC ministry directed.

Membership: Not reported.

Sources:

http://planet-hawaii/dolfinz/.

★76★
North American Old Roman Catholic Church (Rogers)
⅛ James H. Rogers
118-09 Farmers Blvd.
St. Albans, NY 11412

The North American Old Roman Catholic Church (Rogers) dates to October 4, 1916, when the Duc de Landas Berghes, in the United States to escape confinement in England during World War I, consecrated the Rev. Carmel Henry Carfora at Waukegan, Illinois. The Italian-born Carfora had come to the United States to do Roman Catholic mission work among the immigrants in West Virginia, but by 1911 had broken with Rome. In 1912, he sought consecration from Bp. Paolo Miraglia Gulotti, who had been consecrated by Abp. Joseph Rene Vilatte and proceeded to form several independent Old Catholic parishes. After his second consecration, he broke with Bp. W. H. Francis Brothers, also consecrated by Landas Berghes, settled in Chicago, Illinois, and began to organize his own jurisdiction, which he named the North American Old Roman Catholic Church. (Brothers organized the Old Catholic Church in America.) During his lengthy life, Carfora was able to build a substantial church which may have had as many as 50,000

members. He absorbed numerous independent parishes, many of an ethnic nature. He also consecrated numerous bishops (at least 30) most of whom left him to found their own jurisdictions, both in the United States and in foreign lands. In the mid-1920s, a short-lived union with the American Catholic Church was attempted under the name The Holy Catholic Church in America.

Even before Carfora's death in 1958 the North American Old Roman Catholic Church began to collapse, and remnants of what was once a growing ecclesiastical unit now exist as several small jurisdictions. Most have simply disappeared. Splintering began with Samuel Durlin Benedict, who left Carfora a few years after his 1921 consecration to found the Evangelical Catholic Church of New York, a small group that did not survive his death in 1945. In 1924 Carfora consecrated Edwin Wallace Hunter, who in 1929 assumed the title of archbishop of the Holy Catholic Church of the Apostles in the Diocese of Louisiana. This church also died with its founder in 1942. In 1931 Carfora consecrated James Christian Crummey, who, with Carfora's blessing, founded the Universal Episcopal Communion, an ecumenical organization that attempted to unite various Christian bodies (with little success). Crummey broke relations in 1944 and died five years later. The Communion did not continue into the 1950s. This pattern continued throughout Carfora's lifetime. More then 20 jurisdictions trace their lineage to Carfora.

The pattern of Carfora's consecrating priests beyond any ecclesiastical substance to support them, followed by their leaving and taking their meager diocese to create an independent jurisdiction, continued throughout Carfora's life. The major loss of strength by Carfora's N.A.O.R.C.C., however, came in 1952 when 30 parishes under Bp. Michael Donahue moved, with Carfora's blessing, into the Ukrainian Orthodox Church. Donohue was received as a mitered archpriest.

Carfora was succeeded as head of the North American Old Roman Catholic Church by Cyrus A. Starkey, his coadjutor, but before the year was out, the synod met and set aside Starkey's succession. It elected Hubert A. Rogers (1887-1976) who had served for five years as coadjutor but had been deposed by Carfora just a few months before his death. Rogers, while proving a most capable leader, was a West Indian. Most of the nonblack priests and members refused to accept his position and withdrew. This final splintering of the church left it predominantly black in membership, which it remains. H. A. Rogers was succeeded by his son James H. Rogers, the present archbishop.

The N.A.O.R.C.C. advocates a faith in complete agreement with pre-Vatican I Roman Catholicism: "The Old Roman Catholic Church has always used the same ritual and liturgy as the early Church practiced, abiding by the same doctrines and dogmas; following the exact teaching given by the Apostles of Christ, and continuing through valid historical succession down to the present time." In one point it follows Old Catholic rather than Roman Catholic practice: Carfora married, and a married priesthood is allowed at all levels in the N.A.O.R.C.C. The practice has been passed on to those churches that derived from it.

Membership: In 1965, the church reported 30 parishes, 18,500 members, and 112 clergy. However, by 1988 it could report only five parishes, 615 members, and six priests.

Periodicals: *The Augustinian.* Send orders to Box 021647, G.P.O., Brooklyn, NY 11202.

Sources:

Trela, Jonathan. *A History of the North American Old Roman Catholic Church.* Scranton, PA: The Author, 1979.

77

North American Old Roman Catholic Church (Schweikert)
4200 N. Kedvale
Chicago, IL 60641

The North American Old Roman Catholic Church (Schweikert) is one of several Old Catholic jurisdictions which claims to the legitimate successor to the North American Old Roman Catholic Church formed by Abp. Carmel Henry Carfora. Abp. John E. Schweikert (d. 1988) based his claim upon his consecration by Bp. Sigismund Vipartes, a Lithuanian bishop who had served in Westville, Illinois, under Bishop Carfora beginning in 1944.

Archbishop Carfora died in 1958 and was succeeded by Cyrus A. Starkey, his coadjutor. However, the synod of the N.A.O.R.C.C. put aside his succession in favor of Hubert A. Rogers, who had been coadjutor until a few months before Carfora passed away. Starkey left the N.A.O.R.C.C. in 1960, and Richard A. Marchenna claimed that Starkey named him as his successor (see Old Roman Catholic Church (Marchenna)). According to the records of the N.A.O.R.C.C., Schweikert was consecrated by Marchenna on June 8, 1958.

Following Starkey's death in 1965, Schweikert asserted a claim to be his successor against that of Marchenna. He also claimed that Vipartes, not Marchenna, consecrated him in 1958. Through Vipartes (consecrated by Carfora in 1944) and Starkey, Schweikert claimed to be Carfora's legitimate successor.

Headquarters for the church are in Chicago, Illinois, in a building complex that also houses a sisterhood of nuns: the Order of Our Most Blessed Lady, Queen of Peace. The sisters operate a school for retarded children. Belief and practice follow that of the North American Old Roman Catholic Church, though Bishop Schweikert discontinued the practice of an unpaid clergy and promoted a more democratic church structure. In 1962 Schweikert consecrated Robert Ritchie as bishop of the Old Catholic Church of Canada, founded in 1948 by the Rt. Rev. George Davis. The two jurisdictions remain in communion.

Membership: In 1986, the North American Old Roman Catholic Church (Schweikert) reported 133 parishes and missions, 62,611 members, and 150 clergy, figures that reflect the continuing increase in numbers reported during the last decade.

Remarks: It must be noted that during the past decade researchers have been unable to locate any parishes under Archbishop Schweikert's jurisdiction other than the single parish and affiliated mission, both in the Chicago area, over which he serves as pastor. Archbishop Schweikert consistently refused to reveal the names of any priests or the addresses of any parishes under his jurisdiction.

78

North American Old Roman Catholic Church-Utrecht
Succession
Current address not obtained for this edition.

The North American Old Roman Catholic Church-Utrecht succession dates to 1936 when Bp. A. D. Bell, who had been consecrated in 1935 by Abp. W. H. Francis Brothers of the Old Catholic Church in America, accepted reconsecration from Abp. Carmel Henry Carfora of the North American Old Roman Catholic Church. In 1938 Bell consecrated E. R. Verostek who succeeded Bell. Then in 1943 Carfora commissioned Elsie Armstrong Smith (d. 1983) as Abbess of a new order, the Missionary Sister of St. Francis. As an independent order the sisters have conducted a ministry of visiting the sick, offering intercessory prayers and service to the Church—making vestments and publishing pamphlets and prayerbooks. Over the years the congregations under their leadership separated from the main body of the North American Old Roman Catholic Church, though it continues to follow its lead in theology and practice. The Missionary Sisters are headquartered in Mira Loma, California, where they maintain a chapel.

Membership: In the early 1980s, the church reported six parishes with less than 200 members.

79

Old Catholic Church (Anglican Rite)
489 Jasmine St.
Laguna Beach, CA 92651

The Old Catholic Church (Anglican Rite) was founded in 1951 as the Old Catholic Episcopal Church by Jay Davis Kirby (d. 1989), a chiropractor and priest. Kirby had been consecrated in 1970 by Archbishop Herman Adrian Spruit of the Church of Antioch. Affiliated to the church is an order community open to people of other similar church jurisdictions, the Old Catholic Order of Christ the King (Ordo Christus Rex). The order was founded by Fr. Alban Cockeram of Leeds, England and brought to America by Bp. E. Vance Harkness of Atlanta, Georgia. Kirby brought the charter for the order to California. Both the church and the order follow traditional Catholic Christian values and doctrines. During the 1980s, because of its more ecumenical position, the order has been the more active structure and it had developed a ministry through social service in hospitals and other care providing facilities.

In 1978 Kirby consecrated John Charles Maier as his suffragan. In 1988 Kirby retired and entrusted the work to Maier.

Membership: In 1997 there were 638 members, four congregations, eight priests, and two sisters. There are two congregations in Mexico, served by one priest.

Educational Facilities: The church recommends and supports:
Chapman College, Orange, California.
Orange Coast College, Costa Mesa, California.
Graduate Theological Union, Berkeley, California.
San Francisco Theological Seminary, San Amselmo, California.

Periodicals: *Old Catholic Church (Anglican Rite) Newsletter.* Send orders to Box 367, Laguna Beach, CA 92652-0367.

80

Old Catholic Church in America (Brothers)
% Metropolitan Hilarion
1905 S. Third St.
Austin, TX 78704

The Old Catholic Church in America is one of the oldest independent Catholic bodies in the United States, founded in 1917 by W. H. Francis Brothers (1887-1979). Brothers, prior of a small abbey under the patronage of the Protestant Episcopal Church, began to move under the umbrella of several independent Catholic bishops. He was ordained in 1910 by Abp. Joseph Rene Vilatte and the next year took the abbey into the Polish Old Catholic Church headed by Bp. J. F. Tichy. Tichy resigned due to ill health, and in 1914, Brothers became bishop-elect of a miniscule body that had lost most of its members to the Polish National Catholic Church. Then Brothers met the Duc de Landas Berghes, the Austrian Old Catholic bishop, spending the war years in the United States. He consecrated Brothers and then Carmel Henry Carfora (later to found the North American Old Roman Catholic Church) on two successive days in October 1916.

Brothers broke with both Landas Berghes and Carfora, renamed the Polish Old Catholic Church, and assumed the titles of archbishop and metropolitan. He began to build his jurisdiction by appointing bishops to work within ethnic communities. He consecrated Antonio Rodriguez (Portuguese) and attracted Bishops Stanislaus Mickiewicz (Lithuanian) and Joseph Zielonka (Polish) into the church. Most important, former Episcopal Bp. William Montgomery Brown joined his college of bishops. The church grew and prospered, and in 1927, the Episcopal Synod of the Polish Mariavite Church gave Brothers oversight of the Mariavites in the United States. In 1936, the church reported 24 parishes and 5,470 members.

By the 1950s, the once prosperous church began to suffer from the Americanization of its ethnic parishes and the defection of its bishops. In 1962, Brothers took the remnant of his jurisdiction into the Russian Orthodox Church and accepted the title of mitred archpriest. However, five years later he withdrew from the Russian Church and reconstituted the Old Catholic Church in America. He consecrated Joseph MacCormick as his successor. Brothers retired in 1977, and MacCormack organized the synod which administers the affairs of the church. He also began the slow process of rebuilding the jurisdiction. An important step was the acceptance of the Old Catholic Church of Texas, Inc., an independent jurisdiction formerly associated with the Liberal Catholic Church International, and its leader Robert L. Williams, Metropolitan Hilarion, into the church in 1975. Archbishop MacCormack died in 1990 and has been succeeded by Metropolitan Hilarion.

Metropolitan Hilarion serves as resident leader of Holy Name of Mary Old Catholic Church and Saint Hilarion's Monastery in Austin, Texas. The monastery has three resident members and follows the rules of Saint Benedict. The liturgical use is that of Sarum, the restored and historically accurate text which has been published along with its Gregorian music, by the monastery. The Texas church stresses Western Orthodoxy, in remembrance of Abp. Arnold Harris Mathew's union with Antioch in 1911 and in honor of Metropolitan Hilarion's visit with Elias IV, Patriarch of Antioch, in Oklahoma City in 1977.

The Old Catholic Church in America follows the Old Catholic tradition passed to it from Bishop Mathew. The Julian calender is used and kept in publication by the monastery in Texas.

In 1984, Metropolitan Hilarion consecrated Ivan Divalakov as Archbishop of Belgrade (Yugoslavia).

Membership: In 1992 the church claimed four congregations, 500 members, and 12 clergy. Affiliated congregations in Yugoslavia have approximately 2,000 members. In 1992 the parish in Austin reported a membership of 55 and an additional 20 constituents.

Sources:

Brothers, William H. F. *Concerning the Old Catholic Church in America.* N.p. 1925.

___. *The Old Catholic Church in America and Anglican Orders.* N.p. 1925.

LoBue, John. "An Appreciation, Archbishop William Henry Francis Brothers, 1887-1979." *The Good Shepherd* (1980).

★81★
Old Catholic Church in North America (Catholicate of the West)

2118 Wilshire Blvd., Ste. 582
Santa Monica, CA 90403

The Old Catholic Church in North America was established in 1950 by Grant Timothy Billet and several Old Catholic bishops. Billet had been consecrated by Earl Anglin James of Abp. Carmel Henry Carfora's North American Old Roman Catholic Church. Billet established headquarters in York, Pennsylvania, and organized the interdenominational American Ministerial Association which attracted a wide variety of clergy under its umbrella. During the 1970s, he reported a membership of the church at approximately 6,000, a highly inflated figure. Billet died in 1981. He was succeeded by the present archbishop and patriarch, Charles V. Hearn, a psychotherapist and noted counselor on alcoholism. He reorganized the church and reincorporated both it and the American Ministerial Association in California. The church generally follows Roman Catholic doctrine and practice. However, celibacy is not a requirement for the priesthood.

Membership: In 1992 the Church reported 26 churches in the United States with affiliated work in seven countries. There were 43 clergy and 188 members.

Educational Facilities: Trinity Hall College & Seminary, Denver, Colorado.

★82★
Old Catholic Church of Canada

R.R. 1, Inverary Farm
Midland, ON, Canada L4R 4K3

The Old Catholic Church of Canada was founded in 1948 by the Rt. Rev. George Davis. In 1962, Davis' successor, Robert Ritchie, was consecrated by Abp. John E. Schweikert of the North American Old Roman Catholic Church. The church follows Old Catholic doctrine, rejecting papal infallibility and such recent additions to the Roman Catholic Church dogma as the Immaculate Conception of the Virgin Mary. An English-language translation of the Latin Rite is used in worship. Celibacy is optional for all clergy. The present head of the church is the Most Rev. David Thomson, Archbishop.

Membership: In 1997, the church reported 4 congregations and 50 members.

★83★
Old Holy Catholic Church of the Netherlands

4 Briarcliff Ln.
Madison Heights, VA 24572

Alternate Address: International Headquarters: Most Rev. Theodorus P. N. Groenendijk, Primate, Gerard ter Borchstraat 98, 4703 NP Roosendaal, Netherlands.

The Old Catholic movement began in the Netherlands in the former Roman Catholic dioceses of Utrecht, Deventer, and Haarlam. The Old Holy Catholic Church of the Netherlands (Oud Heilig Katholieke Kerk van Nederland) is one in faith with the Old Catholic Church, but administratively is distinct and is not recognized by the Old Catholic Church of Utrecht. It was founded by Abp. Theodorus P. N. Groenendijk. Groenendijk was ordained as a priest in 1971 by A. J. A. Materman of the Liberal Catholic Church International. He was consecrated five years later by Abp. Josef Maria Theissen of the Alt Romanisch Katholische Church (Old Roman Catholic Church), an independent jurisdiction in Germany.

The Old Holy Catholic Church of the Netherlands was established in North America in the mid-1970s by Abp. Rainer Laufers, a French-Canadian whose headquarters are in Montreal. The church operated as the Old Holy Catholic Church of Canada. Under Laufers' direction a United States vicariate, The Vicariate of Colorado, was established by William H. Bushnell, who had been ordained by Laufers in 1979. Bushnell administered the vicariate for two years before moving to the Philippines for a year. Bushnell was consecrated in 1988 as bishop for the Diocese of Pennsylvania, currently the only diocese in North America.

Membership: In 1992, the church reported 1,500 members, nine priests, and five parishes, with an additional two priests and two parishes in Canada. These figures represent the combined figures of the Old Holy Catholic Church and the North American Old Roman Catholic Church (Schweikert) and the Old Catholic Church of Canada, which are in full communion with each other.

Sources:

Ward, Gary L. *Independent Bishops: An International Directory.* Detroit, MI: Apogee Books, 1990.

★84★
Old Roman Catholic Church, Archdiocese of Chicago (Fris)

Current address not obtained for this edition.

In 1970 Abp. Robert A. Burns, of the Old Roman Catholic Church (English Rite), now the Old Roman Catholic Church in North America, consecrated Howard Fris, giving him the right to succession. However, three years later he removed Fris and replaced him with Andrew Johnston-Cantrell. Fris proceeded to found his own church and took some of Burns' small following with him. After Burns' death, the corporation of the Old Roman

Catholic Church (English Rite) lapsed, as no one filed the annual reports during the bickering and in-fighting of that period. Fris revived the corporation and had it assigned to himself.

It is unknown if Burns knew of Fris' personal problems at the time of the consecration in 1970, but there is no doubt that they led to his deposition. They did not stop his continuing to function as the leader of his small flock. Though an alcoholic himself, in the late 1970s Fris opened St. Teresa's Manor, described as a home for alcoholics and wayward men. Because of Fris' ecclesiastical connections, social service agencies in the city began to refer men to the Manor. Then in 1979 Fris was arrested for contributing to the sexual delinquency of a child and the theft of credit cards. In the publicity accompanying his arrest and conviction, it was discovered that both of the priests working with him at the manor also had long records of arrest and conviction for felonies. Fris died in 1981, reportedly of cirrhosis of the liver.

Fris' conviction and the public scandal accompanying it did not destroy his jurisdiction, and he continued to lead his diocese. He performed at least one consecration, and after his death, his coadjutor John Kenelly, succeeded him. St. Teresa's Manor was closed, but Bishop Kenelly heads the Missionaries of St. Jude who minister to the residents of a private hotel for the mentally disturbed, alcoholics, and elderly, located on the north side of Chicago.

Membership: In 1979 the archdiocese claimed 13 clergy and two parishes. It considers the residents of the hotel as lay members.

Sources:

Old Catholic Church (Utrecht Succession). Chicago: Old Catholic Press of Chicago, [1980].

★85★
Old Roman Catholic Church (English Rite)
% Most Rev. Floyd A. Kortenhof
1722 N. 79th Ave.
Elmwood Park, IL 60635-3505

A single church body with two corporate names, the Old Roman Catholic Church (English Rite) is headed by Bp. Robert W. Lane. Lane, a priest in the Old Roman Catholic Church (English Rite) headed by Abp. Robert A. Burns, was consecrated by Howard Fris on September 15, 1974. Both Burns and Lane perceived that Fris had failed to follow the correct form for the ceremony, and later that same day, Burns reconsecrated Lane.

Burns died two months later. Lane left Fris's jurisdiction and placed himself under Abp. Richard A. Marchenna of the Old Roman Catholic Church. Meanwhile, during the last year of his life, Burns had allowed the corporation papers of his jurisdiction to lapse. Lane learned of the situation and assumed control of the corporate title. He was at this time serving as pastor of St. Mary Magdelen Old Catholic Church in Chicago.

According to Lane, in 1978 Marchenna offered him the position of co-adjutor with right to succession. He had, however, developed some disagreements with Marchenna and both refused the position and left the Old Roman Catholic Church. He had previously incorporated his work for Marchenna in Chicago as the Roman Catholic Church of the Ultrajectine Tradition. Upon leaving the Old Roman Catholic Church, Lane formed an independent jurisdiction which continues both former corporations.

The Old Roman Catholic Church (English Rite) and the Roman Catholic Church of the Ultrajectine Tradition are thus two corporations designating one community of faith maintaining a Catholic way of life. It is like the Roman Catholic Church in most of its belief and practice. It retains the seven sacraments and describes itself as "One, Holy, Catholic, Apostolic, and Universal." It differs in that it uses both the Tridentine Latin mass (in both Latin and English translation) and the Ordo Novo. It has also dropped many of

the regulations which govern Roman Catholic clergy, most prominently the provision prohibiting the marriage of clergy.

During the mid-1980s, Lane established six vicariates which function as proto-missionary dioceses. Within each vicariate are one or more quasi-parishes, i.e., communities of the faithful which have not as yet attained parish status. Vicariates are located in Racine, Wisconsin; Topeka, Kansas; St. Charles, Missouri; Lombard, Illinois; and Fullerton, California. In 1992 most Rev. Floyd Akortenhof was name bishop Coadjutor of the jurisdiction with right of succession to Bp. Lane.

Membership: In 1997 Bishop Lane reported 20 congregations in the United States including one Polish-speaking mission in San Diego, California. There was one congregation in Hamburg, Germany.

Educational Facilities: Seminary of St. Francis of Assisi, Chicago, Illinois.

★86★
Old Roman Catholic Church in North America
1207 Potomac Pl.
Louisville, KY 40214

The Old Roman Catholic Church in North America was formed in 1963 as the Old Roman Catholic Church (English Rite) by Bp. Robert A. Burns. Burns was ordained in 1948 by Abp. Carmel Henry Carfora of the North American Old Roman Catholic Church (N.A.O.R.C.C.). He later left the N.A.O.R.C.C. and joined the Old Roman Catholic Church. On April 14, 1961, he was appointed metropolitan vicar general by the church's presiding Abp. Richard A. Marchenna. A month later he was elected bishop-auxiliary and consecrated on October 9, 1961. He left Marchenna's jurisdiction in 1963 and aligned himself with British bishop W. A. Barrington-Evans, Primate of the Old Roman Catholic Church (English Rite). Barrington-Evans appointed Burns archbishop of Chicago.

After Burns' death in 1974, the synod elected Bp. Andrew Johnston-Cantrell, whom Burns had consecrated in 1973, to succeed him. That same synod elected Dr. Francis P. Facione, professor at Wayne State University in Detroit, Michigan, as suffragan bishop. Facione was consecrated several weeks later on St. Andrew's Day. Early in 1975, Johnston-Cantrell resigned due to health reasons, and Bishop Facione was elected by the synod to a 10-year term as presiding bishop. He was also appointed ordinary of the newly created Diocese of Michigan and the Central States. Bishop Facione was re-elected Presiding Bishop in 1985.

At the synod of the Diocese of Michigan and the Central States held on December 3, 1988, Rt. Rev. Raphael John Adams, the diocese's vicar general, was elected suffragan bishop with the title of Bishop of Selbey. He was consecrated on February 8, 1989, by Archbishop Facione assisted by Mt. Rev. John Humphreys of the Old Roman Catholic Church and Archbishop James H. Rogers of the North American Old Roman Catholic Church.

Membership: In 1992, the church reported 900 members in parishes served by 5 priests.

Periodicals: *The Scroll.* Send orders to: Society of St. Mark, PO Box 58273, Louisville, KY 40258.

★87★
Old Roman Catholic Church in the U. S. (Hough)
(Defunct)

Joseph Damien Hough, while under the jurisdiction of Bishop Richard A. Marchenna of the Old Roman Catholic Church, formed a congregation of Oblates of St. Martin of Tours and was designated bishop-elect in 1964. However, following a dispute with Marchenna in 1966, Hough obtained Marchenna's permission to withdraw, and founded the Old Roman Catholic Church in the U.S. In early 1969 Hough was consecrated by Bishop Robert Raleigh of the American Catholic Church (Malabar Succession) with right of succession. Following Raleigh's death, Hough, being the only ultrajectine bishop in California, gathered the faithful into his reorganized church, which combines both Marchenna's and Raleigh's traditions. The ultrajectine element predominates, and worship and belief follow the ultrajectine tradition. Headquarters were established in Venice, California, and all members of the church resided in the state. Both Roman and ultrajectine Catholics were admitted to the services and holy communion. Bishop Hough was in communion with the Old Catholic Church in England, then under Bishop Gerard George Shelley. Hough retired in the early 1980s, and the jurisdiction he headed dissolved.

★88★
Old Roman Catholic Church (Shelley/Humphreys)
5501 62nd Ave.
Pinellas Park, FL 33565

The Old Roman Catholic Church (Shelly/Humphreys) emerged out of a dispute between Abp. Gerard George Shelley (d. 1980), primate of the Old Roman Church in England and America, and Abp. Richard A. Marchenna (d. 1984), head of the jurisdiction in the United States. In 1974, Marchenna consecrated Fr. Robert Clement as bishop of the Eucharistic Catholic Church, an openly homosexual jurisdiction. As a result, Shelley, acting as Marchenna's superior, excommunicated him and those who followed his leadership.

Both those who followed Shelley and those who stayed with Marchenna continued to use the name Old Roman Catholic Church. Following Shelley's death, Fr. Michael Farrell of San Jose, California, was chosen as the new primate. On June 13, 1981, he was consecrated by Bp. John Humphreys, formerly the church's vicar general in the United States, who had been consecrated by Shelley soon after the split with Marchenna. Farrell resigned after only a brief time in his office, and in 1984 Humphreys was elected the new primate.

The church follows the doctrine and practice of the Roman Catholic Church prior to the changes of Vatican II.

Membership: In 1997 the church reported eight parishes.

Remarks: In the 1960s Archbishop Humphreys had briefly worked with Fr. Anthony Girandola, one of the early married Roman Catholic priests. Girandola, who had become somewhat of a celebrity after his founding of an independent parish in St. Petersburg, Florida, interested Humphreys in sharing leadership of the parish so that he could respond to media appearances.

Sources:

Humphreys, John J., ed. *Questions We Are Asked.* Chicago: Old Roman Catholic Information Center, 1972.

★89★
Old Roman Catholic Church-Utrecht Succession
% Roy G. Bauer
21 Aaron St.
Melrose, MA 02176

Abp. Roy G. Bauer was consecrated in 1976 by Bp. Armand C. Whitehead of the United Old Catholic Church and Bp. Thomas Sargent of the Community of Catholic Churches, but served as a bishop under Abp.. Richard A. Marchenna of the Old Roman Catholic Church. In 1977, he, along with Bishops John Dominic Fesi, of the Traditional Roman Catholic Church in the Americas, and Andrew Lawrence Vanore, accused Marchenna of usurping authority, and resigned their positions in the church. Bauer together with Vanore went on to found the Old Roman Catholic Church-Utrecht Succession, following the faith and practice of the parent body. Bauer was elected presiding archbishop in 1979.

The church accepts the Baltimore Catechism and, in general, pre-Vatican II Roman Catholic theology with the exception of the dogmas of papal infallibility, the Immaculate Conception, and the Bodily Assumption of the Virgin Mary. The doctrines on the Virgin

Mary are acceptable as pious belief. The church is headquartered in Boston, and parishes are located in Denver, Colorado; Orlando, Florida; Pennsylvania; California; Texas; and several locations in Massachusetts. In 1984 Bishop Bauer affiliated with the Patriarchial Synod of the Orthodox Catholic Church of America, an association of independent Orthodox and Catholic bishops. Archbishop Bauer is assisted by two auxiliaries: Bishop Andros (Andrew Lawrence Vanore) and Bp. Patrick Callahan.

Membership: In 1995, the church reported approximately 900 members in nine congregations. The archbishop is assisted by two bishops and 16 priests.

★90★
Orthodox Roman Catholic Movement
% Our Lady of Rosary Chapel
PO Box 283
Monroe, CT 06468

Among the first efforts to organize traditionalist members of the Roman Catholic Church was the Orthodox Roman Catholic Movement (ORCM), founded by Fr. Francis E. Fenton. Fenton began holding traditional Latin masses in a private home in Sandy Hook, Connecticut in 1970. In 1972 the group was large enough to purchase a chapel in Brewster, New York. Later they purchased another chapel in Monroe, Connecticut, which has been the headquarters of the movement ever since. Fr. Robert McKenna was installed as pastor of the Monroe church in 1973. Four additional priests joined the ORCM in the fall of 1975, and with the aggressive outreach of the movement, the church began to grow with congregations emerging in Florida, Colorado, and California, as well as in a number of locations in the Northeast.

The movement was controversial even among traditionalists who shared the opinion that the new mass was unsound. Father Fenton was a vocal member of the John Birch Society and was continually criticized for this affiliation. Leaders and members approved of his anti-Communism but not of his membership in a non-Catholic organization. When disagreement among the OCM priests arose over its administration. Fenton and four others left the movement to found the Traditional Catholics of America 1978. Fenton died in Colorado in 1995.

The departure of Fenton and his supporters essentially destroyed the Orthodox Roman Catholic Movement as a national organization. Only the single congregation at Our Lady of Rosary Chapel in Monroe, Connecticut remained. In 1986, its pastor, Fr. McKenna, was consecrated as a bishop by Gerard des Lauriers, a bishop in the lineage of Apb. Pierre Martin Ngo-Dinh-Thuc. McKenna has continued to be active in the circle of Traditionalists in the Thuc lineage primarily through the sporadic publication of a newsletter, *Catholics Forever*.

Periodicals: Catholics Forever.

Sources:

The Essential Roman Catholic Catechism. Monroe, CT: Orthodox Roman Catholic Movement, 1973.

Fenton, Francis E. *The Roman Catholic Church: Its Tragedy and Its Hope.* Stratford, CT: Orthodox Roman Catholic Movement, 1978.

Gasquet, Francis Aidan. *Breaking with the Past.* 1914 Reprint. Stratford, CT: Orthodox Roman Catholic Movement, n.d.

★91★
Our Lady of the Roses, Mary Help of Mothers Shrine
Box 52
Bayside, NY 11361

Our Lady of the Roses, Mary Help of Mothers Shrine emerged from the visionary experiences of Veronica Lueken (b. July 12, 1923), a New York housewife, which began in 1968. Initial visitations from St. Therese of Lisieux (1873-1897) were followed on April 7, 1970, by a visit from the Blessed Virgin Mary. The Virgin announced that beginning April 7, 1970, nine years to the day after the initial apparitions of the Virgin to some children at Garabandal, Spain, she would begin regular visits to Lueken. As announced, she appeared to Lueken outside St. Robert Bellarmine Catholic Church in Bayside, Queens, New York. At the first apparition, the Virgin announced she would return on the eve of the major feast days of the church, especially those dedicated to her. She requested that a shrine and basilica be erected on the grounds occupied by St. Robert's. She revealed herself as "Our Lady of the Roses, Mary Help of Mothers," and designated Lueken as her voicebox to disseminate the future messages.

The messages have focused upon the denouement of many modern trends, especially changes within the Roman Catholic Church. Prediction of an imminent chastisement of the world on the level of the destruction of Sodom and Gomorrah or the flood in Noah's time have added an urgency to the warnings against doctrinal and moral disintegration. Admonitions have been given against abortion, the occult, immodest dress, and freemasonry. Within the church, the messages have denounced the taking of communion in the hand instead of the mouth, the Catholic Pentecostal Movement, the use of recent Bible translations (which replaced the Douay-Rheims version), and religious textbooks which omit vital teachings of the Church.

As the apparitions continued, Lueken's following grew. The Roman Catholic Diocese of Brooklyn instituted an informal investigation and, in an official statement, the chancery office denied any miraculous or sacred qualities to the apparitions and messages. However, the crowds attending the frequent vigils grew beyond the lawn of St. Robert's and into neighboring yards. In April 1975 a restraining order against any outside vigils was obtained, and during the following month St. Robert's refused the use of the building for vigils. This crisis forced the moving of the site away from the location of the mandated shrine. Since that time, gatherings have been held at Flushing Meadows Park in Queens.

The break with St. Robert's was followed by continued polemics. The messages have become increasingly critical of the church. In the fall of 1975, the messages endorsed the idea, popular among some traditionalist Catholics, that an impostor had been substituted for Pope Paul VI. Periodic denunciations of the apparitions came from various Catholic bishops, especially those whose members continued to frequent the shrine. Renewed attempts to vindicate the miraculous nature of the apparitions have centered upon successful prophecies of events, such as the New York blackout and the death of Pope John Paul I and a set of unusual photographs which show what many people believe to be supernatural lights and manifestations. The Bayside apparitions have been widely publicized, and accounts of the events and reprints of the messages have appeared in numerous independent Marian publications. Support for the apparitions has come from These Last Days Ministries in Grand Rapids, Michigan; the Apostles of Our Lady in Lansing, Michigan; Our Lady's Workers in Los Angeles: and Our Lady's Children of Maryland in Millersville, Maryland. For several years (1973-77), the Order of Saint Michael, a Catholic lay group in Quebec, Canada, supported Lueken in its quarterly publication *Michael*, but the group broke with her after a disagreement.

Lueken withdrew from her followers and the public during the mid-1970s. She speaks to no one except her closest followers, though she regularly appears at the site of the apparitions. At such times she is surrounded by a cadre of male followers distinguished by their white berets. Women followers wear blue berets.

Membership: Not reported. Depending upon the weather, as many as several thousand people attend the vigils in Bayside. Schedules are publicized around the United States and Canada. Literature is mailed to many thousands across North America, though the majority remain otherwise members of the Roman Catholic Church. In addition, many people have reported miraculous cures and conversions through the Rose Petals (Blessed) distributed by the Shrine.

Sources:

de Paul, Vincent. *The Abominations of Desolations: AntiChrist Is Here Now.* St. Louis, MO: The Author, 1975.

Grant, Robert. "War of the Roses." *Rolling Stone*, no. 113 (February 21, 1980): 42-46.

Our Lady of the Roses, Mary Help of Mothers. Lansing, MI: Apostles of Our Lady, 1980.

★92★
Polish Catholic Church
(Defunct)

The Polish Catholic Church existed throughout most of the twentieth century as one remnant of the organization begun by independent Polish Bp. Stephen Kaminski which did not join with the Polish National Catholic Church. Kaminiski died without designating a successor or consecrating a bishop for his jurisdiction. Several of his priests, however, continued to serve their parishes awaiting a new opportunity to reestablish Kaminski's diocese. One such priest was Francis Ignatius Boryszewski. During the 1920s, Boryszewski worked under Abp. Carmel Henry Carfora of the North American Old Roman Catholic Church (Rogers) but in 1927 affiliated with the American Catholic Church, headed by Abp. Frederick E. J. Lloyd. Like Kaminski, Lloyd had been consecrated by Abp. Joseph Rene Vilatte. In 1928 Boryszewski began a new parish in New York City, St. Peter and St. Paul Polish Catholic Church. The following year Bishop Lloyd, assisted by Bishops Gregory Lines and Daniel C. Hinton, consecrated Boryszewski to head an independent Polish Catholic Church in communion with the American Catholic Church. (It appears that Polish Mariavite Bp. J. M. P. Prochniewski consecrated Boryszewski a second time in a separate ceremony in 1930.)

The Polish Catholic Church followed Roman faith and practice but rejected the authority of the Roman Catholic Church. The small jurisdiction never grew very large, but Bishop Boryszewski continued to pastor the church in New York City until his death in the 1970s.

Sources:

Church Directory and Year Book. New York: St. Peter and St. Paul Polish Catholic Church, 1933.

Fifth Year Book. New York: St. Peter and St. Paul Polish Catholic Church, 1933.

★93★
Polish National Catholic Church
% Mt. Rev. John F. Swantek
1002 Pittston Ave.
Scranton, PA 18505

In the last decades of the nineteenth century, nationalistic enthusiasms engulfed the Polish communities in the United States. Tension developed from the assignment of non-Polish priests to predominantly Polish parishes. Efforts directed toward autonomy developed in Chicago, Buffalo, and Scranton. In Chicago an independent Polish parish, All Saints Catholic Church, had been established under Father Anthony Kozlowski. In Buffalo an independent congregation was formed and later called Fr. Stephen Kaminski as its priest. Other independent parishes developed in Cleveland and Detroit.

All of these churches were autonomous. On November 21, 1897, Kozlowski was consecrated a bishop by Bishop Herzog of the Old Catholic Church in Switzerland. Kaminski was elected bishop and sought consecration from Abp. Joseph Rene Vilatte. Vilatte consecrated Kaminski on March 20, 1898, and two factions, often bitter rivals, developed.

A third group of Polish nationals emerged in Scranton, Pennsylvania, where the issue was local control of church property. In consultation with Fr. Francis Hodur, their former priest, the Poles constructed an independent church and in 1897 Father Hodur accepted the pastorate. After unsuccessful attempts to remain within the Roman Catholic Church, Hodur was excommunicated in September 1898. A second church was founded in nearby Dickson City.

Other independent congregations followed, and in 1904 a synod met in Scranton. At that time the Polish National Catholic Church of America (PNCC) was organized and Hodur was elected bishop. On January 14, 1907, Bishop Kowalski died. The Old Catholic bishops now consented to consecrate Father Hodur; the consecration was held in St. Gertrude's Old Catholic Cathedral in Utrecht on September 19, 1907. Most of Bishop Kozlowski's followers now aligned themselves with Bishop Hodur and the Scranton movement. Bishop Kaminski died in Buffalo on September 19, 1911, and three years later, the cathedral parish entered into communion with the Polish National Catholic Church.

The Polish National Catholic Church of America differed little from the Roman Catholic Church as it was before the changes brought about by the Second Vatican Council of the 1960s. It has added some feast days and teaches that the preaching and hearing of the Word of God has sacramental power. Bishop Hodur emphasized the love of God and the church hopes and prays that all will be saved. There is local control of property and the congregation does have some say in naming of its pastor. The liturgy, which for many years was said in Polish, has been translated into English. Today English is used in most parishes for the church services.

In 1914 Hodur helped to establish a Lithuanian National Catholic Church and in 1924, he consecrated Father John Gritenas as its bishop. The body became independent but was eventually reabsorbed. The Polish National Catholic Church of America grew steadily through the first half of the twentieth century. It became the only official Old Catholic jurisdiction in communion with the Union of Utrecht in the United States. For many years it was in intercommunion with the Episcopal Church but broke communion after the latter decided to ordain female priests. During the last two decades it has suffered greatly from Americanization, especially the abandonment of the Polish language by younger members, and the mobility of its members, many of whom have moved into areas not served by a PNCC parish.

The PNCC is organized into four American dioceses: Central (Scranton, PA); Eastern (Manchester, NH); Western (Chicago, IL) and Buffalo-Pittsburgh (Lancaster, NY). There is also a Canadian Diocese with the see in Toronto. A very active mission begun after World War I produced a growing National Church in Poland, the Polish Catholic Church. A bishop was appointed in 1924. Today there are three dioceses in Poland; Warsaw, Krakow, and Wroclaw. The PNCC is a member of both the World Council of Churches and the National Council of Churches and is ecumenical dialogue with the Roman Catholic Church and the Episcopal Church.

Membership: In 1998 the church reported a membership of approximately 60,000. There were about 150 parishes and missions in the United States and Canada. An Anglican parish and several Hispanic parishes have come into communion during the 1990s.

Educational Facilities: Savonarola Theological Seminary, Scranton, PA.

Periodicals: *God's Field* (Rola Boza). • *Polka*. Send orders to 104 Pittston Ave., Scranton, PA 18505. • *PNCC Studies*. Send orders to 1031 Cedar Ave., Scranton, PA 18505.

Sources:

A Catechism of the Polish National Catholic Church. Scranton, PA: Mission Fund Polish National Catholic Church, 1962.

Fox, Paul. *The Polish National Catholic Church.* Scranton, PA: School of Christian Living, [1955].

Janowski, Robert William. *The Growth of a Church, A Historical Documentary.* Scranton, PA: The Author, 1965.

Orzell, Laurence. *Rome and the Validity of Orders in the Polish National Catholic Church.* Scranton, PA: Savonarola Theological Seminary Alumni Association, 1977.

Wlodarski, Stephen. *The Origin and Growth of the Polish National Catholic Church.* Scranton, PA: Polish National Catholic Church, 1974.

★94★
Polish Old Catholic Church in America
(Defunct)

The Polish Old Catholic Church in America derived from the Polish Mariavite Church. The Mariavite movement dates from 1893 when Sister Felicia (Maria Franciska Kozlowska), a member of the Third Order of St. Francis, a Roman Catholic order, claimed to have had a vision of the Blessed Virgin. In the vision she was told to establish a mixed order of men and women dedicated to the Blessed Virgin. Thus Sister Felicia founded the Mariavites and the order spread, carried by its strong mystical element. Polish Roman Catholic bishops denounced the vision and labeled it hallucinatory. They ordered the disbanding of the Mariavites, but the members refused to obey. They were excommunicated in 1906. They found support from the Russian Church and were eventually able to obtain priestly orders from the Old Catholic Church at Utrecht. Denied a place in the Roman Catholic Church, the order transformed into a large denomination. Freed from Roman authority, they made several innovations on traditional Roman Catholic practices. They ordained females to the priesthood and episcopacy. They placed a great emphasis upon the veneration of the Virgin. It is estimated that over a half million Mariavites can be found in Poland.

During the first decades of the twentieth century, Mariavites began to migrate to the United States. Many joined the Polish Old Catholic Church of America, founded in 1913 by Joseph Zielonka, a former priest of the Polish National Catholic Church. Zielonka sought consecration from Paolo Miraglia Gulotti, an independent Italian bishop. In 1925 Zielonka brought his jurisdiction into the Old Catholic Church in America, headed by Abp. W. H. Francis Brothers. After fifteen years with Brothers, Zielonka left the Old Catholic Church in America and established the Old Catholic Archdiocese for the Americas and Europe. In 1960 the church had 22 parishes and 7,200 members.

In 1961 Zielonka died and was succeeded by his suffragan Peter A. Zurawetzky, a Ukrainian by birth. His leadership was immediately questioned by Fr. Felix Starazewski, pastor of the parish in South River, New Jersey, who claimed to be Zielonka's true successor. Many of the Polish parishes, opposed to Zurawetzky's attempt to make the Church more inclusive followed Starazewski in founding the Polish Old Catholic Church in America.

In the decades since its creation, the church, consisting originally of a few parishes in the northeast (primarily New Jersey and Massachusetts), found it was unable to overcome the forces of Americanization and a mobile society, and the parishes declined in strength. No evidence of the Polish Old Catholic Church in America had been found during the 1980s, and it is presumed to have ceased to exist.

★95★
Servant Catholic Church
50 Coventry Ln.
Central Islip, NY 11722

The Servant Catholic Church first convened on the Feast of All Saints in 1978 and finalized its polity in January 1980 with the election of its first Bishop-Primate, Robert E. Burns, SSD (d. 1994). Burns was consecrated on July 13, 1980, by Abp. Herman Adrian Spruit of the Church of Antioch. A second bishop, Patricia duMont Ford, served the church from 1980 through 1986, at which time she retired from active ministry to pursue feminist theological studies. In 1993 Ford resumed active ministry due to the failing health of Burns, and succeed him as Premate the following year when he died. The core teaching of the church, termed "eleutheric theology," is rooted in the perception that the essence of the Christian kerygma lies in the proclamation of freedom. All the church's ministries—liturgical, pastoral, sacramental, and social action—reflect this belief system. The church's three-year theological training curriculum centers upon the study of eleutherics. Resonances of this teaching are found in the church's liturgy and in its code of canon law. The church recognizes the sacraments of initiation (baptism), restoration (penance and healing), union (holy, eucharist), instruction (proclamation and teaching), and holy orders. Confirmation and matrimony are designated as sacramental rites.

Though receiving orders from Liberal Catholic sources, the College of Bishops of the Servant Catholic Church has rejected theosophy as "inauthentic teaching." The Servant Catholic Church reaches out ecumenically to other ecclesiastical bodies that share its commitment to peace, justice, effective pastoral ministry, sound theological education, and the admission of women to the three-fold, Catholic-ordained ministry.

Membership: In 1998 the church reported two congregations, one in New York and one in Cicero, Illinois with a total of 50 members.

Educational Facilities: Vilatte Institute, Margate, Florida.

Sources:

The Sacramentary and Daily Office of the Servant Catholic Church. Central Islip, NY: Theotokos Press, 1981.

★96★
Slaves of the Immaculate Heart of Mary
Box 22
Still River, MA 01467

The Slaves of the Immaculate Heart of Mary emerged in the 1940s as one of the first groups protesting the growing accomodation of the Roman Catholic Church to liberal ideas, particularly the acceptance of the possibility of salvation outside of the Roman Catholic Church. Leader of the group was Fr. Leonard Feeney (d. 1978), a Jesuit priest who had become a popular Catholic writer in the 1930s. Feeney taught at Weston College in Cambridge, Massachusetts, but made his second headquarters the Thomas More Bookstore in Harvard Square. The store, opened in 1940 by Catherine Goddard Clarke, become a center for Catholic students. With Feeney's help, it grew into a school in its own right, and from its programs new converts were brought into the church, members for religious orders recruited, and numerous lay people educated in Catholic thinking.

Trouble began in the late 1940s when Feeney began to attack the secularism at Harvard. He broadened his attack to include the liberalism of the church. Fenney charged that some were moving away from the traditional Catholic position which stated that outside the (Catholic) church there was no salvation. Welded together by Fenney's rhetoric and leadership, the core group of the bookstore school became a committed group of dedicated conservative Catholics. The church moved to quiet Feeney by urging him to take a position at the College of the Holy Cross, but he refused to leave the bookstore. Secretly, a group at the bookstore organized a new religious order, the Slaves of the Immaculate Heart of Mary, pledged to Feeney and his attempts to preserve the church in its purity.

Tension increased when four teachers associated with Feeney, who also taught at Boston College (a Jesuit institution), wrote a letter to the General of the Society of Jesus and accused some of their faculty colleagues of heresy. The college fired the four for promoting intolerance and bigotry. When Feeney defended them, Abp. Cardinal Richard Cushing silenced him and then forbade Catholics to associate with the Cambridge center. The Slaves and

Feeney interpreted Cushing's actions as another blow to traditional Catholic faith.

Following the silencing, Feeney was dismissed from the Society of Jesus and in 1953, excommunicated. His excommunication marks the establishment of the Slaves of the Immaculate Heart of Mary as a group independent of the Roman Catholic Church. They saw themselves as a small remnant still holding to the true faith. The group established a residence compound, purchasing several adjacent homes and erecting a high fence around the property. The school lost its accreditation, which led to its loss of funding from the post World War II G.I. Bill and its eventual closing. The Slaves made money by publishing a series of popular books on Catholic themes and selling them door-to-door in the Boston area. They generally spent their Sundays in Boston Commons defending their position within the heavily Catholic community.

In 1958 the Slaves moved from Cambridge to a farm near Still River. An ascetic lifestyle became predominant and eventually all of the adults accepted a vow of ce libacy. Children, which made up half the community's membership, were raised collectively.

After a period of relative quiet, the community went through a series of changes that ended its life as a separated community. In 1974, Fenney led 29 men and women of the community back into communion with the Roman Catholic Church. Then in 1988, the 14 remaining sisters of the group were formally received back into communion and the order regularized. The Slaves of the Immaculate Heart of Mary began a new life as an order recognized by the Roman Catholic Church.

Sources:

The Communion of Saints. Still River, MA: Slaves of the Immaculate Heart of Mary, 1967.

Connor, Robert. *Walled In.* New York: New American Library, 1979.

Feeney, Leonard. *The Leonard Feeney Omnibus.* New York: Sheed & Ward, 1944.

The Holy Family. Still River, MA: Slaves of the Immaculate Heart of Mary, 1963.

Our Glorious Popes. Still River, MA: Slaves of the Immaculate Heart of Mary, 1955.

★97★
Society of St. Pius V
8 Pond Pl.
Oyster Bay Cove, NY 11771

Father Clarence Kelly was among the first American priests to graduate from the seminary established by traditionalist Abp. Marcel Lefebvre (1905-1991) at Econe, Switzerland. In 1973 Lefebvre ordained Kelly, who returned to America with four other priests to found the United States branch of the Society of St. Pius X. Kelly served as United States superior of the society and as superior of the North-East District, when the territory was divided in 1978. In the early 1980s, however, he and Fr. Donald J. Sanborn, superior of St. Thomas Aquinas Seminary in Ridgefield, Connecticut, became concerned about Lefebvre's contacts with Pope John Paul II and his attempts to accomodate the innovations introduced since Vatican II, innovations that had led to the formation of the seminary and the society.

In March 1983, nine society priests, including Sanborn and Kelly, sent a letter to Lefebvre, calling his attention to their objections on a number of issues: 1. The introduction of liturgical changes at St. Thomas Aquinas Seminary; 2. The use of doubtfully ordained priests in missions in the Southwest; 3. The archbishop's desire to introduce the liturgical changes of Pope John XXIII throughout the society; 4. The improper dismissal of priests; 5. The society's usurpation of teaching authority; 6. The need to subordinate loyalty to the fraternity to loyalty to the church; and 7. The liberal acceptance of marriage annulments by Lefebvre. Lefebvre responded to the letter by dismissing Sanborn from his post at the seminary and dismissing all the priests from their place in the society.

Despite disagreements with Lefebvre, the society continued its activities as before, including publication of its two periodicals and services at its churches and missions. In 1984, four priests previously ordained by Lefebvre joined the society, resulting in further expansion. Also that year, Father Kelly founded a congregation of sisters in Round Top, New York, known as the Daughters of Mary, Mother of Our Savior. As of the beginning of 1988, the community had 22 members. The society also operates four elementary schools and two high schools.

The society operated under its founding name until the fall of 1987, when it adopted its present name.

Membership: In 1988 the society reported approximately 50 missions and churches under its care.

Periodicals: *The Bulletin.* • *The Roman Catholic.*

Remarks: In July 1983, the Society of St. Pius X filed a lawsuit asking the court to award them the property of those churches which had been a part of the society before the schism, but which had aligned themselves with the Society of St. Pius V. Parts of that suit have been resolved, the society winning property in Philadelphia and the Roman Catholics of America, property in Norfolk, Virginia. Other property disputes remain to be resolved.

★98★
Society of St. Pius X
℅ Regina Coclihouse
2918 Tracy Ave.
Kansas City, MO 64109

Of the several groups of traditionalist Roman Catholics, the Society of St. Pius X claims the largest number of adherents. Prior to the 1980s, the society was the only traditionalist group which had orders from, and the support of, a Roman Catholic bishop with undisputed episcopal orders—Archbishop Marcel Lefebvre.

Marcel Lefebvre (b. 1905) was raised in a pious Catholic family and spent much of his adult life in Africa as a missionary. After World War II he steadily rose in the African hierarchy as vicar-apostolic of Dakar (1947) and then apostolic delegate for French-speaking Africa (1948). In 1955 Pope Pius XII appointed him archbishop of Dakar. Pope John XXIII appointed Lefebvre to serve on the Central Preparatory Commission of Vatican II. The Council's rejection of all the work prepared by that commission, and the initiation of a number of changes and reforms, disturbed Lefebvre. In 1962, he was appointed by Pope John XXIII as bishop of Tulle (France) and shortly thereafter, was elected superior general of the Holy Ghost Fathers, the religious order of which he was a member. However, Lefebvre found the ruling elite of that order quite accepting of the liberal decisions of Vatican II, and in 1968 resigned his post and retired from public life.

Lefebvre's retirement was soon interrupted by several theological students who, knowing of the Archbishop's opposition to the decisions of Vatican II, sought his assistance. There was no seminary where they could receive traditional Catholic training in theology and spiritual formation. Reluctantly, Lefebvre responded to their overtures for help and in 1969 opened the Fraternite Sacerdotale de Saint Pius X, attached to the University of Fribourg. Fribourg was like other universities, and the Fraternite soon moved to Econe, Canton of Valais, Switzerland, to create a full seminary curriculum. In this venture Lefebvre had the full approval of local bishops. As word spread that a seminary built on pre-Vatican II patterns existed, enrollment increased and growth was rapid.

In 1974, the official attitude toward Econe changed; in November, the French bishops issued a joint statement against adherents of the Latin mass. Informally, the statement was tied to a policy of no longer accepting graduates from Econe into the French dioceses. On May 6, 1975, official approval for Econe was withdrawn by the bishop of Fribourg charging that the seminary opposed the teachings of Vatican II and the authority of Pope Paul VI.

In the wake of the new attitude toward his work, Lefebvre continued his efforts, frequently staying but one step from excommunication. The next major battle began in the spring of 1976 as Lefebvre prepared to ordain some graduates of his seminary. Paul VI publicly rebuked him, but Lefebvre persisted with his plans and ordained 13 seminarians in June. On July 22 Paul VI suspended him from exercising any further priestly functions. Lefebvre responded by traveling to Lille, France, on August 29, 1976, and publicly celebrating mass and denouncing some of the "uncatholic" practices of the Roman Catholic church. His actions led to a personal meeting with Paul VI the following month, which lessened, but did not end, the tension between the two.

Shortly after the meeting with the pope, Lefebvre traveled to England for his first mass there, and the next year he went to the United States. His continued activity inspired the outstanding French theologian Yves Conger to write a book attacking Lefebvre and led Paul VI to threaten excommunication. Since Paul VI's death, Lefebvre has continued to promote the Society of St. Pius X and to negotiate with Pope John Paul II, viewed by many as a very conservative pope. Those negotiations, which produced concessions from Lefebvre, have led some to reject his leadership of the movement.

The Society of St. Pius X had its origin in the United States when several Americans traveled to Econe to study. Upon returning to America, they established centers in East Meadow, New York; Houston, Texas; and San Jose, California. They were soon joined by Fr. Anthony Ward, ordained at Econe in 1975, who founded St. Joseph's Seminary at Armada, Michigan. Fr. Clarence Kelly, one of five Americans ordained in 1973 by Lefebvre, began a periodical entitled *For You and For Many.* It tied together traditionalist supporters around the United States.

By the end of 1975, there were more than 50 congregations served by the priests of the society, and the search for permanent chapel sites was begun. In March 1978, Frs. Kelly, Donald J. Sanborn, and Hector Bolduc met with Lefebvre and decided to divide the work into two districts. Kelly remained superior of the Eastern and Northern Districts and Bolduc was appointed head of the new Western and Southern, headquartered in Houston, Texas. In the Houston suburb of Dickinson, Bolduc founded Angelus Press, which became the major source for literature about Lefebvre and the work of the society.

That same year the society was split by a bitter conflict over the relationship between Lefebvre and the pope. Since the beginning of the society, Lefebvre has continually acknowledged the pope to be the leader of the church, and has tried to obtain the freedom to keep the traditional liturgy and doctrine within the Roman Catholic Church. However, some of his followers in America, including nine priests led by Frs. Kelly and Sanborn, took a more conservative stance. They tended to reject all changes since Vatican II and even some liturgical adjustments made by Pope Pius XII. In 1983, they outlined their complaints in a seven-point letter that included a request for independence from Lefebvre, superior general of the order. In response, Lefebvre, who interpreted their action as evidence of constant disobedience, expelled them from the order. The following year, Father Boldec also left the society. A court suit ensued, in which the expelled priests tried to retain the property of the Northeast District of the society, over which they had previously had control, and bring it into their new organization, the Society of St. Pius X. In 1986 the court returned all the major property, including the seminary, to the society.

In 1987 Archbishop Lefebvre, realizing his aging condition, made last approach to the authorities in the Vatican and initiated negotiations looking toward the formation of a commission of Traditional Catholics with included a provision for him to consecrate three traditionalist bishops to care for the members of the society around the world. These negotiations continued through the winter of 1987-88, but gradually fell apart. Unwilling to delay further, Lefebvre informed the pope of his intention to consecrate four auxiliary bishops which he, assisted by de Castro Meyer of Brazil, did on June 30, 1988. The four bishops were Bernard Fellay, Alfonso Galarreta, Bernard Tissier de Mallerais, and the American Richard Williamson. Both the consecrating and consecrated were immediately excommunicated.

The four bishops were not assigned jurisdictions and there has been not attempt to establish dioceses or to give the appearance of establishing a rival church. While Roman Catholic officials consider the bishops and members of the Society of St. Pius X to be in schism. The members of the society consider themselves good Roman Catholics and acknowledge the authority of the pope through they are currently in conflict with church authorities who are in error following the "reforms" of Vatican II. The society adheres to all Roman Catholic dogma. At each mass said by the society, prayer is offered by name for the pope and the local diocesan bishop. The society's seminaries follow all of the regulations for seminaries as handed down by Vatican II.

The society has avoided all connections with the Old Catholics who deny Papal infallibility. They affirm that the pope is infallible when speaking *ex cathedra*, but is not inerrant (protected from errors of judgment) or impeccable (protected from committing sin). The society also avoids contact with those independent catholic and orthodox jurisdictions which deny various tenets of catholic dogma or traditional practice (such as the ordination of females to the priesthood).

The American District of Society is headquartered in Kansas City, where Angelus Press is also located. There are two seminaries in the United States and a number of elementary and secondary schools. There is also a separate Canadian district.

Membership: In 1988 there were approximately 120 churches, chapels, and missions with 25 priests, 11 nuns, and 15,000 faithful affiliated with the society in the United States. There were 20 congregations in Canada and approximately 250 priests and 150,000 faithful worldwide.

Educational Facilities: St. Thomas Aquinas Seminary, Winona, Minnesota.

Jesus and Mary Seminary, El Paso, Texas.

St. Mary's College and Academy, St. Mary's, Kansas.

Periodicals: *The Angelus.* • *Si Si No No.*

Sources:

Conger, Yves. *Challenge to the Church.* Huntington, IN: Our Sunday Visitor, 1976.

Davies, Michael. *Pope Paul's New Mass.* Dickinson, TX: Angelus Press, 1980.

Davies, Michael Treharna. *Apologia Pro Marcel Lefebvre Part I, 1905-1976.* Dickinson, TX: Angelus Press, 1979.

Hanu, Jose. *Vatican Encounter: Conversations with Archbishop Lefebvre.* Kansas City, KS: Sheel Andrews and McMeel, 1978.

Lefebvre, Marcel. *Liberalism.* Dickinson, TX: Angelus Press, 1980.

★99★
Thee Orthodox Old Roman Catholic Church

Box 49314
Chicago, IL 60649

Thee Orthodox Old Roman Catholic Church is one of several bodies which claims to carry on the work of the Old Roman Catholic Church (English Rite) headed by the late Abp. Robert A. Burns (d. 1974). It was founded by Peter Charles Caine Brown, generally known by his ecclesiastical title, Archbishop Simon Peter. Brown was originally ordained in 1972 by Bp. Anthony Vruyneel of the Orthodox Old Roman Catholic Church of Bellgarden, California. In 1973 he met Mar Markus I (Leo Christopher Skelton) and was consecrated by him. On August 14, 1973, he was enthroned as archbishop. On December 18, 1974, he was appointed chancellor of the jurisdiction headed by Burns. He succeeded to the role metropolitan on December 31, 1974.

Membership: Not reported. In 1983 the church claimed 2,369 members, 19 congregations, and 36 priests.

★100★
Traditional Catholic Church—Conservare et Praedicare

1760 Bush, Ste. 507
San Francisco, CA 94107

The Traditional Catholic Church was founded in 1983 by Thaddeus B. J. Alioto (b. 1934) as the Ancient Tridentine Catholic Church (Catholicate of the West) with the aim of preserving Tridentine Latin liturgy and Gregorian chant, practices then under attack with the spread of changes in the Roman Catholic liturgy following the precepts of Vatican II. The present name was adopted in the late 1980s. The church follows conservative Roman pre-Vatican II beliefs and practices.

Alioto, the brother of San Francisco's former mayor, had been ordained by Wallace D. Ortega Maxey, who carried orders from both Arthur Wolfort Brooks and the Apostolic Episcopal Church and Hugh George de Willmott Newman of the Catholicate of the West. Bp. Robert Ramm, who carried a similar lineage, assisted Ortega Maxey when he consecrated Alioto in 1983.

In 1987, Alioto consecrated Ignatius Mack, who heads an ordered community within the Traditional Catholic Church, the Order of the Holy Spirit.

Membership: Not reported.

Sources:

Pruter, Karl. *The Directory of Autocephalous Bishops of the Apostolic Sucession.* San Bernadino, CA: Brogo Press, 1906. 104 pp.

Ward, Gary. *Independent Bishops: An International Directory.* Detroit: Apogee Books, 1990. 524 pp.

★101★
Traditional Catholics of America

Current address not obtained for this edition.

In the late 1970s, Fr. Francis E. Fenton encountered opposition from some of the leadership in the Orthodox Roman Catholic Movement, due in large part to his membership in, and vocal support of, the John Birch Society. While approving the anti-Communist attitude of Father Fenton, they disapproved of the manner in which he had chosen to express it. As the issue raged, Fenton moved to Colorado and began to reorganize those loyal to him, forming the Traditional Catholics of America. Their beliefs and practices are similar to those of the Orthodox Roman Catholic Movement.

Membership: In 1985 the Traditional Catholics reported eight chapels and missions.

Periodicals: *The Athanasian.* Send orders to Box 6827, Colorado Springs, CO 80934.

Sources:

Fenton, Francis E. *The Roman Catholic Church: Its Tragedy and Its Hope.* Stratford, CT: Orthodox Roman Catholic Movement, 1978.

★102★
Traditional Christian Catholic Church

Current address not obtained for this edition.

The Traditional Christian Catholic Church was founded by Abp. Thomas Fehervary and is built around a group of immigrants from Austro-Hungarian stock who came to Quebec in 1965 following the failure of the Hungarian revolt. Fehervary had been consecrated in 1945 by Abp. R. M. J. Prochniewski of the Polish Mariavite Church, and he had served an independent Hungarian church since 1939. The faith and practice accord with that of the Roman Catholic Church before the Second Vatican Council of the 1960s, and the church opposes the innovations of that Council.

Priests are unsalaried, but (unusual among Old Catholics) they are university-trained.

Membership: In 1972 the church reported one parish in Canada, three missions in the United States, three missions in Western Europe, two missions in Eastern Europe and one mission in Hong Kong. One mission in New York City became independent in 1976 as the Tridentine Catholic Church currently headed by Archbishop Leonard J. Curreri. No current statistics have been reported.

★103★
Traditional Roman Catholic Church in the Americas
% Mt. Rev. Walter Allard
425 E. 11th Ave., Apt. 215
Vancouver, BC, Canada V5T 4K8

History. The Traditional Roman Catholic Church in the Americas was formed in June 1978 by John D. Fesi, a bishop consecrated by Damian Hough, head of the Old Roman Catholic Church in the U.S. Fesi had begun his ecclesiastical career as a Franciscan friar in the Franciscan Provine of Christ the King, a community within the Archdiocese of the Old Catholic Church in America (now known as the Orthodox Catholic Church in America) under the leadership of Archbishop Walter X. Brown. In 1972, Brown created the Vicariate of Illinois and consecrated Msgr. Earl P. Gasquoine as its bishop. Gasquoine in turn appointed Fesi as Vicar of Religious with the title of reverend monsignor. As part of his duties, Fesi managed Friary Press, which printed a quarterly periodical, *The Franciscan,* and pamphlets for the Archdiocese. The community dissolved shortly after Fesi's leaving the Archdiocese in 1973.

After his departure from Brown's jurisdiction, Fesi was approached by Damian Hough, with whom he became associated. On June 30, 1974, Hough, assisted by Bishops Joseph G. Sokolowski and John A. Skikiewicz, consecrated Fesi as a bishop. During this time, Fesi also worked at the Church of St. Mary Mystical Rose, an independent Polish Catholic parish in Chicago. It had originally been founded in 1937 in response to a vision of Maria Kroll, a young Polish immigrant. The parish was, in effect, an independent Catholic jurisdiction headed by Skikiewicz, who had pastored the church for many years. During the 1970s, as his health failed and he could no longer handle the parish work, Fesi was appointed his successor. Though once a strong congregation, support had dwindled and services were being held in the rectory basement hall. After Skikiewicz's death, support further dwindled until the church's board sold the property (which is today the site of a parish of the Polish National Catholic Church). Fesi founded the Traditional Roman Catholic Church a short time later.

Beliefs. The Traditional Roman Catholic Church follows the doctrine and liturgy of the pre-Vatican II Roman Catholic Church. The Tridentine Latin mass is celebrated, and the Baltimore Cathechism is used in teaching. The seven sacraments are kept, and baptism is considered essential for salvation. Veneration of the images and pictures of the saints is promoted. Abortion is condemned. *Organization:* The church is organized hierarchically. Under the bishop, there is an ecclesiastical structure consisting of priests, deacons, subdeacons, acolytes, exorcists, lectors, and doorkeepers. Priests are allowed to marry, unless they belong to a religious order. the priests are organized into a synod that meets annually.

Joseph G. Sokolowski, Hough consecrated Fesi on June 30, 1974. Fesi took his friars into the Old Roman Catholic Church headed by Marchenna. Though *The Franciscan* was discontinued, Friary Press became the church's major publishing arm.

During his years with Brown and Marchenna, Fesi and the Franciscans assisted at the Church of St. Mary Mystical Rose, an independent Old Catholic parish in Chicago. Bishop Skikiewicz pastored the congregation which had been founded in 1937 in response to a vision of Maria Kroll, a young Polish immigrant. The

church was in effect an independent Old Catholic jurisdiction. Eventually, Fesi was appointed associate pastor. Marchenna appointed Fesi head of the Vicariate of Illinois and eventually the Church of St. Mary Mystical Rose became part of the vicariate. Though a strong congregation, after Skikiewicz's death the support dwindled and the building was sold.

The Traditional Roman Catholic Church in the Americas follows the Old Catholic tradition. It keeps the seven sacraments and teaches that baptism is essential for salvation. Veneration of images and pictures of the saints (who are present in a mystical manner in their image) and especially the Blessed Virgin Mary (whose intercession is essential to salvation) is promoted. Abortion is condemned. The church is organized hierarchically. Under the bishop is an ecclesiastical structure which includes priests, deacons, subdeacons, acolytes, exorcists, lectors, and doorkeepers. Priest are allowed to marry. A synod meets annually.

Membership: In 1987, the church reported 14 parishes, 26 priests and 981 members.

Educational Facilities: Our Lady of Victory Seminary, Chicago, Illinois.

Periodicals: *The Larks of Umbria.*

Sources:

Fesi, John Dominic. *Apostolic Succession of the Old Catholic Church.* Chicago: Friary Press, [1975].

___. *Canonical Standing of Religious in Regards to the Sacred Ministry.* Chicago: Friary Press, 1975.

___. *Reasons for Divorce and Annulment in Church Law.* Chicago: Friary Press, 1975.

★104★
Tridentine Catholic Church-Traditional Catholic Archdiocese in America
1740 W. 7th St.
Brooklyn, NY 11223-1301

History. The Tridentine Catholic Archdiocese in America was founded in 1974 as the Tridentine Catholic Church by Fr. Leonard J. Curreri, formerly a priest in the Traditional Christian Catholic Church headed by Abp. Thomas Fehervary. In 1974, Fehervary moved to extend his Canadian-based jurisdiction to the United States by ordaining Fr. Curreri and two other priests. A synod was called in Canada in June of 1975 at which it was decided to call the American branch of the jurisdiction "The Tridentine Catholic Church," a name best symbolizing the affirmations for which the church stood. However, the following year, on April 23, 1977, Curreri was consecrated a bishop by Abp. Francis Joseph Ryan of the Ecumenical Orthodox Church of Christ, thus bestowing on Curreri the Old Calender Greek Orthodox Succession. He was subsequently consecrated conditionally on July 30, 1977, by Abp. Andre Barbeau of the Catholic Charismatic Church of Canada, thus bestowing on him the Brazilian Roman Catholic and other lines of succession. In January 1991, new articles of incorporation for the church were filed and the church adopted its present name.

In 1990 the church was reincorporated as the Traditional Catholic Archdiocese of America, and for a short time used that name. However, some requested a return to the original name. A compromise was reached with the combination of the two names into the one used at present.

Beliefs. The Tridentine Catholic Church Archdiocese follows the doctrines and practices of the of the pre-Vatican II Roman Catholic Church. It rejects the Novus Ordo (the new mass which developed out of the changes initiated by Vatican II). Papal infallibility is also not defined as an article of faith. The ordination of women is rejected in toto. Clerical celibacy is the rule, although there are exceptions.

Concerning the issue of birth control, the church teaches that it is a matter which requires the response of a well-formed conscience. Members are admonished to keep in mind the constant teaching of Catholic Church pertaining to conjugal relations and the responsibilities stemming from them. Contraceptives or the willfull sterilization of a man or woman are not considered valid measures for the prevention of unwanted pregnancies. The only acceptable birth control is self-control, the abstinence from conjugal relations. Abortion is considered the willful killing of a human fetus and never allowable for any reason whatsoever. The Archdiocese teaches that a valid marriage cannot be dissolved while one of the partners is still living. Divorce is not recognized, but for various valid reasons annulments of the marriage may on occasion be arranged. Sacraments are not refused to divorced persons provided they have not remarried.

Membership: In 1997, the church reported 100 members and four priests in the United States.

Sources:

Curreri, Leonard J. *De Sacramentis.* Brooklyn, NY, n.d.

___. *More Questions and Answers on the Tridentine Catholic Church.* Brooklyn, NY, n.d.

___. *Questions and Answers on the Tridentine Catholic Church.* Brooklyn, NY, n.d.

___. *Seccessio Apostolica.* Brooklyn, NY, 1984.

★105★
Tridentine Old Roman Community Catholic Church (Jones)
Current address not obtained for this edition.

The Tridentine Old Roman Community Catholic Church was organized in 1976 by Fr. Jack Alwin Jones, generally known by his church name Jacque A. Jones. Jones was consecrated as a bishop in 1980 by Bishops Lawrence E. Carter of the North American Old Roman Catholic Church-Utrecht Succession and Thomas Sargent of the Community of Catholic Churches. In the mid-1980s, however, Jones resigned his leadership of the single parish of the jurisdiction, St. John the Apostle Church in Bellflower, California, and turned the corporation over to Bishop Charles T. Sutter.

Sutter had recently moved to southern California from Ohio, where he had been the founder of the American Orthodox Catholic Church, Archdiocese of Ohio. He had founded the jurisdiction following his 1979 consecration by Mar Apriam I (Archbishop Richard B. Morrill), head of the Holy Orthodox Catholic Church, Eastern and Apostolic. During the early 1980s, Sutter's jurisdiction had parishes and a religious order in Florida and a school in Arkansas. However, in the summer of 1982, the corporation was dissolved and Sutter later moved to the West Coast.

Membership: In 1988, there was one small parish in Long Beach, California.

★106★
United Catholic Church (UCC)
5115 S. A1A Hwy.
Melbourne Beach, FL 32951

The United Catholic Church (UCC) is a non-papal Catholic jurisdiction founded by Mt. Rev. Dr. Robert M. Bowman, its presiding bishop, with apostolic succession from the Old Catholic Church. It has accepted as its primary mission a ministry to the "millions of alienated or excommunicated Roman Catholics who no longer go to Mass or Communion, for whatever reason." The UCC provides a place for the unchurched, divorced, and excommunicated or people otherwise marginalized. It also considers itself as both a denomination and an interchurch fellowship, and as an interchurch fellowship, the UCC is attempting to bring some unity into the independent Catholic church movement.

The UCC is an Orthodox Christian body in the Western tradition, but relying on the scriptures and the early creeds of the Church as its authority, it does not accept the infallibility of the pope or the canonicity of the Apocrypha, nor does it require belief in any doctrine it finds lacking in biblical support. A prime example of the latter are the various doctrines concerning the Virgin Mary. In like measure it has discarded belief in purgatory, indulgences, and prayers for the dead. The UCC also utilizes the pre-1054 form of the Nicene Creed, without the so-called "filioque clause " ("and the son") words that appear in the Roman Catholic form of the creed. The clause is felt to be an unnecessary obstacle to unity with the Eastern Orthodox. The UCC does affirm the Real Presence of Christ in the Eucharist, but rejects the concept of "transubstantiation" as held by the Roman Catholic Church.

Following what it considers an early church model, the UCC offers ordination without reference to either the gender or marital status of candidates.

Membership: Not reported.

Sources:

http://www.atmnet.net/.

★107★
United Old Roman Catholic Church (Whitehead)
Current address not obtained for this edition.

The United Old Catholic Church resulted from the 1963 merger of three independent jurisdictions, the Catholic Episcopal Church and two other churches. The archbishop and head of the new merged body was Armand C. Whitehead, consecrated in 1960 by Michael A. Itkin, who soon left Itkin's jurisdiction to found the Catholic Episcopal Church. Whitehead was consecrated a second time by James E. Burns in 1970.

In general, doctrine and practice conform to the seven ecumenical councils held between 325 A.D. and 787 A.D., and the canons of the Roman Catholic Church prior to 1880. Distinctive features of the church include a vernacular liturgy, non-obligatory use of the sacrament of penance, and recognition of the primacy (though not the supremacy or infallibility) of the Pope. None of the newer doctrines of the Virgin Mary are accepted, such as her bodily assumption into heaven. Also, "individual bodily parts of our Blessed Lord" such as the "Sacred Heart" are not held in special veneration.

Membership: In 1967, the United Catholic Church reported 3 parishes and approximately 100 members. As of 1984, Archbishop Whitehead was living in semi-retirement and recent information on activities of the church have not been reported.

★108★
Universal Christian Apostolic Church
Current address not obtained for this edition.

In 1947, the Universal Christian Apostolic Church was founded in Vancouver, British Columbia by William F. Wolsey. Wolsey received apostolic succession eight years later when he was consecrated by British Old Catholic bishops Hugh George de Willmott Newman (Mar Georgius) of the Catholicate of the West and Harold Percival Nicholson (Mar Joannes), who had left Mar Georgius to found the Ancient Catholic Church. Wolsey claimed a degree in Bio-Psychology from the Taylor School of Bio-Psychology, out of which he claimed to have developed a psychiatric method compatible with Christianity.

The Universal Christian Apostolic Church believes in the "usefulness" of the original Christian doctrine, but attempted to be nonsectarian in its interpretation. Unique to its perspective are beliefs in Christian doctrine as a living philosophy best manifested in the work of the Christian Ministry and in Jesus as a perfect manifestation of the "Christos," the Christ-Spirit. The Christ-Spirit is thought of as enthusiasm plus, "that something more." Those who are annointed with it reveal the actual presence of Jesus, which gives life to worship and ritual.

Membership: Since Wolsey's death in the 1980s, there has been no sign of the church's continuance. It may be defunct.

Remarks: Wolsey became known during his career as a collector of degrees and a member in a number of honorary societies and orders. These, along with a number of open membership organizations which he had joined, were duly noted on his lengthy curriculum vitae.

Sources:

Somanah, Meernaidoo T. *Mahatma Gandhi and Other Dedicated Souls.* Port Louis, MR, 1968.

___. *The Philosophy and Spiritual Teachings of the Modern Saint, Patriarch-Archbishop Dr. William F. Wolsey.* Port Louis, MR: Standard Printing Establishment, 1971.

Shyam Sundar Agarwal Sarad. *The World Jnana Sadhak Society and Its Founder.* Jalpaiguri, W. Bengal, India: The Author, 1966.

Wolsey, William Franklin. *Vivesco.* North Burnaby, BC: Universal Life Foundation, 1957.

★109★
Universal Episcopal Communion
(Defunct)

The Universal Episcopal Communion was organized in 1930 by James Christian Crummey (d. 1949), a Chicago theosophist, with the hope of uniting the various small and divided Old Catholic jurisdictions of North America and eventually other continents. During the 1920s, Crummey became a priest under Archbishop Carmel Henry Carfora of the North American Old Roman Catholic Church. On March 19, 1931, Carfora consecrated him as a bishop. As a step toward uniting the Old Catholics, he conceived of an additional organization in which bishops could coordinate activity but which would not attempt to control them in their independent ministries. This second body, hardly indistinguishable from the first, was called the Universal Christian Communion. Crummey headed both bodies and kept them within Carfora's jurisdiction until 1944 when he withdrew. At that point, the Universal Episcopal Communion and the Universal Christian Communion became independent entities. Joining him in leaving Carfora were Bishops Mather W. Sherwood and Murray L. Bennett. The two communions lasted until Crummey's death but disolved soon afterwards, neither having attained any significant support from their targeted constituency.

Sources:

Anson, Peter. *Bishops at Large.* London: Faber and Faber, 1964.

Brandreth, Henry R. T. *Episcopi Vegantes and the Anglican Church.* London: Society for Promoting Christian Knowledge, 1947.

★110★
White Robed Monks of St. Benedict
℅ Most Rev. Robert M. Dittler, OSB
Box 27536
San Francisco, CA 94127

The White Robed Monks of St. Benedict is an Old Catholic ordered community that functions as an independent ecclesiastical jurisdiction. It was founded and is led by its abbot, the Most Rev. Robert M. Dittler, who was consecrated as a bishop on November 19, 1991, by Bp. Carlos A. Florido of the Orthodox Catholic Church. He assumed the title of Tituler Bishop of Bodhgaya, India. Members of the order follow the Zen Rule of St. Benedict. The White Robed monks include clerical and lay monks, affiliates, and associates.

The group has developed a ministry of providing the traditional Catholic sacraments and the word to all who seek them. Members have attempted to remove any obstacles in their adherents' spiritual path and have found a particular calling to those Roman Catholics and those who for whatever reason are no longer able to receive the sacraments in the church of their origin.

The White Robed Monks see their mission as letting the world be a more compassionate place. They have adopted a monastic practice of Soto Zen meditation as their monastery is the earth rather than a building. They teach meditation to any who wish to learn. They have as their motto the first word of the Rule of St. Benedict: "Listen." They practice listening through their allusions, delusions, and illusions to better appreciate God's message as offered.

Membership: In 1997 the White Robed Monks of St. Benedict reported a membership of approximately 1,700, of which 1,650 reside in the United States and 11 reside in Canada. Members are also found in South Africa, Singapore, Ecuador, France, Germany, Switzerland, and Australia.

Section 3

Anglicanism

Consult the Contents pages to locate the essay in Part II, Historical Essay Chapters,
that provides an historical discussion of this family

Intrafaith Organizations

★111★

Anglican Consultative Council
6733 Curran St.
McLean, VA 22101

Alternate Address: International Headquarters: c/o Sec. Gen.
Rev. Canon Samuel Van Cullin, Partnership House, 157 Waterloo
Rd., London SE1 8UT, Canada.

The Anglican Consultative Council is the continuing organizational arm of the worldwide Anglican Communion, i.e., those Anglican churches around the world in communion with the Church of England. Most member churches were at one time an integral part of the Church of England but have since become autonomous national churches. Traditionally, the unity of the Anglican Communion has been expressed through the periodic conferences of bishops which met at Lambeth Palace, the headquarters of the Church of England in London. The Lambeth Conference of 1968, in light of the growing number of independent Anglican jurisdictions, suggested the formation of the council.

The council meets every three years, and each member church may send up to three representatives. The council has no legislative authority but facilitates communication and consultation. It may make recommendations and on occasion speak for the Anglican Communion. It also encourages the participation of member churches in the larger ecumenical movement. It conducts ecumenical discussions with similar international organizations of other church groups.

Membership: In North America, the council members include the Anglican Church of Canada and the Episcopal Church.

★112★

Traditional Anglican Communion
℅ Rev. Gregory Wilcox
4510 Finley Ave.
Los Angeles, CA 90027

The Traditional Anglican Communion is the international ecumenical organization serving the Continuing Church Movement which swept through Anglican churches in the 1970s. Following a convention held at St. Louis, Missouri, in 1977, conservative members and priests began to organize traditionalist congregations, establish new jurisdictions, and, utilizing the cooperation of bishops of the Philippine Independent Church, have bishops consecrated. Through the 1980s, independent jurisdictions were established in Canada, Australia, and New Zealand, and it became evident that as a whole, the Anglican jurisdictions worldwide were either approving or tolerant of the changes toward liturgical experimentation and the ordination of females to the priesthood. Thus, in February 1992, the Anglican Catholic Church, the Anglican Catholic Church of Canada, and the Anglican Catholic Church-Australia, and related traditional churches in New Zealand, Hong Kong, and Central America, formed the Traditional

Anglican Communion, a traditionalist counterpart of the jurisdictions in communion with the Church of England.

Membership: North American members include the the Anglican Catholic Church and the Anglican Catholic Church of Canada.

Anglican Churches

★113★

American Anglican Church
10120 Oak Hill Dr.
Port Richey, FL 34666

The American Anglican Church is a small conservative Anglican church headed by Bishop Howard Russell. Though jurisdictionally separate, in belief and practice it is at one with the Continuing Church Movement, which rejects the liturgical changes within the Episcopal Church in the last generation and does not believe in the ordination of females to the priesthood.

Membership: Not reported. In 1995 there were three parishes, all in Florida.

Sources:

Nones, Jane, ed. *1994/95 Directory of Traditional Anglican and Episcopal Parishes.* Tulsa, OK: Fellowship of Concerned Churchmen, 1995.

★114★

Anamchara Celtic Church
432 W. High St.
Wills Point, TX 75169

The Anamchara Celtic Church was founded in 1996 in Wills Point, Texas, by its presiding bishop Thomas J. Faukenbury. He was consecrated by Bp. Ivan MacKillop of the Church of the Culdees (and formerly the Servant Catholic Church). The church views itself as an association of people who follow the prayer and Eucharist in the tradition of the ancient Celtic Church (the pre-Roman Catholic church of the ancient British Isles). Celtic Christianity is distinguished, in part, by an emphasis on community over institutional religion and recognition of the equality of women. The theological work of St. Morgan of Wales (fifth century) and St. John Scotus Eriugena (ninth century) are especially appreciated.

The church affirms the truth of the Holy Scriptures (including the inter-testament writings known as the Apocrypha), the Nicene Creed, and the Seven Ecumenical Councils. It affirms the unity of the church as exemplified by the undivided Catholic church during the first ages of its existence rather than an enforced organizational unity. The church recognizes that all of life is sacramental but also practices the two major sacraments of baptism and Holy Communion, and the five minor sacraments: confirmation (or charismation), penance (or reconciliation), matrimony, holy orders, and unction are recognized. The church is headed by an episcopate in the apostolic lineage though calling is leadership to an attitude of service rather than autocracy.

The church practices open Communion and invites all Christians to partake of the Holy Eucharist. Worship varies from congregation to congregation, but some use the contemporary Celtic-inspired Desert Missel still in process of development. The Celtic calendar is followed as are the feast days of the saints (with special emphasis on Celtic saints). Some congregations mark the seasonal changes at Samhain, Imbolc, Beltaine, and Lammas.

The church is headed by a bishop, but congregations are organized into a loosely affiliated fellowship. The Anamchara Celtic Church is a member of the Celtic Christian Communion and in communion with the Church of the Culdes and St. Ciaran's Fellowship of Celtic Christian Communities.

Membership: In 1997 the church reported 300 members in 11 congregations served by 10 priests in the United States. There was a single congregation in Canada and one each in Scotland and Japan.

Periodicals: *Celtic Fire Newsletter.*

Sources:

http://www.celtchristian.net/.

★115★
Anglican Catholic Church
3841 Veterans Memorial Blvd., Ste. 202
Metairie, LA 70002-5624

While dissent over what many felt was theological and moral drift in the Protestant Episcopal Church led to the formation of several small protesting bodies, large-scale dissent occurred only after a series of events beginning in 1974 gave substantive focus to the conservative protest. In 1974 four Episcopal bishops (in defiance of their colleagues and the church) ordained 11 women to the priesthood. The following year, the Anglican Church of Canada approved a provision for the ordination of women. Then in 1976, with only a token censure of the bishops, the Protestant Episcopal Church regularized the ordinations of the 11 women. It also approved the revised *Book Of Common Prayer* which replaced the 1928 edition most Episcopalians had used for half a century.

The events of the mid 1970s led to the calling of a Congress of Episcopalians to consider alternatives to the Protestant Episcopal Church and to find a way to continue a traditional Anglican Church. In the months leading up to the congress, several congregations and priests withdrew from the Episcopal Church and formed the provisional Diocese of the Holy Trinity. They designated James O. Mote as their bishop elect. Eighteen hundred persons gathered in St. Louis in September 1977 and adopted a lengthy statement, the "Affirmation of St. Louis," which called for allegiance to the Anglican tradition of belief (as expressed in the ancient creeds and the teachings of the church fathers) and practice (as exemplified in the 1928 edition of the Book of Common Prayer). It specifically denounced the admission of women to the priesthood, the liberal attitudes to alternative sexual patterns (especially homosexuality), and both the World Council of Churches and the National Council of Churches. It affirmed the rights of congregations to manage their own financial affairs and expressed a desire to remain in communion with the See of Canterbury.

Throughout 1977 more congregations left the Protestant Episcopal Church, and others were formed by groups of people who had left as individual members. Following the September congress, three more provisional dioceses were established, and bishops elected. The Diocese of Christ the King elected Robert S. Morse; the Diocese of the Southwest elected Peter F. Watterson; and the Diocese of the Midwest elected C. Dale D. Doren. Bishops were sought who would consent to consecrate the new bishops-elect, and four finally agreed. Of the four Paul Boynton, retired suffragan of New York, was the first to withdraw from the consecration service, due to illness. Then Mark Pae of the Anglican Church

of Korea, a close personal friend of Dale Doren, withdrew under pressure from his fellow bishops. But he did send a letter of consent to the consecration. On January 28, 1978, with Pae's letter to confirm the action, Albert Chambers, former bishop of Springfield, Illinois and Francisco Pagtakhan, of the Philippine Independent Church, consecrated Doren. Doren in turn joined Chambers and Pagtakhan in consecrating Morse, Watterson, and Mote.

Having established itself with proper episcopal leadership, the new church, unofficially called the Anglican Church of North America, turned its attention to the task of ordering its life. A national synod meeting was held in Dallas in 1978. Those present adopted a name, the Anglican Catholic Church, and approved a constitution which was sent to the several dioceses (by then seven in number) for ratification. In May 1979, the bishops announced that five of the seven dioceses had ratified the actions of the Dallas synod; thus, the Anglican Catholic Church had been officially constituted.

The early 1980s was a period of flux for the Anglican Catholic Church. It emerged as the single largest body of the St. Louis meeting, claiming more than half of the congregations and members. But along the way, it lost two of its original dioceses and three of its original bishops. The dioceses of Christ the King and the Southeast and their bishops (Morse and Watterson) refused to ratify the constitution. They instead continued under the name "Anglican Church of North America." The Diocese of the Southeast soon broke with the Diocese of Christ the King and became an independent jurisdiction. Then, in 1984, Watterson resigned as bishop and joined the Roman Catholic Church. His action effectively killed the diocese, and member churches were absorbed by the other Anglican bodies, primarily the Anglican Catholic Church.

While dealing with the loss of the dioceses of Christ the King and the Southeast, the church continued to grow as new and independent congregations joined; additions more than made up for losses. Bishop Doren resigned in 1980, but only two congregations followed him. In 1981 several priests and parishes left to form the Holy Catholic Church, Anglican Rite Jurisdiction of the Americas. The largest schism occurred in 1983 when the Diocese of the Southwest under Bishop Robert C. Harvey withdrew and took twenty-one congregations in Arkansas, Texas, Oklahoma, New Mexico, and Arizona. Later that year they joined the American Episcopal Church.

The Anglican Catholic Church describes itself as the continuation of the traditional Anglicanism as expressed in the Nicene and Apostles' Creeds, and it holds to the liturgy of the Book of Common Prayer, 1928 edition. It rejects women in the priesthood and holds to traditional standards of moral conduct, condemning specifically "easy" divorce and remarriage, abortion on demand, and homosexual activity.

At its national convention in 1983, Louis W. Falk, bishop of the Diocese of the Missouri Valley, was elected as the ACC's first archbishop. Falk was succeed by Mt. Rev. William O. Lewis (d.1997) and Mt. Rev. M. Dean Stephens (1990-1998), who died after less than a year in office. Rt. Rev. John T. Cahoon is presently serving as acting Metropolitan until a new election is held in 1999.

Internationally, the church is in communion with the equally conservative Anglican Catholic Church-Australia, which is under Canadian oversight. In what is termed its Original Province, the church has parishes in Puerto Rico, Columbia, and Guatemala. In 1984 a Province for India was created. It has five dioceses and 3,000 members and, as of 1988, Bishop Falk serves as metropolitan for the providence. The American church has also developed direct oversight of a new conservative Anglican movement developing in New Zealand.

Membership: In 1988 the church reported 12,000 members, 200 parishes, and 200 priests in the United States. Worldwide membership included an additional 8,000 members. There are 8 dioceses in the United States and missionary dioceses in Australia, South Africa, Columbia, and the United Kingdom.

Educational Facilities: Holyrood Seminary, Liberty, New York.

Periodicals: *The Trinitarian*. Send orders to 6413 S. Elati, Littleton, CO 80120.

Sources:

A Directory of Churches of the Continuing Anglican Tradition. Eureka Springs, AK: Fellowship of Concerned Churchmen, 1983-84.

Laukhuff, Perry. *The Anglican Catholic Church*. Eureka Springs, AK: Fellowship of Concerned Churchmen, 1977.

Opening Addresses of the Church Congress at St. Louis, Missouri, 14-16 September 1977. Amherst, VA: Fellowship of Concerned Churchmen, 1977.

★116★

Anglican Catholic Church of Canada

℅ Bp. Alfred Woolcock
709 Attersley Dr.
Oshawa, ON, Canada L1K 1P9

The Anglican Catholic Church of Canada grew out of the same movement against changes in the Anglican Church of Canada that had occurred within the Episcopal Church in the United States. In Canada, changes included the allowance of new liturgical forms of questioned orthodoxy, including new sacramental rites, the loosening of the regulations of the marriage canons, and most importantly, the ordination of female priests. The unrest in the church came to a head in 1980 when Carmino J. deCatanzaro, an eminent Anglican scholar who had participated in the 1977 congress of traditionalist Episcopalians in St. Louis, Missouri, left the Anglican Church of Canada and was consecrated by Bp. Lupe Rosete of the Philippine Independent Catholic Church, assisted by a number of other bishops of the Continuing Church Movement. As with its sister church in the United States, the Anglican Catholic Church, the Anglican Catholic Church of Canada considers itself the continuing Anglicanism in Canada, believing that the Anglican Church of Canada has departed from the faith.

The Anglican Catholic Church of Canada was shaken shortly after its founding by deCatanzaro's sudden death in 1983. However, he was succeeded by Alfred Woolcock, who had recently affiliated with the new jurisdiction, and on January 27, 1984, Bp. Louis W. Falk of the Anglican Catholic Church, assisted by Bps. James O. Mote and William O. Lewis, consecrated Woolcock.

The Anglican Catholic Church of Canada follows the traditional Anglican liturgy and belief. It uses the *Book of Common Prayer* (1962, Canadian revision). It is a part of the Traditional Anglican Communion, an association of national Anglican churches in the United States, Australia, New Zealand, Hong Kong, and Central America. Association with the World Council of Churches and the Canadian Council of Churches has been renounced.

Membership: Not reported. In 1995 there were 36 parishes in Canada and one in the state of Washington in the United States.

Sources:

Nones, Jane, ed. *1994/95 Directory of Traditional Anglican and Episcopal Parishes*. Tulsa, OK: Fellowship of Concerned Churchmen, 1995.

★117★

Anglican Church in America

℅ Mt. Rev. Louis W. Falk
4807 Aspen Dr.
West Des Moines, IA 50265

The Anglican Church in America was founded in 1991 following merger talks between the American Episcopal Church and the Anglican Catholic Church (ACC). In the end, leadership of the Anglican Catholic Church was in disagreement with the merger plan and the majority withdrew its support. However, a large segment of the church under Abp. Louis W. Falk did approve, and they subsequently separated from their colleagues in the ACC and merged with the American Episcopal Church. Falk was elected primate of the merged church. Abp. Anthony F. M. Clavier, the leader of the American Episcopal Church, continued as head of the diocese covering the eastern states.

The American Episcopal Church was founded in 1968 by a group of former clergy and members of the Episcopal Church and the Anglican Orthodox Church. They sought a more loosely organized structure than that offered by the Anglican Orthodox Church and formed the new jurisdiction with a congregational polity. The church turned to James Charles Ryan, better known by his Indian name, Joseph K. C. Pillai, of the Indian Orthodox Church, for episcopal orders. Pillai then became the first primate of the new church and merged the Indian Orthodox Church into it. In December 1968, Pillai consecrated James George as Bishop of Birmingham. Bishop George succeeded Pillai as primate following the latter's death in 1970.

On February 11, 1970, George consecrated Clavier as suffragan bishop. Having found the very loose structure of the church unworkable, the pair spearheaded a reorganization plan that led to the adoption of a more centrally organized polity. To accomplish the reorganization, it proved necessary for all of the clergy to resign and to reconstitute the structure. Then the new American Episcopal Church, meeting in a general convention in April 1970, ratified a constitution and canon more in keeping with Anglican tradition. After the reorganization, George resigned as primate and Bishop Clavier succeeded him. In 1981, the bishops of the American Episcopal Church received conditional reconsecration from Bp. Francisco de Jesus Pagtakhan, assisted by Bps. Sergio Mondala and Lupe Rosete, three bishops of the Philippine Independent Church who chose to become involved in the emergence of the Continuing Church Movement in the United States.

In 1982 the American Episcopal Church grew with the addition of two dioceses from the Anglican Episcopal Church, which merged into it. In 1986, churches which had formed in Mexico in the late 1970s were recognized as a diocese. The Rt. Rev. Roberto Martinez-Resendiz, formerly suffragan bishop of Central Mexico of the Episcopal Church, became the first bishop of the new diocese. In addition, the church also entered into communion with the Anglican Church in India and the Anglican Diocese of Pakistan.

The Anglican Catholic Church was one of two bodies that came directly out of the 1977 conference of Episcopalians who met at St. Louis, Missouri, to protest the recent direction of the Episcopal Church and discuss alternatives for those who adhered to the conservative stance regarding the Anglican tradition. After the formation of the church, originally under the name of the Anglican Church of North America, retired Episcopal bishop Albert Chambers and Francisco Pagtakhan of the Philippine Independent Church consecrated the bishops of the new jurisdiction. In 1983, Louis W. Falk, bishop of the Diocese of the Missouri Valley, was elected the ACC's first archbishop.

Beliefs: The Anglican Church in America is theologically conservative and follows the 1928 *Book of Common Prayer* in its liturgy and teachings. It acknowledges the authority of the ancient creeds of Christendom, the teachings of the seven Ecumenical Councils, and the Chicago-Lambeth Quadrilateral of 1886–88. The 1801 text of the Anglican Thirty-nine Articles of Religion are accepted.

Organization: The Anglican Church in America is episcopal in that it is headed by a bishop, but democratic in that laity share in the decision-making process at every level of church life. The church is governed by a General Synod consisting of the House of Bishops, the House of the Clergy, and the House of the Laity. The General Synod meets biannually.

Archbishop Falk resides in Iowa. He is assisted by 7 other bishops whose territory covers the United States and the several foreign dioceses. Four of the eight bishops were reconsecrated conditionally by Bps. Robert Mercer, Robert Mize, and Charles Boynton, thereby providing them with an undisputed Anglican succession of orders and erasing any lingering doubts about the orders which had been earlier passed to the Continuing Church Movement. Three bishops have been consecrated since 1991.

Internationally, the Anglican Church in America is the American Jurisdiction within the Traditional Anglican Communion. Other countries represented by the communion include Canada, Australia, England, Ireland, India, Pakistan, South Africa, Mexico, Puerto Rico, Colombia, and Guatemala. In 1992, Archbishop Falk was elected the primate of the Traditional Anglican Communion.

Membership: In 1997, the Anglican Church in America reported 5,100 members and 196 clergy in the United States.

Educational Facilities: The Traditional Anglican Theological Seminary, Spartanberg, South Carolina.

St. Mary's Theological College, Los Angeles, California.

Periodicals: *Ecclesia*, Box 368, Ivy, VA 22945-0368. • *Anglican Herald*, 4807 Aspen Dr., West Des Moines, IA 50265.

Remarks: In 1995 the Anglican Church in America suffered a severe loss when Archbishop Clavier was charged with sexually abusing several female members of his diocese and subsequently resigned his position. The church quickly moved to minister to the abused women while reaffirming its allegiance to its traditional sexual ethical stance.

Sources:

Falk, Louis W. *The Anglicans: Who Are They? What Is Their Faith?* West Des Moines, IA: Anglican Church in America, n.d.

Nones, Jane, ed. *1994/95 Directory of Traditional Anglican and Episcopal Parishes.* Tulsa, OK: Fellowship of Concerned Clergymen, 1995.

★118★
Anglican Church, Inc.
% Rt. Rev. Frank H. Benning
Box 52702
Atlanta, GA 30355

The Anglican Church, Inc., was founded in the 1980s as the Anglican Church, U.S., a small independent jurisdiction of the Continuing Church movement that had rejected the thrust of the Episcopal Church in the previous generation. In 1988 that church was joined by the former Anglican Diocese of the South of the Anglican Episcopal Church under the leadership of the Rt. Rev. Frank H. Benning.

Bishop Benning, unlike most of the leaders of the independent Anglican movement, was never a priest in the Episcopal Church. He was ordained in 1968 as a priest by James Parker Dees of the Anglican Orthodox Church. In 1972 he went into the Anglican Episcopal Church of North America. In 1973 he was elected suffragan bishop and consecrated by Walter Hollis Adams, assisted by James George and Orlando J. Woodward. In 1975 he was elected coadjutor for the Anglican Episcopal Church. As the Anglican Episcopal Church grew, the church was subdivided into diocese, and Benning was elected bishop of the Diocese of the East in 1980.

For a number of years, Walter Adams had promoted the cause of unity among the several independent Anglican factions. In that cause, the bishops of the Anglican Episcopal Church, including Benning, were consecrated *sub conditione* by Philippine Independent Church bishops Francisco Pagtakhan, Sergio Mondala, and Lupe Rosete in 1981. This action gave each bishop the unquestionably valid orders of the Philippine Church. It also promoted the union of the Anglican Episcopal Church and the American Episcopal Church in 1982. Benning participated wholeheartedly in the merger and his diocese was renamed the Anglican Diocese of the South. He served in that position for six years. In 1988 he withdrew because of administrative canonical changes and joined the Anglican Church, U. S. with his diocese, now renamed the Anglican Episcopal Diocese South. The new jurisdiction retained the same doctrine and practice.

In 1993 the name of the Anglican Church, U.S. was changed to Anglican Church, Inc. In 1994 Benning was elected presiding bishop of the Anglican Church, Inc., while remaining ordinary of the Anglican Episcopal Diocese South.

Membership: In 1995 the Anglican Episcopal Diocese South reported 7 congregations and 11 clergy. Additional parishes of the Anglican Church, Inc., are found in New York and Oregon.

Educational Facilities: St. Georges School of Theology, San Antonio, Texas.

Sources:

Nones, Jane. *1994/95 Directory of Traditioinal Anglican and Episcopal Parishes.* Tulsa, OK: Fellowship of Concerned Clergymen, 1995.

Ward, Gary L. *Independent Bishops: An International Directory.* Detroit: Apogee Books, 1990.

★119★
Anglican Church of North America
% Rt. Rev. Robert T. Shepherd
Chapel of St. Augustine of Canterbury
1906 Forest Green Dr., NE
Atlanta, GA 30329

The Anglican Church of North America traces its origin to the Independent Anglican Church founded in Canada in the 1930s by William H. Daw who was originally a priest of the Church of England in Canada (now the Anglican Church of Canada). Later he led his jurisdiction into the Liberal Catholic Church headed by Bishop Edward M. Matthews and in 1955 was consecrated by Matthews. In 1964 Daw and Bishop James Pickford Roberts left Matthews to found the Liberal Catholic Church International. Daw assumed the role of primate, but retired because of severe health problems. He resumed the primacy in 1979.

In 1981 Daw participated in the formation of the Independent Catholic Church International, which brought together a number of independent Old Catholic, Anglican, and Liberal Catholic jurisdictions in both North America and Europe. Meanwhile, the Liberal Catholic Church International and Daw reasserted its Anglican roots in the wake of the increased liberalization of the national Anglican churches. The Liberal Catholic Church International repudiated all non-orthodox theology and practice and changed its name to the North American Episcopal Church. In 1983 Peter Wayne Goodrich Reynold became primate of the North American Episcopal Church. Goodrich had originally been consecrated by Daw as bishop for the small Independent Catholic Church of Canada.

Goodrich's leadership of the North American Episcopal Church was temporary however, and within a year Archbishop Daw again resumed the primacy. Daw died in 1987. Two bishops, Rt. Rev Robert T. Shepherd and Rt. Rev. M. B. D. Crawford, were consecrated to administer the work of the church in America and Canada respectively. In 1985 Crawford retired to lay life and abandoned his office, which was resumed by Goodrich. The first American parish was established in Atlanta, Georgia, in 1983. In June 1984, the church's name was changed to Anglican Church of North America.

The Anglican Church of North America, as other continuing Anglican Bodies, accepts the 1977 affirmation of St. Louis and follows the practices of the Protestant Episcopal Church and the Anglican Church of Canada prior to the changes of the 1970s. It differs from other continuing Anglican bodies in that it believes that small independent churches, even at the diocesan level, are preferable to a single jurisdiction for all of North America. It also stresses the collegiality of all levels of the clergy and the laity.

Membership: In 1995 the church reported 10 congregations, 5 bishops, 15 priests, and 250 members in the United States and Canada.

Educational Facilities: St. Matthew's Cathedral Seminary, Niagara Falls, Ontario, Canada (a correspondence school).

★120★
Anglican Churches of America
2402 Usery Pass Rd.
Mesa, AZ 85207

The Anglican Churches of America is a small, conservative Anglican church headed by Bp. C. Truman Davis. In belief and practice it is at one with the Continuing Church Movement, which rejects the liturgical changes within the Episcopal Church in the last generation and does not believe in the ordination of females to the priesthood, but is jurisdictionally separate.

Membership: Not reported. In 1995 there were two parishes, one in Arizona and one in Wisconsin.

Sources:

Nones, Jane, ed. *1994/95 Directory of Traditional Anglican and Episcopal Parishes.* Tulsa, OK: Fellowship of Concerned Churchmen, 1995.

★121★
Anglican Episcopal Church
% Rt. Rev. R. H. Hawn
7804 Lyrewood Ln., Ste. 157
Oklahoma City, OK 73132

The Anglican Episcopal Church was founded in 1994 by Bp. Robert H. Hawn and the majority of churches and missions of the former Diocese of the West and Missionary District of the Southwest of the United Episcopal Church in North America. Bishop Hawn had been a leader in the charismatic renewal within the Episcopal Church. He was the first president of the Episcopal Charismatic Fellowship and the original editor of *Acts 29*, the fellowship's magazine. However, he left the Episcopal Church, joined the United Episcopal Church in North America, and in 1992 was consecrated to the episcopacy by Bps. Ogden Miller, Albion Knight, and John Gramley. He was assigned as bishop of the Diocese of the West and had oversight of the Missionary District of the Southwest. By the end of 1993, Hawn had become dissatisfied with what he termed the lack of leadership at the national level within the United Episcopal Church.

As a part of the Continuing Church Movement, the Anglican Episcopal Church adheres to the 1928 edition of the Book of Common Prayer and accepts the Thirty-nine Articles of Religion as its doctrinal standard. The church believes that the Episcopal Church has left the Apostolic Faith and Order. It is most favorable to charismatic congregations and members but is inclusive of noncharismatic Evangelicals and Anglo-Catholics in its membership. It is open to relationships with the other churches, consisting largely of former members of the Episcopal Church constituting the Continuing Church movement.

Membership: In 1994 the church reported approximately 1,000 members, 10 congregations, and 20 clergy members.

★122★
Anglican Episcopal Church of North America
% Walter Hollis Adams
789 Allen Ct.
Palo Alto, CA 94303

The Anglican Episcopal Church of North America was founded in 1972 by Walter Hollis Adams, a veteran of the British Foreign Office who had retired in California. That same year, Adams was consecrated by William Elliot Littlewood of the Free Protestant Episcopal Church. Later that year he was consecrated *sub conditione* by Herman Adrian Spruit of the Church of Antioch, and the next year by Frederick Littler Pyman of the Evangelical Orthodox (Catholic) Church in America (Non-Papal Catholic).

Adams spearheaded efforts in the 1970s to bring together a number of traditional Anglican groups which, by the end of the decade, had either disappeared or merged into the Anglican Episcopal Church. These included, among others, the Anglican Church

of America, the Episcopal Church (Evangelical), and the United Episcopal Church. In 1981 intercommunion was established with the American Episcopal Church (since revoked) and the Holy Catholic Church, Anglican Rite Jurisdiction of the Americas. On September 26, 1981, Adams was the first of several bishops to be consecrated (in Adams case *sub conditione*) by Bishops Francisco Pagtakhan, Sergio Mondala, and Lupe Rosete of the Philippine Independent Church, an effort initiated by Pagtakhan to promote unity among Anglican traditionalists.

In May 1982, the Anglican Episcopal Church and the American Episcopal Church met in Seattle, Washington, to discuss steps towards unity. This effort failed for a variety of reasons (Adams was undergoing emergency surgery at the time of the meeting). However, Anglican Episcopal Church Bishops John M. Hamers and Frank H. Benning withdrew from the church and, taking some of their respective dioceses with them, joined the American Episcopal Church.

In 1983, the Anglican Catholic Church (ACC) initiated discussions with Adams looking toward the merger of the two jurisdictions. At separate synods in 1985, the two formally approved the merger in which the Anglican Episcopal Church would retain its identity as the non-geographical Diocese of St. Paul within the ACC. This union was shortlived, for on July 14, 1986, with the backing of the clergy and parishes, Adams announced the withdrawal of the diocese and the reconstitution of the Anglican Episcopal Church of North America. In a manifesto published two weeks later (July 29, 1986), he accused the ACC heirarchy of intending, contrary to their previous agreement, to eliminate the special status of the Diocese of St. Paul, its bishop, and its clergy.

The Anglican Episcopal Church is traditional Anglican, with roots deeply embedded in the Church of England. It uses the King James Version of the Bible and the 1928 Book of Common Prayer. It believes the Holy Bible to be the inspired Word of God. It accepts the Apostles, Nicene and Athanasian Creeds, and the Thirty-nine Articles of Religion as found in the Book of Common Prayer. The church permits a broad spectrum of ceremonial practice (encompassing both high and low emphases). It has also taken the lead in supporting the recent efforts of the Bishop of London (Great Britain) and the Archbishop of Sydney (Australia) to establish a world-wide unity of faith among traditional Anglicans.

The church has two dioceses, each headed by a bishop. Bishop Adams is the ordinary for the Diocese of St. Paul. In January 1987, Robert Henry Voight, a former priest of the Protestant Episcopal Church in the U.S.A., was consecrated bishop for the Diocese of the Southwest. In that service, Adams was joined by four bishops from the United Episcopal Church of North America and the Anglican Rite Jurisdiction of the Americas.

Membership: In 1988 the Anglican Episcopal Church reported 15 congregations, 1,000 members, and 15 clergy, all in the United States.

Educational Facilities: Laud Hall Anglican Episcopal Seminary, Deming, New Mexico.

Periodicals: *Anglican Episcopal Tidings.* Send orders to Box 1693, Deming, NM 88031.

Remarks: The Episcopal Church (Evangelical) was formed in 1977 by Rt. Rev. M. Dean Stephens and former members of the Protestant Episcopal Church who wished to continue to "teach the faith of Our Father as given to the Church in England and subsequently to the Episcopal Church in America" but which had been abandoned by the Protestant Episcopal Church. Stephens, formerly associated with the American Episcopal Church, had edited their periodical *Ecclesia*. In 1982, Stephens left the Anglican Episcopal Church and was reconsecrated in the Holy Catholic Church, Anglican Rite Jurisdiction of the Americas.

The United Episcopal Church was founded in 1973 by former members of the Anglican Orthodox Church under the leadership of bishops Troy A. Kaichen, Thomas J. Kleppinger, and Russell G. Fry. Under Kleppinger's leadership the church joined the Anglican

Episcopal Council and subsequently merged with the Anglican Episcopal Church. Kleppinger served as suffragan to Bishop Adams and continued to edit the periodical *Episcopal Tidings*, which he had begun several years before. (Most recently, Kleppinger has transferred to the Anglican Catholic Church.)

★123★
Anglican Orthodox Church
323 Walnut St.
Box 128
Statesville, NC 28687

Rev. James Parker Dees, a priest in the Protestant Episcopal Church, was the first of the modern spokespersons to call the members of that church who opposed the changes in liturgy and program to come out and separate themselves from apostasy. A low church Episcopalian, he had trouble with both liberalism, which he felt denied biblical authority, and sacerdotalism among high church members. He therefore left the Episcopal Church and in 1963 formed the Anglican Orthodox Church. The following year he received episcopal orders from autocephalous Ukrainian Bishop Wasyl Sawyna and Old Catholic Bishop Orlando J. Woodward (who later joined the United Episcopal Church of America). Formed in the southern United States in the early 1960s, the North Carolina-based group found its greatest response among Episcopalians who rejected the Protestant Episcopal Church's departure from scriptural teaching and sound biblical doctrine.

The Anglican Orthodox Church follows the low church in a very conservative manner. It adheres to the Thirty-Nine Articles and uses the 1928 edition of the Book of Common Prayer. The polity is episcopal, but local congregations are autonomous and own their own property. Much power has been placed in the hands of the presiding bishop in order to provide a strong center of leadership and reduce the opportunity for error.

The Anglican Orthodox Church was able to bring together many pockets of dissent, however, and has created a strong church. By 1972 it had 37 congregations, though some were lost to other Anglican splinters as the decade progressed. Dees established Cramner Seminary, which in 1977 had four full-time students. He also has brought the church into communion with like-minded churches in Pakistan, South India, Nigeria, the Fiji Islands, Rhodesia (Zimbabwe), Central African Republic, Madagascar, Colombia, South Africa, the Philippines, Japan, and Liberia.

As other Anglican groups have formed, Dees was pressed to draw sharp lines of distinction. He argued against the doctrinal "looseness" and high church tendencies in other groups of Anglicans. He continued his campaign against the growing "apostasy" he saw within the Protestant Episcopal Church, and concentrated his attention upon building the Anglican Orthodox Church as a viable and continuing denomination. Bishop Dees died in 1990. The present bishop is Rt. Rev. Robert Godfrey.

Membership: In 1997 the church reported congregations and members in most of the 50 states. Foreign work, both missionary and with other jurisdictions in communion with the church, has given it a worldwide constituency of over 100,000.

Educational Facilities: Cramner Seminary, Statesville, North Carolina.

Periodicals: *The News.*

Sources:

Dees, James P. *Reformation Anglicanism.* Statesville, NC: Anglican Orthodox Church, 1971.

Anglican Province of America
℅ Saint Alban's Anglican Cathedral
3348 W. State Rd. 426
Oviedo, FL 32765

The Anglican Province of America is a traditional Anglican jurisdiction founded by Rt. Rev. Walter H. Grundorf, who serves as its presiding bishop. It follows the Anglican tradition as passed from the Church of England to the Episcopal Church in the United States, and at one with other churches of the continuing church movement who have left the Episcopal Church in the last two decades, uses the 1928 *Book of Common Prayer*. The church is led by its bishops and adheres to the faith as summarized in the creeds and in the teachings defined by the early church in its councils.

While headed by bishops, the church has developed a democratic format that involves laity in all levels of ongoing decision making, and local church property is owned by the congregation.

Membership: Not reported.

Sources:

http://www.concentric.net/üagape/apa.html/.

★125★
Anglican Province of Christ the King
℅ Robert S. Morse
Box 40020
Berkeley, CA 94704

The Anglican Province of Christ the King shares the history of that larger conservative movement which participated in the 1977 congress at St. Louis and approved the "Affirmation" adopted by the delegates. The Province was one of the four original provisional dioceses that were formed. Its bishop-elect, Robert S. Morse, was consecrated along with the other new Anglican bishops in Denver, Colorado, on January 28, 1978, by Bishops Albert Chambers, Francisco Pagtakhan, and C. Dale D. Doren. However, Bishop Morse and other members of his diocese were among those most opposed to the new constitution adopted by the synod at Dallas in 1978 by the group which took the name Anglican Catholic Church. Neither what was then termed the Diocese of Christ the King nor the Diocese of the Southeast ratified the constitution, preferring instead to work without such a document. They called a synod meeting for Hot Springs, Arkansas, on October 16-18, 1978, two days immediately prior to the opening of the Anglican Catholic Church synod at Indianapolis, Indiana. Those gathered at Hot Springs decided to continue informally to use the name "Anglican Church of North America." They adopted canons (church laws) but no constitution.

The new jurisdiction immediately faced intense administrative pressures. In response to the "Anglican Church of North America" claiming many congregations in California and the South, the Anglican Catholic Church established a new structure, the patrimony, to facilitate the movement of existing congregations into the church and to assist the formation of new congregations in areas not covered by existing diocesan structures. Both Bishop Morse and Bishop Watterson viewed the patrimony as an attempt to steal the congregations under their jurisdiction.

The pressure from the Anglican Catholic Church did not keep the two dioceses in the "Anglican Church of North America" from facing crucial internal issues. Bishop Watterson argued for a strict division of the Anglican Church of North America into geographical dioceses with the understanding that neither bishop would attempt to establish congregations or missions in the other's diocese. The Diocese of Christ the King rejected Watterson's suggestions, and the Diocese of the Southeast became a separate jurisdiction. The Diocese of Christ the King proceeded to initiate work in the South.

Once separated, the Diocese of the Southeast experienced continued internal problems. In 1980, nine congregations withdrew with the blessing of Bishop Francisco Pagtakhan (who was becoming increasingly dissatisfied with the Anglican Catholic Church) and formed the Associated Parishes, Traditional Anglo-Catholic. Pagtakhan named Fr. J. Bruce Medaris as archdeacon. This new jurisdiction dissolved very quickly and merged back into Anglican Catholic Church. Finally, in 1984, Bishop Watterson resigned his office and joined the Roman Catholic Church. His jurisdiction dissolved and the remaining congregations realigned themselves with the other Anglican bodies. The dissolution of the Diocese of the Southeast left the Diocese of Christ the King the only diocese in the "Anglican Church of North America."

At its synod meeting in 1991, the Dicoese of Christ the King voted to completely reorganize as the Anglican Province of Christ the King. The congregations were divided into three dioceses. At subsequent meetings of the new dioceses, George Daniels Stenhouse was elected bishop of the Diocese of Eastern States and James Pollard Clark of the Diocese of Southern States. Morse became bishop of the new Diocese of Western States.

The Anglican Province of Christ the King is at one in faith and practice with the other Anglican bodies, holding to the faith of the undivided primitive church to which Episcopalians have always belonged, as spelled out in the affirmation of St. Louis. It rejects both the National Council of Churches and the World Council of Churches. It differs from the Anglican Catholic Church on several matters of canon law and its insistence that its clergy be seminary trained.

Membership: In 1997 the Diocese of Christ the King reported 62 parishes with an estimated 16,000 members.

Educational Facilities: Saint Joseph of Arimathea Anglican Theological College, Berkeley, California.

Periodicals: *The Province.*

Sources:

A Directory of Churches in the Continuing Anglican Tradition 1983-84. Eureka Springs, AK: Fellowship of Concerned Churchmen, 1983-84.

★126★
Anglican Rite Catholic and Orthodox Church in America
% Most Rev. James N. Meola
9 Abaco St.
Toms River, NJ 08757-3736

The Anglican Rite Catholic and Apostolic Church in America was founded in 1997 by Abp. James N. Meola. Meola had been consecrated in 1986 by Bp. John Riffenbury, then with the United Anglican Church of North America. He has served as a bishop with the Free Protestant Episcopal Church, the Southern Episcopal Church, and the Independent Philippine Catholic Church (IPCC). In 1996 he became the secretary general of the American branch of the IPCC, a position he held until the founding of the Anglican Rite Church.

Membership: Not reported.

Sources:

Barrett, David B. *World Christian Encyclopedia.* New York: Oxford, 1982.

★127★
Anglican Rite Old Catholic Church
PO Box 451006
Houston, TX 77245-1006

The Anglican Rite Old Catholic Church is an independent Old Catholic jurisdiction founded in Houston, Texas, in 1994 by its Metropolitan Abp. William Champion, pastor of St. Albans Catholic Church-Anglican Rite in Houston. He is assisted by Most Rev. Louis Bernhardt, Bishop of South Texas and Mexico. Bishop Louis is executive director of the Internet Catholic Church. The church uses the 1928 edition of the Prayerbook.

The church is a member of the Holy Patriarchate of the Americas and the Federation of Independent Catholic and Orthodox Bishops. It is in communion with the Patriarch of the American Orthodox Church (Russian Orthodox) and the Byzantine Independent Catholic Church of North America.

Membership: In 1997 the church reported 12 congregations, all located in Texas and Oklahoma.

Sources:

http://netministries.org/see/churches/ch01331/.

★128★
Anglican Rite Synod in the Americas
% Rt. Rev. Larry Lee Shaver
195 E. 68th Pl.
Merrillville, IN 46410

Alternate Address: Office of Metropolitan Abp. Herbert M. Grace, 875 Berkshire Valley Rd., Wharton, NJ 07885.

The Anglican Rite Synod in the Americas was founded in 1989 by David Marion-Davis, William C. Thompson, and Rt. Rev. Larry L. Shaver (b. 1936), formerly a bishop with the Holy Catholic Church, Anglican Rite Jurisdiction and the American Episcopal Church. Shaver began his pastoral career as a Methodist minister, but was led first to the Lutheran and then the Anglican tradition by his discovery of and love for Apostolic Faith and other including sacramental theology. He was elected and consecrated a bishop by Abp. Frederick Littler Pyman of the Evangelical Orthodox (Catholic) Church in America (Non-Papal Catholic) while still a Lutheran pastor (1972), and following his retirement from the Lutheran Church (1980), he emerged as Pyman's coadjutant.

In 1985, Shaver was reconsecrated sub conditione by Abp. Gerald Wayne Craig Abp. Robert Q. Kennaugh, and Bp. Ogden Miller of the Holy Catholic Church, Anglican Rite Jurisdiction. That same year (1985) he began to build a congregation (ProCathedral of St. Andrew) in Merrillville, Indiana. In late 1987 he and St. Andrew Church left the Anglican Rite Jurisdiction. In 1989, with the permission of the Philippine Independent Catholic Church, he led in the founding of the Anglican Rite Synod as an independent church body in full communion with the PICC. Cofounders in this effort were Bps. Davis and Thompson, both formerly of the Philippine Independent Catholic Church. Shaver was reconsecrated sub conditione by Philippine Abp. Francisco Pagtakan and Abp. Macario V. Ga. He was elevated to the rank of archbishop with full vote and voice in the Sacred Council of Bishops of the PICC in November 1994 by Abp. Maximo Macario V. Ga.

The Anglican Rite Synod in the Americas is one with several other traditional Anglican jurisdictions, its difference being more administrative than doctrinal, and it is currently engaged in unity talks with other Anglican jurisdictions. A mission in Haiti is supported.

Membership: In 1997 the synod reported 792 members, 19 congregations, and 26 priests in the United States, 15 members in a single congregation in Canada, and 1,078 members in five congregations in Haiti.

Educational Facilities: Geneva Theological College, Merrillville, Indiana.

Sources:

"Profile: Bishop Shaver." *The Evangelist* 3, 4 (June 1985).

Ward, Gary L. *Independent Bishops: An International Directory.* Detroit, MI: Apogee Books, 1990. 524 pp.

★129★
Celtic Evangelical Church
PO Box 90880
Honolulu, HI 96835-0880

The Celtic Evangelical Church is a small Anglican body formed in 1981 by its presbyter-abbot, Wayne W. Gau, and others who had formerly been members of the Celtic Catholic Church. Without necessarily rejecting the authenticity of the episcopal credentials of that church's bishop, Dwain Houser, they had asked numerous questions about it that had remained unanswered.

At its first general synod in November 1981, the church adopted a nine-point doctrinal statement. It is evangelical in its approach and regards the teachings and liturgy of the original Celtic church as authoritative. There are seven sacraments: two major sacraments, baptism and the eucharist, necessary for all Christians; and five minor sacraments, confirmation, penance, holy orders, matrimony, and unction, warranted by scripture but not mandatory. It acknowledges the Real Presence of Christ in the bread and wine of the holy eucharist. The filioque clause in the Nicene Creed is rejected, following the practice of the Eastern Orthodox churches. Worship is conducted in Latin following the ancient Celtic rite.

The Church has nurtured one religious order for men, the Community of St. Columba. Members are engaged in research in the ancient liturgies of Christianity, with special emphasis upon Celtic and Gallican rites. The order's work is directed by Canon James H. Donalson. It accepts associate members from other denominations.

In 1983, the church signed a concordant of intercommunion with the Catholic Apostolic Church of America, a small Anglican jurisdiction with parishes in the southwestern United States. That concordant was terminated in 1985, when the Catholic Apostolic Church united with the Holy Catholic Church, Anglican Rite Jurisdiction of the Americas. However, in 1987, Msgr. James B. Gillespie left the Anglican Rite Jurisdiction and reorganized the Catholic Apostolic Church of America as an independent jurisdiction. The Celtic Evangelical Church reinstituted the concordant with the revived church. In 1992 the church signed a concordat of intercommunion with the Independent Anglican Church-Canada Synod, followed by a similar agreement with the Episcopal Missionary Church in 1993, and the Igreja Catolica Apostolica Ortodoxa do Brasil in 1997.

Membership: In 1995, the church had one congregation in Hawaii.

Educational Facilities: The Iona Institute, Honolulu, Hawaii.

Periodicals: *The Celtic Evangelist.*

★130★
Charismatic Episcopal Church
St. Michael's Pro-Cathedral
107 W. Marquita
San Clemente, CA 92672

The Charismatic Episcopal Church is a conservative Anglican church which differs from other jurisdictions of the Continuing Church Movement by its acceptance and support for the charismatic experience. Members of the church are encouraged to participate in the manifestation of the gifts of the Holy Spirit as mentioned in I Corinthians 12. Such gifts include speaking in tongues, divine healing, and prophecy. The charismatic movement spread through the Episcopal Church in the 1970s, but some charismatics found themselves alienated from the directions being pursued by the church as a whole.

The Charismatic Episcopal Church spread across the United States in the 1990s with parishes in nine states. The church is headed by its presiding archbishop Randolph Adler. A diocese for the southern states is headquartered in Florida and for the midwestern states, in Kansas.

Membership: Not reported. In 1995 the church had 16 parishes.

Sources:

Nones, Jane, ed. *1994/95 Directory of Traditional Anglican and Episcopal Parishes.* Tulsa, OK: Fellowship of Concerned Churchmen, 1995.

★131★
Christian Episcopal Church of Canada
4300 Corless Rd.
Richmond, BC, Canada V7C 1N2

In 1992, some traditionalists within the Anglican Church of Canada who had hoped that the church would reverse what they saw as a growing tolerance for teachings contrary to the Christian faith concluded that their situation had become hopeless. It also became clear to them that the church would not only remain on its present course but would provide no haven for traditionalists within the church community. Their major complaints against the church included its support of Third World liberation movements, the ordination of female priests and bishops, new liturgical and hymn books perceived to be theologically flawed, and the presence (with official approval) of highly offensive "pagan" rites under the guise of feminist and Native spirituality.

Meanwhile in the United States, traditionalists within the Episcopal Church had reached a similar conclusion, and with leadership provided by Rt. Rev. A. Donald Davies, formerly a bishop in the Episcopal Church, they formed the Episcopal Missionary Church. Bishop Davies, who had emerged as a conservative leader in the Episcopal Church while serving as the bishop of Dallas/Ft. Worth (Texas), also assisted the traditionalists in Canada in the creation of the Christian Episcopal Church of Canada. Through Davies and the Episcopal Missionary Church, they received apostolic orders.

The church is theologically conservative and has accepted as its doctrinal standards the Bible, the three creeds of the early Church (Apostles, Nicene, and Chacedonian Creeds), the Thirty-nine Articles of Religion, and the *Book of Common Prayer.* The church uses the 1962 Canadian edition of the *Book of Common Prayer* and the Canadian *Book of Common Praise.* Women are welcomed into the order of deacon but are barred from the priesthood.

Membership: Not reported.

★132★
Church of the Culdees
℅ Most Rev. Ivan B. D. G. MacKillop, OCC
2665 "C" St.
Springfield, OR 97477

The Church of the Culdees was founded in the mid-1990s by the Most Rev. Ivan B. D. G. Mackillop. MacKillop had been consecrated in 1984 by Bp. Robert E. Burns of the Servant Catholic Church and had served as the bishop of its western diocese. While still associated with the Servant Catholic Church, he had founded the Order of the Celtic Cross, which continues as part of the independent Church of the Culdees.

Within the early Culdee (Celtic and Anglo-Saxon) Church, nearly all establishments were monastic, that is to say, that "parish" churches were usually associated with a monastery. Clergy were drawn from monastic ranks, and it was the monastery which served as the seminary for training candidates for Holy Orders. There were a number of "joint" monasteries of both men and women, the most famous being Kildare, founded by St. Brigid and ruled by an abbess. Celibacy was not universal among monastics, even those in Holy Orders.

The contemporary Church of the Culdees is guided and formed by this same style. The Order of the Celtic Cross is open to any man or woman, married or single, who is at least 18 years old and has been a regularly participating member of the church for at least one year and passes an entrance exam. Members of the Order of the Celtic Cross vow: moral purity, apostolic poverty, obedience, and stability. The vow of stability means that they will not leave the jurisdiction of their abbot or abbess without his or her approval, nor may they be forced to leave without their own consent. Although members of the order continue to lead their "secular" lives with jobs, family, and other demands, they are required to pray the Morning, Mid-Day, Evening, and Night Offices every day. They must attend all church functions unless given specific release from their abbot or abbess.

The Church of the Culdees has a leadership composed of deacons, priests, and bishops. It is associated with the Celtic Christian Communion.

Membership: Not reported.

Sources:

http://www.continet.com/culdee/.

★133★
Communion of Evangelical Episcopal Churches
% Rt. Rev. Michael D. Owen
6825 W. Wilshire Blvd.
Oklahoma City, OK 74137

The Communion of Evangelical Episcopal Churches (CEEC) is an evangelical, episcopal, spirit-filled, and liturgical expression of the Episcopal tradition which seeks to be a contemporary church that is nevertheless rooted in the ancient and historical realities of the Church Universal. It was established in 1997 at a meeting of the seven bishops who constituted its original House of Bishops under the leadership of the presiding bishop, Michael D. Owen. The Communion of Evangelical Episcopal Churches considers itself a part of the Holy Catholic Church and attempts to maintain and practice the faith of the apostles passed through the mother church of the worldwide Anglican family, the Church of England. It embodies a communion whose parishes are charismatic and evangelical, as well as liturgical and sacramental.

As evangelical, the communion affirms that the Holy Scriptures are the inspired Word of God, and that they contain all things necessary for salvation and godly living. It also embraces the importance of a personal relationship with Jesus Christ, a holy life, and a commitment to evangelism and missions. As charismatic, it affirms an openness to the work of the Holy Spirit and encourages member parishes to not only allow, but anticipate the Spirit's presence and working through spiritual gifts in both their worship and daily acts of service.

The communion also sees itself as part of what is termed the convergence movement, a movement among Evangelical Protestants which includes an appropriation of both the contemporary charismatic worship renewal and the liturgical renewal movement. The communion is most attuned to what has been termed the "Third Wave" or "Signs and Wonders Movement" which emerged in the late 1970s and wedded charismatic elements of worship, experience, and practice with the evangelical tradition. Participants in the convergence movements characterize their life as focused in: 1. A restored commitment to the sacraments, especially The Lord's Table; 2. An increased appetite to know more about the early church; 3. A love and embrace for the whole church, and a desire to see the church as one; 4. The blending in the practices of the liturgical land signs and wonders movement; 5. An interest in integrating more structure with spontaneity in worship; 6. A greater involvement of sign and symbol in worship through banners, crosses, Christian art, and clerical vestments; and 7. A continuing commitment to personal salvation, biblical teaching, and to the work and ministry of the Holy Spirit.

Doctrinally, the communion affirms the essentials of the faith as revealed in the Apostle's Creed, the Nicene Creed, the 39 Articles of Religion of the Church of England, the Lambeth Quadrilateral II, the Baltimore Declaration and the Chicago Call. Worship is liturgical and sacramental, culminating in the regular celebration of the Holy Eucharist (the Lord's Supper). Existing within the Anglican Spiritual Tradition, worship is best expressed and informed by the Book of Common Prayer.

The communion has a congregational polity. Each CEEC member congregation, regardless of size, shall be autonomous and self-supporting. The clergy and people will endeavor to find the bishop best suited to oversee their ministry. Bishops serve in non-geographical dioceses, allowing parishes to come under the bishop with whom they have the most affinity. Their task is to guard the biblical faith, evangelistic mission, and unity of the church. A bishop need not resign a parochial cure to serve. As with everyone in a leadership position, the bishops are required to affirm the communion's Doctrinal Essentials in writing annually, on Ash Wednesday.

The Communion of Evangelical Episcopal Churches is headed by an episcopate with apostolic succession. Each bishop can organically trace his consecration back to the original Apostles through various lines of succession of Orthodox Catholic bishops. Besides the Anglican succession, other lineage's include: Syrian Malabar (Jacobite) Orthodox Church of Antioch, Roman Petrine Succession through the Roman Catholic Church of Brazil, Metropolitan-Archbishops of Albania, Armenian Catholicate-Patriarchate of Cilicia Catholic Uniate, Patriarchate of Moscow, Greek Melkite Patriarchate of Antioch—Melkite Uniate, Catholic—Patriarchate of Assyria (The East), Chaldean Patriarchate of Babylon of Baghdad—Chaldean Uniate, The Order for Corporate Reunion, Roman Petrine Succession—Utrecht Catholic Church, Ultrajectine, and Old Roman Catholic.

Currently the house of bishops includes: Rt. Rev. Michael D. Owen, Diocese of Saint John (Oklahoma); Rt. Rev. Robert L. Wise, Diocese of Saint John (Oklahoma); Rt. Rev. Wayne Boosahda, Diocese of Saint Patrick (Oklahoma); Rt. Rev. Max Broussard, Province of Christ the Good Shepherd (Louisiana); Rt. Rev. John Kivuva, Diocese of Saint Andrew (Kenya); Rt. Rev. Terry Lowe, Diocese of Saint Peter (Philippines); Rt. Rev. Jim Beckett, Diocese of Saint Antony (Oklahoma); Rt. Rev. Van Gayton, Diocese of St. Paul (New York).

The church is in communion with the American Old Catholic Church and is a member of the Ecumenical Communion of Catholic and Apostolic Churches.

Membership: Not reported.

Sources:

http://ivu.com/ceec/.

★134★
The Continuing Episcopal Church
% Rt. Rev. Colin James III
2080 Kipling
Lakewood, CO 80215

The Continuing Episcopal Church was founded in 1984 by former members of the Episcopal Church who opposed a series of actions taken by, and with the consent of, the leadership. These included the church's participation with other churches in the Consultation on Church Union, the consecration of women as priests and bishops, and the new liturgy of 1979. On June 2, 1984, Colin James III and Henry C. Robbins were consecrated as bishops for the church by Abp. Dismas F. G. Markle of the Eastern Orthodox Catholic Church in America. James was selected presiding bishop.

The Continuing Episcopal Church is a conservative Anglican body. It accepts the traditional 39 Articles of Religion as a doctrinal standard and the Lambeth Quadrilateral of 1888-1889 as authoritative statements of catholicity. It uses the 1928 edition of the *Book of Common Prayer* and the King James Version of the Bible.

Membership: In 1990 the church reported three congregations, three priests (including the two bishops), and 100 members.

★135★
Diocese of the Southwest
(Defunct)

The shortlived Diocese of the Southwest was originally formed in 1978 as a constituent part of the Anglican Catholic Church. In

1982 it left the ACC and for several months existed as an independent jurisdiction. In December 1983 it merged into the American Episcopal Church. It no longer exists as a separate body.

★136★

Episcopal Church
815 2nd Ave.
New York, NY 10017

The Church of England came into the American colonies with the first British settlers. The first church was established at Jamestown in 1607, and in 1619 an act of the Virginia legislature formally declared Virginians to be members of the Church of England. By the time of the American Revolution, more than 400 Anglican parishes were spread along the coast from Georgia to New Hampshire.

The American Revolution created a crisis for the church in the new nation because, in spite of the large number of parishes, the church in the colonies had no bishop. War with England meant England would not be sending a bishop to America, so there was no way to ordain new priests or consecrate future bishops. Further, many priests (already in short supply) sided with England in the Revolution and returned to England. Thus, the war left Anglican congregations highly disorganized. In 1783, the Connecticut churches sent Samuel Seabury to England to be consecrated. But, because he would not swear allegiance to the British Crown, he could not be consecrated. He was finally consecrated by the Nonjuring Church of Scotland in 1784. Upon Seabury's return in 1785, the Connecticut priests held a convocation to organize their parishes.

Meanwhile, a second movement to reorganize the American parishes was undertaken in the Middle Colonies (mainly in Pennsylvania and Virginia) under the leadership of William White. A series of meetings over the next several years resulted in the adoption of the "Ecclesiastical Constitution of the Protestant Episcopal Church in the United States." William White and Samuel Provoost were chosen as bishops. They sailed for England and were consecrated by the archbishop of Canterbury in 1787, after Parliament had rescinded the requirement of an oath of loyalty to the Crown for any consecrated bishop from "foreign parts." In 1789, the new constitution was adopted by all the American churches (including Bishop Seabury's diocese). The Protestant Episcopal Church was born, the church that represents the Anglican tradition in the U.S.

The Protestant Episcopal Church, popularly called the Episcopal Church, grew and became a national body during the nineteenth century. Within its membership three informally organized but recognizable groups developed: the high church of the Anglo-Catholic group; the low church evangelicals; and the broad church party (the group between the high church and low church groups). The differences between these groups was largely based upon their approach to liturgy and the Eucharist. Episcopalians have followed the liturgy of the Prayer Book which is built upon a belief in the Real Presence of Christ in the Eucharist. The Church of England passed to American Episcopalians a repudiation of the particular explanation of that doctrine of the Real Presence called "transubstantiation." High Church Episcopalians have tended to emphasize the forms and ceremonies associated with the Roman tradition and have tended toward a Roman explanation of the Real Presence. In contrast, Low Church Episcopalians have emphasized the "Puritan" element introduced into the Anglican Church after the Reformation. They have opposed the emphasis on outward ceremony, centering their attention upon the reading and preaching of the Word.

During the 1840s the American Church began to receive the influence of the Oxford Movement, a high church revival in the Church of England. Among the personages identified with the movement was John Henry Newman, who later joined the Roman Catholic Church. In the wake of the revival, church architecture and sanctuary furnishings began to change. The Gothic church be-

came common. The typical arrangement of furniture in the sanctuary centered upon a table, and the pulpit was replaced with a center altar, the common arrangement today.

The broad church party, which reached into both high-church and low-church camps was identified mostly by its liberalism in matters of discipline, doctrine, and biblical interpretation. Broad churchmen generally avoided too much emphasis upon ceremony and found their identification in their enclusive spirit. They were open to a variety of creedal interpretations and would often open their pulpit and altar to non-Episcopalians.

During the mid-twentieth century new issues began to become prominent in the church, and these led to new lines of division that cut across the older groupings. Dissent within the church appeared around the issues of laxity in church moral standards (especially an acceptance of sexual immorality), the ordination of women priests, the reported use of funds contributed to the National Council of Churches and World Council of Churches for "far-left" political causes, and the church's involvement in various social crusades (from civil rights and women's liberation to gay liberation). In addition, disagreements evolved over the introduction of extensive revisions of the 1928 edition of the *Book of Common Prayer*, made available in a revised prayer book. These issues came to a head in 1976 when the General Convention of the church approved the ordination of women and the revised *Book of Common Prayer*. Several thousand who disapproved of the changes left the church in the late 1970s. (Following the movement out of the Episcopal Church, the Anglicans, as the conservatives called themselves, tended to split along the older party lines).

Membership: In 1995 the church reported 2,504,682 members in 7,388 congregations served by 15,000 priests.

Educational Facilities: Seminaries:
Berkeley Divinity School at Yale, New Haven, Connecticut.
Bexley Hall-Colgate-Rochester, Rochester, New York.
Church Divinity School of the Pacific, Berkeley, California.
Episcopal Divinity School, Cambridge, Massachusetts.
Episcopal Theological Seminary of the Southwest, Austin Texas.
General Theological Seminary, New York City, New York.
Nashotah House, Nashotah, Wisconsin.
Seabury-Western Theological Seminary, Evanston, Illinois.
Virgina Theological Seminary, Alexandria, Virginia.
Colleges and universities:
Bard College, Annandale-on-the-Hudson, New York.
Hobart and William Smith Colleges, Geneva, New York.
Kenyon College, Gambier, Ohio.
St. Augustine's College, Raleigh, North Carolina.
St. Paul's College, Lawrenceville, Virginia.
Trinity College, Hartford, Connecticut.
University of the South, Sewanee, Tennessee.
Voorhees College, Denmark, South Carolina.

Periodicals: *The Episcopalian*. Send orders to 1930 Chestnut St., Philadelphia, PA 19103. • *The Living Church*. Send orders to 407 E. Michigan St., Milwaukee, WI 53202. • *Historical Magazine*. Send orders to Box 2247, Austin, TX 78705.

Remarks: In 1967 the General Convention adopted the designation "Episcopal Church" as an official alternative name.

Sources:

Gray, William, and Betty Gray. *The Episcopal Church Welcomes You.* New York: Seabury Press, 1974.

Konolige, Kit, and Frederica. *The Power of Their Glory.* Wyden Books, 1978.

Manross, William W. *A History of the American Episcopal Church.* New York: Morehouse-Gorham, 1950.

Parsons, Edward Lambe, and Bayare Hale Jones. *The American Prayer Book.* New York: Charles Scribner's Sons, 1946.

Pittenger, W. Norman. *The Episcopalian Way of Life*. Englewood Cliffs, NJ: Prentice-Hall, 1957.

Shepherd, Massey H., Jr. *The Worship of the Church*. Greenwich, CT: Seabury Press, 1954.

Synder, William. *Looking at the Episcopal Church*. Wilton, CT: Morehouse-Barlow, 1980.

★137★
Episcopal Missionary Church

Box 1294
Aiken, SC 29802

The Episcopal Missionary Church was founded in 1992 by Rt. Rev. A. Donald Davies, formerly a bishop in the Episcopal Church. Bishop Davies had emerged as a conservative leader in the Episcopal Church, and while serving as the bishop of Dallas/Ft. Worth (Texas) had founded the Episcopal Synod, still the organization of traditionalists within the Episcopal Church. By 1992, he had concluded that the Episcopal Church would never be a welcome environment for traditionalists. He left and founded the Episcopal Missionary Church. Initially, several congregations affiliated with it. Then in 1994, the Holy Catholic Church, Anglican Rite Jurisdiction of the Americas (ARJA) dissolved and united with the Episcopal Missionary Church. ARJA brought Los Hermanos Franciscanos de la Providencia, a Franciscan order headquartered in Puerto Rico, into the new church.

The Episcopal Missionary Church follows the traditional Anglican practice and belief. It rejects the recent liturgical changes of the Episcopal Church and does not accept the ordination of females to the priesthood.

Membership: In 1995 the church reported 64 affiliated congregations, including one in British Columbia, Canada.

Sources:

Nones, Jane, ed. *1994/95 Directory of Traditional Anglican and Episcopal Parishes*. Tulsa, OK: Fellowship of Concerned Churchmen, 1995.

★138★
Evangelical Anglican Church in America

2401 Artesia Blvd., Ste. 106-213
Redondo Beach, CA 90278

The Evangelical Anglican Church in America was founded in 1993 when Rev. Craig S. Bettendorf, formerly of the Philippine Independent Church, opened All Saints Parish in Los Angeles. Bettendorf, a gay priest, had had contact over the years with a number of marginalized clergy (both gay and non-gay) and developed the Anglican Institute for Affirmative Christian Studies to unite them through study of its curriculum based on liberation theology. After his election as the first bishop, Bettendorf was consecrated in December 1994 by Abp. G. Stephen Trivoli-Johnson of the Central Orthodox Synod. The church has grown out of the high church traditions of the Anglican Communion and affirms Holy Scripture, believes in tradition, and utilizes reason. It offers the sacraments of baptism and the Eucharist and the rite of confirmation, marriage (and holy union), housewarming blessings, anointing, memorial services, and ordination.

The distinctive role of the church, in relation to other Anglican and Old Catholic jurisdictions, is its inclusivity. The church welcomes all people without reference to gender, marital status, sexual orientation, race, or physical challenges. It welcomes gay men, lesbians, and bisexual people to the ordained ministry, but describes itself as inclusive rather than primarily gay/lesbian. It also advocates the use of inclusive language in its worship and affirms God as Creator, Redeemer, and Giver of Life.

The church has parishes across the United States. Bettendorf is a member of the Federation of Independent Catholic and Orthodox Bishops.

Membership: In 1997 the church reported 19 parishes and missions served by 16 priests. There were approximately 850 members. Parishes are being developed in New Zealand and Nova Scotia.

Educational Facilities: Anglican Institute for Affirmative Christian Studies, Redondo Beach, California.

Periodicals: *Kaleidoscope*.

Sources:

http://www.dir.co.uk/aglo/evengeli.htm/.

★139★
Evangelical Episcopal Church

℅ Rt. Rev. Edward H. Marshall
600 W. 113th St.
New York, NY 10025

The Evangelical Episcopal Church was founded in the 1980s by Bp. Edward Marshall. It is one of a number of churches associated with the Continuing Church Movement among Anglicans who rejected the changes in the Episcopal Church during the last generation. Marshall arrived at his position by a distinct route, as he was never an Episcopal minister. As a young man, he had become a published poet of some note. He was also a lay reader in the Episcopal Church. Then in 1965 he accepted ordination from Abp. Richard A. Marchenna of the North American Old Roman Catholic Church. He was consecrated in 1976 by Bp. James E. Burns of the United Epicopal Church (1945) Anglican/Celtic. Finally in 1989 he was reconsecrated by Francisco Pagtakhan, the bishop of the Philippine Independent Church from whom many in the Continuing Church Movement have their orders.

The Evangelical Episcopal Church has fraternal ties to several other small Anglican jurisdictions of similar faith and practice, especially the Traditional Protestant Episcopal Church and the United Anglican Church.

Membership: Not reported.

Sources:

Ward, Gary L. *Independent Bishops: An International Directory*. Detroit, MI: Apogee Books, 1990.

★140★
Evangelical Episcopal Church (Owen)

17275 E. Goshawk Rd.
Colorado Springs, CO 80908

TheEvangelical Episcopal Church was founded in the mid-1990s by Rt. Rev. Michael D. Owen as an expression of the Anglican/Episcopal tradition that is inclusive, evangelical, and Spirit-filled. The church affirms the sufficiency of the Holy Scriptures and the essentials of the faith as expressed in the Apostles' and Nicene Creeds, the 39 Articles of Religion, and the Lambeth Quadrilateral. The church extols a Christian life marked by the fruits of the Spirit, among which is self-control. Self-control is defined as fidelity in marriage, abstinence from homosexual activity, and continence outside the bonds of marriage.

The church supports an episcopal leadership by congregations that are autonomous and self-supporting, and are encouraged to locate the bishop who is best suited to oversee its ministry. The church has three dioceses: The Provisional Dioceses of St. John and St. James in the United States and the Provisional Diocese of St. Andrew in Kenya.

Membership: Not reported.

Sources:

Pruter, Karl. *The Directory of Autocephalous Bishops of the Apostolic Succession*. San Bernadino, CA: Brogo Press, 1906. 104 pp.

Ward, Gary. *Independent Bishops: An International Directory*. Detroit: Apogee Books, 1990. 524 pp.

Free Church of Scotland on Prince Edward Island
℅ Rev. William R. Underhay
Box 977
Montague, PE, Canada C0A 1R0

The present Free Church of Scotland on Prince Edward Island dates to 1954 when the Church of Scotland congregations were received into the Free Church of Scotland as the Presbytery of Prince Edward Island.

The history of these congregations dates to pioneer times. Rev. Donald MacDonald, a minister of the Church of Scotland, arrived in Prince Edward Island in 1826; and about two years later, following a transforming spiritual experience, his preaching became very effective and bore much fruit. He preached over a large part of the Island, mostly to Scottish immigrants. At the time of his death in 1867 there were about 5,000 followers. While ministers of the Church of Scotland increased in number MacDonald's ministry became largely independent of them, although officially MacDonald and his followers always considered themselves as Church of Scotland.

With the Disruption in Scotland in 1843, a large section of the Established Church (including nearly 500 ministers) withdrew in a protest against the practice of partronage, which interfered with the independence of the church. Chiefly at stake was the induction of ministers against the will of the people. The new body became the Church of Scotland Free. The split in the church also took place in the colonies, including Prince Edward Island. However, Donald MacDonald and his followers, as well as a number of others in Prince Edward Island and elsewhere in the Lower Provinces, did not join the Free Church movement. During the following years, several church unions took place among the Presbyterians in British North America culminating in the Presbyterian Church of Canada in 1875. By this time, Donald MacDonald had died. The Orwell Head congregation, the main center of MacDonald's followers in the eastern part of the Island, was received into the Presbyterian Church of Canada in 1896 and eventually became part of the United Church of Canada. A little over half a century after the union of 1875 more congregations entered the Presbyterian Church of Canada. Thus a significant number of the congregations connected with the ministry of MacDonald and his successors had now departed, leaving a much reduced Church of Scotland populations.

However, in 1954 when the Church of Scotland on Prince Edward Island was received into the Free Church of Scotland, there were still at least 10 church buildings in use. In addition, services were being held in several halls. The congregations were divided into three pastoral charges by the Free Church. At present, there are seven churches where regular services are held. In two others, there are occasional services. Each of the pastoral charges has a pastor.

It may be noted that in the latter part of the nineteenth century and the early part of the twentieth century many people from Prince Edward Island emigrated to Massachusetts, and a Church of Scotland congregation was formed there. This congregation continued until recent years but never became part of the Free Church.

There are three other Free Church congregations in North America. These are located in Livonia, Michigan; Toronto, Ontario; and Edmonton, Alberta. Together they form the Presbytery of the Great Lakes and Western Canada. The history of the formation of these congregations is distinct from that of the congregations on Prince Edward Island. The two presbyteries together make up the Free Church of Scotland of North America. Each presbytery may appoint commissioners to the General Assembly which meets in Edinburgh, Scotland.

The Free Church is conservative in faith, holding to the inerrancy and infallibility of the Bible. It adheres to the Westminister Confession of Faith as its secondary standard to which all ordained office bearers are required to subscribe. The Westminster Large and Shorter Catechisms are also officially recognized. The material for congregational praise is the Scottish Psalter sung without instrumental accompaniment. The Free Church of Scotland does not participate in the World Council of Churches but is a member of the International Council of Reformed Churches (ICRC).

Membership: In 1997 the church's total membership in the three pastoral charges including adherents and children was approximately 300. North American membership, including adherents and children, was approximately 400. Former mission centers in Peru, South Africa, and India have been formed into separate denominations but financial support is still provided and, in the case of South Africa and Peru, missionaries are still sent.

Free Protestant Episcopal Church
℅ Mt. Rev. Benjamin C. Eckardt
430 Elizabeth St.
London, ON, Canada N5W 3R7

The Free Protestant Episcopal Church was established in 1897 by the union of three small British episcopates: the Ancient British Church (founded 1876/77); Nazarene Episcopal Ecclesia (founded in 1873); and Free Protestant Church of England (founded in 1889). Leon Checkemian, an Armenian, the first primate of the new church, was supposedly consecrated by Bishop A. S. Richardson of the Reformed Episcopal Church in 1890, though present claims indicate that he was consecrated in 1878 by an Archbishop Chorchorunian. In either case, no papers have been produced, and the validity of the consecration is questioned by many. In 1952, Charles D. Boltwood became the fifth person to hold the post of primate.

The faith of the Free Protestant Episcopal Church is the same as the Protestant Episcopal Church. The Thirty-nine Articles are accepted. There are, however, seven doctrines condemned as contrary to God's word: 1. That the church exists in only one order or form of polity; 2. That ministers are "priests" in any other sense than that in which all believers are a "royal priesthood;" 3. That the Lord's table is an altar on which the oblation of the body and blood of Christ is offered anew to the Father; 4. That Christ is present in the elements of bread and wine in the Lord's Supper; 5. That regeneration and baptism are inseparably connected; 6. That the law should punish Christians with death; and 7. That Christians may wear weapons and serve in war except in aiding the wounded or assisting in civil defense. In these seven objections, the sacramentalism of Anglo-Catholicism is explicitly denied and conscientious objection to carrying arms in war is elevated to dogma.

The Free Protestant Episcopal Church came to America in 1958 when Boltwood, on a trip to Los Angeles, consecrated Emmet Neil Enochs as archbishop of California and primate of the United States. On the same trip, John Marion Stanley was consecrated bishop of Washington; subsequently four additional bishops were consecrated for the United States. The primate was directly responsible to the bishop primus in London. In 1967 the Free Protestant Episcopal Church reported 23 congregations plus a number of affiliated missions, and there were an estimated 2,000 members in the United States and Canada.

The Free Protestant Episcopal Church dissipated as various bishops passed orders to men who established other jurisdictions. These included such groups as the Autocephalous Syro-Chaldean Church of North America, which received orders from Bishop Stanley; the Anglican Episcopal Church, whose founder was consecrated by a Free PEC bishop, William Elliot Littlewood; and the Apostolic Catholic Church of the Americas, formed by former Free Protestant Episcopal Bishop Gordon I. DaCosta. The last United States Primate Albert J. Fuge, retired without naming a successor. He died in 1982. Boltwood, as Primus Emeritus, named Rt. Rev. Charles Kennedy Stewart Moffatt of Brandon, Manitoba, as the new Primus. Moffatt passed away recently and Boltwood died earlier in the 1980s. Most Rev. Edwin D. Follick of Woodland Hills,

California, is presently serving as Primus. A second bishop, Harry K. Means, resides in Florida.

★143★
Holy Catholic Church, Anglican Rite Jurisdiction of the Americas
(Defunct)

In the several years following the 1977 St. Louis congress, the Anglican Movement grew to encompass more than 200 congregations. However, as it grew, it splintered into several factions due to administrative disagreements as well as the issue of the domination of the Anglican Catholic Church by the Anglo-Catholic (high-church) perspective. Some congregations remained outside of the various diocesan structures altogether. Bishop Francisco Pagtakhan of the Philippine Independent Church, who had participated in the original consecrations of the four Anglican bishops in 1978, became increasingly disturbed at the splintering and lack of unity in the Anglican Movement. In 1980, asserting his role as the ecumenical and missionary officer for the Philippine Independent Church, Pagtakhan decided to create an "umbrella" for those in the Anglican Movement who were searching for a home where they could "belong to a genuinely canonical part of the One, Holy, Catholic and Apostolic Church." Thus in March 1980, in Texas, he initiated the incorporation of the Holy Catholic Church, Anglican Rite Jurisdiction of the Americas.

On September 26, 1981 (with the permission of the supreme bishop of the Philippine Independent Church, the M. Rev. Marcario V. Ga) Bishop Pagtakhan, assisted by retired bishops Sergio Mondala and Lupe Rosete, consecrated Robert Q. Kennaugh, F. Ogden Miller, and Gerald Wayne Craig, all former priests in the Anglican Catholic Church. Kennaugh became head of the Diocese of St. Luke, centered in Corsicana, Texas, and archbishop for the jurisdiction. Miller was named bishop of the Diocese of St. Matthew with headquarters in California. Craig became bishop of the Diocese of St. Mark with headquarters in Columbus, Ohio. In 1982 Herman F. Nelson was consecrated as bishop for the Diocese of St. John the Evangelist with headquarters in Venice, Florida. Shortly thereafter, Kennaugh retired as archbishop, and Craig was named to that post. In 1985 the Anglican Rite Jurisdiction received Bishop Harold L. Trott into the Church as the Bishop of the Missionary Diocese of Reconciliation. Trott had left the American Episcopal Church in 1979 and had formed the Pro-Diocese of Reconciliation (consisting of several congregations in California and New Mexico) while waiting for a larger body with which to affiliate.

In 1986 the jurisdiction accepted Rt. Rev. Lafond Lapointe, a Haitian-born bishop who had been exiled from his homeland for political reasons. In the intervening years he had worked in the Haitian-American community in Chicago, Illinois. After the fall of the dictatorship in Haiti he was able to return as the Bishop of the Anglican Diocese of Haiti. He reconstituted L'Iglise Orthodox Apostolique Haitienne, an independent church established in 1874 by Bishop James Theodore Holley with the approval and backing of the Protestant Episcopal Church. Holley died in 1911 and his church was absorbed into the Episcopal Missionary Diocese in 1913. Also, in recent years, the Anglican Rite Jurisdiction of the Americas has established close ties to Los Hermanos Franciscanos de la Providencia, a Franciscan order in Puerto Rico. Retired Archbishop Robert Q. Kennaugh has become the bishop-protector of the order.

Educational Facilities: Anglican Theological Collegum, Columbus, Ohio.

Sources:

Dibbert, Roderic B. *The Roots of Traditional Anglicanism*. Akron, OH: DeKoven Foundation, 1984.

Official Directory of Bishops, Clergy, Parishes. Akron, OH: Holy Catholic Church, Anglican Rite Jurisdiction of the America, Office of the Secretary of the ARJA Synod, 1985.

The Prologue. Akron, OH: DeKoven Foundation, 1984.

★144★
Holy Celtic Church
% Most Rev. Donald E. Hugh, Presiding Bishop
PO Box 2401
Apple Valley, CA 92307

The Holy Celtic Church traces its history to the ancient Celtic church which preceded the imposition of Roman authority in Celtic lands. Documentation concerning the Celtic church has been lacking because of the destruction of its records and artifacts beginning with the Roman conquests. The modern Holy Celtic Church was reestablished in the 1990s with orders derived from the Order of Corporate Reunion. The order had been founded in 1874 in London, England, to confer valid Apostolic Orders on individuals who were working for the unity of Anglican and Eastern Orthodox churches. In more recent years, it has focused on bringing unity among the many independent Anglican and Orthodox jurisdictions.

The Holy Celtic Church is conservative and adheres closely to basic Christian teachings and the holy Scripture as expressed in the Apostolic Constitution, Teachings and Creed. It recognizes the spirit of the Seven Ecumenical Councils, especially the first three, which were attended by Celtic bishops. The church has a particular affinity with the Coptic Church, especially the spirit of the ancient Desert Fathers who carried Christianity to the fringes of the then-known world. The church's clergy work to visit those unable to attend church services, and to establish small missions, priories, and cell groups.

Membership: Not reported.

★145★
Independent Episcopal Church (Anglican Rite, Old Catholic Church)
5414 W. Pierson St.
Phoenix, AZ 85031

The Independent Episcopal Church (Anglican Rite, Old Catholic Church), also known as the Independent Episcopal Church, International, was founded in 1987 by Most Rev. Steven Styblo, its Primate Bishop. Styblo was consecrated in 1985 by Bishops John Michael Dale, the Bishop Abbot of the Missionaries of Saint John the Beloved, and Western Orthodox Church (Ordinariates within the Evangelical-Eucharistic Catholic Observance). He is assisted in the Church by Bishop Protestant Episcopal Church but has added insights from the Orthodox and Old Catholic traditions. It accepts the 39 Articles of Religion common to Anglicanism and the Lambeth Quadrilateral as approved by the Episcopal Church (1886) and the Church of England (1888) as its standard of doctrine. The Quadrilateral establishes four foundational points of church unity the Bible, the ancient creeds (Apostles' and Nicene), two sacraments of baptism and the Lord's Supper, and the historic episcopate. The Independent Episcopal Church deviates from the Quadrilateral in its acceptance of seven sacraments (rather than the two accepted by Anglicans).

The church is centered in the Diocese of Arizona and the Christ the King Cathedral Mission in Phoenix.

Membership: Not reported. There are three clergy members and a single parish in Phoenix.

Periodicals: *Christ Work: Independent Episcopal News Letter*.

Sources:

Ward, Gary L. *Independent Bishops: An International Directory*. Detroit: Apogee Books, 1990. 524 pp.

★146★
National Anglican Church
401 S. Nacaise Ave.
Bay St. Louis, MS 39520-4429

The National Anglican Church is a small jurisdiction created in the late 1980s by Bp. Montgomery Griffith-Mair. A former priest in the Episcopal Church, Griffith-Mair was consecrated in 1987 by Donald Lee West, a bishop of the Evangelical Catholic Communion. He now serves as premier bishop of the church and ordinary for the Anglican Diocese of the Eastern United States.

Membership: Not reported.

★147★
Old Episcopal Church
Current address not obtained for this edition.

The Old Episcopal Church is a small diocese in the Southwest headed by Rt. Rev. Jack C. Adam, Bishop of Arizona. A former Protestant Episcopal Church priest, he left the Episcopal Church and was consecrated by Archbishop Walter A. Propheta of the American Orthodox Catholic Church in 1972.

Membership: Not reported. There are several parishes in Arizona and New Mexico.

★148★
Old Episcopal Church of Scotland (OECS)
Current address not obtained for this edition.

The Old Episcopal Church of Scotland (OECS) traces its heritage to the pre-Roman Celtic Christian community, which is believed to have existed in the British Isles as early as the first century. This tradition continued in the Celtic monastic communities through the centuries until the Reformation of the sixteenth century when the state-sanctioned Church of Scotland became Presbyterian, i.e., reorganized as a church led by an assembly of elders (the presbytery) rather than bishops. Those who retained the reformed Catholic faith and polity reorganized as the Episcopal Church of Scotland. Problems developed in the Episcopal Church of Scotland in the mid-eighteenth century when King William of Orange and the Church of England attempted to install English bishops over the Scottish church. Those non-jurors opposed to the new policy, who also refused to swear allegiance to the deposed monarch, left and formed the Old Free Episcopal Church of Scotland.

Later, members of the Old Free Episcopal Church of Scotland migrated to Canada. A small community continued through the years and experienced a revival in the 1970s. The present leader of the church is Rt. Rev. Fredrick R. O'Keefe O.S.B. who succeeded Brian G. Turkington in 1983. Turkington, now with the Federation of St. Thomas Christian Churches, had been voted out of office by the church's leadership. O'Keefe had been a priest in the Old Catholic Church of North America. He was loaned to the OECS, which needed additional leadership. In 1981 O'Keefe was consecrated by Abp. Charles V. Hearn of the Old Catholic Church in North America as a bishop for both jurisdictions. An increasing amount of his time was spent with the OECS, and in 1983 he was chosen as its Primus, though he still retains his formal ties to the Old Catholics. He is assisted by Bp. Fonzy J. Broussard. In cooperation with several other small Old Catholic jurisdictions, the church sponsors Incarnation Abbey in Clearwater, Florida, a Benedictine monastic community.

The church has no property and all worship is conducted in the homes of members or in rented facilities. Ministers are unsalaried and usually work at a secular occupation. Both the 1928 and 1979 Episcopal Prayer Books are used, as well as the Eastern Orthodox Peshitta Bible, translated from the Aramaic by George M. Lamsa.

Membership: There are fewer than 50 members and six priests.

Remarks: During the 1970s and early 1980s, in an attempt to move away from their singularly ethnic identification, a number of names were used by different leaders in the church. These names included Free Anglican Church, Free Anglican Church (Iona Conference); Free Anglican Church in America, Free Anglican Church in America and the British Isles; Free Anglican Communion, United Anglican Communion, and United Anglican Communion in America (and the British Isles). The use of such diverse names led to a great deal of confusion, with observers seeing several churches where, in fact, there was only one. The OECS was also confused with other small jurisdictions that used the same or similar names, such as Free Anglican Church. In recent years, the use of the divergent names has ceased.

Also, the relationship of the present-day OECS to the movement founded in the eighteenth century is not entirely clear. At one time it was claimed that the lineage had passed through Bp. Cowan King, the last of the OECS bishops in Great Britain. King supposedly consecrated Harry Edwin Smith in 1970 and Smith passed the lineage to Brian G. Turkington. However, that story has been challenged by O'Keefe.

★149★
Philippine Independent Catholic Church in the Americas
PO Box 6
Glendale, CA 91209

During the 1980s, the Philippine Independent Church, the representative of the worldwide Anglican Communion in the Philippine Islands, was shaken by severe internal disputes. A major issue focused on the church's refusal to reelect Marcario V. Ga as *Obispo Maximo*, Supreme Bishop. Ga had served in that position for several four-year terms. Refusing to accept the decision of the church, he reorganized his following and began what has become an ongoing court fight for recognition in the Philippines. The split in the Philippine Independent Church has had significant repercussions in the United States where several of Ga's close associates have involved themselves since the late 1970s.

In January 1978, Abp. Francisco Pagtakhan took center stage at the consecration of C. Dale D. Doren, Robert S. Morse, James O. Mote, and Peter F. Watterson as bishops for the new church being formed by the conservative Anglicans who had recently left the Episcopal Church. His active participation in the event projected the Philippine Independent Church directly into the affairs of a sister communion by providing legitimacy to a breakaway group.

During the 1980s, Pagtakhan and two other bishops, Sergio Mondala and Lupe Rosete, performed consecrations for several independent Anglican groups, each time further straining relations between the Episcopal Church and the Philippine Independent Church. Following the split in the Philippines, Pagtakhan moved to establish the Ga branch of the Philippine Independent Church in North America. (All of the previous consecrations had been for independent American Anglican jurisdictions.) In April 1986, Pagtakhan consecrated Thomas Gore, an Episcopal minister who was a psychiatrist in Lubbock, Texas. Gore moved to incorporate the church as the Eglesia Filipina Independente, the Philippine Independent Catholic Church in the Americas, as a Texas corporation. Pagtakhan was named president and Gore vicar-general. Pagtakhan and Gore consecrated George Martinus as the church's bishop for Mexico in 1988.

In the few years of the church's existence, it has grown through the addition of independent bishops who have sought association with it. These include Bp. Paul G. W. Schultz (Glendale, California), Bp. Charles Boulton (Texas), Bp. Charles S. J. White (Washington, D.C.) In 1987 Pagtakhan named Abp Bertil Persson, primate of the Apostolic Episcopal Church, as his apostolic representative for Scandinavia and Europe.

Membership: Not reported.

Sources:

Ward, Gary L. *Independent Bishops: An International Directory*. Detroit, MI: Apogee Books, 1990.

★150★
Philippine Independent Church
℅ St. Andrew's Episcopal Cathedral
Queen Emma Sq.
Honolulu, HI 96813

The Philippine Independent Church emerged from the political struggles of the nineteenth century which led to full independence of the Philippine Islands. Following the defeat of the Spanish in 1898, the United States took control of the Philippines, rather than grant it full governmental autonomy. As a result, a revolt led by Emilio Aguinaldo developed against American rule. In that area of the country briefly controlled by Aguinaldo, a military vicar general, Gregorio Aglipay (1860-1940), was appointed to head the Roman Catholic Church. In 1899 the Roman Catholic Archbishop of Manila excommunicated Aglipay, and the church under his control reorganized as the Iglesia Filipina Independiente.

As a guerrilla general, Aglipay became a hero to many, and was the last of the revolutionary leaders to surrender. He retained the loyalty of the members of the new church and spent the remainder of his life guiding it. The progress of the church was checked by a 1906 ruling of the country's supreme court, which awarded most of the church's property to the Roman Catholic Church. Early in the century Aglipay became influenced by Unitarian views (which deny the doctrine of the Trinity), and he led the church in their acceptance. The extent of the theological drift was clearly demonstrated by the 1939 appointment of Dr. Louis C. Cornish, president of the American Unitarian Association, as the honorary president of the church.

The dominance of Unitarian thought was ended after Aglipay's death by his successor as supreme bishop, Isabelo de los Reyes, Jr. A Trinitarian, Reyes led the church to adopt a strong Trinitarian Declaration of Faith in 1947 which included acceptance of the Apostles' and Nicene Creeds. Concurrently, the Protestant Episcopal Church recognized the Philippine Independent Church. The following year the supreme bishop and two other bishops of the Philippine Independent Church were consecrated by the Protestant Episcopal Church, giving them the Anglican lineage of apostolic succession.

The Philippine Independent Church began work in the United States during the years of negotiation, which led to the establishment of full intercommunion with the Protestant Episcopal Church in 1961. With the blessing of the Episcopal bishop in Hawaii, a mission among Filipino-Americans was initiated in 1959. By the mid-1970s three parishes, meeting in Episcopal churches, had been established. Services were held in both the English and Ilocano languages. The church has subsequently established congregations in other states.

The Philippine Independent Church established communion with the Protestant Episcopal Church, the Philippine Episcopal Church, and other Anglican bodies through the terms of the Bonn agreement of 1931, which brought the Church of England and the Old Catholic Church into accord. As of 1985 it maintained communion with a number of Anglican bodies, the Old Catholic Churches in Europe, the Polish National Catholic Church, and the Lusitanian Catholic-Apostolic Evangelical Church. It is a member of the World Council of Churches.

Membership: As of 1985 there were a reported 4,500,000 members, 726 parishes, and 688 priests worldwide, most in the Philippines.

Periodicals: *Aglipayian Review*. Send orders to Box 2484, Manila, Philippines.

Remarks: Since the late 1970s relations between the Protestant Episcopal Church and the Philippine Independent Church have been strained due to the participation of several Philippine bishops in the consecration of bishops for independent conservative Anglican jurisdictions established by former Episcopalians. In 1978 Francisco Pagtakhan, Bishop Secretary of Missions for the Philippine Independent Church, participated in the consecration of several bishops for what became the Anglican Catholic Church, the Diocese of Christ the King, and the United Episcopal Church of North America. Then in 1980, Pagtakhan led in the founding of the Holy Catholic Church, Anglican Rite Jurisdiction of the Americas, and with Bishops Sergio Mondala and Lupe Rosete, consecrated three bishops for the new church. In 1982 he broke relations with that jurisdiction and established rival work in a new Anglican Rite Diocese of Texas.

Sources:

Anderson, Gerald H., ed. *Studies in Philippine Church History*. Ithaca, NY: Cornell University Press, 1969.

Deats, Richard L. *Nationalism and Christianity in the Philippines*. Dallas, TX: Southern Methodist University Press, 1967.

★151★
Provisional Diocese of St. Augustine of Canterbury
(Defunct)

The Provisional Diocese of St. Augustine of Canterbury was formed in 1978 by Canon Albert J. duBois (1906-1980), former head of the American Church Union, and five former parishes of the Diocese of the Holy Trinity (of what is now the Anglican Catholic Church). It was the desire of the parishes to unite with The Roman Catholic Church, though they wished to retain their own liturgy, forms of piety, and their traditional lay involvement in the life of the Church. The group was led by its "senior priest," Canon duBois; the Rev. John Barker, head of the "Clericus," a priests' conference; and Dr. Theodore L. McEvoy, head of its "Laymen's League."

In 1980 Archbishop John Raphael Quinn, Roman Catholic Archbishop of San Francisco, announced a plan by which Anglicans could come into the Roman Catholic Church and keep their own priests, an approved Anglican liturgy, and a common identity. In 1981, James Parker became the first priest to move from the Protestant Episcopal Church to the Roman jurisdiction. By 1985, twenty-three married priests had been re-ordained as Roman priests. Five parishes had been received by the Vatican.

★152★
Reformed Episcopal Church
2001 Frederick Rd.
Baltimore, MD 21228-5599

History. The Reformed Episcopal Church was founded on December 2, 1873, in New York City at the call of the Rt. Rev. George David Cummins, formerly the assistant bishop of Kentucky in the Protestant Episcopal Church in the U.S.A. As an evangelical, Cummins viewed with alarm the influence of the Anglo-Catholic movement within the Episcopal Church. He had come to believe that it had fatally compromised the Protestant character of Anglican doctrine and worship and that it had bred intolerance to evangelical preaching and worship.

Throughout the 1860s, factions within the Episcopal church had been clashing over ceremonial and doctrinal issues, especially concerning the meaning of critical passages of the *Book of Common Prayer*. These clashes reached a climax for Cummins in October 1873, when he was publicly attacked by his fellow bishops for participating in an ecumenical communion service under the aegis of the Evangelical Alliance in New York City. On November 10, 1873, he resigned his office of assistant bishop and on November 15 issued the call to other evangelical Episcopalians to join him in organizing a new Episcopal church for the "purpose of restoring the old paths of the fathers. . ."

Beliefs. At the organization of the new church, a declaration of principles was adopted and the Rev. Charles E. Cheney was elected bishop to serve with Cummins (Cheney was consecrated by Cummins on December 14, 1873). In May 1874, the Second General Council approved a Constitution and Canons for the church and a slightly amended version of *The Book of Common Prayer.* In 1875, the Third General Council adopted a set of Thirty-nine Articles as an explanatory supplement to the Church of England's Thirty-nine Articles of Religion.

Organization. Although Cummins died in 1876, the church had grown to seven jurisdictions in the U.S. and Canada. Although substantial growth ceased after 1900, the Reformed Episcopal Church now comprises three synods (New York-Philadelphia, Chicago, and Charleston-Atlanta-Charlotte) and a Special Missionary Jurisdiction with churches in Arizona and California. It maintains a theological seminary in Philadelphia which offers a three-year curriculum and houses a library and archival resources.

The church is governed by a triennial general council, and elects a presiding bishop from among its serving bishops to be executive head of the church; however, most authority lies at the synodical and parish levels. It has maintained in its doctrine the principles of episcopacy (in historic succession from the apostles), Anglican liturgy, Reformed doctrine, and evangelical fellowship, and in its practice, it continues to recognize the validity of certain non-episcopal orders of evangelical ministry. The church was briefly a member of the Federal Council of Churches at its inception. It is currently a member of the National Association of Evangelicals. It has instituted dialogue in response to invitations from the Episcopal Church in 1920, 1931-41, and in 1987-88.

Membership: In 1995, the church reported 6,084 members in 102 congregations and missions, and 1,607 ministers.

Educational Facilities: The Theological Seminary of the Reformed Episcopal Church, Philadelphia, Pennsylvania.

Cummins Memorial Theological Seminary, Summerville, South Carolina.

Periodicals: *The Evangelical Episcopulian.* Send orders to 3240 Adams Ct. N., Bensalem, PA 29020.

Sources:

The Book of Common Prayer. Philadelphia: Reformed Episcopal Publication Society, 1932.

Carter, Paul A. "The Reformed Episcopal Schism of 1873: An Ecumenical Perspective." *Historical Magazine of the Protestant Episcopal Church* 33, no. 3 (September 1964).

Cheney, Charles Edward. *What Reformed Episcopalians Believe.* N.p. Christian Education Committee, Reformed Episcopal Church, 1961.

Guelzo, Allen C. *The First Thirty Years: A Historical Handbook for the Founding of the Reformed Episcopal Church, 1873-1903.* Philadelphia: Reformed Episcopal Publication Society, 1986.

Platt, Warren C. "The Reformed Episcopal Church: The Origins and Early Development of its Theological Perspective." *Historical Magazine of the Protestant Episcopal Church* 61 (1983).

★153★
St. Ciaran's Fellowship of Celtic Christian Communities
℅ Rt. Rev. Dr. Joseph A. Grenier
PO Box 299
Canadensis, PA 18325-0299

St. Ciaran's Fellowship of Celtic Christian Communities is a contemporary independent Catholic and Orthodox church inspired by the ancient Celtic Church. It adheres to the Seven Ecumenical Councils of the undivided Christian church and the Nicene Creed. It celebrates the seven sacraments (also called Mysteries) of this church, and believes in the real presence of Christ in the Eucharist.

While contemporary Celtic Christian spirituality has held a special appeal to persons of Celtic heritage, St. Ciaran's Fellowship is not an ethnic fellowship and welcomes all who are attracted to the Christian life it offers. The fellowship is comprised of small faith communities, some meeting as "house churches" or in small chapels. Stress is placed on small communities based on family, friends and kin, not in any exclusive way but practicing hospitality. Priesthood is open to both men and women, married or celibate. The bishops are elected by the fellowship's members.

Rt. Rev. Joseph A. Grenier, founder and bishop of St. Ciaran's, was ordained a priest in 1958 in Rome, and has a Ph.D. in Theology from Fordham University in New York City. He is employed as a family therapist.

Membership: There are five member communities in the fellowship.

Sources:

Barrett, David B. *World Christian Encyclopedia.* New York: Oxford, 1982.

★154★
Southern Episcopal Church
℅ Most Rev. Huron C. Manning Jr.
234 Willow Ln.
Nashville, TN 37211

The Southern Episcopal Church was formed in 1953 by 10 families of All Saints Episcopal Church in Nashville, Tennessee. Its constitution was ratified in 1965. The presiding bishop for its first quarter century was Rt. Rev. B. H. Webster. Webster died in 1991 and was succeeded by Bp. Huron C. Manning, Jr. He is assisted by fellow bishops William Green, Jr. and Henry L. Atwell. The church is governed by the National Convention composed of all bishops (House of Bishops) and the lay and clerical delegates. The 1928 *Book of Common Prayer* is standard for worship. The church sponsors an American Indian mission as well as foreign work in four countries, including a mission in India started in the mid-1980s. American parishes can be found in Alabama, the Carolinas, Florida, Georgia, Indiana, New York, Ohio, Oklahoma, and Tennessee.

Membership: In 1984 the church reported 72,000 members in 14 congregations with 17 priests.

Educational Facilities: Holy Trinity College, Nashville, Tennessee.

Periodicals: *The Southern Episcopalian.*

★155★
Traditional Episcopal Church
℅ Most Rev. Richard G. Melli
Rte. 4, Box 1235, Hwy. 19 S.
Palatka, FL 32177

The Traditional Episcopal Church was founded in 1991 by Most Rev. Richard G. Melli, its presiding bishop. In the mid-1970s, Melli was a lay-reader at the St. Edward the Confessor Episcopal Church in Mt. Dora, Florida, a congregation of the Protestant Episcopal Church in the U.S.A. He also studied with the Diocesan Deacon Training Program. Following the formation of the Anglican Catholic Church, a conservative body of former Episcopal priests and lay people, he assisted in the founding of new congregations in central Florida. He was ordained a deacon in 1980 and the following year a priest by Bp. Frank Knutti.

Melli initially served as the diocesan administrative officer and soon was named canon. During these years the Anglican Catholic Church largely established itself as an Anglo-Catholic high church and developed some intolerance for the evangelical wing of the conservative continuing church movement. Following Bishop Knutti's death, Melli left the church and joined the Anglican Episcopal Church of North America under Bp. Walter Hollis Adams. Melli found himself in charge of four parishes and a mission, an ordered community, the Order of Oblates of the Holy Spirit (founded in 1983), and Laud Hall Seminary, an in-house school to provide training for the church's clergy.

When Adams died and the AECNA moved into a period of instability, Melli and the parishes under his leadership began to seek another jurisdiction which was like them—nonpolitical, Christ-centered, spirit-filled, and serving God. They could find no jurisdiction to their liking within the Continuing Church movement and thus in 1991 they decided to form the Traditional Episcopal Church. To insure the validity of his orders, Melli sought consecration by bishops in three different lineages: Bps. Howard Russell (Anglican), Peters (Orthodox), and Roberto Toca (Old Catholic).

The church has experienced steady growth. Formed in succession was a Diocese of the Mid-Atlantic anchored on the St. Charles the Martyr parish in Annapolis, Maryland, and overseas dioceses in Colombia and India. A new Abbot of the Order of the Oblates of the Holy Spirit was consecrated as the fifth bishop sitting in the College of Bishops.

Membership: In 1998, the church reported a membership of 3890.

Educational Facilities: Anglican College of Chaplains, Palaka, Florida.

Laudhall Seminary, Palaka, Florida.

Periodicals: *The Traditional Episcopalian* (on the Internet).

★156★
Traditional Protestant Episcopal Church
6 Derby Ln.
Fairhope, AL 36532

The Traditional Protestant Episcopal Church was founded in 1986 by Bp. Charles Edward Morley. Bishop Morley was raised a Roman Catholic but joined the American Episcopal Church in the 1970s. He was ordained in 1981 by C. Dale D. Doren of the United Episcopal Church of the U.S.A. and consecrated in 1984 by Bp. Richard C. Acker of the United Episcopal Church of America. Morley succeeded Acker as head of the United Episcopal Church.

Instead of continuing the United Episcopal Church, Morley founded a new church. It has one diocese, the Missionary Diocese of the Advent. Morley was consecrated *sub conditione* in 1989 by Abp. Francisco Pagtakhan of the Philippine Independent Catholic Church and Bp. Larry L. Shaver. As its name implies, the Traditional Protestant Episcopal Church is a conservative Anglican body. It adheres to the 39 Articles of Religion of the Episcopal Church and uses the 1928 *Book of Common Prayer* and the King James Version of the Bible. The church also affirms the inerrancy of the Bible. It is evangelical and low church (less liturgical) in its practice of Anglicanism and rejects Anglo-Catholic approaches to understanding the tradition. Associated with the church is Bp. Ed Whatley of Tuscaloosa, Alabama.

Membership: Not reported.

★157★
United Anglican Church
Current address not obtained for this edition.

The United Anglican Church was founded in the mid-1980s by John Riffenbury, Jr., who began his ministerial career in the United Episcopal Church of America. He was originally ordained by Bp. Richard C. Acker, the church's presiding bishop in 1984. The following year he was consecrated by Abp. Edward Marshall of the Evangelical Episcopal Church, and subsequently organized the United Anglican Church. (Several months after Riffenbury's consecration, Acker died unexpectedly and left the United Episcopal Church of America in a somewhat disorganized state.)

The United Anglican Church continues traditional Episcopal belief and practice in a manner similar to the United Episcopal Church.

Membership: In 1990 there were three congregations, four priests, and 50 members in the United States, and two congregations, two priests, and 20 members in Canada.

Educational Facilities: Cranmer Institute for Anglican Studies, Marmora, New Jersey.

Periodicals: *Anglican News and Views.*

Sources:

Ward, Gary L. *Independent Bishops: An International Directory.* Detroit, MI: Apogee Books, 1990.

★158★
United Episcopal Church (1945) Anglican/Celtic
PO Box 1931
Tucson, AZ 85702

History. The United Episcopal Church (1945) Anglican/Celtic (UEC) was formed in 1945 in Plainfield, Illinois, by Bishops Julius Massey, Albert Sorensen, and Hinton Pride. They envisioned a restored church of Anglican/Celtic heritage. St. Paul's Catherdral was designed and built in Plainfield. During the process of its early growth, several previously founded churches affiliated with the UEC, including the Norwegian Seaman's Mission in Chicago. In the mid-1950s, Bishop James E. Burns, who had previously founded several Anglican churches, brought his jurisdiction into the United Episcopal Church. Burns had originally been consecrated by William H. Schneider, who like Massey had been consecrated by Denver Scott Swain of the American Episcopal Church (1940s). Burns also persuaded the Rev. Orlando J. Woodward, pastor of the independent Bethany Presbyterian Church in Fort Orlethorpe, Georgia, to bring his congregation into the jurisdiction. Woodward had been ordained by Archbishop W. H. Francis Brothers of the Old Catholic Church in America, but had introduced the congregation he served to the Episcopal Prayer Book and led it to adopt the Thirty-nine Articles of Religion of the Protestant Episcopal Church in the U.S.A. as its standard of doctrine.

After a period of growth, during which time Woodward served as presiding bishop (1961-1965), the church entered a period of decline. Woodward suffered a near-fatal illness, several of the priests retired, and bishops Massey and Sorensen died. It was during this time with the church nearly moribund that Bishop Burns consecrated Richard C. Acker, who founded the United Episcopal Church of America. However, in the 1980s, Woodward was able to resume his duties as presiding bishop and began reviving the UEC. New parishes were created and in 1988, with the assistance of Karl Pruter, head of Christ Catholic Church, Woodward consecrated Ted D. Kelly as coadjutor bishop with might of succession and bishop of the Southwest. In 1990 Archbishop Woodward died and was succeeded by Bishop Kelly. Rev. Fr. Michael R. Porter is the church's chancellor.

Beliefs. The UEC accepts the Thirty-nine Articles of Religion common to Anglicanism and uses the 1928 edition of the *Book of Common Prayer.* It considers the traditional teachings of the Anglican faith to be binding and not subject to alteration or debate. It also accepts as valid those practices and the liturgical worship as introduced into the ancient British Isles by the Celtic and Gallic monks and missionaries, and which, when integrated into the traditions of St. Augustine of Canterbury, produced the Anglican tradition. The church recognizes two greater sacraments, baptism and the Holy Eucharist, and five lesser ones: confirmation, confession, holy orders, marriage, and unction. It retains the spectrum of high (more liturgical), low (less formal), and broad church emphases in the expression of worship.

Organization. The church follows an episcopal polity. The governance is invested in the National Convention consisting of the all the bishops (the College of Bishops) and all the priests and lay delegates from each parish (the House of Delegates). The presiding bishop presides at the convention meetings. In 1987 Bishop Woodward and Father (now Bishop) Kelly founded the Missionary

Order of St. Jude, dedicated to the assistance of the poor and needy. The church is opposed to the admission of women to the priesthood.

Membership: In 1995 there were 21 parishes, approximately 1,600 members, 14 priests, 6 deacons, and 8 candidates for holy orders worldwide. There were 547 members in the United States and 91 in Canada and affiliated parishes in Mexico, Columbia, India, Puerto Rico, and Africa.

Educational Facilities: The School of Theology, Tucson, Arizona. The School of Clinical Counseling, Nashville, Tennessee.

Periodicals: *The Celt.*

★159★
United Episcopal Church of America
(Defunct)

The United Episcopal Church of America started in 1970 as an independent Anglican parish meeting in the home of Howard Love of Columbia, South Carolina. The congregation decided to affiliate with the American Episcopal Church (AEC) and called former Protestant Episcopal priest Richard C. Acker (d. 1985) to the pulpit. Acker was installed in 1971 by Archbishop Anthony F. M. Clavier, head of the American Episcopal Church. In 1973 the congregation withdrew from the AEC. Over the next few years Acker became acquainted with Bishop James E. Burns of the United Episcopal Church (1945) Anglican/Celtic. Burns' consecration of Acker in 1976 led to the formation of the United Episcopal Church of America over which Acker served as archbishop. Acker was succeeded as head of the church by Charles Edward Morley, whom he consecrated in 1984. Morley disbanded the church which was superceded in 1986 by the Traditional Protestant Episcopal Church.

★160★
United Episcopal Church of North America
% John Gramley
PO Box 9374
Pensacola, FL 32513

In 1980 C. Dale David Doren, senior bishop of the Anglican Catholic Church and head of its mid-Atlantic diocese, resigned. He contended that the Anglican Catholic Church was becoming exclusively "high-church" or "Anglo-Catholic" in its stance. With only two congregations, he formed the United Episcopal Church of the U.S.A. (known since 1985 as the United Episcopal Church of North America.) It adheres to the traditional beliefs and practices of the Protestant Episcopal Church as exemplified in the 1928 *Book of Common Prayer* and the Thirty-nine Articles of Religion.

The UEC tends to the "low-church" end of the Anglican spectrum. Each parish is independent and holds title to properties and control over temporal affairs. The jurisdiction adopted the 1958 Protestant Episcopal Church Constitution and Canons (with specific changes in relation to church properties) as its own. The presiding bishop was given the title of archbishop, but the church vested little power in the office. In 1984 Archbishop Doren consecrated Albion W. Knight as a missionary bishop to assist him in leadership of the jurisdiction's affairs. In the 1980s Doren retired and was succeeded by Knight. Most recently, Knight has retired in favor of Bishop John Gramley.

Membership: In 1995 the UECNA reported 24 parishes across the United States and 40 priests. Membership was estimated to be approximately 2,000.

Periodicals: *Glad Tidings.* Send orders to Box 4538, Pensacola, FL 32507.

Section 4

Eastern Liturgical Family

Consult the Contents pages to locate the essay in Part II, Historical Essay Chapters,
that provides an historical discussion of this family

Intrafaith Organizations

★161★
Federated Independent Catholic and Orthodox Churches
(Defunct)

The Federated Independent Catholic and Orthodox Churches was a short-lived ecumenical organization founded by Bp. Antoine Joseph Aneed (1881–1970) of the Byzantine Universal (Catholic) and Orthodox Church of the Americas. The federation was apparently formed around 1944 following Aneed's consecration by Lowell Paul Wadle of the American Catholic Church and E. R. Verostek of the North American Old Roman Catholic Church-Utrecht Succession. The federation, never very active, did not survive Aneed's death.

★162★
Federation of Independent Catholic and Orthodox Bishops
32378 Lynx Hollow Rd.
Creswell, OR 97426

The Federation of Independent Catholic and Orthodox Bishops (FICOB) emerged in the 1990s as an ecumenical body serving as a meeting ground for Old Catholic, Anglican, Orthodox, and Liberal Catholic bishops. While united by their separation from the older and larger historical liturgical churches, the independent jurisdictions have disagreed with each other on a variety of issues from the ordination of female priests and acceptance/rejection of homosexuals, to various doctrinal and liturgical matters. It has been the suggestion of Archbishop Meri Louise Spruit, matriarch of the Church of Antioch and director of the federation, that FICOB unites people only in Christ's Law of Love. The federation came about in part as a result of independent bishops across North America coming into contact through the Internet.

The federation promotes the idea that all of the churches share in a portion of God's truth and that much is to be gained by a promotion of tolerance, understanding, and an acceptance of diversity. There is also an auxiliary organization, the Friends of FICOB.

Membership: At the start of 1996, FICOB had 93 episcopal members.

Periodicals: *FICOB & Friends.*

★163★
Federation of Orthodox Catholic Churches (FOCC)
Christ Catholic Church International
6160 Barker St.
Niagara, ON, Canada L2G 1Y4

The Federation of Orthodox Catholic Churches was founded in the mid-1990s. Taking the lead in the formation of FOCC was Abp. Seraphim MacLennan of the Holy Orthodox Catholic Church. Other founding members included Abp. Donald William Mullen of Christ Catholic Church International, Archbishop Melchizedek of the Free Orthodox Church International (Eparchy of Lincoln), and Archbishop Ingram of the American Orthodox Catholic Church.

FOCC grew out of an expressed need among some of the smaller Orthodox Catholic jurisdictions to have a meeting place where each group can find recognition and succor without the fear of any loss of identity over its particular expression of the Orthodoxia (correct way). The Orthodox in FOCUS title does not refer to Eastern Orthodoxy, but to the true teachings of Orthodoxia (right theology) and Orthopraxis (correct practice). Members believe themselves to be Orthodox Catholics in belief and practice.

FOCC also provides a synodical covering for those Orthodox Catholic jurisdictions that for one reason or another do not have one. Thus FOCC exists as a synod of synods within which those jurisdictions having an active synod can meet without abandoning that synod, and where those jurisdictions not having a synod can participate without losing their identity. Member churches acknowledge and strengthen core similarities of member jurisdictions without damaging the diversity among members. They share the cup of Communion.

Membership: Members include the Holy Orthodox Catholic Church, Christ Catholic Church International, the Free Orthodox Church International (Eparchy of Lincoln), and the American Orthodox Catholic Church.

★164★
Holy Synod of the Orthodox Catholic Churches of the Americas and Europe
(Defunct)

The Holy Synod of the Orthodox Catholic Churches of the Americas and Europe was a short-lived ecumenical endeavor organized in 1967 by Abp. Peter A. Zurawetzky, then head of the Christ Catholic Church of the Americas and Europe. The synod grew out of a dispute between Zurawetzky and Abp. Cyril John Clement Sherwood, who had succeeded Joseph Klimovich as head of the Orthodox Catholic Patriarchate of America. Zurawetzky, who had cofounded the patriarchate with Klimovich, claimed that Sherwood stole the patriarchate. The new synod included Zurawetzky and the heads of the Autocephalous Greek Orthodox Church of the Americas and Europe (Abp. Joachim Souris), the Greek Orthodox Diocese of America (Archbishop Theoklitos), and the Universal Shrine of Divine Guidance (Abp. Mark Karras).

The synod dissolved in 1975, by which time Sherwood had died and the original charter was inactive. Zurawetzky seized the opportunity to assume corporate control of the patriarchate and revive it around the core of the Orthodox Catholic Churches of the Americas and Europe.

International Federation of Orthodox Catholics United Sacramentally
℅ Mt. Rev. Seraphim MacLennan
R.R. 1, Box 185
Brushton, NY 12916

The International Federation of Orthodox Catholics United Sacramentally (FOCUS) is a federation of sacramental churches which views itself as based on the evangelizing Holy Scriptures and empowered by the Holy Spirit. It is the desire of FOCUS to establish a body that is loving (as commanded by Jesus), forgiving, and united to the glory of God. FOCUS serves as synod of synods, and individual members do not relinquish their own internal structure and governance. Dioceses without a synod may affiliate and FOCUS will provide covering and function as their synod.

FOCUS grew out of a felt need among Orthodox Catholic jurisdictions on the North American continent for a central body for recognition and succor. Members recognize the need to come together in Christ's Holy Name to seek and follow the will of God. It is the stated goal of FOCUS to provide a meeting place where each expression of the ancient Orthodoxia can "come together" and still not fear the loss of individual identity. (The "Orthodox" in the title does not refer to "Eastern" Orthodoxy but rather to the true teachings or Orthodoxia, and the "Catholic" refers to "universal", the original meaning as found in the creeds.) Member jurisdictions are in sacramental communion with each other and can thus provide the sacraments for those individual members of other FOCUS communions who do not reside close to a church or priest of their own jurisdiction.

FOCUS jurisdictions have a wide variety of approved liturgies available for their use, including the Sarum Rite, the Roman Rite (so-called Tridentine Mass) and its revised version of the Novus Ordo, the Liturgy of St. John Chrysostomos, the Liturgy of St. Basil, the Liturgy of St. James, the Western Rite (Sarum) adapted by St. Tikhon, the Gregorian Rite, the Celtic Rite, the Qurbana (conforming to the Councils), and the Gallican Rite.

FOCUS jurisdictions understand that the Holy Church was founded by Jesus Christ who empowered the apostles to bring the church into all the world. In the early centuries, the church grew around five historic centers, the Patriarchates, whose bishops were honored and given special positions as "first among equals". Thus, the church in the world developed as a collegial institution in which the bishops could not exercise jurisdiction or authority beyond their own boundaries or dioceses. The government of the church was conciliar as was demonstrated in the Seven Ecumenical Councils that defined the Christian Faith between the years 325 and 787 C.E.

At present, the Eastern Churches are primarily national churches as manifested in their particular ethnic customs, liturgies, add culture. The great flood of immigrants to America brought this heritage with them, a heritage which in North America has led to a multiplicity of church names, the fragmentation of Orthodoxy, and its isolation into ethnic enclaves. FOCUS affirms the sacramental unity of all Orthodox Catholic jurisdictions who hold to the Faith of Holy Orthodox Catholic Christian Tradition, i.e. Holy Scriptures and the teaching of the Seven Ecumenical Councils and the Holy Fathers. Member jurisdictions regard as sinful the denial and refusing of the Holy Sacraments to believing and practicing Orthodox Catholic Christians who are victims of separation imposed at hierarchical levels.

Member communions may use either the Julian Calendar or the Gregorian Calendar. FOCUS recognizes a hierarchy of spiritual leadership: the bishops, the presbyters, deacons. The highest spiritual office in the church is that of the bishop, and all the FOCUS bishops are equal in authority. Above each bishop is the authority of all the bishops in Council (Synod) under the guidance of the Holy Spirit. While one bishop may preside, such as a metropolitan or archbishop, there is no universal "bishop of bishops".

Membership: The International Federation of Orthodox Catholics United Sacramentally includes the Holy Orthodox Catholic Church, the Metropolitan of the Free Orthodox Church International, the Apostolic Orthodox Catholic Church, Christ Catholic Church International, and the Holy Celtic Church. The ministry of FOCUS members are carried out by 17 bishops and more than 150 clergy and religious among their many ministries.

Educational Facilities: St. Elias School of Orthodox Theology, Lincoln, Nebraska.

★166★
Orthodox Catholic Church in North America
PO Box 321
Monkton, MD 21111-0321

The Orthodox Catholic Church in North America, formerly known as the Holy Eastern Catholic and Apostolic Church in North America, an ecumenical fellowship of various Eastern Orthodox churches, was founded in 1927 and renamed in the 1970s as the Ecumenical Orthodox Catholic Church by Abp. Francis Joseph Ryan (d. 1987). Reportedly, Ryan was consecrated in 1969 by Abp. Walter A. Propheta of the American Orthodox Catholic Church. Originally incorporated as the Ecumenical Orthodox Catholic Church-Autocephalous, the synod continued under that name until 1985 when Ryan was succeeded as Primate-Metropolitan by Abp. Dennis Garrison. It assumed its present name in 1997. Garrison led the synod through a period of expansion. In 1986, he consecrated Renee Bergeron to develop the church in Canada under the name Eglise Equmenique Orthodoxe Occidentale au Canada. In 1988, Garrison was succeeded by Paul Vincent Dolan. Garrison is presently serving his fourth term a Primate.

The Holy Synod of THEOCACNA consists of the bishops of the affiliated churches. Member churches include the American Orthodox Church, the Celtic Orthodox Catholic Church, the Tridentine Orthodox Catholic Church, the Eglise Ecumenique Orthodoxe Occidentle au Canada, the Orthodox Catholic Church— Nigeria, and the Eglise Orthodoxe du Benin.

Membership: Not reported.

★167★
Orthodox Catholic Patriarchate of America
66 N. Brookfield St.
Vineland, NJ 08360

The Orthodox Catholic Patriarchate of America began in 1950 as the Provisional Orthodox Synod of America by the associating together of a number of independent Orthodox jurisdictions. The Provisional Synod in turn authorized the formation of the patriarchate and elected Bp. Joseph Klimovich as its first patriarch. The patriarchate is a coalition of churches joined in faith to the older patriarchal churches headquartered in Antioch, Alexandria, Constantinople (Istanbul), and Jerusalem, but completely separate administratively and not recognized by the older patriarchates. The group was later joined by Abp. Joseph K. C. Pillai of the Indian Orthodox Church.

The driving force in the creation of the patriarchate was Abp. Joseph Klimovich of the American Holy Orthodox Catholic Eastern Church and representatives of the African Orthodox Church, the Autonomous Greek Orthodox Church, the Polish Old Catholic Church in America, and several other small orthodox bodies, including one Canadian Ukrainian jurisdiction. Klimovich died in 1961 and was succeeded by Abp. John Cyril Sherwood, who as patriarch took the name and was thereafter known as Clement I. Following Clement I's death in 1969, Abp. George A. Hyde of the Orthodox Catholic Church of America became the patriarch. He served only until a synod could be called, at which time Archimandrite Pangratios Vrionis was named the new patriarch. Early in 1970 Vrionis was consecrated as Archbishop of the Greek Archdiocese of Vasiloupolis and began his reign as head of the patriarchate. While his church had grown, the patriarchate remained largely an inactive body.

Among the founders of the patriarchate was Peter A. Zurawetzky, a priest consecrated by Klimovich in 1950. In the 1960s he had a dispute with Clement I, whom he accused of stealing the patriarchate. He organized a rival Holy Synod of the Orthodox Catholic Churches of the Americas and Europe. Then in 1975, he discovered that the original charter of the patriarchate had become inactive (as had the patriarchate under Hyde), and he seized the opportunity to take over the corporation, at which time he dissolved his rival body.

Zurawetsky continued to head the minuscule patriarchate, whose member groups were largely paper organizations until his recent death. Among his last acts, in 1993 he turned over his patriarchal authority to the synod of bishops.

Membership: Not reported.

Periodicals: *Our Missionary.*

Sources:

Hyde, George Augustine, ed. *Protocol, The Holy Synod of Bishops, the Orthodox Catholic Patriarchate of America.* Belleair, FL: George Hyde, 1984.

★168★
Standing Conference of Canonical Orthodox Bishops in the Americas
8-10 E. 79th St.
New York, NY 10021

The Standing Conference of Canonical Orthodox Bishops in the Americas was founded in 1960 to express the unity of Orthodoxy in America and to look toward cooperative possibilities among the various ethnic Orthodox communions represented in the United States and Canada. It includes those churches in direct communion with the Ecumenical Patriarch who resides in Constantinople. Due to the spread of Communist governments in many traditionally Orthodox countries, many churches in the West split along political lines over recognition of the various patriarchs then residing under what was seen as hostile and coercive regimes. The Standing Conference represents those churches which remained in communion with the patriarchs through this trying period.

The conference has achieved some measure of success in coordinating activities and reducing duplication of services between member churches in areas such as campus work, Christian education, military and hospital chaplaincies, and ecumenical relationships.

Membership: Membership in the conference includes the following: Albanian Orthodox Diocese of America; American Carpatho-Russian Orthodox Greek Church; Antiochean Orthodox Christian Archdiocese of All North America; Bulgarian Eastern Orthodox Church; Greek Orthodox Archdiocese of North and South America; Orthodox Church in America; Romanian Orthodox Church in America; Serbian Orthodox Church for the U.S.A. and Canada; Ukrainian Orthodox Church of America; and Ukrainian Orthodox Church of Canada.

★169★
Synod of Autonomous Canonical Orthodox Churches in North America
Box 72102
Akron, OH 44372

The Synod of Autonomous Canonical Orthodox Churches in North America was founded in the 1990s as a fellowship of independent Orthodox jurisdictions committed to the faith and gifts given by Christ and the Holy Spirit to the Undivided Church (the Christian community prior to the Great Schism of 1054 C.E. between the Roman Catholic Church and Eastern Orthodoxy). The synod believes it is built on the true Faith and the right administration of the Sacraments, and it stands against the apostasy and Paganism it perceives to be the hallmark of the present age.

Membership: Membership in the synod includes the Orthodox Church of Canada, the Orthodox Catholic Church in North America, the United Orthodox Church in America, and the Celtic Orthodox Christian Church in North America.

Sources:

http://netministries.org/see/churches/ch02059/.

Orthodoxy

★170★
African Orthodox Church
℅ Rt. Rev. Donald A. Smalls
3010 NW 211th St.
Miami, FL 33169

The African Orthodox Church was founded in 1921 following the consecration of Alexander McGuire (1866–1934) as a bishop by Abp. Joseph Rene Vilatte of the American Catholic Church. The ceremony culminated a long search by McGuire, an African American, for recognition for his ministry. McGuire had joined the Episcopal Church in 1895 and was ordained two years later. He served parishes in Cincinnati, Richmond, and Philadelphia before becoming the archdeacon for the Commission for Work Among the Colored People under William Montgomery Brown, the Bishop of Arkansas. In 1911, he became field secretary for the American Church Institute, but two years later left the country for his native Antigua. He remained there for five years as a pastor. Then in 1918 he moved to New York City to participate in the movement led by Marcus Garvey, and the following year left the Episcopal Church to find his own congregation, the Good Shepherd Independent Episcopal Church.

McGuire seems to have settled on the idea of a separate black church with a recognized apostolic succession. He finally obtained that from Vilatte, and upon his return from his consecration was enthroned as the first bishop of the new African Orthodox Church. The new jurisdiction grew quickly, and within two years had parishes in Brooklyn, Pittsburgh, New Haven, and outside the country in Nova Scotia, Cuba, and Santo Domingo, and soon afterwards congregations in Philadelphia, Boston, Florida, and the Bahamas were added. He also initiated an order of deaconesses. Its major appeal was to African Americans of West Indian heritage.

McGuire died in 1934 and was succeeded by William E. J. Robertson. In the wake of the passing of the leadership, the church went through a period of turmoil and several schismatic churches, all now defunct, emerged as bishops left or were suspended from office. However, the time of trouble passed and Robertson remained in the archbishop's throne until his death in 1962. He was succeeded by Richard Grant Robinson (served 1962–1967). Among Robinson's major accomplishments was the reunion he effected with the last remaining group that had left a generation before, the Holy African Church, then under the leadership of Gladstone St. Clair Nurse. Nurse succeeded Robinson as the archbishop of the reunited African Orthodox Church.

Nurse was succeeded in 1976 by William Miller (served 1976–1981) and Stafford Sweeting, the current archbishop.

Membership: In 1983, the church had 17 parishes and reported 5,100 members. Since that time it has not reported, but some of the parishes have left and the church has diminished in size.

Sources:

Newman, Richard. "The Origins of the African Orthodox Church." In *The Negro Churchman.* Millwood, NY: Krause Reprint Co., 1977.

Terry-Thompson, A. C. *The History of the African Orthodox Church.* N.p.: 1956. 139 pp.

Trela, Jonathan. *A History of the North American Old Roman Catholic Church.* Scranton, PA: The Author, 1979. 124 pp.

★171★
African Orthodox Church of New York and Massachusetts
(Defunct)

The African Orthodox Church of New York and Massachusetts was founded in the mid-1930s by Reginald Grant Barrow (1889–1979), a bishop in the African Orthodox Church. Barrow had been born in Barbados but migrated to the United States, where he became one of the founding members of the African Orthodox Church in 1921. In 1925 Barrow became the fourth bishop of the church. In 1934 Abp. George A. McGuire died and was succeeded by Bp. William E. J. Robertson. Robertson resided in Miami, Florida, where the church was incorporated. Church affairs in New York, where the church had its greatest strength, were placed in the hands of Frederick A. Toote, the vicar general. Barrow, Toote, and two bishops, Arthur Stanley Trotman and Robert Arthur Valentine, moved to take control of the church in the northeast by founding a separate jurisdiction, which they called the African Orthodox Church of New York and Massachusetts.

A short time after the founding of the new church, Barrow had a falling out with Trotman, who left to found the African Orthodox Church, Inc. Archbishop Robertson moved legally against both Barrow and Trotman, and in 1938 the court ruled that they were illegitimately using the name African Orthodox Church. Trotman renamed his group the Holy African Church. Barrow soon patched up his differences with Trotman, and his jurisdiction was absorbed into the Holy African Church, which eventually reunited into the African Orthodox Church in 1964.

Sources:

Terry-Thompson, A. C. *The History of the African Orthodox Church.* N.p.: the author, 1956.

★172★
African Orthodox Church of the West
℅ G. Duncan Hinkson
St. Augustine's African Orthodox Church
5831 S. Indiana St.
Chicago, IL 60637

In 1984 Bishop G. Duncan Hinkson, a physician and pastor of St. Augustine's African Orthodox Church, on the southside of Chicago, left the African Orthodox Church and formed a new jurisdiction. While following the teachings and ritual of its parent body, it is administratively independent. Bishop Hinkson consecrated Bishop Franzo King to lead work in San Francisco.

Membership: In 1992, the church had two parishes, one in Chicago and one in California with several hundred members.

Periodicals: *Expression.* Available from One Mind Temple, 351 Divisadero St., San Francisco, CA 94117.

★173★
Albanian Orthodox Archdiocese in America
℅ Metropolitan Theodosius
529 E. Broadway
Boston, MA 02127

The Albanian Orthodox Archdiocese in America can be traced to 1908, when the first Albanian parish in the U.S. was established in Boston. In the same year, an Albanian-American immigrant, Fan Stylin Noli, was ordained to the priesthood by Metropolitan Platon of the Russian Orthodox Church. Father Noli returned to Albania in 1920 where he had a prominent political career, eventually becoming prime minister. He became a bishop in 1923, but in 1930 (due to Turkish domination of Albania), he returned to the United States and organized the American parishes into the Albanian Orthodox Archdiocese in America. The Archdiocese re-

mained in communion with the Church in Albania until after World War II when a Communist government hostile to the Church took control of the country, and, in the eyes of the Archdiocese, subverted the leadership of the Church. While retaining orthodox belief and practice, the Archdiocese became independent. Noli was succeeded by Metropolitan Theodosius.

Membership: In 1996 the archdiocese reported 2 parishes, 1,995 members and 2 priests.

Periodicals: *The Vineyard (Vreshta).* Send orders to 5490 Main St., Trumbull, CT 06611.

★174★
Albanian Orthodox Diocese of America
℅ Rev. Ik. Ilia Katre, Vicar General
6455 Silver Dawn Ln.
Las Vegas, NV 89118

In 1950 His Grace Bishop Mark I. Lipa came to the United States with authority from the Ecumenical Patriarch in Constantinople to organize the Albanian faithful. The following year he formed the Albanian Orthodox Diocese of America. It is a member of the Standing Conference of Canonical Orthodox Bishops in the Americas. Bishop Mark died on March 23, 1982.

Membership: In 1997 the diocese reported 2 parishes, 1,700 members, and 2 clergy.

★175★
All Faiths Ecumenical Diocese of the South and Southwest
℅ Mt. Rev. Leo E. Rondeau
1204-1206 House St.
El Paso, TX 79903

The All Faiths Ecumenical Diocese of the South and Southwest was founded by Bp. Leo E. Rondeau, who was consecrated in 1985 by Bp. Francis Joseph Ryan of the Ecumenical Orthodox Catholic Church-Autocephalous. Rondeau had originally been consecrated by Charles David Luther of the Western Orthodox Church. Rondeau is assisted by Bp. Raymond Hefner, his auxiliary, also ordained by Luther and consecrated by Ryan.

Membership: Not reported.

Sources:

Ward, Gary L. *Independent Bishops: An International Directory.* Detroit, MI: Apogee Books, 1990.

★176★
American Carpatho-Russian Orthodox Greek Catholic Church
℅ Metropolitan Nicholas Smisko
312 Garfield St.
Johnstown, PA 15906

The American Carpatho-Russian Orthodox Greek Catholic Church was founded in the 1930s by a group of former members of the Roman Catholic Church who had migrated to the United States from Carpatho-Russia. Carpatho-Russia had been forcefully converted from Eastern Orthodoxy to the Roman Catholic Ruthenian Rite by a series of rulers who basically followed the Latin Rite. Once in the United States, a process of further Latinizing Ruthenian Rite parishes began. Among other issues, attempts were made to curtail the assignment of married priests to American parishes.

As early as 1891, a Carpatho-Russian Catholic parish sought to return to Eastern Orthodoxy. It was soon joined by others. Then in 1936, approximately forty parishes which had left Roman jurisdiction organized and selected Orestes P. Chornock as their leader. The next year they designated him their bishop-elect and turned to the ecumenical patriarch in Constantinople for recognition. In 1938 the patriarch consecrated Chornock and authorized the American Carpatho-Russian Orthodox Diocese as an independent body. In 1966 the patriarch elevated Chornock to the dignity of a metropolitan. The present ruling bishop is the Metropolitan Nicholas Smisko.

The American Carpatho-Russian Orthodox Greek Catholic Church is an independent autonomous body directly under the authority of the ecumenical patriarch. It has a working relationship with the Greek Orthodox Archdiocese of North and South America, whose archbishop is the exarch of the patriarch. The archbishop intercedes when the appointment of a new bishop is requested by the church and has the task of consecrating him. The church is at one with Eastern Orthodox faith and practice, though its liturgy still retains a few minor peculiarities reflective of its Roman Catholic history. The church is a member of the Standing Conference of Canonical Orthodox Bishops in the Americas.

Membership: In 1992 the Church reported 74 parishes, 100,000 members, and 82 priests.

Educational Facilities: Christ the Savior Seminary, Johnstown, Pennsylvania.

Periodicals: *Cerkovny Vistnik—Church Messenger.* Send orders to 280 Clinton St., Binghamton, NY 13905. • *A.C.R.Y. Annual.* Send orders to PO Box 777, Barton, OH 43905.

★177★
American Eastern Orthodox Catholic Church
5330 Oakhill Dr.
Alger, MI 48610

The American Eastern Orthodox Catholic Church was founded in 1977 by a group of clergy and laity who were Orthodox in faith but who wished to escape the national and political bigotry that they felt characterized the life of the older ethnic Orthodox churches. The group constituted a synod and elected Fr. Martin de Porres as their bishop. He was consecrated on January 29, 1977, by Most Rev. Thomas Ephraim (the ecclesiastical name of Bishop Dennis Smith) of the Reformed Orthodox Catholic Church and Bishop R. Michael Chaffee of the Byzantine Ecumenical Catholic Church. The church was incorporated in 1980 as the Christist Orthodox Catholic Church, but officially changed its name in 1982. The same year, the church sent a letter and papers to the ecumenical Patriarch Demetrios I, the spiritual head of the Eastern Orthodox communion, seeking to come under his jurisdiction. A Holy Antimensia (blessing) was received in return but, to date, no action has been taken on the church's request for union with the Ecumenical Patriarch.

In 1984, the American Eastern Orthodox Catholic Church aligned itself with the Western Orthodox Catholic Church of California headed by Metropolitan Martin J. Hill. Later that year, following concern being raised about the consecration of Bishop Martin de Porres by only two bishops (instead of the usual three demanded in Orthodox lineages), de Porres was consecrated *sub conditione* by Patriarch Andre Barbeau (Andre I), head of the Catholic Charismatic Church of Canada, assisted by bishops Andre Letellier and Bruce Rodgers. In 1990 the union between the Western Orthodox Catholic Church of California and the American Eastern Orthodox Catholic Church came to an end.

The American Eastern Orthodox Catholic Church is Orthodox in faith and practice. It accepts the teachings of the seven ecumenical councils. There are two dioceses, one in Michigan where Bishop de Porres resides, and one in southern California under the leadership of R. Michael Cullinan. Besides its parishes in southern California, the church has established St. Francis of Assisi Orthodox Mission and the Queen of Peace Orthodox Center, an ecumenical project working for world peace and brotherhood, in Alger, Michigan (near Flint). There is also a parish in Detroit, Michigan, and a mission in Seattle, Washington, with a ministry to people with AIDS. Women are welcomed into the ministry of the church which will ordain them to the office of deacon.

Membership: In 1995 the church reported approximately 300 members and 16 priests in the United States and 7 members and one priest in Canada.

Periodicals: *Queen of Peace Orthodox Newsletter.*

Sources:

The American Eastern Orthodox Catholic Church: A Brief History. Alger, MI: American Eastern Orthodox Catholic Church, 1994, 50 pp.

★178★
American Eastern Orthodox Church
(Defunct)

Since the second century, India has had Eastern Orthodox churches that call themselves Mar Thomas churches. They claim that St. Thomas the Apostle founded them. In the 1930s the Church of England was India's state church. When the Christian Missionary Society of the Church of England attempted to convert members of the Mar Thomas churches, a controversy arose. One of its results was that Bishop Anthony Devan left India and came to the U.S. to locate members of the Mar Thomas churches residing there. He succeeded in locating a few families, and he ordained four priests, thus establishing the American Eastern Orthodox Church. It continues the tradition of the Mar Thomas Christians. It is one in faith and practice with the Orthodox churches. St. Thomas is honored on the Sunday after the Resurrection (Easter), July 19 (his birthday), and October 19 (anniversary of his martyrdom). The Liturgy of St. Basil is used.

Membership: In 1973 there were 5 parishes, 5 mission stations and 1,240 members.

Sources:

Following Christ in the American Eastern Orthodox Church. Las Vegas, NV: St. George Monastery, 1967.

★179★
American Exarchate of the True (Old Calendar) Orthodox Church of Greece
℅ St. Gregory Palamas Monastery
Box 398
Etna, CA 96027

Alternate Address: International headquarters: c/o His Eminence, the Most Reverend Cyprian, Metropolitan of Oropos and Fili, Bishop-Abbot of the Holy Monastery of Saints Cyprian and Justina, T. Th. 45004, 135 10 Agrioi Anargyroi (Athens), Greece.

Since World War II, the Old Calendar Movement (which adheres to the old or Julian calendar rather than the more modern Gregorian calendar) has grown within the Church of Greece. One issue that divided the movement, as it separated from the state church, was whether any saving grace (hence efficacious mysteries) remained in the Church of Greece. The Old Calendarists associated with Metropolitan Cyprian are the main group acknowledging that such grace does truly remain with what is otherwise a church that has departed from the faith on various issues.

The monastery headed by Metropolitan Cyprian had originally accepted the Gregorian calendar but returned to the Julian calendar in 1967 and broke relationships with the state church two years later. The monastery accepted the authority of the Old Calendarist officials. Cyprian was consecrated in 1979. The Old Calendar Movement in Greece was disrupted in the early 1980s, and the various factions independently reorganized. The more moderate factions accepted Cyprian as their leader. They look for a possible future reunion with the state church of Greece, seeing a return to the Julian calendar and a rejection of what they view as the excesses as the primary obstacles to a reunion.

Besides its associated parishes in Greece, the church has large missions in Sweden, France, Italy, and Kenya. The work in the United States is centered in St. Gregory Palamas Monastery and the Convent of St. Elizabeth the Grand Dutches of Russia, both in Etna, California, where the church's American exarch headed by Most Reverend Chrysostomos is located. Assisting him is Bishop Auxentios. The church maintains canonical communion with the

Russian Orthodox Church of Russia and the Old Calendarist Churches in Bulgaria and Romania.

Membership: In 1993 the church reported 1,000 members, seven parishes, and 12 priests in the United States, and a Canadian mission in Winnipeg, Manitoba.

Educational Facilities: Center for Traditionalist Orthodox Studies, Etna, California.

Periodicals: *Orthodox Tradition.*

Sources:

Chrysostomos, Archimandrite, with Hieromonk Ambrosios and Hieromonk Auxentios. *The Old Calendar Orthodox Church of Greece.* Etna, CA: Center for Traditionalist Orthodox Studies, 1986.

"Greek Old Calendarists in the U.S.A.: An Annotated Directory." *Orthodox Tradition* 2, 2 (1985): 49-61.

★180★
American Hebrew Eastern Orthodox Greek Catholic Church

Current address not obtained for this edition.

The American Hebrew Eastern Orthodox Greek Catholic Church is a small Orthodox jurisdiction founded by Bp. Gregory Voris following his consecration by Bp. Robert Marshall of the Evangelical Catholic Church on December 21, 1963. Marshall had originally consecrated Voris in 1957, but in 1963 they participated in a ceremony in which they mutually exchanged consecrations. Also associated with Voris are Bps. David R. Vashon, James Griffis, Ronald I. Bessler, and Kenneth L. Hite.

Membership: Not reported.

Sources:

Ward, Gary L. *Independent Bishops: An International Directory.* Detroit, MI: Apogee Books, 1990.

★181★
American Holy Orthodox Catholic Eastern Church
(Defunct)

The American Holy Orthodox Catholic Eastern Church was incorporated in 1933 under the leadership of Cyril John Clement Sherwood, popularly known by his ecclesiastical name, Clement I. His Holiness Clement I had previously belonged to the Benedictine community founded by Archbishop W. H. Francis Brothers of the Old Catholic Church in America. In 1927, however, he received priestly orders from Archbishop Frederick E. J. Lloyd of the American Catholic Church and three years later was consecrated by Bishop William F. Tyarks of the African Orthodox Church. He was then reconsecrated in 1932 by Bishop George A. McGuire of the American Catholic Orthodox Church, and throughout the rest of his life he considered this latter consecration as his true one.

The American Holy Orthodox Catholic Eastern Church followed Eastern Orthodox faith and practice, but it was established as a completely autocephalous jurisdiction, autonomous of all foreign bishops and church bodies. Headquarters of the church were established in Sts. Peter and Paul Church in New York City. For a while Clement issued a periodical, *The Voice of the Community.* Clement founded a coalition of various independent orthodox and catholic bishops, the Orthodox Catholic Patriarchate of America. Clement died in 1969. Following his death, leadership of the Patriarchate passed to Archbishop George A. Hyde of the Orthodox Catholic Church of America. In succeeding years, the already weakened organization ceased to exist (though it has recently been re-established by Archbishop Alfred Louis Lankenau) who succeeded Hyde as head of the Orthodox Church in America. At the same time, the American Holy Orthodox Catholic Apostolic Eastern Church was received into the Orthodox Catholic Church in America as its Eastern Rite Diocese, and it ceased to exist as a separate body.

★182★
American National Catholic Church (Bridges)
Box 472
San Bernardino, CA 92402

The American National Catholic Church was founded in 1976 by Richard W. Bridges, whose episcopal orders were conferred in 1980 by Bishops Gregory Voris, C. Engel, and Hans Kroneberg. It adheres to the faith of the Seven Ecumenical Councils and the Three Ecumenical Creeds, and it is designed to use both Eastern and Western rites. While not open to ordaining females to the priesthood, it is open to receiving homosexuals into Holy Orders. Through the 1980s, the church was known as the American Independent Orthodox Church but adopted its present name around 1990. Archbishop Bridges attained some fame in 1990 when he consecrated Fr. George A. Stallings as the bishop of the African-American Catholic Congregation.

Membership: Not reported. In the early 1980s, the Church claimed 2 parishes, 3 priests and 75 members.

★183★
American Orthodox Catholic and Apostolic Church
PO Box 8041
Charlotte, NC 29202-8041

The American Orthodox Catholic and Apostolic Church was founded in 1922 by Abp. Vladimir Sehorn, formerly a bishop of the Holy Eastern Orthodox Catholic and Apostolic Church in North America. Sehorn had been consecrated in 1987 by Apb. Dennis Garrison, then THEOCACNA's Primate-Metropolitan. The new church follows Orthodox faith and practice, the issues involved in its establishment being administrative.

Membership: Not reported.

★184★
American Orthodox Catholic Church (Healy)
(Defunct)

One of the several jurisdictions formed by clergy who were with Archbishop Walter A. Propheta's American Orthodox Catholic Church, this jurisdiction of the same name was formed by Bishop Lawrence Pierre, formerly the Auxiliary Bishop for New York and the Eastern States. It continued the beliefs and practices as well as the name of Propheta's Church, being bi-ritualistic (i.e, it allowed both Eastern and Western liturgies be used in its parishs' worship services). Archbishop Pierre was succeeded by Archbishop Patrick J. Healy as primate. Upon the death of Healy in 1984, the jurisdiction dissolved.

★185★
American Orthodox Catholic Church (Irene)
851 Leyden St.
Denver, CO 80220

The American Orthodox Catholic Church (Irene) was founded in 1962 and incorporated three years later. Its presiding head is a female-bishop known only as Archbishop Irene, consecrators unknown. Spokesperson of the Church is Bishop Emeritus Milton A. Pritts, who had been consecrated by Archbishop Walter A. Propheta of the American Orthodox Catholic Church.

The Church is Orthodox in faith and practice, accepting the forms presented in the *Service Book* edited by Isabel Florence Hapgood, and the principles enuciated in such standard orthodox volumes as Fr. John Meyendorff's *The Orthodox Church.* The Revised Standard Version of the Bible is used. It differs in the following: 1) It would consider otherwise qualified women and homosexuals for the priesthood; and 2) It believes that apostolic succession is not necessary to the establishment of a valid church or ministry. A resolution passed by the Grant Synod of the Church, January 6, 1979 stated, "We now hold with the Churches of England, Sweden, Congregational, Presbyterian, Lutheran, Methodist, Christian Scientists, and others who are determined to revive lay selection and authority of the congregation to avoid the further creation of hierarchies."

Although renouncing the necessity of apostolic succession and the idea of building further hierarchies, the church has claimed to have a ministry with valid apostolic episcopal orders and claims to have built an elaborate hierarchy. The jurisdiction, divided into 53 dioceses, is spread over all of North America. Apart from Bishop Pritts, the names of Church officers and bishops and the addresses of their diocesan headquarters have not been available for publication.

Membership: Not reported. There is some doubt as to the size of this Church in light of the unverifiable nature of its claims and the inability to locate any parishes associated with Bishop Pritts or Archbishop Irene.

★186★
American Orthodox Catholic Church (Kochones)
810 E. Walnut St.
Pasadena, CA 91101

The American Orthodox Catholic Church was founded in 1969 as the Church of God in the Lord Jesus Christ by Bishop Steven A. Kochones (1931-). Kochones was raised as a member of the Greek Orthodox Archdiocese of North and South America, but left the jurisdiction as a young man. In 1956 he was ordained as a minister in the Independent Assemblies of God, a Protestant church of pentecostal faith, after he had experienced the baptism of the Holy Spirit as evidenced by speaking in tongues. After some years as a pentecostal minister, Kochones was drawn back to his Orthodox heritage and in 1967 accepted ordination as an Orthodox priest by Archbishop Walter A. Propheta of the American Orthodox Catholic Church (Propheta).

In 1969 he established the Church of God in the Lord Jesus Christ, an independent church in fellowship with the American Orthodox Catholic Church (Propheta). It combined Orthodox faith with pentecostal piety and some insights from messianic Judaism. Kochones developed a system of seven sacraments and seven sacramentals. The seven sacraments were baptism and confirmation, confession and absolution, holy eucharist and holy communion, ministry and priesthood, marriage and home life, private and public prayer, and preaching and teaching. The seven sacramentals were: bowing/kneeling to pray/praise; choruses, hymns, and psalms in singing; clapping or uplifted hands in prayer; dancing and singing in the Holy Spirit; music and drama; making the sign of the cross and smiting the breast; and tongues, prophecy, and interpretation. The church used Jewish symbols such as the Star of David in its iconography, and speaks of God as Yahweh. It acknowledged the continuing validity of the seventh-day sabbath, and services are held on both Saturday and Sunday.

The church observes the biblical dietary laws as found in Leviticus. Women, otherwise meeting ordination requirements, may be ordained to the priesthood.

In 1979, following a burglary at the headquarter's church in Pasadena, at which time the corporation papers and seal were stolen, the church's name was changed (for legal reasons) to the Catholic Church of God. The church's symbol combined a latin cross, a star of David, and the Jewish seven-stemmed candelabra. The name chosen also reflected a trend within the church to bring it more in line with the perceptions of the historical and ancient church being made by Kochones. Included in this trend was a new emphasis on apostolic succession, and Kochones began to seek consecration as a bishop. He was consecrated in 1980 by Bishop David Baxter of the Orthodox Church of America.

In 1989 The Catholic Church of God changed its name to the American Orthodox Catholic Church, though it remains separate from the jurisdiction of the same name of late founded by Archbishop Propheta.

Membership: Not reported.
Periodicals: *Orthodox Messenger.*

Sources:

The Christian Liturgy. Pasadena, CA: Church of God in the Lord Jesus Christ, 1977. 9 pp.

The Feast of Passover. Pasadena, CA: Church of God in the Lord Jesus Christ, n.d. 8 pp.

Ward, Gary L. *Independent Bishops: An International Directory.* Detroit, MI: Apogee Books, 1990. 524 pp.

★187★
American Orthodox Catholic Church (Propheta)
Current address not obtained for this edition.

History. The American Orthodox Catholic Church was incorporated in 1965 by Walter A. Propheta (1912-1972), a former Ukrainian Orthodox priest. In 1964 he was consecrated to the episcopacy by Archbishop Theoklitos of Salamis of the Old Calendar Greek Jurisdiction, Greece. The following year he was elevated to archbishop by Archbishop Theodotus and Archbishop Joachim Souris, Old Calendar Greek Jurisdiction, United States. He continued with the task of building an independent and indigenous American Orthodoxy as already initiated by his direct predecessor The Most Rev. Aftimios Ofiesh, Archbishop of Brooklyn, who in 1927 received canonically and formally from the Synod of Bishops of the American Dioceses of the Russian Orthodox Church the mandate to initiate an American Orthodox Catholic Church. As Archbishop and Patriarch Wolodymyr I (as Propheta was ecclesiastically known), he ordained and consecrated a number of clergymen who became part of his jurisdiction. Some of them left the jurisdiction and founded their own autonomous groups and others were received into different jurisdictions as a result of the struggle for the control of the church after Propheta's death.

Archbishop John A. Christian (d. 1984), consecrated to the episcopacy and elevated to archbishop by Archbishops Propheta, Theodotus, and Souris, was elected and enthroned as Propheta's successor in a synod held in 1972.

Archbishop Dom Lorenzo O.S.B., was consecrated to the episcopacy on 1977 by the Most Rev. Ryzy-Ryski, Archbishop of New England and New Hampshire and by the Most Rev. Lawrence Pierre, Archbishop of New York, both of the American Orthodox Catholic Church jurisdiction. Archbishop Christian, on 1978, just before his retirement, elevated him to Archbishop for the Metropolitan See of New York, and appointed him as Apostolic Administrator of the Jurisdiction. The American Orthodox Catholic Church Holy Synod, in 1982, ratified and approved this appointment and confirmed him as the Metropolitan Primate of the Church.

Beliefs. The American Orthodox Catholic Church is Orthodox in doctrine and follows the decrees of the seven Ecumenical Councils. It adheres to the Nicene Creed and requires only adherence to the traditional Orthodox text. It allows the Western text to be used if the disputed filioque clause is understood in an Orthodox sense of a single procession. (Note: The filioque clause, "from the Son," was added to the Nicene Creed by the Roman Catholic Church and is generally not used in Eastern Orthodox Churches. It refers to a complicated theological argument concerning the relation of the Holy Spirit to the Trinity.) The church professes that charity, godliness, and truthfulness are more important than strict doctrinal definitions. A variety of rites are allowed, though the Eastern is most frequently used.

Organization. The church follows an episcopal polity and is governed by the Primate and the Holy Synod. The practice of a celibate clergy is by and large maintained, but secular deacons and priests may be married before ordination. (Special dispensations for marriage after ordination may be granted by the Holy

Synod.) On disciplinary issues, the church follows the canons of the Ecumenical Councils.

Membership: In 1992 the church reported five congregations and two monasteries in the United States, a European Exarcate with several congregations in Italy, and a Latin-American Exarcate with several churches in Brazil and Argentina. Membership is estimated to be several thousand.

Educational Facilities: God's Benevolence Institute, Spokane, Washington.

Remarks: Among the most active centers of the American Orthodox Catholic Church has been God's Benevolence Institute headed by Bishop Patrick McReynolds. The institute is an interdenominational association for ancient studies and practices with the goal of establishing a monastery of "canons regular and secular," the Community of God's Benevolence. McReynolds had originally started the community after being ordained for an independent ministry by Bishop Michael A. Itkin of the Community of the Love of Christ (Evangelical Catholic). In 1975 he was consecrated by Edward C. Payne and became suffragan bishop of the Independent Catholic Church. In 1981 he left Payne and subsequently became a bishop in the American Orthodox Catholic Church.

McReynolds is one of the most educated of the independent bishops, having received his master's degree from Fordham and as of 1988 being enrolled in a Ph.D. program at UCLA. Prior to his moving to Los Angeles, California, McReynolds built the institute's work in Spokane, Washington, where there is a small congregation, God's Benevolence Orthodox Catholic Church. In 1988, there were five fellows and 25 associate fellows in the institute in Spokane and a second chapter being built in Los Angeles.

Sources:

American Orthodox Catholic Church, Ecclesiatical History. Los Angeles: Archdiocese of So. California and the Western Province, 1974.

Propheta, Walter M. *Divine Liturgy for 20th Century Christians.* New York: American Orthodox Church, 1966.

★188★
American Orthodox Church
% Archbishop Aftimios Harold J. Donovan, Exarch
San Antonio, Los Vanos
Laguna 3732, Philippines

The American Orthodox Church was established in 1981 by Harold Donovan as the Orthodox American Catholic Church, Diocese of the Ozarks under a charter from the Orthodox Church of the Philippines. Donovan was originally consecrated by Bishops Howard Fris and John Kenelly of the Old Roman Catholic Church, Archdiocese of Chicago. However, in 1982, Donovan was reconsecrated by Archbishop John A. Christian of the American Orthodox Catholic Church (Propheta) in order to establish formal continuity with the original American Orthodox Church established by Archbishop Aftimios Ofiesh in the 1920s. Donovan took the religious name of the late archbishop and is currently known as Archbishop Aftimios Donovan. On January 1983, Archbishop Christian, in cooperation with the Orthodox Church in the Philippines, established an exarchate known as the North American Synod of the Holy Eastern Orthodox Catholic and Apostolic Church (shortened to its present name the following year).

The Church follows Eastern Orthodox belief and practice. The liturgy of St. Germain is used and sacraments are administered according to the American Rite of St. Germain, an abbreviated and modified formula based upon the Byzantine Rite.

The exarchate retains formal ties to both the Orthodox Church in the Philippines and the American Orthodox Catholic Church headed by Archbishop Christian. Its parish work includes two missions in Los Angeles, one to Oriental-Americans and one to Hispanic-Americans.

Membership: In 1984 the Church reported 3 parishes, 3 clergy, and less than 150 members.

Educational Facilities: Seminary of the Orthodox Catholic Church in the Philippines, Manila, Philippines.

Periodicals: *The Orthodox Catholic.* Send orders to Box 389, Ozark, MO 65721.

Sources:

The Liturgy. Springfield, MO: American Orthodox Church, 1983.

★189★
American Orthodox Church
% Saint Christopher Paris
PO Box 321
Monkton, MD 21111-0321

The American Orthodox Chruch was founded in 1992 by four former bishops of the Holy Eastern Orthodox Catholic and Apostolic Church in North America. Two of the bishops, Dennis Garrison and Paul Vincent Dolan had, at one time, been Primate-Metropolitan of THEOCACNA. The new denomination is Orthodox in faith and practice, and continues the vision an American Orthodoxy first enunciated by Abp. Aftimios Ofiesh.

As organized, the church has four dioceses: Baltimore (Maryland), headed by Archbishop Garrison; Philadelphia (Pennsylvania), headed by Archbishop Dolan; Hickory (North Carolina), headed by Bp. D. Michael Martinat; and the Diocese of the Ozarks, headed by Bp. Victor Prentice.

Membership: Not reported.

★190★
American Orthodox Exarchate: Archdiocese of North America
1829 Coronada Ave.
Youngstown, OH 44504

The American Orthodox Exarchate: Archdiocese of North America was founded in 1989 by the Most Rev. Donald L. Locke (1930-), its Metropolitan Archbishop. Archbishop Locke was ordained to the priesthood by James F. Mondok, who had left the Western Orthodox Church in America the previous year and founded Christ Catholic Orthodox Church. Locke was consecrated as a bishop in Christ Catholic Orthodox Church in February 1988. In December 1988 he was elevated to archiepiscopal status by Most Rev. Andre Barbeau of the Catholic Charismatic Church of Canada.

The Exarchate exists as an autocephalous and autonomous jurisdiction under mandate from the Moscow Patriarchate of the Russian Orthodox Church. Locke is open to relationships with sister orthodox churches and has invited bishops from the Ukranian Eastern Orthodox Church (Most Rev. Ignatius Cash), Apostolic Orthodox Church of Canada (Most Rev. Renee Bergeron), and the Catholic Charismatic Church of Canada (Most Rev. Walter G. Allard).

The Exarchate includes parishes with both an Eastern and Western orientation and congregations may use either the Orthodox liturgy of St. John Chrysostom (in English) or the modified Roman Catholic liturgy. Priests may use both Eastern and Western style liturgical garments as the occasion demands.

Membership: Not reported.

Educational Facilities: The St. Clement's School for Theological Studies, Maine.

Sources:

Ward, Gary L. *Independent Bishops: An International Directory.* Detroit, MI: Apogee Books, 1990. 524 pp.

American Synod: Holy Orthodox Catholic Church
℅ Abp.
12245 E. 14th Ave., No. 110
Aurora, CO 80011

Alternate Address: The Orthodox, Byzantine, Old Calendar Diocese of Berkeley, 1671 Golden Gate Ave. 2, San Francisco, CA 94115.

The American Synod: Holy Orthodox Catholic Church was established in 1969 in Denver, Colorado, by bishops of the earlier existing American Orthodox Catholic Church. The Metropolitan since the Church's inception has been the Most Rev. Colin James Guthrie. The church underwent a reorganization in 1984 and, for a brief while, took the name of the Holy Synod of Denver (1984-1986).

The church has had congregations and ministries in a number of western and midwestern states. During the 1970s, it counted among its members Abp. Bartholomew Cunningham, who was noted for his efforts to extend Orthodoxy among Americans at large and for his positive and friendly contacts with ethnic Orthodox hierarchs.

The American Synod is organized into two dioceses, the Archdiocese of Denver and the Diocese of Berkeley. The latter diocese follows the Old Calendar observance.

The church traces it episcopal orders to independent Old Calendar Greek Archbishop Christopher Contogeorge and Albanian Archbishop Theophan Noli, who in the 1940s established Orthodoxy in New England among people not traditionally or ethnically Orthodox.

Membership: Not reported. In 1992, there were parishes in California, New Mexico, and Washington, D.C.

Sources:

Guthrie, Colin J. *A Brief History of the American Synod, Holy Orthodox Catholic Church.* Denver, CO: Office of the Metropolitan Archbishop, 1991.

American World Patriarchs
℅ Most Rev. Emigidius J. Ryzy
19 Aqueduct St.
Ossining, NY 10562

Uladyslau Ryzy-Ryski (1925-78), a Belarusan priest, was consecrated in 1965 by Archbishop Walter A. Propheta of the American Orthodox Catholic Church as the Bishop of Laconia, New Hampshire and the New England States. During this period he also met Archbishop Peter A. Zurawetzky of the Old Orthodox Catholic Patriarchate of America, who on November 4, 1967, in the presence of a congregation of four, elevated him to the status of Archbishop. Without leaving Propheta's jurisdiction, Ryzy-Ryski began to create archbishops-patriarchs for each national/ethnic group and, quite apart from any laity demanding leadership, to build a hierarchy which he envisioned as international in scope. The World Patriarchate was very loosely structured, and established in large part by the elevation to patriarchial status of other independent bishops not otherwise required to recognize Ryzy-Ryski's authority or come under his jurisdiction. In 1972, as one of the last acts before his death, Propheta excommunicated Ryzy-Ryski from the American Orthodox Catholic Church, an action which merely spurred the growth of the American World Patriarchs, who established patriarchs for Canada, Hungary, Germany, Puerto Rico, Colombia, Haiti, Santo Domingo, Brazil, Peru, Argentina, El Salvador, Nigeria, the West Indies, Norway, Sweden, Formosa, and the Ukraine. Only rarely were new congregations established as a result of a patriarch being named. Occasionally, the new patriarch could claim a small following.

In connection with the American World Patriarchs, Ryzy-Ryski organized the Peoples University of the Americas, an educational center designed to meet the needs of various ethnic and immigrant groups in the Bronx, New York. A well-educated man, with a good academic background, he led a faculty which offered a wide variety of courses in the humanities, and especially in English as a second language. The school also provided the World Patriarchs with a seminary.

Since the death of Patriarch Uladyslau Ryzy-Ryski in 1978, the work has continued under his brother, Archbishop Emigidius J. Ryzy, who holds the title of Apostolic Administrator of All American World Patriarchates. He is assisted by Archbishop Adam Bilecky, Patriarch II of the American World Patriarchate Archbishop Frank Barquera, and Bishop Piot Huszoza.

Membership: In 1988 the church reported 19,457 members, 17 congregations, and 54 priests in the United States. There were also one congregation and three priests in Canada. Affiliated work was to be found in 17 foreign countries. The newest work in Ryzy-Ryski homeland, Belarus. There are a reported 54,542 members worldwide.

Educational Facilities: Peoples University of the Americas, American College and Seminary, Bronx, New York.

Universidad de los Pueblos de las Americas, San Juan, Puerto Rico.

Antiochean Orthodox Christian Archdiocese of North America
358 Mountain Rd.
Englewood, NJ 07631

In 1895, the Russian Orthodox Church began a Syrian Mission in the United States to provide spiritual guidance for Orthodox Christians from the Eastern Mediterranean basin. In 1904, the first Orthodox bishop ever consecrated in North America, Archimandrite Raphael Hawaweeny, became the bishop of the Syrian Mission of the Russian Orthodox Church. Then in 1914 Metropolitan Germanos came to the United States and began organizing Syrian churches. These two efforts paralleled each other until 1925 when an independent church was created. In 1936, Archimandrite Anthony Bashir was elected and consecrated bishop by the American Syrian churches. He became metropolitan of New York and all North America in 1940 and provided leadership for 30 years.

In the 1936 election in which Bashir was elected to the bishopric, Archimandrite Samuel David of Toledo, Ohio, polled the second highest number of votes. On the same day that Abp. Bashir was consecrated in New York, Russian bishops consecrated Samuel David as archbishop of Toledo. Abp. Samuel David was condemned and excommunicated in 1938 but then recognized the following year. The Antiochean Orthodox Archdiocese of Toledo, Ohio, and Dependencies that he led existed as a separate body until 1975.

In 1966, the Mt. Rev. Philip Saliba succeeded Bashir and became primate of the Antiochian Orthodox Christian Archdiocese of New York and All North America. Archbishop Philip has been a leader in promoting the use of English in the liturgy. He has given priority to missions and has emphasized the cause of Orthodox unity in North America and abroad.

In 1958, Archbishop Samuel David died, and hope for reunion of the two Antiochian churches emerged. Abp. Michael Shaheen succeeded Archbishop Samuel and conducted talks toward union, which were finally consummated in 1975. The new Antiochian Orthodox Christian Archdiocese of North America selected Archbishop Philip as head of the church with the title of Metropolitan. There are four auxiliary bishops: Bishop Antoun, Bishop Joseph, Bishop Basil, and Bishop Demetri.

Membership: In 1997, the archdiocese reported 215 parishes and missions, 350,000 members, and 400 priests.

Periodicals: *The Word.* Send orders to 1777 Quigg Dr., Pittsburgh, PA 15241-2071. • *Again.* Send orders to Box 106, Mt. Hermon, CA 95041.

Remarks: In February 1987, the former Evangelical Orthodox Church (EOC) was received as a body into the Antiochian Orthodox Christian Archdiocese of North America, thus ending for its members a pilgrimage that began almost two decades earlier. The Evangelical Orthodox Church had its roots in the late 1960s, when a number of the staff of Campus Crusade for Christ left their positions. Some launched independent ministries; some affiliated with various independent evangelical churches. In the early 1970s seven of these leaders—Peter Gilquist, John Braun, Dick Ballew, Ken Berven, and Jack Sparks—banded together as the New Covenant Apostolic Order (NCAO).

The formation of the NCAO afforded a context for study which led to a concentrated reappraisal of a common view of Evangelical Protestant Christians that the first century church had become corrupted over the centuries until restored by Evangelicals in relatively modern times. Gathering in Chicago in 1979, the leaders of the movement announced the formation of the Evangelical Orthodox Church to supercede the NCAO and to call Evangelicals back to their historic roots. Special emphasis was placed upon ritual, a subject largely neglected in Evangelical circles. The new church immediately turned its attention to a search for valid Orthodox episcopal orders. Initial talks were held with the Orthodox Church in America. While a major obstacle was overcome when the leaders of the EOC professed their belief in the Blessed Virgin Mary as *theotokos*, the Mother of God, the talks eventually reached a stalemate. Finally, the EOC was able to work out an arrangement with the Antiochian Church by which the leaders dropped their designation as bishops and were reordained by Archbishop Philip.

Over the years the leaders of the EOC have written a number of books which received wide circulation within Evangelical circles. Most of these were published by Thomas Nelson, where Gilquist worked as an editor, and included Gilquist's *Why We Haven't Changed the World* and *It Ain't Gonna Reign No More* by Jon Braun. Most notable among them was *The Mindbenders* by Jack Sparks, an anticult book that led to a lawsuit for libel by the Local Church, one of the groups treated in the volume, and its eventual withdrawal by the publishers.

Sources:

Braun, Jon E. *It Ain't Gonna Reign No More.* Nashville, TN: Thomas Nelson, 1978.

The Divine Liturgy of John Chrysostom. Santa Barbara, CA: Evangelical Orthodox Church, Santa Barbara Diocese, n.d.

Sparks, Jack. *The Mindbenders.* Nashville, TN: Thomas Nelson, 1977.

★194★
Apostolic Catholic Church of the Americas
421 Fairmont
Dallas, TX 75219

The Apostolic Catholic Church of the Americas was founded as the American Orthodox Catholic Church in Colorado in 1962, with Robert S. Zeiger as its Archbishop of Denver and Primate. He was consecrated in 1961 by Archbishop Peter A. Zurawetzky as an Orthodox bishop for Westerners.

The Anglican Church of the Americas was found by Gordon A. Da Costa in Indiana in 1971. In 1976, a synod was held at Marion, Indiana, at which Da Costa and others became members of the American Orthodox Catholic Church. At that time, the American Orthodox Catholic Church, in order to avoid confusion with Archbishop Walter A. Propheta's church in New York, took an alternative official name, the Apostolic Catholic Church of the Americas, which became its most commonly used designation.

Da Costa was elected Archbishop Primate of the Apostolic Catholic Church of the Americas. Zeiger, who had resigned as head, was elected chancellor. There was no actual merger of the American Orthodox Catholic Church and the Anglican Church of the Americas. However, Da Costa continued parallel activities as head of the Anglican Church of the Americas for some time in order to carry out responsibilities for those of his clergy who wished to continue as members of that church.

In 1977, Zeiger resigned and submitted to the jurisdiction of the Roman Catholic Church. As a condition for union with Rome, he was required to agree not to exercise his office as bishop or priest. In 1981, Zeiger returned to Orthodoxy. At that time, he became a cofounder of the Holy Synod of Denver in 1984. This venture floundered after a dispute in 1986. At that time, Zeiger returned to the Apostolic Catholic Church of the Americas as Archbishop *ad personam* of Lakewood, Colorado. Zeiger has since been arrested twice in connection with pro-life activities.

Archbishop C. F. Quinn of Dallas, Texas, was elected Archbishop Primate Coadjutor with the right of succession to Da Costa in 1986. Quinn succeeded as primate in 1988, when Da Costa could no longer serve. Da Costa died in 1991, and Quinn continues as Archbishop Primate.

The Apostolic Catholic Church of the Americas employs Western liturgy, accepts as the rule of faith the Sacred Scriptures and Divine Tradition as expressed in the writings of the church Fathers and the dogmatic degrees of the Seven Ecumenical Councils. The church makes clerical celibacy optional, even for bishops. It rejects females as candidates for the priesthood. Church property is held in lay trusteeship. The church is in the Apostolic succession; Catholic, not Protestant; Orthodox, not Roman; and American, not a foreign mission.

Membership: In 1984 the church reported nine parishes, missions, and chaplaincies and had an estimated membership of less than 500.

Periodicals: *The Door.* Send orders to 4201 Fairmount St., Dallas, TX 75219.

Sources:

The Order of Daily Prayer. Dallas: Diocese of Texas, Apostolic Catholic Church, n.d.

★195★
Apostolic Orthodox Catholic Church
PO Box 1834
Glendora, CA 91740

The Apostolic Orthodox Catholic Church was founded by Bps. Richard J. Ingram and Charles Ingram, both former bishops in the Western Orthodox Church in America. Richard J. Ingram had been consecrated on June 17, 1984, by Charles David Luther, assisted by Bps. Peter Paul Brennan and Alan Maxwell Bain. He was also consecrated sub conditione in 1988 by Bp. Luis Fernando Castillo-Mendez, assisted by several of his fellow bishops in the Igreja Catolica Apostolica Brasileira, Josivaldo Pereira de Oliveira, Galvao Barros, and Walbert Rommel Coelho. Richard Ingram consecrated Charles Ingram on September 10, 1989, and before the end of the month, both had resigned from the WOCA. The Apostolic Orthodox Catholic Church is like its parent body in faith and practice, the differences leading to its founding being primarily administrative.

Membership: Not reported.

★196★
Association of Occidental Orthodox Parishes
Current address not obtained for this edition.

The use of the Western Rite in Orthodox Churches has experienced a revival during the twentieth century as Eastern Orthodoxy has flourished in the West. It has a long history, though little noticed due to the predominance of the Roman Rite. It was the opinion of some, verified by such examples as the Western Rite Vicariate within the Antiochean Orthodox Church, that Western Rite parishes do not remain Western within a predominantly Eastern Rite church body. The Orthodox Church of France is a totally Western Rite diocese founded in 1953 by Fr. Evgraph Kovalevsky and several other priests who withdrew from the Russian Orthodox Church. As priests in Lithuania they had followed a Western Rite, and Father Kovalevsky had pastored a Western Rite parish opened in 1944 in Paris. That parish became the source of several others.

After leaving the Russian Orthodox Church, the priests and their parishes affiliated with the Russian Orthodox Church Outside of Russia. Bishop John Maximovitch ordained several new Western Rite priests and saw to the publication of the liturgy, the old Gallican Rite according to Saint Germain, Bishop of Paris (555-576), not to be confused with the eighteenth-century occultist of the same name. The death of Bishop John led to a break with the Russian Church, and, as relations worsened, Kovalevsky, who had been consecrated in 1964, led his followers in forming an autonomous diocese. But he died in 1970 without having a successor consecrated. Finally, in 1972, the Patriarch of Romania agreed to consecrate Pere Gilles Hardy as the new bishop of the Orthodox Catholic Church of France. He is known as Bishop Germain. The Western Rite was reintroduced to America by Fr. Stephen Empson who founded a parish in New York City. In 1981 he organized the Association of Occidental Orthodox Parishes to further promote Western Rite Orthodoxy.

Membership: In 1984 the association had five parishes (New York City; Brooklyn, NY; Chicago; Dorchester, MA; and Fullerton, CA) and a monastery in Jacksonville, Florida. Internationally, the Western Orthodox Church had 60 parishes, most in France, but including two each in Switzerland and Spain and one each in Germany, Belgium, and Argentina.

Periodicals: Unofficial: *Axios*. Send orders to 800 S. Euclid St., Fullerton, CA 92632.

★197★
Autocephalous Greek Orthodox Church of the Americas and Europe
(Defunct)

The Autocephalous Greek Orthodox Church of the Americas and Europe was founded in 1934, according to the church seal. Its bishop was Joachim Souris, who was consecrated in 1951 by Abp. Joseph Klimovich of the Orthodox Catholic Patriarchate of America, assisted by several others. At that time, he also joined Klimovich as a member of the Holy Synod of the Orthodox Catholic Patriarchate of America. In 1967 he associated with the rival Holy Synod of the Orthodox Catholic Churches of the Americas and Europe founded by Peter A. Zurawetzky.

As of the mid-1970s, the single Diocese of Brooklyn and New Jersey of the church consisted of one small parish/mission, the Church of St. Fanourios and Sts. Anargyroi, located in Newark, New Jersey.

★198★
Autocephalous Orthodox Catholic Apostolic Church
Smock, PA

The Autocephalous Orthodox Catholic Apostolic Church is an independent Orthodox jurisdiction founded by Mt. Rev. Paul W. Seese, formerly with the Western Orthodox Church in America. He had been consecrated in 1989 as a bishop by Mt. Rev. Richard J. Ingram of the Western Orthodox Church in America, assisted by Mt. Rev. Patrick M. Cronin of the Independent Catholic Church of America and Timothy W. Browning of the Byzantine Orthodox Catholic Church. The Western Orthodox Church, though an Orthodox body, follows a Western Rite, and Seese, wishing to follow an Eastern Rite, withdrew in 1991.

Membership: Not reported.

Sources:

Pruter, Karl. *The Directory of Autocephalous Bishops of the Apostolic Sucession.* San Bernadino, CA: Brogo Press, 1906. 104 pp.

Ward, Gary. *Independent Bishops: An International Directory.* Detroit: Apogee Books, 1990. 524 pp.

★199★
Autocephalous Slavonic Orthodox Catholic Church (in Exile)
2237 Hunter Ave.
New York, NY 10475

The Autocephalous Slavonic Orthodox Catholic Church (in Exile) dates its existence to the coming of Saint Cyril and Saint Methodius to Moravia in the ninth century. Worship was established according to the Greek Orthodox Church, and in 1620 a jurisdiction of the Podcarpathian Church was founded. It was always a small jurisdiction in a predominantly Roman Catholic land. Following World War I, when Czechoslovakia declared its independence, Orthodox believers asked for their own independent church. Under the Serbian Orthodox patriarch, the church was organized in 1921, and a bishop, Gorazd Pavlik, was consecrated. However, in early 1923, the ecumenical patriarch consecrated a rival archbishop named Sabbazd. Both churches existed side by side until the Nazi occupation and World War II, during which they both disappeared. In 1946 the church reappeared under the patriarch of the Russian Orthodox Church in Moscow who appointed an Exarch to head the small group.

Some perceived the action of the Russian patriarch to be a takeover of the Czechoslovakian church and in 1946 a group of priests and laity formed an underground church movement. In 1968, one of the leaders of this movement, Bishop Filotej, fled the country and settled in America, where he founded the Slavonic Orthodox Church. In 1968 he consecrated Bishop william Andrew Prazsky as his coadjutor archbishop, and after Archbishop Filotej's death in 1970, Archbishop Andrew became the head of the church.

Archbishop Andrew soon established communion with the Ukrainian Autocephalous Orthodox Church in the United States of America and in 1969 accepted provisional reconsecration from Abp. Hryhorij Osijchuk (1898-1985) and Archbishop Hennadij. In 1980, the episcopal leadership of the two churches united their efforts into a single *sobor*, or synod, which had oversight of both churches. Archbishop Andrew stepped aside at that time in favor of Archbishop Hryhorij. In 1985, following the death of Archbishop Hryhorij, Archbishop Andrew was elected Metropolitan Archbishop of the united sobor.

Metropolitan Andrew Prazky passed away on December 16, 1990. The bishop of New York, Alexis Nizza, was elected and enthroned on May 19, 1991, as Archbishop Metropolitan Primate. The leadership is shared with His Grace Efthimious Kontargiris elected as Archbishop co-adjutor the same day. The sobor of bishop withdrew from the Ukrainian Autocephalous Orthodox Church, though the Slavonic church, now a completely independent body, is still in communion with it. A dialogue with the Ecumenical Patriarch has begun in the hope of the eventual union of the Slavonic Orthodox Church with the mother see in Constantinople.

The Slavonic Church is Orthodox in faith and practice. The church's strength is in the Bronx where it ministers to Slavic Americans of various national backgrounds, many first generation immigrants.

Membership: The Slavonic Orthodox Church serves approximately 5,000 families of several Slavic and Greek backgrounds in its congregations in the United States.

Sources:

Clarke, Boden. *Lords Temporal and Lords Spiritual.* San Bernardino, CA: Borgo Press, 1986.

★200★
Autocephalous Traditional Orthodox Catholic Church
Box 17105
St. Bernard, OH 45217

The Autocephalous Traditional Orthodox Catholic Church is a small Orthodox jurisdiction founded in 1963. It is headed by the Mt. Rev. Athanasius K. Armstrong.

Membership: Not reported. There are 41 priests in the United States and seven in Canada. Missionary branches are reported in Japan, the Philippine Islands, Russia, Poland, Singapore, Mexico, and in Africa.

★201★
Bulgarian Eastern Orthodox Church (Diocese of North and South America)
519 Brynhaven Dr.
Oregon, OH

The reestablishment of relations between the Orthodox Church in Bulgaria and the Bulgarian Eastern Orthodox Church (Diocese of North and South America and Australia) and the resultant manifestation of that accord in the joint visitation of North American parishes in 1963 by Bishop Andrey Velichky, metropolitan of the American church and Bishop Preiman, metropolitan of Nevrokop, Bulgaria, led to major protests throughout the Church. Bishop Andrey was accused of violating the declaration made in 1947 that the Bulgarian Church in America would not accept any orders from the Church in Bulgaria. In March 1963, protesting leaders representing 18 churches and missions met in Detroit, Michigan, and reconstituted themselves as the Bulgarian Eastern Orthodox Church (Diocese of the United States of America and Canada) and elected Archimandrite Kyrill Yonchev as their bishop.

They turned to the Russian Orthodox Church Outside of Russia for support. The Russians, also cut off from their homeland by a hostile regime, gave the new Bulgarian jurisdiction their canonical protection and their bishops consecrated bishop-elect Yonchev in 1964 at their monastery in Jordanville, New York.

The Bulgarian Eastern Orthodox Church differs from its parent body only in matters of administration. It lays claim to all properties belonging to the undivided Church in America though it has not been able to take control of them. It is stanchly anti-Communist.

Membership: In the mid-1970s, the church reported 21 parishes and missions.

★202★
Bulgarian Eastern Orthodox Diocese of the USA, Canada, and Australia
℅ Metropolitan Joseph
550 A, W. 50th St.
New York, NY 10019

Bulgarians arrived in the United States throughout the nineteenth century and by 1907 were numerous enough to begin establishing congregations. The first parish was formed in Madison, Illinois. Soon, the Holy Synod in Sofia established a mission to oversee their American members. Finally, in 1937, a diocese was created and Bishop Andrey Velichky came from Bulgaria as its head. Bishop Andrey returned to Bulgaria during World War II and worked on various projects among which was the handling of negotiations between the ecumenical patriarch in Istanbul and the Bulgarian patriarch which led to the healing of a 70 year-old broken relationship.

Soon after the war ended, Archbishop Andrey returned to America. In 1947 he incorporated the Bulgarian Eastern Orthodox Diocese of America, Canada and Australia. The constitutional assembly meeting in March of that year realigned its relationship to the Church in Bulgaria by declaring that while it saw itself as part of the whole of Bulgarian Orthodoxy, it could not accept orders from the church leaders in Sofia as long as a Communist regime ruled their homeland. They then proceeded to formally elect Andrey as their leader. The Holy Synod reacted by declaring the election null and void. The American diocese ignored the Synod and for the next fifteen years the diocese operated independently of the church leaders in Sofia. In 1962 the church in Bulgaria recognized the Metropolia and reestablished a working relationship. In 1969 the jurisdiction was divided into two dioceses, and in 1972 Bp. Joseph Znepolski succeeded Archbishop Andrey as Metropolitan. In 1989 the two dioceses were again merged into one under Metropolitan Joseph.

The Bulgarian Eastern Orthodox Diocese follows standard Orthodox faith and practice. It is a member of the Standing Conference of Canonical Orthodox Bishops in the Americas.

Membership: In 1997 the Diocese reported 13 parishes and 15,000 members. There were 1,000 members in Canada, and 1,000 in Australia.

★203★
Byelorussian Autocephalic Orthodox Church in the U.S.A.
℅ Archbishop Mikalay, Primate
Church of St. Cyril of Turau
524 St. Clarens Ave.
Toronto, ON, Canada

Byelorussia is that section of the U.S.S.R. directly north of the Ukraine and East of Poland. A national church had been organized there in 1291 under Greek jurisdiction. With time, it came under the control of the patriarch in Moscow, the head of the Russian Orthodox Church. In 1922 a split developed in the Byelorussian church when the Minsk Council of clergy and laity, under the leadership of Metropolitan Melchizedek, attempted to organize an autonomous Byelorussian church free of Moscow. Such action met the disapproval of both the government and the patriarch of the Russian Church. Within a short period of time, all the Byelorussian leaders had been arrested and sent to Siberia, and the church reverted to its dependent status. During the Nazi occupation of Byelorussia, the church attempted again to organize independently, but their efforts ended with the defeat of the German occupation forces.

The Byelorussian Autocephalic Orthodox Church in the U.S.A. is one of two Orthodox groups among Byelorussian immigrants. It emerged among refugee Byelorussians in Germany after the War. Their own bishops having returned to the Russian Church, clergy and laity turned to the Ukrainian Church. Metropolitan Polikarp not only blessed the reorganization of an autonomous church among the Byelorussians, but in 1948 granted permission for one of his bishops, Bishop Siarhej, to leave his jurisdiction and join the new church. In 1949, accompanied by his former Ukrainian colleagues, Siarhej consecrated a second bishop for the church, Bishop Vasil. As the church spread among immigrants around the world, two more bishops were consecrated in 1968.

Present Primate of the Church is Archbishop Mikalay, elected in 1984 at a convention at the church in Highland Park, New Jersey. He resides in Toronto, Canada. In the United States, parishes are located in Cleveland, Ohio; Detroit, Michigan; and Dorothy, New Jersey. The Church also oversees parishes in England (3), Belgium, and Australia.

★204★
Byelorussian Orthodox Church
190 Turnpike Rd.
South River, NJ 08882

When refugees and immigrants from Byelorussia came to the West after World War II, some organized as the Byelorussian Autonomous Orthodox Church and elected their own bishops. Others formed independent congregations and sought the canonical blessings of other Orthodox bishops. The Byelorussian Orthodox

Church consists of three congregations who placed themselves under the jurisdiction of Archbishop Iakovos, head of the Greek Orthodox Archdiocese of North and South America, in his role as Exarch in America for the ecumenical patriarch. Besides the congregation in South River, New Jersey, parishes are found in Chicago and Toronto.

Membership: Not reported.

★205★
Byzantine Catholic Church
PO Box 3682
Los Angeles, CA 90078

The Byzantine Catholic Church assumed its present form in 1984 by a merger of the Byzantine Old Catholic Church and the Holy Orthodox Catholic Church, Eastern and Apostolic. The Byzantine Old Catholic Church was an Old Catholic jurisdiction whose history is intimately tied to the career of its leader, Mar Markus I, the duly elected Patriarch.

As a child, Miller had been adopted, and was given the name Oliver W. Skelton by his new parents. In the early 1960s, he joined the American Orthodox Catholic Church (AOCC), in which he was ordained in 1964 after completing his seminary training. He was then given the religious name Father Leo Christopher Skelton by Bishop Christopher Maria Stanley, who was assisted by Bp. John Joseph Frewen, who later consecrated him as his successor for the North American Orthodox Catholic Church in Kentucky in 1965. The church was incorporated in 1964.

In 1966, Stanley commissioned him to work with the Orthodox Old Catholic Church headed by Bishop Claude Hamel in the hopes of engendering expansion and growth among the churches, but a myriad of problems ensued due to conflicts with Hamel's leadership. Thus, Skelton separated his work from Hamel and changed the name of the jurisdiction to the Orthodox Old Roman Catholic Church II, to try to salvage some of the work for expansion in 1967, after Stanley fell ill and died. He then moved to Los Angeles, California, and in 1967, the synod of Bishops unanimously elected Mar Markus to succeed Stanley as Patriarch.

In the mid-1970s, he reorganized the church and changed the name back to the North American Orthodox Catholic Church as it was called when he was originally consecrated. During this period he was moving both theologically and liturgically away from the Old Catholicism toward Eastern Orthodoxy. In April 1975, having respectfully waited until after the deaths of his foster parents, he changed his name legally to Mark I. Miller, the name of his natural parents.

In 1981, the church reorganized again, the result being the formation of the Byzantine Old Catholic Church (BOCC). The reorganization occurred during a period of great flux in the congregations. After the new church was formed, Mar Apriam I (Archbishop Richard B. Morrill), who headed the Holy Orthodox Catholic Church, Eastern and Apostolic (HOCCEA), joined with Archbishop Miller in the formatio of a Sacred Synod of Bishops. Mar Apriam became president of the Synod and Mar Markus vice-president and Chief Justice of the Spiritual Court of Bishops, in addition to his own jurisdiction.

A further merger in mid-1984 united the BOCC and the HOCCEA and led to the formation of the Byzantine Catholic Church. However, before the year was out, Morrill withdrew with approval and reconstituted the HOCCEA. Mar Markus remained as head of the Byzantine Catholic Church, which came into full communion with the reconstituted HOCCEA, their differences being purely administrative.

In 1985, Morrill assumed leadership of the American Orthodox Catholic Church in the United States from Patriarch Christian I (Archbishop John A. Christian), who died in December 1984. He had traveled to Africa in 1977, and became Patriarch of West Africa for the AOCC. While the number grew, the organization suffered. The jurisdiction was scattered and cooperation among bish-

ops difficult to maintain. The possible merger of Morrill's jurisdiction with the Byzantine Catholic Church was again raised and in 1991 a synod was called with that idea on the agenda. However, before it could meet, Mar Apriam died. When the synod did meet, it agreed to unite the various segments of the church previously under Mar Apriam under Mar Markus.

Beliefs. The Byzantine Catholic Church is Orthodox Catholic in faith and practice. It celebrates the Liturgies of St. John Chrysostom and St. Basil in the vernacular of its various jurisdictions. The church also has a growing Western Rite Vicariate directed by Bishop Lawrence Hicks, O.S.B., which is Orthodox Catholic in creed and tridentine in liturgical practice.

Membership: In 1997 the Apostolic Chancery reported 31 congregations in the United States with about 600 members, plus charitable outreaches such as St. Jude Parish under the direction of Fr. Juan Correa, O.S.J. Affiliated congregations are spread throughout the United States. Outside the United States affiliated congregations are found in Canada, Great Britain, France, Italy, Congo, Nigeria, Liberia, Haiti, and have a reported membership of over 100,000.

Educational Facilities: St. John's Theological Seminary, Los Angeles, California.

L'Institute Orthodoxe Ecumenique de St. Jean Chrysostome, Port au Prince, Haiti.

In addition, as the result of a cooperative agreement, clergy can attend

The School of the American Independent Old Catholic Church.

Periodicals: *Byzantine Life.*

★206★
Byzantine Orthodox Catholic Church (Armstrong)
Current address not obtained for this edition.

The Byzantine Orthodox Catholic Church is a small Orthodox jurisdiction founded in the 1980s by Bishop Harry C. Armstrong. On December 3, 1988, assisted by bishops of the Western Orthodox Church in America, consecrated of Timothy W. Browning as a second bishop for the church.

Membership: Not reported.

★207★
Byzantine Orthodox Catholic Church (St. Peters)
6329 E. 55th Pl.
Indianapolis, IN 46226-1647

The Byzantine Orthodox Catholic Church is a small Orthodox jurisdiction founded in 1986 in Cincinnati, Ohio, by Most Rev. Donald St. Peters.

Membership: In 1997 the church had 12 congregations served by 32 priests. Foreign congregations were found in Germany and the West Indies.

Sources:

Pruter, Karl. *The Directory of Autocephalous Bishops of the Apostolic Succession.* San Bernardino, CA: Brogo Press, 1906. 104 pp.

Ward, Gary. *Independent Bishops: An International Directory.* Detroit: Apogee Books, 1990. 524 pp.

★208★
Byzantine Universal (Catholic) and Orthodox Church of the Americas
(Defunct)

The Byzantine Universal (Catholic) and Orthodox Church of the Americas was founded in 1942 by Antoine Joseph Aneed (1881-1970), a Lebanese-American. Though never a large jurisdiction, The Byzantine American Church has played an important role among independent Catholic and Orthodox churches because of Aneed's having possessed Roman Catholic episcopal orders. As a young man, in 1909 Aneed was ordained as a priest in the Roman Catholic Church and served for a short time as secretary of the archbishop of the Melkite-Greek Catholic Patriarchate of Antioch and All the East, one of the uniate Eastern-rite churches within Roman Catholicism. He then moved to the United States and was there in 1911 when Melece Sawoya defied Pope Pius X and came to the United States on a pastoral visit to some of the Melkite parishes.

Aneed was consecrated by Sawoya on October 9, 1911, to serve as his assistant bishop. However, the Vatican did not recognize that consecration. The consecration was recognized by Sawoya's successor and by Abp. S. G. Messmer of Milwaukee, who allowed Aneed to use the title Exarch. During the 1920s, while working within the Syrian community in San Francisco, Aneed began to associate with some of the independent Catholic and Orthodox bishops on the west coast, especially E. R. Verostek of the North American Old Roman Catholic Church-Utrecht Succession and Lowell Paul Wadle of the American Catholic Church. In 1929 he moved to New London, Connecticut, to serve St. Ann's Church. He remained as St. Ann's until 1937, but at some point he left the Roman Catholic Church and in 1942 formed a separate jurisdiction.

The situation became muddled in 1944 when Aneed, in spite of carrying Roman Catholic orders, was consecrated sub conditione by Wadle and Verostek. He engaged in a second important service in 1945 when he exchanged consecrations with Wadle, Henry Joseph Kleefisch, Charles Hampton, and Wallace David de Ortega Maxey. Kleefisch, an independent Orthodox bishop then became a bishop in Aneed's church. In 1946 Aneed was named Patriarch of his church. In 1949 Aneed consecrated Nicolas Urbanovitch and assigned him as bishop of Canada.

The Byzantine Universal Church survived until Aneed's death in 1970 but soon dissolved. His influence remains in those bishops who claim to derive their apostolic authority from him.

Sources:

Aneed, Antoine Joseph. *A Brief History of he Catholic Church of St. George in Milwaukee, Wis., and a Sketch of the Eastern Church.* Milwaukee, WI: The Author, 1919.

Ward, Gary L. *Independent Bishops: An International Directory.* Detroit, MI: Apogee Books, 1990. 524 pp.

★209★
Catholic Apostolic Church in America
Current address not obtained for this edition.

Though officially reconstituted in 1983, the Catholic Apostolic Church in America continues an unbroken existence from 1950 when Stephen Meyer Corradi-Scarella established an American outpost of the Catholic Apostolic Church in Brazil. The Catholic Apostolic Church in Brazil was formed in 1946 by Dom Carlos Duarte Costa, a former bishop of the Roman Catholic Church who had been excommunicated by Pope Pius XII because of his criticism of the church during World War II. Among those who Costa consecrated was Dom Luis F. Castillo-Mendez, who succeeded him as patriarch of the church in 1949. Corradi-Scarella was consecrated by Mendez in 1949 and established the church as an exarchate with headquarters in New Mexico. During the 1960s, following the death of Costa, Corradi-Scarella lost touch with the Brazilian group and began to associate with the various Old Catholics in the United States. By 1970 he called his jurisdiction the Diocese of the Old Catholic Church in America.

The church grew slowly until the 1970s. In 1973 Corradi-Scarella was joined by Francis Jerome Joachim, a priest ordained by Archbishop Bartholomew Cunningham of the Holy Orthodox Church, Diocese of New Mexico. Joachim brought an Eastern Orthodox perspective with him, in contrast to Corradi-Scarella's Catholic tradition, but soon became his chief associate. Corradi-Scarella arranged for Joachim's consecration by Archbishop

David M. Johnson of the American Orthodox Church, Diocese of California, on September 28, 1974. Two months later, on December 1, 1974, Corradi-Scarella, then almost seventy years old, resigned in favor of Joachim.

Under Joachim the small jurisdiction grew, at one point having almost 100 clergy, but lost significant strength due to the defections of many to other independent jurisdictions. In 1980 Joachim renamed his jurisdiction the Western Orthodox Church in America (formerly the National Catholic Apostolic Church in America). At the request of Mendez, Joachim changed the name of the church back to the Catholic Apostolic Church of North America. In 1985, Joachim was name Primate of All North America and the church recognized as the Autocephalous Catholic Apostolic Church in Brazil in North America.

Membership: In 1988 the church reported 5,000 members in 20 parishes served by 25 priests in the United States. There were three parishes in Canada served by two priests, and mission parishes in Australia and Mexico.

Educational Facilities: St. John Chrysostom Theological Seminary, San Francisco, California.
St. Charles Academy of Theology, San Francisco, California.

Periodicals: *Journal Apostolica.*

★210★
Celtic Christian Communion
% Rt. Rev. Joseph A. Grenier
PO Box 299
Canadensis, PA 18325-0299

The Celtic Christian Communion (CCC) is an ecumenical association of independent Catholic and Orthodox jurisdictions which in turn are comprised of small faith communities, many of which meet as either house churches or small chapels. The communion is united in the affirmation of the teachings of the first seven Ecumenical Councils of the undivided Christian Church as summarized in the Nicene Creed. Member jurisdictions celebrate the seven sacraments (also called Mysteries) and believe in the real presence of Christ in the Eucharist.

Christians from every denomination are welcome at services of the communion's member churches and it is not necessary to give up one's denominational affiliation to participate in their services.

While the communion is particularly attractive to persons of Celtic heritage, it does not set any kind of ethnic limitation on membership or participation. Priesthood is open to both men and women, married or celibate. Bishops are elected by church members. The communion has a presiding archbishop who is also elected. Episcopal jurisdictions are based not on geography, as dioceses are, but on spiritual "spheres of influence". Thus, bishops are those who are elected by the very people they serve spiritually, regardless of location, and there could feasibly be several bishops near each other.

There are those in the communion, married and single, who are members of religious communities (not unlike the Third Orders of the Roman Church) and who have added the discipline of monastic prayer to their lives. Personal prayer is strongly encouraged for everyone.

Membership: The CCC includes the Anamchara Celtic Church, the Church of the Culdees, and St. Ciaran's Fellowship of Celtic Christian Communities.

Sources:

http://www.continet.com/culdee/.

★211★
Celtic Orthodox Christian Church in North America
Box 72102
Akron, OH 44372

The Celtic Orthodox Christian Church in North America is an independent Orthodox jurisdiction headed by its bishop elect, Abbot Maelruain Cele De. The church utilizes the Orthodox Celtic Rite represented by the Celtic Liturgy found in the Lorrha "Stowe" Missal, while services for administration of other sacraments, occasional services, daily prayer, and other items use material from Celtic/Gallican documents of the same historical period (seventh-ninth centuries). Since Orthodoxy is primary and its liturgical expression secondary, other Orthodox liturgies may be used where pastoral needs demand. Major clergy (priests, deacons) ordained within the Celtic Orthodox Christian Church are bound to the use of the Celtic Orthodox Rite. Orthodox bishops of other Orthodox rites may affiliate provided they agree to support the primary apostolate of the jurisdiction.

Despite its name, the Celtic Orthodox Christian Church in North America eschews the idea of being simply another ethnic jurisdiction. It seeks rather to follow the preschismatic Faith of the Church (the doctrine prior to the split between Eastern Orthodoxy and the Roman Catholic Church in 1054 C.E.) as the Celtic Fathers did before they were suppressed by Rome. It opposes what it sees as doctrinal drift, especially toward monophysism, in the larger Orthodox churches, and affirms the two natures of Christ as laid out in the Nicene Creed and the decisions of the later ecumenical councils.

The Celtic Orthodox Christian Church in North America is a member of the Synod of Autonomous Canonical Orthodox Churches in North America, consisting of other independent jurisdictions who share its conservative perspectives, and expresses no interest in ties to other churches that might allow views that are condemned by the councils.

Membership: Not reported.

Sources:

http://www.geocities.com/Athens/3374/coccna/.

★212★
Church of Greece
℅ Metropolitan Demetrios
Holy Cross Church
50 Goddard Ave.
Brookline, MA 02140

Alternate Address: International Headquarters: c/o His Beatitude Serephim, Archbishop of Athens and All Greece, Ag Philotheis 21, GR-10556 Athens, Greece.

The Church of Greece, that is, those ancient churches in the Orthodox tradition that used Greek as their dominant language and continued a Greek heritage, operated on a territorial basis from the old patriarchates at Alexandria, Jerusalem, Antioch, and Constantinople (now Istanbul). Over the centuries, each of these churches assumed jurisdiction in different territories and relinquished territories as new autonomous national churches and patriarchates were created. In the twentieth century, with the massive movements of people, the lines between jurisdictions have blurred.

In 1850, the Church of Greece was granted autonomy, and the Ecumenical Patriarchate relinquished jurisdiction over most of the country. However, he retained jurisdiction over the Americas. Thus the Greek Orthodox Archdiocese of North and South America to which most Americans who are Greek Orthodox belong, is affiliated with the Ecumenical Patriarchate. However, over the twentieth century, Greek immigrants who wished to remain attached to the Church of Greece have moved to America and organized a diocese. It is at one in faith and belief with all of Orthodoxy, but administratively separate.

Membership: Not reported.

Sources:

Orthodxy. Regensburg: Ostkirchliches Institute, 1996.

★213★
Church of the True Orthodox Christians of Greece (Synod of Archbishop Andreas)
℅ Holy Trinity Church
38-10 20th St.
Astoria, NY 11105

Alternate Address: International headquarters: His Beatitude, the Most Rev. Andreas, Archbishop of Athens and All Greece, Constantinoupileos 22, Athens, Greece.

The Church of the True Orthodox Christians of Greece dates to the reaction in the state Church of Greece to the adoption of the Gregorian Calendar which replaced the Old (Julian) Calendar which had been used for centuries by the Greek Orthodox Church. Once the new calendar was introduced in 1924, Old Calendarists began to organize, but it was not until 1935 that they had episcopal oversight. In that year, three Church of Greece bishops aligned themselves with the Old Calendar cause. The three bishops quickly ordained four new bishops, among whom was Bishop Matthew of Vrestheni. Within a few years, in part as a result of the attempted suppression, a significant difference of opinion arose among the Old Calendar bishops concerning the status of the state church. Metropolitan Chrysostomos, the head of the Old Calendar Synod, released a statement saying that by adopting the Gregorian Calendar, the state church was in a position of potential schism; however, if no other heretical moves were made, it retained the grace of the Holy Spirit and valid sacraments.

Bishop Matthew rejected Metropolitan Chrysostomos' position. He argued that the Church of Greece was in schism and that grace was no longer present in its sacraments. He separated from the main body of Old Calendarists. In 1948, two years before his death, Bishop Matthew consecrated four other bishops. The other Old Calendar factions did not recognize these consecrations (it taking more than one bishop to perform the ceremony). However, in 1971, the Russian Orthodox Church Outside of Russia acted to regularize them as part of an overall attempt to unite the several Old Calendar factions which had developed. However, the issue of the position of the state church continued to divide the groups. Subsequently, various bishops of the other Old Calendar groups have moved toward the Matthew position, but have as yet been unable to overcome the fragmentation.

The Church of True Orthodox Christians of Greece is headed by Most Rev. Andreas, archbishop of Athens and all Greece. Over the years Old Calendarists in Europe and America have aligned with the church. There are currently parishes in Massachusetts and New York.

Membership: Not reported. In 1985 there were two parishes, one in New Bedford, Massachusetts, and one in Astoria, New York.

Sources:

Chysostomos, Archimandrite, with Hieromonk Ambrosios, and Hieromonk Auxentios. *The Old Calendar Orthodox Church of Greece.* Etna, CA: Center for Traditionalist Orthodox Studies, 1986.

"Greek Old Calendarists in the U.S.A.: An Annotated Directory." *Orthodox Tradition* 2, no. 2 (1985): 49-61.

★214★
Community of James the Just
℅ R. Rev. Clyde Ramon Allee
936 Cedar Ave., No. 15
Long Beach, CA 90813-4231

The Community of James the Just is an autonomous Orthodox jurisdiction formed in 1960 in Los Angeles by then Fr. Clyde

Ramon Allee to serve the spiritual needs of those who could not attend a regularly scheduled Divine Liturgy due to incapacity, location, or vocation. In 1988, after Fr. Allee's consecration by Bp. Alan Bain (assisted by Bsps. John Lester Peace and Morris Saville), the community became fully self-governing. Mar Ramon traces his apostolic succession through the lineages of his consecrators from Antioch (Melkite Greek Catholic and Syrian Orthodox), Constantinople (Ukrainian and Russian Orthodox), and Rome (Utrecht Old Catholic).

Bishops, priests, and deacons now serve in Alaska, Texas, California, Tennessee, and Great Britain. Their ministries include hospitals, convalescent homes, and hospices; prisons, military, and veterans organizations; and parish congregations. English-language translations of Eastern and Western Orthodox liturgies are used as the pastoral needs require. Dialogue with other Orthodox and Catholic jurisdictions seeking reciprocal communion is ongoing.

Membership: Not reported.

Sources:

Ward, Gary L. *Independent Bishops: An International Directory.* Detroit, MI: Apogee Books, 1990. 524 pp.

★215★
Eastern Orthodox Catholic Church in America
Current address not obtained for this edition.

Among the several bodies claiming to carry on the mission of Archbishop Aftimios Ofiesh, the Eastern Orthodox Catholic Church in America can make one of the strongest cases for being the real antecedent body of Aftimios' independent jurisdiction. The first bishop consecrated by Aftimios was Bishop Sophronius Bishira in 1931. Aftimios' retirement and Bishop Joseph Zuk's unexpected death just months after his consecration by Ofiesh, left Sophronius in charge. He turned to Metropolitan Benjamin Fedchenkov of the Moscow Exarch (now the Patriarchal Parishes of the Russian Orthodox Church in the United States and Canada), one of several warring Russian Orthodox factions, and with his blessing, consecrated John More-Moreno in 1933. Sophronius soon left the United States and More-Moreno took up the task of creating an American Orthodox church, in 1951, by forming the Eastern Orthodox Catholic Church in America.

The church follows the practice of Orthodoxy in both liturgy and theology. For many years it published the influential monthly periodical, the *American Review of Eastern Orthodoxy* (suspended in 1980).

Membership: In 1974 the church reported 4 churches, 13 clergy, and 315 members.

★216★
Eastern Orthodox Christian Church in America
% His Eminence, Archbishop Michael
Box 687
New Albany, OH 43054

The Eastern Orthodox Christian Church in America is an Orthodox jurisdiction founded in 1987 by Abp. Michael D. Kirkland, who also serves as pastor of St. Nicholas Orthodox Church in Columbus, Ohio, and leader of the Archdiocese of Columbus, Ohio, and Dependencies. Kirkland was raised a Roman Catholic and attended St. John Vianney Seminary in Miami, Florida, and St. Mary's Seminary and Pontifical University in Baltimore, Maryland. However, he left the Roman Catholic Church and was ordained as a priest in the Antiochean Orthodox Archdiocese of Toledo, Ohio, and Dependencies.

During the 1980s, Father Kirkland became associated with Abp. Peter A. Zhurawetzky, the leader of the Holy Orthodox Catholic Patriarchate of America, an association of Orthodox churches founded in 1951 to manifest the unity and indigenous nature of Orthodoxy in America. The building of an American Orthodoxy which overcame ethnic divisions would call for the naming of a patriarch, the designation of the leader of the Orthodox community in various countries of Europe and the Middle East.

Kirkland was consecrated on September 20, 1986, by Archbishop Peter and the next day elevated to the archepiscopacy. Zhurawetzky was assisted by David Baxter of the Orthodox Church of America and Nikolaus Ilnyckyi of the Ukrainian Autocephalous Orthodox Church in the United States of America Kirkland was installed as Archbishop of Columbus, Ohio, and Dependencies on January 1, 1987. The church is Orthodox in faith and practice. It follows the revised Julian calendar and commonly uses the Greek Liturgy of St. John Chrysostom. The church also has a Western Rite vicariate for those member congregations that wish to follow Western rituals.

Membership: Not reported. There are several parishes in Ohio.

★217★
Ecumenical Orthodox Christian Church
308 Bear Creek Cut-Off Rd.
Tuscaloosa, AL 35405

The Ecumenical Orthodox Christian Church was founded in 1991 with orders from the Russian and Albanian Orthodox Churches. Its leader is His Beatitude, the Most Blessed Sergius (Quilliams), who is assisted by Bps. Yuri Spaeth, Jr. (Florida) and Ignatius Cash (Erie, Pennsylvania). The Ecumenical Orthodox Christian Church is an Old Calendar church adhering to the Julian Calendar in its liturgical practice. It is strictly Orthodox, accepts the teachings of the Seven Ecumenical Councils of the third through seventh centuries, and uses an English translation of the Divine Liturgy of St. John Chrysostom in its celebrations. As with most Orthodox, it rejects the filioque addition to the Nicene Creed made by the Roman Catholic Church in the Middle Ages.

The church has separated itself from most independent Roman, Old Catholic, High Anglican, and Orthodox jurisdictions in which it finds unacceptable doctrine and practice. It does not allow Western Rites within the church, and priests must wear the proper vestments, including a hat indicative of their marital status. The church's "Synodical Statutes" offer detailed instruction on the proper dress of a priest and furnishing of a sanctuary in which the liturgy is to be celebrated. It rejects the doctrines of papal infallibility, papal supremacy, and purgatory. It also rejects the idea of using unleavened bread in the Eucharist. The church adheres to the idea of Mary as theotokos (birth giver of God) and affirms Mary's holy (but not immaculate) conception, her assumption into heaven, and the role as one who can make supplication for the believer, but it rejects the title of Mary as co-redemtrix.

Membership: In 1995 the church reported nine clergy (including the three bishops) and 50 members.

Educational Facilities: Holy Wisdom Correspondence Seminary, Tuscaloosa, Alabama.

★218★
Ecumenical Orthodox Church
Current address not obtained for this edition.

The Ecumenical Orthodox Church is a small jurisdiction founded by Bp. Stanley J. Anjulis, who was consecrated in 1986 by Bp. Denise Mary Michele Garrison of the American Orthodox Church (now the Holy Eastern Orthodox Catholic and Apostolic Church in North America). He remained in Garrison's jurisdiction for only a year, although he was appointed vicar general of the church. In 1987 he left to found his independent work.

Membership: Not reported.

Sources:

Ward, Gary L. *Independent Bishops: An International Directory.* Detroit, MI: Apogee Books, 1990.

★219★

Estonian Orthodox Church in Exile
Current address not obtained for this edition.

In 1944 the Union of Soviet Socialist Republics gained political hegemony over Estonia. Primate of the Estonian Orthodox Church Archbishop Alexander fled to Sweden where he organized The Estonian Orthodox Church in Exile. The church is under the Greek Orthodox Church's ecumenical patriach in Constantinople and at one in faith and worship with the Greek Orthodox Church.

In 1949 the V. Rev. Sergius Samon established the first congregation of the Estonian Church in North America at Los Angeles. Large numbers of Estonians had come to the United States and Canada following World War II. Congregations were subsequently established in San Francisco, Chicago, and New York City. Canadian parishes were established in Vancouver, Toronto, and Montreal.

Membership: In the mid-1970s, the church reported 1,700 members in North America.

★220★

Evangelical Apostolic Church of North America
Current address not obtained for this edition.

The Evangelical Apostolic Church of North America, formerly known as the Autocephalous Syro-Chaldean Church of North America, derives from the Ancient Holy Apostolic Catholic Church of the East through the Metropolitan of India, Mar Basilius, who in 1902, consecrated Mar Jacobus (Ulric Vernon Herford) bishop, to bring the line to England. In 1952, Mar Georgius (Hugh George de Willmott Newman) was brought into the episcopal lineage by Mar Paulus (William Stanley McBean Knight), successor to Mar Jacobus.

Mar Georgius consecrated Charles D. Boltwood bishop in 1952. In 1959, Bishop Boltwood was elevated to Archbishop of the Free Protestant Episcopal Church in England. That same year, Archbishop Boltwood consecrated John M. Stanley bishop of Washington state, in the United States. Bishop Stanley subsequently withdrew from the Free Protestant Episcopal Church and formed the Syro-Chaldean Archdiocese of North America, taking the name of Mar Yokhannan. In 1969, Mar Yokhannan received into the Syro-Chaldean Archdiocese of North America, Mar Jacobus (James A. Gaines), who had received consecration in the Ukranian Orthodox succession.

The series of events which led to the formation of this body began at a meeting of the Holy Synod of the Syro-Chaldean Archdiocese, December 13-14, 1974. The synod designated Archpriest Bertram S. Schlossberg as bishop-elect with the task of organizing a Diocese of New York. By that action, Father Schlossberg came under the direct authority of Mar Jacobus, who had received authority from the Archdiocese for the Eastern half of the United States. Together, on April 16, 1976, they incorporated their new work as the Autocephalous Syro-Chaldean Archdiocese of the Eastern United States of America. On October 31, 1976, Mar Jacobus and Mar Yokhannan consecrated Father Uzziah bar Evyon (Schlossberg). In December, the diocese of the Northeast was erected with Mar Uzziah as bishop.

On April 2, 1977, Mar Yokhannan released Mar Jacobus and Mar Uzziah from "all canonical obedience" and then withdrew from the Syro-Chaldean Archdiocese to join the Patriarchal See Holy Orthodox Catholic Church, Eastern and Apostolic, located in California. Mar Jacobus and Mar Uzziah then recognized all the work within the Eastern Archdiocese and in October 1977 incorporated the Autocephalous Syro-Chaldean Church of North America. Mar Jacobus was archbishop and Metropolitan. Mar Uzziah was bishop of the Northeast. Upon his retirement in 1978, Mar Jacobus elevated Mar Uzziah to be Metropolitan of North America.

Since 1978, the church has grown slowly, concentrating on proclaiming the Gospel to the unsaved and ministering to the broken and wounded in the Spirit of Isaiah 61. The Northeastern Diocese was erected as a mission diocese with the expectation that smaller local dioceses would be carved out of it. The intention was that the church would be organized along small diocesesan lines, each diocese being a city or county. In the years since, the Diocese of Fairfield in Connecticut and the Diocese of Westchester in New York have been created. In addition to New York and New England, the church has work in Florida, a mission parish in the Philippines, and a mission in the Middle East.

In 1991, the Episcopal Synod agreed to change the name of the church from the Autocephalous Syro-Chaldean Church of North America.

The Evangelical Apostolic Church follows the Orthodox theology of the Church of the East. It affirms the Bible as the Word of God and both the Apostle's and Nicene Creeds. It keeps seven sacraments: baptism, confirmation or chrismation, holy communion, reconciliation, annointing for healing, holy matrimony, and holy orders. It uses a simplified English-language version of the Liturgy of Mar Addai and Mar Mari as its official liturgy, but allows parishes freedom in their use of the liturgy. There are several alternative forms which are also authorized. The church is evangelical, believing that all persons need to repent and be converted to Christ; catholic, stressing the historical doctrines, sacraments, and practices of Christianity; and charismatic, emphasizing the ministry of the Holy Spirit. It is strongly opposed to the acceptance of homosexuality and other forms of sexual liberalism that it considers to be a sin. The church stands opposed to the practice of abortion. Women are ordained to the diaconate, but not the priesthood.

Membership: In 1991, the church reported 1,000 members. There were 16 clergy, including three active bishops in three dioceses with five parishes altogether.

Educational Facilities: Christ the King Seminary and School of Discipleship, Rockville, Connecticut.

★221★

Finnish Orthodox Church
Current address not obtained for this edition.

The first Orthodox missionaries reached Finland in the tenth century and founded Valamo Monastery. While the church has remained small, it has persisted. Finland gained independence from Russia in 1919 and a wave of nationalism swept the church. In 1923 the church was given autonomy under the Greek Orthodox Church's ecumenical patriarch in Constantinople. The following year a non-Russian bishop was named primate. The church is Orthodox in faith and practice and uses the Finnish and Russian languages. The selection of archbishops must be submitted to Constantinople for approval.

In 1955 the first attempts to call together Orthodox Finns residing in the United States found most already attached to Russian congregations, but a small mission chapel was established in the Upper Peninsula of Michigan. It was not able to minister to the 1,300 Orthodox Finns and ceased to exist in 1958. A new plan was implemented in 1962 by Fr. Denis Ericson of Lansing, Michigan. Using Lansing as a base, he travels to four worship stations. Services are in English, but Finnish hymns and customs are preserved.

Membership: Not reported.

★222★

Free Orthodox Church International
353 S. 46th St.
Lincoln, NE 68510

The Free Orthodox Church International, formerly known as the Greek Orthodox Eparchy of Lincoln, was founded in 1984 by the Most Rev. Dr. Melchizedek, the Archbishop-Metropolitan. Trained as a Roman Catholic, the future archbishop converted to Orthodoxy in 1983. He affiliated with the Holy Orthodox Synod for Diaspora and Hellas, a free Holy Synod which had been organized in Greece in 1950, and began to work within its jurisdiction. He moved to Lincoln, Nebraska, in 1986 and the following year became the pastor of St. Tikhon's Orthodox Church. He was consecrated in 1993. In 1994 the American work became autocephalous as a step in adjusting to the American situation.

As a free jurisdiction, the church is not affiliated with either the Church of Greece (or any other national jurisdiction) or any of the ancient Patriarchates. Archbishop Melchizedek believes that since society has abandoned patriarchal structures, the church has no scriptural mandate to continue them. It is, however, at one with the Orthodox world in faith and practice and accepts the authority of the Holy Scriptures and the Seven Ecumenical Councils. It recognizes any jurisdiction that teaches and practices the Orthodox faith in nonjudgmental Christian love. Members of the church are encouraged to devote their lives to the service of Christ according to their own life experience.

The church has some opinions that differ from the main body of Orthodoxy. It accepts the authority of the inter-testament books commonly called the Apocrypha. It denies the doctrine of original sin. The church allows bishops to marry. Baptism is by triple immersion in the name of the Father, the Son and the Holy Spirit. The church retains the power to pronounce the forgiveness of sin through the sacrament of forgiveness (confession, penance, and counseling). Life is sacramental but focused in holy baptism, crismation, absolution of sins, the Eucharist, holy anointing of the sick, priesthood, and matrimony.

Various rites have been approved for workshop in the several parishes including the Sarum Rite, the Tridentine Roman Rite, the Liturgy of St. Chrysostomos, the Qurbana, and the Gallican Rite. Worship in the vernacular is recommended but Greek and Latin allowed. Among the structures sponsored by the church is the noncommunal Oblate Order of the Blessed Virgin Theotekos whose members offer themselves to the life of the Blessed Virgin in the spirit of the Magnificat (Luke 1:46-55). When received, the new member is given a blue robe and matching scapular which is worn on special occasions, though on a day-to-day basis members do not dress in special clothing. They are also assigned an individual obedience, in most cases a specific daily prayer to follow.

The church has formal communion with the Diocese of Emmaus, Christ Catholic Church International, the Free Orthodox Catholic Church of Germany, and the Holy Eastern Orthodox Catholic and Apostolic Church in North America, and fraternal relations with the Federation of St. Thomas Christian Churches, the Holy Catholic Apostolic Orthodox Church, and the Shekinah Glory Mar Thoma Orthodox Church. It is a member of the Nebraska Interchurch Ministries and the International Federation of Orthodox Catholics United Sacramentally (FOCUS).

Membership: In 1997 the church reported 13 parishes and missions, and a variety of outreach ministries. There was one parish in New Zealand.

Educational Facilities: St. Elias School of Orthodox Theology, Lincoln, Nebraska.

Periodicals: *The Pilgrim.*

★223★
Greek Orthodox Archdiocese of North and South America
% Archbishop Iakovos, Primate
8-10 E. 79th St.
New York, NY 10021

As early as 1767 Greek Orthodox Christians settled in New Smyrna, Florida. Greek merchants in New Orleans established Holy Trinity, the first Greek Orthodox Church in America, in 1864. Other parishes sprang up across the country. No attempt was made to organize the parishes until 1918 when the Greek Orthodox Archdiocese of North and South America was organized. Archbishop Alexandros headed the archdiocese from 1922. He began the extensive work of bringing the many Greek parishes under his jurisdiction. The greatest progress in this direction was

made by his successor, Metropolitan Athenagoras Spirou, who became the ecumenical patriarch in 1948.

The Greek Orthodox Archdiocese has over the years become the largest in the United States. It has ten districts, each headed by a bishop, and Archbishop Iakovos, as chairman of the Standing Conference of Canonical Orthodox Bishops and Exarch for the ecumenical patriarch, has been a recognized spokesman of the Greek Orthodox community to the outside world.

Currents of change that have flowed through the Orthodox world have made Archbishop Iakovos a subject of intense controversy as he emerged as a founding father of the modern ecumenical movement. As criticism has been directed against the growing openness of Patriarch Athenagoras toward Rome and the World Council of Churches, Archbishop Iakovos has been criticized for approving this openness and initiating contact on his own in the United States with various Protestant and Catholic bodies. Ultra-traditionalists see such ecumenical activity as compromising Orthodox faith. Mt. Athos, the most famous Orthodox monastery, has become a center of traditionalism and at times has been critical of Archbishop Iakovos and of changes in the contemporary church, which has always been done under the aegis of the mother church and headquarters of the Ecumenical Patriarchate in Istanbul, Turkey.

Liturgy being the most important aspect of Orthodox church life, changes affecting liturgy are met with extreme resistance when not in conformity to early church tradition and the esslesiology of the Eastern Orthodox Church. In 1922, the Greek Orthodox Archdiocese of North and South America, following the mandate of the Ecumenical patriarchate, accepted the Geogorian calendar. Some other patriarchates continue to use the Julian calendar. For the canonical orthodox Churches, the calendar controversy has benn a non-issue.

Membership: In 1994 the archdiocese reported 2 million members, 610 churches and 700 priests.

Educational Facilities: Holy Cross School of Theology, and Hellenic College, Brookline, Massachusetts.

Periodicals: *Orthodox Observer.*

Sources:

Constantelos, Demetrios J. *The Greek Orthodox Church.* New York: Seabury Press, 1967.

___. *An Old Faith for Modern Man.* New York: Greek Orthodox Archdiocese, 1964.

The Divine Liturgy of St. John Chrysostom. Brookline, MA: Greek Orthodox Theological Institute Press, 1950.

Litsas, Fotios K. *A Companion to the Greek Orthodox Church.* New York: Department of Communication, Greek Orthodox Archdiocese of North and South America, 1984.

Poulos, George. *A Breath of God.* Brookline, MA: Holy Cross Orthodox Press, 1984.

★224★
Greek Orthodox Church of America
Current address not obtained for this edition.

The Greek Orthodox Church of America was formed on December 1, 1971, at a meeting held in Miami, Florida, for the purpose of forming a federation of independent Greek Orthodox Churches. Many of these churches had grown out of local schisms and were headed by priests who had left the jurisdiction of Archbishop Iakovos. Members object to what they see as a movement "to Catholicize and Protestantize the church." They hope to preserve Greek faith, language, and traditions. They believe in local control of property, not archdiocesan ownership. As of 1974 the church was without episcopal supervision but was seeking it from various sources.

A moving force in the Greek Orthodox Church of America is Fr. Theodore Kyritsis. He was defrocked by Archbishop Iakovos and went under the jurisdiction of Bishop Petros of the Hellenic Orthodox Church in America. Bishop Photios of the Greek Orthodox Diocese of New York was installed as archbishop in Memphis in St. George's Greek Orthodox Church which Kyritsis pastored, and has since then been a vocal opponent of Archbishop Iakovos.

Membership: In the mid-1970s the church had 10 parishes scattered around the United States from Miami to Rhode Island, Pennsylvania, Michigan, and Tennessee.

★225★
Greek Orthodox Church of America
Current address not obtained for this edition.

The Greek Orthodox Church of America (not to be confused with the other church of the same name) was established in the mid-twentieth century as the outpost of the Eastern Orthodox Patriarchate of Alexandria (Egypt). In the first century C.E., Christianity spread among the Greek-speaking residents of Egypt and from them to the Coptic-speaking peoples. In the fifth century C.E., the Patriarch of Alexandria became a monophysite, a position denounced by the Council at Ephesus in 451, and a new Patriarch, Proterios, was installed in his place. The mass of Coptic-speaking peoples followed the deposed patriarch, but a small minority stayed with the Patriarch of Alexandria, whose jurisdiction extended across North Africa. It was substantially reduced by the Muslim conquest of the territory but has survived to the present. The American exarchate was organized among Greekspeaking migrants to North America from North Africa.

In 1964 the exarchate received a young priest into its jurisdiction by the name of Makrogambrakis. He had migrated to America the year previously and served under Bishop Petros of the Hellenic Orthodox Church. In 1983 Makrogambrakis was consecrated as Bishop Dionysios and named Exarchate of the Greek Orthodox Church of America. Several years later, the exarchate was granted autonomy and as Archbishop Dionysios, he became primate of the new church.

Membership: Not reported.

Sources:

Clarke, Boden. *Lords Temporal and Lords Spiritual.* San Bernardino, CA: Borgo Press, 1985.

★226★
Greek Orthodox Diocese of New York
Current address not obtained for this edition.

The Greek Orthodox Diocese of New York was formed in 1964 at Philadelphia, Pennsylvania, by priests and laity formerly under the jurisdiction of Archbishop Iakovos of the Greek Orthodox Archdiocese of North and South America. They objected to the administration of Archbishop Iakovos and are the only Orthodox body in the West which allows the laity the sole right to elect the bishops and to keep the monies of the church under the control of the members. Oxford-educated Bishop Photios was elected archbishop, and Theocletos of Salimis, auxiliary bishop. The installation of the archbishop took place in St. George's Greek Orthodox Church in Memphis, where Archbishop Photios resided for several years.

Archbishop Photios has gathered the largest group of Greek Orthodox followers not under Archbishop Iakovos. In 1965 jurisdiction was extended to Australia. Archbishop Photios was in communion with the late Bishop Dionisije of the Serbian Orthodox Free Diocese of the United States and Canada and Bishop Alexis of Adelaide, Australia, of the Byelorussian Autocephalic Church.

Membership: Not reported.

★227★
Greek Orthodox Missionary Archdiocese of Vasiloupolis
44-02 48th Ave.
Sunnyside/Woodside, NY 11377

The Greek Orthodox Missionary Archdiocese of Vasiloupolis was founded in 1970 when Archimandrite Pangratios Vrionis was elected and consecrated by Romanian Bp. Theofil Ionescu, Russian Patriarchial Dositheus Ivanchenko, and Albanian Apb. Christoforus Rado to serve among the Greek-Americans who had migrated to Long Island from Albania, Romania, and parts of Russia. Vasiloupolis (royal city) refers to Queens, New York, where Metropolitan Pangratios was consecrated. The church grew out of a refugee program started by the late Fr. Alexander Tzulevitch, pastor of St. Nicolas Russian Orthodox Church in New York City. At a "Synod of the Diaspora", Archimandrite Pangratios was chosen to be the archbishop over these people who had declared their desire for a leader who was traditionalist with a multicultural background, an American citizen, and missionary-minded. In addition, he would have to be approved by the exiled royal families of Greece and Romania.

Through the 1970s, Metropolitan Pangratios moved to build the archdiocese which had grown primarily through the addition of conservative ethnic parishes. He is assisted by three titular bishops: Antonios (LeBlanc) of New Bethany, Savvas (Kortmas) of Coronea, and Michael Pangratios (Rouse) of New Carthage. Together with Metropolitan Pangratios they constitute the Hierarchial Consistory.

In the late 1980s, the archdiocese grew significantly by the acceptance into it of former members of the Holy Order of MANS, and indeendent jurisdiction founded by Fr. Paul W. Blighton (d. 1974). This group was catechised and baptized into Orthodoxy largely by Abbot Herman Podmoshensky who himself transferred under the Episcopal Omophorion (authority) of Metropolitan Pangratios along with his monastic communities in 1984. Fr. Herman's order, the Orthodox Brotherhood of St. Herman of Alaska, is well known for its numerous Orthodox books, calendars, and bookstores, as well as the Paisius Missionary School at Forestville, California.

The archdiocese is Orthodox in faith and takes a traditionalist stance, although it does accept and maintain, through a canonical Orthodox manner, Western Rite Orthodox parishes. It is an Old Calendarist group, meaning its liturgical life follows the Julian rather than the Gregorian calendar. It opposes what it considers to be the modernist trends and attempts at liturgical reform represented in the churches which make up the Standing Conference of Orthodox Bishops in America.

Membership: In 1997 the archdiocese reported 115 parishes and 14 monasteries.

Remarks: Among Metropolitan Pangratios' consecrators had been Archbishop Christoforus Rado, who around 1958 had founded the Independent Albanian Orthodox Church of St. Paul. Archbishop Christoforus died in 1974. While some of his parishes joined the Orthodox Church of America, some came under Pangratios who consecrated Stavros Skembi to lead them. Pangratios also inherited the following of Greek-Romanian Bishop Theofil. In 1981 Pangratios consecrated Stephen Degiovanni to minister to a group of Italo-Greek immigrants located on Long Island, New York, and New Jersey.

Sources:

Blighton, Paul. *Memoirs of a Mystic.* San Francisco, CA: Holy Order of MANS, 1974.

Book of the Master Jesus. 3 vols. San Francisco, CA: Holy Order of MANS, 1974.

The Golden Force. San Francisco, CA: Holy Order of MANS, 1967.

★228★
Greek Orthodox Missions to the Americas
Current address not obtained for this edition.

The Greek Orthodox Missions to the Americas was founded in 1963 as a loose confederation of independent Greek parishes. In 1976 Fr. Garasimos Vlosoplos was consecrated as the metropolitan for the church, and the following year it was incorporated. Metropolitan Garasimos heads the small jurisdiction from the church in Astoria, New York. Both Greek and English-language liturgies are used.

Sources:

Clarke, Boden. *Lords Temporal and Lords Spiritual.* San Bernardino, CA: Borgo Press, 1985.

★229★
Hellenic Orthodox Church in America
22-68 26th St.
Astoria, NY 11105

At the time the state Church of Greece adopted the Gregorian calendar in place of the Old (Julian) Calendar it had followed for centuries, pockets of opposition began to arise immediately. Continued adherence to the Old Calendar also emerged among Greek Orthodox believers in the United States. In 1952, Bishop Petros, then a monk from Mt. Athos, arrived in the United States from Greece as the representative of the Old Calendarists to pull together the scattered American believers. In 1962, he was consecrated as bishop of Astoria (New York), where he had established his headquarters, and Exarch of the American work. He was consecrated by two bishops of the Russian Orthodox Church Outside of Russia.

Throughout the years of its existence, the Old Calendar Movement had been split by an ongoing controversy over the presence of grace in the state Church of Greece, given its abandonment of the traditional liturgical calendar. The moderate faction held to the position that grace remained in the state church. In 1974, however, Archbishop Auxentios, the head of the synod of the moderates, issued a statement (seemingly in an attempt to placate the more extreme group which denied the presence of grace in the state church) in which he accepted the essence of the extreme position.

As a result of Archbishop Auxentio's action, Petros left his jurisdiction and reorganized his work independently as the Hellenic Orthodox Church in America. He follows the traditional belief and practice of Orthodoxy. By 1967, he had five churches and some 9,000 members. St. Sincletike Convent is located in Farmingdale, New York. He started a newsletter, *The Voice of Orthodoxy*, and a radio show of the same name. Membership in the jurisdiction is centered among Greek Americans on Long Island.

Membership: Not reported. In 1985 there were parishes in Astoria, Bethpage, and Hensonville, New York.

Periodicals: *The Voice of Orthodoxy.*

Sources:

Chrysostomos, Archimandrite, with Hieromonk Ambrosios, and Hieromonk Auxentios. *The Old Calendar Orthodox Church of Greece.* Etna, CA: Center for Traditionalist Orthodox Studies: 1986.

"Greek Old Calendarists in the U.S.A.: An Annotated Directory." *Orthodox Tradition* 2, no. 2 (1985): 49-61.

★230★
Holy African Church
(Defunct)

The Holy African Church emerged around 1937 under the leadership of Bp. Arthur Stanley Trotman, formerly a bishop of the African Orthodox Church. Following the death of Abp. George A. McGuire in 1934, leadership of the church passed to Abp. William E. J. Robertson, then head of the church's work in Miami,

Florida. The primary membership of the church was in New York and the northeast, and Trotman joined Bps. Reginald Grant Barrow, Robert Arthur Valentine, and Vicar General Frederick A. Toote in the founding of a new church, the African Orthodox Church of New York and Massachusetts, to continue the church apart from the Miami jurisdiction. The new church soon had its own problems as Barrow and Trotman disagreed and Trotman left to found the rival African Orthodox Church, Inc. In the meantime, Robertson filed suit against both churches, claiming that they should not be able to take the name of the African Orthodox Church and confuse people by establishing a rival organization. The court agreed and in 1938 ruled against both Barrow and Trotman. Trotman moved quickly to reorganize his jurisdiction as the Holy African Church. A short time later Barrow and Trotman reconciled, and Barrow merged his work into the Holy African Church.

Trotman was succeeded as head of the church successively by Robert Arthur Valentine (1945), Frederick A. Toote (1954), and Gladstone St. Clair Nurse (1959). Once all the people involved in the schisms of the 1930s were dead, Nurse was able to work out an agreement with the African Orthodox Church by which in 1964 the Holy African Church merged into its parent body.

Sources:

Terry-Thompson, A. C. *The History of the African Orthodox Church.* N.p.: the author, 1956.

★231★
Holy Apostolic Orthodox Catholic Church
(Defunct)

The Holy Apostolic Orthodox Catholic Church was founded in the mid-1960s with headquarters in Fort Lauderdale, Florida. During the 1970s it claimed to have a seminary and an elaborate hierarchy, including two archbishops and one bishop in the United States, and additional archbishops in West Germany, the Canal Zone, Hong Kong, and Switzerland. During the 1980s, no manifestation of the church or its founder Archbishop Mark Cardinal Evans has been seen. The Church professed the Orthodox faith as based in the Nicene Creed without the filoque clause and used the Liturgy of St. John Chrysostom without alteration.

Sources:

Ecclesiatical Proclamation, Divine Liturgy. Home Missions Department of the Holy Apostolic Orthodox Catholic Church, 1965.

★232★
Holy Eastern Orthodox Catholic and Apostolic Church in North America
HC74, Box 419-2
Mountain View, AR 72560

The Holy Eastern Orthodox Catholic and Apostolic Church in North America, better known by its approved shortened name, the American Orthodox Church, traces its history to 1927 and the establishment of an independent non-ethnic synod by action of the Russian Orthodox Church in North America and incorporated in Boston, Massachusetts, in 1928 by Abp. Aftimios Ofiesh and seven others. The new synod was established to serve the English-speaking Orthodox community in "the new world." (Today a number of the independent Orthodox jurisdictions claim to continue the initial effort initiated by Ofiesh.) The Russian Orthodox Church abandoned Ofiesh, who passed his lineage to several bishops who have continued his work.

The American Orthodox Church is headed by Victor I, its primate.

Membership: Not reported.

★233★

Holy Eastern Orthodox Church, Italio-Byzantine
Current address not obtained for this edition.

Orthodoxy established itself in southern Italy and Sicily in the Greek communities which had established themselves in ancient times. Most of these Greek churches came under the authority of the Roman Catholic Church after the Synod at Bari in 1097 A.D. Only two bishops refused to submit and they led their Orthodox followers into what became an increasingly underground church. The church survived in spite of severe measures to convert its members to Catholicism. Cut-off from mainline Orthodoxy, however, it developed several peculiarities, including a married bishopric. It also has a mobile episcopacy, in part due to the persecution it felt, and began to designate their bishops as being "in" a See location rather than "of" a See City. Thus, their present Primate is Bishop Umile Natalino, Bishop in Veneto. The Church became fully autonomous in 1428.

The first Italian Orthodox priests came to America in 1904 and established parishes in Brooklyn, Newark and Philadelphia. Progress was slow until 1979 when two men, Emilio Rinauldi and Luciano Gaudio, were elected Bishop in Newark (NJ) and Las Vegas (NV) respectively. They were consecrated by a deputation of bishops from Italy headed by the late Primate Constantino, Bishop in Catania.

The Church is Orthodox in theology. The two bishops have administrative responsibility for that section of the United States in which they reside. Bishop Gaudio announced plans to build a monastic complex in New Mexico. The Church was affiliated with the Holy Orthodox Church, American Jurisdiction headed by Bishop James Francis Miller which merged into the Orthodox Catholic Church of America.

Membership: Not reported.

★234★

Holy Eastern Orthodox Church of the United States
Current address not obtained for this edition.

The Holy Eastern Orthodox Church of the United States (Orthodox Catholic Archdiocese of Philadelphia, Metropolitan See) dates itself to 1927 and the establishment of the American Orthodox Church under Bishop Aftimios Ofiesh, as authorized by the American bishops of the Russian Orthodox Church. In 1971 Archbishop Trevor Wyatt Moore and the priests under his jurisdiction incorporated the Orthodox Catholic Archdiocese of Philadelphia. Moore had been consecrated in the Ofiesh lineage, on July 11, 1971, by Archbishops Peter A. Zurawetzky and Uladyslau Ryzy-Ryski. A month later Ryzy-Ryski, head of the American World Patriarchs, in his plan to establish a hierarchy of patriarchs representing the various ethnic groups, elevated Moore to archbishop with jurisdiction for the English-speaking world. Then, in 1972, he designated Moore a metropolitan.

From the very beginning, the archdiocese was incorporated independently as a self-protective measure against any irregularities, heterodoxy, or heresy that might develop within the American World Patriarchs. Within a few years, Metropolitan Trevor saw a significant drift within the American World Patriarchs as evidenced by its following an unacceptable pan-ecumenism, developing anti-Russian attitudes, espousing the use of a self-created Western liturgy, and most importantly, failing to perpetuate the necessary conditions set forth by the synod of Russian bishops in 1927 for the American Orthodox Church. Metropolitan Trevor had rigorously followed those conditions in theology, liturgy, and otherwise.

As a result of the irregularities, the archdiocese severed all connections with the American World Patriarchs in 1976, when the official name became the Holy Eastern Orthodox Church of the United States, an abridgement of the original name given to Ofiesh's jurisdiction, the Holy Eastern Orthodox Catholic and Apostolic Church in North America.

Metropolitan Trevor asserts that his jurisdiction is the only remnant of the original jurisdiction headed by Archbishop Ofiesh in that it is the only one which adheres to all of the conditions set forth in the original charter and constitution. It has remained truly Orthodox in all aspects of its life and, while independent, acknowledges the primacy of the Russian jurisdiction and preserves a filial relationship to the Orthodox Church of Russia by the Patriarchial Authority of Moscow and All Russia. [Note: In Orthodox practice, the first Orthodox Church to initiate work in a new couhtry is generally acknowledged to have canonical primacy for that country. In the case of the United States, the Russian Orthodox Church was present for a century prior to any other Orthodox jurisdiction's establishment of a parish.]

Beliefs. The church is strictly Eastern Orthodox in faith and practice and adheres to the Byzantine rite. It holds to the Nicene Creed and follows its Eastern text.

Organization. The church is episcopal in polity. It is organized into the Metropolitan See of Philadelphia, the Orthodox-Greek Catholic Missionary Eparchy of Trenton and All New Jersey, and the Orthodox-Greek Catholic Diocese of Providence and All New England. Congregations can be found in Pennsylvania, New Jersey, Rhode Island, Massachusetts, Virginia, Florida, Illinois, and Nebraska. There is a mission church in Puerto Rico.

The church has been most attuned to the issues that have dominated the established churches in the United States, particularly in matters of social concern. It has spoken out forcefully on peace and nonviolence. It operates a social service center in Philadelphia, Pennsylvania, and through its affiliated Society of the Helpers of Saint Herman of Alaska, a mental health ministry in Florida. It has been active in civil rights and interracial and intercultural efforts, particularly in Spanish-speaking communities. Through it all Metropolitan Trevor has become one of only a few independent Orthodox leaders to gain some recognition from the larger Christian community, through his authorship of several books and service as an editor-at-large for the *Christian Century* magazine.

Membership: In 1988, the church reported 2,400 members in 13 parishes in the United States and one mission in Puerto Rico.

Periodicals: *Tserkobnost.*

★235★

Holy Orthodox Catholic Church
% Paul Gilbert Russell
5831 Tremont
Dallas, TX 75214

This body began in 1965 as the American Orthodox Church but changed its name in 1972 to the Holy Orthodox Catholic Church. It is headed by Bishop Paul G. Russell, who was consecrated on August 22, 1976 by Bishops David Baxter and William Henry. The group accepts the idea of female priests and would ordain a homosexual to Holy Orders, but in all other respects the Church holds to the Orthodox-Catholic faith. It is headquartered in Dallas and claims six priests and three parishes. Membership is unknown.

Membership: In 1983 the church reported 3 parishes and 6 priests.

★236★

Holy Orthodox Catholic Church
% The Order of the Servants of Jesus
PO Box 350
Clarkdale, GA 30020

The Celtic Rite Orthodox Diocese is a rite of the Holy Orthodox Catholic Church that wishes to bring the strength of Celtic spiritual expression into the twentieth century. The diocese considers itself Christian, Orthodox and Celtic; that is, Christian in love and mission; Orthodox in theology, beliefs, and practices; and Celtic in the expression of spirituality and heritage. The diocese uses the vernacular in worship and freely experiments with an array of ancient and modern music. The Order of the Servants of Jesus is a small ordered community affiliated with the diocese. The church is a member of the International Federation of Orthodox Catholics United Sacramentally (FOCUS).

Membership: Not reported.

Sources:

Pruter, Karl. *The Directory of Autocephalous Bishops of the Apostolic Sucession.* San Bernadino, CA: Brogo Press, 1906. 104 pp.

Ward, Gary. *Independent Bishops: An International Directory.* Detroit: Apogee Books, 1990. 524 pp.

★237★

Holy Orthodox Church, American Jurisdiction
238 Overby Dr.
PO Box 415
Antioch, TN 37011-0414

History. The Holy Orthodox Church, American Jurisdiction, though restructured in 1974, was originally established as the American Orthodox Church by the Russian Orthodox Archdiocese of Brooklyn in 1932 under the episcopacy of Archbishop Aftimios Ofiesh for the communicants of Western Rite Orthodoxy. Aftimios' mission, assigned him by the Moscow Patriarchate, was to unite the various ethnic-Orthodox jurisdictions in America into a single American jurisdiction. The unification effort failed due to both foreign and domestic influences and the Russian Church directed Aftimios to abandon the mission, disband the diocese of Brooklyn, and turn over its cathedral and assets to the Syrian Orthodox Church.

Aftimios had established the orthodox Western (Gregorian) Rite in America in January 1932 and ordained the former Episcopal Church priest William Albert Nichols to the orthodox priesthood. With the understanding that he would follow the Gregorian rite, Aftimios assigned him as pastor of the very first canonical Orthodox Western Rite parish in America located in New York City.

As directed, Aftimios began closing down the affairs of the Brooklyn Archdiocese. Among his last actions before turning over the archdiocese to the Syrian Orthodox Church, Aftimios, assisted by Bishop Joseph Zuk and Sophronios Bashira, consecrated Nichols to the episcopacy on September 30, 1932. They named him archbishop of the newly established Western Rite archdiocese under the identity of the American Orthodox church. Nichols took the name "Ignatius" as his episcopal name.

The Society of Clerks Secular of St. Basil, commonly known as the Basilian Fathers, was founded by Aftimios and Nichols as the missionary arm of the newly formed Western Rite apostolate, with Nichols as the superior general. Eventually, as Nichols' health failed, Fr. Tyler Turner, S.S.B., was elected superior-general of the Order and was subsequently consecrated in 1939. Taking the religious name Alexander, he succeeded Ignatius as head of the Western Rite archdiocese of the American Orthodox Church.

In 1960, of the 19 then active members of the Order of Basilian Fathers, four were incardinated as priests in the Antiochean Orthodox Christian Archdiocese of North America, then led by Metropolitan Archbishop Anthony Bashir. Two years previously, the Syrian Orthodox Patriarch of Antioch had authorized Bashir to establish a Vicariate for the Western Rite communicants.

The Basilian Order, as such, did not become part of the Syrian Vicariate. It remained an autonomous entity unto itself committed to the Western Rite apostolate. Nearly two years after Alexander's death, Fr. William Francis Forbes, S.S.B., was elected a superior general of the Order in 1973. In the summer of 1974, following a tenure of 15 years with the Syrian jurisdiction, Father Forbes withdrew from the Vicariate to give full time to the Western Rite apostolate of the Basilians. On October 20, 1974, two bishops within the Aftimios-Ignatius line of succession, Archbishop Thomas Jude Baulmer and Bishop John Chrysostom Martin, consecrated

Forbes to the episcopacy, thus restoring the original line of apostolic succession to the Basilians and the American Orthodox Church. Shortly thereafter, Bishop Forbes restructured both the Basilian Order and the American Orthodox Church. He sold the Basilian Motherhouse in New York and moved the entire operation of the Order and the church to Antioch, a suburb of Nashville, Tennessee, where the Cathedral of St. Basil is located.

Beliefs. The church is thoroughly Orthodox in faith and sacramental practice. It accepts the original Nicene Creed and the doctrinal affirmation of the seven Ecumenical councils. The majority of the parishes are Western Rite. Though the Eastern Rite is allowed, few choose to follow it.

Organization. The ecclesiastical order of the church is vested in its Synod of Bishops which has five members. The Synod has authority over its Metropolitan-Archdiocese of Nashville, the Archdiocese of Boston (Bridgewater) Massachusetts, and the Dioceses of Philadelphia, Louisiana (New Orleans), and Montreal-Quebec. The religious order of Basilian Fathers remains a part of the church. The American (Western Rite) Jurisdiction is responsible for its own ecclesiastical affairs and is not subject to any other Orthodox body, foreign or domestic. It has no connection with any group claiming to American Orthodox and/or deriving authority from either Archbishops Aftimios, Ignatius, or Alexander.

Membership: The jurisdiction maintains a stable membership which has increased slightly since its report of 1,500 in 1988.

Educational Facilities: St. Basil's Seminary, a tutorial structure for preparing priests.

Periodicals: *The Communicator.* • The Reconciler. Send orders to c/o Emmaus House, 27 N. Walker, Taunton, MA 02780.

Sources:

Samuchin, Michael. *A Brief History of the Holy Orthodox Church (American Jurisdiction).* Antioch, TN: Society of Clerks Secular of St. Basil, 1992.

★238★

Holy Orthodox Church, Diocese of New Mexico (Cunningham)
Current address not obtained for this edition.

The Holy Orthodox Church, Diocese of New Mexico was formed by Archbishop Bartholomew Cunningham a former priest of the Roman Catholic Church and seminary professor. Cunningham was consecrated by Bishops Colin James Guthrie and Robert S. Zeiger of the American Orthodox Catholic Church on June 23, 1968 and served under Guthrie until the present Holy Orthodox Church, Diocese of New Mexico, was established in 1970. The church is Orthodox in faith and practice. It is open to the ordination into the priesthood of otherwise qualified homosexuals but rejects females for holy orders.

Archbishop Batholemew died in 1984 and the future status of the Diocese is in question.

Membership: In the early 1980s, the church reported 15 parishes and a few hundred members, primarily in New Mexico and Illinois.

★239★

Holy Orthodox Church in America
PO Box 192-B
Preston Hollow, NY 12469

The Orthodox Church in America grew out of the early interest in Christian Mysticism of Rosicrucian George Winslow Plummer. Plummer had been one of the founders of the Societas Rosicruciana in America, covered in a separate item in this *Encyclopedia*, in 1907 and became its leader when Sylvester Gould died two years later. In the 1920s, Plummer's particular interest in mysticism led him to found the Seminary of Biblical Research through which he issued lessons on Christian mysticism. About this same time he founded the Anglican Universal Church and sought consecration from a Puerto Rican bishop, Manuel Ferrando.

In 1934 Plummer was reconsecrated by Bishop William Albert Nichols of the American Orthodox Church, originally founded by Lebanese Orthodox bishop, Aftimios Ofiesh and took the religious name, Mar Georgius. Following his consecration, he reconsecrated three of his bishops of the Anglican Universal Church and incorporated as the Holy Orthodox Church in America. The Holy Orthodox Church in America (Eastern Catholic and Apostolic) accepted through Nichols the mandate of Bishop Ofiesh to develop an American Eastern Orthodoxy.

The Holy Orthodox Church, while endorsing the canons of the Seven Ecumenical Councils, has remained intimately connected to the Rosicrucian organization which Plummer headed. The original episcopal leadership was drawn from the S.R.I.A. and the original parishes were all located in cities with an S.R.I.A. group. The liturgy of the church is that of St. John Chrysostom, however, a special emphasis is placed upon spiritual healing and special services for that purpose are held weekly.

Plummer died in 1944 and was succeeded by Archbishop Theodotus Stanislaus DeWitow (formerly Witowski). When Dewitow died, the church was without a bishop from 1969 to 1981. The work was carried on by three deaconesses, two of whom, Mrs. G. E. S. DeWitow (a.k.a. Mother Serena), widow of the last archbishop, and Lucia Grosch were consecrated in 1981 by Archbishop Herman Adrian Spruit of the Church of Antioch. Mother Serena died in 1989. She was succeeded by Archbishop Matriarch Lucia Grosch, who is the current presiding bishop.

Membership: In 1997 the church reported that it had two churches, one chapel, and a membership of approximately 100.

Periodicals: *Mercury.*

★240★
Holy Orthodox Church in North America
850 South St.
Box 129
Roslindale, MA 02131

The Holy Orthodox Church in North America is the American branch of the Church of the True Orthodox Christians of Greece (the Synod of Archbishop Maximos). The church was established as a result of the problem that emerged in the State Church of Greece in 1924 when the Gregorian Calendar replaced the older Julian Calendar and ecumenical events between the state church and Non-Orthodox bodies began to occur. Rejecting these developments, the old calendar faithful saw a need to organize separately. In 1963, Archbishop Auxentios (1912–1994) became their leader. The old calendar movement had also found some response in America, and parishes began to emerge there in the 1930s. The State Church of Greece, in the meantime, declared the sacraments of the old calendarists invalid and instituted a persecution by which the faithful were killed and their churches destroyed or confiscated.

In 1974, Archbishop Auxentios issued an encyclical in which he declared that the sacraments of the State Church of Greece were devoid of grace, hence invalid. This encyclical earned him the animosity of the State Church; in the western Hemisphere, his American Exarchate, under the leadership of Bishop Petros, left him. Then in 1987, Archbishop Auxentios jurisdiction in America was again augmented by the addition of a number of parishes that had withdrawn from the Russian Ortodox Church Outside of Russia.

Since its formation following the Russian revolution, the Russian Orthodox Church Outside of Russia had become the bastion of conservative traditionalist eastern orthodoxy. It stood against the subversion of the Russian Church under the hostile antireligious regime and opposed changes in the orthodox community which had entered into the post-World War II spirit of dialogue and ecumenical accommodation with both Protestants and

Roman Catholics. In the United States, priests and believers from a variety of ethnic backgrounds were drawn to this church. Among the issues disturbing twentieth-century Orthodoxy were the increasing ecumenical activities and statements and joint prayers which were contrary to centuries-old Orthodox Church traditions. Many saw the involvement in ecumenism as a serious compromise of the Orthodox Faith, and the Russian church opposed these developments.

In 1986, clergy within the Russian Church, some of whom were Greek-Americans, leveled a series of charges concerning the Russian Churchs change of course and its not disciplining clergy who had participated in extracanonical ecumenical events. This protest was brought to a head by encyclicals published by the Russian bishops which confirmed the charges made by these clergy. As a result, in December 1986, a group of 17 congregations, 25 clergy, and two monasteries, left the Russian Church and placed themselves under Bps. Akakios and Gabriel, two Greek Old Calendar bishops. That arrangement did not work out administratively, and in the fall of 1987, the group placed themselves under Archbishop Auxentios.

In June 1988, Auxentios made his first visit to the United States to meet with his new following. At the churchs Holy Synod in July 1988, Hieromonk Ephrem of Transfiguration Monastery was elected to the Episcopate and consecrated on August 17. In 1991, the Diocese of Toronto was created and Bishop Markarios (consecrated in Greece in January 1991) was placed in charge. Following the death of Archbishop Auxentios in 1994, Archbishop Maximos was selected to succeed him.

Membership: In 1995 the church reported 25 congregations, 41 clergy, and three monastic establishments in the United States and Canada with over 2,000 members. The church is the largest of the Greek Old Calendar Orthodox churches. Affiliated branches are found in Switzerland, Russia, Ukraine, Australia, Italy, and France.

Periodicals: *Orthodox Christian Witness.* Send orders to 10300 Ashworth Ave., N, Seattle, WA 98133-9410; *Orthodox Light.* Send Order to 28 Flintwood Ct., Willowdale, ON Canada M2S 3P2; *The True Vine.* Send orders to Box 129, Roslindale, MA 02131; *The Struggler.* Send Orders to Box 383, Topsfield, MA 01983-0583.

★241★
Holy Ukrainian Autocephalic Orthodox Church in Exile
℅ Rt. Rev. Sirhij K. Pastukhiv
103 Evergreen S.
West Babylon, NY 11704

The Holy Ukrainian Autocephalic Orthodox Church in Exile was organized in New York City in 1951 among immigrants who had left the Ukraine, primarily that part formerly controlled by Poland, as a result of the disruptions of World War II. A diocese was formed under the guidance of Archbishop Palladios Rudenko, former bishop of Krakiv, Lviv and Lemkenland, and Archbishop Ihor Huba, former bishop of Poltava and Kremenchuk, both refugees then living in the United States. The church was incorporated in 1960.

Membership: In 1972 the church had only two parishes, one in West Babylon and one in Syracuse, New York.

★242★
Holy United Catholic and Apostolic Church
PO Box 703
Browns Mills, NJ 08015

The Holy United Orthodox Catholic and Apostolic Church traces its history to 901 C.E. and the founding of the Holy Eastern Orthodox Catholic and Apostolic Church, Order of Saint Gregory of Nyssa by Father Jakot of Worms and Fr. Hugo of Cologne. The occasion for the founding of this Orthodox church in what was nominally Roman Catholic territory was the recovery of the lost writings of Gregory of Nyssa (a fourth-century bishop). In 1065, eleven years after the Great Schism between the Orthodox and Roman Catholic churches, envoys from Constantinople arrived in Cologne and consecrated Bishop Johann as the German Orthodox bishop. The lineage of Bishop Johann was passed on through the centuries.

The relatively small church suffered greatly through the Reformation era (sixteenth century) but survived to the present. The German Orthodox bishops participated in several conferences following the establishment of the Old Catholic Church in the 1870s. In 1873, Abp. Wilhelm Von Strom (1840–1928) was the co-consecrator of German Old Catholic bishop Joseph Hubert Reinkens. He was succeeded by Abps. Otto Stefan Von Strom and Hansel Johnann Von Strom. Abp. Hansel Johann Von Strom consecrated James Stroms as archbishop and enthroned him as Patriarch of the Order of Saint Gregory of Nyssa in 1988. Following Archbishop Hansel's death in 1996, Archbishop Paul II (James Stroms) moved the headquarters to the United States and the following year brought Saint Gregory Seminary from Cologne to Saint Paul Cathedral in Hyder, Alaska. In 1997 he was formally enthroned as Archbishop of the Holy United Orthodox Catholic and Apostolic Church of America (German-American Rite).

The church is Orthodox in faith and practice. The church operates through seven regional divisions, four archdioceses, and three dioceses. The church has been active ecumenically. In 1995, Archbishop Paul II was consecrated into the Order of Saint Gregory of the West African Rite by Patriarch Behazin Optat of Lagos, Nigeria. In 1996 he brought the church into the Holy Patriarchate of the Americas. Archbishop Paul II is also the Commander in Chief of the United Chaplain's Service and Association.

Membership: In 1997 the church reported 70,000 members in 38 congregations worldwide and 20,000 members in five congregations served by 14 priests in the United States. There were 200 members in two congregations in Canada. Foreign congregations were found in Germany, Poland, and Nigeria.

Educational Facilities: Saint Gregory Seminary, Hyder, Alaska.

Periodicals: *Orthodox Newsletter.*

Sources:

Barrett, David B. *World Christian Encyclopedia.* New York: Oxford, 1982.

★243★
Hungarian Greek Catholic Church
Current address not obtained for this edition.

The Hungarian Greek Catholic Church was a short-lived orthodox jurisdiction that grew out of attempts to extend the influence of Eastern Orthodoxy into Hungary. During the chaos of World War I, the patriarch of the Serbian Orthodox Church announced the extension of his jurisdiction into Hungary, a predominantly Roman Catholic country. The action gave an idea to Istvan Theodosius de Nemeth, a Roman Catholic priest, who decided that an independent Hungarian Orthodox church would have a following. However, it would be 20 years before the idea came to fruition.

In 1933 de Nemeth founded the Greek Oriental Hungarian Orthodox Church. He was consecrated as bishop of that church the following year by Moran Mor Ignatius Ephrem I, Patriarch of the Syrian Patriarchate of Antioch and All the East. The small jurisdiction continued through the years. In 1968 de Nemeth consecrated a man named de Nagy as his successor.

The Hungarian Greek Catholic Church was brought to America at some point after World War II by Stefan Boros, a priest who migrated to America from Hungary. For a period he functioned as a priest in the American Catholic Church, but by the early 1960s had established the Hungarian Greek Catholic Church in New York.

Membership: Not reported.

Sources:

Ward, Gary L. *Independent Bishops: An International Directory.* Detroit, MI: Apogee Books, 1990. 524 pp.

★244★
Independent Greek Orthodox Holy Archdiocese of North and South America
Current address not obtained for this edition.

The Independent Greek Orthodox Holy Archdiocese of North and South America was started in 1975 by Archbishop Dorotheos Flengas. Archbishop Dorotheos was born in Greece, and after completing his studies at the University of Athens, he became a priest in the Greek Orthodox Church. He came to America in 1953. He left the Greek Orthodox Church and in 1958 was consecrated as a bishop. He died in 1981. He was succeeded by Metropolitan Andreas. The Archdiocese is aligned with other independent bishops and churches in Greece.

Membership: In 1991 the church reported five congregations, seven priests, and approximately 1,000 members in the United States and 30 churches, 45 priests, and three bishops in Greece.

Educational Facilities: St. Fanourios Greek School, Elizabeth, New Jersey.

★245★
Macedonian Orthodox Church
Current address not obtained for this edition.

Another schism in the Serbian Church occurred in 1947 when under pressure of the government a new church was created to serve the geographic area of Macedonia, now existing in Yugoslavia, Greece, and Bulgaria, though its strength was in South Serbia. In 1959 the patriarchate was "forced" to recognize it as autonomous but under the Belgrade patriarch, and Bishop Dositej was placed at its head. In 1967 Dositej proclaimed separation and independence, an act not recognized by the patriarch (or anyone but Marshall Tito) and thus became schismatic.

The Macedonian Church was begun in Gary, Indiana, in 1961 during a visit of Rev. Spiridon Tanaskovski. Other parishes were established in Syracuse, New York, and Columbus, Ohio. They are under the jurisdiction of Bishop Kiril who resides in Skoplje, Yugoslavia. In 1972 a schism developed in the Sts. Peter and Paul Macedonian Orthodox Church in Gary, Indiana. As a result of disputes, Reverend Tanaskovski left and founded a new church, St. Clement Ohridski, which he claims is loyal to the American flag and not to Tito.

Membership: Not reported.

★246★
Mercian Orthodox Catholic Church
Current address not obtained for this edition.

The Mercian Orthodox Catholic Church (formerly known as Mercian Right Catholic Church) views itself as the continuing church body originally established in the United States by Apb. Joseph Rene Vilatte (1854-1829). Archbishop Vilatte was consecrated in Ceylon (now Sri Lanka) in 1892 by Mar Julius I of the Malankara Syrian Orthodox Church. He returned to the United States to establish the American Catholic Church. Vilatte was succeeded by Frederick E. J. Lloyd (1859-1933), and Lloyd by Daniel C. Hinton. When Hinton died, an era of confusion began in the small, but widely scattered, American Catholic Church. There were several claimants to the leadership, though the corporation eventually fell into the hands of Lowell Paul Wadle, a theosophically oriented bishop who took the American Catholic Church into the orb of the Liberal Catholic Church.

The Mercian Orthodox Catholic Church continues the Eastern or Catholic Orthodox thrust initiated by Vilatte. In this respect, they regard Abp. Joseph G. Sokolowski as the rightful inheritor of

Vilatte's leadership. Sokolowski was consecrated in 1970 by Abp. Joseph John Skureth. He served as a bishop for several years under Francis Xavier Resch in the Archdiocese of the Old Catholic Church in America. However, he broke with Resch's successor, Walter X. Brown, in 1975. Sokolowski founded an independent jurisdiction, St. Paul's Monastery Old Catholic Church. In the late 1970s the jurisdiction began to use the name Orthodox Catholic and gradually added the name Mercian. In 1987, Sokolowski consecrated Stephen Robert Thomas, announced his retirement (at 84 years old), and named Thomas as his successor.

The Mercian Orthodox Catholic Church is a Western Rite Orthodox Church. It adopted the Liturgy of St. Germain for use throughout the church under the leadership of Sokolowski. Through the 1970s and 1980s revisions of the liturgy were undertaken, resulting in a new Mercian Liturgy that was approved in 1987 for the church's worship. The term "Mercian" was adopted by the church in the late 1970s and identifies the jurisdiction with Christ the Merciful while keeping it free from any association with a particular ethnic or national group.

The church is Orthodox in faith and practice. There are seven sacraments, and in Orthodox fashion (as opposed to Roman Catholic practice) the church separates the service of Holy Unction (for the ill) from the service of Last Rites (for the dying).

The Mercian Church experienced significant growth through the 1980s and spread into Canada, Malaysia, Mexico, West Africa, Belgium, and Japan. Two diocese were initially established in the United States: the Primatial Diocese (Colorado Springs, Colorado) and the Diocese of St. Michael (La Porte, Indiana). Later the Missionary Diocese of St. Gregorios was designated in California and the Diocese of St. Peter the Apostle in Minnesota. Besides St. Paul's Monastery in Indiana, the church established several schools including Notre Dame de Lafayette University in Aurora, Colorado. Then in 1994, the upward progress of the church was halted when the state of Colorado's Commission on Higher Education moved against the university and its administration. It was charged with engaging in deceptive business practices in that it was offering degrees in nonreligious subjects beyond the authorizations of their charter and implying to its students, primarily correspondents, that it was an accredited institution.

The action of the state has led to a process of adjudication against the church and Archbishop Stephen Thomas which is continuing as this edition goes to press. The church has continued in its national and international work and has supported those charged in the Colorado case.

Membership: Not reported. In 1990 the church reported 2,500 members, 24 priests, and 18 congregations in the United States. There were two congregations and one priest in Canada.

Periodicals: *The Mercian Messenger.*

Sources:

Thomas, Stephen R. *The Mercian Rite Church: A Catholic Alternative.* Colorado Springs, CO: SCM Publications, 1988. Brochure.

___. *The Mercian Rite of the One, Holy, Catholic, and Apostolic Church.* Colorado Springs, CO: SCM Publications, [1988].

★247★
Old Orthodox Catholic Patriarchate of America
66 N. Brookfield St.
Vineland, NJ 08360

Not all of the independent Polish Catholic Churches founded in the late-nineteenth and early-twentieth century joined with the Polish National Catholic Church. Some of these parishes had associated with independent Old Catholic bodies which had grown out of the work of Archbishop Joseph Rene Vilatte and his American Catholic Church, especially the Old Catholic Church in America headed by Archbishop W. H. Francis Brothers and the Polish Catholic Church of Bishop Stephen Kaminski. In 1937 some of these churches joined with several parishes of Slavic (Lithuanian)

background and came together to form the Polish Old Catholic Church. They incorporated in New Jersey and elected Bishop Joseph Zielonka as their leader. Zielonka had been consecrated some years previously by Paolo Miraglia-Gulotti and had served as a bishop under Brothers.

Under Zielonka's capable leadership the church grew and by the time of his death in 1961 consisted of 22 parishes. Most were located in New Jersey with others in Pennsylvania and Massachusetts. The growth phase under Zielonka, however, was completely reversed under his successor, Peter A. Zurawetzky. Zurawetzky, Zielonka's suffragan, had been consecrated in Springfield, Massachusetts, in 1950. Patriarch Joseph Klimowicz of the Orthodox Catholic Patriarchate of America; Archbishop Konstatin Jaroshevich (a Byelorussian prelate who had been consecrated by Archbishop Fan Stylin Noli of the Albanian Orthodox Church); Archbishop Zielonka; Metropolitan Nicholas Bohatyretz of the Ukrainian Orthodox Church; and Old Catholic Bishop Peter M. Williamowicz participated in the consecration service.

Among his first acts, Zurawetzky changed the name of the Church to Christ Catholic Church of the Americas and Europe, an expression of a desire to move beyond ethnic and language barriers in his jurisdiction so that all nationalities might feel welcome. The future looked promising, but problems began to plague the newly named Church almost immediately. First some churches and clergy did not accept Archbishop Peter's leadership. They also did not like the name change. Second, Fr. Felix Starazewski asserted a claim to be the legitimate successor of the late Bishop Zielonka, and he and his church in South River, New Jersey, refused to honor the jurisdiction of Archbishop Peter. His defection led the way and other congregations departed for either the Polish National Catholic Church or one of the other independent Catholic or Orthodox bodies.

Third, and most importantly, Zurawetzky shifted his attention away from building his jurisdiction through expanding parishes and membership to growth by uniting with other independent Old Catholic and Eastern Orthodox bodies. He thus brought into his jurisdiction the divisiveness which had led to the splintering of these independent groups in the first place, and exacerbated the situation by assuming the title of Patriarch in America. Gradually all of his time and energy were poured into the actualization of a dominating vision, an American Patriarchate. At the same time his churches, consisting largely of Eastern European ethnic parishes, were being further reduced by the inevitable processes of Americanization.

By 1965, the Church having been reduced to a handful of communicants and clergy, a new possibility emerged. Rev. Karl Pruter, who had come from the Free Catholic Movement in the Congregational Church, was ordained by Archbishop Peter, and organized a nonethnic congregation in Boston, out of which a second congregation emerged. The Church of St. Paul was organized in Hobbs, New Mexico, by Fr. Daniel Smith. Then Zurawetzky moved to enlarge the Patriarchate. Assisted by Archbishop Uladyslau Ryzy-Ryski, he consecrated Pruter who consented to the consecration only on the condition that they be set aside as an independent jurisdiction to be called, Christ Catholic Church, Diocese of Boston, now known simply as Christ Catholic Church. Then, Smith was consecrated, but after a short while in Hobbs, he moved to Denver and withdrew from Archbishop Peter's jurisdiction altogether. Another briefly successful venture was the establishment of the Monastery of Our Lady of Reconciliation at Glorieta, New Mexico, in 1969. Fr. Christopher William Jones was a successful author and minister to many of the disenchanted youth of the late 1960s and early 1970s. However, shortly after Archbishop Peter consecrated him, he too left to form an independent, self-governing jurisdiction.

As of the mid-1980s, Archbishop Peter has no congregations in his jurisdiction, but maintains a chapel at Vineland, New Jersey, and a home in Chicago. He continues his efforts to build the Patriarchate.

Membership: As of 1985 there are no parishes in the Patriarchate, though several clergy remain affiliated.

Periodicals: *Our Missionary.* Send orders to 5520 W. Dakin, Chicago, IL 60641.

★248★
Orthodox Catholic Autocephalous Church
Current address not obtained for this edition.

The Orthodox Catholic Autocephalous Church was founded in the 1980s by Bp. James E. Henderson. Henderson had been consecrated by Abp. Trevor Wyatt Moore of the Holy Eastern Orthodox Church in the United States, and for a number of years Henderson functioned as a bishop in that church. The Orthodox Catholic Autocephalous Church resembles its parent body, as the occasion for the split was primarily administrative.

Membership: Not reported.

Sources:

Ward, Gary L. *Independent Bishops: An International Directory.* Detroit, MI: Apogee Books, 1990.

★249★
Orthodox Catholic Church
% Most Rev. Carlos A. Florido, Presiding Bishop
544 Oak St.
San Francisco, CA 94127

The Orthodox Catholic Church was founded in the mid-1980s by Carlos A. Florido. Florido was born in Cuba and became a priest in 1961. He subsequently moved to the United States. In 1983 he was consecrated as a bishop by Lewis S. Keizer of the Independent Church of Antioch and shortly thereafter founded the Independent Catholic Church headquartered at the St Francis of Assisi Church in San Francisco. At a later date that church became known as the Orthodox Catholic Church. In 1990 Florido consecrated Katherine Kurtz as a bishop in charge of an order community, the Third Order of St. Michael, based in Kilmacanogue, County Wicklow, Ireland.

Membership: Not reported.

Sources:

Ward, Gary L. *Independent Bishops: An International Directory.* Detroit: Apogee Books, 1990.

★250★
Orthodox Catholic Church in America
% Walter X. Brown
W 1207 W. River Dr.
Oconomowoc, WI 53066

The Orthodox Catholic Church in America, until recently known as the Archdiocese of the Old Catholic Church of America, began in 1941 when Bishop Francis Xavier Resch, who had been consecrated by Archbishop Carmel Henry Carfora of the North American Old Roman Catholic Church, broke with that jurisdiction and began the independent Diocese of Kankakee, centered upon his parish in Kankakee, Illinois. In a short time he had parishes in Illinois, Indiana, Michigan, and Wisconsin. However, these parishes, consisting primarily of first generation Eastern European immigrants, developed a more broadly based constituency as the second generation became Americanized. In 1963, Resch consecratd Fr. Walter X. Brown to the episcopacy. Brown moved the headquarters to Milwaukee, where the church developed a seminary, several programs for the treatment of alcoholism and drug abuse, and several new parishes.

During the 1980s, under Brown's leadership, the church has moved steadily from an Old Catholic to an Eastern Orthodox position. The church accepts both the Eastern and Western Orthodox tradition of the seven ecumenical councils and the unanimous opinion of the fathers of the Christian Church. The faith, practices, and discipline of the Eastern Orthodox churches has been adopted. The seven sacraments are practiced, and the Nicene Creed is followed in the church's own statement of faith. Individual parishes may use either the Western Gregorian or Eastern Byzantine rites.

The church supports two monastic communities, one Eastern and one Western, in Milwaukee. It became a charter participant in the recently organized Holy Orthodox Synod of America, a council of independent Orthodox jurisdictions in America which seek to facilitate cooperation within the larger American Orthodox community.

Membership: In 1988, the church reported 2,100 members, ten congregations, and 16 clergy in the United States. Churches are located in Dallas and Lubbock, Texas; Erie, Pennsylvania; Chicago, Illinois; Racine, Madison, Watertown, and Milwaukee, Wisconsin; Davenport, Iowa; St. Petersburg, Florida; Ludington, Michigan; Brooklyn, New York; and Ottawa, Ontario, Canada.

Educational Facilities: Holy Cross Theological Seminary, Milwaukee, Wisconsin.

Periodicals: *The Messenger.*

Remarks: In 1986 the Orthodox Catholic Church in America entered into an agreement of intercommunion with the Orthodox Catholic Church of America, headed by Archbishop Alfred Louis Lankenau. The two jurisdictions jointly formed the Holy Orthodox Synod of America, a confederation of independent Orthodox bishops for the purposes of sharing and fellowship.

Sources:

Holman, John Cyprian. *The Old Catholic Church of America.* Milwaukee, WI: Port Royal Press, 1977.

Resch, Francis X. *Compendium Philosophiae Universae.* Lake Village, IN: The Author, 1950.

★251★
Orthodox Catholic Church in America (Verra)
% Michael Edward Verra
238 Mott St.
New York, NY 10012

The Orthodox Catholic Church, known through the mid-1980s as the American Catholic Church, Archdiocese of New York, was established in 1927 by Fr. James Francis Augustine Lashley. Father Lashley, himself an African American, was moved to establish a Catholic jursidiction to serve those African Americans who were drawn to the Roman Catholic faith but felt rejected by the Roman Catholic Church. He also fostered the religious vocation of African American men called to the priesthood who were refused admission to Catholic seminaries because of their race.

In 1932, Bishop William F. Tyarks, of the American Orthodox Catholic Church, consecrated Father Lashley in the lineage of Archbishop of Joseph Rene Vilatte, an episcopal lineage originating in the Syrian Patriarchate of Antioch and the East. Lashley built a substantial jurisdiction, which in the mid-1960s reported 20 congregations (nine in the United States and 11 in the West Indies). Lashley died in the mid-1980s and was succeeded by Bishop Verra.

The Orthodox Catholic Church in America does not consider itself independent but a part of the Body of Christ, the One, Holy, Catholic, and Apostolic Church. The church takes as its standards of faith the Sacred Tradition, the accumulated teachings of the fathers of the Christian Church; the Holy Bible; the truths of the Seven Ecumenical Councils; and the Synod of Jerusalem of 1692, all believed to be inspired by the Holy Spirit. It specifically rejects the universal episcopal jurisdiction and infallibility of the Pope, the Filioque clause in the Apostles Creed; purgatory; indulgences; the immaculate conception of the Virgin Mary; limbo; and the use of unleavened bread in the Divine Liturgy. The church uses a

Western Rite liturgy in conformity with its Orthodox Catholic beliefs concerning the procession of the Holy Spirit from the Father and the changing of the bread and wine into the body and blood of Christ by the holy spirit in the eucharist. Both icons and statues are used. Clergy may marry.

Membership: As of 1997, the church had two parishes and three priests in the United States and two parishes and two priests in Trinidad.

★252★
Orthodox Catholic Church of America
% Alfred Louis Lankenau
PO Box 1222
Indianapolis, IN 46206

Several jurisdictions derive their orders from Archbishop Joseph Rene Vilatte, founder of the American Catholic Church through the orders given to the African Orthodox Church. In 1926 William F. Tyarks, a priest in the American Catholic Church who had been ordained by Vilatte's successor, Archbishop Frederick E. J. Lloyd in 1916, left Lloyd's jurisdiction and with other priests and members formed the American Catholic Orthodox Church. The group applied to the African Orthodox Church for orders and Archbishop George A. McGuire consecrated Tyarks in 1928.

In 1930 Tyarks consecrated one of the priests who had come from the American Catholic Church with him, Cyril John Clement Sherwood (1895-1969). Sherwood soon left Tyarks and was reconsecrated by McGuire in 1932. The next year he formed the American Holy Orthodox Catholic Apostolic Eastern Church. Sherwood's career overlapped that of Archbishop Aftimios Ofiesh's greatest activity, and Sherwood became acquainted with his vision of a united American Orthodoxy. He incorporated it in an ecumenical organization, the Orthodox Catholic Patriarchate of America.

Among Sherwood's bishops was George A. Hyde, whom the Patriarch consecrated in May 1957. Hyde had formed the Eucharistic Catholic Church in Atlanta, Georgia in 1946. This first exclusively gay ministry in America continued until 1959 when Hyde moved to Washington, D.C., and formed the Society of Domestic Missionaries of St. Basil the Great, an order of priests. The following year he left Sherwood and formed the Orthodox Catholic Church of America. He believed that Sherwood was too narrowly Eastern in his approach to liturgy and theology and wanted to restructure the church making it open to Western rite Orthodox practice. In spite of leaving Sherwood's jurisdiction, Hyde continued to participate in the ecumenical Orthodox Catholic Patriarchate of America.

In 1969 Sherwood died. At a meeting of the Synod the next year, Hyde was elected to succeed him as head of the Patriarchate, and the Holy Orthodox Catholic and Apostolic Eastern Church voted to become the Eastern Rite Diocese of the Orthodox Catholic Church of America. Thus Archbishop Hyde took control of all the work begun by Sherwood.

Doctrinally, the Orthodox Catholic Church of America follows the teachings of the Seven Ecumenical Councils and rejects the doctrinal innovations such as purgatory, papal infallibility, the immaculate conception, communion in one kind only, and an unmarried clergy. The Church uses both the Eastern and Western rites in its liturgy. Under Hyde's administration, the Church was active in promoting a ministry to homosexuals and is the ultimate source of the presently existing Eucharistic Catholic Church. After Hyde's retirement, this and other special ministries were discontinued in favor of work directed to all people.

In 1983 Hyde retired and Alfred Louis Lankenau, bishop of the Diocese of Indianapolis and Chicago, was elected to succeed him. Under the new Archbishop, the Orthodox Catholic Patriarchate of America, which had ceased to function during the 1970s, has been revived and several Catholic and Orthodox jurisdictions have affiliated. In 1983, the Holy Orthodox Church, American Ju-

risdiction, headed by Archbishop James Francis Miller, which had broken from the church of the same name headed by Archbishop William Francis Forbes, merged into the Church. Bishop Perry Sills of the Western Rite Orthodox Church was incardinated in 1988.

Membership: In 1995 the church reported parishes located in Maine, New York, Rhode Island, Indiana, Illinois, Georgia, South Carolina, Florida, and New Mexico with mission parishes in Pennsylvania, Ohio, and California. There were 32 priests and 960 members.

Remarks: In 1986 the Orthodox Catholic Church of America entered into an agreement of intercommunion with the Orthodox Catholic Church in America led by Archbishop Walter X. Brown and jointly formed the Holy Orthodox Synod of America. The synod is a confederation that independent Orthodox bishops may join.

Sources:

Bernard, R. J. *A Faith for Americans.* Anderson, SC: Ortho, 1974.

The Divine Liturgy. Elberton, GA: Orthodox Catholic Church of America, 1966.

Hyde, George Augustine., ed., *The Courage to Be Ourselves.* Anderson, SC: Ortho-Press, 1972.

___. *The Genesis of the Orthodox Catholic Church of America.* Indianapolis, IN: Orthodox Catholic Church of America, 1993.

★253★
Orthodox Catholic Church of North and South America
Box 1213
Akron, OH 44309

The Orthodox Catholic Church of North and South America was inspired by the ideal of the American Orthodox Church founded by Archbishop Aftimios Ofiesh under the guidance of Patriarch Tikhon of the Russian Orthodox Church. A new attempt to bring this into reality began with Bishop Joseph W. Alisauskas, Jr. (d. 1980), who had been consecrated in 1968 by Archbishop W. H. Francis Brothers of the Old Catholic Church in America. Early in the 1960s, Brothers had taken his jurisdiction into the Russian Orthodox Church but in 1967 withdrew and reconstituted the Old Catholic Church in America. Alisauskas left Brothers jurisdiction in 1969 and formed the Orthodox Catholic Diocese of Connecticut and New England, a name selected to designate accurately its geographic extent. In choosing the name, he was also drawing upon the impulse of Archbishop Joseph Rene Vilatte, who had ordained Brothers in 1910 and consecrated him in 1913. The church adopted a new constitution in 1976, at which time it assumed its present name.

Associated with Alisauskas was the Holy Protection of the Mother of God Monastic Community of Cleveland co-founded by Roman Bernard, a layman. Bernard was ordained by Alisauskas and in 1978 consecrated Bishop of Ohio City and Cleveland. The same year, Alisauskas was elevated to the rank of metropolitan and, upon his death on August 26, 1980, was succeeded by Archbishop Roman.

The Orthodox Church of North and South America is Orthodox in faith and practice, but follows a variety of liturgical rites including the Orthodox-Byzantine, the Ambrosian-Milanese, a modified (de-protestantized) Anglican, the Gallican (but only in the van der Mensbrugghe translation, approved by the 1985 synod meeting), and the Roman Tridentine.

This jurisdiction grew significantly in 1988 when the Catholic Orthodox Church of Guatemala and Latin America, some 200,000 strong, affiliated with it, bringing several parishes and priests plus a seminary with 46 students. At the 1990 Synod held at Akron, Ohio, a bishop (Jose Imre of Tiquisate, Guatemala) was consecrated by Archbishop Roman and Bishop Emanuel of Montreal, Quebec, for Central America.

In addition to its spiritual activities, this independent Orthodox body has a strong consciousness. Father Andres Giron, once a member of the Guatemalan Parliament, has been a member of the United Nations Human Rights Commission for quite some time. He is also the president and founder of ANACAMPRO, a collective farm system for poor and disenfranchised peasants without land. In the United States there are two facilities caring for the homeless (St. James House in Philadelphia and Holy Cross Home in Cleveland), while N.T.S./St. Paul's Mission in Glassport (Pittsburgh area), Pennsylvania, locates jobs, free of charge, for the unemployed.

Membership: In 1997 the church reported 28 parishes and missions and 11 mission stations, two of which are in the United States (in Warren, Ohio, and Pittsburgh, Pennsylvania), semi-monastic communities (in Pittsburgh, Pennsylvania; Phoenix, Arizona; and Barberton, Ohio), and a Shrine of St. Jude also in Barberton. Among the personnel are two bishops, 13 priests, three sub-deacons, 3 seminarians in the U.S., and nine members of religious communities (including monastics) with a total membership of approximately 214,300.

Educational Facilities: St. Nicholas Seminary, Akron, Ohio. Seminario de San Jose, Nueva Conception, Escuintla Province, Guatemala.

Periodicals: *The Orthodox Catholic Voice* (5/year). • *The Image* (monthly). Send orders to 594 5th Ave. NE, Barberton, OH 44203. • *The Western Orthodox Catholic* (periodic). Send orders to Box 27-406, Willow Station, Cleveland, OH 44127. • *The Clarion.* Available from St. Michael's Monastery, PO Box 8219, Phoenix, AZ 85066.

Remarks: According to Archbishop Roman, Archbishop Brothers had always considered himself head of the Western Orthodox Catholic Church of America and had a large, oval, episcopal ring (used for sealing official documents) which bore that designation. Vilatte, consecrated by the Oriental Orthodox Patriarchate of Antioch, had been permitted to use the title, Exarch of the Old Catholic Church in America, a tacit admission of the Patriarchate's equation of "Old Catholic" and "Western Orthodox." Since that time the name "Old Catholic" has taken on a variety of meanings not envisioned by the Patriarchate in 1892.

★254★

Orthodox Catholic Church of the Americas
Current address not obtained for this edition.

The Orthodox Catholic Church of the Americas is a small independent Catholic jurisdiction founded in 1986 by Msg. Antonio Fuoco. Most of its work is among French Canadians, and it is also known by its French name Eglise Catholique Orthodoxe des Ameriques. Fuoco was consecrated in 1983 by Abp. Andre Barbeau of the Catholic Charismatic Church of Canada, assisted by Andre Letellier and Jean-Marie Breault. He assumed the ecclesiastical name Mar Petros Johannes. In 1985 Fuoco founded the Religious Order of Saint Michael (Communaute Ecclesiale Oecumenique de Saint-Michel), over which he serves as superior general.

Membership: Not reported.

★255★

Orthodox Church in America
% Very Rev. Robert Kondratick, Chancellor
Box 675
Syosset, NY 11791

The Orthodox Church in America is the oldest continuously existing Eastern Orthodox body in North America in general and the United States in particular. As the first Orthodox church began to arrive, it assumed a hegemony over what became in the nineteenth century a multi-ethnic Orthodox community, and many of the presently existing independent Orthodox churches in America

began as parishes and/or a diocese within what is today known as the Orthodox Church in America.

The OCA began in Alaska with the arrival of missionaries of the Russian Orthodox Church. In 1794 eight monks and two novices arrived on Kodiak Island to follow up on the work of converting the Native Americans already begun by a generation of Russian lay people in the Aleutians. Among these ten was Father Herman, later canonized by the church. In 1824 John Veniaminov, a married priest, was sent to the Aleutians. After the death of his wife, he was consecrated the first bishop of a missionary diocese. Bishop Innocent had an outstanding career in Alaska, building the first cathedral at Sitka, among other accomplishments. He was called in 1868 to be the Metropolitan of Moscow, the highest office in the church and finally in 1977 canonized.

The sale of Alaska to the United States left the Missionary Diocese on its own. It moved its headquarters to San Francisco in 1872 and changed its name to the Russian Orthodox Church, Diocese of the Aleutian Islands and North America. The period during the episcopacy of Bishop Nicolas beginning in 1891 was a time of noted growth. The Alaskan Mission was expanded, and the work in Canada and the Eastern United States began.

In 1905 the diocese moved its headquarters from San Francisco to New York City. Its growth was recognized by its elevation to the rank of archdiocese. Under the archbishop was a bishop for Alaska and an Arabic-speaking bishop, Raphael Hawaweeny, who as Bishop of Brooklyn had oversight of Orthodox from the Middle East. Two additional bishops in Cleveland and Pittsburgh were soon added. The church progressed steadily until disrupted by events in Russia during World War I.

The Russian Revolution proved a disaster for the American Russian church. Russian Orthodox Christians had always carried a special loyalty for the royal family which had been executed by the new government in Moscow. Also, money from Russia which had always assisted in the support of the archdiocese was abruptly curtailed, to be almost immediately followed by a wave of immigration by refugees looking to the church for spiritual guidance and support. The patriarch of Moscow was arrested and the American church split over loyalty to him versus acceptance of the new government. Representative of what was termed the Living Church (those supportive of the Communist regime) arrived in the United States in 1923. At a synod of the Russian Church in 1924 in Detroit the credentials of the "Living Church" were rejected and the church asserted its administrative, judicial and legislative independence from Russia. It assumed a new name, the Russian Orthodox Greek Catholic Church of America and declared the imprisoned Archbishop Platon, "Metropolitan of All America and Canada," an action which led then to be popularly called the "Metropolia." Their major loss came in court. Before they were able to legally validate their separation from Moscow, the "Living Church" representatives were able to win the transfer of the title of St. Nicolas Cathedral in New York City into their hands.

In 1925 Archbishop Platon died. He was succeeded by Archbishop Sergius who in 1927 issued a declaration calling for loyalty and cooperation with the new Russian government. Prior to this declaration, the bishops of the Russian Orthodox Greek Catholic Church of America had cooperated with other Russian bishops around the world caught outside of Russia and also cut off by the Revolution. Following the declaration, Metropolitan Platon declared his loyalty to Sergius, but specifically denied him any power to make administrative decisions concerning the American church. In spite of the challenges of the several competing branches of Russian Orthodoxy, one staunchly opposed to any cooperation with the Church under Communist domination (Russian Orthodox Church Outside of Russia), and the other administratively tied to the Patriarch of Moscow (the American Exarchate of the Russian Orthodox Catholic Church), the Russian Orthodox Greek Catholic Church in America retained the support of most American believers.

During the years following the turmoil of the Russian Revolution, the Metropolia assumed the position that it would give recognition to the spiritual authority of the patriarch in Moscow, if he would recognize its administrative autonomy. However, the Church in Russia continued its support of those parishes in the Exarchate who recognized his complete authority. Finally, in 1970, the separation of the Metropolia from the church in Russia was ended when the patriarch of Moscow, His Holiness Alexis, granted autonomous status to the Russian Orthodox Greek Catholic Church of America, renamed the Orthodox Church in America. The Exarchate was dissolved and most of its parishes moved into the OCA.

For quite different reasons, the creation of the Orthodox Church in America created a controversy within the larger American Orthodox community. For many years there had been various attempts to move away from the ethnic divisions within American Orthodoxy. In creating the Orthodox Church in America, the Russian community asserted its status as the oldest Orthodox church in North America and as such the most fitting focus of Orthodox unity. Other Orthodox groups, particularly the Greek Archdiocese, saw the emergence of the OCA as a unilateral effort not deserving of recognition.

The OCA is headed by its archbishop, Metropolitan Theodosius, whose jurisdiction extends throughout the western hemisphere. There are nine dioceses in the United States, one in Canada and an exarchate in Mexico. Also under its canonical jurisdiction are the autonomous Albanian Orthodox Archdiocese and the Romanian Orthodox Episcopate of America. The latter places the OCA in a peculiar position, having a relationship with the Romanian Episcopate while holding membership in the Standing Conference of Canonical Orthodox Bishops which includes the rival Romanian Orthodox Church of America.

Membership: In 1995 the church reported 600 parishes, 2,000,000 members, and 792 priests.

Educational Facilities: St. Tikhon's Orthodox Theological Seminary, South Canaan, Pennsylvania.

St. Vladimir's Orthodox Theological Seminary, Tuckahoe, New York.

Periodicals: *The Orthodox Church*. Send orders to PO Box 675, Rte. 25A, Syosset, NY 11791. • *The Canadian Orthodox Messenger*. Send orders to 369 Alfred St., Kingston, ON, Canada K7K 4H6.

Sources:

Koulomzin, Sophie. *The Orthodox Christian Church through the Ages.* New York: Russian Orthodox Greek Catholic Church of America, 1956.

The Orthodox Liturgy...According to the Use of the Church of Russia. London: Society for Promoting Christian Knowledge, 1964.

Tarasar, Constance. *Orthodox America, 1794-1976: Development of the Orthodox Church in America.* Syosset, NY: Orthodox Church in America, Department of Archives and History, 1975.

★256★
Orthodox Church of America
Current address not obtained for this edition.

The Orthodox Church of America was formed on June 29, 1970 by Bishop David Baxter. Bishop Baxter had been consecrated the previous year by Archbishop Walter A. Propheta of the American Orthodox Catholic Church, assisted by bishops John A. Christian, and Foster Gilead. The church uses the Western Rite, but places emphasis upon its Eastern orders and Eastern spirituality. Its basis of faith is the Nicene Creed, the Seven Sacraments, and the necessity of Orders in the Apostolic Succession.

Membership: In 1983 the church reported 5 parishes, 14 priests, and 214 members.

Educational Facilities: St. Herman Seminary, Morrilton, Arkansas, a correspondence school.

★257★
Orthodox Church of Canada
901-580 Dundas St.
London, ON, Canada N6B 1W9

The Orthodox Church of Canada is an independent conservative Orthodox body whose Primate, Abp. Andrei Brennan, holds orders that derive from the Ukrainian Autocephalous Orthodox Church, the American Orthodox Church, and the former Autocephalous Greek Orthodox Church of the Americas and Europe. It has a stated goal of becoming a national Orthodox body for Canada. It is Orthodox in faith and practice and a charter member of the Synod of Autonomous Canonical Orthodox Churches in North America.

Membership: Not reported. As of 1998, affiliated congregations were primarily in Ontario.

Sources:

http://netministries.org/see/churches/ch051832/.

★258★
Patriarchial Parishes of the Russian Orthodox Church in the U.S.A.
% St. Nicholas Patriarchal Cathedral
15 E. 97th St.
New York, NY 10029

Following the Russian Revolution, the members of the Russian Orthodox Church in both Russia and the United States were split over rejecting or acknowledging the new government which had risen to power. Within the United States, especially after the arrest of the Patriarch of Moscow, the sentiment was largely against any accommodation and the American archdiocese declared itself administratively autonomous of the homeland. Meanwhile, within the Soviet Union, a reorganization of the church by leaders of the so-called "Living Church," those who supported accommodation to the Communist government occurred. With government backing, they assumed control of the Church and elected John Kedrowsky as the new bishop for the West. Kedrovsky arrived in America in 1923 prepared to take up his leadership role. However, at the same synod meeting in 1924 at which the Church declared its autonomy, Kedrovsky's credentials were rejected. As the official representative of the Church in Russia, however, he did find some support, and in 1926 won possession of the headquarters' cathedral in New York City.

Kedrovsky's situation was further complicated in 1933 by the arrival of Metropolitan Benjamin Fedchenkov. In the year that Bishop John had lived in the United States, the Church in Russia had regained some stability and the Living Church faction had died away. Metropolitan Benjamin represented a more acceptable accommodationist position and he gained some support. He established the American Exarchate of the Russian Orthodox Catholic Church. However, for another decade Bishop John, succeeded by his son Nicholas Kedrowsky, whom he had consecrated, kept possession o St. Nicholas Cathedral. Finally in 1945, after the death of both Bishop John and Nicolas, the Kedrovsky faction was left without either support of the Church in Russia or an episcopal leader. Rev. John Kedrovsky, Bishop John's other son signed the cathedral over to the Exarchate.

Negotiations continued sporadically in an attempt to work out differences between the church authorities and the larger autonomous Russian Orthodox Greek Catholic Church of America. These reached fruition in 1970. The Russian Orthodox Greek Catholic Church of America became the Orthodox Church in America and recognized the Patriarch of Moscow as its spiritual authority. The Patriarch, in turn, recognized its autonomous status. As part of the agreement, the Exarchate was disolved. At the time of the disolution of the Exarchate, it was agreed that any parishes which wished to remain under the direct administrative authority of the Moscow patriarchy could remain outside of the Orthodox Church in America. These several parishes reformed as the Patriarchal Parishes of the Russian Orthodox Church in the United States and Canada. A vicar bishop was placed in charge of the approximately 40 parishes. St. Nicholas remained with the Patriarchal Parishes and served as its headquarters. Over the years parishes have been allowed to transfer to the OCA. The church is also a member of the National Council of Churches.

Membership: In 1985, the church reported 9,780 members in 38 parishes served by 45 priests.

Periodicals: *One Church*. Send orders to 727 Miller Ave., Youngstown, OH 44502.

Sources:

Pokrovshy, M. *St. Nicholas Cathedral of New York, History and Legend*. New York: St. Nicholas Cathedral Study Group, 1968.

★259★
Reformed Orthodox Catholic Church
1674 Palm Ave.
San Diego, CA 92154

The Reformed Orthodox Catholic Church is a small Orthodox jurisdiction founded by Most Rev. Thomas Ephraim (the ecclesiastical name of Bishop Dennis Smith). Smith had originally been consecrated on July 1, 1971, in Miami, Florida, by Archbishop Richard E. Drews, head of the Reformed (Slavonic) Orthodox Church of Florida, assisted by Archbishops Mark Karras and George Erline. He later left Drews' jurisdiction.

Membership: Not reported.

★260★
Reformed (Slavonic) Orthodox Church
808 W. Sunrise Blvd.
Fort Lauderdale, FL 33311

The Reformed (Slavonic) Orthodox Church is a small Orthodox jurisdiction founded by Archbishop Richard E. Drews. Drew was originally consecrated on October 4, 1969, at St. Fanourios Orthodox Church, Woodside, New York, by Archbishops Lowell Paul Wadle of the American Catholic Church, assisted by Archbishops Mark Karras and George Erline. He later founded the Reformed Orthodox Church in Florida.

The church is Orthodox in belief and practice. The liturgy is in English.

Membership: Not reported.

★261★
Romanian Orthodox Church of America
℅ Most Rev. Abp. Victorin Ursache
19959 Riopelle
Detroit, MI 48203

The Romanian Orthodox Church of America, officially known as the Romanian Orthodox Missionary Archdiocese in America and Canada, had its beginning in the formation of the first Romanian Orthodox parish in North America, formed at Regina, Saskatchewan, in 1902. It was followed two years later by a parish in Cleveland, Ohio, the first in the United States. These parishes and others to follow functioned under the hegemony of the Russian Orthodox Church. A diocese was created in 1929 and a bishop assigned in 1935. Bishop Policarp Morusca returned to Romania at the beginning of World War II and after the war was detained and finally in 1948 involuntarily retired by the new Romanian government. In 1950 a new bishop, consecrated and sent by the Church in Romania arrived. The appearance of Bishop Andrei Moldovan divided the American church which had a bylaw

providing for the consecration of a bishop only after the election by a diocesan congress.

The majority of the American Romanian Orthodox reject Moldovan. The Romanian Orthodox Church in America began with the 12 parishes that accepted him. They organized as the Canonical Missionary Episcopate in the United States, Canada, and South America. The church is fully Orthodox in faith and practice, a member of the Standing Conference of Canonical Orthodox Bishops in the United States, and differs from the larger Romanian Orthodox Episcopate of America in administration.

Membership: In 1980 the church had 13 parishes and 12,835 members in the United States, with 19 additional parishes in Canada and one in Venezuela.

Periodicals: *Credinta—The Faith*.

★262★
Romanian Orthodox Episcopate of America
℅ Rt. Rev. Nathaniel, Bishop
2522 Grey Tower Rd.
Jackson, MI 49201-9120

The first Romanian Christians came to America at the end of the nineteenth century. A parish of the Romanian Orthodox Church was organized in Regina, Saskatchewan, in 1902, and two years later St. Mary's Church was founded in Cleveland. Individual congregations cooperated with Russian bishops and were related directly to the hierarchy in Romania. After a quarter of a century, a church congress was held in Detroit and in 1929 the Romanian Orthodox Episcopate (diocese) of America was organized. In 1935 the first bishop, His Grace Policarp Morusca, came to the United States and settled in Grass Lake, Michigan.

The second bishop, the Rt. Rev. Viorel (Valerian) D. Trifa, was succeeded by the Rt. Rev. Bp. Nathaniel Popp, the current ruling Bishop of the episcopate. Canonically, the episcopate is under the jurisdiction of the Orthodox Church in America.

Membership: In 1995 the episcopate reported 70 parishes, 100,000 members, and 95 clergy, including 18 parishes and 13 clergy in Canada.

Periodicals: *SOLIA, The Herald*. Send orders to PO Box 185, Grass Lake, MI 49240-0185. • *Lumina Lina*. • *Joyous Light*.

Remarks: In 1939 Bishop Polycarp went to Romania, but due to political events could not return. After World War II, he was detained by the Romanian government and in 1948 placed in retirement. The Romanian patriarchate, without the knowledge or consent of the American diocese, consecrated a new bishop, the Reverend Andrei Moldovan, the parish priest in Akron, Ohio, who had gone to Romania to be consecrated without the concurrence or support of the American parishes. His return to the United States created a major crisis as the status and bylaws of the diocese provided for ordination of bishops only after election by the diocesan congress. The majority party (48 parishes) declared themselves in full separation from the Romanian patriarchate. Later, in 1951, they elected Viorel (Valerian) D. Trifa, who had recently arrived in the United States as their bishop. Through a fraternal tie, Trifa was able to bring the Episcopate under the canonical protection of the Russian Orthodox Greek Catholic Church of America (now the Orthodox Church in America), which recognized Trifa's church as a self-governing body.

The episcopate faced a second major crisis in the 1970s when Bishop Trifa was charged with concealing an alleged role in Nazi atrocities in Romania. In 1980 he surrendered his United States citizenship, and in 1984 went into exile in Portugal. He died there in 1987 and was succeeded by Bp. Nathaniel Popp, the present leader of the episcopate.

Sources:

Beliefs of Orthodox Christians. Jackson, MI: Romanian Orthodox Episcopate, n.d.

Holy Liturgy for Orthodox Christians. Jackson, MI: Romanian Orthodox Episcopate, n.d.

Trifa, Valerian D. *Holy Sacraments for Orthodox Christians.* Jackson, MI: Romanian Orthodox Episcopate, n.d.

★263★
Russian Orthodox Church Outside of Russia
% His Eminence Vitaly, Metropolitan
75 E. 93rd St.
New York, NY 10028

Following the Russian Revolution and the cutting of lines of authority and communication between the Patriarch of Moscow and bishops serving Russian Orthodox communities outside of Soviet control, attempts were made to reorganize the church. In 1921 a conference of Russian Orthodox bishops in exile met at Sremski Karlovtsy, Yugoslavia. Among the participants was Metropolitan Platon, leader of the American archdiocese. Metropolitan Platon continued to work with the Council of Bishops Abroad until 1926 when he ran into conflict over the movement toward autocephalous status of the American church. Metropolitan Platon declared the Council of Bishops an uncanonical organization. The Council dismissed Platon and assigned Bishop Apollinary in his place.

Bishop Apollinary was elevated to archbishop in 1929 and, after a short period of leadership, he died in 1933. He was succeeded by Bishop Vitaly. Efforts to heal the schism between the Church Abroad and the autonomous Russian Orthodox Greek Catholic Church of America (popularly called the Metropolia) led to a temporary reproachment in 1935 which continued through the period of World War II. In the mid-1940s, however, it became evident that the larger body wished some realignment with the Patriarch of Moscow and, in 1946, it broke completely with the Church Abroad. The American followers of the Church Abroad asserted their continuity with Russian Orthodoxy in America and declared the Metropolia schismatic. Since that time the Russian Orthodox Church Outside of Russia has been the major voice of the anti-Soviet faction of Russian Orthodoxy, and it has tried to continue the traditional practices of the Russian Church.

Membership: In 1994 the church reported 177 parishes in the United States, 25 parishes in Canada, and 37 parishes in South America. There were approximately 100,000 members in the United States. There are affiliated congregations on every continent.

Educational Facilities: Holy Trinity Orthodox Seminary, Jordanville, New York.

Periodicals: *Orthodox Life.* Available from Holy Trinity Monastery, Jordanville, NY 13361. • *Orthodox America.* Send orders to Box 3132, Redding, CA 96099.

Sources:

A Cry of Despair from Moscow Churchmen. New York: Russian Orthodox Church Outside of Russia, 1966.

Fiftieth Anniversary of the Russian Orthodox Church Outside of Russia. Montreal: Monastery Press in Canada, 1971.

Rodzianko, M. *The Truth About the Russian Church Abroad.* N.p. 1975.

★264★
Sacred Heart Catholic Church (Arrendale)
Current address not obtained for this edition.

The Sacred Heart Catholic Church was founded in 1980 by Archbishop James Augustine Arrendale and other former members of Archbishop James Francis Augustine Lashley's American Catholic Church, Archdiocese of New York. Arrendale was consecrated on August 10, 1981 by Bishop Pinachio, who was assisted by Bishops Donald Anthony and William Wren. The group adheres to the teachings of the Seven Ecumenical Councils and the three Ecumenical Creeds. Archbishop Arrendale died in 1985 and the future course of the Archdiocese is in doubt.

Membership: In 1983 the church reported three parishes, two priests, and 50 members.

★265★
St. Anne's African Orthodox Church
2485 NW 65th
Miami, FL 33054

The Protestant Episcopal Church, like all American denominations with both episcopal leadership and a significant black membership, faced the problems and pressures related to electing and elevating their first black member to the bishopric. Within the Episcopal Church the cries for a bishop drawn from among black members grew even louder after the Civil War. They were refused, the leadership arguing that, since the church did not recognize racial distinctions, it could not elevate a man to the bishopric just because he was black. A step toward the solution came in 1910 with the creation of black "suffragan" bishops, bishops without right to succession and without vote in the house of bishops.

Among those who complained that suffragans were not enough was Dr. George A. McGuire (1866-1934), an Episcopal priest who had emigrated from the West Indies. In 1921 he left the Protestant Episcopal Church and founded the Independent Episcopal Church. McGuire had had a distinguished career in the Episcopal Church, serving parishes in both the United States and Antigua, and he had been considered for the post of Suffragan Bishop of Arkansas. He declined in order to study medicine at Jefferson Medical College, where he graduated as a Doctor of Medicine in 1910. Upon graduation, he served at St. Bartholomew's Episcopal Church in Cambridge, Massachusetts. He was then called to be the Secretary of the Commission for Work among the Colored People under the Church's Board of Missions.

After several years as Secretary, he moved back to Antigua, where he remained for six years building the church where he was baptized, St. Paul's in Sweets. When fellow West Indian Marcus Garvey formed the United Negro Improvement Association, McGuire returned to the United States to support him. Working with Garvey only strengthened his dissatisfaction in serving a church where black people were systematically denied positions of leadership, and he became determined to pursue an independent course.

On September 2, 1921, in the Church of the Good Shepherd in New York City, a meeting of independent black clergy resolved itself into the first Synod of the African Orthodox Church and designated McGuire as its bishop elect. The synod then entered into negotiations with the Russian Orthodox Church in America in their search for episcopal orders for their newly elected bishop. The Russians indicated a willingness to consecrate McGuire, but only if they controlled the newly created jurisdiction. The idea of non-Black control had no appeal to either McGuire or his followers. They then turned to the American Catholic Church, headed by Archbishop Joseph Rene Vilatte. Vilatte was willing to confer orders and ask little or nothing in the way of control. On September 29, 1921, Bishop Vilatte, assisted by Carl A. Nybladh, consecrated Dr. McGuire in the Church of Our Lady of Good Death in Chicago.

The church experienced slow but steady growth, although most of the individual congregations were small. The priests were seldom full-time clergy, although every church was encouraged to contribute something to their support. McGuire emphasized education and led in the organization of a seminary for the training of clergy. The first class numbered 14 men. The school provided professional training for its students, while accommodating to the generally lower educational level of its applicants. It has not tried to become an accredited degree-granting institution.

Archbishop McGuire led the church until his death in 1934, and it enjoyed peace and stability. After his death the leadership of the church fell into the hands of Archbishop William E. J. Robertson. Shortly after his elevation to the archbishopric, dissatisfaction arose among the group of clergy, and a schism, the Holy African Church, was created. The dissidents were led by Bishop Reginald Grant Barrow, who had been McGuire's closest associate. In time, Barrow was succeeded by Bishop Frederick A. Toote and then Bishop Gladstone St. Clair Nurse. Bishop Nurse led the efforts to reunite the two factions. On February 22, 1964, the two bodies joined together under Robertson, who adopted the Patriarchal name of Peter IV. Just prior to the merger he consecrated several bishops, an obvious effort to insure his continued control of the church. Nurse did not protest Robertson's action, and upon the death of the Patriarch was elected by the bishops to be the new primate of the church. He quickly brought all the elements of the church together, and upon his death, leadership passed very easily to Archbishop William R. Miller, who served as the church's Primate from 1976 until August 1981. At the Annual Synod of the Church, he resigned and was succeeded by Archbishop Stafford J. Sweeting.

The denomination remains small in the United States, but it has affiliated parishes in the West Indies and Africa (Nigeria, Ghana, and Uganda). Recently, the church lost one of its strongest parishes when Bishop G. Duncan Hinkson of Chicago left to found the African Orthodox Church of the West. The church was also formerly known as African Orthodox Church.

Membership: In 1983 the church reported 17 parishes and 5,100 members in the United States.

Educational Facilities: Endich Theological Seminary, New York, New York.

Periodicals: The Trumpet. Available from Rev. Fr. Harold Furblur, Box 1925, Boston, MA 02105.

Sources:

Burkett, Randall K. Garveyism as a Religious Movement. Metuchen, NJ: Scarecrow Press, 1978.

The Divine Liturgy and Other Rites and Ceremonies of the Church. Chicago: African Orthodox Church, 1945.

Newman, Richard. "The Origins of the African Orthodox Church." In The Negro Churchman. Millwood, NY: Kraus Publishing Co., 1977.

Terry-Thompson, Arthur C. History of the African Orthodox Church. New York: The Author, 1956.

★266★
Serbian Eastern Orthodox Church for the U.S.A. and Canada
% Rt. Rev. Mitrofan, Vicar Bishop of Toplica
St. Sava Monastery
Box 519
Libertyville, IL 60048

Few churches have been so affected by the changes in modern Europe as the Serbian Church. Present maps (if they show it at all) reveal Serbia as a part of Yugoslavia, a country welded together out of a number of pre-World War II, pre-Tito states. An independent Serbian Orthodox Church had been established in 1219 under Archbishop St. Sava. A patriarchate was established in the fourteenth century. From 1389 to 1815, Serbia was under Turkish rule and the church suffered severe persecution, but a nineteenth century revival followed independence from Moslem control.

In 1765, Serbian autonomy was ended, and the church returned to the jurisdiction of the ecumenical patriarch in Constantinople, who began a Hellenization program. In 1832 the archbishop of Belgrade was given the title metropolitan, and in 1879, as a result of the Congress of Berlin, the Serbian Church regained autonomy. In 1920 it joined with the independent Serbian churches in Montenegro, Bosnia, Herzegovina, Dalmatia, and Croatia to form the Serbian patriarchate. The seat was established in Belgrade, and its independence recognized by the ecumenical patriarch in 1922.

Immigrants from Serbia began to arrive in the U.S. in significant numbers in the 1890s. In 1892 Archimandrite Firmilian arrived and began to organize parishes. The first was in Jackson, California, but others soon followed in Chicago; Douglas, Alaska; and McKeesport, Steelton, and Pittsburgh, Pennsylvania. All of these early parishes were placed under the jurisdiction of the Russian Orthodox Church in America. The Serbian Church began to seek autonomous status as early as 1913. With Russian encouragement, Serbian Father Mardary was sent to the United States to organize an independent diocese in 1917. In 1919 the Russians elevated him to archimandrite. In 1921 the Serbs separated from the Russian Orthodox Church and Mardary became the administrator. In 1926 he was consecrated bishop for the American diocese. The Serbian Church grew slowly in this country until World War II, when a flood of refugees came into the United States. St. Sava Monastery at Libertyville, Illinois, was built soon after Bishop Mardary's consecration, and the church headquarters are currently established there. On November 14, 1970, King Peter, deposed monarch of Yugoslavia, died; he was buried in the Monastery.

The changes in political structure in Yugoslavia after World War II drastically altered the American diocese. In 1940 Bishop Dionisije Milivojevich was sent to the United States to assume authority for the church. Because Dionisije was a vocal anti-Tito spokesman and defender of the Serbian monarchy, Marshall Tito, the new ruler of Yugoslavia, encouraged the Belgrade patriarch to release Milivojevich of his duties. At the same time, Tito moved against the church by confiscating all church property, thus placing the church under his financial control. The American Archdiocese was divided into three dioceses. Milivojevich was left in charge of the Midwest. He rejected the actions of the patriarch in Belgrade, which he interpreted as coming from an atheist government bent on absolute control of the church. He was suspended from office and excommunicated the following year. He appealed the actions of the Belgrade patriarch to the clergy and laity of the American church and individual congregations, and priests began to take sides. Each side filed suit against the other, and two churches have evolved: the Serbian Orthodox Church in the United States and the Free Serbian Orthodox Church—Diocese for the U.S.A. and Canada.

The Serbian Orthodox Church in the United States of America and Canada is the canonical body loyal to the Mother Church with its Patriarchal See in Belgrade, Yugoslavia. In 1963 it was reorganized into three dioceses. Leading the church is Bishop Firmilian of the Midwestern American Diocese headquartered at Libertyville, Illinois. During the period of the 1960s and 1970s when the headquarters property of the church at St. Sava Monastery was being contested in the court and under the control of Bishop Milivojevich, the Midwestern Diocese erected a large church building in Chicago which served (until 1980) as its temporary headquarters. The Western American Diocese is headquartered in Alhambra, California, and the Eastern American Diocese in Edgeworth, Pennsylvania. In 1983 the Canadian parishes were separated from the Eastern Diocese and organized into a new Canadian Diocese. The Serbian Orthodox Church in the United States of America and Canada is a member of the Standing Conference of Canonical Orthodox Bishops. Through its ties to the church in Belgrade, it is also a member of the World Council of Churches.

In 1992, major steps were taken to heal the division between the two bodies of Serbian Orthodox believers in North America. On February 15, following discussions with the Patriarchate in Belgrade, bishops of the Serbian Orthodox Metropolitanate of New Gracanica, concelebrated the Divine liturgy with Patriarch Pavle. The action formally healed the schism. Only the formalities of working out the legal and administrative issues remained. As of the beginning of 1998, a common Constitution is being worked out for the entire Serbian Church in North America. Once agreed upon and accepted, territorial reorganization of the churches and dioceses will take place, so that administrative unity can follow.

Membership: In 1986 the church reported 67,000 members, 68 parishes and missions, and 82 priests.

Periodicals: *The Path of Orthodoxy.* Send orders to Box 36, Leesdale, PA 15056.

Sources:

Slijepchevich, Djoko. *The Transgressions of Bishop Dionisije.* Chicago: The Author, 1963.

Velimirovich, Nicholai D. *The Faith of the Saints, Catechism of the Eastern Orthodox Church.* Libertyville, IL: Serbian Eastern Orthodox Diocese for the United States of America and Canada, 1961.

___. *The Life of St. Sava.* Libertyville, IL: Serbian Eastern Orthodox Diocese, 1951.

★267★
Serbian Orthodox Metropolitanate of New Gracanica— Diocese for America and Canada
℅ Metropolitan Iriney Kovachevich
Box 371
Grayslake, IL 60030

The Serbian Orthodox Metropolitanate of New Gracanica, formerly the Serbian Orthodox Free Diocese of the United States and Canada, like the Serbian Eastern Orthodox Church in the United States and Canada, claims the history of Serbian Orthodoxy in America since the 1890s. It remains, however, as that branch which remained loyal to Bishop Dionisije Milivojevich after he was defrocked by the Belgrade Patriarch. That action began a lengthy series of court battles between Bishop Dionisije's followers and the appointed representatives of the Belgrade church authorities. In 1978 the courts finally awarded the property at Libertyville, Illinois to the Belgrade representatives. Bishop Dionisije died in 1979, a few months before his followers left the property.

The Free Serbian Church, as it was popularly called, purchased property at nearby Grayslake, Illinois, and began to build a new headquarters complex. The massive Gracanica Monastery was dedicated in 1984. Dionisije was succeeded by Bishop Iriney. Under his leadership the stanch anti-Communist and anti-Tito stance adopted by his predecessor has continued.

On February 15, 1992, after lengthy discussions with the Patriarchate in Belgrade under the guidance of newly elected Patriarch Pavle, Metropolitan Iriney, and Bishop Basil of the Serbian Orthodox Metropolinate of New Gracanica concelebrated the Divine Liturgy with Patriarch Pavle and other bishops of the Serbian Orthodox Patriarchate in Belgrade. This action healed the schism between the Metropolinate and the Belgrade Patriarchate, however, it remained separate administratively from the Serbian Eastern Orthodox Church for the U.S.A. and Canada.

As of the beginning of 1998, a common Constitution is being worked on for the entire Serbian Church in North America. Once agreed upon and accepted, territorial reorganization of the churches and dioceses will take place, so that administrative unity can follow.

Membership: In 1997 the church reported 30,000 members, 53 parishes, and 49 priests.

Educational Facilities: St. Sava Seminary, Lake Villa, Illinois.

Periodicals: *Diocesean Observer.*

Sources:

Dionisije, Bishop. *Patriarch Gherman's Violations of the Holy Canons, Rules and Regulations of the Serbian Orthodox Church in Tito's Yugoslavia.* Libertyville, IL: Serbian Orthodox Diocese in the U.S.A. and Canada (Free Serbian Orthodox Church in Free World), 1965.

Divine Liturgy, Prayers, Catechism. Libertyville, IL: St. Sava Seminary Fund, 1979.

Gracanica. Grayslake, IL: Serbian Orthodox Free Diocese of the United States and Canada, 1984.

A Time to Choose. Third Lake, IL: Monastery of the Most Holy Mother of God, 1981.

Todorovich, Jovan. *Serbian Patran Saint, Krsna Slava.* Merrillville, IN: The Author, 1978.

Velimirovich, Nicholai D. *The Life of St. Sava.* Libertyville, IL: Serbian Eastern Orthodox Diocese for the United States of America and Canada, 1951.

★268★
Turkish Orthodox Church
Current address not obtained for this edition.

The Turkish Orthodox Church was established in 1926 when excommunicated priest Paul Eftymios Karahissaridis claimed to have had his sentence of excommunication lifted by two members of the Holy Synod of the Greek Orthodox Church and that Bishops Cyril of Erdek and Agathangelos of Prinkipo consecrated him. Karahissaridis became popularly known as Papa Eftim. The new church grew out of a controversy begun by Papa Eftim's demanding a Turkish Church independent of the Greek Orthodox ecumenical patriarch in Constantinople. In 1933 Papa Eftin introduced a Turkish language version of the Divine Liturgy and ordained his son Socrates Ermis Karahissaridis and nephew Nicholas Doren to the priesthood. (Ermis became Eftim II.) The relations of the Turkish movement and the ecumenical patriarch have remained shaky and very much tied to Turkish-Greek relations. In 1962 Eftim II succeeded his ailing father as head of the church. Papa Eftim died in 1968.

On December 6, 1966, the Turkish Orthodox Church came to the United States with the appointnment of the Most Rev. Civet Kristof (a.k.a. Christopher M. Cragg) as metropolitan archbishop of New York and patriarchal exarch and primate of the Turkish Orthodox Church in America. Cragg, a well-educated black American of Ethiopian ancestry, had been consecrated by Archbishop Christopher Maria Stanley in 1965 and named Auxiliary Bishop of New York for the American Orthodox Catholic Church headed by Archbishop Walter A. Propheta. He edited the jurisdiction's periodical, the *Orthodox Catholic Herald*, which became the first periodical for the Turkish Orthodox Church. Kristof issued the first copies of *Orthodoks Mustakil*, the new periodical for the Turkish Orthodox Church, in 1969.

Membership: In 1969 the church reported 14 churches and 6 mission parishes.

Remarks: The Turkish Church continued to exist throughout the 1970s but during the early 1980s, Archbishop Cragg moved to Chicago and opened a health clinic. His stationary carried the title, American Orthodox Church, Diocese of Chicago and North America.

Sources:

Kristof, Most Reverend Metropolitan. *A Brief History of the Turkish Orthodox Church in America (Patriarchal Exarchate).* New York: Turkish Orthodox Church in America, Exarchal Office, [1967].

★269★
Ukrainian Autocephalic Church of North and South America
Current address not obtained for this edition.

The Ukrainian Autocephalic Church of North and South America was founded by Abp. Wasyl Sawyna. Sawyna had reportedly been consecrated in 1959 by independent Ukrainian Bp. Evhen Batchynskiy, then a resident of Switzerland. Sawyna came to public attention when in 1964 he participated in the consecration of James Parker Dees, founder and primate of the Anglican Orthodox Church. Subsequently, efforts to obtain information about Sawyna and his jurisdiction, then headquartered in Allentown, Pennsylvania, proved fruitless. While his consecration probably occurred as reported, it also seems likely that his jurisdiction was a paper organization which had no active parishes and is now totally defunct.

Sources:

Piepkorn, Arthur C. *Profiles in Belief.* New York: Harper & Row, 1977.

★270★
Ukrainian Orthodox Church in America (Ecumenical Patriarchate)

St. Andrew's Ukrainian Orthodox Diocese
90-34 139th St.
Jamaica, NY 11435

A new era in the relationship between the Ecumenical Patriarchate and Ukrainians was opened in the late nineteenth century when many immigrants, especially from Western Ukraine, came to the United States and Canada. Prior to World War I, no universally recognized Ukrainian Orthodox jurisdiction existed in North America and many Ukrainians converted back to Orthodoxy under the Russian Church hierarchs in America, with the predictable result that their ethnic heritage was once again submerged.

The movement to re-establish direct ties between the Ecumenical Patriarch and his Ukrainian children received a new impetus on April 9, 1929, when a Church Congress was held in Allentown, Pennsylvania, attended by 15 clergy and 24 laymen. At this meeting, the decision was made to form a separate Ukrainian Orthodox diocese. A second Congress took place in New York in July 1931, when Fr. Dr. Joseph Zuk, was nominated to be the first bishop of the Ukrainian Orthodox Church of America and Canada. Bishop Zuk would be able to serve the diocese until his untimely death in February 23, 1934.

A new bishop, Fr. Bohdan Shpylka, was consecrated on February 28, 1937, in the Greek Orthodox Archdiocesan Cathedral in New York by Archbishop Athenagoras, the future Ecumenical Patriarch. During Bishop Bohdan's tenure, many pastoral visits were made and a Cathedral and adjoining building at 4th Street and Avenue C in New York was acquired along with a monastery in Bridgeport, Connecticut. Bishop Bohdan passed away in November 1, 1965.

On January 28, 1967, Fr. Andrei Kuschak was consecrated in New York by Archbishop Iakovos. Through careful diligent management he was able to improve the precarious financial position of the diocese including the acquisition of the current Cathedral of St. Andrew in Jamaica, New York. His missionary travels included meetings with His All Holiness Patriarch Dimitrios, Patriarch Elia IV of Antioch, Patriarch Maximos of the Bulgarian Orthodox Church, Patriarch Justin of the Romanian Orthodox Church, and Archbishop Michael Ramsey of Canterbury, England. Bishop Andrei was elevated to Metropolitan in 1983 at the same time that Fr. Nicholas Smisko was consecrated as Auxiliary Bishop. Metropolitan Andrei passed away on November 17, 1986.

The current Primate of the Ukrainian Orthodox Church of America and Canada, Bishop Vsevolod of Scopelos, was consecrated on September 27, 1987 by His Eminence Archbishop Iakovos. His efforts have aimed at generating a new spirit of respect among the members for the Orthodox faith and Ukrainian heritage. Special emphasis has been placed on rejuvenated youth program.

Membership: In 1977 the church reported 28 parishes, 25,000 members and 35 priests. A 1980 survey indicated 23 parishes 3,465 confirmed members and an additional 2,000 adherents.

Periodicals: *Ukrainian Orthodox Herald.*

★271★
Ukrainian Orthodox Church of Canada

9 St. John's Ave.
Winnipeg, MB, Canada R2W 1G8

At the time of the Russian Revolution, the Ukrainian National Republic came into existence and Ukrainian Orthodox Christians began asserting their independence. Full separation from the Russian Orthodox Church and the proclamation establishing an autonomous national body came about in 1919. As news of the Revolution spread, immigrants to Canada acted quickly to found an independent jurisdiction. Approximately 150 delegates met in July 1918 at Saskatoon, Saskatchewan. Growth of the new jurisdiction was augmented by the movement of Eastern rite congregations of the Roman Catholic Church into Orthodoxy. At the time Rome was attempting to have the Eastern churches adopt the Latin rite.

In 1919 Metropolitan Germanos of the Antiochean Orthodox Church agreed to take the new church under his jurisdiction as a temporary measure. Rev. S. W. Sawchuk became the administrator. He traveled to Europe to attempt to secure a bishop, but was prevented entry to the Ukraine by Soviet officials. In 1924 Abp. John Theodorovich arrived in the United States to care for the Ukrainian Orthodox. The Canadians accepted him as their spiritual head, though Reverend Sawchuk continued to administer the church. In 1946 Archbishop Theodorovich asked to be relieved of his Canadian obligations. The Council of Bishops of the Ukrainian Autocephalous Orthodox Church in Exile suggested that Bp. Mstyslaw Skrypnyk lead the Canadian work which was growing into the largest segment of Ukrainian Orthodoxy outside of Ukraine. He began his tenure in 1947 and retired in 1950. In 1951 Skrypnyk was succeeded by Metropolitan Ilarion Ohienko and an assistant, Abp. Michael Horoshij. The jurisdiction is currently headed by Metropolitan Wasyly. In 1990 the Ukrainian Orthodox Church of Canada entered into eucharistic union with the Patriarchate of Constantinople.

The church also operates St. Andrew's Theological College, affiliated with the University of Manitoba in Winnipeg. It was the only center for Ukrainian Orthodox theological education of its kind outside of the former Soviet Union and was used by other Ukrainian jurisdictions of the United States, England, and Western Europe. In recent years, several additional Ukrainian Orthodox theological institutions have been opened.

Membership: In 1992 there were 140,000 members in 250 congregations, and 85 priests.

Educational Facilities: St. Andrew's Theological College, Winnipeg, Manitoba, Canada.

Periodicals: *Visnyk.* • *Riona Nyva.*

Sources:

Bilon, Peter. *Ukrainians and Their Church.* Johnstown, PA: Western Penn. Branch of the U.O.L., 1953.

★272★
Ukrainian Orthodox Church of the U.S.A.

Box 495
South Bound Brook, NJ 08880

History. Ukrainian Christians, primarily Roman Catholic followers of the Uniate Eastern Rite, arrived in the United States and organized parishes in the nineteenth century. However, they soon encountered efforts of the Roman Church in America to further Latinize the Uniate parishes. In response, some left and joined the Russian Orthodox Church, in spite of what many felt were imperial designs against Ukrainians. In 1915 a Ukrainian National Church was founded. It placed itself under independent Catholic bishop, Carmel Henry Carfora, head of the National Catholic Diocese in North America and later primate of the North American Old Roman Catholic Church, with an understanding that it would affiliate with the Ukrainian Orthodox Church when and if it was allowed to exist in the Ukraine. In 1917, as the Russian Revolution progressed, the Ukrainian National Republic came into existence and, in 1919, it proclaimed the Ukrainian Autocephalous Orthodox Church the official church of the land. Unable to find a bishop who could give them orders, the clergy and lay leaders assembled at a church council in 1921 and consecrated several candidates for bishop by the laying-on-of-hands of all present. In this manner Archpriests Wasyl Lypkiwsky and Nester Sharayiwsky were elevated to the office of bishop. Lypkiwsky was designated metropolitan.

The Ukrainian-Americans immediately began to establish an independent church. An initial All-Ukrainian Orthodox Council of the American Ukrainian Orthodox Church met in 1922. It petitioned for a bishop and two years later John Theodorovich, who had been consecrated by Metropolitan Lypkiwsky, arrived to head the new church. He established his see in Philadelphia in 1926.

The arrival of Bishop John (who had been consecrated in 1921 in the Ukraine by the Autocephalous Church) led other Uniate congregations to leave the Roman jurisdiction and become Orthodox. In response Rome appointed a bishop over its Ukrainian parishes. However, the new bishop soon came into conflict with many of the members. They broke with Rome and, not yet resolved to become Orthodox, formed the independent American-Ukrainian Greek-Catholic Church. During the 1920s, the parishes decided to become Orthodox and looked to Archbishop Aftimios Ofiesh, head of the American Orthodox Church, for episcopal leadership. In 1932 he consecrated Joseph Zuk (d. 1934) as the bishop of the Ukrainian Orthodox Church of America. He was succeeded by Bishop Bohdan Shpylka.

The Ukrainian Orthodox Church of the U.S.A. and the Ukrainian Orthodox Church of America existed side-by-side for several decades as competitors. Several attempts at union failed. However, in 1948, the Ukrainian Orthodox Church of America elected Mstyslaw Skrypnyk, then head of the Ukrainians in Canada, as their new Archbishop and named Bishop Bohdan as the auxiliary. Resigning from his Canadian post, Skrypnyk took the lead in seeking ways to unite the two churches. Through several gatherings in which members of both churches participated, the barriers to union were removed. As agreed to in the negotiations, Archbishop John was reconsecrated in order to silence any objections to the regularity of his original consecration.

Archbishop John was elected metropolitan of the new church, Archbishop Skrypnyk headed the consistory, and Archbishop Hennadij became the auxiliary bishop. Bishop Bohdan did not join the union, and with several parishes continued to exist separately as the Ukrainian Orthodox Church of America (Ecumenical Patriarch).

Archbishop Skrypnyk emerged as the most potent leader in the new church and eventually succeeded to the post of metropolitan, which he still retains. He developed the Saint Andrews the First-called Memorial Center, the headquarters complex in South Bound Brook, New Jersey which now includes the seminary, St. Sophia Press (the publishing enterprise), a museum and archives, and the Home of Ukrainian Culture.

Beliefs. The church is at one in faith and practice with all of Orthodoxy. It accepts the Nicene Creed. It adheres closely to a rule against instrumental music and uses only vocal music in its worship.

Organization. The church is headed by its primate, Metropolitan Mstyslaw, archbishop of Philadelphia. He is assisted by archbishops in Chicago and New York. The archbishop is also designated the metropolitan of the church in diaspora. In this task he is assisted by archbishops in Paris, France and Australia. Eparchies have been established for Latin America, Great Britain, Western Europe, and Australia and New Zealand. A sobor of bishops meets every two years. In some countries, general sobors of synods of the church meet every three years to establish general and specific administrative policies. The church is also served by the United Ukrainian Orthodox Sisterhoods and the Ukrainian Orthodox League of the USA. The church is in communion with the Ukrainian Greek-Orthodox Church in Canada.

Membership: In 1988 the church reported 85,000 members, 92 congregations and 108 priests in the United States.

Educational Facilities: St. Sophia Orthodox Theological Seminary, South Bound Brook, New Jersey.

Periodicals: *Ukrainian Orthodox Word* (Ukrainian and English editions). • *Bipa (Faith)*. Send orders to 201-63 27th St., Bayside, NY 11360. • *UOL Bulletin.* Available from St. Michael Ukrainian Orthodox Church, 7047 Columbia Ave. Hammond, IN 46324.

Sources:

Bilon, Peter. *Ukrainians and Their Church.* Johnstown, PA: Western Pa. Branch of the U.O.L., 1953.

★273★
United American Orthodox Catholic Church
Rte. 3, Box 31
Excelsior Springs, MO 64024

The United American Orthodox Catholic Church is one of several independent Orthodox jurisdictions that emerged in the 1980s out of the Western Orthodox Church in America. It began in 1988 as a regional meeting of the Western Orthodox Church held at St. Anthonys Monastery in Excelsior Springs, Missouri. Abbot David L. Jones of St. Anthonys and Fr. Michael Kilarsky were chosen as bishops, with Jones selected as presiding bishop. Jones and Kilarsky were consecrated in February 1989 by Bps. Ignatius Cash, Patrick M. Cronin, Max Broussard, and Joseph Turnage.

Early attempts at recognizing a variety of liturgical expressions served only to confuse and frustrate both the clergy and the lay people. Instead of serving to unite people under the teachings of the ancient Christian church, it served to divide. By September of 1992, the organization was reduced to only Bishop David and a handful of clergy and faithful who desired to pursue development of a truly united American Orthodox church. All subsequent activity has centered on reestablishing the work begun early in this century by Bps. Aftimios Ofiesh and Metropolitan Theophan Noli, both of whom appear in Bishop David's succession.

The group continues today to practice the eastern Orthodox faith according to the canons of the ancient and undivided Christian Church. Only the usual Eastern Rite liturgies are used, although Bishop David believes that there is room for a Western Rite liturgy. The church maintains a fraternal relationship with the Orthodox Church of France and steers those interested in Western orthodoxy to that group.

Membership: In 1997 the church reported 60 members in four congregations served by five clergy.

Educational Facilities: The Monastery of St. Anthony coordinates a clergy training program in cooperation with local pastors.

Periodicals: *The Semantron.*

Sources:

Church Manual. Excelsior Springs, MO: United American Orthodox Catholic Church, n.d.

★274★
United Orthodox Church
202 International Ave.
Hyder, AK 99923

The United Orthodox Church, headed by Abp. Gregory Robertson, is an Orthodox church with a Russian Orthodox Church heritage and lineage, but believes that the church was never intended to be structured along ethnic or national lines. It is also a conservative body that rejects what it considers to be the Russian Church's departure from tradition and participation in the larger ecumenical movement. The church staunchly adheres to the Nicene Creed, and rejects prayer or common worship with Christians (deemed heretics). The church also has married bishops (believing that the naming of unmarried bishops was an expedient adopted by the church which is no longer needed) and does not allow women to participate vocally (such as having membership in church choirs) in liturgical worship.

The church is a member of the Synod of Autonomous Canonical Orthodox Churches of North America.

Membership: Not reported.

Educational Facilities: Saint Gregory Seminary, Hyder, Alaska.

Sources:

Pruter, Karl. *The Directory of Autocephalous Bishops of the Apostolic Sucession.* San Bernadino, CA: Brogo Press, 1906. 104 pp.

Ward, Gary. *Independent Bishops: An International Directory.* Detroit: Apogee Books, 1990. 524 pp.

★275★
Universal Shrine of Divine Guidance
% Most Rev. Mark Athanasios Constantine Karras
PO Box 1771
Camarillo, CA 93011

Father Mark Karras, the American-born son of Greek parents, was consecrated in the Church of Saints Damian and Cosmas in Newark, New Jersey, on July 17, 1966, and on the following day elevated to the position of Archbishop of Byzantium by Abp. Peter A. Zurawetsky, Patriarch of the Orthodox Patriarchate of America. He was assisted by independent Greek Apb. Joachim Souris, the American Exarch of the Patriarchate of Alexandria. In the month following his consecration, Archbishop Karras founded the Universal Shrine of Divine Guidance, assisted by Veronica Perweiler (nee Szcente Janos, of the ancient noble House of Hungary), whom he consecrated as "Abbess" the following year.

The Universal Shrine views itself as continuation of the Apostolic Church based upon Pentecost. The first stage was the regulatory period of Judaism and the second the instructional stage of Christianity. In the third stage, a period of fulfillment through enlightenment and grace will ensue. Archbishop Karras promulgates a pure philosophy of faith in God and spiritual values, a universal faith emphasizing moral achievement and merit. At the heart of the doctrine is the Christian teaching of love. To protect the church against ridicule, in 1974 Archbishop Karras moved in the American courts to counter the author, publishers, and filmmakers of the book and film known as "The Exorcist" for the unauthorized use of his name and work.

He is the Supreme Prelate of the ancient (312 C.E.) dynastic Christian Order of Saints Constantine the Great and Helen of the Byzantine House of the Lascaris Comnenus of Constantinople. Under his auspices, the Universal Shrine upholds the princple of the Americas as New Byzantium which is the outcome of Western Christian civilization based upon the influence of the influence of Byzantium.

Membership: Not reported.

Sources:

Karras, Mark. *Christ Unto Byzantium.* Miami, FL: Apostolic Universal Center, 1968.

★276★
Western Orthodox Catholic Church of California
% Most Rev. Martin J. Hill
4109 Louisiana St.
San Diego, CA 92104-1691

The Western Orthodox Catholic Church of California is a small Orthodox jurisdiction founded and led by Bp. Martin J. Hill. Hill was ordained to the priesthood in 1981 by Charles David Luther of the Western Orthodox Church in America and consecrated two years later by Francis Jerome Joachim. Hill subsequently established the Western Orthodox Catholic Church as an independent jurisdiction. The church is Eastern orthodox in faith but follows a Western ritual format.

In August 1993, Hill consecrated Douglas Rees as auxiliay bishop. In 1994 Rees was installed as Bishop of Camarillo and Central California and then elected to succeed Hill as the presiding bishop. Rees also serves as the Superior General of the Order of the Most Holy Trinity and the Director of St. Sergius Seminary. In 1996 Hill founded the interdenominational semi-

comtemplatice Order of Agia Sophia (Holy Wisdon Fathers) for the study and teacing of mysticism for Christians.

Membership: Not reported.

Sources:

Ward, Gary L. *Independent Bishops: An International Directory.* Detroit: Apogee Books, 1990.

★277★
Western Orthodox Church in America
% Mt. Rev. Nickolas Carone
200 Fifth St.
Santa Rosa, CA 95401

The Western Orthodox Church grew out of the Catholic Apostolic Church of Brazil founded by former Roman Catholic Church bishop, Carlos Duarte Costa, which had been brought to the United States by Bishop Stephen Meyer Corradi-Scarella, an independent bishop in New Mexico. In 1973 Corradi-Scarella gave Fr. Charles David Luther, a priest he had ordained, directions to found the Community of the Good Shepherd as a fellowship of priests and priests-in-training. In 1977 the name was changed to Servants of the Good Shepherd. The Community accepts qualified men into the priesthood, trains them and assists them in starting mission churches, usually as worker-priests.

In 1977 Luther was consecrated by Bishop Charles R. McCarthy assisted by Jerome Joachim and Wallace David de Ortega Maxey. In 1974 Joachim had succeeded Corradi-Scarella as head of the National Catholic Apostolic Church in America. In 1980 he renamed his jurisdiction the Western Orthodox Church in America. After his consecration Luther brought the Servants of the Good Shepherd into Joachim's jurisdiction. He became bishop of the Diocese of Altonna and was later (l981) made archbishop. In 1983, however, Joachim and Luther decided to become independent of each other. Joachim and his following became the Catholic Apostolic Church in America, while Luther retained the name, Western Orthodox Church in America.

The Western Orthodox church in America, while possessing Catholic orders, is Orthodox while following a Western Rite. In 1984, Luther consecrated Richard J. Ingram as Bishop of Hobart (Indiana) and James F. Mondok as Bishop of Euclid (Ohio). The Church is affiliated with the Ecumenical Church Federation, a fellowship of independent bishops and other Christian leaders organized by Bishop Alan Bain, Archbishop for the British Isles of the Apostolic Episcopal Church.

Membership: In 1981 there were 25 priests and over 100 seminarians studying for the priesthood affiliated with the Servants of the Good Shepherd.

Educational Facilities: Duarte Costa University, Altoona, Pennsylvania.

Duarte Costa School of Religion, Altoona, Pennsylvania.

Periodicals: *The Herald.* Send orders to Box 2733, Des Plaines, IL 60017-2733.

Sources:

A Brief Description of the Servants of the Good Shepherd. Altoona, PA, [1980].

Non-Chalcedonian Orthodoxy

★278★
Afro-American Orthodox Church
(Defunct)

The Afro-American Orthodox Church was a small liturgical church founded in the late 1930s by Bishop George A. Brooks, who had been consecrated by Reginald Grant Barrow of the African Orthodox Church of New York and Massachusetts. It was similar in faith and practice with the African Orthodox Church. In the

1930s, the church was superseded by the Holy African Church which in the 1960s merged into the African Orthodox Church.

Sources:

Trela, Jonathan. *A History of the North American Old Roman Catholic Church.* Scranton, PA: The Author, 1979.

★279★
Ancient Church of the East
% Mar Emannuel
St. Mary's Church
PO Box 1191
Hughson, CA 95326

Alternate Address: International Headquarters: c/o Mar Addai, Catholicos Patriarch, PO Box 2363, Baghdad, Iraq.

In the 1970s, the schism of the Ancient Assyrian Church of the East split when the Iraqi government recognized Mar Addai as patriarch of the church. The larger faction, led by Mar Dinkha, known in the United States as the Apostolic Catholic Church of the East, North American Diocese, is recognized by the Vatican. The smaller faction, the Ancient Church of the East, continues with the present government's blessing. The two factions of the church are identical in faith and practice, the differences being purely administrative.

In the United States, a diocese of the Ancient Church of the East which acknowledges Mar Addai was formed among America believers in the 1970s.

Membership: Not reported.

Sources:

Orthodxy. Regensburg: Ostkirchliches Institute, 1996.

★280★
Antiochian Catholic Church in America
Box 1061
Campton, KY 41301

The Antiochian Catholic Church in America was founded in 1991 when the former Diocese of Lexington (Kentucky) of the Church of Antioch was granted autocephaly as an independent self-governing jurisdiction. The diocese had been under the leadership of H. Gordon Hurlburt, who was consecrated in 1981 by Abp. Herman Adrian Spruit, Primate of the Church of Antioch. Through the 1980s Hurlburt led his clergy away from the Church of Antiochs theological perspective toward a more Orthodox position, modeled after the Syrian (Jacobite) Church (the principle source of their orders). Following the granting of independence on mutually agreeable terms, Hurlburt was elected the churchs Metropolitan-Primate and took the ecclesiastical name Mar Peter. Metropolitan Gordon Mar Peter is assisted in administrative matters by his Vicar General, Bishop Victor Mar Michael Herron.

In liturgical and theological matters the church generally resembles other churches of the Syro-Antiochene tradition, but prefers the term "Ephesine" to describe their christology over the more controversial term "monophysite" (as defined by the Council of Ephesus in 431 CE). Several of the clergy are engaged in Aramaic biblical and liturgical research and scholarship. The church departs from this Eastern pattern principally in the areas of ecclesiology and womens ordination. Married priests are not barred from the episcopate. The church also actively recruits former Roman Catholic priests, and allows the use of the Tridentine Mass where there is an obvious pastoral need.

All available clergy meet annually with the metropolitan to discuss issues, advise the metropolitan, establish pastoral goals and guidelines, and renew the bonds of fellowship. Clergy are typically bi-vocational.

Membership: The church reports approximately 100 regular communicants in small parishes found in Kentucky, Tennessee,

Ohio, Missouri, and South Carolina. There is one missionary priest who itinerates through several states in the southeast.

Periodicals: *Chrism,* 4250 Bent Rd., Kodak, TN 37764.

Sources:

Ward, Gary L. *Independent Bishops: An International Directory.* Detroit, MI: Apogee Books, 1990. 524 pp.

★281★
Apostolic Catholic Assyrian Church of the East, North American Diocese
% Mar Aprim Khamis
North American Diocese
8908 Birch Ave.
Morton Grove, IL 60053

Alternate Address: His Holiness Mar Dinkha IV, Catholicos Patriarch, Box 3257, Sadoun, Baghdad, Iraq.

Victims of Turkish expansion, the Church of the East was dispursed in the late nineteenth century and its headquarters in northern Kurdistan was abandoned. Scattered members of the church began to arrive in America in the 1890s, but for many years were without organization. Early in this century, there were several visitations by the bishops. They found a flock served by an insufficient number of priests and deacons meeting whenever space was available. All of this changed in 1940 when Mar Eshai Shimun XXIII, the 119th patriarch of the church, moved his headquarters to Chicago. A church-reorganization program was initiated. Priests and deacons were ordained; churches were purchased and built; administration was put in efficient order; and a publishing program, including a new periodical, was begun. The progress of the church has continued under the present patriarch, who has reestablished the international headquarters in Iraq.

Membership: In 1989, the diocese reported 22 churches, 120,000 members, and 109 clergy.

Periodicals: *Voice from the East.* Send orders to Box 25264, Chicago, IL 60626.

Sources:

The Liturgy of the Holy Apostles Adai and Mari. London: Society for Promoting Christian Knowledge, 1893.

O'Dishoo, Mar. *The Book of Marganita (The Pearl) on the Truth of Christianity.* Kerala, India: Mar Themotheus Memorial Printing & Publishing House, 1965.

Rules Collected from the Sunhados of the Church of the East & Patriarchial Decrees. San Francisco: Holy Apostolic and Catholic Church of the East, 1960.

Yulpana M'Shikhay D'eta Qaddishta Washlikhayta O'Qathuliqi D'Mathnkha. *Messianic Teachings.* Kerala, India: Mar Themotheus Memorial Printing & Publishing House, 1962.

★282★
Apostolic Orthodox Church
% Rt. Rev. James H. Hess
2410 Derry St.
Harrisburg, PA 17111-1141

The Apostolic Orthodox Church was founded in 1997 by Bp. James H. Hess. Bishop Hess was consecrated in 1984 by Bp. Brian G. Turkington, then affiliated with the Free Anglican Church in North America. He headed the Arian Apostolic Church (later renamed Nestorian Apostolic Church), superseded by the Apostolic Orthodox Church. The church is a traditional non-Chalcedonian jurisdiction most closely resembling the other Monophysite churches from Armenia, Egypt, and Ethiopia.

The church accepts the authority of Scripture (including the Apocrypha) and Tradition with particular reference to some of the early Christian writings (Didache, Apostolic Constitutions, the letters of Ignatius, the letters of Clement, the Shepherd of Hermes,

Barnabas, and the Martyrdom of Polycarp), the pre-Chalcedonian liturgical books, and the three creeds (Apostles, Nicene, and Athanasian). The Filioque clause in the creeds (which affirms that the Holy Spirit proceeds from the Father and the Son) is accepted. It affirms the two natures (divine and human) of Jesus recognized inseparately (rather than separately as taught at Chalcedon).

The church practices the traditional seven sacraments including the Unction for the Sick. It affirms the real presence of Christ in the Eucharist.

The church rejects homosexuality and abortion and does not ordain women to the priesthood. It also believes that the post-Chalcedonian Roman papacy is the Beast of Revelation, that Protestantism is the image of the Beast, that the church in union with the papacy is the whore of Babylon, that Evangelicalism is the false prophet of Revelation, and that the seven trumpets and vials represent the seven heresies of Sabellianism, Arianism, Macedonianism, Aopollinarianism, Nestorianism, Diophysitism, and Iconoclasm. The phenomena of contemporary miracles and signs (including Marian apparitions and charismatic occurrences) are rejected. It is believed that the signs of the apostolic age were discontinued after the death of the last apostle.

Membership: The church has one congregation.

★283★
Armenian Apostolic Church of America
% Mesrob Ashjian
138 E. 39th St.
New York, NY 10016

In 1933, the Armenian Church in America split along political lines as a result of the Soviet dominance of Armenia. The Armenian Apostolic Church of America preserves the church that began to form in the 1890s among Armenian-Americans and whose members were most commited to a free and independent Armenia. This church existed without official sanction until 1957 when Zareh I, the newly elected catholicos of the See of Cilicia, took it under his jurisdiction. Located in Sis, the capital of Lesser Armenia since the fifteenth century, the See of Cilicia moved to Lebanon in the twentieth century.

In 1972, the Prelacy of the Armenian Apostolic Church of America was divided into the Eastern States and Canada, and the Western States. His Grace, Bp. Mouslegh Mai Sirossian prelate of the Western Prelacy, and His Eminence, Abp. Mesrob Ashjian, of the Eastern. Archbishop Ashjian succeeded Abp. Karekin Sarkissian in 1977.

Membership: In 1996, the church reported 400,000 members in 37 churches with 42 priests in the United States. There were five churches in Canada. Affiliated congregations under the see of Cilicia were located in 10 countries with a reported worldwide membership of 900,000.

Educational Facilities: Armenian Theological Seminary, Bikfaya, Lebanon.

Periodicals: *The Outreach.*

Sources:

Sarkissian, Karekin. "Armenian Church in Contemporary Times" In *The Church in the Middle East*, edited by A. J. Arberry. Cambridge: Cambridge University Press, 1969.

___. *The Council of Chalcedon and the Armenian Church.* New York: Armenian Church Prelacy, 1965.

___. *The Witness of the Oriental Orthodox Churches.* Antelias, Lebanon: The Author, 1970.

★284★
Catholic Apostolic Church at Davis
% Gates of Praise Center
921 W. 8th St.
Davis, CA 95616

The Catholic Orthodox Church at Davis was founded in 1972 by Albert Ronald Coady. Coady was ordained in May 1972 by Archbishop John Marion Stanley of the Orthodox Church of the East. In June 1972 Stanley consecrated Coady at a service in Trichur, India. That consecration was confirmed in July 1972 in a service of enthronement conducted by Archbishops Walter A. Propheta, John A. Christian, Laurence Pierre, and C. Clark, all of the American Orthodox Catholic Church (Propheta). Stanley also participated in that ceremony. Originally known as the Christian Orthodox Church, it became the Eastern Catholic Church Syro-Chaldean Rite before taking its present name in the mid-1980s.

The church is Eastern in its liturgy and accepts the Nicene Creed like the Orthodox Church of the East. It is also charismatic in that it accepts the current manifestation of the gifts of the Spirit (I Corinthians 12) in its worship life.

Membership: Not reported.

★285★
Coptic Orthodox Church
% Gabriel Abdelsayed
427 W. Side Ave.
Jersey City, NJ 07304

Since World War II, an increasing number of Copts have left Egypt because of Moslem discrimination. Many of these have come to the United States. In 1962, the Coptic Association of America was formed to serve the Coptic Eqyptians in New York City and vicinity and to work for the establishment of regular pastoral care. The following year Bishop Samuel, bishop of public, ecumenical, and social services, was delegated to come to the United States by Pope Kyrillos VI to meet with the Coptic Association and implement pastoral care. In 1965 Fr. Marcos Abdel-Messiah was ordained in Cairo and sent as a priest to Toronto to establish the Diocese of North America. In 1967 Fr. Dr. Rafael Younan arrived in Montreal. By 1974 there were nine priests serving four churches in New York, plus other churches in Los Angeles, Houston, Detroit, Jersey City, St. Paul, Indianapolis, Milwaukee, Chicago, and several smaller centers. There are fewer than 2,000 adult Copts in North America. An English translation of *The Coptic Orthodox Mass and the Liturgy of St. Basil* has been produced and educational literature has been initiated by Fr. Marcus Beshai of Chicago.

Membership: In 1992, the church reported 85 churches, 180,000 members, and 68 priests.

Sources:

The Agprya. Brooklyn, Abdelsayed, "The Coptic-American: A Current African Cultural Contribution in the United States of America." *Migration Today* 19 (1975): 17-19.

Ishak, Fayek M. *A Complete Translation of the Coptic Orthodox Mass and Liturgy of St. Basil.* Toronto: Coptic Orthodox Church, Diocese of North America, 1973.

St. Mark and the Coptic Church. Cairo: Coptic Orthodox Partriarchate, 1968.

★286★
Coptic Orthodox Church Apostolic
(Defunct)

The Coptic Orthodox Church Apostolic was chartered in New York City in 1942 by John Hickerson (also spelled Hickersayon). Hickerson, an African American, had one of the more interesting careers in American religion. Little is known of his origin. He first emerged as a preacher in a Pentecostal church in Boston, Massachusetts, shortly after the turn of the century. Then around 1908 he associated himself with Samuel Morris, the leader of a small African-American movement in Baltimore, Maryland. Morris had proclaimed himself God and taken the name Father Jehovia. He was assisted by one George Baker, known as the Messenger, later to reappear as Father Divine.

Around 1911, the team split up. Hickerson had challenged Morris' leadership by arguing that the Spirit of God resided in everyone. Hence all could claim some godhood. Hickerson went to New York and founded a congregation called the Church of the Living God, located on 41st Street. He offered what appeared to be a mixture of Pentecostalism and New Thought. He believed that God lived in everyone and hence none could die. However, the church seems to have disintegrated into a chaotic situation.

Hickerson was also an early advocate of Ethiopianism, the idea that Africans were the true Jews and that Jesus was an African. He is credited with preparing the way for the emergence of Ethiopianism among Blacks in the 1920s in New York City.

In any case, Hickerson was consecrated in 1938 by Bp. Edwin Macmillan Jack, known as Bishop Yakob, head of the Episcopal Orthodox Church (Greek Communion), a small, independent Eastern orthodox jurisdiction with orders from the African Orthodox Church. He had founded his church in 1921 in Cuba and been consecrated a bishop two years later. Bishop Yakob had moved to New York in 1938.

Hickerson incorporated the Coptic Orthodox Church Apostolic in 1942. He seems to have corresponded with His Holiness Abuna Basilios, the head of the Ethiopian Coptic Orthodox Church, but was never received into communion.

Among Hickerson's actions as head of the Coptic Orthodox Church Apostolic was the consecration of Mar Lukos (Denison Quartey Arthur) in 1947. Mar Lukos operated primarily in the Caribbean area but was responsible for passing along Hickerson's apostolic order to several independent Old Catholic bishops, including Primate Hugh George de Willmott Newman (Mar Georgius), who subsequently passed them to a number of others.

Sources:

Anson, Peter. *Bishops at Large*. London: Faber and Faber, 1964.

Harris, Sara. *Father Divine*. New York: Collier, 1971.

Newman, Richard. *Black Bishops: Some African-American Old Catholic's and Their Churches*. New York: The Author, 1992.

★287★
Coptic Orthodox Church (Western Hemisphere)
Current address not obtained for this edition.

The Coptic Orthodox Church is a small African American Orthodox jurisdiction founded in the late 1970s by Samuel Theophilus Garner. Garner had been associated with the American Catholic Church, Archdiocese of New York, whose archbishop, James Francis Augustine Lashley, consecrated Garner in 1976. Garner founded the Coptic Orthodox Church a short time later. The church follows Coptic belief and liturgy, but is not connected with the Coptic Church in either Egypt or Ethiopia.

Membership: Not reported.

Sources:

Ward, Gary L. *Independent Bishops: An International Directory*. Detroit, MI: Apogee Books, 1990. 524 pp.

★288★
Diocese of the Armenian Church of America
% Khajag Barsamian
630 2nd Ave.
New York, NY 10016

Alternate Address: International headquarters: The Holy See of Etchmiadzin, Etchmiadzin, Armenia.

The Armenian Church of America is the American branch of the Armenian Church. It is under the jurisdiction of the See of Etchmiadzin in the Republic of Armenia. It is headed by Abp. Khajag Barsamian, with a western diocese under the leadership of Abp. Vatche Houspeian, and a Canadian dioceses led by Abp. Hovnan Derderian.

Membership: In 1994, the church reported 66 churches, 61 clergy, and 600,000 members. There are approximately 100,000 members and 10 priests in Canada.

Educational Facilities: St. Nersess Seminary, New Rochelle, NY 10804.

Periodicals: *The Armenian Church.*

Sources:

Gulesserian, Papken. *The Armenian Church*. New York: Diocese of the Armenian Church in America, 1966.

Gurlekian, Hogop. *Christ's Religion in Every Branch of Life and the Armenians Really Alive*. Chicago: The Author, 1974.

The Handbook on the Divine Liturgy of the Armenian Apostolic Holy Church. Boston: Baikar, 1931.

Manoogian, Sion. *The Armenian Church and Her Teachings*. The Author, n.d.

★289★
Ethiopian Orthodox Church in the United States of America
% His Eminence Abuna Yeshaq, Archbishop
Holy Trinity Ethiopian Orthodox Church
140-142 W. 176th St.
Bronx, NY 10453

Alternate Address: % His Holiness Abuna Tekle Haimanot, Box 1283, Addis Ababa, Ethiopia.

From its beginning, the Ethiopian Church was affiliated with the See of St. Mark at Alexandria, Egypt. After the death of Frumentius, the first bishop of Ethiopia, Egyptian bishops were appointed to head the Ethiopian church. This practice continued into the twentieth century. However, the changes wrought by the new century, including a new feeling of indepedendency aroused by the leadership of Emperor Haile Selassie, made it desirable to have native bishops. Negotiations began in 1926 and step by step the church moved toward an autonomous status. In 1929, for the first time, native bishops were consecrated, though they were not assigned to specific dioceses and not allowed to perform further consecrations. In 1944 the Emperor established the Theological College in Addis Ababa. Immediately after World War II, in 1948, the Statue of Independence of the Ethiopian Church from the Egyptian Coptic Church was promulgated. That same year the Ethiopian Church joined the World Council of Churches. In 1959, the Ethiopian Church was granted full independence, though it remains in canonical union with the Coptic church. In 1971, the See of Addis Ababa was raised to patriarchal status and Abuna Theophilus was elevated to Patriarch of Addis Ababa.

The 1970s and 1980s have been difficult times for the Ethiopian Church. In 1974, Haile Selassie was overthrown and an atheist Marxist regime came to power. In 1975, the church-state separation was declared and the church placed on its own. In 1976, Abuna Theophilus was removed from office and arrested. He disappeared and was never seen again. The pattern of systematic persecution by the government has only recently been eased. The current Patriarch is Abune Teklte Haimanot.

In 1959, the same year the Ethiopian Church attained independence, Laike Mandefro joined a small group of Ethiopian priests studying in the United States. The group was originally sponsored by Abuna Gabre Kristos Mikael of the Ethiopian Coptic church of North and South America. However, they soon removed themselves from that jurisdiction and placed themselves under Abuna Theophilus, then Archbishop of Harar Provice in Ethiopia. Mandefro gathered an initial congregation in Brooklyn, New York, and soon afterward led in the formation of churches in Trinidad and Guyana. As his efforts bore fruit, he was raised to the rank of archimandrite. In 1970 he moved to Jamaica and over the next seven years established the church in a number of locations across the island.

In 1972, the diocese of the Western Hemisphere was created and Mandefro consecrated as its first bishop. He was elevated to archbishop on 1983. The church, through its international headquarters in Ethiopia, is a member of the World Council of Churches. In Jamaica it is a member of the Jamaica Council of Churches and the Caribbean Conference of Churches. Branch churches of the archdiocese are located in the United States, Guyana, South Africa, and a number of the Caribbean Islands. It is currently led by His Eminence Archbishop Yesehaq.

Membership: In 1992, the archdiocese reported 100,000 communicant members and 75 ordained priests and deacons. Congregations in the United States are located in New York City and the Bronx, New York; Boston, Massachusetts; Washington, D.C.; Atlanta, Georgia; Seattle, Washington; and Fresno, Oakland, and Los Angeles, California.

Periodicals: *Ethiopian Orthodox Church in the United States of America Monthly Bulletin.*

Sources:

Bessil-Watson, Lisa, comp. *Handbook of Churches in the Caribbean.* Bridgetown, Barbados: Cedar Press, 1982.

Molnar, Enrico S. *The Ethiopian Orthodox Church.* Pasadena, CA: Bloy House Theological School, 1969.

Simon, K. M. *The Ethiopian Orthodox Church.* Addis Ababa, Ethiopia, n.d.

Yesehaq, Archbishop. *The Ethiopian Orthodox Tewahedo Church: An Intergrally African Church.* New York: Vantage Press, n.d.

★290★
Ethiopian Orthodox Coptic Church, Diocese of North and South America
Current address not obtained for this edition.

The Ethiopian Orthodox Coptic Church, Diocese of North and South America, was formed by Most Rev. Abuna Gabre Kristos Mikael, an Ethiopian-American who established his jurisdiction under the authority of the Archbishop Walter A. Propheta of the American Orthodox Catholic Church. In 1959, he traveled to Ethiopia, was ordained, and then elevated to the rank of Chorepistopas by Abuna Basilios. late patriarch of Ethiopia. He then served as sponsor for a group of three priests and five deacons sent by Abuna Basilios to the United States for advanced study and to develop an American branch of the Ethiopian Orthodox Church. However, the priests, led by Fr. Laike Mandefro, broke relations with Mikael and centered their efforts on a parish in Brooklyn, New York, later relocated to the Bronx, which was directly under the authority of the Patriarch in Addis Ababa. The Ethiopian Orthodox Coptic Church remains in communion with the American Orthodox Catholic Church, from which some of the clergy were drawn.

In the few years of its existance it has established churches in Trinidad, Mexico, and Pennsylvania; in Brooklyn there are two churches, one with a Latin and one with a Coptic Ethiopian rite, the rite commonly followed by the church. The worship is in English. The priests are both celibate and married, and all bishops are celibate, the common Eastern church practice. Most of the members and clergy are black, but the church made news in 1972 by elevating a white man to the episcopate as bishop of Brooklyn.

Friction has developed between the two "Ethiopian" churches, each questioning the legitimacy of the other.

Membership: Not reported. It is estimated that several hundred members can be found in the three parishes in New York and Pennsylvania.

★291★
Holy Apostolic-Catholic Church of the East (Chaldean-Syrian)
℅ Metropolitan Mar Mikhael OSJ, Ph.D
PO Box 3337
Daly City, CA 94015

The Holy Apostolic-Catholic Church of the East (Chaldean-Syrian) traces its history to the Aramaic-speaking segment of the Christian Church which emerged immediately after the resurrection of Jesus and Pentecost. It has also been known as the Eastern Catholic Church, Coptic, Syriac, and Syro-Chaldean Rites and the Eastern Catholic Archdiocese (Chaldean-Syriac Rite). The Apostles who founded the church were St. Peter, St. Thomas, and St. Jude Thaddeus during the first century C.E. in what is present-day Iran and India. It survived through the centuries that included periods of great expansion and subsequent periods of persecution that saw its almost complete destruction.

In 1934, the Eastern Catholic Church came to the United States in the person of Mar David of Edessa (Stanislaus, Graf von Czernowitz), who served as its first metropolitan. The present metropolitan of the church is Metropolitan Mar Mikhael of Edessa (Heinrich XXVI, Prinz Reuss von Plauen-Brankovic).

The belief and practice of the church is Orthodox. Like the Church of the East, it holds to the doctrines of the first two Ecumenical Councils, affirms the virgin birth of Jesus, His incarnation and sacrificial atonements, and the Holy Trinity. The Bible, consisting of the Old and New Testaments, is the authority for the church, which uses the Peshitta, the Bible version translated directly from the ancient Aramaic texts. In 1951, the Synod of Bishops accepted the spirit of the Theological Decrees of the Third through the Seventh Ecumenical Councils. This jurisdiction differs from some other Eastern bodies in that it has entered into the Charismatic Renewal in 1947 and continues to believe and teach that the gifts of the Holy Spirit (I Corinthians 12) are meant for today.

Membership: In 1994, the church reported 45 parishes, mission stations, nursing mission stations, monasteries, and a daycare center for AIDS babies and children, in the United States, Canada, South America, Australia, and Korea. There are two inpatient hospices for the terminally ill. The ecclesiastical province, which includes North and South America and the Far East. The first official church census was taken in 1972 with a membership of 57,000.

Educational Facilities: Holy Trinity Seminary holds state accreditation and is affiliated with the German University System (Consortium).

Remarks: This author's volume, *The Old Catholic Sourcebook* (Garland, 1983), co-authored with Karl Pruter, incorrectly identified Mar Mikhael with Michael A. Itkin, a bishop since deceased who also resided in the San Francisco Bay area, who had taken the same ecclesiastical name. Itkin, however, headed a church that is openly identified with the homosexual community (The Community of Love). This practice is in direct opposition to the beliefs and practices of the Holy Apostolic-Catholic Church of the East and Metropolitan Mar Mikhael. I am happy to take this further opportunity to dispel any remaining confusion caused by that error.

★292★
Holy Apostolic Catholic Church, Syro-Chaldean Diocese of Santa Barbara and Central California
(Defunct)

The Holy Apostolic Catholic Church, Syro-Chaldean Diocese of Santa Barbara and Central California was founded by Michael Djorde Milan d'Obrenovic (d. 1986). In 1971, d'Obrenovic became the head of a small group in Cornville, Arizona, consisting of former Roman Catholics, Old Catholics, and Serbian Orthodox. Having been chosen the group's pastor, he sought ordination from Christ Catholic Church. The attempt was unsuccessful, and he was later ordained by Archbishop Gerret Munnik of the Liberal Catholic Church, Province of the United States. After a few years he left the Liberal Catholics and was consecrated by Bishops John Marion Stanley, of the Orthodox Church of the East, and Elijah Coady, of the Christian Orthodox Church (now the Catholic Apostolic Church at Davis) in 1977. The Holy Apostolic Catholic Church follows the practice and belief of the Church of the East, without the charismatic-pentecostal emphasis introduced by Stanley and accepted by Coady.

Quite apart from his ecclesiastical career, d'Obrenovic developed a second identity under his birth name, George Hunt Williamson. D'Obrenovic claimed to be a descendent of the Yugoslavian royal family of d'Obrenovic (the last member of which was supposed to have been assassinated in 1903) and he used the name Williamson because it was easier for Americans to pronounce. As George Hunt Williamson, he became one of the first people in the early 1950s to claim direct contact with the entities inhabiting flying saucers. He was present when George Adamski made his initial contact with the Venusian in the California Desert, and eventually as Brother Philip, founded the Brotherhood of the Seven Rays.

Membership: The church had only one parish located in Santa Barbara, California. No evidence of that parish has been found since d'Obrenovic's death in 1986.

Sources:

Philip, Brother [George Hunt Williamson]. *The Brotherhood of the Seven Rays.* Clarksburg, WV: Saucerian Books, 1961.

Williamson, George Hunt. *Other Tongues—Other Flesh.* Amherst, WI: Amherst Press, 1953.

___. *Road in the Sky.* London: Neville Spearman, 1959.

___. *The Saucers Speak.* London: Neville Spearman, 1963.

___. *Secret Places of the Lion.* London: Neville Spearman, 1959.

★293★
Holy Orthodox Catholic Church, Eastern and Apostolic
Current address not obtained for this edition.

The Holy Orthodox Catholic Church, Eastern and Apostolic (HOCC) was established in the 1970s by Mar Apriam (Richard B. Morrill) formerly a bishop of the American Orthodox Catholic Church. He was enthroned as Metropolitan by Patriarch Christian I (John A. Christian or Chiasson) and also named Deputy Patriarch of the American Orthodox Catholic Church (AOCC).

In July 1974, Mar Apriam resigned as Deputy Patriarch of the AOCC and on December 23, 1974. He moved to Nigeria, where the AOCC had some work, and assumed leadership of the Nigerian AOCC. In 1976 (following some internal turmoil in the AOCC), following consultation with the AOCC's new Patriarch Lawrence Pierre, Mar Apriam renounced any claim to a position in the AOCC and founded the Holy Orthodox Catholic Church, Eastern and Apostolic.

In 1977 Mar Apriam merged the HOCC with the North American Orthodox Catholic Church under the direction of Mar Markus I (Mark I. Miller). He assumed the ecclesiastical name Patriarch James VI as head of the merged church. The merger lasted only two years as disagreements arose over the charismatic nature of Mar Apriam's ministry. He was deposed and excommunicated, but left to reestablish the HOCC. In 1984 Mar Apriam and Mar Markus I again reunited their work as the Byzantine Catholic Church. In June of that year he reconsecrated Mar Markus I sub conditione.

After only a few months, Mar Apriam and Mar Markus I again went their separate ways. On Christmas Day 1984, Patriarch Christian I died. In the wake of his passing, Mar Apriam reasserted his role as "Apostolic Administrator" of the AOCC and assumed the role of Metropolitan and Primate of the American Orthodox Catholic Church, Holy Synod of the Americas with headquarters

in Sacramento, California. He died there in 1991 and the present status of his jurisdiction is unknown.

Membership: In 1984 the church claimed seven parishes and missions in the United States. Foreign work was reported in Brazil, Chile, Liberia, Mexico, Nigeria, Trinidad, Zaire, and Zimbabwe. As of January 1983, there were 66 parishes, one school, one mission station, 70 priests, and 106,079 members worldwide.

Educational Facilities: Orthodox Academy of Education, Tarzana, California.

Periodicals: *Maranatha.*

★294★
Malankara Orthodox (Syrian) Church
% His Grace, Dr. Thomas Makarios
Episcopal Diocesan House
1114 Delaware Ave.
Buffalo, NY 14209

The Malankara Orthodox (Syrian) Church dates itself to the arrival of St. Thomas, one of the disciples of Jesus, in India in 52 C.E. St. Thomas worked near southern India and was martyred on St. Thomas Mount, Madras. After existing independently for many centuries, the church developed a relationship with the Roman Catholic Church in 1599 at the synod of Daimper. That relationship ended in 1653 in what is frequently referred to as the "Coonan Cross incident." In a very dramatic action, church members grasping a rope which symbolically tied them to a cross erected at Mattancherry, Cochin, renounced the Roman Catholic faith and the authority of the pope both for themselves and succeeding generations.

The Malankara Church soon affiliated with the Syrian Church of Antioch. After separating from the Roman Church, it was left without a bishop. The Syrian Church refused to consecrate a bishop, but provided for the ordination of priests. In 1772 Thomas Palakomatta IV was consecrated as Dionysius I. A century later, the head of the Indian Church found himself engaged in a quarrel with another bishop claiming authority over the Indian Christians. He asked the Syrian patriarch, who had consecrated the rival, to assist him. In 1975 Mar Peter came to India, excommunicated the rival, and reorganized the Indian Church into seven dioceses, each headed by a bishop subject to him.

The following decades were spent asserting the independent position of the church from both the Syrian patriarch (who tried to assume title to church property) and the followers of the excommunicated rival. Two decisive events ended the controversy: first, in 1912, the Syrian Patriarch cooperated in the creation of the Catholicate of India by declaring the defunct Catholicate of Edessa (Syria) reestablished in India. Second, the last lawsuit was settled in 1958 when the Indian courts recognized the authority of the Indian Catholics in all matters of church administration.

The Malankara Orthodox Church was brought to the United States in the late 1960s by immigrants from southern India. A diocese was created in the 1970s, and in 1980 the first church building, St. George's Orthodox Church, Staten Island, New York, was purchased and dedicated.

The church is similar in faith and practice to the Syrian Orthodox Church of Antioch and the Syrian Orthodox Church of Malabar. The church was a charter member of the World Council of Churches. The present patriarch of the church is His Holiness Moran Mar Basilius Mar Thomas Mathews I, whose chair is located at the Catholicate Palace at Kottayam, Kerala.

Membership: In 1988 the church reported 5,000 families in 37 congregations in the United States and four in Canada. Included were two missions for non-Indians in Spokane, Washington, and Coeur d'Alene, Idaho.

Sources:

Attwater, Donald. *The Christian Churches of the East.* Milwaukee: Bruce Publishing Company, 1962.

Brown, Leslie. *The Indian Christians of St. Thomas.* Cambridge: Cambridge University Press, 1956.

Pamban, Kadavil Paul. *The Orthodox Syrian Church, Its Religion and Philosophy.* Vadayampady, Puthencruz, India: K.V. Pathrose, 1973.

★295★
Orthodox Catholic Synod of the Syro-Chaldean Rite
℅ Bashir Ahmed
100 Los Banos Ave.
Daly City, CA 94014

The Orthodox Catholic Synod of the Syro-Chaldean Rite was formed in 1970 by Bishop Bashif Ahmed and is one of several bodies to continue the tradition of Mar Jacobus (Ulric Vernon Herford), who brought the Syro-Caldean Church to the West in 1902. Raised a Unitarian, Herford journeyed to the Orient on a quest to find a means of uniting East and West. In 1902 he was consecrated by Mar Basilius Soares, Bishop of Trichur, and head of a small body of Indian Christians called the Mellusians. Mar Basilius had been ordained to the priesthood by Julius Alvarez (who had consecrated Joseph Rene Vilatte) and consecrated to the episcopacy by Mar Antonius Abd-Ishu of the Nestorian linage. Upon his return to England, Herford founded the Evangelical Catholic Communion.

The Orthodox Catholic Synod of the Syro-Chaldean Rite derives from a schism of the Evangelical Catholic Communion, an American church founded by Michael A. Itkin. Itkin had led his orgainzation to take a positive activist stance in support of homosexuals. Rejecting Itkin's leadership, Ahmed founded an independent jurisdiction within the same tradition.

Membership: Not reported.

★296★
Orthodox Church of the East
12504 SW 232nd St.
Vashon, WA 98070

History. The Orthodox Church of the East (also known as the Church of the East in America) was founded in 1959 by Bishop John Marion Stanley, and is one of several churches claiming affiliation with the ancient Church of the East through the lineage of its episcopal orders. Stanley was consecrated to the bishopric in 1959 by Charles D. Boltwood of the Free Protestant Episcopal Church as Bishop of Washington. Boltwood also granted Stanley a mandate for an autocephalous body under Boltwood's guidance. Boltwood was originally consecrated by Archbishop William Hall, whom he succeeded as head of the church, but was later consecrated *subconditione* by Hugh George de Willmott Newman of the Catholicate of the West. Newman passed to Boltwood the lineage of Mar Basilius Soares, head of a small body of Indian Christians who have their orders from the Church of the East.

In 1963, Boltwood withdrew from the Catholicate of the West, but remained in communion with Stanley. During this period, Stanley was elevated to metropolitan of the United States by Newman, who gave him the ecclesiastical title of Mar Yokhannan (Aramaic for "Bishop John"). Stanley then experienced the pentecostal baptism of the Holy Spirit accompanied by speaking in tongues. He in turn led his jurisdiction into the acceptance of the pentecostal experience and the exercise of the gifts of the Holy Spirit as mentioned in I Corinthians 12. He also became a popular speaker at the interdenominational Full Gospel Businessmen's Fellowship International conferences.

Also in 1963, Stanley became concerned over the report on Newman in Peter Anson's study of independent bishops, *Bishops at Large.* Under the direction of Metropolitan Archbishop Howard of Portland and the Roman Catholic Archdiocese of Seattle, Stanley, as Mar Yokhannan entered into dialogue with Rome. For five years cathedrals throughout the world were opened to him to celebrate the Eastern rite.

In 1970, in the Catholic Church of the Holy Resurrection in New York City, Patriarch Woldymyr I (Walter A. Propheta) (1912-1972), founder of the American Orthodox Catholic Church, performed an Economia so Stanley could serve as his apostolic delegate for foreign missions. In 1971, Propheta appointed Stanley as exarch plenepotentiary to carry full authority from the patriarch in dealing with problems in church leadership oversees. Stanley's church and clergy remained in his jurisdiction, and he continued in the Church of the East Rite.

Bishop Stanley remained with the American Orthodox Catholic Church until October 24, 1977, when Patriarch Mar Apriam I (Richard B. Morrill) of the Holy Orthodox Catholic Church, Eastern and Apostolic, gave his patriarchial blessing and letter to return the Orthodox Church of the East to an autonomous and autocephalous independent status. Some of the prelates and clergy in Stanley's jurisdiction had previously been under Mar Apriam I. Since that time, the Orthodox Church of the East has remained autonomous, though in dialogue, with the Church of the East in Iraq and the Church of the East in India. It also remains in open communion with the Free Protestant Episcopal Church.

Beliefs. The Orthodox Church of the East in America is Orthodox in faith and practice and accepts the Nicene Creed, using the Eastern text. It follows the Syro-Chaldean (Aramaic) liturgy of the Holy Apostolic Catholic Assyrian Church of the East, but uses an English text based upon the archbishop of Canterbury's committee's translation of Kirbana Kadisha (Holy Eurcharist), the shortened form approved by the Metropolitan of India in 1976 during his visit to Santa Barbara, California. It also follows the Church of the East's Hebraic standards of no statues or pictures in the sanctuary, but does not emphasize the *malka,* i.e., the tradition of dough kept since the Last Supper from which the eucharist is prepared. Members make room for praising in tongues (speaking-in-tongues) following the ancient liturgy's words, "We make new harps in our mouths, and speak a new tongue with lips of fire."

Organization. The Orthodox Church of the East follows an episcopal polity. It keeps the biblical practice of bishops being the husbands of one wife (which the patriarch of the Church of the East reinstated). Women are not admitted to the priesthood but many serve as deaconesses up to the rank of archdeaconess. There is no restriction as to their ministering in the gifts of the Spirit whenever it is appropriate and necessary.

Bishop Stanley also founded the Messianic Believer's Trust, a parachurch organization promoting charismatic (pentecostal) renewal. It cooperates with the Believers Charismatic Fellowship, a similar organization, in the publication of the *The Messianic Messenger.* Another organization under the church is the World Alliance for Peace, which promotes peace amoung the people of God, primarily by developing bridges among Christians, Muslims, and Jews. Recent efforts have included an Israeli Children's tennis match for peace before the 1988 Olympic Games in Seoul, Korea, and the preparation for a Pacific Peace Conference that will include representatives from Nicaragua and Costa Rica.

The church has a bible school and hospital under its direction in India. A mission work in Pakistan cooperates with other churches in relief programs for Afghan refugees and goodwill within the Muslim government. It is also working to develop an accredited graduate school in Pakistan.

Membership: In 1988, the church reported two congregations, one in Bremerton, Washington, and one in Malibu, California. Other congregations formerly in the jurisdiction have become autonomous. There is one congregation each in India and in Pakistan.

Educational Facilities: Suviseshapuram Bible and Technical School, Kerala, India.

Periodicals: *The Messianic Messenger.* Send orders to 3130 Jefferson St.-36, Napa, CA 94558. • *Messiah Letter.* Send orders to 417 Crystal Dr., Cotati, CA 94931.

Syrian Orthodox Church of Antioch (Patriarchal Vicariates of the United States and Canada) (Jacobite)

℅ Eastern U.S. Vicariate
260 Elm Ave.
Teaneck, NJ 07666

Alternate Address: Western U.S. Vicariate, 417 E. Fairmont Rd., Burbank, CA 91501; Canadian Vicariate, 999 Montpellier, No. 102, St. Laurent, PQ, Canada H4L 5E5.

The Syrian Orthodox Church of Antioch (Patriarchal Vicariates of the United States and Canada) dates itself to the beginnings of Christianity in Antioch as recorded in the Acts of the Apostles in the New Testament, but has been greatly affected by two events. In the fifth century, the church refused to accept the decisions of the Council of Chalcedon concerning the Person of Christ and as a result developed a doctrinal position similar to that of the Coptic, Ethiopian, and Armenian churches. In the following century, the church experienced a marked revival of spiritual life under St. Jacob Baradaeus (500–578), and in recognition of his work, has frequently been referred to as the Syrian Jacobite Church.

The church came to the United States through the migration of members in the late nineteenth century. In 1907 the first priest was ordained and sent to work in America. Abp. Mar Athanasius Y. Samuel moved to America in 1949 and was soon appointed patriarchal vicar. The archdiocese was formally created in 1957. Archbishop Samuel received some fame in the 1950s as a result of his having purchased the first of what were to become known as the Dead Sea Scrolls. Samuel died in 1965 and was buried in the Netherlands.

In 1995, the Holy Synod of the Syrian Orthodox Church of Antioch divided the Archdiocese of North America into three separate Patriarchal Vicariates, each under a hierarch of the church.

The church adheres to the faith of the first three ecumenical councils. It accepts the Nicene Creed but not the Chalcedonian formula and its teaching on the two natures of Christ. There are seven sacraments: baptism, chrismation, the Eucharist, confession (and penitence), marriage, ordination to the priesthood, and the anointment of the sick.

The Patriarchal Vicariates are an integral part of the Syrian Orthodox Patriarchate of Antioch and All the East, whose headquarters are located in Damascus, Syria. The church is currently headed by His Holiness Moran Mor Ignatius Zakka I Iwas, the Patriarch of Antioch and All the East.The Patriarchate is a member of the World Council of Churches and the Middle East Council of Churches. The Patriarchal Vicariates of the United States are a member of the National Council of Churches. There is an annual convention of the Patriarchal Vicariates.

Membership: In 1998, Patriarchal Vicariates reported 40,000 members in North America divided between 19 parishes in the United States and five parishes in Canada. There were 26 priests. Worldwide, more than four million believers were related to the Patriarchate.

Periodicals: *SOAYO Speaks and Voice of the Archdiocese.*

Sources:

Anaphora. Hackensack, NJ: Metropolitan Mar Athanasius Yeshue Samuel, 1967.

Ephrem, Mar Ignatious, I. *The Syrian Church of Antioch, Its Name and History.* Hackensack, NJ: Archdiocese of the Syrian Church of Antioch in the United States and Canada, n.d.

Ephrem Barsoun, Mar Severius. *The Golden Key to Divine Worship.* West New York, NJ, 1951.

Ramban, Kadavil Paul. *The Orthodox Syrian Church, Its Religion and Philosophy.* Vadatampady, Puthencruz, India: K.V. Pathrose, 1973.

Samuel, Athanasius Yeshue. *Treasure of Oumran.* Philadelphia: Westminster Press, 1966.

Syrian Orthodox Church of Malabar

℅ Dr. K. M. Simon
Union Theological Seminary
Broadway and 120th St.
New York, NY 10027

From the time of the ancient church, there has existed on the southwest Malabar coast of India a people who by legend were first evangelized by the Apostle Thomas. Relations with the Roman See were established in the Middle Ages. In the fifteenth century when the Portugeuse began to colonize the Malabar coast, they attempted to Latinize the church, and after a period of tension most of the church withdrew from papal jurisdiction in 1653. In 1665 the Syrian Jacobites sent their representative to the Malabar coast and eventually many of the Malabar Christians were brought under the Syrian patriarch of Antioch. A Malabar bishop was consecrated in 1772 and there are approximately 1,500,000 Christians in his jurisdiction today.

The Syrian Orthodox Church of Malabar has established a mission in New York directly under the patriarch of Antioch. There is only one congregation (as of 1967) which meets at Union Theological Seminary every Sunday and on holidays. Its approximate 150 members are drawn from students, diplomatic personnel, and permanent residents. Periodic services are also held in Philadelphia, Washington, DC, and Chicago. Dr. K. M. Simon is the vicar-in-charge.

Membership: Not reported.

Sources:

An English Translation of the Order of the Holy Ourbana of the Mar Thoma Syrian Church of Malabar. Madras, India: Diocesan Press, 1947.

Ramban, Kadavil Paul. *The Orthodox Syrian Church, Its Religion and Philosophy.* Vadayampady, Puthencrez, India: K. V. Pathrose, 1973.

Western Orthodox Church

Current address not obtained for this edition.

The Western Orthodox Church is one of several small jurisdictions which grew out of the ministry of Most Rev. David Stanns (Mar David), an independent bishop who founded the American Coptic Orthodox Church. That church was continued by Archbishop Richard B. Morrill (Mar Apriam) of the Holy Orthodox Catholic Church, Eastern and Apostolic. Joseph Russell Morse established the Western Orthodox Church and its Diocese of the Pacific Coast in 1972. In 1973 he was consecrated bishop and elevated to archbishop in 1974.

The Western Orthodox Church is described as Western because it uses the English language in its worship. It is Coptic in that Archbishop Morrill, who succeeded Archbishop Stanns, gave permission for the establishment of the church with an English-speaking Coptic liturgy. It is charismatic in that the gifts of the spirit are recognized and used in the worship of the church. It is orthodox and acknowledges the Nicene Creed.

Membership: Not reported.

Section 5

Lutheran Family

Consult the Contents pages to locate the essay in Part II, Historical Essay Chapters,
that provides an historical discussion of this family

Intrafaith Organizations

★300★
American Lutheran Conference
(Defunct)

The American Lutheran Conference was a short-lived ecumenical body founded in 1930 soon after the formation of the American Lutheran Church (1930-1960). The American Lutheran Church took the lead in inviting the Augustana Synod, the United Danish Evangelical Lutheran Church (later the United Evangelical Lutheran Church), the Norwegian Lutheran Church in America (later known as the Evangelical Lutheran Church), and the Lutheran Free Church into an associated relationship. Many saw the new structure as designed to facilitate eventual union.

The several member groups quickly moved toward establishing doctrinal consensus and pulpit fellowship, and by the 1950s all but the Augustana were engaged in serious merger negotiations. In the light of these negotiations, the purpose of the conference had been served, and it was disbanded in 1954. The merger in 1960 produced the American Lutheran Church (1960-1988), now a constituent part of the Evangelical Lutheran Church in America.

Periodicals: During most of its life, the conference published *Lutheran Outlook* (originally the *Journal of the American Lutheran Conference*).

Sources:

Dolvin, O. E. *The American Lutheran Conference*. Minneapolis, MN: Augsburg Press, 1935.

Stavig, L. M. "The Genius of the American Lutheran Conference." *AL Conference Report* (1944): 100-115.

Wiederaenders, Robert C., and Walter G. Tillmans. *The Synods of American Lutheranism*. St. Louis, MO: Lutheran Historical Conference, 1968.

★301★
Lutheran Council in Canada
1512 S. James St.
Winnipeg, MB, Canada R3H 0l2

The Lutheran Council in Canada began in 1952 as the Canadian Lutheran Council to serve the churches in Canada affiliated with those Lutheran churches in the United States which were affiliated with the National Lutheran Council (namely the Lutheran Church in America (LCA) and the American Lutheran Church (ALC)). In the early 1960s, the LCA and the ALC entered into negotiations with the Lutheran Church-Missouri Synod, which led to the discontinuance of the National Lutheran Council and the inauguration of the Lutheran Council in the U.S.A. at the beginning of 1967. In anticipation of this action in the United States, the Canadian Lutheran Council disbanded in the summer of 1966 and reformed as the Lutheran Council in Canada. It began to function officially on January 1, 1967, as did its American counterpart.

In 1967 the American Lutheran Church released its Canadian parishes, who organized as the Evangelical Lutheran Church of Canada. In 1986, in anticipation of the merger of the ALC and LCA in the United States, the Evangelical Lutheran Church merged with the three Canadian synods of the Lutheran Church in America to form the Evangelical Lutheran Church in Canada. Then in 1988 the Canadian synods of the Lutheran Church-Missouri Synod became autonomous as the Lutheran Church-Canada. The Lutheran Council in Canada serves these two Lutheran bodies.

Sources:

Wiederaenders, Robert C., and Walter G. Tillmans. *The Synods of American Lutheranism*. St. Louis, MO: Lutheran Historical Conference, 1968.

★302★
Lutheran Council in the U.S.A.
(Defunct)

The Lutheran Council in the U.S.A. was founded on January 1, 1967, at which time it superseded the National Lutheran Council. The National Lutheran Council had been founded in 1918, growing out of the successful cooperative activity of the Lutheran Church in America (then split into a number of autonomous synods) during World War I. Over the next two decades, it provided a nexus for cooperative activities and fellowship and a context in which mergers could and did occur, the primary one being the formation of the American Lutheran Church (1930-1960) in 1930.

World War II led to heightened action in the area of relief efforts, work with refugees, and after the war, the reestablishment of relations with European Lutheran churches through the formation of the Lutheran World Federation. The Lutheran Church-Missouri Synod, though not a member of the council, cooperated with its relief efforts. In the 1960s formal talks were opened with the Missouri Synod on their joining with the National Lutheran Council. After some years of discussion, the way was seen clear to disband the National Lutheran Council in favor of a structure to which the Missouri Synod could relate, the Lutheran Council in the U.S.A.

Through the 1980s events conspired to cause the disbanding of the Lutheran Council in the U.S.A. Most importantly, the Association of Evangelical Lutheran Churches, which had split from the Missouri Synod in 1967, joined with the American Lutheran Church and the Lutheran Church in America to form the Evangelical Lutheran Church in America. That merger was consummated on January 1, 1988. It brought all of the major Lutheran bodies other than the Missouri Synod into a single ecclesiastical organization. In the meantime, the Missouri Synod had taken a more conservative stance, having lost most of its prominent liberal voices in the 1976 split. Thus the need for continuing the Lutheran Council seemed to many to have been dissipated, and it was disbanded.

Sources:

Bonderud, Omar, and Charles Lutz, eds. *America's Lutherans*. Columbus, OH: Wartburg Press, 1955.

Wiederaenders, Robert C., and Walter G. Tillmans. *The Synods of American Lutheranism*. St. Louis, MO: Lutheran Historical Conference, 1968.

★303★

Lutheran World Federation
℅ Office of Ecumenical Affairs
Evangelical Lutheran Church
8765 W. Higgins Rd.
Chicago, IL 60631

Alternate Address: International Headquarters: 160 route de Ferney, 1211 Geneva 20, Switzerland.

The Lutheran World Federation was founded in 1947 but emerged out of the prior work of the World Lutheran Convention, which had first met in 1923. The convention grew out of World War I, during which time many American Lutherans had felt the sting of having originated from Germany—the country America was fighting—or being closely identified with it. As soon as the war ended, they initiated plans to help those ravaged by the war and began relief efforts in 20 European countries. The desire for closer Lutheran association developed in this post-war atmosphere. In 1921 the National Lutheran Council considered the recommendation for a World Lutheran Federation and after consideration launched plans for an international conference of Lutherans, which met in Eisenbach, Germany, in August 1923. After its initial gathering, two additional meetings of the convention were held in Copenhagen, Denmark (1929) and Paris, France (1935). The 1940 meeting, the first scheduled for the United States, was blocked by the beginning of World War II.

The shattered unity caused by the war was reconstituted in 1947 by the organization of the Lutheran World Federation at Lund, Sweden. Forty-nine churches from 22 countries joined in the effort. A Department of Lutheran World Service was created to aid suffering and needy Lutheran groups. However, the federation quickly turned to the broad areas of church life and thought and created work areas for theology, world missions, student life, liturgy, theology, and others concerns. Over the years, increasing interest has been placed on Lutherans in traditionally non-Lutheran settings in the Third World.

The Lutheran World Federation has taken a lead in the modern ecumenical movement and has its headquarters in the World Council of Churches building in Geneva, Switzerland.

Membership: The Lutheran World Federation includes the more liberal wing of Lutheranism worldwide and in North America counts the following among its members: Estonian Evangelical Lutheran Church in Exile; Evangelical Lutheran Church in America; Evangelical Lutheran Church in Canada; Latvian Evangelical Lutheran Church in America; and Lithuanian Evangelical Lutheran Church in Exile.

Periodicals: *Lutheran Reports and Documentation* • *LWF Information*.

Sources:

Bachmann, Mercai Brenne, ed. *Lutheran Mission Directory*. Geneva: Lutheran World Federation, 1982.

Nelson, E. Clifford. *The Rise of World Lutheranism*. Philadelphia: Fortress Press, 1982.

Wolf, Richard C. *Documents of Lutheran Unity in America*. Philadelphia: Fortress Press, 1966.

★304★

Synodical Conference
(Defunct)

The Synodical Conference was formed in 1872 by the more conservative synods of American Lutherans—Missouri, Ohio, Wisconsin, Minnesota, Illinois, and the Norwegian. The synods opposed both liberalizing trends in some of the other Lutheran bodies, which were looking toward union and opposed to Freemasonry. Their initial ambitious plans for cooperation were interrupted in the 1880s by a major doctrinal controversy over predestination, which caused the Ohio Synod to withdraw permanently and others to withdraw for a brief period. Others joined soon after the turn of the century.

In 1950, by which time the majority of American Lutherans were moving toward the mergers that would produce the American Lutheran Church (1960), the Lutheran Church in America (1962), and eventually the Evangelical Lutheran Church in America (1988), the Synodical Conference consisted of the Lutheran Church-Missouri Synod, the Wisconsin Evangelical Lutheran Synod, the Norwegian Synod, the Slovak Church, and a set of African-American parishes that had emerged from a missionary effort in the American South beginning in the 1980s. The conference had also established a mission in Nigeria and welcomed the fellowship of several independent conservative Lutheran churches in Europe.

In the wake of the mergers of 1960 and 1962, the several larger Lutheran bodies, including the Lutheran Church-Missouri Synod, entered into discussions that led to the creation of the Lutheran Council in the U.S.A. In 1963, during the process of approval of this plan, the more conservative members of the conference felt that they could no longer fellowship with the Missouri Synod, and the Norwegian (now known as the Evangelical Lutheran Synod) and Wisconsin Synods withdrew from the Synodical Conference, an action which effectively disbanded it.

Sources:

Meyer, Carl S. *The Synodical Conference—The Voice of Lutheran Confessionalism*. St. Louis, MO: Concordia Publishing House, 1956.

Wiederaenders, Robert C., and Walter G. Tillmans. *The Synods of American Lutheranism*. St. Louis, MO: Lutheran Historical Conference, 1968.

★305★

U.S. National Committee for the Lutheran World Federation
℅ Office of Ecumenical Affairs
Evangelical Lutheran Church
8785 W. Higgins Rd.
Chicago, IL 60631

The U.S. National Committee for the Lutheran World Federation began during World War I. Lutherans found it expedient to cooperate in caring for the spiritual needs of Lutherans serving in the armed forces. Thus in 1917 the National Lutheran Commission for Soldiers' and Sailors' Welfare was founded. Most Lutheran bodies cooperated and the success of the venture led to the suggestion that a more permanent cooperative structure be created. Several meetings led to the formation of the National Lutheran Council in 1918.

The major Lutheran bodies participated in the council. Following the adoption of a constitution by the Lutheran World Federation in 1952, the National Lutheran Council was designated the "National Committee for the Lutheran World Federation in the United States," and the council proceeded in 1956 to establish a Division of Lutheran World Federation Affairs. In 1967 the National Lutheran Council was superseded by the Lutheran Council in the U.S.A., which continued its support of the Lutheran World Federation. With the recent disbanding of the Lutheran Council, the work of the committee has been supported by the Evangelical

Lutheran Church in America, and the committee has its headquarters in that church's Office of Ecumenical Affairs.

Membership: The Lutheran World Federation includes the more liberal wing of Lutheranism worldwide and in North America counts the following among its members: Estonian Evangelical Lutheran Church in Exile; Evangelical Lutheran Church in America; Evangelical Lutheran Church in Canada; Latvian Evangelical Lutheran Church in America; and Lithuanian Evangelical Lutheran Church in Exile.

Sources:

Bonderud, Omar, and Charles Lutz, eds. *America's Lutherans*. Columbus, OH: Wartburg Press, 1955.

Wolf, Richard C. *Documents of Lutheran Unity in America*. Philadelphia: Fortress Press, 1966.

Lutheran Churches

★306★
American Association of Lutheran Churches
PO Box 17097
Minneapolis, MN 55417

The American Association of Lutheran Churches was founded in 1987 by former pastors and members of the American Lutheran Church (ALC) who did not wish to participate in that church's 1988 merger with the Lutheran Church in America (LCA) and Association of Evangelical Lutheran Churches. The church was organized at a gathering in Bloomington, Minnesota, in November 1987. The move by the ALC to merge occasioned the protest of more theologically conservative leaders who did not wish closer association with the more liberal LCA. A major concern was the authority of Scripture, which the conservatives felt should include an affirmation of the inerrancy of the Bible.

With an emphasis upon the inerrancy of Scripture, the new church accepted the position of the ALC, designating the ancient ecumenical creeds (The Apostles, Athanasian, and Nicene), the unaltered Augsburg Confession, and Martin Luther's Small Catechism as its doctrinal statement. It also acknowledged the remaining documents of the *Book of Concord* as the normative presentation of its faith. It called its congregations to a program of solid Bible teaching and evangelism. It also passed strong statements against abortion (except when the mother's life is threatened) and homosexuality. The association has a congregational form of church government.

Membership: By 1996 the association had 90 congregations, 15,140 members and 131 pastors.

Sources:

"American Association of Lutherans Holds Constituting Convention." *The Christian News* (December 14, 1987): 1, 15.

"American Protestantism or Lutheran Orthodoxy?" *The Christian News* (September 28, 1987): 16.

★307★
Apostolic Lutheran Church of America
℅ Rev. George Wilson, President
New York Mills, MN 56567

The Apostolic Lutheran Church of America is the only branch of the Laestadian (Finnish Apostolic Lutheran) Movement to organize formally. Since 1908 the Old Laestadians had held an annual "Big Meeting." It was primarily a time for theological discussions and for affirming consensus. In 1928 the Old Laestadians announced the intention of establishing a national church. In 1929 the constitution and by-laws were adopted, asserting the authority of the Bible and the *Book of Concord*. A congregational government and a mission program were established. The church body ordains ministers, establishes institutions, and helps found new congregations. The Old Laestadians practice the laying-on-of-hands for absolution after the confession of felt sin to a confessor. They also believe in the three baptisms: of water (establishing the covenant between God and his children), of the Holy Spirit (the bond of love), and of blood (godly sorrow).

The Apostolic Lutheran Church is headed by a president and a central board. There are two districts. Congregations are located in Michigan, Minnesota, the Dakotas, Massachusetts, Washington, Oregon, and California.

Membership: In 1995 the church reported 7,700 members, 60 congregations, and 35 ministers.

Educational Facilities: Apostolic Lutheran Seminary, Hancock, Michigan.

Periodicals: *Christian Monthly*. Available from Apostolic Book Concern, Rte. 1, Box 150, New York Mills, MN 56567.

Sources:

Constitution and By-Laws. Finnish Apostolic Lutheran Church of America, 1929.

Saanivaara, Uuras. *The History of the Laestadian of Apostolic-Lutheran Movement in America*. Ironwood, MI: National Publishing Company, 1947.

★308★
Apostolic Lutherans (Church of the First Born)
Current address not obtained for this edition.

The branch of the Apostolic Lutherans, generally called the First Borns, are a continuation of the congregation headed by John Takkinen. They are aligned with the followers of Juhani Raattamaa headquarted at Gellivaara, Finland. They differ from the Old Laestadians (i.e., the Apostolic Lutheran Church) by their emphasis on the simplicity of the Christian life. They turn to the elders of Gellivaara for particular decisions on moral questions. They forbid neckties, pictures on walls, taking photographs, hats on women, Christmas trees, life insurance, and flowers at funerals.

The First Borns were among the first to introduce English in worship and to publish English books. They hold Big Meetings every summer. They print their church news in Valvoju, an unofficial publication circulated among Apostolic Lutherans. By latest count (made in the 1940's) there were approximately 2,000 members. Churches are located in Michigan; Wilmington, North Carolina; Wilmington, Delaware; Brush Prairie, Washington; and Gackle, North Dakota. There are approximately twenty-five congregations.

Membership: Not reported.

Sources:

Saanivaara, Uuras. *The History of the Laestadian or Apostolic-Lutheran Movement in America*. Ironwood, MI: National Publishing Company, 1947.

★309★
Apostolic Lutherans (Evangelicals No. 1)
Current address not obtained for this edition.

That branch of the Apostolic Lutheran Movement generally referred to as the Evangelicals No. 1 began under the inspiration and preaching of Arthur Leopold Heideman who emphasized positive evangelism. Among the Apostolic Lutherans, they lay the least emphasis on confession and sanctification. They use, but do not consider important, public confession. The Evangelicals No. 1 have experienced two splits. In 1921-22 a group led by Paul A. Heideman returned to the beliefs of the Old Laestadians. In 1940 a split occurred over the place of the commands and counsels of Christ and the Apostles and the use of confession. The Evangelicals No. 1 represent those who hold that the commands of Christ are necessary as a norm for Christian living. They believe themselves to be the one church of true believers.

Membership: Not reported.

Sources:

Saavinaara, Uuras. *The History of the Laestadian or Apostolic-Lutheran Movement in America.* Ironwood, MI: National Publishing Company, 1947.

★310★
Apostolic Lutherans (Evangelicals No. 2)
Current address not obtained for this edition.

Formed in 1940 and having broken from the Apostolic Lutherans (Evangelicals No. 1), that branch of the Apostolic Lutheran Movement generally called the Evangelicals No. 2 rejects the need of the commands and counsels of Christ because, they say, the grace of God works in believers to bring about a denial of unrighteousness and worldly lusts, and it works to instill godly and righteous behavior. They reject the confession of sins as a Roman Catholic institution, and they do not emphasize absolution. The law, they believe, should be preached to unbelievers, but only the gospel of free grace, to believers.

Like the Evangelicals No. 1, this group believes itself to be the one true church of Christ. Founders of the group include John Koskela, Victor Maki, John Taivalmaa, and Andrew Leskinen.

Membership: Not reported.

★311★
Apostolic Lutherans (New Awakening)
Current address not obtained for this edition.

Possibly the smallest branch of the Laestadians or Apostolic Lutheran Movement is the New Awakening Group. They teach the "third use of the law," i.e., that Christians must abide by the Ten Commandments in addition to Christ's two laws of love of God and love of neighbor. They also teach a second experience following conversion. The second experience is the "circumcision of the heart," in which one's heart is deeply broken but then experiences a fuller knowledge of Christ's redemptive work and of sanctification.

Membership: Not reported.

Sources:

Saanivaara, Uuras. *The History of the Laestadian or Apostolic-Lutheran Movement in America.* Ironwood, MI: National Publishing Company, 1947.

★312★
Apostolic Lutherans (The Heidmans)
Current address not obtained for this edition.

The Heidemans are the second largest group of Apostolic Lutherans. The group was formed in 1921-22 by members of the Apostolic Lutherans (Evangelicals No. 1) who separated and returned to the Old Laestadian position. Thus they resemble the Old Laestadians group, but they remain outside of its organization. The leader of the group was Paul A. Heideman, son of Arthur Leopold Heideman, who was for many years the only ordained minister in the group. He was assisted by a number of preachers.

Membership: Not reported.

Periodicals: *Rauhan Tervehdys.* • *Greetings of Peace.*

★313★
Association of Free Lutheran Congregations
3110 E. Medicine Lake Blvd.
Minneapolis, MN 55441

History. The Association of Free Lutheran Congregations was formed in 1962 by congregations that refused to enter the merger of the Lutheran Free Church with the American Lutheran Church. Among the organizers was the Rev. John P. Strand, who became president at its founding. The dissenting congregations (about 40 in number) met at Thief River Falls, Minnesota, for the organization. They opposed the American Lutheran Church's membership in the World Council of Churches; the liberal theology reflected in new attitudes toward the Bible and the Roman Catholic Church; compromises of congregational polity; high-churchism; and the lack of emphasis on personal Christianity (including the condoning of social dancing and social drinking).

Beliefs. The association adheres to the traditional Lutheran confessional documents, especially the Unaltered Augsburg Confession and Luther's Small Catechism. The group believes the Bible is the Word of God, complete, infallible, and inerrant, and rejects all affiliations and associations that do not accept the Bible alone as definitive for life and practice. The association specifically rejects the liberal drift of Lutheran theology that accepts modern biblical criticism. It also has refused to make any move toward Roman Catholicism unless the Roman Catholic Church first accepts the Lutheran principles of justification by faith alone and the role of the Bible as the supreme authority for humanity.

The church is rather free in liturgical practice. A variety of biblical translations are used. Simplicity in worship is encouraged and centrality is given to preaching. Founding members cited the "High-church" tendencies in the American Lutheran Church as one cause of their staying out of the merger.

Organization. The association continues the congregational structure of the former Lutheran Free Church. Final human authority rests in local churches, under the Word of God and the Holy Spirit. Representatives of the congregations meet annually in conference. The conference oversees the seminary and bible school, mission work in Brazil and Mexico, and a home mission program.

Membership: In 1988, the association reported 25,250 members, 190 churches, and 139 ministers in the United States. There are four churches and four ministers in Canada.

Educational Facilities: Association Free Lutheran Theological Seminary, Minneapolis, Minnesota.

Association Free Lutheran Bible School, Minneapolis, Minnesota.

Periodicals: *The Lutheran Ambassador.*

★314★
Church of the Lutheran Brethren of America
1007 Westside Dr.
Box 655
Fergus Falls, MN 56537

The Church of the Lutheran Brethren of America was organized December 17, 1900. Five independent Lutheran Congregations met together in Milwaukee, Wisconsin, and adopted a constitution closely patterned to that of the Lutheran Free Church of Norway.

The spiritual awakening in the upper mid-west during the 1890s brought new concerns to the minds of pastors and laymen alike concerning some of the practices of local congregations. These concerns crystallized into convictions that led to the founding of the Church of the Lutheran Brethren. Chief among these concerns were the issues of church membership, communion, confirmation, and church polity.

The Church of the Lutheran Brethren is non-liturgical in worship with central emphasis on the sermon. The primary criterion for church membership is a personal profession of faith in Jesus Christ. The communion service is reserved for those who profess personal faith in Christ. Each congregation is autonomous and the synod serves the congregations in advisory, administrative and cooperative capacities.

Approximately forty percent of the synodical budget goes towards world mission ventures. A growing home mission ministry is planting new congregations in the United States and Canada. The educational mission of the synod dates back to its very beginning. A Bible school was begun in 1903, which continues to this day now under the name of The Lutheran Center for Christian Learning. A seminary department was added during its early years and in 1917 an academy was added. The three schools share adjacent campuses in Fergus Falls, Minnesota.

The administrative offices and Faith and Fellowship Press are located near the school campuses. Affiliate organizations operate several retirement/nursing homes, and conference and retreat centers.

Membership: In 1995, the Lutheran Brethren reported 26,600 members in 125 congregations and a total of 242 ministers in the United States and Canada. The synod supports an extensive world mission program in Cameroon, Chad, Japan, and Taiwan.

Educational Facilities: Lutheran Brethren Seminary. Lutheran Center for Christian Learning.

Periodicals: *Faith and Fellowship*. Send orders to 704 Vernon Ave. W., Fergus Falls, MN 56537.

Sources:

Levang, Joseph H. *The Church of the Lutheran Brethren, 1900-1975*. Fergus Falls, MN: Lutheran Brethren Publishing House, 1975.

Petersen, A. A. *Questions and Answers about the Church of the Lutheran Brethren of America*. Fergus Falls, MN: Lutheran Brethren Publishing Company, 1962.

★315★
Church of the Lutheran Confession
460 75th Ave. NE
Minneapolis, MN 55432

The Church of the Lutheran Confession was organized in 1960 at Watertown, South Dakota, by congregations and clergy who had formerly belonged to the various Lutheran denominations which had comprised the Synodical Conference, a Lutheran ecumenical body. With the loss of doctrinal unity within the Conference, for conscience sake, they felt compelled to leave. At the time of their organization, there were over 30 congregations. This conservative body has experienced a generation of growth and doubled in size over the years of its existence.

Membership: In 1994, the church reported 70 congregations, 8,864 members, and 65 ministers. Missions are supported in India, Nigeria, and Thailand.

Educational Facilities: Immanuel Lutheran College and Seminary, Eau Claire, Wisconsin.

Periodicals: *The Lutheran Spokesman*. Send orders to 2750 Oxford St. N., Roseville, MN 55113. • *Journal of Theology*. Available from Immanuel Lutheran College and Seminary, 501 Grover Rd., Eau Claire, WI 54701.

Sources:

Mark...Avoid...Origin of CLC. Eau Claire, WI: CLC Bookhouse, 1983.

★316★
Concordia Lutheran Conference
Current address not obtained for this edition.

The Concordia Lutheran Conference was formed in 1956 by former members of the Lutheran Church-Missouri Synod who wished to "continue in the former doctrinal position of the Missouri Synod" in the face of what they saw as a deviation. They particularly emphasize the Bible as the inerrant word of God and as the only source and norm of Christian doctrine and life. Like their parent body, they accept the Book of Concord as the proper exposition of the Word of God. The church is nonseparatist in orientation and seeks unity with all other Lutherans and Christians on a basis of unity of faith.

Membership: In 1988, the Concordia Lutheran Conference reported a membership of six congregations, 343 members, and six ministers. There is one congregation each in Illinois, Michigan, South Dakota, Texas, Oregon, and Washington.

Educational Facilities: Concordia Theological Seminary, Tingley Park, Illinois.

Periodicals: *The Concordia Lutheran*.

Sources:

Mensing, H. David. *A Popular History of the Concordia Lutheran Conference*. N.p. 1981.

★317★
Concordia Synod of the West
(Defunct)

The Concordia Synod of the West (also known as the German Evangelical Lutheran Concordia Synod of America), was founded in 1862 by four Lutheran pastors who had left positions in the Ohio, Buffalo, and Missouri Synods: L. F. E. Krause of Winona, Minnesota; F. W. Wier of Washington, Minnesota; C. F. Jung of New Oregon, Iowa; and D. J. Warns of Bethalto, Illinois. The synod apparently met in 1862 and 1864, but afterward it disappeared and no record of it being received into another Lutheran body has been located to date.

Sources:

Wiederaenders, Robert C., and Walter G. Tillmans. *The Synods of American Lutheranism*. St. Louis, MO: Lutheran Historical Conference, 1968.

★318★
Conservative Lutheran Association
3504 N. Pearl St.
PO Box 7186
Tacoma, WA 98407

The Conservative Lutheran Association is the name adopted by the congregations associated with the World Confessional Lutheran Association, a conservative Lutheran advocacy group founded in 1965 in Cedar Rapids, Iowa, as Lutherans Alert National by a group of conservative Lutheran pastors and laypeople concerned with the drift of the larger Lutheran bodies, all of which have now merged into the Evangelical Lutheran Church in America (1988). Chief among their concerns was what they saw as a lessening of the authority of scripture. Lutherans Alert, a nonchurch-forming group, affirmed the inerrancy of the Bible.

In 1969 Lutherans Alert participated in the founding of Faith Evangelical Theological Seminary, a cooperative activity of several conservative denominations. As support for Lutherans Alert continued to grow, it changed its name to World Confessional Lutheran Association in 1984 to acknowledge its international constituency.

The lack of response to the concerns of Lutherans Alert and the move toward the 1988 merger of the larger Lutheran denominations led congregations to attach themselves to the World Confessional Lutheran Association. These merged groups were organized in a separate division called the Conservative Lutheran Association, which slowly emerged as a separate Lutheran denomination. Lutherans Alert National has survived as the apologetics division of the larger World Association. Missions and social concerns are now handled by Lutheran World Concerns.

Membership: In 1988 the association reported 11 congregation, 1,483 members, and 20 ordained ministers.

Educational Facilities: Faith Evangelical Theological Seminary, Tacoma, Washington.

Periodicals: Lutherans Alert National, PO Box 7186, Tacoma, WA 98407.

Sources:

"Oklahoma Church Leaves LCA." The Christian News (October 5, 1987): 1, 22.

★319★
Conservative Lutheran Association
PO Box 7186
Tacoma, WA 98407

The Conservative Lutheran Association (CLA) was formed in 1980 by Lutherans Alert, an organization founded in 1965 by a group of pastors and lay people who were concerned about trends in the American Lutheran Church and other synods which were contrary to what they felt were the historical beliefs and confessions of Lutheranism. The group was originally known as World Confessional Lutheran Association. Its purpose was to affirm the inerrancy of Holy Scripture and to warn the church-at-large of deviations within the various Lutheran bodies. To assist in accomplishing that purpose, Faith Evangelical Lutheran Seminary was founded in Tacoma, Washington, in 1969.

Through the 1970s, the leadership of Lutherans Alert received requests from pastors in need of assistance and identification for their struggling congregations. They did not desire membership in a synod, but did look for Christian fellowship with like-minded people. The Conservative Luthern Association was created as a fellowship of independent congregations who shared a common statement of faith and acceptance of the confessions of the Lutheran Chruch. It has no hierarchical structure. The CLA provides expertise, leadership, fellowship, and assistance to the congregations, its resources being provided to advance the congregation's ministries and to accomplish collectively tasks that could not possibly be undertaken by any single congregations.

The CLA accepts all the canonical books of the Old and New Testaments as a whole and in all their parts as the divinely inspired, revealed, and inerrant Word of God, and submits to this as the only infallible authority in all matters of faith and life. Individual Lutheran congregations who affirm Biblical inerrancy and desire to hold fast to their conservative position are eligible for membership by subscribing to the doctrinal statement. An annual conference is held, and member churches are expected to provide financial support to Faith Evangelical Lutheran Seminary, to encourage one another in their respective ministries, and to develop cooperative plans for the establishment of new mission congregations.

Membership: In 1997 the association reported six churches, 20 ordained pastors, and 1,019 members.

Educational Facilities: Faith Evangelical Lutheran Seminary, Tacoma, Washington.

Sources:

"Oklahoma Church Leaves LCA." *The Christian News* (October 5, 1987): 1, 22.

★320★
Estonian Evangelical Lutheran Church in Exile
% Abp. Udo Petersoo
383 Jarvis St.
Toronto, ON, Canada M5B 2C7

Alternate Address: Bishop Karl Raudsepp, 30 Sunrise Ave., Apt. 216, Toronto, Ontario, Canada M4A 2R3.

The Estonian Evangelical Lutheran Church (in Exile) was instated in 1944 as a free and legal continuation in the free world of the EELC after the occupation of Estonia by Communist forces of the former U.S.S.R. It was to serve Estonian Lutherans who fled their country at that time. Internationally, the church is organized into seven synods. It is a member of the Lutheran World Federation, the World Council of Churches, and the Council of European Churches.

In the years following World War II, Estonians scattered around North and South America and Australia, where they formed congregations, and later synods and a unified church. This international church body is overseen by an archbishop, bishop, and the consistory - previously in Stockholm, Sweden, and since 1991 in Toronto, Canada. The church is conservative, holding *The Book of Concord* (including the unaltered Augsburg Confession) as its standard of faith.

Now, after the collapse of the former U.S.S.R., firm steps are being taken to unite the church in Estonia and that in the West.

Membership: In 1992, the church reported 24 congregations, some 5,000 members, and 18 pastors in the United States; and 15 congregations, 4,500 members, and 12 pastors in Canada.

Educational Facilities: Estonian Evangelical Lutheran Institute of Theology, Toronto, Ontario, Canada.

Sources:

Bachmann, Mercia Brenne. *Lutheran Missionary Directory*. Geneva, Switzerland: Lutheran World Federation, 1982.

★321★
Evangelical Lutheran Church in America
% Rev. Truman Larson
Rte. 1
Jackson, MN 56143

Elling Eielsen was a young Norwegian immigrant who was ordained in America. He led the formation of the Evangelical Lutheran Church in America, the first Norwegian Lutheran synod in the New World, in 1846. Growth of the synod was slow partly due to the demand for proof of conversion prior to admission to membership. Controversy arose as some clergy demanded the admission of all who accepted the Christian faith and led a moral life. In 1876 a constitution revised along these lines was accepted and the name changed to Hauge's Norwegian Evangelical Lutheran Synod (which became part of the American Lutheran Church). At this time Eielsen and his supporters withdrew and formed the Evangelical Lutheran Church in America according to the Old Constitution. Eielsen himself died in 1883 but the Synod has continued as a small body.

Doctrine is at one with other Lutheran bodies. Liturgy is simple. (Eielsen had also protested domination by university-trained clergy, clerical garb, and a too formal liturgy.)

Membership: In 1997, the church reported on two congregations with a total membership of 50. There is one ordained minister, Truman L. Larson, ordained in 1986.

★322★
Evangelical Lutheran Church in America (1988)
8765 W. Higgins Rd.
Chicago, IL 60631

The Evangelical Lutheran Church in America (1988) (ELCA) was formed January 1, 1988, by the merger of the Lutheran Church in America, the American Lutheran Church, and the Association of Evangelical Lutheran Churches. This merger created not only the largest Lutheran body in America, but the fifth largest denomination in America. Through the lineage of the Lutheran Church in America, the Evangelical Lutheran Church in America continues the work of the earliest Lutheran organizations in America: the Philadelphia Ministerium (1748) and the New York Ministerium (1786). It also culminates a process of merger of diverse American Lutheran churches and synods which had been attempting to unite Lutherans since the first half of the nineteenth century.

History. The Lutheran Church in America, the largest body merging into the ELCA, was formed in 1962 by the merger of four Lutheran bodies: The United Lutheran Church in America, the Finnish Evangelical Lutheran Church (Soumi Synod), the American Evangelical Lutheran Church, and the Augustana Evangelical Lutheran Church which for most of its life was known simply as the Augustana Synod. The 1962 merger was the culmination of no fewer than eight previous mergers, the most significant of which was the 1918 merger of the General Synod, the General Council, and the General Synod of the South to form the United Lutheran

Church in America, the largest Lutheran body through most of the twentieth century. The General Synod had in turn been created by the 1820 merger of the older Lutheran associations: the Philadelphia Ministerium, part of the New York Ministerium, and the North Carolina Synod. The membership of the churches in the United Lutheran Church in America tradition was primarily German-American.

The Augustana Synod had originated in 1851 when the Synod of Illinois was established by Lutheran immigrants in the midwest. Around 1860 the Swedish and Norwegian elements in the Illinois Synod withdrew and formed the Scandinavian Augustana Synod. That synod joined with the remainder of the New York Ministerium in 1867 to form the very loosely associated General Council. In 1918, when the General Council merged into the United Lutheran Church in America, the Augustana Synod refused to join in the merger and remained an independent body until 1962.

The Finnish Evangelical Lutheran Church was formed in 1890 in Calumet, Michigan. It used the liturgy of the Church of Finland. The American Evangelical Lutheran Church dated to 1872 when Danish-American Lutherans formed the Kirklig Missions Forening. Through the merger of these Finnish and Danish synods into the larger German, Swedish, and Norwegian bodies, the Lutheran Church in America became the most complete amalgamation of Lutherans across ethnic boundaries and heralded the Americanization of Lutheran immigrant communities (a process through which all immigrant communities in America must eventually pass).

Another body entering into the 1988 merger, the American Lutheran Church, was formed in 1960 by the merger of three Lutheran bodies: The United Evangelical Lutheran Church, the Evangelical Lutheran Church, and the American Lutheran Church (1930-1960). The merged church retained the name of the group formed in 1930 by the merger of the Ohio (1818), Buffalo (1845), Texas (1851) and Iowa (1845) Synods. All of those Synods were of German background. The United Evangelical Lutheran Church was founded in 1896 by the union of two separate synods of Danish background. The Danish Evangelical Lutheran Association was formed in 1884 by pastors seceding from the Norwegian-Danish Conference of 1870. The Danish Evangelical Lutheran Church in North America was created in 1894 by a group which had withdrawn from the Danish Evangelical Lutheran Church of America (which eventually merged into the Lutheran Church in America). The Evangelical Lutheran Church was the result of a merger in 1917 of the different Norwegian Lutheran bodies established in America in the nineteenth century: the United Norwegian Church, the Norwegian Synod, and the Hague Synod. The American Lutheran Church was the first major merger of Lutheran groups across ethnic lines.

The Association of Evangelical Lutheran Churches, the newest and the smallest of the bodies to enter into the 1988 merger, was formed in 1976 by ministers and churches which withdrew from the Lutheran Church-Missouri Synod. The formation of the association followed many years of increased tensions within the Missouri Synod spurred by a series of complaints by conservative members about a perceived liberal drift within the church. Conservatives demanded the withdrawal of pulpit and altar fellowship from the liberal American Lutheran Church. (Pulpit fellowship refers to the practice of exchanging ministers between congregations for Sunday morning worship. Altar fellowship refers to the acceptance of members from other denominations during the practice of holy communion.) Further, conservatives asked for the end of cooperation with both the American Lutheran Church and the Lutheran Church in America in the Lutheran Council in the U.S.A. Most importantly, they demanded an investigation of the Concordia Theological Seminary, whose faculty, they alleged, was teaching doctrine contrary to offical synod standards. Among the key items to which objection was raised was the teaching of modern biblical criticism which, it was claimed, compromised the belief in the inerrancy of the Bible.

The question of the synod's ability to control teaching at the seminary came to a head in 1972. J. A. O. Preus, president of the Missouri Synod, issued a report accusing some of the teachers at the seminary of teaching false doctrines. Seminary president John Tietjen was singled out for particular criticism. This action increased the polarization of the two visible parties in the synod, and the conservative group increased its demands that the synod enforce doctrinal standards, particularly a literal interpretation of the Bible. The liberals, whose strength centered upon the seminary, insisted upon greater freedom to interpret the Bible and teach theology. Following a defeat at the 1973 meeting of the synod, the liberals organized Evangelical Lutherans in Mission (ELIM). Early in 1974 Tietjen was suspended as president of Concordia. In reaction, 43 of the 47 professors went on strike and were supported by three-fourths of the student body who voted to boycott classes. After leaving Concordia, the faculty and students established Concordia Seminary in Exile (popularly known as Seminex). ELIM supported the new seminary and prepared itself to remain as a liberal dissenting group within the synod.

The next two years saw the process of polarization increasing as conservatives, then in control of the synod, pressed for total conformity with traditional doctrinal standards and threatened removal of voices of dissent. The liberals fought a defensive action until 1976 when, feeling no longer able to remain in the fellowship, they left to form the Association of Evangelical Lutheran Churches. While retaining the formal doctrinal standards of the Missouri Synod, the new church emphasized openness, diversity, and ecumenism. It immediately established pulpit and altar fellowship with the American Lutheran Church and the Lutheran Church in America, which it saw as merely a first step to the realization of complete union.

Lutheran work began in Canada in the 1740s, and for many decades the Canadian work was affiliated with the American synods and churches. Congregations affiliated with the American Lutheran Church became an independent body in 1967, and those affiliated with the Lutheran Church in America became an independent body in 1986. (The history of these congregations can be found under the entry for the Evangelical Lutheran Church in Canada).

Beliefs. The Evangelical Lutheran Church in America is the most liberal of Lutheran church bodies in North America. It has as its doctrinal standard the Bible and the Augsburg Confession. It considers the remaining books of the *Book of Concord* as valid interpretive documents to be used in understanding the Augsburg Confession.

Organization. The Evangelical Lutheran Church in America is headed by a presiding bishop. The church is divided into 65 synods, each headed by a bishop. During the final merger process, headquarters for the new church were established in Chicago. Adminstratively, the churchwide organization is divided into units with particular program responsibilities. Fortress Press and Augsburg Press serve the new denomination under the name Augsburg Fortress, Publishers. The church is a member of the National Council of Churches, the World Council of Churches, and the Lutheran World Federation.

In 1997, the ELCA voted intercommunion (allowing exchange of pulpits by clergy and the taking of the sacraments by members) with the Presbyterian Church (USA), the United Church of Christ, and the Reformed Church in America.

Membership: In 1996 the ELCA reported 5,180,910 baptized members, 3,838,750 confirmed members, and 2,563,892 confirmed-communing members in 10,936 congregations.

Educational Facilities: Seminaries:
Lutheran School of Theology at Chicago, Chicago, Illinois.
Lutheran Theological Seminary, Gettysburg, Pennsylvania.
Lutheran Theological Seminary at Philadelphia, Philadelphia, Pennsylvania.
Lutheran Theological Southern Seminary, Columbia, South

Carolina.

Pacific Lutheran Theological Seminary, Berkeley, California.

Trinity Lutheran Seminary, Columbus, Ohio.

Wartburg Theological Seminary, Dubuque, Iowa.

Luther Northwestern Theological Seminary, St. Paul, Minnesota.

Colleges and Universities:

Augsburg College, Minneapolis, Minnesota.

Augustana College, Rock Island, Illinois.

Augustana College, Sioux Falls, South Dakota.

Bethany College, Lindsberg, Kansas.

California Lutheran University, Thousand Oaks, California.

Capital University, Columbus, Ohio.

Carthage College, Kenosha, Wisconsin.

Concordia College at Moorhead, Moorhead, Minnesota.

Dana College, Blair, Nebraska.

Gettysburg College, Gettysburg, Pennsylvania.

Grand View College, Des Moines, Iowa.

Gustavus Adolphus College, St. Peter, Minnesota.

Lenoir-Rhyne College, Hickory, North Carolina.

Luther College, Decorah, Iowa.

Midland Lutheran College, Fremont, Nebraska.

Muhlenberg College, Allentown, Pennsylvania.

Newbury College, Newbury, South Carolina.

Pacific Lutheran University, Tacoma, Washington.

Roanoke College, Salem, Virginia.

St. Olaf College, Northfield, Minnesota.

Suomi College, Hancock, Michigan.

Susquehanna University, Selingrove, Pennsylvania.

Texas Lutheran College, Seguin, Texas.

Thiel College, Greenville, Pennsylvania.

Wagner College, Staten Island, New York.

Waldorf College, Forest City, Iowa.

Wartburg College, Waverly, Iowa.

Wittenberg University, Springfield, Ohio.

Periodicals: *The Lutheran.* • *Lutheran Partners.* • *Lutheran Women Today.* • *Seeds for the Parish.*

Sources:

Chilstrom, Herbert W. *Foundations for the Future.* Minneapolis, MN: Publishing House of the Evangelical Lutheran Church in America, 1988.

Knudsen, Johannes. *The Formation of the Lutheran Church in America.* Philadelphia: Fortress Press, 1978.

Meuser, Fred W. *The Formation of the American Lutheran Church.* Columbus, OH: Wartburg Press, 1958.

Nichol, Todd W. *All Those Lutherans.* Minneapolis, MN: Augsburg Publishing House, 1986.

★323★
Evangelical Lutheran Church in Canada

1512 St. James St.

Winnipeg, MB, Canada R3H 0L2

Lutheranism in Canada dates to the last half of the eighteenth century when German Lutherans began to migrate into Nova Scotia. Periodic migrations, especially from America in the nineteenth century, led to the formation of Canadian parishes attached to what became two of the three largest American Lutheran bodies, the American Lutheran Church and the Lutheran Church in America. The American Lutheran Church, formed in 1960 by a merger of several Lutheran bodies, began an immediate process of facilitating the Canadian congregations' autonomy. They became fully autonomous in 1967 as The Evangelical Lutheran Church of Canada. In 1986 that church merged with the three Canadian synods of the Lutheran Church in America to form the Evangelical Lutheran Church in Canada. This merger anticipated the 1988 merger of the American Lutheran Church, the Lutheran Church in America, and the Association of Evangelical Lutheran Churches to form the Evangelical Lutheran Church in America (1988).

The new Evangelical Lutheran Church in Canada retains a formal working relationship with the Evangelical Lutheran Church in America providing for the exchange of pastors and complete altar and pulpit fellowship. The church meets in convention every two years. Foreign work is supported in Argentina, Colombia, Uruguay, Peru, El Salvador, and Papua New Guinea. The church is a member of the Canadian Council of Churches, the World Council of Churches, and the Lutheran World Federation.

Membership: In 1996 the church reported 196,393 baptized members, 642 congregations, and 858 ordained ministers.

Educational Facilities: Lutheran Theological Seminary, Saskatoon, Saskatchewan, Canada.

Waterloo Lutheran Seminary, Waterloo, Ontario, Canada.

Augustana University College, Camrose, Alberta, Canada.

Luther College, Regina, Saskatchewan, Canada.

Lutheran Colligiate Bible Institute, Outlook, Saskatchewan, Canada.

Periodicals: *Canada Lutheran.*

Sources:

Cronmiller, Carl R. *A History of the Lutheran Church in Canada.* Toronto: Evangelical Lutheran Synod of Canada, 1961.

★324★
Evangelical Lutheran Synod

℅ George Orvick, President

6 Browns Ct.

Mankato, MN 56001

The Evangelical Lutheran Synod was formed at Lake Mills, Iowa, in 1918 by a group of 40 pastors and laymen (the conservative wing of Norwegian Lutherans) who declined to enter the merger of other Norwegian Lutherans deciding instead to establish an independent synod. The name Norwegian Synod of the American Evangelical Lutheran Church was adopted. The present name was assumed in 1957. In 1920 it was received into the conservative-oriented Lutheran Synodical Conference but withdrew along with the Wisconsin Evangelical Lutheran Synod in 1963. It rejects fellowship with all who deny the essence of Lutheran belief.

Doctrine is the same as the Lutheran consensus with a conservative interpretation (similar to the Wisconsin Synod), and the Evangelical Lutheran Synod has in the past used the Wisconsin and Missouri Synods' seminaries for training its ministers. It is congregational in polity. Resolutions passed by the synod are not binding until sent to the congregations for acceptance. The officers of the synod direct the work of common interest. Home missions are conducted in nine states. Foreign mission work is conducted in Peru, Chile, the Czech Republic, and the Ukraine.

Membership: In 1996 the synod reported 22,046 members in 133 congregations being served by 115 ministers.

Educational Facilities: Bethany Lutheran College, Mankato, Minnesota.

Bethany Lutheran Theological Seminary, Mankato, Minnesota.

Centro Cristiano Seminary, Lima, Peru.

Periodicals: *Lutheran Sentinel.* 107 Sunrise Ct., Lake Mills, IA 50450. • *Lutheran Synod Quarterly* Bethany Lutheran Theological Seminary, 6 Browns Ct., Mankato, MN 56001.

★325★
Federation for Authentic Lutheranism

(Defunct)

The Federation for Authentic Lutheranism was formed in 1971 by members of the Lutheran Church-Missouri Synod. They had signaled their intention to withdraw prior to the 1971 meeting of the Missouri Synod if it did not stop fellowship relations with the liberal American Lutheran Church, withdraw from the Lutheran Council in the U.S.A., (which included both the Lutheran Church in America and the American Lutheran Church), and discipline "errorists" in the synod. (An attempt at the latter action has resulted in the recent controversy in the Missouri Synod.) Seven congregations formed the original federation. Eleven more joined within two years.

Theology was extremely conservative and pulpit fellowship was immediately declared with the Wisconsin Evangelical Lutheran Synod and the Evangelical Lutheran Synod. Positions have been taken against women's suffrage, the ordination of women, the Boy Scouts, and military chaplaincies. The federation was congregational in polity and run by a board of directors (half lay and half clerical) elected by the entire federation.

In the late 1970s, after less than a decade of existence, the federation disbanded, and its congregations joined either the Wisconsin Evangelical Lutheran Synod or the Evangelical Lutheran Synod. During its brief existence, it published a periodical, *Sola Scriptura*.

★326★
Fellowship of Lutheran Congregations
% Rev. Robert J. Lietz, President
320 Erie St.
Oak Park, IL 60302

The Fellowship of Lutheran Congregations is a small Lutheran body founded in 1979 by former pastors and members of the Lutheran Church-Missouri Synod who objected to what they saw as liberal trends in the Synod. The group is doctrinally aligned to the Missouri Synod, but adheres to a strict conservative interpretation of the Lutheran doctrinal confessions. Churches are located primarily in Illinois, Missouri, and Minnesota.

Membership: In 1998 there were five congregations, six ministers, and approximately 600 members.

Periodicals: *The Voice.*

★327★
Immanuel Synod
(Defunct)

The Immanuel Synod (of the Evangelical Lutheran Church in North America) is an independent Lutheran body that emerged among German Lutherans in Pennsylvania in the early 1870s. In 1874, the *Lutheran Almanac* reported the existence of an organization called the Bruderbund, with 12 pastors. No Bruderbund is reported in 1875, but in 1876 the Immanuel Synod suddenly appears with six of the pastors of the Bruderbund among its leadership. It appears that the Immanuel Synod evolved out of the Bruderbund. It also appears that at some point in the mid-1880s the Immanuel Synod disbanded and was superseded by a new Immanuel Synod. A report from 1885 indicated that the synod was the result of a desire of several ministers and churches to have greater freedom in church life than was then possible in many other Lutheran synods.

Having survived a generation, the synod took steps to disband, but Pastor J. Frederick was able to garner the necessary support from member churches to keep the doors open. Upon Frederick's death in 1921, however, no one arose to provide further leadership and the synod soon disbanded.

★328★
International Lutheran Fellowship
% President
% Rev. E. Edward Tornow
387 E. Brandon Dr.
Bismarck, ND 58501

The International Lutheran Fellowship is a small Lutheran body founded in 1967 in Fargo, North Dakota. It originally consisted of three congregations grounded in the Bible and the historical confessions of the Lutheran Church but has more recently added four additional churches to its fellowship. Within the confessional

framework, the fellowship allows considerable freedom to each congregation as a fellowship is open to relationships with other Lutheran bodies.

Membership: In 1997 there were seven congregations being served by seven pastors. Congregations were located in North Dakota, Indiana, New York, and Pennsylvania.

★329★
Jehovah Conference
(Defunct)

Hesse is a state in central Germany where Reformed and Lutheran elements vied for ultimate control, but neither obtained it. It was here in the nineteenth century that trends toward the union of Reformed and Lutheran churches were supported by the political rulers. In this climate, a Free Lutheran movement emerged which identified with the traditional Lutheran Confessions and opposed unionism. It found a champion in J. W. G. Vilmar (1804–1884), one of the leading theologians of the day, pastor at Melsungen, and head of the Lower Hessian Mission Association.

In 1886 Rev. Wilhelm C. F. Hartwig (1854–1927) came to America as a representative of the Mission Association and began work around Detroit, Michigan. He was soon joined by several other pastors. About 1893 they organized the Jehovah Conference, over which Hartwig presided for many years. It was distinctive in holding to the Augsburg Confession as the only true confession of the Lutheran Church. The synod was small and in 1926 still had only six congregations and less than 1,000 members affiliated with it. Hartwig died in 1927 and the synod seems to have disbanded a short time later.

Sources:

Lueker, Erwin, ed. *Lutheran Cyclopedia*. St. Louis, MO: Concordia Publishing House, 1975.

Wiederaenders, Robert C., and Walter G. Tillmans. *The Synods of American Lutheranism*. St. Louis, MO: Lutheran Historical Conference, 1968.

★330★
Laestadian Lutheran Church
10911 Hwy. 55, Ste. 203
Plymouth, MN 55441-6114

The Laestadian Lutheran church is one of several associations which have grown up among Finnish Lutheran who were affected by the nineteenth century revival movement begun around Lars Levi Laestadius. It was formed in 1973 in Minneapolis.

Membership: In 1997 the Church reported 1588 members in 27 congregations served by 50 ministers in the United States and 284 members, 6 congregations, and 11 ministers in Canada. There are affiliated churches in Finland, Sweden and Russia.

Periodicals: *The Voice of Zion.* • *Shepherd's Voice.*

★331★
Latvian Evangelical Lutheran Church in America
2140 Orkla Dr.
Golden Valley, MN 55427-3432

The takeover of several European countries by Marxist-Communist governments after World War II placed minority Lutheran Churches in a precarious position. Nationals who had fled Communist rule and refugees who had left during the war and felt unable to return established a church-in-exile with headquarters in Germany. Latvian Lutherans in the United States organized in 1957 as the Federation of Latvian Evangelical Lutheran Churches in America. The churches reorganized in 1975 to become the Latvian Evangelical Lutheran Church in America. It is the North American affiliate of the Lutheran Church of Latvia in Exile. The church supports the School of Theology at the University of Latvia in Riga, Latvia, by providing financial support to raise faculty salaries and sponsoring guest lecturers from the United States and Canada.

The Latvian Lutheran Church follows Lutheran doctrine and affirms the three ancient creeds (Apostles, Nicean, and Athanasian), as well as the unaltered Augsburg Confession, Luther's Small and Large Catechisms, and the other parts of the Book of Concord.

The synod, presided over by the church's president, meets every three years.

Membership: In 1996, the church had 16,900 members in 74 congregations served by 84 ministers in the United States, and an additional 4,649 members, 17 congregations, and 13 ministers in Canada. Most of the Canadian ministers are also members of the Evangelical Lutheran Church in Canada, as it allows double affiliation.

Periodicals: *Cela Biedrs.* • *Lelba Zinas.*

Sources:

Lutheran Churches of the World. Minneapolis: Augsburg Publishing House, 1957.

★332★
Lutheran Church-Canada
3022 E. 49th Ave.
Vancouver, BC, Canada V5S 1K9

In 1988, the former Canadian districts of the Lutheran Church-Missouri Synod were set apart as an autonomous body that took the name, The Lutheran Church-Canada. The Synod's ministry in Canada began with the arrival of Johann Adam Ernst (1817-1882) in Ontario in the 1850s as an outreach of the parish he was serving in Eden, New York. Among the early churches he founded was St. Peter's congregation at Rhineland and the Holy Ghost congregation near Fisherville. The work grew both by the affiliation of previously formed congregations and new congregations to the point that in 1879 the Canadian district was formed with Ernst as the first president. Work soon followed in Western Canada and by the early twentieth century, four districts had been founded. In 1959 a federation of the Canadian districts was created, a step toward the autonomy granted in 1988.

The Lutheran Church-Canada is as one in doctrine with the Lutheran Church-Missouri Synod and follows its conservative perspective on the Lutheran tradition. It has a congregational polity and a convention meets triennially.

Membership: In 1990 the church reported 100 members, 370 congregations, and 350 ministers.

Educational Facilities: Concordia Lutheran Seminary, Edmonton, Alberta; Concordia College, Edmonton, Alberta; Concordia Lutheran Theological Seminary, St. Catherines, Ontario.

Periodicals: *The Canadian Lutheran,* Box 163, Sta. A, Winnipeg, MN R3K 1A1.

Sources:

Cronmiller, Carl Raymond. *A History of the Lutheran Church in Canada.* Evangelical Lutheran Synod of Canada, 1961. 288 pp.

★333★
Lutheran Church-Missouri Synod
International Center
1333 S. Kirkwood Rd.
St. Louis, MO 63122

Of the largest Lutheran bodies, the Lutheran Church-Missouri Synod, often called simply the Missouri Synod, is by far the most conservative. In 1839, a group of Saxon Lutherans, who were fleeing the rationalism which had captured the Lutheran Church in Germany, arrived in New Orleans, Louisiana. They eventually settled south of St. Louis, Missouri on a large tract of land in Perry County. They were led by the Rev. Martin Stephan, who had been

elected bishop. Also among the group was Carl Ferdinand Wilhelm Walther, a young Lutheran minister. Soon after settling in Perry County, Stephan was banished when the colonists discovered he had misappropriated funds to support his opulent lifestyle.

After Stephan's banishment, Walther became the acknowledged leader. He fought what he felt were the theological errors of Stephan's preaching. Chief among these were the beliefs that Lutheran Church was the church, without which there was no salvation; that the ministry was a mediatorship between God and man, hence, ministers were entitled to obedience in all things, even matters not treated by God's Word; and that questions of doctrine were to be decided by the clergy alone. Walther helped found the small school in Altenburg, Missouri, which eventually became Concordia Seminary in St. Louis. In 1841, he went to St. Louis as pastor and in 1844 began to publish the *Lutheraner* which, issue after issue, championed orthodox Lutheranism as opposed to rationalism (a reliance on reason instead of faith). The *Lutheraner* fought for the rights and responsibility of the congregation in the church. In 1847, the Missouri Synod was founded on the principle of the autonomy of the congregation. There were 14 congregations and 22 ministers.

The Synod had been joined by some Franconians in Michigan and Hanoverians in Indiana. Over the years, they were joined by other small synods, including the Illinois Synod (1880) and the English Synod of Missouri (1911). In 1963, the National Evangelical Lutheran Church merged into the Missouri Synod. In 1971, the Synod of Evangelical Lutheran Churches joined the Missouri Synod as one of its districts.

Doctrinally, significant differences exist between the Missouri Synod and the Evangelical Lutheran Church in America, the other larger, American Lutheran body (i.e. concerning ordination of women). Polity is congregational. The nodical convention meets triennially. There are 35 districts represented. The convention elects a president and oversees the vast institutional and missional program. There are two seminaries (including Concordia in St. Louis) and 10 colleges and universities in the United States. A number of hospitals and homes dot the nation.

Membership: In 1996 the Missouri Synod reported 2,601,730 members in 6,099 congregations. There were 8,215 pastors and 8,735 teachers. Mission work is engaged in with missionaries and partner churches in Argentina, Australia, Belgium, Botswana, Brazil, Canada, Chile, Denmark, France, Germany, Ghana, Great Britain, Hong Kong, India, Japan, Korea, Lebanon, Liberia, the Middle East, Mexico, New Guinea, New Zealand, Nigeria, Panama, Paraguay, the Philippines, Sierra Leone, Sri Lanka, Taiwan, Thailand, Togo, Uruguay, and Venezuela.

Educational Facilities: Christ College, Irvine, California.
Concordia College, Ann Arbor, Michigan.
Concordia College, Austin, Texas.
Concordia College, Bronxville, New York.
Concordia University, Mequon, Wisconsin.
Concordia College, Portland, Oregon.
Concordia University, River Forest, Illinois.
Concordia College, St. Paul, Minnesota.
Concordia College, Selma, Alabama.
Concordia College, Seward, Nebraska.
Seminaries:
Concordia Seminary, St. Louis, Missouri.
Concordia Theological Seminary, Ft. Wayne, Indiana.

Periodicals: *The Lutheran Witness.* • *Reporter.*

Remarks: During the 1960s, the Missouri Synod was racked with doctrinal controversy that focused on differing views about how the Bible can be considered the Word of God. The conservatives believe the Bible to be the inerrant Word of God and interpret it quite literally. The more liberal members consider the Bible to bear the Word of God, i.e., Jesus Christ, to the church, and, as such, to be properly the object of historical criticism.

In the end (and for the first time in the twentieth century), the conservative viewpoint prevailed, but only after a decade of discussion. As a result, 200 of the 6,100 congregations, representative of the liberal faction, left the Synod to form the Association of Evangelical Lutheran Churches, which in 1988 merged with the Evangelical Lutheran Church in America.

Sources:

Arndt, W. *Fundamental Christian Beliefs.* St. Louis: Concordia Publishing House, 1938.

Graebner, A. *Half a Century of True Lutheranism.* Chattanooga, TN: J. A. Fredrich, n.d.

Handbook. St. Louis: Lutheran Church-Missouri Synod, n.d.

The Lutheran Annual 1986. St. Louis: Concordia Publishing Company, n.d.

Meyer, Carl S. *A Brief Historical Sketch of the Lutheran Church-Missouri Synod.* St. Louis: Concordia Publishing House, 1938.

★334★
Lutheran Churches of the Reformation
4014 Wenonah Ln.
Fort Wayne, IN 46809

In 1964, several congregations in the Midwest (formerly a part of the Lutheran Church-Missouri Synod) joined to form the Lutheran Churches of the Reformation. These congregations had protested what they considered the growing theological liberalism of the Missouri Synod. They follow the doctrine and life of their parent body but take a conservative position on doctrinal questions.

Membership: Not reported.

★335★
Norwegian Seaman's Church (Mission)
1035 Beacon St.
San Pedro, CA 90731

The Norwegian Seaman's Mission was founded in 1864 in Bergen, Norway to provide mission centers in port cities around the world. Such centers offer a Christian witness and a homelike atmosphere for Norwegian sailors in foreign lands. In many cites the missions have also developed into a community and worship center for first generation Norwegians in foreign lands. Reaching a peak in the nineteenth century of 35 missions worldwide, some of the centers, such as the one in Philadelphia, have closed in recent years. The one in San Pedro, California, opened in 1941. The missions provide services in accordance with the practices of the Church of Norway, the state Lutheran church.

Membership: In 1997 there were 40 Norwegian Seaman's Mission units worldwide. The seven in the United States are located in San Pedro, San Francisco, Houston, New Orleans, Miami, Baltimore, and New York City.

Sources:

Gabriel, Judy. "A Refuge for Scandinavian Seamen." *Los Angeles Times* (December 22, 1985).

★336★
The Protes'tant Conference
1033 Colan Blvd.
Rice Lake, WI 54868

The roots of the Protes'tant Conference can be traced to the appointment of Professor J. Ph. Koehler to the chair of New Testament exegesis, church history, hermeneutics, liturgies, and church music at the theological school of the Wisconsin Evangelical Lutheran Church in 1900. Over the years, the synodical infrastructure grew restive, hesitant to respond to Koehler's theological approach that challenged what he considered their entrenched and ossified tradition. The synod thought of theology merely as the study of a set of intellectual propositions while Koehler taught that the roots of the Gospel, repentance and faith, as emphasized in the Scripture, are the historic basis of church renewal in the synod, its congregations, and its members.

Koehler's emphases were unsettling to many in the synod. Opposition seriously appeared in 1913, 1918, and 1920 from August Piper, a colleague on the seminary faculty and former ally of Koehler. The arguments, heretofore largely confined to the seminary, were given a major public airing in 1926 in an assigned public paper by Pastor W. F. Beitz, "God's Message to Us in Galatians—The Just Shall Live by Faith." Supporting Koehler, but quoting directly from Piper's previous public statements, Beitz charged that the synod was preoccupied with formalism, institutionalism, and membership growth. He called for repentance and a life lived by faith.

Beitz's paper brought the infrastructure of the synod into the controversy and in the ensuing years some 40 professors, teachers, and pastors were ousted from the synod, including Koehler in 1934. The first to be put out formed the Protes'tant Conference in March 1928. They asserted then, as their successors do now, that the conference is an integral element of the synod, even though the synod has refused to recognize them as such. In ensuing years, other Protes'tant-minded pastors have been ousted by the Wisconsin Synod.

Tenets: The doctrinal position of the conference coincides with that of the Wisconsin Synod, but it places special emphasis upon Luther's understanding of the priesthood of believers, as well as the concept of Christian doctrine as truth in action rather than as dogmatic abstraction, while distinguishing between the necessary theological instruction in the dogmatics and the porosis of dogmatism.

Membership: In 1989 the conference reported 1,065 members in eight congregations served by eight pastors.

Periodicals: *Faith-Life.*

Sources:

Koehler, J. P. *The History of the Wisconsin Synod.* St. Cloud, MN: Sentinel Press, 1980.

The Wauwatosa Gospel: Which Is It? Marshfield, WI: Protestant Conference Press, 1928.

★337★
Synod of Evangelical Lutheran Churches
(Defunct)

Lutherans from Czechoslovakia began to migrate to the United States in the 1870s and early congregations were formed at Streator, Illinois; Freeland, Pennsylvania; and Minneapolis, Minnesota. Attempts to organize began in the 1890s, and the Slovak Evangelical Lutheran Synod was finally established at Connellsville, Pennsylvania, in 1902. Theologically, it declared itself at one with the Lutheran Synodical Conference. The move into the Synodical conference proved the first step toward full merger with the Missouri Synod, which was accomplished in 1971. Thus the Synod of Evangelical Lutheran Church ceased to exist as a separate denomination and became a district within the Missouri Synod.

★338★
Wisconsin Evangelical Lutheran Synod
2929 N. Mayfair Rd.
Milwaukee, WI 53222

The Wisconsin Evangelical Lutheran Synod (popularly called the Wisconsin Synod) was established as a result of calls for pastoral service form German immigrants to Wisconsin in the 1840s. Ministers answered the call, and in May 1850, the First German Evangelical Lutheran Synod of Wisconsin was organized under the direction of President John Muelhaeuser at Salem Evangelical Lutheran Church, Milwaukee (Granville), Wisconsin.

In the 1840s, a Michigan Synod had also been organized among the Wuerttembergers by Stephan Koehler and Christoph Eberhardt. A Minnesota Synod was organized by "Father" J. C. F. Heyer and others in 1860. The Wisconsin, Michigan, and Minnesota Synods became conservative theologically and staunch defenders of Lutheran doctrine against the "compromises" of the larger bodies. In 1892, after all three had joined the Lutheran Synodical Conference, they federated to form the Evangelical Lutheran Joint Synod of Wisconsin, Minnesota, and Michigan. A merger in 1917 led to the formation of the Evangelical Lutheran Joint Synod of Wisconsin and Other States. The present name was adopted in 1959.

Doctrinally, the Wisconsin Synod takes a more conservative stance than the Lutheran Church-Missouri Synod. It is opposed to merger without doctrinal unity on all points. It had been active in the Synodical Conference for almost a century but withdrew in 1963.

The Synod meets biennially. It is divided into 12 districts spread across the nation, though membership is concentrated in Wisconsin and the Midwest. There is a network of parochial schools, two synodical preparatory high schools, 20 area high schools, a college, and a seminary. The Northwestern Publishing House in Milwaukee publishes books, Sunday school literature, and religious materials. A vigorous mission program is supported both at home and abroad. Missions are supported in Arizona among both the Apaches and the Latin Americans. Latin American missions are also conducted in Mexico, Columbia, Puerto Rico, and in stateside cities. Overseas missionary endeavors are supported in Brazil, Cameroon, the CIS, Germany, Hong Kong, India, Indonesia, Thailand, Dominican Republic, Bulgaria, Japan, Malawi, Nigeria, Taiwan, and Zambia.

Membership: In 1996 the Wisconsin Synod reported 412,942 members in the United States (with an additional 30,000 outside America), in 1,235 congregations served by 1,604 ministers.

Educational Facilities: Colleges:
Northwestern College, Watertown, Wisconsin.
Dr. Martin Luther College, New Ulm, Minnesota.
Seminaries:
Wisconsin Lutheran Seminary, Mequon, Wisconsin.

Periodicals: *The Northwestern Lutheran.* • *Wisconsin Lutheran Quarterly.* Send orders to 1250 N. 113th St., Milwaukee, WI 53226-3284.

Sources:

Continuing in Word. Milwaukee, WI: Northwestern Publishing House, [1951].

This We Believe. N.p., 1967. Pamphlet.

Section 6

Reformed-Presbyterian Family

Consult the Contents pages to locate the essay in Part II, Historical Essay Chapters,
that provides an historical discussion of this family

Intrafaith Organizations

★339★

**International Association of Reformed and Presbyterian
Churches**
756 Haddon Ave.
Collingswood, NJ 08108

The International Association of Reformed and Presbyterian
Churches was founded in Amsterdam, the Netherlands, in 1962
by delegates and visiting clergymen attending the meeting of the
International Council of Christian Churches (ICCC). The ICCC represents the most conservative wing of twentieth-century Protestantism, usually termed fundamentalism, characterized by its affirmation of the inerrancy and infallibility of the Bible and its
demand for separation from all apostasy and heresy, especially as
it is represented in modernist theology and embodied in liberal
Protestant denominations. The ICCC received much of its early inspiration from a Presbyterian minister, Dr. Carl McIntire of the
Bible Presbyterian Church.

Leading in the formation of the International Association were
McIntire; Dr. A. B. Dodd of Taiwan, the first moderator; and Dr.
J. C. Maris of the Netherlands, the first secretary. The occasion for
the formation of the International Association was the visit of the
moderator of the Church of Scotland to the Vatican for a meeting
with the Pope. At its first gathering, the association also attacked
the World Presbyterian Alliance, whom it accused of departing
from the Reformed creeds and faith, and denounced its friendly relationship with the World Council of Churches. Members of the
alliance are barred from membership in the association.

Meetings of the association are planned to coincide with meetings of the ICCC.

Membership: Not reported. It includes the members of the
ICCC of the Reformed and Presbyterian traditions.

Sources:

Harden, Margaret C., comp. *A Brief History of the Bible Presbyterian
Church and Its Agencies.* Privately published, 1968.

★340★

International Congregational Fellowship
% Richard Kurrasch
1314 Northwood Blvd.
Royal Oak, MI 48073

The International Congregational Fellowship was founded in
1975 in Chrislehurst, England, to provide an international meeting
ground for Congregationalists. It considers itself a successor body
to the International Congregational Council, formed in 1891,
which merged with the World Alliance of Reformed Churches in
1966 to form the World Alliance of Reformed Churches (Presbyterian and Congregational). Some had felt that the World Alliance
did not deal sufficiently with the desires of Congregationalists for
fellowship around their distinctive community lifestyle.

The fellowship has established a network of communication
with Congregationalists around the world and disseminates news
of interest to the community. It also provides a forum for theological discussions, has established a relief service for the needy,
champions the cause of religious freedom, and promotes cooperative activities among Congregationalists.

The fellowship gathers periodically in international conferences. Regional secretaries exist for the United Kingdom, North
America, the Pacific and Australia, Central and South America,
and Africa and Central Europe.

Membership: The fellowship is in contact with Congregationalists in more than 50 countries. The most prominent American affiliate is the National Association of Congregational Christian
Churches.

★341★

Reformed Ecumenical Council
2050 Breton Rd. SE, Ste. 102
Grand Rapids, MI 49546-5547

The Reformed Ecumenical Council was founded in 1946 as the
Reformed Ecumenical Synod. It unites thirty-four Reformed and
Presbyterian denominational bodies in thwenty-three countriese.
They share the same Reformed heritage and have joined together
based on a common confession of faith. These churches represent
a more conservative and evangelical element in the Reformed/
Presbyterian community.

The council meets in general assembly every four years. The
day-to-day affairs are placed in the hands of an interim committee
and permanent secretariat. Through the council, member churches speak on current world issues, coordinate mission programs,
and share ideas.

Membership: The council includes one church based in North
America, the Christian Reformed Church in North America.

Periodicals: *Theological Forum.* • *News Exchange.* • *Mission
Bulletin.* • *Reformed Youth Arena.*

★342★

**World Alliance of Reformed Churches (Presbyterian and
Congregational)**
% Rev. James Dempsey Douglas
Princeton Theological Seminary
Princeton, NJ 80542

Alternate Address: International Headquarters: 150 route de
Ferney, CH-1211 Geneva 2, Switzerland. Caribbean and North
American Area Council: c/o Area Sec.: Rev. Margrete B. J. Brown,
100 Witherspoon St., Louisville, KY 40202.

The World Alliance of Reformed Churches (Presbyterian and
Congregational) was formed in Nairobi, Kenya, by the merger of
the former World Alliance of Reformed Churches and the International Congregational Council. The merger grew out of a recognition of the common heritage of the Reformed, Presbyterian, and

Congregational churches in the Reformation Theology of John Calvin and Ulrich Zwingli.

The alliance represents the more liberal wing of the Reformed tradition theologically such as represented in the United States by the Presbyterian Church (U.S.A.) and the United Church of Christ.

The alliance meets as a general assembly or council at least once every five years, at which time policies and plans are adopted. These are carried out by the Executive Committee, consisting of the alliance's president, three vice-presidents, department heads, and 25 additional members. There are several regional area organizations, including one for the Caribbean and North America.

The alliance shares headquarters with the World Council of Churches, with whom the alliance works on projects of common interest.

Membership: The alliance reports more than 175 member churches from some 75 different countries.

Reformed

★343★
Canadian and American Reformed Churches
PO Box 62053
Burlington, ON, Canada L7R 4K2

Alternate Address: American Reformed Churches: c/o Rev. P. Kingma, 3167 68th St., SE, Caledonia, MI 46316

The Canadian and American Reformed Churches is a conservative reformed church founded in Canada in 1950. It spread to the United States in 1955. It accepts the Bible as the infallible Word of God and finds it is best summarized in the Belgic Confession of Faith (1561), the Heidelberg Catechism (1563) and the Canons of Dort (1618-19). It has a presbyterian polity.

Membership: In 1992 the churches reported 44 congregations, 13,192 members, and 51 ministers.

Periodicals: *Reformed Perspective; The Canadian Reformed Magazine.*

★344★
Christian Reformed Church in North America
2850 Kalamazoo Ave. SE
Grand Rapids, MI 49560

The Christian Reformed Church began in the Netherlands in the 1830s. At that time, some members of the Reformed Church of the Netherlands rejected an attempt to bring the church under the control of the Dutch monarchy. Despite the objections of these churchmen, the church was brought under state control. This led in 1834 to the Sucession (the formation of a church independent from the monarchy). Sucession leaders were Hendrik DeCock, Henrik Scholte, and Albertus C. van Raalte. They saw themselves as defenders of the historical faith that was being lost because of the indifference of the main body of the Reformed Church of the Netherlands. Following persecution and the failure of the potato crop in 1846, the dissidents supporting the Sucession made plans to immigrate.

In 1847 the settlers arrived in western Michigan and by 1848 had formed the Classis Holland. Having been aided by members of the Reformed Church in America with whom they shared the same faith, they affiliated with them in 1850, becoming a classis within the Reformed Church in America. Members of the Classis Holland had the understanding that they could leave the Reformed Church in America if the ecclesiastical connection should prove a threat to their interests. For most it never did. However, one church that belonged to the Classis Holland did leave the classis and the Reformed Church in America in 1857, and others followed, eventually forming the Christian Reformed Church.

The background of the schism starts with Gysbert Haan. Within a few years of the 1850 affiliation, Haan began to suggest that the Reformed Church in America was not sound. In 1857 four documents of Sucession were received by the classis, urging the classis to leave the Reformed Church in America. The documents charged the Reformed Church in America with open communion, the use of a large collection of hymns, and the neglect of catechism preaching. Further, the documents asserted that the Reformed Church in America believed the Sucession in the Netherlands had been unjustified. The classis received but did not approve these documents. One church left the classis in January 1857 and was soon joined by others. In 1859 these congregations became known as the Dutch Reformed Church. Growth was slow at first and came primarily from additional immigration from the Netherlands. Immigration and growth were particularly heavy in the closing decades of the nineteenth century. Through a series of name changes the church became the Christian Reformed Church in 1904 and has retained that name.

The doctrine is strict and based on the Belgic Confession, the Heidelberg Catechism, and the Canons of the Synod of Dort. In 1906 the Conclusions of Utrecht were adopted which recognized that some questions were open for disagreement. Only the children of confessing members are baptized. The church is staunchly anti-lodge. Worship is ordered and derived from the practice of the church in the Netherlands. The early hymnology was largely confined to the Psalms, but an expanded hymnology has developed in the twentieth century. Catechistic instruction is stressed. Polity is presbyterial. The general synod is broadest assemby of the church and is composed of two ministers and two members of each of the 46 classes. There is no intermediate or particular synod between the classis and general synod. Classes meet biannually or triannually.

There is an active mission program. Home missions include an active church planting program, the Reformed Bible College, the Back to God Hour, and Native American Missions. World missions includes work in Nigeria, Japan, Taiwan, Haiti, Central America, France, Sierre Leone, the Philippines, Mexico, Korea, Indonesia, and Guam. There are also a number of hospitals and homes.

Membership: In 1995 the church reported 295,307 members, 985 congregations, and 1,505 ministers. There were 83,974 members in Canada.

Educational Facilities: Calvin College, Grand Rapids, Michigan.
Calvin Theological Seminary, Grand Rapids, Michigan.
Dordt College, Sioux Center, Iowa.
Institute for Christian Studies, Toronto, Ontario.
Redeemer Reformed, Christian College, Ancaster, Ontario.
Trinity Christian College, Palos Heights, Illinois.
Westminister Theological Seminary, Econdido, California and Philadelphia, Pennsylvania.

Periodicals: *The Banner.* • *De Wachter.*

Sources:

One Hundred Years in the New World. Grand Rapids, MI: Centennial Committee of the Christian Reformed Church, 1957.

★345★
Church of the Golden Rule
Current address not obtained for this edition.

The Church of the Golden Rule continues the French Huguenot tradition of the Alsacian Protestants who look to Martin Buber and the city of Strassburg as the source of their faith. A congregation of Alsacian immigrants was formed in 1939 at Hempstead, Long Island, New York, under Pastor Alfred E. Huss. He was authorized by Pastor Boegner of the Alsacian Churches. When Huss died, the congregation relocated in California. In 1971 there were four congregations with about 600 families, all in California, under the leadership of Dr. Pierre Duval. The Church of the Golden Rule is under the Unite Huguenotte Francaise.

Membership: Not Reported.

★346★
Churches of God, General Conference
700 E. Melrose Ave.
Box 926
Findlay, OH 45839

The Churches of God, General Conference was formed by John Winebrenner (1797-1860), a German Reformed pastor of four churches in and around Harrisburg, Pennsylvania. Winebrenner, though a reformer in many areas, never intended to form a new denomination. However, in attempting to reform what he perceived as the spiritual apathy in the Reformed Church, he and other Reformed pastors adopted some of the "new measures" which had become popular during the Second Great Awakening. They began to preach the importance of personal acceptance of Jesus Christ as savior; they introduced prayer meetings in the homes of those concerned about their salvation; they prayed for people by name in their services; they initiated altar calls.

The vestry of the Harrisburg congregation served by Winebrenner took exception to these new devices. Their concern was heightened by their pastor accepting invitations to preach in the local Methodist church and by his refusal to baptize the children of unbelieving parents. He was locked out of the church building in 1823, though he continued to serve other Reformed congregations and remained a member of the synod for several years.

In 1825, a Harrisburg congregation of persons loyal to Winebrenner and others attracted by his preaching was formed. The General Conference dates its beginning from this event. The name Church of God was adopted after a search of the scripture showed it to be the New Testament name of the church. The name was considered to be inclusive of all true believers. (Winebrenner was one of several early nineteenth-century movements which attempted to return to the New Testament model of the church. It was the first of many to follow which adopted the name "Church of God" as an element in their self-reformation.)

The essential teachings of the New Testament Church were taken to be redemption and regeneration through belief in Jesus Christ, justification by faith, and free moral agency. Three "ordinances" instituted by Jesus were followed: believer's baptism by immersion, the observance of the Lord's Supper, and feetwashing. A presbyterial polity was followed, with preachers ordained as "teaching elders," assisted by "ruling elders" and deacons in the local congregation. The first organization of a group of churches into an eldership was accomplished in 1830. For many years the group was known as the Churches of God in North America, General Eldership.

While pastors and elders still participate with each other in the sixteen regional annual business meetings, most are now called "conferences" rather than "elderships." The triennial meeting of ministerial, lay and youth delegates from local conferences and elderships is called the General Conference.

An administrative council functions between the triennial meetings of the General Conference.

Membership: In 1996, the church reported 31,558 members, 350 congregations, and 444 ministers in the United States. There were an additional 4,000 members in missions in India, Haiti, Brazil, and Bangladesh.

Educational Facilities: University of Findlay, Findlay, Ohio. Winebrenner Theological Seminary, Findlay, Ohio.

Periodicals: *The Church Advocate.* • *The Missionary Signal.*

Sources:

Kern, Richard. *John Winebrenner, 19th Century Reformer.* Harrisburg, PA: Central Publishes House, 1974.

We Believe. Findlay, OH: Churches of God Publications, 1986.

Yahn, S. G. *History of the Churches of God in North America.* Harrisburg, PA: Central Publishing House, 1926.

★347★
Free Reformed Church of North America
℅ Rev. P. VanderMeyden
950 Ball Ave. NE
Grand Rapids, MI 49503

The Free Reformed Church of North America was started by post-World War II immigrants whose roots were in the Christian Reformed Churches in the Netherlands (Christelijke Gereformeerde Kerken in Nederland). The first churches of this denomination began to form in 1950, with two U.S. congregations joining in the 1960s. A synod of the churches meets annually in June, usually in Ontario, Canada, where most of the churches are located. The churches fully subscribe to three creeds (i.e., the Heidelberg Catechism, the Belgic Confession, and the Canons of Dort), which are found, together with the liturgical forms used, in the denominational songbook, *The Psalter.* A full corresponding relationship exists with the parent denomination in the Netherlands (C.G.K.N.). The denomination also supports foreign mission work in Cubulco, Guatemala.

Membership: In 1997, the church had 15 congregations (12 in Canada and three in the United States) with 1,038 families. There were a total of 3,748 members, of which 621 were in the United States and 3,127 in Canada.

Periodicals: *The Messenger.*

★348★
Hungarian Reformed Church in America
℅ Rt. Rev. Dr. Andrew Harsanyi
PO Box D
Hopatcong, NY 07843

Hungarian Reformed congregations were established in the United States in the late nineteenth century and in 1904 the Hungarian Reformed Church in America was formed under the care of the Reformed Church in Hungary. Following World War I, however, there was a series of negotiations with the Reformed Church in the United States resulting in the 1921 Tiffin Agreement. This agreement, made at Tiffin, Ohio, joined the Hungarian Reformed Church in America to the Reformed Church in the United States. The merged body is now a part of the United Church of Christ. Three congregations of the Hungarian Reformed Church did not wish to accept the Tiffin Agreement. These congregations and four new ones united to form the Free Magyar Reformed Church in America, which in 1958 adopted the name Hungarian Reformed Church in America.

Doctrinally, the church follows the Second Helvetic Confession and the Heidelberg Catechism. The constitution includes elements of both the presbyterian and episcopal systems. There is a synod headed by a bishop and a lay curator. The New York, Eastern, and Western Classes are headed by a dean and lay curator. The synod meets every four years. The church is a member of the World Alliance of Reformed Churches (Presbyterian and Congregational), the National Council of Churches, and the World Council of Churches.

Membership: In 1995 the church reported 4,195 members, 38 ministers in the United States; 275 members and 12 ministers in Canada.

Periodicals: *Magyar Egyhaz* (Magyar Church). Available from Mr. Stephen Szabo, Synod Chief Elder, 464 Forest Ave., Paramus, NJ 07652.

★349★
Netherlands Reformed Congregations
% J. R. Beeke
2115 Romence, NE
Grand Rapids, MI 49503

The Netherlands Reformed Congregations were formed in 1907 by the merger of two Dutch Reformed denominations. The Churches of the Cross had originated in 1834 by churches that had broken with the Seccession (an earlier group which had broken with the state church). The Ledeboerian Churches had been established under the leadership of Reverend Ledeboer, who had left the state Reformed church at a later date. Doctrinal standards of the church are the Belgic Confession, the Heidelberg Catechism, and the Canons of the Synod of Dort. The church has been very active in publishing and Christian education. It operates seven high schools and elementary schools in the United States.

Membership: In 1992 the church reported 5,300 members in 16 congregations in the United States. There were an additional 4,500 members in 10 congregations in Canada and more than 100,000 members worldwide, primarily in the Netherlands. Foreign congregations and missions were located in Australia, Bolivia, Indonesia, New Zealand, Nigeria, and South Africa.

Educational Facilities: Netherlands Reformed Theological Seminary, Grand Rapids, Michigan.

Periodicals: *Banner of Truth.* Send orders to 1053 Maplegrove NW, Grand Rapids, MI 49504. • *Paul.* Available from the Timothy Christian School, Castleman Rd., Chilliwack, BC, Canada. • *Insight Into.* Send orders to 4732 East "C" Ave., Kalamazoo, MI 49009. • *NRCEA.* Send orders to 1000 Ball Ave. NE, Grand Rapids, MI 49503.

★350★
Orthodox Reformed Church
(Defunct)

In the late 1960s within the Protestant Reformed Churches, charges of sin against some members of the First Protestant Reformed Church of Grand Rapids resulted in the excommunication of some of its members. Feeling the excommunication to be unjust and to be a denial of their rights, members of the First Protestant Reformed Church of Grand Rapids organized the Orthodox Reformed Church (unaffiliated) in the fall of 1970. In doctrine and polity the church was like its parent body though it not "subscribe to the church political policies of the Protestant Reformed Churches after the year 1965." Worship was simple and expressed a love of decency and order.

The leader of the Church until his death in 1984, the Rev. Gerald Vanden Berg, had previously been the stated clerk of the Protestant Reformed Church. He had been active in forming the Fellowship of Reformed Churches, an ecumenical group of independent reformed congregations. Vanden Berg was succeeded by the Rev. Peter J. Breen. The church supported missionary activity in India and Pakistan. The Orthodox Reformed Publishing Society, an independent organization, was informally associated with the church.

Membership: At the beginning of the 1990s, the church consisted of a single congregation of 61 members. In 1992 it voted to disband and the members joined other Reformed Congregations of their choice.

Periodicals: *The Reformed Scope.*

Sources:

VandenBerg, Gerald. *Why Orthodox Reformed?* Grandville, MI: Orthodox Reformed Publishing Society, n.d.

★351★
Protestant Reformed Churches in America (PRC)
4949 Ivanrest Ave.
Grandville, MI 49418

The Protestant Reformed Churches in America (PRC) has its roots in the sixteenth century Reformation of Martin Luther and John Calvin, as it developed in the Dutch Reformed churches. The denomination originated as a result of a controversy in the Christian Reformed Church in 1924 involving the adoption of the "Three Points of Common Grace." Three ministers in the Christian Reformed Church, the Revs. Herman Hoeksema, Henry Danhof, and George Ophoff, and their consistories (Eastern Avenue, Hope, Kalamazoo) rejected the doctrine. Eventually, these men were deposed, and their consistories either deposed or set outside the Christian Reformed Church. The denomination was founded in 1926 with three congregations.

The PRC follows the presbyterian form of church government as determined by the Church Order of Dordt. There is an annual synod. The synodical stated clerk and board of trustees deal with the necessary business of the church between the meetings of synod.

The PRC's doctrinal standards are the Reformed confessions: the Heidelberg Catechism, Belgic Confession of Faith, and Canons of Dordrecht. It maintains the "five points of Calvinism." The doctrine of the covenant is a cornerstone of its teaching. It maintains an unconditional, particular convenant of grace that God establishes with His elect. In practice, the Protestant Reformed Churches maintains the regulative principle of worship, rejects remarriage of divorced persons, and maintains many of its own Christian schools.

Membership: As of 1998, the PRC included some 25 churches in the United States and two in Canada (Edmonton and Lacombe, Alberta) and some 6,000 members. The denomination's seminary is in Grand Rapids, Michigan, where the largest number of churches is located. Over the years the PRC has established numerous mission stations in North America, and has labored in such foreign lands as Jamaica, Singapore, the British Isles, Ghana, and the Philippines.

Educational Facilities: Theological School of the PRC, Grand Rapids, Michigan.

Periodicals: Although the PRC has no official publication, the seminary does publish the *Protestant Reformed Theological Journal,* and several organizations within the denomination publish periodicals: • *Beacon Lights,* • *Perspectives in Covenant Education,* and • *Standard Bearer.* Another organization, the • *Reformed Free Publishing Association,* also publishes religious books both theological and educational.

Sources:

Hoeksema, Herman. *The Protestant Reformed Churches In America.* Grand Rapids, MI: The Author, 1947.

___. *Why Protestant Reformed?* Grand Rapids, MI: Sunday School of the First Protestant Reformed Church, 1949.

★352★
Reformed Church in America
475 Riverside Dr.
New York, NY 10115

History. The first Dutch settlers in America, members of Reformed Church in the Netherlands, brought that church to this country. A minister, the Rev. Jonas Michaelius, arrived here in 1628 and organized the first congregation, now known as the Collegiate Church of the City of New York. Because of a shortage of ministers, some people began to advocate ministerial training in the colonies. Queens College (now Rutgers University) was founded and a theological seminary established there. The independence of the American church was achieved in 1770 when

John Livingston returned from his theological work at Utrecht with a plan of union. In 1792 a constitution was adopted, and in 1819 the church was incorporated as the Reformed Protestant Dutch Church. It took its present name, the Reformed Church in America, in 1867.

The church spread through New York and New Jersey during the colonial era. In the middle of the nineteenth century a new wave of Dutch immigrants arrived. They settled primarily in Michigan and Iowa and from there moved to other states, particularly South Dakota.

Beliefs. Doctrinally the church has remained very conservative and accepted as its standard doctrine the Belgic Confession, the Heidelberg Catechism, and the Canons of the Synod of Dort. Worship is outlined in the *Liturgy* and is supplemented by the church's hymnal, *Rejoice in the Lord*. The liturgies of the Lord's Supper, baptism, and ordination are obligatory; those for the Sunday service and marriage are not.

Organization. The polity is presbyterial. The highest authority is the General Synod, which meets annually in June. A 62-member executive committee functions between sessions. The General Synod is divided into 46 classes. These classes are distributed in eight regional synods made up of lay and clerical members of each classes. The voting members of the classes are all the ministers and an elder from each church in the classes. The ruling body at the congregational level is the consistory, composed of the ministers and elected elders and deacons.

Education has always been given high priority by the Reformed Church, and a Board of Theological Education keeps oversight of its seminaries. The General Synod Council oversees work among American Indians; social services; and foreign work in Mexico, Estonia, several African countries, Japan, Bahrain, Arabia, Kuwait, Oman, India, Taiwan, Hong Kong, the Philippines, Hondaras, Nicaragua, Ecuador, and Venezuela. The church is a member of the National Council of Churches and the World Council of Churches.

Membership: In 1997 the church reported 304,113 members, an additional 190,000 active communicants, 957 churches, and 1,800 ministers. There were 6,535 members in Canada.

Educational Facilities: Seminaries:
Western Theological Seminary, Holland, Michigan.
New Brunswick Theological Seminary, New Brunswick, New Jersey.
Colleges:
Hope College, Holland, Michigan.
Northwestern College, Orange City, Iowa.
Central College, Pella, Iowa.

Periodicals: *The Church Herald.* Send orders to 4500 60th St. SE, Grand Rapids, MI 49512.

★353★
Reformed Church in the United States
% Rev. Vernon Polleme, President
3930 Masin Dr.
Lincoln, NE 68521

In 1934 the Reformed Church in the United States merged with the Evangelical Synod. (In 1961 that merged body joined the United Church of Christ.) One classis of the Reformed Church in the United States, the Eureka Classis in South Dakota, decided not to enter the 1934 merger. So the Eureka Classis adopted the name of its parent body, the Reformed Church in the United States, and stayed separate from all the other classes that joined the 1934 merger. The present Reformed Church in the United States continues the polity and doctrines (adherence to the Heidelberg Confession) of the former Reformed Church in the United States. The classis meets annually.

Membership: In 1997 the church reported 4,120 members, 43 congregations, and 44 ministers.

Periodicals: *The Reformed Herald.* Send orders to Box 276, Eureka, SD 57437.

Presbyterian

★354★
Associate Reformed Presbyterian Church
% Associate Reformed Presbyterian Center
1 Cleveland St.
Greenville, SC 29601

The Associate Reformed Presbyterian Church traces its origin to the preaching of Reformer John Knox in Scotland and the establishment of the Scotch Church as the official church of all Scotland in 1560. Under King William II, in 1688, the Church of Scotland was reorganized into the Established Presbyterian Church of Scotland. In 1733 a pastor, Ebenezar Erskine, led a group of Christians in forming a separate Associate Presbytery. Ten years later, another group of Christians who had come into conflict with the established church organized the Reformed Presbytery.

Both churches spread first to Ireland and then the the United States, where the first Associate and Reformed Presbyteries were formed in the mid-eighteenth century. Formal negotiations between the Associates and Reformeds looking toward union began in 1777 and reached fruition five years later. While some congregations did not join the union, the new church included congregations scattered from Georgia to New York.

In 1790 the Associate Reformed Presbytery of the Carolinas and Georgia was formed in Abbeville County, South Carolina, followed some years later (1803) by the division of the entire church into four synods (Carolinas, Pennsylvania, New York, and Scioto) and one General Synod. Headquarters was established in Philadelphia. In 1822 the Synod of the Carolinas was granted independent status, and by the end of the century was the sole remaining body of the Associate Reformed Presbyterian Church as the remaining synods had been absorbed through several mergers into the former United Presbyterian Church (now a constituent part of the Presbyterian Church U.S.A.).

The remaining Associate Reformed Presbyteries in the Southeast continued on as the Synod of the South, becoming the General Synod in 1935. There are now nine presbyteries in the United States—First (North Carolina), Second (Western South Carolina and Georgia), Northeast, Virginia, Tennessee and Alabama, Mississippi Valley, Catawba, Florida, and Pacific.

The church holds to the Westminister Confession of Faith and the larger and shorter Catechism. The General Synod is the church's highest authority. It is composed of all teachings elders (ministers) and least one ruling elder (lay leader) from each church. The church supports mission work in Mexico, Pakistan, Germany, Russia, and the Middle East; several retirement centers; and an assembly grounds, Bonclarken, at Flat Rock, North Carolina.

Membership: In 1997 the church reported 39,606 members in 227 churches served by 300 ministers in the United States. There were 234 members in seven churches served by five ministers in Canada.

Educational Facilities: Erskine College, Due West, South Carolina.
Erskine Theological Seminary, Due West, South Carolina.

Periodicals: *The Associate Reformed Presbyterian.*

★355★
Bible Presbyterian Church
Haddon and Cuthbert Blvd. S.
Collingswood, NJ 08108

History. The Rev. Carl McIntire (b. 1906) had been a student at Princeton Theological Seminary when J. Gresham Machen left to found the independent Westminster Theological Seminary.

McIntire graduated from Westminster in 1931 and became the pastor of the Presbyterian congregation in Atlantic City, New Jersey. In September 1933, he became pastor of the Presbyterian congregation in Collingswood, New Jersey. He was suspended from the Presbyterian Church in the U.S.A. along with Machen and left with him and others to establish what became the Orthodox Presbyterian Church. In 1937, after the death of Machen, the church divided on three points. The Orthodox Presbyterians refused to take a stand against intoxicating beverages, rebuffed attempts to make it distinctly premillennial in its eschatology, and declined further support of the Independent Board of Presbyterian Foreign Missions in favor of a church-controlled board. (A premillennial eschatology refers to the belief that before the millennium—Christ's predicted thousand-year reign on earth with his saints—Christ will return to earth to fight the Battle of Armageddon and bind Satan.) In 1938, McIntire and his supporters formed the Bible Presbyterian Church.

At times, the personality of McIntire seemed to have been a more significant factor in the formation of the Bible Presbyterian Church than any of his three objections to the Orthodox Presbyterian Church. He has led a zealous crusade against modernism, communism, and pacifism, and called for what he termed the "twentieth century reformation" to root out apostasy and build true churches. Prime targets have been the National Council of Churches and its sister organization, the World Council of Churches. McIntire called all true Christians to separate themselves from the apostasy of members of these councils.

McIntire provided followers with a variety of alternative organizations to support. In 1937, along with others, he founded Faith Theological Seminary. Four years later he was active in organizing the American Council of Christian Churches (ACCC) to bring together separatist churches from across the country. Separatist churches refuse to deal with liberal churches or with conservative churches that cooperate with liberal churches in any way. Just before the Amsterdam meeting of the World Council of Churches in 1948, McIntire joined with others to organize the International Council of Christian Churches (ICCC). because of criticism by some outstanding conservative Presbyterian leaders, the ACCC and ICCC lost much support, and in 1956 were repudiated by some who had been close followers of McIntire. In that same year, a faction of the synod of the Bible Presbyterian Church terminated its support of Faith Theological Seminary, the Independent Board of Presbyterian Foreign Missions, the ACCC, and the ICCC. The seminary and board, though largely supported by Bible Presbyterians, were both separate corporations. The ICCC and ACCC were both interdenominational and had been criticized for some of their activities in the early 1950s such as the Bible balloon project to send religious literature behind the Iron Curtain by balloon. In reputiating these organizations, some of the churches also reputiated McIntire, who had been instrumental in founding the organizations as well as the church. The Bible Presbyterian Church then split into two factions. The larger group, those objecting to McIntire and the organizations, soon changed its name to Reformed Presbyterian Church, Evangelical Synod. It is now a constituent part of the Presbyterian Church in America.

The smaller group, the supporters of McIntire, included the presbyteries of New Jersey (of which he was moderator), California, and Kentucky-Tennessee. They declared themselves independent and free of the 1956 synod. At a meeting in Collinswood they created the new synod of the Bible Presbyterian Church. They returned support to ACCC, ICCC, Faith Theological Seminary, the Independent Board for Presbyterian Foreign Missions. and the Independent Board for Presbyterian Home Missions. However, in 1969, McIntire was removed from the board of ACCC, and he then helped form the American Christian Action Council, now the National Council of Bible-Believing Churches in America.

Beliefs. Doctrinally, the Bible Presbyterian Church accepts the Westminster Confession of Faith and the Larger and Smaller Westminster Catechisms. They are premillennial, which means that they believe Christ will return before the millennium. Premillennialists also look for Christ to come unexpectedly in the near future to fight the Battle of Armegeddon and bind Satan, thus ushering in the millennium. The Bible Presbyterians have also take strong stands against intoxicating beverages, the new evangelicalism, the Revised Standard Version of the Bible, evolution, civil disobedience, and the United Nations.

Organization. The polity is presbyterial, but there is a strong assertion of congregational autonomy. The church supports the Friends of Israel Testimony to Christ; The Five Civilized Tribe Ministry in Oklahoma; Reformation Gospel Publications; The Twentieth Century Reformation Hour, a radio broadcast; The Christian Admiral Bible Conference; and the Cape Canaveral Bible Conference in Florida, all independent corporations. The church also supports the Bible Presbyterian Home in Delanco, Florida.

Membership: Not reported.

Educational Facilities: Independent schools supported by the Bible Presbyterian Church are:

Shelton College, Cape May, New Jersey and Cape Canaveral, Florida.

Faith Theological Seminary, Elkins Park, Pennsylvania.

Periodicals: Unofficial: *The Christian Beacon.* Send orders to 756 Haddon Avenue, Collingswood, NJ 08108.

Sources:

Carl McIntire's 50-Years, 1933-1983. Collingswood, NJ: Bible Presbyterian Church, 1983.

The Constitution of the Bible Presbyterian Church. Collingswood, NJ: Independent Board of Presbyterian Foreign Missions, 1959.

Harden, Margaret G. *Brief History of the Bible Presbyterian Church and Its Agencies.* N.p. 1965.

McIntire, Carl. *Twentieth Century Reformation.* Collinswood, NJ: Christian Beacon Press, 1944.

___. *Modern Tower of Babel.* Collingswood, NJ: Christian Beacon Press, 1949.

___. *Servants of Apostasy.* Collingswood, NJ: Christian Beacon Press, 1955.

★356★

Cumberland Presbyterian Church

Cumberland Presbyterian Center
1978 Union Ave.
Memphis, TN 38104

Before the American Revolution, most of the colonies had state churches, some Congregational, many Episcopal (Anglican). All the colonists supposedly belonged to the state church established by their colony. Immediately after the American Revolution, when state churches no longer existed in America, only fifteen per cent of the new nation chose to belong to a church. The remaining eighty-five percent had no religious affiliation. Around the turn of the nineteenth century, this situation ushered in a great drive to "save the nation," a wave of revivalism usually called the Second Great Awakening. One revivalist was the Rev. James McGready, who worked in Kentucky. While preparing to be a Presbyterian minister, he had a mystical conversion experience and became a strong evangelist. He was licensed by the Redstone Presbytery of the Presbyterian Church and moved to Logan County, Kentucky, where he began to preach regeneration, faith, and repentance. Through his work, revivals flourished and by 1800 spread beyond McGready's congregations. The Great Awakening in Kentucky became ecumenical, including Presbyterians, Methodists, and Baptists. Among the new practices that developed were the group meeting and the anxious seat or mourner's bench. Those in attendance at the revivals exhibited signs of emotional excess, loud, spontaneous behavior, and what today would be called altered states of consciousness (such as trances).

The issue of using unordained, uneducated men to fill leadership posts in the growing church had risen. Some of these men were ordained by the Cumberland Presbytery, which had been formed in 1802 from the Transylvania Presbytery of the Presbyterian Church. Critics of the Great Awakening protested the ordination of uneducated ministers and also complained that ministers did not believe in the Westminister Confession. In 1805 the Kentucky Synod judged against the ordinations of the Cumberland Presbytery and decided to examine those irregularly licensed and ordained and to judge their fitness. The Cumberland Presbytery, however, refused to submit to the Kentucky Synod's judgment. In 1806 the Synod dissolved the Cumberland Presbytery, but Mc-Gready and the ministers continued to function while appeal was made to the General Assembly of the Presbyterian Church. The efforts for appeal went unresolved and finally in 1810, in Dickson, Tennessee, three ministers- Finis Ewing, Samuel King, and Samuel McAdow- constituted a new presbytery, again called the Cumberland Presbytery. In 1813, those still unable to find reconciliation with the Kentucky Synod formed two more presbyteries, Elk and Logan, and created the Cumberland Synod.

Growth was quick and the Cumberland Synod spread in every direction from its Tennessee and Kentucky base. By 1829, when the General Assembly of the Cumberland Presbyterian Church was organized, the church had reached into eight states.

Post-Civil War efforts at reunion came to fruition in 1906 when the main body of the Cumberland Presbyterian Church reunited with the Presbyterian Church in the United States of America, now an integral part of the Presbyterian Church (U.S.A.). From the Cumberland point of view, though, the union was not altogether a happy one. The union carried by only a slight majority of 60 presbyteries to 51, and a large segment of the church refused to go into the united church. They reorganized themselves as the continuing Cumberland Presbyterian Church, and took that name.

The theology of Cumberland Presbyterianism is derived from the Westminster Confession and is described as the middle ground between Calvinism and Arminianism, a theology which defends free will and opposes the belief in strict predestination. The Cumberland Presbyterians deny the five points of Calvinism with the exception of the perseverance of the saints. (The other four points of Calvinism, which this church rejects, are the utter depravity of man, total predestination, limited atonement, and irresistible grace.) The Cumberland Presbyterians have a presbyterian polity. Their General Assembly meets annually.

After 1906 Cumberland Presbyterian missions emerged in Colombia, Hong Kong, Liberia, and Japan. These missions developed into five presbyteries which exist as integral parts of the church. Domestic work includes a Choctaw Indian mission in Oklahoma, and new church developments, some of which are union congregations with the Presbyterian Church (U.S.A.). The church participates in ecumenical Christian education curriculum development.

Membership: In 1994 the church reported 83,733 members, 713 churches, and 736 ministers in the United States. There were an additional 6,392 members in missions in Colombia, Hong Kong, Japan, and Liberia.

Educational Facilities: Bethel College, McKenzie, Tennessee. Memphis Theological Seminary, Memphis, Tennessee.

Periodicals: *The Missionary Messenger.* • *The Cumberland Presbyterian.*

Sources:

Campbell, Thomas J. *Good News on the Frontier*. Memphis, TN: Frontier Press, 1965.

Confession of Faith for Cumberland Presbyterians. Memphis, TN: Frontier Press, 1984.

Hughey, John H. *Lights and Shadows of the C. P. Church*. Decatur, IL: The Author, 1906.

A People Called Cumberland Presbyterians. Memphis, TN: Frontier Press, 1970.

Reagin, E. K. *We Believe So We Speak*. Memphis, TN: Department of Publication, Cumberland Presbyterian Church, 1960.

★357★
Cumberland Presbyterian Church in America
226 Church St.
Huntsville, AL 35801

In the early years of the Cumberland Presbyterian Church, ministers of the church established a mission to African Americans in the South, many of whom were slaves. Many congregations had Black members and some all-Black congregations were formed. By the time of the Civil War, some 30,000 Black members were on the role of the church. After the war, steps were taken to train Black ministers and separate synods were established as a means of organizing (and segregating) the work among African Americans. Between 1871 and 1874, synods were set up in Tennessee, Kentucky, and Texas.

On May 14, 1874, Black members of the Cumberland Presbyterian Church met at Murfreesboro, Tennessee, and organized separately what was for many years called the Second Cumberland Presbyterian Church. For many years, the Cumberland Presbyterian continued some financial support of the new denomination.

Over the years, the church spread across the South and into the Midwest. During the early 1980s, it completed a process of revising its statement of faith and church polity, which it had originally inherited from its parent body. That process was finished in 1984, and a new *Confession of Faith* was issued at that time. More recently, it entered into merger negotiations with the Cumberland Presbyterian Church, but in 1991 voted against the plan of union.

The church is organized into four synods and 16 prebyteries. The general assembly meets annually. The church is a member of the World Alliance of Reformed Churches.

Membership: In 1992, the church reported 10,450 members, 205 ministers (of which 35 are female), and 154 congregations.

Educational Facilities: Educational opportunities and ministerial training are pursued through the schools of the Cumberland Presbyterian Church.

Periodicals: *The Cumberland Flag.*

Sources:

Campbell, Thomas H. *Good News on the Frontier*. Memphis, TN: Frontier Press, 1965.

★358★
Evangelical Presbyterian Church
% Office of the Evangelical Assembly
29140 Buckingham Ave., Ste. 5
Livonia, MI 48154

The Evangelical Presbyterian Church (EPC), established in March, 1981, in St. Louis, Missouri, is a conservative denomination of 11 geographical presbyteries (10 in the United States, and one in Argentina). From its inception with 12 churches, the EPC has grown to 160 churches. In 1991, the General Assembly approved the formation of the newest presbytery, the Presbytery of Mid-America, located in the heartland area of the nation. It held its first meeting in October, 1991.

Planted firmly within the historic Reformed tradition, presbyterian in polity, evangelical in spirit, the EPC places high priority on church planting and development along with world missions. Fourteen missionary families serve in the church's mission at home and abroad.

Working together with the Presbyterian Church of Brazil (IPB), a Joint Committee on Missions was established in 1986, meeting in November each year in alternating sites. Strategies for supporting one another in mission outreach and theological preparation are the ongoing goals of the joint committee.

Based on the truth of Scripture and adhering to the Westminster Confession of Faith plus its *Book of Order*, the denomination is committed to the "essentials of the faith." The historic motto, "In essentials, unity; in non-essentials, liberty; in all things, charity" catches the spirit of the EPC, along with the New Testament theme of "truth in love." The EPC is made up of churches where the range of worship styles move from traditional to contemporary to charismatic (but not Pentecostal). Some churches choose to ordain women as ruling elders, while others do not. The particular church owns and governs its own property.

The EPC does not believe in taking political positions, but does believe the church has an obligation to speak its mind on matters of importance. The General Assembly has adopted position papers on the subjects of abortion, the value of and respect for human life, homosexuality, capital punishment, the ordination of women, and the Holy Spirit.

The Evangelical Presbyterian Church is a member of the World Alliance of Reformed Churches, National Association of Evangelicals, World Evangelical Fellowship, and the Evangelical Council for Financial Accountability. Though not members, observers annually attend the North American Prebyterian and Reformed Churches (NAPARC).

Membership: In 1993 there were 175 churches, 56,000 members, and 387 ministers.

★359★
General Assembly of the Korean Presbyterian Church
1251 Crenshaw Blvd.
Los Angeles, CA 90019

The General Assembly of the Korean Presbyterian church was founded in 1976. It grew out of the migration of numerous Koreans to the United States, especially since the end of the Korean War. Many of these Koreans were Presbyterians, and many chose to align themselves with one of the older American Presbyterian denominations. However, still others found themselves unwilling to affiliate, either because of the barrier created by language or their conservative theology. The General Assembly represents one such group that specializes in serving the Korean-American community.

It is conservative in theology and accepts the Westminster Confession as its doctrinal standard. It has a presbyterian form of government.

Membership: In 1992 the church reported 203 churches, 26,988 members, and 381 ministers.

★360★
Korean American Presbyterian Church
1901 W. 166th St.
Gardena, CA 90296

Many of the Koreans who migrated to the United States in the years following the Korean War were conservative Presbyterians. Once in America, they began to form independent Korean-speaking presbyteries. In 1978, five such presbyteries that had formed in California, the Midwest, New York, Pennsylvania, and Canada came together to create the Korean American Presbyterian Church. The meeting that formed the church was held on February 8–9, 1978, at Westminster Theological Seminary (the school of the Orthodox Presbyterian Church), in Philadelphia, Pennsylvania. Thirty-two ministers attended and the eldest among them, Rev. Jae Lee, was elected to the office of Moderator. Immediate needs were the formation of a seminary and the establishment of relationships with both the General Assembly of the Presbyterian church in Korea and contact with the numerous unaffiliated congregations of Korean Presbyterians known to exist throughout the Western Hemisphere. The Reformed Presbyterian Seminary, now located in Gardena, California, was opened and graduated 68 ministers during its first decade. The church grew quickly from both the ad-

herence of previously formed congregations and the organization of new ones.

The church is staunchly conservative in its theological perspective. It acknowledges an inerrant Bible, the authority of the Westminster Confession of Faith, and both the Larger and Shorter Westminster Catechisms as the most correct interpretations of Scripture.

The church is organized into regional presbyteries. A general assembly of the whole church meets annually.

Membership: In 1990 there were 186 ordained ministers serving approximately 12,000 communicant members in the United States and Canada. There is also a Presbytery of Central South America with congregations in Brazil, Paraguay, Argentina, and Chile.

Educational Facilities: Reformed Presbyterian Seminary, Gardena, California.

★361★
Orthodox Presbyterian Church
607 N. Eastern Rd.
Bldg. E, Box P
Willow Grove, PA 19090-0920

In the early years of the twentieth century the Presbyterian Church in the United States of America became a major focus of the fundamentalist-modernist controversy. Conservatives felt that liberals were leading the church into compromise with the world and away from the witness to the gospel. Conservatives traced liberalism to the Plan of Union of 1801 between Presbyterians and Congregationalists. The Conservatives said that plan aligned Presbyterians with Congregationalists infected with the "New School theology" of Samuel Hopkins. Late in the nineteenth century the issues of compromise with the world and lack of witness to the gospel were raised anew by the heresy trials of Professors Charles Briggs and Henry Preserved Smith. In 1903 doctrinal standards were revised to facilitate the merger with the Cumberland Presbyterian Church.

In reaction against liberal Baptist Harry Emerson Fosdick's preaching in First Presbyterian Church in New York City, a group of conservatives drew up a document presented to and passed by the 1923 General Assembly calling for the ministry to uphold the essentials of the faith, namely the five fundamentals-the infallibility of the Scriptures, the virgin birth of Christ, the substitutionary atonement, Christ's bodily resurrection, and Christ's miracles. Although the assembly passed the conservative document, many of the church leaders were liberals and held key positions on the boards and agencies of the church. In protest of the assembly's vote, they joined with the 1,300 ministers who signed the Auburn Affirmation. This signpost of liberal faith created a storm of controversy, and the two sides were locked in battle.

The publication of *Re-Thinking Missions* by W. E. Hocking in 1932 began the final stage of the church's liberal-conservative battle. Hocking asserted, among other controversial opinions, that missionaries should not take conversions as their only goal, but should provide social services and do medical missionary work in addition to preaching the gospel. J. Gresham Machen, a theology professor at Princeton Theological Seminary, opposed Hocking's suggestion. With other conservative Presbyterians, Machen charged in 1932 that the board of Foreign Missions approved, sent, and supported missionaries who did not teach that Christ is the exclusive, unique way of salvation. The church countered with a mandate comparing non-support of the church boards with refusal to take communion. The fundamentalists replied with charges against other boards, and they condemned participation in the Federal Council of Churches. Machen was tried and convicted of disturbing the peace of the church. Machen and his supporters then left the Presbyterian Church in the United States of America and formed the Orthodox Presbyterian Church.

Doctrine of the new church is the Westminster Confession of Faith and the Westminster Larger and Shorter Catechisms to which all officers are required to subscribe. A general assembly meets annually. Over the years support for the Independent Board for Presbyterian Foreign Missions was dropped and a denominational board created. Great Commissions Publications produces a complete line of church school materials in cooperation with the Presbyterian Church of America. The church participates in the North American Presbyterian and Reformed Council, and for many years belonged to the Reformed Ecumenical Synod. It has more recently joined the International Council of Reformed Churches (ICRC).

Membership: In 1996 the church reported 22,186 members, 192 congregations, 42 mission works, and 366 ministers. There is one congregation in Canada. Missionary work is supported in Korea, Japan, China, Cyprus, Eritrea, Ethiopia, Kenya, and Surinam.

Periodicals: *New Horizons.*

Sources:

Cohen, Gary G. *Biblical Separation Defended.* Nutley, NJ: Presbyterian and Reformed Publishing Co., 1977.

Galbraith, John P. *Why the Orthodox Presbyterian Church?* Philadelphia: Committee on Christian Education, Orthodox Presbyterian Church, 1965.

The Standards of Government, Discipline and Worship of the Orthodox Presbyterian Church. Philadelphia: Committee on Christian Education, Orthodox Presbyterian Church, 1965.

★362★
Presbyterian Church in America
% Stated Clerk
1852 Century Plaza, Ste. 190
Atlanta, GA 30345

History. During the 1960s tensions began to rise between liberals and conservatives within the Presbyterian Church in the United States. Among expressions of this rift was the conservatives' protest of denominational support of the National Council of Churches and involvement in social issues, possible union with the United Presbyterian Church in the U.S.A. (which would put the conservatives in an even smaller minority position and which eventually occurred in 1983), liberal theology in *The Layman's Bible* published by the church, the ordination of women, support of abortion on demand for socioeconomic reasons, and liberal churchmen in positions of authority in the denomination.

In 1972-73 several presbyteries were formed by some 260 congregations with a combined communicant membership of over 41,000 that had left the denomination. These presbyteries were the Warrior Presbytery in Alabama, the Westminster Presbytery in Virginia and East Tennessee, and the Vanguard Presbytery at large. In December 1973, delegates gathered at Briarwood Presbyterian Church in Birmingham, Alabama, and organized the National Presbyterian Church. Rev. Frank Barker, pastor of the Brairwood Church, hosted the gathering.

Organized at a constitutional assembly in December 1973, this church was first known as the National Presbyterian Church, but changed its name in 1974 to Presbyterian Church in America (PCA). It separated from the Presbyterian Church in the United States (PCUS) (Southern) in opposition to the long-developing theological liberalism which denied the deity of Jesus Christ and the inerrancy and authority of Scripture. The PCA held to the traditional position on the role of women in church offices. The PCUS had not only permitted women to serve in offices but began to force all churches to comply. There was also opposition to the PCUS affiliation with the National Council of Churches and World Council of Churches which supported the radical left political and social activism. As conservatives in the southern church, there was opposition to the movement toward merger with the more liberal United Presbyterian Church in the U.S.A. (Northern).

In 1982 the Reformed Presbyterian Church, Evangelical Synod, merged into the Presbyterian Church in America. The Reformed Presbyterian Church, Evangelical Synod, had been formed in 1965 by a merger of the Evangelical Presbyterian Church and the Reformed Presbyterian Church in North America, General Synod.

Evangelical Presbyterian Church was the name taken by the larger segment of the Bible Presbyterian Church following the split in that church in 1956. (See the discussion of the split in the entry on the Bible Presbyterian Church.) The name for the larger group had been adopted in 1961 to avoid confusion with Dr. Carl McIntire's smaller group. At the time of the split, the synod, controlled by the larger group, had voted to establish an official periodical, the *Evangelical Presbyterian Reporter*; a synod-controlled college and seminary, Covenant College and Covenant Seminary in St. Louis; and its own mission board, World Presbyterian Missions. Immediate efforts were directed toward healing the rift with the Orthodox Presbyterian Church and opening correspondence with the Reformed Presbyterian Church in North America General Synod. In 1960 the constitution was amended to allow any view of eschatology, not just premillennialism.

The Reformed Presbyterian Church in North America, General Synod, was of the Covenanter tradition, the church which adhered to the Solemn League and Covenant of 1643 which spelled out the doctrine and practices of Scotch Presbyterians. The General Synod (as the church was often called) dated to 1833 when the Reformed Presbyterian Church split over the issue of participation in civic affairs. One group within the church took the name Reformed Presbyterian Church in North America, General Synod, and allowed its members to vote and hold office. The General Synod also adopted the practice of allowing hymns as well as psalms to be sung at services and allowed instrumental music to be used in worship. Those who did not allow members to vote or hold office, and opposed hymns and instrumental music, are known today as the Reformed Presbyterian Church of North America. In 1965, the Reformed Presbyterian Church in North America, General Synod, merged with the Evangelical Presbyterian Church. The merged body became known as the Reformed Presbyterian Church, Evangelical Synod.

Beliefs. The PCA made a firm commitment on the doctrinal standards which had been significant in presbyterianism since 1645, namely the Westminster Confession of Faith and Catechisms. These doctrinal standards express the distinctives of the Calvinistic or Reformed tradition.

Among the distinctive doctrines of the Westminster Standards and of Reformed tradition is the unique authority of the Bible. The reformers based all of their claims on "sola scriptura," the scriptures alone. This included the doctrine of their inspiration, which is a special act of the Holy Spirit by which He guided the writers of the books of scriptures (in their original autographs). This was so their words should convey the thoughts He wished conveyed, bear a proper relation to the thoughts of other inspired books, and be kept free from error of fact, doctrine, and judgment, all of which were to be an infallible rule of faith and life.

Organization. The church is organized presbyterially. The PCA maintains the historic polity of Presbyterian governance, namely, rule by presbyters (or elders) and the graded courts, which are the session governing the local church, the presbytery for regional matters, and the general assembly at the national level. It has taken seriously the position of the parity of elders, making a distinction between the two classes of elders, teaching and ruling. In addition, on presbyterian governance, it has self-consciously taken a more democratic position (rule from the grass roots up) in contrast to a more prelatical (rule from the top assemblies down). The General Assembly meets annually. The church conducts mission work in 56 countries and is a member of the National Association of Evangelicals.

Membership: In 1995 the church reported 210,758 communicant members, 1,299 congregations and 2,476 clergy.

Educational Facilities: Covenant College, Lookout, Georgia.
Covenant Theological Seminary, St. Louis, Missouri.

Other schools supported by the church and/or its constituent presbyteries include:

Reformed Theological Seminary, Jackson, Mississippi, Orlando, Florida, and Charlotte, North Carolina.

Westminister Theological Seminary, Philadelphia, Pennsylvania, and Escondido, California.

Birmingham Theological Seminary, Birmingham, Alabama.

Chesapeake Theological Seminary.

Atlanta School of Biblical Studies, Atlanta, Georgia.

Greenville Theological Seminary, Greenville, South Carolina.

Sources:

The Book on Church Order of the Presbyterian Church in America. Atlanta, GA: Committee on Christian Education and Publications, 1983.

MacNair, Donald J. *Hallmarks of the Reformed Presbyterian Church, Evangelical Synod.* St. Louis, MO: Presbyterain Missions, n.d.

Richards, John Edwards. *The Historical Birth of the Presbyterian Church in America.* Liberty Hill, SC: Liberty Hill Press, 1987.

Smith, Frank J. *The History of the Presbyterian Church in America: The Continuing Church Movement.* Manasa, VA: Reformation Education Foundation, 1985.

★363★
Presbyterian Church in Canada
50 Wynford Dr.
Don Mills, ON, Canada M3C 1J7

The church today is the continuing Presbyterian body which in 1925 did not merge with the Canadian Methodists and Congregationalists to form the United Church of Canada (UCC). Approximately 30 percent did not enter the United Church. As such, the Presbyterian Church in Canada shares the heritage of Canadian Presbyterianism with the UCC.

The Presbyterian Church in Canada was constituted in 1875 by the Presbyterian Church of the Lower Provinces, the Synod of the Presbyterian Church of the Maritime Provinces, the Synod of Canada Presbyterian Church, and the Synod of the Presbyterian Church of Canada in connection with the Church of Scotland.

Those Presbyterians who disapproved of the merger into the United Church of Canada feared the loss of such Presbyterian distinctives as reformed theology and structures. Theology was being equally threatened by Methodism and a growing liberalism. Many also argued that most of the rewards to be gained from the union could be gained by a federated relationship.

Doctrinally, the church adheres to the Westminster Confession of Faith and both the Longer and Shorter Westminster Catechisms. In 1875, Article 23 of the Confession, concerning civil magistrates, had been explicitly deleted from the Confession accepted by the new church. This issue was resolved in 1955 by the adoption of a "Declaration of Faith Concerning Church and Nation." In 1962 the church also recognized several of the European Reformed confessions, specifically the Belgic, the Second Helvetic, and the Gallican Confessions, as parallel to the Westminster and the Heidelberg Catechisms and permitted their teachings by church elders.

Though more conservative than the United Church of Canada, the Presbyterian Church in Canada has remained a vital part of the larger protestant ecumenical movement. It is a member of both the Canadian Council of Churches and the World Council of Churches. In 1966 it admitted women to the ordained ministry. It conducts international work in Africa; East, South, and Central Asia; the Caribbean and Latin America; and the Middle East.

Membership: In 1997 the church reported 1,010 congregations, 145,328 communicant members, and 1,229 clergy.

Educational Facilities: Knox College, Toronto, Ontario, Canada.

Presbyterian College, Montreal, Quebec, Canada.

Vancouver School of Theology, Vancouver, British Columbia, Canada.

Sources:

Reed, R. C. *History of the Presbyterian Churches of the World.* Philadelphia: Westminister Press, 1912.

Silcox, Claris Edwin. *Church Union in Canada.* New York: Institute of Social and Religious Research, 1933.

★364★
Presbyterian Church of the Lower Provinces
(Defunct)

(The Presbyterian Church of the Lower Provinces no longer exists as a separate entity. It is now a constituent part of the United Church of Canada and the Presbyterian Church in Canada.) The Presbyterian Church of the Lower Provinces (1817-1875) grew out of the Seceders, a faction of Scottish Presbyterianism which emerged during the revivals that swept the Scottish church in the early 1700s. The Seceders were united in their attack upon the patronage system of the established Church of Scotland and its lack of spiritual awareness. They divided into two factions, usually termed Burgher and anti-Burgher, which resulted from the demand of an oath as part of the requirement to hold office in Scotland; the anti-Burgher party refused the oath, claiming it legitimized the established church.

Members of both parties arrived in Canada in the late 1700s. Three members of the Burgher Synod, Daniel Cook, David Smith, and Hugh Graham, organized the Presbytery of Truro in 1786. Almost contemporaneously, James McGregor and two other anti-Burgher ministers began work which culminated in the formation of the Presbytery of Pictou in 1795. Attempts at reconciliation in the new setting eventually led to the merger of the two presbyteries, the creation of a third presbytery (Halifax), and the formation of the Synod of Nova Scotia in 1817.

In 1825 the Church of Scotland organized the Glasgow Colonial Society, which sent missionaries to Canada. Those which settled in Nova Scotia and other Eastern Provinces refused to join the Synod of Nova Scotia. In 1833 the Presbyterian Synod in Connection with the Church of Scotland was organized. This synod prospered until 1843 when the Church of Scotland went through a period of turmoil which led to a number of ministers resigning and forming the Free Church of Scotland. In Canada, the Presbyterian Synod sided with the Free Church faction in the homeland. In 1860 this Free Church Synod merged with the Synod of Nova Scotia to form the Presbyterian Synod of the Lower Provinces.

In the disruption of 1843, one faction of the Presbyterian Church in Connection with the Church of Scotland, the Presbytery of New Brunswick (which had grown to become the Synod of New Brunswick), remained loyal to the established Church of Scotland. It became independent of the Free Synod. Three of its members in New Brunswick then withdrew and formed The (Free) Presbyterian Synod of New Brunswick, which in 1866 became a part of the Presbyterian Synod of the Lower Provinces.

In 1875 the Presbyterian Church of the Lower Provinces merged with three other Presbyterian churches to form the Presbyterian Church in Canada. In 1925 most of that church merged with the Methodist Church, Canada and the Congregational Union of Canada to form the United Church of Canada.

Sources:

Reed, R. C. *History of the Presbyterian Churches of the World.* Philadelphia: Westminister Press, 1912.

Silcox, Claris Edwin. *Church Union in Canada.* New York: Institute of Social and Religious Research, 1933.

★365★

Presbyterian Church of the Maritime Provinces
(Defunct)

(The Presbyterian Church of the Maritime Provinces no longer exists as a separate entity. It is now a constituent part of the United Church of Canada and the Presbyterian Church of Canada.) The Presbyterian Church of the Maritime Provinces (1868-1975) traces its history to the arrival in Canada of ministers of the Church of Scotland in the 1820s. In 1833 the Presbyterian Synod in Connection with the Church of Scotland was organized by a group of ministers, many of whom had been sent to Canada by the Glasgow Missionary Society. At the same time, a Presbytery of New Brunswick had been designated as one of the synod's constituent units. During the next decade the Presbytery of New Brunswick had grown into the Synod of New Brunswick. In 1943 the Church of Scotland had been disrupted by a dispute involving government powers in the appointment of ministers. Those who disagreed with the court's decision in the controversy left the Church of Scotland and formed the Free Church of Scotland. In Canada, the Presbyterian Synod in Connection with the Church of Scotland sided with the Free Church and broke its relation with the established Church of Scotland. The Synod of New Brunswick, however, remained loyal to the established church and became independent. Some members of the new Free Synod wished to return to their connection with the established church, and in 1854 established the Synod of Nova Scotia and Prince Edward Island. These two groups merged in 1868 to form the Church of the Maritime Provinces.

In 1875, the Church of the Maritime Provinces united with three other Presbyterian churches to form the Presbyterian Church in Canada. In 1925 the majority of that church merged with the Methodist Church, Canada and the Congregational Union of Canada to form the United Church of Canada.

Sources:

Reed, R. C. *History of the Presbyterian Churches of the World*. Philadelphia: Westminister Press, 1912.

Silcox, Claris Edwin. *Church Union in Canada*. New York: Institute of Social and Religious Research, 1933.

★366★

Presbyterian Church (U.S.A.)
100 Witherspoon St.
Louisville, KY 40202

The Presbyterian Church (U.S.A.) was formed in 1983 by the union of the United Presbyterian Church in the U.S.A. and the Presbyterian Church in the United States, the two largest Presbyterian bodies in the United States. It continues the beliefs and practices of the two churches, which originally had split over the same issues that divided the United States at the time of the Civil War.

History. The United Presbyterian Church in the United States of America was formed in 1958 by a merger of the Presbyterian Church in the United States of America and the United Presbyterian Church of North America. The Presbyterian Church in the United States of America inherited the tradition of early Presbyterianism in the colonies and is in direct continuity with the first synod organized in 1706. In the 1700s the Presbyterians were split between the revivalism of the Methodist, George Whitefield, who had influenced William Tennent and his brother, Gilbert Tennent, and the more traditional, creedal Calvinism with its ordered worship. The Tennents were the founders of a seminary which later became Princeton University. A split developed in the church in 1741 which lasted until 1758.

The church supported the Revolution and afterward reorganized for western expansion. On the heels of the cooperative Plan of Union of 1801 with the Congregationalists and the Second Great Awakening, the Presbyterians moved West and, in the forty years after the Revolution, grew more than tenfold. The nineteenth century, an era of expansion westward, saw the development of an impressive educational system and large-scale schism over revivalism and slavery. Other schisms would grow out of the fundamentalist debates in the early twentieth century.

The United Presbyterian Church of North America was formed in 1858 by a merger of the Associate Presbyterian Church and the Associate Reformed Presbyterian Church. These two churches continued the Scottish Covenanter and secession movements. The Covenanters were Scotch Presbyterians who seceded from the Church of Scotland, which was Reformed in theology but episcopal in government. The Covenanters formed their independent secession into a church in 1733. The Covenant to which the new church adhered was the Solemn League and Covenant ratified in 1643; it spelled out the doctrine and practices of Scotch Presbyterians.

People who followed the Covenant of 1643 found their way to the American colonies during the seventeenth century. These early Covenanters formed "societies" for worship because they had no minister. The first pastor was the Rev. Alexander Craighead, a Presbyterian attracted to the Covenanters because of their passion for freedom. In 1751, John Cuthbertson landed and began long years of work on a large circuit of Covenanters. He was joined in 1773 by Matthew Linn and Alexander Dobbin, and the three constituted the Reformed Presbyterian Church.

The Covenanters represented one branch of the Scottish secession movement; the Seceders represented another. The Seceders developed from the revival movements of the 1700s in Scotland which attacked the patronage system of the established church and its lack of spiritual awareness. The Seceder Church was not formed in Scotland until 1743, although Seceders began to arrive in the colonies in the 1730s. In 1742 a plea for a minister was issued by a congregation in Londonderry, Pennsylvania. The problem of providing leadership was compounded by the Scottish split into Burgher and anti-Burgher factions. The two parties resulted from the requirement of an oath to hold public office in Scotland. The anti-Burghers felt the oath legitimized episcopacy, and they therefore objected to it; the Burghers saw nothing wrong with taking the oath. Most of the Americans were anti-Burghers. Two anti-Burgher ministers, Alexander Gellatly and Andrew Arnot arrived and, in 1753, organized the Associate Presbyterian Church.

In 1782 the Associate Presbyterian Church and the Reformed Presbyterian Church merged to form the Associate Reformed Presbyterian Church. A few members of both merging churches declined to enter the merger and continued to exist under the names of their respective churches before 1782. Then in 1822, the Associate Reformed Presbyterian Church split into northern and southern branches. The southern branch continues today as the Associate Reformed Presbyterian Church (General Synod). The northern branch continued to be called the Associate Reformed Presbyterian Church. In 1858 this northern branch merged with the majority of the continuing Seceders, called the Associate Presbyterian Church. The new church formed in 1858 took the name the United Presbyterian Church of North America. In 1958, the United Presbyterian Church of North America united with the Presbyterian Church in the United States of America to form the United Presbyterian Church in the United States of America.

The Presbyterian Church in the United States arose out of the same controversies which had split the Methodists and Baptists in the years prior to the Civil War. Presbyterians were able, as a whole, to remain in the same ecclesiastical body until war actually broke. The General Assembly of the Presbyterian Church in the United States of America, meeting in Philadelphia only days after the firing on Fort Sumter and devoid of most southern delegates, declared its loyalty to the United States. Presbyterians in the South claimed the Assembly had no such right to make such a political statement. One by one the Southern presbyteries withdrew, and in December 1861 they organized the Presbyterian Church in the Confederate States (later changed to the Presbyterian Church in the United States).

The war divided the North from the South and feeling created by the conflict did much to keep the churches apart. The two churches had little disagreement on either doctrine or church polity. The southern church tended to be more conservative in its doctrinal stance and adopted a more loosely organized structure. It had replaced the church boards created by the Presbyterian Church in the United States of America with executive committees, unincorporated and devoid of permanent funds.

Beliefs. In 1967 the United Presbyterian Church adopted a new confession of faith. The Confession was a very present-minded document though it begins with a statement of continuity with the Reformed Confessional tradition. It is focused on the reconciling work of Christ through the grace of God. A significant section deals with the mission of the church, particularly in society, and has a vague eschatology. The Confession was published along with the Apostles' and Nicene Creeds, five Reformed Confessions, and the Shorter Catechism in a *Book of Confessions. The Book of Common Worship* contains the liturgical resources.

Organization. The merger of 1983 left many of the important questions of merging geographically overlapping synods and presbyteries and national offices, boards, and agencies to be resolved in the future meetings of the annual General Assembly. In 1986 a structural Design for Mission was adopted by the General Assembly, and in 1988 most of the national offices were consolidated at the new headquarters building in Louisville, Kentucky.

Membership: In 1996, the church reported 2,631,466 members, 20,783 ministers, and 11,328 congregations. Partnership efforts in Christian mission exist with churches in 63 nations.

Educational Facilities: Theological seminaries:
Austin Presbyterian Theological Seminary, Austin, Texas.
Columbia Theological Seminary, Decatur, Georgia.
University of Dubuque Theological Seminary, Dubuque, Iowa.
Johnson C. Smith Theological Seminary, Atlanta, Georgia.
Louisville Presbyterian Theological Seminary, Louisville, Kentucky.
McCormick Theological Seminary, Chicago, Illinois.
Pittsburgh Theological Seminary, Pittsburgh, Pennsylvania.
Presbyterian School of Christian Education, Richmond, Virginia.
Princeton Theological Seminary, Princeton, New Jersey.
San Francisco Theological Seminary, San Anselmo, California.
Union Theological Seminary in Virginia, Richmond, Virginia.
Colleges and Universities:
Agnes Scott College, Decatur, Georgia.
Alma College, Alma, Michigan.
Arkansas College, Batesville, Arkansas.
Austin College, Sherman, Texas.
Barber-Scotia College, Concord, North Carolina.
Beaver College, Glenside, Pennsylvania.
Belhaven College, Jacskon, Mississippi.
Blackburn College, Carlinville, Illinois.
Bloomfield College, Bloomfield, New Jersey.
Buena Vista College, Storm Lake, Iowa.
Carroll College, Waukesha, Wisconsin.
Centre College of Kentucky, Danville, Kentucky.
Coe College, Cedar Rapids, Iowa.
Davidson College, Davidson, North Carolina.
Davis & Elkins College, Elkins, West Virginia.
University of Dubuque, Dubuque, Iowa.
Eckerd College, St. Petersburg, Florida.
College of Ganado, Ganado, Arizona.
Grove City College, Grove City, Pennsylvania.
Hampden-Sydney College, Hampden-Sydney, Virginia.
Hanover College, Hanover, Indiana.
Hastings College, Hastings, Nebraska.
Hawaii Loa College, Kaneohe, Oahu, Hawaii.
Huron College, Huron, South Dakota.
College of Idaho, Caldwell, Idaho.

Illinois College, Jacksonville, Illinois.
Jamestown College, Jamestown, North Dakota.
Johnson C. Smith University, Charlotte, North Carolina.
King College, Bristol, Tennessee.
Knoxville College, Knoxville, Tennessee.
Lafayette College, Easton, Pennsylvania.
Lake Forest College, Lake Forest, Illinois.
Lee Junior College, Jackson, Kentucky.
Lees-McCrae College, Banner Elk, North Carolina.
Lewis & Clark College, Portland, Oregon.
Lindenwood College, St. Charles, Missouri.
Macalester College, St. Paul, Minnesota.
Mary Baldwin College, Staunton, Virginia.
Mary Holmes College, West Point, Mississippi.
Maryville College, Maryville, Tennessee.
Missouri Valley College, Marshall, Missouri.
Monmouth College, Monmouth, Illinois.
Montreat-Anderson College, Montreat, North Carolina.
Muskingum College, New Concord, Ohio.
Occidental College, Los Angeles, California.
College of the Ozarks, Clarksville, Arkansas.
Peace College, Raleigh, North Carolina.
Pikeville College, Pikeville, Kentucky.
Presbyterian College, Clinton, South Carolina.
Queens College, Charlotte, North Carolina.
Rocky Mountain College, Billings, Montana.
St. Andrew's Presbyterian College, Laurinburg, North Carolina.
School of the Ozarks, Pt. Lookout, Missouri.
Schreiner College, Kerrville, Texas.
Sheldon Jackson College, Sitka, Alaska.
Southwestern at Memphis, Memphis, Tennessee.
Sterling College, Sterling, Kansas.
Stillman College, Tuscaloosa, Alabama.
Tarkio College, Tarkio, Missouri.
Trinity University, San Antonio, Texas.
Tusculum College, Greeneville, Tennessee.
University of Tulsa, Tulsa, Oklahoma.
Warren Wilson College, Swannanoa, North Carolina.
Waynesburg College, Waynesburg, Pennsylvania.
Westminster College, Fulton, Missouri.
Westminster College, New Wilmington, Pennsylvania.
Westminster College, Salt Lake City, Utah.
Whitworth College, Spokane, Washington.
Wilson College, Chambersburg, Pennsylvania.
College of Wooster, Wooster, Ohio.

Periodicals: *Presbyterians Today.* • *Church & Society Magazine.* • *Monday Morning.*

Sources:

Jamison, Wallace N. *The United Presbyterian Story.* Pittsburgh: Geneva Press, 1958.

Miller, Park Hays. *Why I Am A Presbyterian.* New York: Thomas Nelson & Sons, 1956.

Minutes of the 195th General Assembly, United Presbyterian Church in the United States of America, 123rd General Assembly, Presbyterian Church in the United States, 195th General Assembly, Presbyterian Church (U.S.A.). Atlanta: Office of the General Assembly, Presbyterian Church (U.S.A.), 1983.

Study Draft, A Plan for Union of the Presbyterian Church in the United States and the United Presbyterian Church in the United States of America. New York: Stated Clerk of the Presbyterian Church in the United States, 1974.

Reformed Presbyterian Church of North America
℅ Louis D. Hutmire, Stated Clerk
7408 Penn Ave.
Pittsburgh, PA 15208

The eighteenth-century Reformed Presbyterian Church was the embodiment of the Covenanter tradition in North America, those adhering to the Scotch Presbyterians' Solemn League and Covenant of 1643. In 1782 the majority of the Covenanter tradition merged with the Seceder Church, originally formed in Scotland in 1743 as a group seceding from the established Church of Scotland. The 1782 merger of Covenanters and Seceders resulted in the Associate Reformed Presbyterian Church, which is now a constituent part of the Presbyterian Church (U.S.A.).

However, some Reformed Presbyterians (Covenanters) did not join the 1782 merger. They remained Reformed Presbyterians, and in 1833 they split over the issue of participation in government, specifically, over whether members would vote and hold office. The New Lights, those who allowed such participation, formed the Reformed Presbyterian Church, General Synod, which merged with the Evangelical Presbyterian Church in 1965. The merged church, the Reformed Presbyterian Church, Evangelical Synod recently merged into the Presbyterian Church in America, discussed above. The Reformed Presbyterian Church of North America is the continuing old school body, the group opposed to the New Lights in the 1833 split.

The Westminster Confession of Faith is the standard of doctrine. Worship is centered on the reading and exposition of the Bible. Hymns are limited to Psalms and there is no instrumental accompaniment. Organization is presbyterian. The synod meets annually. Foreign missions are conducted in Cyprus and Japan.

Membership: In 1993, the church reported 5,657 members in 70 churches being served by 131 ministers.

Educational Facilities: Geneva College, Beaver Falls, Pennsylvania.

Reformed Presbyterian Theological Seminary, Pittsburgh, Pennsylvania.

Periodicals: *The Covenanter Witness.* Send orders to 7408 Penn Ave., Pittsburgh, PA 15208.

Sources:

Adventures in Psalm Singing. Pittsburgh: Christian Education Office, 1970.

Synod of the Canada, Presbyterian Church
(Defunct)

(The Synod of the Canada Presbyterian Church no longer exists as a separate entity. It is now a constituent part of the United Church of Canada and the Presbyterian Church of Canada.) The Synod of the Canada Presbyterian Church (1861-1875) can be traced to 1832 with the arrival of three missionaries into Western Canada as representatives of the independent United Associate Synod of Scotland, one of the factions of Scotish Presbyterianism not connected with the established Church of Scotland. The church offered the missionaries the opportunity to join one of the two existing synods (the Presbyterian Church in Connection with the Church of Scotland or the United Synod of Upper Canada). However, the missionaries turned down the offer upon discovering that these already existing synods were quite willing to accept government support for their work, a position directly opposing that of the United Associate Synod. Therefore, in 1834 the ministers formed the Missionary Presbytery of the Canadas. In 1843 the Presbytery split into three presbyteries and organized the Missionary Synod of Canada.

In 1843, twenty-six ministers of the Presbyterian Church in Connection with the Church of Scotland left the church to found the Synod of the Free Church of Canada. This was done in reaction to ministers in the Church of Scotland who, in protest of govern-

mental influence in clerical matters, resigned from the established church to form the Free Church of Scotland. In 1861 the Synod of the Free Church of Canada and the Missionary Synod of Canada merged to become the Synod of the Canada Presbyterian Church.

In 1875 the Synod of the Canada Presbyterian Church merged with three other Presbyterian churches to form the Presbyterian Church in Canada. The majority of the Presbyterian Church in Canada merged with the Methodist Church, Canada and the Congregational Union of Canada, forming the United Church of Canada.

Sources:

Reed, R. C. *History of the Presbyterian Churches of the World.* Philadelphia: Westminister Press, 1912.

Silcox, Claris Edwin. *Church Union in Canada.* New York: Institute of Social and Religious Research, 1933.

Synod of the Presbyterian Church in Connection with the Church of Scotland
(Defunct)

(The Synod of the Presbyterian Church in Connection with the Church of Scotland no longer exists as a separate entity. It is now a constituent part of the United Church of Canada and the Presbyterian Church of Canada.) The Synod of the Canada Presbyterian Church (1861-1875) began with the arrival of Presbyterians in the eighteenth century into that part of Canada which was termed the Western Provinces (presently Quebec and Ontario). As early as 1796, Rev. John Bethune organized a Presbyterian congregation in Montreal. However, it was not until 1818 that enough growth and development had occurred to organize a presbytery. In that year the Revs. Robert Easton, William Stuart, William Bell, and William Taylor organized the Presbytery of the Canadas. These ministers were associated with the Burgher faction of Scottish Presbyterians who had seceded from the established Church of Scotland. Within a few years the Presbytery reorganized and took a new name, the United Presbytery of Upper Canada, which grew into the United Synod of Upper Canada in 1831.

As the United Synod was taking shape, ministers associated with the established church formed the Presbyterian Church in Connection with the Church of Scotland. In 1840 these two groups merged to become the Synod of the Presbyterian Church in Connection with the Church of Scotland. In 1875 the Synod of the Presbyterian Church in Connection with the Church of Scotland merged with three other Presbyterian Churches to form the Presbyterian Church in Canada. The majority of the Presbyterian Church in Canada merged in 1925 with the Methodist Church, Canada and the Congregational Union of Canada to become the United Church of Canada.

Sources:

Reed, R. C. *History of the Presbyterian Churches of the World.* Philadelphia: Westminister Press, 1912.

Silcox, Claris Edwin. *Church Union in Canada.* New York: Institute of Social and Religious Research, 1933.

Ukrainian Evangelical Alliance of North America
Current address not obtained for this edition.

The Ukrainian Evangelical Alliance of North America was formed in the United States in 1922 by Ukrainian Protestants of several denominations. The purpose of the Alliance was to spread the gospel among Ukrainians in both North America and the Ukraine. The Alliance was thus a missionary organization, and was not meant to be a separate denomination. However, over time the Alliance established mission congregations and in that sense has become a separate denomination. The member congregations typically retain their Ukrainian culture and language and are located in large cities. Most of the Ukrainian Reformed congregations in North America have become members of the larger Presbyterian bodies but two congregations of post-war immigrants, one in Detroit and one in Toronto, carry on the independent tradition and are under the direct guidance of the Ukrainian Evangelical Alliance of North America.

In 1925, the Ukrainian Evangelical Alliance of North America, with the aid of Several Reformed and Presbyterian churches, organized a Ukrainian Reformed Church in what was at that time Polish territory in the Western Ukraine. This church was virtually destroyed by the Communist take-over in World War II.

The Alliance is interdenominational in scope and has passed a resolution declaring denominational missions obsolete and unrealistic in their approach to Ukrainian-Russian relations, especially in their neglect of the native language. The Alliance wishes to be invited to cooperate in all missionary efforts. It has as a major part of its mission, the publication of Ukrainian literature which it distributes in both North America and the Ukraine.

Membership: At last report there were only two congregations solely attached to the Alliance, though congregations consisting of Ukrainian-Russian immigrants of the Reformed faith can be found in several of the larger Presbyterian bodies.

Periodicals: *News Bulletin.*

★371★
Upper Cumberland Presbyterian Church
Current address not obtained for this edition.

The Upper Cumberland Presbyterian Church was formed in 1955 by Rev. H. C. Wakefield, Rev. W. M. Dycus, Lum Oliver, and laymen from Sanderson's, Russell Hill, Pleasant Grove and Poston's Cumberland Presbyterian Churches, all of the Cooksville Presbytery in Tennessee. At the 1950 General Assembly of the Cumberland Presbyterian Church, the Board of Missions and Evangelism reported its application for membership in the Home Missions Council of the National Council of Churches. This application raised the issue of support of the "liberal" social activist theology imposed by the National Council of Churches, and strong opposition to the application developed within the church. In 1952 a Fellowship of Conservative Presbyterians was formed which included Reverend Wakefield and Reverend Dycus. In assembly in the following year, the Fellowship elected a moderator and a stated clerk, urged organization on a presbyterial level, and objected to the Revised Standard Version of the Bible newly issued by the National Council of Churches. Reverend Dycus and Reverend Wakefield were deposed from the ministry of the Cumberland Presbyterian Church. In 1955 they formed the Carthage Presbytery of the Upper Cumberland Presbyterian Church at a session with the Russell Hill Congregation in Macon County, Tennessee. Thus the Upper Cumberland Presbyterians came into existence. At the first session Lum Oliver was ordained.

The Upper Cumberland Presbyterians adopted the Confession of Faith of the Cumberland Presbyterian Church, with the addition of questions on the virgin birth of Christ and his visible return to the church covenant. Ministers must use the King James Bible.

Membership: In 1970 there were 9 churches and 300 members in the Upper Cumberland Presbyterian Church.

★372★
Westminster Biblical Fellowship
Current address not obtained for this edition.

Following the 1969 meeting in which Dr. Carl McIntire was removed from his responsibilities with the American Council of Christian Churches (ACCC), several former leaders of the McIntire-led Bible Presbyterian Church also withdrew support from him. These included J. Phillip Clark, former General Secretary of the Independent Board of Presbyterian Foreign Missions and pastor of Calvary Bible Presbyterian Church in Glendale, California. After the 1969 ACCC meeting, Clark announced the formation of the Westminster Biblical Felllowship in order to provide a vehicle for Bible Presbyterians to remain with the ACCC. Other Bible Presbyterian leaders-Richard E. Smitley, Jack Murray and Arthur Steele-joined Clark. The Westminster Biblical Fellowship continues the faith of the Bible Presbyterian Church in general, but it objects to the strong crusading stance of Carl McIntire.

Membership: Not reported.

Sources:

McIntire, Carl. *A Letter to Bible Presbyterians.* Collinwood, NJ: Bible Presbyterian Church, 1969.

Congregationalism

★373★
Congregational Union of Canada
(Defunct)

(The Congregational Union of Canada no longer exists as a separate entity. It is now a constituent part of the United Church of Canada.) The Congregational Union of Canada was formed in 1906 by the merger of the Congregational Union of Nova Scotia and New Brunswick and the Congregational Union of Ontario and Quebec. Together they represented the Congregational Church tradition which entered Canada from the United States in the eighteenth century.

Congregational beginnings in Canada awaited the British take over of Nova Scotia in 1748. At the invitation of the government, shiploads of settlers arrived from New England to establish towns and begin farming. The first Congregational Church was organized in Chester in 1759; others followed, and two years later a second one was formed in Liverpool. Though never a large and growing movement, these churches passed a generation in peace until, in the 1780s, they were disturbed by the independent revivalistic efforts of Henry Alline, whose preachings led to a split in many congregations. The new congregations, though remaining officially Congregational during Alline's lifetime, eventually became the core of Canadian Baptists in the area. Concurrently, the Methodists began their period of growth under William Black, Jr.. The competition between the Baptists and Methodists, coupled with the difficulties of obtaining ministers after the American Revolution, effectively hampered the future growth of Congregationalism.

At the same time settlements were being established in Nova Scotia, New Englanders traveled to New Brunswick. The first Congregational Church emerged in 1766 at Maugerville. Newfoundland's first congregation came a decade later at St. John's.

Organization of the scattered congregations awaited events in England. In the 1830s the Congregational Union of England and Wales was formed, thus consolidating Congregational efforts in Britain. In 1834 fraternal delegates were sent to Canada. They reported their findings, which led to the formation of the Colonial Missionary Society in 1836. This society, whose purpose was to aid churches through the British Empire, assisted the work in Canada and facilitated the formation of the Congregational Union of Nova Scotia and New Brunswick in 1846.

Congregationalism in Quebec and Ontario grew out of two separate movements. In the years after the American Revolution, settlers from New England began to move northward across the border into Canada. A church was founded at Stamstead as early as 1798. As other churches were founded, ministers were drawn from Vermont. In the 1840s, the Congregationalist-sponsored American Home Missionary Society initiated work in Canada and organized several predominantly black congregations among former slaves who had fled to freedom.

As early as 1801 the British Congregationalists sent a representative of the London Missionary Society to Quebec. Most of that work was lost to the Presbyterians, and the New England-based church were all that survived. British settlers organized a joint Congregational-Presbyterian Church in Elgin County, Ontario in 1819. It survived to become fully congregational, the first in that province.

As with the churches in the Maritime Provinces, those in Quebec and Ontario received a boost from the 1834 delegation from England. Unions were organized in each province, and in 1853 they merged into the Congregational Union of Ontario and Quebec.

In 1807 the Congregational Union of Canada received the Canadian Conference of the United Brethren in Christ into its membership. This German body had become predominantly English-speaking in the late nineteenth century. Rather than becoming another small independent sect after breaking with the American branch, they chose to unite with the Congregationalists.

In 1925 the Congregational Union of Canada joined with the Methodist Church, Canada and the Presbyterian Church in Canada to form the United Church of Canada.

Sources:

Dunning, Albert E. *Congregationalists in America.* New York: J. A. Hill & Co., 1894.

Silcox, Claris Edwin. *Church Union in Canada.* New York: Institute of Social and Religious Research, 1933.

★374★
Conservative Congregational Christian Conference
7582 Currell Blvd., Ste. 108
St. Paul, MN 55125

The Conservative Congregational Christian Conference can be dated to 1935 when Rev. Hilmer B. Sandine, then pastor of First Congregational Church of Hancock, Minnesota, began the publication of the *Congregational Beacon*. Beginning as a monthly parish publication, the *Beacon* became the organ for communication among theologically conservative Congregationalists. Emphasis was placed on Biblical evangelism and evangelical Christianity. Growing concern about liberal theology and social activism within the Congregational and Christian Churches led in 1945 to the formation of the Conservative Congregational Christian Fellowship at Minneapolis. During the previous year a plan of union with the Evangelical and Reformed Church had been published. In 1948, during the lengthy process of the formation of the United Church of Christ, the Conservative Congregational Christian Fellowship became the Conference, a separate body from the Congregational and Christian Churches.

Among Congregationalists, the conference represents the most theologically conservative group. The conference is committed to the five fundamentals: the infallibility of the Scriptures, the virgin birth of Christ, the substitutionary atonement, Christ's bodily resurrection, and Christ's miracles. The conference also emphasizes the historical Puritan beliefs in the sovereignty of God, the sinfulness of man, redemption through Christ, the indwelling Holy Spirit, the sacraments, the life of love and service, and the future life. They restrict membership to those who profess regeneration. The Conservative Congregational Christian Conference is a member of the National Association of Evangelicals and the World Evangelical Congregational Fellowship.

In polity, the Conservative Congregational Christian Conference accepts the interpretation that true Congregationalism is to be identified with the independent or separated Puritan tradition. The local church is the seat of power. It joins in fellowship with other churches for cooperative endeavors. Ecclesiastical bodies or officers have no right to interfere in local church affairs. There is an annual meeting of the conference.

Membership: In 1995, the conference reported 38,241 members, 211 congregations, and 702 ministers.

Educational Facilities: The Conference has endorsed Gordon-Conwell Theological Seminary for its ministerial students.

Periodicals: *Foresee.*

★375★
International Council of Community Churches
% Rev. J. Ralph Shotwell, Executive Director
7808 College Dr., No. 25E
Palos Heights, IL 60463

The International Council of Community Churches was formally organized in 1946, but possesses a history dating from the early nineteenth century when nonsectarian community churches began to appear as an alternative to the formation of separate denominationally affiliated congregations. Such community churches were especially welcomed in communities too small to support more than one viable congregation. Over the years, such congregations have frequently retained a fiercely independent stance. To their number were added other independent congregations that had separated from denominational structures and adopted a nonsectarian stance.

In the wake of the ecumenical movement in the early twentieth century, the most visible symbol being the Federal Council of Churches of Christ formed in 1908, many congregations merged across denominational lines, some forming independent federated or union churches, dropping all denominational affiliation. During this period, some community churches began to see, in light of their years of existence apart from denominational boundaries, that they had a particular role vis-a-vis Christian unity.

A first attempt to build a network of community churches was known as the Community Church Workers of the United States. At a national conference of individuals serving community churches in Chicago in 1923, a committee formed to hold a second conference and outline plans for a national association. Organization occurred the next year and the Rev. Orvis F. Jordan of the Park Ridge (Illinois) Community Church was named as secretary. He later became the first president of the group. The organization continued for over a decade, but died in the 1930s due to lack of support.

A second organization of community churches was also begun in 1923 among predominantly black congregations. Representatives of five congregations gathered in Chicago, Illinois, in the fall of 1923 to form the National Council of the People's Community Churches (incorporated in 1933 as the Biennial Council of the People's Church of Christ and Community Centers of the United States and Elsewhere). The Rev. William D. Cook, pastor of Metropolitan Community Church in Chicago, served as the first president.

Unable to gain recognition from the Federal Council of Churches, the independent community churches began a second attempt at organization in the last days of World War II. The Rev. Roy A. Burkhart, pastor of First Community Church of Columbus, Ohio, led in the formation of the Ohio Association for Community Churches in 1945. The next year representatives from 19 states and Canada met and formed the National Council of Community Churches.

Almost immediately, the black and white groups began to work toward a merger. The merger, accomplished in 1950, created the International Council of Community Churches with a charter membership of 160 churches. By 1957, the several foreign congregations had ceased their affiliation with the council and the word "International" was dropped. In 1969, the name was changed to National Council of Community Churches. In 1983, however, foreign congregations in Canada and Nigeria affiliated, and in 1984 the original name was again assumed.

There is no doctrinal statement shared by the council or its member churches, though most churches share a liberal, ecumenical-minded, Protestant perspective. The council describes itself as committed to Christian unity and working "toward a fellowship as comprehensive as the spirit and teachings of Christ and as inclusive as the love of God."

The council is a loosely organized fellowship of free and autonomous congregations. The national and regional officers facilitate communication between congregations and serve member congregations in various functions, such as representing them at the Consultation on Church Union and coordinating the securing of chaplains in the armed services.

Membership: In 1995, the council reported 217 member congregations serving 250,000 members and 501 clergy ministers. In addition, the council serves more than 1,000 other congregations (membership unknown). The council allows dual membership, and approximately five percent of the congregations have a denominational affiliation.

Educational Facilities: As a matter of policy, the council has no educational institutions or mission projects of its own. It endorses and encourages member churches to support individual schools and missions that meet a council standard of being "postdenominational" and promoting Christian unity while meeting human need.

Periodicals: *The Christian Community.* • *The Pastor's Journal.*

Sources:

National Council of Community Churches, Directory. Homewood, IL: National Council of Community Churches, 1982.

Shotwell, J. Ralph. *Unity without Uniformity.* Homewood, IL: Community Church Press, 1984.

Smith, J. Philip. *Faith and Fellowship in the Community Church Movement: A Theological Perspective.* Homewood, IL: Community Church Press, 1986.

★376★
Korean Christian Missions of Hawaii
1832 Liliha St.
Honolulu, HI 96817

The Korean Christian Missions of Hawaii arose early in this century when Korean immigrants to Hawaii found themselves trapped by a peculiarity of church history. They had been Presbyterians in their home country and wished to organize a Presbyterian judicatory on the island. However, they ran into a longstanding agreement by which Presbyterians and Congregationalists had divided the world and agreed not to organize in areas over which the other had hegemony. Rather than affiliate with the General Council of Congregational Christian Churches (now part of the United Church of Christ), they dropped the word Presbyterian and in 1918 formed Korean Christian churches. Over a period of time they gave up their presbyterianism and moved toward a congregational polity. Thus in recent decades they have emerged as a group that has doctrinal agreement and friendly relationships with both the Presbyterian Church (U.S.A.) and the United Church of Christ.

The church is trinitarian in faith and accepts the Apostles' Creed as its confession of faith. It baptizes by sprinkling.

Membership: Not reported. In 1980 there were three congregations with approximately 500 members.

Sources:

Piepkorn, Arthur C. *Profiles in Belief: The Religious Bodies of the United States and Canada.* Vol. III. San Francisco: Harper & Row, 1979.

★377★
Midwest Congregational Christian Church
Current address not obtained for this edition.

The Midwest Congregational Christian Fellowship was formed in 1958 by former members of the Congregational and Christian Churches. During the years of negotiating the forming of the United Church of Christ, one center of dissatisfaction was in the Eastern Indiana Association. Theologically conservative members of the association were opposed to the church's theologically liberal leadership. They felt there was too much emphasis on social ac-

tion. The first meetings were held in 1957 in which attempts were made to withdraw the entire Association. Having failed, laymen devised a plan by which individual congregations could withdraw. Thirty churches, primarily small rural congregations removed themselves from the rolls in 1958. These quickly organized as the Midwest Congregational Christian Fellowship (now Church).

The doctrinal statement of the church reflects the Puritan heritage, the Christian non-creedal bias, and the evangelical perspective of the members. The statement affirms belief in the Trinity, salvation, the ministry of the Holy Spirit, the resurrection, and the unity of believers. The polity is a loose congregationalism with emphasis on local ownership of property. The church meets quarterly, with one meeting designated the annual meeting. There is an eight-man committee which includes the moderator and officers who oversee the work of the church.

Membership: In 1970 the church reported 33 churches, 23 ordained ministers and 26 licensed ministers. Only three churches had a membership exceeding 100.

★378★
National Association of Congregational Christian Churches
8473 S. Howell Ave.
PO Box 1620
Oak Creek, WI 53154-0620

The National Association of Congregational Christian Churches was formed in 1955 in Detroit, Michigan, by a group of churches and individuals desiring to remain congregational in the face of merger forces that resulted in the formation of the United Church of Christ. The founders came to Detroit in response to a call sent out by the League to Uphold Congregationalist Principles and the Committee for the Continuation of Congregational Christian Churches.

There is little difference between members of the United Church of Christ and those of the National Association. The association leaders saw the United Church of Christ as basically presbyterial, not congregational, in government. In contrast, the polity of the association emphasizes local autonomy and the fellowship of the local churches. The association meets annually. It is seen as purely a spiritual fellowship. While it does not make pronouncements for the member churches, it does undertake a mutually cooperative program.

Today, the association supports programs for the welfare and career development of ministers, theological students, Christian education, spiritual resources, youth of high school age, financial support, building and loan assistance, church development, investment advisory, communications, men's and women's work, and missionary emphasis in the United States and 12 countries worldwide. The association fellowships with a host of "free" or congregationally governed associations including the International Congregational Felassociation reported 430 member churches and 70,000 members in the United States.

Membership: In 1990 the association reported 90,000 members, 400 congregations, and 450 ministers.

Educational Facilities: Olivet College, Olivet, Michigan. Piedmont College, Demorest, Georgia.

Periodicals: *The Congregationalist.* • *News from the NACCC* • *News and Needs.*

Sources:

Burton, Malcolm K. *Destiny for Congregationalism.* Oklahoma City: Modern Publishers, 1953.

Butman, Harry R. *The Lord's Free People.* Wauwatosa, WI: Swannet Press 1968.

Kohl, Manfred Waldemar. *Congregationalism in America.* Oak Creek, WI Congregational Press, 1977.

United Church of Canada
The United Church House
3250 Bloor St. W.
Etobicoke, ON, Canada M8X 2Y4

The United Church of Canada (UCC) was formed in 1925 by the union of the Methodist Church, Canada, the Congregational Union of Canada, the Council of Local Union Churches, and the majority of the Presbyterian Church in Canada. In 1968 the Canada Conference of the Evangelical United Brethren joined the UCC. This church is the most impressive result of the various Christian church union attempts in North America during the nineteenth and twentieth centuries; more than 40 church bodies from two major church families (Reformed and Methodist) were united.

French Huguenots, escaping persecution following the revocation of the Edict of Nantes, brought the Reformed Faith to Canada. But even in the New World their growth and development were restricted. After the ceding of Nova Scotia to England in 1713, and particularly after the ceding of all Canada in 1763 by the Treaty of Paris, the influx of Presbyterians from Scotland and Ireland completely overwhelmed the small French contingent. The first ministers from Scotland were Daniel Cook, David Smith, and Hugh Graham, who organized the Presbytery of Truro in 1786. In 1795, this presbytery was joined by a second, the Presbytery of Pictou, which represented another faction of Scottish Presbyterianism. In 1817 these two groups, joined by a few ministers from the Established Church of Scotland, were able to come together and form the Synod of the Presbyterian Church of Nova Scotia.

Concurrently with the events that led to the formation of the Synod of Nova Scotia, Presbyterians were moving into central and western Canada. As in eastern Canada, they brought the many divisions of the Scottish church with them and established several presbyteries and then synods, the first being the Presbytery of the Canadas in 1818. The establishment of new synodical structures continued through the first half of the nineteenth century, in part due to the importing of schisms within the church in Scotland, the arrival of non-English-speaking (Dutch Reformed) immigrants, and the opening of new territories in the West. By mid-century the trend began to reverse, and in 1875 a series of mergers led to the union of most Presbyterians into the Presbyterian Church in Canada.

Methodism in Canada is traced to Lawrence Coughlan, an Irish Methodist preacher who came to Newfoundland in 1765. At the time of his arrival, he had left Wesley's connection and applied for work with the Anglican Society for the Propagation of the Gospel. Though a Methodist in practice, he became an Anglican minister. Upon his return to England, many of the people he organized openly declared themselves Methodists. Meanwhile, Methodists were migrating from England to Nova Scotia; among them was William Black, Sr.. In 1779, a revival among them led to the conversion of William Black, Jr., then but 19 years old. He began to preach, visiting several nearby settlements, and in 1781 travelled the whole of Nova Scotia to organize Methodist classes. His work expanded greatly two years later as immigrants loyal to Great Britain flowed into Nova Scotia after the American Revolution. In 1784, Black journeyed to Baltimore, Maryland, for the meeting that organized the new Methodist Episcopal Church. The Canadian work that Black had developed was taken under their care. The Canadian work grew and developed as an integral part of the Methodist Episcopal Church until 1828 when it became separate and independent. Meanwhile, Methodists from Great Britain migrated into Canada, and like the Presbyterians from Scotland, brought with them the several divisions of British Methodism. Mergers in 1874 and 1884 resulted in the Methodist Church, Canada being formed.

Congregationalism in Canada originated with the acceptance of the offer made by the British government which promised free land to New Englanders who would relocate in Nova Scotia. In 1759, several hundred immigrants founded new towns and gathered churches; the first was at Chester, and in 1761 the church at Liverpool was formed. In 1760, a colony began at Mungerville, New Brunswick; the first church was organized six years later. The first church in Newfoundland dates to 1777. From these and additional congregations a Congregational Union of Nova Scotia and New Brunswick was organized in 1846. In 1801, the British Congregationalists sent a missionary to organize a church in Quebec. That beginning led to the formation of the Congregational Union of Ontario and Quebec, which merged with the older group in 1906. The newly formed Congregational Union of Canada received the Ontario Conference of the American-based United Brethren in Christ (now part of the United Methodist Church) in 1907.

The final partner in the 1925 merger, the General Council of Union Churches of Western Canada, was the child of the early proposed Plan of Union that led to the founding of The United Church of Canada. A draft proposal of a plan of union was issued in 1908. In November of that year, a new congregation appeared in Saskatchewan that accepted as the basis of its local organization the proposed plan. Others soon followed, and the Congregational, Methodist, and Presbyterian judicatories allowed ministers to participate in the ecumenical experiment. In 1912 the several local congregations formed the General Council to handle practical matters and press forward in implementing the Plan of Union.

The merger in 1925 had one major dissenting voice. Approximately 30 percent of the Presbyterians refused to enter the merger, and continued as the Presbyterian Church in Canada. In 1926, a number of the Canadian congregations of the Christian Church (Disciples of Christ) affiliated with the new church. In 1968, the Canadian Conference of the Evangelical United Brethren, following a favorable vote and anticipating the merger of its parent body into the United Methodist Church, became part of The United Church of Canada. In 1943 a two-decade process of negotiation with the Anglican Church of Canada was initiated. It was joined by the Christian Church (Disciples of Christ). The Plan of Union was adopted by the general commission representing the three churches in 1972, but three years later was rejected by the Anglican Church of Canada. The three bodies remain separate entities, though the UCC and the Anglican Church have several joint enterprises.

The union effected in 1925 originated with merger talks between Methodists and Presbyterians in 1899, joined three years later by the Congregationalists. In the proposed Basis of Union, written between 1904 and 1910, a new doctrinal statement was written, based in large part upon the statements of the Presbyterian Church in the U.S.A. (now a part of the Presbyterian Church (U.S.A.) and the Presbyterian Church in England). It assumes a common affirmation of the Protestant Faith and assumes a position between the classical Calvinistic and Arminian positions, leaving considerable latitude for disagreement on issues such as predestination, election, and God's free grace to all persons.

The church is governed by a General Council that meets biennially. The national church is further divided into conferences and presbyteries. Local churches are administered by an official board. The UCC has retained membership in the Alliance of Reformed Churches (Presbyterian and Congregational), the World Methodist Council, the Canadian Council of Churches, and the World Council of Churches.

Membership: In 1994 the United Church of Canada reported 3,960 churches, approximately 2,000,000 members and adherents, and 4,000 ordained clergy.

Educational Facilities: Atlantic School of Theology, Halifax, Nova Scotia, Canada.
Centre for Christian Studies, Toronto, Ontario, Canada.
Emmanuel College, Toronto, Ontario, Canada.
Queen's Theological College, Kingston, Ontario, Canada.
St. Andrew's College, Saskatoon, Saskatchewan, Canada.
United Theological College, Montreal, Quebec, Canada.

Vancouver School of Theology, Vancouver, British Columbia, Canada.

St. Stephen's College, Edmonton, Alberta, Canada.

University of Winnipeg, Winnipeg, Manitoba, Canada.

Huntington University, Sudbury, Ontario, Canada.

Mount Allison University, Sackville, New Brunswick, Canada.

Victoria University, Toronto, Ontario, Canada.

Iona College, Windsor, Ontario, Canada.

Francis Sandy Native Training Centre, Paris, Ontario, Canada.

Dr. Jessie Saulteaux Native Training Centre, Winnipeg, Manitoba, Canada.

Coughlan College, St. John's, Newfoundland, Canada.

Westminster College, London, Ontario, Canada.

St. Paul's United College, Waterloo, Ontario, Canada.

Periodicals: *United Church Observer;* • Mandate Magazine.

Sources:

Grant, John Webster. *The Canadian Experience of Church Union.* Richmond, VA: John Knox Press, 1967.

Silcox, Claris Edwin. *Church Union in Canada.* New York: Institute of Social and Religious Research, 1933.

★380★
United Church of Christ
700 Prospect Ave. E.
Cleveland, OH 44115-1100

The United Church of Christ (UCC) was formed in 1957 by the merger of the Congregational-Christian Churches and the Evangelical and Reformed Church. The two uniting bodies were themselves products of mergers in the early twentieth century, and any account of the modern UCC must begin with a consideration of the four bodies which are now constituent parts of it: The Congregational Churches, the Christian Church, the Reformed Church in the United States, and the Evangelical Synod of North America.

The Congregational Churches. Through the Congregational Churches, the United Church of Christ reaches back to the first decades of the British presence in North America. They were the fourth church to arrive in the colonies (behind the French Reformed Church, Roman Catholic Church, and the Church of England). Coming from England by way of Holland, the Pilgrims first arrived in the Massachusetts Bay Colony in 1620. The Pilgrims were Separatists, Reformed in theology but believing strongly in the autonomous local congregation. The Puritans arrived a decade later, and for the next century they directed the New England settlement. The Puritans were congregationalists in that they placed most of the ecclesiatical power in the hands of the congregation, but also aligned those congregations to the colonial governments. They hoped to create a theocratic system and were intolerant of competing churches and religious groups. The single Pilgrim congregation at Plymouth was tolerated and eventually was absorbed into the larger body of Congregationalists, though the congregation itself eventually was lost to Unitarianism. Congregationalism was the established church of the New England colonies (except Rhode Island) until the Revolution and remained established in Connecticut until 1818 and in Massachusetts until 1833.

The early Congregationalists were committed to education. They established Harvard University (1636) soon after their arrival, and several generations later as they spread through New England, they founded Yale (1701). These were but the first of a system of institutions of higher education that have made the Congregational Church a major intellectual force in American culture. In 1810 Congregationalists founded the American Board of Commissioners for Foreign Missions, which is not only looked upon as the parent of the nineteenth century missionary thrust in American Protestantism, but which succeeded in taking Congregationalism around the world—to the Sandwich Islands (Hawaii), China, India, Africa, and the Middle East.

During the early years of the nineteenth century, Congregationalists, just beginning to slip from their position as the largest church in the new land, led the crusades to build a Christian land. They initiated organizations and took leadership roles in various movements on behalf of the causes of peace, women, children, immigrants, and the poor, as well as the abolition of slavery. They created a number of social service centers, especially in the Northeast, where most of their strength was concentrated.

Through the early nineteenth century, Congregationalists had only formed statewide associations of churches, but the rapid spread of the the church in the nineteenth century brought the call for a national organization. In 1852 a national council met for the first time and was soon meeting regularly every three years. In 1913, at a meeting of the triennial council in Kansas City, a new Congregational "platform" was adopted which included a preamble, a confession of faith, a form of polity, and a stand on wider fellowships.

Congregationalists have been tied together by a series of doctrinal statements beginning with the Cambridge Platform in 1648 which had affirmed the Reformed theological heritage. The Confession of 1913 adopted at Kansas City declared the "steadfast allegiance of the churches composing this council to the faith which our fathers confessed." But at the same time, the statement, as a whole, reflected the nineteenth-century theological trend usually called Modernism. Some Congregational ministers and theological professors had become the major intellectual pioneers of modernist thought, which placed a great emphasis upon individualism and progress, while stressing God's presence in the world over and against his transcendence, Christ's humanity over and against his divinity, and social activism (the social gospel).

In 1931 the National Council of the Congregational Churches united with the Christian Church to form the General Council of Congregational-Christian Churches.

The Christian Church. The Christian Church which was to become part of the United Church of Christ (there were other groups with the same name which stemmed from similar influences) was the product of the revivals of the post-Revolutionary War period and of the new wave of democratic thinking. In 1792 James O'Kelly withdrew from the Methodist Episcopal Church and formed the Republican Methodist Church, rejecting the strict episcopal authority exercised by Bishop Francis Asbury. Methodist bishops have the power to appoint Methodist ministers to their congregations, and O'Kelly continually objected to Asbury's appointments of him. Two years after leaving the Methodists, O'Kelly and his followers also moved against sectarian labels and resolved to be known as "Christians" only. A similar movement arose among Baptists in New England, where Abner Jones had decided that sectarian names and human creeds should be abandoned and that piety alone should be the test of Christian fellowship. He organized such a "Christian" fellowship in 1800 and was soon joined by others.

In 1819 various churches calling themselves "Christian" held a general conference in Portsmouth, New Hampshire. In 1833 a general convention was organized which in effect formed the Christian Church. The following year the church established a Christian Book Association. Concern for education led to the founding of Elon College in North Carolina. From 1854 to 1890, as a result of the forces that led to the Civil War, and occasioned by the adoption of an anti-slavery resolution by the general convention, the southern branch of the church separated itself from the general convention.

The general convention adopted no doctrinal statement but followed the central affirmations of Reformed Protestantism stressing the authority of the Bible and salvation by grace through faith. Considerable variation was allowed on doctrinal matters, even on the sacramants. The Southern branch of the church tended to favor adult believers baptism (reflecting their Baptists heritage).

Reformed Church in the United States. German-speaking adherents of the Reformed Church came into the United States soon after the founding of Pennsylvania. By 1730 there were more than 15,000 people at least nominally members of the Reformed Church in Pennsylvania. By 1800 the number had grown to 40,000. They had come originally at William Penn's invitation, but were spurred by various negative conditions in their homeland.

Soon after their arrival, these German believers took steps to organize churches. Short of ministers, they often appointed the local school teacher to hold services. One such, John Philip Boehm, eventually sought ordination in 1725 and financial support from the Dutch Reformed Church (which had a strong following in New York). That church sent Michael Schlatter to consolidate the scattered congregations into a denominational mold. In 1747 the clergy of these congregations formed the Coetus of the Reformed Ministerium of the Congregations of Pennsylvania. In 1793 the German Reformed Church in Pennsylvania and adjacent states reorganized as a Synod, independent of the Reformed Church in Holland.

In the mid-1880s the German Reformed Church in the U.S. was torn by a major controversy between the Mercersburg and the Old Reformed movements. The former, stimulated by the leadership of John Williamson Nevin (1803-1886), Philip Schaff (1819-1893), and their associates at the Reformed Seminary that had been established at Mercersburg, Pennsylvania, sought to oppose the inroads being made by revivalism (especially that of Charles G. Finney) and sectarianism. The Mercersburg theologians favored an altar-centered liturgy with responses and chants, ritual forms for the traditional church year, read prayers, and more formal garb for the ministers and choirs. They also stressed the authority of the synod over that of regional and congregational powers, and the minister's authority in matters of local church order. The opponents of the Mercersburg perspective stood for pulpit-centered worship, congregational autonomy, and the control of the churches' order of worship in the hands of lay consistories.

The educational emphasis in the church first emerged in the formation of the seminary at Mercersburg (later moved to Lancaster, Pennsylvania) and the formation of a number of colleges—Heidelberg, Catawba, Hood, Franklin and Marshal, Ursinus, and Cedar Crest. Following the movement of German immigration communities, the church spread from Pennsylvania into 21 states and three Canadian provinces.

Mission work began in 1838 with the formation of the Board of Foreign Missions. For 28 years this board united with the American Board of Commissioners of Foreign Missions and then began to send its own missionaries to China, India, Japan and the Middle East.

The Evangelical Synod of North America. In 1817 King Frederick William II (1797-1840) united the congregations in his realm, some of which had Lutheran and some of which had Reformed leanings into a single Evangelical Church, the Church of the Prussian Union. He enforced one form of worship and one church government. Pietism and a more conciliatory spirit were encouraged and a united front against the inroads of rationalism was created through the development of interconfessional Bible, missionary, and tract societies.

One of these societies, the Basel Missionary Society, sent 288 missionaries as pastors for America, beginning in 1833, in response to appeals from German-American immigrants in the Midwest. The first to arrive were Joseph A. Rieger (1811-1869) and George Wendelin Wall (1811-1867). In 1840 a group of German Evangelical ministers in the St. Louis, Missouri area met and formed Der deutsche evangelische Kirchenverein des Westens (the German Evangelical Church Society of the West). In 1866 the word "Kirchenverein" was changed to "Synod." The society/synod made every effort to avoid rigid institutional organization and to eliminate the bureaucratic features usually associated with synodical bodies. Membership was to consist of ordained pastors, lay delegates, and advisory members. No effort was made at this time to enlist individual churches to the society, and it was explicitly stated that "neither the external nor the internal affairs of local congregations could be made the business of the society."

Reflecting their dual Lutheran and Reformed heritage, catechetical instruction in these Evangelical churches typically used one of several catechisms that were being used in Germany, usually uniting elements of Luther's Smaller Catechism with parts of the Heidelberg Catechism of the Reformed Church.

Contemporaneously with the formation of the Synod of the West, two other like synods were being formed. The United Synod of the Northwest served churches in northern Illinois and southern Michigan. The United Synod of the East stretched from New York to Ohio. As early as 1851, union talks were held between the three bodies. In 1872 they merged to form the German Evangelical Synod of North America (dropping the word "German" in 1927).

Like the Reformed Church in the U. S. and the Congregationalist Churches, the Evangelical Synod placed a strong emphasis upon education, particularly demanding an educated ministry. Eden Seminary was begun in 1850 and Elmhurst College in 1872. Parochial schools were attached to most congregations. The synod was also deeply involved in the revival of the deaconess movement in the last half of the nineteenth century. A deaconess hospital in St. Louis in 1853 spurred other healing efforts in the church, and hospitals were established in Cleveland, Ohio; Evansville, Indiana; Detroit, Michigan; and Chicago, Illinois.

No other German church body, save the Moravians, developed as extensive a missionary effort as did the Evangelical Synod. It formed missions to the American Indian and sent foreign missionaries to India and Honduras. Domestic missions included the Seaman's Mission in Baltimore, Maryland; Caroline Mission in St. Louis; Back Bay Mission in Biloxi, Mississippi; and others in the Ozarks and on Madeline Island, Wisconsin.

The talks leading toward the 1934 merger of the Evangelical Synod and the Reformed Church began in 1929. The new Evangelical and Reformed Church (E&R Church) was in place only a short time before talks began with the newly formed General Council of the Congregational-Christian Churches.

The United Church of Christ. As early as 1941 the Committee on Church Relations of the E&R Church held informal conversations with the corresponding committee of the Congregational-Christian Churches. By 1944 a common procedure was agreed upon for dealing with a formal basis of union and a uniting General Synod was planned for 1950. This, however, was postponed for nearly a decade due to legal challenges within the Congregational-Christian Churches. The formal beginning of the United Church of Christ was the Uniting General Synod in Cleveland in June 1957.

The United Church of Christ adopted a constitution in 1961 that provides for a General Synod as its chief policymaking body. The synod is composed of ministerial and lay delegates from the conferences. The delegates elect an executive council which acts between meetings of the synod. Under the General Synod are a variety of boards and agencies, the most important being the Board of Homeland Ministries, the Board of World Ministries, and the Pension Board of the United Church (all of which continue older organizations and are separately incorporated).

The polity of the church included elements of both congregational and presbyterial styles of government. Local churches are guaranteed the right to own their own property, call their own ministers, and withdraw unilaterally from the denomination. But the associations, in which clergy and denominations hold their denominational standing, can withdraw that standing on their own initiative. Conferences, the General Synod, and instrumentalities can advise local churches and individual members, but their statements and decisions are not binding.

Geographically, the church is divided into 38 conferences (with an additional conference serving Hungarian-American congregations), and each conference is further divided into associations, each related to the other and the General Synod in a covenantal fashion. Local churches are governed by local councils or consistories, variously composed of the pastor, a moderator or president, and other officers.

The statement of faith, adopted by the General Synod of the United Church of Christ in 1959, and rephrased in doxalogical form in 1981, is open to a variety of interpretations, but the Reformed theological background of most ministerial leadership is still evident.

The United Church of Christ has a reputation as one of the most socially liberal and active of American church bodies. At the national level, it has identified with numerous concerns related to peace and justice issues. It is also theologically liberal, continuing its modernist heritage, and maintains a wide variety of theological perspectives. It is broadly ecumenical, yet has developed a variety of specific official partnership commitments to the Christian Church (Disciples of Christ); the Evangelical Church Union (East and West Germany), the Pentecostal Church of Chile, the Presbyterian Church, Republic of Korea, and the United Church of Christ (Philippines). The UCC is a member of the National Council of Churches, the World Council of Churches, and the World Alliance of Reformed Churches (Presbyterian and Congregational).

Membership: In 1996 the church reported 1,452,565 members, 6,110 churches, and 10,311 clergy.

Educational Facilities: College and Universities:
Beloit College, Beloit, Wisconsin.
Carleton College, Northfield, Minnesota.
Catawba College, Salisbury, North Carolina.
Cedar Crest College, Allentown, Pennsylvania.
Deaconess College of Nursing, St. Louis, Missouri.
Defiance College, Defiance, Ohio.
Dillard University, New Orleans, Louisiana.
Doane College, Crete, Nebraska.
Drury College, Springfield, Missouri.
Elmhurst College, Elmhurst, Illinois.
Elon College, Elon College, North Carolina.
Fisk University, Nashville, Tennessee.
Franklin and Marshall College, Lancaster, Pennsylvania.
Grinnel College, Grinnell, Iowa.
Heidelberg College, Tiffin, Ohio.
Hood College, Frederick, Maryland.
Hawaii Loa College, Kenehoe, Hawaii.
Huston-Tillotson College, Austin, Texas.
Illinois College, Jacksonville, Illinois.

Lakeland College, Sheboygan, Wisconsin.
Lemoyne-Owen College, Memphis, Tennessee.
Northland College, Ashland, Wisconsin.
Olivet College, Olivet, Michigan.
Pacific University, Forest Grove, Oregon.
Ripon College, Ripon, Wisconsin.
Rocky Mountain College, Billings, Montana.
Talladega College, Talladega, Alabama.
Tougaloo College, Tougaloo, Mississippi.
Ursinus College, Collegeville, Pennsylvania.
Westminister College, Salt Lake City, Utah.
Seminaries:
Andover Newton Theological Seminary, Newton Center, Massachusetts.
Bangor Theological Seminary, Bangor, Maine.
Chicago Theological Seminary, Chicago, Illinois.
Eden Theological Seminary, St. Louis, Missouri.
Hartford Seminary, Hartford, Connecticut.
Harvard University School of Divinity, Cambridge, Massachusetts.
Howard University School of Divinity, Washington, D.C.
Interdenominational Theological Center, Atlanta, Georgia.
Pacific School of Religion, Berkeley, California.
Lancaster Theological Seminary, Lancaster, Pennsylvania.
Seminario Evangelico de Puerto Rico, Hato Rey, Puerto Rico.
United Theological Seminary of the Twin Cities, New Brighton, Minnesota.
Union Theological Seminary, New York, New York.
Vanderbilt University Divinity School, Nashville, Tennessee.
Yale Divinity School, New Haven, Connecticut.

Periodicals: *United Church News.* • *New Conversation.* • *Prism.*

Sources:

Dunn, David, et al. *A History of the Evangelical and Reformed Church.* Philadelphia: Christian Education Press, 1961.

Gunneman, Louis H. *The Shaping of the United Church of Christ.* New York: Thomas Nelson, 1962.

Horton, Douglas. *The United Church of Christ.* New York: Thomas Nelson, 1962.

Starkey, Marion L. *The Congregational Way.* Garden City, NY: Doubleday, 1966.

Section 7
Pietist-Methodist Family

Consult the Contents pages to locate the essay in Part II, Historical Essay Chapters,
that provides an historical discussion of this family

Intrafaith Organizations

★381★
World Methodist Council
Box 518
Lake Junaluska, NC 28745

The United Methodist Council continues the effort to link different facets of the movement that originated in the ministry of John Wesley in the eighteenth century. By the 1880s, that movement had spread around the world through the missionary endeavors of both British and American Methodists and a number of distinct churches had arisen due primarily to differences over issues of church governannce and reace. The initial efforts to develop a worldwide fellowship among churches of the Wesleyan heritage occurred in 1881 in London at the first Ecumenical Methodist Conference. Thirty Methodist bodies were represented by the 400 delegates. Beginning with that initial conference, similar gatherings were held every decade through the middle of the next century. The 1941 Conference was delayed until 1947, due to World War II. Then in 1951, the Conference changed its name to World Methodist Council and made the decision to meet every five years.

Through the years, the emphases of the council has altered as times have changed. Most importantly, former missionary conferences have grown into autonomous churches and a number of Methodist bodies have merged into national United Protestant bodies (United Church of Canada, Church of South India, United Protestant Church of Belgium). Today, the council endeavors to strengthen internatioanl ties, promote understanding, clarify theological and moral standards, and identify priorities for the Methodist movement. It has developed a program which includes support for Methodist education, worldwide evangelism, publishing, and interchange of clergy and laity between churches. The emphasis on evangelism has led to the formation of a World Evangelism Division which calls member churches to train people for indigenous evangelism and develop new resources for Christian mission, the World Methodist Evangelism Institute as joint project with Emory University in Atlanta, Georgia.

The council is guided by and executive committee which meets annually. It plans the international conference which gathers as many as 3,500 people every five years. The most recent gathering was hosed by the Methodist Church of Brazil in Rio de Janerio in 1996. The council also represents the Wesleyan/Methodist tradition at the annual Conference of Secretaries of Christian World Communions. In like measure, it has initiated and responded to overtures for dialogue with sister organizations such as the Lutheran World Federation and the World Alliance of Reformed Churches. since 1967 it has had regular meetings with the International Joint Committee for Dialogue of the Roman Catholic Church.

Membership: The council links Methodist churches in 108 countries with a combined membership of 33 million. Members in North America include African Methodist Episcopal Church, the African Methodist Episcopal Zion Church, the Christian Methodist Episcopal Church, the Free Methodist Church of Canada, the United Church of Canada, the United Methodist Church, and the Wesleyan Church.

Periodicals: *World Parish.* • *Flame.*

Sources:

Burke, Emory Stevens, ed. *The History of American Methodism.* 3 vols. Nashville, TN: Abingdon Press, 1964.

Scandinavian Pietism

★382★
Evangelical Covenant Church
5101 N. Francisco Ave.
Chicago, IL 60625

The Evangelical Covenant Church has its origins in the pietist movement in the State Lutheran Church of Sweden. The movement was often suppressed but periodically reemerged. In the early nineteenth century a new revival was started by several non-Swedish agents. One of these, George Scott from England, was brought to Sweden to minister to English industrial workers in Stockholm and influenced Carl Olof Rosenius, a layman; Andrew Wilberg, a Lutheran priest; and Oscar Ahnfelt, a musician. Rosenius became editor of *Pietisten*, Scotts periodical. Rosenius also began to hold conventicles, meetings similar to the English religious societies of the early eighteenth century, and aided the development of a revived hymnody. Under Roseniuss leadership a national revival swept Sweden.

Members of the revival movement migrated to America in the mid-nineteenth century. At first, the Swedes joined and attempted to stay within the various Lutheran synods, especially the Augustana Synod of Lutherans in the Midwest. After these attempts failed, the Swedes began to organize their own churches. Two synods were formed, the Swedish Lutheran Mission Synod in 1873 and the Swedish Lutheran Ansgarius Synod in 1884. In 1885 the two synods merged to form the Swedish Evangelical Mission Covenant Church of America. In 1937 the "Swedish" was dropped; in 1957 the word "mission" was dropped; and in 1983 the words "of America" were dropped.

According to the preamble of its constitution, "The Covenant Church adheres to the affirmations of the Protestant Reformation regarding the Holy Scriptures, the Old and New Testament, as the Word of God and the only perfect rule for faith, doctrine and conduct." Although officially non-creedal, the constitution states that the church has "traditionally valued the historic confessions of the Christian church, particularly the Apostles Creed," which is recited by every ordinand. An important volume, *Covenant Affirmations*, was published in 1981 as a means of clarifying the theological heritage and convictions of the Covenant Church. The central affirmations are (1) the centrality of the Word of God; (2) the necessity of the new birth; (3) the church as a fellowship of believers;

(4) a conscious dependence on the Holy Spirit; and (5) the reality of freedom in Christ. Although rooted in "classical Christianity" the Covenant Church has resisted the limitations of creedal and confessional stances for the freedom and authority of the Word of God. "Such a confession," says the foreword to the 1988 shorter form of *Covenant Affirmations*, ". . .does not tell us how little Covenanters believe, but how much they believe." The Covenant Church, then, is an "evangelical" church, committed to proclaiming and living the Gospel as revealed in the Holy Scriptures. Its freedom is illustrated in its openness to both infant and believer baptism.

The church is organized on a connectional congregational polity, which means that local churches operate autonomously in most matters and that congregations call their own ministers. The Covenant holds an annual meeting, and a Covenant Ministerium oversees ordination. There are 10 regional conferences. An executive board of 14 members oversees activities during the year. A Council of Administrators includes the heads of the several boards. The Board of Benevolence oversees two hospitals and twelve continuing care retirement campuses. Covenant Press is the publishing arm.

Membership: In 1996 the church reported 93,136 members (91,823 in the United States and 1,313 in Canada), 621 congregations, and 1,631 ministers. Worldwide there are 220,636 members. Foreign missions are conducted in Colombia, Ecuador, Germany, Japan, Laos, Mexico, Russia, Spain, Taiwan, Thailand, and Congo (Zaire).

Educational Facilities: North Park College and Theological Seminary, Chicago, Illinois;

Covenant Bible College, Strathmore, Alberta, Canada.

Periodicals: *Covenant Home Altar.* • *Covenant Companion.* • *Covenant Quarterly.*

Sources:

Bowman, C. V. *The Mission Covenant of America.* Chicago: Covenant Book Concern, 1925.

Covenant Memories. Chicago: Covenant Book Concern, 1935.

Matson, P., E. B. Larsson, and W. D. Thornbloom, eds. *Covenant Frontiers.* Chicago: Board of Mission, Evangelical Mission Covenant Church of America, 1941.

Olsson, Karl A. *A Family of Faith.* Chicago: Covenant Press, 1975.

★383★

Evangelical Free Church of America

1551 E. 66th St.
Minneapolis, MN 55423

The Evangelical Free Church of America was formed in 1950 by the merger of two Scandinavian independent Pietistic associations of churches which had grown out of nineteenth-century revivals: the Swedish Evangelical Free Church and the Norwegian-Danish Evangelical Free Church Association. The Swedish Evangelical Free Church came into existence in 1884. It was composed of congregations that preferred an association of autonomous congregations rather than a typical denominational structure. These congregations had strong feelings about maintaining their own autonomy, and at the same time desired to sponsor missionary ministry overseas through an association of churches rather than the typical synodical structure. This association was established at a meeting in Boone, Iowa in 1884. An independent religious periodical, *Chicago-Bladet*, established by John Martenson, was a catalyst that brought together the 27 representatives at Boone.

The Norwegian-Danish Evangelical Free Church Association was formed by immigrants from Denmark and Norway who had been influenced by the pietistic revivals in their homeland. The ministry of Rev. Fredrick Franson of Bethlehem Church in Oslo led to the formation of the Mission Covenant Church of Norway, to which some of the immigrants had belonged. In 1889 a periodical

Evangelisten, was launched in Chicago; and in 1891 the Western Evangelical Free Church Association was organized. Later that same year an Eastern Association of Churches was formed. A merger of the Eastern and Western groups was made in 1909, with the church taking the name of the Norwegian-Danish Evangelical Free Church Association.

The church formed in 1950, the Evangelical Free Church of America, adopted a Confession of Faith which stresses the essentials of the Reformation tradition, though the definite influence of evangelicalism is evident. The Bible is declared to be "the inspired Word of God, without error in the original writings." The second coming is seen as personal (meaning Jesus will come in person), premillennial (he will come before the millennium to bind Satan, and he will reign for a thousand years with his saints on earth), and imminent. Polity is congregational. There is an annual conference to oversee the cooperative endeavors of the church, including the credentialing of ministers and a ministerial fellowship.

Mission work is carried on in Austria, Belgium, Brazil, Canada (Quebec), France, Germany, Hong Kong, Japan, Malaysia, Mexico, Peru, the Philippines, Singapore, Venezuela, and Zaire. The church has two children's homes in the United States, and six nursing home facilities. Overseas there are two hospitals, a children's home, a seminary, a Bible institute, and other related institutions.

Membership: In 1992 the church reported 117,165 members, 1,103 churches, and 1,800 ministers in the United States; 5,600 members, 113 churches, and 113 ministers in Canada; and an additional 67,000 members in 14 foreign countries.

Educational Facilities: Trinity Evangelical Divinity School, Deerfield, Illinois.

Trinity College, Deerfield, Illinois.

Trinity Western University, Langley, British Columbia, Canada.

Periodicals: *The Evangelical Beacon.*

Sources:

Norton, W. Wilbert, et al. *The Diamond Jubilee Story.* Minneapolis: Free Church Publications, 1959.

Olson, Arnold Theodore. *Believers Only.* Minneapolis: Free Church Publications, 1964.

___. *This We Believe.* Minneapolis: Free Church Press, 1961.

★384★

Moravian Church in America

Northern Province
1021 Center St.
Box 1245
Bethlehem, PA 18016-1245

The Moravian Church in America dates to the arrival of Bishop August Gottlieb Spangenberg in Georgia in 1735. Due to their pacifism and its incompatability with conscription laws, the Moravians chose to leave Georgia. They traveled to Pennsylvania and began work there, centered in the settlements of Nazareth, Bethlehem, and Lititz. Their primary purpose was the evangelization of Native Americans. Efforts were also made unsuccessfully to bring together Germans of different denominations in Pennsylvania. The church spread as other Moravian settlements were established.

In 1753, Spangenberg began work in North Carolina, where Moravians founded the town of Bethabara. In 1771, Moravians founded Salem, now called Winston-Salem. The town is in what is now Forsyth County. Salem became the headquarters for the Southern Province. Beginning in the 1850s, congregations were established in the American Midwest and Canadian West among the German and Scandinavian immigrants. Suburban growth after World War II, and congregation planting among immigrants from the Caribbean have brought new members in recent decades.

Moravians are considered to have missionary zeal. They were among the first of the Protestant churches to realize that world evangelization was central to the life of the Christian church. Moravians concentrated on people neglected by other Christians. They began work among slaves in the West Indies in 1732, and a main motive in coming to America was to preach to the Indians.

In order to make American Moravians self-supporting, a plan by Spangenberg called the "Economy" was established. It amounted to a communal system with Bishop Spangenberg and a board of directors as supervisors. All the church members placed their time, talents, and labor at the church's disposal. In return they were assured of a home, food, and clothing, as well as the fellowship of the church. By this means affluent agricultural and industrial centers were established, missionaries supported, and books printed and circulated. The missionaries itinerated throughout the colonies and abroad. The "Economy" lasted about two decades, although Moravians maintained closed communities in Pennsylvania and North Carolina into the nineteenth century.

Presently, the church in the United States and Canada is organized into two provinces, Northern and Southern. The North is divided into four geographical districts. Each province is governed by a provincial elders' conference, which includes laypersons and clergy. Each local church has a council of elders (who handle spiritual affairs) and trustees (who handle temporal affairs). Ministers are called through the agreement of congregational boards and the provincial governing board. Every seven years there is a meeting of the Unity, that is, the representatives of all 19 provinces worldwide.

Doctrinally the Moravians follow the motto: "In essentials unity; in non-essentials liberty; in all things love." The church holds to the essentials of Protestant doctrine, which they see to include the Bible as the source of Christian doctrine. Central is "heart religion," a relationship with Jesus Christ. The resultant seeming lack of concern for doctrinal precision has freed the denomination from schism through its five centuries of existence.

The Moravians are distinguished by certain practices that reflect Pietist roots. The love feast, a simple shared meal, became an expression of communal oneness. Moravians follow the pattern of the traditional church year and have developed a simplified liturgy. Infant baptism and holy communion (on certain designated feast days) are practiced. While most clergy do not use clerical vestments, a plain white surplice is worn by ministers for communion. The Holy Week services, which include the entire Passion narrative and culminate in the Easter Sunrise Service, are the height of the Christian year. There is considerable diversity in worship. Music, which was an important part of the Pietist renewal, was furthered among the Moravians by Zinzendorf and James Montgomery, both prolific hymn writers, and expressed itself in numerous compositions of sacred and secular music in the eighteenth and nineteenth centuries.

Half of the American Moravians live in Pennsylvania and North Carolina, the other half are scattered around North America in 15 other states and 2 provinces. The mission tradition is reflected in the fact that four-fifths of the world's Moravians are in Africa or the Caribbean Basin. Both provinces have an active church history and archive program, one of the best among American church bodies.

The Moravian Church is a member of both the National Council of Churches and the World Council of Churches. Affiliated provinces in the Caribbean are affiliated with the Caribbean Conference of Churches. Alaskan Moravians participate in new ecumenical work in Siberia.

Membership: In 1996, the church reported 50,500 members in the U.S. and 4,000 in Canada. Worldwide membership was 736,000.

Educational Facilities: Moravian College and Theological Seminary, Bethlehem, Pennsylvania.
Salem Academy and College, Winston-Salem, North Carolina.
Linden Hall School for Girls, Lititz, Pennsylvania.
Moravian Academy, Bethlehem, Pennsylvania.

Periodicals: *The Moravian.*

Sources:

Allen, Walser H. *Who Are the Moravians.* Bethlehem, PA: The Author, 1966.

Groenfeldt, John S. *Becoming a Member of the Moravian Church.* Winston-Salem, NC: Comenius Press, 1954.

Hamilton, J. Taylor, and Kenneth G. Hamilton. *A History of the Moravian Church—The Unitas Fratrum, 1722-1957.* Bethlehem, PA: Interprovincial Board of Christian Education/Moravian Church in America, 1957.

Neisser, George. *A History of the Beginnings of Moravian Work in America.* Translated by William N. Schwarze and Samuel H. Gapp. Bethlehem, PA: Archives of the Moravian Church, 1955.

Schattschneider, Allen W. *Through Five Hundred Years.* Bethlehem, PA: Comenius Press, 1974.

Weinlick, John R. *The Moravian Church through the Ages.* Moravian Church in America, 1988.

★385★
Unity of the Brethren
% Marvin Chlapek
2513 Revere Dr.
Pasadena, TX 77502

While many of the Moravians fled to Saxony, following the persecutions in the eighteenth century, some remained behind in Moravia and Bohemia. In the mid-nineteenth century, some of these Brethren migrated to Texas. There, under the leadership of the Rev. A. Chumsky and H. Juren, they organized the Evangelical Union of Bohemian and Moravian Brethren in North America. A Mutual Aid Society was organized in 1905, as well as the Hus Memorial School, to train church school teachers, in 1914. In 1924 the Hus Memorial Home was founded in Temple, Texas. An independent group, organized by A. Motycha, joined the Evangelical Union in 1919, and the name Evangelical Unity of Bohemian and Moravian Brethren in North America (later shortened to Unity of the Brethren) was adopted.

Doctrinally, the Unity uses the 1608 Moravian Catechism and the Confessions of the Lutheran and Reformed Churches. It emphasizes the Protestant consensus of theological belief. It practices infant baptism and open communion with all Christians; its ministers are seminary trained. Government is presbyterian, with power invested in a biennial synod of ministers and church delegates. The synod meets in July. Ministers are called by the congregations.

Membership: In 1995, the Brethren reported 27 churches, 3,090 members, and 38 ministers.

Periodicals: *Brethren Journal.* Send orders to 5905 Carleen Dr., Austin, TX 78731.

United Methodism

★386★
United Methodist Church
% Council on Ministries
601 W. Riverside Ave.
Dayton, OH 45406

In 1968, with the formation of the United Methodist Church, for the first time in over a century a majority of those Americans in John Wesley's lineage found themselves in one organization. The United Methodist Church is the successor to five of the larger formerly existing bodies in the Wesleyan tradition, namely the Methodist Episcopal Church, Methodist Episcopal Church, South, United Brethren in Christ, Evangelical Association, and Methodist Protestant Church. (Three of these churches merged in 1939; the other two formed one church in 1946; then those new churches formed the United Methodist Church in 1968.)

History. Apart from the Methodist Episcopal Church, those formed earliest were the Church of the United Brethren in Christ and the Evangelical Association. The United Brethren in Christ formed as a result of the work of Philip Otterbein, a German Pietist, with the help of Martin Boehm. Otterbein and Boehm began evangelistic work among the German immigrants in Pennsylvania. The growth of the work led in 1789 to a first meeting of preachers connected with the work. In 1800 these meetings became an annual affair and the ministers agreed that Otterbein and Boehm should superintend the work. They began to use the name United Brethren in Christ. Otterbein had been associated with Francis Asbury and the Methodists, taking part in the ordination of Asbury, the first bishop of the Methodist Episcopal Church.

A second German-speaking group developed through the work of Jacob Albright in Pennsylvania. A movement gathered around his preaching, and in 1803 a conference of those acknowledging Albright as leader was held. This meeting was the beginning of what became the Evangelical Association.

The Evangelical Association suffered a schism in 1894 when the United Evangelical Church was formed. This schism was largely overcome by the 1922 merger that produced the Evangelical Church. In the 1930s, the United Brethren in Christ entered into merger negotiations with the Evangelical Church, and in 1946 a merger was effected which resulted in the formation of the Evangelical United Brethren.

Within the Methodist Episcopal Church agitation on lay rights and the appointment system (by which a bishop assigns a minister to his church) led to widespread protest, particularly in New England and the Western states. Several dissident periodicals were begun, and leaders such as Asa Shinn, Dennis Dorsey, and Nicholas Snethen pressed for reform along more democratic lines. Following the 1828 General Conference, when it became obvious that the church was not going to move in the direction of reform, schism occurred.

Congregations using the name Associated Methodist Churches were formed. These in turn formed the Methodist Protestant Church two years later. A non-Episcopal form of government termed "connectionalism" was worked out. Lay representation at conference (the legislative body) was given. The annual conference assumed the duty of stationing the ministers, a duty formerly left to the bishop.

A second schism of the Methodist Episcopal Church occurred in 1844, when the General Conference voted to divide itself and form two General Conferences of one church. This split, one of the most unusual in church history, was prompted by heated debates about slavery and the power of bishops. The result was two churches, the Methodist Episcopal Church (North) and the Methodist Episcopal Church, South, and a tremendous amount of animosity existed in those areas where both had congregations. A major issue, long blocking reunion, was the denial by many northern Methodists of the legitimacy of the General Conference action and the right of the Methodist Episcopal Church, South to share the tradition. (In general, until 1939 the Methodist Episcopal Church (North) continued to call itself the Methodist Episcopal Church, and that is how it will be referred to throughout this work.)

Continual attempts at reunion of the Methodist Protestant Church and the Methodist Episcopal Churches, North and South, were frustrated until the 1930s. Finally in 1939 a reunion did occur and The Methodist Church (1939-1968) was organized. It was this body that merged with the Evangelical United Brethren in 1968 to form the United Methodist Church.

Since the middle of the nineteenth century, Methodist women have served their congregations as unordained evangelists. When the Methodist Church was established in 1939, it was decided that women could be trained for the ministry and ordained, but that they could not become "members of conference," that is, ministers guaranteed an appointment to a congregation and thereby guaranteed a salary. In 1956 women were given full ministerial status. Ordained women thereafter could be "members of conference" and received annual appointments to churches.

Schism in Methodism has centered around two issues: centralized government and race. The protest of episcopal and clerical authority was the first issue to disturb the harmony of the Methodists. The first protest centered on the Rev. James O'Kelly, a prominent minister, who refused to accept Asbury's appointments. O'Kelly broke away in 1792 and formed the Republican Methodist Church, which eventually became part of the Christian Church. Other schisms, now defunct, based on protest of the centralized authority of the Methodist Episcopal Church, occurred in 1792 in Charleston, South Carolina, where William Hammett led a group in forming the Primitive Methodist Church, (not to be confused with the presently existing church of the same name); in 1814 with the Reformed Methodist Church led by Pliny Brett of Vermont; and in 1820 in New York City where Samuel Stillwell and his nephew William Stillwell formed the Methodist Society.

During the twentieth century, Methodists became affiliated with the ecumenical movement. This movement, in tune with the reunionist tendencies of Methodism otherwise, became the occasion of schisms, protesting the growth of a "super" church or the loss of Methodist distinctives. In 1939, when the non-episcopal Methodist Protestant Church moved into the Methodist Episcopal Church, a number of congregations remained out of the reunion and formed new denominations.

Race has been the second point at issue among American Methodists. The first blacks joined the Methodist Episcopal Church during Wesley's lifetime; Methodism moved freely among blacks in the 1700s and early 1800s. In the decades prior to the Civil War, the church established a slave mission which brought many thousands of black people into the church. The Methodist Episcopal Church became the major tool for the education of blacks and the development of their organizational skills. The church's very success in evangelizing both slaves and free black people prior to the Civil War made it a victim of the same social upheavals which split the nation at various times. It should be noted that racial schisms have affected American religion whenever a large proportion of non-Caucasians have become part of a family group. Methodists join Baptists, Holiness churches, Pentecostals, and Buddhists in racial separations. Some Methodist churches are segregated; some are integrated. The United Methodist Church is integrated.

During the period 1880-1914, Methodism was rent by a number of schisms related to the Holiness Movement, a revivalistic movement centered on Wesley's doctrine of perfection. According to that doctrine, after a person is saved, he or she should go on to be perfected in love and receive the "second blessing," an experience certifying holiness. The growth of the holiness movement and of its child, the Pentecostal movement, resulted in two new family groups: the holiness churches, discussed in chapter seven, and the Pentecostal churches, discussed in chapter eight.

Beliefs. While affirming the central theological propositions of Western Christianity, Methodists have generally placed greater emphasis upon piety and religious experience than doctrine. While accepting the faith as defined in the Twenty-five Articles of Religion sent by John Wesley to the American church, it has done so in a spirit of freedom, accepting no statement of doctrine as final or free from error. Generally, Methodists accept four landmark documents as definitive of the Wesleyan tradition: the Twenty-five Articles, the early minutes of the British Wesleyan Conference, John Wesley's Sermons (in which he outlined his basic doctrinal stance), and Wesley's *Explanatory Notes on the New Testament*. There are two sacraments, baptism (form optional but usually by sprinkling) and holy communion. Communion is open to all Christians, and congregations vary widely on the number of communion services held (some quarterly, some monthly, and a few weekly). To these are added the General Rules of the Methodist Church, an early definition of Methodist practice. During the twentieth century, the Social Creed, first adopted by the Methodist

Episcopal Church, South and quadrennially revised, has become the major statement of Methodist policy in the political, economic, and social arenas.

Organization. The United Methodist Church is governed by the General Conference, a representative body of an equal number of lay and clerical members, which meets quadrennially. This body legislates for the entire church and its decisions are printed in *The Discipline,* the church's rulebook. It assigns tasks to the various boards and agencies and sets policy within which every organization within the church operates. Between meetings, the Council on Ministries guides and coordinates the church nationally and internationally. The United Methodist Publishing House is a major publisher of religious literature through Abingdon Press.

Geographically, the church is divided into a number of annual conferences, each being assigned the task of implementing the church's programs in a particular area through the numerous congregations. The annual conference has the responsibility, through the bishop and the district superintendents, of appointing all ministers to pastor churches or to various special tasks. Ministers join one annual conference and assume a covenant of reciprocal accountability. The annual conferences have broad freedom for developing their own program within the guideline of *The Discipline.* Annual conferences are organized locally along the same pattern of boards and agencies as established by the General Conference.

Within the United States, conferences are divided into five geographical jurisdictions. A jurisdictional conference meets quadrennially following General Conference. It is assigned the major task of electing new bishops for the jurisdiction. (Conferences outside the United States are organized into seven central conferences which meet for the election of bishops.) Following the jurisdictional conference, the bishops collectively assign each to a particular episcopal area, consisting of one or two annual conferences in the jurisdiction.

The work of the United Methodist Church worldwide is delegated to the Board of Global Ministries. Missionary work is carried on in most countries of the world, though there has been an increasing tendency to grant foreign conferences (of which there were 31 as of 1983) an autocephalous status. In those areas, the Board of Global Ministries works cooperatively under the guidance of local leadership in establishing and staffing any work. Also under the Board of Global Ministries is the United Methodist Committee on Relief (UMCOR) which has gained international acclaim for its ability to respond to emergencies and natural disasters with relief assistance.

The United Methodist Church has been a leader in the ecumenical movement. It is a member of both the National Council of Churches and the World Council of Churches. It has signed a corcordat with the Methodist Church in the Caribbean and the Americas (directly represented in the United States by the United Wesleyan Methodist Church of America, a member of the Caribbean Conference of Churches).

Membership: The church reports a membership of 8,495,378. It also has 36,361 churches, and 53,601 ministers.

Educational Facilities: Theological seminaries:
Boston School of Theology, Boston, Massachusetts.
Candler School of Theology, Atlanta, Georgia.
Drew University, the Theological School, Madison, New Jersey.
Duke University, the Divinity School, Durham, North Carolina.
Gammon Theological Seminary, Atlanta, Georgia.
Garrett Evangelical Theological Seminary, Evanston, Illinois.
Iliff School of Theology, Denver, Colorado.
The Methodist Theological School of Ohio, Delaware, Ohio.
Perkins School of Theology, Dallas, Texas.
Saint Paul School of Theology, Kansas City, Missouri.
School of Theology at Claremont, Claremont, California.

United Theological Seminary, Dayton, Ohio.
Wesley Theological Seminary, Washington, D.C. (Gammon Theological Seminary participates with three other schools in the Interdenominational Theological Center, the largest facility for training black ministers in the United States.)
Predominantly black colleges:
Bennett College, Greensboro, North Carolina.
Bethune-Cookman College, Daytona Beach, Florida.
Claflin College, Orangeburg, South Carolina.
Clark College, Atlanta, Georgia.
Dillard University, New Orleans, Louisiana.
Huston-Tillotson College, Austin, Texas.
Meharry Medical College, Austin, Texas.
Morristown College, Morristown, Tennessee.
Paine College, Augusta, Georgia.
Philander Smith College, Little Rock, Arkansas.
Rust College, Holly Springs, Mississippi.
Wiley College, Marshall, Texas.
Colleges and Universities:
Adrian College, Adrian, Michigan.
Alaska Pacific University, Anchorage, Alaska.
Albion College, Albion, Michigan (no longer affiliated).
Albright College, Reading, Pennsylvania.
Allegheny College, Meadville, Pennsylvania.
American University, Washington, D.C.
Baker University, Baldwin City, Kansas.
Birmingham-Southern College, Birmingham, Alabama.
Boston University, Boston, Massachusetts.
Centenary College, Hackettstown, New Jersey.
Centenary College of Louisiana, Shreveport, Louisiana.
Central Methodist College, Fayette, Missouri.
Columbia College, Columbia, South Carolina.
Cornell College, Mount Vernon, Iowa.
Dakota Wesleyan University, Mitchell, South Dakota.
DePauw University, Greencastle, Indiana.
Dickinson College, Carlisle, Pennsylvania.
Drew University, Madison, New Jersey.
Duke University, Durham, North Carolina.
Emory and Henry College, Emory, Virginia.
Emory University, Atlanta, Georgia.
Ferrum College, Ferrum, Virginia.
Florida Southern College, Lakeland, Florida.
Greensboro College, Greensboro, North Carolina.
Hamline University, St. Paul, Minnesota.
Hawaii Loa College, Kaneohe, Hawaii.
Hendrix College, Conway, Arkansas.
High Point College, High Point, North Carolina.
Huntington College, Montgomery, Alabama.
Illinois Wesleyan University, Bloomington, Indiana.
Iowa Wesleyan College, Mount Pleasant, Iowa.
Kansas Wesleyan, Salina, Kansas.
Kendall College, Evanston, Illinois.
Kentucky Wesleyan College, Owensboro, Kentucky.
LaGrande College, LaGrande, Georgia.
Lambuth College, Jackson, Tennessee.
Lebanon Valley College, Annville, Pennsylvania.
Lycoming College, Williamsport, Pennsylvania.
MacMurray College, Jacksonville, Illinois.
McKendree College, Lebanon, Illinois.
McMurry College, Abilene, Texas.
Methodist College, Fayetteville, North Carolina.
Millsaps College, Jackson, Mississippi.
Morningside College, Sioux City, Iowa.
Mount Union College, Alliance, Ohio.
Nebraska Wesleyan University, Lincoln, Nebraska.
North Carolina Wesleyan College, Rocky Mount, North Carolina.
North Central College, Naperville, Illinois.
Ohio Northern University, Ada, Ohio.

Ohio Wesleyan University, Delaware, Ohio.

Oklahoma City University, Oklahoma City, Oklahoma.

Otterbein College, Westerville, Ohio.

Pfeiffer College, Misenheimer, North Carolina.

Randolph-Macon College, Ashland, Virginia.

Randolph-Macon Women's College, Lynchburg, Virginia.

Rocky Mountain College, Billings, Montana.

Shenandoah College and Conservatory of Music. Winchester, Virginia.

Simpson College, Indianola, Iowa.

Southern Methodist University, Dallas, Texas.

Southwestern College, Winfield, Kansas.

Southwestern University, Georgetown, Texas.

Syracuse University, Syracuse, New York.

Tennessee Wesleyan College, Athens, Tennessee.

Texas Wesleyan College, Fort Worth, Texas.

Union College, Barbourville, Kentucky.

University of Denver, Denver, Colorado.

University of Evansville, Evansville, Indiana.

University of Puget Sound, Tacoma, Washington.

University of the Pacific, Stockton, California.

Virginia Wesleyan College, Norfolk, Virginia.

Wesley College, Dover, Delaware.

Wesleyan College, Macon, Georgia.

Westmar College, Le Mars, Iowa.

Westminister College, Salt Lake City, Utah.

West Virginia Wesleyan College, Buckhannon, West Virginia.

Willamette University, Salem, Oregon.

Wofford College, Spartansburg, South Carolina.

Periodicals: *The Circuit Rider.* Available from United Methodist Publishing House, Box 801, Nashville, TN 37202.

Sources:

Harmon, Nolan B. *Understanding the United Methodist Church.* Nashville: Abingdon, 1977.

Sano, Roy I. *From Every Nation without Number.* Nashville: Abingdon, 1982.

The Structure of the United Methodist Church. Evanston, IL: United Methodist Communications, 1983.

Tuell, Jack M. *The Organization of the United Methodist Church.* Nashville: Abingdon, 1977.

Non-Episcopal Methodism

★387★

Apostolic Methodist Church
Current address not obtained for this edition.

The Apostolic Methodist Church was organized in 1932 in Loughman, Florida, by E. H. Crowson and a few others. In 1931, the Reverend Crowson, an elder in the Florida Conference of the Methodist Episcopal Church, South, had been located (deposed from the itinerant ministry) for "unacceptability." The new group published a *Discipline* in which they complained about episcopal authority and the departure of the Methodist Episcopal Church, South, from its standards of belief and holiness. The Apostolic Methodists believe in the premillennial return of Jesus, his return to earth to bind Satan before his one-thousand-year reign on earth with his saints. The church emphasizes holiness of a "second blessing" type: after being justified or saved, a person can proceed to be perfected in love and have that ratified by a personal religious experience called the "second blessing." In 1933 F. L. Crowson, the father of E. H. Crowson, was tried by the Florida Conference and suspended. He withdrew and joined his son's new group.

The church operates the Gospel Tract Club at Zephyr Hills, Florida.

Membership: At its peak in the 1960s, the church had only a few congregations and less than 100 members.

★388★

Asbury Bible Churches
℅ Rev. Jack Tondee
Box 1021
Dublin, GA 31021

The Asbury Bible Church parallels the John Wesley Fellowship in most ways, but is organizationally separate. Like the John Wesley Fellowship, the Asbury Bible Churches were organized in 1971 by former members of the Southern Methodist Church who withdrew when that church dropped its membership in the American Council of Christian Churches. They follow the same conservative interpretation of Wesleyan doctrine and loose congregational polity and draw on the Francis Asbury Society of Ministers for their pastors. The churches are also members of the American Council of Christian Churches.

Membership: Not reported.

★389★

Association of Independent Methodists (AIM)
Box 4274
Jackson, MS 39216

The Association of Independent Methodists (AIM) was organized in 1965 in Jackson, Mississippi, by former members of the Methodist Church (1939-1968) which, in 1968, merged into the United Methodist Church. The organization rejected the Methodist Church's episcopal polity, the doctrinal liberalism felt to exist in the ecumenical movement of which the Methodist Church was a major supporter, and the neo-evangelicalism in the Sunday school literature, clergy, and church supported colleges and seminaries.

Doctrinally, the church accepts the Twenty-five Articles of Religion of John Wesley common to all Methodists. However, a statement on sanctification and additional articles on the duties of the Christian to the civil authority and the separation of church and state have been added.

Polity is congregational. At each annual meeting, delegates from member churches elect the association's officers including a president, vice-president, secretary, treasurer, and executive director. They serve with standing committee chairs as an executive committee. The executive committee and representatives from each church constitute a board of directors which meets semi-annually.

The church supports Methodist Missions International (MMI). MMI produces the radio broadcasts for the Methodist Bible Hour. The weekly radio broadcasts are heard on six radio stations throughout the Caribbean and Central and South America. Free Bibles and Bible correspondence courses are offered to the listeners of these radio programs.

Membership: In 1995, the association reported more than 3,500 members in 40 congregations with 51 ministers licensed or ordained by the association. Congregations are located in Mississippi, Alabama, Florida, Georgia, Tennessee, Texas, Ohio, and Virginia.

Educational Facilities: Wesley Biblical Seminary, Jackson, Mississippi.

Periodicals: *The Independent Methodist Bulletin.*

Remarks: AIM was established in 1965 as the Methodist Church was beginning the process of eliminating the racially segregated Central Jurisdiction, and as the South was experiencing the height of the civil rights movement. In the original articles of religion of AIM an article was added supporting the social separation of the races as "neither anti-Christian nor discriminatory." More recently, that article has been deleted.

Sources:

Constitution of Churches Organized as Independent Methodist Churches by the Association of Independent Methodists. Jackson, MS: Association of Independent Methodists, n.d.

Howard, Ivan J. *What Independent Methodists Believe.* Jackson, MS: Association of Independent Methodists, n.d.

★390★
Church of Daniel's Band
% Rev. Wesley James Haggard, President
Croll Rd.
Beaverton, MI 48612

The Church of Daniel's Band was formed in 1893 at Marine City, Michigan, as an effort to revive primitive Methodism and continue the class meeting, the regular meeting of small classes for discussion, exhortation, Bible study, prayer, confession, and forgiveness. The doctrine and polity are Methodist with a strong emphasis on evangelism, perfectionism, Christian fellowship, religious liberty, and abstinence from worldly excess. Several articles of faith have been added to the standard twenty-five emphasizing belief in the resurrection and judgment of the dead, divine healing, and the laying on of hands for the gift of the Holy Spirit.

Membership: In 1988 there were four churches, approximately 217 members, and eight ministers.

Sources:

The Doctrine and Discipline of the Church of Daniel's Band. N.p. 1981.

★391★
Congregational Methodist Church
Box 9
Florence, MS 39073

The Congregational Methodist Church was formed by a group of lay people led by local preachers who withdrew from the Georgia Conference of the Methodist Episcopal Church, South. The group met in the home of Mickleberry Merrit on May 8, 1852, and organized. William Farbough was elected chairman, and Rev. Hiram Pinazee was appointed to draw up a *Discipline*, which was approved and published soon afterward. This newly organized group had three main points of contention with the Methodist Episcopal Church, South: the itinerant system, as then practiced, which was plagued with large circuits and weekday preaching to empty pews; the church's neglect of the local preachers who did most of the work with the congregations and received no credit; and the government of the Methodist Episcopal Church, South, which deprived laymen a voice in church business.

On August 12, 1852, a conference was convened. Except for local church conferences, this conference was the first Methodist conference composed of more laymen than ministers, and the first body of Methodists whose total representation was by election of the local congregations. This difference in government remains one of the distinctive features of the Congregational Methodist Church. Local churches call their own pastors, own their own property, elect delegates each year to the annual conferences, and every two years to the general conference.

The Congregational Methodist Church is conservative in its theology, maintaining the doctrines as espoused by John Wesley. Its Articles of Religion are those Wesley presented for his Methodist Church in America. It was not until 1941—and for the purpose of emphasis and clarification, and to show its conservative stance amid the growing trend of liberalism—that articles on regeneration and sanctification were added. In 1957, articles on tithing, eternal retribution, and the resurrection of the dead were added for the same reasons. Congregational Methodists believe in a literal "heaven" and "hell" and in the premillennial second coming of Christ.

Several schisms have occurred within the church. In the late 1880s, when it was estimated that the church had grown to nearly 20,000 members, a move for a merger with other similar church groups resulted in the loss of an estimated two-thirds of the churches. While most of these churches merged with other groups, some of the churches formed the New Congregational Methodist Church of the U.S.A. In 1982 a group of churches withdrew, opposing the realignment of conferences, and formed the Southern Congregational Methodist Church. Some of the those churches have since returned to the Congregational Methodist Church.

In 1945 a Bible School was begun in Dallas, Texas, and eight years later moved to the campus of the old Westminster College at Tehuacana, Texas, and renamed Westminster College and Bible Institute. In 1972 it was moved to Florence, Mississippi, the headquarters of the denomination, and renamed Wesley College in honor of Methodisms founder. Wesley College is accredited as a four-year college offering both a two-year transferable general education certificate and a bachelors degree for those preparing for the ministry.

The Congregational Methodist Church has a missions program with missionaries in Mexico and among Native Americans. It also sponsors missionaries in Central America, South America, and Africa in cooperation with World Gospel Mission.

Membership: In 1995 the church reported 8,544 members served by 317 clergy.

Educational Facilities: Wesley College, Florence, Mississippi.

Periodicals: *Congregational Methodist Messenger.* • *The Harvester.* • *Up-Date of Wesley.*

Sources:

McDaniel, S. C. *The Origin and Early History of the Congregational Methodist Church.* Atlanta: Jas. P. Harrison, 1881.

Minutes of the General Conference of the Congregational Methodist Church, 1869-1945. Tehuacana, TX: Westminister College Print Shop, 1960.

★392★
Cumberland Methodist Church
(Defunct)

The Cumberland Methodist Church withdrew from the Congregational Methodist Church in 1950 because of a disagreement on both polity and doctrine. It was organized at Laager, Grundy County, Tennessee, in the mountainous country near Chattanooga. Membership never reached beyond the several counties in southeastern Tennessee. Since its founder's death, no trace of the existence of the Cumberland Methodist Church has been found.

★393★
Evangelical Methodist Church
68385 Gray Rd.
Indianapolis, IN 46237

The Evangelical Methodist Church was founded by former members of the Methodist Church led by Dr. J. H. Hamblen of Abilene, Texas. In 1945, Dr. Hamblen began serving an independent congregation in Abilene. Calls from other congregations led to the founding of the Evangelical Methodist Church at a Memphis, Tennessee, conference on May 9, 1946. The main cause of dissatisfaction was the "modernism" that had infiltrated the parent body.

At the first Annual Conference at Kansas City, Missouri, in 1946, Dr. Hamblen was elected the first general superintendent. E. B. Vargas brought the Mexican Evangelistic Mission into the new church as the first mission district. In subsequent sessions Lucian Smith and Ralph Vanderwood were elected to the office of general superintendent.

The church holds a conservative theological perspective and believes very strongly the Articles of Religion of the former Methodist Episcopal Church, South, to which it has added an article on "perfect love." In describing themselves, members say, "The Church is fundamental in belief, premillennial regarding the second coming, missionary in outlook, evangelistic in endeavor, cooperative in spirit, and Wesleyan in doctrine."

Organizationally the Church is congregational yet connectional. It is congregational in that each congregation owns its own property and calls its own pastor. It is connectional in that all member churches agree to abide by the *Discipline* of the Evangelical Methodist Church. The denomination, as a whole, is governed by the conference system. The General Conference, presided over by the General Superintendents, is the highest legislative body in the church. It meets every four years and oversees the several district conferences, and the local churches.

In cooperation with the World Gospel Mission and the OMS International, the church has sent more than sixty-five missionaries. The church is also affiliated with both the National Association of Evangelicals and the Christian Holiness Partnership.

Membership: Not reported. In 1997 the church had 8,700 members and 119 churches.

Educational Facilities: Approved schools include: Vennard College, University Park, Iowa.
John Wesley College, High Point, North Carolina.
Western Evangelical Seminary, Portland, Oregon.
Asbury College, Wilmore, Kentucky;
Asbury Theological Seminary, Wilmore, Kentucky;
Wesley Biblical Seminary, Jackson, Mississippi.

Periodicals: *Evangelical Methodist Bulletin.*

★394★
Evangelical Methodist Church of America
Box 751
Kingsport, TN 37662

Largest of several fellowships of independent fundamentalist Methodist churches, the Evangelical Methodist Church of America was established in 1952 by dissenting members of the Evangelical Methodist Church. The issues that led to withdrawal centered around a longstanding doctrinal and organizational disagreement between Dr. J. H. Hamblen and Rev. W. W. Breckbill (d. 1974). Reverend Breckbill and his followers did not accept the doctrine of holiness proposed by Dr. Hamblen. There was also conflict over membership in the National Association of Evangelicals.

The withdrawing body, led by Breckbill, established an organization similar to that of the parent body. Membership was established in the fundamentalist American Council of Christian Churches and International Council of Christian Churches, and close working relations were set up with the Southern Methodist Church, the Fundamental Methodist Church, and the Methodist Protestant Church which jointly sponsored Bible Methodist Missions and the International Fellowship of Bible Methodists. Following the withdrawal of the Southern Methodist Church from the American Council of Christian Churches, the Evangelical Methodist Church still has a close working relationship with other separated groups. These are primarily members of the American Council of Christian Churches and the World Council of Bible Believing Churches.

Missions are conducted in Malawi, Argentina, Chile, Jamaica, and Paraguay.

Membership: Not reported.

Educational Facilities: Breckbill Bible College, Maxmeadows, Virginia.

Periodicals: *The Evangelical Methodist.*

Sources:

Discipline. Altoona, PA: Evangelical Methodist Church, 1962.

★395★
Fellowship of Fundamental Bible Churches
Box 43
Glassboro, NJ 08028

The Fellowship of Fundamental Bible Churches, was founded in 1939 by former members and ministers of the Methodist Protestant Church. As the merger between the Methodist Episcopal Church, the Methodist Episcopal Church, South, and the Methodist Protestant Church approached, some 50 delegates and pastors (approximately one-third of the Eastern Conference) withdrew in protest of the union and what they considered the liberal tendencies of those churches. The congregations represented by those delegates reorganized and continued a separate existence as the Bible Protestant Church. In 1985 the group changed its name to the Fellowship of Fundamental Protestant Churches, a signal of the Fundamentalist theological position they had adopted. Congregations are found in New Jersey, Pennsylvania, New York, Virginia, and Michigan.

As Fundamentalists, the fellowship affirms the infallibility, inerrancy, and literal interpretation of the Bible. It holds to a premillennial theology and a pre-tribulation view of the rapture of the saints. It believes in separation from apostasy and unbelief. The churches hold to two ordinances: baptism by immersion and the Lord's Supper. The fellowship is organized congregationally. It owns and operates Tri-State Bible Camp and Conference Center in Montegue, New Jersey, and oversees a mission board, the Fundamental Bible Missions.

The fellowship is a member of the American Council of Christian Churches.

Membership: In 1998 there were 21 churches, 43 ministers, and 1,500 members.

Educational Facilities: Fundamental Bible Institute. Glassboro, NJ.

Periodicals: *The Messenger.*

★396★
Filipino Community Churches
Current address not obtained for this edition.

The Filipino Community Churches of Hawaii began when the Rev. N. C. Dizon, a Methodist minister, went to Hawaii after World War I to establish a mission. In 1927 he withdrew from the Methodist church and formed the First Filipino Community Church at Honolulu. In 1957 a congregation was added at Wahiawa, and a congregation in Hilo is informally associated. Joseph H. Dizon became pastor of the headquarters church in Honolulu. Its membership consists almost entirely of Filipino-Americans.

Membership: Not reported.

★397★
First Congregational Methodist Church of the U.S.A.
Current address not obtained for this edition.

The First Congregational Methodist Church of the U.S.A. was formed by members of the Congregational Methodist Church who withdrew from that body in 1941. Disagreement had arisen about the addition in 1933 of Articles of Religion on regeneration and sanctification and paragraphs on the duty of pastors' collecting superannuate funds (for retired ministers), ladies' work, youth work, trials of ministers charged with misconduct, and the prohibition of special sessions of the general conference called to reverse action of a regular session. Following eight years of conflict, Rev. J. A. Cook, then president of the General Conference, led a segment of the church to withdraw immediately after the 1941 General Conference, at which a two-thirds majority approved adding the articles and paragraphs in dispute.

The new body adopted the pre-1933 *Discipline* and followed essentially the polity and doctrine of the parent body.

Membership: Not reported. In 1954 the church had 7,500 members in 100 congregations, all in the South.

★398★
Fundamental Methodist Church
1034 N. Broadway
Springfield, MO 65802

The Fundamental Methodist Church was formed by former members of the Methodist Protestant Church who withdrew from the Methodist Church (1939-1968) following the union in 1939. The schism began with John's Chapel Church in Missouri on August 27, 1942, under the leadership of Rev. Roy Keith. Two years later, after having been joined by other congregations, they established an organization.

The church is both congregational and connectional in polity. It is congregational in that the local congregations associate with each other as free and autonomous bodies, and retain the power to hold property and call (appoint) pastors. They are connectional in that their General Conference is the highest legislative body in the church. It is composed of one lay delegate and one minister from each church.

The Fundamental Methodists are fundamentalists theologically. They are members of the American Council of Christian Churches, Bible Methodist Missions, and the International Fellowship of Bible Methodists. They cooperate with other independent fundamentalist Methodist groups in a variety of activities. They are also one of the few Methodist groups to retain the class meeting structure devised by John Wesley, the founder of Methodism. He divided the early societies (congregations) into classes of about 12 members and a class leader. The classes met weekly for mutual discussion, exhortation, prayer, confession and forgiveness, Bible study, and growing in grace. Each person tried to bring to the class a penny a week to help the poor. It is said that some early class leaders supplied the penny for the class member who could not afford to make the contribution.

Membership: Not reported. In 1993 there were 12 churches, 22 ministers, and 682 members. The church supports a mission in Matamoros, Mexico.

Periodicals: *The Evangelical Methodist.*

Sources:

Keith, Roy, and Carol Willoughby, eds. *History and Discipline of the Faith and Practice.* Springfield, MO: Fundamental Methodist Church, 1964.

★399★
John Wesley Fellowship and the Francis Asbury Society of Ministers
Current address not obtained for this edition.

The John Wesley Fellowship and the Francis Asbury Society of Ministers are two structures formed by former ministers and members of the Southern Methodist Church in 1971 following the Southern Methodist Church's withdrawal from the ultra-fundamentalist American Council of Christian Churches. The John Wesley Fellowship is a loose fellowship of independent congregations, and the Francis Asbury Society of Ministers is an association of pastors. While officially two separate organizations, ministers of the Society serve churches of the Fellowship.

The Society has added to the twenty-five Articles of Religion (printed earlier in this chapter) statements on the Bible as the Word of God (an affirmation not specifically made in the original article on the sufficiency of Scripture), separation from apostasy, and the premillennial return of Jesus. *The Guidelines for Independent Methodist Churches*, published by Rev. Thomas L. Baird, serves unoffically as a discipline for the congregations. Beyond the Articles of Religion are seventeen statements which make a significant departure from Wesleyan emphases. The statement on the church defines the invisible church as all who are known of Christ,

"Whether they have joined the visible church or not." The premillennial return of Christ, segregation of the races, and the impossibility of back sliders to be reclaimed (based on Hebrew 6:4-6) are all affirmed. The church has only white members.

The Francis Asbury Society began publication of the *Francis Asbury Society Evangel* in 1971. Both the Society and Fellowship cooperate with Bible Methodist Missions organized by the Evangelical Methodist Church of America. Maranath School of Theology, also sponsored by the Evangelical Methodist Church of America, and Bob Jones University are recommended schools. The Society and Fellowship belong to the American Council of Christian Churches.

Membership: Not reported.

Periodicals: *Francis Asbury Society Bulletin.*

Sources:

Baird, Thomas L., ed. *Guidelines for Independent Methodist Churches.* Colonial Heights, VA: The Author, 1971.

★400★
Methodist Protestant Church
% Rev. F. E. Sellers
Monticello, MS 39654

The continuing Methodist Protestant Church was formed by ministers and members of the Mississippi Conference of the former Methodist Protestant Church who did not wish to join in the 1939 Methodist merger because of the liberalism of the newly formed church, The Methodist Church (1939-1968). They emphasize the Bible as the literal word of God, the indwelling of the Holy Spirit subsequent to regeneration (subsequent to being "born again"), and the premillennial return of Jesus Christ. All members of the church are white and believe that racial segregation best serves the interest of both blacks and whites. The church's motto is, "Earnestly contend for the faith which was once delivered to the saints."

The church has congregations in Mississippi, Alabama, Missouri, Louisiana, and Ohio, in three conferences. Mission work has been established in Korea and in two locations in British Honduras. A church camp is located at Collins, Mississippi. The Church is a member of the American Council of Christian Churches and the International Council of Christian Churches. It is not a member but cooperates with the Christian Holiness Association.

The government is a representative democracy modeled on the United States government. Equal representation is given laymen in all functions of the church. There are no bishops.

Membership: Not reported.

Educational Facilities: Whitworth College, Brookhaven, Mississippi.

★401★
New Congregational Methodist Church
% Bishop Joe E. Kelley
354 E. 9th St.
Jacksonville, FL 32206

Not a direct schism but related to the Congregational Methodist Church is the New Congregational Methodist Church. It was formed in 1881 by members of the Waresboro Mission and others involved in a rural church consolidation enforced by the Board of Domestic Missions of the Georgia Conference of the Methodist Episcopal Church, South. In protest of the consolidation, the group withdrew and formed the new body at Waycross, Georgia, using the constitution of the Congregational Methodist Church as a model. They adopted a loosely connectional system, rejecting particularly the system of annual conference assessments. They also baptized by immersion and allowed foot washing at communion.

An early period of growth was stopped by the death of several leaders and the withdrawal of a number of congregations who joined the Congregational Methodist Church. They have no connections with any ecumenical bodies.

Membership: Not reported. In 1967 there were 13 congregations (7 in Georgia and 6 in Florida).

★402★
People's Methodist Church
Current address not obtained for this edition.

The People's Methodist Church was formed in North Carolina by members of the Methodist Episcopal Church, South, who did not wish to join the Methodist merger of 1939. (That merger united the Methodist Episcopal Church, South, with the Methodist Episcopal Church and the Protestant Methodist Church.) The People's Methodist Church is conservative and stresses "the second blessing," an experience ratifying one's perfection in holiness.

Membership: Not reported.

Educational Facilities: John Wesley Bible School, Greensboro, North Carolina.

★403★
Reformed New Congregational Church
(Defunct)

The Reformed New Congregational Methodist Church was organized in 1916 by the Rev. J. A. Sander and the Rev. Earl Wilcoxen, a minister in the Congregational Methodist Church. A large following was built in southern Illinois and Indiana; however, no data has been located since 1936 when there were eight churches.

★404★
Southern Congregational Methodist Church
Current address not obtained for this edition.

The Southern Congregational Methodist Church was founded in 1982 by a group of churches opposed to the new alignment of conferences that had been undertaken by the Congregational Methodist Church.

Membership: Not reported.

★405★
Southern Methodist Church
% Richard G. Blank
PO Drawer A
Orangeburg, SC 29116-0039

The Southern Methodist Church was formed in 1940 by members of several congregations of the Methodist Episcopal Church, South, who did not wish to participate in the 1939 merger with the Methodist Episcopal Church. They felt that the Methodist Episcopal Church was apostate and full of heresy and infidelity and also that merger, forming The Methodist Church (1939-1968), would eventuate in a powerful centralized ecclesiastical control.

The withdrawing members, meeting in convocation at Columbia, South Carolina, set up plans to perpetuate what they considered to be the Methodist Episcopal Church, South. In attempting to retain local church property and the name "Methodist Episcopal Church, South," the group became the center of a series of landmark court decisions culminating in the mandate of Judge George Bell Timmerman on March 12, 1945. The group lost its case to the merged church, The Methodist Church. The bishops of The Methodist Church were legally established as representatives of the membership of the former Methodist Episcopal Church, South with control over property; and the name "Methodist Episcopal Church, South," was the property of its legal successor, The Methodist Church (now the United Methodist Church). The name Southern Methodist Church was then adopted by the withdrawing group.

The church adopted the Methodist Episcopal Articles of Religion printed earlier in this chapter. The church added statements

of belief on prevenient grace (grace is shed abroad in the hearts of all), the witness of the Spirit, Christian perfection, and the evangelization of the world. It has also added statements on the creation account of Genesis, premillennialism, and Satan.

Departing from its episcopal heritage, the new body is congregational in polity. It has four annual conferences and a general conference, but it has dropped the office of district superintendent and replaced the bishop with a quadrennially elected president.

The Southern Methodist Church was a member of both the American Council of Christian Churches and International Council of Christian Churches but withdrew in 1971. Missions are supported in Cameroon, Cyprus, Ethopia, Italy, Mexico, Peru, Venezuela, and Zimbabwe.

Membership: In 1997, the church reported 127 congregations in four conferences covering territory from Maryland to Florida to Texas. There were 7,976 members and 180 ministers.

Educational Facilities: Southern Methodist Bible College, Orangeburg, South Carolina.

Periodicals: *The Southern Methodist.* Send orders to Foundry Press, Orangeburg, SC 29115.

Sources:

Ballard, Jerry. *To the Regions Beyond.* Orangeburg, SC: Board of Foreign Missions, Southern Methodist Church, 1970.

The Doctrines and Discipline of the Southern Methodist Church. Orangeburg, SC: Foundry Press, 1970.

Black Methodism

★406★
African Methodist Episcopal Church
500 8th Ave. S
Nashville, TN 37203

A short time after the founding of the Methodist Episcopal Church in 1784, friction developed between the blacks and the whites of St. George's Church in Philadelphia. The situation was intensified by the erection of a gallery to which the blacks were relegated. The long-standing grievances came to a head on a Sunday morning in November 1787, when whites tried to pull several blacks from their knees at the altar rail. Richard Allen led the group of blacks out of the church, and they formed a church of their own.

Allen was a former slave whose master had been converted by Freeborn Garrettson (a Methodist preacher). His master allowed Allen to buy his freedom. As a freeman he became a prosperous businessman and a licensed Methodist preacher. After leaving St. George's, Allen purchased an abandoned blacksmith shop, and in 1744 Methodist Bishop Francis Asbury dedicated it as Bethel Church. In 1799 Allen was ordained a deacon, the first black so honored.

Differences continued between the leaders of Allen's Bethel Church and St. George's. The former wished to be independent but with a nominal relation to the Methodists. Finally, in 1816, the issues were settled in a court suit when Bethel was granted full independence.

In Baltimore, blacks at the two white churches formed an independent Colored Methodist Society after they had been put in galleries and not allowed to take communion until after the whites. In 1801 Daniel Coke arrived in Baltimore and took over the leadership of the Society. Through his work an independent Methodist Church, also named Bethel, was formed. A call was issued in 1816 for a national meeting of black Methodists for the purpose of forming an African Methodist Episcopal (AME) Church. The *Discipline*, Articles of Religion, and General Rules of the Methodist Episcopal Church were adopted, and Richard Allen was elected bishop. The AME Church remains close in doctrine, practice and polity to the United Methodist Church, the successor to the Methodist Episcopal Church, with whom it has engaged in some serious merger conversations.

Growth in the church throughout the North and Midwest was steady through 1865. After the Civil War a rapid expansion throughout the South occurred, and conferences were established across the territory of the former confederacy.

A missionary imperative was an early part of African Methodist concern, and in 1827 Scipio Bean was ordained as an elder and sent to Haiti. From that small beginning (and slow growth due to lack of funds), a twentieth-century mission program has emerged with stations in Africa, South America, and the West Indies. The primary work is with other people of African descent.

Publishing was seen as an integral part of the evangelistic, missionary and cultural life of the church from the beginning, and the items published by this church have had a major impact on the black community. The AME Book Concern was the first publishing house owned and operated by black people in America. *The Christian Recorder*, a newspaper begun as *The Christian Herald*, published continuously since 1841, is the oldest black periodical in the world; *The AME Review*, started in 1883, is the oldest magazine published by black people in the world. Education joined publishing as an early concern, and the first AME affiliated college, Wilberforce University, was established in 1856. Educational concerns have been carried to the mission field as well, and the church has established a number of schools from the primary grades through college for its African membership. West Africa Seminary was founded in Sierre Leone.

The church is governed episcopally. An international general conference meets quadrennially. The church is divided into 18 episcopal districts. Districts one through 13 oversee work in the United States, Canada, and Bermuda. The remaining districts oversee foreign work in 20 African countries, Jamaica, Haiti, the Dominican Republic, the Virgin Islands, the Windward Islands, Guyana, and Surinam.

The church is a member of both the National Council of Churches and the World Council of Churches. Affiliated congregations in Barbados and the Caribbean are members of the Caribbean Conference of Churches.

Membership: In 1991 the church reported 3,500,000 members, and 8,000 churches.

Educational Facilities: Payne Theological Seminary, Wilberforce, Ohio.

Wilberforce University, Wilberforce, Ohio.
Allen University, Columbia, South Carolina.
Paul Quinn College, Waco, Texas.
Edward Waters College, Jacksonville, Florida.
Morris Brown College, Atlanta, Georgia.
Kittrell College, Kittrell, North Carolina.
Shorter College, Little Rock, Arkansas.
Campbell College, Jackson Mississippi.
Payne University, Birmingham, Alabama.
Western University, Quindaro, Kansas.

In 1958 Turner Theological Seminary in Atlanta, Georgia joined three other schools to form the Interdenominational Theological Seminary, the largest complex for the education of black Christian ministers in the nation.

Periodicals: *A.M.E. Christian Recorder.* • *A.M.E. Review.* Send orders to 468 Lincoln Dr. NW, Atlanta, GA 30318. • *The Voice of Missions.*

Sources:

Allen, Richard. *The Life Experience and Gospel Labors of the Rt. Rev. Richard Allen.* Nashville: Abingdon Press, 1960.

George, Carol V. R. *Segregated Sabbaths.* New York: Oxford University Press, 1973.

Gomez, Joseph. *Polity of the African Methodist Episcopal Church.* Nashville: Division of Christian Education, African Methodist Episcopal Church, 1971.

Gregg, Howard D. *History of the A M. E. Church.* Nashville: A. M. E. Sunday School Union, 1980.

Singleton, George A. *The Romance of African Methodism.* New York: Exposition Press, 1952.

White, Andrew. *Know Your Church Manual.* Nashville: Division of Christian Education, African Methodist Episcopal Church, 1965.

Wright, R. R., Jr., comp. *Encyclopedia of African Methodism.* Philadelphia, PA: The Book Concern of the AME Church, 1947.

★407★
African Methodist Episcopal Zion Church
Box 23843
Charlotte, NC 28232

In the late 1790s, a movement for independence among New York blacks was begun when a group petitioned Bishop Francis Asbury, the first bishop of the Methodist Episcopal Church, to let them hold separate meetings. They complained of not being allowed to preach or join the conference and itinerate. Asbury granted the request, and meetings were held immediately. In 1801 a charter was drawn up for the "African Methodist Episcopal Church (called Zion Church) of the City of New York." It was to be supplied with a minister from the white John's Street Church. Zion Church was thus assured of regular preaching and the sacraments.

In 1813 Zion Church split and Asbury Church was formed as a second black Methodist congregation. Both churches were being served by William Stillwell of John's Street Church in 1820, when Stillwell left the Methodist Episcopal Church with about 300 white members. Blacks, afraid of losing their property to the Methodist Episcopal Church, separated themselves from John's Street Church. They also voted not to join the African Methodist Episcopal Church. Several independent black churches in New Haven and Philadelphia petitioned them for ministers. A *Discipline*, based upon the one of the Methodist Episcopal Church, was drawn up.

Several attempts at reconciliation were made, the most important being a petition to establish the several black congregations as an annual conference within the Methodist Episcopal Church. This request was refused, and the African Methodist Episcopal Zion (AMEZ) Church emerged. Ordination was accepted from William Stillwell, and in 1822 James Varick was elected the first superintendent.

Doctrinally, the AMEZ Church accepts the Twenty-five Articles of Religion common to Methodists and has an episcopal polity similar to the Methodist Episcopal Church. Church boards implement programs of the quadrennial General Conference. The Publishing House and Book Concern are located in the headquarters complex in Charlotte, North Carolina, and publish a complete line of church school material. The church is a member of both the National Council of Churches and the World Council of Churches.

Membership: In 1997 the church reported 1,252,369 members, 8,000 churches, and 2,767 ministers.

Educational Facilities: Hood Theological Seminary, Salisbury, North Carolina.

Livingstone College, Salisbury, North Carolina.
Clinton Junior College, Rock Hill, South Carolina.
Lomax-Hannon Junior College, Greenville, Alabama.

Periodicals: *Star of Zion.* • *Quarterly Review.* Send orders for both to PO Box 31005, Charlotte, NC 28231.

Sources:

Bradley, David C. *A History of the A.M.E. Zion Church.* 2 vols. Nashville: Parthenon Press, 1956-70.

___. *A History of the A.M.E. Zion Church.* Vol. 2. Nashville: Parthenon Press, 1970.

Walls, William J. *The African Methodist Episcopal Zion Church.* Charlotte, NC: A.M.E. Zion Publishing House, 1974.

★408★
African Union First Colored Methodist Protestant Church
2611 N. Claymont St.
Wilmington, DE 19802

History. The origins of the African Union First Colored Methodist Protestant Church can be traced to 1813 and the formation of the Union Church of Africans, an event that present-day church leaders point to with pride. The Union Church of Africans was the first church in the United States to be originally organized by and afterward wholly under the care of black people.

The Union Church of Africans began in a series of disputes in the Asbury Methodist Episcopal Church, a congregation in Wilmington, Delaware. In 1805, black members under the leadership of Peter Spencer (1782-1843) and William Anderson (d. 1843) withdrew from what had been an integrated congregation, formed an all black congregation, Ezion Church, and erected a building. They cited as reasons for their departure the denial of religious privileges and lack of freedom in exercising their "spiritual gifts." The black members had been segregated in a balcony and made to take communion after white members.

While breaking with the local congregation, Ezion was still a part of the predominantly white Methodist Episcopal Church. However, in 1812, a conflict arose with the white minister who had been assigned to preach to both Wilmington's congregations. The conflict resulted in the minister's dismissing all of Ezion's trustees and class leaders. That action led to a court dispute that ended when the black members withdrew from the church. In 1913, they reorganized independently and elected Spencer and Anderson as their ministers. By 1837, there were 21 congregations.

In the generation after Spencer and Anderson, two events were most important. First, in 1850, a major schism occurred when a group arose in the Union Church that demanded the adoption of an episcopal polity. That group left to found the Union American Methodist Episcopal Church. The Union Church of Africans emerged from this struggle as the African Union Church. Then, after the Civil War, the church merged with the First Colored Methodist Protestant Church to form the present African Union First Colored Methodist Protestant Church.

The First Colored Methodist Protestant Church was formed about 1840 when members of the African Methodist Episcopal Church rejected episcopal leadership and reorganized along the principles of the Methodist Protestant Church, which included no episcopacy and lay representation of local preachers at the general conference. Since the Methodist Protestant Church was very similar to the African Union Church, they united in 1866.

Doctrine. The church accepts the commonly held articles of religion of United Methoidsm, but it has attached the Apostles Creed as the first article and deleted the article on "The Rulers of the United States." It has made a few changes in wording, for example, adding the words "and women" to the article on "The Church," which now reads, "The visible church is a congregation of faithful men and women."

Organization: The church is organized congregationally. Congregations are grouped into three districts: the Middle District, which includes New Jersey, Pennsylvania, New York, Delaware, and Canada; the Maryland District, which includes Maryland, the District of Columbia, Virginia, and all states south and southwest of Maryland; and the Southern and Western Missionary District, which includes all the southern and western states. A general conference meets quadrennially.

In 1966, the church moved to replace the titles of general president and general vice president, the two offices elected by the General Conference, with that of senior bishop and junior bishop. In 1971, the office of presiding elder of the combined districts of the church was created, and a second presiding elder was named in 1979.

There is no foreign mission work, and the home mission work is primarily the providence of the women.

Membership: In 1988, the church reported 6,500 members in 35 congregations served by 50 ministers. There was no membership reported in Canada.

Educational Facilities: AU School of Religion, Wilmington, Delaware.

Sources:

Baldwin, Lewis V. *"Invisible" Strands in African Methodism.* Metuchen, NJ: Scarecrow Press, 1983.

Russell, Daniel James. *History of the African Union Methodist Portestant Church.* Philadelphia: Union Star Book and Job Printing and Publishing House, 1920.

★409★
British Methodist Episcopal Church of Canada
460 Shaw St.
Toronto, ON, Canada M6G 3L3

The British Methodist Episcopal Church traces its beginning to the entrance into Canada of the African Methodist Episcopal Church (A.M.E.) in the 1830s, and more directly to the organization of the Upper Canada Conference in 1840 in Toronto under the leadership of Bp. Morris Brown. At the time, there were 10 preachers and 256 lay members in the conference. Some trouble developed in the early 1850s, which the Canadian members attributed to neglect by the American authorities. In 1854 the conference asked for a discipline in conformity to Canadian laws (rather than those of the United States), and it asked the A.M.E. Church to set it off as a separate body. The 1856 general conference granted the request, and the independent British Methodist Episcopal Church (M.E.C.), under the leadership of Bp. Willis Nazrey, was organized.

During the late nineteenth century, the work prospered. Churches were founded in Ontario and Nova Scotia (where many former slaves had migrated after the Civil War), and a mission was established in Bermuda. The *Missionary Messenger* served the church.

No doctrinal issues existed between the A.M.E. Churches and their Canadian membership, and so the British M.E.C. continued the doctrines of the A.M.E. Church.

Membership: Not reported. The denomination has churches across the province of Ontario.

Sources:

Payne, Daniel A. *History of the African Methodist Episcopal Church.* 2 vols. Nashville, TN: AME Sunday School Union, 1891. Reprint, New York: Johnson Reprint Corp., 1968.

Simpson, Matthew. *Cyclopedia of Methodism.* Philadelphia: Louis H. Everts, 1880.

★410★
Christian Methodist Episcopal Church
564 Frank Ave.
Memphis, TN 38101

From 1844 until the end of the Civil War, slaves formed a large percentage of the membership of the Methodist Episcopal Church. In South Carolina they were in the majority. The proselytizing activity of both the African Methodist Episcopal Church and the African Methodist Episcopal Zion Church claimed many of these former slaves as soon as they were free; others remained with the Methodist Episcopal Church, South (MECS), the southern branch of the Methodist Episcopal Church which had split in 1844. Many white Methodists felt that given the Blacks' new freedom, a new relationship must follow. In 1870, following the wishes of their Black members, the Methodist Episcopal Church, South helped them form a separate church named the Colored Methodist Episcopal Church (CME). In 1954 the church changed its name to the Christian Methodist Episcopal Church.

At the first General Conference nine annual conferences were designated, the *Discipline* of the MECS, adopted with necessary changes, a publishing house established, and a periodical, the *Christian Index*, begun. Two MECS bishops ordained two colored Methodist Episcopal bishops. Throughout its history the Colored Methodist Episcopal Church has been aided financially in its program by the MECS and its successor bodies. Today, the church is very similiar to the United Methodist Church in belief and practice.

One of the keys to Colored Methodist Episcopal success was the 41-year episcopate of Isaac Lane. Besides traveling widely and bolstering the poverty-ridden church, he initiated the educational program by founding the CME High School (now Lane College) in 1882. Education of former slaves and their children, a major enterprise of all Methodists, has been carried through the CME Church in the establishment of a number of schools across the South. Paine College, established with the assistance of the MECS has been a traditional focus of CME and MECS cooperation. Growth and expansion beyond the 200,000 initial members was slowed by lack of funds. Movement northward followed the major migration of Blacks into northern urban centers in the early twentieth century.

The CME Church is a member of both the National Council of Churches and the World Council of Churches.

Membership: In 1983, the church reported 718,922 members, 2,340 churches, and 2,650 ministers.

Educational Facilities: Lane College, Jackson, Tennessee.
Paine College, Augusta, Georgia.
Miles College, Birmingham, Alabama.
Mississippi Industrial College, Holly Springs, Mississippi.
Texas College, Tyler, Texas.
In 1959 Phillips School of Theology moved from Jackson, Tennessee to Atlanta, Georgia to become part of the Interdenominational Theological Center, a complex of four theological schools, the largest educational facility in the nation for the training of black Christian ministers.

Periodicals: *Christian Index.* Send orders to Box 665, Memphis, TN 38101.

Sources:

Harris, Eula Wallace, and Naomi Ruth Patterson. *Christian Methodist Episcopal Church Through the Years.* Jackson, TN: Christian Methodist Episcopal Church Publishing House, 1965.

Johnson, Joseph A., Jr. *Basic Christian Methodist Beliefs.* Shreveport, LA: Fourth Episcopal District Press, 1978.

Lakey, Othal Hawthorne. *The Rise of Colored Methodism.* Dallas, TX: Crescendo Book Publications, 1972.

Savage, Horace C. *Life and Times of Bishop Isaac Lane.* Nashville, TN: National Publication Company, 1958.

★411★
Free Christian Zion Church of Christ
1315 Hutchingson
Nashville, AR 71852

The Free Christian Zion Church of Christ was formed on July 10, 1905, at Redemption, Arkansas, by the Rev. E. D. Brown, a conference missionary of the African Methodist Episcopal Zion Church. He and ministers from other Methodist churches objected to what they considered a taxing of the churches for support of an ecclesiastical system and believed that the primary concern of the church should be the care of the poor and needy.

The doctrine is Wesleyan and the polity Methodist with several minor alterations. The bishop, who is called the chief pastor, presides over the work and appoints the ministers and church officers. Pastors and deacons are the local church officers. There are district evangelists to care for the unevangelized communities.

Membership: In 1965 there were 16,000 members in 60 churches.

Periodicals: *Zion Trumpet.*

★412★
Reformed Methodist Union Episcopal Church
⅟₀ Rt. Rev. Leroy Gethers
1136 Brody Ave.
Charleston, SC 20407

The Reformed Methodist Union Episcopal Church was formed in 1885 by members of the African Methodist Episcopal Church who withdrew after a dispute concerning the election of ministerial delegates to the Annual Conference. The Rev. William E. Johnson was elected the first president. A strong sentiment approving of the non-episcopal nature of the new church was expressed. However, in 1896, steps were taken to alter the polity, and in 1919 after the death of the Reverend Johnson, E. Russell Middleton was elected bishop. He was consecrated by the Rt. Rev. Peter F. Stevens of the Reformed Episcopal Church. Following Middleton's death, a second bishop was elected and consecrated by the laying on of hands of seven elders of the church.

Doctrine was taken from the Methodist Episcopal Church. The polity has moved in the episcopal direction and was fully adopted in 1916. Class meetings and love feasts are also retained. Class meetings are regular gatherings of small groups for exhortation, discussion, confession and forgiveness, Bible study, and prayer. Love feasts are informal services centering on holy communion but also including a light meal, singing, and a talk by the officiating minister.

Membership: In 1983 the church reported 3,800 members, 18 churches, and 33 ministers.

Sources:

The Doctrines and Discipline. Charleston, SC: Reformed Methodist Union Episcopal Church, 1972.

★413★
Reformed Zion Union Apostolic Church
⅟₀ James C. Feggins
416 S. Hill Ave.
South Hill, VA 23970

The Reformed Zion Union Apostolic Church was founded by a group from the African Methodist Episcopal Church interested in setting up a religious organization "to aid in bringing about Christian Union, whose fruit will be Holiness unto the Lord." Led by the Rev. James Howell, the group met at Boydton, Virginia, in April 1869, and organized the Zion Union Apostolic Church with the Reverend Howell as the president. Harmony and growth prevailed until 1874, when changes in polity led to the election of the Reverend Howell as bishop with life tenure. Dissatisfaction with this action nearly destroyed the organization, even though Bishop Howell resigned. In 1882 a re-organization was effected, the four-year presidential structure reinstituted, and the present name adopted.

The representative conference structure is maintained with the law-making power invested in the quadrennial General Conference. Over the years the four-year presidency has again been dropped in favor of life-tenure bishops. A Board of Publication has control over church literature and prints the church school material and the *Union Searchlight*, a periodical.

Membership: Not reported. In 1965 the church reported 1,832 members and 27 churches.

Periodicals: *Union Searchlight.*

Sources:

General Rules and Discipline of the Reformed Zion Union Apostolic Church. Norfolk, VA: Creecy's Good-Will Printery, 1966.

★414★
Union American Methodist Episcopal Church
Current address not obtained for this edition.

The Union American Methodist Episcopal Church is one of two denominations which grew out of the movement within the Methodist Episcopal Church (now a constituent part of the United Methodist Church) led by two African American members, Peter Spencer and William Anderson. They formed the African Union Church (also called the Union Church of Africans) in Wilmington, Delaware, in 1813. At some point, a schism occurred in the African Union Church. According to some accounts, around 1816, 30 congregations of the Union Church separated themselves from the other 24 congregations and that for a number of years the two groups existed side by side, each using the same name. Other accounts say the schism occurred in 1850, after Spencer's death. In any case, by the 1850s, two factions existed. In 1865, one faction united with the First Colored Methodist Protestant Church to become the African Union First Methodist Protestant Church. That same year, the other group incorporated under the name African Union American Methodist Episcopal Church in the United States of America and Elsewhere (now the Union American Methodist Episcopal Church).

The church is Methodist in doctrine and has an episcopal polity. There are two bishops who head four districts. The General conference meets quadrennially. The church not only allows but encourages female minsters. The church is led by Bishops Earl L. Huff and George W. Poindexter.

Membership: In 1990 the church reported 55 congregation and over 12,00 members.

Periodicals: *The Union Messenger.*

Sources:

Baldwin, Lewis V. *The Mark of a Man: Peter Spencer and the American Union Methodist Tradition.* Lanham, MD: University Press of America, 1987.

Payne, Wardell J., ed. *Directory of African American Religious Bodies: A Compendium by the Howard University School of Divinity.* Washington, DC: Howard University Press, 1991.

German Methodism

★415★
Church of the United Brethren in Christ
% Bishop C. Ray Miller
302 Lake St.
Huntington, IN 46750

The United Brethren in Christ grew out of the German pietism and revivalism of such preachers as Philip Otterbein (of the German Reformed Church) and Martin Boehm (of the Mennonite Church), both of whom had been affected by Methodism and eighteenth-century Evangelicalism and who became the first bishops of the United Brethren. Their evangelistic efforts led to the formation of a church in 1800. Its earliest concentration of membership was in Maryland, Virginia, and eastern Pennsylvania.

In 1841 the United Brethren adopted its first constitution. During the next four decades the church was disrupted by the debate over the issues of freemasonry and membership in secret societies and pro rata representation and lay representation at General Conference. The crisis came to a head when the General Conference of 1889 was asked to ratify a new constitution which liberalized the rule against belonging to a secret society, allowed for pro rata and lay representation at General Conference, and altered the Church's Confession of Faith.

The majority ratified the new constitution. They continued to exist as the United Brethren in Christ until 1946 when they merged with the Evangelical Church to form the Evangelical United Brethren, which in turn merged in 1968 with The Methodist Church (1939-1968) to form the United Methodist Church. The

minority objected both to the changes and the method of ratification which they felt were illegal. Bishop Milton L. Wright led the minority in conserving the original United Brethren in Christ along the lines of an allegiance to the original constitution. The minority group tried to claim property, but was unsuccessful. They opened a new publishing house which moved to Huntington, Indiana, in 1897. *The Christian Conservator,* a paper which had supported their cause since its founding in 1885, was adopted as the official newspaper of the church. (In 1954 *The Christian Conservator* was combined with several other periodicals to become the present periodical, *The United Brethren.*)

The continuing minority adhered to the original constitution. They believe in the Trinity and the deity, humanity, and atonement of Christ. Observance of strict scriptural living is required of all members, who are forbidden the use of alcoholic beverages, membership in secret societies, and participation in aggressive nondefensive war. Baptism and the Lord's Supper are observed as ordinances of the church.

Local, annual, and general conferences are held; the general conference meets quadrennially and is composed of ministers, district superintendents (presiding elders), general church officials, bishops, and lay delegates. Both men and women are eligible for the ministry and are ordained only once as elders. Missionary societies administer work in evangelism and church aid in the United States and on foreign fields in Sierra Leone, Jamaica, Honduras, Nicaragua, India, and Hong Kong. Elementary and secondary schools have been opened in Honduras and Sierra Leone. A Bible Institute is operated by the church in Honduras and a Bible college, affiliated jointly with the Missionary Church, Wesleyan Church, and European Baptist Church, is supported in Sierre Leone.

Since 1974, the United Brethren have developed a close relationship with the Primitive Methodist Church and the Evangelical Congregational Church, and they work together with them in a federation arrangement. They share support of missionaries, publish church school literature, and hold seminars and consultations. The church is a member of the National Association of Evangelicals. The Sandusky Conference of the United Brethren is a member of the Christian Holiness Association.

Membership: In 1996 the church reported 24,137 members in 234 churches in the United States. There were also nine churches in Canada. Worldwide membership was 37,692.

Educational Facilities: Huntington College Graduate School of Christian Ministries, Huntington, Indiana.

Huntington College, Huntington, Indiana.

Periodicals: *The United Brethren.*

★416★
Evangelical Congregational Church
100 W. Park Ave.
Box 186
Myerstown, PA 17067

The history of this church goes back to the 1894 schism in the Evangelical Association, now a constituent part of the United Methodist Church. The schismatic church took the name of the United Evangelical Church and reunited with the parent body in 1922, when the two formed the Evangelical Church. The many deep scars created by the 1894 schism, however, were not all healed before the 1922 reunion. Therefore, as efforts toward the 1922 reunion progressed, voices of dissent were raised in the United Evangelical Church, opposing merger. Some United Evangelical Church members were still bitter over the loss of their church buildings to the Evangelical Association in court battles. By the 1920s, congregations of the United Evangelical Church had built new churches, which they did not want to share with or give to those who had taken their buildings in the court cases. After merger was voted, a special session of the East Pennsylvania Conference was called and a motion to refrain from merger passed, and the Evangelical Congregational Church formed. An independent anti-merger periodical, *The United Evangelical*, was taken over as a church organ. Former Bishop W. F. Heil was elected bishop and editor of the church paper.

Doctrinally, the Evangelical Congregational Church is Arminian-Wesleyan, against the theory of predestination and for the theory of free will, the belief that grace is available to all and all can exercise free will to accept grace. The church upholds the Twenty-five Articles of Religion adopted in 1894 by the United Evangelical Church. The polity is episcopal, but the churches are autonomous and the bishops' powers are strictly limited. There are two Annual Conferences divided into districts. Bishops and regional elders/superintendents are elected quadrennially. Ministers are appointed to their charges. Boards and Divisions implement the program of the General Conference.

Missions are located in Australia, Austria, Colombia, France, Germany, India, Indonesia, Japan, Kenya, Liberia, Malaysia, Mexico, New Guinea, the Philippines, Spain, Surinam, Turkey, and Zaire. In the United States, there are missions to the Jews, Latin Americans, and the mountain people in Kentucky. A retirement village is located near the headquarters complex at Myerstown.

In 1974 the Evangelical Congregational Church entered a federation agreement with the Primitive Methodist Church and the Church of the United Brethren in Christ which led to joint support of missionaries, shared production of church school literature, and mutually supported conferences and seminars. More recently the Southern Methodist Church has affiliated with the federation. The church is a member of the National Association of Evangelicals.

Membership: In 1996 the church reported 152 churches and 190 ministers. There were 23,091 members in the United States and more than 100,000 members worldwide.

Educational Facilities: Evangelical School of Theology, Myerstown, Pennsylvania.

Periodicals: *Doors & Windows.* • *Windows on the World.*

★417★
United Christian Church
% Elder John Ludwig Jr.
523 W. Walnut St.
Cleona, PA 17042

The United Christian Church was the second schism of the United Brethren in Christ. Formed also during a war, this time the Civil War, some members felt that the voluntary bearing of firearms was wrong. They had interpreted certain resolutions of the East Pennsylvania Conference as justifying military service. The withdrawing group, led by George W. Hoffman, also opposed infant baptism, secret societies, and human slavery. The withdrawing group also dissented from the position of the United Brethren on the issue of human depravity. A long debate, lasting several years in the Church of the United Brethren, was highlighted by that church's decision to support the doctrine of total depravity in 1853 and to reaffirm its support of the doctrine in 1857. In 1857 reaffirmation became additional cause for the withdrawal of the people who formed the United Christian Church. (The 1857 reaffirmation statement had been adopted by the United Brethren by only one vote.)

Organization of the United Christian Church was informal for more than a decade; then in January 1877, at a meeting in Campbelltown, Pennsylvania, a Confession of Faith was adopted. The name was chosen the following year and a Constitution and Discipline in 1894. The *Discipline* of the 1841 United Brethren in Christ was accepted; the last revision was in 1947. Footwashing is one of the ordinances recognized.

Activities of the church include an annual camp meeting, services in prison and at homes for the elderly, direct support of a mission in Jamaica, and, through the Brethren in Christ, support of missions in Japan. An annual conference has the power to legis-

late for this small church body. The church is a member of the National Association of Evangelicals.

Membership: In 1988 the church reported 11 churches, 12 ministers, and approximately 430 members.

Sources:

History of the United Christian Church. United Christian Church, 1977.

Origin, Doctrine, Constitution and Discipline of the United Christian Church. Myerstown, PA: Church Center Press, 1950.

This We Believe. United Christian Church, 1978.

British Methodism

★418★
Methodist Church, Canada
(Defunct)

(The Methodist Church, Canada no longer exists as a separate entity. It is now a constituent part of the United Church of Canada.) The Methodist Church, Canada (1884-1925) was formed by the merger of the Methodist Church of Canada with three smaller Methodist bodies, two of which had been transported to Canada by representatives of the various divisions of British Methodism (the Primitive Methodist Connection of Canada and the Bible Christian Church), the third a product of a schism within Canadian Methodism in 1833 (the Methodist Episcopal Church of Canada (1833-1884)). The Methodist Church of Canada was formed in 1874 by the merger of several Methodist bodies, the result of American and British Methodists who had completed their efforts to unite.

Methodism in Canada had been taken under the guidance and leadership of the Methodist Episcopal Church as soon as that church emerged as a separate entity in 1784. Itinerants were initially sent to Nova Scotia, but in 1791 William Losee was sent to Kingston, Ontario by the New York Conference and work developed in the Western Provinces under the New York and later the Genesee (Western New York) Conferences. In 1828 this work became independent as the Methodist Episcopal Church in Canada (1828-1833). In 1833 a merger of the Methodist Episcopal Church in Canada (1828-1833) and the British Wesleyan Connection, then still directly tied to the British headquarters, was accomplished. A minority of those formerly associated with the Methodist Episcopal Church in Canada (1828-1833) rejected the merger and reorganized as the Methodist Episcopal Church in Canada (1833-1884). They wanted an independent Canadian church, free of control from England, and they wanted to keep the episcopal polity. (The British had not developed an episcopacy as had the American Methodists.)

An initial conference of the dissenting ministers was held in 1834 and a general conference the following year at which a bishop was selected and the new jurisdiction formally organized. Since most of the meeting halls and members had been lost in the merger, the new church began with almost nothing, but by 1837 reported over 3,500 members. By 1843 there were over 8,000 members, and the single conference was divided into two conferences. A third conference was designated in 1875.

The Primitive Methodist Church of Canada had roots similar to those of the Primitive Methodist Church in the United States, begun in the 1820s. It grew out of the Primitive Methodist Connection in England, a group of Methodists attached to revival and camp meetings and generally known for the emotional displays at their gatherings. In 1829, at about the same time the Primitive Methodist Church began work in New York and Pennsylvania, William Lawson and his family arrived in Toronto. Lawson had been a local preacher in the Wesleyan Methodist Connection, but had been expelled and joined the Primitive Methodists. In Toronto, Lawson organized a class and preached to a small gathering. In 1830 Rev. William Watkins was sent from England to assist in the work. He was replaced a year later by William Summersides, one of the original missionaries sent to America. The Primitive Methodists in Canada formed their conference in 1854. Lawson became the first secretary. The church grew slowly but steadily through the next generation, but welcomed the prospect of union with the rest of Canadian Methodism.

The Bible Christians began in England in the second decade of the nineteenth century out of the work of William O'Bryan, a Methodist local preacher, who continually found himself at odds with his superiors and was twice expelled from the Wesleyan Connection for his operating outside of the discipline of the church. He was an effective preacher, and raised a following in some areas of Cornwall and Devon not otherwise touched by Methodism. O'Bryan organized the first Bible Christian society in October 1815. The first quarterly conference in January 1816 reported 11 societies in the fellowship. At the first conference of the Connection in 1819 16 male and 14 female itinerant preachers were reported, with a following of 2000.

In 1831 the Connection sent two missionaries to Canada to work among Cornish immigrants: John Hicks Eynon to Upper Canada and Francis Metherall to Prince Edward Island. From these small beginnings, other missionaries came and the church grew rapidly. There were over 1,000 members at the first district meeting in 1844. The church slowly became self-supporting and by the time the Canadian conference was organized in 1855, had freed itself from British support. From the time of the formation of the conference until the merger in 1884, the church more than doubled its membership.

Membership: At the time of their merger in 1884, the four uniting churches reported as follows: Methodist Church in Canada, 128,644 members; Methodist Episcopal Church in Canada, 25,671 members; Primitive Methodist Church, 8,090 members; Bible Christian Church, 7,398 members.

Sources:

Centennial of Canadian Methodism. Toronto: William Briggs, 1891.

Davies, Rupert, A. Raymond George, and Gordon Rupp, eds. *A History of the Methodist Church in Great Britain.* Vol. 2. London: Epworth Press, 1978.

Sanderson, J. E. *Methodism in Canada.* 2 vols. Toronto: William Briggs, 1910.

Shaw, Thomas. *The Bible Christians, 1815-1907.* London: Epworth Press, 1965.

Silcox, Claris Edwin. *Church Union in Canada.* New York: Institute of Social and Religious Research, 1933.

★419★
Methodist Church in Canada
(Defunct)

(The Methodist Church in Canada no longer exists as a separate entity. It is now a constituent part of the United Church of Canada.) The Methodist Church in Canada was formed in 1874 by the merger of the Wesleyan Conference of Eastern British North America, the Conference of the Wesleyan Methodist Church in Canada, and the Methodist New Connexion Church in Canada.

The Wesleyan Conference of Eastern British North America continued the earliest Methodist work in Canada. In 1772 a group of Methodists from Yorkshire settled in Cumberland County, Nova Scotia, an area familiar with revivals. In the 1780s it became the site of one initiated by Congregationalist minister Henry Alline, which had split the older Congregational churches and produced a set of rival Separatist congregations. Among the Methodists, 19-year-old William Black, Jr. emerged as a preacher who began to travel through the county and then all of Nova Scotia, organizing small groups of believers. In 1784 he traveled to Maryland to attend the founding conference of the Methodist Episcopal Church and to ask their assistance in the work he had begun. The pros-

pects for Methodism in the Maritime Provinces were enhanced by the migration of many American colonists still loyal to the British government. The first conference was held in 1786.

The work in Nova Scotia and New Brunswick came under the care of the New York Conference of the Methodist Episcopal Church, which appointed ministers throughout the 1790s. However, these ministers experienced open rebuke for their disloyalty to the British government, and the last departed in 1799. That same year Black traveled to England and appealed to the Wesleyan Connexion for ministers. Four returned with him in 1800, others followed. The work spread through the Maritime Provinces. In 1790 a mission in Bermuda was inspired by the efforts of John Stephenson. Until 1855 the work was under the direct supervision of the English Wesleyans and was administered by its London Missionary committee. In that year the work was organized into affiliated conferences and designated the Wesleyan Methodist Connexion of Eastern British America. The British Connexion, besides continuing financial support, retained the right of ratifying the election of the conference president and vetoing actions of the conference. This relationship (tied to the British but independent of efforts further west) remained until 1874.

The Wesleyan Methodist Church in Canada originated with the movement of Methodism into what is today Quebec and Ontario (designated Upper and Lower Canada in the late 1700s). Methodist work began in 1780 with the arrival of a British officer by the name of Tuffey in Quebec. Tuffey was also a Methodist preacher. Six years later Major George Neal, also a Methodist preacher, began preaching in the Niagara area. Their work was taken into an area of Canada organized by former American colonists still loyal to the British government. Among the immigrants were Paul Heck and his wife Barbara Heck, loyalists who had been instrumental in the founding of Methodism in New York prior to the Revolution. They formed a class in Augusta (Ontario) in 1788. The first itinerant, William Losee, arrived in 1790, and in 1791 he led in the organization of a number of classes.

A decade later the Canadian work had grown to become a separate district. In 1810, western New York was separated from the New York Conference and designated the Genesee Conference. The Canadian work was transferred to the Genesee Conference and was also divided into two districts, Upper and Lower Canada. The work was disrupted during the War of 1812, when the area became a battlefield. After the war, the work resumed. The New England Conference developed two charges across the border in Quebec. In 1824 the General Conference separated the Canadian work from the Genesee Conference, and created a new Canada Conference. By this time many of the ministers, including leading minister and presiding elder Henry Ryan, were firmly convinced that full independence of the Canadian Methodists was in order. They worked for that independence during the next four years and in 1828 the General Conference granted it: the Canadian Conference became the Methodist Episcopal Church in Canada. No bishop was ever elected to head the church, which existed only five years.

As the War of 1812 was drawing to a close, the British Methodists appointed a missionary to Canada. John B. Strong arrived in Quebec in 1814 to begin the growth of a rival to the American-based effort. Its growth was augmented by the movement of many Methodists with anti-American sentiments into the new jurisdiction. Competition between and duplication of efforts by the two conferences were somewhat lessened in 1820, when a division of territory was agreed upon. The Americans concentrated on Upper Canada, the British on Lower Canada. In 1833, five years after the Methodist Episcopal Church conference had become independent, a merger between the two finalized. The new Canadian Wesleyan Conference remained in close relationship with the British Methodists, and its polity (which had no bishop) was accepted. The union proved unsatisfactory to many; those committed to an episcopal polity withdrew and formed the Methodist Episcopal Church in Canada (1833-1884).

Of intense concern after the 1833 merger was the reception by the British Methodists of Canadian government funds which were to be used to underwrite Indian missions and to stop the political activities of the Canadian Methodists. The Canadian Methodists were, on the other hand, opponents of state aid to religion. The issues led to a break between the groups in the 1840s. As that break proceeded, some independent efforts developed in Quebec as the Eastern District Meeting. This independent effort merged with the reunited Wesleyans to form the Wesleyan Methodist Church in Canada in 1854. That church continued until 1874. The Methodist New Connexion emerged after the death of John Wesley (1703-1791) in a dispute over the status of Methodism as a dissenting movement. Under Wesley and his immediate successors, Methodists considered themselves Anglicans. They would not schedule meetings to conflict with parish worship, advised their members to have their babies baptized by the local Anglican priest, and encouraged members to receive their sacrament at the local Church of England. William Thom (1751-1811) and Alexander Kilham (1762-1798) disagreed and argued that Methodism should become a dissenting movement and offer the sacraments directly to its members. They also argued for a variety of lay rights in the choice of class leaders (then exclusively the perogative of the preachers) and representation at the annual conference. In 1797 they led in the formation of the Methodist New Connexion.

The Methodist New Connexion Church in Canada began in the 1820s after a wealthy layman, William Ridgeway, visited it and reported its needs to the British Connexion. A short time later a retired minister settled there and began to preach. In 1832 Joseph Clementson traveled to Toronto, only to return and report on the continued needs of the population. Finally, in 1837 John Addyman was sent to formally institute a mission. He was followed two years later by Henry O. Crofts. The work made an immediate advance by its encounter and subsequent merger in 1841 with a small group, the Canadian Wesleyan Methodist Church.

The Canadian Wesleyan Methodist Church was formed in 1829 by Rev. Henry Ryan (1775-1833). Ryan had been a presiding elder working in Canada in the Genesee Conference of the Methodist Episcopal Church. After the War of 1812, he was among the loudest voices appealing for independence for Canadian Methodism from American control. Impatient with the slow process, Ryan became a severe critic of the conference, so much so that after independence was declared in 1828, he led a schismatic movement of several hundred members to the formation of the Canadian Wesleyan Methodist Church. It had grown to approximately 2,000 members when it united with the New Connexion.

The merged church became known as the Canadian Wesleyan Methodist New Connexion, with a direct link to the New Connexion Missionary Society in England through a superintendent appointed by the British leaders. In 1843 the Connexion absorbed the small body of Methodist Protestants, a Canadian conference affiliated with the Methodist Protestant Church which had been organized in 1836. At that time the Methodist Protestants had less than 600 members. In 1864 the Connexion changed its name to the Methodist New Connexion Church in Canada, the name it carried into the union of 1874.

In 1884, the Methodist Church of Canada merged with the Bible Christian Church, the Methodist Episcopal Church in Canada, and the Primitive Methodist Church in Canada to become the Methodist Church, Canada.

Sources:

Centennial of Canadian Methodism. Toronto: William Briggs, 1891.

Davies, Rupert, A. Raymond George, and Gordon Rupp, eds. *A History of the Methodist Church in Great Britain.* Vol. 2. London: Epworth Press, 1978.

Sanderson, J. E. *The First Century of Methodism in Canada.* 2 vols. Toronto: William Briggs, 1908.

Silcox, Claris Edwin. *Church Union in Canada.* New York: Institute of Social and Religious Research, 1933.

★420★
Primitive Methodist Church
1045 Laurel Run Rd.
Wilkes-Barre, PA 18702

The Primitive Methodist Church is one of the two Methodist bodies in the United States which does not trace its history to the Methodist Episcopal Church, an American church, but to the British Wesleyan Methodist tradition. The Primitive Methodist Church grew from the work of two English ministers, the Revs. Hugh Bourne and William Clowes. Out of their evangelistic efforts the new church itself developed in England. Both men became influenced by the great success of the American camp meeting. Under their leadership a camp meeting was held on May 31, 1807. As a result of this meeting and some other camp meetings, both men were dismissed from the Wesleyan Methodist Connection. Since those converted were not welcomed into the Wesleyan Church, Bourne and Clowes found a place of meeting in 1810. Growth was such that in 1812 in Tunstall, they became officially organized as The Society of the Primitive Methodists. The church accepted the polity of the Wesleyan Methodists and did not create bishops.

By 1829 the call for ministers by Primitive Methodists who had migrated to the United States was heard. Four missionaries were sent—William Summersides, Thomas Morris, Ruth Watkins, and William Knowles. Growth was slow and at first confined to New York, New Jersey, Pennsylvania, and Connecticut. In 1840, the American group separated itself from its British parent but kept fraternal relations. Growth increased, particularly in the Pennsylvania coal fields. In 1842, a Primitive Methodist Church was founded in Galena, Illinois, and became the base for a second conference in the Midwest. The conferences existed in close relation but operated autonomously until 1889 when the General Conference was organized and three conferences, Eastern, Western, and Pennsylvania joined and became the legislative body with the conferences remaining as the administrative branches. In 1975, both the annual and general conferences were combined. This combined both the legislative and administrative powers into one conference which meets annually. It is composed of ministers and lay delegates from the six districts. It has direct oversight of all boards and committees. The districts provide administrative guidance along with the district and local church quarterly conference. The conference is presided over by the president, who is elected to a four-year term. There is equal representation of clergy and laity at all levels of administration. There is one full-time officer, the Executive Director, who is in charge of promotion of the denomination. The main mission work is carried on in Guatemala, working in conjunction with the Primitive Methodist National Conference of Guatemala, and in Mexico and the Dominican Republic.

The church is a member of the National Association of Evangelicals and, though not a member, cooperates with the Christian Holiness Association. In 1974, it entered into a federation agreement with the Evangelical Congregational Church and the Church of the United Brethren in Christ, which has led to the mutual support of church conferences, seminars, and missionary activities.

Membership: In 1997 there were 78 churches, 5,019 members, and 75 ministers.

Sources:

Primary Helps and Biblical Instruction for Primitive Methodists. N.p., [1958].

Werner, Julia Stewart. *The Primitive Connection.* Madison: University of Wisconsin Press, 1984.

Wert, Paul R., J. Allan Ranck, and William C. F. Hayes. *The Christian Way.* Dayton, OH: Otterbein Press, 1950.

★421★
United Wesleyan Methodist Church of America
℅ David S. Bruno
270 W. 126th St.
New York, NY 10027

The United Wesleyan Methodist Church of America was formed in 1905 by Methodists who immigrated to the United States from the West Indies and wished to carry on the tradition of the Methodist Church in the Caribbean and the Americas, a Wesleyan church with historical ties to British Methodists. Their doctrine is Wesleyan, and their polity is like its West Indian counterpart (nonepiscopal). A general conference meets biennially. In 1976 the Methodist Church in the Caribbean and the Americas entered into a concordant with the United Methodist Church which aligned their work and led to a number of jointly sponsored projects in the Islands. The church is a member of both the World Council of Churches and the Caribbean Conference of Churches.

Membership: In 1978 there were 4 congregations, all in New York City. In 1982, the church in the West Indies reported 68,898 members.

Sources:

Bessil-Watson, Lisa, comp. *Handbook of the Churches in the Caribbean.* Bridgetown, Barbados: Cedar Press, 1982.

Section 8
Holiness Family

Consult the Contents pages to locate the essay in Part II, Historical Essay Chapters, that provides an historical discussion of this family

Intrafaith Organizations

★422★
Christian Holiness Partnership
% CHP Center
Box 100
Wilmore, KY 40390

The Christian Holiness Partnership (formerly known as the Christian Holiness Association) began in 1867 as the National Camp Meeting Association for the Promotion of Holiness, the prime organized expression of the youthful holiness movement which was revived following the Civil War. The holiness movement had emerged in American Methodism in the decades prior to the war as the champion of the distinctive Wesleyan doctrine of sanctification, the experience of the Christian believer which, by the power of the Holy Spirit, renders him or her perfect in love. As originally formed at the first large post-war camp meeting in Vineland, New Jersey, the association was seen by its leaders as a promotional endeavor operating primarily in the Methodist Episcopal Church.

The work of the association, in holding camp meetings in the Northeast and Midwest, was soon extended to include the South and far West, and in the mid-1870s it ventured to Australia and India for its first international work. The work was altered through the 1880s by the emergence of a number of independent holiness churches and the gradual cooling of enthusiasm for holiness ideas in the Methodist Church (which controlled most of the camp meeting sites regularly utilized by the holiness evangelists). By 1894, when the words "Camp Meeting" were dropped from the association's name, the group had become ecumenical, though much of the leadership was still based in the Methodist Episcopal Church.

The present name was adopted in 1971 and reflects the emergence of a number of strong holiness denominations and the movement of the United Methodist Church away not only from holiness emphases but from conservative Protestant theology. The name change also accommodated Canadian members. The association now serves as a cooperative fellowship for holiness denominations.

Membership: The CHA includes as members the Association of Evangelical Churches, Bible Holiness Movement, Brethren in Christ Church, Church of the Nazarene, Churches of Christ in Christian Union, Evangelical Christian Church, Evangelical Church of North America, Evangelical Friends Alliance, Evangelical Methodist Church, Free Methodist Church in North America, Japan Immanuel Church, Salvation Army, Salvation Army in Canada, United Brethren in Christ Church, and Wesleyan Church.

Sources:

Jones, Charles Edwin. *A Guide to the Study of the Holiness Movement.* Metuchen, NJ: Scarecrow Press, 1974.

★423★
Interdenominational Holiness Convention
Salem, OH

The Interdenominational Holiness Convention (IHC) was founded in 1947 as an expression of the more conservative element in the holiness movement. Its primary moving force was H. E. Schmul, at the time a minister in the Wesleyan Methodist Church. By the end of World War II a variety of developments within the larger holiness denomination were, many felt, leading toward a loss of holiness distinctives. Theological education was becoming standard for ministers. And many of the holiness behavioral standards, especially restrictions on dress and entertainment, were being dropped.

In the 1950s the Church of the Nazarene would be hit with schism as conservatives associated with Glenn Griffith left to found the Bible Missionary Church, and then in 1966–1967 conservatives in both the Wesleyan Methodist Church and Pilgrim Holiness Church founded new denominations in reaction to the merger of the two bodies. The Interdenominational Holiness Convention had been their home and continued to be a focus of fellowship and cooperative activity. He also became well-known for his republication of a number of classic nineteenth-century holiness books.

Membership: Those churches and organizations associated with the IHC include: Allegheny Wesleyan Methodist Connection, Bible Methodist Connection of Churches, Bible Missionary Church, Church of the Bible Covenant, Evangelical Wesleyan Church, Independent Holiness Churches, Pilgrim Holiness Church of New York, Pilgrim Holiness Church of the Midwest, United Holiness Church of North America, Voice of the Nazarene Association of Churches, and Wesleyan Holiness Association of Churches.

Sources:

Jones, Charles Edwin. *A Guide to the Study of the Holiness Movement.* Metuchen, NJ: Scarecrow Press, 1974.

Nineteenth Century Holiness

★424★
American Rescue Workers (ARW)
% Robert N. Coles
National Field Office
1209 Hamilton Blvd.
Hagerstown, MD 21742-3340

Alternate Address: General Claude S. Astin, Jr., Commonder-in-Chief, Operational Headquarters, 643 Elmira St., Williamsport, PA 17701.

Major Thomas E. Moore was national commander of the Salvation Army in the 1880s when a dispute flared between Moore and the armys founder General William Booth. Moore resigned his affiliation with Booth and, due to the fact that the Salvation Army was not at the time an incorporated body, was able to incorporate as the Salvation Army. The name of Moores organization was changed in 1890 to American Salvation Army and in 1913 the current name, American Rescue Workers, was adopted.

The early years of the organization were fraught with instability. Moore only stayed with the group he founded for nine months; he resigned and became a Baptist minister. Col. Richard Holz succeeded Moore, but never formally accepted the title of commander-in-chief. Shortly after taking control, he moved the headquarters from Mohawk to Saratoga Springs, New York. Holz had been leading the organization for only seven months when he was offered a position by Booth and, with some 150 officers, he left to return to the Salvation Army. The ARW then reorganized under Major Gratton, but he soon left and he was succeeded as commander-in-chief by William Duffin, then leader of a large center in Coatsville, Pennsylvania. The young Duffin would lead the organization for over a half of a century, until his death in 1948.

The American Rescue Workers emerged in 1913 as a national religions social service agency that operates on a quasimilitary basis. Membership includes officers (clergy), soldiers/adherents (laity), members of various activity groups, and volunteers who serve as advisors, associates, and committed participants in the organizations service functions.

Motivated by the love of God, the organization has a message based upon the Bible and expressed in its spiritual ministry. Members seek to preach the gospel of Jesus Christ and to meet human needs in His name without discrimination. As a branch of the Christian Church, it has established a diversified program of religious and social welfare services that are designed broadly to meet the needs of all people.

The American Rescue Workers is headed by a general, who holds the title of commander-in-chief, who is elected for a five-year term and can be re-elected. The present general, Claude S. Astin, Jr., is in his first term. Election takes place at the annual grand field councils. A board of managers administers the ongoing affairs of the organization. All properties are held in the name of the organization. Doctrinally, the organization is in agreement with the Salvation Army with the exception of the sacraments (which the army does not observe). The American Rescue Workers believes in equal rights for women.

Membership: In 1997 the American Rescue Workers reported approximately 1,000 members, 15 centers, and 75 officers in the United States.

Periodicals: *The Rescue Herald.*

Sources:

Ritual and Manual. American Rescue Workers, n.d.

★425★
Association of Fundamental Ministers and Churches
Current address not obtained for this edition.

The Association of Fundamental Ministers and Churches, Inc. was formed in 1931 by Rev. Fred Bruffett, Hallie Bruffett (his wife), Rev. Paul Bennett, Rev. George Fisher, and six other former ministers of the Church of God (Anderson, Indiana). Bennett had been disfellowshipped because of his fellowshipping with other churches. The Association believes that the new birth is the only necessity for fellowship.

Doctrine is like that of the Church of God (Anderson, Indiana). Healing is stressed and the ordinances are not emphasized. The Association meets annually and elects four officers to handle business affairs. There are 25 state conventions. Missions are conducted in Guatemala, Hong Kong, and Alaska.

Membership: Not reported.

Periodicals: *The Fundamental News.*

★426★
Bible Fellowship Church
% Pastor W. B. Hottel
404 W. Main St.
Terre Hill, PA 17581

The Bible Fellowship Church was formed in 1947 by churches withdrawing from the Mennonite Brethren in Christ when the Brethren changed their name to the United Missionary Church and dropped all Mennonite connections. Members of the Bible Fellowship Church see themselves as continuing the tradition of the Mennonite Brethren in Christ and date their origin to 1883. Their doctrine follows that of the parent body. They abide by the Dort Confession of Faith (common to most Mennonites), but add statements on sanctification as a second work of grace received instantaneously (the uniquely "holiness" doctrine), divine healing, and the millennium. Baptism is by immersion.

All the churches of the Bible Fellowship Church are in Pennsylvania and are organized into two districts, each headed by a superintendent. There is an annual conference of the entire church. Polity is congregational. Mission work is supported in Colombia, Venezuela, Kenya, and Sweden.

Membership: In 1995 there were 58 churches and 7,132 members and 121 ministers.

★427★
Bible Holiness Church (1995)
600 College Ave.
Independence, KS 67301

The Bible Holiness Church, known until 1995 as the Fire Baptized Holiness Church (Wesleyan), was established in 1890 by holiness people in the Methodist Episcopal Church of southeastern Kansas. The original name, the Southeast Kansas Fire Baptized Holiness Association, was changed in 1945. The church is organized in an episcopal mode taken from the Methodist Episcopal Church. A general assembly meets annually. The Wesleyan holiness doctrine is emphasized, and strong prohibitions exist against alcohol, tobacco, drugs, secret societies, television, immodest clothing, jewelry, and frivolous amusements. Members regularly tithe. The church is aggressively evangelistic. Missions are supported on Grenada, Windward Islands and New Guinea.

Membership: In 1988 the church reported 1,200 members, 50 churches and 92 ministers in the United States.

Educational Facilities: Independence Bible School, Independence, Kansas.
Troy Holiness School, Troy, Missouri.
Holiness School, Afton, Oklahoma.
Brothers School, Grenada.

Periodicals: *Flaming Sword.* • *John Three Sixteen.* Send orders to 10th St. & Country Club Rd., Independence, KS 67301.

★428★
Bible Holiness Movement
Box 223
Postal Sta. A
Vancouver, BC, Canada V6C 2M3

The Bible Holiness Movement, originally called the Bible Holiness Mission, was formed as a church in 1949. It grew out of the earlier work of William J. Wakefield. He and his wife had been Salvation Army officers. Upon their retirement as active officers, due to health, the Wakefields took charge of a city mission (an urban center for transients) in Vancouver, British Columbia. William Wakefield developed several doctrinal emphases distinct from those of the Salvation Army. For example, he believed the sacraments were real means of grace, not just symbolic ordinances. The Salvation Army does not practice the sacraments at all. The Wakefields directed the mission until Wakefield's death in 1947.

Wesley H. Wakefield succeeded his father, William, and formed the Bible Holiness Mission in 1949. The name changed to the Bible Holiness Movement in 1971. Wesley H. Wakefield continues to direct the church as its international leader.

Beliefs. The Bible Holiness Movement continues the traditional holiness theology passed to it from the Salvation Army. It affirms the authority of the Bible, the deity of Christ, and the necessity of a personal experience with Christ for the individual believer. For believers it also offers the hope of total sanctification and directs them to disciplined lives of love, evangelism, and social activism. Movement members are also exhorted to lives of simplicity and holiness, including total abstinence, and no affiliations with secret societies.

Organization: The movement is organized similarly to the Salvation Army. It is headed by its bishop-general, Wesley H. Wakefield. Members of both sexes and all races are admitted to all levels of ministerial leadership. Within its permanent structure there are committees on religious freedom and on racial equality.

From its Vancouver headquarters, the movement has an international outreach. Mission work began as a result of the circulation of movement material around the world. In some cases, people were converted as a result of reading literature, and in others, leaders of independent holiness churches overseas contacted the movement for affiliation. Currently, the church conducts work in Egypt, Ghana, Haiti, India, Kenya, Liberia, Malawi, Nigeria, the Philippines, South Korea, Sri Lanka, Tanzania, Uganda, and Zambia. Its ministry reaches 89 countries in 42 languages through literature, radio, and audio-cassettes. The movement belongs to the Christian Holiness Association, the Evangelical Fellowship of Canada, and the National Black Evangelical Association.

Membership: In 1991, the movement reported 511 members, 29 congregations, and 12 ministers in Canada and the United States. The two congregations in the United States are located in Phoenix, Arizona, and Kent, Washington. The international membership is 75,018.

Periodicals: *Hallelujah!.* • *On the March.*

Sources:

Triumph with Christ. Vancouver: Bible Holiness Movement, 1984.

Wakefield, Wesley H. *Bible Doctrine.* N.p., n.d.

★429★
Christ Holy Sanctified Church of America
5204 Willie St.
Fort Worth, TX 76105

Christ Holy Sanctified Church of America was founded in 1910 in Keatchie, Louisiana, by Sarah A. King and a Bishop Judge. It was incorporated the next year in Memsfield, Louisiana. It grew out of the same movement which had produced Christ's Sanctified Holy Church in Louisiana several years previously. Judge was succeeded by Bishop Ulysses King of Oakland, California, and more recently E. L. McBride, the present leader. The church supports Christ Holy Sanctified School, an industrial school. Headquarters is in Fort Worth, Texas.

Sources:

Payne, Wardell J., ed. *Directory of African American Religious Bodies: A Compendium by the Howard University School of Divinity.* Washington, DC: Howard University Press, 1991.

★430★
The Christian and Missionary Alliance (C&MA)
8595 Explorer Dr.
Colorado Springs, CO 80920

The Christian and Missionary Alliance had its beginning during a summer conference at Old Orchard, Maine, in 1887. A number of Christian men and women connected with various evangelical denominations were organized under the leadership of Dr. A. B. Simpson, a Presbyterian minister. Simpson had begun publishing an interdenominational missionary magazine in 1882 to promote a deeper spiritual life for the support of an aggressive missionary ministry.

Through the magazine and its description of a Bible and missionary convention held in 1884 at the New York Gospel Tabernacle, of which A. B. Simpson was the pastor, there arose a popular demand for similar conventions in other cities. In 1885 five were held in other metropolitan areas. These spread and resulted in two organizations—The Christian Alliance and The Missionary Alliance. The Christian Alliance consisted of local organizations, called "branches," that grew to 300 within 10 years. More than 25 denominations were represented in branch auxiliaries for the support of The Missionary Alliance, the missionary-sending agency. It was a fraternal society with no intent of becoming another church or denomination, although the New York Gospel Tabernacle was organized as a regular independent church.

Again, within 10 years of operation, The Missionary Alliance had more than 200 missionaries on approximately 100 stations in India, China, Japan, Africa, Palestine, the West Indies, and five Latin American countries. A missionary institute, established in 1883, had graduated hundreds of students, many of whom were mature laymen and laywomen who felt they were called by God into the missionary ministry. In 1897, The Christian Alliance and The Missionary Alliance were united as "The Christian and Missionary Alliance."

In doctrine, The Christian and Missionary Alliance stresses the centrality of Christ and His all-sufficiency—Christ as Savior, Sanctifier, Healer, and Coming King. A formal statement of doctrine was adopted in 1965. As the alliance developed in overseas ministries and at home, indigenous policies gave rise to national churches, particularly after World War II. By 1974, the Alliance was completely reorganized in the United States and Canada and declared to be a church and a denomination. Canada, united with the United States until 1980, also became nationally autonomous. Each has its own General Council Assembly resembling a combination of congregational and presbyterian policies.

The United States is presently served by two graduate schools and four colleges. Canada has one college and one graduate school. The United States and Canada each have a seminary fully accredited by the American Association of Theological Schools. An office of alternative education serves 1,591 students.

Membership: Inclusive membership in the United States in 1991 was 267,853 in 1,901 churches. An unusual feature was that 313 of these churches were intercultural (Cambodian, Dega, Haitian, Hmong, Jewish, Korean, Lao, Native American, Spanish, and Vietnamese). Canada, with headquarters in Willowdale, Ontario, reported 76,119 inclusive members and 336 churches, 83 of which were ethnic. Overseas ministries reported 1,931,363 inclusive members in 14,941 churches in 53 countries. In overseas ministries, the United States and Canada are a joint organization with 1,185 missionaries.

Educational Facilities: Nyack College and Alliance Theological Seminary, Nyack, New York.

Simpson College and Simpson Graduate School, Redding, California.

Toccoa Falls College, Toccoa Falls, Georgia.

Crown College, St. Bonifacius, Minnesota.

Canadian Bible College and Canadian Theological Seminary, Regina, Saskatchewan, Canada.

Periodicals: *Alliance Life.*

Sources:

Manual. New York: Christian and Missionary Alliance, 1965.

Simpson, Albert B. *The Four-fold Gospel.* Harrisburg, PA: Christian Publications, n.d.

___. *A Larger Christian Life.* Harrisburg, PA: Christian Publications, n.d.

★431★
Christian Nation Church, U.S.A.
Current address not obtained for this edition.

In 1892, eight young evangelists who called themselves "equality Evangelists" began to work in central Ohio. Their efforts met with success, and in 1895 the Christian Nation Church was incorporated at Marion, Ohio. Doctrinally, the group is related to the Christian and Missionary Alliance, and preaches the four-fold gospel of its founder A. B. Simpson. It is very strict in forbidding worldly amusements, fashionable attire, Sabbath desecration, and divorce. Marriage with non-members is discouraged. Large families are encouraged as being divinely sanctioned.

The polity of the Christian Nation is congregational with district and annual conferences. The pastors' licenses are renewed annually. Camp meetings are an active part of the program.

Membership: In 1989 the church reported 200 members, five churches, and 23 ministers.

★432★
Christ's Sanctified Holy Church (Georgia)
Box 1376
CSHC Campgrounds and Home for the Aged
Perry, GA 31068

History. In the year 1887, Joseph Lynch, a member and class leader in the Methodist Episcopal Church, Chincoteague Island, Virginia, began to preach scriptural holiness, which at that time was in opposition to the direction being taken by the church. Following his conviction, he sought and obtained the experience of sanctification, the second blessing believed by holiness churches to make the believer perfect in love. Assisting him in his early labors was Sarah E. Collins. The resistance of the church to his preaching on this doctrine led Lynch and 58 members to withdraw from the church. In 1892, they established Christ's Sanctified Holy Church; 19 members operated as trustees and were designated Board No. 1. Succesors of Board No. 1 incorporated the church in Chatham County, Georgia, in 1932. The trustee established subservient boards of extension (1938) and a general conference (1950) but reserved the corporate church affairs and management in the hands of Board No. 1.

Beliefs. Christ's Sanctified Holy Church is Trinitarian in its beliefs and centered upon the experience of sanctification as the second work of grace, but differs from most Christians in serveral respects. It does not practice water baptism, but believes in the baptism of the Holy Ghost which is inward and spiritual. It also does not practice the Lords's supper as members believe that no act or ritual is necessary to establish a relationship between God and humans. It does not believe in a bodily resurrection but in a spiritual resurrection through sanctification of the Spirit and a belief in truth. There are no paid ministers, and women share equal participation in all church functions.

Organization. Christ's Sanctified Holy Church has no individual membership nor a congregational form of internal governance. It is governed by a non-congregational trusteeship whereby the church corporation draws from various separate corporate church entities and associations of like religious faith who may gain recognition under prescribed religious qualifications. Congregations are entitled to representation on the governing boards and use of the church's physical facilities for religious worship. At Perry, Georgia, the church owns a campground, a place for internment, and a home for the aged. Camp meeting is held the first Sunday in August of each year.

Membership: In 1995, the church reported approximately 1,500 members, 17 congregations, and 17 ministers.

Sources:

Clelland, E. Joseph. *The Writings of E. Joseph Clelland.* N.p.: The Author, 1989.

★433★
Christ's Sanctified Holy Church (Louisiana)
S. Cutting Ave. at E. Spencer St.
Jennings, LA 70546

In 1903 members of Christ's Sanctified Holy Church (South Carolina) came to West Lake, Louisiana, and proselytized a group of black people, who in 1904 organized the Colored Church South. Among the leaders were Dempsey Perkins, A. C. Mitchell, James Briller, Sr., and Leggie Pleasant. The church soon changed its name to Christ's Sanctified Holy Church Colored. Over the years the church members dropped the word "Colored" from their title and returned to using the same name as their parent body, Christ's Sanctified Holy Church. The parent body is white and has headquarters in South Carolina, whereas the church under discussion here is headquartered in Louisiana. Organization and doctrine are as in the parent body, except that the ministers in Christ's Sanctified Holy Church (Louisiana) are salaried.

Membership: Not reported. At last report (1957) there were 600 members in 30 churches.

★434★
Church of God (Anderson, Indiana)
Box 2420
Anderson, IN 46018

Daniel Warner, a minister of the General Eldership of the Churches of God in North America, now called the Church of God, General Council, was affected by the holiness movement. He became an ardent advocate of sanctification as a second work of grace. For that belief, he was tried and expelled from the church. Warner argued that sanctification led to an identification of the invisible church with the visible church, the concrete embodiment of the spiritual body of Christ.

The new Church of God was organized in 1880 by Warner. Like its parent body, the Church of God has no creed, but it follows the holiness theological consensus. It believes in the inspiration of Scripture, the Trinity, the divinity of Jesus, the indwelling of the Holy Spirit, sin, repentance, and atonement in Christ. There is a distinctive eschatology. While the members look for the second coming of Christ, they hold that it has no connection with a millennial reign. The kingdom of God is here and now. There will be a judgment day with reward for the righteous and punishment for the wicked.

Three ordinances, symbolic of acts of obedience and experience with Christ, are commonly practiced: baptism, the Lord's Supper, and footwashing. Baptism is by immersion. The Communion is open to all believers. Footwashing is usually practiced on Maundy Thursday by separate groups of men and women. These symbolic acts are but highlights of a Christian life of stewardship and high moral and ethical conduct. Prayer for divine healing is practiced, as is tithing.

Warner's distinctive doctrine of the church led to a rejection of the presbyterial system. The church uses a congregational form of government as it allows only the authority of God to operate. No membership is held in a formal way: there is no formal initiation rite for members, and membership lists are not made.

Beyond the local church, there are state and regional associations, and each year a General Assembly is held in connection with the International Convention. Anderson, Indiana, is home to the church. Located there are its national offices, one of its colleges, theological school, and Warner Auditorium (site of the International Convention). There is an active outreach program conducted by the general church. The Christian Brotherhood Hour is heard over three hundred stations, including Spanish, Russian, Arabic, Portuguese, Indian, and Chinese-speaking stations. The Church is resident in 82 countries including Egypt, Lebanon, Greece, Switzerland, Germany, Denmark, England and Ireland, India, Korea, Japan, and throughout Central and South America and the Caribbean. Warner Press publishes many books, pamphlets and tracts, and most of the educational material used by the church. The church is represented in the National Association of Evangelicals and is associated with the Christian Holiness Association.

Membership: No formal membership figures are kept, but an informal count is made periodically. In 1992 the church reported 215,496 members, 2,402 congregations, and 4,396 ministers. There are an additional 299,924 members worldwide.

Educational Facilities: Anderson College, Anderson, Indiana.
Warner Pacific College, Portland, Oregon.
Mid-America Bible College, Oklahoma City, Oklahoma.
Warner Southern College, Lake Wales, Florida.
Gardner Bible College, Camrose, Alberta, Canada.
Bay Ridge Christian College, Kendleton, Texas.

Periodicals: *Vital Christianity.* • *Leader.* • *Missions.* • Shining Light. Available from Warner Press, Box 2499, Anderson, IN 46018.

Sources:

Callen, Barry L., ed. *The First Century.* 2 vols. Anderson, IN: Warner Press, 1979.

Miller, Milburn H. *"Unto the Church of God".* Anderson, IN: Warner Press, 1968.

Sterner, R. Eugene. *We Reach Our Hands in Fellowship.* Anderson, IN: Warner Press, 1960.

★435★
Church of God (Guthrie, Oklahoma)
% Faith Publishing House
7415 W. Monsur Ave.
Guthrie, OK 73044

The Church of God (Guthrie, Oklahoma) was formed by some ministers and laymen of the Church of God (Anderson, Indiana) who separated in 1910-1911 over what they felt had been compromises and changes in doctrine and practice, and drifting into worldliness. Among the new practices coming into the Church of God (Anderson, Indiana) were the segregation of the races and the wearing of neckties. In 1910 C. E. Orr began publishing *The Herald of Truth* in California, advocating the original position of Daniel Warner, founder of the Church of God (Anderson, Indiana). A movement supporting schism developed around Orr.

In doctrine and practice the Church of God (Guthrie, Oklahoma) is almost identical with the Church of God (Anderson, Indiana), but it is stricter in its practice of holiness and refusal to compromise with the world. Like the members of the parent body, the members of the Church of God (Guthrie, Oklahoma) believe in healing and reject the idea of a literal millennium.

In 1923 Fred Pruitt moved from New Mexico to Guthrie and began to print *Faith and Victory* which continues as the organ of the movement. Today from the Faith Publishing House, Wayne Murphy continues his grandfather's work and also publishes many tracts and *The Beautiful Way*, a children's quarterly. A vigorous mission program is supported in the Philippines, Nigeria, Mexico, and India. A national camp meeting has been held each July since 1938. Lesser camp meetings are held across the United States and in Mexico and Canada.

Membership: Not reported.

Periodicals: *Faith and Victory.* • *The Beautiful Way.*

Sources:

Pruitt, Fred. *Past, Present and Future of the Church.* Guthrie, OK: Faith Publishing House, n.d.

Speck, S. L., and H. M. Riggle. *Bible Readings for Bible Students.* Guthrie, OK: Faith Publishing House, 1975.

Susag, S. O. *Personal Experiences.* Guthrie, OK: Faith Publishing House, 1976.

Warner, Daniel S. *The Church of God.* Guthrie, OK: Faith Publishing House, n.d.

★436★
Church of God (Holiness)
7415 Metcalf
Overland Park, KS 66204

History. The origin of the Church of God (Holiness) dates to the very beginning of the "come-out" crisis of the early 1880s, a movement whose leaders advocated coming out of the mainline Protestant churches in order to establish independent holiness congregations. The ideal of the one New Testament church, a divine institution headed by Christ, was opposed in their thinking to what they saw as denominational, man-made organizations. Thus local congregations organized in conformity to the New Testament ideal became the movement's immediate goal. The first independent congregations which were established served primarily those holiness people with no previous church (denominational) affiliation, but eventually included people leaving the older churches.

During the decades when holiness advocates had been welcome in the mainline denominations, holiness associations had formed. These were not churches, but simply groups loosely affiliated with the non-holiness churches. As the come-out movement intensified, these associations fell into disfavor among many holiness proponents. Among those most strongly affected by come-outism were members of the Southwestern Holiness Association covering the states of Kansas, Missouri and Iowa. By 1882 six ministers, leaders of the association, had decided to withdraw from their parent denominational bodies as soon as it was convenient. A minister in the Methodist Episcopal Church, South, A. M. Kiergan, emerged as their leader and spearheaded the drive toward independent holiness congregations. The dominance of the come-outers in the Southwestern Holiness Association caused its dissolution in 1887 and the formation of a new church, the Independent Holiness People, the following year. In 1895 the name was changed to Church of God (known as Independent Holiness People). *The Good Way*, formerly serving the Southwestern Holiness Association, became the church newspaper.

Almost as soon as the church formed, two factions arose. One wanted complete local congregational sovereignty. The other said the elders should interpret doctrine and be spiritual rulers for the church, and should in turn be subject to a presbytery of elders. Kiergan and John P. Brooks, an early leader of the come-outers in Illinois, led the sovereignty faction. The crux of the issue was representation in the annual convention. In 1897 a "Declaration of Principles" was published by the sovereignty faction. The local sovereignty supporters wanted representation of the congregations at the annual meeting, and the others wanted the elders represented. Following the publication of the Declaration, the church split into the Independent Holiness People (sovereignty faction) and Unity Holiness People (elder faction). A reunion of the two factions was accomplished in 1922. The name of the reunited church is Church of God (Holiness). The new church merged with the Missionary Bands of the World, now a contistuent part of the Wesleyan Church, but the merger fell through in 1938.

Beliefs. Four doctrines are central in the Church of God (Holiness)—the New Birth, Entire Sanctification, the one New Testament church, and the second coming followed by a literal millennium. The one New Testament church idea is a distinctive feature of the Church of God (Holiness). The doctrinal statement in the reunited church reads:

The New Testament Scriptures teach that there is one true Church, which is composed only of those who have savingly believed in the Lord Jesus Christ, and who willingly submit themselves to His divine order concerning the ministries of the church through the instrumentalities of God—chosen elders and deacons, ordained in the church by laying on of the hands of the presbytery.

The attributes of the church are unity, spirituality, visibility, and catholicity. (Matt. 16:18; Eph 4:4; Col. 1:18; I Tim. 3: 1-7; Titus 1:5).

The government of the Church of God (Holiness) is congregational, but a delegated annual convention has responsibility for the election of individuals to serve on the various boards of church-wide ministries. The board of publications oversees Herald and Banner Press, the church's publishing house, which publishes the church magazine and a full line of church school materials, "The Way, Truth, & Life Series." The church has a worldwide missions program under the direction of the world mission board. Fields of service include Haiti, Jamaica, Mexico, the Cayman Islands, American and British Islands of the Eastern Caribbean, Bolivia and Nigeria. The home missions board is responsible for encouraging church extension ministries in the United States, including ethnic group ministries among native American Indians, Hispanic, Asian and Haitian immigrants, and blacks. The home and world mission programs are each directed by an executive secretary who is appointed by their respective boards.

Membership: In 1988 the church reported 1,500 members and 120 congregations in the United States and a worldwide membership of 16,000.

Educational Facilities: Kansas City College and Bible School, Overland Park, Kansas.

Fort Scott Christian Heights, Fort Scott, Kansas.

Holiness Bible School, Gravette, Arkansas.

Kirksville Bible School, Kirksville, Missouri.

Mount Zion Bible School, Ava, Missouri.

Mountain State Christian School, Culloden, West Virginia.

Overland Christian School, Overland Park, Kansas.

Periodicals: *The Church Herald and Holiness Banner.* • *Opening the Word.* Send orders to Box 4060, Overland Park, KS 66204.

Sources:

Brooks, John P. *The Divine Church.* El Dorado Springs, MO: Witt Printing Company, 1960.

Cowen, Clarence Eugene. *A History of the Church of God (Holiness).* The Author, 1948.

★437★
Church of God (Northern Indiana Eldership)
(Defunct)

The Church of God (Northern Indiana Eldership) originated as a schism from the Churches of God General Conference, which was generally known in the later-nineteenth century as the Churches of God in North America (General Eldership). It resulted from the influx of holiness experience and theology into the Churches of God. Among its prominent members was Daniel Warner, who served as editor for its newspaper. In 1880 Warner left the group, taking many members with him, and they became the core of the Church of God (Anderson, Indiana). The Church of God (Northern Indiana Eldership) is little heard of after that date and is presumed to have slowly dwindled away.

Sources:

Jones, Charles Edwin. *A Guide to the Study of the Holiness Movement.* Metuchen, NJ: Scarecrow Press, 1974.

★438★
Church of the Living God (Sandford)
Amherst, NH 03031

The Church of Living God (Sandford) was founded in 1894 by Frank Weston Sandford. It began in Brunswick, Maine, where Sandford opened a bible school in the winter of 1894-95. Sandford had been a Freewill Baptist minister, but had left that denomination in 1893 after being strongly affected by the teachings of A. B. Simpson and the Christian and Missionary Alliance and reading Hannah Whitall Smith's *The Christian's Secret of a Happy Life* (1870). Both were representative of the Keswick branch of the Holiness Movement, which called believers to a second experience with the Holy Spirit that granted them entire sanctification. In 1895 the group moved to new headquarters near Lisbon Falls, Maine, which was dubbed "Shiloh." The initial building, which would be greatly enlarged over the years and joined by adjacent buildings, would serve as headquarters of the church for the next quarter century. Shiloh was dedicated in a ceremony in July 1895 in which Sandford ordained his first ministerial assistant William Gleason.

The church followed a theology based on that of the Christian and Missionary Alliance. It was evangelistic and preached the higher sanctified life. There were four ordinances: baptism, healing, the Lord's Supper, and worship. Simpson had been one of the first to emphasize the recovery of divine healing in the church. Sandford deviated from much of the holiness movement by instituting sabbatarian worship (on Saturday). The Lord's Supper was closed to all but the members of the movement, a practice that indicated its separatist stance. In October 1895, without reference to any prior baptisms, Sandford rebaptized all of the members of the group, then some 218 in number.

As churches emerged around New England and, to a lesser extent, the rest of the country, Sandford initiated a system of membership based upon commitment levels. The most committed were those living at Shiloh, who gave up everything and worked full time for the movement. They lived by faith, relying upon God to supply their needs. At a minimum, members were required to tithe.

The most controversial belief of the movement, articulated in 1901, was the belief that Sandford was the prophet Elijah returned, the prophet who was to announce the return of Christ and the beginning of the millennial kingdom. The group began to see itself as the precursor group for the establishment of God's kingdom on earth.

Life at Shiloh was intense and subject to the occasional arbitrary change in direction articulated by Sandford. Some members left and joined forces with other religious leaders in the area to attack the school. However, the movement grew steadily and even developed a small following in Europe, through 1904. That year Sandford was indicted for manslaughter, legal authorities blaming him for several deaths that occurred during the winter of 1902-03. Initially found guilty, the verdict was overturned on appeal. Sanford had escaped momentarily. Then in 1911 he was arrested again and charged with being responsible for several deaths that occurred in the group's missionary ship while on a voyage to Greenland. He was convicted and sentenced to 10 years in prison.

Before leaving to serve his time, Sandford appointed seven ministers to take charge of Shiloh and the movement, but he kept in touch by way of regular letters and the visits of a member who moved to Atlanta and took stenographic notes of their conversations. Released in 1918, he immediately resumed control of the movement. Then in 1920, the state moved against Shiloh claiming that the parents living there were neglecting their children. Threatened with extensive legal proceedings as each family's case was abjudicated, Sandford disbursed the group and closed the center. From that time on, the movement he led has existed in a decentralized state. Sandford continued to lead the church until his death in 1947, but made few personal appearances. The small groups had kept a low profile in the succeeding half century. A small publishing concern, Kingdom Press, is operated from their headquarters in Amherst, New Hampshire.

Membership: Not reported.

Sources:

Murray, Frank S. *The Sublimity of Faith: The Life and Work of Frank W. Sandford.* Amherst, NH: The Kingdom Press, 1981.

Nelson, Shirley. *Fair Clear and Terrible: The Strange Story of Shiloh.* Latham, NY: British American Publishing, 1989. 446 pp.

Sandford, Frank S. *The Art of War for the Christian Soldier*. 1906. Reprint. Amherst, NH: The Kingdom Press, 1966.

___. *The Golden Light Upon the Two Americas*. Amherst, NH: The Kingdom Press, 1974.

___. *The Majesty of Snowy Whiteness*. 1901. Rept.: Amherst, NH: The Kingdom Press, 1963.

★439★
Church of the Nazarene
6401 The Paseo
Kansas City, MO 64131

Most holiness advocates were originally members of the Methodist Episcopal Church and the Methodist Episcopal Church, South, when the hostility of their leaders made the holiness people feel that a new church was their only option. Thus late in the nineteenth century a number of small schisms occurred, and independent holiness congregations and associations came into existence. By the turn of the century these smaller groups were seeking wider fellowship through mergers. The Church of the Nazarene is the result of a set of such mergers.

Phineas Bresee was a leading founder of the Church of the Nazarene. In 1885 Bresee, a former Methodist pastor and presiding elder, organized the First Church of the Nazarene in Los Angeles, California, after leaving the Peniel Missions where he had been preaching for a year. Coincident with Bresee's efforts, the Association of Pentecostal Churches of America was formed in New York. In 1896 this group united with the Central Evangelical Holiness Association (established in 1890) with member congregations located primarily in New England. In October 1907, the Association of Pentecostal Churches of America and the Church of the Nazarene, both having grown into small denominations, merged to form the Pentecostal Church of the Nazarene. On October 13, 1908, the Holiness Church of Christ united with the Pentecostal Church of the Nazarene in a joint assembly at Pilot Point, Texas; the merged body retained the name of Pentecostal Church of the Nazarene. The 1908 date is accepted as the official "anniversary" of the present-day Church of the Nazarene. In 1915 the Pentecostal Church of Scotland and the Pentecostal Mission of Nashville, Tennessee, united with the Pentecostal Church of the Nazarene.

In 1919 the word "Pentecostal" was dropped to avoid confusion with the "tongues" sects. Over the years other groups have united with the Church of the Nazarene including the Laymans Holiness Association (1922); the International Holiness Mission, an English group (1952); the Calvary Holiness Church, also British in origin (1955); the Gospel Workers Church of Canada (1958); and the indigenous Church of the Nazarene (Nigeria) (1988) whose founders were influenced by the 1944 *Manual* of the international Church of the Nazarene.

The Church of the Nazarene views itself as firmly Wesleyan in doctrine and practice and keeps in essence the Articles of Religion and General Rules as sent to America by Methodist founder, John Wesley. The church has, however, added statements on the plenary inspiration of Scripture, regeneration, entire sanctification, divine healing, and eschatology, and has changed completely Wesleys article on the church. The major emphasis is upon entire sanctification subsequent to regeneration and the personal holiness of the believer.

Government in the groups that formed the Church of the Nazarene was of all types: congregational, representative, and episcopal. The final outcome was a representative government. The highest law-making body is the General Assembly, composed equally of ministerial and lay delegates elected by the district assemblies. The general Board, elected by the General Assembly, has oversight of specialized General Assembly concerns: evangelism, missions, publication, education, and ministerial benevolences. The General Assembly, presided over by the general superintendents (who are elected every four years), has final authority in all matters except changes in the convention, which must also be approved by the district assemblies. The district assembly orders the work of the district and supervises the local churches and ministers. The local church calls its own pastor, subject to the district superintendents approval, and conducts its own affairs in accordance with General Assembly guidelines.

Mission in what became the Church of the Nazarene began in 1897 when Mr. and Mrs. M. D. Wood, Carrie Taylor, Lillian Sprague, and Mr. F. P. Wiley sailed for India to begin missionary work. The work has grown and the church is presently at work in more than 110 world areas under the Department of World Missions of the General Board.

Publishing began in 1888 with the *Beulah Christian* and in 1898 with the *Nazarene Messenger*. Early in 1900, the Nazarene Publishing Company was founded to carry on the work of the growing denomination. In 1911, after the merger, plans were made to establish a centrally located Nazarene publishing house. The new publishing concern—dnow Beacon Hill Press of Kansas City, Missouri—is the largest publisher of holiness literature in the world. The Church of the Nazarene is a member of the Christian Holiness Association and the National Association of Evangelicals.

Membership: In 1996 the church reported 5,135 congregations in North America with 608,008 members in the United States and 11,931 members in Canada. There were 1,138,504 members worldwide.

Educational Facilities: Nazarene Theological Seminary, Kansas City, Missouri.
Southern Nazarene University, Bethany, Oklahoma.
Eastern Nazarene College, Quincy, Massachusetts.
Mid-America Nazarene College, Olatha, Kansas.
Mount Vernon Nazarene College, Mt. Vernon, Ohio.
Nazarene Bible College, Colorado Springs, Colorado.
Northwest Nazarene College, Nampa, Idaho.
Olivet Nazarene University, Kankakee, Illinois.
Point Loma Nazarene College, San Diego, California.
Trevecca Nazarene College, Red Deer, Alberta, Canada.
Nazarene Theological College, Manchester, United Kingdom.
Korea Nazarene Theological College, Chonan City, Korea.
Nazarene Theological College, Muldersdrift, South Africa.
Asia Pacific Nazarene Theological Seminary, Manila, Philippines.
Nazarene Bible College, Thornlands, Queensland, Australia.
Luzon Nazarene Bible College, Bagulo City, Philippines.
Caribbean Nazarene Theological College, Santa Cruz, Trinidad.
European Nazarene Bible College, Schaffhausen, Switzerland.
Sekolah Tinggi Theological Nazarene Indonesia, Yogakarta, Indonesia.
Japan Christian Junior College, Chiba Shi, Japan.
Seminario Teologico Nazareno do Brasil, Sao Paulo, Brazil.
Universidad Nazareno de la Americas, San Jose, Costa Rica.
Seminario Nazareno Mexicano, Mexico City, Mexico.
Taiwan Nazarene Theological College, Taiwan, Republic of China.
Visayan Nazarene Bible College, Cabu City, Philippines.
India Nazarene Nurses Training College, Washim, India.
Instituto Teologico Nazareno, Guatemala City, Guatemala.
Nazarene College of Nursing, Mt. Hagen, Papua New Guinea.
Nazarene Nursing College, Manzini, Swaziland.
Seminario Teologico Nazareno Sudamericano, Quito, Ecuador.
Swaziland Nazarene Bible College, Siteki, Switzerland.

Periodicals: *Herald of Holiness*. • *World Missions*. • *El Heraldo de Santidad*. • *Preachers Magazine*. • *Grow*. • *Arauto da Sabtidade*. • *Ministerio*. • *Come Ye Apart*.

Sources:

Brickley, Donald P. *Man of the Morning.* Kansas City, MO: Nazarene Publishing House, 1960.

Girvin, E. A. *Phineas F. Bresee: A Prince in Israel.* Kansas City, MO: Pentecostal Nazarene Publishing House, 1916.

Price, Ross E. *Nazarene Manifesto.* Kansas City, MO: Beacon Hill Press, 1968.

Purkiser, W. T. *Called Unto Holiness, II.* Kansas City, MO: Nazarene Publishing House, 1983.

Redford, M. E. *The Rise of the Church of the Nazarene.* Kansas City, MO: Beacon Hill Press, 1948.

Smith, Timothy. *Called Unto Holiness.* Kansas City, MO: Nazarene Publishing House, 1962.

★440★
Churches of God (Independent Holiness People)
Current address not obtained for this edition.

In 1922 the Church of God (Independent Holiness People) and the Church of God (Unity Holiness People) united to become the Church of God (Holiness). However, some members of the Church of God (Independent Holiness People), those often referred to as the sovereignty faction and most committed to the strong sovereignty of the local congregation, did not join the merger. They reorganized and established headquarters at Ft. Scott, Kansas. The continuing church has no doctrinal differences with the Church of God (Holiness), only distinctive by its firm allegiance to a congregational government. The church has stanchly advocated a pacifist position and has annually at its conventions passed resolutions against Christian participation in war. Membership is concentrated in the Southwest. Missionary work is conducted in Japan and Mexico and among American Indians in South Dakota and Wyoming.

Membership: Not reported. In 1972, 15 churches were represented at the annual convention.

Periodicals: *The Church Advocate and Good Way.*

★441★
Emmanuel Association
% Peoples Bible College
2713 W. Cucharas
Colorado Springs, CO 80904

The Emmanuel Association was formed in 1937 by Ralph G. Finch, a former general superintendent of Foreign Missions of the Pilgrim Holiness Church, now a constituent part of the Wesleyan Church. The Emmanuel Association was run by Finch until his death in 1949. Now, the Association is run by the general conference made up of all ordained and licensed ministers. It establishes all rules and elects the officers. Local churches function under the general conference. There is also a provision for affiliated membership for both ministers and congregations.

Doctrine is like that of the Pilgrim Holiness Church, but with a very rigid behavior code, the "Principles of Holy Living." Members are conscientious objectors, believing that war is murder. Foreign missionary work is carried on in Guatemala.

Membership: Not reported. In the 1970 there were 17 churches in the United States and Canada and an estimated membership of 400.

Educational Facilities: People's Bible College, Colorado Springs, Colorado.

Periodicals: *Emmanuel Herald.*

Sources:

The Guidebook of the Emmanuel Association. Colorado Springs, CO: Emmanuel Association, 1966.

Ralph Goodrich French, the Man and His Mission. Colorado Springs, CO: Emmanuel Press, 1967.

★442★
Evangelical Christian Church (Wesleyan)
Box 277
Birdsboro, PA 19508

The Evangelical Christian Church was born in the holiness revival that occurred spontaneously in various parts of the United States during the latter part of the nineteenth century. In 1882 L. Frank Haas, along with four others, conducted open-air and hall meetings in the city of Philadelphia, Pennsylvania. These efforts resulted in the conversion of many people. Haas and his co-workers assumed spiritual leadership for this rapidly growing fellowship of new Christians.

While the organization of a church was not the original plan, the necessity of organizing was soon realized. The converts needed to be established in holiness of heart and life and opportunities were opening for the expansion of the work into other communities. The name Heavenly Recruit Association was chosen and the new organization was granted a charter by the city of Philadelphia in 1884.

The evangelistic ministry spread rapidly into the areas surrounding Philadelphia. Churches were soon established in Chester and West Conshohocken, Pennsylvania, and Wilmington, Delaware. New missions were organized at other locations in eastern Pennsylvania and in the state of Indiana. At the Annual Conference held at Linwood, Pennsylvania, in 1889, resolutions were passed to establish an itinerant ministry, elect a presiding elder, and station pastors. Haas, president of the association was elected the first Presiding Elder.

Articles of Faith and Bylaws were adopted by the Annual Conference of 1892, which convened at Reading, Pennsylvania. At this time the publication of a church paper was approved. It was called *The Crown of Glory*, and it was first published in Pennsylvania but later was moved to Indiana and was succeeded in 1906 by a new publication, *A Voice From Canaan*. Previous to these publication efforts, *Good News* and *The Heavenly Recruit* had been printed and circulated by the association.

At the tenth Annual Conference, held at West Conshohocken, Pennsylvania, in 1894, the denomination, which had outgrown the limitations of the original charter, voted to reorganize. At this time the church at Philadelphia withdrew, claiming the original charter and name. The conference then adopted the name Holiness Christian Association, elected Rev. C. W. Ruth as Presiding Elder and continued their sessions as the first Annual Conference of the reorganized denomination.

The Annual Conference of 1896, held at Reading, Pennsylvania, authorized the organization of a second Annual Conference in Indiana and a General Conference. The Indiana Conference was duly constituted that same year at Tipton, Indiana, under the direction of Rev. Jonas Trumbauer, the Presiding Elder. The first General Conference convened at Reading, Pennsylvania, in 1897. At this conference the organization modified its name to Holiness Christian Church.

In the period of 1907-1908, the Pennsylvania Conference considered consolidating with the Pentecostal Church of the Nazarene (the word "Pentecostal" was dropped in 1919). Release was requested from the General Conference and was granted. In 1908 several of the churches and ministers did unite with the Church of the Nazarene, forming the nucleus for their Philadelphia District. About an equal number of churches and ministers declined merger, reorganized, and continued as the Pennsylvania Conference of the Holiness Christian Church. In 1916 this conference reunited with the general church then centered in Indiana.

In 1919 at the General Assembly convened in Cincinnati, Ohio, the Holiness Christian Church, with the exception of the Pennsylvania Conference, voted to merge with the International

Apostolic Holiness Church. The Indiana Conference, which provided much of the strength of the new organization, was joined by the Kansas and Oklahoma Conference and the Illinois and Missouri Conference in the union, which selected the name International Holiness Church. A subsequent merger with the Pilgrim Church formed the Pilgrim Holiness Church, which in 1968 united with the Wesleyan Methodist Church to become the Wesleyan Church. The Pennsylvania Conference continued as the Holiness Christian Church.

Annual camp meetings were conducted at various locations throughout the church's history. In 1921 a camp meeting ground was purchased at Seyfert, near Reading, Pennsylvania. This continues to serve as the Conference Center for the denomination. The growth of the church led to the development of congregations beyond the original boundaries of the conference. Presently there are churches in Pennsylvania, Maryland, Delaware, New York, and Virginia, as well as Jamaica. A denominational camp meeting has also been held at Fruitland, Maryland, since 1950. Publication of a church periodical, first called *The Holiness Christian Messenger*, and now *The Christian Messenger*, was begun in 1937.

The church was incorporated under the laws of the Commonwealth of Pennsylvania in 1945. The corporate name, Holiness Christian Church of the United States of America was changed to Holiness Christian Church in 1969. The present name, Evangelical Christian Church (Wesleyan) was approved by the Annual Conference in 1976 and was legally authorized on January 1, 1977.

The Evangelical Christian Church is a member denomination of the Christian Holiness Association and the National Association of Evangelicals. Supportive and cooperative ministeries are also addressed through affiliation with the Evangelical Wesleyan Fellowship, an association of similar holiness denominations.

Throughout its history, the church has been involved in missionary endeavors. Work was conducted in Central and South America, Africa, and other world regions. In 1945, a movement which had begun in Jamaica twenty years previously, united with the Holiness Christian Church. The Jamaican church was incorporated in 1949 and was the focus of evangelistic and missionary activity through the years. Recognized as a District Conference in 1969, the Holiness Christian Church in Jamaica continues its ministry under that name while remaining fully a part of the Evangelical Christian Church.

Missionary outreach has also been accomplished through cooperation with selected international mission organizations. Through its present affiliation with World Gospel Mission, the Evangelical Christian Church is part of a global thrust to bring Christ's love to the nations.

Membership: In 1995 the church reported 1,200 members, 25 churches, and 54 ministers in the United States. There are 2,800 members worldwide.

Educational Facilities: The Church endorses Circleville Bible College, Circleville, Ohio.

Kentucky Mountain Bible College, Vancleve, Kentucky.

Periodicals: *The Christian Messenger*.

Sources:

The Manual of the Evangelical Christian Church (Wesleyan). Birdsboro, PA: Evangelical Christian Church (Wesleyan), 1987.

★443★
Evangelical Missionary Church of Canada
550 1212 - 31st Ave., NE
Calgary, AB, Canada T2E 7S8

The Evangelical Missionary Church of Canada was founded in 1993 by the merger of the former Canadian branches of the Missionary Church and the Evangelical Church of North America. The Evangelical Church in North America was formed in 1968 by ministers and congregations of the former Evangelical United Brethren who refused to participate in the merger of that body with the Methodist Church to form the United Methodist Church. Its Canadian work, under the leadership of Supt. T. J. Jesske, became autonomous in 1970.

The Missionary Church emerged out of various groups in the Mennonite tradition that had been greatly affected by Wesleyan holiness ideas. It had been formed in 1969 by a merger of the United Missionary Church and the Missionary Church Association. Among the formative events in Missionary Church history was a revival among the Mennonites of Ontario in the 1870s. The Canadian conferences of the Missionary Church became autonomous in 1987 and reorganized as the Missionary Church of Canada.

The Evangelical Missionary Church of Canada retains strong fraternal relationships with the two parent bodies in the United States and cooperates with them in various areas, especially foreign missionary work.

Membership: In 1993 the church reported 145 congregations, 12,217 members, and 367 ministers. It is organized into two conferences, East Canada and West Canada.

Educational Facilities: Rocky Mountain College, Medicine Hat, Alberta.

Sources:

Legeer, Eileen. *Merging Streams: Story of the Missionary Church*. Elkhart, IN: Bethel Publishing Company, 1979.

★444★
Faith Mission Church
1817 26th St.
Bedford, IN 47421

Faith Mission Church is a single, independent, holiness congregation founded in 1893. It was formed as a center of the Pentecostal Bands, one of the original holiness associations, later renamed the Missionary Bands of the World. In 1958, the Missionary Bands merged into the Wesleyan Methodist Church (now a constituent part of the Wesleyan Church). Members of the congregation in Bedford, Indiana, which had been originally chartered in the early 1920s, rejected the merger and became independent. Under their pastor, the Rev. Ray Snow, the church adopted its present name in 1963. The church is currently pastored by Leonard Sankey.

Membership: Faith Mission Church is an independent congregation that had approximately 150 members in 1995.

Educational Facilities: God's Bible School and College, Cincinnati, Ohio, is supported by the Faith Mission Church.

★445★
Free Methodist Church of North America
PO Box 535002
Indianapolis, IN 46253

History. The Free Methodist Church of North America was organized in 1860 in western New York by ministers and lay people who had formerly been members of the Genesee Conference of the Methodist Episcopal Church. The Rev. Benjamin Titus Roberts (1823-1893) was the leader of the group and elected general superintendent (later termed bishop). He and other leaders of the conference, both laity and clergy, had been expelled from the church for "insubordination." After an appeal of the case had been denied by the Methodist General Conference in 1860, those excommunicated men and others met to form a new Methodist institution.

Roberts and others had been calling the Methodists to return to what they considered to be the primitive doctrines and lifestyle of Methodism. They especially emphasized the Wesleyan teaching of the entire sanctification of life by means of grace through faith. In their writings and preaching they condemned with vigor their less radical brothers for worldliness and their departure from Methodist doctrine and experience. Because of their strong opposition to secret societies, the leaders of Free Methodism incurred the ill-will of members of the conference who held membership in such lodges and fraternal orders. Also, Roberts and most of his followers were radical abolitionists in the years immediately prior to the Civil War, at a time when many within the Methodist Episcopal Church were hesitant in their condemnation of the practice of slavery. Also important, the early Free Methodists condemned the growing practice of selling pews in Methodist churches and advocated free pews for all, an issue which in part gave them their name.

Beliefs. The Free Methodist Church had little doctrinal quarrel with the Methodist Episcopal Church and originally adopted a modified form of the 25 Articles of Religion. It added an article on entire sanctification and made a few minor changes. However, in 1974, an entirely new and expanded set of articles of religion were adopted by the church. Not only do they cover some issues not touched on in the earlier articles (such as eschatology), they have appended a lengthy set of biblical references which detail the scriptural underpinnings for each statement. The new articles do not in any way deviate in essential content from the earlier set.

From its beginning, the Free Methodist Church has made Christian holiness a significant distinctive of its teaching. The church has interpreted the Bible and the writings of John Wesley to teach that all Christians may be inwardly cleansed from sinful rebellion against God's will. It believes that the sanctification of the affections and will may be experienced instantly, in a moment of faith, when the wholly committed Christian accepts the atonement of Jesus Christ and the fullness of the Holy Spirit for the cleansing of his/her motives and the perfection of his/her love toward God and other persons. According to the church, the sanctification of life is a process of growth and development in holiness through the empowering of the Holy Spirit in the life of the Christian. The Free Methodist Church has endeavored to follow the teachings of Wesley regarding the sanctification of life by forming both general and special rules to guide Christians in the way of holiness. All adult members of the church covenant to refrain from any use of tobacco and alcoholic beverages. They promise to give a tithe of their income to benevolent and Christian causes. They vow to keep themselves free from membership in secret societies, that their loyalities may not be divided. They disavow all racism and political and social discrimination against ethnic minorities. They promise to regard marriage and the family as sacred, and they avoid divorce except for the cause of adultery or desertion.

Organization. The government of the church is a modified episcopacy. From the beginning, when lay leaders and ministers met to form the new denomination, provision was made for equal representation of clergy and laity in all the councils of the church, both local and general. A general conference meets every four to five years to review and establish the polity and programs of the denomination and to elect the bishops. Annual conferences bring together the ministers and delegated representatives of the local congregations in 32 districts in the United States. Pastors are appointed by the annual conference, with the bishop serving as chairman of a ministerial appointments committee. All church property is held in trust for the denomination.

The church is a member of both the Christian Holiness Association and the National Association of Evangelicals.

Membership: In 1996, the church reported 74,855 members, 1050 congregations, and 1,902 ministers in the United States. There were 5,360 members 129 churches and 271 ministers in Canada. Worldwide membership including missions in 34 countries was 358,253.

Educational Facilities: Aldersgate College, Moose Jaw, Saskatachewan, Canada.

Central College, McPherson, Kansas.

Greenville College, Greenville, Illinois.

Roberts Wesleyan College, Rochester, New York.

Seattle Pacific University, Seattle, Washington.

Spring Arbor College, Spring Arbor, Michigan.

The church is affiliated with Asbury Theological Seminary, Wilmore Kentucky.

Western Theological Seminary, Portland, Oregon.

Wesley Biblical Seminary, Jackson, Mississippi.

Azusa School of Theology, Azusa, California, and

Ontario Theological Seminary, Toronto, Ontario. It cooperates with, but does not sponsor, Azusa Pacific University, Azusa, California.

Periodicals: *Light and Life Magazine.* • *Free Methodist World Mission People.* • *The Free Methodist Pastor.*

Sources:

Hogue, William T. *History of the Free Methodist Church.* 2 vols. Chicago: Free Methodist Publishing House, 1918.

Marston, Leslie R. *From Age to Age a Living Witness.* Winona Lake, IN: Life and Light Press, 1960.

Roberts, B. T. *Holiness Teachings.* Salem, OH: H. E. Schmul, 1964.

Taylor, J. Paul. *Holiness, the Finished Foundation.* Winona Lake, IN: Life and Light Press, 1963.

★446★
Independent Holiness Church

% Rev. R. E. Votary, Gen. Supt.
Box 194
Sydenham, ON, Canada K0H 2T0

The Independent Holiness Church dates to the preaching activity of Ralph Cecil Horner (1854-1921). Horner, a member of the Montreal conference of the Methodist Church, Canada, refused to assume his pastoral appointments during the 1890s, preferring to engage in evangelistic activity. He was committed to a holiness perspective (an emphasis upon God's second work of grace which brings sanctification or perfect love to the believer) at a time when sanctification as a progressive process was becoming the dominant perspective in Methodism. In 1895 Horner was discharged from his ministerial duties and formed the Holiness Movement Church. In 1919 the church asked Horner to retire. Instead, he left the Holiness Movement Church and formed the Standard Church of America.

In 1959 the Holiness Movement Church merged into the Free Methodist Church. As the time of the merger approached, several congregations voiced their disapproval by breaking away and reconstituting themselves as the Independent Holiness Church. The doctrinal statement is similar to other holiness bodies, affirming belief in the Trinity, salvation in Christ, and the possibility of entire sanctification for every believer. Members are expected to live a holy life and give evidence of this by refraining from the use of alcohol, tobacco, and drugs, fasting once a week, avoiding worldly entertainments, and dressing modestly. The church promotes tithing and daily scripture reading and is against games of chance and secret societies. Divorce is frowned upon and remarriage after a divorce is not allowed within the voting membership. The church is congregational in organization and has a general conference which meets every two years.

Membership: In 1995 the church had 13 congregations (12 in Canada and one in the United States), and approximately 250 members.

Periodicals: *Gospel Tidings.* Send orders to 1564 John Quinn Rd., Rte. 1, Greecy, ON, Canada K4P 1J9.

★447★
Metropolitan Church Association

323 Broad St.
Lake Geneva, WI 53147

The Metropolitan Church Association was formed in 1894. It grew out of a holiness revival at the Metropolitan Methodist Episcopal Church in Chicago. It was first known as the Metropolitan

Holiness Church and adopted its present name in 1899. Members had a reputation for emotional displays at worship and ascetic behavior patterns. Early in its life, it adopted a communal form of organization, a factor which slowed its growth in the long run.

Besides its early emphasis upon inner city missions, foreign missions were begun around the globe. The one in India has been most productive, and a school and hospital are supported there. Other missions are supported in Mexico and in Cape Town and Swaziland (South Africa). There is an annual camp meeting for revival and fellowship, held since 1971 at the Salvation Army's Camp Wonderland at Camp Lake, Wisconsin. Business is conducted by an annual general assembly.

Membership: Not reported. In the 1970s there were 15 churches and approximately 400 members.

Periodicals: *The Burning Bush.*

Sources:

Henry, G. W. *Shouting: Genuine and Spurious.* Chicago: Metropolitan Church Association, 1903.

★448★
Missionary Christian and Soul Winning Fellowship
350 E. Market St.
Long Beach, CA 90805

The Missionary Christian and Soul Winning Fellowship was formed in 1957 by Rev. Lee Shelley, a minister of the Christian and Missionary Alliance. It continues the evangelistic and missionary interests of the Christian and Missionary Alliance, but its doctrinal statement has deleted any reference to healing, a particular interest of CMA founder, A. B. Simpson.

A missionary program has work in nineteen countries. In the United States there is a single congregation (Christian in Action Chapel) at Long Beach, California. A school provides vocational training for Christian workers. Within the United States a Jewish ministry in Los Angeles led by Abe Schneider is supported, as is an Apache Indian Mission.

Membership: There is a single congregation in California.

★449★
Missionary Church, Inc. (U.S.)
3901 S. Wayne Ave.
Fort Wayne, IN 46807

Missionary Church, Inc. (U.S.) was formed in 1969 by the merger of the United Missionary Church and the Missionary Church Association.

From Defenseless Mennonite roots, the Missionary Church Association was formed in 1898 at Berne, Indiana, under the leadership of J.E. Ramseyer. The group had been influenced by the Christian and Missionary Alliance in both faith and practice.

The United Missionary Church dates to an evangelistic effort in Lehigh County, Pennsylvania, among the Mennonites. In 1858 a conference was founded using the name Evangelical Mennonites. In 1869 Solomon Eby, a Canadian Mennonite minister from Port Elgin, influenced by the Methodist revivals, professed conversion after some years in the ministry and instituted protracted meetings in his effort to spread the new experience of grace. The movement spread and was embraced by a former Mennonite group centered in Elkhart, Indiana, led by Daniel Brenneman, who had also experienced personal conversion. In 1874 the two fellowships took the name Reformed Mennonites. The next year they were joined by a small body located in the Niagara area of Ontario, Canada, called the New Mennonites, and took the name United Mennonites. The United Mennonites and the Evangelical Mennonites merged in 1879 to form the United Evangelical Mennonites. This body merged with a small splinter of the River Brethren in Pennsylvania and Ohio (Brethren in Christ) in 1883 to become the Mennonite Brethren in Christ with churches in both

the U.S. and Canada. The change of name in 1947 to United Missionary Church was a recognition of its move away from its Mennonite background.

In 1969 the United Missionary Church merged with the Missionary Church Association to form the Missionary Church, Inc. The Missionary Church Association had generally followed the four-fold gospel emphasis of A. B. Simpson, founder of the Christian and Missionary Alliance, presenting Christ as saviour, sanctifier, healer, and coming king. The United Missionary Church, influenced by Methodism, emphasized Wesleyan teaching. These have blended and without moving from the truths so held, the Missionary Church, Inc. adopted a more comprehensive presentation of its evangelical conservative and holiness faith.

Membership: In 1987 the Canadian branch of the Missionary Church, Inc. with its 92 churches and 6,400 members (9,500 adherents), chose to separate from the U.S. churches calling themselves Missionary Church of Canada. The two denominations continue to cooperate with each other in their missionary endeavor with missionaries in more than 20 countries. There are 26,700 baptized members included in the 89,100 adherents in these countries.

In 1996 Missionary Church, Inc. (U.S.) reported 46,700 adherents, (of whom nearly 31,550 are members), 325 churches, and 530 active ministers.

Educational Facilities: Bethel College, Mishawaka, Indiana.

Periodicals: *Emphasis.* • *Priority.* • *Ministry Today.* • *World Partners.*

Sources:

Lageer, Eileen. *Merging Streams.* Elkhart, IN: Bethel Publishing Company, 1979.

★450★
Missionary Church of Canada
% Dr. Alfred Rees, Pres.
89 Centre Ave.
North York, ON, Canada M2M 2L7

In 1987, the Canadian conferences of the Missionary Church separated and reorganized as an independent church. The separation, which followed a pattern of a number of their American-based denominations with work in Canada, was amicable and the two organizations still work together closely. One stream of Missionary Church history can be traced to the conversion of a Canadian Mennonite minister, Solomon Eby, of Ontario in 1869. The people affected by his message and experience became known as the Reformed Mennonites. In 1894 this group, having gone through several mergers and known as Mennonite Brethren in Christ, spread to Alberta. Eventually two districts, one centered in Ontario and Quebec and the other in Alberta and British Columbia, would emerge.

The Missionary Church in Canada is at one in faith and practice with the Missionary Church, the separation being entirely an administrative issue.

Membership: In 1987, there were 92 churches, 6,431 members, and 129 ministers.

Sources:

Lageer, Eileen. *Merging Streams: Story of the Missionary Church.* Elkhart, IN: Bethel Publishing Company, 1979.

★451★
Missionary Methodist Church of America
Current address not obtained for this edition.

The Missionary Methodist Church was formed in 1913 in Forest City, North Carolina, by Reverend H. C. Sisk and four other former members of the Wesleyan Methodist Church. (The Wesleyan Methodist Church subsequently merged with the Pilgrim Holiness

Church to form the Wesleyan Church.) The Missionary Methodist Church was originally called the Holiness Methodist Church, but the name was changed upon learning of another group with the same name. The original disagreement that led to the founding of the church was over the number of rules and regulations of the Wesleyan Methodist Church. A two-paragraph Creed includes belief in sanctification, which burns out all inbred sin; living every day above sin; keeping the self unspotted from the world; a personal devil; a literal, burning hell; and the premillennial return of Christ. "There are," states the Creed, "no hard man-made rules to bind one down, you can have freedom in the Missionary Methodist Church. . . ." In 1939 the Oriental Missionary Society was adopted as the missionary agency of the church.

Membership: In 1984 the church reported 1,708 members, 12 congregations, and 32 ministers.

Sources:

Doctrine, Creed and Rules for the Government of the Missionary Methodist Church of America. Morganville, NC, 1969.

★452★
New Testament Church of God
Box 611
Mountain Home, AR 72653

The New Testament Church of God, Inc. was founded in 1942 by G. W. Pendleton and Martha Pendleton, his wife, both former members of the Church of God (Anderson, Indiana). They opposed the Church of God's cooperation and financial support of the National Council of Churches, but kept the doctrines of the parent body. The members hold camp meetings and state and regional conventions, publish gospel literature, and have regular radio broadcasts.

Membership: Not reported. Congregations are found across the United States, but no membership count has been made.

Periodicals: *Seventh Trumpet.*

★453★
Peniel Missions
(Defunct)

The first Peniel Mission was founded by T. P. Ferguson and his wife Manie Ferguson in Los Angeles in 1886. Ferguson had been influenced by the preaching of Charles G. Finney, an early nineteenth century holiness theologian and evangelist. In 1880 he experienced sanctification under some holiness evangelists. Given the success of the Los Angeles work, he established rescue missions in the urban areas of the West Coast in attempts to win the urban masses to Christ. The missions have been marked by intense evangelistic endeavor, spiritual guidance, and stress on sanctification and sinlessness. For a short time, Phineas Bresee, founder of the Church of the Nazarene, worked at the Los Angeles center. By 1900 work had spread north along the West Coast and in Alaska, Hawaii, and Egypt. In 1949 responsibility for the Egyptian mission was assumed by the National Holiness Missionary Society, currently known as the World Gospel Mission, located in Winona Lake, Indiana.

★454★
Salvation Army
615 Slaters Ln.
Alexandria, VA 22313

The Salvation Army is an international religious and charitable movement organized and operated on a quasi-military model. Its juxtaposition of two strong motivations, love of God and a practical concern for the needs of humanity, results in a ministry dedicated to preaching the Christian gospel and disseminating its teaching while actively supplying basic human necessities. It offers personal counseling and a program of spiritual regeneration and physical rehabilitation. This dual focus, and the passion with which it is carried out, have served in the secular community to make the Salvation Army at once a target of popular satire and one of the most respected agencies delivering social services to the community at large.

History: In 1865 William Booth, an independent Methodist minister, began to preach in the slums at the East End of London, England. He organized the East London Christian Mission and began a magazine, the *East London Evangelist*. The mission met a genuine need; within a few years it had spawned 12 others and began to reach beyond London. The name was changed to Christian Mission in 1868. As activities increased over the next decade, Booth began to see the need for a more disciplined core of workers to carry out the demanding program, and he started to think in terms of a "Salvation Army." Step by step the name of the mission was changed, the magazine became the *Salvationist*, the uniform was adopted, and Booth was transformed into "the General." Within two years the Army had spread through England.

As the work of the organization progressed, Booth became aware of the physical needs of the poor among whom the Army had been preaching. His broad investigation of their situation was published in a volume, now a classic of socially concerned Christianity, *In Darkest England and the Way Out* (1890). He proposed a total program of assistance and rehabilitation. This book set the emphases followed by the Army to this day.

The Army was brought to America in 1880 when Commissioner George Scott Railton and seven female officers, known as the "Seven Hallelujah Lassies," arrived in New York City. The Army was brought to Canada two years later by Jack Addie, a convert from Scottish Presbyterianism, and Joseph Ludgate, who started an open-air mission in London, Ontario.

Beliefs. The Army's program of social service has made it famous and respected by many who are quite unaware of its existence as a holiness church body. The Salvation Army was founded as an evangelical organization, dedicated to bringing people into a right relationship with God through Christ. It emphasizes a balanced ministry of social and spiritual work. Its doctrinal basis is that of the Wesleyan-Arminian tradition. It also holds that it is the privilege of believers to be "wholly sanctified." Distinctive to Salvationists is their belief about the sacraments. Salvationists have looked upon the whole of life, the Gospel proclaimed, and the ministry in Christ's name as sacramental, both to the receiver and the giver. Hence, the traditional sacraments of baptism and communion have not been considered by the Army as a necessity to salvation and spiritual growth.

Organization: The Army is organized on a military model. The international leader of the Salvation Army holds the rank of general and operates out of the international headquarters in London, England. The highest ranking officer in the United States is a commissioner. One commissioner serves in the capacity of a national commander over the four territorial headquarters, each operated by a commissioner as a territorial commander. Officers (ministers) begin with the rank of cadet and two years of training at one of the four officers' training schools. Upon graduation, the officer is commissioned (ordained) as a lieutenant and begins to rise in rank.

The Army also is distinguished by its early opening of the ranks of the ordained ministry to females. Catherine Booth, William Booth's wife, had actually been preaching in London before her husband joined her and wrote one of the earliest tracts defending an ordained female ministry. The American work was largely initiated by females. Females have served prominently at every rank and, as of 1994, the Army is headed by General Paul Radar.

The social program of the Army has become one of the most far-reaching of any church organization. It includes feeding, and housing the homeless, disaster relief, alcohol and drug rehabilitation, youth camps and programs, senior citizen camps and programs, hospital and prison visitation, support for unwed mothers, to mention only a sample. These pioneering efforts have provided a model for many other churches.

Membership: In 1995, the Army reported 453,150 members, ,264 churches, and 5,242 officers in the United States. There vere 370 churches, 95,763 members and 2,008 ministers in Canda. Affiliated centers were located in 100 countries and territoies.

Educational Facilities: Salvation Army College/Schools for Oficer Training, Suffern, New York; Chicago, Illinois; Atlanta, Georis; Palos Verdes Estates, California.

Periodicals: *The War Cry.* • *Young Salvationist.*

ources:

\gnew, Milton S. *Manual of Salvationism*. New York: Salvation Army, 1968.

arnes, Cyril. *God's Army*. Elgin, IL: David C. Cook, 1968.

rengle, Samuel Logan. *The Way of Holiness*. London: Salvationist Publishing and Supplies, 1960.

hesham, Sallie. *Born to Battle*. Chicago: Rand McNally & Company, 1965.

McKinley, Edward H. *Marching to Glory*. New York: Harper & Row, 1980.

he Sacraments, the Salvationist's Viewpoint. London: Salvationist Publishing and Supplies, 1960.

andall, Robert. *The History of the Salvation Army*. London: Thomas Nelson, 1947.

Vatson, Bernard. *A Hundred Years' War*. London: Hodder and Stoughton, 1964.

★455★

tandard Church of America
ox 488
rockville, ON, Canada K6V 5V7

Ralph G. Horner had been an evangelist in both the Methodist Church in Canada and the Wesleyan Methodist Church, now a onstituent part of the Wesleyan Church, in the late nineteenth entury, but left them to found his own organization, the Holiness Movement Church, in 1895. As its bishop, he ruled with all the auhority of both a bishop and charismatic personality, and within ve years there were 118 places of worship. Churches were plant-d across Canada, into New York, with foreign work in Ireland, gypt, and China. Then in 1918 the aging bishop was asked to re-ire. Not satisfied with the request of the church, he, with his sup-orters, left and founded the Standard Church of America, incor-orated at Watertown, New York, in 1919. (The Holiness Movement Church eventually merged with the Free Methodist Church, which accounts for that church's large membership in gypt.)

Like the Holiness Movement Church, the Standard Church of America is Methodist in doctrine with a strong emphasis on holiess and evangelism. Polity is episcopal. Pastors are stationed by he annual conferences for four-year terms. There are four confer-nces: Western, Kingston, New York, and Egyptian. A Bible chool and printing establishment are maintained adjacent to the eadquarters. There is missionary work in China and Egypt.

Membership: Not reported.

Educational Facilities: Brockville Bible College, Brockville, Ontario, Canada.

Periodicals: *Christian Standard.*

★456★

Undenominational Church of the Lord
Current address not obtained for this edition.

The Undenominational Church of the Lord was founded at Pla-entia, California in 1918 by Pastor Jesse N. Blakeley, a holiness ninister. Previously, he had helped form the Pentecost Pilgrim Church at Pasadena (which merged into what became the Pilgrim Holiness Church, now a constituent part of the Wesleyan Church).

Blakeley became pastor of the Independent Holiness Mission in Placentia following a revival in Santa Ana. He felt the Holy Spirit leading him south and discovered the pastorless congregation in Placentia praying for the Lord to send them the right person. The Independent Holiness Mission became the Undenominational Church of the Lord.

A second branch of the church was founded in 1920 in Anaheim and became the headquarters. In 1922 the Placentia church was consolidated with the Anaheim church. In 1930 Blakeley was succeeded by Elsie Heughan, and in 1941 the headquarters returned to Placentia.

Doctrine of the Undenominational Church of the Lord is holiness. Evangelism, especially by the printed word, is emphasized. Mission churches have been established in Nigeria, India, and Korea, all of which are now autonomous. Though there are fewer than 100 members in the United States, there are many thousands in the foreign fields.

Membership: At last report (1970s) there were 3 congregations: Placentia, California; Chillicothe, Ohio; and Sheridan, Oregon. There were less than 100 members.

Periodicals: *The Second Comforter.* Send orders to Box 291, Placentia, CA 92677.

★457★

Volunteers of America
3939 N. Causeway Blvd.
Metairie, LA 70002

The Volunteers of America was formed in 1896 by Ballington Booth and Maud Booth, the son and daughter-in-law of William Booth. While very much like the Salvation Army from which it sprang, it differs in several ways; it is more democratic, though keeping the quasi-military organization; it practices both baptism and the Lord's Supper; the early emphasis on sanctification and holiness has lessened in favor of a more general evangelical faith.

Membership: In 1984 the Volunteers reported 70 centers served by 290 ministers.

Periodicals: *The Gazette.*

★458★

Wesleyan Church
Box 50434
Indianapolis, IN 46250-0434

The Wesleyan Church was formed in 1968 by the merger of the Wesleyan Methodist Church and Pilgrim Holiness Church. In the merger two diverse streams of holiness tradition (one pre-Civil War and the other from the late nineteenth century) were brought together.

The Wesleyan Methodist church had been formed in 1843 by ministers and laymen who withdrew from the Methodist Church during the height of the slavery controversy. Reverends Orange Scott, LeRoy Sunderland (later to join the Unitarian Association), and L. C. Matlock were all abolitionists who continually fought the compromise on the slavery issue made by the Methodist Episcopal Church in the early nineteenth century. (A note on that compromise: the eighteenth-century Methodist Episcopal Church did not allow any of its members to have slaves. Over the years, the church reneged on that strong anti-slavery position and allowed slaveholders to membership in the church.) Along with slavery, the reformers also began to attack the abuses of the episcopacy and the failure to teach and practice various forms of piety. By 1843 tension had reached such a level that, feeling no redress of grievances was possible, the reformers withdrew and took twenty-two ministers and 6,000 members and formed the Wesleyan Methodist Church in America. In the first *Discipline*, their book of church order, statements were made against slavery, against the use of alcohol and tobacco, against secret societies, and for modesty in dress. The new structure provided for annual conferences with lay delegates and an elected president (instead of a bishop). There was also a General Conference.

The Pilgrim Holiness Church grew out of the holiness movement of the late nineteenth century. Martin Wells Knapp, a former minister in the Methodist Episcopal Church, and Rev. Seth Cook Rees organized the International Holiness Union and Prayer League in 1897 in Cincinnati, Ohio. The Union was to be a fellowship, not a church. It was established as a completely Wesleyan movement with emphasis on holiness, healing the sick, the premillennial coming of Christ, and evangelization. From a small beginning, rapid growth ensued. The growth of the Union led to a change of character, and the fellowship became a church. It underwent several name changes and, in 1922, finally took the name of the Pilgrim Holiness Church. Other holiness groups that merged with the Union (later called the Pilgrim Holiness Church) were the following (with merger dates): Indiana Conference of the Holiness Christian Church (1919); Pilgrim Church of California (1922); Pentecostal Rescue Mission (1922); Pentecostal Brethren in Christ (1924); People's Mission Church (1925); and Holiness Church of California (1946).

The Wesleyan church has a modified episcopal government headed by the Board of General Superintendents. Globally, each local unit of the denomination serves under one of two general conferences—the North American General Conference or the Philippine General Conference. The general conferences are the supreme governing bodies and elect the general superintendents to four-year term(s). Each general conference has a General Board of Administration, which operates between general conference sessions. The church is divided into districts. North American headquarters of the Wesleyan Church are in Indianapolis, Indiana. The headquarters for the Philippine General Conference are in Manila. The Wesleyan Publishing House located in Indianapolis is responsible for a wide range of books, religious literature, and church school material. The Commission on World Missions oversees a vast foreign mission program, worldwide.

Membership: In 1997 the church reported 119,117 members, 1,578 churches, and 3,140 ministers in the United States. There were 82 congregations and 196 ministers in Canada. There were 248,579 members and 369,312 listed constituents in 49 countries worldwide.

Educational Facilities: Bartlesville Wesleyan College, Bartlesville, Oklahoma.

Southern Wesleyan University, Central, South Carolina.

Houghton College, Houghton, New York.

Indiana Wesleyan University, Marion, Indiana.

Wesleyan Seminary Foundation, Indianapolis, Indiana.

Bethany Bible College, Sussex, New Brunswick.

In addition to the schools listed, the church also approves the following ministerial training programs:

Asbury Theological Seminary, Wilmore, Kentucky.

Evangelical School of Theology, Pine Grove, Pennsylvania.

Nazarene Theological Seminary, Kansas City, Missouri.

Wesley Biblical Seminary, Jackson, Mississippi.

Western Evangelical Seminary, Portland, Oregon.

Periodicals: *The Wesleyan Advocate.* • *Wesleyan World.* • *Wesleyan Woman.*

Sources:

Knapp, Martin Wells. *Holiness Triumphant or Pearls from Patmos.* Cincinnati: God's Bible School Book Room, n.d.

McLeister, Ira Ford, and Roy S. Nicholson. *History of the Wesleyan Methodist Church.* Marion, IN: Wesley Press, 1959.

Thomas, Paul Westphal, and Paul William Thomas. *The Days of Our Pilgrimage.* Marion, IN, 1976.

Twentieth Century Holiness

Calvary Holiness Church
3415-19 N. Second St.
Philadelphia, PA 19140

In 1963, the Brethren in Christ church experienced a split among members; some rejecting what they saw as liberalizing and diversifying trends in the church. Members in the Philadelphia, Pennsylvania, congregation under the leadership of William L. Rosenberry saw the church loosing its stand on separation from the world and practical holiness. This small congregation incorporated in 1964 as the Calvary Holiness Church. It was joined by members who left from Brethren in Christ congregations in Hanover and Millersberg, Pennsylvania, and Massillon, Ohio.

The church follows the general beliefs of the Brethern in Christ, differing primarily in the strictness with which its holds to the beliefs and practices. As with other Wesleyan holiness churches, it believes in the experience of entire santification as a second work of grace in the life of the believer. Members observe the ordinances of baptism in the name of the Trinity, the Lord's Supper, and the washing of the saints' feet. Women wear a veil during worship. The holy kiss (I Peter 5:14) is used as a form of greeting. Believers are admonished to live a life of separation from the follies, sinful practices, and methods of the world, most especially in following a spirit of nonresistance in all matters according to Christ's Sermon on the Mount. Members refrain from use of intoxicating substances, worldly amusements (including television), membership in lodges and secret societies, and activity that does not glorify God on the Lord's Day.

Members wear a version of the "plain people" garb which for men includes a suit of plain material, black or brown shoes, and conservative hats. No neckties or jewelry is allowed. Women wear conservative dresses with full-length sleeves. They may not wear shorts, slacks, socks, jewelry, lace, bows, or artificial means to bedeck the hair or face. During all waking hours they wear a "prayer and prophecy veil" in the shape of a bonnet of white (which is covered with a black bonnet for the out-of-doors).

The church follows a congregational polity. There is an executive council which handles matter of polity, doctrine, and standards at a general church level.

Membership: Not reported. In the early 1970s, there were only two congregations and 38 members, though the church reported a number of constitutency members and the monthly magazine had a circulation of 7,000.

Periodicals: *The Gospel Witness.*

Remarks: This church should not be confused with the Calvary Holiness Church of England (1930-1955) which is now an integral part of the Church of the Nazarene.

Christian Pilgrim Church
Current address not obtained for this edition.

The Christian Pilgrim Church was formed in 1937 by a group of holiness people, including Reverends Fannie Alldaffer, C. W. Cripps, and Tracy Alldaffer. They gathered at Coldwater, Michigan, to build a holiness church that could function without "so much law and order or machinery in the church." Officers were elected for life or as long as they remained in agreement with the Bible and the church.

The doctrine is Trinitarian and holiness (i.e., in essential agreement with the other churches discussed in this chapter). Healing is stressed but speaking in tongues is considered contrary to the Word of God; Baptism by any mode is desired; tithing is insisted upon; secret societies are condemned; Christ's imminent premillennial second coming is expected.

There is a General Assembly which meets annually. The church is divided into districts. A general superintendent has general oversight of the work and is aided by two assistants. Congregations are found in the South and Midwest.

Membership: Not reported. In the mid-1970s, the church had 15 congregations and approximately 250 members.

Periodicals: *The Christian Voice.*

★461★
Church of the Gospel
Current address not obtained for this edition.

The Church of the Gospel was formed in 1911 in Pittsfield, Massachusetts, by the Rev. and Mrs. C. T. Pike and members of the Advent Christian Church. In 1912 the group incorporated as the Church of God but adopted its present name in 1930 to avoid confusion with other groups. Basic doctrinal perspective is drawn from the Wesleyan holiness tradition. The members practice baptism by immersion and believe in the imminent second coming. The church has distributed "Narrow Way" tracts by the thousands across the country.

Membership: Not reported. Never a large body, in the 1940s there were only four or five churches. In 1971 there was only a single congregation in Virginia and scattered remnants in New England.

★462★
Churches of Christ in Christian Union
1426 Lancaster Pike
Circleville, OH 43113

History and Beliefs. The Churches of Christ in Christian Union was formed in 1909 when a small group of ministers withdrew from the annual council of the Christian Union denomination. The cause for withdrawal occurred when the council voted to censure any minister preaching a Wesleyan Holiness doctrine. The doctrine of the CCCU is Wesleyan Holiness with a strong emphasis upon evangelism and the sanctifying work of the Holy Spirit in the life of the believer. The denomination supports a worldwide mission program and the Circleville Bible College, an accredited college specializing in training persons for ministry and other Christian service careers.

In 1952 the Reformed Methodist Church, a 1914 splinter from the Methodist Episcopal Church over episcopal polity, joined the Churches of Christ in Christian Union as the Northeastern District. The Reformed Methodist Church was formed in 1914 in Readsborough, Vermont, by a group of Methodists led by Pliny Brett, a local preacher. At their first conference, February 4, 1914, they adopted the Methodist "Articles of Religion" and some democratic rules for church government. The government was essentially congregational without sharp distinctions between ministers and laymen. While the Methodist system of representative conferences was kept, ministers were delegates only if elected, not ex-officio. The local church was the focus of power, having the right to ordain elders, select its own ministers, and do whatever else was necessary yo carry on its work. Ministers likewise, could pick their field of service.

Organization. Polity is congregational within the limits established by the denominational Constitution and Bylaws. Spiritual officers of the local church are the pastor and elders. Local church business affairs are conducted by a board comprised of the elders, church trustees, and by departmental leaders. The national church officers are elcted by biennial general council and/or annual district councils.

Membership: In 1994 the churches reported 9,598 members.

Educational Facilities: Circleville Bible College, Circleville, Ohio.

Periodicals: *The Evangelical Advocate.*

Evangelical Church of North America
3000 Market St. NE, Ste. 528
Salem, OR 97301

The Evangelical Church of North America was formed in 1968 by members of the Evangelical United Brethren who did not wish to proceed into the merger with the The Methodist Church (1939-1968) that created the United Methodist Church, described in the preceding chapter. The schism in the Evangelical United Brethren involved 50 congregations in the church's Northwest Conference and 23 churches from the Montana Conference. For several decades the Northwest Conference had been a center of holiness theology with many of the pastors being trained in the Western Evangelical Seminary (established in 1945 and firmly holiness in its doctrine and emphases).

Almost as soon as the Evangelical Church of North America was formed, the Holiness Methodist Church, with headquarters in Minneapolis, voted to affiliate, and in 1969 became the North Central Conference of the new church. The Holiness Methodist Church was a result of the "holiness" revival movement that swept the United States in general and Methodism in particular during the late 1800s. The Northwestern Holiness Association was formed at Grand Forks, North Dakota, on March 24, 1909, as a fellowship of those following the holiness way. This informal association changed its name to the Holiness Methodist Church in 1920, recognizing that the association had become a denomination. In 1977 the small Wesleyan Covenant Church, with congregations in Detroit and in Brownsville, Texas, but an extensive Mexican Mission, merged into the Evangelical Church.

The doctrine of the Evangelical Church of North America follows the tradition of Methodism as developed within the Evangelical United Brethren. It includes a special emphasis on entire sanctification.

The Evangelical Church of North America has six annual conferences—the Pacific, the Eastern, the Western, the East Central, the North Central, and the Southeastern. The church is supervised by a general conference that meets quadrennially and the general church council which meets annually. The highest full-time executive office, that of general superintendent, was created in 1976. The work of missions is supervised by the department of missions and a full-time executive director. Fields include Bolivia, Brazil, Germany, New Mexico (among Native Americans), and the Texas-Mexican border. In addition, churches across the denomination participate actively in a number of interdenominational mission agencies such as OMS International, World Gospel Mission, and Wycliffe Bible Translators. Currently there is more than one adult missionary (150) per congregation (140). The church is a member of the National Association of Evangelicals and the Christian Holiness Association.

In 1993 the North West Canada Conference became autonomous and with the blessing of the Evangelical Church of North America merged with the Missionary Church in Canada to become the Evangelical Missionary Church of Canada.

Membership: In 1994, the church reported 13,500 members. This includes 210 ministers and 140 congregations in the United States. Average Sunday morning attendance for the churches totaled 14,000.

Educational Facilities: George Fox College, Newberg, Oregon. Rocky Mountain College, Medicine Hat, Alberta, Canada. Vennard College, University Park, Iowa. Wesley Biblical Seminary, Jackson, Mississippi. Western Evangelical Seminary, Portland, Oregon.

Periodicals: *The Evangelical Advocate.* • *The Challenge.* • *Share.*

Sources:

Pike, John M. *Preachers of Salvation.* N.p., n.d.

★464★
Gospel Mission Corps of the American Rescue Workers
Box 175
Hightstown, NJ 08520

The Gospel Mission Corps was founded by Robert S. Turton III, a graduate of the Pillar of Fire Bible Seminary of Zarephath, New Jersey. He began a mission at Hightstown, New Jersey, which grew into the Gospel Mission Corps in 1962. Its doctrine was like that of the American Rescue Workers (ARW), with which it merged in 1980. Some of its members had previously belonged to the ARW.

★465★
Grace and Hope Mission
4 S. Gay St.
Baltimore, MD 21202

The Grace and Hope Mission was founded in 1914 by Mamie E. Caskie and Jennie E. Goranflo, who opened a gospel mission in Baltimore. The work grew so that by the late 1960s there were 12 centers, mostly in large cities. The doctrine is Wesleyan-Protestant with an emphasis on evangelism, holiness, and the hope of the second coming. The officers, all single females, wear a black uniform with red trimming and the Mission's emblem. There is an annual conference at which the assignments of officers for the coming year are made.

Membership: In 1997 the mission reported ten centers. There is no formal membership, but approximately 800 people participate in the mission's activities.

★466★
Kentucky Mountain Holiness Association
PO Box 2
Vancleve, KY 41385

The Kentucky Mountain Holiness Association was begun in 1925 by Lela G. McConnell, a deaconess in the Methodist Episcopal Church. Following her ordination in 1924, she began a vigorous ministry in the mountains of eastern Kentucky. She preached a Wesleyan-Protestant doctrine with a strong emphasis on sanctification. The association maintains an elementary school, a high school, a four-year Bible college, a radio station, and a campground. J. Eldon Neihof is the current association president.

Membership: In 1997 the association reported 13 churches.

Educational Facilities: Kentucky Mountain Bible College, Vancleve, Kentucky.

Sources:

McConnell, Lela G. *The Pauline Ministry in the Kentucky Mountains.* Jackson, KY: The Author, 1942.

★467★
Lumber River Annual Conference of the Holiness Methodist Church
℅ Bishop C. N. Lowry
Rowland, NC 28383

The Lumber River Annual Conference of the Holiness Methodist Church was organized in 1900 by members of the Methodist Episcopal Church, South, at Union Chapel Church, Robeson County, North Carolina. The members of the Lumber River Annual Conference had an intense interest in the holiness movement with its stress on the second blessing, a religious experience certifying holiness. At the time, the holiness movement was criticized by many Methodists, so the holiness advocates among the Conference decided to form a new church. In addition to their interest in the holiness movement was their concern for home missions.

The church follows Wesleyan-Protestant doctrine and has adopted an episcopal polity. Some features of nineteenth-century Methodism—attendance at class meetings (regular gatherings of small classes for mutual discussion, Bible study, confession and forgiveness, and prayer) and six months' probationary membership—are retained. The itinerant ministry has been dropped.

Membership: Not reported. In the early 1970s there were 7 churches and slightly over 500 members.

★468★
Parkville Bible Church
800 Whisler Rd.
Etters, PA 17319

The Parkville Bible Church, formerly the Holiness Gospel Church was founded in 1945 by former members of the Evangelical United Brethren and the Church in God. Its theology is Wesleyan holiness. The church sponsors camp meetings. The church is a single congregation of 70 members affiliated with the Bahamas Holy Bible Mission headquartered in the Bahama Islands.

Membership: In the 1995 there were 4 congregations and 370 members.

★469★
Pillar of Fire
Zarephath, NJ 08890

The existence of the Pillar of Fire is due in part to the reluctance of the Methodist Episcopal Church to allow female ministers in its churches in the late nineteenth century. Alma White (1862-1946), a Methodist minister's wife, began to preach both in revivals and in her husband's pulpit. Her success led to notoriety and then to opposition from Methodist officials, so she began to organize her converts into independent missions modeled on the early Methodist societies within the Church of England. After initially cooperating with the Metropolitan Church Association, she incorporated the missions in 1902 as the Pentecostal Union, which gradually emerged as a body separate from the association. The name Pillar of Fire was adopted in 1917.

The doctrine of the church is typically Wesleyan holiness, and it adopted a slightly modified form of the Methodist Twenty-five Articles of Religion early in the twentieth century. The church believes in healing, accepts premillinnialism, and advocates a strong stance against participation in war.

The church is organized episcopally and Alma White was its first bishop (among the first women in modern times to assume that role). Women can occupy all ministerial roles. As part of its commitment to women's rights, the church for many years published a periodical called *Women's Chains*.

The headquarters of the church are at Zarephath, New Jersey. The location of the original headquarters, Denver, Colorado, functions as a second major center of activity. At both locations there is a college, Bible seminary, prep school, radio station (KPOF in Denver and WAWZ in Zarepahth), and a branch of the Pillar of Fire Press. A third station, WAKW, and a school are located in Cincinnati, Ohio, and other schools are located in Jacksonville, Florida; Los Angeles, California; and London, England. There is also an active foreign mission program.

Following Alma White's death, her two sons Ray B. White (1892-1946) and Arthur K. White (1889-1981) inherited the leadership of the church. Arthur K. White became the new bishop and directed its activities for more than 30 years. Dr. Donald J. Wolfram is the present bishop and general superintendent.

Membership: Membership is not counted and is unknown. In 1988 there were 20 congregations in the United States and 56 in foreign countries, including Great Britain, India, Liberia, Malawi, Nigeria, the Philippines, Spain, and Yugoslavia.

Educational Facilities: Belleview Junior College and Bible Seminary, Westminster, Colorado.

Pillar of Fire Bible Seminary, Zarephath, New Jersey.

Periodicals: *Pillar of Fire.* • *Mission News Around the Globe Today.* Send orders to 8354 Grove St., Westminster, CO 80030.

Remarks: Alma White was an advocate of a variety of controversial causes, including vegetarianism and women's rights. She was also an active supporter of the Ku Klux Klan in the 1920s. She wrote a book, *Guardians of Liberty*, defending them as God's agent in maintaining the social order, but the church disassociated itself from the Klan many years ago.

Sources:

McRobbie, James. *What the Bible Teaches.* Salem, OH: Schmul Publishing Co., 1983.

White, Alma. *Hymns and Poems.* Zarephath, NJ: Pillar of Fire, 1946.

___. *The New Testament Church.* Zarephath, NJ: Pillar of Fire, 1929.

___. *The Story of My Life.* 6 vols. Zarephath, NJ: Pillar of Fire, 1919-34.

___. *Why I Do Not Eat Meat.* Zarephath, NJ: Pillar of Fire, 1938.

★470★

Sanctified Church of Christ
Current address not obtained for this edition.

The Sanctified Church of Christ was formed in 1937 at Columbus, Georgia, by a group of former members of the Methodist Episcopal Church. The group was led by Brother E. K. Leary and Sister Jemima Bishop, and their purpose was to preserve the rich heritage of true scriptural holiness. Their doctrine was Wesleyan-Protestant with a distinct emphasis upon entire sanctification. Particular rules were made against secret oathbound societies, immodest dress such as shorts, jewelry, make-up, public and mixed bathing, women cutting their hair, television, and divorce. Members are conscientious objectors.

There is an annual conference that elects the general superintendent, secretary, treasurer, and the council of 12 members, which is the chief legislative body of the church. The council approves all candidates for the ministry.

Membership: Not reported. In the early 1970s there were 7 congregations spread across the deep south. There were approximately 1,000 members.

★471★

Wesleyan Tabernacle Association
Current address not obtained for this edition.

The Wesleyan Tabernacle Association is a small holiness church. It was formed in 1936 for the purpose of promoting Christian love and fellowship among godly leaders of various undenominational bodies and to open a greater field of service for holiness evangelistic preachers and singers. The Association asserts belief in the Trinity, salvation and sanctification by God's free grace, divine healing, baptism and the Lord's Supper as ordinances, and the premillennial return of Christ. Polity is congregational. There is an annual Association Convention which elects officers to oversee publications, missions, and cooperative endeavors with like-minded groups. Women are freely admitted to the ministry. The Association supports a children's home and an extensive mission in Haiti.

Membership: Not reported. In the 1970s the association had 26 congregations in the United States. It supports 173 ordained ministers, 53 licensed ministers, 10 song evangelists and 19 commissioned Christian workers, some of whom are under the direction of independent holiness mission agencies.

Periodicals: *The Evangel.*

Sources:

Yearbook. Wesleyan Tabernacle Association, 1965.

Black Holiness

★472★

Associated Churches of Christ (Holiness)
1302 E. Adams Blvd.
Los Angeles, CA 90011

On the West Coast the Church of Christ (Holiness) U.S.A. was formed in 1915 by Bishop William Washington and work was carried on independently of the work in the east and south by the church's founder, C. P. Jones. A few years later, Jones went to Los Angeles and held a revival meeting. At that time the two men worked out an agreement for cooperative endeavor. The agreement was in effect until 1946-47. Because of what the manual of the Associated Churches of Christ (Holiness) calls the "manipulating of some administrative problems in the upper circles of the Church," the West Coast churches withdrew from the Church of Christ (Holiness) U.S.A. They now continue under the original incorporation of Bishop Washington. Doctrine and polity are identical with the Church of Christ (Holiness) U.S.A.

Membership: Not reported. In the early 1970s there were 6 churches and 1 mission in the Associated Churches.

★473★

Christ's Holy Sanctified Church of America
5201 Willie St.
Fort Worth, TX 76105

Christ's Holy Sanctified Church of America is a predominantly black holiness church founded in 1910 in Keatchie, Louisiana, by Bishop Judge and Sarah A. King. Bishop Judge was succeeded by Bp. Ulysses King and later by Bp. J. King and the current bishop, E. L. McBride. The church follows the teaching of the Wesleyan holiness perspective.

The church supports Christ's Holy Sanctified School, an industrial training school.

Membership: Not reported.

Sources:

DuPree, Sherry Sherrod. *African American Holiness Pentecostal Charismatic: Annotated Bibliography.* New York: Garland Publishing, 1992.

Jones, Charles Edwin. *Black Holiness.* Metuchen, NJ: Scarecrow Press, 1987.

King, Abp. J., ed. *Discipline of Christ Holy Sanctified Church of America.* Oakland, CA: Christ's Holy Sanctified Church, n.d.

★474★

Church of Christ (Holiness) U.S.A.
329 E. Monument St.
Jackson, MS 39202

In 1894 C. P. Jones and Charles H. Mason formed the Church of God in Christ as a holiness body, following their exclusion from fellowship with black Baptists in Arkansas. Mason took most of the body into pentecostalism in 1907. Those who remained were reorganized by Jones as the Church of Christ (Holiness) U.S.A. Jones himself, residing in Jackson, Mississippi, became well known as a composer and publisher of holiness gospel songs. Doctrinally, the Church of Christ (Holiness) U.S.A. is very close to the Church of the Nazarene, with which it almost merged. It follows the Methodist Articles of Religion printed elsewhere in this volume, and stresses the second blessing of the Holy Spirit which imparts sanctification to the believer. Race issues prevented close relations between the Church of Christ (Holiness) U.S.A. and predominantly white holiness churches.

The church is episcopal in structure with a senior bishop as the highest official. There are seven dioceses. A convention held every two years is the highest legislative authority. Missionary work is sponsored in Mexico. There is a publishing house in Los Angeles. Present leader of the church is Bishop M. R. Conic.

Membership: In 1984 the church had over 10,000 members and 170 congregations.

Educational Facilities: Christ Missionary and Industrial College, Jackson, Mississippi.

Boydton Institute, Boydton, Virginia.

Sources:

Cobbins, Otho B. *History of the Church of Christ (Holiness) U.S.A., 1895-1965.* New York, 1966.

Jones, C. P. *His Fulness.* Jackson, MS, 1901.

___. *The Story of My Songs.* Los Angeles, n.d.

★475★
Church of God (Sanctified Church)
1037 Jefferson St.
Nashville, TN 37208

In the early years of the Church of Christ (Holiness) U.S.A., discussed elsewhere in this chapter, the church existed as an unincorporated entity called the "Church of God" or the "Holiness Church." It was only after the schism over Pentecostalism in 1907 that the church was incorporated and its present name was adopted. Before the incorporation, one of the ministers, Elder Charles W. Gray, established the church in Nashville, Tennessee, and the surrounding areas. When the Church of Christ (Holiness) U.S.A. incorporated, Gray continued his work independently as the Church of God (Sanctified Church). The doctrine was the same as that of the Church of Christ (Holiness) U.S.A., but the polity was congregational with local churches operating autonomously and appointing their own ministers. The associated churches remained unincorporated. In 1927 there arose a move within the Church of God (Sanctified Church) to incorporate and to consolidate the work under a board of elders. Among those who constituted the newly incorporated church were Elders J. L. Rucker, R. A. Manter, R. L. Martin, M. S. Sowell, B. Smith, and G. A. Whitley. The move to incorporate led to further controversy and a schism. However, under the incorporation, the elders retained the rights to direct the church, and it continues as the Church of God (Sanctified Church). Elder Gray, founder of the church, withdrew to found the Original Church of God (or Sanctified Church).

The Church of God (Sanctified Church) is headed by a general overseer. The first was Elder Rucker. He has been suceeded by Elder Theopolis Dickerson McGhee (d.1965) and Elder Jesse E. Evans. Mission work is conducted in Jamaica.

Membership: Not reported.In the early 1970s the church reported 60 congregations, approximately 5,000 members.

★476★
Church of God (Which He Purchased with His Own Blood)
1628 NE 50th
Oklahoma City, OK 73111

The Church of God (Which He Purchased with His Own Blood) is a predominantly black holiness church founded in 1953 by William F. Fizer following his excommunication from the Church of the Living God (Christian Workers for Fellowship). Fizer had concluded that grape juice or wine, not water, should be used in the Lord's Supper, thus denying one of the major distinctive practices of the Church of the Living God. The first annual convention of the Church of God was held in 1954.

The Church of God distinguishes itself from Pentecostalism and teaches that the Holy Ghost is given to those who obey the Lord. The Lord's Supper is held weekly and grape juice and unleavened bread are used as elements. Foot washing is practiced. Baptism is administered following a trinitarian formula. A holiness code is followed that frowns upon the use of tobacco and alcohol. Divine healing is sought in cases of sickness, but the work of doctors is also affirmed.

The Church of God believes that it is the Body of Christ, following the belief and practice of scriptures; hence it sees itself as the true church as organized originally by Jesus Christ. It is the role of the chief bishop to organize the church by calling people to the true doctrine.

Membership: In 1997 there were seven churches, 800 members, and 10 ministers. These are also members in Nigeria and the Philippines.

Periodicals: *Gospel News.*

Sources:

Fizer, William Jordon. *Bible Doctrine.* Oklahoma City, OK: The Author, n.d. 72pp.

★477★
Church of Universal Triumph/The Dominion of God
% Rev. James Shaffer
8317 LaSalle Blvd.
Detroit, MI 48206

Rivaling Sweet Daddy Grace and Father Divine as charismatic leaders in the black community was the Rev. James Francis Marion Jones, better known as Prophet Jones (1908-1971). Born in Birmingham, Alabama, the son of a railroad brakeman and a school teacher, he was raised in Triumph the Church and Kingdom of God in Christ. Even as a child, he preached (he did so regularly after his eleventh birthday). In 1938 he was sent to Detroit as a missionary and became successful quickly. Tension with headquarters arose before the year was out, however, when members began to shower Jones with expensive gifts. The headquarters claimed them. Rather than surrender his new affluence, Jones left the church and founded the Church of Universal Triumph/the Dominion of God.

The new church, modeled on the parent body, was built upon Jones' charisma. During the 1940s and 1950s he became known for his wealth. His possessions included a white mink coat, a 54-room French chateau which had been built in 1917 by a General Motors executive, five Cadillacs each with its own chauffeur, jewelry, perfumes, and wardrobe of almost 500 ensembles. Jones claimed to be in direct contact with God, who instructed him in the form of a breeze fanning his ear. Among his practices was dispensing solutions to personal problems after inviting individuals to mount his dais and whisper their problems in his ear. Most of Prophet Jones' wealth came from people grateful for Jones' healing ability. Followers were to be found in all the large northern cities. Jones was titled, "His Holiness the Rev. Dr. James F. Jones, D.D., Universal Dominion Ruler, Internationally known as Prophet Jones."

The Church, like the parent body, is very strict. Members are not allowed to smoke, drink, play games of any kind, use coffee or tea, fraternize with non-Dominionitetry, attend another church, or marry without the consent of the ruler of the church. Women must wear girdles and men health belts. The major theological tenet concerns the beginning of the millennium in 2,000 A.D. All alive at that time will become immortal and live in the heaven on earth.

The upward path of Prophet Jones came to an abrupt end in 1956 when a vice raid on his home led to his arrest and trial for gross indecency. He was acquited, but the damage had been done and his following declined from that time. During the year prior to his death in 1971, he commuted between Detroit and Chicago. Following his death, his assistant, the Rev. Lord James Schaffer became the Dominion Ruler. He was named by the Dominion Council and Board of Trustees. Some 20 ministers and 5,000 members attended the funeral of Prophet Jones in 1971.

Membership: Not reported.

★478★
Churches of God, Holiness
170 Ashby St., NW
Atlanta, GA 30314

The Churches of God, Holiness, were formed by Bishop King Hezekiah Burruss (d. 1963), formerly of the Church of Christ (Holiness) U.S.A. Burruss began a church in Atlanta in 1914 that belonged to that organization, and by 1920, the Atlanta congregation was large enough that it hosted the national convention of the Church of Christ (Holiness) U.S.A. Shortly after that Atlanta meeting, however, Burruss formed his own church. Doctrine is like the doctrine of the parent body.

The highest authority is the national convention. There are also annual state conventions. Practically speaking the government developed during the period of strong leadership exercised by the founding bishop. The bishop appoints the state overseers who assign all pastors. The present bishop is Titus Paul Burruss.

Membership: Not reported. In 1967 there were 42 churches, 16 ministers and 25,600 members, mostly along the East Coast.

Periodicals: *The Bethlehem Star.*

★479★
Evangelical Church of Christ (Holiness)
Current address not obtained for this edition.

The Evangelical Church of Christ (Holiness) was founded in 1947 by Bp. William C. Holman, formerly a minister of the Church of Christ (Holiness). As the break was administrative, the doctrine and practice are the same as that of the parent body.

Membership: In 1990 there were approximately 500 members in four churches in Washington, D.C.; Los Angeles, California; Omaha, Nebraska; and Denver, Colorado. There are also two missions in Los Angeles.

Sources:

DuPree, Sherry Sherrod. *African American Holiness Pentecostal Charismatic: Annotated Bibliography.* New York: Garland Publishing, 1992.

★480★
Gospel Spreading Church
2030 Georgia Ave., NW
Washington, DC 20003

The Gospel Spreading Church, sometimes called Elder Michaux Church of God or the Radio Church of God, was founded by Lightfoot Solomon Michaux (1885-1968), a minister in the Church of God (Holiness). At one point he served as the church's secretary-treasurer. However, he came into conflict with C. P. Jones, founder of the Church of God (Holiness) and left to found an independent church in Hampton, Virginia, in 1922, retaining the name he had previously used, the Gospel Spreading Tabernacle Association. In 1928 he moved to Washington, D.C., and established the Church of God and Gospel Spreading Association.

His early success continued in the nation's capital, and he had discovered the potential of radio while in Virginia. In 1929 he began broadcasting on WJSV. Shortly thereafter CBS bought the station and his show expanded through the system. By 1934 he was on over 50 stations nationwide, with an estimated audience of 25,000,000. His show was also carried internationally by shortwave. He was the first black person to receive such exposure. He mixed holiness themes with positive thinking. His magazine was entitled *Happy News.*

From his radio audience, congregations began to form in black communities, primarily in the East. However, by the beginning of World War II his radio ministry had declined and he was heard on only a few stations, in those cities where congregations had formed. In 1964 he reorganized his followers as the Gospel Spreading Church, but most of the congregations continued to call themselves the Church of God.

Membership: Not reported.

Sources:

Lark, Pauline, ed. *Sparks from the Anvil of Elder Micheaux.* Washington, DC: Happy News Publishing Company, 1950.

Webb, Lilian Ashcraft. *About My Father's Business.* Westport, CT: Greenwood Press, 1981.

★481★
Kodesh Church of Emmanuel
% Kenneth O. Barbour
2601 Centre Ave.
Pittsburgh, PA 15219

The Kodesh Church of Emmanuel is a black holiness sect that was formed by Rev. Frank Russell Killingsworth when he withdrew from the African Methodist Episcopal Church in 1929 along with 120 followers. In common with other holiness churches, this church emphasizes entire sanctification as a second definite work of grace conditioned upon a life of absolute consecration. The church forbids use of alcohol, tobacco and prideful dress; membership in secret societies; and profaning the Sabbath. In 1934, a merger was effected with the Christian Tabernacle Union of Pittsburgh.

The church is governed by a quadrennial general assembly. Regional assemblies meet annually. There is mission work in Liberia.

Membership: In 1980 there were five churches, 326 members, and 28 ministers.

★482★
Mount Calvary Holy Church of America
Current address not obtained for this edition.

The Mt. Calvary Holy Church is a small black holiness church headquartered in Boston, Massachusetts, founded by Bishop Brumfield Johnson. Its doctrine is similar to that of the United Holy Church of America. Churches are located in North Carolina; Baltimore, Maryland; New York; Boston; and other cities on the east coast.

Membership: Not reported.

★483★
Triumph the Church and Kingdom of God in Christ
% Rt. Rev. A. Scott, Chief Bishop
213 Farrington Ave., SE
Atlanta, GA 30315

Triumph the Church and Kingdom of God in Christ was founded by Elder E. D. Smith in 1902. The founding followed by five years a divine revelation given to Smith. According to the literature of the church, the 1902 organization of the church marked the time when the revelation was "speeded to earth." Finally, in 1904, the content of the revelation was announced. Headquarters for the church were established in Baton Rouge, Louisiana, then were moved to Birmingham, Alabama, and later to Atlanta, Georgia. The founder was in charge of the church until 1920, when he moved to Addis Ababa, Ethiopia.

The church follows the holiness beliefs common to holiness churches, but also believes in fire baptism, a spiritual experience of empowerment by the Holy Spirit. Fire baptism was first received by the Apostles in the upper room on Pentecost, when tongues of fire appeared above their heads (Acts 2). As practiced by the several nineteenth and twentieth century "fire-baptized" churches, fire baptism is similar to the pentecostal experience of the baptism of the Holy Spirit, except it is typically not accompanied by speaking in tongues. (See separate entry on the Fire-Baptized Holiness Church, Wesleyan.)

Triumph the Church and Kingdom of God in Christ holds a unique view of itself as a church in relation to Christendom, traditionally called the church militant. This view is reflected in the following passage from the church's catechism: *Question* Was there another Church in the earth before Triumph? *Answer.* Yes. Church Militant; *Question* Is there any difference between the Triumph Church and Church Militant? *Answer* Yes. Church Militant is a Church of warfare, and Triumph is a Church of Peace; *Question* What happened to Church Militant when Triumph was revealed? *Answer* God turned it upside down and emptied His Spirit into Triumph; *Question* Is Triumph just a Church only? *Answer* No. It has a Kingdom with it.

Polity is episcopal with bishops elected for life. Under the bishops is a hierarchy of state and local workers. Every four years the church holds an International Religious Congress.

Membership: Not reported. At last report (1972) there were 475 churches, 53,307 members, and 1,375 ministers.

★484★
Triumph the Church in Righteousness
PO Box 1572
Fort Lauderdale, FL 33302

Triumph the Church in Righteousness, a predominantly Black holiness church, was founded in 1951 in Fort Lauderdale, Florida, by Annie Lizzie Brownlee, the church's bishop. She began life as a Baptist and later joined Triumph the Church and Kingdom of God in Christ. Bishop Brownlee began her ministry by founding a mission which served the poor, the old, the mentally ill, and children. She became well known in the black community in Fort Lauderdale where, dressed all in white, she stood on the street corners soliciting financial assistance for her mission work. In 1954 she had a vision which led her to purchase land and start a new church. Over the years she founded five congregations in the Miami-Fort Lauderdale area.

Triumph the Church in Righteousness is a holiness church. Bishop Brownlee has a strict code of appearance for female members, including strictures against straightening hair. She did, however, sanction female ministers.

Membership: In 1990 there were approximately 400 members in five churches.

Sources:

DuPree, Sherry Sherrod. *African American Holiness Pentecostal Charismatic: Annotated Bibliography.* New York: Garland Publishing, 1992.

Glenn Griffith Movement

★485★
Allegheny Wesleyan Methodist Connection
1827 Allen Dr.
Salem, OH 44460

The Allegheny Wesleyan Methodist Connection (Original Allegheny Conference) was formed in 1968 due to the merger of the Wesleyan Methodist Church of America (1843) with the Pilgrim Holiness Church to form the Wesleyan Church. Prominent among the leaders of the new Connection were Reverends H. C. Van Wormer, T. A. Robertson, J. B. Markey, and F.E. Mansell. These men, along with a majority of the Conference, opposed the merger on the grounds that they believed in a congregational form of church governance and in Wesleyan Methodist standards of behavior, which they believed were being abandoned in the new church. Legal technicalities forced them to add the words "Original Allegheny Conference" to their name. Allegheny was one of the original conferences formed by the Wesleyan Methodist Church when it broke away from the Methodist Episcopal Church in 1843.

The Connection follows the traditional holiness doctrine of the former Wesleyan Methodist Church. It emphasizes the belief that the atonement in Christ provides both for the regeneration of sinners and the entire sanctification of believers.

The Connection serves as an agency of the cooperative endeavor. There is a strong thrust in the foreign missions with work in Haiti, Ghana, and Peru. Domestic missions are conducted among the Indians of the Northwestern United States and Canada, and among international university students in Pittsburgh, Pennsylvania.

Membership: In 1997 there were 116 churches, 2,035 members, and 215 ministers.

Educational Facilities: Northwest Indian Bible School, Alberton, Montana.

Allegheny Wesleyan College, Salem, Ohio.

Periodicals: *The Allegheny Wesleyan Methodist.*

Sources:

Discipline of the Allegheny Wesleyan Methodist Connection. Titusville, PA, 1986.

Morrison, H. C. *Baptism with the Holy Ghost.* Salem, OH: Alleghany Wesleyan Methodist Connection, 1978.

★486★
Bible Holiness Church
Current address not obtained for this edition.

The Bible Holiness Church is a small group which separated from the Bible Methodist Connection of Tennessee. The members include a statement on healing among their beliefs, which otherwise are staunchly conservative and holiness in content.

Membership: Not reported. In 1968 there were 9 congregations and approximately 200 members in Tennessee and Virginia.

★487★
Bible Methodist Connection of Churches
1216 Taylor Rd.
Glencoe, AL 35905

Bible Methodist in Alabama and southwestern Ohio organized in 1966 as the Bible Methodist Church and the Wesleyan Connecton of Churches, respectively. In 1970 these two bodies merged to form the Bible Methodist Connection of Churches. The connection is organized congregationally, specifically rejecting centralizing tendencies perceived to exist in the older Holiness bodies.

The connection is a Holiness church whose doctrinal position is contained in 22 Articles of Religion derived from the Methodist Articles of Regligion. They affirm the inspiration and infallibility of Scripture; justification; sanctification, the work of the Holy Spirit which cleanses a believer of inbred sin; and the imminent return of Christ.

Membership: In 1997 there were 45 churches, 1,514 members, and 146 ministers in the United States and 100 members in Canada. The church had a mission and college in both Mexico and the Philippines.

Educational Facilities: The Bible Methodist Connection supports and draws its ministers from God's Bible School and College, Cincinnati, Ohio.

Union Bible College, Westfield, Indiana, and
Hobe Sound Bible Institute, Hobe Sound, Florida.

Periodicals: *Bible Methodist.*

★488★
Bible Methodist Connection of Tennessee
Current address not obtained for this edition.

Protesting both the centralization of authority and the lack of holiness for years in the Wesleyan Methodist Church was D. P. Denton, editor of the *Evangelist of Truth*, an independent monthly out of Knoxvillle, Tennessee. On October 17, 1966, Denton led a meeting in Knoxville with representatives of the various factions opposed to the merger of the Wesleyan Methodist Church and the Pilgrim Holiness Church into the Wesleyan Church, a merger finally effected in 1967. At the Knoxville meeting, representatives opposed to merger decided to organize a new "connection," a new association of churches. The new group would continue the use of Wesleyan Methodist *Discipline* (a book of church order), with the exception that each church would be completely autonomous. The new connection would be formed as the merger was consummated. After the negotiations were completed and those who stayed out of the merger settled on the price of buying their property from the new Wesleyan Church, three new bodies emerged: the Bible Methodist Connection of Tennessee, the Bible Holiness Church, and the Bible Methodist Connection of Churches.

From the former Wesleyan Methodist Church, the members of the Tennessee Conference led by Denton became the Bible Methodist Connection of Tennessee. Denton was elected president. The former Conference paper, *Tennessee Tidings*, became the new church's organ. A campground outside of Knoxville serves the church. The *Evangelist of Truth* continues as an independent monthly. In 1987, following the death of his wife, Denton retired and was succeeded as president of the Connection by Earl Newton.

Membership: Not reported. In 1987 there were 45 churches and 110 ministers.

Periodicals: *Tennessee Tidings.*

★489★
Bible Missionary Church
822 S. Simms
Denver, CO 80211

Following the successful revival led by Church of the Nazarene minister, Rev. Glenn Griffith near Nampa, Idaho, the group of conservative holiness people attracted to Griffith's message were organized into the Bible Missionary Union. Word of the action spread quickly and within ten months congregations of like minded people had been established in twenty states. Joining Griffith were J. E. Cook, Spencer Johnson, and H. B. Huffman. The first general conference of the church was held in Denver in 1956, at which the present name was selected. Membership in the church has been augmented by the failure in 1956 of conservatives to have the Nazarene Council Assembly condemn television.

Like its parent, the Church of the Nazarene, doctrine is Wesleyan with an emphasis on holiness. Entire sanctification, as freedom from original sin and a state of entire devotion to God, is stressed. The future life, heaven and hell, and the premillennial return of Jesus are also central beliefs. The church is understood as "composed of all spiritually regenerated persons whose names are written in heaven." The general rules have also been expanded with the addition of much detail on points of behavior. The difference between the Bible Missionary Church and the parent body, the Church of the Nazarene, is primarily on strictness of personal holiness regulations. The Church has endorsed the King James Version of the Bible for use in its churches and has gone on record against modern versions of the Bible, especially the Revised Standard Version, the Living Bible, the New English Translation, the Readers' Digest Condensed Version, and the New International Version.

The Church is headed by two general moderators who preside over the general conference, the highest law making body for the church. Foreign mission work is supported in Guyana, Venezuela, St. Vincent (West Indies), Canada, Nigeria, Honduras, Japan, the Philippines, Papua New Guinea, Barbados, and Mexico; a home mission project is on the Navaho Reservation at Farmington, New Mexico. A children's home is operated in Beulah Heights, Kentucky.

Membership: Not reported. There are 14 district conferences overseeing churches across the United States.

Educational Facilities: Bible Missionary Institute, Rock Island, Illinois.

Periodicals: *The Missionary Revivalist.*

Sources:

Cook, J. E. *W. M. Tidwell (A Life that Counted).* Ann Arbor, MI: Mallory Lithographing, n.d.

Keene, Mrs. Roy. *"Love-Threads Reaching".* Rock Island, IL: Bible Missionary Church, 1979.

Manual. Rock Island, IL: Bible Missionary Church, n.d.

★490★
Church of the Bible Covenant
Current address not obtained for this edition.

In 1966 four Indiana-based ministers of the Church of the Nazarene (Marvin Powers, Amos Hann, Donald Hicks, and Granville Rogers) formed a steering committee that led to the establishment of the Church of the Bible Covenant the following year at the John T. Hatfield Campground near Cleveland, Indiana. The four invited their former district superintendent, Remiss Rehfeldt, to join them. On August 10, 1967, the new church elected Rehfeldt and Powers as general presiding officers. Those who gathered for that meeting then spread across the country under the leadership of 12 regional presiding officers to develop local congregations.

The Church's doctrine follows essentially that of the Wesleyan-Protestant tradition, with a strong emphasis on holiness and a high code of ethical standards. A general convention meets quadrennially, during which time elections are held and legislation considered. In 1982 Rehfeldt retired and was granted emeritus status. Donald Hicks was elected as new general presiding officer.

Membership: In 1984 the church reported 90 churches in the United States and 75 churches and preaching points overseas. Total membership was 2,000 but approximately 4,000 attended church school each Sunday.

Educational Facilities: Covenant Foundation College, Greenfield, Indiana. The church maintains three Bible-training institutions overseas.

Periodicals: *The Covenanter.* Send orders to New Castle, IN 47352.

Sources:

Articles. Knightsville, IN: Church of the Bible Covenant, 1970.

★491★
Evangelical Wesleyan Church
Current address not obtained for this edition.

The Evangelical Wesleyan Church was formed in 1963 by the merger of the Evangelical Wesleyan Church of North America and the Midwest Holiness Association, both churches composed of members who had left the Free Methodist Church. The Evangelical Wesleyan Church of North America was organized at a convention held near Centerville, Crawford County, Pennsylvania, with a dedication to restore old-time Free Methodism. (The members sought a stricter interpretation of personal moral codes; e.g., they were concerned about women's hair styles, makeup, and the length of dresses.) The Midwest Holiness Association was formed in 1962 as a protest against worldliness and apostasy in the Free Methodist Church. The organizing convention of the Midwest Holiness Association was held in Ansley, Nebraska. The Evangelical Wesleyan Church is set against the compromise of old doctrines and standards of Free Methodism and follows its patterns.

Membership: Not reported. Membership is concentrated in Nebraska, Pennsylvania, and New York.

Educational Facilities: Adirondack Bible College, Northville, New York.

John Fletcher Bible College, Kearney, Nebraska.

Periodicals: *The Ernest Christian.*

★492★
God's Missionary Church
Current address not obtained for this edition.

God's Missionary Church is one of the older conservative holiness bodies. It was formed in 1935 as a result of a dispute in the Pennsylvania and New Jersey District of the Pilgrim Holiness Church.

It has become a conservtive body, very strict in discipline. It is also opposed to participation in war, somewhat reflective of the Quaker influence in the founding of the Pilgrim Holiness Church. The church is congregational, but headed by a general superintendent. There is missionary work in Haiti and among Cuban refugees in Florida. It cooperates with the Interdenominational Holiness Convention.

Membership: Not reported. In 1971 there were 595 members, 532 of which resided in Pennsylvania.

Educational Facilities: Penn View Bible Institute, Penns Creek, Pennsylvania.

Periodicals: *God's Missionary Standard.*

Sources:

Official Handbook and Discipline. Watsontown, PA: God's Missionary Church, 1971.

★493★
Lower Lights Church
Ann Arbor, MI

The Lower Lights Church was formed in 1940 as a single congregation (the Lower Light Mission) in Ann Arbor, Michigan. It subsequently branched out to neighboring communities and now cooperates with the Interdenominational Holiness Convention.

Membership: Not reported. There are several congregations in Michigan and Ohio with several hundred members.

★494★
National Association of Holiness Churches
351 S. Park Dr.
Griffith, IN 46319

The National Association of Holiness Churches was formed at the Singing Hill Camp Ground near Shoals, Indiana, in 1967. H. Robb French (1891-1985), a former pastor in the Wesleyan Methodist Church and one of the founders of the Interdenominational Holiness Convention, was the chief moving force in its founding and early development. He was the first general chairman, a post held until his resignation in 1973. The association exists as a loose confederation of independent ministers and churches formed for purposes of promoting holiness and providing fellowship. An annual camp meeting and association general conference is held in June. Missionary work is supported in Mexico, Brazil, and India.

Membership: In 1995, there were 53 congregations in the association and 51 affiliated ministers in the United States. Many of the ministers and churches affiliated with the association are also affiliated with other conservative holiness church bodies.

Periodicals: *The NAHC Bulletin.* Available from Rev. Dale L. Hallaway, RDI, Box 129, Centerville, PA 16404.

★495★
Pilgrim Holiness Church of New York
32 Cadillac Ave.
Albany, NY 12205

The Pilgrim Holiness Church of New York traces its history to the Pentecostal Rescue Mission organized in 1897 in Binghamton, New York. In 1922 that Mission affiliated as an autonomous district with the International Holiness Church which the following year took the name Pilgrim Holiness Church. During the 1960s the Pilgrim Holiness Church began a process of centralizing authority in the national headquarters and preparing for merger with the Wesleyan Methodist Church (a merger which was completed in 1968 with the creation of the Wesleyan Church). In 1963, asserting its autonomous status, the New York Conference left the Pilgrim Holiness Church and has continued as an independent organization.

The Church is very conservative in doctrine and strict in practice, as are those churches which are affiliated with the Interdenominational Holiness Convention. Missions are directly supported in Brazil, Haiti, and Winnepeg, Manitoba, Canada and other locations through various missionary agencies. Churches are located in New York, New Jersey, Ohio, Pennsylvania, Massachusetts, and Canada.

Membership: In 1988 the church reported 950 members, 54 churches, and 87 ministers in the United States and 275 members, 5 churches, and 5 ministers in Canada.

Educational Facilities: The church has no school of its own, but financially supports and recommends the following:

God's Bible School, Cincinnati, Ohio.

Hobe Sound Bible School, Hobe Sound, Florida (sponsored by the National Association of Holiness Churches).

Allegheny Wesleyan College, Salem, Ohio.

Penn View Bible Institute, Penns Creek, Pennsylvania (sponsored by God's Missionary Church).

Periodicals: *Pilgrim News.*

★496★
Pilgrim Holiness Church of the Midwest
% Union Bible Seminary
434 S. Union St.
Westfield, IN 46074

The Pilgrim Holiness Church of the Midwest was formed in 1970. Three years earlier ten congregations affiliated with the Pilgrim Holiness Church had withdrawn to become the Midwest Conference of the Pilgrim Holiness Church of New York. But the ten congregations eventaully decided to remain independent, though they have stayed friendly with the New York group. They adopted their own *Discipline* (a book of church order). Mission work is through the Evangelical Faith Missions and Evangelical Bible Missions.

Membership: Not reported. In 1969 there were 13 churches and 246 members.

Educational Facilities: Union Bible Seminary.

★497★
United Holiness Church of North America
Current address not obtained for this edition.

The United Holiness Church of North America was formed in 1955 by conservatives within the Free Methodist Church at a camp meeting at Carson City, Michigan. Headquarters are at the Bible College at Cedar. It resembles its parent body, but is more strict in its standards of holiness. The Church cooperates with the Interdenominational Holiness Convention.

Membership: Not reported.

Educational Facilities: Jordan College, Cedar Springs, Michigan.

Periodicals: *United Holiness Sentinel.*

★498★
Voice of the Nazarene Association of Churches
Current address not obtained for this edition.

One focus within the Church of the Nazarene of the post-World II conservative holiness movement was a magazine, *The Voice of the Nazarene*, published at Finleyville, Pennsylvania by W. L. King. Following the 1956 decision in the Church of the Nazarene in favor of television, some groups in the East against watching television associated with King. They formed the Voice of the Nazarene Association of Churches. It is a loosely congregational organization. The literature from the Finleyville headquarters has been characterized by its extreme conservatism, politically as well as religiously. It is strongly opposed to Communism, the National Council of Churches, and the Roman Catholic Church.

Membership: Not reported. In 1967 there were 8 members congregations (plus 18 cooperating congregations) and 31 association evangelists.

Periodicals: *Universal Challenger.* • *Voice of the Nazarene.*

★499★
Wesleyan Holiness Association of Churches
Current address not obtained for this edition.

History. After only four years with the Bible Missionary Church, the Rev. Glenn Griffith left it in protest of its alleged compromise of receiving divorced persons into the membership and/or ministry. He and his supporters felt that there had been a drifting from the old Wesleyan revival fervor and standards. At an informal meeting of ministers and laypeople in August 1959, Griffith was chosen the general leader, and an initials general conference with an accompanying camp meeting was set for the next year at Colorado Springs, Colorado. At that meeting, Griffith was unanimously elected to the post of general moderator (now general superintendent) and the Wesleyan Holiness Association of Churches organized. Among its objectives were to emphasize the doctrine and experience of entire sanctification and to raise the standard of holiness in daily living.

Beliefs. The Association follows a six-article statement of doctrine with the basic affirmations of traditional Wesleyan Christianity. Article IV is concerned with God's plan of redemption and af-firms free will, faith, repentance, and justification. It emphasizes sanctification as a second act of God in believers, whereby they are made free from original sin or depravity and brought into a state of entire "devotement" to God. Sanctification is followed by a continued growth in grace. There are two sacraments: baptism and the Lord's Supper. Baptism may be by sprinkling or pouring, but immersion is preferred. The Association believes in divine healing. It is opposed to drafting females into military service. The Association's general rules establish a strict code of personal conduct.

Organization. The Association is congregationally governed. Each church owns its own property and calls its ministers. Churches are grouped into five districts, each served by a district superintendent. A representative general conference meets biennially. It elects a general board consisting of the general superintendent, assistant general superintendent, general secretary, general treasurer, the district superintendents, and a lay delegate from each district. The Association's home missionary program includes work among American Indians in Arizona and New Mexico; its foreign missionaries can be found in Africa, Bolivia, the Grand Cayman, Guatemala, Taiwan, and New Guinea.

Membership: In 1992, the association reported 36 congregations served by 65 ordained and 25 licensed ministers.

Educational Facilities: The Association has no college, but students are urged to attend Union Bible College, Westfield, Indiana, and God's Bible College, Cincinnati, Ohio.

Periodicals: *Eleventh Hour Messenger.*

Sources:

Declaration of Principles. Dayton, OH: Wesleyan Holiness Association of Churches, 1981.

Griffith, Glenn. *I Sought for a Man.* Phoenix, AZ: The Author, n.d.

Section 9
Pentecostal Family

Consult the Contents pages to locate the essay in Part II, Historical Essay Chapters, that provides an historical discussion of this family

Intrafaith Organizations

★500★

Pentecostal Fellowship of North America
Rev. James M. McKnight, Chairperson
[ ] Overlea Bvd.
[T]oronto, ON, Canada M4H 1A5

At the first meeting of the World Pentecostal Fellowship in [Sw]itzerland in 1947, it was suggested that area fellowships of a [si]milar nature be organized. Thus, in 1948, representatives of [ei]ght Pentecostal churches met in Chicago to organize the North [A]merican Pentecostal Fellowship. That organization was effected [la]ter in the year at a second meeting in Des Moines, Iowa. Partici-[pa]nts included the Assemblies of God, the Church of God (Cleve-[la]nd, Tennessee), the International Church of the Foursquare Gos-[pe]l, the Pentecostal Holiness Church, and the Open Bible [St]andard Church. The Pentecostal Assemblies of Canada was the [on]ly Canadian representative.

Like the World Pentecostal Fellowship, the Pentecostal Fellow-[sh]ip of North America seeks to provide member churches, to dem-[on]strate the essential unity of Pentecostals, and to promote the [co]mmonly held beliefs.

The fellowship is led by a chairperson, two vice-presidents, a [se]cretary, a treasurer, and a board of administration. The officers [co]nstitute an executive committee.

Membership: Members of the Fellowship include the follow-[in]g: Anchor Bay Evangelistic Association; Apostolic Church of [Ca]nada; Assemblies of God; Christian Church of North America; [Ch]urch of God (Cleveland, Tennessee); Church of God of Apostol-[ic] Faith; Church of God of the Mountain Assembly; Congregation-[al] Holiness Church; Elim Fellowship; Free Gospel Church; Garr [M]emorial Church/Carolina Evangelistic Association; International [Ch]urch of the Foursquare Gospel; International Pentecostal [Ch]urch of Christ; International Pentecostal Holiness Church; Ital-[ia]n Pentecostal Church of Canada; Open Bible Standard Church-[es]; Pentecostal Assemblies of Canada; Pentecostal Assemblies of [N]ewfoundland; Pentecostal Church of God; Pentecostal Free Will [Ba]ptist Church; and Pentecostal Holiness Church of Canada.

★501★

Pentecostal World Conference
Dr. Ray H. Hughes
[Bo]x 2430
[Cl]eveland, TN 37320

Alternate Address: International Secretary: Rev. Jakob Zopfi, [H]eimstatte SPM, 6376 Emmetten NW, Switzerland.

The Pentecostal World Conference was founded in 1947 but [it]s roots go back to 1922, a mere two decades after the founding [of] the movement and an initial international European Pentecostal [c]onvention held in Amsterdam. Similar unofficial conventions [w]ere held periodically until the outbreak of war in 1939. Mean-[w]hile, a number of fraternal delegates attended the 1937 meeting

of the Assemblies of God, at which time the General Council called for a world Pentecostal conference to convene in London in 1940. The event was canceled by the war.

In 1946, in the wake of World War II, a group of Pentecostals meeting in Basle, Switzerland, became conscious of the immediate and desperate need of many victims of the war and called for an international gathering of Pentecostals to confront that need. The meeting, held in Zurich, Switzerland, in May 1947, became the catalyst for the organization of a permanent association, the opening of an international office in Basle, Switzerland, and the launching of a periodical, *Pentecost,* under the editorship of Donald Gee. The fellowship's constitution was ratified at a second conference in 1949 in Paris.

The fellowship exists to encourage a fraternal spirit and cooperation among various Pentecostal groups. In addition it assists in the evangelical tasks of the church, manifests the unity of Pentecostal peoples, and upholds the doctrinal consensus of the movement.

The fellowship meets triennially. At its international conferences, a 29-person World Conference Advisory Committee is elected to oversee the planning of the next conference.

Membership: American participants in the fellowship include the following: Anchor Bay Evangelistic Association; Apostolic Church of Canada; Assemblies of God; Christian Church of North America; Church of God (Cleveland, Tennessee); Church of God of Apostolic Faith; Church of God of the Mountain Assembly; Congregational Holiness Church; Elim Fellowship; Free Gospel Church; Garr Memorial Church/Carolina Evangelistic Association; International Church of the Foursquare Gospel; International Pentecostal Church of Christ; International Pentecostal Holiness Church; Italian Pentecostal Church of Canada; Open Bible Standard Churches; Pentecostal Assemblies of Canada; Pentecostal Assemblies of Newfoundland; Pentecostal Church of God; Pentecostal Free Will Baptist Church; and Pentecostal Holiness Church of Canada.

Periodicals: *World Pentecost.*

Sources:

Kendrick, Kalude. *The Promise Fulfilled: A History of the Modern Pentecostal Movement.* Springfield, MO: Gospel Publishing House, 1961.

★502★

United Fellowship Convention of the Original Azusa Street Mission
Current address not obtained for this edition.

The United Fellowship Convention of the Original Azusa Street Mission is an association of Holiness Pentecostal churches, all of which trace their lineage back to William J. Seymour and the beginnings of Pentecostalism in Los Angeles, California, at the Azusa Street Mission. Seymour, formerly a member of the African Methodist Episcopal Church, had entered into the Pentecosta experience in Houston, Texas, under the ministry of Charles Parham, but left to pastor a church in Los Angeles in 1905. Kicked out of his first parish because of his Pentecostal teachings, he began an independent work on Azusa Street which became the center of a worldwide movement during the years 1906–9. However, eventually racism reared its ugly head and the Apostolic Faith Mission which Seymour headed became a predominantly African-American institution.

Around 1909 Seymour and Charles H. Mason, founder of the Church of God in Christ, held a series of revival meetings in Washington, D.C. Among those converted in the meetings was Charles W. Lowe of Handsom, Virginia. He went on to found the Apostolic Faith Church of God, which over the decades of the twentieth century grew and became the source of a number of other churches. In 1987 these churches held a gathering to affirm their shared heritage and common belief.

Membership: Members of the fellowship include Apostolic Faith Church of God, Apostolic Faith Church of God and True Holiness, Apostolic Faith Church of God Live On, Apostolic Faith Churches of God, and Church of Christ Holiness unto the Lord.

Sources:

Payne, Wardell J., ed. *Directory of African American Religious Bodies: A Compendium by the Howard University School of Divinity.* Washington, DC: Howard University Press, 1991.

White Trinitarian Holiness Pentecostals

★503★
Apostolic Faith Church of God and True Holiness
825 Gregg Rd.
Jefferson, OH 44047

In 1946 Charles W. Lowe, founder and for over 35 years leader of the Apostolic Faith Church of God, separated from the main body of the church and with one congregation organized the Apostolic Faith Church of God and True Holiness. He was succeeded by Bishop Levi Butts and more recently by Bishop Oree Keyes. Bishop Keyes has been very active in seeking to unite the various factions that have developed from the original work begun by Bishops Seymour and Lowe. He helped form the United Fellowship Convention of the Original Azusa Street Mission which includes five similar churches.

Membership: In 1990 the Apostolic Faith Church of God in True Holiness reported 24 congregations.

Sources:

DuPree, Sherry Sherrod. *African American Holiness Pentecostal Charismatic: Annotated Bibliography.* New York: Garland Publishing, 1992.

★504★
Apostolic Faith Church of God Giving Grace
Rte. 3, Box 111G
Warrenton, NC 27589

The Apostolic Faith Church of God Giving Grace was founded in the mid 1960s as the New Jerusalem Apostolic Faith Churches of God. Its founders, Bishop Rufus A. Easter and Mother Lillie P. Williams, were formerly associated with the Apostolic Faith Churches of God. There was no doctrinal dispute in the break and the church follows the doctrine of the parent body. Bishop Easter was succeeded by Bishop Geanie Perry, the current leader of the church. The church supports the New Jerusalem Rest Home and a Helping Hand Community Food Bank.

Membership: In 1990 there were 12 churches.

Sources:

DuPree, Sherry Sherrod. *African American Holiness Pentecostal Charismatic: Annotated Bibliography.* New York: Garland Publishing, 1992.

★505★
Apostolic Faith Churches of a Living God
Current address not obtained for this edition.

The Apostolic Faith Churches of a Living God was founded in 1979 when seven congregations in South Carolina which had left the Apostolic Faith Churches of God reorganized as a denomination. The congregations were called together by Bishop Leroy Williams who had in the 1960s been the president of the South Carolina District Young People's Union of the Apostolic Faith Church of God. The present head of the church is Bishop Richard C. Johnson, Sr. The cause of the split was administrative, not doctrinal, hence the churches retain the same holiness pentecostal beliefs and practices of the parent church. The church holds an annual convention each summer.

Periodicals: *Union Newsletter.*

Sources:

Payne, Wardell J., ed. *Directory of African American Religious Bodies.* Washington, DC: Howard University Press, 1991.

★506★
The Apostolic Faith Mission of Portland, Oregon, Inc.
6615 SE 52nd Ave.
Portland, OR 97206

In April of 1906, a small group of people of various denominational backgrounds arranged for prayer meetings in a home located on Bonnie Brae Street in Los Angeles. Their purpose was to seek the infilling of the Holy Spirit, having heard of the Pentecostal experience of believers in the Midwest. When a number received this experience, the word spread, and shortly the meetings were transferred to larger quarters in an old Methodist church on Azusa Street.

Among those attending the meetings on Azusa Street, was Florence L. Crawford, a Methodist laywoman. There she received the experience of sanctification and the power of the Holy Spirit. At her baptism in the Holy Spirit, she related that God "permitted me to speak in the Chinese, which was understood by a Christian Chinese who was present." She also testified to receiving a miraculous healing of her eyes, which had been damaged by spinal meningitis.

A dynamic woman, Crawford entered wholeheartedly into evangelistic work, assisting mission leader William J. Seymour. Thousands of inquiries had begun coming in from people who wanted to know more about the Pentecostal outpouring, so Crawford began putting the record of what was being said in the meetings into a newspaper format. The publication was called *The Apostolic Faith.*

In addition to her efforts in the publishing work, Crawford felt God's call to travel beyond the boundaries of Los Angeles with the Pentecostal message. Her first ministries were along the West Coast where she worked as an intinerant home missionary. In December of 1906, she made her initial visit to Portland, Oregon, where she had been invited to preach in an independent church on Second and Main Street. Subsequently, the pastor of that church offered her his pulpit permanently, and in 1908, Crawford moved to Portland. The Azusa Street ministry turned over the responsibility of publishing *The Apostolic Faith* paper to her, so she and her coworker, Clara Lum, brought that work to Portland with the blessing of the Azusa Street ministry. The publication continued uninterrupted, with the final edition from Los Angeles being printed in June 1908, and the first edition from Portland coming out in July-August 1908.

Portland was established as the headquarters of the growing movement. In 1922, the headquarters building, a landmark in downtown Portland, was erected. A large neon sign with the message "Jesus the Light of the World", first displayed in 1917, was transferred to the new structure.

Through the years, the Apostolic Faith has maintained the doctrines outlined in the first editions of the Apostolic Faith papers printed in 1906. As a Trinitarian church, its doctrinal position centers on a belief in the born-again experience, supports the Wesleyan teaching on holiness, and stresses the need of sanctified believers to receive the Pentecostal experience of the baptism of th Holy Spirit. The church holds to the teaching of salvation rather than the Calvinist belief in predestination and eternal security.

The church is governed by a board of five trustees headed by a general overseer, with Rev. Dwight L. Baltzell being the current general overseer. Both home and foreign missions have emerged on a large scale, with work in 32 countries in Africa, Asia, the West Indies, and Europe. The largest mission fields in Nigeria, where there are approximately 20,000 members. Each local congregation is under the leadership and direction of the international headquarters work in Portland.

Membership: In 1997 the church reported approximately 4,000 members, in 50 congregations with 160 ministers in the United States, and 10 congregations and 25 ministers in Canada. There were approximately 50,000 members in foreign lands. Membership is only an estimate; the church counts those who regularly attend as members.

Periodicals: *Higher Way.* • *The Light of Hope.*

Sources:

A Historical Account of the Apostolic Faith. Portland, OR: Apostolic Faith Publishing House, 1965.

The Light of Life Brought Triumph. Portland, OR: Apostolic Faith Publishing House, 1955.

Saved to Serve. Portland, OR: Apostolic Faith Publishing House, 1967.

★507★
Apostolic Holiness Church of America
Current address not obtained for this edition.

The Apostolic Holiness Church of America was founded in 1927 in Mount Olive, North Carolina, by a group of former members of the Apostolic Faith Church of God originally founded by Bishops William J. Seymour and Charles W. Lowe. The group included Elders J. M. Barns, W. M. D. Atkins, Ernest Graham, J. M. McKinnon, and Sisters Sarah Artis and Emma Spruel. Doctrine is like other branches of the movement, as all the issues at stake in the separation were administrative. In 1973 the church went through a constitutional revision under its present presiding bishop, Isaac Ryals, assisted by W. R. Turner, I. W. Hicks, Jessie Budd, Shirley Clark, and E. V. Ethridge.

Membership: In 1990 it had ten affiliated congregations.

Sources:

Payne, Wardell J., ed. *Directory of African American Religious Bodies: A Compendium by the Howard University School of Divinity.* Washington, DC: Howard University Press, 1991.

★508★
Carolina Evangelistic Association
Garr Memorial Church
7700 Wallace Rd.
Charlotte, NC 28212

Dr. A. G. Garr was the first foreign missionary of the Church of God (Cleveland, Tennessee). He left the church in 1906, immediately after receiving the baptism of the Holy Spirit. He continued to do foreign missionary work until 1912, when he returned to the United States and began to operate as an evangelist in the days when Pentecostals were still a small, scattered group. He was particularly active in the early years of the Angelus Temple, the Los Angeles center for the International Church of the Foursquare Gospel headed by Aimee Semple McPherson. In 1930, he went to Charlotte, North Carolina, to conduct a tent revival. After three

months, those who had been saved, healed, and helped asked him to remain. Fifty-six years old then, he remained and built a tabernacle. An abandoned city auditorium was bought, remodeled, and named Garr Auditorium; it remains as the headquarters of the association. Garr died in 1944 and was succeeded by his wife and son as pastors.

The Carolina Evangelistic Association carries on an active program through Garr Auditorium and Faith Chapel, both in Charlotte. There are missionaries supported by the Association in numerous countries. A regular program of services is conducted in the county jail and the county home. The "Morning Thought for the Day Magazine" radio show is their radio ministry. Camp Lurecrest for youth is located at Lake Lure, North Carolina. The church is a member of the Pentecostal Fellowship of North America.

Membership: Not reported. Approximately 1,000 people regularly attend worship at Garr Auditorium.

★509★
Church of Christ Holiness unto the Lord
1650 Smart St.
PO Box 1642
Savannah, GA 31401

The Church of Christ Holiness unto the Lord was founded in 1926 in Savannah, Georgia, but grew out of the ministry of William J. Seymour of the Apostolic Faith Mission in Los Angeles, the original center from which the Pentecostal movement was disseminated around the United States. It was founded by Bishop Milton Solomon Bishop (d. 1952) and his wife, and Saul Keels and his wife, Dora Brown, as well as others. The present leader of the church is Bishop Moses Lewis who became General Overseer in 1979. The church follows the Holiness Pentecostal teachings as expounded by Seymour.

The church is affiliated with the United Fellowship Convention of the Original Azusa Street Mission which sponsors an annual gathering of those churches in the Eastern United States which grew out of Seymour's evangelistic activity.

Membership: In 1990 it had 35 affiliated congregations.

Sources:

DuPree, Sherry Sherrod. *African American Holiness Pentecostal Charismatic: Annotated Bibliography.* New York: Garland Publishing, 1992.

Payne, Wardell J., ed. *Directory of African American Religious Bodies: A Compendium by the Howard University School of Divinity.* Washington, DC: Howard University Press, 1991.

★510★
Church of God (Cleveland, Tennessee)
Keith St. at 25th St., NW
Cleveland, TN 37311

Most of the Pentecostal churches which bear the name "Church of God" can be traced to a holiness revival in the mountains of northwest Georgia and eastern Tennessee. In 1884, R. G. Spurling, a Baptist minister in Monroe County, Tennessee, began to search the Scriptures for answers to the problems of modernism, formality, and spiritual dryness. An initial meeting of concerned people was held on August 19, 1886, at the Barney Creek Meeting House to organize a new movement that would preach primitive church holiness and provide for reform and revival of the churches. Christian Union was the name accepted by the first eight members enrolled that day. Spurling died within a few months and was succeeded in leadership by his son, R. G. Spurling, Jr..

After ten years of little growth, three laymen influenced by the Spurlings' work claimed a deep religious experience similar to that written about by John Wesley, the founder of Methodism, and as a result began to preach sanctification. (Wesley attended a service at Aldersgate Street in London in 1738 where he "felt his heart strangely warmed." He and his followers interpreted this as a work of God which again sanctified the person who had already experienced a justifying faith in Christ). The three laymen began to hold services at Camp Creek, in Cherokee County, North Carolina, among a group of unaffiliated Baptists. Spurling and the Christian Union moved their services to Camp Creek and united with the group in North Carolina. During the revival that followed this merger, spontaneous speaking in tongues occurred. After searching the Scriptures, the group recognized the phenomena as a Biblical occurrence and as a new outpouring of the Holy Spirit.

The Christian Union, as it grew, suffered from both persecution and fanaticism: as its unrestrained members spoke in tongues and held noisy services, various members of the local community complained. Some leaders of the Christian Union, responding to the criticism, decided to make the services more orderly. They devised a simple plan of government at a meeting in the home of W. F. Bryant. The group's name was changed to the Holiness Church. In 1896, during the revival, Ambrose J. Tomlinson (1865-1943), an Indiana Quaker and agent of the American Bible Society, came to the hill country to sell Bibles and religious literature. In 1903, he cast his lot with the group and became pastor of the Camp Creek Church. This event can be viewed as the real beginning of the Church of God movement. Having been influenced by the Church of God (Anderson, Indiana), Tomlinson persuaded the Holiness Church to accept the Biblical name the Church of God. He is also the probable source for the pacifist emphasis which permeates many Pentecostal churches. Tomlinson began a publishing enterprise and printed for distribution the doctrines of the new church. Headquarters were soon established in his home at Culbertson, Tennessee, and he emerged as the dominant leader. Tomlinson later settled in Cleveland, Tennessee, and eventually led a congregation there to unite with the Holiness Church. The church's period of expansion had begun.

With the establishment of further congregations, the members saw the necessity of an assembly for dealing with questions of mutual concern. The first assembly convened in 1906 at Camp Creek and decisions were made about footwashing—it was to be observed at least annually—and mid-week and family services—they were to be encouraged. At the 1907 assembly, the name was officially changed to the Church of God.

The 1908 assembly was attended by G. B. Cashwell, who was to introduce many holiness people to the baptism of the Holy Spirit and the experience of speaking in tongues which had occurred at the mission of the Pacific Apostolic Faith Movement on Azusa Street in Los Angeles. After the assembly, he preached a revival. Tomlinson received the baptism and spoke in tongues. The following year, in a gesture symbolic of the church's acceptance of the new truth preached by Cashwell and experienced by Tomlinson, he was selected general moderator of the young church, a position he held until 1922. In 1914, he was elected general overseer for life. Accelerated growth, with the exception of losses of schismatic bodies, has continued unabated.

Doctrinally, the Church of God believes in the baptism of the Holy Spirit as an experience subsequent to sanctification. Practices include baptism by immersion, the Lord's Supper, and footwashing. Members believe in holiness-of-life, which excludes the use of cosmetics, costly apparel, and shorts or slacks on women. They accept a premillennial second coming (the coming of Christ to bind Satan before Christ's thousand-year reign on earth with his saints).

Government of the Church of God is centralized. Authority is vested in the general assembly, which meets every two years and is chaired by the general overseer. A supreme council operates between general assemblies, and a general executive committee oversees the boards and agencies. State overseers have charge over the churches in their areas and appoint the pastors. Tithing is a central feature in finances. The height of centralization came in 1914 when the annual elections of the general overseer were discontinued and Tomlinson became overseer for life.

Tomlinson's authority was attacked in the 1920s. In 1922, a committee ordered to investigate the church's finances (which Tomlinson completely controlled) reported unfavorably, and Tomlinson was impeached and removed from office. The overseer's authority had been reduced earlier by the addition of two new offices to control functions previously controlled by Tomlinson (publishing and education). These were supplemented in 1922 by the new constitution, adopted despite Tomlinson's opposition.

The Church of God Publishing House produces a large selection of books, pamphlets and tracts, and a full line of church school material. Missions, both foreign and domestic, are widespread (in seventy-two countries) and supported by the tithe of members. The Church is a member of the National Association of Evangelicals.

Membership: In 1984 the church reported 505,775 members, 5,346 churches, and 9,638 ministers.

Educational Facilities: Lee College, Cleveland, Tennessee. Northwest Bible and Music Academy, Minot, North Dakota. West Coast Bible School, Pasadena, California.

Periodicals: *Church of God Evangel.* • *Lighted Pathway.* Available from Church of God Publishing House, 1080 Montgomery Ave., Cleveland, TN 37311.

Sources:

Conn, Charles W. *Like a Mighty Army.* Cleveland, TN: Church of God Publishing House, 1955.

___. *Pillars of Pentecost.* Cleveland, TN: Pathway Press, 1956.

Hughes, Ray H. *Church of God Distinctives.* Cleveland, TN: Pathway Press, 1968.

Marshall, June Glover. *A Biographical Sketch of Richard G. Spurling, Jr.* Cleveland, TN: Pathway Press, 1974.

Slay, James L. *This We Believe.* Cleveland, TN: Pathway Press, 1963.

★511★
Church of God House of Prayer
% Rev. Charles Mackenin
Markleysburg, PA 15459

Harrison W. Poteat joined the Church of God (Cleveland, Tennessee) in its early years and was an overseer in the Northeast for more than 20 years. In 1933, he established churches on Prince Edward Island. In 1939, he broke with the Cleveland headquarters and founded the Church of God House of Prayer. Many of the churches which Poteat had established went with him. A suit was brought by the parent body, which was able to recover occupancy in many of the church properties, and the loss of the property cut deeply into Poteat's support. Some congregations withdrew from the Church of God House of Prayer and became independent. Doctrine follows that of the parent body. H.W. Poteat remained as Overseer of the Church of God House of Prayer until 1932, when he was succeeded by his sons George Poteat (1952-1955) and Paul E. Poteat (1955-1961). The next general superintendents were Evan Hedglin (1961-1965), Charles McNevin (1965-1991) and Arnold Culleton (1991 to present).

Membership: Not reported. In 1967 the church reported 24 churches in the northeast and two in Canada, with a total membership of 1,200.

Educational Facilities: Markleysburg Bible Institute, Markleysburg, Pennsylvania.

★512★
Church of God (Jerusalem Acres)
% Chief Bishop John A. Looper
Box 1207
1826 Dalton Pike (Jerusalem Acres)
Cleveland, TN 37364-1207

History. The Church of God (Jerusalem Acres) began in 1957 when Grady R. Kent initiated a reformation of the Church of God of Prophecy aimed at a reestablishment of its biblical order. Kent had been a pastor in the church since 1933. In 1943, he was placed in charge of the Church of God of Prophecy Marker Association begun by Ambrose J. Tomlinson, the church's founder, as an auxiliary to locate, mark, beautify, and maintain prominent places in the world connected with the Church of God of Prophecy. One place of particular interest was the Fields of the Wood—a mountainside Bible monument, based on Psalms 132:6 and Habakkuk 2:2-3, located on Burger Mountain in western North Carolina. The monument includes a replica of the Ten Commandments in seven-foot tall letters and an altar on the top of the mountain. The altar marks the spot where Tomlinson prayed, immediately prior to declaring the Church of God to be in existence. Kent also supervised the White Angel Fleet, pilots and airplanes used for public demonstrations of ministry at airports throughout the United States. Between 1948 and 1957, Kent objected to the Church of God of Prophecy replacing the general overseer with the general assembly as the highest authority in the church (which, in effect, repeated the history of the church and led to its formation in the early 1920s). Faced with having to recant his objection to the actions of the general assembly, as well as other controversial ideas he had developed, Kent resigned in 1957. With 300 supporters, many from South Carolina, Kent established a new Church of God, with himself as general overseer.

Beliefs. The Church believes in an experiential understanding of justification by faith, sanctification as a second work of grace, and the baptism of the Holy Spirit evidenced by speaking in tongues. It also believes in the restoration of both ministerial (Ephesians 4:11) and spiritual (I Corinthians 12) gifts to the Church.

In areas of worship and service, the church has developed a comprehensive program termed "New Testament Judaism," a term coined by Kent in 1962 on a visit to Israel. The church observes the biblical (Old Testament) calendar that includes the sabbath as a day of worship; Passover as a time for celebrating communion; Pentecost as a festival for spiritual renewal and dedication to the work of the church; and Tabernacles as a remembrance of the time of Christ's birth and a foreshadowing of his return. Various symbols generally associated with Judaism are used alongside of the cross. The church does not celebrate the holidays of Easter, Halloween, and Christmas.

Organization. The polity is theocratic, government by God through an annointed leader. There is a chief bishop who sits as the final authority (as contrasted to the total authority) in matters of both judicial and executive government. The church has no legislative body, but has a council of apostles and elders, the purpose of which is judicial—that is, to interpret the laws of God in the Bible, both Old and New Testaments, as they relate to the church. The primary officers in the council are the chief bishop, the 12 apostles, the seven men of wisdom, and the 70 elders.

Membership: In 1987, the church reported 10,000 members, 145 churches, and 255 ministers.

Periodicals: *The Vision Speaks.* • *Greater Light.*

Sources:

Introduction to Apostles' Doctrine. Cleveland, TN: Church Publishing Company, 1984.

Kent, Grady R. *Treatise on the 1957 Reformation Stand.* Cleveland, TN: Church Publishing Company, the Church of God, n.d.

Manual of Apostles Doctrine and Business Procedure. Cleveland, TN: Church Publishing Company and Press, n.d.

★513★
Church of God/Mountain Assembly
110 S. Florence Ave.
PO Box 157
Jellico, TN 37762

The Church of God/Mountain Assembly grew out of a holiness revival in 1895 in the South Union Association of the United Baptist Church. From 1895 until 1903, members and ministers who adopted the holiness belief in a second work of grace which imparts sanctification by the power of the Holy Spirit, remained within the United Baptist Church in McCreary County, Kentucky. However, in 1903, the Baptists decided to revoke the licenses of all ministers who were preaching sanctification according to the holiness movement. In 1906, these holiness ministers—Reverends J. H. Parks, Steve N. Bryant, Tom Moses, and William O. Douglas—met at Jellico, Tennessee, with members of their several churches and organized the Church of God. The words "Mountain Assembly" were added in 1911 after the group heard of other Church of God groups. In 1906-07, the group learned of the baptism of the Holy Ghost as evidenced by speaking in tongues and accepted it as a fuller expression of their ideas. Rev. S. N. Bryant was elected as their first moderator. The assembly ascribed to a church covenant, teachings, and declaration of faith.

The doctrine of the Church of God/Mountain Assembly is similar to that of the Church of God (Cleveland, Tennessee). The church professes a conservative trinitarian faith, and the King James Version of the Bible is preferred. Present polity was adopted in 1914. The offices of General Overseer, Assistant Overseer and Missions Director, General Secretary and Treasurer, and District Overseer were established and filled. The Overseers operate in a basically congregational system. The assembly meets annually. The Delegation serves as the legislative body and a Board of Twelve Elders as a judicial body. From its headquarters in Jellico, Tennessee, the Church of God/Mountain Assembly has spread to ten states from Michigan to Florida. A National Youth Campground is located near Winchester, Ohio.

Membership: In 1994, the church reported 116 churches and 5,100 members in the United States, and 350 churches overseas in India, Africa and the Caribbean.

Periodicals: *Gospel Herald.*

Sources:

Gibson, Luther. *History of the Church of God Mountain Assembly.* The Author, 1954.

★514★
Church of God of Apostolic Faith
Current address not obtained for this edition.

The Church of God of the Apostolic Faith was organized in 1914 by four independent Pentecostal ministers who saw the need for some organization and church government. Not wishing to follow the plan of government adopted by the Assemblies of God, which had been formed that year in nearby Hot Springs, Arkansas, the Reverends James O. McKenzie, Edwin A. Buckles, Oscar H. Myers, and Joseph P. Rhoades held a meeting which led to the creation of the Church of God of the Apostolic Faith at Cross Roads Mission near Ozark, Arkansas. They adopted a presbyterial form of government based on Acts 15. The Church also had a doctrinal difference with the Assemblies of God, believing as did the Church of God (Cleveland, Tennessee) that one must seek sanctification before having the baptism of the Holy Spirit. Like the Church of God, healing, tithing, and nonparticipation in war are emphasized.

The general conference of the Church meets annually. It elects the general presbytery of seven ministers, including the general overseer and two assistants. The conference owns all the property and the presbytery controls the ministry. The church is currently divided into five districts. There is a mission in Mexico.

Membership: Not reported. In the mid-1970s there were approximately 1,400 members in 27 congregations.

Periodicals: *Church of God Herald.* • *Christian Youth.*

★515★
Church of God of Prophecy
PO Box 2910
Cleveland, TN 37320-2910

Alternate Address: Canadian headquarters: Eastern Canada: PO Box 457, 1st Line East, R.R. 2, Brampton, ON L6V 2L4. Western Canada: 130 Centre St., Strathmore, AL T1P 1G9.

History. The Church of God of Prophecy traces its beginning to the organization of the Church of God on June 13, 1903, in Cherokee County, North Carolina. Ambrose J. Tomlinson was selected as pastor. New churches in other areas were organized under his pastoral leadership.

Although it was understood that the small group was operating as the Church of God, it was in the second assembly held at Union Grove, Bradley County, Tennessee, in 1907, that the name Church of God was formally adopted by the assembly and entered into the records. In 1952, the suffix "of Prophecy" to the name came about to distinguish the church from other organizations using the same "Church of God" in business and secular activities.

The first general assembly of its membership was called for January 1906, in Cherokee County, with A. J. Tomlinson serving as moderator and clerk. He continued to hold this dual office until the title was changed to general overseer in the fifth assembly in 1910.

The leadership of A. J. Tomlinson was marked by making the Church of God a national, then an international body, and by the development of various educational, social, and ecclesiastical programs. He continued as general overseer until his death in 1943. At that time, his youngest son, Milton A. Tomlinson, was duly selected by the overseer leadership and approved by the assembly body.

M. A. Tomlinson's tenure as general overseer continued until April 30, 1990, when due to ill health, he vacated the office. In a meeting of the state and national overseers, Billy D. Murray, Sr. was selected to serve as interim general overseer until the annual assembly in August. At that official conclave of the church membership, Murray was confirmed as general overseer; he continues in that position.

During Tomlinson's tenure as general overseer, the church was noted for its call for unity and fellowship not limited socially, racially, or nationally. The church is integrated on all levels and various leadership positions are occupied by women. The following ministries were developed under his leadership: radio and television, youth camping, servicemen's outreach, world mission corps, youth mission teams, international orphanages, and Tomlinson College.

Church history includes a strong emphasis on youth ministries, national and international missions, and various parochial education ministries.

The church has developed a biblical-theme park, known as Fields of the Wood near Murphy, North Carolina, the site where the first congregation was organized in 1903. It includes the world's largest cross, the Ten Commandments depicted in five-foot letters, and biblical markers that portray the message of Christ. The park is visited by more than 100,000 visitors annually.

Beliefs. The Church of God of Prophecy accepts the authority of the whole Bible as the Word of God and hence has no creed. However, it has summarized what it considers to be "Twenty-Nine Important Bible Truths" which show it to be in basic agreement with traditional trinitarian Christian beliefs. It places special emphasis on sanctification (holiness of the believer) and the doc-

trine of Spirit-baptism that includes speaking-in-tongues as initial evidence. Other prominent doctrinal commitments include: an eschatology that involves a premillennial return of the risen Jesus, which, according to the church, will be preceded by a series of events; a call for sanctity in the home that includes denial of multiple marriages; practice of baptism by immersion, the Lord's Supper and washing the saints' feet; total abstinence from intoxicating beverages and tobacco; a concern for modesty in all dimensions of life; and an appreciation for various gifts of the Holy Spirit with special attention to divine healing.

Organization. The church is headed by its general overseer. An biannual general assembly is held where various doctrinal and business concerns as come before it are considered. To be adopted, all resolutions must receive unanimous consent of all male members in attendance. These resolutions are then ratified by each local congregation. The general assembly concludes with the general overseer appointing all national and international leaders, who in turn are responsible for appointing the various leaders under their jurisdiction.

In 1916, the church developed the Assembly Band Movement, now known as the Pastoral Care Department, a unique program which organizes cell groups of eight to twelve people fostering religious commitment and growth. These groups resemble the classes organized in the nineteenth century by the early Methodists.

In 1933, the church adopted an official church flag which is on display in all church facilities.

Membership: The church is organized in 99 countries of the world and in every state of the United States. In 1994, the church reported 303,034 members in 5,717 churches and 1,345 missions. There were 3,009 members in 43 Canadian churches.

Educational Facilities: Center for Biblical Leadership, Cleveland, Tennessee. World Harvest Institute, Cleveland, Tennessee.

Periodicals: *White Wing Messenger.* • *The Happy Harvester.* • *Victory.*

Remarks: The problems which led to the withdrawal of A. J. Tomlinson from the Church of God (Cleveland, Tennessee) in 1922 are described quite differently by the two groups. According to Homer Tomlinson, one of A. J. Tomlinson's sons, the occassion of the schism was the desire of some church elders to organize a Golden Rule Supply Company to operate as a co-op for members, and to use the profits to support the church's mission program. Reportedly, the Rev. Joe S. Lewellyn and others campaigned against Tomlinson, which undermined his support and the confidence in his leadership. In any case, Tomlinson strongly objected to the church's reorganization in 1921 which substantially stripped many of the powers from the office of general overseer.

Sources:

Davidson, C. T. *Upon This Rock.* 3 vols. Cleveland TN: White Wing Press, 1973-76.

Duggar, Lillie. *A. J. Tomlinson.* Cleveland, TN: White Wing Publishing House, 1964.

Pruitt, Raymond M. *Fundamentals of the Faith.* Cleveland, TN: White Wing Publishing House and Press, 1981.

Stone, James. *The Church of God of Prophecy: History and Polity.* Cleveland, TN: White Wing Press, 1977.

★516★
Church of God of the Original Mountain Assembly
Current address not obtained for this edition.

In 1939 Steve N. Bryant, longtime leader of the Church of God of the Mountain Assembly died. He was succeeded by A. J. Long, who led the Church in a reorganization in 1944. However, in 1946, Long was not reelected as moderator. That same year, with his supporters, he left and founded the Church of God of the Original Mountain Assembly. Approximately one fourth of the membership (fifteen ministers, eight deacons, and approximately 300 people) established the new church on the original structure of the parent body. The church is headed by a general overseer and a council of twelve. The first meeting of the Church of God of the Original Mountain Assembly was held at Williamsburg, Kentucky. The doctrine of the parent body was adopted, from the covenant originally made when it was incorporated in 1917, but articles were added on the need for harmony between pastors and deacons (lay leaders), the subordinate role of women and opposition to snake handling.

Membership: Not reported. In 1967 there were 11 churches and 17 ministers.

★517★
Church of God of the Union Assembly
Box 1323
Dalton, GA 30720

The Church of God of the Union Assembly is a small schism formed in 1920 from the Church of God of the Mountain Assembly. It began when the congregation in Center, Jackson County, Georgia withdrew. The immediate occasion for the split was the issue of tithing. The Union Assembly rejects the tithing system established in 1919 by the Mountain Assembly, believing it to be an Old Testament practice not taught by Jesus or his apostles. The group also believes the kingdom of God is a spiritual kingdom; that David's throne is established in heaven, not on earth; and that Christ's coming will be followed by the end of time, not the millennium (Christ's reign on earth for 1,000 years with his saints). The Union Assembly's present leader is Jesse Pratt, who has written a number of pamphlets disseminated through the church. Congregations have spread to seventeen states.

Membership: Not reported.
Periodicals: *Quarterly News.*

★518★
Church of God (World Headquarters)
1270 Willow Brook SE, Apt. 2
Huntsville, AL 35802

Ambrose J. Tomlinson, founder of the Church of God (Cleveland, Tennessee) and the Church of God of Prophecy died in 1943. Before his death, however, he designated his eldest son Homer Tomlinson, his successor as general overseer. However, the General Assembly set aside that appointment and selected the younger son, Milton A. Tomlinson as the new general overseer. Homer Tomlinson rejected their action, called his followers to a meeting in New York and reorganized the Church of God, generally distinguished from other similarly-named groups by the additional phrase, "World Headquarters." A struggle in court over control of the church resulted in Milton and his followers being recognized as The Church of God of Prophecy which was awarded all properties and trademarks. Homer continued as head of the group of loyal followers and rebuilt the church which he led until his death in 1969. He was succeeded by Voy M. Bullen.

The doctrine, which follows closely that of the other Church of God bodies, is contained in the *Book of Doctrines/1903-1970.* The only doctrinal divergence in the entire Church of God movement occurs in the Church of God (World Headquarters). Its members replace the premillennialism of the other branches with a belief that the Church of God has the keys to bring the kingdom of God on earth, and that the kingdom will come by the setting up of the saints of God in the governments of the nations of the world now, here upon earth. Saints are encouraged to become responsible rulers and to preach the gospel of the kingdom. This doctrine was based upon the Bible as interpreted by A. J. Tomlinson, who gave Homer a commission to plant the church flag in every nation of the earth. Given that commission, Homer established the "World Headquarters" of the Church of God in Jerusalem.

After Bishop Homer's death in 1969, the American headquarters was moved from Queens, New York, to Huntsville, Alabama, a location more central to the congregations. The church's administrative offices are there. An annual assembly is held at Choffee, Missouri. A vigorous mission program, attributed in part to Homer's tireless traveling, has seen affiliated Churches of God established in Barbados, Canada, Egypt, England, Ghana, Greece, Haiti, Jamaica, Kenya, Liberia, Nigeria, Panama, the Philippine Islands, Scotland, the Virgin Islands, and Zambia. The Theocratic Party, associated with the church, runs candidates for both state and national offices in the United States.

Membership: Not reported. In 1973, there were 2,035 churches, 75,890 members, and 2,737 ministers worldwide.
Periodicals: *The Church of God.*

Sources:

Book of Doctrines, 1903-1970. Huntsville, AL: Church of God Publishing House, 1970.

Tomlinson, Homer A. *The Shout of a King.* Queens Village, NY: Church of God, 1968.

★519★
Congregational Holiness Church
3888 Fayetteville Hwy.
Griffin, GA 30223

In 1920 a controversy over divine healing arose in the Georgia Conference of the Pentecostal Holiness Church, now known as the International Pentecostal Holiness Church. One faction contended that the healing provisions in the atonement were sufficient, and that human aids (doctors) were unnecessary. While this faction admitted the therapeutic value of effective remedies, such remedies were not considered necessary for God to heal. The other faction, led by Rev. Watson Sorrow, insisted that God had placed medicine on earth for man's use. The group against doctors relied on the Biblical phrase about Christ's passion, "By his stripes you are healed."

The names of the Rev. Watson Sorrow and Hugh Bowling were dropped from the ministerial roll of the Pentecostal Holiness Church without their first being tried by the board of the Georgia annual conference of which they were members. A number of ministers withdrew with them, and together they organized the Congregational Holiness Church. They expressed differences with their parent body on the concentration of power in a few hands, so they attempted to democratize the church government. Consequently their polity is not episcopal, like that of the Pentecostal Holiness Church. Their polity is a moderate connectional system: local churches are grouped in associations which elect delegates to a general association with legislative powers. Pastors are called by vote of the congregation. Men and women may be ordained. Mission work is going forth in Cuba, Costa Rica, Brazil, Mexico, Honduras, Guatemala, India, Nicaragua, and Spain.

Membership: In 1995 the church reported 7,000 members, 175 churches, and 429 ministers.
Periodicals: *Gospel Messenger.*

Sources:

Cox, B. L. *History and Doctrine of the Congregational Holiness Church.* Gainesville, GA: The Author, 1959.

___. *My Life Story.* Greenwood, SC: C. H. Publishing House, n.d.

★520★
Door of Faith Church and Bible School
1161 Young St.
Honolulu, HI 96814

The Door of Faith Church and Bible School was founded by Mildred Johnson Brostek. Raised a Methodist, she experienced the baptism of the Holy Spirit in an Assemblies of God church in Florida. She later joined the Pentecostal Holiness Church (now known as the International Pentecostal Holiness Church), which licensed her to preach. She graduated from the Holmes Theological Seminary and soon thereafter went to the Hawaiian Islands where she had earlier felt a call from God to go as a missionary. In 1937, she began to hold evangelistic services on Molokai in the home of a native Hawaiian. The services prospered and in 1940, the Door of Faith Churches of Hawaii was chartered and the work soon spread to the other islands.

The church is headed by the Reverend Brostek who is the church's overseer. There is an annual conference. A daily radio ministry is broacast over two stations, one in Honolulu and one in Hilo, Hawaii.

Membership: Not reported. There are churches at a number of locations in Hawaii and a prosperous mission has developed in the Philippines, where a Bible college has been opened. There is one church in New York. In 1979, there were 40 churches and 3,000 members in Hawaii and missions work in Okinawa and Indonesia.

Educational Facilities: Door of Faith Bible School, Honolulu, Hawaii.

Sources:

Donovan, Robert D. *Her Door of Faith*. Honolulu, HI: Orovan Books, 1971.

★521★
Emmanuel Holiness Church
Box 818
Bladenboro, NC 28320

In 1953, controversy over standards of dress among the members of the Pentecostal Fire-Baptized Holiness Church led to a vote to divide the church. One issue which occasioned the split was the use of neckties, which the Pentecostal Fire-Baptized Holiness Church explicity forbids. Those who voted for the split elected Rev. L. O. Sellers chairman and formed the Emmanuel Holiness Church. It differs from its parent body only on minor points of dress, a more congregational form of government, and tithing which is required of members. A general assembly of all ministers and one delegate from each church has limited legislative powers.

Membership: Not reported. In 1967 there were 72 congregations and 118 ministers.

Periodicals: *Emmanuel Holiness Messenger.*

★522★
Emmanuel Tabernacle Baptist Church Apostolic Faith
329 N. Garfield Ave.
Columbus, OH 43203

The Emmanuel Tabernacle Baptist Church Apostolic Faith began in 1916 (incorporated 1917) in Columbus, Ohio. Columbus was an early center of the non-Trinitarian Apostolic movement which had originated in 1913 and spread through the still youthful Pentecostal movement. The new church was founded by Rev. Martin Rawleigh Gregory (later Bishop) (1885-1960). Gregory had been called to the ministry as a 17 year old youth. He was educated at Colgate University and became a Baptist minister in 1903. In 1914 he moved to Columbus, Ohio, where he encountered Pentecostalism in its Apostolic form. His adoption of Pentecostalism led to a break with the Baptist Church.

Gregory was assisted in the founding of the Emmanuel Tabernacle by two females who had worked with him in the Baptist Church, Lela Grant and Bessie Dockett. He came to believe very early that women should share equally in the preaching of God's word, and as bishop of the church, Gregory opened the ordained ministry to women, the first Apostolic church to do so. As the church grew and a board of bishops was created, women were elevated to the episcopacy.

The church holds to an Apostolic non-Trinitarian theology. Jesus is the name of the One God and baptism is done in the name of Jesus only. The church also practices foot washing. The current leader, Bishop H. C. Clark, is a female. An annual meeting is held each summer in Columbus.

Membership: In 1990 there were approximately 30 congregations.

Sources:

Payne, Wardell J., ed. *Directory of African American Religious Bodies: A Compendium by the Howard University School of Divinity*. Washington, DC: Howard University Press, 1991.

★523★
Evangelistic Church of God
Current address not obtained for this edition.

The Evangelistic Church of God was incorporated at Denver, Colorado in 1949. It grew out of the work of Norman L. Chase, former minister of the Church of God (Cleveland, Tennessee) and of the (Original) Church of God. By 1955 the group claimed 774 members in twelve churches. The general assembly meets annually.

Membership: Not reported.

Periodicals: *The Church of God Final Warning.*

★524★
First Interdenominational Christian Association
Calvary Temple Holiness Church
1061 Memorial Dr., SE
Atlanta, GA 30315

In 1946, the Rev. Watson Sorrow, who had been one of the founders of the Congregational Holiness Church, formed the First Interdenominational Christian Association, centered upon his own congregation, Calvary Temple in Atlanta. The Association is like the Congregational Holiness Church but less definite in doctrine. The parent body's statements on war, eschatology, and the forbidding of varying doctrinal beliefs among ministers were dropped. Retained were statements on healing, footwashing, and Pentecostalism. Several churches have joined Sorrow by adopting the congregational polity and policies of Calvary Temple.

Membership: Not reported. In the late 1960s, Calvary Temple had about 100 members.

★525★
Free Will Baptist Church of the Pentecostal Faith
Current address not obtained for this edition.

The Free Will Baptist Church of the Pentecostal Faith was formed in the 1950s when some members of the South Carolina Pentecostal Free Will Baptist Church Conference decided not to participate in the reorganization that led to the formation of the Pentecostal Free Will Baptist Church. Those who abstained adopted a constitution and chose a new name. They are at one doctrinally with the other Pentecostal Free Will Baptists.

The polity is congregational. The annual conference is to approve teachings, methods and conduct, and to encourage fellowship and evangelism. A general board headed by the conference superintendent functions between conference meetings. The Foreign Missions Department oversees work in Costa Rica. Camp meetings are periodically sponsored.

Membership: Not reported. In 1967 there were 33 congregations and 39 ministers.

Sources:

Faith and Government of the Free Will Baptist Church of the Pentecostal Faith. N.p. 1961.

★526★
Full Gospel Church Association
Box 265
Amarillo, TX 79105

The Full Gospel Church Association, Incorporated, was organized by the Rev. Dennis W. Thorn at Amarillo, Texas, in 1952 for the purpose of bringing together a number of small, independent Pentecostal churches and missions, most of them with fewer than 100 members in the South and Southwest.

Doctrinally, the Full Gospel Church is similar to the Church of God (Cleveland, Tennessee). It emphasizes healing, tithing, and a literal heaven and hell, and uses only the King James Version of the Bible. It practices footwashing. Bearing arms is a matter of individual judgment. It does forbid disloyalty, insubordination, and criticism of the Association by its individual members. One unique element is the requirement that each church have an "Altar of God" in its building as a condition of its recognition by the Association.

The Association is congregational in polity. A general convention meets regularly. The general board of directors meets quarterly; its executive directors are the supreme council of the Association. Mission workers were active in Mexico, the Philippines, and Africa.

Membership: Not reported. In 1967 there were 67 churches with a total combined membership of 2,010.

★527★
General Conference of the Evangelical Baptist Church
Kavetter Bldg.
3400 E. Ash St.
Goldsboro, NC 27530

The General Conference of the Evangelical Baptist Church was organized in 1935 as the Church of the Full Gospel, Inc. It is Pentecostal and holiness in emphasis, following a theology close to that of the Pentecostal Free Will Baptist Church. It stresses spiritual gifts, healing, and the pretribulation, premillennial return of Christ. Four ordinances are recognized—baptism by immersion, communion, the dedication of children, and tithing. The dedication of children is a form of christening that is distinct from baptism.

The polity is congregational. There is an annual conference which elects officers. In the local church, the pastor is the chief officer. He is elected by the congregation and has the power to appoint or nominate all church officers.

Membership: Not reported. In 1952 there were 31 churches, 2,200 members and 37 ministers.

Educational Facilities: Evangelical Theological Seminary, Goldsboro, North Carolina.

William Carter College, Goldsboro, North Carolina.

Periodicals: *Evangelical Baptist.*

Sources:

Discipline of the General Conference of the Evangelical Baptist Church. N.p., n.d.

★528★
Holiness Baptist Association
Current address not obtained for this edition.

The Holiness Baptist Association can be traced to 1893 when, because of their teaching on "sinless perfection," two congregations and several ministers were expelled from the Little River Baptist Association. The next year, together with two additional newly-organized churches, representatives met at the Pine City Church in Wilcox County, Georgia and formed the Association. The Association mixes the Wesleyan understanding of sanctification with traditional Missionary Baptist standards of faith and decorum. Tongues-speech, while permitted by the group, is not regarded as evidence of the baptism of the Holy Spirit. The Association operates a campground on the Alma Highway seven miles east of Douglas, Georgia. Association business is transacted there annually during camp meeting.

Membership: Not reported. In the mid-1970s there were 46 congregations (all in Georgia and Florida) and approximately 2,000 members.

★529★
Holiness Church of God
% Bishop B. McKinney
602 E. Elm St.
Graham, NC 27253

The Holiness Church of God was formed in 1920 by members from several holiness churches which had received the baptism of the Holy Spirit. Three years before, a revival, called the Big May Meeting, led by Elder James A. Foust had occurred in Madison, North Carolina. The entire membership of several congregations became Pentecostals, including the Kimberly Park Holiness Church in Winston-Salem. The church incorporated in 1928. Churches are found in New York, Virginia and West Virginia.

Membership: Not reported. In 1968 there were 28 congregations and 927 members.

★530★
Holy Church of God
PO Box 6455
115 W. 49th St.
Savannah, GA 31405

The Holy Church of God is a Holiness Pentecostal church founded early in the twentieth century. It affirms a belief in the Trinity, salvation by faith in the shed blood of Jesus, sanctification of the believer, and the baptism of the Holy Ghost for the sanctified. The initial evidence of the baptism of the Holy Ghost is speaking in tongues. The church practices baptism by immersion, the Lord's Supper, and foot washing. It also believes in divine healing and tithing.

Marriage is considered a sacred state in the church. Divorce is allowed, when the offending party has committed adultery, but each divorce is decided on a case by case basis. Women may take leadership roles in the church, including evangelist, missionary, and temporary pastor, but are not allowed to assume a role that allows them to usurp authority over males. All of the business matters of the church are to be managed by the men. Members must refrain from the use of alcohol, tobacco, and narcotics, and are required to dress modestly. The church is headed by a board of overseers, a board of directors, and a delegated convention. The three-person board of overseers has charge of all matters except those dealing with finances and real estate, the concern of the board of directors. The annual convention includes all ministers and delegates from the local churches. Local churches are self-governing but must restrict themselves to pastors licensed by the Holy Church of God.

Membership: Not reported.

Sources:

Constitution and By-laws of the Holy Church of God. Savannah, GA: Holy Church of God, n.d. 31 pp.

★531★
Holy Temple of God
Big Apple Rd.
East Palatka, FL 32077

The Holy Temple of God is a holiness Pentecostal church founded in 1973 by Walter Camps, formerly an evangelist and presiding district elder with the Church of God by Faith. At the time he left to found the new church, he supervised a district of

18 churches in the Gainesville, Florida, area. During the 1970s Camps established new congregations in Central Florida and launched a radio ministry.

Membership: In 1990 there were approximately 1,000 members in the church.

Sources:

DuPree, Sherry Sherrod. *African American Holiness Pentecostal Charismatic: Annotated Bibliography.* New York: Garland Publishing, 1992.

★532★

International Pentecostal Church of Christ

PO Box 439
2245 U.S. 42, SW
London, OH 43140

The International Pentecostal Church of Christ was formed in 1976 by a merger of the International Pentecostal Assemblies and the Pentecostal Church of Christ. The International Pentecostal Assemblies was formed in 1936 by the merger of the Association of Pentecostal Assemblies and the National and International Pentecostal Missionary Union. The former body was an outgrowth of a periodical, *The Bridegroom's Messenger*, which had been founded in 1907. The Association of Pentecostal Assemblies was founded in 1921 in Atlanta by Elizabeth A. Sexton, Hattie M. Barth, and Paul T. Barth. The National and International Pentecostal Missionary Union was founded in 1914 by Dr. Philip Wittich.

In 1908, evangelist John Stroup of South Solon, Ohio, received the baptism of the Holy Spirit, signified by his speaking in tongues. In 1913, he began to travel through southeastern Ohio and the adjacent territory in Kentucky and West Virginia, organizing churches in that area. In 1917 at Advance (Flatwoods), Kentucky, a group of ministers met, organized the Pentecostal Church of Christ, and appointed Stroup bishop. In 1927, the Pentecostal Church of Christ was incorporated.

The doctrine of the merged church follows closely that of the Church of God (Cleveland, Tennessee). Members believe in healing, the premillennial return of Christ, a personal devil, Sunday as the Lord's rest day, and two ordinances—baptism and the Lord's Supper. Footwashing is optional for local assemblies and believers.

Organization of the small church is congregational with a general overseer elected every two years. Women are admitted to the ordained ministry. *The Bridegroom's Messenger* continues as the official periodical and is now the oldest continuously published Pentecostal publication. Missions are supported in Brazil, India, Mexico, Kenya, the Philippines, and Uruguay.

Membership: In 1997 the church reported 5,541 members, 71 churches, and 168 ministers. There were 160,000 members worldwide.

Educational Facilities: Beulah Heights Bible College, Atlanta, Georgia.

Periodicals: *The Pentecostal Leader.* Send orders to PO Box 439, London, OH 43140. • *The Bridegroom's Messenger.* Send orders to 121 Hunters Trail W, Elizabeth City, NC 27909.

★533★

International Pentecostal Holiness Church

PO Box 12609
Oklahoma City, OK 73157-2609

Alternate Address: Their Canadian headquarters is located at 16293 104th Ave., Surrey, BC V4N 1Z7.

In addition to those Pentecostal churches that derive from the Rev. Charles Parham and the Apostolic Church and the Topeka Bible School, which he founded, there is a Pentecostal group that begins with Benjamin Hardin Irwin. He was a Baptist who had received the experience of sanctification under the influence of the Iowa Holiness Association, a group made up mostly of Methodists.

As a holiness minister, he began to delve into Methodist writings, in particular those of John Fletcher, the eighteenth-century Wesleyan divine. In Fletcher he found what he felt to be an experience for sanctified believers, described as a "baptism of burning love." Eventually Irwin claimed to have received this "baptism of fire," and he began to teach and preach about it. Also called "fire baptism," the experience was related to the Apostles' reception of the Holy Spirit in the form of tongues of fire on Pentecost, as recorded in the Acts of the Apostles. Irwin's preaching of a third experience beyond justification and sanctification (called the "second blessing" in the holiness churches) led to controversy. He and his followers were the objects of intense criticism.

The "third blessing" spread across the Midwest and South. In 1895, the Fire-Baptized Holiness Association was organized in Iowa. Other state and local organizations followed. Irwin exercised authority over each and appointed the presidents. From July 28 to August 8, 1898, a First General Convention was held at Anderson, South Carolina, and formal organization of the Fire-Baptized Holiness Association occurred. Among those in attendance was W. E. Fuller, who later founded the Fire-Baptized Holiness Church of God of the Americas. The 1898 convention adopted a *Discipline*, which provided for life tenure for the general overseer who was given wide-ranging authority and control over the work. The association soon took the name of the Fire-Baptized Holiness Church. Within two years, involved in a personal scandal, Irwin left the church and turned it over to Joseph H. King, a former Methodist minister who had been assisting him in running the church.

Contemporaneous with the ministry of Irwin was that of A. B. Crumpler. Crumpler, a Methodist minister in North Carolina, had received the second-blessing sanctification experience the "second blessing" was the basic distinguishing mark of the holiness movement. Crumpler received his sanctification experience through the ministry of the Rev. Beverly Carradine, a famous Southern Methodist holiness preacher. He became the leading exponent of the "second blessing" in North Carolina, and in 1896, a great holiness movement began there. In 1899, Crumpler was tried for ignoring some of the organizational rules of the Methodist Church. He withdrew and the following year formed the Pentecostal Holiness Church at Fayetteville, North Carolina.

In 1906, the Rev. G. B. Cashwell, a Pentecostal Holiness minister, attended the Pentecostal revival services which were occurring on Azusa Street in Los Angeles, California, and received the baptism of the Holy Spirit evidenced by his speaking in tongues. Cashwell headed eastward to introduce the experience to his brothers and sisters. On New Year's Eve, 1906, he began a revival at Dunn, North Carolina, and introduced the experience to the Pentecostal Holiness Church. He also led J. H. King into the experience. Not without controversy, both the Pentecostal Holiness Church and the Fire-Baptized Holiness Church accepted the new experience in 1908. A merger under the name of the former occurred in 1911. It became the International Pentecostal Holiness Church in 1975.

The Pentecostal Holiness Church insists that the Pentecostal experience of the baptism of the Holy Spirit, signified by speaking in tongues, is valid only as a "third blessing." In other words, the Pentecostal experience can come only to those who have already been justified (accepted Jesus as their personal savior) and sanctified (received the "second blessing" which was the key experience of the holiness movement). By contrast, most Pentecostals believe the baptism of the Holy Spirit is available to any believer at any time and brings with it power for a holy life. Most Pentecostals seek only "two experiences," while the Pentecostal Holiness Church seeks three.

The Pentecostal Holiness Church is a direct outgrowth of the holiness movement: that explains why it retains the "second blessing." The church also has a Methodist heritage, so it derives its doctrinal statement from the Methodist Articles of Religion. In line with its Methodist roots, the church is among the few Pentecostal bodies to allow baptism by methods other than immersion. Footwashing is optional.

The polity of the Pentecostal Holiness Church is episcopal. One bishop elected by the general conference and other officers form a general board of administration to administer the affairs of the denomination. Under the administrative board are various other boards and agencies. Among the boards are those on education, evangelism, missions, and publication. The Board of Education oversees the work at the three colleges. The World Missions Board, created in 1904, oversees missions in 72 countries. Foreign work in those countries has been set off as autonomous churches that remain aligned ideologically and filially: the Pentecostal Wesleyan Methodists of Brazil, the Pentecostal Methodist Church of Chile, and the Pentecostal Holiness Church of Canada which became autonomous in 1971. A vigorous publishing program is pursued by Lifespring Resources.

Membership: In 1997 the church reported 171,000 members, 1,700 congregations, and 3,000 ministers in the United States and 1,200 members in 34 churches in Canada. There were an additional 2.5 million members overseas, including affiliates.

Educational Facilities: Emmanuel College, Franklin Springs, Georgia.

Southwestern College of Christian Ministries, Oklahoma City, Oklahoma.

Pacific Coast Bible College, Sacramento, California.

Periodicals: *Issachar File0.* • *The Helping Hand.* • *Worldorama.*

Sources:

Beacham, A. D., Jr. *A Brief History of the Pentecostal Church of God.* Franklin Springs, GA: Advocate Press, 1983.

Campbell, Joseph E. *The Pentecostal Holiness Church, 1898-1948.* Franklin Springs, GA: Publishing House of the Pentecostal Holiness Church, 1951.

King, Joseph H. *Yet Speaketh.* Franklin Springs, GA: Publishing House of the Pentecostal Holiness Church, 1949.

Synan, Vinson. *The Old Time Power.* Franklin Springs, GA: Advocate Press, 1973.

★534★
(Original) Church of God
PO Box 592
Wytheville, PA 24382

The first schism in the Church of God (Cleveland, Tennessee) occurred in 1917, and was led by the Rev. Joseph L. Scott, a pastor in Chattanooga. Among the issues involved were local autonomy, the tithe (obligatory versus voluntary), and the reception of divorced persons into the church. After the schism a less centralized government was established in the newly formed church. Each congregation is autonomous and takes the name of its location; for example, "The Church of God at Chattanooga." Above the local church is a general office which serves as headquarters and publishing house, which publishes Sunday school literature and the church's two periodicals. A presbytery has oversight of the ministry. The official name of the church includes the word "Original" in parentheses.

There are five ordinances in the (Original) Church of God, Inc.— baptism by immersion, Biblical church government, footwashing, the Lord's Supper, and tithing. Previously divorced persons can be accepted by pastors as church members.

Membership: Not reported. In 1971 there were 70 churches (including one in Trinidad), 20,000 members and 124 ministers.

Periodicals: *The Messenger.* • *The Youth Messenger.*

Sources:

Manual or Discipline of the (Original) Church of God. Chattanooga, TN: General Office & Publishing House, 1966.

★535★
Pentecostal Fire-Baptized Holiness Church
Current address not obtained for this edition.

The enforcement of discipline in the Pentecostal Holiness Church, now the International Pentecostal Holiness Church, led in 1918 to a schism by those who wanted stricter standards concerning dress, amusements, tobacco, and association between the sexes. In the Pentecostal Fire-Baptized Holiness Church, the schismatic church, women's dresses are to be at least mid-calf in length; women are not to bob or wave their hair, or wear jewelry, gold, or costly apparel. Men are not to wear neckties. Attending fairs, swimming pools, and theaters is forbidden. The strict group was joined by a few who never approved the 1911 merger of the Pentecostal Holiness Church and the Fire-Baptized Holiness Church. The pre-1911 name was adopted and the word "Pentecostal" added. The group also was joined in 1921 by the North Carolina Conference of the Pentecostal Free Will Baptist Church.

The church had 1,929 members in 85 churches in 1952. However, the next year more than half the members left to form the Emmanuel Holiness Church. That schism began a period of unabated decline.

The polity is connectional. A general convention meets biennially, with power to legislate. A seven-member board of missions, elected at the general convention, oversees work in Haiti and Mexico. A campgrounds and printing establishment are owned at Toccoa Falls, Georgia, where the church headquarters are located.

Membership: By 1981 the church had decreased to 298 members.

Periodicals: *Faith and Truth.* Send orders to Box 212, Nicholson, GA 30565.

★536★
Pentecostal Free Will Baptist Church
Box 1568
Dunn, NC 28334

The Pentecostal Free Will Baptist Church was formed in a merger and reorganization of several Free Will Baptist Associations, mainly in North Carolina. Pentecostalism had entered the Free Will Baptist Church through the efforts of the popular evangelist G. B. Cashwell. In 1907 he conducted a revival in Dunn, North Carolina, and persuaded many members of the Cape Fear Conference of the Free Will Baptist Church of the truth of his position. The Conference accepted a Pentecostal doctrine, but remained within the national Free Will Baptist Association. In 1907, the Cape Fear Conference split into two geographic associations; the second body became the Wilmington Conference, and the first retained the original name. In 1911, a third association was formed in southeastern North Carolina as the New River Conference. The following year, the Cape Fear Conference split over the Pentecostal issue. Finally, in 1912 a South Carolina Conference was organized.

In 1943, a group of ministers and laymen of the four Pentecostal conferences: Cape Fear, Wilmington, New River, and South Carolina Conferences, met. They formed a general conference but the organization proved unsatisfactory. In 1959, it was decided to dissolve all the conference structures and organize under one charter and one name. Thus, in 1959, the Pentecostal Free Will Baptist Church was formed.

The doctrine is almost identical to that of the Church of God (Cleveland, Tennessee), and includes belief in three experiences of grace: baptism by immersion, footwashing, and premillennialism. It is this group's position that Benjamin Randall, the founder of the Free Will Baptist Church, taught sanctification as an instantaneous act of God.

The church is congregational in structure with a biannual conference. The general superintendent heads an executive board for implementing the program. There are four districts; the World Missions Board oversees missions in Costa Rica, Puerto Rico, Mexico, Venezuela, Nicaragua, and the Philippines. Churches are primarily in North Carolina, with congregations in South Carolina, Virginia, Georgia, and Florida.

Membership: In 1996 the church reported 16,000 members and 157 churches served by 250 ministers.

Educational Facilities: Heritage Bible College, Dunn, North Carolina.

Periodicals: *The Pentecostal Free-Will Baptist Messenger.*

Sources:

Carter, Herbert. *The Spectacular Gifts, Prophecy, Tongues, Interpretations.* Dunn, NC: The Author, 1971.

Discipline of the Pentecostal Free Will Baptist Church. N.p. 1962.

Faith and Practices of the Pentecostal Free Will Baptist Church, Inc.. Franklin Springs, GA: Advocate Press, 1971.

Sauls, Don. *The Ministerial Handbook of the Pentecostal Free Will Baptist Church.* N.p. 1971.

★537★
Romanian Apostolic Pentecostal Church of God
(Defunct)

The Romanian Apostolic Pentecostal Church of God had its origins in the influx of the Pentecostal awakening within the Romanian-American community in the early twentieth century. The first congregation was founded in Detroit, Michigan, in 1922. Eventually more than 40 congregations were part of a loose fellowship. However, in 1981, the majority of these congregations joined the Church of God (Cleveland, Tennessee) and five more have joined the Assemblies of God. Some remain independent. One congregation in California of about 50 members continues to use the name of the older fellowship.

The Church of God congregations work together as the Romanian Pentecostal Ministries and publish a periodical, *Propovaduitorul.* The Rev. Ioan J. Buia, pastor of the original Detroit congregation (now located in Dearborn Heights, Michigan), conducts a Romanian radio ministry, Maranatha, that is heard over one station in Michigan and one in Kitchner, Ontario. There is also a continuing annual convention of the Romanian Pentecostal congregations. In 1987, it met in Detroit and in 1988, in Portland, Oregon.

Sources:

Buia, Ioan J. *Pine Pe Unde* (Bread on Waves). Detroit, MI: Romanian Pentecostal Church of God, 1987.

Romanian Pentecostal Church of God, 1937-1987, Semicentinar. Detroit, MI: Romanian Pentecostal Church of God, 1987.

White Trinitarian Pentecostals

★538★
American Indian Evangelical Church
Current address not obtained for this edition.

During the early twentieth century, conditions forced many American Indians into the cities. By 1945, 8,000 had settled in the Minneapolis/St. Paul metropolitan area. In that year a group of Indians organized the American Indian Mission. In 1956, the Mission became the American Indian Evangelical Church, and Iver C. Grover (a Chippewa) was elected president. He was joined by seven others. In 1959, a committee on ordination was appointed to facilitate the development of an Indian ordained ministry, and four men were ordained.

Doctrine is in line with fundamental evangelicalism. The doctrinal statement of the church begins with the Apostles' Creed and moves on to affirm the Trinity, the divinity of Jesus, and the conscious suffering of the wicked. Baptism by immersion and the Lord's Supper are practiced. The polity is congregational, but the pastor is viewed as the spiritual overseer of the congregation.

Membership: Not reported.

★539★
Anchor Bay Evangelistic Association
Box 188
New Baltimore, MI 48047

Roy John Turner and his wife Blanche A. Turner became Pentecostals in 1916. Dr. Turner was a medical doctor and his wife a nurse, and they continued to function as medical professionals while leading prayer meetings. Following a revival campaign in 1918 by evangelist, Mrs. M. B. Woodworth-Etter, a church was formed in New Baltimore. In 1923, Dr. Turner was ordained and became pastor of the congregation. The old opera house in New Baltimore, Michigan, was purchased and remodeled as Bethel Temple. From 1938 to 1940, Turner served as an executive with the International Church of the Foursquare Gospel, the congregation in New Baltimore remained independent. Finally, in 1940, the Turners left the Foursquare Gospel and the Anchor Bay Evangelistic Association was formed and incorporated. After the Turners' deaths, they were succeeded by their daughter, Lucy Evelyn Turner.

The doctrine of the Anchor Bay Evangelistic Association is like that of the International Church of the Foursquare Gospel. Mission work is conducted in Belize, Turkey, the Philippines, South India, West Africa, Indonesia, and Mexico. The church is a member of the Pentecostal Fellowship of North America.

Membership: In the late 1960s there were 320 ministers and 115 churches worldwide.

Educational Facilities: Anchor Bay Institute, New Baltimore, Michigan.

★540★
Apostolic Church
142 N. 17th St.
Philadelphia, PA 19103

Alternate Address: California headquarters: 10841 Chapman Ave., Garden Grove, CA 92640; Canadian headquarters: 27 Castlefield Ave., Toronto, On, Canada M4H 1G3.

The Apostolic Church grew out of the Apostolic Faith Church founded in England in 1908 by W. O. Hutchinson. The Apostolic Faith Church was one of the first Pentecostal bodies in England, and it had roots both in the Azusa Street revival in Los Angeles, and the Welsh Revival led by Evan Roberts that began in 1904. Distinctive of the Apostolic Faith Church was to give precedence to the Holy Spirit in everything, and an accompanying belief that one of the primary purposes for the exercise of spiritual gifts is to bring a revelation from God, through either prophecy or speaking-in-tongues and the interpretation. Prophecy could then be used in matters such as the selection of church officers and the making of various decisions. To some people, the practice produced only fanaticism and intolerable excesses. Thus the Rev. Daniel Powell Williams led a group of members out of the Apostolic Faith Church to found what in 1916 became the Apostolic Church. From its headquarters in Wales, within a decade it had circled the globe, especially in British colonial lands.

The church came to North America in 1924 when a church was founded in Canada. From that original congregation, churches have been formed in Pennsylvania and California, which operate as two separate districts. The Canadian churches support missions in Brazil, Barbados, and Jamaica, but the North American churches remain part of the worldwide church headquartered in Wales.

Membership: Not reported. In the 1970s, there were 700 members in 13 churches in Canada and 250 members in seven churches in the United States.

★541★

Apostolic Church of Pentecost of Canada
200—809 Manning Rd. NE
Calgary, AB, Canada T2E 7M9

The Apostolic Church of Pentecost of Canada was founded in 1921 by evangelist Franklin Small (1873- ?). As a young man, Small had been healed by the prayer of a visiting clergyman. Several years later, in Winnipeg, he heard Rev. A. H. Argue preach. Argue had just returned from Chicago where he had received the baptism of the Holy Spirit and spoke in tongues. Eventually Small was also baptized. In 1912, when Argue left for Los Angeles, Small took over his pulpit. Small went to Los Angeles in 1913 and was present at the famous camp meeting at Arreyo Seco at which the controversy over baptism in the name of Jesus (rather than the trinitarian formula of Father, Son, and Holy Ghost) emerged. Initially unimpressed with the new teaching, Small did not consider and accept it until later that year when he heard R. E. McAleister preach the "Jesus Only" doctrine at a convention in Winnipeg. Two years later he was finally baptized in that manner. Seven years later he led in the founding of the Apostolic Church of Pentecost of Canada.

The Apostolic Church affirms belief in the verbal inspiration of the Bible, the one God, salvation by grace alone, water baptism by immersion in the name of Jesus, the gifts of the spirit, divine healing, and the personal return of Jesus Christ. The church has a presbyterian polity, though each church is autonomous and owns its own property. The church conference meets annually. Missionary work is carried on in India, Malawi, Zimbabwe, Zambia, Japan, Taiwan, Guatemala, Nicaragua, Burkina Faso, South Africa, Estonia, Trinidad, and Mexico.

Membership: In 1997 the church reported 13,000 members, 450 ministers, and 160 churches in Canada. These was a single congregation in the United States and approximately 1000 worldwide.

Sources:

Larden, Robert A. *Our Apostolic Heritage.* Calgary, AL: Apostolic Church of Pentecost of Canada, 1971.

★542★

Apostolic Faith (Kansas)
1009 Lincoln Ave.
Baxter Springs, KS 66713

In 1898, the Rev. Charles Parham (1873-1929) left the Methodist Episcopal Church and established a home for divine healing in Topeka, Kansas. That same year he began to publish a periodical, *Apostolic Faith,* and two years later opened Bethel Bible College. It was at Bethel that Agnes Ozman had the initial experience of speaking in tongues, an event from which the modern Pentecostal movement is dated. After Mrs. Ozman's experience and its acceptance by others, Parham began to spread the word of modern Pentecostalism in Kansas, Oklahoma, Missouri, and Texas. In 1905, he established a Bible school in Houston, Texas. Among those who attended was William J. Seymour, a black holiness preacher affiliated with the Church of God (Anderson, Indiana), who related the experience at Azusa Street, Los Angeles, California.

Parham is hardly mentioned in pentecostal history after 1906. The split between he and the emerging leadership of the movement began toward the end of that year when he arrived in Los Angeles to observe firsthand the revival about which he had read. He did not like what he saw. He felt that the revival had taken on elements of fanaticism and was quick in his words of reproof. The disagreement led to his immediate split with Seymour and the leaders of the revival in southern California. Then early in 1907 he also resigned his role as "Projector of the Apostolic Faith Movement," as a means of opposing the spirit of leadership and the attempts to organize the movement.

Returning to the East and Midwest, he took up his ministry and continued to preach. However, he was soon faced with accusations of scandalous personal behavior which further ruined his reputation within the movement. Though he remained active until his death, his efforts were cut off from the movement as a whole. Those who received his ministry were eventually consolidated in a very loose fellowship centered on Baxter Springs, Kansas. The Apostolic Faith was not incorporated until 1976. No membership records have ever been kept, but there is a directory of churches and ministers.

In 1950, Baxter Springs also became the permanent site chosen for the group's Bible college. Following Parham's direction, the college charges no tuition, but operates on a freewill offering plan. No salary is paid to the faculty, who are also supported by freewill offerings.

Beliefs of the Apostolic Faith are similar to those of the Assemblies of God, and include a strong emphasis on spiritual healing. Footwashing, baptism, and the Lord's Supper are observed as ordinances. No collections are taken, the ministry being supported by tithes. Organization is informal and congregational. There is a seven-person board of trustees which oversees the Bible college.

Membership: No membership records are kept by the Apostolic Faith. These are an estimated 10,000 adherents. In 1988 there were 100 churches and 118 ministers.

Educational Facilities: Apostolic Faith Bible College, Baxter Springs, Kansas.

Periodicals: *Apostolic Faith Report.* Send orders to Box 653, Baxter Springs, KS 66713.

Sources:

Carothers, W. F. *The Baptism with the Holy Ghost.* Zion City, IL: The Author, 1907.

Parham, Charles F. *A Voice of One Crying in the Wilderness.* Baxter Springs, KS: Apostolic Faith Bible College, 1910.

Parham, Sarah E. *The Life of Charles F. Parham.* Joplin, MO: Hunter Printing Company, 1930.

★543★

Association of Vineyard Churches
Box 18329
Anaheim, CA 92817

The Association of Vineyard Churches was formed in 1986 but dates to an earlier Bible study group in Yorba Linda, California, formed in 1978 by John Wimber (d. 1997). The original group of approximately 150 affiliated with Calvary Chapel Church, an evangelical church in Costa Mesa, California, which had developed a number of affiliates throughout the United States. After a brief period of association, Wimber felt that his work, which included an emphasis upon the manifestation of the gifts of the Spirit to all age groups, was distinct from that of Calvary Chapel.

Closely approaching Wimber's perspective was the Vineyard Christian Fellowship, a congregation which had originated from a Bible study group formed by Kenn Gullikson in 1974. In 1982 Wimber changed his congregation's name to Vineyard Christian Fellowship of Yorba Linda. The following year he moved it to Anaheim, California, and within a short time over 4,000 were attending Sunday services. By 1992 over 6,000 attended regularly. Several other congregations merged with the two Vineyard fellowships, and Vineyard Ministries International was created to direct the outreach of the movement (John Wimber's international and interdenominational outreach). Wimber became the object of much media attention, especially after his being asked to teach a course at Fuller Theological Seminary in Pasadena, California, concerning divine healing. In the wake of the publicity, the movement grew rapidly as both independent pastors and congregations, at first mostly in southern California, affiliated. However, the movement lacked a structure to deal with the increased size and geographic spread of the movement. Very basically, the church needed a means to ordain pastors and credential churches and ministers. In 1986 leaders in the movement organized the Association of Vineyard Churches. Vineyard Ministries International continues as the facilitator of John Wimber's numerous programs and seminars centered upon church growth, Christian life, and gifts of the Spirit.

The churches affiliated with the association are similar in doctrine to Calvary Chapel, but have a distinct emphasis upon the ministry of the gifts of the Spirit and a strong program of church growth and evangelism. At the time of the association's formation, Wimber was appointed International Director. Kenn Gullikson now serves as National Director. Regional Overseers and Area Pastoral Coordinators, designated from among the ministers who are leading stable Vineyard congregations, oversee its church government. It is their task to guide emerging fellowships and to foster a collegiate relationship between the churches in the association. Todd Hunter now serves as the national director of the Association of Vineyard Churches.

Membership: In 1992 the association reported approximately 100,000 members in 315 Vineyard congregations, including a number of international congregations, in Brazil, Canada, Costa Rica, England, Mexico, Scotland, South Africa, Switzerland, and Germany.

Periodicals: *VOV Vocie of the Vineyard.* Send orders to Box 18379, Anaheim, CA 92817.

Sources:

Loftness, John. "A Sign for Our Times!" *People of Destiny Magazine* 3, no. 4 (July/August 1985).

Wimber, John, with Kevin Springer. *Power Evangelism. Praise Offerings.* Anaheim, CA: Vineyard Christian Fellowship, 1977.

★544★
Bethel Temple
2033 Second Ave.
Seattle, WA 98121

The Bethel Temple was formed in 1914 as the first Pentecostal congregation in the state of Washington. Its doctrine is like that of the Assemblies of God. Loosely affiliated with the temple are eight congregations, seven in the state of Washington, and one in Alaska. There are also 10 congregations in Holland and missions are conducted in Japan and Indonesia. The Indonesian Pentecostal churches, the Gereja Pantekosta de Indonesia, look to Bethel Temple as their founder. A Bible school opened in 1952 was discontinued in 1987.

Membership: In 1987 there were approximately 300 members in eight congregations in the United States.

Periodicals: *Pentecostal Power.*

★545★
Bible Church of Christ
1358 Morris Ave.
Bronx, NY 10456

The Bible Church of Christ is a small Pentecostal body founded on March 1, 1961, by Bishop Roy Bryant, Sr. The church is trinitarian and accepts the authority of the Bible as the inspired Word of God. Members receive the baptism of the Holy Spirit and deliverance and miracles of healing are frequently experienced. Congregations are reported in the West Indies, India, and Africa.

Membership: In 1993 the church reported 3,768 members, six churches, and 52 ministers. Congregations are located in New York, Delaware, and North Carolina.

Periodicals: *The Voice.*

★546★
California Evangelistic Association
Current address not obtained for this edition.

The California Evangelistic Association began in 1933 (incorporated, 1934) as the Colonial Tabernacle of Long Beach, California. The tabernacle had been established by Oscar C. Harms, a former pastor in the Advent Christian Church. Additional assemblies became associated with it, and in 1939, it assumed its present name. It is in essential doctrinal agreement with the Assemblies of God, except that it is amillennial. Polity of the Association is congregational, with affiliated congregations remaining autonomous. Churches are found along the West Coast. The California Evangelistic Association supports missionaries in Italy, Zambia, Brazil, Colombia, and Mexico.

Membership: Not reported. In the 1970s there were 62 associated congregations and approximately 4,700 members.

Sources:

Constitution and By-Laws. Long Beach, CA: California Evangelistic Association, 1939.

★547★
Calvary Chapel
3800 S. Fairview Rd.
Santa Ana, CA 92704

In 1965, Chuck Smith, an independent minister, who was the pastor of a fairly large and growing congregation in Corona, California, accepted a call to pastor a very small congregation (25 adults), Calvary Chapel, in Costa Mesa, California. At that particular time, many "hippies" populated the ocean front near Costa Mesa. His outreach to these people lead to the conversion of thousands of young people. He instituted a series of discipleship homes where they received training. Services were held every night of the week at a small building in Costa Mesa. This church became known as a center of the "Jesus People Revival" that moved across the United States in the early 1970s. As membership and fame grew, other Calvary Churches began to be established in different communities and individuals who had visited the church began congregations model that follow the Calvary. At present there are more than 600 Calvary Chapel Churches worldwide with several of the congregations numbering some 6000 members.

A very simple statement of belief has been developed that emphasizes the nondenominational character of Calvary Chapel. The church refuses to overemphasize those doctrinal differences that have divided Christians in the past. Agape (God's Divine Love) is held as the only true basis of Christian fellowship. Emphasis is placed upon a "verse by verse" expository type of biblical teaching. The church believes in the continuance of the Gifts of the Holy Spirit for today, but there is no emphasis placed upon speaking-in-tongues as the necessary sign of baptism of the Holy Spirit. Prophesy in the scripture is one of the focal points and many of Pastor Smith's books relate the expectation of seeing some of the predicted events take place in this generation.

Calvary Chapel has developed a variety of outreach ministries. The most notable is "The Word For Today," which includes cassettes, video tapes, books, and other literature, radio shows, and other communicative sources for teaching the Bible.

Membership: The present membership of Calvary Chapel of Costa Mesa is well over 20,000 formal members with more than 35,000 constituents who claim Calvary Chapel of Costa Mesa as their home church.

Educational Facilities: Calvary Bible College, Costa Mesa, California.
Calvary Chapel School of Ministry, Costa Mesa, California.

Sources:

Ellwood, Robert S., Jr. *One Way.* Englewood Cliffs, NJ: Prentice-Hall, 1973.

Smith, Church. *Charisma vs. Charismania.* Eugene, OR: Harvest House Publishers, 1983.

___. *The Final Curtain.* Costa Mesa, CA: Word for Today, 1984.

___. *Future Survival.* Costa Mesa, CA: Word for Today, 1980.

___. *What the World Is Coming To.* Costa Mesa, CA: Word for Today, 1980.

★548★

Calvary Ministries, Inc., International

Box 365
4450 N 50W
Angola, IN 46703

Calvary Ministries, Inc., International (CMI) was founded in 1971 as an umbrella organization for those congregations and ministries developed from the work of Calvary Temple, an independent Pentecostal church in Fort Wayne, Indiana. Calvary Temple was begun in 1956 by Dr. Paul E. Paino, a graduate of the Assemblies of Gods Central Bible Institute in Springfield, Missouri. Under his leadership, CMI's membership grew to 5,000. In 1978 a new building complex was erected to house the expanding program.

In 1969 six men approached Paino for training in the ministry and ordination. The next year several more came for the same reason. In 1972 a more permanent means of training was established with the Christian Training Center and the Paul and Timothy Internship program. Among the early graduates of the center were those ready to begin pastoral ministry and plant new congregations. In part, Calvary Ministries, Inc., International was created to facilitate these students' ordinations and credentialing as well as provide structure for the planting and establishing of new congregations.

CMI follows a blending of episcopal and presbyterian polity with each member church completely selfgoverning and autonomous.

During the early years of the Jesus People Revival—a national interdenominational revival movement among young adults that began on the west coast in the late 1960s—the church in Fort Wayne sponsored a Jesus People coffee house ministry called Adams Apple. The Apple produced quality music ministry among whom were Nancy Honeytree, Petra, and Jeoff Benward. In addition, a number of CMIs early church planters came from the ranks of Adams Apple members. The Apple no longer exists, but, in its place are several thriving youth ministries around the tri-state area.

Calvary Ministries statement of faith is very close to that of the Assemblies of God, from which Paino came, and differs only in that it does not include the additional statements on ministry adopted by the Assemblies of God in 1969.

CMI has now expanded from Indiana to 15 other states. Regional offices now exist in New Castle, Pennsylvania (Northeast); Dayton, Ohio (Ohio Valley); Fort Wayne, Indiana (Great Lakes); and Clearwater, Florida (Southeast). In 1991 CMI departmentalized in order to facilitate the membership, offering Home, Training and Development, Missions, and Camp (Oakhill) departments, with full-time directors in the Home and Training departments. Oakhill Conference and Retreat Center in Angola, Indiana, situated on a 220-acre site, houses the four departments of CMI as well as hosting summer camps for all ages, spring and fall retreats, and other year-round conferences for CMI and other denominational and non-denominational groups.

Membership: In 1997 CMI reported more than 124 affiliated congregations and 250 ministers in the United States, Japan, South Africa, United Kingdom, Italy, Sweden, and the Dominican Republic.

Educational Facilities: Christian Training Center, Fort Wayne Indiana; Clearwater, Florida; Harbor Springs, Michigan.

Periodicals: *Together.*

★549★

Calvary Pentecostal Church

(Defunct)

The Calvary Pentecostal Church was formed in 1931 by a group of Pentecostal ministers in the northwestern United States who were dissatisfied by what they regarded as "a sad departure from the entire dependence on the power of God that had brought the Pentecostal revival." They formed a ministerial fellowship in Olympia, Washington, which was the following year named the Calvary Pentecostal Church. What was originally intended as an interdenominational fellowship became a denomination as churches began to affiliate.

The doctrine was like that of the Assemblies of God. Healing was emphasized. Adult baptism by immersion was practiced, but when parents requested it, infants were dedicated to God (not baptized). The literal second coming was awaited. The church was governed in a loose presbyterial system headed by a presbyterial board and the general superintendent. A general meeting of all ministers and local church delegates was held annually. The local churches were governed by the minister, elders, and deacons. The church supported a home for the aged in Seattle and foreign work in Brazil and India.

By the early 1970s, there were 22 churches and 8,000 members, however, internal problems disrupted the church and led to its disbanding.

★550★

Churches of the Kingdom of God

Current address not obtained for this edition.

The Churches of the Kingdom of God is a small pentecostal body that emphasizes Jesus' message of the kingdom as the basic proclamation of the gospel. According to Elder F. H. Reese, a prolific writer for the churches, Jesus came preaching the kingdom which he declared to be "at hand." It is entered by repentance and being born again and is open to all. The kingdom was prepared for us from the foundation of the world, but it came in power only at Pentecost when the Spirit descended upon the early disciples. During the 1960s, Reese wrote a series of tracts on the kingdom of God theme.

Membership: Not reported.

Sources:

Reese, F. H. *Entering into the Kingdom of God.* Gravette, AK: Churches of the Kingdom of God, n.d. 8 pp.

___. *The Gospel of the Kingdom of God.* Gravette, AK: Churches of the Kingdom of God, n.d. 16 pp.

___. *The Promise of the Father.* Gravette, AK: Churches of the Kingdom of God, n.d. 12 pp.

★551★

Congregational Bible Churches International

PO Box 165
Hutchinson, KS 67501

Congregational Bible Churches International is a full gospel pentecostal body founded in 1977 by the merger of the Way Open Door Church and the Independent Holiness Church. Formerly known as the Congregational Bible Holiness Church, it adopted its present name in 1988. The Independent Holiness Church began in 1922. The Way Open Door Church—formerly affiliated with the General Council of Congregational Christian Churches— included congregations that had severed ties with that organization when it merged with the Evangelical and Reformed Church to become the United Church of Christ. Dr. M. L. Webber, president of the Open Door Church at the time of the 1977 merger, has continued to serve as international president of the Congregational Bible Churches since its formation.

The Churches' doctrine is similar to that of the Assemblies of God and asserts a faith in the Bible as the infallible Word of God, the Trinity, the deity of Jesus Christ, the baptism of the Holy Spirit, and the sanctification of Christians by the Holy Spirit. Members believe in the future rapture of the church, in which Christians will be taken from the earth before the period of Great Tribulation, and the eventual resurrection of all to heaven or eternal punishment.

The church is headed by a national and an international board over which the president of the church sits as chairman.

Membership: In 1990 the church had approximately 100,000 members in 500 churches worldwide, of which 10,000 members and 60 churches served by 100 ministers were in the United States. Missionary work is pursued in Guyana, Jamaica, Haiti, Puerto Rico, Singapore, India, Nigeria, Ghana, and Liberia.

Periodicals: *Congregational Bible Revival News.*

★552★
Elim Fellowship
7245 College St.
Lima, NY 14485

In 1924, the Rev. and Mrs. Ivan Q. Spencer opened a pentecostal Bible institute in Endicott, New York, to train young men and women for full-time revival ministry. Graduates of the Elim Bible Institute formed the Elim Ministerial Fellowship in 1932, which eventually became the Elim Fellowship in 1972. In 1951, the school moved to Lima, New York, where it occupies the campus of the former Genesee Wesleyan Seminary, founded in the nineteenth century by the Methodist Church.

The doctrine of the Fellowship is similar to that of the Assemblies of God, with a strong emphasis upon the Holy Spirit-filled and sanctified life of the believer. Spencer was strongly affected by the Latter Rain revival which began in Canada in 1948. He and others brought the revival to the school, publicized it in the *Elim Herald*, and took a leadership role in spreading the renewed emphasis upon the gifts of the Spirit being poured out on God's people in the last days.

The fellowship is governed congregationally. An annual meeting is held each spring at Lima. Elim Fellowship-sponsored missionaries are currently at work around the world, on all continents. The founder's son, I. Carlton Spencer succeeded his father in the leadership of the fellowship, overseeing it from 1947 to 1985. Rev. Elmer A. Frink is the current general overseer. The Fellowship holds membership in the Pentecostal Fellowship of North America, the Network of Christian Ministries, and on the North American Renewal Service Committee.

Membership: In 1988, the fellowship reported 21,038 members, 170 congregations, and 357 ministers in the United States. There were 20 congregations in Canada and 5,500 congregations worldwide in 11 countries.

Educational Facilities: Elim Bible Institute, Lima, New York. Lima Trade School, Lima, New York. Nairobi Pentecostal Bible College, Nairobi, Kenya. Instituto Biblico de Elim, Belen, Costa Rica.

Periodicals: *Elim Herald.* • *Single Impact.* • *The Elim Bell Tower.*

Sources:

Meloon, Marion. *Ivan Spencer, Willow in the Wind.* Plainfield, NJ: Logos International, 1974.

★553★
Fellowship of Christian Assemblies
% Henry Jauhiainen, Chairman
Heritage Committee
520 N. 34th Ave., E.
Duluth, MN 55804

The Fellowship of Christian Assemblies (FCA), an unincorporated fellowship of evangelical Pentecostal churches, began in 1922 when three small Scandinavian-oriented groups joined ranks under the banner Independent Assemblies of God. Several of the original key figures had Scandinavian Baptist backgrounds. The group stresses both local church autonomy and voluntary interchurch cooperation as "biblical norms". Its first period emphasized autonomy; its more recent history has seen a quest for intentional cooperative ministries. A watershed in the fellowship's history occurred in the late 1940s when a number of churches defected to what was termed the Latter Rain movement which, among other factors, emphasized the restoration of the prime role of apostles and prophets. This event stimulated a search for a clearer identity and more cohesive processes in the remaining main body of the group. The group retains its strong adherence to local autonomy and its recognition of the roles of model-churches within various geographical areas. The current name was adopted in 1973.

Fellowship Press, a publishing society with membership open to any FCA congregation, publishes the monthly *Fellowship Today.* Both Fellowship Today and the Heritage Committee serve as sources of information for inquirers. National gatherings, which include the FCA of Canada, are planned by annually chosen conference committee. Regional conferences and ministerial clusters give attention to mutual concerns and projects.

New ministers and churches seek recognition and directory listing through recommendation by two currently listed ministers. Ministers and missionaries are credentialed by their local churches.

Membership: The fellowship lists approximately 330 ministers and missionaries in the United States and 270 in Canada. About 125 churches in the United States are formally listed, and 90 in Canada. A number of cooperating churches are unlisted. Missionaries from FCA churches work in 48 countries, but there are no churches outside of the United States and Canada listed in the FCA directory.

Periodicals: *Conviction.*

★554★
Filipino Assemblies of the First Born
1229 Glenwood
Delano, CA 93215

The Filipino Assemblies of the First Born was founded at Stockton, California, by the Rev. Julian Barnabe, an immigrant to the United States. The organization took place at a convention which met June 26 to July 4, 1933. Headquarters was established in Fresno and moved to San Francisco in 1942 and to Delano, California, in 1943. Doctrine and practice are like those of the Assemblies of God; the group is primarily an ethnic church with preaching often done in the Filipino language.

Membership: Not reported. In 1969 there were 15 churches in California and 17 in Hawaii.

★555★
Free Gospel Church, Inc.
% Rev. Chester H. Heath
Box 477
Export, PA 15632

The Free Gospel Church was founded in 1916 as the United Free Gospel and Missionary Society by two brothers, the Reverends Frank Casley and William Casley. It adopted its present name in 1958. An early emphasis upon missions led to initial efforts in Guatemala, though the work was lost to the Church of God (Cleveland, Tennessee) and China, closed after the communists come to power in 1948. In doctrine, it is similar to the Assemblies of God. Missions are conducted in Sierra Leone, India, and the Philippines.

Membership: Not reported. In the early 1970s there were approximately 25 churches and 2,000 members.

Educational Facilities: Free Gospel Institute, Export, Pennsylvania.

Free Gospel Bible Institute, The Philippines.

Free Gospel Bible Institute, Sierra Leone.

★556★
Full Gospel Evangelistic Association
PO Box 1122
Cleveland, TN 77327-0122

In the late 1940s a controversy developed in the Apostolic Faith Church over issues of taking offerings in church, visiting churches not in fellowship, foreign mission work, and using doctors. Some who supported these activities formed the Ministerial and Missionary Alliance of the Original Trinity Apostolic Faith, Inc., for which they were disfellowshipped. In 1952, they formed the Full Gospel Evangelistic Association. Except for the points at issue, the doctrine is like that of the Apostolic Faith.

Headquarters, established at Kuty, Texas, were moved to Webb City, Missouri, in 1967. The association supports missions in Mexico, Peru, Guatemala, and Taiwan. Annual camp meetings are held in Oklahoma and Texas.

Membership: Not reported. In the mid-1970s there were 30 congregations and approximately 4,000 members.

Educational Facilities: Midwest Bible Institute, Houston, Texas.

Periodicals: *Full Gospel News.*

★557★
Full Gospel Truth, Inc.
304 3rd St.
PO Box 886
East Jordan, MI 49727

Full Gospel Truth, Inc., is a Pentecostal church founded in 1951 in Michigan by Harley R. Barber, a Pentecostal minister. Full Gospel Truth was formed after Barber withdrew from his previous denominational affiliation. It quickly spread to neighboring states and by the mid-1950s was functioning in California.

Full Gospel Truth is a Trinitarian Pentecostal church whose doctrine is very similar to that of the Assemblies of God. It teaches the practice of baptism by immersion, footwashing, divine healing, and tithing. It advises members to become conscientious objectors to war. It teaches that persons of both sexes should have the privilege of ministering to the fullest, except in those areas of church life that call for the exercise of authority. Women should not exercise authority over men. The church expects the imminent return of Christ.

The church follows what it sees as a biblical organization following Rom. 12:4, Eph. 4:11, and I Cor. 12:28. It thus recognizes seven offices to be filled: apostles, prophets, evangelists, pastors, teachers, governments, and helps. Nationally the church is organized theocratically under the guidance of a national superintendent. The national officers meet annually in conference.

Membership: In 1995 the church reported 750 members in 12 congregations served by 70 ministers.

Periodicals: *Yours and Mine Share Paper.*

Sources:

Constitution and By-Law of the Full Gospel Truth, Inc. East Jordan, MI: Full Gospel Truth, n.d.

★558★
General Assemblies and Church of the First Born
Current address not obtained for this edition.

The General Assembly and Church of the First Born, formed in 1907, is a small Pentecostal body without church headquarters or paid clergy. It has about 30 congregations across the country. Congregations are concentrated in Oklahoma and California, with individual congregations at Montrose and Pleasant View, Colorado, and Indianapolis, Indiana. Members believe in the Trinity, deny original sin, believing that we will be punished only for our own sin, and assert that man can be saved by obedience to the laws and ordinances of the gospel. There are four ordinances—faith in Jesus Christ, repentence, baptism by immersion, and laying-on-of-hands for the gift of the Holy Spirit. The group makes use of all of the gifts of the Spirit and holds the Lord's Supper in conjunction with footwashing, but does not seek the help of doctors.

Elders oversee the local congregations, which are organized very informally. Some elders are ordained and serve as preachers. No membership rolls are kept. The Indianapolis church has published a hymnal. There is an annual campmeeting in Oklahoma each summer.

Membership: Not reported. In 1976 there were approximately 6,000 members.

Remarks: In 1976 the Church of the First Born was involved in a controversy following the death of a member's child after medical treatment was withheld. A district court in Oklahoma made a second child a ward of the court, ruling that the state had a right to intervene when religious beliefs might lead to harm of a minor.

★559★
General Council of Christian Church of North America
Rte. 18 & Rutledge Rd.
Box 141-A, R.D. 1
Transfer, PA 16154

The Christian Church of North America traces it origins to the spread of the revival that started at the Azusa Street Mission in Los Angeles and moved to Chicago in 1907. There it found some response in the Italian community, and among those who began a ministry soon afterward were some who gathered in 1927 in Niagara, New York, to formally organize the Christian Church of North America. The church places evangelism and especially mission work (including efforts to evangelize its homeland) as its top priority, a fact that is vividly illustrated in its finally incorporating in 1948 as "The Missionary Society of the Christian Church of North America."

By 1963, in recognition that the original movement had transcended its roots representing a single ethnic group and had become a multiethnic church, the movement was renamed, as the "General Council" of the Christian Church of North America. The church resembles the Assemblies of God in its doctrinal stance.

Membership: Not reported. In 1998, it had work in more than 40 countries of the world.

Periodicals: *Vista.*

★560★
General Council of the Assemblies of God
1445 Boonville Ave.
Springfield, MO 65802

The General Council of the Assemblies of God was formed in Hot Springs, Arkansas, in April 1914 at a convention of Pentecostal ministers and churches. The poeple came together to adopt a common body of doctrinal standards and to consolidate missionary, ministerial, educational, and publishing efforts. *The Word and Witness*, edited by E. N. Bell, was the first official periodical of the denoination; a forerunner of today's weekly *Pentecostal Evangel.*

The church's governmental structure is congregational on the local church level and presbyterial at the national level, where the General Council has centralized control over missionary, educational, ministerial, and publishing concerns. A 15-member Executive Presbytery serves as the church's board of directors and meets every other month. The church has over 1,800 missionaries serving in 148 nations of the world. At home, the Division of Home Missions oversees ministries to intercultural groups, military personnel, secular college campuses, Teen Challenge (a program for those with life-controlling problems such as drugs and alcohol), and the opening of new churches. The Gospel Publishing House, the printing arm of the church, is one of the major publishers of Christian literature in the United States.

The church's cardinal doctrines include the Bible as the Word of God, the fall of humanity, and God's provision of salvation only through the death of His Son Jesus Christ, water baptism by immersion, divine healing, and the imminent return of Jesus for those who have accepted Him as Savior. The church's distinctive doctrine is the belief in the baptism of the Holy Spirit, an experience following salvation which is accomplished by speaking in other languages. The assemblies of God has more than 2 1/2 million members and adherents in the United States and over 250 million worldwide.

The assemblies is in fellowship with the Pentecostal Assemblies of Canada. It is a member of the Pentecostal Fellowship of North America and cooperates with the Pentecostal World Conference.

Membership: In 1997 the assemblies reported 2,467,588 members in 11,884 congregations served by 32,314 ministers in the United States. There were 25,362,718 members, 146,348 churches and 159,780 ministers worldwide. Missionaries are now stationed in 148 countries.

Educational Facilities: Assemblies of God Theological Seminary, Springfield, Missouri.

American Indian College of the Assemblies of God, Phoenix, Arizona.

Berean University of the Assemblies of God, Springfield, Missouri.

Bethany College of the Assemblies of God, Scotts Valley, California.

Central Bible College, Springfield, Missouri.

Central Indian Bible College, Mobridge, South Dakota.

Evangel College, Springfield, Missouri.

Latin American Bible Institute, San Antonio, Texas.

Latin American Bible Institute of California, La Puente, California.

North Central Bible College, Minneapolis, Minnesota.

Northwest College of the Assemblies of God, Kirkland, Washington.

Southeastern College of the Assemblies of God, Lakeland, Florida. Southern California College, Costa Mesa, California.

Southwestern Assemblies of God University, Waxahachie, Texas.

Trinity Bible College, Ellendale, North Dakota.

Valley Forge Christian College, Phoenixville, Pennsylvania.

Western Bible Institute, Phoenix, Arizona.

Periodicals: *Pentecostal Evangel.* • *Assemblies of God Heritage.* • *Enrichment Journal.* • *Christian Education Counselor.*

Sources:

Brumback, Carl. *Suddenly from Heaven.* Springfield, MO: Gospel Publishing House, 1961.

Carlson, G. Raymond. *Our Faith and Fellowship.* Springfield, MO: Gospel Publishing House, 1977.

Hoover, Mario G. "Origin and Structural Development of the Assemblies of God". Master's thesis, Southwest Missouri State College, 1968.

Menzies, William W. *Annointed to Serve.* Springfield, MO: Gospel Publishing House, 1971.

Perkin, Noel, and John Garlock. *Our World Witness.* Springfield, MO: Gospel Publishing House, 1963.

★561★
International Church of the Foursquare Gospel
1100 Glendale Blvd.
Los Angeles, CA 90026

Alternate Address: Canadian headquarters: Foursquare Gospel Church of Canada, 7895 Welsley Dr., Burnaby, BC V5E 3X4.

History. The International Church of the Foursquare Gospel was founded by Aimee Semple McPherson (1890-1944), the flamboyant and controversial pastor of Angelus Temple in Los Angeles, California. Aimee's mother, a member of the Salvation Army, had promised God to dedicate her daughter to the ministry. At the age of 17, the teenage Aimee was converted, baptized with the Holy Spirit, and soon married to evangelist Robert James Semple. In 1910, the couple traveled to China as missionaries, and while serving there, Robert Semple died of malaria, just one month before the birth of their daughter, Roberta. With her daughter, Aimee returned to the United States where she later married Harold S. McPherson and to them was born a son, Rolf Kennedy McPherson. Together the McPhersons began to conduct independent itinerant pentecostal evangelistic meetings. Following her divorce from McPherson, Aimee continued the ministry which had already begun. In 1917, she began a periodical, *Bridal Call*, which served her ministry for many years.

Unsupported and berated by other ministers who did not believe in women speaking from a pulpit, Aimee won success through her oratorical abilities, her charisma, her expounding the teaching of the Foursquare Gospel, and her use of unusual and heretofore untried methods which brought widespread publicity. During her early ministry, she spent much time with T. K. Leonard and William H. Durham, both early pentecostal leaders. In 1918, Aimee settled in Los Angeles and with the help of those who had responded to her ministry, built and dedicated Angelus Temple in 1923. Throughout the remainder of her ministry, the temple became the focus of numerous spiritual extravaganzas, including religious drama, illustrated messages, and oratorios, which brought Sister Aimee, as she was affectionately called, a reputation for the unconventional. In 1926, Aimee disappeared for more than a month and upon her return, she said that she had been kidnapped. A major controversy developed, with critics claiming that she had disappeared of her own volition, yet no proof was substantiated to disprove her claim.

An evangelistic and training institute was opened even before the temple was dedicated and it began to educate leaders who went on to found numerous Foursquare churches. The creation of some 32 churches in southern California by 1921 spurred the formation of the Echo Park Evangelistic Association, and in 1927, the International Church of the Foursquare Gospel was incorporated. The church also built and began operation of KFSG, the third oldest radio station in Los Angeles. It currently operates 24 hours daily in southern California.

Work expanded to Canada; first to Vancouver and then eastward to Ontario. The Western Canada District was set off from the Northwest District in 1964. The Church of the Foursquare Gospel of Western Canada was established as a provincial society in 1976. A federal corporation was created in 1981 and the Foursquare Gospel Church of Canada emerged as a autonomous sister church.

Beliefs. The church has adopted a lengthy declaration of faith which affirms the authority of scripture and the traditional beliefs of protestant evangelical Christianity. There are two ordinances, baptism and the Lord's Supper. The baptism of the Holy Spirit is emphasized, but along with an equal emphasis upon the Spirit-filled life and the gifts and fruits of the Spirit. Tithing is acknowledged as the method ordained of God for the support of the ministry.

Organization. The organization of the church is vested in the president, a position held by Aimee until her death in 1944. She was succeeded by her son who held the post until his retirement in 1988. The third president is John R. Holland. A board of directors, which includes the president and other appointed or elected members, serves as the highest administrative body for the denomination's business affairs. The Foursquare cabinet and executive council advise the board of directors and the president. The Convention Body has the sole power to make or amend the Bylaws of the "ICFG" in keeping with the Articles of Incorporation. The convention body is comprised of representatives from Foursquare Churches and the credentialed ministers of the International Church of the Foursquare Gospel. Throughout the United States, the church is divided into nine districts with each area overseen by a district supervisor.

Membership: In 1994, the church reported 218,534 members, 1,710 churches, and 4,124 ministers in the United States. The affiliated Foursquare Gospel Church of Canada reported 2,760 members, 51 churches, and 98 ministers. Worldwide membership in the church was approximately 1.95 million in 31,564 churches in 72 countries.

Educational Facilities: L.I.F.E. (Lighthouse of International Foursquare Evangelism) Bible College, Los Angeles, California.

L.I.F.E. Bible College East, Christiansberg, Virginia.

The Foursquare Gospel Church of Canada sponsors:

L.I.F.E. Bible College of Canada, Vancouver, British Columbia.

There are also more than 247 Bible colleges and institutes in foreign mission fields around the world.

Periodicals: *The Foursquare World Advance Magazine.*

Sources:

Cox, Raymond L., ed. *The Foursquare Gospel.* Los Angeles: Foursquare Publications, 1969.

Duffield Guy P., and Nathaniel M. Van Cleave. *Foundations of Pentecostal Theology.* Los Angeles: L.I.F.E. Bible College, 1983.

Mavity, Nancy Barr. *Sister Aimee.* Garden City, NY: Doubleday, 1931.

McPherson, Aimee Semple. *The Story of My Life.* Waco, TX: Word Books, 1973.

Thomas, Lately. *The Vanishing Evangelist.* New York: Viking Press, 1959.

★562★
Italian Pentecostal Church of Canada
6724 Fabre St.
Montreal, PQ, Canada H2G 2Z6

Italian Presbyterians were the first of the Italian-Canadians to receive the baptism of the Holy Spirit and experience speaking-in-tongues. Though some Italians in Chicago became Pentecostals as early as 1907 and began missionary work in the United States, the Canadian work had an entirely independent origin, beginning in 1913 in Hamilton, Ontario, with the ministry of a Christian-Jewish missionary named Cohen. In 1914, two of the men who had received the baptism, Charles Pavia and Frank Rispoli, took the experience to Toronto, where they visited door-to-door in the Italian community. By 1920, the fervor spread to Montreal and other Italian-Canadian communities. Among the early leaders of the movement were Luigi Ippolito and Ferdinand Zaffuto.

Upon his return to the United States, evangelist Cohen informed the Italian Pentecostals in Chicago of the Canadian group, and a delegation visited the Hamilton and Toronto churches. The doctrine and practice of the Italian Pentecostal Church of Canada is similiar to that of the Pentecostal Assemblies of Canada, with whom they share fraternal relations. A missionary program is supported in Australia, Argentina, Brazil, England, France, Germany, Italy, and Switzerland.

Membership: In 1997, the church reported 23 congregations and 40 ministers in Canada. There were 5,000 members worldwide, of which approximately 3,300 were in Canada.

Educational Facilities: Eastern Pentecostal Bible College, Peterborough, Ontario, Canada.

Italian Bible Institute.

Periodicals: *Voce Evanglica* (Evangel Voice).

Sources:

De Caro, Louis. *Our Heritage.* Sharon, PA: General Council, Christian Church of North America, 1977.

Zucchi, Luigi. *The Italian Pentecostal Church of Canada: Origin and Brief History.* Montreal: Italian Pentecostal Church of Canada, 1993. 26 pp.

___. *Origin and Brief History.* Montreal: Italian Pentecostal Church of Canada, 1987.

★563★
Lamb of God Church
612 Isenburg St.
Honolulu, HI 96817

The Lamb of God Church was founded in 1942 by Rev. Rose H. Kwan. It is a small church with its several congregations located on Oahu, and Nolokai, Hawaii. The faith and practice are Pentecostal. The churches primarily serve native Hawaiians.

Membership: In 1997 there were four congregations, seven minister, and approximately 300 members.

Educational Facilities: Lamb of God Bible School, Honolulu, Hawaii.

★564★
Mt. Zion Sanctuary
21 Dayton St.
Elizabeth, NJ 07202

The Mt. Zion Sanctuary was formed in 1882 by Mrs. Antoinette Jackson, a member of the Baptist Church. Rejecting the idea that she was suffering as an invalid for the glory of God, she sought healing by prayer and fasting, and was instantly cured on July 14, 1880. She became blessed with the gifts of the Spirit, particularly healing, and others who were blessed by her ministry gathered around her.

Mt. Zion Sanctuary members believe in the Trinity as God the Father, God the Son, and the Holy Spirit who is the executive power of God. Humans find deliverance from sin and sickness in the vicarious sacrifice of Jesus. Believers are sanctified as they obey the truth. Baptism by immersion is practiced and the sabbath is kept. The church is considered to be the society of born-again believers who live a holy life. Church members believe in Christ's premillennial second coming, i.e., Christ will return to find Satan prior to His 1,000-year reign on earth with His saints.

Mrs. Jackson was succeeded by Pastor Ithamar Quigley, who was healed under her ministrations. The current President is Pastor Theodore Jordan.

Membership: In 1992 the sanctuary reported 100 members in two centers led by two ministers in the United States. Internationally, there were 10 churches in Nigeria and 11 in Jamaica. Two formerly affiliated congregations in England have become independent.

★565★
Music Square Church
PO Box 398
Alma, AK 72921

History. Music Square Church (also known as the Holy Alamo Christian Church Consecrated) began in 1969 as a street ministry in Hollywood, California, by Susan Alamo (born Edith Opal Horn) (d. 1982), an independent Pentecostal minister, and Tony Alamo (born Bernie Lazar Hoffman), her husband, whom she had converted. They began a ministry in Hollywood in the mid-1960s and opened a church there in 1969 where their first converts gathered. The church was originally known as the Tony and Susan Alamo Christian Foundation, but in 1981 Music Square Church was incorporated and in 1982 superceded the foundation.

During its formative years, the church became known as one segment of the Jesus People movement, however, it remained separate organizationally. As much of the larger movement was incorporated into various Baptist and Pentecostal churches, it survived as an independent organization heavily committed to an evangelistic street ministry. In the early 1970s, the church became quite controversial and was heavily criticized because of the format its ministry had developed. Church members (associates of the foundation's ministry) generally worked the streets of Hollywood inviting potential converts to evening services at the church which had, by that time, been established at Saugus (a rural community approximately an hour's distance). The mostly young recruits were taken by bus to Saugus for an evangelistic meeting and meal. Many of those who did convert remained in Saugus to be taught the Bible and become lay ministers.

In 1976, as the foundation grew, it purchased land at Alma and Dyer, Arkansas, where Susan Alamo grew up and where it transferred its headquarters. There it developed a community of several hundred foundation associates and established printing facilities, a school, and a large tabernacle. As part of its rehabilitation program it began to develop several businesses in which associates (many of whom were former drug addicts) could begin a process of reintegration into society. As the organization expanded further, churches (evangelistic centers) were opened in cities around the country (including Nashville, Tennessee; Chicago, Illinois; Brooklyn, New York; Miami Beach, Florida.) Associated with the church in Nashville, a retail clothing store was opened.

Beliefs. Music Square Church is a Pentecostal church with doctrine similar to the Assemblies of God. It accepts the authority of the Bible (using only the King James Version) and places its emphasis upon the preaching of Jesus Christ as the son of the Living God who died for humanity. The church adheres to a strict moral code, and members condemn drugs, homosexuality, adultery, and abortions. Both Susan and Tony Alamo were Jewish and they developed a special interest in evangelism of Jews.

Organization. Music Square Church has developed as an ordered community of people dedicated to evangelism. Converts who wish to remain associated with the church (i.e., to receive its training and participate in its ministry) take a vow of poverty agreeing to turn over all their real property to the church. In return the church agrees to provide the necessities of life (housing, clothes, food, medical assistance), including the education of children through high school. The church is headed by a three-person board presided over by Tony Alamo, the church's pastor. Alamo and the board set the policy and direction for the ministry.

Approximately half of the associates of the church reside on church property near Alma. Others reside at the several church centers around the United States. The headquarters complex includes housing units for the associates, a Christian school for grades one through 12, a large community dining hall, and offices. Periodically associates are sent out on evangelistic tours around the United States, frequently using the established church centers as bases of operation. Services are held daily at each of the church centers and generally free meals are served.

The church publishes a variety of evangelistic tracts which are passed out in the street witnessing and are mailed around the country and to a number of foreign countries as requested. The church also distributes numerous tapes of sermons by former pastor Susan Alamo and present pastor Tony Alamo. Among those associated with the church are a number of talented musicians and the church had produced a set of records and tapes featuring Tony Alamo and other members. A national television ministry begun in the 1970s has been largely discontinued.

Membership: Not reported. Church centers are located in Alma, Arkansas and Saugus, California.

Remarks: In 1985 a series of actions taken against the church severely disrupted its life. To suppport itself, the communal-style church had developed a number of businesses. Some former members who had aligned themselves with the anti-cult movement filed a complaint that they should be paid led to a series of lawsuits. That same year, the Internal Revenue Service stripped the church of its tax-exempt status. The church went to court to fight the IRS action. As the cases proceeded, Alamo was accused of beating an eleven-year-old boy. Charges were filed against him and he disappeared.

During the next three years, Alamo remained a fugitive from justice. During this time, he moved around the country and frequently called radio talk shows for interviews. He was finally arrested in 1991. While most of the charges, including the one of child abuse, were withdrawn, he was eventually tried and convicted in 1994 on charges arising from the church's loss of tax exemption. The church continues to function in his absence and he is expected to resume his former leadership role as soon as he is released.

Sources:

Ellwood, Robert S., Jr. *One Way.* Englewood Cliffs, NJ: Prentice-Hall, 1973.

We're Your Neighbor. Alma, AK: Holy Alamo Christian Church Consecrated, [1987].

★566★
Open Bible Standard Churches, Inc.
2020 Bell Ave.
Des Moines, IA 50315-1096

The Open Bible Standard Churches, Inc., was founded in 1935 by the merger of two evangelistic movements, both of which had their roots in the Azusa Street Mission, in Los Angeles and the spreading Pentecostal revival—the Open Bible Evangelistic Association and Bible Standard, Inc.. The former body had been founded by John R. Richey in Des Moines, Iowa, in 1932 and the latter in Eugene, Oregon, by Fred Hornshuh in 1919. At the time of the merger there were 210 ministers.

Doctrinally, the churches affirm the Bible as the infallible Word of God, the Trinity, the deity of Christ, and the believers experience of the holiness, healing, and the baptism of the Holy Spirit as evidenced by speaking in tongues. The church is governed by a biennial representative convention which elects a national board of directors. It is a member of the National Association of Evangelicals and the Pentecostal/Charismatic Churches of North America, and supports the Pentecostal World Conference. Missions are conducted in 36 countries around the world.

Membership: In 1997 the churches reported 41,00 constituents, 371 congregations, and 1,035 ministers. There were also 1,000 members in Canada and 45,00 members overseas in over 700 international congregations.

Educational Facilities: Eugene Bible College, Eugene, Oregon.

Periodicals: *Message of the Open Bible.*

Sources:

Mitchell, Robert Bryant. *Heritage & Horizons.* Des Moines, IA: Open Bible Publishers, 1982.

Policies and Principles. Des Moines, IA: Open Bible Standard Churches, 1986.

★567★

Pentecostal Assemblies of Canada
6745 Century Ave.
Mississauga, ON, Canada L5N 6P7

Among the people drawn to Los Angeles by the news of the Pentecostal revival which had broken out at the little mission on Azusa Street in 1906 were several Canadians, most prominently Robert McAleister. McAlister brought the revival to Ottawa. In addition, A. H. Argue encountered the first wave of the revival which swept Chicago, and he returned to Winnipeg with its message. In 1907 he began a magazine, *The Apostolic Messenger*, to spread the word. Within a few years Pentecostal assemblies had been established across Canada.

Organization proceeded slowly, though as early as 1909 a Pentecostal Missionary Union was formed. In 1917 ministers from the eastern part of Canada met at Montreal and formed the Pentecostal Assemblies of Canada. Two years later, ministers in the west formed the Western Canada District of the Assemblies of God, attached to the United States group headquartered in Springfield, Missouri. In 1921 the eastern group also affiliated with the Assemblies of God. In 1922 the government charter was finalized.

Soon after the affiliation with the American Pentecostals, the Canadians began to see that they were at a disadvantage and gradually they moved to separate themselves and assume the original name of the eastern organization. Headquarters were reestablished in Ottawa and later moved to Toronto. Several reasons for the organizational split (which implied no break in fraternal relations) are generally given. First, the Canadians placed less emphasis upon doctrine and were thus open to more latitude of belief. Second, there was a greater ethnic diversity, with one out of ten congregations not speaking English. Third, there was the influence of such Canadian voices as James Eustace Purdie, who argued for Canadian autonomy.

Doctrinally, the Canadian assemblies largely agree with the Assemblies of God. They advocate tithing and have strict rules about divorce, especially among ministers. They are also fraternally related to the Pentecostal Assemblies of Newfoundland, with whom they share the same doctrinal statement.

Membership: In 1994 there were 1,068 churches, 226,678 members, and 2,815 ministers. There are over one million members worldwide.

Educational Facilities: Berea Bible Institute, Pierrefonds, Quebec, Canada.

Canadian Pentecostal Correspondence College, Clayburn, British Columbia, Canada.

Central Pentecostal College, Saskatoon, Saskatchewan, Canada.

College Biblique Quebec: Formation Timothee, Charlesbourg Quest, Quebec, Canada.

Eastern Pentecostal Bible College, Peterborough, Ontario, Canada.

Northwest Bible College, Edmonton, Alberta, Canada.

Western Pentecostal Bible College, Abbotsford, British Columbia.

Periodicals: *The Pentecostal Testimony.*

★568★

Pentecostal Assemblies of Newfoundland
57 Thorburn Rd.
PO Box 8895, Sta. "A"
St. John's, NF, Canada A1B 3T2

Pentecostalism spread to Newfoundland in 1910 and on Easter Sunday, 1911, the first assembly, Bethesda Mission, opened at St. John's. The work was incorporated in 1925 as the Bethesda Pentecostal Assemblies of Newfoundland, the name by which it was known until it assumed its present name in 1930. That same year, using a ship, *The Gospel Messenger*, the assemblies moved into towns in Laborador.

The assemblies are separate from the Pentecostal Assemblies of Canada, but maintain close fraternal ties and hold to the same doctrinal position.

Membership: In 1998 the assemblies reported 142 churches, 40,000 members, and 425 ministries.

Periodicals: *Good Tidings.*

★569★

Pentecostal Church of God
4901 Pennsylvania
Joplin, MO 64802

History. The Pentecostal Church of God was formed in Chicago, Illinois, in 1919 by a group of pentecostal leaders. They chose the Rev. John C. Sinclair as their first moderator and the Pentecostal Assemblies of the USA as their name. That name was changed to the Pentecostal Church of God in 1922. The words "of America" were added in 1936 and then dropped in 1979. The church enjoyed a steady growth over the years. It moved its headquarters to Ottumwa, Iowa, in 1927. The following year the Pentecostal Young Peoples Association was organized. The expansion of the youth ministry was further manifested in the issuance of the first Sunday school material published by the church in 1937. Missionary support began as early as 1921 and was formalized in a church department in 1929.

Beliefs. The church's beliefs follow the central affirmation of evangelical Pentecostal Christianity. It affirms the authority of scripture, the Trinity, the deity of Christ, and humanity's need of salvation in Christ. The ordinances of the Lord's Supper and baptism by immersion are practiced. The church affirms the baptism of the Holy Spirit received subsequent to the new birth (faith in Christ) which is evidenced by the initial sign of speaking-in-tongues. Foot washing is observed at the discretion of local congregations. Prayer for divine healing of bodily ills is a regular part of church life. The church is not pacifist, but supports conscientious objectors in their search for alternative service. Tithing is advocated.

Organization. The church is headed by the general superintendent, assisted by the general secretary, director of world missions, director of Indian missions, director of home missions/evangelism, president of the Pentecostal Young Peoples Association, and the director of the women's ministries. The church is divided into districts headed by district superintendents, district presbyters, and district secretary-treasurers. The general convention meets biennially with most district conventions meeting annually.

Membership: In 1997, the church reported 45,200 members, 1,230 congregations, and 3,214 ministers. There was a reported constitutency of 111,900 in the United States. There were 350,000 members worldwide in 38 countries.

Educational Facilities: Messenger College, Joplin, Missouri.

In the mission field, there are 15 resident Bible schools and 29 extension training centers.

Periodicals: *The Pentecostal Messenger.* • *The Missionary Voice.* • *The Harvester.* • *The Spirit.* Send orders for any of the above to Box 850, Joplin, MO 64802.

Sources:

General Constitution and By-Laws. Joplin, MO: Pentecostal Church of God, 1984.

Moon, Elmer Louis. *The Pentecostal Church.* New York: Carleton Press, 1966.

Wilson, Aaron M. *Basic Bible Truth.* Joplin, MO: Messenger Press, 1988.

★570★

Pentecostal Church of New Antioch
Current address not obtained for this edition.

The Pentecostal Church of New Antioch is a trinitarian Pentecostal church founded 1953 in New Antioch, Ohio, by Marshall

M. Bachelor. Bachelor later moved the headquarters to Cleveland, Ohio. At the founding conference, he was elected president and general superintendent for life. The church professes belief in the baptism of the Holy Spirit as evidenced by speaking in tongues; spiritual gifts; the practice of baptism by immersion; the Lord's Supper, and foot washing; divine healing; the imminent coming of Jesus Christ; and the resurrection of the dead. The church does not approve of divorce and remarriage.

The church is headed by its president assisted by six vicepresidents, a secretary, and a treasurer. There is an annual national conference.

Membership: Not reported. In 1966 there were approximately 300 ministerial members serving churches across the United States and in Manitoba and Ontario, Canada, Jamaica, and England.

Sources:

Constitution and By-Laws o the Pentecostal Church of New Antioch, Inc. N.p.: 1959. 18 pp.

★571★
Pentecostal Church of Zion
% Zion College of Theology
Box 110
French Lick, IN 47432

As a youth in Kentucky, Luther S. Howard was converted by an independent Pentecostal minister and, in 1920, was ordained a minister of the Holy Bible Mission at Louisville. He served as a minister and then vice-president. Upon the death of its founder, Mrs. C. L. Pennington, the Mission was dissolved. Its ministers felt the need to continue their work and, in 1954, formed a new organization, the Pentecostal Church of Zion, Inc. Elder Howard was elected president and, in 1964, bishop. Since most of the work of the Holy Bible Mission was in Indiana, the new organization was headquartered at French Lick, Indiana.

The Pentecostal Church of Zion is like the Assemblies of God in most of its doctrine but differs from it on some points. The group keeps the ten commandments, including the Saturday Sabbath, and the Mosaic law concerning clean and unclean meats. (Cows and sheep are clean and may be eaten; pigs and other animals with cloven hooves may not be eaten because they are considered unclean). Most important, the group does not have a closed creed, but believes that members continue to grow in grace and knowledge. Anyone who feels that he has new light on the Word of God is invited to bring his ideas to the annual convention, where they can be discussed by the executive committee. By such a process, a decision was made in the 1960s to drop the Lord's Supper as an ordinance. The church now believes in the celebration of Passover by daily communion with the Holy Ghost.

Polity is episcopal. There is one bishop with life tenure and an assistant bishop elected for a three-year term. An annual meeting with lay delegates is held at the headquarters.

Membership: Not reported. In 1974 there were 5 congregations in Indiana and 1 in Oregon.

Educational Facilities: Zion College of Theology, French Lick, Indiana.

Periodicals: Zion's Echoes of Truth.

★572★
Pentecostal Evangelical Church
Current address not obtained for this edition.

The Pentecostal Evangelical Church was founded in 1936. Its first bishop, G. F. C. Fons, had been the moderator of the Pentecostal Church of God of America in the period directly preceeding the formation of the new body. Its doctrine is similar to that of the Pentecostal Church of God of America, and its polity is a mixture of congregationalism and episcopal forms. Each local church is

autonomous. The general conference meets every two years and elects a general bishop (for a four-year term), a vice-president (for two years), and a district superintendent (as an assistant bishop). Missions are supported in the Philippines, Bolivia, India and Guyana.

Membership: Not reported.

Periodicals: Gospel Tidings.

★573★
Pentecostal Evangelical Church of God, National and International
Current address not obtained for this edition.

The Pentecostal Evangelical Church of God, National and International was founded at Riddle, Oregon in 1960. It holds to beliefs similar to those of the Assemblies of God. It ordains women to the ministry. A General Convocation meets annually.

Membership: Not reported. In 1967 there were 4 congregations and 14 ministers.

Periodicals: Ingathering. • Golden Leaves.

★574★
Seventh-Day Pentecostal Church of the Living God
1443 S. Euclid
Washington, DC 20009

The Seventh-Day Pentecostal Church of the Living God was founded by Bishop Charles Gamble, a Pentecostal who had adopted some of the Old Testament practices including the seventh-day Sabbath. Gamble was a Roman Catholic and Baptist before becoming a Pentecostal. The church follows the Jesus-Only non-Trinitarian theology of the Apostolic churches.

Membership: Not reported. In the early 1970s there were 4 congregations with an estimated membership of less than 1,000.

★575★
United Apostolic Faith Church
2 Delbert Dr.
Scarborough, ON, Canada M1P 1X1

The United Apostolic Faith Church is one of several churches that grew out of the early Pentecostal movement in the British Isles. In 1908 the Apostolic Faith Church had been founded under the leadership of W. O. Hutchinson. During the next decade, the church spread across Great Britain, but experienced a major schism just as World War I was beginning. In 1916 the congregations in Wales broke away and reorganized as the Apostolic Church. The original organization, which included churches in Scotland and England, reorganized as the United Apostolic Faith Church.

In 1912, prior to the schism, a congregation of the Apostolic Faith Church had been established in Toronto, Ontario. It existed as a vital congregation for many years, but all but died out during World War II. Revived in 1947, the congregation associated itself with the United Apostolic Faith Church.

The United Apostolic Faith Church is a trinitarian pentecostal body whose doctrine is similar to that of the Assemblies of God. It affirms the free salvation of Christ and the baptism of the Holy Spirit evidenced by speaking in tongues for all believers. It practices baptism by immersion and the Lord's Supper. Members believe strongly in divine healing, deliverance, and the casting out of demons. They tithe and attempt to manifest both the gifts and fruits of the Spirit in their daily life.

The original Apostolic Church had emphasized the centrality of the activity of the Holy Spirit who manifested God's will through the gifts of the Spirit. The leaders tended to seek direction from either prophecy or interpretation and speaking in tongues, especially in the appointment of church leaders and in making decisions about the guidance of the church. That practice led to some degree of fanaticism and underlay the schism of 1916. U.A.F.C. attempted to respond to its critics over the years and developed a biblical form of ministerial leadership based upon the five-fold ministry of Ephesians 4:11. The local church is led by a presbytery of a pastor and elders. The church in Toronto is known as Dayspring Christian Fellowship.

Membership: In 1997 there were two congregations of the United Apostolic Faith Church in Canada, both in Ontario, with approximately 300 members.

Sources:

Piepkorn, Arthur C. *Profiles in Belief: The Religious Bodies of the United States and Canada.* Vol. III. San Francisco, Harper & Row, 1979.

★576★
United Full Gospel Ministers and Churches
Current address not obtained for this edition.

The United Full Gospel Ministers and Churches was incorporated May 16, 1951. Arthur H. Collins was the first chairman. Within a few years it had grown to include more than fifty clergy and a number of congregations. The church is governed by four executive officers, one of whom faces election at each annual meeting. The group has an affiliate in India—the Open Bible Church of God, founded by Willis M. Clay, who at one time also served as treasurer of the United Full Gospel Ministers and Churches.

Membership: Not reported.

★577★
United Fundamentalist Church
Current address not obtained for this edition.

The United Fundamentalist Church was organized in 1939 by the Rev. Leroy M. Kopp of Los Angeles. It was at one time a member of the National Association of Evangelicals and accepts the Association's doctrinal position. In addition, it is Pentecostal, and prophecy and healing are emphasized. Members are expected to believe that "The divine healing of the sick is not only to honor the prayer of faith (James 5:14, 15) but is to be a sign to confirm the word as it is preached at home and abroad (Mark 16:15-20)." Signs are given until the end of this age, when they will no longer be needed.

The general officers of the United Fundamentalist Church, together with the territorial supervisors and state district superintendents, constitute a council which settles all doctrinal disputes. Zion Christian Mission is sponsored in Jerusalem. Proselyting other Christian denominations is not practiced. A radio ministry was begun in 1940 by Kopp and still continues. The Rev. E. Paul Kopp has succeeded his father as head of the group.

Membership: Not reported. In 1967 there were approximately 250 ministers and missionaries.

Deliverance Pentecostals

★578★
Branham Tabernacle and Related Assemblies
% The William Branham Evangelistic Association
and The Branham Tabernacle
Box 325
Jeffersonville, IN 47130

Alternate Address: The Voice of God Recordings, Inc., Box 950, Jeffersonville, IN 47130

William M. Branham (1909-1965) was a Baptist minister who, as a child, began to hear the voice of one he claimed to be an angel of the Lord. Healed as a young man in a Pentecostal Church, he became a preacher and his success led to the building of a tabernacle in his home town of Jeffersonville, Indiana. Another angel-

ic visitation in 1946 launched his evangelical career as a seer with a healing ministry. He spoke of being called by God to pray for the sick, and the angel told him that he had been sent with a gift. He began to travel around the country leading revival services. He met Gordon Lindsay, a young Assemblies of God pastor in Oregon, who joined Branham and in 1948 began *The Voice of Healing* to publicize Branham's work and bring supporters together. As Branham's tours and fame spread nationally and internationally, other ministers with a gift for healing associated themselves with him and *The Voice of Healing*. During the 1950s, Branham led the revival in healing that would project such people as Oral Roberts, Morris Cerullo, and A. A. Allen into the spotlight as leaders of their own organizations.

Around 1960, Branham became separated from the majority of the healing evangelists when he allowed divergent opinions, which he had always held but rarely spoken about, to become frequent topics in his sermons. He denounced denominationalism as the mark of the beast of the Book of Revelation. He openly denounced trinitarian doctrine, which led many to see him as an advocate of "Jesus Only" nontrinitarian theology. Jesus Only Pentecostals believe that Jesus is the name of the One God, and that Father, Son, and Holy Spirit are not distinct persons in the Godhead. They baptize in the name of Jesus. Branham, however, did not agree with the "Jesus Only" position, teaching that the Father, Son, and Holy Spirit were each a manifestation of the One God. He also held that baptism was to be in the name of the "Lord Jesus Christ." Then in 1963, he began to emphasize the message of Malachi 4:5, that God had promised to send his prophet, Elijah. While never identifying himself as that messenger, he left the door open for his followers, many of whom came to believe that he was the one spoken about by Malachi. This issue alienated Branham from many of his former followers. He died in a car accident two years later.

Those who followed Branham's message and believed him to be the one with the spirit of Elijah, began immediately to preserve and perpetuate his message. Copies of sermon tapes and transcripts of sermons were reproduced and circulated by Spoken Word Publications and The Voice of God Recordings, Inc., both of which were headquartered a few blocks from the tabernacle in Jeffersonville. In 1986 Spoken Word merged into The Voice of God, which now houses the most complete archive of Branham's tapes and written material. The Voice of God regularly sends out copies of Branham's sermons which it is publishing one-by-one as a series of pamphlets under the general heading *The Spoken Word*. The Voice of God is headed by Joseph M. Branham, Branham's son.

The Rev. Billy Paul Branham, another of Branham's sons, now heads the William Branham Evangelistic Association, formed to perpetuate the missionary work of Branham's ministry. The Branham Tabernacle in Jeffersonville, Indiana, is pastored by Rev. Willard Collins. Besides the Branham Tabernacle, there are a number of independent churches which follow the message initiated by Branham. There is no association, no bishops or overseers, and only an informal fellowship. Many of these churches regularly order materials from The Voice of God and offer financial support of its work. Besides the following in the United States and Canada, support comes from many countries around the world. The literature is regularly translated into more than 30 languages.

Membership: In 1995 the William Branham Evangelistic Association reported approximately 70,000 members in the United States, 5,000 in Canada over 700,000 worldwide. There are more than 300 affiliated churches in North American and affiliated congregations in 29 countries.

Periodicals: *The Witness.* Send orders to Box 950, Jeffersonville, IN 47130.

Sources:

Branham, William. *Footprints on the Sands of Time.* Jeffersonville, IN: Spoken Word Publications, n.d.

Branham, William Marrion. *Conduct, Order, Doctrine of the Church.* Jeffersonville, IN: Spoken Word Publications, 1974.

Harrell, David Edwin, Jr. *All Things Are Possible.* Bloomington, IN: University of Indiana Press, 1975.

Lindsey, Gordon. *William Branham, A Man Sent From God.* Jeffersonville, IN: William Branham, 1950.

Sproule, Terry. *A Prophet to the Gentiles.* Blaine, WA: Bible Believers, n.d.

Weaver, C. Douglas. *The Healer-Prophet, William Marrion Branham: A Study in the Prophetic in American Pentecostalism.* Macon, GA: Mercer University Press, 1987.

★579★

Deliverance Evangelistic Church
2001 W. Lehigh Ave.
Philadelphia, PA 19132

The Deliverance Evangelistic Church was founded in 1960 as an independent prayer group that engaged in evangelistic endeavors in Philadelphia. After a year of informal activity, the group, under the leadership of Rev. Dr. Benjamin Smith, Sr., settled in a permanent location and formally organized as the Deliverance Evangelistic Church. As the movement grew, other churches were founded primarily in Pennsylvania and New Jersey.

The church has set itself three goals: to evangelize people to Christ, to teach the word of God so that believers might mature spiritually, and to prepare believers for worship and service. Service to the community has been especially emphasized and as the church grew it developed a broad spectrum of social ministry to the poor through the redistribution of clothing, food, and shelter, and through visitation to hospitals, prisons, nursing homes, and shut-ins.

The church has developed a radio broadcast and has founded the Deliverance Evangelistic Bible Institute and a youth Bible School. The church choirs have produced several albums. Smith, the founder, continues as the pastor of the organization. There is an annual convention each summer. Smith has envisioned the construction of "Deliverance Village," a building complex that would include a 7,000-seat auditorium, a Christian medical center, a Christian elementary and high school, and a home for the aged. To date, a part of the complex has been completed and opened, and construction on the auditorium began in 1989.

Membership: In 1990 the church reported 32 congregations and 83,000 members. Missionary work is supported in Liberia, Haiti, and India.

Periodicals: *Evangel.*

Sources:

Payne, Wardell J., ed. *Directory of African American Religious Bodies: A Compendium by the Howard University School of Divinity.* Washington, DC: Howard University Press, 1991.

★580★

Fellowship of Inner-City Word of Faith Ministries
℅ Crenshaw Christian Center
7901 S. Vermont Ave.
Los Angeles, CA 90044

The Fellowship of Inner-City Word of Faith Ministries, founded in 1990, is an association of ministers, ministries, and congregations that grew out of the ministry of Frederick K. C. Price, the Crenshaw Christian Center, and the center's Ministry Training Institute. Price, while a pastor of a congregation of the Christian and Missionary Alliance, read one of the books of Pentecostal healer Kathryn Kuhlman, which led him into the Pentecostal baptism of the Holy Spirit as evidenced by speaking in tongues. He later became associated with Kenneth Hagin, with whom he found himself in essential doctrinal agreement. In 1976 Price was awarded an honorary degree from the Rhema Bible Training Institute which Hagin founded.

In 1973 Price founded the Crenshaw Christian Center. The church is built upon the message of faith, that in asking the Lord in faith for what is desired and His will, it will be forthcoming. The church, serving primarily African Americans, prospered, and membership steadily increased. In 1978 Ever Increasing Faith, an evangelistic ministry of Crenshaw Christian Center, was begun and found its major expression in a television program (now seen internationally in the Caribbean and West Africa). In 1981, the former campus of Pepperdine University was purchased to house the growing congregation (over 5,000) and its associated ministries. The move allowed the founding of a School of Ministry (1985), School of the Bible (1988), Helps Ministry Summer School (1989) and Correspondence School. Most recently the center completed construction of the Faithdome, a sanctuary which can hold the more than 10,000 people who gather for Sunday worship.

As the ministry work initiated by Price spread, and as ministers graduated from the School of Ministry, other Word-Faith ministries grew up in Southern California and other cities, most working in inner-city African-American communities. The Fellowship of Inner-City Word of Faith Ministries provides a place for ministers and lay leaders involved in various Word of Faith ministries to fellowship and share their knowledge of the work. They are tied together by their mutual acceptance of the Word of Faith perspective. Many are graduates of the School of Ministry.

Membership: Not reported.

Sources:

Price, Frederick K. C. *How to Obtain Strong Faith.* Tulsa, OK: Harrison House, 1980.

★581★

First Deliverance Church of Atlanta
Current address not obtained for this edition.

The First Deliverance Church was founded in Atlanta in 1956 by the Reverends Lillian G. Fitch and William Fitch, two deliverance evangelists. The church teaches three experiences (justification, sanctification, and baptism of the Holy Spirit), emphasizes healing, and practices tithing. Fasts are an important feature of church life. Occasionally members hold a shut-in fast, when they stay at the church for three days over the weekend. Among distinctive practices is their kneeling in prayer upon entering the church. Congregations headed by licensed ministers are located in Georgia, Florida, Oklahoma, and California.

Membership: Not reported.

★582★

Full Gospel Fellowship of Churches and Ministers International
4325 W. Leadbetter Dr.
Dallas, TX 75233

In the early 1960s, Gordon Lindsay, founder of the Christ for the Nations Institute, in Dallas, Texas, and publisher of the *The Voice of Healing* magazine, called together a group of independent Pentecostal ministers. The ministers expressed a desire to give expression of the unity of the Body of Christ under the leadership of the Holy Spirit, a unity that would go beyond individuals, churches, or organizations. Thus the Full Gospel Fellowship of Churches and Ministers International was formed in 1962.

The Fellowship has adopted a set of "Suggested Articles of Faith" that they offer to member churches. While assuming an essential doctrinal agreement among member churches and ministers, individual churches may choose to revise the articles. The articles affirm belief in the Bible as the inspired Word of God, the Trinity, the need of people for salvation, sanctification, the second coming and millennial reign of Christ, heaven, and hell. Baptism of the Holy Spirit with the initial evidence of speaking in tongues is strongly advocated.

The Fellowship is an organized association of independent churches and is designed to perform only those services that churches cannot easily or conveniently provide for themselves. Individual churches, groups of churches, and organizations of churches may be recognized within the Fellowship. Each church is free to carry out its own program and missionary work and to ordain and/or license ministers as it deems necessary. Those ministers recognized by the Fellowship are subsequently issued a membership card and certificate of ministerial status. Annually, an international and several regional conventions are held to provide opportunities for fellowship and to support the objectives and goals of local and national ministries. The business meeting is held during the international meeting each July.

While the Fellowship is not a governing body, it has been recognized by the Internal Revenue Service as an organization qualified to offer independent congregations tax-exempt status under its group exemption umbrella.

Membership: In 1988 the Fellowship reported 1,493 clergy members and 765 congregation members in the United States. There were 18 clergy members from Canada and 249 clergy members from 42 countries worldwide.

Periodicals: *Fellowship Tidings.*

Remarks: Gordon Lindsay (1906-1973), whose efforts were so important in initiating the fellowship's organization, was a former pastor in the Assemblies of God, and, in the late 1940s, a close associate of evangelist William M. Branham. He served as president of the Voice of Healing Publishing Company and edited *The Voice of Healing*, a magazine that publicized and coordinated the activities of many of the prominent healing evangelists of the 1950s. In 1949 he called together the first meeting of the evangelists and ministers who supported the healing emphases that had grown from Branham's original efforts. The last of these annual conventions was held in 1961, the year before the formation of the Full Gospel Fellowship of Churches and Ministers International. Lindsay's work has been carried on by his widow, Freda Lindsay, through Christ for the Nations and its affiliated activities.

Sources:

Lindsay, Freda. *My Diary Secrets.* Dallas: Christ for the Nations, 1976.

Lindsay, Gordon. *Bible Days Are Here Again.* Shreveport, LA: The Author, 1949.

___. *The Gordon Lindsay Story.* Dallas: Voice of Healing Publishing Company, n.d.

★583★
Hall Deliverance Foundation
Box 9910
Phoenix, AZ 85068

The Hall Deliverance Foundation was established in 1956 in San Diego, California, as the focus of the ministry of the Rev. Franklin Hall (d. 1993), an independent Pentecostal minister, who began his ministerial career in 1946 as a Methodist. Hall also founded and pastored the International Healing Cathedral in San Diego, California. During the years in the Pentecostal ministry prior to the organization of the foundation, Hall was closely connected with the evangelist Thelma Nickel.

Hall taught what he termed "body-felt" salvation. It was his belief that salvation is for the body as well as the biblical text, "By his stripes you are healed" and also by his own obtaining of the full baptism of the Holy Ghost (or Spirit) and Fire, as mentioned in Matthew 3:11. According to Hall, this teaching was alluded to by Jesus in Acts 1:8. The Holy Ghost power coming upon the physical body keeps the body well and healed, just as long as the believer keeps that portion of the Holy Spirit called the "Fire" upon the physical body. The believer, therefore, has "body-felt" salvation, as there is no sickness. Those who participate in the body-felt salvation also participate in a miracle ministry and find its demonstration in a wide variety of healings and deliverance from natural disasters and dangerous situations. Also, the experi-ence of the Holy Spirit when it comes upon the person is felt tangibly as a pleasant warmth to heal the body or to bring healing protection energy. This sensation is related to the fire portion of the Holy Spirit baptism (Acts 2:3), which Jesus urged his disciples to obtain (Acts 1:8). Hall also recommended prayer and fasting. The latter enabled one to become a powerful conductor of divine and spiritual forces, according to Hall.

Hall died in 1993. His widow, Rev. Helen Hall, continues to pastor the International Healing Cathedral and travels around the world teaching and holding meetings. The Foundation distributes numerous pieces of literature and both audio and video tapes. Affiliated work takes place in Mexico, Canada, the Bahamas, Australia, New Zealand, Great Britain, West Germany, Finland, France, Sweden, the Philippines, Nigeria, Ghana, the Ivory Coast, Ethiopia, Tanzania, Kenya, Malaya, South Africa, and India.

Membership: Not reported.

Educational Facilities: Glory Knowledge Bible School, Phoenix, Arizona.

Periodicals: *Miracle Word.* • *The Healing Word News.*

Sources:

Hall, Franklin. *Atomic Power with God.* San Diego, CA: The Author, 1946.

___. *The Baptism of Fire.* San Diego, CA: The Author, 1960.

___. *The Body-Felt Salvation.* Phoenix: Hall Deliverance Foundation, 1968.

___. *Our Divine Healing Obligation.* Phoenix: The Author, 1964.

Nickel, Thelma. *Our Rainbow of Promise.* Tulsa, OK: Vickers Printing Co., 1950.

★584★
International Convention of Faith Ministries
10801 Executive Center Dr., Ste. 502
Little Rock, AR 72211

The International Convention of Faith Ministries (known until 1985 as the International Convention of Faith Churches and Ministers) was founded in 1979 by Dr. Doyle Harrison and a number of independent Pentecostal pastors and evangelists, some of whom head their own national and international ministries, and a few of whom had become very well known for their work on Christian television—Kenneth Hagin, (Tulsa, Oklahoma), Kenneth Copeland (Fort Worth, Texas), Frederick K. C. Price (Los Angeles), Norvel Hayes (Cleveland, Tennessee), Jerry J. Savelle (Fort Worth, Texas) and John H. Osteen (Houston, Texas). Hagin is pastor of RHEMA Bible Church and heads Kenneth Hagin Ministries, Inc.. Copeland, assisted by Gloria Copeland, his wife, heads Kenneth Copeland Ministries and Publications. Price, a black minister, heads Ever Increasing Faith Ministries and pastors Crenshaw Christian Center. Savelle heads Jerry Savelle Ministries and founded the Overcoming Faith Churches of Kenya in Africa. Osteen heads the John Osteen World Satellite Network. Norvel Hayes, a successful businessman, is also an independent healing evangelist. Doyle Harrison pastors Faith Christian Fellowship International Church in Tulsa.

Not only does their work center upon healing, but they subscribe to the "faith confession" doctrine which holds that a child of faith can publically confess or claim something from God and be assured of getting it. The convention admits both churches and individuals to membership. Many of the students trained at RHEMA Bible Training Center, started in 1974 by Hagin, have created new congregations partially drawing upon listeners of the television programs of the convention founders. In 1975 Harrison founded Harrison House, a book concern, which publishes many of the healing evangelists' materials.

Membership: In 1985 the convention had over 800 ministers and churches on its rolls.

Educational Facilities: RHEMA Bible Training Center, Tulsa, Oklahoma.

Crenshaw Christian Center School of Ministry, Los Angeles, California.

Periodicals: *International Faith Report.* • Unofficial (periodicals issued by ministries associated with the convention): *The Word of Faith.* Available from Kenneth Hagin Ministries, Box 50126, Tulsa, OK 74150. • *Ever Increasing Faith Messenger.* Available from Crenshaw Christian Center, Box 90000, Los Angeles, CA 90009. • *Believers Voice of Victory Magazine.* Available from Kenneth Copeland Ministries, Box 2908, Fort Worth, TX 76113.

Remarks: Some of the leading ministers of the convention (Hagin, Copeland, Price) are among a group of evangelists-teachers who have been attacked by other Pentecostal leaders for what has been termed "faith formula theology," that is a belief that by publically confessing (claiming) something from God, believers will be given it according to their faith.

Sources:

Copeland, Gloria. *God's Will for You.* Fort Worth: Kenneth Copeland Publications, 1972.

Hagin, Kenneth E. *How You Can Be Led by the Spirit of God.* Tulsa, OK: Kenneth Hagin Ministries, 1978.

Hayes, Norvel. *7 Ways Jesus Heals.* Tulsa, OK: Harrison House, 1982.

Osteen, John H. *This Awakening Generation.* Humble, TX: The Author, 1964.

Price, Frederick K. C. *How to Obtain Strong Faith.* Tulsa, OK: Harrison House, 1980.

★585★
International Deliverance Churches
Box 353
Dallas, TX 75221

Among the deliverance evangelists associated with William M. Branham was W. V. Grant (1913-1983). After several years as an active evangelist, he settled in Dallas because of health problems and became a prolific writer of deliverance literature. He became pastor of the Soul's Harbor Church in Dallas and the leading force in the International Deliverance Churches.

From the Dallas Center, annual conventions have been held each summer since 1962. During this period, classes are held for two weeks, and ministers are ordained. Following his death Grant was succeded by his son, W. V. Grant, Jr.. Grant has emerged as one of the better known healing ministers among Pentecostals with his national radio and television broadcasts.

Membership: Not reported. There is foreign work in Haiti, Ghana, Nigeria, and India.

Educational Facilities: Eagle Bible Institute, Dallas, Texas.

Periodicals: *Where Eagles Fly.*

Sources:

Grant, W. V. *Faith Cometh.* Dallas: The Author, n.d.

___. *The Grace of God in My Life.* Dallas: The Author, 1952.

___. *The Truth About Faith Healers.* Dallas: Faith Clinic, n.d.

★586★
Leroy Jenkins Evangelistic Association
Current address not obtained for this edition.

Leroy Jenkins is a healer who has become known as "the man with the golden arm" for his healing work. When he was five years old, so the story goes, the Lord spoke to him in an audible voice. Four years later, God spoke to him again and he levitated and floated through the air. In an accident in 1960, his arm was almost cut off. He was healed instantly (after refusing amputation) in a

meeting conducted by A. A. Allen in Atlanta. With Allen's encouragement, he began to preach and his evangelistic association was formed in 1960. Originally headquartered in Tampa, Florida, he moved to Delaware, Ohio, where a large tabernacle was build in the 1970s. In 1971, his radio ministry was being heard over 57 stations.

In 1977 Jenkins moved to Greenwood, South Carolina, and opened the Spirit of Truth Church. However, in April 1979 Jenkins was arrested and convicted on two counts of conspiracy to commit arson related to the burning of a state trooper's home in Ohio. Jenkins protested his innocence, but was sentenced to serve 12 years. He was paroled in June 1985 and has since resumed his ministry.

Membership: Not reported. The magazine of the association is mailed to over 100,000 supporters.

Periodicals: *Revival of America.*

Sources:

Jenkins, Leroy. *God Gave Me a Miracle Arm.* Delaware, OH: Leroy Jenkins Evangelistic Association, 1963.

___. *How I Met the Master.* Delaware, OH: Leroy Jenkins Evangelistic Association, n.d.

___. *How You Can Receive Your Healing.* Delaware, OH: Leroy Jenkins Evangelistic Association, 1966.

Randi, James. *The Faith Healers.* Buffalo, NY: Prometheus Books, 1987.

★587★
Kathryn Kuhlman Foundation
(Defunct)

Kathryn Kuhlman emerged in the 1970s as the most famous and sought-after spiritual healer in the country. Born in Concordia, Missouri, and reared in the Methodist Church, she could not preach for the Methodists because she was a woman, so she became a Baptist and was ordained by the Evangelical Church Alliance. While she pastored a church in Franklin, Pennsylvania, spontaneous healings began to occur. These were coincidental with some personal mystical/psychical experiences of Mrs. Kuhlman, experiences that included a trancelike state in which her consciousness left her body. From that time on, spectacular healing activity was characteristic of her services. She was reported to have cured such illnesses as muscular dystrophy, emphysema, terminal cancer, and blindness. In 1947, she moved to Pittsburgh where her work was later institutionalized as the Kathryn Kuhlman Foundation. She died in 1976.

Kuhlman was pastor of a congregation in Pittsburgh and once a month held Sunday morning services in Los Angeles. She was a popular speaker for the Full Gospel Businessmen's Fellowship International. In 1970, the Foundation was subsidized by approximately 21 churches in countries around the world. The Foundation operated a vigorous radio and television ministry, a food assistance program, and a college scholarship program.

Sources:

Hosier, Helen Kooiman. *Kathryn Kuhlman.* Old Tappan, NJ: Fleming H. Revell, 1971.

___. *God Can Do It Again.* Englewood Cliffs, NJ: Prentice-Hall, 1969.

Kuhlman, Kathryn. *I Believe in Miracles.* Englewood Cliffs, NJ: Prentice-Hall, 1962.

___. *Nothing Is Impossible with God.* Englewood Cliffs, NJ: Prentice-Hall, 1974.

Spraggett, Allen. *Kathryn Kuhlman, The Woman Who Believes in Miracles.* New York: New American Library, 1970.

★588★
Miracle Life Fellowship International
11052 N. 24th Ave.
Phoenix, AZ 85029

Asa Alonzo Allen was born of a poor Arkansas family, saved in a Methodist revival, and later baptized with the Holy Spirit in a Pentecostal meeting. He joined the Assemblies of God and felt called to preach. In the early 1940s, he began to seek a ministry of signs and wonders, particularly healing. He had what amounted to a theological conversion when, during a prayer time, he formulated the thirteen requirements for a powerful ministry. He became convinced that he could do the works of Jesus, and do more than Jesus did; that he could be flawless and perfect (in the Biblical sense), and should believe all the promises. During World War II, his throat became, according to one throat specialist, "permanently ruined," but Allen was healed.

In 1951, he purchased a tent and began the crusade in earnest. Headquarters of A. A. Allen Revivals, Inc., were established in Dallas and *Miracle Magazine* was begun. From that time until his death, Allen was an immensely popular evangelist speaking both to integrated and predominantly black audiences. As early as 1960, he was holding fully integrated meetings in the South. In 1958, he was given 1,250 acres near Tombstone, Arizona, which were named Miracle Valley and which became the international headquarters. Allen died in 1970 and was succeeded by Don Stewart, who chose the new name for the organization: Miracle Revival Fellowship.

Miracle Valley was created as a totally spiritual community. Allen founded a Bible school and publishing house, located adjacent to radio and television studios, the healing pool of Bethesda, and the headquarters. He also operated a telephone Dial-a-Miracle prayer service. The church seats 2,500. As a result of Allen's accomplishments and success, missionary churches were begun and independent ministers have become associated with him. Miracle Revival Fellowship, (now Miracle Life Fellowship International) at first a department of A. A. Allen Revivals, was established as a ministerial fellowship and licensing agency. After Allen's death, the Bible college was turned over to the Central Latin American District Council of the Assemblies of God and is now known as Southern Arizona Bible College. A. A. Allen Revivals became the Don Stewart Association.

Membership: In 1988, the fellowship of ministers had 350 clergy members in the United States and an additional 50 in other countries.

Periodicals: *Feed My People Magazine.* • *Miracle Magazine.* Send orders to Box 2960, Phoenix, AZ 85062-9984.

Sources:

Allen, A. A. *My Cross.* Miracle Valley, AZ: A. A. Allen Revivals, n.d.

Allen, A. A., with Walter Wagner. *Born to Loose, Bound to Win.* Garden City, NY: Doubleday, 1970.

Stewart, Don. *Blessings from the Hand of God.* Miracle Valley, AZ: Don Stewart Evangelistic Association, 1971.

___. *How You Can Have Something Better Through God's Master Plan.* Phoenix, AZ: Don Stewart Evangelistic Association, 1975.

Stewart, Don with Walter Wagner. *The Man from Miracle Valley.* Long Beach, CA: Great Horizons Company, 1971.

★589★
Miracle Life Revival, Inc.
Box 20707
Phoenix, AZ 85036

Independent Pentecostal evangelist Neal Frisby became known in the early 1960s for possessing a gift of prophecy. In 1967 he began regularly to release prophetic scrolls; by 1974 there were 60 and they were published in book form, and by 1995 the number had grown to 223. In 1972 Capstone Cathedral, a large pyra-mid-shaped church was completed on the outskirts of Phoenix, Arizona. It serves as a publishing center and headquarters. The church also houses a television studio and produces films concerning worldwide events. In recent years, Frisby has released a number of pictures in which strange, "supernatural" lights are said to have appeared. He appears weekly on the World Harvest T.V. and Satellite Network.

Membership: Not reported. Besides the congregation in Phoenix, there is a mailing list of "special partners" around the United States who regularly support the ministry.

Sources:

Frisby, Neal. *The Book of Revelation Scrolls.* Phoenix: The Author, n.d.

Grant, W. V. *Creative Miracles.* Dallas: Faith Clinic, n.d.

★590★
Mita's Congregation
Calle Duarte 235
Hata Rey, PR 60919

Mita's Congregation orginiated in Puerto Rico. Founded in 1940 in the city of Arecibo, the congregation also expanded to the United States in 1948 by a preacher who was sent to the city of New York. The founder of the church, Mrs. Juanita Garcia Pereza, who after being ill for a long period of time, prayed to God and asked him that if He healed her, she would always serve Him. She had a revelation from God that He chose her body as the dwelling place for the Holy Spirit and commanded her to establish this church following the doctrinal principles of the Primitive Christian Church. It is their biblical understanding that Jesus Christ's Church was only one, and today the Holy Ghost is preparing his people in order to lead them towards salvation. According to the Holy Scriptures, of the many that are called, He would join the chosen together.

Pereza was considered to be the prophet and instrument of God, and through her God healed the sick and entirely changed and improved peoples lives as He did in ancient times, according to the Holy Scriptures.

Moreover, she was commended in the beginning of the church to preach the Triple Message: Love, Liberty, and Unity. Love, because God is love, and He called His people so they could love Him above all things and to love thy neighbor as thyself. Liberty, because He came to free His people from sin. And Unity, because Christ came to unify His people and unite them in one unique feeling.

Mita's name, which signifies "Spirit of Life," was revealed by God to various spiritual brothers and herself. For its followers, Mita's name is the fulfillment of the biblical prophecies that say that the Lord would return with a new name (Isaiah 52.6 and 62.2 and Revelation 2.17 and 3.12). They also believe Jesus promised that Christ would come as the promised Comforter (John 14:26).

On February 23, 1970, Peraza passed away in the city of Hato Rey, Puerto Rico. In her place and with the same attributes, Teofilo Vargas Sein Aaron remains. Since his childhood, Aaron had accompanied her and was annointed of the Lord for this ministry when he was 15 years old. Under his guidance, the church has extended to other places in the United States (New Jersey, Connecticut, Chicago, Orlando, Miami, Washington, New York, Boston) and overseas to the Dominican Republic, Mexico, Colombia, Venezuela, Costa Rica, El Salvador, Curacao, Panama, and Canada.

In 1990, Mita's Congregation celebrated its fiftieth anniversary and inaugurated a new House of Worship, necessary because of the increasing number of members. It has the capacity of seating more than 6,000 people.

The principal church is located in Hato Rey and religious services are regularly held every Tuesday, Thursday, Saturday, and Sunday.

The congregation possesses a Pastoral Home, where people reside who are devoted and have dedicated their lives to God. There is also a home for the elderly which accommodates 89 people, a private educational institution, Colegio Congregacion Mita, ranging from pre-school to high school, a social work and counseling office, and an Orientation and Social Assistance Office, which offers social work services to all people.

Membership: In 1997, the Congregation reported six congregations and 1,500 members in the United States and 63 congregations and 46,730 members worldwide. There is one congregation in Canada.

★591★
Salvation and Deliverance Church
37 W. 116 St.
New York, NY 10026

The Salvation and Deliverance Church was begun in 1975 by Rev. William Brown as a ministry of the African Methodist Episcopal Church. Brown had been raised as a Roman Catholic and had become a businessman. He later entered the ministry. In the 1980s he separated from the African Methodist Episcopal Church in favor of developing an international, interracial Holiness ministry. In a very short time, the church has developed an enormous program which currrenly reaches more than forty countries. Emphasis in the membership is placed on developing Holy living rather than doctrinal uniformity.

Apostle William Brown has led the church in the development of a multidimensional program. It includes an award-winning drug rehabilitation center in Harlem; a youth ministry, the International Youth Movement for Christ; schools (both elementary and bible schools); and work with the physically retarded. The church maintains a retreat center in the Catskill Mountains with special facilities for those involved in the ministry to the retarded. The church supports five Bible colleges including Saint Paul's Bible Institute in New York.

Membership: The church's more than 140 affiliated congregations included churches in Haiti, Nigeria, Jamaica, Liberia, India, and Canada.

Educational Facilities: St. Paul's Bible Institute, New York, New York.

Sources:

Payne, Wardell J., ed. *Directory of African American Religious Bodies: A Compendium by the Howard University School of Divinity.* Washington, DC: Howard University Press, 1991.

Apostolic Pentecostals

★592★
Apostolic Assemblies of Christ, Inc.
26798 Sumter Rd.
Belleville, MI 48111-9629

The Apostolic Assemblies of Christ was formed in 1970 by former members of the Pentecostal Churches of Apostolic Faith led by Bishop G. N. Boone. During the term of presiding bishop Willie Lee, questions of his administrative abilities arose. In the midst of the controversy, he died. In the organizational disaray the church splintered, and one group formed around Bishop Boone and Virgil Oates, the vice-bishop. The new body is congregational in organization and continues in the doctrine of the parent body, since no doctrinal controversy accompanied the split.

Membership: In 1980 the Assemblies had approximately 3,500 members, 23 churches and 70 ministers.

★593★
Apostolic Church of Christ
2044 Martin Luther King, Jr. Dr.
Winston-Salem, NC 27107

The Apostolic Church of Christ was founded in 1969 by Bishop Johnnie Draft and Elder Wallace Snow, both ministers in the Church of God (Apostolic). Draft, for many years an overseer in the church and pastor of St. Peter's Church, the denomination's headquarters congregation, expressed no criticism of the Church of God (Apostolic); rather, he stated that the Spirit of the Lord brought him to start his own organization. The church differs from its parent body in its development of a centralized church polity. Authority is vested in the executive board, which owns all the church property. Doctrine follows that of the Church of God (Apostolic). Bishop Draft serves as the church's Chief Apostle.

Membership: In 1992 the Apostolic Church of Christ had six churches, 400 members, nine ministers, six elders, two licensed missionaries, and one bishop.

★594★
Apostolic Church of Christ in God
℅ Bethlehem Apostolic Church
1217 E. 15th St.
Winston-Salem, NC 27105

The Apostolic Church of Christ in God was formed by five elders of the Church of God (Apostolic): J. W. Audrey, J. C. Richardson, Jerome Jenkins, W. R. Bryant, and J. M. Williams. At the time of the split, the Church of God (Apostolic) was formally led by Thomas Cox, but, due to his ill health, Eli N. Neal was acting as presiding bishop. The dissenting elders were concerned with the authoritarian manner in which Neal conducted the affairs of the church as well as with some personal problems that Neal was experiencing. Originally, three churches left with the elders, who established headquarters in Winston-Salem, North Carolina. J. W. Audrey was elected the new presiding bishop.

The new church prospered and in 1952 Elder Richardson was elected as a second bishop. In 1956 Audrey resigned and Richardson became the new presiding bishop. Under his leadership the Apostolic Church enjoyed its greatest success. He began The *Apostolic Gazette* (later the *Apostolic Journal*) which served the church for many years. He also instituted a program to assist ministers in getting an education. However, his efforts were frustrated by several schisms that cut into the church's growth, most prominently the 1971 schism led by former-bishop Audrey.

The church retained the doctrine and congregational polity of the Church of God (Apostolic).

Membership: In 1980 the church had 2,150 members in 13 congregations being served by five bishops and 25 ministers.

★595★
Apostolic Church of Jesus
Current address not obtained for this edition.

The Apostolic Church of Jesus was founded by Antonio Sanches, who had been converted in an evangelistic meeting led by Mattie Crawford in Pueblo, Colorado in 1923, and his brother George Sanches. The Sanches brothers began to preach to the Spanish-speaking population of the city and in 1927 organized the first congregation of the Apostolic Church of Jesus. In subsequent years, congregations were established throughout the state and elsewhere and can now be found in Denver, Westminister, Fountain, Walsenbury, and Ft. Garland, Colorado; Palo Alto, California; San Luis, Trinidad; and Velarde, New Mexico. The group, presently under the leadership of Raymond P. Virgil, has a weekly radio ministry.

Membership: Not reported.

Periodicals: *Jesus Only News of the Apostolic Faith.*

★596★
Apostolic Church of Jesus Christ
Current address not obtained for this edition.

The Apostolic Church of Jesus Christ is a second body that grew out of the Pentecostal Assemblies of the World after the death of Garfield Thomas Haywood (1880-1931), who founded the "oneness" work in Indianapolis, Indiana. The Church believes in the indispensability of baptism for salvation.

Membership: Not reported.

Periodicals: *The Voice of the Wilderness.*

★597★
Apostolic Faith (Hawaii)
1043 Middle St.
Honolulu, HI 96819

The Apostolic Faith Church, known in Honolulu for the neon sign proclaiming "JESUS COMING SOON" on the rooftop, was founded by the late Pastor Charles Lochbaum and his wife Ada Lochbaum, who felt called by the Lord to come to Hawaii from California in 1923. They held revival services in a tent where many came and witnessed preaching of the "Gospel of Jesus Christ, gifts of the Holy Spirit, and Divine healing." This early ministry was very successful and within a year, a permanent church was erected. An evangelistic tour of the island was started, and after four years more than 4,000 converts were baptized.

The church is currently headed by a board of trustees consisting of the Chief Pastor and Chairman of the Board William M. Han, Sr., Pastor Rodney S. Asano, Sr., Pastor Leonard K. Y. Asano, Sr., Edwin H. Sproat, Sr., Evangeline L. Han, and associate trustee William M. Han, Jr.. In addition, the church is a self-sufficient and independent organism from any affiliation with other national and independent church groups. One of its tenets admonishes members to "Stand for the Name of Jesus Christ, not to join up with any other organization, and not to compromise the Gospel Truths found in Gods Word, the Bible."

The first branch church was built in the district of Kaimuki, on the island of Oahu in 1930. In 1944, the Pukoo, Molokai branch was built, and in 1953 the Maui branch was constructed at Lahaina. A temple sanctuary with a seating capacity of 1,000 was built as the headquarters in 1959. In 1964, the late Pastors Charles and Ada Lochbaum were succeeded by the current Chief pastor William M. Han, Sr. In 1970, a branch of the church was initiated at Kaunakakai, Molokai, and the complex consisting of a parsonage, church office, and classrooms was dedicated in 1973. Subsequently a prayer tower some seven stories high was completed and dedicated to the Lord for daily prayer services and weekly tarrying services. In the ensuing years, branch churches have been established in Hilo, Hawaii; Koloa, Kauai; and two branches in Cotabato, Mindanao, Philippine Islands. Currently the Honolulu church is undergoing a major expansion and renovation that will include the establishment of a television studio, air conditioning, and additional parking.

In the 1960s, the church began a radio broadcast over KIKI in Honolulu. Television broadcasts began around 1980 on KIT each Sunday morning. That broadcast is currently aired on seven stations in California, Arizona, and Oregon.

Membership: In 1995 the church reported 144,000 members worldwide.

Periodicals: *Kingdom of God Crusader.*

Sources:

Kingdom of God Crusader. Honolulu: Apostolic Faith Church of Honolulu, 1969.

★598★
Apostolic Faith Mission Church of God
3344 Pearl Ave. N
Birmingham, AL 36101

Among the people who visited the early Pentecostal revival which occurred in 1906-08 in Los Angeles was Frank W. Williams (d. 1932), a black man from the deep south. He received the baptism of the Holy Spirit under the ministry of William J. Seymour and returned to Mississippi to establish an outpost of the Apostolic Faith Mission. Not having great success, he moved to Mobile, Alabama, where a revival occurred under his ministry. Among those converted was an entire congregation of the Primitive Baptist Church. The members gave him their building as the first meeting house for the new mission parish. The church was organized on July 10, 1906.

In 1915, Bishop Williams became one of the first to adopt the Oneness or non-Trinitarian theology which had been espoused through Pentecostal circles. He broke with Seymour and renamed his church the Apostolic Faith Mission Church of God. He incorporated the new church on October 9, 1915. The church continues to place a strong emphasis upon divine healing, allows women preachers, and practices footwashing with communion. Baptism is in the name of the "Lord Jesus Christ," and without the use of the name, the baptism is considered void. Intoxicants, especially tobacco, alcohol, and drugs are forbidden. Members are admonished to marry only those who have been "saved." The church is headed by the Senior Bishop and a Cabinet of Executive Officers composed of the bishops, overseers, and the general secretary.

Membership: In 1989 the church reported 18 congregations (most of which were in Alabama), 6,200 members, and 32 ministers.

★599★
Apostolic Gospel Church of Jesus Christ
Current address not obtained for this edition.

The Apostolic Gospel Church of Jesus Christ was founded in Bell Gardens, California, in 1963 by the Rev. Donald Abernathy. During the next five years, four other congregations, all in the Los Angeles area, were added and a new denomination emerged. In 1968, Abernathy reported a series of visions in which it was revealed to him that the entire West Coast of North America would be destroyed in an earthquake. He reported the vision to the other congregations, and one pastor, the Rev. Robert Theobold, reported a confirming vision. As a result, the five congregations decided to move East. Abernathy took his congregation to Atlanta. The church at Avenal went to Kennett, Missouri; the church at Porterville to Independence, Missouri; the church at Port Hueneme to Murfreesboro, Tennessee; and the Lompoc congregation to Georgia.

The church accepts "oneness" doctrines, identifying Jesus with the Father. It does not approve of the use of medicines, doctors, or hospitals—only divine healing. Footwashing is practiced. Members are pacifists. There is a strict code of dress that prohibits bathing suits, slacks, shorts, tightly fitting or straightcut skirts, dresses with hemlines shorter than halfway between the knee and ankle, jewelry, and short hair for women. Long hair, short sleeves, and tightly fitting pants are prohibited for men.

The church is ruled by bishops (or elders) and deacons, and includes in its structure apostles, prophets, evangelists, pastors, and teachers. The attempt is to build a perfect church to which Christ will return. The perfect church will manifest both the fruits and gifts of the Spirit.

Membership: There are five congregations.

★600★
Apostolic Overcoming Holy Church of God
1120 N. 24th St.
Birmingham, AL 35234

History. The Apostolic Overcoming Holy Church of God was founded by William Thomas Phillips (1893-1973), the son of a Methodist Episcopal Church minister. However, at a tentmeeting service in Birmingham, Alabama, Phillips was converted to the message of pentecost and holiness under the ministry of Frank W. Williams of the Faith Mission Church of God. Williams ordained Phillips in 1913, and three years later Phillips launched his career as an evangelist in Mobile, Alabama. In 1917, he was selected by the people who has responded to his ministry as the bishop of the Ethiopian Overcoming Holy Church of God. The new organization was incorporated in 1920. It adopted its present name in 1941 in realization that the church was for all people, not just Ethiopians, a popular designation for black people in the early twentieth century.

Beliefs. The AOH Church of God follows the Oneness theology. It believes in One God who subsists in the union of Father, Son, and Holy Spirit. The church, however, rejects any hint of tritheism and believes that the One God bears the name of Jesus, a name that can express the fullness of the Godhead. Out of this belief, the church baptizes members in the name of Jesus. Baptism is by immersion and considered necessary for salvation.

The church teaches that God acts in the believer both to baptize in the Spirit (which will be signified by speaking-in-tongues) and progressively over a lifetime to sanctify (make holy). Besides baptism, there are two other ordinances—the Lord's supper and foot washing. The church also teaches divine healing and exhorts members to tithe.

Organization. The AOH Church of God has an episcopal polity though each church manages its own affairs. Churches are grouped into districts presided over by bishops and overseers. A General Assembly, to which all churches send representatives, convenes annually. It is led by the presiding bishop. After serving the church for 57 years, Bishop Phillips was succeeded by Bishop Jasper Roby, the present senior presiding bishop. He is assisted by eight associate bishops. The church's periodicals are published by the church's publishing board. Missions are supported in Haiti and Africa.

Membership: In 1995, the church reported 12,369 members, approximately 419 churches, and 750 ministers.

Educational Facilities: Berean Christian Bible College, Birmingham, Alabama.

Periodicals: *People's Mouthpiece.* • *Young Educator.*

Sources:

Arrington, Juanita R. *A Brief History of the Apostolic Overcoming Holy Church of God, Inc. and Its Founder.* Birmingham, AL: Forniss Printing Company, 1984.

Doctrine and Discipline. Birmingham, AL: Apostolic Overcoming Holy Church of God, 1985.

★601★
Assemblies of the Lord Jesus Christ, Inc.
875 N. White Station Rd.
Memphis, TN 38122

The Assemblies of the Lord Jesus Christ was formed in 1952 by the merger of three "Jesus only" groups which had sprung up around the country—the Assemblies of the Church of Jesus Christ, the Jesus Only Apostolic Church of God, and the Church of the Lord Jesus Christ. The Assemblies closely resembles the United Pentecostal Church in doctrine. The group preaches two experiences—justification and the baptism of the Spirit, emphasizes healing, washes feet, tithes, and forbids participation in secret societies. While holding respect for the civil government, members

do not participate in war. Worldly amusements are forbidden, as are school gymnastics and clothes which immodestly expose the body.

The government is congregational in form. There is an annual general conference. A general board oversees the church during the year. The church is divided into state districts which are located in the South, Midwest, and Southwest. The Foreign Mission Committee oversees the mission program in Chile, Mexico, Australia, Nigeria, Russia and New Guinea.

Membership: In 1997 these were 50,000 members in 600 congregations served by 1,000 ministers in the United States and 300 members in 5 churches served by 8 ministers in Canada. These were an addition 10,000 members worldwide.

Periodicals: *Apostolic Witness.*

★602★
Associated Brotherhood of Christians
PO Box 3256
Hot Springs, AR 71914-3256

Described as an "association of churches and ministers working together for the up-building of the Church of the Lord Jesus Christ, and the Spread of the New Testament Gospel," the Associated Brotherhood of Christians is a "oneness" Pentecostal body. It was formed under the leadership of E. E. Partridge and H. A. Riley to facilitate fellowship among all "blood-bought" people, those who believe Christ atoned for sins through the blood he shed in the crucifixion. Formation of the Associated Brotherhood of Christians was necessary because other Pentecostal churches were refusing fellowship to the ministers who eventually formed this church. The other Pentecostal churches objected to the ministers' divergence from the churches' doctrines. The original meetings to consider forming the Associated Brotherhood of Christians were held in 1933, with the incorporation taking place during World War II. (This facilitated exemption from military duties for ministers.)

While attempting to facilitate wider fellowship, the group has a definite doctrinal perspective. The "oneness" Pentecostalism of this church is of the "two-experiences" variety, focusing on justification and the baptism of the Holy Spirit. Baptism in Jesus' name is the only ordinance; the church's statement of beliefs includes a specific article on why foot-washing is not practiced. The group accepts the so-called "Bread of life" message, or what is termed spiritual communion. The emphasis of the message is not on the literal eating of literal elements but on the proper discernment of the body of Christ in the church. The church is pacifist, and conscientious objection is recommended to members.

Polity is congregational. There is an annual conference. The association is headed by an official board of three members: a chairman, vice-chairman, and secretary-treasurer. State presbyters are appointed by the official board. Churches are located across the South and Midwest and along the Pacific Coast.

Membership: Not reported. In the early 1970s there were 40 congregations, approximately 2,000 members and 100 ministers.

Periodicals: *Our Herald.*

★603★
Bethel Ministerial Association
4350 Lincoln Ave.
Evansville, IN 47715

The Bethel Ministerial Association is a fellowship of ministers founded in 1934 by the Rev. Albert Franklin Varnell as an outgrowth of his desire to offer fellowship to ministers who held similar doctrinal views without the organizational pressures of that day on the local church. Varnell began his ministry as a tent evangelist. In 1933, the church to which he belonged decided that all members should believe that speaking in tongues was the first evidence of the reception of the Holy Spirit. Varnell opposed this teaching.

He believed that the new birth and the baptism of the Holy Spirit were the same and that the filling of the believer by the Spirit was a subsequent event which occurred when the born again believer yields to the Spirit. Varnell felt speaking-in-tongues was a supernatural manifestation of the Spirit among those who had been filled with the Spirit.

The association also teaches that God manifests in the flesh as Jesus. Jesus is the name of the One God. It denies the traditional doctrine of the Trinity (God as three persons) but affirms that the One God (Jesus) expresses Himself in the Trinity personalities of Father, Son, and Holy Spirit. It accepts the Bible as the Word of God. Water baptism is by immersion in the name of Jesus.

Organization. Bethel churches are independent and self-governing, and membership in the association is available to ministers only. The association has a publishing house in Evansville, Indiana. An aggressive missionary program supports over 50 missionaries around the world. The association also operates Circle J Ranch, a youth camp facility in southern Indiana, and the Bethel Ministerial Academy, a ministerial training program.

Membership: In 1988, the association had 120 ministers, missionaries, evangelists, and administrators as members. There are approximately 35 associated churches in the United States and more than 120 churches in other lands.

Educational Facilities: International Bible Institute, San Antonio, Texas.

Periodicals: *The Bethel Link.*

Sources:

It Does Make a Difference What You Believe! Decatur, IL: Bethel Ministerial Association, n.d.

★604★
Bible Way Church of Our Lord Jesus Christ World Wide
1130 New Jersey Ave., NW
Washington, DC 20001

The Bible Way Church of Our Lord Jesus Christ World Wide was founded in 1957 by former members of the Church of the Lord Jesus Christ of the Apostolic Faith. Prior to 1957, some leaders of the Church of Our Lord Jesus Christ of the Apostolic Faith decried what they saw as the autocratic leadership of Robert Clarence Lawson, the church's bishop. They had suggested that Lawson consider sharing the leadership and consecrate more bishops for the growing denomination. Lawson refused and thus a number of the leading ministers and their churches left to form the Bible Way Churches of Our Lord Jesus Christ. Among the leaders of the new church were Smallwood E. Williams (1907-1991), John S. Beane, McKinley Williams, Winfield S. Showell, and Joseph Moore. They were consecrated by John S. Holly, a bishop of the Pentecostal Assemblies of the World. They selected Williams, for many years the general secretary of the parent body, as their presiding bishop. The name of the church derives from the name of the congregation Williams had led in Washington, D.C., since the 1920s.

Williams has been credited with taking the lead among Apostolic Pentecostal groups in the development of a social service and social justice ministry. He led the church to become involved in Washington politics, sponsored the construction of a supermarket near his church, encouraged the development of a housing complex, and worked for more job opportunities within the African American community. His book, *Significant Sermons* (1970), was largely concerned with a Christian response to social problems. Williams also emphasized education as signaled by his opening and maintaining a Bible school adjacent to the headquarters church in Washington, D.C. In this effort he was greatly aided by Dr. James I. Clark, remembered as the denomination's great pioneer educator.

The church follows the non-Trinitarian Pentecostal doctrine of its parent body which emphasizes the sole divinity of Jesus and thus baptizes in the name of Jesus only.

Membership: In 1988 the church reported approximately 250,000 members in 250 churches.

Educational Facilities: Bible Way Training School, Washington, D.C.

Periodicals: *The Bible Way News Voice.*

Sources:

Official Directory, Rules and Regulations of the Bible Way Church of Our Lord Jesus Christ World Wide, Inc. Washington, DC: Bible Way Church of Our Lord Jesus Christ World Wide, 1973.

Richardson, James C., Jr. *With Water and Spirit: A History of Black Apostolic Denominations in the U.S.* Winston-Salem, NC: The Author, 1980.

Williams, Smallwood Edmond. *Significant Sermons.* Washington, DC: Bible Way Church Press, 1970.

___. *This Is My Story.* Washington, DC: Wm. Willoughby Publishers, 1981.

★605★
Bible Way Pentecostal Apostolic Church
Current address not obtained for this edition.

The Bible Way Pentecostal Apostolic Church was founded by Curtis P. Jones. Jones began as a pastor in North Carolina in the Church of God (Apostolic), but left that church to join the Church of Our Lord Jesus Christ of the Apostolic Faith under Robert Clarence Lawson. He became pastor of the St. Paul Apostolic Church in Henry County, Virginia. Jones left during the internal disruption within Bishop Lawson's church in 1957, but did not join with Smallwood E. Williams' Bible Way Church of Our Lord Jesus Christ. Rather, in 1960, with two other congregations in Virginia, he founded a new denomination. A fourth church was soon added.

Membership: In 1980 the church had four congregations, all in Virginia.

★606★
Church of God (Apostolic)
3683 Old Lexington Rd.
Winston-Salem, NC 27107-5262

The Church of God (Apostolic) was formed in 1877 by Elder Thomas Cox at Danville, Kentucky, as the Christian Faith Band. It was one of a number of independent holiness associations of the late nineteenth century. In 1915, it voted a name change, and in 1919 became the Church of God (Apostolic). In 1943, Cox was succeeded by M. Gravely and Eli N. Neal as co-presiding bishops. Headquarters were moved to Beckley, West Virginia. Two years later Gravely divorced his wife and remarried. He was disfellowshipped from the church. In 1964 Neal was succeeded by Love Odom who died two years later and was succeeded by David E. Smith. These two bishops did much to put the national church in a firm financial condition. They were suceeded by the present general overseer, Ruben K. Hash.

It is a strict church, opposing worldliness and practicing footwashing with the monthly Lord's Supper. Baptism by immersion is in the name of Jesus. The church is headed by a board of bishops, one of whom is designated the general overseer who serves as the church's executive head. There is a general assembly annually.

Membership: In 1980 the church had 15,000 members, 43 congregations and approximately 75 ministers.

★607★
Church of God in Christ Jesus (Apostolic)
Baltimore, MD

The Church of God in Christ Jesus (Apostolic) was founded in 1946 in Baltimore, Maryland, by Randolph A. Carr and Monroe

R. Saunders, both former ministers in the Pentecostal Assemblies of the World. The doctrine followed that of the parent body.

The church had very strict standards concerning divorce and remarriage which led to complaints by Saunders that the standards were not being uniformly enforced. The controversy led him to break with Carr and take the majority of members to found the United Church of Jesus Christ (Apostolic). Carr continued to lead the Church of God in Christ Jesus (Apostolic) until his death in 1972.

Membership: Not reported.

Sources:

DuPree, Sherry Sherrod. *African American Holiness Pentecostal Charismatic: Annotated Bibliography.* New York: Garland Publishing, 1992.

Richardson, James C., Jr. *With Water and Spirit.* Martinsville, VA: The Author, n.d.

★608★
Church of Jesus Christ (Bloomington)
Current address not obtained for this edition.

The Church of Jesus Christ (Bloomington) emerged when several churches withdrew from the Church of Jesus Christ (Kingsport) in the late 1940s. It is similar in belief and practice to its parent body. It is under the leadership of its presiding bishop, Ralph Johnson.

Membership: In the 1980s there were approximately 500 members, twelve ministers, and eight congregations.

★609★
Church of Jesus Christ (Kingsport)
5836 Orebank Rd.
Kingsport, TN 37664

The Church of Jesus Christ (Kingsport) grew out of the Pentecostal ferment in eastern Tennessee associated with the Church of God (Cleveland, Tennessee). While tracing its origin to 33 A.D. and the crucifixion and resurrection of Jesus Christ, the church appeared as a separate chartered organization in 1927 under the leadership of Bishop M. K. Lawson. Formed at Cleveland, it moved its headquarters to Kingsport, Tennessee, in 1975.

The church differs from the Church of God due to its belief in the one God, Jesus Christ, and its practice of baptizing members in "the name of Jesus Christ" (rather than the trinitarian formula, in the name of "Father, Son, and Holy Spirit"). The church is similar to the United Pentecostal Church in its doctrinal stance. It holds to the literally infallible Bible as its creed. It believes that the Bible teaches justification by faith, baptism of the Holy Spirit evidenced by speaking in tongues, and the imminent second coming of Jesus. It practices baptism by immersion, the Lord's Supper, and foot washing in connection with the Lord's Supper. Wine (rather than grape juice) is used at the Lord's Supper. The church believes in divine healing and calls members to holy living. Members refrain from the use of tobacco and alcohol and do not wear jewelry. While generally following the laws of the state, members do not bear arms or take oaths before a magistrate. They do not join secret societies.

Local churches are autonomous, but are organized in fellowship over state bishops and nationally, a presiding bishop. There is an annual state convention, and each August, a national convention. The term "reverend" is not used in connection with "ministers," who are referred to as "elders," "pastors," and "evangelists" (all biblical terms).

Membership: Not reported. In 1974 it reported 37,500 members. The church has a vigorous church education program and many more attend sunday school than appear on the church rolls. Missionary work is supported in Africa, India, Australia, Haiti, Jamaica, Israel, Mexico, Panama, England, and the Dominican Republic.

Periodicals: *The Messenger,* Dublin, Georgia.

★610★
Church of Jesus Christ Ministerial Alliance
Current address not obtained for this edition.

The Church of Jesus Christ Ministerial Alliance was formed in 1962 by members who withdrew from the Church of Jesus Christ (Kingsport) following the death of the founder and long-time leader, Bishop M. K. Lawson. There are no doctrinal differences between the two groups, their distinctions being solely administrative. In recent years there has been a friendly fellowship between the Church of Jesus Christ Ministerial Alliance and its parent body.

Membership: In 1990 there were 85 congregations, 300 ministers and 6,000 members. Missionary work is supported in Canada, Jamaica, Trinidad, the Bahamas, England, and Australia.

Periodicals: *The Church of Jesus Christ Message of Hope.*

★611★
Church of Jesus Christ of Georgia
℅ Elder Wilbur Childres
Rte. 1
Ranger, GA 30734

The Church of Jesus Christ of Georgia is a small group which, under the leadership of Elder Wilbur Childres, withdrew from the Church of Jesus Christ (Kingsport) in the early 1960s. The church is similar to the parent body and still cooperates with its foreign mission program. It differs in its strict policy regarding marriage and divorce. It demands any minister who was divorced and remarried before conversion to the church to either return to their original spouse or live alone.

Membership: Not reported. There are two congregations, both in Georgia.

★612★
Church of Our Lord Jesus Christ of the Apostolic Faith
2081 Adam Clayton Powell Blvd.
New York, NY 10027

The Church of Our Lord Jesus Christ of the Apostolic Faith was founded in New York City, in 1919 by Robert Clarence Lawson (d. 1961), who as a pastor in the Pentecostal Assemblies of the World had founded churches in Texas and Missouri. At one point in his early life when he was ill he had been taken to the Apostolic Faith Assembly Church, a leading church of the Pentecostal Assemblies, and its pastor, Garfield Thomas Haywood. Healed, Lawson joined the Assemblies and adopted their non-trinitarian theology. However, in 1919 he left Haywood's jurisdiction and, moving to New York City, founded Refuge Church of Christ, the first congregation in his new independent church. Given Lawson's effective leadership, the organization grew quickly. Other congregations were established and a radio ministry, a periodical, a day nursery, and several businesses were initiated. In 1926 he opened a bible school to train pastors.

In the 1930s, Lawson began a series of trips to the West Indies, which led to congregations being formed in Jamaica, Antigua, the Virgin Islands, and Trinidad. His lengthy tenure as bishop of the church was a time of steady growth, broken only by two schisms by Sherrod C. Johnson, (Church of the Lord Jesus Christ of the Apostolic Faith, 1930) and Smallwood E. Williams, (Bible Way Church of Our Lord Jesus Christ, 1957). Lawson was succeeded by Hubert Spencer and by the present presiding apostle, Bishop William Lee Bonner.

Doctrine is like the older Pentecostal Assemblies of the World. Footwashing is practiced and the baptism of the Holy Spirit is believed to be necessary for salvation. The church is headed by the presiding apostle, who is assisted by six regional apostles. There is an annual convocation. Affiliated churches can be found in the West Indies, Africa, England, and Germany.

Membership: In 1992, the church reported 30,000 members in 500 churches.

Educational Facilities: Church of Christ Bible Institute, New York, New York.

Periodicals: *The Contender for the Faith.* Send orders to 2081 7th Ave., New York, NY 10027.

Sources:

Anderson, Arthur M., ed. *For the Defense of the Gospel.* New York: Church of Christ Pub. Co., 1972.

★613★
Church of the Lord Jesus Christ of the Apostolic Faith (Philadelphia)
22nd & Bainbridge Sts.
Philadelphia, PA 19146

The Church of The Lord Jesus Christ of the Apostolic Faith was founded in 1933 by Bishop Sherrod C. Johnson, formerly of the Church of Our Lord Jesus Christ of the Apostolic Faith. Johnson protested what he felt were too liberal regulations espoused by Bishop Robert Clarence Lawson in regard to the appearance of female members. Lawson allowed the wearing of jewelry and make-up. Johnson insisted upon female members wearing cotton stockings, calf-length dresses, unstraightened hair and head coverings. Johnson also opposed the observance of Lent, Easter and Christmas. Upon Bishop Johnson's death in 1961, he was succeeded by S. McDowell Shelton, the "Bishop, Apostle, and Overseer of the Church." This church has been most aggressive and has approached its parent body in members hip.

The doctrine is a typical "oneness" doctrine, though the church is known for its conservatism. It does demand that baptism must be in the name of the "Lord Jesus" or "Jesus Christ," but not just "Jesus." This exacting formula is to distinguish the Lord Jesus from Bar Jesus (Acts 13:6) and Jesus Justas (Col. 4:11), two other Biblical characters. The church members also believe one must be filled with the Holy Ghost in order to have the new birth. The church's conservatism is most manifest in its rigid behavior code. Prohibited are women preachers and teachers, remarriage after divorce, dressing like the world, and wearing costly apparel.

The church is episcopal. There is a national convention annually at the national headquarters in Philadelphia. Lay people have an unusually high participation level in the national church, holding most of the top administrative positions. There is an active radio ministry, "The Whole Truth," carried on 50 stations. Missions are conducted in Liberia, West Africa, England, Honduras, Jamaica, Haiti, Bahamas, Jordan, Portugal, and the Maldives.

Membership: In 1980 there were approximately 100 congregations.

Periodicals: *The Whole Truth.*

★614★
Churches of the Lord Jesus Christ of the Apostolic Faith
Current address not obtained for this edition.

The Churches of the Lord Jesus Christ of the Apostolic Faith was founded in Hartsville, South Carolina, in 1946 by Bp. L. Hunter, who is currently the chief apostle of the group. Hunter was a minister with the Churches of the Lord Jesus Christ of the Apostolic Faith. At the direction of that church's founder, Bp. Sherrod C. Johnson, he moved to South Carolina and began preaching in Darlington County. He operated out of a tent until a congregation was assembled and a church building purchased in 1948 in Hartsville. Hunter pastored the growing church and gradually split from the Churches of the Lord Jesus Christ of the Apostolic Faith.

Hunter's ministry spread throughout the state and reached outward to New York, Virginia, the District of Columbia, Ohio, Georgia, and Florida. He began a radio show in 1956 which led to the formation of the Apostolic Faith Radio Network that supports a na-

tionwide radio ministry. Since 1980 the church has owned The White House for Senior Citizens, a home for the elderly.

Hunter followed the doctrine of the parent body. He was strongly opposed to female ministers.

Membership: Not reported.

Periodicals: *The Whole Truth Gospel Herald.*

Sources:

DuPree, Sherry Sherrod. *African American Holiness Pentecostal Charismatic: Annotated Bibliography.* New York: Garland Publishing, 1992.

★615★
Evangelical Churches of Pentecost
Current address not obtained for this edition.

The Evangelical Churches of Pentecost emerged out of the early pentecostal revivals that occurred in Saskatchewan in 1913 as the Oneness nontrinitarian perspective spread through the West. A camp meeting was founded at Trossachs. Some men converted at Trossachs became ministers and founded churches in various communities of the province. These ministers and churches were brought together in 1927 through the efforts of Rev. Alan H. Gillett (1895-1967), pastor at Radville, who secured a charter for the group as the Full Gospel Mission. Churches and ministers credentialed by the mission spread to the neighboring provinces of Alberta, Manitoba, and British Columbia.

The Full Gospel Mission evolved into a substantial body by the end of World War II, and in 1946 it incorporated as the Evangelical Churches of Pentecost. In 1953 the Evangelical Churches of Pentecost merged into the other major Oneness church in Canada, the Apostolic Church of Pentecost. At the time of the merger, some of the ministers and churches of the Evangelical Church of Pentecost declined to enter the merged body. They were concerned that some of the affiliated churches would lose their sovereignty. Also, being amillennialists, they rejected the premillennial eschatology of the Apostolic church. Amillennialism is a position that suggests that the millennium talked about in the book of Revelation is a metaphorical time period rather than an actual thousand-year period to be expected to occur in the near future. Those who stayed out of the merger reorganized and continued as the Full Gospel Ministerial Fellowship, but in the 1960s reincorporated and reassumed their earlier name.

Apart from its position on the millennium, the Evangelical Churches of Pentecost is similar to the Apostolic Church of Pentecost and the United Pentecostal Church. It believes in the One God, whose name is Jesus; baptism by immersion in the name of Our Lord Jesus Christ; the baptism of the Holy Spirit evidenced by the believer speaking in tongues; the living of a Spirit-filled life of holiness; and divine healing.

The Evangelical Churches of Pentecost is organized as a fellowship of ministers, evangelists and missionaries. Theirs is a strong belief in the autonomy of the local church and the congregations affiliated with the church are independent assemblies who happen to welcome pastors credentialed by the fellowship.

Membership: Not reported. In 1980 the churches reported approximately 50 ministers who served 19 churches in Canada and three in the United States with a combined membership of approximately 3,000. These churches support missionaries in Mexico, South India, and Upper Volta.

Sources:

Piepkorn, Arthur C. *Profiles in Belief: The Religious Bodies of the United States and Canada.* Vol. III. San Francisco, Harper & Row, 1979.

★616★
First Church of Jesus Christ
1100 E. Lincoln St.
Tullahoma, TN 37388

The First Church of Jesus Christ is a Pentecostal group chartered in Tullahoma, Tennessee, in 1965 by Bishop H. E. Honea (b. 1938), who has served as its chairman for thirty years. Honea grew up in Taft, Tennessee, and was called to ministry as a teenager. He began to preach when he was 16 years old and pastored churches in Alabama, Louisiana, Indiana, and Illinios before becoming pastor of the church in Tullahoma, Tennessee, in 1961. He remains pastor of that church.

The church is composed of those ministers, missionaries, and deacons licsensed by the church and the members of the local congregations affiliated with it. It is their belief that the Church of Jesus Christ is a company of company of baptized believers who adhere to the form of doctrine preached by Jesus and his Apostles, who have associated in the faith and fellowship of Jesus Christ, who are governed by the rules of the New Testament church, and who possess the gifts of ministry (Romans 12:6–8). The church continues the revival begun on the Day of Pentecost, 33 A.D. (Acts 2). The Church of Jesus Christ is the name of God's church and the incorporation and charter make no provision for ever changing its name.

The church affirms the One True God. Jesus Christ is the name of the One True God. He reveals himself as the Father, the Son, and the Holy Ghost. The Holy Ghost is not considered the third person of the Godhead, but rather the manifestation of the Spirit of God (the creator) coming to dwell in the hearts and lives of men. This position is generally termed "oneness" or "Jesus only." The church practices the ordinances of the Lord's supper, foot washing, tithing, and baptism in the name of Jesus Christ. The church does not allow membership in secret societies and specifically decries the teachings of snake handling, the seed in the serpent doctrine, the spiritualizing of the ordinances of baptism and the Lord's supper, the denial of a denial of a physical resurrection, and the denial of marriage. This doctrine is similar to that of other Apostolic pentecostal churches, such as the Church of Jesus Christ (Kingsport).

The First Church of Jesus Christ is headed by the Chairman, assisted by the Vice-Chairman, Assistant Vice-Chairman, and the state bishops. Together they constitute the board of bishops. The board of bishops holds the property of the church in trust. Missionary work is carried out in Jamaica, Haiti, and the Philippines.

Membership: In 1997 the church reported 7,000 members and 175 ministers in the United States and an additional 8,000 members and 175 ministers on the mission field.

Periodicals: *Banner of Love.*

Sources:

Articles of Faith and By-laws of the First Church of Jesus Christ, Inc. Tullahoma, TN: First Church of Jesus Christ, n.d.

★617★
Free Gospel Church of the Apostle's Doctrine
Current address not obtained for this edition.

The Free Gospel Church of the Apostle's Doctrine (also known as the Free Gospel Church of Christ and Defense of the Gospel Ministries) was founded in 1964 in Washington, D. C., by Bp. Ralph E. Green, formerly of the Way of the Cross Church of Christ. The church is similar in doctrine and practice to its parent body. The church is built around a large, 2,500-member congregation in Washington which Green pastors. He has developed an aggressive outreach ministry which includes a prison visitation program, a publishing concern, and a popular radio ministry. The prison ministry publishes a periodical, *From Prison to Praise*, and a variety of tract literature. Green has recorded over 1,000 sermons, and

the church choir has made several records. The church has a retreat center in King George, Virginia.

Membership: Not reported. In 1990 there were five congregations, including one in Jamaica.

Periodicals: *Defense of the Gospel Newsletter.*

Sources:

Payne, Wardell J., ed. *Directory of African American Religious Bodies: A Compendium by the Howard University School of Divinity.* Washington, DC: Howard University Press, 1991.

★618★
Glorious Church of God in Christ Apostolic Faith
Current address not obtained for this edition.

The Glorious Church of God in Christ Apostolic Faith was founded in 1921 by C. H. Stokes, its first presiding bishop. He was succeeded in 1928 by S. C. Bass who was to head the church for over a quarter of a century. However, in 1952, after the death of his first wife, Bass remarried a woman who was a divorcee. It had been taught for many years that marrying a divorced person was wrong. Bass' actions split the fifty-congregation church in half. Those who remained loyal to Bishop Bass retained the name, but the founding charter was retained by the other group, which took the name Original Glorious Church of God in Christ Apostolic Faith.

★619★
God's House of Prayer for All Nations
Current address not obtained for this edition.

God's House of Prayer for All Nations, Inc., was founded in 1964 in Peoria, Illinois, by Bishop Tommie Lawrence, formerly of the Church of God in Christ. The doctrine is "oneness" Pentecostal, identifying Jesus with the Father, and the polity is strongly episcopal. Great stress is placed on healing as one of the signs of the spirit and there is much fellowship with the churches of the Miracle Revival Fellowship founded by the late A. A. Allen.

Membership: Not reported. There are several congregations, all in northern Illinois.

★620★
Highway Christian Church of Christ
436 W St. NW
Washington, DC 20001

The Highway Christian Church of Christ was founded in Washington, D.C. in 1929 by James Thomas Morris, (1892–1959), formerly a minister with the Pentecostal Assemblies of the World. Morris had been raised a Methodist and was called to the ministry in 1918. He received the Pentecostal gift of the Holy Spirit in 1923 under the ministrations of Bp. Samuel Kelsey, a leader in the Church of God in Christ. He was later baptized in the name of Jesus Christ and affiliated as a minster with the PAW. After the founding of the Highway Church, he remained on cordial terms with his PAW colleagues. After a decade of service to his church, during which time it moved out of a tent and store into its own building, PAW Bp. J. M. Turpin consecrated Morris to the bishopic. Following Morris' death, he was succeeded by his nephew, J. V. Lomax, formerly a minister of the Church of Our Lord Jesus Christ of the Apostolic Faith under Bp. Robert Clarence Lawson. Lomax is assisted by Vice Presiding Bp. Samuel Redden, who currently resides in Newport News, Virginia.

The church is among the most conservative of Pentecostal bodies. Members are encouraged to dress modestly as becoming the holy life and to be baptized in Jesus' name and filled with the Holy Spirit as in Acts 2:38. The church will install women as Deaconesses and will accept ordained women from othe denominations, but will neither ordain nor install women as pastors.

Membership: In 1997 there were 13 congregations and about 3,000 members.

★621★
Holy Temple Church of the Lord Jesus Christ of the Apostolic Faith
2075 Clinton Ave.
Bronx, NY 10457

The Holy Temple Church of the Lord Jesus Christ of the Apostolic Faith was founded in 1947 in the Bronx, New York, by Randolph Goodwin. Who originally was a minister of the Church of the Lord Jesus Christ of the Apostolic Faith. Goodwin had been a barber and founded his church in the building behind his shop. By 1965 the congregation had grown to the point that it was able to move into a new building. The congregation drew members from across the New York City metropolitan area and northern New Jersey.

Bishop Goodwin now oversees a large congregation and a radio ministry. There is only one congregation in the United States, but a mission has been launched in Jamaica where several congregations have been formed.

Membership: Not reported. There is one congregation in the Bronx.

Periodicals: *The Holy Temple Bible Truth: A Magazine of Understanding.*

Sources:

DuPree, Sherry Sherrod. *African American Holiness Pentecostal Charismatic: Annotated Bibliography.* New York: Garland Publishing, 1992.

★622★
International Ministerial Association
9455 Lackland Rd.
St. Louis, MO 63114

The International Ministerial Association, Inc. was formed in 1954 by W. E. Kidson and twenty other pastors formerly with the United Pentecostal Church. It practices baptism by immersion and foot-washing. Tithing is believed to be the financial plan of the church. A strong belief in the Second Coming is taught, and the group believes in a distinct judgment where believers only will be rewarded.

An annual international conference is the place for fellowship of the ministers, who hold credentials through the Association and the members of the autonomous congregations which accept the statement of faith. Herald Publishing House is located in Houston, Texas.

Membership: Not reported. In the early 1970s, there were 440 ministerial members and 117 affiliated congregations.

Periodicals: *The Herald of Truth.*

★623★
Mount Hebron Apostolic Temple of Our Lord Jesus of the Apostolic Faith
Mt. Hebron Apostolic Temple
27 Vineyard Ave.
Yonkers, NY 10703

The Mount Hebron Apostolic Temple of Our Lord Jesus of the Apostolic Faith was founded in 1963 by George H. Wiley III, pastor of the Yonkers, New York, congregation of the Apostolic Church of Christ in God. As his work progressed, Wiley came to feel that because of his accomplishments for the denomination he should be accorded the office of bishop. He had had particular success in the area of youth work, and his wife, Sister Lucille Wiley, served as president of the Department of Youth Work. However, the board of the Apostolic Church denied his request to become a bishop. He left with his supporters and became bishop of a new Apostolic denomination.

Wiley has placed great emphasis upon youth work and upon radio work, establishing an outreach in New York, one in North Carolina, and another in South Carolina. The temple continues the doctrine and polity of the Apostolic Church of Christ in God and has a cordial relationship with its parent organization.

Membership: In 1980 the temple reported 3,000 members in nine congregations being served by 15 ministers. There are two bishops.

★624★
New Bethel Church of God in Christ (Pentecostal)
Current address not obtained for this edition.

In 1927, the Rev. A. D. Bradley was admonished by the board of bishops of the Church of God in Christ to refrain from preaching the "Jesus only" doctrine. (The Church of God in Christ was the oldest and among the largest of the predominantly-black trinitarian Pentecostal churches.) He refused, and with his wife and Lonnie Bates established the New Bethel Church of God in Christ (Pentecostal). Bradley became the church's presiding bishop. Doctrine is similar to other "Jesus only" groups. The three ordinances of baptism, the Lord's Supper, and foot-washing are observed. The group is pacifist but allows alternative noncombatant positions to be held by law-abiding church members. The group disapproves of secret societies and of school activities which conflict with a student's moral scruples.

The presiding bishop is the executive officer and presides over all meetings of the general body. A board of bishops acts as a judicatory body and a general assembly as the legislative body.

Membership: Not reported.

★625★
Original Glorious Church of God in Christ Apostolic Faith
995 Foster Ave.
Elyria, OH 44035

The Glorious Church of God was founded in 1921. However, in 1952 its presiding bishop, S. C. Bass married a divorced woman. Approximately half of the fifty-congregation church rejected Bass and reorganized under the leadership of W. O. Howard and took the name Original Glorious Church of God in Christ Apostolic Faith. The term "Original" signified their claim to the history of the church, demonstrated by their retention of the founding charter. Howard was succeeded by Bishop I. W. Hamiter, under whose leadership the church has grown spectacularly and developed a mission program in Haiti, Jamaica and India. Hamiter has also led in the purchase of a convention center for the church's annual meeting in Columbus, Ohio.

Membership: In 1980 the church had 55 congregations in the United States, 110 congregations overseas, 200 ministers and approximately 25,000 members worldwide.

★626★
Pentecostal Assemblies of the World
% Paul A. Bowers, Bishop
1150 W. Galbraith Rd.
Cincinnati, OH 45231

Oldest of the Apostolic or "Jesus Only" Pentecostal churches, the Pentecostal Assemblies of the World began as a loosely-organized fellowship of trinitarian pentecostals in Los Angeles in 1906. J. J. Frazee (occasionally incorrectly reported as "Frazier") was elected the first general superintendent. Early membership developed along the West Coast and in the Midwest. From 1913 to 1916, the annual convention was held in Indianapolis, soon to become the center of the organization. Growth in the organization was spurred when it became the first group of pentecostals to accept the "Jesus Only" Apostolic theology, which identified Jesus as the Jehovah of the Old Testament and denied the Trinity. Many ministers from other pentecostal bodies joined the assemblies when the group within which they held credentials rejected Apostolic teachings. In 1918, the General Assemblies of the Apostolic Assemblies, a recently formed Apostolic body, which included such outstanding early movement leaders as D. C. O. Opperman and H. A. Goss, merged into the PAW.

From its beginning the Pentecostal Assemblies of the World was fully integrated racially, though predominantly white in membership. In 1919, following the influx of so many ministers and members, especially the large newly-merged body, the Pentecostal Assemblies reorganized. Four of its 21 field superintendents were black, among whom were Garfield Thomas Haywood (1880-1931), who would later become presiding bishop. In 1924, most of the white members withdrew to form the Pentecostal Ministerial Alliance, now an integral part of the United Pentecostal Church. The remaining members, not totally, but predominantly black, reorganized again, created the office of bishop, and elected Haywood to lead them. He remained presiding bishop until his death in 1931.

Shortly after Haywood's death, the Apostolic Churches of Jesus Christ, a name briefly assumed by the former Pentecostal Ministerial Alliance that was then in a phase of consolidating various Apostolic groups into a single organization, invited the Assemblies to consider merger. The merger attempt failed, but the assemblies again lost individual congregations and members to the Apostolic Churches of Jesus Christ, and a large group who formed a new church, the Pentecostal Assemblies of Jesus Christ, as a prelude to the merger which failed. In the face of the new losses, a third reorganization had to occur in 1932. For several years, the church was led by a small group of bishops, enlarged to seven in 1935. Two years later, Samuel Grimes, a former missionary in Liberia, was elected presiding bishop, a post he retained until his death in 1967. Under his guidance, the Pentecostal Assemblies Church experienced its greatest era of expansion. Contrary to most black Pentecostal bishops, Grimes did not also serve a parish, hence he was able to devote himself full-time to his episcopal duties.

Doctrine of the Assemblies is similar to that of the Assemblies of God except that it does not believe in the Trinity. Holiness is stressed and the group believes that for ultimate salvation, it is necessary to have a life wholly sanctified. Wine is used in the Lord's Supper. Healing is stressed and foot-washing practiced. Members are pacifists, though they feel it is a duty to honor rules. There is a strict dress and behavior code. Divorce and remarriage are allowed under certain circumstances.

There is an annual general assembly which elects the bishops and the general secretary. It also designates the presiding bishop, who heads a board of bishops. The church is divided into 30 districts (dioceses) headed by a bishop. The assemblies are designated joint members of each local board of trustees. A missionary board oversees missions in Nigeria, Jamaica, England, Ghana, and Egypt.

Membership: In 1994 the Assemblies had reported 1,000,000 members/constituents in 1,760 churches served by 4,262 ministers, divided into 43 districts, each headed by a bishop. There are approximately 1,000 churches in the foreign missionary field.

Educational Facilities: Aenon Bible School, Indianapolis, Indiana.

Periodicals: *Christian Outlook.*

Sources:

Dugas, Paul P., comp. *The Life and Writings of Elder G. T. Haywood.* Portland, OR: Apostolic Book Publishers, 1968.

Golder, Morris E. *History of the Pentecostal Assemblies of the World.* Indianapolis: The Author, 1973.

___. *The Life and Works of Bishop Garfield Thomas Haywood.* Indianapolis: The Author, 1977.

Tyson, James L. *Before I Sleep.* Indianapolis: Pentecostal Publications, 1976.

★627★
Pentecostal Church of God
9244 Delmar
Detroit, MI 48211

The Pentecostal Church of God (not to be confused with the Pentecostal Church of God of America headquartered at Joplin, Missouri) is a predominantly black Pentecostal body founded by Apostle Willie James Peterson (1921-1969). Peterson grew up in Florida, and though his family attended the Baptist church there, he was never baptized. The course of his life was interrupted in his early adult years by a dream in which he was in the presence of God and His angels. Peterson began a period of prayer, after which God called him to preach. He became an independent evangelist and had come to believe in the Apostolic or non-Trinitarian position. He began to preach that doctrine in 1955 in Meridian, Mississippi, and to raise up congregations across the South. At the time of his death, Peterson was succeeded by the four bishops of the church, William Duren, J. J. Sears, C. L. Rawls, and E. Rice.

It is the belief of the Pentecostal Church of God that Peterson was an apostle, annointed by God for his task through revelation. The essence of the revelation was an understanding of the Kingdom of God. Peterson taught that conversion meant turning away from worldliness (the kingdom of this world ruled by Satan) to godliness (the kingdom of Heaven). Peterson identified the Roman Catholic Church with Babylon, the Mother of Harlots, spoken of in Revelation 17:3-5. Satanic doctrine was taught in that church and in its daughter churches, Protestantism. To accept the gospel of the kingdom is to turn from the false teachings of the Babylonish churches to God's truths which include repentance as godly sorrow for one's sins; baptism by immersion in the name of Jesus Christ; a rejection of the unbiblical doctrine of the Trinity; an understanding of heaven as the realm of God and his angels and hell as a place of confinement; the nonobservance of holidays such as Christmas, Easter, and New Year's Day; nonparticipation in human government (which includes pacifism, not saluting the flag, and not voting); and holy matrimony performed by a holy minister.

Membership: Not reported.

Sources:

Faison, Jennell Peterson. *The Apostle W. J. Peterson.* Detroit, MI: Pentecostal Church of God, 1980.

★628★
Pentecostal Churches of Apostolic Faith
14 S. Ashland
Chicago, IL 60607

The Pentecostal Churches of Apostolic Faith was formed in 1957 by former members of the Pentecostal Assemblies of the World under the leadership of Bishop Samuel N. Hancock. Hancock was one of the original men selected as a bishop of the Assemblies following its reorganization in 1925. In 1931 he was one of the leaders in the attempt to unite the Assemblies with the predominantly white Pentecostal Ministerial Alliance, and he helped form the Pentecostal Assemblies of Jesus Christ, a body whose polity was more acceptable to the Alliance. Within a few years, Hancock returned to the Assemblies as an elder and was elected as a bishop for the second time.

However, soon after Hancock's return, it was discovered that he had deviated on traditional Apostolic doctrine in that he taught that Jesus was only the son of God, not that he was God. His position forced the Assemblies to issue a clarifying statement of its position, but Hancock's teachings were tolerated. Hancock also felt that he should have become the presiding bishop. Disappointment at not being elected seems to have fueled the discontent felt throughout the 1950s. Hancock carried two other bishops into the new church formed in 1957, including Willie Lee, pastor of Christ

Temple Church, the congregation pastored by Garfield Thomas Haywood, the first presiding bishop of the Assemblies. Lee succeeded Hancock as presiding bishop of the Churches upon the latter's death in 1963. The following year, a major schism occurred when the majority of the Churches rejected the doctrinal position held by Hancock and also taught by Lee. Elzie Young had the charter and claimed the support of the Churches to become the new presiding bishop. The church returned to the traditional Apostolic theology.

The Pentecostal Churches of the Apostolic Faith are congregational in polity, and headed by a presiding bishop (Elzie Young) and a council of bishops. Under Young's leadership, the Churches have grown and stablized their original shaky financial condition. A mission program developed, and the Churches support missionaries in Haiti and Liberia, where they have built a school.

Membership: In 1980 the Churches had approximately 25,000 members, 115 churches and 380 ministers.

★629★
Primitive Church of Jesus Christ
% Bethel Church of Jesus Christ
Hwy. 19 N.
Inglis, FL 34449

The Primitive Church of Jesus Christ resulted from a split in the Church of Jesus Christ (Kingsport). The occasion of the split was the decision by the Church to move the location of the Mid-Season Convention from Inglis, Florida, to Homosassa, Florida, a move opposed by many of the Florida members. The church shares doctrine and practice with its parent body, the split being purely administrative. The church holds an annual Bible conference each June. It is headed by Elder John Wilson.

Membership: Not reported.

★630★
Pure Holiness Church of God
St. Timothy's Pure Holiness Church
408 McDonough Blvd., SE
Atlanta, GA 30315

Rev. John Isaac Woodly was an early and outstanding leader of the Church of God in Christ (COGIC). Through the 1920s he had become the general evangelist for the states of Alabama, Georgia, and Florida. During these years, the non-Trinitarian beliefs of the Apostolic Pentecostal movement spread through the South, and Woodly and a number of the COGIC leaders associated with him accepted the new perspective in 1927. As a result, Woodly, Mother Lilla Pittman, Mother Mary Rowe, Elder Ed Lee Blackwell, and an Elder Brysen left to found the Pure Holiness Church of God with headquarters in Anniston, Alabama.

In addition to the acceptance of the Apostolic position on the Godhead, the group differed on several other concerns with COGIC. Most importantly, they ordained women, a practice opposed by COGIC founder Charles H. Mason. Pittman and Rowe became prominent ministers in the church. They also structured the church under the leadership of an unmarried presiding bishop and unsalaried pastors. Woodly led the church for the first five years during which time it spread to Florida. He was succeeded by Bishop John Grayhouse who led the church through the difficult years of recovery from the Depression, but then left to the church to return to COGIC. He was succeeded by Bishop Charles White who saw the church spread throughout the South.

Following White's death in 1947, Bishop Ed Lee Blackwell, one of the founders, became the presiding bishop. During his term, women's work expanded. The Women's Missionary Society was founded and Mother Luzole Tigner was selected as its first president. Mother Jessie Simms was appointed as the church's hymnal chairman and she authored 54 hymns which constitutes the church's unique music. Blackwell also moved to develop a more democratic structure and for the first time ministers were permitted to vote in the church's convocations. He also supported the removal of the rule that presiding bishops must be unmarried.

In 1958 Charles Frederick Fears, the church's Sunday school director, succeeded Blackwell as presiding bishop. During his term he promoted the system by which pastors became salaried. He was succeeded by Bennie G. Isem. During his term, in 1964 the church founded both the Pure Holiness School of Theology and a denominational periodical, *The Triumph of Truth Newsletter*, under the editorship of Sister Wilma Ringer. In 1978 Isem, a widower, married Ringer. He resigned in 1984 and was succeeded by Bishop Edward Ackley.

Membership: In 1990 the Pure Holiness Church of God reported 24 churches in the United States and four congregations in Jamaica.

Educational Facilities: Pure Holiness School of Theology.

Periodicals: *The Triumph of Truth Newsletter*.

★631★
Redeemed Assembly of Jesus Christ, Apostolic
% Bishop James F. Harris
7556 Hudgins Rd.
Richmond, VA 23228

The Redeemed Assembly of Jesus Christ, Apostolic was formed by James Frank Harris and Douglas Williams, two bishops of the Highway Christian Church who rejected the leadership of that church by Bishop J. V. Lomax. They complained of his control, by-passing other bishops and pastors and making decisons in conference with the elders of the congregation he headed in Washington, D.C. The new church is headed by a presiding bishop, assistant presiding bishop, and an executive council consisting of the bishops and all the pastors. There was no doctrinal conflict in the split.

Membership: In 1980 the church had six congregations, one in Richmond, Virginia, one in New York City, and four in the Washington, D.C., area.

★632★
Shiloh Apostolic Temple
1516 W. Master
Philadelphia, PA 19121

The Shiloh Apostolic Temple was founded in 1953 by Elder Robert O. Doub, Jr., of the Apostolic Church of Christ in God. In 1948 Doub had moved to Philadelphia to organize a new congregation for the Apostolic Church of Christ in God. He not only succeeded in building a stable congregation, Shiloh Apostolic Temple, but assisted other congregations throughout the state to organize. In light of his accomplishments, Doub felt that he should be made a bishop and so petitioned the church. He believed that the state overseer was taking all the credit Doub himself deserved. Doub's petition was denied. He left with but a single congregation in 1953 and incorporated separately in 1954.

The energetic work that characterized Doub's years in the Apostolic Church of Christ in God led Shiloh Apostolic Temple to outgrow its parent body. Doub began a periodical and purchased a camp, Shiloh Promised Land Camp, in Montrose, Pennsylvania. He also took over foreign work in England and Trinidad. The doctrine, not at issue in the schism, remains that of the parent Church of God (Apostolic) from which the Apostolic Church of Christ in God came.

Membership: In 1980 the church had 4,500 members of which 500 were in the congregation in Philadelphia. The church reported 23 congregations, of which 8 were in England and 2 in Trinidad.

Periodicals: *Shiloh Gospel Wave*. Send orders to 1516 W. Master, Philadelphia, PA 19121.

★633★
True Jesus Church
11236 Dale St.
Garden Grove, CA 92841

The True Jesus Church was established in 1917 in Beijing, China, after three of the early workers, Paul Wei, Ling-Shen Chang, and Barnabas Chang, once affiliated with other denominations, had received the Holy Spirit and the revelation of the perfect Truth concerning salvation. The True Jesus Church spread through missionaries who were commissioned and by gospel newsletters published and distributed to various provinces throughout China. The church spread to Taiwan and through Southeast Asia in 1926 and 1927 respectively, and in 1926, the headquarters of the church was established in Nanjing, China, and relocated to Shanghai the following year. The first workers reached the United States— Hawaii— in 1930.

Like other churches, the True Jesus Church suffered following the Communist takeover of China in 1949, but survived and prospered after moving its headquarters to Taiwan. The growth led to the formation of the International Assembly of the True Jesus Church by delegates at the World Conference in Taiwan in 1975. In 1985, the principal office of the international assembly was relocated from Taiwan to Los Angeles, California. Subsequently, under the jurisdiction of the international assembly, four evangelical centers were established: the America Evangelical Center (AEC), the Europe Evangelical Center (EEC), the North-East Asia Evangelical Center (NEAEC), and the South-East Asia Evangelical Center (SEAEC).

The True Jesus Church considers itself the restored Apostolic Church of the End Time. The church has received what it believes to be the divine revelation of the Truth through the Holy Spirit, which has been confirmed through signs and miracles. Its name, "True Jesus Church" also has a spiritual significance. The word "True" denotes that God is true (John 3:33, 17:3; 1 Thessalonians 1:9) and that Jesus referred to Himself as the Truth (John 14:6), or the true Vine (John 15:1), just as He was regarded as the true Light (John 1:9).

Since church founders believed that God called and established the church (Acts 15:14-18), they also believed that the church bears His name. The Holy Bible indicates that God's name was Jesus (Matthew 1:21; John 17:11, 26). The church exalts the name of God (Jesus). The church is the body of Christ, and the church rightly has "Jesus" as her name.

Doctrinally, the church is aligned with that of the non-trinitarian Apostolic or "Jesus Only" movement which practices baptism in "Jesus' Name." Baptism is by full immersion in living water, but unlike most pentecostal churches, infants are baptized. The church practices foot washing (as a third sacrament beside baptism and the Lord's Supper) and worships on the Sabbath.

It is believed that the reception of the Holy Spirit is necessary for entering the kingdom of God, and that speaking in tongues is the sign of that reception.

Membership: As of 1997 the church reported approximately 79,000 members in the free world, found in some 20 different countries on five major continents. In 1995, reliable sources indicated that the membership in the People's Republic of China had grown to approximately 1,000,000 members.

Sources:

The Five Biblical Doctrines. Garden Grove, CA: Words of Life Publishing House, 1995. 27 pp.

Return to the True Church. Garden Grove, CA: Words of Life Publishing House, 1995. 30 pp.

Speaking in Tongues: A Biblical Perspective. Garden Grove, CA: Words of Life Publishing House, 1996. 33 pp.

★634★
True Vine Pentecostal Churches of Jesus
Current address not obtained for this edition.

Dr. Robert L. Hairston had been a pastor in several trinitarian Pentecostal groups and had been a co-founder with William Monroe Johnson of the True Vine Pentecostal Holiness Church. However, in 1961 Hairston accepted the Apostolic "Jesus Only" teachings. He left the church he had founded and formed the True Vine Penetcostal Churches of Jesus. Also causal factors in the formation of the new denomination were differences between Hairston and Johnson over church polity and Hairston's marital situation. Hairston rejected the idea of local congregations being assessed to pay for the annual convocation of the church. Also, he had divorced his first wife and remarried, an action frowned upon in many Pentecostal circles.

The Church follows standard Apostolic teachings. Women are welcome in the ministry. Growth of the group was spurred in 1976 by the addition of several congregations headed by Bishop Thomas C. Williams.

Membership: In 1980 the church reported 10 churches and missions, two bishops, 14 ministers and approximately 900 members.

★635★
United Church of Jesus Christ
Current address not obtained for this edition.

The United Church of Jesus Christ withdrew from the Church of Jesus Christ (Kingsport) in 1948. The occasion for the split was a controversy over baptism. The United Church believes that not only should baptism be in the name of Jesus Christ, but that the words should be said over the candidate while the person is under the water. In referring to ministers, the word "bishop" is not used, but the term "reverend" is employed. Also, the church mixes water and wine (not grape juice) in the Lord's Supper. Otherwise, the church follows the belief and practice of the parent body. The church is under the leadership of a chairman, currently W. C. Gibson, elected at their annual convention.

Membership: Not reported. In the 1980s there were approximately 1,250 members, 100 ministers, and 25 congregations. There is no foreign mission work.

★636★
United Church of Jesus Christ Apostolic
2226 Park Ave.
Baltimore, MD 21217

The United Church of Jesus Christ Apostolic was founded in 1963 by Bishop James B. Thornton, formerly a minister of the Church of Our Lord Jesus Christ of the Apostolic Faith. During the early 1960s the Church of Our Lord Jesus Christ went through a significant period of turmoil due to the death of its founder and long-time leader Robert Clarence Lawson. Lawson was succeeded in Hubert Spencer who served during a two-years transition period prior to the election of William Lee Bonner. Bishop Thornton rejected the post-Lawson leadership.

The church follows the non-Trinitarian Jesus Only perspective of the parent body, as there was no doctrinal conflict involved in the break. It teaches the concept of the One God whose name is Jesus and baptizes members in the name of Jesus only rather than with the traditional baptismal formula of Father, Son, and Holy Ghost.

Membership: In 1990 there were five congregations and approximately 1,000 members.

Sources:

Payne, Wardell J., ed. *Directory of African American Religious Bodies: A Compendium by the Howard University School of Divinity.* Washington, DC: Howard University Press, 1991.

★637★
United Church of Jesus Christ (Apostolic)
% Bishop J. R. Ziglar
606 2nd St.
Martinsville, VA 24112

The United Church of Jesus Christ (Apostolic) traces its history to 1945 when Randolph A. Carr an Overseer in the Church of God in Christ, withdrew because of doctrinal differences, and formed the Church of God in Christ (Apostolic). Carr had come to believe in the Apostolic doctrine concerning the Oneness of the Godhead (as opposed to the Church of God in Christ's adherence to the doctrine of the Trinity).

In 1965, Monroe R. Saunders, Sr., then the General Secretary and a member of the Board of Bishops of the church, expressed serious difficulties with some contradictions between belief and action by the church's leadership, specifically as related to the teaching on marriage and divorce and the actions of Bishop Carr. His actions had become a matter of concern throughout the church. Carr forced Saunders out of the church. Many of the members and leaders left with Saunders and joined him in the formation of the United Church of Jesus Christ (Apostolic).

Saunders carefully and prayerfully put together a Book of Church Order and Disciple to guide the administration of the church. The church is operated by a board of bishops, one of which is the presiding bishop or president, and one the vice-bishop or vice-president. The Church observes the ordinances of baptism, holy communion, and foot washing.

Saunders has served as president since the church's founding in 1965. One of the more educated leaders in the Apostolic Movement, Saunders completed his post-graduate studies and has led in the cause of an educated ministry. He formed the Center for a More Abundant Life, which serves as an umbrella for a variety of social and educational services, such as the Center for Creative Learning, an early childhood educational facility; the Monroe R. Saunders School for elementary school children; and two high rise houses for the elderly and handicapped.

Membership: The church reports 80 congregations, 100,000 members, and 150 ministers in the United States and Canada, and it has missions in England, Africa, and the West Indies.

Educational Facilities: Institute of Biblical Studies, Baltimore, Maryland.

Sources:

Saunders, Monroe R., Sr. *The Book of Church Order and Discipline of the United Church of Jesus Christ (Apostolic).* Washington, DC, 1965.

★638★
United Churches of Jesus, Apostolic
Current address not obtained for this edition.

The United Churches of Jesus, Apostolic was formed by several bishops of the Apostolic Church of Christ in God who rejected the leadership of presiding bishop J. C. Richardson, Sr. Richardson had married a divorced woman. The church is headed by a general bishop, J. W. Audrey (one of the founders of the Apostle Church) and a board of bishops. Doctrine is like the parent body.

Membership: In 1980 the United Churches had 2,000 members, 20 churches, 30 ministers and six bishops.

★639★
United Pentecostal Church International
8855 Dunn Rd.
Hazelwood, MO 63042

History. The United Pentecostal Church International was formed in 1945 by a merger of the Pentecostal Church, Inc. and the Pentecostal Assemblies of Jesus Christ. Both organizations dated to a 1924 schism of the Pentecostal Assemblies of the World. During the early 1920s, ministers within the Assemblies had become convinced that, due in part to various laws in the South about the mixing of blacks and whites, its interracial make-up was hindering its functions. Members who left eventually formed three separate organizations.

Members who left the Pentecostal Assemblies of the World met in a separate hall before leaving the 1924 Chicago, Illinois, conference at which the split occurred to lay plans for a new organization. That organization was chartered the next year as the Pentecostal Ministerial Alliance. It continued to function under that name until 1932, when it became the Pentecostal Church, Inc.

Some who had participated in the formation of the Pentecostal Ministerial Alliance were upset over the final organization as it provided only for the ministers and not for the members of the congregations. Meeting in Texas in October 1925, they formed Emmanuel's Church in Jesus Christ. A third group gathered in St. Louis and formed the Pentecostal Churches of Jesus Christ. In 1927, these two groups merged to become the Pentecostal Church of Jesus Christ.

In 1931, the Pentecostal Church of Jesus Christ voted to merge with the Pentecostal Assemblies of the World, the body from which it had orginally derived. The newly merged interracial body was called the Pentecostal Assemblies of Jesus Christ. However, as the decade proceeded, racial tensions again arose. For example, many Southerners (who constituted a significant part of the group) were concerned that the church's conferences could never be in the South because of racial laws. Beginning around 1936, black ministers and predominantly black congregations began to resign and return to the Pentecostal Assemblies of the World, eventually leaving the Pentecostal Assemblies of Jesus Christ an all-white body. As such it entered the 1945 merger.

The distinctive doctrines of water baptism in the name of Jesus Christ and the oneness of God were taught in 1913-14 by early Pentecostal leaders such as Frank J. Ewart, Robert McAleister, Glenn A. Cook, and Garfield Thomas Haywood. Many of these men became members of the Assemblies of God but left that organization in 1916 when differences arose over these doctrines.

Beliefs. According to the statement of faith issued by the church, its basic and fundamental doctrine is "repentance, baptism in water by immersion in the name of the Lord Jesus Christ for the remission of sins, and the baptism of the Holy Ghost with the initial sign of speaking with other tongues as the Spirit gives utterance." The statement also affirms belief in the one true God who manifested Himself in the flesh as Jesus Christ and who also manifests Himself as the Holy Spirit. The church practices footwashing and healing and follows a holiness code which includes disapproval of secret societies, mixed bathing, women cutting their hair, worldly amusements, home television sets, and immodest dress. While strongly affirming loyalty to the government, the church is against bearing arms or taking human life.

Organization. Government of the church is basically congregational with presbyterial elements. A general conference meets annually. A general superintendent, two assistants, and a secretary-treasurer are members of a general board consisting of district superintendents, executive presbyters, and division heads. A foreign missions division oversees missions around the world in about 125 countries. Under the name Word Aflame Press, the Pentecostal Publishing House in Hazelwood, Missouri, publishes books, Sunday school material, and a wide variety of religious literature. The church is divided into 50 districts that include churches in every state and all Canadian provinces and territories. The church supports nine Bible colleges, the Tupelo, Mississippi, Children's Mansion, the Lighthouse Ranch for Boys, the Spirit of Freedom Ministries, and Compassion Services.

Membership: In 1991 the church reported 500,000 constituents and 3,635 churches in the United States and Canada served by 7,581 ministers. There were 1.5 million constituents worldwide.

Educational Facilities: Apostolic Bible Institute, St. Paul, Minnesota.

Apostolic Missionary Institute, Oshawa, Ontario, Canada.

Christian Life College, Stockton, California.

Gateway College of Evangelism, Florissant, Missouri.

Indiana Bible College, Indianapolis, Indiana.

Jackson College of Ministries, Jackson, Mississippi.

Kent Christian College, Dover, Delaware.

Texas Bible College, Houston, Texas.

United Pentecostal Bible Institute, Fredericton, New Brunswick, Canada.

Periodicals: *The Pentecostal Herald.* • *The Global Witness.*

Sources:

Clanton, Arthur L. *United We Stand.* Hazelwood, MO: Pentecostal Publishing House, 1970.

Foster, Fred J. *Their Story: 20th Century Pentecostals.* Hazelwood, MO: World Aflame Press, 1981.

Urshan, Andrew D. *My Study of Modern Pentecostals.* Portland, OR: Apostolic Book Publishers, 1981.

★640★
United Way of the Cross Churches of Christ of the Apostolic Faith
Current address not obtained for this edition.

The United Way of the Cross Churches of Christ of the Apostolic Faith was founded by Bishop Joseph Adams of the Way of the Cross Church of Christ and Elder Harrison J. Twyman of the Bible Way Church of Our Lord Jesus Christ World Wide. The new church was formed when the two founders, both pastors of congregations in North Carolina, discovered that God had given each a similar vision to form a new church. Also, Adams, a bishop in North Carolina for the Way of the Cross Church of Christ, had developed some concerns with the administrative procedures of the church. The church grew, in part, from the addition of pastors and their congregations who had previously left other Apostolic bodies.

Membership: In 1980 the United Way of the Cross Churches had 1,100 members in 14 churches. There were 30 ministers and four bishops.

★641★
Universal Church of Jesus Christ
Current address not obtained for this edition.

The Universal Church of Jesus Christ was founded in the 1950s by the withdrawal of some members of the Church of Jesus Christ (Kingsport). The immediate occasion of the split concerned the Lord's Supper. The withdrawing members argued that communion was spiritual and that there was no mandate to continue the Lord's Supper, or the accompanying practice of washing feet, as an outward ceremony. They also dropped several beliefs considered important by the Church of Jesus Christ (Kingsport) including the rapture of the saints and the imminent second coming of Jesus. It also does not believe in Sunday school programs.

There is no fellowship between the Universal Church of Jesus Christ and the other Apostolic churches.

Membership: Not reported.

★642★
Way of the Cross Church of Christ
% Bishop Leroy H. Cannady Sr.
600 E. 43rd St.
Baltimore, MD 21212

The Way of the Cross Church of Christ was founded in 1927 by Henry C. Brooks, an independent black Pentecostal minister. Brooks had founded a small congregation in Washington, D.C. which became part of the Church of Our Lord Jesus Christ of the Apostolic Faith founded by Robert Clarence Lawson. At that time there was another small congregation under Bishop Lawson in Washington headed by Smallwood E. Williams, and Lawson wanted Brooks' congregation to join Williams'. Brooks rejected the plan, left Lawson's jurisdiction and founded a separate organization. A second congregation in Henderson, North Carolina, became the first of several along the East Coast. Brooks pastored the mother church for forty years and built a membership of over 3,000.

The Way of the Cross Church is headed by a presiding bishop. John L. Brooks, the son of the founder, succeeded to that post. He is assisted by twelve other bishops. Missions are supported in Ghana and Liberia.

Membership: In 1980 the Way of the Cross Church of Christ had 48 affiliated congregations and approximately 50,000 members.

★643★
Yahweh's Temple
Current address not obtained for this edition.

Yahweh's Temple was founded in 1947 as the Church of Jesus and has through the decades of its existence sought the name that best expressed its central doctrinal concern of identifying Jesus with the God of the Old Testament. In 1953 the Church became The Jesus Church, and it adopted its present name in 1981. The Temple is headed by Samuel E. Officer, its bishop and moderator, a former member of the Church of God (Cleveland, Tennessee). The Temple follows the "oneness" doctrine generally, but has several points of difference from other bodies. From the Sacred Name Movement it has accepted the use of the Hebrew transliterations of the names of the Creator. It also keeps the Saturday Sabbath. It derives its name from a belief that Jesus is the "new and proper name of God, Christ, and the church." Specifically rejected are names such as "Church of God," "Pentecostal," and "Churches of Christ." The organization of the Temple is based upon an idea that all the members have a special place to work in a united body. From Ezekiel 10:10, a model of four wheels within wheels has been constructed. Each wheel consists of a hub of elders, spokes of helpers, a band for service, and the rim of membership. At the center is the international bishop, who exercises episcopal and theocratic authority. There are national and state bishops, and local deacons.

Membership: Not reported. In 1973 there were approximately 10,000 members.

Periodicals: *The Light of the World.*

Black Trinitarian Pentecostals

★644★
African Universal Church, Inc.
2336 SW 48th Ave.
Hollywood, FL 33023

The African Universal Church, Inc. is one of two churches which grew out of the ministry of Laura Adorkor Koffey (or Kofi), better known as Mother Koffey. Mother Koffey preached throughout the South for several years (1926-1928) until her assassination in 1928 in Miami. Following the assassination, some of her followers in Florida and Alabama reorganized.

The history of the group during its early decades is fragmentary, but many of the local centers became autonomous churches disconnected from the movement as a whole. Emerging as a prominent leader continuing to keep alive Koffey's teachings and memory during the 1930s was E. B. Nyombolo, an African who had been attracted to the Church while living in America. He headed what was termed the Missionary African Universal Church, founded, the Ile-Ife Institute in Jacksonville, Florida, and edited a periodical, *The African Messenger.* He also published the *African Universal Hymnal, Mother's Closet Prayer Book, Mother's Sacred Teachings,* and a volume of *Mother's Sayings.* In keeping with the church's message of self-help, an intentional community was created near Daphne City, Alabama, in the 1940s Adorkaville, a second church community, was opened in Jacksonville.

In 1953 a reorganization of the churches, which had over the years drifted apart, occurred and three churches came together in a new corporate structure: St. Adorkor African Universal Church, Miami, Florida; St. Adorkor African Universal Church, Hollywood, Florida; and the african Universal Church, Jacksonville, Florida. Elder John Dean was elected as the first chairman of the general assembly. He served until 1958 and was succeeded by Deacon Clifford Hepburn (1958-1970), Sister Gloria Hepburn (1970-74) and Deacon Audley Sears, Sr. (1974-present).

The doctrine of the African Universal Church, Inc. is like that of the African Universal Church. An important new area of the church's life began in 1968 when Ernest Sears, a member, traveled to Ghana in an attempt to locate Mother Koffey's family. An earlier attempt in the 1930s had left unanswered charges that Koffey had lied about her African background. However, Sears was able to make contact with the family, who had never been informed of the assassination in 1928. Upon his return, Sears brought Koffey's nephew with him.

Membership: In 1990 the African Universal Church, Inc. reported seven affiliated congregations in Florida and Alabama.

Sources:

African Universal Hymnal. Jacksonville, FL: Missionary African Universal Church, 1961.

Bantu Prayerbook. Jacksonville, FL: Adorkaville, n.d.

The Church: Why Mother Established the Church and What It Stands For. Jacksonville, FL: The Ile-Ife, n.d.

Kofi, Laura Adorka. *Mother's Sacred Teachings.* Jacksonville, FL: The Mafro Ile-Ife, n.d.

___. *Mother's Sayings.* Jacksonville, FL: Missionary African Universal Church, n.d.

Payne, Wardell J., ed. *Directory of African American Religious Bodies: A Compendium by the Howard University School of Divinity.* Washington, DC: Howard University Press, 1991.

★645★
Alpha and Omega Pentecostal Church of God of America, Inc.
Current address not obtained for this edition.

The Alpha and Omega Pentecostal Church of God of America, Inc., was formed in 1945 by the Rev. Magdalene Mabe Phillips, who withdrew from the United Holy Church of America and, with others, organized the Alpha and Omega Church of God Tabernacles, soon changed to the present name. Like the Church of God (Cleveland, Tennessee), the church's doctrine reserves the baptism of The Holy Spirit for the sanctified.

Membership: Not reported. In 1970 there were three congregations, six missions, and approximately 400 members, all in Baltimore.

★646★
Apostolic Faith Church of America
Fremont, NC 27830

The Apostolic Faith Church of America was founded in 1922 by former members of the Apostolic Faith Churches of God. The split was possibly occasioned by the death of California-based William J. Seymour who had inspired the founding of the original congregation of the Apostolic Faith Churches of God. The new organization subsequently grew into a denomination under its bishop Isaac Ryles. While organizationally separate, the church continued the holiness Pentecostal perspective of its parent body.

Membership: In 1990 the church had 10 congregations.

Sources:

DuPree, Sherry Sherrod. *African American Holiness Pentecostal Charismatic: Annotated Bibliography.* New York: Garland Publishing, 1992.

★647★
Apostolic Faith Church of God Live On
2300 Trenton St.
Hopewell, VA 23860

The Apostolic Faith Church of God Live On is one of several groups which originated in the Apostolic Faith Church of God founded in 1909 by Bishop William J. Seymour and Charles W. Lowe. It was founded in 1952 by Bishop Jesse Handshaw, Bishop Willie P. Cross, and Elder R. T. Butts, all formerly of the Apostolic Faith Church of God and True Holiness, the branch of the church headed by Lowe at that time. No doctrinal matters were at issue, and the church follows the beliefs and practices of its parent body. Bishop Handshaw was succeeded by Bishop Richard Cross, the present leader of the church. The Church has joined with other branches of the Apostolic Faith Church to form the United Fellowship Convention of the Original Azusa Street Mission which meets annually.

Membership: In 1990 the church had approximately 25 affiliated congregations.

Periodicals: *The Guiding Light.* • *Crusade.*

Sources:

DuPree, Sherry Sherrod. –African American Holiness Pentecostal Charismatic: Annotated Bibliography–. New York: Garland Publishing, 1992. Payne, Wardell J., ed. –Directory of African American Religious Bodies–. Washington, DC: Howard University Press, 1991. 363 pp.

★648★
Apostolic Faith Churches of God
700 Charles St.
Franklin, VA 23851

The Apostolic Faith Churches of God traces its history to 1909 when William J. Seymour, under whose leadership the original pentecostal revival in Los Angeles, California, visited Washington, D.C. From the the mission on Azusa Street in Los Angeles which Seymour pastored, the Pentecostal Movement spread around the United States. Accompanying Seymour on his visit was Charles H. Mason, founder of the Church of God in Christ.

Among the people affected by their new teachings of Pentecostalism was Charles W. Lowe of Handsom, Virginia, who in turn founded the Apostolic Faith Church of God, which was loosely affiliated with Seymour's organization in Los Angeles. Over the years other congregations were founded, some of which became the sources of new denominations. The church was finally chartered in Maryland in 1938 (the same year the Los Angeles center was permanently dissolved).

In 1945 Bishop Lowe separated from the main body of the Apostolic Faith Church of God and and established himself as leader of a new organization, the Apostolic Faith Church of God and True Holiness. The main body of the church then reorganized and elected Bishop Rossie Cleveland Grant, who was succeeded by Bishop George Buchanan White. Following White was Bishop George W. Parks. Parks discontinued the previous corporation and operated as an unincorporated fellowship of churches. His successor, Bishop Lois Cleveland Grant, reincorporated as the Apostolic Faith Churches of God. Bishop Grant was succeeded by Bishop Abraham Urquhart and Stephen Douglas Willis, Sr., the present presiding bishop.

The Apostolic Faith Churches of God have joined with other branches of the church originally founded by Seymour and Lowe in the United Fellowship Convention of the Original Azusa Street Mission. The church holds an annual convention each August.

Azusa Interdenominational Fellowship of Christian Churches
8621 S. Memorial Dr.
Tulsa, OK 74133-4312

The Azusa Interdenominational Fellowship of Christian Churches was founded in 1990 by Carlton D. Pearson, the head of Higher Dimensions Ministries in Tulsa, Oklahoma. Pearson, a prominent African American Charismatic minister, had been given what he felt was a Divine mandate to establish such a cooperative fellowship that might speak to the issue of racial and ethnic divisions that have split the larger Pentecostal/Charismatic movement. In 1977 Pearson founded Higher Dimensions Ministries as a traveling evangelistic team that grew through the 1980s into a significant, multifaceted ministry that included the Higher Dimensions Family Church, a megachurch of more than 5,000 members, and a variety of community services from a meals-on-wheels program to an adoption agency. The church and its program serve a multiethnic and multiracial constituency.

By the end of the 1980s, the larger Charismatic movement was beginning to raise significant questions about its racial division and finding ways of healing the organizations split along racial lines. At the same time, Pearson had concluded that an effort towards unity is a key ingredient in understanding the beauty of diversity resident in the Body of Christ, a principle he had felt he had already established in his ministry. Out of a desire to see the large unity within the larger fellowship, in 1988 he hosted the first annual Azusa Conference. This conference served to bring together people of diverse races, cultures, and theologies. Azusa Fellowship was born at the third Azusa Conference in 1990. He found a keynote for the new fellowship in II Corinthians 11:28. "Besides everything else, I face daily the pressure of my deep concern and care for all the churches."

The fellowship is organized as a coalition of Christian churches and ministries which recognizes the need for networking, accountability, fellowship, and resource facilitation.

Membership: In 1998, there were more than 500 congregations affiliated with the fellowship.

Periodicals: *Dimensions Digest.*

★650★
Azusa Street Apostolic Faith Mission of Los Angeles
(Defunct)

The Pentecostal Movement, begun in Topeka, Kansas, under the leadership of Charles Parham, was brought to the West Coast by William J. Seymour, a black holiness minister and former member of the Church of God (Anderson, Indiana). He established work in a renovated building on Azusa Street in Los Angeles, California, from which the movement would spread across the North American continent and into many foreign lands between 1906 and 1909. Before the first year was out, however, Parham charged Seymour with distorting the teachings and practices of the movement and the two broke. Seymour reorganized the mission under his sole leadership.

During the next few years, Seymour personally spread the movement across the nation, especially in black communities. On trips to the East, his evangelistic activities led to the founding of a number of congregations that associated with the Los Angeles mission. Others who visited Azusa Street took the revival back home with them. Then, in the midst of the spreading movement, several disasters struck which led the initially interracial work to split along racial lines. In 1907, Florence L. Crawford took the mailing list of the mission's newspaper with her to Oregon where she established an independent organization, the The Apostolic Faith Mission of Portland, Oregon, Inc.. In 1909, Seymour broke with William H. Durham over the issue of sanctification, and most of the remaining white members left.

Seymour had inherited a Wesleyan holiness approach to Pentecostalism. He taught a succession of three major spiritual experiences for the believer: justification, sanctification, and baptism in the Holy Spirit. The first brought the new believer into a relationship with God. The second infused perfection in love, while the third brought the indwelling of the Holy Spirit. This three-experience approach was denied by Durham who taught that the baptism of the Holy Spirit was for any believer and that holiness of life came gradually through Christian living.

Seymour led the congregation in Los Angeles and the several affiliated congregations around the country. The revival, whose guidance in Los Angeles was under Seymour's organization, quickly burst beyond his Azusa Street Mission. People who received the baptism of the Holy Spirit there returned to their homes to found numerous new churches never organizationally tied to Azusa Street. Seymour continued to lead the Los Angeles congregation for the rest of his life, but few looked to him for leadership around the United States, and his organization folded soon after his death in 1922.

Sources:

The Doctrine and Discipline of the Azusa Street Apostolic Faith Mission of Los Angeles. Los Angeles: W. J. Seymour, 1915.

Lovett, Leonard. "Black Origins of the Pentecostal Movement." In *Aspects of Pentecostal Charismatic Origins.* Edited by Vinson Synan, 123-213. Plainfield, NJ: Logos International, 1975.

Nelson, Douglas J. *For Such a Time as This; The Story of Bishop William J. Seymour and the Azusa Street Revival: A Search for Pentecostal/Charismatic Roots.* Ph.D. diss., University of Birmingham, Birmingham, England, 1981.

Tinney, James S. "Black Origins of the Pentecostal Movement." *Christianity Today.* 16 (October 8, 1971): 4-6.

★651★
Church of God in Christ
272 S. Main St.
Memphis, TN 38103

The Church of God in Christ was established in 1894 in Jackson, Mississippi, by Charles H. Mason, at that time an independent Baptist minister who four years previously had been affected by the holiness movement and sanctified. With a colleague, Elder C. P. Jones, he had founded the Church of Christ (Holiness) U.S.A.. He had as a child of twelve been healed suddenly of a sickness that almost killed him. In 1907, two events further changed his life. Elder Jones convinced him that he did not yet have the fullness of the Holy Spirit, for, if he did, he would have the power to heal the sick, cast out devils, and raise the dead. He also heard of the meetings at Azusa Street in Los Angeles, went there, was baptized in the Spirit and spoke in tongues.

In August, 1908, the new doctrine and experience was presented to the representatives of the Church of Christ (Holiness) U.S.A. convention in Jackson. At a meeting of those who accepted Pentecostalism, a General Assembly of the Church of God in Christ was organized. Mason was elected general overseer. (This brief history is at odds with the history presented in the item elsewhere in this *Encyclopedia* on the Church of Christ (Holiness) U.S.A.; the two churches involved tell two different stories.)

The Church of God in Christ was organized in an ascending hierarchy of overseer (pastor), state overseer, and general overseer. There are annual state convocations which decide on disputed matters and assign pastors, and a general convocation for matters of the general church.

Upon the death of Bishop Mason in 1961, a series of reorganizational steps began. Power reverted to the seven bishops who made up the executive commission. This group was extended to twelve in 1962 and O. T. Jones, Jr., was named "senior bishop." An immediate controversy began over the focus of power and a constitutional convention was scheduled. In 1967, a court in Memphis ruled that the powers of the senior bishop and executive board should remain intact until the constitutional convention in

1968. That year reorganization took place and power was invested in a quadrennial general assembly and a general board of twelve with a presiding bishop to conduct administration between meetings of the general assembly.

Doctrine is similar to that of the International Pentecostal Holiness Church. The group believes in the Trinity, holiness, healing, and the premillennial return of Christ. Three ordinances are recognized: baptism by immersion, the Lord's Supper, and foot-washing.

.

Membership: In 1987 the church reported 3,000,000 members, 10,500 congregations and 31,896 ministers in the United States. There were 21 congregations and 33 ministers in Canada and an additional 700,000 members in 43 countries around the world.

Educational Facilities: Charles H. Mason Theological Seminary, Atlanta, Georgia.

In addition to the seminary in Atlanta (now part of the Interdenominational Theological Center), the church supports the C. H. Mason System of Bible Colleges which includes a number of schools attached to local congregations both in the United States and abroad.

Periodicals: *Whole Truth.* • *The Voice of Missions.* Send orders to Box 329, Memphis, TN 38101.

Sources:

Cornelius, Lucille J. *The Pioneer History of the Church of God in Christ.* The Author, 1975.

Mason, Mary Esther. *The History and Life Work of Elder C. H. Mason and His Co-Laborers.* Privately printed, n.d.

Patterson, J. O., German R. Ross, and Julia Mason Atkins. *History and Formative Years of the Church of God in Christ with Excerpts from the Life and Works of Its Founder—Bishop C. H. Mason.* Memphis, TN: Church of God in Christ Publishing House, 1969.

Patterson, W. A. *From the Pen of W. A. Patterson.* Memphis, TN: Deakins Typesetting Service, 1970.

★652★
Church of God in Christ, Congregational
1905 Bond Ave.
East St. Louis, IL 62201

The Church of God in Christ, Congregational, was formed in 1932 by Bishop J. Bowe of Hot Springs, Arkansas, who argued that the Church of God in Christ should be congregational, not episcopal, in its polity. Forced to withdraw, Bowe organized the Church of God in Christ, Congregational. In 1934, he was joined by George Slack. Slack had been disfellowshipped from the church because of his disagreement with the teaching that if a saint did not pay tithes, he was not saved. He was convinced that tithing was not a New Testament doctrine. He became the junior bishop under Bowe. In 1945, Bowe was wooed back into the Church of God in Christ, and Slack became senior bishop.

Doctrine is like that of the Church of God in Christ, but with disagreements on matters of polity and tithing. Members are conscientious objectors.

Membership: Not reported. In 1971 there were 33 churches in the United States, 4 in England, and 6 in Mexico.

Sources:

Slack, George, William Walker, and E. Jones, *Manual.* East St. Louis, IL: Church of God in Christ, Congregational, 1948.

★653★
Church of God in Christ, International
% Rt. Rev. Carl E. Williams, Presiding Bishop
170 Adelphi St.
Brooklyn, NY 11205-3302

In 1969, following its constitutional convention and reorganization, a major schism of the Church of God in Christ occurred when a group of fourteen bishops led by Bishop Illie L. Jefferson rejected the polity of the reorganized church, left it and formed the Church of God in Christ, International, at Kansas City. The issue was the centralized authority in the organization of the parent body. The new group quickly set up an entire denominational structure. The doctrine of the parent body remained intact.

Membership: In 1982 the Church reported 200,000 members, 300 congregations and 1,600 ministers.

Periodicals: *Message.* • *Holiness Code.*

★654★
Church of the Living God (Christian Workers for Fellowship)
% Bishop W. E. Crumes
434 Forest Ave.
Cincinnati, OH 45229

The Church of the Living God (Christian Workers for Fellowship) was formed in 1889 by a former slave, the Rev. William Christian (1856-1928) of Wrightsville, Arkansas. Christian was an early associate of Charles H. Mason, also a Baptist minister who left the Baptist Church to form the Church of God in Christ. Christian claimed to have had a revelation that the Baptists were preaching a sectarian doctrine and he left them in order to preach the unadulterated truth. He created the office of "chief." Mrs. Ethel L. Christian succeeded her husband after his death and was, in turn, succeeded by their son, John L. Christian. Mrs. Christian claimed that the original revelation came to both her husband and herself.

The doctrine is trinitarian and somewhat Pentecostal. The group rejects the idea of "tongues" as the initial evidence of the baptism of the Holy Spirit, although "tongues" are allowed. However, "tongues" must be recognizable languages, not "unintelligible utterance." Footwashing is a third ordinance. Salvation is gained by obeying the commandments to hear, understand, believe, repent, confess, be baptized, and participate in the Lord's Supper and in foot-washing.

The Church of the Living God also has a belief that Jesus Christ was of the black race because of the lineage of David and Abraham. David in Psalms 119:83 said he became like a bottle in the smoke (i.e., black). The church members also hold that Job (Job 30:30), Jeremiah (Jer. 8:21), and Moses' wife (Numbers 12:11) were black. These teachings were promulgated at a time when many Baptists were teaching that blacks were not human, but the offspring of a human father and female beast. The Church of the Living God countered with the assertion that the saints of the Bible were black.

The polity is episcopal and the church is modeled along the lines of a fraternal organization. Christian was very impressed with the Masons, and there are reportedly many points of doctrine known only to members of the organization. Tithing is stressed. Churches are called temples.

Membership: In 1985 the church reported 170 churches, 42,000 members, and 170 ministers.

Periodicals: *The Gospel Truth.* • *Fellowship Echoes.*

★655★
Church of the Living God, the Pillar and Ground of the Truth, Inc.
4520 Hydes Ferry Pike
Box 80735
Nashville, TN 37208

Alternate Address: % Meharry H. Lewis, Gen. Sec., Church of the Living God, PGT, Inc., PO Box 384, Tuskegee, AL 36083-0384.

The Church of the Living God, the Pillar and Ground of the Truth, Inc. traces its beginning to 1903 when Mary L. Tate (1871-1930), a black woman, began to preach the gospel first at Steel Springs, Tennessee, and Paducah, Kentucky, and then other states in the South. By 1908, when a number of holiness bands had been formed by people converted under her ministry, she was taken ill. Pronounced beyond cure, she was healed and given the baptism of the Holy Spirit and spoke in tongues. She called an assembly in Greenville, Alabama, during which the Church of the Living God, the Pillar and Ground of Truth was organized. She was selected Chief Apostle Elder and chief overseer. The church grew quickly in the states of Georgia, Florida, Tennessee, and Kentucky and by the end of the next decade had congregations across the eastern half of the United States. Bishops were introduced into the church in 1914.

In 1919, the first of two major schisms occurred. Led by the church in Philadelphia, Pennsylvania, some members left to found the House of God Which Is the Church of the Living God, the Pillar and Ground of Truth. Then, in 1931, following Mother Tate's death, the church reorganized, and three persons were ordained to fill the office of chief overseer. The three chosen were Mother Tate's son F. E. Lewis, M. F. L. Keith (widow of Bishop W. C. Lewis), and B. L. McLeod. These three eventually became leaders of distinct church bodies. Lewis' following is the continuing Church of the Living God, the Pillar and Ground of the Truth, Inc. Keith's group became known as the House of God Which Is the Church of the Living God, the Pillar and Ground of Truth Without Controversy.

Bishop McLeod's organization is known as the Church of the Living God, the Pillar, and Ground of Truth which He Purchased with His Own Blood, Inc. The church affirms the central doctrines of traditional Christianity including the Holy Trinity and salvation through Christ. It teaches that people are justified and cleansed by faith in Christ and glorified and wholly sanctified by receiving the Holy Ghost and Fire. Evidence of the reception of the Holy Ghost is speaking in tongues. The unknown tongue is a sign of God's victory over sin. There are three ordinances: baptism by immersion, the Lord's Supper, and foot washing.

Organization. The church is headed by a bishop, designated the chief overseer. After the death of Bishop F. E. Lewis in 1968, Bishop Helen M. Lewis, the present head of the church, became the chief overseer. She administers the affairs of the church with the assistance of the general assembly, which meets annually, a board of trustees, and the supreme executive council consisting of the other bishops and seven elders. The New and Living Way Publishing House is the church's publishing arm.

Membership: In 1988, the church reported approximately 2,000 members and approximately 100 ministers.

Periodicals: *The True Report.*

Sources:

The Constitution, Government and General Decree Book. Chattanooga, TN: New and Living Way Publishing Co., n.d.

Lewis, Helen M., and Meharry H. Lewis. *75th Anniversary Yearbook.* Nashville, TN: Church of the Living God, Pillar and Ground of Truth, 1978.

★656★
Deliverance Evangelistic Centers
505 Central Ave.
Newark, NJ 07107

The initial Deliverance Evangelistic Center was formed in Brooklyn, New York in the 1950s by Arturo Skinner (d. 1975). Skinner had been stopped from committing suicide by what he believed to be the voice of God which told him, "Arturo, if you but turn around, I'll save your soul, heal your body, and give you a deliverance ministry." He was twenty-eight years old at the time, and though he had a full gospel background, he had never heard of anything termed a "deliverance ministry." In a period of retreat following his encounter with God, Skinner fasted and had a number of visions and dreams. He also consecrated his life to the ministry to which he had been called. After the founding of the first center, others were founded and pastors ordained to care for them. Women have been accepted into the ordained ministry as both evangelists and pastors.

The statement of belief of the centers includes an affirmation in the authority of the Bible as inspired and infallible, the Trinity, Jesus Christ as redeemer, the Holy Spirit who empowers and baptizes believers, speaking-in-tongues as evidence of the baptism of the Holy Spirit, creation, the necessity of repentence, sanctification, and water baptism by immersion. Skinner was the church's first Apostle. He was succeeded by Ralph Nickels.

Membership: There are centers in Brooklyn and Poughkeepsie, New York; Philadelphia; Washington, D.C.; Orlando, Florida; and Asbury Park and Newark, New Jersey.

Periodicals: *Deliverance Voice.*

★657★
Faith Tabernacle Council of Churches, International
7015 NE 23rd Ave.
Portland, OR 97211

The Faith Tabernacle Council of Churches, International was founded as the Faith Tabernacle Corporation of Churches in Portland, Oregon, in 1962 by Bishop Louis W. Osborne, Sr. Osborne began the organization after a vision in which he caught and carried a light which gradually grew in intensity, thus allowing him to lead them down the correct pathway.

The council is basically an Apostolic Pentecostal organization, but Osborne has emphasized the need for the preaching of the gospel and for fellowship and freedom. He has organized it as an association of autonomous congregations. The council charters congregations and ordains minister, but conformity of belief by ministers and churches is not demanded. While the council provides congregations with a set of "Guidelines for Christian Development," there is no requirement that the Guidelines be followed.

Membership: In 1990 it reported 55 congregation including several churches in South Africa and Zimbabwe.

Periodicals: *The Light of Faith.*

Sources:

Payne, Wardell J., ed. *Directory of African American Religious Bodies: A Compendium by the Howard University School of Divinity.* Washington, DC: Howard University Press, 1991.

★658★
Fire-Baptized Holiness Church of God of the Americas
Current address not obtained for this edition.

W. E. Fuller (1875-1958), the only black man in attendance at the 1898 organizing conference of the Fire-Baptized Holiness Church, became the leader of almost a thousand black people over the next decade. Feelings of discrimination led to their withdrawal and they organized the Colored Fire-Baptized Holiness Church at Anderson, South Carolina, on May 1, 1908. The white body gave them their accumulated assets and property at this time

Reverend Fuller was elected overseer and bishop. Doctrine is the same as in the International Pentecostal Holiness Church, the body that absorbed the Fire-Baptized Holiness Church.

Legislative and executive authority are vested in a general council that meets every four years and in the eleven-member executive council (composed of bishops, district elders, and pastors). Mission work is under one of the bishops.

Membership: Not reported. In 1968 the church reported 53 churches and 9,088 members.

Periodicals: *True Witness.*

Sources:

Discipline. Atlanta: Board of Publication of the F. B. H. Church of God of the Americas, 1962.

★659★
Free Church of God in Christ
Current address not obtained for this edition.

The Free Church of God in Christ dates from 1915 when J. H. Morris, a former pastor in the National Baptist Convention of the U.S.A., Inc., and a group of members of his church experienced the baptism of the Holy Spirit and spoke in tongues. The group, mostly members of Morris' family, founded a Pentecostal group which they called the Church of God in Christ. They chose as their leader the founder's son, E. J. Morris, who believed he was "selected" for the role. In 1921, the group united with the larger body led by Bishop Charles H. Mason, which had the same name. The union lasted for only four years, and Morris' group adopted its present name when it again became independent in 1925. It has the same doctrine and polity as the Mason body. By the late 1940s the church had 20 congregations.

Membership: Not reported.

Remarks: No direct contact has been made with the Church since the 1940s and its present condition is unknown. It may be defunct.

★660★
Full Gospel Baptist Church Fellowship
3030 Canal St.
New Orleans, LA 70119-6306

The Full Gospel Baptist Church, founded in 1995, is a fellowship of predominantly African American charismatic Baptist churches. Through the 1970s and 1980s, the Pentecostal experience spread through African American churches, including the Baptists. The Baptists have been among the most resistant to continuing fellowship with charismatic pastors and congregations. The mother church of the organization of the charismatic churches has been the St. Stephens Baptist Church in New Orleans. The congregation had been founded in 1937 and grown steadily through the years. In 1974, following the death of Percy Simpson, then pastor of the church, the assistant pastor, Paul S. Morton, succeeded him. He led in the building of a 2,000-seat sanctuary in 1980 and the acquisition of a 4,000-seat sanctuary in 1988. In 1991, the church changed the name to reflect a newly acquired level of spiritual growth. It became Greater St. Stephen Full Gospel Baptist Church. More recently, the School and College of Ministry was formed to educate minister and church leaders. In February of 1993, Elder Debra B. Morton, the wife of Pastor Morton, became the co-pastor of the ministry.

In March of 1993, Elder Paul S. Morton, Sr., accepted the office of bishop (an office not found in most Baptist groups), and became the First Presiding Bishop of the Full Gospel Baptist Church Fellowship. The first conference was held in New Orleans at the Louisiana Superdome in 1994 with over 30,000 in attendance.

Membership: Not reported. In 1998, there were approximately 50 congregations affiliated with the fellowship.

Educational Facilities: *College of Ministry.*

Sources:

1997 Ministries Newtworking Directory. Lake Mary, FL: Strang Communications, 1997.

★661★
Full Gospel Pentecostal Association
1032 N. Sumner
Portland, OR 97217

Alternate Address: c/o Tabernacle of Evangelism Community Church, 1300 N. La Brea Ave., Inglewood, CA 90302.

The Full Gospel Pentecostal Association is a predominantly black Pentecostal church founded in 1970 by Bp. Adolph A. Wells, Rev. Edna Travis, and Bp. S. D. Leffall. It is a loosely organized association of independent Pentecostal congregations that supports a prison ministry, a national women's organization (Full Gospel Pentecostal Association for Women on the Move), and an international fellowship with similar Pentecostal groups in Africa. It is one of several similar bodies that belongs to the ecumenical Federated Pentecostal Church International led by Bishop Leffall, who also serves a church in Seattle, Washington.

Membership: Not reported.

Periodicals: *The Epistle.* • *Full Gospel News.* • *Truth.*

Sources:

Dupree, Sherry Sherrod. *African American Holiness Pentecostal Charismatic: Annotated Bibliography.* New York: Garland Publishing, 1992.

★662★
Healing Temple Church
660 Williams St.
Macon, GA 31201

Healing Temple Church is a predominantly black Pentecostal church with a special emphasis on the ministry of healing. It was founded in 1955 in Macon, Georgia, by Bp. P. J. Welch, a native of Georgia who had begun a tent ministry in 1950 in New Jersey. He took his ministry around the country during the nationwide Pentecostal healing revival which had been launched by such evangelists as William M. Branham, Oral Roberts, and A. A. Allen. The church grew out of Welch's itinerant ministry. Welch was assisted in his work by his wife, L. R. Welch, who served as a missionary, supervisor, and instructor in the church.

Though the leader of a growing denomination, Welch continued to travel with his healing ministry, and more congregations were founded. The belief is Trinitarian and believers consider speaking in tongues as a sign of the baptism of the Holy Spirit.

Membership: In 1990 there were 17 congregations.

Sources:

DuPree, Sherry Sherrod. *African American Holiness Pentecostal Charismatic: Annotated Bibliography.* New York: Garland Publishing, 1992.

★663★
House of God, Holy Church of the Living God, The Pillar and Ground of Truth, the House of Prayer for All People
548 Georgetown St.
Lexington, KY 40508

The House of God, Holy Church of the Living God, The Pillar and Ground of Truth, The House of Prayer for All People is a predominantly black Pentecostal group that has adopted Sabbatarianism and the perspective of the Sacred Name Movement. That perspective includes the adoption of the Old Testament dietary regulations, the observance of the Old Testament feast days (rather than Christmas and Easter), and the use of "Yahweh" as the name of the Almighty God. The church was founded in 1914 in Beaufort, South Carolina, by Bp. R. A. R. Johnson. It supports the belief in the baptism of the Holy Spirit as evidenced by speaking in

tongues as a cardinal tenet and practice. It has also adopted the use the *Holy Name Bible* published by the Scripture Research Association.

The church follows 24 principles, including baptism by immersion, the washing of feet, the equality of the races, and sanctification. Women are accepted into the ministry. Women generally dress in white, especially from Passover to the harvest festival (through the agricultural growing season).

Membership: In 1990 the church reported 100 congregations and approximately 2,500 members.

Remarks: The first female member of the church was Mamie Gaye, the grandmother of popular singing star Marvin Gaye.

Sources:

DuPree, Sherry Sherrod. *African American Holiness Pentecostal Charismatic: Annotated Bibliography*. New York: Garland Publishing, 1992.

Traina, A. B. *Holy Name Bible*. Brandywine, MD: Scripture Research Association, 1980.

★664★
House of God Which Is the Church of the Living God, the Pillar and Ground of Truth
Current address not obtained for this edition.

Not to be confused with the church of the same name which derives from the movement begun by Mary L. Tate known as the Church of the Living God, the Pillar and Ground of Truth, the church presently under discussion derives from the work begun by William Christian. In the early twentieth century, the Church of the Living God (Christian Workers for Fellowship), which Christian founded, was splintered on several occasions. In 1902, a group calling itself the Church of the Living God, Apostolic Church, withdrew and, six years later under the leadership of Rev. C. W. Harris, became the Church of the Living God, General Assembly. It united in 1924 with a second small splinter body. In 1925, a number of churches withdrew from the Church of the Living God (Christian Workers for Fellowship) under the leadership of Rev. E. J. Cain and called themselves the Church of the Living God, the Pillar and Ground of Truth. The Harris group joined the Cain group in 1926 and they later adopted the present name. The Church is one in doctrine with the Church of the Living God (Christian Workers for Fellowship). Polity is episcopal and there is an annual general assembly.

Membership: Not reported.

Remarks: The last independent source on this body is the 1936 *Census of Religious bodies*. Later sources often confuse it with the Philadelphia-based group of the same name. Its present location and strength is unknown.

★665★
House of God Which Is the Church of the Living God, the Pillar and Ground of Truth, Inc.
6107 Cobbs Creek Pkwy.
Philadelphia, PA 19143

In 1919 the Church of the Living God, the Pillar and Ground of Truth founded by Mary L. Tate, experienced a schism led by the congregation in Philadelphia. The new group, the House of God, the Church of the Living God, the Pillar and Ground of Truth continues the doctrine and episcopal polity of the parent body, but is administratively separate. The general assembly meets annually.

Membership: Not reported. In the early 1970 the church reported 103 churches and 25,860 members.

Periodicals: *The Spirit of Truth Magazine*. Send orders to 3943 Fairmont St., Philadelphia, PA 19104.

★666★
House of God Which Is the Church of the Living God, the Pillar and Ground of Truth Without Controversy (Keith Dominion)
℅ J. W. Jenkins, Chief Overseer
Box 9113
Montgomery, AL 36108

In 1931, following the death of founder Bishop Mary L. Tate, the Church of the Living God, the Pillar and Ground of the Truth, Inc., appointed three chief overseers. Eventually, each became the head of a distinct segment of the church and then of an independent body called a dominion. One of the three chief overseers was M. F. L. Keith, widow of Bishop Tate's son, W. C. Lewis. Her dominion became known as the House of God Which is the Church of the Living God the Pillar and Ground of Truth Without Controversy (Keith Dominion).

The church is headed by a Chief Overseer (Bishop J. W. Jenkins succeeded Bishop Keith in that post) and a Supreme Executive Council.

Membership: Not reported.

★667★
House of the Lord
Current address not obtained for this edition.

The House of the Lord was founded in 1925 by Bishop W. H. Johnson, who established headquarters in Detroit. The doctrine is Pentecostal but departs on several important points. A person who enters the church is born of water and seeks to be born of God by a process of sanctification. The Holy Ghost may be given and is evidenced by speaking in tongues. But sanctification is evidenced by conformity to a very rigid code which includes refraining from worldly amusements, whiskey, policy rackets (the "numbers game"), becoming bell hops, participating in war, swearing, secret organizations, tithing, and life insurance (except as required by an employer). A believer is not sanctified if he owns houses, lands, or goods. Water is used in the Lord's Supper. Members are not to marry anyone not baptized by the Holy Ghost.

The church is governed by a hierarchy of ministers, state overseers, and chief overseer. There is a common treasury at each local church from which the destitute are helped.

Membership: Not reported.

★668★
Latter House of the Lord for All People and the Church of the Mountain, Apostolic Faith
Current address not obtained for this edition.

The Latter House of the Lord for All People and the Church of the Mountain, Apostolic Faith, was founded in 1936 by Bishop L. W. Williams, a former black Baptist preacher from Cincinnati. The founding followed an enlightenment experience and spiritual blessing realized in prayer. The doctrine is Calvinistic, but adjusted to accommodate Pentecostal beliefs. The Lord's Supper is observed, with water being used instead of wine. The Church members are conscientious objectors. The chief overseer is appointed for life.

Membership: Not reported. In 1947 there were approximately 4,000 members.

★669★
Mount Calvary Pentecostal Faith Church, Inc.
Current address not obtained for this edition.

Mount Calvary Pentecostal Faith Church, Inc., also known as the Emmanuel Temple Pentecostal Faith Church, Inc., and the Mount Assembly Hall of the Pentecostal Faith of All Nations, is a predominantly African-American Pentecostal group founded in 1932 in New York City by Bp. Rosa Artemus Horne. The work has been continued by Mother Horne's adopted daughter, Bp. Gladys Brandhagan.

Sources:

Payne, Wardell J., ed. *Directory of African American Religious Bodies: A Compendium by the Howard University School of Divinity.* Washington, DC: Howard University Press, 1991.

★670★
Mount Sinai Holy Church
1469 N. Broad St.
Philadelphia, PA 19122-3327

Ida Robinson grew up in Georgia, was converted at age seventeen, and joined the United Holy Church of America. She moved to Philadelphia where she became the pastor of the Mount Olive Holy Church. Following what she believed to be the command of the Holy Spirit to "Come out on Mount Sinai," she founded the Mount Sinai Holy Church in 1924. Women have played a prominent role in its leadership from the beginning.

The doctrine is Pentecostal, with sanctification a prerequisite for the baptism of the Holy Spirit. One must be converted before becoming a member. Bishop Robinson believed that God ordained four types of human beings: the elect or chosen of God, the compelled (those who could not help themselves from being saved), the "who so ever will" who can be saved, and the damned (ordained for hell). Spiritual healing is stressed. Foot-washing is practiced. Behavior, particularly sexual, is rigidly codified and rules are strictly observed. Short dresses, neckties, and worldly amusements are frowned upon.

The Mt. Sinai Holy Church is episcopal in government. Bishop Robinson served as senior bishop and president until her death in 1946. She was succeeded by Bishop Elmira Jeffries, the original vice-president, who was, in turn, succeeded by Bishop Mary Jackson in 1964. Assisting the bishops is a board of presbyteries, composed of the elders of the churches. There are four administrative districts, each headed by a bishop. There is an annual conference of the entire church, and one is held in each district. Foreign missions in Cuba and Guinea are supported.

Membership: Not reported. In 1968 there were 92 churches, and approximately 2,000 members.

★671★
Mt. Zion Spiritual Temple
Current address not obtained for this edition.

King Louis H. Narcisse (1921-1989), founder of Mt. Zion Spiritual Church, was one of the most colorful of the Spiritual church leaders. Baptized in Mt. Zion Baptist Church, his singing abilities made him a choir soloist and a winner of five radio auditions. During World War II, he moved to San Francisco, California, and found an $85-a-week job as an electrical worker in a shipyard. He also spent some time as a bank janitor, living in the Hunter housing project in South San Francisco.

In 1945, Narcisse had a vision which impelled him to found the Mt. Zion Spiritual Temple, which began as a simple prayer meeting among a handful of people. It soon grew to a large church on 14th Street in Oakland, through a combination of his personal charisma and the success of his radio program, "Moments of Meditation," which developed a national audience of as many as 1.5 million. He further increased his visibility with a number of single records, such as "Without the Lord," and "Jesus, I Can't Forget You" cut for such labels as Jaxyson, Modern, Hollywood, Music City, Veltone, and Peacock. His signature theme song and church motto was, "It's Nice to be Nice."

King Narcisse maintained his "International Headquarters" in Oakland, California, and his "East Coast Headquarters" in Detroit, Michigan. In addition to these two temples, the association has seven other congregations, including a second temple in Detroit and temples in Sacramento and Richmond, California; Houston, Texas; Orlando, Florida; New York City; and Washington, D.C.

On March 9 each year, he held a mass prayer meeting in Oakland Park with city officials and citizens, and the mayor of Oakland proclaimed it Prayer Day. In September 1955 a coronation ceremony was performed at the municipal auditorium by the Right Reverend Frank Rancifer in which he was officially given the title "His Grace, the King of Spiritual Church of the West Coast."

For those occasions when King Narcisse could not be with his flock at the King Narcisse Michigan State Memorial Temple, a large picture of "His Grace" faced the congregation, reminding its members of their spiritual leader. A sign below the picture reads as follows:

GOD IS GREAT AND GREATLY TO BE PRAISED IN THE SOVEREIGN STATE OF MICHIGAN IN THE KING OF "HIS GRACE KING" LOUIS H. NARCISSE, DD, WHERE "IT'S (sic) NICE TO BE NICE, AND REAL NICE TO LET OTHERS KNOW THAT WE ARE NICE."

Part of his appeal was his flamboyant style; he was literally treated as royalty. He wore a crown, diamond rings, and other jewels, and wherever he went in his Rolls Royce, a red carpet was rolled out in front. He lived in a 24-room palace in Oakland's Piedmont district, known as "The Light on the Hill," with numerous personal attendants. He often received followers in a "throne room," with a copy of federal income tax regulations sitting nearby. Narcisse explained that all the finery was not just for himself, but was a means of attracting those who are not yet ready for the purely spiritual. It also served as a symbol of the earthly achievements and prizes to which he called his followers. His church was also known for its many charity functions in the community.

Membership: Not reported.

Sources:

Baer, Hans A. *The Black Spiritual Movement: A Religious Response to Racism.* Knoxville, TN: University of Tennessee Press, 1984.

"His Grace King; the West Coast's Most Colorful Religious Leader." *Sepia* 9 (February 1961): 4247.

Robinson, Louie. "The Kingdom of King Narcisse." *Ebony* 18 (July 1963): 112-118.

★672★
Original United Holy Church International
Current address not obtained for this edition.

The Original United Holy Church International grew out of a struggle between two bishops of the United Holy Church of America. The conflict led to Bishop James Alexander Forbes and the Southern District being severed from the organization. Those put out of the church met and organized on June 29, 1977, at a meeting in Raleigh, North Carolina. The new body remains in essential doctrinal agreement and continues the polity of the United Holy Church.

The Original United Holy Church is concentrated on the Atlantic coast from South Carolina to Connecticut, with congregations also found in Kentucky, Texas, and California. Bishop Forbes also serves as pastor of the Greater Forbes Temple of Hollis, New York. The church supports missionary work in Liberia. On January 24, 1979, in Wilmington, North Carolina, an agreement of affiliation between the Original United Holy Church and the International Pentecostal Holiness Church was signed, which envisions a close cooperative relationship between the two churches.

Membership: In 1985 the church had approximately 210 congregations and over 15,000 members.

Educational Facilities: United Christian College, Goldsboro, North Carolina.

Periodicals: *Voice of the World.*

★673★
Sought Out Church of God in Christ
Current address not obtained for this edition.

The Sought Out Church of God in Christ and Spiritual House of Prayer, Inc., was founded in 1947 by Mother Mozella Cook. Mother Cook was converted in a service led by her physical mother, an ecstatic person who was once hauled into court to be examined for lunacy because of her mystical states. Mother Cook's mother seemed to go into trances and was "absent from this world while she talked with God." Mother Cook moved to Pittsburgh and there became a member of the Church of God in Christ founded by Charles H. Mason, but left it to found her own church, which she formed in Brunswick, Georgia, after feeling a divine call.

Membership: Not reported. In 1949 the church had four congregations and 60 members.

★674★
Tabernacle of Prayer for All People
Jamaica, NY

The Tabernacle of Prayer for All People was founded in 1986 in Brooklyn, New York, by Johnnie Washington, a former member of the Christian Church (Disciples of Christ). Beginning with 15 people, the congregation grew swiftly, and in the early 1970s moved into successively larger buildings and began a school for church members. Washington conducted a number of tent revivals during the 1970s through which many thousands were reported to have had been saved. The evangelistic outreach led to the founding of a number of congregations, first along the East Coast, and then along the Pacific Coast. Washington died in California while leading the work there.

The church is led by a seven-member Apostles Council. The current church leader is Rev. Ira Davison.

Membership: In 1990 there were 49 churches and approximately 4,000 members.

Sources:

DuPree, Sherry Sherrod. *African American Holiness Pentecostal Charismatic: Annotated Bibliography.* New York: Garland Publishing, 1992.

★675★
True Fellowship Pentecostal Church of God of America
4238 Pimlico Rd.
Baltimore, MD 21215

The True Fellowship Pentecostal Church of God of America was formed in 1964 by the secession of the Rev. Charles E. Waters, Sr., a presiding elder in the Alpha and Omega Pentecostal Church of God of America, Inc.. Doctrine is like the Church of God in Christ, differing only in the acceptance of women into the ministry as pastors and elders. Bishop Waters and his wife operate a mission for those in need in Baltimore.

Membership: Not reported. In 1948 the church reported three congregations and about 120 members, all in Baltimore.

★676★
True Grace Memorial House of Prayer
205 V St., NW
Washington, DC 20001

In 1960 after Bishop Marcelino Manoel de Graca (Sweet Daddy Grace) died, Walter McCollough was elected bishop of the United House of Prayer for All People, but approximately six months later criticism was directed at him for his disposal of church monies without explanation to the other church leaders. The elders relieved him of his office and a lawsuit ordered a new election, at which time he was re-elected. Complaints continued that he was assuming false doctrines, such as claiming that he and

only he was doing God's work or that he had power to save or condemn people. Shortly after the second election, he dismissed a number of the church leaders. Twelve dissenting members, with Thomas O. Johnson (d. 1970) as their pastor, formed the True Grace Memorial House of prayer in Washington, D.C. (Elder Johnson had been dismissed after 23 years of service as a pastor.) In 1962 the church members adopted a church covenant in which they agreed to assist one another in loving counsel, prayer, and aid in times of sickness and distress; to do all good to all, in part, by assisting them to come under the ministry of the church; to avoid causes of divisions, such as gossip; and to refrain from any activity that might bring disgrace on the cause of Christ. The present head of the church is Elder William G. Easton.

Membership: Not reported. In the 1970s there were eight congregations which could be found in Washington, D.C., Philadelphia, New York City, Baltimore, Savannah, Hollywood, Florida and in North Carolina.

★677★
True Vine Pentecostal Holiness Church
929 Bethel Ln.
Martinsville, VA 24112

The True Vine Pentecostal Holiness Church was founded in the 1940s in Winston Salem, North Carolina, by William Monroe Johnson and Robert L. Hairston. Johnson served as bishop and Hairston as vice bishop. The church grew peacefully until the early 1960s when Hairston became the center of an intense multi-faceted controversy. First, Hairston had come to accept the non-trinitarian "Jesus Only" doctrine concerning the Godhead. Second, he was heavily criticized for his divorce. Hairston had also become an advocate of women ministers, a cause Johnson opposed. In 1961 Hairston was removed as vice bishop and he left the church with his supporters and founded the True Vine Pentecostal Churches of Jesus (Apostolic Faith).

The True Vine Pentecostal Holiness Church is a holiness Pentecostal body. Johnson continued to lead the church until succeeded by his son Sylvester D. Johnson, the present bishop.

Membership: Not reported.

Sources:

DuPree, Sherry Sherrod. *African American Holiness Pentecostal Charismatic: Annotated Bibliography.* New York: Garland Publishing, 1992.

★678★
United Church of the Living God, The Pillar and Ground of Truth
Los Angeles, CA
Alternate Address: 601 Kentucky Ave., Fulton, KY 42021

The United Church of the Living God, The Pillar and Ground of Truth was founded in 1946 in Los Angeles, California, by Bp. Clifton "O.K." Okley. Raised a Baptist, Okley became a minister in the Church of the Living God, The Pillar and Ground of Truth (Jewell Dominion) and a leading figure in the church on the West Coast. In 1946 Okley had a disagreement with his bishop, M. Jewell, who wanted him to move to Florida. Okley refused to move and left the church; with his supporters he founded a new denomination.

Because the church was formed as a result of an organizational dispute, it still adheres to the doctrine of its parent body. It has established congregations in California and Kentucky and missions in Germany, Haiti, and Africa.

Membership: Not reported.

Sources:

DuPree, Sherry Sherrod. *African American Holiness Pentecostal Charismatic: Annotated Bibliography.* New York: Garland Publishing, 1992.

★679★
United Crusade Fellowship Conference
Current address not obtained for this edition.

The United Crusade Fellowship Conference is a small, independent Pentecostal de nomination founded by Bp. Richard E. Taylor. It has an active program that includes support of the Christian Bible Institute and a children's daycare center. It is a member of the Federated Pentecost Church International, an ecumenical group.

Membership: In 1990 there were six congregations.

Sources:

DuPree, Sherry Sherrod. *African American Holiness Pentecostal Charismatic: Annotated Bibliography.* New York: Garland Publishing, 1992.

★680★
United Holy Church of America
825 Fairoak Ave.
Chillum, MD 20783

The United Holy Church of America was formed as the outgrowth of a holiness revival conducted by the Rev. Isaac Cheshier at Method, North Carolina (near Raleigh), in 1886. In 1900, the group became known as the Holy Church of North Carolina (and as growth dictated, the Holy Church of North Carolina and Virginia). In the early twentieth century, the church became Pentecostal and adopted a theology like the Church of God (Cleveland, Tennessee). The present name was chosen in 1916.

Membership: Not reported. In 1970 there were approximately 50,000 members in 470 churches and over 400 ministers.

Periodicals: *The Holiness Union.*

★681★
The United House of Prayer for All People of the Church on the Rock of the Apostolic Faith
1721 1/2 7th St. NW
Washington, DC 20001

The United House of Prayer was founded in the 1920s by the late Bp. C. M. Grace (1882?–1960), who built the first House of Prayer in 1919 in West Wareham, Massachusetts, with his own hands. National attention began to focus on the United House of Prayer during the Great Depression, when Bishop Grace, popularly known as "Sweet Daddy" Grace, fed the poor, held services for integrated congregations in southern cities, built churches in poverty-stricken areas for the downtrodden, and gave hope to thousands of distraught people. Over a period of 31 1/2 years of preaching, he established over 100 Houses of Prayer across the nation with a membership that grew into the millions. In the process he became one of the most controversial religious leaders in the African American community and the subject of numerous news articles on both his family life and the various properties he purchased and the projects he initiated.

The United House of Prayer was eventually incorporated in Washington, D.C., on June 20, 1927. The purpose of the organization was to establish, maintain, and perpetuate the doctrine of Christianity and the Apostolic Faith throughout the world among all people and to erect and maintain houses of prayer and worship where all people may gather for prayer and to worship the Almighty God in Spirit and in Truth, irrespective of denomination of creed.

The church affirms the Apostolic Faith and takes its name from the biblical passages Isaiah 56:6-7, Matthew 21:13, Mark 11:17, and Luke 19:46. It affirms belief in God as Creator, in Jesus as the virgin-born savior of humanity, water baptism for repentance, the rebirth in the Holy Spirit, and holiness of life. The church is organized hierarchically.

Following Bishop Grace's death in 1960, Bp. Walter McCollough was elected to the position of Bishop of the United House

of Prayer. He started the McCollough Scholarship College Fund, which has awarded more than 1,000 grants, many of whose recipients have gone on to careers in medicine, law, engineering, and education. He also inaugurated a nationwide building program of new "Houses of Prayer" and "new and affordable housing," which resulted in, among other accomplishments, the 90-unit McCollough Canaanland Apartment, the 190-unit McCollough Paradise Gardens, and the McCollough Haven for senior citizens along the District of Columbia's 7th Street, well known as a former site of riots. Additional housing units were constructed in Charlotte, North Carolina; Norfolk Virginia; New Haven, Connecticut; and Los Angeles, California.

Upon Bishop McCollough's passing in 1991, he was succeeded by S.C. Madison as bishop. During his first six years in office, he led in the erection of over 100 new "Houses of Prayer". In addition, he has continued his predecessor's efforts to build new, affordable, multifamily housing, parsonages, day care centers, commercial/retail malls, and senior citizen's housing, all without private mortgages or federal or local government assistance. The church pays cash for the total costs of construction for all of its developments. Also, the purchase of several new, interstate buses have expanded the outreach of the church.

In keeping with the distinctive architectural "signature and style," the church's structures are adorned with the "Sweet Blessing Angel," This "Sweet Blessing Angel" and other indicia of the United House of Prayer are currently the focus of historians and and investigators with the Smithsonian Institution. An exhibit focused upon the urban church outreach and housing programs of the United House of Prayer and their impact on the neighborhood environment is scheduled for display in 1998 at the Arts and Industries Building on the National Mall.

Membership: In 1997, the church reported 135 congregations and 875 ministers in the United States.

Sources:

Davis, Lenwood G., comp. *Daddy Grace: An Annotated Bibliography.* Westport, CT: Greenwood Press, 1992. 130pp.

Whiting, Albert N. *The United House of Prayer for All Peope: A Case Study of a Charismatic Sect.* Washington, D.C.: Ph.D. dissertation, American University, 1952. 319 pp.

★682★
Universal Christian Church
2140 Martindale Ave.
Indianapolis, IN 46202

The Universal Christian Church was founded in 1955 by Bishop Sallie M. Swift (d.1970), an independent African American pentecostal Bible teacher, in Indianapolis, Indiana. The church is noteworthy for the prominent role it has given to female leaders. Prior to the church's founding, Swift led Bible classes in her home and in the homes of associates for some 15 years. One of those who regularly attended her classes spoke for the group and asked her to organize a church and be their pastor. After a time of prayer, she consented. Swift served as bishop until her death in 1970. She was succeeded by Bishop Clara M. Roberts.

During Bishop Swift's time as head of the church, one additional congregation was opened in Nashville, Tennessee, and an older congregation, the Church of Jesus Christ, in Louisville, Kentucky, pastored by Mother Mattie Walker, affiliated with the Universal Christian Church.

Membership: Not reported. There are three congregations.

★683★
Universal Christian Spiritual Faith and Churches for All Nations
Current address not obtained for this edition.

The Universal Christian Spiritual Faith and Churches for All Nations was founded in 1952 by the merger of the National David

Spiritual Temple of Christ Church Union (Inc.) U.S.A., St. Paul's Spiritual Church Convocation, and King David's Spiritual Temple of Truth Association. National David Spiritual Temple of Christ Church Union (Inc.) U.S.A. had been founded at Kansas City, Missouri, in 1932 by Dr. David William Short, a former Baptist minister. He became convinced that no man had the right or spiritual power "to make laws, rules or doctrines for the real church founded by Jesus Christ" and that the "denominational" churches had been founded in error and in disregard of the apostolic example. Bishop Short claimed that the temple was the true church, and hence dated to the first century.

The merged church differs from many Pentecostal churches in that it denies that only those who have spoken in tongues have received the Spirit. It does insist, however, that a full and complete baptism of the Holy Ghost is always accompanied by both the gift of "tongues" and other powers. The members of the church rely on the Holy Spirit for inspiration and direction. The church is organized according to I Corinthians 12:1-31 and Ephesians 4:11. It includes pastors, archbishops, elders, overseers, divine healers, deacons, and missionaries. Bishop Short is the chief governing officer. In 1952, he became archbishop of the newly merged body. He is assisted by a national executive board which holds an annual assembly.

Membership: Not reported. In the mid-1960s there were reportedly 60 churches and 40,816 members.

Educational Facilities: St. David Christian Spiritual Seminary.

Periodicals: *The Christian Spiritual Voice.*

★684★
Universal Church of Christ
19-23 Park St.
PO Box 146
Orange, NJ 07050

The Universal Church of Christ was founded in 1972 by Rev. Dr. Robert C. Jiggetts, Jr., with the assistance of Elders Nathaniel Kirton and Carl Winckler. The first center was in Orange, New Jersey. The church has been very service oriented and in 1984 initiated a soup kitchen program which mobilized church volunteers, govern grants of money and food surpluses, and donations from local businesses. By the beginning of the 1990s, it was serving 1,300 meals a month to the poor and homeless.

The church accepted the Apostolic Pentecostal position which identifies Jesus as the one God of the Bible and denies the Trinity. It has three ordinances: baptism, the Lord's Supper, and holy matrimony. It affirms a belief in the infallibility of the scripture and divine healing. Jiggetts heads the church as its Chief Apostle, president, and overseer.

Membership: In 1990 had approximately 20 congregations in the Northeast United States and in the West Indies.

Sources:

Payne, Wardell J., ed. *Directory of African American Religious Bodies: A Compendium by the Howard University School of Divinity.* Washington, DC: Howard University Press, 1991.

Signs Pentecostals

★685★
Church of God with Signs Following
Current address not obtained for this edition.

The Church of God with Signs Following is a name applied to an informally organized group of Pentecostal churches, ministers and itinerant evangelists popularly known as snake-handlers, who are distinguished by their practice of drinking poison (usually strychnine) and handling poisonous serpents during their worship services. Among those who handle snakes and drink poison, the actions are called "preaching the signs." The terms "signs" refers

to Jesus' remarks in Mark 16: 17-18: "And these signs will accompany those who believe: in my name they will cast out demons; they will speak in new tongues; they will pick up serpents; and if they drink any deadly thing, it will not hurt them; they will lay their hands on the sick, and they will recover." The practice, an object of curiosity scorned and ridiculed by outsiders, is a commonplace to believers.

The practice of snake-handling began with George Went Hensley, a minister with the Church of God (Cleveland, Tennessee) in the very early days of the spread of the Pentecostal message throughout the hills of Tennessee and North Carolina. Converted, Hensley erected a brush arbor at Owl Holler outside of Cleveland and began to preach. One day during a service in which he was preaching on Mark 16, some men turned over a box of rattlesnakes in front of Hensley. According to the story, he reached down, picked up the snakes and continued to preach.

Ambrose J. Tomlinson, then head of the Church of God, having become convinced that his ministry was a further proof of the pouring of power on the Church in the last days , invited Hensley to Cleveland to show church members what was occurring. By 1914 the practice had spread through the Church of God, though practiced by only a small percentage of members. Hensley settled in Grasshopper Valley, near Cleveland, and pastored a small congregation. A number of years later, after a member almost died from a bite, Hensley moved to Pine Mountain, Kentucky.

Meanwhile, the Church of God was growing and in the 1920s, after Tomlinson's leaving the Church, the early support for the practice of snake-handling turned to strong opposition. In 1928 the Assembly of the Church of God denounced the practice, and it became the activity of a few independent churches, primarily scattered along the Appalachian Mountains. It was largely forgotten until the 1940s.

During the 1940s new advocates of snake-handling appeared. Raymond Hays and Tom Harden started the Dolly Pond Church of God with Signs Following in Grasshopper Valley not far from where Hensley had worked two decades earlier. Over the years since, that church has been the focus of the most intense controversy concerning the practice and become the best known congregation of the signs people. In 1945 Lewis Ford died of a bite received at the Dolly Pond Church. His death led to the passing of a law against the practice by the state of Tennessee and the subsequent suppression of the group by authorities. Persecution against and demonstrations for the group led to the arrest of Hensley in Chattanooga (convicted of disturbing the peace in 1948) and the disruption of an interstate convention of believers in Durham, North Carolina in 1947. Following these events the group again withdrew from the public eye, and, except for the death of Hensley, bitten in a service in Florida in 1955, was forgotten for several decades.

Then in 1971 the group again was in the news when Buford Peck, a member of the Holiness Church of God in Jesus' Name, a second snake-handling church located not far from the Dolly Pond Church, was bitten. Though he did not die, he did loose his secular job. Over the next few years three persons in Tennessee and Georgia died, two, including Peck and Jimmie Ray Williams, his pastor, from strychnine poison taken during a service. Subsequent court battles, in part to test the law against the practice, led to a 1975 ban on snake-handling and the drinking of poison in public religious services by the Tennessee Supreme Court. Followers vowed to continue the practice.

Members of the snake-handling churches are Pentecostals who accept the basic theology by which people seek and receive the baptism of the Holy Spiirt, evidenced by speaking in tongues. The snake-handlers, however, go beyond the Pentecostals in their belief that snake-handling and the drinking of poison (and for some the application of flames to the skin) are a sign of an individual's faith and possession by the Holy Spirit. It should be noted that the handling of snakes and the drinking of poison are done only while the believer is in an ecstatic (trance-like) state, referred to by members as being "in the Spirit." Scholars who have examined the movement have frequently questioned the low frequency of bites, given the number of occasions the snakes are handled and the generally loud atmosphere of the services.

The snake-handlers accept the rigid holiness code of the Pentecostal and holiness churches. Dress is plain. The Bible is consulted on all questions having to do with the nature of "worldly behavior." The kiss of peace is a prominent feature of gatherings. Worship is loud, spontaneous and several hours in length.

Congregations of signs people can be found from central Florida to West Virginia and as far west as Columbus, Ohio. Each church is independent (and a variety of names are used, mostly variations on the Church of God). They are tied together by evangelists who move from one congregation to the next. They produce no literature.

Membership: Observers of the snake handlers estimate between 50 to 100 congregations and as many as several thousand adherents.

Sources:

Carden, Karen W., and Robert W. Pelton. *The Persecuted Prophets.* New York: A. S. Barnes, 1976.

Collins, J. B. *Tennessee Snake Handlers.* Chattanooga: The Author, [1947].

Holliday, Robert K. *Test of Faith.* Oak Hill, WV: Fayette Tribune, 1966.

La Barre, Weston. *They Shall Take Up Serpents.* New York: Schocken Books, 1969.

★686★
Original Pentecostal Church of God
Current address not obtained for this edition.

Rarely recognized by observers of snake-handling groups, the Original Pentecostal Chruch of God represents a significant departure from the commonly accepted belief and practice of signs people. They do not believe in "tempting God" by bringing snakes into church services. However, should the occasion arise where the handling of a serpent provides a situation for a test and witness to one's faith, it is done. Members recount times in which they have encountered rattlesnakes or copperheads outside the church and have picked them up as they preached to those present.

The Original Church of God emerged from the Free Holiness people, the early Pentecostals, in rural Kentucky during the first decade of the twentieth century. Tom Perry and Tom Austin founded churches in rural Tennessee. Perry carried the Pentecostal message to Alabama and in 1910 converted P. W. Brown, then president of the Jackson County Baptist Association. Brown became the pastor of the Bierne Avenue Baptist Church in Huntsville, Alabama, one of the leading congregations of the Original Pentecostal Church. There is little formal organization nor are there "man-made rules." Congregations are scattered throughout the deep South.

Membership: Not reported.

Spanish-Speaking Pentecostals

★687★
The Assembly of Christian Churches, Inc.
% Bethel Christian Temple
7 West 110th St.
New York, NY 10026

The Assembly of Christian Churches, Inc. grew out of the Concilio Olazabal de Iglesias Latino Americano shortly after the death of that church's founder Francisco Olazabal (18861937). In 1939, Bp. Carlos Sepúclveda, pastor of the Bethel Christian Temple in Manhattan invited various Spanish-Speaking pentecostal churches in the city to unite in an evangelistic crusade. The effort proved so fruitful that some of the cooperating congregations created a

new permanent denomination. In 1940 they extended their work to Puerto Rico where they operated as La Asamblea de Iglesias Cristianas. Their work spread rapidly and within the first generation it not only spread across the United States and throughout Puerto Rico, but to the Virgin Islands, Dominican Republic, Central and South America, and India.

The doctrine of the assembly is like that of the parent body, there being no doctrinal issues involved in the establishment of the assembly. The church is led by a bishop elected by the membership.

Membership: Not reported. In 1980 there were approximately 60 congregations with 800 members. There were 54 churches and 1,200 members in Puerto Rico, and additional churches in Central and South America. There was one English-speaking congregation in the Virgin Islands and one in India.

Sources:

Piepkorn, Arthur C. *Profiles in Belief: The Religious Bodies of the United States and Canada.* Vol. III. San Francisco, Harper & Row, 1979.

★688★
Concilio Olazabal de Iglesias Latino Americano
1925 E. 1st St.
Los Angeles, CA 90033

The revival on Azusa Street in Los Angeles which launched the Pentecostal movement soon spread and attracted some Spanish-speaking Christians. Most were affiliated with the Assemblies of God, formed in 1914. Among the early leaders was the Rev. Francisco Olazabal (1886-1937). Mexican-born Olazabal had became a Methodist minister and worked among the Methodists of southern California. In 1917, however, he received the baptism of the Holy Spirit in a prayer meeting in the home of George Montgomery and his wife Carrie Judd Montgomery. As a minister in the Christian and Missionary Alliance, George Montgomery had had a direct influence on Olazabal's conversion and entry into the ministry. By 1917 the Montgomerys had become Pentecostals. He left the Methodists and became an Assemblies pastor. He experienced great success in establishing new churches and recruiting pastors. Then in 1923 he led a movement out of the Assemblies, which he had come to feel had placed an insensitive Anglo in charge of the Spanish-speaking work. With his supporters he began independent work along the West Coast and the Mexican border. In 1931, he came to New York, after which he made visits to Mexico City and in 1934 to Puerto Rico. In 1936 he organized the Concilio Olazabal de Iglesias Latino Americano. In 1937, Rev. Olazabal died and was succeeded by Rev. Miguel Guillen. The present name was adopted after Olazabal's death as a means to honor his life work.

Reverend Olazabal had close contact with Ambrose J. Tomlinson and his son Homer Tomlinson then with the Church of God of Prophecy, and he noted Olazabal's natural affinity to Church of God doctrine rather than that of the Assemblies of God. Olazabal followed the emphasis upon the three experiences of justification, sanctification and the baptism of the Holy Spirit. The Assemblies position negated the necessity of sanctification prior to the baptism. The Council is also, like the Church of God, pacifist in orientation.

Membership: Not reported. In 1967 there were seven churches with 275 members with an additional four churches in Mexico.

Periodicals: *El Revelator Christiana.*

Sources:

DeLeon, Victor. *The Silent Pentecostals.* Taylor, SC: Faith Printing Company, 1979.

Tomlinson, Homer A. *Miracles of Healing in the Ministry of Rev. Francisco Olazabal.* Queens Village, NY: The Author, 1939.

★689★
Damascus Christian Church
% Rev. Enrique Melendez
170 Mt. Eden Pkwy.
Bronx, NY 10473

The Damascus Christian Church is a small Pentecostal body formed in 1939. It grew out of the work of Francisco Rosado and his wife Leoncai Rosado in New York City. By 1962 it had spread to New Jersey, with foreign affiliated congregations in Cuba and the Virgin Islands. The Church is headed by a bishop who is assisted by a council of officers and a mission committee.

Membership: Not reported. In 1962 the church had 10 congregations and approximately 1,000 members.

★690★
Defenders of the Faith
PO Box 2816
Bayamon, PR 00621-0816

The Defenders of the Faith was formed in 1925 by an interdenominational group of pastors and laymen headed by Dr. Gerald B. Winrod, an independent Baptist preacher. Winrod gained a reputation in the 1930s not only for his fundamentalism but also for his support of right-wing political causes. The Defenders of the Faith became the instrument by which Winrod promoted his ideas, and during his lifetime it was a large organization. After Winrod's death in 1957, the group lost many members. However, in 1963, it began a three-year revival under Dr. G. H. Montgomery, who died suddenly in 1966. Since then, it grew slowly and steadily under Dr. Hunt Armstrong, its new leader.

Its main program consists of publishing a magazine, *The Defender*, and numerous pamphlets and tracts; administering six retirement homes in Kansas, Nebraska, and Arkansas; maintaining a school (opened in 1957) and headquarters in Kansas City; and conducting a vigorous mission program.

The Defenders of the Faith was not intended to be a church-forming organization nor to be associated with Pentecostalism. In 1931, however, Gerald Winrod went to Puerto Rico to hold a series of missionary conferences. He met Juan Francisco Rodriguez-Rivera, a minister with the Christian and Missionary Alliance. Winrod decided to begin a missionary program and placed Rodriguez in charge. A center was opened in Arecibo, and *El Defensor Hispano* was begun as a Spanish edition of *The Defender*. Rodriguez's congregation became the first of the new movement. In 1932, Rodriguez accompanied Francisco Olazabal founder of the Concilio Olazabal de Iglesias Latino Americano on an evangelistic tour of Puerto Rico. The Defenders of the Faith received many members as a result of the crusade and emerged as a full-fledged Pentecostal denomination. A theological seminary was opened in 1945 in Rio Piedras. Members of the Defenders of the Faith migrated to New York in the late 1930s. In 1944, the Defenders' first church in New York was begun by J. A. Hernandez. From there the movement spread to other Spanish-speaking communities in the United States.

Doctrinally, the churches are not specifically Pentecostal; e.g., they do not insist that speaking in tongues is the sign of the baptism of the Holy Spirit. They are fundamentalist, believing in the Bible, the Trinity, salvation by faith, and the obligation of the church to preach the gospel, to carry on works of charity, and to operate institutions of mercy. Baptism is by immersion. Beyond the basic core of theological consensus, there is a high degree of freedom. Many congregations have become Pentecostal. Others are similar to Baptist churches. Premillennialism is accepted by most.

A central committee directs the work of the Defenders of the Faith. An annual assembly is held. Ties to the national office in Kansas City, which in 1965 discontinued all specific direction for the Spanish-speaking work, are very weak. It does continue support of missionaries and pastors. American congregations are located primarily in the New York City and Chicago metropolitan areas.

Membership: Not reported. In 1968 there were 14 churches and approximately 2,000 members in the United States, and 68 churches and 6,000 members in Puerto Rico.

Educational Facilities: Defenders Seminary, Kansas City, Missouri.

Periodicals: *The Defender*. Send orders to 928 Linwood Blvd., Kansas City, MO 64109.

★691★
Iglesia Evangelica Congregacional, Inc., de Puerto Rico
Box 396
Humacao, PR 00792

The Iglesia Evangelica Congregacional, Inc., de Puerto Rico resulted from the spread in the mid-1930s of the Pentecostal experience of the baptism of the Holy Spirit and the associated speaking in tongues within a congregation of the nonpentecostal Iglesia Evangelica Unida in Barrio Aguacate de Yabucoa, Puerto Rico. The congregation split and the pentecostal members created a council they called Hermanos Unidos de Xristo (United Brothers in Christ). Their work prospered and by 1948 a number of additional congregations had been formed. That year the council was dissolved and the work reorganized as the Iglesia Evangelica Congregacional, Inc., de Puerto Rico. Over the next decades, the church followed the migration of Puerto Rican members to the continental United States and in the 1970s work was established in Gary, Indiana, and Chicago.

The church is a holiness pentecostal organization that believes that sanctification in this life is a condition for entering the kingdom of God. They depart from most pentecostal groups in that they believe that speaking in tongues is not the only sign of the baptism of the Holy Spirit. The church practices baptism by immersion and the Lord's Supper. Infants are not baptized but are presented for a dedication service. The church specifically rejects the Roman Catholic practice of saying novenas and prayers for the deceased.

Members follow a strict dress code. Men must not wear neck chains, nor loose shirts, nor shirts with short sleeves or large collars. Women must dress modestly, in such a way as to not show much skin. They should not cut their hair and should avoid wearing jewelry, adornments, and expensive fabrics. Women who allow themselves to be sterilized and husbands who consent are to be expelled from the church.

Membership: Not reported. In 1980 there were two churches in Chicago, one in Gary, Indiana, and seven in Puerto Rico. The total membership was approximately 600.

Sources:

Piepkorn, Arthur C. *Profiles in Belief: The Religious Bodies of the United States and Canada*. Vol. III. San Francisco, Harper & Row, 1979.

★692★
La Iglesia de Dios, Inc.
Current address not obtained for this edition.

La Iglesia de Dios was founded at Fajardo, Puerto Rico, by a small group of nine Pentecostal believers in 1939. It spread throughout the island during its first generation. In the years after World War II, as Puerto Rican members moved to the continental United States, members of La Iglesia de Dios also arrived, and in the 1970s the church extended its work along the Eastern seaboard and into the Midwest, as well as to the Virgin Islands.

The church's doctrine is similar to that of the Assembly of God. It believes in the Trinity, repentance and the new birth, the baptism of the Holy Spirit, the gifts of the spirit, divine healing, and the premillennial second coming of Christ. The church is sabbatarian, believing Saturday to be the only biblical day of rest. Baptism, the Lord's Supper, and foot washing are observed as ordinances. Women are to dress modestly. They may serve as deaconesses and missionaries, but not in the ordained ministry. They have shown special concern to oppose witchcraft, which has been noted to be quite popular in sections of Puerto Rico.

Membership: Not reported. In 1980 the church had approximately 70 churches in Puerto Rico, 18 churches in the continental United States (in Spanish-speaking communities in New York, New Jersey, Connecticut, Pennsylvania, Ohio, California, Illinois, and Florida). There were two churches in the Virgin Islands. There were 5,500 members 12 years and older.

Sources:

Piepkorn, Arthur C. *Profiles in Belief: The Religious Bodies of the United States and Canada.* Vol. III. San Francisco, Harper & Row, 1979.

★693★
Latin-American Council of the Pentecostal Church of God of New York
115 E. 125th St.
New York, NY 10035

The Latin-American Council of the Pentecostal Church of God of New York, Inc. (known also as the Concilio Latino-Americano de la Iglesia de Dios Pentecostal de New York, Incorporado) was formed in 1957 as an offshoot of the Latin American Council of the Pentecostal Church of God. (The latter is a Puerto Rican church without congregations in the U.S., and therefore not discussed in this encyclopedia.) Work in New York had begun in 1951 and the New York group became autonomous in 1956, though it remains loosely affiliated with the Puerto Rican parent body.

Doctrinally, it is like the Assemblies of God. Healing, tithing, and a literal heaven and hell are stressed. The matter of participation in war is left to the individual members. Secret societies are forbidden and no political activity is advised beyond voting. An unaccredited three-year school of theology with an average enrollment of 500 trains Christian workers. Mission activity is carried on in Central America and the Netherland Antilles, among other places.

Membership: Not reported. In 1967 there was an estimated 75 churches, most in the New York metropolitan area.

★694★
Soldiers of the Cross of Christ, Evangelical International Church
636 NW 2nd St.
Miami, FL 33128

The Soldiers of the Cross of Christ, Evangelical International Church was founded as the Gideon Mission in the early 1920s in Havana, Cuba. Its founder, affectionately known among his followers as "Daddy John," was Wisconsin-born Ernest William Sellers. He was assisted by three women—Sister Sarah, Mable G. Ferguson, and Muriel C. Atwood. Successful efforts led to the spread of the mission throughout Cuba. In 1939, the periodical *El Mensajero de los Postreros Dias* (*Last Day's Messenger*) was begun. Until 1947, Daddy John functioned as the bishop. But at the annual convention of that year, he was named apostle, and a three-man board of bishops was selected. In 1950, the church sent out its first missionaries, Arturo Rangel Sosa, to Panama, and Arnaldo Socarras to Mexico.

Prior to his death in 1953, Daddy John named Bishop Angel Maria Hernandez y Esperon as his successor. During Hernandez's eight years as an apostle, special attention was given to overseas missions, which were started in nine countries. Plans for starting a mission in the United States were also made.

After the death of Apostle Angel M. Hernandez, Bishop Arturo Rangel became the third apostle. He was in office during the

Cuban revolution and the persecution of the church by the Castro government. The periodicals were cancelled and many churches were closed and/or destroyed. In 1966, the same year the American mission was opened, Apostle Rangel, one bishop, and one evangelist disappeared and have not been heard of since. The remaining members of the board took control of the church, and in 1969 moved its headquarters to Miami, Florida.

The Soldiers of the Cross of Church is a sabbatarian pentecostal body. Members believe in keeping the Law of God (the Ten Commandments) and the dietary restrictions on unclean food (Genesis 7:2; Leviticus 11). They believe in baptism as the first step to salvation, the Lord's Supper as commemorating Christ's death (not his resurrection), and washing the feet as a sign of humility. They believe in the Second Coming of Jesus, and have a strong belief in the gifts of the Spirit, especially prophecy and revelation by means of dreams and visions. Ministers are not to be involved in politics.

After Apostle Rangel disappeared, Bishops Florentino Almeida and Samuel Mendiondo headed the church. They were designated archbishops in 1971. They revived *The Last Day's Messenger.* In the United States, because of the similarity of the church's name with that of the Gideons International, the Gideon Mission used the name Gilgal Evangelistic International Church. At the annual convention held in Jersey City, New Jersey in 1974, the church adopted its present name.

The church conducts work in twenty Latin American countries as well as Spain and Germany. Much of the work is in the Spanish language.

Membership: In 1984 the church reported 23 congregations, 75 ministers, 1,500 members in the United States, and 100,000 members worldwide.

Periodicals: *The Last Day's Messenger.*

Latter Rain Pentecostals

★695★
AEGA (Association of Evangelical Gospel Assemblies) International
2152 Hwy. 139
Monroe, LA 71203

AEGA (Association of Evangelical Gospel Assemblies) Ministries International is a Pentecostal/charismatic fellowship of ministers and churches founded in 1976 in Monroe, Louisiana, by Dr. Henry A. Harbuck, originally as Christian Ministries. In 1988 the corporation was reorganized and the present name assumed. The AEGA sees itself primarily as a ministry to ministers; it credentials qualified ministers who accept its statement of belief and charters otherwise independent congregations. It provides a variety of traditionally "denominational" services, such as Bible college education, for its affiliated ministers and congregations.

The church has centrist Pentecostal beliefs which emphasize the authority of the inerrant Bible, the Trinity, and salvation in Christ by repentance and faith. The church is seen as an agency for evangelizing the world, a place for fellowship and worship, and an instrument through which God is building a body of saints perfect in the image of His Son. Two ordinances are recognized: baptism by immersion and the Lord's Supper. Each member should seek and receive the baptism of the Holy Spirit as evidenced by his or her speaking in tongues. The AEGA is organized according to the fivefold ministry of Ephesians 4:11. Women are accepted into the ordained ministry. The AEGA also affirms the pre-millennial second coming of Christ and the resurrection of the dead.

The AEGA is led by its founder, who also serves as the general overseer and president. He is assisted by a board of bishops and the general executive presbytery. Congregations chartered by the organization must accept its regulation and receive their tax-exempt status through the AEGA corporate exemption. Independent congregations, not chartered by the AEGA, may affiliate but are not covered by the exemption. The association is divided into areas, with a coordinator in each.

Members are expected to remain free of involvement in secret societies or occultic organizations and to renounce racism and allow it no place in the fellowship. While upholding standards of holiness, members are admonished to refrain from legalism having to do with strictures on minor matters.

The association has extended its outreach through its National Youth Ministries, the Christian Leadership and Church Growth Institute, and its extensive foreign missions program. The association meets annually for an international conference. Also affiliated with AEGA is the International Association of Christian Counselors and Therapists.

Membership: In 1997 the association reported approximately 1,500 members served by 350 ministers in the United States and approximately 300,000 members and an additional 600 ministers in 41 countries throughout Europe, Africa, and Asia. There were 35 chartered congregations and 25 affiliated independent congregations in the U.S.A.

Educational Facilities: Evangal Christian University of America;

Omega Bible Institute and Seminary, Louisiana.

Periodicals: *The Grapevine.* • *The Omegan.*

★696★
Apostolic Christian Churches, International
Box 3966
Florence, SC 29502

The Apostolic Christian Churches, International, was founded in the 1980s as the Gloryland Fellowship of Churches and Ministers, International. The present name was adopted in 1988. It is a charismatic church that emphasizes the fivefold ministry of Ephesians 4:11 as the proper means of ordering church life with apostles, prophets, evangelists, pastors, and teachers.

Membership: Not reported.

Educational Facilities: Gloryland Bible College, Florence, South Carolina.

★697★
Assemblies of God International Fellowship (Independent/Not Affiliated)
8604 Commerce Ave.
San Diego, CA 92121

The Assemblies of God International Fellowship (Independent/ Not Affiliated) emerged in 1986 when the Independent Assemblies of God, International voted to dissolve its old corporation and reorganize under its present name. The Assemblies of God International Fellowship traces its origin to the early days of the Pentecostal revival and its spread among Scandinavian believers during the second decade of this century. As early as 1911 Pastor B. M. Johnson founded the Lakeview Gospel Church in Chicago. A. A. Holmgren, a Baptist minister, was affected by the movement in Chicago and began *Sanningens Vittne,* which became the voice of the independent assemblies of Scandinavian Pentecostals.

An extreme congregationalism dominated the attitude of the early Scandinavian pentecostal leaders and most stayed separate from the General Council of the Assemblies of God, which formed in 1914. However, associates slowly began to form, the first being the Scandinavian Assemblies of God in the United States, Canada, and Other Lands in 1918. A second association of independent congregations was formed in St. Paul, Minnesota, in 1922. Pastor Johnson in Chicago took the lead in forming a third group, the Independent Assemblies of God. These three groups united in 1935 as the independent Assemblies of God. The group began the slow process of Americanizing and moving beyond any ethnic exclusivity.

In 1947-48, there was a division in the Independent Assemblies of God over participation in the ''Latter Rain'' Movement, the revival that swept western Canada and became known for its extreme doctrines and practices in some phases. The words ''Latter Rain'' refer to the end of this order of things, when God will pour out his Spirit upon all people. One group accepted the revival as the present movement of God, as God's deliverance promised in the Bible. This group, under the leadership of W. A. Rasmussen, became the Independent Assemblies of God International, now the Assemblies of God International Fellowship.

Membership: Not reported. In the mid-1970s there were approximately 300 congregations affiliated with the assemblies. Missions are supported in some 20 countries around the world.

Periodicals: *The Mantle.*

Sources:

Rasmussen, A. W. *The Last Chapter.* Monroeville, PA: Whitaker House, 1973.

★698★
Body of Christ Movement
% Foundational Teachings
Box 6598
Silver Spring, MD 20906

Along with the neo-Pentecostal movement of the 1960s, there deveoped what can be termed the Body of Christ movement, focused in the ministry of Charles P. Schmitt and Dorothy E. Schmitt of the Fellowship of Christian Believers in Grand Rapids, Minnesota. The basic idea is that God has moved among his people in each generation and has poured out his Spirit upon them in a vital manner. In the eighteenth century, this outpouring occurred through the Wesleyan revival, and in the early twentieth century, through the Pentecostal revival. In the late 1940s, the ''Latter Rain'' movement swept Canada. According to Schmitt, the outpouring on the present generation is the most momentous of all because this is the last generation and in it shall be manifest the full intent of God (I Cor. 4:1).

Initiation into the ''mysteries'' is through the baptism of the Holy Spirit. The central mystery of the church as the Body of Christ is that God is preparing a glorious church for himself. God is pouring out his Spirit in every denomination to bring forth the bride of Jesus Christ in this hour. The church as the Body of Christ is the very fullness of Jesus, who fills everything, everywhere with himself.

Doctrine, beyond the core of Pentecostal and Protestant affirmation, is not emphasized. The true basis of fellowship is in God and Jesus Christ. The Body of Christ Movement is organized on a family model, under the care of the responsible brethren (elders) and the ones possessed of spiritual gifts (I Cor. 12:11-14).

The Body of Christ Movement originated in Grand Rapids, Minnesota. Fellowship Press was established and it has issued numerous pamphlets on a wide variety of topics. The Schmitts began a tape ministry and a literature ministry, ''Foundational Teachings''. From Grand Rapids, ministers were sent out to cities across the United States. Centers were rapidly established. In the early 1980s, the Schmitts moved to Silver Springs, Maryland, near Washington, D.C., where a strong following had developed under the name of Immanuel's Church. Camp Dominion in rural northern Minnesota was the scene of national gatherings during the summer until recently.

Membership: In 1988 there were several hundred congregations and tens of thousands of people involved in the movement.

Periodicals: *Foundational Teachings.*

★699★
Bold Bible Living
International Headquarters
5774-132 A St.
Surrey, BC, Canada 98230

Alternate Address: American headquarters: Box 2, Blaine, WA, 98230.

The Bold Living Society is the organization facilitating the worldwide ministry of evangelist/missionary Don Gossett. Gossett had been the editor of *Faith Digest*, the magazine of the T. L. Osborn Evangelistic Association. While editor, Gossett was also an evangelist who toured North America, holding evangelistic campaigns and working as a radio minister. During the 1950s, his desire to become a full-time radio evangelist grew, and in 1961 he moved to British Columbia and organized the Bold Living Society.

During the 1950s Grossett became a devoted student of the writings of the late E. W. Kenyon, an early radio evangelist on the West Coast, and founder of the New Covenant Baptist Church in Seattle. After his death, Kenyon's daughter continued to publish his books through the Kenyon Gospel Publishing Society in Fullerton, California. Gossett obtained a copy of Kenyon's *The Wonderful Name of Jesus* in 1952 and eventually obtained an entire set of his writings. Kenyon emphasized the power of the Word, the Bible, and the power of confessing that Word as a means of exercising faith and bringing God's promises into visible reality.

Gossett emerged in the 1970s as a major exponent of what has been termed the "positive confession" perspective, a popular emphasis within the larger Pentecostal community. He maintains the Bible is the Word of God, and that people need to affirm the Bible's truth. It is through the confession of the believers' lips that Jesus gives life and love. Gossett applies Biblical promises for physical healing and contends God will supply people's every need. Confession of negative states traps individuals in sickness and poverty.

Gossett's radio work began in Canada and reached out to the United States. In 1964 he began broadcasting from stations in Puerto Rico and Monte Carlo, and soon a second office was opened in Blaine, Washington. As the audience grew, he wrote and published *School of Praise*, a home Bible study course, and numerous books and booklets. Besides the two congregations in British Columbia which are affiliated with the society, Gossett has a world-wide ministry which takes him on evangelistic campaigns around the world; his radio show is aired in over 100 countries.

Membership: There are two congregations with an approximate membership of 100, both in British Columbia. There are affiliated churches in Barbados. In 1988 there were 4,000 partners who support the ministry scattered across the United States and 3,000 others in Canada and the West Indies.

Sources:

Gossett, Don. *I'm Sold on Being Bold*. Springdale, PA: Whitaker House, 1979.

___. *There's Dynamite in Praise*. Springdale, PA: Whitaker House, 1974.

___. *What You Say Is What You Get*. Springdale, PA: Whitaker House, 1976.

Gossett, Don, and E. W. Kenyon. *The Power of the Positive Confession of God's Word*. Cloverdale, BC: Don Gossett, 1981.

Kenyon, E. W. *In His Presence*. Seattle, WA: Kenyon's Gospel Publishing Society, 1969.

★700★
Christian International Network of Prophetic Ministries
PO Box 9000
Santa Rosa, CA 32459

The Christian International Network of Prophetic Ministries, founded in 1988 by Dr. Bill Hamon (1934-), is one of the more recent outgrowths of the Latter-Rain Revival that swept through Pentecostalism in the late 1940s. That revival began in western Canada in 1948 and within a few years found a response among Pentecostal leaders across the continent. The revival emphasized such concepts as the laying-on-of-hands to receive the Holy Spirit, organization around a biblical five-fold ministry, and the role of prophecy. Prophecy, as understood within Pentecostalism, is believed to be a present word from God that is spoken by a person called by God and given the gift of prophecy. Prophecy, which goes beyond Scripture and often offers very specific direction to groups and individuals, should, however, never contradict Scripture.

Bill Hamon was converted to Christianity on his sixteenth birthday in 1950 at a revival meeting in rural Oklahoma and several days later was baptized with the Holy Spirit and spoke in tongues. He began attending a Latter Rain or Restoration church. In 1953, while struggling with a call to the ministry, he was given a word of personal prophecy indicating that he would soon emerge as a prophet himself. Hamon moved to Portland, Oregon, and began to attend a Latter-Rain bible college. In 1954, after graduation, he became a pastor. He left the pastorate in 1960 and served as an evangelist for three years. He served on the faculty of a bible college in San Antonio, Texas from 1964 to 1969.

In 1967, prior to his leaving college teaching, he incorporated Christian International Correspondence Bible College to provide an education for ministers who could not leave their work to attend school. The development of the college consumed his time for the next few years. In 1970 he developed the extension program to assist local churches in founding a bible college in their facilities. The college headquarters moved to Arizona in 1981 and then to Florida in 1984. It has since matured into the Christian International School of Theology. Through the years, Hamon has been responsible for training many Pentecostal ministers and introducing them to the prophetic ministry. In 1988 a number of the ministers he had trained and the churches they served banded together in a loose association, the Christian International Network of Prophetic Ministries. He was consecrated bishop of the network in 1989.

In his role as leader of the network, Hamon has authored three important books expounding on the concept and work of a prophet: *Prophet's and Personal Prophecy, Prophets and the Prophetic Movement*, and *Biblical Principles to Practice and Personal Pitfalls to Avoid*. The Network sponsors an annual National Prophetic Conference.

Membership: Not reported.

Sources:

Hamon, Bill. *The Eternal Church*. Point Washington, FL: Christian International Publishers, 1981.

___. *Prophets and Personal Prophecy*. Shippensburg, PA: Destiny Image Publishers, 1987. 218 pp.

___. *Prophets and the Prophetic Movement*. Shippensburg, PA: Destiny Image Publishers, 1990. 227 pp.

★701★
Church of the Living Word
Box 858
North Hollywood, CA 91603

The Church of the Living Word, often informally called "The Walk," was founded by John Robert Stevens (1919-1983), formerly a pastor with the International Church of the Foursquare Gospel. Because of Stevens' interest and involvement with the new Latter Rain Revival, the Church of the Foursquare Gospel defrocked him in 1949. A few months later he was admitted to the Assemblies of God. However, the Assemblies developed a growing dislike of the developing Latter Rain movement, and in 1951 also revoked Stevens' credentials. That year he opened an independent chapel in South Gate, California, the first congregation of the Church of the Living Word. The church gained strength quickly when a congregation of the Foursquare Gospel in Iowa, led by his father, affiliated with Stevens' new church.

The beliefs of the Latter Rain movement are similar to those of traditional Pentecostals, as represented by the Assemblies of God, differing more in emphasis than in doctrine. Those who became a part of the movement firmly believed that they were living at the end of time when God was giving new knowledge and gifts to restore the church to what it should be in the last days. Among the first things to be restored was the five-fold ministry of Ephesians 4:11; the church is headed by apostles, prophets, evangelists, pastors, and teachers, Stevens is considered to be an apostle and a prophet. Especially coming to the fore during the last days was the gift of prophecy (Acts 2). The Latter Rain and the Church of the Living Word have emphasized this role to bring forth the word of God in particular situations.

Through the Church of the Living Word, members believe God is rejecting Babylon and denominational Christianity, and restoring the Divine Order among his chosen last day remnant. Leadership will be exercised by his instruments. It is the duty of Christians to submit to that Order. As the Church of the Living Word moved into the New Divine Order, it developed a variety of ideas which have separated it from other Pentecostal groups. One such idea is termed "aggressive appropriation." Prayer, according to the church, is part of God's system of self-imposed limitation. God works through human beings who are consecrated to him, and who actively and aggressively appropriate God's promises and blessings. This appropriation will lead them above and beyond the Apostles and the Bible into the "greater works" mentioned in John 14:12.

The Church of the Living Word is organized as a fellowship of congregations tied together by their acceptance of the apostolic authority of John Robert Stevens and the ministering authority of those called to the five-fold ministry. A retreat center is located in Kalona, Iowa. Communication centers have been established in Panorama City, California, and Des Moines, Iowa. An extensive tape ministry, consisting primarily of Stevens' sermons, functions through the church from four distribution centers in Virginia, Iowa, California, and Hawaii.

Membership: In the mid-1970s there were 75 congregations across the United States and an additional 14 congregations in Brazil, Canada, Germany, Ghana, Guam, Japan, Mexico, the Netherlands, the Philippine Islands, and South Africa.

Periodicals: *This Week.* Send orders to Box 958, North Hollywood, CA 91603.

Remarks: As the Church of the Living Word has developed under the ministry of prophecy, many critics have complained that it strayed into occultic practices and doctrines which have denied basic Christian affirmations.

Sources:

It Shall Be Called Shiloh. North Hollywood, CA: Living Word Publications, 1975.

Stevens, John Robert. *Baptized in Fire.* North Hollywood, CA: Living Word Publications, 1977.

___. *Living Prophecies.* North Hollywood, CA: Living Word Publications, 1974.

___. *The Lordship of Jesus Christ.* North Hollywood, CA: Living Word Publications, 1969.

___. *Present Priorities.* North Hollywood, CA: Living Word Publications, 1968.

★702★
Community Chapel and Bible Training Center
18635 8th Ave. S.
Seattle, WA 98148

Community Chapel and Bible Training Center grew out of the Charismatic movement of the late 1960s. Some individuals with a variety of denominational backgrounds began to meet in the home of Pentecostal minister Donald Lee Barnett for Bible study. The study led to the formation of a church in 1967. Meeting at first in members' homes, the group outgrew available facilities and in 1969 began construction of a church building. At about the same time a Bible college was begun. Within a decade the church facility, expanded to seat over a thousand, was inadequate, and in 1979 a new sanctuary with seating for 2,200 was completed. Enrollment in the Bible college grew to approximately 900. The center has a lengthy statement of faith which affirms belief in the authority and inerrancy of the Bible; God as Father and Creator; Jesus Christ as fully God and fully human; the Holy Spirit; the necessity of repentance; water baptism by immersion for the remission of sins; the Lord's Supper as a memorial feast; strict church order led by pastors, elders and deacons; tithing; divine healing for the body; the gifts of the Holy Spirit; and a premillennial eschatology. There is no clear affirmation of the Trinity.

The center is led by the pastor, who has complete authority in spiritual matters. Administratively, the center is led by a four-member Board of Senior Elders. Over 125 people are on the paid staff of the center which includes the college, a Christian school (kindergartern through high school), a music program, recording studios, and a number of evangelical and social outreach ministries in the greater Seattle area. Members are encouraged to participate in one or more of the 150 active ministries. Community Chapel Publications has published a number of booklets by Barnett and a set of cassette tapes reflecting the center's music program.

Membership: In 1984 there were 2,800 members of the center in Seattle, and a number of affiliated congregations around the United States. Foreign work is conducted in Greece, the Philippines, Sweden, and Switzerland.

Periodicals: *Balance.*

Remarks: During the early 1980s, Community Chapel faced a variety of widely-publicized charges from former members. These charges include accusations that Barnett asked members to shun the businesses of former members, that former longtime members suffered mental problems related to their association with the church and its understanding of demon possessions, and the disruption of marriage relations due to the encouragement of close "spiritual connections" (which do not include any sexual liaison) between men and women apart from their spouses. The latter accusation is directly related to a church practice of dancing with one's spiritual connection during church services. Members of the center have staunchly defended the pastors and church leaders from such charges and from additional charges of leaders from other churches that the group is a "cult." Several lawsuits are currently under ajudication.

★703★
Endtime Body-Christian Ministries, Inc.
Miami, FL

The Endtime Body-Christian Ministries Inc. (a.k.a. the Body of Christ Movement and Maranatha Christian Ministries) was founded in the early 1960s by Sam Fife (d. 1979). A former Baptist minister, Fife became a Pentecostal after his involvement in the Latter Rain Movement, a Pentecostal revival movement which began in Canada in the late 1940s. Fife founded his organization in New Orleans, but soon moved to Miami where he had formerly worked as a contractor and singer. Fife's messages emphasized what he believed was the approaching end of the world. One sign of the end was the emergence of visions among Christians. In one vision, he was told that he would father a child who would be a great prophet. The woman designated as the mother was not his wife; however, with the consent of his wife and the church, he lived with her for a year, until he became convinced of the error of the vision.

Fife also called his members to prepare for the second coming of Christ by separating themselves from the world. They are in the process of preparing a perfected bride (i.e., church body) for Christ to find upon his return to earth. To accomplish this task, he organized a series of commuanl farms in the United States, Canada and Latin America. Many of the church members have sold their possessions and moved into these rural communities. The group also established a set of parochial schools for its children. The process of separation from the world led to the disruption of many families, especially where only one spouse was a strong member of the group. Also, the presence of single young adults in the group, often living at rather primitive (by middle class standards) levels, in the 1970s led to several deprogrammings and the focus of attention on the group by segments of the anti-cult movement.

Sam Fife died in 1979 in a plane crash. He was 54 years old. He was succeeded by C. E. "Buddy" Cobb, pastor of the Word Mission in Hollywood, Florida.

Membership: Not reported. There were reported to be between 6,000 and 10,000 members at the time of Fife's death. Approximately 25 communal farms had been established.

★704★
Independent Assemblies of God, International
24411 Ridge Rte. Dr.
Laguna Hills, CA 92653

Among the many independent Pentecostal churches that did not join the Assemblies of God in 1914, were congregations consisting primarily of Scandinavian immigrants, converts of the Scandinavian Pentecostal movement. Petrus Lewi Johanson of Stockholm and Thomas Ball Barrett of Oslo were the dominant figures in the Scandinavian Pentecostal movement. The Scandinavians were extreme congregationalists and believed that all discipline, even of ministers, should be vested in the local level.

In the United States, the extreme congregationalism worked for a while, but gradually loose federations began to develop. In 1918, a Scandinavian Assemblies of God in the United States, Canada and Other Lands was formed in the northwestern states. In St. Paul, Minnesota, in 1922, a fellowship of independent churches was formed. A third group, the Scandinavian Independent Assemblies of God, was formed around Pastor B. M. Johnson, who had founded the Lakeview Gospel Church in Chicago in 1911, and A. A. Holmgren, who published the *Scanningens Vittne*, a periodical for Scandinavian Pentecostals. In 1935, the latter group dissolved its corporation, and the three groups united to form the Independent Assemblies of God. They began to Americanize and to move beyond their ethnic exclusiveness.

In 1947-1948, there was a division in the Independent Assemblies of God over participation in the "Latter Rain" Movement, a revival that swept western Canada and which became known for extreme doctrine and practices in some phases. The words "Latter Rain" refer to the end of the world when God will pour out his Spirit upon all people. One group accepted the revival as the present movement of God, as God's deliverance promised in the Bible. This group, under the leadership of A. W. Rasmussen, became the Independent Assemblies of God, International. Missions are supported in seventeen countries around the world.

Membership: Not reported. In the mid-1970s there were approximately 300 congregations affiliated with the Assemblies.

Periodicals: *The Mantle.*

Sources:

Rasmussen, A. W. *The Last Chapter*. Monroeville, PA: Whitaker House, 1973.

★705★
Independent Churches of the Latter-Rain Revival
Current address not obtained for this edition.

Alternate Address: Important centers: Faith Temple, 672 N. Trezevant, Memphis, TN 38112; Glad Tidings Temple, 3456 Fraser St., Vancouver, BC V5V 4C4; House of Prayer Church, Box 707, Springfield, MO 65801; Bethesda Missionary Temple, Box 4682, Detroit, MI 48234; Praise Tabernacle, Box 785, Richlands, NC 28574; Restoration Temple, 2633 Denver St., San Diego, CA 92110.

History. The Latter-Rain Movement emerged after World War II among Pentecostals who had come to believe that the Pentecostal Movement which had grown from the revival at Azusa Street in Los Angeles, California, earlier this century had reached a low ebb. The movement had divided into a number of warring factions, and worship had become dry and formalized. In February 1948, a spiritual revival brokeout at the Sharon Bible College, an independent Pentecostal school at North Battleford, Saskatchewan, headed by George Hawtin, a former minister with the Pentecostal Assemblies of Canada. The revival was characterized by the development of a number of doctrinal innovations and new practices, including the laying-on-of-hands for the reception of the baptism of the Holy Spirit, the five-fold ministry, a recognition of the importance of the Jewish feast of Pentecost and Tabernacles; a distrust of denominations and denominationalism; and the manifestation of the sons of God. There was also a renewed emphasis upon the gifts of prophecy and healing in contrast to the older Pentecostal churches where they had largely disappeared.

As the revival spread, ministers and leaders from the older churches came to Battleford to see what was occurring. Their news about the doctrinal emphases and the variant practices led to a break between the revival's leaders and promoters with the Pentecostal Assemblies of Canada and the Assemblies of God, the two largest Pentecostal bodies in Canada and the United States respectively. Pastors and denominational officials who continued to participate in the revival and spread its doctrines were expelled from the Assemblies. Their break with the older Pentecostal bodies merely served to increase their dislike of denominational powers. Many of these became itinerate evangelists while others established independent congregations. These congregations rejected any formal denominational life. Many remained as simple small independent churches (frequently sharing a pastor with his secular job). Many of these new independent congregations, over subsequent decades, developed into a fellowship of associated congregations, and hence became, in effect, a new denomination. Included in this category would be the Body of Christ Movement, the Endtime Body-Christian Ministries, Inc., The Independent Assemblies of God, and the Church of the Living God. However, many congregations have remained free and independent through the last four decades. Together they form a distinct group of Pentecostal churches and will be the possible seedbed for new circles of fellowship. These congregations have developed an informal relationship through the sharing of publications, speakers, and various special events. Thus each church remains completely autonomous, keeping is own name and issuing its own literature, while relating to other congregations which grew out of the revival through support of locally promoted national conventions, camp meetings, shared publications, and missionary tours by prominent elders. Several hundred such independent congregations exist in North America, and form a circle of interlocking fellowship. A very few of the prominent centers are discussed below.

Beliefs. The Latter-Rain Movement accepted the basic beliefs of Pentecostalism. It did not so much reject any of the doctrines of the Assemblies of God and the Pentecostal Assemblies of Canada as it added to them and added in such a way as to create a new way of understanding the faith. Decisive for the movement was its understanding of history and of the present time being the final climax to history, i.e., the "latter days." Members of the movement view Christian history as a movement of disintergration and restoration. Following the apostolic era, the church began to fall away from the pristine nature of the original generations. That process gained ascendency through the Roman Catholic Church. However, beginning with Luther, God began a process of restoring the church. That process continued through John Wesley and the Methodists and more recently the Pentecostals. The Latter-Rain continues the Restoration process. The unique teachings and practices of the movement restore at least a remnant of the church to its destined state, the purity and holiness necessary for it to be the bride of Christ.

Most of the new ideas emerged during the original revival in North Battleford. Undergirding these new ideas as a whole was an interpretation of Isaiah 43: 18-19, which equated the "new things" mentioned in the verses with revelation yet to come. The new move of God included the following:

(1) The practice of laying-hands on people so that they could receive the baptism of the Holy Spirit and initiate the exercise of various gifts of the Spirit (I Corinthians 12:4-11). This practice contrasted sharply with the common practice in Pentecostalism to advise those seeking the baptism to tarry or wait upon God until it was given as God willed.

(2) The acceptance of the local church (as opposed to denominational structures) and the basic unit of church life. From Ephesians 4:11-12, the revival saw a divinely appointed church order in the five-fold ministry of apostles, prophets, missionaries (or evangelists), pastors, and teachers. The controversy surrounded the addition of apostles and prophets. The apostles were people who operated on a trans-local church context as divinely appointed leaders, as opposed to denominational executives. Prophets brought immediate inspired words of revelation to the congregation of believers. Almost from the beginning of the revival, the prophets spoke "directive prophecies," i.e., words understood as direct messages from God which offered particular advice and/or admonition to people and groups.

(3) The restoration of all nine gifts of the Spirit of I Corinthians 12. Through the Christian and Missionary Alliance, the gift of healing had been restored, and through the Pentecostal Movement, the gift of tongues. However, as the revival proceeded, all of the gifts, especially the gift of prophecy, began to operate.

(4) The modern fulfillment of the Jewish "feast of tabernacles." This teaching, ascribed to George Warnock, saw the three great feasts of Israel being fulfilled in the Church, the New Israel. The feast of Passover was fulfilled in Christ's death and resurrection. The feast of Pentecost was fulfilled in the creation of the Church and the giving of the Spirit. Yet to be fulfilled was the prayer of Jesus recorded in John 17:21 concerning the bringing together of the body of Christ free of spots and wrinkles.

(5) The idea of the manifested sons of God. Members of the movement believed that God would in the near future glorify individual people who would in turn be invested with authority to set creation free from its present state of bondage and decay. Those so prepared would be fit vessels as the bride of Christ.

Prominent Ministries. As is to be expected the Latter-Rain Movement spread first throughout Western Canada. Reg Layzell, pastor of Glad Tidings Temple in Vancouver, British Columbia, attended meetings at North Battleford in the summer of 1948, and in November invited Hawtin and others from Sharon to bring their message to his church. As a result, Glad Tiding Temple accepted the new truths and became a major center for disseminating the message throughout the continent. Layzell authored several important books and developed a particular emphasis within the movement as a whole upon the praise of God as a special activity for believers. He was suceeded by B. Maureen Gaglardi as senior pastor.

The Bethesda Missionary Temple in Detroit, Michigan, was among the first congregations in the United States to join in the revival. When in November 1948, Hawtin and others from the school carried the Latter-Rain message to Glad Tidings Temple, in Vancouver, Myrtle D. Beall, a pastor of the Assemblies of God, was present and became an enthusiastic supporter of the revival. Returning to Detroit, a revival brokeout in her church which attracted many future converts and leaders of the movement including Ivan Q. Spencer, head of the Elim Missionary Assemblies and Stanley Frodsham, prominent leader in the Assemblies of God. In 1949 Beall led in the construction of a larger church building which could seat 3,000 people. The new building was completed in time to encounter the first major attacks by the Assemblies of God on the Latter-Rain Movement and the church soon became independent. In 1951 Beall began the Latter Rain Evangel, which helped spread the Latter-Rain across the United States.

Today the Bethesda Missionary Temple is pastored by James Lee Beall who succeeded his mother as pastor. The church operates the Bethesda Christian Schools which provide education for first grade through high school. The church sponsors two annual festivals each spring and fall which bring many outstanding Pentecostal ministers to Detroit each year. Plans for a new sanctuary in Sterling Heights, a Detroit suburb, have been announced.

Among the oldest of Latter-Rain churches is Faith Temple in Memphis, Tennessee. The Rev. Paul N. Grubb and his wife, the Rev. Lula J. Grubb, were dropped from the ministerial list of the Assemblies of God in December 1949 (at the same time that Myrtle Buell was dropped). They were possibly the first spokespersons for the revival in the south and have continued to head the church he founded almost forty years ago. Grubb also established a bible school and sponsors an annual national convention each summer. He leads two influential books, *The End-Time Revival* and *Manifested Sonship.*

Restoration Temple in San Diego, California, is pastored by Graham Truscott, and his wife, Pamela Truscott. Graham Truscott is from New Zealand, where he was raised a Methodist. He became a lay minister but while in college he heard about and then accepted the baptism of the Holy Spirit. He became a missionary to India in 1960. Upon his return to the United States he began Restoration Temple. Truscott is best known in the Latter-Rain circles as the author of *The Power of His Presence*, a lengthy treatment on the feast of tabernacles. The church distributes this book and others he has authored, as well as numerous cassette tapes on Latter-Rain or Restoration themes.

The House of Prayer Church was started in Springfield, Missouri, in the early 1960s by Bill Britton (1918-1986), a former Assemblies of God Minister. Following several years as a marine in World War II, Britton attended Central Bible College and in 1949 was ordained by the Assemblies. However, having become involved in the Latter-Rain revival, he left the Assemblies and denominationalism the following year. For the next decade he worked as an evangelist, during which time he spent one important semester as an instructor at the bible school operated by Faith Temple in Memphis. (Faith Temple was also an important early Latter-Rain congregation, led for many years by Paul Grubb.) While in Memphis, Britton developed his understanding of the "overcomers." He came to feel that the church would have to go through the times of tribulation in the last days, as opposed to many of his colleagues who believe that the church will be raptured out of the world before this last terrible time for the earth. Shortly after leaving the school, he also developed the idea of a plurality of leadership in the local church. He felt that the church should be headed by a group of elders who mutually submit to each other rather than by a single autocratic pastor. This idea was later instituted in his congregation.

Britton became a popular speaker and writer in Latter-Rain circles. Voice of the Overcomer, the literature ministry established even prior to the congregation, regularly distributes numerous tapes, books, and tracts. He also initiated a correspondence course, and Park Avenue Christian School, a Bible school for kindergarten through high school. Semiannual national conventions are held in March and October. The church supports missionaries in 10 countries. Since Britton's death, the family, particularly Britton's son Philip Britton, and the Voice of the Overcomer staff continued the evangelistic and pastoral work.

Praise Tabernacle in Richlands, North Carolina, was founded in 1978 by Kelley H. Varner (b. 1949), a close associate of the late Bill Britton. Varner is one of the best educated leaders in the Latter-Rain Movement having several graduate degrees and having been for seven years a former Bible school teacher. It was during the years he taught that he accepted the truth of the Restoration message and left his teaching position to become pastor of congregation. Varner has become one of the major advocates of the Latter-Rain emphases through his radio ministry and the broad distribution of numerous tapes (many of his radio show) and writings across the United States. He publishes an extensive catalog of tapes and books biannually.

Membership: There are several hundred congregations which have developed out of the Latter-Rain Movement in the United States and Canada, but no census of the membership has been attempted.

Educational Facilities: Overcomer Training Center, Springfield, Missouri.

Periodicals: *Good News*. Available from Praise Tabernacle, Box 785, Richlands, NC 28574. • *Foibles, Fables and Facts*. Available from Bethesda Missionary Temple, 7616 E. Nevada, Detroit, MI 48234.

Remarks: The Latter-Rain Movement was opposed almost from the beginning by the Assemblies of God and the Pentecostal Assemblies of Canada. In the 1980s, it has joined the list of groups attacked by the Christian counter-cult spokespersons and organizations. Of particular concern has been the doctrine of the manifested sons of God. Critics of the Latter-Rain have accused them of teaching that humans who enter into the sonship experience are considered essentially divine themselves, thus obscuring the distinction between creature and Creator, a vital part of orthodox Christian thought. Latter-Rain spokespersons deny any such attempt to assume the role of God, but state that sonship is an actual gaining of the image and likeness of Christ by members of the His church as stated in I Corinthians 15 :45-47.

Sources:

Beall, Myrtle. *The Plumb Line*. Detroit, MI: Latter Rain Evangel, 1951.

Britton Volz, Becky. *Prophet on Wheels*. 10 vols. Springfield, MO: Bill Britton, n.d.

Graham, David. *The Doctrine of Sonship, A Theological Investigation*. Springfield, MO: Bill Britton, n.d.

Grubb, Paul N. *The End-Time Revival*. Memphis, TN: Voice of Faith Publishing House, n.d.

Hawtin, George R. *Pearls of Great Price*. Battleford, SK: The Author, n.d.

Hoekstra, Raymond G. *The Latter Rain*. Portland, OR: Wings of Healing, [1950].

Riss, Richard Michael. "The Latter Rain Movement of 1948 and the Mid-Twentieth Century Evangelical Awakening". M.C.St. thesis, Regent College, Vancouver, BC, 1979.

Truscott, Graham. *The Power of His Presence*. San Diego, CA: Restoration Temple, 1969.

Varner, K. H. *Prevail*. Little Rock, AR: Revival Press, 1982.

Warnock, George H. *The Feast of Tabernacles*. Springfield, MO: Bill Britton, n.d.

★706★
International Evangelical Church (IEC)
13901 Central Ave.
Upper Marlboro, MD 20772-8636

The International Evangelical Church (IEC) is a fellowship of Pentecostal churches formed in 1964 as the International Evangelical Church and Missionary Association. As originally constituted, the association was a corporation designed to legalize the Italian mission of John McTernan. Very early, McTernan became associated with John Levin Meares (b. 1920), the pastor of an independent Pentecostal Church in Washington, D.C. Though still largely a foreign movement, the United States branch of the church has become an important structure within the African American Pentecostal community. The origin of the church in the United States can be traced directly to Meares' decision in the mid-1950s to establish a ministry within the Black community of Washington, D.C.

Meares was a promising young minister in the Church of God (Cleveland, Tennessee) and the nephew of the general overseer. He was in the midst of a successful pastorate in Memphis, Tennessee, in 1955, when he decided to resign and go to Washington to assist independent evangelist Jack Coe in a series of revival meetings. He liked the city and decided to stay and build a church, the Washington Revival Center. He also started a radio show, "Miracle Time." From the beginning, the major response to his ministry was from African Americans. He thus found himself as the White minister of an integrated congregation in which the majority of members were Black, affiliated with a White-controlled denomination with very Southern attitudes about the races. He was forced to choose between his ministry and his denomination, resulting in his leaving the Church of God. The congregation grew and in 1957 settled in an abandoned theatre as the National Evangelistic Center.

The center faced a series of problems which were increased by the tumultuous social changes going on around it. Meares changed the emphasis of his ministry from one of miracles to one of teachings. Several evangelists raided the membership. All of the problems climaxed in the riots following the assassination of Martin Luther King, Jr. in 1968. Almost of all of the remaining White members left at this time. While the changes were going on around him, Meares became the vice-president of the International Evangelical Church and Missionary Association.

In the early 1970s, 300 remaining members reorganized and decided to built a $3 million facility. The renewed congregation opened the Evangel Temple in 1975. As the building was being completed, McTernan died in 1974 and Meares inherited the corporation, which at some point became simply the International Evangelical Church. Since then, the story of the International Evangelical Church has been the story of its international development and its expansion within the African American community. Internationally, the IEC began with some Italian churches and then reached out to include a group of Brazilian churches under Bishop Robert McAleister, and churches in Nigeria led by Bishop Benson Idahosa. Today more than half the congregations associated with the church are in Africa. In 1972 the church joined the World Council of Churches.

In 1982 the church also became the instrument of the founding of a new Pentecostal ecumenical organization, the International Communion of Charismatic Churches. It includes the various branches of the International Evangelical Church and several other church groups such as the Gospel Harvesters Church, founded by Earl P. Paulk in Atlanta, Georgia. That same year, the bishops of the Communion, McAleister, Paulk, and Idahosa, consecrated Meares as a bishop.

In the United States, Evangel Temple expanded and a ministry of people ordained by Meares emerged. Other independent Pentecostal congregations affiliated with the church. Through the 1980s, Meares emerged as a leader in a mediating position between the Black and White Pentecostal communities which, for several generations, had gone their separate ways. In 1984 he began the annual Inner-City Pastor's Conference which draws together the pastors (primarily African American) of the many churches of the association. Meares has also become a major voice raising the issue of the White Pentecostal churches' role in the African American community.

Membership: The IEC has approximately 500 congregations worldwide, more than 400 of which are in Africa. There are approximately 50 in South America, 20 in Italy, 20 in the United States and one in Jamaica.

Sources:

Burgess, Stanley M., and Gary B. McGee, eds. *Dictionary of Pentecostal and Charismatic Movements*. Grand Rapids, MI: Zondervan Publishing House, 1988.

Evangel Temple's 30th Anniversary Historical Journal. Washington, DC: Evangel Temple, 1985.

Meares, John L. *Bind Us Together*. Old Tappan, NJ: Chosen Books, 1987.

___. *The Inheritance of Christ in the Saints*. Washington, DC: Evangel Temple, 1984.

★707★
International Evangelical Church and Missionary Association

% Evangel Temple
13901 Centural Ave.
Upper Marlboro, MD 20772

The International Evangelical Church and Missionary Association is a charismatic fellowship of churches formed in the early 1980s under the leadership of John Levin Meares, pastor of Evangel Temple in Washington, D.C. Meares was raised in the Church of God (Cleveland, Tennessee), the nephew of the general overseer. After serving several Church of God congregations, Meares went to Washington, D.C., in 1955 to begin the Revival Center (soon renamed the National Evangelistic Center), a new Church of God outreach for the city. However, he soon encountered controversy within the Church of God because he had started an unlicensed ministry. This led to his disfellowshipping in May 1956. He continued his independent ministry, however, which emerged in new quarters as Evangel Temple in 1957. Membership of the integrated congregation was approximately two-thirds black.

In the early 1960s, Meares became aware of Bethesda Missionary Temple, one of the principle congregations of the Latter-Rain movement. From his observation of the life of the temple, he picked up a new emphasis on praise and the gift of prophecy which he introduced to Evangel Temple. This coincided with the heightened tensions of the civil rights movement which climaxed for Meares and the temple in the rioting that followed the assassination of Martin Luther King. Most of the white members withdrew, and Meares emerged in the early 1970s as the white pastor of a largely black church. Membership dropped to several hundred. The church slowly rebuilt, however, and in 1975 moved into new $3 million facilities. In 1991 Evangel Temple relocated to suburban Maryland. Their new facilities house a 2,000-seat sanctuary and their Bible school.

During his years in Washington, many independent Pentecostal pastors had begun to look to Meares for leadership and guidance. The International Evangelical Churches and Missionary Association emerged out of that relationship. In 1982, Bishops Benson Idahosa of Nigeria, Robert McAleister of Brazil, and Earl P. Paulk, Jr. of Atlanta, Georgia, all members of the International Communion of Charismatic Churches, consecrated Meares a bishop.

Over the years, Meares and Evangel Temple have become major voices in the Pentecostal community speaking to the issues of racism. Since 1984, Evangel Temple has become the site of an annual national Inner City Pastors' Conferences, attended primarily, but by no means exclusively, by black Pentecostal pastors from around the United States and Canada. More than 1,000 pastors attended the 1987 conference.

Membership: Not reported. Evangel Temple has over 1,000 members.

Educational Facilities: Centural Bible School, Upper Marlboro, Maryland.

Sources:

Evangel Temple's Thirtieth Anniversary. Washington, DC: Evangel Temple, 1985.

Haggerty, Steve. "A Spiritual Powerhouse." *Charisma* 10, no. 10 (May 1985).

Meares, John. *Bind Us Together*. Old Tappen, NJ: Chosen Books, 1987.

Meares, John L. *The Inheritance of Christ in the Saints*. Washington, DC: Evangel Temple, 1984.

★708★
Maranatha Christian Churches

Box 1799
Gainesville, FL 32602

History. Maranatha Christian Churches began in 1972 as a campus ministry. It founders were Bob Weiner, a former youth pastor for the Assemblies of God, and his wife, Rose Weiner. Bob Weiner had dropped out of Trinity College, the school of the Evangelical Free Church at Deerfield, Illinois, and joined the U.S. Air Force. However, a chance encounter with Albie Pearson, a former baseball player turned evangelist-pastor, led to his receiving the baptism of the Holy Spirit. Weiner finished his commitment to the Air Force and soon became involved with a coffeehouse ministry. With Bob Cording he formed Sound Mind, Inc. to evangelize youth, and in 1971 began to tour college campuses as an evangelist. He eventually settled at the Christian Life Center in Long Beach California. In 1972, he moved to Paducah, Kentucky, (where his wife's father was a minister in the United Methodist Church) and began a campus ministry at Murray State University.

As campus minister, Weiner sought to convert students and train them in the fundamentals of the Christian faith. While focusing on Murray State, he continued to travel as an evangelist and develop other ministries. By the end of the decade 30 Maranatha Campus Ministries had been established. As national ministries grew and members finished their college careers, Maranatha Campus Ministries became part of the larger work which was named Maranatha Christian Churches.

Beliefs. The doctrine and practice of Maranatha follow the common affirmations of Protestant Christianity and Penetcostalism, but have developed a few distinctives of practice. Weiner emphasizes a "scriptural pattern" for church organization based upon Ephesians 4:11, and attempts to build each center as a strong fellowship and training ground for practical discipleship. In previous years each center had a dorm in which converts could live while attending college, but that is no longer the case. General meetings of the fellowship are held weekly and most members also participate in small group fellowships. Prophecy is an important practice in Maranatha and is seen as ongoing confirmation of God's present activity in the church.

Organization. Maranatha's work is focused in the campus ministry, and all the congregations are adjacent to a college or university. The Weiners have written a series of books published by Maranatha Publications, which are used as textbooks in the discipleship training work. Maranatha Leadership Training School, often featuring a variety of charismatic leaders not otherwise associated with Maranatha, offers more advanced training for people on a national basis.

There is also a world leadership conference every two years. In 1985, Maranatha began a satellite TV network show as a televised prayer meeting in which 60 churches, tied together for the broadcast, pray for specific requests phoned in by viewers.

Membership: In 1988, the churches reported 5,000 members, 150 churches (campus outreach locations), and 300 ministers in the United States. There was one Canadian center, work in 17 foreign countries, and 7,000 members worldwide.

Educational Facilities: Maranatha Leadership Institute, Gainesville, Florida.

Periodicals: *The Forerunner.*

Remarks: During the early 1980s, Maranatha became the center of a variety of accusations centered around their intense program for training their new members. Many of these accusations proved unfounded and in other cases program adjustments made which have largely put the controversies in the past. Most importantly, a program of parent-student contact was broadly implemented thus reducing the problems which had arisen because of lack of knowledge by parents of Maranatha and the life shared by new members, most of whom are students.

Sources:

Andrews, Sherry. "Maranatha Ministries." *Charisma* 7, no. 9 (May 1982).

Weiner, Bob and Rose Weiner. *Bible Studies for a Firm Foundation.* Gaineville, FL: Maranatha Publications, 1980.

___. *Bible Studies for the Life of Excellence.* Gainesville, FL: Maranatha Publications, 1981.

___. *Bible Studies for the Lovers of God.* Gainesville, FL: Maranatha Publications, 1980.

★709★
Network of Kingdom Churches
4650 Flat Shoals Rd.
Decatur, GA 30034-5095

The Network of Kingdom Churches was founded in 1961 as the Gospel Harvesters Evangelistic Association in Atlanta, Georgia, by Earl P. Paulk, Jr. and Harry A. Mushegan, both former ministers in the Church of God (Cleveland, Tennessee). Mushegan is a cousin of Demos Shakarian, founder of the Full Gospel Businessmen's Fellowship International, while Paulk's father had been the General Overseer of the Church of God. Each man began a congregation in Atlanta. Gospel Harvester Tabernacle, founded by Paulk, moved to Decatur, an Atlanta suburb, and changed its name to Chapel Hill Harvester Church. The Gospel Harvester Chapel, begun by Mushegan, became Gospel Harvester Church, and in 1984 Gospel Harvester Church World Outreach Center, at the time of its move to suburban Marietta, Georgia. To traditional Pentecostal themes, inherited from the Church of God, the Gospel Harvesters have added an emphasis upon the message of the end-time Kingdom of God. According to Paulk, creation has been aiming at a time when God will raise up a spiritually mature generation who will be led by the Spirit of God speaking through his prophets. Given a clear direction from God, that generation, represented by the members of the Network of Kingdom Churches and others of like spirit, will overcome many structures in society opposed to God's will.

The congregations in the network developed a variety of structures to make visible the kingdom. The churches have supported Alpha, a youth ministry; House of New Life, for unwed mothers (an alternative to abortion); a drug ministry; a ministry to the homosexual community; and the K-Center, a communications center.

The government of the network is presbyterial, though the two senior pastors-founders have been designated bishops. They are members of the International Communion of Charismatic Churches, formerly the World Communion of Pentecostal Churches, that includes congregations in Brazil, Nigeria, and Jamaica. Bishop John Levin Meares, pastor of the Evangel Temple in Washington, D.C. and head of the International Evangelical Church and Missionary Association, is also part of the Communion.

Membership: In 1984 there were two churches in the United States; the church in Marietta had 1,000 members, and the one in Decatur, 6,000. In 1995 there were approximately 200,000 people affiliated with the network worldwide.

Periodicals: *The Fire.* Available from Gospel Harvester Church, 1710 DeFoor Ave. NW, Atlanta, GA 30318. • *Harvest Time.*

Available from Chapel Hill Harvester Church, 4650 Flat Shoals Rd., Decatur, GA 30034.

Remarks: In 1985 Bishop Paulk became the object of attack by popular (non-Pentecostal) evangelical writer, Dave Hunt. Hunt labeled Paulk one of a number of "seductive forces within the contemporary church." Paulk was included along with a number of popular pentecostal leaders including Oral Roberts, Kenneth Hagin, Kenneth Copeland and Frederick K. C. Price. Hunt, one of several who have attacked Paulk's kingdom message, was quickly answered by Pentecostal leaders, who came to Paulk's defense.

Sources:

Mushegan, Harry A. *Water Baptism.* Atlanta: Gospel Harvester World Outreach Center, n.d.

Paulk, Earl. *Satan Unmasked.* Atlanta: K Dimensions Publications, 1984.

___. *Ultimate Kingdom.* Atlanta: K Dimensions Publications, 1984.

★710★
New Covenant Churches of Maryland
804 Windsor Rd.
Arnold, MD 21012

The New Covenant Churches of Maryland is a fellowship of churches which emerged in the mid-1970s. The fellowship was originally centered upon the New Life Christian Center in Arnold, Maryland. Most notable among the leaders of New Life Christian Center is Robert Wright, a retired Naval officer and director of the center. He was instrumental in building the early association which, by 1977, included five congregations. He assumed the office of apostle (senior presbyter) for the affiliated churches and has engaged in a ministry of founding new churches and strengthening local churches who have joined the fellowship.

The New Covenant Church accepts the basic Pentecostal perspective, including the contemporary operation of the charismatic gifts (I Corinthians 12). Further, while accepting the main body of doctrine agreed upon by other trinitarian Pentecostal churches, the New Covenant Churches are among those groups which believe in restoring the fivefold ministry of apostle, prophet, pastor, evangelist, and teacher according to Ephesians 4:11, an emphasis which grew out of the Latter Rain Revival in the late 1940s.

The New Covenant Churches have been active in the development of Christian parochial schools. In 1983 these schools were removed from the Maryland Association of Christian Schools, the Maryland branch of the American Association of Christian Schools, an organization representing conservative evangelical church schools headed by fundamenatalist leaders. The schools were put out of the organization, a decision later accepted by the national organization, as a rejection of the Pentecostal doctrine of the supporting churches. In reaction, Wright has led in the formation of a National Federation of Church Schools.

Membership: In 1984, there were 24 congregations in the fellowship of churches.
Periodicals: *Koinonia.*

Sources:

Wright, Robert. "Key Questions Concerning Apostles." *People of Destiny Magazine* 2, no. 1 (January/February 1984).

★711★
People of Destiny International
7881-B Beechcraft Ave.
Gaithersburg, MD 20879

People of Destiny International, under the direction of an apostolic team of men, is a fellowship given to the planting and re-building of local churches and the proclamation of Christian teachings through churches, conferences, leadership training, worship and teaching tapes, books, and a magazine.

History. Larry Tomczak committed his life to Christ and received the baptism of the Holy Spirit in the early 1970s. Initially, he was active within the Roman Catholic phase of the Charismatic Movement as an evangelist and author. Tomczak and C. J. Mahaney (who now leads the PDI apostolic team) led a weekly teaching ministry called TAG (Take and Give) in Washington, D.C. in the late 1970s. As they studied the book of Acts, Tomczak and Mahaney began to see that members of the Church universal (those people who have become genuine followers of Christ and have personally appropriated the gospel) are called to be a vital and committed part of a local church. In this context they are called to live out the New Covenant as the people of God and demonstrate the reality of the kingdom of God. They further came to believe that the ascended Christ had given gift ministries to the church (Ephesians 4:11—apostles, prophets, evangelists, pastors and teachers) for the equipping of Christ's body that it might mature and grow. Through the gift ministries, all members of the Church are to be nurtured and equipped for the work of ministry. In the context of the local church, God's people receive pastoral care and leadership and the opportunity to employ their God-given gifts in his service, in relation to one another and to the world.

Tomczak and Mahaney have been influenced by British apostles Arthur Wallis, author of *The Radical Christian* (1981), Bryn Jones, and Terry Virgo. Jones and Virgo lead apostolic teams in Great Britain which provide oversight to churches in Wales, South Africa, and other countries.

In 1978, Tomczak and Mahaney established what is now called Covenant Life Church in the northern suburbs of Washington, D.C. In 1981 they sent out their first church-planting team and organized a team of men who function as apostles to help lay foundations in the church (Ephesians 2:20). Each apostle is a man of proven character and ministry commissioned by his local church for the work of an apostle, establishing churches and offering oversight to them through leadership training. New churches are usually founded by church-planting teams sent out from established churches. (In some rare cases PDI may "adopt" an already-established church with a history of relationship to one of the apostles and which has sought to become a People of Destiny team-related church.) Apostles are seen as builders and servants, giving general care and oversight to the various churches. Prophets are people who have a special gift from God to speak his word creatively and immediately to the church, consistent with the written Word of God. In PDI, the apostolic and prophetic offices are exercised with an emphasis on *relationship* rather than organization. The senior pastor of each church is personally overseen by one of the four apostles who comprise the apostolic team. Pastors are cared for and trained as friends and fellow servants in the Lord.

Tomczak and Mahaney founded People of Destiny International in the mid-1980s to provide resources and training for church growth and care. In 1985 they began publishing *People of Destiny* magazine as a vehicle of communication for the churches.

Membership: In 1992, there were 26 churches and 5,000 adult members related to the PDI Apostolic Team.

Educational Facilities: School of Ministry, Washington, D.C. Cross-Cultural Training School, Pasadena, California.

Periodicals: *People of Destiny Magazine.* • *People of Destiny Update.*

Sources:

Tomczak, Larry. *Clap Your Hands.* Plainfield, NJ: Logos International, 1973.

___. *Divine Appointments.* Ann Arbor, MI: Servant Publications, 1986.

★712★
Resurrection Church and Ministries (RCM)
Current address not obtained for this edition.

Resurrection Church and Ministries (RCM) grew out of the ministry of John Kelly, a Charismatic evangelist. In the early 1980s he came to question the scriptural nature of his own successful work. One day while in a period of quiet prayer, he received a message from the Holy Spirit which, he believed, directed him to "Go and wash the feet of the young men who will become the patriarchs of the end-time move of My spirit." Based upon this new calling, he reoriented his ministry to developing a nurturing network of ministers and ministries according to the New Testament pattern of local churches with a global vision. Kelly saw God's provision of the vision as the fivefold ministry of Ephesians 4:11: apostles, prophets, evangelists, pastors, and teachers. Kelley now functions as an apostle of the local churches that make up the RCM fellowship.

When Resurrection Church was formally established, it united churches in Pennsylvania, New York, New Jersey, and Michigan. In the next decade churches in Delaware, South Carolina, Florida, and Illinois were added. Foreign congregations exist in Haiti, Belize, England, and Russia. Headquarters in South Carolina were established in 1987. RCM sponsors Team World Outreach, which allows local congregations to send shortterm missions in various foreign and domestic mission fields. RCM's Apostolic Teams are composed of church leaders who move into a given country to strengthen local congregations.

Membership: Not reported.

Periodicals: *Covenant Communique.*

★713★
SHEM Ministries International
13232 Ambaum Blvd. SW, Ste. 102
Seattle, WA 98146

SHEM Ministries (Servant House Evangelistic Ministries), an outgrowth of Servant House Fellowship, was founded in 1996 by Glenn Smith, a Pentecostal minister. Smith attended Portland Bible College, Sterling Academy and received his Doctorate of Theology from St. John's University in Acre, Israel. He worked closely with the ministry of Vickie Walber at Ministries of the Living Stones in Anchorage, Alaska. SHEM Ministries International, a prophetic and apostolic ministry, began in Anchorage, Alaska, in 1990. In March 1993 Smith moved to Renton, Washington, and established a new congregation and an associated television ministry. His ministry attracted the attention of a variety of independent ministers who came to appreciate his work and his call for unity in the church. He produced and distributed a variety of books, tapes, and videos.

His ministry also brought him in contact with a number of people who were doing the work of a minister but had never asked for nor been offered ordination. After several ministers requested ordination, an ordination council for SHEM Ministries International was formed and the first ordinations occurred. The council grew into SHEM Ministerial Fellowship out of the additional desire that the ministers associated with SHEM be able to draw on the strengths of their colleagues and share their talents and experience where needed.

Membership: Not reported.

Sources:

http://www.harvestnet.org/SHEM/.

Other Pentecostals

★714★
Alpha and Omega Christian Church
96-171 Kamahamaha Hwy.
Pearl City, HI 96782

The Alpha and Omega Christian Church was formed in 1962 by Alezandro B. Faquaragon and other former members of the Pearl City Full Gospel Church. A congregation, primarily of Filipino nationals, was established in Pearl City. Four years later, a few members of the church returned to the Philippines and established a congregation at Dingras, Ilocos Norte. In 1968 a flood struck Pearl City and destroyed the meeting hall of the church. Many of the members withdrew after that event, though the church has survived and been rebuilt. The group is small, restricted to the Hawaiian Islands, and completely independent.

Membership: There are only two congregations, one in Hawaii and one in the Philippines.

Educational Facilities: Alpha and Omega Bible School, Pearl City, Hawaii.

★715★
American Evangelistic Association
PO Box 1954
Lake City, FL 32056-1954

The American Evangelistic Association was founded in 1954 in Baltimore, Maryland, by Dr. John E. Douglas, its president, and seventeen other independent ministers. Many of these had been affected by the Latter Rain Movement which had begun in Canada in the late 1940s. It licenses independent pastors, mostly Pentecostals, but also some other conservtive evangelical ministers. Government is congregational, with congregations affiliating with the national headquarters. The Association is headed by a five-man executive committee. The association was formed to promote doctrinal, ethical, and moral standards for independent ministers and churches, many of whom had come out of Pentecostal "denominations."

The American Evangelistic Association is missionary in outlook and oversees more than 1,000 workers outside of the United States, mostly in India, Korea, Hong Kong, and Haiti. Headquarters for the Association are in Baltimore, and for the missionary department, World Missionary Evangelism, in Dallas. Its periodical, *World Evangelism*, primarily an informational and promotional work for its many missions, circulates over a half-million copies The group sponsors the annual Christian Fellowship Convention.

Membership: Not reported. In 1968 there were a reported 2,057 ministers whose congregations had over 100,000 members.

★716★
B'nai Shalom
Current address not obtained for this edition.

During the 1950s, Elder Reynolds Edward Dawkin, an elder in the Gospel Assemblies (Sowders), had several visions, among them one in which he was instructed to begin work in Palestine, looking toward the restoration of Israel and the end of the Gentile age which began in 1959. Following the death of William Sowders, founder of the Gospel Assemblies, the movement reorganized with a presbyterial form of government. Dawkins rejected that polity in favor of an apostolic order of the five-gifted ministry of Romans 13, the church led by pastor, teacher, evangelist, and prophets, and (over all) the apostle. Dawkins was accepted by his followers as an apostle and his revelations are highly revered.

Dawkins died in 1965 and was succeeded by Elder Richard Tate. He leads a core membership called "overcomers," members who have given three years in living wholly for the body of Christ or who give at least fifty-one percent of their time, money and life for the body. Membership has spread to Jamaica, the Netherlands,

Hong Kong, India, Nigeria and Israel. The Peace Publishers and Company serves as the body's financial and publishing structure.

Membership: Not reported. In the early 1970s, there were 8 congregations in the United States and 11 outside, with a total membership of approximately 1,000.

Periodicals: *B'nai Shalom.* Send orders to 6401 8th Pl., Phoenix, AZ.

★717★
The Body (Bro. Evangelist)
Current address not obtained for this edition.

The Body is the name of a nomadic Jesus People group founded by Jimmie T. Roberts (b. 1939), known within the group as Brother Evangelist. Roberts was born and raised in Paducah, Kentucky, and following high school joined the marines. Roberts emerged as a religious leader following his times in the Marine Corps and founded The Body around 1969. The first converts consisted primarily of young adults, many previously part of the street people subculture of the era, and college students who had dropped out of school.

Brother Evangelist taught a separatist Bible-oriented pentecostal Protestantism. Members rejected the world and all personal wealth. They shun education, medicine, and bathing. Clothing is plain and simple. Sex is not allowed for singles, and sexual activity is discouraged among the married. They do not work, but gain a large portion of their food from what is thrown away by groceries and restaurants (a practice that earned them the label, "garbage eaters"). Women in the group are subordinate to the men.

The group kept a low profile, and its existence only became widely known in 1975 when some 35 members were involved in an accident near Fayetteville, Arkansas. A truck in which they were riding overturned and members of the group called attention to themselves by refusing to allow any medical personnel to tend to their wounds. One baby who was in the truck later died, though it was determined that medical aid could not have saved her. The accident led to several attacks upon the group by parents wishing to pull their sons and daughters from their affiliation with it. Over the next five years, members were kidnapped and deprogrammed by people associated with various anti-cult organizations that were attempting to counter the group's activity. However, the nomadic lifestyle kept the group constantly on the move, and made monitoring it difficult. While occasional reports of the group surfaced through the late 1970s, since the 1980s virtually no mention of its appearance has been noted, and the present status of the group is not known.

Membership: Not reported. In the late 1970s there were approximately 100 members.

Sources:

Martin, Rachael. *Escape.* N.p., n.d.

Sneed, Michael. "America's Bizarre Cult of Nomads." *Chicago Tribune* (June 1970).

———. "'Brother Evangelist': Hypnotic Shepherd of a Wandering, Ragtag Flock." *Chicago Tribune* (June 11, 1979).

★718★
Christ Faith Mission
6026 Echo St.
Los Angeles, CA 90042

Christ Faith Mission continues the work begun in 1908 by Dr. Finis E. Yoakum, a Denver Methodist layman and medical doctor. In Los Angeles in 1895 following a near fatal accident, he was healed in a meeting of the Christian and Missionary Alliance, the holiness church founded by A. B. Simpson, which had been among the first modern churches to emphasize divine healing. As a result of his healing, he dedicated himself to the work of the Lord and began his efforts among the derelicts, outcasts and street people of the city. In 1908 he opened Old Pisgah Tabernacle in Los Angeles. He began to hold gospel services and to provide meals for the hungry. In 1909, he began to publish the *Pisgah Journal*.

Yoakum had a utopian spirit, and envisioned a series of communities that would embody the life of the early church. He opened Pisgah Home for the city's hungry and homeless; Pisgah Ark in the Arroyo Seco, for delinquent girls; and Pisgah Gardens in the San Fernando Valley for the sick. His most famous experiment was Pisgah Grande, a model Christian commune established near Santa Susana, California in 1914. The community attracted people from across the United States, including some who had formerly lived at Zion, Illinois, the community built by John Alexander Dowie, several decades earlier. Piscah Grande, already weakened by charges of financial mismanagement and unsanitary conditions, was thrown into further confusion by Yoakum's death in 1920. They eventually incorporated and took control of the Los Angeles property. They bought property in the San Bernadino Mountains and then moved to Pikesville, Tennessee.

. In 1939 James Cheek, formerly the manager of Pisgah Grande, took control of the Pisgah Home property in Los Angeles and founded Christ Faith Mission, continuing the heritage of Yoakum's inner city work. He began a periodical. In 1972, the surviving Pisgah group in Tennessee united their work with that of Cheek and merged their periodical into *The Herald of Hope*, which he published.

Under Cheek's leadership, the old Pisgah movement reborn as Christ Faith Mission has become a world-wide full gospel (Pentecostal) ministry. He continued the healing emphasis, and the present-day mission sends out prayer cloths to any sick person who requests them. The Mission operates the Christ Faith Mission Home near Saugus, California, and the Pisgah Home Camp Ground at Pikeville, Tennessee. A radio ministry is heard over stations in Los Angeles and Long Beach, California. Foreign language editions of *The Herald of Hope* are sent to mission stations in Korea, Mexico, India, Indonesia, and Jamaica.

Membership: Not reported. In 1984 several hundred attended the headquarters center in Los Angeles.

Periodicals: *The Herald of Hope.*

Sources:

Kagan, Paul. *New World Utopias*. Baltimore: Penguin Books, 1975.

★719★
Church of God by Faith
3220 Haines St.
Jacksonville, FL 32206

The Church of God by Faith was organized in 1919 by Elder John Bright and chartered in 1923 at Alachua, Florida. Its doctrine is like that of the Church of God (Cleveland, Tennessee). It believes in one Lord, one faith and one baptism, and in the Word of God as the communion of the body and blood of Christ. Members isolate willful sinners from the church. Polity is episcopal and officers consist of the bishop, general overseer, and executive secretary. A general assembly meets two times a year. The church experienced significant growth through the 1980s and now has congregations in 13 states.

Membership: In 1992, the church reported 10,000 members, 200 congregations, and 250 ministers.

Periodicals: *The Spiritual Guide.*

★720★
Church of Jesus and Watch Mission
(Defunct)

The Church of Jesus and Watch Mission was a small Pentecostal church founded in the home of Bp. George A. Luetjen in Long Island City, New York. Luetjen had been converted, according to his own account, in 1910 following a period of depression and

guilt brought on by some family problems. One day in December of that year, while walking the streets of New York smoking a cigar, he tossed his cigar away, found his new relationship to God, and received the baptism of the Holy Spirit.

Luetjen began preaching some 12 years later and by the mid1940's reported ministers in eight states and Canada. He published a tract recounting his conversion and a periodical, *Prophetic Age*. Closely associated with the group was the Mizpah Mission of Taft, Florida, and the Israel Gospel Church, also of Long Island City.

In recent years no sign of the small mission has been found and it is presumed defunct.

Sources:

Clark, Elmer T. *The Small Sects of America*. Nashville, TN: Abingdon Press, 1949.

★721★
Church of the Little Children
Current address not obtained for this edition.

The Church of the Little Children was formed in 1916 by John Quincy Adams (1890-1951) in Abbott, Texas, following his withdrawal from the Baptist ministry. In 1930, he transferred his headquarters to Gunn, Alberta. After his death, his widow succeeded him, remarried, and returned to the United States (Black Rock, Arkansas).

The church is "oneness" Pentecostal—denying the Trinity and identifying Jesus with the Father—and has picked up elements of doctrine from a number of traditions. The writings of Adams constitute the sole source of doctrinal teachings. The group practices foot-washing. Wine is used in communion. The Trinity, Sunday Sabbath, Christmas, Easter, shaving the male beard, wearing neckties, and using the names of the pagan deities for the days of the week are viewed as vestiges of pagan phallic worship. Conscientious objection is required and no alternative service allowed. Healing is emphasized and modern medicine is rejected. There is a major thrust toward acts of love for little children; members try to prevent any child from suffering want or hunger.

The church is headed by a superintendent. Organization is loose and informal. Congregations are located in Arkansas, Missouri, Nebraska, Montana, Wyoming, and Saskatchewan. Each congregation is quite small and meets in a home. Contact between congregations is by correspondence.

Membership: Not reported. In the early 1970s there were eight congregations and fewer than 100 members.

★722★
Colonial Village Pentecostal Church of the Nazarene
Current address not obtained for this edition.

The Colonial Village Pentecostal Church of the Nazarene grew out of an independent congregation founded in 1968 by Bernard Gill, a former minister in the Church of the Nazarene. There followed an attempt to form the true church composed solely of "wholly sanctified holy people with the gifts of the Spirit operating among them," who then accepted as their goal and mission the reformation of the parent denomination.

Gill had begun to think of himself as "God's Prophet of the Latter Rain," and he received numerous revelations directly from God, as did one of the members, Mescal McIntosh. These were published in a periodical, the *Macedonian Call* in 1974. In the July 3rd issue, a resurrection was predicted. Two weeks later, Gill died. On August 11 a letter to readers of the *Macedonian Call* announced the belief of Gill's faithful followers that the prophecy obviously applied to their pastor, and that they were waiting in faith.

Membership: Not reported. No recent information has been received and the present status of the church is unknown.

★723★
Evangelical Bible Church
2436-44 Washington Blvd.
PO Box 7476
Baltimore, MD 21227

The Evangelical Bible Church was founded by the Rev. Frederick B. Marine in 1947. The doctrine is similar to that of the Assemblies of God discussed earlier in this chapter, but great emphasis is placed on the three baptisms for New Testament believers—the baptism into Christ when a person is "born again," water baptism, and Spirit baptism. The church teaches that any doubtful practice that is not forbidden in the New Testament should be left to individual judgment. There are definite statements on meat, drinks, days for worship, and dressing for show. The church teaches conscientious objection and is against worldly organizations that would inhibit spiritual growth, character, and commitment to God. A pretribulation, premillennial eschatology is taught.

The polity is congregational and there is an annual convention of both ministers and laity. Officers of the church include the general superintendent, the assistant general superintendent, and the general secretary. There are three orders of ministers—exhorter, evangelist, and ordained minister. Foreign missions are conducted in the Philippines where the Church is known as the Evangelical Bible Church of Cotabato, Philippines, and in Nigeria where it is known as the Soul Winners Christian Mission.

Membership: Not reported. In 1992 there were six churches (four in Maryland, one in West Virginia, and one in Pennsylvania) and 300 members.

★724★
Faith Assembly
Current address not obtained for this edition.

Faith Assembly was founded by Hobart E. Freeman (1920-1984), originally a minister with the Southern Baptist Convention. Among other things, Freeman began to criticize the Baptists for the celebration of Christmas and Easter, which he felt were Pagan holidays. In 1959 he entered Grace Theological Seminary at Winona Lake, Indiana, the seminary of the Fellowship of Grace Brethren Churches, which he joined. After receiving his doctorate in 1961, Freeman joined the faculty to teach Old Testament. He became increasingly critical of the Brethren Church, especially on the issue of holidays, and in 1963 was dismissed from the seminary and excommunicated from the Fellowship of Grace Brethren Churches. Fellowship meetings held in Freeman's home became the Church at Winona Lake, Indiana. It soon moved to Claypool, Indiana. The initial beliefs of the church were similar to those of the Brethren, though they espoused a concept of closed worship.

In 1966, in Chicago, Freeman experienced the baptism of the Holy Spirit. He began to read the works of popular charismatic leaders such as Kenneth Hagin, Kenneth Copeland, and John Osteen, as well as those of the late E. W. Kenyon. He also met Mel Greide, who owned a large barn near North Webster, Indiana, which was converted into a church hall. From 1972 to 1978 Faith Assembly, as the church had been renamed, met at "Glory Barn." After a split with Greide, Freeman moved the assembly to Warsaw, Indiana, until a facility could be built at Wilmot. During the 1970s, Freeman began to write many books and booklets which circulated through the larger charismatic movements and he frequently spoke at charismatic conventions. His books and tapes led to the formation of home groups around the Eastern half of the United States, with a concentration in the Midwest.

The beliefs of Faith Assembly are similiar to those of the Assemblies of God, differing more in emphases than in doctrine. Freeman taught what is popularly called "positive confession" or "Faith-formula theology." Freeman, like other faith-formula teachers, taught that when genuine faith is exercised by the believer and accompanied by a positive confession of that faith, anything is possible, especially physical healing. Unlike such faith-formula teachers as Kenneth Hagin or Kenneth Copeland, Freeman taught that medicine was Satanic and he forbade members from using the services of doctors. Assembly members remove seat belts from their cars and do not take immunization shots or use medicines. He also emphasized a rigid behavioral code which included personal separation from smoking, alcohol, drugs, and popular entertainment such as movies. Members do not borrow money. Young adults are counseled to not work at careers in law, medicine, insurance, or pharmacology. Abortion was also forbidden, and natural childbirth recommended.

Membership: There are approximately 2,000 members of the main church in Wilmot, Indiana and an estimated 15,000 in an unknown number of other congregation in 20 states. There are also members in Canada, Australia, Switzerland, and Germany.

Remarks: During the 1970s, family members of people associated with Faith Assembly congregations began to complain of its disturbing family relations. Several deprogrammings occurred. In 1983 a major controversy erupted around the Faith Assembly when charges were made that a number of people, many of them children, had died of medically treatable ailments. In 1984 several parents were convicted of child neglect and reckless homicide, and Freeman was indicted on felony charges for responsibility in the death of an assembly member's child. He died before going to trial.

Sources:

Crowell, Rodney J. *The Checkbook Bible: The Teachings of Hobart E. Freeman and Faith Assembly*. Miamisburg, OH: The Author, 1981.

Freeman, Hobart E. *Angels of Light?*. Plainfield, NJ: Logos International, 1969.

___. *Charismatic Body Ministry*. Claypool, IN: Faith Publications, n.d.

___. *Deeper Life in the Spirit*. Warsaw, IN: Faith Publications, 1970.

___. *Positive Thinking & Confession*. Claypool, IN: Faith Publications, n.d.

★725★
Full Gospel Assemblies International
% Dr. Anna Mae Strauser
PO Box 1230
Coatesville, PA 19320-1230

Full Gospel Assemblies International was founded in 1972 by Dr. Charles E. Strauser, an independent charismatic minister. Some years earlier, Strauser had founded the Full Gospel Bible Institute to train ministers. The Full Gospel Assemblies provided an affiliation for the ministers as they began to pastor churches. Over the years, as the charismatic movement has blossomed, pastors and churches not otherwise affiliated with the school have become part of the assemblies fellowship. Notices of the existence of the school and association have appeared monthly in *Charisma* magazine for a number of years.

Membership: In 1995 the assemblies reported 3,960 members in 44 churches, served by 290 ministers.

Periodicals: *The Charisma Courier*. Send orders to PO Box 1230, Coatesville, PA 19320.

★726★
Full Gospel Defenders Conference of America
Current address not obtained for this edition.

The Full Gospel Defenders Conference of America is a small Pentecostal body with headquarters in Philadelphia. Its emphasis is on evangelism and Christ's authority as manifested by the miracles and signs.

Membership: Not reported.

★727★
Full Gospel Minister Association
Current address not obtained for this edition.

The Full Gospel Minister Association is a fellowship of Pentecostal ministers and churches believing in the infallibility of the Bible, the Trinity, the fall of man and his need for redemption in Christ, the necessity of holy living, and heaven and hell. Members are conscientious objectors to war. The group sees ministry as being two-fold: the evangelism of the world and the edifying of the body of Christ and the "confirming of the Word with Signs Following and evidence of the power of God." The Association meets annually and elects officers. It issues credentials for both churches and ministers.

Membership: Not reported.

★728★
Glad Tidings Missionary Society
3456 Fraser St.
Vancouver, BC, Canada

The Latter Rain Movement, a revival movement within the larger Pentecostal movement, began in 1948 in a bible school in North Battleford, Saskatchewan. Among the first places which leaders of the new movement were invited to speak was the Glad Tiding Temple in Vancouver, British, Columbia, where Reg Layzell pastored. Layzell became an enthusiastic supporter of the revival and the Temple became a major center from which the revival spread around the continent. The Glad Tidings Missionary Society began as an extension of the Glad Tidings Temple of Vancouver, British Columbia. Over the years, other congregations affected by the Latter Rain (in Canada and the state of Washington) became associated with the Temple through it. It has become a primary religious body itself. Mission work is conducted in Africa, Taiwan, and the Arctic.

Membership: Not reported. In the 1970s there were eight churches, three in Washington and five in Canada.

★729★
Gospel Assemblies (Jolly)
Current address not obtained for this edition.

In 1952, Elder Tom M. Jolly became pastor of the Gospel Assemblies (Sowders) congregation in St. Louis, succeeding Dudley Frazier. In 1965, Jolly led supporters to separate from the older, larger Gospel Assemblies group. Under his leadership there has been a marked tendency to centralized congregations in or near major urban areas, followed by the centralization of funds in preparation for the purchase of land upon which the congregations can settle away from the evil influences of contemporary cities. Twice yearly, members gather for pastoral conferences, fellowship meetings and youth rallies. Doctrine follows that of the parent body. The number of congregations (originally twelve) had more than doubled in the first five years.

Membership: Not reported. In 1970 there were approximately 30 congregations and 4,000 members.

★730★
Gospel Assemblies (Sowders/Goodwin)
Gospel Assembly Church
7135 Meredith Dr.
Des Moines, IA 50322

History. William Sowders (1879-1952) was one of the early Pentecostal leaders in the Midwest. He was brought into the movement through the labors of Bob Shelton who had established a work in Olmstead, Illinois. In 1912, Sowders, a former Methodist, was converted and received the baptism of the Holy Spirit on a gospel boat which Shelton was operating on the Ohio River. In 1914, Sowders began preaching at various locations, finally settling in Evansville, Indiana, in 1921.

In 1923, Sowders conducted his first camp meeting at Elco, Illinois. Here he began to introduce the distinctive teachings that were to separate him from the main body of Pentecostals and lead to the emergence of what became known as the Gospel of the Kingdom movement or the Gospel Assembly Churches movement. Sowders developed his position in the context of the debates between the trinitarian Pentecostals and the Apostolic or Oneness Pentcostals, whose ideas denying the traditional doctrine of the Trinity had been spread through the Midwest by Thomas Garfield Haywood, founder of the Pentecostal Assemblies of the World. Sowders proposed a middle position and suggested that there were two persons in the Godhead,

God the Father, a Spirit being, and Jesus the Son, a Heavenly Creature. The Holy Ghost was not a person, it was the essence or Spirit of God which filled all space. Since the Son possessed the same name as the Father, God's name was Jesus. Jesus was the name given to the family of God in Heaven and in earth. Baptism was, therefore, in the name of the Father, Son and Holy Spirit, i.e., Jesus. He also emphasized that the formula for baptism was not as important as the action, that baptism became an action done in Jesus' name and for his sake, but could not be done in Jesus' name if one belonged to Babylon.

In 1927, Sowders relocated in Louisville, Kentucky, where he lived for the rest of his life. In 1935, he purchased a 350-acre tract near Shepherdsville, Kentucky, which became the Gospel of the Kingdom Campground, a place for camp meetings and annual ministerial gatherings. Estimates vary, but as many as 200 ministers and 25,000 members in 31 states were associated with the movement at the time of Sowders' death in 1952.

Following his death there were attempts by several ministers to assume leadership and several schisms emerged. The larger fellowship continued until 1965 under the direction of Tom M. Jolly. The movement continued, however, as a loose fellowship of ministers who pastored independent gospel assemblies. Among these men was Lloyd L. Goodwin (d.1996), a young minister at the time of Sowders passing, whose parents had been among the early converts of Sowders' ministry. In 1963, Goodwin moved to Des Moines, Iowa, to pastor the Gospel Assembly Church, a congregation of less than 30 members. Over the next decade he built it into a large stable congregation. In the late 1960s, due to his missionary activities, new congregations were started around the United States. In the early 1970s, Goodwin began to encounter tension with the larger fellowship of Gospel of the Kingdom ministers who rejected some of the doctrines which Goodwin believed had been revealed to him by God through his study of the scriptures. The break with the fellowship came in 1972.

After the break with the larger fellowship, a new movement began to grow around Goodwin beginning with those few ministers and congregations who sided with him. In 1973, he outlined a six-point program to his congregation in Des Moines. It included the development of the local assembly, the dissemination of Goodwin's teachings in print and sound media, and the sending of ministers to found other assemblies both in the United States and abroad. In 1974, the Gospel Assembly Christian Academy, a Christian elementary and high school, was opened. The following year foreign work was initiated in Toronto, Canada, and Poona, India. Africa, Singapore, and the Philippines soon followed. A book and tape ministry was launched in 1977. Goodwin has written a number of substantial volumes which detail his distinct Bible teachings, especially on eschatological matters. A radio ministry begun on one station in 1981 had grown by 1987 to 17 stations that reached most of the eastern half of the United States and the West Indies.

Beliefs. Apart from the distinctive ideas about the Godhead first articulated by Sowders, the Gospel Assemblies have a statement of faith which affirms many of the traditional evangelical Christian beliefs in the authority of the Bible, creation, the fall of humanity, the vicarious substitutionary atonement of Christ, the baptism of the Holy Spirit, water baptism, and the imminent second coming.

It is the belief of the movement that Christ will come while some who are alive today are still living. The ordinance of holy communion is also recognized and observed.

Organization. The Gospel Assemblies is described as a fellowship of ministers and saints around the world, where no church is organized above the local level, and yet where each assembly is in fellowship with all, and all acknowledge and are part of each in the fellowship. The churches recognize five ministerial offices in the church. First, apostles establish the work throughout the body of Christ. According to the Gospel Assemblies, "There is not another office in the ministry as authoritative as that of the apostle. The apostle stands next to Christ." Goodwin is such an apostle. Second, the prophet exhorts, edifies, and comforts. Third, the evangelists preach the news of salvation. Fourth, the pastors shepherd the saints. Fifth, the teachers instruct the church in doctrine. The five offices are not appointed, but recognized as possessed by some as gifts of God. A single individual may hold several of these offices. Appointed to handle the temporal affairs of the local church are deacons under the supervision of elders. There are regular conventions of the churches around the world, the main convention being held at Des Moines each May.

Prior to his death, Goodwin began to call for the healng of the divisions in the fellowship of churches that originated under Sowders. He proclaimed that the end-time church will confront organized religion and an apostate state; and further that the fellowship of churches that orginated with William Sowders, or a remnant of that fellowship, will be raised up by God to give a final witness to the world. Since his death in 1996, there has been increasing communication and fellowship between the various divisions of the movement that originated with William Sowders.

Membership: In 1997, there were an estimated 250 congregations and approximately 50,000 members. Gospel assemblies in fellowship with the Gospel Assembly Church in Des Moines can now be found across the United States (including Hawaii), Canada, Ukraine, Russia, Poland, Norway, England, India, Singapore, Australia, the Philippines, South America, and throughout the continent of Africa.

Periodicals: *The Gospel of Peace Newsletter.*

Sources:

The Former Days: A Brief History of the Body of Jesus Christ in These Last Days. Des Moines, IA: Gospel Assembly Church, n.d., 21 pp.

Goodwin, Lloyd L. *Prophecy Concerning the Church.* 2 vols. Des Moines, IA: Gospel Assembly Church, 1977.

___. *Prophecy Concerning the Resurrection.* Des Moines, IA: Gospel Assembly Church, 1976.

___. *Prophecy Concerning the Second Coming.* Des Moines, IA: Gospel Assembly Church, 1979.

Gospel Assemble Churches. Worldwide Fellowship, Pentecostal-Nondenominational. Des Moines, IA: Gospel Assembly Church, 1995.

Gospel Assembly, Twenty-Five Years, 1963-1988. Des Moines, IA: Gospel Assembly Church, 1988.

Ministers' Address Directory. Norfolk, VA: Gospel Assembly Ministers' Fund, 1970.

★731★

Gospel Crusade Ministerial Fellowship (GCMF)
1200 Glory Way Blvd.
Bradenton, FL 34202

Gospel Crusade Ministerial Fellowship (GCMF), founded by Charismatic evangelist/pastor Gerald G. Derstine, is a connectional organization and support group for ministers, churches, and ministries. The fellowship was created to facilitate and enable believers to develop their God-given vision for ministry and become successful in the fulfillment of their vision and calling.

GCMF has a Presbyterian form of government, with a group of presbyters who form the board of directors and are the corporate officers. There are 23 geographic districts, each with a leader called a district coordinator. The district coordinators are the elders of the fellowship and meet twice a year as an advisory council. They are committed to facilitate, assist, counsel, support, and help augment the ministry of the Gospel Crusade Ministerial Fellowship.

Each member (minister) is expected to attend the conferences and fellowship activities in his or her district, to attend the annual convocation at Christian Retreat, Florida, to support GCMF with monthly contributions amounting to one percent of his or her personal income which is considered dues, and to submit an annual report of his or her ministry when he or she files the annual credential renewal forms.

Over 100 Canadian clergy hold their credentials through the Gospel Crusade Ministerial Fellowship, and there are also members in Nigeria, Trinidad, the Philippines, Tanzania, Haiti, and Honduras.

Membership: The GCMF has over 900 ministers, and 67 affiliated churches and ministries in the United States and abroad.

Educational Facilities: International Training Center, Bradenton, Florida.

★732★

Gospel Harvesters Evangelistic Association (Buffalo)
Current address not obtained for this edition.

A second Pentecostal body, identical in name to the church headquartered in Atlanta and completely separate in organization, is the Gospel Harvesters Evangelistic Association in Buffalo, New York, founded in 1962 by Rose Pezzino. No information on doctrine or polity is available. Foreign work has been started in Manila and India.

Membership: Not reported. There are two congregations, one in Buffalo and one in Toronto. There are individual believers in the South. In the mid-1970s, there were an estimated 2,000 adherents.

★733★

Grace Gospel Evangelistic Association International Inc.
(Defunct)

The Grace Gospel Evangelistic Association International, Inc. was formed in the mid-1930s by Pentecostals of a Calvinist (predestinarian) theological background who rejected the Arminian (free will) theology of the main body of Pentecostals. The association was organized congregationally. By the early 1970s the association had approximately 70 ministers and missionaries, and foreign congregations could be found in Canada, Jamaica, Colombia, Formosa, Japan, and India. A periodical, *Grace Evangel*, was published. In the late 1980s, however, the association was disbanded and many of the formerly affiliated congregations merged into other pentecostal groups or became independent churches.

★734★

Integrity Communications (and related ministries)
Box Z
Mobile, AL 36616

In the midst of chaos in the emerging pentecostal/charismatic movement of the early 1970s, a group of experienced pastor/leaders stepped forward with a proposed solution. They suggested that submission, discipline, and respect for law and order were needed, and that the movement stood under a divine mandate to develop a program for discipleship and the development of Christian maturity along Biblical principles. They suggested that the New Testament norm was that each believer become directly accountable for others as a shepherd or spiritual guide that would demonstrate the Christian life. This concept became popularly known as discipling/shepherding.

Leading proponents of the discipling/shepherding concept were Charles Simpson, a former minister with the Southern Baptist Convention, Bob Mumford, former Dean of Elim Bible Institute; Ern Baxter, formerly a colleague of healer William M. Branham; Derek Prince, an independent leader of a radio ministry; John Poole, pastor of a church in Philadelphia; and Don Basham, a former minister with the Christian Church (Disciples of Christ). In 1970 these six men made a personal covenant with each other and began the task of making disciples who could, in turn, become shepherds engaged in making disciples. In their many travels they established local presbyteries of elders who became leaders of congregations related to the six ministers. These elders then fulfilled roles as apostolic leaders for those congregations. (The relationship between the local congregational elders and the leaders in Fort Lauderdale has been referred to as a "translocal" relationship.) Simpson, Mumford, Baxter, Prince, and Basham then founded Good News Church in Fort Lauderdale, Florida, and began Christian Growth Ministries. A magazine, *New Wine*, disseminated their teachings. Numerous books and tapes were produced which dealt with various aspects of church life and Christian growth. While working together, some of the original group also developed independent ministries under different names, such as Bob Mumford's Life Changers.

In 1975 the issues raised by the group became a matter of intense controversy within the larger charismatic community, and major steps were taken to resolve the differences. Critics were concerned over the abuse of authority which occurred in the shepherding relationship; shepherds interfered in the personal affairs of those whom they were leading. In the more extreme cases, anticultists attempted deprogrammings of people in congregations which were organized around the shepherding principles. Several meetings between the leaders of Christian Growth Ministries and other Charismatic movements resulted in the resolution of the many misunderstandings which had grown out of rumors and unverified accusations. Differences on the shepherding principle remained, however.

In 1978 Christian Growth Ministries and *New Wine* were moved to Mobile, Alabama. At that time, Derek Prince, who had served as chairman of the board, stepped down in favor of Simpson. Simpson initiated a new congregation, Gulf Coast Covenant Church, and Christian Growth Ministries became Integrity Communications. Leaving the Fort Lauderdale work in local hands, Basham, Mumford, and Baxter joined Simpson in Mobile. Prince remained in Fort Lauderdale as head of his own Derek Prince Ministries. As early as January 1975, following a visit by Simpson to Costa Rica, a Spanish-speaking congregation was established and elders were appointed. Christian Growth Ministries immediately initiated *Vino Nuevo*, the Spanish edition of *New Wine*. By 1980 it was being sent to believers in fifteen countries.

In 1984 Derek Prince announced his withdrawal from Integrity Communications. Among his reasons, he cited his disagreement with the opinion that every Christian should have a personal human pastor, and the practice of one pastor overseeing another translocally.

It has been the stated goal of the leaders of Integrity Communications not to allow the congregations associated with it, or the elders who derive authority from them, to develop into a "denomination." However, those churches and congregations have formed a distinct grouping within the larger Pentecostal community. In 1986, the four remaining leaders of Integrity Communications decided to decentralize their ministries as a means of stopping a trend toward "denominationalism." With this decision, Baxter moved to San Diego, Mumford to San Rafael, California, and Basham to Cleveland. *New Wine* was discontinued and replaced with *Christian Conquest*, edited by Simpson, who has remained in Mobile, Alabama. The group continues to meet periodically.

Membership: In 1986, *New Wine* had a circulation of 55,000, though its audience went far beyond the members of the church due to an oversight at Intergrity Communications.

Periodicals: *Christian Conquest.*

Sources:

Basham, Don. *A Handbook on Holy Spirit Baptism.* Monroeville, PA: Whitaker Books, 1969.

___. *Ministering the Baptism of the Holy Spirit.* Monroeville, PA: Whitaker Books, 1971.

Mumford, Bob. *Take Another Look at Guidance.* Plainfield, NJ: Logos International, 1971.

Simpson, Charles. *A New Way to Live.* Greensburg, PA: Manna Christian Outreach, 1975.

Vintage Years. Mobile, AL: New Wine Magazine, 1980.

★735★
Interdenominational Ministries International (IMI)
PO Box 2107
Vista, CA 92085-2107

The Interdenominational Ministries International (IMI) originated in a series of home prayer groups initiated by the Rev. Dr. Rocco Bruno and his wife Rev. Dr. Mary Bruno in Vista, California (north of San Diego). Their work was incorporated in 1983 and the following year missionary teams began work in Mexico. Within a few years the work outgrew the small home-based groups with which it began, and the present day name adopted to reflect its new status. As those who desired to work with the I.M.I. manifested a need for training, the IMI Correspondence School of Ministry emerged around a curriculum focused in Bible study, theology, and preaching. The school evolved into the present IMI Bible College and Seminary with students drawn from many denominations, though most are from Pentecostal and Charismatic churches.

The IMI is committed to an Orthodox Christian perspective with an affirmation of the baptism of the Holy Spirit, divine healing, and the necessity of holy living. Both baptism and the Lord's Supper are practiced. The Bible is taught as the Word of God.

Today IMI offers ordination and credentials to ministers (especially those who have completed a course of study at the IMI school) for a variety of independent ministries. Licenses are now held by ministers on every continent.

IMI is affiliated with the Chaplaincy Full Gospel Churches.

Membership: Not reported.

Educational Facilities: IMI Bible College and Seminary, Vista, California.

★736★
International Christian Churches
2322-22 Kanealii Ave.
Honolulu, HI 96813

The International Christian Churches, founded in 1943 by Rev. Franco Manuel, is a pentecostal group formed by former members of the Christian Church (Disciples of Christ) in Hawaii. Members consider themselves "Disciples by Confession and Pentecostal by Persuasion." They accept the pentecostal doctrines and place emphasis on the life in the Spirit.

In Honolulu, where there is a single congregation consisting mainly of Filippino-Americans. There are, however, an additional seven churches in the Philippines. The church functions on the loose congregational polity typical of the Disciples of Christ.

Membership: Not reported. In the 1970s there was one congregation with several hundred members.

★737★
International Evangelism Crusades
14617 Victory Blvd.
Van Nuys, CA 91411

The International Evangelism Crusades was founded in 1959 by Dr. Frank E. Stranges, its president, and Revs. Natale Stranges, Bernice Stranges, and Warren MacKall. Dr. Stranges has become well-known as president of the National Investigations Committee on Unidentified Flying Objects and for his claims that he has contacted space people. The International Evangelism Crusades was formed as a ministerial fellowship to hold credentials for independent ministers. As a denomination, it is organized as an association of ministers and congregations and unhampered by a dictating central headquarters.

The doctrine of the organization is similar to the Assemblies of God. A Canon of Ethics is stressed, the breaking of which constitutes grounds for expulsion from the fellowship.

Membership: In 1997 the International Evangelism Crusades reported 85 congregations and 125 ministers in the United States and a worldwide membership of 350,000. Associated foreign congregations can be found in Canada, Mexico, Korea, Jamaica, and Africa.

Educational Facilities: The International Evangelism Crusades formed the International Theological Seminary, Van Nuys, California.

Three seminaries serve the congregations in Asia:
Heavenly People Theological Seminary, Hong Kong.
International Christian Seminary, South Korea.
International Theological Seminary, Indonesia, with five branches in New York City and South Korea.

Periodicals: *IEC Newsletter.* • *Inner Circle Newsletter.*

Sources:

Stranges, Frank E. *Like Father-Like Son.* Palo Alto, CA: International Evangelism Crusades, 1961.

___. *My Friend from Beyond Earth.* Van Nuys, CA: I.E.C., 1960.

___. *The UFO Conspiracy.* Van Nuys, CA: I.E.C. Publishing Co., 1985.

★738★
International Ministerial Fellowship
PO Box 32366
Fridley, MN 55432-0366

Founded in 1958, the International Ministerial Fellowship is a charismatic fellowship that offers credentials to independent Pentecostal ministers. Ministers may serve churches or work in non-congregational chaplaincies and ministries. The fellowship also charters independent congregations. Affiliated members are found across North America and in several foreign countries.

Membership: Not reported.

★739★
International Ministers Forum
PO Box 1717
433 Oak St.
Dayton, OH 45401-1717

The United Ministers Forum is a Pentecostal fellowship founded in 1950 by Rev. Louise Copeland. As an international organization, it ordains and grants licenses to ministers serving independent churches, serving churches affiliated with other fellowships, or engaging in special ministries.

The forum affirms the Bible as the infallible Word of God, the Trinity, the deity of Christ, the indwelling of the Holy Spirit signified by speaking in tongues, and the unity of believers. The fellowship acknowledges all Christians who have been saved by the blood of Jesus Christ, to be members of the body of Christ.

The fellowship holds an annual convention in Dayton at the United Christian Center, where its headquarters is located. The fellowship is currently headed by its president, Rev. Doris J. Swartz. Members are found in Mexico, Romania, Honduras, India, Africa, Brazil, Guatemala, and Russia.

Membership: In 1997, the fellowship reported 450 ministerial members in the United States and an additional 150 in other countries.

★740★
Jesus People Church
(Defunct)

The Jesus People Church grew out of a "discipleship ministry" led by Dennis Worre, Roger Vann, and four other young men who created a Christian home in order to become better established in the Christian life. Worre and Vann led weekly Bible study meetings for what became formally known as Disciple Homes, when a girl's home was added a year later. As the ministry grew, a church building was purchased for Sunday services and, with fifty charter members, Jesus People Church begun. The church grew steadily through the 1970s and by the early 1980s two Sunday services were required to hold the congregation. Over 7,000 received the monthly bulletin, and a number of smaller churches began in the St. Paul-Minneapolis area.

The Jesus People Church was Pentecostal in belief. Its statement of faith affirmed belief in the Bible as infallible and authoritative, the Trinity, the Deity of Christ, healing from the redemptive work of Christ on the cross, the present-day reality of the baptism of the Holy Spirit as recorded in Acts 2, and the resurrection.

The Jesus People Church created a variety of outreach programs. Worre, a former actor, organized the Academy of Christian Theatre Sciences which put on periodic professional drama for the public. Jesus People Institute was a lay educational program conducted through the week. A radio show, "Today's Walk in the Spirit," heard over several area stations. The church owned a retreat center, Shepherd's Inn, located ninety miles north of Minneapolis, and operated Hesed and Fishnet, ministries to high school and junior high students. Foreign missionaries were supported in Canada, Germany, Haiti, Mexico, the Philippines, South Africa, and Thailand. There was also a missionary in Hawaii, and a domestic mission among Cambodian refugees.

In the mid-1980's, the Jesus People Church's pastors became the center of a scandal involving improper sexual activity. Subsequently, new leadership changed the name of the church and led the remaining members into affiliation with the Assemblies of God.

Educational Facilities: Jesus People Institute, Minneapolis, Minnesota.

Remarks: The Jesus People Church suffered a major setback in 1983 when Dennis Worre admitted to several indiscretions with women. Worre was asked to step aside from his leadership role, though he soon returned to active duty as senior pastor. The indiscretions did not include adultery.

★741★
Kingdom and World Mission of Our Lord Jesus Christ
5039 Franklin Ave.
Los Feliz, CA 90027

The Kingdom and World Mission of Our Lord Jesus Christ was incorporated in 1984 by Elie Khoury. Born and raised in Egypt, Khoury was given a message from God in 1960 concerning the war between Egypt and Israel that would occur in 1967. Following the delivery of this message to the Jews in 1965, he was imprisoned and tortured by the Egyptian government. He was released in 1968 but was arrested again. After a second period in prison, he migrated to the United States and opened the mission.

The mission is centered upon a single congregation in southern California. Khoury is a Pentecostal and preaches the baptism of the Holy Spirit as evidenced by speaking in tongues, the laying on of hands for the sick, and the other gifts of the Spirit. The Mission is dedicated to the cause of support for Israel and peace between Israel and its neighbors, and exists to serve people in the name of Jesus Christ. Among its primary services, it assists refugees to settle and become permanent residents in the United States.

Membership: The Mission claims over 5,000 members in the United States served by five ministers. Worldwide, the Mission claims some 65,000 members, most of whom reside in Lebanon and Egypt.

Educational Facilities: Kingdom and World Mission of Our Lord Jesus Christ School of Theology, Los Angeles, California.

★742★
Kingsway Fellowship International
3707 S.W. 9th St.
Des Moines, IA 50315-3047

Kingsway Fellowship International, a Pentecostal fellowship of independent ministers and missionaries, was founded in 1966 by Dr. D. L. Browning, who serves as its president. The fellowship offers ministerial services, counsel, and religious nonprofit status with the IRS to its members. It also seeks to mobilize its members as leaders in a worldwide evangelism/missionary effort.

The fellowship is incorporated and headed by a 13-member board of directors who appoint regional, district, and national superintendents to assist in the evangelism program. It offers credentials to Christian workers, lay-exhorters, and ordained ministers. It also charters churches and related ministries. It sponsors an annual conference, providing fellowship among its members.

Membership: Not reported. There are several thousand members.

Sources:

http://www.kingsway.edu/.

★743★
Liberty Fellowship of Churches and Ministers
2732 Old Rocky Ridge Rd.
Birmingham, AL 35216

The Liberty Fellowship of Churches and Ministers was organized in 1975 in Pensacola, Florida, by Ken Sumrall and twenty other ministers. Sumrall, a former pastor in the Southern Baptist Convention, received the baptism of the Holy Spirit in February 1964. The following month he organized Liberty Baptist Church (later Liberty Church) as a congregation for Spirit-filled Baptists. At first the work grew slowly, but membership increased markedly in 1966, the year the college began adjacent to the church. In 1972 land was purchased on the edge of Pensacola, and a building complex was constructed. During the 1970s, other independent charismatic pastors who saw the need of oversight for themselves, and their congregations began searching for a proper structure. In that search, they were influenced by other Pentecostal leaders who had been influenced by the Latter-Rain Movement. Such leaders as Bill Britton of Overcomers Fellowship in Springfield, Missouri, believed the church was properly led by a five-flood ministry of apostles, evangelists, prophets, pastors, and teachers (Ephesians 4:11-12).

The fellowship's doctrine is close to that of the Assemblies of God, including belief in the triune God, salvation through Christ, two ordinances (baptism and the Lord's Supper), divine healing, the present-day operation of the gifts of the Holy Spirit (I Corinthians 12), and the baptism of the Holy Spirit as an immediate possibility for the believer.

The fellowship is governed by a presbytery headed by the president. The first president, Sumrall, is considered the apostle of the fellowship. He will serve in that capacity until he dies or retires. The presbytery ordains and appoints pastors to local churches and within its membership the entire five-fold ministry is represented. Local congregational affairs are administered by elders and deacons elected by the congregation and confirmed by the presbytery.

Membership: Congregations within the fellowship are scattered throughout the South.

Educational Facilities: Liberty Christian College, Pensacola, Florida.

Sources:

Sumrall, Ken. *New Wine Bottles.* Pensacola, FL: Liberty Creative Press, 1976.

___. *Practical Church Government: Organized Flexibility.* Pensacola, FL: The Author, 1982.

★744★
Lighthouse Gospel Fellowship
Current address not obtained for this edition.

The Lighthouse Gospel Fellowship is a Pentecostal church founded in 1958 by Drs. H. A. Chaney and Themla Chaney of Tulsa, Oklahoma. There are a set of beliefs held in common by ministers and members. The fellowship is trinitarian. It believes in the virgin birth, the bodily resurrection of Jesus, baptism of the Holy Spirit evidenced by speaking in tongues, the laying on of hands for the confirmation of ministry and imparting of the gifts of the Spirit. However, the group also conceives of itself as nonsectarian and hence home to a variety of views on less essential beliefs.

Membership: Not reported.In the 1970s there were approximately 100 congregations and 1,000 members.

★745★
The Neverdies
Current address not obtained for this edition.

Known locally in the communities of West Virginia as the Church of the Living Gospel or the Church of the Everlasting Gospel, the Neverdies are Pentecostals who believe in immortality not only of the soul but also of the body. The soul, they believe, returns to earth in a series of reincarnations until it succeeds in living a perfect life. At that point, the body can live forever. The origin of the group has been lost, but among the first teachers was Ted Oiler, born in 1906, who in 1973 was still traveling a circuit through the mountains of Virginia and North Carolina. The congregations are rather loosely knit, held together by their acceptance of what is a rather unusual doctrine for the mountain area. Among the leaders is Rev. Henry Holstine of Charleston, West Virginia.

Membership: Not reported.

★746★
Pentecostal Full Gospel Church
212 East 25th St.
Baltimore, MD 21211

Membership: The Pentecostal Full Gospel Church was founded in 1922 as the Apostolic Churches of Christ. It is a trinitarian church (though its articles of faith do not treat such basic theological concerns as the doctrine of God, Christ, or the Holy Spirit). There is an emphasis upon the baptism of the Holy Spirit as evidenced by speaking in tongues, healing out of the atonement of Jesus, three ordinances (baptism by immersion, the Lords's Supper, and foot washing), tithing, and the imminent return of Christ to reign on earth for a thousand years. At the Lord's Supper unleavened bread and unfermented grape juice is used. There is a strong aversion to divorce and remarriage, and no ministerial credentials can be issued to divorced and/or remarried people.

The church is headed by a president elected at the annual convention. He appoints ministers to the local congregations. Pastors appoint local elders, deacons, and deaconesses. Not reported.

★747★
Pentecostal 7th Day Assemblies
% Elder Garver C. Gray, Chairman
4700 NE 119th St.
Vancouver, WA 98686

The Petecostal 7th Day Assemblies, formerly known as the Association of Seventh-Day Pentecostal Assemblies (incorporated in 1984) had existed as an informal fellowship of congregations and ministers since 1931. It is an association headed by a chairman and a co-ordinating committee. The committee has a responsibility for joint vetures, but has no authority over local church programs or affairs. Doctrinally, the association has taken a nonsectarian stance, affirming some minimal beliefs commonly held but leaving many questions open. Ministers hold an non-Trinitarian position. Baptism is by immersion, but a variety of formulas are spoken. The association believes in sanctification by the blood, Spirit and the Word, the baptism of the Holy Spirit, the Ten Commandments (each of equal worth) and the millennium. The association is congregationally organized. Each local church is autonomous and sets its own policy and mission. The association supports missions in Canada, Ghana, and Nigeria, and works in other countries through its congregations.

Membership: Not reported.

Educational Facilities: The assemblies support a college in Kumasi, Ashanti, Ghana.

Periodicals: *The Hour of Preparation.* Send orders to 16826 118th Ave. NE, Bothell, WA 98011.

★748★
The Rock Church
640 Kempsville Rd.
Virginia Beach, VA 23464

The Rock Church was founded in Norfolk, Virginia, in 1966 by John Gimenez, a former drug addict, and his wife and fellow evangelist, Anne Gimenez. John Gimenez had been saved from his drug addiction in 1965 and began touring the country with seven other former addicts in *The Addicts,* a dramatic presentation of their stories. The play was also made into a movie, and Gimenez published his accounts in a book, *Up Tight.* While on tour he met his future wife who was holding evangelistic services in Indianapolis. They married in 1966. During the early phase of their combined ministry, they associated with Pat Robertson's *700 Club,* which brought them to the Tidewater Area of Virginia where they discovered an abandoned church building in Norfolk. Within a few years, the church proved too small to hold the growing congregation, and they built a new building in nearby Virginia Beach. They called the new church the Rock Church, based upon the passage in the Gospel of Matthew 16:18, ". . . upon this rock I will build my church." They soon added a school, the Rock Academy.

The church expanded its ministries and grew spectacularly during its first decade, and by 1979 the church had 23 additional affiliated congregations.

Membership: Not reported. In 1998 there were more than 300 congregations associated with the Rock Church.

Sources:

Gimenez, Anne. *The Emerging Christian Woman.* N.p., n.d.

Gimenez, John. *Up Tight.* N.p., n.d.

★749★
United Christian Church and Ministerial Association
Box 700
Cleveland, TN 37311

The United Christian Ministerial Association was founded in 1956 by the the Rev. H. Richard Hall as an association of independent Pentecostal ministers. The local church in Cleveland, Tennessee, was formed in 1972 at which time the name of the organization was changed to United Christian Church and Ministerial Association. Doctrinally the church is described as fundamental and pentecostal.

The association is headed by Hall and a board of directors. Ministerial training is offered for resident students through the United Christian Church and for nonresident students though a correspondence institute. The association offers exhorter and ordination licenses to all charismatics and pentecostals who are called to preach in any one of 16 categories including apostles, bishops, pastors, teachers, missionaries, and ministering through the various gifts of the Spirit as outlined in I Cor. 12. There is an annual minister's convention in Cleveland during which one day is set aside for the ordination of ministers and one for graduation for students of the United Christian Bible Institute.

Membership: In 1997, the association reported more than 18,500 licensed and ordained ministers worldwide and 150 affiliated congregations in the United States.

Educational Facilities: United Christian Bible Correspondance Institute, Cleveland, Tennessee.

Periodicals: *Shield of Faith.*

Sources:

Sims, Patsy. *Can Somebody Shout Amen!* New York: St. Martin's Press, 1988.

★750★
United Evangelical Churches
Current address not obtained for this edition.

The United Evangelical Church was formed in 1960, one of the first structural responses to the neo-Pentecostal revival. It is made up especially of those ministers and laymen from mainline churches who, since their baptism with the Holy Spirit, have not felt free to remain in their mainline churches. As a fellowship, they hope to avoid some of the evils of institutionalism, namely, the excessive control of man that prevents control by the living Spirit of God. Because of its origin, the church continues to be open to charismatics who choose to remain in their own churches.

The tenets of faith of the United Evangelical Church profess belief in the Bible as the Word of God, the Trinity, the virgin birth and resurrection of Christ, the inability of man to save himself, salvation in Christ, regeneration by the Holy Spirit, the present ministry of the Holy Spirit which empowers Christians and manifests itself in gifts and ministries, and the judgment of Christ.

The church is governed by an executive council and there is a conference of the church every two years. Churches are divided into three regions-Western, Central, and Eastern. Churches (in 1970) were found in twenty-four states. Foreign work was located in India, Korea, Formosa, Hong Kong, Singapore, Japan, Ghana, Kenya, Jamaica, Guatemala, El Salvador, Colombia, Mexico, Costa Rica, Honduras, and Iran.

Membership: Not reported.

★751★
The United Network of Christian Ministries and Churches
Current address not obtained for this edition.

The United Network of Christian Ministries and Churches was founded in 1985 by Rev. Don Pfotenhauer, formerly a pastor in the Lutheran Church-Missouri Synod. Pfotenhauer had become affiliated with the larger Charismatic movement which occasioned his being expelled from his denomination. As that process proceeded, out of meetings and prayer with his supporters, he felt called to an "apostolic" ministry. The vision for this ministry articulated through prophetic utterances of several people included the establishment of local churches which would operate as the body of Christ in their community and unite believers in a loving fellowship where each member is rightly related to Christ and each other.

Local churches are autonomous; transcongregational leadership, though, is supplied to the churches affiliated with the fellowship by several apostolic teams. These teams are seen as "coaches" who prepare the body of Christ for the work of the ministry. They are viewed as authorities delegated by the Holy Spirit who govern the church. The apostolic team visits each member church at least once annually. Pfotenhauer serves as the apostolic director of the fellowship.

Membership: In 1997 there were 25 congregations with 3,300 members affiliated with the fellowship in the United States and an additional 14 churches worldwide in Tanzania; Manitoba, Canada; and India.

★752★
Universal Church, the Mystical Body of Christ
Current address not obtained for this edition.

The Universal Church, the Mystical Body of Christ, is an interracial Pentecostal group which emerged in the 1970s. It is distinguished by its belief that in order to serve God freely, members must come out of a corrupt government, society, and churches of this land, and establish a separate government on another continent where a theocratic system can be constructed. Only then, can perfection exist in society. Members call upon all Christians to join them. They believe that these are the end-times and that God is calling together his 144,000 mentioned in Revelation.

The church has a strict moral code and disapproves of short dresses for women, long hair for men, and women preachers and elders. Women cover their heads during worship. The group fasts, uses wine and unleavened bread at the Lord's Supper, and believes in baptism for the remission of sins, divine healing, speaking in tongues, and the unity of the church. The Universal Church is headed by Bishop R. O. Frazier. Members do not think of themselves as another denomination, but as the one true body of Christ.

Membership: Not reported.

Periodicals: *The Light of Life Herald.* Send orders to Box 874, Saginaw, MI 48605.

★753★
Universal World Church
123 N. Lake St.
Los Angeles, CA 90026

The Universal World Church was formed in 1952 by former Assemblies of God minister Dr. O. L. Jaggers, its president. It differs from other Pentecostal bodies primarily in organization and its doctrine of the sacrament. Under Jaggers are twenty-four elders who form the governing executive body. Their role is taken from Exodus and from Revelations 4:4, 10; 5:6-8. The elders' custom of wearing robes and golden crowns is based on these texts. There are 144 bishops, one for each state of the United States and the rest for the various countries of the world. Elders and bishops must be graduates of the University of the World Church.

One is received into the church by baptism following repentance and faith in Jesus Christ as personal Lord and savior. The reception is the first process of new birth and new creation. Following the new birth, one may receive the genuine baptism with the Holy Spirit of resurrection power and fire, a baptism called the second process. After the second process, one is allowed to partake of the third, the transubstantiation communion which is offered once every three months. At that time twenty-four elders, by

faith in Christ and the power of God, perform the miracle of changing bread and wine into the sacred body and blood of the Lord Jesus Christ. This act is done before the golden altar of the church in Los Angeles.

The World Church has come under considerable attack for its flamboyance, which some feel smacks more of showmanship than religion. In spite of these attacks, however, the church has grown. There were 11,315 members of the mother church in 1969. There were approximately 800 congregations in the United States and around the world. The 3,170 ministers are organized into the World Fellowship of the World Church. The World Church schools operate on the elementary and high school levels, and the university on the college level. All ministers are university graduates.

Membership: Not reported. In 1969, the church reported 11,315 members in the mother church in Los Angeles. There were 800 congregations in the United States and the world, with 3,170 ministers organized into a World Fellowship of the World Church. These figures have been questioned by many who claim that the movement consists merely of the single congregation in Los Angeles.

Educational Facilities: University of the World Church, Los Angeles, California.

★754★
Victory Fellowship of Ministries (V.F.M.)
7700 S. Lewis
Tulsa, OK 74136-7700

Victory Fellowship of Ministries (V.F.M.) was founded and organized in January 1980 as an outreach ministry of Victory Christian Center (formerly Sheridan Christian Center), a large charismatic church in Tulsa, Oklahoma. It provides a fellowship for a number of like-minded ministers and churches, especially many who have been trained and sent out from Victory Bible Institute.

Membership: In 1998, there were 85 affiliated assemblies in the United States and one each in Canada, Germany, France, Albania, the Czech Republic, Russia, Argentina, and Scotland.

Educational Facilities: Victory Bible Institute, Tulsa, Oklahoma.

Sources:

http://www.victory.com/.

★755★
Zion Fellowship
PO Box 79
Waverly, NY 14892

Zion Fellowship is a worldwide Pentecostal/Charismatic fellowship of churches, colleges, and ministries that includes orphanages, clinics, and feeding programs in several countries. The fellowship's primary work is in education and embodied in the Zion Ministerial Institute in Waverly, New York, and the Distance Education Degree Program through Zion University in Albuquerque, New Mexico, and an additional 15 colleges around the world.

Zion Fellowship affirms a belief in the Triune God, salvation through the work of Jesus Christ, the Bible as the authoritative Word of God, water baptism by immersion, the baptism of the Holy Spirit, divine healing as provided by Christ's atoning work, and the miraculous work of the Holy Spirit. It is also the fellowship's belief that God will visit His Church in unusual ways before Christ's second coming, bringing multitudes into His kingdom. As a matter of principle, it is felt that since divorce and remarriage are contrary to God's will, anyone who has been divorced and remarried is not permitted to hold ministerial credentials. Pastors are asked not to solemnize such remarriages.

Membership: Not reported. There are Zion churches across the United States and Canada and around the world.

Educational Facilities: Zion Ministerial Institute, Waverly, New York.
Zion University, Albuquerque, New Mexico.

Periodicals: *Zion Ministries.*

Sources:

http://zionfellowship.org/.

Section 10

European Free-Church Family

Consult the Contents pages to locate the essay in Part II, Historical Essay Chapters,
that provides an historical discussion of this family

Intrafaith Organizations

★756★

Friends World Committee for Consultation
% Office of the Executive Secretary
Section of the Americas
1506 Race St.
Philadelphia, PA 19102

Alternate Address: World Office: 4 Byng Pl., London WC1E 7SH, England.

Following World War I, members of the Society of Friends gathered in international conferences in 1920 in London and first recommended the formation of an organization to give expression to the sense of fellowship among Friends around the world. In 1937, at the Friends World Conference, the Friends World Committee for Consultation was formed. It was to have a consultative capacity but also to promote cooperation and interaction between Friends in various groups around the world. As war soon broke out, it met irregularly through the 1940s and only gained some stability in the early 1950s. It has become the major instrument through which Friends relate to the larger Christian world and the international ecumenical movement.

Since 1952, the committee has met triennially. It has international offices in London and regional offices on every continent. Periodically it sponsors world conferences of Friends. It also publishes a directory of the different Friends Meetings in each country.

The work of the committee in North America is carried out through its office in Philadelphia, Pennsylvania. The American Section was formed soon after the founding of the committee. The section publishes a directory of all of the Friends congregations (termed monthly meetings, churches, and worship groups) in the Western Hemisphere.

Membership: Most Friends denominations in the United States and Canada support the committee.

Sources:

Finding Friends Around the World. London: Friends World Committee for Consultation, 1982.

FWCC Friends Directory. Philadelphia: Friends World Committee for Consultation, 1987.

★757★

Mennonite World Conference
465 Gundersen Dr., Ste. 200
Carol Stream, IL 60188

Alternate Address: International Headquarters: c/o Exec. Sec. Larry Miller, 7 ave. al Foret-Noire, 67000 Strassbourg, France.

The Mennonite World Conference was founded in 1925 but grew out of a proposal first published and circulated prior to World War I. The first gathering of Mennonites internationally, held at Basel, Switzerland, occurred on the anniversary of the first

Mennonite baptism in 1625 and was attended primarily by German, Swiss, French, and Dutch representatives. One person attended from the United States, but the two Russian delegates were unable to obtain a visa to enter Switzerland. The conference became more active after World War II and has grown steadily in its representation of Mennonites in both North America and the Third World.

The conference seeks to further the Christian witness of Mennonites with a particular emphasis on loving interaction between various Mennonite churches, ethical concerns, and the peace witness. It seeks to maintain a network of communication and information for member organizations, establish task forces, and facilitate education, theological studies, and publications. It publishes the *Mennonite World Handbook* following each meeting of the conference.

Membership: Members of the Conference in North America include the following: Beach Amish Mennonite Fellowship; Bergthaler Churches of Alberta and Saskatchewan; Brethren in Christ General Conference; Chortitzer Mennonite Conference; Church of God in Christ, Mennonite; Conference of Mennonites in Canada; Eastern Pennsylvania Mennonite Church; Evangelical Mennonite Church; Evangelical Mennonite Conference (Canada); Evangelical Mennonite Mission Conference; General Conference Mennonite Church; General Conference of Mennonite Brethren Churches; Hutterian Brethren; Hutterian Brethren of New York; Markham-Waterloo Conference; Mennonite Church; New Reinland Mennonite Church of Ontario; Old Colony Mennonite Church Alberta; Old Colony Mennonite Church-British Columbia; Old Colony Mennonite Church-Manitoba; Old Colony Mennonite Church-Ontario; Old Colony Mennonite Church-Saskatchewan; Old Order Amish; Old Order Mennonites; Old Order River Brethren; Reinland Mennonite Church; and Sommerfeld Mennonite Church.

Sources:

Mennonite World Handbook: Mennonites in Global Mission. Carol Stream, IL: Mennonite World Conference, 1990.

German Mennonites

★758★

Brethren in Christ
PO Box 290
Grantham, PA 17027-0290

Alternate Address: Canadian Headquarters: 2619 Niagara Pkwy., Fort Erie, ON Canada L2A 5M4.

The Brethren in Christ Church (originally called River Brethren) formed in the 1770s within the intense religious atmosphere of Lancaster County, Pennsylvania. The brethren, many of whom were Mennonites, had been influenced by the Dunker tradition and accepted triune immersion as the proper mode of baptism. Among the first to be immersed in this manner were Jacob Engel and Peter Witmer. The original group of about 14 met in the upper room of Engel's home in Stackstown, Pennsylvania.

Soon after this meeting, organization was effected and Engel was elected bishop. Triune immersion was a central feature. Doctrine was otherwise drawn from the Anabaptist-Brethren consensus but with an emphasis on evangelism. Over the years, it was also positively affected by the Wesleyan Holiness movement which taught a doctrine of sanctification that included the belief that individual believers could become and should expect to become perfect in love in this early life. In the mid-nineteenth century, three groups emerged from the original one because of doctrinal and accomodationist differences. The three groups were the Brethren in Christ, the Old Order River Brethren (earlier referred to as the Yorker Brethren), and the United Zion's Children, later called United Zion Church.

The Brethren in Christ represented the largest wing of the River Brethren. The name was adopted in 1863 although the church was not incorporated until 1904. Through migration of members in search of better economic opportunities, the church has spread across the United States and Canada. Since the 1950s the church has tripled through its evangelist thrust.

The Brethren in Christ is congregationally organized and eight regional conferences and a general conference serve to carry out churchwide programs. A Board of World Missions oversees work in Colombia, Cuba, England, Honduras, India, Japan, Malawi, Mexico, Nepal, Nicaragua, South Africa, Spain, Venezuela, Zambia, and Zimbabwe. The Board of Media Ministries operates Evangel Press, located in Nappanee, Indiana, and publishes books as well as other Brethren in Christ literature. Two retirement centers, Messiah Village in Mechanicsburg, Pennsylvania, and Upland Manor in Upland, California, are supported by the church. Ministries to the marginalized include Lifeline in San Francisco, California, and Paxton Ministries in Harrisburg, Pennsylvania. Several camps are owned and operated regionally. The Brethren in Christ Church is a member of the National Association of Evangelicals, the Christian Holiness Association, and the Mennonite Central Committee.

Membership: In 1996 the brethren reported 18,424 members, 193 congregations, and 353 ministers. The Canadian Conference reported 3,219 members, in 38 congregations served by 78 ministers. There were 65,000 members worldwide.

Educational Facilities: Messiah College, Grantham, Pennsylvania.

Niagara Christian Collegiate, Fort Erie, Ontario. Canada.

Periodicals: *Evangelical Visitor.* • *Shalom.* • *Therefore. Evangelical Visitor.* • Hostetler, Paul, ed. *Perfect Love and War.* Nappanee, IN: Evangel Press, 1974. • *Manual for Christian Youth.* Nappanee, IN: Evangel Press, 1959. • *Manual of Doctrine and Government.* Nappanee, IN: Evangel Press, 1968. • *Shalom* • *Therefore* • Wittlinger, Carlton O. *Quest for Piety and Obedience.* Nappanee, IN: Evangel Press, 1978.

★759★
Church of God in Christ, Mennonite
420 N. Wedel
Moundridge, KS 67107

John Holdeman, a member of the Mennonite Church, had, at the age of 21, an intense religious experience which changed his life. Following his baptism, he began a period of serious study of the Bible and of the writings of Menno Simons. As a result of his studies, he came to believe that his church had departed from the true way. Holdeman emerged as a young powerful leader and visionary.

He began to hold meetings at his home, and spread his concerns through the writing and publishing of his major books. He felt that the Mennonite Church had grown worldly and departed from the true faith; it did not rigidly screen candidates for baptism to insure that they had been born again; the avoidance of the ex-

communicated was neglected, members took part in political elections and the proper training of children was neglected. He also objected to choosing ministers by lot. He also felt it was wrong to receive money on loans. While he found much agreement with his observations, few would join him in reformative action.

Growth of his church was slow until the late 1870s when he encountered the German-speaking immigrants who had just arrived from Russia. In 1878 the first church was built, and the first conversion of many people to his church occurred in the Lone Tree Community of McPherson County, Kansas. Holdeman became the first minister to successfully introduce revivalism into a Mennonite framework. Revivals accounted for much of the rapid growth of his movement in the late nineteenth century, especially in the immigrant communities in Kansas and Manitoba. A slow and steady growth period followed through the early twentieth century, followed by a rapid expansion in both North America and abroad after World War II. The greatest concentration of members is in Kansas and Manitoba.

The church follows the Anabaptist-Mennonite doctrinal concensus with strong emphasis upon repentance and the new birth, a valid believer's baptism, separation from the world, excommunication of unfaithful members, a humble way of life, nonresistance, plain and modest dress, the wearing of the beard for men and devotional covering for women.

The church is headed by a delegated General Conference which meets when the need arises. It is composed of all ministers and deacons (all unsalaried) and lay people. Its decisions are binding on the congregations. It oversees the Gospel Tract and Bible Society, Gospel Publishers (the publishing arm of the church), three mission boards, and numerous other functions. There are congregations in 29 states, eight Canadian provinces, Brazil, Belize, the Dominican Republic, Ghana, Guatemala, Haiti, India, Jamaica, Kenya, Malawi, Mexico, Nigeria, and the Philippines. Most North American congregations have an elementary parochial school attached to them. The church supports one hospital, seven nursing homes, and four children's homes.

Membership: In 1994 the church reported 10,742 members in the United States and 3,729 in Canada. There were a total of 16,188 members worldwide in 170 congregations and approximately 60 mission stations.

Periodicals: *Messenger of Truth.* • *Christian Mission Voice.*

Sources:

Hiebert, Clarence. *The Holdeman People.* South Pasadena, CA: William Carey Library, 1973.

★760★
Congregational Bible Church
℅ Congregational Bible Church
Marietta, PA 17547

The Congregational Bible Church was formed in 1951 at Marietta, Pennsylvania, as the Congregational Mennonite Church. The name was changed in 1969. The original members of the church were from six congregations of the Mennonite Church. The statement of faith is at one with Mennonite belief, but includes a statement on anointing the sick and emphasizes separation from the world. The group has an aggressive evangelistic ministry. The church is organized with a congregational government as a fellowship of like-minded churches. The bishop or pastor is the chief officer.

Membership: Not reported.

★761★
Conservative Mennonite Fellowship (Non-Conference)
Box 36
Hartville, OH 44632

The Conservative Mennonite Fellowship (nonconference) was the result of a protest movement in the main branches of the Mennonite Church in the mid-1950s. The conservatives were concerned that Mennonites were conforming to the world (e.g., women were neglecting to cover their hair or were letting it fall down to their shoulders instead of being tied into a knot), that Mennonites were not resisting the military (e.g., the young men were joining the Army as noncombatants instead of staying out of the Army), and that Mennonites were becoming involved in civil affairs (e.g., they were voting or holding office or becoming policemen). The conservatives were also concerned about the growing acceptance of neo-orthodox theology in Mennonite circles. The fellowship was formed in 1956. It added to the prior disciplinary standards (the Apostles' Creed, the Dordrecht Confession, and the Schleitheim Confession) the Christian Fundamentals, which emphasize strict discipline and separation from the world. These were adopted at a fellowship meeting in 1964.

Membership: Not reported. In 1967 there were 23 congregations with 980 members and an additional 50 cooperating congregations with 2,400 members.

★762★
Markham-Waterloo Conference (Mennonite)
% Clare Frey
Rte. 2
Elmira, ON, Canada N3B 2Z2

The Markham-Waterloo Conference came into being in 1939 as the culmination of a modernization movement among some of the members of the Old Order Mennonites of Ontario. Among the concerns was the purchase of automobiles by members. Such members were known as the "black bumpers," as they painted over the chrome on the cars to avoid any sign of ostentation. However, a second issue arose in the person of Bp. Jesse Bauman, a leader who had been chosen by lots. Bauman's preachings attracted many, but disturbed others who had little appreciation for his adoption of a more evangelical style, which he hoped would keep the younger people from straying to nearby non-Mennonite churches. In 1939 in the face of growing criticism, Bauman withdrew from the group. About the same time, the "black-bumper" people in Markham and Waterloo joined forces and created a new conference.

The Markham-Waterloo Conference continues as a very conservative Mennonite group, but less so than the Old Order, which does not allow the use of cars and telephones.

Membership: In 1997 the group reported 10 congregations, 1,250 baptized members (and an additional 600 constituency), and 28 ordained preachers, deacons, and bishops.

Sources:

Epp, Franklin H. *Mennonites in Canada, 1920–1940*. Toronto: Macmillan of Canada, 1982.

Lichdi, Diether Gotz. *Mennonite World Handbook 1990: Mennonites in Global Mission*. Carol Stream, IL: Mennonite World Conference, 1990.

★763★
Mennonite Church
421 S. 2nd St., Ste. 600
Elkhart, IN 46516

The largest and oldest of the Mennonite bodies in North America is the Mennonite Church. Many other U.S. Mennonite groups derive from it. Organization within the church was slow since each congregation tended to be autonomous. In 1725, a conference of Pennsylvania congregations was called to consider, among other things, an English translation of the Confession of Dordrecht. Other conferences were called in particular regions to deal with controversy. Formal conferences began to emerge in the nineteenth century. At present, a biennial General Assembly meets as an advisory body for the entire church. District conferences counsel and provide resources at a local level.

Developing autonomously, but cooperating with the conferences, have been various service and mission agencies. The Mennonite Board of Missions now supervises a program that includes North American volunteer ministries (that engage more than 80 volunteers), media ministries, and church development. Overseas ministries including district conference programs engage over 300 workers in more than 50 countries. Herald Press is the publishing arm of the church and operates under the Publication Board. The Board of Education oversees the several colleges and seminaries. Other services are provided by the Board of Congregational Ministries and the Mennonite Mutual Aid Board. A General Board coordinates and oversees the five program boards.

While still holding to Anabaptist separatist practices—pacifism, a disciplined membership, believers' baptism—the church has endeavored to minister to urban society. It carries on a vast mission program with congregations on every continent. In the United States, home mission work is conducted among Native Americans, African Americans, Jews, the Spanish-speaking, Asian refugees, and the deaf.

Membership: In 1995 the church reported 110,308 members, 1,110 churches, and 2,692 ministers.

Educational Facilities: Goshen Biblical Seminary, Elkhart, Indiana.

Eastern Mennonite Seminary, Harrisonburg, Virginia.
Eastern Mennonite College, Harrisonburg, Virginia.
Goshen College, Goshen, Indiana.
Rosedale Bible Institute, Irwin, Ohio.
Hesston College, Hesston, Kansas.
Conrad Grebel College, Waterloo, Ontario, Canada.

Periodicals: *Gospel Herald.* • *Mennonite Historical Bulletin.* • *Mennonite Quarterly Review.*

Sources:

Horsch, James E., ed. *Mennonite Yearbook.* Scottdale, PA: Mennonite Publishing House, n.d.

An Invitation to Faith. Scottdale, PA: Herald Press, 1957.

Wenger, J. C. *The Mennonite Church in America.* Scottdale, PA: Herald Press, 1966.

★764★
Old Order (Reidenbach) Mennonites
% Henry W. Riehl
Rte. 1
Columbiana, OH 44408

During World War II, the issue of the draft was of great concern to the Old Order Mennonites. There was a consensus that all the draft-age youths should be conscientious objectors. However, among the Old Order (Wenger) Mennonites there developed a group who felt that prison, not alternative service (medical work, etc.) should be the only course in reaction to the draft. This group further insisted that those youths who accepted alternative service should be excommunicated.

This group was not supported by the majority of the Wengerites. Thirty-five members of the group began to build a separate meeting house near Reidenbach's store in Lancaster County (hence the name). They remain the most conservative of the Pennsylvania Mennonites. They still use candles instead of coal oil for lighting. Rubber tires on carriages are prohibited. They are the only Pennsylvania group which currently opposes the use of school buses.

Among the Reidenbach Mennonites there are a number of specific regulations to keep them separate from the world. Farm equipment is restricted; for example, manure spreaders are not allowed. Children go only to the one-room school and not beyond the elementary grades. The group has only one congregation.

Membership: Not reported. There is only one congregation, in Lancaster County, Pennsylvania.

★765★
Old Order (Wenger) Mennonites
% Henry W. Riehl
Rte. 1
Columbiana, OH 44408

Among the Old Order (Wisler) Mennonites of Southeastern Pennsylvania, several schisms have developed over the continuing issue of accommodation to change. In the 1930s, the use of the automobile on a limited basis was advocated by Bishop Moses Horning. Bishop Joseph Wenger rejected the idea, believing automobiles should not be used for either occupational transportation or coming to worship. Wenger's group became the more conservative wing of the Old Order Mennonites. The group holds no evening services and uses only German in the pulpit. Jail, rather than alternative service, is advocated for boys of draft age.

Membership: Not reported. There are an estimated 1,000 members in southeastern Pennsylvania.

★766★
Old Order (Wisler) Mennonite Church
% Henry W. Riehl
Rte. 1
Columbiana, OH 44408

In the 1860s the Yellow Creek congregation of the Mennonite Church, located near Elkhart, Indiana, found itself caught between two vocal leaders. Daniel Brenneman demanded a progressive policy and the adoption of such innovations as English preaching, Sunday schools, protracted meetings, and four-part singing. He was opposed by Jacob Wisler, who opposed all innovations and deviations. Wisler began to place under the ban anyone deviating from the past. Wisler's arbitrary manner of enforcing his ideas resulted in a church trial and he was removed from his office. He then took his followers and formed a new congregation in 1870.

During the following decades, other churches of like perspective were founded and then these united with Wisler's group. A group in neighboring Medina County, Ohio, was the first. A Canadian group headed by Bishop Abraham Martin from Woolwich Township, Waterloo County, Ontario, who opposed speaking in English, sunday schools, evening meetings , "falling"-top buggies, and other modernisms, formed a separate church and later allied itself with the Wislerites. In 1901 followers of Bishop Jonas Martin and Gabriel D. Heatwole formed a church; that church later joined the Wislerites. Bishop Jonas Martin had been the leader of the Mennonite Church in Lancaster County, Pennsylvania, until controversy arose about installing a new pulpit in the church. Martin opposed the new pulpit because he was against innovations, and with a third of the congregation he left the Mennonite Church. A separate group of Mennonites in Rockingham county, Virginia, led by Gabriel D. Heatwole, joined Martin's group and then this church joined the Wislerites.

As a group, the Old Order Mennonites remain among the most conservative in dress, forms of worship, and social customs. They are very close to the Amish in their thinking, but meet in church buildings instead of homes and do not wear beards.

Membership: Not reported. In 1972 they reported 38 congregations, 8,000 members and 101 ministers.

★767★
Old Order Yorker River Brethren
Current address not obtained for this edition.

The Old Order (or Yorker) River Brethren separated in 1843 from their parent church, the River Brethren (now known as the Brethren in Christ), protesting what they saw as laxity in matters of nonconformity to the world and non-resistance to the military. The group was led by Bishop Jacob Strickler, Jr., of York County, Pennsylvania (hence the nickname). It was joined in the 1850s by a Franklin County group headed by Bishop Christian Hoover, who had been expelled for being "too orthodox."

The Old Order River Brethren remain the smallest of the River Brethren groups, having only four congregations, all in southeastern Pennsylvania. Three small independent congregations have split off at various times in disputes over modes of transportation. All worship is conducted in home, not in churches. The Old Order River Brethren are also agriculturists.

Membership: Not reported. In 1963 there were 4 congregations and 340 members.

Sources:

Breckbill, Laban T. *Doctrine, Old Order River Brethren.* The Author, 1967.

___. *History of the Old Order River Brethren.* Lancaster County, PA: Breckbill & Strickler, 1972.

★768★
Reformed Mennonite Church
% Bishop Glenn M. Gross
602 Strasburg Pike
Lancaster, PA 17602

The oldest splinter from the Mennonite Church that still survives dates from 1812. It grew out of a previously existing separatist congregation headed by Francis Herr, who had been expelled from the church for irregularities in a horse trade. After Herr's death, his son John Herr, never a religious man, took up his father's faith, became convicted of sin, was baptized, and soon rose to a position of leadership. He was then chosen bishop. John Herr and his associates immediately began to issue a set of pamphlets charging the Mennonite Church with being worldly and corrupt. They complained of laxity in enforcing discipline and separation from the world. Based on Herr's ideas, the Reformed Mennonite Church was created.

In relation to the Mennonite Church, the Reformed Mennonites emphasize the exclusive claims of their particular faith, practices and community. All who are not Reformed Mennonites are considered to be of the world. The Reformed Mennonites practice the ban and avoidance rigidly. They dress plainly and tend to live in plain surroundings. Membership is located primarily in southeastern Pennsylvania.

Membership: Not reported. In 1993 there were 10 churches, 20 clergy and approximately 346 members in the United States and several hundred in Canada.

Sources:

Bear, Robert. *Delivered Unto Satan.* Carlisle, PA: The Author, 1974.

Christianity Defined. Lancaster, PA: Reformed Mennonite Church, 1958.

Funk, John F. *The Mennonite Church and Her Accusers.* Elkhart, IN: Mennonite Publishing Company, 1878.

The Reformed Mennonites, Who They Are and What They Believe. Lancaster, PA: Reformed Mennonite Church, n.d.

★769★
Stauffer Mennonite Church
℅ Bishop Jacob S. Stauffer
Rte. 3
Ephrata, PA 17522

Jacob Stauffer, a minister in the Mennonite Church at Groffdale, Pennsylvania, was the leader of a group in a progressive-conservative split. The issue was the ban, which Stauffer and colleague Joseph Wenger of the Old Order (Wenger) Mennonites believed should be applied more strictly. About forty members withdrew from the Mennonite Church, demanding that when the ban was used there should be no communion between the church and the offender.

The Stauffers have continued in their conservative ways. They are part of the horse and buggy culture but, unlike the Amish, are cleanshaven and will ride trains on long trips. They prefer the one-room school and refrain from politics (even voting). Though never large, and hurt by one major schism, the group has grown steadily by maintaining a rather high birth rate.

Membership: Not reported. There are three congregations (Lancaster County, Pennsylvania; Snyder County, Pennsylvania and St. Mary's County, Maryland) and approximately 750 members.

★770★
United Zion Church
℅ Bishop Luke Showalter
181 Hurst Dr.
Ephrata, PA 17522

The United Zion's Children originated in 1855 following the expulsion of Bishop Matthias Brinser from the River Brethren (i.e., the Brethren in Christ) for building and holding services in a meetinghouse. Other than the use of church buildings, there were no doctrinal differences. An annual conference is held but the government is congregational. The United Zion's Children was strengthened within a few years by some churches formed by Henry Grumbein and Jacob Pfautz. These groups accepted Brinser because of a revelation, but remain a separate unit within the church. They constitute one of three districts which send representatives to the annual conference. Mission work is supported through the Brethren in Christ. One home for the aged is maintained.

During the twentieth century several attempts have been made to improve the relationship between the United Zion Church and the Brethren in Christ, and even to look toward a future reunion. In 1967 the Brethren in Christ passed a resolution asking for the forgiveness of the United Zion Church for the action of the Church's council in 1855 and the continued lack of humility on their part which has kept the two groups apart. The next year the United Zion Church issued a formal statement offering complete forgiveness. These resolutions became the basis for cooperative action on the mission field and in higher education. A member of United Zion Church currently sits on the board of Brethren in Christ-founded Messiah College.

Membership: In 1993 there were 13 churches, 852 members, and 23 ministers.

Educational Facilities: Messiah College, Grantham, Pennsylvania.

Periodicals: *Zion's Herald.*

Sources:

A History of the United Zion Church, 1853-1980. N.p. 1981.

Wittlinger, Carlton O. *Quest for Piety and Obedience.* Nappanee, IN: Evangel Press, 1978.

★771★
Weaver Mennonites
Current address not obtained for this edition.

The one schism affecting the Stauffer Mennonite Church was occasioned by the issue of the strictness of the ban. In 1916, the son of aged Bishop Aaron Sensenig married outside the faith. The girl was received into the Stauffer Mennonite Church but later returned to her earlier heritage. The church was split over the strictness of the ban to be applied to the girl. The lenient group, led by Sensenig and John A. Weaver, left and began a new congregation and constructed a meeting house near New Holland, Pennsylvania.

Membership: Not reported. There is one congregation of approximately 60 members.

★772★
Weaverland Conference Old Order (Horning or Black Bumper) Mennonites
Current address not obtained for this edition.

Bishop Moses Horning (1870-1955) established a liberal wing of the Old Order (Wisler) Mennonites. His followers use automobiles, but only for necessary purposes. The car must be black and without "frivolous" trim. Most of the members cover the chrome with black paint to avoid further ostentation.

Membership: Not reported. There are five congregations, all located in southeastern Pennsylvania, and approximately 1,700 members.

Russian Mennonites

★773★
Chortitzer Mennonite Conference
Box 968
Steinbach, MB, Canada R0A 2A0

During the 1870s a number of German Mennonites who had been residents of Russia for several generations settled in southern Manitoba on two tracts of land on either side of the Red River, referred to as the East Reserve and the West Reserve. They were often named for that area of Russia in which they had resided and/or that area of Germany from which they had originated. Among those who settled on the East Reserve were a group from Chortitza, a German colony in Russia, some of whom founded the village of Chortitz. Bp. Gerhard Wiebe emerged as the leader of this group. Wiebe was known for his desire to live in peace with his neighbors, both Mennonite and non-Mennonite. This was made difficult in part by the restrictions placed by some Mennonite leaders on their members in an attempt to hold their communities together and continue their life as it had been in Russia.

Over the years the Chortitzer Mennonites remained a separate body, founded a separate conference, and adopted a statement of faith. The church believes in the Trinity, the Bible as the infallible authority for faith and life, and the church as the body of Christ—which has the duty of preaching, teaching, and discipling. The church has a particular task of keeping itself pure by disciplining members who fall into gross sin. The church celebrates two ordinances, baptism and communion. It recognizes the legitimacy of government but also feels the duty of church members to refrain from mortal strife and contentions in all areas of life (such as war).

The conference is currently led by Bp. Wilhelm Hildebrandt. It is organized congregationally and composed of those churches that accept its constitution and bylaws.

Membership: In 1997 the church reported 2,500 members in 14 congregations served by 23 ministers. There were 70 members in these congregations in the United States.

Educational Facilities: Steinbach Bible College, Steinbach, Manitoba.

Periodicals: *CMC Chronicle.*

Sources:

Epp, Frank H. *Mennonites in Canada, 1786-1920: The History of a Separate People.* Toronto: Macmillan of Canada, 1974. 480 pp.

___. *Mennonites in Canada, 1920-1940: A Peoples' Struggle for Survival.* Toronto: Macmillan of Canada, 1982.

★774★
Conservative Mennonite Church of Ontario
Current address not obtained for this edition.

Among the Mennonite population of Canada in the early twentieth century, three tendencies arose. Some Mennonites, most of whom had migrated from Europe, sought means of accommodating the new situation of living in Canada. Others resisted any form of accommodation. Many, however, took a "middle-of-the-road" position, accommodating where necessary, and only in ways that did not threaten the faith. This latter group was generally called the Old Mennonites. In Ontario, the Old Mennonites were of Swiss and southern German origin. During the 1950s part of the Old Mennonite faction, some of whom were members of the General Conference Mennonite Church, decried the departure of fellow members and leaders from traditional standards of faith and practice. They disapproved of liberal views on biblical inspiration and moral latitude. Bishops Moses H. Roth and Curtis C. Cressman became the spokespersons of the traditionalist position. They and the ministers and congregations which followed them were expelled in 1959, whereupon they formed the Conservative Mennonite Church of Ontario.

In 1952 the Conference adopted a Constitution and a Faith and Practice which affirmed the Dordrecht Confession of 1632 and the "Christian Fundamentals," which were adopted by the General Conference in 1921. Much of the attention of the Conference was directed to a definition of the believers' stance in relation to secular society which has been spelled out in a series of prohibitions. Members are prohibited from participation in war (including any type of military service), politics (including voting and jury duty), and membership in worldly organizations (such as secret societies, life insurance societies, etc.). Members refrain from strong drink, tobacco, worldly amusements (such as movies and organized sports), television, jewelry (such as wedding bands and gold watches), and remarriage after divorce. Members may use radios, but may not listen to programs which are not conducive to holiness. All are called to simple modest dress, which for women includes uncut hair and veiled heads. Churches do not use instrumental music, nor do they allow floral displays at weddings or funerals.

Membership: In the 1970s there were 8 congregations with less than 300 members.

★775★
Evangelical Mennonite Conference (Kleine Gemeinde) (EMC)
Box 1268
440 Main St.
Steinbach, MB, Canada R0A 2A0

The Evangelical Mennonite Conference (EMC) came about as a result of a renewal movement among a small group of Mennonites in Southern Russia in 1812. Their leader was Klaas Reimer, a Mennonite minister. Reimer believed that the Mennonite church had become lax in discipline and that it condoned such practices as card playing, smoking, and drinking. He also felt that the church had become too closely aligned with the Russian government as evidenced by its contributions to the war against Napoleon. Around 1812 Reimer and several others began to hold separate worship services. By 1814 the Reimer group had separated entirely from the main body of Mennonites. They became known as the Kleine Gemeinde (small fellowship).

Increasing pressure on the group from the Russian government in such matters as military conscription finally led to a migration in 1874-75 of the entire membership to North America. A total of 158 families settled in Manitoba, Canada, while 36 settled near Jansen, Nebraska. The Nebraska group eventually seceded from the conference.

The name Evangelical Mennonite Conference was chosen in 1952 to replace the earlier designation. The group saw itself as evangelical, i.e., standing for the true gospel message of Jesus Christ; Mennonite in that it holds to the traditional characteristics of Mennonite faith; and as a conference that works together to carry out its ministry.

The conference membership is now spread over five Canadian provinces. To facilitate fellowship, growth, and administration, the congregations have been grouped into nine regions. A Bible college in Manitoba educates many of the church's ministers, missionaries, and volunteer lay workers. The church developed a strong missionary program that had, as of June 1997, some 128 workers in 20 countries under the guidance of the board of missions and several approved independent faith missions. In Mexico, Nicaragua, and Paraguay, the conference churches have organized as national autonomous conferences.

Membership: In 1997 the church reported 6,683 members, 53 churches, and 123 ministers in Canada.

Educational Facilities: Steinbach Bible College, Steinbach, Manitoba, Canada.

Periodicals: *The Messenger.*

Remarks: The members of the Kleine Gemeinde that settled in Nebraska were gradually, over a period of several decades, lost to other Mennonite bodies, primarily the Evangelical Mennonite Brethren Conference. The last congregation, which had moved to Kansas, dissolved in 1944.

Sources:

The Golden Years, The Mennonite Kleine Gemeinde in Russia (1812-1849). Steinbach, MN: D. F. P. Publications, 1985.

★776★
Evangelical Mennonite Mission Conference
526 McMillan
Winnipeg, MB, Canada R3C 2G1

The conference was born in 1937 as the result of a revival movement in the Sommerfelder Mennonite Church in Manitoba. Four young ministers became the leaders of a new group that met in the school district of Rudnerweide for their organizational meeting. They called themselves the Rudnerweider Mennonite Church. Rev. W. H. Falk was elected as the first bishop.

The church stressed personal conversion, teaching of children in Sunday School, youth programs, and missions. The first missionary, John Schellenberg, went to Africa under the Africa Inland Mission in 1942.

The revival spread to Saskatchewan where several congregations were established. In 1959, the congregations in Manitoba and Saskatchewan organized as the Evangelical Mennonite Mission Conference. Mission work among Mennonites returning from Mexico led to the establishment of four congregations in Ontario during the 1960s. During this decade also, mission work began in Belize and Bolivia and more recently in Texas and Mexico. In 1986, the conference joined the Africa Inter-Mennonite Mission. Numerous workers serve with various independent missionary agencies in several countries.

This conference is characterized by a strong emphasis on evangelism and missions. A full-time evangelist is on staff. A Low-German radio broadcast ministry is based in Saskatoon, Saskatchewan. It is active in the Mennonite Central Committee and the Mennonite World Conference.

Membership: In the 1990 there were 27 congregations with a total membership of 3,528. Internationally, including Canada, there were 3,928 members in 36 congregations.

Educational Facilities: Steinbach Bible College, Steinback, Manitoba, Canada.

Aylmer Bible School, Aylmer, Ontario, Canada.

Sources:

Epp, Frank H. *Mennonites in Canada, 1920-1940*. Toronto: Macmillan of Canada, 1982.

★777★
Fellowship of Evangelical Bible Churches
5800 S. 14th St.
Omaha, NE 68107

The Fellowship of Evangelical Bible Churches grew out of a merger in 1889 of two conservative Mennonite groups that had been founded by Elders Isaac Peters (1826-1911) and Aaron Walls (1834-1905) respectively. Peters had migrated from Russia in 1874, settled in Henderson, Nebraska, and joined the Bethesda Mennonite Church. As an elder he began to voice some of the ideas that had previously led to a break with the church in Russia. He was a vigorous proponent of evangelism and all the means to accomplish that task, including lively preaching, indoctrination of the youth, prayer meetings, and Bible study. He saw a separated life as a sign of regeneration. With a minority of the Henderson congregation, he withdrew in 1880 and formed the Ebenezer congregation.

Walls had migrated from Russia in 1875 and settled near Mountain Lake, Minnesota. After his election in 1876 as elder of the Bergfelder Church, he stressed the need for regeneration and the new life in Christ to an extent that he and his followers felt compelled to leave the Bergfelder Church. In 1889 he founded an independent congregation. In October of that year, he led in the union of the congregation with that led by Peters and the resulting formation of the United Mennonite Brethren of North America. The name was soon changed to Defenseless Mennonite Brethren of Christ in North America. In 1937, the name was changed to Evangelical Mennonite Brethren Conference. At the annual conference in 1987 the present name was adopted.

Born in an evangelical awakening, the fellowship gave early emphasis to church schools and world missions. From early congregations in Nebraska, Minnesota, and South Dakota, the church spread throughout the Midwest and Canada. Missions are currently supported in Europe, Africa, Southeast Asia, Japan, Taiwan, and South America. The church is a member of the National Association of Evangelicals.

Membership: In 1996 the fellowship reported 15 congregations, 2,228 members, and 19 ministers in the United States. Worldwide membership is 4,039. There are 26 congregations in Canada, Argentina, and Paraguay.

Periodicals: *Gospel Tidings.*

★778★
General Conference Mennonite Church
722 Main St.
Newton, KS 67114

History. John H. Oberholtzer was an educated young minister in the Franconia District (located in Pennsylvania) of the Mennonite Church. Oberholtzer being of a progressive nature, encountered trouble soon after entering the ministry by protesting the plain, collarless coat worn by most ministers. He felt that the coat was an arbitrary requirement from outside the Mennonite creed. He next asked for the Conference of the Franconia District to adopt a written constitution so proceedings could be conducted more systematically. The result of Oberholtzer's agitation was a parting of the ways. He withdrew in 1847 from the Franconia District at the same conference which proceeded to expel him. With 16 ministers and several congregations, he led in the organization of a new conference. A major thrust of Oberholtzer's movement

was the union of all Mennonite congregations. New practices were initiated, including a more liberal view of the ban, open communication, intermarriage with persons of other denominations and, within a short time, a salaried clergy. Oberholtzer proved a zealous advocate and founded the first Mennonite paper in America, the *Religioeser Botschafter* (later *Das Christliche Volksblat*).

Meanwhile, with the influx of thousands of Mennonite immigrants in the mid-1800s, other leaders were emerging and bringing into existence new churches. Daniel Hoch, a minister to several Mennonite churches in Ontario, had joined hands with an Ohio congregation led by Rev. Ephraim Hunsberger to form, in 1855, the Conference Council of the Mennonite Communities of Canada-West and Ohio. In Lee County, Iowa, two congregations found themselves in isolation, banded together, and called for united efforts in evangelism among members who had settled at some distance from the main body in the East. At a meeting in 1860 in Iowa, representatives of some of the above groups met and invited Oberholtzer to attend. He was chosen chairman and the General Conference Mennonite Church was organized. Their vision was the union of all Mennonite congregations in the United States and Canada.

Beliefs. The belief of the General Conference is in accord with many other Mennonite bodies. The "Confession of Faith in a Mennonite Perspective" was adopted by the General Conference Mennonite Church and the Mennonite Church in 1995.

Organization. Polity is congregational. A Commission on Education oversees Faith and Life Press and Mennonite Press, and provides resources to congregations. The Commission on Home Ministries oversees multi-cultural ministries, as well as peace and justice, and voluntary service work. The Commission on Overseas Missions sponsors work in over 20 countries in Latin America, Africa, Asia, and Europe. Canadian members have organized as the Conference of Mennonites in Canada. The South American Conference includes churches in Brazil, Paraguay, and Uruguay.

Membership: In 1996, the church reported 35,335 members, and 265 congregations in the United States. Worldwide there were 63,620 members.

Educational Facilities: Associated Mennonite Biblical Seminary, Elkhart, Indiana.

Bethel College, North Newton, Kansas.

Bluffton College, Bluffton, Ohio.

Periodicals: *The Mennonite.* • *Der Bote.*

Sources:

Constitution and Charter of the General Conference Mennonite Church. Newton, KS, 1984.

Kaufman, Edmund G. *General Conference Mennonite Pioneers.* North Newton, KS: Bethel College, 1973.

Krehbiel, H. P. *The History of the General Conference of the Mennonite Church of North America.* 2 vols. Newton, KS: The Author, 1889-1938.

___. *The History of the General Conference of the Mennonite Church of North America.* Vol. 2. Newton, KS: The Author, 1938.

Pannabecker, Samuel Floyd. *Open Doors, A History of the General Conference Mennonite Church.* Newton, KS: Faith and Life Press, 1975.

Waltner, James H. *This We Believe.* Newton, KS: Faith and Life Press, 1968.

Yost, Burton G. *Finding Faith and Fellowship.* Newton, KS: Faith and Life Press, 1963.

★779★

Mennonite Brethren Church of North America (Bruedergemeinde)

3155 Lincoln
PO Box V
Hillsboro, KS 67063-0155

In the mid-1800s, Pastor Edward Wuest, a fiery evangelical preacher, toured the German colonies in Russia. His message was the free grace of God and the need for a definite religious experience. His influence led a number of Mennonites to become dissatisfied with the formality of their church meeting. They also felt themselves too pure to participate in the communion with others and demanded a separate sacramental service. When the elders refused their request, they began to hold secret sacramental meetings. When they were discovered, opposition was intense and they withdrew, and on January 6, 1860, wrote a statement of protest. After bitter controversy, the government accepted their separate existence and they took the name Mennoniten Bruedergemeinde (Mennonite Brethren). They were one in doctrine with other Mennonites, but did emphasize religious experience. Among the Russian Mennonites they introduced footwashing (with the Lord's Supper) and baptism by immersion (backwards), the latter a unique practice among Mennonites. The Bruedergemeinde members began to arrive with the first immigrants in America. In 1879, Elder Abraham Schellenberg arrived and began to tour the settlements and organize strong congregations. By 1898, the group was supporting a German Department at McPherson College and in 1908, founded Tabor College in Hillsboro, Kansas. A vigorous mission program was established.

As the Brudergemeinde was developing, Jacob Wiebe, a member of the Kleine Gemeinde, now the Evangelical Mennonite Conference, in the Crimea, organized in 1869 the Crimean Brethren, similar in nature to the Bruedergemeinde. The Crimean Brethren came to America in 1874 and settled in Kansas. They were similar to the Mennonite Brethren but had a few differences. They prohibited excessive worldliness, buying of land, and attendance at public amusements. They took Biblical positions against life insurance, voting, and oaths. Marriage with non-members was forbidden. In 1960, the Mennonite Brethren Church absorbed the Krimmer Mennonite Brethren Church (as the Crimean Brethren became known).

The church is a member of the National Association of Evangelicals.

Membership: In 1997 the church had 160 churches, 20,830 members, and 243 ministers.

Educational Facilities: Fresno Pacific Unviersity, Fresno, California.

Mennonite Brethren Biblical Seminary, Fresno, California.

Tabor College, Hillsboro, Kansas.

Periodicals: *The Christian Leader.*

Sources:

Fundamentals of Faith. Hillsboro, KS: Mennonite Brethren Publishing House, 1963.

Lorenz, John H. *The Mennonite Brethren Church.* Hillsboro, KS: Mennonite Brethren Publishing House, 1950.

Wiebe, Katie Funk. *Who Are the Mennonite Brethren?* Hillsboro, KS: Kindred Press, 1984.

★780★

Old Colony Mennonite Church

℅ John P. Wiebe, Bishop
Box 601
Winkler, MB, Canada R6W 4A8

The Old Colony Mennonite Church continues the traditions of the Reinlaender Mennonites who came into Canada from Russia in 1875 and settled in South Central Manitoba, on an area designated as the Western Reserve, immediately north of the American border. Approximately 3,240 individuals made up the Reinlaender Mennonite Church. It was among this group that a revival movement would start in the 1880s, leading some to form the Mennonite Brethren Church. Through the decades, little by little, the outside world began to encroach upon the Mennonite settlements in the Western Reserve. These encroachments came to a head in the conflict over public school in the years immediately following World War I. In 1921 the group was able to work out an agreement with Mexico that granted them religious freedom, including the right to private schools, and the majority of the group moved out of Canada.

The move to Mexico was made a condition of continued membership in the church, and everyone was required to reregister as a member and indicate the intention to migrate. Of the 4,526 members in Manitoba, 3,340 migrated, and of the 7,182 members in Saskatchewan, 5,180 left for Mexico. Those who remained had no sense of direction, and some members drifted off to other churches. Finally in the early 1930s, efforts were made to reorganize the remnants. A new membership book was created, and in 1930 a bishop, Johann Loeppky, was chosen and ordained for the Saskatchewan group, and he ordained the new bishop for Manitoba, Jacob J. Froese, in 1936. Their numbers grew as members returned from Mexico.

Today the Old Colony Mennonite Church exists in five sections: Saskatchewan, Alberta, British Columbia, Manitoba, and Ontario.

Membership: In 1990 the Old Colony Mennonites reported 17 congregations and approximately 8,700 members.

Sources:

Epp, Franklin H. *Mennonites in Canada, 1920–1940.* Toronto: Macmillan of Canada, 1982.

Lichdi, Diether Gotz. *Mennonite World Handbook 1990: Mennonites in Global Mission.* Carol Stream, IL: Mennonite World Conference, 1990.

★781★

Reinland Mennonite Church

PO Box 96
Rosenfeld, MB, Canada R0G 1X0

The Reinland Mennonite Church was founded in 1958 by some 10 ministers and 600 members of the Sommerville Mennonite Church in Manitoba who separated and founded an independent body. A short time later 200 of these members and four of the ministers left Canada for Bolivia.

Membership: In 1992 the church reported 780 members in seven congregations served by nine ministers. Six of the congregations are in Manitoba and one is in Ontario. Several hundred members reside in Bolivia.

★782★

Sommerville Mennonite Church

Current address not obtained for this edition.

During the 1870s a number of German Mennonites who had been residents of Russia for several generations settled in southern Manitoba on two tracts of land on either side of the Red River, referred to as the East Reserve and the West Reserve. One group, which had settled on the Western Reserve, came under the leadership of the independent-minded Bp. Johann Funk, who in 1887 had been ordained by Bp. Gerhard Wiebe, leader of the Chortitzer Mennonites in the Eastern reserve and appointed as his assistant in the West. Funk had one of the more progressive outlooks of all the Mennonite leaders in the area and he welcomed the coming of the railroad and the integration of the community into the larger Canadian society, as opposed to the establishment of isolated Mennonite conclaves. However, Funk met significant opposition and in 1893 four churches in the Western Reserve asked Wiebe to ordain another bishop to lead them. He ordained Abraham Doerksen from the village of Sommerfeld and those groups that came under him quickly became known as Sommerfelder or Sommerville Mennonites as opposed to the Bergthaler Mennonites led by Funk. The Sommerville Mennonites soon emerged as the largest of several related groups, claiming some 80 percent of the Western Reserve following, formerly under Funk, and was twice as large as the Chortitzer Mennonites under Wiebe.

The Sommerville Mennonites continue as a separate group.

Membership: Not reported.

Sources:

Epp, Frank H. *Mennonites in Canada, 1786-1920: The History of a Separate People.* Toronto: Macmillan of Canada, 1974. 480 pp.

___. *Mennonites in Canada, 1920-1940: A Peoples' Struggle for Survival.* Toronto: Macmillan of Canada, 1982.

Amish

★783★
Beachy Amish Mennonite Churches
9650 Iams Rd.
Plain City, OH 43064

A split in the Pennsylvania Amish was occasioned by the refusal of Bishop Moses Beachy to pronounce the ban and avoidance on some former Old Order Amish who left to join a Conservative Mennonite congregation in Maryland. The conservative element withdrew fellowship with the bishop, who then, with his supporters, separated and formed a new association. The Beachy Amish have become more accommodating to modern culture. Churches have been built, and in recent years, the automobile has been allowed, as are tractors and electricity. Missionary-aid work for needy people has become a project in contrast to the strictly separatist Old Order group.

Membership: In 1996 the Beachy Amish reported 8,399 members, 138 congregations, and 425 ministers.

Periodicals: *Calvary Messenger.*

Sources:

Yoder, Elmer S. *The Beachy Amish Mennonite Fellowship Churches.* Hartville, OH: Diakonia Ministries, 1987.

★784★
Conservative Mennonite Conference
℅ Ivan J. Miller
Grantsville, MD 21536

After the establishment of the Old Order Amish Mennonite Church, more liberal Amish gradually began to separate from the church. Some of these congregations became associated and, in 1910, met at Pigeon, Michigan, for a first general conference. These congregations took the name Conservative Mennonite Conference. They introduced innovations to the Amish community such as the use of meeting houses, Sunday schools, protracted meetings, and English language services. Conservative Mennonites are located primarily in the Midwest, but congregations are located as far away as Florida, Arizona, and Delaware.

Membership: Not reported.

Sources:

Miller, J. Ivan. *History of the Conservative Mennonite Conference, 1910-1985.* Grantsville, MD: Ivan J. and Della Miller, 1985.

★785★
Evangelical Mennonite Church
1420 Kerrway Ct.
Fort Wayne, IN 46805

The Evangelical Mennonite Church was formed in 1866 out of a spiritual awakening among the Amish in Indiana, and was first known as the Egly Amish, after its founder Bishop Henry Egly (1824-1890). A preacher in an Amish congregation in Berne, Indiana, Egly underwent a spiritual experience in 1864 and began to emphasize regeneration, separation, and nonconformity to the world. His willingness to rebaptize anyone who had been baptized without repentance created a split in his church, prompting him to gather a new congregation in 1866. The conference, which has met annually since 1895, united a number of other congregations of like mind. This group adopted the name The Defenseless Mennonite Church in 1898, and became known as the Evangelical Mennonite Church in 1948.

Membership: In 1997, the church reported 4,348 members, 30 churches, and 78 ministers.

Periodicals: *EMC Today.*

Sources:

Nussbaum, Stan. *A History of the Evangelical Mennonite Church.* The Author, 1980.

★786★
Old Order Amish Mennonite Church
Pathway Publishers
Rte. 4
Aylmer, ON, Canada N5H 2R3

The Old Order Amish are in practice the continuation of the original Amish who settled in America. They are strictly conservative and may be identified by their horse-and-buggy culture. The men must grow beards but moustaches are forbidden. The plain dark blue, gray, brown, or black suit for men and bonnet and apron for women are uniforms. Buttons are used on men's shirts and pants, but none are allowed on suit coats, vests, or coats. Marriage with non-Amish is forbidden.

The Amish society is a rural community in which church life and worldly life are not separated. Symbolic of their life are the Amish barn raisings in which the congregation gathers to build a member's barn, usually in several days. Worship is held in the homes of the members every other Sunday on a rotating basis. During the three-hour service, the congregation is divided according to sex and marital status.

Schooling beyond the "3R's" is frowned upon within the church, and prior to a Supreme Court ruling in 1972 trouble with various state governments (such as Wisconsin, Indiana, Ohio) became a major cause of immigration to more lenient states (such as Missouri). Ministers are chosen by lot from a nominiated few. Since this is not a missionary church, new members generally come into the community from the children of members. In the last generation there have been converts, some highly educated, and recent studies have shown that approximately eight percent of the present membership is made up of descendents of such converts.

Membership: Not reported. In 1995 there were approximately 30,000 members in the United States and 900 in Canada. No statistics are kept. The total Amish population is estimated at 139,000, but only adults are baptized and full church members.

Periodicals: *The Dairy.* Send orders to PO Box 98, Gordonville, PA 17529. • *Die Botschaft.* Send orders to 200 Hazel St., Lancaster, PA 17601. • *The Budget.* Send orders to 134 N. Factory St., Sugarcreek, OH 44681. • *Herald der Wahrheit.* Send orders to 2010 110th St., Kalona, IA 52247. • *Blackboard Bulletin.* • *Family Life.* • *Young Companion.* All available from Rte. 4, Aylmer, ON Canada N5H 2R3.

Sources:

Amish Life in a Changing World. York, PA: York Graphic Services, 1978.

Browning, Clyde. *Amish in Illinois.* The Author, 1971.

Hoestetler, John A. *Amish Society.* Baltimore: Johns Hopkins University Press, 1968.

Rice, Charles S., and Rollin C. Steinmetz. *The Amish Year.* New Brunswick, NJ: Rutgers University Press, 1956.

Schreiber, William I. *Our Amish Neighbors.* Chicago: University of Chicago Press, 1962.

Brethren

★787★
Association of Fundamental Gospel Churches
9189 Grubb Ct.
Canton, OH 44721

The Association of Fundamental Gospel Churches was formed in 1954 by the coming together of three independent Brethren congregations: Calvary Chapel of Hartsville, Ohio; Webster Mills Free Brethren Church of McConnellsburg, Pennsylvania; and Little Country Chapel of Myersburg, Maryland. Prime leader in the new association was G. Henry Besse (d.1962), a former member of the Reformed Church who had in 1937 become a minister among the Dunkard Brethren. He withdrew from their fellowship in 1953 complaining about their strictures agains wearing neckties, wristwatches and jewelry and their demands that women always wear the prayer veil or cap. Former members of the Church of the Brethren were also opposed to that Church's participation in the National Council of Churches.

In general, members of the association follow Brethren doctrine and practice. They reject as unbiblical participation in war, but allow members to accept noncombatant military service. They do not allow the taking of oaths, suing at law (including for reason of divorce), or wearing ornamental adornment. They do not practice the kiss of peace.

The association meets annually to elect officers and conduct business. Ministers are chosen from among the congregation's members. They are not required to have advanced education. G. Henry Besse was succeeded by his two sons, Lynn Besse and Clair Besse, both of whom have pastored Calvary Chapel.

Membership: In 1980 there were an estimated 150 members in three congregations.

★788★
Bible Brethren
Current address not obtained for this edition.

The Bible Brethren was formed in 1948 by a small group who withdrew from the Lower Cumberland (Cumberland County, Pennsylvania) congregation of the Church of the Brethren. Clair H. Alspaugh (1903-1969), a farmer and painter who had been called to the ministry in the congregation in 1942, led the group that assumed a traditional Brethren posture. Alspaugh protested the Church of the Brethren's association with the Federal Council of Churches (now the National Council of Churches) and the failure of the Brethren to endorse doctrinal preaching as inspired by the Holy Spirit.

The original group constructed a church building following simple nineteenth-century Brethren patterns (with a long preachers' desk and straight-back pews) at Carlisle Springs, Pennsylvania. A second congregation was formed at Campbelltown, Pennsylvania. It was strengthened by the addition of a group under Paul Beidler which had withdrawn from the Dunkard Brethren, but was lost when Biedler led the entire congregation away in 1974 to form Christ's Ambassadors. A third congregation of Bible Brethren formed in 1954 at Locust Grove Chapel, near Abbotstown, York County, Pennsylvania.

Membership: In 1979 there were approximately 100 members of the Bible Brethren in two congregations.

Sources:

Gleim, Elmer Q. *Change and Challenge: A History of the Church of the Brethren in the Southern District of Pennsylvania.* Harrisburg, PA: Southern District Conference History Committee, 1973.

★789★
Brethren Church (Ashland, Ohio)
524 College Ave.
Ashland, OH 44805

Agitation among the German Baptist Brethren began in the late nineteenth century against what some considered outmoded practices. The lack of educational opportunities, an unlearned clergy, and the plain dress were main objections. The crisis came to a head with the expulsion in 1882 of Henry R. Holsinger of Berlin, Pennsylvania. Holsinger leader of the Progressives in the church, had objected to the authority of the annual meeting over the local congregation. Others left with him and in 1883 formed the Brethren Church.

The Brethren Church is like the Church of the Brethren in many respects, with the exceptions of having been the first to move toward an educated and salaried ministry, modern dress, and missions. While generally conservative in theology, and expecting a high degree of doctrinal consensus among its ministers, the church has refused to adopt a statement of faith (though it does have a doctrinal statement) on the grounds that the New Testament is its creed. During the 1930s, a group supportive of a dispensational fundamentalist doctrinal position left the church to found the National Fellowship of Brethren Churches, now the Fellowship of Grace Brethren. The church practices baptism by trine immersion, a communion service usually in the evening which includes footwashing, and the laying on of hands for ordination and for confirmation, and anointing and laying on of hands for healing. Elders (ordained ministers) lead the church in spiritual affairs.

The church follows a congregational polity and an annual conference conducts common business. Missionary activity is supported in Argentina, Colombia, India, Malaysia, Peru, Paraguay, and Mexico. The church is a member of the National Association of Evangelicals.

Membership: In 1995 the church reported 13,028 members in 103 churches.

Educational Facilities: Ashland Theological Seminary, Ashland, Ohio.

Ashland University, Ashland, Ohio.

Periodicals: *The Brethren Evangelist.* • *Insight into Brethren Missions.*

Sources:

The Task Force on Brethren History and Doctrine. *The Brethren: Growth in Life and Thought.* Ashland, OH: Board of Christian Education, Brethren Church, 1975.

★790★
Christ's Ambassadors
Current address not obtained for this edition.

Christ's Ambassadors traces its origin to a dispute in 1968 within the Dunkard Brethren congregation at Lititz, Pennsylvania. Leaders in the congregation protested an unauthorized prayer meeting conducted by some of the members under the leadership of Paul Beidler. Beidler led the members in withdrawing and forming an independent congregation. The small group affiliated with the Bible Brethren congregation at Campbelltown, Pennsylvania, in 1970. However, four years later Beidler led the entire congregation to withdraw from the Bible Brethren and formed Christ's Ambassadors. The group follows traditional Dunkard Brethren practice and beliefs, but places great emphasis upon the freedom of expression in worship.

Membership: In 1980 Christ's Ambassadors had approximately fifty members meeting in two congregations, one at Cocalico and one at Myerstown, Pennsylvania.

★791★
Christ's Assembly
Current address not obtained for this edition.

Krefeld, Germany, in the lower Rhine Valley, was one place that dissenting Pietists found relative safety and toleration during the eighteenth century, and several groups, including the one which would later become the Church of the Brethren upon its arrival in America, had members among the Krefeld residents. In 1737 two Danes, Soren Bolle and Simon Bolle, visited Krefeld and joined the Brethren. They soon returned to Copenhagen and began to preach and gather a following. While they had been baptized by the Brethren, they had been influenced as well by other Pietist Groups, most notably the Community of True Inspiration (which later migrated to America and formed the colonies at Amana, Iowa). The movement under the Bolles, Christ's Assembly, spread through Sweden, Norway, and Germany.

During the 1950s Johannes Thalitzer, pastor of Christ's Assembly in Copenhagen, learned of the continued existence of the Brethren in America through his encounter with some remnants of the recently disbanded Danish Mission of the Church of the Brethren. He initiated contact with several Brethren Groups, especially the Old German Baptist Brethren, who sponsored a visit by Thalitzer to the United States in 1959. In subsequent visits he became acquainted with all of the larger Brethren factions, but felt each was deficient in belief and/or practice. In 1967 he organized a branch of Christ's Assembly at a love feast with nine Brethren (from several Brethren groups) at Eaton, Ohio.

Christ's Assembly largely follows Brethren practice, but like the Community of True Inspiration places great emphasis upon the revealed guidance of an apostolic leadership. In more recent years it has been further influenced by the Pentecostal (Charismatic) Movement which has swept through most major denominations.

As Christ's Assembly grew it included members from four states and all the major Brethren branches. A second congregation was formed in the 1970s in Berne, Indiana.

Membership: Christ's Assembly has two congregations and an estimated 100 members.

Sources:

Benedict, F. W., and William F. Rushby. "Christ's Assembly: A Unique Brethren Movement." *Brethren Life and Thought* 18 (1973): 33-42.

★792★
Church of the Brethren
1451 Dundee Ave.
Elgin, IL 60120

The Church of the Brethren developed out of the wave of radical Pietism in early eighteenth century Germany. Hearing William Penn's invitation to come to the American colonies, most of the Brethren immigrated; those who remained were absorbed into the Mennonite movement. Their first American congregation was instituted in Germantown, Pennsylvania, on Christmas Day 1723. Important leaders of the first generation included Alexander Mack, Sr. (1679-1735), the first recognized minister; Christopher Sauer II (1721-1784), a noted colonial printer; Alexander Mack, Jr. (1712-1803); and Peter Becker (1687-1758). Until the early twentieth century, Brethren were commonly known as "Dunkers" (or Tunker), after their manner of thrice-fold immersion baptism. The formal name, German Baptist Brethren, used during most of the nineteenth century, was changed to the current designation on the anniversary of the church's bicentennial in 1908.

In colonial Pennsylvania, the Brethren shared with the Mennonites a German cultural background and Anabaptist theology, and with the Friends (Quakers) a commitment to peace and simplicity. All of these groups sought a separation from secular influences, wore distinctive plain dress, and opposed slavery. Brethren practiced strong church discipline (although not the ban), selected leaders who were not salaried or expected to obtain theological education, and refrained from voting, taking oaths, or entering lawsuits. One of the most distinctive features of Brethren worship has been their observance of the love feast, a communion service that includes foot washing, a love meal, and the taking of unleavened bread and wine/grape juice.

As one of the historic peace churches, Brethren were opposed to military service in the American Revolution and the Civil War. This resulted in limited persecution, including fines and imprisonment. The program of alternative service has been available to conscientious objectors in World War II and later conflicts.

Although the early Brethren were open to urban life, most preferred an agricultural setting and followed the farming frontier across the continent. Congregations were established in Kentucky and Ohio during the 1790s, Missouri and Illinois during the 1810s, and California and Oregon during the 1850s. Brethren settlement of the West at the turn of the century was greatly aided through colonization programs of the transcontinental railroads. The small movement of Brethren into Canada was aided by the Canadian Pacific Railroad, encouraging immigration in the early twentieth century. Between 1903 and 1922 as many as twelve congregations, mostly in Alberta and Saskatchewan, were founded. By 1968 only two of these congregations remained and they became part of the United Church of Canada.

The Brethren began to meet in a yearly meeting for worship and business during the 1740s, although no minutes were recorded until the 1780s. By the 1840s a delegated conference of lay representatives and ministers had become the highest authority in the church. Following the Civil War, the church took an active interest in missionary work (foreign and domestic), publishing, and education. Foreign mission efforts began in Denmark in the 1890s. Fields were also opened in India, China, Nigeria, and Equador. The Brethren Press, founded in 1897, produced a supply of books, periodicals, church school materials, and other literature. Numerous educational institutions were founded, six of which evolved into fully accredited independent liberal arts colleges and a university. The church also supported a theological seminary.

Tensions within the denomination in the late nineteenth century produced a painful three-way division. In addition to the original group, an "old order" movement that opposed innovation and venerated the tradition of earlier Brethren organized the Old German Baptist Brethren in 1881. A "progressive" faction organized the Brethren Church (Ashland, Ohio) in 1883.

The twentieth century has seen rapid change in Brethren life. Following an important decision on dress at the annual conference of 1911, the distinctive dress of the church has virtually disappeared. The free, plural ministry was transformed into salaried, professional pastoral leadership. Women became eligible for ordination in 1957. Efforts at evangelism and new church development have produced a more inclusive membership that includes several black, hispanic, and Korean congregations.

The extensive world mission program began a process of dramatic change in 1955, resulting in the creation of indigenous and independent religious bodies. The Ecuadorian congregations joined the United Evangelical Church of Ecuador in 1965; the India mission program merged into the Church of North India in 1970; and the Nigerian churches became the independent Brethren Church of Nigeria in 1973. The mission program in China folded when western missionaries were sent home in 1950.

Perhaps Brethren have been best known around the world for their efforts in relief and rehabilitation work in Europe following World War II. Brethren service projects later stretched into India and China and fostered ecumenical organizations such as Heifer

Project International, founded by layman Dan West, Christian Rural Overseas Program (CROP), and International Christian Youth Exchange (ICYE). The denomination also organized and administers SEERV (Salves Exchange for Refugee Rehabilitation Vocations), the largest marketing program of its type for third world handicrafts.

Since 1946 a general board of 25 members elected by the annual conference employs a program and administrative staff in the areas of parish ministries, world ministries and disaster response, publishing, and stewardship. The general offices and Brethren Press are located in Elgin, Illinois; a service center is operated in New Windsor, Maryland. The church is a founding member of both the World Council of Churches and the National Council of Churches. The Brethren Church of Nigeria is also a member of the World Council.

Membership: In 1996 the Brethren reported 141,811 members, 1,106 congregations, and 1,946 ordained ministers in the United States and Puerto Rico.

Educational Facilities: Bethany Theological Seminary, Oak Brook, Illinois.

Bridgewater College, Bridgewater, Virginia.
Elizabethtown College, Elizabethtown, Pennsylvania.
Juniata College, Huntingdon, Pennsylvania.
Manchester College, North Manchester, Indiana.
McPherson College, McPherson, Kansas.
University of La Verne, La Verne, California.

Periodicals: *Messenger.* • *Brethren Life and Thought.* Available from Bethany Theological Seminary, Butterfield and Meyer Rds., Oak Brook, IL 60521.

Sources:

Book of Worship, The Church of the Brethren. Elgin, IL: Brethren Press, 1964.

Durnbaugh, Donald F., ed. *The Brethren Encyclopedia.* 3 vols. Philadelphia, PA: Brethren Encyclopedia, 1983.

Mallot, Floyd E. *Studies in Brethren History.* Elgin, IL: Brethren Publishing House, 1954.

Manual of Brotherhood Organization and Polity. Elgin, IL: Church of the Brethren, General Offices, 1965.

Sappington, Roger E., ed. *The Brethren in the New Nation.* Elgin, IL: Brethren Press, 1976.

★793★
Conservative German Baptist Brethren
Current address not obtained for this edition.

The Conservative German Baptist Brethren is a small Brethren body body which dates to the 1931 withdrawal of a group under the leadership of Clayton F. Weaver and Ervin J. Keeny from the Dunkard Brethren Church in Pennsylvania. In 1946 Loring I. Moss, a prominent exponent of the conservative element of the Brethren Movement and one of the organizers of the Dunkard Brethren Church, withdrew and formed the Primitive Dunkard Brethren. Noting the similar concern to keep stricter Brethren standards, Moss led his new group into the Conservative German Baptist Brethren, though personally, he later withdrew and joined the Old Brethren.

Membership: In 1980 the Conservative German Baptist Brethren had two congregations, one at New Madison, Ohio, with ten members and one at Shrewsbury, Pennsylvania, with twenty-five members.

★794★
Dunkard Brethren Church
℅ Dale E. Jamison, Chairman
Board of Trustees
Quinter, KS 67752

The Dunkard Brethren Church grew out of a conservative movement within the Church of the Brethren which protested what it saw as a worldly drift and a lowering of standards in the church. The movement formed around *The Bible Monitor*, a periodical begun in 1922 by B. E. Kesler, a minister who had joined the Church of the Brethren in the first decade of the twentieth century. He was one of seven people chosen to write the report on dress standards adopted by the church in 1911. However, in the ensuing decade he saw the dress standards being increasingly ignored. Men began to wear ties and women were adopting fashionable clothes and modern hair styles. Kesler also protested the acceptance of lodge and secret society membership, divorce and remarriage, and a salaried educated ministry (which was pushing aside the traditional lay eldership).

The emergence of the *Bible Monitor* movement led to much tension within the Church of the Brethren. In 1923 Kesler was refused a seat at the annual conference. That same year he met with supporters at Denton, Maryland, to further organize efforts to reform the church. Subsequent meetings were held in different locations over the next few years. However, by 1926 it became evident that the church would not accept the movement's perspective, and at a meeting at Plevna, Indiana, the Dunkard Brethren Church was organized.

The Dunkard Brethren Church follows traditional Brethren beliefs and practices, and until recently has rebaptized members who joined from less stict branches of the church. The Dunkard Brethren adopted and enforces the dress standards accepted by the Church of the Brethren in 1911. Modesty and simplicity (though not uniformity) of dress is required. No gold or other jewelry is worn. Women keep their hair long and simply styled. They generally wear a white cap. Men cut their hair short. Divorce and remarriage are not allowed. Life insurance is discouraged. No musical instruments are used in worship.

The church has three orders of ministry. Elders marry, bury, and administer the ordinances; ministers preach and assist the elders in their sacramental role; deacons attend to temporal matters. All are laymen elected by their local congregations. The standing committee, composed of al1 the elders of the church, has general oversight of the church. Together with the ministers and elders elect ed by the local churches as delegates, they form the general conference, the highest legislative body in the church. Its decisions are final on all matters brought before it. The church is organized into four districts which meet annually.

The Dunkard Brethren Church also supports the Torreon Navajo Mission in New Mexico.

Membership: In 1980 the Dunkard Brethren reported 1,035 members in twenty-six congregations.

Periodicals: *The Bible Monitor.* Available from the editor at 1138 E. 12th St., Beaumont, CA 92223.

Sources:

Dunkard Brethren Church Manual. Dunkard Brethren Church, 1971.

Dunkard Brethren Church Polity. N.p. 1980

Minutes of the General Conference of the Dunkard Brethren Church from 1927 to 1975. Wauseon, OH: Glanz Lithographing Company, 1976.

★795★
Emmanuel's Fellowship
Current address not obtained for this edition.

Emmanuel's Fellowship was formed in 1966 by members of the Old Order River Brethren, under the leadership of Paul Goodling of Greencastle, Pennsylvania. Goodling rejected the Brethren's insistence on baptism by immersion and their allowing members to accept social security benefits. The fellowship baptizes by pouring, as the candidate stands in water. There are very strict dress requirements.

Membership: Not reported. In 1967 there was one congregation of 15 members.

★796★
Fellowship of Grace Brethren Churches
Winona Lake, IN 46590

The movement which led to the founding of the Fellowship of Grace Brethren Churches developed within the Brethren Church (Ashland, Ohio) during the 1930s. Conservatives within the Church voiced concern over liberal tendencies within the church and more particularly at the church-supported school, Ashland College. Led by ministers such as Alva J. McClain, the National Ministerial Association drew up and adopted the "Message of the Brethren Ministry," a statement of the Brethren position. The entire church refused to adopt the statement on the grounds that it seemed to be a substitute for their adherence to the New Testament as their only creed.

Conservatives scored a second victory in 1930 when a graduate school of theology opened at Ashland under McClain's leadership. However, in 1937, both McClain, then dean of the school, and Professor Herman A. Hoyt were dismissed. Their supporters organized Grace Theological Seminary as a new institution for ministerial training, which set the stage for a confrontation at the 1939 General Conference of the Church. After the exclusion of some of the new seminary's supporters, all walked out and formed the National Fellowship of Brethren Churches, which in 1976 assumed its present name.

The new church adopted the 1921 "Message of the Brethren Ministry" as its doctrinal position. That document was replaced in 1969 by a revised and expanded "Statement of Faith." The new statement affirms the conservative evangelical theology of the original document but adds a lengthy statement on various eschatological issues such as the premillennial return of Christ, eternal punishment for nonbelievers and a belief in a personal Satan. The church practices baptism by triune immersion and a threefold communion that includes footwashing, a meal, and partaking of the elements of bread and the cup.

The Fellowship adopted a congregational polity. The Conference of the Fellowship meets annually and oversees the several schools and a vigorous mission program. The Foreign Mission Society operates in Argentina, Brazil, Africa, France, Germany, Hawaii, Mexico, and Puerto Rico. The National Council of Churches is stanchly opposed.

Membership: In 1996 the fellowship reported 34,500 members, 270 congregations, and 562 ministers.

Educational Facilities: Grace Theological Seminary, Winona Lake, Indiana.
Grace College, Winona Lake, Indiana.

Periodicals: *Brethren Missionary Herald.*

Sources:

Baumann, Louis S. *The Faith.* Winona Lake, IN: Brethren Missionary Herald Co., 1960.

Hoyt, Herman A. *Then Would My Servants Fight.* Winona Lake, IN: Brethren Missionary Herald Co., 1956.

Kent, Homer A., Sr. *Conquering Frontiers: A History of the Brethren Church.* Winona Lake, IN: BMH Books, 1972.

McClain, Alva J. *Daniel's Prophecy of the Seventy Weeks.* Grand Rapids, MI: Zondervan Publications, n.d.

★797★
Fundamental Brethren Church
Current address not obtained for this edition.

The Fundamental Brethren Church was formed in 1962 by former members of four congregations of the Church of the Brethren in Mitchell County, North Carolina, under the leadership of Calvin Barnett. The doctrinally conservative group adopted the "Message of the Brethren Ministry," a statement written by some ministers in the Brethren Church (Ashland, Ohio) in the 1920s as their doctrinal standard. Among the issues involved in their leaving the Church of the Brethren, its participation in the National Council of Churches and use of the Revised Standard Version of the Bible were prominent. The group added to its doctrinal statement that the King James Version of the Bible is authoritative. It also adopted a fundamental premillennial dispensational theological stance. By 1967, there were four congregations with 200 members.

Membership: In the 1970s there were 3 congregations of less than 200 members.

★798★
Independent Brethren Church
Current address not obtained for this edition.

The Independent Brethren Church was formed in 1972. On February 12 of that year, the Upper Marsh Creek congregation at Gettysburg, Pennsylvania, of the Church of the Brethren withdrew and became an independent body. Later that year, members from the Antietam congregation left and established the independent Blue Rock congregation near Waynesboro, Pennsylvania. These two congregations united as the Independent Brethren Church. They are conservative in their following of Brethren belief and practice. They have kept the plain dress and oppose any affiliation with the National Council of Churches.

Membership: In 1980 the Independent Brethren Church had approximately 85 members in two congregations.

★799★
Old Brethren Church
Current address not obtained for this edition.

The Old Brethren Church, generally termed simply the Old Brethren, is a name taken by two congregations which split from the Old German Baptist Brethren in 1913 (Deer Creek congregation in Carroll County, Indiana) and in 1915 (Salida congregation in Stanislaus County, California). Though widely separated geographically, the two congregations banded together and in 1915 published *The Old Brethren's Reasons,* a twenty-four page pamphlet outlining their position. The Old Brethren dissented from the Old German Baptist Brethren's refusal to make annual meeting decisions uniformly applicable and from their allowing divergences of practice and discipline among the different congregations. Also, the Old Brethren called for greater strictness in plain dress and called for houses and carriages shorn of any frills which would gratify the lust of the eye.

In particular, the Old Brethren denounced the automobile and the telephone. Use of either caused a believer to be hooked into the world and inevitably led to church members being yoked together with unbelievers. In practice, over the years, the Old Brethren have been forced to change and have come to closely resemble the group from which they originally withdrew. Even prior to World War II, they began to make accommodation to the automobile.

Members of the Old Brethren meet annually at Pentecost, but keep legislation to a minimum. They allow the congregations to retain as much authority as possible.

Beginning with two congregations, the Old Brethren Church has experienced growth in spite of a schism in 1930 that led to the formation of the Old Brethren German Baptist Church. A third meeting house was built in the 1970s.

Membership: In 1980 the Old Brethren had approximately 130 members and three congregations (Salida, California; Deer Creek, Indiana; Gettysburg, Ohio). Individual members could be found in Tennessee, Mississippi, and Brazil (where a group of Old German Baptist Brethren had settled in 1969).

Periodicals: *The Pilgrim.* Send orders to 19201 Cherokee Road, Tuolumne, CA 95379.

★800★
Old Brethren German Baptist Church
Current address not obtained for this edition.

The Old Brethren German Baptist Church originated among the most conversative members of the Old Brethren Church and the Old Order German Baptist Brethren Church. Around 1930 members of the Old Brethren Deer Creek congregation near Camden, Indiana, began to fellowship with the Old Order Brethren in the Covington, Ohio, area. However, by 1935 the traditionalist Old Brethren found themselves unable to continue their affiliations with the Ohio Brethren. They continued as an independent congregation until they made contact with a few Old Order Brethren near Bradford, Ohio, who met in the home of Solomon Lavy. In 1939 the two groups merged and adopted the name Old Brethren German Baptist Church. They were joined in 1953 by a group of Old Order Brethren from Arcanum, Ohio.

The Old Brethren is the most conservative of all Brethren groups. They use neither automobiles, tractors, electricity, or telephones. Their only accommodation to modern mechanization is that they do permit occasional use of stationary gasoline engines and will hire nonmembers for specific tasks requiring machinery. Members follow a strict personal code of nonconformity to the world. Homes and buggies are plainly furnished and simply painted. No gold or jewelry is worn. Farmers do not raise or habitually use tobacco. Members do not vote or purchase life insurance.

Membership: Among the smallest of Brethren groups, the Old Brethren, in 1980, reported 45 members in three congregations: Camden and Goshen, Indiana and Arcanum, Ohio.

★801★
Old German Baptist Brethren
% Elder Clement Skiles
Rte. 1, Box 140
Bringhurst, IN 46913

The Old German Baptist Brethren represents the conservative wing in the Brethren movement. This group withdrew in 1881, the year before Henry R. Holsinger, a leader of what became known as the Progressive Brethren (now the Brethren Church (Ashland, Ohio)) was expelled from the Church of the Brethren. The group was protesting innovative tendencies and was opposed to Sunday schools, missions, higher education, and church societies and auxiliaries. It has lessened its opposition to higher education among members and now sponsors parochial schools. No missions are supported, and children attend the regular services of the church instead of having a church school.

The Old German Baptist Brethren retain plain garb and are committed to non-participation in war, government, secret societies, and worldly amusements. They also object to participation in government (i.e., voting) even by members whose conscience otherwise allows it. They remain conservative on oaths, lawsuits, non-salaried ministry, and veiled heads for women at worship.

Membership: In 1997 the Brethren reported 5,671 members in 56 churches served by 236 ministers.

Periodicals: *The Vindicator.* Send orders to 701 St., Rte. 571, Union City, OH 45390.

Sources:

Fisher, H. M., et al. *Doctrinal Treatise.* Covington, OH: Little Printing Company, 1954.

★802★
Old Order German Baptist Church
Current address not obtained for this edition.

As the Old German Baptist Brethren continued to deal with questions of accommodating to a fast-moving society in the early twentieth century, a group of members withdrew in 1921 because of the departure of the Old German Baptist Brethren from the established order and old paths. The petitioners, as they were informally called, could be found throughout the brethren, but were concentrated in the congregations at Covington and Arcanum, Ohio.

Staunchly set against most modern conveniences, the Old Order German Baptists have over the year been forced to accommodate. Automobiles are forbidden, but tractors are now allowed for farm work. Members do not use electricity or telephones. Increasingly, younger members have been forced to leave the farm and seek employment in nonfarm occupations.

Membership: In 1980 the church had less than 100 members and three congregations, all in Ohio (Gettysburg, Covington, and Arcanum).

Quakers (Friends)

★803★
Alaska Yearly Meeting
% Walter E. Outwater
Box 687
Kotzebue, AK 99752

As early as 1897 Quaker missionaries from the California Yearly Meeting, an independent programmed meeting of Friends, began work among the Eskimo people in Alaska. In 1970 the work had grown to the point that it was organized as a yearly meeting affiliated with the California Meeting, which maintained a Bible Training School. A goal of turning the work of the Meeting entirely over to its Eskimo constituency was completed in 1982 when the last of the missionaries were withdrawn and the Alaska Yearly meeting became fully independent. The California Meeting has joined the Friends United Meeting.

Membership: In 1981 there were 11 congregations and 2,860 members.

Educational Facilities: Bible Training School.

★804★
Central Yearly Meeting of Friends
% Ollie McCune, Supt.
Rte. 1, Box 226
Alexandria, IN 46001

The Central Yearly Meeting of Friends was formed in 1926 by several meetings in eastern Indiana who were protesting the liberalism of the Five Years Meeting. Doctrinally, the Central Yearly Meeting of Friends is evangelical and very conservative in matters of personal holiness. Worship is programmed. Churches of this small body are found in Indiana, North Carolina, Arkansas, and Ohio. Missionary work is sponsored in Bolivia.

Membership: In 1981 the meeting reported 11 congregations (monthly meetings) organized into 3 quarterly (district) meetings and 446 members.

Educational Facilities: Union Bible College, Westfield, Indiana.

Periodicals: *Friends Evangel.* Send orders to 5601 E. Co. Rd. 6505, Muncie, IN 47302.

★805★

Evangelical Friends Church, Eastern Division
5350 Broadmoor Circle, NW
Canton, OH 44709

Prior to 1971 known as the Ohio Yearly Meeting of Friends, the Evangelical Friends Church is that branch of the Friends most influenced by the holiness movement. The Evangelical Friends have a programmed worship service with a minister who preaches. Formed in 1813, the Ohio Yearly Meeting of Friends supported the Gurneyites, followers of Joseph John Gurney, a promoter of beliefs in the final authority of the Bible, atonement, justification, and sanctification. After the Civil War, the Ohio Yearly Meeting became open to the holiness movement through the activities of such workers as David Updegraff, Dougan Clark, Walter Malone and Emma Malone. The latter founded the Cleveland Bible Insititute (now the Malone College) in 1892, and it now serves an interdenominational holiness constituency.

The Evangelical Friends Church, never a member of the Five Years Meeting, has become a haven of conservative congregations who have withdrawn from the Friends United Meeting in both the United States and Canada. Mission work is sustained in Taiwan and India. The church participates in the Evangelical Friends Alliance.

Membership: In 1990 there were 8,610 members in 93 churches.

Educational Facilities: Malone College, Canton, Ohio.

Periodicals: *The Facing Bench.*

Sources:

DeVol, Charles E. *Focus on Friends.* Canton, OH: Missionary Board of the Evangelical Friends Church—Eastern Division, 1982.

Faith and Practice, the Book of Discipline. Canton, OH: Evangelical Friends Church—Eastern Region, 1981.

★806★

Evangelical Friends International
3823A S. Genoa Circle
Aurora, CO 80013

The Evangelical Friends International came into being in 1990 when it superseded the former Evangelical Friends Alliance. The alliance had existed as an association of four autonomous Quaker groups, the Evangelical Friends Church, Eastern Division, the Rocky Mountain Yearly Meeting of Friends, the Mid-America Yearly Meeting of Friends, and the Northwest Yearly Meeting of Friends. These groups represented the most theologically conservative element in the Friends movement, much of it having been influenced by the holiness movement of the nineteenth century. The Evangelical Friends Alliance had been founded in 1965 but was restricted at the end of the 1980s in recognition that the four affiliated groups in fact had come to exist as a single denomination. The members of Evangelical Friends International attribute their change to the general evangelical renewal within Christianity, the new scholarly recognition of the evangelical nature of early Quakerism, and the cooperative work of the Evangelical Friends Alliance.

The Evangelical Friends Church, Eastern Division, which existed for many years as the Ohio Yearly Meeting of Friends, was formed in 1813. As the work developed, members became attracted to the preaching of Joseph John Gurney, who had been deeply affected by Methodist holiness doctrines. Most active in promoting the holiness movement in Ohio were David Updegraff, Dougan Clark, Walter Malone, and Emma Malone. The Malones founded Cleveland Bible Institute (now Malone College) in 1892.

A generation after their movement into Ohio, Friends moved into Kansas and from there into Oklahoma, Texas, Nebraska, and Colorado. A Kansas Yearly Meeting (since the 1970s, the Mid-America Yearly Meeting) was formed in 1872. In 1900 it affiliated with the Five Years Meeting but withdrew in 1937 as more conservative elements came to dominate the Meeting. In 1934 the Kansas Meeting established a mission in the Congo (now Burundi) and later founded Camp Quaker Haven at Arkansas, Kansas, for its youth.

The Northwest Yearly Meeting of Friends Church dates to the movement of Friends into the Willamette Valley of Oregon in the late-nineteenth century. The first settlers had been from Iowa and they continued their affiliation with the Iowa Yearly Meeting, but by 1893 they had grown sufficiently so that an independent Oregon Yearly Meeting could be set apart. As work expanded into Washington and Idaho, the present name was assumed. From 1902 to 1936, the Oregon Yearly Meeting was affiliated with the Five Years Meeting but withdrew because of the growing conservative theological stance of Friends in the Northwest.

The Northwest Meeting sponsors four campground facilities, Friendship Manor (a retirement home), Barclay Press (a printing company), George Fox College, and several elementary and high schools.

The Rocky Mountain Yearly Meeting was established in 1957 from congregations formerly affiliated with the Nebraska Yearly Meeting. The Nebraska Meeting was affiliated with the Friends United Meeting, and the Rocky Mountain Meeting did not continue that relationship. It sponsors a campground near Woodland Park, Colorado.

Missionary work of Evangelical Friends is located in Barundi, Mexico, Rwanda, Taiwan, Peru, Bolivia, India, and among Native Americans in Arizona.

Membership: In 1982 Evangelical Friends International reported 217 congregations, 24,095 members, and 483 clergy.

Educational Facilities: Malone College, Canton, Ohio; Friends Bible College and Academy, Haviland, Kansas; Friends University, Wichita, Kansas; Houston Graduate School of Theology, Houston, Texas; George Fox College, Newberg, Oregon.

Periodicals: *Evangelical Friends*, Box 232, Newberg, OR 97132. • *The Facing Bench*, 5350 Broadmoor Circle, NW, Canton, OH 44709.

Sources:

Barrett, Paul W. *Educating for Peace.* Board of Publication, Kansas Yearly Meeting of Friends, n.d.

Choate, Ralph E. *Dust of His Feet.* The Author, 1965.

DeVol, Charles E. *Focus on Friends.* Canton, OH: Missionary Board of the Evangelical Friends Church-Eastern Division, 1982.

Discipline. Kansas Yearly Meeting of Friends, 1966.

Faith and Practice of the Rocky Mountain Yearly Meeting of Friends Church. Pueblo, CO: Riverside Printing Co., 1978.

Faith and Practice, the Book of Discipline. Canton, OH: Evangelical Friends Church-Eastern Division, 1981.

The Story of Friends in the Northwest. Newberg, OR: Barclay Press, n.d.

25th Anniversary Committee. *Friends Ministering Together.* Pueblo, CO: Riverside Printing Co., 1982.

★807★

Friends General Conference
1216 Arch St., 2B
Philadelphia, PA 19107

The Friends General Conference is an association of otherwise autonomous yearly meetings in the United States and Canada, most of which emphasize the authority gained through the direct experience of God, are open to theological diversity and the enrichment it can bring, and follow an unprogrammed pattern of worship. In general the yearly meetings which make up the conference continue the tradition most associated with Elias Hicks (1748-1830).

History. Elias Hicks ministered among the American Quakers in the 1820s. He was an eloquent preacher, but as his ideas developed, his emphasis upon asceticism, rationalism, and subjectivism irritated many of the Quaker faithful. Hick's followers assigned a most significant role to the Inner Light, even to the extent of considering all outward forms useless and possibly harmful. Worship should be unprogrammed, not planned ahead of time. Hicks also attacked the divinity of Christ and expounded an exemplary theory of Christ's saving work. He was strong in his condemnation of amusements and other activities for self-gratification.

Controversy over Hicks' views became public in 1823 at the Philadelphia Yearly Meeting, where complaints were lodged by some more "orthodox" members. Four years of tension ensued in which many non-theological factors (sociological differences and personal feelings, among others) led to further polarization of the pro-Hicks and anti-Hicks factions. In 1827 the pro-Hicks faction made what was termed a "quiet retreat" from the controversy. They called a conference and organized a separate yearly meeting. Separations followed in New York, Ohio, and across the East and Midwest. Seven "Hicksite" yearly meetings were soon established.

In 1868 a Sunday school conference began efforts to coordinate and communicate among the various Hicksite yearly meetings, and in 1900 the General Conference emerged to aid in their common witness. Originally, four coordinating organizations merged to form the conference, including the First-Day School Conference and the Friends Union for Philanthropic Labor (organized in 1882). The conference is for fellowship and service only, and has no legislative authority over the participating yearly meetings.

Organization. The conference held biennial conferences until 1968, ever since that time it has held an annual "FGC Gathering of Friends." At constituent yearly meetings, members are appointed to a central committee and to an executive committee which are responsible for the direction and administration of the conference's year-round program.

The program in carried out by six standing committees: Advancement and Outreach, Christian and Interfaith Relations, Long Range Conference Planning, Ministry and Nurture, Publications and Distribution, and Religious Education. The Friends Meeting House Fund, Inc., which holds funds for meetings in need of buying, building or remodeling buildings, operates with a separate board of directors appointed by the central committee. The *Friends Journal*, an independent publication, is closely identified with FGC.

Included in the conference are the Baltimore, Canadian, Illinois, Lake Erie, New England, New York, Northern, Ohio Valley, Philadelphia, South Central, and Southeastern Yearly Meetings; the Southern Appalachian Yearly Meeting and Association, Piedmont Friends Fellowship (NC), Central Alaska Friends Conference, and six monthly meetings.

Membership: In 1997 the conference reported approximately 32,000 affiliated Quakers in 600 meetings and worship groups. Of these members, 1,200 were in Canada.

Periodicals: *FG Connections.* • Related: *Friends Journal.* Send orders to 1216 Arch St., 2-B Philadelphia, PA 19107.

Sources:

Bacon, Margaret Hope. *Mothers of Feminism.* San Francisco: Harper & Row, 1986.

Boulding, Elsie. *My Part in the Quaker Adventure.* Philadelphia: Religious Education Committee, Friends General Conference, 1858.

Doherty, Robert W. *The Hicksite Separation.* New Brunswick, NJ: Rutgers University Press, 1967.

Jones, Rufus M. *The Latter Periods of Quakerism.* 2 vols. Westport, CT: Greenwood Press, 1970.

Rushmore, Jane P. *Testimonies and Practice of the Society of Friends.* Philadelphia: Friends General Conference, 1945.

★808★
Friends United Meeting
101 Quaker Hill Dr.
Richmond, IN 47374

The largest of all the North American Quaker bodies, the Five Years Meeting of Friends was formed in 1902 as a loose coordinating agency by 12 yearly meetings. By the addition of programs and agencies, a full denominational structure has developed. There are now 27 yearly meetings in what became in 1965 the Friends United Meeting.

The Friends United Meeting represents the continuation of the "orthodox" Friends who had survived the Hicksite (Friends General Conference) and Wilburite (Religious Society of Friends Conservative) schisms, but who had existed throughout the nineteenth century as independent, geographical yearly meetings. Most worship is programmed. Ecumenical efforts began in the 1880s and a series of conferences every five years led to the formation of the Five Years Meeting.

The statement of faith of the Meeting, based upon the teachings of Jesus as "we understand them," includes beliefs in 1. true religion as a personal encounter with God rather than ritual and ceremony; 2. individual worth before God; 3. worship as an act of seeking; 4. essential Christian vitures of moral purity, integrity, honesty, simplicity, and humility; 5. Christian love and goodness; 6. concern for the suffering and unfortunate; and 7. continuing revelation through the Holy Spirit.

Organization. The work of the meeting is carried out through its general board. The department of World Ministries oversees missions in Cuba, Jamaica, Belize, West Bank in Israel, Kenya, Uganda, Tanzania, and the United States. The department of Meeting Ministries serves the needs of the local congregations promoting spiritual development, church planting, evangelism, and Christian education programs. Friends United Meeting also operates a retail bookstore and a book publishing enterprise called Friends United Press. Member Yearly Meetings are: Baltimore, Canada, Cuba, East Africa, East Africa (South), Elgon, Indiana, Jamaica, Iowa, Nairobi, Nebraska, New England, New York, North Carolina, Southwest, Southeastern, Western, Wilmington, Bwase, East Africa (North), Kaka Mega, Luggri, Malava, Nandi, Tanzania, Uganda, Vokoli, and Canadian Central. It is a member of both the World Council of Churches and the National Council of Churches.

Membership: In 1996, the meeting had 46,789 members in the United States and 1,129 members in Canada, with an additional 100,000 members in Africa, Cuba, Jamaica, Mexico, and Israel.

Educational Facilities: Earlham College, Richmond, Indiana.
Earlham School of Religion, Richmond, Indiana.
Guilford College, Greensboro, North Carolina.
William Penn College, Oskaloosa, Iowa.
Friends Theological College, Tiriki, Kenya.

Periodicals: *Quaker Life.*

Sources:

Hall, Francis B., ed. "Friends United Meeting". In *Friends in the Americas.* Philadelphia: Friends World Committee, Section of the Americas, 1976.

★809★
Intermountain Yearly Meeting
℅ Martin Cobin
1720 Linden Ave.
Boulder, CO 80304

In the early 1970s, the Pacific Yearly Meeting devised a plan to divide its widely scattered membership into more geographically workable units. Members in Arizona and New Mexico joined with otherwise independent friends in Arizona, New Mexico, and Colorado, as well as Colorado Friends who had withdrawn from the Missouri Valley Yearly Meeting, to form the Intermountain Yearly Meeting. The group had its first annual session in 1975. Most congregations are unprogrammed. The Mexico City congregation affiliated with the Pacific Yearly Meeting also participates in the Intermountain fellowship.

Membership: In 1991 the meeting reported 997 members in 17 monthly meetings and 18 worship groups.

★810★
Iowa Yearly Meeting of Friends
% Del Coppinger, Gen. Supt.
Box 657
Oskaloosa, IA 52577

The Iowa Yearly Meeting of Friends was established in 1877 by Conservative Friends who separated from the Iowa Yearly Meeting, which is now a part of the Friends United Meeting established in 1863. It keeps unprogrammed meetings for worship and operates the Scattergood School, a coeducational college-preparatory high school, in West Branch, Iowa.

Membership: In 1992 there were 601 members in nine monthly meetings.

Sources:

Hall, Francis B., ed. *Friends in the Americas.* Philadelphia, PA: Friends World Committee, 1976.

★811★
Missouri Valley Friends Conference
Current address not obtained for this edition.

The Missouri Valley Friends Conference was formed in 1955 as an association of unprogrammed Quaker meetings in the Midwest which were not affiliated with any other established yearly meeting. The conference meets annually. Over the years some of the local groups have affiliated with the yearly meetings and discontinued participation in the conference. At the same time, new unaffiliated meetings have joined the conference, so attendance has remained fairly constant.

Membership: In 1988 the conference reported approximately 150 members in eight congregations.

★812★
North Carolina Yearly Meeting of Friends (Conservative)
% Lloyd Lee Wilson, Clerk
536 Carnaby Ct.
Virginia Beach, VA 23454

The North Carolina Yearly Meeting of Friends (Conservative) is the result of a separation among Friends in North Carolina at the beginning of the century. At that time there was a move to form what would become the Five Years Meeting (now known as the Friends United Meeting). As part of the developments, a new book of discipline was adopted. The Cedar Grove Monthly Meeting opposed the new trends it saw emerging and placed special emphasis on the retention of the unprogrammed meetings for worship. In 1904 they formed a separate yearly meeting and over the years other monthly meetings have been added. They have found fellowship with the other conservative Friends in the Ohio and Iowa Yearly Meetings, and periodically gather with them for fellowship.

Conservative Friends, also called Wilburites, place special emphasis in their faith and practice on the direct, unmediated experience of the presence and guidance of God. Their worship consists of waiting silently for this presence to become manifest, and vocal ministry is limited to those words the speaker feels confident are inspired by God. They do not act on any matter until moved of God; but after that, are not easily or soon dissuaded.

Membership: In 1991 there were 450 members in eight monthly meetings.

Educational Facilities: Guilford College, Greensboro, North Carolina.

★813★
North Pacific Yearly Meeting of the Religious Society of Friends
3311 NW Polk
Corvallis, OR 97330

In the early 1970s the Pacific Yearly Meeting, which had congregations spread over a cumbersome distance, divided into several yearly meeetings. In 1972 members in Oregon and Washington became the North Pacific Yearly Meeting and held the first session in 1973. Since its formation groups have been added in Idaho and Montana. The Meeting keeps close ties with the parent body with whom it jointly supports a periodical. The Meeting is governed in a non-hierarchical fashion. A steering committee provides continuity and a clerk convenes its gatherings, records its minutes, and represents it to to others.

Membership: In 1997 the meeting reported 18 monthly meetings, four quarterly meetings, and 32 worship groups gathered in the quarterly meetings. There were approximately 761 members.

Periodicals: *Friends Bulletin.* Send orders to 5238 Andalusia Ct., Whittier, CA 90601.

Sources:

Faith and Practice. Corvallis, OR: North Pacific Yearly Meeting of the Religious Society of Friends, 1986.

★814★
Northwest Yearly Meeting of Friends Church
200 N. Maridian St.
Newberg, OR 97132-2714

Quaker settlers in the northwest first gathered in the fertile Willamette Valley in Oregon in the late nineteenth century. These early settlers were from Iowa and associated with the Iowa Yearly Meeting. In 1893 they were officially established as an independent yearly meeting by the Iowa Yearly Meeting with the name Oregon Yearly Meeting of Friends. Because some churches were located in Washington and Idaho, the name was changed to Northwest Yearly Meeting of Friends. From 1902 to 1936, the Oregon Yearly Meeting was a part of the Five Years Meeting, but has in more recent years affiliated with the Evangelical Friends International.

The doctrine of the Northwest Yearly Meeting (NWYM) is biblically based with a central message of the Lordship of Jesus Christ. The emphasis of salvation through the Lord coupled with a strong sense of social commitment have been the two dominant themes of the meeting.

NWYM maintains a relationship with four camping facilities, Friendsview Manor (a retirement home), Barclay Press (a printing company), George Fox University, and several elementary and high schools. Missionary work is carried out in cooperation with the Evangelical Friends International. A joint mission program is supported in Mexico, Rwanda, Burundi, Taiwan, Peru, and Bolivia.

Membership: In 1997 NWYM reported 7,054 members, 57 churches, including four extension churches, and three mission points.

Educational Facilities: George Fox University, Newberg, Oregon.

Periodicals: *The Friends Voice.* Send orders to 110 S. Elliott Rd., Newberg, OR 97132.

Sources:

This Story of the Friends in the Northwest. Newberg, OR: Barclay Press, n.d.

★815★
Ohio Yearly Meeting of the Society of Friends
61830 Sandy Ridge Rd.
Barnesville, OH 43712

History. The Ohio Yearly Meeting of the Religious Society of Friends was established in 1813 and originally included most of the Friends west of the Alleghany Mountains. The meeting was also one of those most affected by the the conflict in the 1840s between English Quaker Joseph John Gurney and John Wilbur. Gurney had absorbed much from the British Methodists, and Wilbur saw Methodist doctrine replacing the traditional Quaker reliance on the Inner Light. Beginning in 1845, Wilbur's supporters began to separate from the main body of Quakers and are generally known as Conservative Friends. The Ohio Yearly Meeting aligned itself with the Conservative cause.

Beliefs. The Ohio Yearly Meeting places great emphasis upon providing a form of worship which is simple, pure, and spiritual. They advocate the unprogramed meetings in which believers wait in silence for the movement of the Spirit. The yearly meeting has taken a strong stand in opposition to capital punishment, the taking of oaths, participation in war, racial discrimination, and the use of intoxicants.

Organization. The yearly meeting, composed of representatives of the monthly meetings, provides general oversight of the society. Each monthly meeting appoints two members of each gender to act as overseers to have responsibility for pastoral care of members and spiritual oversight of the meeting for worship; two elders to have oversight of the ministry; and ministers as are called.

The yearly meeting is a member of the Friends World Committee for Consultation. Fellowship is kept with the other two remaining Conservative Yearly meetings—North Carolina and Iowa—and there are periodic gatherings of members from the three groups. There is no direct missional program, but a number of service projects are supported through the American Friends Service Committee.

Membership: In 1997 the meeting reported 537 members in 10 monthly meetings.

Periodicals: *Ohio Conservative Friends Review.* Send orders to 8106 Sherbrooke Ct., Springfield, VA 22152.

★816★
Pacific Yearly Meeting of Friends
℅ Eric Moon
2151 Vine St
Berkeley, CA 94709

Quakers began to establish congregations on the West Coast in the 1880s. In 1931, with impetus from Howard H. Brinton and Anna Brinton, a meeting was called which led to the formation of the loosely organized Pacific Coast Association of Friends. In 1947, the Pacific Yearly Meeting was established within the Association. Over the next decade it grew to include forty congregations as far apart as Mexico City, Honolulu, and Canada. As a result, a committee recommended the division of the meeting into three meetings which led to the establishment of the North Pacific Yearly Meeting (1972) and the Intermountain Yearly Meeting (1973). Though each is independent, there are close familial ties and they jointly publish a periodical.

Its worship is unprogrammed. Membership though concentrated in California includes congregations in Mexico City and Honolulu.

Membership: Not reported. In 1981 the meeting reported 1,452 members in 35 congregations. In 1996 there were 48 congregations in California and Nevada.

Periodicals: *Friends Bulletin.* Send orders to Friends Bulletin Corporation, 5238 Andalucia Ct., Whittier, CA 90601-2222.

Sources:

Brinton, Howard H. *Guide to Quaker Practice.* Wallingford, PA: Pendle Hill Publications, 1955.

Faith and Practice. San Francisco: Pacific Yearly Meeting of the Religious Society of Friends, 1973.

★817★
Rocky Mountain Yearly Meeting
3350 Reed St.
Wheat Ridge, CO 80033

The Rocky Mountain Yearly Meeting was established in 1957 by separation from the Nebraska Yearly Meeting and did not continue the latter's affiliation with the Friends United Meeting. Worship is programmed. Mission work is carried out by the Navajo Indians at the Rough Rock Friends Mission near Chinle, Arizona and by other individuals through cooperation with Evangelical Friends Mission. Quaker Ridge Camp is maintained north of Woodland Park, Colorado.

Membership: In 1997 the meeting reported 1,162 members in 20 congregations located in Colorado, New Mexico, Nebraska, and Arizona. These include four Navajo churches in the Rough Rock area.

Educational Facilities: Barclay College, Haviland, Kansas.
Friends University, Wichita, Kansas.
George Fox College, Newberg, Oregon.

Periodicals: *The Traveling Minute.* • *Friends Voice.* Send orders to 600 E. 3rd St., Newberg, OR 97132.

Sources:

Faith and Practice of the Rocky Mountain Yearly Meeting of Friends Church. Pueblo, CO: Riverside Printing Co., 1978.

25th Anniversary Committee. *Friends Ministering Together.* Pueblo, CO: Riverside Printing Co., 1982.

★818★
The Rogerenes
(Defunct)

The Rogerenes were a small religious group which began as Baptists but were strongly influenced by members of the Society of Friends. They were orginally led by John Rogers (1648?-1721). James Rogers, John's father, had settled in New London, Connecticut, in 1656 and soon became one of the wealthiest men in the colony. Then in 1674 John and his wife Elizabeth withdrew from the Congregational Church and joined the Seventh-Day Baptist Church at Newport, Connecticut. Soon afterward, Elizabeth's father pursuaded her to leave her husband and return home, a separation that became permanent. But other members of the family joined him, and they began a Baptist congregation in New London. John Rogers became the pastor. He actively attacked the state-supported Congregational Church, especially its support of infant baptism and the forced payment of church taxes. As Rogers ideas became more radical, the congregation also broke its ties to the Baptists in Newport around 1677. One of the radicalizing influences was the visits in 1675 between John and members of the congregation and William Edmundson, a Quaker from Ireland visiting America. Out of these discussions, the Rogerenes, as they were soon to be known, dropped the sabbatarian beliefs. But though they worshipped on Sunday, they felt that all days were alike. Rogers especially attacked idolatry which for him included many of the practices of the Congregational Church, such as a salaried ministry and the use of elaborate titles of respect. The group adopted plain clothes, refused to use oaths, and opposed war and violence. John Rogers became a shoemaker as a means of demonstrating the belief that ministers should make their own living.

They also opposed contemporary medical practice, replacing it with clean living, good nursing, homemade remedies, and prayer. The group continued to disagree with the Quakers on the issue of sacraments. They baptized new members and celebrated the Lord's Supper annually.

Almost from the beginning the group was persecuted and John Rogers seems to have spent as much as one-third of his life in jail for his religious beliefs. It should be noted that the group did little to decrease the tension with the state church. Members refused to pay church taxes. They would travel on Sunday to attend meetings in defiance of state regulations. They periodically staged demonstrations against idolatrous practices. For example, they would attend the Congregational services and bring work with them. They would interupt and contradict the minister. Gordon Saltonstall, the Congregational minister in New London and later governor of Connecticut, led the persecution until his death in 1724. A final period of intense persecution occurred in the mid-1760s.

John Rogers was succeeded in leadership of the group by his son John Rogers, Jr. (d.1853) and he by John Walterhouse, John Bolles, Samuel Whipple, and Jonathan Whipple (1794-1877). Bolles was an early abolitionist who had freed his slaves in the 1720s. In 1735 a group of Rogerenes moved to Morris County, New Jersey, and established a colony. Three years later they moved to Monmouth County, New Jersey, near present-day Ocean City. The settlement died out by the end of the century. During the 1740s, land was purchased near Groton and Mystic, Connecticut, and over a generation the group migrated eastward. Its prosperity in spite of difficulties during the Revolution and the War of 1812 is shown by the erection of a new large meetinghouse in 1815 and an even larger one in the post-Civil War era.

The twentieth century saw the decline of the church. Some families had moved west before the turn of the century, and others drifted to other churches. By the 1940s only a small group was left in Mystic and a smaller group in California. A generation later, while some descendents of former Rogerene families still identified themselves with the group, it seems to have ceased to exist as a church body.

Sources:

Brinton, Ellen Starr. "The Rogerenes." *The New England Quarterly* 16 (March 1943): 3-19.

Randolph, Corliss Fitz. "The Rogerenes." In *Seventh Day Baptists in Europe and America*. Plainfield, NJ: Seventh Day Baptist General Conference, 1910.

★819★
Southeastern Yearly Meeting
Current address not obtained for this edition.

The Southeastern Yearly Meeting is a small body established in 1962 and is composed mostly of Friends who migrated south to Florida. They support a retreat and study center near Orlando, Florida. In 1967, there were ten congregations, one of which was in Georgia, with a membership of 389. Membership is from various Friends' traditions.

Membership: In 1981 the meeting reported 445 members and 22 congregations and worship groups.

Periodicals: *SEYM Newsletter*. Send orders to 1375 Talbot Ave., Jacksonville, FL 32205.

★820★
Southern Appalachian Yearly Meeting and Association
℅ Peggy Bonnington, Clerk
408 Coy Circle
Clarksville, TN 37043

The Southern Appalachian Yearly Meeting and Association of Friends was formed in 1970 at Crossville, Tennessee. It was established by congregations in Alabama, Tennessee, Georgia, Kentucky, West Virginia, South Carolina, and North Carolina, some of which had been associated together as early as 1940 in the South Central Friends Conference (and later in the Southern Appalachian Association of Friends). Congregations are unprogrammed, and there are no paid ministers. Annual meetings, held in May, center on silent worship, a search together on a chosen theme, and social concerns. While existing for some years as an independent Meeting, the Southern Appalachian Association has recently become a constituent part of the Friends General Conference.

Membership: See Friends General Conference (separate entry). In 1991 there were an estimated 433 members.

Periodicals: *Southern Appalachian Friend*. Send orders to 3848 Wilmot Ave., Columbia, SC 29205.

Other European Free Traditions

★821★
All-Canadian Union of Slavic Evangelical Christians
Current address not obtained for this edition.

The All-Canadian Union of Slavic Evangelical Christians traces its roots to a variety of independent evangelical Protestant activities in Russia in the late nineteenth century. Among them was what came to be known as the Shtundist movement, which began among German residents in the Ukraine in the 1860s. Two Reformed ministers, Johann Bonekmper and his son Karl Bonekmper, began to conduct devotional Bible study sessions with the idea of improving the spiritual life among the church members. Lay people who mastered the format their ministers had taught them began to conduct similar meetings elsewhere among members of other churches Mennonite, Molokon, and especially the Orthodox. As the movement grew, developed, and absorbed ideas from the various churches, a split occurred with the Russian Orthodox Church and the Shtundists became an independent sect. The Church persecuted them, and they in turn forbade many of the popular element of Orthodox piety, including the veneration of the Virgin Mary and the saints, prayer for the dead, and attendance at Orthodox worship.

As the Shtundists were emerging in the Ukraine, Martin Kalweit, also a German, began to spread his Baptist faith in Tiffis, Georgia. Beginning with the first baptism in 1867, the faith spread throughout Germany. Slightly later, in the 1870s, Granville Augusta William Waldgrave Baron Radstock (1833-1913), an English Wesleyan (Methodist) converted some members of the nobility in St. Petersburg. Possibly his most important convert was Col. Vasili Petrovich Pashkov. A wealthy member of the Imperial Life Guards, Pashkov devoted time and energy (until banished by the Emperor in 1884) to the union of evangelicals Shtundists, Baptists, Molokons, and Wesleyans. His efforts were continually blocked by differences on the practice of baptism, but one of his converts, Ivan Prokanov organized the All-Russian Evangelical Christian Union in 1909.

Russian Evangelical believers migrated into Canada and the United States beginning in the 1880s, until slowed by World War I and the immigration restrictions imposed in the 1920s. Many of these believers found their way into various Baptist churches, but others formed congregations that were both independent and resistant to anglicizing forces. In 1930 a number of these congregations founded the All Canadian Union of Slavic Evangelical Christians and established headquarters in Toronto.

The union uses the "Confession of Faith of Evangelical Christians" written by Prokanov in 1910. It is a simple faith consisting of major Protestant affirmations of faith in a trinitarian God and salvation through Jesus Christ. Baptism by immersion is practiced. Russian Evangelicals had largely accepted the pacifism of author Leo Tolstoy who had befriended them early on, but have in more recent years moved away from that ideal. Some have suggested that serving in the military was part of the taxes that Christians were to pay the government (Romans 13:7).

As the union developed, it suffered most from continued tension between conservative and anglicizing forces. In 1958 a large number of members and congregations left to join in the formation of the Union of Slavic Churches of Evangelical Christians and Slavic Baptists of Canada. They have had a steady loss of younger members who have felt alienated from traditional Russian beliefs and language.

The union is in communion with the Union of Russian Evangelical Christians, which works among Russian-Americans. They have also developed missionary work in Poland and Argentina, as well as among the Doukhobors of western Canada.

Membership: Not reported. In 1980 there were eight congregations scattered across five provinces with a membership of 225.

Sources:

Piepkorn, Arthur C. *Profiles in Belief: The Religious Bodies of the United States and Canada.* Vol. III. San Francisco: Harper & Row, 1979.

★822★
Apostolic Christian Church (Nazarean)
Current address not obtained for this edition.

The Apostolic Christian Church (Nazarean) traces its history to the movement begun by Samuel Heinrich Froelich (1803-1857), a Swiss clergyman who led a revival in the late 1820s. In 1830, he was deprived of a pulpit by the Swiss state church for preaching the "Gospel of reconciliation in its original purity." The movement, called "Nazarean" on the Continent, spread throughout Europe and was persecuted. Many immigrants flocked to America and congregations were established: Froehlich himself came in 1850 and began immediately to organize his followers as the Apostolic Christian Churches of America. Around 1906/1907 some members of the Apostolic Churches withdrew over several points of doctrine. They adopted the designation "Nazarean," the popular name by which the group is known on the Continent.

Members of the church believe in Christ, are baptized in the name of the Father, Son and Holy Spirit, and form a covenant with God to live a sanctified life and to seek to become rich in good works. They reject the priesthood, infant baptism and transubstantiation, and refuse to be bound with oaths or to participate in war. The church consists only of baptized believers, but affiliated with it are "Friends of Truth," those being converted. Apart from refusing to bear arms and kill in the country's wars, the church is completely law-abiding.

The church is congregationally governed. Elders serve the local church with powers to baptize, lay on hands, administer the Lord's Supper and conduct worship. The Apostolic Catholic Church Foundation is a service organization. It recently moved from Akron, Ohio to its present location.

Membership: In 1985, the church reported 2,799 members, 48 congregations, and 178 ministers.

Periodicals: *Newsletter.*

★823★
Apostolic Christian Churches of America
% Bill Schlatter
14834 Campbell Rd.
Defiance, OH 43512

The Apostolic Christian Churches of America began in the protest of a new catechism introduced in 1830 by the Reformed Church in Switzerland. Samuel Heinrich Froehlich (1803-1857), a Reformed minister, rejected the new catechism as too rationalistic and in the resulting controversy was dismissed. Rebaptized by Mennonites, he organized the community of Evangelical Baptists. The nonresistance stance (including refusal to bear arms) adopted by the Community led to considerable tension with the govern-

ment and occasioned the migration of many members beginning in the 1840s.

The first congregation in America began among members of the Old Order Amish Mennonites of Lewis County, New York. They requested leadership from Froehlich, and he sent an elder, Benedict Weyeneth, to found a congregation at Croghan. He ordained Joseph Virkler to the ministry and returned to Switzerland. He soon returned to the United States and established a second congregation in Woodford County, Illinois. Growth came slowly, primarily from German-speaking immigrants to the Midwest.

Following Froehlich, the church draws upon the Anabaptist concensus of the Reformed and Mennonite churches. It preaches the salvation of souls, the change of heart through regeneration, a life of godliness and simplicity guided and directed by the Holy Spirit, and a striving for entire sanctification. Members are noncombatants, but loyal to the laws of the United States. A mission in Japan is supported.

Membership: In 1996, the church reported 12,220 members, 85 congregations, and 291 ministers.

Periodicals: *The Silver Lining.*

Sources:

Footsteps to Zion, A History of the Apostolic Christian Church of America. N.p., n.d.

Froehlich, S. H. *The Mystery of Godliness and the Mystery of Ungodliness.* Apostolic Christian Church, n.d.

___. *Individual Letters and Meditations.* Syracuse, NY: Apostolic Christian Publishing Co., 1926.

★824★
Christian Apostolic Church (Forest, Illinois)
Forrest, IL 61741

The Christian Apostolic Church grew out of unrest within the German Apostolic Christian Church during the 1950s. Elder Peter Schaffer, Sr., one of the founders of the German Apostolic Christian Church, protested the attempts of church leaders in Europe to direct the life of the American congregations. Beginning with members in Illinois and Oregon, he organized congregations in Forest and Morton, Illinois; Silverton, Oregon; and Sabetha, Kansas in 1955. Doctrine and practice of the parent body were continued.

Membership: In 1988 the church reported four congregations with several hundred members.

★825★
Christian Apostolic Church (Sabetha, Kansas)
Sabetha, KS 66534

The Christian Apostolic Church was founded in the early 1960s when members of the German Apostolic Christian Church in Illinois and Kansas withdrew under the leadership of William Edelman. The members were protesting several points of "interpretation of the statues and customs" of the Church.

Membership: Not reported. There are three congregations.

★826★
Christian Community and Brotherhood of Reformed Doukhobors (Sons of Freedom)
Site 8, Comp. 42
Cresent Valley, BC, Canada V0G 1HO

The Christian Community and Brotherhood of Reformed Doukhobors, better known as the Sons of Freedom, emerged within the larger Doukhobor community in Canada in the early twentieth century. They were the ardent supporters of Peter Verigin (d. 1924) who was the leader of the Doukhobors at the time of their migration to Canada in 1899. Verigin was left behind in prison, but was released in 1902 and rejoined the community. The Sons of Freedom were that element of the group most loyal to Verigin and most opposed to the Canadian government's varied attempts to integrate the Doukhobors into the larger social context. They particularly opposed the establishment of public schools and the government imposing secular education on Doukhobor children.

For many years they existed as an integral part of the Doukhobor community. They supported the leadership of Peter Christiakov Verigin who succeeded the elder Verigin in 1924. During his tenure in office the number of the Sons of Freedom greatly expanded, and by the early 1930s, there were more than 1,000. The actual break with the larger community came in 1933, occasioned by a letter from P. P. Verigin, at the time in prison, asking all Doukhobors to refrain from paying any dues to the directors of the Christian Community of Universal Brotherhood (CCUB). They followed Verigin's orders, and the CCUB expelled them from the larger body. The break was healed for a short while during World War II when the Sons of Freedom were invited into the Union of Doukhobors of Canada. Formed in 1945, the Union soon fell apart, and the Sons of Freedom emerged as a fully independent group.

The Sons of Freedom were particularly critical of John Verigin who succeeded to the leadership of the larger group of the Union of Spiritual Communities of Christ (Orthodox Doukhobors in Canada) after the death of P. P. Verigin in 1939. His plans to accomodate government pressure were denounced as a distortion of Doukhobor faith. They were especially resistant to any introduction of public schools which they felt would simply educate people into an acceptance of war and the exploitation of working class people, and lead to the distruction of families and communities.

In 1950 Stephan Sorokin, an immigrant from Russia and former member of the Russian Orthodox Church, came to the Doukhobors to claim a leadership role. After fleeing from Russia, he wandered from many years and successively joined the Plymouth Brethren, the Lutherans, the Baptists, and the Seventh-day Adventist Church. He came to Canada in 1949 and lived among the members of the Society of Independent Doukhobors in Saskatchewan, learning the ways of the community, particularly their songs. He also learned of the story of Peter P. Verigin (Christiakov), the leader who died in 1939. It would have been the place of his son, Peter Verigin III to assume the role as spiritual leader of the Doukhobors, but it was assumed that he was in a Russian prison camp. Though it was later learned that he had died in prison in 1942, many in the community awaited the arrival of the "lost" son of Peter P. Verigin (Christiakov).

Sorokin arrived among the Doukhobor settlements in April 1950. He was introduced among the Sons of Freedom by one of their prominent leaders, John Lebedoff, who departed three months later to begin serving a two year prison term. Under Lebedoff's period of influence, there was heightened violence and tension between the Sons of Freedom and the state. However, the majority of the Sons of Freedom accepted Sorokin as the lost spiritual leader and reorganized themselves as the Christian Community and Brotherhood of Reformed Doukhobors.

Over the years of their existence, the Sons of Freedom had gained a reputation for more extreme forms of civil disobedience in their attempts to prevent the loss of Doukhobor ideals by accomodation to the government, and the late 1940s and early 1950s were years of heightened anti-government protests. The Sons of Freedom were accused of bombings and arson (of new school buildings), and periodically underscored their displeasure with demonstrations in the nude. When tried and convicted of actions associated with their protests, many of the group served prison terms. However, under the leadership of Sorokin, the group began restraining from participation in such activities, which lessened the overall tension level between the Doukhobor community, its neighbors, and the Canadian government. Stephen Sorokin died in 1984, and no new leader has been designated as his successor.

Membership: Not reported.

Periodicals: Istina.

Sources:

Lebidoff, Florence E. *The Truth about the Doukhobors*. Crescent Valley, BC: The Author, 1948.

A Public Indictment of J. J. Verigin. Krestova, BC: Christian Community of Reformed Doukhobors, (Sons of Freedom), 1954.

Woodcock, George, and Ivan Avakumovic. *The Doukhobors*. Toronto: Oxford University Press, 1968.

★827★
German Apostolic Christian Church
Current address not obtained for this edition.

The German Apostolic Christian Church is the result of a schism in the Apostolic Christian Churches of America. During the 1930s the pressure to discard the German language in worship, pressure which had greatly intensified since World War I, led the majority of the church to begin to use English. A group led by Elder Martin Steidinger protested that the loss of German would be accompanied by a loss of piety and lead to the influx of worldliness. With the encouragement of some European church leaders, he led members in the founding of the German Apostolic Christian Churches with initial congregations in Sabetha, Kansas; Silverton and Portland, Oregon; and several locations in Illinois. Support came primarily from first generation immigrants. Doctrine and practice are like that of the parent body.

Membership: Not reported. There are an estimated 500 members.

★828★
Molokan Spiritual Christians (Postojannye)
841 Carolina St.
San Francisco, CA 94107

The Postojannye are those Molokan Spiritual Christian who reject the practice of enthusiastic jumping during worship services which characterize their Pryguny Molokans. The split in the Molokan community into the Postojannye (the Steadfast) and the Jumpers occurred in the mid-nineteenth century in Russia. The Postojannye also reject the authority of the charismatic- prophetic leaders who arose at that same time, such as Maksim Gavrilovic Rudometkin. Otherwise the beliefs and practices of the Postojannye and Pryguny are similiar.

The first Postojannye came to the United States in 1905. They tried to work in the sugar field of Hawaii, but in 1906, shortly after the earthquake, moved to San Francisco and settled on Potrero Hill.

Membership: Not reported. There were an estimated 2,000 Postojannye Molokans in the mid 1970s. They live in San Francisco, the greater Bay area, and in Woodburn, Oregon.

Sources:

Dunn, Ethel, and Stephen P. Dunn. "Religion and Ethnicity: The Case of the American Molokans." *Ethnicity* 4, no. 4, (December 1977): 370-79.

★829★
Molokan Spiritual Christians (Pryguny)
Current address not obtained for this edition.

Among numerous free evangelical groups which derived from the Russian Orthodox Church, only a few have come to the United States. Among these few are the Molokans, founded by Simeon Uklein (b.1733). He was a son-in-law of a leader of the Doukhobors, a mystical Russian group which is now found in western Canada. Forsaking mysticism, Uklein returned to the Russian Orthodox Church, and began to preach a Bible-oriented faith. He claimed that the church fathers had diluted the true faith with pagan philosophy. The true church, which existed visibly until their time, disappeared and survived only in scattered and perse-cuted communities. Uklein taught a form of unitarianism and gnosticism. Both the Son and the Holy Spirit were seen as subordi-nate to the Father; Christ was clothed in angelic, not human, flesh. Uklein tended to be anti-ritualistic and denied the sacraments and rites. Baptism means hearing the word of God and living accord-ingly; confession is repentance from sin; and the anointing of the sick is prayer. A ritual was constructed from Scripture and hymns. Molokans drink milk during Lent (from which the name Molokans or Milk Drinkers is derived), a practice forbidden in the Russian Orthodox Church. Uklein also adopted some of the Mosaic di-etary law.

In the 1830s a great revival, an outpouring of the Holy Spirit, began in the Molokan community. It led to much enthusiastic reli-gious expression, especially the jumping about of worshippers and the appearance of a number of charismatic prophetic leaders, the most popular one being Maksim Gavrilovic Rudometkin (d.1877). The acceptance of these new emphases which grew out of the revival split the Molokans into the Postoiannye (the Stead-fast) who reject the practice of jumping and the teachings of Rudo-metkin and the Pryguny (jumpers). The urge to migrate to America began among the Molokans after the introduction of universal mil-itary service by the Russian government in 1878, but came to a head with their refusal to bear arms during the Russo-Japanese War. Over 2,000 left, primarily between 1904 and 1914 (when Russia stopped legal immigration) and settled in California. After World War I, some 500 more who had originally settled in the Middle East were allowed into the United States.

The Pryguny Molokons, the largest group to migrate to the United States, settled in Los Angeles from which they have moved into surrounding suburbs and communities. Various studies of the community found an estimated 3,500 (1912), 5,000 (late 1920s), and then 15,000 (1970). Churches can be found in Kerman, Porterville, Sheridan, Shafter, Delano, Elmira, and San Marcos, California. There is also a group in Glendale, Arizona and a small group in Baja California.

Membership: Not reported. There are an estimated 15,000 to 20,000 Prygun Molokons as of the mid-1980s.

Sources:

Dunn, Ethel, and Stephen P. Dunn. *The Molokan Heritage Collection. I, Reprints of Articles and Translations.* Berkeley: Highgate Road Social Science Research Station, 1983.

Moore, Willard Burgess. *Molokan Oral Tradition.* Berkeley and Los Ange-les: University of California Press, 1973.

Samarin, Paul I., comp. *The Russian Molokan Directory.* Los Angeles: The Author, n.d.

★830★
Schwenkfelder Church in America
Pennsburg, PA 18073

A surviving group of the followers of Caspar Schwenckfeld (1489-1561) left Silesia in 1734 because of persecution and came to America. In 1782 they organized the Schwenkfelder Church. The present general conference is a voluntary association of five churches, all in southeastern Pennsylvania. It meets semi-annually.

The Schwenkfelders follow the spiritual-mystical lead of their founder. Schwenckfeld, at one time a wealthy German nobleman, came to believe that all externals, though to be used, are of the perishable material world, and he sought to discover the spiritual imperishable reality behind them. He found them in the inner word, the church of those redeemed and called, the invisible spiri-tual sacrament, faith, and liberty—all emphasized by contempo-rary Schwenkfelders. Baptism is for adult believers only, but com-munion is open to all. No distinctive dress is worn. Both public office and military service is allowed (a practice which separates them from many of the Pennsylvania German groups).

Membership: In 1992 there were five churches, 2,700 mem-bers, and 17 ministers.

Periodicals: *The Schwenkfeldian.* Send orders to 1 Seminary St., Pennsburg, PA 18073.

Sources:

Erb, Peter C. *Schwenckfeld in His Reformation Setting.* Valley Forge, PA: Judson Press, 1978.

Kriebel, Howard Wiegner. *The Schwenkfelders in Pennsylvania.* Lancas-ter, PA: Pennsylvania-German Society, 1904.

Schultz, Selina Gerhard. *A Course of Study in the Life and Teachings of Caspar Schwenckfeld von Ossig (1489-1561) and the History of the Schwenkfelder Religious Movement (1518-1964).* Pennsburg, PA: Board of Publication of the Schwenkfelder Church, 1964.

★831★
Smith Venner
% Lothar Dreger
470 Ediron Ave.
Winnipeg, MB, Canada R2G 0M4

The Smith Venner, more popularly known as the "friends" of Johann Oskar Smith (b. 1871), is a loosely-organized Norwegian group which emphasizes piety and living the Christian life as op-posed to the emphasis placed on doctrine by the Norwegian state church. Smith Venner spread as Norwegians migrated to other countries around the world. In the 1970s, some 3,500 where re-ported to have attended the annual meetings, representing some 20 nations. Membership in the United States is centered in the Northwest, with additional members spread across the western half of Canada. During the 1970s, the group was served by two periodicals, *Skjulte Skatter* (in Norwegian) and *The Way* (in En-glish), but published in Salem, Oregon. In 1979 *The Way* was su-perceded by *Hidden Treasures.*

Membership: Not reported.

Periodicals: *Hidden Treasures.*

★832★
Society of Independent Doukhobors
Current address not obtained for this edition.

The Doukhobors migrated to Canada from Russia beginning in 1899. There, a communal organization, the Christian Community of Universal Brotherhood, was implemented. A number of mem-bers of the community, people who otherwise accepted Doukho-bor belief, soon rejected the communal lifestyle. In addition, these individuals came to reject the special role of the community's spir-itual leader, Peter Verigin, though they continued to live on the edge of the community and interact with its members.

The issue of the Independents, as they had come to be called, came into sharp focus as World War I began. Verigin, angered by their dissent, cut them off from the protection provided by the Na-tional Service Act of 1917. In 1918 the Independents organized the Society of Independent Doukhobors. Following the death of Peter Verigin, the society was briefly reconciled to the leadership of Verigin's son, Peter Christiakov Verigin, and cooperated in the formation of the Society of Named Doukhobors. In 1937, as the communal structures were dissolving, the Independents de-nounced Verigin and broke relations with his organization. Dur-ing World War II, the Independents briefly joined in with the Union of Spiritual Communities of Christ, the successor to the So-ciety of Named Doukhobors, and the Sons of Freedom (a third fac-tion) to form the short-lived Union of Doukhobors of Canada. It fell apart when the Union of Spiritual Communities of Christ with-drew. The Independents expelled the Sons of Freedom. Since that time the Independents have existed separately. Not bound by communal economic restraints, they have spread across western Canada as far east as Manitoba.

Membership: In the mid-1970s the society had 23 affiliated centers in British Columbia, Alberta, and Saskatchewan, and one center in Manitoba.

★833★
Sons of Freedom (Doukhobors)
Krestova, BC, Canada

Soon after the arrival of the Doukhobors in Canada from Russia, Peter Verigin's leadership was protested. Some felt he was compromising the teachings of his letters, which had guided the group during his exile in Siberia. They marched through the early settlements in Saskatchewan, preaching the renunciation of the world and calling themselves "Svobodniki," literally "Freedomites," but generally referred to as "Sons of Freedom." To call the members of the community to the simple life and to dramatize their own God-given Adamic nature, they marched naked. They were eventually arrested and some sent to an asylum. Through the next few decades, though often disapproving of its actions, they remained a part of the larger Doukhobor community.

In 1923 a public school in the community was burned to the ground shortly after opening. The Sons of Freedom have been blamed for that burning and the many others that have occurred over the years. The school burnings represented a new motif in the protests which had previously been directed at other community members. They began protesting outside forces, government regulations that were against the Law of God.

The Sons of Freedom initially accepted the new leadership of Peter Christiakov Verigin III, who succeeded his father as spiritual leader of the Doukhobors in 1924. But as he proceeded with the reorganization of the communal life and dealt with the governmental demands of the province, the Sons of Freedom began to voice their dissent. In 1928 they issued an open letter denouncing, among other things, the acceptance of public schools (which had been forced upon the community) and the payment of taxes.

The Sons of Freedom gained support during the 1930s as the communal corporation disintegrated and as the main body of community members formed the Society of Named Doukhobors. The Sons of Freedom were excluded from the larger body when they did not pay their annual dues. The apparent break was healed for a short time during World War II, when the Sons of Freedom were invited into the Union of Doukhobors of Canada. Formed in 1945, the Union soon fell apart and the Sons of Freedom emerged as a fully independent group. The succeeding decades have been a time of the rise and fall of leaders, periodic protests by the Sons of Freedom (including fires, bombings, and nude demonstrations), and periods of relative calm.

In 1950 the Sons of Freedom experienced a schism when Stephan Sorokin appeared among them. A former member of the Russian Orthodox Church, Sorokin appeared as a leader capable of reuniting the loosely organized group. His main rival was John Lebedoff, who in July 1950 began a prison term. Subsequently, many of the Sons of Freedom accepted Sorokin and left to found the Christian Community and Brotherhood of Reformed Doukhobors. When Lebedoff returned in 1952, he was unable to become the sole leader of the remaining Sons of Freedom. They have remained loosely and informally organized. They have also remained in a high degree of tension with both the government of British Columbia and the surrounding non-Doukhobor society (tension ably demonstrated by the 1965 polemic against the Sons of Freedom by Simma Holt, *Terror in the Name of God*).

Membership: There are three centers in British Columbia, one at Agassiz, Gilpin, and Krestova, and several hundred adherents.

Sources:

Holt, Simma. *Terror in the Name of God*. New York: Crown Publishers, 1965.

Woodcock, George, and Ivan Avakumovic. *The Doukhobors*. Toronto: Oxford University Press, 1968.

★834★
Union of Russian Evangelical Christians
Current address not obtained for this edition.

The Union of Russian Evangelical Christians was founded in the 1920s as an American branch of the All-Russian Evangelical Christian Union, headquartered in St. Petersburg (then Leningrad). At a later date it became an independent association. It shares a common history with, is in communion with, and is theologically identical to the All-Canadian Union of Slavic Evangelical Christians.

Membership: Not reported. In 1980 there were eight churches scattered through Pennsylvania, New York, New Jersey, Illinois, and California with an active membership of approximately 300.

Sources:

Piepkorn, Arthur C. *Profiles in Belief: The Religious Bodies of the United States and Canada*. Vol. III. San Francisco, Harper & Row, 1979.

★835★
Union of Spiritual Communities of Christ (Orthodox Doukhobors in Canada)
℅ USCC Central Office
Box 760
Grand Forks, BC, Canada V0H 1H0

The Union of Spiritual Communities of Christ is the oldest and largest of several Doukhobor, or "Spirit Wrestler," groups in western Canada. The Doukhobors originated out of the great schism in the Russian Orthodox Church which began in the reforms of Patriarch Nikon. Nikon assumed control of the church in 1652. Over the years a number of sectarian groups appeared, including the Khlysty, or People of God, who originated in the early eighteenth century and perpetuated a mystical doctrine of the inner guiding light and the dwelling of God in the human soul. The Khlysty developed some extreme doctrines, especially those surrounding the claims to godhood by several early leaders. In the mystical life of the Doukhobors there was no place for water baptism, only spirit baptism. They seemed to have originated from the Khlysty, though they drew strongly from the Unorthodox Unitarian Protestantism that had also penetrated Russia from Poland.

The exact origins of the Doukhobors as a separate "sect" is a matter of controversy. But by 1730, when Sylvan Kolesnikoff formed a community of followers in the village of Nikolai, Ekaterinoslav, the Doukhobors had been established. Kolesnokoff was succeeded by Ilarion Pobirokhin as the new leader of the group. During his tenure, which ended in his exile in Siberia, Ambrosia, the Russian Orthodox bishop of Ekaterinoslav, gave the group its name, Doukhobors. Ambrosia intended "Doukhobor" to be a derisive term, implying the group's defiance of the Spirit of God in the Russian Church; the group interpreted the term as denoting their wrestling against spiritual pride and lust by the Spirit of God.

The next century saw the Doukhobors experiencing alternate periods of persecution and toleration. After Pobirokhin's exile, Sabellius Kapustin assumed leadership. In 1802, with the blessing of Czar Alexander I, Kapustin organized the Doukhobors in Molochnyne Valley, where they had been exiled in isolation from the Orthodox. He established a communal system, the memory of which periodically reappears in the larger Doukhobor community.

In 1886 Peter Verigin (d. 1924) became the leader. He was opposed by a minority group led by Alesha Zubkov, who created a schism in the community. Zubkov was also able to have Verigin arrested and exiled to Siberia. From Siberia, however, Verigin was able to stay in contact with the group and continued to exercise leadership. He also learned of Leo Tolstoy, through whom he led the group to accept pacifism and to deny the state's right to register birth and marriage. Communal ownership of property was reasserted. With Tolstoy's financial assistance and the aid of American and British Quakers, the Verigin group migrated to Canada, the first Doukhobor arriving in January 1899. They settled in Saskatchewan, and in 1902 the Russian government released Verigin so he could also migrate. He led the group until 1924 when his son, Peter Christiakov Verigin, succeeded him.

Even as plans began to be made for the migration, the Doukhobors reorganized as a communal group, named the Christian Community of Universal Brotherhood. In Saskatchewan the Christian Community was almost immediately reestablished. But in 1907, when the group members refused to acknowledge the Oath of Allegiance, as required by the Homestead Act, the government took back the land upon which they had settled. A new settlement in British Columbia was begun.

Under Verigin's son, in 1928, the C.C.U.B. was reorganized as the Society of Named Doukhobors. In 1934 a Declaration outlining Doukhobor belief and practice was published. The decade proved a financial disaster for the communally organized C.C.U.B. Beset by schism of its more activist members and a slow recovery from the Depression, the CCUB went bankrupt in 1940. The land was taken over by the government, who payed the debts and became its "trustee." it was also at this time that the Union of Spiritual Communities of Christ superceded the Society of Named Doukhobors.

Peter Christiakov Verigin died in 1937; his son was in Russia in prison. In his absence John Verigin, a nephew, became the group's leader, but never assumed the role of "spiritual leader," the position of his uncle. Under his leadership, a plan for reclaiming the land was pursued, and most was returned to the group in 1963.

The Union of Spiritual Communities of Christ was able to retain the loyalty of the majority of Doukhobors, though challenged by several factions in the 1930s. The Union has no creed, but its beliefs find expression in the Doukhobor Psalms and the Declaration of 1934. In the Psalms, God is seen as an eternal spiritual being, the creator. God frequently chooses to speak through the mouths of men, historically the Doukhobor leaders. Christ was the savior of whom God spoke most perfectly. Within the human self God places a divine spark, and it is the believer's duty to recognize and nurture it. Believers best approach God through worship and by following the inward law of God. The spiritual knowledge attained from this inward divinity is the sustaining force in times of persecution. The Declaration identifies the Doukhobors as of "the Law of God and Faith of Jesus." They advocate pacifism and refuse to vote, but consider themselves law-abiding in all matters not contrary to the Law of God and Faith of Jesus. They strive toward a communal life. They have taken an activist stance in the peace movement, and have frequently come into conflict with the govenment by defending their beliefs against what they consider government interference.

Membership: In the mid-1970s the Union had 36 community branches, all within a seventy-mile radius of Grand Forks, British Columbia.

Periodicals: *Iskra.*

Remarks: The U.S.C.C. is to be distinguished from the most activist and often violent wing of the Doukhobor movement, the Sons of Freedom, which became quite controversial in the early 1960s for their public demonstrations against Canadian-government policy.

Sources:

Maude, Aylmer. *A Peculiar People*. New York: Funk & Wagnalls, 1904.

Mealing, F. M. *Doukhobor Life*. Castlegar, BC: Cotinneh Books, 1975.

Tarasoff, Koozma J. *A Pictorial History of the Doukhobors*. Saskatoon, SK: Modern Press, 1969.

Woodcock, George, and Ivan Avakumovic. *The Doukhobors*. Toronto: Oxford University Press, 1968.

Section 11

Baptist Family

Consult the Contents pages to locate the essay in Part II, Historical Essay Chapters, that provides an historical discussion of this family

Intrafaith Organizations

★836★
Baptist World Alliance
6733 Curran St.
McLean, VA 22101

The Baptist World Alliance is an international fellowship of Baptist conventions, associations, and unions which was created at a meeting of Baptists from around the world in London in 1905. It is a voluntary organization whose objectives are to show forth the basic unity of Baptists, to inspire Baptists everywhere, and to promote a spirit of fellowship, service, and cooperation within the Baptist community. The alliance makes no attempt to usurp the work or prerogatives of any of its member organizations or of local congregations. It has emerged as the champion of those Baptists who exist as a small minority in a hostile environment and a force in the fight for religious freedom.

The idea of an international Baptist conference had been generated in America, and an invitation was extended by several Baptist leaders in London to meet during the summer of 1905. Alexander Maclaren, a prominent British minister, presided at the first session, where a committee was appointed to draw up a draft constitution and set of by-laws.

The Alliance meets every five years, at which time it elects a president and general secretary and names an executive committee. Those members of the executive committee who live reasonably close to the headquarters are named as the administrative committee. Headquarters remained in London until the beginning of World War II, when it was moved to Washington, D.C. The move was made a permanent one in 1947.

The alliance has expanded activities into every area of the globe where a Baptist community exists. It seeks to provide communication between Baptists, had developed a program to provide relief and aid to the needy, speaks out on issues of religious freedom, and sponsors conferences on various aspects of church life and Christian development.

Membership: The Baptist World Alliance is a fellowship of 1991 Baptist unions and conventions comprising a membership of more than 42 million baptized believers and a community of more that 100 million Baptists in every country. The North American membership in the Baptist World Alliance includes the following: American Baptist Churches in the U.S.A.; Baptist General Conference; Czechoslovak Baptist Convention of the USA and Canada; General Association of General Baptists; Lott Carey Baptist Foreign Missionary Convention, USA; National Baptist Convention of America; National Baptist Convention, U.S.A., Inc.; National Missionary Baptist Convention of America; North American Baptist Conference; Progressive National Baptist Convention, Inc.; Russian-Ukraine Evangelical Baptist Union, U.S.A., Inc.; Seventh Day Baptist General Conference, USA and Canada; Southern Baptist Convention; and Union of Latvian Baptists in America.

Periodicals: *The Baptist World.*

Sources:

Gaver, Jessyca Russell. *"You Shall Know the Truth": The Baptist Story.* New York: Lancer Books, 1973.

Nordenhaug, Josef, and Cyril Eric Bryant. "Baptist World Alliance." In *Baptist Advance.* Forrest Park, IL: Roger Williams Press, 1964.

★837★
North American Baptist Fellowship
6733 Curran St.
McLean, VA 22101

The North American Baptist Fellowship is a cooperative body of Baptist conventions and associations in North America. Though its membership is slightly different from that of the North American membership of the Baptist World Alliance, the fellowship functions as the alliance's regional body in North America. The fellowship emerged from the celebration of the Baptist Jubilee (celebrating the 150th anniversary of the founding of the first national Baptist organization in America). The spirit engendered in the cooperative effort of planning the event led the leaders to petition the Baptist World Alliance to establish a continuing North American organization, which occurred in 1964. The first president of the fellowship was Dr. V. Carney Hargroves, also generally recognized as its founder.

Its specific program objectives are to promote fellowship and cooperation among the Baptists of North America and to further the aims of the Baptist World Alliance in the North American context.

The fellowship meets annually for fellowship and consultation on matters of interest that cross denominational lines. It has no powers to legislate or establish programs for its representative bodies, but it does encourage cooperative work among congregations of different Baptist denominations located in the same city or county.

The fellowship shares office space with the World Baptist Alliance.

Membership: The total membership of the bodies represented in the fellowship is 28 million. It includes the following: American Baptist Churches in the U.S.A.; Canadian Baptist Federation; General Association of General Baptists; National Baptist Convention of America; National Baptist Convention, U.S.A., Inc.; North American Baptist General Conference; Progressive National Baptist Convention; Seventh-Day Baptist General Conference; and Southern Baptist Convention.

Sources:

Gaver, Jessyca Russell. *"You Shall Know the Truth": The Baptist Story.* New York: Lancer Books, 1973.

Calvinist Missionary Baptist

★838★
American Baptist Association
4605 N. State Line Ave.
Texarkana, TX 75501

No sooner had the Southern Baptist Convention (SBC) been formed than it became disturbed by the controversy over what came to be called "Old Landmarkism." Dr. James R. Graves, editor of *The Tennessee Baptist*, in an attempt to restore Apostolic purity to the churches, called on them to reject Protestants, who could not rightly be considered New Testament churches. This view was shared by Dr. J. M. Pendleton of Bowling Green, Kentucky, and a number of churches that did not join the Southern Baptist movement.

The issues of "Old Landmarkism" centered on alien baptism, pulpit affiliation, closed communion, and missions. Supporters of Landmarkism opposed recognition of any baptism by a non-Baptist, the allowing of non-Baptists to join in the Lord's Supper, the exchange of pulpits with non-Baptist ministers, and missions controlled by boards beyond the local church. The Southern Baptist Convention never accepted Landmarkism, but for many years supporters of Landmarkism remained a dissenting minority within the SBC, strongly affecting its policy toward centralization. The Landmark position involved a theory of a succession of Baptist churches from the time of Christ to the present. The succession begins with the biblical church and continues through the Montanists, Novatians, Donatists, Paulicians, Waldenses, and Anabaptists.

Until 1899, when the Missionary Baptist Association of Texas was formed, Landmarkism remained unorganized. In 1905, however, churches both inside and outside the SBC formed a Landmark denomination, the General Association, which in 1924 became the American Baptist Association (ABA). It is doctrinally like the SBC, except for the Landmark ideals.

The ABA is congregationally governed. It maintains a publishing concern in Texarkana, Texas, and campgrounds at Bogg Springs, Arkansas and Pine Springs, Texas. The several Bible institutes and seminaries recognized by the ABA are locally owned and controlled, as are several periodicals.

Membership: In 1987 the association reported 250,000 members, 1,705 churches, and 1,740 ministers in the United States. There were five churches in Canada.

Educational Facilities: The schools recognized by the American Baptist Association are owned and operated by local churches rather than the association as a whole.

Aba Mexican Baptist Institute, Pharr, Texas.
Antioch Missionary Baptist Seminary, Manuthy, Trichur, India.
California Missionary Baptist Institute, Bellflower, California.
Calvary Mexican Baptist Institute, Juarez, Mexico.
Davao Missionary Baptist Institut and Seminary, Davao City, Philippines.
Florida Baptist Schools, Lakeland, Florida.
Fresno Missionary Baptist Institute, Fresno, California.
Gulf Coast Baptist Institute, Theodore, Alabama.
Historic Baptist Bible Institute, Scarborough, Ontario, Canada.
Landmark Correspondence School, Lookeba, Oklahoma.
Landmark Missionary Baptist Institute, Mauldin, South Carolina.
Louisiana Missionary Baptist Institute and Seminary, Minden, Louisiana.
Mid-South Baptist Institute and Seminary, Bogalusa, Louisiana.
Missionary Baptist Institute of Costa Rica, Guadalupe, San Jose, Costa Rica.
Mission Valley Mission Schools, San Antonio, Texas.
Missionary Baptist Seminary and Institute, Little Rock, Arkansas.
Monterrey Bible Institute, Santa Catarina, Mexico.

Northwest Baptist Institute, Bend, Oregon.
Oklahoma Missionary Baptist Institute, Marlow, Oklahoma.
Oxford Baptist Institute, Oxford, Mississippi.
Peru Missionary Baptist Institute, Trujillo, Peru.
Philippine Missionary Baptist Seminary, Davao City, Philippines.
Seoul Missionary Baptist Institute, Seoul, South Korea.
Somerset Baptist Bible Institute, Somerset, Kentucky.
Tennessee Missionary Baptist Institute, Nashville, Tennessee.
Texas Baptist Institute and Seminary, Henderson, Texas.
Washington Missionary Baptist Institute and Seminary, Auburn, Washington.
West Florida Baptist Institute, Pensacola, Florida.

Sources:

Nevins, William Manlius. *Alien Baptism and the Baptists*. Ashland, KY: Press of Economy Printers, 1962.

★839★
American Baptist Churches in the U.S.A.
Valley Forge, PA 19481

History. The organization of Baptists in America proceeded in stages. While the first churches were organized in the 1600s, they were too few to formally organize above the congregational level. In 1707, however, five churches (three in Philadelphia and two in the countryside) organized the Philadelphia Baptist Association. That association at one point included churches from as far away as Connecticut and South Carolina. Then, in 1751, the Charleston (South Carolina) Association was formed. The number of Baptists began to grow significantly after the American Revolution. The association became the typical structure by which Baptist congregations affiliated. Tensions emerged among those who saw the association strictly for fellowship and those who saw it as a structure through which the congregations could extend their ministry. Most Baptists have been content to emphasize the autonomy of the local church, while assigning specific tasks such as higher education and foreign missions (not generally possible for a congregation) to the association.

The next major step in Baptist organization was spurred by the new missionary zeal that emerged in the early nineteenth century. Among the first missionaries sent out by the Congregational Church were Adoniram Judson, his wife Ann Judson, and Luther Rice. Rice soon converted to the Baptist perspective and as a result felt he could not work with Congregationalists. Rice returned to America to organize support among the Baptist churches. As a result of his efforts, the General Missionary Convention of the Baptist Denomination in the United States for Foreign Missions was organized in 1814. This organization was the first to draw support from Baptists nationally. It met every three years and became popularly known as the Triennial Convention. The Baptist General Tract Society was founded in 1824. In 1832, it was joined by the American Baptist Home Mission Society, which directed its activity primarily toward the western United States. A third major national society, the Woman's American Baptist Home Mission Society, was formed in 1877.

Over the next decades, Baptists were served by several mission agencies, each of which developed its own program and appealed to individual congregations. The need for coordination and the elimination of duplicated efforts was evident. In 1845, when the congregations in the South organized the Southern Baptist Convention, a cohesive convention structure had finally been formed. In 1907, the Northern Baptist Convention was organized, and the several missionary agencies became cooperating organizations of the convention. While retaining their official autonomy, the mission boards agreed to hold their regular meetings at the same time and place and to accept representatives of the congregations as voting delegates. The convention gave new national coherence to the majority of Baptists. The Northern Baptist Convention became known as the American Baptist Convention in 1950, and it assumed its present name in 1972.

Beliefs. Doctrinally, Baptists grew out of the Puritan-Reformed tradition in England. The reliance upon the Puritans is visible in the early Baptist confessions of faith, the First and Second London Confessions (1677 and 1689), the Philadelphia Confession (1742), and the New Hampshire Confession (1833). The first major break with the Reformed theological heritage came after the Revolution when attempts were made to move away from a strong doctrine of predestination. The theology of Andrew Fuller was among the most prominent statements of Baptists attempting to provide a place for the free response of men and women to the gospel. This changing emphasis was embodied in the New Hampshire Confession. Eventually, however, confessional statements fell into disuse. The need for doctrinal uniformity was no longer emphasized, and a variety of theological opinions appeared.

The lack of theological unity allowed several new perspectives to become prominent among American Baptists. An emphasis upon social reform in the cities merged with the new discipline of sociology to produce the social gospel movement. Baptists such as Walter Rauschenbush became leading exponents. Prominent Baptist scholars were among the first to absorb the new German higher criticism of the Bible. As both movements gained support within the denomination, the reactions of conservatives threatened the very existence of the new Northern Baptist Convention. It became one of the most heated and bitter battlegrounds for what became known as the fundamentalist-modernist controversy in the early twentieth century. The losses of conservatives at the convention meetings and the resultant decrease of influence in the mission societies led to several major schisms as well as the formation of such bodies as the General Association of Regular Baptist Churches and the Conservative Baptist Association.

Organization. The American Baptist Churches in the U.S.A. (ABC) is organized congregationally. Delegates from the individual churches and regional organizations meet biennially. Between meetings, a general board oversees the affairs of the denomination. The work of the ABC is delegated to the boards that have charge of foreign missions, home missions, education and publication, and ministerial and missionary benefits. Under each of the boards are a variety of specialized divisions. Judson Press is the publishing arm of the ABC.

Membership: In 1996, the ABC reported 1,503,267 members, 5,807 congregations, and 7,929 ministers.

Educational Facilities: Seminaries:
American Baptist Seminary of the West, Berkeley, California.
Andover Newton Theological Seminary, Newton Centre, Massachusetts.
Central Baptist Theological Seminary, Kansas City, Missouri.
Eastern Baptist Theological Seminary, Philadelphia, Pennsylvania.
Northern Baptist Theological Seminary, Lombard, Illinois.
Colgate Rochester/Bexley Hall/Crozer, Rochester, New York.
Evangelical Seminary of Puerto Rico, Hato Rey, Puerto Rico.
Morehouse School of Religion, Atlanta, Georgia.
The School of Theology, Richmond, Virginia.
Colleges and universities:
Alderson-Broaddus College, Phillipi, West Virginia.
Benedict College, Columbia, South Carolina.
Eastern College, St. Davids, Pennsylvania.
Florida Memorial College, Miami, Florida.
Franklin College of Indiana, Franklin, Indiana.
Judson College, Elgin, Illinois.
Kalamazoo College, Kalamazoo, Michigan.
Keuka College, Keuka Park, New York.
Linfield College, McMinnville, Oregon.
Ottawa University, Ottawa, Kansas.
University of Redlands, Redlands, California.
Shaw University, Raleigh, North Carolina.
University of Sioux Falls, Sioux Falls, South Dakota.
Virginia Union University, Richmond, Virginia.
William Jewell College, Liberty, Missouri.
Bacone College, Muskogee, Oklahoma.

Periodicals: *American Baptist in Mission.* • *The Secret Place.* Send orders to Box 851, Valley Forge, PA 19482.

Sources:

Bailey, Ambrose M. *Manual of Instruction for Baptists.* Philadelphia: American Baptist Publication Society, 1951.

Harrison, Paul M. *Authority and Power in the Free Church Tradition.* Princeton, NJ: Princeton University Press, 1959.

Maring, Norman H. *American Baptists, Whence and Whither.* Valley Forge, PA: Judson Press, 1968.

Maring, Norman H., and Winthrop S. Hudson. *A Baptist Manual of Polity and Practice.* Valley Forge, PA: Judson Press, 1963.

Straton, Hillyer H. *Baptists: Their Message and Mission.* Chicago: Judson Press, 1941.

★840★
Association of Evangelicals for Italian Missions
314 Richfield Rd.
Upper Darby, PA 19082

The Association of Evangelicals for Italian Missions was formed by sixteen Baptist ministers meeting in New York City in 1899 as the Italian Association of America. The new association was the product of mission work among Italian immigrants undertaken by the Northern Baptist Convention, now the American Baptist Churches in the U.S.A., after the Civil War. The association became the Italian Baptist Association of America and recently adopted its present name. The association remains on good terms with its parent body, but carries on a mission to Italian-Americans. *The New Aurora* is published five times yearly. Most churches are in the North and East. There is an annual conference that elects officers.

Membership: Not reported.
Periodicals: *The New Aurora.*

★841★
Association of Reformed Baptist Churches
28 Meadows Rd.
Lafayette, NJ 07848

The Association of Reformed Baptist Churches was formed in 1997 at what became the first General Assembly at which 24 churches from 14 states affiliated. The group of pastors and congregations who formed the association represent a wing of the generally loosely organized Reformed Baptist movement who desired a slightly stronger degree of national organization for purposes of ministerial training, church planting, and publication. These churches had also disagreed with other pastors who exercised a heavier degree of pastoral oversight of members (a practice sometimes called shepherding) than was accepted by all.

The churches follow a particular Calvinist understanding of salvation (which suggests that Christ died for the elect) and adhere to either the 1689 or 1644 Baptist Confession of Faith. Their position is similar to that of the Sovereign Grace Baptist Churches and they have fraternal relations with the Reformed Baptists in Great Britain.

Membership: In 1997, there were 24 affiliated congregations.

★842★
Association of Regular Baptist Churches (Canada)
130 Gerrard St., E
Toronto, ON, Canada M5A 3T4

The Association of Regular Baptist Churches (Canada) continues the tradition of the conservative fundamentalist Baptist perspective that gathered around Thomas Todhunter Shields (1873-1955) in the 1920s. Shields, pastor of the Jarvis Street Baptist Church, had been put out of the Baptist Convention of Ontario and Quebec (now part of the Canadian Baptist Federation), and with his supporters founded the Union of Regular Baptist Churches (now part of the Fellowship of Evangelical Baptist Churches). In 1949, after the union failed to reelect him its president, Shields and the Jarvis Street Church withdrew from the union completely. Shields and his assistant H. C. Slade then formed the Conservative Baptist Association of Canada (now the Association of Regular Baptist Churches (Canada)).

The association is committed to a historic Baptist position and affirms the belief in the inerrant Bible. Also asserted are the doctrines of the Trinity, creation, the deity and vicarious atonement of Christ, the personal and visible return of Christ, and eternal punishment of the unsaved. Following Baptist tradition, the association defines the church as the voluntary association of believers who have been immersed (baptized). The association's position is seen as in general agreement with earlier Baptist confessions (the London, Philadelphia, and New Hampshire).

The association has a congregational polity. Missions are supported in Belgium, France, Jamaica, Martinique, St. Lucia, Spain, Fiji, Madagascar, the Philippines, and Switzerland.

Membership: In 1992 there were 15 churches in the association with 10 other supporting churches cooperating in the mission work.

Educational Facilities: Toronto Baptist Seminary and Bible College, Toronto, Ontario, Canada.

Periodicals: *The Gospel Witness.*

★843★
Baptist Bible Fellowship
Box 191
Springfield, MO 65801

The Baptist Bible Fellowship was begun in 1950 by former members of the World Baptist Fellowship, including Rev. Beauchamp Vick, who had succeeded J. Frank Norris as pastor of the Temple Baptist Church in Detroit. In 1948 he was made president of the debt-ridden Bible Baptist Seminary. Within two years he was able to wipe out most of the debt. He also discovered that Norris retained and would not surrender to him the ultimate power to run the school. In 1950 Vick was dismissed, and open schism soon occurred as pastors and churches lined up behind either Norris or Vick. Vick led in the founding of a new school, the Baptist Bible College, and a new periodical, the *Baptist Bible Tribune.*

Doctrinally, the Bible Baptists are in the main line of traditionally Baptist beliefs. They are strong fundamentalists and believe in both personal and ecclesiastical separation. Congregations and pastors have no fellowship with individuals and groups deemed to be infidels, idolaters, and/or immoral. There is a firm statement on the supernatural inspiration and verbal inerrancy of Scripture. Their Calvinism is very mild. The Bible Baptists believe in God's electing grace, but also teach that blessings of salvation are made free to all by the gospel. The main way in which the Bible Baptists differ from some other Baptists is in their ecclesiology. They emphasize the autonomy of the local church combined with the placing of strong authority in the pastor as "shepherd of his flock". Any congregation which accepts the doctrinal statement may affiliate with the fellowship. The fellowship acknowledges two ordinances, baptism by immersion and the Lord's Supper. The government is to be supported and obeyed in all matters not opposed to the "will of Jesus Christ."

Work of the denomination is centered on its colleges, its periodical, and, primarily, its missions. A part of the doctrinal statement is a belief in the command to give the gospel to the world. Also, scriptural giving is one of the fundamentals of faith. A director of missions and a mission committee oversees responsibility for the mission work of the fellowship. In 1997 there were 858 missionaries operating in 107 countries. The Baptist Bible Fellowship has grown tremendously both through its evangelistic activities and by acquisition of independent congregations who choose to join. Among its member churches are some of the largest in the country; their congregations have almost one-fourth of the 100 largest Sunday schools in the country. Congregations are concentrated in the South and Midwest and are divided into 48 fellowship districts.

Membership: In 1997 the fellowship reported over 1,600,000 members in 3,500 churches.

Educational Facilities: Baptist Bible College, Springfield, Missouri.
Baptist Bible College East, Boston, Massachusetts.
Atlantic Baptist Bible College, Chester, Virginia.
Baptist Christian College, Shreveport, Louisiana.
Spanish Baptist Bible College, Miami, Florida.
Pacific Coast Baptist Bible College, San Dimas, California.
Baptist Bible Graduate School of Theology, Springfield, Missouri.

Periodicals: *Baptist Bible Tribune.* Send orders to Box 309, Springfield, MO 65801. • *Global Partners Magazine,* P.O. Box 191, Springfield, MO 65801.

★844★
Baptist Missionary Association of America
716 Main St.
Little Rock, AR 72201

In 1949, a protest was lodged within the American Baptist Association (ABA) against the practice of seating some messengers to association meetings who were not members of the churches which elected them. The matter was referred to the churches. In 1950, the issue was ignored. After that session, a call meeting of the "church equality" people was held at the Park Place and Temple Baptist Churches in Little Rock, Arkansas, and the North American Baptist Association was organized. It changed its name in 1969 to the Baptist Missionary Association of America. It varies from the ABA only in designating that the association will recognize three messengers chosen from the membership of its member churches.

Headquarters were established in Little Rock. A publication board oversees the publishing of books, Sunday school material, and Spanish literature. A vigorous mission program has 80 workers in the field.

Membership: In 1989 the association reported 229,315 members, 1,339 congregations, and 2,648 ministers.

Educational Facilities: North American Theological Seminary, Jacksonville, Texas.

Periodicals: *The Advancer.* Send orders to 712 Main St., Little Rock, AR 72201. • *Baptist Trumpet.* Send orders to Box 9502, Little Rock, AR 72209.

Sources:

Harmon, Sherman, comp. *A Fire Was Kindled.* N.p., n.d.

Jackson, D. N. *Studies in Baptist Doctrines and History.* Little Rock, AK: Baptist Publications Committee, n.d.

★845★
Canadian Baptist Ministries (CBM)
7185 Millcreek Dr.
Mississauga, ON, Canada L5N 5R4

Canadian Baptist Ministries was formed on January 1, 1995, through the merger of the Canadian Baptist Federation and Canadian Baptist International Ministries. The purpose of Canadian Baptist Ministries is "to unite, encourage and enable Canadian Baptist Churches in their national and international endeavors to fulfill the commission of our Lord Jesus Christ, in the power of the Holy Spirit, proclaiming the gospel and showing the love of God to all peoples."

History. Like Congregationalists, Baptists came to Canada from New England following the British takeover of the land in 1748. Their initial settlements were in Nova Scotia where the oldest Baptist churches were organized in Sackville (now in New Brunswick) in 1763, and at Horton (now called Wolfville) in 1765 under the leadership of the Rev. Ebenezer Moulton. Both churches were lost when many of their members returned to New England in the 1770s. However, the continuous history of the Baptists can be traced to the ministry of independent Congregationalist evangelist Henry Alline (1748–1784), who began to travel throughout Nova Scotia in the 1770s. Finding little support from either Congregationalists or Presbyterian leaders, his converts founded a number of independent ("New Light") Congregational churches, most of which later became Baptist churches. Alline also participated in the reconstitution of the Horton church in 1788 under a new pastor, Nicolas Pierson. In 1798, the Baptists and the Alline churches formed the Baptist and Congregational Association, which became the Nova Scotia Baptist Association in 1800.

As Baptist work spread through the three Maritime provinces, the Nova Scotia Baptist Association became the fountainhead of a number of new associations. In 1846, the association formed the Baptist Convention of Nova Scotia, New Brunswick and Prince Edward Island, shortened in 1879 to the Baptist Convention of the Maritime Provinces. The African Association, consisting of 17 black churches, dates back to the 1830s, and in 1884 it affiliated with the convention.

Contemporaneous with the growth of the Regular (Calvinistic) Baptist churches that made up the Baptist Convention of the Maritime Provinces, Free Baptists from New England arrived in Nova Scotia. Asa McGray and Joseph Norton led in the formation of these Free Baptist churches, the first organized at Barrington in 1795. In 1834, a Free Baptist Association was formed. Not a part of this association, a group led by Norton organized the Union of Free Christian Baptists. In 1867, these two groups merged to become the Free Christian Baptist Conference. An association of New Brunswick Free Baptists, consisting largely of immigrants from Maine, was formed in 1832. Known at first as the New Brunswick Christian Conference, the name was changed to Free Christian Baptists in 1847 and in 1896 to Free Christian Baptist Conference.

In 1905 and 1906, the two streams of Baptist, Regular and Free Will, merged to form the United Baptist Convention of the Maritime Provinces. When Baptist congregations were planted in Newfoundland, the name was changed to the United Baptist Convention of the Atlantic Provinces in 1963.

Baptists began to move into Upper and Lower Canada (Quebec and Ontario) from the United States following the American Revolution, but the first churches were not formed until the 1790s (Calwell's Manor in the Eastern Townships, Lower Canada, in 1794, and a church near Beamsville, Upper Canada, in 1796). These churches were formed by American ministers in those areas closest to the American-Canadian border. The development of the Baptist church was stimulated after 1815 by the arrival in the Ottawa Valley of Scottish Highlanders who had experienced the ministry of Robert Haldane (1764–1842) and his brother James Haldane (1768–1851), Scottish Baptist evangelists. Cooperation between the various Baptist churches in the province was hindered primarily by disagreement over communion. Those original churches formed in the later eighteenth century tended to practice closed communion (excluding all but correctly baptized church members from participating in the Lord's Supper). In 1888, a merger of two regional bodies led to the formation of the Baptist Convention of Ontario and Quebec. Meanwhile, beginning in the 1820s, slaves, who had settled in Canada after their escape from slavery, formed a set of black Baptist congregations. In the 1830s, French-speaking immigrants from Switzerland settled in Quebec and

Henriette Fuller (1800–1868) began Baptist work in Montreal and the Eastern Townships. In 1869, the French congregations organized the Union d'Eglises Baptistes Francaises au Canada (Union of French Baptist Churches in Canada).

In 1873 the Rev. Alexander McDonald began Baptist work in Winnipeg, Manitoba. The planning of other churches led to the formation of the Baptist Convention of Manitoba and the Northwest in 1884. Extensive work among non-English-speaking immigrant communities was pursued by the Baptists in Western Canada, as a result of which a number of ethnic congregations were incorporated into the new convention.

Work on the Canadian West Coast had progressed since 1876, partially with help from the United States. In 1897, Baptists organized the Baptist Convention of British Columbia. In 1907, churches in the four western provinces joined to form the Baptist Convention of Western Canada, reorganized as the Baptist Union of Western Canada in 1909.

In 1944, the Baptist Federation of Canada was established as a loose affiliation of the three autonomous conventions/unions. The Union d'Eglises Baptists Francaises au Canada has participated in the federation since 1970. The name was changed to Canadian Baptist Federation in 1983.

The Canadian Baptist work overseas began as early as 1814, when Baptist churches in Atlantic Canada gave financial support to the American Baptist Missionary Union. When Canadian Baptists began to volunteer as missionaries, the American Baptist Missionary Union seemed to be the logical way to send them. The first Canadian Baptist missionaries overseas, Rev. and Mrs. Richard E. Burpee went to Burma in 1845 to work among the Karen people.

In 1865, the Maritime Baptist Convention incorporated a Foreign Mission Board. In 1867, this Mission Board made history by sending a single woman, Minnie DeWolfe, to Burma. She was the first single woman sent overseas by any Baptist Board in the world.

In 1866 Baptists in Ontario and Quebec formed a "Canadian auxiliary" to the American Baptist Missionary Union, an organization to which they had been making contributions for several years. In 1870 this auxiliary was reorganized as the Regular Baptist Foreign Mission Society of Canada, and in 1889 the name was changed to the Board of Foreign Missions of the Regular Baptist Convention of Ontario and Quebec.

By 1875, Canadian Baptist missionaries from both the Maritime and the Ontario and Quebec boards were working in the same area of India, but under their respective boards. In addition to their efforts in evangelism and church planting, the early missionaries sought to address the poverty they encountered in India. One response was to establish schools. By 1890, thirty village schools were in operation. High schools, boarding schools, vocational training institutes and teacher training schools followed, and by 1940, there was a total of 440 schools in operation.

In 1898, another need was addressed with the opening of the Star of Hope Hospital at Akividu, under the direction of Dr. Pearl Smith. Over the next thirty years, a total of eight other hospitals were founded in India by Canadian Baptists.

Also in 1898, Canadian Baptists from Ontario and Quebec became involved in another mission field—Bolivia—with the arrival of Archibald Reekie in Oruro. He established contact with the Bolivians by opening an English-language school, an approach that was also followed by missionaries in La Paz and Cochabamba. In 1905, freedom of worship was granted in Bolivia, largely because of the favorable example set by the Canadian Baptist missionaries.

On a number of occasions between 1875 and 1910 attempts were made to unite the two mission boards in Canada. Finally in 1911, stimulated by the formation of Baptist Unions in western Canada and the frustration of the missionaries working cooperatively in India but under separate boards, the Canadian Baptist Foreign Mission Board was formed. It brought together the Foreign Mission Board of the Maritime Baptist Convention and the Board of Foreign Missions of the Regular Baptist Convention of Ontario and Quebec, uniting Canadian Baptists in their administration of overseas mission. On May 1, 1970, a revised constitution changed the name to the Canadian Baptist Overseas Mission Board. In 1990, the board's name was changed again to Canadian Baptist International Ministries, reflecting changes in attitudes in some countries to the missionary enterprise.

Canadian Baptist Ministries currently has personnel in 17 different countries, including Canada. One of its ministries is The Sharing Way, which focuses in the areas of relief, development, and refugees. CBM also operates a program for short-term ministries called the Canadian Baptist Volunteers.

Beliefs. A majority of Canadian Baptists accept moderate Calvinism with an Arminian (free will) minority active as well. Canadian Baptist Ministries is non-creedal but has a statement of mission that addresses both basic theological issues as well as questions of purpose, service and fellowship.

Organization. The Council, which is the delegated governing body of Canadian Baptist Ministries meets semiannually. The churches meet triennially for celebration and for fellowship. A congregational polity is practiced in Canadian Baptist churches. Local Baptist churches are self-governing but cooperate in missionary and other activities through the conventions/unions.

Canadian Baptist Ministries is a member of the Baptist World Alliance. It declined invitations to participate in the formation of the United Church of Canada. It was a member of the Canadian Council of Churches until 1980 when it withdrew, although the Baptist Convention of Ontario and Quebec continues to be a member. The Baptist Union of Western Canada and many individual Baptist congregations are members of the Evangelical Fellowship of Canada.

Membership: In 1993, Canadian Baptists reported 130,000 members and 1,150 churches that worship in over 20 different languages on any given Sunday.

Educational Facilities: Acadia Divinity College, Wolfville, Nova Scotia. Atlantic Baptist College, Moncton, New Brunswick. McMaster Divinity College, Hamilton, Ontario. Baptist Leadership Educational Center, Whitby, Ontario. Baptist Leadership Training School, Calgary, Alberta. Carey Theological College, Vancouver, British Columbia. Centre d'Etudes Theologiques Evangeliques, Montreal, Quebec.

Periodicals: *The Canadian Baptist*, 195 The West Mall, Suite 414, Etobicoke, Ontario M9C 5K1. *The Link and Visitor*, 195 The West Mall, Suite 414 Etobicoke, Ontario M9C 5K1. *The Atlantic Baptist*, Box 756, Kentville, Nova Scotia B4N 3X9. *The Enterprise*, 7185 Millcreek Dr., Mississauga, Ontario, Canada L5N 5R4. *Tidings*, 1006 George St., New Minas, Nova Scotia B4N 4E1.

Sources:

McBeth, H. Leon. *The Baptist Heritage*. Nashville, TN: Broadman Press, 1987.

Torbet, Robert G. *A History of the Baptists*. Valley Forge, PA: Judson Press, 1973.

Zeman, Jarold Knox. *Baptists in Canada*. Burlington, ON: G. R. Welch, 1980.

★846★
Canadian Convention of Southern Baptists
℅ Rev. Allen E. Schmidt, Executive Dir.-Treasurer
Postal Bag 300
Cochrane, AB, Canada T0L 0W0

The Canadian Convention of Southern Baptists was organized in Kelowna, British Columbia, in May 1985. It cooperates with the Southern Baptist Convention in Home and Foreign Missions.

Membership: In 1997 there were 115 churches, 7,957 members, 103 ministers, and 3 families in foreign missions in Nigeria, Malaysia, and Chile.

Educational Facilities: Canadian Southern Baptist Seminary, Cochrane, Alberta, Canada.

Periodicals: *The Baptist Horizon.*

★847★
Central Baptist Association
309 Lebanon Rd.
Kingsport, TN 37663

The Central Baptist Association was founded in 1956. It is conservative fundamentalist in theological perspective, and member churches hold to the absolute authority of the King James Version of the Bible and practice baptism by immersion. The association exists to maintain a common standard of doctrine and practice among member churches. It also operates a summer camp in Jasper, Virginia.

Membership: In 1994 the association reported 33 member churches in four associations located in Virginia, Kentucky, Indiana, and South Carolina.

★848★
Christian Unity Baptist Association
℅ Elder Thomas T. Reynolds
Thomasville, NC 27360

The Christian Unity Baptist Association dates to 1901, when the Mountain Union Regular Association passed a resolution dropping from membership all churches which practiced open communion. Those who opposed the action walked out and for many years functioned as independent congregations. Over the years, only two ministers, F. L. Sturgill and Eli Graham, and three churches survived. In 1932, these churches organized as the Macedonia Baptist Association. In 1935, they were joined by other churches who had left the Mountain Union Regular Association, and the Christian Unity Baptist Association was organized.

Doctrinally, a mild Calvinism prevails. The article on the security of the believer was amended to read that all who are saved and endure to the end shall be saved. Footwashing and open communion are practiced. The polarity is congregational and the association acts in an advisory role.

Membership: Not reported. In 1965, there were eleven churches in the association in Virginia, Tennessee, and North Carolina, with 623 members and 17 ministers.

★849★
Conservative Baptist Association
25W560 Geneva Rd.
Box 66
Wheaton, IL 60189-0066

The Conservative Baptist Association (CBAmerica) dates its beginnings to 1946, the year Northern Baptists (now American Baptist Churches) met in Grand Rapids, Michigan. The conflict between modern religious liberalism and theological conservative leadership within the convention dates back to the 1920s. Earlier breakaways from the convention over the same issues included the General Association of Regular Baptists in 1932. The Conservative Baptist Foreign Mission Society, (now CB International), founded in December 1943, was finally excluded from the convention in 1945.

At the Grand Rapids meetings, theological conservatives made one final attempt to change the liberal course of the convention. Failing in this attempt, Dr. Albert Johnson, Hinson Baptist Church, Portland, Oregon, introduced the resolution calling for the exploration of affiliation with other Baptist groups. The final conclusion of the "Committee of 15" called for regional conferences that gave overwhelming endorsement to the formation of the Conservative Baptist Association of America. This action was considered at Atlantic City in May 1947, and finalized at Milwaukee in 1948.

Actions in Milwaukee included the appointment of a general director and three regional evangelists, a committee to consider and report on the formation of a Home Mission Society in 1949 at San Francisco, and the adoption of a constitution.

Following a move from Chicago to Elk Grove, Illinois, in 1963, the Association built a new headquarters adjacent to the Home and Foreign Mission Society in Wheaton, Illinois, in 1968.

The association ministers in cooperation with the two mission agencies and shares in ministry with 23 state associations, three seminaries located in Portland, Oregon; Denver, Colorado; and Dresher, Pennsylvania, and three colleges located in Honolulu, Hawaii; Phoenix, Arizona; and South Portland, Maine. There are presently 1200 churches affiliated with the CBAmerica.

The present ministries of CBAmerica include Church Growth, Chaplaincy, Financial Services, Church and Pastoral Referral, Women's and Youth Ministries, Communications, which publishes *Spectrum*, the national newsletter, and Churchmart (formerly CB Press), which supplies churches with ministry resources.

Membership: In 1994, the association reported 210,000 members, 1,324 senior ministers, 1200 associate ministers, and 1,166 churches, with 15 congregations in Canada.

Educational Facilities: Denver Seminary, Denver, Colorado.
Southwestern College, Phoenix, Arizona.
Western Conservative Baptist Seminary, Portland, Oregon.
International College and Graduate School of Theology, Honolulu, Hawaii.
Seminary of the East, Doesher, Pennsylvania.
New England Bible College, South Portland, Maine.

Periodicals: *Spectrum*. • *Impact*. Send orders to Box 5, Wheaton, IL 60189.

Sources:

A Baptist Primer in Church Discipline. Chicago: Conservative Baptist Fellowship, n.d.

Founded on the Word, Focused on the World. Wheaton, IL: Conservative Baptist Foreign Missionary Society, 1978.

Pegg, Walter A. *Historic Baptist Distinctives*. Wheaton, IL: Conservative Baptist Foreign Missionary Society, 1952.

Shelley, Bruce R. *Conservative Baptists*. Denver, CO: Conservative Baptist Theological Seminary, 1962.

Tulga, Chester E. *The Independence of the Local Church*. Chicago: Conservative Baptist Fellowship, 1951.

★850★
Duck River (and Kindred) Association of Baptists
% Elder Wayne L. Smith, Moderator
Duck River Association
Rte. 1, Box 429
Lynchburg, TN 37352

The Duck River (and Kindred) Association of Baptists separated from the Elk River Association in 1825. The issue was the atonement, and the "liberals" who believed in a general atonement withdrew from the Elk River Association, which was a member of the Triennial Convention, the initial missionary organization which later evolved into the American Baptist Churches in the U.S.A.. Another issue soon divided churches in the Triennial Convention, the issue of compulsory mission support. In 1843 that issue caused some people to withdraw from churches in the Triennial Convention and from another Duck River Association. With further divisions within churches associated with the Triennial Associations, more Duck River Associations were formed. Now there are four Duck River Associations and three Kindred Associations included in the general association. Most of the churches are in Tennessee. All mission work is local. Doctrine is mildly Calvinistic. Members practice footwashing. Polity is congregational. Letters are a standard means of communication. Ministers are ordained by two or more of their colleagues.

Membership: Not reported. In 1975 there were 85 churches, 8,632 members, and 148 ministers.

★851★
Fellowship of Evangelical Baptist Churches in Canada
Current address not obtained for this edition.

After World War I, a fundamentalist-modernist controversy split the Baptist Convention of Ontario and Quebec (now a constitutent part of the Canadian Baptist Federation). Leading the fundamentalists was Thomas Todhunter Shields (1873-1955), pastor of the Jarvis Street Baptist Church in Toronto. Shields was intimately involved with the World's Christian Fundamentals Association and hosted the annual meeting in 1926. He helped found the Baptist Bible Union, a fundamentalist Baptist organization, and led it for nine years.

In Canada, Shields focused the fundamentalist controversy on McMaster University, the Baptist school in Toronto. He led an attack on the school through his periodical, the *Gospel Witness*. As a result, in 1927 Shields was ousted from the Convention for lack of harmony and cooperation with the Convention's work. With his supporters, he founded the Union of Regular Baptist Churches, which reported approximately seventy churches its first year, and the Toronto Baptist Seminary, to compete with McMaster. However, internal controversy began to divide the Union. In 1933 a group left and formed the Fellowship of Independent Baptist Churches. After Shields led the Jarvis Street Church and other supporters out in 1949, the Union remained with little of its original substance.

Rebuilding of the divided fundamentalist structures began in 1953 when the Union of Regular Baptist Churches united with the Fellowship of Independent Baptist Churches to form the Fellowship of Evangelical Baptist Churches. In the 1960s the fellowship absorbed two other fundamentalist groups which had existed independently since their formation in the western provinces. The Regular Baptist Missionary Fellowship of Alberta, formed in 1930, joined the fellowship in 1963 and the Regular Baptists of British Columbia, formed in 1927, joined in 1965.

Beliefs of the fellowship are fundamental and resemble those of the General Association of Regular Baptist Churches. It supports missionaries in India and Japan through its own missionary board, and several hundred through a variety of approved independent missionary-sending agencies.

Membership: In 1983 the fellowship reported 445 churches and 53,285 members.

Periodicals: *The Evangelical Baptist*. • *Intercom*.

Sources:

Dollar, George W. *A History of Fundamentalism in America*. Greenville, SC: Bob Jones University Press, 1973.

★852★
Fundamental Baptist Fellowship
Current address not obtained for this edition.

The Fundamental Baptist Fellowship was formed as a result of conflict and controversy in the Conservative Baptist Association. At issue was what was termed the "new evangelicalism," a trend in conservative Christian circles toward cooperation and accommodation to certain modern situations, without giving up any essentials of the faith. However, some within the Conservative Baptist Association (CBA) saw the new evangelicalism as a departure from Baptist traditions. The critics also believed in a premillennial eschatology and in separation from those who do not hold to fundamentalist doctrine. The controversy centered on the Denver Conservative Baptist Seminary in Denver, Colorado, founded in 1950 and strongly staffed with exponents of the new evangelicalism.

During the 1950s, controversy centered on attempts to control the seminary by the Separatists. Conservative Baptist churches in Colorado began to take sides. The separatist strength was concentrated in the Conservative Baptist Fellowship, one of the constituent agencies of the CBA. The CBF was headed by Research Secretary Chester Tulga, who spelled out the separatist position in a number of "Case" booklets which attacked modernist and centralizing trends. The new evangelical position was concentrated in the CBA and the Conservative Baptist Foreign Missionary Society. During the 1950s, the distance between the two sides grew. The Colorado Conservative Baptists withdrew support from the seminary, and individual churches and leaders began to support either the CBA or the CBF.

The split became final in 1961 when the leadaers of the CBF formed the World Conservative Baptist Mission. An aggressive stance toward the CBA was taken, and pre-CBA convention sessions were held to try to woo churches to the CBF position. The name was eventually changed to the Fundamental Baptist Fellowship.

The Fundamental Baptist Fellowship established headquarters in Denver from which it issued the *Information Bulletin*, its periodical. The Baptist Bible College offers a two-year curriculum. Close relations are kept with the Minnesota Baptist Convention as a sister organization.

Membership: Not reported.

Educational Facilities: Baptist Bible College, Denver, Colorado.

★853★
General Association of Regular Baptist Churches
1300 N. Meacham Rd.
Schaumburg, IL 60173

Rmong the conservative elements in the Northern Baptist Convention (now the American Baptist Churches in the U.S.A.) were a number whose main concern was doctrine. After the failure in 1922 of the convention to adopt the New Hampshire Confession of Faith, Thomas Todhunter Shields of the Jarvis Street Church in Toronto led in the formation of the Baptist Bible Union, a union of individuals interested in the purging of modern elements in the Convention. In 1932, the Baptist Bible Union gave way to the General Association of Regular Baptist Churches (GARBC), formed in Chicago by delegates from eight states.

The GARBC considers itself an association of sovereign Bible-believing Baptist churches. The New Hampshire Confession of Faith was used as a model for the Articles of Faith, though emphasis is placed on the fundamentalist issues of the Bible and Christology. A single article concerns the "Resurrection, Personal, Visible Premillennial Return of Christ, and related events."

The GARBC is also a vocal exponent of separation. Churches in the fellowship are required to withdraw fellowship from and refuse cooperation with any organization or group which permits modernists in its ranks. Their separatist position was included in the name of the GARBC; the term "Regular" was adopted to oppose the other, "irregular" Baptist churches.

Missions are promoted through eight independent mission agencies which hold to the GARBC doctrinal position. They are the Association of Baptists for World Evangelism, Baptist Church Planters, Baptist Mid-Missions, Evangelical Baptist Missions, Baptist Missionary Builders, Western Baptist Home Mission, and Continental Baptist Missions. Together, in 1997, they supported more than 2,000 missions. There are seven independent college/seminaries which are approved by the GARBC. Five social ministries, two children's homes, a senior citizen's home, and a residential school for the retarded are also approved.

Membership: In 1997 the association reported 157,522 members, 1,541 congregations, and 1,600 ministers.

Educational Facilities: Approved educational facilities include the following:

Baptist Bible College of Pennsylvania and Baptist School of Theology, Clarks Summit, Pennsylvania.
Cedarville College, Cedarville, Ohio.
Faith Baptist Bible College, Ankeny, Iowa.
Grand Rapids Baptist College and Seminary, Grand Rapids, Michigan.
Northwest Baptist Seminary, Tacoma, Washington.
Spurgeon Baptist Bible College, Mulberry, Florida.
Western Baptist College, Salem, Oregon.

Periodicals: *Baptist Bulletin*.

Sources:
Barndollar, W. W. *The Validity of Dispensationalism*. Des Plaines, IL: Regular Baptist Press, 1964.

The Biblical Faith of Baptists. 3 vols. Des Plaines, IL: Regular Baptist Press, 1966.

Hull, Merle R. *What a Fellowship?* Schaumburg, IL: Regular Baptist Press, 1981.

[R. T. Ketcham]. *The Answer: What Are Non-Convention Baptists Doing?* Waterloo, IA: General Association of Regular Baptist Churches, 1943.

Murdoch, J. Murray. *Portrait of Obedience*. Schaumburg, IN: Regular Baptist Press, 1979.

★854★
Independent Baptist Church of America
Current address not obtained for this edition.

The Independent Baptist Church of America dates to the 1870s, when Swedish Free Baptists emigrated to the United States and settled in the Midwest. In 1893, an annual conference began to be held under the name Swedish Independent Baptist Church, later changed to Scandinavian Independent Baptist Denomination of America. In 1912, a split occurred when part of the group incorporated. The incorporated group called themselves the Scandinavian Independent Baptist Denomination in the United States of America. The unincorporated group continued as the Scandinavian Free Baptist Society of the United States of America. In 1927, the two groups united at a conference at Garden Valley, Wisconsin, and adopted their present name.

Doctrinally, the churches are pietistic and evangelical. Like the Six-Principle Baptists, they practice the laying-on-of-hands at the time a member is received into the church. Members believe in the authority of and obedience to the civil government in all of its demands, except those contrary to the Word of God, such as participation in war.

Membership: Not reported. In 1965 there were two congregations and 70 members (down from 13 congregations in 1926).

Periodicals: *The Lighthouse*. Send orders to 2646 Longfellow, Minneapolis, MN 55407.

★855★
Independent Bible Baptist Missions
Current address not obtained for this edition.

Among the organizations to evolve out of the latter stages of the fundamentalist-modernist controversy was the Independent Bible Baptist Missions founded in Colorado in 1949. By this time the World Council of Churches had been formed and the liberal Protestant-based Federal Council of Churches had announced the formation of its successor body, The National Council of the Churches of Christ in the U.S.A. Also, among more conservative Protestants a new movement had arisen called Neoevangelicalism, which, without giving up any of the doctrinal affirmation of fundamentalism, had a new openness toward the academic world, science, and cooperative endeavors with liberal Protestants.

Among the many conservative Baptists who rejected both liberal Protestantism and Neoevangelicalism was Harvey H. Springer, a pastor at Englewood, a suburb of Denver, Colorado. He called together 12 colleagues who shared his basic perspective and in December 1949 they organized the Missionary Fellowship of Baptist Churches. At this organization's first assembly in 1950, it adopted the name, Independent Bible Baptist Missions. Headquarters were established in Colorado Springs, Colorado.

Doctrinally, the organization followed traditional Baptist beliefs as set forth in the Philadelphia Confession. It held to a premillennial dispensational eschatology. It also specifically forbade members any affiliation with the National Council of Churches or the National Association of Evangelicals, the primary organizational expression of Neoevangelicalism. Organization is congregational and there is an annual general assembly. Foreign missions were established in Brazil, Uruguay, and Mexico.

Membership: Not reported. In 1980 there were approximately 25 churches and 3,000 members.

Sources:

Piepkorn, Arthur C. *Profiles in Belief: The Religious Bodies of the United States and Canada.* Vol. IV. San Francisco: Harper & Row, 1979.

★856★
Kyova Association of Regular Baptists
Current address not obtained for this edition.

The Kyova Association of Regular Baptists was formed in 1924 from the New Salem Association of Regular Baptists. In the 1940s, a controversy arose over whether the United Mine Workers (or any union) was in fact a secret society. As a result of this controversy, the Kyova Association dropped correspondence with the New Salem Association in 1945 and then splintered. Some churches moved into other Regular Baptist Associations. The group uses the King James version of the Bible and forbids members to belong to secret societies.

Membership: Not reported. In 1960 the association had 4 congregations and 140 members.

★857★
Liberty Baptist Fellowship
Candler's Mountain Rd.
Lynchburg, VA 24502

Liberty Baptist Fellowship is an association of independent fundamentalist Baptist churches and ministers founded in 1981 that grew out of minister Jerry Falwell's Thomas Road Baptist Church in Lynchburg, Virginia. Falwell founded Thomas Road Baptist Church in 1956. The work prospered, and in 1971 he founded Liberty Baptist College with 141 students. Two years later Liberty Baptist Theological Seminary was opened. Both the college and seminary grew as people responded to the television ministry of Falwell's "Old Fashioned Gospel Hour." By 1983 650 graduates were pastoring churches, each of whom had been taught the aggressive evangelism techniques used by Falwell to build Thomas Road. When Liberty Baptist College became Liberty University, the seminary program was integrated into the university's overall structure.

Liberty Baptist Fellowship follows the fundamentalist faith for which Falwell has become a major national spokesperson. It holds to separatism from religious groups that deny the fundamentals of the faith. The fellowship affirms, within a framework of traditional Christian beliefs, the inerrancy of the Bible, the creation of the earth in six literal days, and the imminent return of Jesus Christ. Evangelism is emphasized; the fellowship believes salvation can come only through the acceptance of Jesus as one's personal savior.

Liberty Baptist Fellowship was formed as the school's graduates began to assume professional positions as pastors across the United States. It has a goal to form 5,000 churches by the end of the twentieth century. It is headed by Falwell, chairman of its executive committee, A. Pierre Guillermin, also president of Liberty University, and Elmer Towns, also vice-president of Liberty University and professor of systematic theology. It has a congregational polity.

Membership: In 1987 the fellowship reported 510 congregations, 200,000 members, and 1,500 ministers (many serving churches not affiliated to the fellowship).

Periodicals: *Liberty Journal.* • *Fundamentalist Journal.*

Sources:

Falwell, Jerry. *The Fundamentalist Phenomenon: The Resurgence of Conservative Christianity.* Garden City, NY: Doubleday & Company, 1981.

___. *Stepping Out on Faith.* Wheaton, IL: Tyndale House Publishers, 1984.

___. *Strength for the Journey: An Autobiography.* New York: Simon and Schuster, 1987.

Falwell, Jerry, and Elmer Towns. *Church Aflame.* Nashville, TN: Impact Books, 1971.

Lee, Ron. "Falwell's College Strives to Become a Fundamentalist University Serving 50,000." *Christianity Today* (November 25 1983): 40-43.

★858★
Minnesota Baptist Association
% Richard L. Paige Jr., Executive Secretary
5000 Golden Valley Rd.
Minneapolis, MN 55422

As the fundamentalist debate arose anew in the 1940s, Minnesota emerged as one of the few areas where, under the leadership of such men as William Bell Riley (1861-1947), conservatives were in the majority. Controversy developed over support of the mission program of the Northern Baptist Convention (now the American Baptist Churches in the U.S.A.), and in 1944 a "special account" was created by the Minnesota Convention to channel funds to the Conservative Baptist Foreign Missionary Society (CBFMS). Other objections to the Northern Baptist Convention's program were focused on ecumenism, youth work, and the distribution of funds in the unified budget. The break came in 1948 when the Minnesota Convention became independent of the Northern Baptist Convention.

After the formation of the Conservative Baptist Association in 1947, there was a period of cooperation between it and the Minnesota Convention. Individual churches and leaders (such as Dr. Richard V. Clearwaters) were active in both. The Minnesota Convention continued to function, for the CBA accepted only churches (not conventions) as members.

Cooperation with the CBA continued, but the Conservative Baptists were criticized in 1955 when an article in a Minnesota Convention magazine complained that CBFMS missionaries did not believe in the pretribulation, pre-millennial return of Christ. Later that year, a pretribulation position was adopted by the Minnesota Convention. The convention began to move in a separatist direction; criticism of the CBA continued. The CBA was accused of interfering with local autonomy in the churches and of allowing inclusivist thinking in the early 1960s. (Inclusivist thinking pertained to association with those in liberal associations.) The break between the Minnesota Convention and the Conservative Baptist Association was completed in 1963. The name was officially changed to the Minnesota Baptist Association in 1974.

The association publishes a church school curriculum and as well as various tracts and booklets through the publication ministry of North Star Baptist Press.

Membership: In 1997 there were 62 churches and approximately 80 ministers.

Educational Facilities: Pillsbury Baptist Bible College, Owatonna, Minnesota.

Periodicals: *The North Star Baptist.*

Sources:

Becklund, David. *A History of the Minnesota Baptist Convention.* Minneapolis: Minnesota Baptist Convention, 1967.

Riley, Marie Acomb. *The Dynamic of a Dream.* Grand Rapids, MI: William B. Eerdmans Publishing Company, 1938.

★859★

New England Evangelical Baptist Fellowship

% Dr. John Viall
40 Bridge St.
Newton, MA 02158

The New England Evangelical Baptist Fellowship is a small body in the Northeast. It is a conservative body and was formally a member of the National Association of Evangelicals. The president in 1965 was Dr. John S. Viall of Boston.

Membership: Not reported. In 1965 there were 10 churches, 20 pastors and 1,022 members.

★860★

New Testament Association of Independent Baptist Churches

1079 Westview Dr.
Rochelle, IL 61068

The New Testament Association of Independent Baptist Churches was formed in 1965 at a meeting in Denver. Twenty-seven churches affiliated at the organizational meeting. A previous meeting had been held in 1964 by members of the Conservative Baptist Association (CBA) who supported a premillennial, pretribulationist, separatist position. Among leaders of the newly formed association was Dr. Richard V. Clearwaters of the Minnesota Baptist Convention (now the Minnesota Baptist Association). The polity is a loose congregationalism. An annual meeting is held in which each pastor and five lay delegates have voting power. They elect a president, other officers, and members of a board of trustees to implement Association programs.

Doctrinally, the Association resembles the Conservative Baptist Association. The New Testament Association has adopted a Confession of Faith based on the New Hampshire Confession, but with emphasis on separation and pre-tribulation eschatology. The group is opposed to speaking in tongues. The schools of the Minnesota Baptist Association are approved for students.

Membership: Not reported.

Periodicals: *New Testament Testimonies.*

Sources:

Clearwaters, Richard V. *The Great Conservative Baptist Compromise.* Minneapolis, MN: Central Seminary Press, n.d.

___. *The Local Church of the New Testament.* Chicago: Conservative Baptist Association of America, 1954.

___. *The Ten Commandments.* Minneapolis, MN: Central Seminary Press, 1975.

★861★

North American Baptist Conference

1 S. 210 Summit Ave.
Oakbrook Terrace, IL 60181

The North American Baptist Conference originated in the early nineteenth century with German-speaking Americans who had been influenced by English-speaking Baptists to work among the growing number of German immigrants. While tracing their history to a number of efforts begun independently of each other, the German Baptists look to Konrad Anton Fleischmann as the first of their number. A Bavarian, Fleischmann had been converted in Switzerland and joined a separatist church molded on the English model. On a request from George Mueller of Bristol, England, he traveled to America and became pastor of a German Protestant church at Newark, New Jersey, in the spring of 1839, but was fired for refusing to baptize infants. In October, he baptized three people, his first converts, and sent them to an English Baptist church. He traveled throughout eastern Pennsylvania and New York, where he established groups of believers and preaching stations. In 1843, he drew up a series of ''Articles'' for use by the church at Philadelphia which he founded. It was Baptist in all points except closed communion.

Other missionaries were also at work in the 1840s. Aided by the American Baptist Home Missionary Society, John Eschmann was working in New York City. Alexander Von Puttkamer was converted by English Baptists at Lawrenceville, New York, and began to organize a German Baptist Church in Buffalo while an agent of the American Tract Society. Churches in the Midwest were begun in the late 1840s.

The first conference of German Baptists met in 1851 representing eight churches and 405 members. With the cooperation of the American Baptist Publication Society, they were able to produce a hymnal and a German translation of the New Hampshire Confession. A Western Conference was formed in 1859, and a Trienniel Conference met in 1865.

Doctrinally, the North American Baptists affirm the standard Baptist faith as embodied in the New Hampshire Confession, though only a brief statement has been adopted. Polity is congregational. There is a triennial conference every three years, with 19 associations in the United States and Canada. Higher education has been a major concern from the beginning, and as early as 1858, August Rauschenbusch went to the Baptist Seminary at Rochester and became one of the outstanding exponents of the social gospel. Missions are carried on in Mexico, Eastern Europe, Cameroon, Nigeria, the Philippine Islands, Japan, and Brazil. Home missions are directed toward various multi-cultural groups and planting new churches in areas of need. The conference is affiliated with the Baptist World Alliance.

Membership: In 1996 the conference reported 61,000 members and 400 congregations.

Educational Facilities: North American Baptist Seminary, Sioux Falls, South Dakota.

North American Baptist College, Edmonton, Alberta, Canada.

Edmonton Baptist Seminary, Edmonton, Alberta, Canada.

Periodicals: *NAB Today.* • *Intercessor.*

Sources:

Kerstan, Reinhold Johannes. *Historical Factors in the Formation of the Ethnically Oriented North American Baptist General Conference.* Ph.D. diss., Northwestern University, 1971.

Ramaker, Albert John. *The German Baptists in North America.* Cleveland, OH: German Baptist Publication Society, 1924.

Woyke, Frank H. *Heritage and Ministry of the North American Baptist Conference.* Oakbrook Terrace, IL: North American Baptist Conference, 1979.

★862★

Orthodox Baptists

Current address not obtained for this edition.

The Orthodox Baptists originated among the most conservative fundamentalist element of the Southern Baptist Convention in the 1940s. The movement was founded by W. Lee Rector (1883–1945), a former professor at Baylor University, who in 1931 became pastor of the First Baptist Church of Ardmore, Oklahoma. In the early 1940s he resigned from the Southern Baptist Convention and organized the first Orthodox Baptist Church in Ardmore, and he was soon joined by several other likeminded ministers and congregations. In 1944 he opened the Orthodox Bible Institute to train ministers. The church has remained staunchly fundamentalist, and members refrain from association with apostasy, liberalism, neo-evangelicalism, and compromise on doctrinal matters.

Rector died in 1945. In the 1960s, the Orthodox Bible Institute closed and a new Orthodox Baptist College, located in Dallas, Texas, (now the Independent Baptist College), succeeded it. The Texas school was founded by James L. Higgs, then pastor of Trinity Baptist Temple.

Membership: Not reported. In the early 1970s there were approximately 300 congregations associated with the Orthodox Baptists.

Educational Facilities: Independent Baptist College, Dallas, Texas.

Sources:

Dollar, George W. *A History of Fundamentalism in America*. Greenville, SC: Bob Jones University Press, 1973.

★863★
Regular Baptists
Current address not obtained for this edition.

In the 1740s during what was called the Great Awakening in the American colonies, the new Baptists were divided into Regular Baptists and Separate Baptists. The Separatists were former Congregationalists who had been affected by the revival and particularly the preaching of George Whitefield. Regular Baptists were members of the Philadelphia Association and adhered to the Philadelphia Convention. The Separate and Regular Baptists spent the second half of the eighteenth century engaging in polemics and attempting union. In 1765, the first Regular Baptist Association was formed by churches in Virginia and given the name Ketocten. The Regular Baptists spread into Kentucky and the surrounding states.

In 1801, the Separate and Regular Baptists were able to overcome their differences and merge. They formed various associations with the terms "united" in the association names. Some second generation members of these associations, however, became dissatisfied with the term "united" and many associations dropped it from their name. Larger Baptist bodies absorbed many of these associations.

Toward the middle of the nineteenth century, a move to reconstitute the Regular Baptists began. In 1854, the New Salem Association of United Baptists changed its name to the New Salem Association of Regular Baptists. In 1870 this association adopted another name, Old Regular Baptists. In 1867 the Burning Springs Association of United Baptists changed the term "united" in its name to "regular." Other associations followed suit. Regular Baptists now live in all sections of the country, with the heaviest concentration of them living in the area from Virginia to Indiana.

The reason for the formation of the Regular Baptists is not clear. By the end of the nineteenth century, though, they clearly represented a rejection of the organizational and methodological innovations of most nineteenth-century Baptists. The group rejects Sunday schools, a trained ministry, secret societies, missionary societies, and organization beyond the associational level.

A doctrinal consensus exists among the Regular Baptists, a body of beliefs very close to the doctrine of the United Baptists. Most statements of the beliefs of Regular Baptists affirm adherence to the Trinity, the Bible as the written word of God, election, man's depravity, the eternal security of the believer, believers' baptism by immersion (often specified as "back foremost," so water covers the whole person), closed communion, the resurrection, and a properly ordained ministry. Beyond that consensus, there is a wide variety of freedom and belief. The statements on salvation and justification are so worded as to be open to both Calvinistic and Arminian interpretations. (Calvinists say the number and identity of the elect was predetermined before the world began; Arminians say salvation is possible for all who, by free will, choose to follow the gospel.) However, the Regular Baptists have no fellowship with those who reject their statements of beliefs. Government is extreme congregationalism with no central headquarters and no structure beyond the association. Among the periodicals serving the churches are *The Regular Baptist* from Laurel, Maryland, and the *Regular Baptist Messenger* of Whitestown, Indiana.

The Regular Baptists have allowed Arminianism but not hyper-Calvinism, and in the 1890s, they split over absolute predestination. (See separate entry on Regular Baptists-Predestinarian.) The following Regular Baptist associations are in correspondence with each other, display doctrinal similarity, and reject absolute pre-

destination: the New Salem, Union, Indian Bottom, Mud River, Sardis, Friendship, Philadelphia, Thornton Union, and Northern Salem Associations.

Membership: Not reported. In the early 1970s there were an estimated 266 churches and 17,186 members.

Periodicals: *The Regular Baptist*. Send orders to 9023 Contee Rd., Laurel, MD 20810.

Sources:

Perrigan, Rufus. *History of Regular Baptists and their Ancestors and Accessors*. Haysi, VA: The Author, 1961.

Short, Ron. "We Believed in the Family and the Old Regular Baptist Church." *Southern Exposure* 4, no.3 (1976): 60-65.

Wallhausser, John. "I Can Almost See Heaven From Here." *Katallagete* 8, no. 3 (Spring 1983): 2-10.

★864★
Regular Baptists (Predestinarian)
Current address not obtained for this edition.

In 1894, the Union Association of Regular Baptists split over the question of predestination. The majority was Calvinist, holding to strict predestination. Both the majority and minority groups continue with the same name, the Union Association of Regular Baptists, and have equal claims on the pre-1984 history.

The Sandlick Association of Regular Baptists was formed in 1876 from the New Salem Association of Regular Baptists. In 1896, it became involved in the Calvinist controversy. The Calvinist majority prevails in the Sandlick Association. The Arminian minority, holding that salvation is possible for all, formed the Indian Bottom Association.

Other associations were also racked with the controversy. In 1893, the Mates Creek Association of Regular Baptists was divided, the Arminian group becoming the Sardis Association. Although called Regular Baptists, the following groups are strongly predestinarian and fit the description of Regular Baptists (Predestinarian): the Union Association, the Sandlick Association, and the Mages Creek Association. Most members of these associations live where the Regular Baptists live, that is, from Virginia to Indiana. The predestinarian associations have grown, though some have possibly been lost to the Primitive Baptists.

Membership: Not reported. There are no current statistics; figures quoted (22 associations, 7,000 members) in the *Encyclopedia of Southern Baptist* may refer only to Calvinistic associations.

★865★
Russian-Ukrainian Evangelical Baptist Union of the U.S.A., Inc.
Current address not obtained for this edition.

The Russian/Ukrainian Evangelical Baptist Union of the U.S.A., Inc., dates from 1901 when Baptists migrated from Russia to Kiev, North Dakota. During the next twenty years, the Baptists absorbed other evangelical groups, many of which were lost in transition to English-language worship. In 1919, the Union was organized at Philadelphia. Missionary work was begun worldwide among Russian immigrants. A Slavic missionary society supported 21 missionaries in Western Europe, South America, and Australia. An English branch works among English-speaking Slavic people. The Evangelical Baptist Camp Home for the Aged is operated by the Union.

Membership: Not reported. In 1968 there were approximately 40 churches of Russian/Ukrainian-speaking Americans.

Periodicals: *Evangelical Baptist Herald* (in English). • *The Sower of Truth* (in Russian).

★866★
Separate Baptists in Christ
℅ Rev. Roger Popplewell, Moderator
Rte. 5
Russell Springs, KY 42642

The Separate Baptists emerged in the "First Great Awakening" of the eighteenth century as a result of the hostility of the majority of Congregationalists to the revivalism that swept New England. Some former Congregationalists were rebaptized, including Isaac Backus, who became an outstanding theologian and historian. The Separatist movement spread, but the Separatists were not for a long time accepted by many other Baptists, in part because of their acceptance of those baptized but not immersed. However in 1801, a union was effected between the Regular and Separate Baptists. Some Separatists did not accept the union, and continued to exist west of the Allegheny Mountains as independent congregations and associations. In 1912, several of these associations came together as the General Association of Separatist Baptists.

The Separatist Baptists are similar to the Regular Baptists. A mild Calvinism is generally held. There is no universally accepted creed. Footwashing is an ordinance. Immersion is the only form of baptism. The government is congregational. Sunday schools and home missionary work are supported on a local level. Education is more highy rated than with the Regular Baptists.

Membership: In 1982 the Separate Baptists reported 8,800 members, 100 congregations, and 160 ministers.

Periodicals: *The Messenger.*

★867★
South Carolina Baptist Fellowship
℅ Dr. Richard Hughes
Tabernacle Baptist Church
3931 Whitehorse Rd.
Greenville, SC 29611

The South Carolina Baptist Fellowship was formed at a meeting in 1954 in Greenville, South Carolina, called by the Rev. John R. Waters and the Rev. Vendyl Jones. It was known as the Carolina Baptist Fellowship until its incorporation in 1965. Eleven independent Baptist pastors were present at the 1954 meeting. Reverend Waters was editor of *The Baptist Bible Trumpet,* and in 1955 at the fellowship meeting, it was adopted as the official organ. Doctrine is fundamental and premillennial; polity is congregational. Meetings of the fellowship are held monthly. Some are affiliated with the International Council of Christian Churches and the Southwide Baptist Fellowship or Baptist Bible Fellowship. Missions are supported through independent fundamentalist faith mission organizations such as Baptist Mid-Missions.

Membership: In 1987 there were approximately 300 churches with a membership of approximately 52,000 affiliated with the fellowship, though no formal membership list is kept.

Educational Facilities: Approved educational facilities:
Bob Jones University, Greenville, South Carolina.
Tennessee Temple University, Chattanooga, Tennessee.
Tabernacle Baptist College.

Periodicals: *The Baptist Bible Trumpet.* Send orders to 1607 Greenwood Rd., Laurens, SC 29360.

★868★
Southern Baptist Convention
℅ Executive Committee
901 Commerce St., Ste. 750
Nashville, TN 37203

History. The Southern Baptist Convention was formed in 1845 by the Baptist congregations in the southern United States. Underlying the separation of the southerners were the variety of tensions that would fifteen years later divide the nation and lead to the Civil War. Some of those tensions had become focused in the American Baptist Home Mission Board which many felt had neglected the south and southwest in the appointment of missionaries. The immediate occasion for the separation of the southern Baptists was the refusal in 1844 of the American Baptist Foreign Mission Board to appoint a slaveholder as a missionary and American Baptist Home Mission Board to appoint a slaveholder to a mission in Georgia. These refusals seemed to violate longstanding practice and the agreement of the Triennial Convention (the meeting of the foreign mission board), that cooperation in the foreign mission enterprise would sanction neither slavery nor anti-slavery.

Delegates met in Augusta, Georgia, in May 1845 to form the convention which would in turn coordinate the churches as a whole in the propagation of the gospel. A constitution was adopted and both a foreign and domestic mission board established. Thus, from the beginning, the southerners, without infringing upon traditional Baptist emphases concerning congregational polity, provided a more unified approach in structuring their denominational work. After several attempts to establish a publishing concern failed, a Sunday school board was created in 1891. It provided a single set of materials for the churches' educational program, a major force in unifying southern Baptist thought.

Significant in the life of the convention was the adoption in 1925 of the Cooperative Program by which all the boards, commissions and programs (with the exception of the Sunday School Board) supported by the churches came under a unified budget. The program provided stable financial support for all the church's ministries and eliminated competitive fund-raising among the congregations.

Beliefs. Southern Baptists inherited the Puritan-Reformed theological tradition which had been passed through the Baptist confessions of London (1677 and 1689), Philadelphia (1742) and New Hampshire (1833). The New Hampshire Confession was slightly revised and adopted by the convention as the Baptist Faith and Message in 1925, and it was again slightly revised in 1963. These statements, which place Southern Baptists clearly within the Reformed theological tradition, are balanced on the one hand by the frequently articulated belief in the freedom of the individual to interpret Scripture not bound by any creedal statement, and on the other hand by the theological perspective of fundamentalism which has the support of many Southern Baptist leaders.

During the twentieth century, the convention has been embroiled in a series of battles between those who have championed a variety of innovative perspectives that the more conservative elements of the convention have seen as deviating from traditional Baptist standards of doctrine. The controversy over evolution which began before the turn of the century sharply divided Baptists during the 1920s but gradually gave way to an accomodation to the several forms of theistic evolution as a means of reconciling science with Genesis. During the early 1960s, conservatives attacked *The Message of Genesis,* a book by Midwestern Baptist Theological Seminary professor Ralph H. Elliott. Elliott advocated a critical view of Genesis which sees it as a compilation of various documents rather than a unitive volume written by Moses. In the resulting controversy, Elliott was forced out of his teaching position.

Crucial to Baptist thought has been the authority of the Bible. The Baptist Faith and Message declares the Bible to be divinely inspired with God as its author. In recent decades that belief as been interpreted by some in terms of Biblical inerrancy. Among conservatives that has led to debates on exactly how inerrancy is to be defined. More moderate and "liberal" positions have rejected inerrancy as a means of defining Biblical inspiration.

Organization. The Southern Baptist Convention has a congregational polity. Congregations are related sucessively to three levels of cooperative affiliation. Associations operate on the county level. State conventions include churches in one or more states. Nationally, the annual convention is composed of from one to ten messengers from each congregation which cooperates with the work of the convention and contributes to its support. The national convention has oversight of the national boards and commissions: the Annuity Board, the Foreign Mission Board, the Home Mission Board, the Sunday School Board, the Brotherhood Commission, the Christian Life Commission, the Education Commission, the Historical Commission, the Radio and Television Commission and the Stewardship Commission. It also oversees six seminaries. Broadman and Holman Press, one of America's major publishers of religious literature, is officially the Sunday School Board's publishing arm. The foreign mission program has over 4,000 missionaries in over 130 countries, and almost 5,000 missionaries in the United States.

The Southern Baptist Convention has not been among the most active church bodies in the twentieth-century ecumenical movement that has drawn so many of the larger denominations into cooperative actions. It has preferred to work cooperatively within the larger Baptist family and has been active in the Baptist World Alliance until 1991 it helped fund and staff the Baptist Joint Committee on Public Affairs. It has, however, refrained from participation in such organizations as the World Council of Churches, the National Council of Churches or the National Association of Evangelicals.

Membership: In 1996, the Convention reported 15,691,964 members, 40,565 congregations, and 71,257 ministers.

Educational Facilities: Seminaries:
Golden Gate Baptist Theological Seminary, Mill Valley, California.
Midwestern Baptist Theological Seminary, Kansas City, Missouri.
New Orleans Baptist Theological Seminary, New Orleans, Louisiana.
Southeastern Baptist Theological Seminary, Wake Forest, North Carolina.
Southern Baptist Theological Seminary, Louisville, Kentucky.
Southwestern Baptist Theological Seminary, Fort Worth, Texas.
State Baptist convention cooperating with the Southern Baptist Convention sponsors the following colleges and universities:
Anderson College, Anderson, South Carolina.
Averett College, Danville, Virginia.
Baylor University, Waco, Texas.
Belmont University, Nashville, Tennessee.
Blue Mountain College, Blue Mountain, Mississippi.
Bluefield College, Bluefield, Virginia.
Brewton-Parker College, Mt. Vernon, Georgia.
California Baptist College, Riverside, California.
Campbell University, Buies Creek, North Carolina.
Campbellsville College, Campbellsville, Kentucky.
Carson Newman College, Jefferson City, Tennessee.
Charleston Southern University, Charleston, South Carolina;
Chowar College, Murfreesboro, North Carolina;
Clear Creek Baptist Bible College, Pineville, Kentucky.
Cumberland College, Williamsburg, Kentucky.
Dallas Baptist University, Dallas, Texas.
East Texas Baptist University, Marshall, Texas.
Florida Baptist Theological College, Graceville, Florida.
Furman University, Greenville, South Carolina.
Gardner-Webb University, Boiling Springs, North Carolina.
Georgetown College, Georgetown, Kentucky.
Grand Canyon University, Phoenix, Arizona.
Hannibal-LaGrange College, Hannibal, Missouri.
Hardin-Simmons University, Abilene, Texas.
Houston Baptist University, Houston, Texas.
Howard Payne University, Brownwood, Texas.
Judson College, Marion, Alabama.
Louisiana College, Pineville, Louisiana.
Mars Hill College, Mars Hill, North Carolina.
University of Mary Hardin-Baylor, Belton, Texas.
Mercer University, Macon, Georgia.

Meredith College, Raleigh, North Carolina.
Mississippi College, Clinton, Mississippi.
Missouri Baptist College, St. Louis, Missouri.
University of Mobile, Mobile, Alabama.
North Greenville College, Tigerville, South Carolina.
Oklahoma Baptist University, Shawnee, Oklahoma.
Ouachita Baptist University, Arkadelphia, Arkansas.
Palm Beach Atlantic College, West Palm Beach, Florida.
University of Richmond, Richmond, Virginia.
Samford University, Birmingham, Alabama.
Shorter College, Rome, Georgia.
Southwest Baptist University, Bolivar, Missouri.
Stetson University, DeLand, Florida.
Truett-McConnell College, Cleveland, Georgia.
Union University, Jackson, Tennessee.
Virginia Intermont College, Bristol, Virginia.
Wayland Baptist University, Plainview, Texas.
William Carey College, Hattiesburg, Mississippi.
William Jewell College, Liberty, Missouri.
Williams Baptist College, Walnut Ridge, Arkansas.
Wingate College, Wingate, North Carolina.

Periodicals: *SBC Life.* • *Missions USA.* • *The Commission.* Send orders to PO Box 6767, Richmond, VA 23230.

Sources:

Baker, Robert A., ed. *A Baptist Source Book.* Nashville, TN: Broadman Press, 1966.

Hastings, C. Brownlow. *Introducing Southern Baptists, Their Faith and their Life.* New York: Paulist Press, 1981.

McClellan, Albert. *Meet Southern Baptists.* Nashville, TN: Broadman Press, 1978.

Wallace, O. C. S. *What Baptists Believe.* Nashville, TN: Sunday School Board of the Southern Baptist Convention, 1934.

Wardin, Albert W., Jr. *Baptist Atlas.* Nashville, TN: Broadman Press, 1980.

★869★
Southwide Baptist Fellowship
% John R. Waters
Faith Baptist Church
1607 Greenwood Rd.
Laurens, SC 39360

In 1955 at the meeting of the Carolina Baptist Fellowship at Aiken, South Carolina, Dr. Lee Roberson, pastor of the Highland Park Baptist Church of Chattanooga, Tennessee, the main guest speaker, was asked to lead in the formation of a fundamental Baptist church that would draw from the entire South. At a conference the following year at Dr. Roberson's church, and with the support of the South Carolina group, such a fellowship was formed as the Southern Baptist Fellowship. One hundred and forty-seven clergy and laymen registered as charter members. Though heavily supported by the Carolina Fellowship, the Southern Baptist Fellowship became a separate body. Many of the South Carolina churches are members in both bodies. The present name was adopted in 1963.

A statement of faith continues the Baptist consensus and emphasizes the autonomy of the local church. The group professes belief in premillennialism. It also holds that the Revised Standard Version of the Bible is a "perverted translation." It demands separation from all forms of modernism, especially the National Council of Churches.

The headquarters of the Southwide Baptist Fellowship is in Laurens, South Carolina. The fellowship cooperates with the Commission on Chaplains of the Associated Gospel Churches. Fellowship churches are found in all the Southern states, Wyoming, New Mexico, Iowa, Maine, Oregon, New York, New Jersey, and Wisconsin. Foreign work is being carried out in Ghana, Nigeria, Puerto Rico, Canada, Nassau, Nicaragua, Brazil, Japan, St. Lucia, Cayman Islands, and Spain.

Membership: In 1987 these were over 285 churches on the *Trumpet* list of independent Baptist Churches in South Carolina. The *Trumpet* is the newspaper of the Highland Park Baptist Church.

★870★
Sovereign Grace Baptist Churches
Calvary Grace Baptist Church
Box 7464
Pine Bluff, AR 71611-7464

Out of the post-World War II theological liberalism which many saw as having permeated the churches of the Reformed theological tradition (particularly the large Baptist and Presbyterian denominations), there arose a reaction which emphasized Calvinist theological distinctions, particularly the sovereign grace of God. In 1966, Grace Baptist Church in Pine Bluff, Arkansas, invited people known to be sympathetic to what was becoming a growing movement to a conference at Carlisle, Pennsylvania. The conference became the focus around which cooperative action by otherwise independent churches and pastors could begin. Most of those attending had come out of either the Southern Baptist Convention or, to a lesser extent, the Presbyterian churches. A few were from independent evangelical congregations. Approximately 100-250 ministers attended the Pennsylvania Conference. By 1969, the loosely organized movement had grown large enough to initiate regional conferences, and no less than three periodicals emerged.

Doctrinally, Sovereign Grace congregations are Calvinistic, accept the Philadelphia Baptist Confession of Faith of 1772, and use the great works of the Reformed theologians such as Calvin, Edwards, and Charles Hodge. An extreme congregational polity has been accepted. Local churches are headed by pastors (who are seen as teaching elders) and ruling elders (lay elders).

Besides the annual conference in Pennsylvania, other conferences have grown up, including ones at Ashland, Kentucky, and Pine Bluff, Arkansas. E.W. Johnson, pastor of Calvary Baptist Church in Pine Bluff, edits *Sovereign Grace Message*. The Trinity Reformed Baptist Church of Allentown, Pennsylvania, publishes *The Sword and Trowel*. Among the most substantive of the Sovereign Grace periodicals is the quarterly *Baptist Reformation Review*, begun by Nobert Ward of Nashville, Tennessee. Ward identifies with the Sovereign Grace Movement as a result of his former position within the Primitive Baptist Church. Before 1972, as a Primitive Baptist, he edited *Inquirer*.

Membership: In 1996 there were approximately 300 Sovereign Grace congregations, 3,000 members, and 400 ministers.

Educational Facilities: Spurgeon Theological Seminary, Memphis, Tennessee.

Periodicals: *The Sovereign Grace Message.* • *Searching Together.* Send orders to Box 548, St. Croix Falls, WI 54024. • *Reformation Today.* 2817 Dashwood St., Lakewood, CA 90712.

Sources:

Green, Jay. *God's Everlasting Love for His Chosen People.* Marshallton, DE: Sovereign Grace Publishers, n.d.

Johnson, E. W. *Questions Concerning Evangelism.* Pine Bluff, AR: Sovereign Grace Publishers, 1988.

★871★
Strict Baptists
℅ Zion Strict Baptist Church
1710 Richmond NW
Grand Rapids, MI 49504

Alternate Address: International headquarters: Gospel Standard Strict Baptist Churches, c/o H. Mercer, Hampton, Highworth, Swindon, Wilts., England SN6 7RL.

The Strict Baptists is the American branch of the Gospel Standard Strict Baptist Churches, a division among Baptists that arose in England during the nineteenth century. During the seventeenth century, British Baptists emerged as one segment of the larger Puritan movement, an effort to "purify" the Church of England by appeal to a more literal allegiance to biblical doctrine and practice. Baptists participated in the Puritan debates during the Commonwealth Period, and Baptists were among the leaders of Oliver Cromwell's government. As such, the Baptists had accepted a basic Calvinist theological perspective, which they shared with the Presbyterians. They departed from the Presbyterians (who were in the majority) over church government, the Baptists championing the authority of the local church and the independence of the church from any affiliation with the state. Baptists were further differentiated from fellow Puritans by their acceptance of adult baptism by immersion as the proper mode of initiation of members into the church.

Baptists split into two branches following the theological lines of the controversy among Dutch Calvinists over predestination. General or Arminian Baptists accepted the opinions of Jacob Arminius that allowed for some free will. Particular Baptists believed that God chose or predestined those who would be saved out of sinful humankind. Strict Baptists arose out of the Particular Baptists and might be said to have begun with the founding of *The Gospel Standard, or Feeble Christian's Support* by John Gadsby. *The Gospel Standard* became the vehicle of several prominent Baptist ministers including William Gadsby (father of the magazine's founder), John Warburton, and John Kershaw. The immediate occasion for the founding of the periodical was the appearance of another shortlived magazine advocating the pre-existence of the human soul, however, Gadsby's magazine was in full force in the 1840s when a more serious controversy arose among the Particular Baptists over the nature of the divine sonship of Jesus Christ. The appearance of views denying the eternal sonship of Christ prompted articles in defense of the teaching in *The Gospel Standard* as early as 1844. However, the controversy reached a new level of intensity in 1860 following the publication of a sermon by a Rev. Crowther entitled "The Things Most Surely Believed Among Us, as to the Person, Mission, and Work of Christ." Crowther suggested that Jesus became the son of God as a result of his supernatural begetting in the womb of Mary. By the end of the year the first resolution in support of the eternal sonship was issued by a church in London. Other resolutions followed in 1861 and a gradual separation occurred between those churches that held to the doctrine of Christ's eternal sonship and those that allowed the preaching of the opposite position.

By the 1870s the Strict or Gospel Standard Baptists were recognized as a distinct group within the larger Baptist movement. The Strict Baptists consisted of a number of independent congregations who accepted the basic views espoused by *The Gospel Standard* magazine, and who met in association separate from other Particular Baptists.

The doctrinal controversy of the British Particular Baptists did not transfer to the United States, a nation then caught up in the problems of a Civil War. However, during the late-twentieth century several congregations formally related to the Gospel Standard Baptists have arisen under the name Strict Baptists.

Membership: There are three congregations of Strict Baptists in the United States—one each in Michigan, Montana, and Wisconsin. There are also four congregations in Australia with the main body of Gospel Standard Baptists located in England.

Periodicals: *Gospel Standard Magazine; Friendly Companion* (both published in England and distributed through the church in the United States).

Sources:

Articles of Faith and Rules of Church Order. Grand Rapids, MI: Zion Strict Baptist Church, n.d. 15 pp.

Gosden, J. H. *Believers' Baptism and the Lord's Supper.* Harpenden, Herts, England: Gospel Standard Baptist Trust, 1977. 22 pp.

Paul, S. F. *Historical Sketch of the Gospel Standard Baptists.* London: Gospel Standard Publications, 1945. 86 pp.

Ramsbottom, B. A. *New Testament Church Order.* Grand Rapids, MI: Zion Baptist Church, n.d. 11 pp.

★872★
Ukrainian Evangelical Baptist Convention
% Olexa R. Barbuiziuk
6751 Riverside Dr.
Berwyn, IL 60402

The Ukrainian Evangelical Baptist convention (UEBC) was formed in 1945 as the Ukrainian Missionary and Bible Society by a group of Ukrainian Baptists meeting at Chester, Pennsylvania. The first official assembly was in 1946; the present name was adopted in 1953. The Rev. Paul Bartkow was the first president, serving in that post for twenty years. The UEBC is the conservative branch of the Ukrainian Baptists and is a member of the separatist American Council of Christian Churches.

In line with the anti-communist stance of the American Council of Christian Churches, the convention has developed a program aimed at Iron Curtain countries. Misssionaries have been sent behind the Iron Curtain, and in 1966, the Ukrainian Voice of the Gospel, a biweekly radio program over Trans World Radio in Monte Carlo, began. A publishing House, Doroha Prawdy (The Way of Truth), established in 1954, is operated in cooperation with the sister organization in Canada. Missionary work is carried on among Ukrainian communities in Argentina, Brazil, Paraguay, Australia, France, and Germany. The UEBC supports the Ukrainian Bible Institute in Argentina.

Membership: Not reported. In 1970 there were more than 20 churches scattered across the United States.

Periodicals: *The Messenger of Truth.* Send orders to 690 Berkeley Ave., Elmhurst, IL 60126.

★873★
Ukrainian Evangelical Baptist Convention of Canada
Current address not obtained for this edition.

After the Russian government permitted the British and Foreign Bible Society into Russia to distribute their literature, Baptists began migrating to the Ukraine. In the late nineteenth century, along with other Russian Christian minorities, Ukrainian Baptists began to migrate to Canada. In the early years of the twentieth century, organization proceeded at a swift pace, especially in the western provinces. By 1903 a church was organized at Winnipeg, another a year later at Overstone, Manitoba. In 1907 a congregation was formed in Toronto, and a missionary from England, John Kolesnikoff, arrived to begin work. In 1908 an intercongregational meeting convened at Canora, Saskatchewan.

For a number of years the Canadian-Ukrainian Baptists cooperated directly with the American-based Ukrainian Evangelical Baptist Convention, but in 1950 they reorganized the all-Canadian Ukrainian Evangelical Baptist Convention of Canada. Though independent, the convention remains in fellowship with the United States Ukrainian Baptists. While conservative in belief, the convention is less strict doctrinally than the Union of Slavic Churches of Evangelical Christians and Slavic Baptists of Canada, Inc.

Membership: In 1961 there were 25 churches and 3,200 members.

Sources:

Bolshakoff, Serge. *Russian Nonconformity.* Philadelphia, PA: Westminister Press, 1950.

★874★
Union of Slavic Churches of Evangelical Christians and Slavic Baptists of Canada, Inc.
Current address not obtained for this edition.

As Russian and Ukrainian Baptists moved into Canada they began to divide theologically. Though both groups were conservative, those who were most strict and fundamental in the eastern provinces organized the Russian-Ukrainian Evangelical Baptist Union of Eastern Canada in the late 1920s. Other Canadian-Ukrainian Baptists organized the Ukrainian Evangelical Baptist Convention of Canada. At about the same time, a similar organization was formed in the western provinces, the Union of Slavic Evangelical Christians. Members of the two groups established fraternal ties very quickly. In 1958 a number of the churches of the Slavic Union joined with the Evangelical Baptists to form the Union of Slavic Churches of Evangelical Christians and Slavic Baptists of Canada. The new union was incorporated in 1963.

The union holds to a conservative fundamental Christianity which emphasizes the full inspiration of the Bible, a premillennial eschatology, and eternal punishment for the unsaved. It is affiliated with the Russian-Ukrainian Baptist Union in the United States of America. Mission work is supported in Argentina, Australia, and Europe.

Membership: In the early 1970s there were 11 congregations and approximately 500 members.

★875★
World Baptist Fellowship
3001 W. Division
Arlington, TX 76012

The World Baptist Fellowship emerged around the followers of J. Frank Norris (1877-1952), longtime pastor of First Baptist Church of Fort Worth (1909-1952) and Temple Baptist Church in Detroit (1934-1948). During the 1920s, Norris arose as one of the most charismatic leaders of the fundamentalist movement. Then in 1926, he killed a Fort Worth businessman, the climax to a quarrel he was waging with Roman Catholics in Texas. Though acquitted in court, his name was dropped from the officiary of the Bible Baptist Union. That act, which cut him off from a large segment of the movement, did not stop his active work which only ended with his death in 1952.

The fellowship was organized around an annual meeting held at Norris' Fort Worth Church. In 1939 he began the Bible Baptist Institute which later moved to Arlington, Texas, and became the Bible Baptist Seminary. After Norris' death, the headquarters of the fellowship moved on campus. In early the 1970s they reported over 550 churches with 800 more supporting the work. The main strength is in Texas and Ohio. Most recently the Seminary has added a liberal arts curriculum and is now known as the Arlington Baptist College.

Doctrine is Baptist, with an extremely conservative-fundamentalist approach assumed. Mission work is carried out through Fellowship Missions. Polity is congregational.

Membership: Not reported. In 1995, there were approximately 500,000 members.

Educational Facilities: Arlington Baptist College, Arlington, Texas.

Periodicals: *The Fundamentalist.*

Sources:

Norris, J. Frank. *Practical Lectures on Romans.* Fort Worth, TX: First Baptist Church, n.d.

Russell, C. Allyn. *Voices of American Fundamentalism.* Philadelphia: Westminister Press, 1976.

Primitive Baptists

★876★
Black Primitive Baptists
% Primitive Baptist Library
Rte. 2
Elon College, NC 27244

Until the Civil War, blacks were members of the predominantly white Primitive Baptist associations and worshipped in segregated meeting houses. After the Civil War, the blacks were organized into separate congregations, and associations were gradually formed. In North Alabama, the Indian Creek Association was formed as early as 1869. Among the leaders was Elder Jesse Lee. He was ordained after the War, and in 1868, organized the Bethlehem Church in Washington, Virginia. In 1877, he became the moderator of the newly formed Second Ketocton Association.

Doctrine and practice of the Black Primitive Baptists are like those of the Regulars. They have no periodical. *The Primitive Messenger,* partially underwritten by Elder W. J. Berry, editor of *Old Faith Contender,* lasted only four years in the early 1950s.

Membership: Not reported. In the early 1970s there were 43 associations which averaged approximately five churches per association and 20 members per church. There are approximately 3,000 members.

★877★
Covenanted Baptist Church of Canada
Current address not obtained for this edition.

The Covenanted Baptist Church of Canada traces its roots to Daniel McArthur, a young Presbyterian of Cowal, Scotland. Converted in the early nineteenth century, he began preaching with great success. However, his Bible study led him to become a Baptist and he was baptised and ordained a minister by Elder McFarland of Edinburgh. Among McArthur's converts was Dougald Campbell, who migrated from North Knapdale, Scotland to Aldboro, Elgin County, Ontario in 1818. He joined with the regular Baptists and was ordained. A few years later, however, Campbell felt the Baptists were departing from the strict Calvinism of his Scottish heritage, and he withdrew to organize the Covenanted Baptist Church of Canada. By the 1850s there were five congregations in Aldboro, Dunwick, Lobo, Ekfurd, and Orford (Duart), all in Ontario.

The Covenanted Baptists fellowshipped with no other groups until the mid-1850s, when copies of the American Primitive Baptist periodical *Signs of the Times* arrived in Canada. Gilbert Beebe, editor of the periodical, was the leading voice of Primitive Baptists in the northern United States. Correspondence led to the visit of Elder William McColl, who had been ordained by Beebe, and other Primitive Baptists in Dundas, Ontario. McColl's visit was followed by that of Beebe and other prominent elders, and fellowship between the two churches was established. Fellowship with the Absolute Predestinarians continues to this day.

The Articles of Faith of the Covenanted Baptists affirms belief in the Trinity, Jesus Christ as Lord and Redeemer, righteousness that saves as imputed to the sinner by God's grace, absolute predestination, free and permanent election, the sufficiency of the Holy Scriptures, and believers baptism by immersion. In keeping with their position on predestination, the articles disallow preaching that includes a general call for sinners to repent and respond to the Gospel. The attendance at meetings of other religious groups is frowned upon.

Membership: There are less than 100 members in several churches in Ontario.

Sources:

Hassell, Cushing Briggs. *History of the Church of God.* Middletown, NY: Gilbert Beebe's Sons, 1886.

★878★
National Primitive Baptist Convention of the U.S.A.
6433 Hidden Forest Dr.
Charlotte, NC 28213

Around the turn of the century, there was a movement among the Black Primitive Baptists to organize a national convention. In 1906, Elders Clarence Francis Sams, George S. Crawford, James H. Carey, and others called on their colleagues to join them in a meeting at Huntsville, Alabama, in 1907. Eighty-eight elders from seven Southern states responded. In organizing the convention, of course, the members departed from a main Primitive Baptist concern-that there should be no organization above the loose associations that typically cover several counties.

Doctrinally, the National Primitive Baptist Convention follows the Regular Primitive Baptists. The Convention's creeds profess belief in the "particular election of a definite number of the human race." Footwashing is practiced. The organization is congregational, and at the local level there are two offices-pastor (elder) and deacon or deaconness (mother). The convention meets annually and sponsors Sunday schools and a publishing board.

Membership: Not reported. In 1975, it claimed 606 churches with 250,000 members and 636 ministers.

Sources:

Discipline of the Primitive Baptist Church. Tallahassee, FL: National Primitive Baptist Publishing Board, 1966.

★879★
Primitive Baptists-Absolute Predestinarians
% Primitive Baptist Library
Rte. 2
Elon College, NC 27244

The smallest of the three larger groups of Primitive Baptists is composed of those who differ from the Regulars only on the issue of predestination. While all Primitive Baptists believe that god chose the elect before the foundation of the world, the "Absoluters," as they are often called, believe that God decreed in Himself from all eternity all things that will come to pass from the greatest to the smallest event. A lengthy exposition of their belief, including numerous Scriptural references, is found annually in the Upper County Line Association Minutes. Only a few of the Absolute Predestinarians practice footwashing.

Most Absoluters are to be found in Texas, Alabama, North Carolina, Virginia, and the Northeast. Among the periodicals reflecting the Absolute Predestination position are *Zion's Landmark* issued in Wilson, North Carolina, and *Signs of the Times,* the oldest Primitive Baptist periodical, begun in 1832 and now issued from Danville, Virginia. Elder E. J. Berry has been a major force in Primitive Baptist circles for many years. He developed the Primitive Baptist Library in Elon College, North Carolina, and edits the *Old Faith Contender.*

Membership: Not reported. Fifty-one associations have been located. There are approximately 10 churches to each association, but the average is only about 17 members per church. Thus, a rough estimate of Absoluters would be approximately 8,500, with several hundred in independent churches.

Periodicals: *Signs of the Times.* Send orders to Rte. 1, Box 539, Beechwood Ln., Danville, VA 24541. • *Zion's Landmark.* Send orders to 117 N. Goldsboro St., Wilson, NC 24065. • *Old Faith Contender,* Rte. 2, Elon College, NC 27244.

★880★
Primitive Baptists-Moderates
% Primitive Baptist Library
Rte. 2
Elon College, NC 27244

Alternate Address: No central headquarters. For information: Elder S. T. Tolley, Box 168, Atwood, TN 38220

The largest single grouping of Primitive Baptists is composed of the moderate Calvinist Regulars. They are to be found throughout the South and Midwest, and are most heavily concentrated in North Carolina, Michigan, West Virginia, Georgia, Alabama, and Tennessee. They believe in the depravity of man, often stated as the imputation of Adam's sin to his posterity. The chosen are elected before the foundation of the world; are called, regenerated and sanctified, and are kept by the power of God. Good works are the fruits of faith and are evidence of salvation. In general, evangelism is not engaged in, since God will call his elect. Most practice footwashing. They oppose secret orders, missionary societies, Bible societies, theological seminaries, and related institutions, and will not fellowship with churches which are connected with those organizations.

Among the periodicals serving the Moderates are *The Christian Pathway*, monthly from Atlanta, Georgia; *Baptist Witness*, from Cincinnati; *The Christian Baptist*, from Atwood, Tennessee; and the *Primitive Baptist*, from Thornton, Arkansas. Besides publishing the *Baptist Witness*, Elder Lasserre Bradley, Jr., publishes the *Primitive Baptist Directory*, with more than 1,000 churches listed, and broadcasts the "Baptist Bible Hour" over stations in the South, Midwest, and California. Elder S. T. Tolley is compiling a library at Atwood, Tennessee.

Membership: Not reported. No recent census of Primitive Baptists has been made. In the 1970s, 150 Moderate associations were located. They vary in size from two churches to more than 20. The average size is seven. The average church has fewer than 50 members, all baptized. On that basis, there are more than 50,000 members, not including the membership of almost five hundred churches of the Moderate position which are not affiliated with any associations. Those churches would add another 25,000.

Periodicals: *The Christian Pathway*. Send orders to Box 601, Paris, AR 72855. • *Baptist Witness*. Available from Baptist Bible Hour, Box 17-37, Cincinnati, OH 45217. • *The Primitive Baptist*. Available from Cayce Publishing Co., Thornton, AR 71766. • *The Christian Baptist*. Send orders to Box 168, Atwood, TN 38220.

Sources:

Berry, W. J. *Tracing the True Worship of God*. Elon College, NC: Primitive Publications, 1971.

Bradley, Lasserre, Jr. *What Do Primitive Baptists Believe?*. Cincinnati, OH: Baptist Bible Hour, n.d.

Historical Facts on the Origin of "Campbellism". Atwood, TN: Christian Baptist Library, n.d.

Rives, Samuel Lee. *Meditations Upon Religious Subjects*. Elon College, Primitive Baptist Publishing House, n.d.

Wood, A. D. *The Book of Acts*. Atwood, TN: Christian Baptist Publishing Concern, n.d.

★881★
Primitive Baptists-Progressive
% Pat McCoy
PO Box 69
Culloden, GA 31016

The most easily defined group of Primitive Baptists are the Progressives. In doctrine, Progressives are similar to the Regulars, but differ in their acceptance of innovative forms of congregational life. Included in the congregational life are youth fellowships and Bible study classes, men's brotherhoods and women's societies,

vacation Bible schools, and youth camps. The Progressives' periodical has carried ads for books not written by Primitive Baptists. Beyond the church, the Primitive Baptist Foundation is a non-profit corporation underwriting denominational projects. The Primitive Baptist Builders helps new and struggling churches to build and purchase. In the summer, Bible conferences are held in Georgia and Indiana. "The Lighthouse" is a radio ministry heard in all parts of Georgia and eastern Alabama. Two Bethany Homes—one for men in Millen, Georgia, and one for women in Vidalia, Georgia—serve senior citizens.

Progressive churches are predominantly in Georgia, with scattered congregations in Florida, Alabama, Tennessee, Indiana, Mississippi, Texas, Louisiana, Missouri, and Illinois. A ministerial association functions among the non-associational churches of Florida. A music workshop is held annually for all church musicians and choirs.

Membership: In 1997 there were 128 churches 7,650 members, and 133 ministers reported.

Periodicals: *The Banner Herald*. Send orders to 403 Oaklawn Dr., Swainsboro, GA 30401. • *Quarterly Ministry Report*. Available from Multimedia Ministry, PO Box 69, Culloden, GA 31016. • *Donetsk Report*, PO Box 69, Culloden, GA 31016.

Sources:

Primitive Baptist Church Manual. Jesup, GA: Banner Publications, n.d.

Black Baptists

★882★
Assembly of Free Spirit Baptist Churches
3627 Mt. Elliott
Detroit, MI 48207

The Assembly of Free Spirit Baptist Churches (AFSBC) was founded in 1985 by former ministers and members of the older Baptist churches who had adopted a spontaneous worship style commonly associated with Pentecostalism (but not Pentecostal doctrine) and who felt excluded from other Baptists. Baptists have, as a whole, adopted a more staid worship format and have questioned the freewheeling and expressive worship associated with traditional gatherings within African American churches. The assembly has an outreach ministry using inspirational audiotapes.

Membership: In 1994 the church reported 85,000 members.

★883★
Fundamental Baptist Fellowship Association
Current address not obtained for this edition.

The Fundamental Baptist Fellowship Association was formed in 1962 by black members of the General Association of Regular Baptist Churches (GARBC). The black members came into the GARBC as a result of missionary work but felt that the GARBC would not accept them into the full fellowship. They presently cooperate with the Conservative Baptist Association.

Membership: Not reported. In the early 1970s there were approximately 10 churches.

★884★
National Baptist Convention of America
% National Baptist Publishing Board
7145 Centennial Blvd.
Nashville, TN 37209

In 1915, an issue arose in the National Baptist Convention of the U.S.A., Inc. over the ownership of the publishing house. Early in the Convention's life, the Rev. R. H. Boyd, a brilliant businessman, was made corresponding secretary of the publication board. Under his leadership, the publishing house did over two million dollars in business in the first decade. As time passed, however, some members of the Convention realized that the publishing interest had been built on Boyd's property, and all the materials had been copyrighted in his name. Further, no proceeds were being donated to other Convention activities.

In a showdown, the 1915 Convention moved to correct its mistake by adopting a new charter which clarified the subservient position of the boards. Refusing to comply, Boyd withdrew the publishing house from the Convention and made it the center of a second National Baptist Convention, called the National Baptist Convention of America. Because of its refusal to accept the charter, it is usually referred to as "unincorporated." Missions are carried on in Jamaica, Panama, and Africa. Ten colleges and seminaries are supported.

Membership: Not reported. The latest statistics are from 1956 when there were a reported 2,668,799 members, 11,398 churches, and 28,574 ministers.

Educational Facilities: Central Baptist Theological Seminary, Indianapolis, Indiana.

Morehouse School of Religion, Atlanta, Georgia.

Sources:

Boyd, R. H. *Boyd's National Baptist Pastor's Guide.* Nashville, TN: National Baptist Publishing Board, 1983.

_____, ed. *The National Baptist Hymn Book.* Nashville, TN: National Baptist Publishing Board, 1906.

Pius, N. H. *An Outline of Baptist History.* Nashville, TN: National Baptist Publishing Board, 1911.

★885★
National Baptist Convention of the U.S.A., Inc.
% Dr. T. G. Jemison, President
915 Spain St.
Baton Rouge, LA 70802

The National Baptist Convention of the U.S.A. came into existence after the adoption of a resolution before the Foreign Mission Baptist Convention of the U.S.A. to merge itself, the American National Baptist Convention, and the Baptist National Educational Convention. To these three would be added a publications board for Sunday school literature. The Convention was formed in Atlanta, Georgia, in 1895. Elected president and corresponding secretary of foreign missions were Rev. E. C. Morris and Lewis G. Jordan, respectively. Both were able men; the National Baptist Convention's survival, stability, and success were in no small part due to their long terms in office.

Doctrine and government were taken over from the white Baptists. The congregational form of church life allowed a ready adaptation to the black culture, which used religious forms as a socially accepted way to express their frustration and to protest their conditions. The worship developed a high degree of emotional expression, making little reference to traditional liturgical forms. (While freed from the rituals of their white parents in the faith, the local church developed its own "forms," which seem spontaneous to the occasional visitor. In fact, the black Baptists allowed themselves to create a new religious culture, the pattern of which they follow weekly in their service.)

Within two years of its founding, the new National Baptist Convention ran into trouble when Jordan moved its offices from Richmond to Louisville. The Virginia Brethren, fearing a loss of power, withdrew support. They formed the Lott Carey Missionary Convention, which still exists as an independent missionary society. A more serious disagreement split the denomination in 1915.

For twenty-nine years (1953-1982) the National Baptists were led by J. H. Jackson. He was succeeded in 1982 by T. J. Jamison, the son of the convention's president from 1941-1953, D. V. Jemison. The current president is Henry J. Lyons. There is mission work in Africa and the Bahamas. The group operates five colleges, a theological seminary, and a training school for women and girls.

Membership: Not reported. In 1984 there were an estimated 7,000,000 members in over 30,000 congregations.

Educational Facilities: Shaw University, Raleigh, North Carolina.

Shaw Divinity School, Raleigh, North Carolina.
National Baptist College, Nashville, Tennessee.
Central Baptist Theological Seminary, Indianapolis, Indiana.
Morehouse School of Religion, Atlanta, Georgia.
Selma University, Selma, Alabama.
American Baptist Theological Seminary, Nashville, Tennessee.

Periodicals: *National Baptist Voice.* Send orders to 2900 3rd Ave., Richmond, VA 23222.

Remarks: In the summer of 1997 Convention President Henry J. Lyons became involved in what has been a growing controversy after his wife was accused of setting fire to a house owned by Lyons with another woman. She eventually confessed and was sentenced to five years probation. The incident, however, led to an investigation of Lyons and charges of widespread misuse of Convention funds including the diversion of funds intended for the rebuilding of black churches. In September 1997, he survived three no-confidence votes at the Convention's annual meeting. However, his problems did not go away. Early in 1998 he was indicted for theft and racketeering. Lyons has pleaded innocence and adjudication of the charges continues as this edition goes to press.

In the midst of the investigation, charges have also been leveled that the claims by the Convention to have more than eight million members is false and that the true membership of the convention is closer to one million.

Sources:

Jackson, J. H. *A Story of Christian Activism.* Nashville, TN: Townsend Press, 1980.

___. *Unholy Shadows and Freedom's Holy Light.* Nashville, TN: Townsend Press, 1967.

The National Baptist Pulpit. Nashville, TN: Sunday School Publishing Board, 1981.

Pegues, A. W. *Our Baptist Ministers and Schools.* Springfield, MA: Wiley & Co., 1892.

Pelt, Owen D., and Ralph Lee Smith. *The Story of the National Baptists.* New York: Vantage Press, 1960.

★886★
National Baptist Evangelical Life and Soul Saving Assembly of the U.S.A.
441-61 Monroe Ave.
Detroit, MI 48226

The National Baptist Evangelical Life and Soul Saving Assembly of the U.S.A. was founded by A. A. Banks in 1920 in Kansas City, Missouri. It was begun as a city mission and evangelical movement within the National Baptist Convention of America, with which it remained affiliated for 15 years. Differences arose in the mid-1930s, and in 1936 at Birmingham, Alabama, the Assembly declared itself independent. Centers were established in cities across the nation.

No official statements regulate the doctrine of the Assembly, but generally the doctrine follows that of the National Baptist Convention of America. Relief work, charitable activity, and evangelizing are the main concerns of the Association. Each member hopes to add one member to the kingdom annually. Correspondence courses have been developed in evangelism, missions, pastoral ministry, and the work of deacons and laymen. Degrees are awarded for these studies.

Membership: Not reported. In 1951 there were 57,674 members, 264 churches and 137 ministers.

★887★

National Missionary Baptist Convention of America
719 Crosby St.
San Diego, CA 92113

The National Missionary Baptist Convention of America was founded in 1988 as the result of a schism in the National Baptist Convention of America. The crux of the conflict was the National Baptist Publishing Board. The Board, which had been established in the 1890s by R. H. Boyd, had operated as an independent corporation headed by Boyd and his descendants. In 1915, a disagreement over the relationship of the Board to the National Baptist Convention led to a split and to the formation of the National Baptist Convention of the U.S.A., Inc., which wished to have a publishing concern under its own control, and the National Baptist Convention of America, which continued the relationship with the Boyd family's National Baptist Publishing Board.

Over the years, the Board supplied many services to the Convention. Among these has been an annual summer Sunday School Congress, a teacher training school which drew more than 20,000 students. However, the Board made no accounting of the profits from such activities nor did the Convention share in the revenues.

In the mid 1980s, voices began to rise within the Convention calling for a reordering of the relationship between it and the Publishing Board. At a meeting in the summer of 1988, a majority of the attendees at the annual meeting of the National Baptist Convention of America voted to break ties with the Publishing Board and to begin conducting an independent Sunday School Congress. As a result, those who disagreed with the decision met in Dallas, Texas, in November 1988, and organized the National Missionary Baptist Convention. They have remained loyal to the Publishing House and will continue to support its annual Sunday School Congress. Rev. S. M. Lockridge of San Diego, California, was elected as the first president of the Convention.

Organizers of the new Convention claim their share of the history of the National Baptists for the last century. It is too early yet to see what percentage of the five million plus members will adhere to the continuing National Baptist Convention of America or to the National Missionary Baptist Convention, though the majority has seemed to favor the new convention.

Membership: Not reported. At the time of the schism, there were approximately 5 million members of the National Baptist Convention of America. It is not yet known haw many will adhere to the new convention though churches with a cummulative membership of over a million have indicated their allegiance.

Sources:

Waddle, Ray. "Baptists' Split Intensifies Over Rival Publishing Boards." *Nashville Tennessean* (March 11, 1989).

★888★

Progressive National Baptist Convention, Inc.
601 50th St., NE
Washington, DC 20019

The Progressive National Baptist Convention was formed in 1961 following a dispute over the tenure of the presidency at the 1960 meeting of the National Baptist Convention of the U.S.A., Inc. In 1957, Dr. J. H. Jackson, who had been elected president in 1953, declined to step down and ruled the four-year tenure rule out of the Constitution. Prior to the adoption of the rule in 1952, presidents had served for life. At the 1960 Convention session, dissatisfaction came to a head in the attempt to elect Dr. G. C. Taylor as Dr. Jackson's successor. The failure of Dr. Taylor's supporters led in 1961 to the call for a meeting to form a new National Baptist Convention by Dr. L. V. Booth of Zion Baptist Church, Cincinnati, Ohio. He was elected the first president of the new Progressive National Baptist Convention.

Also at issue in the 1961 break was denominational support for the Civil Rights Movement, then gaining momentum in the South.

Those who formed the new convention represented the strongest backers of Martin Luther King, Jr., who was among those who left to join the Progressives, who in turn gave King their full support.

The convention is in agreement on doctrine with its parent body, the disagreements being concerned with organization and social policy. It has organized nationally with two-year terms for all officers, except the executive secretary, who has an eight-year term. The women's auxiliary was formed in 1962 and a Department of Christian Education, Home Mission Board, and Foreign Mission Bureau were soon added.

Membership: In 1995 there were 2,000 churches and 2,500,000, members.

Educational Facilities: Central Baptist Theological Seminary, Indianapolis, Indiana.

Morehouse School of Religion, Atlanta, Georgia.

Periodicals: *Baptist Progress*. Send orders to 712-14 Quincy St., Brooklyn, NY 11221.

Sources:

King, Martin Luther, Jr. *Strength to Love*. New York: Harper & Row, 1963.

___. *Why We Can't Wait*. New York: Harper & Row, 1964.

General Baptists

★889★

Baptist General Conference
2002 S. Arlington Heights Rd.
Arlington Heights, IL 60005

Gustaf Palmquist was a Swedish Lutheran preacher and teacher who migrated to America in the mid-nineteenth century. In 1852, shortly after his conversion and baptism in an English-speaking Baptist church in Galesburg, Illinois, he baptized three immigrant Swedes in the Mississippi River and organized a Swedish Baptist Church in Rock Island, Illinois. Other churches of immigrant Swedish Baptists were organized wherever immigrant Swedes settled—in rural areas as well as in large cities in the Medwest and Northeast. By 1864 there were 11 such churches.

Doctrine is predominantly Arminian Baptist with some Reformed Baptist emphases. There are two ordinances, baptism and the Lord's Supper. The polity is congregational. There is an annual delegated meeting of the churches. A 25-member board of overseers is drawn from representatives of the various denominational boards and the thirteen districts. The boards implement the program of the Conference. The home missions board (now Global Church Planting) oversees work in the Virgin Islands, and among American Indians. The board of foreign missions was first appointed in 1944. Before that time, mission work had been carried on through various independent agencies and the American Baptist Foreign Mission Society. Since 1944, work has been established in India, Japan, the Philippines, Ethiopia, Mexico, Cameroon, Ivory Coast, Brazil, Argentina, Thailand, Uruguay, the Middle East, Central Asia, Bulgaria, France, Slovakia, and Vietnam.

Membership: In 1997 the conference reported 134,795 members, 879 churches, and 1,700 ministers.

Educational Facilities: Bethel College, St. Paul, Minnesota. Bethel Theological Seminary, St. Paul, Minnesota, and San Diego, California.

Periodicals: *The Standard*. • *Alive in Christ*. • *New Life*.

Sources:

Ericson, C. George. *Harvest on the Prairies*. Chicago: Baptist Conference Press, 1956.

Guston, David, and Martin Erikson. *Fifteen Eventful Years*. Chicago: Harvest Publications, 1961.

Johnson, Gordon H. *My Church*. Chicago: Harvest Publications, 1963.

Olson, Adolf. *A Centenary History*. Chicago: Baptist Conference Press, 1952.

★890★
Colorado Reform Baptist Church
% Bishop William T. Conklin
Box 12514
Denver, CO 80212

The Colorado Reform Baptist Church was formed in 1981 by a small group of Baptist congregations that agreed to share a mutual commitment to a loose and free association in order to further common aims, including cooperation in mission and educational work. The church finds its basis in the reformist tradition of Roger Williams and Anne Hutchinson. Not to be confused with Reformed theology, the reformist tradition is Arminian and stresses the mission of Christ to correct and address the social condition of humanity. Tenets of civil rights and religious liberty are strongly affirmed.

The church is Trinitarian in its theology. It departs from many Baptists by its observance of seven ordinances: baptism, the gifts of the Holy Spirit, marriage, repentance, healing, communion (the Lord's Table) and spiritual vocations (ordination). The church has a congregational polity. A conference, representing all the congregations, meets annually. It selects a board of directors and a bishop to lead the church and oversee the boards and agencies. A very active social action ministry to address the problems of racism, sexism, hunger, poverty, political prisoners, and other issues is supported. Ecumenical activities are carried out through the Association of Baptist Fellowships.

Membership: In 1987 the church reported 38 member congregations with 43 ordained ministers. Each of the approximately 2,015 members is considered a lay minister. Missions are currently supported in Costa Rica, Mexico, Colombia, Grand Cayman, and West Germany.

Educational Facilities: Reform Baptist Theological Seminary, Denver, Colorado.

Periodicals: *Baptist Voice.* • *Roger Williams Review.*

★891★
General Association of General Baptists
100 Stinson Dr.
Poplar Bluff, MO 63901

The General Association of General Baptists dates to the work of Benoni Stinson. He was a member of a United Baptist group formed in Kentucky in 1801 by the union of Separate Baptists and Regular Baptists. These United Baptists adopted an article of faith that allowed Arminian preaching, which emphasized free will, not predestination. Stinson was baptized in 1820, joined a United Baptist Church in Wayne County, Kentucky, and was ordained in 1821. He then moved to Indiana. The Wabash United Baptist Association, however, would not tolerate his Arminian free-will views, so he organized the independent New Hope Church near Evansville, Indiana. He soon had a thriving congregation. Tension with Indiana's predominantly Calvinistic Baptists led to the founding of other churches with an Arminian perspective.

The articles of the second church, Liberty Church, professed faith in the unlimited atonement which must be apprehended through faith and the final perseverance through grace to glory. The church practiced closed communion. In 1824, the churches that followed Stinson's Arminian tenets organized the Liberty Association of General Baptists. The associations's growth was sporadic for a decade but became steady in the 1830s. The movement spread south and west.

Doctrinally, the General Baptists are similar to the Methodists. They believe in a general atonement and practice open communion. Some churches also practice footwashing. The polity is congregational, and churches are organized in local and state associa-

tions. A general association was organized in 1870. Ordinations are approved by local bodies of ministers and deacons.

The general association is the highest cooperative agency in the church. The association's program is implemented by the Council of Associations elected by local associations. The Council publishes the *General Baptist Messenger*. The foreign mission board conducts work in Guam, Saipan, Jamaica, and the Philippines, and there is a Bible college at Davao City in the Philippine Islands. The association sponsors two nursing homes, one in Campbell, Missouri, and the other in Mt. Carmel, Illinois.

Membership: In 1989 the association reported 70,461 members, 801 congregations, and 1,477 ministers. There were an additional 14,820 members overseas in churches in Jamaica, India, the Philippine Islands, and the Marianas.

Educational Facilities: Oakland City College, Oakland City, Indiana.

General Baptist Bible College, Davao City, Philippines.

Periodicals: *General Baptist Messenger.* • *Capsule.* • *Voice.*

Sources:

Doctrines and Usages of General Baptists and Worker's Handbook. Poplar Bluff, MO: General Baptist Press, 1970.

Latch, Ollie. *History of the General Baptists.* Poplar Bluff, MO: General Baptist Press, 1954.

★892★
General Six-Principle Baptists
Rhode Island Conference
350 Davisville Rd.
North Kingstown, RI 02852

In 1652, the historic Providence Baptist Church, once associated with Roger Williams, split. The occasion was the development within the church of an Arminian majority who held to the six principles of Hebrews 6:1-2: repentance, faith, baptism, the laying-on-of-hands, resurrection of the dead, and a final judgment. Soon other churches were organized, and conferences were formed in Rhode Island, Massachusetts, and Pennsylvania.

The distinctive doctrine of the six principles is the laying-on-of-hands. This act is performed when members are received into the church, as a sign of the reception of the gifts of the Holy Spirit. Polity is congregational, but the conference composed of delegates of the various churches retains specific powers. A council of the ordained ministers approves all ordinations. Decisions of the conference on questions submitted to it are final. Never a large denomination, the Six-Principle Baptists had dwindled to three congregations, all in Rhode Island, by 1969. There were 134 members.

Membership: Not reported. In 1970, there were 7 churches, 175 members and 7 ministers.

★893★
National Association of Free Will Baptists, Inc.
PO Box 5002
Antioch, TN 37011-5002

The National Association of Free Will Baptists dates to 1727 when Paul Palmer organized a church at Perquimans, Chowan County, North Carolina. The church grew and spread. A yearly meeting was formed in 1752 and included 16 churches. A general conference was formed in 1827; a doctrinal statement was issued in 1834. For many years, these churches were in communion with the Free Will Baptists in the North. But most of the northern brethren were absorbed by the inclusive Northern Baptist Convention, now the American Baptist Churches in the U.S.A.

In 1916, the general conference expanded by the addition of non-aligned churches in Oklahoma, Texas, Missouri, Kansas, and North Carolina, and formed the General Association of Free Will Baptists. Controversy developed between the churches in Tennessee and North Carolina over footwashing as an ordinance, and in 1921, the churches in the South withdrew and formed the Eastern General Conference. Working out a settlement took 14 years, but in 1935, the National Association of Free Will Baptists was formed.

The Free Will Baptist movement developed in the maritime provinces of Canada in the early nineteenth century. In 1932, a number of groups came together to form the Christian Conference Church, which became the Free Christian Baptists in 1847. Among the ministers in the latter half of the century was the capable George W. Orser of Carleton County, New Brunswick. Orser found himself in the middle of controversy as he began to call for an "apostolic" or "primitive" church order. He opposed salaries, and, in large part, education for ministers. In the 1870's, Orser withdrew from the church and formed the Primitive Baptist Conference of New Brunswick, Maine, and Nova Scotia. Headquarters were eventually established as the Saint John Valley Bible Camp at Hartland, New Brunswick. In 1981, after a century of independent existence, the conference voted to join the National Association of Free Will Baptists and became the Atlantic Canada Association of Free Will Baptists.

Beliefs. In 1935, the association adopted a statement of "The Faith of Free Will Baptists," which, with minor amendments added over the years, remains its position. It affirms a belief in an infallible and inerrant Bible, God as Father, Son and Holy Spirit, a universal atonement in Christ, salvation by grace through faith, the possibility of a believer falling from a state of grace into unbelief, tithing, the resurrection, and final judgment. There are three ordinances—baptism, the Lord's Supper and foot washing.

Organization. The association is organized by congregations who freely associate together in district, state and the national associations. The National Association conducts foreign missions in Spain, Panama, Cuba, Brazil, Uruguay, France, the Ivory Coast, India, and Japan. North American missions are sponsored in Canada, Mexico, Alaska, Hawaii, Puerto Rico, and the Virgin Islands.

Membership: In 1997 the association reported 210,305 members, 2,489 churches, and 4,705 ministers in the United States. There are 12 congregations and 323 members in the Atlantic Canada Association.

Educational Facilities: Free Will Baptist Bible College, Nashville, Tennessee.

Hillsdale Free Will Baptist College, Moore, Oklahoma.

California Christian College, Fresno, California.

Southeastern Free Will =Baptist College, Wendell, North Carolina.

Periodicals: *Contact.* • *Heartbeat.* • *Co-Laborer.* • *Attack.* • *Mission Grams.*

Sources:

Buzzell, John. *The Life of Elder Benjamin Randall.* Hampton, New Brunswick: Atlantic Press, 1970.

Cox, Violet. *Missions on the Move.* Nashville, TN: Woman's National Auxiliary Convention, [1966].

Davidson, William F. *The Free Will Baptists in America.* Nashville, TN: Randall House Publishers, 1985.

Picirilli, Robert E. *History of Free Will Baptist Associations.* Nashville, TN: Randall House Publications, 1976.

A Treatise of the Faith and Practices of the Free Will Baptists. Nashville, TN: Executive Office of the National Association of Free Will Baptists, 1981.

★894★
Original Free Will Baptists, North Carolina State Convention
Box 39
Ayden, NC 28513

History. General Baptists, most known as Free Will Baptists after they arrived in the American colonies, came into North Caro-

lina in the late seventeenth century from England. The first congregation in the Southern colonies was a house church at Cisco Crossroads near Edenton, North Carolina, organized by the Rev. Paul Palmer and some 30 others. Palmer went on to do evangelistic work throughout the colony and organized other churches. In 1852, an association was organized, though most of the churches became apart of the Calvinistic Baptists, and a reorganization of the remaining five churches had to take place. By the early 1800s, the churches were meeting as a general conference (of North Carolina). In 1886, this conference divided into a western and eastern conference. Other conferences were formed in part drawing on work in South Carolina. In 1913, a state convention was organized. It developed a number of projects including the Free Will Baptist Press, an orphanage, an assembly grounds, a college, and a seminary.

For many years the North Carolina Convention was part of the larger Free Will Baptist work and joined in the formation of the National Association of Free Will Baptists in 1935. However, over the years several areas of tension emerged between the convention and the national association. For example, when the national association decided to establish a college, it was placed in Nashville, Tennessee, rather than in North Carolina. Soon, it was noted, activities began to shift toward Nashville. The North Carolina Baptists had owned and operated a press and published both Sunday school material and the periodical for the denomination. A struggle for control between the press and the national association (and its college graduates) developed and was never fully resolved. Finally, in 1958, the North Carolina Convention and the national association came into open conflict when they took opposite sides in a disturbance in the Edgemont Church at Durham, North Carolina. A law suit developed and in 1961, the convention withdrew from the national association. It became an independent body and eventually assumed its present name.

Beliefs. The Original Free Will Baptists are at one in doctrine with other Free Will Baptists. The articles of faith affirm human free will and that the status of the elect is conferred on all who have faith in Christ. Three ordinances are observed, baptism by immersion, the Lord's Supper, and foot washing. The church covenant calls upon members to avoid all appearance of evil; to abstain from all sinful amusements; to not engage in the buying, selling or using of intoxicating beverages; and to be honest in all matters.

The convention is congregational in polity. The convention, however, reserves the right to settle disputes within the local churches where such disputes cannot be settled locally. Churches are organized into conferences and the conferences makeup the state convention. The convention oversees the Cragmont Assembly at Black Mountain, a children's home at Middlesex, and its several boards and agencies. The Free Will Baptist Press, founded in 1873, is the oldest ministry program. Foreign missions are conducted in Austria (in conjunction with the Slavic Gospel Association), Mexico, the Philippines, and India. Home mission programs include work among Laotian refugees in six states and Canada, and Spanish-speaking work in Florida.

Membership: In 1987, the convention reported 40,000 members, 275 congregations, and 384 ministers.

Educational Facilities: Mount Olive College, Mount Olive, North Carolina.

Palawan Bible Institute/College, Palawan, Philippines.

Periodicals: *The Free Will Baptist.*

Sources:

The Articles of Faith and Principles of Church Government for Original Free Will Baptists (of the English General Baptist Heritage). Ayden, NC: Free Will Baptist Press Foundation, 1976.

Barfield, J. M., and Thad Harrison. *History of the Free Will Baptists of North Carolina.* 2 vols. Ayden, NC: Free Will Baptist Press, [1959].

Cherry, Floyd B. *An Introduction to Original Free Will Baptists.* Ayden, NC: Free Will Baptist Press Foundation, 1974.

Picirilli, Robert E. *History of the Free Will Baptist State Associations.* Nashville, TN: Randall House Publications, 1976.

★895★
United Baptists
No central headquarters

The United Baptists were formed by a union of the Separate Baptists and the Regular Baptists in 1786. The Separate Baptists were former Congregationalists who became Baptists. The Regular Baptists claimed to represent the Baptists before dissension over Calvinist and Arminian beliefs split many Baptist bodies. In 1772, the Kehukee Association of Regular Baptists made the first overtures toward union with the Separate Baptists. Because there was little difference between the groups, union was consummated in 1786. Most of the United Baptist groups dropped the term "united" after awhile, and they exist within the larger Baptist bodies. But several associations in Kentucky, West Virginia, and Missouri persist.

The churches follow a congregational polity and are organized into eleven associations. They follow the early Baptists in doctrine; they lean toward Arminianism. They practice footwashing. Communion is closed. The Cumberland River Association supports the Eastern Baptist Institute in Somerset, Kentucky.

Membership: Not reported. At last report, there were 63,641 members in 568 churches in 26 associations.

Educational Facilities: Eastern Baptist Institute, Somerset, Kentucky.

★896★
United Free-Will Baptist Church
Current address not obtained for this edition.

Racial division did not escape the Free Will Baptists, but did wait until the twentieth century. The predominantly black United Free Will Baptist Church was established in 1901. Like its parent body, it is Arminian in theology and practices footwashing and anointing the sick with oil. The congregational polity was modified within a system of district, quarterly, annual, and general conferences. The local church is autonomous in regard to business, elections, and form of government, but the conferences have the power to decide the questions of doctrine.

Membership: Not reported. In 1952 there were 836 churches and 100,000 members.

Educational Facilities: Kingston College, Kingston, North Carolina.

Periodicals: *The Free Will Baptist Advocate.*

Seventh Day Baptists

★897★
Seventh Day Baptist General Conference USA and Canada
Seventh Day Baptist Center
3120 Kennedy Rd.
PO Box 1678
Janesville, WI 53547

The English-speaking Sabbatarian Baptists organized their conference in 1801. Headquartered in Janesville, Wisconsin, the conference is composed of autonomous churches which meet together annually. The conference is divided into eight associations. They differ from other Baptists only in the keeping of the Sabbath.

The Seventh-Day Baptists established a headquarters for the first time in the 1920s in the Seventh-Day Baptist Building in Plainfield, New Jersey. In 1982 the headquarters were moved to Janesville, Wisconsin, and the Plainfield property sold. The new center houses the various denominational agencies, including the publishing house. The American Sabbath Tract Society, a major distributor of Sabbath literature in America and the world, merged into the General Conference in 1986. The General Conference supports an active historical society, missionary society, and board of Christian education.

Affiliated Seventh-Day Baptists are also found in 20 countries of Europe, Africa, Asia, and Latin America. The General Conference is a member of the Baptist World Alliance, the North American Baptist Fellowship, and the Baptist Joint Committee on Public Affairs. It was formerly a member of the World Council of Churches and the National Council of Churches, but has withdrawn.

Membership: In 1995 the conference reported 4,500 members, 86 churches, and 77 ministers. There are more than 50,000 members worldwide.

Periodicals: *The Sabbath Recorder.*

Sources:

A Manual for Procedures for Seventh Day Baptist Churches. Plainfield, NJ: Seventh Day Baptists General Conference.

Saunders, Herbert E. *The Sabbath: Symbol of Creation and Re-Creation.* Plainfield, NJ: American Sabbath Tract Society, 1970.

Seventh Day Baptists in Europe and America. 3 vols. Plainfield, NJ: Seventh Day Baptist General Conference, 1910-72.

Stillman, Katl G. *Seventh Day Baptists in New England, 1671-1971.* Plainfield, NJ: Seventh Day Baptist Historical Society, 1971.

Thomsen, Russel J. *Seventh-Day Baptists—Their Legacy to Adventists.* Mountain View, CA: Pacific Press Publishing Assn., 1971.

★898★
Seventh Day Baptists (German)
Current address not obtained for this edition.

In 1764, as the work of Johann Beissel at the Ephrata colony declined, a group of German Seventh Day Baptists settled at Snow Hill, Pennsylvania. In 1800, a society was organized. From here, other congregations were organized (five by 1900). The German Baptists differ from their English counterparts in their practice of triune forward immersion, footwashing at the communion service, the anointing of the sick, the blessing of infants, and induction into the ministry by a personal request for ordination rather than election by the congregation. They are also non-combatants. An annual delegated general conference is held.

Membership: Not reported.

Christian Church

★899★
Amended Christadelphians
% Christadelphian Book Supply
14651 Auburndale
Livonia, MI 48154

In 1898, the prominent Birmingham, England, ecclesia of the Christadelphians accepted an amended text of the statement of faith which affirmed that some who had not been justified by the blood of Christ would be resurrected for judgment by Christ prior to His establishment of His kingdom. The revised text had been drawn up by Robert Roberts, the editor of *The Christadelphian*, the group's leading periodical. The majority of Christadelphians accepted Roberts' position. It is their belief that those judged to be unworthy to receive immortality and life in the kingdom will be annihilated. *The Christadelphian* remains the prime organ among those who accept the amended statement.

In the United States, the majority also accepted the amendment. During the twentieth century the position was championed for many years by *Christadelphian Tidings of the Kingdom of God*, published by Donald H. Styles, of Franklin, Michigan. Other periodicals include *The Sunday School Journal* published in Meridian,

Connecticut, and *The Watchman* published in Austin, Texas. Located at San Mateo is the Christadelphia Retirement Community, Inc., supported by the Amended ecclesias. Week-long, regional Bible schools are held around the country. A mail-order library is operated by the Christadelphian Book Supply, located at the address given above.

Affiliated amended assemblies in Australia publish materials through the Gospel Publicity League.

Membership: In 1992, there were approximately 4,000 members in 90 amended assemblies in the United States. There were an estimated 50,000 members worldwide.

Periodicals: *Christadelphian Tidings.* Send orders to Box 250305, Franklin, MI 48025.

Sources:

Christadelphian Hymn Book. Birmingham, England: Christadelphian, 1964.

A Declaration of the Truth Revealed in the Bible. Birmingham, England: Christadelphian, 1967.

One Hundred Years of The Christadelphian. Birmingham, England: Christadelphian, 1964.

★900★
Christian Church (Disciples of Christ)
222 S. Downey Ave.
Box 1986
Indianapolis, IN 46206

Continuing the thrust of the International Convention of Christian Churches (described in the introductory material for this volume) is the Christian Church (Disciples of Christ). At the 1968 annual assembly of the International Assembly, a restructuring of the Convention was accomplished. The Convention was voted out of existence and was replaced with a strong international structure. The Disciples were no longer a loosely formed confederation of individuals and congregations with a delegated general assembly. The change is a recognition by the Disciples that they have become another denomination.

The general assembly meets every two years and is composed of representatives from each congregational region and all ministers. It elects the general board of 250 members, which in turn elects an administrative committee to implement programs.

Membership: In 1990, the church reported 1,043,943 members, 4,105 congregations, and 6,854 ministers.

Educational Facilities: Barton College, Wilson, North Carolina. Bethany College, Bethany, West Virginia. Brite Divinity School, Fort Worth, Texas. Chapman College, Orange, California. Christian Theological Seminary, Indianapolis, Indiana. Columbia College, Columbia, Missouri. Culver-Stockton College, Canton, Missouri. Drake University, Des Moines, Iowa. Eureka College, Eureka, Illinois. Hiram College, Hiram, Ohio. Jarvis Christian College, Hawkins, Texas. Lexington Theological Seminary, Lexington, Kentucky. Lynchburg College, Lynchburg, Virginia. Northwest Christian College, Eugene, Oregon. Phillips University, Enid, Oklahoma. Texas Christian University, Fort Worth, Texas. Tougaloo College, Tougaloo, Mississipppi. Transylvania University, Lexington, Kentucky. William Woods College, Fulton, Missouri.

Periodicals: *The Disciple.* Send orders to Box 179, St. Louis, MO 63166.

Sources:

Garrison, Winfred. *Heritage and Destiny.* St. Louis, MO: Bethany Press, 1961.

Harrell, David Edwin, Jr. *The Social Sources of Division in the Disciples of Christ, 1865-1900.* Atlanta, GA: Publishing Systems, 1973.

McAllister, Lester G., and William E. Tucker. *Journey in Faith.* St. Louis, MO: Bethany Press, 1975.

Short, Howard Elmo. *Doctrine and Thought of the Disciples of Christ.* St. Louis: Christian Board of Publication, 1951.

Sprague, William L., and Jane Heaton, eds. *Our Christian Church Heritage: Journeying in Faith.* St. Louis, MO: Christian Board of Publication, [1978].

★901★
Christian Churches and Churches of Christ
No central address. For information:
North American Christian Convention
4210 Bridgetown Rd.
Cincinnati, OH 45811

Christian churches and churches of Christ constitute one branch of the restorationist movement which emerged among protestant and free church leaders in the early nineteenth century on the American frontier. Prominent leaders of the movement included Barton Stone (a former Presbyterian), Thomas Campbell and his son Alexander Campbell (both also former Presbyterians), and evangelist Walter Scott (a former Baptist). The movement was originally centered in Ohio, Pennsylvania, and Kentucky.

As the movement developed, the leaders rejected denominational structures and labels, preferring to call themselves simply Christians or disciples of Christ and the congregations as churches of Christ or Christian churches. Accepting the New Testament as the sole authority of faith and resting on the scriptural affirmation that Jesus Christ is the Son of God and head of all things for His church, they accepted no creeds and wrote no formal confessions, though they certainly held two strong positions on various sectarian issues drawn from their reading and interpretation of the Bible. They practiced baptism by immersion. The ordinance of the Lord's Supper was observed weekly each Lord's Day (Sunday). They were organized congregationally. Each congregation was considered autonomous and led by self-chosen elders and deacons. Periodicals, schools, and the various benevolence enterprises tended to be private self-supporting concerns, the congregations eschewing any formal overall coordinated cooperative activities. Individuals and individual congregations frequently and informally cooperate on a variety of concerns.

Tensions within the movement in the early twentieth century led to its division into three major branches. The introduction of organs of the church in the late nineteenth century became a major issue that led many congregations to separate around 1906 and they are today known as the Churches of Christ (Non-Instrumental). In the ensuing years they have further divided into a number of factions. Disagreements over issues of polity led to a second division. One group, without giving up its congregational polity, began to develop a central office and official structures for coordination of activity and the collection of money, and a convention representative of all the congregations in the fellowship. That process of centralization continued through most of the twentieth century and culminated in 1968 with the restructuring of what is now known as the Christian Church (Disciples of Christ). Those who rejected that move toward centralization are now known as the Christian churches and churches of Christ. The churches are known for their biblical conservatism in relation to the more liberal Christian Church (Disciples of Christ) and have made no attempt to relate to the National Council of Churches and World Council of Churches.

Working from the voluntary activity of members and congregations and without any central office, the churches have been able to build an impressive ministry beyond the local churches. They support approximately 1,500 missionaries in 53 countries. They have established 38 colleges and three graduate seminaries. They maintain 40 homes for children, 20 homes for the aged, eight nursing homes, and three hospitals in the United States, plus a variety of related facilities in other countries. None of these agencies are official, none are supported by all the congregations. Each has arisen as individuals have seen a need and have been able to solicit support within the fellowship. They are primarily supported by those congregations which choose to avail themselves of their services. In like measure, the churches support numerous Christian camps, campus ministry programs, and radio and television ministries.

The same approach operates at various national, regional, and state conventions and rallies that bring together people for inspiration, instruction, and fellowship, and without the adoption of any positions or the transaction of any business. Among the major conventions nationally is the North American Christian Convention, which met occasionally from 1927 to 1948 and has met annually since 1950. An office in Cincinnati, Ohio, exists merely to manage the mechanics of the convention, which is a significant effort, since some 20,000 persons regularly attend its four-day program. A National Missionary Convention serving the same constituency with a mission-oriented program has met annually since 1947.

A number of publishers serve the Christian churches and churches of Christ. Among the most important is Standard Publishing in Cincinnati, which produces books and study material especially directed to their needs. It also publishes two major periodicals, *Christian Standard* and *The Lookout*. Mission Services Association in Knoxville, Tennessee, publishes many items concerned with missions.

Membership: In 1995, the churches reported 1,100,000 members in 5,579 churches served by 6,596 ministers in the United States. There are 6,000 members and 68 churches in Canada. There are sister churches on every continent.

Educational Facilities: Alaska Christian Bible Institute, Houston, Alaska.
Alberta Bible College, Calgary, Alberta.
Atlanta Christian College, East Point, Georgia.
Bluefield College of Evangelism, Bluefield, West Virginia.
Boise Bible College, Boise, Idaho.
Central Christian College of the Bible, Moberly, Missouri.
Christian Institute of Biblical Studies, Louisville, Kentucky.
Cinncinnati Bible College and Seminary, Cincinnati, Ohio.
Colegio Biblico, Eagle Pass, Texas.
College of the Scriptures, Louisville, Kentucky.
Dallas Christian College, Dallas, Texas.
Eastern Christian College, Bel Air, Maryland.
Emmanuel School of Religion, Johnson City, Tennessee.
Floria Christian College, Kissammee, Floria.
Great Lakes Christian College, Lansing, Michigan.
Grundy Bible Institute, Grundy, Virginia.
Johnson Bible College, Knoxville, Tennessee.
Kentucky Christian College, Grayson, Kentucky.
Lincoln Christian College and Seminary, Lincoln, Illinois.
Louisville Bible College, Louisville, Kentucky.
Manhattan Christian College, Manhattan, Kansas.
Maritime Christian College, Charlottetown, Prince Edward Island.
Mid-South Christian College, Memphis, Tennessee.
Midwestern School of Evangelism, Ottumwa, Iowa.
Milligan College, Milligan, Tennessee.
Minnesota Bible College, Rochester, Minnesota.
Nebraska Christian College, Norfolk, Nebraska.
Northwest Christian College, Eugene, Oregon.
Northwest College of the Bible, Portland, Oregon.
Ontario Christian Seminary, Toronto, Ontario.
Ozark Christian College, Joplin Missouri.

Pacific Christian College, Fullerton, California.
Platte Valley Bible College, Scottsbluff, Nebraska.
Puget Sound Christian College, Edmonds, Washington.
Roanoke Bible College, Elizabeth City, North Carolina.
St. Louis Christian College, Florissant, Missouri.
San Jose Christian College, San Jose, California.
Summit Theological Seminary, Peru, Indiana.
Winston-Salem Bible College, Winston-Salem, North Carolina.

Periodicals: Periodicals serving the churches include: *Christian Standard*. • *The Lookout*. Both available from Standard Publishing, 8121 Hamilton Ave., Cincinnati, OH 45231. • *The Restoration Herald*. Available from Christian Restoration Association, 5664 Cheviot Rd., Cincinnati, OH 45147. • *Horizons*. Available from Mission Services Association, Box 2427, Knoxville, TN 37901-2427. • *One Body*. Available from College Press Publishing Co., Box 113, Joplin, MO 64802.

Sources:

Dowling, Enos E. *The Restoration Movement*. Cincinnati, OH: Standard Publishing, 1964.

Leggett, Marshall. *Introduction to the Restoration Ideal*. Cincinnati, OH: Standard Publishing, 1986.

Murch, James DeForest. *Christians Only*. Cincinnati, OH: Standard Publishing, 1962.

NACC, History and Purpose. Cincinnati, OH: North American Christian Convention, 1973.

Walker, Dean E. *Adventuring for Christian Unity*. Cincinnati, OH: Standard Publishing, 1935.

Weishimer, P. H. *Concerning the Disciples*. Cincinnati, OH: Standard Publishing, 1935.

★902★
Christian Congregation
℅ Ora Wilbert Eads, General Supt.
804 W. Hemlock St.
La Follette, TN 37766

History. The Christian Congregation claims to be the oldest denominational evangelistic association in the United States. Its work as an unincorporated religious society dates to 1789. It was formally constituted in 1887 during a period when leaders such as Isaac V. Smith, John Chapman, and John L. Puckett were active in the Ohio River Valley. During the early nineteenth century, the group became loosely identified with the Barton Stone movement that later institutionalized as the Christian Church (Disciples of Christ) though never organically associated. The first Christian Congregation was formally organized in Kokomo, Indiana, by former members of the Christian Church. They sought a means of union on a noncreedal and nondenominational basis. Beginning with the new commandment of John 13: 34-35, they asserted that the church is founded not upon doctrinal agreement, creeds, church claims, names, or rites, but soley upon the individual's relation with God.

Beliefs. The basis of this Christian fellowship is love toward one another. The church has doctrinally taken on a universalist, but strongly biblical, perspective. Ethically activated, the perspective has led to a central emphasis upon respect for life and a resultant condemnation of abortion, capital punishment, and all warfare.

Organization. The Christian Congregation follows a congregational polity, as a "centralized congregational assembly." Local congregations are semiautonomous. The Bible Colportage Service distributes bibles, Bible helps, and literature for field workers. Most congregations are located in either the inner-city areas of metropolitan complexes or in relatively neglected rural and mountainous regions.

Membership: In 1997, the church reported 114,685 members, 1,437 congregations (scattered in all 50 states), and 1,435 ministers in the United States. Affiliated congregations, found in 18 countries, have an additional 2,149 members.

★903★
Churches of Christ (Non-Instrumental)
No central headquarters
For information:
% Gospel Advocate
Box 150
Nashville, TN 37202

A non-structured religious movement, churches of Christ (Non-Instrumental) emerged from the more encompassing Stone-Campbell (the American Restoration Movement) tradition in 1906. Paralleling much of the Fundamentalist thrust of late nineteenth century, churches of Christ continue to represent the most conservative elements of the American Restoration Movement.

Prior to the Civil War, the motto developed by Thomas Campbell—"Where the Scriptures speak, we speak; where the Scriptures are silent, we are silent"—began to be interpreted in two ways. The more conservative (strict) interpretation led to eventual separation over such issues as the missionary society and the use of an instrument of music in worship. Tolbert Fanning's *Gospel Advocate* and Benjamin Franklin's *American Christian Review* gave direction to the conservatives during the years following the American civil conflict.

Unquestionably, the Civil War hastened the division within the Stone-Campbell movement. Historically, churches of Christ have been more numerous south of the Ohio River. Disciples, both North and South, gave their allegiance to their section of the nation. However, the strict and loose interpretations of the Bible, developed before the civil conflict, must be recognized as the prime causes of the ultimate separation among Disciples. The emergence of higher criticism impacted the Stone-Campbell movement as it did other American religious groups. Northern Disciples turned toward a more progressive stance on most issues. John W. McGarvey led the opposition to higher criticism through the pages of the *Christian Standard*. David Lipscomb, who became editor of the *Advocate* in 1866, gave leadership to conservative Disciples during the last years of the nineteenth century and into the twentieth century.

The specific issue that triggered Lipscomb's move toward separation was the wider use of women in worship. Unable to share the cultural interpretation placed on the biblical statements concerning women, he believed many of his Disciple brethren had abandoned the Scriptures in favor of their own positions. Add to this the controversy over becoming associated with the National Federation of Churches and Christian Workers and the perceived liberal stance of James H. Garrison and his associates on the *Christian-Evangelist*, the division Lipscomb had opposed he now supported. This division became reality with the census of 1906.

To suggest unity among those who became designated churches of Christ would not be true. The most important issue was rebaptism, i.e., a person who does not understand baptism for the remission of sins is not scripturally baptized. A large segment of the Stone-Campbell tradition, including Alexander Campbell and David Lipscomb, emphasized baptism as obedience to a command of God. Austin McGary, founding editor of the *Firm Foundation*, urged rebaptism. So strong was McGary's position that it dominated churches of Christ in the 1930s.

Heir to Benjamin Franklin's *American Christian Review* was Daniel Sommer. Although not sharing McGary's views on rebaptism, the two men did oppose the support of schools and other institutions supported by local churches. Because Lipscomb and other *Advocate* writers supported such organizations, they were criticized for their liberal positions.

Churches of Christ grew substantially from the 159,000 reported in the 1906 census through the 1950s. Missionaries were sent to Africa and Japan prior to World War II. After 1945, churches sent teachers to Germany, Italy, and Japan in increased numbers. Domestically, the war years spread churches of Christ to most corners of the United States. Although the numbers were not accurate, reports appeared that suggested there were over two million members early in the 1960s.

Since 1906, churches of Christ have experienced division within the ranks. Although all segments continue to wear the name Churches of Christ, the major groups are: 1. Premillennial; 2. Non-Sunday school; 3. One-communion cup; and 4. Non-institutional. These groups, with the exception of the non-Sunday school and the one cup, do not share fellowship. The larger body of Churches of Christ do not adhere to these positions, even though some of the congregations would hold variant positions of fellowships.

Membership: In 1990, the churches of Christ reported 1,284,056 members in approximately 13,000 churches. This represents a 3.5 percent growth since 1980. In nations other than the United States, the membership was 747,568 in 13,908 churches.

Educational Facilities: Abilene Christian University, Abilene, Texas.

Columbia Christian College, Portland, Oregon.
David Lipscomb University, Nashville, Tennessee.
Faulkner University, Montgomery, Alabama.
Freed-Hardeman College, Henderson, Tennessee.
Harding Graduate School of Religion, Memphis, Tennessee.
Harding University, Searcy, Arkansas.
Lubbock Christian University, Lubbock, Texas.
Michigan Christian College, Rochester, Michigan.
Northeastern Christian College, Villanova, Pennsylvania.
Ohio Valley College, Parkersburg, West Virginia.
Oklahoma Christian University, Oklahoma City, Oklahoma.
Pepperdine University, Malibu, California.
York College, York, Nebraska.

Periodicals: *Firm Foundation.* Send orders to PO Box 690192, Houston, TX. • *Gospel Advocate.* • *Image.* Send orders to 3117 N. 7th St., West Monroe, LA 71291. • *Old Paths Advocate (One Cup).* • *Guardian of Truth (Non-institutional).* Send orders to PO Box 9670, Bowling Green, KY 42102. • *Gospel Tidings (Non-Sunday school).* Send orders to PO Box 4355, Englewood, CO 80155. • *The Word and Work (Premillennial).* Send orders to 2518 Portland Ave., Louisville, KY 40212.

Sources:

Brownlow, Lerow. *Why I Am a Member of the Church of Christ.* Fort Worth, TX, n.d.

Churches of Christ Around the World. Nashville: Gospel Advocate Company, 1990.

Churches of Christ in the United States. Compiled by Lynn Mac. Nashville: Gospel Advocate Company, 1990.

De Groot, A. T. *New Possibilities for Disciples and Independents.* St. Louis: Bethany Press, 1963.

Hooper, Robert E. *Swift Transitions: Churches of Christ in the Twentieth Century*, (tentative title). Compiled by Lynn Mac. West Monroe, LA: Howard Publishing Company, 1992.

Reed, Forest. *Background of Division, Disciples of Christ and Churches of Christ.* Nashville, TN: Disciples of Christ Historical Society, 1968.

West, Earl. *Search for the Ancient Order.* 4 vols. Nashville, Indianapolis, and Germantown, TN: Gospel Advocate Company and Religious Book Service, 1950-87.

Winkler, Herbert E. *Congregational Cooperation of the Churches of Christ.* Nashville, TN: The Author, 1961.

★904★
Churches of Christ (Non-Instrumental, Conservative)
% Florida College
119 Glen Arven Ave.
Tampa, FL 33617

With the growth of institutions serving large segments of the Churches of Christ (Non-Instrumental), voices arose protesting church support for institutions and various projects. The dissent became a movement in the 1950s, and became a separate discernible "group" in the 1960s. *The Gospel Guardian* of Lufkin, Texas, remains a major voice of the group, but its initial effort has been joined by a dozen more periodicals. Conservatives vary from total isolation from non-conservatives, to fellowshipping with individual non-conservatives on the basis of attitude.

Missions are supported in numerous areas around the world. Florida College at Temple, Florida, and the associated CEI bookstore serve the Conservatives. The college's annual lectureship serves as a time for many members to gather around conservative issues. They hold strongly to the pattern principle, that is, that the sum total of what God has said about any matter becomes the pattern for it. Patterns are discovered in the Bible by considering direct commands (such as the command to go into the whole world and preach the gospel), approved example (such as monogamy), and necessary inference from Scriptural passages (such as inferring from Scripture that the Trinity exists.)

Membership: Not reported.

Educational Facilities: Florida College, Tampa, Florida.

★905★
Churches of Christ (Non-Instrumental, Non-Class, One Cup)
% Old Paths Advocate
Box 10811
Springfield, MO 65808

Following a growing trend in American Protestantism, Church of Christ minister G. C. Brewer introduced the use of individual cups in the communion (as opposed to one cup for all communing) into the churches of Christ in the congregation at Chattanooga, Tennessee, in 1915. Over the next three decades the practice spread, not without controversy, and became dominant, especially in newly-formed congregations. In 1913, a periodical, *The Apostolic Way*, was founded by Dr. G. A. Trott, H. C. Harper, and W. G. Rice, to fight what they considered the intrusion of Sunday schools into the worship of the churches of Christ. This same periodical took up the fight against individual cups. In 1928 Harper founded a second periodical, *The Truth*, which in 1932 changed its name to *Old Paths Advocate*. The one cup faction within the larger Churches of Christ movement remains a small minority with congregations spread across the United States and in several foreign countries.

Membership: In 1995, the churches reported 450 congregations in the United States and 1,500 congregations spread through Africa, Australia, the Philippines, Mexico, England, Scotland, and Malaysia.

Periodicals: *Old Paths Advocate*.

★906★
Churches of Christ (Non-Instrumental, Non-Sunday School)
% Gospel Tidings
500 E. Henry
Hamilton, TX 76531

The issue of Sunday schools has plagued the Churches of Christ during the entire twentieth century. An increasingly smaller group of leaders held that anything practiced by the church without command, example, and/or necessary inference from Scripture was wrong, particularly Sunday schools. In 1936, *Gospel Tidings*, edited by G. B. Shelburne, Jr., was begun in support of the non-Sunday school cause. Jim Bullock has succeeded Shelburne as ed-

itor. It has been joined by the *Christian Appeal* and the *West Coast Evangel*. Churches are concentrated in Texas, Oklahoma, Arkansas, Indiana, California, and Oregon. Missions are supported in Malawi, India, Mexico, and Germany.

Membership: Not reported. There are an estimated 500 to 600 congregations and 25,000 to 30,000 members.

Educational Facilities: West Angelo School of Evangelism, San Angelo, Texas.

Periodicals: *Gospel Tidings*.

★907★
Churches of Christ (Non-Instrumental-Premillennial)
Current address not obtained for this edition.

Premillennialism became a major issue in American Protestantism in the late nineteenth century as fundamentalism developed. Premillennialism means Christ will return before the end of the world and the establishment of his thousand year reign. In the first quarter of the twentieth century it invaded the Churches of Christ and a periodical, *Word and Work*, emerged in Louisville, Kentucky, with a premillennialist perspective. A radio show, "Words of Life," begun in the early 1930s, is now heard in many of the eastern United States.

Among premillennialist congregations, several schools and one Christian home are supported. Missionaries are active in Africa, Japan, the Philippines, Hong Kong, and Greece. Approximately 100 congregations support the annual Louisville Christian Fellowship Week every August. Churches are concentrated in Indiana, Kentucky, Louisiana, and Texas.

Membership: Not reported. There is an estimated 12,000 members.

★908★
Churches of Christ (Pentecostal)
Conference on Spiritual Renewal
Box 457
Missouri City, TX 77459

As the Charismatic movement moved through the major denominations in the late 1960s, it began to attract both ministers and laity in congregations of the Churches of Christ. Among the early Charismatics was singer Pat Boone, who in 1971 was disfellowshipped from his congregation in Inglewood, California. Among the early ministers to receive the baptism of the Holy Spirit and subsequently speak-in-tongues (the definitive experience of members of the Charismatic movement) were Dean Dennis, Dwyatt Gantt, and Don Finto. In 1976 a group of 12 ministers met in Nashville, Tennessee, where Finto led the Belmont Church of Christ and organized the first Conference on Spiritual Renewal. The conference, which still meets annually, provided a unifying structure for those involved with the movement.

Like other segments of the Churches of Christ, the Charismatic churches are loosely organized in a congregation-free church polity. There is no central headquarters or governing structure. Intercongregational gatherings are for fellowship and inspiration only. Prominent congregations identified with the charismatic Churches of Christ include Orange Park Christian Church, Jacksonville, Florida; Calvary Chapel, Atlanta, Georgia; and Quail Ridge Church of Christ, Houston, Texas. Some of these congregations deviate from the main body of the Churches of Christ by their introduction of instrumental music. Popular recording star Amy Grant is a member of Belmont Church of Christ in Nashville, Tennessee.

Membership: In 1984 over 300 people, representing congregations across the United States, attended the Conference on Spiritual Renewal.

Sources:

The Acts of the Holy Spirit in the Church of Christ Today. Los Angeles, CA: Full Gospel Business Men's Fellowship International, 1971.

Ambrose, George. "God Said It. I Believe It. That Settles It." *Charisma* 9, no. 11 (July 1984).

Buckingham, Jamie. "The Music of Spiritual Awakening." *Charisma* 9, no. 11 (July 1984).

"Amy Grant, How the Word Is a Light Unto Her Path." *Charisma* 11, no. 12 (July 1986).

★909★
International Churches of Christ (ICC)
3530 Wilshire Blvd., Ste. 1750
Los Angeles, CA 90010

The International Churches of Christ (ICC) dates its history from June 1979, when a group of members in a small and declining congregation of the Churches of Christ (Non-Instrumental) in Lexington, Massachusetts (a Boston suburb), made a new commitment to devote their lives to restoring the Christianity of the Bible. Their new minister, Kip McKean, challenged the 30 members of the small congregation to totally commit their lives to Christ and to hold that same commitment as a biblical standard for all of the people they would convert to Christ. He soon developed a series of Bible lessons called First Principles, and asked the members of the church to learn them and teach the Scriptures to others. This process became the bedrock of a program of transforming nominal church members into active disciples. Prior to being baptized, new members were asked to commit themselves to becoming disciples, not just people who warmed a church pew. Previously baptized Christians who had not made such a commitment prior to their baptism, were rebaptized. The church came to believe and teach that a true Church of Christ was composed totally of disciples. As disciples, each member was expected to be evangelistic.

As the church grew, it moved into Boston proper and took the name the Boston Church of Christ. It met for Sunday worship and midweek services in rented facilities, thus allowing it to redirect its financial resources to ministry rather than buildings. A new Christian was assigned an older member as a discipleship partner and invited into a discipleship group that met weekly. A special program was developed by Elena McKean and Pat Gempel to meet the needs of the female disciples and to avoid possible temptations in the dynamics of men and women in personal counseling. Due to deep convictions and consistent with Churches of Christ interpretations of the Scriptures, only males occupy the positions of elder, deacon, and evangelist. Couples, however, always lead together and the women have the full responsibility of the women's ministry. One of the most successful programs of the ICC has been its Woman's Day seminars held around the world. In 1997, 9,000 women attended this event in Los Angeles alone.

Imitating the spread of the New Testament church, in 1981, McKean developed a plan that he believed would allow for the evangelism of the world in one generation. This plan envisioned sending a small group of disciples to key urban centers. They would grow a congregation and it would become the pillar from which teams of disciples would be sent to each of the world's capitals. From the capitals, the movement would move on to the other, smaller cities, until the world would be evangelized in one generation. This plan was introduced to the Boston Church of Christ as a whole in October 1981. In 1982, the first churches were planted in Chicago and London. Over the next few years additional churches were planted in New York City, Toronto, and Providence, Rhode Island. In 1986, churches were opened in Johannesburg, Paris, and Stockholm. In the meantime some older Churches of Christ congregations and ministries became affiliated with the growing movement. In order to do this each church went through a process termed "reconstruction," and each of the former members were called upon to decide if they wanted to be a disciple.

The implementation of this plan, with its direction coming from the leadership in Boston, represented a major departure in organization from that traditionally followed by the Churches of Christ (Non-instrumental). The Boston Church of Christ leadership saw their movement as creating one church family. The churches would start churches that would plant other churches and they would all remain unified. The implementation of this plan led to a separation by the traditional Churches of Christ denomination from the new movement. Due to the rapid growth of the movement, men were set aside as "world sector leaders" and given responsibility for evangelizing different regions of the world. In 1990, McKean moved to Los Angeles to build new churches, and the international movement has been centered in that city since that time.

In 1994, Kip and Elena McKean, the World Sector Leaders, and their wives signed the Evangelization Proclamation stating their intent to, by the year 2000, plant a church in every nation that has a city of at least 100,000 in population. The International Churches of Christ had 146 churches in 53 nations at the time of the Evangelization Proclamation. By the end of 1997, it had 312 churches in 124 nations and was on track to meet its goal.

Doctrinally, the International Churches of Christ shares a Bible-based free church perspective with the traditional Churches of Christ (Instrumental), but has developed several unique beliefs. While the International Churches of Christ does not believe it is the exclusive home of Christians, it believes that it is God's movement for this period of history. It also holds that each member should be a disciple, obey the Scriptures according to Matthew 28:18–20, and be a part of evangelizing the world in this generation. The ICC has organized a volunteer program, HOPE Worldwide which conducts a variety of social service projects in 125 countries around the world. In 1996 HOPE Worldwide was granted special consultative status with the Economic and Social Council of the United Nations and registered with USAID. HOPE has since become a separate benevolent organization. Discipleship Publications International is the ICC publishing concern.

In 1996, *Church Growth Today,* edited by Dr. John Vaughn, named the Los Angeles church the fastest growing church in North America (non-Catholic) for the second year in a row. The International Churches of Christ placed nine churches in the top 100. At the end of 1997, the Los Angeles church had an average Sunday attendance of 12,000 (though segments of the congregations met in different locations). The New York church had 8,000 and the Boston church nearly 7,000.

The ICC is divided into regions called sectors headed by a sector leader (all male) assisted by his wife. They appoint lead evangelists to head local churches. Churches are organized congregationally following the discipleship pattern that has emerged over the years of the Churches' existence. Each member has a personal discipleship partner with whom s/he is in contact weekly to discuss their progress in the Christian life, their efforts in evangelism, and any personal issues which they face.

Membership: As of October 1997, the ICC reported 93,000 members, with a worldwide Sunday attendance of over 155,000. There were 312 congregations in 124 countries.

Periodicals: *LA Story.* • *Kingdom Network News* (a video magazine).

Remarks: While the International Churches of Christ formally began in 1979, it originated out of an older movement variously known as the Discipling movement, an pan-denominational movement which emerged among Evangelical Christians in the 1960s. It was distinguished by its attempts to transform nominal Christians to active disciples and was characterized by the assignment of each new Christian to an older, more mature Christian with whom they met regularly, at least weekly. The older Christian had the responsibility of mentoring the younger disciple and encouraging the steady progress in the life of faith.

The Discipling movement came into the Churches of Christ through the Crossroads Church of Christ, a congregation in Gainesville, Florida. By adopting a form of the Discipleship program in its campus outreach, it grew spectacularly. Among the people led into the ministry through the Crossroads Church was Kip McKean.

The Discipling movement spread through the Churches of Christ and became quite controversial. As members of a conservative movement, many with the Churches of Christ rejected the changes brought by the new movement and a number of publications denouncing it appeared. Eventually, the Crossroads Church withdrew its support from the movement and the remnants of it within the Churches of Christ tended to reorient its allegiance to the Boston Church of Christ. As the Boston Church of Christ grew, its opponents among the Churches of Christ (Non-instrumental) were joined by members of the anti-cult movement, and the ICC was accused of being a destructive cult growing its membership through brainwashing. That opposition based upon the brainwashing hypothesis has waned as the Cult Awareness Network was dismantled.

Sources:

The Disciple's Handbook. Los Angeles: Discipleship Publications International, 1997. 177 pp.

Ferguson, Gordon. *Discipleship: God's Plan to Train and Transform His People.* Los Angeles: Discipleship Publications International, 1997. 251 pp.

___. *Prepared to Answer.* Los Angeles: Discipleship Publications International, 1995. 219 pp.

Geissler, Rex. *Born of Water: What the Bible Really Says about Baptism.* Long Beach: Grand Commission International, 1996. 140 pp.

Giambalvo, Carol, and Herbert L. Rosedale, eds. *The Boston Movement: Critical Perspective on the International Churches of Christ.* Bonita Springs, FL: American Family Foundation, 1996. 243 pp.

Jacoby, Doug. *True & Reasonable.* Los Angeles: Discipleship Publications International, 1994. 109 pp.

Nelson, Robert. *Understanding the Crossroads Controversy.* Fort Worth, TX: Star Bible Publications, 1986.

★910★
National Association of Free, Autonomous Christian Churches
Current address not obtained for this edition.

Among the people who strongly opposed the restructuring of the Christian Church (Disciples of Christ) in the 1960s was Dr. Alvin E. Houser, pastor of a large congregation at Centex, Texas. As the debate on restructuring continued, he formed the National Association of Free Christians. His position was conservative theologically and focused on the radical congregationalism of traditional Christian Church thinking. After restructuring became inevitable, the Association of Free Christians became the National Association of Free, Autonomous Christian Churches, with most of its strength in the Southwest.

★911★
Tioga River Christian Conference
℅ Rev. Calvin Duvall
RD 1, Box 134
Cherry Valley, NY 13320

The Tioga River Christian Conference was formed in 1844 at Covington, Tioga County, Pennsylvania. It was for many years a constituent part of the Christian Church. In 1931, however, the Conference rejected the merger of the Christian Church with the Congregational Church. The Conference adopted articles of faith manifesting belief in the Trinity, the Bible as the Word of God, sin and salvation, the local church, Satan, resurrection, and eternal life. There is an annual meeting of the conference for fellowship and business. A nine-man mission board oversees missions in Bolivia, Peru, and India. *His Messenger* is a quarterly periodical. There are 13 churches in New York and Pennsylvania. Headquarters are in Binghamton, New York.

Membership: Not reported. There are approximately 13 congregations located in New York and Pennsylvania.

Periodicals: *His Messenger.*

★912★
Unamended Christadelphians
℅ Edward W. Farrar
4 Mountain Park Ave.
Hamilton, ON, Canada L9A 1A2

Alternate Address: Christadelphian Advocate Publishing Committee, 9420 Stanmore Place, Richmond, VA 23236.

In 1898, the prominent Birmingham, England, Ecclesia of the Christadelphians adopted an amendment to the Statement of Faith then in use, whose purpose was to define, more precisely, who will be raised for a resurrectional judgement at the second coming of Jesus Christ. The original unamended statement had read: "That at the appearing of Christ, prior to the establishment of the Kingdom, the responsible (faithful and unfaithful) dead and living of both classes, will, be summoned before his judgment seat..." The Amendment suggested "That at the appearing of Christ prior to the establishment of the Kingdom, the responsible (namely those who know the revealed will of God and have been called upon to submit to it) dead and living—obedient and unobedient—will be summoned before the judgment seat..."

The introduction of this amendment caused a division throughout the movement. Those who retain the Unamended Statement refuse to define with certainty of a resurrectional judgment, any others than those (in this dispensation) who have entered into a covenant relationship with God by baptism. Those who adopted the amendment believe that the basis of resurrection is response to enlightenment, understanding, and knowledge of God's Word.

As of 1992, virtually all of the Unamended Christadelphians reside in North America. They are served by a monthly periodical, *The Christadelphian Advocate.* This publication was begun in 1885 by Thomas Williams who was opposed to the Amendment as who indefatigably tried to heal the division by proposing a more satisfactory definition of the basis for resurrectional judgment.

Talks looking toward reunion of the two groups of Christadelphians were pursued in the 1970s and 1980s. Agreement was reached on various points which had come to distinguish them concerning fellowship, inspiration, baptism, and the nature of man. However, in the end, no agreement was reached on either the primary issue of resurrectional responsiblity or new differences which had developed on matters related to Christ's atonement. As of 1992, reunion does not appear to be imminent.

Christadelphians are organized congregationally, the authority in all matters resting in the collective hands of the members of each local ecclesia (congregation). There is no central headquarters, but the periodicals serving the fellowship as a whole form a network to keep the ecclesias in communication with each other. Each congregation elects serving brethren to perform various tasks, there being no paid clergy.

Membership: In 1997 there were approximately 2,000 baptized adults in about 95 ecclesias in Canada and the United States.

Periodicals: *The Christadelphian Advocate.* Send orders to 9420 Stanmore Pl., Richmond, VA 23236.

Sources:

The Christadelphian Statement of Faith. Quincy, MA: Christadelphian Advocate Publications, n.d.

Roberts, Robert. *A Guide to the Formation and Conduct of Christadelphian Ecclesias.* Birmingham, England: Christadelphian, 1922.

Roberts, Robert, and J. J. Andrew. *Resurrectional Responsibility.* Birmingham, England: The Authors, 1894.

Section 12
Independent Fundamentalist Family

Consult the Contents pages to locate the essay in Part II, Historical Essay Chapters,
that provides an historical discussion of this family

Plymouth Brethren

★913★
Christian Brethren (Open or Plymouth Brethren)
Interest Ministries
218 W. Willow
Wheaton, IL 60187

The Christian Brethren (Open or Plymouth Brethren) came to the United States in the mid-nineteenth century and grew by evangelistic efforts. They prospered in part because John Nelson Darby's ideas on eschatology were being accepted by many mainline American Protestants, and dispensational thinking was spreading. In some cases, the Open Brethren increased by the movement of Exclusive Grant Brethren churches into their ranks.

While there is no generally accepted statement of faith for the Open Brethren, one statement used in some assemblies affirms the Bible as the inerrant Word of God; the Trinity; the depravity of man, and the necessity of salvation by grace through faith; the church as composed of all true believers in Jesus Christ; two ordinances, baptism by immersion and the Lord's Supper; the security of the believer (once a person is truly a child of God, that status is secure for all time); and pretribulation premillennialism (that is, Christ will return before the tribulation and before the millennium.) (For a discussion of various positions on the millennium see the introductory material for this volume.) Brethren assemblies (congregations) are usually led by elders recognized by the local congregation. Assemblies celebrate a weekly communion service, at which many are encouraged to speak or pray. Concerted efforts to fellowship with like-minded Christians in such other groups as InterVarsity Fellowship and the Billy Graham crusades are characteristic. Open Brethren see themselves as a part of mainstream evangelicalism.

Some Open Brethren assemblies were originally a part of the Plymouth Brethren (Grant Brethren), named after Frederick W. Grant. He was a nineteenth-century leader among the Exclusive Brethren in the northeast. The Loizeaux Brothers, Bible Truth Depot, long identified with the Grant Brethren as a publishing house, also identified with the Open Brethren.

There are no central headquarters for the Open Brethren, but several structures have become the focus of the assemblies' cooperative endeavor. The extensive foreign missionary work of the Open Brethren is publicized and served by Christian Missions in Many Lands, Inc. (U.S.A.) and Missionary Service Committee (Canada), who jointly publish a periodical *Mission* from central offices in Wall, New Jersey. The corporations do not designate missionaries, a function left to local assemblies, but do transmit funds and facilitate relations with foreign governments. Other missionary agencies include Workers Together of Wheaton, Illinois, which publishes a newsletter that bears its name. International Teams operates a missionary center and sponsors teams of short-term missionaries from its headquarters in Prospect Heights, Illinois.

Walterick Publishers of Kansas City, Kansas, is a main publisher and book distributor for the Open Brethren. It also publishes an annual directory of assemblies in North America and the Caribbean. Truth and Praise, Inc., of Belle Chasse, Louisiana, publishes three Open Brethren hymnals. There are a number of additional small, independent publishers who produce a variety of tracts and booklets. Emmaus Bible College, Dubuque, Iowa, founded in 1945, provides a three-year Associate of Arts program in a Bible-related curriculum as well as four-year degrees in basic and elementary education. Mount Carmel Bible of Edmonton, Alberta, and Kawartha Lakes Bible School in Peterborough, Ontario, provide a one-year Bible curriculum. Many ministers attend one of several conservative evangelical seminaries such as Dallas Theological Seminary or Trinity Evangelical Divinity School or Talbot School of Theology for further training. *The Address Book*, published by Walterick Publishers, lists 19 homes for the elderly and one children's home. Open Brethren operate 54 summer camps in the USA and Canada. In Great Britain, the Open Brethen are served by the publishing firm of Pickering & Inglis of Glasgow and London which publishes a directory of assembles worldwide.

Membership: In 1998 there were 850 assemblies in the United States and 430 in Canada. Additional assemblies listed in the annual address books were located in Antigua, the Bahamas, Barbados, Bermuda, Cuba, Dominica, Grenada, Jamaica, Mexico, Nevis Island, Puerto Rico, St. Lucia, St. Vincent, Tobago, Trinidad, and the Virgin Islands. Missions are located around the world.

Educational Facilities: Emmaus Bible College, Dubuque, Iowa.
Mount Carmel Bible School, Edmonton, Alberta.
Kawartha Lakes Bible School, Peterborough, Ontario.

Periodicals: *Missions*, Christian Missions in many Lands, PO Box 13, Spring Lake, NJ 07762. • *Uplook*, P.O. Box 2041, Grand Rapids, MI 49501.

Sources:

Barker, Harold B. *Why I Abandoned Exclusivism*. Fort Dodge, IA: Walterick Printing Company, n.d.

Conrad, William W. *Family Matters*. Wheaton, IL: Interest Ministries, 1992. 138 pp.

Darms, Anton. *The Abundant Gospel*. New York: Loizeaux Brothers, Bible Truth Depot, 1941.

MacDonald, William. *What the Bible Teaches*. Oak Park, IL: Emmaus Correspondance School, 1949.

North American Missions: 1995 Resource Guide. Wheaton, IL: Interest Ministries, 1995. 144 pp.

Porter, Carol, and Mike Hamel, eds. *Women's Ministry Handbook*. Wheaton, IL: Victor Books, 1992. 272 pp.

Smart, John. *Historical Sketch of Assembly Missions*. New York: Christian Missions in Many Lands, 1966.

A Younger Brother [A. Rendle Short]. *The Principles of Christians Called "Open Brethren"*. Glasgow, Scotland: Pickering & Inglis, 1913.

★914★
Churches of God in the British Isles and Overseas (Needed Truth)
Current address not obtained for this edition.

In the 1870s questions began to arise among the Plymouth Brethren (Open Brethren) as to just how far they should go in their openness. Discussions led to several separations by groups with different solutions. One strict group formed around the periodical *Needed Truth*, which began in 1889. The bulk of separations of *Needed Truth* supporters began in 1892-1893. Early in the present century, the movement spread from England to North America, primarily to Canada. The Needed Truth groups, called Churches of God, are most properly described as open, in that they will fellowship with likeminded believers who are not members of the Churches of God, and constitute a bridge between the Open and the Exclusive Brethren groups.

The distinctive teaching of the Churches of God concerns ecclesiology. This group believes that the "church which is Christ's body" is composed totally of believers in Christ. The fellowship of the Churches of God in the British Isles and Overseas is composed of those who received the Word and who live in obedience, having been baptized by other disciples (Churches of God elders) and having been "added" by the Lord. "Addition" means that a believer is associated with the churches where the proper authority of Christ is expressed, i.e., with churches in fellowship with the Churches of God. There is a tendency toward exclusivism in that assemblies of the Churches of God feel that all brethren (ultimately, all Christians) ought to be a part of their fellowship. Members live a strict life. Television is frowned upon, though radios are tolerated. Members marry within the group. They are conscientious objectors.

The Churches of God constitute the only group of Brethren who have developed what approaches a presbyterial polity. Elders of the Churches of God have powers similar to those of presbyters in the Presbyterian Church, with the duty of leading the worship services, setting doctrinal standards, ruling on governmental matters, and teaching. Government in the Churches of God is placed in the hands of a united elderhood. Local assemblies function as the constituencies of elders who operate on both the local and regional levels. A premium is placed on consensus of the elders. The elders or overseers form a self-perpetuating body. They appoint deacons, and from the deacons, choose new elders. Regular meetings of the overseers occur.

Membership: Not reported. While the Churches of God became a substantive movement in England, there were in the 1970s only eight churches in North America, all but one in Canada. The single United States congregation was in Trinidad, Colorado. There is some question of its continued existence.

Periodicals: *Needed Truth.* Available from Needed Truth Publishing Office, Assembly Hall, George Lane, Hayes, Bromley, Kent, Great Britain.

Sources:

Willis, G., and B. R. Wilson. "The Churches of God: Pattern and Practice." In *Patterns of Sectarianism.* Edited by Bryan R. Wilson. London: Heinemann, 1967.

★915★
Plymouth Brethren (Ames Brethren)
% Christian Literature, Inc.
Box 1052
Anoka, MN 55303-1052

History. Among the several factions which developed among the Plymouth Brethren are those designated the Ames Brethren. This grouping originated with a preacher named Ames, who worked among the Plymouth Brethren (Booth Brethren), now a constituent part of the Plymouth Brethren (Reunited Brethren). He distrusted the teachings and practice of the Plymouth Brethren (Glanton Brethren), a group with whom the Booth Brethren cooperated in England. Those supporting his opinions separated from the Booth Brethren in 1949.

Beliefs. The Brethren believe the Bible to be the Word of God. While holding to no creed, they believe that the Scriptures teach the fall of humanity and humans lost condition, the love of God in providing a savior, the perfection of Christ, atonement of Christ on the cross, the resurrection, the need of a new birth, the assurance of present salvation, and a future of heaven for the saved and eternal punishment for unbelievers. Believers' hope is not to be placed in the improvement of the world but in the coming of Christ.

Organization. Essential to Brethren belief and life is the gathering unto Christ as a divine center over against all human centers. No sectarian names are assumed. The church is guided by the Holy Spirit and has no need of an ordained priesthood or ministry. No salary is paid to preachers of the word and no collections are taken at public meetings. Meeting halls are modest in appearance.

As a corrolate to belief in the communion of the saints, the Brethren maintain the necessity of godly order, meaning that no one assembly can be owned as independent and apart from all the assemblies. They believe in holiness and truth that includes the putting away of evil doers, the refusal to hear unsound teachers and the marking and avoiding of those who cause division. Each local assembly is seen as an expression of the whole assembly of God.

Several publication centers serve the Brethren, especially Christian Literature, Inc. in Minneapolis and Moments with the Book in Bedford, Pennsylvania. Don Johnson, the printer and editor from Pennsylvania, also conducts a weekly radio show, "Moments with the Book," which has been heard over 22 stations in the United States and one in the Bahamas. Bible conferences are held annually in Iowa and Pennsylvania.

Membership: Not reported. Membership records are not kept.

Periodicals: *Moments with the Bible.* • *Moments for Youth.* Send orders for the above to Box 322, Bedford, PA 15522. • *Words of Truth.* • *Fellowship Letters.* Available from Aldridge F. Johnson, Rte. 1, Box 33, Isanti, MN 55040.

Sources:

Smith, Hamilton. *Perspectives on the True Church.* Minneapolis, MN: Christian Literature, n.d.

★916★
Plymouth Brethren (Ex-Taylor Brethren)
Current address not obtained for this edition.

In 1960, several assemblies left the Plymouth Brethren (Raven-Taylor Brethren) because of the restrictions enunciated by the James Taylor, Jr. faction. This group is small, probably divided among itself, and is in correspondence with some similar assemblies in Britain.

Membership: Not reported.

★917★
Plymouth Brethren (Raven-Taylor Brethren)
Current address not obtained for this edition.

In 1905, after the death of F. E. Raven, James Talyor, Sr., a New York businessman, assumed leadership of this group. Under Taylor's leadership the group became more and more separatist. The elder Taylor was succeeded by his son, James Taylor, Jr., who demanded a rigorous separation from the world. The Taylor Brethren prefer a secluded separatist existence. They refuse to list their centers in the telephone directories. They encourage their members to withdraw from professional associations, to resign offices in business corporations, and dispose of stock. They refuse to eat with any not in their fellowship. Taylor's critics have claimed he advocates divorce if any member of a household loses religious fervor. They have made him a public figure with their fervent denunciation of him. One British newspaper, reporting his return to the United States from England in 1969, commented, "The harsh tenets of this sect have broken up homes and led to misery and suicide. Now he has gone home, Britain's parting message is 'good riddance and don't come back.'"

The strength of the Taylor Brethren is in New York and California. Other congregations are located in the Northeast and Midwest, while a very few are located in the South. Stow Hill Bible and Tract Depot has been their publisher in England for many years. This group is "IV" in the 1936 *Religious Census* list.

Membership: Not reported.

Sources:

F.E.R. [F.E. Raven]. *Readings and Addresses in the United States*. Kingston-on-Thames: Stow Hill Bible and Tract Depot, 1902.

Gardiner, A. J. *The Recovery and Maintenance of the Truth*. Kingston-on-Thames, England: Stow Hill Bible and Tract Depot, n.d.

____. *The Substantiality of Christianity*. Kingston-on-Thames, England: Stow Hill Bible and Tract Depot, 1954.

____. *The Recovery and Maintenance of the Truth*. Kingston-on-Thames, England: Stow Hill Bible and Tract Depot, n.d.

Taylor, James. *Administration in the Assembly*. London: Stow Hill Bible and Tract Depot, 1937.

____. *Christ's Personal Service for the Saints*. Wellington, NZ: Whitcombe & Tombs, Printers, 1925.

Wilson, Bryan. "A Sect at Law." *Encounter* 60, no. 1 (January 1983): 81-87.

★918★
Plymouth Brethren (Reunited Brethren)
No central headquarters. For information:
Grace and Truth
210 Chestnut St.
Danville, IL 61832

The Plymouth Brethren (Reunited Brethren) was formed by the coming together of a number of Exclusive Plymouth Brethren groups which had divided into factions in the nineteenth and early twentieth century. Their story is told in two segments, first as one of division and then one of reunion.

History. One of the earliest schisms of the Brethren centered upon the popular and zealous William Kelly (1820-1906). Kelly, an Irishman, was editor of the *Bible Treasury* for 50 years and also of the *Collected Writings* of John Nelson Darby, the prominent early leader of the Brethren. In the 1870s, however, Darby became associated with a party in the movement known as New-Lumpism. Members of this group attacked the worldliness they saw in the Brethren of their day and looked with disfavor upon the evangelism that was swelling their ranks with new converts. They yearned for a pure fellowship and advocated the high church principle, namely, that the assembly has the supreme judicial power and its decisions, which are in accord with scripture, must be accepted. Kelly and his supporters separated in 1881, the year before Darby's death. The group was limited to England and the West Indies.

Just four years after the Kelly schism, Clarence Esme Stuart and the few congregations who adhered to him were expelled from the main body of the Exclusive Brethren because of what were considered his mystical teachings on Christian position and condition. In 1885 a division that began in Montreal had the effect of separating the supporters of Frederick W. Grant, a well-known teacher and writer, from Brethren in most countries of the world.

Not many years afterward, around 1890, the majority of assemblies in continental Europe separated. They were the surviving Exclusive Brethren who did not accept either Frederick W. Grant or F. E. Raven (d. 1906), a popular Exclusive Brethren teacher of the

late nineteenth century (see separate entries). Also, they sided with C. Strange and W. J. Lowe in 1909 in the Tunbridge Wells controversy (see Plymouth Brethren (Tunbridge Wells)). While strongest on the Continent, these Brethren had assemblies across America. In the 1936 *Religious Census*, they were called "III."

In 1928, the Grant Brethren, remnants of which are now a constituent part of the Plymouth Brethren (Open Brethren), divided into three factions as the result of a controversy that erupted in Philadelphia, Pennsylvania. One reason for the controversy was the alleged heresy of James Boyd, a visiting British preacher who had written a tract denying that Christ had a human spirit. A second controversy developed between two people within the Philadelphia assembly, C. A. Mory and his business partner C. V. Grant. The partner was accused of deceit, fraud, and misuse of funds. The assembly's refusal to excommunicate the partner or to brand Boyd's teachings as heresy led to schism. Adding fuel to the fire of controversy was the contemporaneous movement of some Grant Brethren toward the Open Brethren.

One small group of assemblies (labeled "VII" by the *Religious Census*) withdrew fellowship from Boyd and any who did not agree with their strong stand. One leader of this faction was R. J. Little, editor of *Holding Fast and Holding Faith*, though he later joined the Open Brethren and the faculty at Moody Bible Institute.

A larger group of assemblies was led by A. E. Booth, who accepted Boyd's retraction of his "heretical" position but rejected the Grant Brethren in the move toward the Open Brethren position. He led the formation of the Erie Bible Truth Depot, in Erie, Pennsylvania. In 1932, he began *Things Old and New*. (The Booth Brethren were numbered "VIII" in the *Religious Census*.)

The mergers of the separated Brethren occurred in 1926, 1940, 1953, and 1974. The first, in 1926, resulted in the union of the Kelly and Continental Brethren. This action was effective in England, the West Indies, Europe, Egypt, and North America. Then in 1940, the Kelly-Continental Brethren and the British section of the Tunbridge Wells Brethren reunited. However, the American section of the Tunbridge Wells group remains separate to this day and has undergone several internal divisions in the course of the years.

In 1953, the Kelly-Continental Brethren united with the Stuart Brethren and also took in the Mory faction of the former Grant Brethren. This reunion affected assemblies around the world. Finally, in 1974, the previously reunited Brethren merged with the Glanton Brethren (a splinter from the Plymouth Brethren (Raven-Taylor Brethren)) and the Booth Brethren which had previously become associated with the Glanton Brethren.

Beliefs. The reunion changed little doctrinally with the various segments of the Brethren who reunited, as few of the earlier schisms had a strong doctrinal element, and those few doctrinal questions previously at issue had become academic. The reunited assemblies now seek to maintain the unity of the Spirit of God and to function as assemblies gathered in the name of the Lord Jesus Christ on the ground of the One Body of Christ in contrast to acting as independent assemblies. They acknowledge Christ as their only head and the Holy Spirit as the only administrator of the church.

Organization. The assemblies are organized congregationally and tied together by their mutual like-mindedness and cooperative activities in which they participate. Missionaries are supported in Africa, South America, the Caribbean Islands, India, and the Philippines. Grace & Truth, Inc. and Believers Bookshelf of Sunbury, Pennsylvania, are the major publishers for the Reunited Brethren in the United States; there are numerous others in other countries.

Membership: In 1995, there were 94 congregations in the United States and 28 in Canada. Worldwide membership was unknown, but there are an estimated 1500 congregations altogether.

Periodicals: *Grace & Truth.* • *Assembly Bulletin. Missionary Bulletin.* • *Come & See.*

Sources:

Campbell, R. K. *The Christian Home.* Sudbury, PA: Believers Bookshelf, 1982.

___. *The Church of the Living God.* Sudbury, PA: Believers Bookshelf, n.d.

___. *Reunited Brethren: A Brief Historical Account Including a Brief Statement of Some Vital Principles of Faith.* Danville, IL: Grace & Truth, 1990.

Kelly, William. *Lectures on the Church of God.* Oak Park. IL: Bible Truth Publishers, n.d.

★919★

Plymouth Brethren (Tunbridge Wells Brethren)
No central headquarters. For Information:
% Bible Truth Publishers
59 Industrial Rd.
PO Box 649
Addison, IL 60101

The Plymouth Brethren (Tunbridge Wells Brethren) designates a group of the Plymouth Brethren which dates from 1909 when there was an act of discipline in the assembly in Tunbridge Wells, London, England, involving Mr. C. Strange. After moving to that city and establishing a business there, his conduct and participation in meetings, both at home and elsewhere, ultimately resulted in his being excluded. W. J. Lowe, a prominent brother in London, took the lead in rejecting the action of the Tunbridge Wells assembly and in forming a group, later identified by his name as the Lowe Brethren, which included those sympathetic to Strange. Ironically, Strange was a member of that group for only a brief period. However, Lowe found support among the Continental Brethren who also aligned themselves against the action at Tunbridge Wells.

In 1940, the Tunbridge Wells Brethren were invited to forget the past differences and amalgamate with others who had already been participating in a reunion process. The sponsoring group included the now-merged former (William) Kelly, Lowe, Continental, Stuart, and Glanton Brethren as well as some of the Grant Brethren. Most of the Tunbridge Wells Brethren in England accepted the invitation and now are a constituent part of the Plymouth Brethren (Reunited Brethren). In North America, however, the brethren felt that no true reunion could be be accomplished without a consensus judgment on the root cause of the 1909 and earlier divisions. They have remained separate.

The Tunbridge Wells Brethren are a worldwide fellowship with assemblies in North, Central, and South America, as well as Australia, Europe, Asia, and Africa. Bible Truth Publishers in Addison, Illinois, is an independent operation, but owned and managed by members of the groups and publish materials especially for it. It issues three periodicals, and a number of books, pamphlets and tracts, including reprints of a number of the nineteenth-century brethren and the *Collected Writings* of John Nelson Darby. There is a similar operation known as Bibles and Publications in Montreal, Quebec. A number of smaller publishers issue tracts, not only in English, but in a variety of foreign languages.

Membership: Membership figures are unavailable. In 1997, there were over 180 assemblies.

Periodicals: *Echoes of Grace.* • *Messages of God's Love.*

Sources:

Hayhoe, H. E. *Present Truth for Christians.* St. Louis, MO: Bible Truth Publishers, 1950.

Price, G. H. S. *Church History.* Addison, IL: Bible Truth Publishers, 1982.

Stanley, Charles. *The Church of God.* Oak Park, IL: Bible Truth Publishers, n.d.

Wilson, Paul. *A Defense of Dispensationalism.* Oak Park, IL: Bible Truth Publishers, n.d.

Wolston, W. T. *The Church, What Is It?* Oak Park, IL: Bible Truth Publishers, 1971.

Fundamentalists

★920★

Aggressive Christianity Missions Training Corps
Klamath Falls, OR 97601

The Aggressive Christianity Missions Training Corps is an Evangelical communal ministry founded in 1982 by Jim Green and his wife Lila Green as the Free Love Ministry. They saw the group as an endtime army brought together to fight sin, especially what they saw as some of the major evils running rampant in society—pornography, homosexuality, rock music, etc. Inspired in part by the Salvation Army, they developed a disciplined military lifestyle, and members wore uniforms and assumed a rank in the corps. Several businesses were developed to support the group financially.

The progress of the corps was blocked in 1987 when a former member sued, claiming that the group brainwashed her. The leaders of the corps ignored the suit and did not appear when the case came up in court. The former member received a million-dollar default judgment, which led to the loss of the corps' California property. Headquarters were moved to Oregon in 1989.

The corps teaches a fundamentalist Protestant Christianity.

Membership: Not reported. There were approximately 25 members in the late 1980s. The corps supports an orphanage in India and a medical center in the Philippines.

Periodicals: *Battle Cry.*

Sources:

"Onward Christian Soldiers." *Herald and News* (Klamath Falls) (November 12, 1989).

★921★

American Coalition of Unregistered Churches
Current address not obtained for this edition.

The American Coalition of Unregistered Churches was founded in 1983 as a fellowship of fundamentalist Christian congregations (many Baptist in faith) that exist as unincorporated entities and have organized to resist government pressures that appear to encroach upon their religious liberties and attempt to reshape their ministries. The Association grew out of a meeting of pastors from some 25 states who gathered in Chicago, August 8-9, 1983, to discuss what they saw as attacks on many phases of church ministries. Among the major underlying considerations was the government's attempt to force schools attached to churches to be licensed and conform to state educational regulations. Most in attendance felt that the attack they had been facing was due in part to the government's acceptance of a humanist position in place of a biblical perspective, which they felt had traditionally guided government action.

The gathering passed a set of resolutions that rejected government attempts to license church ministries, regulate churches, or impose taxation. One resolution specifically rejected state jurisdiction to inspect church property on issues of health, fire prevention, or safety. They also passed a resolution rejecting any use of force in defending their ministries.

Following the meeting, Greg Dixon, pastor of the Indianapolis Baptist Temple and head of the Indiana moral majority, resigned his leadership position with the Moral Majority to become chairman of the new Association. Dr. Everett Sileven, pastor of the Faith Baptist Church in Louisville, Nebraska, was elected co-chairman. Sileven had become well known for his ongoing fight over his arrest and the seizure and padlocking of his churchsponsored school.

The association has no doctrinal statement, but most of its member congregations are very conservative fundamentalist churches. It does not think of itself as a denomination, but as an association assisting independent churches. Most recently, in 1993, Dixon found himself in jail for refusing to respond to a subpoena to produce his church's financial records.

Membership: In 1993 there were 500 congregations affiliated with the association.

Periodicals: *The Trumpet.*

★922★
American Evangelical Christian Churches
Waterfront Dr.
Pineland, FL 33945

The American Evangelical Christian Churches was founded in 1944 as an interdoctrinal ecclesiastical body. It has tried to remain open to both Calvinist and Arminian theological trends, with the Calvinists believing in predestination and the Arminians insisting that people can exercise free will and choose to follow the gospel. Each church member must accept the seven articles of faith that are seen as the "essentials." They are the Bible as the written word of God; the virgin birth; the deity of Jesus, the Christ; salvation through the atonement; the guidance of our life through prayer; and the return of the savior. All other points are optional.

The polity is congregational, and the American Evangelical Christian Churches seems to function primarily to offer orthodox evangelical ministers a chance to preach without the "restrictions of man-made doctrines imposed by so many religious bodies today." A retreat center known as Pala Mar is located on an estate at Pineland, Florida. The Bible school specializes in home-study courses. There are five regional offices in the United States and one in Canada. Headquarters were moved from Chicago to Pineland, Florida, in the 1970s.

Membership: In 1988, the church reported 54 full-time pastor members, 49 other ministers, 12 retired ministers, and one missionary in the Philippines.

Educational Facilities: American Bible College, Pineland, Florida.

Sources:

Directory. Pineland, FL: American Evangelical Christian Churches, 1988.

★923★
American Mission for Opening Churches
6419 E. Lake Rd.
Olcott, NY 14126

The American Mission for Opening Churches was organized in 1943 for the purpose of opening churches that had been closed and establishing soul-saving Gospel ministries. The work began as a prayer meeting of Western New York businessmen and pastors. The organization has specialized in reaching rural areas and areas with no witness for Christ. Once churches are self-supporting, they are turned over to the community, and the American Mission shifts its activity elsewhere.

The doctrinal statement of the mission includes the fundamental affirmations in the divine inspiration of scripture, the Trinity, the deity of Christ and his supernatural (virgin) birth, the sinfulness of man and his need for a savior, the atonement, the bodily resurrection and ascension of Christ, the bodily resurrection of both the just and unjust at the end of time, and heaven and hell.

Membership: In 1988 the mission had oversight of 30 congregations, with 39 missionary families providing the leadership for the mission and its projects.

★924★
Armenian Evangelical Union of North America
% Rev. Yessayo Sarmaziam
42 Glenforest Rd.
Toronto, ON, Canada M4N 1Z8

During the nineteenth century, Protestant missionaries, primarily those with a Presbyterian background, established work in Armenia and began to draw members from the older national church of the Armenians. During the early twentieth century, as Armenians began to migrate to North America, many Protestants were among them. They established independent ethnic churches, many of which joined what today is either the United Church of Christ, the United Church of Canada, or the Presbyterian Church (U.S.A.). Others have remained independent, being more theologically conservative than the large liberal Protestant denominations.

In 1960 the Armenian Evangelical Union of North America was created as a fellowship of Armenian Christians in the United States and Canada. It includes both the majority of congregations and those congregations that are formally attached to other denominations, and serves as the denominational home for the independent congregations.

Membership: Not reported.

Periodicals: *Canada Armenian Press.*

★925★
Associated Gospel Churches
1919 Beach St.
Pittsburgh, PA 15221

The Associated Gospel Churches (AGC) was begun by about 25 congregations of the Methodist Protestant Church which refused to enter the merger in 1939 which led to the formation of the Methodist Church, now the United Methodist Church. The congregations against merger adopted the name American Bible Fellowship. Their leader was Dr. W. O. H. Garman, a former minister of the United Presbyterian Church and later president of the Independent Fundamental Churches of America. Dr. Garman led the Associated Gospel Churches into the fundamentalist family. He had been president of the American Council of Christian Churches (ACCC), but the AGC is not affiliated at present with the ACCC.

Doctrinally, the AGC accepts the fundamental dispensationalist theology (though there is no article on human depravity) and believes in the maintenance of good works. Baptism is by immersion. Separation from apostasy is adamantly affirmed. Polity is congregational with the central headquarters serving as a service agency for chaplains, missionaries, pastors, and schools. A major function is to represent fundamentalist chaplains in the armed forces. Member churches are located in more than 20 states, and overseas work is supported in Italy, Spain, the Philippines, Sri Lanka, Kenya, Nigeria, South Africa, and South America.

Membership: Not reported.

Periodicals: *The AGC Reporter.*

★926★
Associated Gospel Churches (Canada)
3430 S. Service Rd.
Burlington, ON, Canada L7N 3T9

The Associated Gospel Churches (AGC) (not to be confused with several groups based in the United States with the same name) traces its history to the mid-nineteenth century and to the growth liberal theological thinking in the major Canadian denominations. In the face of the rising torrent of liberal teachings, some churches and pastors arose to uphold the final authority of the Scriptures in all matters of faith and conduct. In the first two decades of the twentieth century their actions resulted in a movement to evangelical ministry under the authority of the inspired Word of God and a defense of the belief that "All Scripture is given by inspiration of God". They became part of the movement to stay true to the traditional fundamentals of the faith and were labeled "fundamentalists". Foundational to their movement, along with a belief in the inspiration and literal interpretation of Scripture, was a commitment to the virgin birth of Christ, salvation by Christ's shed blood, Christ's bodily resurrection, and His second coming as the blessed and "imminent" hope of the church.

One can notice the beginnings of a movement in the 1890s. A strong evangelistic thrust in the Toronto-Hamilton area of Ontario resulted in the formation of several independent churches which joined together as the Christian Workers' Churches of Canada. By 1922 they desired a more structured union for purposes of both fellowship and doctrinal stability. Dr. P. W. Philpott (1866–1957) of the Gospel Tabernacle in Hamilton and Rev. H. E. Irwin of the Missionary Tabernacle in Toronto took the lead in forming the union of like-minded churches. In 1925 the name was changed to Associated Gospel Churches which subsequently spread across Canada from British Columbia to Nova Scotia.

Very early the AGC participated in the Bible Conference movement; for 17 years it sponsored the Oakland Bible Conference held on the shores of Burlington Bay, Ontario. It was succeeded by Fair Havens Bible Conference, still one of the best-know conferences among Evangelical Christians in North America.

The Western Region of the AGC was founded in 1940 under the leadership of Rev. A. N. Lambshead. In the years immediately after World War II The AGC spread eastward with English-speaking churches in Quebec, then into the Maritime Provinces (1962), and finally among the French-speaking areas of Quebec (1969). In the wake of this growth, in 1989, the AGC restructured into a fully regionalized format.

Membership: In 1997 the AGC reported 10,239 members in 137 churches served by 313 ministers. Average Sunday attendance was almost double the membership figures.

Periodicals: *Advance.*

Sources:

Redinger, Lauren. *A Tree Well Planted: The Official History of the Christian Workers' Church of Canada and the Associated Gospel Churches, 1892-1993.* Burlington, ON: Associated Gospel Churches, 1995. 124 pp.

★927★
Association of Torah-Observant Messianics
% Rabbi Yeshayahu Heiliczer
PO Box 578
Bowie, MD 20715

The Association of Torah-Observant Messianics was formed to provide a home for Messianic Jews and non-Jews to live a life in observation of the Torah (i.e., the biblical law) which association members were given by the Creator as a perfect standard for His people. While it is clear from the Scriptures that salvation is an undeserved and unearned gift from the Creator through His grace, and that human works and effort cannot earn salvation, the Scriptures also teach that the Creator is a righteous and just deity who never changes.

Taking their cue from Matthew 5:17-19, association members believe that the Torah as given to the Jewish people has never been abolished and thus stands as a true test of humanity's love for Him. Thus, without judging other believers, the association provides a link between those who would like to fellowship with other observant Messianic believers.

Membership: Not reported.

Periodicals: *Teshuvah Online Magazine.*

Sources:

http://www.teshuveh.com/.

★928★
Berachah Church
2815 Sage Rd.
Houston, TX 77056

Berachah Church was founded in 1935 as a nondenominational local church. Berachah is the Hebrew word for "blessing" (2 Chron. 20:26). The churchs purpose is stated in Article II of its constitution: "to present isagogical, categorical, and exegetical Bible teaching, standing unequivocally for the fundamentals of the faith as contained in the Holy Scriptures; and through the teaching of the Word in this church, the sending out of missionaries, and the ordaining of pastor-teachers, present the Gospel of the Lord Jesus Christ both at home and abroad." The mission of Berachah Church is to evangelize the unbeliever and teach the believer to fulfill Gods plan, will, and purpose for his life.

History: C. W. Colgan, an oil company executive who transferred to Houston from Philadelphia in the early 1930s, founded Berachah Church to teach fundamental Christian doctrine. When he was transferred back to Philadelphia in 1936, the independent Dallas Theological Seminary recommended J. Ellwood Evans, who became the full-time pastor from 1936 to 1940. The church constructed a small auditorium at 171 Heights Boulevard and remained there until 1948. Richard Seume, also a graduate of Dallas Theological Seminary, was pastor from 1941 until 1946. He was followed by William F. Burcaw. In 1948 the congregation moved to 502 Lamar Street, near downtown Houston.

Robert B. Thieme, Jr., an ordained minister with the Conservative Baptist Association, was recommended by Dallas Theological Seminary to become pastor of Berachah Church in 1950. He has continued as pastor to the present. Thiemes academic background includes the University of Arizona (magna cum laude, phi beta kappa) and Dallas Theological Seminary (summa cum laude). His graduate studies were interrupted by World War II during which he rose to the rank of Lieutenant Colonel in the Army Air Corps. Thieme returned to Dallas Theological Seminary in 1946 to resume preparation for the ministry. His extensive training in Greek, Hebrew, theology, history, and textual criticism became the foundation for his demanding professional life of studying and teaching the Word of God. As a student he became the interim pastor of Reinhardt Bible Church, Dallas, Texas. He was ordained on July 15, 1948, by the First Baptist Church of Tucson, Arizona. Upon graduating summa cum laude with a Master of Theology in May 1949, he continued to pastor at Reinhardt until April 1950.

Beliefs. Thieme brought the fundamental dispensational theology taught at Dallas Theological Seminary to a congregation that already had accepted that theological perspective. The eighteen-article statement of beliefs of Berachah Church agrees with the twenty-one articles of the doctrinal statement of the seminary. Since 1969 Thieme has become the target of theological controversy because of his doctrinal positions on certain issues. This disagreement with his exegesis created some disharmony within the larger independent fundamentalist movement toward Thieme, Berachah Church, and Thiemes extended congregation around the United States.

The prime point of controversy concerns Thieme's position on the nature and effects of Christ's death. Thieme teaches that Christ's spiritual death marked the completion of His bearing our sins on the cross. Christs spiritual death, i.e., His separation from God while being judged for our sins, was substitutionary and, hence, efficacious for the salvation of humanity. The Lord's physical death, while essential for His resurrection, ascension, and session, was not the means of salvation but occurred only after His substitutionary work was *tetelestai*, "finished" (John 19:30). This position leads Thieme to further assert that the phrase "blood of Christ" is a representative analogy for the work of Christ for salvation.

Thieme has also taken a biblical position in favor of Christian participation in the military. He denounces anti-Semitism as condemned by God and incompatible with biblical Christianity.

Thieme teaches from the original languages of Scripture in light of the historical context in which the Bible was written. His ministry has become noteworthy for the development of an innovative system of vocabulary, illustrations, and biblical categories designed to communicate the truths of God's Word. The unique focus of his ministry concentrates on the procedures for living the Christian way of life.

Organization: His development for the concept of the role of the pastoral minister is reflected in the constitution of Berachah Church. He teaches that the leadership of the local congregation is vested in the pastor "whose absolute authority is derived from Scripture" with an advisory board of deacons to administer church business.

Since coming to Berachah Church forty-eight years ago, Thieme has recorded over eleven thousand hours of Bible classes covering much of the Bible verse by verse. Berachah Church has responded to demands to publish and distribute Thiemes Bible teaching by establishing R. B. Thieme, Jr., Bible Ministries. This nonprofit organization is a grace ministry designed to extend and distribute biblical teaching in the form of books, tracts, sermon transcripts, tapes, and Bible conferences. All are available at no charge. The ministry also provides information on classes that meet regularly throughout the country where his lectures can be heard either on audiotape, videotape, or by live telephone transmission. A radio series that includes over three hundred half-hour lessons on general biblical subjects is broadcast on stations in various areas of the United States, Puerto Rico, and the Philippines.

As a result of the response to his teaching, congregations and groups of Christians have formed across the United States. Each congregation, like Berachah Church, is independent. Thieme speaks regularly at Bible conferences sponsored by these local congregations and coordinated by R. B. Thieme, Jr., Bible Ministries.

Membership: In 1993 Berachah Church reported approximately 1,360 members in the United States and Canada.

Sources:

King, George William. *Robert Bunger Thieme, Jr.'s Theory and Practice of Preaching*. Ph.D. diss., University of Illinois, Urbana, 1974.

Thieme, R. B. *Anti-Semitism*. Houston, TX: Berachah Tapes and Publications, 1979.

___. *Blood of Christ*. Houston, TX: Berachah Tapes and Publications, 1979.

___. *Freedom Through Military Victory*. Houston, TX: Berachah Tapes and Publications, 1973.

___. *The Integrity of God*. Houston, TX: Berachah Tapes and Publications, 1979.

Thieme, R. B., Jr. *The Divine Outline of History: Dispensationalism and the Church*. Edited by Wayne F. Hill. Houston, TX: R. B. Thieme, Jr., Bible Ministries, 1989. 163 pp.

Walker, Robert G. *The False Teachings of R. B. Thieme, Jr.*. Collinwood, NJ: Bible for Today, 1972.

Wall, Joe Layton. *Bob Thieme's Teaching on Christian Living*. Houston, TX: Church Multiplication, 1978.

★929★
Berean Fundamental Churches
Box 6103
Lincoln, NE 68506

The Berean Fundamental Churches were formed in 1936 by Dr. Ivan E. Olsen, a graduate of Denver Bible Institute. Olsen had moved to North Platte, Nebraska, to do independent work following graduation. They are fundamental in theology and evangelical in program, and are non-pentecostal. They are governed by a church council composed of each pastor and one lay delegate from each church. Congregations are located in Nebraska, Kansas, Colorado, Wyoming, California, and South Dakota. Due the small size of the fellowship, the churches have not developed their own denominational structures but have developed their program by utilizing the services of various faith missions, fundamental-conservative seminaries and Bible schools, and church school literature.

Membership: In 1995 the church reported 6,900 members, 50 churches, and 67 ministers in the United States. There were two affiliated congregations in Canada.

Periodicals: *The Communicator.*

★930★
Bethany Bible Church and Related Independent Bible Churches of the Phoenix, Arizona, Area
6060 N. 7th Ave.
Phoenix, AZ 85013-1498

The Bethany Bible Church, a single congregation, was begun in the 1950s by members of some Baptist and Presbyterian churches who felt that these churches had deviated from their traditional theological stance. The members called Dr. John Mitchell, a graduate of the conservative Dallas Theological Seminary, to be their minister. As the church grew ministers (now 9 in number) from a variety of evangelical seminaries have joined the staff. Meanwhile, other graduates of Dallas Theological Seminary, with the assistance of Bethany, founded similar churches in the Phoenix, Arizona, area. While each church is entirely independent, these churches have an informal fellowship based upon the unity of their doctrinal perspective. There are no formal organizational ties between the several congregations.

Bethany's doctrine is dispensational and evangelical. There is a strong belief in the verbally inspired and inerrant Bible, and both individual and corporate Bible study is stressed. Most preaching and teaching is derived from the New American Standard Bible, with periodical use of the New International Version. Baptism by immersion is practiced and the ordinance of the Lord's Supper is held monthly. Missions are supported through independent faith missionary agencies.

Membership: At the end of 1994 Bethany reported 1,312 members. There were several thousand members in the other independent evangelical congregations in addition.

Periodicals: *Window on Bethany.*

★931★
Central Alaskan Mission
Glennallen, AK 99588

Central Alaskan Missions was founded in 1936 by former Methodist Vincent J. Joy (1914-1966) as an independent faith mission. Missionary efforts began among the residents of the isolated Copper Valley in south-central Alaska via airplane. The airborne effort slowly gave way to a more conventional movement on the ground as the roads were built through the area. A medical program led to the founding of a hospital in 1956. The mission also sponsored a radio station and the Alaska Bible College.

The mission is fundamentalist in faith and affirms a belief in the Trinity, the verbal inspiration of the bible, salvation by grace through faith in Jesus Christ, and Christ's imminent premillennial return. It practices the Lord's Supper and believer's baptism by immersion. Members are exhorted to separate themselves from anything that would dishonor God, bring discredit to His cause, or weaken their testimony.

Membership: Not reported. In 1980 the mission had nine affiliated mission congregations.

Educational Facilities: Alaska Bible College, Glennallen, Alaska.

Sources:

Piepkorn, Arthur C. *Profiles in Belief: The Religious Bodies of the United States and Canada*. Vol. IV. San Francisco, Harper & Row, 1979.

★932★
Christ's Apostolic Church of North America
% Most Rev. Ronald D. Nowlan, D.D.
Chancery Office
316 Hullett St.
Long Beach, CA 90805-3424

Christ's Apostolic Church of North America is a small Old Catholic jurisdiction whose primate, Most Rev. Ronald D. Nowlan, holds lines of apostolic succession derived from the Roman Catholic Church, the Old Catholic Church of Utrecht and the Brazilian National Catholic Church. The church was founded with the intention of establishing independent ministries, most operating out of private homes, throughout the United States.

The church uses an Old Catholic liturgy, but others are acceptable. Archbishop Nowlan is assisted by the Vicar General for North America, Most Rev. Irwin Young, and the diocese's chancellor, Rt. Rev. Msgr. Harvey Beagle. The church has good relations with the Independent Catholic Church of America headed by Most Rev. Maurice McCormick.

Membership: Not reported.

★933★
Church of Christian Liberty
502 W. Euclid Ave.
Arlington Heights, IL 60004

Paul Lindstrom, a graduate of Trinity Seminary in Deerfield, Illinois, founded the Church of Christian Liberty in 1965 with the combined purposes of preaching salvation, contending for the faith, and defending God-given liberties. Since that time, both the pastor and the church have been involved in controversy. Lindstrom identified himself with several right-wing political causes which can be grouped under the heading "anti-communist." He received an award from the Republic of China, and the Anti-Communist League of America gave him a statue of John Birch. He has featured in his pulpit conservative leaders such as Dr. Charles S. Poling, Richard Wurmbrand, and George Bundy.

Pastor Lindstrom's activism in forming the "Remember the Pueblo Committee" brought national headlines. (The Pueblo was an American ship seized by North Korea in January 1968.) Lindstrom formed the committee in the summer of 1968, and by 1971 another committee developed from the Remember the Pueblo Committee. The second committee was the Douglas MacArthur Brigade, formed to seek the release of prisoners of war in Vietnam. In 1972, Lindstrom formed the Christian Defense League to take up the defense of persecuted Christians behind the Iron Curtain.

Doctrinally, the Church of Christian Liberty is reformed fundamentalist, and it has adopted a seven-article statement of faith, adding the following four articles on "Responsibilities of the United States of America":

"l) We believe that we have been endowed by our Creator 'with certain unalienable Rights, that among these are Life, Liberty, and the Pursuit of Happiness.' 2) We believe in a Constitutional Republic as set up by our founding fathers and the responsibilities inherent in such upon its citizens. 3) We believe that individual responsibility and a free economy is the best way to achieve the highest standard of living among all men. 4) We believe in combating Socialism, godless Communism, and all forms of collectivistic tyranny alien to our way of life."

There were, in 1974, three congregations. The first was formed in Prospect Heights, Illinois, with others added in Milwaukee, Wisconsin, and Rockford, Illinois. Parochial schools (Christian academies) are attached to each church and take children through the eighth grade. The supplementary Basic Education Associates, a home-study course, has also been developed. Half the offerings at the church go to missions, and missionaries are supported in Japan, India, Kenya, Mexico, Surinam, and Arizona (Indians).

Membership: Not reported.
Periodicals: *The Christian Educator.*

Sources:

Lindstrom, Paul. *Armageddon, The Middle East Muddle.* Mt. Prospect, IL: Christian Liberty Forum, 1967.

★934★
Community Churches of America
% United Community Church
Box 90
Glendale, CA 91209

Community Churches of America is the corporate expression of the various ministries headed by William Stuart McBirnie, a conservative evangelical minister. Canadian-born McBirnie, a graduate of Bethel Theological Seminary and Southwestern Baptist Theological Seminary, began his ministerial career with the Southern Baptist Convention. During the 1950s he served Trinity Baptist Church in San Antonio, Texas, but in 1959 he broke with the Convention and moved to California. After a period at First Congregational Church in Los Angeles, he accepted the pastorate of the independent United Community Church in suburban Glendale.

He built the small church into a large congregation and from it launched the many associated ministries that lifted him into prominence in both the United States and Canada. In 1961 he launched the Voice of Americanism (VOA), a daily radio program standing against communism, socialism, and religious and racial prejudice. Through VOA, McBirnie attacked many of what he considered Marxist-oriented organizations functioning in America, and dealt with a variety of social problems from marijuana to pornography and sex education in the public schools. In 1969 he founded the California Graduate School of Theology. In the mid1970s he founded World Emergency Relief, through which funds were channelled to a number of relief efforts overseas. In 1977 the growth of the congregation led to the building of a new sanctuary for worship.

The ministries have been further expanded through Frontline Missions, which sends literature to the "frontlines" where Christians face Communist aggression such as Korea, Taiwan, Hong Kong, and Thailand. Forest Springs, a mountain retreat in the Angeles forest near Los Angeles, is used for retreats and training seminars for both adults and youth. Students Against Violence in Education (S.A.V.E.) is a youth organization sponsored by VOA.

The Churches hold to a staunch conservative Protestant faith based upon the authority of the Bible. McBirnie has become most known for his application of Christian thought to social questions, especially communism and socialism. He has authored more than 150 booklets, several of which, such as "What It Means to Accept Christ," and "Should Christian Fight Communism?," have been frequently reprinted and distributed worldwide.

The various national and international ministries operate under the aegis of the Community Churches of America. The United Community Church is a single congregation affiliated with the ministries.

Membership: Not reported. In 1983 the United Community Church had approximately 1,400 members.

Educational Facilities: California Graduate School of Theology.

Sources:

McBirnie, William S. *An Awareness of Consequences.* Glendale, CA: Voice of Americanism, n.d. 16 pp.

___. *Should a Follower of Christ Be a Capitalist or a Socialist?* Glendale, CA: The Author, n.d. 18 pp.

___. *The Truth about the New Sex Education in the Schools.* Glendale, CA: The Author, (1968). 39 pp.

★935★
Evangelical Church Alliance
% Dr. George Miller, President/CEO
205 W. Broadway, PO Box 9
Bradley, IL 60915

The Evangelical Church Alliance (ECA) is an interdenominational organization of ministers who have united to promote evangelical Christianity throughout the world. What is known today as the Evangelical Church Alliance began in 1887 as the World's Faith Missionary Association. In October 1931 the name Fundamental Ministerial Association was chosen to reflect the organization's basis of unity. On July 21, 1958, during its annual convention, the name was changed to the Evangelical Church Alliance.

The ECA is conservative Protestant and strictly holds to its Renets of Faith, however, at the same time it attempts to reach beyond doctrinal differences to experience Christian unity. The ECA provides ministerial credentials for individuals who otherwise qualify and associate memberships for churches and nonprofit organizations. The ECA also provides military, prison, and hospital chaplain endorsement. The ECA holds an annual international convention that is currently held in Chicago, Illinois. In addition there are regional conventions throughout the United States and an annual Canadian convention.

Membership: In 1996 the ECA reported 2,184 clergy members.

Periodicals: *The Evangelical Church Alliance Evangel.*

★936★
Evangelical Ministers and Churches, International, Inc.
Current address not obtained for this edition.

The Evangelical Ministers and Churches, International, Inc. was formed in 1950 by a group of independent ministers. They are evangelical and fundamentalist in belief. Government is congregational, but the fellowship is headed by an executive board elected by the national convention. Missions are conducted in South Korea, Portugal, and Spain.

Membership: Not reported. In the 1970s there were approximately 150 affiliated ministers.

Educational Facilities: Colorado Bible College and Seminary.

Periodicals: *EMCI Herald.* Send orders to 106 Madison, Chicago, IL 60602.

★937★
Evangelistic Messengers' Association (EMA)
PO Box 4018
Cleveland, TN 37320

The Evangelistic Messengers' Association (EMA) is a fellowship of independent evangelical pastors/ministers founded in Chicago, Illinois, in 1933 by Mr. and Mrs. Walter Willis and Revs. Sales Malcomb Smith, Erobert Askins, and O. L. Ford. The association was designed to avoid the limitations of most denominations and maintain its existence through bonds of love and fellowship. Ministers who would become a part of the association would believe that "In essentials we must have unity, in non-essentials liberty, and in all things, charity". A brief statement of belief drawing heavily from the Apostles' Creed was adopted. As word of the association spread, membership applications began to arrive from across the United States and several foreign lands.

Today, the association licenses unordained Christian workers and pastors and provides credentials of affiliation for local churches. Ministers pay an annual fee to maintain their credentials. As the association expanded, educational facilities were established. The More than Conquerors School of Theology and Bible Institute offers both on-campus classes and correspondence courses (utilizing videos of class lectures). While ministers from many countries hold EMA credentials, particular missionary work is focused in Africa, Romania, and the Ukraine. Work in the Ukraine began in

1993 after Rev. J. David Ford, the present leader of the EMA, visited the city of Uzhgorod and realized its central location for ministry in the five countries whose borders were all less than 50 miles away.

Membership: In 1997 there were more than 500 ministers affiliated with the association in North America and that same number in countries scattered around the world.

Educational Facilities: More than Conquerors School of Theology, Cleveland, Tennessee.

More than Conquerors School of Theology, Africa.

More than Winner School of Theology, Uzhgorod, Ukraine.

Periodicals: *Operation Breakthrough Newsbreak.* • *EMA World Changer.* • *EMA NewsBreak.* • *Operation Breakthrough Messenger.*

Sources:

Barrett, David B. *World Christian Encyclopedia.* New York: Oxford, 1982.

★938★
Evangelistic Missionary Fellowship
5405 W. 1st Ave.
Lakewood, CO 80226

The Evangelistic Missionary Fellowship is a Fundamentalist Protestant church founded in 1926 as the Radio Prayer League. It began with the efforts of Rev. S. H. Patterson who wanted to initiate a ministry on the then relatively new media of radio. He started a church in Denver, and through the years other like-minded congregations were started around the United States. Patterson served as president of the fellowship until 1964, when he was succeeded by Rev. Gordon K. Peterson. Subsequent fellowship presidents have been Norman K. Peterson (1982), Ronald T. Scheimo (1987), and Cleon Laughlin (1993), the present head of the organization. The league took its present name in 1971.

The fellowship affirms the Bible as the inerrant Word of God, the Trinity, Christ as Savior, the depravity of humanity, and the reality of Satan. It also believes in supporting the government but in times of war seeks noncombatant status for all members and ministers.

The fellowship is headed by the president and a five-member board of directors elected by the delegates to the annual convention consisting of all ministers and two delegates from each local church. Churches are organized into districts, each headed by a district superintendent. All property is held in trust for the benefit and purposes of the fellowship as a whole. Local churches call their pastors, but must elect a pastor affiliated with the fellowship. Missionary congregations are found in Iran, Turkey, Guinea Bissau, Mexico, and New Guinea. There is an extensive ministry in Alaska which includes both a radio and a television station.

Membership: In 1997 the fellowship reported 3,000 members in 25 congregations served by 80 ministers in the United States and an additional 15 congregations served by 10 ministers in other countries.

Periodicals: *Update.*

Sources:

Barrett, David B. *World Christian Encyclopedia.* New York: Oxford, 1982.

★939★
Fellowship of Independent Evangelical Churches
Current address not obtained for this edition.

The Fellowship of Independent Evangelical Churches was formed in 1949 by independent fundamentalist ministers, including Dr. L. P. McClenny of Wheaton College Church in Illinois. The group is fundamentalist and premillennial, and professes a belief in angels and Satan. Members hold to separation from evil in all forms. Government is congregational. There is an annual meeting which elects officers.

Membership: Not reported. In 1970 there were 45 ministers and 10 churches, most in the South or Midwest.

★940★
Great Among Nations
Current address not obtained for this edition.

Great Among Nations, a small conservative Evangelical Christian church, was founded in Santee, California, in 1984 by Benjamin Altschul. Altschul, a Danish Jew born during World War II, converted to Christianity as a young man and migrated to the United States in 1972. He began teaching Bible classes in Los Angeles and San Diego in the early 1980s, and eventually a group attracted to his teaching formed an independent ministry. The small group emphasized Bible study and generally met in members' homes. Altschul then felt a calling into televangelism and began to create a set of videotapes as part of an evangelism ministry. The group had approximately 30 members when in the late 1980s it was attacked as a "cult" and became the subject of a series of deprogrammings, the majority carried out by Clint Daniels. The pressure of the deprogrammings led the group to move from Santee to Carlsbad, and then in March 1989 to Coronado, California. The last deprogramming, which occurred in 1989, led to a highly publicized trial in which the victim, Ginger Brown, accused Daniels and her parents of kidnapping, false imprisonment, and battery. The trial resulted in a hung jury and the judge dismissed the case. Since that time the ministry has continued its work while assuming a low profile.

Membership: Not reported. In the late 1980s there were approximately 20 members.

★941★
Greater Gospel World Outreach
6025 Moravia Park Dr.
Baltimore, MD 21206

The Greater Gospel World Outreach, formerly known as the Bible Speaks, can be traced to 1964 and the organization of a 15-member group at a Baptist church in Wiscasset, Maine by Carl H. Stevens. Under Stevens, a graduate of Moody Bible Institute in Chicago, the group grew quickly and soon built their own church near Wiscasset and Stevens began a radio broadcast over a station in Portland, Maine. There were more than 1,000 members when in 1971 the group relocated to South Berwick, Maine. While there, a Bible school was started. The group moved to South Lenox, Massachusetts in 1976. By this time, the missionary-minded organization had developed congregations in various locations along the Eastern United States and begun missionary work overseas in Europe, Kenya, and Nicaragua.

During the 1970s, the group came under attack from critics who claimed that it was brainwashing its members, however, it continued to prosper until a 1987 court ruling forced it into bankruptcy. From 1983 to 1985, Elizabeth Dovydenas, the daughter of a wealthy retail store owner, had given the church more than $6 million. In 1985, Dovydenas went through a deprogramming process and afterwards turned against the church and sued to regain her money. The court ordered the sale of the church property in Massachusetts in order to meet the judgment. At that time Stevens and many of the church members relocated to suburban Baltimore, Maryland. A short time afterward, the name of the group was changed to its present name. Even though the lost property included the church's radio broadcasting equipment, Stevens soon resumed his program, "Grace Hour," on stations in Maryland and surrounding states.

The church is a fundamentalist Christian church with a strong belief in the authority of the Bible. Stevens believes himself called to a ministry and his members consider him especially anointed by God to direct that ministry. There is a strong missionary emphasis and missionaries are supported in a number of countries.

Membership: Not reported. In 1987 the church claimed 16,000 members worldwide. Missions were conducted in 12 countries.

Educational Facilities: Maryland Bible College, Baltimore, Maryland.

Periodicals: *Wings of Glory.*

Sources:

Fisher, Marc. "Controversial Cult Moves Pastor, Dog, Stock, Flock to Maryland Suburb." *Los Angeles Times* (October 3, 1987).

Freebairn, William. "The Bible Speaks Alive in Baltimore." *Republican* (Springfield, MA) (September 17, 1989).

★942★
Rex Humbard Ministry
Box 3063
Boca Raton, FL 33431

Rex Humbard came out of a radio preacher's family. The Humbard family had broadcast over the Mutual network for more than 30 years. At age 15, Rex became the master of ceremonies. He was ordained by his father. In 1952, the Humbard family stayed for five weeks in Akron, Ohio, and Rex decided to remain there. Having been impressed with the power of television to communicate, he decided to build a congregation, go on television with its services and expand the coverage around the world. With brother-in-law Wayne Jones, he created Calvary Temple and built a stable congregation. Calvary Temple was superceded by the Cathedral of Tomorrow founded in 1958, and Humbard began the erection of the $3.5 million building. The cathedral was to be the center of a large complex, which was to include a retirement home, television station, library, and youth park.

The center of the cathedral's activity became the weekly worship service, which by 1971 was televised over 335 stations. One of the unique practices of the cathedral was the communion service held periodically and televised. Its uniqueness lay in that a week before the broadcast, the television audience was invited to participate, and participants were given instructions on preparing the elements in their homes. The cathedral had approximately 2,000 families who worshiped at the cathedral from the Akron area.

Doctrinally, Humbard is evangelical and conservative, but refuses to be pinned down on a specific creed. He opposed the cathedral's pushing any "sectarian" ideas. During Humbard's tenure as pastor, the cathedral was operated by a six-person board of trustees which included Humbard and his wife. Humbard's salary was not paid by the cathedral, but by the television outreach ministry. There were eleven ministers on the staff. As the Humbard ministry grew, the cathedral issued a monthly magazine, *The Answer.* Humbard kept a busy schedule of traveling, preaching and writing. By the end of the decade, the cathedral services were broadcast over 350 television stations in North America, 700 radio stations, and 293 foreign stations on every continent. In 1976, a special Christmas program became the first religious program carried worldwide by satellite.

In 1983, Humbard resigned as pastor of the Cathedral of Tomorrow and was succeeded by Wayne Jones. He separated the Rex Humbard Ministry from the church, though he continues as pastor emeritus. The ministry is now focused in the worldwide evangelistic preaching services, quarterly television specials supported by the Prayer-Key Family Partners, aimed at supporting and rebuilding family life. The cathedral has developed a broad program of service to the Akron community.

Membership: Not reported.

Periodicals: *Rex Humbard Family Ministry.*

Sources:

Humbard, A. E. *My Life Story.* Akron, OH: Cathedral of Tomorrow, 1945.

Humbard, Rex. *The Ten Commandments Plus 1*. Akron, OH: Cathedral of Tomorrow, n.d.

___. *Where Are the Dead?* Akron, OH: Rex Humbard World Outreach Ministry, 1977.

★943★

Independent Bible Church Movement

Current address not obtained for this edition.

During the early twentieth century as the Fundamentalist-Modernist controversy reached its peak, many independent fundamentalist Bible churches were founded, as congregations withdrew from the older denominational bodies and isolated groups formed new congregations. While many of these congregations affiliated with one of the fundamentalist associations, others have remained independent and have affiliated informally over the years with various congregations, publishing houses, missionary enterprises, and schools as deemed expedient. Among the most popular schools have been the Moody Bible Institute (Chicago, Illinois) and Dallas Theological Seminary (Dallas, Texas).

During the 1970s the number of independent Bible churches increased and leadership from the more prominent fundamentalist colleges and seminaries added impetus to the movement to plant independent fundamentalist congregations throughout the United States. Among those taking the lead in this new impulse, Church Multiplication, Inc., was formed in 1977 by people associated with Dallas Theological Seminary. It grew directly out of the New Church Development Committee of the Spring Branch Community Church in Houston, Texas. Its purpose has been to enchance church growth and assist in the formation of new independent Bible Churches. Operating in the Southwest, it has a primary focus in Texas, Arkansas, Louisiana, Oklahoma and New Mexico.

Independent Bible churches are fundamentalist in theology and believe in the infallibility of the Bible and the deity of Christ (exemplified in his virgin birth, his substitutionary atonement, literal resurrection from the dead, and his premillennial second advent). They basically accept the dispensational approach to Scripture as outlined in the *Scofield Reference Bible*. Most distinctively, such churches are congregationally unaffiliated to any denomination or congregational association.

Membership: Unknown. The directory published by Church Multiplication, Inc., in 1983 lists 248 congregations in the states of Texas, Oklahoma, Arkansas, Louisiana, and New Mexico.

★944★

Independent Christian Churches International

Current address not obtained for this edition.

Independent Christian Churches International was founded in 1984 by Dr. Donald Hicks, pastor of the Metroplex Bible Chapel of Dallas, Texas, and other conservative evangelical ministers who recognized that "faithfulness to the commands of God toward a true ministry will put them in a bitter conflict with the established church world." The Independent Christian Churches International provides a place for ministers and churches that wish to be separate from the world, yet have the necessary legal standing in the American system. Hicks serves as the churches' president and presiding bishop.

The churches' doctrinal statement sets forth the affirmations of fundamentalist Protestantism, but allows considerable freedom on most issues. The statement affirms the inspiration and infallibility of the Bible, the Trinity, redemption in Jesus Christ, salvation evidenced by a life of righteousness, baptism by immersion, the Lord's Supper, divine healing, the resurrection, the millennium, and punishment in hell for the wicked. The church is congregationally organized and is opposed to denominational labels.

Membership: In 1984 the churches reported 12,000 members, 101 congregations, and 147 ministers. There were 23,000 members worldwide.

Educational Facilities: Independent Christian Bible Training Center, Mesquite, Texas.

★945★

Independent Churches Affiliated

% Dr. Robert E. Mayer
810 E. Canal St.
Lebanon, PA 17042

Independent Churches Affiliated is a small fundamentalist body founded in 1953 by several independent congregations and ministers. It holds to a fundamentalist Christian faith, is loosely organized, and has no central headquarters. It also has no publishing concern but draws its literature form other fundamentalist organizations such as the General Association of Regular Baptist Churches. It is a member of the American Council of Christian Churches.

Membership: Not reported. In 1960 there were a reported 14,100 members.

Sources:

Piepkorn, Arthur C. *Profiles in Belief: The Religious Bodies of the United States and Canada.* Vol. IV. San Francisco, Harper & Row, 1979.

★946★

Independent Fundamental Churches of America

Box 810
Grandville, MI 49468

The Independent Fundamental Churches of America is one of the oldest and largest of the fundamental church groups. It dates to 1922 when Dr. R. Lee Kirkland, pastor of Lake Okoboji Community Tabernacle in Arnold's Park, Iowa, organized the American Conference of Undenominated Churches. Kirkland had previously participated in the Conference of Union, Federated, and Community Churches, but he opposed its modernism. In 1930, a number of Congregational Churches joined with the American Conference of Undenominated Churches to form the Independent Fundamental Churches of America (IFCA). At the organizational meeting at the Cicero Bible Church in Cicero, Illinois, O. B. Bottorff was elected president of the IFCA. For a time, the IFCA was a member of the American Council of Christian Churches (ACCC), but he left in 1953 in a dispute over differences in personalities and policies.

Doctrine of the IFCA follows five fundamentals closely: the beliefs in the inspiration of the Bible; the depravity of man; redemption through Christ's blood; the true church as a body composed of all believers; and the coming of Jesus to establish his reign. The IFCA is dispensationalist, but it rejects the ultra-dispensational views of Ethelbert W. Bullinger regarding the sacraments and soul-sleep, the belief that the soul exists in an unconscious state from death to the resurrection of the body. Whereas Bullinger said the church should not practice water baptism or the Lord's Supper, the IFCA practices both as ordinances. The total depravity of man and the eternal security of the believer (once the believer becomes a child of God, that status is secure forever) are emphasized. The IFCA believes that ecumenism, ecumenical evangelism, neo-orthodoxy, and neo-evangelicalism are contrary to faith. It believes strongly in separatism from religious apostasy. In 1970, an addition to the statement of faith was made affirming the ordinances of baptism and the Lord's Supper, and the theory of dispensationalism as divinely ordered stewardships by which God treats man according to his purpose. Polity is congregational; independent churches organize for fellowship and mutual helpfulness. The IFCA meets in convention annually. Each church can send two or more male delegates. A twelve-man executive committee plus the president are active between annual conventions. The national executive director and the editor of the *Voice* magazine are ex-officio members of the executive committee. Missions are conducted through the 20 missionary agencies approved and affiliated with the IFCA.

Membership: In 1995, the churches reported 1,600 ministerial (including students in training and missionaries) and 670 affiliated congregations. There were 69,857 lay members in the affiliated churches.

Educational Facilities: There are seven schools affiliated with the IFCA, including the following:

Appalachian Bible College, Bradley, West Virginia.

Southeastern Bible College, Birmingham, Alabama.

Carver Bible College, Atlanta, Georgia.

San Diego Bible College and Seminary, San Diego, California.

Sacramento Bible Institute, Sacramento, California.

Grand Rapids School of the Bible and Music, Grand Rapids, Michigan.

Other independent colleges of a similar doctrinal position are accepted and used by IFCA members.

Periodicals: *The Voice.* Send orders to 1860 Mannheim Rd., Westchester, IL 60153.

Sources:

Henry, James O. *For Such a Time as This.* Westchester, IL: Independent Fundamental Churches of America, 1983.

Martin, Dorothy. *The Story of Billy McCarrell.* Chicago: Moody Press, 1983.

This We Believe. Wheaton, IL: Independent Fundamental Churches of America, 1970.

★947★
Independent Fundamentalist Bible Churches
Current address not obtained for this edition.

The Independent Fundamentalist Bible Churches was formed in 1965 by a group of leaders active in the American Council of Christian Churches (ACCC). Among the founders were Dr. Marion H. Reynolds, the first president, the Rev. W. E. Standridge, the Rev. Henry Campbell, and the Rev. Kenneth L. Barth. Reverend Reynolds, formerly of the Independent Fundamental Churches of America (IFCA), was president of the ACCC, an organization from which the IFCA withdrew. Doctrine in the new church is, as the name implies, fundamentalist and Bible-oriented. It differs from the Independent Fundamental Churches of America only on its stand on the necessity of purity of doctrine in the church and on the separation of the church from all "apostasy and scripturally-forbidden alliances" (cooperation with unbelievers). Government is completely congregational (i.e., churches are independent) and the Independent Fundamentalist Bible Churches is composed of those congregations which accept its doctrinal statement.

Membership: Not reported. In 1967 there were 11 churches and 1,700 members.

★948★
International Alliance of Messianic Congregations and Synagogues
Box 417
Wynnewood, PA 19096

One of two major groupings of Messianic Jewish congregations, the International Alliance of Messianic Congregations and Synagogues was founded in 1986. Through it publications and programs it promotes the welfare of Messianic ministries and provides for the ordination of clergy. Member congregations follow the practices and traditions of Judaism, but believe that Yashua (Jesus) of Nazareth is the Jewish Messiah.

Membership: In 1994 there were 42 affiliated congregations.

Periodicals: *IAMCS Newsletter.*

Sources:

Goble, Philip E. *Everything You Need to Grow a Messianic Synagogue.* South Pasadena, CA: William Carey Library, 1974.

Rausch, David A. *Messianic Judaism.* New York: Edwin Mellen Press, 1982.

★949★
International Ministerial Federation, Inc.
Current address not obtained for this edition.

The International Ministerial Federation was founded in 1930 by Dr. J. Kellog and Dr. W. E. Opie as a fellowship of independent ministers. It has as its purpose the giving of "ministerial status and authorization to whoever wants it without affiliating with a specific denomination." There is a strong antidenominational bias. Members must be "Evangelical believers in the basic Christian concepts," but there is no statement of doctrine by which that concept could be made specific. The president of the International Ministerial Federation is Dr. Sidney Cornell of St. Petersburg, Florida, and the executive director is Dr. Opie of Fresno, California.

Membership: Not reported. In 1968 there were over 400 members, all ministers.

★950★
Moody Church
1630 N. Clark
Chicago, IL 60614

The Moody Church is named for famed evangelist Dwight L. Moody (1837-1899). In 1858 Moody began a Sunday school in an old Chicago saloon building, which later moved to Illinois Street. That initial group formally became the Illinois Street Church in 1864, and J. H. Harwood served as the first pastor. The unordained Moody served as deacon. After the Chicago fire, a temporary structure was used until a new tabernacle was built on Chicago Avenue Church in 1873-74. The church assumed its present name in 1901 to honor Moody, who had died in 1899. About 1915, construction was begun on the present church, which was dedicated in 1925. It has been the pulpit for some of the leading fundamentalist/evangelical voices in the land, including Charles A. Blanchard, R. A. Torrey, A. C. Dixon, Paul Radar, Harry A. Ironside, Alan Redpath, George Sweeting (current chancellor of Moody Bible Institute), and Warren Wiersbe.

Doctrinally, the church basically follows dispensationalism, which Moody learned from the Plymouth Brethren. Members are asked to give their assent to an eight-article doctrinal statement which includes belief in the depravity of man and the eternal security of the believer. The members also accept the responsibility to win others to Christ. Approximately 100 church members serve as missionaries on five continents. Polity is congregational.

The church sponsors the weekly "Songs in the Night" radio show, begun in 1943 and heard over some 400 stations as of 1995. Other radio broadcasts include "The Moody Church Hour" (weekly) and "Running to Win" (daily). Present pastor of the church is Dr. Erwin W. Lutzer. Associated with Moody Church, but completely separate in operation, are the Moody Bible Institute and the *Moody Monthly*, the prominent fundamentalist periodical.

Membership: In 1997 the church reported 1,100 members and supported a ministerial staff of 17.

Periodicals: *Inside Moody.* Send orders to 1609 N. La Salle St., Chicago, IL 60614.

★951★
Ohio Bible Fellowship
Current address not obtained for this edition.

The Ohio Bible Fellowship was formed in 1968 by thirteen former members of the Independent Fundamental Churches of America (IFCA) (see separate entry.) The Ohio Bible Fellowship rejected the IFCA's failure "to see the dangers inherent in mediating positions" and claimed it had "wavered under the pressure of the prevailing cooperative spirit of the age." Doctrinally, there is little difference between the fellowship and the IFCA. The pre-1970 IFCA statement of faith was adopted. To it was added a statement on baptism, professing belief in immersion as the proper mode of baptism, although baptism is not seen as essential for salvation. At least three fellowship conferences are held each year. A campground is being developed near Chesterville, Ohio. The Ohio Bible Mission aids new churches.

Membership: Not reported.

Periodicals: *The Ohio Fellowship Visitor.*

★952★
Oriental Missionary Society Holiness Church of North America
3660 S. Gramercy Pl.
Los Angeles, CA 90018

The Oriental Missionary Society Holiness Church of North America began in 1920 among several Japanese-American Christian ministerial students in Los Angeles. In that year, six seminarians—Henry T. Sakuma, George Yahiro, Paul Okamoto, Aya Okuda, Toshio Hirano, Hatsu Yano, and Hanako Yoneyama—formed a prayer fellowship with the goal of evangelizing Japanese-Americans. In 1921 they formed the Los Angeles Holiness Church. Sadaichi Kuzuhara (1886-1988) became the pastor of the group and was revered for his promotion of the cause of Japanese-American ethnic churches and his solid biblical teaching. The work spread to Japanese communities throughout California, the neighboring states, and Hawaii. In 1934 the Oriental Missionary Conference of North America was formed to oversee the work of the several congregations. Though completely disrupted by the internment of Japanese during World War II, the conference (now Church) reconstituted itself at the end of the war. After the war, Kuzuhara moved to Chicago to found the Lakeside Japanese Christian Church.

Beliefs of the church are summarized in a four-point statement. The church affirms the Trinity, the deity of Christ, the authority of the Bible, salvation of humans through Christ, and the church as consisting of all who have been regenerated through faith in Christ. There are two sacraments, baptism, and holy communion.

The church is directed by an annual conference. A ten-person executive committee implements the decisions of the annual conference.

Membership: In 1995 the church reported 2,500 members, 13 congregations, and 28 ministers in the United States.

Periodicals: *The Voice.*

Remarks: Because of its name, the church is continually associated with the Oriental Missionary Society, a holiness missionary organization founded in the early twentieth century. There has been a fraternal relationship between the church and the society, but there is no official connection. The church also has a fraternal connection with the OMS Holiness Church of Japan, from which it has drawn several of its ministers.

★953★
The Peoples Church
374 Sheppard Ave. E
Toronto, ON, Canada M2N 3B6

The Peoples Church is an independent evangelical work, founded by Dr. Oswald J. Smith in 1928 in Toronto, Ontario, Canada. It stands predominently for the conversion of souls, the edification of believers, and worldwide evangelism, emphasizing especially the four great essentials: salvation, the deeper life, foreign missions, and the return of Jesus Christ. It has been noteworthy among Evangelical Christians for its efforts, by every means, to get its message to the "Christless" masses, both at home and abroad, in the shortest possible time.

Smith was one of 10 children born to a railway telegrapher in Erneston, Ontario. Raised in the village of Embro, near London,

Ontario, he was a sickly child suffering from bouts of prolonged, undiagnosed illness. At 16 years of age, while attending an evangelistic meeting in Toronto's Massey Hall, under the ministry of R. A. Torrey, he committed his life to Christ, and dedicated his life to the single purpose of preaching the gospel to those who had never heard of Jesus Christ. At 18 he enrolled in night classes at Toronto Bible College and at the end of the term he applied for a mission posting. He was turned down, the church assuming that this 6-foot, 119-pound youth would never pass the physical examination. He went to work for the upper Canada Bible Society selling Bibles door-to-door in Ontario's Muskoka District, some 90 miles north of Toronto. There he had his first opportunity to preach, in a small Methodist church at Severn, and while there he purchased a notebook to keep a "Record of Sermons Preached." That book later contained more than 12,000 entries.

The Bible Society next asked him to go Western Canada, and at the age of 19 under the auspices of the Shantymen's Christian Association, he began a trek through the forests taking Bibles to Indian villages and lumber camps. During the summers he traveled the Kentucky mountains by horseback and muleback preaching the gospel. His experience led to his penning the words and music to "Into the Heart of Jesus, Deeper and Deeper I Go."

Smith graduated from McCormick Theological Seminary (Presbyterian) in Chicago, but found upon his return to Toronto that once again his church would not send him as a missionary. They citied as their reason that "with your poor health you could never stand the rigors of a foreign field." After the Presbyterian Church of Canada turned him down for the fourth time, Smith vowed, "If I cannot go, I will burn out my life sending others."

In 1915 at the age of 25 Smith was ordained and appointed associate pastor of the fashionable Dale Presbyterian Church in Toronto. There he met and married deaconess Daisy Billings. His burning passion for missions caused him difficulties when he lifted the missionary program of the church out of the hands of the women's missionary, society, being convinced that missions were the task of the whole church. He was asked to leave the church. He moved to British Columbia but after some six months returned to Toronto, where he turned to writing. As a result of an article for the *Toronto Globe and Mail* concerning the political unrest and famine in Armenia, the readers gave more than a quarter of a million dollars for Armenian relief. Still wanting to preach, Dr. Smith began to hold services in a rented YMCA auditorium and in 1921 the Christian and Missionary Alliance Church asked him to merge his fledgling YMCA work with its struggling Parkdale congregation.

Within 18 months the congregation moved to Christie Street Tabernacle to accommodate the 2,500 who attended service after service. In 1928 Smith launched his own independent work under the name "Gospel Tabernacle" but when it was found that the name had already been incorporated and could not be used officially, the elders of the church unanimously decided to change the name to "The Peoples Church," under which name it was officially incorporated in 1933.

Services were initially held in Massey Hall but in 1930 moved to St. James Square Church on Gerrard Street East. Every night for the first week Smith preached on missions. In July 1934, the congregation moved to the 1,500-seat Methodist Church at 100 Bloor Street East. The publisher of the *Globe and Mail* gave $20,000 toward the purchase of the building, and Dr. Smith sold the elegant pipe organ for $40,000. The two amounts almost met the purchase price of $65,000. So large were the crowds that the church soon has to stop advertising.

Smith became famous for this concept of giving to missions based on the "Faith Promise." The high point of the church year was the month-long Missionary Convention. He challenged young and old to carry the gospel to those "in the back rows" still in heathen darkness. The grand finale of the Missionary Convention was the closing Sunday when Smith announced the total of the Faith Promise. Each year it increased. In 1936 the Missionary

Medical Institute (now called Missionary Health Institute) was founded to provide prospective missionaries with a year's training in tropical diseases and in 1943 the Russian Bible Institute, offering a three-year Bible course, was established.

By 1952 the church was partially supporting 296 missionaries, with a missions budget at $258,000. Seventy percent of every dollar given to the church went to missions and the remaining 30 percent remained to maintain the home base. In 1962 the congregation of The Peoples Church moved from its downtown location on Bloor Street to newer, larger facilities on Sheppard Avenue.

Smith died on January 25, 1986 at 96 years of age, having ministered in Toronto since 1915. He was the author of 35 books, published in 128 languages, exceeding six million copies. As a poet and hymnwriter he wrote over 1,200 hymns, poems, and gospel songs, including "Then Jesus Came," "God Understands," "The Glory of His Presence," "The Song of the Soul Set Free," "Saved," and "Joy in Serving Jesus." As a missionary statesman, he led his church in a missionary program giving toward the support of over 500 missionaries and nationals worldwide. Since the church was founded, the church has raised well over 50 million dollars for global missionary support. As an editor, Dr. Smith published a magazine for over 50 years, and wrote many tracts and pamphlets. As a radio and television preacher, he was heard in Toronto and other cities since 1930 and over some 42 stations.

In 1952 the board of managers had invited Paul B. Smith, Smith's younger son, to join the staff as assistant pastor, thus freeing Smith to minister across Canada and in other countries. In 1959 Paul Smith became the senior pastor of The Peoples Church, and continued the ministry initiated by his father. He authored several books and traveled widely. During his tenure, The Peoples Christian School School (Junior Kindergarten through Grade 6) opened (1971), and The Peoples Academy (for Grade 7 through OAC) established (1975). Paul Smith died in 1995.

Dr. John D. Hull succeeded Smith as senior pastor of The Peoples Church in 1994. He had previously founded a growing church in Marietta, Georgia, in a pattern similar to that of The Peoples Church.

Membership: In 1998 there were an estimated 3,000 active members of The Peoples Church in a single center in Toronto.

Educational Facilities: Missionary Health Institute, Toronto, Ontario.

Russian Bible Institute, Toronto, Ontario.

Periodicals: *The Peoples Magazine.*

Sources:

Hall, Douglas. *Not Made for Defeat.* Grand Rapids, MI: Zondervan Publishing House, 1969.

Neely, Lois. *Fire in His Bones.* Wheaton, IL: Tyndale House Publishers, 1982.

Smith, Oswald J. *The Clouds Are Lifting.* London: Marshall, Morgan & Scott, 1936.

___. *Man's Future Destiny.* Grand Rapids, MI: Zondervan Publishing House, 1940.

___. *The Story of My Life.* London: Marshall, Morgan & Scott, 1962.

Smith, Paul B. *The Senders.* Burlington, ON: G. R. Welch Company, 1979.

★954★
River of Life Ranch and Ministry of Truth
Current address not obtained for this edition.

The River of Life Ranch and Ministry of Truth was founded in 1978 by Ed Mitchell, a Christian layman who had been working as a manager of a supermarket. He gathered his first members in Thousand Oaks, California, but the original group disintegrated following the death of a member from insulin deficiency. Mitchell had preached a doctrine of divine healing that precluded the use of doctors. The core of followers purchased property in Apple Val-

ley, California, and created a commune, the River of Life. Then in 1980 and 1981, Mitchell with the assistance of commune members Jody Scharf and Dori Webster, wrote several books that were widely distributed in Christian bookstores, *The Mystery of Babylon Revealed* (1980), *The Truth* (1980), and *The 1,981 Tribulation Report.* These books, written from an Evangelical Christian and pentecostal perspective, detailed a belief in the fast approaching disintegration of the social system and the end of the present order of things.

The idyllic life of the community, however, was disrupted in 1980. One of the members, Linda Marshall, was deprogrammed and began to complain of physical child abuse within the group. Then on February 21, 1981, deprogrammers hired by Skip Webster, who had gained some fame as the producer of the popular television series "Fantasy Island," entered the commune and kidnapped Webster's son Dennis Webster (aged 36) and two grandchildren, Todd (aged 9) and Benjamin (aged 9 months). The elder Webster had become concerned after hearing Marshall's testimony. The police stopped the kidnappers and released Webster and his two children. In the wake of the controversy, the members of the commune admitted to using corporeal punishment, but said that they did not beat their children.

In the wake of the controversy, membership in the group dwindled from 50 to around 20. Also, spokespersons for the Christian Research Institute, an Evangelical anti-cult group, took it upon themselves to contact Christian bookstores and ask them to remove the River of Life books from their shelves. That action severely cut into the cash flow of the group, which moved to sell their property. Since that time the group has taken a low profile and its present status is unknown.

Sources:

Mitchell, Ed, and Jody Scharff. *The Mystery of Babylon Revealed.* Palm Springs, CA: Victory Press, 1980. 210 pp.

___. *The Truth.* Palm Springs, CA: Victory Press, 1980. 184 pp.

——, and Dori Webster. *The 1981 Tribulation Report.* I & II. Palm Springs, CA: Victory Press, 1981.

★955★
Union of Messianic Jewish Congregations
6304 Beltline Rd.
Dallas, TX 75240

Messianic Judaism is a movement which began among American Jewish converts to Christianity in the 1960s, though it is a perspective which has periodically found expression within the larger context of Hebrew Christianity throughout the twentieth century. It has been the dominant position among Jews who become Christians that they lose their Jewish religious (if not ethnic) identity and become members of congregations of various Christian denominations. Overwhelmingly Jewish Christians have blended into mainline Christian churches and are visible primarily through the numerous independent evangelical Jewish missionary ministries they support. Among the most well-known of the Hebrew-Christian organizations which carries out a missionary program to Jews, but which does not establish separate Jewish congregations, is Hineni Ministries, better known as Jews for Jesus, founded in 1973 by Moishe Rosen, formerly with the American Board of Missions to the Jews, the largest of the Jewish missionary organizations.

Messianic Judaism, in contrast to the more popular Jewish missionary perspective, believes that Jews can still identify with Jewish culture and religious forms and be Christians. They see Christianity as completing Judaism, not a religion in stark contrast to it. While rarely assuming any organized form, Messianic Jewish thinking was always present among people associated with Jewish missions. In the 1960s it led to the formation of at least one Messianic synagogue, the Congregation of the Messiah in Philadelphia. In 1970, Martin Chernoff founded Beth Messiah in Cincinnati. The movement found its first major organizational support, however, in Chicago.

Within the Chicago-based Hebrew Christian Alliance, one of the oldest Hebrew Christian organizations in America, Messianic sentiments began to grow among the leaders of the Young Hebrew Christian Alliance in the early 1970s, partially a fallout from the Jesus People revival. By 1975 the Messianists became the majority of the Young Hebrew Christian Alliance's membership, voted in a name change, and reoriented the organization's direction as the Messianic Jewish Alliance of America. Since that time, the alliance has sponsored an annual gathering that has served as the major meeting ground for fellowship for Messianic Jews, both those within Messianic synagogues and those in more traditional gentile congregations.

In the summer of 1979, as the number of Messianic congregations increased, leaders from 33 such congregations met to form an umbrella congregational organization, the Union of Messianic Jewish Congregations. The charter meeting was held at the 1979 annual gathering of the Messianic Jewish Alliance of America, Messiah '79. Daniel C. Juster and John Fischer were the first president and vice-president respectively. Nineteen congregations joined the first year, and by 1982 there were 25.

The union set as its goals the advocacy of Messianic Judaism, the development of Messianic synagogues, and the training of Messianic leaders. In 1981, the union adopted the statement of faith of the National Association of Evangelicals, with the appropriate changes in terminology for Jewish Christians. That statement is in line with earlier guidelines which affirmed the Bible as the absolute authority in matter of belief; the divinity of Jesus, normally called by his Hebrew name, Yeshua; and salvation by grace through faith in Yeshua's atonement. Congregations generally have services on either Friday evenings or Saturday mornings in addition to Sunday worship. Worship varies considerably but each congregation's worship bears a distinctly Jewish flavor.

The union is very loosely organized with a congregational polity. To join, a congregation must have been in existence for one year and have at least 10 Messianic Jews among its members. Typically, congregations have a large number of non-Jews who are also members.

Membership: In 1987 there 57 congregations affiliated with the union, several of which are in Canada.

Educational Facilities: UMJC Yeshiva, Gaithersburg, Maryland.

Periodicals: *Messianic Judaism Today*. Send orders to 905713 Gaither Rd., Gaithersburg, MD 20877. • Unofficial: *Shofar Shalom*. Available from Beth Ha Shofar, 13001 37th Ave. S. Seattle, WA 98168. • *The American Messianic Jew*. Send orders to Box 1055, Havertown, PA 19083. • *The Messianic Outreach*. Send orders to Box 37062, Cincinnati, OH 45222.

Remarks: The Messianic movement has emerged as part of a period of aggressive Jewish evangelism and has had to face the growing activism of the Jewish religious community, which opposes any attempts by evangelical Christians to evangelize within the Jewish community. The existence of Messianic synagogues has been a particular affront to many Jewish leaders who have seen them as further attempts to destroy Judaism, deceptive in their appearance (Christian "wolves" in Jewish "sheep's clothing"). The polemic has led to a number of confrontations, the most intense having occurred in Toronto as Jews picketed Congregation Melech Yisrael, the union's center in that city.

Sources:

Fischer, John. *The Olive Tree Connection*. Downers Grove, IL: InterVarsity Press, 1983.

Goble, Phillip E. *Everything You Need to Grow a Messianic Synagogue*. South Pasadena, CA: William Carey Library, 1974.

Rausch, David. A. *Messianic Judaism*. New York: Edwin Mellon Press, 1982.

Yellow Pages. Rockville, MD: Union of Messianic Jewish Congregations, 1982.

Grace Gospel Movement

★956★
Berean Bible Fellowship
Current address not obtained for this edition.

Centered in the Pacific Southwest is the Berean Bible Fellowship. It accepts only two vast dispensations but otherwise is in concert with Charles Welch and Ethelbert W. Bullinger (whose views are discussed in the essay section of this volume). Faith in God in Christ is stressed and is differentiated as faith that receives Christ, faith that motivates the believer to walk in love, faith that constrains believers to set their minds on things above, and faith that is humble-minded when believers have among themselves the mind that was in Christ. The Phoenix center operates the Berean Tape Ministry, which distributes more than 1,000 different tapes by Oscar M. Baker (founder of the Truth for Today Bible Fellowship), Welch, Stuart Allen, Arthur E. Lamboune (the leader of the Fellowship), and others. Associated with the fellowship is Scripture Research, Inc., formerly the Ewalt Memorial Bible School, of Atascadero, California, and the Bible Fellowship Church of South Holland, Illinois.

The use of the word "Berean" by this church and a number of other groups stems from the Bible. The Acts of the Apostles mentions that members of the church at Berea in Greece were students of the Scriptures. Because the Bible is so important in the fundamentalist movement, many fundamentalist groups adopted the name "Berean."

Membership: Not reported.

Periodicals: Unofficial: *Scripture Research, Inc.* • *The Scripture Research Greek Tutor*. Send orders for both to Box 518, Atascadero, CA 93423.

Sources:

Bullinger, E. W. *The Book of Job*. Atascadero, CA: Scripture Research, 1983.

Morgan, Harold P. *Christian Values and Principles*. 3 vols. Atascadero, CA: Ewalt Memorial Bible School, n.d.

★957★
Berean Bible Fellowship (Illinois)
PO Box 6
Collinsville, IL 62234

The Berean Bible Fellowship is a fellowship of conservative fundamentalist churches founded in 1968 under the leadership of Conelius R. Stam (of Chicago, Illinois) and Win Johnson (of Denver, Colorado). Both men had been leaders in the Grace Gospel Fellowship from which they separated because of perceived permissive and liberal trends. Grace Gospel Fellowship of Wyoming, Michigan, was a focal point of the inroads of said departures.

The formal doctrinal statements of the Berean Bible Fellowship and Grace Bible College are essentially the same. Both present a basic and fundamental Christianity with a special emphasis on the distinctive apostleship and teachings of Paul and his ministry to all nations. The fellowship teaches that the church, the body of Christ, was established by the risen glorified Lord after the salvation and call of Paul (Cf. Acts 9), not at Pentecost (Acts 2) as most Christians assume. The implication of this understanding is that water baptism belongs to the earthly ministry of Christ toward Israel and was properly continued by Peter and the 12 apostles. Paul, not sent to baptize, was raised up to preach the gospel of the grace of God, a message distinct from that proclaimed by Christ and the 12 to Israel. The hope of the church is believed to be the coming of the Lord in the air, commonly called the "rapture", which will conclude the present dispensation by His gathering said church to heaven to be "forever with the Lord".

In 1940, prior to the founding of the Berean Bible Fellowship, Stam had founded the Berean Bible Society through which he had published a number of books and a periodical, *Berean Searchlight*. In 1996 the society moved from Chicago to Germantown, Wisconsin. Win Johnson had founded Grace Gospel Publishers in Denver, Colorado, where it remains to the present. Although separate organizations, both are closely related to and supportive of the Berean Bible Fellowship. The fellowship enlists membership worldwide, sponsors local and national Bible conferences, and maintains Bible study literature.

Membership: Not reported.

Periodicals: *BBF News & Notes*.

Sources:

Stam, Cornelius R. *The Controversy*. Chicago: Berean Bible Society, 1963.

___. *Satan in Derision*. Chicago: Berean Bible Society, 1972.

___. *Things That Differ*. Chicago: Berean Bible Society, 1951.

___. *True Spirituality*. Chicago: Berean Bible Society, 1959.

★958★
Bible Churches (Classics Expositor)
% Dr. C. E. McLain
1429 NW 100th St.
Oklahoma City, OK 73114

In Oklahoma, there are four churches (three in Oklahoma City and one in Moore) which are associated with C. E. McLain, pastor of the Northside Bible Church and editor of *The Classics Expositor*. A radio ministry by the Rev. David Webber was heard over eight stations in the South Central states in 1968. *The Classics Expositor* is republishing some dispensational items formerly out of print.

Membership: Not reported.

Periodicals: *The Classics Expositor*.

★959★
Concordant Publishing Concern
15570 Knochaven
Santa Clarita, CA 91330

Adolph Ernst Knoch (1874-1965), as a young believer, was briefly associated with the Plymouth Brethren (discussed elsewhere in this volume). After a time he was disfellowshipped from this group due to his differing views on points of scriptural interpretation. In 1909, the first issue of *Unsearchable Riches* appeared as an instrument of Knoch's ideas. It was printed in Minneapolis by Vladimir M. Gelesnoff, its co-editor, who soon moved to southern California, where permanent headquarters were established. Knoch launched his life-work, which was to be a new translation of the Scripture called the Concordant Version. The first part, Revelation, was published in 1919; other portions followed until 1926, when the entire New Testament was issued. In 1939, a German version was issued. Though he had finished the early phases of his translation work, Knoch lived to see only two portions of the Hebrew Scriptures published before his death: Genesis in 1957 and Isaiah in 1962.

The thrust of the Concordant Version is: 1. To correct the faults of past translations, particularly the King James, American Revised (1901), and the Revised Standard versions; 2. To determine the meanings of the inspired words of Scriptures; and 3. To produce a "literal" translation within the bounds of good diction. In the process, a new Concordance, which became the basis of the translation, was produced. The appearance of the Concordant Version created a great deal of controversy in conservative evangelical circles. While it is generally most actively used by those people associated with Knoch through *Unsearchable Riches*, it is used (often quite actively) by believers from most denominations.

Knoch's study of the Scripture, bolstered in part by his correspondence with British dispensationalist scholar Ethelbert W. Bullinger, led to a new form of dispensationalism based upon the eons (a transliteration of the Greek word usually translated "ages"). Our knowledge of God begins in his decrees before eonian times. The first eon is from creation to the disruption of Gen. 1:2. The eonian times begin with Adam and continue through five periods: innocence (Adam), conscience (Seth), government (Noah), promise (Abraham), law (Moses). The sixth period, that of Jesus' life, begins the eon of the fullness of times (Gal. 4:4). After Jesus comes the era of the nations, which includes the periods of Pentecost, transition (with Paul as priest), and the secret (with Paul the prisoner) or Grace. Currently, we are in the period of the secret. Yet to come is the period of indignation (the tribulation) and the eschatological events of the oncoming eons, which includes the binding of Satan, the millennial kingdom, the white throne judgment, the new heavens and earth, and the consummation when God is All in all (I Cor. 15:28).

Knoch's thinking had become centered upon Paul, who, Knoch was convinced, had been commissioned directly by Christ to reveal further truths; truths that Jesus had not already revealed to his original disciples. These truths concern the glories of Christ and appear throughout Paul's epistles, especially his prison epistles. From these writings, a "creed" can be constructed. Paul believed in the deity of God (Rom. 11:36), the glories of Christ (Col. 1:25), the believer's share in that glory (Eph. 1:3-5), the justification of all mankind (Rom. 5:18-19), the reconciliation of all (Col. 1:18-20), the abolition of death (I Cor. 15:20-26), and the subjection of all to God (I Cor. 15:27-28), including Satan (Eph. 1:10; Col. 1:29). Knoch thus departed from most of his former brethren by a belief in universal salvation. He felt that the believer is justified when he believes, and that the unbeliever must wait until the consummation.

Unsearchable Riches found readers who grouped around it as a tool for Bible study, and thus a national following of the eonian interpretation of Scripture developed. A song book, *Scriptural Songs*, was produced for these groups.

Membership: The Concern is not a membership organization. In 1995, *Unsearchable Riches* listed 23 independent groups in the United States, and an additional 33 groups in 15 countries. More than half of the foreign groups were to be found in Canada, Australia, and Great Britain. These groups, which include approximately 2,000 people, are informally associated with the Concern.

Periodicals: *Unsearchable Riches*.

Sources:

Adolph Ernst Knoch, 1874-1965. Saugus, CA: Concordant Publishing Concern, 1965.

Concordant Literal New Testament. Saugus, CA: Concordant Publishing Concern, 1966.

The Concordant Version in the Critics' Den. Los Angeles: Concordant Publishing Concern, n.d.

Scriptural Songs. Saugus, CA: Concordant Publishing Concern, n.d.

★960★
Grace Gospel Fellowship
2125 Martindale SW
PO Box 9432
Grand Rapids, MI 49509

The Grace Gospel Fellowship is an organization of autonomous churches that preach dispensational theology from what is termed a Pauline perspective. J. C. O'Hair was an early exponent of this theological position in Chicago, Illinois. There have been several developmental stages. First, in 1938, a group of pastors and laypersons met to formulate a structure to implement the spread of this message at home and abroad. A doctrinal statement was agreed upon: a constitution was formulated, and in January

1939, the World Wide Grace Testimony (later Grace Mission and now Grace Ministries, International) came into being.

In 1944, the Grace pastors met in Evansville, Indiana, and formally organized the Grace Gospel Fellowship. J. C. O'Hair and Charles Baker continued as prominent leaders. At first a ministers' fellowship, it was later opened to laymen. Charles O'Connor became its first full-time president in 1971. Roger G. Anderson, a pastor for 33 years and a graduate of Grace Bible College succeeded him in October 1991.

In 1945 the Milwaukee Bible Institute was founded by the organization and Charles Baker, a fundamentalist pastor and was operated as a function of the local congregation. This school developed a full curriculum in the late-1940s, and in 1961, it moved to Grand Rapids, Michigan, as Grace Bible College. The school has since received accreditation from both North Central Accrediting and the AABC.

The doctrine of the Grace Gospel Fellowship follows a limited Calvinistic view with emphasis on the total depravity of man and eternal security (once a person is a child of God, that status is secure but not in the concept of limited atonement). Specific doctrine affirms the temporary nature of both the gifts of the Spirit (I Cor. 12:4-11) and baptism. There is no connection with the beliefs of Ethelbert W. Bullinger and Charles Welch regarding observation of the Lord's Supper, annihilationism, or a two Body concept. Eschatologically the group adheres to the pre-millennium, pretribulation concepts of John Nelson Darby, founder of the Plymouth Brethren.

Membership: In 1997 the fellowship reported 143 churches, and 286 ministers in the United States and 1,400 additional churches worldwide.

Educational Facilities: Grace Bible College, Grand Rapids, Michigan.

Periodicals: *Truth.*

Sources:

Baker, Charles F. *Bible Truth*. Grand Rapids, MI: Grace Bible College, Grace Gospel Fellowship, Grace Mission, 1956.

___. *Dispensational Relations*. Grand Rapids, MI: Grace Line Bible Lessons, n.d.

___. *God's Clock of the Ages*. Grand Rapids, MI: Grace Line Bible Lessons, 1937.

Egemeier, C. V., ed. *Grace Mission Story*. Grand Rapids, MI: Grace Missions, 1967.

★961★
Last Day Messenger Assemblies
(Defunct)

Nels Thompson, born in Denmark, immigrated to the United States in the early 1900s and, in 1912, was converted in a meeting of the Plymouth Brethren (Grant Brethren) under the leadership of Harry A. Ironside, later pastor of Moody Church. Thompson became an evangelist, but a conflict arose with the Brethren over the control of his evangelical activity. He also accepted the Grace Gospel position and dropped water baptism (as of the Jewish dispensation). He founded an assembly at Oakland, and, soon, others were formed.

The Gospel Tract Distributors was founded as an independent, but associated, publishing concern, and began publishing *Outside the Camp* (now *Last Day Messenger*) as a nondenominational dispensational periodical. Each issue carried a seven-point statement of belief in the verbal inspiration of the Bible, the Trinity and the deity of Christ, total depravity, redemption by grace, the security of the believer, the personality and punishment of Satan, and the pretribulation second coming. The group did not practice baptism and was opposed to celebrating Christmas and Easter. Headquarters for Gospel Tract Distributors remain in Portland, Oregon. The assemblies were disbanded in the mid-1990s.

Periodicals: *Last Day Messenger.*

★962★
Timely Messenger Fellowship
℅ Pastor Charles Wages
Grace Bible Church
1450 Oak Hill Rd.
Fort Worth, TX 76112

The Timely Messenger was begun in 1939 by Pastor Ike T. Sidebottom of Fort Worth, Texas, as a periodical expounding the Grace Gospel position in the Southwest. Sidebottom had been a student at Moody Bible Institute in Chicago and served as an associate pastor for J. C. O'Hair, the early Grace Gospel pastor in Chicago. Sidebottom returned to Fort Worth in 1928 with the intention of establishing himself as a radio evangelist. His following in a Bible class, however, grew into a church on College Avenue. Work continued to grow from the pulpit of College Avenue Church (rebuilt in 1950), the periodical, and the radio program. Through College Avenue Church, other men were prepared for the ministry, and independent congregations began to emerge. Most ministers work full-time at a secular job and serve as pastors on the weekends. In 1980, the congregation of the College Avenue Church built a new building, and in their new location became known as Grace Bible Church.

The Timely Messenger Fellowship is an informal, cooperative endeavor. It differs from the Grace Gospel Fellowship, discussed elsewhere in this chapter, in that it neither baptizes nor partakes of the Lord's Supper. Mission work is done through Grace Ministries International and Things to Come Mission. The Timely Messenger Fellowship sponsors summer camps and mid-winter conferences for high school and college students.

Membership: No formal "membership" is maintained.

Periodicals: *The Timely Messenger.*

★963★
Truth for Today Bible Fellowship
Box 6358
Lafayette, IN 47903

The dispensational Bible teachings of Ethelbert W. Bullinger and Charles Welch were passed to Stuart Allen, who succeeded Welch as pastor of the Chapel of the Opened Book in London. He edits *The Berean Expositor* and has written a number of books and pamphlets. In the United States, Welch's theological disciples are grouped in local fellowships built around several periodicals. One such periodical, *Truth for Today*, was begun in 1948 by Oscar M. Baker (1898-1987) of Warsaw, Indiana. Baker had been a student of Dr. S. E. Long, an early follower of Bullinger and an extension teacher at Moody Bible Institute. He began his preaching in an abandoned church in Lulu, Michigan. Baker distributed Bullinger's, Welch's, and Allen's books, and supported a tape ministry located in Indianapolis, Indiana.

Baker was succeeded by Joseph L. Watkins, current editor of *Truth for Today*. The Fellowship sponsors a radio ministry that is heard over stations in Vancouver, Washington, and Phoenix. The correspondence course is distributed from Lafayette, Indiana. Congregations in fellowship with the fellowship are located in Alabama, Tennessee, Illinois, Iowa, Indiana, Wisconsin, Michigan, New York, Oklahoma, California, and Canada. A very active group associated with the Berean Chapel in Mobile has radio ministries in Dallas, Lansing (Illinois), and Mobile. *Truth for Today* is mailed to all 50 states and over 38 foreign countries.

Membership: Not reported. In 1988, *Truth For Today* circulated more than 5,700 copies per issue.

Periodicals: *Truth for Today.*

★964★
The Way International
PO Box 328
New Knoxville, OH 45871

The Way International was founded by Victor Paul Wierwille (1916–1985) in 1942 as the "Vesper Chimes," a radio ministry over a station in Lima, Ohio. Wierwille was a minister in the Evangelical and Reformed Church (now a constituent part of the United Church of Christ) into which he had been ordained the previous year. The radio ministry later was renamed "The Chimes Hour" and then incorporated as "The Chimes Hour Youth Caravan." During these years Wierwille became an avid student of the Bible. In 1951 he manifested the reception of God's Holy Spirit by way of speaking in tongues, one of the nine manifestations of the one gift(I Corinthians 12:7). All of his study culminated in the first Power of Abundant Living Class, a series of sessions presenting his basic perspective on Biblical truth, in 1953. Two years later his ministry was chartered as The Way, Inc. (changed to The Way International in 1975). In 1957 Wierwille resigned from the Evangelical and Reformed Church to devote himself full-time to his growing work. The Wierwille family farm outside New Knoxville, Ohio, was donated to the ministry as its headquarters.

The Way, Inc., grew steadily during the 1960s and then experienced a sudden growth in the 1970s as the "Jesus People" revival spread across the United States. The facilities at New Knoxville were expanded and hosted the first national Rock of Ages festival, the annual gathering of people associated with the ministry, in 1971. The Way considers itself to be a biblical research, teaching, and household fellowship ministry. It neither builds nor owns any church buildings but holds its meetings in home fellowships. Often overlooked by those who write about The Way's development is the role that Wierwille's research in Aramaic has played. He was spurred on by his personal relationship and contact with Dr. George M.Lamsa, translator of the Lamsa Bible. Among the activities of the The Way have been the establishment of a large Aramaic facility (completely computerized) and the training of a group of scholars in the Aramaic (Syrian) language.

Like other Grace Gospel churches, The Way teaches a form of dispensationalism, although Wierwille preferred the term "administration." According to Wierwille, present believers live under the church administration that began at Pentecost. Scripture from before Pentecost is not addressed to the Church but is for the believer's learning. Pre-Pentecost scripture includes the Old Testament and the four Gospels. Acts serves as a transition volume from the Old Testament to the New Testament. The Book of Acts chronicles the rise and expansion of the first-century Church.

Doctrinally, The Way could be considered both Arian and Pentecostal. It rejects the trinitarian orthodoxy of most of Western Christianity. It believes in the divinity of Jesus Christ, the divine conception of Jesus by God, and that he is the Son of God but not God the son. It also believes in receiving the fullness of the Holy Spirit, God's power, which may be evidenced by the nine manifestations of the spirit: speaking in tongues, interpretation of tongues, prophecy, word of knowledge, word of wisdom, discerning of spirits, faith (believing), miracles, and healing.

The Way International is organized on the model of a tree, from the root (international headquarters) to trunks (national organizations) to limbs (state and province organizations) to branches (organizations in cities and towns) to household fellowships (small, individual fellowship groups). Administratively, the ministry is directed by a three-member board of trustees. Founding president Wierwille was succeeded by Rev. L. Craig Martindale. Currently, Martindale serves with Rev.Rosalie F. Rivenbark, the vice president, and Mr. Howard R. Allen, the secretary-treasurer. The board appoints the cabinet which oversees the Headquarters complex. Each of the ministry's two properties in the United States (located in New Knoxville, Ohio and Gunnison, Colorado) is a designated Root location. American Christian Press is The Way's publishing arm.

Those desiring the research, teaching, and fellowship may take a basic 12-session course called "The Way of Abundance and Power" developed by Rev. Martindale, building on Dr. Wierwille's work. Several options are open to graduates of the course. Many continue to attend home fellowships. Others may avail themselves of the Disciples of the Way Outreach Program, which is designed to build quality of life based on The Way's biblical teachings. The Way of Abundance and Power has run all over the United States and in Europe, Australia, Asia, South America, and Africa and recently has been translated into French and Spanish.

Membership: Not reported. Outside of the United States, The Way International currently has work in over 30 countries and U.S. territories.

Educational Facilities: The Way College, Emporia, Kansas. The Way College of Biblical Research, Rome City, Indiana.

Periodicals: *The Way Magazine.*

Remarks: Criticism of The Way has been mounting and intense. Most has focused on the standard anti-cult theme, accusing The Way of brainwashing youthful members and Wierwille of growing rich from the movement. In addition, critics claim that Wierwille has been training The Way members in the use of deadly weapons for possible future violent activity against the group's enemies. This criticism derived from The Way College's cooperation with the State of Kansas program to promote hunting safety, in which all students had the choice (but were not required) to enroll. No evidence of any violent motivations, intent, or actions has been produced to back up this criticism.

In 1985 the U.S. Internal Revenue Service revoked The Way International's tax exempt status. The case is under appeal.

Sources:

Juedes, John P., and Douglas V. Morton. *From "Vesper Chimes" to "The Way International."* Milwaukee, WI: C.A.R.I.S., n.d.

Morton, Douglas V., and John P. Juedes. *The Integrity and Accuracy of The Way's Word.* St. Louis, MO: Personal Freedom Outreach, [1980].

Whiteside, Elena S. *The Way, Living in Love.* New Knoxville, OH: American Christian Press, 1972.

Wierwille, Victor Paul. *Jesus Christ Is Not God.* New Knoxville, OH: American Christian Press, 1975.

___. *Jesus Christ, Our Promised Seed.* New Knoxville, OH: American Christian Press, 1982.

___. *Power for Abundant Living.* New Knoxville, OH: American Christian Press, 1971.

___. *Receiving the Holy Spirit Today.* New Knoxville, OH: American Christian Press, 1972.

Williams, J. L. *Victor Paul Wierwille and The Way International.* Chicago: Moody Press, 1979.

Other Bible Students

★965★
The Church (in Augusta, Maine)
Current address not obtained for this edition.

The Church (in Augusta, Maine) is a fellowship that grew up around the ministry of Gene Edwards. Edwards, a graduate of Southwestern Baptist Theological Seminary, was on his way to becoming an outstanding Southern Baptist minister, but during his early years in the pastorate became discouraged with the way the denomination treated people, which led to the further conclusion that Christianity, in general, was dead. Reading a copy of *The Normal Christian Church Life* by Watchman Nee led him to the Local Church (a Chinese movement that had developed out of the Plymouth Brethren) and through the rest of the decade he associated himself with Witness Lee.

In 1969 Edwards moved to Santa Barbara, California, where he associated with a group of independent Christians formerly affiliated with Campus Crusade for Christ, an independent Evangelical campus ministry. While living in Santa Barbara, Edwards broke with Witness Lee. The small group became known as the Church in Isla Vista (the name of the unincorporated community adjacent to the University of California-Santa Barbara). By the spring of 1973 there were approximately 225 members, but the group was decimated with internal discord, and a split cost it the great majority of support. The remaining members formed a commune and held all their possessions in common.

In 1976 many of the older members left Santa Barbara for various spots around the world (Belgium, Germany, Switzerland, Hawaii, Thailand, and Nepal) where they began missionary work. Edwards worked for a year in Canada. Then in 1981, Edwards dissolved the work in Isla Vista and moved with some of the members to Maine. By this time, communal living had been abandoned. In Maine, Edwards established a new congregation. He also authored a number of books that have been widely circulated through Christian bookstores.

The Church in Augusta (and affiliated groups) follows a conservative dispensational Evangelical faith that carries with it the strong critique of denominational Christianity, which the Plymouth Brethren passed to the Local Church. Part of that critique included the unwillingness to accept any name other than "the Church" with some geographical designation to distinguish it from other groupings.

Membership: Not reported.

Sources:

Edwards, Gene. *The Divine Romance.* Gardiner, ME: Christian Books Publishing House, 1984. 207 pp.

___. *The Early Church.* Isla Vista, CA: Christian Books, 1974.

___. *How It 'All Began.* Isla Vista, CA: The Church in Isla Vista, (1975). 37 pp.

___. *Letter to a Devastated Christian.* Augusta, ME: Christian Books, 1984. 47 pp.

___. *Our Mission.* Gardiner, ME: Christian Books, 1980. 211 pp.

★966★
The Church Which Is Christ's Body
Current address not obtained for this edition.

The nondenominational theme which was so pronounced in Plymouth Brethren thinking found an ally in the person of Maurice M. Johnson, a former minister with the Methodist Episcopal Church, South (MECS). Licensed to preach in Texas in 1912, he moved to Los Angeles, California, in 1921 as assistant pastor at Trinity, the congregation of Robert Schuler, the Methodist pastor. In 1925, he withdrew from the MECS, objecting to the Church's church-school literature and its ministerial training course. With seventy-five followers, he established an independent Maranatha Tabernacle, but two years later withdrew from it and from his role as a salaried pastor and "began to preach only as a minister of Jesus Christ in the church which is Christ's Body." As he traveled about preaching, a fellowship of Christians, both members and those called to preach, emerged.

The distinctive feature of this fellowship is its refusal to be known by "any denominational name," even such a nondescript name as the "brethren." The group also refuses to incorporate. Members do not use any titles, such as "Reverend," which would distinguish clergy and laity, though they do recognize divinely given offices of pastor, evangelist, teacher, elder, and deacon. In this age, there are no longer apostles and prophets. Members believe that all people who have been convicted of their sins, have personal faith in Christ, and have been added to his body are fellow-members of the church which is Christ's Body. Members of the fellowship think of themselves as merely "some members of the church which is Christ's Body," outside all man-made organizations. Whenever two or more Christians gather for fellowship

they constitute a Christian assembly, a local manifestation of the church.

The fellowship teaches fundamental Christianity, including belief in the Trinity, the incarnation of Christ and his finished work on the cross, and the Bible as the only guide. Members see the Bible interpreted in terms of God's successive dispensations. We live in the dispensation begun at Pentecost, when believers began to be baptized by the Lord with one Spirit into one body. Ordinances of baptism and the Lord's Supper are not practiced in the present dispensation. Ordination is considered an act of recognition by an assembly that God has called an individual to the office of elder. Members do not object to saluting the flag and do not endorse conscientious objection to military service.

Assemblies are centers of aggressive evangelism. Ministers are supported by the assemblies, but do not receive a regular salary. A vigorous tract and radio ministry has been established. Maurice Johnson received mail in Orangeville, California, though there are no formal headquarters of the autonomous assemblies. Other leaders include Berl Chisum of Los Angeles, James Cox of Charlottesville, Virginia, and Jack Langford of Fort Worth, Texas. There are assemblies in Los Angeles, San Diego, Riverside, San Luis Obispo, Sacramento, and other places in California; Fort Worth, Texas; Tulsa, Oklahoma; and Charlottesville, Virginia. No membership records are kept because identifying church members is considered a prerogative of God, the head of the church.

Membership: No membership records available.

Sources:

A Federal Court Acknowledges Christ's True Church. Fort Worth, TX: Manney Company, [1963].

★967★
The (Local) Church
% Living Stream Ministry
1853 W. Ball Rd.
Anaheim, CA 92804

The group that is variously known as the Little Flock or the Local Church was founded in the 1920s in China by Ni Shu-tsu, popularly known by the English translation of his name, Watchman Nee (1903-1972). Nee was born into a Chinese Christian family, his grandfather serving as a Congregationalist minister and his parents faithful Methodists. He changed his given name, Ni Shu-tsu (Henry Nee) to To-Sheng (Watchman), as a constant reminder to himself that he was a bell-ringer whose purpose was to raise up people for God.

From a nominally religious youth, he was converted by Dora Yu, a Methodist evangelist, and soon afterward began working with Margaret E. Barber, an independent missionary through whom he discovered the writings of John Nelson Darby and the exclusive Plymouth Brethren. He adopted Darby's nondenominational approach to church organization and soon emerged as the leader of a small band of evangelical Christians. By the end of the decade he had made contact with that branch of the Brethren led by James Taylor and at their invitation visited England in 1933. They, however, soon broke relationships with Nee because of his unauthorized fellowship with the Honor Oak Christian Fellowship, a non-Brethren group headed by T. Austin Sparks.

From its modest beginning in Foochow, Nee's movement spread through China. During the 1930s, he traveled widely and founded congregations based upon his idea that there should be only one local church (i.e., congregation) in each city as the basic expression of the unity of Christianity (in the face of divisive denominationalism). More than two local churches were raised up by his ministry between 1922 and 1952 (when the Chinese revolution ended the spread of Christianity). Nee also authored more than 50 books, mostly on Christian life and church life. His mature view of the church is found in his most famous book, *The Normal Christian Church Life.* He also authored the *The Spiritual Man,* in which he developed his understanding of the tripartite nature of human beings as body, soul, and spirit.

The new People's Republic of China, following its rise to power in 1949, accused Nee (and by association the churches affiliated with him) of being a spy for the Americans and the Nationalist government. He was first exiled from Shanghai and then in 1952 imprisoned. He died in prison in 1972.

During the 1930s, Nee gained a follower in the person of Witness Lee, a former Protestant minister who founded, established, and became an elder of the church at Chefoo. He joined Nee in the ministry in 1932 and within a few years was among Nee's most valuable assistants. After a three-year absence fighting tuberculosis, Lee rejoined Nee in full-time work in 1948, on the eve of the Chinese Revolution. Nee sent Lee to Taiwan where the church was to flourish and spread around the Pacific Basin.

Members migrating to the United States brought the movement to the West Coast. Lee moved to America in 1962 and founded Living Stream Ministry. He has since been recognized as the leading full-time worker among the local churches, and has provided overall direction for the spread of the Local Church. He also has been a source for innovation in the movement by his introduction of several theological emphases not found in the writings of Watchman Nee and his initiation of several practices such as "pray reading" and "calling upon the name of the Lord," both of which have become the subject of controversy.

Organization. The Local Church affirms the unity of the church, the corporate nature of church life, and the direct headship of Christ over the church. Great emphasis is thus placed on church life, meeting together (several times a week), and the function and responsiblity of each member in keeping alive a relationship with God and sharing the duties of congregational life. In rejecting the clergy-laity distinction, a pattern for the practical expression of the church's life has been established.

The Local Church is organized as a fellowship of autonomous congregations, one in each city. Each congregation is led by a small group of elders, two to five men drawn from the congregation's recognized leaders, who teach, preach, and administer the congregation's temporal affairs. There are also a small number of men who have an apostolic function, who travel among the local churches as teachers and leadership trainers and start new congregations in those cities where the Local Church is not yet organized. Such men, designated workers, organize their efforts, more or less formally, as an independent ministry. In the case of Witness Lee, for example, his work is incorporated as the Living Stream Ministry, and is currently the most prominent apostolic endeavor among the Local Churches.

As with the Plymouth Brethren, the adoption of Darby's "nondenominational" stance created a problem as Nee's movement took no name by which to be denominated. The Local Church sees itself as simply the Church. The term "local church" is a convenient designation but not a name. Local congregations call themselves "The Church in (name of the city)."

The Local Church has generally spread through the happenstance movement of members who would organize a congregation in a new city or the efforts of the apostolic workers. The church in the United States was initially started by members who migrated from Taiwan. However, in recent years, with Lee's encouragement, the Local Church has adopted a new strategy, which they call the "Jerusalem Principle," by which church members as a small group migrate to a new locale for the single purpose of seeding a new congregation.

Beliefs. The local churches follow the teachings found in the voluminous writings of Watchman Nee and Witness Lee. A convenient summary is found in a booklet, "The Beliefs and Practices of the Local Churches" (reprinted in *The Encyclopedia of American Religions: Creeds*). The statement professes a belief in fundamental Christianity, similar to that if the Plymouth Brethren, and affirms belief in the Trinity, the deity of Christ, the virgin birth of Jesus, the substitutionary atonement, the resurrection of Jesus, His second coming, and the verbal inspiration of the Bible.

Particular attention, as might be expected, is given to a treatment of the unity of the Church, the Body of Christ. Sectarianism, denominationalism, and interdenominationalism are all rejected, and the oneness of all believers in each locality affirmed.

The Local Church sees itself in a history of recovery (or restoration) of the biblical church. Since apostolic times the full life and unity of the Church was lost but a recovery began with Martin Luther and the Protestant Reformation and has continued through the pietist recovery of Count Zinzendorf and the Moravians, John Wesley and the Methodists, and more recently the Plymouth Brethren. Through the local churches the Christian experience of the riches of Christ (i.e., the enjoyment of Christ as life), and the practice of church life according to the Scripture are being recovered. Some elements of the recovery have become the focus of controversy.

"Pray reading" is a devotional practice that uses the words of Scripture as the words of prayer. Individuals or groups will, when praying, repeat words and phrases from the Scripture over and over, frequently interjecting words of praise and thanksgiving, as a means of allowing the Scripture to impart an experience of the presence of God in the person praying. "Calling upon the name of the Lord" as the very name of the practice indicates, is an invocation of God by the repetition of phrases such as "O Lord Jesus."

"Burning" is a term to denote a close contact with God. When a person impresses another with the message of the Gospel, that person is seen as having been "burned." "Burning" is also an occasional practice by which objects symbolic of a person's pre-Christian existence or of a phase of lesser commitment are destroyed in a fire. Like "burning" objects from a rejected past, "burying," literally a rebaptism, is symbolic of a newer level of Christian commitment, and members of a local church might be baptized more than once.

Membership: In 1991 the Local Church listed congregations on six continents. The largest numbers are in the Pacific rim countries. Taiwan has 200 churches with 60,000 members. The combined United States and Canadian membership is 15,000 in 265 churches. There are 16,500 members in Spanish-speaking congregations in South and Central America. There are also churches in Europe, Africa, Australia, and New Zealand. In spite of the intense persecution, it appears that congregations have survived in mainland China, and that the movement actually spread over the last decades to include tens of thousands of people.

Since the demise of the Soviet Union, the Local Churches have initiated evangelical work in Eastern Europe and Russia. As of 1992 the Local Church had congregations in Moscow and St. Petersburg and was developing work in other countries as well.

Periodicals: *Voice.* Available from Living Stream Ministry, Box 2121, Anaheim, CA 92804.

Remarks: A controversy that emerged in the 1970s between the Local Church and some prominent voices within the larger Evangelical Christian community culminated in a series of legal actions in the mid-1980s. Different writers, some known for their battle against some of the new religions, the so-called "cults," attacked the Local Church for heresy and its development of unique forms of Christian piety. Several books were written and several items on the Local Church appeared in the Christian "anti-cult" literature. Claiming libel and unable to get an apology for what it felt were unjust criticisms that were harming its ministry, the Local Chruch instituted several lawsuits which brought retractions and apologies from all but one organization, the Spiritual Counterfeits Project, which had published a book attacking the church. That case went to court and in 1985 an $11 million judgement for libel was rendered against the Spiritual Counterfeits Project.

Sources:

The Beliefs and Practices of the Local Churches. Anaheim, CA: Living Stream Ministry, 1978.

Duddy, Neil T., and the Spiritual Counterfeits Project. *The God-Men.* Downers Grove, IL: InterVarsity Press, 1981.

Ford, Gene. *Who Is the Real Mindbender?* Anaheim, CA: The Author, 1977.

Freeman, William T. *In Defense of the Truth.* Seattle, WA: Northwest Christian Publications, 1981.

Kinnear, Angus I. *Against the Tide.* Ft. Washington, PA: Christian Literature Crusade, 1973.

Lee, Witness. *Gospel Outlines.* Anaheim, CA: Living Stream Ministry, 1980.

___. *How to Meet.* Taipei, Taiwan: Gospel Book Room, 1970.

___. *The Practical Expression of the Church.* Los Angeles: Stream Publishers, 1970.

Melton, J. Gordon. *An Open Letter Concerning the Local Church, Witness Lee and the God-Men Controversy.* Santa Barbara, CA: Institute for the Study of American Religion, 1985.

Nee, Watchman. *The Normal Christian Church Life.* Washington, DC: International Students Press, 1969.

Roberts, Dana. *Understanding Watchman Nee.* Plainfield, NJ: Haven Books, 1980.

Sparks, Jack. *The Mind Benders.* Nashville, TN: Thomas Nelson, 1977.

★968★
The Two-by-Two's
Current address not obtained for this edition.

The group of Christians called "Two-by-Twos" in this text are also referred to as Cooneyites, Go Preachers, and Tramp Preachers, but they claim no name but Christian. All of these names have been placed upon this somewhat anonymous group by outsiders. The group itself, though numbering in the tens (some suggest hundreds) of thousands of members in the United States, has remained virtually invisible. Members shun publicity, refuse to acquire church property, and issue no ministerial credentials or doctrinal literature, believing that the Bible (King James Version) is the only textbook and that, to be effective, the communication of spiritual life must take place orally, person-to-person. The only printed documents are hymnals. The distinctive feature of the movement has been sending forth, two by two, unmarried teams of preachers who, "as they go, preach" (Matt. 10:7).

The Two-by-Two's originated with William Irvine (1863-1947), a Scotsman and member of the Faith Mission founded in 1886 by Mr. John George Govan (1861-1927). The mission, which worked in neglected rural communities, spread to Ireland. Irvine was a leader at Menagh in County Tipperary. Taking his direction from a literal reading of the Gospel of Matthew, chapter 10, Irvine began to feel that the Faith Mission's practices related to renouncing the world were not as strict as called for in the scripture. By 1899 he had begun independent work and in 1901 formally severed any connection with the Faith Mission. Among the young preachers who joined him was Edward Cooney, a strong leader and zealous worker, from whom one of the derisive names comes. Cooney and Irvine, unfortunately, had differences, and Cooney withdrew from working with Irvine.

In 1903 Irvine held a convention at which the pattern for the next decades were set. Ministers were to give over their possessions to the work, renouncing their former life. They took vows of poverty, chastity, and obedience. Following the meeting, ministers were dispersed to carry the gospel around the world—Australia, New Zealand, South Africa, China, South America, and the European mainland. Irvine, George Walker and Irving Weir brought the movement to the United States. They were soon joined by Jack Carroll, his sister Mae Carroll, William Cleland, Tom Clarke, George Beatty, Tom Grooms, John Burns, and Alfred Magowan. By the end of the decade the movement had spread across the eastern half of the United States. In the South, black preachers added their efforts. By 1923, the movement reached Hawaii.

During the years just prior to World War II, Irvine began to predict the end of the dispensation of grace in 1914. His prophetic zeal, as well as conflict over his role as a general overseer of the movement, led to schism and the ouster of Irvine from leadership of the movement which has since been led collectively by the overseers in the various fields. Irvine moved to Jerusalem and lived there for the rest of his life, supported by a small number of followers.

The Two-by-Two's originated not as a doctrinal movement, but as a response by young Christians to follow the example and admonitions of Christ in their life. Membership in the group involved the acceptance of a pattern of renunciation of the world rather than allegiance to a creed. Beginning with the evangelical faith common to free church Protestants in England at the turn of the century, the group took the Bible as their only creed and have allowed considerable variation in expression and belief. The most orthodox presentation of their faith appears in their hymnbook. Critics, primarily former members, have published excerpts of sermons of leading preachers which indicate that a unitarian theology which denies the Trinity and emphasizes the role of Jesus and human example is a prominent perspective and that further doctrinal variation from evangelical belief is present. Two ordinances are observed: adult believers baptism by immersion (including rebaptism of those who come from other church bodies) and the Lord's Supper, which is observed weekly. Most emphasis is placed upon a holy life indicated by modes of dress, no jewelry (except wedding rings), and generally, no television. Women wear no makeup and do not cut their hair. Conscientious objection to war is general, but not mandatory.

The fellowship has an "episcopal" polity. The United States and Canada are divided into fields, typically a state or province, each with an overseer (also called "senior servant" or "elder brother"). The overseers acting in fellowship exercise general supervision of the movement as a whole. The members are organized into house churches of from 12 to 20 members presided over by a bishop (or local elder). Members meet on Sunday for the breaking of bread and during the week for Bible study.

The missionary and evangelistic arm of the movement is supplied by the preachers. These unmarried "servants" travel in teams of two as successors of the Apostles (Matt. 10:1-7). They move into a new community, hold evangelistic services and gather a following. Members of the house churches will support any evangelistic services in their area. The preachers do not draw a salary, but are supported by the free-will gifts of the members.

There is an annual group meeting, or convention, of each field. It typically is held on a large farm, with members camping while in attendance. In these meetings, matters of work, doctrine, discipline, and policy are aired, and decisions are made. There are house churches in all 50 states and throughout Canada. George Walker, the last of the original preachers in America, died in 1981.

Reportedly, Edward Cooney, following his break with Irvine, came to the United States and began his own variation on Irvine's movement. Recent reports indicate that a few members survive, some in North America, but that there are no preachers, and that it is a dying group.

Membership: Not reported. In the mid-1980s there were 96 annual conventions held in the United States, with an average attendance of from 500 to 2,000 each. That attendance would indicate between 10,000 and 100,000 members in the United States, and possibly twice that number in other countries.

Remarks: Only in the late 1970s did substantive literature on the Two-by-Two's become available. Since that time, individual researchers have appeared who have gathered the scant literature (such as notices of conventions). To date only one book, by an ex-member and his wife, has appeared (though at least one other major study is projected). In the United States, Threshing Floor Ministries, headed by a former member, is collecting data (which has been reviewed in preparing this item for the *Encyclopedia*).

Critics of the movement have charged that it has concealed its origins, especially hiding its association with Irvine and its recent origin, and that it has presented a false front of evangelical orthodoxy when in fact it is completely heterodox. Because of the difficulty in gaining authoritative material about the group, and the contradictory reports on its normative beliefs, no assessment of the doctrinal issue is possible. There is, however, little doubt of its rejection of its early (and to some extent) unhappy history.

Sources:

Crow, Keith W. *The Invisible Church*. Master's thesis, University of Oregon, Eugene, 1964.

Hymns Old and New. Glasgow, Scotland: R. L. Allan and Son, 1951.

Parker, Doug, and Helen Parker. *The Secret Sect*. Pandle Hill, N.S.W., Aust.: The Authors, 1982.

Paul, William E. *They Go About "Two by Two."* Denver, CO: Impact Publications, 1977.

★969★
Witness and Testimony Literature Trust and Related Centers
Current address not obtained for this edition.

Theodore Austin-Sparks, a former member of the Baptist Church, left to found an independent meeting place in the Honor Oak suburb of London, England, for Christians who wished to fellowship together around the Lord Jesus Christ and not men. That ministry was conceived to be apart from and above traditional denominational barriers. The nondenominational approach manifests the influence of Plymouth Brethren. Austin-Sparks was also influenced by Jessie Penn-Lewis (1861-1927), a popular speaker and writer on the "deeper Christian life." The group that gathered under Austin-Sparks' ministry became known as the Honor Oak Christian Fellowship. The fellowship's distinctive emphasis, somewhat derived from Penn-Lewis, was upon the subjective work of the Cross in the Christian's life, an emphasis that many evangelical Christians saw as distracting from the prime work of witnessing to the faith. In the mid-1920s, Austin-Sparks began the publication of a periodical, *A Witness and a Testimony*, and later established the Witness and Testimony Literature Trust. The magazine was discontinued in 1972. Over the years, he published a number of books and pamphlets, most compiled from his spoken ministry. In 1939-40, he discovered his close agreement with Watchman Nee, Chinese founder of an evangelical movement popularly called the Little Flock or the Local Church. Nee spent 18 months with Austin-Sparks while the first edition of his most important books, *The Normal Christian Life* and *Concerning Our Mission* (later reissued as *The Normal Christian Church Life*) were translated with the assistance of the fellowship's members. While Austin-Sparks' ministry was never merged into that of Watchman Nee, the group remained on cordial terms for many years. Austin-Sparks shared many of Nee's emphases such as those of the two-fold expression of the church (local and universal) and the importance of the local assembly, which are reflected in his writings. However, he saw himself as part of an even more loosely organized movement of God that had many centers of like-minded Christians. Over the years such centers have been tied together filially and distinguished by their circulation of the literature of an informally "approved" set of teachers. When in England, such teachers would speak at the Honor Oak Centre, and Austin-Sparks would speak at their centers when traveling around the world, but no direct "responsibility" was shared for the separate ministries. The various ministries would also circulate the literature produced by Austin-

Sparks and other associated writers. Some of these teachers, such as Bakht Singh, popular Indian leader, were associated with Watchman Nee but not with Witness Lee, the recognized leader of the largest segment of Nee's movement.

Austin-Sparks' materials began to reach America soon after the fellowship was organized, and he made his first visit to the United States in 1925. Among the early centers of his support was the Hepzebah House in New York City and the Almquist Christian Book Nook in Northfield, Minnesota, which distributed Austin-Sparks literature. By the 1960s the trust regularly recommended three American centers which distributed its literature: M.O.R.E. (Mail Ordering Religious Education), the Westmoreland Chapel in Los Angeles, California, and Convocation Literature Sales in Norfolk, Virginia. M.O.R.E. was headed by Dean Baker of Indianapolis, Indiana. It absorbed the Northfield work as well as a periodical, *The Ultimates*, edited by DeVern Fromke, an early friend and supporter of Austin-Sparks. M.O.R.E. was supported by the Sure Foundation. Westmoreland Chapel was an independent congregation in Los Angeles, pastored for a decade by Mr. Carl B. Harrison, formerly of the Honor Oak Centre. Convocation Literature Sales, now known as Testimony Book Ministry, was headed by Ernest L. Chase, who also organized the Atlantic States Christian Convocation, held annually since 1966 to 1972 at Camp Wabanna, Mayo, Maryland. The Testimony Book Ministry is a nonprofit organization that reprints the heritage left by Austin-Sparks. As of 1988 approximately 40 titles have been kept in print. More loosely affiliated was the Rev. John Myers and Voice Christian Publications of Northridge, California. During the 1960s and 1970s Myers edited a quarterly, *Voice in the Wilderness. The Voice* (after 1970, *Recovery*) promoted the views of both Nee and Austin-Sparks, but is not limited to supporting them.

Austin-Sparks was in fellowship with Nee for a while but did not follow Nee's ideas completely on the local church. He broke off relations with Witness Lee's followers in 1958. In recent years literature has been reprinted primarily by Christian Fellowship Publishers of Richmond, Virginia. Testimony Book Ministry also distributes the books of Bakht Singh. In England, long-time associate of Austin-Sparks, Harry Foster, currently publishes *Toward the Mark*, a periodical originating in Weston-Super-Mare, Avon.

Those congregations and centers most closely associated with Honor Oak and the Witness and Testimony Literature Trust are distinguished from the local church founded by Watchman Nee in that the former generally does not accept the writings and teachings of Witness Lee.

Membership: Not reported.

Periodicals: *A Witness and A Testimony*. Available from Witness and Testimony Literature Trust, 39 Honor Oak Rd., London, England, S.E.23. • *Toward the Mark*, 26a Lower Bristol Rd., Weston-Super-Mare, Avon, BS23, England.

Sources:

Austin-Sparks, T. *The Battle for Life*. Washington, DC: Testimony Book Ministry, n.d.

___. *The Centrality and Supremacy of the Lord Jesus Christ*. Washington, DC: Testimony Book Ministry, n.d.

___. *The Recovery of the Lord's Testimony in Fullness*. Washington, DC: Testimony Book Ministry, n.d.

___. *The Work of God at the End Time*. Washington, DC: Testimony Book Ministry, n.d.

Myers, John. *Voices from Beyond the Grave*. Old Tappan, NJ: Spire Books, 1971.

No Other Foundation. Indianapolis, IN: Sure Foundation, 1965.

Roberts, Frances. *Dialogues with God*. Northridge, CA: Voice Christian Publications, 1968.

Singh, Bakht. *David Recovered All*. Bombay: Gospel Literature Service, 1967.

"This Ministry," *Messages Given at Honor Oak, London.* 2 vols. London:
   Witness and Testimony Literature, n.d.

Section 13

Adventist Family

Consult the Contents pages to locate the essay in Part II, Historical Essay Chapters,
that provides an historical discussion of this family

Intrafaith Organizations

★970★
Bible Sabbath Association
RD 1, Box 22
Fairview, OK 73737

The Bible Sabbath Association was established in 1943 by several sabbatarians (those who believe Saturday to be the biblical sabbath and day set aside for worship) from different churches who felt the need for mutual support and closer fellowship. An office was established in Pomona Park, Florida, and later moved to Fairview, Oklahoma. The association has as its goals the promotion of the seventh-day sabbath, the encouragement of the repeal of blue laws (which inhibit activity on Sunday); and the facilitation of fellowship among sabbath keepers on a nonsectarian basis.

The organization periodically publishes a *Directory of Sabbath-Observing Groups*, which lists those with Adventist, Baptist, Pentecostal, and Latter-day Saint backgrounds.

Membership: In 1986 the association reported approximately 1,000 individual members. The latest directory lists several hundred groups, including denominations and independent congregations.

Periodicals: *The Sabbath Sentinel.*

Sources:

Directory of Sabbath-Observing Groups. Fairview, OK: Bible Sabbath Association, 1986.

Sunday Adventists

★971★
Advent Christian Church
Box 23152
Charlotte, NC 28212

Among the earliest attempts to organize the scattered believers in William Miller's message of the second coming of Christ after the Great Disappointment in 1844 (when Christ failed to appear as predicted) were those of John T. Walsh, who began preaching in Wilbraham, Massachusetts, in the late 1840s. Walsh had some distinctive ideas—namely, that the wicked dead would not be resurrected and that the millennium had already occurred. The saints were now in a period of waiting for Christ's return. After the advent, the earth would be renovated and become the home of the righteous.

At about the same time (following the Great Disappointment), a party arose which believed Miller was in error by ten years in his calculations and that Christ would return in 1854. Simultaneously, there arose a third party which did not believe in the immortality of the soul. This latter party held that man had lost his potential immortality after the fall. They believed that the dead were in an unconscious state in the grave—a belief contrary to the notion that the body dies and the immortal soul lives on. The second party was headed by Jonathan Cummings and the third by George Storrs, editor of *The Bible Examiner*. These two forces united in the late 1840s. Following the failure of Christ to return in 1854, an attempt to unite the Adventists who had split off because of the date-setting failed because of the immortality issue. Those who believed in immortality formed the Evangelical Adventist Church.

In 1855, those who believed in conditional immortality formed the Advent Christian Church, headed by Cummings. Cummings, who followed the independent Bible study of Philadelphia businessman Henry Grew, taught that the Christian's hope of immortality was in Christ's atoning death alone and was not inherent in humankind. Furthermore, he believed that immortality was conditional—it would apply only to those who through faith in Christ could qualify for it. Finally, immortality and its subsequent rewards would be withheld until Christ's second coming.

In the late 1850s, George Storrs began to accept and publicize the peculiar ideas of Walsh, particularly the non-resurrection of the wicked. He left the Advent Christian Church and, with Walsh, formed the Life and Advent Union in 1863. For many years, the two groups existed as separate bodies, though the Life and Advent Union remained small and was confined to New England. In 1964, a merger was effected and the Life and Advent Union became part of the parent body.

Doctrinally, the Advent Christian Church continues Miller's views about the imminent coming of Jesus, with the exception of the date-setting aspects. It recognizes baptism by immersion for believers and has recently tended toward a more reformed theological perspective (while allowing for diversity on this issue). Members of the Advent Christian Church worship on Sunday. They are opposed to setting new dates, but believe that Christ's return is imminent, a belief based on the fact that "Bible prophecy has indicated the approximate time of Christ's return."

Organizationally, a congregational government is most prominent. The general conference meets triennially and has charge of the mission and education program. Missions are currently under way in Ghana, Liberia, Nigeria, Japan, the Philippines, China, Malaysia, Mexico, Honduras, Croatia, Romania, New Zealand, and India. Two retirement centers—Vernon Advent Christian Home, Vernon, Vermont, and the Advent Christian Village, Dowling Park, Florida—are supported by the denomination. In 1987 the church joined the National Association of Evangelicals.

Membership: In 1997 the church reported 26,236 members, 311 churches and 525 ministers in the United States, and 286 members 7 churches and 7 ministers in Canada. There were an additional 28,478 members worldwide.

Educational Facilities: Aurora University, Aurora, Illinois. Berkshire Christian College, Haverhill, Massachusetts. The Berkshire Institute for Christian Studies, Lenox, Massachusetts.

Periodicals: *Advent Christian Witness.* • *Maranatha Devotions.* • *Advent Christian News.* • *Henceforth....*

Sources:

The Advent Christian Manual. Charlotte, NC: Venture Books, 1987.

Dean, Dana A. *Resurrection: His and Ours.* Charlotte, NC: Venture Books, 1976.

Hewitt, Clarence H. *The Conditional Principle in Theology.* Boston: Clyde and Robert Hewitt, 1954.

Hewitt, Clyde E. *Midnight and Morning.* Charlotte, NC: Venture Books, 1983.

Kearney, Clarence J. *The Advent Christian Story.* The Author, 1968.

★972★
Church of God General Conference (Abrahamic Faith)
5823 Trammell Rd.
PO Box 100000
Morrow, GA 30260

History. As early as 1816, there appeared among American Protestants independent congregations which took the name "Church of God." They believed this name to be the only scriptural designation of God's gathered people. The first such Church of God appears to have been formed in Lancaster, Pennsylvania, by John Elliot. By 1828, a Church of God congregation had been established as far west as Old Union, Indiana. Some, but by no means all, of these early Churches of God congregations came into the association under the leadership of John Winebrenner. Others were among those congregations most affected by the Adventist movement under the leadership of William Miller in the 1830s and 1840s. In the years after the Great Disappointment of 1844, when Christ failed to return as predicted by the Millerites, some of these Church of God congregations, learning of each other's existence through various Adventist periodicals, begun to associate together.

They gathered initially in 1858 at a conference of Adventist believers that included the Churches of God and congregations later to become part of the Advent Christian Church. This initial unity of Advent believers in the Midwest was shattered over doctrinal disagreements. Those who later joined the Church of God General Conference held another conference in 1869 in Chicago, followed by annual conferences for several years. These conferences were somewhat informal, very loosely constituted, and soon ceased.

A renewed call for a conference was not issued until 1888. Meeting in Philadelphia, Pennsylvania, the conferees established the General Conference of the Churches of God in Christ Jesus in the United States and Canada. At a conference the following year in Chicago, Illinois, however, a disagreement over the rights of the congregations versus the rights of the national conference led to an abandonment of the conference organization established in 1888 and the refusal of the congregational representatives to gather again for a number of years. Finally, in 1910, a conference was held in Waterloo, Iowa, where the group's "Articles of Faith" were adopted. But a full decade elapsed before another conference, met in Waterloo, Iowa, in 1921 and created a corporation, the National Bible Institution, to handle the corporate matters of the Churches of God. Headquarters were located in Oregon, Illinois. In 1968, the National Bible Institution was renamed and became the Church of God General Conference. In 1991, the headquarters were moved to Morrow, Georgia, out of Atlanta suburbs.

The Church of God differs from other Adventists in its views on Christology and eschatology. As it had become increasingly common among Adventists, the church emphasizes the one God, denying the Trinity, and seeing Jesus as the Son of God, distinct from the Father. The church believes Jesus came into existence when born to the Virgin Mary. Members believe that when Jesus returns he will set up his reign as king in Jerusalem, and the church will be his joint heir. Israel will be established in Palestine as the head of nations. The Christian, through repentance, faith, and baptism for the remission of sins, enters into a covenant with God. A persevering life of faith in Jesus Christ, results in a life of usefulness and good works which leads to a position of honor in the coming earthly kingdom.

Organization. A congregational government is the accepted polity. A general conference meets annually. Missions are operated in Nigeria, Ghana, England, the Philippine Islands, India, and Mexico.

Membership: In 1996 the church reported 5,096 members, 82 ministers, and 89 congregations.

Educational Facilities: Atlanta Bible College, Morrow, Georgia.

Periodicals: *The Restitution Herald.* • *Progress Journal.* • *A Journal from the Radical Reformation.*

Remarks: Affiliated with the Church if God is the Restoration Fellowship, an organization founded in England in 1981 by Anthony Buzzard. In 1982 Buzzard moved to the United States and joined the faculty of the Oregon Bible College (now Atlanta Bible College). In the United States, the fellowship works with the Church of God as an educational ministry supplying written material in support of the church's doctrinal position. In England, a small group remains in existence as a single fellowship.

Sources:

Buzzard, Anthony. *The Kingdom of God—When & Whence?* Oregon, IL: Restoration Fellowship, 1980.

___. *What Happens When We Die?: A Biblical View of Death and Resurrection.* Oregon, IL: Restoration Fellowship, 1986.

___. *Who Is Jesus?: A Plea for a Return to Belief in Jesus, the Messiah.* Oregon, IL: Restoration Fellowship, n.d. *Historical Waymarks of the Church of God.* Oregon, IL: Church of God General Conference, 1976.

Huffer, Alva C. *Systematic Theology.* Oregon, IL: Church of God General Conference, 1961.

Mattison, James. *The Abrahamic Covenant and the Davidic Covenant.* Oregon, IL: Restitution Herald, 1964.

★973★
Church of the Blessed Hope
7450 Wilson Mills Rd.
Cleveland, OH 44143

The Church of the Blessed Hope, now somewhat aligned with the Christadelphian movement, began with missionary efforts of the Church of God movement (now organized in the Church of God General Conference Abrahamic Faith) in Cleveland, Ohio. In 1863 14 believers in Cleveland formed a Church of God congregation. At the time, the Church of God was a pacifist group and in 1865 the church affirmed its adherence to that belief. Over the next decades the Cleveland congregation had been responsible for the establishment of similar congregations in Unionville and Salem, Ohio. In 1888, the same year the Church of God formed a General Conference, these three churches incorporated independently as the Church of the Blessed Hope, though they continued to receive ministers from the Church of God into the 1920s. In 1922 the churches received a pastor from the Christadelphians and from that time forward adopted Christadelphian beliefs and practices and began to use a Christadelphian hymnal.

The church is non-trinitarian. There is one God, and Jesus is His son and advocate. All who accept Christ will be resurrected to live with Christ. The unsaved will remain in the grave. The church practices baptism by immersion and observes the memorial meal of breaking bread and drinking wine weekly. The church retains its prohibition of participation in war, though some congregations allow members to accept noncombatant service in the armed forces.

The church has articulated its own understanding of the Kingdom of God, which its sees as a political entity that will be established by Christ in the future. Its initial members will be a small number of those who are alive when Christ returns (primarily infants, children, a few well-disposed individuals, and the saved believers) and who survive God's judgment. They will be joined by the resurrected saints. Christ will destroy all human government and all competing religions. War and premature death will be abolished. The kingdom will last for a thousand years after which the righteous will be granted immortality and God's direct authority will supersede that of Christ.

Through the twentieth century, other congregations, some Christadelphian in background, affiliated with the Church of the Blessed Hope. The church has tried to establish cordial relationships with the Christadelphians and opens their communion service to them, though that openness has not been returned.

Membership: Not reported. In 1980 there were seven affiliated congregations.

Sources:

Piepkorn, Arthur C. *Profiles in Belief: The Religious Bodies of the United States and Canada.* Vol. IV. San Francisco, Harper & Row, 1979.

★974★
Primitive Advent Christian Church
℅ Donald Young
1640 Clay Ave.
South Charleston, WV 25312

The Primitive Advent Christian Church developed out of a controversy centering on the preaching of a Reverend Whitman, a minister of the Advent Christian Church in Charleston, West Virginia. The Reverend Whitman opposed both footwashing and rebaptizing reclaimed backsliders. Proponents of these two practices organized the Primitive Advent Christian Church. On these two points alone, they differ doctrinally from the parent body.

An annual delegated conference meets to carry on the business of the church. It ordains ministers and elects officers. The pastor is the presiding officer in the local church. There are also deacons and elders. The church is small, and all the congregations are in central West Virginia.

Membership: In 1984 the church reported 10 churches, 546 members, and 11 ministers.

Seventh Day Adventists

★975★
Branch Davidians
Current address not obtained for this edition.

The small, relatively unknown Branch Davidians, more properly called the Branch Seventh-Day Adventist or Branch SDA's, suddenly burst out of obscurity into the national spotlight on February 28, 1993, when agents of the Bureau of Tobacco, Alcohol, and Firearms, raided their church center outside of Waco, Texas. The raid failed as church members resisted the agents' assault, and in the ensuing gunfight, BATF agents and church members were killed. Several days later the FBI took over what had developed into a siege. The siege ended on April 19 when most of the people inside the compound died following a second assault on the church complex by FBI agents.

History: The Branch Davidians carry on the work begun by Victor T. Houteff, a member of the Seventh-Day Adventist Church, in Los Angeles. In 1930, Houteff had come to see himself as a divinely inspired messenger of God with the special task of calling for a reformation and the gathering of the 144,000 mentioned in the biblical Book of Revelation 7:4. Some of his basic ideas were put together in a book, *The Shepherd's Rod* (2 volumes, 1930, 1932). In 1935 he moved with 11 of his followers to Waco, Texas, and established the Mount Carmel Center, originally designed as a temporary assembling point for the 144,000. Their ultimate goal was to reach Palestine, where they would establish the Davidic

kingdom with a theocratic regime and direct the closing work of the gospel age prior to the second coming of Christ.

Houteff's movement was tolerated within the Seventh-day Adventist Church for a number of years, though increasingly congregations began to disfellowship Houteff's people. The growing level of tension increased dramatically following the attack upon Pearl Harbor and the United States' entrance into World War II. The Seventh-day Adventist Church, traditionally a pacifist church, began to call for conscription and refused to back members who claimed conscientious objection status or asked for ministerial deferments to military service. In the crisis, Houteff hastily organized, issued membership certificates, and distributed ministerial credentials. The movement, now an independent church, organized theocratically with Houteff as the leader, and assumed the name the Davidian Seventh-day Adventist Association.

Some 125 members came to reside at the Mount Carmel Center with other followers still in Los Angeles and scattered around the country. Houteff died in 1955. Soon afterward, Benjamin Lloyd Roden, then residing in Odessa, Texas, began championing the idea that the Davidians should continue to be led by inspiration (i.e., by a prophet). During September and October he wrote seven letters which he claimed had been dictated by God to Lois Houteff, Victor's widow, calling for reform. They were signed "The Branch." Lois countered Roden through her announcement that on April 22, 1959, the 1,260 days of Revelation 11 would be completed and that on that day, God would intervene in Palestine. He would clear out both Arabs and Jews and create a situation into which the Davidic kingdom could enter. She called for the faithful to gather at an assembly beginning April 16, 1959, and to arrive in Waco ready to move immediately to the Holy Land.

In the meantime she began to sell off Davidian property and to buy a new parcel of land, some 900 acres east of Waco, where she erected a new Mt. Carmel. In 1958 Roden moved his followers to Israel and began to work out an agreement by which other Davidians could move there. In 1959 some 900 Davidians gathered in Waco to await the fulfillment of Lois Roden's prophecy. When Roden arrived to present his option of moving to Israel, he was again rejected.

The failure of Lois Houteff's prophecy became a traumatic event in the movement. Splintering began, and while some joined Roden, several new alternative groups emerged. In December 1961, Lois Houteff admitted her errors, formally dissolved the Davidian Seventh-day Adventist Association, and put Mount Carmel up for sale. The property was purchased by Roden in 1965. He called his faction the Branch Davidian SDA's. Houteff had declared himself the fourth angel (mentioned in Revelation 8:12). Roden declared himself the fifth angel (Revelation 9:1). He headed the Branch until his death in 1978. The previous year, the Branch Davidians had accepted Lois Roden, Benjamin Lloyd Roden's wife, as a prophet and as having new light on the issue of the femininity of the Holy Spirit. She assumed the role of the sixth angel of Revelation 9:16 and withstood the attempt of her son George Roden, to succeed his father. Another potential successor was a relative newcomer, Vernon Howell, who had emerged as a talented leader. He had joined the group in 1981 and by 1983 had been put forth by Lois as the group's next prophet. However, in 1984 George Roden forced Howell and his followers out of Mount Carmel.

With his followers, Howell settled in Palestine, Texas. Roden was arrested in 1987 and in 1988 was sentenced to six months for contempt of court, a charge growing out of some grossly obscene documents he had filed with the court. With Roden in jail, Howell assumed control of the property and the group. Roden moved to Odessa, Texas, following his release. There, in 1989, he shot a man he claimed Howell had sent to kill him. In a trial he was found not guilty by reason of insanity and as of 1994 remains in confinement in a mental hospital.

Beliefs: Howell took over the group, and in the tradition of previous leaders set about the task of discerning his role in the scheme of the Book of Revelation, the key to his most unique additions to the Branch Davidian teachings. His understanding was still under development at the time of the siege, and is not fully understood. However, important outlines survived in his final speech and writings. From Isaiah 45, he assumed the name David Koresh (Koresh being a form of Cyrus). Cyrus was the only non-Israelite who was given the title "anointed" or "a messiah" or in Greek, "a christ." As a modern-day Koresh, he saw his role as that of the Lamb mentioned in Revelation 5. While traditionally this Lamb has been identified as Jesus Christ, Koresh dissented and claimed that the Lamb was identical with the rider of the White Horse who appeared in Revelation 6:1-2 and 19:7-19. The rider was clearly not Jesus.

Koresh made the identification of the Lamb and the rider from his reading of Psalm 45. Here, a warrior king was anointed, "made a christ," and rode his horse triumphantly. This warrior king would marry and his princess would be but one among many of his women. Koresh accepted as his own the role of the Lamb. The Lamb's job was to loose the seven seals and interpret the scroll (Revelation 5:2), i.e., bring the endtime revelation of Jesus Christ to the world. By accomplishing that task, people would know his identity. Also, the warrior king's polygamous situation in Psalm 45 undergirded Koresh's assumption of special husbandly prerogatives toward the women of the group.

Organization: Mount Carmel was organized communally. Agriculture provided some of its resources, while several residents had outside jobs and businesses, including some dealing with guns. In fact, a stockpile of weapons, some related to a gun business operated by one member, was crucial in the government's plan to move against the church. Other members of the group lived in several locations around the United States, most prominently in suburban Los Angeles.

Recent Events: A significant number of members died in the fire of April 19, 1993. Some of those who survived were placed on trial. While acquitted of the more serious charge of conspiracy to murder, most were convicted of lesser charges growing out of the siege and will spend some years in jail. Others, including some members not involved in the siege, are regrouping and continuing as a church. It is not yet evident what shape that reorganized movement will take.

Membership: There are 30 to 50 surviving members including several recent converts.

Remarks: The raid, siege, and fire raised many questions about the nature of life among the Davidians, the reasons for the ill-planned and disastrous raid by the BATF, and the deaths of the Davidians following the FBI assault on the church building. Many of these questions will never be answered, the possibility having been destroyed by the fire and the further destruction of the site several days later. Other issues were resolved by the BATF and FBI reports on the affair and the trial of the survivors. In the meantime, some have attempted to identify the Branch Davidians with Jonestown and to take the event into an anti-cult context. Others have tried to defend the group against what they consider outlandish and unproven claims.

This brief entry has limited itself to an outline of the group's history and beliefs. Space has not allowed even a beginning to the discussion of the many charges made by Koresh's critics and his responses and counter charges. Readers wishing to pursue these questions are encouraged to obtain a copy of the government reports and the scholarly responses available in Lawrence Sullivan's report and the more recent compilation by Lewis.

Sources:

Very little was published by (or about) the Branch Davidians during the years of Koresh's leadership. Soon after the fire at Mount Carmel several hastily written books appeared. Madigan's book is important primarily for its reprinting of Koresh's speech broadcast over several Texas stations shortly after the initial BATF raid. Breault's volume details the effort of an ex-leader who worked for several years to destroy the group

and who is an important additional source on the events which overtook the Branch Davidians in the months before the raid. Lewis has compiled a major collection of scholarly writings that appeared in the months after the fire, and Sullivan has produced a most insightful response to the raid. Official findings by the BATF and FBI teams investigating the events surrounding the raid, siege, and fire were released in a series of reports by the Department of the Treasury and the Department of Justice.

Breault, Marc, and Martin King. *Inside the Cult.* New York: New American Library, 1993. 375 pp.

Heymann, Philip B. *Lessons of Waco: Proposed Changes in Federal Law Enforcement.* Washington, DC: U.S. Department of Justice, 1993.

Lewis, James S., ed. *From the Ashes: Making Sense of Waco.* Lanham, MD: Rowland and Littlefield, 1994. 269 pp.

Madigan, Tim. *See no Evil: Blind Devotion and Bloodshed in David Koresh's Holy War.* Fort Worth, TX: Summit Group, 1993. 300 pp.

Recommendations of Experts for Improvements in Federal Law Enforcement after Waco. Washington, DC: U.S. Department of Justice, 1993.

Report of the Department of the Treasury on the Bureau of Alcohol, Tobacco, and Firearms Investigation of Vernon Wayne Howell also known as David Koresh. Washington, DC: U.S. Government Printing Office, 1993.

Report to the Deputy Attorney General on the Events at Waco, Texas, February 28 to April 19, 1993. Redacted Version. Washington, DC: U.S. Department of Justice, 1993.

Sullivan, Lawrence E. *Recommendations to the U.S. Department of Justice and the Treasury concerning Incidents such as the Branch Davidians Standoff in Waco, Texas.* Cambridge, MA: Center for the Study of World Religions, Harvard University, 1993. 20 pp.

★976★
Branch SDA's

Current address not obtained for this edition.

The Branch SDA's carry on the work begun by Victor T. Houteff, a member of the Seventh-Day Adventist Church in Los Angeles. In 1930, he wrote a book, *The Shepherd's Rod*, from which the group derived its popular name. Houteff considered himself a divinely inspired messenger of God with the task of calling for reformation and the gathering of the 144,000 mentioned in Revelation. In 1935, Houteff and eleven followers moved to the Mount Carmel Center, established near Waco, Texas, as a temporary assembling point of the 144,000. Their goal was Palestine, where they would establish the Davidic kingdom with a theocratic regime and direct the closing work of the gospel prior to the second coming of Christ.

Though denounced by the Seventh-Day Adventist Church in which many congregations were disfellowshipping adherents to *The Shepherd's Rod*, Houteff and his followers tried to remain within the Seventh-Day Adventist Church until the beginning of World War II. After the attack on Pearl Harbor, members began to be called for conscription, and the Seventh-Day Adventists refused to back up the requests for conscientious objector status or ministerial deferment. In a crisis, Houteff hastily organized, issued membership certificates, and distributed ministerial credentials. A formal theocratic organization was created, with Houteff as its leader, and in 1942 the name of the organization was changed to the Davidian Seventh-Day Adventist Association

At its height, there were 125 members at Mount Carmel. Houteff died in 1955 and was succeeded by his wife. She, inturn, announced that on April 22, 1959, the 1,260 days (Revelation 11) would end and that, on that day, God would intervene in Palestine. He would clear out both Jews and Arabs and set the state for the entrance of the Davidic kingdom. In answer to an official call, the faithful gathered for an assembly during April 16-22, 1959, in readiness to move to Palestine. They never recovered from the disappointment, and splintering occurred. On December 12, 1961, Mrs. Houteff acknowledged her error and the lack of soundness of the group's teachings. In March 1962, she and her associate leaders resigned, declared the Davidic SDA's dissolved, and put the Mount Carmel property up for sale.

The Branch SDA's were one of several splinters which broke with the main body of Davidic SDA's following Houteff's death. They did not accept Mrs. Houteff, opposing her leadership and prophecies. Many of her followers joined them in 1959. At one point, the Branch sent colonizers to Israel, but their attempts were unsuccessful. They continued as a small body with headquarters near Waco. Annual convocations following the Old Testament feast days (Leviticus 23) are held at the center. They also manage an organic gardening and farming experimental station for the production of foods free of pesticides and commercial fertilizer.

Membership: In 1986 there were eight congregations in the United States and Canada and an additional 20 foreign congregations.

Periodicals: *Shekineh Magazine.*

Sources:

Houteff, V. T. *The Great Controversy Over "The Shepherds Rod".* Waco, TX: Universal Publishing Association, 1954.

★977★
Davidian Seventh-Day Adventist Association
Bashan Hill
Exeter, MO 65647

History. The Davidian Seventh-Day Adventist Association continues the work of Victor T. Houteff (1885-1955), a Bulgarian-born convert to the Seventh-Day Adventist Church. He became a prominent member in Los Angeles, California, in the 1920s. In 1930, he wrote a 255-page book, *The Shepherd's Rod.* Volume One, a detailed doctrinal exposition concerning the harvest of mankind, led to a lengthy controversy. His second volume, published in 1932, was a prophetic analysis; the publication of these books created considerable controversy and led to his dismissal in 1934. Undaunted, he organized the Shepherd's Rod Publishing Association (which later became the Universal Publishing Association) to propogate his views. In May 1935, he moved to Waco, Texas, with 12 members to begin construction of a new headquarters named Mt. Carmel Center. They saw themselves as an association within the Seventh-day Adventist Church and, reflecting this view, went under the name The Shepherd's Rod Seventh-day Adventists until 1943. During World War II, the Shepherd's Rod Adventists held to the view of conscientious objection to war, whereas the Seventh-day Adventist Church held the more relaxed view of noncombatancy service. This, along with internal pressures from the Adventist Church, forced the Shepherd's Rod adherents to formally incorporate as the General Association of Davidian Seventh-day Adventists in 1943.

At Waco, Mt. Carmel Center spread rapidly on 385 acres and grew to include a school, publishing facilities, and a home for the aged. It had approximately 125 residents at the time of Houteff's death in 1955. During the next decade, the association passed through a series of crises. In 1959, Houteff's widow, despite strong internal opposition from Davidian leaders, prophesied that on April 22, God would directly intervene in Palestine and remove both Jews and Arabs in preparation for the establishment of the Davidic empire. Her misguided interpretation of the prophecy failed, which led to widespread disillusionment among the membership. The association rapidly divided into two groups, one led by her, and another led by editor M. J. Bingham, which strongly opposed what it saw as her doctrinal and prophetic speculations.

The latter group, though not large, was vocal and instrumental in her decision to discontinue as leader of the association. In December 1961, she admitted the failure of her prophecy and along with several leaders of the Waco faction, resigned and put the assets of the association in court-appointed receivership.

Despite this setback, there were a number of leaders and members who had opposed her views and desired to continue the association. The reorganized in 1961 in Los Angeles, taking the name Davidian Seventh-day Adventist Association. In less than a year, they moved to Riverside, California, where they remained headquartered until May 1970, when they moved their new center to land purchased in rural Missouri.

Beliefs. The Davidian Seventh-day Adventist Association has no disagreement with the doctrine of the Seventh-day Adventist Church and accepts all of its fundamental beliefs. Rather, it added to those beliefs based on end-time prophecies, a set of convictions about its particular role in history. The association is dediated to the work of announcing and actually bringing forth the restoration of the Kingdom of David (the biblical king) upon whose throne Jesus, the Son of David, will sit (though not literally, but spiritually) in the last days. The association's members consider themselves the vanguard, remnant drawn out from the descendants of the early Christians. With the appearance of the sealed people, the Kingdom reign begins. Part of its special task is to sound the "Eleventh Hour Call" mentioned in the *Testimonies for the Church,* a series of prominent books by Ellen G. White, one of the founders of the Seventh-day Adventist Church. The association's work is internalized to the Adventist Church preparatory to sounding the everlasting to every nation, tongue, and people with the intent of gathering the saints into the Davidic Kingdom. *Organization.* The Association is headed by Jemmy E. Bingham, the current president and pastor general and also has a seven-member Executive Council. The community in Missouri has a strong agricultural emphasis, based in part upon the belief that agriculture is an essential foundation of education. The 549-acre tract contains an administration building, an apartment complex, several houses, a printing plant, a 300-seat auditorium, a cafeteria complex, and a ministerial school. Members are found on nearly every continent.

Membership: Since most of the association's members also hold membership in the Seventh-day Adventist Church, it does not make a formal census of its adherents; therefore, current membership is unknown, though members are found in 25 countries.

Educational Facilities: The Davidic-Levitical Institute, Exeter, Missouri.

The Bashan School of Prophetic Theology, Exeter, Missouri.

Periodicals: *The Bashan Tidings.* • *The Timely Truth Educator.* • *The Communicator.* • The Report and Analysis Series. Available from The Universal Publishing Association, Bashan Hill, Exeter, MO 65647.

Sources:

Fundamental Beliefs and Directory of the Davidian Seventh-day Adventists. Waco, TX: Universal Publishing Association, 1943.

Houteff, V. T. *The Great Controversy Over the Shepherd's Rod.* Exeter, MO: Universal Publishing Association, 1954.

___. *The Shepherd's Rod.* Vol. 1. Waco, TX: Universal Publishing Assn., 1945.

The Whirlwind of the Lord. War!. Exeter, MO: Universal Publishing Association, 1987.

★978★
General Association of Davidian Seventh-Day Adventists
Box 450
Salem, SC 29676

The General Association of Davidian Seventh-Day Adventists is one of several groups that look to the ministry of Victor Tasho Houteff (1885–1955) as their heritage. Houteff, a member of the Seventh-Day Adventist Church, began his mission in 1929, and founded the General Association of the Shepards Rod Seventh-Day Adventists in 1934. In 1942 he changed the name to the General Association of Davidian Seventh-Day Adventists. Because he claimed the title "David," his followers were called "Davidians."

After his death in 1955, the association was headed by his widow, Florence Houteff.

Florence Houteff sold the property near Waco, Texas, which Houteff had built up as the associations headquarters and which he had named Mt. Carmel, and purchased land near Elk, Texas; an act many saw to be unauthorized in her husband's teachings. She then predicted an event for 1959, again not authorized by Houteffs teachings, and called all the groups members to the new Mt. Carmel center for its preparation. When her prediction did not prove true, she gave up the work and left the property to be sold. In 1961 Ben L. Roden acquired the property and established his faction of Branch Davidians there. Roden was succeeded by his wife Lois Roden who led the branch until her death in 1986. George Roden, her son, then led the group for three years after which David Koresh assumed leadership until the fire in 1993 when Mt. Carmel was burned to the ground.

In 1961, the most conservative remnant of the original association that still adhered to the Shepherds Rod teachings of Victor Houteff reorganized and elected new leaders. At that time, the General Association of Davidian Seventh-Day Adventists was formed in Los Angeles and headquarters were established at Riverside, California. In 1970 the headquarters were moved to Salem, South Carolina, to continue the publishing of Houteffs writings. Shortly before the move, some members separated and moved to Missouri and established headquarters for the Davidian Seventh-Day Adventist Association.

The General Association is headed by a vice-president, and Houteff is considered the last president. The vicepresidency is currently held by Don Adair, who moved to South Carolina in 1972. He had originally joined the General Association in 1951 and subsequently moved to the original Mt. Carmel Center (1952–1954) to study for the ministry. Under his leadership, the General Association has moved to put all of Houteffs writings into print.

Membership: Not reported.

Sources:

Adair, Don. *The Fall of the Protestant Nations!* Salem, SC: Expose, Press, 1986.

Houteff, V. T. *The Shepherd's Rod Series.* Salem, SC: General Association of the Davidian Seventh-day Adventists, 1990.

___. *The Symbolic Code Series.* Salem, SC: General Association of the Davidian Seventh-Day Adventist, 1992.

★979★
People's Christian Church
Current address not obtained for this edition.

Elmer E. Franke (1861-1946), a member of the Seventh-Day Adventist Church, rejected the claims of Ellen G. White as a prophetess and, in 1916, left to found the People's Christian Church in New York City. Seven years later, a second congregation was founded in Schenectady, New York, and, the following year, a third congregation was established in New Bedford, Massachusetts. The beliefs are similar to those of the Seventh-Day Adventists. Members believe in God, Jesus as one in nature with the Father, and the Holy Spirit as one with the Father and Son. Baptism by immersion is practiced, and the Lord's Supper is celebrated as an ordinance on the first Sabbath of each month. While accepting the Ten Commandments, members believe man was released from the Mosaic Ceremonial law.

Each church is autonomous, though the New York congregation is spoken of as the mother church. Ministers, deacons, and elders are ordained. There were four churches in 1968, two in New York and two in Massachusetts, with members in California, Florida, Maryland, and elsewhere. There were approximately 1,000 members, in all, in 1968. Present (1985) leader of the church is A. Warren Burns, pastor of the congregation in Schenectady. In 1986, the church's periodical *Light*, was discontinued.

Membership: In 1987 there were two congregations and approximately 1,000 members.

Sources:

Burns, A. Warren. *Civilization.* Schenectady, NY: Peoples Christian Church, n.d.

Franke, E. E. *Pagan Festivals in Christian Worship.* Schenectady, NY: People's Christian Church, 1963.

___. *The "2300 Days" and the Sanctuary.* Schenectady, NY: People's Christian Church, 1964.

★980★
The Registry
Current address not obtained for this edition.

The Registry was founded in 1967 by Cecil Shrock and others of the "Adventist complex" in general believing in the Seventh-day Sabbath and prophetic authority of Ellen G. White as a means of providing fellowship and cooperation among independent missionary efforts in the United States. Shrock had previously worked as a medical missionary in rural Alaska, where he had become aware of the problems of lack of fellowship with among Christians and the need for cooperation. Hearing other missionaries express the same concerns led to the development of the idea of an association and a newsletter which would publicize the various efforts, share needs and problems, highlight employment opportunities, monitor legal changes that could affect the work, and, in general, spread news. The most immediate need was the overcoming of a sense of separateness and isolation. Thus, the Registry began as an association of Christian workers but with an open membership to all who accepted its basic teachings.

The Registry follows the teachings of the Seventh-day Adventist Church in believing in the seventh-day sabbath; the Spirit of prophecy that manifested through Ellen G. White, co-founder of the Seventh-day Adventist Church; the soon visible return of Jesus; the necessity of striving to develop a perfect character; a desire to engage in service to others; work to reduce the use of drug medication in favor of natural remedies; and the desire for cooperation with others who hold the principles.

The Registry is not incorporated, owns no property, and has no organizations (only individuals as correspondents). Co-workers oversee missionary efforts, some of which are incorporated and which are regularly featured in items in the newsletter. The House of Health, conducted by Cecil Shrock, a natural health center in Marshal, Arkansas, offers public health care and trains lay workers. There is also work in the Philippines and Africa. The Registry is supported entirely by donations of associates and friends.

Membership: As of 1995 there were several hundred correspondents.

Educational Facilities: The House of Health.

Periodicals: *The Registry Case-file.*

★981★
Seventh-Day Adventist Church
12501 Old Columbia Pike
Silver Spring, MD 20904

History. The Seventh-Day Adventist Church (SDA) is an evangelical sabbatarian church whose teachings have been supplemented by insights drawn from the prophecies and visions of its founder, Ellen G. White. The church views the ministry and writings of White as prophetic gifts of the Holy Spirit. After the Great Disappointement of October 22, 1844, when Christ's second coming did not occur as William Miller had predicted, a group including White, her husband James White, Hiram Edson, Joseph Bates, Frederick Wheeler, and S. W. Rhodes, led the group. The visionary White saw in a trance the Adventists going straight to heaven. She was soon accepted as a prophetess by the disheartened Adventists. About the same time, under the influence of a member of the Seventh-Day Baptist Church, whose opinions were confirmed by their own Bible study, the group accepted the idea of a Saturday Sabbath. White further confirmed the correctness in a vision she had of Jesus and the tables of stone upon which the Ten Commandments were written. The fourth commandment, on keeping the sabbath holy, was surrounded by light.

White also confirmed for the group the interpretation, as originally proposed by Hiram Edson, of the 1844 date set by William Miller for the return of Christ. Taking a clue from Hebrews 8:1-2, Edson proposed that Miller was correct in his date, but wrong in the event. Christ came not to cleanse the earthly sanctuary, i.e., did not come in visible presence to earth, but initiated the cleansing of the heavenly sanctuary discussed in the text. After his heavenly work is completed, in an indeterminable but short time, he would visibly return to earth.

In 1850, at Paris, Maine, the Whites began the *Review and Herald*, a periodical advocating sabbatarianism and attempting to tie the loose band of Millerites together. In 1860, as those who accepted sabbatarianism and White's teachings were distinguished from other Adventists, the name Seventh-day Adventist Church was adopted. The church, which originally included approximately 3,500 members in 125 congregations, was officially organized in 1863.

Beliefs. Along with their belief in the seventh day and the sanctuary work of Christ, the Seventh-day Adventists accept a general protestant faith, which they had received from their background as Methodists and Baptists. A statement of belief includes acceptance of the Bible as the rule of faith and practice, the Trinity, creation ex nihilo (from nothing), baptism by immersion, and salvation by the atonement of Jesus Christ. They believe that Christ's soon return will be followed by a thousand year period (the millennium). They do not believe in the innate immortality of the soul; they believe that the dead await the resurrection in an unconscious state. Their acceptance of the seventh-day Sabbath has been followed by an emphasis upon the Old Testament health laws such as the distinction between clean and unclean meats. They abstain from alcohol and tobacco.

Organization. The church is organized as a representative democracy. Authority for administering the church is delegated through a system of conferences beginning with the local churches which form local conferences. In turn, these conferences combine into larger, regional (termed union) conferences which meet every five years. The general conference, which also meets every five years, and the executive committee of the general conference, which continues between conference sessions, are the highest administrative bodies of the church. They set policies and manage the extensive missionary, educational, benevolence, and publishing activities. The church has work in 208 countries plus home mission activities among a variety of ethnic groups. The church's educational system includes 15 colleges and universities, 95 secondary schools, and 1,049 primary schools in the United States and Canada. The church has attained an outstanding reputation for its hospitals (46 in the United States) and work in health related activities. Three publishing houses—Pacific Press Publishing Association (Nampa, Idaho); Review and Herald Publishing Association (Hagerstown, Maryland); and Christian Record Services (Lincoln, Nebraska) publish books, and periodicals. The affiliated Religious Liberty Association has continued the church's concern for church-state issues and publishes a leading periodical in the field, *Liberty*.

Membership: In 1994, the church reported 775,349 members, 4,303 congregations, and 3,192 ministers in the United States, and 43,840 members, 331 churches, and 222 ministers in Canada. There were 8,382,558 members worldwide.

Educational Facilities: Andrews University, Berrien Springs, Michigan.
Atlantic Union College, South Lancaster, Massachusetts.
Canadian Union College, College Heights, Alberta, Canada.

Columbia Union College,
Florida Hospital College of Health Sciences, Orlando, Florida.
Home Study International/Griggs University, Silver Spring, Maryland.
Kettering College of Medical Arts, Kettering, Ohio.
La Sierra University, Riverside, California.
Loma Linda University, Loma Linda and Riverside, California.
Oakwood College, Huntsville, Alabama.
Pacific Union College, Angwin, California.
Southern Adventist University, Collegedale, Tennessee.
Southwestern Adventist University, Keene, Texas.
Union College, Lincoln, Nebraska.
Walla Walla College, College Place, Washington.

Periodicals: *Adventist Review.* • *Liberty.* • *Listen.* • *Message. Ministry.* Available from 55 W. Oak Ridge Dr., Hagerstown, MD 21740. • *Signs of the Times.* Send orders to Nampa, ID 83707.

Sources:

Damsteegt, P. Gerard. *Foundations of the Seventh-day Adventist Message and Mission.* Grand Rapids, MI: William B. Eerdmans Publishing Company, 1977.

Land, Gary, ed. *Adventism in America: A History.* Grand Rapids, MI: William B. Eerdmans Publishing Company, 1986.

Maxwell, C. Mervin. *Tell It to the World.* Mountain View, CA: Pacific Press Publishing Association, 1977.

Schwarz, Richard W. *Light Bearers to the Remnant.* Mountain View, CA: Pacific Press, 1979.

Seventh-Day Adventist Church Manual. Washington, DC: General Conference of the Seventh-day Adventists, 1986.

Seventh-day Adventists Believe...A Biblical Exposition of 27 Fundamental Doctrines. Washington, DC: Ministerial Association, General Conference of Seventh-day Adventists, 1988.

★982★
Seventh-Day Adventist Reform Church (Rowenite)
(Defunct)

The Seventh-Day Adventists Reform Church (Rowenite) was founded out of the visionary experiences of Margaret Rowen, a member of the Seventh-Day Adventist church in Los Angeles. Her initial vision of coming events occurred on June 22, 1916. Her visions attracted more attention than they might have otherwise because the Seventh-Day Adventist Church had given great authority to the visions of its founder, Ellen G. White, who died the previous year. Some who witnessed the early visions suggested that God had chosen another prophetess to guide the church. Several church leaders, especially Dr. B. E. Fullmer, became active supporters. They were affected by Rowen's sincerity, her striving for moral uprightness, and the sufferings she seemed to be enduring.

Concerned, the Southern California Conference conducted an initial investigation, which reached inconclusive results, but did note that some of the teachings were out of harmony with the Bible and the message of Ellen G. White. In 1918 Adventist Church official A. G. Daniells reported that those who had investigated Rowen had unanimously concluded that her visions did not come from heaven. In 1919 Rowen and Fullmer were disfellowshipped. Meanwhile, a periodical, *The Reform Advocate and Prayer Band Appeal* was launched to create a network of followers of Rowen's visions.

The next year, in order to legitimize her role, Rowen created a document, which she signed with Ellen G. White's signature, and slipped into the files at White's northern California home. The document, dated 1911 would have, if genuine, placed White's authority on Rowen. However, when examined, the poorly produced document was immediately recognized as a forgery.

Rowen's visions led to some doctrinal innovations. She suggested that Christ had been created as an angel and later elevated as the Father's son. She predicted a worldwide famine in 1916 and in 1923 predicted the end of the world for 1925. The latter prediction led to actions by followers to prepare for the endtime. The failure of the prediction led to a falling away of followers. Even Fullmer, her strongest supporter and editor of the movement's periodical, fell away. In the March 1926 issue, he declared his belief that Rowen was a charlatan and apologized for his role in attracting people to her claims. In the most bizarre event in the movement's history, Rowen conspired to murder Fullmer. The attempt was botched, however, and she and her co-conspirators were arrested and convicted of assault with attempt to injure. The movement, which had peaked at around a thousand followers, died away.

Sources:

Fullmer, B. E. *Bearing Witness*. Los Angeles: The Reform Press, 1923.

Rowen, Margaret W. *A Stirring Message for the Time*. Pasadena, CA: The Grant Press, 1918.

White, Larry. "Margaret W. Rowen: Prophetess of Reform and Doom." *Adventist Heritage* 6, 1 (Summer 1979): 28-40.

★983★
Seventh-Day Adventist Reform Movement
Box 7239
Roanoke, VA 24019

At the beginning of World War I, a controversy arose among members of the Seventh-day Adventist Church in Europe when the European leaders committed the membership of the church to total combatancy in opposition to the historic position of the church of non-participation. This brought repercussions through the church in Europe involving most countries. Many could not accept this reversal and as a result a two percent minority were officially disfellowshipped.

After the war, those who had been cut off from the church met and tried to have corrections made, but without result. In 1920 a meeting was convened at Friedensau, Germany, at which the world leaders of the Seventh-Day Adventist Church and representatives of the separated members met to discuss the problems. The result was that the SDA leaders took a backward step by repudiating the first clear stand of non-participation and accepting a position of freedom of conscience for all members while advocating noncombatancy.

Those who had been summarily disfellowshipped sent representatives to the General Session of the SDA Church held in San Francisco in May of 1922, but without result. The members who had been expelled from the church felt that they had no other recourse but to organize themselves into the present body. They did so officially at a conference held at Gotha, Germany, in July of 1925.

Membership: The Seventh-Day Adventist Reform Movement now exists in 78 countries with a worldwide membership in excess of 24,000.

Periodicals: *Reformation Herald*. • *Youth's Messenger*. • *Standard Bearer*.

Sources:

Church Manual. Denver, CO: International Missionary Society, Seventh-day Adventist Reform Movement, General Conference, n.d.

International Missionary Society. *Bible Study Handbook*. Denver: Religious Liberty Publishing Assn., 1974.

The Principles of Faith of the Seventh-day Adventist Church "Reform Movement" and Her Church By-laws. Mosbach/Baden, West Germany: General Conference, Seventh-day Adventist Church, Reform Movement, n.d.

★984★
Seventh-Day Christian Conference
246 W. 138th St.
New York, NY 10030

The Seventh-Day Christian Conference was founded in 1934 in New York City as an independent Trinitarian Sabbath-keeping body. The Bible (Old and New Testament) is its only rule of faith and practice. It observes three ordinances: baptism by immersion, the Lord's Supper and fellowship. Members tithe. The church holds that war is immoral and members are conscientious objectors. Only males may hold positions of leadership—bishop, pastor or elder.

Membership: In 1986 there were two congregations, one in New York City and one in Montclair, New Jersey. There were also four affiliated congregations in Jamaica.

★985★
Unification Association of Christian Sabbath Keepers
255 W. 131st St.
New York, NY 10027

In the early 1940s in Manhattan a movement was started among black Adventists to unite independent Sabbath-keeping congregations. It was begun by Thomas I. C. Hughes, a former minister in the Seventh-Day Adventist Church and pastor of the Advent Sabbath Church, formed in 1941 in Manhattan. The missionary-minded Hughes conceived the idea of both home and foreign endeavors and began to gather support from his congregation. In 1956, the Unification Association of Christian Sabbath Keepers was formed, bringing together Hughes's parish and the New York United Sabbath Day Advent Church. Others joined, including the Believers in the Commandments of God.

There is a wide range of doctrinal belief in the various churches. Immersion is practiced and the Sabbath kept. A general adventist theology prevails. The polity is congregational. There are annual meetings for fellowship and general conferences every four years for business. At the second general conference, the title "bishop" was created, but there is no episcopal authority accompanying that title. A twenty-three member board of evangelism operates between general conferences.

The Unification Association is very missionary-minded. Missions had been established by its founders even before the Association was formed. Affiliated fellowships can be found in Nigeria, Liberia, Jamaica, Antigua and Trinidad.

Membership: As of 1986 only one congregation remained in the United States, at Elizabeth, New Jersey. There were scattered affiliated congregations in Africa and the West Indies.

Periodicals: *Unification Leader*.

Church of God Adventists

★986★
Assembly of God in Christ Jesus
Box 770537
Lakewood, OH 44107

The Assembly of God in Christ Jesus was founded in the early 1990s by Bill Phillips, formerly associated with John W. Trescott and the Church of God (Anadarko). Trescott had come to believe that he was possibly one of the two endtime witnesses mentioned in the biblical Book of Revelation 11:3. Phillips came to believe that he was a messenger from God, possibly Elijah, the prophet, and has come to believe that the voice of God speaks through him. He terms his teachings Christian Judaism.

Membership: Not reported.

Periodicals: *End of the World Report Newsletter*.

★987★
Associated Churches, Inc.
Box 4455
Rolling Bay, WA 98061

As schism developed in 1974 and ministers were either disfellowshipped or quit, a national fellowship of former Worldwide Church of God ministers and laypeople developed. Headquarters were established at Columbia, Maryland. While making note of the accusations against the ministry of Garner Ted Armstrong, son of the founder of the Worldwide Church of God, as part of the reason for their leaving the fellowship, they placed greater emphasis upon doctrinal issues. Among their first actions, they established a committee to review all of the various theological questions under dispute at the time of their leaving. They issued a 24-item doctrinal statement, which continued many Worldwide Church of God emphases, but rejected tithing in favor of financing by free-will offering and offered a congregational church government instead of the theocratic government of the Worldwide Church of God. Questions on other issues were assigned to a Biblical Studies Committee for discussion and review.

Congregations initially made up of former Worldwide Church of God members were established across the United States and a periodical, *Impact*, and a radio ministry were begun. In 1977 an evangelistic-teaching auxiliary organization, the Association for Christian Development (ACD), was formed and much of the work beyond the local congregations shifted to it. Through ACD, the Associated Churches issue a newsletter and numerous booklets, circulate cassette tapes, conduct radio broadcasts, and offer a Bible course (all of which introduce nonmembers to the doctrine of the Associated Churches).

Membership: In 1986 the churches reported 1,500 members in ten congregations in the United States and Canada. There was one congregation in Africa and a few members in Australia and New Zealand.

Periodicals: *ACD Newsletter.*

Sources:

Christian Giving or Tithing? Columbia, MD: Associated Churches of God, 1974.

Fundamental Beliefs of the Associated Churches of God. Columbia, MD: Associated Churches of God, 1974.

What Is Christ's Commission to His Church? Columbia, MD: Associated Churches of Christ, 1974.

★988★
Associates for Scriptural Knowledge (ASK)
PO Box 25000
Portland, OR

Associates for Scriptural Knowledge (ASK) was founded in 1984 by Ernest L. Martin, former chairman of the theology department at Ambassador College and founder of the Foundation for Biblical Research. After leaving the Worldwide Church of God in the early 1970s, Martin served as president, director, and chairman of the board of the Foundation for Biblical Research for over a decade. He wrote most of its publications, which included booklets, a monthly newsletter, and biblical and theological studies. In December 1984, however, a conflict arose between Martin and the two other members of the board. At a board meeting called to revise corporation by-laws, a major discussion developed concerning the openness of the foundation to alternative opinions. Several members of the board accused Martin of perpetuating a dogmatism, while Martin argued that there were some prime doctrinal teachings of the New Testament that were fundamental and should not be ignored.

As the meeting progressed, the board removed Martin from office and elected Ken Fischer as his replacement. Before the end of the month, Martin, with the assistance of several supporters, founded the Associates for Scriptural Knowledge as a tool to assist in the restoration of the truth of the Holy Scriptures that is to be accomplished in the days immediately prior to the Second Advent of Jesus Christ. Headquarters of the new organization were established in Hemet, California, but moved to Alhambra, California, in 1986.

Associated with A.S.K. is the Academy for Scriptural Knowledge, a home study course which offering a systematic presentation of the essential teachings of the Bible.

Membership: In 1987 the membership was approximately 1,000, of which 800 were in the United States and 100 in Canada.

Periodicals: *The A.S.K. Exposition.* • *Prophetic Encounter.* • *The Communicator.*

Sources:

Martin, Ernest L. *The Divine Titles and Their Christian Significance.* Hemet, CA: Associates for Scriptural Knowledge, 1985.

___. *Human Destiny and the Crucifixion.* Hemet, CA: Associates for Scriptural Knowledge, 1985.

___. *The Law of Moses, the Passover, and the Lord's Supper.* Hemet, CA: Associates for Scriptural Knowledge, 1985.

___. *The Sanctity of Marriage.* Hemet, CA: Associates for Scriptural Knowledge, 1985.

★989★
Biblical Church of God
Box 1234
Santa Cruz, CA 95061

The Biblical Church of God was incorporated in 1979 by a group of former members of the Worldwide Church of God under the leadership of Fred Coulter. A radio ministry was initiated, and several churches along the west coast and one in Canada affiliated with the new organization. Then in 1982 Coulter left to found the Christian Biblical Church of God. Eventually the Canadian congregation disagreed on church policy and became independent as the Biblical Church of God, Canada, but remained in fellowship otherwise.

The church is in general agreement with the Worldwide Church of God. It believes God is a family consisting of the Father and the Son, and denies that the Holy Spirit, the power of God, is a third member of a Trinity. Members are expected to follow God's plan of salvation which involves repentance, faith baptism by immersion, the reception of the Holy Spirit by the laying-on-of-hands, and overcoming and growing in grace and knowledge until the resurrection. The church is sabbatarian, and follows the Old Testament feast days. It also follows the Worldwide Church of God in its belief that the descendents of the people of ancient Israel are the Anglo-Saxon people, not modern-day Jews.

Membership: In 1986, the church had three congregations (San Jose and Castroville, California, and Portland, Oregon) and approximately 150 members. Associated were the First Century Church of God, an independent congregation in Napa, California, and the Biblical Church of God, Canada, Oshawa, Ontario.

Periodicals: *The Bible Answers Magazine.* • *Biblical Church of God Newsletter.*

Sources:

Coulter, Fred. R. *The Biblical Truth About Jesus Christ's Crucifixion and Resurrection.* Monterey, CA: Biblical Church of God, n.d.

Coulter, Fred R., and James Sorenson. *When Was Jesus Born?* Monterey, CA: Biblical Church of God, n.d.

★990★
A Candle
(Defunct)

A Candle was a small Sabbatarian body which became known in the 1960s for its wide circulation of a number of one-page tracts, which detailed its theological perspective. A Candle's beliefs were similiar to those of the Worldwide Church of God and advocated the observance of the Old Testament law, the seventh-day Sabbath, and the Hebrew feast days. A Candle opposes evolution, voting, healing by medicine, the Good Friday hoax, Christmas, and Easter. Members believe that hell is the grave, baptism is necessary for salvation, and that parts of the Bible (specifically those books mentioned in the Old Testament, but not preserved) are missing. Headquarters of A Candle were in Lehigh Valley, Pennsylvania.

★991★
Church of God (Anadarko)
900 W. Alabama St.
Anadarko, OK 73005

The Church of God (Anadarko) was founded in 1986 by John W. Trescott, previously a minister with the Worldwide Church of God and the Church of God Evangelistic Association. It continues the basic doctrinal perspective of the Worldwide Church of God, though it disagrees on a number of particular points. Trescott has come to believe that he is possibly one of the two witnesses mentioned in the biblical Book of Revelation 11:3.

Trescott teaches that the contemporary Jews are not from the ancient tribe of Judah but are Edomites (from the ancient land of Edom). The Church of God follows the Jewish festival cycle but believes that Passover should, if possible, be observed in the home rather than in large gatherings. Trescott rejects the Hebrew calendar and dates Passover from current observation of the moon. The church has also developed a more open attitude toward government and Trescott rejects pacifism and advocates members voting in elections.

The Church of God is engaged in a ministry of witness and warning. It publishes tracts which members pass out on the street, especially in Washington, D.C. There is an expectation of the imminent return of Christ, and a belief that the period of the tribulation mentioned in the Bible has already begun.

Membership: Not reported.

Periodicals: *Light of Truth.*

★992★
Church of God, Body of Christ
Rte. 1
Mocksville, NC 27028

The Church of God, Body of Christ, is a sabbatarian adventist group, which, unlike many adventist bodies, believes in the Trinity. In common with other Church of God adventists, members do believe in baptism by immersion, keeping the ten commandments, celebrating the Lord's Supper annually on the day corresponding to the fourteenth day of the Hebrew month of Nisan, and in the bodily, personal, and imminent return of Christ, as well as in tithing, gifts of the spirit, divine healing, abstaining from pork, and the holy life. The church, as the Body of Christ, is organized into a general assembly and state assemblies, with a general overseer and state overseers.

Membership: Not reported.

Periodicals: *The True Gospel Advocate.*

Sources:

Church of God, Body of Christ Manual. Mocksville, NC: Church of God, Body of Christ, 1969.

★993★
Church of God Evangelistic Association
Current address not obtained for this edition.

The Church of God Evangelistic Association is an association of Church of God congregations formed in 1980. Initially four congregations supported the association leadership of David J. Smith, the editor of *Newswatch Magazine*. Smith has produced numerous booklets, a Bible correspondence course, and many cassette tapes and videos for distribution. Evangelistic efforts have been assisted by a radio show heard on stations across the United States.

The Church of God Evangelistic Association follows the non-Trinitarian beliefs of other adventist Church of God groups. The association teaches that God's church is a spiritual organization and not limited to any one earthly organization. Christian believers should be organized to effectively serve God and carry out their commission of evangelism, baptising those who repent, and of teaching, but such organizations should not impede the individual's spiritual growth or subvert personal conscience. The association is sabbatarian and observes the annual Passover feast as a time to partake of the memorial Lord's Supper.

Membership: The association does not report membership figures, but in 1987 it reported 93 fellowship groups supporting the association. The periodical circulated 10,000 copies to all 50 states and 31 countries.

Periodicals: *Newswatch Magazine.* • *Restoring Knowledge of God.*

Remarks: The association was originally organized by former members of the Worldwide Church of God, with which it shares most of its beliefs. Working with the association in its formative years and authoring some of its early teaching material John W. Trescott left to found the Church of God at Anadarko, Oklahoma.

★994★
Church of God, International
Box 2525
Tyler, TX 75710

In the summer of 1978, following his second suspension from the Worldwide Church of God, Garner Ted Armstrong, son of Herbert W. Armstrong, formed the Church of God, International. From his leadership role in the Worldwide Church of God, particularly his years of speaking on its television program, he carried a large following which he began immediately to consolidate and organize. He began broadcasting over the radio from San Antonio. Though not yet gaining a membership approaching that of the Worldwide Church, the Church of God, International has grown quickly into a strong organization in the United States and an international body with membership in Jamaica, Europe, Australia, Canada, and South Africa. The radio and television ministry has been rebuilt and Garner Ted Armstrong is seen and heard across North America. A vast body of literature, including two periodicals, doctrinal booklets, and Bible study material, is supplemented by a cassette tape ministry.

The Church of God, International follows Worldwide Church of God doctrine closely but dropped much of the hierarchical structure. It denies the ruling apostolic authority of Herbert W. Armstrong. While not discouraging tithing by members, the Church does not require and does not monitor membership giving. The feasts are kept and in 1991 five feast sites in the United States and one in Canada were required for the membership.

Membership: In 1991, the church reported 3,000 members in 100 congregations in the United States. There were 600 members and eight congregations in Canada and 200 members in six foreign congregations.

Periodicals: *Twentieth Century Watch.* • *The International News.*

Remarks: In November 1995, Garner Ted Armstrong was accused of sexually assaulting a woman in July of that year. Armstrong denied the allegations, but stepped aside as head of the Church of God, International as the spokesperson of the church's TV broadcast. The issue came to a head in 1997 when the church's board and the ministerial council sought the retirement of the 68-year-old church leader and his ceasing his evangelistic and ministerial activity. Armstrong found their proposal unacceptable and withdrew form the church and in 1998 founded the Intercontinental Church of God. Apart from the departure of some members to the new church, the Church of God International has continued on its previous course.

Sources:

Armstrong, Garner Ted. *Sunday— Saturday...Which?* Tyler TX: Church of God, International, 1982.

___. *Where Is the True Church.* Tyler, TX: Church of God, International, 1982.

___. *Work of the Watchman.* Tyler, TX: Church of God, International, 1979.

Constitution and Bylaws. Tyler, TX: Church of God, International, 1979.

★995★
Church of God (Jesus Christ the Head) (UNICO)
% Pastor M. L. Bartholomew
Box 02026
Cleveland, OH 44102

The Church of God (Jesus Christ the Head) was founded in 1972 by a group of Sabbatarian Church of God members who hoped to unite the various factions of the Church of God following the principles of the church in the New Testament. They stood opposed to all divisions and sectarianism. They also opposed all forms of control above the local church. Hence, the Church of God follows a loose congregational polity; each church is completely autonomous. There are no denominational officers or general governing board. Christ is seen as the only head, and all who are in Him are considered members. Regular unity conventions are held for fellowship among the members around the United States. Each congregation is allowed their opinion on all doctrine. The Lord's Supper is celebrated annually at Passover.

Membership: Not reported. Members can be found throughout the United States and affiliate congregations in Nigeria, India, Canada, Jamaica, and the Philippines.

Periodicals: *The Voice of Unity.*

★996★
Church of God (O'Beirn)
Box 81224
Cleveland, OH 44181

The Church of God, currently under the administrative leadership of presiding elder Carl O'Beirn, was founded in 1970. Members consider Jesus Christ the founder of the church. O'Beirn was formerly a minister of the Worldwide Church of God and while a leader in that organization argued for the observation of not only the Old Testament (Jewish) Sabbath and feast days, but also for the monthly new moon days. His pressing of the moon days issue (as well as the proper observance of the Feast of Booths) led to his being excommunicated. He subsequently calculated what he believed to be the more correct calculation of Abib, the first month of the Old Testament year. O'Beirn's concerns have been embodied in the teachings of the Church of God and have become the subject of various widely circulated booklets.

The church has a worldwide ministry and O'Beirn has published open letters, supplying information on the correct days for celebrating the various feast days. O'Beirn's ministry has also been extended through a weekly radio broadcast.

One special aspect of the church's ministry is termed Psalmos. Members are taught to sing all of the psalms as a daily act of worship.

Membership: Not reported. The counting of members and adherents is contrary to the churchs beliefs based upon *I Chronicles* 21.

Sources:

Abib. Cleveland, OH: Church of God, 1976.

The Israel Mystery. Cleveland, OH: Church of God, 1975.

Understanding the Law. Cleveland, OH: Church of God, 1974.

★997★
Church of God, Philadelphia Era
Box 371
Pasadena, CA 91102

The Church of God, Philadelphia Era, was founded by David Fraser in 1986 following the death of Herbert W. Armstrong, founder and apostle of the Worldwide Church of God. Fraser believes that only he and the Church of God, Philadelphia Era, are truly following in Armstrong's footsteps, especially given the doctrinal changes in the Worldwide Church in the post-Armstrong era. The term "Philadelphia Era" refers to the messages to the seven churches found in the biblical book of Revelation 2-3. The Church at Philadelphia (Revelation 3:7-13) is praised for its faithfulness in the difficult times before Christ's return. It is a church with but "little strength" which has not denied Christ's name.

Fraser publishes a set of "Qwikread" booklets setting out the teachings of the church.

Membership: Not reported.

★998★
Church of God (Sabbatarian)
Current address not obtained for this edition.

In 1969, there was an unsuccessful attempt to unite the various factions of the Church of God (Seventh Day), initiated by members of the Denver body led by Elder Roy Marrs of Los Angeles and his uncle, Elder B. F. Marrs of Denver. The issue of local autonomy, denied to the congregations by the General Conference of the Church of God had originally led to schism. In Denver, the group became known as the Remnant Church of God, and in Los Angeles, as the Church of God (Sabbatarian). Missions are supported in India, Nigeria, and the Philippines.

Membership: Not reported. In the mid 1970s there were 7 congregations.

Periodicals: *Facts of the Faith.*

★999★
Church of God (Seventh-Day, Salem, West Virginia)
79 Water St.
Salem, WV 26426

The loosely affiliated congregations of the Church of God that adhered to the Ten Commandments, especially the keeping of the seventh-day Sabbath, had organized a general conference in 1887. At the conference meeting in 1933, a prime issue became the move to reorganize the church from its congregational pattern into one following what was considered an apostolic pattern with 12 apostles, 70 prophets, and seven financial stewards. The move was defeated. However, the main supporters of the reorganization issued a call for a general meeting to be held at Salem, West Virginia, on November 4, 1933. Those gathered, being in unanimous agreement and having resigned from the General Conference of the Church of God, reorganized as a new congregation, the Church of God (Seventh Day, Salem, West Virginia), selecting the 12, 70, and seven by lot (after the pattern of Acts 2:23-26). The church considered itself the true successor of the Sabbath-keeping Church of God tradition.

During the 1940s, several proposals called for the merger of that church with the General Conference. In 1947, merger talks were begun and the merger consummated in 1949. However, following the merger, some members rejected the merger claiming that those taking part from the Salem church acted without any official authority from their congregation and without following the procedure established in the church's constitution. Those rejecting the merger continued the national Church of God organization despite the loss of the majority of ministers and members. Spearheading the opposition was the church at Salem, which retained control of the publishing house. A new periodical, *The Advocate of Truth*, was begun in 1950.

Membership: In 1970, the church had seven congregations, nine ministers, and approximately 2,000 members.

Periodicals: *The Advocate of Truth*. Send orders to Box 328, Salem, WV 26426.

Sources:

Nickels, Richard C. *A History of the Seventh Day Church of God.* The Author, 1977.

★1000★
Church of God, the Eternal
Box 755
Eugene, OR 97440

Because of the controversies within the Worldwide Church of God in the early 1970s, several doctrinal changes were authorized. Pentecost was changed to Sunday and, under certain circumstances, remarriage was allowed for those who had divorced. Some saw these changes as a sign of a general doctrinal decline. Among those who disagreed with the changes, in favor of the "faith once delivered," was Raymond C. Cole. In 1975 he was put out of the Worldwide Church of God and several weeks later formed the Church of God, the Eternal, with headquarters in Eugene, Oregon, where Herbert W. Armstrong had founded the original Radio Church of God in 1934.

It is Cole's position that God revealed the truth to Armstrong in the early years of the Radio Church of God and appointed him to a special position to teach that truth. Such truth is unchangeable, and no allegiance is owed to a church organization that departed from truth. From the headquarters in Eugene, the church sends out a monthly newsletter with much content on the feast days, numerous doctrinal papers and tapes to an unspecified number of members across the United States. Foreign offices are located in Vancouver, British Columbia, Canada, and Lausanne, Switzerland. The church sponsors an annual Feast of Tabernacles gathering each fall.

Membership: In 1995 the church reported two congregations in the United States (Eugene and Portland, Oregon) and one in Canada (Vancouver, British Columbia) served by five ministers. Other groups met informally at points around the United States. There were three foreign congregations, in Switzerland, France, and Nigeria.

Periodicals: The church publishes a newsletter.

★1001★
Church of God's Truth
Box 2109
Corona, CA 91718-2109

The Church of God's Truth was founded in 1991 by James Russell, formerly associated with the Worldwide Church of God, with which it shares a basic doctrinal perspective. Russell has developed a different belief on a set of issues concerning the Hebrew calendar and the setting of the date for observation of the church's festivals (the Jewish festivals as described in the Jewish Bible, the Christian Old Testament). Russell rejects the Hebrew calendar and relies upon present observation of the moon to set the date of the festivals (hence they tend to occur a day earlier than the date set for Jewish observation). Russell also rejects the year 31 C.E. as the time of Christ's death, opting for 30 C.E. instead. He thus believes that Jesus was born on the day of the Feast of Trumpets in 5 B.C.E.

Russell also teaches that the seven churches described in the biblical book of Revelation 2-3 refer to eras in the life of the church. The last two churches described, Philadelphia and Laodicea, refer to the present faithful and apostate church.

Membership: Not reported.

Periodicals: *Prove All Things*.

★1002★
Church of the Great God
Box 471846
Charlotte, NC 28247-1846

The Church of the Great God was founded in 1992 as an end-time ministry by John Ritenbaugh, Richard Ritenbaugh, Martin Collins, Andy Benedetto, and Richard Nickels, all formerly associated with the Worldwide Church of God, whose doctrinal perspective is basically accepted. Members of the church do not believe in evangelization or proselytizing but understand their present commission to be to feed the present flock of Christians (including those still in the Worldwide Church of God and associated movements). A large part of this church is currently in a Laodicean phase, referring to the church of Laodicea discussed in the biblical book of Revelation 3:14-19. God says to the church that it is lukewarm and that since it is neither hot nor cold He will spew it out of His mouth.

Membership: Not reported.

Periodicals: *Forerunner*.

Remarks: Richard Nickels operates the Giving and Sharing Book Service in Neck City, Missouri.

★1003★
Congregation of God (Biblical Church of God)
Box 612440
San Jose, CA 95161

The Congregation of God (Biblical Church of God) was founded in 1979 by C. E. Barrett, formerly with the Worldwide Church of God, whose general doctrinal perspective is accepted. There are some beliefs unique to the church. Barrett teaches that prior to the flood, there was no universal language. He also believes that some of the Essenes were Christians and that the Apostle James (Jesus' brother) was invested with an office in the early church similar to the presidency and that Peter and John were his deputies.

Members assemble on the new moons rather than every Saturday. The church does not advocate tithing.

Membership: Not reported. Associated with the church is the First Century Church of God in Vallejo, California.

★1004★
Congregation of God, Seventh Day
Box 2345
Kennesaw, GA 30144

The Congregation of God, Seventh Day, is a small association of congregations founded in 1992 by former members of the Worldwide Church of God, whose general doctrinal perspective it accepts. It was founded by John Pinkston, Hubert Neil, Rick Allen, and Norman Rowe.

Membership: Not reported.

Periodicals: *The Herald*.

★1005★
Congregation of Yah
Current address not obtained for this edition.

The Congregation of Yah was founded as the Church of God 7th Era in July, 1973, by Larry Johnson, a former member of the Worldwide Church of God. He had been disfellowshipped in January, 1973, after sending a 160-page manuscript detailing his opinions on the organization of the Church to the Pasadena headquarters. In December, 1973, Johnson left his home in Buffalo, Missouri, and traveled to California to meet Herbert W. Armstrong, the Church's founder and apostle. He hoped to explain that, just as the Worldwide Church of God claimed to be the Church of Philadelphia (spoken of in Revelation 3:7-13) and claimed Herbert W. Armstrong one of the two witnesses of Revelation 11:3, Johnson was the other witness. Rebuffed, he continued for several years to contact Armstrong. As the internal turmoil disturbed the Church, and Garner Ted Armstrong (Herbert Armstrong's son) was disfellowshipped, Johnson began to revise his understanding of the meaning of the Book of Revelation. He concluded that the Worldwide Church of God was not the Philadelphia Church, but the Church of Sardis (Revelation 3:1-6) and that Garner Ted Armstrong, not Herbert Armstrong, was the witness. Over the years he also absorbed some Sacred Name Movement ideas and, in 1978, changed the name of the Church of God 7th Era to the Congregation of Yah. To date, Garner Ted Armstrong and the Church of God International have made no acknowledgement of Johnson. The Congregation of Yah is built around an inner family of supporters and a far larger group who receive Johnson's mailings. The Feast of Tabernacle is celebrated annually.

Membership: Not reported. In 1978 about 400 people supported the Congregation as coworkers. A smaller number were active supporters. About 7,000 people receive Johnson's material with some regularity.

Periodicals: *Activity Bulletin.* Send orders to Box S, Beebe, AR 72012.

★1006★
Foundation for Biblical Research
Current address not obtained for this edition.

Among the most popular of the Worldwide Church of God leaders was Dr. Ernest L. Martin, former chairman of the theology department at Ambassador College. With several colleagues and a group of supporters in the Pasadena area, he formed the Foundation for Biblical Research and began to circulate tapes and literature on such topics as tithing, marriage, the Sabbath, and church government. A monthly Foundation Newsletter was established, now called the *Foundation Commentator*, and regular research papers are issued on a wide variety of topics. Bible history, theological topics, and Christian living have been emphasized. The Foundation program encourages small groups of believers to meet in their homes regularly for prayer and study. Dr. Martin and his associates also travel widely, speaking to believers around the country. Exact membership figures have not been reported.

The Foundation has departed from Worldwide Church of God doctrine on several points: they believe in congregational church government and see autocratic forms as being condemned by Christ; doctors are allowed; tithing has been dropped in favor of free-will offerings; baptism is no longer practiced.

In 1985 the Board of the Foundation voted to change the format of publication to reflect a broader set of opinions and publish a much higher percentage of material not authored by Martin. This occasioned a split in the Foundation with Martin leaving to found the Associates for Scriptural Knowledge (ASK). The new arrangement represented not so much a change in doctrinal perspective as a new administrative order.

Membership: Not reported. In 1988 there were over 2,000 on the foundation mailing list receiving its publications.

Periodicals: *The Foundation Commentator.*

Sources:
Church Government and Church Organization. Pasadena, CA: Foundation for Biblical Research, 1974.

Martin, Ernest L. *Passover, Lord's Supper, Communion.* Pasadena, CA: Foundation for Biblical Research, 1975.

___. *The Tithing Fallacy.* Pasadena, CA: Foundation for Biblical Research, 1979.

The Sabbath and the Christian. Pasadena, CA: Foundation for Biblical Research, 1974.

★1007★
Fountain of Life Fellowship
Current address not obtained for this edition.

The Fountain of Life Fellowship was organized in 1970 by James L. Porter, a former member of the Worldwide Church of God. Five years previously he had published a study of the feast days of the Old Testament and the seventh-day sabbath. The study began with a discussion of his discovery of what he felt to be the proper method of entering the Kingdom of God, calling directly upon the name of Jesus in prayer. (This method of prayer had led to his being disfellowshipped from the Worldwide Church of God in 1958.) In 1972 Porter began a study of the doctrine of the baptism of the Holy Spirit which led him to believe in the necessity of Christians' having the baptism of the Holy Spirit with the accompanying sign of speaking in tongues. He places an emphasis upon the centrality of all nine gifts of the Spirit (I Corinthians 12) and the fruits of the Spirit (Galatians 5:22-23).

The fellowship was organized as a fellowship of believers. Initially Porter began a radio program but soon dropped it in favor of printing and circulating a periodical. The fellowship is headed by a board. No membership roll is kept, but supporters gather annually for the Feast of Tabernacles. Believers meet locally in fellowship groups. Teachings follow Church of God emphases. Worship is weekly on the sabbath, and the Old Testament festivals are celebrated annually. Porter travels around the United States to meet with believers.

Membership: Not reported. Several hundred people receive regular mailings from the fellowship.

Sources:
Porter, James L. *Knowing the Father through the Spring Feasts.* Valley Center, KS: Fountain of Life, 1985.

___. *The Sabbaths of God.* New York: Exposition Press, 1965.

Porter, Virginia. *The Gifts of the Spirit.* Valley Center, KS: Fountain of Life Fellowship, 1984.

___. *Man's Substitute Gifts of the Spirit.* Valley Center, KS: Fountain of Life, 1985.

★1008★
General Conference of the Church of God (Seventh-Day)
% General Conference Offices
Box 33677
Denver, CO 80233

During the two decades following the Great Disappointment of 1844, the followers of William Miller became grouped into what became the larger Adventist churches. However, numerous Adventists remained independent of the larger churches. Many sabbatarians, in particular, rejected the "visions" of Ellen G. White of the Seventh-Day Adventist Church. Some of these independents associated together in 1863 around a periodical, *The Hope of Israel*, published in Hartford, Michigan. Enos Easton, Samuel Davison, and Gilbert Cranmer were among the leaders. *The Hope of Israel* continued intermittently for several years and, in 1866, was formally established at Marion, Iowa, under the aegis of the Christian Publishing Association. By this time, the name Church of God was in general use and was eventually adopted as the "denominational" name.

During the nineteenth century, the movement grew around the periodical and the evangelical endeavor of its leaders. In 1889, the headquarters were moved to Stanberry, Missouri. The periodical continues as *The Bible Advocate*. In 1906, the associated congregations registered as the Church of God (Adventist) Unattached Congregations.

The General Conference of the Church of God (Seventh-Day), as the church is known today, has emerged with a moderate Old Testament emphasis. It believes that the Christian will lead a life of obedience to God, which includes the observance of the Ten Commandments, and the Sabbath. The use of tobacco, alcohol, and narcotics is discouraged. Christmas, Easter, Lent, Good Friday, and Sunday are considered pagan holidays. The group believes that tithing is the method of church financing. The church is popularly called the Church of God (Seventh-Day), and will be referred to by that title frequently in this chapter.

Organization is congregational, and a general conference meets every two years. A ministerial council oversees ministerial licensing. The Bible Advocate Press publishes numerous booklets, church school materials, and several periodicals. Missions are supported in 25 countries.

Membership: In 1998 the conference reported 170 congregations, 127 ministers, and 10,000 members in the United States and 400 members, ten congregations, and five ministers in Canada. There were approximately 130,000 members worldwide.

Educational Facilities: Summit School of Theology, Broomfield, Colorado.

Periodicals: *Bible Advocate.*

Sources:

Church Manual of Organization and Procedure. Stanberry, MO: Church of God Publishing House, 1962.

Coulter, Robert. *The Story of the Church of God (Seventh Day).* Denver: Bible Advocate Press, 1983.

Doctrinal Beliefs of the Church of God (Seventh Day). Denver: Bible Advocate Press, 1974.

Nickels, Richard. *A History of the Seventh Day Church of God.* The Author, 1977.

The 2300-Day Prophecy of Daniel Eight. Stanberry, MO: Bible Advocate Press, 1960.

★1009★
General Council of the Churches of God
1827 W. 3rd St.
Meridian, ID 83642-1653

In the summer of 1950, a meeting in Meridian, Idaho, four former members of the Gemeral Conference of the Church of God who wished to continue the congregational polity followed by the church in the years before its 1949 merger with the Church of God (headquartered at Salem, West Virginia) and the church's subsequent adoption of some aspects of the "apostolic" church government of the Salem body. The doctrine remained without change, but a spirit of freedom in the Lord is emphasized. Mission work is supported in Jamaica, St. Vincents (West Indies), the Philippines, Great Britian, Austrailia, Burma, Brazil, and Africa.

Membership: In 1988 there were 25 congregations in the United States, two in Canada, and three in the West Indies, plus some independent congregations which unofficially associate with the council.

Educational Facilities: Maranatha College, Meridian, Idaho.

Periodicals: • *Acts. The Fellowship Herald.* Both available from the Church of God Publishing House, 1827 W. 3rd St., Meridian, ID 83642-1653.

Sources:

A Declaration of Things Most Commonly Believed Among Us. Meridian, ID: Church of God Publishing House, 1963.

Nickels, Richard C. *History of the Seventh Day Church of God.* The Author, 1977.

Walker, Frank M. *The Beast, His Image, and the Two-Horned Beast.* Meridian, ID: Church of God Publishing House, n.d.

★1010★
Global Church of God
Box 501111
San Diego, CA 92150-1111

The Global Church of God grew out of the doctrinal changes that began to occur in the Worldwide Church of God in the months immediately after the death of church founder Herbert W. Armstrong in 1986. Among the founders were Roderick Meredith and Raymond McNair, both prominent leaders in the Worldwide Church. They opposed the changes initiated by Joseph W. Tkach, Armstrong's successor who has dropped many of the church's distinctives, especially during the 1990s. The Global Church of God retains the doctrines and practices of the Worldwide Church prior to 1986.

Membership: Not reported. In 1995 the church had approximately 7,000 members.

Periodicals: *World Ahead Magazine.* • *Global Church News.*

★1011★
Harmony of Life Fellowship
1434 Fremont Ave.
Los Altos, CA 94022

The Harmony of Life Fellowship was founded in 1955 by Dr. Roy B. Oliver, formerly a minister with the Unity School of Christianity. Using a basic metaphor of harmony and balance, the fellowship seeks to awaken humanity's hidden faculties and assert what it perceives to be the timeless spiritual values undergirding human life. The purpose of life is the achievement of a brilliance of mind, a nobility of character, a perfection of the body, and an exaltation of spirit. Each of these can be attained through the ancient wisdom taught as the inner truth in all religions through the application of specific techniques of meditation and concentration, study and reflection, worship, and a devotion to the highest ideals. The fellowship was incorporated in 1957, and during the 1960s its work was extended through the formation of the Harmony College of Applied Science, the International University, and the International Society of Naturopathy.

The fellowship finds truth in the mystical Christianity of the first three centuries, before the church lost its spiritual mooring in a literal interpretation of that which was meant to be understood metaphorically and allegorically. The inner mystical interpretation of the scripture leads to the same basic truth found in all religions. Each individual is a soul on a journey of growth through a series of incarnations and lives among an assembledge of souls whose evolution is being guided by the Great White Brotherhood, the spiritual hierarchy.

The fellowship assumes a nondogmatic approach to Truth. It is to be found in the searching by each individual. The fellowship tries to create an environment where every individual can discover the Truth in his or her own unique manner. The fellowship believes that humans are inherently divine, and as they pursue spiritual reality, they perceive the oneness of life expressed on the seven levels of reality. Being divine, they should seek to express the perfection of God. Service, expressed in facilitating the healing of self and others, is encouraged. The universe is the body of God and operates according to immutable spiritual laws.

The development of the individual is best accomplished through group endeavor. Group worship is encouraged by the fellowship as is the formation of shareview groups (six or more people who meet in homes to share their views on important matters). The seven traditional Christian sacraments are practiced according to an esoteric interpretation.

To aid the progress of the individual, the society offers a variety of study materials organized into courses. Through the college, both basic and advanced degrees may be secured in a variety of subjects. The college is structured in an alternative off-campus style with each student proceeding at his/her own pace. Students may seek ordination as Harmony of Life ministers and then choose to begin a chapter of the fellowship. Ministers may choose to become members of the Harmony Ministerial Alliance. The fellowship is affiliated with the Union of Christian Universal Churches headquartered in France.

Membership: Not reported.

Educational Facilities: Harmony College of Applied Science; International University, Los Altos, California.

Sources:

Harmony of Life. Los Gatos, CA: Harmony of Life Fellowship, 1991.

The Master Key: A New Faith for the New Age. Los Altos, CA: Harmony of Life Fellowship, n.d.

★1012★
Intercontinental Church of God (ICG)
PO Box 1117
Tyler, TX 75710

During the mid-1970s, Garner Ted Armstrong, founder of the Church of God International, had been in tension with the board and the ministerial council of the church over charges which surfaced in 1994 concerning his conduct. While denying the charges against him, Armstrong stepped down as the head of the church. Then, in 1997, the ministerial council moved to permanently retire him and seek his agreement to cease functioning as a minister/evangelist. Armstrong found their plan unacceptable and withdrew from the church and in January 1998 founded the Garner Ted Armstrong Evangelistic Association (PO Box 747, Flint, MI 75762) as a structure to continue his evangelistic endeavors. He also soon discovered that many of the members of the Church of God International wished to continue in a church relationship with him and a few months later he founded the Intercontinental Church of God (ICG).

The ICG continues the doctrinal stance of the former body, the differences being purely administrative.

Membership: Not reported. Members are found in Great Britain, Ireland, Norway, Canada, Australia (including Tasmania), and the Philippines.

Periodicals: *Worldwatch.*

Sources:

http://www.coginterlink.org/.

★1013★
Philadelphia Church of God
PO Box 3700
Edmond, OK 73083

The Philadelphia Church of God emerged out of reactions to perceived changes in the Worldwide Church of God following the death of its founder, Herbert W. Armstrong, and the emergence of his successor, Joseph W. Tkach. These changes involved dropping some distinctive beliefs of the church and its movement toward the doctrinal stance of Evangelical Protestantism. This move was signalled by the removal of many publications from print, including those written by Armstrong. Many members and leaders of the Worldwide Church of God opposed those changes. Among those who challenged the changes were two ministers, Gerald Flurry and John Amos, and as a result of their protest in 1989 they were disfellowshipped and founded the Philadelphia Church of God. Flurry and Amos published an apology, *Malachi's Message,* which they began to mail out in January 1990. In February they published the first issue of a new magazine, *The Philadelphia Trumpet,* as the official organ of the church.

Flurry and Amos developed their rationale for founding the church from their reading of the biblical book of Revelation, chapters 2 & 3, which includes the messages to the seven churches. These chapters have often been interpreted as a prophetic outline of history, an interpretive perspective adopted within the Worldwide Church of God. Church members viewed Herbert W. Armstrong as having been raised up by God to begin a new era, the Philadelphia Church era (Rev. 3:7-13). It is the opinion of the Philadelphia Church of God that under Tkach the Worldwide Church of God has veered from the Philadelphia stance articulated by Armstrong and has become the Laodicean church. People faithful to the Philadelphian stance have had to reorganize to continue their life.

The Philadelphia Church of God continues the doctrines of the Worldwide Church of God prior to 1986, and it has been at pains to document each change through a booklet *Worldwide Church of God Doctrinal Changes and the Tragic Results* and in articles in *The Philadelphia Trumpet.* It has also moved to put Armstrong's books back in print, beginning with *The United States and Britain in Prophecy* and *Mystery of the Ages.*

The church continues the teachings of the larger Church of God movement. It is non-Trinitarian, and observes the seventh-day Sabbath, recognizing two ordinances, baptism and the annual observance of the Passover, which includes foot washing. The Old Testament festivals are observed and the more familiar holidays—Christmas, Easter, Halloween, and Valentine's day—denounced. The church also holds to the special position in cosmic history held by Herbert W. Armstrong, who they believe is the Elijah figure mentioned in such biblical passages as Matthew 17:10-13.

The church also has a strong belief in British Israelism, a belief in the prophetic significance of Britain and the United States as the literal descendants of ancient Israel. British Israelism has been played down in recent years by the Worldwide Church of God. The church emphasizes prophecy and believes that most prophetic passages of the Bible are being fulfilled in this generation.

The Philadelphia Church of God found immediate support both among people who had been disfellowshipped and others who had left the Wordlwide Church. It quickly developed support in Canada, Europe, New Zealand, the Philippines and Australia. It also launched a radio show and a television program, the "Key of David," which is aired on cable in the United States, Canada, Asia, and Europe.

Membership: In 1997 the Church reported approximately 5,000 baptized members and 98 congregations in the United States. Additionally, the church has congregations across Canada and in England, other European countries, New Zealand, and Australia, South Africa, and throughout Latin America.

Periodicals: *The Philadelphia Trumpet.* • *Royal Vision.* • *Philadelphia News.*

Sources:

Flurry, Gerald. *The Ezekiel Watchman.* Edmond,OK: Philadelphia Church of God, 1992. 71 pp.

___. *Jeremiah: Prophet of Doom or Hope?* Edmond,OK: Philadelphia Church of God, 1993. 43 pp.

___. *Lamentations and the End-Time Laodiceans.* Edmond,OK: Philadelphia Church of God, 1993. 37 pp.

-___. *Malachi's Message.* Edmond, OK: Philadelphia Church of God, 1992. 162 pp.

★1014★
The Pure Truth
Lock Box 126
Hamilton, TX 76531

The Pure Truth is a ministry and fellowship of believers founded in Pasadena, California, in 1979 by Richard Scott, formerly associated with the world wide church of God and the

Church of God International. Scott came to believe that he was a prophet sent to speak especially to former and present members of the Worldwide Church and its offshoots. He received his commission to preach from several visions and vivid dreams which also gave him insight into some future events, many of which subsequently occurred. He believes that he is the only true heir to Herbert W. Armstrong and his work of proclaiming the truth.

While generally following the beliefs of the Worldwide Church of God as it was prior to Armstrong's death in 1986, Scott has developed some distinctive ideas. He employs the sacred name in speaking of the Creator and Savior. He accepts some of the tenets of the British Israel idea but believes that the United States, not Great Britain, is to be identified with the scriptual Ephraim. He believes that the first (preparation) day of the Feast of Unleaven Bread (an important date in the Worldwide Church of God annual calendar) is on the 14th of the first solar calendar month, but that the Feast proper begins on the 15th. He rejects the idea of the lunar month as having anything to do with the sacred calendar.

Membership: Not reported.

Educational Facilities: APT School of Scripture and Truth.

Periodicals: *The Pure Truth Magazine.* • *Ephesian Messenger Newsletter.* • *The Prophetic Notebook Newsletter.*

★1015★
Restoration Church of God
Current address not obtained for this edition.

The Restoration Church of God was founded in 1993 by M. John Allen, a former member of the Worldwide Church of God, whose general doctrinal perspective is accepted by the Restoration Church. Allen teaches that Herbert W. Armstrong, the late founder/apostle of the Worldwide Church, was a modern day Elijah, but that the church he founded has departed from the Truth. Today, Allen believes, the Restoration Church is the only work of God that is building on God's foundation.

Membership: Not reported.

Periodicals: *The Clear Truth.*

★1016★
Seventh-Day Church of God
Box 804
Caldwell, ID 83606-0804

The Seventh-Day Church of God was formed in 1954 by several ministers of the Church of God (Seventh-Day) headquartered in Salem, West Virginia. They rejected that church's stance on divorce (allowing divorced and remarried ministers and/or spouses to continue as ministers). They also embraced the observance of the seven annual Holy Days. Otherwise the church follows most of the doctrine commonly known to the sabbatarian Church of God groups. The church is headed by a chairman and secretary, apostles, elders, evangelists, and teachers. Mission work is supported in several countries.

Membership: Not reported. The church believes that membership records are in the *Lambs Book of Life* and thus no earthly records as such are kept.

Educational Facilities: Zion Faith College.

Periodicals: *The Herald of Truth.*

Sources:

Nickels, Richard C. *A History of the Seventh Day Church of God.* The Author, 1977.

★1017★
Triumph Prophetic Ministries (Church of God)
Box 292
Altadena, CA 91003

The Triumph Prophetic Ministries (Church of God) was founded in 1987 by William Dankenbring, Nick Wood, and James Rector, all former members of the Worldwide Church of God, whose general doctrinal framework is accepted. However, the church disagrees on a variety of particular points. Most importantly, the church does not believe that Herbert W. Armstrong, the founder/apostle of the Worldwide Church, was a modern-day Elijah figure. It does believe that the seven churches described in the biblical book of Revelation 2-3 are indicative of seven church eras to the present. The Church of God is the faithful Philadelphia remnant, and most of the other Worldwide splinter groups belong to the Laodicean era of lukewarm believers.

As to the Jewish feats, the church teaches that Passover should be kept according to the Hebrew calendar on Nisan 15 (not 14), and Pentecost on Sivan 6, the dating being a matter of great concern to Worldwide Church members. Passover should include the eating of a Passover meal. The Feast of Tabernacles should only be celebrated in Jerusalem and kept in actual booths as described in the Bible. The church accepts the British Israel theology but believes that the United States is to be identified with ancient Ephraim, not Manassah as is commonly done.

The church teaches that we are living in the end times and preparing for the battles which shall characterize that period. Among the prophetic personages who have appeared are the King of the South (Egypt); the King of the North (coalition of Arab-German-Eastern European nations); the Beast (Saddam Hussein); and the Man of Sin (Joseph W. Tkach, the successor to Herbert Armstrong as the head of the Worldwide Church of God). There will be a New World Order under the United Nations. Saddam Hussein will build a modern Babylon the Great.

Membership: Not reported.

Periodicals: *Prophecy Flash.*

★1018★
Twentieth Century Church of God
Current address not obtained for this edition.

Among the church leaders to leave the Worldwide Church of God in 1974 was Al Carrozzo, regional director of the western half of the work in the United States and director of the Counseling and Guidance Office in Pasadena. He accused Garner Ted Armstrong, son of founder-apostle Herbert W. Armstrong, of adultery (citing numerous instances over a period of years) and continued to raise the issue in his monthly *Newsletter.* He also had pushed for a change in the church's demand that people living with a second spouse following a divorce and remarriage leave their spouse because they would be living in adultery.

After leaving the church, Carrozzo formed the Twentieth Century Church of God, began a tape and literature ministry, started a radio show over several stations, and traveled around the country talking to groups who had left the Worldwide Church of God. The monthly newsletter contained two sections. One part discusses continuing concerns within the Worldwide Church of God. The other part centers upon the Twentieth Century Church of God's main emphases-spiritual growth, prayer, Christian living, and preaching the gospel of reconciliation. These emphases emerge within a context of general agreement with Worldwide Church of God doctrine.

Membership: Not reported.

Periodicals: *Newsletter.* Send orders to Box 129, Vacaville, CA 95688.

Sources:

Carrozzo, Al. *Christmas.* Vacaville, CA: Twentieth Century Church of God, n.d.

___. *How to Study the Bible.* Vacaville, CA: Twentieth Century Church of God, n.d.

___. *Who Is Qualified to Be Your Minister?* Vacaville, CA: Twentieth Century Church of God, n.d.

Our Christian Responsibilities. Vacaville, CA: Twentieth Century Church of God, n.d.

★1019★
Twentieth Century Church of God (Pennsylvania)
Box 25
Ninevah, PA 15344

The Twentieth Century Church of God was founded in 1990 by C. Kenneth Rockwell and David E. Barth, Jr., both former members of the Worldwide Church of God. The church (not to be confused with the other church of the same name) accepts the basic doctrinal perspective of the Worldwide Church of God, especially as it existed prior to the doctrinal changes of the early 1990s. It is very close to the position of the Church of God International and the Triumph Prophetic Ministries (Church of God), with whom it cooperates. In regard to the church festivals, it teaches that Passover should be kept in Nisan 15 and Pentecost on Sivan 6. It rejects tithing.

Membership: Not reported.

Periodicals: *Voice from Afar Newsletter.*

★1020★
United Biblical Church of God
Box 547
Crystal River, FL 32623

The United Biblical Church of God was formed in 1992 as an association of autonomous congregations by Charles Kimbrough, Mark Carr, and Chris Patton, all former members of the Worldwide Church of God. The general doctrinal perspective of the Worldwide Church of God is accepted, but the church has a number of specific disagreements with it. Most importantly, the church has departed from the sabbatarianism of the Worldwide Church and has concluded that Jesus was resurrected on Sunday, not Saturday. The church keeps to the Jewish festivals but rejects the Hebrew calendar. Thus it celebrates the festivals a month later than other groups. It also observes the new moon.

Membership: Not reported.

Periodicals: *The Jerusalem Sentinel.*

★1021★
United Seventh-Day Brethren
Current address not obtained for this edition.

The United Seventh-Day Brethren was formed in 1947 by two independent congregations and several individuals who banded together for greater effect in the fields of evangelism, publication, Sabbath promotion, and fellowship. Each local church in the fellowship remains autonomous. Views held generally in common include the following: the Bible is the inspired Word of God and the final authority in faith and conduct; there is one God; Jesus is God's son, who was born of a virgin, died, was resurrected, and ascended; man has no hope apart from the blood of Christ; the Sabbath Day remains in effect, as do the Ten Commandments; and the local church is autonomous. Members deny the immortality of the soul. They do not use unclean meats.

For several years, *The Vision* was the official periodical for the group, though it was owned privately. In 1966, it was bought by W. Allen Bond and, soon after, the official relationship was ended. *The Vision* continues to reflect Seventh-Day Brethren ideology, however.

Membership: Not reported. In 1980 there was only one congregation.

★1022★
Universal Church of God
Rte. 1, Box 52
Manna, OK 74845

The Universal Church of God was founded in 1981 by Ray Lampley, formerly associated with John W. Trescott and the Church of God Evangelistic Association, and Arthur Fields. The general perspective of the Worldwide Church of God under the leadership of Herbert W. Armstrong is accepted. The church believes that we are living in the last days and that the events described in the biblical book of Revelation are now occurring. Lampley operates as a prophet and believes that future events have been revealed to him. Lampley and Fields are identified as the two witnesses of Revelation 11:3. The period of great tribulation began in 1991. The Beast is identified with the United Nations and the Whore of Babylon with apostate Christianity.

Lampley rejects the Hebrew calendar and thus celebrates the Hebrew festivals a month later than most. He also observes the new moon (visible crescent moon). He rejects pacifism and believes that it is a God-given right to own a gun or other weapon of one's choice.

Membership: Not reported.

Periodicals: *The News of the Watchman.*

★1023★
World Insight International
Current address not obtained for this edition.

World Insight International was formed in 1977 by Kenneth Storey, a former administrator of the Worldwide Church of God who had been associated with the Foundation for Biblical Research, as a Christian service organization offering insight into the full scope of God's plan for the world. A strong evangelistic program was announced as well as provision for the establishment of local fellowship groups. Underlying World Insight International was the discovery by Storey and his wife of the manifestation of the spiritual gifts discussed in I Corinthians 12. The first mailing from the new organization announced both the beginning of the Latter Reign of the Holy Spirit before the end of time and warned against counterfeits (which he believes are manifest throughout the contemporary Charismatic Movement). While looking for the manifestation of spiritual gifts, Storey rejected the basic Pentecostal idea of the primacy of speaking in tongues.

Over the years, Storey received support from other prominent Worldwide Church of God leaders such as David Orr, who had initiated the work of the Foundation for Biblical Research in England, Brian Knowles, and Richard Plache. Since its founding, a program of biblical research and publication has led World Insight into fellowship with more orthodox Christians and has produced a critique of Worldwide Church of God ideas. There is a strong emphasis upon prophetic themes and the inner life.

Membership: Not reported. There is a mailing list of several thousand and fellowship groups around the United States.

Periodicals: *World Insight.*

Sources:

Storey, Ken. *Love Feasts of the Church.* Pasadena, CA: World Insight International, 1978.

___. *Worldwide Church of God in Prophecy.* Pasadena, CA: World Insight International, 1979.

★1024★
Worldwide Church of God
300 W. Green St.
Pasadena, CA 91129

The Worldwide Church of God (originally known as the Radio Church of God) was formed in 1933 by Herbert W. Armstrong (1892–1986) and approximately 20 people in Eugene, Oregon.

Armstrong had been a member of a small independent sabbtarian group, Oregon Conference of the Church of God when he first began to function as a minister in the late 1920s.

The Armstrong Era. Herbert W. Armstrong and his wife, Loma Armstrong, moved to Oregon in the mid-1920s. Shortly after the move, Loma began to absorb the teachings of the Church of God from Ora Runicorn, who taught her about Sabbath observance. Catching the enthusiasm of his wife, Armstrong became an avid bible student and eventually was convinced of the truth of the Church of God. Without formally joining it, he became an active participant in 1927, and the following year preached his first sermon. He was ordained by the Oregon Conference in 1931.

After his ordination, Armstrong began to preach regularly and became the pastor to a small group in Eugene. In 1933, while still a member of the Church of God, he began an independent radio ministry, "The World Tomorrow" broadcast, and issued the first copies of a periodical, *The Plain Truth*. This ministry was incorporated as the Radio Church of God. By this time, Armstrong had come to accept a belief in the modern identity of the ancient tribe of Israel. Though never accepted by the General Conference of the Church of God as a whole, the belief had been present among the ministers for a generation.

At the time Armstrong began his radio ministry, the Church of God was being split on a national level by disagreements over church government and the observance of the Jewish (Old Testament) feasts. Armstrong sided with the minority faction that argued for the observance of the feast days and the abandonment of democratic procedures for the selection of church leaders. As such, he participated in the formation of the Church of God (Seventh-Day), headquartered in Salem, West Virginia. He was chosen as one of its 70 leaders in 1933. The Salem faction, however, after observing the feast days for a few years, dropped the practice. They also denounced the belief in British-Israelism. About this same time, in 1937, Armstrong withdrew from further participation in any Church of God activities. His ministry continued under the corporate title of Radio Church of God.

Following World War II, Armstrong moved to Pasadena, California, and in 1947 launched Ambassador College. From this point, the ministry grew steadily. In 1953, the Radio Church of God spread to Europe. A television ministry was added in the 1960s and the voice of Garner Ted Armstrong, the son of the founder, became a familiar sound in many American homes. The work expanded greatly, both in North America and overseas, especially in Western Europe, Australia, and South Africa. In 1968, the name of the work was changed to the Worldwide Church of God. By the mid-1970s the circulation of *The Plain Truth* (which was distributed freely) had jumped to over 2,000,000.

The last fifteen years of Armstrongs expanding ministry proved a time of intense controversy. Within the church, a debate arose over the dating of the Feast of Pentecost and a number of ministers began to question the absolutist approach to the ban on divorce and remarriage. As the debates proceeded, Garner Ted Armstrong was involved in a public scandal that took him off the air and eventually led to his disfellowship from Worldwide Church of God and his founding the Church of God, International. The internal discontent also led to the departure of some prominent ministers and several thousand members, some of whom established the first of several splinter churches. One group of former members began an anti-Worldwide Church of God newsletter, *The Ambassador Report*, which critically discussed trends in the church.

The controversies came to a climax in 1978 when several former members filed a lawsuit against the church. Gaining the cooperation of the California states attorney, they were able to have the church placed in receivership pending trial. The action of the court thoroughly disrupted the church's life for a period of months, before the lawsuit was abruptly brought to an end by new legislation that prohibited such actions by the states attorney. During this time, other churches, recognizing the threat inherent in the courts

preemptive action, came to the Worldwide Church of God's defense. A final ruling in the court on the action stated that the initial lawsuit was from its ". . . inception constitutionally infirm and predestined to failure."

Some peace returned to the church in the few years immediately prior to the death of Herbert Armstrong in 1986. He was succeeded by Joseph W. Tkach, whom he had chosen as the church's new Apostle.

The Tkach Era. After settling into office, the new pastor general, responding to some Evangelical Christian spokespersons, some of whom had labeled the Worldwide Church of God a "cult," opened the church to a largescale reexamination of the doctrinal stance and practices initially taught by Armstrong. In 1987, Tkach announced a doctrinal review to prepare a Statement of Beliefs, and subsequently issued a new doctrinal manual. Changes began to be noticed by the end of the 1980s when pieces of Armstrongs writings (which had been published in a series of booklets) were one-by-one withdrawn from circulation, and the very popular Bible correspondence course was dropped from distribution as it went through a complete revision. The editorial format of *The Plain Truth* was changed in 1990 to focus more on biblical and spiritual matters rather than comment on world affairs. Two years earlier, a second magazine, *Good News*, had been discontinued.

The changes in the Worldwide Church of God came to a head in 1994–95 as major steps were taken toward dropping significant unique teachings of the church and move toward mainstream Evangelical Christian beliefs. The most significant changes included the adopting of the doctrine of the Trinity, and the dropping of requirements that church members triple tithe, observe the Sabbath (Saturday) as a "holy time" and keep the annual festivals, and practice the dietary restraints as outlined in the Levitical law. Church leaders also dropped the belief that the Worldwide Church of God had an exclusive relationship to God as the remnant of true believers in the last days of history.

The doctrinal changes have been hailed by the Evangelical Christian community, but rejected by many leading ministers and long-time church members who had organized their life around these beliefs and practices. Almost one-third of the membership withdrew and formed a variety of new churches, the two largest being the Global Church of God and the United Church of God. The resulting financial disruption following the dropping of tithing requirements in January 1995 forced the church to divest itself of some capital assets and to cut back on staff. Then in the midst of these changes, in September 1995, Tkach died of cancer. He was succeeded by his son, Joseph Tkach, Jr.

Beliefs. Under Armstrongs leadership, the Worldwide Church of God accepted the basic doctrinal stance of the larger Church of God movement. It accepted the authority of the Bible. It was non-Trinitarian, with Armstrong proposing the idea that God could be thought of as a "family" of multiple "spirit beings" into which humans may be born. Armstrong was seen as God's chosen apostle-messenger and he and the church he led had a special place in human history. Drawing on an interpretation of the biblical book of Revelation, chapters 2–3, he saw the Worldwide Church as God's church of the last days. It was the Philadelphia church described in Revelation 3:7–14.

The church was sabbatarian and its members were expected to keep the Sabbath as a "holy time." Christmas, Easter, and other popular holidays were denounced and the ancient Jewish feasts kept. Members were expected to tithe twenty percent of their income annually (ten percent being given to the church and ten percent used for the celebration of the annual major feast) and every third year an extra ten percent. Jewish dietary laws were also kept.

Among the major beliefs of the church was British Israelism, an understanding that the nations of northern and western Europe and those countries largely founded by them (such as Australia, South Africa and especially the United States) were the descendants of the Ten Lost Tribes of Israel. Often the first piece of church literature read by people who encountered it was a booklet by

Armstrong entitled *The United States and British Commonwealth in Prophecy.*

Marriage was deemed a onetime affair, to be kept inviolate until the death of one of the marriage partners. Divorce and remarriage was not allowed. Couples who joined the church after a second marriage were forced to separate, a fact that pained many ministers who were forced to deliver the church's teachings. Interracial marriage was forbidden.

During the Armstrong years, the high-profile church was labeled as a "cult" by numerous Evangelical Christian writers. A large number of anti-Armstrong books appeared through the 1970s and 1980s. However, through the years of Joseph Tkachs and Joseph Tkach, Jr.'s leadership, all of these unique doctrines have been dropped and *The United States and British Commonwealth in Prophecy* has joined the pieces of literature which have been withdraw from circulation. The church is going through a significant period of transition as members consider the new doctrinal perspective.

Organization. Herbert W. Armstrong served the church for many years as its Apostle. As the chief administrator, he made all of the policy decisions and held the power to appoint all church officers and ministers. He was the chief teacher of the church and guided its development through a regular column in *The Plain Truth* and several hundred books and booklets published and regularly revised over the years. While most of these materials were distributed freely to any who asked for them, some were reserved for members only.

"The World Tomorrow" broadcast and the widespread distribution of *The Plain Truth* led to tens of thousands of people joining the church. Initial contact was either by individuals contacting the national headquarters or by chance knowledge of a church member. Admission to membership was by baptism by immersion. Congregations are established across North America but meet in rented facilities; thus they are virtually invisible in the larger religious landscape. Local congregations do not advertise their presence and only rarely are telephone numbers listed in local directories. Today, pastor's names and telephone numbers may be obtained from the church's internet site.

Eventually some of church's programs were discontinued due to financial difficulties. Ambassador Foundation, a cultural, humanitarian, and educational program, has since shut down. Ambassador College has also been discontinued, and *The Plain Truth* magazine was turned over to a new corporation, Plain Truth Ministries.

Membership: In 1992 the church reported 68,918 members, 462 congregations, and 1,227 ministers in the United States, and 83 congregations in Canada. World membership was 98,532 in 122 countries. As of 1995 membership is in flux and an estimated loss of as much as one-third of the membership has been reported in the wake of the recent doctrinal changes.

Educational Facilities: Ambassador College, Big Sandy, Texas.

Periodicals: *The Plain Truth.* • *Youth.*

Remarks: The Worldwide Church of God is among those religious bodies which have since the early 1970s been attacked as a "cult." Numerous pieces of literature, primarily from a conservative evangelical Protestant perspective, have been produced about it. The concentration of criticism has concerned its departure from traditional Christian affirmations on such issues as the Trinity. Almost no objective studies have been produced about the church, and there has been a constant complaint by church leaders that the anti-church literature fails to portray their position accurately.

Sources:

Hopkins, Joseph. *The Armstrong Empire.* Grand Rapids, MI: William B. Eerdmans Publishing Company, 1974.

Armstrong, Herbert W. *The Autobiography.* Pasadena, CA: Ambassador College Press, 1967.

___. *The United States and British Commonwealth in Prophecy.* Pasadena, CA: Worldwide Church of God, 1980.

Bjorling, Joel. *The Churches of God, Seventh Day, A Bibliography.* New York: Garland Publishing, 1987.

McNair, Marion J. *Armstrongism: Religion or Rip-off.* Orlando, FL: Pacific Charters, 1977.

Nichols, Larry, and George Mather. *Discovering the Plain Truth: How the Worldwide Church of God Encountered the Gospel of Grace.* Downers Grove, IL: InterVarsity Press, 1998. 141 pp.

Rader, Stanley R. *Against the Gates of Hell.* New York: Everest House, 1980.

Robinson, David. *Herbert Armstrong's Tangled Web.* Tulsa, OK: John Hadden Publishers, 1980.

This Is the Worldwide Church of God. Pasadena, CA: Ambassador College Press, 1971.

Tkach, Joseph. *Transformed by Truth.* Sisters, OR: Multnomah Books, 1997. 207 pp.

Tuit, John. *The Truth Shall Make You Free.* Freehold Township, NJ: Truth Foundation, 1981.

Bible Student Groups

★1025★
Back to the Bible Way
(Defunct)

Long-time pioneer for the International Bible Students Association and the Jehovah's Witnesses, Roy D. Goodrich was excommunicated in 1944. To put his case before the public and to serve as a rallying point for other "free" Bible Students, he began publishing a periodical, *Back to the Bible Way*, in 1952. Goodrich departed from the main body of Bible Students at two points. He denied that Charles Taze Russell, founder of the Bible Student movement, is to be considered the "wise and faithful servant" of Matthew 25: 45-47. He also rejected Russell's thinking relative to the ransom, and to the significance of 1914. Headquarters were established in Fort Lauderdale, Florida, from which a large amount of literature was distributed to a mailing list of as many as 3,000.

Goodrich died in 1977 and the movement centered upon him dissolved.

Periodicals: *Back to the Bible Way.* (Published in Fort Lauderdale, Florida, from 1952-1973.)

★1026★
Christian Believers Conference
% Berean Bible Students Church
5930 W. 29th St.
Cicero, IL 60650

Since Charles Taze Russell (whose work led to the founding of the Jehovah's Witnesses), raised the issue of the atonement in a most "unorthodox" way, it was no surprise that dissent from a more "orthodox" perspective would appear. J. H. Paton was the first to break with Russell. Paton promulgated his own speculations in both a book and a magazine. In 1909 a significant challenge to Russell arose from three prominent leaders (pilgrims) within his movement—H.C. Henninges, M.L. McPhail, and A.E. Williamson. They rejected Russell's teaching on the ransom atonement in that it elevated the church to the place of Christ as the redeemer and mediator for humanity. They said Russell's theology spoke of Christ as only a part of the sin-offering presented to God. They also rejected Russell's identification of himself with "that servant" of Matthew 25:45-47.

In the midst of the controversy, which lasted for some two years, Henninges led many of the Australian brethren out of Russell's Millennial Dawn Bible Students and McPhail and Williamson led out groups in New York and Chicago. In America, the groups took the name of the Christian Believers Conference. Continuing polemics by descendants of Henninges and McPhail have brought into focus the sharp distinction which the Christian Believers draw between themselves and Russell. They reject the idea of the elect being limited to 144,000 as "mere assumption." They insisted the Lord did not come in 1914 (or 1925) invisibly; he has always been present (Matthew 18:20).

The Christian Believers Conference is structured very loosely, being held together by its peculiar doctrine. For many years a Publications Committee published *The Kingdom Scribe*, discontinued in 1975. The most active ecclesia as of the 1980s is the Berean Bible Students Church in Cicero, Illinois, which publishes the main periodical serving the group nationally. Since 1910 an annual conference has been held, in most recent years in Grove City, Pennsylvania. The conferees meet for mutual edification and Bible instruction, and they have no legislative authority.

Membership: Not reported. In the early 1970s there were 13 ecclesias scattered across the United States from Massachusetts to Wisconsin and Florida.

Periodicals: *The Berean News.*

Sources:

McPhail, M. L. *The Covenants: Their Mediators and the Sin-Offerings.* Chicago: The Author, 1919.

What Say the Scriptures about the Ransom, Sin Offering, Covenants, Mediator, Scapegoat? Melbourne, Australia: Covenant Publishing Company, 1920.

★1027★
Christian Bible Students Association
(Defunct)

Gradually separating from the Dawn Bible Students Association in the late 1960s was the Christian Bible Students Association headquartered in Warren, Michigan. This group began publication of the periodical *Harvest Message* in 1969 and subsequently published several booklets and tracts. Like the Dawn Bible Students Association and the Pastoral Bible Institute, the group emphasized the writings of Pastor Charles Taze Russell and carried the same statement of beliefs. A radio program, "The Harvest Message Broadcast," was heard in Chicago, Nashville, and Detroit. The group disbanded in 1978, and members were absorbed back into the Dawn and other Bible Student groups.

★1028★
Christian Millennial Fellowship
307 White St.
Hartford, CT 06106

Three groups are in agreement theologically but separate administratively. They are the Christian Millennial Fellowship, the Western Bible Students, and the Christian Believers Fellowship. The former began as the Italian Bible Students Association of l'Aurora Millenniale. In 1928 following a break with the International Bible Students Association due to doctrinal and service problems, the Italian Bible Students were incorporated in Connecticut in 1948. It later became known as the Millennial Bible Students Church and under such name was granted bulk mailing privilege by the United States Postal Service and reorganized as a non-profit religious organization for tax purposes by the Internal Revenue.

Since the beginning of its monthly publication of *The New Creation* magazine in January 1939, the group was also known as the New Creation Bible Students. Founded by Italian-American Gaetano Boccaccio, who also edits the magazine, the Fellowship is centered on a single congregation in Hartford with nationwide membership.

The fellowship is an independent lay movement headed by a board of directors elected annually by the membership. Officials of affiliated member churches of Bible classes are elected by their congregations to the office of elder, deacon, secretary, and treasurer. No officers receive a salary, as all work is volunteered. Besides the monthly magazine, a special *African Newsletter* is also published (as part of the magazine) for all the African readership. Three different Bible correspondence courses and a variety of Christian literature is distributed free to any who request it. The voluntary donation of the membership and readership undergird the fellowship's efforts. Besides the magazine, it publishes literature in Spanish, Nigerian, Mala-wian, and Tulugo (India).

Italian-American Bible Students in Connecticut and Massachusetts began work in Italy in 1939. A periodical, *L'Aurora Millenniale*, was begun in Hartford and mailed to subscribers in the homeland. Growth of the work allowed the periodical to be transferred to Italy for publication in 1962. It is now known as *La Nuova Creatione* and is published by the Chiesa Christiana Millenarista at Pescara, Italy. Its present editor is Mario Celenza.

During the 1980s, fellowship groups have been established in Great Britain, Ghana, Nigeria, Ivory Coast, Cameroon, Liberia, Malawi, Mozambique, and Zambia. There is also work in the Philippines, Guyana, and India.

Membership: No membership records are kept.

Educational Facilities: Christian Millennial College, Ghana.

Periodicals: *The New Creation.* • *African New Creation.*

Sources:

"We Believe". Hartford, CT: Christian Millennial Church, 1980.

★1029★
Christian Prophets of Jehovah
Current address not obtained for this edition.

The Christian Prophets of Jehovah was formed in the 1970s by Timothy Tauver, a former member of the Jehovah's Witnesses. Trauver was a typesetter in the Witnesses headquarters in Brooklyn, New York, before his questioning of various doctrinal questions led to his disfellowshipping. After a period of intense Bible study, he came to feel that God had ordained him a prophet. While commissioned to speak to the nations, Tauver has a special word to the Witnesses and has on several occasions been arrested for refusing to leave their meeting halls.

During the early 1980s, Tauver outlined a prophetic timetable calculated from the biblical books of Daniel and Revelation: on October 5, 1982, Babylon the Great (Revelation 17:5) will be established as the greatest power on earth; during 1983, over a million people were to suffer a premature death; Antichrist was to reign until 1989; God will deliver his judgment on the entire "world system" in 1989. Tauver has spread his message through constant travels, advertisments in newspapers, and media coverage of his attempts to confront Jehovah's Witnesses. He has also written a series of open letters to United States President Ronald Reagan.

Membership: Not reported.

★1030★
Dawn Bible Students Association
199 Railroad Ave.
East Rutherford, NJ 07073

The Dawn Bible Students Association grew up among younger members of the Brooklyn ecclesia of the Pastoral Bible Institute (PBI) in the late 1920s. Some energetic members led by former radio broadcaster W. N. Woodworth, who had worked with Charles Taze Russell, wished to begin a radio ministry. Without any hostility toward the work, the PBI felt genuinely unable to sponsor it. The group, joined by some recent additions who had left the IBBA (International Bible Students Association) led by Judge J. F. Rutherford (soon to be renamed the Jehovah's Witnesses), withdrew, formed the Dawn Publishers, and began radio work. The very popular "Frank and Ernest" radio show has become a major outreach effort and has more recently been joined by a television show, "The Bible Answers."

The Dawn carries on the most extensive outreach ministry of any of the Bible Student groups other than the Jehovah's Witnesses. Their monthly periodical, *The Dawn*, was begun in 1932. Over the years, the group has published numerous booklets and pamphlets and a few books. The Association is among the most avid reprinters of Russell's works and keeps most of the other Bible Students supplied.

Doctrinally, the Dawn is at one with the PBI, differing only in being more strict concerning doctrinal divergences among its members. The PBI is much more open to fellowship with other Bible Students groups. The Dawn carries in each issue the same statement of beliefs as the PBI's *Herald of Christ's Kingdom*.

The Dawn is a service organization supplying literature and services to independent Bible Student congregations (ecclesias) across the country. These congregations and the Dawn conduct an extensive outreach program. The Dawn magazine is circulated for only a token subscription cost of $3.00 per year (or with no price) beyond membership. The radio and television programs cover the United States and Canada, and extend overseas to South America, Europe, Africa, and parts of Asia. A tract and literature ministry is pursued, including Spanish language work in South America and Mexico. Foreign work reaches Great Britain, Australia, New Zealand, France, Greece, Germany, Italy, Poland, Romania, Moldavia, Finland, Argentina, Chile, and Brazil. Australian work is coordinated through the Berean Bible Institute, headquartered in Melbourne; and Canadian work through the Canadian Bible Students Association in Vernon, British Columbia. The South India Bible Students Committee headquartered in Bangalore, has developed a working relationship with the Dawn Bible Students through the Northwest India Committee for supplying literature. The Africa Bible Students Committee also uses the Dawn for supplies of literature.

Membership: No membership statistics are maintained since membership is not a requirement in any of the congregations. A rough estimate as of 1997 is that the attendance in congregations worldwide is about 9,000 with about 3,000 in the United States.

Periodicals: *The Dawn.* Send orders to East Rutherford, NJ 07073.

Sources:

The Book of Books. East Rutherford, NJ: Dawn Bible Students Association, 1962.

The Creator's Grand Design. East Rutherford, NJ: Dawn Bible Students Association, 1969.

Our Most Holy Faith. East Rutherford, NJ: Dawn Bible Students Association, 1948.

When Pastor Russell Died. East Rutherford, NJ: Dawn Bible Students Association, 1946.

★1031★
Epiphany Bible Students Association
Box 97
Mount Dora, FL 32757

After the death of Paul S. L. Johnson in 1950, the Layman's Home Missionary Movement began to experience troubles in its leadership. In the spring of 1955, charges of fraud and dishonesty in business were circulated against John J. Hoefle (1895-1984), a prominent leader who had spoken at Johnson's funeral. Hoefle, in turn, accused the leadership of the Layman's Home Missionary Movement of slander and lying, and, in the ever growing polemics, some doctrinal distinctions between Hoefle and Raymond Jolly, who had succeeded Johnson as head of the organization, began to appear. They disagreed on the nature and validity of John's baptism (Acts 19:1ff), which Hoefle saw as an excuse for

Jolly to accuse him of being out of harmony with both Johnson and Charles Taze Russell, founder of the Bible Student Movement. Hoefle was formally disfellowshipped on February 8, 1956.

Hoefle began to publish the correspondence on the controversy and his opinions on the ongoing administration of Jolly. By the end of 1957, these letters had become a regular monthly publication. In 1968, the title Epiphany Bible Students Association began to appear on the masthead. Hoefle continues in the Russell/Johnson theological school with only minor differences with the Laymen's Home Missionary Movement, primarily of an administrative nature and concerning variations on the interpretation of specific texts. For example, both the LHMM and the Hoefle taught of two classes of individuals who would appear in the future Kingdom of God: the Ancient Worthies who would rule (Ps. 45:16) and the Youthful Worthies who would be in partnership with them. The LHMM under Jolly, were teaching that as of 1954, all of the Youthful Worthies had been won and began to speak of a new class of people, the Consecrated Epiphany Campers. Hoefle rejected this teaching, claimed that no such class existed, and that the Youthful Worthies would be won until the time of restitution.

The Epiphany Bible Students Association is organized around individuals who receive the monthly newsletters. There are regular meetings for Bible study at the Mount Dora Bible House, the headquarters in Florida. Other study groups around the country meet in private homes. Leonard E. Williams has succeeded Hoefle as president of the association, and Emily Hoefle, his widow, remains active as the secretary.

Membership: There is no formal membership. In 1997, there were approximately 1,400 people in the United States receiving the mailings and an additional 250 in foreign countries.

Periodicals: The association publishes an untitled newsletter.

★1032★
Jehovah's Witnesses
25 Columbia Heights
Brooklyn, NY 11201

Jehovah's Witnesses are a worldwide Christian society of people noted for their use of Jehovah as the name of God. Their purpose is to bear witness regarding God and his purposes for mankind and do God's will as revealed in the Bible. According to the Witnesses, in the Bible all faithful worshipers, such as Abel, Noah, Abraham, and Jesus, were called witnesses of God (Hebrews 11:1–12:1; Revelation 3:14). A prominent Witness in modern times was Charles Taze Russell (1852–1916). Though his parents were Presbyterians of Scottish-Irish descent, Russell joined the Congregational Church. However, in 1870 he organized a Bible study group in Allegheny (Pittsburgh), Pennsylvania, for the purpose of promoting the basic teachings of the Bible. It was his desire to return to the beliefs of first-century Christianity. In 1879 he began to publish the results of his research, bound by "no creed but the Bible" in the magazine *Zion's Watch Tower and Herald of Christ's Presence*, today called *The Watchtower*, which would be bound by "no creed but the Bible."

The basic teachings of the Witnesses go back to the early Bible studies of Russell. Because of what he learned from the Bible, Russell rejected the belief that hell is a place of eternal torment. He understood it to be mankind's common grave. Benefiting from existing Bible research by nineteenth-century scholars, Russell learned that the Greek word translated "coming" (*parousia*) in the King James Version of the Bible actually meant "presence," and so he and his associates realized that the return of Christ was to be invisible (Matthew 24:3). As these continued their study of the Scriptures and progressed in their knowledge of them, they harmonized their teachings with their deeper understanding. In 1882 Russell wrote: "The Bible is our only standard, and its teachings our only creed, and recognizing the progressive character of the unfolding of Scriptural truths, we are ready and prepared to add to or modify our creed."

Just as did Russell, Jehovah's Witnesses today accept the entire Bible as the inspired Word of truth. Not being Trinitarians, they believe that God, "whose name alone is Jehovah," is the Most High (Psalm 83:18). Jesus said: "My Father is greater than I." He is the Son and the Redeemer of believing mankind (John 14:28). The holy spirit is God's active force for accomplishing His will. God's Kingdom is a heavenly government made up of Jesus Christ as King along with 144,000 corulers taken from earth (Revelation 14:1–4). The nearly six million Witnesses worldwide (1997) proclaim the Kingdom as the only hope for mankind and warn that we are living in "the last days" of this present system. The Kingdom, or heavenly government, will soon exercise dominion over the earth and remove wickedness from the earth, transforming it into a paradise in which true worshipers will live forever. There will be a resurrection of the dead into that Paradise.

The Bible Students, as Jehovah's Witnesses were then known, met together in classes (congregations). Yet, they felt an obligation to share their beliefs with others, so they distributed millions of copies of tracts, books, and booklets. Russell determined that these preaching activities should depend entirely on volunteer workers. To this day, the house-to-house ministry, home Bible study activity, and distribution of literature by Jehovah's Witnesses are done voluntarily.

In 1884 they formed a nonprofit corporation, now the Watch Tower Bible and Tract Society of Pennsylvania, with Russell as the elected president. Branch offices of the society were established in Britain, Germany, and Australia in the early 1900s. The number of countries with branches has steadily increased, and in 1997 there were 104 branches.

The headquarters of the society was moved from Allegheny to its present location in Brooklyn, New York, in 1909. Printed sermons by Russell were syndicated in newspapers, and by 1913 they appeared in more than 2,000 newspapers in the United States, Canada, Europe, South Africa, and Australia, reaching an estimated 15,000,000 readers.

A few months after Russell's death in 1916, Joseph F. Rutherford (1869–1942) was unanimously elected president of the society, on January 6, 1917. In 1918, because of the pressure from prominent clergymen, Rutherford and seven other members of the headquarters staff were imprisoned on the false charge of sedition. However, in 1919 they were released, and eventually they were fully exonerated. Rutherford initiated a great expansion of the preaching work, giving greater emphasis to the door-to-door evangelizing activity. A companion periodical to *The Watchtower*, first known as *The Golden Age* and now called *Awake!*, was introduced during that year.

In 1931 the Bible Students embraced the name Jehovah's Witnesses, based on Isaiah 43:10, which states: "Ye are my witnesses, saith Jehovah, and my servant whom I have chosen." (American Standard Version) During the 1930s and 1940s, there were many arrests of Witnesses because of their preaching activity. A period of intense legal battles ensued in which the Witnesses fought for freedom of speech, press, assembly, and worship. Of the 59 cases they brought before the Supreme Court of the United States, the Witnesses won 43. These victories had a profound impact on the development of constitutional law and preserved freedom of speech, press, and religion for all.

A concerted program of training and global expansion began when Nathan Homer Knorr (1905–1977) followed Rutherford as president in 1942. A training school for missionaries, called the Watchtower Bible School of Gilead, was established in 1943. By 1992 more than 6,500 graduates had been sent to well over 200 lands and island groups. In 1995 this school was moved to the newly constructed Watchtower Educational Center at Patterson, New York. This complex of 28 buildings—including school facilities, an office building, and residence buildings for 1,500—was built entirely by volunteers.

In 1961 the Witnesses released the entire New World Translation of the Holy Scriptures, a modern-English Bible translated from original-language texts. By 1997 over 80 million copies had been printed. The New World Translation has been translated in whole into 17 languages and in part (the "New Testament") into 13 additional languages, making it available in the native tongues of upwards of one fourth of the earth's population.

After the death of Knorr in 1977, Frederick W. Franz (1893–1992) became the next president of the society, to be followed by Milton G. Henschel (b. 1920) in 1992, the current president. Five men have served as president of the Watch Tower Society, a legal instrument used by the Witnesses, but their worldwide activities in 232 countries are coordinated by a Governing Body made up of a group of men, presently 10 in number, located at their world headquarters in Brooklyn, New York. The members of the Governing Body and all others who work full-time in the preparation and production of Bibles and Bible literature at the New York-based headquarters receive only their room and meals and a small reimbursement for expenses.

Conventions are an integral part of the Witnesses' activities. In the early 1890s, these were held in Allegheny, Pennsylvania. In 1893 the first one outside that locality was held in Chicago, Illinois. It was attended by 360 persons, and 70 adults were baptized. The largest single international convention convened in New York City in 1958, using both Yankee Stadium and the nearby Polo Grounds (since demolished). Peak attendance was 253,922; those baptized numbered 7,136. Since then, there have been large international conventions in scores of lands. Smaller regional conventions are normally held each year in many cities throughout the world. In the United States during 1997, some 190 of these were held.

Although the Witnesses are politically neutral, they are interested in their communities. In 1997 they conducted individual weekly Bible study sessions in over 4,500,000 households, thereby helping many in their communities to learn and apply Bible standards of honesty, morality, and family values. In the summer of 1994, a team of Witness volunteers from Europe rushed to help refugees of the civil war in Rwanda. Well-organized camps and field hospitals were set up for the refugees. Huge quantities of clothing, blankets, food, and Bible literature were flown in or shipped to them by other means. More than 7,000 afflicted persons—nearly three times the number of Jehovah's Witnesses in Rwanda at the time—benefited from the relief effort.

Witnesses respect government officials as the "superior authorities" and have a reputation of being law-abiding citizens (Romans 13:1). While respecting the flag of any country, they consider the saluting of a flag to be an act of worship. When ill, they seek medical treatment, including, when necessary, transfusions of non-blood products. However, because they are careful to follow the apostolic edict to "abstain from blood," they refuse blood transfusions (Acts 15:29). Their membership has more than doubled since 1975. Worldwide, there are over 85,000 congregations, each presided over by a body of elders. The elders, assisted by ministerial servants, receive no payment for their services. Most congregations hold their meetings in Kingdom Halls, usually built by the Witnesses themselves. The Witnesses take literally Jesus' command: "Go therefore and make disciples of people of all the nations, baptizing them" (Matthew 28:19, 20). All Witnesses accept this responsibility to share their beliefs with their neighbors, especially by preaching from "house to house" (Acts 20:20).

Literature is distributed without cost to those who show interest in reading it. The expense of publishing and distributing literature worldwide is covered by voluntary donations. No collections are taken at meetings. No dues or tithes have to be paid.

Membership: By the end of 1997, nearly six million Witnesses (5,599,931) in 85,256 congregations were active in 232 lands. During that year 375,923 were baptized. For the annual Memorial of Christ's death in 1997, worldwide a total of 14,322,226 were present. That same year the United States reported 974,719 publishers (active members), associating in 10,883 congregations; 45,220 new ones were baptized; and 2,135,167 attended the annual Memorial of Christ's death. Witnesses have been especially active in Europe and as the twentieth century comes to a close, they are either the second or third largest religious body (next to the traditional state church) in most of the European countries.

Educational Facilities: Watchtower Bible School of Gilead, Patterson, New York.

Periodicals: *The Watchtower.* • *Awake!.*

Sources:

Bergman, Jerry. *Jehovah's Witnesses and Kindred Groups, A Historical Compendium and Bibliography*. New York: Garland, 1985.

Botting, Heather, and Gary Botting. *The Orwellian World of Jehovah's Witnesses*. Toronto: University of Toronto Press, 1984.

Gruss, Edmond Charles. *Apostles of Denial*. Nutley, NJ: Presbyterian and Reformed Publishing Co., 1970.

Jehovah's Witnesses: Proclaimers of God's Kingdom. Brooklyn, NY: Watchtower Bible and Tract Society of New York, 1993.

Jehovah's Witnesses in the Divine Purpose. Brooklyn, NY: Watchtower Bible and Tract Society, 1959.

"Make Sure of All Things". Brooklyn, NY: Watchtower Bible and Tract Society, 1957.

Organization for Kingdom-Preaching and Disciple Making. Watchtower Bible and Tract Society, 1972.

Organized to Accomplish Our Ministry. Brooklyn, NY: Watchtower Bible and Tract Society, 1983.

Rogerson, Alan Thomas. *Millions Now Living Shall Never Die*. London: Constable & Co., 1969.

The Truth that Leads to Eternal Life. Brooklyn, NY: Watchtower Bible and Tract Society, n.d.

White, Timothy. *A People for His Name*. New York: Vantage Press, 1967.

★1033★
Laodicean Home Missionary Movement
Rte. 38
9021 Temple Rd., W.
Fort Myers, FL 33912

John W. Krewson was a member of the Layman's Home Missionary Movement who withdrew in protest over the leadership of Raymond Jolly, who had succeeded Paul S. L. Johnson. In 1955, within months of Johnson's death, Krewson was disfellowshipped and soon began to publish a periodical, *The Present Truth of the Apocalypsis*. He offered LHMM members an option to John J. Hoefle, who had also been disfellowshipped and had formed the Epiphany Bible Students Association. They began to argue, each casting doubt on the other's right to preach and asserting that the other was not a pilgrim (preacher with proper credentials). As time passed, Jolly, Hoefle and Krewson have continued the intrafamily feud; sometimes Jolly and Krewson agree against Hoefle, and sometimes Hoefle and Jolly agree against Krewson. Krewson and Hoefle disagreed on Johnson's status as the last saint, Hoefle arguing that Charles Taze Russell's appointments of other pilgrims (who were still alive) was ample refutation. Both Hoefle and Jolly joined in refuting Krewson's teaching on the apocalypse.

The Laodicean Home Missionary Movement is loosely structured around Krewson's periodical by individuals and small groups who use it for study and edification.

Membership: Not reported. Readership of the magazine is estimated in the hundreds.

Periodicals: *The Present Truth of the Apocalypsis.*

★1034★
Layman's Home Missionary Movement
Chester Springs, PA 19425

Shortly before Pastor Charles Taze Russell died in 1916, Paul S. L. Johnson, a Jew who had become first a Lutheran minister and then a Bible Student pilgrim (teacher/preacher), was sent to England to straighten out troubles among the British students. In order to facilitate Johnson's work, Russell gave him "enlarged powers." Johnson, in November, proceeded to England and, under the authority received from Russell, fired two of the managers of the London office. Judge J. F. Rutherford, confirmed as president of the Watch Tower corporation while Johnson was in still in England, saw Johnson as a major threat to his consolidation of leadership control. Johnson believed that the "special authority" given by Russell was still valid.

The issue came to a head at the 1918 board meeting of the Watch Tower Bible and Tract Society, the corporate entity of the Bible Students, at which Rutherford's authority was decisively confirmed. Johnson, Raymond Jolly, and a host of Bible Students withdrew from the Rutherford-led organization and joined in the formation of the Pastoral Bible Institute (PBI). Differences soon arose among the PBI leaders, so Johnson left and formed the Layman's Home Missionary Movement. The major strength was in the Philadelphia ecclesia. Two periodicals, *The Herald of the Epiphany* (for general readership) and the *Present Truth*(an in-group periodical and major polemic organ), were begun.

The Layman's Home Missionary Movement believes Russell was that faithful and wise servant of Matthew 25:45-47 and was labelled by Johnson the "parousia messenger." As Russell brought word of the presence, so Johnson, as the "epiphany messenger," brought word of Christ's appearance. Raymond Jolly, Johnson's successor, was the "epiphany scribe." Like Russell, Johnson published voluminously. During Johnson's lifetime, fifteen of the seventeen volumes of the *Epiphany Studies in the Scriptures*, volumes following the format and appearance of Russell's *Studies in the Scriptures*, appeared. Jolly published two additional volumes during the 1970's.

The Layman's Home Missionary Movement remains one of the "orthodox" Bible Student groups which still uses Russell's writings and follows Russell's pattern of finding Biblical types of current events and groups. Other Bible Student groups were typed as divisions of the tribes of Levites (Num. 3:17-37). PBI students were seen as Shimite Gershonites, revolutionists changing Russell's charter into an ecclesiastical, clerical document. Johnson's main disagreement with the PBI and the Dawn Bible Students Association, which he saw merely as the PBI masked under another name, concerned the harvest. Johnson believed that, in 1914, the door of salvation (Luke 13:24-25) closed as an entrance into consecration and spiritual-begettal for high calling purposes. The door, he believed, is closed for entrance into the spiritual kingdom. The PBI believed that the door was still open. In essence, the Layman's Home Missionary Movement pointed to the closing of the inner circle, but allowed new members.

Membership: Not reported. There are conflicting claims on membership, ranging from 10,000 to 50,000. The lower estimate more closely approaches the LHMM's real strength.

Periodicals: *The Bible Standard and Herald of Christ's Kingdom.* • *The Present Truth and Herald of Christ's Epiphany.*

Sources:

Johnson, Paul S. L. *Gershonism*. Chester Springs, PA: Layman's Home Missionary Movement, 1938.

___. *Meratiism*. Chester Springs, PA: Layman's Home Missionary Movement, 1938.

Jolly, Raymond. *The Chart of God's Plan*. Chester Springs, PA: Layman's Home Missionary Movement, 1953.

★1035★
Pastoral Bible Institute
1425 Lachman Ln.
Pacific Palisades, CA 90272

"Harvest siftings" was a term used by the Bible Students led by Charles Taze Russell to describe a period of controversy which resulted in the loss of doctrinal or organizational dissidents. Such a period followed the death of Russell, whose work with Bible Students eventually led to the formation of the Jehovah's Witnesses. Judge J. F. Rutherford, who succeeded Russell as president of the Watch Tower Bible and Tract Society, the Bible Students' corporate entity, was opposed in his rise to power by a number of board members, including R. H. Hirsh, I. F. Hoskins, A. I. Ritchie, and J. D. Wright. They opposed Rutherford's issuance of Volume VII of the *Studies in the Scripture*, the first six volumes of which had been Russell's central teaching materials. They fought Rutherford's power until the elections at the convention in 1918. After his decisive victory, they withdrew and with some 50 colleagues and supporters set up the Pastoral Bible Institute (PBI). A committee of seven was appointed to supervise the work and R. E. Streeter was made editor of a new periodical, *The Herald of Christ's Kingdom*.

Doctrinally, the PBI is the most conservative of the Bible Student groups. Each issue of the *Herald* carries a creed-like statement summarizing the truths which "To us the Scriptures Clearly Teach." These include the following:

"That the church is the 'Temple of the Living God'—peculiarly 'his workmanship'; that its construction has been in progress throughout the Gospel Age—ever since Christ became the world's Redeemer and the chief corner stone of this Temple, through which, when finished, God's blessings shall come to 'all people,' and they find access to him. I Cor. 3:16, 17; Eph. 2:20-22; Gen. 28:14; Gal. 3:29.

"That meantime the chiseling, shaping, and polishing of consecrated believers in Christ's atonement for sin, progresses, and when the last of these 'living stones, elect and precious,' shall have been made ready, the great Master Workman will bring all together in the first resurrection; and the temple shall be filled with his glory, and be the meeting place between God and men throughout the Millennium. I Pet. 2:4-9; Rev. 20:4,6.

"That the basis of hope for the church and world lies in the fact that 'Jesus Christ, by the grace of God tasted death for every man,' 'a ransom for all,' and will be 'the true light which lighteth every man that cometh into the world,' in due time. Heb. 2:9; John 1:9; I Tim. 2:5,6.

"That the hope of the church is that she may be like her Lord, 'see him as he is,' be a 'partaker of the divine nature,' and share his glory as his joint-heir. I John 3:2; John 17:24; Rom. 8:17; II Pet. 1:4.

"That the present mission of the church is the perfecting of the saints for the future work of service to develop in herself every grace, to be God's witnesses to the world; and to prepare to be the kings and priests in the next age." Eph. 4:12; Matt. 24:14; Rev. 1:6, 20:6.

"That the hope for the world lies in the blessings of knowledge and opportunity to be brought to all by Christ's Millennial Kingdom-the restitution of all that was lost in Adam, to all the willing and obedient, at the hands of their Redeemer and his glorified Church-when all the willfully wicked will be destroyed." Acts 3:19-23; Isaiah 35.

The import of the statement for PBI comes in its belief that the membership in the church is still open. The harvest is not yet closed, and evangelism, not just the perfecting of those believers left in 1918, is a major thrust. The invitation is to the fullness of the heavenly hope, not just to an earthly paradisiacal state, as with the Jehovah's Witnesses. Because of their evangelistic endeavors, PBI and related groups are the largest of the Bible Student bodies other than the Witnesses.

Organization of the PBI is very loose, with individuals and autonomous local ecclesias affiliated through the *Herald* and an annual membership meeting at which the seven-member board and five-member editorial committee are elected. Affiliated ecclesias are found in 30 countries. Active correspondence and interchange with the British Bible Students of the Bible Fellowship Union are promoted.

Membership: Not reported. In 1992 the institute's periodical circulated sightly more than 3,000 copies in the United States and Canada, and slightly less than 1,000 overseas. The church had affiliate congregations (ecclesias) in England, and continued in fellowship with the Berean Bible Institute in Australia.

Periodicals: *The Herald of Christ's Kingdom.*

Sources:

Streeter, R. E. *Daniel the Beloved of Jehovah.* Brooklyn, NY: Pastoral Bible Institute, 1928.

___. *The Revelation of Jesus Christ.* 2 vols. Brooklyn, NY: Pastoral Bible Institute, 1923-1924.

★1036★
Philanthropic Assembly
Current address not obtained for this edition.

F. L. Alexander Freytag (1870-1947) was in charge of the Swiss Bureau of the International Bible Students Association. Though an able leader, he was never an exponent of founder Charles Taze Russell's theology, and in 1917 he began to criticize Russell's main teaching books, the six-volume *Studies in the Scripture*. Then in 1920 he published the *Message of Laodicea* as an attack on the society, and Judge J. R. Rutherford, who succeeded Russell, took up the debate in *The Harp of God*, his first major book, before the year was out. In 1921, Freytag withdrew and set up the Church of the Kingdom of God, also known as the Philanthropic Assembly of the Friends of Man, taking with him many Swiss, German, and French Bible Students.

Freytag concentrated on the religious problem of death. He believed that he had found the answer in his intimate relationship with the person of Christ. One overcomes death by conforming to the form of Jesus. By eschewing sin and following Jesus, one escapes the wages of sin. Freytag's message of death conquered was set within a framework of Russell's theology. He added an important point: eternal happiness is God's goal for all mankind, without exception. The replacement of death with hell's torment was not good enough for Freytag, who demanded the conquering of death itself. The idea is further supported by allegiance to the Universal Law-"God is love." This characteristic is the supreme fact of creation.

Freytag's movement main strength was in central Europe (Switzerland, Germany, France, Spain, Austria, Belgium and Italy), but it found some adherents among Bible Students in the eastern United States. The American headquarters circulates English-language editions of Freytag's books and two periodicals.

Membership: Not reported. American adherents are estimated to be in the hundreds. Internationally, the *Monitor*, the main periodical, circulates 120,000 copies in several languages.

Periodicals: *The Monitor of the Reign of Justice.* • *Paper for All.* Available from L'Ange de l'Eternal, Le Chateau, 1236 Cartigny, Switzerland.

Sources:

Freytag, F. L. Alexander. *The Divine Revelation.* Geneva, Switz.: Disciples of Christ, 1922.

___. *Eternal Life.* Geneva, Switz.: Messenger of the Lord, 1933.

___. *The New Earth.* Geneva, Switz.: Bible and Tract House, 1922.

★1037★
Western Bible Students Association
Current address not obtained for this edition.

The Western Bible Students Association centered in Seattle, Washington, is at one in doctrine with the Christian Believers Conference but administratively separate. It holds an annual conference at Mission Springs, Santa Cruz, California.

Membership: Not reported.

Sacred Name Groups

★1038★
Assemblies of the Called Out Ones of Yah
Current address not obtained for this edition.

The Assemblies of the Called Out Ones of Yah began in 1974 when Sam Surratt, a believer who had previously been convinced that "Yah" was the correct name of the Creator and "Yeshuah" that of His son, the Messiah, felt compelled to create a unity of the truly Called Out Ones of Yah. Surratt felt that the true church would be guided by Yah through Yeshuah and the Holy Spirit, rather than by one leader, and that leaders would be chosen by casting lots. Following a Biblical pattern, the Called Out Ones are led by twelve apostles, the seven, and the seventy. The seven, which constitute the officers for the assemblies, are elected for two-year terms and, together with the seventy (directors at large), comprise the board of directors for the assemblies.

The assemblies follow the main ideas of the Sacred Name Movement and are very clear in their rejection of both the Trinitarian position and the "Oneness" or "Jesus Only" position of some Pentecostals. The assemblies teach the importance of the baptism of the Holy Spirit and the reception of the gifts of the Spirit (1 Corinthians 12). Members of the assemblies refrain from military duty but will accept alternative humanitarian government service. Members tithe ten percent of their increase (net income) annually. A second tithe is given at the annual feast days (Deuteronomy 14: 22-26), and every third year there is a poor fund tithe. Baptism is by immersion. Weekly worship is on the Sabbath.

In the early 1970s Surratt began to send literature to Sacred Name and Sabbatarian believers across the United States and into foreign fields. He built a mailing list of many thousands that has produced some new members who have begun local assemblies. Branch chapters were designated wherever two or more of the Called Out Ones gathered. Surratt died in 1990 and the present status of the church is unknown.

Membership: Not reported. According to the assemblies, the Called Out Ones of Yah consists of the great multitude (which no one can number) from all nations being called out by Yah from all Babylonish religions to serve with Yeshuah in the coming kingdom. It numbers more than 144,000.

Periodicals: *Called Out Ones Bible Thought Provoker Messenger.*

Sources:

Surratt, Sam. *"Judge" or "Be Judged," That's the Question.* Jackson, TN: Assemblies of the Called Out Ones of Yah, n.d.

___. *The Point of No Return.* Jackson, TN: Assemblies of the Called Out Ones of Yah, n.d.

___. *Virgin Lamps.* Jackson, TN: Assemblies of the Called Out Ones of Yah, 1977.

★1039★
Assemblies of Yah
(Defunct)

The Assemblies of Yah was a small Sacred Name group headquartered in Albany, Oregon. Its aims were to present Yah's name to the world; to teach the laws, statutes and judgments of the Most High; and to foster growth of the Assemblies throughout the world. During the 1960s, it published a periodical, *The Word.*

★1040★
Assemblies of Yahweh
Bethel, PA 19507

Jacob O. Meyer, a former member of the Church of the Brethren, left the church of his childhood and began a spiritual pilgrimage that led him to a small independent Sacred Name assembly meeting in Hamburg, Pennsylvania. In 1964 he moved to Idaho to become assistant editor of the *Sacred Name Herald.* In 1965 at a Feast of Tabernacles meeting in Nevada, Missouri, he was consecrated for the ministry. Then in 1966, after having previously moved to Bethel, Pennsylvania, near to his birthplace, he began his radio ministry. The Sacred Name Broadcast first aired over a station in Baltimore, Maryland. A magazine, *The Sacred Name Broadcaster*, was begun in 1968. In 1969, to facilitate the preaching of the Sacred Name message, he founded the Assemblies of Yahweh. Ten elders were ordained. As the membership grew, a second periodical for members only, *The Narrow Way*, was added. Under Meyer's leadership the Assemblies has grown into the largest Sacred Name organization in the world. The Assemblies also publishes its own version of the Sacred Scriptures.

Doctrinally, the Assemblies of Yahweh has concepts at variance with Christianity. Members affirm "that in order to interpret correctly the Inspired Scriptures, we must use the Old Testament as a basis of our faith." This hermeneutical position toward the dominance of the Old Testament in biblical interpretation is related to the basic Israelite faith and Judaism. The Assemblies teaches the necessity of believers' affirming the divine names Yahweh and Yahshua, the marks of the Divine Father that stand in contrast to the mark of the beast (Rev. 13: 16-17). A non-Trinitarian position is maintained. All the Old Testament commandments, including the feast days and excepting only the ritual and annual sacrifice laws, must be kept. Tithing is stressed. Women cover their heads for worship and wear modest dress. Nonviolence and conscientious objection to war are stressed.

The Assemblies of Yahweh is headed by the directing elder as the earthly shepherd under the Savior, Yahshua the Messiah. Under his direction are the ordained preaching elders who serve in spiritual matters and the deacons who handle temporal affairs. Under these members (who are always males) are the senior missionaries and missionaries (who may be either male or female). Affiliated assemblies are located in 50 countries around the world. The missionary thrust, both foreign and domestic, is concentrated through the Sacred Name Broadcast, heard over 24 stations across the United States (as of 1995) and in 75 foreign countries, over shortwave radio station WMLK owned and operated by the Assemblies of Yahweh. The Sacred Name Telecast, a half-hour program, is aired weekly over several networks. Listeners may receive a wide variety of literature and enroll in a correspondence course. Foreign offices are maintained in England, the Philippines, and Trinidad. Affiliated members are found in 115 countries.

Membership: The Assemblies does not count members but (as of 1992) estimates the number to be several thousand. There are 75 congregations and six elders (ministers).

Educational Facilities: Obadiah School of the Bible, Bethel, Pennsylvania.

Periodicals: *The Sacred Name Broadcaster.* • *The Narrow Way.*

Sources:

Meyer, Jacob O. *Exploding the Inspired Greek New Testament Myth.* Bethel, PA: Assemblies of Yahweh, 1978.

Meyer, Jacob O. *The Memorial Name—Yahweh.* Bethel, PA: Assemblies of Yahweh, 1978.

Psalms, Anthems, Spiritual Songs for the Assemblies of Yahweh. Bethel, PA: Assemblies of Yahweh, n.d.

The Sacred Scriptures, Bethel Edition. Bethel, PA: Assemblies of Yahweh, 1981.

Statement of Doctrine. Bethel, PA: Assemblies of Yahweh, 1981.

★1041★
Assemblies of Yahweh (Eaton Rapids, Michigan)
Box 102
Holt, MI 48842

The Sacred Name movement began among members of the Seventh-Day Church of God during the 1930s. Possibly the oldest surviving assembly is the Assembly of Yahweh, of Eaton Rapids, Michigan, originally chartered as the Assembly of YHWH in 1939. Among its charter members were Joseph Owsinski, John Bigelow Briggs, Squire LaRue Cessna, Harlan Van Camp, George Reiss, Daniel Morris, William L. Bodine, John M. Cardona, Edmond P. Roche, and Marvin Gay. The original charter allowed some variation in the spelling of the Sacred Name, but Yahweh came to be accepted. It associated with other independent assemblies, in large part through the efforts of C. O. Dodd, an early Sacred Name advocate.

Dodd founded a magazine, *The Faith*, at Salem, West Virginia, in 1937, originally to promote the observance of Yaweh's feasts (as described in the Old Testament) among the members of the Seventh Day Church of God. In 1938 he organized the Faith Bible and Tract Society. Within a few years Dodd had become convinced of the Sacred Name position and began using it on the pages of *The Faith*. The magazine tied together the growing movement and became a major instrument in its spread. After Dodd's death it was passed to several assemblies until 1969 when the assembly at Eaton Rapids took responsibility for publishing it. The Faith Bible and Tract Society was continued by Dodd's family in Amherst, Ohio.

A lengthy statement of faith asserts the Assemblies' aim to remove the names substituted by man for the true names: Yahweh, the Father, and his son, Yahshua the Messiah. The Assemblies uphold the Ten Commandments, including the seventh-day Sabbath, and practice footwashing, baptism by immersion, and the festivals according to Leviticus 23. The Old Testament food laws are advocated, as are tithing and divine healing. The assembly is non-Trinitarian. The Assembly of Yahweh at Eaton Rapids is autonomous, but has fellowship and communication with like assemblies across the United States and in some 30 countries around the world.

Membership: Not known. The assembly is in fellowship with other assemblies across the country and around the world.

Periodicals: *The Faith.*

Sources:

Snow, E. D. "A Brief History of the Name Movement in America." *The Faith* 45 (January-February 1982).

★1042★
Assembly of Yahvah
Box 89
Winfield, AL 35594

History. Among the first to accept the idea of the Sacred Name movement were Elder Lorenzo Snow (b. 1913) and his wife, Icie Lela Paris Snow (b. 1912), members of the Seventh Day Church of God at Fort Smith, Arkansas. They affiliated with the original Assembly of Yahweh led by C. O. Dodd, and L. D. Snow was licensed to preach by the church in the early 1940s. In 1945, he began publishing *The Yahwist Field Reporter.* Four years later, he moved to Emory, Texas, where he and other sacred name believers attending a camp meeting formed the Assembly of Yahvah. They used the spelling of the Creator's name that Snow had come

to believe was most correct. Elder Snow served as overseer until 1961, since which time a number of people have served in that capacity including Howard Jefferson, James Pridmore, and Wilburn Stricklin. During this time, Snow served two additional terms. From 1945 to 1961, Snow also served as editor of the *Reporter* (now *The Elijah Messenger*). In 1970, he began a second periodical, *The World Today*, which also serves the assembly.

Beliefs. The Assembly of Yahvah differs from most sacred name groups on two points. First, it spells the name of the Creator, Yahvah, and the name of the Creator's Son, Yahshua. Second, it teaches that the baptism of the Holy Spirit and the nine gifts of the Spirit (I Cor. 12) are operative for believers today. The assembly further affirms the necessity of keeping all Ten Commandments, including worship on the Sabbath (Saturday). It affirms the virgin birth of Yahshua, salvation by faith in Yahshua, and the necessity of sanctification. Water baptism by immersion is practiced. Members are required to dress modestly and abstain from all intoxicating substances.

Organization. The church has been headed since 1984 by an assembly council consisting of assembly ministers and elders. There is an annual camp meeting in July.

Membership: In 1988, the assembly reported less than 200 members in its two congregations in Jackson Gap and Winfield, Alabama. There were six ministers. Affiliated members could be found in Africa, India, Jamaica, and the Philippines.

Periodicals: *The Elijah Messenger.*

Sources:

Major Beliefs of the Assembly of Yahvah. Winfield, AL: Assembly of Yahvah, 1977.

★1043★
Assembly of YHWHHOSHUA
% Pastor Laycher Gonzales
1998 - 58th Ln.
Boone, CO 81025

The Assembly of YHWHHOSHUA is a small Sacred Name groups in Colorado. It differs from other Sacred Name groups in its designation of YHWH (as opposed to Yah, Yahweh, or Yahvah) as the true revealed name of the Almighty and YHWHHOSHUA (YHWH plus HOSHUA) for the name of the Messiah (as opposed to Yahshua or Yahoshua). The Assembly of YHWHHOSHUA is not affiliated with any other Sacred Name body.

The assembly is one of several Sacred Name Groups to accept the Pentecostal emphases on the baptism of the Holy Spirit. It believes in water baptism along with receiving the gift of the Holy Spirit, evidenced by speaking in new tongues and shown by a marked improvement in life as manifested by the fruits of the Spirit (Gal. 5: 22-23). It also teaches the Oneness of YHWH—Father, Son, and Holy Spirit—rather than the Trinity. The assembly has developed a strict mode of living, and members strive to be a daily witness and example of the things taught by YHWHHOSHUA, beginning with modest dress, the eating of pure natural foods, and abstaining from sin and the lusts of the world.

The assembly teaches that the Roman Catholic Church, along with her daughter churches, are the Great Whore spoken of in Rev. 17 and that the United States of America is modern Babylon (Rev. 18). Out of that belief, members do not pay taxes, and do not pay social security (in accordance with Mat. 6: 19-21). Social Security numbers are believed to be a form of governmental control leading to the mark of the Beast (Rev. 14: 16, 17).

Such traditional holidays as Christmas, New Year's, Easter, and Halloween, which have their origin in Pagan holidays, are not celebrated. However, members keep Passover, in remembrance of YHWHHOSHUA'S sacrifice for redemption. Members rely on prayer and faith healing, rather than depend on doctors. Along with other commandments, the assembly firmly believes in keeping Saturday, the Seventh Day, as the sabbath; on that day members refrain from work, buying, and selling.

Women in the assembly are believed to be the keepers of the home and the teachers of children (Titus 2: 3-5). Only men may become ministers. The assembly also supports its own parochial school to provide its children with a sound education, upright morals, and a religious background.

Membership: Not reported. There are also members in the Philippines.

★1044★
Bible Study Association
28877 Summerville Rd.
Eugene, OR 97405

The Bible Study Association is a small Sacred Name group with roots in the Worldwide Church of God, with which it shares a basic doctrinal perspective. It was founded in 1980 by Davis B. Northnagel, Sr. and Donald Goddard. The group does not believe in evangelizing and focuses its efforts upon in-depth research on the Bible and personal growth.

Membership: Not reported.

★1045★
Church of God (Jerusalem)
Box 10184
91101 Jerusalem, Israel

Elder A. N. Dugger was one of the leaders of the Church of God (Seventh-Day) who advocated a more biblical form of church government and who helped organize the Church of God with headquarters at Salem, West Virginia, in 1933. For several years he edited that church's periodical, *The Bible Advocate.* In spite of the controversies in which he was involved, the Church of God had, in 1931, sent Dugger to Jerusalem to begin work on moving the world headquarters there when possible. The work was established with the help of Elder Henry Cohen, a Hebrew Christian. At the reorganization meeting at Salem in 1933, a resolution passed to reaffirm movement of the headquarters to Jerusalem, and money was collected for a headquarters building. Then in the late 1930s Dugger became closely identified with C. O. Dodd, editor of the independent magazine *The Faith,* founded to promote the observance of the Old Testament feast days and then the Sacred Name movement. However, unlike Dodd, Dugger did not leave the Church of God. In 1950, following the merger of the Salem organization with the Church of God (Seventh-Day), Dugger became a leader of one faction of the "Back to Salem" Movement, a small group which rejected the merger. However, the Seventh-Day Church of God, reestablished in Salem, voted to reject the idea of a headquarters in Jerusalem. It was Dugger's goal to implement the original resolution looking toward the establishment of such a world headquarters. Spurred by Israel becoming an independent state, Dugger formed his own group, which goes under various names—Church of God, Congregation of Elohim, and Family of Elohim. He moved to Jerusalem and, in 1953 began to publish *The Mount Zion Reporter.*

Dugger represented a middle ground between the Church of God (Seventh-Day) and the Sacred Name movement. While accepting basically the same theology as C. O. Dodd, with whom he coauthored an important apology for the Church of God (Seventh-Day), and using the Sacred Names, he did not emphasize the names as do other branches of the movement. He noted his distress at the various names for the mighty Creator and his Son which were being used in the Holy Land. "This is surely not pleasing to them, or to the Holy Angels in their presence. . .These names are in the Hebrew language."

Dugger's emphasis was much more on eschatology, particularly as it relates to the prophetic significance of reestablished Israel. According to Dugger's interpretation of prophecy, the Abomina-

tion of Desolation (Daniel 11:31) occurred in 622, the date of Mohammed's choosing of his disciples and beginning of his flight from Mecca. The exact date is either 622 or 632. Moslem calendars begin at that point, the Hegira. From that time, there would be 1,290 days (or years) until the consummation. In 1912, World War I began in the Balkans. After this began, there could be only one generation (45 years) until the end. Thus, the end is imminent.

In Jerusalem, Dugger began a Hebrew-Christian ministry and publishing concern which prints books, numerous booklets and tracts, church school material, a correspondence course, and several periodicals. Members are scattered around the world. Following Dugger's death in 1975, the work of the church passed into the hands of his wife, Effie Dugger, his daughter Naomi Dugger Fauth, and his son-in-law, Gordon Fauth. They keep in touch with members and assemblies around the world and in the United States through their regular mailing and voluminous correspondence.

A. N. Dugger's son Charles Andy Dugger broke with the family and began another group, Workers Together with Elohim.

Membership: In 1986 the church reported more than 40,000 members and 300 congregations worldwide.

Periodicals: *The Mount Zion Reporter.*

Sources:

Dugger, A. N. *A Bible Reading for the Home Fireside.* Jerusalem: "Mt. Zion" Press. Reprint. Decatur, MI: Johnson Graphics, 1982.

Dugger, A. N., and C. O. Dodd. *A History of the True Religion.* Jerusalem: Mt. Zion Reporter, 1968.

★1046★
House of Yahweh (Abilene, Texas)
Box 2498
Abilene, TX 79604

Among the people with whom Jacob Hawkins, founder of the House of Yahweh (Odessa, Texas), communicated during his inspired discovery of the Name of the true organization of the Called out one of Yahweh was his brother Yisrayl B. Hawkins in Abilene, Texas. Yisrayl joined Jacob in building the sanctuary of the House of Yahweh even while Jacob was in Israel. However, in 1980, Yisrayl Hawkins began to hold Sabbath services in a mobile home refurbished as a sanctuary outside Abilene, Texas, when he became convinced of the necessity of establishing the House of Yahweh according to the prophecies of Micah 4:1-2 and Isaiah 2:2. He asserted that the chartering of the House of Yahweh in Abilene by the State of Texas (and its subsequent recognition by the Internal Revenue Service) was the fulfillment of prophecy of the establishment of Yahweh's House in the last days, with the coming of Yahshua Messiah. It would fulfill the prophecies in Micah 4:2 and Isaiah 2:2 that the House of Yahweh would be exalted above every other form of government and religion.

Yahweh himself is the head of the House of Yahweh. Yahshua Messiah is second in command under His Father, and is the High Priest over the House of Yahweh. The overseer of the international headquarters of the House of Yahweh, Abilene, is Yisrayl B. Hawkins, who is assisted by the elders, deacons, and deaconesses. Weekly worship is held in the sanctuary building in Abilene each Saturday morning. Holy days, including those commanded in Leviticus 23 are celebrated: Yahshua's Memorial, Yahweh's Passover, the Feast of Unleavened Bread, the the Day of Pentecost, the Feast of Tabernacles, and the Last Great Day. Adjacent to the sanctuary is a campground for those attending the feasts from out of town.

The House of Yahweh carries on an active publishing program that includes a monthly magazine, a number of booklets on various doctrinal subjects, and a new holy name version of the Holy Scriptures, *The Book of Yahweh.*

Membership: In 1997 the House of Yahweh reported 4 congregations, 23 minister and 5,500 members in the U.S. The subscription list of *The Prophetic Word* now reaches over 15,000 and the magazine is sent to most foreign countries outside of the former Soviet bloc. These is a single Canadian congregation, and also one each in Trinidad, the Philippines, Nigeria, England, Mexico, Australia, and Burma.

Periodicals: *The Prophetic Word.*

Sources:

The Book of Yahweh. Abilene, TX: House of Yahweh, 1987.

Hawkins, Yisrayl B. *True Stories About Christmas.* Abilene, TX: House of Yahweh, n.d.

The House of Yahweh Established. Abilene, TX: House of Yahweh, n.d.

Who Do You Worship? Abilene, TX: House of Yahweh, n.d.

Yahweh's Passover and Yahshua's Memorial. Abilene, TX: House of Yahweh, n.d.

★1047★
House of Yahweh (Odessa, Texas)
% Jacob Hawkins
Box 4938
Odessa, TX 79760

The House of Yahweh was founded in 1973 in Nazareth, Israel, by Jacob Hawkins, an American who had gone to Israel in 1967 to work on a kibbutz in the Negev. Hawkins learned of the discovery in 1973 of an ancient sanctuary dating to the first century that had "House of Yahweh" engraved over its entrance in Hebrew. In his own study of Scripture, he had determined that the name of the people called out by Yahweh was the "House of Yahweh." Thus he was led to found Yahweh's House anew. He began to correspond with people about his discovery and his subsequent actions. In 1975 he returned to the United States and built a sanctuary of the House of Yahweh in Odessa, Texas.

Members of the House of Yahweh direct their worship to Yahweh the Father, whose title is Elohim, and His son Yeshua, whose title is Messiah. Yahshua's shed blood cleanses believers from sin if they keep the Ten Commandments, Yahweh's law. Members tithe one-tenth of their income to the support of the ministry. They are sabbatarians.

The House of Yahweh observes the Old Testament feast days as mentioned in Leviticus 23. Further, it teaches that all believers must come together for the feasts of Passover, Pentecost, and Tabernacles, and members travel from around the United States and the world for these events. In like measure, holidays such as Christmas, Easter, Halloween, and Sunday as a day of worship are condemned as pagan and un-Biblical. Yahshua was born in the spring (around Passover), not in December.

The House of Yahweh is organized on a Biblical pattern with twelve apostles and seventy elders. They meet to conduct business each new moon.

Membership: The House of Yahweh does not keep membership records. In 1980 the House of Yahweh reported congregations in the United States, Israel, India, South Africa, West Africa, Burma, Australia, and Belgium.

Educational Facilities: Ministers Training School, Odessa, Texas.

Periodicals: *The Prophetic Watchman.*

Sources:

Directory of Sabbath-Observing Groups. Fairview, OK: Bible Sabbath Association, 1980.

★1048★
Missionary Dispensary Bible Research
Box 5296
Buena Park, CA 90622

Associated with the Assembly of Yahvah is the Missionary Dispensary Bible Research, headquartered in Buena Park, California.

The group is responsible for the production of *The Restoration of Original Sacred Name Bible* which used Yahvah, Elohim, and Yahshua for the Sacred Names. It is based on Joseph B. Rotherham's translation but uses the King James Version's form of paragraphing. Rotherham included a paragraph entitled "The Name Suggested" in the introduction to his translation. No reference is made to *The Holy Name Bible* translated by A. B. Traina of the Scripture Research Association.

Membership: As of 1988, there were centers in Ward, Arkansas; Winfield, Alabama; Winston, Ontario, Canada; and several in Texas. There are several hundred affiliated members.

★1049★
New Life Fellowship
(Defunct)

The New Life Fellowship was formed by nine ministers, representing four Sacred Name congregations, who gathered at Van Buren, Arkansas, and drew up the doctrinal statement "A Declaration of Those Things Most Commonly Believed Among Us." This group differed from most other Sacred Name organizations in its adoption of a Pentecostal perspective that places strong emphasis upon the gifts of the Spirit as outlined in Corinthians 1:12 and initially evidenced by speaking in tongues. They also believed in the organization of the church under the five-fold ministry as outlined in Ephesians 4:11: apostles, prophets, evangelists, pastors, and teachers lead the church fellowship as a whole. Locally, elders and deacons lead individual congregations.

At the time of the fellowship's formation, a 260-acre tract of land near Natural Dam, Arkansas, was purchased for the purpose of establishing an intentional community. The New Life Community was attached to the congregation at Van Buren. The New Life Fellowship accepted the Sacred Name emphases and acknowledged Yahweh as the Father Creator and Yahshua as His son and humanity's Savior. Weekly worship is on the seventh-day Sabbath (Saturday), and the Old Testament feasts were kept. The annual feast of tabernacles was a time for members of the fellowship to gather from around the United States. Missionary work was supported in Haiti and Europe.

Membership: The fellowship began with four congregations in Van Buren, Arkansas; Henryetta, Oklahoma; Murrysville, Pennsylvania; and Jim Falls, Wisconsin. In 1983 a congregation in Eaton Rapids, Michigan was added. However, in 1986, the Fellowship disbanded.

Sources:

Directory of Sabbath-Keeping Groups. Fairview, OK: Bible Sabbath Association, 1980.

★1050★
Scripture Research Association
14410 S. Springfield Rd.
Brandywine, MD 20613

The Scripture Research Association was founded in January 1950 by A. B. Traina, pastor of the Kingdom Truth Assembly, an independent Sacred Name congregation in Irvington, New Jersey. During the years prior to the formation of the association, Traina had been frequent contributor to *The Faith* magazine, the original Sacred Name periodical, published in Salem, West Virginia, by C. O. Dodd. The association has as its goal the ascertaining of a clearer translation of the Scriptures, especially in restoring to them the name of the Creator, Yahweh, and of His Son, Yahshua, the Messiah. It was Traina's opinion that the New Testament was written in Aramaic and Hebrew, rather than Greek as is commonly assumed. He also believed that the Nicolaitans (Revelation 2:6) were responsible for the substitution of the name of Greek deities "Kurios" (commonly translated "Lord") and "Theos" (commonly translated "God") for the sacred names.

The association published the results of Traina's work in two installments. *The Sacred Name New Testament* appeared in 1950 and the complete *Holy Name Bible* in 1963. It also publishes tracts on a variety of related subjects. The association is governed by a board of trustees.

Membership: Not reported.

Sources:

Traina, A. B. *The Holy Name Bible.* Brandywine, MD: Scripture Research Association, 1980.

★1051★
Workers Together with Elohim
Box 14411
Jerusalem, Israel

Following the death of A. N. Dugger, his son Charles Andy Dugger had a disagreement with the board of the Church of God (Jerusalem). With his followers, he quickly established his own organization and began to publish *The Jerusalem Reporter*, similar in appearance and format to *The Mount Zion Reporter* published by his father's church. He called his new group Workers Together with Elohim.

Workers Together with Elohim are thorough-going Sacred Name people and use all of the Hebrew transliterations in referring to the deity. (Elohim is the Hebrew word commonly translated as "God" in most English-language Bibles.) Church members also follow the Old Testament ritual and food laws. In particular, they take quite literally the admonition in Num. 15:38-40 and add blue fringes to all their garments.

Operating out of Jerusalem, the Workers Together with Elohim continue to operate an organization quite similar to the Church of God (Jerusalem), and they relate to an American constituency. In Jerusalem, they have a strong mission which distributes Bibles in both Hebrew and Russian languages.

Membership: Not reported.

Periodicals: *The Truth.*

★1052★
Yahweh's Assembly in Messiah
Rte. 1, Box 364
Rocheport, MO 65279

Yahweh's Assembly in Messiah was incorporated in 1980 as the Assemblies of Yahweh in Messiah in Kansas, by former elders of the Assemblies of Yahweh, led by Jacob O. Meyer. Following the settlement of a lawsuit for trademark infringement, the Assembly took its present name in 1985. The Assembly follows the doctrine of its parent body. There were only administrative disagreements leading to the formation of the new organization. The Assembly is led by a Board of Directors.

The Assembly initiated a publication program which includes a correspondence course, a number of booklets, and several magazines. Video and cassettes of Sabbath messages are sent to those not affiliated with a local assembly, and traveling elders meet regularly with scattered members. Affiliated assemblies are found across the United States and Canada, and in 20 foreign countries.

Membership: In 1998 there were 500 members in 5 congregations in the United States and one congregation in Canada.

Periodicals: *The Master Key.* • *Beginning Anew.* Send orders to 401 N. Ruby Farm Rd., Rocheport, MO 65279.

Sources:

The Heavenly Father's Great Name. Columbia, MO: Assemblies of Yahweh in Messiah, n.d.

Southcottites

★1053★
Israelite House of David
Box 1967
Benton Harbor, MI 49023

The Israelite House of David was founded in 1903 by Benjamin Purnell (1861-1927), believed by his followers to be the seventh messenger of Revelation 10:7. Preceding Purnell were six other messengers beginning with Joanna Southcott. She was followed by Richard Brothers, George Turner, William Shaw, John Wroe and James Jershom Jezreel. While each of the messengers had their part to play in the "life-of-the-body," each was independent of the other and very little of the writings of the former messengers is to be found in those of Brother Benjamin. Members of the Israelite House of David believe that in this present age the work of ingathering is occurring around the message of the seventh messenger (Gen. 49:10).

For several years, Purnell and his wife Mary travelled around the Midwest before finally settling in Benton Harbor, Michigan, in 1903. They purchased land and began the Israelite House of David. In 1907 an additional 30 acres were purchased and turned into an amusement park that opened in 1908 and for many years attracted people both from surrounding communities and far away. In 1914 the auditorium was built and lectures were regularly held there for visitors to the community.

In 1904 a cablegram was received from some members of the Christian Israelite Church (the church originally founded by John Wroe) in Melbourne, Australia. Having read some books by Purnell, they had accepted him as the seventh messenger spoken of in Revelation. They asked for instructions and in response, Purnell and several members of the House of David traveled to Melbourne and preached among the Christian Israelite Church centers. As a result, 85 people migrated to Benton Harbor and some members of the House of David stayed in Australia to become a permanent presence there.

The Israelite House of David considers itself a Christian organization founded upon the Scripture. It holds to the King James version of the Bible and Apocrypha insofar as Jesus quoted from it (the Book of Enoch and the books of Esdras). It is organized communally according to the Apostolic plan (Acts 2). Jesus is considered the members' Pattern and Waymark. The group is celibate and, following Jesus' example, have taken a Nazarite vow, hence they do not cut their hair. They are vegetarians and pacifists.

Purnell is identified as the seventh messenger. The new truths he brought include an identification of the true Israelites, who will be gathered from both Jews and Gentiles. Israel is the elect of the Jews and Gentiles who will be called out from among them. The elect are now and always have been scattered among all of the Christian denominations (a fact that leads members of the House of David to have a high regard for other churches). Purnell also asserted that Jesus Christ came to abolish death and that it was possible to attain bodily immortality (I Corinthians 15:23). They believe that salvation of the soul, as preached by most Christian groups, is a free gift of God, but by striving in this life, it is possible to never taste death.

The House of David is headed by a Board of Pillars that is assisted by an Advisory Board. There is an annual general assembly that elects both boards. After Purnell's death in 1927, there was a division in the membership and property, which was settled out-of-court.

Membership: In 1997 the group, once having an excess of 500 members, reported less than 60, some of whom still reside in Australia.

Periodicals: *Shiloh's Messenger of Wisdom.*

Remarks: The emergence of the Israelite House of David is difficult to understand without some knowledge of the prior movements that set the context for Purnell's ministry.

After the death of John Wroe, founder of the Christian Israelites, other leaders appeared in England to claim his followers. Among these were a Mr. and Mrs. Head, leaders of the New House of Israel. Another leader was James White, known to his followers as James Jershom Jezreel, a name derived from Hosea's son (Hosea 1:4,11). Jezreel was the author of a book, *The Flying Scroll* (Zech. 5:1). In it, he asked of himself if he was Shiloh, the son whom Joanna Southcott had awaited. He answered "No!" Rather, he identified Shiloh with the seventh angel of the Book of Revelation. Jezreel was the sixth angel. A seventh angel (messenger) was yet to come. Jezreel's message prepared the way for Benjamin Purnell.

The Flying Scroll was addressed to the ten lost tribes of Israel. In it, creation was described. When the world was made and Satan rebelled (Isaiah 14:12), some spirits joined him willingly and some joined him through ignorance; others remained loyal to God. All these spirits are on earth today. The first are redeemable; the second can be saved by repentance; the third will be rewarded by redemption of the body. They will escape death and reign with Christ as the 144,000 Israelites during the millennium. Jezreel's followers become known for their long hair, looped in back and tucked under violet caps.

In his ideas about God, Jezreel departed from his orthodox precedessors. He taught that the Great Father-Spirit descended on Christ at baptism and left him on the cross. Jezreel's main emphasis, however, was the Divine Mother. Drawing on a number of Biblical texts (for example Gal. 4:23), he talked of a Great Mother-Spirit who shall help men and women withstand Satan's power.

Among Jezreel's converts was Clarissa Rogers, a fifteen-year-old. In 1878, three years after her conversion, she declared a voice had told her to go to America; thanks to her beauty and zeal, many converts were won. A second trip, this time with Jezreel, was made in 1880. Progress was rapid until Jezreel died in 1885 and splintering began.

In Detroit, Michael Keyfor Mills, a Baptist businessman, was converted. He sold everything, sent his money to England, and began a career selling *The Flying Scroll* door-to-door. In 1891 he had a Spirit baptism experience in which he fell into a trance and, along with other unusual happenings, his beard fell to the floor. He arose from this trance believing it his duty as Michael the Archangel to gather the 144,000 for the battle of Armageddon mentioned in Revelation. His belief was strengthened by the discovery that he possessed the power of healing. He gathered the Jezreelites into a commune, with himself as leader.

Detroit was stirred by his miracles, but even more by his proclamation that as Eve had seduced Adam into sin, he would seduce women into virtue. He was arrested, and when he refused to explain his meaning, was sentenced to four years' imprisonment. After being released, he took what followers were left to England. Though not considered a messenger, Mills introduced Purnell to the movement.

Sources:

Fogarty, Robert S. *The Righteous Remnant*. Kent, OH: Kent State University Press, 1981.

Purnell, Benjamin. *The Book of Dialogues*. 3 vols. Benton Harbor, MI: Israelite House of David, 1912.

___. *The Book of Wisdom*. 7 vols. Benton Harbor, MI: Israelite House of David, n.d.

Thorpe, Francis. *House of David Victory and Legal Troubles Reviewed*. Benton Harbor, MI: The Author, n.d.

The What? Where? When? Why? and How? of the House of David. Benton Harbor, MI: Israelite House of David, 1931.

★1054★
Israelite House of David as Reorganized by Mary Purnell
Box 187
Benton Harbor, MI 49023-0187

Following the death of Benjamin Purnell, co-founder with his wife Mary Purnell of the Israelite House of David, members were divided between their loyalty to Mary, and the prominent leader H. T. Dewhirst. Following her being locked out of some of the group's facilities, Mary Purnell filed suit. In 1930, an out-of-court settlement awarded Mary some of the colony's farm property, with headquarters property just immediately east of the present House of David. With her followers, Purnell formed a new organization incorporated as the Israelite House of David as Reorganized by Mary Purnell.

Beliefs generally follow those of the Israelite House of David with the exception of the opinions held concerning the role of Mary Purnell. She is considered, together with Benjamin Purnell, the seventh messenger to follow the birth of Shiloh to Joanna Southcott in 1814. Her books are now generally distributed, along with those of her husband, by the group. She died in 1953. The Mary Purnell groups are often referred to as the City of David to distinguish them from the House of David.

Membership: There were less than 50 members in the 1997.

Periodicals: *The New Shiloh Messenger*.

Sources:

Adkin, Clare E. *Brother Benjamin: A History of the Israelite House of David*. Berrien Springs, MI: Andrews University Press, 1990.

Fogarty, Robert S. *The Righteous Remnant*. Kent, OH: Kent State University Press, 1981.

Purnell, Benjamin. *Shiloh's Wisdom*. 4 vols. Benton Harbor, MI: Israelite House of David as Reorganized by Mary Purnell, n.d.

Purnell, Mary. *The Comforter, The Mother's Book*. 4 vols. Benton Harbor, MI: Israelite House of David, 1926.

Thorpe, Francis. *House of David Victory and Legal Troubles Reviewed*. Benton Harbor, MI: The Author, n.d.

★1055★
Yahweh's New Covenant Assembly
PO Box 50
Kingdom City, MO 65262

Yahweh's New Covenant Assembly is a fellowship and ministry dedicated to a return, as closely as possible, to the true and pure teachings of the scriptures. Integral to that process is the adoption of the true name of the Heavenly Father, Yahweh, and of his Son, Yahshua, generally termed God and Jesus by most professing Christians. It is believed that the true names were hidden by misdirected Bible copyists and translators.

The assembly affirms that the Bible is inspired by Yahweh; the Father is the sole Master Designer of all creation, which was carried out by His Son at the beginning of His creation; that Yahshua is the correct name of the Savior (a contraction of the combination of "YAHweh" and "HoSHUA"); that He emptied Himself of His celestial glory and took upon Himself the form of a human, was born of a virgin, lived a sinless life, was resurrected from the dead by the Father, and has now ascended into heaven sitting on the right hand of Yahweh. Yahshua is now considered humanity's Advocate, Mediator and High Priest, and through Him only can we approach the Heavenly Father.

The assembly also affirms that the Holy Spirit (Ruach) is the invisible dynamic force, the mind, the power emanating from the Father and shared by the Son. This invisible essence or power is placed within the believer through the Son, by laying on of hands of the presbytery following baptism into Yahshua's saving Name. Correlative to this view of the Spirit, the assembly believes that the Trinity doctrine is not scriptural but is from paganism.

The assembly practices baptism as a single act of backwards immersion in water and into the saving Name of Yahshua as a necessary act of consecration. The assembly believes that Yahweh's grand plan of salvation for mankind is only through His Son Yahshua the Messiah and is revealed through observing Yahweh's holy Sabbaths and Feast Days. The seventh day of the week (called Saturday) is the day Yahweh has set apart, and is a memorial of His omnipotent creative power. The Sabbath day is a holy day of rest. The commemoration of the sacrifice of Yahshua the Messiah is observed annually on the evening (beginning) of the 14th of Abib, as the 13th ends, according to the original Passover in Egypt when the death angel came over on midnight of the 14th.

After partaking of the Passover, members of the assembly strive to live a sin-free life of obedience in observing the following seven days of Unleavened Bread. Unleavened bread is eaten for these seven days, allowing members to symbolically take in the unleavened bread of sincerity and truth. The day of Pentecost (Shavuoth) or Feast of Weeks is a Sabbath day and the third Annual Sabbath that is counted from the day after the weekly Sabbath that falls during the days of Unleavened Bread. The Day of Trumpets, the fourth Annual Sabbath, begins the seventh month and is a holy convocation leading to the rejoicing upon the return of Yahshua at the last trump. The Day of Atonement, the fifth Annual Sabbath, points to Yahshua's atoning work. Historically it is the holiest day of the year.

The Feast of Tabernacles shows the righteous one-thousand-year reign of the soon-coming King Yahshua and is observed for seven days starting on the 15th day of the seventh month (Tishri 15 through 21). The first day is the sixth Annual Sabbath. The final culmination of the plan of Yahweh is completed in the great harvest. Known as the White Throne Judgment, it is prefigured by the eighth day of the Feast of Tabernacles, the seventh Annual Sabbath called the Last Great Day.

The assembly believes that the scriptural months are delineated by the appearance of the thin crescent of the visible new moon. Scripture indicates that the new moon days will begin from the actual area where the new moon is spotted for that particular month. The scriptural day begins and ends with sunset and will be kept in the Kingdom.

Assembly members consider it an act of worship to support the work with tithes (10 percent of one's income) and offerings.

The assembly believes that after death, human beings are unconscious in their graves in the sleep of death awaiting the resurrection. Immortality is something humans seek which is made available through the work of Yahshua. Humans do not have an immortal soul; they can die.

Yahshua the Messiah is the foundation and cornerstone of His Body—the ecclesia, the assembly—consisting of the called-out Body of believers since Pentecost of Acts 2, who have accepted the sacrifice of Yahshua and changed their lives according to Yahweh's word. The assembly trains and prepares believers for the coming Kingdom. In accordance with the custom of the early assembly in the Apostle Paul's time, the sisters of the assembly wear a headcovering during worship. On earth, males reflect Yahweh's glory and stand bareheaded before Him. Woman, on the other hand, is the glory of man and therefore is to have her head covered or veiled (katakaluptos).

Yahweh's New Covenant Assembly publishes numerous booklets on a wide variety of biblical subjects, especially Yahweh's name and the sabbath and Holy Days. It sponsors a radio show, "Back to the Ter'uth," heard on stations across the United States. International offices are found in England, the Philippines, and on Guadeloupe and Dominica in the West Indies.

Membership: Not reported.

Periodicals: *Light.*

Other Adventists

★1056★
Christian Nations—Eagle Warriors
% Rev. St. Michael Doc Balzarini
Box 5002
Caliptris, CA 92233-5002

Christian Nations—Eagle Warriors was founded by Rev. St. Michael Doc Balzarini in Panorama City, California, in 1994 as the Universal World Federation but soon adopted its present name. The church affirms a belief in God, Jesus Christ as God manifest in the flesh, and the Holy Spirit. Its holds as its authority the Bible as the verbally inspired Word of God. Satan is a real personality, a fallen angel and the enemy of believers. Regarding humanity, the church teaches what is termed the "Teeter-Taughter Principle" that humans consist of Mind, Body, and Spirit.

The church teaches that the laws of the Jewish scriptures (the Old Testament), except those dealing with blood sacrifice and the levitical priesthood, are still in effect and applicable to present-day Israel. Christians are part of present-day Israel. In the near future a new confederation of 10 Western nations, all formerly a part of the old Roman Empire, will occur, a sign of the approaching endtime, referred to in *Daniel* 2:7 and *Revelation* 13:1. Following the organization of this confederation, the New World Order, a world dictator will emerge.

Membership: Not reported.

★1057★
Church of God (Reinertsen)
% Olaf Egge
33738 McKenzie Vw. Dr.
Eugene, OR 97401

The Church of God (Reinertsen) began in 1883 in Chicago, Illinois, when Aanen Reinertsen, a Norwegian immigrant, declared through a set of pamphlets and a periodical, *Domsbasumen* (The Judgment Trumpet), that he had been called out and sent by the Lord to declare that the great day of the Lord was at hand. A major theme in his writings was the apostasy of the contemporary Christian churches.

Reinertsen believed that the Church had fallen away in the year 666 and that Satan was given the power to work his deceptions for 1,260 years. Luther brought the truth of God through, but the wound he gave to Rome was soon healed. Eventually all the Christian sects fell into the same apostasy. With the time of Satan coming to an end, the kingdom of God would again rise up.

Reinertsen identified himself as the sixth angel of the tenth chapter of the biblical Book of Revelation. The angel was identical with the stone that smites the mountain (false Christianity) in Daniel 2:34-35. The stone shall become a great mountain, the kingdom of God which replaces the false church. The angel comes from heaven with the strength of God and is the cloud with which Jesus clothes himself as he comes to his people. Jesus dwelt in him, worked through him, and guided him. The angel also has an open book, i.e., the Book of Revelation, by which he can see the whole plan of God.

When the sixth angel comes and the church of God arises, the war in heaven begins between Christ and the church and the dragon and the society of the dragon. The church will win this war. The church shall exist for 1,260 years in the land of the Gentiles. Then shall the church be suppressed for about three and one-half years, to be followed by the seventh angel and the woes that he brings. The church shall then relocate to Israel. The entire historical Israel shall be saved and brought into the kingdom of God. Then shall ensure another thousand years of the millennial reign. Thus through Reinertsen, the millennial reign of Christ begins and the church he builds shall never fall again.

Reinertsen gained a small following within the Norwegian-American community which has survived to the present.

Membership: Not reported.

Sources:

Reinertsen, Aanen. *The Testimony of the Man-child.* Eugene, OR: Church of God, n.d. 23 pp.

★1058★
Kingdom of God on Earth Within Man
% Kingdom of God Headquarters
PO Box 77659
Los Angeles, CA 90007

The Kingdom of God on Earth Within Man was founded in 1973 by Eugene Emmanuel Purnell, an African American pastor known among the members of the Kingdom as Pastor Emmanuel. He has received the teachings of the kingdom of God through Jesus by the instrument of a host of angels who have guided and informed him in Spirit. Pastor Emmanuel, in turn, published these teachings in a series of books.

The Kingdom understands God to be Good, the totality of all Good, the Creator, Maker, Ruler, and Owner of all things. Thus all things are a part of God and inseparable from God, though no person or thing is God. The opposite of God is Evil—the devil, the consciousness of scarcity. Heaven is the throne of God. It is not a physical place, but a spiritual place. The government of heaven is the kingdom of God within the minds of the saints. In the kingdom all people are rich, free, secure, happy, mentally healthy, at peace, and immortal. They all recognize God as the creator and owner of all. The opposite of heaven is the world, the realm of lies, sin, and the devil (consciousness of scarcity). Angels exist as messengers of God or the devil to bring spirits (words, concepts) to us. All persons are messengers either of God or the devil.

The good people are being organized into the kingdom of God, the structure of which was first revealed to Pastor Emmanuel in 1973. It is designed as the perfect social system and the solution to all the individual and social problems that today beset humankind. Basic to understanding the kingdom is the truth that God creates, makes, and owns everybody and everything. The sinful person is guided by the devil—the law of scarcity—to acts of war, murder, slavery, destruction, in the false understanding that man creates, makes, rules, and owns nature, laws, persons, lands, and things.

The Kingdom of God moves to organize and coordinate all of the general activity of humankind, including the gathering and distribution of all of the appointed spiritual and material things needed to dress, feed, and shelter people. Its concerns include justice, housing, transportation, education, health, communications, and other areas of life. It comes first in one person, Jesus, and then grows through the coming of the saints. As it grows, a social transformation will occur as God transfers governmental stewardship from the governments of the world to the Kingdom of God. It is Pastor Emmanuel's observation that most of the structures of the world are permeated by the devil, i.e., the consciousness of scarcity. Included in this evil realm are all of the world's governments, religious organizations, school systems, and marriages.

In each generation God's anointed prophet, the one whom God has ordained to serve as His chief coordinator of the return of God's saints to Paradise on earth is designated the Son of God. Pastor Emmanuel is that person and he is calling the saints to the kingdom. The kingdom will be led by a hierarchy of the Council of Elders (24 or more leaders), the Assembly of Elders (15,00 in number) and coordinators of the twelve ministries: Justice, Food, Housing, Transportation, Education, Health, Clothing, Accounting, Music, Communication, Human Resources, and Material Resources. The official language of the kingdom will be English and its physical headquarters will be in the United States.

Membership: Not reported.

Sources:

Catechism One. Los Angeles: Kingdom of God Press, 1981. 56 pp.

God's Eternal Kingdom, Laws and Judgments: Official Guidelines for the Day of Judgment, Resurrection of the Dead and Immaculate Social Transformation. Los Angeles: Kingdom of God Press, 1983. 103 pp.

★1059★
Leatherwood God, Followers of the
(Defunct)

The story of the man who came to be known as the Leatherwood God began in August 1828, in the small community of Salesville, Ohio. He quietly joined a group that had gathered for a camp meeting and—during a pause in the proceedings, when the preacher had called for repentance—he interrupted the service with a loud shout of "Salvation!" People turned to look at the then strangely dressed man. He wore a black silk, beaver-skin hat. He seemed to be approximately 50 years old. The people later learned his name was Joseph C. Dylks. During the next few weeks he moved through the town as a rather mysterious personage. At times he preached and on occasion interrupted others with his shout.

As days passed, he revealed his claim that he was the true messiah and that he had arrived to establish the millennial kingdom. He further claimed that he was immortal, that his kingdom would never end, and that all who joined him would not die. He had a decisive encounter with the devil after which he declared his work done and never again shouted. He also appointed a man named McCormick as his associate leader. A short time after announcing his claims, the majority of the village had become adherents and took control of the local church building, rededicating it for the use of Dylks followers. At the service, Dylks proclaimed, "I am God, and there is none else. I am God and the Christ united. . . " Angry detractors now challenged Dylks, demanding a miracle. He promised one but did not deliver. Finally, someone grabbed him and pulled a handful of hair from his head (He had said that not a hair on his head could be touched.). He was arrested, but a judge could find no crime to charge him with.

In October 1828, a mere three months after his appearance, he announced that Philadelphia, not Salesville, would be the center of the New Jerusalem. He would depart and while he was away preparing the new site, the faithful should remember him by facing east (toward Philadelphia) when they prayed. He departed with McCormick and two other disciples. However, several miles from Salesville, Dylks departed from his disciples and said that they would meet again in Philadelphia when the New Jerusalem began to appear. However, Dylks did not reappear. The men searched Philadelphia for him, and finally returned to Ohio to tell their story to the congregation.

The disappointment at Dylks' departure without actually founding the millennium did not deter the congregation, and most of the members remained faithful. Some seven years after the journey to Philadelphia, one of the three men, a former minister, told the church members that he had recently seen Dylks ascend to heaven and that he would soon return to set up his kingdom. The next day the man disappeared. McCormick remained faithful through the rest of his life, dressing in a manner similar to Dylks when he first appeared. The church slowly dissolved as the members died off, there being few new converts. Around 1850, a man named Moses Hartly appeared in the neighborhood and claimed that he had seen Dylks and that Dylks would reappear before the end of the century. Dylks, however, was never seen again.

Sources:

Kummer, George. "Introduction." In *The Leatherwood God* by Richard H. Tannyhill. Gainesville, FL: 1966.

Taneyhill, Richard H. *The Leatherwood God.* Cincinnati, OH: N.p., 1870.

★1060★
Matthias, Followers of
(Defunct)

There appeared in Albany, New York, in 1830 a man calling himself Matthias who declared that he was the Christ and had come to judge the world. Matthias had been born Robert Matthews, but little is known of his life before assuming his religious persona. He dressed in unusual, expensive clothes pontifical robes lined with silk and velvet, carrying a rule in one hand and a sword in the other. He claimed the sword was the Sword of Gideon, but it was identified by onlookers as merely a common U.S. Army issue. He identified himself with Matthias, the apostle chosen to take the place of Judas (Acts 1:21-26). The new Matthias was the Spirit of Truth that had disappeared from the earth with the death of the first Matthias. With his sword he would pronounce judgment and with his rule he would measure the New Jerusalem.

Soon after his appearance, he declared that Albany would be destroyed and warned residents to flee. He left on what became a grand apostolic tour (though Albany was not destroyed) and made his way west toward the Ozark Mountains. He then went into the deep South through Tennessee and Georgia. He soon returned to New York, having gathered a small following. He became a public figure walking around New York City in his apostolic costumes. At one point, around 1833, he was briefly committed to Bellevue Hospital for the Insane. A short time later, when his wife became pregnant, he announced that a holy son would be born. The child turned out to be a girl.

He left New York and was last seen visiting with Joseph Smith, Jr., and the members of the Church of Jesus Christ of Latter-day Saints in Kirkland, Ohio. When he explained his message, Smith had him ejected from their community. From that time on the fate of Matthias and his small following is unknown.

★1061★
Remnant Church
Current address not obtained for this edition.

The Remnant Church originated in the early 1950s in the visions of Mrs. Tracy B. Bizich of Sewickley, Pennsylvania. In 1951, Ellen G. White, founder of the Seventh-Day Adventist Church reportedly appeared and told her that that church had backslidden beyond recovery. She was also told that her spiritual name was "the Bee" and that she would soon be joined by a man whose spiritual name would be "the Fly." Together, they would begin to gather the 144,000 mentioned in Revelation 14:1-3, who would be the only ones to enter the new earth after its destruction, which is imminent.

In 1957, Mrs. Bizich met Elsworth Thomas Kaiser (b. 1901), a railroad worker from Rochester, New York. He, too, had many visionary experiences, which Mrs. Bizich was able to interpret for him. She recognized him as "the Fly" and designated him an elder and the first minister of the Remnant Church. That same year, a congregation was founded in Rochester.

According to the Remnant Church, 1957 marked the beginning of the end of the world. In 1962, the first angel blew his trumpet (Rev. 8:7); 1965 brought a foretaste of the burning up of all the green grass. The Remnant Church is very strict. Members are required to be obedient to superiors, observe the Sabbath, dress modestly, share a community of goods, live in sinless purity, eat without question the food placed before them, clean their quarters, be diligent in study, and wear uniforms (gray for women and tan for males). Members are forbidden to go to physicians (although the use of herbs and leaves is permitted, since these are for the healing of the nations); take others to court except in defense of the Remnant; make distinctions on the basis of race; use drugs, alcohol, or tobacco; or attend other church services. The Lord's Supper is celebrated annually. Baptism is by immersion, and full baptism includes baptism with the Spirit.

The 144,000 will perform active spiritual work in the world until they are all caught up in the Spirit. Some souls have already risen from their graves and have preached in the spirit to friends and relatives.

Membership: Not reported. When last encountered in the mid-1970s, the church had only a few members.

★1062★
Restored Israel of Yahweh
Current address not obtained for this edition.

The Restored Israel of Yahweh was founded in McKee City, New Jersey, in 1973 by Leo Volpe (b. 1916). Volpe is considered to be the resurrected Prophet Jeremiah. According to the Restored Israel, the Bible tells of the resurrection of the prophets in the last days, who should be sought because they would have a true understanding of the Bible. Volpe is said to be one of these prophets and others are expected in the near future. Volpe began his study of the Bible under the guidance of Yahweh (a transliteration of the Hebrew name of God) in 1940. The year 1973 is marked as the beginning of God's Kingdom on earth.

The group believes that Yahweh deals only with the nation of Israel. In the past he dealt with the fleshly nation which was rejected for its disobedience. However, he has promised to restore Israel, which will be composed of those who fulfill the name Israel by placing Yahweh above all else. Chosen out of all the nations of the earth, the true Israel is composed of individuals with righteous hearts. This is the end time when Satan's world system will be destroyed. Yahshua (Jesus Christ) made his Second Presence in 1913. At that time he resurrected his 144,000 Body members. These people are kings and priests who have begun to reign with Yahshua in heaven. In 1917 Yahshua began his period of 1,000 years rulership of earth and will bring the events of earth to a rapid climax. The final ten years of the system will begin with a 1,260-day period of preaching, during which time the Restored Israel of Yahweh will be heard and become known around the world. Everyone will have a chance to accept or reject the message. The 1260 days will be followed by the abomination of desolation which is the union of the United States, Russia, and the papacy into a world government. Israel will be silenced and will retreat into self-sufficent communities. The union will last only another 1290 days. The pope will be cast out of power and war will soon follow. More will respond to the message of Israel and will become, with Israel, the third of humankind to survive the war and establish Yahweh's beautiful kingdom on earth (these prophecies are derived in part from a reading of Daniel, Zechariah, and Revelation). Those who survive will have life everlasting here on earth.

The Restored Israel of Yahweh gathers twice weekly for Bible study. Other periods are spent in evangelistic activity, including speaking and distributing literature. A major activity of the group is gathering in public places with large signs upon which scripture quotations and a portion at their own writings are written. Interested persons are allowed to speak with members about their message. The group runs its own school (kindergarten through high school) open to children of baptized members. There is no instruction in evolution, patriotism, or competition. As of 1985, the group was constructing a self-sufficient community, the first of many, seen as the beginning of God's kingdom on earth. At the beginning of 1988, the community had a functional saw mill, cabinet shop, auto mechanics shop, auto-body shop and four homes.

Membership: In 1988 there were approximately 50 members in the one group in New Jersey.

★1063★
Shiloh True Light Church of Christ
Rte. 1, Box 426
Indian Trail, NC 28079

History. The Shiloh True Light Church of Christ grew out of the work of Cunningham Boyle (1831-1884), a former Methodist preacher who had received a message believed to come from heaven. He declared that the existing churches had so deviated from Christ's teachings that they had become irretrievably lost. In the 1870s he left Methodism and began to preach in the area around Lynchburg, South Carolina, establishing several churches. He also authored a book, *A Key to the Bible* which delineated his teachings. The Shiloh Church, near Charlotte, North Carolina, was founded around 1900.

Beliefs. The beliefs of the church are summarized in its articles of faith. The church affirms the living God, a personal spiritual Being whose perfection consists of his attributes of mercy, justice, truth, omniscience, omnipresence, omnipotence and immutability. The Bible is the inspired Word of God. Jesus Christ, God's Son, possesses the same attributes. The Son existed in an embryo state until the beginning of creation, at which time the Son was separated from the Father and made equal to Him. The devil is also a personal spiritual being who is co-eternal with God. The devil possesses seven attributes of unmercifulness, injustice, untruthfulness, wisdom, power, omnipresence, and immutability. Humans are essental souls (personal spiritual beings) who exist in the body and impart life to it.

The church teaches that all spiritual and immaterial things are non-created, hence cannot be annihilated. Besides God and the devil, the uncreated reality includes time and space, and the souls of human beings. Souls are the offspring of God, existing from all eternity. Souls were separated from God on the sixth day of creation to go through a period of probation. God created human beings in His own image, but when they fell to temptation, the Spirit of God (the image) was lost and humanity received the spirit of the devil. The work of Christ was to provide salvation and the recovery of the Spirit of God for humanity.

Members believe that there is one true church of Christ, and membership in it, gained by repentence of sin and faith in God through Christ, is essential for salvation. The church observes two ordinances, baptism (by either sprinkling, pouring, or immersion) and the Lord's supper. Members are conscientious objectors to war. Alcohol and tobacco are forbidden.

The church teaches that 7,000 years was the period allotted by God from creation to judgment, and that 6,000 years is the time allotted for the probationary period. The last generation began in 1870 and before this generation passes (i.e., the end of the 6,000 years), Christ will return. Without specifically naming the date, the church believes that it is living in the last years before Christ's return, possibly by the end of the twentieth century.

Organization. There is but one congregation of the True Light Church. It is led by a head elder and assistant elders, who teach, minister to the members, and handle the financial affairs of the congregation. None of the leadership is salaried.

Membership: In 1988 there were approximately 1,200 members in the single congregation. While most of the members live in the vacinity of the church building, some are to be found in communities in adjacent states.

Remarks: In 1970 the church was split by a schism when a member, Herman Flake Braswell (b. 1926), claimed to be the successor to the late-head elder. That position was challenged by James Rommie Purser. The issue went to court which decided in Purser's favor. The Braswell faction then formed a second church called the True Light Church of Christ.

During 1986, the Shiloh church became the subject of controversy in a still continuing conflict with the U.S. Department of Labor over a program of vocational training it had instituted among the youth members of the church. In 1971, the church had won the right to school its children in the homes of the members. As an extension of its educational program, it launched a vocational training program which saw a number of younger members working at a masonry company. The labor department has instituted legal proceedings, and as of mid-1988, the issue remained unresolved.

Sources:

Boyle, Cunningham. *A Key to the Bible or the Book of Truth.* Lynchburg, SC, n.d.

★1064★
Star of Truth Foundation
(Defunct)

The Star of Truth was the ministry of Ruth H. Lang and V. Jean Mallatt of Galena, Kansas. It was their belief that the fullness of time had come (Eph. 1:10, Mk. 16:7), and a new age was upon us. Each new age (or period of administration) is initiated by God's representatives giving birth to the Christ. The previous age was begun by Mary, who conceived and brought forth the Son of the most high God. This Son was not a physical birth, but a spiritual being which she conceived within the consciousness of her own being. As God's representative, Mary was told to go and tell the brethren (Matt. 28:7), and a new pattern was set for the age.

It was the Foundation's belief that This period was the day for a new birthing of the Christ. The representative of God for this new birth would be Ruth Lang. In the passing dispensation, the Comforter was given; in the new age, the Spirit of truth which will abide forever would be given. Paul ran ahead of time and saw this new age. He is thus the establisher of it. At one time, Ruth thought of herself as a reincarnation of Paul. She then came to see him as the resurrected one in Christ, who has come in her to resurrect her also.

The Star of Truth Foundation published *The Sparkler* bimonthly. Ms. Lang also wrote a number of pamphlets. The publications tied together the small band of believers, who were scattered across the United States. The Star of Truth Foundation was disbanded in the early 1980's.

★1065★
True Church
Current address not obtained for this edition.

The True Church began in 1930 in the home of Mina Blanc Orth in Seattle, Washington. Ms. Orth, the daughter of Baptist home missionaries in Julian, California, had opened her home to George J. Sherwin (b. 1879) to teach a Bible class. In 1937, she took over leadership of the group, becoming the authoress of a dozen books and pamphlets which contain the basics of the True Church's teaching. Beginning in 1950, she engaged in an extensive radio ministry.

The beliefs of the True Church were based upon an allegorical (spiritual) interpretation of Scripture. The church taught that God's Word is understood in "God's three-way light," the literal light, the historical light, and the symbolic, or spiritual light. Numbers are a focus of the interpretation which holds that the Bible is "formed over a numeric system divisible by seven," the number of perfection. Typical elucidation of texts is seen in the Song of Solomon 6:8, an allegorical description of churchanity: "There are sixty queens (Catholicism) and eight concubines (Protestantism) and maidens without number (Modernism). God is Father and Son. The personhood of the Holy Spirit is denied."

There was a strong expectancy of the imminent return of Christ. During the 1940s, a date between 1950 and 1967 seemed a possible time for that return. World War III, the third War of Revelation 11:14, would begin in the near future. Churchanity would be destroyed; only a remnant of Anglo-Saxon nations (Israel) and the Jews in Palestine would survive. Upon Christ's return, he would destroy all systems of men in opposition to him and set up a new government, symbolized by Job's seven new sons (Job 43:13) to rule during the millennium.

Membership: Not reported. The True Church is organized into small groups meeting in homes. There were an estimated 600 such centers in the United States and Canada in 1968. Headquarters were in Seattle.

★1066★
True Light Church of Christ
Current address not obtained for this edition.

In 1969, a dispute arose within the leadership of Shiloh True Light Church of Christ when Elder Herman Flake Braswell and Mr. Clyde M. Huntley claimed to have been elected bishop and elder, respectively, of the church. At a meeting on December 26, 1969, Braswell was elected bishop and appointed Huntley as elder. James Rommie Purser, the church's elder, disputed Braswell's claims. The court ruled in Purser's favor. It declared that Shiloh True Light Church was congregationally ruled and enjoined Braswell from disturbing its life and worship.

The disruption occurred just prior to the date in which a 100-year-old prophecy made by Cunningham Boyle, founder of the Shiloh True Light Church of Christ, was to be fulfilled. Jesus was to appear in 1970. The Braswell faction of the church approached the date of Christ's coming in a more radical way that did the main body. Braswell closed his upholstery business; others left their jobs. Huntley committed suicide in May 1970, apparently because of the failure of the prophecy. After the failure, some left the church, but most tried to reestablish their normal church activities and secular activities. Braswell, at last report, had reopened his business.

Membership: Not reported. There is estimated to be less than 100 members.

British Israelism

★1067★
Anglo-Saxon Federation of America
Box 177
Merrimac, MA 01860

The longest-lived and largest group of the Anglo-Israel movement is the Anglo-Saxon Federation of America headed by Howard B. Rand, lawyer and Bible student. Rand started a small Anglo-Saxon group in his home in 1928, and as the group grew he began to publish *The Bulletin* as a periodical. He also met W. C. Cameron (editor of Henry Ford's *Dearborn (Michigan) Independent*) who, by 1933, had become president of the newly founded Anglo-Saxon Federation. With Cameron's help, a convention of the Anglo-Israelite groups met in Detroit under Rand's leadership. While unable to unite the groups, Rand was able to launch the Federation.

The position of the Federation is spelled out in *The Pattern of History*, an introductory pamphlet. The Bible is the central document; it is to be understood as the history of Israel, past, present and future, and therefore presents quite literally a pattern of history. The key item in Biblical interpretation is identifying Israel. The history of Israel really begins with God's covenant and promises to Abraham (Genesis 15ff.) and passes on through Isaac, Jacob (who was given the name Israel), and the ten tribes. The covenant was especially focused in Joseph's sons, Ephraim and Manasseh, who were to become the head of all of Israel (Genesis 48). Present-day Israel is found by determining which nation or race fulfills God's promises made in the Old Testament. Israel was to be a powerful nation living northwest of Palestine, a mistress of the earth who holds a great heathen empire in dominion, the chief missionary power of the earth, a nation immune to defeat in war. Part of Israel was to have split off and become a great people in its own right. Such a description can fit only Great Britain and the United States, who split off from her.

In the 1930s and 1940s, groups affiliated with the Federation could be found around the country. From the Destiny Publishers, a large number of books and pamphlets were produced, as were the monthly issues of *Destiny Magazine*. The contents of these materials dealt largely with current events interpreted in terms of the British-Israelite stance. As of the mid-1970s, most of this following had dissolved. Precise statistics are not available. *Destiny Maga-*zine ceased publication in 1969 and has been replaced with a much more modest newsletter. Books are still published and distributed, and membership is still open in the Federation.

Membership: In 1988 the federation reported several thousand members and associated groups in all Anglo-Saxon countries.

Periodicals: *Monthly Newsletter.*

Sources:

The Covenant People. Merrimac, MA: Destiny Publishers, 1966.

Gayer, M. H. *The Heritage of the Anglo-Saxon Race.* Haverhill, MA: Destiny Publishers, 1941.

The Pattern of History. Merrimac, MA: Destiny Publishers, 1961.

Rand, Howard B. *Digest of Divine Law.* Haverhill, MA: Destiny Publishers, 1943.

★1068★
British-Israel-World Federation (Canada) Inc.
313 Sherbourne St.
Toronto, ON, Canada M5A 2S3

Among the oldest of the British-Israel groups, the British-Israel-World Federation dates to 1919, when a number of older organizations in Great Britain affiliated. Some of these groups date themselves to study groups that were formed in the 1860s in response to the early theoretical books by John Wilson (*Our Israelitish Origins*, 1840) and George Moore (*The Ten Tribes*, 1861). In the 1870s, Edward Hine formed the British Israel Identity Corporation to be followed by the Metropolitan Anglo Israel Association in 1878, and the Imperial British Israel Association in 1902. The federation's Covenant Publishing Company has been a major publisher of British-Israel books and pamphlets. Its periodical, *The National Message*, was founded in 1922. From England, the federation has spread around the world, primarily throughout the British Commonwealth.

A Canadian branch of the British Israel Association was organized in 1907 in Victoria, British Columbia, by Edmund Middleton. The Vancouver branch was opened in 1909. Edward Odlum was its first president. Odlum took the work of the association to the radio in 1926. Over the decades the radio work spread across Canada and is currently heard in every province. The federation was established in Canada in the 1920s and held its first convention toward the end of the decade.

The federation conceives of itself as an interdenominational organization, not a church. Rather than competing with other churches, its membership is composed of members from other churches who are admonished to remain in those churches. Meetings are scheduled so as not to compete with the normal Sunday worship hours of most Christian churches. The federation affirms the most basic conservative Protestant Christian beliefs including the authority of the Bible as the Word of God, the deity of Christ, the Virgin Birth, Christ as Savior and Redeemer of Israel and Savior of humankind, and His Second Coming. It clearly affirms belief in the Trinity.

The federation does, however, affirm a variety of doctrines not acceptable to the mainline Christian churches. Primarily, it teaches that the Anglo-Celto-Saxon people are the present-day physical descendents of ancient Israel, the kingdom of 10 tribes spoken of in the Bible.

Membership: In 1992 the federation reported 1,300 members in nine centers across Canada. The radio program "The Voice of British Israel" is heard on 19 stations including short-wave to other continents on WWCR. It is associated with sister organizations in Great Britain, Australia, South Africa, New Zealand, and Kenya.

Periodicals: *The Prophetic Expositor.*

Sources:

Allen, J. H. *Judah's Septre and Joseph's Birthright.* Boston, MA: A. A. Beauchamp, 1930.

These Are the Ancient Things. Fort Langley, BC: Association of Covenant People, n.d.

★1069★
Calvary Fellowship, Inc.
Box 128
Rainier, WA 98576

Calvary Fellowships, Inc., founded in 1960, is a ministry centered upon Woodbrook Chapel pastored by the Rev. Clyde Edminster in Rainier, Washington. Edminster was one of several graduates of Dayton Theological Seminary, a shortlived seminary in Dayton, Ohio, in the 1940s. The Fellowship was originally built among the seminary graduates and other ministers of like mind. The magazine, *Christ Is the Answer*, began in 1967, and for several decades the chapel was the center of a vigorous movement. Edminster had previously begun the Woodbrook Soul Winning and Missionary Training School, and the magazine tied together the growing fellowship. Each summer a Western Bible Conference brought together followers throughout the Northwest and British Columbia.

Calvary Fellowships differed from other Anglo-Israel groups in that it has allowed Pentecostalism and an understanding of grace to become established in its midst—it advocates the present experience of the baptism of the Holy Spirit as signified by speaking-in-tongues, and do not feel bound by the laws of Moses.

During the 1980s, the annual conference has been discontinued and the school closed. Only the chapel and magazine remain of the fellowship ministries. Edminster the authored of numerous books which are circulated to the periodical's readers. He returned in 1995 and was succeed by pastors John and Judy Smith. He continues to edit *Christ Is the Answer*.

Membership: There is currently what is described as one small "elite" congregation.

Periodicals: *Christ Is the Answer.*

Sources:

Edminster, Clyde. *Is It Law or Grace?* Rainier, WA: Woodbrook Chapel, 1987.

★1070★
Christian Conservative Churches of America
Box 575
Flora, IL 62839

The Christian Conservative Churches of America was founded in 1959 by John R. Harrell, but because of several occurrences did not begin to function effectively until 1975. In 1961, law enforcement officials arrived at church headquarters looking for a deserter from the U.S. Marines. In 1964, just before his scheduled appearance at an Internal Revenue Service hearing, Harrell disappeared, only to be arrested the following year. He pleaded guilty to charges related to the 1961 incident and jumped bail. He served four years of his 10-year sentence, but was not allowed to activate the church again until his period of parole was completed in 1975.

It is Harrell's belief that the present governmental system in the United States is fragile and likely to collapse in the near future. Therefore, Harrell encourages members of the Christian Conservative Churches of America and the larger Identity (British-Israel) movement to band together for the survival and preservation of the white race. Harrell has designated an area in the middle of the United States as the survivalist stronghold. He terms this area the "Golden Triangle," the prime area which survivalists can colonize and defend when and if a disaster occurs.

Beliefs. The doctrine of the church is summarized in its Articles of Religion. These include belief in the traditional Protestant affirmations: the Trinity; creation by God; the Bible as an instrument of divine revelation; Jesus Christ's virgin birth, act of atonement, resurrection and second coming; the necessity of faith for salvation; the two sacraments of baptism and the Lord's Supper; and the

kingdom of God and judgment at the end of this age. The articles show a Methodist influence in an affirmation that a certain goodness, as evidenced by conscience, remains in fallen humanity and the idea of the Witness of the Spirit to believers that confirm the biblical promise of God. The church has also been influenced by Pentecostalism in affirming the role of the gifts of the spirit (I Corinthians 12-13).

The articles, in distinction from the majority of Protestants, affirm much in common with the Anglo-Israelite movement, though in a manner somewhat different from the other Identity churches. For example, it specifically denies a popular British-Israel belief that the British monarchs have descended in unbroken succession from the kings of ancient Israel. The church also identifies the descendants of ancient Israel with neither the Jews nor the nations of Western Europe, but with those "peoples who have been gathered into the North American continent, the true land of regathered Israel." It also affirms that any person, race, or nation may be grafted spiritually into the Israel of God by accepting Christ; those who are literal physical descendants of ancient Israel have a distinct role to defend the new chosen land of gathering.

Headquarters of the church is located on an estate at Louisville, Illinois, formerly owned by Harrell and given by him to the churches at the time of their formation in 1959. The life-size replica of Mt. Vernon located on the estate is a popular tourist attraction in southern Illinois.

Membership: Not reported. The church is small with only a few centers in operation.

Remarks: The Christian Conservative Churches of America has often been associated with a number of other organizations through the activities of its founder, John R. Harrell. In 1979, Harrell founded the Citizens Emergency Defense System and the Christian Patriots Defense League. The former organization is a private standing militia on alert status, should the collapse of government become imminent. The league is a dues-paying organization that educates and organizes Christian Patriots to ready them for the government collapse. A third organization, the Paul Revere Club is primarily a fund-raising structure that supports the other two. Church leaders have pointed out that while the church endorses these several organizations, they are completely separate from it.

The church has also been included in lists of rightist organizations affiliated with the Ku Klux Klan. Such organizations as the Anti-Defamation League of B'nai B'rith have noted that Harrell served as the leader of the Committee of Ten Million, along with Robert dePugh of the Minutemen and Robert Shelton, Imperial Wizard of the United Klans of America. Church leaders assert that, whatever Harrell's personal actions and affiliations may be, the church has no relation to the Klan.

Sources:

Harrell, John R. *The Golden Triangle.* Flora, IL: Christian Conservative Church, n.d.

Hate Groups in America. New York: Anti-Defamation League of B'nai B'rith, 1982.

★1071★
Christian Identity Church
Box 1779
Harrison, AK 72601

The Christian Identity Church was founded in 1982 by a group of independent believers in the Identity message under the leadership of Pastor Charles Jennings. It grew out of the work of Wesley Swift who first introduced Sacred Name themes (the use of Yahweh and Yashua as names of the Creator and his son) into Christian Identity churches. The church teaches that YHVH (Yahweh) is the one true God who manifests as a Trinity of Father, Son (Yahshua), and Holy Spirit, and that the Bible is the inerrant Word of God. Yahshua came to redeem God's people, Israel, identified as the "White, Anglo-Saxon, Germanic and Kindred people." It also teaches that Israel now makes up the Christian nations of the earth and is considered far superior to other peoples in their calling as a servant race.

In addition, the church teaches that Satan is a real being who also has a literal seed or posterity on earth, identified with the Jews, believed to be children of Satan through the bloodline of Cain, and the eternal enemy of the chosen people. The chosen race should not partake of the wickedness of the world system, and thus should live a segregated existence apart from all non-white races.

Ideally, the church believes, Christians should live in a theocracy under the laws of God. World problems are due to disobedience of these laws. Ultimately the Kingdom of God will be established on earth. America is the prophesied place where Israel is to be regathered, which is to be a center of the dissemination of truth to the other nations until the kingdom is established.

Fred Demoret is the current pastor of the church. The church annually sponsors a "Family of God Reunion," a national Christian Identity conference over Pentecost weekend.

Membership: The Christian Identity Church consists of one congregation.

Remarks: For a brief period (1985-1986) the Christian Identity Church was pastored by Thom Robb, one of the more controversial figures in the larger Identity movement. Robb, a chaplain for the Ku Klux Klan, established several Identity periodicals such as *Robb's Editorial Report* and *The Torch*.

★1072★
Christian Research
℅ Dan Gentry, Dir.
PO Box 385
Eureka Springs, AR 72632

Christian Research is a Bible-centered ministry, teaching that the Bible is not only for the individual, family, church, and school, but for local, county, state, and national governments. The ministry's purpose is to preserve our Christian heritage, and pursue our destiny in the Kingdom of God on earth. Christian Research teaches the Saxon, Celtic, Scandinavian, Slavonic, and kindred peoples are the physical progeny of ancient Israel, while the majority of Jews today are not Israelites, but anti-semitic Khazars.

Christian Research publishes a quarterly newsletter emphasizing God's law as the answer to our national problems. It also publishes and distributes books, including *More Light*, and occasional booklets and tracts. Christian Research has an active prison ministry and provides educational materials to students and home-school groups at a discount. It also has book tables at various fairs and conferences.

Membership: Christian Research is not a membership organization.

Periodicals: *Facts For Action.*

Sources:

Hall, Verna N., comp. *Christian History of the Constitution.* San Francisco, CA: American Christian Constitution Press, 1960.

★1073★
Church of Israel
Box 62 B3
Schell City, MO 64783

History. The Church of Israel originated in the early 1970s, born of a controversy in the Church of Christ at Halley's Bluff (a.k.a. the Church of Christ at Zion's Retreat), located in rural Vernon County, Missouri (discussed elsewhere in this volume). This church was a splinter of the Church of Christ (Temple Lot) which claims to be the original Church of Christ founded by Joseph

Smith, Jr., the Latter-day Saint prophet. Little, if any, of the Latter-day Saint background remains in the present-day Church of Israel.

Dan Gayman, founder of the Church of Israel, was the son of one of the founders of the Church of Christ at Halley's Bluff. During the 1960s, he became a pastor in the church and was appointed to edit the church's periodical, *Zions Restorer.* Gayman came into open conflict with other church leaders because he promoted views which they considered to be racist. He was charged with inviting white supremists to the churches youth camp and using the facilities for training individuals in the use of weapons and military defense.

The tension culminated in 1972 when Gayman called a church meeting at which two bishops were deposed and new church officers elected. The name of the church's periodical was changed to *Zion's Watchman,* and the priesthood dissolved. The meeting's action led to a law suit, resulting in the court awarding the two deposed bishops the bulk of the church's land. Gayman and his supporters were awarded 20 acres and was denied use of the name "Church of Christ." In 1974 they incorporated as the Church of Our Christian Heritage and adopted the present name in 1981. In 1977-78 a chapel was erected at Nevada, Missouri, and both Christian Heritage Academy, an elementary school, and a ministerial training school were opened. Gayman also developed a home study program which by 1982 had enrolled approximately 125 people.

Beliefs. The beliefs of the church are summarized in its *Articles of Faith and Doctrine.* The Bible is accepted as the infallible Word of God (Yahweh). While the 66 books of the Bible are sufficient for building Christian doctrine, the Apocrypha and the Pseudapigrapha (writings authored somewhat contemporaneously with the Biblical books, but not included in the canon of either the Jewish Bible or Christian Testament). The church's doctrine of God follows the traditional affirmation of orthodox Christianity, but differs in matters of election and salvation. Yahweh (God) exists as the Trinity of Father, Son, and Holy Ghost. Jesus Christ is seen as both God and man, who died as a sacrifice for human sin. The church affirms the Apostles, Nicene, and Athanasian Creeds.

The Church of Israel teaches that God chose a race (the Elect in Christ) who are identified as the Seed of Abraham and as the Israelites of the Old Testament. They are God's workmanship and entirely passive in the matter of their salvation. The Seed are made willing and repentent vessels by the grace of Christ and made holy by his atoning blood. The Law was given as a mirror to expose the sin of the Israelites and thus demonstrate that salvation was not earned by the work of people. The Israelites of the Bible are identified with the present-day Caucasian nations of Europe, Scandinavia, America, Canada, South Africa, New Zealand, Australia, and wherever the seed of these people have been dispersed.

Integral to the understanding of the church's doctrine of salvation is the theory of the two seeds, a variation on the two-seed-in-the-spirit doctrine first popularized by Baptist preacher Daniel Parker in the nineteenth century. Basing his interpretation on Genesis 3:15, Parker argued that Abel and Cain represented two seeds carried by the human race, the former of God and Adam, and the latter of Satan. Every person was born of the two seeds and thus predestined from the beginning to be part of God's family or Satan's dominion. Gayman has developed Parker's ideas along racial lines. He teaches that Caucasians have descended from Seth (the substitute for the murdered Abel). Blacks and Jews have descended from Cain, a product of Satan's impregnating Eve.

As an organization, the church opposes social security, innoculation and the use of vaccines and harmful drugs (narcotics), females serving in the military, the use of violence, and abortion. The church teaches that the goal of history is the establishment of the kingdom of God. In that light, members keep the festivals as established by God for the ancient Israelites—Passover, Pentecost, the Feast of Trumpets, the Day of Atonement, and the Feast of Tabernacles. They also keep the seven sacraments of the ancient church—baptism, communion, confirmation, matrimony, ordination, repentence, and unction (or healing).

Organization. In 1981, when the present name of the church was adopted, a total reorganization of the church occurred. The church was envisioned as 12 dioceses, each named for and representative of one of the 12 tribes of Israel. There was no diocese for Joseph; rather, there are two dioceses for Joseph's sons, Ephraim and Manasseh. There is also no diocese for Levi (the priestly tribe). The Levites are scattered throughout the nation (or church) as a continuing priesthood. Each diocese is to be headed by a bishop.

To date, only the diocese of Manasseh has been activated and Gayman serves as its bishop. Each of the ancient tribes is identified as one of the nations of Europe and North America. Manasseh is identified as the United States and Ephraim as the British Commonwealth.

Membership: In 1988 the church reported several hundred members in five congregations served by 10 ministers.

Periodicals: *The Watchman.*

Remarks: In response to the charges that the Church is a white supremist organization, the Church has included a statement in their articles of faith explicitly denying white supremacy. They do affirm that white people are the Israelites of the Bible and hence called to be the servant people of God. The church denies any goal of white separatism or hatred toward any races. They do believe in the segregation of the races, and seek to live, dwell, work, play, worship and educate children in a segregated environment.

Sources:

Articles of Faith and Doctrine. Schell City, MO: Church of God at Schell City, 1982.

Gayman, Dan. *Do All Races Share in Salvation?* Schell City, MO: The Author, 1985.

___. *The Holy Bible, the Book of Adam's Race.* Schell City, MO: Church of Israel, n.d.

___. *One True and Living Church.* Schell City, MO: Church of Israel, n.d.

___. *The Two Seeds of Genesis.* Nevada, MO: Church of Our Christian Heritage, 1978.

★1074★
Church of Jesus Christ Christian, Aryan Nations
Box 362
Hayden Lake, ID 83835

The Church of Jesus Christ Christian, Aryan Nations dates to the late 1940s when Wesley Swift founded a congregation, the Church of Jesus Christ Christian, in Lancaster, California. Swift had emerged as one of the most prominent voices of pro-White Christian and anti-Marxist Jewish perspectives. Swift died in 1970 and his widow succeeded him as head of the congregation.

After Swift's death, Richard Girnt Butler, a pastor in the church, moved to Hayden Lake, Idaho, and in 1974 began an independent branch of the church. During the 1980s, Butler and the church became the focus of national attention because of his association with factions of the Ku Klux Klan and the American Nazi movement. As early as 1979 he hosted the Pacific States National Identity Conference, and in 1982 he hosted the first World Aryan Congress, an organization periodically reconvened. The congress brought together a wide variety of white-separatist groups and has called for the establishment of an all-white nation in the Pacific Northwest.

The Church of Jesus Christ Christian, Aryan Nations follows the Christian-Israel identity message which believes that modern Anglo-Saxons, Scandinavian, Germanic, Celtic, Basque, Slavic, Lombard, and kindred peoples are the physical descendants of ancient Israel, and hence heir to the promises of the Bible which refer to Israel as a whole. The church is adamantly pro-White.

Membership: In 1995 the church reported over 700 members in Idaho and some 11,000 members throughout the United States

and Canada. There were 12 ministers in the United States and two in Canada. Affilicated branches are found in Australia, Denmark, Italy, France, and Germany.

Periodicals: *Calling Our Nation.* • *The Way.*

Remarks: Increasing public concern about the Church of Jesus Christ Christian, Aryan Nations is the activity of a group called The Order, composed of former members of the church. The Order has been credited with the 1984 murder of Jewish radio talk-show host Alan Berg, in Denver, and a number of crimes in the Seattle, Washington, area. A massive manhunt for members of The Order resulted in the death of the leader Robert Mathews, killed in gun battles with police, and the arrest, trial, and conviction of 11 on charges of racketeering. Richard Butler, while noting the former affiliation of The Order's leaders and sympathizing with their frustrations, rejected their violent and illegal activities.

Because of The Order, as well as the connections between the church and several Klan and Nazi organizations, the group has come under close observation by the media and groups such as the Anti-Defamation League of B'nai B'rith. In 1987 Butler was indicted by the federal government for sedition. He was later found innocent.

Sources:

Coates, James. *Armed and Dangerous.* New York: Hill and Wang, 1987.

Haberman, Frederick. *Tracing Our White Ancestors.* Phoenix, AZ: Lord's Covenant Church, 1979.

Hate Groups in America. New York: Anti-Defamation League of B'nai B'rith, 1982.

Swift, Wesley A. *God, Man, Nations, and the Races.* Hollywood, CA: New Christian Crusade Church, n.d.

___. *Testimony of Tradition and the Origin of Races.* Hollywood, CA: New Christian Crusade Church, n.d.

★1075★
Covenant, the Sword and the Arm of the Lord
(Defunct)

The Covenant, the Sword and the Arm of the Lord (C.S.A) was founded in the mid-1970s by James D. Ellison, an Identity minister in San Antonio, Texas. He had had a vision of the coming collapse of the American society and decided to flee the city and establish a survivalist community in the Ozark Mountains. He moved to Elijah, Missouri, and then in 1976 purchased a 224-acre tract of land in Arkansas, adjacent to the Missouri border, near Pontiac, Missouri. The commune, called Zarephath-Horeb, was viewed as a purging place, the name having been adopted after its Biblical counterpart.

The C.S.A. taught the Kingdom Identity Message, i.e., it identified the white Anglo-Saxon race as the literal descendents of Ancient Israel and hence the heir to the covenants and promises God made to Israel. The Anglo-Saxons have been called to be the light of the world, and black people were created for perpetual servitude. The C.S.A. also believed the Bible teaches that the two-edged sword of God's Spirit is coming soon in judgment to the earth, and God's Arm will be manifest to administer that judgment. The C.S.A. will be that Arm of God. In preparation for the difficult times ahead, the community stored food and stockpiled weapons and ammunition.

The C.S.A., in line with Ellison's vision, expected the imminent collapse of America, the sign of judgment, and an ensuing war. In that war (Armageddon), whites would be set against Jews, blacks, homosexuals, witches, Satanists, and foreign enemies. At that point, the settlement in Arkansas would have become a Christian haven.

The community was largely self-supporting. A farm produced much of the food. Education and medical services were provided internally, and most families lived without electricity or plumbing.

Since its founding, the C.S.A. had been a matter of concern for law-enforcement officials. Following a revelation in 1978, the group began to acquire sophisticated weaponry adequate for modern warfare. In 1981, it opened a survival school and gave training to the public in the use of firearms and survivalism. In 1984, a warrant was issued for Ellison's arrest when he failed to appear before a grand jury investigating the murder of an Arkansas state trooper. A gun found in the possession of the accused was registered to Ellison. In spite of a splintering in the winter of 1981-82 over the continuance of paramilitary training and the departure of those most in favor, the tension that grew out of the C.S.A.'s potential for violence remained an unresolved concern.

In April 1985, agents of the F.B.I. surrounded C.S.A. and arrested Ellison and several members on federal racketeering charges. Following the raid, the group disbanded. Subsequently, four members of C.S.A. were sentenced to prison terms. Ellison received 20 years for racketeering. Others receiving lesser terms were Kerry Noble, Kent Michael Yeats, and William Thomas.

Sources:

Schwartz, Alan M., et al. "The 'Identity Churches': A Theology of Hate." *ADL Facts* 28, no. 1 (Spring 1983).

★1076★
House of Prayer for All People
Box 837
Denver, CO 80201

The House of Prayer for All People was founded in Denver, Colorado, by William Lester Blessing (1900-1984) in 1941. A member of the Church of the United Brethren in Christ, he withdrew in 1927 and became an independent evangelist. He began to use the name House of Prayer for All People as early as 1932. He identified his audience as "Anglo-Saxon, Cymric, and Scandinavian Israelites" with a definite interest in establishing the Kingdom politically and economically on earth. The goal of his work was the restoration of the church (The temple of Yahveh) in the heart of Israel and the earth as his dominion. Great Britain and the United States are the latter-day Israel of Yahveh.

Blessing considered himself, the House of Prayer, and *Showers of Blessing*, the monthly periodical established in 1942, to be together the Voice of the Seventh Angel (VOTSA) of Revelation 10:7 and 11:15. VOTSA will usher in the reestablishment of the Church and the Kingdom of Yahveh. Early in his work he had been influenced by the Sacred Name movement and decided that Yahveh and Yahshua to be the proper name of the Creator and Messiah respectively (see the discussion of the Sacred Name movement elsewhere in this volume).

According to Blessing's teachings, the First Recovery of Israel took place between the birth of Yahshua (Jesus) and 70 C.E. After His crucifixion, Christ and 12,000 members from each tribe of Israel were resurrected. They returned in power on Pentecost, and the Apostolic ministry was begun. During this time, all of the New Testament was written under the work of the Holy Spirit, the Mother. The second coming occurred in 70 C.E., at which time the temple in Jerusalem was destroyed, the dead raised, and the saints raptured. The age came to an end. Since that time, there has not been a true church of Christ on earth; the world has existed in the "times of the Gentiles." However, there has been a remnant on earth, through whom Yahveh has spoken. In 1809, the first of the seven angels began to be heard in the person of Alexander Campbell. He was followed by Joseph Smith, Jr., Ellen G. White, Charles Taze Russell, Benjamin Purnell, and A. P. Adams. In 1962 the desolation was ended according to the prophecy of Daniel 12:12, and mankind is now in the wilderness, the time between the end of the present evil world and the coming of the righteous world. In the near future is a One World government—Babylon, the Mother of Harlots. Yahshua, the messiah, is also already here and will before 2000 A.D. reestablish the kingdom, to be administered by the remnant of his people.

The House of Prayer for All People believes that salvation is a contact between Yahveh and the believer. Baptism is the last step in the plan of salvation. Members practice tithing and the kingdom meal, and worship on Sunday. Blessing had an interest in the Great Pyramid, unidentified flying objects, the hollow earth theory, and the psychical, and wrote on all of these.

From the headquarters in Denver, two periodicals are sent to adherents around the United States. Members have established local congregations. The minimum number for each congregation is 70 adults, but ideally this includes 70 heads of family. Each local congregation is headed by seven servants and two bishops who are ordained by the evangelist, the head of the church. Blessing was succeeded by his son, John David Blessing, the present head of the ministry.

Membership: Not reported.

Periodicals: *Showers of Blessing.* • *Blessing Letter.*

Sources:

Blessing, William Lester. *Hallowed Be Thy Name.* Denver, CO: House of Prayer for All People, 1955.

___. *More About Jesus.* Denver, CO: House of Prayer for All People, 1952.

___. *The Supreme Architect of the Universe.* Denver, CO: House of Prayer for All People, 1956.

___. *The Trial of Jesus.* Denver, CO: House of Prayer for All People, 1955.

___. *VOTSA.* Denver, CO: House of Prayer for All People, 1965.

★1077★
Kingdom Identity Ministries
PO Box 1021
Harrison, AK 72602

Kingdom Identity Ministries is an independent Christian ministry that generally follows the Christian Identity teachings with which it has mingled insights of the Sacred Name movement. Kingdom Identity Ministries seeks to establish God's heavenly Kingdom upon this earth; to proclaim the Gospel of the Kingdom; to identify the true Children of Israel, God's chosen people; to further the spiritual growth and development of the Saints and to actively encourage each individual calling within the Elect. The ministries reaches out both nationally and internationally via the distribution and publication of books and tracts; the Herald of Truth radio broadcast; the American Institute of Theology Bible Correspondence Course; a prison ministry; and meetings of various types.

Kingdom Identity Ministries affirms a belief in YHVH as the one and only true and living eternal God who is manifested in three beings: God the Father, God the Son, and God the Holy Spirit, all one God, and in Yahshua the Messiah (Jesus the Christ) as the incarnate begotten Son of God. The entire Bible, both Old and New Testaments, as originally inspired, is considered the inerrant, supreme, revealed Word of God.

The ministries teaches that God chose unto Himself a special race of people who are above all people upon the face of the earth. These children of Abraham through the called-out seedline of Isaac and Jacob were to be a blessing to all the families of the earth who bless them and a cursing to those who curse them. The descendants of the 12 sons of Jacob, called "Israel," have not been cast away. The New Covenant was made with the Children of Israel, and the white, Anglo-Saxon, Germanic, and kindred people are believed to be God's true, literal Children of Israel and only this race fulfills Biblical prophecy concerning Israel and continues in these latter days to be heirs and possessors of the covenants, prophecies, promises, and blessings of YHVH. This chosen seedline making up the "Christian Nations" of the earth stands far superior to all other peoples in its call as God's servant race, the ministries teaches. Only these descendants of the 12 tribes of Israel scattered abroad have carried God's Word, the Bible, throughout the world, have used His Laws in the establishment of their civil governments, and are the "Christians" opposed by the satanic anti-Christ forces of this world who do not recognize the true and living God.

The ministries believes that the man Adam (a Hebrew word meaning: ruddy, to show blood, flush, turn rosy) is father of the white race only. As a son of God, made in His likeness, Adam and his descendants, who are also the children of God, can know YHVH God as their creator. Adamic man is made trichotomous; that is, not only of body and soul, but having an implanted spirit giving him a higher form of consciousness and distinguishing him from all the other races of the earth. As a chosen race, elected by God, the members of the white race are not to be partakers of the wickedness of this world system, the ministries teaches. This includes segregation from all non-white races, who are prohibited in God's natural divine order from ruling over Israel. Race-mixing is an abomination in the sight of Almighty God, a satanic attempt meant to destroy the chosen seedline, and is strictly forbidden by His commandments, according to the ministries.

The ministries also affirms the existence of a being known as the Devil or Satan and called the Serpent (Gen. 3:1; Rev. 12:9), who has a literal "seed" or posterity in the earth commonly called Jews today. These children of Satan through Cain have throughout history always been a curse to true Israel, the Children of God, because of a natural enmity between the two races. The ministries teaches that the Jews do the works of their father the Devil, please not God, and are contrary to all men, though they often pose as ministers of righteousness. The ultimate end of this evil race whose hands bear the blood of the Savior and all the righteous slain upon the earth, the ministries believes, is divine judgment.

The ministries believes that God gave Israel His Laws for their own good. Theocracy being the only perfect form of government, and God's divine Law for governing a nation being far superior to man's laws, individuals are not to add to or diminish from His commandments. The ministries teaches that homosexuality is an abomination before God and should be punished by death.

Additionally, the United States of America fulfills the prophesied place where Christians from all the tribes of Israel would be regathered, according to the ministries. It is here that God made a small nation a strong one, feeding His people with knowledge and understanding through Christian pastors who have carried the light of truth and blessings unto the nations of the earth. The ministries believes that North America is the wilderness to which God brought the dispersed seed of Israel, the land between two seas, surveyed and divided by rivers, where springs of water and streams break out and the desert blossoms as the rose. The ultimate destiny of all history, according to the ministries, will be the establishment of the Kingdom of God upon this earth.

Membership in the church of Yahshua or Messiah (Jesus Christ) is by divine election. The ministries believes that God foreknew, chose, and predestined the Elect from before the foundation of the world according to His perfect purpose and sovereign will. Yahshua the Messiah (Jesus the Christ) came to redeem (a word meaning purchase back according to the law of kinship) only His people Israel who are His portion and inheritance. Baptism is by immersion for the remission of sins, baptism being ordained by God a testimony to the New Covenant as circumcision was under the Old Covenant.

Membership: The ministries believes that membership in the body of Christ is considered to be by divine election only, not by man's appointment, and therefore it does not maintain membership rolls nor issue any membership cards.

Sources:

http://www.kingidentity.com/.

★1078★
LaPorte Church of Christ
3206 E. Country Rd. 52
LaPorte, CO

The LaPorte Church of Christ is an independent Christian church that generally follows what is termed the Anglo-Israelite or Christian Identity position. It was founded in the mid-1970s and moved to its present location in 1977. The church is pastored by Peter J. Peters, who also serves as the evangelistic head of Scriptures for America Ministries Worldwide, a national outreach ministry dedicated to preaching the Kingdom of Jesus Christ and revealing to the Anglo-Saxon, Germanic, and kindred (white) Americans their true Biblical Identity.

The church affirms the Bible as the Word of God and the incarnation and atonement of Jesus Christ. It also affirms that Jesus Christ came to the descendents of Abraham and in the process of establishing a covenant with them purchased the world. Believers are to be light to the world and a force against evil. The anti-Christ people are seen as children of darkness who appear outwardly righteous but hinder the Kingdom of Christ (Matthew 23). Followers of Christ, in opposing evil, are to hold up His Laws, Statutes, and Judgements as His answer to man's problems.

Peters graduated from the Church of Christ Bible Training School in Gering, Nebraska, with a Bachelor of Sacred Literature degree. He extends the church's mission as a popular writer and speaker and edits *Scriptures for America* newsletter. He has developed a sizeable national audio tape ministry. He has a weekly radio show.

Membership: Not reported.

Sources:

http://www.identity.org/.

★1079★
Ministry of Christ Church
Current address not obtained for this edition.

The Ministry of Christ Church is a national ministry headed by William Potter Gale. It has taken a prominent place in the larger Identity movement because of Gale's activism and involvement with several associated organizations. A retired army officer, Gale served on General Douglas MacArthur's staff during World War II. After his retirement Gale became associated with several groups, including the Church of Christ Christian founded by Wesley Swift. In 1960 he organized the California Rangers, a paramilitary group condemned by the office of that state's attorney general. During the 1970s, he started his own church in Glendale, California, and later moved it to Mariposa, California. While the church is centered on the small congregation at Mariposa, the major work of the church is in the distribution of tapes and literature across the country to members of the church and the Identity movement.

The church follows the consensus of beliefs of the Identity movement. It is segregationist and strongly opposed to interracial marriage. It has a survivalist orientation and has circulated tapes condemning the Internal Revenue Service and the idea of income tax. Gale was a member of the Posse Comitatus, a tax-protest group with strong ties to the Identity movement.

The work of the Ministry of Christ Church was slowed by the conviction in 1987 of Gale and Fortunato Parrino, a minister of the church, on 10 counts of attempting to interfere with the administration of internal revenue laws and the mailing of threatening communications to IRS agents and a state judge. These convictions arose out of Gale's involvement with a tax protest group called the Committee of the States.

Membership: There is one congregation of the Ministry of Christ Church with approximately 30 attendees, but the tapes and written materials distributed by the church are sent to members around the country.

Periodicals: *Identity.*

Sources:

Gale, William P. *Racial and National Identity.* Glendale, CA: Ministry of Christ Church, n.d.

Schwartz, Alan M. and Gail L. Gans. "The Identity Churches: A Theology of Hate," in *ADL Facts* 28, 1 (Spring 1983).

★1080★
National Association of Kingdom Evangelicals
% Gospel Temple
PO Box 72
Hopkins, MN 55343

The National Association of Kingdom Evangelicals arose out of the ministry of C. O. Stadsklev in the 1930s. Stadsklev had been a minister with the Christian and Missionary Alliance but left that organization when he came to accept the perspective of British Israelism, the idea that the Anglo-Saxon, Celtic, Nordic, and related peoples of Northern and Western Europe were the literal descendants of the ancient nation of Israel, the 10 tribes that formed a separate kingdom from the tribe of Judah and who were lost to history after the nation was conquered and its leaders deported. As with most British Israel leaders in the United States, Stadsklev also saw the United States, like the nations of Europe, as having a special scheme in the prophetic plan of God.

Stadsklev emerged as one of the most prominent proponents of British Israelism in the years after World War II. He saw the former Soviet Union as the primary enemy of God's people, the standard bearer of Communism, and believed that at some point it would attack the United States. He opposed what he saw as the "Babylonian money system" that undergirded the present economy. He advocated a system in which money could be loaned interest free and backed by the nation rather than by gold. Among the many British Israel ministers, some wished to associate with Stadsklev's special emphases, and thus the National Association of Kingdom Evangelists was founded, though Stadsklev's writings circulated within the larger movement far beyond the National Association.

The National Association is generally conservative and orthodox in its belief. It affirms the Trinity (a doctrine not held by many who believe in British Israelism). It varies from Evangelical emphases by its belief that God has chosen an earthly servant race through whom he works in a special way to bless humankind and its disavowal of a doctrine of a hell of eternal torment.

The association is a loose fellowship of autonomous congregations who meet annually in a national conference. For many years Stadsklev had a radio show, "America's Hope." The Gospel Temple which Stadsklev served for most of his adult life, circulates his writings and tapes.

Membership: Not reported. In 1980 there were seven affiliated congregations.

Periodicals: *Truth and Liberty Magazine.*

Sources:

Piepkorn, Arthur C. *Profiles in Belief: The Religious Bodies of the United States and Canada.* Vol. IV. San Francisco, Harper & Row, 1979.

Stadsklev, C. O. *Our Christian Beginnings.* Hopkins, MN: America's Hope Broadcasts, n.d. 15 pp.

___. *Personal Salvation.* Hopkins, MN: America's Hope, n.d. 18 pp.

___. *What Happened at Calvary.* Hopkins, MN: America's Hope, n.d. 27 pp.

★1081★
New Beginnings
Box 228
Waynesville, NC 28786

New Beginnings is a movement that brings together aspects of Pentecostalism and British-Israel Covenant-keeping teachings.

New Beginnings was founded by Eldon Purvis, the former editor of *New Wine*, a Pentecostal-Charismatic magazine associated with the ministry of Robert Mumford, Charles Simpson, and Derek Prince in Ft. Lauderdale, Florida. During the 1960s, Purvis began to disagree with the leaders of the *New Wine* ministry over their advocacy of shepherding; leaders in the *New Wine* ministry began to disagree with Purvis over his absorption of British-Israel theories. Purvis taught modern Anglo-Saxons to identify with ancient Israel. Purvis also used the sacred names, transliterated from the Hebrew, Yahweh and Yahshua, for the Creator and the Saviour (whom most Christians term God and Jesus).

During his years of association with *New Wine*, Purvis identified with the Latter Rain revival, a Pentecostal movement that originated in Canada in the late 1940s. Among its emphases were the spiritual gifts of healing and prophecy, the restoration of the church, and the manifestation of the sons of God. It was widely taught through the Latter Rain movement that God was preparing the church for the second coming of Jesus. He was bringing into visible manifestation a group of people dwelling on earth in the image of God. They are overcomers of the world destined to rule and reign with their Everlasting One when he returns to establish His Kingdom on Earth. Integral to this restoration was the reinstitution of the Tabernacle of David, a restoration of God's presence with his people and a return to the Davidic pattern of praise. These teachings are presented in depth in the 1969 book by Graham Truscott, pastor of Restoration Temple in San Diego, California, *The Power of His Presence.* It is Purvis' belief that the revival gave birth to the sons and daughters of Yahweh.

In the late 1960s, after leaving *New Wine*, Purvis who had established the Holy Spirit Teaching Ministry, later founded Heartbeat, Inc., and more recently New Beginnings. In the early 1970s, he began a periodical and a book distribution service. In 1981, he organized the New Beginnings Church of Jesus Christ. An annual gathering of people associated with the movement celebrate the feast of Tabernacles near New Beginnings' headquarters. There are also gatherings for Passover and Pentecost.

Since the death of Eldon Purvis in 1990, his wife Nancy Purvis has continued the publishing of the monthly *New Beginnings* and continues to interpret scripture as it is read in the light of current events of the day.

Membership: In 1995, New Beginnings reported 2,000 members in the United States, 150 in Canada, and an additional 50 worldwide. The magazine is sent to readers in Finland, France, Great Britain, Germany, Northern Ireland, Denmark, the Netherlands, and Switzerland.

Periodicals: *New Beginnings.*

Sources:

Henderson, A. L. *The Mystery of Yahweh.* Waynesville, NC: New Beginnings, n.d.

Truscott, Graham. *The Power of His Presence.* San Diego, CA: Restoration Temple, 1982.

★1082★
New Christian Crusade Church
Box 426
Metairie, LA 70004

The New Christian Crusade Church was formed in 1971 by James K. Warner. In the 1960s Warner had been a member of the American Nazi Party headed by George Lincoln Rockwell. He broke with Rockwell and later associated himself with the National States Rights Party led by J. B. Stoner and with the Knights of the Ku Klux Klan. The New Christian Crusade Church teaches that all white people are the descendents of the ancient Israelites and thus it distinguishes its belief from British Israelism, which identifies the present day Anglo-Saxon people as the literal racial descendents of Ancient Israel. The church believes that the present-day Jews come from the Khazars, a warrior people of Turkish-Mongol origin who inhabited the Volga River valleys near the Black Sea in the tenth century. The church is both anti-Semitic and antiblack.

Associated with the church is the Christian Defense League, an open membership organization founded by Warner for individuals who support the church's racial policies. Warner also established the Sons of Liberty, a publishing and literature-distribution company.

Membership: Not reported. The New Christian Crusade Church consists of a single independent congregation, which serves as the literature and information dissemination center for other independent British-Israel Churches in North America. Through its affiliated Christian Defense League, the church is in direct contact with people who share its beliefs throughout North America.

Periodicals: *The CDL Report.* • *Christian Vanguard.*

★1083★
Prophetic Herald Ministry
(Defunct)

The Northwest has been a center of British-Israelite activity partly because of a strong concentration of believers in Vancouver, British Columbia, Canada. Bethel Temple in Spokane, Washington, was one of the most active British-Israel centers serving, as headquarters of the Prophetic Herald Ministry and its leader, Alexander Schiffner. Founded in 1933, the ministry has concentrated on anti-Communism and anti-Roman Catholicism as major themes in its British-Israel message.

Schiffner taught that the United States is "branded as God's servant nation, Israel." Jacob gave his name "Israel" to both Ephraim and Manasseh, making thirteen tribes instead of the original twelve. The number thirteen is prominent in the history and founding of the United States. *The Prophetic Herald* proclaimed the new consummation of history, at which time true Israel and true Judah (Romans 2:28-29) will be restored as the terrestrial kingdom and head of nations over unrepentant Gentiles and heathen nations. The ministry also advocated the celestial restoration of true Israel to be joint heir with Christ. In an emphasis missing in other British-Israel ministries, Schiffner taught that "only those who receive God's Holy Spirit through repentance and faith in the Lord Jesus Christ" can be a part of the "chosen people," and that a consecrated life is essential to celestial glorification.

In 1970 approximately 40 radio stations carried the Prophetic Herald broadcasts from coast to coast. The monthly *Prophetic Herald* is mailed out to subscribers around the nation. Schiffner wrote a variety of pamphlets and booklets. His death ended the ministry, and in 1973 Bethel Temple was sold.

★1084★
Remnant of Israel
11303 E. 7th
Opportunity, WA 99206

The Remnant of Israel is a small movement that originated in the Church of God (Seventh Day) by G. G. Rupert (1847-1922). Originally a Methodist, Rupert joined the Seventh-Day Adventist Church and for over 30 years served as a minister. Though blind for most of that period, he had an outstanding career, serving as president of the Southwest Union Conference until his resignation in 1902. Several years later he associated with the Church of God headquartered in Stanberry, Missouri (then known as the Church of God (Adventist) Unattached Congregations and today known as the General Conference of the Church of God headquartered in

Denver, Colorado), but was among a number of "independents" who rejected the church's organization. Rupert wrote several articles for the *Bible Advocate*, the church's periodical.

During these years he absorbed the British-Israel thought that had emerged among the Church of God ministers. In the early 1900s he wrote a book on prophecy entitled *The Yellow Peril*. Rupert also came to believe a number of doctrines that gradually separated him from his colleagues in the Church of God. To the practice of keeping a Saturday sabbath he added a belief in the continuing validity of Old Testament feast days, advocating their observance in place of such Babylonish holidays as Easter, Christmas, Ash Wednesday, and Good Friday. Most importantly, he came to believe that there was only one true church, undenominational, invisible, and headed by Christ directly. This belief led him to reject the Church of God organization and to label all the visibly organized churches as false. Besides these ideas, Rupert also believed in tithing, divine healing, speaking in tongues, and pacifism.

Rupert began a periodical, *The Remnant of Israel*, in 1915. It was originally published at Britton, Oklahoma, but was moved to Oklahoma City a short time later. Rupert traveled widely, gathering support for his cause, and small congregations of supporters emerged. In 1919 a national conference of his supporters was held in Pasadena, California. After his death in 1922, his daughter, Lucille Rupert, edited the paper and the work was continued to mid-century by I. C. Sultz, her husband, whom Rupert had ordained in 1916. Sultz ordained William J. Walker as director of the Remnant of Israel in 1967. Walker continued to issue the periodical for several years, but it was discontinued for lack of financial support. Since then, Walker has issued a number of tracts, pamphlets, and Bible studies.

As a correspondence minister, Pastor Walker takes Rupert's ideas a step further: he discounts all church organization and teaches that the true children of Israel (the white race) consists of those whose names are written in Heaven. He believes there is no true church, organized or otherwise; the Saviour is not the head of any church, rather he is the head of his elect, the called-out ones; the modern term "church" is a mistranslation of the Greek "ecclesia" meaning "called-out chosen ones." In like measure, "Christ" is a pagan title of an Eastern sun-deity known as Kristos (Christos). Today, the Remnant of Israel is a small organization supported by a few people who receive the literature produced from its headquarters in Opportunity, Washington.

The contemporary supporters of the Remnant of Israel continue to observe the sabbath and the Old Testament feast days, though the thrust of the work and literature is centered upon the heralding of the "Remnant Message" (British-Israelism) to modern Israel (the white race).

Membership: The Remnant of Israel is not a membership organization. Believers in the Remnant of Israel message can be found throughout the United States (i.e., the land of modern Israel, the new Jer*USA*lem), Canada, Great Britan, Australia, and other predominantly white Anglo-Saxon nations.

Sources:

Nickels, Richard C. *The Remnant of Israel.* Sheridan, WY: Giving and Sharing, 1972.

Walker, William J. *History of the Remnant of Israel.* Opportunity, WA: Remnant of Israel, n.d.

___. *Remnant Message to Modern Israel.* Opportunity, WA: Remnant of Israel, n.d.

Section 14

Liberal Family

Consult the Contents pages to locate the essay in Part II, Historical Essay Chapters, that provides an historical discussion of this family

Intrafaith Organizations

★1085★

Congress of Religion
(Defunct)

The Congress of Religion was founded in 1895 in Chicago, Illinois, as the American Congress of Liberal Religious Societies. It was a direct outgrowth of the 1893 World's Parliament of Religions held two years previously in Chicago. The congress provided a meeting ground for liberal leaders among Reform Jews, Unitarians, Universalists, Ethical Culturalists, and others in more conservative denominations who were beginning to feel the changes in thought brought about by the new science, critiques of denominationalism, biblical criticism, and a faith in progress.

A moving force in the organization was Unitarian minister Jenken Lloyd Jones, who had for some years published a periodical, *Unity*, and had led in the planning of the Unitarian participation at the parliament. The idea of a congress of religious liberals had first been broached during the planning for that gathering.

Some 200 attended the first meeting of the congress in 1895. Many members expressed concern about the group's name—American Congress of Liberal Religious Societies—and it became a topic of consideration for the next several meetings. It was finally changed in 1900 to simply Congress of Religion, which dispelled any suggestion that it was a delegated congress or looking toward the formation of a new denomination.

The congress met for the first time in the deep South in 1897 in Nashville, Tennessee. By the early twentieth century, the need for the congress seemed to have faded. Most of the Jewish members joined the American Ethical Union. National meetings were discontinued, and only a few state meetings persisted, primarily in the Midwest. *Unity* was published into the early 1920s but survived on its own merit, not in connection to the congress. By 1909, the thrust of the congress would be picked up in the East in the National Federation of Religious Liberals.

Sources:

Miller, Russell E. *The Larger Hope: The Second Century of the Universalist Church in America, 1870–1970.* Boston, MA: Unitarian Universalist Association, 1985.

★1086★

International Association for Religious Freedom
North American Office
576 Fifth Ave.
New York, NY 10036

Alternate Address: International Secretariat, 2 Market St., Oxford OX1 3FF, UK.

The International Association for Religious Freedom was organized in 1900 in Boston, Massachusetts, as the International Council of Unitarian and Other Liberal Religious Thinkers and Workers. Known through much of the early twentieth century as

the International Council of Religious Liberals, it is the oldest of the several currently existing international interfaith organizations. The original organizers assembled in Boston from around the world for the purpose of attending the seventy-fifth anniversary of the founding of the American Unitarian Association. Prominent in the formation of the council was Samuel A. Eliot, the president of the American Unitarian Association, and in attendance was Protap Chunder Mozoomdar, the first of the numerous Indian spiritual teachers who would migrate to the United States through the new century.

The following year, the first international congress was held in London, England. The council continued to meet until gatherings were interrupted by World War I. After the war, the council resumed meeting into the 1930s, but it seemed to have served its purpose and did not regain the enthusiasm from the pre-war years. Thus it was that the initiative was revived in England and then the Netherlands, where it was reorganized as the International Association for Liberal Christianity and Religious Freedom. Its headquarters returned to the United States briefly before settling permanently in Germany. In the post-World War II global climate, it has attracted an interfaith coalition from across Europe and Asia, as well as North America. Periodically, the Triennial World Congress returns to the United States, where regional conferences are also held. The U.S. chapter meets annually in conjunction with the Unitarian Universalist Association's general assembly.

Membership: Membership from North America includes the American Humanist Association, Canadian Unitarian Council, Fellowship of Religious Humanists, Meadville Theological Seminary, Thomas Starr King School for Religious Leadership, Unitarian Universalist Association, Unitarian Universalist Christian Fellowship, and Unitarian Universalist Service Committee.

Periodicals: *IARF World.*

Sources:

Bowie, W. Copeland. *Liberal Religious Thought at the Beginning of the Twentieth Century: Addresses and Papers at the International Council of Unitarian and Other Liberal Religious Thinkers and Workers, Held at London, May 1901.* London: Philip Green, 1901.

Miller, Russell E. *The Larger Hope: The Second Century of the Universalist Church in America, 1870–1970.* Boston, MA: Unitarian Universalist Association, 1985.

★1087★

International Humanist and Ethical Union
% IHEU Secretariat
47 Theobald's Rd.
London WC1X 8SF, England

The International Humanist and Ethical Union is a worldwide association of humanists founded in 1952 at a conference in Amsterdam, the Netherlands. Among the seven founding members were the American Ethical Union and the American Humanist Association. The congress was organized as part of an attempt to offer to the public an alternative to religions based on revelation and on totalitarian political systems. Humanism was seen as a system built around the conviction of respect for humans as spiritual and moral beings. In an original statement adopted in 1952, the union defined humanism as a way that was democratic, ethical, and aimed at the maximum possible fulfillment through creative and ethical living. It affirmed the use of science creatively and demanded the alignment of concern for personal liberty and social responsibility.

In 1966 the union issued a more definitive statement on what it saw as its unitive position, ethical humanism. It affirmed the primal concern for taking responsibility for human life in the world. Humanist morality acknowledges human interdependency and the need for human beings to respect one another. The union saw human progress being made as freedom of choice was extended and saw justice coming in the realization of equality.

The union maintains open lines of communication with the United Nations and the Council of Europe.

Membership: Among the full members of the union are the American Ethical Union, American Humanist Association, and Council for Secular Humanism. Extra-ordinary members include the Humanist Society of Canada and North American Committee for Humanism. Cooperating groups include the American Rationalist Association, Committee for the Scientific Investigation of the Claims of the Paranormal, and Unitarian Universalist Association.

Periodicals: *International Humanist,* c/o Don Page, ed., RR 1, Smith Falls, ON K7A 5B8 Canada.

★1088★
National Federation of Religious Liberals
(Defunct)

The National Federation of Religious Liberals was formed in Philadelphia, Pennsylvania, in 1908 by a coalition of Unitarians, Universalists, Reform Jews, liberal Quakers, Ethical Culturalists, and a few members of some mainline Christian denominations. The organization picked up the thrust of the Congress of Religion, which had operated primarily in the Midwest in the 1890s, and could be seen as a national expression of the International Council of Unitarian and Other Liberal Religious Thinkers and Workers (later the International Council of Religious Liberals). The International Council held its second American meeting in Boston, Massachusetts, in 1907, and the National Federation was in large part an attempt to consolidate the gains and good feeling generated by it.

The purpose of the federation was ''. . . to promote the religious life by united testimony for sincerity, freedom, and progress in religion, by social service, and with a fellowship of spirit beyond the lines of sect and creed.'' Those who participated represented the most liberal wing of the religious community who had become positively influenced by science, committed to a social ethic of reform, and had little use for the confines of denominational strictures.

The first gathering of the federation was held in 1909 in Philadelphia. Many who had formerly supported the Congress of Religion (which still had a formal existence) attended and became active in the federation's work. In 1913, following some communication with the Federal Council of Churches of Christ in America, which represented the more liberal wing of Protestant Christianity, the federation adopted the council's social program as its own. The federation continued to meet biannually until 1932. Along the way it absorbed the MidSouthern Federation of Religious Liberals, which it had fostered following World War I.

The federation disbanded in 1933. Having lost most of its money at the time of the national bank closing, it was broke. Also, the two groups that supplied the largest amount of support, the Universalists and Unitarians, had adopted a plan by which they organized the Free Church, a cooperative arrangement in which the two churches operated in fellowship while remaining autonomous as to governance and creed. The Free Church idea took most of the winds from the federation's sails.

Sources:

Miller, Russell E. *The Larger Hope: The Second Century of the Universalist Church in America, 1870–1970.* Boston, MA: Unitarian Universalist Association, 1985.

National Federation of Religious Liberals. Seventh Congress: Program, Proceedings, and Papers. Boston: National Federation of Religious Liberals, 1919.

Wendte, Charles W. *The Unity of the Spirit: Proceedings and Papers of the First Congress of the National Federation of Religious Liberals.* Boston: National Federation of Religious Liberals, 1909.

★1089★
North American Committee for Humanism
28611 W. 12 Mile Rd.
Farmington Hills, MI 48018

The North American Committee for Humanism was founded in 1982 to establish a solidarity among the Humanist organizations of the United States and Canada. Its first major project was the establishment of the Humanist Institute, the first school in North America for the training of professional Humanist leaders (the equivalent of clergy in other religious groups). Under the leadership of Howard Radest, more than 25 outstanding Humanist scholars, serving in a part-time capacity, constitute the faculty. In 1987 the committee organized an association of Humanist professionals to deal with problems of recruitment, training, and professional standards.

The committee sponsors an annual Humanist Weekend at which Humanists can gather and celebrate their life, hold discussions, and engage in creative problem solving. The committee shares headquarters facilities with the Society for Humanistic Judaism.

Membership: The groups brought together by the committee include the American Ethical Union; American Humanist Association; Council for a Democratic and Secular Humanism; Fellowship of Religious Humanists; Humanist Association of Canada; and Society for Humanistic Judaism.

Liberal

★1090★
American Association for the Advancement of Atheism
Box 2832
San Diego, CA 92112

The oldest of the several atheist bodies in the United States is the American Association for the Advancement of Atheism founded by Charles Lee Smith (1887-1964) as an anti-religion/anti-God body. Smith, a lawyer, was converted to atheism from his reading of freethought books. After World War I he began to write for *The Truth Seeker,* an independent freethought journal published in New York City. In 1925, with his friend Freeman Hopwood, he founded the Association. Starting with little support and surrounded by a hostile environment, Smith engaged in a number of controversial activities, beginning with his involvement in the debates over Arkansas's antievolution law in 1928. He debated Christian ministers when the opportunity arose, the most famous being Aimee Semple McPherson, the flamboyant leader of the International Church of the Foursquare Gospel. From the publicity given his various activities, the Association grew. It peaked with approximately 2,000 members, and chapters could be found on some 20 college and university campuses. It sponsored periodic lectures, the Ingersoll Forum (named for Robert G. Ingersoll, the famous nineteenth-century freethinker), in New York City. In 1930 Smith purchased *The Truth Seeker,* which remained independent but closely identified with the Association. Hard hit by the Depression, the Association shrank, and most of his organized activities disappeared, though Smith continued to publish the magazine monthly.

Around 1950 Smith began to let his dislike of Jews and blacks become visible on the pages of *The Truth Seeker*, which began to publish an increasing number of racist and anti-Semitic articles. These led to further loss of support and the isolation of the Association from other atheist organizations. In 1964 Smith sold *The Truth Seeker* to James Hervey Johnson, and he moved it and the Association to San Diego. A few months later, Smith died and Johnson has continued as head of the Association and editor of the magazine.

The association believes religion to be a fraud and God nonexistent. It also teaches that the civilized white race is superior to Jews and blacks and actively distributes such books as *The Biological Jew*, by Eustace Mullins, *The International Jew*, by Henry Ford, *The Protocols of the Learned Elders of Zion*, and *Our Nordic Race*, by R. K. Hoskins. The he association also stands for law and order, honest government, real liberty, freedom of the press and of speech, absolute separation of religion and government, and taxation of churches. All members must be atheists, a requirement which distinguishes the AAAA from many freethought organizations.

During the 1970s there were approximately 200 members, but no regular meetings. As with most atheist groups, there are too few members in most cities to support a separate meeting, thus members attend any local freethinkers' gathering available to them. In San Diego, the freethinkers gather on the birthdays of Thomas Paine (January 29) and Robert Ingersoll (August 7).

Membership: Not reported. It is estimated that there are only a few hundred members. In 1968 *The Truth Seeker* had about 1,000 subscribers.

Periodicals: *The Truth Seeker.*

Sources:

Cardiff, Ira D. *"If Christ Came to New York."* New York: American Association for the Advancement of Atheism, [1932].

Dalgliesh, Malcom. *The Sage of San Diego Said Choose Quality and Reason.* New York: A New Enlightment, n.d. 100 pp.

Graves, Kersey. *The World's Sixteen Crucified Saviors.* New York: Truth Seeker, 1875.

Johnson, James Hervey. *"Charles Smith: 1887-1964."* *The Truth Seeker* 91, no. 11 (November 1964).

___. *Superior Men.* San Diego: The Author, 1949.

McPherson, Aimee Semple, and Charles Lee Smith. *Debate: There Is a God!* Los Angeles: Foursquare Publications, n.d.

Swancara, Frank. *Separation of Religion and Government.* New York: Truth Seeker Company, 1950.

★1091★
American Atheists, Inc.
Box 2117
Austin, TX 78767

Possibly the most famous contemporary atheist in the United States is Madalyn Murray O'Hair (b. 1919). She founded American Atheists, Inc. on July 1, 1963, in Austin, Texas. O'Hair became a national figure in 1963 when the Supreme Court upheld her suit, which had been joined with a second like case, and ruled against the recitation of the Lord's Prayer and the Bible in the public schools, often mistakenly reported as outlawing prayer in the public schools. She next instituted a suit aimed at eliminating tax-exempt status for church-owned property. Soon after the second suit was filed, she moved from Baltimore to Honolulu, where she formed the International Free Thought Association of America. She eventually settled in Austin, Texas, where she founded Poor Richard's Universal Life Church, the Society of Separationists, and the Charles E. Stevens American Atheist Library and Archives. The

Society of Separationists was superceded by American Atheists, Inc., the headquarters of which moved into the American Atheist Center in Austin, Texas in 1977. During the 1970s, O'Hair emerged as a popular and controversial speaker on atheism, frequently debating ministers in public meetings and on television. She instituted a number of lawsuits built around atheistic concerns, most of which failed. Her activities also led to many false rumors, including one that she had petitioned the U.S. Federal Communications Commission to ban religious broadcasting, the persistency of which forced several formal retractions by the FCC. In the midst of building American Atheists, she discovered members who rejected what they considered her autocratic leadership. She dropped some of these from membership, and they, joined by others who left, formed other atheist groups, the most prominent being the Freedom from Religion Foundation.

The group stands free from theism, which is equated with religion. Religion is viewed as a crutch which healthy people do not need. It is called superstitious and is considered to be supernatural nonsense. O'Hair has become deeply involved in various social causes: civil rights, peace, etc. She is actively anti-religous and specifically anti-Christian and rejects the historicity of Jesus, a life after death, and the authority of the Bible.

The American Atheists' library, founded in 1965 and now housed at the Atheist Center, has more than 40,000 volumes and related material. The American Atheist Radio Series (1968-1973) was being heard on over 20 stations in 12 states at its peak. American Atheists is organized into a number of local chapters. Members in Petersburg, Indiana have opened an atheist museum. The organization promotes an annual national convention.

At the annual convention in 1986, O'Hair resigned as president of American Atheists and was succeeded by her son, Jon G. Murray. She continues to serve as presiding officer of its board of directors. American Atheists, Inc. recently founded the American Atheists General Headquarters, a building complex to house the library, archives, and printing facilities (American Atheist Press). It has also established United World Atheists as a network of international atheists organizations.

Membership: Not reported. In 1997 there were an estimated 2,400 members in 30 chapters across the United States.

Periodicals: *The American Atheist.*

Remarks: On September 4, 1995, 76-year-old Madalyn Murray O'Hair, her son Jon, and granddaughter Robin Murray O'Hair left their home without prior warning. Jon Murray kept in contact with the organization for a few weeks and offered some instructions on keeping it going while they were away. Eventually, all contact stopped and none of the three have been seen since. They did not take their passports, but they seemed to have left in the midst of breakfast with more than $600,000 in funds are missing from a New Zealand bank account. Some months later, Robin's car was found at the local Austin Airport. Some have speculated that she put money away in a foreign bank account and the three disappeared with it. Others have suggested foul play.

In 1996, the organization reorganized and Ellen Johnson was selected to succeed O'Hair as president of American Atheists. She, along with Ron Barrier have assumed leadership of the organization's cabel television show, "The Atheists Viewpoint."

Sources:

Conrad, Jane Kathryn. *Mad Madalyn.* Brighton, OH: The Author, 1983.

Murray, William J. *My Life without God.* Nashville, TN: Thomas Nelson, 1982.

O'Hair, Madalyn Murray. *Bill Murray, the Bible and the Baltimore Board of Education.* Austin, TX: American Atheist Press, 1970.

___. *What on Earth is an Atheist.* Austin, TX: American Atheist Press, 1969.

Wright, Lawrence. *Saints and Sinners.* New York: Random House, 1993. 266 pp.

★1092★
American Ethical Union
2 W. 64th St.
New York, NY 10023

Alternate Address: International Humanist and Ethical Union, Ouderhof 11, 2512 GH Utrecht, The Netherlands.

Felix Adler (1851-1933) was born in Alzey, Germany, and came to the United States at an early age. The son of the rabbi at Temple Emmanuel in New York City, he returned to Germany to study for the rabbinate at the University of Heidelberg, and made plans to succeed his father. During this time, he encountered neo-Kantian idealism and its critique of religion, which left him with a strong sense of duty and a zeal to implement his ethical ideals. Adler came to believe that morality could be established independently of any theological system. For Adler, the autonomy and the centrality of ethics became the philosophical basis for an ethical culture. He added a philosophical complement to Emerson's call for a purely ethical religion and to America's moralistic religious tradition. On his return to the United States, he taught Hebrew and oriental languages and literature at Cornell University (1874-76) and returned to New York City to found the Ethical Culture Society on May 15, 1876. This was the first of the ethical culture societies in America, later nationally federated as the American Ethical Union and internationally in the International Humanist and Ethical Union.

Under Adler's direction, the society was dedicated to the principle of "deed before creed," and both education and social reform were seen as necessary deeds. In Adler's view, creeds about God were not important and, socially responsible deeds were the one way people had of affirming the worth and dignity of every human being. Thus, in 1877, the District Nursing Department, now the Visiting Nurse Service, and the Tenement House Building Committee were started. In 1878, the first free kindergarten, later (1880) to grow into the Workingman's School, was opened. The Mother's Society to Study Child Nature, started in 1888, became the Child Study Association in 1915. Adler was elected president of the Free Religious Association in 1878, but resigned in 1882 because of the lack of commitment to social action and social and political reform. He was founder and chairperson of the Child Labor Committee from 1894 to 1921, and the Visiting and Teaching Guild for Crippled Children was started in 1889. For almost two decades (1902-1921), he served as professor of political and social ethics at Columbia University.

In 1882, Adler formed a second ethical culture society in Chicago, Illinois. Another emerged at Philadelphia, Pennsylvania, in 1885 and a fourth in St. Louis, Missouri, the following year. In 1887, the first international society was formed in London, England. Eventually some 20 countries would have groups included in the International Humanist and Ethical Union which includes groups associatied with the American Humanist Association.

Religion, seen as a way of life in this world, has led the union into social involvement on a number of issues related to racism, war and peace studies, adult education, citizenship, and language training for refugees in America. Union members were instumental in establishing the American Civil Liberties Union (ACLU), the National Association for the Advancement of Colored People (NAACP), and the Legal Aid Society. They participate in the United Nations programs as a Non-Governmental Organization (NGO).

Membership: In 1988, there were 21 ethical culture societies in the United States. Groups from more than 20 countries participated in the International Humanist and Ethical Union.

Periodicals: *Ethical Platform.* • *AEU Reports.*

Sources:

The Fiftieth Anniversary of the Ethical Movement, 1876-1926. New York: A. Appleton and Company, 1926.

Friess, Horace Leland. *Felix Adler and Ethical Culture, Memories and Studies.* New York: Columbia University Press, 1981.

Kraut, Benny. *From Reform Judaism to Ethical Culture.* Cincinnati, OH: Hebrew Union College Press, 1979.

Muzzey, David Saville. *Ethical Religion.* New York: American Ethical Union, 1943.

Radest, Howard B. *Toward Common Ground.* New York: Frederick Unger Publishing Co., 1969.

★1093★
American Humanist Association
7 Harwood Dr.
Box 8188
Amherst, NY 14226-7188

In the early twentieth century, an aggressive humanist orientation developed among supporters of the American Unitarian Association, the Free Religious Association, and the American Ethical Union. At the time, members of these groups were still mostly theistic. By the 1920s, however, some Unitarians had become non-theists. Their greatest spokespersons were John H. Dietrich, a Unitarian minister in Minneapolis, and Curtis W. Reese, secretary of the Western Unitarian Conference. Using ideas from science and pragmatic philosophy, the non-theists saw humanism as the only possible alternative to traditional religion. While Dietrich and Reese remained within the Unitarian structure, others of like mind left to found humanistic societies. The first two were founded in 1929, in New York by Charles Francis Potter and in Hollywood by Theodore Curtis Abell.

In 1933 eleven prominent humanist leaders issued "A Humanist Manifesto," the definitive statement of the movement. Among its signers were John Dewey, Harry Elmer Barnes, C. F. Potter and John Herman Randall. The statement called for a radical change in religious perspectives. Religion was seen as a tool for realizing the highest values in life. A religion adequate to the twentieth century regards the universe as self-existing, not created, and regards humanity as part of evolved nature. Mind-body dualism, supernaturalism, theism, and even deism are rejected. The goal of life is the complete realization of human personality. Social ethics and personal fulfillment are priority items. Social control is a means to the abundant life for all. That statement was updated in 1973 by a "Humanist Manifesto II," which adds an additional emphasis on human responsibility toward humanity as a whole.

To bring some coordination and fellowship nationally to the various independent humanist efforts, the American Humanist Association was formed in 1941. It accepts the basic perspective of the two Humanist Manifestos, especially their call for the use of science for social welfare. Its social program has included a defense of human rights, religious liberty, and freedom of thought; separation of church and state; population growth control; death with dignity; penal reform; ecology; and the United Nations.

The American Humanist Association is organized democratically; board members are elected by the general membership. Chapters are located across the country. An annual conference is held in a different city each year. Certified leaders of the association, analogous to ministers or rabbis, are termed "celebrants". The association is also a member of the International Humanist and Ethical Union.

Membership: In 1997 the association reported approximately 10,000 members in 70 chapters. There were 120 celebrants in the United States, one in Canada, and one in Australia.

Periodicals: *The Humanist.* • *Free Mind.* • *Humanist Living.*

Remarks: Among the counselors of the association is Paul Kurtz, former editor of *The Humanist* who has developed a number of enterprises which, while entirely independent of the American Humanist Association, serve the humanist cause as a whole. He founded and heads Prometheus Books, the major American publisher of humanist and freethought literature in recent decades. During the 1970s he led in the formation of the Committee for the Scientific Investigation of the Paranormal, whose quarterly *Skeptical Inquirer* is a major voice in the debunking of psychic and paranormal phenomena. Around 1980 he formed the Council for a Democratic and Secular Humanism and began *Free Inquiry*. He also became a leading force in the formation of the Academy of Humanism, an organization formed to disseminate humanist ideals and beliefs and to recognize outstanding humanists, and in the Religion and Biblical Criticism Research Project, which disseminates the results of biblical criticism (especially claims many humanists consider unfounded, such as the divine inspiration of the Bible and the historicity of Jesus).

Sources:

Blackham, H. J. *Modern Humanism.* Yellow Springs, OH: American Humanist Association, 1964.

Humanist Manifestos I and II. Buffalo, NY: Prometheus Books, 1973.

Kurtz, Paul, ed. *The Humanist Alternative.* Buffalo, NY: Prometheus Books, 1973.

Lamont, Corliss. *Voice in the Wilderness.* Buffalo, NY: Prometheus Books, 1975.

Reese, Curtis W. *Humanism.* Chicago: Open Court Publishing Company, 1926.

_____, ed. *Humanist Sermons.* Chicago: Open Court Publishing Company, 1927.

★1094★
American Rationalist Federation
Current address not obtained for this edition.

The American Rationalist Federation, formed in 1955 by a number of rationalist groups (mostly limited to a single urban area) and individuals, continues the organized rationalist movement in America which dates to the middle of the nineteenth century. As early as 1857 (St. Louis), German-America rationalists had begun to organize local societies. (That early St. Louis group may have grown out of an even earlier group called Licht-freunde, formed in 1832.) In 1859 several such societies came together to form the Bund der deutschen Freien Gemeinden von Nordamerika (the Federation of German Free Communities of North America). At the time of the second national convention in 1871, societies could be found in Hoboken, New Jersey; New York City; Milwaukee, Painesville, and Maryville, Wisconsin; Frankfurt, Missouri; and New Ulm, Minnesota. The organization of the German-American rationalists was followed by the Czechs and a number of English-speaking groups such as the Friendship Liberal League. These groups seemed to thrive in the late-nineteenth century, but by the time of the formation of the Federation, had dwindled noticeably, many finding it difficult just to continue to exist.

In 1947 many of the surviving rationalist groups had banded together in the United Secularists of America. However, many members began to protest the secretive financial policies adopted by the Secularists, and in 1955 most of the local societies in the United States withdrew and reorganized as the American Rationalist Federation. Representatives of twelve societies gathered in Chicago, in the building owned by the Czech Rationalist Federation (and previously used as the address of the United Secularists) for the organizing convention.

Rationalism is defined as the mental attitude which "unreservedly accepts the supremacy of reason and aims at establishing a system of philosophy and ethics verifiable by experience and experiment and independent of all arbitrary assumptions of authority." The Federation believes in the complete separation of church and state; in free public education; and that the improvement of civilization can come only by combating all forms of political, social, religious, and economic tyranny.

At the organizing meeting of the American Rationalist Federation, delegates from Chicago and St. Louis formed the Rationalist

Association, Inc., whose main task has been the publication of *The American Rationalist*, a bimonthly periodical and the circulation of rationalist-atheist books and literature. Through the years the magazine, though completely independent, has been closely associated in the public mind with the Federation and is often mistakenly seen as its official organ.

Included within the American Rationalist Federation are several surviving German groups and the Czech Rationalist Federation of America, centered in Chicago where a monthly periodical, *Vekrozumu*, is published. Local organizations of rationalists are also found in San Francisco, Chicago, and Cleveland (Czech).

Membership: Not reported. Their were 11 independent rationalist-freethought organizations and 20 state organizations in the Federation in the early 1980s.

Periodicals: *The American Rationalist* is an unofficial publication of the rationalist movement.

Sources:

Capek, Thomas. *The Czechs in America.* Boston: Houghton Mifflin Company, 1920.

School, Eldon, and Walter Hoops. "Going Back to the Beginning: Twenty-five Years Ago." *The American Rationalist* 25, no. 1 (May-June 1980): 17-19.

★1095★
American Secular Union
(Defunct)

The American Secular Union, one of the most prominent freethought/atheist organizations at the beginning of the twentieth century, grew out of the efforts of Francis Ellingwood Abbot, who in 1872 published "The Nine Demands of Liberalism" in his paper, *The Index*, then published in Toledo, Ohio. The "Demands" virtually defined freethought's agenda at the time and called for the complete separation of church and state and the total secularizing of tax-supported institutions. Abbot's call for separation implied the doing away with chaplains, the dropping of the Bible from school curricula, the withdrawal of support for religious holidays, the end of Sunday blue laws, and the end of tax exemption for religious organizations.

Several "liberal" societies were formed by Abbot's readers, and in 1875 delegates met in a convention in Philadelphia, Pennsylvania, and chose Abbot as their president. That meeting also issued a call for a national convention to be held the following year for the purpose of creating a national organization. The convention gathered in Philadelphia on July 1, 1876, and formed the national Liberal League.

The league met annually and chartered chapters across the United States. It was soon hit by a controversy over the enforcement of the so-called Comstock Laws, aimed against the trafficking in obscene literature. Postal official Anthony Comstock expanded the scope to include anti-religious materials. In 1878 he conspired to have R. M. Bennett, editor of *The Truth Seeker*, arrested. Some liberals began to agitate for the repeal of the Comstock Laws. Abbot argued for their revision. The debate, in which the majority stood for repeal, led to Abbot's pulling out of the organization. In 1879, Robert G. Ingersoll championed a proposal in defense of Bennett which called for rewriting the Comstock Laws while decrying obscene literature; many included the Bible on their list of obscene materials. The league also called for the complete separation of church and state.

At the convention in 1883 the league changed its name to National Secular Union. Ingersoll was elected president of the organization and served for two years.

In 1892 Samuel P. Putnam, a prominent freethinker, called for the formation of a national organization that would push for the liberal program in a political arena. The result was the formation of the Freethought Federation of America. Two years later it merged into the National Secular Union and Putnam was named president of the merged organization, which became known as the American Secular Union. It had little success in gaining legislative support for its views.

The union continued into the 1920s.

Sources:

Putnam, Samuel P. *400 Years of Freethought*. New York: The Truth Seeker, 1894.

Warren, Sidney. *American Freethought, 1860–1914*. New York: Gordian Press, 1966.

★1096★
Americans First, Inc.
(Defunct)

Kent Meyer was a member of the Society of Separationists, now known as the American Atheists, Inc., but he resigned in 1969 and formed his own organization. The small group operated within the state of Oklahoma as an atheist/freethought organization. Within weeks of the founding of Americans First, Meyer made national headlines for his instigation of a lawsuit to have a fifty-foot lighted cross removed from the state fairgrounds in Oklahoma City. He charged that the presence of the cross is a violation of the state constitution. No recent information on Americans First has been forthcoming and it has been reported defunct.

★1097★
Atheist Alliance Inc. (AAI)
PO Box 6261
Minneapolis, MN 55406

The Atheist Alliance Inc. (AAI) is a democratic association formed in 1995 by independent, autonomous atheist societies most of whom had formerly been associated with American Atheists, Inc. Members of the alliance see blind religious mania as a rising threat that seeks to repeal the advances made in establishing civil rights and civil liberties for all citizens. It seeks to abolish First Amendment rights to freedom of and especially from religion. In response, they believe they see the need for a concerted atheist influence on society and the application of reason and common sense to solving problems. Atheism, given its human centered vision and a reality-based approach to problem solving, leads toward intellectual growth, personal freedom, and social, environmental and scientific progress.

The alliance offers the possibility of unified atheist action on a national scale, but notes that they consider themselves independent thinkers. It attempts to affirm the freedom of members by refraining from the establishment of a strong controlling centralized power structure. The alliance works through the diverse member groups to facilitate common purposes. The group believes it gives atheism an effective voice in public affairs to persuade legislators and the public to recognize the danger to freedom of basing laws and policies on religious doctrines.

The alliance seeks to establish a strong, democratic atheist organization in every state and provides brochures on atheism and issues of concern to atheists. It also provides seed money for organizational development. It holds a national convention every year so atheists can gather to exchange information, participate in programs, and fellowship with unbelievers from around the country.

The Alliance seeks to reclaim a heritage of the struggle of men and women who defied the superstitions of their day and in so doing advanced culture and provide the facts of history to the public to dispel ignorance about atheist contributions to civilization. They oppose what they see as the obscuring of atheism in discussions in schools, noting that even such an important reference tool as the *Encyclopedia Britannica* has, since the Eleventh Edition, presented a negative twist to atheism.

Membership: As of 1997, the Alliance had 13 local atheist groups including: Atheist Centre (Vijayawada, India), Atheist Co-

alition (San Diego), Atheists and Agnostics of Wisconsin, Atheists and Other Freethinkers (Sacramento), Atheists of Colorado, Atheists of Florida, Atheists of the San Francisco Region, Atheists United (Los Angeles Chapter), Freethought Society of Greater Philadelphia, Metroplex Atheists (Dallas - Fort Worth), Minnesota Atheists, Rationalist Society of Saint Louis, and the Society Against Religion.

Periodicals: *Secular Nation.*

★1098★
Atheists United
14542 Ventura Blvd., Ste. 211
Sherman Oaks, CA 91403

Atheists United was formed in 1981 by atheists in Los Angeles, and is the major organization for unbelievers on the West Coast. It promotes two goals: the separation of church and state and the furtherance of atheism, primarily through education. Educational efforts are focused in meetings throughout southern California, the publication of a newsletter, a set of atheist literature a "Dial-an-Atheist" telephone service, and a weekly radio show in Los Angeles.

Members of Atheists United consider themselves nontheists. They accept only ideas confirmed by evidence, and even these are subject to reconsideration. All superstitions, especially religions, are rejected.

Membership: Atheists United does not release membership information. There is an estimated 1,500 members. Meetings were held regularly throughout Southern California from Ventura to San Diego.

Periodicals: *Atheists United Newsletter.* Send orders to 12542 Ventura Blvd., Suite 211, Sherman Oaks, CA 91403.

★1099★
Bund der deutschen Freien Gemeinden von Nordamerika
(Defunct)

During the mid-nineteenth century, several freethought organizations were formed in German-speaking communities in the United States. Among the earliest was one called Lichtfreunde (Light Friends), of St. Louis, Missouri. During the 1850s, several suggestions emerged that a national organization be created. Thus at a gathering of German freethought leaders in Philadelphia, Pennsylvania, the Bund der deutchen Freien Gemeinden von Nordamerika (Federation of German Free Communities of North America) came into existence. The Philadelphia Freie Gemeinde became the organizational center of the group, and seven of its members were the first directors.

The start of the Civil War largely curtailed the new organization's work; however, Friedrich Schuenemann-Pott, the editor of *Blaetter fur freies-religioeses Leben* (Sheets for a Free-Religious Life), authored a widely distributed pamphlet, *Die freien Gemeinden*, for the new organization in 1861. Chapters appeared along the East Coast and as far west as Milwaukee and Sauk City, Wisconsin. Among the early accomplishments were the appointment of several "secular" chaplains in the Union Army and the development of a corresponding relationship with European freethought groups.

The first national convention was held in 1866, and contact was established with the Free Religious Association. The national organization continued to be active into the twentieth century. By the end of the 1920s only three centers remained: Chicago, Milwaukee, and St. Louis. The St. Louis group finally closed in 1970 and deeded its assets to the St. Louis Ethical Society.

Sources:

Hempel, Max. *Was sind die Freien Gemeinde?* St. Louis, MO: 1902.

Stein, Gordon. *Encyclopedia of Unbelief*. 2 vols. Buffalo, NY: Prometheus Press, 1985.

★1100★
Canadian Atheist Society
PO Box 41613
923 12th St.
New Westminster, BC, Canada V3M 6L1

The Canadian Atheist Society is a small atheist organization formed in the mid-1990s in British Columbia under the leadership of Ray Blessin and Fern Wayman. In 1994 they launched *The Canadian Atheist* as a quarterly magazine and moved to incorporate as an educational organization. Though based on the Canadian West Coast, they quickly gained a following across the country. The also launched an effort urging the removal of the god references from the preamble of the Canadian Constitution and the National Anthem. They feel that these national symbols should unite all Canadians, not just religious Canadians.

Membership: Not reported.

Periodicals: *The Canadian Atheist.*

★1101★
Canadian Secular Union
(Defunct)

The Canadian Secular Union emerged from the Toronto Freethought Association, the earliest organized expression of freethought in Canada. It was formed in 1873 by a small group of rationalists, secularists, and atheists who dedicated themselves to challenging Christian beliefs, removing sabbath laws, and promoting evolution. In 1877 the association was reorganized under the leadership of Ick Evans and a periodical, the *Freethought Journal*, was launched though it folded after only a few issues. The organization's name was changed in 1881 to Toronto Secular Society. Some have argued that the name change suggested an emphasis on sabbath laws might serve to mobilize members from the public who had shown some lack of interest in freethought philosophy.

In 1884 the society's president, Alfred Piddington, invited freethought lecturer Charles Watts, newly arrived from England, to address the citizens of Toronto. Watts had been one of the founders of the National Secular Society in England in 1866. The lectures were a great success, and eventually Watts settled in the city. In 1885 the society was again reorganized, this time by William Algie, and emerged as the Canadian Secular Union, following the English model. The growth in the society allowed branches to form in neighboring towns and the revival of a periodical, *Secular Thought* (which ran through some 30 volumes).

The union, according to its prospectus of 1887, affirmed a "constructive Secularism," which found expression in agnosticism, the destruction of the influence of the errors "born of priestcraft, dogmatism, and perpetuated prejudice," and the championing of free speech and inquiry.

The union seems to have run out of steam around the beginning of World War I.

Sources:

Putnam, Samuel P. *400 Years of Freethought.* New York: The Truth Seeker, 1894.

Stein, Gordon. *Encyclopedia of Unbelief.* 2 vols. Buffalo, NY: Prometheus Press, 1985.

★1102★
Christian Universalist Church of America
(Defunct)

The Christian Universalist Church of America was founded in 1964 by Universalists with a Christian emphasis. Headquarters of this small organization was in Deerfield Beach, Florida. In 1967 there were reported an estimated 200 churches and missions (some of which were also affiliated with the Unitarian Universalist Association) located in 21 states with more than 15,000 members.

The subsequent disappearance of the Church has cast some doubts on the reported figures.

★1103★
Church of Eternal Life and Liberty
Current address not obtained for this edition.

The Church of Eternal Life and Liberty is a libertarian church founded on June 2, 1974, by Patrick A. Heller, Anna Bowling, and James Hudler. It has no creed but espouses a noncoercive libertarian philosophy. Confirming its strong belief in individual freedom, the church has offered support for tax protesters, draft resistance, and alternative schooling for children in the home. The church also has a strong interest in cryogenics, the practice of freezing the body at death in hopes of its being brought back to life at a future point in time when science has conquered physical death and disease.

The church cooperates with other libertarian churches, particularly the Church of Nature, with whom it holds regular joint meetings. Since the early 1980s, the church has engaged in a constant battle with the U.S. Internal Revenue Service, which has questioned the group's legitimacy as a church body and has moved to deny it tax-exempt status.

Membership: In 1984 the church reported approximately 100 members in three congregations, two in Michigan and one in California.

Periodicals: *Live and Let Live.*

Sources:

Heller, Patrick A. *As My Spirit Beckons.* Pontiac, MI: Church of Eternal Life and Liberty, 1974.

___. *Because I Am.* Oak Park, MI: Church of Eternal Life and Liberty, 1981.

★1104★
Church of Nature
(Defunct)

The Church of Nature was founded in 1979 in Dryden, Michigan, by Rev. Christopher L. Brockman. It was a libertarian humanist church that espoused a naturalistic philosophy. The church placed a high value upon individual freedom and believed that "living up to one's best nature as a human being is the standard of goodness." Freedom was seen as essential to goodness. The church established two sacraments: marriage and affirmation. The latter consisted of providing a ceremonial context in which an individual (or group of individuals) could offer an affirmative statement of some truth or concern to members of the church.

The church attempted to provide an ethical and religious context within the larger Libertarian Movement and cooperated with organizations such as the now disbanded United Libertarian Fellowship and the American Humanist Association to encompass libertarianism and humanism under a single, consistent ethical philosophy. In 1988, the church reported 150 members in two congregations (Michigan and Virginia) served by two ministers.

Periodicals: *Exegesis.*

★1105★
Church of Reason
Current address not obtained for this edition.

The Church of Reason was founded in the early 1970s by Robert M. Dunn and other reason devotees in northern Ohio, with associates then in Massachusetts, New York, and Tennessee. It is dedicated to several basic principles that appear in its creed. Members seek knowledge; see reason as the faculty that identifies and integrates the materials provided by the senses; and as only means to knowledge; and agree to attempt to act on that knowledge. They also pledge to initiate neither force nor fraud, and understand that their right to life depends upon their recognition of the same right in others.

Unlike many rationalists and atheists, members of the Church of Reason are not inimical to religion. Rather, they view religion, as quoted by a character in Ayn Rand's novel *The Fountainhead*, as "the great aspiration of the human spirit toward the highest, the noblest, the best. The human spirit as the creator and the conqueror of the ideal." As such, by reason of the volitional and conceptual nature of human consciousness, religion is inherent in human nature. Organized religion assists individuals in forging a worldview and helps them to act accordingly. The Church of Reason promotes the discovery and dissemination of information concerning ultimate and ulterior issues by providing a forum for the study and sharing of fundamental ideas. It also provides a forum for the celebration of life cycle events, a place to meet and share life with like-minded people, and an efficient means of accomplishing goals.

Members of the Church of Reason see the faculty of reason, operating on the evidence of the senses, as the basic tool of human survival, and thus see it as the cardinal virtue; rationality implying productivity, independence, integrity, honesty, justice, and earned pride as correlative virtues.

Membership: Not reported.

Sources:

Welcome to a Good Look at the Religion of Reason. Cleveland, OH: Church of Reason, 1989. 19 pp.

★1106★
Church of the Creator
Current address not obtained for this edition.

The Church of the Creator was founded in 1973 by Ben Klassen. In that same year, his book, *Nature's Eternal Religion*, which contained the principles of the laws of nature, was published. While accepting the idea that religion is necessary and beneficial, all belief in deities, heaven and hell, and worship as such are rejected, as is atheism, which is considered purely negative. Instead, these ideas are replaced by a positive belief in the eternal laws of nature, in the lessons of history, and in logic and common sense. According to the church, the objective of creativity is the survival, expansion, and advancement of the white race.

The church believes that Nature teaches each species to expand and upgrade itself according to its abilities. The white race is considered by the church to be Nature's finest achievement, while blacks and Jews are considered enemies. Members are urged to comit themselves to making a lasting contribution to their race, as well as making it their first priority. Members give preferential treatment in business to white people and oppose miscegenation.

Membership: In 1988, the church reported approximately 3,000 members and 100 ordained ministers. Members can be found in Great Britain, South Africa, Australia, and in small numbers in South America.

Periodicals: *Racial Loyalty.*

Sources:

Klassen, Ben. *Building a Whiter and Brighter World* Otto, NC: Church of the Creator, 1986.

___. *Nature's Eternal Religion.* Lighthouse Point, FL: Church of the Creator, 1973.

___. *The White Man's Bible.* Lighthouse Point, FL: Church of the Creator, 1981.

★1107★
Church of the Humanitarian God
Current address not obtained for this edition.

The Church of the Humanitarian God was founded in 1969 in St. Petersburg, Florida, as an alternative to yielding to the prevailing military-industrial complex. The church teaches that it is man's purpose in this life to aid his fellow man as best as he can. Such service to others establishes man's status in the life hereafter. Sustaining life is the natural law of God. Therefore, only self-defensive aggression can be participated in by members of the church. Nonviolent change is part of the new direction in which the church wishes to lead people.

The church says introspection is man's means of facing himself and allowing his conscience to guide him. Thus, questions of sex, nudity, divorce, drinking, and smoking are largely left to individuals. Drug use is disapproved. Ministers must be 18 years old, but there are no other restrictions because of age, sex, or marital status.

Membership: Not reported.

★1108★
Confraternity of Deists, Inc.
Current address not obtained for this edition.

The Confraternity of Deists was begun in 1967 in St. Petersburg by Paul Englert, a former Roman Catholic. Deism is belief in one God, the supreme intelligence, as contrasted with belief in Scripture or atheism. Without God, believes the Deist, man is defenseless against himself. The Creed of Confraternity includes the beliefs that the constructive exercise of human intelligence contributes to the glorification of God; that all man-made Scriptures are mere literary works, without religious, historical or chronological value; that the church of the Deist should constitute the free university, disseminating scientific knowledge and nurturing the arts; and that the social duty of the Deist is to work for the spiritual and temporal elevation of the people.

Membership: Not reported. In 1969 there were 3 centers of the Confraternity, one at the headquarters and two at universities.

★1109★
Council for Secular Humanism
Box 664
Amherst, NY 14226-0664

At the end of the 1970s, Paul Kurtz, an outstanding humanist intellectual and controversialist, and the American Humanist Association, parted company. At that time Kurtz was head of Prometheus Books, a prominent humanist/atheist publishing concern, and the driving force behind the Committee for the Scientific Examination of the Paranormal, a skeptical watchdog group dedicated to debunking unfounded claims of psychic, occult, and ufological phenomena. With supporters, he led in the establishment of the Council for a Democratic and Secular Humanism now known as the Council for Secular Humanism. Whereas the American Humanist Association is representative of the broad range of humanist thought, the council emphasizes the most secular aspect of humanism.

Kurtz had been prominent in the execution and circulation of "Humanist Manifesto II" in 1973. In 1980 he wrote and circulated "A Secular Humanist Declaration," which outlined the position of secular humanism and to which a number of prominent liberal thinkers appended their signatures. According to Kurtz, secular humanism is committed (1) to the application of reason and science in the understanding of the universe and to the solving of human problems and to stand against perceived efforts to denigrate human intelligence, (2) to seek to understand the world in supernatural terms, and (3) to look outside of nature for salvation. It is committed to the scientific nature of inquiry, a belief that nature is intelligible to human reason and explainable by means of causal hypotheses, and a naturalistic ethics that exists quite apart from any theological or metaphysical base. It differs from other forms of humanism in its confidence in humanity's ability to apply science and technology for the betterment of human life. Like atheism it rejects the supernatural but also offers a positive program for constructing an ethical value system.

The council sponsors the Academy of Humanism to recognize distinguished humanists and disseminate humanist ideals and beliefs. The Committee for the Scientific Examination of Religion attempts to examine critically the claims of religion, both East and West, in the light of scientific inquiry. The Biblical Criticism Research Project was founded to disseminate the results of biblical scholarship, which it believes undercuts many of the claims of both the Jewish and Christian faiths.

The council founded *Free Inquiry* magazine, and through it sponsors the Alliance of Secular Humanist Societies, a network for mutual support that assists the organization of local and regional societies of secular humanists. Such groups are now found across the United States. Also related is Secular Organizations for Sobriety, a humanist alternative to Alcoholics Anonymous.

The council is a full member of the International Humanist and Ethical Union.

Membership: Not reported.

Educational Facilities: Center for Inquiry Institute, Amherst, NY.

Periodicals: *Free Inquiry*.

Sources:

Kurtz, Paul. *Forbidden Fruit: The Ethics of Humanism.* Buffalo, NY: Prometheus Books, 1988.

___, ed. *The Humanist Alternative: Some Definitions of Humanism.* Buffalo, NY: Prometheus Books, 1973.

___. *In Defense of Secular Humanism.* Buffalo, NY: Prometheus Books, 1983.

___ et al. *A Secular Humanist Declaration.* Privately printed, 1980.

___. *Transcendental Temptation: A Critique of Religion and the Paranormal.* Buffalo, NY: Prometheus Books, 1986. 500 pp.

★1110★
Deistical Society of New York
(Defunct)

The Deistical Society of New York was the first expression, other than the very ephemeral Universal Society of Philadelphia, Pennsylvania, of what was to become a tradition of organized freethought in the United States. It was formed in 1794 by a group of liberal thinkers who responded to a lecture given by Elihu Palmer. Palmer, a former Presbyterian and Baptist minister, had become a deist, a fact he announced publicly in Philadelphia in 1791 with a lecture attacking the divinity of Jesus Christ. That very lecture sealed the fate of the newly formed Universal Society, before which it was given. Palmer was forced out of the city, and he left the ministry and read law for several years and traveled about. He was on his way to Connecticut when prevailed upon to lecture in New York.

The Deistical Society of New York espoused the religion of nature and opposed all forms of what it termed fanaticism and superstition. It affirmed the existence of One God, worthy of adoration, and believed that humans possess the necessary moral and intellectual faculties sufficient for the improvement of life. It also believed that the religion of nature emerges out of the moral relationships in society and is aligned with progressive improvement and the common welfare. The society opposed religious persecution and championed civil and religious liberty.

The society barely survived for the next few years, but found new life with the election of Thomas Jefferson, himself a deist, to the presidency of the United States. It launched a periodical, *The Temple of Reason.* By this time, Palmer was lecturing every Sunday evening at a hall on Broadway. The society became Palmer's headquarters for the rest of his life, but he also traveled south to Philadelphia and Baltimore to lecture and raise funds. The Society died soon after Palmer passed away in 1806.

Sources:

Gay, Peter. *Deism: An Anthology.* Princeton, NJ: Van Nostrand, 1968.

Koch, G. Adolf. *Republican Religion.* New York: Henry Holt and Company, 1933. Reprinted as *Religion of the American Enlightenment.* New York: Thomas Y. Crowell, 1968.

★1111★
Free Religious Association
(Defunct)

The Free Religious Association (FRA) emerged at the end of the Civil War in reaction to the solidifying of Unitarianism into a denomination as the American Unitarian Association and its affirmation of the supernatural lordship of Jesus (though the association had repudiated the doctrine of the trinity and the deity of Jesus). The more radical elements among the Unitarians looked for an alternative to denominationalism and the theological boundaries such an organized life represented. Thus it was in October 1866 that eight Unitarian leaders gathered in the home of Charles A. Bartol in Boston, Massachusetts, to discuss the situation. At a second gathering a few weeks later, William Potter, Francis Ellingwood Abbot, and Edward C. Towne presented a draft constitution for a Free Religious Association. A public meeting was held on May 30, 1867, at which a constitution was presented and accepted. Octavius Brooks Frothingham was elected president and Potter, secretary. Ralph Waldo Emerson was the first member enrolled. Other officers included Robert Dale Owen and liberal Rabbi Isaac M. Wise.

The Free Religious Association was designed as a home of theistic radicals, people who believed in God but who held opinions that often put them at odds with other institutions with which they were in association. It was designed especially to assist the more left-wing Unitarians who did not want to break with the FRA but found it impossible to accept its doctrinal guidance. Initially, the organization affirmed its allegiance to what was termed "pure religion," defined as the worship of God. This definition of pure religion was challenged in 1872 and theism dropped as a core idea. At this time Felix Adler (who later left to form the American Ethical Union) and Benjamin Franklin Underwood joined the FRA. Underwood led in 1885 to the organization's dropping any reference to pure religion. As such, the FRA was committed to ". . . the scientific study of religion and ethics, to advocate freedom in religion, to increase fellowship in the spirit, and to emphasize the supremacy of practical morality in all of the relations of life." The change, representing a resolution between the contradictory goals of defining a rationalistic religion and the infinite divergences among radical free speculative theologians, was in the latter's favor.

The FRA was continually threatened with dissolution from the very different souls who constituted its membership. Its survival through the nineteenth century was largely credited to the organizational zeal of William Potter. Potter died in 1894, by which time the FRA had seemingly run its course and been left behind by developments in the larger religious community. It continued to operate into the twentieth century but slowly dwindled into nonexistence.

Sources:

Persons, Stow. *Free Religion.* New Haven, CT: Yale University Press, 1947. Reprint, Boston: Beacon Press, 1963.

★1112★
Freedom from Religion Foundation
Box 750
Madison, WI 53701

The Freedom from Religion Foundation, incorporated in 1978, is a North American association of freethinkers (atheists, agnostics, and skeptics of various pedigrees). Many of the founders had formerly been members of American Atheists, Inc. who had left in protest of what they saw as undemocratic policies. It has among its priority goals the education of the public on matters of nontheism and the promotion of the principle of church/state separation which is interpreted as disavowing any religious participation in government matters and government expressions of favorable attitudes toward religion, even in a nonsectarian fashion. Since its founding, the foundation has been under the leadership of Anne Nicole Gaylor and has grown into the largest Freethought group on the continent.

The foundation acts on what it sees as violations of the separation of church and state and in recent years has intervened in situations involving prayers in public schools, payment of public funds for religious purposes, government favoritism toward religious institutions, illegal activities conducted in the name of religious charities, and religious efforts to deny civil rights to women, gays, and lesbians.

In 1983, it filed a suit challenging President Ronald Reagan's declaration of that year as the "Year of the Bible". It has gone to court to halt the U.S. Postal Service's practice of giving cancellations to a Roman Catholic group, ended commencement prayers at a major university, stopped federal subsidy to the "Virgin of the Rockies" chapel, and in 1996 won a court decision overturning a Wisconsin law declaring Good Friday to be a state holiday. The federation also succeeded in posting the first atheist placard to be displayed in a state capitol over the Christmas holidays, in protest of religious activities hosted there. One of its more active chapters, the Alabama Freethought Association, has moved to stop religion in the state's parks and has become a plaintiff in the case against Judge Roy Moore, who has allowed questionable religious practices in his courtroom.

At its annual convention, the federation awards a "Freethinker of the Year" to a successful litigant working for church/state separation, and an annual "Freethought Heroine", presented to Ann Druyan, the widow of Carl Sagan in 1997. Additionally, for two decades it has sponsored an annual essay competition for students, awarding cash grants, and now offers a similar scholarship program for college-bound high school seniors. The federation publishes a variety of books in the Freethought tradition.

Membership: In 1997 the federation reported more than 3,800 members and subscribers throughout the United States and Canada.

Periodicals: *Freethought Today.*

Sources:

Gaylor, Annie Laurie. *Betrayal of Trust: Clergy Abuse of Children.* Madison, WI: Freedom from Religion Foundation, 1988.

Gaylor, Annie Laurie, ed. *Women without Superstition: No Gods—No Masters.* Madison, WI: Freedom from Religion Foundation, 1997. 696 pp.

___. *Woe to Women—the Bible Tells Me So.* Madison, WI: Freedom from Religion Foundation, 1981.

Green, Ruth. *Born Again Skeptic's Guide to the Bible.* Madison, WI: Freedom from Religion.Foundation, 1979.

Hurmence, Ruth. *The Book of Ruth.* Madison, WI: Freedom from Religion Foundation, 1982.

Rejecting Religion. Madison, WI: Freedom from Religion Foundation, 1982.

Stein, Gordon. *An Anthology of Atheism and Rationalism.* New York: Prometheus Books, 1980.

★1113★
Freethinkers of America
(Defunct)

The Freethinkers of America was a small freethought group founded in New York in 1915. Around 1920 Joseph Lewis (1889-1968), destined to become one of the leading exponents and pop-

ularizers of atheism in the United States, moved from his home in Alabama to New York. Already an atheist, he joined the group and became its leader. During the next decade he wrote several classic statements of the atheist position, all published by the Freethought Press Association which he had founded: *The Tyranny of God* (1920); *The Bible Unmasked* (1926) and *Atheism and Other Addresses* (1930). During this period he also became interested in the study of sexuality, and in the early 1930s he initiated a second publishing concern, Eugenics Publishing Company, which published low-cost books on sexology written by specialists.

Lewis's books addressed a host of major atheist concerns. He attacked religion, particularly the Judaism he had forsaken early in life. He denied the necessity of religion as a basis for either the individual moral life or social order. He argued for the separation of church and state. He publicized the life of America's founding fathers as a means of arguing for the patriotic role of freethought.

Lewis continued to write into the 1950s. Possibly his two most important books appeared after World War II, *The Ten Commandments* (1946) and *An Atheist Manifesto* (1954). The Freethinkers of America were headquartered in New York, though Lewis lived in Miami for a brief period (and frequently appeared on local radio programs to speak on atheist themes). In the 1960s there were branches in San Diego and Milwaukee and as many as several thousand members. The size of the group had shrunk significantly after the exclusion of the Communists, rejected because they tended to dominate meetings with their own brand of atheism. The Freethinkers had close relations with the American Association for the Advancement of Atheism for many years, but differed in that it did not demand members to be atheists. The Freethinkers published a periodical, *Age of Reason*, which ceased publication after Lewis's death in 1968. The organization survived Lewis's death only a few years.

Sources:

Howland, Arthur H. *Jeseph Lewis—Enemy of God.* Boston: Stratford, 1932.

Lewis, Joseph. *An Atheist Manifesto.* New York: Freethought Press Association, 1954.

___. *The Bible Unmasked.* New York: Freethought Press Association, 1926.

___. *The Ten Commandments.* New York: Freethought Press Association, 1926.

___. *The Tyranny of God.* New York: Freethought Press Association, 1921.

★1114★
Goddian Organization
(Defunct)

The Goddian Organization was formed in 1965 by Lawrence A. Whitten of Portland, Maine. It was begun as a back-to-God movement, started because other religious organizations were not doing their work of bringing people back to God. Whitten consolidated all religious belief into one affirmation—God as the creator. He sought the union of all people in one brotherhood of man. That union could be achieved if each person will stop insisting that those who differ from him must believe as he does.

There were no ministers or churches. Whitten attempted to unite all Goddians through the headquarters in Portland around a mutual allegiance to the program of good works. In the monthly periodical, *The Goddian Message,* an attack upon Christianity and the Bible followed traditional free thought ideas. While people from around the country responded to ads about the organization, it never received enough support to make it a viable concern. After a few years, it was discontinued.

★1115★
Humanist Association of Canada
Box 3726, Station C
Ottawa, ON, Canada K1Y 4J8

Humanism and people identifying themselves as humanists emerged in the early twentieth century amid the larger freethought movement in Canada. Among the earliest groups to take the name was the Winnipeg Rationalist Society, which in the 1930s changed its name to the Winnipeg Humanist Society. That group dwindled following the death of its long-time leader Marshall Jerome Gauvin (1881–1978), but other groups, primarily in Victoria, British Columbia, and Montreal, emerged. In 1967, the Victoria and Montreal groups formed the Humanist Association of Canada. At that time they also combined their two periodicals, the *Victorian Humanist* and the *Montreal Humanist*, into *Humanism in Canada*.

The association provides a focus and forum for the broad range of humanist thought in Canada and is similar in beliefs and practice to the American Humanist Association. It is also a member of the International Humanist and Ethical Union.

Membership: Not reported. There are chapters in Ottawa, Montreal, and Toronto.

Periodicals: *Humanism in Canada*.

Sources:

Stein, Gordon. *Encyclopedia of Unbelief*. 2 vols. Buffalo, NY: Prometheus Press, 1985.

★1116★
National Alliance of Pantheists
Current address not obtained for this edition.

Founded in the mid-1980s, the National Alliance of Pantheists is a network of individuals who hold pantheistic beliefs. Pantheism is a belief that god is everything and everything is God. It stands in contrast to the idea of theism that God is the transcendent Creator who stands over and apart from creation. Pantheism assumes that the world, nature, and humanity are all an intimate part of the Divine being. Most pantheists recognize philosopher Baruch Spinoza as the grandfather of their perspective, but claim such diverse thinkers as Ralph Waldo Emerson, Pierre Teilhard de Chardin, and Mahatma Ghandi as fellow pantheists.

While pantheism is an ancient belief, no attempt to organize its believers as a religious group has previously occurred. Pantheism tends to be a very individualistic philosophy; it has no dogma and is not immediately suggestive of corporate worship or united action. However, the Alliance was founded as a religion especially suitable for the modern world, i.e., the New Age. It works to end bigotry and religious discrimination through its belief that ultimately all people are involved in the Divine Essence. Thus, no one religion can be the "true faith" as all religious expressions exist within the one consciousness of the Divine.

The Alliance has established itself as a place where pantheists can discover each other, thus leading to the formation of local groups and churches. It ordains clergy and charters churches, but has no hierarchy. While it encourages the individual expression of the member's relationship to God, the Alliance notes that many Pantheists keep the ancient agricultural festivals at the solstices and equinoxes (and halfway between them) as a means of calling attention to the intimate connection between God and nature. They also tend to be environmentalists. The Alliance holds an annual celebration of Lammas in August.

Membership: Not reported.

Periodicals: *Nap Time*.

★1117★
Northeast Atheist Association (NAA)
Box 63
Simsbury, CT 06070

The Northeast Atheist Association (NAA) was founded in 1992 to promote atheism in the Northeast United States. It is headed by Franklin Marshall (president) and Howard Palmer (vice-president) and publishes a newsletter.

Membership: In 1997, the association reported approximately 150 members.

Educational Facilities: The association supports the Center for Inquiry Institute, PO Box 703, Amherst, NY 14226-0703.

Periodicals: *The Northeast Atheist*.

★1118★
Society of Evangelical Agnostics
(Defunct)

The Society of Evangelical Agnostics was founded in 1975 by William Henry Young. Young had called himself an agnostic for several years and had harbored a hope that an agnostic organization would emerge. After developing the idea of the society, he placed ads in a number of liberal, religious journals such as *The Humanist* and mass circulation periodicals such as *Nation* and the *Saturday Review*. He also began to champion the cause of agnosticism, frequently speaking to audiences on the subject and writing letters to periodicals whenever he thought agnosticism had been misrepresented. He also began a newsletter, *The SEA Journal*.

The society defined agnosticism by reference to a tradition of outstanding freethinkers who called themselves by that label, most notably Thomas Henry Huxley (who coined the term), Bertrand Russell, and Robert G. Ingersoll. Its principles consist of three statements: One should approach all questions and issues with an open mind; One should avoid advocating conclusions without adequate or satisfactory evidence; One should accept not having final answers as a fundamental reality in one's life. According to Young, agnosticism is to be distinguished quite strongly from atheism. The latter flatly denies the existence of God while the former affirms God is both unknown and an unknowable factor. Atheism, like Christianity, violates the second principle of agnosticism by advocating conclusions without adequate evidence.

The society was headed by a board of directors and its administrator, William Henry Young. Young was also the librarian of the Cedar Springs Library, in Auberry, California, which had developed a special collection of freethought literature. The library was the official archive of the society and distributed numerous inexpensive items related to the society's concerns. The society reprinted many classic statements of agnosticism as well as original material writtten by its members. Membership was open to all who considered themselves agnostics and who contributed a modest annual membership fee. Members were also encouraged to form chapters and hold meetings in their local neighborhoods. The society was dissolved in 1987 at the request of its founder after enrolling more than 1,150 members.

Sources:

Huxley on Agnosticism. Auberry, CA: Cedar Springs Library, n.d.

Ingersoll, Robert G. *Ingersoll's Greatest Lectures*. New York: Freethought Press Association, 1944.

Stephens, Leslie. *An Agnostic's Apology*. New York: G. P. Putnam's Sons, 1903.

Young, William Henry. "The Agnostic as Prophet." *Faith and Thought* 1, no. 2 (Summer 1983): 27-31.

★1119★
Unitarian Universalist Association
25 Beacon St.
Boston, MA 02108

Unitarian Universalist Association was formed in 1961 by the merger of the American Unitarian Association and the Universalist Church in America. The merger represents the coming together of the two oldest and most conservative segments of the liberal tradition. (See introductory material for historical survey). Within that tradition, it is the only body that affirms its base within the Judeo-Christian heritage. Many of its ministers can be found in local ministerial associations.

The basis of modern Unitarian belief is the free search for truth. Truth is found in the universal teachings of the great prophets and teachers of all ages and traditions, but summarized in the Western tradition as love of God and man. Members believe in the worth of every human and in the democratic method in human relationships. A world community based on brotherhood, justice, and peace is the goal of all actions. While varying widely in belief structures, Unitarian Universalists generally believe in God as the source of mind and spirit, Jesus as a great prophet, the Bible as a collection of valuable religious writings, science as a source of knowledge, and prayer as a means to lift the mind beyond the ordinary. There are no sacraments.

Following the pattern of their Congregational parents, the Unitarian Universalists are congregationally governed. A national Association meeting is held annually and each minister and local church is represented. The Unitarian Universalist Service Committee was established in 1940 to aid refugees of Nazi persecution and has continued as a means to embody social concerns. Beacon Press is a major publisher of religious books.

During the 19th century, both Universalists and Unitarians engaged in foreign missionary activity, the former most noticeably in Japan and the latter in India and Japan. Ties to liberal religionists in these countries have been retained (long after any understanding of a missionary-mission relationship existed) and fellowship with similar groups in other lands has been established. Currently, there are affiliated congregations of Unitarian-Universalists in Argentina, Australia, Belgium, Canada, France, Japan, West Germany, Mexico, the Netherlands, New Zealand, the Philippines, Puerto Rico, and the Virgin Islands.

Membership: In 1991, the association reported 191,317 members, 978 churches, and 1,250 ministers in the United States, and 6,167 members and 42 churches in Canada.

Periodicals: *UU World.*

Sources:

Ahlstrom, Sydney E., and Jonathan S. Carey. *An American Reformation.* Middletown, CT: Wesleyan University Press, 1985.

Cheetham, Henry H. *Unitarianism and Universalism.* Boston: Beacon Press, 1962.

Tapp, Robert B. *Religion Among the Unitarian Universalists.* New York: Seminar Press, 1973.

Wilbur, Earl Morse. *Our Unitarian Heritage.* Boston: Beacon Press, 1963.

Williams, George Huntston. *American Universalism.* Boston: Beacon Press, 1976.

Wintersteen, Prescott B. *Christology in American Unitarianism.* Boston: Unitarian Universalist Christian Fellowship, 1977.

★1120★
United Libertarian Fellowship
(Defunct)

The United Libertarian Fellowship was incorporated in 1975 in Los Altos, California, by William White, Kathleen J. White, and C. Douglas Hoiles. The fellowship was organized as a religious order enspousing libertarian ideals of individual freedom and responsibility within a religious context. It offered a broad framework within which libertarians could develop religiously following their own initiative and perspectives.

The fellowship had a simple statement of beliefs. God was acknowledged as the fundamental force in the universe. Human beings possessed the capacity to think and act. That capacity placed a duty upon people to search for truth and to act in accord with that truth. Individuals, being capable of influencing their own destiny, also accepted responsibility for their actions and the consequences which flow from them. The guidance of personal conduct began in refraining from the initiation of the use of force or fraud on another person and the general assumption that others are free and should be allowed that freedom to develop their own religious nature.

The fellowship described worship as "focusing the mind in search for truth." Five sacraments were observed as outward manifestations and public observances of the sacred realm in human life. Affirmation, parallel to confirmation in other churches, was a declaration of adulthood and acceptance of adult responsibility. Marriage was contracted to share lives. Consecration was the dedication of a person or property to sacred purposes. The final two sacraments attempted to integrate religious ideals into everyday life by infusing otherwise mundane activity with sacred worth. Transformation was the act of changing physical materials into a new form with more utility and/or value than the original materials possessed. Exchange was the voluntary giving and receiving of objects or labor.

The direction of the fellowship was in the hands of a board, officers, and its ministers. A three-person board of elders manages the fellowship. The board appointed the officers: a president who directed the religious work, a secretary-treasurer who kept the records, and bishops who managed the temporal affairs. The board also appointed and ordained ministers who had sacramental functions and could, if they chose, establish churches. In keeping with libertarian principles, neither bishops nor ministers were assigned tasks; rather, they were encouraged to work in accordance with libertarian beliefs and spread its fellowship as their individual creativity dictates. After functioning for several years, the fellowship ran into problems with the Internal Revenue Service. It was declared non-religious and eventually its elders were tried and convicted of tax evasion.

Sources:

The United Libertarian Fellowship, A Religious Order. Los Altos, CA: United Libertarian Fellowship, 1982.

★1121★
United Moral and Philosophical Society for the Diffusion of Useful Knowledge
(Defunct)

The United Moral and Philosophical Society for the Diffusion of Useful Knowledge was founded in 1836 at Saratoga Springs, New York, as the response of a convention of freethinkers to the call for the establishment of a national organization. Prominent among its supporters were Abner Kneeland and Benjamin Otten. Kneeland (1774–1844) was a former Universalist minister turned atheist and beginning in 1830 the editor of an atheist journal, the *Boston Investigator*, and lecturer for the First Society of Free Inquirers. The society lasted for five years and held annual conventions. After its demise, a second attempt at a national organization was made with the formation of the Infidel Society for the Promotion of Mental Liberty, which lasted for three years (1845–48).

Sources:

Post, Albert. *Popular Freethought in America, 1825–1850.* New York: Columbia University Press, 1943. Reprint, New York: Octagon Books, 1974.

★1122★
United Secularists of America
(Defunct)

The United Secularists of America was formed in 1946 as an anti-God, anti-religion organization by William McCarthy. It is the secularists' belief that religion is a great hoax, and the organization opposed the "dangerous" encroachments of religion in education and other areas of life. Among the group's outstanding members was ex-priest Joseph M. McCabe, one of the major popularizers of atheism in the twentieth century. Prior to his death in 1955, he had written more than 200 books against the church and translated 30 others. Titles include *The Sources of Morality of the Gospel*, *Crime and Religion*, and *A Rationalist Encyclopedia*.

The United Secularists of America advocated the complete separation of church and state; the right not to believe as part of freedom of religion; the exclusion of all religion from public schools; and the taxation of church property. Opposing all supernaturalism and superstition, the United Secularists of America believed in the free intellectual growth of man and the advancement of society toward a rational civilized existence.

During its first decade, the United Secularists were among the largest of the rationalist/atheist bodies, drawing support from many independent rationalist and secularists societies. In 1947 they had begun a magazine *Progressive World*. However, in the early 1950s, protests against secretive financial policies led most of the groups to withdraw and in 1955 form the American Rationalist Federation. After that year, the United Secularists lacked support to even hold an annual meeting. By 1970 there were only three centers, 1,000 active members, and 1,000 at-large members. Over the decade the United Secularists steadily lost their remaining support. In 1981 they finally disbanded and the magazine ceased publication.

★1123★
Universal Pantheist Society
PO Box 265
Big Pine, CA 93513

The Universal Pantheist Society was founded in 1975 to provide a spiritual home for people who are attracted to a Pantheistic worldview. Traditionally, pantheism is defined as a belief that the universe taken as a whole is God. Members of the society would expand upon that definition by noting that the universe is a creative process, thus it is our (humanity's) Creator, but at the same time we are part of it. The religious feeling derives from a relationship with the surrounding universe and may be romantic, mystical, or personal. Thus pantheism can be distinguished from both theism (belief in a supreme being that created the universe) and atheism. For the pantheist, humans are not separate from Nature/God, but Nature forms the ultimate context for human existence. While different forms of pantheism exist, all agree that anthropocentrism—the idea that the world was basically created for humanity's benefit—is incorrect. Rather, they support a reverential attitude toward the earth and its nonhuman inhabitants.

Pantheists promote three basic approaches to acknowledging the sacredness of the world: knowledge, devotion, and works. In integrating these three approaches to nature, the unity of body, mind and spirit is also experienced. Thus pantheists study nature and engage in art and other activities that show appreciation, and participate in environmental efforts. A sacerdatal policy outlines guidelines for holding celebrative activities for natural events such as the solstices and equinoxes.

The society is headed by a president, currently Derham Giuliani, and a board of directors.

Membership: Not reported. There are members in both the United States and Canada.

Periodicals: *Pantheist Vision.*

Sources:

Burroughs, John. *Accepting the Universe.* N.p., n.d.

The Pantheist World View. Big Pine, CA: Universal Pantheist Society, 6-page tract. n.d.

Haeckel, Ernst. *The Riddle of the Universe.* New York: Harper and Brothers, 1900.

Thomas, Henry, and Dana Lee Thomas. *God, Humanity, and Pantheism.* N.p., 1941.

Thomas, In. *God and Belief: The Pantheist Alternatives.* Big Pine, CA: Universal Pantheist Society, 1986.

Wood, Harold W., Jr. "Modern Pantheism as an Approach to Environmental Ethics." *Environmental Ethics* 7 (Summer 1985).

★1124★
Universal Society
(Defunct)

The Universal Society was the first organization in America to give expression to the deist/freethought religiousphilosophical perspective. It was founded in Philadelphia, Pennsylvania, in 1791. Philadelphian Benjamin Franklin was a deist theologically, but his prominence did little to assist the young society.

Elihu Palmer, a blind Baptist minister in the city, was fired from his position, not for his disability, but for holding and preaching heretical views. At about that same time, John Fitch, the inventor of the steamboat, had organized the Universal Society to which Palmer and his few supporters adhered. Palmer became the minister of the society and in one of his first discourses broached the subject of the divinity of Jesus, which he proceeded to deny. Bp. William White, the Episcopal Church authority in the city, then applied pressure to the society's landlord to refuse to rent to the group and mobilized public hostility against Palmer. Palmer left town and the society collapsed.

Thus the first freethought organization in the United States came to an end in a matter of weeks. It became the foundation, however, upon which a more successful organization, the Deistical Society of New York, would be built in the early years of the new century.

Sources:

Koch, G. Adolf. *Republican Religion.* New York: Henry Holt and Company, 1933. Reprinted as *Religion of the American Enlightenment.* New York: Thomas Y. Crowell, 1968.

Mail Order Churches

★1125★
American Fellowship Church
225 Crossroads Blvd., No. 345
Carmel, CA 93923

The American Fellowship Church (originally named the Mother Earth Church), was formed in 1975 by T. H. Swenson, as an independent church which believes in individual responsibility for spiritual growth and development. Described as a church without walls whose members are widely scattered, ministers are invited to unite daily in prayer and meditation at 7 a.m. and 7 p.m. (Pacific Standard Time). The International Clergy Association is a division of the church open only to ordained ministers. It publishes a directory of members and offers correspondence courses.

Membership: In 1991, there were approximately 15,000 members of AFC chartered churches.

Periodicals: *Newsletter.*

★1126★
Brotherhood of Peace and Tranquility
(Defunct)

The Brotherhood of Peace and Tranquility was a fellowship of semi-autonomous churches which included local autonomous congregations and a "Church of the Brotherhood," a single world-wide congregation of individuals. Individual churches varied widely in belief and practice. The brotherhood operated the Academy of the Brotherhood, its teaching arm, which offered training to ministers as well as courses for members who wish merely to improve their religious knowledge. Both resident and nonresident instruction was offered, and the curriculum was slanted toward the psychic. Both the academy and the church were headquartered in Costa Mesa, California.

★1127★
Calvary Grace Christian Church of Faith
Current address not obtained for this edition.

The Calvary Grace Christian Church of Faith was formed in 1961 by the Rev. Dr. Herman Keck, Jr. of Ft. Lauderdale, Florida, who began his ministry as a member of the Calvary Grace Churches of Faith. In 1962, he began calling himself the international superintendent and established Faith Bible College. The Church resembles its parent body.

Membership: Not reported.

Educational Facilities: Faith Bible College, Fort Lauderdale, Florida.

Faith Theological Seminary, Fort Lauderdale, Florida.

Sources:

Bruns, Bill. "Praise the Lord and Pass the Diploma." *Life* (November 14, 1970): 69-78.

★1128★
Calvary Grace Churches of Faith
Current address not obtained for this edition.

Among the first of the mail-order churches is the Calvary Grace Churches of Faith formed in 1954 (chartered in 1958) by Angelo C. Spern of Irwin, Pennsylvania. It issues ordination certificates on application to "worthy Christians who have accepted (the) Lord Jesus Christ as the Savior." The International Chaplain's Association functions as the churches' missionary arm.

Membership: Not reported. In 1984 there were a reported 70 congregations.

Educational Facilities: Calvary Grace Bible Institute, Rillton, Pennsylvania.

★1129★
The Church of Holy Light
(Defunct)

The Church of Holy Light was a small mail-order church that ordained ministers and chartered congregations. The church asked only that candidates felt called to preach. An initial $50.00 offering was asked of new applicants. Nothing has been heard of this church for many years and it is presumed to be defunct.

Membership: Not reported.

★1130★
Church of the Holy Monarch
Current address not obtained for this edition.

Describing itself as a "church without walls," the Church of the Holy Monarch is headed by Dr. Robert Walker and Archbishop R. M. LeRoux. It was founded in 1976 and ordains ministers and charters churches. Ministers are asked to respond to a nominal accessment to remain active clergy in the church.

Membership: Not reported.

Periodicals: *The Monarch Messenger.* Send orders to Box 116, Port Orange, FL 32019.

★1131★
Church of Transition
210 NE 48th Terr.
Miami, FL 33137

The Church of Transition emerged in the 1980s as a nondogmatic, nonpolitical, and loosely organized association of ministers and churches. It was founded by Bruce Cole, designated as First Minister. The church initially provides credentials for ministers who follow a spiritual path and wish to assist others from their spiritual orientation. The church has no requirements of belief, and practice and ministers are prohibited from requiring the members of their congregations to adhere to any particular belief or practice. Ministerial candidates, who must have the equivalent of a masters degree in a helping profession (social work, counseling, etc.), are privately tutored by one of the present ministers prior to ordination. Most ministers come out of a Western mystical tradition.

Membership: In 1991 there were approximately 20 ministers in the United States, two in Canada, and one in Mexico. Several of the ministers had formed congregations, but no count on members had been taken.

★1132★
Church of Universal Brotherhood
Current address not obtained for this edition.

The Church of Universal Brotherhood offers (for $10.00) a kit that includes an ordination certificate, a Doctor of Divinity certificate, and complete instructions on forming a church. The Church was founded by Michael Valentine of Hollywood, California, with the purpose of helping people become aware that they are in charge of their own beliefs. The Church admonishes members to love themselves, love their brothers and sisters as they do themselves, and take control of their lives as they see fit. Their Church believes that all is one. The goals of life are best attained, according to the Church, by getting high and staying there, raising the vibes, cherishing the world, and praising God for his grace.

Freedom is a keynote with the church, which encourages ordinations as a means of releasing power for good. Members of the Church say people are in prison, but they deserve to be free and must get the necessary help. The prime virtue is the constant striving for self-mastery. Three tools available to aid the seeker are mirrors, water beds, and hypnosis.

Membership: Not reported.

★1133★
Crown of Life Fellowship
Current address not obtained for this edition.

The Crown of Life Fellowship was formed in 1967 at Pullman, Washington, by the Rev. D. H. Howard. It functioned for several years as a fellowship at the University of Washington and then moved to Spokane, and more recently to Oregon. In 1970, the small Spokane group began to place advertisements offering ordination and, by 1972, had ministers in most of the states and provinces. The Fellowship functions as an association of ministers drawn from a diverse theological spectrum. There are no doctrinal requirements for membership.

The church supplies a short course leading to a Doctor of Divinity degree. Through its periodical, *Crown of Life Fellowship News*, it informs members of their privileges as ordained ministers. Many of the churches function as house churches and study groups.

The Crown of Life Fellowship sees itself as continuing the work of A. K. Mozumdar, who began a teaching ministry in Spokane in 1914. For the next 40 years, from the southern California headquarters of the Messianic World Message, Mozumdar preached a "universal message" of the God within. His teachings represented an attempted synthesis of Hinduism and Christianity. The Fellowship has sponsored the republishing of Mozundar's major work, *The Triumphant Spirit*.

Membership: Not reported.

Periodicals: *The Universal Message*. Send orders to Rte. 2, Box 190, Albany, OR 97321.

Sources:

Mozumdar, A. K. *The Triumphant Spirit*. Marina Del Rey, CA: DeVorss & Co., 1978.

★1134★
Hilltop House Church
(Defunct)

On November 1, 1971, newspapers across the United States carried pictures of Sadie, a Labrador retriever in Terre Linda, California, who has been ordained a minister in the Hilltop House Church by Archbishop Ben F. Gay, its founder. Gay, former president of Holiday Magic, Inc., a cosmetics firm founded by the late William Penn Patrick, founded the Hilltop House Church in 1970 in San Rafael, California. He had formerly been ordained by the Missionaries of the New Truth, a Chicago-based group. The guiding precepts of the Hilltop House Church were the golden rule and John 8:32, "Ye shall know the truth and the truth shall set you free."

Inherent within the Hilltop House Church was a certain cynicism toward religion as a whole. Ministers were ordained for $15.00 and a registration form. They were then promised promotions for recruiting other ministers (a structure quite similar to Holiday Magic's program). The church's stated goal was to ordain 48 bishops, 24 monsignors, and 12 vicars. Ministers were offered ordination simply because of all the benefits ordination brings.

On January 8, 1973, after a year of protesting tax shelters offered to churches, Gay, in a letter to the U.S. Internal Revenue Service, asked that the tax-exempt status of his church be canceled. This act was a dramatic protest of the large, nonreligious, tax-free holdings of other churches.

★1135★
Holy Gospel Church IV, Inc.
Current address not obtained for this edition.

The Holy Gospel Church IV, Inc., was founded in 1977 in New Port Richie, Florida, by Rev. Mario J. Sautte, the church's patriarch. It is described as a liberal church organization without any traditional doctrine. It is the belief of the church that each clergy person has a right to serve god in his own way according to their own religious convictions. It is Christian, interfaith, and nondenominational. The Church accepts belief in God, the divinity of Christ, and the power of prayer, but these are not required beliefs by those ordained by the church.

The church is prepared to ordain anyone who professes a call to the ministry. There are no educational nor creedal requirements. The church also issues doctor of divinity degrees upon application. The church charters congregations, but does not cover individual congregations with its tax-exempt umbrella. Local churches must gain tax exemption on their own. Foreign members can be found in the United Kingdom, Ireland, Germany, France, Spain, Italy, Ghana, Lebanon, Haiti, and Mexico.

Membership: In 1992 the church reported approximately 10,000 members, 1,000 clergy, and 33 congregations in the United States. There were approximately 20 clergy and five congregations in Canada. There were some 10,000 members in 12 countries around the world.

★1136★
Life Science Church
Current address not obtained for this edition.

Similar to the Universal Life Church is the Life Science Church, formed by Archbishop Gordon L. Cruikshank. He offers to ordain "those gifted people that have been called to the ministry and for various reasons have been denied the right to fulfill their mission because of lack of formal education and/or college or seminary training." Ministers may be ordained by sending in $25, an application form, and a short thesis on "what the Ministry means to me and how I can serve." All ministers receive an ordination certificate and a Doctor of Divinity degree from the Life Science College. Churches are chartered for $35.00. Ministers may become bishops by recruiting others for ordination.

According to Cruikshank, the science of life consists of learning to live to the fullest. Freedom is the most important part of life, especially freedom of religion. Although the church is not doctrinally oriented and stresses freedom of belief, each minister makes a "non-denominational affirmation of faith."

Since the 1970s, the Life Science Church has become associated with the Posse Comitatus, a right-wing tax protest group in the Midwest. Ministers have been accused of using the church as a tax-dodge and of involvement in several violent confrontations between members of the Posse and the legal authorities.

Membership: Not reported.

★1137★
Missionaries of the New Truth
(Defunct)

The Missionaries of the New Truth was formed in 1969 by Frederich W. Zurndorfer and David A. Muncaster of Chicago. The organization immediately began to advertise, offering respondents ordination and a Doctor of Divinity degree. Advantages offered included the right to ordain others in the church's name, the authority to conduct weddings, tax exemption, cash grants for doing missionary work, draft exemption, and reduced rates for ministers at hotels, theaters, and on public transportation. A statement of belief says man is a seeker of truth. The church urges its ministers and members to seek truth, recognizing that subjective truth will differ from person to person. The higher truth is synonymous with God. By 1971, the Missionaries of the New Truth had ordained 7,000 ministers, signifying the church's success. However, the organization was beset with problems. Following an expose in the *Chicago Tribune*, the Illinois state's attorney general filed suit, charging the group with fraud in soliciting funds to establish schools and churches that never materialized. In addition, Muncaster and several leaders of the church were seized in a drug raid and were accused of running the largest hallucinogenic drug factory in the Midwest. Following their conviction, the church dissolved.

★1138★
Omniune Church
Current address not obtained for this edition.

The Omniune Church was formed by the Rev. M. S. Medley, former international president of public relations for the Life Science Church. The Omniune Church is based upon the ideal of building a church from the bottom up, democratically. Individual member participation is stressed. Beliefs are drawn from ethical liberalism and include emphasis on freedom of belief. The Omniune Church Creed asserts the following: "Believe what ye will, so long as ye do good to thy fellow man: for verily, he that doeth Godly deeds is a Godly man: and he that hath loving kindness in his heart hath God in his soul." The seven great laws of life further enlarge the Omniune perspective: 1) do unto others what you would have done unto you; 2) give the world love and kindness, for you reap what you sow; 3) believe in your own worth and turn from error toward improvement; 4) take nothing which the owner has need of, neither his property nor his life; 5) love and honor God and your fellow man—harm neither by word or deed; 6) seek wisdom, justice, peace and a better life for all; and 7) live joyfully, simply, naturally, sharing God's bounty, moderate in all but love of God and God's creation.

The church stresses function over form in organization and advises congregations, instead of hiring a paid minister, to divide the minister's duties and appoint unpaid volunteers to fulfill those duties. Any person can then become the speaker, conductor, clerk, organizer, instructor, steward, or counselor. These seven officers are designated elders and any assistants are deacons. Congregations are small and close-knit. They are advised to split rather than become too big. In 1973, there were 17 missionary ministers. There were missions in Los Angeles, Houston, Chicago and Atlanta. There were approximately 500 members. Headquarters are in Breckenridge, Texas.

Membership: Not reported. In 1973 there were approximately 500 members and 17 missionary ministers with missions in Los Angeles, Houston, Chicago, and Atlanta.

★1139★
United Church of the Apostles
Current address not obtained for this edition.

The United Church of the Apostles is a small mail order church that charters congregations and ordains ministers. The Church believes in freedom of religion. It sees its purpose as seeking to unite people and to open them to the beauty and great handiwork of God in everyday life.

Membership: Not reported.

Periodicals: *Church Newsletter*, Lindenhurst, NY 11757.

★1140★
Universal Free Life Church
Current address not obtained for this edition.

The Universal Free Life Church was formed in 1969 by the Rev. Dr. Arthur H. Fox, assisted by the Rt. Rev. Richard H. Kerekes and the Rev. Diane Fox. There is no doctrine; the Free Life Church recognizes the individual's right to his own beliefs. In 1970, the Church reported 1,100 centers in the United States (912 on college campuses) and 43,000 members. No verification of these claims was ever made, and no centers of the church's activity have been located during the 1980s.

★1141★
Universal Life Church
601 Third St.
Modesto, CA 95351

Kirby J. Hensley (b. 1911) was an illiterate Baptist minister from North Carolina. He educated himself and, in the process, was influenced by his readings in world religion. Over the years, he conceived the idea of a universal church that would bring people of all religions together, rather than separating them. In 1962, he founded the Universal Life Church, having previously opened a "church" in his garage in Modesto, California. Though Hensley had his own ideas about theology, he felt others had a right to their own theories. He began to ordain ministers for no fee, for life, without question. He would present a signed ordination certificate and a one-page information sheet covering the ordination ceremony merely for the asking.

In the late 1960s, Hensley attained the status of a minor folk hero as the media discovered his activity and gave it national news coverage. He would often address large college classes and ordain the audience instantly and en masse. Though ordination was free, a Doctorate of Divinity cost $20 and was offered with ten lessons explaining how to set up and operate a church. In the state of California, however, he was enjoined from issuing a degree from an unaccredited institution, so the Church's Department of Education was moved to Phoenix, Arizona.

While the Universal Life Church has no doctrine of its own, Hensley has developed an eclectic theology that includes the following beliefs: people are reincarnated; the soul is the continuing essence of man; God is substance manifest in natural laws; Jesus was a man more intelligent than most men; heaven is nothing more or less than the position of having what you want; and hell is when you do not have what you want. He has also developed an elaborate concept of history. According to Hensley, two thousand years before the Biblical flood man began to multiply on the earth, and church and state became separate. Thus began a 6,000-year spiritual dispensation which will end in thirty years of turmoil around 2000 A.D. By that time, the church and state will be reunited under the Universal Life banner. To implement his ideas, Hensley has formed the People's Peace Prosperity Party and has run for both governor of California and president of the United States. Hensley has also initiated several "reforms" by marrying a couple in a trial marriage and marrying two females at the 1971 Universal Life Church Festival.

The Church is organized very loosely. An annual convention is held. Subsidiary structures include the Universal Life Church Press Association. By 1974, churches belonging to the Universal Life Church were functioning in most states, and ministers were located in every state and many foreign countries. By 1977, the Universal Life Church claimed to have ordained more than six million ministers, some 25,000 of which had reportedly formed congregations that met regularly, usually as small groups in house churches.

Membership: In 1998 the church reported "missions" of members in the United States, 17,000,000 million worldwide, and more than 60,000 churches.

Educational Facilities: Universal Life University, Modesto, California.

Periodicals: *The ULC News*.

Remarks: The Universal Life Church has remained a constant source of controversy, having been targeted by the U.S. Internal Revenue Service as a tax-dodge. Congregations that claimed a Universal Life charter and ministers that claimed a Universal Life ordination have been carefully scrutinized, and charges of profit-making businesses and various clandestine organizations operating under the Universal Life Church's protection have been periodically reported. The Church has responded to the IRS and resulting negative image of the Church by filing suits against the IRS, moving to overturn denials of state-tax exemption and seeking recognition of its ministers to perform marriages. While the problems with the Internal Revenue Service have done little to slow the Church nationally, they have led many congregations originally chartered by the Church to seek their own charters.

Sources:

Ashmore, Lewis. *The Modesto Messiah*. Bakersfield, CA: Universal Press, 1977.

Hensley, Kirby J. *The Buffer Zone*. Modesto, CA: Universal Life Church, 1986.

___. *A New Life*. Modesto, CA: The Author, 1983.

★1142★
Universal Life Mission Church
Current address not obtained for this edition.

The Universal Life Mission Church, also known as the General Council of the Apostolic Sabbatarian Baptist Churches of America, Inc., was founded by Kenneth Russell Lyons, its bishop. The Church was originally chartered by the Universal Life Church, but in 1977 the Church was independently incorporated. The Church is a sabbatarian group. It believes in the Bible as its only guide, preferring the New International or World Version published by the Jehovah's Witnesses.

Membership: In 1984 there were 4 congregations.

★1143★
World Christianship Ministries (WCM)
PO Box 8041
Fresno, CA 93947

World Christianship Ministries (WCM) is a worldwide Christian ordination outreach ministry which through the 1980s and 1990s was providing an alternative to seminary for individuals who wished to be ordained immediately and initiate their own ministry. WCM offers a number of needed resources for such ministries, including materials on the Bible, music, organization, getting started, and religious freedom laws. It also offers "true to the Word" Bible study courses and various ministerial handbooks.

WCM ordains by application through the mail. It also invites the ministers who receive ordination from it to be a part of the World Christianship International Association.

Membership: Not reported.

Sources:

http://www.psnw.com/üwcn/.

Section 15

Latter-day Saints Family

Consult the Contents pages to locate the essay in Part II, Historical Essay Chapters, that provides an historical discussion of this family

Utah Mormons

★1144★

Aaronic Order
Box 57095
Murray, UT 84157-0095

The Aaronic Order was organized by followers of Dr. Maurice Lerrie Glendenning. While still a young man, Glendenning began to receive messages and insights pertaining to God's work for Israel and for Levi and Aaron. Some of these messages, together with some of his letters and epistles, were later assembled into a book known as the *Levitical Writings*. (This book is also referred to as the *Book of Elias* or the *Record of John*.) The Bible, however, is considered the basic scripture of the Aaronic Order and the final authority in all matters of doctrine and practice. The *Levitical Writings* are seen as consistent with and supportive of the Biblical revelation. The order considers itself a Christ-centered and Bible-based church.

In 1928 he and his family moved to Provo, Utah where he continued to receive revelations from Elias (Elijah) and to share them with interested people, many of whom became convinced of their divine origin. His followers increased over the years, and in 1942 incorporated the Aaronic Order under the laws of the State of Utah.

The order has a Chief High Priest who functions primarily in the spiritual area; a First High Priest who functions primarily in the temporal area; a Second High Priest who is in charge of ordinance and ceremonial work; and a Branch Priest who is appointed over each congregation. The ruling legislative body is the Supreme Council of seventy members.

The order stresses discipleship and consecration which require full members to relinquish title to all goods and property. Any property or goods held by a full member constitutes a stewardship under direction of the Supreme Council of the Aaronic Order. The church also has several communal settlements, known as Levitical communities, which practice the Biblical teachings of "all things common." These practices are in harmony with the ministry of Levi and Aaron in early Israel which required that this tribe could have no ownership or inheritance of the temporal things in Israel. The priesthood and the service at the altar were the heritage of Levi and Aaron for all time.

According to the order's teachings, the beginning of the Levitical priesthood dates to 1736 B.C.E., when the priesthood was granted to Levi and his descendents forever. The priests were known as Levites, Aaronites, Zadokites and Essenes at various times, and many of them became Christians in the New Testament period. One line of the Aaronic priesthood continued through the Middle Ages by lineage of Robert Bruce, king of Scotland, and through one branch of his family known as Glendowyn, brought to America by the Glendennings (or Glendonwyns) in 1742. This family maintained a constant awareness of their lineage and priesthood heritage and passed this on from father to son by written blessings, some of which are in possession of the order.

The headquarters and a branch of the order are located in Murray, Utah (a Salt Lake City suburb). Other branches are located in Provo and Partoun, Utah, and in Independence, Missouri. One of the most important thrusts of the work, however, is in the Levitical community of Eskdale, Utah, which was established in 1956 in the western desert area near the Utah-Nevada Border. In the 1980s, the Order came into contact with a Sacred Name group, Bet HaShem Midrash, headed by Shmuel ben Aharon of New Haven, Indiana. The Indiana group merged into the Order and increased awareness of the Hebrew names of the deity and of Jesus into the larger community. Members not associated with a branch are located across the United States.

Membership: The order does not believe in keeping membership figures. In 1995 there were six centers of the order approximately 1,000 members, and 20 ministers.

Periodicals: *Aaron's Star.* A. O. Publishing, 1100 Circle Dr., Esk Dale, UT 84728-9702. •*Pathlight*, c/o Ken Hill, 550 Trout Creek, UT 84083.

Remarks: The Aaronic Order is not affiliated with the Church of Jesus Christ of Latter-day Saints nor does it consider itself as having been derived from it. It should be noted, however, that Glendenning was a member of the church, and was excommunicated from it because of his revelations. Also, the *Levitical Writings* begin with chapter 137 while the LDS edition of the *Doctrine and Covenants* ends with section 136.

Sources:

Beeston, Blanche W. *Now My Servant.* Caldwell, ID: Caxton Printers, 1987.

——. *Purified as Gold and Silver.* Idaho Falls, ID: The Author, 1966.

Erickson, Ralph D. *History and Doctrinal Development of the Order of Aaron.* Master's thesis, Brigham Young University, Provo, UT, 1969.

Levitical Writings. Eskdale, UT: Aaronic Order, 1978.

★1145★

Church of Christ (Brewster)
(Defunct)

The Church of Christ (Brewster) was a Latter-day Saint-inspired communal group founded by James C. Brewster in 1848 soon after the martyrdom of Mormon prophet Joseph Smith, Jr., the resulting disruption of the Mormon community at Nauvoo, Illinois, and the movement of the majority of the saints to Utah. Prior to the founding of the church, Brewster had a lengthy career as a would-be prophet. In 1836, when the Church of Jesus Christ of Latter-day Saints was but a few years old, a 10-year-old Brewster claimed that he had communicated with the Angel Moroni (from whom Smith claimed he had originally obtained the *Book of Mormon*). Church leaders disfellowshipped Brewster.

Two years after his being put out of the church, Brewster began writing a book eventually finished and published in 1842 as *The Words of Righteousness to All Men, Written from One of the*

Books of Esaras, Which Was Written by the Five Ready Writers, In Forty Days, Which Was Spoken of by Esaras, in His Second Book, Fourteenth Chapter of the Apocrypha, Being one of the Books Which Was Lost, and Has Now Come Forth, by the Gift of God, In the Last Days. Over the next few years, Brewster wrote additional books criticizing Smith's new revelations and the direction taken by the church he headed. Brewster was not far away when the Mormon settlement was disrupted, and in 1848 he began to work directly among those members who had not joined the exodus westward. As the church was being organized, a periodical, *The Olive Branch, or, Herald of Peace and Truth to all Saints,* began to appear from Kirkland, Ohio, where the church's headquarters had been established. Brewster claimed that by 1842 Smith had been led astray and that a reorganization of the church was needed.

Among the first converts to Brewster's cause was Hazen Aldrich, a former member of the First Council of Seventy in the church at Nauvoo. When the church was formally organized, Aldrich was named president, with Brewster and Jackson Goodale as counselors. Other members filled out the remaining hierarchy of the church. Brewster guided the church with a series of communications from the spirit world. Brewster designated an area in the Rio Grande Valley as the gathering place for the saints, and he and Goodale migrated there while Aldrich remained behind in Kirkland.

The church held together for several years, but in 1851 Aldrich proclaimed his belief that Brewster had misconstrued the writings from Esaras. Brewster answered Aldrich's charges with a revelation suggesting that Aldrich had improperly usurped authority. Meanwhile, Goodale was found guilty of a transgression and put out of the church. In the midst of the infighting, the church fell apart. A short time later, Brewster moved to California and became a lecturer for Spiritualism, which found strong support among California Mormons. He remained a Spiritualist the rest of his life.

Sources:

Brewster, James C. *An Address to the Church of Christ, and Latter Day Saints.* Springfield, IL: The Author, 1848. 24 pp.

___. *A Warning to the Latter Day Saints, Generally Called Mormons. An Abridgement of the Ninth Book of Esdras.* Springfield, IL: The Author, 1845. 16 pp.

___. *The Words of Righteousness to All Men, Written from One of the Books of Esaras, Which Was Written by the Five Ready Writers, In Forty Days, Which Was Spoken of by Esaras, in His Second Book, Fourteenth Chapter of the Apocrypha, Being one of the Books Which Was Lost, and Has Now Come Forth, by the Gift of God, In the Last Days.* Springfield, IL: Ballad and Roberts, Printers, 1942. 48 pp.

Shields, Steven L. *Divergent Paths of the Restoration.* Los Angeles: Restoration Press, 1990. 336 pp.

★1146★
Church of Christ (Whitmer)
(Defunct)

David Whitmer was one of the original witnesses to the authenticity of the *Book of Mormon,* and during the early years of the Church of Jesus Christ of Latter-day Saints was a close associate of the church's founder, Joseph Smith, Jr. However, he had disagreements with Smith in the 1830s and he separated from the main body of the church. In the late 1840s he refused to assume the leadership of a group of Mormons who did not move to Utah. Afterwards, little was heard from him for many years, however, in the years after the Civil War he gathered a small following and by the mid-1870s formed an independent church organization. He commissioned missionaries who went out to preach and assemble groups of believers. He remained active until his death in 1888.

Among Whitmer's last activities was the writing and publication of a booklet, *An Address to all Believers in Christ* (1887). In this work he not only attested to his belief in the authenticity of the *Book of Mormon,* but expressed his opinion that Joseph Smith, Jr. was called to translate the *Book of Mormon* and to preach the restored gospel, but was never called to receive revelations or to lead a church.

After Whitmer's death, the movement seems to have been headed by John J. Snyder. In 1889, Ebenezer Robinson began to edit a periodical, *The Return,* which was published intermittently until 1900 when it was superseded by *The Messenger.* A hymnal was issued in 1890 and an edition of the *Book of Mormon* under the title *The Nephite Record,* in 1899, and the *Book of Commandments* in 1903. The church seems to have continued until 1925 when Snyder led the membership of several hundred members in Missouri, Iowa, and Kansas, to unite with the Church of Christ (Temple Lot).

Sources:

Brown W. P. *Defense of the Church of Christ; and Exposure of the Errors of Mormonism.* Newton, KS: Democrat Publishing House, 1887. 30 pp.

Shields, Steven L. *Divergent Paths of the Restoration.* Los Angeles: Restoration Press, 1990. 336 pp.

Snyder, John J. *The Solution to the Mormon Problem.* Independence, MO: Zion's Advocate, 1926. 16 pp.

Whitmer, David. *An Address to All Believers in Christ. By a Witness to the Divine Authenticity of The Book of Mormon.* Richmond, MO: The Author, 1887. 75 pp.

★1147★
Church of Jesus Christ (Bulla)
Current address not obtained for this edition.

Art Bulla joined the Church of Jesus Christ of Latter-day Saints around 1970. While a member he had come to believe that he was the "One Mighty and Strong" who was spoken of in Mormon scriptures who was to come and set God's house in order. He organized the Church of Jesus Christ in the early 1980s.

Membership: Not reported.

Sources:

Bulla, Art. *The Revelations of Jesus Christ.* Salt Lake City, UT: The Author, 1983.

★1148★
Church of Jesus Christ of Israel
(Defunct)

The Church of Jesus Christ of Israel was founded in 1936 by J. H. Sherwood, a former member of the Church of Jesus Christ of Latter-day Saints residing in Los Angeles, California. Sherwood had come to believe that he was a literal descendent of the Biblical Aaron, the older brother of Moses, and the first high priest of Israel. As a result of his relation to Aaron, Sherwood demanded that the Church give him the office of Presiding Bishop. That demand was refused and thus he claimed that on September 13, 1936, the priesthood authority was withdrawn from the LDS Church and all ordinances performed by the church's priests after that date were invalid. Sherwood was excommunicated and founded the Church of Jesus Christ of Israel. His small but dedicated following persisted quietly over the next few decades.

The Church of Jesus Christ of Israel followed the basic belief and practices of its parent body, Sherwood's issue being primarily administrative. His allegiance to Latter-day Saint practice was demonstrated in 1954, at which time Sherwood briefly emerged out of his obscurity when he requested the use of the facilities of the temple in Salt Lake City for a service of baptism for the dead. His request was denied and he performed the service at a lake near Ventura, California. The service consisted of a proxy baptism for all of the dead, which Sherwood claimed would do away with the necessity of putting so much time and energy into genealogy.

The church was organized around two levels of membership. Members of the church partaking in the celestial glory were required to live communally according to the united order. All the members of the priesthood were of the celestial order. Those of the lesser glory, the terrestrial, were required merely to tithe. In recent decades nothing has been heard from the church and it is presumed to be defunct.

Sources:

Shields, Steven L. *Divergent Paths of the Restoration.* Los Angeles: Restoration Press, 1990. 336 pp.

★1149★
Church of Jesus Christ of Latter-day Saints
50 E. North Temple
Salt Lake City, UT 84150

The main body which carries the history and theology of the Latter-day Saints tradition described in the introductory material in this chapter is the Church of Jesus Christ of Latter-day Saints (LDS), headquartered in Salt Lake City, Utah.

History. After the assassination of Joseph Smith, Jr. in 1844, the Saints were forced to evacuate Nauvoo, Illinois, and most of them moved to Iowa. Brigham Young (1801-1877), the former president of the Council of Twelve Apostles under Smith, became their leader and three years later was formally installed as president of the church at the reorganization of the First Presidency. Young led the Saints across the Plains states to the Rocky Mountains, where in 1847, they settled the present site of Salt Lake City. Under Young's leadership the Saints colonized more than 300 settlements from Canada to Mexico.

During the early years in Utah, polygamy, which had begun to be practiced among church leaders in Nauvoo, became openly discussed, practiced, and advocated. Possibly more than any other issue, polygamy thwarted Young's plans for a western state of Deseret, the original name proposed for Utah, while bringing the power of the federal government down on the church. During the 1880s, laws were passed against polygamy. Church leaders were obligated by law to move against the practice and to move against those church members who continued to participate in plural marriages. Since 1890, the church has been officially opposed to polygamy.

In 1849, they stepped up their worldwide mission previously initiated in Nauvoo. They concentrated on Western Europe, primarily England and Scandinavia. The many converts they made constituted the basis for the spectacular spread of the church throughout the world in the twentieth century. While becoming an international religion of some importance, the church spread along the Rocky Mountains from Phoenix, Arizona to Boise, Idaho and westward to the Pacific. From their western base, the Saints have gradually spread across the United States and currently have congregations in every section of the country.

For many years, the church was criticized for its stance on admitting black people to the lay priesthood, an essential structure in the church for male members. That condition was changed in 1978, following a revelation given to President Spencer W. Kimball.

Organization. The church is organized along patterns revealed to Joseph Smith Jr. Leading the church internationally is the First Presidency, comprising three men (the president and two counselors) who are assisted by the Council of Twelve Apostles. Young succeeded Smith, the first president of the church. Since Young's tenure, the church has been served successively by the following: John Taylor (1880-1887); Wilford Woodruff (1889-1898); Lorenzo Snow (1898-1901); Joseph Fielding Smith (1901-1918); Heber J. Grant (1918-1945); George Albert Smith (1945-1951); David O. McKay (1951-1970); Joseph Fielding Smith (1970-); Harold B. Lee (1972-1973); Spencer W. Kimball (1973-1985); and Ezra Taft Benson (1985-1994); Howard W. Hunter (1994-1995); and Gordon B. Hinckley (1995-present).

The First Presidency and the Twelve Apostles regulate the affairs of the church generally. The Quorums of the Seventy, including a seven-man presidency and (in 1995) 73 additional members, administer the affairs of 22 "areas" of the world, under the direction of the First Presidency and the Twelve. The Presiding Bishopric (three men) has charge of the temporal affairs of the church, including the building and welfare programs. The structure of the international organization is somewhat repeated in structures at the regional (stakes) and local (wards) levels.

Integral to the belief and practice of the church are temples. Such structures are used for special weekday ceremonial work rather than being centers for the weekly gathering of worshippers. The four main services performed in the temple are the baptism for the dead, in which the living are baptized as proxies for those who died in generations past; the temple endowments; temple marriage; and sealings, which establish family structures in the life beyond earthly existence.

The church has expanded rapidly, especially in the decades since World War II. It now has missions in most countries of the world. Wherever the church is, its ministry is assisted by the Relief Society (the woman's auxiliary organization), the Primary Association (a children's organizations), the Young Women and Young Men organizations, and the Church Welfare Services Program (to assist church members in need).

Membership: In 1997, the church reported 4.8 million members and over 10,000 congregations in the United States, and an estimated 140,000 members and 420 congregations in Canada. There were more than 9 million members worldwide in 160 countries and territories.

Educational Facilities: Brigham Young University, Provo, Utah and Laie, Hawaii.
Ricks College, Rexburg, Idaho.
LDS Business College, Salt Lake City, Utah.

Periodicals: *Deseret News.* Send orders to Box 1257, Salt Lake City, UT 84110. • *The Ensign.* • *New Era.* • *The Friend.* Send orders to 50 East Temple, Salt Lake City, UT 84150. • *The Church News.* Send orders to PO Box 1257, Salt Lake City, UT 84110.

Remarks: Beginning with the polygamy era, the Church of Jesus Christ of Latter-day Saints has been the object of evangelical Protestant Christian missionaries. Since the 1960s, efforts to convert Mormons and to denounce the church have increased in proportion to the church's growth. Currently, the single largest number of Christian counter-cult organizations operating in the United States are focused entirely on Mormonism. Prominent among anti-Mormons have been Jerald Tanner and Sandra Tanner, former Mormons who head Utah Lighthouse Ministry in Salt Lake City, and Baptist minister Walter Martin of Christian Research Institute in San Juan Capistrano, California. The vast outpouring of anti-Mormon literature has led to the production of literature defending the church and countering the attacks on the faith. Besides that material produced by the church specifically for the use of missionaries, Mormon Miscellanies prints a variety of shorter works and Robert L. Brown and his wife, Rosemary Brown have produced a set of substantive polemical texts which attempt to answer the attacks of the Tanners and Martin. The literature on Mormonism is vast, and has been greatly increased in the past decade due to the work of the Mormon History Association.

Sources:

Arrington, Leonard J., and Davis Bitton. *The Mormon Experience.* New York: Alfred A. Knopf, 1979.

Bitton, David, and Maureen Ursenbach Beecher, eds. *New Views of Mormon History.* Salt Lake City, UT: University of Utah Press, 1987.

Bushman, Richard L. *Joseph Smith and the Beginnings of Mormonism.* Urbana, IL: University of Illinois Press, 1984.

Church History in the Fullness of Times. Salt Lake City, UT: Church of Jesus Christ of Latter-day Saints, 1989.

Richards, LeGrand. *A Marvelous Work and a Wonder.* Salt Lake City, UT: Deseret Book Company, 1968.

Shipps, Jan. *Mormonism.* Urbana, IL: University of Illinois Press, 1985.

Smith, Joseph S. *Gospel Doctrine.* Salt Lake City, UT: Deseret Books Company, 1969.

★1150★
Church of Jesus Christ of Latter-day Saints (Walter Murray Gibson)
(Defunct)

Among the most colorful leaders in Latter-day Saints history is Walter Murray Gibson. He arrived in Hawaii in 1861 for a stopover on his way to Japan as a missionary for the Church of Jesus Christ of Latter-day Saints. He found the remnant of a small Mormon mission which had succeeded in getting the *Book of Mormon* translated into Hawaiian in 1855 and had since turned its attention to converting the native Hawaiians. Unfortunately, the missionaries had been withdrawn in 1858 because of the impending War Between the States. Gibson stayed in Hawaii rather than continuing his journey. He reorganized the remaining Mormons and established headquarters on Lanai which he saw as the future center of the kingdom of God. He designated himself "Chief President of the Islands of the Sea and the Hawaiian Islands for the Church of Latter-day Saints." He raised money for his various concerns through simony (the selling of church positions). One of his concerns was building a temple, and he chose a site on the island for the future erection of the temple.

In 1864 a delegation of Mormon leaders arrived from Salt Lake City to investigate Gibson's mission. As a result, they decided to excommunicate him. Initially, most of his followers stayed with him, and Gibson continued on his course. His plans for expansion, however, were somewhat shattered by the lack of necessary water on the area of the island he owned. After a number of unsuccessful schemes to develop his property on Lanai, his following dwindled away and Gibson moved to Honolulu.

Since Gibson's church leadership career was over, he turned to politics and in 1882 became prime minister of Hawaii. For the next five years he was the most powerful white man in the islands, an articulate spokesperson for the cause of keeping "Hawaii for the Hawaiians." He was toppled in the revolution in 1887 and fled to California. He died there the following year.

Sources:

Adler, Jacob, and Robert M. Kamins. *The Fantastic Life of Walter Murray Gibson: Hawaii's Minister of Everything.* Honolulu: University of Hawaii Press, 1986.

Gibson, Walter Murray. *The Diaries of Walter Murray Gibson, 1886, 1887.* Edited by Jacob Adler and Gwynn Barrett. Honolulu: University Press of Hawaii, 1973.

Joesting, Edward. *Hawaii: an Uncommon History.* New York: W. W. Norton, 1972.

Shields, Steven L. *Divergent Paths of the Restoration.* Los Angeles: Restoration Research, 1990.

★1151★
Church of Jesus Christ of Saints of the Most High
(Defunct)

The Church of Jesus Christ of Saints of the Most High, a short-lived Mormon group of the 1860s, was founded by Joseph Morris (1824-1862). Morris converted to the Church of Jesus Christ of Latter-Day Saints in 1848. Prior to his 1853 relocation to Utah, Morris lived in St. Louis and affiliated with the Congregation of the Presbytery of Zion, another Mormon splinter. He became known for his piety, which some considered "excessive." Then, in 1857, he had a revelation in which he was told he was a prophet of God. In a series of letters written to Brigham Young, president of the Church of Jesus Christ of Latter-Day Saints, Morris proclaimed

God's rejection of the church leaders and His desire that the saints unite around Morris. Morris believed he was a reincarnation of the Biblical Seth and Moses. He identified himself with the seventh angel of the Book of Revelation. He also opposed the Mormon practice of polygamy.

In 1860, Morris moved to South Weber, Utah, and began to attract a few followers, including the bishop of the South Weber Ward. In 1861, along with 17 followers, Morris was excommunicated, a rebuff that led to the formal organization of the Church of Jesus Christ of the Most High in April 1861. The following month Morris issued a call for people to move to his settlement on the Weber River, predicting the imminent appearance of Jesus. In the meantime, the group would live communally; over 300 responded.

In 1862, in the midst of a legal dispute, the militia was ordered to Morris' settlement. In a brief skirmish, Morris was killed. Following his death, the church splintered into several factions as new prophets arose. It is believed the largest group became a part of the Church of the First Born (Prophet Cainan), a faction led by George Williams, also known as the Prophet Cainan.

Sources:

Morris, Joseph. *The Spirit Prevails.* San Francisco, CA: George S. Dove and Company, 1886.

★1152★
The Church of the First Born (Dove)
(Defunct)

The Church of the First Born (Dove) was a short-lived Mormon group founded in the mid-1870s by George S. Dove. Dove was a follower of George Williams, the Prophet Cainan, who founded the Church of the First Born (Prophet Cainan). In the early 1870s Dove, whose father James Dove had been an active worker on behalf of Cainan, began receiving revelations. He did not claim to be a prophet, but he assumed pastoral functions and baptized five people, including his father. He began to proselytize among the former followers of Joseph Morris and over the next several decades gathered a small following primarily in California and Montana. With his father, Dove also published many of the revelations of Joseph Morris.

The beliefs of the Church of the First Born were outlined in its Articles of Religion. They follow the beliefs of the Church of Jesus Christ of Latter-Day Saints in many areas, but also make several important departures. The Godhead is believed to consist of God and Jesus Christ, the Holy Ghost being identified with angels of God. The church advocated a second chance for sinners through reincarnation, rather than through punishment in hell.

This small faction seems to have existed into the 1890s, fading by the end of the century.

Sources:

Anderson, C. Leroy. *For Christ Will Come Tomorrow: The Saga of the Morrisites.* Logan, UT: Utah State University Press, 1981.

Dove, George S., and James Dove. *A Voice from the West.* San Francisco, CA: Church of the Firstborn, 1879.

Dove, James. *A Few Items in the History of the Morrisites.* San Francisco, CA: Church of the Firstborn, 1892.

★1153★
Church of the First Born (Prophet Cainan)
(Defunct)

George Williams (1814-1882), a pious Mormon, participated in the religious revival which swept Utah in 1857; he had been rebaptized as a sign of his commitment. In April 1862 he received a revelation telling him to prepare to follow the ministry of Joseph Morris, a prophet who had established a colony on the Weber River in Utah. Morris had been receiving and publishing revelations for several years. He rejected the leadership of the Church of Jesus Christ of Latter-Day Saints and, after founding his settlement near South Weber, Utah, was excommunicated. In spite of official disapproval, over 300 joined him in his new church, the Church of Jesus Christ of Saints of the Most High. In June 1862 the militia attacked his settlement, and Morris was killed in the battle.

At the time of Morris's death, Williams was not involved with the Church of Jesus Christ of Saints of the Most High. Then in the fall of 1862, he began to circulate a manuscript entitled, "A Description of Interviews with Celestial Beings." Subsequently, he was ordained by two spiritual beings, Elias and Enoch. Williams was identified as a reincarnation of an angel, Cainan, and of the Old Testament priest, Melchisedec (or Melchizedek). He assumed the title and became known as the Prophet Cainan.

From his home in Salt Lake City, Cainan began to visit the Morrisite settlement. Some of those who accepted his revelations moved to Montana and settled at Deer Lodge Valley. In 1868 Cainan announced his intention of joining them. After only a year, however, he appointed William James as leader of the church, and returned to England, his birthplace. Cainan led the group in Montana through his letters, until his death in 1892. The group remained in existence into the twentieth century. James was eventually suspended from membership in the church for rebelling against its teachings. He was succeeded by George Thompson (d. 1894) and Andrew Hendrickson, one of the church's bishops. Hendrickson served as president until his death in 1921. The last leader was George Johnson (d. 1954). By the 1940s less than a dozen members were reported.

Sources:

Anderson, C. LeRoy. For Christ Will Come Tomorrow: The Saga of the Morrisites. Logan, UT: Utah State University Press, 1981.

Eardley, J. R. Gems of Inspiration. San Francisco, CA: Joseph A. Dove, 1899.

★1154★
Church of Zion
(Defunct)

The Church of Zion was a short-lived, but important, movement that grew out of a major disagreement over economic policy in postCivil War Utah. In late 1868, William S. Godbe, Elias L. T. Harrison, and some associates began to receive revelation confirmed by various spiritual manifestations that instructed them to oppose some of the new policies being introduced by church president Brigham Young. The revelations represented a direct challenge to Young's power. The focus of the dissent by Godbe was the newly organized Zion's Cooperative Mercantile Institute, a structure to coordinate the economic resources of Utah Mormons. All Mormon business were ordered to join it and faithful Mormons were to do their buying through it. Young saw ZCMI as a step in building a self sufficient Mormon community.

Godbe and the Church of Zion members believed in an open economy of free enterprise and opposed the controlled economy exemplified by ZCMI. Godbe looked to the future integration of Utah into the United States as a whole and argued for industrialization, the bringing of Gentile (non-Mormon) culture to Utah, and an openness to non-Mormons in general. Godbe had no doctrinal quarrel with the Church of Jesus Christ of Latter-day Saints, including its doctrine of plural marriage.

The Godbeite movement flourished for only a few years. A periodical, the Utah Magazine, lasted for two years (January 1868-December 1869); Godbe continued to publish into the early 1870s. However, it soon became evident that his views were not shared by a significant minority of Utah residents and the church disbanded.

Sources:

Godbe, William S. Manifesto from W. S. Godbe and E. L. T. Harrison. Salt Lake City, UT: The Authors, 1869. 4 pp.

___. Polygamy; its Solution in Utah A Question of the Hour. Salt Lake City: Salt Lake Tribune, 1871. 16 pp.

Shields, Steven L. Divergent Paths of the Restoration. Los Angeles: Restoration Research, 1990. 336 pp.

Walker, Ronald W. "The Commencement of the Godbeite Protest: Another View." Utah Historical Quarterly 42 (Summer 1974): 216-44.

★1155★
Kingdom of Heaven
(Defunct)

One of the most unusual groups in Mormon history, the Kingdom of Heaven was established by William W. Davies (b. 1833). Davies was a British Methodist who converted to the Church of Jesus Christ of Latter-Day Saints and migrated to Utah in 1847. He became dissatisfied with the church leadership, and in 1861 joined the Church of Jesus Christ of Saints of the Most High, founded by the prophet Joseph Morris. Davies was present at the Morrisite settlement on the Weber River in June 1862 when Morris was killed by the militia. In subsequent years he associated himself with the Church of the First Born (Prophet Cainan) and migrated to Montana. Eventually he settled at Deer Lodge Valley, where a number of the followers of George Williams (also known as the Prophet Cainan) resided.

When Williams moved to Montana in 1868, Davies had departed. In 1866 Davies had a vision which convinced him that he had been chosen as an instrument through which God would speak His will to humanity. He was directed to begin the millennial Kingdom of Heaven near Walla Walla, Washington. With forty followers, Davies migrated there in 1867, purchased 80 acres, and established a communal life. The group was joined over the next few years by a few additional converts, including John Livingston, one of the original apostles of the Church of Jesus Christ of Saints of the Most High.

In the Kingdom of Heaven, reincarnation and the designation of the true identity of some of the more illustrious residents became central to the life of the group. Davies claimed to be Michael the Archangel, a reincarnation of Adam, Abraham, and King David. Following the birth of his son Arthur on February 11, 1868, Davies revealed that he (Arthur) was Jesus Christ returned. Soon after the announcement, the size of the community doubled. A second child, David, was revealed to be none other than "God, the Eternal Father of Spirits." Both children were believed to be incarnate members of the Godhead, which, among various factions of the Morrisites, consisted only of God the Father and Jesus Christ.

The colony survived for a decade, but a series of events in 1879-80 led to disaster. First, Davies' wife died. Then, in the winter of 1880, both of the divine children died from diphtheria. The disgruntled members of the community turned upon Davies; one sued him and received a $3,200.00 judgment. The Kingdom's land was sold to satisfy the judgment and court costs. The loss of the land effectively destroyed the Kingdom of God. Davies moved to Mill Creek, Washington, with a few followers, remarried, and proclaimed that the daughter born to his second wife was the reincarnation of his first wife. A short time later he abandoned all semblance of rebuilding the Kingdom and moved to San Francisco, dying in obscurity.

Sources:

Anderson, C. Leroy. For Christ Will Come Tomorrow: The Saga of the Morrisites. Logan, UT: Utah State University Press, 1981.

★1156★
LDS Scipture Researchers
(Defunct)

Also known as the Believe God Society and Doers of the Word, the LDS Scipture Researchers was a small group headed by Sherman Russell Lloyd, a music teacher in Salt Lake City. They believed that the present age is the time for the promised return of Joseph Smith, Jr., in the flesh reincarnated. He was believed to be a member of their group. While accepting the basic Mormon scripture, they also read the writings of Emanuel Swedenborg. The group was organized under the authority of the one spoken of in Third Nephi 20:23, who would come forth with fabulous information. They did not publish a periodical but did publish several pamphlets.

★1157★
Restored Church of Jesus Christ of Latter-day Saints
Current address not obtained for this edition.

The Restored Church of Jesus Christ of Latterday Saints was founded in 1971 under the leadership of F. Elwood Russell of San Diego, California. For several years during the late 1960s Russell had been receiving revelations that suggested that the Church of Jesus Christ of Latter-day Saints had lost the priesthood during the presidency of Joseph Fielding Smith (p. 1901-1918). Russell was directed by God to restore the power of the priesthood to the church. The Church rejected his claims and excommunicated him, the immediate occasion of the founding of the Restored Church.

The members of the Restored Church believe Russell to be the Messenger of the Covenant as foretold by the prophet Malachi. That messenger was to lead in the restoration of all things from which the Latter-day Saints had fallen and to prepare for the return of Jesus Christ to earth. It is their belief that the Latter-day Saints had fallen by changing the ordinances and breaking the covenants. In particular, the Church's general authorities had led in the fall by setting up a salaried ministry and by investing church funds in secular businesses.

At the time of its founding, the Restored Church believed that Jesus had already returned and was living quietly on earth making ready for his appearance. The keys of the priesthood, having been withdrawn from the Latter-day Saints, have been given to the Restored Church. San Diego County is believed to be the place designated by earlier prophecies as the New Jerusalem. It is the place where the Saints should gather as a place of refuge from the times of trouble and war, which will continue until the endtime. The leadership of the church believes itself to have been selected to save the constitution of the United States and eventually to establish theocratic rule in the land.

Membership: Not reported.

Sources:

Shields, Steven L. *Divergent Paths of the Restoration.* Los Angeles: Restoration Press, 1990. 336 pp.

★1158★
School of the Prophets
PO Box 396
Salem, UT 84653

The School of the Prophets was organized March 1982 in response to a revelation from the Lord. This revelation was one of many received on a continuing basis, dating from 1961 by R. C. Crossfield, a Canadian Melchizedek Priesthood holder in the Church of Jesus Christ of Latter-day Saints, which was first published in 1969 as the *Book of Onias*

Before this school was set up, several individuals who believed in the book eventually gathered in Boise, Idaho. They published a monthly newsletter called *Restorers*. In 1980 the majority of these early believers broke with Crossfield, some started their own organization, one couple joined Fred Collier's Church of the Firstborn, and others followed different paths.

Yet, a few remained and the school was organized. Early in 1984 it was moved to the Salem area in Utah. The revelations are now entitled *The Second Book of Commandments* and are received in an ongoing basis, with the latest one being Section 172.

Among other things, they contain continual instructions to His servants that will eventually be elaborate enough to establish God's true Zion upon the earth. They recognize that the only true church is the one established in Salt Lake City, known as the Church of Jesus Christ of Latter-day Saints. However, they instruct that this church has now been polluted by the Gentiles, whose times have now been fulfilled, and that the church will soon be restored to its purity by God's true Israel, whose identity has now begun to be revealed.

The school's belief is that Joseph Smith not only set up the church, but three other distinct organizations: 1. The School of the Prophets—which is the Educational arm of Zion; 2. The Kingdom of God—Political Arm; 3. The United Order—Economic arm; and lastly 4. The Church—which is the Missionary arm. The arms are what constitute the four Squares of God's true Zion.

The Second Book of Commandments reveals many truths, laws, and ordinances that will be needed to set up the coming millenial society of Zion. Prime examples of outstanding revelations are: Section 51, a revelation on the law of Adoption; section 61, which reveals the United Order covenants, and identifies the Four-square organization of Zion; Section 135, which reveals many of the powers of the Adversary, and instructs how we may be able to overcome them; Section 46 which explains the New and Everlasting Covenant of Marriage in clarity, allowing patriarchal plural marriages by revelation only.

The school recognizes that John Koyle, the prophet of the Salem, Utah Dream Mine, was a true instrument in God's hands to provide a means of survival at a time yet to come when great destructions and chaos will encompass the earth. Much of the present work of the school is to prepare places of refuge for those who will be guided to them when the calamities begin to fall upon the present nations.

"And ye Shall set up the School of the Prophets first, for from it cometh all truth and authority upon the face of the earth, and from it shall go forth the power to set all things aright, both temporally and spiritually." (2nd BC 75:6)

Membership: The school does not consider itself a church, consequently those who study under its aupices are free to retain membership in their present denomination. Records of the students are not made public in order to protect their church affiliation. Some of the students are members of the Church of Jesus Christ of Latter-day Saints.

Periodicals: *The Restorer Newsletter.* Send orders to PO Box 396, Salem, UT 84653.

Sources:

Crossfield, R. C. *Book of Onias.* New York: Philosophical Library, 1969.

Shields, Steven L. *Divergent Paths of the Restoration.* Los Angeles: Restoration Research, 1990.

★1159★
School of the Prophets (Wood)
Current address not obtained for this edition.

The School of the Prophets (Wood) was founded in 1986 by Archie Dean Wood, a former member of the Church of Jesus Christ of Latter-day Saints. On June 12, 1986, Wood was one of 13 people visited by Jesus Christ. Within a few weeks Wood produced a booklet, *The Grand Delusion,* in which he both affirmed the legitimacy of the position of Ezra Taft Benson as president of the Church of Jesus Christ of Latter-day Saints and complained of mistakes coming into the church. Wood also had received a set of personal revelations that were gathered together as *The Book of Azrael.*

Wood and the members of the school see their purpose as preparing Latter-day Saints for the second coming of Jesus Christ; they seek to train members to become prophets, seers, and revelators. They also wish to correct the errors that have become a part of Latter-day Saint life.

Membership: Not reported. There are fewer than 100 members.

Sources:

Shields, Steven L. *Divergent Paths of the Restoration.* Los Angeles: Restoration Research, 1990.

Wood, Archie Dean. *The Grand Delusion.* Pocatello, ID: The Author, 1986.

★1160★
United Outcasts of Israel
(Defunct)

The United Outcasts of Israel was a small, short-lived Mormon group that emerged in the 1950s under the leadership of Noel B. Pratt. Pratt, a descendent of Parley Pratt, a first generation leader of the Church of Jesus Christ of Latter-day Saints, left that church and joined the polygamy-practicing Church of the First Born of the Fullness of Times soon after its founding in 1955. In 1957 he became the editor of *The Rolling Stone,* a periodical for the Church of the Firstborn. However, by the end of 1958, Pratt's opinion of the church's founder, Joel LeBaron, had changed dramatically, and in the December 1958 issue of *The Rolling Stone,* he attacked LeBaron and his brothers, who were working with him. As a result, Pratt was excommunicated from the church and, with a small following, founded the United Outcasts of Israel headquartered in Alexandria, Virginia.

Pratt emerged as the champion of a barter system of economics and he advised people to put all of their money into tangible assets, especially in real estate. He founded a credit association, a bank, and a political party to further embody his ideals. Then as quickly as he emerged, Pratt quit, for reasons not altogether clear, but possibly from a lack of support. In November 1960 he announced, "My records and books are burned, as a testimony that I no longer shall seek to set myself up as a light unto the world." The united Outcasts of Israel was dissolved.

Within a year, however, Pratt developed a new cause, the restoration of Native Americans—the present outcasts and rightful heirs of Israel—to their proper place in the world. In this regard he founded American Indians Restoration Enterprises, an organization dedicated to the organization of American Indians into a self-governing body. In that effort he published a new edition of the *Book of Mormon* under the title, *The Indian Bible.* In the introduction he presented the book as a history of Native Americans. He suggested that in the near future Native Americans would be restored to their white skin and would subsequently build a great city centered upon a temple to the Great Spirit. In so doing the Indians would save the present white people from selfdestruction. Like the United Outcasts, American Indian Restoration Enterprises lasted only a few years.

Pratt pursued at least two further efforts to find a following. In the mid-1960s he emerged in Independence, Missouri and called attention to his preaching through some advertisements in the local newspaper. His presence was noted because of his prediction that the leadership of the Reorganized Church of Jesus Christ of Latterd-day Saints would be killed b lightning. His prediction was not fulfilled and he returned to a period of obscurity. In the mid-1980s he emerged in Salem, Massachusetts, as the head of Praetorian Press. After several years, the Press was relocated to Maine.

Sources:

Pratt, Noel B. *An Apology of Conscience.* N.p.: The author, 1959. 24 pp.

Shields, Steven L. *Divergent Paths of the Restoration.* Los Angeles: Restoration Press, 1990. 336 pp.

★1161★
Zion's Order, Inc.
Rte. 2, Box 104-7
Mansfield, MO 65704

In 1938, Dr. Merl Kilgore felt called by the Lord to work among the older Mormon churches; the Church of Jesus Christ of Latter-day Saints, the Reorganized Church of Jesus Christ of Latter Day Saints, and the Church of Jesus Christ (Strangite). He wanted to call them back to the United Order, the communal structure practiced in the early days of the church, which must be lived when Christ returns (D.C. 104). He worked with the LDS Church until 1950 when differences with his bishop led him to join the Aaronic Order. He moved to Bicknell, Utah, to aid a Mr. Taylor in his sawmill. Once there, he persuaded Taylor to leave the Aaronic Order and help him form a new church, which they called "Zion's Order of the Sons of Levi." After several moves, they bought a farm near Mansfield, Missouri, in 1953. There are slightly over fifty members governed by a presidency, counselors, a bishop, and a patriarch. They use all the Mormon scripture with the exception of Section 132 of the Doctrine and Covenants. They have adopted a communal lifestyle.

Zion's Order claims more than 650 revelations through Mr. Kilgore since 1951. Most of these have to do with the particularities of the life of the group. They claim the site of their commune as the place referred to by Isaiah (2.2) where the Lord's house should be built. They have tried to have other groups join them in building Zion anew, but these attempts have been unsuccessful to date. However, Kilgore resigned as president in 1969 to do mission work among Indians in the Southwest, which has brought a number of members into the church. Zion's Order of the Sons of Levi became known simply as Zion's Order, Inc. in 1975.

Membership: In 1988 the order reported 55 members and six ministers at the single location in Missouri.

Polygamy-Practicing

★1162★
Apostolic United Brethren
3139 W. 14700 S., No. A
Bluffsdale, UT 84065

History. The Apostolic United Brethren has its roots in a major split in the largest of the polygamy-practicing groups, generally referred to as the United Order Effort. In 1951 leadership of the group had passed to Joseph White Musser (1872-1954) who became president upon the death of John Y. Barlow. Musser had become a polygamist in the early twentieth century and was among the original leaders who had organized around Lorin C. Woolley. Over the years Musser had arisen as a major writer-apologist for polygamy. He ran Truth Publishing Company in Salt Lake City, Utah, from which he published a number of books and a periodical, *The Truth.*

Musser began almost immediately to encounter trouble with the other elected leaders of the group, most of whom resided in Short Creek (now Colorado City), Arizona. They mistrusted his leadership, while he felt they were changing doctrines and ordinances from the original fact and intent as taught by Joseph Smith, Jr., the founder of the Church of Jesus Christ of Latter-day Saints. The tensions were heightened following Musser's stroke in 1953 which left him incapacitated. He appointed two new members to the ruling elite, Margarito Bautista and Rulon C. Allred. As resistance to Musser's decisions increased, he dismissed the leadership and appointed a new set of leaders, consisting entirely of his supporters. At this point, most of the members followed the leadership at Short Creek, but several thousand followed him. Allred, his chief assistant, became the presiding elder of Musser's followers in 1954. The group considered itself the continuing church founded by Joseph Smith, Jr. The group finally incorporated in 1975 as "The Corporation of the Presiding Elder of the Apostolic

United Brethren,'' to assist in its working with and conforming to the tax laws. The group is generally known as the Apostolic United Brethren.

During the period of Rulon Allred's leadership, the Apostolic United Brethren grew several times over. A respected naturopathic physician in the Salt Lake City suburb of Murray and a polygamist since the 1930s, Allred moved quickly to consolidate the Apostolic United Brethren among polygamists, particularly in Mexico. He led in the establishment of a colony in Pinesdale, Montana, where a large meeting hall was dedicated in 1970. His leadership came to an abrupt end on May 10, 1977, when members of another polygamist group, the Church of the Lamb of God, led by Ervil LeBaron, assassinated him. He was succeeded by his brother, Owen Allred.

Beliefs. The Apostolic United Brethren believe that the leaders of the Church of Jesus Christ of Latter-Day Saints in this century have in a very real sense disqualified the leadership of Joseph Smith, Jr., Brigham Young, John Taylor, and the early leaders of the church, by their rejection of their teachings. The more recent leaders of the church have implied that Smith and his associates made serious errors that they can now correct as they see fit. The Brethren cannot accept recent instructions to disregard the teachings of the church's founding prophet. The Brethren cite as one major error the giving of the priesthood to black men. They believe that since ancient time the priesthood was denied the descendents of Cain (black people), and the church does not have the authority to change that reality. It has also criticized the church for changes in both the temple service and the garments worn during the temple services. They are opposed to granting the priesthood to women, though women have many other leadership functions.

Membership: In 1992 the Brethren reported approximately 7,000 members in five centers in the United States and foreign membership in England and Mexico.

Sources:

Allred, Rulon C. *Treasures of Knowledge*. 2 vols. Hamilton, MT: Bitteroot Publishing Co., 1982.

Bradlee, Ben, Jr., and Dale Van Atta. *Prophet of Blood*. New York: G. P. Putnam's Sons, 1981.

The Most Holy Principle. 4 vols. Murrary, UT: Gems Publishing Co., 1970-75.

Musser, Joseph W. *Celestial or Plural Marriage.* Salt Lake City: Truth Publishing Co., 1944.

___. *Michael Our Father and Our God.* Salt Lake City: Truth Publishing Company, 1963.

★1163★
Christ's Church
Current address not obtained for this edition.

Christ's Church, also known as the "Branch" Church, was formed in 1978 at Provo, Utah by Gerald W. Peterson, Sr. (d. 1981). Peterson, a former leader with the Apostolic United Brethren, acted in accord with a revelation he had received. He had come to believe that the Church of Jesus Christ of Latter-day Saints had become apostate and no longer taught the true principles of Christ's church. The decline into apostasy began with the presidency of Heber J. Grant, when the keys of priesthood authority were removed, culminating with the acceptance of a black man into the priesthood.

Peterson did not see his new organization as a replacement of the Mormon Church. The purpose of Christ's Church is to provide a righteous branch so those who choose to follow the Lord completely can find the correct organization, experience the gifts of the spirit, and be served by the fullness of the ordinances. In establishing the church, Peterson is fulfilling the prophecy from Mormon scripture concerning the setting of God's house in order under Joseph Smith, Jr. The beliefs and practices are similar to those of the Apostolic United Order, except for the belief that Peterson had been given the keys to the priesthood and is President Prophet of it. At the time of Peterson's death, his son, Gerald W. Peterson, Jr., received the keys to the priesthood. He currently leads the church.

Membership: Not reported.

Periodicals: *The Branch.* Send orders to Box 1329, St. George, UT 84770.

★1164★
Church of Jesus Christ of the Saints in Zion
Current address not obtained for this edition.

The Church of Jesus Christ of the Saints of Zion emerged in 1984 among a group of Mormons headed by Roger Billings, who had moved from Utah to Blue Springs, Missouri in 1979. They had planned to build a community, but it was disrupted by the introduction of teachings on polygamy and other beliefs which disagreed with those of the Church of Jesus Christ of Latter-day Saints. As a result of his teaching activity, Billings and his supporters were excommunicated from the church. They organized independently.

It is the position of the Church of Jesus Christ of the Saints in Zion that polygamy was condoned by God, though it is not practiced by the group. However, new relationships based upon the addition of multiple "spiritual wives" (women who will be married for all eternity to their spiritual husbands), have been created. Billings, as head of the church, performs spiritual marriage ceremonies.

Membership: There is only one congregation, with less than twenty members.

★1165★
Church of the First Born
(Defunct)

When Joel LeBaron, founder of the Church of the First Born of the Fullness of Times, claimed Patriarchal Priesthood for himself, his brother, Ross Wesley LeBaron, rejected Joel's claim in favor of himself. He thus left his brother's church and formed the Church of the First Born. The statement of beliefs published by Ross Lebaron emphasized belief in Michael, the Eternal Father, and in his Son, Jesus Christ, and in Joseph Smith, the witness and testator. The Church of the First Born was established originally by Adam and restored in Joseph Smith. A belief in One Mighty and Strong to come was firmly held. LeBaron disincorporated the church in the early 1980s.

Sources:

LeBaron, Ross W. *The Redemption of Zion.* Colonia LeBaron, Chih., Mexico: Church of the First-Born, [1962].

LeBaron, Verlan M. *The LeBaron Family.* Lubbock, TX: The Author, 1981.

★1166★
Church of the First Born of the Fullness of Times
5854 Mira Serana
El Paso, TX 79912

Church of the First Born of the Fullness of Times dates to the participation among Mormon fundamentalist groups of the LeBaron family—Alma Dayer LeBaron, his sons Floren LeBaron, Benjamin F. LeBaron, Alma LeBaron, Jr., Ross Wesley LeBaron, Ervil LeBaron, Joel LeBaron, Verlan M. LeBaron, and a cousin, Owen LeBaron. Alma Dayer LeBaron who, with his family, was a member of the Church of Jesus Christ of Latter-day Saints was affiliated with polygamist leader Joseph White Musser as early as 1936. In 1934, Benjamin claimed to be the One Mighty and Strong, the prophetic figure mentioned in the Mormon writings (*Doctrines and Covenants 85*), and he convinced several members of the family to substantiate his claims as a prophet. In 1944 the LeBaron family was excommunicated. From then until 1955, most of the family associated with the "fundamentalist" colony in Mexico directed by Rulon C. Allred, leader of the Apostolic United Brethren. The LeBaron family members were in the process of setting up a united order (a communal economic style of living) when, in 1955, they decided to leave Allred's Mexican colony.

Joel, Ross Wesley, and Floren worked out the basic order of their own church and incorporated on September 1, 1955, under the name of the Church of the First Born of the Fullness of Times. Joel claimed to have the "Patriarchal Priesthood" and had a revelation directing Allred to become his councilor. Allred rejected the invitation. Both Benjamin and Ross Wesley also rejected his claims.

Joel claimed a line of priesthood succession through his father, Alma, Sr., to Alma's grandfather, Benjamin F. Johnson, who was secretly ordained by Joseph Smith. (Mormon authorities point out that Johnson accepted the Manifesto of 1890 abolishing polygamy.) Joel claimed that the priesthood was superior to the presidency of the church, the apostles, and seventies.

Joel LeBaron led the Church of the First Born of the Fullness of Times until he was murdered in 1972. He was succeeded by his brother Verlan, who was killed in an automobile accident in 1981. The current leader of the Church is Siegfried Widmar. For a number of years the Church issued a magazine, *Ensign*, in which most of its doctrinal and polemical works were published.

Membership: The group is small, containing several hundred members at most. Most of the membership is located in Mexico.

Sources:

LeBaron, Verlan M. *Economic Democracy Under Eternal Law*. El Paso, TX: Church of the Firstborn of the Fullness of Time, 1963.

___. *The LeBaron Story*. Lubbock, TX: The Author, 1981.

Priesthood Expounded. Mexican Mission of the Church of the Firstborn of the Fullness of Times, 1956.

Richards, Henry W. *A Reply to "The Church of the Firstborn of the Fullness of Times"*. Salt Lake City: The Author, 1965.

Silver, Stephen M. "Priesthood and Presidency, An Answer to Henry W. Richards." *Ensign* 2, no. 11 (January 1963): 1-127.

Widmar, Siegfried J. *The Political Kingdom of God*. El Paso, TX: The Author, 1975.

★1167★
Church of the Lamb of God
Current address not obtained for this edition.

The Church of the Lamb of God was formed in 1970 by Ervil LeBaron, who had held the second-highest office in the Church of the First Born of the Fullness of Times, founded by his brother, Joel LeBaron. In that year Ervil was dismissed from the Church of the First Born of the Fullness of Times. As the leader of his new church, he claimed full authority over all of the polygamy-practicing groups, and asserted an authority to execute anyone who would refuse to accept him as the representative of God.

Beginning at the time of the establishment of the Church of the Lamb of God, a string of murders and felonious attacks plagued the polygamy-practicing Mormons. On August 20, 1972, Joel LeBaron was shot to death in Ensenada, Mexico. On June 16, 1975, Dean Vest, an associate of Joel LeBaron, was killed near San Diego. On May 10, 1977, Dr. Rulon C. Allred, leader of the Apostolic United Brethren, a rival polygamy group, was brutally murdered in his chiropractic office in Salt Lake City while attending patients. On May 14, 1977, Merlin Kingston, another polygamy leader, narrowly survived an attempt on his life. At least thirteen other polygamy-practicing Mormons were killed before Ervil was arrested, tried, convicted, and sentenced in 1980 for the death of Allred. He died in prison the following year of natural causes.

After Ervil LeBaron's death, his son Aaron LeBaron emerged as the new leader of the group. Deaths associated with the group continued, mostly prominenly the the 1988 slayings of Ed Marston, Mark and Duane Chynoweth, and Duane's eight-year-old daughter, Jenny. In 1997, Aaron LeBaron was convicted of conspiracy to commit murder and racketeering in connection with these deaths. Reportedly, these former members were killed because the church's belief that anyone who left the group had to be killed before the members could inherit God's kingdom on Earth.

Membership: Not reported. Since the death of Ervil LeBaron, there have been conflicting reports of the disbanding of the Church. Its present status is unknown.

Sources:

Fessier, Michael, Jr. "Ervil LeBaron, the Man Who Would Be God." *New West* (January 1981): 80-84, 112-17.

LeBaron, Ervil. *An Open Letter to a Former Presiding Bishop*. San Diego: The Author, 1972.

___. *Priesthood Expounded*. Buenaventurea, Mexico: Mexican Mission of the Church of the Firstborn of the Fullness of Times, 1956.

★1168★
Church of the New Covenant in Christ
Box 3910
Salem, OR 97302

The Evangelical Church of Christ was founded in 1975 as the Church of Christ Patriarchal by John W. Bryant (b. 1946), a former member of the Apostolic United Brethren. Bryant was baptized into the Church of Jesus Christ of Latter-Day Saints in 1964 and became a missionary to Japan a short time later. However, in the early 1970s he became convinced of the truth of polygamy and joined the polygamy-practicing order headed by Rulon C. Allred.

In 1974 Bryant began to receive new revelations (he had received periodic revelations since childhood.) He was visited by John the Beloved Disciple (one of Jesus' original twelve disciples), who instructed him to form an "Order of the Ancients" among those who would be led of the Holy Spirit. In 1975 he was taken to the City of Enoch where, in the presence of Joseph White Musser, founder of the Apostolic United Order, and Joseph Smith, Jr., founder of the Church of Jesus Christ of Latter-Day Saints, he received the fullness of keys to the Kingdom of God (i.e., the priesthood, patriarchy, and presidency of the church). Bryant received some immediate support from other fundamentalist Mormons, and in 1979 the group moved to the Fair Haven Ranch near Las Vegas, Nevada to establish a communal life together. The ranch was lost when they were unable to keep up payments, and in 1981 Bryant, five of his six wives, and a number of members moved to a farm near Salem, Oregon.

During the early 1980s, Bryant continued his religious development. He began to question what he saw to be problems in fundamentalism: focus upon polygamy and male dominance, rather than Christ. That questioning led to what he termed a "born-again" relationship with Christ, a change reflected in the change of the church's name. Not wanting to split up the family, Bryant remained a polygamist, but reoriented family life away from its patriarchal structure. He has also vowed to take no more wives and ceased promoting the idea.

By the mid 1980s, over 100 church members moved into the Salem area. Attempts to convert the large barn on the Bryant farm into a church have been blocked by neighborhood action. In the wake of problems both internal and external, Bryant left the church and it soon disintegrated. However, he reorganized many of the former members into the Church of the New Covenant in Christ, which continues many of the teachings of and utilizes many of Bryant's writings issued by the former Evangelical Church of Christ.

Membership: In 1985 there were approximately 120 families and one congregation.

Sources:

King, Marsha. "Changing Beliefs Led Family to Rearrange Plural Union." *The Seattle Times* (October 13, 1985).

★1169★
Confederate Nations of Israel
% Alexander Joseph, Presiding King
Long Haul, Box 151
Big Water, UT 84741

Alexander Joseph was a member of the Apostolic United Brethren. He withdrew in 1975 and led a group of 13 families in homesteading a colony in southern Utah. Then he moved to Glen Canyon City, now Big Water, Utah, where he founded the Church of Jesus Christ in Solemn Assembly and, in 1978, the Confederate Nations of Israel, which eventually superceded the other church. Joseph envisions the Nations as composing an operational government of 144 seats, each to be filled by a current king of the particular nation that owns the seat. The nations are divided into three quorums: judges (24), senate (70), and the Council of Fifty (50). Each kings acts as an independent sovereign and acts upon his own patriarchical authority.

The confederacy convenes formally twice every year for public business meetings at the vernal and autumnal equinoxes. As of 1988, the quorums had 71 of 144 seats filled; among those holding seats were Dennis Short and Ogden Kraut (independent writers known for their defense of polygamy). Two late members of the Church of the First Born of the Fullness of Times, Norman LeBaron and Keith Batemen, had been slated to hold a seat.

Joseph has issued a brief statement of belief, "Alexander's Creed," which espouses belief in posterity, reality, freedom, responsibility, justice, grace, and patriarchial government. The church teaches polygamy, and many members enter celestial marriage contracts, but it is not a requirement for members. The church does teach that the kingdom of God is fully comprehended in the marriage relationship and cannot be fully comprehended apart from it. Joseph has married over 20 times, and as of 1984 he had 18 children.

There are two independent organizations founded by church members, the Order of the Rainbow and the Order of Diana. The former, for men, has as its constitution the statement, "The father presides." The latter, founded by Joseph's wife, Elizabeth Joseph, for women, has as its constituting statement, Isaiah 4:1.

Membership: In 1988 the Confederate Nations reported 250 members and 1 congregation with 70 ministers.

Educational Facilities: University of the Great Spirit, Big Water, Utah.

Periodicals: *The Laws That Govern the Confederate Nations of Israel.*

Sources:

Fulton, Gilbert A., Jr. *That Manifesto*. Kearns, UT: Deseret Publishing Co., 1974.

Joseph, Alexander. *Dry Bones*. Big Water, UT: University of the Great Spirit Press, 1979.

Kraut, Odgen. *Polygamy in the Bible*. Salt Lake City, UT: Kraut's Pioneer Press, 1983.

Short, Dennis R. *For Men Only*. Sandy, UT: The Author, 1977.

★1170★
Millennial Church of Jesus Christ
Current address not obtained for this edition.

Claiming to be the spiritual successor to Ervil LeBaron, founder of the Church of the Lamb of God, Leo Peter Evoniuk LeBaron organized the Millennial Church of Jesus Christ in the mid-1980s. According to a revelation given him in 1984, Ervil LeBaron was delivered by the Lord God from his enemies and now sits on God's right hand. The keys held by Ervil LeBaron have passed to Leo LeBaron. The revelation asserted the necessity of the restoration of the Melchizedek Priesthood and the Patriarchial Order, or damnation will follow. LeBaron and his associate Grand Patriarchs, Paul L. Gardunio, Bill Rios, and Raul Rios, have inherited the sealing keys formerly held by Ervil LeBaron. Their task is to seal the 144,000 Grand Patriarchs of the Twelve Tribes of Israel, whom God had hidden from the world previously. They are the only persons entrusted with that sealing power.

Evoniuk disappeared suddenly in 1987. It is feared that, like others in the dissident polygamy community, he has become the victim of foul play.

Membership: Not reported.

★1171★
Perfected Church of Jesus Christ Immaculate Latter-Day Saints
(Defunct)

Among the most unusual of the polygamy-practicing churches was the Perfected Church of Jesus Christ Immaculate Latter-Day Saints, founded by William C. Conway, D.D., of Redondo Beach, California, who claimed to be "the scribe and goodwill ambassador for 500,000 Indians," members of the Perfected Church. Conway claimed that when the Church of Jesus Christ of Latter-day Saints rejected the six commandments given to Joseph Smith (concerned with the united order and plural marriage primarily), Jesus Christ walked out of the church to Walker Lake, Nevada. There, in the spring of 1890, directed by visions and dreams, several hundred Indians had assembled. Jesus re-established the kingdom as it was in pre-Edenic days and gave Joseph Smith's authority to one of their members, a young white Indian from Yu-ka-tan, named Eachta Eacha Na. He is identified with the One Mighty and Strong, the prophetic personage mentioned in the Mormon scriptures, the *Doctrines and Covenants 85*. The reincarnated Joseph Smith and Angel Moroni (an angel mentioned in the Book of Mormon) are with the One Mighty and Strong.

In 1930, additional keys of authority were transferred by Lorin C. Woolley, founder of the United Order Effort, largest of the Mormon fundamentalist groups. Woolley was supposedly one of the five authorized to continue plural marriage by President John Taylor of the LDS Church.

Mr. Conway also claims that Moroni "succeeded in perfecting a plan of instruction that abolished mensturation among the woman folk," and that Jesus had explained the technique of immaculate conception. Babies conceived immaculately stay for twelve months in the womb and are immune to all disease.

Membership: This church is presumed to be defunct as of 1985.

★1172★
Suns Ahman Israel-I:A:O:
Chevrah B'Qor Community
HC 65, Box 535
Canebeds, AZ 86022

Suns Ahman Ishrael was founded at Saratoga Hot Springs, Utah, at dawn on January 25, 1981, by presiding Patriarch David Asia Israel and four other former members of the Church of Jesus Christ of Latter-day Saints. The group believes in the continued visitation of and revelation by angels, and Davied Israel regularly receives such revelations in the form of morning and evening oracles. Besides the Bible and the *Book of Mormon*, a wide variety of materials are accepted as scripture, including ancient apocryphal writings (such as the *Gospel of Thomas*, the *Gospel of Philip*, the *Book of Enoch*, the writings found at Nag Hammadi) and modern Mormon revelations (such as the *Oracles of Mohonri* and *The Order of the Sons of Zadok*). Members believe in a secret oral tradition which passed from Moses to the Essenes, the Gnostics, and eventually to Joseph Smith, Jr. That tradition is preserved in such books as the *Pistis Sophia*, an ancient Gnostic text, and the *Sephir Yetzira*, a prime text from Hassidic Judaism.

A 22-item statement of "S.A.I. Beliefs" affirms belief in a heavenly hierarchy consisting of a Heavenly Father and Mother, their son, Jesus Christ, the Holy Spirit, angels and archangels, and ministers of the flame (just men made perfect). Human beings are the literal offspring of the heavenly parents and have come into earthly existence to experience the mystery of mortality. Redemption for humans comes only through surrendering their life to Yeshu-Maria the Christ and subsequently developing a relationship to them in the holy temple ordinances and ritualistic ceremonies. The Suns Ahman Ishrael also follows the Old Testament feasts and holy days.

The Suns Ahman Ishrael had absorbed much of its ritual practice from the Christian Kabbalah. A monthly ritual cycle begins with each new moon when baptisms are held. On the second lunar day, charisms (holy annointings) are made and on the third day a eucharistic supper is prepared. The fourth through the fifteenth days are for participation in ceremonial priesthood rituals. The full moon is a time for a monthly feast.

The Suns Ahman Ishrael is headed by a presiding patriarch and matriarch, under whom function (when the organization is at full strength) a first presidency (of three people), a council of twelve apostles, seven arch seventies, and twelve stake princes. Each stake is headed by twelve high counselmen, a quorum of seventy, and twelve bishops. The church believes in the perfect equality of the sexes. Women are accepted into the priesthood on an equal basis with men. During the 1980s, SAI has developed an international following with branches in England (Independent Church of Jesus Christ of Latter Day Saints), Switzerland, Norway, Japan and the Netherlands.

Membership: In 1995 SAI had three centers in the United States with a combined membership of less than 100.

Educational Facilities: School of the Prophets, Canebeds, Arizona.

Periodicals: *Stone Magazine.*

Sources:

The Sacred Scrolls of the Sons Ahman Israel. LaVern, UT: Sons Ahman Israel, n.d.

★1173★
United Order Effort
Colorado City, AZ 86021

The United Effort Order, the largest of the polygamy-practicing groups among the Mormons, began in 1929 when Lorin C. Woolley organized a council of people dedicated to seeing that no year passed without at least one child being born within a plural marriage. Woolley, who claimed to have been commissioned by Mormon Church President John Taylor in 1886, acted only after all of the others present at that time were dead. Woolley had been actively publishing and spreading the story of the authority he and others had from the late-president of the Church of Jesus Christ of Latter-day Saints since 1912 but experienced only modest success until 1929, when Joseph White Musser compiled the various accounts of the 1886 revelation and published them. He also joined J. Leslie Broadbent, John Y. Barlow, Charles Zitting, Legrand Woolley, and Louis Kelsh as a member of the council.

Lorin Woolley died in 1934. He was succeeded by Broadbent, who died a few months later, who in turn was succeeded by Barlow, the man most known for his early leadership of the group and of its main colony in rural Arizona, Short Creek (presently known as Colorado City). Short Creek had become a haven for polygamists who had gathered there in the late 1920s to escape the problems created by both law enforcement agents and the increased discipline of the Church of Jesus Christ of Latter-Day Saints. Soon after becoming leader of the group, Barlow contacted some of the more vocal advocates of polygamy at Short Creek and worked out

an agreement between them and the council. Eventually he moved to Short Creek with some of his followers, and within a few years the polygamists dominated the settlement. Barlow created the United Trust, incorporated formally in 1942 as the United Effort Plan, but commonly known as the United Effort Order. Meanwhile, Musser, who remained in Salt Lake City, began publication of *The Truth*, the periodical for the group, and the most influential organ promoting polygamy by any group.

Under Barlow's leadership the colony at Short Creek flourished and the United Effort spread throughout Mormon communities in the West, particularly in Idaho, Montana, and Southern California. Many of the polygamists who had fled to Mexico in previous years also accepted Barlow's authority. Having survived a 1935 raid which attempted to destroy the Short Creek community, the only major trouble for the United Effort came in 1944 when an anti-polygamy crusade swept through Salt Lake City. Musser and other leaders were arrested and spent several months in jail while the crusade lasted.

Barlow's death in 1951 led to internal crisis and schism within the United Effort. Musser, the new president of the ruling council, was in poor health, and many people rejected his appointments of his physician, Rulon C. Allred, and a Mexican leader, Margarito Bautista, to fill council vacancies. In response, Musser disbanded the entire council and appointed a new one made up of his supporters. That action split the group, the majority of which supported the leadership at Short Creek. The older members of the council elected a new president, Charles Zitting, while Musser organized his following as the Apostolic United Brethren.

Zitting died within months of his election and was succeeded by Leroy Johnson, a council member added by Barlow. Johnson was almost immediately plunged into a new crisis. On July 26, 1953, the governor of Arizona conducted a massive raid on Short Creek. Most of the men were arrested and the women and children placed in the state's custody. Only after several months, during which time the governor realized the political and financial disaster of his actions, were the colonists allowed to return to their homes where they have lived quietly in recent decades.

The United Effort Order is among the strictest of the several polygamy-practicing groups. It approves of sex only for the intention of producing children and demands abstinence while a female is either pregnant or breast-feeding.

Membership: Not reported. Of the approximately 30,000 polygamists, it is estimated that 7,000 to 10,000 are affiliated with the United Order Effort. Several hundred reside at the colonies at Colorado City, Arizona, and nearby Hilldale, Utah.

Sources:

Anderson, Max J. *The Polygamy Story: Fiction or Fact.* Salt Lake City: Publishers Press, 1979.

Bradlee, Ben, Jr., and Dale Van Alta. *Prophet of Blood.* New York: G. P. Putnam's Sons, 1981.

Musser, Joseph White. *Celestial or Plural Marriage.* Salt Lake City: Truth Publishing Co., 1944.

Young, Kimball. *Isn't One Wife Enough.* New York: Henry Holt and Company, 1954.

★1174★
The Watchmen on the Towers of Latter Day Israel
Current address not obtained for this edition.

The Watchmen on the Towers of Latter Day Israel was formed in the early 1970s by Elders Henry Braun, Arno Mittenberg, and others who were excommunicated from the Church of Jesus Christ of Latter-day Saints because of their protest of changes in doctrine and practice within the Church, especially on the issue of polygamy. As a result of their problems with the church, the elders of the Watchmen began a study of the position of the church in the nineteenth century as opposed to its present beliefs and practices and have concluded that modern Mormonism is completely apostate.

Membership: Not reported.

Sources:

Braun, Henry. *Celestial Marriage: For All Time and All Eternity.* Salt Lake City, UT: The Author, 1984. 987 pp.

___. *Thoughts of a Mormon Convert, Pro and Con.* 3 vols. Salt Lake City, UT: Watchmen on the Towers of Latter Day Israel, 1974-76.

Mormon Fundamentalism and the LSD Church. 2 vols. Salt Lake City, UT: Watchmen on the Towers of Latter Day Israel, 1975.

Shields, Steven L. *Divergent Paths of the Restoration.* Los Angeles: Restoration Research, 1990. 336 pp.

Missouri Mormons

★1175★
Center Branch of the Lord's Remnant
709 W. Maple
Independence, MO 64050

Among the people who left the Reorganized Church of Jesus Christ of Latter Day Saints following the 1984 revelation given by President Wallace B. Smith on women's ordination were Robert E. Baker and members of the church's Seventy. Because of Baker's longtime dissent to the direction the church was taking, he was silenced. In the fall of 1984 he withdrew and established the Gathering Center, a center, as the name implies, to facilitate the latter-day gathering of the Saints into the Center Place (Independence, Missouri). Alternative church services are held at the Gathering Center and a number of services for members are provided.

More recently, Baker has left the Center Branch which continues as an indpendent Restoration congregation in Independence. It holds regular church services and has a program for feeding and clothing the needy.

Membership: Not reported. It is estimated that several hundred people are affiliated with the single congregation in Independence, Missouri.

Sources:

Baker, Robert E. *As It Was in the Days of Noah.* Independence, MO: Old Path Publishers, 1985.

★1176★
Church of Christ at Halley's Bluff
Schell City, MO 64783

The Church of Christ at Halley's Bluff, also known as the Church of Christ at Zion's Retreat, was founded in 1932 by former members of the Church of Christ (Temple Lot) who left in a dispute over the messages of Otto Fetting. A group centered in Denver, Colorado, and led by E. E. Long and Thomas B. Nerren had accepted Fetting's messages but had remained within the Temple Lot when the majority of his followers had left. The original congregation was located in Denver, Colorado, but by the end of the decade five other congregations had joined the small denomination. Nerren began to receive revelations. In 1941, in response to such a revelation, the church moved its headquarters to Zion's Retreat, a 441-acre tract of land in northeast Vernon County, about seventy miles south of Independence, Missouri, the site of Zion according to Mormon prophet Joseph Smith, Jr.

In 1942 the congregation in Cranston, Rhode Island, moved to Zion's Retreat. They were soon joined by the remaining members in Denver, and the group in Independence came in 1946. The remaining congregation, located in Delevan, Wisconsin, separated from the group in Missouri in 1966 and continues to exist today as an independent congregation.

The peace within the church in Missouri was disturbed in the 1960s after Daniel Gayman, one of its pastors, became editor of the church's periodical. He began to advocate strong racist and antiblack sentiments. Then in 1972 Gayman called a meeting of the church, deposed several bishops, and had himself elected to lead the church. The deposed bishops, General Hall and Duane Gayman, and their supporters filed suit and the court returned the property and the use of the church's several names to them. Meanwhile, the Hall-Gayman group had reincorporated as the Church of Christ at Halley's Bluff.

With the loss of its members in Wisconsin and the defection of Daniel Gayman's supporters, the Church of Christ at Halley's Bluff remains as but a small remnant within the family of Latter Day Saint Churches.

Membership: There are less than 100 members.

★1177★
Church of Christ (David Clark)
PO Box 126
Oak Grove, MO 64075

The Church of Christ (David Clark) was founded in 1985 by David B. Clark, a former member of the Reorganized Church of Jesus Christ of Latter Day Saints, and his wife Gwyn Clark. The Clarks had come to feel that the Reorganized Church had drifted far away from the standards and teachings of the Bible and the Book of Mormon and were actually teaching doctrines in contradiction to them. The Clarks teach that the church was established on May 15, 1829, when an angelic messenger bestowed ministerial authority upon Joseph Smith, Jr., and Oliver Cowdery, who subsequently baptized each other. The Church of Christ that was established in 1829 has continued as a remnant though the larger organization fell away into apostasy.

The Church of Christ began in November 1985 when the Clarks began to hold a scripture study in their home. They developed a small following, acquired a meeting house, and in May 1987 began to issue a newsletter, *The Return.*

While adhering closely to the King James Version of the Bible and the *The Record of the Nephites,* (Book of Mormon), the church does not consider other Mormon scripture, the Doctrine and Covenants, the Pearl of Great Price, or the Inspired Version of the Bible, to be authoritative.

Periodicals: *The Return.*

Sources:

Clark, David. *The Path Which Leads to the Kingdom of God.* Oak Grove, MO: The Church of Christ, 1991.

Shields, Steven L. *Divergent Paths of the Restoration.* Los Angeles: Restoration Research, 1990.

★1178★
Church of Christ (Fetting/Bronson)
1138 E. Gudgell
Independence, MO 64055

On February 4, 1927, Otto Fetting, one of the twelve apostles of the Church of Christ (Temple Lot), claimed that John the Baptist had appeared to him and told him that it was time to build the temple. Other messages gave instructions concerning the building of the temple.

The twelfth message became the matter of lengthy controversy. It said, "Let those who come to the church of Christ be baptized, that they may rid themselves of the traditions and sins of men." The members of the Temple Lot church had great difficulty with this passage. Many had come into the church by transfer from the Reorganized Church of Jesus Christ of Latter Day Saints, and had not been baptized upon entering the Temple Lot church. They intepreted the message to call for a rebaptism of the entire church membership. A conference held in October 1929 denounced the idea of rebaptizing the church. Fetting was not allowed to speak on the baptism question. After the conference, he was silenced and told to wait for a referendum vote at the conference the following April. For whatever reason, he did not wait, and after the conference, he, Apostle Walter L. Gates, and Thomas B. Nerren were baptized. Others also received a new baptism and in the fall of 1929, all who had been baptized were disfellowshipped. The Church of Christ (Fetting) was begun by Fetting's followers, approximately 1,400 or about one-third of the Temple Lot church at the time.

Fetting continued to report receiving messages until his death in 1933. There were thirty messages in all. Several years after Fetting's death, a member in Colorado, W. A. Draves, began to report receiving messages. At first, these messages were accepted by the larger body of the church. However, some members, especially those in Louisiana and Mississippi, rejected Draves almost from the beginning and before the end of the decade reorganized as the Church of Christ (Restored). Eventually, in 1943, the church rejected Draves. After a court suit, which the Draves' supporters lost, they reorganized as the Church of Christ with the Elijah Message.

During years following the departure of Draves' supporters, leaders of the Fetting church began to advocate the keeping of the Saturday Sabbath. The issue was debated for many years until 1956, when the Twelve Apostles, having reached an agreement on the issue, adopted sabbatarianism for the entire church. The church is organized like the Church of Christ (Temple Lot). The church uses the *Book of Mormon* (1908 edition), but does not accept either the *Book of Commandments* or the *Doctrine and Covenants*, used by other Restoration groups.

Membership: In 1988, the church reported approximately 1,500 members, 24 ministers, and 12 congregations in the United States and an additional 500 members in Nigeria.

Periodicals: *The Voice of Warning.*

Sources:

Fetting, Otto. *The Midnight Message.* Independence, MO: Church of Christ (Temple Lot), [1930].

Smith, Willard J. *Fetting and His Messenger's Messages.* Port Huron, MI: The Author, [1936].

The Word of the Lord. Independence, MO: Church of Christ, 1935.

★1179★
Church of Christ Immanuel
Current address not obtained for this edition.

The Church of Christ Immanuel orginated in a split in the Flint, Michigan, congregation of the Church of Christ (Temple Lot). C. W. Morgan, the pastor of the group and one of the apostles in the Temple Lot church, began to teach that there was but one person in the Godhead (rather than the idea of multiple persons common to most Mormon churches) and in the 1930s was silenced. Under Morgan's influence, this group left the Church of Christ (Temple Lot) and sued for the local church property. In an out-of-court settlement, the new church, which became known as the Church of Christ Omnipotent, abandoned its original building and constructed a new meeting house. During this period they became familar with the Church of Christ (Bible and Book of Mormon) led by Pauline Hancock (d. 1962) in Independence, Missouri, which had been established for similar reasons. From them they absorbed some practices, such as using fermented wine in their communion services instead of grape juice.

After a period, some of the members formed a second congregation at Davison, Michigan, under the leadership of Leland Cory, Harold Graves, and Atwood Shelley. The new congregation was merely a convenience for members who did not wish to drive all the way to Flint. However, in 1975 C. W. Morgan died, and the small group of members in Flint, without a leader, sold their property and began to meet with the group in Davison, which had taken the name Church of Christ Immanuel.

Membership: Not reported. There are less than 100 members.

★1180★
Church of Christ (Leighton-Floyd/Burt)
Current address not obtained for this edition.

The Church of Christ (Leighton-Floyd/Burt) was founded in 1965 by former members of The Church of Christ "With the Elijah Message," Established Anew in 1929. That church had been established in 1943 as the Church of Christ Established Anew. However, between the 1964 and 1965 assemblies of the church, Elder W. A. Graves, whose messages from Elijah were guiding the church, reincorporated the church under its present name. Although nondoctrinal, that action led to a disagreement at the 1965 assembly. Apostle Howard Leighton-Floyd and Bishop H. H. Burt rejected the name change and led a withdrawal of members. The membership of the new church they established centered on an agricultural cooperative near Holden, Missouri, where Leighton-Floyd resided.

Shortly after the formation of the Church of Christ, Leighton-Floyd resigned from the new church and joined the Church of Christ (Temple Lot), leaving the small body without an apostle. It is their belief that someday Christ will restore the apostleship to them. After Leighton-Floyd's withdrawal, Burt assumed leadership of the group. He resides in Colorado Springs, Colorado. From 1965 to 1968 the church published a periodical, *The Banner of Truth.*

The church accepts the Bible, the *Book of Mormon,* the messages of Otto Fetting and some of the messages of W. A. Graves (up to the split in 1965). It also accepts some of the *Doctrines and Covenants* (without some of the recent additions by the Reorganized Church) and parts of the *Book of Commandments.* They have a strong belief that in the near future the Lord will take the lead in the building of a temple in Independence, Missouri. The church practices baptism by immersion and uses the sacramental prayers in the book of Mormon (Moroni 4 & 5) in the ordinance of the Lord's Supper. Wine is used in the Lord's Supper.

Membership: Not Reported. At last report, some 35 members resided at the cooperative in Holden, Missouri.

Sources:

Shields, Steven L. *Divergent Paths of the Restoration.* Los Angeles: Restoration Press, 1990. 336 pp.

★1181★
Church of Christ, Nondenominational Bible Assembly
(Defunct)

The Church of Christ, Nondenominational Bible Assembly, grew out of a splintering movement among former members of the Reorganized Church of Jesus Christ of Latter-Day Saints and the Church of Christ (Temple Lot) in the 1940s. The church was founded and led in its first generation by Pauline Hancock. Hancock was the daughter of a leader in the Reorganized Church. In the mid-1920s she sided with those church members who protested the realignment of authority in the Reorganized Church into the church president's hands and in 1926 she joined the Church of Jesus Christ (Protest Group). She was the church's secretary for most of the years of its existence, but also worked within a congregation of the Church of Christ (Temple Lot). In 1931, when the Protest Church disbanded, she followed the majority of members in joining the Church of Christ (Temple Lot). Hancock continued as a powerful figure and teacher in the congregation of the former Protest group.

Over the years Hancock began to absorb the idea of the single Godhead, a more orthodox Christian understanding of God, as opposed to the generally accepted understanding of Mormonism of God as being several personages. This was an opinion which some Mormons held, but was not generally taught within the church. During the 1940s, she also began to lead a Friday evening study group which researched apparent discrepancies in the Bible, the Book of Mormon, and the Doctrine & Covenants (the third

Mormon scripture). Gradually, the group began to believe that the Reorganized Church taught a number of ideas which contradicted the Bible and the Book of Mormon.

Underlying her teaching role, Hancock had experienced several visions over the years. In January 1950, responding to another vision, she baptized a number of the people attending her church. She began to assume the full duties as pastor of the congregation, including leadership of the Sunday meetings. She cited Joseph Smith's ''ordination'' of Emma Smith, his wife, as precedent for her assuming the pastoral role. Asked to leave the church property, the new Church of Christ purchased a lot at Crysler and Linden streets in Independence, Missouri. The congregation became known as the Church of Christ (Bible and Book of Mormon Teaching). Over the next decade Hancock and the church departed from numerous doctrines held by most Mormons.

The early 1970s became a critical period in the history of the group. During 1973 the group discovered and accepted as factual evidence that Joseph Smith, Jr. was a fraud. At that point the group decided it must discontinue any use of the Book of Mormon. On November 24, 1973, the church issued a statement which appeared in the local newspaper to the effect that the Book of Mormon was not of divine origin and that the group would henceforth rely solely upon the Bible.

In subsequent years the church moved toward an orthodox evangelical Christian position. It taught the exclusive authority of the Bible, the Trinity, the deity of Christ, and the destiny of humanity in an afterlife in heaven or hell. Dissenting from Mormon beliefs, the church denied that the gospel was ever taken from the earth and hence there has been no need for a restoration. Baptism by immersion has been retained. After a generation of activity the church disbanded in the early 1990s and its members moved into other evangilical churches.

Sources:

Correspondence between Israel Smith and Pauline Hancock on Baptism for the Dead. Independence, MO: Church of Christ, [1955].

Hancock, Pauline. The Godhead, Is There More Than One? Independence, MO: Church of Christ, n.d.

___. Whence Came the Book of Mormon? Independence, MO: Church of Christ, [1958].

Wood, Samuel. The Infinite God. Fresno, CA: The Author, 1934.

★1182★
Church of Christ/Order of Zion
(Defunct)

The Church of Christ/Order of Zion was organized in Kansas City, Missouri, in 1918 by John Zahnd, a former member of the Reorganized Church of Jesus Christ of Latter-day Saints. Zahnd emerged during World War I as a critic of church organization. He rejected the idea of a First Presidency, seeing it as an umbilical office, and suggested that the church should be headed by the Twelve Apostles. His conclusions led him to believe that Joseph Smith, Jr., the prophet to whom Mormons look as their founder, should never have taken the authority to assume the presidency of the church, though he was undoubtedly a prophet of God. Equally important, Zahnd believed that the entire church should be living according to the united order, that is, communally.

The church was organized in September 1918. He began a periodical, The Order of Zion. The next month Zahnd received a revelation designating him an apostle (elder) and naming several men as priests and apostles. Two men were also named as bishops to handle the temporal affairs of the church. At the annual meeting of the church, 12 men among the elders were chosen by casting lots as the Twelve Apostles to head the church.

The church seems to have survived approximately a decade in the Kansas City area.

Sources:

Zahnd, John. All Things Common. Kansas City, MO: Church of Christ/Order of Zion, 1919. 68 pp.

___. The Old Paths. Kansas City, MO: Church of Christ/Order of Zion, 1920. 28 pp.

___. The Order of Zion. Kansas City, MO: Order of Zion, n.d. 89 pp.

★1183★
Church of Christ (Restored)
% Uel Sisk
609 C Lilac Pl.
John Knox Village
Lee's Summit, MO 64063

The Church of Christ (Restored) is one of several groups which grew out of the Church of Christ (Temple Lot) and the revelations received by Otto Fetting (1871-1933). Fetting was a member of the Church of Christ (Temple Lot) in 1927 when a heavenly Messenger, who identified himself as John the Baptist, began to appear to him. These messages, which concerned the building of the temple in the lot owned by the church, they were received warmly. However, the twelfth message ordered that all new members, including those transferring from the Reorganized Church of Jesus Christ of Latter Day Saints be rebaptized. This admonition led to great controversy. Eventually, in 1929, Fetting and his followers left and founded the Church of Christ (Restored). Fetting continued to receive messges, 30 in all.

Two significant events for the Church of Christ (Restored) were initiated in 1938. First, W. A. Draves claimed to have received messages from the same source as Fetting. The Church received these messages until 1943 when the majority of the church membership rejected them. Draves' supporters withdrew and founded the The Church of Christ, ''With the Elijah Message,'' Established Anew in 1929. Second, A. C. DeWold, being uninterested in Draves' mesages had left Missouri for Mississippi. He began to make converts and build the church in the South.

After the departure of Draves, the church enjoyed a period of relative calm until the late 1950s. At this time, Apostle S. T. Bronson began to advocate the keeping of the seventh-day sabbath. This proved unacceptable to some, and the church split the Independence, Missouri, area established the Church of Christ (Fetting/Bronson).

Beliefs. The Church of Christ (Restored) have teachings similar to the Church of Christ (Temple Lot), except that it accepts the revelations of Otto Fetting. These are published in a small volume entitled, The World of the Lord. Worship is on Sunday.

Organization. The Church is headed by the Quorum of Twelve Apostles and the several bishops. There is an annual assembly at which church business is conducted. Congregations are found in the South, in Missouri, along the West Coast. Foreign affiliated work can be found in Wales, Germany and the Netherlands.

Membership: In 1984 the church reported approximately 300 members in the United States. There were eight congregations and 16 ministers. There were also approximately 25 foreign members in Wales, Germany, and the Netherlands.

Periodicals: The Gospel Herald.

Sources:

Daniel, William A. Rediscovering the Messages. N.p., n.d.

Fetting, Otto. The Word of the Lord. Independence, MO: Church of Christ, 1938.

★1184★
Church of Christ (Restored)
4717 NE 15th Ave.
Vancouver, WA 98663

The Church of Christ Restored was founded in 1976 following the formal silencing of Paul Fishel, a patriarch/evangelist with the Reorganized Church of Jesus Christ of Latter Day Saints in Vancouver, Washington. The action by the reorganized church culminated a seven-year battle which had begun when the church published a set of position papers in 1969. These papers reflected the rise of a set of theologically trained leaders in the Independence, Missouri, headquarters. It was the opinion of conservative leaders, such as Fishel, that, among other problems, the papers presented a deviant concept of God and questioned the authority of the Book of Mormon. Fishel became a vocal critic of the "apostasy" he saw in the church leadership; he was warned by the church to stop his agitation.

Finally in 1976, the Reorganized Church formally silenced Fishel, disorganized the congregation, and established a new mission. With his supporters Fishel reorganized his congregation and, for a while, tried to remain within the reorganized church structure. Eventually, however, he incorporated the Church of Christ Restored. Hearing of the action in Vancouver, Robert Buller, a conservative leader in Michigan, contacted Fishel and subsequently opened several centers in that state. In 1984 Fishel traveled to Australia, and as a result congregations were formed in the states of Victoria and South Australia.

Membership: In 1992 the church reported several hundred members in the United States and approximately 50 in Australia.

Sources:

"Church of Christ Restored." *Restoration* 4, no. 3 (July 1985): 7.

Shields, Steven L. *Divergent Paths of the Restoration.* Los Angeles: Restoration Research, 1990.

★1185★
Church of Christ (Temple Lot)
Temple Lot
Independence, MO 65051

In the winter of 1852, a number of Latter Day Saints members met in the home of Granville Hedrick near Bloomington, Illinois. Word of polygamy in Utah had reached these Saints, and they withdrew their fellowship from the Utah brethren. Over the next few years they met sporadically, and in 1857 Granville Hedrick was set apart as their presiding elder. The group further declared their belief in the Book of Mormon and the 1835 *Doctrine and Covenants.* They took their stand against polygamy and baptism of the dead as practiced in Utah, and against the idea of "lineal succession of the presidency," which the Reorganized Church of Jesus Christ of Latter Day Saints (then called the New Organization) advocated. They adopted the name of the Church of Christ.

In 1863, Hedrick was elected president, and shortly thereafter he received a revelation that the Saints should be gathered back to Missouri, specifically to Independence, Missouri, which had been declared by Joseph Smith, Jr. to be the headquarters of the New Zion (Doctrine and Covenants 57:3). The Saints had been driven out of Independence, 1838-39, but while most of the Saints settled in Nauvoo, Illinois, some returned to their earlier homes near Bloomington, Illinois, in Woodford County, Illinois. These believers were the ones organized around Granville Hedrick and who, in the winter of 1866-67, began quietly to return to Independence and individually purchase the land that had been designated by Joseph Smith, Jr., the church's founder, for the building of the temple. On that land, they put up a small structure that now serves as the headquarters. The church grew slowly and steadily and in good relations with the Reorganized Church until the 1890s. At that time, the Reorganized Church took the Church of Christ to court to try and recover the temple lot. To do this, the Reorganized

Church produced a false deed which had supposedly been made out to Oliver Cowdery's children. Eventually, the Church of Christ was able to furnish proof that the deed was false.

In 1925, the Church of Christ voted to accept the 1833 *Book of Commandments* instead of the 1835 edition used prior to that time. Finding no mention of a first presidency, they abolished that office in favor of the 12 apostles.

The church reached its highest membership of approximately 4,000 about 1930. This followed some dissension in the Reorganized Church. In 1884, the Church of Christ had recognized other churches of the Restoration and declared their baptism valid. Thus, members of the Reorganized Church could easily transfer.

The influx of members was a short-lived boon as the church was immediately thrown into turmoil over the revelations of one of its 12 apostles, Otto Fetting. Fetting had reported receiving revelations since 1927. The church had acknowledged the revelation that centered upon instructions to begin building the temple. Excavations were begun on the temple in 1929 and corner stones were uncovered. In 1930, a revelation was received that was interpreted to mean that all the church members who had transferred from the Reorganized Church would have to be rebaptized. After this revelation, the church refused to accept Fetting, and in 1930 disfellowshipped him and his followers. In 1990, the church building on the Temple Lot was burned by an arsonist. Subsequently, a new building was erected and dedicated in 1991.

The Church of Christ (Temple Lot) is presided over by 12 apostles, a secretary, a few bishops, evangelists, and other officers. In 1864, a periodical, *The Truth Teller,* was begun. Its name was changed to *The Search Light* (1896) and then to *The Evening and Morning Star* (1900). The present periodical took its name in 1922.

Membership: At last report (1972), the church had 2,400 members, 32 congregations, and 188 ministers. At present, there are affiliated congregations in Mexico and The Netherlands.

Periodicals: *Zion's Advocate.* Send orders to Box 472, Independence, MO 64051.

Sources:

A Book of Commandments for the Government of the Church of Christ. Independence, MO: Church of Christ (Temple Lot), 1960.

Flint, B. C. *Autobiography.* Independence, MO: Privately printed, n.d.

___. *An Outline History of the Church of Christ (Temple Lot).* Independence, MO: Board of Publication, Church of Christ (Temple Lot), 1953.

___. *What About Israel?* Independence, MO: Board of Publication, Church of Christ (Temple Lot), 1967.

Smith, Arthur M. *Temple Lot Deed.* Independence, MO: Board of Publication, Church of Christ (Temple Lot), 1963.

Wheaton, Clarence L., and Angela Wheaton. *The Book of Commandments Controversy Reviewed.* Independence, MO: Church of Christ (Temple Lot), 1950.

★1186★
The Church of Christ "With the Elijah Message," Established Anew in 1929
608 Lacy Rd.
Independence, MO 64050

The Church of Christ (Fetting/Bronson) (discussed elsewhere in this chapter) received no revelations from 1933, when Otto Fetting died, to 1937. In October 1937, however, an elder, W. A. Draves, in Nucla, Colorado began to experience visits from John the Baptist (from whom Fetting had also claimed to have received his messages). These messages were officially accepted, at least through Message 56. Message 48 placed Draves among the church's 12 apostles. Then in 1943 some doubt was raised about the messages. He was accused of attaining information about members to use in the messages. A battle over control of the church's assets began at the 1943 assembly and led to a court suit in which those who supported the message lost. They continued on, however, and incorporated as the Church of Christ, Established Anew.

The Church of Christ is similar to the Church of Christ (Temple Lot). It shares the same history of the Temple Lot Church until 1930 and the history of the Church of Christ (Fetting/Bronson) until 1943. They worship on Sunday. They have also published their own edition of the Book of Mormon under the title, *The Record of the Nephites*. The Church has twelve apostles who reside in various areas of the country. A council of seven bishops manages the church property through the council's secretary. The church supports an active mission program and has congregations in India, Uganda, Kenya, Nigeria, France, Germany, and Italy.

Membership: In 1987 the church reported 2,500 members, 15 churches, and 125 ministers in the United States. There were 12,500 members worldwide.

Periodicals: *The Voice of Peace.*

Sources:

The Record of the Nephites. Independence, MO: Board of Publication, Church of Jesus Christ, "With the Elijah Message," Established Anew in 1929, 1970.

The Word of the Lord. Independence, MO: Board of Publication, Church of Jesus Christ, "With the Elijah Message," Established Anew in 1929, 1971.

★1187★
Church of Christ with the Elijah Message (Rogers)
Current address not obtained for this edition.

The Church of Jesus Christ with the Elijah Message was founded by Daniel Aaron Rodgers, who had been named an elder in The Church of Jesus Christ "With the Elijah Message," Established Anew in 1929, and while a member published a short work defending the inspiration of the messages of its prophetic messenger, W. A. Draves. The following year he was removed from the church, but he continued to preach under the same name as his former church. He accepted the doctrines and practices of his former church, and continued to circulate the *Record of the Nephites* (that church's edition of the Book of Mormon) by covering the church's address in Independence, Missouri, with that of his own. He also began a periodical, *The Missionary Newsletter* (later *The Standard*).

Rogers gained some fame as an evangelist who had absorbed some themes from popular pentecostalism. He emphasized faith-healing and the gifts of the Holy Spirit. During this period, he made the news when he unsuccessfully attempted to resurrect his mother whom he had kept frozen for a month following her death in February 1978. He briefly reconciled with the Church of Christ with the Eliajah Message parent body in 1983, but was soon operating independently again.

Membership: Not reported.

Sources:

Roger, Daniel Aaron. *The Angel Spoken of in Rev. 14:6 Speaks, Warning All People of the Second Coming of Christ.* Harrison, AR: The Author, n.d. 6 pp.

Shields, Steven L. *Divergent Paths of the Restoration.* Los Angeles: Restoration Press, 1990. 336 pp.

★1188★
Church of Jesus Christ of Latter-day Saints (William Smith)
(Defunct)

William Smith was the brother of Joseph Smith, Jr., the prophet and founder of the Church of Jesus Christ of Latter-day Saints. Following the death of both Joseph and Hyrum Smith (another brother), William emerged as the leading member of the family in the church. However, he had significant disagreements with Brigham Young who succeeded Joseph Smith as the new president of the church following Smith's assassination in 1844. When Young demoted William Smith, who had been the church's patriarch, Smith responded by publishing a statement comparing Young to Pontius Pilate. On October 19, 1845, Young excommunicated Smith.

Cut off, Smith associated with James Jesse Strang for a while, but reappeared in 1847 with the announcement that he was the church's new president. He excommunicated the leadership that had acknowledged Young. Smith's actions, occurring as Young was moving with a large group of the Saints to Utah, were intended to call together those who had remained behind in the Midwest. He called for a gathering in Lee County, Illinois. He was assisted by Aaron Hook whom he had appointed his counselor. A second center developed in Covington, Kentucky, but was lost in the controversy following Smith's acknowledgement that he was open to the practice of polygamy. In 1849 Smith gained the support of Lyman Wight, and his colony in Texas came into Smith's church.

Smith's following never stabilized and within a few years dissolved. The majority of the membership, including Smith, joined the Reorganized Church of Jesus Christ of Latter Day Saints, which had been organized in 1852.

Sources:

Shields, Steven L. *Divergent Paths of the Restoration.* Los Angeles: Restoration Research, 1990.

___. *The Latter Day Saint Churches: An Annotated Bibliography.* New York: Garland Publishing, 1987.

★1189★
Church of Jesus Christ (Protest Movement)
(Defunct)

The Church of Jesus Christ (Protest Movement) was founded in 1926 by Thomas W. Williams (1975-1931) and others who protested the actions of Frederick M. Smith, then president of the Reorganized Church of Jesus Christ of Latter Day Saints. In 1924 in what became known as the "Supreme Directional Control Controversy," Smith asked for more direct managerial authority over the programs of the church. Many saw his request as a move to gain power at the expense of members and other leaders. Several hundred members signed and presented to the 1925 church general conference a formal document opposing the governmental changes. When their protest was rebuffed and further attempts to be heard seemed lost, they held a conference in February 1926 to form a new church. The group survived for several years, but at the end of the decade Williams, the acknowledged leader, moved to Los Angeles, California. He died there in 1931. After his death, the church was disbanded. The largest number of protest group members joined the Church of Christ (Temple Lot).

★1190★
Church of Jesus Christ Restored
(Defunct)

The Church of Jesus Christ Restored began in 1979 when a group of members from the Reorganized Church of Jesus Christ of Latter Day Saints separated from that church and began to hold independent meetings. They called Stanley M. King to lead the restored church, which began a vigorous outreach program. King has received a number of revelations which became part of the church's scripture. A mission in Independence, Missouri, was opened in the mid-1970s, as well as churches in India and the Netherlands.

The church believed that it is necessary for Christians to be a part of the true church on earth and that both the Church of Jesus Christ of Latter-day Saints and the Reorganized Church of Jesus Christ of Latter-day Saints had apostacized. The Church of Jesus Christ Restored was God's chosen church which preached the fullness of the gospel. The church was organized under a First Presidency, a Council of Twelve Apostles, the Standing High

Council of the Church, a Presiding Bishopric, and a Presiding Patriarch.

The purpose of the church was the perfection of its human members. In order to reach perfection, life must be lived in the stakes of God. Stakes are communities built around a central temple, the place for the performance of the high ordinances of the church. Each member's task is to become independent of, and above, every creature and system of this world.

The church accepted the Book of Mormon (the inspired version of the Bible as revised by Joseph Smith, Jr.), the Doctrines and Covenants, and the additional prophecies received by King.

In 1987 Stanley King died. Following his death, church members kept his body out of the ground for three days hoping it would be reserrected. It was then buried. Subsequently, the leadership of the group collapsed and the church soon dissolved. The majority of members, the Mission India, affiliated with the Restoration Church of Jesus Christ of Latter-day Saints.

Membership: Not reported.

★1191★
Church of Jesus Christ (Toney)
Current address not obtained for this edition.

Forrest Toney (b. 1945) was a member of the Reorganized Church of Jesus Christ of Latter Day Saints and was raised in the church in Spokane, Washington. He later moved to Independence, Missouri, where, in 1977, he began to receive visions. In one of these visions in 1980 he was ordained to the high priesthood. A few months prior to the ordination he had resigned his job to devote full time to preaching. Since the Reorganized Church would not allow him to preach, he began to hold services in the Blue Hills Elementary School in Independence and to place advertisements in the local newspaper. Toney claims to offer prophetic insight into the Biblical books of Daniel and Revelation. He says of himself, "I am the Elijah and the only High Priest." He denounces money and worldly goods.

Membership: Not reported.

★1192★
Church of Jesus Christ (Williams)
(Defunct)

The Church of Jesus Christ emerged out of what was called the "Supreme Directional Control" controversy within the Reorganized Church of Jesus Christ of Latter-day Saints. The controversy flared in 1924 when Frederick M. Smith, president of the Reorganized Church, requested more managerial authority in directing the program agencies of the church. Some members, including Thomas W. Williams (1875-1931), immediately objected as they saw in the request a dangerous move to centralize power in the president's hands with a resultant loss of democratic controls by the members. Leaders of what became known as the protest held a prayer meeting that lasted for 10 days prior to the 1925 general conference at which the request would be considered.

At the close of the prayer meeting, approximately 25 people signed a statement protesting what they saw as granting "supreme directional control" which would "fundamentally change the established order of the church." The conference sustained President Smith's request, and many of the protest leaders left the church. While the largest group that withdrew transferred their membership to the Church of Christ (Temple Lot), others called a conference to meet in Independence, Missouri, in April 1926, at which they organized the Church of Jesus Christ. Williams was among the several men elected to the executive committee which headed the new church.

The Church of Jesus Christ generally followed the beliefs and practices of the Reorganized Church, the issue being entirely administrative, though the church issued its own statement of doctrine. The church moved away from acceptance of the *Doctrine*

and Covenants and replaced it with the older *Book of Commandments*. More importantly, in reaction to the centralized structure of the Reorganized Church, the new church had an extremely loose organization. While biennial church conferences were held regularly for a few years, the issue that called the church into existence faded in prominence, and the leadership's commitment to the church declined. Williams, the church's primary leader, for example, moved to California before the end of the decade and his death in 1931 seemed to seal the fate of the new church. It soon disbanded and the majority of the members went into the Church of Christ (Temple Lot).

Sources:

Shields, Steven L. *Divergent Paths of the Restoration.* Los Angeles: Restoration Press, 1990. 336 pp.

Williams, T. W. *The Protest Movement: Its Meaning and Purpose.* Independence, MO: The Church of Jesus Christ, 1926. 28 pp.

★1193★
Church of Jesus Christ (Zion's Branch)
108 S. Pleasant
Independence, MO

The Church of Jesus Christ (Zion's Branch) is one of several groups organized by former members of the Reorganized Church of Jesus Christ of Latter Day Saints in 1984 following the revelation of the church's president Wallace B. Smith concerning the ordination of women. The members believe that the Reorganized Church has become an apostate body. Among the leaders of the church is Robert Cato who played an important role in the International Elders Conference, a 1986 gathering of former Reorganized Church leaders from some 20 separate factions. The new church follows the traditional beliefs and practice of the Reorganized Church.

Membership: In 1986 there were six branch congregations and about 200 members in the church in Independence, Missouri.

★1194★
Churches of Christ in Zion
Current address not obtained for this edition.

The Churches of Christ in Zion was formed in 1979 by Bishop Robert W. Chambers. It was originally known as the National Association of American Churches. Integral to the life of the church was an economic system called "Zionomics." The system called for large-scale investment of tithes and gifts to the church in various commercial, residential, and agricultural ventures. The goal of these investments was the reclamation of the waste places of Zion, the area around Independence, Missouri, which, according the the Book of Mormon, will be the center of the future Kingdom of God and the gathering place of the saints. Parishoners, most of whom worship in house churches, have been exhorted to establish "Minicipals in Zion" to accomodate the gathering of people at the time of Christ's second coming. It is hoped that the investments will have an immediate effect of creating both new jobs and homes in the new metropolitan villages. In 1982 the Missouri state legislators adopted a resolution applauding Zionomics.

David Roberts, now head of the True Church of Jesus Christ Restored was at one time president of the National Association of American Churches. He also attended the church's seminary Continental College, which was open for several years in the early 1980s.

Membership: Not reported. In 1980 there were more than 40 missions all in the greater Kansas City metropolitan area, 28 of which were in Independence, Missouri. Because of adverse rulings from the Internal Revenue Service on the church's tax exempt status, its membership has dropped through the 1980s.

Remarks: The Churches of Christ in Zion have encountered opposition from the Internal Revenue Service since the beginning of its existence. The IRS accused the association of being a tax dodge which has helped its members convert their homes into nonprofit church missions. It denied the church tax exempt status in 1981 and again in 1984 because the church was not exclusively a church and because it had provided assistance to church members in their dealings with the IRS. Chambers, the head of the church, is a tax consultant. Sponsors of the legislative resolution have claimed that it was not passed in any effort to provide substantive support to the church's programs.

★1195★

Independent Church of Jesus Christ of Latter Day Saints
% Mark Cortez, Pres.
22 Homas Pl., Apt. C
Destrehan, LA 70047

Alternate Address: International Headquarters: Bergliengate 14, 0354 Oslo 3, Norway.

The Independent Church of Jesus Christ of Latter Day Saints was founded in Oxford, England, in the mid-1980s under the leadership of Christopher C. Warren Also known by his religious name, Lev-Zion haEphrayim, Warren was a former member of the Church of Jesus Christ of Latter-day Saints, and was assisted by Erik Danielson. HaEphrayim had received a revelation in 1977 of the apostasy that had crept into the church, a vision which was confirmed by his own observations in the next months. In 1981 he left the church and began a study of the various factions of Latter-day Saints, finding in each an admixture of truth and error. He joined the Reorganized Church of Jesus Christ of Latter Day Saints in 1984, but left in 1986 to organize the Independent Church of Jesus Christ of Latter-day Saints as a new restored church. The church quickly spread through Europe and back to the United States, but enjoyed its greatest success in Norway where the church's headquarters were soon relocated.

During 1988 and 1989, haEphrayim had a series of over 150 revelations that were published as the *Covenants and Commandments*, a sequel to the *Doctrines and Covenants*, one of the standard Latter-day Saints scriptures. One of the tasks the Independent Church has undertaken is the compilation of an authoritative edition of the *Doctrines and Covenants* that would contain all of Joseph Smith, Jr.'s, revelations and delete those made by church leaders in the intervening years. It is the contention of the Independent Church that both the Latter Day Saints church in Utah and the Reorganized Church fell into apostasy that none of the various factions had been able to reverse. The Independent Church believes it represents a new beginning.

The Independent Church has developed cordial relations with Sons Ahman Israel and its leader David Israel. The church accepts as authoritative scripture the translations by Israel claimed to be the sealed portions of the Book of Mormon plates.

Membership: Not reported. There are centers in Norway, Denmark, and the United States.

Periodicals: *Messenger and Advocate.*

Sources:

Covenants and Commandments. Vetlandveien, Norway: Independent Church of Jesus Christ of Latter Day Saints, 1989.

Shields, Steven L. *Divergent Paths of the Restoration.* Los Angeles: Restoration Research, 1990.

★1196★

Lundgren Faction
(Defunct)

In 1986 Jeffrey Lundgren, a member of the Reorganized Church of Jesus Christ of Latter Day Saints, formed a study group from church members in the Kirkland, Ohio, area. It became the core of a small new religion Lundgren founded in 1988 after he was stripped of his priesthood and subsequently withdrew from the church. Then in January 1990, newspapers across the country were filled with the news of five bodies whose deaths were attributed to Lundgren and the members of his group.

Jeffrey Lundgren (b. 1950) was born and raised in the Reorganized Church in Independence, Missouri, where the church is headquartered. In 1983 he was ordained a priest in the church (a ceremony through which most male members pass). The following year, however, he moved to Kirkland, Ohio, to work at the Kirkland Temple, the original temple constructed by Joseph Smith, Jr., the prophet upon whose writings the church is built. The Kirkland Temple is a popular tourist site, especially for Mormons, and Lundgren served as a tour guide.

Within a few years Lundgren began to give voice to several ideas at variance with the teachings of the Reorganized Church. He shared his ideas with people he showed around the temple and by 1986 had gathered a small study group. During 1987 officials in the church became aware of his heterodox notions and began to monitor his work with the tourists. Thus in January 1988 church officials stripped him of his priesthood, silenced him, and fired him from his position at the temple. On October 21, he and his wife formally withdrew from the church, and with his followers, organized separately. Lundgren proclaimed himself a prophet, and approximately 30 people followed him into a communal living arrangement.

Over the next several months Lundgren claimed to have found a chamber holding the golden plates from which the *Book of Mormon* was written and a sword of Laban spoken of in that book. He believed that Kirkland was to be the center of the new Zion and developed plans to gather several hundred followers, take over the Kirkland Temple, and from there await the return of Christ.

Before the group could take over the temple, however, Lundgren deemed necessary some purifying and ritual cleansing actions, including a period in the wilderness. On April 17, 1989, five people, Dennis and Cheryl Avery and their three children, were executed as an act of cleansing. Some 20 people were involved in some way with the murders, though Lundgren actually pulled the trigger. After the murders the group moved to Davis, West Virginia, for a period and then to Chillowee, Missouri. In December the group appears to have split up as some members began to disagree on Lundgren's status as a prophet.

The bodies of the Averys were discovered the first week of January 1990. Within a few days, most of those involved were arrested; Lundgren and his wife were found in San Diego, California. At a trial later that year, Lundgren was sentenced to death and his wife to life imprisonment. Other members of the group received lesser sentences. By these legal proceedings, the remnant of the group was effectively disbanded.

Sources:

Earley, Pete. *Prophet of Death.* New York: William Morrow and Company, 1991.

★1197★

New Jerusalem Church of Jesus Christ
(Defunct)

The New Jerusalem Church of Jesus Christ was founded in Independence, Missouri, in 1975 by Barney Fuller, a former member of the Reorganized Church of Jesus Christ of Latter-day Saints. For more than a decade Fuller had been protesting the spread of liberalism in the reorganized church and as early at 1967 had published a book, *Have You Received the Holy Ghost?*, in which he and his co-authors argued that the Holy Ghost had been withdrawn from the church. In 1969, he joined with other people concerned about what they agreed were unwelcome trends in the Reorganized Church to form World Redemption to protest the changes in the church. At this time the church was experiencing some dissent from changes in church school curricula, the attendance at a Methodist seminary of some ministerial leaders, and the promotion of the cause of female ordination.

Fuller and the other leaders of the group were silenced by the Church's leadership, but made their views known through a periodical, *Zion's Warning* (1970-75). World Redemption continued until 1975 when it was superseded by the New Jerusalem Church. The new church adopted the *Book of Mormon*, the *Book of Commandments*, and the Inspired Version of the Bible as scripture and gained some popular support from conservative members of that church. However, in 1976, Fuller renounced the Latter Day Saint scriptures, and the majority of his supporters withdrew. A short time later, the church was disbanded.

Sources:

Fuller, Barney R. *Stick of Joseph*. Pasadena, CA: Tri Tech Publications, 1969. 118 pp.

——, Glen Stout, and William Spilsbury. *Have You Received the Holy Ghost?*. La Mirada, CA: The Authors, 1967. 81 pp.

Shields, Steven L. *Divergent Paths of the Restoration*. Los Angeles: Restoration Press, 1990. 336 pp.

★1198★
Reorganized Church of Jesus Christ of Latter Day Saints
The Auditorium
Box 1059
Independence, MO 64051

History. Few churches have as complicated an early history as the Reorganized Church of Jesus Christ of Latter Day Saints. It was formed in 1860 by remnants of the Latter-day Saint movement left in the East and Midwest after the larger group migrated to Utah; the prime movers of the new church were Jason Briggs, Zenos Gurley, and William Marks.

Briggs had been an elder in the Church of Jesus Christ of Latter-day Saints (LDS) at Nauvoo, Illinois, and remained loyal until the trek West. He then joined James Jesse Strang in 1848. He soon rejected Strang and joined in William Smith's short-lived church in 1850. In 1851, he left Smith and in November claimed a revelation in which the Lord affirmed that He had not cast off His people and that in due time, from the seed of Joseph would come forth one mighty and strong (II Nephi 2:46-47).

Zenos Gurley was senior president of one of the seventies in Nauvoo. He remained loyal to Brigham Young until a few days before the departure west. He joined Strang and was a bishop, but like Briggs he left Strang in 1852. He claimed a revelation similar to Brigg's concerning Joseph's son.

William Marks was the Nauvoo stake president who was excommunicated when he supported the leadership claims of Sidney Rigdon, who founded the precursor to the Church of Christ (Bickertonite). Marks joined Rigdon, then Strang, then several other Mormon groups.

In 1852 Gurley and Briggs came together to form the New Organization, basically from some of Strang's followers. They decided that Joseph Smith III should lead the new church. The organization was effected in 1853 and Briggs was chosen to preside. Young Joseph refused the presidency at first, but in 1859 accepted it. In 1859, William Marks was admitted to the New Organization, and it was he who ordained Smith president. On April 6, 1860, the New Organization became the Reorganized Church of Jesus Christ of Latter Day Saints with 300 members.

The Reorganized Church agrees with the Utah Church in a number of important points. Members of the Reorganized Church accept all the scriptures that Joseph Smith wrote and their statement of belief is very close to that of the Utah brethren. In particular, they accept the idea of the restoration of the ministerial, priestly, and prophetic offices in the nineteenth century; the gifts of the Spirit; and salvation by faith, repentance, baptism by immersion, and the laying on of hands.

Beliefs. The Reorganized Church draws sharp distinctions on several points on which it feels the Utah Church has fallen into error. The Reorganized Church rejects polygamy, and all the associated doctrines-sealing of marriages for eternity and marriage by proxy to persons deceased-are rejected most strongly. The doctrine that "As man is now is, God once was; as God now is, so man may become," the Adam-God theory, is felt to conflict plainly with the monotheism of the Bible. The members of the Reorganized Church consider abhorrent the practice of "blood atonement" as enunciated by Brigham Young, by which apostates were killed to save them from damnation. In the Reorganized Church, there are no closed temples nor services from which the public is barred, nor any special temple garments.

The most significant difference in the Reorganized Church is its adoption of a hereditary prophetic office in the descendants of Joseph Smith, Jr. Since 1860, the president-prophets of the church have been successively Joseph Smith III (1860-1914), Frank Madison Smith (1914-1946), Israel Alexander Smith (1946-1958), and W. Wallace Smith (1958-78) and Wallace B. Smith (1978-). The president-prophets have, unlike the Utah Church presidents, added periodic revelations which appear as additions to the *Doctrine and Covenants*.

In the 1990s, the RLDS faced a crisis in that no descendant of Joseph Smith, Jr. was waiting to take over the leadership of the church following the dealth/retirement of present leader Wallace Smith. The problem was resolved in 1996, when the church's World Conference designated 48-year-old W. Grant McMurray as Smith's successor. Until such time as Smith vacates his office, McMurray remains a member of the First Presidency.

The Reorganized Church is described as a theocratic democracy-a government of God directed divinely under the law of "common consent" of the people. There is a world conference held every two years in the church headquarters auditorium, located across the street from the Church of Christ (Temple Lot) in Independence, Missouri. The church has been the most open of all Mormon bodies to mainline Protestantism and one finds books by outstanding Protestants (of a noncontroversial nature) in the catalogue of the church book service. Herald House serves as both the publishing arm of the church and as a retail book distributor. Foreign work is being conducted in Nigeria, Japan, South Korea, Okinawa, South India, the Philippines, Brazil, Mexico, Haiti, New Zealand, Australia, French Polynesia, England, and Germany.

Membership: In 1996 the church reported 245,000 members.
Educational Facilities: Graceland College, Lamoni, Iowa.
Periodicals: *Saints Herald*.

Sources:

Edwards, F. Henry. *Fundamentals, Enduring Convictions of the Restoration*. Independence, MO: Herald Publishing House, n.d.

Knisley, Alvin. *Infallible Proofs*. Independence, MO: Herald Publishing House, 1930.

Koury, Aleah G. *The Truth and the Evidence*. Independence, MO: Herald Publishing House, 1965.

MacGregor, Daniel. *A Marvelous Work and a Wonder*. The Author, 1911.

★1199★
Restoration Branches Movement
No central address. For information:
Price Publishing Co.
915 E. 23rd St.
Independence, MO 64055

The Restoration Branches Movement arose in the 1980s within the Reorganized Church of Jesus Christ of Latter Day Saints in an attempt to coordinate the conservative dissent which had grown within the church over the previous two decades. Dissent had been focused upon a number of changes which had moved the church from what some members have felt to be traditional church perspectives. Issues of change arose with the introduction of a new church school curriculum in the 1960s, an action which caused additional concern because of the use of authors who were nonchurch members. The introduction of the new curriculum highlighted the development within the church of a "liberal" leadership composed of people theologically trained in liberal Protestant seminaries. These leaders were introducing a variety of ideas whose overall effect would be to move away from the distinctive truths held by the church. This new position of the church was stated in a series of "position papers" produced in 1967-68 by the church's Department of Religious Education. Conservatives also complained that these leaders were aligning the church to the National Council of Churches and the World Council of Churches.

The ordination of women became the most controversial of the important new doctrines introduced during the 1970s. Discussion within church periodicals moved into the highest leadership by the mid-1970s. In 1976 the First Presidency of the church introduced a resolution calling for the reversal of previous church action forbidding the ordination of women. Finally in 1984, President Wallace B. Smith issued a new revelation (to be added to the *Doctrines and Covenants* as item no. 156) calling for women's ordination and a restructuring of the priesthood. The first women were ordained the following year. At the same time a number of dissenting members of the priesthood were silenced. Using guidelines issued in January 1985, a review of the priests commenced. These guidelines were rejected by the conservative members and leaders.

Using guidelines issued in January 1985, a review of the priests commenced. These new guidelines were rejected by the conservative members and leaders.

The cause of conservative dissent within the church was championed by a number of individuals around the country and several organizations, most headquartered in Independence, Missouri. Prominent among the organizations were the Restoration Foundation, Price Publishing Company, Mothers in Israel, and the Concerned Members Committee. Even prior to the revelation of 1984 and its implementation the following year, independent congregations, having anticipated the future course of the church, had separated and formed new churches. A gathering of approximately 20 such independent groups occurred in Independence in April 1986.

In the wake of the actions of 1984-85 by the Reorganized Church of Jesus Christ of Latter Day Saints and the formation of numerous new church groups, a number of conservative church members, most prominently Richard Price and Rudy Leutzinger, began to call for the formation of autonomous branches (congregations) which would stay within the Reorganized Church but be independent of the "apostate" hierarchy of the world headquarters. In 1985 Leutzinger led in the formation of such a branch, the Independence Branch. Price wrote and published guidelines for such independent branches which began to form wherever Reorganized Church congregations were found.

Such branches are to refrain from participation with the separate groups, especially those which have proposed new beliefs in the authority of their leader as a prophet. They are to follow traditional Reorganized Church doctrine and accept the Epitome of Faith as a true doctrinal statement. Special emphasis is placed upon the authority of the Book of Mormon, the Doctrine and Covenants (without item No. 156), and the Inspired Version of the Bible (as revised and translated by Joseph Smith). Such branches are to withdraw support, both spiritual and financial, from the world headquarters. It is the movement's belief that it is one remnant of the true church, within the continuing Reorganized Church of Jesus Christ of Latter Day Saints. Members of the independent branches are to stay members of the Reorganized Church awaiting the day when God will act through them to complete the present Restoration.

Membership: Not reported. A directory, published in 1991, listed 72 branches and groups in the United States, one group in Ontario, Canada, and one in Australia.

Periodicals: Unofficial: *Restoration Voice.* Send orders to Box 1611, Independence, MO 64055. • *Quarterly Report.* Available from the Restoration Foundation, Box 1774, Independence, MO 64055. • *Vision.*

Remarks: As this volume goes to press, the Restoration Branches Movement appears to be one of the strongest segments of the recent dissent in the Reorganized Church of Jesus Christ of Latter Day Saints. It is also one of the most fluid and will, by its own projections, grow and develop as affiliated branches become stable and an ackowledged leadership emerges.

Sources:

Leutzinger, Rudy. *Branch Organization and the History of the Independence Branch.* Independence, MO: Restoration Foundation, 1985.

Price, Richard. *Restoration Branches Movement.* Independence, MO: Price Publishing Co., 1986.

___. *The Saints at the Crossroads.* Independence, MO: Price Publishing Co., 1974.

Price, Richard, and Larry Harlacher. *Action Time.* Independence, MO: Price Publishing Co., 1985.

★1200★
Restoration Church of Jesus Christ of Latter-day Saints
801 W. 23rd St.
Independence, MO 64055

The Restoration Church of Jesus Christ of Latter Day Saints was founded in 1991 by former members of the Reorganized Church of Jesus Christ of Latter Day Saints who rejected what they saw as a drift toward liberal Protestant theology and an abandonment of distinctive teachings by Joseph Smith, Jr. in the 1830s and 1840s. Changes within the Reorganized Church had been a matter of controversy for several decades. The members of the Restoration Church had fought to stop the changes into what they considered apostasy but finally concluded that such efforts were in vain. Beginning in the mid-1980s, individuals and congregations began to withdraw and in 1991 "reorganized" under the leadership of some former members of the Quorums of Seventy of the Reorganized Church.

Once the Restoration Church was established, a set of Apostles and other priesthood Quorums were designated, and in 1993 a Prophet/President was ordained. The Prophet/President is Marcus Juby, a Native American. The naming of Juby is seen as fulfilling a prophecy from the *Book of Mormon* (2 *Nephi* 2:45-47, Reorganized Church edition). The Restoration Church grew quickly by gathering into membership a number of small independent groups that had separated from the Reorganized Church over the years. They opened a mission in Nepal and have received into membership several thousand people in India who were formerly members of the now-defunct Church of Jesus Christ Restored.

The Restoration Church holds to the same doctrines of the Reorganized Church prior to the changes initiated in the 1970s. They identify those doctrines with the original teaching of Joseph Smith, Jr., and of early Christianity which survived through such groups as the Donatists until the sixth century C.E. The church acknowledges One God and the substitutionary atonement of Jesus Christ, which is effective in the lives of all who come to Christ in baptism, accept the ministry of Christ's true church, and lead a life of repentance. The church believes that children are not accountable for their life until the age of eight, ant that those who die having never heard the gospel will have the opportunity to accept it in the next life.

The church accepts the authority of the Bible (the Inspired Version of Joseph Smith, first published in 1867), the *Book of Mormon*, the *Doctrines and Covenants*, and such additional revelations as may be given to the church's Prophet/President. The church rejects polygamy, secret rites, blood atonement, ecumenism, and White supremacy.

The church practices the ordinances of baptism by immersion for the remission of sins; and the laying on of hands in confirmation to bestow the gift of the holy Spirit, for ordination to the priesthood, and with oil for the anointing of the sick. Revelatory "Patriarchal Blessings" are given to individuals by ordained Patriarchs.

Membership: In 1995 the church reported 65 branches, missions, and groups in 32 states of the United States. Outside of the United States, there are members in Australia, Canada, Nepal, and India.

Periodicals: *The Restoration Advocate.*

Other Mormons

★1201★
Church of Jesus Christ (Bickertonite)
6th & Lincoln Sts.
Monongahela, PA 15063

Sidney Rigdon had been the First Counselor to Joseph Smith, Jr. during the early years of the church. In spite of his health problems which began with the incident in which he and Smith were tarred and feathered and his falling out with the Church over Smith's proposing plural marriage to his daughter, Rigdon retained his formal position in the church. Based upon his office in the church, after Smith's assassination, he claimed to be his successor. Though rejected by the other church leaders, Rigdon found some followers which he led to Pennsylvania. In 1844 he reorganized the church which had but a short life. In the fall of 1846 disagreements appeared that led to its disintegration.

William Bickerton, who never knew Joseph Smith, had joined Sidney Rigdon's church in 1845. Left without a church by the disintegration of Rigdon's following, he joined the Church of Jesus Christ of Latter-day Saints congregation at Elizabeth, Pennsylvania, in which he became an elder. Sometime shortly after the public announcement of the doctrine of polygamy, Bickerton denounced Brigham Young and the Utah apostles and left the church. He formally organized a new church in July, 1862, claiming he did so in obedience to a revelation. Bickerton gathered some of Rigdon's followers as his first members.

The small Church of Jesus Christ has had a rather tumultuous history. A branch was established in Kansas in 1875, and Bickerton moved there with the church headquarters. Friction arose between the Pennsylvania and Kansas branches, and Bickerton, accused of adultery, was disfellowshipped from his own church. (He returned in 1902.) William Cadman was elected president. In 1904, the year before Cadman's death, a reorganization took place. In 1907, further friction resulted in half the leaders leaving and forming the short-lived Reorganization Church of Jesus Christ. A second schism occurred in 1914.

The doctrine of the Bickertonite Church follows closely that of the Church of Jesus Christ of Latter-Day Saints prior to Joseph Smith's death. The members are strongly opposed to polygamy. They do practice the Lord's Supper weekly (a reflection of Sidney Rigdon's continued attachment to the ideas of Alexander Campbell), the washing of feet, and the holy kiss. The church is ruled by a president, two councilors, a secretary, financial secretary, and treasurer. There is an annual conference of elders which elects officers.

Membership: In 1989 the church reported 2,707 members, 63 congregations, and 262 ministers.

Periodicals: *Gospel News.* Send orders to 8423 Boettner Rd., Bridgewater, MI 48115.

Sources:

Cadman, W. H. *A History of the Church of Jesus Christ.* Monongahela, PA: Church of Jesus Christ, 1945.

Cadman, William. *Faith and Doctrines of the Church of Jesus Christ.* Roscoe, PA: Roscoe Ledger Print., 1902.

McKiernan, F. Mark. *The Voice of One Crying in the Wilderness: Sidney Rigdon, Religious Reformer, 1793-1876.* Independence, MO: Herald House, 1979.

★1202★
Church of Jesus Christ (Cutlerite)
807 S. Cottage St.
Independence, MO 64050

Alpheus Cutler was an elder in the LDS Church and gained some prominence for his efforts in building the Nauvoo Temple. In 1841, he was by revelation (D.C. 12:132) appointed to the Nauvoo State High Council. After Joseph Smith's death, Cutler began a mission to the Indians. Cutler claimed later that he was given the call by Joseph Smith, Jr., who had given him sole authority to preach the gospel to the Lamanites, the American Indians. When the group under Young went to Utah, Cutler stayed behind and claimed authority from Smith to carry on as an elder in the church.

As a recent church member wrote: "Joseph Smith had organized a group of men into an order of seven, a kingdom order. Joseph was number one in that order and Alpheus Cutler was number seven, and Joseph ordained all six of those men to hold the keys, powers and authorities which he held. So they each held the kingdom authority. As time went on all of the men in that order of seven except Alpheus Cutler either died or joined some of the factions. Alpheus Cutler was number seven and he waited his turn to work. He had been promised he would be given a sign, a certain sign when it was time for him to begin his work, and when he received that sign he began to prepare for organization."

In 1849, Cutler and some followers established a settlement in Iowa which was named Manti. A formal organization of the Church of Jesus Christ followed in 1853, after a number of saints from Council Bluffs swelled the growing community. There was constant fluctuation in membership during the remainder of Cutler's lifetime because of periodic arguments with other groups of Mormons operating in the Midwest.

In 1864, following Cutler's death, Chauncey Whiting, Cutler's successor, led a group to Minnesota (according to a revelation which Cutler had received) where the town of Clitherall was established. Here they tried to establish a an order of all things common (the United Order) but were unsuccessful at first. In 1910, Isaac Whiting, who succeeded to the presidency following the death of Chauncey Whiting in 1902, called all to return to the United Order, which was accomplished in 1913. Isaac Whiting died in 1922 and Emery Fletcher then became president, having been Isaac's first counselor.

In 1928, a branch of the church was established in Independence, Missouri, the site of Zion (*Doctrine and Covenants* 57:3). A home and a church building were paid for by the United Order in Clitherall, Minnesota, and about half the group took possession of them. Conflict arose almost immediately, and Emery Fletcher, the then church president, returned to Clitherall. In 1952, he convinced the Minnesota group to excommunicate the Missouri group, including Erle Whiting, the first councilor. The excommunication was not recognized by the Missouri group. Then in 1953 Emery Fletcher died. The Minnesota groups elected Clyde Fletcher as the new president. The Missouri group rejected the election and recognized Erle Whiting (d. 1958), who as first councilor had the assumed right of succession to that office. This set of events completed the separation between the two groups.

Erle Whiting served as president until 1958 and was succeeded by Rupert J. Fletcher (d. 1974) and Julian Whiting (1974). Clyde Fletcher served the Minnesota group until his death in 1969. During the 1970s the Minnesota congregation dwindled steadily and eventually had no one to perform priesthood functions. In recent years it has been reconciled to the Missouri group. During the years of the separation, the Minnesota group referred to itself as the True Church of Jesus Christ.

The main distinctive mark of the Church of Jesus Christ is a belief in the authority of Alpheus Cutler. The president or chief councilor and his first and second councilors are the main officers. Upon the death of the first councilor, the second succeeds him if approved by the vote of the church members. Besides believing in the authority of Cutler, the Church of Jesus Christ believes that the Lord rejected all Gentiles who did not accept Joseph Smith's message and therefore there is to be no preaching to them unless called by revelation. They are the only group besides the LDS Church in Utah to perform temple rites; Cutler had known them from his days at Nauvoo.

Membership: In 1995 the church reported 29 members. The congregation in Missouri continues services. The few members in Minnesota moved to Missouri and joined with that congregation.

Sources:

Fletcher, Daisy Whiting. *Alpheus Cutler and the Church of Jesus Christ.* Independence, MO: The Author, 1970.

Fletcher, Rupert J. *The Scattered Children of Zion.* Independence, MO: The Author, 1959.

___. *The Way of Deliverance.* Independence, MO: The Author, 1969.

★1203★
Church of Jesus Christ (Drew)
35315 Chestnut
Burlington, WI 53105

Theron Drew (d. 1978) formerly associated with the Church of Jesus Christ of Latter-day Saints (Strangite), lived in a house formerly owned by Wingfield Watson, a leader in the church from 1897 to 1922. Watson left his farm, located adjacent to the original Strangite church, to three trustees to handle as they saw fit. One of these trustees, Barbara Drew (wife of Theron) had a third control of the property.

In the early 1950s. Theron Drew met Merl Kilgore. He saw in Kilgore the answer to a basic problem of the Church of Jesus Christ of Latter Day Saints (Strangite), its lack of a head, i.e., a prophet-translator-seer-revelator, since the death of Joseph Smith, Jr., the church's founder. Since Strang's death, and especially since the death of the apostles he had appointed, leadership had been exercised by people periodically appointed to take charge of meetings of the members. Drew came to believe that Kilgore, then head of Zion's Order of the Sons of Levi, was the "One Mighty and strong," prophesied to come and set the house of God in Order in the last Days (Doctrine and Covenants, 85). He allowed Kilgore to baptize him. Within a month, however, he became convinced that he had erred, and he returned to the Church of Jesus Christ of Latter-day Saints, only to find that he was not wanted. At a 1965 church conference, he was dismissed from membership.

Drew, his family, and a small number of supporters, began to hold meetings in the old church building on the Wingfield farm, the larger body having built a new church building a short distance away. The Church of Jesus Christ of Latter-day Saints (Strangite) filed suit against Drew to reclaim some of the church documents in his possession, but were not successful in their suit. Management of the farm and church building and the role of taking charge of the meetings of the Church of Jesus Christ (Drew) has now passed to Richard Drew, Theron's son.

Membership: As of 1995, there was one congregation with approximately 15 members.

Sources:

Couch, Edward T. *Evidences of Inspiration.* Bay Springs, MI: The Author, 1980.

___. *The Sabbath and the Restitution.* Bay Springs, MI: The Author, 1891.

Drew, Richard, ed. *Revelation to the Priesthood.* Voree, WI: Church of Jesus Christ of Latter Day Saints, 1986.

___. *Word of Wisdom.* Voree, WI: Church of Jesus Christ of Latter Day Saints, [1986].

★1204★
Church of Jesus Christ of Latter Day Saints (Strangite)
℅ Vernon Swift
Box 522
Artesia, NM 88210

James Jesse Strang (1813-1856), a Baptist and a lawyer, first heard of Joseph Smith, founder of the Mormons, in 1843 while living at Voree, Wisconsin. In February, 1844, Strang was baptized by Joseph Smith, Jr., and was ordained elder in the Melchizedek Priesthood. The church asked him to survey the Burlington, Wisconsin, area as a possible new home for the Saints. While Strang was on this mission, Smith was killed (June 27, 1844). On this day, Strang later claimed, an angel of the Lord appeared to him, saluted him and said, "Fear God and be strengthened and obey him for great is the work which he hath required at thy hands." The angel then touched him with oil. On July 9, 1844, Strang claimed that he received a letter (dated June 18, 1844) from Joseph Smith. The letter named Strang as his successor, appointed Aaron Smith as Strang's councilor, and designated Voree as the new gathering place of the Saints. Strang first presented his claims at a meeting held August 5, 1844, at Florence, Michigan. The twelve apostles at Nauvoo, Illinois, after receiving a report, excommunicated Strang.

The organization of the Church of Jesus Christ was effected June 5, 1845, at Voree. A dispute with the supporters of Brigham Young arose when Strang attempted to discourage the Saints from traveling West. After the trek West began, Strang received new members who did not join the march. Dissension developed, however, and Strang decided to take his loyal followers and go to Beaver Island, Michigan. Here he set up a theocracy, with himself at its head. More than 2,000 Saints came to Beaver Island, and Strang emerged as the most politically powerful man in the area. By 1856, the Church of Jesus Christ was the largest of the Mormon groups that did not follow Brigham Young. The church suffered a severe setback in 1856 when Strang was shot and died several weeks later in Voree, where he had been taken by his followers.

Strang's death cost the church most of its members, many of whom joined the Reorganized Church of Jesus Christ of Latter Day Saints. Further, Strang failed to name a successor. The five apostles carried on without a leader. Finally, L. D. Hickey, the last surviving apostle, began to function as their leader. The small group held together under the successive leadership ordained by Hickey before his death in 1897. Wingfield Watson served from 1897 to 1922 and was succeeded by Samuel H. Martin, Moroni Flanders, Lloyd Flanders, and the present head, Vernon Swift.

The Strangite Church currently works out of two centers—Artesia, New Mexico, and Voree (Burlington), Wisconsin. A periodical, *The Gospel Herald*, published at Voree in the 1970s has been discontinued.

Membership: In 1984 the church reported 200 members in 2 congregations. The were 3 priests.

Remarks: Though not accepted by the church, charges of fraud and/or forgery have been leveled by historians from Dale Morgan to, more recently, Lawrence Foster. They have accused Strang of forging the letter upon which his authority rests.

Sources:

The Book of the Law of the Lord. Rept.: Voree, WI: Church of Jesus Christ of Latter-day Saints, 1991.

Foster, Lawrence. "James J. Strang: The Prophet Who Failed." *Church History* 50, no. 2 (June 1981): 182-92.

The Revelations of James J. Strang. Church of Jesus Christ of Latter Day Saints, 1939.

Shepard, William, Donna Falk, and Thelma Lewis, eds. *James J. Strang, Teaching of a Mormon Porphet.* Burlington, WI: Church of Jesus Christ of Latter Day Saints (Strangite), 1977.

Strang, James J. *The Prophetic Controversy.* Lansing, MI, 1969.

Strang, Mark A., ed. *The Diary of James J. Strang*. East Lansing, MI: Michigan State University Press, 1961.

★1205★
Church of the Messiah
(Defunct)

The Church of the Messiah was formed in 1861 in Springfield, Massachusetts, by George J. Adams. Adams had become a follower of Mormon prophet Joseph Smith, Jr. in 1840. During the Nauvoo, Illinois years (the 1840s) of the Church of Jesus Christ of Latter-day Saints, he took several mission journeys to England and to Massachusetts. He was in Nauvoo when Smith was assassinated, an event which deeply affected him. Discouraged, Adams soon fell into conflict with Brigham Young, who had emerged as the new president of the church. In 1845 Young excommunicated Adams. Adams then associated for a time with James Jesse Strang. He put his theatrical knowledge to the task of staging the coronation of Strang as "King of the Kingdom of God." Then in 1856 he was excommunicated from the Strangite church.

Adams emerged from obscurity in 1860 and began to identify himself as a minister of the Church of the Messiah. He published a short work on a traditional Mormon theme—a *Lecture on the Destiny and Mission of America and the True Origin of the Indians*. However his essential message was the imminent return of Jesus Christ and the redemption of Israel. To that end, he founded the Church of the Messiah in 1861 and issued a Church Covenant that some 43 persons signed. The next year he began a periodical, *The Sword of Truth*, issued from his home in South Lebanon, Maine.

In the summer of 1865, Adams acted on revelations he had received and moved to the Holy Land. The following year 156 church members joined him in the attempt to establish a colony. The effort failed in a few years from lack of local government cooperation and scarce water resources. By 1870, Adams and his following had returned to the United States. He reestablished his Church of the Messiah in Philadelphia, Pennsylvania, and pastored it for the rest of his life. He died in 1880 and the church soon dissolved.

Sources:

Holmes, Reed M. *The Forerunners*. Independence, MO: Herald Publishing House, 1981.

Shields, Steven L. *Divergent Paths of the Restoration*. Los Angeles: Restoration Research, 1990.

★1206★
Congregation of Jehovah's Presbytery of Zion
(Defunct)

The Congregation of Jehovah's Presbytery of Zion was founded in 1847 by Charles Blanchard Thompson (b. 1814), a former member of the Church of Jesus Christ of Latter-Day Saints. Blanchard, among the first to respond to the message of Mormon prophet Joseph Smith, Jr., joined the Mormons in the 1830s in Kirkland, Ohio. After Smith's murder, he joined the Church of Jesus Christ (Strangite), a Mormon faction led by James Jesse Strang, but left it and moved to St. Louis. He soon began to receive revelations which became the basis of his new church.

On New Year's Day, 1848, Thompson issued a revelation which accused the Latter-Day Saints of failure in God's eyes for not completing the temple abandoned at Nauvoo, the Mormon settlement in Western Illinois. The Congregation of Jehovah's Presbytery of Zion was to be a temporary substitute for the real Zion to be established in Independence, Missouri. A few weeks later he denounced the polygamy practices instituted among the saints. Because of Smith's actions, Thompson's progeny could not inherit the keys to the kingdom, which had been transferred to him. By 1853 approximately fifty families had affiliated with the congregation. They purchased a tract of land in Monona County,

Iowa, and began to build Preparation, a communal settlement. The settlement failed in 1857, just after Thompson had issued his collection of revelations. Thompson was also accused of mismanaging funds. Driven from the community, he returned to St. Louis to reestablish the congregation there. A small following developed. During this time, he published another book, *The Nachash Origin of the Black and Mixed Races*. It was an elaborate anthology which included a defense of slavery. But his hopes of rebuilding were dashed by the lawsuit over the Iowa property, which was awarded to the former members in 1867. Thompson moved to Philadelphia where for the third time, he rebuilt the congregation and began a newspaper, *Cyips Herald*. In 1888 this group also disintegrated as the result of an internal dispute. Thompson died in obscurity a few years later.

Sources:

Arbaugh, George Bartholemew. *Revelation in Mormonism*. Chicago: University of Chicago Press, 1932.

Thompson, Charles Blanchard. *The Nachash Origin of the Black and Mixed Races*. St. Louis: George Knapp & Co., 1860.

★1207★
Holy Church of Jesus Christ
Current address not obtained for this edition.

The Holy Church of Jesus Christ was founded in the 1970s by Alexandre Roger Caffiaux. Caffiaux initiated correspondence with the Church of Jesus Christ (Strangite) in 1963 and subsequently traveled to the United States. He was baptized and ordained to the priesthood by the leadership in Wisconsin. On the return flight to France, Caffiaux had a revelation that he was to become the head of the church. He wrote a letter to that effect to those who had just ordained him. Early in 1964, he journeyed to Iran. While there, he experienced yet another revelation. A vision of an angel ordained him to the "First Presidency of the High Priesthood of Melchizedek," calling him to be a prophet, seer, and revelator to this generation. He asked that a general conference of the church be called to consider his claims. The small band of Strangites in France voiced their complete confidence in him.

The claims of Caffiaux were argued in the church for a number of years without resolution. At a conference in France, members voted to change the name of the Strangite church to the Holy Church of Jesus Christ. Finally in 1978, the Strangite Church, meeting in conference, formally voted to reject his claims and agreed that acceptance of his revelations and authority were incompatible with membership in the Church of Jesus Christ (Strangite).

Membership: There is a small following of the Holy Church of Jesus Christ in the United States, primarily in New Mexico.

Sources:

Johnston, Stanley L. *The Call and Ordination of Alexandre Roger Caffiaux*. N.p. 1966.

★1208★
Primitive Church of Jesus Christ (Bickertonite)
(Defunct)

In 1914 a schism occurred in the Church of Jesus Christ (Bickertonite). A schismatic group, led by James Caldwell, formed the Primitive Church of Jesus Christ at Washington, Pennsylvania. They were joined shortly by another Bickertonite schism, the Reorganization Church, which had formed in 1907 under the leadership of Elder Allen Wright. Caldwell was succeeded by his nephew, Lawrence Dias. The Primitive Church largely followed the beliefs and practices of the parent body, but held that the institution in 1830 of the office of the first presidency was an introduction of an alien institution. The members opposed polygamy, plurality of gods, and baptism for the dead.

By the 1970s, the church has dwindled to a single congregation in Erie, Pennsylvania. More recently the congregation disbanded; some of the members rejoined the parent group.

★1209★
Reorganized Church of Jesus Christ (Wright)
(Defunct)

The Reorganized Church of Jesus Christ (Wright) was founded in 1907 by Allen Wright, formerly a member of the Twelve Apostles of the Church of Jesus Christ (Bickertonite). At the Bickertonite general conference in 1907, Wright's pamphlet in which he had expressed some dissenting opinions on the millennium and the return of Jesus Christ to earth, was publicly condemned. The conference passed a resolution suspending any who believed in Wright's ideas. Wright and five other church apostles refused to sustain the conference actions and as a result were removed from office and excommunicated. Several months later, with their supporters, Wright and the other apostles held a conference and founded a reorganized church. Except for the issue that occasioned the split, the Reorganized Church followed the beliefs and practices of its parent body. One of the former apostles, William T. Maxwell, was named as president. The church seems to have continued into the mid-1930s, when it disintegrated and its members either returned to the Bickertonite church or other Mormon bodies.

Sources:

Armburst, J. L. *Reformation or Restoration, or Which Is the Church? Jesus Christ Established but One Visible Church.* N.p.: Reorganized Church of Jesus Christ, 1929. 4 pp.

Maxwell, W. T. *A Statement Issued by the Re-Organized Church of Jesus Christ, July 4th, 1908.* Youngwood, PA: Re-Organized Church of Jesus Christ, 1908. 6 pp.

Shields, Steven L. *Divergent Paths of the Restoration.* Los Angeles: Restoration Press, 1990. 336 pp.

Wright, Allen. *A Conversation on the Thousand Years' Reign of Christ.* St. John, KS: The County Capital, 1907. 24 pp.

★1210★
The Restored Church of Jesus Christ (Walton)
Box 1851
Independence, MO 64055

The Restored Church of Jesus Christ was founded by Eugene O. Walton following a revelation in 1977. Walton, raised a Baptist, had joined the Reorganized Church of Jesus Christ of Latter-day Saints, but had increasing problems with what he saw as a growing liberalism and a discarding of the essentials of the faith. His opposition to the churchs president led to his excommunication. He joined the Church of Jesus Christ (Cutlerite), and was ordained an elder. While with the church he oversaw the printing of a three-volume compendium of writings entitled *The Book of Commandments.* It contained the 1835 edition of the *Doctrine and Covenants,* one of the Restoration scriptures, and some doctrinal materials by Walton.

In 1977 Walton received a revelation that he was the "one mighty and strong" predicted in the churchs history to come to set the house of God in order. In 1978 three witnesses were raised up by the Lord in the state of Maine, about 2,000 miles away from Independence, Missouri. They knew nothing of the revelation received by Walton in 1977. The three—Joyce R. Crowley, Barbara E. Overlock, and Louise B. Young—received word on the same day, by the Holy Spirit, that Eugene Walton was the "one mighty and strong," the promised prophet to come to set up the city of Zion, after the death of Joseph Smith, Jr., the founder of the Church of Jesus Christ of Latter-day Saints.

This revelation also gave Walton the keys to the kingdom and named him the successor prophet to Joseph Smith, Jr., and at the same time instructed him to be rebaptized without hands (i.e., without the hands of any man) even as Adam and Nephi had been baptized. He was also instructed to rebaptize all the other members entering into a new and everlasting covenant by command of God. This revelation led to disagreements with the Cutlerite church membership. In 1978 Walton and two other elders left and formed Restorationists United. Following a revelation to Walton at the beginning of 1979, his small band of followers held a general conference at which Walton was ordained Apostle-High Priest and Prophet. Jack Winegar and James Rouse were named First and Second Counselor respectively. By further revelation, Restorationists United became The Restored Church of Jesus Christ.

The church espouses belief in a Godhead of two personages: God the Father and Christ the Son. The Holy Ghost is seen as the life and power of God. Members are called to follow and believe the doctrine of Jesus Christ: faith in God and Christ, repentance, baptism by immersion, laying on of hands for the gift of the Holy Ghost, the resurrection of the dead, and eternal life in the Celestial Kingdom of God. The church practices "All Things in Common" (i.e., communalism), a necessary step in the establishment of Zion. Christ will not return until Zion is established. Members look forward to the temple of Zion being built in Independence, Missouri. The *Inspired Version of the Bible* (as revised by Joseph Smith, Jr.) is used and called by Gods revelation to them as "The Stick of Judah."

The Restored Church, following the reception of revelation, renamed all three books of scripture common to the restoration movement. They were reprinted in order with names derived from the biblical book of *Ezekiel* 37: 16-20 (*Inspired Version*) *The Stick of Joseph* (better known as the *Nephite Record* or the *Book of Mormon*); *The Stick of Ephraim* (*Doctrine and Covenants*), which is an open canon of scripture; *The Stick of Judah* (*Inspired Version of the Bible*); and also several more revelations printed in two other supplements of *The Stick of Ephraim.*

All revelations that come to the prophet, Walton, are accepted by common consent. As of 1995 there were approximatley 100 such revelations. The first prophet, Joseph Smith, Jr., received 106 revelations during his lifetime. Joseph Smith III received three revelations and Brigham Young one revelation.

Membership: Not reported.

Educational Facilities: School of the Prophets, Independence, Missouri.

Periodicals: *Zions Trumpet.*

Sources:

The Book of the Lord's Commandments. 3 vols. Independence, MO: Restored Church of Jesus Christ, n.d.

★1211★
True Church of Jesus Christ Restored
Current address not obtained for this edition.

David Roberts was ordained to the priesthood in 1966 in the Church of Christ Established Anew (now called the Church of Christ with the Elijah Message). While visiting the congregation in Wellston, Michigan, in 1967 he had a visitation by the Angel Nephi who told him of a future as a healing evangelist and told him to preach baptism in Jesus' name. Later that year he went to Independence, Missouri, for the first time and visited the temple lot, the location where, according to the Mormon scriptures, the temple of Zion is ultimately to be built. In another visit by the angel, he was told to rededicate the temple lot. He returned to his home in Columbus, Ohio. Seven years later, in 1974, he and his wife, Denise Roberts, were visited by the Prophet Elijah, who came to give David Roberts the keys to the salvation of the dead and ordained him to the office of Moses and king over the kingdom of God until Jesus returns to earth. At Elijah's bidding, they began new work in Newark, Ohio, out of which the True Church of God Restored emerged.

Roberts came to feel that his ordination represented a third restoration of the Church of Jesus Christ, the first two having been through Joseph Smith, Jr. and James Jesse Strang. Roberts is the successor to both. The True Church uses the Bible, the Book of Mormon, *The Book of the Lord's Commandments*, *The Book of Abraham*, *The Voree Plates* (translated by Strang), and *The Oracles of God Book* (revelation given through Roberts).

The Church is sabbatarian. Roberts also preaches the baptism of the Holy Ghost and Fire, which brings a new birth to the body. This blessing, also called body-felt salvation, changes the body in such a way as to prevent sickness and tiredness. It is experienced as a general feeling of comfort and completeness and the continuous healing process become established in the body.

Membership: Not reported. There is one congregation in Independence.

Periodicals: *The Voice of Eternal Life.*

Remarks: Robert's concept of body-felt salvation is very close to that of Pentecostal evangelist Franklin Hall, discussed elsewhere in this volume as the founder of the Hall Deliverance Foundation.

Sources:

Articles of Religion. Independence, MO: True Church of Jesus Christ Restored, n.d.

Roberts, David L. *The Angel Nephi Appears to David L. Roberts.* Independence, MO: True Church of Jesus Christ Restored, [1974].

Section 16

Communal Family

Consult the Contents pages to locate the essay in Part II, Historical Essay Chapters,
that provides an historical discussion of this family

Communal — Before 1960

★1212★
Adonai-Shomo
(Defunct)

Adonai-Shomo was an Adventist communal group founded in 1861 at Athol, Massachusetts, by Frederick T. Howland, a Quaker who had accepted the Adventist perspective on the imminent second coming of Jesus. Among the beliefs Howland taught the group of some 30 members was Sabbatarianism (worship on Saturday—then becoming a popular perspective within Adventist circles) and the equality of men and women. Howland also believed in physical immortality. The group faced a major crisis when Howland was killed in an accident a few years after the group was formed.

A short time after Howland's death, a man named Cook arrived and announced that God had sent him to become the new leader of the group. He was accepted as leader, but when he tried to institute some unconventional sex practices, the group revolted and had the local grand jury indict him. The next leader, a man named Richards, headed the group for many years. Under Richards, the group prospered for a generation, and the colony moved to a large house on an 840-acre tract of land near Petersham, Massachusetts.

By the 1890s the group had dwindled since many of the original members died and the younger members moved away. The end of Adonai-Shomo came in 1896 when a group of the young ex-members sued Richards in an attempt to gain some equity in the property. They won, but when the land was sold there was nothing left after the community's debts and legal fees were paid. The charter which had been granted in 1876 was dissolved and the group formally disbanded.

Sources:

Communities of the Past and Present. Newllano, LA: Llano Cooperative Colony, 1924.

Webber, Everett. *Escape to Utopia: The Communal Movement in America.* New York: Hastings House Publishers, 1959.

★1213★
Altruria
(Defunct)

Altruria was a communal experiment that grew out of the attempt of merging liberal Protestantism with the communal thought of William Dean Howells. Howells was the author of *A Traveler from Altruria* (1894), a utopian novel in which he described his vision of the ideal society. It inspired the thinking of Rev. Edward Biron Payne, a Unitarian pastor in Berkeley, California, who had been advocating a form of Christian socialism in his sermons. Of the essence of Christian socialism was the idea of the immanence of God in the social context and a program of saving people by reorganizing society in such a way that the sinful structures perpetuated by capitalism would be discarded. Humanity would im-prove by learning to live in a more just society that emphasized brotherhood, cooperation, and good will.

Payne and a small group of idealists met in 1894 to draft plans for a cooperative colony based on democratic suffrage and equality of community goods with some retention of private ownership of personal possessions. A site was selected near Fountain Grove, California, and in October, 18 adults and six children moved onto the land. A community periodical, the *Altrurian,* kept the larger community of supporters informed of its progress and promoted the formation of Altrurian clubs across the state. Clubs emerged in San Francisco, Oakland, Berkeley, San Jose, Pasadena, and Los Angeles. The clubs began to establish cooperative ventures and served as screening agencies for people desiring to move into the colony.

While attracting a number of new members, Altruria suffered from under-capitalization and poor financial planning. Within a year it was evident that bankruptcy was imminent, and in June 1895 a reorganization plan was announced. The colony's assets were liquidated and the entire effort restructured into several smaller units. Sixteen members moved to a new colony near Cloverdale, a second group moved into Santa Rosa, and a few remained at the original site. However, the restructuring only postponed the inevitable, and the next year all three of the sub-units had disbanded.

Sources:

Hine, Robert V. *California's Utopian Colonies.* San Marino, CA: Huntington Library, 1953. 209 pp.

★1214★
Amana Church Society (Community of True Inspiration)
% Kirk Setzer, President
PO Box 103
Middle Amana, IA 52307

The Amana Church Society, also known as the Community of True Inspiration, originated in Germany in the year 1714 among the Pietists who rejected Lutheran state- church polity and ritualism, as well as state laws on military service and oath taking. Their leaders were Eberhard Ludwig Gruber and Johann Friedrick Rock. These men gathered a following attracted to the notion that the divine revelation and prophecy were as operative in their day as in biblical days. All the sayings of the spiritual leaders were recorded and circulated among the faithful.

The eighteenth and early nineteenth centuries were times of persecution of nonconformists, so in 1842, Christian Metz was placed in charge of a Committee of Four to find a new home in America. An initial tract of land was purchased in New York and Ebenezer Society organized. In 1845 a communal system of property ownership was established. After twelve years, the Society outgrew its land. In 1855, the move began to Iowa, and Amana was first settled. Then five other villages——West Amana, South Amana, High Amana, East Amana, and Middle Amana-were established on a 26,000-acre tract. A new constitution, similar to the Ebenezer Constitution, was adopted in 1859. In 1861, the land of the whole community of Homestead was purchased in order for the society to have a community on the railroad line.

In addition to a complete faith in the Holy scriptures, the belief of the Amana Society is summarized in the *Twenty-four Rules forming the Basis of the Faith*, a short document channeled through J. A. Gruber. Subsequent revelations, paricularly those of Metz and his later contemporary, Barbara Heinemann, also have been published. Except for the orientation on the "Instruments" of revelation, the Amana Church Society's beliefs closely resemble those of the German Brethren. The *Twenty-four Rules* deal with the strict observance of the holy life and the christian community ethic.

In 1932, the Amana Society went through a thorough reorganization which separated the church and the temporal enterprises. The community system was abandoned, and each member of the community was given a share in the business enterprises, a very successful appliance corporation and farming. The community assets were distributed to members of the society in the form of stock certificates, in proportion to years of service. A community representative system of church government was adopted and power invested in a thirteen-member board of directors elected by the members.

The Amana Church Society continues as a church consisting of the members who live in the seven Amana communities. Economic communalism has been replaced by a wage system and private enterprise.

Membership: In 1997 the society reported 500 members in 1 congregation. There were 12 elders.

Periodicals: *Amana Church Society Newsletter*. Send orders to Box 103, Middle Amana, IA 52307.

Sources:

The Amana Church Hymnal. Amana, IA: Amana Church Society, 1992. 238 pp.

Barthel, Diane L. *Amana, From Pietist Sect to American Community*. Lincoln: University of Nebraska Press, 1984.

Rettig, Lawrence. *Amana Today*. South Amana, IA: The Author, 1975.

Scheuner, Gottlieb. *Inspirations—Histories*. 2 vols. Trans. by Janet W. Zuber. Amana, IA: Amana Church Society, 1976-77.

Shambaugh, Bertha M. H. *Amana That Was and Amana That Is*. Iowa City, IA: State Historical Society of Iowa, 1932.

Zuber, Janet W., trans. *Barbara Heineman Landmann Biography/E. L. Gruber's teaching on Divine Inspiration and Other Essays*. Lake Mills, IA: Graphic Publishing Co., 1981.

★1215★
Association of Beneficents
(Defunct)

The Association of Beneficents was established at Kiantone, Chatauqua County, New York in 1953 by John Murray Spear and a group of Spiritualists. Three years earlier, a blacksmith at Kiantone had gone into a trance in which information came forth that the area around a spring in the community had once been the site of a perfect society. Free love was one element in that perfection. The blacksmith sent samples of the water, which he believed had special magnetic and healing properties, to various prominent Spiritualists including Spear. A former Universalist, Spear had received communication from the spirit world instructing him to initiate some radical changes in society. He was told to inaugurate a model community and was even given the location, the design for domiciles, and a program for social reform. He decided that the site at Kiantone conformed to the information he had been given and would be an ideal location for building a city of universal harmony. In the spring of 1893 he constructed 10 small oval and octagonal homes, each approximately 10' x 14' and attracted up-

ward of 40 members, though most wintered away from the site. The colony was also known as the Domain, Harmonia, and the Kiantone Community.

Those attracted were feminists and believers in Spiritualism and free love. These were all espoused in a large convention held on the site by Spiritualists in 1858.

In 1859 the colonists abandoned the site and headed down the Mississippi River to promote a "planetary congress" to bring peace on earth. At the beginning of their journey, they reorganized as the Sacred Order of Unionists. Their journey was interrupted by a side trip to Patriot, Indiana, where in early 1860 they established a second colony that survived until 1863.

Sources:

Duino, Russell. "Utopian Themes with Variation: John Murray Spear and His Kiantone Domain." *Pennsylvania History* (April 1962).

Fogarty, Robert S. *Dictionary of American Communal and Utopian History*. Westport, CT: Greenwood Press, 1980. 271 pp.

★1216★
Bethel-Aurora Communities
(Defunct)

The communities of Bethel (Missouri) and Aurora (Oregon) were the result of the leadership of William Keil (1812-1877), a former Methodist minister who launched his first communal experiment in 1844. Keil, an Austrian by birth, arrived in the United States as a young man. He became a tailor and then a Methodist preacher at Phillipsburg, Pennsylvania. Along the way he came to see himself as one of the endtime witnesses mentioned in the biblical book of Revelation. In the early 1940s some former members of the Harmony Society—at the time headquartered not far away at Economy, Pennsylvania—left and joined Keil's church. From them he possibly developed the idea of forming a community.

In the spring of 1844, with his congregation of 200 members (all German-speaking), Keil moved onto a 2,560-acre tract in northern Missouri. He named the new community Bethel, after the old biblical town. The town grew rapidly and tripled in size over the next three years. The colonists built a church in which Keil preached a simple Christianity that centered upon primary Christian affirmations and the Golden Rule. Keil preached at the monthly church services.

A first branch colony was founded at Nineveh, Adair County, Missouri, in 1847. At its height it housed some 150 people on 2,000 acres. In 1856 a second group left Bethel for the far West. They settled in the Willamette River Valley about 30 miles from Portland and build another town, Aurora. Keil chose to move with the group to Oregon.

The Bethel and Aurora communities prospered through the 1870s. However, Keil died in 1877 and soon afterward both groups dissolved their communal structures. Historic museums survive at both sites today to interpret the history to visitors and tourists, and many descendants of the colonists still live in the two towns.

Sources:

Hendricks, R. J. *Bethel and Aurora*. 1933. Reprint, AMS Press, New Y ork, NY.

Hinds, William Alfred. *American Communities and Cooperative Colonies*. Chicago: Charles H. Kerr & Company, 1908. 608 pp.

★1217★
Bishop Hill
(Defunct)

Bishop Hill was a pietistic Christian community that originated in the independent preaching of Eric Janson in the 1830s in Sweden. The Church of Sweden showed little patience with Janson and charged him with spreading heresy. Janson had rejected the writings of Luther and professed to preach the Bible alone. Members of the group refused to attend their parish church, a fact that brought them (and their leader) to the attention of the authorities. In he face of continuing repression, they commissioned one of their number Olaf Olson to search out possibilities of a new life in America. He arrived in 1845 and purchased land in Henry County, Illinois. Janson also came in 1845 (to avoid a jail term) and the group, 1,200 strong, arrived the next year.

In 1850 Janson was shot by a disgruntled former member of the community who had been prevented by Janson from marrying a community member. The community continued without him. It was not until 1853 that they surmounted the legal difficulties to their organizing as a corporation and formally established the community. The community was loosely organized. It was led in its business dealings by a board of trustees, and several foremen organized the work. There were several preachers among them who shared the Sunday preaching duties but otherwise labored with the rest of the men through the week. Two worship services consisting of hymn singing, prayer, Bible reading, and preaching, were held each Sunday.

The simple community life continued until a significant number of youth reached adulthood and complained of boredom with the life and disbelief in the religion. In several steps during 1861 and 1862, the communal organization was abandoned and the property divided among the members. The church gave way to two new congregations, the members becoming either Methodists or Adventists.

Today, the buildings of the old Bishop Hill community are open to the public, and a historical museum has been created to interpret the story of Bishop Hill to tourists and visitors.

Sources:

Nordhoff, Charles. *The Communistic Societies of the United States.* 1875. Reprint. New York: Schrocken Books, 1965. 439 pp.

★1218★
Brotherhood of the New Life
(Defunct)

The Brotherhood of the New Life was the collective name given to the followers of prophet and visionary Thomas Lake Harris, whose movement took on a number of different organizational forms during his lifetime. Harris was born in England in 1823. He was raised a strict Baptist, but as a young man became a Universalist. At some point he migrated to the United States and in 1844 emerged as the pastor of the Fourth Universalist Church of New York City. While serving that church, however, he read the writings of Emanuel Swedenberg and converted to the Church of the New Jerusalem, and in 1847 became pastor of a Swedenbergian congregation in New York. Swedenbergianism led him into Spiritualism, which was spreading across the nation during the decade. In 1851 he became involved in the short-lived Spiritualist Mountain Cove Community in Fayette County, Virginia.

In the years after the failure of the Mountain Cove experiment, Harris became a writer and editor and a champion of Christian Spiritualism (the Spiritualist community having been divided into Christian and non-Christian factions). He founded the Brotherhood of the New Life in 1861 in Wassaic, New York. The community moved to Armenia, New York in 1865, to Brocton, New York in 1868, and to Santa Rosa, California in 1875. The Brocton community remained active through 1881 and became a screening place for people before moving to Fountain Grove, as the California center was called.

Harris' teachings evolved out of Swedenbergianism and Spiritualism. In the attempt to live out of the spiritual world, two ideas came to the fore. Harris believed himself to have been singled out as the core person to be the priest/king of a new society. His community would consist of people who had learned to breathe in harmony with himself, the "pivotal man." They would then become the vortex of divine power. The special breathing techniques en-

abled people to inhale what was believed to be a divine vapor and to repel evil spirits seen as pervasive in the atmosphere.

Harris became best known for his doctrines on sexuality. God, he taught, was bisexual, and he found sexuality expressed throughout nature. However, Harris called for a spiritualized sex life. Harris believed that one came closest to God when united with one's sexual counterpart. One's true counterpart existed in the spirit world and was able temporarily to inhabit a human body, but rarely did it inhabit the body of one's earthly spouse. Union with the counterpart could be obtained only in exalted states of consciousness reached through the breathing technique he taught.

His arcane doctrine was perfectly attuned to the separation of spouses living in the community and the living of celibate lives. Harris fathered two children by his first wife, but lived a celibate life with his second and third wives. However, Harris' writings were filled with sexual language that was easily misunderstood by the average reader who did not understand the metaphysical system out of which Harris operated. On several occasions, the community life was disturbed by accusations of sexual improprieties.

Harris came under strong attack in 1891 when Margaret Oliphant, whose cousin Laurence Oliphant had been a member of the Brotherhood, and Alzire A. Chevaillier both published accounts of the community. Oliphant accused Harris of sexual immorality and improper financial maneuvering. Chevaillier centered her attack on Harris' strong control over the community, but also hinted at sexual wrongdoings. Harris left and settled in New York and attempted to manage the community from across the country. It continued after Harris' death in 1906. Gradually, the spiritual teachings of the group died out and in the 1920s the property reverted to Kanaye Nagasawa, the last of the community members.

Sources:

Fogarty, Robert S. *Dictionary of American Communal and Utopian History.* Westport, CT: Greenwood Press, 1980. 271 pp.

Hine, Robert V. *California's Utopian Colonies.* San Marino, CA: Huntington Library, 1953. 209 pp.

★1219★
Bruderhof Communities in New York, Inc.
PO Woodcrest, Rte. 213
Rifton, NY 12471

History. Bruderhof Communities in New York, Inc. (formerly known as the Hutterian Brethren of New York, Inc. and the Society of Brothers) was formed in post-World War I Germany around the leadership of Eberhard Arnold (1883-1935). Arnold had had a background in the Christian Socialist Movement and the Student Christian Movement, out of which he began to preach a radical form of Christianity based upon the demands of the Sermon on the Mount (Matthew 5-7). In 1920 he rented Sannerz Villa where work on both publishing and gardening began and the writings of the Anabaptists and Hutterian Brethren studied. Upon learning of the continued existence of the Hutterian Brethren in the United States and Canada, the small group instituted a fellowship with them that led in 1930 to a merger. This union continued until 1956.

In 1935 Arnold died and a collective leadership emerged. His death was followed by moves to England (1936), Paraguay (1940), and the United States (1954). The group's initial move from Germany was forced by the Gestapo, who would not allow the Bruderhof to sustain either its pacifist stance or communal way of life. Both the break with the Hutterian Brethren and the move to the United States spurred changes. Some Hutterite forms were abandoned. At this time the Bruderhof consisted of 1,717 residents in nine communes in the United States, Paraguay, Uraguay, Germany, and England.

The first settlement in the United States was on a 100-acre site near Rifton, New York, named Woodcrest. The group was joined almost immediately by half of the members of another already existing commune, Macedonia, who brought with them a light industry, Community Playthings. It soon became the major source of income for the Bruderhof. In 1955, the Forest River, North Dakota, colony of he Hutterite Brethren-Schmieldeleut decided to join the Bruderhof. A third colony was begun at Oak Lake (now New Meadow Run) near Pittsburgh, Pennsylvania. In 1958 Evergreen, now Deer Spring Bruderhof, was established near Norfolk, Connecticut.

The early 1960's were years of crisis for the Bruderhof. The realization came more and more that the movement had wandered far from the enthusiastic beginnings in Germany and there was a great wish to find these early radical Christian roots again. In the process many left (though over the following years many of these returned to the renewed brotherhoods.) From the nine *hofs* (centers) in 1956, only four remained. Membership was consolidated in the United States and the lone British colony. About this same time, Eberhard Arnold's son, Heini Arnold (d. 1982), was unanimously appointed elder of all four communities. He remained in that position for the next two decades as the Bruderhof movement experienced an increasing appropriation of the Spirit in which it was founded. During this time Darvell Bruderhof in East Sussex, England, was established (1971) and the Eastern colonies were reunited with the Western Hutterian movement (1974) through mutual reconciliation, and took on once more much of the dress and customs of the older movement. This has led to much interchange with the Western colonies including many intermarriages and mutual aid. More recently the following Bruderhofs have been started: Pleasant View, Ulster Park, New York (1985), Michaelshof, Germany (1988), Spring Valley, Pennsylvania (1990), Catskill, Elka Park, New York (1990).

Beliefs. The Bruderhof remains in the Anabaptist theological tradition of the Hutterites, taking a strong stand on community of goods, nonviolence, and nonresistance, and faithfulness in marriage and sexual purity. The common life, which the Bruderhof believes is ordained of God and has Him as its center, is demonstrated in work, learning, play, and worship.

Worship is centered in the Gemeindestunde (a brotherhood gathering, very much like a prayer meeting) which is held most evenings. It includes a talk by a servant of the Word, silent prayer waiting in the Spirit (resembling a Quaker meeting), and a closing prayer by the servant. The religious experience of the Bruderhof is joy, expressed in singing and the closeness of life together.

Organization. Bruderhof is governed by a chief servant or "Vorsteher," the elders or servants of the Word (usually three in each colony), and the stewards, witness brothers, and house mothers. Great emphasis is placed, however, upon the consensus of the community in decision making.

The differing work loads that sustain the community are distributed to the different hofs. Community Playthings and Rifton Equipment for the Handicapped are located in sections at all bruderhofs, Woodcrest, New Meadow Run, Deer Spring, Pleasant View, and Darwell, and supply the basic financial support for the community. Plough Publishing House is located at Spring Valley Bruderhof, Farmington, Pennsylvania. In recent years it has published ten new books per year.

Membership: In 1997 there were approximately 2,500 residents of the five Bruderhof communities, of whom 250 live at the two centers in England.

Periodicals: *The Plough.* Send orders to Plough Publishing Company, Spring Valley Bruderhof, Farmington, PA 15437.

Sources:

Arnold, Eberhard. *Foundation and Orders of Sannerz and the Rhoen Bruderhof.* Rifton, NY: Plough Publishing Company, 1976.

___. *Why We Live Communally.* Rifton, NY: Plough Publishing House, 1976.

Arnold, Ebehard, and Emmy Arnold. *Seeking for the Kingdom of God.* Rifton, NY: Plough Publishing House, 1974.

Arnold, Emmy. *Torches Together.* Rifton, NY: Plough Publishing House, 1971.

Eggers, Ulrich. *Community for Life.* Scottsdale, PA: Herald Press, 1988.

Hutterian Society of Brothers, and John Howard Yoder, eds. *God's Revolution.* New York: Paulist Press, 1984.

Mow, Merrill. *Torches Rekindled: The Bruderhof's Struggle for Renewal.* Ulster Park, NY: Plough Publishing, 1989.

Zablocki, Benjamin. *The Joyful Community.* Baltimore, MD: Penguin Books, 1971.

★1220★
Celestia
(Defunct)

Celestia was a nineteenth century communal group that grew out of the Adventist excitement over the predicted imminent return of Christ. Among those affected by the preaching of Christ's return were Peter E. Armstrong and his wife Hannah Taylor Armstrong, who together operated a paper store in Philadelphia, Pennsylvania. Armstrong became convinced that Christ had been rejected during his life on earth because the people had not been prepared for his arrival. In his study of the Bible, he was drawn to Isaiah 40:3, "In the wilderness prepare ye the way of the Lord." He saw this passage as a personal message to himself and he began to act upon it literally. In 1850 he purchased a tract of land in Sullivan County, Pennsylvania, and began to lay plans for the building of a city modeled upon the one described in Revelation 21:6. Eventually other pieces of land were added, bringing the total to some 600 acres by 1860.

Celestia (the new city) was to be on a mountain top and to be laid out in a set of squares. The people attracted to the new city would live in a theocracy apart from human law. The theocracy included a communal lifestyle. Armstrong moved onto the property in 1860; Celestia was formally organized in 1863. The group was supported by farming and the operation of a few businesses. In 1864, Armstrong, in his most remembered action, deeded the land to God. Armstrong also created a second village which served as a probationary stopover for people inquiring about joining Celestia.

The community survived through the 1870s, though it never prospered. In 1876, the local county treasurer demanded the back taxes from God's property. The land was sold; Armstrong's son became the legal owner. Armstrong died in 1887 and the community faded away. His widow settled in Philadelphia.

Sources:

Bender, D. Wayne. *From Wilderness to Wilderness: Celestia.* Dushore, PA: Sullivan Review, 1980.

Miller, Timothy. *American Communes, 1860-1960: A Bibliography.* New York: Garland Publishing, 1990.

★1221★
Chapter of Perfection
(Defunct)

The Chapter of Perfection, frequently referred to as the Woman in the Wilderness community, was a pietistic Rosicrucian group founded in Germany in the seventeenth century by Johannes Jacob Zimmerman. The original members were primarily Lutheran scholars ready to delve into the inner mystical mysteries of life. Zimmerman had also been affected by two female seers who, drawing upon their personal psychic visions, had published their speculations about the return of Jesus, possibly in 1694.

Zimmerman proposed that the members of the chapter leave the relatively hostile atmosphere of Germany and accept the offer of land tended by William Penn, should they migrate to the new colony of Pennsylvania. There they would await the second coming. Zimmerman died in 1693, before the group finished preparations for leaving, and was succeeded by Johannes Kelpius. The group arrived in Philadelphia on June 24, 1694, just in time to celebrate the summer solstice on St. John's Eve.

The group settled in Germantown north of Philadelphia, adjacent to Wissahickon Creek. There they constructed a headquarters building, shaped as a cube, each side being 40 feet in length. Numerologically, 40 was believed to be a perfect number. The building had a sanctuary, study room, and a mediation room. On the roof they established their astronomical laboratory where during the evenings they scanned the sky for evidence of the soon appearance of Christ. In the meantime, the brothers (all the members were male) founded a school for the neighborhood children, served as doctors for the community, and did astrological work for any who requested it.

The community lived through a series of disappointments when Christ did not return in 1694 or in 1700. Matthias died in 1708 after a lengthy illness. The chapter began to disintegrate after Matthias' death. The surviving members remained in the area as individual healers and psychic practitioners. Their work seems to have led directly to the practice of the hexen-meisters, magical practitioners who can still be found in rural southeastern Pennsylvania.

Sources:

Holloway, Mark. *Heavens on Earth: Utopian Communities in America, 1680-1880*. London: Turnstile Press, 1951. 240 pp.

Melton, J. Gordon. "Pioneers. . . in Land, in Knowledge, in Astrology!" *American Astrology* 41, 10 (December 1973): 18-21,

★1222★
Christian Commonwealth Colony
(Defunct)

Among the more important experiments in Christian socialism, the Christian Commonwealth was formed by the merger of two previously existing efforts, the Willard Cooperative Colony and the Christian Corporation. It was organized for the purpose of demonstrating to the world the desirability of Christian cooperative activity as a means to building a Christian civilization. The Willard Cooperative colony had been formed in 1895 at Harriman, Tennessee, by a group of some 50 prohibitionists who sought an alternative to capitalist society. Frances Willard, then the prominent president of the Women's Christian Temperance Union, lent her name and support to the project. After its founding, the colonists settled on land near Andrews, North Carolina. The Christian Corporation was founded in 1896 by George Howard Gibson. The colony was located in Lincoln, Nebraska, and included some 26 members.

Both colonies experienced some instability, but in 1896 merged their efforts into a new colony in Muskogee County, Georgia, and were united by a vision of Christian brotherhood, a belief in making Christianity practical, and the desire to continue the cooperative life. Members of the two older colonies were joined by new members attracted by accounts of its plans in *The Kingdom,* a socialist magazine. The colonists began their own periodical, *The Social Gospel.*

The colony was supported by the Right Relationship League, a socialist group headquartered in Chicago, which advanced it some initial capital. The colonists began a textile mill and publishing concern. By 1898 the mill was producing and selling towels.

The colony ran into trouble in 1899. The textile business failed, and several ex-members began to vocalize charges of mismanagement. In 1900, the Right Relationship League took steps to secure its investment. By the summer of 1900 the corporate assets went into receivership and the colony effectively disbursed. At its height, some 90 people resided in the community.

Sources:

Hinds, William Alfred. *American Communities and Cooperative Colonies.* Chicago: Charles H. Kerr & Company, 1908. 608 pp.

★1223★
Christ's Church of the Golden Rule
Ridgewood Ranch
16100 N. Hwy. 101
Willits, CA 95490

Christ's Church of the Golden Rule emerged in 1944 following conversations between a group of Christian men and women who shared a concern about existing religious and economic practices and their perceived failure to meet the spiritual and material needs of humanity. These conversations were held in the context of the Bible and the teachings of Jesus Christ, especially The Golden Rule and Jesus' words, "Seek ye first the kingdom of God and his righteousness (right-use-ness) and all these things will be added unto you" (Matthew 6:33). These men and women concluded that these directions had not, to their knowledge, been followed since the days of the early Christian church described in Acts 2:44 and Acts 4:32. They agreed that they should respond to Jesus' words and actually attempt to live Jesus' teachings and thus demonstrate to their contemporaries whether living such principles would overcome poverty, war, and insecurity, and in the process make possible a worldwide brotherhood of humanity.

They investigated the manner to best structure their ideals and concluded that the formation of a church was the best way both to embody their understanding in a community and meet the necessary legal requirements that would allow them the greatest freedom of action. They formed Christ's Church of the Golden Rule in January 1944.

The church's creed is the Golden Rule, "Therefore all things whatsoever ye would that men should do to you, do ye even so to them" (Matthew 7:12). The church understands the Rule as working in one direction; it never applies to the manner in which others treat you, but always the way you treat others. The church's goal is stated in its vision, "A World free from want, with liberty and justice for all, and with understanding love toward God and one another. This day's work is dedicated to the end that we may prove that it is more blessed to give than to receive, and that it is true that giving does not impoverish nor does withholding enrich."

The teachings of the church are summarized in its brief "Declaration of Faith." It affirms belief in the one true God, conceived as Father-Mother; Jesus of Nazareth who came to reveal God to humankind and who was possessed of the eternal Christ (Truth); the authority of the Holy Bible; and salvation by repentance and regeneration through the Truth, the mind of God which was in Christ Jesus. The church teaches that the essence of true religion is to love God and to do unto others as we would have them do unto us. It also teaches that equality in economic affairs is the only foundation upon which to build a humane world.

Through 1944 and 1945 some 850 people signed up as founding members of the church and gave up their personal wealth, family, and social ties, and moved onto the church's property. At the same time, some 100 pieces of property, primarily along the West Coast, were donated and a few additional pieces purchased for church use. Resident training centers were established on these properties.

By 1945 the church's property was valued at approximately three million dollars. That same year some of the founding members decided that they did not wish to remain church members. They withdrew and began legal proceedings to retrieve property they had donated. California's attorney general joined that effort and moved to place the church into a receivership. The church responded by filing voluntary bankruptcy proceedings in federal court. The legal battle, which finally went in favor of the church, lasted for six years, and was costly. Not only did many members leave, but much of the church's property was sold during this period and the value of the church's holdings was reduced from three million to several hundred thousand.

In 1951, the church, in effect, had to begin anew to build the working model with which they had begun. In 1953, the church's seminary in San Francisco, an important training center, was sold and property purchased near Bolinas, California. In the early 1960s that property was included in a government plan to create the Point Reyes National Seashore Park. Thus in 1962 the church sold its property and moved to Mendicino County onto the large Ridgewood Ranch. Over the next few years the church's other centers, including ones in Colorado and Wyoming, were closed and consolidated at the ranch. Over the next two decades the property was improved to house up to 100 residents. Private housing for students, a chapel-dining room complex, a social lounge, a food processing unit, business and accounting office, a publications department, school building, and library were all erected. Facilities are available to welcome people making inquiry about church membership and other visitors.

The church was legally recognized as a church in 1964. It is directed by an Advisory Board of Elders. All resident members of the church live communally. No property or income came inure to any individual and all is used for the benefit of the church. No outside donations are solicited, though gifts are accepted for the spread of the church's message, especially through its publications. The church operates a variety of business enterprises which have allowed the community to be self-supporting. Members of the church are active in the larger community. The church's facilities are available to different religious, cultural, and educational groups in the county and the group has been especially supportive of the local 4-H club and the Willits Jr. Horsemen.

Membership: In 1994 there were several hundred members, between 50 and 100 residing at the ranch in Willits at any one time. The non-resident adherents subscribe to the church's teachings but reside around the country, primarily in the western states.

Remarks: The Church has often been associated with a previously existing movement, Mankind United. Leaders of the church strongly deny any such connection beyond the bare fact that some of the founding members had been associated with that movement and the two organizations happen to share some concerns for the economic injustice present in society. However, the church was founded quite independently of that movement and has through its 50 years of existence demonstrated its adherence to its religious teachings.

Sources:

The Essence of Our Teachings. Willits, CA: Christ's Church of the Golden Rule, 1971. 35 pp.

Our Golden Rule Crusade. 2 vols. Willits, CA: Christ's Church of the Golden Rule, 1963.

Our Golden Rule Way of Life. Willits, CA: Christ's Church of the Golden Rule, 1967. 53 pp.

★1224★
Church of Jesus Christ of Latter-day Saints (Wight)
(Defunct)

Lyman Wight was one of the Twelve Apostles of the Church of Jesus Christ of Latter-day Saints during the Nauvoo, Illinois, years in the 1840s. With the formation of Texas as a new independent republic, Mormon prophet Joseph Smith, Jr. had considered it as a possible place of refuge for the embattled Saints. He commissioned Wight as the leader of a company to explore the opportunities in Texas, but the plan was postponed while Smith campaigned for president of the United States. It was further delayed by Smith's assassination in 1844. Brigham Young, who succeeded Smith as president of the church, disapproved of the plan. But Wight felt he had a commission from Smith and led a group of approximately

150 church members to Austin, Texas. The group settled near Fredericksburg and built a new town, Zodiac, in 1847. In 1848, Wight issued his sole statement relating his position to that of the church as a whole and defending himself against accusations made by Brigham Young. On January 1, 1849, the group formally organized a new church and elected Wight as its president. Young excommunicated Wight a month later. A temple was dedicated on February 17, 1849, though little is known of how much of the temple ceremony from the Nauvoo period was carried over. A communal life was adopted.

Meanwhile, events were moving swiftly in the Midwest. William Smith, the brother of Joseph Smith, Jr. and patriarch of the church at the time of the assassination, fell out with Brigham Young and was excommunicated in 1845. In 1847 Smith emerged as the president and patriarch of a new church. During 1849 Smith began to look toward Texas as a place of refuge, and in 1850 he attempted to consolidate his work with that of Wight. As the two groups merged, Wight was named as Smith's counselor. Smith, because of his fraternal relationship to Joseph Smith, Jr., was granted the leadership of the church.

The church that Smith had created in the Midwest was never stable and had suffered a major controversy because of Smith's openness to polygamy. In the months following the merger, the organization completely fell apart and most of the membership, including Smith, moved into the Reorganized Church of Jesus Christ of Latter Day Saints, which had been constituted in 1852. With the disintegration in the Midwest, Wight's colony simply returned to its premerger organization.

Wight's colony prospered through the 1850s. Having to move because of flooding in 1851 and 1853, the group eventually settled near Bandera, Texas. In 1858 Wight suddenly died. No new leader arose, and a short time later the colony united with the Reorganized Church.

Sources:

Hunter, J. Melvin. *The Lyman Wight Colony in Texas.* Bandera, TX: The Author, n.d.

Shields, Steven L. *Divergent Paths of the Restoration.* Los Angeles: Restoration Research, 1990.

Wight, Lyman. *An Address by Way of an Abridged Account and Journal of My Life from February 1844 up to April 1848, with an Appeal to the Latter Day Saints, Scattered Abroad in the Earth.* Austin, TX: The Author, 1848.

★1225★
Church of the Brotherhood
Current address not obtained for this edition.

The Church of the Brotherhood is a Hutterite-like body which no longer professes any formal or ethnic ties with the Hutterite Brethren. The two groups hold in common the fundamental doctrines: adult confession and baptism, reliance on Scripture rather than theology or doctrine, pacifism, and the effort to duplicate the communal Apostolic church. The Church of the Brotherhood differs from the Hutterites in its belief that communities must maintain their apartness while living in the world and transacting business with non-believers, all the while giving witness to the gospel. Members believe it idolatrous to adopt any practice which makes symbols, not life, the means of giving and maintaining identity. Thus they speak a contemporary language and wear no special clothing. Full members live in complete discipline, and dedicate all work and wealth to the community. Confessional members devote a minimum of a tithe of goods and wealth and a full day of work in service projects.

Ministers work in secular pursuits and are not salaried. No separate worship houses are built. Love feasts, washing of feet, and baptism are ordinances. The group operates four centers for emotionally disturbed children and has created more than fifty centers for slum families and migrants, which operate as autonomous facilites.

Membership: Not reported. In 1969 there were 200 disciplined members and 30,000 confessional members.

★1226★
Church of the Covenant
(Defunct)

The Church of the Covenant was one name for the religious community that arose in the larger community founded in the 1870s at Preston, California, under the leadership of Emily Preston. It was also referred to as the Church of Heaven or the religion of inspiration. The church began soon after H. L. Preston purchased some land several miles north of Cloverdale, California, and moved there in 1869. Over the next few years he purchased some 1,500 acres. After the railroad was extended to Cloverdale, other people began to arrive in the area and settled on or near the Preston land. Thus arose a town that came to be built around Emily Preston's healing and preaching work.

At Preston, a church building was erected and Emily became the preacher. As people moved to the community, attendance at the Sunday and Thursday church services was one requirement. Preston had learned some of the secrets of herbal medicine during her youth, and in the years before her marriage, Emily had worked as a healer in San Francisco. She gave up her healing work after her marriage, but her husband saw a need for it and encouraged her to begin again after they moved to Preston. Many were drawn to Preston for either a brief visit or as residents following their receipt of some healing potions sent to them through the mail.

Preston seems to have preached a simple, practical faith built around the worship of God and the Golden Rule. She believed that how one led one's life determined whether they would go to heaven or hell after death. Worship consisted of a time of singing, of quiet meditation, and Preston's preaching. She taught that verbal prayer was not needed as God knew what to do better than any humans did. It was proper to be thankful to God at all times. Her thoughts on religion were gathered in a book, *The Hell and the Heaven,* published in 1902. Preston had a peculiarity in generally referring to God as a Man (rather than a spirit). She referred to Christ as the Son of Man.

H. L. Preston died in 1887; Emily followed in 1909. At the time of her death some 100 people lived at Preston, either on the Preston land or adjacent property. For several decades through the early twentieth century, people continued to gather at the church for periods of singing and silent meditation. Many of the structures at Preston continued to stand and be used into the 1980s. In 1988 a fire swept through the area and destroyed many of the buildings.

Sources:

Miller, Timothy. *American Communes, 1860-1960: A Bibliography.* New York: Garland Publishing, 1990. 583 pp.

Preston, Mrs. H. L. *The Hell and the Heaven.* The Author, 1902.

Votruba, M. J. "The Preston Story." Unpublished paper in the collection of the Institute for the Study of American Religion, 1971. 40 pp.

★1227★
Church of the Saviour
2025 Massachusetts Ave., NW
Washington, DC 20036

The Church of the Saviour was formed in 1946 in Washington, D.C., by a group of nine, headed by Gordon Cosby, a former Baptist. The vision of the new ministry was one of ecumenicity and evangelism, and total commitment of life and resources to Christ. The new communal existence was seen as representative of new humanity-reconciled and reconciling men and women. The result has been a community dedicated both to the nurture of the inner spiritual life and to the outward life of service.

The church has identified four missional thrusts: to Christ's church throughout the world, to the poor and oppressed, to the stranger in our midst, to the building of our common life. To carry out its missions, it has divided itself into nine faith communities, an Ecumenical Service, and the Ecumenical Council which coordinates and oversees the communities. Located in Washington, D.C. in the same headquarters as the council is the Seekers Church. Also located in Washington at various locations are the Eighth Day Church, the Jubilee Church, the Christ House Church, the Festival Church, the Lazarus House Church, the New Community Church, and the Potter's House Church. In Maryland is the Dayspring Church. Each of the nine faith communities has a number of mission groups which involve the members in corporate ministries. For example, Dayspring, through its Wellspring mission groups provides programs and a newsletter which attempt to build and nurture church growth among Christians not necessarily affiliated with the Church of the Saviour. The Jubilee Church ministers within the Jubilee apartments, a multi-family dwelling established and managed by Jubilee Housing. Other missional thrusts are concerned with peace, the rights of the elderly, health care for the homeless, and education of underprivileged youth.

Each faith community is under the guidance of one or more elders. Each community has its own worship services during the week, and there is an ecumenical service on Sunday mornings.

Membership: In 1992 the church reported 165 full members and 600 in its worshipping community.

Educational Facilities: The Servant Leadership School, Washington, D.C.

Periodicals: *Wellspring.* Send orders to 11301 Neelsville Church Rd., Germantown, MD 20874. • *The Potters House Book.* • *The Servant Leadership Press.* • *Service Newsletter.* Send orders to 1658 Columbia Rd. NW, Washington, DC 20009.

Sources:

Cosby, Gordon. *Handbook for Mission Groups.* Washington, DC: Potter's House, 1973.

O'Connor, Elizabeth. *Call to Commitment.* New York: Harper & Row, 1963.

___. *Cry Pain, Cry Hope.* Waco, TX: Word Books, 1987.

___. *Eighth Day of Creation.* Waco, TX: Word Books, 1971.

___. *Journey Inward, Journey Outward.* New York: Harper & Row, 1968.

___. *The New Community.* New York: Harper & Row, 1976.

★1228★
The Colony
Burnt Ranch, CA 95527

The Colony was begun August 18, 1940 by its prophet and founder, Brother John Korenchan (1886-1982), and eighteen members who settled on the Trinity River near Hawkins Bar, California. Brother John had his spiritual awakening in 1912, when, after five days of fasting and prayer, he was made to feel as a child without fault or law-breaking against the Creator. He wandered through the Siskiyou and Trinity Counties for years, and spent a few months in jail for his pacifism during World War I. As World War II began, he gathered a group of followers in Seattle. This group was finally led to California. Over the years, the group turned the area into a bountiful farm. Brother John was succeeded by Sister Agnes, the only surviving member of the original group.

There are no rules, not even grace at meals. Moderation, not abstinence, is the goal. Brother John taught that religion is meaningless unless it comes from within and is lived. Emphasis is placed on the guidance of the Power. The Power guided members to the Colony, brings in new members as it will, and discerns who is ready for the Truth, Christ.

Membership: In 1988 there were 13 residents of the Colony, all of whom had lived there at least 12 years. Others come in regularly for group activities.

★1229★
Dorrilites
(Defunct)

Among the first of the nonconventional religions founded among the European colonists in North America occurred in New England in the years after the American Revolution (1775-83). A former British Army officer named Dorril claimed to be a prophet of God and to be receiving revelations from him. He worked in Massachusetts and Vermont and gathered groups of followers during the 1790s. At its height, membership was approximately 40.

Dorril organized his followers communally. There was not private property. Vegetarianism was strictly observed, and leather shoes were not allowed. It also appears that the group did away with marriage vows and practiced a form of free love, though the records of their exact patterns of behavior have not survived. They were attacked for their sexual license by one contemporary minister, the Rev. Joseph Lathrop of Springfield, Massachusetts, who also noted that they disregarded the laws of the land and worked on the Sabbath.

The end of the small band is reported to have been brought on by a confrontation between Dorril and a local unbeliever. Dorril had told his followers that he was immune to pain. He was challenged by a man who proceeded to hit him several times. The man did not stop until Dorril announced not only his pain, but also promised not to make any further supernatural claims. The group disbursed shortly after the incident.

Sources:

Ludlum, David M. *Social Ferment in Vermont, 1791-1850.* New York: Columbia University Press, 1939.

★1230★
Ecumenical Institute
4750 N. Sheridan Rd.
Chicago, IL 60640

The Ecumenical Institute, formed in 1957, grew out of a World Council of Churches meeting in Evanston, Illinois, in 1954, which called for the formation of regional institutes modeled on the Ecumenical Institute at Bossey, Switzerland. In 1957, an American regional institute was formed in Evanston, with Walter Leibrecht as its director. It existed as a center for continuing ecumenical discussion. At about the same time, The Christian Faith and Life Community, formed in Austin, Texas, as a lay institute, was inspired by direct visitation to many such institutes in Europe. Joseph Wesley Mathews, brother of Bishop James K. Mathews of the United Methodist Church, was its dean of studies from 1956 to 1962.

In 1962, the Joseph Mathews family and seven other families were called by the Church Federation of Greater Chicago to become the staff of the Ecumenical Institute in Evanston. Within a year, the work that had been previously focused on curriculum for local church clergy and laity had taken on the task of community development in a ghetto neighborhood on the west side of Chicago, Illinois, where the staff relocated. The staff discovered that there was a group of people, many of whom were in the church, committed to being a leading force in the "movement to create the future." The Institute defined its task as providing structure, training, and models of possibility in order to bring about needed changes in a most practical manner.

The staff reorganized itself to operate as a family religious order—with a common economic, political, and cultural life, and with a common understanding of embodying the vows of poverty, chastity, and obedience. A unique theology for the twentieth century was developed by integrating major themes from the teachings of Deitrich Bonhoeffer, H. Richard Niebuhr, Rudolf Bult-

mann, Paul Tillich, Karl Barth, and Soren Kierkegaard, all leading modern Protestant theologians. The programs were designed to be applicable to any person regardless of race, religion, or nation, and a variety of people found them effective in making a difference in their local situations.

Beginning in 1968, institute staff were deployed outside of Chicago, starting with Australia and Malaysia. The Institute of Cultural Affairs, a program division of the institute, was separately incorporated in order to work more effectively in non-Christian settings. Between 1975 and 1978, human development projects were established around the globe with a central emphasis on the "human factor world development." These projects were celebrated as demonstrations of comprehensive, integrated human development in 1984 at the International Exposition of Rural Development in New Dehli, India. This exposition, which brought together the wisdom of local developments in some 50 nations, was sponsored by the Institute of Cultural Affairs and included the co-sponsorship of the United Nationa Development Program, the United Nations International Children's Education Fund, the World Health Organization, and the International Council of Women.

The staff is organized around 18 units with resident centers in 23 nations and a work in 50 nations. Work in each nation is incorporated separately and is headed by a national board of directors and a national board of advisors. These national groups are part of the Institute of Cultural Affairs International, registered as a charitable association in Belgium.

In 1972 the Ecumenical Institute separately incorporated in Illinois as The Institute of Cultural Affairs (ICA). Through this new corporation the institute could work with local communities in rural villages and urban neighborhoods in non-Christian countries. The work was focused on comprehensive economic and social development including local commerce and industry, community identity and organization, education of all ages, both preventative and curative health. As this work developed in the 1970s, it was found that the basic methods could also be applied and adapted for work with organizations such as corporations, hospitals, schools, government agencies, and other not-for-profit organizations.

Membership: In 1997 the Ecumenical Institute reported 200 staffs in 23 countries worldwide plus an additional 20,000 associates and affiliates. There were 1,000 members in 10 centers in the United States and 200 members in one center in Canada (Toronto).

Periodicals: *Highlights* (quarterly)—newsletter. • *Image.* Available from ICA India, 13 Sankli St., 2nd Fl., Bombay 400-008, India. • *Edges.* Available from ICA Canada, 577 Kingston Rd., Toronto, ON, Canada M4E 1R3. • *Initiatives* (quarterly)—newsletter. Available from ICA West, 4220 N. 25th St., Phoenix, AZ 85016. • *The Network Exchange* (monthly)—newsletter. Available from ICA Brussels, rue Amedee Lynen 8, B-1030 Brussels, Belgium.

Sources:

Cryer, Newman. "Laboratory for Tomorrow's Church." *Together* 10, no. 3 (March 1966).

★1231★
Esoteric Fraternity
Box 37
Applegate, CA 95703

The Esoteric Fratenity was founded in 1887 in Boston, Massachusetts, by Hiram Erastus Butler (d. 1916). Butler, after losing several fingers in a saw-mill accident, became a hermit in a New England forest for fourteen years and, as a hermit, began to receive revelations from God. In the late 1880s, he began to tell these revelations to others, gathering around him a dozen followers, all single men and women. They pooled their resources, moved to Applegate, California, and established a monastic-like community. The basic ideas of the Fraternity was that to believe in God one must live the life of a celibate. When man gives up the sex act, the kingdom of God will be established on earth. This belief has tended to keep the group small. At its height, around the beginning of this century, there were only forty members.

The Esoteric Faternity teaches Esoteric Christianity. Members believe in reincarnation and that the population of the world remains constant, as old souls are constantly reborn. They believe that the Fraternity consists of the chosen ones, the Order of Melchizedek as prophesied in the Book of Revelation. They will grow to be 144,000 in number and then the kingdom of God will begin. They would be rulers of the earth for eternity.

Following Butler's death, Enoch Penn, a prolific writer (as was Butler), succeeded him. Penn was editor of the *Esoteric Christian*, the popular periodical of the fraternity which ceased when Penn died in 1943. The next leaders were Lena Crow (d.1953), William Corecco (d.1972), and Fred Peterson, the current president. Peterson, a former Mormon, had converted to the group in the 1950s. A large business in Butler's and Penn's books continues.

In August 1973, one elderly male member of the fraternity was murdered. His killer has not been apprehended.

Membership: Not reported. In 1981 there were only three members.

Sources:

Butler, Hiram E. *The Goal of Life*. Applegate, CA: Esoteric Publishing Company, 1908.

___. *The Narrow Way of Attainment*. Applegate, CA: Esoteric Publishing Company, 1901.

___. *The Seven Creative Principles*. Applegate, CA: Esoteric Publishing Company, 1950.

___. *Special Instructions for Women*. Applegate, CA: Esoteric Fraternity, 1942.

Penn, Enoch. *The Order of Melchisedek*. Applegate, CA: Esoteric Fraternity, 1961.

★1232★
Fruitlands
(Defunct)

Fruitlands was a communal experiment established as a visible expression of the Transcendentalist Movement in nineteenth-century New England. Transcendentalism was an idealistic spiritualized philosophy, the end product of the questioning of Christian orthodoxy that began in Unitarianism. Whereas Unitarianism had found its base in rational thought, Transcendentalism was based much more clearly in the affections. Its main exponent was Ralph Waldo Emerson, who admonished the readers of his many essays to embrace the spiritual realities that stand behind the visible world and to come to a comprehension of the oneness of spiritual reality. His thoughts would, in the late-nineteenth century, lead directly to Christian Science and New Thought.

Fruitlands began in the idealism of Bronson Alcott, the father of Louisa May Alcott and an associate of Emerson. In 1842 Emerson loaned the financially embarrassed Alcott money to visit England, where a school had been established on a model of the school Alcott had established in Boston. While in England, Alcott met three men who shared his ideals and his vision of an ideal society. When he returned to America, two of the men (Henry Wright and Charles Lane) and Lane's son William, accompanied him. They also brought a large occult library. Charles Lane put up the initial capital to obtain the land upon which Fruitlands could be founded.

The young idealists and the Alcott family moved to Fruitlands, a 90-acre farm about two miles from Harvard, Massachusetts.

The first goal of the Fruitlands program was personal reform, which was focused in a number of behavior changes. The group accepted a strict vegetarian diet that banished even milk and butter. They did not drink coffee, tea, or alcoholic beverages and ex-

isted on a diet of apples, bread, cereal, herbs, and roots. The life at Fruitlands was to be a simple one that allowed for the nurturance of culture. However, the group rejected the idea of using animals to assist in farming and soon found that their leisure time was taken up in the realities of farm life. Culture soon was limited to after-meal conversations. No form of religion was adopted, Transcendentalism being best expressed in individual mystical appropriation of a spiritual vision.

A communal dress was adopted. It consisted of linen tunics and shoes made of cork and canvas (rather than leather). The men had trousers and hats; the women wore bloomers. Daily baths were taken in unheated water.

While many came to see what Alcott had established, few stayed to join. They were unwilling to don the strange dress and accept the rigid diet. In the winter after the first year, the capital was used up and the community was forced to close. The land was sold at the beginning of 1844. At its height it had approximately 20 members.

Sources:

Hinds, William Alfred. *American Communities and Cooperative Colonies*. Chicago: Charles H. Kerr & Company, 1908. 608 pp.

Lawson, Donna. *Brothers and Sisters All Over This Land: America's First Communes*. New York: Preager Publishers, 1972. 142 pp.

Webber, Everett. *Escape to Utopia: The Communal Movement in America*. New York: Hastings House Publishers, 1959. 444 pp.

★1233★
Harmony Society
(Defunct)

The Harmony Society was a prominent communal group that originated in the pietistic preaching of a farmer, George Rapp, who began to preach to his neighbors in a rural area of Wrttemburg, Germany. He was one of a number of unofficial preachers and Bible teachers who had emerged as purveyors of a popular pietistic religious faith to supplement the rather dry and ritualistic experience many had in the local Lutheran parish church. The Lutherans viewed such movements, such as those led by Rapp, as challenges to authorities rather than the natural outgrowth of faith. Rapp and some of his followers were fined, imprisoned, and subjected to various attempts to discourage their assembling. Such activity merely led to the group's expansion.

In 1803 Rapp left for America in an attempt to find land where the group could settle. He initially purchased land north of Pittsburgh in southwest Pennsylvania, and the next summer the group of more than 700 people migrated. They survived on their own through the winter of 1804–05, but in 1805 they assembled on the land Rapp had purchased and formally organized the Harmony Society. At this time the group adopted a communal order that included a common purse, a simple form of dress, and a plan to care for the elderly and the children. They then turned to the task of building a community based upon farming and some related industries: a saw-mill, a tannery, a distillery, and a winery. Following a wave of religious fervor that swept the community in 1807, they adopted celibacy (though not nuclear family life) and gave up tobacco.

In 1814 the community bought 30,000 acres of land along the Wabash River in southern Indiana, and the following year the entire community in Pennsylvania moved and founded the town of New Harmony. In 1818 the group renewed their communal commitment, signaled by their burning all the records of what each person and family had originally contributed to the group more than a decade earlier. However, New Harmony, while a great success financially, was less than what the group had hoped, and in 1824 and 1825 the group moved back to Pennsylvania on land near their earlier location and created the town of Economy. Robert Owen purchased New Harmony and built his own community there. Economy prospered, as had the previous communities, and was disturbed only by a schism in 1832 when several hundred members were drawn away by a rival leader.

The community was built around the pietistic Lutheran faith espoused by George Rapp, usually called Father Rapp by his followers. He was ably assisted by an adopted son, Friedrich Rapp (d. 1832), who handled much of the practical business and administrative affairs of the group. When Father Rapp died in 1847, he was succeeded by Romelius Baker and Jacob Henrici. In the late nineteenth century John Duss became the leader and during his tenure in the 1890s, the community suffered from a number of bad investments. Their economic problems led to a series of lawsuits and severe internal disputes that finally resulted in the colony disbanding in 1898.

After the end of the communal life, many of the colonists continued to reside in Economy and perpetuated the group's religious life into the first decades of the twentieth century. By World War I, however, almost all signs of the group had faded away.

Sources:

Arndt, Karl J. R. *George Rapp's Harmony Society, 1785-1847.* Cranbury, NJ: Farleigh, Dickinson 1965.

___. *George Rapp's Successors and Material Heirs, 1847-1916.* Fairleigh Dickinson, 1972.

Duss, John. *The Harmonists: A Personal History.* Pennsylvania Book Service, 1943. Reprint, Philadelphia, PA: Porcupine Press, 1973.

Holloway, Mark. *Heavens on Earth: Utopian Communities in America, 1680-1880.* London: Turnstile Press, 1951. 240 pp.

★1234★
Heaven City
(Defunct)

Heaven City was a communal group founded by Albert J. Moore (d. 1963) in 1923 in Harvard, Illinois. Moore was born in Wales and migrated to Chicago as a young man. Claiming miraculous powers to assist people, he founded an organization called the Life Institute. In 1922 he was charged with fraud, and though initially convicted, his case was overturned on appeal. Shortly thereafter, he and 28 followers established a community on a 130-acre farm near Harvard. The colony practiced a community of consumption, but was largely financed by the jobs held by some members who worked outside it. In the 1930s, Heaven City moved to Mukwonago, Wisconsin, where the group operated a motel, restaurant, and bar. Membership reached a peak of 75 in the mid-1930s.

Along with a strict communalism, the group started its own school. Sexual relationships were rather free, though marriages did occur. Moore believed that the sex instinct was the creative force of the world. Heaven City continued until Moore's death, though it had begun to decline. The motel was managed by his secretary Shirley P. Talcott who died in 1978 at the age of 95. She willed the hotel to two of its employees who have continued to manage it as a business.

Following Talcott's death some of Moore's family tried to lay claim to the motel property, and even briefly reorganized the Heaven City religion, but their effort failed in court.

Sources:

Zahn, Michael. "Heaven City Dies with Founder." *Milwaukee Journal* (August 14, 1979).

★1235★
Holy City Brotherhood
(Defunct)

The Holy City Brotherhood was founded in 1914 in Los Angeles as the Perfect Christian Divine Way by William Edward Riker (1873-1969). Riker, a native Californian who moved to San Francisco as a young man, was an avid reader of occult and New

Thought metaphysical literature, out of which he began to develop his own metaphysical world. Soon, he began to think of himself as The Comforter, the biblical name for the Holy Spirit sent by God to humankind. He started to travel the country preaching what he called the Perfect Christian Divine Science. In 1914, with a core of five close disciples, Riker established headquarters of the Perfect Christian Divine Way in Los Angeles. A second group emerged in San Francisco. Incorporation followed in 1918. Among his unique ideas was a racial understanding of humanity on the analogy of the human body, with Jews representing the mind (head) and Christians the heart (chest). Black people made up the legs and oriental races the arms. He felt humanity's great sin was race mixing.

In 1991 Riker purchased some 200 acres in the Santa Cruz Mountains and moved there with his followers, who set about building Holy City. They created a self-sufficient community complete with an electric generator, barber shop, laundry, and cafe. They raised much of their own food and built a soft drink bottling company. Holy City itself was built on the road from San Jose to Santa Cruz and became a popular tourist stop. Riker ran for governor on several occasions.

Through the 1930s, Holy City prospered with 38 permanent members and up to several hundred who passed through for short stays. It began a long process of decline in the years after World War II as members moved away and few new members took their place. By 1956 only eight members (seven males and one female) remained. That year Riker sold the property to Maurice Kline, but the members were allowed to stay on the property. Riker and Kline soon disagreed over the future of the community and Riker sued to regain control of the property, but lost in court in 1958. Meanwhile, he passed the leadership of the Perfect Christian Divine Way to Robert Clougher. The property finally passed into the hands of the H. C. Development Company. In the late 1950s several fires destroyed much of the community. Finally, in 1966, the few remaining disciples were thoroughly alienated from Riker when he suddenly converted to Roman Catholicism. He died three years later, still a member of the Catholic Church.

Sources:

"Holy City Brotherhood." *Fortnight* (March 2, 1955): 1617.

Plate, Harry. "Riker: from Mechanic to Messiah." *California Today* (August 30, 1978).

★1236★
Hutterian Brethren-Dariusleut
% Rev. Elias Walter
Surprise Creek Colony
Stanford, MT 59479

The second group of Hutterites to settle in the United States purchased a section of land in South Dakota on Silver Lake, north of the original Hutterite colony. (For the early history of the Hutterites, see separate entry on Hutterian Brethren-Schmiedeleut.) Under the leadership of Darius Walter, this second colony and those which sprang from it took his name. While establishing seven colonies in South Dakota, they had also spread to Montana (two colonies) and Manitoba, Canada (one colony) by the beginning of World War I. Abandoning all of their colonies, they moved to new colonies in Alberta, Canada. Not until 1935 did they reestablish a colony in the United States, in Montana. Since then they have become the most geographically spread out of the leuts, having colonies in Washington and Montana and Alberta, Saskatchewan, and British Columbia in Canada. There is also an affiliated colony in Japan. The Dariusleut affiliated with the Society of Brothers for a short period (1931-1950).

The Dariusleut is the most loosely affiliated leut, as symbolized by the ability of new colonies to be founded without prior consent. Hooks and eyes are required on clothing. The minister is the first to enter the worship service.

Membership: In 1988 there were 133 Dariusleut colonies.

Sources:

Allard, William Albert. "The Hutterites, Plain People of the West." *National Geographic* 138, no. 1 (July 1970): 98-125.

Flint, David. *The Hutterites.* Toronto: Oxford University Press, 1975.

Gross, Paul S. *The Hutterite Way.* Saskatoon, SK: Freeman Publishing Company Limited, 1965.

Holzach, Michael. "The Christian Communists of Canada." *Geo* 1 (November 1979): 126-54.

★1237★
Hutterian Brethren-Lehreleut
% Rev. Joseph Kleinsasser
Milford Colony
Wolf Creek, MT 59648

The Lehrerleut dates to 1877, when the third group of Hutterites to migrate to America in the 1870s settled near Parkston, South Dakota. (For information on the early history of the Hutterites, see the item on the Hutterian Brethren-Schmiedeleut.) Upon arrival in the United States, the group decided to live communally under its leader, Jacob Wipf. Wipf was an accomplished teacher (lehrer), and the group derived its name from his ability. Slow to expand, the group had only four colonies at the beginning of World War I. Like the other leuts, however, it abandoned the American colonies and migrated to Alberta. Only after World War II was a new American colony established, in Montana. Present-day colonies are scattered across Alberta, Saskatchewan, and Montana.

The Lehrerleut is the most liberal of the Hutterite leuts. From their founder's formal education, members have inherited a preference for high German, in which they are thoroughly schooled. They wear buttons on their clothes. Unlike ministers of other leuts, the Lehrerleut minister is the last to enter worship services.

Membership: In 1983 the Lehrerleut had 82 colonies.

Sources:

Horst, John. *The Hutterian Brethren, 1528-1931.* Cayley, Alberta: Macmillan Colony, 1977.

The Hutterian Brethren of Montana. Augusta, MT: Privately Printed, 1965.

★1238★
Hutterian Brethren-Schmiedeleut
% David D. Decker
Tachetter Colony
Olivet, SD 57052

The Hutterite Brethren are the only surviving group which adopted communal living in response to an Anabaptist vision of establishing a Christian community in which private property would be abolished. They were founded in 1528 among a group of Anabaptist refugees fleeing to Austerlize. (A word on the Anabaptists: They believed the church was the society of adult believers gathered together freely. They thus opposed infant baptism and protested the state church of any area in which they resided. They were continually persecuted by state churches. Menno Simons, founder of the Mennonite Church, was an Anabaptist. He did not urge a communal lifestyle, however.) For the early Hutterites, the introduction of "community of goods" was at the time a religiously sanctioned necessity. The first colony or Bruderhof (common household) was founded in Austerlitz in Moravia. The group is named for Jacob Hutter. Not the founder, he became an early leader and organizer and was martyred at the stake in 1536. The pattern of persecution in Moravia became a common one for several centuries. Hutterites were tolerated, became successful and grew in numbers, were objects of jealousy, and finally were persecuted because of their success and their pacifism. This pattern repeated itself in Slovakia, Wallachia, and the Ukraine.

In the nineteenth century, living in close proximity to the Mennonites in Russia, the Hutterites' ideal was lost for a time, but in the 1850's, a renewal of communal living developed around the person and ministry of Michael Waldner. Waldner was a visionary, noted for his trances and psychic experiences. In a vision, an angel told him to reinstitute the *Gemeinschaft* of the Holy Spirit after the pattern of Jesus and the apostles. The phrase *Gemeinschaft* has no exact English equivalent; loosely translated, it is a brotherhood, a very closely knit group. The renewal took place in Hutterdorf, a Hutterite village in the Crimea. Two communal groups were established, one at each end of the village, and they became the basis of the division of the Hutterites into leuts (people) or colonies. The renewal of communal living among the Hutterites ran up against a renewal of nationalism in Russia. In 1871, universal compulsory military service was introduced and the Hutterites' requests for exemption were ignored. In 1874, migration to the United States and Canada was accomplished.

The Hutterites' beliefs arise from the Anabaptist tradition and in general follow the Schleitheim Confession. Like the Amish, the Hutterite Brethren adopted a plain dress. Some of them use hooks-and-eyes instead of buttons, a tradition symbolizing their rejection of the soldiers, their persecutors, who wore large buttons on military uniforms. The Hutterites use electricity, drive cars, have powered farm equipment and telephones. However, they have no televisions and dancing, smoking, and playing musical instruments are forbidden. They are pacifists and follow the radical Anabaptist theology. While there is a similarity among all Hutterites, the three leuts (discussed below) show marked distinctions in dress and discipline, and they do not intermarry.

Approximately 800 Hutterites migrated to America between 1874 and 1876. Approximately one half of these homesteaded family farms and eventually affiliated with Mennonite churches and ceased to be part of the Hutterite community. The remainder settled in three colonies in South Dakota. These three colonies gave rise to the three "leuts" (people), each named for its founder. Each leut developed its own pecularities and each serves as an organizing unit for fellowship, discipline and administering the religious life of the colonies. The oldest of the luets is the Schmiedeluet.

The Schmiedeleut dates to the original renewal under Michael Waldner and was named for Waldner, who was called "Schmied-Michel" because he was a blacksmith. Upon arrival in the United States, Waldner's people settled the Bon Homme County in South Dakota in 1874. Waldner's continual visions remained a major motivating force in the communal patterns. By 1918, the Schmiedeleut had founded nine colonies. With the coming of World War I, the Hutterites German background combined with their pacifism led to heightened tension. One by one they abandoned their colonies and relocated in Manitoba. Only in 1934 did a group settle a new American colony (Rockport, near Alexandria, South Dakota).

Among the Hutterites, the Schmiedeleut is considered the most conservative, though it has dropped the requirement for hooks and eyes as a means of fastening clothes. In its worship, the minister is the first to enter the gathering place. Colonies are tied closely together, and the consent of all is required before a new one can be created.

Membership: In 1983 there were 138 Schmiedeleut colonies.

Sources:

Cobb, Douglas S. "The Jamesville Bruderhof: A Hutterian Agricultural Colony." *Journal of the West* 9, no. 1 (January 1970): 60-77.

Peters, Victor. *All Things Common.* New York: Harper & Row, 1971.

Sturdivant, Lori. "The People of Jacob Hutter." *The Minneapolis Tribune* (October 16, 1977).

★1239★
Jerusalem
(Defunct)

Jerusalem was the religious community founded in 1788 near Seneca Lake, New York, by Jemima Wilkerson, known to her followers as the Public Universal Friend. Wilkerson, raised as a Quaker, was deeply affected by the preaching of traveling evangelist George Whitefield, and by the New Light Baptists. Around 1774 Wilkerson became ill, and eventually fell into a coma. When she came out of the coma she claimed that Jemima Wilkerson had died and her soul had ascended to heaven. In its place was the "Spirit of Life" sent by God to warn the world, as the Methodists were preaching, to flee from the wrath to come. She told everyone that she was now to be called the Public Universal Friend and would no longer answer to her birth name. She began to preach to all who would listen.

Soon after her change, she acquired a small following, and with the band, toured Rhode Island and Connecticut. She travelled on a white horse and wore men's clothes over which she draped a flowing robe. Work was slow during the years of the American Revolution, but by 1782 she had three churches. As her evangelistic endeavors continued, she became a controversial figure when one member of a family who joined her was not followed by the rest of the household. In 1788, she obtained land in western New York to build a community. A faithful vanguard began to clear the land and prepare it for the movement of the main body of members. Jerusalem grew and prospered through the 1790s and by 1800 had received some 250 residents. It survived peacefully into the 1820s, but began a rapid decline after Wilkerson's death in 1819.

Sources:

Holloway, Mark. *Heavens on Earth: Utopian Communities in America, 1680-1880*. London: Turnstile Press, 1951. 240 pp.

★1240★
Joyful
(Defunct)

Joyful, a Christian utopian community, was funded in 1884 by Isaac B. Rumford, and his wife Sara Rumford, in Kern County, California. As early as 1880 Rumford had a visionary dream in which he pictured a heaven-like land where Christian love ruled. Already involved in a variety of reformist efforts, the Rumfords now felt inspired to create a community that would express their ideals of a simple Christian life. Integral to their vision was a new "Edenic" diet, a vegetarian diet based on the consumption of raw foods. Rumford had concluded that cooking destroyed the vital life of food substances. The Rumfords adopted the Edenic diet in 1881 and ascribed to it their continuing good health.

The Rumfords took steps to realize their communal vision in 1884 with the publication of the *Joyful News Co-operator*. "Joyful" was the name they had already given their fruit farm near Bakersfield, California. They also published a constitution for what they termed the Association of Brotherly Co-operators, the corporate name for the colony. Recruitment meetings were held in San Francisco, and a small number of converts moved to the farm. However, the movement never really got off the ground, and by the end of the year, the experiment was discontinued. The Rumfords continued active as reformers and advocates of the raw food diet.

Sources:

Hine, Robert V. *California's Utopian Colonies*. San Marino, CA: Huntington Library, 1953. 209 pp.

★1241★
Koreshan Unity
(Defunct)

The Koreshan Unity was formed in 1888 in Chicago by the followers of Cyrus Read Teed (1839-1906), a physician and metaphysician who developed a religious system termed the cellular cosmology. The group was organized as a celibate religious organization. The followers of Koresh (Hebrew for Cyrus) moved into a home and, the next year, began to publish the *Guiding Star*, which after six months became the *Flaming Sword*. In 1894, a colony was established in Estero, Florida, where the climate was mild and communal living was tolerated. In 1903, the entire group arrived from Chicago. At its height the organization had more than 300 residents on 6,000 acres, and more than 4,000 followers throughout the United States. A press was established, and numerous books, pamphlets, and periodicals were produced up until 1949, when the press was destroyed by fire.

The cellular cosmology is based upon the belief that the earth's surface is concave and that man lives on the inside of a sphere, not on a ball in space. The earth is not four and one-half billion years old, but eternal. God is an eternal being dwelling in the central brain cells of aggregate humanity. God is both male and female, in one eternal form. Jesus Christ is God perpetuating himself in an individual person formed by parthenogenesis (virgin birth).

The cellular cosmology contains theories on the macrocosm and the microcosm. The macrocosm is viewed as a cosmic egg, a hollow egg. The inside of the "eggshell" is the surface of the earth; in the hollow center of the egg floats the sun, from which flow light, heat and the influence of gravity. The shell of the earth forms a limitation to the effects of the sun, expressed in the materialization of metallic and mineral substance. In a reciprocal relation, the shell of the physical cosmos gives forth the energies, decomposed from material substance, which by Levic force (the opposite of gravity) move toward the sun. By such reciprocity, eternal perpetuity is ensured.

Mankind is a microcosm of the macrocosm, having as its central sun, God, who has his eternal habitation in the enviromental circumference of humanity. From God, flow truth and love, which are reciprocated by worship-the highest and purest moral thoughts.

Membership: The membership of the Koreshan settlement in Florida peaked soon after the turn of the century and the departure of 30 members in 1906 signaled the beginning of a long period of decline. By 1940 the Unity had been reduced to 36 members. In 1960 the presidency of the group passed to Hedwig Michel, a Jew who had escaped from the Holocaust and joined the Unity in December 1941. She reorganized the small band of worshipers and led in the deeding of 300 acres of the group's land to the State of Florida in 1961. It became a state park in 1967 and was later designated a national historic site.

In 1965 Michel revived the former periodical, *The American Eagle*, and on the small amount of land remaining to the Koreshans, prepared for the emergence of the Koreshan Unity Foundation. She led in the building of a library/museum to house and preserve the community publications and artifacts. She died in 1982 and was considered to be the last Koreshan. The foundation has continued to preserve the property and open it to scholars and the general public. It also publishes *The American Eagle* which includes articles on Koreshan histoy and current events celebrative of the community's heritage.

Today the former community is open to the public as two sites, one a public part and the other the headquarters of the foundation. The foundation may be reached at Box 97, Estero, FL 33928.

Sources:

Koresh [Cyrus R. Teed]. *Cellular Cosmology, or, the Earth a Concave Sphere*. Estero, Lee County, FL: Guiding Star Publishing House, 1922.

Koreshanity, the New Age Religion. Miami, FL: Koreshan Foundation, 1971.

Landing, James E. "Cyrus R. Teed, Koreshanity, and Cellular Cosmology." *Communal Societies* 1 (Autumn 1981): 1-17.

Teed, Cyrus R. *The Alchemical Laboratory of the Brain.* Chicago: Eta Company, n.d.

★1242★
The Lord's Farm
(Defunct)

The Lord's Farm was founded in 1877 by Mason T. Huntsman. At some point in the 1870s, Huntsman, who had been raised an orphan, underwent a religious conversion. He took the name Paul Blandin Mnason, and settled in Westwood, New Jersey. He assumed some messianic pretensions and was known to his followers as the "New Christ." Members of the Lord's Farm lived communally and supported themselves by raising crops on their 23 acres of land and operating a furniture moving business. They had a policy of welcoming anyone to their farm and inviting them to partake of the community's activities and resources (food and shelter).

Mnason came to public attention in 1887 after he launched a vocal assault on the nearby village of Park Ridge, New Jersey, which he accused of being a corrupt and evil place. Residents, unappreciative of his words, manifested their disgust by attacking Mnason and cutting off his beard and long hair. Their actions did not stop Mnason, however, and he continued to preach and gather a following. However, he now faced a series of continued community reactions to his efforts. Between 1890 and 1893, members were harassed with a series of court actions on charges ranging from violation of sabbath laws to fraud. In 1893 Mnason was imprisoned for running a disorderly and immoral house. In 1899 he was convicted under New Jersey blasphemy laws for "impersonating the Saviour," and abducting two young girls (among his early followers).

The group continued until around 1910. At its height, it had 35 adult resident members, though there were always others living there for longer or shorter periods. The group was vegetarian, celibate (in spite of continued charges of nudity and sexual misconduct), and sought to live a simple life following their inner guidance. Mnason referred to the colony as "The City of God, Land of Rest and Peace, State of Eternal Bliss." In the end, Mnason's brother took control of the property and evicted the group.

Sources:

Fogarty, Robert S. *Dictionary of American Communal and Utopian History.* Westport, CT: Greenwood Press, 1980. 271 pp.

Hinds, William Alfred. *American Communities and Cooperative Colonies.* Chicago: Charles H. Kerr & Company, 1908. 608 pp.

Miller, Timothy. *American Communes, 18601960: A Bibliography.* New York: Garland Publishing, 1990. 583 pp.

★1243★
Mount Zion Overcoming Body of Christ—The True Bride
Rte. 1
Crescent City, FL 32012

Mount Zion Overcoming Body of Christ—The True Bride was founded in 1944 in New York City by Mother Essie M. MacDonald. The founding of the group was directly connected to McDonald's recovery from a near fatal illness. Once recovered, she began to dress in white and refused to wear either a coat or cape. She carried a dive, the symbol of the Holy Spirit. For a time, she was affiliated with the Church of God in Christ (the largest of several predominantly black Pentecostal denominations), but the church eventually rejected her unconventional dress code.

She eventually moved to Florida, her original home, where her mother gave her a tract of land. Here she opened a mission house in a 100-room "ark" to which she invited the aged, infirm, the homeless, and any others simply in need of help. Some, attracted by her work, moved to the ark as resident members of the church.

The church is pentecostal in emphasis. Members believe in the baptism of the Holy Spirit as evidenced by speaking in tongues. They also have a strong belief in healing and invite the sick to receive the ministrations of Mother MacDonald. Worship is conducted daily, though Saturday is designated the Sabbath. The church is organized communally. The resident chambers, separate for men and women, are designated by names associated with the bride's chamber. Mother MacDonald is viewed as the "Bride of Christ" and in that role wears a white gown with a Star of David on its skirt. She teaches what is termed the "Female Principle," a belief in the important role of females on the earth. As part of communal life, members grow their own food. Members wear white clothes and no shoes. They have also painted the seats of the sanctuary white.

Membership: The group does not consider itself a denomination or organization, but as a house of prayer for all people.

Sources:

DuPree, Sherry Sherrod. *African American Holiness Pentecostal Charismatic: Annotated Bibliography.* New York: Garland Publishing, 1992.

★1244★
Mountain Cove
(Defunct)

The Mountain Cove community was a commune founded in 1851 at Mountain Cove, Virginia by James L. Scott and Thomas Lake Harris. The original members of the community came from Auburn, New York, and the idea seems to have originated from the spread of Spiritualism from western New York where it had emerged in the mid1840s. Spiritualism mixed with idealism over the possibility of founding a perfect Edenic society. Among the circle of Spiritualists was Ira S. Hitchcock who made the trip to Virginia and found the land at Mountain Cove. He believed that the spot was the site of the original Garden of Eden and that no humans had set foot on it since Adam and Eve were driven from the garden. An open letter dated December 14, 1851, called people to participate in the new community. It was described as a place of refuge to escape the vales of death. Among the participants at Mountain Cove was Thomas Lake Harris who would, a decade later, found the Brotherhood of the New Life as a Spiritualist communal movement.

The Mountain Cove community was led by Scott and Harris who acted as mediums and professed direct communication and inspiration from God. They gave guidance to the movement from their "channelings" from the divine. Members were required to donate their real property to the community and live from the community treasury. The temporal life of the colony was based upon agriculture.

In spite of the claims of divine guidance, the community soon found itself divided by internal bickering. Some rejected the arbitrary nature of leadership provided by Scott and Harris, and even suggested that members had become the equivalent of slaves to work the community farm. Others complained about the financial and property arrangements. As a result of the discord, the experiment collapsed in 1853.

Sources:

Hinds, William Alfred. *American Communities and Cooperative Colonies.* Chicago: Charles H. Kerr & Company, 1908. 608 pp.

Noyes, John Humphrey. *History of American Socialisms. 1870.* Rept. as *Strange Cults and Utopias of 19th-Century America.* New York: Dover Publications, 1966. 678 pp.

★1245★
New Jerusalem
(Defunct)

New Jerusalem was a communal group established near Cairo, Illinois, in the mid-nineteenth century. It was founded by Cyrus Spragg, who had been a member of the Church of Jesus Christ of Latter-day Saints. Expelled from a congregation (stake) in Michigan, he gathered a few followers and led in the founding of a commune noted for its disavowal of polygamy and its practice of nudism. It reportedly failed because of the bitter winter weather.

Following the collapse of his community in Michigan, Spragg led the remnant of his following to Illinois and organized New Jerusalem near Cairo. He had come to believe himself the Messiah, and had an ark built which was to save group members when a flood, predicted to occur in the near future, would overrun Cairo and the sight of the commune. In fact a heavy rain brought a flood, but it did not do the damage or reach the extent predicted. A short time later Spragg moved into the ark, announced that he was the Invisible Presence of God, and would never be seen again. He remained in touch with the members of the group through a window that had been cut in the side of the ark. He received food, and each evening he was visited by a virginal member of the group, one of whom, it was predicted, would become a Madonna, the mother of a messiah.

The new arrangement worked for some months, several children being born to the young women. Then a man who fell in love with one of the sacred virgins broke into the ark and claimed to have shot Spragg before fleeing the community. That night the young woman appointed to visit the leader reported that he had not been shot but was very much alive. The community resumed its normal course until Spragg's daughter-in-law accused her husband Obadiah Spragg and his brother Jared Spragg of having gone into the ark, disposed of their father's body, and having assumed his role each evening. Members of the community then went into the ark and discovered that Spragg was not there. The revelation led to the collapse of the community.

Remarks: No contemporary records of New Jerusalem exist. The site of the community is unknown and the main account, which appeared in the 1920s, was a "biography" of Spragg's daughter written in the form of a novel. Some have suggested that the story of New Jerusalem is a folk account derived from the account of James Jesse Strang, the Mormon leader on Beaver Island, Michigan. The parallels in Spragg's and Strang's lives are striking. Presently, there is no way to resolve the issue.

Sources:

Bloomfield, Louis. *Strange Case of Miss Annie Spragg.* New York: Frederick A. Stokes Co., 1928.

Muncy, Raymond Lee. *Sex and Marriage in Utopian Communities: 19th Century America.* Bloomington, IN: Indiana University Press, 1973.

Randolph, Vance. *Americans Who Thought They Were Gods: Colorful Messiahs and Little Christs.* Girard, KS: Haldeman-Julius Publications, 1943.

Webber, Everett. *Escape to Utopia: The Communal Movement in America.* New York: Hastings House Publishers, 1959.

★1246★
Oneida Community of Perfectionists
(Defunct)

The Oneida Community of Perfectionists was a religious community founded in 1841 at Putney, Vermont, by John Humphrey Noyes (1811-1886). It was inspired by the spread in early nineteenth century America of both Methodist perfectionist thought and communal idealism. Having become something of a religious skeptic during his college days, Noyes was soundly converted in a revival in 1830 and a short time later felt a call to preach. He attended seminary but found the atmosphere cold and uninviting and he turned to personal Bible study. He concluded that Christians were called to be perfect. He also believed that Christ had made perfection humanly possible and as part of that perfection had taken away the need to observe earthly laws. He graduated from seminary, but the Congregationalists took back his license to preach.

During the next few years Noyes wandered around Vermont and New York and gathered a small following. He began a periodical, *The Witness,* and in 1837 he began an informal Bible study group in Putney. He instituted the practice of mutual criticism he had earlier learned at the seminary. In a very structured situation, members would allow the community to freely censure them and offer suggestions for change and improvement. All members underwent such criticism. Among the ideals that Noyes slowly espoused to the group was a new sexual order that put aside regulations against fornication and adultery. His wife Harriet and his converts also accepted the concept of a community of wives.

Noyes was greatly affected by the painful experiences of his wife, who had several miscarriages. He thought that celibacy would be the only alternative to preventing her further distress for unwanted pregnancies, but then discovered what he would term "male countenance." Male countenance was his name for an older technique widely practiced in some Asian cultures by which males were able to engage in lengthy sexual intercourse without reaching a climax. The technique, also called coitus reservatus and karezza, would later become the basis of the Oneida community's new sexual order.

In 1841 the group was formally organized as the Putney Society. As was Nayes' goal to initiate the establishment of the kingdom of God on earth, he restructured the group by the imposing a system of complex marriage. Briefly stated, Noyes assumed (as did most of his contemporaries) that in the heavenly society monogamous marriages would be abolished. However, he departed from most other Christian thinkers by assuming that sexual relations would continue. For such to occur, sexual relations would have to continue without benefit of marriage. In the heavenly society, all the men would be "married" to all the women. The attempt to actualize such a situation, however, presented new problems. How would one keep from falling into mere libertinism? How did one regulate the random pregnancies and children that would result? To deal with these problems, Noyes developed the system of complex marriage.

In Noyes' system, the men and women of the community regularly changed partners, but instead of making random choices based upon momentary attractions, partners were assigned each month (according to the women's menstrual cycles). Men requested their partner for the next month, but the actual choices were made by the older women. Thus during any one month, a woman would have relationships with only one man. In case of an accidental pregnancy, the father would be known. Also, every person in the community had a new sexual partner each month, and pains were taken to see that no exclusive relationships developed that would distract individuals from their commitments to the community.

In 1848, under pressure from legal authorities in Putney who complained of the immoralities among the Noyes group, the community moved to Oneida, New York. Here they built one of the most successful community experiments. The economy of the community came off of the sale of traps, silk, and horticultural products. In the 1870s they started a silverware industry that became their most successful business and continues to the present day.

At Oneida the practice of complex marriage was so successful that only a very few unplanned pregnancies occurred. The success led to further speculation on sexuality and the development of a new eugenics program—stirpiculture—centered upon children produced by the union of two "scientifically selected" parents. Some 51 children were born following implementation of the stirpiculture plan.

The community at Oneida lasted for more than three decades. Its long and successful existence is credited to Noyes, who became an astute student of the communal life and wrote one of the first books describing America's communal experiments, *History of American Socialisms* (1870). Through most of its existence it averaged some 300 members/residents. In 1851 it founded a second community in Wallingford, Connecticut. However, for reasons still not fully understood, on January 1, 1881, the community came to an end and reorganized the economic segment of the community to a joint stock company. Many of the former members then settled in Oneida in nuclear families.

Sources:

Carden, Maren L. *Oneida: Utopian Community to Modern Corporation.* Baltimore: John Hopkins University Press, 1969.

Foster, Lawrence. *Women, Family, and Utopia: Communal Experiments of the Shakers, the Oneida Community, and the Mormons.* Syracuse, NY: Syracuse University press, 1991. 353 pp.

Noyes, John Humphrey. *History of American Socialisms.* 1870. Rept. as *Strange Cults and Utopias of 19th-Century America.* New York: Dover Publications, 1966. 678 pp.

Noyes, Pierrepont B. *A Godly Heritage.* New York: Rinehart, 1958.

Robertson, Constance Noyes, ed. *Oneida Community: An Autobiography, 1851-1876.* Syracuse, NY: Syracuse University Press, 1970.

★1247★
The Peace Mission Movement
% The Woodmont Estate
1622 Spring Mill Rd.
Gladwyne, PA 19035

The Peace Mission Movement was founded as an organization in the early twentieth century by the Rev. Major J. Divine, better known as Father Divine. He was one of the most colorful and controversial leaders of a new religious movement in American history. By his own choosing, and in accord with his own religious conviction, Father Divine's life and activity are veiled in obscurity until just prior to 1919 in Brooklyn, New York, where he was known to be preaching about Jesus Christ and the coming of the kingdom of God.

From his own writings and the testimonies of those who knew him, it is believed that Father Divine left Brooklyn and went south just after the Jim Crow Law was passed in Grover Cleveland's administration. While in the South, he was in the hands of 32 lynch mobs because of his stand for brotherhood, eternal life, and salvation being free and without the payment of money. The first Mother Divine and others were witnesses of his treatment in the hands of lynch mobs. In the name of the Rev. Major J. Divine, he married Mother Peninniah Divine on June 6, 1882.

Father Divine appeared as an intinerant preacher on the east coast of the United States who found fellowship with others who were preaching that the Christ could be manifested as God in man. Samuel Morris, known as Father Jehovah, and John Hickerson, known by his followers as Bishop St. John the Divine, were two of these. Because of jealous rivalry, it is believed, Hickerson fabricated the story that Father Divine's name was really George Baker. Hickerson also is responsible for other biographical misinformation.

To remove himself from the turmoil, Father Divine went into seclusion in the little Long Island fishing village of Sayville, New York. It was here that his residence became known as "The Rescue Home for the Poor Only." He attracted those in need of food, clothing, shelter, and employment, as well as seekers who were drawn by the demonstration at the Sayville residence of "supernatural" abundance in the midst of seeming scarcity. Father Divine's work commanded more and more attention, and ever greater numbers flocked to Sayville to banquet with him, listen to his sermons, and receive healings of mind, body, and spirit, all gratis to everyone who came.

The influx of numbers of people into the town disturbed the residents. Their hostility led to a court case against Father Divine in 1931, the events of which created worldwide publicity. Although the local county court convicted Father Divine, fined him, and sent him to jail for 30 days, Appellate Division of the Supreme Court of New York later condemned the proceedings as erroneous and prejudicial.

The vindication notwithstanding, Father Divine chose to move his headquarters to Harlem in 1933, where he could direct his activity to the masses, especially the African Americans who had gathered there after World War I. While gaining a large following from the Harlem public, he experienced continual harassment from the authorities, so that in 1942 he moved again, this time to Philadelphia, Pennsylvania.

The Peace Mission Movement is primarily of a religious nature, but its tenets have strong social, economic, and patriotic ramifications. Its members believe in the principles of Americanism, brotherhood, Christianity, democracy, and Judaism, and that all true religions are synonymous. Members believe that Father Divine fulfills the scriptural promise of the Second Coming of Christ, is the personification of God in a bodily form, and that heaven is a state of consciousness. This state is being materialized, in as much as the members believe that America is the birthplace of the Kingdom of God on Earth, which will be realized when everyone lives the life of Christ.

Father Divine founded the churches under the Peace Mission Movement which were incorporated in 1940 and 1941. Mother Divine, with the recognition of Father Divine's Ever Presence, became the Spiritual Head in 1965. There are no ministers and is no prescribed ritual in the church services. Those in attendance are free to testify, sing, read scripture or the Words of Father Divine or Mother Divine, or offer praise to God as they are led to do from any inner prompting. Services feature congregational singing. The only sacrament is Holy Communion, served daily as a full-course meal to which all are welcome. There are also two holidays: April 29, which is the celebration of Father Divine's marriage to His Spotless Bride (Mother Divine) to bring about the universal brotherhood of man and the propagation of virtue, honesty, and truth; and September 10-12, which is the consecration and dedication of Woodmont to universalize the Woodmont Estate as a symbol of the highest spiritual state of consciousness.

The mission stands for the absolute fatherhood and motherhood of God and the universal brotherhood of man. Its members believe that a person is a person—not a specified race, color, nationality, or religion, and they live integrated together as brothers and sisters in the family of God and as members only of the human race. They avoid all reference to color or race.

Members of the mission live communally in the churches and affiliated sorority and fraternity houses. They are strictly celibate men and women living in separate houses and on separate floors of the larger facilities. They observe Father Divine's International Modest Code which states: "No smoking, No drinking, No obscenity, No vulgarity, No profanity, No undue mixing of sexes, and No receiving of gifts, presents, tips or bribes." It is understood to include abstinence from all drugs.

The Peace Mission Movement was most active in the post-depression era when Father Divine preached peace, health, happiness, and abundance, and demonstrated that his teachings were practical as he provided food and shelter for all those in need at no cost to them. To others in dire circumstances, but who had a poverty-level income or less, Father Divine offered 15-cent meals and one dollar-per-week shelter, so that they could hold up their heads with a sense of individual worth and independence, since they were able to pay for their sustenance. The same abundance was manifested in the churches and extensions in various countries as well as those in the United States, where elaborate banquets are the custom.

After Father Divine's passing, his wife Sweet Angel, known to members as Mother Divine, assumed leadership of the movement.

She had married Father Divine in 1946, and currently resides at Woodmont. The movement has a long history of being integrated, as was the marriage.

Membership: In 1995 the movement reported that it owned and operated two hotels in Philadelphia. Branches exist in Canada, Germany, Switzerland, Austria, Australia, Central America, Great Britain, and Nigeria. No membership statistic are kept.

Periodicals: *The New Day. Enlightenment.*

Sources:

Burnham, Kenneth. *God Comes to America*. Boston, MA: Lambeth Press, 1979.

Harris, Sara. *Father Divine*. New York: Collier Books, 1971.

Hoshor, John. *God Drives a Rolls Royce*. Philadelphia, PA: Hillman-Curl, 1936.

Mother Divine. *The Peace Mission Movement*. Philadelphia, PA: Imperial Press, 1982.

Weisbrot, Robert. *Father Divine and the Struggle for Racial Equality*. Urbana, IL: University of Illinois Press, 1983.

★1248★
People of the Living God
Rte. 2, Box 423-46
McMinnville, TN 37110-9512

The People of the Living God was formed in 1932 by Harry Miller (a former minister in the Assemblies of God) and his father-in-law (a former minister in the Presbyterian Church). They saw their action as a stand against sectarianism, and they opened a Bible training school in Los Angeles to prepare "non-sectarian" missionaries. During the next four years (1937-1941), some of them lived in Kentucky operating a free school in a bankrupt county and then moved into the mountains of Tennessee. The group finally settled in New Orleans, where it remained for many years.

Sectarianism is defined as holding doctrinal agreement a necessary requirement for fellowship. To keep free from it, the group maintains an open pulpit, from which laymen and ministers who wish to contest doctrinal beliefs can speak. Conduct, not opinion, is the rule in matters of fellowship (Acts 15:28-29). The doctrinal consensus of the group is close to the beliefs of the Assemblies of God. Members are Trinitarian Pentecostals and practice two ordinances-baptism by immersion and the Lord's Supper (which is open to all). They believe that speaking in tongues is a sign of receiving the baptism of the Holy Spirit.

The fellowship remains small. Headquarters moved from New Orleans to rural Tennessee in 1982. Members work inside the group, with a common treasury. All buying is done by a purchasing agent. Members receive no personal allowance. They run a free Christian school which any child may attend. The simple lifestyle allows a large percentage of money to be put into literature and into the support of nonsectarian missionaries overseas. The group publishes a series of booklets, mostly of a controversial nature, which is sent throughout the world.

Membership: In 1997 there were two centers and approximately 75 resident members. There are affiliated members in the Philippines.

Periodicals: *The Testimony of Truth*. Send orders to Rte. 2, Box 423, McMinnville, TN 37110.

Sources:

Miller, Harry R. *Community, A Way of Life*. New Orleans, LA: People of the Living God, n.d.

___. *Enchantments*. New Orleans, LA: People of the Living God, n.d.

___. *A Man of Like Passions*. New Orleans, LA: People of the Living God, n.d.

★1249★
The Pilgrims
(Defunct)

The Pilgrims were a small group that arose in Quebec, in an area just north of the Vermont border in 1816. They were formed by Isaac Bullard, who recovered from a long illness with a determination to follow Christ. He began to preach and to gather a following that he organized along what he saw as a primitivist pattern. The group lived communally out of a common purse and became known for their constant prayer and frequent fasts. However, the most remembered characteristic by those who encountered them was their refusal to bathe. They also discarded their civilized "manufactured" clothing and donned animal skins. Their clothing—coupled with their refusal to bathe—led to their exuding an offensive smell.

In the summer of 1817, Bullard received a revelation to migrate toward the American southwest in a pilgrimage to a Promised Land. Meanwhile, Bullard had married and named his first child, a boy, Christ. As the pilgrimage began, the Pilgrims numbered approximately 55. As they traveled across New England, they were heard to mutter a prayer, "My God, My God, What wouldst thou have me do? Mummyjum, Mummyjum." As a result they were often dubbed the Mummyjums.

The pilgrimage took the better part of a year. They journeyed through New York, New Jersey, Ohio, and Missouri. As they traveled, members dropped out, some because they fell ill, others because they came to reject the message preached by Bullard. Still others left to join the Shakers. When the group reached Arkansas in 1881, only about 10 people were left. They settled on an isolated island and the Pilgrims soon passed into obscurity.

Sources:

Fogarty, Robert S. *Dictionary of American Communal and Utopian History*. Westport, CT: Greenwood Press, 1980. 271 pp.

Ham, F. Gerald. "The Prophet and the Mummyjums: Isaac Bullard and the Vermont Pilgrims of 1817." *Wisconsin Magazine of History* (Summer 1973).

★1250★
Shiloh Trust
℅ James Janisch
Sulfur Springs, AR 72763

The Rev. Eugene Crosby Monroe (1880-1961) was a businessman who in 1923 was ordained in the Apostolic Church, a British-based pentecostal body. Monroe served as a pastor of the Apostolic Church in Philadelphia until ill health forced his retirement from both his pastoral duties and his business career, which he had continued. He settled on a farm near Sherman, New York, to which young men and women came to continue under his ministry. Out of this situation evolved Shiloh Trust, a self- supporting Pentecostal community, also known as the Church of Shiloh. A large-scale food business was established, through which baked goods, cheese, and other foods were distributed to retail outlets.

Monroe died in 1961, by which time Shiloh Trust had grown into a sucessful operation. He was succeeded by his son, who was later killed in a plane crash. James Janisch is the current Trustee. In 1963, the wholesale distribution of health foods to retail stores began to dominate the group's business interests. In 1968, headquarters were moved to Sulphur Springs, Arkansas. Members of the community gather daily for meetings. Beliefs are similar to those of the Apostolic Church.

Membership: As of 1988, there were 84 beneficiaries of the Shiloh Trust in Arkansas.

★1251★
Societas Fraternia
(Defunct)

The Societas Fraternia was a communal group founded in 1878 by George Hinde on land he had purchased near Fullerton, California. Hinde settled on the land in 1876, but the beginning of the community followed the arrival of Spiritualist, Dr. Louis Schlesinger, two years later. The major beliefs and practices seem to have been derived from those of Isaac B. Rumford and the Joyful Community, which had advocated a form of Christian Spiritualism and a diet of raw food named for the Garden of Eden. Buildings were erected on a circular pattern to allow the better circulation of air.

In 1879 Schlesinger was forced into court to answer charges that a child at the farm was being starved to death on a diet of apple, rice, and barley water. The case (in which Schlesinger was convicted and then later acquitted) initiated a period of controversy that led him to leave the colony in 1882. Hinde vanished the following year. Leadership was then assumed by Walter Lockwood, who led the group for almost 40 years until his death in 1921. During its years of existence, the colony's dietetic commitments led to its participation in the development of the fruit and vegetable industry in southern California. The colony dissolved a short time after Lockwood's death.

Sources:

Hine, Robert V. *California's Utopian Colonies.* San Marino, CA: Huntington Library, 1953. 209 pp.

★1252★
The Society of the Separatists of Zoar
(Defunct)

The Society of the Separatists of Zoar originated in a dissenting religious movement led by George Bimeler (originally Baumeler), a German weaver. The group, which grew up around the unofficial preaching of Bimeler, ran into conflict with state church authorities. They refused to send their children to the Lutheran Church-controlled schools and the young men refused to serve in the army. Most annoyingly, they refused to recognize the authority of government officials. They soon found themselves on the receiving end of church and government repression.

In 1817, with some money contributed by British Quakers, Bimeler was able to purchase 5,600 acres in northeast Ohio, and the group settled there in 1818. They had no plans to establish a communal society, but in 1819 they formally adopted a new corporate structure as a means of better group survival. They struggled until 1827 when many of the men were employed to work on the new canal that was being built through their county. The money their labor brought in provided the necessary capital to lift them out of poverty. In 1832 the group was incorporated as the Society of the Separationists of Zoar. Leadership was invested in a three-man board of trustees.

The Zoarites practiced a simple, quietist faith based upon the Sermon on the Mount. They did not use audible prayer, did not baptize or celebrate the Eucharist, and tended to avoid all ceremony. They had no religious functionaries except for Bimeler who delivered "discourses" (not sermons) at the Sunday gatherings. Hymns and music seemed to have been their chief form of entertainment. Like the Quakers, they tended to address people in the familiar tense with "thou." Originally they were celibate, but began to marry and have children in the 1830s, though the married Bimeler contended that celibacy was the better way.

The Zoarite experiment lasted into the 1890s when internal disputes among the aging group led to its dissolution; there were some 221 adult members at the time. Some have attributed the dissolution to a lessening of religious faith and zeal among the leaderless members (Bimeler having died in 1853).

Sources:

Holloway, Mark. *Heavens on Earth: Utopian Communities in America, 1680-1880.* London: Turnstile Press, 1951. 240 pp.

Randall, E. *History of the Zoar Society.* N.p., 1904.

★1253★
Straight Edge Community
(Defunct)

The Straight Edge Community was a Christian Socialist community founded in 1899 in New York City by Wilbur F. Copeland and his wife. Its rather unusual name was derived from a line of reasoning that suggested that Jesus was a carpenter and that a carpenter's rule is a straight edge. Chapman placed an ad in the *New York Herald* asking for responses from any who might want to take the teachings of Jesus Christ seriously and to work in a cooperative endeavor based upon the Golden Rule.

The Golden Rule became the constitution of the group and a set of bylaws were adopted from applicable Bible verses:

> 1. Thou shalt love thy neighbors as thyself. 2. In honor preferring one another. 3. Lay not up for yourself treasures upon earth. 4. I am in the midst of you as he that serveth. 5. Take heed that ye do not let your righteousness before men to be seen of them. 6. Whatsoever things are true, honest, just, pure, of good report, virtuous, praiseworthy, think on these things.

The Straight Edge Community emerged as a school of methods for the application of the teachings of Jesus to business and society. A periodical, *The Straight-Edge,* was initiated. The Copelands' home became the center of the community, and a farm was purchased on Staten Island and several small industries were begun in Manhattan. The community averaged some 18 people at any one time, but more than 200 people passed through it during the years of its existence. Many entered out of poverty, but left with a skill and ready for financial independence. Workers were not paid a salary, but shared in the earnings of the corporation according to a complex point system that allowed some incentive for improving work skills and staying with the community. The community continued for more than a decade, but seems to have been disbursed soon after the turn of the century.

The Straight Edgers developed a school and camp program for the children of its member-workers where young people could learn the simple life without paying large sums of money. Children received a practical education that prepared them for work in industry.

Sources:

Hinds, William Alfred. *American Communities and Cooperative Colonies.* Chicago: Charles H. Kerr & Company, 1908. 608 pp.

★1254★
Temple Society
% Dr. Richard Hoffman
152 Tucker
Bentleigh, Australia

The Temple Society, known earlier as the Friends of Jerusalem, was founded by Christopher Hoffmann (1815-1885) in 1861 in Wurttemberg, Germany. Hoffmann had attacked the established church conventicles (meetings) as being unable to heal the spiritual decay in the church. Hoffmann's alternatives were a literal adherence to the Old Testament prophecies and a demand that the kingdom of God as preached by Jesus be reestablished as the only avenue to a moral and spiritual reformation. Hoffmann began to gather the true followers and prepare them to go to the Holy Land, but the political situation delayed settlement.

In the settlement of Kirschenhardthof, a society which became the prototype of the New Jerusalem was organized in Germany. A co-worker named Hardegg claimed to possess the gifts of the

Spirit. In a series of writings, Hoffmann presented a version of Christianity very much viewed from what he considered to be the actual teachings of Jesus. His main works were *Sendschreiben uber den Temple und die Sakramente; Das Dogma von der Dreieinigkeit und von der Gottheit Christi; and Die Versohnung der Menschen mit Gott.* He ridiculed some commonly held Christian views, including belief in the trinity and the deity of Christ and the Holy Spirit. The incarnation is viewed as the expression of God's creative thought in the mind and body of Christ. Through the resurrection, Christ became a "man-made God." Christ showed the possibilities of human nature, changed humanity's attitude toward God, and thus established his kingdom as a better mental and social relationship among people. Sin is a disorder; faith is obedience to Christ and the courage to improve the world despite many obstacles. A socialized theocratic state is the goal. The sacraments are rejected. The true sacrament is manifested when a society decides to dedicate all its resources (time, talents, and material goods) to spreading Christ's kingdom.

Beginning in 1869, three colonies were planted in Palestine before Hoffmann's death. Amazingly, a total of six settlements survived until 1948 when the state of Israel was founded. Within the first decade after the 1861 founding of the Temple Society, German immigrants to America founded communities and formal organization occurred in 1866. By 1890, there were four congregations. This number had dwindled to two by 1916. These two congregations survived into the 1970s. Earlier, American Templers had been formally advised to join the Unitarians as World War made communications among Germans difficult. Today there are no known Templers left in the United States.

Membership: Not reported.

★1255★
United Society of Believers in Christ's Second Appearing
Sabbathday Lake, ME 04274

Mother Ann Lee (1736-1787) was a psychic-visionary who gathered a group of followers around her while still in her native England. Included in her teaching was a deep sense of the sinfulness of humanity. After the death of her four children in infancy, she began to manifest her sense of sin by a vocal attack on the indecent act of sexual union. The name given to the group was the United Society of Believers in Christ's Second Appearing; the members are popularly called the Shakers.

In the 1750s Mother Ann Lee became associated with a group of Quakers who had been influenced by the French Prophets, people who prophesied and sometimes had visions. She gradually became their leader. Her leadership led to the group's acceptance of celibacy as a sign of folowing Christ. In 1774, encouraged by persecution, the group sailed for America. Because of their pacifism, Shakers became the object of scorn during the Revolution.

After the Revolution, they began to prosper, especially under the leadership of Joseph Meacham, who came to power in 1787 following Ann's death. The Shakers established communities across America. At the height of their development around 1830, they had 19 communities stretching from southern Kentucky to Maine, with 6,000 resident members. Books were being published and widely circulated. Products of various community interests further spread their reputation.

Shaker theology centers upon the belief that in the coming of Ann Lee, Christ had appeared. They accepted the common millennialist use of the 2,300-days prophecy (Daniel 8:14). They dated the beginning of this prophecy from 533 B.C. when it was given, and 2,300 years brought them to 1747, when James Wardley and his wife began their work in Manchester. It was out of this independent French Prophet/Quaker Society that Ann Lee rose to prominence. The most famous activity of the Shakers and the one from which they got their nickname was ecstatic dance. This activity was ritualized in to a communal exercise and has often been viewed as sublimation of the prohibited sexual activity.

The United Society has become an important aspect of American history, and one of its abandoned communities at Pleasant Hill, Kentucky, is being reconstructed. A museum exists in the Shaker church at South Union, Kentucky, and at Old Chatham, New York. The community at New Lebenon, New York, was sold to the Sufi Order headed by Pir Vilayat Khan.

Membership: In June 1988, Gertrude Soule, one of the eight remaining members of the United Society of Believers died at the age of 93. Her death left seven remaining members (all females), two of which reside at Canterbury, New Hampshire, and five of which live at Sabbathday Lake, Maine. In 1965 all the remaining Shakers had agreed to admit no new members. Recently, the Sabbathday Lake group has broken that agreement and has admitted three new members, not recognized by the remaining members at Canterbury. In 1990, Bertha Lindsay, the last of the Shaker eldresses, died. There are now only four full and four additional members who keep the Shaker life alive.

Sources:

Andrews, Edward Deming. *The Gift to Be Simple.* New York: Dover, 1962.

Barker, R. Mildred. *Poems and Prayers.* Sabbathday Lake, ME: Shaker Press, 1983.

___. *The Sabbathday Lake Shaker.* Sabbathday Lake, ME: Shaker Press, 1978.

Desroche, Henri. *The American Shakers.* Amherst: University of Massachusetts Press, 1971.

Faber, Doris. *The Perfect Life.* New York: Farrar, Straus and Giroux, 1974.

★1256★
WFLK Fountain of the World
(Defunct)

Francis H. Pencovic (1911-1958) was born in obscurity, but as Krishna Venta; he died a martyr's death amongst followers who still thought of him as the reincarnated Christ. Pencovic spent part of his early life in Utah, where he both married his second wife, Ruth, and became enamored of Joseph Smith and the *Book of Mormon.* According to belief, as Krishna Venta, he landed in America from the Himalayas in 1932. He had been sent from heaven to work among the Indians one hundred and forty-four years previously. Krishna established his group in Box Canyon in the San Fernando Valley of California, where it gained a reputation for fire-fighting activities. Venta was rumored to have developed an openly promiscuous sexual life, which seems to have been his downfall, for on December 10, 1958, two dissident sexual partners of Venta set off an explosion in the group's administration building, killing themselves, Venta, and seven others.

Members of the Fountain of the World believed that Venta was the latest of a series of "saviors" of mankind who have come from heaven. The first was Adam, then Enoch, Methuselah, Noah, Abraham, Moses, Elijah, Jesus, Constantine, Abraham Lincoln, and Joseph Smith. One by one, each gave up in disgust as the sins of men overcame them both spiritually and physically. Members lived communally, turning over any prior possessions to the group. Thus, they became united with one another spiritually, mentally, and through sharing their belongings. They were called upon to practice the virtues of wisdom, knowledge, faith, and love. The Fountain was headed by Krishna and twelve apostles.

Krishna's death in 1958 was a setback, but it did not destroy the group. Mother Ruth Pencovic assumed leadership of the Fountain of the World. The group survived into the early 1980s near Canoga Park, California. There was also second center near Homer, Alaska, set up by Krisha before his death.

Sources:

Mathison, Richard. *Faiths, Cults and Sects of America.* Indianapolis, IN: Bobbs-Merrill, 1960.

Orrmont, Arthur. *Love Cults & Faith Healers*. New York: Ballantine Books, 1961.

★1257★
Woman's Commonwealth
(Defunct)

The Woman's Commonwealth was a communal society organized by Martha McWhirter in the late 1860s, in Belton, Texas. In the years immediately after the Civil War, the Holiness Movement, which offered to believers the possibility of entire sanctification, spread through all parts of Methodism. The movement was initially carried by informal prayer bands, many of those led by women. Thus it was that McWhirter, a life-long Methodist, called together a few women to meet for prayer, Bible study, and an exploration of the meaning of the sanctified life. They soon experienced sanctification and, as occurred elsewhere, their experience and the resulting censure they made of unsanctified church members split the local congregation. It also split families, McWhirter's included. Many of the women were cut off from any financial support. The idea of living together communally arose and was adopted.

To keep themselves together financially, the women began several businesses, including a boarding house and a laundry. Initially, many of the women worked at day jobs until the community businesses were prosperous enough to support all of them. As they prospered, initial hostile opinions gave way to more favorable ones. By the 1890s they had become an economic force in the small community and McWhirter was elected to the town council.

In 1898 the entire group relocated to Washington, D.C. In 1902 the group, consisting of approximately 24 members, was incorporated as the Woman's Commonwealth of Washington, D.C. McWhirter died in 1904 and was succeeded by Fannie Haltzclaw.

The group followed a Methodist Holiness theology. Believers could receive the Holy Spirit and be sanctified, and as most of the women had experienced sanctification prior to the community's establishment, the group lived as a community of the sanctified, and were frequently referred to as the Sanctificationists, a designation members did not find inappropriate. They believed that communal living produced the important virtues of honesty, sobriety, spirituality, happiness, and justice. They tried to organize their life according to the Golden Rule. As there were no men in the community, celibacy was a way of life. They also lived separate from involvement in local churches, though they had a positive view of the role and work of government.

In the end, because of their celibacy and reluctance to take in new members, the group died out, though remnants survived on their farm in rural Montgomery County, Maryland, into the 1930s.

Sources:

Fogarty, Robert S. *Dictionary of American Communal and Utopian History*. Westport, CT: Greenwood Press, 1980. 271 pp.

Hinds, William Alfred. *American Communities and Cooperative Colonies*. Chicago: Charles H. Kerr & Company, 1908. 608 pp.

Miller, Timothy. *American Communes, 1860-1960: A Bibliography*. New York: Garland Publishing, 1990. 583 pp.

Communal — After 1960

★1258★
Aquarian Research Foundation
5620 Morton St.
Philadelphia, PA 19144

The Aquarian Research Foundation, an outgrowth of the work and vision of Arthur Rosenblum, combines radical politics, Christian communalism, and intuitive insights with a scientific approach to the future of the world. A product of 20 years of communal living with the Hutterian Brethren (Societ of Brothers) and other groups, Rosenblum formed the foundation in 1969. The goal of the research is to assist a new age of love to come to the planet and thus avoid the chaos as present systems decline.

In order to do the research, which includes life in community, the total commitment of the individuals is required. The foundation's intimate communal structure allows members to help each other with personal problems that make people afraid to do something different. Drugs and smoking are excluded.

According to Rosenblum, God is the universe. Just as matter may be seen as concentrated energy, so energy may be seen as concentrated spirit (love). God and the universe consist of love, energy, and matter, and are the same entity. The "kingdom of God" is the rulership of love.

As an expression of the foundation's commitment, in 1986 Rosemblum traveled to Moscow, where he met with Prof. Georgi Arbatov, a high-level Soviet advisor on American affairs. The object of the meeting was to seek new ways of ending the arms race. As a result of the meeting, Rosenblum sponsored a tour by Soviet researcher Dr. Peter Gladkov, a scholar of American contemporary communal societies. It is Rosenblum's opinion that communal societies work and have worked in a way that demonstrates the basis of a new social order, solving today's social problems through a loving approach. Rosenblum believes that most social problems are caused by people's unhappiness due to lack of loving relationships with others.

Membership: In 1995, the foundation had approximately 20 members.

Periodicals: *Aquarian Alternative*.

Remarks: One longterm project pursued by the foundation has been the exploration of methods of natural birth control. With interest begun by Rosenblum's becoming aware of the research of Dr. Eugen Jonas of Czechoslovakia on the relation of female fertility and astrological cycles, the foundation has continued to update the research and report experiences of women using the method in a book currently in its sixth edition.

Sources:

Rosenblum, Art. *Aquarian Age or Civil War?* Philadelphia, PA: Aquarian Research Foundation, 1970.

___. *The Natural Birth Control Book*. Philadelphia, PA: Aquarian Research Foundation, 1984.

___. *Unpopular Science*. Philadelphia, PA: Running Press, 1974.

★1259★
Bride of Christ Church
330 SE Sabbath Way
PO Box 885
Canyonville, OR 97417

The Bride of Christ Church began in 1980 in Las Vegas, Nevada, following the ordination of Thomas Clyde Smith, Jr. by Dr. G. J. Soriano, founder of the Faith Restoration Center, a Philippine Islands Christian organization. According to Smith, in 1965 he was convicted of molesting his nine-year-old daughter. Following his jail sentence he spent a year in a mental hospital. While there he had a conversion experience and became a Christian. He later decided to become a minister and start the church. Smith advocated a form of what he termed Christian socialism, which included communal living. After four years in Nevada, he moved with the members of the church to rural Oregon.

The Bride of Christ Church existed quietly until 1987 when there was an attempt to kidnap and deprogram a church member. The attempt was foiled when the deprogrammers were caught breaking into property at the church headquarters and arrested. A year later Smith invited Lawrence Singleton to join the group on its farm near Azalea. Singleton had been convicted in California for a particularly heinous crime, raping a 15-year-old girl and severing both her arms. Smith said he identified with Singleton, who reportedly had repented for his crime and become religious during his years in prison. However, public outrage prevented Singleton's moving in with the church.

The Church is organized communally. Men work in two group-owned businesses to support the members. Women work at the center in Azalea.

Membership: There are approximately 65 members of the church.

Sources:

Tims, Dana. "Azalea Sect Riles Region." *Oregonian* (April 7, 1988).

★1260★
Christ's Household of Faith
355 Marshall Ave.
St. Paul, MN 55102-1898

Christ's Household of Faith is a large urban Christian communal group which dates to 1965 when the group's founder and pastor, Donald Alsbury, was suspended from the ministry of the Lutheran Church-Missouri Synod. Alsbury had been the pastor of a small church serving the communities of Giese and McGrath, Minnesota. A conflict arose in the church over a woman who was seeking membership in the church. Some of the lay people, citing her bad reputation, wanted Alsbury to condemn her from the pulpit. Alsbury said the congregation should encourage her to repent and join the congregation. This conflict became the occasion for other issues to emerge. Following Alsbury's suspension, the majority of the congregation left the synod and established worship services at Mora, Minnesota. In 1970 the congregation was joined by a group of approximately 75 people who had moved to Minnesota from St. Helen's, Oregon, under the leadership of Vernon Harms, an old friend and colleague of Alsbury's.

The Harms' group joined the older group as it was in the midst of an intensive period of Bible study and selfreflection characterized by the members' attempt to share all of their past sins and to begin to divest themselves of their material goods in expectation of Christ's second coming. At one point in 1970, the business at which many of the group were employed burned, and the group left Mora and resettled in St. Paul. They found temporary lodging in houses in one of the poorer sections of the city. They survived by developing a maintenance fix-up business, living off of the abundance of a throw-away culture, and living frugally. In 1976 they were able to purchase an abandoned convent which became the group's new home. They started a school for their children, and much as The Farm did in rural Tennessee, have prospered.

Leadership in the community is invested in Alsbury, Harms, and a group of elders. A finance committee makes key business decisions. All money earned from outside the community (in the community-managed business) is put into a common pool from which major purchases are made. Each member receives a monthly allowance. A farm in a nearby rural community is used for the production of food and provides both employment and a learning experience for the youth during the summer. There is a strong emphasis on the nuclear family as a working unit within the community as a whole.

Sunday is a day of worship and fellowship during which the entire community is together.

Membership: In 1995 the group had approximately 500 members, of which 300 were minors.

★1261★
Church of Jesus Christ at Armageddon
14724 184th NE
Arlington, WA 98223

The Church of Jesus Christ at Armageddon was founded by Love Israel in 1968. According to its charter, it was established "to fulfill the New Testament as revealed to Love Israel in the form of visions, dreams, and revelations received by members of the Church. The members of the Church have all had heavenly visions without which we would never understand our purpose on this earth or our relationship with each other." The name of the church is based on Revelation 16:16 where Armageddon is mentioned as the gathering place of the end-time. The members of the church refer to themselves as the Love Family, drawn together out of the world and recognizable by their love for one another. They believe that their relationships are eternal, and that through their love and commitment to one another, they create the opportunity for Christ to express his personality in them.

New members contribute all their possessions upon joining and begin a new life with a new name. Since Israel is the name of God's people, Israel is the surname of all members of the church. A biblical name or a "virtue" name such as "Abishai" or "Honesty" is assumed as a first name and former names are abandoned. Although they live in traditional family units or expanded households, they consider themselves married to one another in the universal marriage of Jesus Christ and are not bound by "worldly traditions of matrimony." The father is respected as the "head" of each household and represents his household in the Family government. The affairs of the larger Family are governed through close communication and frequent informal meetings.

The church sees itself as being the beneficiary of the Old Testament promises to Israel and committed to practicing the beliefs and lifestyle of the New Testament as created by Jesus Christ. Rules are replaced by love, agreement, moderation, and common sense. Eating and drinking are considered sacramental, with the understanding that all food and drink are the body and blood of Jesus Christ. Water baptism represents the opportunity to be freed from the past and become a new personality that has an eternal place within the Body of Christ.

During the 1970s the church enjoyed a steady growth, reaching a residential population of around 300 members by 1983. Their unorthodox appearance and lifestyle made them the object of considerable controversy and a target for anti-cultists and deprogrammers. For a short while, they participated as "observers" in the Church Council of Greater Seattle. Their headquarters was a handmade mansion on Seattle's Queen Anne Hill, surrounded by a compact "village" of residences, gardens, and shops. They maintained a 24-hour Inn, where guests were freely housed and fed, and from which food from their farms and fishing boat were distributed to needy neighbors. They operated numerous small businesses and maintained satellite communities in several places throughout Washington, Alaska, and Hawaii.

In 1984, an internal power struggle and a lawsuit by a former member severely disrupted the church community and resulted in the relocation of the core members to a 300-acre ranch near Arlington, Washington. This ranch has become the new headquarters for Love Israel and the church, and provides a cultural center for those members who remain dispersed throughout the region. Here, and in the other small satellite communities, members continue to live and work together to fulfill their original vision of harmonious interdependence.

The church defines its continuing ministry as follows: "Our purpose is to reform our relationships and our patterns of relating until they conform to the truth of our Oneness in Jesus Christ. We understand that this is how we can best help fulfill Christ's purpose on this earth. The fruits of our labors are the comfort, the happiness, and the harmony which we achieve with one another in our daily lives together. WHEN THE SEERS COME TOGETHER, THEN THE WATCHERS WILL SEE."

Membership: Not reported. There were approximately 300 members in 1980.

Remarks: Recently, a major split (following several years of internal dispute) was being reported. Some predicted the end of the Church, following intense criticism of Love Israel. It appears that a smaller core of his following is reorganizing and continuing at the group's major compound in Seattle.

Sources:

Allen, Steve. *Beloved Son.* Indianapolis: Bobbs-Merrill Company, 1982.

Israel, Love. *Love.* Seattle: Church of Armageddon, 1971.

★1262★
Circle of Friends

Current address not obtained for this edition.

The Circle of Friends is a small New Age communal group built around the teachings of George Jurcsek. Born in Hungary around 1920, Jurcsek migrated to America in 1950. Over the years he absorbed a variety of Eastern and occult teachings from the writings of Rudolf Steiner and Edgar Cayce and a trip to India. He came to believe that a catastrophe would overwhelm the earth in the near future and that civilization would end. Jurcsek began lecturing in the late 1960s. The Circle was formed in 1973 and at its height in the late 1970s had approximately 75 members. Members of the group believe they will emerge as leaders in the New Age.

Soon after its formation, the Circle came under attack by anti-cult groups for its intensive lifestyle. The charges focused on the communal life, requiring members to live on a minimal allowance (above their room and board) and pool their money for investments for the group. There were also charges that Jurcsek manipulated the lives of people, dictating to whom they should be wed. Several deprogrammings occurred with mixed success. In 1979 Jurcsek dropped out of sight, reappearing several years later in central North Carolina, where the group had purchased property.

The Circle encountered severe problems a few years later when Jurcsek and Mary O'Rourke, one of the group's leaders, were indicted for fraud involving student loans. Both were convicted in 1988 and given seven-year prison sentences. Both appealed their convictions; Jurcsek's appeal is still under adjudication. Meanwhile, O'Rourke has renounced the group, withdrawn her appeal, and applied for a lessened sentence.

Membership: There were approximately 50 members at last report.

Remarks: Information on the Circle of Friends has been difficult to attain. The group itself has kept a low profile and published little. Media coverage has centered on the claims of former members, most of whom have associated with the anti-cult network, and have adopted their terminology. Hence, it is difficult to objectively assess their testimony.

★1263★
The Family

14118 Whittier Blvd., Ste. 116
Whittier, CA 90605

Alternate Address: International Headquarters: World Services, Postfach 241, Zurich, Switzerland 8021.

The Family, an international network of Christian communes, was founded in 1968, originally going by the name Teens for Christ, but later dubbed the Children of God (COG) by the media. They were one of the original Jesus People groups. The Children of God originated from the West Coast ministry of David Berg, a former Christian and Missionary Alliance minister. From 1953 to 1965 Berg had been associated with Fred Jordan's Soul Clinic, an independent ministry founded in 1944. Teen Challenge, a national youth ministry which had been established by Assemblies of God minister David Wilkerson, turned over to Berg's teenage children the use of their Christian coffeehouse in Huntington Beach, California, known as the Light Club.

The work of the Light Club, ministering primarily to surfers and hippies, changed directions dramatically in 1969. Berg, agreeing with revelations received by other members that California was threatened by an earthquake, decided the club members should leave. Berg and those who chose to follow him split into three groups and crisscrossed North America for eight months, an event

which the group compared to the Exodus of the Hebrew children under Moses. During this period the group acquired the name Children of God (COG) and Berg became known as Moses David.

In early 1970 the COG accepted the hospitality of the Soul Clinic, and Jordan gave them the use of the abandoned Soul Clinic ranch near Thurber, Texas. Shortly afterwards he also granted them the use of the Soul Clinic mission building in downtown Los Angeles, as well as a property he owned near Coachella, California. The membership grew, adding converts encountered on the streets of various cities and many former drug users. Slowly, from the small group around Berg, a disciplined community emerged. By 1971 the COG had become a national organization. Over the next few years they became well known for their public witnessing activity which occasionally included demonstrations involving an element of apocalyptic warning.

During the early 1970s the life of the Children of God was altered by the growing opposition of the parents of the youthful members (most in their late teens and early 20s). Many of these people had disappeared on the streets only to emerge after a period of isolation from their family as a missionary for the Children of God. Some parents were opposed to Berg's teachings and communal practices and claimed that COG was a destructive cult. The parents organized FREECOG (Free Our Children from the Children of God), the first of the contemporary anti-cult groups. As pressure built against the COG in the United States and new mission opportunities opened in Europe through the mid-1970s, the membership largely left the United States. Though some members remained in America, all visible signs of their presence disappeared.

In 1976 Berg introduced a new ministry he had been testing to the now large, scattered group. He suggested that the female members of the groups (most then in their mid-20s) begin "flirty fishing," to use their feminine charms to allure men and set up an opportunity for witnessing God's love to others. In the most extreme cases, such activity could, and frequently did, lead to the women having sexual relationships with the men, the "fish," and developing long-term relationships with them.

In 1978 the organization went through the first of several radical organizational changes, the RNR (Reorganization, Nationalization, Revolution). As the organization had grown and spread internationally, a strong hierarchical system had been put in place headed largely by Berg's own children and their spouses. Berg became aware of a variety of leadership abuses, including the imposition of unauthorized tithes going into some leaders' pockets. Thus in 1978 he removed all of the leaders and the organization moved into a period of organizational anarchy. Many members left or dropped their communal lifestyle. The name Children of God was abandoned and the group became known as the Family of Love, a short time later shortened to The Family. The chaos of the RNR only abated in the spring of 1981 with what was termed the Fellowship Revolution, in which a semblance of order began to be restored. A new structure arose out of the reestablished communal homes: local area fellowships, district fellowships, greater area fellowships and national fellowships. Shepherds were elected to serve at each level of administration.

During the RNR period the organizational chaos was accompanied by a liberalization of sexual mores and many adult members—especially those who continued to live in communal homes and in those cities with a concentration of members—had multiple sexual contacts. Following the Fellowship Revolution, herpes began to spread through the group and sexual contacts were limited. Later, the "flirty fishing" ministry was curtailed, not only because of problems of disease but due to the need to divert attention to the care of a growing number of children.

Doctrine: The Family developed out of the evangelical Protestantism of the Jesus People movement. It differed from other Jesus People on three points. First Father David, as he was affectionately known in the movement, noted that he had contacts with spirit entities, especially with one named Abrahim the Gypsy King. Other evangelicals condemned the group for practicing (or tolerating) spiritism. Secondly, the group identified Father David as the prophet of the endtime and associated him with the "David" referred to in Ezekiel 34 and 37, Hosea 3, and Jeremiah 30. Thirdly, the COG advocated "forsaking all" and dropping out of the "system" in order to live a communal lifestyle dedicated to God's service.

Through the 1970s Father David also developed the concept of the Law of Love as the over-arching ethical principle, based on the Gospel of Matthew 22:36-40. The Law of Love views love as the great commandment that overrides and frees individuals from the strictures of the Mosaic Law. The Law of Love was articulated as a means to undergird the practice of flirty fishing, seen as a sacrificial activity to bring people to the saving truth of the gospel, but also applied to all sexual relationships. Sexual contacts were condoned among consenting adults as long as they met the conditions of love (unselfishness) and did not fall into mere lust.

The developing doctrinal perspective has recently been formally presented in "Our Statement of Faith." The Family follows the Evangelical Protestant consensus believing in the Bible as the inspired Word of God, the Trinity, and salvation through Jesus Christ received by faith in him and receiving him into our hearts. Once saved, the believer will be kept by God forever. The Family is Pentecostal and believes in the baptism of the Holy Spirit as a baptism of love that empowers the believer. Speaking in tongues does not necessarily accompany the baptism, but baptized believers do manifest the gifts of the Spirit (such as healing, miracle working, prophecy, and speaking in tongues). Believers should also manifest the fruits of the spirit as noted in Galatians 5:22-23 (love, joy, peace, long-suffering, gentleness, goodness, faith, meekness, and temperance). The Family believes in a literal creation (as depicted in the Book of Genesis), angels, Satan, divine healing, and the soon end of the world. They are opposed to abortion.

Family members gather for worship daily in the morning and often in the evening. Periodically, days are set aside for prayer and self-examination. The ordinance of the Lord's Supper is held regularly, usually every Sunday evening. A special candlelight service is held on New Year's Eve, the most liturgical of The Family's worship life.

Family members live communally, and with very few exceptions do not hold secular jobs. Most children are schooled at the communal homes. Evangelism is seen as the member's primary calling and vocation. Thus their daily life is spent in witnessing to their faith and in "provisioning," gathering resources (food, clothing, shelter, finances, etc.) to support the evangelical ministry. Since most people reached by their evangelism are not ready for communal living, converts are generally referred to other evangelical churches.

Organization: The Family is built around communal homes usually comprising several families and a few unmarried adults. Families tend to be large and couples with 10 or more children are not unusual. Each home with children houses a home school. It is led by a team of at least three shepherds elected by the adult and older teen members. A leadership structure of Area Shepherds provides guidance and counsel; assists in formulating, interpreting, and enacting policy; and helps homes with problems they cannot solve by themselves.

In 1994 The Family was in transition. Late that year Berg died. He was 83 years old. He was succeeded by his wife Maria who had been the active administrative head for some years. Announcement of his death to the larger world in early 1995 was soon followed by the announcements of significant changes in organization. In February 1995, The Family adopted a new constitution, "The Love Charter," declared to be Berg's parting gift to the group. It outlined the basic rights and responsibilities of members as well as as the beliefs and behavior standards to which members were expected to adhere. Soon thereafter, Maria announced her marriage to Peter Amsterdam who had been an important assistant to Berg for many years.

The Charter takes great pains to spell out not only the responsibilities, but the rights of individual members. This includes the rights of self-determination, personal initiative, development of gifts and talents, choice of place of residence, and choice of medical care. All adult members may vote on matters before their home and be considered for leadership positions. Parents are assigned responsibilities for the care of their children and the home sees that parents have the time and resources to care for their children properly. One day a week is usually set aside specifically for parents to spend in a relaxed atmosphere with their children. Each home takes collective responsibility for the education through the secondary-school level of all of the minors living in the home.

Membership: In 1997 the Family reported 9,937 full-time members worldwide of which approximately 6,000 are children and youth. There are 749 Family communities in 85 countries of the world. In the United States family homes are found in suburban Los Angeles, San Diego, Chicago, Houston, and Washington D.C. In addition to the 9,000 full members, there are some 20,000 members who do not reside in Family homes, though many did at one time. These members, designated TRF supporters, tithe to support The Family's work and receives The Family's literature.

Periodicals: *The Family in Action!* (The periodicals are prepared by Wordl Services in Zurich, and distributed through The Family's homes.) • *Family Specials News Magazine!* • *The Hope of the Future.* • *The New Good News.* • *The Persecution Endtime News.*

Remarks: Over the years, as many as 40,000 people have been live-in members of The Family. Beginning in the early 1970s a small number of ex-members vocally opposed the organization. Following the introduction of "flirty fishing" and the disbanding of the leadership in 1978, a more intense core of former members arose, among them Deborah Davis, the eldest daughter of David Berg. Many of these former members organized in a group, No Longer Children, which has focused a continuing attack upon The Family, though there is a current movement for reconciliation between The Family and its disaffected members.

While the thrust of the attack upon The Family has generally followed standard anti-cult rhetoric, in the 1990s that attack has concentrated on accusations of child abuse. Critics of The Family have charged it with institutionalizing child abuse during the RNR period. The Family's leadership has responded by denying any widespread child abuse (while admitting that some cases of adult/minor sexual contact were brought to their attention in the mid-1980s and, oncee aware of the problem, they instituted strong rules barring any such activity). In the wake of these accusations, government child protection services agencies have moved against the Family in Australia, Argentina, Spain, France, and England. As a byproduct of such action, more than 600 children of The Family have been examined by either government-appointed or private physicians and therapists. To date, the charges have proved unfounded, and as of early 1994 not a single case of child abuse has been discovered among the youth and children.

Sources:

The Family has a vast literature, most of which was published over the years as a series of "MO" Letters sent to the membership and containing the majority of policy statements. In recent years such communications have been included in the periodical, *The New Good News.* After a drought of scholarly study of the groups, a new volume of recent historical and social science studies has been compiled by James Lewis. Deborah Davis's book is typical of the several anti-Children of God books.

David, Moses (David Berg). *The Basic Mo Letters.* Gold Lion Publishers, 1976.

Davis, Deborah (Linda Berg). *The Children of God.* Grand Rapids, MI: Zondervan Publishing House, 1984.

Lewis, James R., ed. *Sex, Slander, and Salvation: Investigating The Family/Children of God.* Goleta, CA: Center for Academic Publication, 1994.

"Mo" (David Berg). *The True Story of Moses and the Children of God*. Children of God, 1972.

Pritchett, W. Douglas. *The Children of God, Family of Love: An Annotated Bibliography*. New York: Garland Publishing, 1985.

★1264★
The Farm
100 The Farm
Summertown, TN 38483

The Farm grew out of the weekly Monday-evening teaching sessions in the 1960s and 1970s in San Francisco, California, led by Stephen Gaskin, at that time, known simply as Stephen. He soon became a well-known spiritual philosopher and published two books, *Monday Night Class* and *Caravan*. Attendance at the Monday class increased from a handful to more than 1,000. In October 1970, about 250 of the class in 50 converted school buses and vans joined Stephen in a cross-country tour, dubbed Caravan. In four months, the Caravan criss-crossed the country, gathering additional converts as it went. At the end of the tour, about 350 from the Caravan and the class decided to set up a communal religious community with Stephen and settled on 1,000 acres near Summertown, Tennessee.

During the 1970s, ten other independent communities (including one in Canada) formed around Stephen's teachings. Though administratively autonomous, they considered themselves familially tied to The Farm. All these associated communites have disbanded.

From 1971 to 1983, The Farm had a traditional communal economy like the Shakers or Hutterites. Everyone joining the community gave everything they owned to the common treasury and anything developed or received by any member belonged to the whole group. Trying to do too much with too little for too long brought about a severe financial crisis. In October 1983, The Farm reorganized its communal economy. In addition to allowing individuals to own property, members were made responsible for providing for their own living expenses and contributing to the support of the community, which included paying off a large debt. Because of austerity measures after 1981, the inability of many members to earn a living in one of the poorest areas in Tennessee, and other contributing factors, the population decreased from its peak of about 1,400 in 1981 to its present population.

Currently the Farm is a cooperative community of 60 households, of more than 230 people, including children, living on 1,750 acres (750 additional acres were purchased in 1973). The Farm was settled to establish a strongly cohesive, outwardly-directed community, a base from which the members could, by action and example, have a positive effect on the world. The members try to use agreement and mutual respect to generate a friendly working environment. The members recognize that there are many paths toward recognizing personal ideals and that people have a wide range of social values, but as a group, they do not accept the use of violence, anger, or intimidation for solving problems. The fabric of the community is created by their friendship and respect for one another. The institutions developed to operate the community have changed over the years and will probably continue to change.

The Farm is a nondenominational church of people who consider themselves "free thinkers" because they discuss religion and philosophy in terms that do not exclude any possibilities. People come to The Farm from a variety of religious traditions and disciplines and find those views treated with honor and respect. While individual practice is an on-going, free-ranging discussion. In keeping with their deep reverence for life, the members are pacifists, conscientious objectors, and most are vegetarians. An emphasis on natural healing led to participation in a national revival of midwifery. Stephen's wife, Ina May Gaskin, editor of *The Birth Gazette*, has become a prominent author and advocate of the practice.

The Book Publishing Company, one of the first businesses on The Farm, publishes vegetarian and vegan cookbooks, Native American books, and books on the environment, gardening, and lifestyle. Other businesses built by Farm members include Total Video, SE International, and The Farm Building Co.. Most residents work with one of the Farm's business.

The Farm has attempted to contribute to the solving of world problems. PLENTY, founded on The Farm in 1974, aims to provide food and health self-sufficiency for the world. Projects were established in the Bronx, New York, Bangladesh, Guatemala, the Caribbean, and Lesotho. The multiplication of food protein by vegetarianism is a basic principle of PLENTY's approach. It is recognized as a United Nations nongovernmental agency.

Membership: In 1995 there were approximately 230 residents at The Farm.

Periodicals: *The Birth Gazette*. Send orders to 42 The Farm, Summertown, TN 38483. • *Plenty News*. Send orders to PO Box 394, Summertown, TN 38483. • *Natural Rights*. Send orders to PO Box 90, Summertown, TN 38483. • *ENNA, the Journal of the Ecovillage Network of North America*. Send orders to PO Box 90, Summertown, TN 38483.

Sources:

Gaskin, Ina May. *Spiritual Midwifery*. Summertown, TN: Book Publishing Company, 1978.

Gaskin, Stephen. *The Caravan*. New York: Random House, 1972.

___. *Monday Night Class*. San Francisco: Book Publishing Company, [1974].

___. *Rendered Infamous*. Summertown, TN: Book Publishing Company, 1981.

___. *Volume One*. Summertown, TN: Book Publishing Company, 1975.

Popenoe, Cris, and Oliver Popenoe. *Seeds of Tomorrow*. San Francisco: Harper & Row, 1984.

★1265★
The Finders
Current address not obtained for this edition.

The Finders is a communal group founded in the late 1960s by George Marion Pettie, the teacher of an eclectic religious philosophy that combines elements of the human potentials movement, Eastern religion (especially Taoism), and New Age thought. The Washington, D.C.-based group was thrust into the public eye when several members were arrested in Tallahassee, Florida. The arrests followed anonymous calls to the police after the members, two men and six children, were seen in a Tallahassee park. As later reported, the children were described as unwashed and covered with insect bites. A short time later a number of newspaper articles appeared describing the men as possible members of an international child pornography ring or a Satanic cult.

Pettie's followers, mostly young adults, established their community in a residential area of the District of Columbia and engaged in an intense interactive lifestyle aimed at shedding delusions and inhibitions. Integral to the group's program was the use of fantasy role-playing games. Along the way, around 1980, the group decided to create a new generation of children who would be raised on a model developed from their knowledge of the Indians of the plains, tough and strong. Each child would be raised by the group as a whole rather than the biological parents.

After an investigation that lasted some six weeks, all charges against the two men arrested in Florida were dropped, there being no evidence of wrongdoing. Since that time, the group has assumed a low profile and its present status is unknown.

Membership: Not reported.

Sources:

Mintz, John, and Marc Fisher. "Ex-Finders Tell of Games, Complex Beliefs." *Washington Post* (February 8, 1987).

★1266★
Jesus People USA
4707 N. Malden
Chicago, IL 60640

History. Jesus People USA is one of several groups which grew out of the Jesus People revival of the early 1970s. It is also among the few which have retained the communal lifestyle so prominent in the movement's early years. The group began in June 1972 as an itinerant evangelistic outreach of a parent body informally known as the Milwaukee Jesus People. The Milwaukee Jesus People originated with six people in February 1971, under the leadership of Jim Palosaari. By 1972, it had grown to about 150-200 members, with three pastors, and published *Street Level*, an early Jesus People paper. Most of the followers lived communally. In April 1972, Jim and 30 core members of the Milwaukee Jesus People went to Europe with a Jesus rock band, "The Sheep."

In June 1972, Pastor John Herrin left with a team of 30 members, traveling south and east across the United States in a caravan of three cars and a reconverted school bus (hence the "USA" part of the name). While they were on the road, they issued a Jesus paper, *Cornerstone*, filling out their evangelistic endeavor with a Jesus rock band, Resurrection, and the Holy Ghost Players, a street-theater drama troupe. Meanwhile, in late 1972, the parent body in Milwaukee, Wisconsin, closed down in the wake of more than 60 members leaving to become the Jesus People Traveling Tent Revival Show, now known as Christ Is the Answer under the leadership of evangelist Bill Lowery. In the winter of 1972, Jesus People USA (now numbering about 40 followers) traveled through Illinois, Michigan, and Wisconsin, conducting rallies and revivals. They settled in Chicago, Illinois, in January 1973, where they have been headquartered ever since. In 1976, the group incorporated as Jesus People USA Full Gospel Ministries and was chartered as a church by the Full Gospel Church in Christ, a San Jose, California-based Pentecostal organization. In 1990, Jesus People USA became affiliated with the Evangelical Covenant Church and now exists as a community within its worldwide fellowship.

Beliefs. Jesus People USA has adopted a 10-point statement of belief which emphasizes its agreement with conservative evangelical Protestantism. It asserts a belief in the infallibility and inerrancy of the Bible, the Trinity, the deity of Christ, humanity's need of salvation in Christ, the imminent second coming of Christ, and the work of the Holy Spirit manifest in the gifts of the Spirit. There is no specific reference to the Pentecostal baptism of the Holy Spirit and the necessity of speaking-in-tongues. There are two ordinances: baptism by immersion and the Lord's Supper.

Organization. Leadership of the ministry is exercised by nine copastors (elders), each with equal authority, though the prime spokesperson for the group in recent years has been Glenn Kaiser. There are also deacons assigned to various community tasks, who act as spiritually mature leaders for newer members. The group lives communally, and members of the community generally do not own real property beyond a few personal items. Members work in a covenant relationship with the community as a whole. New members are admitted upon consent of the elders. The group sponsors a number of ministries including its periodical, *Cornerstone*, which has emerged as a major evangelical voice; street evangelism; chaplaincy in adult and youth correctional houses; visitation in nursing homes; cult ministry; a food program; crisis pregnancy center; and housing for the homeless. Rez (Resurrection Band) is a Christian rock band. There is an annual Cornerstone Festival which draws up to 10,000 people. Support is provided through a number of businesses such as construction, roofing, home repair, second-hand merchandise, and painting.

Membership: In 1988, more than 450 people were members of Jesus People U.S.A., living in five residence buildings. There is also a farm in rural Missouri.

Periodicals: *Cornerstone.* • *Rez Rag.*

★1267★
Katharsis
(Defunct)

Kartharis was established in 1971 by a group wishing to establish an alternative community with an emphasis on harmony and spiritual growth. In 1974, the members purchased twenty acres near Nevada City, California, for their community and research center. The goals of Katharsis include the following: 1) spiritual growth and self-realization through the study of yoga and related sciences; 2) the development of a natural lifestyle based on diet; 3) cooperative living; and 4) promotion of the practice of astrology as an aid to a fuller life. The group annually published the "Solar Lunar Calendar" and a line of related astrology products. After several years Katharsis disappeared and no sign of their existence has surfaced for several years. The organization is presumed to be defunct.

★1268★
Kerista Commune
PO Box 410068
San Francisco, CA 94141-0068

The Kerista Commune can be traced to 1956 to a mystical revelatory experience of John Presmont, a former businessman, now known as Brother Jud. The experience initiated a search for meaningful religiousness and communal living. The attempt to resolve issues of sexual attitude restucturing and sexual liberaltion were also a persistent element in what became a lengthy life quest. Several different efforts to organize a communal lifestyle were tried in New York and outside the United States in Central America and the Caribbean. Each effort failed, the victims of internal problems. In the beginning of 1971, at the end of the Flower Children era, Brother Jud was in San Francisco, California. He met a young woman Eve Furchgott, known as Even Eve, also a communalist, and with several others of like mind, founded the New Kerista Tribe. Eve and Jud discovered that they shared many common insights about communal life and became convinced that together they could create the next great world religion, the next new family structure, and the first viable utopian culture. They were soon joined by Wat, an old friend of Eve's, and Geo Logical, a psychiatric nurse. (All group members have taken new names.)

The distinctive characteristics of Kerista life were initiated early in its existence. The early members formed what they termed a living school residence group, later renamed a superfamily, then a polyfidelitous closed group, currently termed a best friend identity cluster. Polyfidelity, the new form of family life practiced at Kerista is seen as combining the best features of monogamous marriage and its extended companionate family unit with the idea of non-monagamy. Kerista members are ideally members of a best friend identity cluster, an intimate family unit loyal to the members of their cluster (ideally 36 people: 18 women and 18 men), and relate to all of them on an equal basis. Members of Kerista not yet part of a cluster are celibate. Members and clusters may be either heterosexual, bi-sexual or homosexual. To date all clusters have been heterosexual, though there have been attempts to form a homosexual cluster. The oldest cluster is known as The Purple Submarine. In 1988, it had nine adult females and seven adult males. Some members of the cluster had been together for 17 years.

Sexuality in the community is placed in the context of loving mutual reciprocity. Group sex, sado-masochistic sexuality, bestiality, pedophilia, incest, and sexual exhibitionism are not allowed. Overt public displays of physical attraction between members of the Kerista tribe are minimized.

The Keristians organized the Kerista Consciousness Church. They believe in a pantheistic Divinity, a Totality, called Kyrallah. Kyrallah, It, is the one and only reality. They have faith in an ongoing evolution of the human species from blue-green algae to an animal-like nature to a utopian paradise. In developing their theology, they invented a deity as a symbol of a megaintelligence field to express the connection between the individual and the Totality. She is named Sister Kerista, and is pictured as a hip black woman with a pair of sneakers—an embodiment of women's liberation, poetic justice, and the four Keristan ideals of humor, equality, liberation, and love (hell). Sister Kerista, in the Keristan mythology, is the daughter of the Black Madonna and Queen Mother Granny Nanny, the folk heroine of the Eastern Maroons of Jamaica.

Through the 1980s the Kerista Commune organized as a potential worker's paradise with horizontal democracy, worker self-management, and with exacting kibbutz-type communal and equalitarian structures. Sexism, ageism, and racism are not tolerated. Each person is treated as an economic equal and policy decision-making is by majority rule of the general assembly. Children are raised by the entire community and education is provided by their own school called the EZ Learning Academy. Integral to the ongoing life of the community is the Gestalt-O-Rama process, the process for generating group commitment and motivation, solving conflicts, and enhancing self-esteem within the communal life. In both formal and informal settings, members are encouraged to foster a passionate sense of mission and to avoid and transcend negative behavior and attitudes, while cultivating and reinforcing positive traits. Members are encouraged to be verbal and personally accountable for feelings, thoughts, and behavior, and open to continual growth. The Gestalt-O-Rama, Mental Health Maintenance Process revolves around 88 basic behavior standards. Rap groups are also open to non-Keristans who want to participate in the growth process.

Several structures developed to further the community's goal of creating a scientific utopian society. These include the Club Utopia Growth Co-op, the Performing Arts Social Society (which publishes several of the group's periodicals), the Alliance for Creative Philanthropy, the New School of Utopian Psychology, and the Node Unity Alliance. Keristans hope to create a transnational kibbutz movement whose members, like themselves, will reduce per capita costs via cooperative living and use the surplus to fund philatropic projects aimed at solving global problems. A project was initiated in Jamaica as a model for the future interaction of distant human communities along scientific utopian lines.

In November 1991 the Kerista Community as it had existed through the 1980s went through a major disruption when Eve Furchgott and a group of members left Kerista. Their departure effectively disrupted the settled life, including the computer business, which they had enjoyed in San Francisco. Jud quickly moved to constitute the remaining members as the World Academy of Keristan Education to continue to perpetuate the Keristan ideals. The small group has reorganized as a theater arts repertory company and to build a larger network of support to spread the Keristan program for a prosperous future.

Membership: Following the disruption of 1991, less than 15 members remained in the case group. In 1993, Brother Jud reported some 200 in the immediate support group.

Sources:

Chapman, Paul, ed. *Clusters*. Greensboro, NC: Alternative, 1975.

Gruen, John. *The New Bohemia*. New York: Grosset & Dunlap, 1966.

O'Lee, Lil, and Even Eve, eds. *Polyfidelity*. San Francisco, CA: Performing Arts Social Society, 1984.

★1269★
Lama Foundation
Box 44
San Cristobal, NM 87564

The Lama Foundation, located on a mountain near San Cristobal, New Mexico, serves as a coming-together point for the New Age mystical/psychical/Eastern religious perspectives which spread so widely in the counterculture in the 1960s. The foundation began when Steve Durkee, his wife, and three children settled

on the one-hundred-and-fifteen acre tract in the Sangre de Cristo Mountains in 1967. Eventually, a community of approximately 20 adults and their children gathered at the foundation. Adherents follow different paths, including yoga, Buddhism, Judaism, Zen, Sufism, Native American Church, and Christianity. During the summer, the community enlarges to more than 50 people, and a vigorous teaching program is maintained. A wide variety of spiritual teachers spends time at the Lama Foundation.

Identified strongly with the Lama foundation is Baba Ram Dass (formerly known as Richard Alpert). Through the foundation, he published *Be Here Now*, Lama's first publication venture. Sufism has been a strong influence. Murshid Samuel L. Lewis is buried at Lama. The foundation also published *Towards the One* by Pir Vilayat Khan, head of the Sufi Order.

Activities at the foundation center on the main Dome, which includes a library, prayer room, and bath house. The residents gather daily for meditation and prayer sessions. Work is spread among the residents and includes construction and maintenance of the various buildings, the preparation of food, gardening, car maintenance, childcare, and working for Flag Mountain (which sells rubber stamps, books, and silk-screened Tibetan prayer flags).

Membership: Approximately 18 people live year round at Lama Foundation and approximately 50 in residence through the summer.

Sources:

Dass, Baba Ram. *Be Here Now*. San Christobal, NM: Lama Foundation, 1971.

Gardner, Hugh. *The Children of Prosperity*. New York: St. Martin's Press, 1978.

Hedgepeth, William, and Dennis Stock. *The Alternative*. New York: Macmillan, 1970.

Houriet, Robert. *Getting Back Together*. New York: Avon, 1972.

★1270★
Messianic Communities of New England
Box 443
Island Pond, VT 05846

History. The origins of the Messianic Communities of New England can be traced to Chattanooga, Tennessee. There, in 1972, Gene Spriggs and his wife Marsha Spriggs opened their home to youth and young adults, as well as the homeless poor in the area. Around this core group of young people, a community composed of various ages began to form during the spreading Jesus People Revival. Those who received the gospel they preached gave up all their own possessions and moved into households together, sharing all things in common after the patterns described in the biblical book of Acts 2:37-47 and 4:32-35. Settling in several large homes on Vine Street in Chattanooga, the group became known as the Vine Christian Community and operated a restaurant known as the Yellow Deli. Eventually in response to invitation from residents in nearby towns, the Vine Community sent workers to establish other communities; and by 1978 a dozen communal households had emerged in Tennessee, Georgia, and Alabama. They operated six Yellow Delis, a bakery, and a restaurant and meeting house called Areopagus. At the time, there were approximately 150 members.

In 1978, workers went to Vermont to help a group of eight Vermont families establish a community in Island Pond, Vermont, in a geographical area known as the Northeast Kingdom, and was for a time called the Northeast Kingdom Community. They soon opened a business together known as the Common Sense Wholesome Food Store and Restaurant.

Meanwhile, as the cult controversy developed during the late 1970s, parents of some of the young people who had joined the Chattanooga community began to criticize it for its communal lifestyle and the authority represented by the elders. In the midst of the controversy, a number of deprogrammings were attempted.

The Community also incurred the enmity of some christian leaders and was spoken against by some local churches and Christian colleges in the area. In the midst of the controversy, fewer and fewer people responded to the preaching of community members, and in 1979, the Vermont community opened its doors for the members in the South to move there.

Selling their properties and businesses in the South, the various communities began relocating in Vermont, where they lived together in large extended families with shared households throughout the village of Island Pond. Here they diversified into a number of service oriented businesses. Their lifestyle sought to openly demonstrate the unity of the body of Christ in a practical, daily manner. Within a few years, the community had grown to more than 300 people, approximately one-fifth of the population of the village.

Soon, however, some local opposition arose from the group's stance regarding the necessity of a disciple's (i.e. member's) separation from the world system. Criticism was leveled at the apparent submission of women, the children's nonattendance at public schools, and the group's dress (adopted with concerns of modesty in mind). Members of the community were accused of many things, from underbidding local contractors for a series of government projects to mistreating their children. The primary focus of media concern, however, was the disciple of the children, an issue initially raised in a custody battle between a member and a spouse who had left the movement.

Then, in 1984, a member of the community left and accused the members of child abuse. As a result, approximately 90 state troopers raided the community, and 50 social workers seized the 112 children of the community. The raid was officially declared unconstitutional and "grossly unlawful" by Vermont District Court Judge Frank Mahady. The children were found to show no signs of child abuse. A brief time later, the complainant admitted to fabricating the allegations of child abuse due to pressure to do so from a local organization which was boycotting the community's businesses in an effort to drive them from the area. He was later forgiven and rejoined the community.

During the 1980s, the community in Island Pond sent workers to various locations in New England, as well as France, Canada, New Zealand, Brazil, and the midwestern United States at the invitation of people in those areas who had become believers. The communities thus established also began to send out workers to establish communities themselves. The communities in New England refer to themselves as the Messianic Communities of New England. As the communities have entered the 1990s, they have drawn further criticism for their stand against homosexuality. They claimed it was a sin worthy of eternal punishment, according to Revelation 21:8, Romans 1:26-27, I Corinthians 6:9-11, and other biblical passages.

Beliefs. The community receives the traditional affirmations of evangelical Christianity, but is unrelated to any particular denominational family. It believes in an authoritative and inerrant Bible, the Trinity, the incarnation of Christ, and His atonement. They look for the return of Christ. Members affirm the fall of humanity, salvation by grace, and justification by faith. While recognizing the validity and necessity of all the spiritual gifts (I Corinthians 12), especially prophecy, they do not consider themselves specifically pentecostal or charismatic.

The community refers to Him who most term Jesus as Yahshua, the Hebrew name given to Him in Matthew 1:21 and by Him in Acts 26:14-15.

The communities place heavy emphasis on obedience to the commands of the Son of God, and not merely belief in his atonement. They believe that such obedience, particularly in loving one another as their Savior loved them (John 13:34), is necessary for a person to enter the kingdom of heaven (Matthew 7:21). They recognize that, while a person is irreversibly saved from eternal damnation by grace through faith (which is a gift from God), participation in the Millennial kingdom and the first resurrection must be striven for and attained, according to Luke 13:24-28 and Philippians 3:8-12. They believe that this is what the Son of God was referring to when he said, "If anyone keeps my word, he shall never see death". (John 8:31-32, 51).

Organization. The Messianic Communities in New England are each established according to a New Testament pattern, and share their goods as did the church at Jerusalem, following the words of the Master in Luke 14:33. A council of elders oversees each local setting, while a regional council coordinates the interaction between communities. There is no central headquarters, nor do the individual communities consider themselves to be part of a denomination. Each one derives its name from the geographical location, and thus known simply as the Community in Island Pond, Dorchester, etc.

Membership: As of 1995, the membership of the Messianic Communities is estimated at 650 in the United States and an additional 200 in France, and less than 100 each in Canada, New Zealand, and Brazil.

Periodicals: *New England Freepaper*.

Sources:

The Constitution, Abiding Laws or Empty Words. Island Pond, VT: Island Pond Freepaper, 1987.

Nori, Don. "Persecution at Island Pond." *Charisma* 10, no. 4 (November 1984).

Wanted: the Answer to Abortion. Island Pond, VT: Island Pond Freepaper, [1987].

★1271★
Mu Farm
Current address not obtained for this edition.

Mu Farm is named for the ancient continent of Lemuria or Mu, made famous in theosophical lore. It was begun in 1971 when Fletcher Fist and two other people purchased land near Yoncalla, Oregon. A goat-milk farm was established as an economic base, and other works are developing. The beliefs of Mu Farm are eclectic and derive from the many psychical and mystical teachings that developed in the 1960s. The group lists sources of belief as the Bible, the I Ching, the *Aquarian Gospel of Jesus Christ* by Levi, and the writings of Martin Buber, Swami Yogananda, Einstein, and others. The golden rule is emphasized as replacing a set of specific rules and regulations.

Membership: Not reported. In 1988 there were approximately 30 resident members.

Periodicals: *Mu Eggs Press*.

★1272★
Padanaram Settlement
R.R. 1, Box 478
Williams, IN 47470

Padanaram Settlement, also known as God's Valley, is an intentional community in south central Indiana founded in 1966 by a small group under the leadership of Daniel Wright. Wright, an independent thinker and minister, was raised in the Brethren Church. His life was punctuated with periodic religious experiences which led to the building of Padanaram as a microscopic city, the first of many to be created in the millennial order of "Kingdomism".

In 1960, Wright heard a voice that said to him, "I will show you My valley." He got in his car and allowed the Spirit to guide him to the present site of the Padanaram Settlement. With a group of five men, three women, and four children, he purchased the former Smokey Valley Farm in 1966. A sawmill, which became the backbone of the community's growth, was purchased in 1968. The businesses have continued to expand into compost, bark mulch, organic farming, and other areas. Padanaram started a communal school (K-12) in 1972, a preschool in 1975, and a nursery in 1978. Meals are eaten three times daily in the communal dining area.

Five principles emerged from the building of Padanaram Settlement: 1. As one would that others do, do unto others; 2. Hold all things in common, count nothing one's own; 3. Distribution to each according to the need; 4. Of one who has much, much is required; and 5. One that won't work, shall not eat. Guided by these principles, a flourishing community developed and overcame the initial hardships of establishing an economic base and unfriendly feelings in the area. Today, two conventions are held annually (May and October), and an open house in October brings individuals of the surrounding towns for a visit.

Members of the community see themselves as a part of a "Kingdomism" movement and look to the day when people will live communally. They see hope in the emergence of many similar communal groups around the United States and the world. They are not separatists. To the contrary, they actively promote their form of "utopian" living and see a society governed by the simple principles by which they have become successful as necessary for the survival of humanity. The International Communal Utopia is the name given to the future order. According to its teachings, many villages like Padanaram Settlement will be formed as self-sufficient villages. The group believes that together, they will lead humanity out of its jungle-like past into a world of economic cooperation, peace, and security.

Membership: Approximately 200 people reside at the Padanaram Settlement as of 1992.

Periodicals: *Millennial Chronicles.*

Remarks: Wright and Padanaram have been heavily criticized for establishing a patriarchal and sexist social order. In return, Wright has defended the differentiation of gender roles at Padanaram as proper, biblical, and in keeping with both the equality of the sexes as well as their inherent differences.

Sources:

Faith Babies. Williams, IN: Padanaram Press, 1987.

Kingdomism. Williams, IN: Padanaram Press, 1990.

Padanaram. Williams, IN: Padanaram Press, [1980].

Wagner, Jon. "A Midwestern Patriarchy." In *Sex Roles in Contemporary American Communes.* Bloomington, IN: Indiana University Press, 1982.

Wright, Daniel. "Open Letter to the National Historical Communal Societies Association." N.p. 1988. Mimeo.

___. *Utopian Concepts for Social Revolution.* Williams, IN: Padanaram Press, 1987.

★1273★
Rainbow Family of Living Light
Current address not obtained for this edition.

Growing out of the counterculture movement of the late 1960s and conceptualized in the thinking of the Rev. Barry Adams (also known as Barry Davis), the Rainbow Family of Living Light is a loosely organized network of individuals, informal groups, and communes which share in common an attachment to what is termed New Age consciousness. The Family is truly a rainbow in its eclectic mixture of differing beliefs, concerns, and practices, but united in its vision that humanity is passing into a new age of spiritual consciousness. The Rainbow Family sees itself and is seen as a harbinger of the new age and a major component of the New Age movement which has its exponents in many of America's alternative religions.

The major activity of the Family since the early 1970s has been the sponsorship of an annual "gathering of the tribes." (New Age people often describe the essence of community as a new tribal consciousness.) These annual meetings began with a small "Vor-

tex" gathering in Oregon around 1970. The first large gathering to attract several hundred attendees (and significant media coverage) was held in 1972 at Strawberry Lake, east of Granby, Colorado. It called together the "tribes" to give honor and respect to anyone or anything that has aided in the positive evolution of humankind and nature upon this, our most beloved and beautiful world.

The belief world of the Rainbow Family centers upon ecology and the psychic/spiritual world much discussed in the 1960s. Basic is a nature-pantheism expressed in the belief, "God is you, God is me, God is the World, God is the Sky, God is the Sun." The ecological emphasis is expressed in a love of nature and of the out-of-doors. Adherents believe that everything in nature was placed there for man's use (not abuse). Marijuana is one of the God-created herbs, and it viewed as having sacramental value. All forms of pollutants are opposed.

The psychic world view is expressed in the incorporation of numerous practices from various bodies. The great invocation (channeled through Alice Bailey) is freely used, as is the distinction between Jesus the man and the mystic Christ consciousness. Followers believe in reincaration but with a distinct, this-worldly interest. Christ consciousness is a mystic state, but it is signalled by a person's making others happy, doing good, and giving more than is taken.

Love is an important goal. Loving someone is equated with heaven, and hating someone is equated with hell. Sex is considered to be an expression of love. Legal aspects of marriage are no longer considered necessary, for when two people love each other, they are thought to be married. There are no formal acts of worship, and the formality of most religious acts is condemned. A wide mixture of Hindu chants, Christian hymns, and meditative techniques are employed to reach God consciousness.

Membership: No membership roles are kept, but a directory of the family's network is published irregularly. Several thousand people are involved. The family claims as many as 10,000 among those who share its free lifestyle. In 1984, 28,000 attended the Family's summer gathering in Modoc County, California. In the late 1970s Rainbow Family gatherings emerged in Australia and New Zealand in around 1982 in Europe.

Periodicals: *The Guide.*

Sources:

Garlington, Phil. "The Return of the Flower Children." *California* 9, no. 10 (October, 1978): 81-83, 137-38.

The Rainbow Nation Cooperative Community Guide. McCall, ID: Rainbow Nation, 1972.

★1274★
Reba Place Church and Associated Communities
727 Reba Pl.
Evanston, IL 60602

Reba Place Church began in 1956 with a group of Mennonite students at Goshen College in Goshen, Indiana, and started as an off-campus fellowship. The members were reacting against the sterility of the church and were operating out of a vision of the church as a disciplined brotherhood in small communities of spiritual consensus. Among the leaders were John Miller, Don Mast, and Virgil Vogt. In 1957 the fellowship moved to 727 Reba Place, Evanston, Illinois, from whence the original group took its name. Growth in the church/fellowship was steady, as like-minded individuals, spurred by the communal thrust of the 1970s were drawn to Reba Place. Other buildings were purchased, and community activity accelerated.

Prior to 1980 membership in the church (the religious structure) and the fellowship (the communal living arrangement) were one and the same. Every person who became a member of the Reba Place Church also commited her/himself to participation in a common purse. In 1980 that definition changed, and church membership was opened to people outside the fellowship. As of the late 1980s, about two-thirds of the members were living outside the communal arrangements. The Reba Place Fellowship now exists as a subgroup of Reba Place Church.

As Reba Place was progressing, however, other communal experiments were also beginning. In 1971, the Plow Creek Fellowship was established by three families of the Reba Place Fellowship. They purchased a 190 acre farm in Bureau County, Illinois, and by 1974 it had grown into an independent congregation in its own right. The Fellowship of Hope was formed by nine people at the Mennonite Seminary at Elkhart, Indiana. From their struggle to find meaning in their church participation, and partially inspired by the Reba Place model, a communal life emerged. In 1971, three families in Newton, Kansas, joined together to "concentrate resources for the work of peacemaking and care for the families at the same time." In 1974, the communes in Bureau County, Illinois, Elkhart, Indiana, and Newton, Kansas joined with Reba Place in a mutual covenant of dependency. According to the covenant, the basis for membership is a commitment to Jesus and to his radical teaching. Membership specifically involves renunciation of property; love as an alternative to anger, violence, and war; faithfulness in marriage as the context for sex; a servanthood stance in all human relationships; and a communal organization of personal affairs. Each community is seen as a local church, with all the rights and privileges thereof. Within the circle of communities, encouragement is given to the sharing of spiritual gifts and resources, responding to words of correction, visiting between communities, allowing transfer of members between communities, sharing finances, and scheduling occasional intracommunal gatherings.

Each of the associated communities has grown out of a Mennonite base, though strong emphasis is place on the multi-traditional nature of their present membership. A general Mennonite theological perspective remains, along with concerns for peace and social service. Emphasis is placed on the radical teachings of Jesus in the Sermon on the Mount. The impetus to communal forms has also been present in Anabaptism, partially as a means of survival in a hostile world. At Reba Place, it is seen as a positive means to fulfill the teachings of Jesus. The communes differ from their Mennonite neighbors primarily in their spontaneous style of worship, which includes guitars, folk music, and the free expression of emotion. Priority is given to learning to live together in a family-like existence. Basic teachings are found in the *Christian Way*, by John Miller, one of the founders.

Members of the fellowships work at jobs within the surrounding communities. A group associated with the Plow Creek Fellowship, The Builders, helps finance the group through various kinds of construction work. Income is pooled, and each individual or nuclear family receives an allowance. Social structures supported by the Reba Place Church include a day nursery and apartment rentals. Support is also given to indiviuals in the community. Reba Place is located in a racially mixed neighborhood, and it includes black, Asian, and Puerto Rican Americans in its Fellowship. The Church is administered by four senior elders: Virgil Vogt, John E. Lehman, Julius Belser, and James C. Croequert.

Membership: Not reported. In 1988 there were 160 members/residents at Reba Place; 45 at Plow Creek; approximately ten at New Creation in Newton, Kansas, and 30 at Fellowship of Hope at Elkhart, Indiana.

Periodicals: *Life Together.* Send orders to Box 6017, Evanston, IL 60204. • *RPC Information Exchange.* Send orders to Box 6016, Evanston, IL 60204.

Sources:

Jackson, Dave, and Neta Jackson. *Glimpses of Glory, Thirty Years of Community.* Elgin, IL: Brethren Press, 1987.

___. *Living Together in a World Falling Apart.* Carol Stream, IL: Creation House, 1974.

Miller, John W. *The Christian Way.* Scottdale, PA: Herald Press, 1969.

★1275★
REMAR International
% Angel Jimenez
917 S. Western Ave.
Chicago, IL 60612

REMAR International grew out of the religious experience of Miguel Dias, a Spaniard. A compulsive gambler, Dias had a conversion experience to conservative evangelical Christianity in 1982 and founded a communal Christian group which he named for its goal of REhabilitating MARginal people. It is also the case that, in Spanish, remar means "to row," and the community views itself as being in a boat rowing out into the sea to save people drowning in their addictions. The community has a four "pillared" program that includes evangelism, discipleship, social work, and the development of Christian businesses. It accomplishes its first task both by going into the streets of the urban centers in which its communities are located and finding addicts and by inviting homeless people to take up residence in their homes and utilize the opportunity to turn their lives around. In the United States, as might be expected from their point of origin, REMAR communities have been active in the Hispanic communities.

REMAR is a conservative charismatic (Pentecostal) group. Worship is lively and spirited and punctuated with testimonies of those whose lives have been changed by their coming to the community. A leader, Angel Jimenez, has been appointed to oversee the communities in America, and he in turn has appointed a leader over each local community. Besides gifts from people in the larger secular community who appreciate their work, the individual REMAR centers have founded businesses, especially thrift stores, which they feel are in line with their goals of Christian living and assisting people to rehabilitate themselves.

Membership: Not reported. In 1996, there were more than 200 REMAR communities in 21 countries. There were five communities in the United States.

Sources:

Jansen, David. *Fire, Salt, and Peace: Intentional Christian Communities Alive in North America.* Evanston, IL: Shalom Mission Communities, 1996. 207 pp.

★1276★
Renaissance Church of Beauty
Current address not obtained for this edition.

The Renaissance Church of Beauty and the Renaissance Community was founded in 1969 as the Brotherhood of the Spirit near Leyden, Massachusetts, by Michael Metelica. Still in his teens and having just returned from California, he built and moved into a tree-house. Soon he was joined by eight friends. They began to work for farmers for wages of food or goods instead of money. When vandals burned down the tree-house, they moved into a cottage on the land of a farmer for whom they had been working. The Brotherhood was born there.

Metelica, who chose the name Michael Repunzal, by which he is currently known, was greatly influenced by Spiritualist medium Elwood Babbitt, who also introduced him to *The Aquarian Gospel of Jesus the Christ* by Levi Dowling, a major source of group beliefs. Babbitt specializes in psychically providing information about an individual's previous incarnations on earth. The beliefs center upon the seven immutable laws: order within the universe; balance of the mind (positive) and brain (negative); harmony (a direct alignment with all vibration of electrical energy); growth from carnal to celestial; God-perfection; spiritual love; and compassion. From the early days of vegetarianism and abstinence from alcohol, a much less strict diet has been adopted.

During the first years of the 1970s the group expanded rapidly, numbering 365 by 1973. By 1972, the movement decentralized and moved into new centers near four northwest Masschusetts towns. To provide an economic base, several businesses were created. Though most eventually failed, several have survived: Rockets, which outfits buses for touring musicians, and Renaissance Builders and Renaissance Excavating supply most of the current income. By 1974 two separate organizational structures emerged. The Renaissance Church of Beauty was created so that all residents and nonresidents could participate in the support of the beliefs and practices of the former Brotherhood of the Spirit. The Renaissance Community, consisting of the resident members, was then created for church members who wished to practice the church's beliefs on a full-time basis.

In 1975 a eighty-acre tract at Gill, Massachusetts, was purchased. The group began to reassemble there and construct the 2001 Center, conceived in part as a haven against the coming time of troubles predicted by Edgar Cayce as the twentieth century comes to an end. An organic farm has been started on the property.

Membership: In 1983 there were approximately 105 members of the Community.

Periodicals: *The Renaissance Community Newsletter.* Send orders to 71 Avenue A, Turners Falls, MA 01376.

Sources:

Borowski, Karol. *Attempting an Alternative Society.* Norwood, PA: Norwood Editions, 1984.

Hapgood, Charles H. *Voices of Spirit.* New York: Delacorte Press, 1975.

Popenoe, Cris, and Oliver Popenoe. *Seeds of Tomorrow.* San Francisco: Harper & Row, 1984.

★1277★
Salem Acres
7419 E. Brick School Rd.
Rock City, IL 61070

Salem Acres is an eclectic commune founded in the late 1960s. It combines elements of Pentcostalism and Sacred Name Adventism. Its founder was Lester B. Anderson, a former Baptist minister. The purpose of creating Salem acres was to provide a place where a group could grow in the Spirit and be free to accept new truth as it came. From the Pentecostals, the group at Salem Acres has accepted an emphasis on the baptism of the Spirit and speaking in tongues, and it has adopted a New Testament church order. The various gifts of the spirit are manifest and these ministries are functioning. Women partake in the minsitry but not over men. Spirited singing, testimonies, and prayer for the sick characterize services. The group has derived an emphasis on the Old Testament laws, particularly keeping the Sabbath and diet. Both the Lord's Supper and baptism by immersion are practiced. The group operates Lakeview Academy for grades 4-12.

Membership: Not reported. There were approximately 50 residents in 1992. The group is loosely affiliated with like-minded congregations in other countries.

Periodicals: *Yahweh Nissi.*

★1278★
Shepherdsfield Community
777 Shepherdsfield Rd.
Fulton, MO 65251-9473

Shepherdsfield Community, also known as New Christian Life Fellowship, is an independent communal Christian fellowship that grew out of the Jesus People revival that began in the late 1960s. Some affected by the revival in 1971 in La Jolla, California, founded an independent church, the Bird Rock Fellowship. Within a year the groups had become five congregations serving various sections of the greater San Diego metropolitan area. In 1977, two of the pastors within the fellowship, John Welker and Elliott Sterns, saw a need for a deeper level of fellowship as described in the New Testament, specifically the adoption of a communal life-

style. A period of study and learning about contemporary Christian community as represented in such groups as the Reba Place Fellowship and the Society of Brothers, prepared members of the fellowship to found a new Christian community. In 1979 the group purchased a former sheep farm near Fulton, Missouri, which they named Shepherdsfield. The group of approximately 70 people arrived in Fulton on Pentecost Sunday, June 9, 1979, the date recognized as the founding date of Shepherdsfield Community.

Shepherdsfield is organized communally. Members relinquish personal property to the group. The majority of meals are eaten together, and membership comes only after a period of testing of one's commitment to the ideals of the communal life. Families live in separate family dwellings and nuclear family units are recognized and nurtured within the communal structure. The community is supported by a variety of businesses—the Shepherd's Company, the Shepherd's Bakery, and the Shepherd's Brethren. Children attend a community school.

The community holds to a conservative evangelical Christian faith and affirms belief in the Bible as the infallible word of God, the Trinity, the deity of Christ, and the spiritual unity of believers. The community also affirms the necessity of baptism and the acknowledgment of the believer having received forgiveness of sins in Jesus Christ.

Membership: As of 1995 there were approximately 100 residents at Shepherdsfield.

★1279★
Shiloh Youth Revival Centers
(Defunct)

The Shiloh Youth Revival Centers was one of the most successful of the groups to emerge out of the Jesus People Revival of the 1970s. The movement originated in a vision of John J. Higgins, Jr. (1939-), to extend the Jesus People Movement, then centered in California, into Oregon. A drug addict, he was converted to Christianity in the mid-1960s by reading the Bible. He began attending Calvary Chapel in Costa Mesa, California. With others like himself, in 1968 he founded a Jesus People commune called the House of Miracles. His work attracted people and very soon a string of similar houses could be found around southern California.

In April, 1969, Higgins and some 30 young people moved to Pleasant Hill, Oregon, where the first house to bear the name Shiloh was opened. The new name reflected a belief that Shiloh (Jesus) would soon return. Over the summer the group tripled in size and purchased 70 acres of land near Dexter, Oregon, upon which a discipleship training center was erected. They incorporated as the Oregon Youth Revival Centers, later changed to Shiloh Youth Revival Centers. From that point forward they centered their life work on building the center, evangelizing, and founding centers across the country. By 1974 they had founded some 163 Shiloh centers, though most were short-lived and only half that number were in existence at any one time.

Shiloh was communal in nature. Members made a commitment to Christ to forsake all and follow him. The movement took care of basic needs of the members. The group also believed in working to support themselves rather than asking for donations. In that process they built a number of very successful businesses from canning to construction, and from printing to carpet cleaning. Eugene, Oregon, became their second central focus of activity, and they opened the Shiloh Fellowship there for regular public worship services.

The organization went through a severe upheaval when the board questioned Higgins' autocratic leadership and fired him. There followed a period of turmoil when many members left. Higgins left to become a pastor with Calvary Chapel. Meanwhile, the Internal Revenue Service began to question the tax status of the group and its numerous business ventures. The group reorganized and began a lengthy fight with the IRS. Slowly the many communities around the country closed and by 1986 none were left. The first trial on taxes occurred in 1986 and the following year the court ruled that the businesses were not tax exempt and hence taxes were owed. That decision effectively bankrupted the organization, and two years later it formally disbanded.

A final reunion was held was held in the summer of 1987. By this time most of the members had drifted into other similar movements.

Sources:

Peterson, Joe V. *Jesus People: Christ, Communes and the Counterculture of the Late Twentieth Century in the Pacific Northwest.* Eugene, OR: M.A. thesis, Northwest Christian college, 1990. 160 pp.

Richardson, James T., Mary W. Stewart, and Robert B. Simmons. *Organized Miracles: A Study of a Contemporary Youth, Communal, Fundamentalist Organization.* New Brunswick, NJ: Transaction Books, 1979. 368 pp.

★1280★
Shivalila
Current address not obtained for this edition.

Shivalila was founded in Bakersfield, California, in the 1970s by Gridley Lorimer Wright IV (1934-1979). Wright, a Yale graduate and former stockbroker, left his career during the 1960s and joined the counterculture movement on the West Coast. He became an active user of LSD and brought around him a group which explored the effects of its use. Shivalila grew out of this experimental group.

Wright had reasoned that the foundation of society emerged from the relationship of mother and child and hence that relationship is the dimension in which microcosm and macrocosm intersect. Western society, based upon the nuclear family, grows out of the child's relationship with the One Source of the Energy of Life, the mother. The One-Source imprint leads to competitiveness and an expectation of partiality. In contrast, in communal societies, children respond to many Sources which make it less competitive and better able to adjust to broad life experiences. Wright had first experienced and was attracted to the collective communal aspect of culture during the 1960s. Thus adding to their experiments in psychedelic drugs, members of the group traveled and gained experience by living in various communal societies in both the United States and abroad. During this period of exploration, some members of the group studied with both Buddhist and Hindu tantric masters who taught them some of the tantric secrets, including some left-hand sexual techniques.

As Shivalila emerged in the 1970s, it included an emphasis upon the use of psychedelic drugs, a communal lifestyle, and the practice of tantric yoga. Added emphasis was placed upon the raising of children in an ideal environment, and the group often referred to itself as the Children's Liberation Front. The emphases led to group members' assuming a four-point social contract, the Covenants of Shivalila. They agreed to practice *ahimsa*, nonviolence; *sattva ava*, the recognition of the relative nature of truth; *bhramcari*, nonparticipation in the ownership of private property and denial of relationships that involve privacy or secrecy (including the marriage contract); and *tantra*, participation in sexual relationships only after the other party has manifested an identification with nature and babies. To Wright, these characteristics meant the recreation of a society similar to that of the Stone Age.

Shivalila enjoyed a brief moment of fame after its publication of its beliefs and practices in a book, *The Book of the Mother*, in 1977. After finding that the closest approximation to their ideal lifestyle was being practiced by the Tasaday tribe in the Philippines, they moved to the islands. However, the Philippine government forced them to move in March 1978, and the group immigrated to India. Burying their American passports, they asked for political asylum. The group chose an area in a rural part of Rajasthan state to create their new society. Unfortunately, in Decem-

ber 1978, several months after their settling in, Wright was stabbed and died of complications of the injuries some weeks later.

Membership: Not reported. In 1979 the group had 18 members. Its present status is unknown.

Sources:

The Book of the Mother. Bakersfield, CA: Children's Liberation Front, 1977.

★1281★
Sirius
Baker Rd.
Shutesbury, MA 01072

Sirius, a center for Evolution of Consciousness, is an intentional community founded in 1978 by several former members of the Findhorn Community, the pioneering Scottish New Age community. Among the founders were Corrinne McLaughton and Gordon Davidson. It was named after the star which many believe, in an esoteric sense, to be the source of love and wisdom on Earth. Resident members see themselves as part of a network of light groups and individuals around the world working for the uplifting of consciousness. They place great emphasis on the development of a planetary consciousness that honors the interconnectedness and sacredness of all life.

Sirius is located on a 90-acre tract of land. Members believe that they are stewards of the land and that they should live as lightly on the earth as possible. They strive to create a sustainable abundance through the growth of an organic, pesticide-free, vegetable and herb garden and environmentally sound construction.

In their group life, members seek to honor the Divine presence in each person. They strive to serve the good of the whole and balance the needs of the individual and group. Decisions are made by consensus of the general meeting or core group. Meditation is used both for individual growth and as an aid in building consensus. Daily life is a spiritual teacher.

Sirius has developed a program of community outreach through workshops for visitors to the community, open houses, sponsoring seasonal celebrations, and resident apprenticeships. Nonresidents may become associate members in the community.

Membership: In 1997 there were approximately 25 resident members.

Sources:

McNaughton, Corinne, and Gordon Davidson. *Builders of the Dawn: Community Lifestyles in a Changing World.* Shutesbury, MA: Sirius Publishing, 1986.

★1282★
Solar Logos Foundation
PO Box 2008
Buellton, CA 84110

The Solar Logos Foundation is composed of a group of spiritual seekers who have found guidance in the teachings of Norman Paulsen, a direct disciple of Paramahansa Yogananda and the author of *The Christ Consciousness.* The path that Paulsen encourages is guided by his direct experiences with "I Am That I Am" as the First Light of Creation, the Solar Logos, and combines elements of living consistent with many of the world's wisdom traditions.

In the 1970s, prior to being involved with the Solar Logos Foundation, Paulsen had founded the Brotherhood of the Sun, an experiment in communal living in the vicinity of Santa Barbara, California. The community members practiced an eightfold path of right living, which included meditation twice daily, and the pursuit of a virtuous life. The use of drugs, alcohol, and tobacco was not permitted. The communal experiment ended in 1986. Pualsen and some of the members of the brotherhood moved to northeastern Nevada and Paulsen became associated with The Builders, an educational organization through which he continued to teach meditation and right living.

In 1993, Paulsen became the leading force in the founding of the Solar Logos Foundation, which superseded The Builders. The foundation is designed to promote the teachings of Paulsen's book, *The Christ Consciousness*. Shortly thereafter he moved back to southern California. Unlike the brotherhood, the foundation members do not live communally, but they do live in close proximity to one another in order to strengthen their commitment and to facilitate the opportunity to meditate together daily. It is believed that through the collective energy derived from meditating and working together, each aspirant's development is quickened by becoming more conscious of the presence of God within and around them as they go about their daily activities. They strive to live a life of self-discipline, service, and kindness to all, and endeavor to walk an eightfold path of right living and virtues in daily life. This practice is intended to harmonize the inner life with the outer life and prepares a foundation for entry into the Pure Self within, the Christ Consciousness; this is self-realization.

The foundation teaches that we are all sons and daughters of the same Divine Source; we have all been gifted with life on this planet; and we should desire only to help humanity and ourselves to realize our true nature, and then to use that knowledge to help Mother Nature make this planet a healthy garden again for all life forms—minerals, plants, animals, and people, all living in harmony again and in true understanding of each other as it was intended to be.

Once a person has established direct mental and visual communion with God in meditation, his or her mental compass needle will always swing toward the Polestar, the light at the end of the inner-dimensional tunnel, the Solar Logos. The attainment of constant communion with God is that Pearl of Great Price that Jesus spoke of, that divine possession which cannot be bought with any amount of material wealth. The attainment of this state of consciousness by a man or woman can truly have a positive effect on all of humanity, and would be an important contribution to that cause.

As of the beginning of 1998, the foundation members were creating a sanctuary near Point Conception, California, north of Santa Barbara. It is projected as a quiet place for reflection and meditation and the promotion of God-Realization; a place to feel the subtle energies of God; a place where the outer sanctuary can reflect the inner sanctuary in each one. It will be a place to conduct meditation seminars where one can receive the teachings of the Solar Logos and experience the beauty of the Spirit in undisturbed Nature. It will provide an atmosphere conducive to the contemplation and cultivation of the Eightfold Path and the twelve Virtues.

Membership: Not reported. There are approximately 100 members.

Sources:

Duquette, Susan. *Sunburst Farm Family Cookbook*. Santa Barbara, CA: Woodbridge Press Publishing Company, 1978.

Hansen-Gates, Jan. "Growing Outdoors: The Brotherhood of the Sun." *Santa Barbara Magazine* 1, no. 3 (Winter 1975-76): 64-71.

Paulsen, Norman. *Sunburst, Return of the Ancients*. Goleta, CA: Sunburst Farms Publishing Farms, 1980. Revised and retitled as *Christ Consciousness*. Salt Lake City, UT: The Builders Publishing Company, 1984.

Weaver, Dusk, and Willow Weaver. *Sunburst, A People, A Path, A Purpose*. San Diego, CA: Avant Books, 1982.

★1283★
The Synanon Church
Current address not obtained for this edition.

The Synanon Church began in 1958 as Synanon Foundation, Inc., a therapeutic group for alcoholics and drug addicts. Charles E. Dederich, a former member of Alcoholics Anonymous, began

the organization informally in his apartment in Ocean Park, California. As the group grew and began to experience some benefits, it rented a clubhouse and incorporated. The following year it moved to Santa Monica and over the next few years gained a reputation for reeducating drug addicts. From its base in Santa Monica, during the 1960s Synanon communities formed along the West Coast, particularly San Francisco, Marin County, and Oakland, and outposts opened in the East, Midwest, and Puerto Rico. Residents totaled 1,400 by decade's end. In 1968 Dederich moved to Marin County, where within a few years three rural Synanon communities developed near the town of Marshall.

The religious nature of Synanon, coming as it did out of another religious organization, Alcoholics Anonymous, had been tacitly recognized from almost the beginning of its existence. However, Dederich also recognized that many of the people Synanon was attempting to assist had rejected organized religion; therefore, Synanon was not formally called a religion. Those outside Synanon tended to view it as another therapeutic community. As community life developed, the religious nature of Synanon life could not be denied. Discussions of Synanon's role as a religion in the 1960s led to a change of Articles of Incorporation in January, 1975, which designated the Synanon Foundation as the organization through which the Synanon religion and church is manifest. On November 17, 1980, the present name, The Synanon Church, was formally adopted.

Synanon derives its theological perspective from Eastern thought (Buddhism and Taoism) and from those Western mystics who had absorbed a prominent Asian religious component in their teachings, most notably Ralph Waldo Emerson and Aldous Huxley. As a community, Synanon seeks to manifest the basic principles of oneness, and members seek to manifest that integration (or oneness) in themselves and in their relations with each other. The Synanon Game, described as the group's central sacrament, is the principal tool utilized in adherents' search for unity. Similar to encounter groups, the Synanon Game is "played" by a small group of people who meet together as equals in a circle to share in an intense and emotionally expressive context. When successful, the game leads to mutual confession, repentence, and absolution while providing overall pastoral care.

Synanon residents follow the golden rule, and helping others is basic in the practical philosophy that all residents attempt to follow. Residents also believe that the most effective way to redeem humanity from alienation and achieve unity and integration is to form religious communities based upon the beliefs of the Synanon religion and church.

The Synanon Church is organized hierarchically. It is headed by an eight-member executive committee of the board of directors. The board is composed of the ministers of the church. The ministers oversee the communities, schools, and offices of the church, besides performing their normal ministerial functions.

Membership: In 1988 the church reported two communities, both at Badger, California. Approximately 860 adherents reside there. Other nonresident members can be found across the United States.

Educational Facilities: Synanon College, Badger, California. Charles E. Dederich School of Law, Badger, California.

Remarks: Since its earliest days, Synanon has been subject to controversy. In December, 1961, Dederich went to jail, for the first time, on a zoning code violation. Synanon has also been attacked in articles by individuals who disagreed with its practices and techniques. One such attack, considered particularly defamatory, led to a libel suit against the *San Francisco Examiner*. Synanon received not only a large cash settlement but an additional $2,000,000 in damages from the Hearst Corporation, the newspaper's publisher for, among other things, burglarizing the Synanon offices.

Possibly the most controversial event affecting Synanon occurred in 1978 when an attorney, representing a person suing The

Synanon Church, was bitten by a rattlesnake. In the year following this incident, Dederich, who along with two church members had been charged in the case, suffered three strokes. As the trial date approached, and with Dederich's health failing and unable to pursue the defense of the case, those charged settled the case by pleading no contest.

During the last several years, over forty people associated with The Synanon Church have been indicted on various charges by grand juries. None of these well-publicized indictments went to trial, as charges were dropped in each case for lack of evidence. (It is the position of The Synanon Church that, had Dederich's health permitted a trial, he and the others charged in the rattlesnake incident would also have been found innocent). As of 1988, The Synanon Church continues a process of adjudication of charges leveled by various government agencies.

Sources:

Dederich, Charles E. *The Tao Trip Sermon.* Marshall, CA: Synanon Publishing House, 1978.

Endore, Guy. *Synanon.* Garden City, NJ: Doubleday, 1968.

Garfield, Howard M. *The Synanon Religion,* Marshall, CA: Synanon Foundation, 1978.

Gerstel, David U. *Paradise Incorporated: Synanon.* Novato, CA: Presidio Press, 1982.

Mitchell, Dave, Cathy Mitchell, and Richard Ofshe. *The Light on Synanon.* New York: Seaview Books, 1980.

Olin, William. *Escape From Utopia.* Santa Cruz, CA: Unity Press, 1980.

Yablonsky, Lewis. *The Tunnel Back: Synanon.* New York: Macmillan, 1965.

★1284★
Universal Industrial Church of the New World Comforter
PO Box 1447
Windsor, CA 95492

The Universal Industrial Church of the New World Comforter was formed by Allen Michael Noonan, who in 1947 in Long Beach, California, was contacted by extraterrestrial intelligences for the first time. According to Noonan, generally known simply as Allen Michael, in that first contact he (i.e., the entity within his body) was transported up a beam of light to what he later recognized as a spaceship. While aboard, he was given the choice to be a channel of the "everlasting gospel," fulfilling Jesus' prophecy in John 16: 7-14 of "the Comforter" that would come. He accepted the mission, and since that time has devoted his life to channeling (through automatic writing) Spirit God's plan for the transformation of this planet.

Twenty years later, in 1967, the first members of the One World Family Commune came together in San Francisco's Haight/Ashbury District, inspired by the truth they recognized being channelled through Allen Michael and sharing with him the vision of eliminating money and bringing about a world of sharing and serving (love). They felt that the usury money system perpetuated subjugation of materiality in a duality of consciousness, and limited progress toward the synthesis of "one for all and all for one," which according to Michael, would have been the next stage in the evolution of consciousness had Article I, Section 8, paragraph 5 of the United States Constitution been upheld.

The commune also recognized that a change in diet to one of natural food was basic to higher consciousness and health. As a means of supporting themselves, as well as a service to the community, members operated the Here and Now Natural Food Restaurant in Haight/Ashbury. In 1971, the commune moved to Berkeley, California, where they opened the One World Family Natural Food Center on Telegraph Avenue, which included a large restaurant, a pizzeria, a bakery, a handmade clothing shop, and an entertainment hall.

While still in Berkeley, in 1973, the group founded the Universal Industrial Church of the New World Comforter, in recognition of themselves as the "church of God rising out of the people." They viewed Michael as the channel of energies described by the archangel in Daniel 12:1. Michael is believed to have been given the keys to prophecy in the Bible therein, so that these days of tribulation might be shortened for the sake of the elect, and, with the World Master Plan, people will arise out of subjugation to materiality into a world sharing economy and God-consciousness.

The means they advocated for ending the dying world order and bring about the New World Order of the Ages (the "Novo Ordo Seclorum" pictured on the Great Pyramid seal on the American dollar bill) is through the World Wide Work Stoppage 30/30 Plan. Michael suggests that all businesses that provide no real service or anything of true value, be stopped and that people begin to rotate on a 30-day cycle with half the people providing all the goods and services to the other half, who travel, rest, and recreate. This action would automatically lift the vibrational energies (consciousness) out of duality into synthesis—"one for all and all for one"—which is Spirit God's prophesied heaven on earth, the kingdom of God.

The church has, through its publishing arm, Starmast Publications (Box 1241, Santa Rosa, CA 95402), produced a series of books which detail the teachings of the church as channeled through Michael. It has also produced a popular natural foods cookbook and a series of video tapes for airing on cable television.

Membership: In 1988, the church had approximately 200 members.

Periodicals: *Galatic Messenger.*

Sources:

Allen Michael. *ETI Space Beings Intercept Earthlings.* Starmast Publications, 1977.

___. *The Everlasting Gospel, God, Unlimited Mind Speaks.* Stockton, CA: Starmast Publications, 1982.

___. *The Everlasting Gospel, to the Youth of the World.* Berkeley, CA: Universal Industrial Church of the Divine Comforter, 1973.

___. *UFO-ETI World Master Plan.* Starmast Publications, 1977.

Hannaford, Kathryn. *Cosmic Cookery.* Stockton, CA: Starmast Publications, 1974.

★1285★
West Coast Communities
℅ Church of the Sojourners
866 Potero
San Francisco, CA 94110

West Coast Communities is a fellowship of conservative Christian communities located along the West Coast of the United States from Washington to Southern California that emerged in the 1980s. The fellowship consists of a number of largely autonomous communities with varying Christian traditions dominating from community to community. They have a program with twin foci of development of a strong intimate fellowship and outreach in the community. Formal leadership is elected, but in practice leadership is demonstrated by individuals as new issues arise and affirmed informally by the community.

West Coast Communities is a conservative Christian community and largely apolitical, though individual members may be politically active. The groups tend to be anti-abortion and anti-homosexuality, and in favor of home schooling.

Membership: Not reported. In 1996, there were four communities affiliated with the West Coast communities.

Sources:

Janzen, David. *Fire, Salt, and Peace.* Evanston, IL: Shalom Communities, 1996.

Section 17

Christian Science-Metaphysical Family

Consult the Contents pages to locate the essay in Part II, Historical Essay Chapters,
that provides an historical discussion of this family

Intrafaith Organizations

★1286★
Affiliated New Thought Network (ANTN)
% New Thought Center, San Diego
5520 Ruffin Rd., Ste. 101
San Diego, CA 92123

The Affiliated New Thought Network is a cooperative fellow-ship of independent New Thought Centers in the state of California. ANTN seeks to assist affiliated centers with practical knowledge concerning their development as an organization designed to provide mental, spiritual, emotional, and physical fulfillment. While creedless, the centers share an appreciation for the New Thought tradition as found in the writings of the Transcendentalists, Ralph Waldo Emerson, and Ernest S. Holmes.

Membership: In 1997 there were five centers associated with ANTN.

Educational Facilities: Emerson Institute.

Sources:

http://www.newthought.org/.

★1287★
International New Thought Alliance (INTA)
5003 E. Broadway Rd.
Mesa, AZ 85206

The International New Thought Alliance was founded in 1914 as an ecumenical expression of the merging New Thought movement. It recognizes Phineas P. Quimby (1802-1866) as the "Father of New Thought."

The alliance, a successor to some earlier attempts at developing the New Thought, formed as an umbrella organization to further the work of the numerous groups and individuals. It adopted what is called a "Declaration of Principles." Believers in the New Thought have a primary mission to heal the sick through prayer. Individuals affirm their faith through the "Divine Nature"—health, wisdom, love, life, truth. power, peace, beauty, and joy. People are considered to be invisible spiritual dwellers within human bodies and will unfold as spiritual beings beyond the change called physical death.

Membership: There are more than a hundred congregations. Members are found in the United States, Canada, Australia, the Bahamas, Jamaica, Trinidad, Costa, Rica, New Zealand, the Philippines, Great Britian, and South Africa.

Periodicals: *New Thought.*

Christian Science

★1288★
Church of Christ, Scientist
Christian Science Center
Boston, MA 02115

The Church of Christ, Scientist grew out of the experiences, work and writings of Mary Baker Eddy. Following her healing in 1866, which happened concurrently with her discovery of God as the sole reality of life, Eddy began a period of Bible study which involved testing the practicality of her new discovery, as well as questioning the earlier teachings on mental healing she had received from Phineas P. Quimby. The result was the development of her thought, first expressed in a booklet, *The Science of Man* (1870) and later embodied in her textbook, *Science and Health with Key to the Scriptures* (1875). She began almost immediately to apply the precepts of Christian Science to healing and to teach them informally to others. Her work led her to seek a letter of dismissal from the Congregational Church in which she was raised, and in 1876 she founded the Christian Science Association, the first organization for her students.

The next 16 years were ones of the development of a variety of organizational expressions, some temporary, some lasting. A final reorganization in 1892 and the development of the church's by-laws in the *Church Manual* (1895), resulted in the church as it is known today. These 16 years were punctuated by the formation of the Church of Christ, Scientist in 1879; Eddy's ordination in 1881; the dissolution of the church in 1889; and its reorganization in 1892. This reorganization placed the governance of the Christian Science movement in the First Church of Christ, Scientist, of Boston, generally known as The Mother Church. The remainder of Eddy's life was spent in perfecting the textbook of the movement which went through several revisions and in completing by-laws as codified in the *Church Manual.* The texts of these two volumes remain the prime sources of the church's doctrine and polity.

The beliefs of the Church of Christ, Scientist are summarized in the Tenets printed in both *Science and Health* (p. 497) and the *Church Manual* (p. 15). The Church defines itself as Christian in essence, a major difference between it and most other "metaphysical" churches with which it is often compared. The Tenets affirm the Church's allegiance to the inspired Word of the Bible as the sufficient guide to Life; one God; God's Son; the Holy Ghost; and man as being in God's likeness and image. Forgiveness for sin comes in spiritual understanding that casts out evil as having no God-ordained reality. Jesus is acknowledged as the Way-shower. His atonement, as the evidence of God's love and salvation, comes through the Truth, Life, and Love he demonstrated in his healing activity and by his overcoming sin and death.

Healing activity following the principles laid down in the Bible and in *Science and Health* has been the keynote of the Christian Science movement. Christian healing is a normal practice among members—some giving their full time to the ministry of spiritual healing. This is in accord with Eddy's experience of the allness of God. It is distinct from other forms of healing, especially psychic or magnetic healing.

Eddy is held in high regard by Christian Scientists. The church does, however, carefully distinguish Eddy's status and role as the discoverer of Christian Science from that of Jesus as the Savior of humanity. In like measure, while acknowledging the essential and central role of the Christian Science textbook, it does not understand *Science and Health with Key to the Scriptures* to be a second Scripture or a revelation equal in authority to the Bible. Rather, *Science and Health* is considered a tool for understanding the Bible.

The governance of the Christian Science movement is vested in The Mother Church, whose rules of operation are spelled out in the *Church Manual*. Administration is placed in a five-member self-perpetuating board of directors. The board charters branch churches, which are run according to their own democratic control (apart from any matters covered in the *Church Manual*). Worship in all branch churches is conducted by elected readers, each of whom must be a member in good standing of The Mother Church. Services in the branch churches consist of readings from scripture and *Science and Health*. The exact passages for each week are delineated in *The Christian Science Quarterly*.

Publications of the Church are produced by the Christian Science Publishing Society and its Board of Directors. Included in its publications are its award-winning newspaper, *The Christian Science Monitor*, its prime foreign language periodical *The Herald of Christian Science* (published in 12 languages and braille for the blind), and numerous books and pamphlets. Eddy's writings are controlled and published by the Trustees Under the Will of Mary Baker Eddy. Under the Board of Directors of The Mother Church is a Board of Lectureship which approves speakers who travel the world offering free public lectures on Christian Science. The Committee on Publication is charged with correcting false information about the church and injustices done to Mrs. Eddy, The Mother Church, and Christian Scientists.

Headquarters of the church are in the Christian Science Church Center, a large complex in Boston, Massachusetts, which has become one of the city's most-visited tourist stops. Branch churches are found in more than 70 nations of the world (though approximately 73 percent of the membership is in North America).

Membership: In 1997 there were approximately 2,300 Christian Science congregations worldwide with 1,800 congregation in the United States and 54 in Canada.

Educational Facilities: Unofficial: Principia College, Elsah, Illinois.

Periodicals: *The Christian Science Monitor.* • *The Christian Science Journal.* • *Christian Science Sentinel.* • *Christian Science Quarterly.* • *The Herald of Christian Science*—in 12 languages. Available from One Norway St., Boston, MA 02115.

Remarks: Since its founding, the Church of Christ, Scientist, has been the subject of intense controversy. Its healing emphasis brought criticism from a variety of perspectives, both those who shared the emphasis but followed a different set of teachings and practice, and those who disapproved of any form of spiritual healing. The most intense criticism found its way into various legal proceedings and has led to an extensive body of legal opinion defining the rights and limits of Christian Science practice. Courts have defined Christian Science healing as a legally protected activity of the church as a form of worship. Deductions for some Christian Science services are allowed by the U.S. Internal Revenue Service. Various state-level committees on publication have issued handbooks defining the legal rights and obligations of Christian Scientists in some detail.

During the 1880s Eddy was accused of drawing her teachings from Phineas P. Quimby, first by Annetta Dresser and her husband, Julius Dresser who, like Eddy, had been students of Quimby, and later by numerous members of what became known as the New Thought movement. An examination of Eddy's writings and the publications of the Church of Christ, Scientist, reveals an essential difference between Eddy's teachings on healing and those of Quimby and finds the major similarity to be in the area of terminology, and the attempt to struggle with some of the same questions of religion and health.

The Church of Christ, Scientist has maintained over the years that there is a basic gulf between its teachings and those of the New Thought movement. This difference is highlighted in Eddy's rejection of Quimby's adherence to magnetic healing and the movement's abandonment of Eddy's essential Christian orientation. The Church also disapproves of the emphasis in the movement on prosperity and the openness to various psychic and occult practices most evident in some of the larger New Thought groups. Christian Science retains a focus on healing and has denounced Spiritualism and animal magnetism, the forms of the occult most evident in Eddy's lifetime, from its earliest years. Some obvious differences between New Thought and Christian Science can be seen by comparing the Tenets of the Church with the Declaration of the International New Thought Alliance (INTA). Despite these differences, the two movements are historically related. New thought was, to a great extent, built upon the work of Eddy's early students, particularly Emma Curtis Hopkins, and used *Science and Health* as a major sourcebook. Today New Thought groups vary considerably, from those who are close to Eddy's teaching to those who more closely follow Quimby while developing their own form of metaphysical thought.

Finally, over the years the Church has had to face formal and informal challenges to its authority, beginning with the various individuals and groups claiming to have inherited Mary Baker Eddy's authority. These challenges led to the formation of several movements, such as the Christian Science Parent Church, none of which prospered more than a few years. There is, of course, a small but steady stream of practitioners who have left the church and who continue to practice independently. Many have built a successful personal following (possibly the most prominent being Joel S. Goldsmith). Most, however, have been anti-organization and their following has continued only briefly after their retirement and/or death.

Sources:

Braden, Charles S. *Christian Science Today*. Dallas: Southern Methodist University Press, 1958.

Christian Science: A Sourcebook of Contemporary Materials. Boston: Christian Science Publishing Society, 1990.

Eddy, Mary Baker. *Church Manual of the First Church of Christ, Scientist, in Boston, Mass.* Boston: Trustees Under the Will of Mary Baker Eddy, 1908.

___. *Science and Health with Key to the Scriptures*. Boston: Trustees Under the Will of Mary Baker Eddy, 1906.

Gottschalk, Stephen. *The Emergence of Christian Science in American Religious Life*. Berkeley: University of California Press, 1973.

Peel, Robert. *Mary Baker Eddy*. 3 vols. New York: Holt, Rinehart and Winston, 1971.

Swihart, Altman K. *Since Mrs. Eddy*. New York: Henry Holt and Company, 1931.

★1289★
Church of Integration
(Defunct)

The Church of Integration was founded in 1935 as the Society of Life, but has roots that go back to 1912 and the formation in London, England, of a small group of former members of the Church of Christ, Scientist around Annie C. Bill (1865?-1937). Bill, a member of the Third Church of Christ, Scientist, in London, resigned after a friend of hers, R. L. Rawson, was excommunicated. The church took exception to Rawson's book, *Life Understood*, which Bill had a hand in writing. Rawson would later found a prominent British New Thought group, the Society for the Propagation of True Prayer. In the meantime, a few months after Bill resigned, Mary Baker Eddy, founder of the church, died and left no successor. Bill became convinced that she was the true successor and in 1912 organized what became known as the Christian Science Parent Church. After World War I she moved to the United States and in 1924 established the church in America.

At the time Bill became active in America, the Church of Christ, Scientist was involved in an intense controversy which had grown out of varying interpretations of Eddy's instruction to the church once she had died. Her church acquired members from among the losers in that battle, the most prominent being John V. Dittemore. About the same time, she made a most significant convert, A. A. Beauchamp, who turned over the services of his publishing house, including his magazine, *Watchman of Israel*, to the new church. The new church grew steadily. In the 1926 *Census of Religious Bodies* it reported 29 churches and 582 members in the United States. By 1928 there were 44 branches, including churches in Great Britain, Australia, and Canada, with approximately 80 branches and 1,200 members by 1930.

The last major development of Bill's church occurred around 1930. During the 1920s Bill had become convinced that many of the criticisms leveled by Eddy's critics were true. In particular, she came to believe that Eddy had been a frequent user of morphine and that she had derived many of her teachings from Phineas P. Quimby, the healer who had been her teacher in the 1860s. Bill concluded that Eddy no longer deserved the central role the parent church had accorded her and that Eddy's textbook, *Science and Health with Key to the Scriptures*, was no longer a valid textbook. She authored a new textbook, *The Science of Reality* (1930), which replaced *The Universal Design of Life* (1924), the older volume that acknowledged Eddy's authority. She also reorganized the parent church into the Church of Universal Design and *The Watchman* became *The Universal Design, A Journal of Applied Metaphysics*.

Two ideas dominated the new church. First, Bill suggested the possibility of conscious spiritual evolution by direct intention and in accordance with a universal design of Life which impels periodic transformations. The design is based upon the prior recognition that Mind is God and that the universe unfolds from Mind. This unfoldment follows a sevenfold pattern. Secondly, response to the design was also built into the new organization. When the church's recognized leader died, the church entered an interim period during which church directors appointed deputy leaders to carry on the services of the church until a new leader emerged who demonstrated that s/he had made the discovery of the next successive step in the design of Life.

Bill adopted several controvesial ideas which took prominence in the church's beliefs. A. A. Beauchamp had been an advocate of British-Israelism, the idea that the modern Anglo-Saxon people of northern and western Europe and North America were the descendents of the ancient 10 tribes of Israel. His magazine, published on behalf of British-Israelism, became the magazine of the parent church and the central perspective adopted by Bill. She also came to believe in pyramidology, the idea that the measurements and geometric design of the Great Pyramid in Egypt had religious and prophetic significance.

The transition from the Church of Universal Design to the Church of Integration occurred following Bill's death in 1937 in a manner quite similar to the pattern she had proposed. In 1934 Francis J. Mott (b. 1901), who had been with Bill since 1922, withdrew from the Church of Universal Design. Claiming new light on the spiritual process, he organized The Society of Life. Following Bill's death he presented his new findings and new organization to the leaders of the Church of Universal Design and won their support. They voted to dissolve the church and urged all the members to join the society. Overwhelmingly they did, though there

were a few exceptions, such as Dittemore who wrote a letter to the Church of Christ, Scientist, recanting his association with Bill.

Over the next decade, the society evolved and in several years emerged as the Church of Integration. As evolved, the church saw itself still in continuity with the Church of Christ, Scientist. It tenets acknowledge one God who creates according to One Plan. Particular reverence is given to the "Seed in the Church," that is the discoverer of the new, often at first looked upon as a heretic, who is actually the bearer of a new birth for the church. Mott also believed that the new Seed need not wait until the death of the present leader before addressing the mind of the church.

Mott initially published his views in a several books (published by A. A. Beauchamp) and over a decade issued at least four editions of the covenant of the new church. The British branch of the church was destroyed in the chaos of World War II. In America the church survived and briefly revived after the war. A new magazine, *Integration*, was issued from the church's headquarters in Washington, D.C., beginning in 1946. Eventually, however, the church, which was never numerically strong, dissolved.

At least one follower of Bill who opposed Mott's leadership, Mary Sayles Atkins, continued to write, under her pen name, Mary Sayles Moore, about Bill and during the 1950s published several volumes with A. A. Beauchamp, who had left the Church of Integration in the 1940s. Her most important volume was *Conquest of Chaos*, which reviewed Bill's career and the rise of Mott.

Remarks: The organization headed by Annie C. Bill frequently changed names, a fact that can be confusing to anyone seeking information on the church. Founded orginally as the Central Assembly of the Church of Christian Science in 1913 in England, it became the New Church of Christ, Scientist, the Mother Church in 1916. The following year the name became the New Church, the Leading Christian Science Church. In the United States in 1922 it was briefly known as the New Community of Christian Scientists, the Parent Community. In 1924 it became the Christian Science Parent Church of the New Generation but was also known as the Church of the Transforming Covenant. It eventually became known as the Church of Universal Design, by which it was known until Bill died.

Sources:

Bill, Annie C. *The Universal Design of Life*. Boston: A. A. Beauchamp, 1924.

Mott, Francis J. *Christ the Seed*. Boston: A. A. Beauchamp, [1939].

———. *Consciousness Creative*. Boston: A.A. Beauchamp, 1937.

———. *The Universal Design of Birth*. Philadelphia: David McKay Company, 1948.

Spiritual Organization. New York: Integration Publishing Company, 1946.

Swihart, Altma K. *Since Mrs. Eddy*. New York: Henry Holt and Company, 1931.

★1290★
Infinite Way
Box 2089
Peoria, AZ 85380-2089

The Infinite Way is the name given to the teachings of Joel S. Goldsmith (1892-1964). A nonpracticing Jew, Goldsmith encountered Christian Science as a young man. The father of a woman he was dating was a practitioner. When Joel's father was healed by that practitioner in 1915, Joel began seriously to study Christian Science. Later, consulting a practitioner for help with a cold, he found himself cured not only of the cold, but also of smoking and drinking. The experience changed his life. He began to pray for people, and to his amazement, they were healed. He joined the Church of Christ, Scientist, and became a practitioner, a practice he pursued for sixteen years. In the early 1940s, however, he began to feel the pressure of the organization, and in 1946 withdrew from the Church. He began working on the book which became *The Infinite Way*. Reluctantly at first, he accepted invitations to teach and lecture, primarily on the West Coast and in 1950 for the first time in Hawaii.

In 1946, a year after withdrawing from Christian Science, he experienced a mystic "initiation" which lasted over several months and which has been described as lifting him to a new dimension of life, a God-experience. Most of the Infinite Way emphases derive from that incident. The Infinite Way represents a mystical form of Christian Science. Without rejecting healing or prosperity demonstration, Goldsmith centered his teaching on the experience of God. "The Infinite Way is not to give the world a new teaching, but to give the world an experience." It was Goldsmith's belief that the seeker of truth begins with solving problems and overcoming discords. When these endeavors become futile, he can then perceive that one can transcend them. Desiring to improve his human condition, he moves out of the less pain/more pleasure syndrome into spiritual consciousness.

Methodologically, spiritual consciousness is attained by meditation. Contemplative meditation, the primal step, is the holding of spiritual truth in the consciousness. Pure meditation is the state of complete silence within. God is within. We cannot make it so; we can only come to the realization.

God is the one, hence he is all-presence, all-power and all-wisdom. To establish a relationship with the god within is to be able to tap the ready supply of all that makes life worthwhile. God appears as the many, but appearance must not be confused with reality. Christ is the activity of truth within each individual consciousness. The revelation brought by Jesus is the revelation of the Christ.

Goldsmith rejected the idea of founding another organization, and during his lifetime the "Infinite Way " existed only as an informal circle of his students. However, he did fall into a pattern of offering regular classes which were taped and transcribed (an later became the bases for several books). A weekly (later monthly) newsletter was begun and provided a means to keep the scattered students in regular contact. The first of several Infinite Way study centers appeared in Chicago in 1954. For several years after Goldsmith's death, his wife, Emma Goldsmith, continued to issue the newsletter from Hawaii, with the editorial assistance of Lorraine Sinkler, a longtime student. She has more recently moved to Arizona, and with the assistance of Geri MacDonald, her daughter (by a previous marriage), continues to make available the tapes of his lectures. The majority of Goldsmith's material has been edited by Sinkler and published in book form. Individual students such as Sinkler travel around the United States lecturing to groups of people who follow Goldsmith's teaching and others facilitate gatherings which make Goldsmith's material available to local audiences.

Membership: The Infinite Way is not an organization. Rather, it is a designation given to Goldsmith's teachings and, collectively, to the unnumbered people who have accepted them.

Periodicals: *Aloha Nui.*

Sources:

Goldsmith, Joel S. *The Art of Spiritual Healing.* New York: Harper & Row, 1959.

___. *The Infinite Way.* San Gabriel, CA: Willing Publishing Company, 1961.

Sinkler, Lorraine. *The Alchemy of Awareness.* New York: Harper & Row, 1977.

___. *The Spiritual Journey of Joel S. Goldsmith.* New York: Harper & Row, 1973.

International Metaphysical Association
Current address not obtained for this edition.

Among the various independent Christian Science groups, the International Metaphysical Association (IMA), formed in 1955, is perhaps the largest and most influential. It was formed by a number of ex-members of the Church of Christ, Scientist, who saw that the often individual, fragmentary and undisciplined study of independent followers of Mary Baker Eddy was inadequate. The Association has as its purposes to bring to public notice Eddy's scientific revelation, and to encourage students of Christian Science to regard the teachings as a science and approach them in an orderly way.

To accomplish these goals, it sponsors television and radio work, lectures and special schools, and publishes a number of pamphlets and books. Closely associated is the independent Rare Book Company, which has reprinted the first three editions of *Science and Health* by Mary Baker Eddy and serves as a clearinghouse and distributor of much Christian Science literature.

The IMA is headed by a seven-member board of trustees which included Ethel Schroeder, a popular speaker and writer. In 1966, it sponsored its first international conference, which featured popular independent Christian Scientists from Europe: Peggy Brook, Max Kappeler and Gordon Brown. A second conference was held in California in 1968. The mailing list of the IMA includes students from around the United States, some of whom are banded into study groups which use IMA material.

Membership: Not reported.

Periodicals: *Independent Christian Science Quarterly.*

Sources:

Brown, W. Gordon. *Christian Science Nonsectarian.* Haslemere, Surrey, England: Gordon & Estelle Brown, 1966.

Kappeler, Max. *Animal Magnetism—Unmasked.* London: Foundational Book Company Limited, 1975.

Schroeder, Ethel. *Science of Christianity.* New York: International Metaphysical Association, n.d.

Margaret Laird Foundation
(Defunct)

Margaret Laird was a practitioner at the first Church of Christ, Scientist, in Evanston, Illinois. In the late 1930s, she was accused of erroneous teachings. These charges led to a decade of negotiations between the board of directors of the mother church and herself, ending with the removal of her name from the list of practitioners. In 1957 she resigned from the Mother Church. Mrs. Laird continued to teach and operate as an independent Christian Science practitioner. Then in 1959, she incorporated the Margaret Laird Foundation in California. The stated purposes were research into the science of being and dissemination of the results of such research. A world-wide fellowship with other independent Scientists was established and centers were opened in Liverpool and Bombay. The British group published *The Liverpool Newsletter of the Margaret Laird Foundation* a bimonthly periodical.

Among the former Christian Scientists associated with Laird was Harold Woodhull Lund of Bridgeport, Connecticut. Lund published *The Lund Re-View* beginning in 1963 and authored a number of pamphlets. He maintained a cordial relation with the Margaret Laird Foundation and each distributed the other's writings.

Sources:

Laird, Margaret. *Christian Science Re-explored.* Los Angeles: Margaret Laird Foundation, 1971.

___. *The Personal Concept.* Los Angeles: Maragret Laird Foundation, 1969.

Lund, Harold Woodhull. *Four Steps in the Evolution of Religious Thought.* Bridgeport, CT: The Author, 1964.

★1293★
William Samuel Foundation
307 N. Montgomery St.
Ojai, CA 93023

Among the popular metaphysicians in the United States is William Samuel. Since 1968 Mr. Samuel has been publishing *Notes from Woodsong* (originally *Notes from Lollygog*), which is sent to an unspecified number of students across the United States. In several areas groups have formed to study the letters and/or Mr. Samuel's books, most notably *A Guide to Awareness and Tranquility.* Mr. Samuel professes a profound sense of well-being and a surprising abililty to pass that well-being on to others. He asserts that tranquility is acquired not through step-by-step methods but rather by simplicity and honesty in a childlike approach.

Periodicals: *The Child Within, A Journal.*

Sources:

Samuel, William. *The Child Within Us Lives!: A Synthesis of Science, Religion and Metaphysics* Mountain Brook, AL: Mountain Brook Publications, 1986.

___. *A Guide to Awareness and Tranquility.* Lakemont, GA: CSA Press, 1967.

___. *The Melody of the Woodcutter and the King.* Palo Alto: Seed Center, 1976.

___. *2 Plus 2=Reality.* Lakemont, GA: CSA Press, 1963.

★1294★
Truth Center
566 Crestview Dr.
Ojai, CA 93023

Truth Center was founded in Los Angeles, California, in 1970 by W. Norman Cooper. Born in Winnipeg, Canada, in the 1920s, Cooper moved as a youth with his family to Los Angeles in 1939. He received his college degree from Chapman College and a Doctor of Divinity degree from Eastern Nebraska Christian College (associated with the Congregational Church of Practical Theology and now superceded by St. John's University, Ponchatoula, Louisiana). An active church worker, he withdrew from church life in 1965 and spent three years largely in meditation. After his years of withdrawal he began to hold one-day seminars to share his discoveries and later initiated Sunday services. This activity led to the organization of Truth Center.

Cooper's teachings emphasize two principal aspects. He teaches the Bible and Bible history (primarily the Gospels) as illustrative of the inner life. In this process he has come to believe that the apocryphal *Gospel of Thomas* provides the purest presentation of Jesus' teachings. Secondly, he emphasizes the inner search for one's divine Self. He advises daily meditation. The inward search should lead to a realization of the individual's oneness with the Source, i.e., God. Cooper also stresses the need for activity in the world as opposed to merely a self-centered mysticism.

Membership: There is one center in Los Angeles where most of Cooper's students reside. However, some of Cooper's students are scattered across the United States.

Sources:

Cooper, W. Norman. *Dance with God.* Marina del Rey, CA: DeVorss & Company, 1982.

___. *The Non-Thinking Self.* Marina del Rey, CA: DeVorss & Company, 1980.

Field, Filip. *W. Norman Cooper, a Prophet for Our Time.* Marina del Rey, CA: DeVorss & Company, 1979.

Witt, Roselyn. *W. Norman Cooper, A View of a Holy Man.* Marina del Rey, CA: DeVorss & Company, 1982.

★1295★
United Christian Scientists
Current address not obtained for this edition.

United Christian Scientists was founded in 1975 in New Jersey by a group of independent students of Christian Science. The following year David James Nolan of San Jose, California, was elected to serve as chairman of the religious education foundation. The prime issue raised by the United Christian Scientists concern the polity of the Church of Christ, Scientist. They filed a suit seeking to have the text of the writings of Mary Baker Eddy declared in the public domain and were successful. More recently they have begun a probe into the issues involved in the establishment of centralized control at the Boston, Massachusetts, headquarters of the Church of Christ, Scientist, in what they consider to be flagrant disregard of Eddy's instructions to dissolve such control at the time of her passing.

The United Christian Scientists operate within the context of the larger movement of independent Christian Scientists, continuing their work individually in much the same way as they did prior to leaving the Church of Christ, Scientist.

Membership: Not reported

New Thought

★1296★
Altrurian Society
(Defunct)

The Altrurian Society was founded by L. A. Fealy in 1911 in Birmingham, Alabama. In 1892, Fealy had a vision of a life work in which he was told to "go heal the sick" and to seek, through laws which would be revealed, a plan in which all might know the "freedom from the bonds of matter and have Health, Happiness, and Abundance." He studied the hidden and latent forces of the inner self and became a successful healer. His success led to an "Initiation into Apostolic Powers," and as a bishop he was able to establish churches and commission others as ministers and healers. By 1902 he was actively traveling, preaching, and healing.

The Altrurian Society had as its goals, "To Heal, Teach Abundance and Happiness, and otherwise perform the ordinances of God." The society taught a belief in One God. By strict obedience to law, individuals could become conscious of God within. Jesus Christ is the Son of God, as is potentially every person. Christ healed the sick and did other mighty works as a demonstration of the way of salvation; what he did, anyone can do. Healing the sick and abundance from God are a part of the Christian's inheritance.

The society followed seven ordinances: belief, faith, repentence, baptism, remission of sin through confession and work, divine consciousness, and the transmission of the power of the Holy Ghost by the laying-on-of-hands. The Kingdom of God is present when persons comply with the law of God in belief, acceptance, faith, intention, contemplation, meditation, and conviction.

The Altrurian Society was administered by a board of trustess with a president, vice-president, secretary, and treasurer. Spiritually it was led by a hierarchy of apostles, bishops, ministers, deacons, and disciples. The members were called upon to demonstrate healing, happiness, and opulence. The society is known today primarily by several pamphlets which have survived. It seems to have disappeared in the 1930s.

Remarks: The Altrurian Society was hindered in its work by the arrest of Fealy in 1916 for violating the medical practice acts of the state of Alabama. While his conviction slowed the society, it did not prove fatal.

Sources:

Fealy, L. A. *Love's Way*. Birmingham, AL: Altrurian Society, 1927.

McCulloch, Bonnie. *Fealy Aphorisms*. Birmingham, AL: Altrurian Society, 1913.

Rubenstein, I. H. *Law on Cults*. Chicago: Ordain Press, 1981.

★1297★
American School of Mentalvivology
Current address not obtained for this edition.

The American School of Mentalvivology was founded in the 1960s by Dr. Merle E. Parker. It grew out of the Foundation for Divine Meditation founded in 1948 and headquartered in Santa Isabel, Calfornia. Mentalvivology is described as a science of mind and a practical application of the law of mind. The goal of mentalvivology is producing whole men and women. The basic course involves teaching the student to produce any sensation at will, the use of mind to effect "faith healing," the use of the inner mind to set goals and accomplish them, and the practical application of mind. Advanced courses deal with mysticism and the ritual magic of the ancient wisdom. These advanced lessons were originally published by the now-defunct Aquarius School of the Masters, also of Santa Isabel, California. All courses are by correspondence.

Membership: Not reported. Students are found around the country.

Sources:

Parker, Merle E. *Instant Healing Now!* Santa Isabel, CA: Foundation for Divine Meditation, 1955.

___. *The Mentalvivology Story*. Thornfield, MO: The Author, 1969.

★1298★
Antioch Association of Metaphysical Science
Current address not obtained for this edition.

The Antioch Association of Metaphysical Science is a metaphysical church founded in 1932 by Dr. Lewis Johnson of Detroit, Michigan. It serves a predominantly black membership.

Membership: Not reported. In 1965 there were 6 churches.

★1299★
Applied Power
(Defunct)

Applied Power was the name given to the metaphysical ministry of Jane Hanford Hopkins and Charles Henry Hopkins, two metaphysical teachers during the 1920s. C. H. Hopkins had been a successful businessman and his wife a teacher of oratory and drama. After a career in the city, the Hopkins forsook urban life and moved to Les Cheneaux Islands, Michigan, for a life centered on nature and self-expression. In this rustic setting revelations began to flow through Jane Hopkins. Applied Power grew out of these revelations, which the Hopkins compiled into a book, *Applied Power*.

Leaving behind the conception of an anthropomorphic deity, the Hopkins begin with God who is described as Pure Spirit, Perfect Life, Love, Truth, Law and Harmony, and All Wise, Knowing, Powerful, Perfect, and Immanent. Man is a threefold being consisting of body or matter, mind or soul, and spirit. While fully acknowledging their physical and mental aspect, most individuals only partially acknowledge their spiritual aspect. While everything in the universe is an expression of Spirit, humans are vaguely aware of that fact. As an expression of God, humans are conceived in power (not sin), and there is virtually no limit to a human's power short of the infinite.

The universe operates under three great laws: love, the creative force in the universe; life, the expression of cooperation between God and man; and liberty, freedom from limitations as one comes into a realization of God. Success depends upon the full harmonious working of the whole human being.

The Hopkins' lived at Cedarville on Les Cheneaux Islands. Theirs was a personal ministry, rendered through one-to-one relationships with pupils. They invited their students to gather at Cedarville each summer for intensive study based upon their textbook. The rest of the year they spent touring the county teaching and lecturing.

Sources:

Hartmann, William C. *Who's Who in Occultism, New Thought, Psychism and Spiritualism*. Jamaica, NY: Occult Press, 1927.

Hopkins, Jane Hanford, and Charles Henry Hopkins. *Applied Power*. Cedarville, MI: The Authors, 1926.

★1300★
The Aquarian Ministry
(Defunct)

The Aquarian Ministry, founded by George B. Brownell (d. 1945) and Louise B. Brownell (d. 1967) in Brookline, Massachusetts, in 1918, was a major force within the larger New Thought metaphysical community for half a century. Organized around a magazine, *The Aquarian Age*, and correspondence lessons, it gathered members from across the United States and around the world. Shortly after its founding, the ministry moved to California, finally settling in Santa Barbara in 1920. The heart of the ministry was a daily prayer time each morning during which the Brownells prayed for each person who wrote them for help on matters of either health or financial distress. The prime teaching work was done through a 52-part correspondence course. The Prosperity League (later the Mutual Blessing League), an integral part of the ministry, was organized by the Brownells to assist members in financial and career goals.

The ministry established itself on the left wing of the emerging New Thought metaphysical community, and freely included various theosophical and occult teachings. The Brownells believed strongly in reincarnation, and astrology was given a special emphasis. However, the ministry departed from theosophy in its main work of healing. [Healing was offered as the central work of the Brownell's ministry. In light of each person's Divine heritage, healing is an immediate possibility, and anyone can rise above hereditary, environmental, and karmic influences]. In particular, the Brownells opposed the theosophic admonitions against healing work as interfering with an individual's karma. During the early years of the ministry, a special emphasis was placed upon assisting young mothers during the months of their pregnancy and the event of childbirth.

Following the death of her husband in 1947, Louise Brownell enlisted the help of James Dodds (d. 1951), a pastor of the Church of the Truth in Portland, Oregon, and a noted author in his own right, to head the ministy and edit the magazine. Under his leadership, the magazine, heretofore written primarily by the Brownells, featured articles by many of the leading New Thought authors. Also, the emphasis upon astrology, so prominent in the Brownells' ministry, virtually disappeared. Following his untimely death four years later, there was a succession of editors, until 1958 when Lionel Kenworthy, also a pastor in the Church of the Truth, assumed control. In 1963 he moved the ministry headquarters to Atascadero, California. The ministry survived only a few years after this final relocation.

Sources:

Brownell, George B. *Reincarnation*. Santa Barbara, CA: Aquarian Ministry, 1946.

Brownell, Louise B. *Life Abundant for You*. Santa Barbara, CA: Aquarian Ministry, 1928.

___. *Your Destiny in the Zodiac*. Santa Barbara, CA: Aquarian Ministry, 1925.

Brownell, Louise B., and George B. Brownell. *Lessons in Truth*. Santa Barbara, CA: Aquarian Ministry, n.d.

Dodds, James E. *Conscious Immortality*. Santa Barbara, CA: Aquarian Ministry, 1942.

★1301★
Association of Independent Ministries (AIM)
(Defunct)

The Association of Independent Ministries (AIM) is a fellowship of independent New Thought ministers and churches founded in 1984 under the leadership of Dr. Margaret Stevens, pastor of the Santa Anita Church in Arcadia, California. Stevens was ordained in 1966 by the Church and School of Christian Philosophy in Phoenix, Arizona. She became the pastor of the Santa Anita Church the following year. In 1977 she founded the Santa Anita Center for Ministerial and Spiritual Studies, a school and seminary.

While many independent New Thought ministers value their autonomous status, they also feel the need for support and joint efforts in accomplishing tasks too big for any one congregation. At an initial meeting in 1984, the organization was created, a newsletter, *On Target*, was planned, and future conferences slated. Conferences have been held semiannually since. In addition, AIM provides a home for New Thought ministers in noncongregationally oriented chaplaincy ministries. AIM has also established a speakers bureau and a prayer ministry. By the end of the decade, two of the leading ministers retired and in the absence of fresh leadership, the association disbanded.

Sources:

Stevens, Margaret. *Prosperity Is God's Idea*. Marina del Rey, CA: DeVorss & Co., 1978.

★1302★
Christ Truth League
2409 Canton Dr.
Fort Worth, TX 76112

The Christ Truth League was founded in 1938 by Alden Truesdell (d. 1985) and his wife, Nell Truesdell (d. 1971), as an independent ministry and fellowship of students seeking what they believed to be the right application of the law of life as taught and lived by Jesus Christ. The Truesdells were closely aligned with the teachings of Harley Bradley Jeffery (1872-1954).

Jeffery was a popular New Thought author and lecturer for most of the first half of the twentieth century. He had come into New Thought through the efforts of Charles Brodie Patterson and studied with Emma Curtis Hopkins, with whom he collaborated while she was writing her classic study, *High Mysticism*. He studied in England with Thomas Troward and was associated for a period with the Unity School of Christianity. During his mature years he produced a number of books developed out of the concepts of *High Mysticism*, including: *The Principles of Healing* (1939), *Coordination of Spirit, Soul and Body* (1948), and *Mystical Teachings* (1954).

After Jeffery's death, the Truesdells acquired rights to his works and, for more than 30 years, carried on his ministry, published his books, and saw to their distribution. The Truesdells have been succeeded by Dr. Robert Applegate, the current minister and president of the league. The magazine *Spiriticity*, has recently resumed publication. The league is a member of the International New Thought Alliance (INTA).

Membership: The league is a free fellowship with no formal membership. There is one center, in Fort Worth, Texas, where Sunday services and weekly classes are offered. There is affiliated work in Benin, Nigeria, and the Philippines.

Sources:

Jeffery, H. B. *Coordination of Spirit, Soul and Body*. Fort Worth: Christ Truth League, 1948.

___. *Mystical Teachings*. Forth Worth: Christ Truth League, 1954.

___. *The Principles of Healing*. Fort Worth: Christ Truth League, 1939.

___. *The Spirit of Prayer*. Cambridge, MA: Ruth Laighton, 1938.

★1303★
Christian Assembly
PO Box 6120
San Jose, CA 95150

Among the most specifically Christian of the several New Thought groups is the Christian Assembly. It was founded by William Farwell in 1900 in San Jose, California, as a branch of the Home of Truth, the loose association of centers led by Annie Rix Militz. Around 1920 Farwell's congregation separated from the Home of Truth and took its present name. The Christian Assembly believes Christianity is founded upon the doctrines of Jesus Christ and the Bible, and these are used by the Assembly as a source of teaching. The Bible contains a spiritual sense within its historical/literal sense, and this spiritual meaning can be discerned by the Spirit of truth working upon the understanding.

Unlike many New Thought groups, the Christian Assembly has attempted to produce a summary statement of its beliefs. The fundamental principles of the teaching of the Christ include: God is Spirit, whose nature is love and wisdom; the kingdom of God is within; Jesus is the Christ, the Son of the living God; he is divine and human (a perfect unity) and, as the risen Lord, he abides in his kingdom within; true faith comes from God and makes all things possible; evil has no power from God; love is the fulfillment of the law which is constitutional to man; Christian healing is properly a part of the gospel; the kingdom is known through works of faith and love. The work of the Christian Assembly is centered upon a weekly Sunday morning worship service, prayer groups, and Bible classes and truth lectures through the week. The sacraments have been discontinued so that concentration can be upon inner meaning.

Over the years, branches of the Christian Assembly were established in the San Francisco Bay area. Ministers trained and ordained by the Christian Assembly are pastors of branch churches in Gilroy, Palo Alto, Oakland, Redwood City, and San Jose (2). Farwell was also a prolific writer, and the assembly has published much of his material.

Membership: Not reported. In 1971 there were 6 congregations.

Sources:

Farwell, William. *Be Thou a Blessing*. San Jose, CA: First Christian Assembly, 1936.

___. *The Paraclete*. San Jose, CA: Christian Assembly, 1928.

★1304★
Church of Hakeem
Current address not obtained for this edition.

The Church of Hakeem was founded by Clifton Jones, better known to his followers as Hakeem Abdul Rasheed, in Oakland, California, in January 1978. Jones, a Detroit-born black man, attended Purdue University as a psychology major. In the mid-1970s he ran a weight-reduction clinic, which was closed in 1976 when the state Board of Medical Quality Assurance reported that he was using "psychology" rather than diet and exercise to treat clients. He was practicing psychology without a license.

Hakeem turned from weight-reduction to religion and assumed his new name. Like his colleague, Rev. Frederick Eikerenkoetter II (Reverend Ike), founder of the United Church and Science of Living Institute, Hakeem built upon New Thought emphases that health, wealth, and happiness came from positive mental attitudes put into positive action. He emphasized positive action as a means to wealth. In contrast to Reverend Ike, however, Hakeem implemented his teachings through a variation of what is known as the Ponsie game, a standard confidence scheme. Members paid into the church with the promise of a 400 percent return within three years. Members would in turn recruit further investors. The early investors receive their promised return. People who joined last receive nothing, not even their original investment. Such schemes are illegal.

In May 1979 Hakeem was indicted and later convicted on six counts of fraud. A group of members signed a class action suit against the church, and the Internal Revenue Service moved against the church for taxes. The cummulative effect of these actions have paralyzed the Church of Hakeem, and its future is doubtful.

Membership: By 1979 congregations of the church had been established in San Diego, Los Angeles, San Francisco, and Sacramento, California. There were an estimated 5,000 to 10,000 members.

★1305★
Church of Inner Wisdom
Current address not obtained for this edition.

The Church of Inner Wisdom was founded in San Jose, California, in 1968 by a metaphysician, Dr. Joan Gibson. Prior to 1968, she had been a member of the Rosicrucians (Ancient Mystic Order of the Rosy Cross) and had studied with Clark Wilkerson, founder of the Institute of Cosmic Wisdom. The church combines the teachings of New Thought with a major secondary emphasis on the psychic. The teachings are described as "macro-ontology," the study of the nature of a child of God, forgiveness, expansion of awareness, Jesus and the major religious prophets as examples for living, and sharing truth received. The psychic is seen as a tool in expanding awareness and as spiritual. However, without the perspective of metaphysics, it becomes a means of mere ego-gratification. Lessons, which may be taken in classes or by correspondence, are the main means of disseminating the church's teachings. The church is governed by a board of directors, Dr. Gibson being the permanent chairman. An annual business meeting is open only to officers, directors and ministers.

Membership: Not reported. In 1972 ministers of the church were at work in Alameda, Alhambra, Concord, and Burlingame, California; Phoenix, Mesa, and Wickenburg, Arizona; Chicago, Illinois; Erie, Pennsylvania; and Atlanta, Georgia.

Periodicals: *The Voice.* Send orders to Box 4765, San Jose, CA 95126.

★1306★
Church of the Fuller Concept
Current address not obtained for this edition.

The Church of the Fuller Concept is a New Thought group headed by Dr. Bernese Williamson, a doctor of metaphysical science. Dr. Williamson teaches that we live in the God dispensation. God is our Father and Mother, our natural parents being God caring for us. God has a body (I Cor. 11:30) and is manifested in body-form on earth. Man's body is the image and likeness of God. In recognizing God's body, man can have the blessing of a healthy, whole body. Members of the church do not carry insurance, because in God, where man lives and moves and has his being (which is the body of God), there can be no illness. Dr. Williamson teaches that every meal is a communion and that what one visualizes as he eats and drinks will materialize.

Headquarters of the church are at the Hisacres New Thought Center in Washington, D.C. Members live by a pledge to remember their spiritual nature. They greet each other with the word, "Peace." They adopt spiritual names, because they want to acquire the nature, characteristics and attributes of God. All students sign a pledge to give honest service to their employer for their pay, not accepting tips or vacation-with-pay, nor using intoxicants on the job. This pledge is given to the employers.

Membership: Not reported.

★1307★
Church of the New Civilization
(Defunct)

The Church of the New Civilization was founded by Julia Seton (1862-1950), who emerged as one of the most energetic exponents of New Thought metaphysics during the early twentieth century. Her early bouts with tuberculosis led her into medicine, and she became a doctor, doing postgraduate work at Tufts Medical College in Boston, Massachusetts. She also became a theosophist and was briefly married (1903-1914) to New Thought lecturer-writer F. W. Sears, during which time her books appeared under her married name, Julia Seton Sears. Her healing practice led her to concentrate first on preventive medicine and finally in 1905 to leave her medical work for a career in metaphysical healing. Her teachings blended theosophy (represented in her books on numerology, the aura, an d the emanation on body) and more traditional New Thought metaphysical themes (healing and prosperity).

The first center of the Church of the New Civilization was founded in Boston in 1905. In 1907 Seton moved to New York City and began a second congregation as the New Thought Church and School and within a few years had affiliated centers in Brooklyn, Hempstead, and Buffalo, New York; Boston, Salem, and Brockton, Massachusetts; Cleveland, Ohio; Chicago, Illinois; Denver, Colorado; and California. Classes were taught in healing, abundance, graphology, the tarot, and numerology. As World War I was beginning, Seton began a period of travel to England (where an affiliate center had developed soon after the first Boston work) and Australia. Upon her return to America she settled in Kansas City, Missouri. Around 1937, she purchased land near Ocala, Florida, and began to build the New Civilization school, the Ocala Post-graduate School of Metaphysics. Unfortunately, the location was commandeered by the army during World War II, and the day after she reclaimed her property all but one building burned in a massive fire. Seton, then in her 80s, retired from active leadership in the movement she had led, and it dwindled away after her death in 1950.

The basic perspective of the church was presented systematically in the student's manual, *Fundamental Principles of the New Civilization.* Seton proposed a reordering of human life around the basic principle that "God Is All." Humans are Individualized God on a self-imposed pathway. Seeing life as a whole, people can see themselves as part of the larger system and know that there is no evil. What people call evil is but undeveloped good.

Sources:

Seton, Julia. *Fundamental Principles of the New Civilization.* New York: Edward J. Clode, 1916.

___. *The Key to Health, Wealth and Love.* New York: Edward J. Clode, 1917.

___. *The Mystic's Goal.* London: William Rider & Son, 1924.

___. *The Science of Success.* New York: Edward J. Clode, 1914.

___. *Western Symbology.* Chicago: New Publishing Company, 1929.

★1308★
Church of the Science of Religion
(Defunct)

The Church of the Science of Religion was founded in 1922 by the Rev. Carolyn Barbour Le Galyon, a former practitioner with the Church of Christ, Scientist, who had been healed of a broken wrist. She became a student of various New Thought leaders—Charles S. Fillmore, Ernest S. Holmes and others. The Church of the Science of Religion teaches an eclectic New Thought perspective drawn from the numerous early metaphysical teachers. Headquarters were in Cleveland, Ohio, at the New Thought Temple of Christ. The Church dissolved following Le Galyon's death in the 1970s.

Sources:

LeGalyon, Carolyn Barbour. *All Things New*. New York: Analysts' Publisher, 1963.

★1309★
Church of the Trinity (Invisible Ministry)
Box 4608
Salem, OR 97302-8608

Friend Stuart (i.e., A. Stuart Otto) was a West Coast publisher who, in 1954, had a religious awakening that started his metaphysical search. Over the next few years, he was able to study with many of the outstanding New Thought leaders. In 1957, a series of additional enlightenment experiences began, culminating in 1963 with an inward ordination in what is called the invisible ministry. Three years later, Stuart began to conduct private metaphysical practice under the name "Invisible Ministry," and, in 1967, obtained a charter and began issuing *Tidings* as a quarterly bulletin. Work was primarily by mail at a distance, though classes were held at the Invisible Ministry center. In 1972, Church of the Trinity was established as an outgrowth of the healing ministry.

The theology of Church of the Trinity is based upon the work of James Allen, Henry Drummond, Emmet Fox and Friend Stuart. The church is grounded in the faith that the Christian doctrine of the Father, Son and Holy Spirit is the ultimate spiritual truth, and that all things proceed from these three aspects of almighty God. The church calls its theology the science of dominion, the Christ-Jesus way. According thereto, man fulfills his destiny by achieving dominion and glorifies God in so doing. Jesus came to overcome death, and, as we recognize truth, we are freed of disease, disharmony and lack. Those on the way are members of the fifth kingdom. The Church of the Trinity thus is similar to the Unity School of Christianity in its emphasis on specifically Christian tenets which are allegorized in a New Thought framework. However, the church is strictly trinitarian, an aspect not strongly emphasized by Unity.

The Church of the Trinity is purely spiritual and refrains from involvement in secular matters. It enjoins its members to obey the law and to be good citizens. Healing is the major concern, and the church sees itself as a balancing influence with Christ's church as a whole. Seven sacraments are practiced by members: baptism, confirmation, communion, matrimony, holy orders, cognition of divine life, and expiation. As of 1972, there was only one center of the Church of the Trinity, but others were imminent and a school of theology has been opened.

Membership: Not reported, but in 1992 the *Tidings* newsletter reported a circulation of 400 copies. The church considers all baptized Christians as members. In 1992 there were two ministers and one center with an affiliated work in Nigeria and the Philippines led by lay members. Affiliated individuals and supporters of the ministry, especially those involved in the healing work, can be found across the United States. They stay in contact through the mail.

Educational Facilities: Trinity School of Theology, San Marcos, California.

Periodicals: *Tidings.* • *Theologia 21.* • *Master Thoughts.* • *The Theologia 21 Encyclopedia.*

★1310★
Comforter League of Light
(Defunct)

The Comforter League of Light grew out of the intense religious experience of Florence Gloria Crawford, who, around 1913, was "given the Comforter message." The Comforter is a reference to one of the last sayings of Jesus to his disciples, "It is expedient for you that I go away; for if I go not away, the Comforter will not come unto you." (John 16:7) Traditionally, the Comforter has been interpreted by Christians as the Holy Spirit. Crawford interpreted both the Holy Spirit and the Comforter as the Christ Consciousness. From the time of her experience, Crawford acted as one entrusted with a message for all the world. She opened the Irvington Center of Truth in Portland, Oregon, which became the core congregation of the Comforter League of Light. A major step in the emergence of the league occurred in the months following the beginning of World War I as Crawford was led to focus upon the work of the the Christ Consciousness as bringing a message of love, peace, and comfort to the word. Thus in December 1914, she issued the first copies of a new magazine, *The Comforter*.

Crawford taught the central New Thought affirmations. God was defined as the great life-power, substance, and intelligence. Humans bring God into active expression. Crawford believed that she was in regular contact with Jesus, from whom she received teachings. Included in her revelatory writings were her commentaries on Jesus' parables and a lenghty book on peace. She also placed an emphasis upon prosperity, which she believed to be immediately available to people as they expressed their highest ideals following the universal laws.

During the years of her ministry, Crawford was a popular speaker for ecumenical New Thought gatherings. In 1921 the league moved to San Francisco, California, and there continued for another decade. Healing groups were formed along the West Coast. Integral to the league's work was the Comforter Healing Circle. Each morning at 10 a.m. Crawford and others at the San Francisco headquarters prayed individually for those requesting their assistance. Members and readers of the magazine around the country were invited to join them for a half hour of silence at that time. Following the healing prayers, members were invited to participate in the Comforter Study Hour, for which materials were published in the magazine.

Remarks: Among the members of the Comforter League of Light was Baird Spalding, author of the classic occult volumes the *Life and Teachings of the Masters of the Far East*, the first chapters of which were originally published in *The Comforter* in 1922.

Florence Gloria Crawford should not be confused with Florence L. Crawford, founder of the Pentecostal denomination the Apostolic Faith, also headquartered in Portland, Oregon, during the years of the Comforter League of Light.

Sources:

Crawford, Florence Gloria. *The Christ Ideal for World Peace.* San Francisco: Comforter League of Light, 1925.

★1311★
Disciples of Faith
Current address not obtained for this edition.

Similar to the Life-Study Fellowship (see separate entry) is the Disciples of Faith of Nashville, Tennessee. As with Life-Study Fellowship, no mention of the leadership is made in the group's literature. Members are related through the mail and by printed testimonials. United prayer with a world-wide prayer fellowship is stressed. Members are asked to rate themselves according to health, prayer life, use of time, faith and relation to God. Members work on receiving the full abundance of God.

Central to the Disciples of Faith are lessons which train the member to prepare the prayer-time, to understand the power of prayer, and to know the laws of abundant living, faith and spiritual healing. The mystical teachings of Jesus on the necessity of prayer as "holy communion" are stressed. Miracles happen to people after their prayers are offered in Jesus' name.

Membership: Not reported.

★1312★
Dispensable Church
Box 8444
Santa Fe, NM 87504-8444

The Dispensable Church was founded in 1985 as an instrument to facilitate the teaching work of Hugh Prather. Prather had been raised a Christian Scientist and for a year attended Principia College. As his thought developed, however, he found himself more in tune with the teachings of a New Age spiritual text called *A Course in Miracles*. Through the 1970s, Prather issued a series of books containing reflections on his inner explorations and pilgrimage, that became popular metaphysical and new age texts. The first, *Notes to Myself* (1970), became a best seller and was followed by *I Touch the Earth, the Earth Touches Me* (1972) and *Notes on Love and Courage* (1977). Each book offers a set of brief entries from Prather's diary, seemingly random reflections upon his reactions to mundane events. However, though the numerous brief entries an understanding of the nature of the world and advice on a way of existing in the world emerged.

Prather, by his example, made note of an underlying spiritual reality and projected a means of living at peace with that reality. He sought to be in touch with his feelings as a means of living in the present. Spending too much time reflecting on the past or projecting oneself into the future was dehumanizing and a way of holding on to unhappiness. Prather also asserted that a major problem with society was the tendency to continually analyze events in life rather than simply experience and learn from them.

Prather's vision was subjective in the extreme. He saw the need for self-exploration and self-knowledge as a means to freedom and happiness. He saw body states, especially illness, as the projection of inner states and attitudes into visible expression. As he became intimate with his own inner state and conscious of his actions and reaction in community, he began to develop a series of games and exercises to assist others in the same explorations with a goal of producing a life of consistent happiness. Happiness is consistent with a life of simplicity, peace, gentleness, forgiveness, humor, trust, and fearlessness.

The Dispensable Church provided a means for Prather to interact with the people who had been attracted by his writings. Prather spoke and led attendees in the mental exercises he had developed. The name of the church indicated that attendance was not a necessary activity but gatherings might be useful for a while. Tapes of Prather's sessions were recorded and distributed to people across the country and around the world.

Membership: Not reported.

Sources:

Prather, Hugh. *A Book of Games: A Course in Spiritual Play*. Garden City, NY: Doubleday & Company, 1981. 142 pp.

___. *I Touch the Earth, the Earth Touches Me*. Garden City, NY: Doubleday & Company, 1972. Unpaged.

___. *Notes on How to Live in the World. . . and Still Be Happy*. Garden City, NY: Doubleday & Company, 1986. 271 pp.

___. *Notes on Love and Courage*. Garden City, NY: Doubleday & Company, 1977. Unpaged.

___. *Notes on Myself*. N.p., n.d.

★1313★
Divine Science Federation International
1819 E. 14th Ave.
Denver, CO 80218

Divine Science continues the merger of two streams of early metaphysical teachings both of which began in the 1880s and both of which had derived from the initial work of Emma Curtis Hopkins, the founder of what today is termed New Thought. The first stream began in 1886 with Kate Bingham of Pueblo, Colorado. Bingham went to Chicago, Illinois, hoping to find some cure

for her illness. She found that healing under the ministration of Mabel MacCoy, a student of Hopkins, who sent Bingham to her teacher for classes. Bingham would eventually complete the ministerial course at the Christian Science Theological Seminary and be ordained by Hopkins. Meanwhile, however, after completing her basic class work with Hopkins, she returned to Colorado in 1887 to teach a class attended by two sisters Nona Brooks (1862-1945) and Althea Small. Brooks experienced a healing as a result of the class. At about the same time, MacCoy held a class in Denver, Colorado, which was attended by yet a third sister, Fannie James. By the summer of 1887 the Hopkins School of Christian Science was flourishing in Denver. It continued active until the mid-1890s when Hopkins retired from her work in Chicago and moved into private work in New York.

At about the same time Bingham was offering her class in Pueblo, Hopkins traveled to San Francisco, California, and held a class in April 1887 attended by more than 200 people. Among those in attendance were Miranda Rice and Melinda Elliot Cramer (1844-1906). Miranda Rice had been an early student of Mary Baker Eddy but had left the Church of Christ, Scientist, moved to San Francisco, and opened the first Christian Science practitioners office in the west coast. Melinda Cramer had moved to San Francisco in 1870 hoping that the climate would be a cure for the ill health she had suffered for the preceeding decade. She found that cure in 1885, probably under the ministration of Miranda Rice. In any case, both women attended Hopkins' class, and in May 1888 she opened the Home College of Spiritual Science, with which Rice affiliated. Later that year Cramer began publishing *Harmony*, one of the most prominent early New Thought periodicals.

The Denver and San Francisco streams began to flow together in 1889 when William McKendree Brown, a student of Hopkins from Iowa, moved to Denver and became the local agent for distributing *Harmony*. In early 1890, Cramer came to Denver and taught a number of classes which were well received. Brooks attended the classes and discovered a close affinity with Cramer. In 1892 she formed the International Divine Science Federation, originally an attempt to built a fellowship association for the early New Thought centers in the West and Midwest. Annie Rix Militz of the Home of Truth served as the first vice president. The first convention was held in San Francisco in 1894. The association continued to hold meetings through the end of the century.

In the early 1890s Nona Brooks moved to Denver where Fannie James had organized a separate metaphysical group. Over the years the sisters had developed several important differences with Kate Bingham and the ideas taught her by Hopkins. They also began to remold Hopkins' basic teaching around the central concept of the omnipresence of God. For example, they rejected any notion of prayer as supplication and centered their work on meditation as contemplation of God's omnipresence. They discarded any distinction between a mortal mind-immortal mind, present in both Eddy's and Hopkins' thought, in favor of a simple reliance on omnipresence. They disagreed with the idea of "chemicalization," an idea Hopkins passed on from Eddy, which explained what happened when some patients seem to get worse before getting better. They also rejected Hopkins' use of alternating denials and affirmations in treating patients as well as the multiple six-day healing treatment which utilized them. They preferred a single method treatment which merely affirmed the omnipresence of God.

In the mid-1890s, Althea Small also moved to Denver. Brooks and James were already holding classes and doing healing from the latter's home. However, by 1896 the work required them to open an office in downtown Denver. In 1898 they incorporated as the Divine Science College. Brooks received her ordination from Cramer that year, and on Sunday, January 1, 1899, Brooks opened the first church chartered by the college. James served as president of the college until her death during World War I, after which Brooks succeeded her. The formal organization of the work in Denver was vital to the survival of the movement, as the work in San Francisco was destroyed by an earthquake in 1906. Cramer herself died from injuries sustained in the disaster.

Following the demise of Cramer, Nona Brooks came to the forefront as the leader and dominated it until her second retirement in 1941. She was, however, ably assisted over the years by some of the most talented teachers in the New Thought field. During the early twentieth century W. John Murray and Ernest S. Holmes (later to found Religious Science) were ordained by Divine Science. Emmet Fox, at one time the preacher for the largest New Thought congregation in America, was a Divine Scientist. More recently Joseph Murphy, who had the largest New Thought audience in Southern California, built up the Los Angeles church.

Beliefs. The keystone of Divine Science is the affirmation of the Limitless Being of God, equally present everywhere. God is pure Spirit, manifesting at all phases at all times. Creation is the emanation of life and substance from God, i.e., God in self-manifestation. Spirit and Substance are but two aspects of the same reality. Matter is divine energy manifest as form. Humans are in essence divine and one with their Creator. These basic ideas are summarized in Divine Science's Statement of Being, "God is all, both invisible and visible. One Presence, One Mind, One Power is all. This One that is all perfect life, perfect love, and perfect substance. Man is the individualized expression of God and is ever one with this perfect life, perfect love, and perfect substance."

In the absence of the individual's realization that each person is an individualized center of God's activity, the possibility of all manner of confusion, turmoil, and adverse circumstances (illness, poverty) can manifest. These circumstances are reversed by an inward turn to the Christ to unfold a consciousness of our oneness with the father—Divine Omnipresence.

Organization. As the work of Divine Science grew rather informally, the need for closer fellowship between the emerging churches became evident, and in the early 1920s a federation was created as a center for coordination of the otherwise autonomous Divine Science organizations. Then in 1957 the Divine Science Federation International was formed. It is governed by a house of delegates composed of representative of the various churches. A general council of five members handles administrative matters between meetings of the house of delegates. The federation licenses practitioners, ordains ministers, charters churches, operates a school for the training of practitioners and ministers, and prints material for use in all the churches. *Daily Studies* continues *Daily Studies in Divine Science*, begun in 1915, the oldest of the New Thought daily devotional guides. Brooks Divinity School supercedes the Colorado College of Divine Science founded by Brooks.

Membership: In 1995, the federation reported 32 congregations, 131 practitioners, and 72 ministers in the United States and one center and three ministers in Canada. There was also one center in New Zealand and one in South Africa.

Educational Facilities: Brooks Divinity School, Denver, Colorado. Divine Science School, Washington, D.C.

Periodicals: *Daily Studies.*

Sources:

Brooks, Louise McNamara. *Early History of Divine Science.* Denver, CO: First Divine Science Church, 1963.

Dean, Hazel. *Powerful Is the Light.* Denver, CO: Divine Science College, 1945.

Divine Science, Its Principle and Practice. Denver, CO: Divine Science Church and College, 1957.

Gregg, Irwin. *The Divine Science Way.* Denver, CO: Divine Science Federation International, 1975.

★1314★
ESP Picture Prayers
Current address not obtained for this edition.

ESP Picture Prayers is headed by Murcie P. Smith of Gary, Indiana. Like the Life-Study Fellowship (see separate entry) ESP Picture Prayers offers printed prayers based upon the idea of God as a loving father. The ESP Picture Prayers organization offers private ESP readings to members as an added incentive. Included in the prayers are special ones for those in the armed services, a "Blessed Sacred Heart of Jesus Christ Prayer" (with a picture of the Sacred Heart included), and a "Blessed Sacred Eyes of Jesus Christ Prayer" (with a picture of the sacred eyes included).

★1315★
First Church of Divine Immanence
Current address not obtained for this edition.

The First Church of Divine Immanence was founded in 1952 by Dr. Henry Milton Ellis (d. 1970). Ellis was a journalist who studied at the College of Divine Metaphysics, from which he received a doctorate. He was for a while a Religious Science practitioner. He became aware that no New Thought group was serving the scattered believers not close to urban areas, so he founded the First Church of Divine Immanence as a mail order denomination. Ellis wrote *Bible Science: the Truth and the Way* as a textbook. At its height, before Ellis' death, the church numbered close to 1,000 members, but with a much larger constituency. Ellis sent a newsletter, *From the Pastor's Study*, regularly to the membership.

Teachings of the church, Bible Science, draws heavily upon the works of Ernest S. Holmes, founder of the Church of Religious Science. God is Spirit, the original life-essence. "Infinite mind" is the animative life principle, and we think, decide and act with this omniscient mind. Man is an expression of God in activity. The law of mind is the power of authority in the natural order of law. Man enters the kingdom of heaven by being "born again," in Greek, metanoia, changing the mind. That change occurs when man realizes his true nature.

Membership: Not reported.

★1316★
Foundation for *A Course in Miracles* **(FACIM)**
1275 Tennanah Lake Rd.
Roscoe, NY 12776-5905

Among the prominent centers perpetuating *A Course in Miracles*, the work channeled by Dr. Helen Schucman from an entity she believed to be Christ, is the Foundation for *A Course in Miracles*, established in 1983 by cofounders Kenneth Wapnick and his wife, Gloria Wapnick. Dr. Kenneth Wapnick, a clinical psychologist, was a close friend and associate of Helen Schucman and William Thetford, the two people whose joining together was the immediate stimulus for the scribing of *A Course in Miracles*. Together with Schucman he prepared the *Course* manuscript for publication and sits on the executive board of the Foundation for Inner Peace, the book's publisher. Gloria Wapnick is a former social studies instructor and high school dean of students who has been working with *A Course in Miracles* since 1977.

In 1984 the Foundation for *A Course in Miracles* (FACIM) evolved into the Teaching and Healing Center in Crompond, New York, which was quickly outgrown. In 1988 the Wapnick's opened the Academy and Retreat Center in upstate New York, and in 1995 began the Institute for Teaching Inner Peace Through *A Course in Miracles* (ITIP-ACIM), an educational corporation chartered by the New York State Board of Regents. The institute operates under the aegis of the foundation, administering workshops and academy courses.

The foundation's statement of purpose affirms its purpose as to foster spiritual development through the study and practice of *A Course in Miracles*, a set of three books channeled by Jesus, that teach that the way to remember God is by undoing guilt through forgiving others. The corporation has as its specific aims to teach the *Course*, helping those interested to integrate the *Course* principles into their personal lives, that they may better realize their true identity, shared with all people, as children of God; to teach and train those who wish to teach the *Course*, to others; to teach the *Course*'s reinterpretation of traditional Christian principles such as sin, suffering, forgiveness, atonement, and the meaning of the Crucifixion; to further understanding of the *Course* by means of educational and training programs, seminars, and publications.

As they worked with the *Course*, the Wapnicks concluded that it was not the simplest of thought systems to understand, not only in the intellectual grasp of its teachings, but in the application of these teachings to personal lives. Additionally, Schucman shared a vision of a teaching center that the Wapnicks understood to be a place where the person of Jesus and His message in *A Course in Miracles* would be manifest. The foundation has been partially inspired by Plato (and his mentor Socrates), and it is hoped that the foundation could function in a manner similar to Plato's Academy, a place where people studied his philosophy in an atmosphere conducive to their learning, and then returned to their professions to implement what they were taught by the great philosopher.

It is the Wapnicks' belief that Jesus gave *A Course in Miracles* at this particular time in this particular form for several reasons, including: 1. the necessity of healing the mind of its belief that attack is salvation; this is accomplished through forgiveness, the undoing of our belief in the reality of separation and guilt. 2. the needed emphasis upon the importance of Jesus and/or the Holy Spirit as our loving and gentle Teacher, and developing a personal relationship with this Teacher. 3. a need to correct the errors of Christianity, particularly where it has emphasized suffering, sacrifice, separation, and sacrament as being inherent to God's plan of salvation.

Membership: Not reported.

Periodicals: *The Lighthouse.*

Sources:

Barrett, David B. *World Christian Encyclopedia.* New York: Oxford, 1982.

★1317★
Home of Truth
1300 Grand St.
Alameda, CA 94501

There is only one congregation remaining of what was for several decades in the early twentieth century the largest New Thought group in the world. The Homes of Truth were founded by Annie Rix Militz (1856-1924) and her sister Harriet Rix in 1888. They grew directly out the early ministry of Emma Curtis Hopkins. In April 1887, Hopkins came to San Francisco, California, and held what was for many years the largest Christian Science class ever held. Among the students were the Rix sisters. Annie, a school teacher, was completely transformed by the class and felt that she had found her role in life. She founded the first Home of Truth in San Francisco. A second one was started in Alameda, California, a few years later. Annie also accepted an invitation from Hopkins to join the faculty of her Christian Science Theological Seminary in Chicago, Illinois, where she met and married Paul Militz and came to know many of the early New Thought leaders, including Myrtle Fillmore and her husband Charles S. Fillmore, who were also students at the seminary.

After the dissolution of the seminary and the retirement of Hopkins to New York City in the mid-1890s, Militz returned to California. Finding the work in the Bay area stable, she moved to Southern California and opened a Home of Truth in Los Angeles, California. She also developed close ties to the Fillmore's who had started the Unity School of Christianity, and became one of the important contributors to their magazine, *Unity*. She wrote one of the first sets of Unity basic lessons, later republished as *Primary Lessons in Christian Living and Healing* and an early volume on prosperity, the only book still in print in the 1980s.

During the last two decades of her life, Militz traveled widely (including several around-the-world tours) on behalf of New Thought. She was an early and avid supporter of the International New Thought Alliance (INTA) and gave much of her energy to it. She also developed the Homes of Truth along the Pacific coast as well as in Chicago and Boston. At the time of her death, there were no less than 12 Homes of Truth. Militz also founded the Master Mind Publishing Company which published New Thought books and, beginning in 1911, *The Master Mind*, one of the most prominent metaphysical magazines into the 1930s.

Militz, along with the Fillmores and other early New Thought leaders, had a strong belief in the possibility of physical immortality. At the time of her death, her closest disciples refused to bury her body until the city of Los Angeles intervened, an action which brought some unwanted press coverage to the movement. In spite of the loss of Militz, the movement remained vital for another generation, but began to decline after World War II. By the 1970s there were only two congregations. One of these, the Boston Home of Truth, died with its longtime leader, Eleanor Mel. During the agreement with its basic principles. It draws eclectically upon and attempts to integrate a variety of New Thought systems, including Unity and, more recently, New Age emphases such as *The Course in Miracles*.

Membership: There is one congregation of the Home of Truth with several hundred members.

Periodicals: *The Channel.*

Sources:

Militz, Annie Rix. *Both Riches and Honor.* Kansas City, MO: Unity School of Christianity, 1945.

___. *Primary Lessons in Christian Living and Healing.* New York: The Absolute Press, 1909.

___. *The Renewal of the Body.* Holyoke, MA: The Elizabeth Towne Co., 1920.

Rix, Harriet Hale. *Christian Mind Healing.* Los Angeles: Master Mind Publishing Co., 1918.

★1318★
Inner Powers Society
Current address not obtained for this edition.

The Inner Powers Society was founded by Alfred Pritchard, its president. Metaphysician Pritchard contacts prospective members through advertisements in metaphysical and psychic publications. The Society is organized by members relating to the home office in Yucca Valley, California. It offers courses which Pritchard wrote on a wide variety of New Thought topics. Pritchard teaches that one must become attuned to the "inner environment" of "cycling cosmic forces." As these forces of inner powers flow through mankind, the distortions of past reversals of truth will be eliminated, and a new age of super-intelligence will be established. Man is entering a new age, an occurrence which is repeated every 2,155 years.

Membership: Not reported.

Sources:

Pritchard, Alfred W. *Man...God's Helpmate.* Los Angeles: Inner Powers Society, 1958.

★1319★
Institute of Esoteric Transcendentalism
Current address not obtained for this edition.

Dr. Robert W. C. Burke is a New Thought teacher in Los Angeles. In 1956, he founded the Robert Burke Foundation and, nine years later, Christology. These were combined in 1969 as the Institute of Esoteric Transcendentalism. There is no formal statement of belief. The right to hold divergent religious tenets is acknowledged.

The basis of the Institute's teachings is Christology, the science of the knowledge of Christ, which rests alone upon the words credited to Jesus. All else in the Bible is considered history and stories for guidance and inspiration. Jesus is described as the man who spoke the illumined Word, Christ, and laid before mankind a foundation for spirituality. Mankind is a creature of divinity and thus "of God." He has within him the divine power that moves the universe, but man misuses the abundant gift of God. Intellectual awareness is the first step in building toward a spiritual consciousness. When spiritual consciousness is put into action, complete self-awareness occurs. Meditation is emphasized as a way to spiritual consciousness.

The program of the Institute is centered upon its headquarters at the William Penn Hotel, Whittier, California, where a full program of lectures, classwork and individual counseling is offered. The two periodicals, both of which follow a lesson format, are mailed to several states.

Membership: Not reported. The Whitter location is the only center.

Periodicals: *The Christext.* • *The Transcendentalist.*

★1320★
Institute of Infinite Science
(Defunct)

Dr. Roman Ostoja was a Polish nobleman who discovered as a teenager that he was telepathic. After finishing his medical degree, he traveled to India and Tibet to learn yoga and improve his psychic skills. He returned to the West and offered himself to many psychical researchers for testing. Included in the tests were not only demonstrations of his psychic abilities, but of yogic austerities including being buried alive for several hours without air, lying on a bed of nails, and sticking a nail through his hand. He came to America in the 1920s and worked with Dr. William McDougall at Harvard. He also studied in the early 1920s with Swami Paramahansa Yogananda, founder of the Self-Realization Fellowship. Shortly thereafter he opened the Institute of Infinite Science in Los Angeles, California. Ostoja offered a variety of nonmedical forms of healing at the institute, and became well-known for the cures he facilitated. But he primarily thought of himself as a Westernized yogi, combining the teachings of the East with the new Western psychology, thus providing a form of Hinduism acceptable to modern Westerners. He shared his multiple healing techniques with students as an integral part of his spiritual and metaphysical teachings.

The teachings of Ostoja combined the yoga teachings of Yogananda with New Thought metaphysics. The object was to produce both self-mastery and the identity of the deepest level of the self with the Infinite One, Mind, Self of All, God. The primary method to achieve those goals is concentration and will power. He taught the yoga disciplines, especially *pranayana* (breathing) for the development of the will and the use of suggestion and autosuggestion as a means of projecting ideas into the mind. Once in the mind, ideas could be a force for good, such as controlling the body in the cure and prevention of disease.

Ostoja continued to head the Institute into the late 1940s, but in the ensuing years he died and the Institute dissolved. Former students can still be found in southern California. The Ostoja Laboratories of Reseda, California, manufacture and distribute the Peruvian Healing Balm, made from Peruvian Tree Oil, developed by Ostoja more than a half century ago.

Sources:

Ostoja, Roman. *Body and Mind Control.* Santa Barbara, CA: J. F. Rowney Press, 1949.

___. *Mind Made Visible.* Santa Barbara, CA: J. F. Rowney Press, 1928.

Sinclair, Upton. *Dr. Roman Ostoja Demonstrations.* N.p., n.d.

★1321★
Interfaith Fellowship
459 Carol Dr.
Monroe, NY 10950

Interfaith Fellowship was founded in New York City in 1977 as Interfaith, Inc. by Rabbi Joseph H. Gelberman of the New Synagogue, Rev. Jon Mundy (a United Methodist minister), and Swami Satchidananda of Integral Yoga International. As originally conceived, Interfaith provided a meeting ground where people from various faiths could meet together for dialogue, sharing, and mutual worship and celebration. It was built upon the idea that the experiences of joy, love, serenity, wisdom, and healing, which all religions share in common, was more important than those elements of theology and ritual which divided. The mystical relationship to transcendent reality was emphasized. Interfaith, Inc., held a meeting one Sunday afternoon each month until 1993. Interfaith Fellowship emerged out of Interfaith, Inc., as a church which began to hold weekly worship services.

Taking the lead in Interfaith Fellowship have been Revs. Mundy and Diane Burke. Both have a longtime involvement with *A Course in Miracles*, a metaphysical text channeled by Dr. Helen Schucman. The perspective of the Course is strongly evident in the fellowship's literature. Also growing out of Interfaith, Inc., was the New Seminary, which carried the spirit of the evolving fellowship into the training of ministers, counselors, and practitioners for work in local communities. Joining Rabbi Gelberman and Reverend Mundy in the creation of the seminary was Fr. Giles Spoonhour. Graduates of the seminary have banded together in the Association of Interfaith Ministers.

The Interfaith Fellowship is built upon the idea that inclusiveness is better than exclusivity, and people of all religious and spiritual backgrounds are welcomed. The literature and wisdom of all faiths are utilized in worship. There is neither a creed nor a set of beliefs to which members must give consent. Emphasis is placed upon each person having a direct loving relationship to God, humanity, and all creation. Members seek an understanding and appreciation of all different kinds of people, confident that the process will bring them closer to the Spirit within each person.

Membership: As of 1995 there was one congregation of approximately 250 members; however, the New Seminary has graduated and ordained some 700 ministers, some of whom stand ready to start additional congregations affiliated with the fellowship.

Periodicals: *On Course.*

Sources:

About Interfaith Fellowship. Monroe, NY: Interfaith, 1992.

★1322★
International Alliance of Churches of the Truth
690 E. Orange Grove Blvd.
Pasadena, CA 91104

The International Alliance of Churches of Truth was formed in 1987 out of the remnants of what had been a loose fellowship of congregations of the Church of the Truth, also known informally as the Church of Truth. The church was formed in 1913 when Albert C. Grier, pastor of a Universalist Church in Spokane, Washington, resigned from the church and, with most of his congregation, formed a new congregation which taught Divine Science or New Thought. Later that year he began *Truth,* for many years an important New Thought periodical. Grier had become converted to New Thought after reading a pamphlet written by Clara T. Stocker, a student of Emma Curtis Hopkins, who worked as a practitioner in Spokane and in Cascade, British Columbia. Grier's work expanded quickly as he became a popular lecturer and as other

New Thought leaders were drawn into his fellowship. In 1914, work began in nearby Coeur d'Alene, Idaho, and within a few years affiliated centers spread across the Northwest.

Grier also developed close ties with Nona Brooks and the Divine Science Church in Denver, Colorado. He joined them, and along with Ernest S. Holmes of the Metaphysical Institute, they formed the Truth Association in 1918 as a competing ecumenical group to the recently formed International New Thought Alliance (INTA). After the alliance made changes in its declaration of principles to accomodate the association members, they dissolved the association and joined the alliance in 1921. Grier became an honorary president and, in 1922, a field lecturer, a duty that began to consume much of his time. In 1924 he was granted a year's leave of absence from his pulpit and spent the year traveling for INTA and organizing a new church in Pasadena, California. In 1925 he moved to New York to become pastor of the Church of the Healing Christ, a prominent independent New Thought congregation formerly headed by W. John Murray. Early in 1925, after only a few months in his new post (to be succeeded by Emmet Fox), he resigned and formed a new Church of the Truth congregation, for many years the church's largest. That church was later pastored for several decades by Erwin Seale.

Grier was succeeded in the Spokane pastorate by Erma Wells, who became the leader of the church after Grier's death in the 1930s. Wells, outstanding in her own right, founded the University of Metaphysics to train New Thought ministers, and was president for three years of the INTA. Her career was cut short by an automobile accident. The university was moved to Portland, Oregon, and the Spokane congregation eventually affiliated with the Association of Unity Churches. Leadership of the loosely-organized group shifted to the Pasadena church. During its first generations the church produced a number of outstanding New Thought leaders such as Elizabeth Towne, James Dodds, and H. Edward Mills. However, after Wells' accident, much of the organizational glue was lost, the informal fellowship began to collapse, and many of the congregations became independent or were lost to other New Thought organizations.

Beliefs. Grier brought little hostility toward organized religion with him in creating the new Church of the Truth, and showed no reluctance in composing statements of belief and church mission so evident in many New Thought circles. Almost immediately after the church was formed, he published a church covenant and a "Statement of the Truth" in which he affirmed the allness of God, the primacy of thought, Love as the essence of the Divine Omnipresence, and the ability to know and utilize the power of Divine Omnipresence through thinking God's thoughts. While drawing heavily upon Divine Science, he hoped to build a broader, more universal faith capable of withstanding the ravages and changes of time. The intellectual thrust of his ministry was manifest in the University of Metaphysics created by Erma Wells and in the theological text written by his daughter, *Foundation Stones of Truth.*

Organization. The Church of the Truth has always existed as a loose supportive association of like-minded ministers and churches tied together by *Truth* magazine. In recent decades, the fellowship dwindled to only a few churches. During the tenure of Pasadena pastor, Judi D. Warren, (1979-89) the attempt was made to revive the church's common life and to breathe new vitality into the organization. While creating a broad program of activities, including a Wellness Center, at the Pasadena location, Warren opened a ministerial training school and developed a new generation of mission-oriented pastors. In 1987, she led in the founding of the International Alliance of Churches of Truth and launched an aggressive program of creating new congregations and inviting independent like-minded congregations into the alliance.

Unfortunately, following Rev. Warren's retirement from the Church of Truth in Pasadena in 1989, the International Alliance became dormant. Most recently, however, Rev. Deborah Coleman of the Deborah Coleman Ministries in Ontario, Canada, has assumed a leadership role and is reactivating the organization. In the meantime, Rev. Kathleen S. Myers, who succeeded Warren as pastor of the Church of Truth in Pasadena, has continued to nurture the Albert Grier Ministerial School which has 3 1/2 year program to train people for the ordained ministry in the Church of Truth.

Membership: In 1988 the fledgling alliance had three congregations, Pasadena, California; Coeur d'Alene, Idaho; and Victoria, British Columbia; and reported approximately 1,000 members. In 1992, there were a reported 11 congregations.

Educational Facilities: Albert Grier School of Religious Studies, Pasadena, California.

Periodicals: *Open Heart.*

Sources:

Grier, Albert C. *Truth's Cosmology.* Spokane, WA: Church of the Truth, n.d.

Grier, Albert C., and Agnes M. Lawson. *Truth and Life.* New York: E. P. Dutton, 1921.

Grier, Gladys C. *Foundation Stones of Truth.* Los Angeles: Williang Publishing Company, 1948.

Seale, Ervin. *Ten Words That Will Change Your Life.* New York: William Morrow & Company, 1954.

Stocker, Clara T. *Realization through Concentrated Attention.* Pasadena, CA: Church of the Truth, n.d.

★1323★
Life Study Fellowship Foundation, Inc.
Noroton, CT 06820

The Life Study Fellowship Foundation, Inc. was begun in 1939. It differs from other New Thought groups in that its members are related to each other and to the headquarters only through the literature sent out regularly. Recent literature carries no mention of the founders or present leaders, but often quotes from testimonials of members who have been helped. Several of the more substantial early books were written by Herbert R. Moral. Basis of the Fellowship is the "new way of prayer," which, while simple, will open the power of prayer to all.

The new way is based on "Unity Prayer," the thrice daily prayer by all members for others in the Fellowship. The prayer to be used at each period is printed in the bimonthy *Faith* magazine. At 8 a.m., the prayer is for God's guidance, at 12 noon, for prosperity, and at 9 p.m., for healing. A second aspect of the "new way of prayer" is the special printed prayers which are sent to members with problems in particular areas. These prayers articulate needs, requests for blessings, and affirmations. They are to be read daily at a regular prayer-time. The third part of the new way is the special-help department devoted to short-term special problems. Members may write to headquarters for help at any time. Members of the Fellowship are urged to use the prayers as a means for problem-solving and obtaining particular goals. A golden key is distributed for good fortune. Each key has letters which can bring good luck when understood and used.

Membership in the Fellowship is solicited in numerous ads in the printed media. Members fill out a lengthy form. The work is supported by offerings of the members. The Teachings Department has, since the mid-1960s, published a series of books and booklets containing prayers on particular themes of prosperity, healing, and peace of mind.

Membership: Not reported.

Periodicals: *Faith.* Send orders to Noroton, CT 06820.

Sources:

Moral, Herbert R. *How to Have Better Health through Prayer.* Noroton, CT: Life Study Fellowship, n.d.

[Moral, Herbert R.?] *"With God All Things Are Possible."* Noroton, CT: Life Study Fellowship, 1945.

Power for Peace of Mind. Noroton, CT: Life Study Fellowship, n.d.

★1324★
Miracle Distribution Center
1141 East Ash Ave.
Fullerton, CA 92831

A Course in Miracles is a three volume channeled textbook which offers a set of teachings very close to traditional New Thought metaphysics. The material in the *Course* was received by Dr. Helen Schucman (d. 1981), a psychologist at the Neurological Institute at Columbia University in New York City. Born into a Jewish family, Schucman had become an atheist, but in 1965 began to receive the material for the *Course* as dictated by an inner voice. The dictations continued over a seven-year period and the speaking voice claimed to be Jesus Christ.

In 1975 Dr. Schucman met Judith Skutch, a well-known leader in New York City's psychic-metaphysical community and head of the Foundation for Parasensory Information. During the next year Skutch read the material and was so impressed that she established the Foundation for Inner Peace. During that year she also met Saul Steinberg, owner of Coleman Graphics, a printshop on Long Island, who offered to print the book. It was published in 1976 without any mention of Dr. Schucman. Though given little fanfare and informally promoted, largely by word of mouth, it quickly found an audience. By 1977 groups studying *A Course in Miracles* sprang up from New York to California. In addition to Coleman Graphics, Steinberg founded a publishing company, Miracle Life, Inc. (now Miracle Experiences, Inc.), and began a newsletter, *Miracle News*, which promotes the *Course* through conferences and workshops and has fostered the emergence of a network of study groups.

The movement which grew around the *Course* soon attracted leaders from among people already accepting of New Thought metaphysics, including some medical and psychological professionals previously aligned with the human potential movement. Several of these professionals, most notably Dr. Gerald G. Jampolsky, founder of The Center for Attitudinal Healing in Tiburon, California, have become national promoters and spokespersons for the *Course.*

As the movement grew, Saul Steinberg emerged as the national conference coordinator and national group coordinator for the Course. During the 1980s a national network of study groups emerged and Miracle Experiences, Inc., headed by Steinberg coordinated and promoted national and regional conferences. Numerous independent centers and teachers of the *Course* material become focus of a loosely connected Miracles community across North America and in Europe. Through the 1990s new teachers and centers continued to emerge. Prominent teachers included Tara Sigh, Jon Mundy, and bestselling author Marianne Williamson. Coming to prominence as a nurturing and organizing center fo the community was the Miracles Community Network. It publishes *Miracles Magazine*, provides coordination for the network of *A Course in Miracles* students and study groups, and sponsors conferences.

Founded in 1978, the Miracle Distribution Center has distributed the Course in Miracles and related materials, fostered study groups, and become the nexus of the worldwide network of students of the Course.

Membership: In 1998 these were more than 2,200 Course in Miracle study groups in the United States, Canada and around the world. Over 100,000 copies of *A Course in Miracles* had been sold.

Periodicals: *Miracle News.* • *Miracles.* Available from San Francisco Miracles Foundation, 1040 Masonic Ave., No. 2, San Francisco, CA 94117. • *Inner Peace.* Available from Coleman Publishing, 99 Milbar Blvd., Farmingdale, NY 11735. • Unofficial: *Miracles Magazine.* Send orders to PO Box 418, Sante Fe, NM 87504-0418. • *On Course.* 459 Carol Dr., Monroe, NY 10950.

Sources:

A Course in Miracles. 3 vols. New York: Foundation for Inner Peace, 1975.

Koffend, John. "The Gospel According to Helen." *Psychology Today* 14 (September 1980): 74-78.

Ray, Sondra. *Drinking the Divine.* Berkeley, CA: Celestial Arts, 1984.

Skutch, Robert. "A Course in Miracles, the Untold Story." Parts 1, 2. *New Realities* 4, nos. 1,2 (July/August, September/October 1984): 17-27; 8-15, 78.

★1325★
New Thought Science
Current address not obtained for this edition.

New Thought Science is a New Thought organization founded by Dr. Crist V. Bass in Los Angeles. Described as a worldwide metaphysical movement, it is very close to the Church of Religious Science and uses the writings of Ernest S. Holmes and Frederick Beals as primary texts.

Common to most New Thought churches, New Thought Science affirms that all phenomena of nature, both physical and spiritual, are the expression of one Infinite Intelligence. Members believe that the basic truth of all religions is similar, and that if understood and applied in daily life, that truth brings health and prosperity to the individual. They also adhere to the teachings of Christ found in the New Testament, especially that the kingdom of Heaven is within us, that we are one with the Father, that we should not judge, that we should love each other, that we should return good for evil, that we should minister to each other, and that we should be perfect as the Father is perfect. New Thought Science is open to all and exists as a racially integrated fellowship.

Founded in Nevada, New Thought Science was reincorporated in California in 1954. Bass also founded and led Searchlight University, the church's ministerial training school. The university offers instruction leading to designation as a practitioner, master metaphysician, minister, or bishop. New Thought Science also offers home study courses.

Membership: Not reported.

Educational Facilities: Searchlight University.

★1326★
Noohra Foundation
Current address not obtained for this edition.

The Noohra (Light) Foundation was founded in 1970 by Dr. Rocco A. Errico, a student of George M. Lamsa (1892-1975), an Assyrian-born Bible scholar and translator. The Noohra Foundation grew out of and supercedes the Aramaic Bible Society, founded by Lamsa in 1927. Lamsa had migrated to the United States in 1917. He attended Virginia Theological Seminary (Episcopal) and the University of Pennsylvania, and then began his career as a Bible translator. It was Lamsa's claim that Greek was not the original language of the Scriptures. He believed that Jesus and the Apostles spoke Aramaic, that they wrote in Aramaic, and that the Eastern Peshitta Bible was the original version. He feels that only by understanding the Aramaic background could the many idioms of the New Testament be understood. Most important, Lamsa claimed that the language, customs, and manners of his home country, Assyria (the current Assyrian language is the modern form of Aramaic), have not changed since the time of Jesus and could be studied for direct light on Scripture.

Lamsa's scholarship has been embodied in a series of translations of biblical literature and commentaries on the New Testament which deal with Aramaic customs. The Aramaic Bible Society was created to teach Lamsa's insights and distribute his writings. In 1970 Errico founded the Aramaic Bible Center in San Antonio, Texas (where Lamsa resided during the 1960s), as an educational organization to expand knowledge of Lamsa's work and do further work on Aramaic texts. At the time he was co-pastor of the Calvary Missionary Church, which served briefly as a "branch office" of the society, and co-editor of *Light for All*, the society's magazine. Two years later he resigned his position at the church to devote his full attention to the center.

During the 1960s and 1970s, Lamsa's work was increasingly identified with metaphysical movements and his interpretation of Scripture leaned toward a more metaphysical worldview associated with New Thought. During this time he became a popular speaker for New Thought groups, especially the Unity School of Christianity and its affiliated churches. As Lamsa's health failed during the 1970s, Errico became the spokesperson for his ideas. In 1977 the center took its present name and the following year moved its operations to California, first to Newport Beach and more recently to its present location. The foundation's stated purpose is to encourage humanity's potential through the study of the scriptural, mystical, and practical aspects of Truth, using the Lamsa translation of the Bible. Besides its regular ongoing classes at various locations in southern California, Errico is a popular speaker-teacher and has attracted members to the foundation from across the nation.

The Noohra Foundation is associated with other Aramaic study centers such as St. Ephrem's Institute in Solna, Sweden, and the Lamsa Foundation in Germany. Errico also frequently speaks at the Church of Daily Living, an independent congregation which shares facilities with the foundation in Costa Mesa. The Center of Creative Living in Westminister, Colorado, pastored by Mary Beth Olson, is an affiliate branch of the foundation. Both the foundation and the center in Colorado are members of the International New Thought Alliance (INTA).

Membership: Not reported.

Periodicals: *Noohra-Light*.

Sources:

Alyes, Tom. *The Life of George Lamsa*. St. Petersburg, FL: Aramaic Bible Society, 1966.

Lamsa, George M. *The Kingdom on Earth*. Lee's Summit, MO: Unity Books, 1966.

___. *My Neighbor Jesus*. Philadelphia: Aramaic Research, 1932.

___. *New Testament Commentary*. Philadelphia: A.J. Holman, 1945.

★1327★
"Now" Folk
(Defunct)

"Now" Folk was formed by people drawn around Henry Harrison Brown (1864-1918), a New Thought leader in San Francisco, California, at the beginning of the twentieth century. Brown, a Civil War veteran and former Unitarian minister, had become an independent lecturer in the 1890s and in 1900 launched *Now*, a New Thought periodical, in San Francisco. It was his belief that the most important task to be accomplished in his day was teaching humanity to know itself as an expression of Infinite Energy (i.e., everything theologians mean by God and everything scientists mean by energy). The key to knowledge of humanity's real essence was, according to Brown, suggestion, by which anyone could direct his/her subconscious (the real self) and thereby control the outward expression of the self and thus produce life according to present desire. Brown's belief was expressed in an affirmation which became the group's motto, "Man is spirit here and now, with all the possibilities of Divinity within him and he can consciously manifest these possibilities Here and Now."

Brown developed a broad program of what he termed "soul culture," the education of people in the use of their spiritual facul-

ties. In this regard, he produced a series of booklets which became the basis of a variety of correspondence courses on such topics as suggestion, the art of living, psychic development, self-healing, concentration, and psychometry. Brown lectured regularly in San Francisco, and organized home meetings through out the Bay Area.

Brown also offered a critique of the turn-of-the-century society which he saw characterized by "competition through concentration," by which he meant that individuals were lost within various social structures whose members saw fellow members as brothers and all outsiders as aliens. To this competitive society he offered a vision of brotherhood and cooperation, the practical application of the Golden Rule. To that end, in 1906 he organized a short-lived cooperative community in Glendale, California.

Brown died in 1918, and the "Now" Folk did not survive his death. However, *Now*, the magazine he founded, continued for many years as a prominent independent New Thought periodical under its new editor Sam E. Foulds.

★1328★
Phoenix Institute
Current address not obtained for this edition.

The Phoenix Institute was founded in 1966 in San Diego by metaphysician Kathryn Breese-Whiting, its president. It has three stated purposes: to teach the inner creative action of science, art, and religion; to encourage an intercultural atmosphere; and to provide a place for those who wish to live a life of dedicated service. It implements these goals through a basic course in mind science and through its affiliated structures, the School of Man, the International Friendship Club and the Church of Man. The Church of Man is the specifically religious aspect of the Institute; its statement of belief forms the basis for the Institute's ideals.

The church believes that there is only one presence, God; that God and man cannot be separated; that man hungers for oneness with the self of his own being; that this "one" acts reciprocally and man is the evidence of this action; that man experiences the finding of himself; that every man is the church; and that the principle "Ye are Gods" is verified by both esoteric and exoteric experience.

Membership: Not reported.

Sources:

Breese-Whiting, Kathryn. *The Phoenix Rises*. San Diego: Portal Publications, 1971.

★1329★
Psychiana
(Defunct)

Psychiana, one of the first mail-order religious groups, was founded by Frank B. Robinson (1886-1948), the son of a Baptist minister and a former Baptist minister himself. His bad experiences with what he termed "orthodox" churches led Robinson away from his Baptist faith while concurrently spurring his search for God. While working in a pharmacy in Portland, Oregon, he had an encounter with God which became a life changing event for him. Shortly after that event, he enrolled for the 1915-1916 school year at the College of Divine Metaphysics, an early New Thought school in Indianapolis. Around 1928 he moved to Moscow, Idaho, where he worked in a pharmacy and began to teach metaphysics. He authored a series of correspondence lessons and in 1929 founded Psychiana as a new religion. Developing a national advertising campaign, he gathered students who took his lessons by mail.

The lessons quickly became a success and within a few years were being sent out to all 50 states and to some 70 countries. During the peak of the movement he was receiving more than 1,000 letters daily. Periodically, Robinson would travel around the country to lecture. In the late 1930s, he began to establish offices in other countries to facilitate distribution of his writings, but lost most of them during World War II. He also founded the *Psychiana Quarterly* magazine. As the work grew, Robinson, as founder/teacher of the organization, appointed himself archbishop. By the late 1940s, he was assisted by four bishops in leading the organization. Members became a part of the Psychiana Brotherhood.

Robinson's lessons expounded a naturally revealed religion that rejected all supernaturalism. God worked through immutable Law and was identical with that Law. Rather than a personal deity, Robinson described God as the Spiritual Law (usually referred to as the God-Law). The Law was equated with the invisible power and intelligence behind the physical universe. Matter is a visible expression of that power. By understanding and using the Law people could rid themselves of poverty, sickness, and unhappiness. Thought was considered the manifestation of God in human life.

Robinson was also opposed to the deification of Jesus, a popular subject in several of his books. He denounced religion based upon the life of a "crucified God." Rather, he felt that emphasis should be placed on the message of Jesus: that the power of the God-Law is real. The Life Spirit could be used to produce health, wealth, and happiness. The evil in the world could be attributed to Humanity's ignorance of the God-Law.

Robinson died in 1948. His son carried on the work for several years, but eventually it dissolved. During the last years of his life Robinson encouraged the formation of Psychiana groups, something he had actively discouraged during most of his years as a writer. During the 1970s there was a brief attempt to revive Psychiana by a former student in California, but it lasted only a brief time.

Sources:

Bach, Marcus. *He Talked with God*. Portland, OR: Metropolitan Press, 1951.

Braden, Charles Samuel. *These Also Believe*. New York: Macmillan, 1949.

Robinson, Frank B. *The God Nobody Knows*. Moscow, ID: Psychiana, 1941.

___. *The Pathway to God*. Moscow, ID: Psychiana, 1943.

___. *The Strange Autobiography of Frank B. Robinson*. Moscow, ID: Psychiana, 1949.

★1330★
Psychophysics Foundation
(Defunct)

The Psychophysics Foundation was headed by Ingra Raamah and taught the science of abundant living. Psychophysics teachings centered upon the great laws of being which, when known and practiced, lead to healing, success, and fulfilled dreams. In the most ancient times, the Golden Age, man lived in direct contact with God and in accord with his laws. Since that time, man's history has been one of losing his interior contact with the Word. Truth has remained alive, however, in every age and was made available through psychophysics. Psychophysics accepted a particular mission, seeing the mid-twentieth century as the time immediately preceeding the return of a second Golden Age, at the very time when humanity seemed to have lost hope of such an event.

Psychophysics was a mixture of metaphysics and concern for bodily health. New students were given exercises and adjustments in diet from the beginning of their affiliation. The basic law of the universe was seen to be love. Headquarters of the Psychophysics Foundation were in Glendora, California.

Sources:

Raamah, Ingra. *The Science and Fine Art of Creative Living*. Glendora, CA: The Psychophysics Foundation, n.d.

___. *The Science of Abundant Life*. Glendora, CA: The Psychophysics Foundation, n.d.

★1331★
Religious Science International
W. 1636 1st Ave.
Spokane, WA 99204

Religious Science International (RSI) continues the original fellowship of Religious Science ministers and churches, the International Association of Religious Science Churches, organized in 1949. In 1954, at the annual meeting, Ernest S. Holmes presented a plan for reorganizing the Religious Science movement which involved disbanding the association and realigning each individual church as an affiliate church to the Church of Religious Science (the name assumed in 1953 by the Institute of Religious Science, which trained all Religious Science ministers). That church is now known as the United Church of Religious Science. A number of the ministers and churches refused to affiliate with the new church and continued as the association. In all ways other than organization, the association, now known as Religious Science International, is like the United Church, following the teachings and practice of founder Ernest Holmes and using his textbook, *The Science of Mind*. The organization and its affiliated congregations are major supporters of the International New Thought Alliance (INTA) and the Association for Global New Thought.

Membership: In 1997 the church had 113 churches and study groups includiing 13,101 members in the United States and nine churches and 1,130 members in Canada. An additional two churches and groups were located in Jamaica and South Africa.

Periodicals: *Creative Thought*. • *RSI Reporter*.

Sources:

Bitzer, Robert H. *How to Make Your Mental Computer*. Hollywood, CA: The Author, 1963.

Keyhoe, Merle A., ed. *A Fountain of Truth*. Marina del Rey, CA: DeVorss & Co., 1980.

Whitaker, Claudine. *God Is in This Place*. Chicago: First Church of Religious Science, 1974.

Whitehead, Carleton. *Can You Keep a Secret?* Wakefield, MA: Montrose Press, 1955.

★1332★
School of Esoteric Christianity
(Defunct)

The School of Esoteric Christianity was a coalition of independent Science-of-Mind (Religious Science) churches in the Denver, Colorado, area. The School offered classes for both interested lay students and those seeking licenses as practitioners and ministers at several churches in metropolitan Denver. Among the leading ministers was Dr. Helen V. Walker, pastor of the Esoteric Truth Center in suburban Englewood and publisher of *The Esoterian News*. In the 1970s there were churches in Englewood (1), Pueblo (1), and Denver (3). Though the School is defunct, the participating congregations continue as independent churches.

★1333★
School of Truth
Box 5582
Johannesburg, Republic of South Africa

New Thought invaded the Union of South Africa in the 1930s through the influx of literature and the visits of various leaders. One person affected was Dr. Nicol C. Campbell, who, in 1937, founded the School of Practical Christianity in Johannesburg. It later changed its name to School of Truth. By the late 1960s, it had saturated South Africa and moved into Rhodesia. In the early 1960s, a center was opened in Los Angeles.

The teachings of the School of Truth are more heavily drawn from the Bible than are those of many New Thought bodies. The basis is "Seek first the kingdom of God" (Matt. 6:33). The kingdom of God is within. Jesus longed for the manifestations of the king-dom, which in latent form is within every person. Finding the king-dom is a state of awareness, the consciousness of love's omnipresence. As we attune to love, we bring the kingdom into expression on earth. Love is the omnipresent law that rules supreme. Live the law by thinking and feeling good thoughts: love, health, happiness, peace and goodwill to all men, and you will reap their benefits in your own life.

All the literature and meetings of the School of Truth are offered without charge. The two monthly periodicals are sent world-wide without request of subscription. Members of the School of Truth are taught to tithe, and it is from their gifts and tithes that the work is sustained. Affiliated centers and study groups are found in England and several African countries. The School is a member of the International New Thought Alliance (INTA).

Membership: Not reported. As of 1985 there were no centers in the United States (the Los Angeles center having closed). Adherents kept in contact through periodicals.

Periodicals: *The Path of Truth.* • *Young Ideas.*

★1334★
Seicho-No-Ie
North American Missionary Headquarters
14527 S. Vermont Ave.
Gardena, CA 90247

New Thought was organized in Japan through the efforts of Dr. Masaharu Taniguchi. Dr. Taniguchi (b. 1893), as a youth, was a student of English literature at Waseda University, where he became a devotee of Omoto, one of the new religions of Japan. He took a job as an editor of Omoto's publications and used his leisure time to continue his education in Western philosophy, spirituality, Buddhism, and psychotherapy. In 1921, he left Omoto and, among other things, edited a magazine on psychic phenomena. Then in 1928, he obtained a copy of *The Law of Mind in Action* by Fenwicke Holmes, brother of Ernest S. Holmes, founder of Religious Science. Putting the principles into practice, he was able to improve his financial situation and heal his daughter. He also had a mystical experience with an influx of a brilliant light.

In 1930, Seicho-No-Ie (the home of infinite life, wisdom, and abundance) was begun, and Taniguchi inaugurated a periodical. Material from the magazine was later collected into a book, *Seimei No Jisso (Reality in Life)*, now comprising some 40 volumes. In 1931, the Holy Sutra, Nectarean Shower of Holy Doctrine, now recited by all the members, was given to Taniguchi by an angel. Seicho-No-Ie's growth has slowed only during a period after World War II, when Dr. Taniguchi was stopped from teaching because of his expression of extreme Japanese nationalism during the war.

Seicho-No-Ie's teaching is similar to that of Religious Science, but it is unique in its use of Shinsokan, the art of prayerful meditation. Members gathered together, or in the privacy of their own homes, began each day by reciting the Holy Sutra. It is described as a means of self-remembering to clear the mind so that the real man can shine forth. Shinsokan begins in a correct posture, sitting with the palms together in prayer and contemplating reality. A closing prayer ends the session. Elements from many sources which Taniguchi has encountered during his studies mold the basic New Thought thrust.

Seicho-No-Ie came to the United States in 1938 when Masaharu Matsuda, Tsuruta Yojan and Mrs. Taneko Shimaza began work among the Japanese Americans on the West Coast. These leaders had been through the 15-day training session, an intensive experience in the divine nature through which all leaders are trained. After the war, a church was opened in Los Angeles, which was later moved to suburban Gardena, serving as its headquarters. Other churches were founded in Seattle, Washington, Honolulu, Hawaii, and San Jose, California. By 1974, approximately 7,000

members and 24 missionaries were under the leadership of Rev. Paul K. Kumoto, appointed by Dr. Taniguchi.

Membership: In 1991 Seicho-No-Ie reported 10 centers in the United States and three in Canada.

Periodicals: *Seicho-No-Ie Truth of Life.*

Sources:

Davis, Roy Eugene. *Miracle Man of Japan.* Lakemont, GA: CSA Press, 1970.

Tanaguchi, Masaharu. *The Magic of Truth.* Gardena, CA: Seicho-No-Ie Truth of life Movement, 1979.

___. *Recovery from All Diseases.* Tokyo: Seicho-No-Ie Foundation, 1963.

___. *Seimei No Jisso.* Denver: Smith-Brooks Printing Company, 1945.

___. *Wondrous Way to Infinite Life and Power.* Gardena, CA: Seicho-No-Ie Truth of life Movement, 1977.

★1335★
Society of Pragmatic Mysticism
R.R. 1
Box 800
Pawlet, VT 05761

The Society of Pragmatic Mysticism was formed by Mildred Mann, a metaphysical teacher in New York City. She was the author of several books, lesson pamphlets and tracts. She died in 1971 and was succeeded by a group which is carrying on her work and teaching. The society has one meeting center in New York City, where a library, bookstore and offices are located. Teaching work is centered upon the textbook, *How to Find Your Real Self,* and several lesson-series. Members in a corresponding relationship are located around the country.

Metaphysics, the combination of science and religion, is taught by the society. Metaphysics teaches that man is a child of God, the great mind, and has been given everything he needs for complete self-expression and dominion over his own life. The only issue in life is the self's dealing with its own acceptance and belief. Love and fear are the two emotions from which other issues derive. Our task is to express love and overcome fear. Fear arises from the belief that we will lose. When one changes his belief to love and acts on that belief and self-acceptance, he finds that God is life.

Membership: In 1995 the society reported 30,000 members worldwide with the majority residing in Nigeria.

★1336★
Today Church
504 Business Pkwy.
Dallas, TX 75081

The Today Church was formed in 1969 as the Academy of Mind Dynamics by Bud Moshier and his wife, Carmen Moshier in Dallas, Texas. Bud Moshier was a former Southern Baptist minister who was influenced by New Thought ideas, particular the secular ideas concerning success motivation. Carmen Moshier was a music teacher in the public school and formerly a minister with the Unity School of Christianity. The present name of the Moshier's church was adopted in 1970.

The theology is like that of the Unity School of Christianity, and much Unity material is used in teaching. The oneness of God and the Christ within are affirmed. Man's problems are considered to be due to his having lost sight of his spiritual origin and of his dominion over thought and feelings. Man manifests oneness in three phases-spirit (Christ mind), soul (awareness) and body (vehicle of expression). Man is responsible for finding the inner awareness of God that leads to prosperity, peace and health.

The Today Church is governed by the members while the program is implemented by the pastors and board of trustees (and a vigorous program of classes and book-publishing has developed). The weekly periodical circulates around the country. A tape library of lessons and lectures has been established, and copies are available on request. The aim of the program is to help people help themselves. The Moshiers have developed a new liturgy and hymnology to express the work of the church. They have authored syllabi for the classes on some of the classic books of the New Thought tradition.

Membership: Not reported.

Periodicals: *The Voyager.*

Sources:

Moshier, Bud, and Carmen Moshier. *Freeing the Whole Self.* Dallas, TX: The Today Church, 1971.

A Syllabus for the Study of "Science of Succeeding." Dallas, TX: Academy of Mind Dynamics, n.d.

Moshier, Carmen. *Success Programming Songs for You!* Dallas, TX: Academy of Mind Dymanics, 1970.

★1337★
United Church and Science of Living Institute
4140 Broadway
New York, NY 10033

The United Church and Science of Living Institute was formed in 1966 by the Rev. Frederick Eikerenkoetter II, a former Baptist minister, popularly known as Reverend Ike. After graduating from the American Bible School in Chicago in 1956, Reverend Ike spent a time in evangelism and faith healing and became influenced by New Thought. "Science of Living" is the term used to describe the teachings of Reverend Ike, which focus upon the prosperity theme in New Thought thinking. He believes the lack of money is the root of all evil.

Reverend Ike emphasizes the use of mind-power. Members are urged to rid the self of attitudes of "pie-in-the-sky," and postponed rewards. Instead, they should begin thinking of God as the real man in the self. Turning one's attention to the self allows God to work. Believing in God's work allows one to see the self as worthy of God's success. Visualization is a popular technique to project desires into the conscious mind as a first step to the abundant life. A prosperity "blessing plan" emphasizes believing, giving, and prospering. Reverend Ike developed an extensive media ministry and is heard over 89 radio and 22 television stations in the Eastern half of the United States and in California and Hawaii.

Membership: Not reported. In 1974 there were two congregations, one in New York (over 5,000 average attendance) and one in Boston. Today Rev. Ike's ministry is focused in the New York Center with outreach across America.

Periodicals: *Action.*

Sources:

Eikerenkoetter, Frederick. *Health, Happiness and Prosperity for You!.* New York: Science of Living Publications, 1982.

★1338★
United Church of Religious Science
3251 W. 6th St.
Box 75127
Los Angeles, CA 90075

History. The United Church of Religious Science grew out of the work of Ernest S. Holmes (1887-1960), a metaphysical teacher in Los Angeles, California, during the early twentieth century. Born in rural Maine where his family attended the Congregational church, he was educated in the public schools until the age of 15. Several years later, he moved to Boston, Massachusetts, and soon enrolled in a school for public speaking. Continuing his own education through extensive reading, he encountered the writings of both philosopher Ralph Waldo Emerson and Mary Baker Eddy, founder of the Church of Christ, Scientist, which introduced him to the realm of metaphysical thinking. He became an avid student,

consuming the writings of the leading thinkers such as Ralph Waldo Trine and Christian D. Larson.

In 1912 he moved to California, where his brother Fenwicke Holmes had settled as the Congregational minister at Venice. Several years later, at a local metaphysical library, he discovered the writings of Thomas Troward, the outstanding British New Thought writer, whose approach freed Holmes to develop the mature perspective that would become known as the Science of Mind.

In 1916 Holmes organized the Metaphysical Institute, under whose umbrella he began to give public lectures and with his brother started a magazine, *Uplift.* He received ordination for his work through the Divine Science Church in Denver, Colorado. For several years he cooperated with Divine Science and the Church of the Truth in Spokane, Washington, in the organization of the Truth Association, a short-lived New Thought ecumenical organization which had formed in opposition to the International New Thought Alliance (INTA). The Truth Association disbanded as soon as their objections had been met by the INTA, and the Metaphysical Institute affiliated with it. In 1919 Holmes published his first book, *Creative Mind,* and spent the next few years traveling as a lecturer.

In 1924 Holmes moved to New York for a brief period where he became the last student of Emma Curtis Hopkins (1853-1925), who introduced him to the mystical element which became so prominent in his later thought. In 1925 he returned to Los Angeles and the following year published his most important work, *The Science of Mind,* a textbook which systematically presented the fundamental teachings of Religious Science. In 1927 he founded the Institute of Religious Science and School of Philosophy, Inc., under whose banner he spoke each Sunday and taught classes during the week. In 1935 the organization incorporated at the Institute of Religious Science and Philosophy, the same year it moved to its present headquarters. Holmes was speaking to more than 2,800 people each Sunday.

Organized Religious Science proceeded through several stages. In the 1930s graduates of the Institute began to open teaching centers (chapters) and teach Religious Science. Soon, a few began to designate their centers as "churches," and the "ministers" began meeting as the Annual Conference of Religious Science Chapters and Churches. In 1949 the conference was transformed into a more permanent organization, the International Association of Religious Science Churches. The association, a representative body, established a working arrangement with the institute, which trained the ministers. Then in 1953, the Institute of Religious Science became the Church of Religious Science, and a new reorganization began. Designating the various centers as affiliated churches, the new church asked each center to resign from the association and formally affiliate with the church. This change led to the most severe opposition from some ministers who refused to align themselves and their congregations with the new church. Many continued as the International Association of Religious Science Churches, eventually taking their present name, Religious Science International. Others simply became independent as leaders of nonaffiliated Science of Mind churches. The Church of Religious Science added the word "United" to its name in 1967.

Beliefs. The United Church describes its teachings as a correlation of the laws of science, opinions of philosophy, and revelations of religion applied to human needs and the aspirations of man. The church's essential philosophy is spelled out in the first four chapters of *The Science of Mind* textbook and is built around some basic beliefs that people are made in the image of God and are thus forever one with infinite Life; that all life is governed by spiritual laws; and that people create their experiences by their thoughts and beliefs.

The teachings of Religious Science, or Science of Mind, as it is also known, featured two distinctions within the New Thought movement of the early twentieth century. While accepting the basic ideas of the International New Thought Alliance that Mind or Spirit was the one absolute and self-existent Cause (God) which manifested Itself through all of creation, Religious Science developed an emphasis upon the understanding of "mind" as taught by Thomas Troward. Troward recognized a distinction between what he termed objective mind (waking consciousness) and subjective mind (or subsconscious, most clearly visible when a person was hypnotized). The subjective mind, when impressed with the images of healing and wholeness by the objective mind, could bring health to individuals. Practitioners are trained in the process of using the Universal Subjective Mind to bring healing to others.

The church also teaches a method of affirmative prayer called spiritual mind treatment. Integral to the treament is a five step process, developed by Holmes, of accomplishing the desired results. As outlined in his textbook, the five steps are: 1. Recognition of God as Omnipotent, Omniscient, and Omnipresent; 2. Unification with the One Reality; 3. Realization and acceptance of the good one is seeking; 4. Thanksgiving, even before a visible manifestation of healing, for the answered prayer; and 5. Release, knowing that all is well. Going through these five steps in relation to specific concerns, which may include a variety of problems from physical sickness, to financial distress, to tension in one's relations with others, is termed "treating" the problem. As can be seen, the purpose of the treament is not to placate, convince, or persuade God to grant one's desires, but rather to change one's own beliefs to conform to Divine reality.

Integral to the ministry of the church are the many practitioners, individuals trained in the art of spiritual mind treatment, who make themselves available to assist members and the general public with their problems. Ministers are drawn from the ranks of practitioners.

Organization. At the national level, the church is governed by the board of trustees, which is elected by delegated district business meetings which are convened at the annual convention. The annual convention serves primarily an advisory function in its receiving reports from and making recommendations to the board of trustees. The Board sets general policy, provides leadership in directing the church's mission and goals, and provides oversight to the management of the church. It also elects the ecclesiastical head of the church, the president, who serves a two year term. The president acts as the ecclesiastical spokesperson for the church.

The day-to-day administration is delegated to a chief operating officer who is appointed by the board. The board provides for the ordination and regulation of ministers and licensed practitioners, and charters local churches. Member churches are governed congregationally in accord with an agreement signed at the time of affiliation. They own their own property and organize themselves locally as seems suitable.

The church oversees the Ministry of Prayer, located at the church's headquarters, which offers a 24-hour assistance to the ill and those in spiritual need through a widely-advertised toll-free telephone number. The educational program of the church is directed through the office of Growth Education and Ministries which maintains the records of Science of Mind classes taught in local churches. Ministerial training is conducted through the Holmes Institute, A Graduate School of Consciousness Studies which was founded in 1972 as the Ernest Holmes College School of Ministry. Science of Mind Publications produces books, periodicals, cassette tapes, and other materials for local churches and the general public. The principal publication is the magazine *Science of Mind*, which circulates more than 100,000 copies per issue and has been in continuous publication since 1927.

United Church congregations remain among the major supporters of the International New Thought Alliance.

Membership: In 1992 the church reported 270 churches and study groups in the United States, Canada, Costa Rica, Brazil, Nigeria, South Africa, India, the Philippines, Australia, Belgium, Great Britain, Germany, Sweden, Switzerland, Russia/Commonwealth of Independent States and Tonga. There are approximately 90,000 members.

Educational Facilities: Holmes Institute, A Graduate School of Consciousness Studies, Los Angeles, California; Huntington Beach, California; Seattle, Washington; and Denver, Colorado.

Periodicals: *Science of Mind.*

Sources:

Armor, Reginald. *Ernest Holmes, the Man.* Los Angeles: Science of Mind Publications, 1977.

Awbrey, Scott. *Path of Discovery.* Los Angeles: United Church of Religious Science, 1987.

Holmes, Ernest. *The Science of Mind.* New York: Dodd, Mead and Company, 1944.

Holmes, Fenwicke L. *Ernest Holmes, His Life and Times.* New York: Dodd, Mead and Company, 1970.

Practitioner's Manual. Los Angeles: United Church of Religious Science, 1967.

★1339★
Unity School of Christianity
1901 NW Blue Pkwy.
Unity Village, MO 64065-0001

Alternate Address: Association of Unity Churches, Box 610, Lee's Summit, MO 64063.

History. The Unity School of Christianity and the affiliated Association of Unity Churches are two aspects of the Unity movement founded in the 1880s by Charles S. Fillmore (1854-1948) and his wife, Myrtle Fillmore (1845-1931). Unity originated with the attendance of the Fillmores, then living in Kansas City, Missouri, at a lecture by Eugene B. Weeks, a representative of the Illinois Metaphysical College, an independent Christian Science school founded by George B. Charles in Chicago, Illinois. At the time, Myrtle was afflicted with tuberculosis. She left the lecture remembering and frequently repeating a phrase used by Weeks, "I am a child of God and therefore do not inherit sickness." From this beginning, over a period of months, she made a thorough recovery. Myrtle Fillmore soon was using the same techniques which had brought her health on other people. In 1890 she had the idea of an organization to offer prayer for those in need and led in the formation of the Society of Silent Help. Skeptical at first, Charles Fillmore slowly accepted the new metaphysical ideas and in 1889 left the real estate business to devote full time to their pursuit and promulgation. He began a magazine, *Modern Thought*, and led gatherings of interested students in Kansas City. He opened a lending library of metaphysical books. In 1890 he sponsored lectures by Emma Curtis Hopkins in Kansas City, and then both Fillmores traveled to Chicago to take classes at her Christian Science Theological Seminary. Won over to Hopkins' presentation of metaphysics, he renamed his magazine *Christian Science Thought*. Then in June 1891, the Fillmores were ordained by Hopkins.

Over the years, the Fillmores had been searching for a name to tie together their various activities, and in the spring of 1891, while completing their studies with Hopkins, chose the name Unity. A new magazine, *Unity*, was begun. The Society of Silent Help became Silent Unity, by which name it is known today. Publishing activity was placed under the Unity Book Company. The first steps at expanding the organization came in late 1891 when the Fillmores called for local societies of Silent Unity to be formed by interested persons. By the mid-1890s more than 6,000 people had been issued memberships. As Silent Unity grew, the Fillmores instituted a free-will offering plan for those seeking assistance from Unity prayer, a plan which set them apart from many of the metaphysical groups whose practitioners charged a set fee for their healing assistance work.

During the 1890s, the demand for a more systematic presentation of the ideas taught by Unity led to the appearance in the magazine of the two most important teachers in the early years of Unity, Dr. Harriet Emilie Cady and Annie Rix Militz, both Hopkins' students. Cady published a series of articles later put together as a book, *Lessons in Truth*, which became Unity's introductory text. Militz began to write a Bible column commenting upon the weekly International Sunday School Lessons which introduced most readers to the metaphysical interpretation of the Bible. She also wrote articles that became important Unity textbooks, *Primary Lessons in Christian Living and Healing* and *Both Riches and Honor*, on prosperity. In 1894, the advertisments placed in the magazine by various metaphysical healers was dropped in favor of a column of approved teachers and healers with whom they were in basic agreement.

Through the years, Charles Fillmore had begun to teach locally, holding regular Sunday meetings and occasionally teaching classes. In 1905 he began to publish his own lessons in the magazine which appeared the next year as his first book, *Christian Healing*, which joined Cady's text as the second definitive work of the Unity perspective. He turned soon afterwards to writing a Unity correspondence course. About that same time, he reorganized the movement in Kansas City, and at a service in August 1906, the Fillmores and seven other students were ordained as Unity ministers.

In 1914, a most important organizational development in the Unity movement occurred when the literature distribution arm of the movement, the Unity Tract Society and Silent Unity were incorporated together as the Unity School of Christianity. The following year a field department was organized as a liaison between the school and the teachers and healers around the country affiliated with it and as a coordinating center for Unity groups. Out of the correspondence course, a training school for teachers and ministers developed. Originally a two week summer intensive course, by 1980 it developed into the Unity School of Religious Studies with a wide variety of programs for ministerial training, the education of teachers and lay people, and the conducting of national retreats.

In 1923 the first annual Unity convention was held. Attended by most Unity teachers and healers, it led to a growing awareness that all manners of teachings were occurring in the field. Concerned about occult and spiritualist ideas being offered in Unity's name, at the third annual meeting in 1925, a Unity Annual Conference was formed to govern teaching and regulate leaders of local Unity groups. Chartered in 1934, the conference would pass through several reorganizations to become the Unity Minister's Conference (1946) and eventually emerged in 1966 as a separate organization, the Association of Unity Churches. The Association headquartered in nearby Lee's Summit, Missouri, now has charge of the training and oversight of all Unity ministers and the servicing of all churches in the United States.

Beliefs. While offering a liberal degree of freedom of belief among its members, Unity teaches what it terms "practical Christianity," a return to what is believed to be the primitive Christianity of Jesus and the Apostles. Unity teaches a belief in one God and in Christ, the Son of God, made manifest in Jesus of Nazareth. Jesus is believed to be divine, but divinity is not confined to Jesus. Since all people are created in the image of God, all are potentially divine. Jesus is regarded as the great example, the Wayshower, in the regeneration of each person. Jesus created an "at-one-ment" between God and humanity and, through Jesus, each person can regain his or her estate as a son or daughter of God.

The authority of the Bible is accepted, but Unity follows a metaphysical interpretation of it (as exemplified in Charles Fillmore's *Metaphysical Bible Dictionary*), which offers a somewhat allegorical approach to Scripture. For example, the 12 apostles are seen as representing 12 powers in humans that can be used for the salvation of the world. The kingdom of God is seen as the harmony within each individual.

Unity has become identified with several practices within the larger context of New Thought metaphysics. It has long emphasized the form of prayer termed "entering into the silence," which begins with a quiet inwardness and establishment of a state of receptivity. Unity has also emphasized the use of affirmations, the repetition of positive statements that affirm the presence of a condition desired but not yet visible. In the development of the prayer life, in 1924, Unity began what has become its most widely circulated periodical, *Daily Word*, a daily devotional magazine that has readers far beyond the bounds of Unity or even the New Thought movement as a whole.

Organization. Today Unity is headquartered at Unity Village, a 1,400-acre tract adjacent to Lee's Summit, Missouri, about 20 miles from Kansas City. It moved to that location permanently in 1949. Connie Fillmore Bazzy, the great-granddaughter of Charles and Myrtle Fillmore, currently heads the Unity School of Christianity.

The village is headquarters for the Unity School of Christianity. Located on the grounds are Silent Unity, the Unity School of Religious Studies, the Village Chapel, the Unity School Library and Heritage Rooms, and a publishing concern that produces books, cassette tapes, and radio and television programs. Silent Unity offers a 24-hour a day prayer service. Within the Silent Unity building, a prayer vigil is kept without interruption.

Unity is a major publisher of religious materials. *Daily Word* is now printed in 13 languages and circulated in 153 countries. *Unity* magazine contains inspirational articles aimed at effective spiritually-based living. Unity also publishes a wide range of books and pamphlets. Because it sends out more than 34 million pieces of mail annually, it has its own postal ZIP code.

Though the largest of the New Thought bodies in the United States, Unity has had only nominal relations with the organized New Thought movement. It briefly participated in early conferences organized by Divine Science in the 1890s. It was also a member of the International New Thought Alliance (INTA) for a few years, but withdrew in 1923 because of Charles Fillmore's feeling that the INTA embraced too many beliefs that Unity could not support. Individual Unity churches have been free to affiliate, and many are staunch supporters of INTA.

Membership: In 1995, the Association of Unity Churches reported 628 ministries (congregations) and 172 satekkute nubusterues in North America. In addition, there were 75 ministries and 100 study groups in foreign countries. There are approximately 115,000 members.

Educational Facilities: Unity School for Religious Studies, Unity Village, Missouri. Unity Training School, San Juan, Puerto Rico.

Periodicals: *Unity.* • *Daily Word.* • *USRS Newsletter.* Available from Unity School of Christianity, 1901 N.W. Blue Parkway, Unity Village, MO 64065-0001. • *Children on the Quest.* • *Minister Letter.* • *Variety of Ministry Manuals.* • *Contact.* Available from the Association of Unity Churches, Box 610, Lee's Summit, MO 64063.

Sources:

Bach, Marcus. *The Unity Way of Life*. Unity Village, MO: Unity Books, 1972.

D'Andrade, Hugh. *Charles Fillmore*. New York: Harper & Row, 1974.

Freeman, James Dillet. *The Story of Unity*. Unity Village, MO: Unity Books, 1978.

A Manual of Special Unity Services. Unity Village, MO: Association of Unity Churches, 1976.

Witherspoon, Thomas E. *Myrtle Fillmore, Mother of Unity*. Unity Village, MO: Unity Books, 1977.

★1340★
Universal Church of Scientific Truth
1250 Indiana St.
Birmingham, AL 35224

The Universal Church of Scientific Truth is headed by its founder, Dr. Joseph T. Ferguson, and headquartered in Birmingham, Alabama. Ferguson also operates the Institute of Metaphysics, in Birmingham. It offers both resident and correspondence courses on a wide variety of metaphysical topics, including metaphysical healing, philosophy, sacred theology, and psycho-vaxeen. Dr. Ferguson is the author of the textbooks from which the material for lessons comes. In 1970, the church had congregations in Birmingham and Harrisburg, Pennsylvania, and Dallas, Fort Worth, Brownsville and Waco, Texas.

Metaphysical healing is the major thrust of the church's program. A basic course explains the laws and principles as well as the disciplines and techniques by which the individual attains the "superconscious mind" wherein all is attained. The church offers a Christ universal healing service which involves the sacrament of Christ healing. In the service, the inner light or divinity is released in the individual.

Membership: Not reported.

Educational Facilities: Institute of Metaphysics, Birmingham, Alabama.

Sources:

Ferguson, Joseph T. *Manual on Metaphysical Healing.* Birmingham, AL: Institute of Metaphysics, 1959.

★1341★
Universal Foundation for Better Living
11901 Ashland Ave.
Chicago, IL 60643

The Universal Foundation for Better Living was founded in 1974, but grew out of the ministry begun in Chicago, Illinois, in 1956 by Dr. Johnnie Colemon, then a minister with the Unity School of Christianity and one of the first black New Thought ministers. In 1953, she learned that she had an incurable disease. She moved to Kansas City, Kansas, and enrolled in the Unity School of Christianity. In a few months she was healed. Moving to Chicago, she founded the Christ Unity Temple, which first met in the Y.M.C.A. building on South Cottage Grove. She became a prominent Unity minister and was the first black to be elected president of the Association of Unity Churches. However, in 1974 she withdrew from the association and renamed her congregation Christ Universal Temple. That same year, she founded the Johnnie Colemon Institute as an educational arm of the church for both lay and professional education. The first ministers were graduated and ordained in 1978. In 1981, she began a television ministry with the "Better Living with Johnnie Colemon" show that aired on 13 stations across the United States.

In 1985, the growing ministry reached a major plateau with the opening of the Christ Universal Temple complex on the far south side of Chicago. The church, which also serves as headquarters from the foundation and institute, seats 3,500 in its sanctuary, the largest in Chicago. The building also houses the UFBL Bookstore and the Prayer Ministry, which offers a 24-hour call-in service for those in need.

The beliefs of the foundation are in harmony with that of the Unity School of Christianity, the break being largely a matter of so-

cial policy, not doctrine. A statement of belief emphasizes that it is God's will for everyone to live a healthy, happy, and prosperous life and that such a life is attainable for each person. The kingdom within can be brought to visible expression by following the principles of Jesus Christ, the Wayshower. The key is right thinking followed by right action. Specifically cited is a belief that rather than making a primary effort to provide for the needy, the church should provide the teaching which will allow each person to provide for themselves.

The foundation is a member of the International New Thought Alliance (INTA).

Membership: In 1995 the foundation had 17 member churches and study groups in the United States, and one each in Canada, Trinidad, and Guyana. There were 20,000 members in the United States, 350 in Canada and an additional 1,650 members worldwide.

Educational Facilities: Johnnie Colemon Institute, Chicago, Illinois.

Periodicals: *Daily Inspiration for Better Living.*

Sources:

Coleman, Johnnie. *The Best Messages from the Founder's Desk.* Chicago: Universal Foundation for Better Living, 1987.

___. *It Works If You Work It.* 2 vols. Chicago: Universal Foundation for Better Living, n.d.

Harrell, Allison D. *Follow Me.* Chicago: Universal Foundation for Better Living, 1981.

___. *Prosperity for Better Living.* Chicago: Universal Foundation for Better Living, n.d.

Nedd, Don. *Practical Guidelines for Better Living.* Chicago: CSA Press, 1983.

★1342★
Wisdom Institute of Spiritual Education
Current address not obtained for this edition.

The Wisdom Institute of Spiritual Education (WISE) was founded by Frank and Martha Baker in Dallas, Texas. Martha Baker, the Institute's president, is a prolific writer and poet. Associated with WISE is the Allison Non-profit Press, which publishes the church's materials. From the Dallas headquarters, lessons and books are distributed locally and nationally through correspondence courses and mail order.

WISE teaches the "life message," aimed at perfection of the spirit, mind and body, and offers techniques to accomplish this perfection. Self-knowledge of the power within is stressed. In classes, pupils are taught to control their thoughts and feelings and to locate their inner selves and God.

Sources:

Baker, Martha. *Sermonettes in Rhyme.* Little Rock, AK: Allison Press, 1960.

___. *Wake Up the God In You and Live.* Dallas, TX: Allison Press, 1958.

Section 18
Spiritualist, Psychic, and New Age Family

Consult the Contents pages to locate the essay in Part II, Historical Essay Chapters,
that provides an historical discussion of this family

Swedeborgian Groups

★1343★

General Church of the New Jerusalem
⅁ Rt. Rev. L. B. King, Executive Bishop
Bryn Athyn, PA 19009

The Rev. Richard de Charms, a pastor in Cincinnati, began in 1836 a magazine, the *Precursor*. In its pages, he began to agitate for what he considered true New Church principles. He protested the adoption of an episcopal form of government. In 1838 the General Convention of the New Jerusalem adopted a rule which required all societies to organize under the same rules of order. This rule led to schism. De Charms, then pastor of the New Church in Philadelphia, pulled his church out of the General Convention and, in 1840, led in the founding of the Central Convention. In part, the cause of the schism was a growing conflict between Boston and Philadelphia. The Boston church had proposed a theory of the General Convention as spiritual mother, to which all owed allegiance. Since New England votes (primarily Bostonian votes) controlled the General Convention, the theory was interpreted as an attempt by the New Englanders to run the church. The Philadelphia Society also was moving toward the view that the works of Swedenborg were the only authority of the new dispensation and contained no contradiction or untruth. This was a view opposed by many General Convention members.

The General Convention reacted to the growth of the Central Convention by loosening its rules. The rules of order were declared merely recommendations; closed communication was rejected; a new system of equitable representation was established; and the assumption of any spiritual authority by the General Convention was renounced. The Central Convention was formally dissolved in 1852, but some of its key ideas led eventually to the foundation of a new group within the General Convention—the Academy Movement.

In 1859, William Benade, a younger contemporary of De Charms, proposed the formation of an Academy as an inner circle of scholars devoted to the study of Swedenborg, the propagation of the belief in divine origins and the training of young men for the priesthood. Most members of the General Convention were opposed to the idea of "priesthood," even though it was contained in Swedenborg's writings. The Academy was begun on an informal basis in 1874. To carry the movement, a periodical, *Words for the New Church*, was begun. A theological school and children's day schools were proposed. The Academy students were pulled together in Philadelphia.

Benade, unlike his elder sponsor, was an advocate of episcopal authority and, in 1882, became bishop of the General Church of Philadelphia, the reorganized Philadelphia Association with its seven societies. Others soon joined. Tension developed between the General Church of Philadelphia and the General Convention with which it associated. In 1890, the General Church of Philadelphia made the final break with the General Convention. The General Church of Philadelphia is now called the General Church of the New Jerusalem, a name often shortened to General Church.

Polity of the General Church is episcopal; only the bishop has the power to ordain. There are three bishops. The Executive Bishop is elected at the general assembly and is assisted by a council of the clergy, and the directors of the corporation (laymen). A director of General Church Religious Lessons oversees production of church school course material on New Church themes. An active book-publishing program is also pursued. Affiliated congregations are found in Canada, England, New Zealand, Australia, Denmark, Sweden, Ghana, Japan, Korea, Holland, South Africa, and Brazil.

Membership: In 1997 the church reported 3,036 members, 36 congregations, and 47 ministers in the United States. There were 412 members in four congregations served by 5 minutes in Canada. These were an additional 1,032 members worldwide.

Educational Facilities: Academy of the New Church College, Bryn Athyn, Pennsylvania.

Academy of the New Church Theological School, Bryn Athyn, Pennsylvania.

Periodicals: *New Church Life.* • *New Church Home.*

Sources:

de Charms, George. *The Distinctiveness of the New Church.* Bryn Athyn, PA: Academy Book Room, 1962.

——. *The Holy Supper.* Bryn Athyn, PA: General Church Publication Committee, 1961.

The General Church of the New Jerusalem, A Handbook of General Information. Bryn Athyn, PA: General Church Publication Committee, 1965.

Liturgy and Hymnal. Bryn Athyn, PA: General Church of the New Jerusalem, 1966.

What the Writings Testify Concerning Themselves. Bryn Athyn, PA: General Church Publication Committee, 1961.

★1344★

General Convention of the New Jerusalem in the United States of America
48 Sargent St.
Newton, MA 02158

The oldest of the several Swedenborgian churches in America is the General Convention, formed in 1817 at Baltimore, Maryland. A call was issued by the Philadelphia Society to the 17 societies then in existence. Plans were laid for regulating ordination and missionary work west of the Allegheny Mountains. The convention is governed by its executive council, an executive committee elected by ministers and delegates, but local affairs are in the hands of the congregation. The convention meets annually. Any member may attend and speak, but only ministers and delegates may vote.

The doctrine of the convention follows Emanuel Swedenborg's writings on the Bible and Christian doctrine. Convention members believe in the Trinity, but not of distinct individuals, and teach that the words and even the letters of the Bible were inspired by God but are not necessarily infallible in every respect. Most important, the Bible contains a spiritual sense. God came to earth to overcome the demonic powers dominating the human race. Salvation is open to all who cooperate with God with faith, love and a life of uses. When a person dies, that person passes into the spiritual world and ultimately into either heaven or hell, depending on the spiritual character acquired on earth. Both baptism and the Lord's supper are administered. Worship, formerly liturgical, now varies considerably from congregation to congregation. Chants are no longer used extensively.

The convention elects a president and other officers and oversees a board of trustees. Foreign work is supported in Europe, Japan, Guyana, and Canada. In 1966, the convention joined the National Council of the Churches of Christ in the U.S.A.

Membership: In 1996 there were 2,096 members worldwide, of which 1,674 members reside in the United States and 354 in Canada. There is one affiliate branch in Guyana.

Educational Facilities: Swedenborg School of Religion, Newton, Massachusetts.

Urbana College, Urbana, Ohio.

Periodicals: *Our Daily Bread.* • *The Messenger.*

Sources:

Zacharias, Paul. *Insights into the Beyond.* New York: Swedenborg Publishing Association, n.d.

★1345★
The Lords New Church
1725 Huntingdon Rd.
Box 7
Bryn Athyn, PA 19009

The Lord's New Church (formerly known as the Lord's New Church Which is Nova Hierosolyma) was formally established in 1937 as a result of new insights among some members of the General Church of the New Jerusalem regarding the authority and understanding of Swedenborg's writings. In Holland, in 1929, articles by New Church priests and lay persons began to appear in a periodical, *De Hemelsche Leer* "The Celestial Doctrine", taking the position that the writings of Swedenborg were like the Bible in being both authoritative (divine revelation) and having an internal sense. A primary task was to come to an understanding of the internal sense (or inner meaning) of Swedenborg's writings, in order that the spiritual development of regeneration of every person receptive to the Lord's leading might be facilitated. Thus viewed, the doctrine of the New Church is seen to be from the Lord, and not merely of human production. A corollary to that position is the belief that as understanding deepens and the church follows the Lord, there can be growth and development of these ideas to eternity. When the General Church rejected that doctrinal position, a split occurred, the consequences of which was the formation of the Lord's New Church.

Societies of the church were soon formed in various countries around the world. In the United States, the Rev. Theodore Pitcairn was the main exponent. His efforts initially led to the formation of two congregations, in Bryn Athyn, Pennsylvania, and in Yonkers, New York, the latter having closed after the death of its pastor. The church operates a theological school to train men for the priesthood. The Swedenborg Association, the church's publication division, publishes books and a quarterly journal.

Membership: As of 1997, there were three North American congregations, one each in Charleston, South Carolina, Asheville, North Carolina, and Bryn Athyn, Pennsylvania. Individual members are scattered around North America unattached to a congregation they can attend. Additional congregations can be found in Holland, Japan, Sweden, and South Africa.

Periodicals: *Arcana: Inner Dimensions of Spirituality.* • *Stella Matutin* (South Africa). • *Varldarnas Mote* (Sweden).

Sources:

Handbook of the Lord's New Church Which Is Nova Hierosolyma. Bryn Athyn, PA: Lord's New Church Which Is Nova Hierosolyma, 1985.

Pitcairn, Theodore. *The Bible, or Word of God, Uncovered and Explained.* Bryn Athyn, PA: Lord's New Church Which Is Nova Hierosolyma, 1964.

___. *The Book Sealed with Seven Seals.* Bryn Athyn, PA: Cathedral Book Room, 1927.

___. *My Lord and My God.* New York: Exposition Press, 1967.

___. *The Seven Days of Creation.* Bryn Athyn, PA: Lord's Church Which Is Nova Hierosolyma, 1940.

Spiritualism

★1346★
Agasha Temple of Wisdom
Current address not obtained for this edition.

The Agasha Temple of Wisdom was founded in 1943 by the Rev. Richard Zenor (1911-1978), an intertransitory medium for the Master Teacher, Agasha. Zenor had begun to show paranormal abilities as a child in Terre Haute, Indiana. During the first decade of the temple's existence, Zenor attained recognition and fame from being featured in *Telephone Between Two Worlds* (1950), by popular writer , James Crenshaw. The temple became the center from which Zenor traveled and spread the message of Agasha.

Two years after Zenor's death, the Rev. Geary Salvat was chosen to continue his work. Salvat, an intertransitory medium for the Master Teacher Ayuibbi Tobabu, had, like his predecessor, manifested psychic abilities from his early life.

While activity at the temple includes communication with the departed, it is primarily directed toward master teachers, advanced individuals who communicate teachings from the other side. From Agasha, Ayuibbi Tobabu, and other teachers, a distinct philosophy has been developed: the Universal Understanding of the God Consciousness. Its keynote is individual responsibility and spiritual democracy within the plan of Universal Laws. The basic laws include the Golden Rule: Do unto others as you would have them do unto you; and the law of compensation: For every action, there is an equal and opposite reaction. Individuals spend many lifetimes seeking to understand these laws by which their life is governed. During the 1980s the teachings received from Agasha became the subject of a series of books by longtime temple student William Eisen, and a volume on the teachings of Ayuibbi Tobabu is projected.

Membership: During most of the life of the temple, its work has been centered on the single temple in Los Angeles, but in the mid-1980s, a second United States center opened in New Jersey and a foreign center started in Japan.

Periodicals: *Agasha Temple Newsletter.*

Sources:

Crenshaw, James. *Telephone Between Two Worlds.* Los Angeles: DeVorss & Co., 1950.

Eisen, William. *Agasha, Master of Wisdom.* Marina del Rey, CA, 1977.

___. *The English Cabalah.* 2 vols. Marina del Rey, CA: DeVorss & Co., 1980-82.

_____, ed. *The Agashan Discourse.* Marina del Rey, CA: 1978.

Zenor, Richard. *Margie Answers You.* San Diego, CA: Philip J. Hastings, 1965.

★1347★
Aquarian Fellowship Church
(Defunct)

The Aquarian Fellowship Church was formed in 1969 by the Rev. Robert A. Ferguson, who was until that time president of the Universal Church of the Master, one of the larger Spiritualist organizations. Ferguson founded the new church as a result of inspiration received through dreams. He also felt a growing concern about the doctrine of reincarnation, which most ministers in the Universal Church of the Master accepted but which he, their leader, denied.

The Aquarian Fellowship Church centered its teachings upon Bible, the writings of Andrew Jackson Davis (the founder of modern spiritualism) and the writings of Ferguson as primary sources of belief. Ferguson has initiated a project of reprinting Davis' works. Like Davis, Ferguson rejected the Christian beliefs in the Trinity and the deity of Christ, but considered Jesus the most perfect of men and a pattern for all to copy. This life is the beginning of a process of continual growth. After death, individuals go to one of seven heavens, to which they gravitate according to their earthly character, and from where they continue to work out their salvation. Communication with those in "summerland" (the afterworld) is emphasized. There are no sacraments, though infant dedication occurs.

The headquarters of the Aquarian Fellowship Church was in San Jose, California, and in 1972, there were three congregations, one each in Los Angeles, San Jose, and Dayton, Ohio. Lessons in Spiritualism were offered on a correspondence basis. Ferguson authored several books on psychic themes. Sometime during the 1980s, the church seems to have dissolved.

Sources:

Ferguson, Robert A. *Adventures in Psychic Development*. London: Regency Press, 1972.

___. *Universal Mind*. West Nyack, NY: Parker Publishing Company, 1979.

Ferguson, Walter F., as told to Robert A. Ferguson. *The Celestial Telegraph (A Message from Beyond)*. New York: Carlton Press, 1974.

★1348★
Aquarian Foundation
315 - 15th Ave. E.
Seattle, WA 98112

The Aquarian Foundation was founded in 1955 by Rev. Keith Milton Rhinehart, a Spiritualist minister. The foundation combines elements of Spiritualism, Theosophy, and Eastern philosophy into an eclectic occult perspective. It existed for many years as an independent Spiritualist congregation in Seattle. During the 1960s, however, Rhinehart became known for his "materialization" seances and later claimed contact with those same "ascended" masters originally contacted by Helena P. Blavatsky, founder of the Theosophical Society.

The Aquarian Foundation does not have a statement of belief, which it feels would serve to prevent growth into greater knowledge. Aquarians draw inspiration from, and identification with, all of the major religious traditions though the elements of Spiritualism and Theosophy are most evident. "Mediums," individuals with an ability to regularly communicate with the "so-called" dead, are valued. However, the foundation does not focus upon regular contact with dead relatives and friends. Instead, contact is made primarily with Masters of the Great Brotherhood of Cosmic Light (also known as the Great White Brotherhood). The foundation believes in many of the concepts passed on by this Brotherhood through the Theosophical Society—karma and reincarnation, the evolution of the soul, the law of cause and effect, mastery of life and death, and the eventual attainment of personal mastery. Rhinehart, the primary medium for the foundation, has trance sessions, through which the Masters speak, regularly recorded from playback at the foundation's many centers.

The foundation is committed to the Great Plan enunciated by the Masters, who are viewed as ascended and evolved beings guiding the evolution of humanity and ushering in the present Aquarian Age. Prominent among the Masters who have regularly spoken over the last decades through Rhinehart are Saint Germain, Morya, Sanat Kumara, and Djwal Kul (D. K.), popular figures in the Theosophical and I AM Religious Activity presentation of the spiritual hierarchy. Rhinehart also serves as the medium for many other "Masters" including the Angel Moroni, who gave Joseph Smith Jr. the Book of Mormon; Mahatma Ghandhi; Ashtar, first contacted by George Van Tassel, an early UFO contactee; Clarion, a UFO entity contacted by Truman Betherum in the 1950s; and the Master Immanuel, from South American Spiritualism. Rhinehart gained his early fame in Spiritualism because of his well-publicized materialization seances conducted in the 1950s. More recently he has claimed to possess the stigmata, a paranormal appearance of the wounds of Christ, which is said to have appeared on his body before hundreds of witnesses.

Membership: During the 1970s the foundation spread from its Seattle base to become both a national and international organization. Churches are located in Honolulu, New York City, Miami Beach, Anchorage, Hollywood, Dallas, San Francisco, and Portland, Oregon. Study groups are found in Hilo, Hawaii; Ft. Lauderdale; Tacoma; West Palm Beach, Florida; Austin, Texas; and Atlanta. Foreign groups are located in Vancouver; British Columbia; and Johannesburg, South Africa.

Sources:

Rhinehart, Keith Milton. *Soul Mates and Twin Rays*. Seattle, WA: Aquarian Foundation, 1972.

★1349★
Believers' Circle
% Rev. Estel Merrill
7437 Bear Mt. Blvd.
Bakersfield, CA 93313

The Believers' Circle was founded in the early 1980s by the Rev. Estel Peg Merrill. Merrill had been a student of metaphysical and esoteric studies for many years before she became aware of a gift of healing. She also intuited several spirit guides, and began to go into trances and to channel messages from the spirit world. These guides/teachers were affiliated with a group called the Council, which was seen as part of the Group Mind, which in turn was a part of the Spiral Unihood (formerly known as the Brotherhood). The council expressed its concern for humankind. Merrill's primary guide is named Levi, formerly a scribe in his earthly incarnation, famous as the same entity who directed Levi Dowling in the transcription of *The Aquarian Gospel of Jesus Christ*. Her spirit control is HiChing, formerly an astrologer in China during the Ming Dynasty.

In 1979 Merrill began to receive lessons that became the basis of the teachings of the Believers' Circle. These teachings have been collected together in several books. They affirm God as the supreme Power and designer of the universe. Neither male nor female, God is "Uni," and exists in and around all of creation. God's energy is available for healing the mind and body. Humans are a form of God consciousness who are in this present life to learn God's absolute laws and correct past mistakes. Following death humans make a transition to spirit existence and continue their learning.

The Believers' Circle is headquartered in Bakersfield, California, but members are scattered across the continent. Members relate to Merrill primarily through the reception of the Circle's lesson through the mail. Beginning students start through three volumes entitled *Spiritual Understanding* and progress to more advanced lessons in *God's Prevailing Laws, God's Energy through Thoughts,* and *God's Laws of Love and Life*.

Membership: Not reported.

★1350★
Christian Spirit Center
Box 114
Elon College, NC 27244

The Christian Spirit Center is headed by S. J. Haddad, its president, and is centered in Elon College, North Carolina. The Center is primarily devoted to translating messages received by Brazilian mediums from Portuguese into English. It also publishes books and distributes literature on spirit doctrines. Spiritualism came into Brazil through the writings of French writer and medium Allen Kardec. His particular teachings were distinctive, at the time, by their introduction of reincarnation into Spiritualism.

The main tenets of the Center are the continuity of life after death (first taught and demonstrated by Christ in his own resurrection, and now proven by mediumship), the laws of reincarnation and cause and effect ("karma"), and people's free will and responsibility for their actions.

In accordance with the words of Christ, "Freely ye have received, freely give," and based upon spirit teachings to the same effect, the center advocates mediumship as a free service. The same principle is applied to lectureships and other spiritual work. Active followers of the Spirit doctrine earn their living in secular occupations.

Membership: Not reported.

★1351★
Church of Cosmic Science
Current address not obtained for this edition.

The Church of Cosmic Science is a small Spiritualist body formed in 1959 at Rialto, California, by the Rev. William Dickensen, Reginald Lawrence, and Josephine Dickensen of Jamul, California. For many years, the associated Cosmic Light Press issued the monthly *Cosmic Light*, which was widely circulated among the independent Spiritualist churches. They use it for advertising. The group also circulates *Awareness for Cosmic Truth*, lessons in psychic development. The headquarters in Jamul, California, grant ordinations, healer's certificates, and church charters to otherwise autonomous ministers.

Membership: Not reported. In 1970 there were 500 members and 7 churches.

★1352★
Church of Essential Science
Box 62284
Phoenix, AZ 85082

The Church of Essential Science was founded in Detroit, Michigan, in 1965 by the Rev. Kingdon L. Brown, a medium ordained originally by the National Spiritual Aid Association. Brown was an early member and developed in an informal study group with the Detroit-area chapter of the Spiritual Frontiers Fellowship. In January 1964, he received his first message from the Silent Brotherhood of Ascended Masters. Eventually, one of their number, Master Manta Ru, became Brown's guide and teacher. Brown slowly became noted for his mediumistic ability, and followers were drawn to him. They became the original members of the new church.

From Manta Ru were received the basic principles of Essential Science, the system taught by the church. Essential Science is a religion responsive to the new data available to twentieth century man—parapsychology, philosophy, sociology, metaphysics and mysticism. God is seen as the cause that sustains and protects all who seek God. Man comes to know God as the Divine Mind Power as he widens his awareness to include spiritual impressions. Man is body, mind, and soul. The soul is man's divine inheritance, a part of divinity. Through the soul, man aligns himself with the God power, the basic atomic pattern structure of the universe itself, the basic energy of the universe. A significant part of creation is the Silent Brotherhood, the fellowship of all seekers of truth. Some are in the body, some have ascended. The ascended ones become our teachers as we decide to put our spiritual development above all else.

Headquarters of the Church of Essential Science are in Scottsdale, Arizona, where Brown became pastor of the Desert Shadows Church. Other centers are located in Detroit; Chicago, Illinois; New York, New York; Columbus and Tijeras, New Mexico; Little Rock, Arkansas; Fort Wayne, Indiana; and Palo Alto, California. Foreign centers are in Curacao, Canada, and Nigeria. Members are scattered around the country. Many were drawn to the church by the numerous personal appearances of Brown, who in recent years changed his name to Brian Seabrook.

In 1987, the church began a new public outreach with a mystical system dictated by the Silent Brotherhood known as the Knights Templar Aquarian. The purpose of this degree system of spiritual knowledge is to prepare humankind for the Aquarian dispensation about the year 2000 C.E. It is based on the metaphysical interpretation of the Christian Bible, and the origianl mission of the Master Jesus. Highly symbolic and transformative, this system incorporates a new understanding of traditional esoteric practices. The aim is to bring the individual into direct contact with the Divine Essence of all earthly life. Techniques such as channeling, healing, and meditation are central to Knights Templar Aquarian initiation.

Membership: In 1997 there were 132 ministers associated with the church.

Periodicals: *Monthly Reminder*.

Sources:

Brown, Kingdon L. *The Power of Psychic Awareness*. West Nyack, NY: Parker Publishing Company, 1969.

The Metaphysical Lessons of Saint Timothy's Abbey Church. Grosse Pointe, MI: St. Timothy's Abbey Church, 1966.

★1353★
Church of Metaphysical Christianity
2717 Browning St.
Sarasota, FL 34237

The Church of Metaphysical Christianity was founded in 1958 by the Revs. Dorothy Graff Flexer and Russell J. Flexer, two prominent mediums in the Spiritualist Episcopal Church. Dorothy Flexer had led the Spiritualist Episcopal Church in its break with Camp Chesterfield in 1956, which resulted in a number of churches and ministers leaving the church. She also became independent two years later.

Metaphysical Christianity, a combination of religion, philosophy and science, disseminates the spiritual truths as manifested in the life and teachings of the master, Jesus. It seeks to study the laws of nature—mental, physical and spiritual. Obedience to these laws is said to constitute the highest form of worship. The church also teaches and gives evidence of the continuity of life after death, encouraging each member to develop his own gifts of the spirit so that communion between the two worlds will become natural.

The basic spiritual laws are: the law of life, the law of love (the creative force of life), the law of truth or right thinking, the law of compensation, the law of freedom, the law of abundance, and the law of perfection. After death, the spirit continues and has a possibility of communicating with those still on the earth-plane. Healing is emphasized as a spiritual art.

Headquarters of the church is in Sarasota, Florida. In 1973, there were on the rolls some 25 spiritual healers.

Membership: In 1997 the church reported 125 members.

Periodicals: *The Metaphysical Messenger*.

Sources:

Davis, Charles [spirit speaking through Dorothy Graff Flexer]. *A New Way of Life*. Sarasota, FL: Church of Metaphysical Christianity, 1989.

___. *Spirit Speaks*. Sarasota, FL: Church of Metaphysical Christianity Press, 1988.

Wade, Alda Madison. *At the Shrine of the Master*. Philadelphia: Dorrance & Company, 1953.

★1354★
Church of Revelation (California)
Current address not obtained for this edition.

The Church of Revelation was formed in 1930 at Long Beach, California by the Rev. Janet Stine Lewis (Wolford) (d. 1957). It is not to be confused with the church of the same name formed in 1974 by Harrison Roy Hasketh in Honolulu. In 1945, the headquarters were moved to Hanford, California. The church teaches the Old Christian Initiate, a set of beliefs which the church calls a world-religion and a non-sectarian philosophy. The Old Christian Initiate, based on scientific truth, shows how to find spirit, understand the natural law and have everlasting life without death. The Old Christian Initiate teaches that people survive death in a conscious state, that they can communicate with mortals through mediumship, that as a man sows on earth he will reap in the life to come, that the future life is constructive, social and progressive, and that peace and brotherhood are to be extolled and war decried. After the Reverend Wolford's death in 1957, she was succeeded by the Rev. Winifred Ruth Mikesell.

Membership: Not reported. There has been no information since a 1966 report which listed congregations in Hanford, Sacramento, Burlingame and Apple Valley, California; Toccoa, Georgia; Phoenix, Arizona; and Toledo, Ohio. There were approximately 500 members and 30 ministers. Recent attempts to locate congregations have been unsuccessful.

★1355★
Church of Revelation (Hawaii)
21475 Summit Rd.
Los Gatos, CA 95030

The Church of Revelation was founded in Honolulu 1974 by Harrison Roy Hesketh. It is an eccletic mystical Spiritualist group whose teachings center upon the one God, who is all in all as all. Hesketh calls his higher or transcendental consciousness "Tattenaiananda," generally shortened to "Tat," the name by which most of his students refer to him. The centers connected with the church teach a wide variety of psychic development techniques, among the most important being the Rainbow Bridge Meditation, by which the leaders take students over the rainbow bridge (that part of the inner consciousness which connects the conscious self with the spiritual realms) to the White Light of God. Tat is also in contact with the ascended masters, those spiritual beings spoken of by Guy Ballard, founder of the "I AM" Religious Activity.

The church is headed by a board of directors. Hesketh is the president of the church. In 1983 the headquarters were moved to Los Gatos, California. The educational arm of the church is the Astral Physics School. Affiliated centers and churches are found in Honolulu; Seattle, Washington; Vancouver, British Columbia, Canada; and Pambrook East, Bermuda.

Membership: Not reported. In 1984 there were 5 centers/churches.

Periodicals: *The New Spirit*.

★1356★
Church of the Four Leaf Clover
(Defunct)

The Church of the Four Leaf Clover was founded in 1925 by the Rev. M. E. Claas. The four leaf clover is a symbol of humility, its four leaves standing for eternal life, everlasting light, divine love and truthfulness. The church emphasized the fatherhood of God, the brotherhood of man, the Ten Commandments and the Sermon on the Mount. The church was among the early Spiritualist bodies which taught reincarnation and karma. There were, in the 1950s, four churches, all on Long Island. Headquarters were at Jamaica, New York.

★1357★
Church of Tzaddi
Current address not obtained for this edition.

Amy Merritt Kees was a semi-invalid cripple, victim of an accident to the spine as a teenager. Shortly after the birth of her first child in 1936, however, she began to experience contacts from the spirit world. In 1958, Amy was healed completely. She dedicated her home as a center for study, meditation and healing and, in 1959, formed a study group, "The Open Door of Love." She also became a student of Unity School of Christianity, the Universal Church of the Master, and the Self-Realization Fellowship. The growth of her work, along with the spiritual communications received through her daughter, Dorothe, led in 1962 to the founding of the Church of Tzaddi. (Tzaddi is the 18th letter of the Hebrew alphabet and is identified with the Aquarian Age.)

The purpose of the Church of Tzaddi is "to teach sciences, ancient wisdom, ideals and principles, philosophy, psychology, psychometry, and spiritual truths; to promote the brotherhood of man, the universal law of truth and all educational subjects; to solemnize marriages and officiate at funerals; to perform and administer divine healing, give inspirational counsel and communications and prophesy." An extensive course for the ministry includes material drawn from Unity School of Christianity, the Bible, parapsychology, Hermeticism, and world religion. It may be taken by correspondence. Headquarters of the church recently moved from Orange, California to Colorado. Branches are located around the country, among the most prominent being the church in Phoenix, Arizona. Its pastor, Dr. Frank Alper, is also the founder of the Arizona Metaphysical Society.

Membership: Not reported.

Sources:

Alper, Frank. *An Evening with Christos*. Phoenix, AZ: Arizona Metaphysical Society, 1979.

___. *Exploring Atlantis*. 3 vols. Farmingdale, NY: Coleman Publishing, 1982.

Johnson, Amy (Kees), and Dorothy Blackmere. *Developing Spiritually*. Garden Grove, CA: Bishop of the Church of Tzaddi, 1980.

Slate, Ann B. "Your Daughter Shall Prophecy." *Fate* 23, no. 4 (August, 1970): 68-78.

★1358★
Churches of Spiritual Revelation Association
Current address not obtained for this edition.

The Churches of Spiritual Revelation Association was a small fellowship of Spiritualist churches and mediums functioning in the 1970s. Though possessing a loosely organized structure, they had an episcopal polity. Most of the churches were in the Northeast and headquarters were in Reading, Pennsylvania, at the residence of Bishop Edward M. Leighton. No evidence of the continuance of the association in the 1980s had been available.

★1359★
Cosmic Church of Life and Spiritual Science
Current address not obtained for this edition.

The Cosmic Church of Life and Spiritual Science is a small Spiritualist body headed by a Rev. M. Russo of San Francisco, California. Ordinations and healing certificates are granted.

Membership: Not reported.

★1360★
Eclesia Catolica Cristina
2123 Grand Ave.
New York, NY 10453

The Eclesia Catolica Cristina evolved from the Spiritualist Christian Church, was founded in March 1956 by His Holiness Delfin Roman-Cardona. It was incorporated as the Eclesia Catolica Cristina in June 1969, the name being changed to differentiate the church from spiritist centers, and in keeping with the fact that its liturgical rituals more closely resembled traditional Roman Catholic practice.

Delfin Roman-Cardona was born to Roman Catholic parents in Utuato, Puerto Rico, on December 14, 1918. An ability at clairvoyance manifested when he was but three years old. From the age of seven to 14 he served as an acolyte at the Church of Saint Michael the Archangel in Utuado. During these years, when he was 12, he visited a neighbor who was suffering from a recurrent migraine headache, and, as if by instinct, he placed his hands on her head. The woman was cured. From that time, he developed as a clairvoyant and healer, never charging for his services. He eventually moved to New York in obedience to what he felt was a divine mandate.

In line with many congregations throughout South America, the Eclesia Catolica Cristina follows the practices of exorcism, prophecy, channeling, and psychic healing, the rites being modeled on those of the ancient Hebrews and Christians. The church draws upon the spiritism of Allen Kardec, the tenets of which it has mingled with those of Judaism, Christianity, and Eastern religions in an effort to preach a universal Catholicism. It does not identify with the New Age movement, but believes its practices and rituals are closer to those of ancient Christianity.

The church is organized on the model of the Roman Catholic Church with a pontiff, cardinals, archbishops, bishops, and priests. The church ordains both men and women to the priesthood, a practice which it is claimed derives its precedence set in Atlantis when women were held as equal to men, and were granted the same ecclesiastical positions.

The college of priests elected Delfin as its first Pontiff on April 25, 1965. The Pontifical elevation occurred in 1976. In the meantime, in 1972, His Holiness entered a state of renunciation. After considering hundreds of testimonials and listening to many witnesses attesting to miracles performed by His holiness, the members voted to proclaim Delfin a Living Saint on October 28, 1978. He has since been known as Saint Delfin the first.

Delfin has been reported as healing a variety of illnesses including a number that were considered terminal. He also taught many others to do healing and exorcisms and anointed them to carry on their ministries. He also prohibited the exploitation of their abilities. The church holds weekly celebrations of the Mass and services of healing and exorcism, all without charge. Members pay a membership fee of ten dollars per month to assist in the church's upkeep with additional tithes and offerings being voluntary.

Twenty-five years after his renunciation, the church felt led to pronounce Delfin as a Pure and Divine Avatar and the spirit of a Solar Angel, who is the promised Comforter. He was proclaimed the Second Savior and New Messiah of this planet by the Spirit of the Lord Jesus Christ, on August 31, 1997. As the Second Savior, the college of priests and the faithful understand His Holiness' messianic mission to be to restore the teachings of Christ, to clarify his parables, and to define God and creation through enlightened reason and logic.

Olga Roman, the wife of His Holiness, was ordained as a priest on June 21, 1959, and was elevated to pontifical cardinal on January 6, 1976. Her Eminence will become the church's second pontiff following the death of Saint Delfin I. Cardinal Roman was born in Puerto Rico in 1938, and moved to New York as a young woman. She is also the mother of three sons.

Membership: As of 1997, the church operated out of a single center in New York City. There were approximately 1,500 members, 1,000 of whom resided in the United States. There were 18 priests.

★1361★
Foundation for Science of Spiritual Law
Current address not obtained for this edition.

The Foundation for Science of Spiritual Law was founded in 1968 at Tonopah, Arizona, by Dr. Alfred Homer and the Rev. Gladys A. Homer. From Tonopah, they tour the country as spiritualist mediums, teaching and speaking to small groups of followers. The winter is spent at Tonopah (the Foundation headquarters are only a short distance from the Sun Spiritualist Camp).

Membership: Not reported.

Periodicals: *Foundation Newsletter.* Send orders to Tonapah, AZ 85354.

★1362★
General Assembly of Spiritualists
27 Appleton St.
Rochester, NY 14611

The General Assembly of Spiritualists is a sovereign, self-governing ecclesiastical body. Its history as an organized religious body goes back to November 15, 1897, at which date it was incorporated as the New York State Association of Spiritualists. At the Convention in Rochester, New York, on June 20, 1914, the delegates, by unanimous vote, authorized changing the constitution, by-laws, and name to the General Assembly of Spiritualists to conform with the Laws of New York, 1914, Chapter 485, Section 1, Chapter 53 of the Laws of 1909, entitled "an act in relation to religious corporations, constituting Chapter 51 of consolidated laws," adding Article XII, Spiritualist Churches, section 262 to 273, inclusive. By this act Spiritualism for the first time was recognized by law as a religion with distinct powers conferred by the Legislature upon the General Assembly of Spiritualists. The original charter of the General Assembly of Spiritualist was signed and recorded in Monroe County, New York, on October 15, 1915.

At the convention in Buffalo, New York, June 19, 20, and 21, 1931, the delegates, in order to preserve what they saw as the principles expressed by the pioneers of Spiritualism, especially that of universal brotherhood, and to protect the movement against a felt threat from the encroachment of prejudice and sectarianism, voted to sever its affiliation with other Spiritualist groups. The necessary legal steps were duly consummated and papers signed, thus establishing the General Assembly of Spiritualists as a sovereign, self-governing ecclesiastical body, with executive power vested in a Board of Directors. Jurisdiction extended to several states in the United States and to Canada.

The General Assembly believes in the advancement of the Spiritualist religion as an idealistic, humanitarian, and inspiring movement, that gives aid to the sick, through spiritual healing, and aid to the sound of body, by wellfounded hope and faith. The General Assembly is firmly and permanently opposed to all fraudulent and dishonest imitation of real mediumship and to the sensational display thereof. The ideal of the General Assembly is to continue to raise the standards of the Spiritualist movement and to encourage study classes, reading courses, the dissemination of Spiritualist literature, and research work, to the end that others may learn the reality of the Spirit World and its meaning to humankind.

Membership: Not reported.

Periodicals: *How Shall We Teach Spiritualism?* • *Jesus of Nazareth.* • *The Nature of the Spirit World.* • *Spiritualism Fact or Fiction.* • *Voice of Spirit.* • *What is Spiritualism?*

Sources:

General Assembly of Spiritualists, State of New York. New York: Flying Saucer News, n.d.

Lomaxe, Paul R. *What Do Spiritualists Believe?*. New York: General Assembly of Spiritualists, 1943.

★1363★
Hallowed Grounds Fellowship of Spiritual Healing and Prayer
(Defunct)

The Hallowed Grounds Fellowship of Spiritual Healing and Prayer was established in 1961 by the Rev. George Daisley, an outstanding British medium who settled in Santa Barbara, California. Beginning with a mailing list of 1,500 names accumulated on previous lecture tours, Daisley traveled around the country teaching Spiritualism and issued *The Witness*, a small quarterly journal. Only one center was opened, but adherents and supporters were found across the country. *The Witness* ceased with the December, 1973 issue.

Emphasis of Daisley's teachings was a form of Christian Spiritualism with particular interest in the nature of the next life. The new insights were derived from material received in spirit communication. The Bible was interpreted in Spiritualist terminology. It was believed that the next life is a discarding of the physical body and a manifesting of its duplicate spiritual body. After death, the soul continues on several planes of existence, each of a higher vibration, hence invisible. Those with a gift of discerning spirits can communicate. Spirit life is much like this life.

Membership: The fellowship dissolved in 1994 following Daisley's retirement due to ill health.

★1364★
Holy Grail Foundation
Current address not obtained for this edition.

The Holy Grail Foundation was founded in Fresno, California, in the early 1940s by the Rev. Leona Richards. The Reverend Richards was one of a group of twelve who sat in meditation, seeking guidance. Messages received were recorded, and the Foundation grew out of this shared experience. In the early 1960s, the headquarters were moved to Santa Cruz, California. Messages emphasize man's essential divinity and the awareness of the divine as a part of one's life. Classes, using the messages received from spirits, teach self-development by spiritual enlightenment. The goal is that each member will know the presence of God within, the Holy Grail, and his or her own personal guardian angel.

There are three centers of the Foundation, in Fresno, Santa Cruz, and Portland, Oregon. Heading the Foundation are its officers: President Leona Richards, Vice-president Robert Isaacson, Secretary Gerry Isaacson and Treasurer Ruth Musiel. The foundation is affiliated with the International Spiritualist Alliance, headquartered in Vancouver, British Columbia, Canada.

Membership: Not reported.

★1365★
Independent Associated Spiritualists
Current address not obtained for this edition.

The Independent Associated Spiritualists was incorporated in 1925. It is headquartered in New York City, but has churches across the country. Notable among its members was the late psychic surgeon Tony Agapoa of Bagio City, Philippines.

Membership: Not reported.

Sources:

Valentine, Tom. *Psychic Surgery*. Chicago: Henry Regnery Company, 1973.

★1366★
Independent Spiritualist Association of the United States of America
℅ Rev. Harry M. Hilborn
5130 W. 25th St.
Cicero, IL 60650

The Independent Spiritualist Association of the United States of America was formed in 1924 by Amanda Flowers, who with others withdrew from the National Spiritualist Association of Churches because of her objection to the rule which forbade NSAC mediums to work in non-NSAC churches. She also wanted greater freedom to express her own theosophical views, which went beyond beliefs of the NSAC.

Membership: In 1988 there were 120 member mediums.

Sources:

Basic Course of Study. Cicero, IL: Independent Spiritualist Association of the United States of America, n.d.

★1367★
International Church of Ageless Wisdom
Box 280
Wyalusing, PA 18853

The International Church of Ageless Wisdom was founded by Beth R. Hand (1903-1977), a spiritualist minister, in the 1920s. She was also an early student of Paramahansa Yogananda, the founder of the Self-Realization Fellowship, one of the first Hindu organizations established in America. From Yogananda, who came to the United States in 1924, and other studies. She became convinced of the truth of reincarnation and karma. The Spiritualists requested her resignation, and she was forced to abandon the three churches she had founded in New Jersey. She moved to Philadelphia and opened the first Church of Ageless Wisdom in 1927.

Soon after the formation of the Church of Ageless Wisdom, Hand met the Rev. George Haas, leader of the Universal Spiritual Church, a British Spiritualist body which shared Hand's ideas about reincarnation. She brought her church into commmunion with his. She later sought, but did not receive, a formal charter from that church. Meanwhile, in 1956, Haas was consecrated a bishop by John Beswarick, bishop of the Catholic Apostolic Church (United Orthodox Catholicate), an independent British Orthodox-Catholic body, who had received orders from the famous independent bishop, Hugh George de Willmott Newman. In 1958 he consecrated Hand. In spite of the consecration, the inability to receive a formal charter led Hand to become independent of the Universal Spiritual Church. In 1962 she received a charter from the State of Pennsylvania. Subsequently, she consecrated other bishops of the Church, one of whom, Muriel E. Matalucci, succeeded her as Archbishop Primate in 1977. That same year Archbishop Metalucci changed the name of the organization to its present designation.

The Church's teachings are eclectic, drawing upon Spiritualist, Hindu, Buddhist and ancient occult wisdom teachings, though there is a primary emphasis upon Christianity. It teaches that God is the father of all that exists; that all men are brothers (hence no discrimination is allowed); souls are immortal and there is always the opportunity for reformation; reincarnation and karma; and the planet and humanity can be saved by the power of prayer and love. God is not conceived in anthropomorphic terms. Jesus is considered the Wayshower, who manifested the way for individuals, all of whom are sons of God, to become one with God. Humans evolve by following the Universal laws of the universe. Finally, the church believes in and uses the wide variety of psychic gifts as tools for human progress and service in God's work.

The Church is headed by the Archbishop Primate, assisted by the other archbishop, one bishop, the canons-of-states and the canons-at-large, which together comprise the Holy Synod. There is an annual meeting.

Membership: In 1980 the the church reported 2,000 members in 5 congregations.

Educational Facilities: The International Church of Ageless Wisdom Esoteric Seminary, Wyalusing, Pennsylvania.

Periodicals: *Aquarian Lights.*

Remarks: Associated with the International Church of Ageless Wisdom is the Michigan Metaphysical Society, headed by popular Detroit-area psychic teacher, Sol Lewis, who was ordained by Hand. Another famous member of the church is popular occult lecturer Col. Arthur Burks.

Sources:

Barrett, Lawrence R. *10 Principles.* Atlanta, GA: The Author, 1982.

Ritual Book. Wyalusing, PA: International Church of Ageless Wisdom, 1979.

★1368★
International General Assembly of Spiritualists
Current address not obtained for this edition.

The International General Assembly of Spiritualists (IGAS) was incorporated in 1936 in Buffalo, New York, by the Rev. Arthur A. Ford (1897-1971), Fred Constantine and eight other Spiritualist ministers. Arthur Ford was the first president. The Rev. Fred Jordan, a retired Navy commander, was ordained by Ford in 1937 and served as president of the IGAS from 1938 to 1974. Rev. Jerry Higgins was elected to succeed Jordan, but died before assuming the post. The Rev. Fred Jordan, Jr., the vice-president, was then elected to succeed his father.

In 1946, the IGAS adopted a "Declaration of Principles" which is word-for-word that of the National Spiritualist Association of Churches. Emphasis is placed on prayer, healing, and spiritual unfoldment and development. Communion is served regularly. There are affiliated congregations in Africa, and Nepal.

Membership: In 1987 the church reported 35 congregations, 410 members and 103 ministers in the United States and an additional 190 members worldwide.

Educational Facilities: Shrine of the Healing Master, Ashtabula, Ohio.

Periodicals: *The I.G.A.S. Journal.*

Sources:

Ford, Arthur. *Why We Survive.* Cooksburg, NY: Gutenberg Press, 1952.

Ford, Arthur, with Margueritte Harmon Bro. *Nothing So Strange.* New York: Harper & Row, 1958.

Royce, Clifford M., Jr. *To the Spirit...From the Spirit.* Chicago: The Author, 1975.

Spraggett, Allen, with William V. Rauscher. *Arthur Ford: The Man Who Talked with the Dead.* New York: New American Library, 1973.

★1369★
International Spiritualist Alliance
Current address not obtained for this edition.

The International Spiritualist Alliance is a Canadian-based Spiritualist church headquartered in Vancouver, British Columbia. It was founded to "bring into closer Brotherhood and Unity Spiritualists the world over." Churches are located across Canada and the British Isles and include two churches in California, one in San Bernardino and the Holy Grail Foundation in Santa Cruz. There is an annual convention. The current president is the Rev. Beatrice Gaulton Bishop.

The Alliance has a loose belief-structure, accepting as "Principles of Spiritualism" seven affirmations on the fatherhood of God, the brotherhood of man, the immortality of the soul, communion with the departed, personal responsibility, compensation for good and evil, and eternal progress of the soul. Members are Christian, accepting the belief in God and the creator, who is love, and in

Jesus, the Lord who was incarnated for the salvation of men. Jesus became perfected in suffering and thus became both Lord and Christ.

Membership: Not reported.

Periodicals: *International Spiritualist News Review.* Send orders to 3371 Findlay St., Vancouver, BC, Canada.

★1370★
Lotus Ashram
℅ Rev. Noel Street
264 Mainsail
Port St. Lucie, FL 33452

The Lotus Ashram was established in 1971 in Miami, Florida, by Noel and Coleen Street. Noel is a medium originally from New Zealand and ordained by the Universal Church of the Master. Coleen is a yoga teacher. Noel became a popular figure in the psychic community in the United States through his annual tour and his many books and writings. He specializes in psychic healing, which he learned from the Maori natives of New Zealand, and past-life reading by which he is able to trace an individual's previous incarnations on earth. Coleen's work stresses physical fitness through yoga, vegetarianism, and food preparation.

In 1975 a second center for the Ashram was opened in Chillicothe, Ohio and named "Springtime." A chapel, healing sanctuary and bookstore are part of the complex. In 1977 the Ashram headquarters moved to Texas, at a location near the Mexican border. The Ashram is governed by an eight-person board of directors.

Membership: Not reported.

Periodicals: *Lotus Leaves.* Send orders to Box 39, Fabens, TX 79838.

Sources:

The Story of the Lotus Ashram. Miami, FL: Lotus Ashram, n.d.

Street, Noel. *Karma, Your Whispering Wisdom.* Fabens, TX: Lotus Ashram, 1978.

___. *Reincarnation, One Life-Many Births.* Fabens, TX: Lotus Ashram, 1978.

★1371★
Metaphysical Episcopal Church
Current address not obtained for this edition.

The Metaphysical Episcopal Church was founded as an independent Episcopal jurisdiction in 1974 in Titusville, Florida, by Fr. R. D. Finzer, II, its bishop primate. The church describes itself as "metaphysical" in philosophy and theology. It also believes in the unity of religion and that religious paths eventually lead to God. The creedal statement included in the church's liturgy affirms belief in the fatherhood of a God and the brotherhood of man. It follows the teaching of the Master Jesus and the guidance of angels. Spiritualist influence is manifested in the affirmation of communication with those who have passed through the experience of death and the future progress of the soul after death.

The church is decidedly Christian and follows a liturgy derived from the Book of Common Prayer.

Membership: Not reported.

Sources:

Fenzer, F. D. *The Missal of the Metaphysical Episcopal Church.* N.p.: Metaphysical Episcopal Church, 1975. 18 pp.

★1372★
Metropolitan Spiritual Churches of Christ, Inc.
Current address not obtained for this edition.

The Metropolitan Spiritual Community Churches of Christ, Inc., was founded in 1925 by Bishop William Taylor and Elder Leviticus Lee Boswell. The word "spiritual" in the church's name indicates its basic Christian beliefs and its practice of the spiritual gifts according to I Corinthians 12. The church is trinitarian and baptizes people in the name of the "Father, the Son and the Holy Ghost." It affirms the Apostles Creed, but replaces the word "catholic" with the word "universal." The Gospel is described as foursquare: preaching, teaching, healing, prophecy. Incarnation, not reincarnation, is taught. The churches believe that "all men (humankind) are incarnations of the one Spirit regardless of race, creed, or condition, with full belief in creation."

Bishop Taylor was succeed by the Rev. Clarence Cobb (b. 1979), founder and pastor of the First Church of Deliverance in Chicago, Illinois. In the 1970s he brought additional churches in Accra, Ghana, and Monrovia, Liberia, into the fellowship of the Metropolitan Spiritual Church of Christ. Cobb was succeeded by Dr. I. Logan Kearse, pastor of the Cornerstone Church of Christ in Baltimore, Maryland, the current international president.

Membership: Not reported. In 1965 there were 125 churches and 10,000 members. Currently there are a number of churches in the eastern half of the United States.

★1373★

National Colored Spiritualist Association of Churches
Current address not obtained for this edition.

Shortly after World War I, the growing black membership in the National Spiritualist Association of Churches separated from the parent body and, in 1922, formed the National Colored Spiritualist Association of Churches. Doctrine and practice follow closely those of the parent body. Churches are located in Detroit, Chicago, Columbus (Ohio), Miami, Charleston (South Carolina), New York City, Phoenix and St. Petersburg.

Membership: Not reported.
Periodicals: *The Nationalist Spiritualist Reporter.*

★1374★

National Federation of Spiritual Science Churches
(Defunct)

The National Federation of Spiritual Science Churches was a Spiritualist association founded in 1927 whose member churches were primarily on the West Coast. In the 1930s, a periodical, *Spiritual Science Magazine,* was inaugurated. In the 1940s, churches were to be found in the states of California and Washington. The federation taught a form of Christian Spiritualism and affirmed a belief in God revealed in Nature, the teaching of Jesus the Christ, and the worthiness of the Bible as a source of inspirational truth (to be tested by reason and the Laws of God). Spiritual healing was emphasized as was spirit communication. The small federation granted ordination and church charters and offered study courses to the ministry. The mother church was in Los Angeles; however, no sign of its continuance has been observed in recent years. It is presumed to be defunct.

Sources:

Textbook of Spiritual Science. Los Angeles: National Federation of Spiritual Science Churches, 1932.

★1375★

National Spiritual Aid Association
Current address not obtained for this edition.

The National Spiritual Aid Association, Inc. was formed in 1937 and incorporated at Springfield, Illinois. It functions as a central office to certify and hold certification credentials for otherwise independent Spiritualist ministers. Beliefs are not specified beyond the insistence that Spiritualism is the true religion that God sent Christ on earth to teach. Headquarters are in St. Petersburg, Florida, where its president, Charles E. Lyons, resides.

Membership: Not reported.

★1376★

National Spiritual Alliance of the U.S.A.
RFD 1
Lake Pleasant, MA 01347

The National Spiritual Alliance of the U.S.A. was formed in 1913 by the Rev. G. Tabor Thompson, previously a medium with the National Spiritualist Association of Churches, and an advocate of belief in reincarnation, an opinion at variance with the NSAC. Otherwise, the Alliance is similar to its parent body. Baptism is practiced. An annual convention is held at Lake Pleasant, Massachusetts. Polity is congregational. An official board of directors conducts missionary work.

Membership: In 1992 there were 34 churches, 3,230 members, and 54 ministers.

★1377★

National Spiritual Science Center
409 Butternut St., NW, Ste. 1
Washington, DC 20012

The National Spiritual Science Center was established in Washington, D.C., in 1941 by Rev. Alice Welstood Tindall. Reverend Tindall was trained at the Spiritual Science Mother Church, headquartered at Carnegie Hall Studios, New York City, which was founded by Rev. Julia O. Forrest on May 29, 1923. For many years it was an active part of the Ecclesiastical Council of the Spiritual Science Mother Church and also a charter member in the Federation of Spiritual Churches and Associations, an ecumenical organization of Spiritualist groups which was organized by Reverend Tindall. In 1969, while attending a Federation meeting, Reverend Tindall suffered an accident which disabled her and led her to turn the center over to two people she had trained over the 1960s, Reverends Henry J. Nagorka and Diane S. Nagorka.

During the 1970s the Nagorkas reorganized the center, independent of the Spiritual Science Mother Church, moved the headquarters at 5605 16th St. NW, and under their leadership, the center emerged as a prominent national Spiritual Science organization. ESPress, Inc. was created which became a significant Spiritualist publishing concern, and for 16 years Rev. Henry Nagorka served as its publisher and president of the center's Board of Directors. Rev. Diane S. Nagorka founded the School of Spiritual Science and with her colleague and assistant, Rev. Margaret Moum, established the curriculum and theology for metaphysical studies for which the school became known. She served as its director for many years. After Rev. Henry's death in 1986, ESPress, Inc. ceased its publishing activities, and Rev. Diane S. Nagorka assumed management of the operations of the center and school as its president and director until her retirement in June 1989.

The baton of leadership passed to the Board of Directors, and during this transition, the office and school moved to its present location in Washington, D.C. Healing and Worship Services are held every Sunday evening at 1611 16th St. NW. The Board of Directors, the governing body of the Center, meets on a regular basis to determine policy and to administer the services and activities of the center. The School of Spiritual Science continues its program of metaphysical studies under the guidance of the Director of Education, who is appointed to the position, and presents a four-year course of study leading to certification as Graduate of Spiritual Science of Minister of Spiritual Science.

Beliefs of the center are summarized in a nine-point statement which affirms belief in God as the Universal Creative Energy, the dynamic growing nature of the universe; the drive of every entity to unite with God; the immortality of the soul; individual free will; wisdom as the latent power of God within; the reality of communication with spirit; soul-unfoldment and service as the purpose of life; and God as a just, accepting and impersonal Force, drawing all to perfection.

Membership: In 1991 the center reported 20 chartered affliated centers and more than 125 Ministers of Spiritual Science.

Educational Facilities: School of Spiritual Science, Washington, D.C.

Periodicals: *Psychic Observer.*

Sources:

Moum, Margaret R. *Guidebook to the Aquarian Gospel of Jesus the Christ.* Washington, DC: ESPress, 1974.

Nagorka, Diane S. *Spirit as Life Force.* Washington, DC: ESPress, 1983.

★1378★
National Spiritualist Association of Churches
℅ Morris Pratt Institute
11811 Watertown Plank Rd.
Milwaukee, WI 53226

Oldest and largest of the Spiritualist churches is the National Spiritualist Association of Churches (NSAC) formed in 1893 at Chicago. Among its leaders were Harrison D. Barrett and James M. Peebles, both former Unitarian clergymen, and Cora L. Richmond, an outstanding medium and author. The association was formed both for fellowship and to deal with fraudulent mediumship. The association is also important for its adoption of a number of statements on Spiritualism which have become a standard to which other Spiritualist bodies more or less adhere.

In 1899, a six-article "Declaration of Principles" was adopted. (Three other articles were added at a later date.) Because of its significance in setting the beliefs of modern Spiritualism, all nine articles are quoted in full below. (The influence of Unitarianism is obvious in the definition of God in article one.)

l. We believe in Infinite Intelligence; 2. We believe that the phenomena of Nature, both physical and spiritual, are the expression of Infinite Intelligence; 3. We affirm that a correct understanding of such expression and living in accordance therewith constitute true religion; 4. We affirm that the existence and personal identity of the individual continue after the change called death; 5. We affirm that communication with the so-called dead is a fact, scientifically proven by the phenomena of Spiritualism; 6. We believe that the highest morality is contained in the Golden Rule: "Whatsoever ye would that others should do unto you, do ye also unto them." 7. We affirm the moral responsibility of the individual, and that he makes his own happiness or unhappiness as he obeys or disobeys Nature's physical and spiritual laws; 8. We affirm that the doorway to reformation is never closed against any human soul here or hereafter; 9. We affirm that the precept of Prophecy and Healing contained in the Bible is a divine attribute proven through Mediumship.

Over the years, other statements have been adopted on "What Spiritualism Is and Does" and "Spiritual Healing." A set of "Definitions" has also been approved. The two issues of "reincarnation" and the relation of Spiritualism to Christianity have been the major questions dividing Spiritualists. Differing answers to these two questions have split the NSAC on several occasions, and dissent led independent Spiritualists to form their own organizations instead of joining the NSAC. Reincarnation, gaining popularity through theosophy, began to find favor among some mediums in the early twentieth century, but was specifically condemned by the NSAC in 1930. "Are Spiritualists also Christians?" was debated by the NSAC and generally decided in the negative. While the NSAC has drawn heavily on the Christian faith, from which most members came, it identifies its members as Spiritualists. The specifically "Christian" Spiritualists were found in other bodies such as the Progressive Spiritualist Church. [It should be noted that most Spiritualists differentiate between primitive Christianity, which they believe themselves to be following and practicing, and contemporary orthodox Christianity, which they strictly differentiate from both primitive Christianity and Spiritualism.]

The polity of the association is hierarchical. There are loosely organized state associations and an annual national convention. Among Spiritualists, the association has the highest standards for ordination. The NSAC is noteworthy as the only Spiritualist body to attempt to develop work among youth. The lyceum was originally promoted and shaped by Andrew Jackson Davis in 1863. Children's materials have been developed and many churches have an active lyceum (Sunday school) program. Such efforts have given the NSAC a stability lacking in most Spiritualist bodies.

Membership: In 1992 the association reported 144 member congregations. There are ten state associations and 11 camps. There were also four affiliated congregations of the National Spiritualist Churches of Canada in Ontario and Quebec.

Educational Facilities: Morris Pratt Institute, Milwaukee, Wisconsin.

Periodicals: *The National Spiritualist Summit.* Send orders to 668 E. 62nd St., Indianapolis, IN 46220.

Sources:

Barrett, H. D. *Life Work of Cora L. V. Richmond.* Chicago: Hack & Anderson, 1895.

Holms, A. Campbell. *The Fundamental Facts of Spiritualism.* Indianapolis: Stow Memorial Foundation, n.d.

Kuhnig, Verna Kathryn. *Spiritualist Lyceum Manual.* Milwaukee: National Spiritualist Association of Churches, 1962.

One Hundredth Anniversary of Modern American Spiritualism. Chicago: National Spiritualist Association of Churches, 1948.

★1379★
Order of the White Rose
(Defunct)

The Order of the White Rose was a Spiritualist organization founded in Chicago, Illinois in the 1890s by Jesse Charles Fremont Grumbine (1861-1938). Around 1900 Grumbine moved the headquarters to Boston, Massachusetts, where it was to remain for the next two decades. Around 1921, Grumbine moved to Cleveland and two years later to Portland, Oregon. The order was described as mystical and Rosicrucian in nature, pure spiritualism. It was composed of two branches, the Spiritual Order of the Red Rose, the exoteric or outer branch, and the Spiritual Order of the White Rose, the esoteric or inner branch. Both branches led members to the celestial branch of the order.

Grumbine began his understanding of spiritualism by distinguishing universal spirit and personal individual spirits. Universal spirit does not exist as a God outside of the universe, but is the radiant center from which spirits draw life. Matter is the substance of form. Form defines and limits spirits, which are temporal, relative, and finite. Spiritualism is the revelation of the being of God within each person. The message of excarnate spirits through mediums is the divinity of each spirit. Psychic abilities such as clairvoyance, telepathy, healing, and prevision were seen as innate divine powers, which, when properly used and controlled, could check evil and produce a divine manhood and womanhood.

The order had as its primary task the establishment of the Universal Spiritual as defined in Grumbine's many books. Members were organized into chapters around the United States. No estimate of the size of the order is available. Grumbine wrote a number of books which continued to appear into the mid-1920s.

Sources:

Grumbine, J. C. F. *Clairaudience.* Boston, MA: Order of the White Rose, 1911.

___. *Clairvoyance.* Boston, MA: Order of the White Rose, 1911.

___. *Melchizedek or the Secret Doctrine of the Bible.* Boston, MA: Order of the White Rose, 1919.

★1380★
Progressive Spiritual Church
Current address not obtained for this edition.

The Progressive Spiritual Church was formed in 1907 by the Rev. G. V. Cordingley, who had been one of the organizers of the Illinois State Spiritualist Association of the National Spiritualist Association of Churches. The Reverend Cordingley had rejected the NSAC's adoption of a ''Declaration of Principles'' instead of a ''Confession of Faith'' based upon the authority of the Bible. An aggressive policy of proselytization brought steady growth during the first decade of the Progressive Spiritual Church.

The doctrine of the church is derived from Christian affirmations as modified by divine revelations received through spirit communication. The Confession of Faith affirms belief in communication with spirits, the resurrection of the soul (but not of the body), God as absolute divine spirit, and angels or departed spirits, who communicate through mediums. Members further hold that Jesus was a medium, that spirits have desires, that the Bible is the inspired word of God, and that heaven and hell are conditions, not locations. Four sacraments are practiced: baptism, marriage, spiritual communion and the funeral.

A mother church was established. Officers—a supreme pastor, a board of trustees, a secretary and a treasurer—are elected by it. Individual congregations elect their own officers, but are subject to the mother church. Churches are located mainly in the Midwest.

Membership: Not reported. Multiple attempts in recent years to contact individuals associated with the church have proved futile. It is not known if the church is still functioning.

Sources:

McArthur, Paul. *Text Book, Ritual, Valuable Data and Selected Poems.* Progressive Spiritualist Association of Missouri, 1908.

★1381★
Pyramid Church of Truth and Light
Current address not obtained for this edition.

The Pyramid Church of Truth and Light was formed in 1941 by the Revs. John Kingham and Emma Kingham in Ventura, California. They continued at its head until 1962, when the leadership was passed to Dr. Steele Goodman. During the pre-1962 era, four churches were chartered, but none has survived. The teachings of the church center upon individual unfoldment. The church says the basic principle of the universe is vibration or love, which is manifest in many laws. In 1973, there were two churches, the headquarters church in Sacramento and a second in Phoenix, headed by Isaiah Jenkins, a black man and popular medium. A third church is projected for Santa Ana.

Membership: Not reported.

★1382★
Roosevelt Spiritual Memorial Benevolent Association
Current address not obtained for this edition.

The Roosevelt Spiritual Memorial Benevolent Association was formed in 1949 by a group of independent Spiritualists. Its main purpose in forming was to provide a home for otherwise independent mediums and churches, which it certifies and charters. Doctrinally it is Spiritualist, believes in communication as taught in the Bible and promotes psychical research. It does provide, for any seeking it, a study course in Spiritualism. President of the Association is the Rev. Nellie M. Pickens.

Membership: Not reported.

★1383★
St. Paul's Church of Aquarian Science
Current address not obtained for this edition.

The Rev. Harold C. Durbin is a Spiritualist medium and was formerly a pastor in the Spiritualist Episcopal Church. In the 1960s, he became independent and founded St. Paul's Church of Aquarian Science in St. Petersburg, Florida. In 1970, his book, *Someone Asked, He Answered*, was published. The name of the church is derived from the zodiacal sign of Aquarius. According to the church, humanity is now moving into the Aquarian Age. The ''man with the waterpot,'' Aquarius, is referred to by Jesus in Mark 14:13-15.

The church teaches that God is Universal Spirit with the attributes of power and intelligence; that God is a trinity of Father (creator), Son (created), and Holy Spirit (the process of creation); that man is a trinity of body, soul or mind, and spirit; that Jesus the master gave the highest teachings, and we grow as we practice these teachings; that man is divine creation, with all the divine attributes and access to God through Jesus; that all life is eternal and must grow and evolve; that the door of reformation is never closed; and that by developing the divine attributes, attunement of the world of spirit (mediumship) is developed. Reincarnation is accepted.

Besides the original congregation in St. Petersburg, a second congregation was established in Tampa, and, in 1970, a third was projected for Sarasota. However, in the late 1970s, headquarters were moved to Texas.

Membership: Not reported. There were over 800 people affiliated with the several congregations prior to the move to Texas.

Sources:

Durbin, Harold C. *Someone Asked, He Answered*. Lakemont, GA, 1970.

★1384★
Society of Christ, Inc.
Current address not obtained for this edition.

The Society of Christ is a small spiritualist body founded by Bishop Harriette Leifeste and Bishop Dan B. Boughan, the president. Teachings are derived from the Bible and the ''wisdom teachings of all the great religions,'' which are interpreted esoterically. God is seen as infinite intelligence manifested in nature and as love and goodness. Members believe in the moral responsibility and free choice of the individual; that science and religion have proved the continuity of life after death, as demonstrated through mediumship; that the highest morality is the golden rule; that the possibility of reformation is never closed, and that man can unfold and manifest the gifts of the spirit. The church grants ordinations, healing certificates and church charters.

Membership: Not reported. At last report there were 2 congregations and 4 ministers.

★1385★
Spiritual Israel Church and Its Army
Current address not obtained for this edition.

The exact origin of the Spiritual Israel Church and Its Army is unknown, but it draws heavily upon two older African American religious traditions—Black Judaism and Spiritualism. Leaders of the Spiritual Israel Church, such as Bishop Robert Haywood (the ''King of All Israel'') and Bishop George Coachman (the association's ''Overseer''), placed its establishment in the late 1930s, with some organization precedents going back to the 1920s. The forerunner of the Spiritual Israel Church was the Church of God in David, which was established by Derks Field in Alabama. At some point, either in Alabama or Michigan, Field met W. D. Dickson, who had arrived at similar ideas. After Field's death, Dickson took on the title of the ''King of All Israel'' (a title also carried by his successors) and pulled Spiritual Israel ''out of David'' upon instructions from the Spirit. Spiritual Israelites credit both Field and Dickson with "restoring" the teachings of the ancient Israelites. Apparently after the Field's death, a power struggle for the leadership of the association occurred among Dickson and the surviving Field brothers, Doc and Candy. Each of the Field brothers established a separate organization, and several other groups, all containing the word "Israel" in their names, later broke away from the Spiritual Israel Church. Because of the severe Michigan winters, Dickson moved the sect to Virginia for a while, but returned to Detroit upon further instructions from the Spirit. Dickson was succeeded in his leadership by Bishop Martin Tompkin and Bishop Robert Haywood.

Members of Spiritual Israel Church and Its Army view themselves as spiritual descendants of the ancient Israelites or "Spiritual Jews," and their association as a restoration of the religion of the ancient Israelites. They maintain that "Ethiopian" is the "nationality" name of Black people whereas "Israel" is their "spiritual" name. They believe that the first human beings were Black, starting with Adam, who was created from the "Black soil of Africa" and that all of the great Israelite patriarchs and prophets were Black men. In time, however, with the sons of Isaac, a division in humanity developed. Jacob became the progenitor of the Ethiopian nation and Esau of the Caucasian nation. Spiritual Israelites maintain that most whites who identify themselves as "Jews" are actually the descendants of Gentiles who intermarried with the original Jews or Israelites.

Spiritual Israelites maintain that they belong to the "one true Spiritual church" and that the Spirit dwells in all people. Like most other Spiritual groups, they believe that heaven and hell are projections of the human mind. The Christ Spirit, which is simply the "anointed power" of God, has occupied the bodies of many kings of Israel.

Membership: In 1982 the group reportedly had 38 temples and missions, with a concentration of them in southeastern Michigan (namely the Detroit metropolitan area, Flint, Ann Arbor, and Lansing). There were also congregations in New York City; the Chicago area; Milwaukee, Wisconsin; Philadelphia, Pennsylvania; Minneapolis, Minnesota; Washington, D.C.; Louisville, Kentucky; New Orleans, Louisiana; several cities in Indiana (Gary, Fort Wayne, and Muncie); and a small city in Ohio, as well as five congregations in the Southeast (New Orleans, Florida, Georgia, Alabama, and Mississippi).

Sources:

Baer, Hans A. "Black Spiritual Israelites in a Small Southern City." *Southern Quarterly* 23, no. 3 (1985):103-124.

___. *The Black Spiritual Movement: A Religious Response to Racism.* Knoxville, TN: University of Tennessee Press, 1984.

★1386★
Spiritual Prayer Home, Inc.
Current address not obtained for this edition.

The Spiritual Prayer Home was incorporated in 1939 in California as a Spiritualist organization. The Home issues ordinations and charters, and offers students training courses. The president during the 1970s was Norman C. Fredriksen and the headquarters were in San Dimas, California. Recent attempts to locate the church have failed.

Membership: Not reported.

★1387★
Spiritual Science Mother Church
Current address not obtained for this edition.

Mother Julia O. Forrest, a former Christian Science practitioner, became a Spiritualist and, with Dr. Carl H. Pieres, organized a new body modeled on the Christian Science Mother Church in Boston. The Spiritual Science Mother Church is headquartered in New York City. From its ruling ecclesiastical council, it issues charters and runs the Spiritual Science Institute for training ministers. Forrest was succeeded by Glenn Argoe as president of the council and pastor of the mother church in New York City.

From Christian Science the idea of the mother church is retained, as is the concept of demonstration of spiritual realities in this life. Three principles of demonstration are emphasized: preaching, or the giving out to each one through messages (clairvoyance) what God has for him to do; communications from other realms, and healing through the channelling of healing power. Spiritual Science is specifically Christian in its orientation, holding that Jesus Christ is lord and master and dispenser of the law of love. The Trinity of God the Father and creator, the virgin-born Son and Holy Spirit is affirmed. Man is a free agent on a spiritual path which has included past reincarnations. A major emphasis is on soul-unfoldment. Salvation comes as a cleansing process through intelligent prayer.

Membership: Not reported. In the 1970s there were approximately 40 churches.

Educational Facilities: Spiritual Science Institute, New York, New York.

★1388★
Spiritualist Episcopal Church
Current address not obtained for this edition.

The Spiritualist Episcopal Church was formed in 1941 by the Revs. Clifford Bias, John Bunker and Robert Chaney, all prominent mediums at Camp Chesterfield in Indiana. Bias and Bunker were members of the Independent Spiritualist Association and Chaney was a member of the National Spiritualist Association of Churches (NSAC). The founders expressed dissatisfaction with an overemphasis on phenomena within Spiritualism; they wanted a greater emphasis on philosophy, particularly that channeled from the spirit realm.

The beliefs of the church resemble those of the NSAC. Reincarnation is not accepted. Inspiration is drawn from the world's religions, especially Christianity and Buddhism. For many years, the summer seminary at Camp Chesterfield was conducted by the Spiritualist Episcopal Church, and lessons leading toward ordination were developed. The Rev. Ivy Hooper was prominent in the production of this material, which while basically Spiritualist, incorporates material from the Rosicrucian and theosophical traditions.

Significant in the history of the Spiritualist Episcopal Church was the disruption in 1956. In that year, a morals charge was brought against a prominent medium, a candidate for a church office. Camp Chesterfield, where the church had its headquarters, was split between those supporting and those opposing the medium. After attempting to dissuade the medium from seeking office, the Rev. Dorothy Graff Flexer moved the church headquarters to Lansing, Michigan, hoping to keep the divisiveness at Camp Chesterfield from spreading throughout the church. The break between the camp and the leaders of the Spiritualist Episcopal Church was complete when the church was forbidden to hold classes at the camp's summer seminary, and the church's mediums were forbidden to work there.

Membership: Not reported.

Sources:

Chaney, Robert G. *"Hear My Prayer".* Eaton Rapids, MI: Library, The Spiritualist Episcopal Church, 1942.

Development of Mediumship. Dimondale, MI: Spiritual Episcopal Church, n.d.

★1389★
Superet Light Doctrine Church
2516 W. Third St.
Los Angeles, CA 90057

The Superet Light Doctrine Church was founded in Los Angeles in 1925 by Dr. Josephine De Croix Trust (d. 1957), called Mother Trust by her followers. According to Superet Light belief, Mother Trust was a Light Scientist who found Jesus' religion because she had the gift to see the light, vibration and aura of Jesus' words. At the age of four, Mother Trust was able to see auras. Twelve years later, she developed tuberculosis. In a vision, Jesus healed her and gave her the mission of bringing to the world his light teachings. She gained a reputation around New York City as a miracle healer. She also began to study the Bible and discovered that only Jesus' words shone with light.

Soon she began to realize the secret of the Mother God. In a revelation, she was told, "This is the new name, Superet, which is the everlasting Fire in God's sacred purple Heart." She discovered that there are two purple hearts united in one, and that the Holy Ghost is the Mother God. This doctrine was not heretofore revealed, because men looked upon women only as breeders.

The Superet Science is the manifestation of God's light through our light atom aura. All substances that possess magnetism, especially all life, have an aura, an invisible emanation. Mother Trust, as an aura scientist, was able to see both the outer and inner aura (or light of the soul). The light atom aura, capable of receiving God's light, is produced by developing one's inner aura. Through use of the aura light, healing is effected and people are made successful in their daily lives.

New affiliates of the church may take one of several lesson series which explain basic Superet Light beliefs, such as "The Superet Light Lessons" or the "Golden Test Lessons." Mother Trust wrote over 25 books, most of which are available to the general public. Also associated is the Prince of Peace Movement, inaugurated by Mother Trust on Christmas Day, 1938, in Bethlehem. It is considered a movement for people of all religions.

Membership: Not reported. In 1988 there were three churches in the United States (Los Angeles, California, Washington, D.C., and Reynoldsville, Pennsylvania) and one in Prince George, British Columbia. There were also churches in Mexico (one), Nigeria (13), and Panama (one). There were eight Prince of Peace clubs in the United States, two each in Nigeria and Panama, and one each in Jamaica, Trinidad, Mexico, and the Bahamas.

Periodicals: *Newsletter of the Superetist Brotherhood and Sisterhood.* Send orders to 1516 W. Third St., Los Angeles, CA 90057.

Sources:

Miracle Woman's Secrets. Los Angeles: Superet Press, 1949.

Superet Light Doctrine Ministry. Los Angeles: Superet Press, 1947.

Trust, Josephine C. *Bible Mystery by Superet Light Science.* Los Angeles: Superet Press, 1950.

___. *Superet Light.* Los Angeles: Superet Light Center, 1953.

___. *Superet Light Doctrine.* Los Angeles: Superet Press, 1949.

★1390★
T.O.M. Religious Foundation
Box 52
Chimayo, NM 87522

The T.O.M. Religious Foundation was founded in the 1960s by the Rev. Ruth Johnson of Velarde, New Mexico. The Reverend Johnson achieved her leadership through knowledge gained from study, experience and previous lives. In 1970, the Foundation was moved to Canon City, Colorado. The Teachings are transmitted primarily through the correspondence studies, "Moon Time Studies in Spiritual Culture." Students receive instructions in dreams and the Bible, ESP and psychic development, and "Atlantis" and "Original Christianity." God is conceived as the divine one, or Whole, or Spirit, who knows, loves and cares for us. He manifests his love through spiritual guidance. Students learn the language of the soul, which supplies lines of communication with the spirit world. Graduates may be ordained as ministers and receive a franchise from the foundation.

Membership: Not reported.

★1391★
Temple of Universal Law
5030 N. Drake
Chicago, IL 60625

The Temple of Universal Law was founded in 1936 by the Rev. Charlotte Bright. The Reverend Bright is a medium under the guidance of Master Nicodemus, the control and directing voice who speaks through the Reverend Bright. In 1965, a temple was erected in Chicago on the North Side. Teachings were given through the Reverend Bright by the Masters of the Great White Brotherhood. The Reverend Bright passed away in 1989, but the control and directing voice, as well as other masters of the brotherhood, speak through her son and successor, the Rev. Robert E. Martin.

The Temple describes itself as a nondenominational church based in metaphysical Christianity. Members believe in God who expresses himself as a Trinity. God the Father is the universal law of life which creates, sustains, and progresses to eternal life. Christ is the perfect demonstration of divine mind. The Holy Spirit is the action of divine mind within. Worship can come in many forms. Truth is found in the Bible and in all spiritual traditions. Man in immortal. The essential duty of man is to look within and begin to awaken the Christ Spirit. Only by learning and understanding universal law can we come into oneness with God. The Lord's Supper is celebrated on the first Sunday in each month.

A complete program of classes, special workshops and lectures, and various services emphasizing communication with spirits supplement the Sunday worship. A library is maintained, and numerous booklets have been published. A branch temple is located in Wisconsin near Winter.

Membership: In 1988, the church reported two congregations with more than 200 members served by 11 minister-mediums. There were also 12 missionaries (channels) affiliated with the church.

Periodicals: *Temple Messenger.*

★1392★
United Spiritualist Church
813 W. 165th Pl.
Gardena, CA 90247

The United Spiritualist Church was founded in 1967 by the Rev. Floyd Humble, Edwin Potter, and Howard Mangan. The Reverend Humble had earlier served several independent Spiritualist Churches. The United Spiritualist Church differs from most Spiritualist churches by its adoption of a centralized form of government. Power is invested in the presidency which includes the president, first advisor-secretary and second advisor-treasurer. Under the presidency is the board of governors. There is also a board of publication, education, and church extension and missions. There is a general conference which elects the board of governors.

The beliefs and practices of the church are out of the consensus of Spiritualism. Members believe in mediumship, both mental and physical, and follow the practices of Jesus in preaching, healing, teaching and prophecy. Man is considered immortal; the unfoldment and development of individuals are means to bring the kingdom of God on earth.

Membership: Not reported.

Periodicals: *The Spiritual Outlook.* Send orders to 809 W. 165th Place, Gardena, CA 90247.

Sources:

Humble, Floyd. *Bible Lessons.* Gardena, CA: United Spiritualist Church, 1969.

★1393★
Universal Christ Church, Inc.
Current address not obtained for this edition.

The Universal Christ Church was formed in 1970 by the coming together in fellowship of several Spiritualist churches in the Los Angeles area. Doctrine is Spiritualist, and reincarnation is accepted. There is an element of ritualism in the worship; the clergy wear clerical vestments. The Rev. Anthony Benik is the head of the church.

Membership: Not reported. In 1971 there were 5 churches, all in the Los Angeles area, and one 500-member congregation in Australia.

Periodicals: *U.C.C. Spokesman.* Send orders to 1704 Venice Blvd., Los Angeles, CA 90006.

★1394★
Universal Church of Psychic Science
Current address not obtained for this edition.

The Universal Church of Psychic Science is a small Spiritualist body headquartered in Philadelphia and headed by W. L. Salisbury, its president, and Clarence Smith, its secretary. The group is limited to the states of New Jersey, Maryland and Pennsylvania. The Church issues ordinations and church charters.

Membership: Not reported.

★1395★
Universal Church of the Master
National Headquarters
501 Washington St.
Santa Clara, CA 95050

The Universal Church of the Master (UCM) was formed in 1908 in Los Angeles, California, and was incorporated in 1918. Until recently, it was largely a West Coast association of ministers and churches, but it began to spread across the nation in the 1960's. Among its early leaders was Dr. B. J. Fitzgerald, author of *A New Text of Spiritual Philosophy and Religion*, the basic book of the UCM. In 1930, the headquarters were moved to Oakland and then, in 1966, after Dr. Fitzgerald's transition (death), to San Jose.

The church sees itself as both Christian and Universal in its religious philosophy. While it uses much out of liberal Christianity, it also is eclectic, allowing a wide range of beliefs to exist. Its ten-point statement, drawn from the *Text*, affirms belief in the fatherhood of God and the brotherhood of man, the laws of nature and living in harmony with them, life after death, commmunication with the unseen world, the golden rule, individual responsibility and the continual possibility of improvement, prophecy, and the eternal progress of the soul. The emphasis on the laws of nature denies any supernaturalism or miraculous nature in the communication phenomena. The church also uses *The Aquarian Gospel of Jesus the Christ* by Levi Dowling as a source for its teachings.

The UCM is headed by a governing board including the president, other officers and trustees. There is an annual membership meeting. An examining committee approves all ordinations and certifications. The board of trustees grants charters. The polity is congregational.

Membership: In 1997 the church reported 176 congregations, 850 ministers and 8,987 lay-members.

Periodicals: *UCM Quarterly Magazine.*

Sources:

Dowling, Levi. *The Aquarian Gospel of Jesus the Christ.* Los Angeles: Leo W. Dowling, 1925.

Fitzgerald, B. J. *A New Text of Spiritual Philosophy and Religion.* San Jose, CA: Universal Church of the Master, 1954.

Universal Church of the Master, History and Principles. Santa Clara, CA: Universal Church of the Master, 1995.

★1396★
Universal Hagar's Spiritual Church (UHSC)
Current address not obtained for this edition.

The Universal Hagar's Spiritual Church (UHSC) was founded by Father George Willie Hurley, a contemporary of Father Divine and also a self-proclaimed god. Hurley was born in 1884 in Reynolds, Georgia, and received his early training as a Baptist minister, though he later became a Methodist. After moving to Detroit, Michigan, with his wife in 1919, he joined a small Holiness sect called Triumph the Church and Kingdom of God in Christ and actually became its Presiding Prince for the state of Michigan.

Then in the early 1920s, Hurley became a minister in the National Spiritual Church, probably a predominantly White organization, which brigded his transition into the leader of his own church established in Detroit on September 23, 1923. In 1924 he established the School of Mediumship and Psychology, which eventually became a secret auxiliary in each congregation affiliated with UHSC. Father Hurley maintained that the school is a branch of the Great School of the Prophets, which Jesus attended during the eighteen years of his life that are not accounted for in the Bible. He also established the Knights of the All Seeing Eye, a Masonic-like auxiliary open to both men and women. By the eve of Hurley's death on June 23, 1943, UHSC had grown to an association of at least 37 congregations (eight in Michigan, eight in Ohio, six in Pennsylvania, seven in New Jersey, five in New York City, and single congregations in West Virginia, Delaware, and Illinois).

Similiar to other Black Spiritual groups, UHSC inherited a eclectic religious heritage, drawing elements from Spiritualism, Catholicism, African-American Protestantism, and possibly Voodoo or hoodoo. Father Hurley also incorporated concepts from the *Aquarian Gospel of Jesus Christ*, astrology, Ethiopianism, and other belief systems in his church. Sometime around 1933 if not earlier, Father Hurley began to teach his followers that his "carnal flesh" had been "transformed into the flesh of Christ." He maintained that just as Adam had been the God of the Taurian Age, Abraham the God of the Arian Age, and Jesus the God of the Piscean Age, he was the God of the Aquarian Age. Unlike most Spiritual churches, which have assumed an apolitical posture and refused, for example, to participate in the Civil Rights Movement, Hurley took unequivocal stands on a number of social issues, particularly the status of African Americans in the larger society, and urged his followers to vote for Franklin D. Roosevelt. Since Hurley's death the strongly nationalist and critical rhetoric of his church has been considerably tempered.

Father Hurley's successors as head of UHSC have included Prince Thomas Surbadger, Mother Mary Hatchett, Prince Alfred Bailey, and Rev. G. Latimer, a daughter of Hurley. The Wiseman Board, which has consisted primarily of women in recent decades, serves as UHSC's governing body. Over the years, the heaviest concentrations of Hagar's congregations have been in southeastern Michigan, where the association's headquarters is located, and in the New York-New Jersey megalopolis. The affiliations of individual member congregations have changed considerably over the years, and especially since the early 1960s, UHSC has experienced significant fluctuations in the number of its congregations in the East and Midwest, somewhat offset by the spread of the church to California and the Southeast.

Membership: In 1965 UHSC had 41 congregations in eight states. In 1980 it had 35 congregations in 11 states.

Sources:

Baer, Hans A. *The Black Spiritual Movement: A Religious Response to Racism.* Knoxville, TN: University of Tennessee Press, 1984.

★1397★
Universal Harmony Foundation
5903 Seminole Blvd.
Seminole, FL 33542

The Universal Harmony Foundation grew out of and superceded the Universal Psychic Science Association, founded in 1942 by the Rev. Helene Gerling and her husband, J. Bertram Gerling. Both had been prominent mediums at Lily Dale Spiritualist Camp near Rochester, New York. Headquarters were later moved to St. Petersburg, Florida, where a seminary was opened, offering nine courses leading to ordination as minister, healer, missionary, or teacher. Headquarters are now in Seminole, Florida.

Teachings of the foundation are eclectic, drawn from the universal revelation and the tested teachings of all the world's prophets. Study is directed toward metaphysics, healing, comparative religion, Bible, yoga, and mysticism. The seven affirmation-tenets present a religion premised upon the religious and scientific demonstrations of the talents and powers of the Living Spirit. They affirm the fatherhood of God and brotherhood of man, the eternality of life, the power of prayer, spiritual healing, the reality of the psychic, soul-growth as the purpose of life, and fraternal service as the way of life. The Torch of Truth, the symbol of universal harmony, is lighted at the beginning of all services.

There is a mother church, the first chartered by the foundation, and members are encouraged to join it by participation in an annual free-will offering. Ministers are organized into a ministerial fellowship. They may apply for temple (i.e., congregation) charters. Rev. Gerling is the author of correspondence lessons offered through the seminary and a number of books. Rev. Gerling retired in 1988 and was succeeded by Rev. Nancy Castillo.

Membership: In 1997 the church reported 125 members all in the United States. There were five affiliated congregations.

Educational Facilities: Universal Harmony Foundation Seminary, Seminole, Florida.

Periodicals: *The Spiritual Digest.*

Sources:

Gerling, Helene A. *Healthy Intuitive Development.* New York: Exposition Press, 1971.

★1398★
Universal Religion of America
% Christ Universal Church
295 N. Tropical Trail
Merritt Island, FL 32952

The Universal Religion of America was founded in 1958 by the Rev. Marnie Koski, pastor of a church in Kenosha, Wisconsin, and a former minister of the Spiritual Science Mother Church. The body is Spiritualist and Pentecostal, and emphasizes ESP and the spiritual gifts such as speaking in tongues. Koski is also known to her followers as Soraya (meaning a "Solar Ray"), because she has served as a medium for some contemporary messages from Jesus. Leaving the Kenosha congregation to assistants, Koski moved the headquarters to Rockledge, Florida, and then more recently to the Metaphysical Center in Merritt Island.

Membership: Not reported. In 1968 there were 500 members. There are two congregations, one in Wisconsin and one in Florida.

Sources:

Koski, Marnie. *Person Talks with Jesus.* Washington, DC: ESPress, 1979.

★1399★
Universal Spiritualist Association
4905 W. University Ave.
Muncie, IN 47304-3460

The Universal Spiritualist Association was founded in 1956 at the suggestion of Mabel Riffle, long-time secretary of Camp Chesterfield (Indiana Association of Spiritualists). The occasion for the founding of the "Universal" was the break between Camp Chesterfield and the Spiritualist Episcopal Church which had been in charge of the theological training institutes held each summer as an important part of Camp Chesterfield's program. Most of the founders of the Universal Spiritualist Association had been members of the Spiritualist Episcopal Church. Clifford Bias (1910-1987) was installed as the Universal's first president, a post he held until his death in 1987. He was succeeded by Warren Smith who retired from his Spiritualist activities in 1990. He was succeeded by the current President, T. Ernest Nichols, who is also Director of the Maple Grove Spiritual Retreat.

From 1956 until 1970, the Universal's work, headquarters, and ministerial training programs, now called the Institute for Holistic Studies, were centered around Camp Chesterfield. As the result of a dispute between the two organizations, the Institute sessions were held at a variety of locations around the USA, and Camp Chesterfield began to develop its own system of spiritual studies. In 1985, the headquarters of the Universal Spiritualist Association were permanently housed in a five-acre tract called the Maple Grove Spiritual Retreat, a property with housing, food services, auditorium, and class facilities appropriate for conducting the Institute for Holistic Studies sessions.

The Universal Spiritualist Association is composed of people who believe in and practice Spiritualism, described as "the Science, Philosophy, and Religion of continuous life, based upon the demonstrated fact of communication by means of channeling (mediumship) with those who live in the Spiritual World." The Association and its churches affirm the belief of the Creatorship of God, the oneness of all life everywhere, the leadership of the Christ, salvation by character, and the progression of humanity upward and onward forever.

Maple Grove Spiritual Retreat is located in Anderson, near Indianapolis, Indiana, and established in 1984 by Clifford Bias as the international headquarters and educational center of the Universal Spiritualist Association and sanctuary of the Metaphysical Gnostic Church of the New Age. Teaching, Preaching, and Practicing the Great Religions, including Buddhism, Christianity, Hinduism, and Judaism as well as the Esoteric Faiths of Esotericism, Native American Spirituality, Rosicrucianism, Spiritualism, Sufism, and Theosophy as a Serene Way of Life in a troubled world. A Spiritual Retreat for the devotees and adherents of the Mystic, the Psychic, the New Age, the Metaphysical, and the Traditional.

The Universal Spiritualist Association is among the very few Spiritualist organizations still attempting the demonstration of the "physical phenomena of Spiritualism," the traditional Phases of physical mediumship. Among the Phases demonstrated are precipitation on silk, independent card writing, direct and independent voice, apportation, spontaneous art, as well as the various forms of materialization and trumpet.

The Association is led by a general board consisting of a president, vice president, secretary, treasurer, and three trustees. There is now a Board of Regents which controls the activities of the Institute for Holistic Studies. Its government includes a dean, registrar, and treasurer besides four regents. The general board is elected by the Membership-At-Large meeting held annually. The board of regents is, at present, elected by the general board. The general board has the power to charter churches as well as license ministers and mediums. There are three institute sessions at Maple Grove as well as one in Canada and another in California. Ministerial students now receive their licensing with institute studies in conjunction with the Universal Spiritualist Association's Home Study System.

Within the association, there is a society, the Ancient Mystical Order of Seekers, consisting of clergy and the more serious students who wish to learn and understand "the esoteric arts and sciences." The subject matter extends far beyond that common to most spiritualist practices. During his lifetime, Clifford Bias authored a series of manuals, *The Path of Light*, and published several books representative of their work. There is also a monthly newsletter for which there is no charge to members.

Membership: In 1992 the association reported 512 members in good standing in the United States and Canada including ministers, spiritual healers, and mediums as well as 13 churches in the United States and one church in Windsor, Ontario, Canada.

Educational Facilities: Institute for Holistic Studies, Muncie, Indiana.

Periodicals: *The Banner of Light*. Send orders to PO Box 379, Pendleton, IN 46064-0379.

Sources:

[Bias, Clifford]. *The A. M. O. S. Path of Light*. 19 vols. Anderson, IN: The Ancient and Mystical Order of Seekers, n.d.

___. *The Way Back*. York Beach, ME: Samuel Weiser, 1985. *Universal Spiritualist Manual*. Manor Grove, IN: Universal Spiritual Church, n.d.

Wallace, Austin D. *Thistle Presents Prince Nikeritis*. Eaton Rapids, MI: Transcendental Science Publications, 1950.

★1400★
University of Life Church
℅ Richard Ireland
5600 Sixth St.
Phoenix, AZ 85040

The University of Life Church was formed by renowned psychic Richard Ireland of Phoenix, Arizona. After serving a number of Spiritualist churches in the Midwest and East, he moved to Phoenix in 1955. Ireland gained a reputation during the 1960's as a nightclub entertainer, conducting ESP shows in which he read serial numbers of dollar bills while blindfolded. At the church he is a full trance medium; several guides, a Dr. Ellington and an Indian, speak through him. They answer questions for members and visitors, prophesy future events and give spiritual teaching. Reincarnation is stressed.

The center of the church is the congregation in Phoenix, which has 1,450 members. A healing shrine is being built in South Mountain in Phoenix. Lessons written by Ireland and/or his guides are sent out around the country. Ireland tried unsuccessfully to inherit the estate of James Kidd of Miami, Arizona, who willed his money for research on the existence of the human soul. The money went to the American Society of Psychical Research.

Membership: Not reported.

Sources:

Ireland, Richard. *The Phoenix Oracle*. New York: Tower Books, 1970.

Channeling

★1401★
Anthropological Research Foundation
(Defunct)

In 1967 William Ralph Duby, the leader and channel for the Organization of Awareness (see Cosmic Awareness Communications), died. Over the several years following his death, the organization splintered into several groups. The Anthropological Research Foundation was founded in the early 1970s in San Diego by Jack T. Fletcher and Pat Fletcher. Among the members of the group was Danton Spivey, a trance medium who claimed to be a continuing voice for "Cosmic Awareness", the universal mystical voice who spoke through Duby. In 1972, the foundation began to

issue a magazine, *Aware*, and announced plans for the organization based upon the messages given through Spivey.

The foundation saw itself as composed of ordinary people who had been exposed to extraordinary information. It viewed its task to expose those forces which divide humans from each other and from the divine, and to discover the new culture which is characterized by wholeness. To this end it proposed projects that looked at ancient cultures, especially those of Atlantis and Lemuria.

There is no indication thet the foundation survived more than a few years.

★1402★
Aspects of Light
12540 Braddock Dr., Ste. 218B
Los Angeles, CA 90066

Aspects of Light is a channeling center built around the messages of a group of entities termed collectively the Counsel of Light as channeled by Cherryl Lynn Taylor. Taylor began channeling in the mid-1980s and established the present center in 1991. The counsel members have indicated that they have appeared to assist individuals to get in touch with their soul urges, to discover higher identities and bring those into manifestation. Human beings are Divine but often live in a state of separation from that Divinity. Such separation produces fear and leads to all variety of pain and suffering. The answer to fear is learning to love the self. To facilitate the process of learning to love, Taylor has prepared a set of tapes of dictations from the counsel that include both teachings and meditative exercises that the students learn and use in their life. Students also learn to picture themselves in three major aspects, physical, emotional, and mental, and to use the techniques as they monitor each aspect.

Aspects of Light carries on an intensive program that includes weekly healing and development classes and group channeling sessions. Tapes of a wide variety of previous channeling sessions are available.

Membership: Not reported.

Periodicals: *The Counsel of Light.*

★1403★
Association for the Understanding of Man
(Defunct)

The Association for the Understanding of Man (AUM) was formed in 1971 as an organization to focus the psychic accomplishments of Ray Stanford (b. 1938). He is the brother of noted parapsychologist Rex Stanford. Ray Stanford began to manifest psychic abilities in his youth. In 1960, meeting with a meditation group, he slipped into an unconscious trance-like state from which he was able accurately to answer questions by group members. The next year he began giving readings to the general public. Over the years, five types of readings evolved: self-help, question-and-answer, dream-interpretation, group-help and research-reading. The self-help readings include reflections upon past lives; research-readings explore various issues in depth. In 1972, a book containing the research-readings on the Fatima prophecy was published. The book discusses the significance of the appearance and words of Mary, the mother of Christ, at Fatima, Portugal, in 1917.

The "Source" of the Stanford readings is not a disincarnate entity, but is described as the unconscious and superconscious of Stanford, which contacts the object of the reading (the person the reading concerns). Recordings of all the readings have been kept. While no creed or dogma has been established, a consistent world-view has emerged. It includes Hindu concepts. The basic psychic/spiritual nature of man and the universe is accepted. Transcending the earth plane are various spiritual regions, including the lower astral and causal planes and, at the top, the "Abode of the Most High." From the higher planes emanates Aum, the great sound, and the music of the spheres, the audible life stream which underlies and sustains all creation, called by Hindus, "Nam." Among the inhabitants of the high planes are the Great White Brotherhood, beings advanced beyond the need of reincarnation.

Man is a spiritual entity, spirit individualized. Soul is the enduring vehicle of individual form which records all past experiences. Component parts of the self are the seven psychic centers (chakras) which serve as contact points between soul and body. The third-eye center (in the forehead, above the nose) is a point of contact with higher levels of consciousness.

Headquarters of AUM were established in Austin, Texas. Members could be found across the country and were of two kinds: recipient and full-participant members. Both a newsletter and the *Journal of the Association for the Understanding of Man* were published, as were a number of books and booklets. AUM was disbanded in the early 1980s.

Remarks: Stanford also possessed a lifelong interest in UFOs (Unidentified Flying Objects). As teenagers in the 1950s, both he and his brother had professed contact with the space beings. Associated with AUM during its years of existence was Project Starlight International (also established by Ray Stanford), a sophisticated UFO detection system in Austin, Texas. It published the shortlived *Journal of Instrumented UFO Research*.

Sources:

McCoy, John, Ray Stanford, and Rex Stanford. *Ave Sheoi...From Out of This World.* Corpus Christi, TX: The Authors, 1956.

Speak Shining Stranger. Austin, TX: Association for the Understanding of Man, 1975.

Stanford, Ray. *Fatima Prophecy, Days of Darkness, Promise of Light.* Austin, TX: Association for the Understanding of Man, 1974.

___. *The Spirit Unto the Churches.* Austin, TX: Association for the Understanding of Man, 1977.

___. *What Your Aura Tells Me.* Garden City, NY: Doubleday, 1977.

★1404★
The Association of Love and Light
3399 Bennett, No. 28
Hollywood, CA 90068

The Association of Love and Light was founded in the 1980s to facilitate the work of Lyssa Royal, the channel for an entity named Raydia, described as a multi-dimensional consciousness system. Royal, a former secretary, began channeling in 1985. More recently she has also worked for Shirley MacLaine's Higher Self Seminars. Raydia is a non-physical entity who is seen as assisting people to discover their own potentials and the possibilities of ecstasy and joy. The work of Raydia is a natural part of the process of human evolution that occurs over many lifetimes. Individuals are seen as a part of the God force that exists immanently within each person rather than as an outside force. Each person can, by turning within, connect with Universal Energy.

The Association of Love and Light offers weekly events at various locations in the greater Los Angeles area including group channeling sessions, basic and advanced channeling classes, and a support group. Tapes of previous channeling sessions, including sessions on after death experiences, AIDS, and extraterrestrial contact, are circulated.

Membership: Not reported.

★1405★
Church of Amron
2254 Van Ness
San Francisco, CA 94109

The Church of Amron is a metaphysical church growing out of a spiritualist tradition founded in San Francisco in the mid-1980s. Its program is built around spiritual healing and channeling (medi-

umship). It holds weekly worship services each Sunday and mid-week activities that include a Tuesday evening forum, healing circles, and an AIDS support group.

Membership: Not reported. In the late 1980s there were two congregations, both in San Francisco.

★1406★
Church of the White Eagle
% Rev. Jean Le Fevre
% Star Center for the Americas
St. John's Retreat Center
9 St. Beulah Rd.
Montgomery, TX 77356

Alternate Address: International headquarters: New Lands, Rake, Liss, Hampshire, England GU33 7HY.

History. The Church of the White Eagle Lodge was establised in England in 1934 by Grace Cooke (d. 1979), affectionately known as Minesta, and her husband, Ivan Cooke (d. 1981), known in the lodge as Brother Faithful. For many years, Minesta worked as a medium in the Spiritualist church of England, primarily associated with the Stead Borderland Library in London. In 1930 she was contacted by a member of the Polaire Brotherhood from France, who informed her that a recently deceased author and Spiritualist, Arthur Conan Doyle, had chosen her as an instrument through whom he wished to speak. She was also given a six-pointed star, symbolic of the Christ star (perfect balance) and asked to train men and women to work with and through the light of Christ to help the world through the "years of fire" into the coming of the "golden age." The star became the symbol of the lodge.

Clairvoyant from childhood, Minesta had long been guided by one whom she knew as White Eagle. Instead of giving personal spirit messages, as is commonly done in Spiritualist churches, she was used to transmit (or channel) a vast series of teachings, which provided the base of the training she had been asked to do. White Eagle, it is believed, is the symbol of St. John, the Beloved Disciple, a sign of the "age of brotherhood," the golden age, and a title given by the American Indians to a spiritual teacher of great wisdom.

The work spread to the United States in the 1950s and eventually a lodge was established in Texas. More recently lodges were opened in California and in Canada.

Beliefs. The church is built around the teachings of White Eagle. They convey the teaching of the Great White Brotherhood and emphasize the coming of a golden age when human intuition will arise as a greater force in human affairs. White Eagle's teachings are summarized in the "principles" of the lodge and include a belief in God as Father and Mother; the Cosmic Christ whose light shines in the human heart; and the five cosmic laws of reincarnation, cause and effect (karma), opportunity, correspondences, and compensation. The church teaches that every man, woman and child has in their heart a little spark of light which is the Christ Light, the spirit of Divine love.

To church members happiness is a realization of God and a quiet, tranquil realization of God's love for all of life. They seek a life which is gentle and in harmony with natural and spiritual laws. The basic law which controls life is love—love for God, for humanity, and for the animals and nature. A vegetarian diet is encouraged. Since God is the creative power within all life, individuals can look within and learn to contact the love of God, the Christ within their own hearts, and use that love to comfort and heal others. As one gives oneself in a life of service, joy and blessings from God are received.

Organization. The work in the United States is headquartered at the daughter lodge located on a 70-acre rural tract, the St. John's Retreat Center, where both spiritual guidance for humans and a sanctuary for wildlife is provided. The Texas lodge is one of 15 daughter lodges located around the world. Among other services, it provides training for center group leaders. The American daughter lodge oversees centers located in various parts of the United States, as well as work in Canada, Brazil, Chile, Japan, and Mexico. Conferences and retreats are held on a regular basis.

Membership in the church and lodge is open to all who feel in harmony with the basic teachings. Meditation and healing are an integral part of the work and there is a special program for children. Sacramental services are held around baptism, marriage, and funerals (with an understanding that there is no death, only eternal life). Members are encouraged to set aside a time daily for prayer using the six-pointed star, the Christ Star, as a focus while sending out the light of Christ. Members may also apply for the brotherhood, an order of men and women within the church who are committed to trying to follow a spiritual way of life and discipline while still living and working in the outer world. The work of the brotherhood includes using and working with the Christ Light for the healing of the planet as well as individuals. The motto of the lodge is "I Serve."

Membership: In 1997 the church reported 1,200 full members and 3,000 active supporters in 18 United States centers. There was one minister. There were four centers in Canada. Worldwide membership was more than 15,000.

Periodicals: *Stella Polaris*. Send orders to Newlands, Brewells Lane, Rake, Liss, Hampshire, England GU33 7HY. • *Newsletter for the Americans*. Send orders to 9 St. Beulah Rd., Montgomery, TX 77356.

Sources:

Cooke, Grace. *The Illuminated Ones*. Liss, Hampshire, England: White Eagle Publishing Trust, 1966.

Cooke, Grace. *Minesta's Vision*. Liss, Hampshire, England: White Eagle Publishing Trust, 1992. 60 pp.

Cooke, Ivan, ed. *The Return of Arthur Conan Doyle*. Liss, Hampshire, England: White Eagle Publishing Trust, 1956.

Lind, Ingrid. *The White Eagle Inheritance*. Wellingsborough, Northamptonshire: Turnstone Press, 1984.

The Living Word of St. John. Liss, Hampshire, England: White Eagle Publishing Trust, 1985.

The Story of the White Eagle Lodge. Liss, Hampshire, England: White Eagle Publishing Trust, 1986.

The Wisdom of White Eagle. Liss, Hampshire, England: White Eagle Publishing Trust, 1967.

★1407★
Church of Universal Love (Texas)
(Defunct)

The Church of Universal Love (Texas) is a New Age organization founded in 1968 and chartered in 1972. It was built around the channeling of Rev. Linda Forman, its founder. Forman channeled from the Cosmic Masters, believed to be extraterrestrials. Some of the channeled material is published for church members in the bimonthly newsletter, *Cosmic Channelings*. Members are scattered around the country and have access to Powers through private channelings, which are recorded and sent to members via mail. The single church center in El Paso offers a weekly schedule of worship and healing services, classes, and study groups.

Remarks: The Church of Universal Love (Texas) has no connection with the church of the same name which is headquartered in Washington state.

★1408★
Circle of Inner Truth
(Defunct)

Marshall Lever was a Presbyterian seminarian who developed the ability of trance mediumship. As a medium, he began to receive messages from a guide, Chung Fu. Chung Fu is viewed as a spirit last incarnated as a student of Lao Tzu in China. The Circle of Inner Truth was begun in 1970 by Marshall and his wife, Quinta Lever, as an instrument for the expression of Chung Fu's work and teaching. Through counseling in trance, Chung Fu offered help to individuals on personal problems, particularly health, and works with groups to teach spiritual truths. Health readings resembled those given through Edgar Cayce, the founder of the Association for Research and Enlightenment.

Lever taught that man has an immortal spirit within, which has evolved through many life forms and previous incarnations. This spirit is continually reincarnating until it breaks the cycle of reincarnations; man must identify with his spiritual self or God-Force during an earth cycle, after which he is spiritually free, eternal and universal, and will not again incarnate. To aid its members, circles were developed for inner awareness through affirmative meditation, nutrition and health, and direct lessons from Chung Fu.

During the 1970s, the Levers had no home and spent all their time traveling among the several groups of the Inner Circle, which were widely scattered across the United States. One was located in London, England. A monthly, *Our News and Views*, was issued from San Francisco and mailed to approximately 600, of which 400 were in the United States. During the 1980s the Circle has ceased to exist and the Levers have moved into other psychic endeavors.

Sources:

Fu, Chung. *Evolution of Man*. Circle of Inner Truth, 1973.

★1409★
Circle of Power Spiritual Foundation
Current address not obtained for this edition.

The Circle of Power Spiritual Foundation was established during the 1980s to spread the teaching of Tawa, a spiritual entity, who speaks through Rey Fletcher. During the 1960s, when the Fletchers lived in a Chicago suburb, Rey's wife, Candy R. Fletcher, began a spiritual search that led her to reading metaphysical books and experimenting with the ouija board and hypnosis. Thus it was on August 22, 1968, that Tawa first made contact during a session in which Candy had convinced Rey to join her in asking questions of the ouija board. Tawa identified himself as a Blackfoot Indian in a previous incarnation though currently in a disembodied state. He also asked if he could speak using Rey's vocal cords. Prior to this time, Rey had also proved himself a good subject for hypnotism, and in the future Tawa spoke to him while he was in a hypnotic trance. Tawa's first spoken communication was on September 3, 1968.

Tawa continued to speak through Rey until the end of 1970, but for a time the material was put aside as he pursued a successful career. Meanwhile Candy considered writing a book based upon the teachings Tawa had given them. She began work on the text in 1979. Shortly thereafter, the Circle of Power Spiritual Foundation was formed. In 1984 the book was published at about the same time the Foundation moved to Victor, Montana. Assisting the Fletchers are Richard and Bobbie Graham who head the Foundation branch in Las Vegas, Nevada.

Tawa identified himself as a contemporary of Jesus and the person who served as Jesus' original spiritual teacher. He remained with Jesus through his life, death, and resurrection. The resurrection was the proof that Jesus had been sent by God. According to Tawa, Jesus was reborn in the flesh somewhere in the Orient in 1962. At the time of Tawa's dictations, the reincarnated Jesus was not aware of his mission as Messiah. However, at some point in the near future he will take on his Christ essence and reveal himself to the world. This time he will be fully accepted. However, prior to his coming forth, the anti-christ, a person now residing in England, will exert power for one year.

The Fletchers see themselves as part of a chosen circle of followers who will be the messengers of the coming Messiah. The

Foundation is bring together an initial group of 52 families/persons who will become the spearhead of the mission leading to Christ's next appearance. The Foundation plans to establish a network of lodges from which the message can be disseminated.

Membership: Not reported.

Sources:

Bjorling, Joel. *Channelling: A Bibliographic Exploration.* New York: Garland Publishing, 1992. 363 pp.

Fletcher, C. R. *Spirit in His Mind.* Victor, MT: Circle of Power Spiritual Foundation, 1984. 618 pp.

★1410★
Cosmerism
(Defunct)

Cosmerism was the name of a short-lived group which began in September, 1972, when the *Book of Cosmer* was channeled by seven angels, the most important of whom was named "Ashram." Receiving the communications were a couple simply known as Luke and Mark (the latter a female). In accordance with the entities' instructions, an original group of thirteen was collected and each member received a Cosmerite name: Matthias, Matthew, Judas Secarius, Josephus, Ananda, Peter, James the Elder, Thomas, Paul, Thaddeus, John the Beloved, and Luke and Mark. In the summer of 1974, the first circle to begin the formal study of the *Book of Cosmer* was held, and the first issue of *The Moon Monk*, a periodical, was issued.

Cosmerites termed their message "the Way" of Cosmer, the creative force, innate in all things and the source of creation. The power of Cosmer focuses in small groups and goes out with them into the world. The Way is a beginning toward peace, both external and internal. Under the oversight of Cosmer, man is on a path toward final absorption, or the building into oneness of men and angels creative force.

Headquarters of Cosmerites in 1974 were at Winter Park, Florida, and the small group of followers was drawn from eastern Florida and Canada. Plans included the building of Ichikama, a wilderness Ashram (a secluded retreat) of peace and tranquility. These plans were never brought to fruition as a brief time later the group's address became obsolete and the periodical discontinued. No sign of the group has appeared since the mid-1970s, and it is presumed to have disbanded.

★1411★
Cosmic Awareness Communications
Box 115
Olympia, WA 98507

In 1962 a voice describing itself as "From Cosmic Awareness" began to speak through the body of ex-army officer, William Ralph Duby. In response to the question, "What is Cosmic Awareness?" the group with Duby was told it was "total mind that is not any one mind, but is from the Universal Mind that does not represent any unity other than that of universality."

As the voice continued to speak, its words of wisdom were collected. In 1963, instructions were received for the formation of an Organization of Awareness as a means of giving to individuals the teaching of the voice. The real organization is said to be composed of 144 entities on that inner plane known as Essence.

Communications from Awareness have covered the whole scope of subjects about which people have questions, but, through it all, a few central ideas have emerged. God is seen not as a personal deity, but as natural cosmic law. The spiritual life is stressed, as is compassion in our dealings with men. Man's purpose is to move toward cosmic awareness.

A summary of the voice's stance is contained in the "Laws and Precepts of Cosmic Awareness," printed below.

The Universal Law is that knowledge, that awareness, that all living things, all life has within it that vitality, that strength to gather into it all things necessary for its growth and its fruition.

The Law of Love is that law which places the welfare and the concern and the feeling for others above self. The Law of Love is that close affinity with all forces that you associate with as good. The Law of Love is that force which denies the existence of evil in the world, that resists not evil.

The Law of Mercy is that law which allows one to forgive all error, to forgive equally those who err against you as you err against them. This is to be merciful. To be merciful is akin to the Law of Love, and if one obeys the Law of Mercy there can be no error in the world.

The Law of Gratitude is that sense of satisfaction where energy which has been given receives a certain reward.

Judge Not. Be Humble. Never Do Anything Contrary to the Law of Love. Resist Not Evil. Do Nothing Which Is Contrary to the Law of Mercy.

Duby died in 1967 and a major splintering occurred in the organization. No fewer than seven bodies were formed, each claiming to be the continuation of the original. Disagreement over the publication of materials which some thought should remain secret was one major issue in the schisms. Largest of the several splinters is Cosmic Awareness Communications, which continues the 1963 organization. About four months after Duby's death, a channel emerged through which Cosmic Awareness continued to speak. In the late 1960s, messages received through this new channel, Paul Shockley, both clarified and altered the older material. The new voice revealed that the Organization of Awareness has helped to accomplish a vast shift of consciousness—a return to the Godhead, which for thousands of years Essence has willed would eventually occur. The return to the Godhead is equated with the return of Lucifer, the fallen angel of light.

Membership: Not reported, but in 1995 the newsletter reported a circulation of 3,000 copies. In the 1970s, Cosmic Awareness Communications claimed 75 centers (including three in Canada) and 144,000 members.

Periodicals: *Revelation of Awareness.*

Sources:

Cosmic Awareness Speaks. Olympia, WA: Servants of Awareness, n.d. Vol. II & III. Olympia, WA: Cosmic Awareness Communications, 1977, 1983.

★1412★
Divine Word Foundation
Current address not obtained for this edition.

The Divine Word Foundation was founded in 1962 by Dr. Hans Nordewin von Koerber (1886-1979), formerly professor of Asiatic studies at the University of Southern California. The purpose of the Foundation is to disseminate the revelation of Jakob Lorber (1800-1864). An Austrian-born musician, Lorber in his fortieth year heard a voice in his heart, "Jakob, get up, take your pencil and write." Obeying, he began to function as the scribe to this Voice, which he believed to be none other than the Lord Jesus Christ. Through Lorber, the Voice dictated twenty-five books and other, shorter works. The revelations did not end with Lorber. In 1870, Gottfried Meyerhofer (1807-1877), a retired Army officer living in Trieste and a student of the Lorber literature, heard the Voice, which began to dictate through him. Since Meyerhofer's death, others have continued in succession: Leopold Engel, Johanne Ladner, Bertha Dudde, Johannes Widmann, Max Seltmann, Johanna Henzsel, George Riehle, Johannes Friede, and others.

The works of Lorber were published primarily by Christoph Friedrich Landbeck of Bietigheim, West Germany, who headed the Neutheosophischer Verlag (after 1907 Neusalems-Verlag or New Jerusalem Publication House). In 1924, the Neusalem Gesellschaft (New Jerusalem Society) was formed. Adolf Hitler suppressed the Lorber work, but it was quickly re-established. The Society became the Lorber Gesellschaft and the publishing arm, the Lorber Verlag. In 1921, the Lorber revelations were discovered by Dr. von Koerber. As he accepted them, he began to translate them into English and introduce them to others.

The new revelation fills 42 volumes of approximately 450 pages each. For Lorber, God is the Infinite Spirit behind the universe. The Holy Spirit is the "external life ether" that permeates the universe. The universe is the expression of God, made up of tiny spiritual primordial sparks created to grow into the divine likeness. It is God's desire to create a society of living love.

The plan of God was thwarted by Lucifer who revolted with the spirits below him and became entrapped in matter: impure spirit condensed. God is using matter as a filtering plant through which the impure spirits can be purified. Earth is the place where the rebellious spirits are being given the chance to return voluntarily to God. God became man in Jesus to accelerate the redemptive process. The cross is a perfect example of love.

A human being is intended to learn, through the imitation of Christ, to love God and his neighbor as himself. He thus achieves rebirth and is allowed to participate in the work of redemption. At death, each soul discards the body and begins life as a spirit. It ascends, beginning from its point of development in the body, ultimately to the New Jerusalem. Christ will return in the near future to recreate the earth and establish the millennium, the first signs of which are worldly conflict and turmoil. The present period will culminate in Lucifer's making his final choice and a war of destruction of the most rebellious ones.

The membership of the Lorber Society is concentrated in German-speaking Europe, but has spread to every free continent. In the United States, individuals around the country study the revelation in the books published by the Divine Word Foundation. Study groups are located in San Diego and Newark, California; Denver, Colorado; and Salt Lake City, Utah. Since Dr. von Koerber's death, his widow, Hildegard von Koerber, has continued his translating efforts. There is also a translator residing in Salt Lake City. Dr. Fred S. Bunger, the Foundation's first president, died in 1979 and was succeeded by Earl G. Fox of Melba, Idaho. Bunger co-authored with Dr. von Koerber the Foundation's basic text, *A New Light Shines Out of Darkness.*

The Foundation has a friendly relationship with the Lorber-Verlag in Germany, though organizationally independent. It is also associated with another English-language translator in Great Britain.

Membership: There were in 1984 approximately 200 people studying the Lorber material in several study groups in the United States and another 100 people worldwide.

Sources:

Bunger, Fred S., and Hans N. Von Koerber. *A New Light Shines Out of the Present Darkness.* Philadelphia: Dorrance Company, 1971.

Lorber, Jakob. *The Three-Days-Scene at the Temple of Jerusalem.* Bietigheim, Wuerttemberg, Germany: Neu-Salems-Society, 1932.

★1413★
Doctrine of Truth Foundation
Current address not obtained for this edition.

The Doctrine of Truth Foundation was established in the mid1970s to promulgate the research and ideas of Lewis E. Cook, Jr., and Junko Yasui, as contained in their book *Goldot: Guidebook of Life and Doctrine of Truth.* Following the Korean War, Cook (1925-) worked in Korea as part of the reconstruction program and stayed on as head of a construction company. In 1964 he moved to Japan to establish a prefabricated-home business. There he met and fell in love with Junko Yasui. They were married in 1967, and soon afterward moved to the Philippines. In the islands, both began a period of heightened attention to their spiritu-

al lives. They began to practice yoga, read metaphysical and occult books, and meditated.

The couple moved to the United States in 1970 and immediately began to teach all that they had learned in the Orient. They assembled a summary of their ideas in *Goldot,* and founded the Doctrine of Truth to disseminate those ideas. *Goldot* is acclaimed as the modern Bible and Guidebook for humanity. It covers all dimensions of life beginning with its origins. Creation was, it teaches, an emanation from Spirit. Spirit beget the Oversoul, which in turn led to the development of universal mind, the universe, light, darkness, heaven (the astral universe), and earth (the material universe). The astral light entered the material universe and all life forms resulted. God then released the individual soul within Itself, and these "gods of creation" then created the world and all of the plant, vegetable, and human life within it. The human life was in their image and likeness. The Astral gods took on physical bodies. However, the God Men violated their own divine mandate and began to intermingle with that segment of the human race who were not God Men.

According to *tGoldot,* earthly life is governed by Truth, universal principles and laws. The principles produce life while the laws govern it. Underlying reality is Unity-Equilibrium, the infinite eternal presence within all phenomena, also known as Spirit or God. Unity-Equilibrium manifests as Mind, the essence of all phenomena. The Unity-Equilibrium particle of each human manifests as pure mind, also known as soul or ego. The universe is the result of the creative expressions of the Universal Mind, the collective ego of all souls. Every instant and every detail of an individual's life is the result of mental creative activity. Life equals creativity. We experience life through sensory perception. Our limited perceptions in the material realm create illusion.

The Life and its sensory experiences are governed by the laws of harmony, duality-polarity, cycles, cause-effect, and karma. The universe exists in harmony, disrupted only by human ignorance. Humans should strive for harmonious life and relationships. Since harmony undergirds the universe, in order for it to be perceived, it must manifest as either the negative or positive aspect of a neutral equilibrated image. Thus phenomena functions to produce the illusion of our world. The world of illusion goes through cycles of formation and dissolution. The ongoingness of the cycles follows a pattern of cause and effect. The law of cause and effect in human life manifests as karma, the consequences of the thoughts, words, and deeds, of individuals.

The Doctrine of Truth Foundation builds upon the basic principles and laws of life and disseminates teachings that explain the meaning of these principles and laws for all of life. In this endeavor, it publishes *Goldot* and other related literature. Related to the Foundation are the Doctrine of Truth Church, the Doctrine of Truth School, and the Doctrine of Truth Research Center.

Membership: Not reported.

Sources:

Cook, Lewis E., Jr., and Junko Yasui. *Goldot: Guidebook of Life and Doctrine of Truth.* Oceanside, CA: Doctrine of Truth Foundation, 1976. Unpaged.

★1414★
EarthStar Alliance
3416 Waco St., Apt. 4
San Diego, CA 92117-6350

EarthStar Alliance was founded in the mid-1990s by Sara Mattoon and Scott Myrom to assist what they believe to be a planetary transformation now occurring on Earth. They view themselves as two of a number of masters who have incarnated on Earth during this generation who, having lived some years as just a normal human being, now have become aware of their task to aid in the creation of Heaven on Earth. They believe that Earth is in the process of becoming a star as the planet moves from one of dense physical reality into a radiant body of light. The movement produces stress in humans' dense earth bodies, and EarthStar Alliance provides a way of viewing the world, specific techniques, and new technologies to support the body during this change. These include bodywork, channeling sessions, and group events.

EarthStar Alliance teaches that each individual is both of the One, or God, as well as a separate unique individual. As being of the One, persons exist in one reality or dimension; as a separate individual, persons exist in a multitude of realms or dimensions. Most individuals live totally in the third (physical and mental) and fourth (astral) dimensions where the game of good and evil is played out. Individuals also exist in various nonphysical dimensions from the fourth (light) to the twelfth (experience of the One). Understanding the multiple existence of oneself on these various dimensions (including the lower ones) assists in one's comprehending one's divine nature. On the eighth and ninth dimensions, individuals see their Spirit manifesting as individual identities that represent groups, i.e., as part of a group soul. Individuals from various group souls are now on planet Earth.

In shifting one's perspective on who one is, the illusion of reality is also shifted and the manifestation of who one is in other dimensions begins to manifest in the third and fourth dimensions. Basic to the new view of the self is a shift of identity from that of struggling human to that of multi-dimensional divine self, and from that of student to that of master. Also, each should shift the way of measuring reality from the beliefs and feelings of the third and fourth dimensions to a fifth-dimension perspective (based in our knowingness and inner authority).

Members of EarthStar Alliance and those who resonate with its work are considered part of one group soul now manifesting on planet Earth. This group soul has a specific task in the period of transition as pathcutters bringing light, information, and energy from the more expanded dimensions.

Membership: Not reported. The alliance supports regular meetings in San Diego and is reaching out to other communities along the Pacific Coast.

Periodicals: *True Reality.*

★1415★
The Eloists, Inc.
Drawer O
Duxbury, MA 02331

The Eloist Ministry (named shortened to The Eloists, Inc., in 1972) was founded at the beginning of the twentieth century by Walter de Voe. At the time, de Voe was a New Thought practitioner and the author of several books including *Healing Currents from the Battery of Life* and *Mystic Words of Mighty Power.* The growth of his ministry led to its incorporation in 1918 in Brookline, Massachusetts. As he grew along with his work, de Voe came to a series of realizations, beginning with an understanding that most physical ailments were derived from the state of the individual's mind and that permanent healing needed to be accomplished by a change of lifestyle.

De Voe also came to see that effective physical healing had to include the healing of the individual's spirit as well as the lifting of lower spiritual entities that often surrounded those who were ill. The change in perspective led the ministry to emphasize the rescue, education, and revival of what Spiritualists term earth-bound spirits, who were perceived to be a burden on the planet as a whole.

Then in the mid-1930s, an elevated angelic presence manifested to the group. The members of the ministry were told that the spiritual work they had been doing would be appropriated by an angelic overshadowing that had undertaken a specialized task relating the arrival of a new era that had commenced in 1848. They were directed to read a new book *Oahspe,* and to adopt a vegetarian diet. From that time the work of the ministry followed two avenues: an inner council worked directly with this angelic presence,

and an outer council continued with education, healing, and publishing, much as before. Following De Voe's death in the late 1950s, the outer council work was largely abandoned for a generation. However, it was revived in 1983 and incorporated the publication of a new journal, *Radiance.*

The Eloists, Inc., does not consider itself a church, but rather a spiritual family that emphasizes attunement with the One Creator who is ever present in all of Creation. Each individual is a new creation at birth and destined for eternal growth and progression through eternity. The Creator dwells as a center of light within the human soul. Consequently, service to others is service to the Creator. Violence to others is compatible with this understanding, and pacifism and vegetarianism are logical conclusions of this point of view. The Creator may be contacted personally by listening to one's inner Light, and while Eloists set their primary source of inspiration coming from within, they also value *Oahspe,* and members are expected to have a comprehensive understanding of the book. The Eloists do not proselytize, but are willing to instruct, if asked.

In public outreach, members customarily maintain a degree of casual anonymity, not because they are a secret society, but because they prefer to emphasize the message, not the messenger.

Membership: Not reported. There are no clergy.

Periodicals: *Eloist Focus.* • *Radiance.*

Sources:

DeVoe, Walter. *Healing Currents from the Battery of Life.* N.p.

———. *Mystic Words of Mighty Power.* New York: Gordon Press Publishers, 1991.

The Eloists. Duxbury, MA: Eloist Ministry, 1990.

Oahspe: A New Age Bible. Los Angeles: Essenes of Kosmon, 1950.

★1416★
Family of Abraham
Box 690070
San Antonio, TX 78269

In the early 1980s channel Esther Hicks began to receive messages from Abraham, the name assumed from a group of evolved noncorporeal entities. In 1986, with the assistance of her husband, Jerry Hicks, who had received the initial messages, she began to inform some close friends and business associates of what was occurring and the messages they were receiving. These people began to offer questions to Abraham and found his answers useful and meaningful. Receiving a positive response, the Hickses made Abraham's teaching available to the general public, primarily through the circulation of tapes of the channeling sessions.

Abraham has spoken to a wide variety of issues of concern to the New Age community, such as coming earth changes, but has centered his message on the need for individuals to become conscious co-creators of their reality. This process is assisted by one's becoming aware of the laws of the universe and learning to move in accordance with them. Most important is the law of attraction, by which one can attract whatever he or she desires. It is used in connection with the law of allowing, by which one becomes free of the negativity that binds our life.

The Hickses have established a schedule of regular weekend "Dialogues" with Abraham around the country, and over the years Abraham study groups have formed across the United States. Those responding to the messages from Abraham have been informally dubbed the Family of Abraham. A quarterly newsletter, *Abraham Speaks,* was begun. It was superseded by the more substantive *The Leading Edge* in 1994.

Membership: In 1994 there were nine Abraham study groups and an unreported number of individuals receiving *The Leading Edge.*

Periodicals: *The Leading Edge.*

★1417★
Father's House
(Defunct)

Ralph F. Raymond (d. 1984) was a channel for spirit teachers. In the late 1960s he operated the Universal Link Heart Center in Los Angeles. In 1968, he was sent by the "Master" to England and Scotland to visit all the Universal Link centers and people. The centers in the United States were included in the tour. His findings were published in a booklet, *The Universal Link Concept.* Upon his return to the United States, he established the Father's House. The original seven-person board of trustees included several of the Link personalities.

The Father's House published *The Father's House Quarterly* and, through its pages, tied together the several hundred subscribers. A plan was initiated in 1973 to acquire a Center for Healing and Meditation. Brother Francis, as Raymond was commonly known, was joined in this endeavor by Ms. Carole Freeman. These plans had not materialized at the time of Brother Francis' death. Foreign affiliated groups were to be found in New Zealand and England.

The thrust of Brother Francis' thought was to provide guidance and leadership as the earth moves into the Aquarian Age. Though the Father's House was independent of other Link groups, informal contact was frequent. Selections of writings from other Link writers appeared in each issue of the quarterly. For example, Tarna Halsey regularly submitted articles channeled from the space people (beings in outer space). Brother Francis also circulated *The Three Day Scene,* one of the books of Jakob Lorber, whose American followers have founded the Divine Word Foundation. Almost every issue carried material from Illiana of New Age Teachings.

Sources:

[Raymond, Brother Francis Ralph]. *Universal Link Concept.* Los Angeles: Universal Link Heart Center, 1968.

★1418★

Fellowship of the Inner Light
℅ The Fellowship Center
620 14th St.
Virginia Beach, VA 23451

The Fellowship of the Inner Light was formed in Atlanta, Georgia, in October, 1972, by psychic Paul Solomon and his associates. In February, 1972, in a hypnotic trance, Solomon began to speak in a stern voice, a voice later to be labeled "the Source." As the trance sessions continued and Solomon began a vigorously disciplined life, the material which came through the readings began to provide for treatment of disease, prophecies which proved accurate, spiritual philosophy and a complete system for the development of "Inner Light Consciousness." The Fellowship was organized as a structure to further the work of Solomon and to disseminate the Inner Light Consciousness. In 1974, the Fellowship moved to Virginia Beach, Virginia, the home of Edgar Cayce, to whom Solomon is likened by his followers. Cayce founded the Association for Research and Enlightenment, discussed elsewhere in this volume.

The material in the transcripts of the Solomon readings cover a wide range of topics—Atlantis, diet and health, healing, reincarnation, sex, spiritual development, and prophecies. The worldview closely parallels that of the Cayce readings. Man is a son of God trapped in material forms which had their first manifestation on Atlantis. By spiritual growth, the cleansing of the body and evolvement, the trapped soul can come back to be one with God. Also in the material are those who came to aid those who are trapped and who wish to return. Reincarnation allows time for the growth of the soul.

The Source for the information coming through Solomon is the Universal Mind and the Akashic records. All thoughts and actions are said to be recorded on the "universal ethers" of the Akashic records, and psychics "tap into" those records to obtain information. In the Fellowship of the Inner Light, contact with spirits is discouraged. From the readings, a course that places the student on the mystic path to cosmic consciousness has been constructed. The course emphasizes the Light Within (or Holy Spirit). Consciousness of the Light is the key to overcoming the limitations of the material. The methods of the course, including relaxation, meditation, prayer, self-control, occult law and psychic development, lead to mastery of one's psychic nature, to integration of the total person and to spiritual development.

The Fellowship is conceived of as a religious association serving the needs of the New Age community. During the 1970s, the Fellowship was headquartered in Virginia Beach, from where a vigorous local program was offered. Closely affiliated was the Heritage Store and Heritage Publications, which issued the material from the readings, the first volume of which appeared in 1974. Heritage Store began in 1969 to make available the remedies suggested in the Cayce readings to the general public. In 1978, however, a thirteen-acre tract of land near New Market, Virginia, was dedicated as "Carmel-in-the-Valley." Headquarters shifted to the rural site, and ambitious plans for the development of a new age community as the center of the fellowship were announced. Publication offices remained in Virginia Beach. Affiliated fellowships can be found across the United States, and in England, Holland, and several other countries.

Membership: Not reported.

Periodicals: *Reflections on the Inner Light.* Send orders to Rte. 1, Box 141, Timberville, VA 22853.

Sources:

A Healing Consciousness. Virginia Beach, VA: Master's Press, 1978.

Spiritual Unfoldment and Psychic Development through Inner Light Consciousness. Atlanta, GA: Fellowship of the Inner Light, n.d.

★1419★

Fellowship of Universal Guidance
Current address not obtained for this edition.

The Fellowship of Universal Guidance was founded in 1960 by Dr. Wayne A. Guthrie and Dr. Bella Karish, both of whom serve as channels for the "great sources of light," teachers from the spirit world who guide Fellowship activities. The Fellowship has been associated with the Universal Link on occasion, but the thrust of the Fellowship's concern is the harmonizing of the three levels of consciousness. The Fellowship teaches that there are three separate entities within each person—the high self, the conscious self, and the basic self. The ultimate goal is to bring them into alignment for the eventual good of the karmic pattern by blending them for physical, emotional, mental and spiritual development. The high self is part of the super conscious structure and is located about three inches above the head. The conscious self functions in interpersonal relationships, and the basic self is that part that just evolved from the animal kingdom, according to the Fellowship.

Man reincarnates on earth once but is re-embodied until his goal is reached. The high self chooses where to incarnate. The basic self carries memory, emotions, and the masculine/feminine consciousness. Unfulfilled karma from previous embodiments can cause the basic self to open to negative forces that can cause disease, which can be healed only by discharging the karmic pattern. The Fellowship offers a "Three Selves Evaluation" to aid the individual in growth.

The insights of the Fellowship are given to the world through several series of lessons, beginning with the *Wisdom Workshop Series I.* Students may take these lessons by correspondence, and groups have formed to study the material collectively.

Membership: Not reported. As of 1974, fellowship chapters were located in San Francisco and San Diego, California. Groups in the process of becoming chapters are functioning in Phoenix, Arizona; Omaha, Nebraska; Mooresville, North Carolina; and Summerville and St. John's Island, South Carolina.

Periodicals: *Uniguidance.* Send orders to 1674 Hillhurst Ave., Los Angeles, CA 90027.

Sources:

Master Apollonius Speaks. Los Angeles: Fellowship of Universal Guidance, 1970.

The Prophetic Word. Revelation Number Two. Los Angeles: Fellowship of Universal Guidance, [1980]

Wisdom Workshop Lessons. Series 1. 12 vols. Los Angeles: Fellowship of Universal Guidance, n.d.

★1420★
Foundation Church of Divine Truth
Box 66003
Washington, DC 20035-6003

The Foundation Church of Divine Truth supersedes the former Foundation Church of the New Birth, based upon the writings of James Edward Padgett (1852-1923). Padgett, an attorney and Methodist Sunday school teacher, became interested in Spiritualism after the death of his wife in 1914. He was told by a medium to begin practicing automatic writing (writing or typing words believed to be dictated by spirit entities), and in a short time he became proficient. Within a year, Padgett began to receive messages purporting to be from Jesus of Nazareth, urging him to pray for the inflowing of the Father's divine love. On October 5, 1914, Jesus (Master of the Celestial Heavens) told Padgett that he had been selected to disseminate the Father's Truths to humankind. The result was some 1,500 messages received from Jesus, other high celestial spirits, and a variety of spirits either progressing through the Spiritual Heavens or stagnating in the lower spheres of the spirit world. The most important messages were published in four volumes, the first of which was printed in 1940. The sum total of these messages from Jesus were said to constitute his Second Coming to earth. Padgett received the messages between the years 1914 and 1923. After his death, the manuscripts were left in the custody of a close associate, Dr. Leslie R. Stone. Stone and others interested in the messages incorporated the Foundation Church of the New Birth in 1958 in Washington, D.C.

In 1982 the Rev. John Paul Gibson, the sole surviving founding trustee of the Foundation Church of the New Birth, died and was succeeded by Victor Summers. Soon afterward a reorganization of the church occurred with all working in an official capacity for the church located in the Washington, D. C. metropolitan area. However, in October 1983, Victor Summers moved the headquarters of the church to San Diego, California, and then to Lake Helen, Florida. He resigned from any leadership role in the work the following year and the church disbanded. A group of members, primarily in the Washington, D.C. area, reorganized as the New Birth Christian Healing Sanctuary. They received permission to receive the mail from the former church's mailbox. In December 1985, nine former members (eight of whom were ordained ministers) of the Foundation Church of the New Birth formed the Foundation Church of Divine Truth to carry forward the work of the former Foundation Church of the New Birth.

Beliefs. Since their initial publication, the volumes of messages have been variously titled: *Book of Truths*; *Messages from Jesus through James E. Padgett*; *Messages from Jesus and Celestials*; *True Gospel Revealed Anew from Jesus*; and most recently *Angelic Revelations of Divine Truth*. A summary of the material is found in the tenets of the church, given as direct revelation by Jesus of Nazareth and his disciples from the Celestial Heavens. True to the Spiritualist heritage, the first tenet concerns the continuity of the soul after death. The soul enters the spirit world and continues to progress until it reaches the Sixth Sphere, which is the Paradise of the Old Testament, or the Kingdom of the Perfect Natural Man, be-

yond which no further progress occurs. Should the soul seek to be filled with the Divine Love of the Creator, however, its progress takes it to the Celestial Heavens, where it continues to receive inflowings of the Divine Essence of the Father and is conscious of its immortality. These heavens are open only to those souls who seek the Divine Love. Jesus' mission on earth was to teach that this love had been bestowed by the Father and was available to all; that true salvation of soul (the realization of immortality) comes through obtaining sufficient quantity of the Father's Divine Essence of Love through earnest, sincere prayer to Him for its inflowing into the soul, thus filling the soul with its Divine Nature, which is immortal. The potentiality for receiving this Love had been lost with the fall of the first created parents.

Organization. The church is governed by a board of trustees which has the power to ordain ministers and charter churches. Members relate to the church primarily through the mail. Church services are occasionally on Sunday evenings in the homes of the ministers.

Membership: In 1995, the church reported 50 members and 17 ministers in the United States, 25 members and three ministers in Canada, and 125 members in three centers in Nigeria, Republique du Togo, and England. There are two churches in Washington, D.C.

Sources:

Padgett, James E. *True Gospel Revealed Anew by Jesus.* 4 vols. Washington, DC: Foundation Church of the New Birth, 1958-1972.

★1421★
Foundation Church of the New Birth
Box 996, Benjamin Franklin Sta.
Washington, DC 20044

The Foundation Church of the New Birth, reestablished in 1991, is a through-the-mail church organization that continues the work of the organization by the same name originally founded in 1958. The earlier church was built around the channeled messages of James Edward Padgett (1852–1923) who received numerous messages from Jesus via automatic writing between 1914 and his death in 1923. These messages were published by the church in four volumes under the title *True Gospel Revealed Anew by Jesus.* During the mid-1980s, the church passed through a period of organizational disruption, and it was disbanded. An attempt to reorganize led, in December 1985, to the formation of the Foundation Church of Divine Truth, by nine of the former members. In 1991, another group of former members reorganized under the original name. The church is led by its trustees, with Rev. Jocelyn Harleston serving as current administrative head. They continue to reprint the first two volumes of *True Gospel Revealed Anew by Jesus.*

The church seeks to inform mankind of the availability of the Heavenly Father's Divine Love which is received into the soul when earnestly sought for through prayer and soul longings. Its inflowing is felt as a radiant glow in the heart region. Upon obtaining a sufficient abundance of this love, it will transform the soul from the image of the Father into His very substance, which is not only Divine but immortal.

The church teaches that Jesus of Nazareth brought this love to light during his public ministry on earth and continues to teach its availability today, from the realm of spirit.

Membership: Not reported.

Periodicals: *New Birth Commentary.*

Sources:

Padgett, James D. *True Gospel Revealed Anew by Jesus.* 4 vols. Washington: Foundation Church of the New Birth, 1958-72.

★1422★
Foundation for the Realization of Inner Divinity
PO Box 458
White City, OR 97524

The Foundation for the Realization of Inner Divinity was founded in 1990 by Swami Paramananda Saraswatti, and supersedes an earlier organization, MAFU Seminars. The founding of the foundation followed an intense religious experience by Penny Torres Rubin, a New Age channel (medium) of the entity MAFU. During the late 1980s, Torres Rubin had emerged as one of the most popular channels within the growing New Age Movement. She started channeling in 1986 when she began to communicate with the disincarnate personage, MAFU. Within a few months she was channeling regularly in public sessions in Los Angeles and Santa Barbara, California. Torres Rubin's organization, MAFU Seminars, circulated cassettes and videotapes of the channeling sessions around the world.

MAFU is characterized as a 32,000-year-old entity who has incarnated on earth at least 17 times. His enlightened messages insist that each person is, in essence, divine. God is equated with the power of life. Thus all things are of God and in God. The goal of life is to realize one's own divine nature, by which knowledge one becomes a master.

Towards the end of 1989, Torres Rubin traveled to Hardiwar, India, in the Himalayan foothills. She took the vows of a *sannyassi* (accepting the renounced life), and also accepted a mission as the "ordained leader of spirituality" for the present age. Here, she received her new name, Swami Paramananda Saraswatti. Upon her return to the United States, Saraswatti established the Foundation for the Realization of Inner Divinity and its subsidiary, The Center for God Realization, which now disseminates MAFU's teaching materials and regularly conducts seminars and retreats for thousands of seekers.

The Foundation has brought together all of the wisdom received from MAFU and presents it as a distinct path to God consciousness. The organization has purchased a campground near Ashland, Oregon, as a retreat center. It has also developed a mastery course that introduces people to MAFU's spiritual path.

Membership: In 1992 the foundation reported an active membership of 15,000.

Sources:

Torres, Penny [Mafu]. *And What Be God?*. Vacaville, CA: Mafu Seminars, 1989.

___. *Reflections on Yeshua Ben Joseph*. Vacaville, CA: Mafu Seminars, 1989.

★1423★
Freewill Foundation
(Defunct)

The Freewill Foundation was founded to facilitate the public's contact with the channeling activity of Gerry Bowman and the channeled teachings of the entity John. Bowman's channeling dates to the evening of January 22, 1976, when a group of people gathered to contact the spirit world through a ouija board. During the evening members of the group had previous lives described and were told how those lives affected their present life. Bowman, one of the people in attendance, was told that in the future he would become verbal and have no more need of the ouija board. It was some five years later, on August 2, 1981, that Bowman first went into a light trance and John announced his presence with the words, "We are known as John. We are here to assist you, and any who are willing to listen, to discover who, and more importantly, what you are." John was believed to be identical to the biblical Apostle John, the Brother of James, and follower of Jesus.

Bowman was assisted by Joe Albani, a former radio talkshow host, who transcribed what became weekly sessions with Bowman and John. Albani also contacted Los Angeles radio station KIEV and in 1984 arranged for a weekly talk show, "The Out-of-the-Ordinary Show," each Sunday evening at midnight in which people called in and talked to John. The show was a success and Bowman and Albani created a series of workshops/seminars at which John periodically makes public appearances.

Within a general New Age framework, John's teachings centered upon a means to personal power through compassion, humility, and confidence. He also taught a simple technique to enhance the natural healing powers of the body through relaxation and concentration.

The foundation was composed of Bowman, Albani, and John. People who wished to relate to John were able to may arrange private sessions with him or attended groups sessions. Tapes and transcripts of the seminars were also circulated by the foundation.

★1424★
Grail Movement of America
2081 Partridge Ln.
Binghamton, NY 13903

Alternate Address: International headquarters: Grals Verwaltung-Vomperberg, A-6134, Vomp., Tirol, Austria.

The Grail Movement of America is supported by the Grail Foundation, which is the structure for disseminating the teachings of Oskar Ernest Bernhardt (1875-1941) of Bischofswerda, Germany. In 1924, Bernhardt moved to Bavaria, where he began to write lectures under the pen name Abd-ru-shin. In 1928, he settled in Austria, where he wrote *In the Light of Truth, the Grail Message*. He continued writing until he was expelled by the Nazis in 1938. The first center in America was formed about 1939 at Mt. Morris, Illinois. Abd-ru-shin's message is termed the Grail Message, a reference to the Holy Grail as the power center of creation.

According to Abd-ru-shin, God created man equal and set him in search of self-consciousness and maturity. In his search, man was led to the world of gross matter. The physical bodies were fashioned for our true selves to function within while on Earth. The purpose of man is to learn to live in harmony with the divine laws that brought forth the creation and now maintain it. Eventually, man could return to the spiritual realm as a mature human spirit, ready to enter life-eternal as a fully seasoned and self-conscious entity capable of serving the Creator as a true human spirit.

The Grail Message is contained in the three volumes of *In the Light of Truth*. There are also other writings by Abd-ru-shin. They are circulated in North America by the foundation through its two headquarters in Binghamton, New York, and Quebec, Canada, formerly located in Mt. Morris, Michigan, and Lapeer, Michigan. The International Grail Movement also works in most European countries, Australia, and New Zealand. There is some work in South America, Asia, and Africa.

Membership: In 1997, the movement reported 300 active adherents in the United States and 900 in Canada. Worldwide the movement has some 18,600 adherents.

Sources:

Abd-ru-shin. *Awake! Selected Lectures*. Vomperberg, Tyrol, Austria: Maria Bernhardt Publishing Co., n.d.

___. *In the Light of Truth*. Vomperberg, Tyrol, Austria: Maria Bernhardt Publishing Co., 1954.

★1425★
HomeWords
Box 57396
Salt Lake City, UT 84157

HomeWords is the outreach vehicle for New Age channeler Sheradon Bryce (born Susan Johnson). Since 1987 Bryce has channeled an entity named Philip, whose teachings have been compiled in a book, *JoyRiding the Universe* (1993). Bryce is a full-trance channel (medium) who has moved to demystify the channeling process. She suggests that while channeling it is possible that the individual's mind taps into a larger body of knowledge than that known to the waking consciousness and then creates a new personality to hold that new knowledge. Perhaps channeling is simply a way of giving the self permission to do what it would not normally allow itself to do.

Each person, according to Bryce, is a god spark. That god spark inhabits a physical body as a vehicle for expression. It is common for individuals to put the power of the god spark outside of the self, to externalize it. That process occurs whenever individuals believe that they are not god. Whenever one worships a god apart from oneself, one has externalized one's god spark. The externalization also coincides with irresponsibility, the claim that one is not accountable for one's circumstances. One creates victims by externalizing one's godly power and then not understanding one's sense of powerlessness. To become fully functioning individuals, persons must first accept their status as gods in embodiment.

Bryce has been a prolific channeler and distributes her work via both tapes and written transcripts of channeled sessions. She offers periodic retreats and workshops, leads tours to "power" places of the world, and infrequently holds private sessions with Philip. Her channeled material, over 2,000 hours of sessions, covers a wide variety of New Age topics from earth changes to ascension, kundalini and sexuality, and prosperity consciousness.

Membership: Not reported.

Periodicals: *HomeWords*.

Sources:

Bryce, Sheradon. *JoyRiding the Universe: Snapshots of the Journey*. Salt Lake City, UT: HomeWords, 1993.

★1426★
Inner Circle Kethra E'Da Foundation, Inc.
Box 1722
San Diego, CA 92112

The Inner Circle Kethra E'Da Foundation, Inc. was established in 1945 by Mark Probert (d. 1969) and his wife, Irene Probert of San Diego, California. Mark Probert, an orphan with little formal education, one evening began to speak aloud in his sleep. As described by his wife, he spoke in foreign languages and sang arias from operas. Dr. Meade Layne, founder-director of the Borderland Science Research Society, a large southern California psychic organization, recognized Probert as a trance medium and helped guide his development. Gradually, teachers from the spirit world began to contact Probert. One afternoon, five of his teachers appeared to him and told him that they wished to bring their teaching to the world using him as their channel. Many of the teachings were published in 1954 and 1955 in *Mystic, the Magazine of the Supernatural* and later collected in a book, *The Magic Bag*.

In all, 11 teachers manifested themselves in light bodies (figures similar to shining, brilliant ghosts), and Mark was able to make sketches of them. The three main ones were Professor Alfred Luntz, a Anglican clergyman, Ramon Natalli, a contemporary of Galileo, and Yada di Shi'ite, who lived half a million years ago in the ancient civilization of Yu in the Himalayas. These teachers are members of an Inner Circle, having been one time in a previous reincarnation, together with Probert, on earth. Eternal life expressive is at the heart of the teachings of the Inner Circle. The goal of life is to attain one's original state as a divine being. Earth experiences are seen as movement through a series of initiations into higher and greater states of awareness. When one attains a state where there is no break in consciousness, freedom is accomplished and there is no necessity to return to the physical. Work with love and sincerity is the way to awareness. Yoga practices, secret mantras, sitting in meditation, and deep concentration are considered futile attempts to hurry progress. The basic entity in the universe is the individual. The plan of the universe lies within the individual, as he solves his own riddle of the universe. God, or the

Creative Force, is said to be the impersonal soul with which one becomes aware of the unification.

The foundation has preserved the numerous tapes of Probert's trance-lectures and disseminates them in both cassettes and transcripts. Members gathered on Friday evening for dictation prior to Probert's death in 1969, and now gather to listen to tapes and for discussions.

Membership: There is no formal membership. In 1997 there were three centers in the United States.

Sources:

Probert, Mark. *Excerpts from the Mark Probert Seances: 1950 Series*. 3 vols. San Diego: Inner Circle Press, 1950.

___. *The Magic Bag*. San Diego: Inner Circle Kethra E'Da Foundation, 1963.

Wassen, Ralph, ed. *Yada Speaks*. San Diego: Kethra E'Da Foundation, 1985.

★1427★
International Organization of Awareness
(Defunct)

In 1967, William Ralph Duby, leader of the Organization of Awareness (see Cosmic Awareness Communications) died. Within a short time, the organizations splintered into a number of factions. The International Organization of Awareness was one such, founded in Honolulu by Edward Young. This small body survived into the 1970s.

★1428★
Lifelight University
Current address not obtained for this edition.

Lifelight University, an esoteric college of Light, grew out of the channeling activity of Arlene Nelson. Since 1983 Nelson has channeled an entity named Sinat Schirah, who is generally referred to more simply by the nickname Stan. Nelson is a fulltrance medium. In 1986 a new intensity of the channeling work, described as pure channeling, began and now occurs one weekend a month from January to May each year. During these pure channeling sessions, Stan completely takes over and Nelson has no memory of the sessions. Nelson is married to Mervin Colver and believes that she, Stan and Colver have been reunited for present work because of their association together in previous incarnations.

Lifelight University opened in 1987 to assist people in assuming greater responsibility for their own spiritual, mental, and physical growth. It offers a year-round program of seminars, workshops, classes, and retreats for New Age seekers. Off-campus two-day intensives and introductory sessions are offered at which Stan gives instructions on a variety of topics. New students are invited to take introductory courses in meditation and then proceed through a set of progressive intensives. Material channeled through Nelson from Stan has been published in tapes and books. Weekly devotional sessions called "affirmative sharing" are held each Sunday.

Membership: Not a membership organization.

Periodicals: *Lifelight Newsletter; 7 Rays*.

★1429★
Light of the Universe
Current address not obtained for this edition.

The Light of the Universe group was formed in the early 1960s as a psychic interest group in Tiffin, Ohio. Its investigations included ESP, health foods, and UFOs. Gradually, a more formal organization emerged, and a teacher, Helen Spitler, known publicly as Maryona (one who has received teachings of light from a higher source) became the leader. In 1965, Maryona published a book, *The Light of the Universe* I, and in 1966, a quarterly periodical began. In December 1969, the first branch of the group was formed in Cortland, Ohio. Others have organized since then. Correspondence lessons are mailed to students around the country.

Behind the L.O.T.U. group lie a number of books that influenced both members and teacher. These books include *The Aquarian Gospel* by Levi Dowling, *The Life and Teachings of the Masters of the Far East* by Baird Spalding and *Breathing Your Way to Youth* by Edwin John Dingle (of Mentalphysics). A strong emphasis is placed upon helping those dissatisfied with false and outmoded traditions and upon teachings that include the problems in translating the Bible, information on the hidden years of Jesus, and corrections in Christian teachings, especially some corrections previously asserted in the *Aquarian Gospel*.

Great emphasis is placed on the great cosmic law of reincarnation. The soul progresses through various experiences and lessons. It is Maryona's teachings that a soul never goes backward; progress is ever upward. Each person is a master within himself, possessing unlimited power and potential. The god within is pointed to in the words of the Old Testament, ''Ye are Gods.'' This power within, a shining inner presence, man's true self, the divine soul, rules the universe. As man turns from the mud and filth in which he is mired, he can turn to the light and claim his divine birthright. To accomplish this turning, a series of cleansing exercises and meditation techniques is offered to students.

Membership: Not reported. In 1988, there were two ministers. Members were scattered around North America and a few were located in Europe and Africa.

Periodicals: *The L.O.T.U.S.*. Send orders to 161 N. Sandusky, Tiffin, OH 44883.

Sources:

Maryona. *The Light of the Universe I and II*. Tiffin, OH: Light of the Universe, 1965-76.

___. *Mini-Manual for Light Bearers*. Tiffin, OH: Light of the Universe, 1987.

★1430★
Lighting the Way Foundation
Current address not obtained for this edition.

In the early book about Jeanne Dixon, *A Gift of Prophecy* by Ruth Montgomery, Dixon reported in a vision she had on February 5, 1962, that an exalted master was born somewhere in the Middle East. That same vision was given to Helena Elizabeth Ruhnau, a new Age channel. In 1969, Dixon, under heavy pressure from critics—primarily conservative Christian ministers—reversed her earlier claim. In *My Life and Prophecies* she suggested that the vision concerned the advent of the Anti-Christ. In the wake of Dixon's retraction, Ruhnau emerged as a champion of the original vision, and claimed that Dixon had allowed her human consciousness and lower mind to hold sway and reinterpret it. Ruhnau asserted her role as the Messenger of the New World Avatar, and founded the New World Avatar Link in Colorado Springs, Colorado.

In 1951, Ruhnau had an experience in which she felt someone tap her on the shoulder and a voice (later identified as that of the Christ) say, ''Come, follow Me.'' In 1954 she had the experience of dying and leaving her body. However, she was returned to her body by the Christ. She spent the next 15 years studying theosophy and metaphysical writings and became a channel. She channeled from the Spirit of God, the masters of the Great White Brotherhood, and her own God Self. Her first book, *Light on the Mountain*, appeared in 1966. Along the way it was revealed to her that she was, in one of her past lives, Akhenaten, the Egyptian pharaoh who brought the religion of the one God to his people.

After her own vision of the new Avatar born in 1962, she was given a picture of him reportedly taken when he was four years old. She also reported that as he grew older, the image in the picture changed. It was not until 1970, however, that she was told what her mission in life would be and why she had been returned

to her body in 1954. Having been related to the new Avatar in a previous life, it would be her task to explain to the world who he really was.

According to Ruhnau, an Avatar comes whenever evil increases and law and order break down. His coming was marked by the great conjunction of sun, moon, and planets in the sign of Aquarius in 1962. He would set affairs in order and teach the brotherhood of man to all nations. The idea of brotherhood is based upon the knowledge of the one God. There is only one true religion, the worship of the one God (ala Akhenaten) and the keeping of right relations with all.

Over the next few years she was given information on forthcoming catastrophic earth changes. In 1974 she began publishing a newsletter, *Lighting the Way,* in which she recorded the information she was receiving. All of this material was compiled in 1978 in her book, *The Return of the Dove.* She noted that the Avatar will make his appearance prior to the coming catastrophes and give time for people to move away from those portions of the planet that will be most adversely affected.

During the 1980s, Ruhnau relocated from Colorado City to Ava, Missouri, and the New World Avatar Cosmic Link was superseded by the Lighting the Way Foundation. Colleasius Press is an affiliated publishing concern.

Periodicals: *Lighting the Way.*

Sources:

Ruhnau, Helena Elizabeth. *Let There Be Light: Living Water of Life for the New Age.* Ava, MO: Lighting the Way Foundation, 1987. 171 pp.

___. *Light from the Fifth Dimension (The Heaven World).* Colorado Springs, CO: Colleasius Press, 1982. 171 pp.

___. *Light on a Mountain.* Riverside, CA: The Author, 1966. 168 pp.

___. *Mirror of a Soul.* Colorado Springs, CO: Colleasius Press, 1981. 80 pp.

___. *Reappearance of the Dove.* Colorado Springs, CO: Colleasius Press, 1978. 203 pp.

★1431★
Michael Educational Foundation
10 Muth Dr.
Orinda, CA 94563

In the years since the original contact of ''Michael,'' the collective entity who has been communicating with the Michael Teachings group in the San Francisco Bay area, and especially since the publication of Chelsea Quinn Yarbro's original book on Michael in 1978, several other teachers also claiming contact with Michael have appeared. Among these, J. P. Van Hulle and Aaron Christeaan founded the Michael Educational Foundation in 1984. While in basic agreement with the Michael Teaching group, the Michael Educational Foundation has expanded its teachings in some very different directions than that of the Michael Teachings group.

According to the foundation, Michael is the name of a group of 1050 souls, all people who have lived many previous lifetimes on Earth. These souls have come together as a single entity to share their vast experience with humanity and speak to the challenge of being human. Michael speaks through a number of human channels, offers guidance and mentorship to those who choose to listen, and offers a cosmic perspective on life.

Unlike the more anonymous Michael Teachings group, the foundation has carried on a high profile public program, has published a number of books and tapes drawn from the weekly channeling sessions, and sponsors various public events in the San Francisco Bay Area. It has nurtured the formation of Michael study groups at different locations around the United States. The group's newsletter, *The Progress,* is distributed nationally as well as in Scotland, Sweden, and Nepal.

Membership: Not reported.

Periodicals: *The Progress.*

Sources:

Baumbach, Emily. *Michael's Cast of Characters.* Orinda, CA: Affinity Press, 1989.

Christeaan, Aaron, JP Van Hulle, and M. C. Clark. *Michael: The Basic Teachings.* Orinda, CA: Affinity Press, 1988.

Pope, Joya. *The World According to Michael.* San Mateo, CA: Sage Publishing, 1987.

Steven, Jose, and Simon Warwick-Smith. *Essence and Personality: The Michael Handbook.* Orinda, CA: Warwick Press, 1987.

★1432★
Michael Teachings
Current address not obtained for this edition.

"Michael," a disembodied reunited entity, first manifested in 1970 during a dinner party in the home of Walter and Jessica Lansing, a couple living in the San Francisco Bay area. The couple was playing with a ouija board when a simple message appeared, "We are here with you tonight." When inquiry was made as to the identification of the "we," the response received was "Each soul is part of a larger body, an entity. Each entity is made up of about one thousand souls, each of which enters the physical plane as many times as necessary to experience all aspects of life and achieve human understanding. At the end of the cycles on the physical plane, the fragments once again reunite as we have reunited." Michael went on to indicate that he/they comprised an ancient entity that would come to those who requested valid assistance and instruct them in the nature of human evolvement.

Michael described a universe created by evolution from the Tao into seven planes of existence (buddhaic, messianic, mental, akaskic, causal, astral, and physical) similar to the Gnostic/theosophical understanding. Michael resides on the causal plane. He/they call attention to the individual's personal life plan with particular emphasis upon aspects of choice. Understanding is centered upon agape, an all-embracing and selfless love.

The Lansings and their guests, Craig and Emily Wright, stayed at the board for the next five hours that first night. They were joined on subsequent occasions by Lucy North (the group's typist) and Leah and Arnold Harris. During the first six months the group steadily grew until it numbered around thirty members. In 1978, popular novelist Chelsea Quinn Yarbro, who had long been a part of the group, took the material that had accumulated over the eight years of its existence and edited the book *Messages from Michael* (1979), which first brought widespread public attention to the Michael teachings. The initial group has remained together, and continuies to meet twice monthly. Yarbro has edited three subsequent volumes that expand upon the teachings.

Membership: There is one group of some thirty people who meet regularly to receive the messages. The much larger number of those who have received and found guidance from the teachings, especially since the publication of Yarbro's books, are unnumbered.

Sources:

Yarbro, Chelsea Quinn. *Messages from Michael.* Chicago: Playboy Press, 1979.

___. *Michael for the Millennium.* New York: Berkley Books, 1995.

___. *Michael's People.* New York: Berkley Books, 1988.

___. *More Messages from Michael.* New York: Berkley Books, 1986.

★1433★
Morse Fellowship
(Defunct)

The Morse Fellowship was founded in 1959 by Louise Morse of Silver Springs, Maryland, and was named for Elwood Morse, her husband, who had died the year before. In 1961, the headquarters were moved to Alamogordo, New Mexico. Mrs. Morse began to travel, teach and publish lessons, mostly of material which had been channeled through her. In 1967, she met and married James Spence and, in 1968, they moved to Richardson, Texas (a suburb of Dallas). Two years prior to the founding of the Fellowship, Mrs. Morse had begun to publish the lessons.

The "Portals of Light" was the name given to the ministry of Mrs. Morse, who was seen as a channel for the Holy Spirit. Her ministry was also seen as a fulfillment of Biblical prophecy concerning the last days when the spirit of truth would be poured out on all flesh. The whole range of psychic issues has been dealt with in the lessons given by the celestial teachers. The teachers, who have spoken through Mrs. Morse while she was in trance, were never identified, but were of both sexes.

According to the teachings, man had come forth from the God nature. The disobedience in the Garden of Eden had allowed sin to enter the race, for, through disobedience, the consciousness was lowered. The race entered the kingdom of Satan. In Jesus, man is given the chance to enter God's kingdom through obedience. By consciously identifying with Jesus, man is drawn back into the nature of God. The way back is through love. The reorientation to God's will allows one to become aware of the still, small voice within. As this voice becomes clearer and one follows it, one will be moving closer to God's will.

Mrs. Morse gave weekly trance sessions with a more or less stable group of sitters from the 1950s into the 1970s. The lessons are made available on tape and in printed form. By 1968, approximately 250 persons were receiving the lessons regularly. During the last years of her work, Morse was able to receive messages from the spirit world without going into trance.

Sources:

The Living Water. Richardson, TX: Morse Fellowship, 1970.

★1434★
New Age Teachings
Current address not obtained for this edition.

New Age Teachings was established in 1967 in Brookfield, Massachusetts, by Anita Afton (b. 1922), better known as Illiana, the name she uses as a channel. Illiana is referred to as the "soul which is in this body." In the beginning of her work as a channel, she reports, entities from a planet called Jamal spoke through her, but after a few years, as her own consciousness was "uplifted", the "I AM THAT I AM" was and remains the only voice that speaks through her.

Illiana had become influenced by Eastern philosophy while attending a Unitarian Church. She later joined the Self-Realization Fellowship of Paramahansa Yogananda (discussed in the chapter on Hinduism) and went through the entire set of lessons in Kriya Yoga. She learned of her past lives in India and how to meditate. In 1965, while in meditation, she received her first message as a channel. It was a rather mundane message concerning a lecture topic. A second, later message was a complicated code-like message drawn from several languages. Messages began to be received regularly from then on.

At the request of the cosmic being who issued messages through her, Illiana began to publish regular bulletins. They carry the messages from the cosmic hierarchy, the "I AM THAT I AM," which emphasizes the increasing Light coming into earth as a result of the New Age vibrations being poured forth upon the planet.

From the headquarters in Massachusetts, the bulletin and other publications are mailed to followers across the United States and around the world to every continent. Some members have formed study groups and centers from which the bulletins can be circulated locally. The bulletin is considered a "Universal Organ for World Upliftment though study and spiritual understanding." In 1976, a Spanish edition of the bulletin appeared and segments of the messages are regularly translated into several languages.

Headquarters for the Spanish-language work are in Houston, Texas.

In the mid-1980s, a music ministry was begun. It is believed that music is a Universal Vibrational Aspect of the LIGHT and can assist in bringing people "in tune" with their higher selves. Each person, it is believed, has his or her own keynote, which, when sounded, brings harmony, peace, and openness. Individuals using the ministry receive a chart, a cassette tape of a complete life song, and a composition based upon the life song channeled by Illiana. The chart is based upon the person's birth data and birth name.

Membership: As of 1992, approximately 2,000 people in the United States received *New Age Teachings*. There are 30 study groups who use the material channeled by Illiana. It is mailed to some 3,500 followers in 35 countries around the world.

Periodicals: *New Age Teachings.*

★1435★
Open Channel Resources, Unlimited
Current address not obtained for this edition.

Open Channel Resources, Unlimited is the organization that facilitates the channelling work of Katar Schoenstadt, a channel of various ascended masters, collectively referred to as the Guides. The primary entities who speak through her include Tsen Tsing of the Council, Ariana, the Goddess of Truth, Clark, Seth, and Favor. They bring a message of the basic divinity of each human being. In the sessions students are linked to a network of energies that allow the acceleration of the individual's growth as limiting ideas and other blockages are removed. Ariana, the goddess of Truth, provides special contact with feminine energies.

Katar began channeling in the early 1970s and developed into a full body trance medium. During sessions her consciousness departs and the various entities speak through her. She is assisted by her husband Darryl Schoenstadt, who conducts the channeling sessions, leads students in discussions of the Guides' teachings, and assists in sharing their techniques for personal development. Primary in the techniques are the mastery of breath and the "Sword of truth," that each person carries in their hand "to cut the strings of attachment that cause us to feel separate from our Creation."

Open Channel Resources, Unlimited offers a wide variety of classes and "playshops" and personal sessions at which individuals may talk with the Guides. Cassette tapes of the Guides' teachings are also available.

Periodicals: *Open Channel-A Journal with Spirit.*

★1436★
Organization of Awareness (Calgary)
(Defunct)

In 1967 the Organization of Awareness which had formed in the early 1960s splintered when its main leader and spiritual channel, William Ralph Duby, died. Three branches retained the name of the original group, among them a small group in Calgary, Alberta headed by Nick Chwelos. It survived into the 1970s.

★1437★
Organization of Awareness (Federal Way)
(Defunct)

The Organization of Awareness (Federal Way) was one of several groups which splintered from the original Organization of Awareness after the death of its leader and spiritual channel, William Ralph Duby, in 1967. This branch was headed by Frances Marcx and headquartered in Federal Way, Washington. It was a small body which survived into the 1970s.

★1438★
Organization of Awareness (Olympia)
Current address not obtained for this edition.

One of several splinters of the original Organization of Awareness formed in the early 1960s (see Cosmic Awareness Communications which retained the name under which the organization operated until the death of its main spiritual channel, William Ralph Duby). In 1967, this branch was formed and headed by David DeMoulin. It was a small group headquartered in Olympia, Washington. It survived into the 1970s.

★1439★
Radiant School of Seekers and Servers
(Defunct)

The Radiant School of Seekers and Servers was founded in 1963 by a small group led by Kenneth Wheeler at Mt. Shasta, California. The mystic mountain had brought them together the previous year and, as a group, they moved to the village at the mountain's base. In the 1890s, an entity, Phylos the Tibetan, had begun to speak through Frederick Spencer Oliver, his amanuensis. The material by Phylos was collected into a book, *A Dweller on Two Planets*, published in 1899. It described the existence of a mystic brotherhood of survivors of Atlantis, who live inside the mountain. The existence of Phylos was further highlighted in 1940 by the appearance of *An Earth Dweller Returns*, a second book by Phylos. The Radiant School began channeling from Phylos in 1963 and offered to its members the material from Phylos in lesson form.

The material advocated belief in God's divine plan, which is for all and enwrapped in the "folds of every life pattern." Every life pattern is interwoven in a great universal pattern. Each person is expected to unfold his plan in full. There is opportunity to meet all others with whom we have interfered and created karma. Each divine plan includes the rights to health, happiness and prosperity.

Man resides in his physical body as a "Temple" and the Temple is the means of contacting the higher self. The self is overshadowed by angels and is thus never alone. Prayer is the expression of desires. Abundance comes in longing to know the great love of God. To be patient, willing, forgiving and enduring is the key to the soul's progress of perfection.

Headquarters of the Radiant School were in Mt. Shasta, California. The School was run by a six-person board of directors, a president, bishop and assistant bishop. Members received monthly lessons from Phylos. The school disbanded in the early 1980s.

Sources:

Phylos the Tibetan [Frederick Spencer Oliver]. *A Dweller on Two Planets.* Los Angeles: Borden Publishing Co., 1899.

Van Valer, Nola. *My Meeting with the Masters on Mount Shasta.* Mount Shasta, CA: Radiant School, 1982.

★1440★
Ramtha's School of Enlightenment
Box 519
Yelm, WA 98587

Ramtha's School of Enlightenment was founded in 1988 by JZ Knight, who channels Ramtha, a spiritual entity. Born Judith Darlene Hampton in 1946, Knight was living in Tacoma, Washington, in 1977, when she had her first encounter with Ramtha. He appeared to her in her kitchen and told her simply, "I am Ramtha, the Enlightened One. I have come to help you over the ditch." She did not initially understand, but allowed him to begin to speak through her. Over the next few years she became a channel. During her channeling, she is in a full trance and Ramtha emerges as a second complete personality.

Ramtha has described himself as a person who lived on earth some 35,000 years ago. Since that time he has not again incarnated into a human body. According to the accounts of his earthly life, he was born among a group of survivors of ancient Lemuria. He grew up among the Lemurians, then a despised minority living at Onai, the port city of Atlatia (Atlantis). He hated the dominant Atlantians and eventually left the city and led a successful revolution against them. He emerged as a powerful warrior/conqueror but his career was interrupted by a would-be assassin's sword which almost killed him. During his lengthy recovery period he had time to contemplate the unknown God initially manifest in the life force all around him and wondered what it would be like to be the unknown God. He was led to consider the wind, the powerful unseen force free of boundaries, limits, or form. After several years of contemplation of the wind, he discovered the ability to separate his consciousness from his body. Further contemplation led to further change; he was able to become one with light and to change his entire body. Eventually he ascended with his body into a new level of existence.

Knight first publicly operated as a channel in November 1978, to a small group in Tacoma. She found an immediate public response. During 1979 Ramtha began to speak through her on a regular basis. The number of Dialogues, as the channeling sessions were called, increased dramatically in 1980, and by the mid-1980s the practice of holding two-day weekend Dialogues became common.

Knight was the most prominent of the channelers of the decade. Ramtha books, cassettes, and videos could be found in metaphysical bookstores across North America, and several celebrities became his students. Knight enjoyed great success through the mid-1980s, and culminated her first decade as Ramtha's channel in 1987 with the publication of her autobiography, *A State of Mind*. However, it was recognized that the Dialogue format had exhausted its potential and was limiting the progress of the work. Through the Dialogues, Ramtha had been able to engage students with his philosophy but not with the processes of the kind of transformation which he had suggested was possible for each individual. Thus, in 1988 Knight ceased holding Dialogues and turned her attention to the School of Enlightenment, formally initiated in May 1988. Classes and other activities have since been conducted at her ranch in rural Yelm, Washington.

Beliefs and Practices. Ramtha's teachings derived from the Gnostic tradition that began with such ancient teachers as Valentinus and Plotinus and were continued through modern movements such as Rosicrucianism, Freemasonry, and Theosophy. According to Ramtha, what we know as the universe originated in a sea of pure potentiality called the Void. In the Void, no thing existed, but from which everything that exists derived. In the timeless past, the Void contemplated itself and as a result an original point of consciousness, generally referred to as Point Zero, appeared. Point Zero received the command to realize the potential of the Void. Point Zero then contemplated itself and as a result a second point of awareness appeared in the Void. Between the two points appeared space and time. In the atmosphere resulting from the separation a flux emerged in which could be found the original particles of energy; the universe was created from the particles of energy (analogous to sub atomic particles). Existence was then characterized by the very high frequency at which the points of awareness (entities) and the particles of energy vibrated. At some point, desiring to explore the Void further, the points of awareness moved further away from Point Zero. That movement led to the formation of a second level of existence characterized by the slowing of the frequency at which the points of awareness and the particles of energy vibrated. In a similar fashion, five additional levels were formed, each characterized by an increasingly slower rate of frequency. The universe which resulted from the entities following their original directive can be pictured as a triangle with Point Zero at the top. Once some entities came to the first level, they began the process of creation and evolution which has resulted over the millions of years in our present existence as human be-

ings on Earth. Our present gross material existence is at the first level along the bottom, the slowest level of frequency.

Ramtha considers the teachings concerning the creation of the world, the evolution of humanity, and the understanding of humans as gods who have forgotten their origin, as mere "philosophy." The adoption of that philosophy is a precondition to masters (students) recovering their divine status, however, change occurs as the philosophy is turned into truth. Truth is apprehended when the philosophy is experienced and believed. That is accomplished through the practice of the several spiritual disciplines taught at the School of Enlightenment. The basic spiritual practice at the school is termed Consciousness & Energy (C&E). Various additional disciplines provide a means of practicing C&E in different game-like settings with specific goals to be accomplished as a means of training the self in the new reality being proposed by Ramtha.

Organization. Ramtha's School of Enlightenment is organized as an esoteric academy with students progressing through a graded curriculum. New students start with a Beginning Weekend at which they are introduced to Ramtha's philosophy and to the practice of C&E. Over the next year, they attend several additional events at which they are given a more complete and detailed overview of the schools teachings and the various disciplines. They may then join the larger student body. To retain their status as a current student after the first year, students must attend two events a year, one in the spring and one in the fall. There are also a number of additional events that students may attend and many, especially those who reside near the school, take advantage of these opportunities. Ramtha calls the students attention to the general instability of the world, both the fluctuating economic climate, and the natural environment (symbolized in natural disasters); students are advised to structure their personal lives in such a way as to be prepared in the face of unexpected adversity.

Membership: As of the mid-1990s, there were slightly more that 3,000 students, approximately half of whom live in the northwest corner of the state of Washington. The others are scattered across North America, Europe, Australia, and New Zealand.

Educational Facilities: Ramtha School for Enlightenment.

Periodicals: *Windworks...Ideas for Awakening Masters.* Send orders to Box 576, Rainier, WA 98576.

Remarks: During the early years of the school, Knight experienced a period of intense criticism, much of it directed at her channeling, an activity considered by many as inherently questionable. Some within the New Age movement, unaware of what was occurring within the school, suggested that Knight's withdrawal from the public spotlight signaled a change of focus toward an darker apocalyptic future. However, as she has again become relatively public, that image has been gradually dissipated. Also in the 1980s, Knights love of horses led her to begin a business of raising and selling Arabian horses. The business prospered until at one point in the mid 1980s, the Arabian horse market fell apart and the business went bankrupt. Knight was plunged into debt and a number of students who had invested in the business lost their investments; many had done so with an understanding that Ramtha had approved and sanctioned their investment. As Knight recovered financially, she offered to pay back all of the students (as well as the other investors) any money they had lost; while some refused her offer, she eventually returned the investment to all who accepted it.

Sources:

Kerins, Deborah, editor. *The Spinner of Tales: A Collection of Stories as Told by Ramtha.* Yelm, WA: New Horizon Publishing Co., 1991.

Knight, J. Z. *A State of Mind.* New York: Warner Books, 1987.

MacLaine, Shirley. *Dancing in the Light.* New York: Bantam Books, 1985.

Melton, J. Gordon. *End Enlightenment: Ramtha's School of Ancient Wisdom.* Hillsboro, OR: Beyond Words Publishing, 1998. 216 pp.

___ (as Ramtha). *I Am Ramtha*. Ed. by Cindy Black, Richard Cohn, Greg Simmons, and Wes Walt. Portland, OR: Beyond Words Publishing, 1986.

Weinberg, Steven L., ed. *Ramtha*. Eastsound, WA: Sovereignty, 1986.

___. *Ramtha: An Introduction*. Eastsound, WA: Sovereignty, 1988.

★1441★
Robin's Return
1008 Lamberton St., NE
Grand Rapids, MI 49505

Dorothy and Ray Davis founded Robin's Return from their home in Grand Rapids, Michigan. In the mid-1960s, they began to receive messages from Paramahansa Yogananda (discussed in the chapter on Hindus). At the time, they did not know who Yogananda was. Then, in 1965, Robin, Dorothy Davis' son by a previous marriage, was killed when his bomber was shot down over Vietnam. After his death, both Ray and Dorothy began to receive messages from him, as well as from Yogananda and other masters. They gathered the messages together and began to publish them, first as a booklet entitled *Robin's Return* and then in a newsletter sent to a contact across the United States. During the last six months of 1966, *Chimes*, the Spiritualist magazine, ran a series of articles by the Davises on their experiences. Reader response led to the establishment of a national network of people who receive the Davis material. Though many of the early messages were from Robin, over the years the majority came from master spiritual teachers and a divine Spirit usually referred to as "I AM."

According to the Davises, light and love are the basic reality of the universe. The soul is evolving toward God through a series of incarnations in which the attempt is made to raise the vibrations of the soul. As one moves in the light of God, one is growing spiritually. Death is the gateway to a new sphere of light. Love is a means of raising one's vibrations, thus creating a channel of communication with the masters. The purpose of life is to become a living expression of love. Growth through the light and love are the essence of the great plan of the universe. Although Ray died in 1976, Dorothy continues spreading their beliefs.

The Davises have been close friends of Nellie Cain of the Spiritual Research Society and Illiana of New Age Teachings (discussed elsewhere in this chapter), and have moved freely in the Universal Link circles.

Membership: Several hundred people receive mailings from the Davis home in Grand Rapids, Michigan.

★1442★
School of Natural Science
25355 Spanish Ranch Rd.
Los Gatos, CA 95030

The School of Natural Science is an organization of men and women devoted to the study and application of natural laws as these operate in all realms of life. The general purpose is to conduct education along moral, ethical, and spiritual lines, the basis of which is outlined in text books known as the Harmonic Series, written by John E. Richardson. Its specific purpose is to help individuals live in harmony with the Constructive Principles of Nature, thereby attaining self-unfoldment, self-mastery, and resultant health and peace. By achieving these goals, people become, in turn, wholesome units in the aggregate of individuals who comprise nations. The School of Natural Science makes no charge for its instruction—it is a Gift to those deemed qualified to receive it.

The School of Natural Science teaches that the Universal Intelligence is revealed through his immutable laws, that nature is engaged in the evolvement of individual intelligences, that nature impels individuals to higher levels of consciousness, that the soul is immortal and passes successively into physical and spiritual bodies, that man's free will works within a law of compensation (karma), that willing conformity to the laws of nature leads to self-

mastery, poise and happiness, and that by living the laws of nature, people come to know instinctively that spiritual reality exists and that life continues after death. Correspondence courses based upon these teachings are offered to students.

Membership: As of 1997, there were approximately 1,000 members in the United States and around the world.

Periodicals: *Life In Action.*

Remarks: The School of Natural Science was established in Stockton, California, in 1883 by John E. Richardson, a practicing attorney. According to Richardson, in the summer of 1883, he was encountered by a stranger at the Grand Central Hotel in Stockton. He had been drawn by a voice telling him, "There is someone at the hotel who wants to see you." The stranger, who identified himself as Hoo-Kna-Ka, told Richardson that he had known him all his life and had come over continents and oceans to see him. He described Richardson's spiritual journey from Baptist to Spiritualist to the decision that both hypnotism and mediumship were the results of the same destructive process. Hoo-Kna-Ka then invited Richardson to become an initiate of the School of the Master, headquartered in India, on the condition that he would begin an education movement of that school in the Western world. He was taught by Hoo-Kna-Ka without pay, and was instructed always to give the teachings as a gift: "By an endless chain of Gifts shall the Great Work be established."

In 1894 Richardson (popularly known as "TK") moved to Chicago and associated himself with Mrs. Florence Huntley. In 1907 he founded the Indo-American Book Company which became the publishing arm of the "Great Work," the name of the movement that spread Hoo-Kna-Ka's teachings. The company issued the Harmonic Series, still the basic teaching materials of the School of Natural Science. In 1916, after what was termed "certain disclosures," (which included charges of financial mismanagement), TK withdrew from the School in Chicago and the Great Work, and moved to California. In California, he reestablished the School and continued to teach and publish his books.

Sources:

Leech, W. Stuart. *The Great Crystal Fraud or the Great P.J.*. Chicago: Occult Publishing Company, 1926.

Richardson, J. E. *The Great Message*. Great School of Natural Science, 1950.

___. *The Great Work*. Chicago: Indo-American Book Co., 1907.

___. *Who Answers Prayer?*. Great School of Natural Science, 1954.

West, Sylvester A. *TK and the Great Work in America*. Chicago: The Author, 1918.

★1443★
Servants of Awareness
(Defunct)

In 1967, following the death of William Ralph Duby, the Servants of Cosmic Awareness (see Cosmic Awareness Communications) split into several groups. The Servants of Awareness was formed by David E. Worcester and was headquartered in Seattle. It continued into the 1970s with several groups around the United States, but has not been heard from in the 1980s. It is presumed defunct.

★1444★
Seth-Hermes Foundation
Current address not obtained for this edition.

Seth is a spirit entity originally channelled through Jane Roberts, a New York housewife. Her channeled material, which appeared in a host of books beginning with the 1966 volume, *How to Develop Your ESP*, stood at the fountainhead of the modern New Age movement in America, and is generally seen as one beginning point of modern channeling (mediumship). Among the people who responded to Seth was Thomas Massari. As early as 1972, Massari also began to channel Seth. Born and raised in Chicago, Massari moved to Los Angeles as a musician. A short time later, unplanned, he began to channel.

Seth first began to speak through Massari in 1972, but Massari eventually came to understand that prior to this incarnation he had made an agreement with Seth to be his voice. During the mid-1970s he taught in the ESP school managed by his sister in Milwaukee, and then founded his own organization, The Parapsychology Center. He moved back to Los Angeles in 1977 and in 1981 formed the Seth-Hermes Foundation. Through the foundation, individuals can relate to Seth who gives lectures and classes, leads retreats, and makes himself available for private consultations. A monthly mastery class is held for advanced students.

The Seth-Hermes Foundation views itself as dealing with the realities people create for themselves. It contends that most people simply create a world without knowing what they are doing or taking responsibility for it. Seth calls attention to the potentials humans possess for creating their world and the need to take action to make that world as positive as possible.

Membership: Not reported.

★1445★
Seth Network International
Box 1620
Eugene, OR 97440

Seth Network International is a network of people who follow and promote the teachings articulated by "Seth," a spirit entity who spoke (was channeled) through Jane Roberts (Mrs. Robert Butts). The network was founded in 1979 as the Austin Seth Center by Dr. Maude Caldwell. Following her death in 1992, the headquarters were moved to Eugene, Oregon, and the present name was adopted. The network is currently headed by Lynda Dahl.

Seth described himself as an "energy personality essence." Jane Roberts Butts (1929–1984) was a housewife and writer who began her life as a channel following some experiments with a ouija board in 1963. Seth first spoke through the board, and as often occurs, was soon speaking through an entranced Roberts, whose husband taped the sessions. Three years later, the first of what would become 22 books appeared based upon Seth's words, *How to Develop Your ESP Power* (1966), later retitled *The Coming of Seth* (1976). In these and the later books, Seth taught a metaphysical system that emphasized some basic ideas including the following: People form their experience through their thoughts, feelings, expectations, and focus; each individual is a multidimensional whole; together, human beings are cooperating in forming our present reality.

The network has as its goal the bringing of the Seth ideas into the mainstream of global consciousness. It hosts an annual conference, SethNet, which centers upon the reform of world society in a manner discussed in Roberts' book, *Psychic Politics* (1976). Human Journeys is a project to make Seth's teachings available in countries where the books are not yet distributed and in languages into which they have not yet been translated.

Membership: Not reported. As of 1993 members are found in 17 countries.

Periodicals: *Reality Change: The Global Seth Journal.*

Sources:

Melton, J. Gordon. *Religious Leaders of America.* Detroit: Gale Research, 1991.

Roberts, Jane. *Adventures in Consciousness: An Introduction to Aspect Psychology.* Englewood Cliffs, NJ: Prentice-Hall, 1975.

___. *Dreams, "Evolution," and Value Fulfillment: A Seth Book.* 2 vols. Englewood Cliffs, NJ: Prentice-Hall, 1986.

___. *The God of Jane: A Psychic Manifesto.* Englewood Cliffs, NJ: Prentice-Hall, 1981.

___. *How to Develop Your ESP Power.* New York: Frederick Fell, 1966. Rept. as: *The Coming of Seth.* New York: Pocket Books, 1976.

___. *Seth, Dreams and Projection of Consciousness.* Stillpoint Publishing, 1986.

___. *The Seth Material.* Englewood Cliffs, NJ: Prentice-Hall, 1970.

___. *Seth Speaks: The Eternal Validity of the Soul.* Englewood Cliffs, NJ: Prentice-Hall, 1972.

___. *The Nature of Personal Reality: A Seth Book.* Englewood Cliffs, NJ: Prentice-Hall, 1974.

Watkins, Susan. *Conversations with Seth: The Story of Jane Roberts's ESP Class.* 2 vols. Englewood Cliffs, NJ: Prentice-Hall, 1980-81.

★1446★
Sisters of the Amber
(Defunct)

As the message of the Universal Link spread in the United States, a number of informal centers developed. Some evolved into independent teaching organizations built around a single teacher-spiritual channel-writer, which published independently, though the teachings remained similar to those of the Universal Link. During the 1970s, the name most connected with the Universal Link operation in North America was Merta Mary Parkinson (d. 1983). Parkinson was, like Liebie Pugh, the British leader of the Link, a journalist and writer and, because of her interest in metaphysics, became an early devotee of the Link.

Parkinson created two more-or-less informal organizations to tie together students. The more general audience received material from the Dena Foundation. Many of the women were brought together as the Sisters of the Amber. Ms. Parkinson became intrigued with amber after a friend asked help in locating some for healing purposes. The Sisters are linked to each other by their dedication to loving service to each other and by the amber each has been given by Ms. Parkinson. She was directed by inner light to begin the work.

★1447★
SOL Association for Research
Box 2276
North Canton, OH 44720

The SOL Association for Research (SOLAR) is dedicated to preserving and disseminating the spiritual insights gained through the deep catatonic trances of psychic William Allen LePar. Paranormally gifted since childhood, LePar shunned these abilities until his early 30s, when he began to enter into periods of trance, at first involuntarily. In 1974 SOL was founded, and in the early 1980s was expanded to SOLAR.

While LePar is in the deep trance state, a voice identified as a union of 12 souls known as The Council speak through him. Considered especially significant in this situation is the exalted level of growth reached by those on The Council. They reportedly speak from the "Celestial Level of the God-Made Heavenly Realms," and they state that this is the only time in history that humanity has been directly contacted by beings in the God-Made Realms. More than 1.25 million words of dialogue with The Council have been recorded, covering virtually all areas of the human condition. This material constitutes one of the most extensive bodies of psychically derived (channeled) material available to mankind.

SOL, non-profit and tax exempt, offers a membership program with a lending library and a quarterly newsletter. Monthly meetings are held in Canton, Ohio, and LePar and SOL associates are available for lectures, presentations, interviews, etc. As of 1995, the organization had produced a dozen books, two video documentaries, and numerous audio tapes. SOLAR has several hundred members in the United States and in several foreign countries.

Membership: In 1995, SOL reported several hundred members in the United States.

Periodicals: *SOLAR Newsletter of the SOL Association for Research.*

★1448★
Spiritual Education Endeavors—The Share Foundation
1556 Halford Ave., No. 288
Santa Clara, CA 95051

Spiritual Education Endeavors (S.E.E.)—The Share Foundation was founded in the mid-1980s by Virginia Essene. In 1984 Essene had allegedly been contacted by The Christ, the same entity who had walked the earth almost 2,000 years ago as Jesus, and she was asked to be the instrument through which he brought his present message to humanity. She worked intensively over a six-month period in 1985 to receive his message via mental telepathy and produced what became a book, *New Teachings for an Awakened Humanity,* published in 1986.

In the book, The Christ issued a warning that failure to acknowledge God in our lives had given humankind a war-like mentality that threatened not only grave harm to the planet but posed the threat that weapons would be taken into outer space. He called for a new peace consciousness and called upon all to join together as light workers in a Light Corps to work for peace on earth. He was placing his Christ energy at humanity's disposal in this endeavor.

The Christ was also preparing for his Second Coming and a new Golden Age. By the end of this century, every loving soul would be given the opportunity to achieve self-mastery. Light workers were to choose a spiritual path that forewent all desire for war and hatred. To bring about this reality, The Christ proposed that each light worker meditate daily and gather with a group to meditate at least once a week. He also called upon people to join with others in efforts to influence governments to embody peace in all they did and intended.

Spiritual Education Endeavors was formed to help mobilize and organize the Light Corps, which could respond positively to Christ's call. It published *New Teachings for an Awakened Humanity* and through the Light Corps has sought to distribute it internationally. Especially for those just beginning in the work, a *Newsletter* was issued nine times annually. Since that time Essene has regularly received messages expanding upon the original words from The Christ and commenting upon ongoing earth changes. These messages have been published in several subsequent books and released in seminars. The period from 1987 to the mid1990s has been designated a period of the awakening of humanity to the new age that is dawning. Shortly after beginning her work, Essene was joined by Ann Valentin who also channels from the Light realm.

Membership: Not reported.

Periodicals: *Newsletter.*

Sources:

The Christ (through Virginia Essene). *New Teachings for an Awakened Humanity.* Santa Clara, CA: Spiritual Education Endeavors Publishing Company, 1986. 197 pp.

Essene, Virginia. *Secret Truths for Teens & Twenties.* Santa Clara, CA: Spiritual Education Endeavors Publishing Company, 1986. 120 pp.

Valentin, Ann, and Virginia Essene. *Cosmic Revelation.* Santa Clara, CA: Spiritual Education Endeavors Publishing Company, 1987. 160 pp.

___. *Descent of the Dove.* Santa Clara, CA: Spiritual Education Endeavors Publishing Company, 1988. 185 pp.

★1449★
Spiritual Research Society
(Defunct)

Edwin Cain, Sr., was the son of a Spiritualist medium. Shortly after their marriage, he and his wife, Nellie Cain recognized some spirit rappings (rhythmic noises made by spirits to communicate messages), which led to a "developing circle" and the emergence of Mr. Cain's mediumship in the early 1940s. Mrs. Cain also began to develop and to contact a group of Masters from the White Brotherhood (spirits who were once human and who, after death, evolved to levels of spiritual excellence and teach humans about spiritual reality). She was accepted by them as a novice and was presented with the robe of the initiate. The Cains founded the Spiritual Research Society, which evolved from the original circle.

The teachings, which came through the Masters, are based upon the evolution and progression of life and of the soul. The universe is organized on an upward spiral from electronic and mineral to vegetable, animal and human, to Christ-Buddhic or divine. The levels are likened to the rising frequency of the musical scale. The soul also evolves to higher levels of consciousness. The universe is organized on seven-fold structures and according to the universal laws of vibration, correspondence, cause and effect, rhythm, polarity and gender.

Following the publication of the first book on the Masters, a copy was sent to Merta Mary Parkinson of the Sisters of the Amber and an American representative of the Universal Link. Parkinson then forwarded a copy to Liebie Pugh, of the Universal Link in England. Subsequent correspondence brought the Cains into close association with Parkinson and Pugh. They were both disappointed by the nonoccurrence of the momentous event predicted for Christmas, 1967. They soon came to view the period since then as a time of great siftings in every area of man's life, a time of renewal and reevaluation and spiritual discoveries. In 1971, they received a message that the Linking had been completed on the outer levels, and the work now is one of radiating light in a collective "Nuclear Evolution" Operation.

Sources:

Cain, Nellie B. *Exploring the Mysteries of Life.* Grand Rapids, MI: Spiritual Research Society, 1972.

___. *Gems of Truth from the Masters.* Grand Rapids, MI: Spiritual Research Society, 1965.

★1450★
Star of Isis Foundation
Current address not obtained for this edition.

The Star of Isis Foundation is a mystery school established in the 1980s by Christine Hayes, better known by her spiritual name, Chrystine StarEagle. Hayes is a channel and the Foundation is built upon the material she has channelled and continues to channel on a regular basis. The Foundation is built around the ancient myth of Isis retrieving the body parts of her slain and mutilated husband, Osiris, recast in the light of present planetary transformations. The purpose of the Star of Isis Foundation is to lead individuals in the "gathering" of the parts of their self into a whole entity/consciousness that leads to a future resurrection of the archetypical Logos/Mind. Through this assemblage, the souls of people can ascend in a Phoenix-like flame, emancipated from earth, and reborn in a realm of Light and Air.

The Foundation initiates individuals into a specific form of meditation (termed Matrix) and teaches the initiate to tap the source of personal co-creative power. The foundation expounds the way to access the ancient archetypes of our spiritual-genetic memories that leads to the premise that all goodness comes from God and that God is found within (not outside) ourselves.

Chrystine StarEagle has channelled one volume, *Magi from the Blue Star,* from Elvis Presley. This book recounts Presley's past incarnation and his spiritual journey since the end of his earthly life.

The volume also recounts his conversations with long-time friend Wanda June Hill and includes stories of his extraordinary effect upon people who knew him.

Membership: The foundation has one center, the Church of the Johannine Origin, in San Antonio, Texas, and in 1992 reported approximately 50 members

Periodicals: *Temple Doors Doctrine of Mysteries.*

★1451★
Trilite Seminars
Current address not obtained for this edition.

Trilite Seminars is an organization that facilitates the work of a channel known as Shaari. Shaari is described as a walk-in, that is a soul that moved into the body of a person who had decided to leave their body. The personality who inhabited Shaari's present body before the walk-in took place had been a trance medium who channeled two entities named Abraham and Malaya. Shaari continues to channel these two entities.

Shaari describes herself as an extraterrestrial entity from Star Command who has a conscious memory of interdimensional and universal knowledge. She also operates as a "holographic" healer. She integrated into the body of the former trance medium in 1989 after that person had requested to leave her body following and automobile accident. Shaari now works to understand the complexities of communication between humans and the Star Command.

Abraham, whom Shaari channels, is described as a member of the Light Brotherhood and the Intergalactic Command whose teachings provide a practical understanding of individuals as dynamic beings in the Universe. Malaya, a feminine entity, brings forth a New Ray of Consciousness, and assists individuals in integrating the new information into their lives. Together, Shaari, Abraham, and Malaya form the triad of the Trilite Seminars.

Shaari holds regular workshops around the United States and Canada, triennial four-day retreats, and private sessions with individuals. Once or twice a year she offers sacred journeys to places considered power sacred sights such as the pyramids in Egypt or Machu Picchu, the Incan center in Peru. These journeys have a twin focus on healing the planet and individual growth.

Membership: Not reported.

★1452★
Trinity Foundation
7410 Montgomery Blvd. NE, Ste. 206
Albuquerque, NM 87109-1574

The Trinity Foundation was founded in 1991 by Norma J. Milanovich, a channel who in 1981 had begun receiving messages from entities who identified themselves as originating from the Great White Brotherhood (the spiritual hierarchy that guides the affairs of the planet) and the Galactic Command, a group that rules this segment of space. Those who began to give messages to Milanovich bore names familiar to theosophists and those who were familiar with the world of flying saucers and the New Age—Kuthumi, Moinka, and Soltec. Much of this material was circulated informally, but a growing response led to the publishing of selected portions received from some entities who claimed to have visited earth from the star system of Arcturus. *We, the Acturians,* appeared in 1990. At about the same time, Milanovich was invited to share the material from the masters with the members of the United Nations Parapsychology subcommittee. These two events occasioned the inauguration of a newsletter, *Celestial Voices,* in October 1990.

Kuthumi, a representative of the Tribunal Council of the Space Command, has emerged as the major voice speaking through Milanovich. He delivered the first message to the United Nations Parapsychology Committee. He noted that the Space Command had made themselves available to assist humanity in transforming

the earth into a world of peace and prosperity for all. The Space Command is composed of individuals who have completed their journey through earth incarnations and have learned the curriculum earth had to teach. They now exist at a higher frequency and now seek to bring the Light to the earth.

In subsequent messages, Kuthumi outlined his vision of coming changes. During the next 20 years (1991-2011) earth will be birthed into a star and individuals will emerge from the three-dimensional world in which we now live into the fifth dimension. To prepare for this change, Kuthumi released a Curriculum of Thought manifestation, containing the material that must be mastered for entry into the fifth dimension. This world is composed of solidified energy perceived through the five senses. To move to the fifth dimension, one must first accept the possibility that other realities synchronized with the physical world exist and can be perceived as one raises their consciousness.

Also, one must learn that we create reality. Reality is created by thoughts, will, emotion, and actions. The path to higher consciousness is one of choosing right thought, right will, right emotion, and right action. As one changes consciousness, one changes reality. Consciousness creates with Light energy. Light is found by looking within.

On September 24, 1991, Kuthumi delivered an important message. He made public a project he had initiated two years previously, The Templar. It was imbedded in an understanding of the earth as an energy system with certain power points similar to the chakras in the tantric understanding of the human body. The United States represents the crown chakra at the top of the head. The crown chakra is being prepared to receive the energies from the Most High. The point of the earth that will actually receive the new energies is in process of being prepared to receive a structure known as the Templar. The Templar is designed to realign earth with the heavens and to stabilize it as it moves through the transition. The Templar will be a pyramid with a base of approximately 500 square feet and a height of 450 feet. Its face will be pink granite and its capstone will be obsidian. It will be surrounded by a six-sided wall.

Milanovich founded the Trinity Foundation to support the building of the Templar. Shortly thereafter, the foundation received a grant of land at Crestone, Colorado, upon which to build the pyramid. The proposed structure has become a major item of controversy in the small community. Meanwhile, Milanovich has published several other books detailing the Masters messages: *Sacred Journey to Atlantis* and *Many Paths, One Way.*

Membership: Not reported.

Periodicals: *Celestial Voices.*

★1453★
Universal Association of Faithists
% Pahspe Publishingq
6115 LaSalle Ave., Ste. 215
Oakland, CA 94611

John Ballou Newbrough (1828-1891) was a Spiritualist medium. In 1881, he received by automatic writing on a typewriter a revelation published under the title *Oahspe.* He rose early each morning for 50 weeks and, as the "lines of light" rested on his hands, he typed for an hour. The first edition of the resultant book was published in September 1882. The next year a convention was held in New York City to work toward founding a communal group to care for orphans and foundlings, as directed in *Oahspe.* A colony was founded in New Mexico, but failed after only a couple of years. Since that time, small bands of followers have kept *Oahspe* in print. The recently published *Inside the Shalam Colony* (1991) by Elnora Wiley is a partly romantic, partly historical account of the original colony.

Oahspe is a large volume, written in the style of the King James version of the Bible. It contains the story of human creation about 78,000 years ago and the upward struggle of the race. Humanity originated on Pan, a Pacific continent much like Lemuria, which was the sole victim of the Biblical flood. Religion evolved through 11 prophets, beginning with Zarathustra and continuing through Joshu (Jesus). All religion and effort have been guided by angelic forces toward the Kosmon Era. During this era, which began in the nineteenth century, a new people will emerge, and will transform the world into a place of joy and beauty.

Over the decades, a wide variety of Faithist groups have emerged and disappeared. The movement is sustained through a number of independent groups who stay in touch through several informal networks and periodicals. The most active center is the Universal Faithists of Kosmon (a church). Its headquarters is in Riverton, Utah, with affiliated centers in Colorado, Utah, California, and West Virginia. It publishes a newsletter, *Kosmon Voice*. The Faithists also sponsor a committee, the Global Council, which carries out various projects suggested and inspirited by *Oahspe*, and holds an annual conference. The leaders of the committee meet monthly through a conference call.

The Eloists, Inc., headquartered in Henniker, New Hampshire, is another active *Oahspe* group. It publishes a periodical, *Radiance*. *The Faithist Journal* is published by Oahspe followers in Arizona. During his mature years, Ray Palmer, the founder/publisher of *Search Magazine* became an enthusiastic believer in Oahspe and added "The Oahspe Circle" as a column to the magazine. The "Circle" carried news of *Oahspe* groups, discussed its main ideas, and promoted networking among the scattered believers. *Search* is now published by Judith M. Statezny at Owl Press in Rosholt, Wisconsin, but still carries "The Oahspe Circle."

Worship among Faithists follows the format suggested in *The Kosmon Church Service Book*, kept in print by some British Faithists. It includes liturgy for worship, baptisms, weddings, and funerals. Ministerial training is offered and ordinations of new ministers scheduled as appropriate.

Membership: Unknown. There are several hundred people who have identified themselves with the Faithists and have agreed to have their name published in their directory. Many more have purchased *Oahspe* (over 20,000 in the last decade) and, though unaffiliated with any of *Oahspe* groups, are sympathetic to the movement's teachings. Groups active in the informal networks can be found in Australia, New Zealand, Great Britain, the Nigeria, and Ghana.

Periodicals: *The Faithist Journal*. Send orders to Drawer 4670, Hualapai, AZ 86412. • *Kosmon Voice*. • *Radiance*. Send orders to Box 83, Henniker, NH 03242. • *Kosmon Unity*. Available from Kosmon Press, BM/KCKP, London, England WC1N 3XX. • *Global Council Newsletter*. • *Four Winds Village News*. Send orders to Rte. 1, Box 2120, Tiger, GA 30576.

Sources:

Dennon, Jim. *Dr. Newbrough and Oahspe*. Kingman, AZ: Faithist Journal, 1975.

___. *The Oahspe Story*. Kingman, AZ: Faithist Journal, 1975.

Oahspe. Los Angeles: Essenes of Kosmon, 1950.

Stowes, K. D. *The Land of Shalam, Children's Land*. Evansville, IN: Frank Molinet Print Shop, n.d.

★1454★
Universal Life: The Inner Religion
PO Box 3549
Woodbridge, CT 06525

Alternate Address: International Headquarters: Universelles Leben, Postfach 5643, 97006 Wuerzburg, Germany. Canadian Headquarters: Universal Life: The Inner Religion, PO Box 54002, Toronto, ON, Canada M6A 3B7.

Universelles Leben or Universal Life: The Inner Religion is a worldwide free Christian movement that originated in 1975, when, as those affiliated with the movement believe, Christ en-

tered the life of Gabriele Wittek, a woman and mother, revealed to her His plan to use her as His instrument on earth. Since then, she has served as His prophetic instrument and ambassadress in fulfilling this plan, which is to show His children the way back into their eternal home and to build up His Kingdom of Peace on earth. In 1980, the first Original Christian Gathering Places for All Godseekers, The Cosmic School of Life emerged— formerly called the Inner Spirit Christ Church—where people came together as in early Christianity to hear the prophetic word, to pray together, and to speak openly with each other about all questions of life, using the Sermon on the Mount and the Ten Commandments as a basis.

In the same year, the movement believes that Christ also called into being the spiritual, mystical schooling path within to the divine self, the Homebringing Mission of Jesus Christ. In this schooling, the Spirit of God teaches all seekers on this earth the Inner Path, the path to experiencing God in one's own inner being. On this Inner Path, the person attains the spiritual expansion of consciousness, becoming one with Christ, God and all forms of nature, by gradually overcoming sinfulness step by step with the power of Christ. On this foundation, in 1984, Universelles Leben was established through the prophetic word.

In the late 1990s, a community of inner Christianity has emerged again. Adherents consider themselves Original Christians who strive for an inner religion, a religion of the heart, an inner striving for the liberation from sin and for gradually becoming one with Christ in the innermost being. They believe that all people are the temple of God and that the Spirit of the Christ of God, which is a spirit of freedom, dwells in everyone. It is a religion without human leaders, rituals, dogmas, or temples of stone, and is not tied to denominations, dogmas, rites, or institutions. Such movements of inner Christianity are not new. They believe that since the time of Jesus of Nazareth, there have been groups of people who took seriously the high ethics of Jesus the Christ's teaching, who with His life gave mankind an example of how to live in the Spirit of God in unity with our neighbor, with the animals, with nature, with all of creation, by observing the Sermon on the Mount and the Ten Commandments.

Universal Life is based on the prophetic word of this generation, given in the form of revelations. These revelations are seen to deepen and clarify the divine laws of God and their application in daily life, explaining many basic spiritual principles such as the why and how of our earthly existence, eternal damnation, reincarnation, the law of sowing and reaping, active faith, health and illness, life after death, man's relationship to the cosmos, and much more. This information is made available to all who desire it through the books and tapes produced by Universelles Leben, whose members believe that only the actualization of the laws of God makes us free, glad, healthy, and loving persons.

Membership: Universal Life is not a membership organization. In 1997 there were three centers in the United States and two in Canada, and an unnumbered number in Europe. Additional centers have opened in Africa, Australia, South America, and Asia.

Periodicals: *The Prophet*.

Remarks: Universal Life has emerged as one of the more controversial groups in German-speaking Europe as a growing concern over new religions has swept across central Europe. Several books denouncing Universal Life have appeared from an anti-cult perspective.

★1455★
Universal Link
1, St. Georges Sq.
St. Annes, Lancs., England

The Universal Link and the Universal Foundation are two closely related British organizations which trace their history to April 11, 1961, to the visionary experience of Richard Grave of Worthing, England. While working on a newly-rented house, he saw "a bearded Christlike figure" who blocked his path. Pointing to a picture, the figure touched the glass, causing it to explode and pulverize, driving fragments into the picture. The being then disappeared in a blaze of orange light. The picture, a representation of an angel announcing the birth of Jesus, soon gained reknown as the "Weeping Angel of Worthing" as salty drops of moisture formed on its surface.

The being, who called himself "Truth," visited Grave often after that and left him a series of messages. The messages were apocalyptic, concentrating on the imminent second coming of the Christ as mankind seems on the brink of disaster. The message and events were carried in a *Psychic News* article on May 4, 1961. Liebie Pugh, an artist of St. Anne's, England, heard of Grave through the articles. After meeting Pugh, Grave realized the spiritual being that had visited him was the one portrayed in a sculpture by Ms. Pugh which she called simply "Limitless Love."

Ms. Pugh is regarded as the architect of the Universal Link, a linking of a number of individuals and groups to the Highest, who in this period is breaking through in an ever-increasing way. The Link developed as an informal fellowship of like-minded individuals centered upon a number of "channels." These channels were delivering revelations of the cosmic operation ushering in the new age.

The critical period in the revelation was from 1961 to 1967. An early revelation through Grave said the following: "No one can know the day nor the hour of MY COMING, or when the great Universal Revelation will be enacted; however by Christmas morning 1967, I will have revealed myself through the medium of nuclear evolution. This is MY PLAN which is absolute."

During the six years, a major effort was made to spread the message and tie together other channels, primarily through the travel and work of Anthony Brooke. Brooke, a descendant of Sir James Brooke, the first "White Rajah of Sarawak," ruled that land before it became a British colony in 1946. In the mid and late 1960s, Brooke traveled widely, locating and tying together individuals and groups. In England, the Universal Foundation was formed, with Brooke and Monica Parish at its head.

As December, 1967 approached, a great feeling of expectancy pervaded the movement. There was hope for an objective event, a spectacular change-over in universal thinking, which would signal the coming new age. When no event occurred, a spiritualized explanation was sought. For Brooke, attention was focused on the purpose of Liebie Pugh. Liebie had become identified with the entity known as Limitless Love, and, as early as 1964, the hypothesis had been put forth that Limitless Love was Liebie herself in the form of a constellated fragmentation of her own personality. Liebie was, reasoned Brooke, "an extension or a projection—a secondary personality, if you like—of Truth or Limitless Love." In January, 1966, Liebie was given a prophecy of her death in December, 1966. After she died in December, members of the Universal Link groups discovered that "Limitless Love is appearing with ever greater frequency in the actions and to the vision of more and more people."

Thus the work of the Universal Foundation became the linking together of groups and individuals who were working toward the spiritual evolution of mankind around the world. These people form a vanguard who are attuned to the cosmic lights and are awaiting the yet-to-appear day of manifestation which will mark the Christing of the whole earth and the beginning of the Golden Age.

The Universal Link was brought to the United States in the late 1960s, primarily through the visits of Anthony Brooke. Initial centers were formed in Elkins, Pennsylvania; Grand Rapids, Michigan; Kansas City, Missouri; Brookfield, Massachusetts; Denver, Colorado, and Los Angeles, California. During the 1970s several of these centers died out, but others became independent centers in their own right, publishing their own books and newsletters. In effect, their work superceded that of the Foundation for North America, though they remained more or less loosely affiliated with the work in England and acknowledged their debt to it. In Grand

Rapids, Nellie Cain and Edwin Cain, Sr. developed the Spiritual Research Society. In Kansas City, Merta Mary Parkinson began to issue material under the name of the Sisters of the Amber and the Dena Foundation. In Brookfield, Illiana (Anita Afton) developed an international network receiving her New Age Teachings. From Los Angeles, Brother Francis (Ralph F. Raymond) moved the Universal Link Heart Center to Santa Monica, where it was renamed the Father's House and then later in the decade to Santa Clara, California, where it existed for many years. Each of these centers is covered elsewhere in this chapter.

Membership: Not reported. There is no direct affiliate of either the Universal Foundation or Universal Link currently functioning in America.

Sources:

Brooke, Anthony. *The Universal Link Revelations.* London: Universal Foundation, 1967.

Pugh, Liebe. *Nothing Else Matters.* St. Anne's-by-the-Sea, Lanc.: The Author, 1964.

[Raymond, Brother Francis Ralph]. *The Universal Link Concept.* Los Angeles: Universal Link Heart Center, [1967].

★1456★
Universalia
Box 6243
Denver, CO 80206

Universalia is a New Age channeling group which grew out of a study group that formed in Denver, Colorado, in 1981. Meeting weekly, the group began to channel by a technique that it termed "thought plane transference," i.e., clearing one's mind, being open to whatever information comes, and writing it down as it enters the consciousness. As a mass of information was accumulated, the group incorporated and in May 1985 released the first issue of a newsletter, *The Universalian.*

Universalia means "of the universe." Information from the process of channeling comes through the individual members of the group from such energies as Kyros, the Brotherhood, Archangel Michael, and so on. Two books of channeled works by Universalia members have been published: *The Kyrian Letters; Transformative Messages for Higher Vision* by Sandra Radhoff and *The Wisdom Teachings of Archangel Michael* by Lori Flory as told to Brad Steiger. The thrust of Universalia's teaching is toward the expansion of conscious awareness and follows the main affirmation of New Age philosophy. God, the I AM, resides within each person. Spiritual life is perfect; the physical dreamspace dimension is illusionary. Having created illusions, humans tend to believe in them and empower them. Hence, they follow outward form instead inward reality. Members are taught that they are the loved and beautiful expressions of God and have unlimited potential. As they are connected to all of creation, service is an integral part of their life.

Membership: In 1998, the 14th year of publication, the circulation of the newsletter is 800, and it is sent nationally and internationally. In 1998, there was only one active group in Denver, although past and present members still submit channeled material to Universalian, which continues to be presented quarterly on a freewill offering basis.

Periodicals: *The Universalian.*

Flying Saucer Groups

★1457★
Aetherius Society
6202 Afton Pl.
Hollywood, CA 90028

The Aetherius Society was begun in London in 1954 by George King, medium and long-time student of occultism and yoga. He was told to prepare himself to become the voice of the Interplanetary Parliament. In 1955, he was named by Master Aetherius of Venus as the "primary terrestrial mental channel." Since that time, he has regularly channeled messages form Aetherius and the Master Jesus. They and other members of the Great White Brotherhood oversee the activities of the Society. A center was opened in Los Angeles within a year of the first messages. King's teachings are the focus of the Society.

According to the Aetherius Society, earth is engaged in a cosmic warfare focused on the activities of certain "black magicians" seeking to enslave man. The cosmic brotherhood, the space hierarchy, wages war on these magicians. Members of the Society cooperate with the Brotherhood by channeling spiritual energy to particular concerns. Channeling activities are centered on certain periods when a space ship orbits earth and sends out special power. These periods are termed "spiritual pushes," and all members help direct the energy. These pushes are typically given military titles, such as Operation Bluewater, which ended on November 27, 1976. During this operation, the cosmic masters poured vital spiritual power into a psychic center through a spiritual-power radiating instrument at sea.

Still celebrated is Operation Starlight, begun at Holdstone Down in England in 1958 and continued for three years and one month. During this time, King, directed by a vision of the Master Jesus, climbed eighteen designated mountains to charge them with spiritual power, to be used by anyone making a pilgrimage to them. August 23 is the date of the annual convention.

The most important date in the annual calendar is July 8, commemorating the 1964 initiation of earth by a gigantic space ship and the ship's manipulation of cosmic energies. Other days in the annual calendar are King's birthday, the end of Operation Karmalight (a phase of Armageddon) and the Master Jesus' birthday. The push dates are announced annually and are usually for periods of three to four weeks.

As described by King, the Interplanetary Parliament is headquartered on Saturn, the tribunal of the solar system. The agents from Mars and Venus are making a metaphysical survey of earth. The saucers have also saved earth from the damage of terrestrial scientists to earth's ionosphere.

King has accepted consecration as an archbishop through the Independent Liberal Catholic Church headed by Richard Earl Quinn. He has also received a number of titles and awards, most of them conferred by the "cosmic" sources or the Society which he heads. He has been a prolific writer, the author of several books and numerous pamphlets, all published by the Aetherius Society.

Membership: Not reported, but in 1987 the *Cosmic Voice* newsletter reported a circulation of 650 copies. There are two centers of the society in the United States, one in Hollywood and one in Detroit, Michigan. Several hundred members are involved. The Society has several centers in England.

Periodicals: *Cosmic Voice.* • *Spiritual Healing Bulletin.*

Sources:

King, George. *A Book of Sacred Prayers.* Hollywood, CA: Aetherius Society, 1966.

___. *The Nine Freedoms.* Los Angeles: Aetherius Society, 1963.

___. *The Practices of Aetherius.* Hollywood, CA: Aetherius Society, 1964.

___. *The Twelve Blessings.* London: Aetherius Press, 1958.

___. *You Are Responsible.* London: Aetherius Press, 1961.

The Story of the Aetherius Society. Hollywood, CA: Aetherius Society, n.d.

★1458★
Ashtar Command
Current address not obtained for this edition.

In 1980 Thelma B. Terrell, through the publication of the book *World Messages for the Coming Decade,* announced that she had been in contact with a group of space beings known collectively as the Ashtar Command. They described themselves as residing in a set of thousands of spaceships that hovered above the planet. Through Tuella, the name assumed by Terrell as a channel for the members of the Ashtar Command, the command asserted its desire to speak with world leaders concerning the crisis of the planet. The command explained that it acted as representatives of the Intergalactic Council that derived its authority from the spiritual hierarchy of the solar system. A number of the members of this council and hierarchy were previously known and described by theosophists as members of the theosophical spiritual hierarchy. The head of the hierarchy as described in the material channeled by Tuella is Sananda, better known as Jesus Christ.

While concerned about the imminent world crisis, members of the council are forbidden to interfere in the life of the planet without the approval of the governments, but have to date been unable to confer with such leadership.

According to the command, the planet is soon to go through a period of cleansing, to begin with a tilting of the earth and widespread destruction, and then to enter a new age of Light. The Ashtar Command has as part of its mission the evacuation of those souls who are already walking in the light, during this period of cleansing. The program of world evacuation was announced in Tuella's second book. The sign of the coming transition will be the tilting of the earth's axis. As the tilting begins, the computers on the spaceships will lock on the people of Light and lift them off the planet along with the children—those not yet old enough to be accountable. The command wants to meet with the governments to facilitate the most orderly evacuation.

The head of the mission to earth is Ashtar, a space being first channeled and made famous by George Van Tassel, founder of the Ministry of Universal Wisdom. In the intervening years, a number of contactees have brought forth messages from Ashtar, including Oscar Magocsi, Ethel B. Hill, Franklin Thomas, and European contactee Eugenio Siragusa.

Guardian Action Publications was founded to publish and disseminate the messages of the Ashtar command. Along with the several books produced through the 1980s, a newsletter, *Ashtar's Golden Circle,* was also issued. In 1988, Ashtar made it known that his work of announcing the mission and the future cataclysm and evacuation had been completed. He would retire until the time of the evacuation. In the meantime, Tuella would continue to disseminate the message to those who had yet to hear and concentrate on working directly with Sananda in bringing forth energies from the spiritual hierarchy, from the very throne of the Father Mother God, to the people of the planet. This new work was signaled by the first issue of a new periodical, *The Throne Connection.*

Membership: Not reported.

Periodicals: *The Throne Connection.*

Sources:

Tuella (Thelma B. Turrell). *Ashtar: A Tribute.* Durango, CO: Guardian Action Publications, 1985. 178 pp.

___. *On Earth Assignment.* Salt Lake City, UT: Guardian Action International, 1988. 179 pp.

___. *Project World Evacuation.* Salt Lake City, UT: Guardian Action International, 1982.180 pp.

___. *World Messages for the Coming Decade: A Cosmic Symposium.* Deming, NM: Guardian Action Publications, 1980. 128 pp.

★1459★
Association of Sananda and Sanat Kumara
Box 35
Mount Shasta, CA 96067

The Association of Sananda and Sanat Kumara is headed by Sister Thedra (Dorothy Martin), for many years a channel for the ascended masters. Very early in her career, she became the object of a famous sociological study, *When Prophecy Fails*. She also reports that in 1954 that she was healed and restored to a life of usefulness by Sananda, an ascended master, and she was instructed to go to Peru and Bolivia, where for the next five years she experienced great trials and tribulations. She spent some time at the monastery established by the Brotherhood of the Seven Rays headed by George Hunt Williamson. During this period she lived with the natives, observing and experiencing their hardships, squalor and unbelievable poverty. Through this period of training under the tutelage of the masters, she learned the "true meaning of divine love towards human beings, regardless of their status in life." The ensuing years were interspersed with moments of ecstastic communication with the masters—Sibors, the Elohim (council of Gods), John the Beloved, the Angel Moroni (mentioned in the *Book of Mormon*), beings from other planets, and, primarily, Sananda, who most people know as the Christ. Thedra was given the prediction of the reincarnation of the Angel Moroni, which occurred in 1965. The child was to begin to manifest his powers in August, 1975.

While still in Peru, Thedra began to send the inspired messages back to interested people in the United States. Through her, Christ continues to reveal and call out to those who wish wholeheartedly to come to Him. These people will be sibored—illumines of the Father. A sibor is a teacher in the higher realms.

Sister Thedra returned to the United States from South America in 1961 and established the association in 1965. The material channeled through her is sent across the United States and to a number of foreign countries to those students who request it. The basic material is contained in three sets of material: "The Sibors Portions," "The Fundamentals," and "The Order of Melchezdek." These are constantly supplemented by ongoing revelation from the masters. In 1985, the association hosted the first annual Gathering of the Children of Light, a convocation of individuals who receive Sister Thedra's material and/or are related to similar groups.

Membership: The association does not keep statistics on the number of students who regularly request material channeled by Sister Thedra. It is estimated to be in the thousands. There is one center in Mt. Shasta.

Educational Facilities: University of Melchezedek, Castleton, Virginia.

Sources:

Festinger, Leon, Henry W. Riecken, and Stanley Schachter. *When Prophecy Fails*. New York: Harper & Row, 1956.

Sananda, as recorded by Sister Thedra. *I, the Lord God Say Unto Them*. Mt. Shasta, CA: Association of Sananda and Sanat Kumara, [1954].

Thedra. *Excerpts of Prophecies from Other Planets Concerning Our Earth*. Mt. Shasta, CA: Association of Sananda and Sanat Kumara, [1956].

Thedra, Sister. *Mine Intercome Messages from the Realms of Light*. Sedona, AZ: Association of Sananda and Sanat Kumura, [1990].

Watkins, Edward L. *The Teachings and the Liberation*. Mt. Shasta, CA: Association of Sananda and Sanat Kumara, 1977.

★1460★
Blue Rose Ministry
Blue Rose Starlight Spiritual Center
Box 332
Cornville, AZ 86325

The Blue Rose Ministry was founded by Robert E. Short, a channel for flying saucer entities. Short became a channel in the 1960s and emerged into public notice in 1967 at the contactee convention at Giant Rock, California, hosted by George Van Tassel. On Saturday evening, October 14, as Short was being introduced to the assembled audience, a reddish-orange craft flew overhead and was seen by all for approximately two minutes. Short then chan-

neled a message from "Korton," who described himself as a resident of the planet Jupiter who flew over Earth in a mother ship. The light the people saw was described as a space craft from that mother ship. While Korton is the main entity who speaks through Short, others also at times have spoken.

The goal of the ministry is the preparation and closer atunement with all enlightened being in the cosmos. Short has authored several books and his lectures are available on audio tapes. He also conducts private channeling consultations. The ministry has periodic Solar Space Circle seminars.

Membership: Not reported. The ministry has two centers, one in Cornville, Arizona, and one in Joshua Tree, California.

Periodicals: *Solar Space-Letter*.

★1461★
Brotherhood of the Seven Rays
(Defunct)

Among the early contactees was George Hunt Williamson (1926-1986), an archeologist and student of Theosophical literature. He and his wife were among those who watched from a distance as George Adamski made his first contact with a Venusian in the California desert on November 12, 1952. Then, in 1953, Williamson published his own story, *The Saucers Speak*, in which he claimed contact with Martians by way of automatic writing (writing what a spirit dictates) as early as August 2, 1952. The messages were, initially, from Kadar Laqu, the head of the Interplanetary Council-Circle. The messages called for cooperation to prevent the death of human civilization. The Telonic Research Center was established by Williamson to study the new science of space-visitation.

All of Williamson's interests were brought together in the Brotherhood of the Seven Rays. Besides contact with the space beings, Williamson had been in touch with the ascended masters, those mysterious beings first described by Guy Ballard, founder of the "I AM" Religious Activity. As early as 1955, Lake Titicaca had been mentioned as a sanctuary of the Great White Brotherhood, the hierarchy of ascended masters who were once human and who now as spirits teach humans about spiritual realities. In 1956, it was decided that an outer retreat of the sanctuary (as well as the others around the world) would be established by dedicated individuals. The inner sanctuaries for full-fledged members date to the submergence of Lemuria, when the secrets of that advanced civilization were deposited in secluded centers the world over. Araru-Muru, now an ascended master in the spirit world, was in charge of Titicaca. The other retreat, or abbey, was to be located near the inner sanctuary on the Peruvian side of Lake Titicaca, and was to have priories at spots around the world as contact points with the populace.

In December, 1956, Williamson, under his religious name, Brother Philip, and others made a trip to Peru to establish the Abbey of the Seven Rays, Lord Muru's primary outer retreat. The expedition extended through most of 1957. The ruins of the area were viewed as partially the result of contact and cooperation between the Great White Brotherhood and the space masters. The contact has continued, and is focused in the Brotherhood of the Abbey. It was Williamson's belief that "the space confederation has a gigantic base there near the remains of the lost cities," which survived from the time of the original contacts.

The Brotherhood of the Seven Rays, referring to the spectrum of light rays administered by the ascended masters, was established at the time of the destruction of Lemuria between 10,000 and 12,000 B.C., but not until 1956 did it have outward expression in a monastic system in which students could come together. Since each student would be most attuned to one of the seven rays, the grouping of students would bring a harmony of the seven colors symbolic of the spiritual life of the monastery. The monastery was established in the 1960s and continued into the 1970s. Students who came to live at the center in Peru had to accept the cosmic Christ as one who came to earth and who is due to return in the near future. The Essene way of life—meditation, fasting, and contemplation—was followed. The communal meal, or supper, of the Essenes was observed daily. Novices underwent water-baptism by immersion before becoming friars and were anointed with oil before becoming monks. No narcotics or stimulants (including chocolate) were used, and monks were vegetarians. Hair was worn long. Both sexes were welcome to all levels, and marriage was acceptable.

Associated with the Brotherhood were its two orders. The Order of the Red Hand was dedicated to the preservation of the arcane knowledge through the ages, particularly through the Scriptorium at the Monastery in Peru. The Ancient Amethystine Order was the prime group associated with the Brotherhood and has reference to the vibrations of the seventh ray of violet, into which the earth is moving. Its hoped-for effects were to be the cure of humanity's ills and earth's drunken state. United States headquarters of Williamson's small following was in Corpus Christi, Texas.

Remarks: It was Williamson's claim that his real name was Michael d'Obrenovic and that he was a descendent of a Yugoslavian royal family. During the last years of his life, Williamson reasserted that claim and, as Michael Djorde Milan d'Obrenovic, was consecrated to the episcopacy by an unnamed bishop claiming orders from the Nestorian (Syro-Chaldean) Church. He moved to Santa Barbara, California and established an independent jurisdiction called the Holy Apostolic Catholic Church, Syro-Chaldean Diocese of Santa Barbara and Central California. There was but one small parish which existed for several years in the early 1980s.

Williamson was also profiled in several issues of *Who's Who* in which he claimed degrees from at least three institutions of higher learning which deny ever having issued degrees to him.

Sources:

McCoy, John. *They Shall Be Gathered Together.* Corpus Christi, TX: The Author, 1957.

Williamson, George Hunt [Brother Philip]. *The Brotherhood of the Seven Rays.* Clarksburg, VA: Saucerian Books, 1961.

___. *Road in the Sky.* London: Neville Spearman, 1959.

___. *The Saucers Speak.* London: Neville Spearman, 1963.

___. *Secret Places of the Lion.* London: Neville Spearman, 1959.

★1462★
Cosmic Circle of Fellowship
4857 N. Melvina Ave.
Chicago, IL 60630

The Cosmic Circle of Fellowship was formed in 1954 by William A. Ferguson, Edward A. Surine, and Edna I. Valverde and was incorporated in Illinois in 1955. Ferguson, a former mail carrier, learned the techniques of absolute relaxation and became adept at relaxing his body, mind, and conscious spirit. In 1937, he wrote *Relax First* and later began to teach relaxation techniques to others.

Ferguson reported that, on July 9, 1938, while lying on his sofa in a state of absolute relaxation, his body was charged by a powerful Current of Life—Pure Intelligent Energy—and carried away to the Seventh Dimension. During his two-hour stay in the Seventh Dimension, he held the key to all knowledge and his soul became illuminated. Upon his return back to the Earth's Third Dimension (normal waking consciousness), he found that his physical body was no longer on the sofa, and, according to the account, he could not be seen nor heard by his wife and his friend. He placed his noncorporal being back on the sofa, and soon he regained his physical, three-dimensional form.

Ferguson claimed that he experienced the Sixth Dimension on July 16 of the following week, when he was carried away to the center of all Creation. There he saw Creation in action—the rays

of Pure Intelligent Energy were of all forms and colors and were flowing throughout a cube of Pure Universal Substance. Other experiences were to follow.

According to Ferguson, in 1947, Khauga, the chief uniphysicist of our solar system, took Furguson on a trip to Mars. Upon his return to Earth, members of his family and a friend could neither see nor hear him. In his eagerness to tell his experience, he had not first allowed himself to return to three dimensions. Realizing what was occurring, he went into the next room, lay on a cot, and was transformed into three dimensions. He then went into the next room and told his account.

Ferguson reported that the matter of the physical body had been raised into a four-dimensional frequency, and that he had been teleported to Mars at the speed of consciousness. He returned with a message that the Martians were sending an expedition to Earth. Within a few months, many UFOs were reported, and several people claimed that they had made personal contacts with their inhabitants.

In 1954, Ferguson revealed that he was taken aboard a Venusian spacecraft and given a message from the Oligarchs of Venus for the people of earth. They noted that spacecraft normally function in four dimensions (and are hence invisible), but can also function in three dimensions by changing their frequency or their density. When they disappear suddenly, they have merely changed back into the fourth dimension.

In the 1940s, Ferguson began to gather a group primarily related to the cosmic healing techniques and the "clarified water device" taught to Ferguson by Khauga. The device, thought to impart healing properties to water, got Ferguson in trouble with the American Medical Association. Eventually, he was convicted of fraud in 1947 and served a year in prison. Upon his return from prison, he decided to go public with his story and organized the Cosmic Circle. In 1958, he commenced a journey to found circles in other cities, gaining a following in Washington, Philadelphia, New York, and San Francisco.

According to Ferguson, at the center of creation are the Father and Mother of creation. A sphere of pure intelligent energy exists inside a cube of pure universal substances. Creation commences as the rays of life of the Father impregnate the substance of the Mother. Khauga is described as the Comforter, the Spirit of Truth, the angel who gave the Book of Revelation to St. John, a perfected being from the Holy Triune. Khauga is the leader in the Universal Brotherhood of the Sons of the Father, members of which are drawn from the various solar systems. They are preparing earth for the next evolutionary step—the second coming of Jesus.

Members believe that a war of consciousness, symbolized by the war in heaven of Revelation 12, has been created as man makes the next step in evolution. As the New Age comes in, the dragon of materialism and evil will be overthrown. It will be replaced as man is lifted into a fourth-dimensional consciousness. Ferguson had been a long-time teacher of relaxation, and his techniques remain the major way to consciousness expansion.

Ferguson died in 1967. Leadership passed to the Chicago group, which still publishes his booklets. Associated with it is the Cosmic Study Center, headed by Cloe Driscoll of Potomac, Maryland.

Membership: In 1997, the circle reported 41 members in the Chicago area.

Sources:

The Comforter Speaks. Potomac, MD: Cosmic Study Center, 1977.

Ferguson, William. *A Message from Outer Space.* Oak Park, IL: Golden Age Press, 1955.

___. *My Trip to Mars.* Chicago: Cosmic Circle of Fellowship, 1954.

___. *The New Revelation.* The Author, 1959.

___. *Relax First.* Chicago: Bronson-Canode Printing Co., 1937.

★1463★
Cosmic Star Temple
Current address not obtained for this edition.

The Cosmic Star Temple was founded in 1960 by Violet Gilbert of Santa Barbara, California, who claims that her first contact with the space brothers was in 1937. Prior to that time, she was a student of Theosophy and "I AM" Religious Activity, and is described as having a "rich background of service for the Brotherhood since childhood." As an adult, she was made aware of the space brothers in 1937 and in January, 1939, after an eight-month preparation, she was given a three-and-one-half-week excursion to Venus. This trip was a physical visit. Her initial contact had been arranged by her previous teachers, following a request for healing. She received a complete physical healing. Since her initial visit, she has returned in the astral (not physically, but through her consciousness). She also acquired a control, Dr. Winston of the Ashtar Command. Her first trip to Mars was in 1955. She was not allowed to go public until 1960.

While on Venus, she was given instructions in healing, which forms a major aspect of the Temple's works, and in reading the Akashic records. (The Akashic records are the records of all that has happened, and are inscribed on the "universal ethers.") Mrs. Gilbert reads the Akashic records of individuals, which give information about their previous incarnations. The teachings of the Temple are eclectic and include material from the New Thought metaphysics, Spiritualism and the dominant Theosophy. Color-healing has become a major emphasis.

Mrs. Gilbert teaches that the coming of the space brothers is entirely beneficial. Their overall purpose is to keep us from destroying ourselves and to share their advanced knowledge. Mankind now is in a transition to a new age and is currently experiencing a cleansing in preparation.

Membership: Not reported.

Sources:

Gilbert, Violet. *"Love Is All."* Grants Pass, OR: Cosmic Star Temple, 1969.

___. *My Trip to Venus.* Grants Pass, OR: Cosmic Star Temple, 1968.

★1464★
Delval UFO, Inc.
948 Almshouse Rd.
Ivyland, PA 18974

Delval UFO, Inc. is a New Age UFO contactee group founded in 1972 by its current directors, Anthony Volpe and Lynn Volpe. Members seek to commune with the Space Brothers and Sisters on all levels of existence. They hope to be an instrument in the process of preparing humanity for the New Age, which is seen as imminent.

There is one group which meets monthly at the Pennsylvania headquarters. Through its periodical, the group maintains contact with people across the United States, Canada, and Japan.

Membership: In 1992 Delval UFO reported 400 members in the United States and additional adherents in Japan and Australia.

Periodicals: *Awakening.*

Sources:

Clark, Jerome. "UFOs in the 1980s" in *The UFO Encyclopedia,* Volume 1. Detroit, MI: Apogee Books, 1990.

Volpe, Anthony, and Lynn Volpe. *Principles and Purposes of Delval UFO, Inc.* Ivyland, PA: The Authors, n.d.

★1465★
Extraterrestrial Earth Mission
PO Box 959, No. 0432
Kihei, HI 96753

The organization today known as Extraterrestrial Earth Mission can be traced to March 3, 1986, when an extraterrestrial spirit named Avinash walked into the body of a person named John in the Mission's literature. John was a channel and teacher of metaphysics in the Seattle, Washington, suburb of Bellevue. He had previously been channeling an entity named Elihu.

The concept of a "walk-in" was popularized by Ruth Montgomery, who described situations in which the spirit of an individual would, for whatever reason, abandon a body and a disembodied spirit would walk-in and take over. In that change, the memory of the person who left would remain, but the personality of the new entity would take over. Thus it was that Avinash walked-in and took over John's body. Shortly after Avinash appeared, he moved to Hawaii. He was accompanied by a second walk-in, a female named Alezsha. In Hawaii they met a third walk-in, Ashtridia. During the remainder of 1986, the primary teaching that is channeled by Avinash, concerns the concept of mastery of limitation. The universe, he taught, tended to rearrange itself according to one's concept of reality. By changing one's reality, removing a sense of limitation, the world began to change.

The three also have contact with a huge extradimensional spaceship resulting in their becoming conscious of their ability to operate in other dimensions. Before the year is out, the three decided to move to Sedona, Arizona. Soon after relocating they met a fourth walk-in, Arthea. Avinash and Arthea soon discovered that they were divine design mates, i.e., a couple divinely created to work together. Through 1987 the group of walk-ins grew to 12 but disbanded as each found their mission elsewhere. By October, only Avinash, Arthea, and a third person, Alana, remained.

The three remaining people would experience what is not a totally unique occurrence, but certainly an uncommon one. Over the next years a series of new entities would walk-in to their body and others depart; thus the same body would become known by different names. Thus John, now known as Avinash, would soon become known as Aktivar, Alarius, Savizar, and most recently ZaviRah. Arthea became known as Akria, Polaria, Silarra, and most recently Ziva'rah. Alana became known as Akrista and then as Tantra. It is believed that each of these names refer to an extraterrestrial person who inhabits the body of the earth person. The emergence of Aktivar, Akria, and Akrista occurred at the end of the summer of 1987. During the last three months of 1987 into 1988, these three entities toured the United States during which time Extraterrestrial Earth Mission began to make an initial public impact. The three made a videotape on humanity's role as co-creators of heaven on earth and a series of cassette tapes aimed at overcoming particular individual dysfunctionalities.

In March 1988 a new phase of work began when Aktivar, Akria, and Akrista left and were replaced by three new walk-ins, Alarius, Polaria, and Tantra. Shortly thereafter Tantra exited from the trio and began to work separately. Alarius and Polaria described their work as temporary, preparing the way for Savizar and Silarra. Under the guidance of the couple known as Savizar and Silarra, Extraterrestrial Earth Mission matured into a New Age organization announcing the planetary shift of humans from dense physical bodies into bodies of light. According to Savizar and Silarra, there are many masters present on the earth today. It was their job to awaken these masters to the nature of their true selves and to cooperate with them in the co-creation of a new earth. Assisting in this process, the pair taught the superconscious technique, which, when used, allows people to manifest their desires by altering their picture of reality.

In 1990, Savizar and Silarra were replaced by ZaviRah and Ziva'rah. Each change is believed to announce a new phase in the mission. In this case, the newcomers represented a change from an exclusive emphasis on opening and awakening to one of mobilization. Those who have been awakened to their true nature should begin the process of creation and manifestation. In 1993 Zavirah and Ziva'rah were replaced by Drakar and Zrendar, and very soon after their appearance Extraterrestrial Earth Mission moved from Arizona to Hawaii. Included in the new phase of the mission is the ChristStar Project, the work of a group of people on

Maui to built a prototype of the new civilization. Public events have been developed to present techniques (usable technologies) of consciousness that assist individuals to see the divinity is all life and to manifest their own role as co-creators of Heaven on Earth.

In response to the lectures, workshops, and the printed, audio, and video material published by the mission, groups have formed around the United States and Canada to share in the mission's work. Currently, ChristStar Project Mastery Events are being held at which many extraterrestrial entities speak through Drakar and Zrendar to the assembled group. Extraterrestrial Earth Mission has been chartered through the Universal Life Church in Arizona.

Membership: Not reported.

Periodicals: *ChristStar.*

Sources:

Savizar and Silarra. *Conscious Channeling.* Sedona, AZ: Earth Mission Publishing, 1989. 82 pp.

___. *Extraterrestrial Earth Mission. Book I: The Awakening.* Sedona, AZ: Earth Mission Publishing, 1989. 155 pp.

___. *The Superconscious Technique.* Sedona, AZ: Earth Mission Press, 1989. 43 pp.

★1466★
GAF International/Adamski Foundation
Box 1722
Vista, CA 92085

The first person to become widely known for his claims to having talked to the beings who flew the flying saucers and who taught what was purported to be their wisdom was George Adamski (1891-1965). On November 20, 1952, he claimed to have conversed with a human-like man from Venus, the first of several contacts and subsequently wrote three of the most popular flying saucer books ever penned: *Flying Saucers Have Landed* (co-authored with Desmond Leslie); *Inside the Space Ships* (reprinted as *Inside the Flying Saucers*); and *Flying Saucers Farewell* (reprinted as *Behind the Flying Saucer Mystery*). The two most important of the several groups which emerged to perpetuate his teachings were the now former George Adamski Foundation and the UFO Education Center.

Polish-born Adamski first assumed a role as a metaphysical teacher in the 1930s when he issued several publications from the Royal Order of Tibet, an order which he claimed to represent and for whom he lectured. He was also briefly associated with the Order of Loving Service, another metaphysical group centered on Laguna Beach, California. For many years he lived in Southern California and lectured to interested audiences.

Soon after his contact with the space people and his first two books appeared (1953 and 1955), Adamski attained a broad following among people not only interested in his contact stories, but the wisdom which the space brothers had to offer. In 1957 he organized his following into the International Get Acquainted Club. The next year his metaphysical teachings, the cosmic wisdom of the saucer people, began to appear first in a telepathy course and then in its more systematic form in *Cosmic Philosophy* (1961) and the *Science of Life Study Course* (1964).

Adamski, while a popular lecturer, was not organizationlly minded. He turned his early organization over to C. A. Honey, who broke with Adamski shortly before his death. However, in 1965, Alice Wells (d. 1980), Adamski's daughter, and Charlotte Blob, his secretary and editor, both formed organizations to keep his teachings alive. GAF International brought together the largest group of Adamski followers. After Wells' death, Fred Steckling, a longtime associate of Adamski, became head of the Foundation. The UFO Education Center with headquarters in Valley Center, California and Appleton, Wisconsin has a similar program to to the Foundation.

Membership: Not reported.

Remarks: Adamski was plagued throughout his life by charges of fraud. In the 1950s several expose articles claimed that Adamski had faked the photographs he claimed to have taken of the flying saucers. Noting the resemblance of his *Inside the Space Ships* to a science fiction novel he wrote in the 1940s led to further accusations. The most damaging attack upon Adamski's credibility came from his close associate, C. A. Honey. He published material from Adamski's own copy of Royal Order of Tibet materials (edited for reissuance in the *Science of Life Study Course*) as if it originated from the space brothers.

Sources:

Adamski, George. *Cosmic Philosophy.* Freeman, SD: Pine Hill Press, 1971.

George Adamski, Questions and Answers by the Royal Order of Tibet. Laguna Beach, CA: Privately Printed, 1936.

Leslie, Desmond, and George Adamski. *Flying Saucers Have Landed.* London: T. Werner Laurie, 1953.

Steckling, Fred. *Why Are They Here?* New York: Vantage Press, 1969.

Zinsstag, Lou. *UFO...George Adamski: Their Man on Earth.* Tucson, AZ: UFO Photo Archives, 1990.

Zinsstag, Lou, and Timothy Good. *George Adamski, The Untold Story.* Beckenham, Kent: Ceti Publications, 1983.

★1467★
Interplanetary Connections
℅ Bashar Tapes, Inc.
7210 Jordan Ave., Ste. B53
Canoga Park, CA 91301

Interplanetary Connections is the organization promoting the channeling activity of Darryl Anka. Anka, the brother of singer Paul Anka, is an illustrator and designer who began to channel two entities, Bashar and Anima, in 1983. Previously he had been reading on mediumship and sitting in a class learning how to be a medium. Bashar and Anima are thought of as beings from an extraterrestrial society that communicates totally by telepathy. They do not have names in the same way that humans do, so they simply chose two names for the sake of convenience. *Bashar* is an Arabic word meaning commander, and *Anima* is a Jungian psychological term referring to the feminine aspect expressed through a masculine individual.

Twice in a single week in the early 1970s—each time in the company of other people—Anka saw a flying space craft at relatively close range. He described it as being triangular in shape and approximately 40 feet on each side and eight feet thick. However, it was a decade later—when Bashar began to channel through Anka—that he concluded that the craft he saw was in fact Bashar's spaceship.

Bashar proclaimed he was from the planet Essassani, located approximately 500 light years away in the direction of the constellation Orion. However, the planet is located in a different dimension, and its solar system is thus invisible to normal sight. Bashar described himself as approximately five feet tall with whitish-gray skin and no hair. Bashar, when he channelled, also emphasized that he was speaking as a single voice for the collective voices of his society who had tuned into him as he spoke through Anka.

Bashar manifested in order to begin an interaction between worlds and assist this world through a time of transition. An essential element in the message of Bashar and his colleagues (collectively called the Association) is the message of overcoming limitation. According to the message, a basic problem of human society is guilt. Guilt perpetuates limitation and keeps people from realizing their own empowerment. Further, guilt prevents our claiming our birthright—happiness, ecstasy, and creativity. Human beings are by nature infinite creators like the Infinite Creator who created them.

By 1984, Anka was channeling once a week and then two to three nights a week over the next few years. The sessions were tape recorded. By 1987 more than 200 people were coming to sessions each Thursday evening to listen to the channeling. Interplanetary Connections was founded to organize the channeling session, to care for the tapes, and to publish transcripts. A volume with summaries of the information and highlights from the more important sessions was compiled and released in 1990 as *Bashar: Blueprint for Change, A Message from Our Future.* Anka has become a popular person at New Age events at which he frequently lectures and leads workshops.

Membership: Not reported.

Sources:

Anka, Darryl. *Bashar: Blue Print for Change, A Message from Our Future.* Simi Valley, CA: New Solutions Publishing, 1990. 302 pp.

___. *Miracles.* Encino, CA: Interplanetary Connections, 1987. 49 pp.

___. *The New Meta-Physics.* Beverly Hills, CA: Light & Sound Communications, 1987. 95 pp.

___. *Orion and the Black League.* Encino, CA: Interplanetary Connections, 1985. 72 pp.

Perry, Lee, and Michwel Heril. "Interview with Darryl/Bashar." *Meditation* (Winter 1985/86): 34-44.

Waldron, Caryline. "Bashar: An Extraterrestrial Among Us." *Life Times* 3.

★1468★
Last Day Messengers
Current address not obtained for this edition.

The Last Day Messengers is a small group centered in Fort Lauderdale, Florida, headed by Dave W. Bent. Bent became interested in psychic phenomena and began to develop his psychic consciousness. During this process, he encountered the material from the Mark-Age Meta Center and other groups in contact with the spiritual hierarchy. He became a channel for the White Brotherhood, and formed the Last Day Messengers. It is his belief that we are in the last days prior to Christ's physically cleansing the earth. Man must cleanse his consciousness before that time. The Messengers point to positive signs of the New Age: technological progress, the youth who are seeking love and simplicity in life, the spread of psychic development and healing, the popularity of reincarnation and the flying saucers.

Membership: Not reported.

★1469★
Mark-Age, Inc.
Box 290368
Fort Lauderdale, FL 33329

Mark-Age was initiated by spiritual revelations received in 1956 by Charles Boyd Gentzel and formally organized in 1960 by Gentzel and Pauline Sharpe to channel the messages of the "Hierarchal Board" (the spiritual government for the solar system) during the last 40 years of this century (1960-2000 B.C.E.). This is the transition coordinating group for the movement from the Piscean Age to the Aquarian. The original leaders of the group included several psychics who channeled the data from the Hierarchy. The primary channel, Nada-Yolanda (Pauline Sharpe), has channeled most of the messages. In 1962, the Mark-Age Meta Center, Inc., now Mark-Age, Inc., incorporated in Miami. As early as 1949, the name Mark-Age was revealed. A subsequent revelation in 1955 concurred in its significance.

Mark-Age sees itself as one of numerous focal points of contact with the higher spiritual forces. By automatic writing and telepathic communications, the Hierarchy speaks. Messages have come through from Gloria Lee (founder of the Cosmos Research Foundation and early contactee who died during a fast in 1962), famous individuals such as John F. Kennedy, and the Theosophical masters El Morya, Lady Nada, Sananda (Jesus), and Djual Khool. Mark-Age was corresponding with Lee just prior to her death in 1962. After her death, their communications with her and the publication, *Gloria Lee Lives*, were major steps forward in Mark-Age's growth.

Space craft are one means of communication between the Hierarchal Board and earth. They include both physical craft, and other craft from the etheric realms. Jesus (Sananda) has been in orbit around earth since 1885 in the etheric realms and will take on material form as the planet is cleansed. Through telepathy with the spaceships, contact is made with beings of other planets.

Since 1960, Mark-Age has published a large amount of teaching material, much of which is condensed in the standard introductory book, *MAPP to Aquarius: Mark-Age Period and Program.* The content of the messages, besides outlining the minimal organization of Mark-Age, has been toward a defining of the roles of the hierarchy (which, apart from the emphasis on flying saucers, is very theosophical) and raising man's spiritual consciousness as the Aquarian Age dawns in preparation for the second coming, expected around the year 2000. The latter involves a process of meditation and psychic development. Instructions for groups associated with Mark-Age have also been published. In 1979 a site near Ft. Lauderdale, Florida, was purchased as a site for a headquarters complex.

Membership: Not reported.

Periodicals: *Mark-Age Inform-Nations (MAIN).* • I AM Nation News.

Sources:

1000 Keys to the Truth. Miami, FL: Mark-Age Meta Center, 1976.

Group Guidelines for New Age Light Centers. Miami, FL: Mark-Age Meta Center, 1971.

"History of Mark-Age." *Mark-Age Inform-Nations.* 22 (June-July 1975) (special issue).

How to Do All Things. Miami, FL: 1970.

Nada-Yolanda [Pauline Sharpe]. *Angels and Man.* Miami, FL: 1974.

___. *Mark Age Period and Program.* Miami, FL: Mark-Age, 1970.

___. *Visitors from Other Planets.* Miami, FL: Mark-Age, 1974.

Plan a Nation. Miami, FL: Mark-Age, 1975.

★1470★
Ministry of Universal Wisdom
(Defunct)

Among the most important of the 1950s contactees was George Van Tassel (19101970). A former employee of Howard Hughes, in 1957 he moved to Giant Rock, California, and started an airport to service the burgeoning postwar air industry. Beginning in 1949, he and his wife Doris Van Tassel, held weekly meditation sessions during which he would go into an altered state and channel messages. In January 1952 he began to receive channeled messages from several entities who identified themselves as space commanders, entities from outer space. Among these entities was one named Ashtar, commandant quadra sector, patrol station Schare. By this time flying saucers had become an item of popular national interest and the first people were coming forward to claim contact with the space beings they stated inhabited the saucers, which they believed to be spacecraft from other worlds. Ashtar and his colleagues revealed their mission as one of saving humanity from self destruction, which loomed closer with the discovery of atomic power.

The record of the initial contacts were published in the booklet, *I Rode a Flying Saucer.* Van Tassel also received information on constructing a building in which people were going to be able to be rejuvenated and their aging stopped or significantly reduced. The building was called the Integratron. There was also some hope that the devices in the building would be able to turn cosmic energy into useful electricity, allow time travel, and supply a means to nullify gravity. Beginning in the 1950s, Giant Rock became the site for a popular annual flying saucer convention.

Through the channeled messages, Van Tassel developed a theological perspective. God was continuously creating the universe. Man had been a part of that creation (humans did not evolve), but were created on another planet. Adam, or more properly the Adamic race, came from outer space to inhabit this planet. God finished his creative work on humans and rested. Then another entity, called "Lord God" in the Bible entered the picture. According to Van Tassel, the Lord God was a member of the Adamic race. He created Eve, a female counterpart of the all-male Adamic race. Eve was an animal, not human. One of the Adamic race mated with Eve and created the hybrid hu-man. Thus each of us has an Adamic constructive aspect and a destructive physical aspect. We have degenerated from following our bestial tendencies. The space brothers, pure Adamic beings, have some concern for us because we were created by one of their number having sexual relations with Eve.

Van Tassel founded the Ministry of Universal Wisdom as the corporate form through which he disseminated the messages of the space brothers. He had an associated College of Universal Wisdom that controlled the research conducted with the Integratron. According to Van Tassel, Ashtar and his colleagues constituted what was known as the Council of Seven Lights, space beings who operated from a space station called Schare.

Van Tassel died in 1970 and for a while his work was carried on by his widow. However, he had leased the land and it was eventually reclaimed by the government, which also took possession of the items inside the Integratron. The ministry was continued by Doris Van Tassel into the 1980s but eventually died out. The metaphysical work has been carried on by a number of channels who claim contact with Ashtar.

Sources:

Van Tassel. George. *The Council of Seven Lights.* Los Angeles: DeVorss & Co., 1958. 156 pp. Reprinted as: *Religion and Science Merged.* Yucca Valley, CA: Ministry of Universal Wisdom, 1968. 156 pp.

___. *I Rode a Flying Saucer.* Los Angeles: New Age Publishing Co., 1952. 44 pp.

___. *Into This World and Out Again.* Yucca Valley, CA: The Author, 1956. 94 pp.

___. *When Stars Look Down.* Los Angeles: Kruckeberg Press, 1976. 198 pp.

★1471★
Semjase Silver Star Center
Current address not obtained for this edition.

The Semjase Silver Star Center is the American branch of the Freie Interessengemeinschaft fur Grenz- und Geisteswissenschaften und Ufologie-Studien (Free Community of Interests in the Border and Spiritual Sciences and UFO Studies) headquartered in Hinterschmidruti, Switzerland. The Free Community was founded in the late 1970s by Eduard "Billy" Meier (b. 1936), who in 1975 experienced the first of a series of contacts with a flying saucer. Meier claimed the UFO had come from the Pleiades to visit him at several locations near his home in Canton Zurich, Switzerland. Its purpose was to spread the voluminous teachings which Meier received from the Pleiadean "cosmonauts." Meier wrote the story of his contact and published some of the material from the encounters soon after they began, and the Free Community was organized among people who responded to the teachings. Knowledge of Meier's contacts was spread in America primarily by Wendelle Stevens, who wrote two articles on them for *Argosy UFO* in 1977. In 1979 he published a book, complete with many pictures taken by Meier of the flying saucers.

Meier has noted that he had his first UFO experience in 1942, during World War II, when he was but five years old. He saw a metallic disc fly over his house and a few months later had contact with a person from a saucer who invited him for a ride. Beginning in 1944 he experienced regular telepathic contact with an entity named Sfath, who also took him for a ride in the spaceship. Other unusual experiences occurred throughout his life, which led him into the study of the psychic and to Spiritualism. The 1975 contact began while he was attempting to elicit spirit messages from a tape recorder, a manner made famous by psychical researcher Konstantin Raudive. Meier received a message that instructed him to go outside with a camera. He traveled down the road to an unpopulated area and had his initial contact with Semjase, a woman cosmonaut who claimed to be from the Pleiades star cluster. He took a number of pictures. Semjase told Meier that she and others had come to develop a voice "channel" through which they could speak and thus assist humanity out of its present ignorance.

According to entities from the Pleiades, the Solar System is entering the Waterman Era (the Aquarian Age) which will signal a powerful upheaval in the spiritual realm. Basic to understanding our life is the Creation, the Being and Non-Being of life. Creation is the immense mass of Spiritual energy in the universe, Spirit in its purest form—Wisdom, Knowledge, Love, and Harmony in Truth. Meier has arisen as the herald of the Truth, the one who is to spread the Creation's Universal Laws. Integral to his message are the Twelve Bids, the things Creation bids us do. The twelve admonitions, analogous to the Ten Commandments, provide guidance in ways to keep from violating the Creation.

Membership: Not reported.

Remarks: Once they were published in 1979, the claims of Eduard Meier caused an immediate controversy in the ufological community. In 1980 an article reporting on an examination of his claims pronounced him a fraud. Evidence cited included photo analysis of the pictures he took which revealed strings holding what appeared to be model flying saucers. An analysis of objects Meier claimed to have received from the flying saucer entities were in fact mundane earth objects. Letters from people who substantiated Meier's claims were also fraudulent. Wendelle Stevens, who first reported on Meier's claims, has remained a supporter in the ufological debate. Besides a number of articles, he has produced two additional books on Meier. As the debate over Meier raged, Stevens has also published a set of volumes representing the claims of a wide variety of UFO contactees and presents their stories of visits from a number of planets and star systems.

Sources:

Korff, Karl K. "The Meier Incident: The Most Infamous Hoax in Ufology." *Mufon UFO Journal* 154 (December 1980).

Meier, Eduard "Billy." *Decalogue or the Ten Bids.* Alamogordo, NM: Semjase Silver Star Center, 1987.

___. *The Psyche.* Alamogordo, NM: Semjase Silver Star Center, [1986].

Stevens, Wendelle C. *UFO Contact from the Pleiades.* Phoenix, AZ: Genesis III Productions, 1979.

★1472★
Solar Light Retreat
7700 Avenue of the Sun
White City, OR 97503

Aleuti Francesca is the Director and Tele-thought contactee for the Solar Light Retreat, established in 1966 in the foothills in southern Oregon, 20 miles outside of Medford. Francesca (originally known as Marianne Francis; she changed her name legally in 1975) became interested in UFO's in 1947 in London, England where she was born and grew up. In 1954 Francesca moved with her American husband, Kenneth Kellar to Santa Barbara, California where she also studied Hatha Yoga with Indra Devi and Baala Krishna. Telepathic and highly sensitive all her life, her sensitivity increased as she and Kenneth Kellar conducted experiments with Light Beam apparatus aimed at contacting outer space intelligences.

In forming the Santa Barbara Space Craft Research Society, Kenneth Kellar and the then Marianne Francis arranged many lectures for leading figures in the UFO field. At this time they met and became associated with Gayne and Roberta Myers and Richard Miller, the originators of the Solar Cross Fellowship. They moved to Oregon in 1965, and the following year the Solar Light Center was incorporated as a non-profit organization (the name was later changed to Solar Light Retreat as Fancesca's lecture work and tours increased). Kenneth Kellar and Francesca were quietly and amicably divorced in 1969 but remained friends after Kenneth's remarriage and relocation first to Washington state and then Nevada. Keller died in 1994.

Francesca's contact is mainly with the XY7, a mother craft from the Saturn Command. Ray-mere and Sut-ko of the Saturn Council are two of the main communicators. Information given over many years has indicated that all life in this and many other solar systems functions at the physical etheric level not the physical dense (as it does here on Earth). This is a physical plane level of functioning and has nothing to do with the spirit world per se.

Principles of the Solar Light Retreat are focused on knowledge of a spiritual hierarchy of beings, the Great White Brotherhood working under Christ, angelic contact and the reality of the infinite Creator, the "All Knowing One," "Our Radiant One" as the space beings call God. The eternal truths given by world Avatars such as Jesus Christ, Buddha, Krishna, and other spiritual masters are the basis of the teachings. The reality of advanced space beings from the Light Commands is the focus Francesca's lectures. She is now an international speaker having recently participated in the UFO Conference in Cairo, Egypt and last October at the Channelling Conference in Crete. Extensive speaking engagements throughout the United States and Canada, and in England, as well as plus hundreds of radio and television appearances have made Francesca a clear and committed spokesperson for the Space Commands.

Since 1975 Francesca has also given workshops and private regression consultations (more than 3,000) on the subjects of "Sex and the Soul" and "Transmutation of Consciousness." The private regressions have been designed to assist individuals seeking to clear energy blocks as we move towards the end of this cycle. Reincarnation, (the Law of Karma: cause and effect) is the basis for these workshops and counselling. A freedom of attitude toward the Infinite Creator, the self and others, as well as the Law of Personal Responsibility, is the basis for all lectures, workshops, and counselling. The end of this 2600-year major cycle is upon the planet and a cleansing is now taking place as a result of increased light energies. This heralds a new heaven and a new Earth and the beginning of the Golden Age of Light.

Membership: The retreat is not a membership organization.

Periodicals: *Starcraft—Newsletter.*

★1473★
Star Light Fellowship
Current address not obtained for this edition.

The Star Light Fellowship was founded in 1962 in New York City by Sterling Warren and Jackie Altisi as a "continuing Spiritual Education Program, initiated, directed and transmitted by Etheric Master Teachers of this and Other Planets, Galaxies and Realms of the Universe." Mrs. Altisi functions as Jackie White Star and is the main direct-voice channel of messages from the spirit world, but is assisted by Phyllis Veronica. Messages have been received from departed spirits, the ascended-master hierarchy, and the space brothers, including Gloria Lee (discussed elsewhere in this volume). One of the central communications has been from Christopher, aide to the King of the Moon and spokesman for the Luna Moon Government Headquarters of United Cosmic Planets. Ch

ristopher described the moon as a "complete authority in itself, but working with an interplanetary confederation."

Within the context of emphasis on communication with the space brothers, the general "ascended master" theology is accepted, and there is much correspondence with the "I AM" ascended master groups (discussed elsewhere in this volume). Ascended masters were once human and now, as spirits, teach humans about spiritual realities. During the 1970s, activities of the Fellowship were centered in New York City, where regular meetings were held and a semi-annual periodical, *The Star Light Messenger*, was published.

Membership: Not reported.

★1474★
Unarius-Science of Life
143 S. Magnolia
El Cajon, CA 92022

Unarius was founded in 1954 by Ernest L. Norman (d. 1971), a former Spiritualist medium, shortly after his meeting with Ruth Norman (d. 1993), his future wife. Ernest, the Unarian moderator, is described in the Unarius literature as "the greatest intelligence ever to come to earth" and is believed to be a reincarnation of the entity who was also Pharaoh Amenhotep IV and Jesus. Mrs. Norman, in previous lives, had been the pharaoh's mother, the betrothed of Jesus, the woman who found Moses in the bullrushes, and the woman who sat for Leonardo da Vinci as Mona Lisa. The beginning of Ernest's mission was on ancient Atlantis and Lemuria, to which Ernest came via a space ship. The mission is also seen as the return of Jesus and the renewal of his work, so abruptly cut off 2,000 years ago. During his life, Ernest dictated material which Ruth copied and published.

The teachings of Unarius are encompassed in the many books channeled by Ernest after he met Ruth, the books written through Ruth since Ernest's death, and the Unarius lessons which contain teachings not otherwise published. Ernest's mission began when he materialized on earth and was guided by the evolved beings, now residing on other planets. From these teachers, he dictated seven books, which contain information about and teachings from the planets Venus, Mars, Hermes, Eros, Orion and Muse. The teachings comprise the true science of life and deal with spiritual development and healing. Healing is accomplished by Ray-Booms, the projected light beams from the great intelligences on the higher worlds. Besides detailed descriptions of the various planets in Ernest's books, Ruth has given a picture of the Intergalactic Confederation. The Confederation consists of planets, advanced beyond earth, with which Ruth has been in touch. As the Confederation was formed, earth was invited to join. The polarization (joining) of earth occurred on September 14, 1973, with Ioshanna (Ruth) as the central contact. Earth is progressing more rapidly since it became part of the Confederation.

Since Ruth Norman's passing in 1993, Unarius has been headed by Charles L. Spiegel. The organization's program has been centered upon two courses of lessons, "The Psychology of Consciousness" and the more advanced "Self Mastery, the Infinite Concept of Cosmic Creation," primarily accessed through correspondence, designed to bring forth the powers believed latent in each human being. The course facilitates people in attaining self-knowledge and then assuming responsibility for their past thus allowing corrections of current conditions which have resulted from past actions and prevent any new ones from surfacing. Integral to the lessons is a study of what is termed the physics of reincarnation. The student is presented with a picture of the ever evolving nature of life and our true purpose as spiritual beings. Knowledge of self leads to a knowledge of the Infinite Creative Intelligence, the ever generative source of life.

The word Unarius is an acronym standing for "universal articulate interdimesional understanding of science."

Membership: Not reported.

Periodicals: *Unarius Light.*

Sources:

Ioshanna [Ruth Norman]. *A Space Woman Speaks from Outer Space.* El Cajon, CA: Unarius, n.d.

Norman, Ernest L. *The Elysium.* Pasadena, CA: Unarius, 1956.

___. *The Voice of Venus.* Santa Barbara, CA: Unarius-Science of Life, 1956.

Norman, Ruth E. and Vaughn Spaegel. *Who Is the Mona Lisa?* El Cajon, CA: Unarius-Science of Life, 1973.

Pathway to Light: An Introduction to the Unarius Science of Life. El Cajon, CA: Unarius Academy of Science, 1995. 44 pp.

The Universal Hierarchy. *A Pictorial Tour of Unarius.* El Cajon, CA: Unarius Educational Foundation, 1982.

★1475★
United States Raelian Movement
Box 611793
North Miami, FL 33261

Alternate Address: Canadian Raelian Movement, PO Box 86, Youville Sta., Montreal, PQ, Canada H2P 2V2. International Raelian Movement, CP 225, CH-1411 Geneva 8, Switzerland.

On December 13, 1973, a French journalist by the name of Rael was contacted by an extraterrestrial being. During this encounter, the extraterrestrial dictated a series of messages for humankind and requested that an embassy be built in Jerusalem, if possible, where they will officially land and bring with them all the prophets announced by every religion. These messages explain that in the original Hebrew Bible (the opening book of *Genesis*) the opening phrase "In the beginning *Elohim...*" (not "God"), literally translates to "Those who came from the sky." "Elohim" is plural. Thus, Rael was told by the ETS that *Genesis* is a written account of how people from another planet created all life on Earth. The messages dictated to Rael explain how the Elohim, through their mastery of genetics, scientifically created life using DNA.

The messages go on to explain that all the great prophets, including Buddha, Moses, Jesus, and Mohammed were messengers of these extraterrestrials. Jesus was born from the union of one of these extraterrestrials and a daughter of man and his task was to spread the biblical Genesis throughout the world in anticipation of the age in which we are now living, the predicted Age of Apocalypse.

According to popular belief, humanity entered the Age of Apocalypse in 1945. The word "apocalypse" comes from the Greek "apocalupsis" and means "revelation." It is the time in which our scientific development allows us to understand the true origin of humanity. With this same level of technology we can also either destroy or liberate our world. This age of apocalypse has been anticipated by every religion.

According to the Raelians, the Elohim contacted Rael in modern times because the human race can finally rationally understand its origins. They have asked him to make these messages known throughout the world and to build an embassy for them where they will meet with the leaders of the world officially. They are not invaders. They have shown their desire to come, but they respect Earth's choice to say no. It is up to humanity to invite them, and the invitation is the "Embassy." In Raelian belief, its the least humanity can do; they created mankind, and without them mankind would not exist.

According to the Raelians, the Elohim taught Rael the techniques of "sensual meditation" so that mankind can awaken its mind by awakening its body and realizing the true potential. It is an instruction manual given to mankind to help harmonize all the possibilities that lie within our collective brain and written by those best placed to know how it works since they created it. As human beings, we are linked by our receptors, the senses, to the infinite which surrounds and composes us. Every year, on every continent, members of the Raelian Movement are able to participate in sensual meditation seminars. On the American continent, the seminars are held in Quebec, starting the third week of July, now a campground where naturalism is permitted.

The Raelian Movement is a non profit, international organization. Rael has written a number of books which have now been translated into 25 languages.

Membership: In 1997 the movement reported 35,000 members worldwide, 250 in the United States, and 5,000 in Canada.

Educational Facilities: Les Jaedins Du Prophete, Quebec, Canada; Eden, France.

Periodicals: *Apocalypse.* • *The Contact.* • *Le Raelian.*

Remarks: The movement has been criticized for its emblem, a stylized swastika inside of a Star of David. Rael explains it is a symbol of infinity, but others complain that it has racial connotations.

Sources:

Palmer, Susan J. "The Raelian Movement International." Robert Towler, ed. *New Religions and the New Europe.* Aarhus, Denmark: Aarhus University Press, 1995.

Rael. *Let's Welcome Our Fathers from Space: They Created Humanity in Their Laboratories.* Tokyo: AOM Corporation, 1986.

___. *Sensual Meditation.* Tokyo: AOM Corporation, 1986.

___. *Space Aliens Took Me to Their Planet.* Liechtenstein: Foundation pour l'Accueil des Elohim, 1978.

★1476★
Universariun Foundation
Current address not obtained for this edition.

The Universariun Foundation was formed in 1958 and for many years headquartered in Portland, Oregon. Among the small group, Zelrun Karsleigh and his wife, Daisy Karsleigh, then still in her teens, began to receive telepathic material. Meetings were held regularly in their home, and the work grew steadily. For several decades, the Karsleighs remained the primary channels of messages from the spirit world, though eventually others have developed within the group.

Messages have been received from both the ascended masters and the masters from outer space. The principle communicators have been Sri Soudah, Koot Hoomi, and Lord Michael. The material follows the perspective of the "I AM" Religious Activity and is aimed at the illumination and emancipation of earth from its fear, chaos, and confusion.

The Universariun Foundation is governed by a board of seven directors elected by the membership at an annual meeting. The board oversees publication of the monthly periodical. A sanctuary for weekly meditation and telepathic channeling and a bookstore are maintained in Tucson. The recommended reading list of books, sold on a mail-order basis, includes a wide variety of metaphysical works.

Membership: Not reported.

Periodicals: *The Voice of Universarius.*

Sources:

How the Forces of Love Can Overcome the Forces of Hate. Portland, OR: Universariun Foundation, n.d.

Khul, Djwhal. *The Prophecies of the Tibetan.* Tucson, AZ: Universariun Foundation, 1983.

Oh! Urantia. Portland, OR: Universariun Foundation, [1967].

Prins, Ethera. *Miracle of Love and Life.* Portland, OR: Universariun Foundation, 1974.

Universarius as Given in Space Messages of 1960. Portland, OR: Sadhana-Western Publishers, 1961.

★1477★
Universe Society Church (UNISOC)
Current address not obtained for this edition.

The Universe Society Church (UNISOC) was founded in 1951 as the Institute of Parapsychology. It was also known as the Universe Society prior to taking its present name in the early 1980s. The church was founded by Hal Wilcox (b. 1932), who had had a number of psychic experiences as a child. He was later ordained as a Spiritualist minister. In the early 1950s, along with several other individuals with mediumistic abilities, Wilcox learned of Master Fahsz and other ascended teachers of the Great White Brotherhood (termed TABOF or The Ancient Brotherhood of Fahsz). Wilcox and the other oracles began to channel messages from these teachers/masters who taught the group about the nature of the universe and humanity's role in it.

According to the TABOF the universe was created by God, described as "The Father, The Ultimate One, The Force behind All Force, The Ultimate Cause behind All Cause." God permeates the universe, which is divided into seven sectors. Our sector, under Master Brsgv, contains seven galaxies. Our galaxy is in seven groups of seven planets each, making a total of 50 principal colonies including Fahsz's home planet of Narvon in the Altair system. UFOs are simply spacecraft used to colonize our galaxy and stay in touch with the inhabited planets, or galactic colonies in the Milky Way. Contacts from 1951 to 1961 were maintained by shel services, a method the group was taught in order to facilitate regular communications. It consists of a brief ceremony in which a mantrum, "Ino Pazis Gnurum," is chanted, followed by a 30-minute message channeled by one of UNISOC's 12 oracles for directions. The short service, it is believed, activates the pineal gland, and connects it with either the INO, a galatic computer bank, of one of the space brothers within Fahsz's command.

In 1963 physical contacts started with Zemkla, a man who governs planet Selo, in the Bernard Star system. According to the information received over the years, humanity's goal is governance, wherein all the people of this galaxy are to learn via reincarnation and karma to live according to God's spiritual laws.

In the 1950s UNISOC began work on seven Project Tests. In the process of completing the test projects, Wilcox discovered the results of past covenants, the first of which was a new 1838 Japanese religion, Tenrikyo. Since that time, Wilcox has discovered many other teachings that came from the same source but which were presented according to humanity's changing cultural understanding. After UNISOC completed Project-1 in 1963, Wilcox was ordained as a Tenrikyo priest, before moving on to Project-2. During the process of completing six projects he wrote approximately 60 books to expound the emerging truth. As of 1987 UNISOC had completed six of the seven text projects. The seventh text, upon which UNISOC is currently expending its efforts, corresponds roughly with America's third test of destiny.

UNISOC holds weekly classes and has expanded their shel services to include an interfacing computer network that in 1978 produced a printout of extraterrestrial communications. the associated Galaxy Press has published Wilcox's books, several levels of instructional material, booklets, and a newsletter.

Membership: As of 1988 there was only one center, in Hollywood, but graduates of the work are being encouraged to start their own units in other states and/or countries. Several of the books have been translated into other languages.

Periodicals: *UNISOC Newsletter.*

Sources:

Wilcox, Hal. *Contact with the Master.* Hollywood, CA: Galaxy Press, 1984.

___. *Gateway to the Superconsciousness.* Hollywood, CA: The Author, n.d.

★1478★
White Star
Box 307
Joshua Tree, CA 92252

Located close to Giant Rock in the Yucca Valley of California is White Star, founded by Doris C. LeVesque of Joshua Tree, California. (Giant Rock is the location of the Ministry of Universal Wisdom founded by George Van Tassel, a center discussed elsewhere in this chapter.) LeVesque began to channel messages from unseen entities in the mid-1950s after having read a book on saucers in 1954. In 1957, she began publication of the *White Star Illuminator.* She developed contact with the Ashtar Command, previously contacted by Van Tassel.

Ms. LeVesque teaches that earth is in a transition period created by the atomic age. Cataclysm is to be avoided by moving away from the destruction of nature. Universal laws, especially that of divine love, must be expressed. Love is the prime motivating force in the universe. The universe is organized on the principles of density and substance. Man evolves by assuming more density which vibrates at high rates. Life on all planets is at differing points of evolvement. A key evolutionary concept is light, which is said to be created by vibration traveling in substance. Evolvement to higher spiritual levels accompanies the presence of more light. Followers are encouraged to meditate and to visualize the coming of the light into various needful situations.

Membership: Not reported. Mailings go out to followers across the United States.

Periodicals: *Times of the Signs.*

★1479★
World Understanding
Current address not obtained for this edition.

Daniel Fry, an explosives technician and employee of Aerojet General Corporation, became one of the most famous of the flying saucer contactees following his experience on July 4, 1950. Out walking on a hot evening near the Organ Mountains and White Sands Proving Grounds, New Mexico, he saw an "ovate spheroid about thirty feet in diameter." He encountered a space-being, A-Lan, and took a ride in the saucer. The trip to New York and back took less than an hour. The purpose of the visit was to determine the basic adaptability of the earth-race to concepts completely foreign to the customary mode of thinking. Fry was described as open. The entire visit was discussed in a book, *The White Sands Incident,* in 1954. The following year, Understanding, Inc., was founded.

Understanding, Inc. has been one of the most eclectic of UFO groups but has been very much shaped by the teachings of A-Lan through Daniel Fry. Major purchases are the charting of the area of worldwide agreement in "spiritual" science and those tenets accepted as valid by all races and creeds, leading toward a guide for the behavior of man. Hypnotism has been highly recommended when properly used. The group has promoted the UFO cause generally, and Fry is a popular speaker in psychic circles.

During the 1970s headquarters of Understanding, Inc. were moved from Oregon to Tonapah, Arizona, where the Universal Faith and Wisdom Association, founded by the Rev. Enid Smith (and centered upon some saucer-shaped buildings adjacent to Sun Spiritualist Camp) was absorbed into Understanding, Inc. More recently the headquarters moved to New Mexico. The organization is administered by its officers who are elected in the annual membership meeting.

Membership: Not reported. During the 1970s, there were approximately 60 units worldwide.

Periodicals: *Understanding.*

Sources:

Fry, Daniel W. *Alan's Message: To Men of Earth.* Los Angeles: New Age Publishing Co., 1954.

___. *Atoms Galaxies and Understanding.* El Monte, CA: Understanding Publishing Co., 1960.

___. *The Curve of Development.* Lakemont, GA: CSA Printers and Publishers, 1965.

___. *To Men of Earth.* Alamagordo, NM: El Cariso Pub. Co., 1973.

___. *The White Sands Incident.* Los Angeles: New Age Publishing Co., 1954.

Drug-Related Groups

★1480★
The Church of Sunshine
Current address not obtained for this edition.

The Church of Sunshine was founded in 1980 by Jack McCall and his wife Mary Jo McCall. The McCalls, who had been members of the Neo-American Church through most of the 1970s rejected what they considered the absolute and autocratic nature of the leadership of the Neo-American Church by Art Kleps, its founder. That autocratic rule, in their opinion, had led to the creation of dogma or a "party line" on many issues and tended to isolate Kleps behind his close associates.

Jack McCall further disagreed with Kleps's belief in solipsistic nihilism. Kleps believed that the psychedelic experience led to the conclusion that life was a dream, a conclusion shared by McCall. However, Kleps also believed that ultimately life was a very personal dream, which he spoke of as "my dream," and thus not a shared dream that could be spoken of as "our dream." McCall thought it was meaningless to speak of the nature of the dream.

In establishing the Church of Sunshine, the McCall's limited their beliefs to two items. The Church affirms that psychedelic substances, primarily LSD and related psycho-active substances, bring salvation, i.e., liberation from ignorance and/or illusion and a sense of deliverance from danger, hence the peak psychedelic experience is the most profound experience imaginable. Second, the Church affirms that it is under the authority of no person, group of persons, or special writings, but derives its authority solely from the logical analysis of experience. Thus while McCall serves as an administrative focus, he does not dictate policy or particular beliefs.

Initially, congregations of the church of Sunshine were established in Whittier, California, by the McCalls, and in Frankfurt, Germany, by Peter Akwai. Members were invited to become ministers and establish additional congregations, but were required to go through a period of "seminary" training at one of the churches.

Membership: Not reported. The church is quite small (less than 100 members) especially in light of the numerous judicial ruling against psychedelics in the years since the church's founding.

Periodicals: *The L Train.*

★1481★
Church of the Awakening
(Defunct)

The Church of the Awakening was formed in 1963 by John W. Aiken and Louisa Aiken, both retired physicians. The Aikens lost their sons in 1951 and 1957, and were led into the realm of the psychic to seek an answer to why their sons were taken from them. They also began to experiment with peyote, using it as early as 1955. The year after the Church of the Awakening was formed, they sold their home and became active in speaking to psychic and psychedelic groups around the country.

The church had no formal statement of doctrine, but six affirmations formed a common core of accepted ideas: the unity of mankind, the reality of man's spiritual nature, the importance of experiencing that reality, the importance of the properly directed psychedelic sacrament as a means of achieving the unitive experience, the practical application of the unitive experience in every-day life, and the extension of the awareness of the reality as a factor in the solution of both personal and world problems. A great deal of control was exercised over the taking of the sacrament. Members were required to make application, after which an experienced monitor was secured, and a proper environment arranged.

The church was a loosely organized fellowship. Ten or more members of the church in a given area could apply for a charter to operate as a branch. Among the outstanding members were Dr. Huston Smith, professor of religion at Massachusetts Institute of Technology, and Dr. Walter Houston Clark, professor emeritus of the psychology of religion at Andover-Newton Theological Seminary. Clark has remained a major advocate of the religious psychedelics.

The Church suffered heavily from the 1966 ruling which made psychedelic drugs illegal. In 1969, looking for a status like that of the Native American Church, the group had a hearing with the Bureau of Narcotics, but received a negative verdict. Further rulings against the church later in the decade proved fatal to it. In 1970, there were 400 members, nationwide.

Sources:

Clark, Walter Houston. *Chemical Ecstasy: Psychedelic Drugs and Religion.* New York: Sheed & Ward, 1969.

___. "What Light Do Drugs Throw on the Spiritual and the Transpersonal?" *The Journal of Religion and Psychical Research* 4, no. 2 (April 1981): 131-37.

★1482★
Church of the Psychedelic Mystic
Current address not obtained for this edition.

The Church of the Psychedelic Mystic was founded in 1978 by a small group of people who described themselves as mystics and used psychedelic drugs in their search for a direct personal experience of the Divine. The church was founded at a time when the use of psychedelic drugs for any purpose, religious or otherwise, was illegal, and the church did not use illegal substances at any church function. However, the church was dedicated to overturning those drug laws that prevented their use of psychedelics for religious purposes. The church also recognized that many individuals, including church members, might continue to use psychedelics regardless of their legal status. The church also opposed the use of consciousness altering drugs administered without the consent of the individual for the purpose of social control.

The church considers its members to be mystics and as such teaches them to seek the Divine in very individualized ways. There is no external authority in the church, no sacred books, and no church buildings. While aware of the vast literature on psychedelic mysticism, the church recognizes the very individual interpretations of psychedelic experiences and the new syntheses of knowledge as a result of continued use of drugs. The church proposes its own four noble truths:

(1) God is One; Praise the Lord; (2) The kingdom of God is within us, perceived through our individual selves; (3) It is possible for any of us to directly experience this divinity within; (4) It is desirable for us to do so.

The Church was originally chartered by the Universal Life Church. In the early 1980s, it was headquartered in Encinatas, California, from which its periodical, *Mystic Vibes,* was published. Through the 1980s, not only was no progress made in liberalizing laws for the use of psychedelic mystics, but ruling consistently went against any who tested them. Nothing has been heard from the church in recent years, and it is likely that the church is now defunct.

★1483★
Church of the Tree of Life
Current address not obtained for this edition.

Apart from the Native American Church, the only psychedelic church to survive into the 1980s with its legal status intact has been the San Francisco-based Church of the Tree of Life, formed in 1971. It is a non-dogmatic church believing that each person is sovereign of his or her own mind and body and must have the right to do with himself or herself, or with any consenting adults, whatever he or she pleases, as long as those actions do not violate the rights of others. This sovereignty includes the use of psychedelic drugs.

It is the belief of the church that all substances are God's gifts, to be used as one may elect. However, since LSD and marijuana are illegal, they are not "officially" embraced as sacraments, rather a number of alternative legal mind-altering substances are listed as sacraments. They include nutmeg, kava, soma, peyote, ginseng, and calamus. The church feels a responsibility to impart information to members and has published *The First Book of Sacraments* as a guide to legal mind-alterants. Ritual is practiced in connection with the individual's taking of psychedelic substances as a means of organizing one's life and thus gaining the most from the experience.

Membership: Not reported. In 1972 the church reported 1,500 members.

Periodicals: *Bark Leaf.* Send oders to 451 Columbus Avenue, San Francisco, CA 94133.

Sources:

Mann, John, ed. *The First Book of Sacraments of the Church of the Tree of Life.* San Francisco: Church of the Tree of Life, 1972.

★1484★
Ethiopian Zion Coptic Church
PO Box 1161
Minneola, FL 34755-1161

The Ethiopian Zion Coptic Church was founded in Jamaica in 1914 by Marcus Garvey and orginially came to America in 1920 as part of his reformist efforts in the black community. However, the church died out in the United States and became a small body in Jamaica. Then in 1970, several Americans in Jamaica encountered the church, joined it, and brought it back to Star Island, off Miami Beach, Florida. A second center was started in New Jersey. The leader of the group was Thomas Reilly, Jr., generally known by his religious name, Brother Louv.

Church members believe in God who is experienced through the smoking of ganja, i.e., marijuana. Smoking marijuana is described as making a burnt sacrifice to the God within. The ceremonies for smoking the ganja utilize a specially made pipe. Coptics smoke ganja in such quantities that they hope it will reorganize their body chemistry around THC, the psycho-active ingredient in the plant, and they will thus survive the end of this world to live in God's new world. The new world is seen as a time in which there will be plenty for all without the necessity of an eight-hour work day. Peace and brotherhood will reign, and life will be lived at the horse-and-buggy pace. Ceremonially smoking ganja is the major sacramental act of church members, and members quote the Bible (Genesis 1:29; Exodus 3:2-4; Psalm 104:14; and Hebrews 6:7) in support of their use of marijuana.

Coptics also have a strong code dictating relations between the sexes. Women sit separately for the sacramental service and are not allowed to fill their own pipe. Sexual activity is strongly regulated. Homosexuality, oral sex, birth control, and abortion are prohibited. The only recognized purpose for sex is procreation.

Even prior to the church being granted tax exemption in 1975, it has fought an intense battle with government authorities. As early as 1973, authorities had seized 105 tons of marijuana from the group. In 1977 tax exemption was revoked. The church filed a lawsuit demanding the religious right of its members to smoke marijuana, a case lost in late 1978. Immediately after the court ruling, Reilly and five other church leaders were arrested in a raid on the Star Island headquarters. They were indicted and in 1981 convicted for drug smuggling. In 1982, Reilly, serving time in the Metropolitan Corrections Center in Miama, sued U.S. Attorney General William French Smith for the right to his daily sacrament of at least an ounce of marijuana.

In 1981, a group of approximately 20 members of the church moved to rural Wisconsin and established a settlement in an isolated valley near Soldiers Grove. They had moved from Iowa because of local harassment as a result of their refusal to have their children immunized as required by state law. Investigation stimulated by the group's use of marijuana led to arrests of church leaders in 1985. The arrest and conviction of church leaders has disrupted the life of the church, and the courts in the United States have persistently refused to allow the use of controlled substances by church organizations (apart from the Native American Church). The present status of the church is in doubt.

International headquarters of the church are in White Horses, Jamaica, where it had incorporated in 1976. They operate a 4,000 acre farm in St. Thomas Parish. Leader of the church in Jamaica is Keith Gordon (religious name, "Nyah").

Membership: Not reported. There are an estimated 200 members in the United States.

Periodicals: *Coptic Time.*

Sources:

Marijuana and the Bible. Hialeah, FL: Ethiopian Zion Coptic Church, n.d., 38pp.

★1485★
Native American Church
% Douglas Long, President
Rte. 1, Box 67
Osseo, WI 59758

Long before the white man came to America, psychedelic substances were used by the various American Indian tribes that came into what is now the United States from Mexico. Some time prior to 1870, the use of psychedelic drugs entered the United States by way of the Mescalero Apaches. The practice spread northward to the Kiowa, Comanche, and Caddo. Its spread followed the demise of the Ghost Dance, for which it substituted. The prime psychedelic source was peyote, a small, spineless, carrot-shaped cactus which grows wild in the Southwest. The dried peyote button is ingested during the ceremony and produces effects similar to those of LSD. Rpa1 Legal measures and hostility of both whites and fellow Indians led to the quest for legally guaranteed security of worship. In the second decade of the twentieth century, Jonathan Koshiway, son of an Oto mother and a former missionary for the Church of Jesus Christ of Latter-day Saints, discovered in peyotism a way of affirming both his Indian heritage and his Christian tendencies. He viewed peyote as one of God's creations, which he pronounced "good," seeing the button and the peyote tea as a reflection of sacramental bread and wine. Under his leadership, the First Born Church of Christ was formed in 1914 with 411 members. This group was later absorbed by the Native American Church.

The Native American Church dates to 1906, when a loose intertribal association of peyote groups in Oklahoma and Nebraska was formed. In 1909, the name "Union Church" was adopted. In 1918, the U.S. Bureau of Indian Affairs began a campaign to declare peyote illegal. In reaction to this effort, the Native American Church was incorporated. Present at the formation was Jonathan Koshiway, who attempted to get the group to join the First Born. Koshiway's church was rejected as too Christian; eventually, Koshiway joined the Native Americans.

Although the actual practices of the Native American Church vary widely, there is a considerable core of commonality. The central figure is the shaman, who keeps the peyote buttons and controls their use. As with all mediumistic figures, he is endowed with psychic powers. Peyote ritual begins with the pilgrimage by members of the tribe to collect the buttons, which are returned to the shaman.

The ceremony occurs in the evening in a tepee. The "father peyote" is placed on a crescent-shaped mound. The mound is in the West, with the crescent horns facing East. Before participants eat the peyote, prayer and smoking occur, and singing and drumming follow. The ritual lasts until morning.

Legal battles for peyote began as early as 1899, when Oklahoma outlawed its use. Following the conviction of three Indians in 1907, the law was repealed in 1908. Anti-peyote laws were passed in Colorado, Utah and Nevada in 1917. Similar laws were passed in other Western states. A significant case was that of Mary Attakai, arrested for peyote use in 1960. In his decision, the judge ruled that peyote was non-habit forming and not a narcotic, and found the anti-peyote statute unconstitutional. In 1964, the California Supreme Court ruled that the Native American Church could not be deprived of peyote for religious ceremonies. Finally, when the psychedelic drugs were made illegal by federal law in 1966, peyote and the Native American Church were excluded from the strictures of the law. Since the court rulings of the 1970s, many non-Indians have attempted to affiliate with the church. In reaction, it has tended to exclude non-Indians from its rituals, both to protect its special status and to keep people believed to be merely seeking a drug experience from distorting its rituals.

The church is headed by a national president elected for a two-year term. An annual convention elects officers and is the church's highest legislative body. State and local chapters are autonomous.

Membership: Not reported. In 1977 the church had approximately 225,000 members.

Sources:

Aberle, David F. *The Peyote Religion among the Navaho.* New York: Wenner-Glen Foundation for Anthropological Research, 1966.

Anderson, Edward F. *Peyote, the Divine Cactus.* Tucson, AZ: University of Arizona Press, 1980.

Artaud, Antonin. *The Peyote Dance.* New York: Farrar, Straus and Giroux, 1976.

La Barre, Weston. *The Peyote Cult.* New York: Schocken Books, 1969.

Roseman, Bernard. *The Peyote Story.* No. Hollywood, CA: Wilshire Book Company, 1963.

★1486★
The Original Kleptonian Neo-American Church
Box 3473
Austin, TX 78764

The Original Kleptonian Neo-American Church (OKNeoAC) was founded in 1965 at Star Lake, New York, by Art Kleps, the Chief Boo-Hoo. The church has had three principles: 1. The psychedelic substances, such as cannabis and LSD, are religious sacraments since their ingestion encourages Enlightenment, which is the recognition that life is a dream and the externality of relationships an illusion. 2. The use of the psychedelic sacraments is a basic human right and all interference therewith is an assault on this right. 3. We do not encourage the ingestion of the greater sacrament such as LSD or mescaline by those who are unprepared and we define preparedness as familiarity with lesser sacraments such as cannabis and nitrous oxide and with solipsist-nihilist epistemological reasoning based on such models as David Hume (an eighteenth-century British philosopher) and Nagarjuna (second-century Indian philosopher).

The church was incorporated in December 1967. Kleps, Timothy Leary, William Mellon Hitchcock, Joseph Gross, Michael Duncan, and William Haines (also known as Sri Sankara) formed the original Board of Toads (directors). The church was head-quartered at Millbrook, in upstate New York, until dispersed in 1968 when law enforcement agents moved against the group. The church was reincorporated in 1973. Through the next decade Kleps and other church members fought a losing battle with federal authorities over the religious use of psychedelic substances. Following a conviction in 1985, Kleps served a year in prison. He has continued to fight for the right to use psychedelic drugs, in spite of the massive legal barriers that have been erected throughout North America and Europe against their use.

Kleps described Neo-American philosophy as Solipsistic Nihilism. He identifies it as similar to the thought of Heraclitus, David Hume, Nagarajuna and Zen Buddhism. He denies the externality of relations, space, time, and multiplicity. He believes that life is a dream and truth is found by ridding oneself of illusions through the ingestion of psychedelic drugs under the proper conditions. Yoga and meditation are believed by Kleps to be used more often than not to prevent awareness of the Truth.

The church is headed by Kleps as an absolute monarch. His wife Joan Kleps, has been designated his successor. He has appointed a Board of Toads (directors). There are three levels of membership: upper, middle, and lower. Lower class members are those who have subscribed to former versions of the three principles. Middle and upper class members subscribe to the three principles as presently stated. Upper class members apply in writing for their status. Only upper class members may be ordained. All members are expected to pay nominal annual dues. Members in a local area may be organized into a vortex or an affiliate church, either of which is headed by a boo hoo general.

Currently there are two affiliate churches, the Original Kleptonian Neo-American Church of California headed by Robert Funk and the Neo-American Church of Texas and Sahib Kevin, Lord Sanford. There are also foreign affiliates in Finland and Ireland.

Membership: Not reported. In 1990 the church reported 15 members and 15 congregations in the United States.

Periodicals: *Divine Toad Sweat.*

Sources:

Brown, Robert E., et al., eds. *The Psychedelic Guide to Preparation of the Eucharist.* Austin, TX: Linga Shirira Incense Co., 1975.

Dwyer, Ed, and Robert Singer. "Interview: Art Kleps, Chief Boo Hoo, Neo American Church." *High Times* 8 (March 1976): 21-24.

Kleps, Art. *The Boo Hoo Bible.* San Christobal, NM: The Author, 1971.

___. *Millbrook.* Oakland, CA: Bench Press, 1977.

Kleps, Arthur. "Synchronicity and the Plot/Plot." *Psychedelic Review* 8 (1966): 123-24.

★1487★
Peyote Way Church of God
Star Rte. 1, Box 7X
Willcox, AZ 85643

The Peyote Way Church of God was founded in 1977 by the Revs. Immanuel Pardeahtan Trujillo, Eugene Yoakum, and William Russell. Trujillo, the son of an Apache and his French-American wife, joined the Native American Church in 1948. This church is the main body carrying on the traditional use of peyote among Native Americans. However, Trujillo arose as a voice of dissent over the church's policy of excluding from membership, and hence participation in the ritual use of peyote, anyone who was not at least 25 percent Native American. Trujillo considered that policy racist. He also had believed some of the teaching of Joseph Smith, Jr., the founder of the Church of Jesus Christ of Latter-day Saints. He left the Native American Church in 1966 and established an independent group. That group evolved over the years under various names including the Church of Holy Light Pentecostal Indian Mission.

At the time of the founding of the church in 1977, Trujillo, Matthew S. Kent, and Anne L. Zapf registered a declaration of intent with the recorder of Graham County, Arizona, stating their practice of growing, using, and distributing peyote as a holy sacrament of their church. The new church placed an emphasis on Section 89 of the *Doctrines and Covenants,* one of the scriptures of the Church of Jesus Christ of Latter-day Saints that specifically forbids the use of a number of harmful substances such as alcohol and tobacco, while commending the use of "all wholesome herbs." Church members believe that passage speaks directly to their concern about peyote, a wholesome herb.

The church uses peyote in what is termed a "Spirit Walk." The member planning to ingest the sacrament comes to the church land, fasts a minimum of 24 hours, and spends a period of time in the desert in prayer and self-examination. The peyote is taken while alone rather than in the communal context common to Native American Church practice. Peyote, the church teaches, cleanses both body and spirit, produces a visionary state of consciousness, and allows users to contact the light of Christ within.

From the beginning, the church's leaders were particularly concerned with building a presence in South Texas, the only place peyote cactus occurs naturally in the United States. Their plans have been continually thwarted by Texas authorities and anti-drug laws. In 1988 a court upheld both the federal and state statutes that the church had tried to overturn on constitutional grounds. In 1990 the court refused to expand its exemption of the Native American Church from drug laws relative to peyote to include any non-Indian groups, among them the Peyote Way Church of God. At present, the church has a legal standing in Arizona, and may use peyote on its property, but is unable to obtain peyote from Texas through the same legal channels that the Native American Church has available to it. More recently, the church faced another setback when its cottage industry, MANA Black Rim Earthenware was denied tax exemption and accessed for back taxes.

Resident members of the Peyote Way Church of God participate in the United Order, a system originally instituted by early Mormon Joseph Smith, Jr. Members take a vow of poverty and consecrate all their time, talents, wealth, and property to the kingdom of God. This consecration is symbolized by their deeding all their property to the church. The church then deeds the property back to the donor who serves as steward. Excess wealth is used by the church to support the poor.

The church is guided by a ministry graded into degrees from first to fourth, the latter being the highest level. The church is headed by its president, who serves a nine-year term. In 1984 Anne L. Zapf succeeded Trujillo as president of the church. She was in turn succeeded by Matthew Kent in 1993. Zapf continued as the Apostle and secretary/treasurer of the church. The president and apostle are assisted by a board of stewards elected annually at the church membership meeting. The church is centered on the 160 acres of land it owns in southern Arizona.

Membership: In 1992 the church reported 95 active members worldwide including 20 clergy members in the United States and two in Canada. During the 1980s the church had reported more than 200 members, but like all churches that have proposed the use of psychedelic substances, they have suffered a loss of support under anti-drug court rulings. Approximately 100 individuals incarcerated for various non-peyote-related offenses receive The Sacred Record and are recognized as honorary members.

Periodicals: *The Sacred Record.*

Sources:

Garcia, Joseph. "Peyote: a Drug or a Sacrament?" *Tucson Citizen* (January 3, 1989).

Other Psychic New Age Groups

★1488★
The Afro-American Social Research Association
Box 2150
Jacksonville, FL 32203

The Afro-American Social Research Association was formed by a black man who has taken the religious name, The Spirit of Truth. In the 1970s he began to receive messages from the Creator, many of which were incorporated into a book entitled *"The Spirit of Truth." Doom Days!*. The content of the messages was a word of warning and judgment, an important aspect of which was the necessity of doing away with the monetary system. According to The Spirit of Truth, the earth was given as a divine inheritance, but in time the wicked took control of everyone's divine inheritance, the monetary system being a tool in that takeover. He has predicted an astronomic catastrophe in the near future in which a comet will strike the moon which will in turn strike the sun. The earth will then move out of orbit and take a new position in the center of the universe. Most of earth's people will be destroyed in the process and a new world system, the United Countries of the Solar System, will then be established. The New Jerusalem will be built upon the exact spot where the first Jerusalem was built.

Membership: Not reported.

★1489★
American Universalist Temple of Divine Wisdom
Current address not obtained for this edition.

The American Universalist Temple of Divine Wisdom was founded in 1966 by a group of esoteric Christians living in the vicinity of Escondido, California. It is known as a Christ-centered point of light from which the love of God pours forth. It was prophesied by John the Revelator on the Isle of Patmos, who established the Order of the Golden Grail for the preservation of the original, unadulterated Christian doctrine of the inner life. The teachings of the Temple are "clairsentiently" received from ascended beings, and the Temple has instituted courses based upon the divine wisdom as a means of reaching sincere seekers of spiritual truth. The Temple is governed by a board of trustees.

Membership: Not reported. In 1968 there were 2 centers, one in California and one in Chicago.

★1490★
The Aquarian Academy
Current address not obtained for this edition.

The Aquarian Academy was founded in 1972 by Robert E. Birdsong (1912-) to assist people through was is believed to be the transition period into the Aquarian Age and to teach the principles of what it terms Adamic Christianity, a form of gnostic wisdom.

According to the academy's teachings, the first act of creation occurred when God emanated an image of Its own nature as the first Adam of Life, Spirit, Soul and Body of the Creator. The first human beings were microcosmic replicas of the first Adam. A second group of human entities, this time differentiated into male and female were created in order to balance the activity of Spirit (wisdom) and Soul (Love). Some of these human entities became trapped in the gross material plane of animal existence resulting in the earthly humans we know today.

The divine plan calls for the eventual extraction of the humans from their material captivity. The Lord God ordained that those humans so trapped would have to undergo a period of training and would be released from the body when the lessons of physical experience were mastered. The supervision of the plan was turned over to the divine emanations personified as male and female. The female Divine Soul assumed responsibility for the reproduction, growth, and emotional stability of humanity, while the male Divine Spirit (Wisdom) was assigned responsibility for the education and mental stability of humanity. Individual humans would progress through a series of human embodiments until the lessons were mastered. The Divine Soul maintained her mission as the constantly present Mother Nature and the Divine Spirit periodically reappeared as a avatar/teacher. The last avatar was Jesus. The crucifixion of Jesus represented the reunion of Divine Spirit and Divine Soul and the appearance of the androgynous Christ as the Indwelling Spirit of Earth.

It is the belief of the Academy that the teachings of the various avatars, while not lost, have been obscured by the religious leaders of the world. Adamic Christianity is a restatement of the avataric truth in language suitable to the present generation.

In the beginning, humans were divided into five races (brown, yellow, red, white, and black), each one of whom lived upon one of five great continents isolated from each other. The first avatars brought a message of guidance to each continent. However, these messages were largely ignored. On the continent of Mongolia, where now the Gobi Desert is located, a remnant of people who accepted and lived by the message of the avatars built a retreat, Shambhala (later relocated to Tibet), to keep the truth alive. The Divine powers assigned to this group of advanced humans the task of perpetuating the truth and recruiting initiates into it. The group at Shambhala later became known as the Great Brotherhood of Light. The brotherhood established wisdom schools on each of the five continents. These schools have now given way to a set of twelve wisdom centers, described as vibratory vortexes or spheres of influence. In addition there is a thirteenth center, the central hub, to which the other wisdom centers owe allegiance. It brings together all of the specialized wisdom of each of the other centers into a single body of truth. That thirteenth center, located near Mt. Shasta, California, is the Aquarian Academy.

As part of its work, the Academy publishes a set of books written by Birdsong, which embody the truths of Adamic Christianity and cover the wide range of subjects embraced by its teachings, the basic text being *The Revelations of Hermes*. It also publishes a set of monographs that explore selected subjects in great detail. There are no classes nor correspondence lessons as Birdsong believes that in this generation each person is responsible for searching out the truth.

Membership in the Academy is open to all who ask. As individuals read the literature and progress in their understanding of its truth, Birdsong offers his guidance. Members are encouraged to establish discussion groups both as a means of spreading the teachings and becoming more established in the truths.

Membership: Not reported.

Sources:

The Aquarian Academy. Eureka, CA: Sirius Books, 1978. 12 pp.

Birdsong, Robert E. *Fundamentals of Adamic Christianity.* San Francisco, CA: Sirius Books, 1974. 30 pp.

___. *Mission to Mankind: A Cosmic Autobiography.* Eureka, CA: Sirius Books, 1975. 122 pp.

___. *The Revelation of Hermes: An Exposition of Adamic Christianity.* Eureka, CA: Sirius Books, 1974. 278 pp.

___. *Steps on the Path: Daily Words of Wisdom.* Eureka, CA: Sirius Books, 1975. 64 pp.

★1491★
Association for Research and Enlightenment (ARE)
Atlantic Ave. at 67th St.
Box 595
Virginia Beach, VA 23451

Edgar Cayce (1877-1945), one of the great psychics of the twentieth century, was born in 1877 in Hopkinsville, Kentucky. At the age of 21, he cured himself of a throat condition by taking advice given while in an altered state of consciousness. He developed a reputation for being able to "tune in" to others, even at great distances, and diagnose medical ailments and prescribe remedies for them. He began to attract subscribers to what was called "his work."

In 1923, during a reading for Arthur Lammers, a Theosophist, astrologer, and student of Eastern religions, Cayce began to talk about reincarnation and to describe what he claimed were the past lives on earth of various individuals. The "life readings," as these were called, was an additional area of exploration. Most unusual for psychics in his day, Cayce had all of his readings recorded and transcribed. The Association for Research and Enlightenment Inc. (A.R.E.) was founded in 1931 to preserve, research, and act upon the readings. When Cayce died, he left records of more than 14,000 readings given to more than 8,000 people. Seventy percent of his readings are medical in nature; thirty percent explore metaphysics, Christianity, and comparative religion.

Since Cayce's death, the A.R.E. has been cross-indexing, publishing, and presenting the teachings of the readings. A number of biographies of Cayce, books on various topics in his thought, and numerous pamphlets have been produced. Interest shifts between the health readings and the various remedies recommended for different illnesses, and the metaphysical readings which center on reincarnation and a theosophical cosmology.

Today, three Cayce organizations survive in Cayce's Virginia Beach home. The Association for Research and Enlightenment, chartered in 1931, is a worldwide membership organization with a general mailing list in excess of 100,000. Members attend cnference and workshops organized through the ten regions in the United States as well as at the headquarters in Virginia Beach. The A.R.E. supports a number of community and member related activities including a children's and adult summer camp located in Rural Retreat, Virginia. Considered the most significant spiritual growth and development opportunity provided by A.R.E. was built in the 1960s and 1970s under the leadership of Edgar Cayce's son, Hugh Lynn Cayce (1907-1982). He was succeeded by his son Charles Thomas Cayce (b. 1942).

The Edgar Cayce Foundation received its charter in February 1948. It is the physical and legal custodian of the Edgar Cayce readings and their related documentation and emeorabilia. The foundation computerized the readings in a seven-year project culminating in the publication of the CD-ROM of the Edgar Cayce readings from the A.R.E. Press. It has published medical studies from the readings through its *Research Bulletin*. It has maintained active contact with those who had readings from Cayce and has provided updated reports that have been published behind each reading. In depth and scholarly presentation of pharmacological, anthropological, geological, and other subject matter are published under the series entitled *Special Collections*. An active preservation and acquisitions program enriched the foundation's holdings for researcher and authors.

Atlantic University, chartered in 1930, offers a master's degree in Transpersonal Studeies. It provides both resident courses and correspondence study. Its current president is Thomas Wallace.

Membership: In 1997 A.R.E. report 40,000 full members. Center are now open in England, Japan, Sweden, Poland, Germany, and France.

Educational Facilities: Atlantic University, Virginia Beach, Virginia.
Harold J. Reilly School of Massage Therapy, Virginia Beach, Virginia.

Periodicals: *Venture Inward.* • *The New Millennium.* • *The Atlantean.* • *A.R.E. Library Newletter.*

Remarks: The Association for Research and Enlightenment does not consider itself a religion. It is included in this volume, however, because, like other organizations which also do not consider themselves a religion (World Plan Executive Council, Ancient and Mystical Order of the Rosae Crucis), it meets the definition of religion being used by this volume. A.R.E. does present through its publications a distinct spiritual-religious worldview, unique in its derivation from the Cayce readings, and a program of action analogous to the other groups and organizations included throughout this volume. Many of the members of the A.R.E. are also members of other churches and religious groups.

Sources:

Bolton, Brett, ed. *Edgar Cayce Speaks*. New York: Avon, 1969.

Cayce, Hugh Lynn, ed. *The Edgar Cayce Reader*. 2 vols. New York: Paperback Library, 1969.

Bro, Harmon Hartzell. *A Seer Out of Season: The Life of Edgar Cayced*. New York: New American Library, 1989.

Cayce, Hugh Lynn, ed. *The Edgar Cayce Reader*. 2 vols. New York: Paperback Library, 1969.

Puryear, Herbert B. *The Edgar Cayce Primer*. New York: Bantam Books, 1982.

Smith, Robert A. *Hugh Lynn Cayce: About My Father's Business*. Norfolk, VA: Donning Company, 1988.

Stern, Jess. *Edgar Cayce, the Sleeping Prophet*. New York: Bantam Books, 1968.

___. *A Prophet in His Own Country: The Story of the Young Edgar Cayce*. New York: William Morrow & Company, 1974.

Sugue, Thomas. *The Story of Edgar Cayce*. New York: Dell Publishing Company, 1945.

★1492★
Astrological, Metaphysical, Occult, Revelatory, Enlightenment Church

Current address not obtained for this edition.

The Astrological, Metaphysical, Occult, Revelatory, Enlightenment Church (AMORE) was formed in 1972 by the Rev. Charles Robert Gordon, formerly a minister of the African Methodist Episcopal Zion Church. His father was Bishop Buford Franklin Gordon of the AMEZ Church. The church is Bible-based and views Jesus as the embodiment of cosmic consciousness. The AMORE Church believes in using the occult arts as a means to enlightenment in the coming Aquarian Age. Headquarters of the AMORE Church were established in Meriden, Connecticut. In recent years the church has moved and no contact has been made. Its present status (1985) is unknown.

Membership: Not reported.

★1493★
AUM Temple of Universal Truth
(Defunct)

The Aum Temple of Universal Truth was founded by Elizabeth Delvine King (1858-1932) as the Church Truth Universal-Aum in 1925 in Los Angeles. A metaphysician for many years, in 1907, as an answer to prayer, she received "the infilling of the Holy Spirit, which is the New Birth." Three days after her experience, "The Voice of the Infinite" spoke to her, saying, "Child, thy ministry is to be among what is called advanced thinking people." Over the next seven years, she wrote five books, which are the basic texts of the movement. In 1912 she headed a center for Practical Christianity in Manhattan Beach, California and in 1916 moved to Los Angeles and began a ministry of "Primitive Christian Teachings." In 1925, the first Sunday services were held.

Work progressed, and, by 1930, 22 ministers had been ordained. In 1929, the idea of a temple in the LaCrescenta Valley outside Los Angeles led to the beginning of construction. An Ashram was built as an adjunct of the Temple. At the time of Dr. King's death, there were two centers in Los Angeles and one in the Valley. Dr. King was succeeded by Dr. E. W. Miller and he, by Nina Fern Brunier (Dennison), who has served as the leader beginning in 1940. Under her guidance, the later name of the church was adopted and, in 1956, she relocated the temple in the Mojave De-

sert where she had found a site for a new sanctuary and retreat complex. In 1964, the move was made to Newberry Springs, California, the La Crescenta Temple having previously been sold. In 1967, a new temple was completed. The center at Newberry Springs served the group through the 1970s, but in the early 1980s, the Temple was disbanded.

The Aum Temple taught Esoteric Christianity as given by the Great White Brotherhood, of which Jesus Christ is the active head. Truth is the light and wisdom divine, given to assist men to the kingdom of God. To enter the kingdom, the self must be cleansed and purified through scientific prayer, renunciation of carnal beliefs and meditation. By cleansing, not bodily death, one escapes the cycle of reincarnation in the dense material world and the law of cause and effect.

Aum is God's own name for himself, is God in unmanifested and manifested form. The repetition of the name of God attunes one to the vibration of the spirit. In speaking the word, one wields the power of the universe. The word is but part of the "Secret Heart Way," the discipline of mind, body, and spirit through which one attains union. It is the path of Bhakti Yoga, first taught in the United States by Baba Premanand Bharati, a Krishna devotee who worked in the United States from 1902 to 1907. Healing is an integral aspect of the work.

The Sanctuary and Retreat in Newberry Springs housed a self-contained community of disciples, who lived their love and devotion and kept an organic garden, bee hives, goats and chickens. Besides the disciples, there were a few members of the Temple who did not reside at Newberry Springs, but supported the work and frequently attended the weekly services on Sunday and Thursday. At various times periodicals, *The Greeting Messenger* and *AUM, The Cosmic Light* were published.

Sources:

Althma, Leh Rheadia. *The Garden of the Soul*. Newberry Springs, CA: AUM Temple of Universal Truth, 1943.

Brunier, Nina. *The Path to Illumination*. Highway Highlands, CA: The Author, 1941.

King, Elizabeth Delvine. *The Flashlights of Truth*. Los Angeles: AUM Temple of Universal Truth, 1918.

King, Elizabeth Delvine. *The Lotus Path*. Los Angeles: J. F. Rowny Press, 1917.

New Age Songs. Newberry Springs, CA: AUM Temple of Universal Truth, 1972.

★1494★
The Awakened, A Fellowship in Christ
(Defunct)

The Awakened, A Fellowship in Christ was founded on Easter Sunday 1932 in Los Angeles, California by Melvin L. Severy. He had been a student of popular religious literature, including books about the Great Pyramid of Egypt and the possible prophetic significance of its architecture. Concerned about the state of the world, he began to envision an organization for human betterment, an idea which matured over several decades. Finally in 1932, he was invited to view a new painting of Christ done by Los Angeles artist Charles Sindelar. Deeply impressed by the picture, Severy became convinced that the picture should be used as a standard around which to rally the people of the earth into a Christ-minded fellowship. Severy enlisted Sindelar to design a membership button and a membership certificate, and called together an initial group.

The fellowship was designed to ready the world for the coming new dispensation promised in the Bible, the Great Pyramid, and more recent prophets and seers. Rallying around the portrait was seen as hastening to advent of the new age. Once the body of believers is formed, it would await a sudden call, the time and nature of which Severy never divulged. Much of the future of the fellowship awaited further revelation as it matured. Unfortunately, the group never matured, the thrust of its program being assumed by another organization soon after the formation of the initial group and the publication of a small pamphlet calling for other groups to form.

In the mid 1930s, Guy Ballard, founder of the "I AM" Religious Activity, visited the Sindelar Studios and was equally impressed with the portrait of Christ, identifying it with the same Master Jesus with whom he had been in communication. Sindelar, equally impressed with Ballard, joined the resources of his artistic establishment with the "I AM." His studio on Hoover Street, which had served as the headquarters of the fellowship, became the "I AM" movement's West Coast headquarters. Sindelar did the art work and published the magazine for the "I AM." The fellowship survived only a brief time and most of its resources were absorbed by the newer movement.

Sources:

The Awakened. Los Angeles: Awakened, [1933].

★1495★
Chirothesian Church of Faith
% Chirothesian Way Chapel
23548 Lyons Ave., Unit E
Newhall, CA 91321

The Chirothesian Church of Faith was formed in 1917 in Los Angeles by the Rev. D. J. Bussell, its president and senior bishop. Chirothesia is described as a natural religion based on the original form of the law of God. A Chirothesian is one who observes and obeys the law of God. The law of God was laid down in the beginning, has always had its followers and accepts Jesus as a modern messiah presenting the law of God in a more modern manner and adapting them to a more modern world. The four Gospels and the Books of James and Jude contain the presentation of the law, according to Chirothesians. The account of creation in Genesis illustrates the law of God: "A fully concentrated thought must produce its kind." Man was created according to this law. Man is body (earthly) and soul and spirit (godly). The physical part of man is to be subject to the intellectual part. As an expression of God, "Man becomes what he thinks." The way of the law is the way of harmony and indicates a way back for any who has missed the original plan. Practicing the law allows one to overcome discord, unrighteousness, and disease. Healing has been especially emphasized.

The Chirothesian Church does not proselytize, is not evangelistic, and does not invite membership. However, the church is open to those who seek membership, and most meetings are open to the public. Closed meetings are business meetings and classes of instruction in which prior sessions are necessary to understand the class subject. Headquarters are in Los Angeles, with branch churches across the United States.

Membership: Not reported. There are several congregations across the United States.

Sources:

Bussell, D. J. *Chirothesia.* Los Angeles: Chirothesian Church of Faith, n.d.

___. *Co-Ordinating Knowledge.* Los Angeles: National Academy of Metaphysics, n.d.

___. *First Steps in Metaphysics.* Los Angeles: National Academy of Metaphysics, n.d.

Garlichs, E. E. *The Life Beautiful.* Long Beach, CA: Aquarian Church of Chirothesia, [1946].

★1496★
Christ Ministry Foundation
Current address not obtained for this edition.

The Christ Ministry Foundation was established in 1935 by Eleanore Mary Thedick (1883-1973) of Oakland, California. Ms.

Thedick received her initial vision in 1926, when she was told that she would be a channel for a "spiritual broadcasting station." As the plan unfolded, the ministry was seen to illustrate the Christ-Light within. The outer foundation was to have 48 dual sects, each to be named for the Christ-qualities displayed in persons. Over the years, Ms. Thedick wrote several books. In 1970, Ms. Thedick merged her efforts with those of one of her students, Woods Mattingley. Mattingley had been involved in psychic/spiritual work for many years and had founded the Seeker's Quest. As the merger of efforts occurred, the Seeker's Quest Ministry was seen as being in an exoteric role, and the Foundation as being in an esoteric one.

The Christ Ministry Foundation teaches a form of esoteric Christianity. Christ is the great teacher who brought love into the world. The soul is envisioned as growing slowly toward at-one-ment with the Father. This process takes many incarnations, but, as with the prodigal, all will eventually return. During incarnation, we attempt to overcome character weakness, pay karmic debts and bear witness to the Light of God. Healing is a major practice; it is done by channeling the Light of God, often envisioned as the Triune Ray (Father, Son, and Holy Spirit). In 1970, Ms. Thedick retired from active work, and the ministry was headed by Mattingley. In 1972, she gave her students, Geneva D. Seivertson and her husband, Wayne Seivertson, charge over the Foundation, and Mattingley's Seeker's Quest Ministry became independent, though affiliated, in San Jose. He continued to publish his quarterly periodical.

Membership: Not reported.

Periodicals: *The Seeker's Quest Newsletter.* Send orders to Box 8188, San Jose, CA 95155.

Sources:

Seivertson, Genevah D. *The Christ Highway.* Marina del Rey, CA: DeVorss & Company, 1981.

Thedick, Eleanor. *The Christ Highway.* Oakland, CA: Christ Ministry Foundation, n.d.

___. *Jewels of Truth and Rays of Color.* Oakland, CA: Christ Ministry Foundation, n.d.

___. *Light on Your Problems.* Oakland, CA: Christ Ministry Foundation, n.d.

★1497★
Christian Institute of Spiritual Science
(Defunct)

The Christian Institute of Spiritual Science, founded by Hanna Jacob Doumette, functioned in the Los Angeles area in the early 1960s. It taught a form of esoteric Christianity that included attention to mystic and occult philosophy. The institute believed in one God, considered as the Creator and Heavenly Father, the Spirit of Life. God is experienced by human consciousness as a Trinity, as Father, Mother, and Son and/or as Creative Spirit, Holy Spirit, and Christ Spirit. The Trinity lives in humans as their true identity. The Divine Father Principle is a person's spirit, the Mother Principle is the soul, and the Christ Principle is the mind and consciousness. Humans are the idea of God manifest in creation.

Humans possess all the powers of God. Individuals may receive the Gift of the Holy Spirit (a spiritual experience). It is attained by faith, purity of heart, renunciation of all negation, fervent devotion, and constant concentration and meditation upon the indwelling Christ Self. Thus the individual attains spiritual transformation (resurrection), which in turn brings a quickening and mastery of spiritual and psychic powers, especially the power of healing. In this state of Divine Presence there are no negatives, only life, righteousness, immortality, and goodness.

The institute was headquartered in Santa Monica, California. There is no information on its size or the years of its existence. Doumette authored a number of books and booklets expounding the institute's teachings.

Sources:

Doumette, Hanna Jacob. *After His Living Likeness.* Santa Monica, CA: Christian Institute of Spiritual Science, n.d. 12 pp

___. *Jesus the Man.* Santa Monica, CA: Christian Institute of Spiritual Science, n.d. 12. pp.

___. *The Sun of Higher Understanding.* N.p., n.d.

★1498★
Church of Basic Truth
Current address not obtained for this edition.

The Church of Basic Truth was founded in 1961 in Phoenix, Arizona and is headed by Dr. George H. Hepker. It teaches huna (power), the beliefs of the pre-Christian religious leaders of Hawaii, with an emphasis on healing via "Meda-Physical Dynamics." This therapy was developed on the theory that any disorder the mind can allow to develop can be controlled and often cured.

Membership: Not reported. A second center was in Gary, Indiana.

★1499★
Church of Divine Man
% Berkeley Psychic Institute
2018 Allston Way
Berkeley, CA 94704

The Church of Divine Man and the Berkeley Psychic Institute, its seminary workshop, were founded in 1973 by psychic Lewis Bostwick (1918-1995), the church's archbishop. A psychic for many years, Bostwick saw the need for a structure in which others like himself could find community, validation for their work, and a spiritual atmosphere in which to work. There was also the need for the training and development of latent psychic gifts. Graduates of the institute may be ordained as ministers by the church, and during the first decade of its existence the church grew rapidly as newly ordained ministers began to spread along the West Coast. The development of the church was spurred in 1976 by the opening of an affiliate in Seattle by Revs. Menuard Slusher and Mary Ellen Flora, bishops of the church in the Northwest. They established the Washington Psychic Institute which now has branch centers in Oregon. The Washington group has separated from the California organization and has become an independent church, retaining the same name. Graduate ministers have formed their own churches in other cities, states, and nations.

The church is not doctrinally oriented and is very loosely organized. Its creed affirms "psychic freedom" and decries the need for ideologies and dissenting philosophies which divide and destroy communication. It stresses living the mystic life in the inward infinity and cosmic consciousness. It tenets are based upon the miracles of Jesus and his statement, "What I can do, you can do and greater things than these shall you do." The church does accept the realm of psychic reality, and the institute, which functions as the church's seminary, offers courses in the wide variety of psychic experience—healing, meditation, kundalini energy, aura reading, and related topics. A clairvoyant intensive religious training course is offered for those who wish to pursue a career as a minister. Reincarnation is accepted and many of the psychic readers specialize in past-life readings.

In 1980 the church launched a periodical, *This Is Your Psychic Life*, and the following year nurtured the independent incorporation of Deja Vu Publishing Company to manage its production. The magazine was discontinued in 1986 and replaced by a monthly newspaper, *The Psychic Reader.*

Membership: In 1998 the Berkeley Psychic Institute reported branches in Berkeley, Santa Rosa, Mountain View, Marin, Sacramento, and Pleasanton, California. The Church of Divine Man is affiliated with the Church of the Rose/Southern California Psychic Institute in Anaheim, California. The Institute reported over 3,500 graduates. More than 50,000 associate members have completed beginning clairvoyant training classes in psychic meditation and healing.

Educational Facilities: Berkeley Psychic Institute, Berkeley, California.

★1500★
Church of Eductivism
Current address not obtained for this edition.

Jack Horner (b. 1927) worked from 1950 to 1965 with L. Ron Hubbard, founder of the Church of Scientology. A prominent member of the church, he was awarded the first Doctor of Scientology degree. Then in 1965, he left the church over what he considered an authoritarian ethics policy. After a period of non-association with Scientology, he began to develop Dianology, viewed as an improved Scientology drawing from a number of various sources. In 1970, Horner moved to Los Angeles and founded the Personal Spiritual Freedoms Foundation. In 1971 he changed the name Dianology to Eductivism with emphasis placed on "educing" latent potentials and uncovering what is hidden. The Church of Eductivism, formerly the Church of Spiritual Freedoms, is the religious adjunct to the Foundation; both are aspects of the umbrella corporation, the Association of International Dianologists.

Eductivism is an applied philosophy aimed at evoking the individual's infinite spiritual potentials. Individuals (usually referred to as "life sources") are infinitely capable of total creation and total cessation, simultaneously. But individuals do not use that potential. Through classes and exercises, the potentials are released in a meaningful context.

The creed of the church emphasizes the freedoms believed to be implicitly denied in the Church of Scientology—to seek God, however he may be perceived; to create alternatives, to possess opinions, thoughts and sanity; to communicate freely with others, and to join voluntary associations. Like Scientology, the Horner teaches that humans are basically "well disposed" and that "occlusions which mar and blemish the human spirit can be removed by the application of Spiritual technology."

Horner had an immediate response to his efforts, and associated centers have been established and independent clearing consultants trained. Horner is a leader in the California Association of Dianetic Auditors, a fellowship of independent cousultants.

Membership: Not reported.

Sources:

Horner, Jack. *Clearing.* Santa Monica, CA: Personal Creative Freedoms Foundation, 1982.

___. *Dianology.* Westwood Village, CA: Association of International Dianologists, 1970.

___. *Eductivism and You.* Westwood, CA: Personal Creative Freedoms Foundation, 1971.

Horner, Jack, and J. Rey Geller. *What an Eductee Should Know.* Santa Monica, CA: Personal Creative Freedoms Foundation, 1974.

★1501★
Church of General Psionics
Current address not obtained for this edition.

The Church of General Psionics was founded by John L. Douglas and Henry D. Frazier. Douglas was an amateur hypnotist and student of the psychic. Over the decade preceding the church's founding in 1968, Douglas had been evolving a pragmatic view of "psi"—the psychic. "Does it work?" became his criterion for things psychic. Then, in a visionary experience in 1968, a new understanding of the nature and purpose of humanity was given and a group was formed by those who were of like mind.

The purpose of Psionics is to help a person develop his own philosophy. Since the path to enlightenment is loaded with obstacles, General Psionics aids the individual by offering training to help him to become aware of his immortality. Man is a soul inhabiting a body, as it has inhabited other bodies previously. The various techniques of becoming aware are termed psionics engineering. New members of the church, before they are introduced to psionic engineering, are asked to agree to the "code of an immortal." The code acknowledges the dignity of all entities, quite apart from the body, and the fight of each entity to self-determination. From the church center in Redondo Beach, California, a program of classes, workshops, and counseling is offered.

Membership: Not reported. There was only a single center in the 1970s.

★1502★
Church of Loving Hands
Current address not obtained for this edition.

The Church of Loving Hands is a New Age church founded in 1979 by Rev. Rosalind Beal-Ojala. Beal-Ojala was ordained in 1979 by the Mother Earth Church and her church was chartered in 1980 by the same. Beal-Ojala began her studies in psychic awareness in 1968 with the Inner Peace Movement, the year after her graduation from the University of Arizona. Through the early 1970s she worked with Universal Communications, an organization founded by her father, Robert L. Beal, in Phoenix, before moving to Mill Valley, California, in 1975. By this time, natural healing had become the keystone of her work and she began to concentrate on various forms of healing activity from Swedish massage to diet to spiritual healing by the laying-on-of-hands.

Beal-Ojala is also part Native American, a Meti, and a member of the National American Metis Association. She has found a convergence between New Age teachings and healing practices and those of Native Americans. Much of the work of the church is conducted under her Native American name, Skyhawk. The church also sponsors sweat lodge ceremonies, medicine circles, and wilderness vision quests. Along with theosophical texts, the church considers such books of Native American teachings as *The Book of the Hopi, Black Elk Speaks,* and *Warriors of the Rainbow* as authoritative texts for its members.

The church is dedicated to the research, teaching, and ministering of Natural Earth Healing, which combines the Ancient Ways of Native Americans and New Age techniques. The church shares these teachings with all in the hope of rekindling connections between people and the spirit power and Mother Earth. It also supports the Cross Cultural Shamanism Network, Berkeley, California, and the XAT Medicine Society, Nashville, Tennessee.

Membership: In 1991 the church reported 2,000 members in four congregations.

Educational Facilities: Rosebud College, Sioux Falls, South Dakota is sponsored by the church.

Periodicals: *Medicine Ways.*

★1503★
Church of Mercavah
Box 66703
Baton Rouge, LA 70896

Mercavah is a small New Age church founded in 1982 by Rev. James R. Montandon. Montandon has a decade-long background in metaphysical and spirtualist training. He graduated from the International Spiritualist University, and finished a course of study with a variety of educational structures: The University of Metaphysics, the Neotarian Fellowship, the New England Academy of Hypnosis, and the Natural School of Healing. He has also been a member of a variety of metaphysical and spiritualist organizations and has lectured widely in meditation and spirituality. He has served as a chaplain at one of the Louisiana state prisons.

The church is headed by a board of deacons, composed of ten ministers who serve for life. A wide spectrum of opinion is encour-

aged in the church concerning matters of belief. The church's doctrinal statement centers upon a belief in the spiritual nature of human beings. As spiritual beings, individuals must find their path to self-knowledge. Emphasis is placed upon the freedom of the search for truth. The openness of the church allows it to cooperate locally with a variety of esoteric organizations.

Future ministers and members may study with the church via correspondence, and as of 1992 there are several students studying with the church's College of Applied Arts from neighboring states and one in London, England.

Membership: In 1995 the church reported 19 ministers and 612 members internationally.

Educational Facilities: College of Applied Arts.

Sources:

Book of Service: The Book of Guided Group Worship for the Church of Mercavah. Baton Rouge, LA: Church of Mercavah N.D. 99 pp.

★1504★
Church of Scientology
℅ Church of Scientology International
6331 Hollywood Blvd., Ste. 1200
Los Angeles, CA 90028-6329

History. Few of the new religious bodies of the 1950s and 1960s have grown as much as the Church of Scientology, first founded in Los Angeles, California, in 1954. Due to its fast growth and its new teachings or methods (its religious technology, as it's called in the church), it has also found itself the target of attacks and controversy; not unlike other new religious movements. In the face of controversy, the church has aggressively defended its rights and vigorously worked to correct and/or refute any charges or what it considers false statements about itself, its teachings, or the founder of Scientology, L. Ron Hubbard (1911-1986).

L. Ron Hubbard first became a public figure as an explorer and adventure/fiction writer, becoming most widely known through his science fiction books and stories. Throughout his early years Hubbard was most fascinated with what made man tick and how man could better himself and his fellows. As early as 1949 he had established a small organization to help him respond to the inquiries made concerning his emerging ideas about the human mental processes. The growing number of inquiries led Hubbard, in 1950, to write *Dianetics: The Modern Science of Mental Health.* The book became a bestseller and has sold more than 15 million copies. *Publishers Weekly* carried it in its bestseller lists for more than 100 weeks and included it among the top five longest running paperback bestsellers of 1990. It is still a basic text of the present Church of Scientology.

Hubbard wanted to offer Dianetics as a mental health discipline, so in the summer of 1950 he journeyed to Washington, D.C., and made a presentation to a group of psychiatrists and educators. Shortly after the presentation, the American Psychological Association called upon psychologists not to use Dianetics therapy. Dianetics techniques also came under attack by the American Medical Association. During this period, considered by Scientologists a time of persecution motivated by self-interests, Hubbard continued his research, lectured, and helped establish Dianetic Research Foundations in Los Angeles, and Wichita, Kansas, all the while dealing with several internal disputes. More importantly he continued to expand the more practical and mundane areas of concern covered by Dianetics into the more metaphysical speculations which became Scientology. Finally, in 1954, as other churches were established, Scientologists in Los Angeles founded the Church of Scientology. (This first church became the Church of Scientology of California.)

Scientology is the logical extension of Dianetics. Just as Scientology was outlined, and the Church founded, Hubbard moved to Washington, D.C., where the Founding Church of Scientology of

Washington, D.C., was established in 1955. This evolution of the movement had the added effect of creating a new religion.

Beliefs. Dianetics theory is described as a science leading to the source of all psychosomatic ills and human aberrations. Hubbard postulates the existence of the mind in two aspects. The Analytical Mind perceives, reasons, and remembers. The Reactive Mind simply records "engrams," completely detailed impressions of perceptions present in a past moment of pain and unconsciousness. (Other moments of severe loss or trauma can be recorded in the Reactive Mind, but draw their aberrative effects from the engrams.) Significant engrams are lodged by the fetus before birth at moments when the mother is experiencing injury or severe stress or trauma, such as an attempted abortion or a blow to the mother's stomach. _Dianetics: The Modern Science of Mental Health_ provided techniques for helping people discover and rid themselves of engrams (and thus aberrations). The person who has rid himself of all his engrams is called a Clear. One becomes clear by going through a series of courses leading to self-discovery, and through a process called auditing. Auditing is the application of Dianetics and/or Scientology technologies to an individual by a practioner trained in the use of the E-Meter. The auditor takes him through various drills, all aimed at freeing one from engrams.

Either before or after receiving Dianetics, one proceeds to various levels of Scientology. Scientology is concerned with the isolation, description, handling, and rehabilitation of the human spirit. Hubbard discovered the means of separating the human personality from the body and mind (a process called exteriorization, not to be confused with astral travel). This personality, or the being himself, which is separate from the body and mind, is called the "thetan," after the Greek letter, theta. The thetan has the power to create MEST, that is, Matter, Energy, Space, and Time, or the basic elements of existence. In Scientology terminology, a highly aware thetan who has the ability to handle the affairs of life in this exterior state is called an Operating Thetan. The thetan has lived and can continue to live through a series of lifetimes. The Church's beliefs are uniquely presented in the christening ceremony which is seen as a means to get the thetan oriented after its taking over a new body.

The religious credentials of Scientology have frequently been questioned in the court both in the United States and around the world. Overwhelmingly (in 68 countries as of 1992) Scientology has been acknowledged as a new religion, and the church established as a legal entity. These court victories have had important implications for Scientology, as different countries grant religious rights and privileges only to such legally established religious bodies. They have also served to establish the church's religious bona fides in the face of frequent intense criticism from the media and anti-cult spokespersons.

Organization. General oversight of the Church of Scientology is invested in the Church of Scientology, International, headquartered in the large church complex in Los Angeles. It is accorded a variety of tasks, not the least of which is ensuring that the teachings and practice of the church follow the strict procedures prescribed in the various books written by Hubbard and/or issued by the church. The office charters the various churches, missions (small parishes), and other units of the church.

Over the years, the church has also organized its thrust into social concerns, having fostered other structures (many now independent): Narconon (drug rehabilitation), the Citizens Commission on Human Rights, the Committee on Public Health and Safety, American Citizens for Honesty in Government, Applied Scholastics, and the National Commission on Law Enforcement and Social Justice.

There are senior churches in the United States, Great Britain, Europe, and Australia that deliver the advanced levels of Scientology instruction and counseling (auditing). One of these, the Flag Service Organization, is an advanced religious retreat maintained in Clearwater, Florida. It is called "Flag" out of tradition for the years this retreat was located on an ocean-going ship named Apol-

lo and nicknamed Flag as it was the "flagship" headquarters for the Sea Organization. The Sea Organization is an elite dedicated fraternity of Scientology staff who supported Hubbard (prior to his death) in his continuing research and development of Scientology. The top management of the church is composed of Sea Org members. The Sea Org continues to operate an ocean-going mission for advanced level Scientology courses.

Membership: In 1992, the church reported more than 1,100 churches, missions, and affiliated groups located in over 80 countries serving an estimated eight million members. The total number of L. Ron Hubbard's books exceeds 100 million copies. His books have been translated into 31 languages.

Periodicals: _The Auditor._ • _Freedom._ Both available from the Church of Scientology Western United States, 1404 N. Catalina St., Los Angeles, CA 90027. • _Advance._ Available from Advanced Organization of Los Angeles, 1306 N. Berendo St., Los Angeles, CA 90027. • _Cause._ Available from the American Saint Hill Organization, 1413 N. Berendo St., Los Angeles, CA 90027. • _Source._ Available from the Church of Scientology Flag Service Org, Inc., PO Box 31751, Tampa, FL 33631-3751.

Remarks: The years since the founding of the church in 1954 have seen periods of intense controversy. Controversy first began in the 1950s when the new Dianetics techniques ran head-long into the teeth of the "established" practices used by the professions of psychiatry and organized medicine. At the urging generally of psychiatric or mental health organizations, branches of some Western governments became hostile to Scientology. In 1963, officers of the U.S. Food and Drug Administration raided the Washington, D.C., church and seized all of its E-Meters. It wasn't until 1969 that a decision was reached that E-Meters and auditing were valid religiously, and the confiscated E-Meters and books were returned.

In 1968, the British Home Office placed a restriction on all non-English nationals who were entering the country just to study or practice Scientology. This ban was later relaxed in practice, and was officially lifted in July 1980. The 1965 ban on Scientology by the Australian government led to a lengthy legal battle which was resolved in the church's favor in 1983 by the Australian High Court. (Additionally, this landmark decision drew upon many United States legal precedents and defined "religious freedom" for the first time in Australia.)

One pattern repeated frequently in the Scientology controversies has been strong assertions against the church (or Hubbard), followed by press exposure, lawsuits, and the attempt to clearly establish the falsity of the original assertions. Such assertions filled several early books on Scientology. The church has also been raided several times by government agencies. Partially in response to the build-up of questionable documents on the church in various government files (the direct cause of some raids), the church has become one of the most vigorous users of the Freedom of Information Act (FOIA). The church has even published a booklet aimed at helping individuals and church members gain access to files on themselves through the FOIA.

During the 1970s, the church pursued a variety of legal procedures to stop government action (particularly action by the U.S. Internal Revenue Service) against it and to defend itself against the attacks of hostile ex-members and other opponents. Prior to the 1980s, the church won a majority of such cases. However, during the first half of the 1980s, the church suffered some major defeats in court. Criminal charges filed against a few church leaders and staff following a raid of church offices in 1977 led eventually to their conviction. Those sentenced for stealing government documents included the church's (then) top administrative official, Guardian Jane Kember and Hubbard's wife, Mary Sue Hubbard. In 1981, the church reformed the Guardian's Office, and then dissolved it altogether. In 1984 the Church of Scientology of California's tax-exempt status was taken away in a federal tax court decision. The trial, which highlighted the financial dealings of the church, created a significant amount of bad publicity, and led the church to place ads in newspapers asking for those with information on illegal actions by the Internal Revenue Service to come forward. (The ads did result in current and former IRS employees and agents coming forward with reported abuses by the IRS.) Most of the other United States Scientology churches are recognized as tax exempt religious organizations.

During the 1980s, two juries also awarded multi-million dollar judgements against the church. In the case of ex-member Julie Christofferson, the court ruled that the original trial violated the church's religious freedom. The case was heard again and resulted in a mistrial. Eventually, the case was settled out of court. In a second case, a large judgement given to ex-member Larry Wollershein was reduced substantially after review. The case is still under appeal by the church. Apart from the judgement, the Wollershein case had further ramifications, as testimony and subsequent court records provided new data for the church's critics and provided a focus for uniting various pockets of opposition. One result was a May 6, 1991, cover story in *Time* magazine that attacked the church as "The Cult of Greed." The church responded with a series of full-page ads in *USA Today* and a lawsuit, yet to be argued, accusing *Time* of libel.

Sources:

Hubbard, L. Ron. *Dianetics, The Modern Science of Mental Health.* New York: Hermitage House, 1950.

Meldal-Johnson, Trevor, and Patrick Lusey. *The Truth About Scientology.* New York: Tempo Books, 1980.

Scientology: A World Religion Emerges in the Space Age. Los Angeles: Church of Scientology Information Service, Department of Archives, 1974.

Scientology, What Is It? Los Angeles: Church of Scientology International, 1988.

Wallis, Roy. *The Road to Total Freedom.* New York: Columbia University Press, 1977.

What Is Scientology. Los Angeles: Church of Scientology of California, 1978.

★1505★
Church of the Gentle Brothers and Sisters
Current address not obtained for this edition.

Frank Douglas was a trance medium in New York City who moved to London to continue his work. While in London in January of 1971, he received messages through other mediums that Mexico was an ideal place to begin a spiritual center and healing group. He arrived at Puerto Angel and there met Martin Myman, who agreed to join forces in forming a center. Healing work commenced, and the center's fame spread throughout both Mexico and California. A community formed around Douglas. Healing was done by a combination of spiritual healing, zonal therapy, counseling, massage and even drugs. After two years, the Mexican government began to suppress the efforts, and the center moved to San Francisco, where it incorporated as the Church of Gentle Brothers and Sisters. Because of legal restrictions, the laying-on-of-hands has been the main method employed in healing since the move. Prior to healing, palm readings are done on patients. The group is Theosophic in outlook and studies the Alice Bailey books. Emphasis is placed on spiritual unfoldment (religious growth), as opposed to psychic development (through telepathy, clairvoyance, etc.).

★1506★
Church of the Gift of God
(Defunct)

The Church of the Gift of God was a nonsectarian group whose prime manifestation occurred through the New England Conser-

vatory of Health headquartered in Magnolia, Massachusetts. There, the Conservatory operated a retreat house that offers a program "dedicated to restoring your natural and spiritual good health." The church was headed by Professor James A. Dooling II, who based it upon the teachings of St. Luke, St. Benedict and St. Dorothy. It was Dooling's belief that good health is within the reach of all who will merely abide by the laws of the creator of nature.

Various healing techniques were offered at the Conservatory. They ranged from the more accepted medical and physical therapy practices to less orthodox approaches such as medical astrology, color therapy and psychic healing. Emphasis is placed on natural diet and exercise, and on human ecology as the correct ordering of the total environment of physical and spiritual man. The Church seems to have dissolved in the early 1980s.

★1507★
Church of the Lord Jesus Christ (Ishi Temple)
(Defunct)

The Church of the Lord Jesus Christ (Ishi Temple) was founded by bishop Robert N. Skillman, known to his followers as the Prophet Saoshyant. The church was described as Christoid, that is, in the image of Christ. It honored the holy name of God, Ishi (Hosea 2:16), meaning "My Husband." It was a church which recognized the necessity of having living prophets to govern it: "Saoshyant" is the name in Avestan (Zoroastrian) literature of the great coming Prophet. The church also taught that miracles were needed to demonstrate the power of God in extraordinary ways and that revelation was needed as a vehicle for bringing greater truth to the world today. Finally, the church taught the truth of the Latter Rain, the movement from the divine light of the Sixth Ray to the Seventh Ray (a reference to theosophic teaching on the light which emanantes from the divine).

Skillman was assisted in the Ishi Temple by Archdeacon Robert S. Kimball. Headquarters were established in Brisbane, California, from where a periodical, *The Christoid Evangel*, was published irregularly. The church offered correspondence lessons in "prosperity" and distributed talismans for a variety of needs. Saoshyant authored several booklets—*The Grand Affirmation*, *The Healing Affirmation* and *The Sayings*.

★1508★
Congregational Church of Practical Theology
31916 University Circle
Springfield, LA 70462

The Congregational Church of Practical Theology was formed in 1969 by Dr. E. Arthur Winkler, a former United Church of Christ and United Methodist minister. There are no creeds, though there is a set of beliefs that members and ministers are asked to use as guidelines for individual spiritual search. God is seen as continually revealing Himself in the open-minded search for truth. The Bible is a textbook for truth, but not the final word. Jesus is divine, but each person is also a divine child of God. The theology is practical and seeks to apply religion to all of life. The dignity of all people is affirmed; service to individuals and society is extolled. Ministers are seen as catalysts to the spiritual quest of individuals.

The church was founded not for the purpose of establishing congregations (though it has chartered a number of congregations), but to provide a ministry of guidance for all people who seek its varied forms of ministry, as well as to promote the dignity and love of all humankind—people of all colors, races, religions, social backgrounds, and economic levels. Ministers are ordained for the purpose of putting their religion into action in all areas of their life. Ministers, being needed in all professions, are not necessarily pastors of congregations but may be counselors, psychologists, medical doctors, hypnotherapists, lawyers, law officers, or in any other occupation. Affiliated with the church are the American Counselor's Society and the National Society of Clinical Hypnotherapists, both professional associations headquartered in Springfield, Louisiana.

Membership: In 1988 the church reported 251 ministers and 34 chartered congregations. Membership figures are not kept. Affiliated members can be found in Canada, Sweden, the West Indies, and Africa.

Educational Facilities: St. John's University, Springfield, Louisiana.

Periodicals: *Attain: Health, Happiness and Success.* • *Minister's Tips.*

Sources:

The Congregational Church of Practical Theology. Springfield, LA: Congregational Church, n.d.

Winkler, Arthur. *Hypnotherapy.* Valley, NB: Eastern Nebraska Christian College, 1972.

___. *New Age Minister's Manual.* Springfield, LA: St. John's University Publications, 1994.

★1509★
Coptic Fellowship of America
1735 Pinnacle, SW
Wyoming, MI 49509-1339

The Coptic Fellowship of America was founded in Los Angeles, California, in 1937 by Hamid Bey (d. 1976). Bey was born in Egypt and, as a five-year-old child, met the masters of the hidden temples of the Christian religion. According to Bey, due to persecution and the destruction of early Christian temples, Christians built many hidden temples that could not be found. The churches remained as mere outside schools. In the temple, Bey was trained in self-control, in how to subdue the body, concentration, the essentials of personality, and clairvoyance. The most important temple is the Head Masters Temple, which is 9,000 years old and hewn out of rock on the Nile. It is headed by the Great Eleven Ring Master. Having finished his temple education, Bey was sent to America to show that Houdini's claim to be able to reproduce any occult phenomenon was false. Though Houdini died soon after Bey's arrival, Bey stayed to tour the country, demonstrating his yogic abilities, particularly the feat of being buried for several hours.

The Coptic Fellowship teaches an esoteric Christianity—the laws of successful balanced living. The universe expresses polarity. Eastern and Western civilizations are manifestations of the polarity. Egypt is of the East. Nature is the handiwork of the creator. The human is the epitome of creation. The purpose is to bring into manifestation latent potential powers of conscious awareness—cosmic consciousness. Christ was one of the major teachers of the one law, and beheld the law more completely than any other master. In Christ, we see the essentials of the upward path—health of the physical body, work, science, and love. It is the belief of the fellowship that truth is eternal and eternally available. All of life, creation, progress, and evolution emanate from God's love, the same reality that leads humans and societies to perfection. Individual souls grow through a continuous progression (reincarnation and karma), but are often hidden from truth by ignorance and misdirection.

During the 1970s, the fellowship became aligned to the New Age Movement, and saw its work as a catalyst in the transformation to a new planetary civilization the Spiritual Unity of Nations (SUN). SUN was founded in England by Joseph Busby with the purpose of uniting spiritual powers to bring about a world spiritual bonding of nations. SUN's American headquarters are located at the fellowship's headquarters.

Bey was suceeded as head of the fellowship by John Davis, formerly its Midwest Director. The fellowship is guided by a board of directors. Work within the fellowship is divided among three orders: the Light Ministry is a body of teachers who publicly dissemi-

nate the orders' teachings, often through opening centers; the World Service Order; and the Devotional Order, an inner order of people who follow a meditative discipline. Correspondence lessons are offered for new members.

Membership: In 1992, the fellowship reported 3,500 members in several centers in the United States. There is one branch center in Nigeria. Most members are not affiliated with a center.

Sources:

Bey, Hamid. *My Experiences Preceding 5000 Burials.* Los Angeles: Coptic Fellowship of America, 1951.

★1510★
Embassy of the Gheez-Americans
Mt. Helion Sanctuary
Rock Valley Rd., Box 53
Long Eddy, NY 12760

The Embassy of the Gheez-Americans is headed by Empress Mysikiitta Fa Senntao, who runs the Mt. Helion Sanctuary at Long Eddy, New York. She is also titled "The Ambassadress of the Sun God and Resurrector of the Gheez-Nation [Ethiopia]." She is believed to have come from the sun in a space ship, leaving her husband behind and taking over a body upon arrival. Her mission is to redeem her people, who have been lost on earth for thousands of years and during that time have reincarnated in many nationalities.

According to Her Majesty, Satan and his brother, Tao, the god of love, fought for control of earth. After man chose Satan and the tree of good and evil in the garden, Satan took control. The tree of life (wisdom) was hidden among the few occult. Taoism, the wisdom of eternal life, came to Ethiopia at the beginning of the Age of Taurus. From there, it went to Egypt and survived the flood with Noah. Of Noah's sons, only one, Ham, accepted the ministry of the wisdom, a burden Hamites have had to bear. With Egyptian decline, Abraham and Israel were chosen the custodians of the wisdom. When Moses saw his people, who were worshipping Taurus, not able to keep the law, he gave them a lesser law.

The empress is calling together the ancient Gheez-Nation. Members are united by a common language (Gheez), a history, culture and a cosmic link of God. Her Majesty has bound Satan on the planet Uranus. The chosen people, the Gheez-Nation, will become the leaven in lifting all of humanity. The new nation learns the Gheez language, engages in ecstatic dancing and practices the martial arts of the Priest Kurahti. Most members are black people and number in the hundreds. Her Majesty functions as a psychic and a teacher of occult wisdom.

Membership: Not reported.

★1511★
Emissaries of Divine Light
5569 N. Country Rd. 29
Loveland, CO 80537

The Emissaries of Divine Light was formed in 1932 in Tennessee by Lloyd Arthur Meeker (d. 1954). Meeker, who wrote under the penname Uranda, established Sunrise Ranch, a community and home base of Emissaries, in rural Colorado, near Loveland. He was succeeded by Martin Cecil (d. 1988). In 1954, a second community was begun at 100 Mile House, British Columbia.

The basic stance of the Emissaries is spelled out in a pamphlet, "The Divine Design." According to the Emissaries, man was created in the image and likeness of the body of God, i.e., he was created to manifest the divine design. God is the one focus of all being. Distortions appear when the mind allows evil influences (fear, hate, jealousy, anger, resentment, etc.) to gain control. Since man has free will, the mind can select the influences that will be allowed to enter and control his body. The mind can choose to accept divine control.

Collectively, mankind manifests the distortions of evil influences in societal problems. But the return to divine control is the immediate possibility of every individual. The re-emergence of the divine design is called healing. Ontology, defined as the science of true being, is the art of manifesting reality in the world of chaos. That reality (God) manifests as truth (the design of form) and love (the power of life). Form is constantly in process, a fact which allows for healing.

A goal of the Emissaries is to experience reality, to know the identity of one's true being, to know oneness. The experience of oneness is an experience of the image and likeness of God in the present, without reference to past or future.

The Emissaries are centered in twelve communities around the world as well as in 160 meeting locations in 23 countries. The Emissaries do not proselytize. Members have been active in cooperative activities with other groups of like mind and purpose. One structure for such cooperative endeavor is Emissary Foundation International, which supports a variety of programs such as the Association for Responsible Communication, Renaissance Business Associates, Renaissance Educational Associates, the Stewardship Community, and Whole Health Institute.

Membership: In 1988 the Emissaries reported approximately 3,000 people closely affiliated worldwide.

Periodicals: *Integrity International.* Send orders to Box 9, 100 Mile House, British Columbia, Canada V0K 2E0.

Sources:

Aumra. *As of a Trumpet.* Loveland, CO: Eden Valley Press, 1968.

Cecil, Lord Martin. *Being Where You Are.* New Canaan, CT: Keats Publishing, 1974.

___. *On Eagle's Wings.* New York: Two Continents Publishing Group, 1977.

Cecil, Michael, et al. *Spirit of Sunrise.* London: Mitre Press, 1979.

Exeter, Martin. *Beyond Belief: Insights to the Way It Is.* Loveland, CO: Foundation House Publications, 1986.

___. *Thus It Is.* Denver, CO: Foundation House Publications, 1989.

★1512★
Essene Center
(Defunct)

The Essene Center was founded in 1972 in Hot Springs, Arkansas, by the Rev. Walter Hagen. In 1970 Hagen had a vision of Christ, and the stigmata (marks similar to those in Jesus' hands after the crucifixion) were placed on his hands as a sign of his acceptance of his mission. In other visions, he was given the power to work miracles. Hagen is also a prophet and regularly made predictions of coming events.

According to Hagen, Jesus was an Essene, and the order of Essenes actually dates to the time of Moses. The House of Prophets on Mt. Carmel was the center of the order. Essenes were characterized by abstinence from slavery, by communal living, disdain for commerce and industry, longevity, belief in reincarnation, healing by God's power, and psychic abilities. As modern-day Essenes, Hagen taught his followers to believe that war is wrong, that waste is a misuse of what God had given, that all religions are acceptable to God, that respect for the rights of all men includes disdain of slavery, and that it is a duty to help other Essenes. He accepted the Dead Sea Scrolls and believed that the coming messiah will arise from among the Essenes.

During the 1970s there was only one Essene group, that one associated with the Center at Hot Springs, but members were located around the country. They were tied together by *The Guide*, a monthly periodical. Hagen's workshops and a variety of services were offered through the Center. No evidence of the continuance of the center into the 1980s has been found.

★1513★
Essene Fellowship of Peace/Spiritual Church of Ataraxia
Current address not obtained for this edition.

The Essene Fellowship of Peace and the Spiritual Church of Ataraxia are two names for the same organization established in 1942. "Ataraxia" is a Greek word meaning "house of peace." The church believes in God as the One Source, Law, Light, and Love and in humans as spiritual beings. Jesus is considered the Way-shower, though the path he shows manifests quite differently for each person.

According to the church, individuals live on after death and their possibilities for further development and unfoldment is limitless. To assist, help from the higher planes is available. The door to reformation is never closed.

Three members of the church, George and Mary Weddell and Miriam B. Willis, have put together a book, *Creative Color*, which discusses the various esoteric meanings of color and how to put color to practical use in one's life. This volume has become a major instrument of the church reaching the public.

Membership: Not reported.

Sources:

Creative Color. Hemet, CA: Fellowship of Peace, 1989. 204 pp.

★1514★
Essene Foundation
2536 Collier Ave.
San Diego, CA 92116

The Essene Foundation, formerly known as First Christians' Essene Church, was founded in 1937 as the Essene School, the name by which it was known until the mid-1980s. Its founder was Edmond Bordeaux Szekely (d. 1980), a descendent of Hungarian royalty, world traveller, and author-scholar. In the 1920s, Szekely discovered an ancient manuscript which proported to be the collection of Jesus' teachings as written down by His disciple John in the original Aramaic (the language Jesus actually spoke). In 1937, he published the translation of part of the text as *The Essene Gospel of Peace*. (The remainder of the text was published in four subsequent volumes beginning in 1971.) Soon afterward he founded several cooperatives in southern France whose members attempted to follow the Essene way. It was Szekely's belief that Jesus was a member of the Essene brotherhood, and hence the first Christians were Essenes.

In 1939, forced out of Europe by the rise of Hitler, Szekely settled in Tecate, a town in Mexico just across the border from San Diego, California. He opened the Essene School on his ranch estate in Mexico and he eventually became a Mexican citizen. The school attempted to teach broad Essene concepts which included the essence of healthful life which he had termed biogenic living. The center, Rancho La Puerta, became famous as a health spa and attracted many of the wealthy and famous. In 1958 a second center, the Golden Door, was opened in Escondido, California, and also became well known as a health and beauty center, attracting many movie stars. During the remainder of his life Szekely continued to travel widely and authored numerous books expounding upon the Essene ideal as he had come to understand it. He founded the International Biogenic Society to perpetuate his teachings on healthful living and the Academy of Creative Living, which published many of his books. For many years he edited *The Essene Quarterly*, the school's periodical.

Following Szekely's death, the Essene School was reorganized as the First Christians' Essene Church under the leadership of Archbishop Garry A. White, a longtime colleague of Szekely's. Beliefs are summarized in the church's creed which affirms the fatherhood of God, the motherhood of Nature, and the brotherhood of Man, and advocates a natural creative lifestyle. Members are encouraged to follow a path to enlightenment which begins in developing bodily, mental, and emotional health. Vegetarianism is advocated as is the use of natural foods. A form of daily meditation, the "Essene Communions," which exemplify the unity between humans and the visible and invisible universe, is taught. It is the church's opinion that the discovery of the Dead Sea Scrolls has strengthened their beliefs about the Essene nature of early Christianity, and the Scrolls are cited as authoritative texts from which church teachings are derived.

In the mid-1990s the organization's corporate name was changed to The Essene Foundation. The First Christian's Essene Church now exists as the mother church. In 1992 Garry White retired as archbishop and was succeeded by Dr. Emmanuel M. Winocur, and White was named patriarch of the church. The foundation has a number of affiliated missions scattered across the West Coast of the United States (California, Oregon, Arizona), New York, and Arkansas.

Holistic healing continues to be a primary concern. Study groups sponsored by the foundation emphasize the importance of purity of every body beginning with a strict avoidance of flesh eating, emotional equanimity, mental clarity, and spiritual awareness. Among the prominent members is Bp. Patricia Bragg, the daughter of the famous naturopathic physician, Paul Bragg.

Membership: The church is not a membership organization. They estimate that as many as three million people worldwide follow the Essene way of life.

Periodicals: *Scroll.* Send orders to Box 16103, San Diego, CA 92116.

Remarks: A serious charge of fraud was leveled at Szekely concerning the two original manuscripts from which *The Essene Gospel of Peace* was translated, one of which (in Aramaic) he claimed was to be found in the Vatican Library and the other (in Old Slavonic) was reportedly in the library of the Hapsburg emperors in Vienna. After diligent search, neither manuscript has been located, and doubt has been expressed of their existence. On the other hand, Bishop Purcell Weaver, a longtime associate of Szekely's, testifies to having assisted in the complicated process of producing the English translation.

Sources:

Beskow, Per. *Strange Tales About Jesus.* Philadelphia: Fortress Press, 1983.

Mazzanti, Deborah Szekely. *Secrets of the Golden Door.* New York: William Morrow & Co., 1977.

Szekely, Edmond Bordeaux. *The Essene Gospel of Peace.* San Diego, CA: Academy of Creative Living, 1971.

___. *The Essene Way, Biogenic Living.* Cartago, Costa Rica: International Biogenic Society, 1978.

___. *Talks.* San Diego, CA: Academy of Creative Living, 1972.

★1515★
Essenes of Arkashea
21450 SW 240th St.
Homestead, FL 33031

The Essenes of Arkashea claim a heritage dating to an ancient order founded by Pharaoh Akhenaten in the year 1354 B.C.E. Akhenaten is famous for his belief in one God (as opposed to the polytheism of the older Egyptian tradition) and his attempt to suppress the old religions in favor of his new faith. He was eventually murdered and much of his work destroyed by his successors. After his death many of his followers fled Egypt. The Essenes of Arkashea believe that members of their order and many other tribes of the land reentered Egypt and became laborers for the pharaohs. They were the source of the Hebrew tribes. The Essenes of the first century C.E. were derived from the older Egyptian order.

The modern Essenes of Arkashea claim that the original Egyptian order has survived secretly over the centuries and that they are part of it. They became publicly known only in 1993 with the publication of *The Discovery*, the story of a woman's discovery and

initiation into the Order in the 1980s. She had found its monastery, which at that time was located in Alabama. The order is headed by Reginald Therrien, the regent of Arkashea, who offers services to the public as a psychic counselor.

The term Arkashea refers to the history of what each individual has done as s/he reincarnates from life to life. The Essenes attempt to explore this history that is written within each person and use the Arkashea as a toll for change toward self-realization. Thus the resident members of the Essenes' monastery study themselves. Students search through the Arkashea in order to become free of the mire of maya (illusion). To assist this process, the monastery publishes a series of monographs that teach the Laws of Creation.

The Monastery of Arkashea is both a community for members and a place from which they offer their assistance to people. It exists in two aspects; the Cloister is for residents who have taken a vow of poverty and celibacy, while the Commonwealth is the name for that part of the membership who do not assume a monastic life. The Hamlet is a section of the Commonwealth for people who have taken a vow of poverty but not of celibacy, meaning they can marry and have children. The Hoblet is the section of the Commonwealth that receives new arrivals at the monastery and introduces people to its teachings. People who want to relate to the monastery, but take neither a vow of poverty nor chastity, remain affiliated through the Hoblet. The Magic Circle is a for-profit corporation that was created to handle much of the monastery's income.

Membership: Not reported. Membership includes people across North America and in several foreign countries.

Sources:

Nier, Susan. *The Discovery.* Homestead, FL: OmniTouch, Inc., 1993. 548 pp.

★1516★
Etherian Religious Society of Universal Brotherhood
Current address not obtained for this edition.

The Etherian Religious Society of Universal Brotherhood was formed in 1965 in California by its director, the Rev. E. A. Hurtienne, and has its source in the mental visions given Mr. Hurtienne earlier in his life. While no being or form was seen in these visions, there were present waves of love and the awareness of universal consciousness. The purpose of the Society is to minister through love so as to insure dignity, equality and justice for all mankind throughout the universe and help establish the future root races (developmental stages) of mankind upon earth and assure the entrance of earth into the Planetary Federation of Light of our solar system.

The basic philosophy of the Society recognizes a consciousness that is divine and manifested in four principles of omnipresence, omnipotence, omniscience and love. It further holds that all men are brothers throughout the universe; all forms of life on all planes are related; all religions, though under the direction of God, are man-made; love is the unifying force and must become a living reality, for only through it can eternal life by achieved; karma and reincarnation are universal laws, man is divine and is entitled to free thought and action; man is a spiritual being with seven complete bodies, and all life is to be held in reverence. Behavior is to center upon sincerity, tolerance, integrity, kindness and affection.

The Society has among its immediate goals the establishment of primary classes in metaphysics and esoteric studies and the formation of light and meditation groups for healing, unity, and harmony between nature and mankind. Membership is open to all; after a year, members may become a part of the Brotherhood of Light, an inner group with the Society. The group circulates copies of *Man, Know Thy Divinity*, published by the Living Christ Movement of New Zealand. Among future goals are the establishment of a university, a healing center and a religious community of advanced spiritual beings.

Membership: Not reported.

Periodicals: *The Etherian Bulletin.*

Sources:

Man, Know Thy Divinity. Auckland, NZ: Living Christ Movement, n.d.

★1517★
Fifth Epochal Fellowship
529 Wrightwood Ave.
Chicago, IL 60614

The Fifth Epochal Fellowship was founded in 1989, but continues the work begun by the URANTIA Brotherhood in 1955. The Brotherhood was originally founded by people who had read *The URANTIA Book*, a 2,097-page collection of material received from numerous celestial beings. The Book had first been published by the URANTIA Foundation in 1955. For many years the Brotherhood and the Foundation worked together amicably. However, in 1989, the Brotherhood moved to become an independent organization. As a result, the URANTIA Foundation withdrew from the Brotherhood the right to use the name "URANTIA" and its associated symbols. The Brotherhood changed its name to Fifth Epochal Fellowship (the URANTIA Book being the revelation of the Fifth Epoch) and continued the programs and affiliation with study groups as before. David Elders was chosen as president of the Fellowship.

Membership: Not reported. A year after its formation, the Fellowship announced that 17 of the 21 societies formerly associated with the Brotherhood had voted to remain affiliated with the new Fellowship.

★1518★
First Century Church
(Defunct)

The Rev. David N. Bubar was a Southern Baptist minister and graduate of New Orleans Baptist Theological Seminary. After a seven-year pastorate during which he became more and more aware of his psychic abilities, he resigned his parish and, in 1969, opened the Spiritual Outreach Society (later renamed the First Century Church). During the 1970s, he developed a national reputation as a clairvoyant, prophet, and psychic counselor, and he kept a heavy schedule of lectures around the country.

In 1975 Bubar was involved in the arson case of the Sponge Rubber Plant in Shelton, Connecticut. Plant owner Charles Moeller had been a longtime client of Bubar's and Bubar had predicted a plant "disaster" shortly before it was bombed. As of 1977, Bubar was serving a prison term following his conviction as a participant in the arson.

There was only a single congregation of the First Century Church, but it had a significant outreach through its nationally circulated periodical, *Flaming Sword.* Weekly services and classes were held at the church, which survived only a short time after Bubar began his long sentence.

★1519★
Foundation Faith of God
Current address not obtained for this edition.

The Foundation Faith of God was formed in 1974 when the majority of the leaders of the Process Church of the Final Judgment rejected the direction being taken by Process prophet Robert de Grimston, withdrew their support, and reorganized as the Foundation Church of the Millennium. Subsequently it has progressed through several doctrinal positions and internal reorganizations reflected in the change of names, first to the Foundation Faith of the Millennium (1977) and then to its present name (1980).

A dissatisfaction with the growing emphasis upon what was perceived as an esoteric, somewhat gnostic, doctrine of the unity of Christ and Satan was the immediate problem leading to the ousting of de Grimston and the formation of the Foundation Faith by most of the following of the Process Church. A hierarchical order has been retained. Heading the Faith is a nine-member Council of Luminaries who in turn delegate temporal administration to the Office of the Faithful. Ministers are ranked from luminaries and celebrants (both ordained) to mentors and covenanters. Those preparing for the ministry are termed witnesses. The uniforms, consisting of a blue suit with a white shirt, so evident in the 1970s, have been largely abandoned. Laity is composed of aides and disciples.

The church always possessed of a strong emphasis upon Christian themes, has moved steadily toward an orthodox Christian belief, expressing belief in the Trinity, the deity of Jesus, salvation from sin, the necessity of the new birth, and the second advent. There is also a strong emphasis upon the impending second coming of Christ and the establishment of the Kingdom of God.

The church has established centers and missions across the United States. The church is also spread through prayer fellowship and outreach ministries. There is a wide and diverse program of social programs, conceived as part of a healing ministry. Spiritual healing has been a consistent part of the Faith's belief and practice, and ministers make themselves available for healing prayer at all Faith centers. Spiritual consultations are also offered for their healing value.

Periodicals: *Newsletter.* • *Best Friends Magazine.*

Sources:

Hymns and Chants. Las Vegas, NV: Foundation Faith of God, 1977.

Hymns and Chants. Las Vegas, NV: Foundation Faith of the Millennium, n.d.

★1520★
Foundation of Human Understanding
Box 811
Grants Pass, OR 97526

The Foundation of Human Understanding was founded in Los Angeles, California in 1961 by Roy Masters. Masters was born in England in 1928 and during his early life studied hypnosis. He later spent a period of his early adulthood in South Africa observing the witchdoctors and further spurring his interest in the nature of the mental healing processes. In 1949 he moved to the United States and became a successful diamond cutter and expert, finally settling in Houston, Texas. Then in the mid-1950s, as the phenomena surrounding the case of Bridey Murphy made reincarnation and hypnosis of great popular interest, friends discovered Masters' work in hypnosis and beseiged him for help. These sessions led to his quitting the diamond business and founding the Institute of Hypnosis, the forerunner of the foundation. He stayed in Houston for two more years during which time he perfected psychocatalysis, a meditation technique which was to become the most important aspect of his teachings, and then moved to Los Angeles, where the foundation was started.

Once in Los Angeles, Masters developed a successful radio talk show and wrote *Your Mind Can Keep You Well*, which appeared as both a book and a record. It is Masters's conclusion from his work in hypnosis that what was wrong with people was that they were already hypnotized by the mass of pressures put on them by life. Hypnotized people act in irrational ways and possess strong components of anxiety and guilt. The answer to hypnosis is psychocatalysis, the meditation technique taught by Masters. By using the technique people can be cured of diseases and learn to cope with life. It can lead many into a transformed life which quickly takes on a religious and mystical quality. The foundation became a place that not only taught meditation but where people whose lives had been changed could gather to continue their spiritual growth.

During the 1960s and 1970s, Masters gained an extensive following in southern California. His radio show, originally on a local station in Los Angeles, was eventually syndicated across the United States and Canada. Periodically he left Los Angeles to lecture around the country. Soon groups of people who followed his meditation teachings and appreciated his approach to life's problems emerged, particularly on the West Coast. During the 1970s the foundation was registered as a religious organization with the Internal Revenue Service which then refused to recognize it as a church. In 1980 Masters filed a lawsuit seeking such recognition which was finally granted in 1987. About 1985 the headquarters of the foundation was moved to Grants Pass, Oregon, where it operates a religious retreat and ranch.

Membership: Not reported.

Educational Facilities: Brighton Academy, Grants Pass, Oregon.

Periodicals: *New Insights.* Send orders to PO Box 1009, Grants Pass, OR 97526.

Sources:

Masters, Roy. *How to Conquer Suffering Without Doctors.* Los Angeles: Foundation of Human Understanding, 1976.

___. *No One Has to Die!.* Los Angeles, CA: Foundation of Human Understanding, 1977.

___. *The Satan Principle.* Los Angeles: Foundation of Human Understanding, 1979.

___. *Secret of Life.* Los Angeles: Foundation of Human Understanding, 1972.

___. *Sex, Sin and Salvation.* Los Angeles: Foundation of Human Understanding, 1977.

___. *Your Mind Can Keep You Well.* Los Angeles: Foundation of Human Understanding, 1968.

Wolff, William. *Healers, Gurus, and Spiritual Guides.* Los Angeles: Sherbourne Press, 1969.

★1521★
Future Foundation
(Defunct)

The Future Foundation was formed in 1969 in Steinauer, Nebraska, by Gerard W. Gottula, an associated group which had been meeting for several months. The history of the group actually dates to the 1950s and the healing works of Jennings Ruffing, who lived in a small Wyoming town. Ruffing discovered that one of his patients was clairvoyant and, under the direction of Ruffing, could give psychic readings. The eight members of the original foundation group gathered for a reading from Ruffing and his associate, at which time the formation of the Foundation was announced to them.

The first issue of the *Future Foundation*, a newsletter, appeared in 1969. A board of 12 members was formed to govern the work, which would consist of giving health, life, and guidance readings.

Membership: The foundation grew through the 1970s and 1980s; however, it faced continual conflict with new regulations from the FDA and in 1991 disbanded.

Sources:

Prophecies of Cyrus. Steinauer, NE: Future Foundation, 1970.

★1522★
Haikim International Meditation Society
(Defunct)

The Haikim International Meditation Society is/was a small group headquartered in Houston, Texas, and headed by Mary Be-

atrice Gunn, its director/counselor. Its world headquarters were in Zurich, Switzerland. No sign of its continuance into the 1980s has been observed.

★1523★
Heart Consciousness Church and New Age Church of Being
PO Box 82
Middletown, CA 95461

In 1972 the Harbin Hot Springs Retreat Center was purchased by Robert Hartley. Because the resort needed repairs, he brought in friends to make it fit for public use again. Some of these people met in 1974 and agreed that they were in alignment with the emerging New Age Movement. They defined that movement as consisting of three basic elements: universal spirituality, the Human Potential Movement, and the Holistic Natural Movement. They affirmed that there is a fundamental agreement in all religions, there is a need for honest, open, and spontaneous relationships, and there is a desire for a holistic natural approach to health and healing. This core of agreement became the basis of a religious fellowship that was incorporated in 1975 as the Heart Consciousness Church. Hartley turned Harbin Hot Springs over to the church. The New Age Church of Being was founded in 1985 as a more ceremonial and "churchy" organization. It administers a ministerial training program.

The church sees itself as serving the cause of the New Age Movement by hosting various new age events, including conferences, seminars, and workshops, and by acting as a unifying force among the various groups. The use of the resort by outside groups is a primary means of financial support.

New members may join the group by residing at the retreat center and working with the present church members. They are required to have a personal goal that is compatible with that of the church and to contribute labor or money toward their own support. The group has a loose structure. It makes group life decisions by a process called "spiritual anarchy" and attempts to resolve differences in a spirit of love and oneness. However, ultimate control of the property is by a board of directors.

Because of the opportunities at Harbin Hot Springs, it is the goal of the church to develop a new alternative economy to allow people who have no financial assets to be integrated into the life of the church and to foster similar satellite communities in other locations.

Membership: In 1997 there were 150 church members living at Harbin Hot Springs, and another ten in the first satelitte center, Sierra Hot Springs, Sierraville, California. Sierra Hot Springs is operated by the New Age Church of Being.

Periodicals: *Harbin Hot Springs Quarterly Catalog/Magazine.*

Sources:

Klages, Ellen. *Harbin Hot Springs: Healing Waters, Sacred Land.* Middletown, CA: Harbin Hot Springs Publishing, 1991.

Living the Future. Middletown, CA: Harbin Hot Springs Publishing, 1993, 16 pp.

★1524★
Holy Order of Ezekiel
(Defunct)

The Holy Order of Ezekiel was founded in 1969 by Dr. Daniel Christopher. Dr. Christopher was a student of Dr. Judith Tyberg, who had been a disciple of Sri Aurobindo and later taught at the East-West Cultural Center in San Francisco, California. Christopher graduated from the Center and later studied in Europe at the Prasura Institute and the Guggenheim Academy. The Order, founded upon Christopher's return to the United States, was composed of two parts, the Celestial and Terrestrial Circles. The Celestial Circle, composed of three masters, seven practitioners and other initiates, is the center of guiding light that radiates celestial illumination to every attuned being. The masters are the spiritual gurus of all members. Christopher was the First Master. The Terrestrial Circle consisted of the scribes, secretaries and members and was to be the growing branch of the Order. Members who manifest assimilation of and dedication to the precepts of the Order were welcomed as initiates.

The Order's basic teachings centered upon the knowledge of God's power and the techniques of achieving personal success and fulfillment through that power. The Divine Life Lessons distributed by the Order prepared the seeker to receive the power promised by Christ. These include instruction in meditation, breathing, the use of "Aum" (a mantra), mystical symbolizing, spiritual healing and numerology. There was a strong belief in reincarnation and karma. The masters were seen as helpful in the student's progress. The Order taught that God assumes one-half of the student's burden and the master, one-fourth. The members must generate the initial spark.

In the 1970s, headquarters of the Holy Order were in Glendale, California. From there, the lessons were sent out to students across the country.

★1525★
Holy Spirit Association for the Unification of World
   Christianity
4 W. 43rd St.
New York, NY 10036

The Holy Spirit Association for the Unification of World Christianity was brought to the United States in 1959 from South Korea. After a period of slow growth, it mushroomed during the early and mid-1970s and became a controversial and significant religious force because of its nonconventional beliefs, accusations of improper recruitment techniques, and its attempts to build coalitions of scholars and world leaders around the church's idealistic programs and ideals. The church first gained national attention as a result of a speaking tour that its founder, the Rev. Sun Myung Moon, made across the country in 1972. The Unification Church, as it is usually called, came to the United States in the person of Young Oon Kim, who produced the first expression of the founder's teachings. The basic scripture of the church through Moon, the Divine Principle, was translated into English in 1972 by Mrs. Won Bok Choi. A revised translation, Exposition of Divine Principle, by Jin Keum Kim and Andrew Wilson, was published in 1995. During its early years in America, the church was the subject of one major sociological study, and Moon was proclaimed a voice for the New Age by Spiritualist medium Arthur A. Ford.

The Reverend Moon was born in 1920 in what is now North Korea. During his youth, the family converted to Christianity and joined the Presbyterian Church. In 1935, he had a vision of Jesus in which he was told to carry out Jesus unfinished task. The vision occurred and was nurtured at a time when Korean Pentecostal Christians were predicting a Korean messiah. In 1945 Moon began to collect a following and two years later founded the Broad Sea Church. He also spent six months at Israel Soodo Won (Israel Monastery), established by Baek Moon Kim, a self-proclaimed messiah, and changed his name from Yong Myung Moon to Sun Myung Moon (meaning someone who has clarified Word or Truth). From 1946 to 1950, Moon was in prison in North Korea much of the time for his refusal to cooperate with Kim Il Sung's regime and in 1950 became a refugee. He eventually settled in Pusan, and in 1954 he founded the Unification Church in Seoul. The new church grew slowly, but by 1957 a Korean edition of the Divine Principle was in print. Meanwhile, church members established several corporations dealing in such varied products as ginseng tea and titanium. Missionaries were sent to Japan where they had their greatest success.

In December 1971, Moon moved to the United States. During the early 1970s, as the church began to grow, a variety of buildings were purchased to house its expanding program. Facilities for the Unification Theological Seminary were acquired near Barrytown, New York; an estate used for training sessions was purchased in Tarrytown, New York; and a conference center, which also serves as Moon's American residence, called "East Garden," is located at Irvington, New York. In Manhattan, a headquarters building and mission center (the former New Yorker Hotel) completed its major organizational facilities.

Beliefs: Unification belief is built around three basic concepts of Creation, Fall, and Restoration. The Principle of Creation asserts that God created the world and by that act became known. The world, reflective of God, has two expressions as *Sung Sang* (internal, causal) and *Hyung Sang* (external, resultant). It also has a second set of dual characteristics, masculine and feminine. These two kinds of relations are quite distinct and express different qualities of the created order. Sung Sang and Hyung Sang express the relatedness of spirit or mind and matter while masculinity and femininity express the complementarity between male and female or yang and ying. God created the world out of His inner nature, His heart, and His impulse to love and to be united in love. The purpose of creation is to experience the joy that comes from loving.

The principle of The Fall began with Adam and Eve's lack of realization of God's original purpose in creation. They fell away from God because of disobedience resulting in a premature sexual relationship (a misuse of love) and their resultant inability to create a perfect family. Their failure placed the fallen archangel, Satan, in control of the world. Since that time God has been trying to restore His primal intention and replace the order of selfish love with the ethic of true love.

The Principle of Restoration outlines the conditions necessary for restoration to occur. Since God created humankind with free will and some measure of responsibility, the restoration process has been repeatedly prolonged because of human failure. God's ultimate design is to send one sinless man, the Messiah, through whom humankind can be engrafted and achieve salvation. The Messiah must meet a variety of qualifications.

According to the church's beliefs, the Messiah must be born on earth as a substantial, physical being, since the Messiah must accomplish the original task of becoming an ideal person, the person who has perfected his character, and thus has fulfilled the First Blessing, to be fruitful (Gen. 1:28). He can carry out this responsibility only in the flesh. He must also take a bride and realize the ideal family that God has desired, and thus become the True Parent, one who has realized God's Second Blessing, to multiply (Gen 1:28). His parental heart will implant God's Heart and love in the hearts of everyone following him and will help them to perfect themselves by giving rebirth to them and showing each one how to accomplish true marriage and family life. This is how all humans can achieve complete physical and spiritual salvation, and create the Kingdom of God on earth, fulfilling the Third Blessing (Gen. 1:28)

Members believe that due to the failure of the chosen people (chiefly, John the Baptist and the religious leaders) to accept and follow him 2,000 years ago, Jesus was not able to complete these tasks. Instead, he was killed, contrary to God's original will. Nevertheless, through his resurrection, Jesus established the possibility of spiritual salvation for all humankind. Thus, if human beings accept Jesus as their savior, they can attain spiritual salvation and live with Jesus in Paradise. This spiritual salvation does not provide complete and physical salvation for humans on earth. Therefore Christ must come again to complete the salvation process on the earth. He will come to fulfill the Lords Prayer: "Thy Kingdom come on earth as in Heaven." This will be a world where there is no sin, no Satan, and where humankind will live in peace and harmony as God's children.

The Reverend Moon has come to fill the conditions of the Lord of the Second Advent. In 1960 he married Hak Ja Han, with whom he has parented 14 children (two of whom, Hye Jin Moon, a daughter, and Heung Jin Moon, a son, have died). Through Rev. and Mrs. Moons's fulfillment of the position of True Parents, according to Unification belief, God has brought the opening of complete restoration. Couples participate in the restoration by their marriage blessing. Many are at first called to a period of sacrificial work and personal celibacy. At the end of that period, church members are engaged and blessed in marriage in a public ceremony conducted by Moon and his wife. The events surrounding the marriage are the primary events in the messianic mission. As part of their engagements, members participate in a holy wine ceremony (somewhat analogous to Christian communion) whereby their original sin is conditionally absolved. Couples are married in large mass ceremonies, the most recent having been in 1997 (39.6 million couples on November 29, 1997) celebrated in Washington D.C. with 28,000 couples present and broadcast to over 50 satellite locations worldwide. After the wedding, the couples may separate for no less than 40 days before the union is consummated. The so-called three-day ceremony, during which consummation occurs, ritually dramatizes the restoration.

Organizations: The Unification Church is headed by the Reverend and Mrs. Moon who have complete authority over major decisions. The American church is advised by church elders who reside in America. The board appoints the various national presidents; currently Dr. Tyler Hendricks heads the church in America. To carry out the Messiahs program for restoration and bring forth the kingdom of God, Rev. Moon has created a variety of evangelistic, political, cultural, charitable, and religious programs.

Evangelistic programs include the Collegiate Association for the Research of Principles (referring to the church's basic principles), a prime educational outreach on the nations campuses. Church families around the United States reach out through "Tribal Messiahship." The Church's theistic beliefs lead members to advocate a strong ideological opposition to Communism, a prominent part of the church's public expression through the 1980s. One reason Korea is identified as the land in which the New Lord will appear is that it is on God's front line as well as Satan's. The 38th parallel is referred to as the confrontation line between Communism and democracy. The major expression of the critique against Communism in the 1970s, the Freedom Leadership Foundation, was replaced by CAUSA, which found significant success in Latin America. CAUSA has finished it mission and Rev. Moon has turned his attention to the creation of true families through the non-sectarian Family Federation for World Peace and Unification (FFWPU).

A cultural program is promoted under the International Cultural Foundation, the most important aspect being the International Conference on the Unity of the Sciences, which is one of the Unification community's most successful programs and annually brings scientists together to discuss the convergence of science, morals, and values. Growing out of the Conference has been the Professors World Peace Academy and the Washington Institute for Values in Public Policy. The various ecumenical religious programs were reorganized in the early 1980s under the International Religious Foundation (IRF) and under the Inter-Religious Federation for World Peace (IRFWP) in the 1990's. Some of its major programs include ecumenical conferences for theologians and other scholars (New Ecumenical Research Association), conferences for clergy (True Family Values Ministry), and the Religious Youth Services (RYS).

The prime charitable activity, finding its greatest response in the urban minority community and the developing world, is the International Relief Friendship Foundation (IRFF), which later spawned the United to Serve America organization.

The church grew very slowly until 1972. By 1976 it had grown from a few hundred to approximately 6,000 members. It also began a worldwide expansion that has seen church centers opened in many countries on every continent. In the United States and western Europe, the church became an object of controversy and public hostility. Church membership in the United States dropped below 5,000 by the end of the decade and continued to decline. During the early 1980s, centers were established in every state; most, however, remain small.

Membership: In 1998 the church reported an estimated core membership of 50,000 in America, and some 3 million worldwide. However, in addition to this membership, more than 70 million couples worldwide have received the holy wine and Rev. Moon's marriage blessing, though they often remain in their own faith.

Educational Facilities: Unification Theological Seminary, Barrytown, New York.
University of Bridgeport, Bridgeport, Connecticut.
Sun Moon University, Korea.

Periodicals: *Dialogue and Alliance.* • *Todays World.* • *True Family Times.* • *Unification News.*

Remarks: Alarmed by the growth of the Unification Church in the early 1970s, opponents have organized and carried on a steady program of opposition that has succeeded in making the church an object of continued controversy. By the 1970s the church had become the prime reference for the popular derisive term "cult." Attacks have been launched from a variety of sources. These attacks culminated in the conviction of Moon for tax evasion. For details on other controversies the church has been involved in, please refer to the volumes listed below as well as other titles covering the church and/or contemporary cult controversies.

Sources:

Barker, Eileen. *The Making of a Moonie.* Oxford: Basil Blackwell, 1984.

Breen, Michael. *Sun Myung Moon: The Early Years, 1920-53.* Hurstpierpoint, UK: Refuge Books, 1997. 191pp.

Bromley, David G., and Shupe, Anson D., Jr. *Moonies' in America.* Beverly Hills, CA: Sage Publications, 1979.

Divine Principle. New York: Holy Spirit Association for the Unification for World Christianity, 1973.

Durst, Mose. *To Bigotry, No Sanction.* Chicago: Regnery Gateway, 1984.

Outline of the Principle, Level 4. New York: Holy Spirit Association for the Unification of World Christianity, 1980.

★1526★
Huna International
PO Box 663
Kilauea, HI 96754

Huna International was founded in 1973 as a religious order for the teaching of the Huna philosophy of ancient Hawaii as understood by Serge Kahili King. King was introduced to kahuna philosophy by his father Harry King, a member of a still secret network that King calls The Organization. Through Serge Kahili King's contacts he was given training and as a young man initiated as a kahuna in the Order of Kane. After working with a relief and development program in Africa, he returned to the United States and studied with his adoptive Hawaiian uncle, a kahuna (1971 to 1975), which led to his founding Huna International.

He defines huna as "that which is hidden" and refers to it as the Hidden Knowledge or Secret Reality. A kahuna is the transmitter of the secret, and the motto of Huna International is "Let that which is unknown become known." The ancient kahunas of Hawaii were divided into three orders, the Ku, the Lono, and the Kane. The Kane Order was known for its intuitive approach to the world and its use of what today are called alternate states of consciousness and psychic abilities.

The basic teachings of the Huna philosophy have been summarized in seven statements, each represented by a Hawaiian keyword:

> *Ike,* "The world is what you think it is." That is, we create our world by our beliefs, judgments, and expectations. We can create illness and poverty or we can create health and prosperity. *Kala,* "There are no

limits." Anything is possible if we believe it. *Makia,* "Energy flows where attention goes." Energy is directed to the things about which we think. If we change our thinking, our world will be remade. *Manawa,* "Now is the moment of power." We are not bound by the past or future, and can thus change in the present. Healing, change, development, or any other desired goal is dependent upon our keeping our attention focused in the present. Looking to the past or future misdirects energy away from present actions. *Aloha,* "To love is to be happy with." Love the great healer and the change agent is freed as we become happy with ourselves and our surroundings. Happiness is accentuated by acts of forgiveness, tolerance, and self-acceptance. *Mana,* "All power comes from within." Outside forces only have power as one believes and submits. Real power is that which operates from the inner resources of the self. *Pono,* "Effectiveness is the measure of truth." Effectiveness, another name for harmony, comes from an integrated working of mind, body, and spirit.

There are also three chartered branches of Huna International: Aloha International, its networking and project supervision arm; Voices of the Earth, a forum for native peoples; and Finding Each Other International, which conducts relationship training. Through Aloha International, the huna philosophy is shared through various programs, termed projects. The Network Project nurtures local chapters and service networks. The Hawaiiana Project supports the spread of knowledge of Hawaiian culture through museums, shops, and a mail order service for Hawaiiana. The Training Project provides Hawaiian Shaman Training as taught by King and other leaders, self development workshops of a wide variety, and teacher and counselor training for leaders. There is an annual gathering each November for the Mahakiki Festival on Kauai.

Membership: In 1994 Huna International reported approximately 7,000 members, 35 ordained *alakai* (clergy), and some 20 affiliated centers.

Periodicals: *The Aloha News,* c/o Aloha International, Box 599, Kauai, HI 96746.

Sources:

King, Serge. *The Aloha Spirit.* Kilauea, HI: Aloha International, 1990. 16 pp.

___. *Kahuna Healing.* Wheaton, IL: Theosophical Publishing House, 1983. 173 pp.

"Making the Good the Most Important." *Threshold Quarterly* 14, 4 (Nov 1996): 12-16.

___. *Mastering Your Hidden Self.* Wheaton, IL: Theosophical Publishing House, 1983.

___. *Urban Shaman.* New York: Simon & Schuster, 1990.

★1527★
Huna Research, Inc.
1760 Anna St.
Cape Girardeau, MO 63701-4504

The religion of ancient Hawaii, i.e., before 1820, was primarily ritualistic observance performed in *heiaus* (temples) by *kahunas* ("priests"). Control of the people was effected by strictly enforced *kapu* (taboo), which reserved most privileges and wealth for the royal families and their religious leaders. Severe punishments were exacted from those who violated the innumerable prohibitions of the kapu system. Each heiau was dedicated to one of the many gods and goddesses, of which the four major ones were Kane, the creator; Ku, the war god; Kanaloa, the god of the sea and of death; and Lono, the fertility god. Mana ("divine" power) was

a special privilege of royalty and the kahunas and was jealously guarded.

The ancient kahuna religious practices virtually ceased when Hewahewa, the kahuna nui ("high priest") of Kamehameha anticipated the coming of the "new" religion and abolished the temple observances. Most Hawaiians did not adapt well to the white man's religion and went back to their old ways, even after they were outlawed by the missionaries, who gained political and financial control of the Islands. Often Hawaiians professed Christianity, while retaining many of the older beliefs and practices.

Many heiaus have been restored and are preserved as historical monuments by the government. A few modern day "kahunas" have maintained some of the rituals and practices, primarily using *mana* ("divine" power) for healing. Sam Lono, living on ancestral lands, maintained an ancient healing heiau on Oahu until his death a few years ago. David "Daddy" Bray, Sr. (1889-1968), a recognized practitioner, was known as a "kahuna," and passed on to his students the ancient religious practices near Kona on the Big Island. His son, David, Jr., continues in that tradition. Charles Kenn on Oahu was a specialist in the kahuna lore, including the inner meanings (kaona) of the Hawaiian language, but did not leave any record of his knowledge.

The great student of the Hawaiian religion of the twentieth century was Max Freedom Long (1898-1971), who went to Hawaii in 1917 as a teacher. He became fascinated with the traditional lore and religious practices of the kahunas, especially their methods of performing certain apparent "miracles," such as healing. He met a wall of secrecy wherever he tried to discover the secrets of their accomplishments. He left the Islands in 1931, thinking the secrets would never be known.

Four years later, he awoke in the middle of the night with the clue that would lead to the rediscovery of the ancient "magic." The secrets of the kahunas were hidden and preserved in coded form in the Hawaiian language itself. He chose the name "Huna" (the Hawaiian wording meaning "secret") for the "workable, psycho-religious system" that resulted from his investigations into what he called the Huna Code. It combined the best of both psychology and of religion.

As a psychological/religious practice Huna is distinguished from the ancient kahuna religion discussed above. Huna was never an attempt to restore or reconstruct those practices. Huna has neither *kapu* nor *heiau.* It is a practical way of life, based on the harmonious relationship of the three levels of consciousness, called the three "selves." These are *unihipili* (the inner, emotional, intuitive self), *uhane* (the waking consciousness or rational self), and *aumakua* (the High Self or connection with the "divine"). Huna considers *mana* the vital life force that vivifies and empowers each person and not the special prerogative of the privileged few. *Mana* is transmitted via invisible aka substance.

To Long, Huna is "magic" based on the knowledge of how our three selves function, using mana not only to heal body, mind, and circumstance, but also to attain our goals and live effective lives.

After his first books (1936, 1948) explained the history of his discoveries, Long wrote textbooks to teach readers how to accomplish the things they desired by using the Huna way of life, e.g., *The Secret Science at Work* (1954). In *The Huna Code in Religions* (1965) he explored the Huna parallels in world religions, especially Buddhism, Yoga, and Christianity. Many later books on Huna have been written by students on Long, notably *Huna: The Ancient Religion of Positive Thinking,* by William R. Glover, which is probably the best introduction for new readers.

The Huna Research organization was established in 1945, because of the responses of readers of his first book. Members, called Associates, were from all walks of life and several countries, especially Australia and England. As a teaching that emphasizes a practical philosophy or psychology that all can use for themselves, the organization has maintained a steady but growing membership. Many learned what they needed, quietly continued to live according to the Huna principles, but did not continue as official members of Huna Research.

Long died in 1971 and was succeeded by Dr. E. Otha Wingo at the request of Long himself. The Huna headquarters was moved to Missouri, where Dr. Wingo was a professor at a university. In 1985, a headquarters building was purchased in Missouri.

Membership: With active Huna teachers and affiliated groups (Huna fellowships) throughout the United States and Canada, and in Australia, England, Germany, Switzerland, and Brazil, Huna currently has more followers than at any time in the organization's 50-plus year history. There are members in more than 50 countries. Huna Research, Inc. does not exert central control over affiliated organizations, but rather seeks to give guidance and assistance in the dissemination of Huna teachings. There are some 5,000 persons in Germany and Switzerland who have received the Huna teachings through the affiliate organization in Zurich, Huna Forschungs-gesellschaft, directed by Heinrich Krotoschin. Major Huna publications are available in the German language. Another major branch is Associacao de Estudos Huna in Brazil, directed by Ceres Elisa da Fonseca Rosas, where Huna books are available in Portuguese. Spanish editions are being produced currently in this country by Edgardo Torralvo of Torralvoma Holistic Center in New York.

In addition, a number of independent "Huna" organizations have sprung up in various locations based on the extensive research and experimentation of Max Freedom Long and his Huna Research Associates, but whose teachings are often mixed with other related concepts and which do not maintain affiliation with Huna Research, Inc.

An annual International Huna Seminar and meeting are held in various areas of the United States and Canada.

Periodicals: *The Huna Work.* • *The Aka Cord.* • *Huna Arbeit—* bulletin/newsletter; published in Switzerland in the German language.

Sources:

Hoffman, Enid. *Huna, A Beginner's Guide.* Rockport, MA: Para Research, 1976.

Long, Max Freedom. *Introduction to Huna.* Sedona, AZ: Esoteric Publications, 1975.

___. *Recovering the Ancient Magic.* Cape Girardeau, MO: Huna Press, 1978.

___. *The Secret Science at Work.* Vista, CA: Huna Research Publications, 1953.

___. *The Secret Science Behind Miracles.* Vista, CA: Huna Research Publications, 1954.

Wingo, E. Otha. *The Story of the Huna Work.* Cape Girardeau, MO: Huna Research, 1981.

★1528★
Inner Light Foundation
Box 750265
Petaluma, CA 94975

The Inner Light Foundation was founded in the 1969 by mystic and psychic Betty Bethards, with the objective of developing in all people a conscious awareness of God. It is Bethards' belief that within each individual are intuitive faculties, the development of which can lead to the greater brotherhood of man. The foundation teaches that for individuals to tap into their own inner guidance and insight, they need only three tools-dreams, affirmations, and visualizations/meditation. The foundation teaches a simple powerful meditation technique. This process of quieting allows for inner awareness, mystic development, and the emergence of spiritual abilities.

The foundation has grown steadily. It now holds regular lectures at several locations in the San Francisco Bay area and Los Angeles. Bethards remains a popular lecturer and worship leader

and has written nine books presenting the foundation's teachings. She offers private readings to individuals.

Membership: In 1995, the foundation reported 10,000 members in the United States, 100 in Canada, and an additional 400 worldwide.

Periodicals: *Inner Light Foundation Illuminations.*

Sources:

Bethards, Betty. *Relationships in the New Age of Aids.* Novato, CA: Inner Light Foundation, 1988.

___. *The Sacred Sword.* Novato, CA: Inner Light Foundation, 1972.

___. *Sex and Psychic Energy.* Novato, CA: Inner Light Foundation, 1977.

___. *There Is No Death.* Novato, CA: Inner Light Foundation, 1975.

★1529★
Inner Peace Movement
Box 4897
Washington, DC 20008

Francisco Coll had been a student of the psychic and spiritual most of his life. In the early 1960s, he became involved with medium Arthur A. Ford in the ecumenical church-psychic group Spiritual Frontiers Fellowship. In 1964, he established the Inner Peace Movement (IPM) to help people unfold their abilities by awakening the potentials of the inner man. IPM was founded in Washington, D.C. and soon a camp conference center and head office facilities were established in Osceola, Iowa. The program developed based in the communities, with lectures, workshops, groupwork, and personal spiritual counsellings. (Counseling is considered a method through which an individual can clarify his communication subliminally, as acknowledged by angelic messengers in the quickening of the flesh.)

The basic perspective of IPM is contained in Colls book, *Man and the Universe*, and in *Discovering your True Identity*, the text for the IPM groupwork. Individuals are shown with techniques and meditation how to unfold their own true reality and uniqueness, based on the premise they are a soul with a physical body, not a physical body with a soul. A soul is believed to be essentially spiritual electro-magnetic energy, and, as this energy is eternal, never dies. We are the sum total of every thought and experience throughout lifetimes and this becomes the essence and identity of each soul. It is this reality that acknowledges man as a feeling being. For every feeling we need an interpretation. For every interpretation, a feeling. Being in balance with his inner self, and with organization in the physical world, man can achieve his goals and life purpose with harmony and a oneness of self.

In 1972 the headquarters of IPM was moved to Washington, D.C. IPM is governed by a board of directors that meets annually. Although Coll is the founder, a new executive board and president is elected each year. Among the several related organizations, also founded by Coll, are: The Americana Leadership College, Inc. and Peace Community Church. The Americana Leadership College provides the leadership training for those that work with IPM in the communities. It also has 300 plus in-depth courses that cover a wide variety of spiritually related topics in several departments of study.

Membership: Over 90,000 people have been involved in the United States and an additional 35,000 people in 21 countries are trained to be leaders of IPM in the communities.

Educational Facilities: American Leadership College. Locations in the United States are based in: Iowa, Texas, Alaska, Florida, Nevada, California, New Mexico, Washington, New York, and Puerto Rico. Internationally IPM is represented in over 10 countries on an active basis.

Periodicals: *The Times Communicator and Expression Magazine.*

Sources:

Coll, Francisco. *Discovering Your True Identity*. Osceola, IA: American Leadership College, 1968.

___. *Discovering Your True Identity Leadership Training Manual*. Osceola, IA: American Leadership College, 1972.

___. *The Gifts of Intuition, Vision, Prophecy and Feeling in the Seven-Year Cycles*. Washington, DC: American Leadership College, 1981.

★1530★
Institute of Cosmic Wisdom
3528 Franciscan Ln.
Las Vegas, NV 89121

The Institute of Cosmic Wisdom was founded by the Rev. Clark Wilkerson. It combines New Thought metaphysics with the magical religion of the huna. Wilkerson began as a metaphysician, and the main class offered students of Cosmic Wisdom was in "Mental Expansion." Wilkerson's teachings differ from those of most metaphysicians in his emphasis on the use of the mind to gain control of not only the self but others. He also believes that mastery of metaphysics comes in the deep meditative or hypnotic state.

In the early 1950s Wilkerson began to emphasize Hawaiian huna (the ancient magical practices of Hawaii) as an occult science which leads to success and happiness with less effort. The course emphasizes concentration and entering into the meditative silence as well as adjusting the mind to open concepts. Exercises are offered in how to enter the silence and use this ability.

Members of the Institute are drawn primarily through advertisements, mostly in psychic periodicals. Most students begin with correspondence courses in metaphysics or huna. Classes taught by Wilkerson are held periodically. Students who have completed the courses become the core of continuing members. An Inner Circle of ordained ministers constitutes the leadership.

Membership: Not reported.

Sources:

Wilkerson, Clark L. *Celestial Wisdom*. Gardena, CA: Institute of Cosmic Wisdom, 1965.

___. *Hawaiian Magic*. Playa Del Rey, CA: Institute of Cosmic Wisdom, 1968.

★1531★
Institute of Mentalphysics
59700 29 Palms Hwy.
Joshua Tree, CA 92252
Alternate Address: Mailing Address: PO Box 1000, Joshua Tree, CA 92252.

The Institute of Mentalphysics was founded in 1927 in New York City, New York, by Edwin John Dingle (1881-1972). An editor and explorer in early life, he was one of the few American metaphysical teachers to have actually studied in Tibet prior to 1927. Once in Tibet, Dingle described his meeting with a master who helped him recall his memory (i.e., of previous incarnations). He was taught proper breathing and the remaining disciplines, which became the basis of the Science of Mentalphysics. In 1927, he gave a series of lectures in New York City. Some who attended asked that he share the wisdom he had learned in the East. That class is viewed as the beginning of the institute and of the new career of Ding Le Mei (Dingles' religious name). The institute was incorporated in 1934, in California.

Dingle combined the spiritual wisdom of the East with religious knowledge of the West to form a Super Yoga. The teachings of mentalphysics combine universal truths, breathing exercises, diet control, recognizing and working with one's individual chemistry, exercises, and meditation. New students are introduced to the universal laws of the creator which, if followed, are believed to lead to mastery on oneself and all of life. A vegetarian diet is recom-

mended. Proper breathing is a key; it is the means of extracting prana, the energy of life, from the air. The healthy body prepares one to develop mind and spirit toward one's highest potential.

The Science of Mentalphysics teaches that prana or life energy, is substance, a subtle form of energy that animates life. It is universally distributed and is what the soul uses to think with. Using the mind-substance, as activated through breathing, one is able to activate the creative powers within. Students are also instructed in meditation, which leads toward tapping universal wisdom and development as a mystic. As a mystic one understands truth, life, and one's potential through experience.

The Science of Mentalphysics begins with the Initiate Group Course which consists of 26 basic lessons. There are 124 additional advanced lessons, and a Teachers or Preceptor Course which assist developed persons to share their knowledge and experience with seekers on all levels.

Headquarters, which serves the world-wide student body is located at the Mentalphysics Teaching Center and Spiritual Retreat, in Joshua Tree, California. The 385 acre facility can house up to 250 delegates. Most of the buildings are Frank Lloyd Wright designed. Main buildings such as the Caravansary of Joy, Meditation Building, and the Preceptory of Light are used to not only teach the Science of Mentalphysics, but serve sponsored groups dedicated to the elevation of human consciousness. Sunday services are held in the First Sanctuary of Mystic Christianity.

The non-profit organization is irrevocably dedicated to humanity and is operated by a board of trustees.

Membership: As of 1995 the active mail list is 6,003 and 222,307 students have been enrolled. This includes students in the U.S.A., Canada, Mexico, Iceland, India, Spain, England, Trinidad, and Ecuador. Seven centers serve seekers around the world.

Periodicals: *Light of the Logos.*

Sources:

Dingle, Edwin John. *Borderlands of Eternity*. Los Angeles: Institute of Mentalphysics, 1939.

___. *Breathing Your Way to Youth*. Los Angeles: Institute of Mentalphysics, [1931].

___. *The Voice of the Logos*. Los Angeles: Institute of Mentalphysics, 1950.

★1532★
Interfaith Church of Metaphysics (ICOM)
Windyville, MO 65783

The Interfaith Church of Metaphysics (ICOM) was founded in 1976 as the religious branch of the School of Metaphysics, an educational and service organization founded by Jerry L. Rothermel (1926-) in 1973. The school is dedicated to study and research on what it considers to be the Universal Laws that govern creation and the development of humanity's spiritual consciousness. The school offers a comprehensive three-tiered program of study in the causal principles underlying humanity's existence. While the program is comparable in some ways to those found in traditional schools of higher education, it goes beyond the limitation inherent in physical study alone. It teaches how learning occurs as a sequence of thought, as well as how the application of the knowledge gained. Through the practice of spiritual disciplines, students transcend what they understand to be the pairs of opposites manifesting in the physical world and are led to the discovery of the origin of unity in religion and science, philosophy and conduct, freedom and responsibility, and peace and discipline.

In 1976 the board of directors of the School of Metaphysics, in response to the growing need for spiritual knowledge upon the part of those who had a more religious rather than a scholastic inclination, created the International Church of Metaphysics. Designed to offer truth, inspiration, and guidance to humans in their search to know and understand their relationship to their Creator, ICOM provides various means for spiritual renewal and association. An interfaith church, ICOM members believe that all Holy Scriptures of the world embody truths that are universally applicable to all of humanity. When interpreted in the "Universal Language of Mind," all scriptures, regardless of the religion arising from them, offer insight and instruction into the origin and reason for humanity's existence. Because of this belief, ICOM eschews dogma, and church members are not required to drop previously held religious beliefs or membership in any religious group at the time they affiliate with ICOM.

ICOM members believe that each human is a spiritual being given existence and free will by the Creator; that the Creator set in motion principles and laws that function throughout our universe governing creation; that each human is made in the likeness and image of the Creator and thus possesses the freedom and responsibility of creating thought; that each human being is striving to know Truth that is Universal and to become compatible with his/her maker; that thought is cause and everything else is sub cause; that the temporal life is a choice made by the soul for the acceleration of spiritual progression; that all individuals have every possible opportunity for a spiritually enriching existence if only they will choose to envision it; that the destiny of each individual is an Enlightened state of being, a possibility demonstrated by singular individuals throughout history; that this Enlightened spiritual maturity can be aspired to through everincreasing awareness through disciplining our minds by meditation, prayer, and positive thinking; and that as this destiny is manifest in the individual's progression, it will become manifest for all people, and the evolution of the race is accelerated.

Church pastors have completed at least the first series of lessons in the program of study at the School of Metaphysics. These pastors serve as apprentices under the guidance of an ordained minister in the church. SOM students in the third and final series of lessons can elect to pursue a Doctorate of Divinity degree from the school and become ordained ministers in the church.

In 1993, ICOM was one of the many co-sponsors of the centennial Parliament of the World's Religions held in Chicago. Two board members, Rev. Dr. Daniel R. Condron, president of the ICOM Ordination Board, and Rev. Dr. Barbara Condron, addressed the Parliament and the church's choir gave a performance. As a result of this participation, the ordination board of the church elected to change the name to the Interfaith Church of Metaphysics, as a designation more clearly describing the ideal, purpose, and activity of the membership. Members of the church support the document released by the conference, "Toward a Global Ethic," as a pledge toward understanding one another and toward the realization of a more socially beneficial, peace-fostering, and nature-friendly way of life.

Members are dedicated to an ever-increasing awareness of Truth, a personal communication with the Creator, and a deepening understanding of self and of others. They are committed by thought and action to being of service to their neighbors and all of humankind. Through the School of Metaphysics, the church publishes and distributes worldwide a selection of books and tapes. Audiotapes offer musical presentations, sermons by church leaders, and courses on meditation and the Universal Language of Mind.

Membership: : Not reported. The Church offers regular services in 16 major cities across the United States.

Educational Facilities: School of Metaphysics, Windyville, Missouri.

Periodicals: *Thresholds Quarterly.*

Sources:

Condron, Barbara. *Kindalini Rising: Mastering Creative Energies.* Windyville, MO: SOM Publishing, 1992. 212 pp.

Condron, Daniel. *Dreams of the Soul: The Yogi Sutras of Patanjali.* Windyville, MO: SOM Publishing, 1991. 204 pp.

___. *Permanent Healing: Includes Quantum Mechanics of Healing.* Windyville, MO: SOM Publishing, 1993. 214 pp.

Fuller, Laurel Jan. *Shaping Your Life: The Power of Creative Energy.* Windyville, MO: SOM Publishing, 1994. 214 pp.

Rothermel, Jerry L. *Meditation: The Answer to Your Prayers.* Windyville, MO: S. O. M. Publishing, 1987. 99 pp.

___. *Symbols of Dreams.* Springfield, MO: School of Metaphysics, 1976. 79 pp.

★1533★
International Church of Spiritual Vision, Inc. (Western Prayer Warriors)
Current address not obtained for this edition.

The International Church of Spiritual Vision, Inc., was formed by Dallas Turner who as Nevada Slim became a country-music star in the 1960s. In 1959, he received the Pentecostal "baptism of the Holy Spirit" and spoke in tongues, in an actual foreign language. A long-time student of psychical metaphysics, numerology and hypnotism, Turner has built an eclectic system of belief which combines elements of the psychic, Pentecostalism and Sacred Name Adventism in a blend called Aquarian Metaphysics.

The essence of the church's beliefs are included in the Yahwist Creed: "I believe in Yahweh the Father Almighty, creator of all things. And in Yahoshua—whom the world knows as Jesus Christ—Yahweh's only begotten Son our Savior; who was conceived by the Holy Ghost, born of the blessed virgin, suffered under Pontius Pilate, was crucified, died and was buried. He descended into hell; preached to the spirits in prison. The third day He arose from the physical dead. He ascended into the World of Spirit, sits at the right hand of Yahweh the Father Almighty; from there He shall come to judge the living and the so-called dead. I believe the original message of our Saviour and Wayshower. I accept the Scriptural and Metaphysical Truths of all religions. I give no place to the devil. I believe that Yahweh is the only power that exists. I believe in the Holy Ghost, the nine gifts of the Spirit, the communion of believers, the resurrection of the spiritual body, and life everlasting. Amen." Members relate to the church through the mail. Turner solicits the prayer concerns from members and sends blessed cloths (Acts 19:12) and includes absent members in metaphysical healing prayers. He also offers lessons in Aquarian Metaphysics.

Membership: Not reported.

★1534★
Kabalarian Philosophy
5912 Oak St.
Vancouver, BC, Canada V6M 2W2

The Kabalarian Philosophy was developed by Alfred J. Parker (1897-1964). Parker was born in England, but his family moved to British Columbia in his youth, settling in Vancouver. Though raised an Anglican, Parker began to search through the various philosophies available to him and studied for a time with a Hindu swami. He developed what became known as the Kabalarian Philosophy during the 1920s, and began publicly expounding it through personal contacts and newspaper articles in the 1930s. He started classes in his living room, later moving into a hall constructed in his basement. He began to rent lecture halls for Sunday evening lectures.

The Kabalarian Philosophy is a scientific practical knowledge based upon the definite divine laws which teach humanity's relationship to the two basic laws of life: mathematics and language. God is in all things, the one Spiritual Principle embodied in all religions. All persons are created equal in the eyes of God the Principle. Intelligence, as universal power, is expressed consciously through language and is limited according to the medium of expression, the alphabet. Like a musical scale, there is a scale of conscious power known as qualities of intelligence. There are nine

735

gradations (hence the Mathematical Principle of Nine) in the scale of conscious expression: individuality, diplomacy, artistic expression, technical detail, analytical research, responsibility, philosophical depth of thought, organization, and universal love and understanding.

Each individual is dual in nature. The inner nature of a person is determined by the quality of Universal Consciousness incorporated in the individual through the first breath. That inner nature is measured by the date of birth. The outer nature of a person is created by the mind which in turn is determined by the person's name. Each can be analyzed by numerological analysis. By assigning a numerical value to each letter in the name and birth month, both the name and the birth date can be reduced to a single figure by simple addition. The philosophy teaches how to relate and balance the inner and outer natures.

There is also an emphasis upon a proper vegetarian diet which includes vegetables, eggs, and some dairy products. Fish and shell fish are eaten sparingly, but members do not eat meat. The use of refined products such as flour and sugar is discouraged.

Parker died in the 1960s and was succeeded by Ivon Shearing. Today various centers offer classes in the philosophy, and a correspondence course has been developed. Basic to people wishing to avail themselves of the philosophy's benefits is a life analysis based upon the laws of mathematics and language.

Membership: In 1997, the seven centers of Kabalarians were located in Calgary and Edmonton, Alberta; Saskatoon, Saskatchewan; Vancouver, and Powell River, British Columbia; Oxnard, California; and the Netherlands. These were approximately 1,500 members in Canada.

Periodicals: *Kabalarian Courier.*

Remarks: In the fall of 1997, Kabalarian leader Ivon Shearing was tried on counts of rape and sexual assault brought by 11 female complainants. Though he was found guilty (as this edition goes to press, the case is on appeal), he has continued to profess his innocence and members of the society have remained supportive of him.

★1535★
Karin Society
2531 Braircliff Rd. NE, Ste. 217
Atlanta, GA 30329

The Karin Society was founded in the 1980s as an association of people seeking their spiritual growth through the *kabbalah*. It grew out of the Karin Kabalah Study Course written by Shirley Chambers and published in 1984. It is Chambers' belief that the kabbalah, often thought of as a particularly Jewish form of mysticism, embodies an understanding that is more ancient than either Christianity or Judaism. From that understanding flowed all of the world's religions, and as humanity proceeds to a new level of progress, a reinterpretation of the kabbalistic wisdom is both possible and necessary. The Karin Kabalah is such a modern reinterpretation. "Karin" is a Hindustani word meaning "light" or more literally, "rays of the sun."

The Kabalah presents a mystical system that leads the student to Truth; not an intellectual Truth, but an experienced Truth that cannot be explained in words. The Karin Kabalah Course is offered as a correspondence course with monthly lessons. In 1988 Chambers established the Karin Kabalah Center in Atlanta, Georgia, where a two-year course in kabbalistic wisdom is taught along with related subjects such as astrology, hatha yoga, psychic and spiritual development, and eastern philosophy. The society developed out of the expanding work of the correspondence course and center.

Membership: Not reported.

Periodicals: *Karin Journal.*

★1536★
Light Institute
HC-75, Box 50
Galisteo, NM 87540

The Light Institute was founded in 1985 to facilitate the teachings of Chris Grissom, popular New Age writer and teacher. Grissom's preparation as a teacher began in Mexico while attending the University of Mexico and using her spare time to explore the rural countryside. She became the student of a *curandera*, a village healer, who introduced her to the presence of god in nature. Throughout the 1960s she spent nine years in El Salvador, Bolivia, and Paraguay in the Peace Corps, where people further taught her their esoteric traditions. She came to believe that nature, even the rocks, were alive with energy. Upon her return to the United States, she studied with Silva Mind Control and a variety of individual teachers. During this period she emerged as a spiritual healer. She later studied massage and acupuncture and throughout the early 1980s developed her healing work. She came to feel that the primary experience needed by people in the present era is the clearing of the emotional body.

It is Grissom's opinion that the self is composed of four bodies—the physical, astral, emotional, and spiritual. The emotional body is described as the emotional vehicle of consciousness which vibrates at a low frequency. It is also her belief that now is a time of spiritual awakening which will lead humankind into a new, more enlightened, cosmic human reality. From her initial insights, she has expanded the teachings to cover all aspects of life and through the institute offers a variety of courses teaching people to apply the spiritual teaching in their lives. Grissom is now assisted by a number of facilitators whom she has trained. In 1988 she also founded the Nizhoni School for Global Consciousness as a day school for people age three to adult focused around exploring the individual purpose in the global context.

The institute has an affiliated center in Brazil and contact persons in France, Holland, and Germany.

Membership: Not reported.

Sources:

Grissom, Chris. *Ecstasy Is a New Frequency: Teachings of the Light Institute.* New York: Simon & Schuster, 1988.

___. *Time Is an Illusion.*

★1537★
Lorian Association
(Defunct)

The Lorian was an association of people dedicated to the vision of the New Age, defined as the spirit of wholeness upon the earth. Members believed that humanity was striving for a new level of completeness expressed in a new sense of partnership with creation, the emergence of a wholistic spirit within individuals, and a new covenant between God and the godliness in each person.

The catalyst for the formation of the Lorian Association was the return of David Spangler (b. 1945) to the United States in 1973 after three years as the co-director of the Findhorn Community in northern Scotland, a New Age community founded by Peter Caddy, his wife, Eileen Caddy, and Dorothy McLean. Along with the Universal Link, Findhorn has been one of the most important groups fostering the larger New Age Movement. Spangler led in the founding of the association soon after his arrival in America. Over the next few years, he authored several books which for many people provided the definitive statements of the New Age vision.

The beliefs of the association were summarized in their 15-part "Statement of Interdependence" which committed members to a dedication to sacred, cooperative decision making, the process of growth, one world, harmless interaction with the environment, the building of a planetary village, conservation and wise use of energy, diversity in cultural expressions, an open social order, and the communication with and learning from preaterhuman intelligences who also inhabit earth. Since the 1960s, Spangler has been in contact with a spiritual entity named "John," and he views much of his literary production as a synthesis of John's insight and his words.

In the mid-1980s, the association moved from Wisconsin to a new center in Washington. An active program was built around educational events for the public, publication of new age literature, encouragement of music and the arts and networking with people who share one or more common concerns. The association was made up of a small and dedicated community and encouraged the development of like-minded groups over the growth of the association. It disbanded in the late 1980s.

Sources:

Spangler, David. *Festivals in the New Age*. Forres, Moray, Scotland: Findhorn Publications, 1975.

___. *Reflections on the Christ*. Forres, Moray, Scotland: Findhorn Publications, 1977.

___. *Revelation, the Birth of a New Age*. San Francisco: Rainbow Bridge, 1976.

___. *Towards a Planetary Vision*. Forres, Scotland: Findhorn Foundation, 1977.

Spangler, David, ed. *Conversations with John*. Elgin, IL: Lorian Press, 1980.

★1538★
Mahanaim School of Interpretation
(Defunct)

The Mahanaim School of Interpretation was founded around 1900 in Chicago, Illinois, by George Chainey (b. 1851). Prior to founding the school, Chainey had a long ministerial career first as a Methodist, and after 1877, as a Unitarian. He spent much of the 1880s touring the world as an independent author and lecturer on religion and mysticism. He settled in Chicago during the 1890s and devoted himself to writing an interpretation of the Bible. In 1901 he began publishing *The Interpreter*, a monthly magazine through which he announced the school's programs and publicized its teachings. The first volumes of the projected 30-volume series, *The Unsealed Bible*, his occult-metaphysical commentary on the scriptures were published in 1902.

As the school's "conductor," Chainey saw three main purposes in the school: to teach (1) the knowableness of God, the distinctiveness of the manifest life of God in revelation from the unmanifest God, (2) the true relation between God and humanity, and (3) the law of immortal life, which is to be in an embodied state. Chainey viewed his task to be that of interpreter of God's language of revelation. Revelation was of the essence or *amrit* of God. Present living revelation was to be appropriated through the interpretation of past revelation, hence Chainey's efforts to compose interpretative volumes on the various books of the Bible.

In the formative years of the school, Chainey conducted worship weekly on Sunday mornings and public classes on most weekdays. He also accepted a few private students who did more intense study in a resident home situation, the summer being spent in a resort center in Wisconsin. Chainey's work continued over the next two decades, eventually moving its center to Burnett, California, and in the 1920s to Long Beach, California. By this time, the work expanded to become the Amrita University, which consisted of the Chainey's Mahanaim School of Interpretation, which he personally headed; The School for Parents under the direction of Walt de Noir Church; the Emersonian Delsarte School of Life and Expression; and the School of Metaphysics, Psychology and Healing, headed by Dr. Fredoon C. Birdi. Chainey retained the pattern of interaction with students, most of whom studied through his correspondence course. Only a few actually resided at the school to work under his personal direction.

The final disposition of the school is unknown.

Sources:

Chainey, George. *Deus Homo*. Boston, MA: Christopher Publishing House, 1927.

___. *Time's Garland of Grace*. San Diego, CA: Charles Gardner, 1918.

___. *The Unsealed Bible*. London: Kegan Paul, Trench, Truebner & Co., 1902.

★1539★
Mindstream Church of Universal Love
Current address not obtained for this edition.

The Mindstream Church of Universal Love began in 1979 with a charter from the Universal Life Church of Modesto, California. It is headed by the Rev. Kenneth Donabie-Dixon and Wendie Gilmour Donabie-Dixon. The church has no set doctrine. Its prime mission is to assist members in discovering their own path in life. God is seen as a living part of all that is. Man's purpose is to return to the Godhead. This may be accomplished by living the Law of Love. This Law, the basic truth of existence, is "God is Law, Law is Love, and Love is God." Love for humans means providing the opportunity for others to do for themselves.

The church provides practical tools to assist members. These tools take the form of classes and individual sessions on dream study, development of psychic skills, meditation, spiritual healing, relaxation, goal setting, age regression and reincarnation, and motivation. Age regression is done without hypnosis. Under the direction of the church, monies are set aside to assist the development of self-sufficient communities across North America.

Membership: Not reported.

Periodicals: *Spiritual Growth and Psychic Awareness*. Send orders to R.R. 2, Sutton West, ON, Canada L0E 1R0

★1540★
New Age Church of Truth
(Defunct)

Gilbert N. Holloway (b. 1915) began his career as a lecturer and metaphysical teacher in the 1930s. He became aware, as a result of studies in Rosicrucianism and Theosophy, that he had psychic powers. In the 1960s, he became prominent as a psychic on radio and television, and large audiences flocked to hear his lectures and to obtain readings (the statements he uttered while in a psychic state). In 1967, he received a Pentecostal experience and spoke in tongues. In the mid-1960s Holloway established a community and center in Deming, New Mexico. After his conversion, this center became the Christ Light Community.

Through the 1970 and 1980s, Holloway and his wife, June Holloway, who specialized in healing work, continued to travel, lectured and gave psychic demonstrations. They built the Deming community into a New Age Center. There was a free movement in the programming between Pentecostal and psychic categories. Holloway wrote books and booklets and published a monthly newsletter for members and friends of the church. He was particularly adept at prophecy; predictions of future events composed much of the content of his publications.

Membership: Not reported.

Periodicals: *Newsletter*.

Sources:

Holloway, Gilbert N. *E.S.P. and Your Super-Conscious*. Louisville, KY: Best Books, 1966.

___. *Let the Heart Speak*. Los Angeles: DeVorss & Co., 1951.

___. *New Ways of Unfoldment*. Deming, NM: New Age Truth Publications, n.d.

___. *Seven Prophetic Years*. Deming, NM: New Age Truth Publications, 1969.

___. *This Way Up.* Deming, NM: New Age Church of Truth, 1975.

★1541★
New Age Community Church
6418 S. 39th Ave.
Phoenix, AZ 85041

The New Age Community Church is an ecclesiastical expression of the New Age, the Age of Aquarius. It is like the new religious consciousness of the older or Picean Age, which made its definitive expression in Catholicism, in that it draws on all of the major religions of the present time. The New Age fulfills Christianity (and all the other world religions). It believes that the differences between the nine major religions are relatively unimportant, though it does oppose perspectives that emphasize fear and hatred. More important are the many pathways or systems of expression of a relationship with the Divine worship that appear in the different systems. Each of these pathways appears in a variety of the presently existing religions and each one will lead to God. The nine pathways are: social—through relationships and society meditation—through mental discipline revelation—through channeling and psyche karma—through good deeds and service ecstasy—through dance and music ritual—through magic and sacrament knowledge—through wisdom and understanding physical—through yoga, diet, and health worship—through devotion and adoration.

The New Age Community Church speaks of God as all there is. God is not personal and does not reside in a place called heaven. The universe can be thought of as God's physical body. Christ is thought of as the Logos or Higher self. Humans are currently trapped on the wheel of reincarnation. We continually eat of the tree of believing in good and evil and creating emotional values based on that belief. When we cease create such emotional values the karma can no longer hold us and we will ascend to the level of the divine.

Membership: Not reported.

★1542★
New Age Samaritan Church
Current address not obtained for this edition.

The New Age Samaritan Church was incorporated in 1961 by the Rev. Ruth McWilliams of Everett, Washington. The doctrine is eclectic, a combination of material from the New Testament, New Thought, metaphysical beliefs, Theosophy, Zen and Spiritualism. The church espouses no system of beliefs, but professes to help its students and members to discover for themselves the spiritual laws. Its goals include helping the poor in body and spirit, relieving the suffering in the world, eliminating prejudice and teaching the interrelation of all creatures. It practices the various psychic arts, including "treasure mapping" as a means to achieving your heart's desire. This involves visualizing what you want and how to get it.

Membership: Not reported. In 1967 there were 4 study groups and students engaged in correspondence across the United States. Attempts at contact have not been successful for several years and the present status of the church is unknown.

★1543★
New Psychiana
% Psychiana Study Group
4069 Stephens St.
San Diego, CA 92103

The New Psychiana was formed in 1967 by Jack E. Gardner of San Diego, California. Gardner was an early student of Frank B. Robinson, the founder of Psychiana, a popular New Thought group which had its greatest growth in the 1930s and 1940s. Gardner completed both the regular and advanced courses. Gardner accepted the role of the student who would arise to continue Robinson's work following his death in 1948. In the years since Robinson's death, the whole field of ESP has emerged, and Gardner added teachings on conscious evolution to Psychiana to bring it up to date.

Conscious evolution is the "divine cybernetics to spiritual growth." It teaches techniques of becoming fully aware of the powerful God-presence within you. By learning to control this power, one can heal bodily and spiritual wounds, bring peace and break free from poverty and defeat.

Membership: Not reported.

★1544★
The Only Fair Religion
Current address not obtained for this edition.

The Only Fair Religion was founded by Saint Kenny and a group of his followers. Neither the identity of Saint Kenny, nor any of his group, is disclosed in the literature. The group teaches modern reincarnationism. The universe is in constant flux, governed by natural laws. Souls progress through lower life-forms to higher ones. When a being evolves to a point of gaining a sense of awareness, it simultaneously acquires an immortal soul. It then moves through a series of incarnations which are necessary for its development. It eventually evolves to become a planetary ruling spirit. The system is the "Only Fair Religion" because it assures a balance of woe and happiness, explains evil and assures eventual salvation for all.

New groups form for the discussion of issues in light of modern reincarnationism. Members seek to unite in their concept of God and in their concern for justice, and true communion results. Telepathy and psychic phenomena will often occur during this process.

Membership: Not reported. In 1972, the "Only Fair Religion" claimed 10,000 members in Southern California, a figure based on the number of people successfully qualified to be group leaders.

★1545★
People's Temple Christian (Disciples) Church
(Defunct)

The People's Temple Christian (Disciples) Church was formed in 1955 in Indianapolis by the Rev. Jim Jones. (Though formally a member congregation in the Christian Church (Disciples of Christ), the People's Temple, in the 1970s, developed beliefs and practices that were very much different than those of its parent body.) Jones emerged in the 1960s as a charismatic leader who cared for the poor and the black people of the city and preached a message of equality, brotherhood and socialism.

In 1965, a year after being ordained in the Christian Church (Disciples of Christ) he migrated with his following to Ukiah, California. From there the People's Church became a communal group modeled on the Peace Mission of Father Divine, whom Jones had known and revered. Though white himself, Jones gathered a largely black following who came to view him as a prophet and miracle worker. By 1972 Jones claimed that over forty people had been raised from the dead. Church services featured psychic readings and healings by Jones, spirited singing, testimonies and sermons. A wide range of social services was supported.

By 1972 congregations flourished in San Francisco, Los Angeles, and Indianapolis and followers were to be found in cities around the United States. That same year Jones leased land in Guyana which became a farming community, Jonestown. Jones became a prominent, controversial, but powerful figure in the California religious community, but also became an object of government investigation because of reports of violence directed toward ex-members and abuse of children under his care. Coincidental with the publication of several major media reports on the church and with the filing of several lawsuits, Jones moved with many of his members to Guyana.

By 1977 when Jones moved to Guyana, Jonestown had swelled to a thousand residents. This town was the scene, in 1978, of the murder of Congressman Leo J. Ryan and several of his party, who came to Jonestown to investigate the charges which had been brought against it. Immediately following Ryan's murder was the mass suicide/murder of over 900 of the town's residents, including Jones. In 1978 the church was formally disbanded by the remaining members in California.

In the years since the deaths in Guyana, the People's Temple and its leader have become symbols of the possibilities inherent in religious groups and have frequently been invoked as the end result of cultic practice. As most of the papers assembled for the investigation of Congressman Ryan's death have remained unpublished, the likelihood of substantive future revelations about Jones, the temple, and the deaths in Guyana remains high.

Sources:

Feinsof, Ethan. *Awake in a Nightmare*. New York: W. W. Norton & Co., 1981.

Klineman, George, and Sherman Butler. *The Cult That Died*. New York: G. B. Putnam's Sons, 1980.

Mills, Jeanne. *Six Years With God*. New York: A & W Publishers, 1979.

Reiterman, Tim, with John Jacobs. *Raven*. New York: E. P. Dutton, 1982.

Yee, Min S., and Thomas N. Layton. *In My Father's House*. New York: Holt, Rinehart & Winston, 1981.

★1546★
Planetary Light Association
Current address not obtained for this edition.

The Planetary Light Association was founded by Jann Weiss, a psychic medium who, in January 1983, began to channel messages from a spirit entity named Anoah. Anoah is considered to be a member of the Melchizedek Order of the White Brotherhood. His work is to assist in a smooth transition from the old age into the new. Under Anoah's direction, Golden Circle sessions were initiated. Each session consisted of a planetary meditation, a dissertation that Anoah delivered through Weiss, and a question and answer period. In July 1983 the Planetary Light Association was formed. It is dedicated to the uplifting of the planet through positive thought, word, and activity. By the fall of 1983 the association had a program that included psychic development workshops, books by Anoah, and a line of "Be Your Light and Be in Peace" products. A regular schedule of events in Texas and Washington was established. Through the cassette tapes and literature derived from the Golden Circle sessions, the organizations spread throughout the country. By 1986 the "Anoah Material" was being communicated internationally.

Membership: In 1987 the association reported 2,700 members in the United States and an additional 500 internationally.

Periodicals: *Planetary Beacon*.

Sources:

Achad, Frater. *Melchizedek Truth Principles*. Phoenix, AZ: Lockhart Research Foundation, 1963.

Weiss, Jann. *Reflections by Anoah*. Austin, TX: Planetary Light Association, 1986.

★1547★
Process Church of the Final Judgment
Current address not obtained for this edition.

The Process Church dates to 1963, when a group began to gather around the charismatic Robert de Grimston, then a resident of London. The group was primarily psychologically oriented to begin with, but its search led to a spiritual quest. In 1966, members spent several months at Xtul, Yucatan, which is viewed as a place of miracles and a shared religious experience. Those who went were welded into a closely-knit group. Over the next seven years, a theology-in-process developed, primarily through the continued revelations of de Grimston. Development was rapid; significant changes could be noted annually and with each issue of the irregularly-issued *Process*.

As the theology appeared in 1973, the central emphasis was a dualism of Christ and Satan overcome by a reconciliation expressed in the formula, "The Unity of Christ and Satan is Good News for You. If that conflict can be resolved, then yours can be too." Behind this theme was a belief in the four deities: Jehovah, Lucifer, Christ and Satan—each representative of a personality-type and a spiritual path. All doctrine was set within the context of a Biblical apocalypticism.

To perpetuate the teaching, a strong hierarchical organization was established. Topping the hierarchy with de Grimston was a twelve-member Council of Masters. Ministers were called messengers. Initiated lay members were disciples, and joined the ranks of the Inside Processeans, as opposed to the Outside Processeans who lived according to process teaching without initiation. Inside Processeans dressed in the black uniform and wore the cross with a snake entwined upon it.

The Process Church was delt a fatal blow in 1974 when the majority of the Council of Masters rejected de Grimston's prophetic leadership (particualrly his emphasis on Satanic themes) and reorganized as the Foundation Church of the Millennium (now the Foundation Faith of God). Most of the members, including de Grimston's wife, aligned themselves with the new church.

The Process Church did not die completely with the schism. De Grimston reorganized the Process in a loose fashion and attempted to gather the remnant of followers into a very loose organization. He sent an open letter to his followers from his new home in New Orleans, encouraging them to form local autonomous groups around his teachings. Chapters formed in Boston and Toronto and smaller groups in Chicago, New Orleans, New York City, San Francisco, and London, England. A periodical, *The Process*, was published from the Boston headquarters. After several years in which it became evident that the organization could not be rebuilt, de Grimston returned to England and obscurity and all sign of the Process disappeared before the end of the decade.

After a period without public manifestation, a remnant of the Process Church reappeared in the late 1980s. It is composed of a small number of former Process members who have remained believers in spite of the reverses of the 1970s. They attempted to establish contact with other members now scattered around the country, but then again disappeared from public sight. Their present status is unknown.

Membership: Not reported.

Sources:

Assemblies and Hymns. Process Church of the Final Judgment, n.d.

Bainbridge, William Sims. *Satan's Power*. Berkeley and Los Angeles: University of California Press, 1978.

de Grimston, Robert. *Exit*. Letchworth, Herts., England: Garden City Press, 1968.

___. *The Gods and Their People*. Chicago: Process Church of the Final Judgment, 1970.

Facts and Figures, Some Questions and Answers about the Process Church. Chicago: Process Church, 1973.

★1548★
Quartus Foundation for Spiritual Research
PO Box 1768
Boerne, TX 78006

The Quartus Foundation for Spiritual Research was founded in 1981 by John Randolph Price and his wife, Jan Price. It is a New Age organization whose goal is to expand the human mind to its divine origin and thus affect a measurable change in the collective consciousness of humanity. Such a change of consciousness will usher in a new world of harmony and divine order.

To fulfill the foundation's purpose, Price has written a number of books. The first was *The Superbeings* (1981) in which he called attention to the appearance of a new species of human that had overcome limitations and had become Masters to raise the level of human consciousness. In 1984 Price announced the Planetary Commission, that would have 500 million people consent to the healing of the planet and 50 million people mobilized to meditate for that healing at the same time, noon Greenwich time. December 31, 1986, was designated the first World Healing Day. The event was successful enough to become an annual tradition among New Age groups around the world.

Price views the Quartus Foundation as a research laboratory in spirituality and is continually developing new approaches to bring in the New Age. Among the most recent was a 1988 experiment in which he invited several hundred people to live for two months in the realm of the "fourth dimension," i.e., the realm of spiritual causation. It is the Foundation's position that causation basically originates in the spiritual world, hence change comes from identifying with that world. The results of this experiment became the subject of his book, *A Spiritual Philosophy for the New World* (1990).

The Quartus Foundation is a member of the International New Thought Alliance (INTA).

Membership: In 1990 the foundation reported 1,700 members, including 300 outside the United States. There is one center in Texas, though members are scattered around the country.

Periodicals: *The Quartus Report.*

Sources:

Price, John Randolph. *The Planetary Commission*. Austin, TX: Quartus Foundation for Spiritual Research, 1984.

___. *A Spiritual Philosophy for the New World*. Boerne, TX: Quartus Foundation for Spiritual Research, 1990.

___. *The Superbeings*. Austin, TX: Quartus Foundation for Spiritual Research, 1981.

___. *With Wings as Eagles*. Austin, TX: Quartus Foundation for Spiritual Research, 1987.

★1549★
Quimby Center
Current address not obtained for this edition.

The Quimby Center dates to 1946 when its founder, Dr. Neva Dell Hunter (d. 1978), began working in the field of ESP. Though part of her spiritual work assignment from the beginning, the Center did not materialize until 1966 in Alamogordo, New Mexico. The purpose of the Center, besides being a vehicle of Dr. Hunter's continued work, was fourfold: to promote the fatherhood of God and the brotherhood of man, to promote spiritual understanding among men, to provide education by holding classes and to provide facilities for the general public. Like its namesake, Phineas P. Quimby, the founder of New Thought, the Center teaches that man is a direct expression of God. By applying metaphysical teachings, man can gain self-mastery.

Man lives within a universe governed by spiritual laws. These impersonal cosmic laws hold man responsible for every choice. Through the cycle of reincarnation, man becomes aware of the nature of life, assumes his responsibility and becomes attuned to the oneness of life. He realizes that there is life on other planets. He realizes that the present upheavals are preparation for movement into the Aquarian Age.

The Center programs stress workshops, seminars and lectures. A large library is maintained, and books, records and tapes are available to members on loan. One of the unique practices of the Center is a form of spiritual healing called "aura balancing," in which healers work on the patient's auric emanations. (Auras are

invisible waves of psychic energy that bodies project.) A booklet on the work, *The Auric Mirror*, by Ellavivian Power, has been published. Dr. Hunter was a psychic with a wide reputation in the psychic community. She gave karmic live-readings and psychic counseling both at the Center and at her many lectures around the country. When in Alamogordo, she gave weekly channeled classes.

The Center is run by a president-director, a vice-president, treasurer, secretary and nine-member board. Hunter was succeeded as president by Robert D. Waterman. Members are found both in Alamogordo and scattered around the United States in small study groups. Study groups have focused on aura-balancing. An annual Memorial Day picnic is held in Michigan by the Midwestern members.

Membership: Not reported.

Periodicals: *Quimby Center Newsletter.* Send orders to Box 453, Alamogordo, NM 88310.

★1550★
Religious School of Natural Hygiene
PO Box 1011
Boulder Creek, CA 95006

The Religious School of Natural Hygiene was founded in 1979 by Arthur D. Andrews, Jr., its first minister and president. During most of its first decade, the church was headquartered at its California Health Sanctuary located on a farm near Hollister, California.

As spelled out in its primary text, the church teaches a very positive faith that affirms humanity's creation by a loving God. According to the text, God created humans to carry out His will—to become caretakers of ourselves, each other, the other life forms on the planet, and the planet itself. This way is called stewardship. Humans are free to choose to live out God's will or not. The church is officially against all forms of violence, including war and capital punishment.

The major practical conclusion to be drawn from this theological perspective is that God wants humans healthy and has built a plan so they can live out healthy lives. That plan, or Natural Hygiene, involves following both a spiritual program of prayer, the laying-on-of-hands, and a process of fasting and diet derived from the Bible. This method allows God's power to work through us to bring healing. The recommended diet centers on uncooked fruits, nuts, and greens.

The school encountered major opposition to its work in 1987 when the state of California Board of Medical Quality Assurance charged the institution and Andrews with practicing medicine without a license. The state was particularly concerned with the lengthy fasts Andrews oversaw for people staying at the school. In addition, several former students filed suit for damage received from adherence to the regimen (though the suits were subsequently dismissed). While working through these challenges to its program, the church moved from Hollister to Boulder Creek.

Membership: In 1995 the school reported approximately 1,000 members in three centers in the United States and 25 members in Canada.

Periodicals: *Naturally, The Hygiene Way.*

Sources:

Major Tenets: Heed My Words. Hollister, CA: Religious School of Natural Hygiene, n.d.

★1551★
Savitria
2405 Ruscombe
Baltimore, MD 21209

Savitria, formed in 1970 by a group led by artist Robert Hieronimus, is dedicated to sowing the seeds for the Aquarian

Age. The spiritual heart of Savitria is a three-and-one-half-acre estate in North Baltimore, Maryland, which houses the core communal group, the Aum Esoteric Study Center and the New Morning School. Hieronimus began with a meditation group at Johns Hopkins University. Savitria was an outgrowth of that group.

It is Savitria's belief that man is a dual being, both mental and immortal. Man's goal is to allow the immortal aspect of being to overshadow the mental. This goal is accomplished through the study of esoteric sciences, which allow man to understand the cosmic process, and meditation, which raises his consciousness without the use of drugs. The high consciousness allows the two aspects of man to work in harmony and will lead to the era of the brotherhood of man and fatherhood of God, the golden age spoken of in all ancient esoteric writings.

Hieronimus had, in the early 1970s, gained a reputation in the psychic community because of his interest in the esoteric history of the United States. He believes that the Masons and Rosicrucians had a large part in the founding of the country. Evidence of their influence is to be found in the reverse of the Great Seal of the United States (found on the back of the one-dollar bill), which features the eye of God in the great triangle, a Rosicrucian symbol.

The Aum Esoteric Study Center is a state-approved institution and functions as a branch of the World University, founded by Howard John Zitko headquartered in Tucson, Arizona. It was formed as the first step in providing a total alternative education curriculum for all grades through college. At this point, the center has a three-year curriculum, with classes on the mystic arts, occult sciences and religion metaphysics. Certificates are offered in each area. New Morning School was formed in 1971 as a day-care/nursery school for pre-school children. In the mid-1970s, the Savitria community included approximately 15 people, who follow a strict code of conduct which includes meditation before sunrise and abstinence from drugs, extramarital sex, and wearing shoes in the house.

Membership: Not reported.

Sources:

Hieronimus, Robert. *The Two Great Seals of America.* Baltimore, MD: Savitriaum, 1976.

Zitko, Howard John. *New Age Tantra Yoga.* Tucson, AZ: World University Press, 1974.

★1552★
Society of Novus Spiritus
35 Dillon Ave.
Campbell, CA 95008-3001

The Society of Novus Spiritus was founded by spirit medium Sylvia Browne who has been channeling a spirit, Francine, since the 1960s. The society was created to disseminate the teachings which have been received over the past 30 years. Novus strives to uncover all of the "mysteries" regarding the nature of life, death, God, and the role humans play in life's scheme. To its understanding, God never withholds information; it is humans who choose to ignore it. The society exists to help prepare individuals for receiving God's wisdom.

Novus affirms the existence of an all-loving God and is dedicated to eliminating what it considers the false concepts of Satan, hell, sin, guilt, and the fear of God, all of which are contrary to its understanding of a benevolent Creator. The pain of life is not punishment from God; rather, it is a learning tool, and a very necessary one in the larger scheme of life.

Observing that nearly everything in nature exhibits a dual nature, most notably in the pairing of male/female, members of the society understand that this pattern extends even to the Most High, to God. They believe in a Mother God as well as a Father God, who reflect the patterns of nature. While God the Father holds creation in a constant state of being, God the Mother actively works with and through human beings for learning and perfection. Each

is a distinct entity, not just a nebulous force, and they are addressed as Om (male) and Azna (female).

The society teaches that knowledge provides the key needed to unlock the mind, and considers the society to be a Gnostic organization, by which it means that members are seekers after truth (gnosis). God is the source of all truth, available to all who are ready to receive it. The society seeks to promote a community of people who desire to be guided by the Light and dedicated to living a spiritual life.

The society also affirms that after "death," the human soul goes to the Other Side, which is better known as heaven. This place is the true reality, as opposed to the temporal planet Earth. The Other Side is eternal, a place of total harmony, no physical limitations. The individual's identity is intact. Life exists in its most wondrous and joyous form on the Other Side.

According to the society, even though the Other Side is total beauty and happiness, the soul may not be at peace and will still seek to better itself. This seeking drives an urge again to enter life on Earth to experience God's knowledge, gaining perfection in the process. Each soul decides how much experience it wants. While some may never have a life on Earth, others will choose 50 or more lives.

The society also holds weekly celebration services in Campbell, California, and Seattle, Washington. The work of the society is expanded through study groups which utilize a series of books written by Browne, *Journey of the Soul*, a set of 16 volumes based upon Browne's mediumship, her seminars, and her sermons. Each month study groups receive two cassette tapes by Browne to assist them. Those who complete the *Journey of the Soul* lessons may choose to take more advanced lessons leading to becoming a deacon and ordained minister of the society.

Membership: Not reported.

Sources:

Browne, Sylvia. *Journey of the Soul.* 16 vols. Campbell, CA: Society of Novus Spiritus, 1991-1994.

___. *Meditation Book I.* Campbell, CA: Society of Novus Spiritus, 1994.

★1553★
Teaching of the Inner Christ, Inc.
℅ International Center
4444 Zion Ave., Ste. A
San Diego, CA 91220-2328

The Teaching of the Inner Christ, Inc. (previously known as the Society for the Teaching of the Inner Christ) was founded in 1965 and incorporated in 1977 as the Inner Christ Administration Center. The founders were the Reverends Ann Meyer Makeever and Peter Victor Meyer. Makeever, who is a "sensitive," claims constant contact with the master teachers, Jesus and Babaji, and with her own I AM Self. The ministers and members accept guidance from these masters and from their own I AM Selves. Counseling, in which the counselor contacts the deeper levels of spirit through the invisible teachers, and a wide range of classes in prayer therapy and inner sensitivity, the Bible, and leadership and ministerial concerns are offered.

Headquarters of the center are in San Diego. The group supports a World Healing Ministry. There are centers and study groups in San Diego, Long Beach, Los Angeles, Oakland, and San Luis Obispo, California; Salt Lake City, Utah; Las Vegas, Nevada; and Edmonton, Alberta.

Membership: In 1998 the center reported 500 active members in 10 centers. There were 17 ministers and a number of licensed teachers and counselors.

Periodicals: *Double Heartline Newspaper.* • *Monthly International Center Bulletin.*

Sources:

God's Will. San Diego, CA: Brotherhood, 1968.

Jesus' Love. San Diego, CA: Brotherhood, 1964.

Meyer, Ann. *Ann, A Biography.* San Diego, CA: T.I.C. Books, 1982.

Meyer, Ann, and Peter Meyer. *Being a Christ!.* San Diego, CA: Dawning Publications, 1975.

★1554★
Teleos Institute
PO Box 12009-418
Scottsdale, AZ 85267

Teleos Institute, formerly the Love Project, headed by Arleen Lorrance and Diane K. Pike, is an outgrowth of the Foundation for Religious Transition, founded originally in 1969 by Episcopal Bishop James A. Pike and his wife, Diane Pike. The formation of the foundation came after Pike's well-publicized problems throughout the 1960s with a traditional statement on Christian doctrine, the accusations of heresy, his remarriage, and his involvement in the psychic. Bishop Pike's main doctrinal disagreements with orthodox Christianity centered on the doctrine of the Trinity and the inerrancy of the Bible. In the spring of 1969, the Pikes decided to leave the institutional church and begin a ministry to other "church alumni and those on the 'inside edge' of the church." The foundation's program was multi-faceted, with major themes in such diverse areas as social activism, parapsychology, clergy-training, and the study of Christian origins.

The death of Bishop Pike in September 1969, less than a year after the formation of the foundation, necessitated a reorientation. The name was changed to the Bishop Pike Foundation, but during the next two years it became increasingly clear that, without the bishop, the specific missions of the foundation were not materializing. In 1972, the foundation was merged into a structure already being formed by Arleen Lorrance, the Love Project. The Love Project grew out of a teacher-student experience of sharing which turned a violence-ridden ghetto into a center of love, concern, and positive action after the 1970-71 school year. This experience led to a realization of the distinction between inspiring people with a story and facilitating the emergence of love. As the Love Project matured, it was conceived as an active process of creating love.

The Teleos Institute creates an alternative to negative, destructive, violent living and a way in which all seekers of such alternatives may link energies in a universal chain of caring—a chain forged with the strength of the uniqueness of each individual. The way of the seeker is to make his or her very life an alternative, that of being change rather than seeking to change others. The institute has various structures—workshops, group travel experiences, and training people in learning to love universally and unconditionally. Advance work is offered in the School of Consciousness Classes (both in person and by cassette) and in an intensive Theatre of Life program focused upon bringing forth creativity in daily living. Recent programs have focused on "Life as a Waking Dream," a method that facilitates the awakening process by looking at ordinary life experiences as if they had been dreams. The nature of the institute keeps seekers on the move.

Membership: The institute is not a membership organization, but has a network of people who attend institute-sponsored events across the United States and Canada.

Periodicals: *Emerging.*

Sources:

Lorrance, Arleen. *Buddha from Brooklyn.* San Diego, CA: LP Publications, 1975.

___. *The Love Project.* San Diego, CA: LP Publications, 1972.

___. *Why Me? How to Heal What Is Hurting You.* New York: Ranson Associates Publishers, 1977.

Lorrance, Arleen, and Diane Kennedy Pike. *The Love Project Way.* San Diego, CA: LP Publications, 1980.

Pike, Diane Kennedy. *Cosmic Unfoldment.* San Diego, CA: LP Publications, 1976.

★1555★
Theocentric Foundation
Current address not obtained for this edition.

The Theocentric Foundation was founded in 1959 in Phoenix, Arizona, but is the successor to a series of prior structures dating to the 1920s: The Shangrila Missions of Ojai, California, the Eden Foundation, the Manhattan Philosophical Center and the Theocentric Temple. The basic teachings of the Foundation are Hermetic, based on the writing of Hermes Mercurious Trismegistus. The Bible and other metaphysical books are also used.

The Theocentric Foundation teaches basic truth, the understanding of the divine self. In this understanding, the seventy-three "Gods of the walking dead," such as anger, fear, grief, domination, limitation, prejudice, etc., and the five basic questions (What am I? What is my origin? Why am I here? Where do I go? and What am I doing about it?) can be dealt with. Before man can recognize his divine origin, he must become fully human and possess attributes such as affection, discrimination, enthusiasm, justice, kindness and tenderness. These attributes lead into the attributes of pure awareness, possessed by the self-governing identity. The self-governing identity has conquered the outside forces that would dominate a person and embodies love, certainty, consideration, understanding, empathy and admiration.

The headquarters of the Theocentric Foundation are in Phoenix. It has established branch centers around the country, and classes are offered in Hermetic theology. Degrees are issued after completion of the courses. Inner-order courses of ten degrees are also offered to students.

Membership: Not reported.

Sources:

Orpheus. *The Poimandres of Hermes Mercurius Trimegistus.* Phoenix, AZ: Theocentric Foundation, 1960.

★1556★
True Church of Christ, International
Box 2, Sta. G
Buffalo, NY 14213

The True Church of Christ, International, was formed by Christian Weyand of Buffalo, New York. It is described as the "nonprofit establishment of religion authorized by ecclesiastical authority of the True Bible Society International" (also headed by Weyand) and "the only existing Christian Church founded upon and teaching the True Complete Christian Bible and the True Complete Teachings and Scriptures of God and Christ." The church has published the True Complete Bible, which contains the Old and New Testaments translated from Aramaic; the True New Testament, containing the secret unwritten teachings of Jesus; the *Lost Books of the Bible* and the *Forgotten Books of Eden*, a collection of apocryphal writings, and the *Apocrypha*.

The True Church teaches psychic development and mediumship, and that the reason why no miracles occur in today's churches is because churches limit themselves to the Old and New Testament. The True Church believes Jesus taught hypnosis, miracle power and ESP. Man's soul, his life spirit, is part of God, the great creative intelligence. Psychic powers are natural to the soul and it is through these powers that all miracles are wrought. The church believes also that the water baptism of John has been replaced with spirit baptism.

The True Church advertises widely and offers its members around the country correspondence courses in the True Scriptures, hypnotism and the psychic. The church also has formed the World Roster of Psychic Contact, a prayer group.

Membership: Not reported.

★1557★
The United Spiritual Church of the Spiritual Advisory Council
14345 SE 103rd Terr.
Summerfield, FL 34491

The United Spiritual Church of the Spiritual Advisory Council is an ecclesiastical body associated with the Spiritual Advisory Council, an open-membership united spiritual society of friends. The council was founded in Chicago in 1974 by Paul V. Johnson (1924-1996) and Robert Ericsson, both former leaders in the Spiritual Frontiers Fellowship, a church-related organization that explored psychic and spiritual experiences. The council differed from the fellowship in its adoption of a mystical perspective within which to operate. Soon after its formation, Johnson relocated to Florida and in 1979 opened the New Age Centre for Alternative Realities in Orlando. The council sponsors several national conferences annually and has nurtured the formation of study groups.

Among the members of the Spiritual Advisory Council were some who had manifested leadership in their abilities as teachers and in the exercise of various spiritual gifts, especially in spiritual healing and offering psychic readings and counsel. The United Spiritual Church of the Spiritual Advisory Council emerged for those who saw the council as their spiritual home and who wished to exercise their ministry within its context. The first ministers were ordained at the council meeting in Chicago in 1979.

The church has no organized creed or dogma, but generally accepts a metaphysical, esoteric perspective. Ministers are encouraged to continue their growth in understanding of spiritual truth and to develop their awareness for channeling healing energies to those in suffering, pain, or want. The council exists as a national body with many members and the church as a smaller fellowship within the council. Following Johnson's death, leadership of the church has been assumed by David Beede.

Membership: In 1995 the Church reported approximately 1,000 members and 56 ministers.

Periodicals: *Spiritual Advisory Council Out-Reach Newsletter.*

★1558★
Universal Brotherhood
Current address not obtained for this edition.

The Universal Brotherhood is an occult group headquartered in New York City and headed by the Rev. Ureal Vercilli Charles. The Order is under the guidance of the Great White Brotherhood and offers lessons on the "Seven Immutable Laws of the Universe," man's key to health, success, and happiness. These laws are the laws of gender, cause/effect, rhythm, polarity, vibration, correspondence, and mentalism. Mr. Charles runs the First Church of Spiritual Vision in New York City. Other centers of the Brotherhood are in Jamaica, New York City, and the Bronx. *Lessons from the Great Masters* is a correspondence course taken by students across the United States. The Brotherhood also publishes *Wake Up and Learn!*, a series of pamphlets by Krishnahara, a Master of the Great Lodge who dictates through Elizabeth Dean.

Membership: Not reported.

Periodicals: *The Light Beyond.* Send orders to Box 366, Grand Central Station, New York, NY 10017.

★1559★
URANTIA Foundation
533 Diversey Pkwy.
Chicago, IL 60614

The URANTIA Foundation was founded in 1950 in Chicago, Illinois, for the dissemination of the teachings of *The URANTIA Book*. The book is a 2,097-page collection of messages received from numerous celestial beings; the name of the person who received these messages has never been revealed. It represents the first major revelation since the coming of Christ. The contents, according to the Foundation, "differ from all previous revelations, for they are not the work of a single universe personality, but a composite presentation of many beings." *The URANTIA Book* was first published in 1955, the twelfth printing being issued in 1995. It has been translated into French, Spanish, Finnish, Russian, and Dutch, with Korean, Swedish, Estonian Italian, Chinese, and German translations underway as of 1997.

The URANTIA Book is divided into four parts. Part I describes the nature of Deity, the reality of Paradise, the organization and working of the central and superuniverse, the personalities of the grand universe, and the high density of evolutionary mortals. Part II deals with the local universe, the handiwork of a Creator Son of the Paradise order of Michael. Our world, Urantia, belongs to a local universe whose sovereign is Michael, the Son of God and the Son of Man, known on this world as Jesus of Nazareth. Part III is a history of Urantia, the geologic development, the establishment of life, and the evolution and history of man. Part IV contains a biography of Jesus Christ, including a detailed discussion of the hidden years (from birth to the beginning of his public ministry). According to *The URANTIA Book*, Jesus was born August 21, 7 b.c.e., had an excellent education, became a skilled carpenter, began a Mediterranean tour in his twenty-eighth year, and began his public ministry in 27 c.e. After more than three years, his ministry ended in the crucifixion and resurrection. Objectives of the URANTIA Foundation include promoting the teachings of Jesus, primarily the appreciation of the fatherhood of God and the brotherhood of Man, in order to increase the comfort, happiness, and well-being of Man.

The foundation is a tax-exempt, common-law, educational foundation operating under a Declaration of Trust. It is managed by a board of five trustees who are appointed for life and serve without compensation. The duties of the foundation are to publish *The URANTIA Book*, "to perpetually preserve inviolate the text of *The URANTIA Book*," and "to retain absolute and unconditional control of . . . media for the printing and reproduction of *The URANTIA Book* and any translation thereof." The URANTIA Foundation is headquartered in Chicago and has additional offices in England, France, Spain, Finland, and Australia.

Associated with the foundation is the International URANTIA Association (IUA), a reader membership organization also headquartered in Chicago. The purpose of IUA is the in-depth study of *The URANTIA Book* and the orderly dissemination of its teachings. The association's long term task is to encourage the formation of study groups, and to foster and facilitate the voluntary transformation of stable and mature study groups into URANTIA Associations. These Associations function on a regional level and operate with great autonomy. The Association emphasizes its nonsectarian nature, and maintains that members of diverse religions may be students of *The URANTIA Book* and receive its revelations as an enrichment to rather than a contradiction of their own faith. It is a fraternal organization with a spiritual objective.

Membership: In 1997 the International URANTIA Association comprised three national associations (Australia-New Zealand, Finland, and the United States) and fourteen local associations in the United States.

Periodicals: • *JOURNAL URANTIAN NEWS* (URANTIA Foundation). (of the International URANTIA Association).

Remarks: Since 1955, the Foundation has protected the text of *The URANTIA Book* through its ownership of the copyright. In addition, since 1950, in order to preserve the unique identity of *The URANTIA Book* and the URANTIA Foundation, the Foundation established and began using the "URANTIAN," the concentric-circles symbol that was registered in 1952 as a service mark and in 1971 as a trademark. The use of the circles by the Foundation in association with *The URANTIA Book* assures a prospective reader that he or she has the original text. The Foundations ownership of the marks will continue in perpetuity, which means that after the copyright expires, only those copies of *The URANTIA Book* published by the URANTIA Foundation can bear the concentric-circles symbol, assuring future readers of the authenticity of the text.

Sources:

Bedell, Clyde. *Concordex to the URANTIA Book.* Laguna Hills, CA: The Author, 1980.

Faw, Duane L., comp. *The Paramony.* Malibu, CA: The Author, 1986.

Myers, Martin W. *Unity, Not Uniformity.* Chicago: URANTIA Foundation, 1973.

Renn, Ruth E. *Study Aids for Part IV of The URANTIA Book, The Life and Teachings of Jesus.* Chicago: URANTIA Foundation, 1975.

Special Report to the Readers of THE URANTIA BOOK: URANTIA Foundation Ends Its Relationship with the Former URANTIA Brotherhood. Chicago: URANTIA Foundation, 1990.

The URANTIA Book. Chicago: URANTIA Foundation, 1955.

★1560★
World Catalyst Church
Current address not obtained for this edition.

The World Catalyst Church seeks to be a catalyst in moving from old ideas to new. The church believes that there is an inner light that is beyond ourselves in wisdom, power and scope. The church's job is to lead men from their present ignorant state to the eternal something within. Man's forward movement can be accomplished through his own efforts. Man is bound, however, by natural law and by his oneness with others. No man will enter eternal perfection until all are able to. Man is a microcosm of the macrocosm. He is reincarnated in any given dimension long enough to learn the necessary lessons. Prayer and meditation are useful tools in learning to live.

The World Catalyst Church has members around the country, drawn from those who have taken the basic correspondence study course, "That Man May Find Himself." The course also is the beginning material for any who wish to become teachers for the church. The church refuses to put money into religious edifices. There is no charity assistance of a material nature. All monies go into communities. The church was formed in 1967 at Butte, Montana by Helen Muschell (author of *Wells of Inner Space*), Margot Jones, Ese Jasper, Ernest Hanson, Ruth Adams, Beata Kamp, and Matt Gleason.

Membership: Not reported.

Section 19

Ancient Wisdom Family

Consult the Contents pages to locate the essay in Part II, Historical Essay Chapters, that provides an historical discussion of this family

Intrafaith Organizations

★1561★
Synod of Independent Sacramental Churches
℅ Abp. Julian Gillmon
Box 227
Dulzura, CA 92107

The Synod of Independent Sacramental Churches was founded in 1984 following a disruption in the Federation of St. Thomas Christian Churches, an organization which had served as an ecumenical home for many of the smaller independent liturgical churches that had developed an esoteric, gnostic, or theosophical perspective, many of which had a lineage tracing back to either the Liberal Catholic Church or the American Catholic Church. Much of the motivation for the formation of the new group came from Bp. Michael G. Zaharakis of the Mesbarim Fellowship, though Zaharakis died suddenly before the synod was fully organized.

The synod served as a point of unity for independent churches with a valid apostolic succession for the purpose of mutual aid and education. It imposed no doctrinal unity. The synod was fully in accord with the acceptance of women into all levels of the ministry and selected as its first chairperson Bp. Rosamonde Miller of the Ecclesia Gnostic Mysteriorum. While based in sacramental Christianity, it professed acceptance of the authenticity and validity of other religions and the ongoing nature of revelation.

Also included among the original member churches were the Independent Church of Antioch, the Independent Catholic Church International, the New Church of the East, the Johannine Catholic Church, the New Church Universal, the Church of the Seven Seals, the Apostolic Order of the Christos, and the Mesbarim Fellowship.

Periodicals: *SISCOM.*

Rosicrucianism

★1562★
Ancient and Mystical Order of the Rosae Crucis
San Jose, CA 95191

[It should be noted that the Ancient and Mystical Order of the Rosae Crucis does not consider itself a religion and points out that its membership includes persons of every religion and creed. It is in this encyclopedia for two reasons. First, it is a major disseminator of the ancient wisdom teachings, the subject of this chapter, which are a significant element of what has, over the last century, become a new religious tradition in the West. Second, the order accepts as its own the same history (detailed in the introductory section of this volume) as the other Rosicrucian groups. Its inclusion has seemed necessary in order to present a full picture of the Rosicrucian presence in North America. The order is the largest of the several Rosicrucian bodies, and throughout its history it has

been forced to interact with other organizations that have taken the Rosicrucian name.]

The Ancient and Mystical Order of the Rosae Crucis (AMORC) was founded in 1915 by H. Spencer Lewis (1883-1939) in New York City, as an esoteric fraternal order. Lewis was a young occultist who had been associated with the various British occult orders and who met Aleister Crowley. Active attempts to establish the Rosicrucian Order began in 1909. In that year, Lewis states he met French members of the International Rosicrucian Council in Toulouse. He was initiated, returned to America, and began holding meetings. In 1915, the order was firmly established, and the massive publicity campaign, which has made this branch of the Rosicrucian the best known to the general public, was begun.

Lewis' early affiliations with various occult groups, especially the Ordo Templi Orientis (O.T.O), headed by Crowley for many years, is clearly reflected in his frequent inclusions of material from them in the teachings and symbolism of the AMORC. For example, the Rose Cross emblem was taken from the *Equinox* III (Crowley's periodical), and other emblems were borrowed from other issues. (Lewis was not above pure plagiarism; whole chapters of his *Mystic Life of Jesus* were taken from the *Aquarian Gospel of Jesus* by Levi Dowling.) In 1916, after the German O.T.O. split with Crowley over *The Book of the Law*, it gave its recognition to the AMORC in a document Lewis proudly displayed (in spite of O.T.O.'s association with the practice of sex magic, which AMORC has never advocated).

Rapid growth led to conflict with the other Rosicrucian bodies. In 1928, shortly after the move of the AMORC to San Jose, the older Fraternitas Rosae Crucis launched an attack on Lewis, challenging the Order's right to the designation "Rosicrucian." Lewis accused R. Swinburne Clymer, a lifelong advocate of alternative healing practices, of receiving an M.D. from a diploma mill and fraudulent behavior. An intense polemic, which at times has involved the Rosicrucian Fraternity in Oceanside, California, has continued to the present.

The teachings of the Rosicrucians center on God's purpose for life. Rosicrucians believe God created the universe according to his immutable laws. Man's success is through mastership, the ability to bring into material expression one's mental imaging. The techniques taught to students lead to mastery. For example, students are taught to "image" or imagine such things as health, wealth, and happiness, and thereby draw those things to themselves. Progress in the teaching and knowledge of the accompanying practices comes through a series of correspondence lessons mailed regularly to members. Completion of a set of lessons admits students to a higher degree in the work and makes available the next, more advanced, set of lessons. Members may also attend local centers (designated lodges, chapters, or pronaoi, depending upon their strength) for group activities.

The AMORC sees itself as a continuation of the ancient mystery schools of Amenhotep IV and Solomon; listed among famous Rosicrucians are Isaac Newton, Rene Descartes, Benjamin Franklin, and Francis Bacon. The Fraternity works on 180-year cycles, first acting in silence and secrecy and then in public. A new public cycle began in 1909. Head of the order is the Grand Imperator, a post held by Ralph M. Lewis (1904-1987), Spencer Lewis' son, from 1939 to 1987. Following the death of Ralph M. Lewis, Gary L. Stewart was chosen as the new Grand Imperator. However, three years later he was removed from office by vote of the Order's board and stands accused of embezzling $3.5 million which he had transferred from a bank account in California to one in the small European country of Andorra. Stewart was succeeded by Christian Bernard who currently serves as the Grand Imperator.

Internationally the AMORC is headed by the Supreme Grand Lodge headquartered in San Jose, California. Its directors include the Grand masters of each of the twelve grand lodges which have been established to serve various geographical regions and language groups. Grand Lodges serve Portuguese, French, German, Greek, Italian, Japanese Dutch, and the Nordic Languages. Two England-language Grand Lodges serve the Americas and Europe/Africa respectively and two Spanish-language Grand Lodges serve the Americas and Europe/Africa/Australasia respectively.

Lewis was interested in Egypt, and, through the Rosicrucian Egyptian Museum in San Jose, which he founded, made many significant contributions to Egyptology. The museum is located in Rosicrucian Park, a square block in San Jose that houses the other departments of the order and which has become a major tourist stop in California. The museum celebrated its 65th anniversary in 1992.

Membership: Not reported, but in 1990 the order claimed over 250,000 members worldwide. In 1995 the Order listed 98 chartered lodges, chapters, and pronaoi in the United States, including Puerto Rico. There were 36 groups in Canada, and more than 1,200 worldwide. Members were reported in 86 countries around the world. In 1991 the *Rosicrucian Digest* circulated over 40,000 copies per issue. The members only *Rosicrucian Forum* circulates approximately 10,700 copies.

Educational Facilities: Rose-Croix University, San Jose, California.

Periodicals: *Rosicrucian Digest*. Send orders to Rosicrucian Park, San Jose, CA 95191. • *Rosicrucian Forum* (available to members only).

Sources:

Bernard, Raymond. *Messages from the Celestial Sanctum*. San Jose, CA: Supreme Grand Lodge of AMORC, 1980.

Lewis, H. Spencer. *Cosmic Mission Fulfilled*. San Jose, CA: Supreme Grand Lodge of AMORC, 1973.

___. *The Mystical Life of Jesus*. San Jose, CA: Supreme Grand Lodge of AMORC, 1929.

___. *Rosicrucian Manual*. San Jose, CA: Rosicrucian Press, 1941.

___. *Rosicrucian Questions and Answers*. San Jose, CA: Supreme Grand Lodge of AMORC, 1969.

___. *Yesterday Has Much to Tell*. San Jose, CA: Supreme Grand Lodge of AMORCS, 1973.

★1563★

Ausar Auset Society
℅ Kamit Publications
140 Buckingham Rd.
Brooklyn, NY 11226

The Ausar Auset Society is a Rosicrucian body serving the black community of the United States. It was founded in the mid-1970s by R. A. Straughn, also known by the name Ra Un Nefer Amen, formerly head of the Rosicrucian Anthroposophical League in New York City. He is the author of several occult texts in spiritual science, each offering methods drawn from the Kabbalah and eastern religions to facilitate the orderly transition to the enlightened state.

The Society has directed its program to blacks and *Metu Neter* (formerly *The Oracle of Thoth*) regularly features, alongside of its occult articles, items of general interest and concern to black people. The Society advocates the appropriation of the positive accomplishments of African ancestors by the contemporary black community. The Society offers free public classes in a variety of occult topics. Currently such classes are being held in New York City, Brooklyn, Chicago, Philadelphia, New Haven, Washington, DC, and Norfolk, VA.

Membership: Not reported.

Periodicals: *Metu Neter*.

Sources:

Ra Un Nefer Amer [R.A. Staughn] *Metu Neter*. Vol. 1. Bronx, NY: Khamit Publishing Co., 1990.

Straughn, R. A. *Black Woman's, Black Man's Guide to a Spiritual Union*. Bronx, NY: Oracle of Thoth, 1981.

___. *Meditation Techniques of the Kabalists, Vedantins and Taoists*. Bronx, NY: Maat Publishing Company, 1976.

___. *The Oracle of Thoth: The Kabalistical Tarot*. Bronx, NY: Oracle of Thoth Publishing Company, 1977.

___. *The Realization of Neter Nu*. Brooklyn, NY: Maat Publishing Company, 1975.

★1564★

Fraternitas Rosae Crucis
Beverly Hall
Quakertown, PA 18951

This, the oldest of the several existing Rosicrucian bodies, dates to 1858 when it was founded by Paascal Beverly Randolph (1825-1875). The first lodge was established in San Francisco three years later. On three occasions, the grand lodge was closed and reestablished: first in Boston (1871), then in San Francisco (1874), and finally in Philadelphia (1895). Randolph was succeeded by Freeman B. Dowd who in turn was succeeded by Edward H. Brown (1907) and R. Swinburne Clymer (1922). Clymer was recently succeeded by his son, Emerson M. Clymer. Randolph, a physician, had for many years lectured upon issues of sexuality. The inner teachings of the order he established included a system of occult sexuality, which he termed Eulistic, a word derived from the Greek Eleusinian mysteries, which Randolph believed to be mysteries of sex. In 1874 he established a Provisional Grand Lodge of Eulis in Tennessee, but he had to dissolve it because of internal problems among the membership. Translations of Randolph's writings, disseminated through his European followers, became a source for the sex magick system developed by the Ordo Templi Orientis. As presented in the English-speaking world by Aleister Crowley, the O.T.O.'s sex magic stood in contradiction to Randolph's teachings at several points, particularly on the moral level. Randolph had advocated the practice of his teachings only by married couples. Twentieth-century followers of Randolph have denounced the O.T.O. teachings as black magick.

In the Fraternitas Rosae Crucis, the member begins his work and is taught the basic ideas of the "secret schools," which include reincarnation and karma, and the Law of Justice and the non-interference with the rights of others. He begins to learn the process of transmutation (of the base self into the finest gold) and the acquisition of health and strength by casting out thoughts of weakness and age. He is also taught to contact the hierarchies of the heavenly realm. Members believe in the fatherhood of God and the ultimate brotherhood of man. The inner circle of the Fraternity is the Aeth Priesthood, in which is taught "the highest occultism known to man."

Associated with the fraternity is the Church of Illumination, an outer court group, which means it interacts with the public and from which a select few may be chosen to join the inner group. The church emphasizes the establishment of the "Manistic" Age, which began in the late nineteenth century and follows the previous Egyptian and Christian ages. Manisism is the recognition of the equality of man and woman. It is also the name of the new world leader who teaches the divine law with its five fundamentals: As ye sow so shall ye reap; talents as gift and responsibility; the golden rule; honesty; and the new birth as the awakening of the Christos or divine spark within.

"Many are called but few are chosen" is a watchword with the Fraternitas Rosae Crucis, which does not advertise in the manner associated with the Ancient and Mystical Order of the Rosae Crucis (AMORC). Numerous books by R. Swinburne Clymer, who revived the all but moribund fraternity in the early twentieth century, have attracted members. Authority of the Fraternity rests with the Council of Three. The highest office is held by the Hierarch of Eulis. The Beverly Hall Corporation in Quakertown, Pennsylvania, handles the distribution of literature. Continuing the lifelong health concerns of R. Swinburne Clymer, like Randolph, a physician, are the Humanitarian Society and the Clymer Health Clinic, both located at the fraternity's headquarters complex in Quakertown.

Membership: Not reported.

Sources:

Clymer, R. Swinburne. *The Age of Treason*. Quakertown, PA: Humanitarian Society, 1959.

___. *The Rose Cross Order*. Allentown, PA: Philosophical Publishing Co., 1916.

___. *The Rosicrucian Fraternity in America*. 2 vols. Quakertown, PA: Rosicrucian Foundation, 1935.

___. *The Rosy Cross, Its Teachings*. Quakertown, PA: Beverly Hall Corporation, 1965.

Randolph, Paschal Beverly. *Eulis, Affectional Alchemy*. Quakertown, PA: Confederation of Initiates, 1930.

★1565★
Holy Rosicrucian Church
(Defunct)

The Holy Rosicrucian Church was a small shortlived Rosicrucian body known primarily through a single literary remain, a booklet, *Rosikrucianism*, published in 1915. The Church, and its associated orders were founded by a person known only as Sergius Rosenkruz and headquartered in Los Angeles. The Church and Brotherhood taught a method of liberation, the awakening to the knowledge of unity with the One. The Church advocated a series of preparatory methods which included study, twice daily baths, the practice of charitable works, the avoidance of frivolous activities, and the adoption of a variety of occult meditative techniques. The associated Order of the Knights of the Golden Circle which through rites and ceremonies prepared members for either a favorable reincarnation, or safety in the beyond.

Sources:

Rosenkruz, Sergius. *Rosikrucianism*. Los Angeles: The Author, 1915.

★1566★
Lectorium Rosicrucianum
Western North American Headquarters
Box 9246
Bakersfield, CA 93389

Alternate Address: International headquarters: Bakenessergracht 11-15, 2011JS Haarlem, The Netherlands; Eastern North American Headquarters: Box 334, Chatham, NY 12037.

The Lectorium Rosicrucianum was founded in Holland in 1924 by a small group of people most of whom formerly had been members of the Rosicrucian Fellowship. The spiritual leaders of the group wrote under the pen names Jan Van Rijckenborgh and Ca-

therose de Petri. The organization remained small until 1940, when it was forced to shut down until after the war. Since its reopening it has become a worldwide organization. It came to the United States in the early-1970s, and headquarters were established in Bakersfield, California.

The Lectorium Rosicrucianum describes itself as a gnostic, transfiguristic spiritual school. By gnostic is meant, "coming from the Logos," i.e., from God the source of all things. Transfiguration is the name of the path of return to the gnosis (knowledge or divine wisdom) for humans who are seen as fallen from a divine state and now in need of reawakening and unfolding of the spirit-spark atom, the rose of the heart, located in the center of ones microcosmic self. People are aided in this process by the Universal Brotherhood, the divine spiritual hierarchy. The Universal Brotherhood consists of those of the human life wave who either never fell from the original immortal nature order or who have returned through a process of building a New Soul Body, through the process of Transfiguration. The Light of the Universal Brotherhood is transmitted through a transfiguristic spiritual schools power field into a usable source of energy thus making it possible for individuals to break the wheel of birth and death (reincarnation after reincarnation). Thereby one can return to humanity's original sphere, the Sixth Cosmic Region.

The Lectorianum is differentiated from other groups using the name Rosicrucian by its concept of the two Nature Orders. Their philosophy explains that humans are born into this Nature Order, the seventh Cosmic region, the world of nature that individuals perceive and experience as mortal beings. But humans also carry a remnant of the original nature order, the Sixth Cosmic Region, as a human immortal seed, the Christ principle in the center of the microcosm. Thus, the purpose of an individuals life in this nature order is to cooperate with the blossoming of the rose of the heart, the Christ within, through the process of Transfiguration, in order to return to the immortal nature order to which s/he originally belonged.

The Lectorium Rosicrucianum has initiated a broad publication program that includes not only the publication of over forty of the schools books, but their translation into various languages. The spiritual school's journal, *Pentegram*, appears in Dutch, English, German French, Portuguese, and Swedish editions.

Membership: In 1995 the group reported four centers in the United States and two in Canada. There were 17,000 members worldwide.

Periodicals: *Pentegram*.

Sources:

Van Rijckenborgh, Jan. *The Coming New Man*. Haarlem, Neths.: Rozekruis- Pers, 1957.

___. *Elementary Philosophy of the Modern Rosecross*. Harlem, Neths: Rozekruis-Pers, 1961.

The Way of the Rosecross in Our Times. Haarlem, Neths.: Rozekruis-Pers, 1978.

★1567★
New Age Bible and Philosophy Center
1139 Lincoln Blvd.
Santa Monica, CA 90403

The New Age Bible and Philosophy Center was founded by Mary Elizabeth Shaw in May 1931. It consisted of a school dedicated to basic Christian spiritual teachings of the Ancient Wisdom. It included classes in Theosophy and the Rosicrucian teachings. The center, now in its 67th year, was always closely associated with the works of Max Heindel and Corinne Heline. Its two main courses are aligned to Corinne Heline's seven volumes of the *New Age Bible Interpretation* and Max Heindel's *Rosicrucian Cosmo-Conception*.

Heline was born in Atlanta, Georgia, in 1875 as Corinne S. Dunklee. Following the death of her mother in 1891, Heline moved to California where she met and became the close student of Max Heindel (1865-1919), founder of the Rosicrucian Fellowship. After Heindel's death, she remained for many years a leading member. In 1922, she received an "inner Commission" to begin work on interpreting the Bible in the Light of the Esoteric tradition. The project would consume the remainder of her life. Her early efforts were published in the Fellowship periodical, *The Rosicrucian Magazine*. During this period she met and married Theodore Heline (d. 1971). Both the Helines were prodigious authors who published books and booklets which have a broad circulation around the world.

Mary Elizabeth Shaw was succeeded by Rev. Gene Sande, who had served at the center since its beginning. She was the head of the center for more than 50 years. The present head of the center is Rev. Patricia Talis, assisted by Rev. Patricia Tinker.

Besides Sunday services, there are monthly Full Moon Services and various classes offered weekly. A bookstore and library are open daily Wednesday through Friday. The correspondence courses in the Bible and Philosophy are mailed to students who request them. The New Age Bible and Philosophy Center publishes the Corinne and Theodore Heline books.

Membership: There is one center with 100 people affiliated and an unknown number of class attendants and correspondence students.

Periodicals: *Quarterly Bulletin*.

Sources:

Heline, Corinne. *Mysteries of the Holy Grail*. Los Angeles: New Age Press, 1977.

___. *The Mystery of the Christos*. Los Angeles: New Age Press, 1961.

___. *New Age Bible Interpretation*. 7 vols. Los Angeles: New Age Press, 1938-54.

Heline, Theodore. *As in the Days of Noah*. Los Angeles: New Age Press, 1946.

___. *The Redemptive Feminine*. Los Angeles: New Age Press, n.d.

★1568★
Rosicrucian Anthroposophical League
Current address not obtained for this edition.

The Rosicrucian Anthroposophical Society was formed in 1932 by Samuel Richard Parchment (b.1881), a former leader in the San Francisco Center of the Rosicrucian Fellowship. Parchment, continuing the astrological emphasis of the Fellowship, wrote a classic textbook, *Astrology, Mundane and Spiritual*, and even before leaving the Fraternity began writing the books which were to guide the League: *The Just Law of Compensation, The Middle Path, the Safest, Ancient Operative Masonry*, and *Steps to Self-Mastery*. Early centers were in California and New York. (In the late 1970s the surviving New York City center broke away to become the Ausar Auset Society.)

The principles of the League commit it to an investigation of occult laws, the brotherhood of man, the dissemination of spiritual truth, and the attainment of self-conscious immortality. Recent contact with the League has not been made and its present status is uncertain.

Membership: Not reported.

Sources:

Parchment, S. R. *Ancient Operative Masonry*. San Francisco: San Francisco Center-Rosicrucian Fellowship, 1930.

___. *Astrology, Mundane and Spiritual*. San Francisco: Anthroposophical Rosicrucian League, 1933.

___. *The Just Law of Compensation*. San Francisco: San Francisco Center-Rosicrucian Fellowship, 1932.

___. *Steps to Self-Mastery*. Oceanside, CA: Fellowship Press, 1927.

★1569★
Rosicrucian Fellowship
2222 Mission Avenue
Oceanside, CA 92054

The Rosicrucian Fellowship was founded as a Christian organization in 1909 by Carl Louis von Grasshoff, better known under his pen-name as Max Heindel (1865–1919). Born in Denmark, Heindel eventually moved to the United States and, in 1903, settled in Los Angeles, California. He became active in that citys branch of the Theosophical Society serving as its vice-president for three years.

According to Heindel, while in Germany in 1907, he encountered a being later identified as an Elder Brother of the Rosicrucian Order who appeared in his room. After submitting Heindel to a test to determine his integrity and fitness for being a messenger of the Western Wisdom Teachings, the being promised to reveal to him the esoteric knowledge he sought. Heindel was given directions to the Temple of the Rose Cross, near the GermanBohemian border, where he was given the material to be used in his first book, *The Rosicrucian CosmoConception*, the basic textbook of the fellowship.

Returning to the United States, he proceeded to rewrite the book, as the Elder Brother had told him he would, and publish it. Soon he became a popular speaker, lecturing in Columbus, Ohio; Seattle, and North Yakima, Washington; Portland, Oregon; and Los Angeles, California, which led to the formulation of centers and study groups in these and many other locations. Subsequently, the teachings of this book spread internationally.

The Rosicrucian Cosmo-Conception puts forth a view of the cosmos from an esoteric Christian standpoint and advocates the adoption of Jesus Christ as the aspirants ideal. Heindel also advocates the intelligent use of spiritual astrology as a tool for self-knowledge and moral development. He also introduced new formats for temple, healing, marriage, and memorial services, now published in the fellowships *Manual of Forms*.

In 1911, the fellowships international headquarters were established at Mount Ecclesia in Oceanside, California, for the purpose of best implementing its two principal goals of healing the sick and disseminating esoteric Christian teachings. A chapel, administrative offices, residents quarters, a vegetarian cafeteria, and a healing temple were erected on the grounds. An abundance of literature in the form of correspondence courses, books, pamphlets, and monthly mailings issue from Mount Ecclesia. The fellowship became a major force in the spread of astrology in the twentieth century, and many astrologers not connected with the organization use the single-year, decade and 100-year ephemerides and the *Table of Houses*, most of which are published on site.

Membership is open to all, provided they are not professional astrologers, mediums, hypnotists, or palmists. After a two-year term of being a regular student of the fellowship, a person who abstains from all flesh food, tobacco, mind-altering drugs, and alcohol may apply for Probationership in the fellowship. Upon his death in 1919, Heindel was succeeded in leadership by his wife, Augusta Foss Heindel (d. 1949), an accomplished occultist in her own right. Mount Ecclesia remains the headquarters of the fellowship; the work is carried on there in the same tradition established by the founders. The Rosicrucian doctrine is preserved in its pristine purity and the service rendered to humanity throughout all departments retains its original quality of faithful, anonymous dedication.

Membership: In 1995 the fellowship reported 8,000 members worldwide, 700 of which are in the United States. Members are found on every continent.

Periodicals: *Rays from the Rose Cross*.

Sources:

Heindel, Max. *Rosicrucian Cosmo-Conception*. Oceanside, CA: Rosicrucian Fellowship, 1937.

___. *Rosicrucian Philosophy in Questions and Answers*. Oceanside, CA: Rosicrucian Fellowship, 1922

___. *Simplified Scientific Astrology*. Oceanside, CA: Rosicrucian Fellowship, 1928.

Heindel, Mrs. Max [Augusta Foss]. *The Birth of the Rosicrucian Fellowship*. Oceanside, CA: Rosicrucian Fellowship, n.d.

★1570★
Societas Rosicruciana in America
Box 192-3
Preston Hollow, NY 12469

Sylvester Gould was an early member of the Societas Rosicruciana in Civitatibus Foederatis, the masonic Rosicrucian society. He was admitted into the Boston College in 1885. However, it was his desire to create a Rosicrucian organization that would admit non-Masons. In 1907, with the assistance of George Winslow Plummer (1876-1944) he created the Societas Rosicruciana in America (S.R.I.A.) adapting the masonic materials for general use. He also began *The Rosicrucian Brotherhood*, a periodical. Gould died in 1909. Plummer succeeded to the leadership role, a position he held until his death.

Plummer incorporated the S.R.I.A. in 1912 and four years later founded the Mercury Publishing Company and *Mercury*, a quarterly magazine for the society. During the decade six colleges were chartered in the United States and one in Sierre Leone. In 1921 two more were added. Plummer authored the lessons and other material distributed by the society. His interests in Christian mysticism and ritual also led him to create a Seminary of Biblical Research (through which he wrote and published a series of lessons on Christian mysticism) and to found two churches: the Anglican Universal Church and the Holy Orthodox Church in America, treated elsewhere in this encyclopedia. These organizations were intimately intertwined with the S.R.I.A. Colleges, and church congregations were frequently located in the same cities with the church's members being drawn primarily from society adherents.

The booklet, *Principles and Practices of the Rosicrucians*, by Plummer details the affirmations and duties of members. The group affirms the existence of one infinite intelligence, the incarnation of Spirit in matter, the continuousness of all life in evolution, the possibility of the mental attaining knowledge of the spiritual while yet incarnate, and reincarnation. Each student is expected to experiment and to demonstrate knowledge of concentration, meditation, contemplation, prayer, dietetics, exercise, rest, rituality, sexual faculties, healing, cheerfulness, fasting, and individual development; vegetarianism is not demanded, but alcohol is forbidden. New members in the Societas Rosicruciana in America are called postulants. After a year, they become fraters (brothers) or sorores (sisters). Progress is through ten degrees.

Following Plummer's death, the society and the Holy Orthodox Church in America were headed by Stanislaus Witowski (de Witow), who married Plummer's widow, Gladys Plummer. Gladys Plummer de Witow, also known as Mother Serena, became head of the society and the church after her second husband's death. Mother Serena died in 1989 and was succeeded by Sister Lucia Grosch.

Membership: In 1991 the newsletter reported a circulation of 1,000 copies. Only one small center of the S.R.I.A. remains, and it is located in Preston Hollow, New York. There is an associated membership from many countries.

Periodicals: *Mercury*.

Sources:

Plummer, George Winslow. *The Art of Rosicrucian Healing*. New York: Society of Rosicrucians, 1947.

___. *Esoteric Masonry*. Kingston, NY: Society of Rosicrucians, 1988.

___. *Principles and Practice for Rosicrucians*. New York: Society of Rosicrucians, Inc., 1947.

___. *Rosicrucian Healing*. Kingston, NY: Society of Rosicrucians, 1988.

Serena. *Lettergrams*. New York: Society of Rosicrucians, Inc., 1976.

Serena, Mother. *Victorinus Teaches*. Kingston, NY: Society of Rosicrucians, 1988.

★1571★
Societas Rosicruciana in Civitatibus Foederatis
Current address not obtained for this edition.

The Societas Rosicruciana in Anglia was formed in England in 1865 by Robert Wentworth Little. It seems to have been based on eighteenth-century Rosicrucian texts. Among its members were Kenneth R. H. Mackenzie, William Wynn Westcott and W. R. Woodmen, who were among the founders of the Hermetic Order of the Golden Dawn, the group most credited with initiating the revival of magic in the twentieth century. Members of the Societas were required to be masons prior to beginning their work. During the late nineteenth century, colleges were opened in London (1867), Bristol (1869), Manchester (1871), Cambridge (1876), Sheffield (1877), Middlesex (1877), and Newcastle (1890). In 1873 the East of Scotland College was inagurated in Edinburgh.

News of the formation of the Rosicrucian organization spread through masonry to the American lodges. In 1878 a group led by Charles E. Meyer (1839-1908) of Pennsylvania traveled to England and were initiated at Sheffield. They applied for a charter, but getting no response, turned to Scotland and received a charter from the college in Edinburgh in 1879. A second charter was granted for a college in New York and in 1880 the two colleges formed the Society Rosicruciana Republicae Americae. A Boston and a Baltimore college were chartered later that year. The organization's name was changed to the Societas Rosicruciana in the United States of America, also known as the Societas Rosicruciana in Civitatibus Foederatis. Later charters were granted for Duluth, Minnesota (1911), Texas (1918), New Jersey (1931), North Carolina (1932), Virginia (1933), Illinois (1934), Colorado (1935), Long Island, New York (1935), Nova Scotia, Canada (1936), and Ontario, Canada (1937). Membership from the 1930s to the 1950s remained steady at between 200 and 300 members. Membership has remained small and, like the British and Scottish counterparts, it is limited to masons. From 1951 to 1973, the society issued a biannual report, *The Rosicrucian Fama*. Recent information on the society has not been available.

Membership: Not reported. In 1973 the society reported 31 members.

Sources:

Voorhis, Harold V. B. *Masonic Rosicrucian Societies*. New York: Press of Henry Emmerson, 1958.

Occult Orders

★1572★
Astara
792 W. Arrow Hwy.
Box 5003
Upland, CA 91785

Astara was formed in 1951 by Robert and Earlyne Chaney, both former Spiritualists. Robert Chaney had been active at Camp Chesterfield and instrumental in the founding of the Spiritualist Episcopal Church. While still a Spiritualist, he became interested in Theosophy and began to profess a belief in reincarnation, which was, in the 1940s, still a minority idea within Spiritualist circles and which met with strong disapproval at the camp. Earlyne, as a child clairvoyant, had held conversations with a being she called simply "Father." When she asked his name, he replied "Kut-Hu-Mi." When she later discovered Koot Hoomi in Theosophical literature, he revealed that he had chosen her for special hierarchical work—to write the teachings of the ancient wisdom for the new age. After resigning from their church in Eaton Rapids, Michigan, the Chaneys moved to Los Angeles, California, and began their independent endeavor.

Astara is one of the most eclectic of bodies. The eclecticism is a reflection of the varied strong influences on the Chaneys at points in their lives: Spiritualism, Theosophy, yoga, Christianity, as well as the expressed desire to allow Astara to be a center of all religions and philosophies. These various tendencies have found unity, however, in the teaching of Hermes Mercurious Trismegistus, the ancient Egyptian Ptoh said to have organized the mystery schools from which all others have derived. Astara conceives of itself as a mystery school in the Hermetic tradition. The name is from the Greek goddess of divine justice, Astraea, and was chosen as a sign of the renewal of the Golden Age.

Hermes taught of God, the cosmos, and man, each in relation to the others. God is the only uncreated who emanates his seven attributes and all that is. He also taught seven laws. Basic is the matical law of correspondence, "As above, so below." According to Hermes, our world is a microcosm of the macrocosm, the universe. This law is the basis of alchemy. The law of vibration says everything is in motion. Other laws deal with polarity, cycles, cause and effect, gender, and mind.

These laws encompass a number of practices. Lama Yoga is a consciousness-expanding method taught originally to Earlyne Chaney by the masters. The chanting of the holy name, "Om," is encompassed under the law of vibration. A natural food diet, preferably vegetarian, is encouraged. The arcane rhythm techniques include numerous yogic practices and breathing techniques.

For many years, the center for Astara was a congregation in Los Angeles where regular Sunday services were held. The real heart of Astara, however, has always been the correspondence lessons called the Book of Life. It is Astara's belief that written instructions by a mystery school can function as a guru in teaching the student. Astarians are led through ascending degrees of twenty-two lessons each. An active healing ministry is conducted by both Earlyne and Robert Chaney and their appointed representatives. In 1976 the headquarters were moved from Los Angeles to Upland, California. Astara has become well known through its large ads in major psychic periodicals such as *Fate Magazine*. The Chaneys are also popular seminar teachers and prolific authors, both having published many books on varied mystical and esoteric subjects.

Membership: In 1995 there were approximately 15,000 Astara students worldwide.

Periodicals: *Voice of Astara.*

Sources:

Chaney, Earlyne. *Beyond Tomorrow.* Upland, CA: Astara, 1985.

___. *The Book of Beginning Again.* Upland, CA: Astara, 1981.

___. *Remembering.* Los Angeles: Astara's Library of Mystical Classics, 1974.

___. *Shining Moments of a Mystic.* Upland, CA: Astara, 1976.

Chaney, Earlyne, and William L. Messick. *Kundalini and the Third Eye.* Upland, CA: Astara's Library of Mystical Classics, 1980.

Chaney, Robert. *Mysticism, the Journey Within.* Upland, CA: Astra's Library of Mystical Classics, 1979.

Chaney, Robert Galen. *The Inner Way.* Los Angeles, CA: DeVorss & Co., 1962.

★1573★
Brotherhood of the White Temple
PO Box 966
Castle Rock, CO 80104

The Brotherhood of the White Temple was formed in Denver in 1930 by Doreal, a long-time student of occultism and a "channel for bringing the ancient wisdom to the Western Student." Doreal claims contact with the Great White Lodge, the Elder Brothers

of man (figures similar to the ascended masters, spirits who were once human and now teach humans about spiritual reality). Doreal is the agent for the coming Golden Age in which the brotherhood of man will be established on earth. Integral parts of the Brotherhood of the White Temple are the White Temple Church, which emphasizes the "Original Gnostic Teachings of Jesus," and the Shamballa Ashrama, a tract of 1,560 acres at Sedalia, Colorado, where a community of Brotherhood members is housed and the headquarters are located. From the publishing plant the numerous booklets and lessons written by Doreal are printed and distributed. The booklets cover the whole range of occult topics.

The teachings of the Brotherhood come from the central core of occult teachings, drawing heavily on Kabbalistic images. (The Kabbalah is a Jewish magical system.) God is conceived as the all-pervasive one, and man is a spark of the divine. The soul is incarnate for the purpose of overcoming negation and darkness and changing itself into order and light. The fall of man was caused by his being overwhelmed by inharmony after his creation. The teachings of the White Brotherhood emphasize methods of establishing harmony and cover various topics in the occult tradition (Atlantis, Lemuria, the Masters of Tibet and the Great Pyramid). In keeping with the occult tradition, an allegorical approach to the Bible is offered.

From the headquarters in Sedalia, booklets and lessons are offered by correspondence to members around the country. Lessons are divided into four neophyte grades and twelve temple grades. After completion (approximately four and one-half years), a member is invited into the inner work.

Membership: Not reported. Approximately 50 families live at the Ashrama, and corresponding students are located across the United States.

Periodicals: *Light on the Path.*

Sources:

Doreal, M. *Maitreya, Lord of the World.* Sedalia, CO: Brotherhood of the White Temple, n.d.

___. *Man and the Mystic Universe.* Denver: Brotherhood of the White Temple, n.d.

___. *Personal Experiences amongthe Masters and Great Adepts in Tibet.* Sedalia, CO: Brotherhood of the White Temple, n.d.

___. *Secret Teachings of the Himalayan Gurus.* Denver: Brotherhood the White Temple, n.d.

★1574★
Christian Fellowship Organization
(Defunct)

Among the most outstanding of the occult-metaphysical teachers in Southern California in the decades immediately before and after World War II was Edward Lewis Hodges, a San Diego physician. He claimed to be the representative and earthly head of the Secret Order of the Christian Brotherhood and School of Christian Initiation. The order consists of those evolved beings who had in ages past spiritualized their body, perfected their wisdom and understanding, and had been given the keys to the Kingdom Universal to rule the earth (similar to what other groups term the Great White Brotherhood). Hodges, as an initiate of the order, was given its teachings and told to propagate them. He founded the Christian Fellowship Organization and in 1938 published the *Teachings of the Secret der of the Christian Brotherhood.*

According to Hodges, the order taught how to achieve liberation from death through the restoration and spiritualization of the body. Knowledge of the spiritualization processes is as old as humanity, but is periodically almost forgotten. At one point Jesus, head of the order, appeared to teach that the great secret of life was God the Universal All expressed through the Christ which is simply the mortal body. The Christ within the human form is what saves. The first step on the path of initiation is realizing oneness with that Christ within.

New students of the Christian Fellowship Organization were invited to place themselves under the "cultural condition of the Christian Brotherhood," by invoking its presence. They were also taught a series of formulas, i.e. affirmations, to bring about health, prosperity, and eventually the spiritualization of the body. Hodges claimed that the use of the formulas would lead to a rejuvenation of the body and ultimately to a state in which the individual can take his/her body to the heaven worlds capable of returning to earth as situations warrant.

Hodges continued to publish into the early 1950s, but no evidence of the persistence of the Christian Fellowship Organization in recent years has been uncovered.

Sources:

Hodges, Edward Lewis. *Be Healed...A Remedy That Never Fails.* San Diego: Christian Fellowship Organization, 1949.

___. *Teachings of the Secret Order of the Christian Brotherhood.* Santa Barbara, CA: J. F. Rowney Press, 1938.

___. *Wealth and Riches by Divine Right.* San Diego: Christian Fellowship Organization, 1945.

★1575★
Church of Light
2341 Coral St.
Los Angeles, CA 90031

Alternate Address: Alternative address is: Church of Light, Canada, 337 Bain Ave., Toronto, ON, Canada M4J 1B9.

The Church of Light was incorporated in 1932 in Los Angeles by Elbert Benjamine (also known by his pen name, C. C. Zain), but actually dates to 1876, when Emma Harding Britten (who the year previously had participated in the founding of the Theosophical Society) published the teachings of the occult Brotherhood of Light in her book, *Art Magic*. The Brotherhood of Light was, according to the Church of Light tradition, formed in 2400 B.C. by a group which separated from the theocracy of Egypt. It has existed since that time as a secret order and is called the source of the science upon which Western civilization rests. Its initiates are said to have included Thales, Pythagoras, and Plato. It has continued to exist on the inner planes as well as the outer. (The outer plane is the one people live on; the inner plane contains ghostly bodies and is visible only to psychics.)

In the nineteenth century, one M. Theon was the head of the Brotherhood of Luxor in Europe. He was contacted by T. H. Burgoyne (1855–1894), a Scot, who originally contacted the brotherhood on the inner plane. He came to America in the 1880s. Joining him was Captain Norman Astley, a retired British army officer who married Genevieve Stebbins, a member of the Brotherhood in New York. Burgoyne, while living with the Astleys in Carmel, California, wrote an original series of lessons, *Light of Egypt*, Vol. I. With the help of Dr. Henry Wagner and Mrs. Belle M. Wagner, a branch of the Brotherhood, the Hermetic Brotherhood of Light was formed. The Hermetic Brotherhood was always governed by a scribe, an astrologer and a seer. Burgoyne was the original scribe. In 1909 when Minnie Higgins, the original astrologer, died, Elbert Benjamine was called to the home of a Mrs. Anderson, the seer, to become the council's astrologer.

The teaching of the Brotherhood was the ancient Religion of the Stars, and Benjamine was appointed to prepare a complete system of occult studies by which humankind could become conversant with the religion of the stars in the coming Aquarian Age. He was guided in this task by members on the inner plane, and wrote the twenty-one series of lessons covering three branches of occult science astrology, alchemy, and magic. In 1915, he began to hold classes, which were opened to the public in 1918. The lessons were completed in 1934. In 1913, the Hermetic Brotherhood of Luxor was closed and its mission was turned over to Benjamine.

The Church of Light teaches that there are two orders of truth—religion and science—between which there can be no true antagonism. The only book infallible in interpreting the will of deity is the book of nature. There is but one religion, nature's laws. Astrology is stressed as a means of interpreting nature, though all occult arts are recognized. The main program of the church consists of twenty-one courses. The member is given a Hermeticism certificate upon completion of the 21 courses. Service to others is stressed as a means to evolution from man to angel. The life of service to others is the life of the Spirit. Reincarnation is not a belief of the church.

The Church of Light is headed by a president. Upon Benjamine's death in 1951, he was succeeded by Edward Doane. The present president is Paul M. Brewer. There are a vice-president and secretary-treasurer. An annual meeting of the church is held at the headquarters in Los Angeles. Ordained ministers may establish branch churches where interest warrants, and individual members taking correspondence courses are located across the United States.

Membership: In 1995 the church reported approximately 1,000 members worldwide of which 900 were in the United States. Most of the foreign members are in Australia.

Periodicals: *The Church of Light Quarterly.*

Remarks: According to occult historian A. E. Waite, Thomas Burgoyne is a pseudonym adopted by one Thomas Henry Dalton, a convicted felon (on fraud charges) who actually came to America to escape a scandal concerning the Hermetic Brotherhood. M. Theon, also according to Waite, was a man named Peter Davidson, possibly identical with Norman Astley.

Sources:

Astrological Research & Reference Encyclopedia. 2 vols. Los Angeles: Church of Light, 1972.

Burgoyne, Thomas H. *The Light of Egypt.* 2 vols. Albuquerque, NM: Sun Publishing Company, 1980.

Gibson, Christopher. "The Religion of the Stars: The Hermetic Philosophy of C. C. Zain." *Gnosis* 38 (Winter 1996): 58—63.

Godwin, Joscelyn, Christian Chanel, annd John P. Deveney. *The Hermatic Brotherhood of Luxor.* York Beach, ME: Samuel Weiser, 1995.

Wagner, H. O., comp. *A Treasure Chest of Wisdom.* Denver, CO: H. O. Wagner, 1967.

★1576★
Gnostic Association of Cultural and Anthropological Studies
Box 291488
Los Angeles, CA 90029

The Gnostic Association of Cultural and Anthropological Studies was formed in 1952 by Columbian native Samuel Aun Weor (d. 1977), described by his followers as the Kaiki Avatar of the Age of Aquarius. During his early years he studied with Dr. Arnold Krumm Heller, a German esotericist, and over the years as he continued his studies became a master of the esoteric realms in his own right. He began to prepare his own synthesis of esoteric teachings based upon his investigation of other planes of consciousness, out of which he authored a number of books. The basic teachings are embodied in a 1961 volume, *The Perfect Matrimony*. The association spread through South America and then to Europe, Japan, Ireland, Australia, France, Spain, Portugal, Africa, Canada, and the United States. The first American centers were opened in Los Angeles and New York in 1970.

While accepting a basic theosophical framework for his teachings, Weor wrote about the practical synthesis of all religions, schools, orders, sects, lodges, and yogas. His findings, which he experienced directly, were presented in *The Perfect Matrimony*. The essence of the system is called "el sexo yoga" in Spanish and "sexual alchemy" in English. Weor taught that the redemption of humanity is in the transmutation of the sexual energies. (The practice taught by Weor draws heavily from Hindu Tantric and Chinese Taoist sources, and is to be sharply distinguished from the "sex magic" of Aleister Crowley and his followers in the Ordo Templi Orientis.)

Weor taught that God manifested as both Father (knowledge) and Mother (love). The "Perfect Matrimony" is the union of two persons who know how to love. With the fire of love, individuals can transform themselves into gods. The secret of the fire is discovered in the sexual act. During the sexual act, participants are charged with universal magnetism. True white magicians stop the act before any semen is spilled. To transmute the creative energies, so that orgasm does not occur and therefore the semen is not released, is equated with the commitment of the act of sexual magic. The kundalini, the latent energy believed by Hindu Tantrics to reside at the base of the spine, awakens and travels upward. Thereby the individual awakens consciousness.

After its arrival in the United States, the association opened centers in Spanish-speaking communities in several cities. Though most instruction is still in Spanish, there are several centers that now provide free lectures in English, and most of Weor's books have been translated. The first issues of the English-language periodical appeared in 1987. The first International Congress of the association was held in Montreal in 1986.

Membership: In 1988 the association reported 5,000 members in more than 20 centers in the United States and more than 10,000 members in 50 centers in Canada. Foreign centers were located in 25 countries worldwide.

Periodicals: *The Gnostic Arhat.*

Sources:

Almarez, Anita Ford. *Simple Introduction to the Ancient Science of Gnosis.* Chicago: Gnostic Association, n.d.

Weor, Samuel Aun. *The Awakening of Man.* Chicago: Gnostic Association of Anthropological and Cultural Studies, n.d.

___. *Fundamental Education.* Los Angeles: Gnostic Association, 1987.

___. *Manual of Practical Magic.* Los Angeles: Gnostic Association, 1988.

___. *Manual of Revolutionary Psychology.* Los Angeles: Gnostic Association, 1987.

___. *The Perfect Matrimony.* New York: Adonai Editorial, 1980.

___. *Zodiacal Course: Hermetic Astrology.* Los Angeles: Gnostic Association, 1986.

★1577★
Lemurian Fellowship
Box 397
Ramona, CA 92065

The Lemurian Fellowship was founded on September 16, 1936, by Dr. Robert D. Stelle, who claimed to be operating under the direction and guidance of the Lemurian Brotherhood, one of the original mystery schools of this human era. The Lemurian Fellowship considers itself the mundane channel of the Lemurian Brotherhood and is affiliated with no other group or organization.

The fellowship was first formed in Chicago, establishing its permanent headquarters on two properties in Ramona, California, in 1941. One property houses the headquarters of the Lemurian Fellowship. The other is the home of the Lemurian Order, the only student organization sponsored or recognized by the Lemurian Fellowship, the membership of which has passed through an extended study of the Lemurian Philosophy.

Since its inception and incorporation as a California nonprofit religious corporation, the fellowship has offered a course of balanced religious instruction called the Lemurian Philosophy. The Philosophy is based upon the teachings of Christ with its primary purpose that of helping people recognize, understand, and apply God's Universal Laws and Principles.

The Lemurian Philosophy is released through a series of printed lessons. The main program of the fellowship is its correspondence school, through which individual instruction by printed word is geared to fit the needs and capabilities of the individual student. Students are encouraged to face life rather than try to escape it. This is accomplished by working with such practical areas as health, finances, and the human association encountered in family, marriage, work, and community. Moderation and the balancing of the three sides of human nature (the physical, mental, and spiritual), along with service to others, are taught as vital parts of the purpose of human life. In applying cosmic principles, students are helped to work with their everyday problems, discovering that their greatest learning opportunities come through their associations with other people. The building of a more noble character is the goal of all of its members.

Background subjects include the origin of man, civilizations, human relationships, the life of Christ, and Cosmic or Universal Principles, including the laws of cause and effect, transmutation, compensation, and precipitation. The study of virtues such as patience, tolerance, charity, and kindness (and others) emphasize the need to work on self through attention to the needs of, and assistance to, others. The continuity of human life, or reincarnation, is a basic precept of the Lemurian Philosophy.

Since the founder's death in 1952, the work of the Lemurian Fellowship has been carried on by a staff who live and work on fellowship property in Ramona. All responsibility for the administration and conduct of the Lemurian Fellowship rests with a Board of Governors. Lemurian Fellowship publications include *Into the Sun* a brochure that introduces the Lemurian Philosophy, and *The Sun Rises* which details the early developments of the Mukulian civilization. The fellowship also holds the copyright of *An Earth Dweller's Return.*

According to the fellowship, the Great Being, Christ, first taught humanity when he appeared as Melchizedek on the continent of Mu (Lemuria), now submerged in the Pacific Ocean. Christ, as Poseidonis, appeared for a second time many thousands of years later on Atlantis, once again to help humanity recognize its true purpose. A complete record of these and subsequent civilizations up to our own is stored in the archives of the Lemurian Brotherhood. Only when correct use is made of the information that has thus far been released, will the succeeding phase of the brotherhood's Plan be made known.

The goal for which the fellowship strives is the eventual realization of the Kingdom of God on earth. While such a concept is common to many religions, the Lemurian Philosophy makes no predictions or prophecies about when such an advanced society may come into being. The Lemurian Fellowship stresses to its students that it will be a steady, sure effort at building more noble characters on the part of many that will enable mankind to eventually experience a better world.

Membership: Not reported.

Periodicals: *Lemurian View Point.*

Sources:

de la Torre, Teofilo. *Psycho-Physical Regeration, Rejuvenation and Longevity.* Milwaukee: Lemurian Press, 1938.

The Lemurian Scribe. *Be It Resolved.* Milwaukee: Lemurian Press, 1940.

Phylos the Tibetan. *An Earth Dweller Returns.* Milwaukee: Lemurian Press, 1940.

Stelle, Robert D. *The Sun Rises.* Ramona, CA: Lemurian Fellowship, 1952.

★1578★
Mayan Order
Box 2710
San Antonio, TX 78299

The Mayan Order, it is claimed, was founded by people who had rediscovered the teachings of an ancient group of holy men

(H'Men) who dominated Mayan culture and to whom the greatness of the civilization was due. These men possessed great knowledge of astrology, the calendar, medicine, mathematics and occult wisdom. Only a few H'Men survived the Spanish conquest, and only three copies of the ancient books have survived. What is known of the ancient wisdom is preserved today by the Mayan Order.

Mayan material is distributed in degree-lessons through correspondence. Early in the work, the student is taught a very simple code; in succeeding lessons, key words are printed in that code. Reincarnation is stressed within a framework of New Thought metaphysics, with the New Thought emphasis on light, mind, and the power of positive thinking. Psychokinesis in practiced by each student. Appropriate rituals are learned at each initiation; content is heavily biblical.

Like Astara, the Mayan Order has become known through its ads in various psychic periodicals. It is under the guidance of Rose Dawn, the registrar and supreme leader.

Membership: Not reported.

Periodicals: *Daily Meditation.*

Sources:

Dawn, Rose. *The Miracle Power.* San Antonio, TX: Mayan Press, 1959.

___. *The Search for Happiness.* Mayan Order, 1966.

★1579★
Philosophical Research Society
3910 Los Feliz Blvd.
Los Angeles, CA 90027

The Philosophical Research Society was founded in 1934 by Manly Palmer Hall (1901-1990), the most prolific and widely-read occult writer of the twentieth century. He began as a young occult scholar and lecturer in the 1920s as a leader in the Church of the People in Los Angeles. During these years he began to publish his own books under the imprint of the Hall Publishing Company. The Philosophical Research Society was the culmination of a dream to establish a philosophical/religious institution modeled on the ancient philosopher/religious schools of Pythagoras, Plato, and the Serapeum of Alexander. Its goals include research, application of the occult heritage to modern problems, and the dissemination of the ancient wisdom by a variety of means.

Hall's basic position was closely related to an Eastern idealism. Life is eternal, it is an endless unfoldment towards the real. It has its beginnings in the immeasurable past and its ultimates in the immeasurable future. Man's present individual existence is but one episode of innumerable ones. Law brings us into life and is the purpose of living. The seven laws of life are evolution, cause and effect, polarity, reincarnation, harmony and rythym, generation, and vibration. Man may come into harmony with these but they are immutable. All of Hall's lecturing and writing has been an explication of this perspective. He has also published a number of historical studies of occultism and occultists.

The Philosophical Research Society is centered at its headquarters complex in Los Angeles. Included are a research library, bookstore and publishing facilities. Books, booklets, and lecture transcripts are distributed across the United States. Correspondence courses are offered in a wide variety of topics. Regular classes and Sunday morning services are offered weekly. Through his publications, Hall continues to make a significant impact on the psychic/occult community.

Membership: The PRS is not a membership organization.

Periodicals: *Ancient Wisdom for Modern Living.*

Sources:

Hall, Manly P. *Growing Up with Grandmother.* Los Angeles: Philosophical Research Society, 1985.

___. *Man, the Grand Symbol of the Mysteries.* Los Angeles: Philosophical Research Center, 1947.

___. *The Mystical Christ.* Los Angeles: Philosophical Research Society, 1951.

___. *Questions and Answers.* Los Angeles: Philosophers Press, 1937.

___. *Reincarnation, the Cycle of Necessity.* Los Angeles: Philosophical Research Society, 1946.

★1580★
Sabian Assembly
℅ Sabian Publishing Society
PO Box 7
Stanwood, WA 98292

The Sabian Assembly evolved from a class in astrology led by Marc Edmund Jones in New York City as the culmination of a decade of work that included a "meeting with a master." The following year, he held a second class in Los Angeles, California. On October 17, 1923, with a group of his students who had found some direction in the occult truths and who wished to test them in their lives, he created the Sabian Assembly. His charter called for the group to be "experimental" in nature. The astrological emphasis broadened to a synthesis of philosophy, psychology, and religion against a background of occult insights. In 1925, Jones published *Key Truths of Occult Philiosophy*, which he revised and reissued in 1948 as *Occult Philosophy*. His *Ritual of Living* was published in 1930 and revised in 1957 as *The Sabian Manual*. From 1923 through 1943, Jones wrote 3,000 lessons which are circulated and studied weekly by members of the Sabian Assembly. The Sabian Assembly has continued as a group, oriented to the Philosophy of Concepts as enunciated by Jones. After World War II, it gradually spread with the increasing popularity of Jones' books and lectures. A free-lance writer and ordained Presbyterian pastor, who earned his doctorate in philosophy from Columbia University in 1948, Jones emerged as, intellectually, one of the strongest occultists in the eyes of the public.

The Sabian Assembly is an openly eclectic body. Jones acknowledged that he had drawn from New Thought, Theosophy, Kabbalism, and Spiritualism, as well as from Eastern and Western theological and philosophical traditions. This reformulation of the ancient wisdom is seen as a special way of understanding and self-dedication. The Sabian project is basically the application of Cabala, as Jones interpreted it, to all of life. Since the occult is easily warped into a structure of illusions, the group effort reinforces the student's need for verifiable experience in direct proportion to spiritual realization.

The Sabian Assembly is a solar group whose occult discipline derives its authority from within the self (as opposed to lunar groups who see authority as represented outwardly by a hierarchical system). Sabian students maintain individual "work in consciousness" with a consistent focus on spiritual healing.

Rituals were developed at the request of the sponsors, the invisible council of the Assembly. Rituals are provided for healing, for the initiatory discipline, for the quarterly reviews of progress, and for specific occasions such as the dedication of a life (baptism), a departure (funeral), or a partnership, such as marriage.

The Sabian Assembly continues as a loosely organized fellowship of aspirants, each pursuing his or her own course of study in Jones' material, with the support of Sabian study groups where possible. Prime working principles of the fellowship are "respect for personality" and MYOB, or "mind your own business." Membership is open to any who wish to participate in this approach to the Solar Mysteries. After two years as a neophyte, a new student may choose to participate in the five-year acolyte discipline, which requires work in consciousness and a course of spiritual exercises as well as specific volunteer work for the Assembly. Beyond that, students may continue with three years of legate studies, although the group gives no outward recognition of inward status.

Marc Edmund Jones served as chancellor of the Sabian Assembly until shortly before his death in March 1980. He has not been replaced as chancellor. The work of the Assembly continues, without a central headquarters or staff, on the basis of volunteer work coordinated by an unpaid administrator. New students receive copies of *Sabian Manual* and *The Sabian Book*, which is a collection of short essays characteristic of the Sabian approach. Sabian lesson materials are re-edited and distributed by students.

Membership: In 1997 there were more than 100 regular students in North America and Europe.

Periodicals: *Sabian News Letter.* • *Sabiana Journal.*

Sources:

Jones, Marc Edmund. *Occult Philosophy.* Standwood, WA: Sabian Publishing Society, 1971.

___. *The Ritual of Living.* Los Angeles, CA: J. F. Rowny Press, 1930.

___. *The Sabian Book.* Stanwood, WA: Sabian Publishing Society, 1973.

___. *The Sabian Manual.* New York: Sabian Publishing Society, 1957.

___. *The Scope of Astrological Prediction.* Stanwood, WA: Sabian Publishing Society, 1969.

★1581★
Soulcraft
Box 192
Noblesville, IN 46060

William Dudley Pelley (1890-1965), the elucidator of the Liberation-Soulcraft philosophy, was a New England newspaperman in 1918 when he was sent by the Methodist Episcopal Church to the Far East to report on foreign missions. He also was commissioned at that time by the YMCA to venture into Siberia to report on the Russian Revolution. In the early 1920s, he gained a national reputation as a magazine writer. By the end of the decade, he had turned to Hollywood and produced several movie scenarios. One of his novels, *Drag*, was produced as one of the first sound movies.

It was during this time, in 1928, that he had an out-of-body experience (an experience of one's consciousness becoming separated from the body). He described the experience in an article for the popular *American Magazine* in the March 1929 issue. This unsought out-of-body experience led him into the world of extrasensory perception and the recording or "channeling" of remarkable messages from higher intelligences, called mentors. These messages form the basis of the Soulcraft philosophy: Every human spirit-soul is a part of the Godhead and, therefore, related to every other spirit-soul. Spirit-souls come to the classroom of Earth in physical form to become aware of themselves and their relationship to others and to God through many lives. The questions opened by this basic premise form the subject matter of the more than two dozen books written by Pelley. He also recorded messages from a source wishing to be called the Elder Brother, which are found in a book entitled *The Golden Scripts* (1941). Pelley refused to found a church on this philosophy for fear of its becoming crystalized and dogmatic and losing its open-endedness. Fellowship Press, Inc. serves as the distributor of the Soulcraft books, thus keeping the philosophy alive.

After Pelley's death, his daughter, Adelaide Pelley Pearson, and son-in-law, Melford Pearson, have continued to print and distribute his metaphysical books and also his book outlining the blueprint for a healthier and sounder economic system, *No More Hunger*. Soulcraft itself is not incorporated. Fellowship Press is a corporation owned and operated by the Pearson's for the purpose of printing Pelley's books.

Membership: Soulcraft is not a membership organization; rather, it serves as a center of dissemination for the Soulcraft teachings.

Remarks: During the 1930s, Pelley became well known in a second and even more controversial area of public life. During the 1930s he formed an organization he called the Silver Shirts. It was avowedly anti-Communist, anti-New Deal, and against what Pelley believed to be the undue Jewish influence in government, banking, and the media. His operation came under scrutiny of the government as Adolf Hitler rose to power and war clouds gathered in Europe. Remaining adamant in his beliefs, even after Pearl Harbor, he was arrested and tried for sedition in 1942. Convicted, he was sentenced to 15 years in federal prison, but was then immediately included with a number of other defendants in a "mass sedition trial" in Washington, D.C. That trial continued for a number of years. In the end it was thrown out by the Supreme Court which termed it a "travesty of justice." Meanwhile, Pelley served over seven years on his prior conviction. The last years of his life were spent on his metaphysical work.

Sources:

The Golden Scripts. Noblesville, IN: Soulcraft Chapels, 1951.

Pelley, William Dudley. *The Door To Revelation.* Asheville, North Carolina: Foundation Fellowship, 1936.

___. *No More Hunger.* Noblesville, IN: Aquila Press, 1961.

___. *Seven Minutes in Eternity.* Noblesville, IN: Soulcraft Chapels, 1954.

___. *Star Guests.* Noblesville, IN: Soulcraft Press, 1950.

Strong, Donald S. *Organized Anti-Semitism in America.* Washington, DC: American Council on Public Affairs, 1941.

★1582★
Stelle Group
127 Sun St.
Stelle, IL 60919

The Stelle Group, named for Robert D. Stelle, founder of the Lemurian Fellowship, and its sister society, the Adelphi Organization, were founded by Richard Kieninger (b. 1927). As early as 1953, Kieninger had been associated with the Lemurian Fellowship, from whom he received his initial occult training, but in 1963 he broke from it and formed the Stelle Group. The same year the group was formed, *The Ultimate Frontier*, written by Kieninger under a pen-name, Eklal Kueshana, was released. It is an autobiography and discussion of the basic philosophy of the Stelle Group. In 1966, the Lemuria Builders was formed to acquaint the public with the group's philosophy and to recruit new members. Stelle School was opened in 1968. Originally the headquarters of the Group were in Kieninger's home in Chicago, but in 1973, with the official founding of the community of Stelle, Illinois, the offices shifted there.

Essential to an understanding of the Stelle Group is the reported experience of its leader. Kieninger claims his first contact with several mysterious beings was on his 12th birthday. The initial contact, a Dr. White, taught reincarnation, told Kieninger of his past lives, including ones as the biblical King David and Pharaoh Akhnaton, and began to explain Kieninger's mission to found a new nation. Later that year, he was given a secret name, permanently incised into his skin, and at the same time was taught of the 12 Brotherhoods (five greater and seven lesser). In 1945, Dr. White gave him the place of the ideal community—Stelle City. Stelle is a community near Kankakee, Illinois, to which the activity and life of the group gradually shifted over the 1970s. As an intentional community, it is seen as one preparatory model of the new society that will be formed in the next decades. From 1973 to 1982, the focus of the Stelle Group was upon the community of Stelle. However, in 1976, Kieninger formed a sister organization to the Stelle Group, the Adelphi Organization. It purchased 78 acres of land 35 miles east of Dallas, Texas, upon which a community open only to a dedicated core of disciples of Kieninger's teachings (i.e. members of either the Adelphi Organization or the Stelle Group) was being developed. Residents must have lived in the vicinity of either Stelle or Dallas to attend a weekly orientation for a year prior to their moving into the community. Then, in 1982, the headquarters of the Stelle group were moved to Dallas and the community of Stelle was opened to nonmembers who nevertheless wanted to participate in the experimental community life. The Stelle Community Association was chartered in 1982.

Kieninger wrote in *The Ultimate Frontier* that, at the end of the twentieth century, a massive natural catastrophe leading to a rearrangement of the land masses will be triggered by the alignment of the planets in this solar system on May 5, 2000 A.D. It will be preceded by an economic depression that was to begin after the 200th birthday of the United States, but prior to the 201st birthday, and by the Battle of Armageddon, an atomic war to end in 1999. The people of Stelle and Adelphi will be among the ten percent of the world's population to survive this catastrophe. After the worst is past, members of the brotherhood will rebuild a new Philadelphia.

The Stelle Group is now seen as a school offering basic training in the philosophy of the Brotherhoods. It leads individuals into the Adelphi Organization and the future community of Philadelphia.

Kieninger has not been associated with either the Stelle Group or the Adelphi Organizations since 1986. Both the Stelle Group and the Adelphi Organization have separately elected boards that manage their affairs. Both are orienting their activities around preparation for the troubles believed due at the end of the century and the development of resources and skills to rebuild the new society.

Membership: In 1988, the Stelle Group reported approximately 200 members nationally, with an additional 6,000 who follow the progress of the group. There were 47 residential units at Stelle City with slow growth proceeding.

Periodicals: *The Stelle Group Newsletter.* Send orders to Box 75, Quinlan, TX 75474. • *The Philosopher's Stone.* Send orders to Stelle Administration Building, Stelle, IL 60919.

Sources:

Kieninger, Richard. *The Hidden Christ.* Dallas, TX: Paragon Press, 1989.

___. *Observations.* 4 vols. Chicago: Stelle Group, 1971-79.

___. *Spiritual Seekers' Guidebook and Hidden Threats to Mental and Spiritual Freedom.* Quinlan, TX: Stelle Group, 1986.

Kueshana, Eklal [Richard Kieninger, psued.] *The Ultimate Frontier.* Chicago: Stelle Group, 1963.

Valentine, Tom. *The Great Pyramid: Man's Monument to Man.* New York: Pinnacle Books, 1975.

Theosophy

★1583★
Aquarian Foundation
(Defunct)

Not to be confused with the presently existing Spiritualist reorganization of the same name, the theosophical Aquarian Foundation was established in 1927 by Edward Arthur Wilson. The previous year, Wilson reported that he had been "translated in spirit to the higher realms in order to meet the eleven masters of Wisdom." As head of the foundation, Wilson assumed the name "Brother XII." Wilson initially placed his work in the context of the major program of the Theosophical Society of the time, the announcement of the arrival of the World Teacher in the person of Jiddu Krishnamurti. Brother XII denied Krishnamurti's assigned role and suggested instead that preparation for the coming World Teacher would be made through the foundation. A community was established in British Columbia in Canada. Over 100 theosophists left England with him at the beginning of 1927 to become the community's initial residents. Brother XII authored several books detailing the foundation's basic theosophical teachings and perspective.

The foundation was planted near Nanaimo, on Vancouver Island. Residents turned over their worldly possessions, and many friends of the work contributed additional sums. The colony flourished in spite of the introduction of some new teachings not otherwise disclosed in Brother XII's books. The immediate goal of the foundation was to give birth to a new generation of advanced human beings. To accomplish this end, each of the colony females, no matter what their present marital status, was to have sexual relations with Brother XII, and the resultant children raised by the colony were to be the individuals who would actually receive the coming World Teacher in 1975. Brother XII also designated one colonist, Myrtle Baumgartner, as the mother of the World Teacher. Baumgartner did not produce a male child, however, and was soon replaced by Mabel Skottowe, known to her fellow colonists as Madame Zee.

The work continued until 1934, when two former members filed suits claiming that Wilson had treated them harshly and had misused the funds entrusted to him. The trials, which received sensational coverage in the press, were both decided for the plaintiffs, who were awarded both property and money. Wilson and Madame Zee soon disappeared, and the colony dissolved.

Sources:

Brother XII. *Foundation Letters and Teachings.* Akron, OH: Sun Publishing Co., 1927.

___. *The Three Truths.* Akron, OH: Sun Publishing Co., 1927.

Oliphant, John. *Brother Twelve: The Incredible Story of Canada' False Prophet.* Toronto: Mc Clelland & Stewart, 1992.

___. "The Teachings of Brother XII." *Theosophical History* 4, 6/7 (April/July 1993): 194–219.

Santucci, James. "The Aquarian Foundation." *Communal Societies* 9 (1989): 39–61.

Wilson, Herbert Emmerson. *Canada's False Prophet.* Richmond Hill, ON: Simon & Schuster, 1967.

★1584★
Hermetic Society for World Service
Current address not obtained for this edition.

The Hermetic Society of World Service was founded in 1947 for the study of the Hermetic gnosis or ancient wisdom. While much of the teaching of the society is esoteric, and hence reserved for members only, its general perspective includes several basic truths. The society asserts human brotherhood, irrespective of race or nationality as a realizable condition essential for life on earth. Humans evolve through the process of reincarnation, and the moral order is dictated by the law of karma, the law of ethical causation. Salvation is attained only by the conscious effort of the individual through a process of spiritual growth over a number of lifetimes. The Society is headed by its hierophant and spiritual guru who is believed to be in contact with the Sirian Brotherhood, the spiritual hierarchy dedicated to the dissemination of the Light of Spiritual Knowledge throughout the world.

The society maintains that earth is in a period of change into the New Age, which is operating in the world process and is bringing about changes in science, religion, philosophy, civilization, and the way of life for humanity. What was termed the Battle of Armageddon in the Bible is currently being fought out on the Inner (invisible) Planes between the righteous and unrighteous and will soon descend to the visible realm and manifest in a period of war, tribulation, and crisis. The Society offers resources for individuals to live through the changing times and proceed to greater levels of attainment. Those without these resources will be cast aside from the mainstream of human evolution. Those who adopt the New Age spiritual techniques will have the opportunity to prepare themselves for entry into the Spiritual Universe as partakers of the Divine Nature.

The Society seeks to return humanity from the Path of Outgoing (directed away from their divine origins) to the Path of Return to God and the soul's eternal home. In this endeavor, the society teaches a technique of soul immortalization and methods to manifest the powers latent in the individual human soul, and the law governing the technique and disciples required to bring about the regeneration of human nature, preparatory to the gaining of liberation from the necessity of reincarnation and the operation of the law of karma. To achieve liberation, the individual must atone and liquidate the effects of past sins of body, mind, and speech, and undertake a process of spiritual regeneration. In the end the individual soul will gain immortality. Immortality must be sought for in accordance with the principles of esoteric science.

America has a special place in the New Age. It is the place designated as the new Holy Land of Earth. It is the domain designated by the spiritual hierarchy who guide human destiny for the preservation of the seeds for the continuation of human life. It is the grail that will hold the Great Cosmic Light that will illumine the whole world.

Membership: Not reported.

Sources:

Browne, Robert T. *Introduction to Hermetic Science and Philosophy.* Hermetic Society, n.d. 4 page tract.

★1585★
International Group of Theosophists
(Defunct)

The International Group of Theosophists is a small group which grew out of the American Theosophical movement in southern California. It was founded in the 1940s by Boris Mihailovich de Zirkoff (1902-1981), the grand-nephew of Helena Petrovna Blavatsky. Its objectives were to uphold and promote the original principles of the modern Theosophical movement and to disseminate the teachings of the esoteric philosophy as set forth by Blavatsky and her teachers. The group has tried to operate outside of the disagreements of the more established lodges and has cooperated with them in Zirkoff's major life work, the editing and publishing of Blavatsky's collected writings. For over thirty years it published *Theosophia,* a quarterly journal (1944-1981), but issued a final volume in the summer of 1981 as a tribute issue to its founder.

★1586★
Temple of the People
Box 7095
Halcyon, CA 93420

The Temple of the People began in Syracuse, New York, during the period of the disruption of the American branch of the Theosophical Society following the death of founders Helena Petrovna Blavatsky and William Q. Judge. Following Judge in the leadership of the American Society was Katherine Tingley, who many, including the group in Syracuse, rejected. Under the leadership of William H. Dower (1866-1937) and Francis A. LaDue (1849-1922), they became independent and formed the Temple of the People in 1898. Within a few years, they purchased a tract of land at Halcyon, California, (near Pismo Beach) and moved there in 1903. In 1904, Dower opened a sanatorium, which became famous during the generation of its operation for its treatment of tubercular patients, alcoholics, and drug addicts. In 1903, the Temple organized the Temple Home Association as a cooperative colony. The Temple Home Association existed through 1949 when it was reorganized as set forth in its original bylaws into the Home of the Temple Associated, Inc. The HTA was dissolved in 1992 and all properties are administered by the Temple Corporation.

The Temple began with the contact from the Mahatmas, or Masters, through LaDue and Dower, known respectively as "Blue Star" and "Red Star," the designations given them by the Masters.

They were told to abandon the Tingley-led society, and through their reception and publishing of continuing materials from the Masters, to carry on the work begun by Madame Blavatsky. Over the years, they produced an impressive set of materials, including a large volume, *Theogenesis,* a third volume of commentaries on the Stanzas of Dyzan. Madame Blavatsky wrote *The Secret Doctrine,* the two volumes of which were entitled *Anthropogenesis* and *Cosmogenesis,* as a commetary on those parts of the Stanzas that were known to her.

According to the Temple, the spiritual hierarchy is led by the Central Spiritual Sun, the Christos, the expression of the Infinite Godhead. Other Masters, members of the Great White Brotherhood, embody aspects of the divine light, key members being the Masters of the Seven Rays (of the color spectrum). Integral to the original teachings given to the Temple's founders from the Master Hilarion, Regent of the Red Ray, was a prophecy concerning the soon-to-occur birth of an avatar, an incarnation of the Christos, an event which only happens every 2,000 years. The first generation of the Temple was to a great extent motivated by that expectation and the belief that members were the spearhead of the Messianic Age into which humanity was moving. These emphases, which still undergird the Temple's understanding of its educational mission and work in the world, are summarized in the three *Teachings of the Temple* volumes.

During the first generation, the life of the community at Halcyon revolved around the sanitorium and the building of the Temple. Groups that received and studied the material produced through the Temple sprang up around the country, and every summer a national convention was held. Dower succeeded LaDue as guardian-in-chief of the Temple. He was in turn succeeded by Pearl F. Dower, and she by Harold Forgostein. The present Guardian-in-Chief is Eleanor L. Shumway. The Temple has kept the material originally received by Dower and LaDue in print and their work revolves around it.

The Temple of the People is still headquartered in the community at Halcyon, which has consistently been home to approximately 100 residents. There is a lively group following in both England and Germany, and individual members around the world. The Temple is led by the guardian-in-chief (Eleanor L. Shumway) and a board of four officers appointed yearly.

Membership: An estimated 350 people are actively participating in Temple activities worldwide as of 1997.

Periodicals: *The Temple Artisan.*

Sources:

Burns, Bob, et al. *The Temple of the People.* Halcyon, CA: California Polytechnic State University, 1972.

From the Mountain Top. 3 vols. Halcyon, CA: Temple of the People, 1974-1985.

Kagan, Paul. *New World Utopias.* Baltimore: Penguin Books, 1975.

Teachings of the Temple. 3 vols. Halcyon, CA: Temple of the People, 1947-1985.

Theogenesis. Halcyon, CA: Temple of the People, 1981.

★1587★
Theosophical Society
PO Box C
Pasadena, CA 91109-7107

The Theosophical Society (TS), with international headquarters in Pasadena, California, looks to Helena Petrovna Blavatsky (1831-1891) and her teachers for its beginnings and goals. The first preamble and bylaws of the Theosophical Society, adopted on October 30, 1875, listed one, all-embracing objective: "To collect and diffuse a knowledge of the laws which govern the universe." Within a few years, the aims of the society included a Universal Brotherhood of Humanity and two further objectives in the study of the philosophies, religions, and sciences of the world, and the investigation of the powers innate in humanity and nature.

When Blavatsky died in 1891, William Q. Judge, a cofounder of the TS and general secretary of its American Section, became joint head of the esoteric work with Annie Besant, while Henry S. Olcott continued his post as president of the Society internationally. During the next few years, a number of problems concerning leadership and administration arose between Judge on the one hand and Olcott and Besant on the other. These problems eventually led to the American Section's declaration of complete autonomy at its annual convention in April 1895, and its election of Judge as president for life. This action led to the cancellation of the membership by President Olcott. The resulting division in the society reached into all sections.

After Judge's death in 1896, Katherine Tingley became head of the esoteric work and E. T. Hargrove president of the society. Within a month, Tingley laid the groundwork for a school for the revival of the lost mysteries of antiquity, and shortly thereafter formed the International Brotherhood League to implement her humanitarian concerns. In 1898, in order to give greater expression to practical altruism, she founded the Universal Brotherhood Organization and the society became known as the Universal Brotherhood and Theosophical Society of which she was the leader and official head. In 1900, she moved the headquarters from New York City to Point Loma, California (a peninsula across the bay from San Diego), where she founded a school for children, a college, and in 1919, the Theosophical University. Education for all residents of Point Loma included a balanced development of physical, mental, moral, and spiritual qualities, with emphasis on character training, music, drama, and the arts. Tingley paid regular visits to members in the United States and abroad. While lecturing to capacity audiences during her travels, she also pursued her philanthropic activities, among them the rehabilitation of prisoners. The Point Loma enterprise drew prominent educators, musicians, and artists from around the world, attracted by her leadership in cultural and humanitarian endeavors.

Tingley died in Sweden in 1929 following an auto accident in Germany. Her successor, Gottfried de Purucker, was an able leader and scholar whose literary legacy of thesophic literature is well known. Under his leadership, the original name of "The Theosophical Society" was resumed and new groups and lodges formed. In June 1942, he moved the society's headquarters, including the press, university, and library facilities to Covina, near Los Angeles, where he died a few months later.

Arthur L. Conger followed de Purucker as leader in 1945. Conger had joined the society while at Harvard during the time of Judge, was private secretary to Katherine Tingley in New York, and president of the American Section under de Purucker. Under Conger's leadership a strong publishing program was maintained and lodges and groups promoted. In 1950 he led the acquisition and move of the headquarters into new facilities in the Pasadena area. He closed the esoteric section as a means of preventing crystallization.

Conger also fostered a more practical expression of theosophy, a policy continued after his death in 1951 by his successor, James A. Long. Long founded the magazine Sunrise as a bridge between the public and the deeper teachings of theosophy and featured articles that focused upon their altruistic application. He urged members to express these truths in their daily lives and in simple nontechnical language. Following the 20 years of service by Long, Grace F. Knoche became leader of the society, and in 1972 opened the specialized collections of Theosophical University Library to the public.

Today, the society continues to pursue the principles set forth in the original program. Toward this end, the headquarters and national sections sponsor translation and publishing activities, library centers, public discussions, and study groups. Theosophical correspondence courses in the U.S. and abroad are offered free of charge except for study materials and postage, and cassette ver-

sions of Sunrise magazine and growing numbers of books are made available gratis to the visually impaired. Theosophical University Press and its overseas agencies feature the theosophic classics of Blavatsky, Judge, de Purucker and long among other writers, while adding new titles to their lists. In addition to Fellows-at-Large worldwide, national sections exist in Australasia, Finland, Germany, Great Britain, the Netherlands, Nigeria, Scandinavia, South Africa, and the United States.

Periodicals: *SUNRISE: Theosophic Perspectives* (also in Dutch, Swedish, and German editions). • *Teosofiskt Forum*—in Swedish.

Sources:

de Purucker, Gottfried. *Fountain-Source of Occultism.* Pasadena, CA: Theosophical University Press, 1974.

___. *H. P. Blavatsky.* San Diego: Point Loma Publications, 1974.

Judge, William Q. *Echoes of the Orient.* San Diego: Point Loma Publications, 1975.

___. *The Ocean of Theosophy.* Point Loma, CA: Aryan Theosophical Press, 1926.

Ryan, Charles J. *H. P. Blavatsky and the Theosophical Movement.* Pasadena, CA: Theosophical University Press, 1974.

Tingley, Katherine. *Theosophy: the Path of the Mystic.* Pasadena, CA: Theosophical University Press, 1977.

★1588★
Theosophical Society (Hartley)
% Blavatskyhius
de Ruyterstratt 74
NL-2518 AV Gravenhage, Netherlands

In 1951, the Theosophical Society, headquartered in Pasadena, California, split. The former leader of the society, Arthur L. Conger (d. 1951) had designated William Hartley (d.1956) to be his successor. However, the society's ruling council rejected Hartley in favor of James A. Long. Long and his supporters retained control of the society and its library and properties; thus Hartley and his followers were forced to reorganize. New headquarters were established in Covina, California. This branch gained few members from among American theosophists and eventually died out in the United States. But it found some measure of support in the Netherlands, and there it survives. Hartley was succeeded as head of the group by D. J. P. Kok. The present leader is Herman C. Vermeulen.

The society has these objectives: to diffuse among people a knowledge of the laws inherent in the universe; to promulgate the knowledge of the essential unity of all that is and to demonstrate that this unity is fundamental in nature; to form an active brotherhood among people; to study ancient and modern religion, science, and philosophy; and to investigate the power innate in humanity. The society promulgates its teachings in strict accordance with *The Secret Doctrine* by Madame Helena Petrovna Blavatsky and the writings of the other original leaders.

The society flourishes in Holland, with an active program of public lectures, classes, and lodge work. Much effort is being made to translate theosophical works into other languages and to publish theosophical material. Blavatskyhuis, the headquarters, houses a library. Publishing is done through the Society's corporation, the International Study Center for the Independent Search for Truth.

Membership: Not reported. In 1987, there were five lodges, all in The Netherlands.

Periodicals: *Lucifer.*

★1589★
Theosophical Society in America
Box 270
Wheaton, IL 60189-0270

Alternate Address: International headquarters: Adyar, Madras 600 020, India.

History. The Theosophical Society in America is the American Branch of the international Theosophical Society headquartered in Adyar, Madras, India. It was founded in 1875 by Helena Petrovna Blavatsky, Col. Henry S. Olcott, William Q. Judge and others. In 1879, the two principal founders, Olcott and Blavatsky, moved to India, and in 1882 established the international headquarters in Adyar. Olcott, as the first president of the society, took the lead in administrative duties and during his lifetime it became a truly international organization with lodges that circled the globe. Blavatsky became the great teacher of the movement and the founder of an independent sister organization called the Esoteric Section (associated primarily by the requirement that one must be a theosophist to be a member). The international headquarters chartered the American Section in 1886, and Judge organized the then scattered branches at an organizational convention in Cincinnati, Ohio. Following Blavatsky's death, Judge led a movement among American members to become independent of the international headquarters, and persuaded most members to join with him in the formation of what is now known in the United States as simply the Theosophical Society, with headquarters in Pasadena, California. Those lodges that remained loyal to the international headquarters were known as the American Section of the Theosophical Society.

Beginning with 14 lodges, the American society rebuilt through the first decades of the twentieth century reaching a peak in the late-1920s at around 8,000 members. During these years the society was led internationally by Annie Besant who had succeeded first Blavatsky and then Olcott in the top leadership positions of the society and the Esoteric Section. The low point of the society came as World War II began when membership was slightly more than 3,000. It resumed a slow growth after the war and reached a second peak about 1972 with more than 6,000 members.

Beliefs. The society emphasizes its nondogmatic nature and the freedom it allows members in interpreting theosophical teachings. However, it does present in its literature an explicit worldview which is generally shared by theosophists and is taught in classes, seminars, and lectures by the leadership. The worldview affirms that One life pervades the universe and keeps it in existence. The universe is an expression of an eternal Principle with transcends human perception. Ultimate Reality manifests in two aspects, generally referred to as spirit (or consciousness) and matter. Spirit, matter, and their interaction, constitute a trinity which produce a multitude of universes.

Every solar system is governed by natural law with the planets being the densest aspect. There are also exceeding fine material parts of the system, the whole of which is undergoing a process of evolution. The spirits (or souls) of humans are in essence identical with the supreme Spirit and undergoing a process of unfolding the essential divine nature. That process is by a means called reincarnation in which the spirit passes through periods of activity (embodiments) followed by periods of rest/assimilation. Closely related to reincarnation is the Law of Karma, in which each soul creates its fate by its actions. The spirit's pilgrimage begins in unity, moves to an experience of the manyness of this life and back to conscious union with the One Divine Source of all.

Organization. Olcott, the administrative center of the American Section is located in Wheaton, Illinois, on a 40-acre tract purchased in the 1920s. The society is headed by a president and a board of directors consisting of the first and second vice presidents and district directors elected regionally. The board oversees a number of administrative departments and the national program. Also located at the headquarters complex is the Olcott Library and Research Center, now housing more than 20,000 volumes on a wide variety of subjects on theosophy and related topics. The Theosophical Publishing House is a major publisher of esoteric literature and has in recent decades extended its influence through a series issued under the imprint of "Quest Books," made possible by generous donations by the Kern Foundation. A string of bookstores, Quest Bookshops, are located in Wheaton, New York City, Seattle, and elsewhere.

The society is an open membership organization, and anyone who is in sympathy with its general principles may join. Also nonmembers may join its library and benefit from its use. The current president of the society in America is John Algeo. Among those who have served as president are Alexander Fullerton, Weller Van Hook, A. P. Warrington, L. W. Rogers, Sidney A. Cook, James S. Perkins, Henry A. Smith, Joy Mills, Ann Wylie, Dora Kunz, and Dorothy Abbenhouse.

Membership: In 1995, the society reported 4,300 members and 140 centers in the United States, and approximately 400 members and 18 centers in Canada. There were 30,000 members worldwide.

Educational Facilities: The Olcott Institute, Wheaton, Illinois.

Periodicals: *The American Theosophist.* • *The Quest.* • *The Messenger.*

Remarks: There are several organizations closely associated with the Theosophical Society in America which, while largely composed of members of the society, are in fact completely independent of it. These include the Esoteric Section, Krotona School of Theosophy, and the Theosophical Order of Service. The Esoteric Section and the Krotone Institute now serve the society as an educational arm.

Sources:

Ellwood, Robert. *Theosophy.* Wheaton, IL: Theosophical Publishing House, 1986.

Mills, Joy. *100 Years of Theosophy.* Wheaton, IL: Theosophical Publishing House, 1987.

Perkins, James S. *Through Death to Rebirth.* Wheaton, IL: Theosophical Publishing House, 1973.

Rogers, L. W. *Elementary Theosophy.* Wheaton, IL: Theosophical Press, 1929.

★1590★
United Lodge of Theosophists
245 W. 33rd St.
Los Angeles, CA 90007

The United Lodge of Theosophists (U.L.T.) is an association of students of theosophy founded by a small group of Theosophists dissatisfied with what they perceived as organizational formalities and distractions within the larger Theosophical movement. The conception of U.L.T. as a vehicle for Theosophical work derived mainly from the experience and insight of Robert Crosbie (1848–1919), who through his many years with the movement witnessed the schisms and divisions that he attributed to conflicting organizational claims, controversy over authority, and the conceptions of personal leaders. In 1909, with the help of a few others who had come to share his "unsectarian" view of Theosophy, Crosbie founded the United Lodge of Theosophists—an organization defined by a simple statement of policies and intentions—and set about the task of restoring the record of Theosophical teachings available to the public and inaugurating a program of practical Theosophical education. The statement of purpose, called the "Declaration," has remained unchanged to the present, and the modes of work established by Crosbie have remained unaltered in principle.

Beliefs. The lodge teaches that there is but one life; all life is spirit or consciousness evolving toward greater individualization and toward a greater awareness of identity and unity; and this evolution proceeds under an inherent law—an order that is native to human understanding. Believing that the mind, in its highest sense, is the place of realization and growth, individual students come to regard these general principles as meaning that human life is a continuous process of learning, and that this learning involves unceasing revision of the terms of individual understanding as men gain awareness of its operations.

Organization. According to its "Declaration" the U.L.T. is devoted to "the cause of Theosophy without professing attachment to any Theosophical organization. It is loyal to the great Founders of the theosophical movement, but does not concern itself with dissensions or difference of individual opinion." The basis of union among Theosophists is a similarity of aim, purpose, and teachings, and to that end, the U.L.T. has neither a constitution, by-laws, nor officers. Those affiliated with the lodge sign a statement of sympathy with the "Declaration" at the time of their becoming an associate (member) of the U.L.T. Members may found autonomous lodges.

The U.L.T. considers the original and pure message of Theosophy to be recorded in the writings of Helena Petrovna Blavatsky and William Q. Judge, co-founders of the Theosophical Society. The U.L.T. make their works, and other works deemed consistent with them, including a monthly magazine, available to the public.

Membership: There is no formal membership as the lodge is an informal association of students. In 1995 there were 11 lodges in the United States and 11 in other countries.

Periodicals: *Theosophy.* Send orders to 245 W. 33rd St., Los Angeles, CA 90007. *Hermes.* Available from the Universal Theosophy Fellowship, Box 1085, Santa Barbara, CA 92102. *The Theosophical Movement.* Available from the Theosophy Hall, 40 New Marine Lane, Bombay 400 001, India.

Remarks: Among the prominent centers affiliated with the U.L.T. is the center in Santa Barbara, California, which was built up through the 1970s and 1980s by the late Rhagavan N. Iyer, formerly a professor of political science at the University of California–Santa Barbara. It is currently headed by his widow, Nandini Iyer, an instructor in religious studies at UCSB. The center is home to the Concord Press, which pursues an aggressive program of publishing material on theosophy, Eastern religion, and classical philosophy, and the Institute of World Culture, which promotes dialogue on classical traditions, modern science, art, and social structures as they attempt to relate to world culture. The center also issues a periodical, *Hermes.*

Sources:

Crosbie, Robert. *The Friendly Philosopher.* Los Angeles: Theosophy Company, 1934.

___. *Answers to Questions on the Ocean of Theosophy.* Los Angeles: Theosophy Company, 1937.

The Theosophical Movement, 1875-1950. Los Angeles: Cunningham Press, 1951.

The United Lodge of Theosophists, Its Mission and Its Future. Los Angeles: Theosophy Company, n.d.

★1591★
Voodoo Spiritual Temple
828 N. Rampart St.
New Orleans, LA 70116

The Voodoo Spiritual Temple is an important center of voodoo located on the northern edge of the French Quarter in New Orleans. Its importance lies in its openness to people not of African lineage, especially visitors to New Orleans, and its willingness to introduce outsiders to the often secret world of voodoo (or voudou). The temple was founded by Priestess Miriam Chamani, who came to voodoo out of the Spiritual movement. She was ordained a bishop in the Angel All Nations Spiritual Church in Chicago. Her husband, Oswan Chamani, was born in Belize where he studied with

several teachers of the Obeah tradition and specializing in herbal and healing practices.

To Priestess Miriam, Voodoo worship is centered upon the Voudon, the invisible power that created all things, and the Loa (or Orisha), intermediary spiritual beings who operate much like the saints in traditional Roman Catholicism. The Loa interact with human beings to create and maintain spiritual balance.

In its interaction with the general public, the temple offers consultations (including card and palm readings), participation in rituals, and various potions.

Membership: The small temple has one center.

Periodicals: *Voodoo Realist Newsletter.*

★1592★
The Word Foundation, Inc.
Box 180340
Dallas, TX 75218

Harold W. Percival (1868-1953) was an early theosophist, having joined the Theosophical Society in 1892. The society seemed to serve as a springboard for his own development, and the year after his joining he had a profound experience which he described as being "conscious of Consciousness" during which "Light greater than that of myriads of suns opened in my head. In that instant or point, eternities were apprehended." By a process he called "real thinking", he was able to select any subject, focus the Conscious Light upon it, and when the Light was brought to a focus on a subject, have complete knowledge of that subject.

While a member of the Theosophical Society, but several years after the death of its leader, William Q. Judge, he withdrew and founded the Theosophical Society Independent. He also organized the Theosophical Publishing Company of New York and started a magazine, *The Word*, which he published from 1904 to 1917.

It was during his years as editor of *The Word* that he began to outline materials for what was to become his most important work. By the process of "real thinking," Percival wrote *Thinking and Destiny*, an exhaustive survey of humanity and the world. The text was dictated (primarily to an assistant, Benoni B. Gattell) since his body had to be very still while he thought. He spent more than 30 years dictating and refining the material in *Thinking and Destiny.*

Thinking and Destiny sets forth an impressive system in which humans are at the center of a universe created by their own thinking and thoughts. In this system, each human being is descended from a Triune Self (Thinker, Knower, and Doer) and is living in a self-induced hynosis and ignorance in a human body. One of the goals of life is to teach beings to awaken to knowledge of themselves and of their purpose, that purpose being to become conscious in ever greater degrees until one knows the ultimate, Consciousness.

Every doer so embodied is bound by the law it has made for itself by its thinking and action. The universal law causes the everyday acts, objects, and events to exteriorize around one's self as destiny. By self-dehynoptization and thinking, one gains an understanding and acquaintance with these inner realities. As one becomes free of the states of feeling and desire that bind one to nature, the way to conscious immortality is shown.

In 1946, Percival and some associates formed The Word Publishing Company and released *Thinking and Destiny*. In 1950 the foundation was formed to perpetutate Percival's teachings. The next few years saw the publication of three smaller books which provide a more detailed discussion of selected subjects. The foundation, primarily dedicated to the publication and distribution of Percival's writings, became an open membership organization in 1986. That same year, it also revived *The Word* magazine.

Membership: In 1995, the foundation reported approximately 1,000 members and subscribers worldwide.

Sources:

Percival, Harold W. *Adepts, Masters and Mahatmas*. Dallas: Word Foundation, 1993.

___. *Democracy Is Self-Government*. New York: Word Publishing Company, 1952.

___. *Man and Woman and Child*. New York: Word Publishing Company, 1951.

___. *Masonry and Its Symbols*. New York: Word Publishing Company, 1952.

___. *Thinking and Destiny*. New York: Word Publishing Company, 1950.

Alice Bailey Groups

★1593★
Aquarian Educational Group
Box 267
Sedona, AZ 86336

The Aquarian Educational Group is a religious and educational orgnaization founded by the Rev. Torkom Saraydarian (1915-1997) and based upon his studies of the world's religions, in relation to both the philosophy of the ages and the findings of modern science. The group studies all branches of the Ageless Wisdom tradition and attempts to be an inclusive response to human aspirations and needs. The Ageless Wisdom is defined by the group as the treasury of human knowledge and experience in all fields of human endeavor. Members are advised to study all the religions of the world and the teachings of the East and West such as the Puranas, Vedas, and Upanishads (of the Hindus), and the works of Helena Petrovna Blavatsky, Alice Bailey, and Helena Roerich. Strong emphasis is also given to the study of the teachings of Christ.

Members are also advised to consider the discoveries of modern science and are educated through various regular meetings, seminars, correspondence lessons, and regular scientific meditation. The group also performs services for Christian baptism, matrimony, and last rites.

The group is headed by a nine-person Board of Trustees. During his lifetime, Saraydarian, who had authored numerous books, as well as the teaching materials of the group, also served as its president. The group is identified by a symbol described as a five-pointed star surrounded by three concentric circles. The circles stand for the infinity of light, love, and beauty. The points of the star symbolize Beauty, Goodness, Righteousness, Joy, and Freedom. Within the star is an arrow pointed upward, a symbol of the striving toward perfection.

Membership: In 1995 there were approximately 150 members.

Periodicals: *Fiery Synthesis*.

Sources:

Saradarian, Haroutiun. *The Magnet of Life*. Reseda, CA: Aquarian Educational Group, 1968.

___. *The Science of Meditation*. Reseda, CA: Aquarian Educational Group, 1971.

Saraydarian, Torkom. *Christ the Avatar of Sacrificial Love*. Agoura, CA: Aquarian Educational Group, 1974.

___. *A Commentary on Psychic Energy*. West Hills, CA: T.S.G. Enterprises, 1989.

___. *The Flame of Beauty, Culture Love, Joy*. Agoura, CA: Aquarian Educational Group, 1980.

___. *Sex, Family, and the Woman in Society*. Sedona, AZ: Aquarian Educational Group, 1987.

___. *The Symphony of the Zodiac*. Agoura, CA: Aquarian Education Group, 1980.

___. *Woman: Torch of the Future*. Agoura, CA: Aquarian Educational Group, 1980.

★1594★
Arcana Workshops
Box 605
Manhattan Beach, CA 90266

Among the largest of the groups promoting the teachings of Alice Bailey in Southern California is Arcana Workshops. The group has developed a meditation training-program based upon Bailey's writings and the Agni Yoga Series (published by the Agni Yoga Society). It offers meditation training via its home page on the Internet. Through the workshops, offered in the Los Angeles area, groups of people around Southern California have formed full-moon meditation groups. Through correspondence courses, numerous pamphlets, books, and regular mailings, the organization has been able to establish a network around the country. The Arcana Workshops pioneered the intergroup cooperation that led to the annual celebration of the three linked festivals of Aries, Taurus, and Gemini among occult groups in southern California every spring.

Sources:

The Full Moon Story. Beverly Hills, CA: Arcana Workshops, 1974.

For Full Moon Workers. Beverly Hills, CA: Arcana Workshops, n.d.

What Is Arcana? Beverly Hills, CA: Arcana Workshops, n.d.

★1595★
Arcane School
113 University Pl., 11th Fl.
Box 722, Cooper Sta.
New York, NY 10276

The original group continuing the work and thought of Alice Bailey is the Arcane School, founded by Alice and Foster Bailey. It remains the largest of the full-moon meditation groups. All of the Alice Bailey books are published through its Lucis Publishing Trust, which publishes her books for the entire movement.

Several subsidiary programs were created to implement the program of the hierarchy. Triangles was founded in 1937 to build groups of three people who would unite daily in a mental chain radiating energy into the world. World Goodwill was established in 1932 with the purpose of establishing right human relations in the world. It is an "accredited non-governmental organization" with the United Nations in New York and Geneva.

Students of the Arcane School are now found in all the major countries of the world but relate to the school through one of the three headquarters in New York, London, or Geneva. The Alice Bailey books have risen in circulation as a result of recent paperback editions. Beginning in 1923, Alice, with the help of some leading students, began the preparation of correspondence lessons which are now mailed out to students internationally. They are based on Alice's books and lead the student through various degrees. Following Alice's death in 1949, Foster Bailey took charge of the work. Mary Bailey assumed the leadership role after Foster's death in 1977.

Membership: Not reported.

Periodicals: *The Beacon*. • *World Goodwill Newsletter*. Available from World Goodwill, 113 University Place, 11th Floor, Box 722, Cooper Station, New York, NY 10276.

Sources:

Bailey, Alice A. *The Unfinished Autobiography*. New York: Lucis Publishing Company, 1951.

Sinclair, John R. *The Alice Bailey Inheritance*. Wellingsborough, Northamptonshire: Turnstone Press, 1984.

Thirty Years' Work. New York: Lucis Publishing Company, n.d.

★1596★
Meditation Groups, Inc.
Box 566
Ojai, CA 93023

One of the several groups inspired by the writings of Alice Bailey, Meditation Groups, Inc. (MGI) assumed the task mentioned in *Discipleship in the New Age* of establishing a worldwide group devoted to mediation on the Laws and Principles that prepare the world for the coming new order and the jurisdiction of the Christ. It was formed in 1950 by Florence Garrique (1888-1985) and was headquartered in Greenwich, Connecticut. With the assistance of Ray Whorf MGI was moved to a mountain precipice overlooking the Ojai (California) Valley in 1968, and the site became known as Meditation Mount. The Mount has held full-moon meditation gatherings every month since its dedication in 1971. The overall purpose of Meditation Groups, Inc., is to promote meditation on the Laws and Principles of the New Age as an act of service to the world.

While following the same teachings as the Arcane School, that centered its activities on the books of Alice Bailey, Meditation Groups, Inc., has developed three major programs: Meditation Groups for the New Age (MGNA), Group for Creative Meditation (GCM), and Specialized Groups. MGNA is the instructional arm of Meditation Groups, Inc. It teaches an introductory three-year course in meditation, as a service to Humanity, introducing the student to an esoteric perspective on life from the books Alice Bailey received telepathically from the Tibetan Master of the Spiritual Hierarchy, with whom she had extensive contact. After completion of the three-year course, students may elect to continue with the work of GCM, which offers a more intensive course of occult study and meditation. MGNA holds an annual fall symposium at Meditation Mount and communicates every tow months with MGNA members and study groups across the world.

The Group for Creative Meditation encompasses worldwide meditation groups actively working on a program of service to Humanity, the Spiritual Hierarchy, and the Christ. The world group follows a cycle of meditation based upon the call of the Tibetan Master, for unanimous and simultaneous meditation on the Laws and Principles that must condition the consciousness of Humanity and usher in the New Age. The group provides a number of materials for conducting full-moon meditation group gatherings (Community Meditation Service, Meditation at the Time of the Full Moon, etc.) and meditation calendar (Ritual of the Year) with full information on the exact time of the full moon with the various time zones in the United States. More importantly, the group publishes a continuing course based upon the Alice Bailey books and a *Bimonthly Newsletter* mailed to members every two months, and holds an annual spring conference at Meditation Mount.

Conceived as the subject of the three activities, the specialized groups combine disciplined meditation with a focus upon a particular area of endeavor, one of ten originally discussed by the Tibetan: Telepathic Communication, Recognition of Reality, Heling, Education, Politics, Religion, Science, Psychology, Finance, and Creativity. Advanced students of GCM are invited to take part in the work of one of these specialized groups.

Membership: In 1997 Meditation Groups, Inc., reported 5,000 coworkers scattered around the world. Affiliated members and groups are found on every continent. Materials produced by Meditation Groups, Inc., are being sent to 80 countries (including the Eastern Eurpean nations), and many have been made available in Spanish and Portuguese editions.

Sources:

Moore, Frances Adams. *A View from the Mount*. Ojai, CA: Group for Creative Meditation, 1984.

Whorf, Raymond B. *The Tibetan's Teaching*. Ojai, CA: Meditation Groups, n.d.

★1597★
School for Esoteric Studies
58 Oak Terrace
Arden, NC 28708-2820

The School for Esoteric Studies was established in 1956 by former close co-workers of Alice Bailey. The School is located in New York City and offers training for discipleship in the New Age. Its courses, given via correspondence to English speaking students throughout the world, focus on study of the ageless wisdom teachings, meditation, and service as a way of life. Discipleship is seen not as devotion towards any individual or group, but as intelligent cooperation with the Spiritual Hierarchy (i.e., the Masters of the Wisdom or the Christ and His Disciples) towards the working out of the Plan of Light and Love within humanity.

The curriculum of the school is based on the methods and various texts by Alice Bailey and others. Apart from the courses for students, the school has made available a series of small introductory booklets for the interested public on such subjects as the Spiritual Hierarchy - Inner Guidance of the World; There is a Plan - Cooperation of Humanity with the Spiritual Hierarchy; the Externalization of the Hierarchy; and Building and Bridging - the New Group of World Servers.

Membership: As of 1992, the student body fluctuates between 200 and 400 students of which approximately 80 percent resided in the United States and Canada. It is not organized into local groups.

Sources:

Building and Bridging. New York: School for Esoteric Studies, n.d.

Gregor, Norman. *Whither Man?*. New York: School for Esoteric Studies, n.d.

★1598★
School of Light and Realization (Solar)
Current address not obtained for this edition.

The School of Light and Realization (Solar) dates to 1969, when the concept of the school emerged in a conversation between Hamid Bey of the Coptic Fellowship in America and Norman Creamer, the founder of Solar. Following the conversation, Creamer, who had been searching for the right course for his life, and his wife, Katy Creamer, purchased a farm north of Traverse City, Michigan. The vision of Solar emerged largely out of a reading of the works of Alice Bailey and Theosophy. There is strong belief in the imminent reappearance of the Christ and coming of the Aquarian Age. Solar is conceived to be one of the "New Group of World Servers" that will create the new society on the principles of goodwill and basic human character.

Solar's program is centered upon training men and women for life in the new age, and training them to raise the level of consciousness in order to come in touch with the world of ideas and intuition. Solar teaches the growth of the communal ideal; the coming of the one Christ; the removal of limitations and the development of potentials; that there is no original sin, that each individual has his own set of liabilities, assets and responsibilities; that to give the soul its freedom is the goal of human life, that discipline is self-imposed and that Eastern philosophy is useful for Western man.

A school for both children and adults is being established on the farm near Traverse City. The first session of the adult training school was held in the summer of 1972. Centers for the dissemination of Solar concepts are being established across the country; the first is in St. Petersburg, Florida. Solar offers correspondence lessons in its teachings.

Membership: Not reported.

Periodicals: *The Solarian*.

Sources:

Creamer, Norman. *The Aquarian Cosmic Vision.* Suttons Bay, MI: School of Light and Realization, n.d.

___. *Song of Solar.* Sutton's Bay, MI: School of Light and Realization, 1972.

★1599★
Tara Center
Box 6001
North Hollywood, CA 91603

Alternate Address: Affiliate offices: Share International, Box 41877, 1009 DB Amsterdam, Netherlands; and Box 3677, London NW4 1RW, United Kingdom.

Within the Theosophical tradition, Charles W. Leadbeater and Annie Besant first promoted the expectation of a world teacher whose appearance was equated with the Second Advent of Christ and the arrival of Lord Maitreya, the Buddhist bodhisattva who would assist humanity in making its next evolutionary step. They identified Jiddu Krishnamurti as the vehicle for the world teacher and organized the Order of the Star of the East to communicate their message. In 1948, almost two decades after Krishnamurti had renounced his messianic role, Alice Bailey, founder of the Arcane School, published *The Reappearance of the Christ,* in which she argued that the time was ripe for the appearance of a new world teacher (avatar) who would come as both Son of God and head of the Spiritual Hierarchy, the group of exalted beings believed by Theosophists to stand behind and oversee the evolution of the planet. She also suggested that preparatory work for the appearance would begin in 1975.

In 1959, Benjamin Creme, an artist born Scotland (1922) but residing in London, made contact with the Spiritual Hierarchy when he received a message telepathically from one of its masters. A short time later he was informed that Maitreya, the Christ, would return to earth some 20 years in the future. In 1975, having been offered the task of announcing Maitreyas appearance, he began to state that truth publicly. In 1977, he began to receive telepathically and speak messages from Maitreya to the general public. The messages suggested that humanity had reached a dangerous crisis and must either change course or face self-destruction. Humans must begin to manifest their divinity through love and justice, and specifically by sharing the worlds resources with the poor and starving. In 1980 Creme came to the United States for the first time to speak of behalf of Maitreya. At that time, the Tara Center was founded by some of those who responded to his message.

It is the general teaching of Tara Center and the other affiliated groups responding to Cremes message that humanity is one and united with all life. All religions reflect spiritual truth and as such all are acknowledged and respected. It is also possible for those who have no religion to come to truth. In common with theosophy, Tara Center teaches that the evolution of earth and its people is guided by a Spiritual Hierarchy made up of individuals who have evolved from humanity. Maitreya is considered the head of the hierarchy.

According to Creme, Maitreya manifested 2000 years ago by overshadowing his disciple Jesus. Maitreya, himself, reappeared in the world in 1977, as did other members of the Spiritual Hierarchy, an event described in theosophical literature as the externalization of the hierarchy. The externalization process comes, in part, as a response to the unconscious invocation by humanity.

On April 24–25, 1982, through advertisements taken out of a number of the worlds prominent newspapers, Creme announced that Maitreyas "Day of Declaration" would occur within two months. Followers expected it on or before June 21, 1982. When Maitreya did not appear as anticipated, Creme pointed to disinterest in the subject by the media as a sign of general human apathy. He also announced that the Day of Declaration was still imminent and could take place any time the sincere interest of the media— as humanitys representatives—drew Maitreya forward. In the meantime, followers were urged to continue their main task of announcing that Christ is in the world, and is soon to appear.

In August 1987, Creme announced that Maitreya was working to bring about a breakthrough in international relations. During the next month a new armament agreement was announced by the United States and the U.S.S.R. Since that time major political totalitarianism has disintegrated throughout the world, as exemplified by the collapse of the Soviet Union, the reunification of Germany, the ending of apartheid and introduction of democracy in South Africa, and steps toward the establishment of a Palestinian homeland. Next to go, according to Creme, will be economic totalitarianism, beginning with the collapse of the Japanese stock market.

In 1988 Maitreya appeared in Kenya and allowed himself to be photographed. That picture has subsequently been reproduced and widely circulated. Meanwhile, Maitreya has appeared to hundreds of fundamentalist religious groups worldwide, while simultaneously potentizing water sources near each location with healing properties. Many other signs of Maitreyas presence are being documented (and/or exploited) by the still-skeptical media as unexplained phenomena or miracles. Such "signs" include visions of the Virgin Mary, angelic encounters, "crosses of light," crop circles, and the September 1995, worldwide Hindu "milk miracle."

Those who wait in expectation of Maitreyas appearance do not postulate that he will build a new religion around himself but that he will teach humanity the art of self-realization, the first steps of which are honesty of mind, sincerity of spirit, and detachment. Maitreya has also communicated through Creme a strong social concern with specific priorities that include an adequate supply of food and shelter for all, and health care and education as a universal right. It is the movements belief that sharing is the key to proper human relations and is reflected in their motto, "Share and save the world."

Membership: Tara Center is not a membership organization. As of 1996 there was an 8,000 name mailing list for the United States and over 100 transmission meditation groups. Affiliated groups are currently functioning in Canada, England, Holland, Germany, France, Belgium, Italy, Spain, Sweden, Greece, Romania, Poland, Japan, Mexico, New Zealand, Australia, the Philippines, and Taiwan.

Periodicals: *The Emergence.* • *Share International.* • *The Emergence Quarterly.*

Sources:

Bailey, Alice. *The Reappearance of the Christ.* New York: Lucis Publishing Company, 1848.

Creme, Benjamin. *Maitreya's Mission.* Amsterdam, Netherlands: Share International Foundation, 1986.

___. *Messages from Maitreya the Christ.* Los Angeles: Tara Press, 1980.

___. *The Reappearance of the Christ and the Masters of Wisdom.* Los Angeles: Tara Center, 1980.

___. *Transmission, A Meditation for the New Age.* North Hollywood, CA: Tara Center, 1983.

A Master Speaks: Articles from Share International. Amersterdam, Netherlands: Share International Foundation, 1985.

Update on the Reappearance of the Christ. North Hollywood, CA: Tara Center, 1983.

★1600★
Upper Triad
Current address not obtained for this edition.

The Upper Triad project was begun in Albuquerque, New Mexico, in January 1974 by a group of twelve students of the Alice Bailey material. Originally a meditation group, they began the *Upper Triad Journal,* which became the major group effort. In 1976 the headquarters was moved to New Brunswick, New Jersey, and incorporated the following year. In 1979 headquarters were moved to Virginia.

The Upper Triad follows the general Alice Bailey emphases on world goodwill, right human relations, and the awareness of humanity. It has not been the group's intention to compete with or duplicate other theosophical groups, and it has limited the circulation of its *Journal* to serious students rather than use it as an instrument for promulgating the esoteric philosophy. The assumptions upon which the teachings are based include an affirmation of the unity of all life, the evolution of consciousness as the purpose of life, reincarnation and karma, the relativity of truth which may be perceived at many levels, the problem of life as the elimination of illusion and glamour, the essence of the self in the soul as opposed to the personality, and the higher stages of human evolution as being on the spiritual path.

Members of the Upper Triad conduct a meditation program which includes daily personal meditation, several weekly meditations, and the monthly full moon meditation. Those individuals who receive the *Journal* are invited to coordinate their meditation with the group's meditation. Members of the group in Virginia periodically give classes and lectures, and hold public meditation sessions. Besides the *Journal*, the group has published a series of brief commentaries on the esoteric philosophy.

Membership: Formal members consist of a small number of workers in the Upper Triad project, all of whom reside in close proximity to the headquarters. Informal members who receive the *Journal* (numbered in the hundreds) live around the United States and the world.

Periodicals: *Upper Triad Journal.* Send orders to Box 280, Springfield, VA 22150.

Liberal Catholic Churches

★1601★
American Catholic Church
% Most Rev. Simon Eugene Talarczyk
430 Park Ave.
Laguna Beach, CA 92651

On December 29, 1915, as one of the first acts after founding his fledgling American Catholic Church, Joseph Rene Vilatte, consecrated Frederick E. J. Lloyd (1859-1933), an Episcopal clergyman whose distinguished career included his election and then rejection of the post of Bishop Coadjutor of Oregon. In 1915, after four years as pastor of Grace Episcopal Church in Oak Park, Illinois, he resigned to go with Vilatte. In 1920 at a Synod of the Church held in Chicago, Vilatte retired and turned the Church over to Lloyd who assumed the titles of Primate, Metropolitan and Archbishop.

Lloyd proved to be an able leader, but, following the pattern of other independent bishops, he attempted to build the American Catholic Church by drawing priestly colleagues around him and consecrating them to the episcopacy. He hoped that bishops would generate a jurisdiction, and appointed them before there were congregations over which they could give oversight. Among the eight bishops he consecrated Gregory Lines (1923), Francis Kanski (1926), Daniel C. Hinton (1927) and Ernest Leopold Peterson (1927). Each of these would at one point leave the American Catholic Church and establish a different jurisdiction.

Lloyd was succeeded in 1932 by Hinton. Hinton in turn consecrated Percy Wise Clarkson the following year. Clarkson opened a very successful church in Laguna Beach, California, but he was a Theosophist and brought a Theosophical theological perspective which came to dominate American Catholic Church life and thought.

Bishop Lines had problems with Hinton. He withdrew from the American Catholic Church in 1927 in reaction to Hinton's consecration as Bishop-Auxiliary to Lloyd, and formed the Apostolic Christian Church. He returned a few years later only to leave again

when Hinton became Primate. During his first year separated from the Church, he consecrated Justin A. Boyle (a.k.a. Robert Raleigh). In 1930 Raleigh consecrated a Theosophist, Lowell Paul Wadle. Wadle soon left Raleigh and placed himself under Clarkson who had succeeded Hinton. In 1940 Wadle succeeded Clarkson, and served as Primate of the American Catholic Church for the next twenty-five years. During these years the Theosophical perspective initially brought in by Clarkson became the only perspective in the church and interaction with the Liberal Catholic Church branches has been strong. Wadle participated in a number of Liberal Catholic consecration services. In 1965 Wadle was succeeded by Hanlon Francis Marshall, who served only one year before being replaced by Hugh Michael Strange. The present Primate is Archbishop Simon E. Talarczyk.

During this same period, the other bishops, now separated from Clarkson and Wadle, initiated their new jurisdictions: The American Catholic Church (Syro-Antiochean) (Peterson); The Church of Antioch (Lines/Raleigh); the Traditional Roman Catholic Church in the Americas (Kanski): and the Apostolic Episcopal Church (Kanski).

The beliefs of the American Catholic Church are very close to that of the Liberal Catholic Church. It views itself as holding to an "orthodox" faith but interpreting it in the light of some basic truths: that our ignorance of God and nature is due to the lack of the spirit and life of God within us; that the way to the divine knowledge is the way of the gospel that leads to a new birth; and that the way of new birth is totally within the will of man to grasp.

Membership: Not reported. There are only one or two churches and several hundred members remaining in the church.

Sources:

Barry, Odo A. *Outline History of the American Catholic Church.* Long Beach, CA: American Catholic Church, 1951.

The Holy Liturgy. Long Beach, CA: American Catholic Church, 1955.

Wadle, Lowell Paul. *In the Light of the Orient.* Long Beach, CA: The Author, 1951.

★1602★
Canadian Catholic Church
(Defunct)

The Canadian Catholic Church was a short-lived Liberal Catholic jurisdiction founded in 1948 by Odo Acheson Barry as an independent sister church of the American Catholic Church. A priest of the Liberal Catholic Church, Barry was originally consecrated by Antoine Joseph Aneed of the Byzantine Universal (Catholic) and Orthodox Church of the Americas on July 26, 1946. He was consecrated again three days later by Charles Hampton, a liberal Catholic bishop, assisted by several other bishops including Lowell Paul Wadle of the American Catholic Church. In 1948 he was consecrated sub conditione by Wadle.

A short time after establishing the Canadian Catholic Church, Berry moved to Sri Lanka (Ceylon). He also lived for a while in New Zealand and England and only returned to Canada in 1960. Little was heard of his jurisdiction during the years he was away and it did not develop any substantial membership after his return. Berry died in 1968 and the church folded afterward.

Sources:

Ward, Gary L. *Independent Bishops: An International Directory.* Detroit, MI: Apogee Books, 1990. 524 pp.

★1603★
The Catholic Church of the Antiochean Rite
% Archbishop Primate
2008 Chesapeake Dr.
Odessa, FL 33556

The Catholic Church of the Antiochean Rite is a small jurisdiction founded in 1980 by the Most Rev. Roberto Toca (b. 1945), archbishop for Florida and exarch for Latin America. Toca was consecrated as bishop in 1976 by Abp. Herman Adrian Spruit of the Church of Antioch who also consecrated him as archbishop in 1982. He was elevated to Archbishop Primate in 1987 and took the religious name Sar Mar Roberto. The church has developed a ministry within the Hispanic community in Florida. While independent of the Church of Antioch, it generally follows its beliefs and practices. Along with the Bible, the church recognizes the Apocryphal writings such as the Gnostic texts found at Nag Hammadi, as authoritative literature. Worship is primarily in Spanish. The church is headquartered in the Holy Trinity Cathedral and Gnostic Orthodox Abbey, Odessa, a suburb of Tampa, Florida.

Archbishop Toca has assumed a leadership role in the Cuban community in the Tampa Bay area. He has won awards for his ethnic television series, "University on the Air," "Popular Academy," "From the Point of Light," "University of the Soul," and most recently, "The Prophet of the Mysteries of Beyond." He has also won a number of awards for his writings from the National Association of Cuban Journalism, and is the head of a magical order, the Ordo Templi Orientis Antiqua. He has written several books in Spanish on esotericism, magick, parapsychology, and political issues.

Membership: In 1997, the church claimed 1,000 members, 25 congregations and 29 priests in the United States and a worldwide membership of approximately 12,000. Members are scattered in 196 congregations, mostly in Cuba, Spain, and Latin America.

Educational Facilities: International University of Theology and Parapsychology, Odessa, Florida.

★1604★

Church of Antioch
% Mt. Rev. Meri Louise Spruit
32378 Lynx Hollow Rd.
Creswell, OR 97426

During the 1930s the American Catholic Church on the West Coast became thoroughly infused with Theosophical metaphysics. One instrument for moving the Church in that direction was Justin A. Boyle, more popularly known as Robert Raleigh. Boyle, a Roman Catholic priest, joined the Apostolic Christian Church, a splinter of the American Catholic Church schism formed by Gregory Lines in 1927. Lines consecrated Boyle on April 7, 1928, and appointed him coadjutor with right of succession. Lines returned for a few years to Lloyd's Church, but seceded again upon Lloyd's retirement. After Lines' death Raleigh continued as head of his independent jurisdiction. Over the years he also headed several Christian metaphysical organizations, St. Primordia's Guild and the Mystical Prayer Shrine.

At the time of Bishop Raleigh's retirement in 1965, his coadjutor was Herman Adrian Spruit (b. 1911). A pastor in the Methodist Church (1939-1968), Spruit left the church in 1951. He was inclined to follow the metaphysical movement in certain respects, and feeling that the Methodists were unable to accept his perspective, he joined the Church of Religious Science. At the outset, he became the executive secretary of the church and taught homiletics in the school of ministry. He left in 1953 to become vice president of the Golden State University in Hollywood, California.

Spruit, having become familiar with Liberal Catholicism, sought out Archbishop Charles Hampton, who ordained him to the deaconate in 1955 and to the priesthood the following year. Archbishop Hampton was joined by Archbishop Lowell Paul Wadle and Bishop Francis Marshall in consecrating Spruit to the bishopric in 1957. Spruit then interacted with Wadle and the American Catholic Church Wadle headed, but joined himself to Raleigh's independent jurisdiction, the Christian Catholic Church. In 1968, three years after Spruit succeeded Raleigh, he changed the name of the church to the Church of Antioch, Malabar Rite, to affirm the church's orders through Archbishops Joseph Rene Vilatte and Frederick E. J. Lloyd, the first bishops of the American

Catholic Church, who brought the Antiochean succession to America.

In faith and practice the church emphasizes a Gnostic Catholic perspective. In the interpretation of scriptures, it follows a liberal bent and relies upon the Ecumenical Creeds. It is quick to state that "it seeks further light on the mystery and wonder of the faith by searching in the spirit of disciplined scholarship for those aspects of Christian evidences that preceded and followed the Apostolic Period." The church was among the first Christian groups to ordain women to the priesthood, and in 1976 Spruit consecrated Helene Seymour as the first woman bishop in modern times. In 1980 he consecrated his wife Meri Louise Spruit as archbishop, and on January 26, 1986, she was enthroned as Matriarch of the Church of Antioch, the feminine counterpart of the Patriarch, with equal rights, powers, and responsiblities.

Archbishop Spruit resigned in 1991 due to health problems and recently passed away. Mt. Rev. Meri Louise Spruit continues to head the church and has been an active leader in the formation of the Federations of Independent Catholic and Orthodox Bishops.

Membership: Not reported. In 1988 there were an estimated several thousand members served by 123 priests. Parishes under the juridiction of the church are scattered throughout North America and Australia, where four priests currently reside.

Educational Facilities: Sophia Divinity School, Mountain View, California.

Periodicals: *Prism*.

Sources:

Spruit, Herman A. *Constitution and Statement of Principles*. Mountian View, CA: Church of Antioch Press, 1978.

___. *The Sacramentarion*. Mountain View, CA: The Author, n.d.

Spruit, Mary, ed. *The Chalice of Antioch*. Mountain View, CA: Archbishop Herman Adrian Spruit, 1979.

Sullivan, Edward C. *A Short History of the Church of Antioch and Its Apostolic Succession*. Bellingham, WA: Holy Order of the Rose and Cross, 1981.

Van Campenhout, W. John Kooistra. *Apostolic Succession in the Catholic and Apostolic Church of Antioch*. Scarborough, ON: Institute for Johannine Christianity Press, 1993. 86p.

★1605★

The Church of Gnosis (Ecclesia Gnostica Mysteriorum)
3437 Alma, No. 23
Palo Alto, CA 94306

The Church of Gnosis, (Ecclesia Gnostica Mysteriorum), founded in the 1970s by Bishop Rosamonde Miller, began as a center of the Church of the Sacred Wisdom, a small jurisdiction founded and headed by Bishop Neil Jack. It was later associated with the Ecclesia Gnostica led by Bishop Stephan A. Hoeller. In 1983 the Ecclesia incorporated as a separate entity. Bishop Miller had been ordained in 1974 by Bishop Hoeller, assisted by Bishops Neil Jack, Forest Barber, and Herman Adrian Spruit of the Church of Antioch. Bishops Hoeller, Jack, and Barber consecrated Miller as a bishop in 1981.

Bishop Miller claims a primal apostolic succession through the Mary Magdalene lineage. According to her account, Mary Magdalene had received her "hierophantic power" in the Isis Mystery schools of Egypt and later at the hands of Christ, as did the other apostles. Later she was the first to see the resurrected Christ. Unable to function in the immediate area because of sexist attitudes, she traveled west with Joseph of Arimathea, first to England and later to the Continent, where she lived out her life. She left behind a secret sisterhood that survives to this day. During the 1960s, Miller made contact with this sisterhood and was consecrated in it. She promised to keep her association confidential until after she had received the more recognized male lineage. She has now, however, ordained the first male priests in the Mary Magdalene

Order. Teachings of the church are taken from the Mary Magdalene Order, gnostic writings, her own experience of gnosis, and other sources. A liturgy was developed based upon the writings of the Mary Magdalene Order, Miller's own writings, and quotations from George Mead's collection of gnostic texts, *Fragments of a Faith Forgotten*. The church is unconcerned with reviving any doctrine or system, including Gnosticism, and does not consider itself Christian even though it uses a male/female Christos mythology as basis for its ritual. It is concerned with the elimination of doctrines and systems altogether in order to free the mind to experience "gnosis."

Membership: As the church does not operate in a jurisdictional system, no parishes or branches exist. However, there are several ordained priests with their own churches throughout the world and 17 local clergy. Membership is not counted, but as of 1997 approximately 400 people regularly attend services throughout the year and approximately 1,000 are loosely connected.

Periodicals: *The Gnostic.*

Sources:

The Gnostic Holy Eucharist. Palo Alto, CA: Sanctuary of the Holy Shekinah, 1984.

Mead, George R. S. *Fragments of a Faith Forgotten.* New Hyde Park, NY: University Books, 1960.

Miller, Rose. *The Gnostic Holy Eucharist.* Palo Alto, CA: Ecclesia Gnostica Mysteriorum, 1984.

Segal, Robert, and Iyne Singer. *Allure of Gnosticism.* LaSalle, IL: Open Court, 1994.

★1606★
Ecclesia Gnostica
4516 Hollywood Blvd.
Los Angeles, CA 90027

Stephan A. Hoeller has for many years been a popular writer of occult literature and has written extensively on gnosticism and the wisdom tradition. Early in his career, he became acquainted with the writings of James Morgan Pryse. Pryse, a leader of the independent Theosophical movement in New York City early in the century, later moved to Los Angeles and became a popular lecturer and writer on the occult and gnosticism. The Ecclesia Gnostica continues, in a religious vein, the gnostic tradition of the Gnostic Society founded by Pryse in 1928. The society is now a chartered lay organization of the church.

In 1959 Hoeller was appointed to oversee the work of the Brotherhood and Order of the Pleroma and the Pre-Nicene Church as the American representative of Richard, Duc de Palatine. After de Palatine's death, he and many members of the Order left and formed the Ecclesia Gnostica. Hoeller had been consecrated in 1967 by de Palatine, assisted by Bishops John Martyn-Baxter and Gregory F. E. Barber. He was reconsecrated sub-conditione by Archbishop Herman Adrian Spruit (of the Church of Antioch), assisted by Bishop Barber and Neill P. Jack, Jr., in 1972.

The Ecclesia Gnostica continues the teaching of the Brotherhood and Order of Pleroma, but has a much more open approach. From the headquarters, the Sophia Gnostic Center in Hollywood, California, regular classes and lectures and weekly worship is offered to the public, and a worshipping community has gathered. The Church has been in the forefront of welcoming women to the priesthood and has one female bishop.

Membership: In 1997 the church reported approximately 300 affiliated lay people, 14 priests, and five congregations worldwide.

Sources:

Hoeller, Stephan A. *The Enchanted Life.* Hollywood, CA: Gnostic Society, n.d.

___. *The Gnostic Jung.* Wheaton, IL: Theosophical Publishing House, 1982.

___. *The Royal Road.* Wheaton, IL: Theosophical Publishing House, 1975.

___. *The Tao of Freedom: Jung, Gnosis and a Voluntary Society.* Rolling Hills Estates, CA: Wayfarer Press, 1984.

Pryse, James M. *Spiritual Light.* Los Angeles: The Author, 1940.

★1607★
Edta Ha Thoma
Current address not obtained for this edition.

Edta Ha Thoma is a small jurisdiction formed just before the disruption of the Federation of St. Thomas Christian Churches in 1984. It was founded by Abp. James A. Dennis, a bishop in the Ecumenical Catholic Communion. He established a ministry at San Bruno, California. In the mid-1980s the jurisdiction was strengthened by the absorption of the Mesbarim Fellowship, which had been formed in 1976 by several former priests of the Church of Antioch. On Thanksgiving Day 1976, one of the priests, Michael G. Zaharakis (1946-1984) was consecrated by Lewis P. Keizer of the Independent Church of Antioch to lead the fellowship. An initial congregation of 22 members was formed at Santa Cruz, California.

The fellowship shared the gnostic-mystical perspectives of the Church of Antioch, but had placed its priorities on social action and community service. In Portland, Oregon, for example, a ministry to alcoholics was initiated, and in Santa Cruz, an outreach to migrants led to the development of a jail ministry. A variety of outreach projects flowed from these initial efforts. Basor Press was founded as a publishing arm of Mebasrim. Edta Ha Thoma, like the Federation of St. Thomas Christian Churches, recognizes the *Gospel of Thomas* as having scriptural authority.

In 1980, the fellowship affiliated with the ecumenical Federation of St. Thomas Christian Churches, an older organization that was attempting to tie together the scattered esoteric Christian churches. Zaharakis provided much of the leadership for the federation during the remaining few years of his life. The year 1984 proved traumatic for the fellowship. Due to internal disputes, the federation was disrupted and the fellowship withdrew its support. Zaharakis threw his support behind the formation of a new organization, the Synod of Independent Sacramental Churches, which included many of the churches formerly in the federation. However, before the synod could reorganize, Zaharakis died.

The fellowship supported the synod, but much of its work was assumed by Bp. Ismael Ford of the New Age Universal Church. Among the new members of the synod was Edta Ha Thoma. Within a short time the remaining remnant of the Mebasrim fellowship merged into that jurisdiction, in which it now functions as an order. Basor Press is now the publishing arm of Edta Ha Thoma.

Membership: Formal membership is not required of those who are involved with Edta Ha Thoma.

Educational Facilities: St. Thomas Institute, San Bruno, California.

Western Orthodox Theological Institute, San Bruno, California.

Periodicals: *Basor.*

Sources:

Keizer, Lewis S. *Initiation: Ancient & Modern.* San Francisco: St. Thomas Press, 1981.

★1608★
Federation of St. Thomas Christian Churches
℅ Joseph Vredenburgh
134 Dakota, No. 308
Santa Cruz, CA 95060

The Federation of St. Thomas Christian Churches was founded in 1963 by its Archbishop and Patriarch, Joseph L. Vredenburgh, a former Congregationalist minister. Vredenburgh was ordained in the Reformed Church in America in 1958 and for several decades served congregations in California culminating in a year's work in British Samoa (1977-78). However, in 1963 he was also consecrated as a bishop by another Congregationalist minister carrying Old Catholic episcopal orders, Howard E. Mather, and Cyrus A. Starkey. Through Mathers, Vredenburgh inherited orders from the Syrian Church of Antioch, the church of the St. Thomas Christians of India. Upon his return from Samoa, Vredenburgh settled in Santa Cruz and activated the Federation of St. Thomas Christians as a fellowship of independent and autonomous churches. A number of small jurisdictions, many of which has derived from the Church of Antioch, affiliated with the federation. By 1983 there were approximately 30 ministries and churches in the federation including the MeBasrim Fellowship, the Ecclesia Gnostica Mysteriorum, and the Independent Church of Antioch.

Disruption of the Fellowship began in 1984. That year Bishop Michael G. Zaharakis, a leading member of the federation died, and presiding Bishop Joseph L. Vredenburgh, who had moved to Hawaii, and Bishop Lewis S. Keizer, of the Independent Church of Antioch, had a disagreement on policy which led to a disintegration of the federation as it was then constituted. Many of the member churches withdrew and formed the Synod of Independent Sacramental Churches. Vredenburgh reorganized the federation as an umbrella for the remaining independent ministries. In 1984 the Reformed Catholic Church in America, led by Most Rev. Brian G. Turkington, its founder, merged into the federation. Turkington was named Archbishop-Metropolitan of the Federation and shares leadership with Vredenburgh. An annual synod convenes on the July 4th weekend.

The federation professes belief in the "True Light", which enlightened the Lord Jesus Christ and brings salvation, and acknowledges the necessity of a personal commitment to Christ. Members look to the Universal Divine Gnosis (Wisdom). The Gnostic *Gospel of Thomas* is accepted as scripture along with the Bible.

The federation has grown steadily as it has become the umbrella for a variety of churches and ministries across North America. In 1997, for example, the church added to its fold the congregations of Zoe Ministries in New York City, the Skekinah Glory Mar Thomas Orthodox Church in Fresno, California; Christ Cathedral in Chesterfield, Virginia; and Mar Georges Ministries in Augusta, Georgia. A new ministry for bikers has been developed in Flagstaff, Arizona, and a seminary program has emerged in Atlanta, Georgia.

Membership: In 1997 the federation reported 1,500 members, 94 churches, 98 clergy persons in the United States, 84 members in four churches served by two priest in Canada, and an additional 500 members in churches in Barbados, Western Samoa, Australia, and the United Kingdom.

Educational Facilities: College of Seminarians, Santa Cruz, California and Atlanta Georgia.

American Apostolic University, Santa Cruz, California.

St. Andrews Pastoral Institute, Alta Monte Springs, Florida.

Periodicals: *Basor*. Send orders to 123 Bixby St., No. 1, Santa Cruz, CA 95060.

★1609★
Free Liberal Catholic Church
107-111 E. Locust
San Antonio, TX 78212

The Free Liberal Catholic Church was founded in 1975 by a group of Liberal Catholic priests including Bishops Donald M. Berry (1935-) and John Russell (1920-1985). Bishop Berry was consecrated by Bishop William H. Daw of the Liberal Catholic Church International. Bishop Russell was consecrated by Bishop William A. Henley of the American Orthodox Catholic Church. Archbishop John Shelton Davis, vicar general at the time of the formation of the Free Liberal Catholic Church, is currently the presiding bishop. Davis was consecrated by Berry in 1979.

The Free Liberal Catholic Church follows the Liberal Catholic tradition. The Bible is accepted as the guide and rule of life by members and priests, but no one is required to subscribe to a creedal summary or to a particular formulation of faith. Freedom of inquiry is encouraged. There are seven sacraments that operate by the power of the Holy Spirit and depend for their efficacy on the clear conscience of the supplicant.

Membership: In 1995 the church reported approximately 100 members and 16 priests. It also had a ministry to the Spanish-speaking population of Texas.

★1610★
Gnostic Orthodox Church of Christ in America
Box 75, Rte. 1
Geneva, NE 68361

The pilgrimage of Abbot George Burke and the group of monastics that surround him at the Holy Protection Grostic Orthoday Monastery outside Geneva, Nebraska (including the convent for women in Geneva) is among the most fascinating of all of the independent apostolic churches. Burke was raised a conservative Protestant but among people with a mystic bent who had prophetic powers and practiced spiritual healing. As a young adult he discovered the *Bhagavad Gita*, the ancient Hindu scripture from India, to which he was immediately attracted. He began a study of Eastern religious literature. He finally traveled to India where he became a disciple of Sri Sri Ananda Mayi Ma (b. 1895), a famous female guru, and was initiated into the classical Hindu monastic order of Shankaracharya.

He returned to the United States and resided for three years in a Greek Orthodox monastery where he discovered the convergence of mystical Eastern Christianity with much Hindu spirituality. Upon leaving the Monastery he gathered a small group around him and in 1968 they went to India. Upon their return in 1969, they settled in Oklahoma City and created the Sri Ma Anandamayi Monastery and began publishing a magazine called *Ananda Jyoti*. As disciples of Anandamayi they practiced japa (or mara) yoga, a spiritual discipline which requires the repetition of a mantrum, word(s) of power. The practice leads to the spiritual liberation that all seek.

Then in the early 1970s Burke, known then as Swami Nirmalananda Giri became acquainted with Archibishiop Robert Williams of the Liberal Catholic Church International. On August 23, 1975 he was consecrated by and Robert L. Williams of the Liberal Catholic Church International, Bishop Jay Davis Kirby working with a letter of concurrence from Archbishop E. R. Verostek of the North American Old Roman Catholic Church-Utrecht Succession.

During the mid- and late 1970s Burke and the Monastery functioned under the episcopal authority of Bishop Williams as the American Catholic Church. They created Rexist Press, from which flowed some of the most substantive material produced by Old Catholics in America. Burke's catechetical text, *Faith Speaks*, remains the most complete theological text produced by any American Old Catholic. He also wrote several booklets, reprinted several classical Old Catholic works, produced a series of *Bible Guides*, and in 1976 began *The Old Catholic* (later renamed *The Good Shepherd*) which gave Old Catholicism one of its few high-quality periodicals. During this period Burke's writings were traditional Catholic in its theological perspective and widely read and appreciated by Old Catholics.

More recently, Burke has openly moved toward Liberal Catholicism in belief, while the early attunement to Eastern Orthodoxy has asserted itself in practice. He remains a member of the Shankaracharya Order and has sought an affiliation that will provide an ideological compatibility. The concept of reincarnation and karma are integral to his theology. Finally, in 1984 he founded the Gnostic Orthodox Church. It is in communion with the Liberal Catholic Church, Province of the United States.

Membership: In 1997, these were six monks residing at the monastery and these nuns in the convent of St. John in Geneva. These are no secular (non-monastic) members nor external mission work. The nine members of the church concentrate on developing the monastic live and operating St. George Press which publishes Gnostic Christian book.

Sources:

Burke, George. *Faith Speaks.* Oklahoma City, OK: Rexist Press, 1975.

___. *Magnetic Healing.* Oklahoma City, OK: Saint George Press, 1980.

Sullivan, Edward C., and Jeffrey A. Isbrandtsen. "An Interview with Abbot George Burke." Parts 1, 2. *AROHN* 3, no. 3 (1980): 26-29, 24-30.

★1611★
Independent Catholic Church International
℅ Mt. Rev. R. V. Bernard Dawe
1260 American Canyon Rd., No. 148
Vallejo, CA 94589

The Independent Catholic Church International was formed in 1981 as both a new jurisdiction out of the Anglican heritage and an ecumenical body which related a variety of independent episcopal bodies, some out of the theosophical Liberal Catholic tradition. The first primate was Peter Wayne Goodrich. Goodrich resigned in 1983 and was succeeded by R. V. Bernard Dawe (b. 1925), who had been consecrated in 1980 and had served as the church's international legate.

As constituted, the small jurisdiction has freely developed interchanges with a variety of Old Catholic and Anglican jurisdictions and has remained open to theosophical currents. It is a member of the Synod of Independent Sacramental Churches.

Membership: Not reported.

Sources:

Ward, Gary L. *Independent Bishops: An International Directory.* Detroit, MI: Apogee Books, 1990.

★1612★
Independent Catholic Church of Canada
℅ Mt. Rev. William Hains-Howard
4520 Huron St., Apt. 602
Niagara Falls, ON, Canada l2E 6Y0

The Independent Catholic Church of Canada is a Catholic jurisdiction founded in the late 1970s, one of a set of fraternally related independent Anglican, Catholic, and Liberal Catholic jurisdictions which would associate in 1981 in the Independent Catholic Church International (ICCI). Peter Wayne Reynold Goodrich, consecrated in 1978 by William H. Daw of the Liberal Catholic Church International, became the first primate. Goodrich also headed the ICCI. He resigned both positions in 1983 to become primate of the North American Episcopal Church and was succeeded by William V. P. Hains-Howard.

Hains-Howard had been consecrated in 1970 by Earl Anglin James of the North American Old Roman Catholic Church. He also heads the Order of St. Gilbert of Sempringham, an ordered community.

Membership: Not reported.

Sources:

Ward, Gary L. *Independent Bishops: An International Directory.* Detroit, MI: Apogee Books, 1990.

★1613★
Independent Church of Antioch
℅ The New Church Center
350 Santa Cruz St.
Boulder Creek, CA 95006

The Independent Church of Antioch is a small jurisdiction founded by its Primate, Bishop Robert Branch. Branch was consecrated by Archbishop Herman Adrian Spruit of the Church of Antioch, but left that jurisdiction to found the Independent Church of Antioch. The new jurisdiction became known in the 1970s through the varied activities of its regional bishop, Lewis S. Keizer.

Keizer, a former Episcopal priest, received his doctorate from the Graduate Theological Union in 1973. In the late 1960s, while serving as a deacon at St. Mark's Episcopal Church, he met Jeannie Maierader, a teacher of esoteric wisdom known affectionately as Mother Jeannie. She convinced Keizer to resign from the Episcopal Church, and on March 30, 1975 he was ordained and made Vicar General of the Church of Antioch by Archbishop Spruit. Two weeks later he was consecrated bishop by Spruit. Soon after that consecration, Keizer left Spruit's jurisdiction and aligned himself with Bishop Branch and the Independent Church of Antioch. Besides authoring a number of books and scholarly papers, Keizer has founded and directed a nationally recognized school for gifted children, and has attained fame as a jazz and classical musician.

The Independent Church of Antioch functions not so much as a traditional body of believers, but as an association of five theosophically-inclined teacher-bishops. Besides Branch and Keizer, the bishops are Dr. Daniel Fritz, a close associate of Manly Palmer Hall and Omraam Michael Aivanhov; Warren Watters, head of the Center for Esoteric Studies in Santa Barbara, California, and editor of the *Esoteric Review*; and Torkom Saraydarian, head of the Aquarian Educational Group.

Membership: Not reported.

Periodicals: *Esoteric Review.* Send orders to 533 E. Anapamu St., Santa Barbara, CA 93013.

Sources:

Keizer, Lewis S. *The Eighth Reveal the Ninth: A New Hermetic Initiation Disclosure.* Seaside, CA: Academy of Arts and Humanities, 1974.

___. *Initiation: Ancient & Modern.* San Francisco, CA: St. Thomas Press, 1981.

___. *Love, Prayer and Meditation.* Santa Cruz, CA: The Author, n.d.

___. *Priesthood in the New Age.* Santa Cruz, CA: The Author, 1985.

★1614★
International Free Catholic Communion
PO Box 3454
Clearwater, FL 34630

The International Free Catholic Communion is a liturgical Christian church founded in 1991. On Pentecost 1991, the first synod of the Communion was held at Bremerton, Washington, by Bishop Timothy Barker (1953-), Bishop-elect Michael Milner (1954-), and his wife, Rev. Maru Milner. The Statement of Union was completed at that synod. Bishop Barker had been consecrated in 1989 by Patriarch Herman Adrian Spruit of the Church of Antioch and served as the bishop of the church's diocese of New England. Bishop-elect Milner was consecrated in 1991 by Barker, assisted by Bishops Brian G. Turkington and Joseph P. Sousa, and Louis Boynton. Milner had an eclectic background, having studied Taoism, served as a Pentecostal minister, and worked with the Roman Catholic Church prior to a brief period with the Church of Antioch.

The International Free Catholic Communion follows the Free Catholic tradition earlier exemplified in the Church of Antioch. It sees itself as a viable sacramental alternative to the Eastern Orthodox, Roman Catholic, and Protestant traditions. It accepts the traditional Apostles' and Nicene Creeds as the basis of Christian unity but also emphasizes the right and privilege of individual freedom of thought. The church offers seven sacraments: baptism, confirmation, the holy Eucharist, reconciliation, anointing the sick, matrimony, and holy orders. Women are admitted to all orders of the ministry: deacon, priest, and bishop. In like measure, married people are also admitted to all levels of ministry. The Eucharist is open to all, whatever their religious affiliation.

The Communion has formal intercommunion agreements with the Federation of St. Thomas Christian Churches and the Orthodox Church of the East. Bishop Barker also founded the Koinonia Institute to foster communication among independent Catholic, Anglican, and Orthodox jurisdictions.

Membership: Not reported. There are two dioceses with headquarters in Florida and California.

Periodicals: *Free Catholic Communicant,* 1250 Grand Ave., 10, Arroyo Grande, CA 93420.

★1615★
International Liberal Catholic Church
(Defunct)

The International Liberal Catholic Church was founded in 1966 by Bishop Edmund Walter Sheehan and others who left the Liberal Catholic Church branch led by Bishop Edward M. Matthews. He had previously served as an auxiliary bishop under Bishop Charles Hampton. His disagreement with Matthews concerned administrative matters.

Sheehan linked the International Liberal Catholic Church to the Brotherhood of the Blessed Sacrament, a Dutch group which had broken with the British headquarters of the Liberal Catholic Church. The Brotherhood had originally sided with Matthews but had broken relations with him in 1962.

The International Liberal Catholic Church followed the Matthews faction in doctrinal and liturgical matters. While reporting 9 bishops, 25 clergy, and 3,000 members in 1969, the International Church dwindled to only a few parishes during the 1970s, and in the early 1980s was disbanded.

Sources:

International Liberal Catholic Church, Origins, Principles, Worship, Theology, Sacraments. Ojai, CA: St. Raphael's Printing Guild, 1968.

Sheehan, Edmund. *Teaching and Worship of the Liberal Catholic Church.* Los Angeles, CA: St. Alban Press, 1925.

★1616★
Johannine Catholic Church
Rancho Vista Mobile Home Estates
13490 Highway 8 Business, Space 143
Lakeside, CA 92040

The Johannine Catholic Church was organized in 1968 (incorporated in 1971) by J. Julian Gillman and his wife, Rita Anne Gillman, as a ministry to those rejected by or disillusioned with the traditional churches. Initially it was directed to the hippie culture of the late 1960s. Gillman was consecrated "sub-rosa" by a 'renegade' (unnamed) Episcopal bishop, but in 1977 both he and his wife were consecrated by H. Ernest Caswell of the North American Old Roman Catholic Church-Utrecht Succession.

The church is described as new age in orientation, open to clergy of both sexes and making no distinctions due to sexual preferences. The designation Johannine refers to the Gospel of John and its central message of love. Love, not theology, is considered the overriding principle of Christianity.

The church sponsors several religious orders, all open to men and women, both married and single. The Order of Saint John the Evangelist is the order of clergy whose ministry is to the rejected. The Order of Saint John Bernadone is a street ministry to street people. The Paracelsian Order is a new age community seeking to develop an alternative life style. The church is a member of the Synod of Independent Sacramental Churches. Gillman edits *SISCOM*, the journal of the synod. Saint Dionysius' Press is the church's publishing arm.

Membership: In 1988 the church reported approximately 100 members in four congregations served by eight priests. The church centers were located in San Diego, Santa Barbara, Dulzura, and San Francisco, California.

Periodicals: *The Madre Grande Journal.*

Sources:

Nihle, William. *A True History of Celtic Britain.* San Diego, CA: Saint Dionysius Press, 1982.

The People's Liturgy. San Diego, CA: Johannine Catholic Church, 1968.

★1617★
Liberal Catholic Church International
741 Cerro Gordo Ave.
San Diego, CA 92102

The Liberal Catholic Church (being the American Province of the Liberal Catholic Church International) was constituted in 1983 by the merger of the Liberal Catholic Church and the Liberal Catholic Church International. The Liberal Catholic Church was one of two groups claiming to continue the original Liberal Catholic Church incorporated in 1928. In that church (under the second regionary bishop Charles Hampton) a strong division of opinion developed. Hampton articulated an independent stance regarding the Theosophical Society. As a result, he was deposed in 1944.

Most clergy and congregations supported him, and a schism was created. Then, the Presiding Bishop of the Church, F. W. Pigott (d. 1956), in London appointed John T. Eklund as the new regionary bishop. Eklund in turn consecrated two priests as bishops without obtaining the required approval of the priests and deacons of the Province. This act precipitated a second schism under Bishop Ray Marshall Wardall (d. 1954). A majority of the clergy and congregations in the United States supported Wardall.

In response to the Eklund consecrations, Wardall consecrated Edward M. Matthews (1898-1985), whom the Eklund faction had deposed from his position as Dean of the Liberal Catholic Cathedral in Los Angeles. Nevertheless, Matthews retained possession of the Cathedral. In 1950 Matthews succeeded Wardall as head of those clergy and congregations under his control. At that point, the Eklund faction filed suit against the Wardall-Matthews faction asking the court to deny Matthews use of either the name Liberal Catholic Church or the title Regionary Bishop. In 1955 Matthews exercised his powers as head of the jurisdiction by consecrating two priests to the episcopacy, William H. Daw and James Pickford Roberts.

The litigation took over a decade, by which time Pigott, Eklund, Hampton and Wardall had all died. The court ruled in favor of Matthews, who it declared to be the Presiding Bishop of the Liberal Catholic Church. However, during the years of litigation most of the clergy and congregations were now aligned with other jurisdictions. (Also, detached from the organizational strength of the Theosophical Society, the Matthews' faction had lost a major source for new members.) In 1964, shortly after the ruling, Bishops Daw and Roberts left the Mathews' jurisdiction to form the Liberal Catholic Church International.

Matthews eventually sold the Los Angeles Cathedral property and moved his headquarters to Miranda, California, where it remained until 1976, at which time Matthews reported 8 churches, 8 clergy, and 4,000 members. (In fact the church had only two parishes, one in Miranda and one in San Diego, California, and several priests.) The church splintered and Matthews, along with the congregation in Miranda, returned to the Liberal Catholic Church, Province of the United States. The San Diego parish under the leadership of then Very Rev. Dean Bekken, Vicar General of the Province, retained the corporate structure, and began to rebuild the Church.

Meanwhile, the Liberal Catholic Church International had picked up strength internationally. In 1974, Daw, the presiding bishop resigned in favor of Joseph Edward Neth.

On July 4, 1983, the Liberal Catholic Church merged with the Liberal Catholic Church International and became its American Province. Neth remained as the Presiding Bishop but also became the Provincial Bishop for the United States. The present presiding Bishop is the most Rev. Dean Bekken. Affiliated parishes are reported in England, Canada, and the Netherlands.

Among the important documents produced by Bishop Matthews, the 1959 Encyclical *"Freedom of Thought"* outlined the distinctives of this branch of Liberal Catholicism. Matthews attempted to move the Church away from Theosophical distinctives by affirming traditional Catholic ones. He specifically attacked the doctrine of reincarnation and noted that Liberal Catholicism does not now, nor ever has at any time, insisted or prescribed the dogma or teaching of the principle known as reincarnation, ''Christian'' or otherwise, as a tenet of belief and practices. Reincarnation is often a basic ''text'' belief in one's acceptance or rejection of Theosophy.

Membership: In 1997 the church reported 6,000 members in the United States, 12 priests, and six congregations in the United States.

Educational Facilities: St. Alban Theological Seminary, San Diego, California.

Sources:

The Holy Eucharist and Other Services. San Diego, CA: St. Alban Press, 1977.

Matthews, Edward M. *''Freedom of Thought,'' An Encyclical.* Los Angeles: Liberal Catholic Church, 1959.

___. *The Liberal Catholic Church and Its Place in the World.* Los Angeles: St. Alban Book Shop, n.d.

Statement of Principles. San Diego, CA: Liberal Catholic Church, 1977.

★1618★
Liberal Catholic Church, Province of the United States
9740 S. Avers
Evergreen Park, IL 60642

Bishop James Ingall Wedgewood brought The Liberal Catholic Church to the United States on the round-the-world tour he took his first year as Primate. Crossing the United States and meeting with Theosophists, he ordained as priests Charles Hampton (Los Angeles, August 19, 1917), Dr. Edwin Burt Beckwith (Chicago, September 16, 1917), and Ray Marshall Wardall (New York City, October 4, 1917). In 1919 Charles W. Leadbeater joined Wedgwood in consecrating Irving Steiger Cooper as the first regionary bishop for the United States. That consecration led to a war of words. Independent American Theosophists, especially those led by Katherine Tingley, used the emergence of the Liberal Catholic Church as an opportunity to denounce the Annie Besant-led Theosophists for selling out to Catholicism.

The Liberal Catholic Church prospered and spread under Cooper, but ran into trouble under its second regionary bishop, Charles Hampton (d. 1958). Hampton questioned the necessity of the provincial board and its beliefs. As the controversy continued, Hampton was deposed, and John T. Eklund was appointed to succeed him. Eklund's consecration of Newton A. Dahl and Walter J. Zollinger led to a second schism by priests led by Bishop Wardall, who objected to the legality of the action. Among those opposed to Eklund was Edward M. Mathews, the priest in charge of the leading congregation of the church in Hollywood, California. Eklund instituted suit against the schismatic group in hopes of denying it use of the Church's name. The suit was lost in a ten-year court battle, but in spite of the loss, most Liberal Catholics adhered. In 1973 it could report 29 congregations, 61 clergy, and 2,393 members. The church retained the recognition of the international church headquartered in London, but it was forced to re-incorporate in 1962 in Maryland in order to continue the use of its original name in the United States.

This branch of Liberal Catholicism is most closely tied to the Theosophical Society. The cathedral church of Our Lady and All Angels is located in Ojai, California. It is aligned with the world headquarters of the Church now located in South Africa. International leader of the church is Rt. Rev. Johannes Van Alphen. In 1985, Rt. Rev. Lawrence J. Smith of Chicago became the Regionary Bishop for the Province of the United States, succeeding Rt. Rev. Gerret Munnik.

Membership: In 1997, the church reported 2,400 members, 25 congregations, and 60 priests.

Educational Facilities: Liberal Catholic Institute of Studies, (LCIS).

Periodicals: *Ubique.* Available from The Liberal Catholic Church, Box 1117, Melbourne, FL 32901. • *The Voice of the Synod.* Send orders to Very Rev. Lloyd Worley, 1232-24th Ave. Ct., Greeley, CO 80631.

Sources:

Cooper, Irving S. *Ceremonies of the Liberal Catholic Rite.* London: St. Alban Press, 1964.

Leadbeater, Charles Webster. *The Science of the Sacraments.* Los Angeles: St. Alban Press, 1920.

The Liturgy of the Liberal Catholic Church. London: St. Alban Press, 1983.

Norton, Robert. *The Willow in the Tempest: A Brief History of the Liberal Catholic Church in the United States from 1917-1942.* Ojai, CA: St. Alban Press, 1990.

Pitkin, William H. *Credo, First Steps in Faith.* Ojai, CA: St. Alban Press, 1977.

Wedgewood, James Ingall. *The Beginnings of the Liberal Catholic Church.* Lakewood, NJ: Ubique, 1967.

★1619★
New Order of Glastonbury
Box 285
Yellow Jacket, CO 81335

The New Order of Glastonbury began in 1979 when seven independent Old and Liberal Catholic priests decided to establish an ordered community. The previous year, one of their number, Frank Ellsworth Hughes, had been consecrated by Archbishop Herman Adrian Spruit of the Church of Antioch. The group incorporated in 1980 and only later decided to add a Protestant-style ministry as a means of serving the lay public. A number of the clergy have established churches and ministries.

The order is very eclectic but generally follows a Liberal Catholic perspective. Their statement of principles espouses a belief in One God, manifest as the Creator; the Cosmic Christ, the Son; and the Holy Spirit, the Comforter. In life and worship, the order combines emphases from Catholic (apostolic succession, seven sacraments); Protestant (freedom of belief and mode of worship); and Metaphysical (the study of comparative religion, occult and psychic reality) traditions. A variety of liturgies are approved from the more orthodox (such as the Tridentine Latin or Byzantine) to the theosophical liturgy of the American Catholic Church written by Lowell Paul Wadle.

The order is governed by a seven-member board of directors. Most Rev. Frank Ellsworth Hughes was elected as the first presiding bishop. The order admits both men and women married or unmarried to all levels of its ministry. Fr. Merle D. Mohring, Sr. served as the first president of the board of directors, while his wife, Most Rev. Martha Theresa (Martha Jo Mohring Shultz) served as secretary-treasurer, and in 1985 she was appointed presiding bishop.

Membership: In 1997 the order reported ten congregations and 300 members served by 52 priests and ministers.

Educational Facilities: Seminary of Our Lady, Yellow Jacket, Colorado and Boulder, Colorado.

The order also offers a correspondence study program leading to ordination.

Periodicals: *Gateways.*

Sources:

The New Order of Glastonbury, History and Apostolic Succession. Rialto, CA: New Order of Glastonbury, [1980].

★1620★
Old Catholic Church of British Columbia
715 E. 51st Ave.
Vancouver, BC, Canada V5X 1E2

The Old Catholic Church of British Columbia traces its history to 1919 when a Father Love began a Catholic mission in Vancouver. The mission grew under the leadership of Love's successor, Father Barney, a former member of the Roman Catholic Order of Oblates, who in 1934 opened St. Raphael's Old Catholic Church. In the early 1970s, Gerard LaPlante, a member of the congregation, was ordained as a priest and became the church's pastor. At that time the congregation was affiliated with the Liberal Catholic Church. Several years later, in order to move toward a more traditional orthodox position, the church left the denomination and organized as a separate jurisdiction. In September 1979, LaPlante was consecrated as a bishop by Liberal Catholic bishops Donald M. Berry and H. V. Russell. Subsequently, the church moved into communion with the Liberal Catholic Church of Ontario and U.S.A. In more recent years other congregations have affiliated with the church.

A Liberal Catholic liturgy is used in the church. There are seven sacraments. Confession is not required before communion. The church is opposed to the ordination of both females and homosexuals. LaPlante pastors the church in Vancouver, which has a weekly mass in English and French, but which also serves a number of non-English-speaking residents. Church membership also includes several hundred French-Canadians. Affiliated congregations are found in France, Great Britain, Austria, Germany, and the United States. The church is in communion with Christ Catholic Church International.

Membership: In 1998, the church reported 12 Canadians congregations and 14 congregation in the United States.

★1621★
Old Holy Catholic Church, Province of North America
℅ Mt. Rev. Alvin Lee Baker
3600 E. 7th Ave., No. 34
Flagstaff, AZ 86804

The Old Holy Catholic Church, Province of North America was founded in 1979 by the Rev. George W. S. Brister. Brister had been ordained to the priesthood by Bishop James A. J. Taylor of the Order of St. Germain, Ecclesia Catholica Liberalis in 1969. He headed the Maranatha Ministry Church and the Order of St. Timothy, Ecclesia Catholica Liberalis, both in Oklahoma City, Oklahoma. By 1975, Maranatha Churches could also be found in Tulsa and Las Vegas. He was consecrated by Bishop Stephan A. Hoeller of the Ecclesia Gnostica in 1980. His church, as is true of Liberal Catholic congregations, was quite eclectic and combined teaching drawn from Theosophy, Buddhism, New Age metaphysics, and Religious Science.

In June 1987, Brister retired as archbishop primate of the church and appointed Bishop Alvin Lee Baker to succeed him. Besides his role as archbishop emeritus of the church, Brister now serves as vicar general of the Liberal Catholic Church (Oklahoma Synod) with which the Old Holy Catholic Church is in commu-

nion. Baker now serves as pastor of St. Timothy's Church in Oklahoma City, Oklahoma.

The Old Holy Catholic Church affirms the Nicene Creed, and the beliefs of the undivided church in Christ and redemption, though it understands them with a Liberal Catholic interpretation. It affirms its oneness with the one church founded by Christ that consists of the Roman Catholic Church, all the independent Catholic hierarchical churches, the Eastern churches such as the Orthodox, Coptic, and Armenian. The church condemns moral permissiveness, immodest dress during worship, homosexuality, and, in general, conforming to the "spirit of this world."

The church follows the liturgical year in its worship and emphasizes fasting during penitential seasons (such as Lent). It advocates the use of pious images, the rosary, and Gregorian chants.

Membership: In 1988 there were six congregations and approximately 400 members served by five priests and two bishops.

Periodicals: *The Lamp.*

★1622★
Order of St. Germain, Ecclesia Catholica Liberalis
(Defunct)

The Order of St. Germain, Ecclesia Catholica Liberalis was founded in 1969 as the Order of St. Germain. Its more recent name was adopted two years later. Its founder was James A. J. Taylor, also known as James Matthews, a former member of the Holy Order of MANS, an esoteric-metaphysical group modeled on the structure of a Roman Catholic religious order. Like traditional orders, the Order of St. Germain had no lay members, but is made up entirely of priests, ministers and "practitioners." Taylor asserted that although he "was consecrated by a Bishop (unnamed) of the Liberal Catholic Church, the Order claims no genetic connection with that Church."

The Order existed to forward the work of the Masters, the Christs, in the world. It was a sacramental church but differed in that it attempted to offer the widest latitude in matters of intellectual liberty and respect for individual conscience. Theologically it was Liberal Catholic in perspective.

The small order was headed by the Archbishop, assisted by other bishops appointed to administer state jurisdictions. A board of directors assisted in administrative matters. The order never grew beyond northern California.

★1623★
Order of the Americas
Current address not obtained for this edition.

The Order of the Americas is a Gnostic religious jurisdiction founded in 1994 by Bp. Michael von Stambach Bruce. The order can be traced to a series of lectures offered by Bruce in 1992 at several locations in Atlanta, Georgia. Out of the positive response to his lectures, the Gnostic Academy, a school of Gnostic studies was formed. In the meantime, Bruce became a seminarian at Sophia Divinity School, the seminary of the Church of Antioch, and in 1993 he attended the American College of Seminarians, the school of the Federation of St. Thomas Christian Churches. He was ordained by Abp. Joseph Vredenburgh on October 31, 1993. He was consecrated in 1994 by Bp. Louis P. Keizer of the Independent Church of Antioch, and the following day (April 26) founded the Order of the Americas. On January 1, 1995, he participated in a service of cross-consecration with Bp. Russell Hill of the Ecclesia Gnostca Spirtualis and the NeoPythagorean Church. He was elevated to the office of archbishop in April 1995.

The Order of the Americas is a non-creedal Gnostic church. The Gnostic perspective rejects the God of Judaism and Christianity, which it considers a tribal deity. The highest expression of God to the Gnostic is an impersonal God as Ineffable, i.e., consciousness at rest, and has not thought of Itself. God can not be expressed in images, but can be experienced. Salvation is an act of awakening from the dream of life in matter and remembering who one really is, a spiritual being. Jesus is seen as the personification of the Logos, an impersonal principle of reason. As a person awakens, Logos operates to translate the new knowledge of the self.

The Order of the Americas, as an independent episcopal jurisdiction, is organized as a chivalric order and offers a course in religious knighthood. Knighthood is considered an archetypal role model. Through the gnostic academy, ministers are trained for the orders of deacon and priest. Priests are also eligible for consideration for the office of bishop. Ministers organize study groups and lead Sunday worship services. Services are conducted on a democratic basis and include meditation, readings from Gnostic scriptures, communion, and healing. Currently, the primary worship center is at the Gnostic shrine of Sophia in Atlanta. Worship services are open to all.

Membership: In 1995 the order reported approximately 300 members and eight clergy. The great majority of members are in the United States, but there are members in Great Britain, New Zealand, and Canada.

Educational Facilities: Gnostic Academy, Atlanta, Georgia.

Periodicals: *Gnostica.*

Sources:

Gregorious, Tau, Russell Slay Hill, and Michael von Stambach Bruce. "European Esoteric Lineages." *Gnostic* 1, 9 (February 1995): 1–5.

"Questions and Answers." Atlanta, GA: Order of the Americas, 1995.

★1624★
Paracletian Catholic Church
(Defunct)

The Paracletian Catholic Church was founded in 1982 by Leonard R. Barcynski and Vivian Barcynski, two bishops in the Church of Antioch. The Barcynskis had become well-known during the 1970s for their many books on magick and the occult written under their pseudonms, Melita Denning and Osborne Phillips. They have been leaders for over a decade in the Aurum Solis, a ritual magick organization which they helped reconstitute in 1971.

In 1978 the Barcynskis moved to the United States and soon after met Archbishop Herman Adrian Spruit, who in June 1982 consecrated them and established a Diocese of St. Paul (Minnesota) which the Barcynskis jointly administered. However, in October of that year, they broke with the Church of Antioch and established an independent jurisdiction. The Church never became firmly established, however, and several years later they abandoned any further effort to establish its parishes.

The articles of association of the Paracletian Catholic Church indicated that the church's main purposes were "to spread the love and knowledge of Christ, to administer the sacraments of the Catholic and Apostolic tradition in their plenitude, and to perform charitable works." The church was an attempt to give expression through the forms of the Catholic liturgical tradition to the teachings of Western Occultism as transmitted through the Aurum Solis. As defined by the Aurum Solis, the purpose of life in this world is to discover one's True Will and to do it. God is envisioned as the Divine Spark within, which motivates people to search out their true Vocation or Will.

★1625★
Pre-Nicene Church (de Palatine)
% Most Rev. Seiji Yamauchi
23301 Mobile St.
Canoga Park, CA 91307-3322

The Brotherhood and Order of the Pleroma was founded in 1953 in England by Ronald Powell, better known by the name he adopted, Richard, Duc de Palatine. The year previous to his founding of the Order he had been given the office of archon

(ruler) of an Italian-based order, The Ancient Mystical Order of the Fratis Lucis. The Church is a liturgical community open only to members of the Order. It has its apostolic succession from Hugh George de Willmott Newman, who consecrated de Palatine in 1953.

The Order and Church differs from many Liberal Catholic groups by their emphasis upon gnosticism. The Gnostics were second century Christians who rejected the humanity of Jesus. They said he never became human, i.e. fleshly, and only seemed to have a material body. "Gnosis" means "knowledge," and the Gnostics sought salvation through the secret knowledge (occult wisdom) teachings.

The Order and Church emphasize a Western approach to the ancient wisdom, as opposed to Theosophists who draw heavily upon Eastern occultism.. It emphasizes Jesus' role as the bringer of gnosis and de-emphasizes the Oriental yogic disciplines. It is an active system, calling members to strive for enlightenment and push aside any self-abnegation. God is identified with nature and is pictured as fragmented into billions of parts, which are the spiritual selves, sparks of the divine, which man is. This spark is buried in the tomb of flesh. Humanity's task is to realize his God-nature and actualize his divine potentials. Reincarnation is a part of this scheme of actualization.

The method of actualization is the arcane (hidden) discipline, a way known to mystics of all ages. It includes the esoteric sacramental rituals of the Church which are based upon the allegorical interpretation of Holy Scripture.

The Order and Church are headquartered in London. The Sanctuary of the Gnosis is the corporate body created to give legal and civil status to the Order in America. The present President of the Sanctuary is George Ricci. The apostolic succession was passed by Powell to John Martyn-Baxter, who has passed it to the present bishop leaders of the Church.

Membership: Not reported. There are only a few hundred members of the Order in America and no more than 1,000 worldwide.

Sources:

Duc de Palatine, Richard John Chretien. *The Inner Meaning of the Mystery School.* London: Pre-Nicene Publishing House, 1959.

___. *You and Reincarnation.* Sherman Oaks, CA: Aeon Press, 1976.

I AM Groups

★1626★
Ascended Master Fellowship
(Defunct)

The Ascended Master Fellowship was founded in 1972 by the Rev. Theodore M. Pierce, a former minister in the Cosmic Church of Life and Spiritual Science. In 1954, he had been called by Ascended Master Saint Germain through a vision in which he was shown the word "Freedom" written across the universe. The basic teachings of the church are found in two volumes written by A. D. K. Luk, *Law of Life.* The volumes are a variation on the original "I AM" teachings as presented by Guy Ballard, founder of the "I AM" Religious Activity. Volume II includes a minute description of the spiritual hierarchy and the personages that fill the positions. The Fellowship worked especially under Saint Germain, the Chohan of the Aquarian Age, but also was in cooperation with Ascended Masters Jesus and Mother Mary.

The Reverend Pierce entered the realm of spiritual healing, and practiced cosmic surgery through several spirit doctors. According to the Fellowship, in January, 1969, during a healing session, he was taken out of his body and taken back in time so as to be able to release "misqualified energy" (karma) from the individual. Pierce subsequently became a karmic eraser, one who can remove the consequences of evil that was done in former incarnations.

Regular services were held at the headquarters at Yarnell, Arizona. Affiliated groups were located in South Carolina, North Carolina, and Phoenix; Arizona; and individual members were found across the United States, and in Canada, New Zealand, and Saudi Arabia. For a number of years, Pierce published a periodical, *Temple Notes* The fellowship was discontinued when the demand on Pierce for past life readings began to take all of his time.

Sources:

Luk, A. D. K. *Law of Life.* 2 vols. Baltimore, MD: The Author, 1959-60.

Pierce, Ted M. *Healer Extraordinaire.* Yarnell, AZ: Top Publishers, 1987.

★1627★
Ascended Master Teaching Foundation
Box 466
Mount Shasta, CA 96067

The Ascended Master Teaching Foundation was founded in 1980 by Werner Schroeder and other students of the Ascended Masters. Of particular interest are messages received by Guy Ballard, co-founder of the "I AM" Religious Activity in the 1930s, and Geraldine Innocente, a messenger with the Bridge to Freedom in the 1950s. It is the goal of the foundation to gather, cross index, make available to students, and translate into foreign languages the messages received by these two students. In addition, the foundation encourages the formation of study groups for people who wish to learn the teachings and initiate spiritual practice through decrees, songs, and visualizations. Within its first decade it has reprinted and/or published 32 books and 21 tapes.

It is the belief of the foundation that in the 1930s, Ascended Master Saint Germain initiated a "New Age" dispensation through Guy W. Ballard and his wife Edna Ballard. To them he expounded cosmic law in precise terms. For the first time since the sinking of the continent of Atlantis, the knowledge of the I AM Presence, (the spiritual body), and the practice of invoking the Violet Flame (which erases karma) was made public. Ballard spread the messages until his "ascension" (death) in 1939. In the ensuing years, the books were no longer freely available until the mid-1980's, and the books have never been permitted to be translated into other languages. In 1951 the Masters began to give additional messages through Geraldine Innocente. After her death in 1961 most of her messages were no longer published.

The effort begun in the 1930s is the last effort to free mankind. The Masters plan to increase the light to earth so that humanity can go through future planetary changes with the least amount of suffering possible. They plan to redeem the earth quickly and bring all humanity into contact with the Ascended Masters.

Membership: Not reported. Affiliated members can be found in Austria, Italy, Greece, Sweden, Nigeria, Tanzania, Jamaica, Venezuela, and Canada.

Periodicals: *The Spiritual Caravan.*

Sources:

King, Godfre Ray. "Guy Ballard". *Unveiled Mysteries.* Mount Shasta, CA: Ascended Master Teaching Foundation, 1986.

Prinz, Thomas Geraldine Innocente. *Memoirs of Beloved Mary, Mother of Jesus.* 1855 Reprint. Mount Shasta, CA: Ascended Master Teaching Foundation, 1986. 178 pp.

___. *The Seventh Ray.* 1953 Reprint. Mount Shasta, CA: Ascendee Master Teaching Foundation, 1986. 123 pp.

Schroeder, Werner. *Man—His Origin, History and Destiny.* Mount Shasta, CA: Ascended Master Teaching Foundation, 1984.

★1628★
The Bridge to Spiritual Freedom, Inc.
Box 333
Kings Park, NY 11754

This Activity, incorporated in the early 1950s under the name, the Bridge to Freedom, was later called The New Age Church of the Christ. At the present time, the name, The Bridge to Spritual Freedom, has been reinstated, as it more accurately describes the Activity of the Ascended Masters. Its origins can be traced to 1944, when Geraldine Innocente, then a member of the "I AM" Religious Activity, was contacted by the Ascended Master El Morya. This marked the beginning of a series of dictations from the Maha Chohan, other members of the Great White Brotherhood, and Cosmic Beings. These instructions formed the foundation upon which The Bridge to Spiritual Freedom is based.

During the following years, the messages received through Geraldine Innocente were published under the sponsorship of Master El Morya. Using the psuedonym Thomas Printz, he directed the editing and compilng of these communications. This name appears on most of the publications released up to the present day. This includes a periodical called *The Bridge to Spiritual Freedom Journal* and weekly letters from various Ascended Masters called *The Shamballa Letter*, which are published at the worldwide headquarters on Long Island, New York.

Geraldine Innocente made her transition in June 1961. Her duties as Contact for the Ascended Masters and President of this organization were given to Lucy W. Littlejohn. Mrs. Littlejohn served in this capacity until her retirement on December 31, 1989. At the present time, following the instructions of Master El Morya, the Contact is to remain anonymous. The Activity serves as a bridge of consciousness between the physical octave and the Heirarchy of Ascended Masters, through which cooperative work may take place to raise the consciousness of all the people on Earth.

The goals are brotherhood and peace between all people and nations, and the elevation of humanity above disease, limitation, and imperfection. Students are taught about the use of the Sacred Fire through various methods, including the decrees, rhythmic breathing, and constructive visualization.

Since the beginning of the era of spiritual freedom in 1954 under the direction of the Ascended Master Saint Germain, attention has been focused on the activities of the Seventh Ray and the use of the Violet transmuting Flame.

In addition to publishing, activities at Headquarters include three regularly scheduled services each week, plus ongoing training programs as needed. There are also conferences scheduled each year, which are open to the entire membership.

Membership: Not reported. Outpost groups are located throughout the world, and it is estimated that many thousands of students now follow the teachings of the Ascended Masters as released through the Bridge.

Periodicals: *The Bridge to Spiritual Freedom Journal* (monthly). • *The Shamballa Letter* (weekly). • *Ascended Master Discourses* (annual).

Sources:

Kuthumi, Ascended Master. *The Wisdom of the Ages.* 2 vols. St. James, NY: Bridge to Freedom, n.d.

Printz, Thomas. *Memoirs of Beloved Mary, Mother of Jesus.* Philadelphia: Bridge to Freedom, 1955.

___. *The Seven Beloved Archangels Speak.* Mount Shasta, CA: Ascended Master Teaching Foundation, 1986.

___. *The Student's Handbook.* King's Park, NY: Bridge to Freedom, 1972.

The Violet Transmuting Flame. Kings Park, NY: Bridge to Freedom, 1968.

★1629★
Church Universal and Triumphant
Box 5000
Livingston, MT 59047

History. The Church Universal and Triumphant had its beginnings in the Summit Lighthouse, founded in 1958 in Washington, D.C., by Mark L. Prophet under the direction of the Ascended Master El Morya. Prophet had previously been associated with the Lighthouse of Freedom, a Philadelphia-based organization headed by Frances K. Ekey.

The Summit Lighthouse had as its primary purpose the publication and dissemination of the teachings of the Ascended Masters, described as "Immortal, God-free beings" who have mastered the circumstances of their lives by victoriously passing all of their tests and trials on earth. These Illuminaries, such as Jesus Christ, Mother Mary, Moses, Zarathustra, and Gautama Buddha, are the saints, revolutionaries, mystics, wise men, and women of all ages who have fulfilled their reason for being, balanced their karma and ascended to God, free at last from the round of rebirth. El Morya, an Ascended Master, is considered to be the Chief of the Darjeeling Council of the Great White Brotherhood. The brotherhood is thought to be an order of Western saints and Eastern masters. (The word white refers not to race, but to the aura (halo) that surrounds the masters and their embodied disciples). The primary method of disseminating the messages is a periodical, *Pearls of Wisdom*, published weekly since 1958, and numerous books and tapes.

In 1961, Prophet was joined by Elizabeth Clare Wulf, whom he later married and who eventually received the mantle of Messenger from Saint Germain, which (the Church teaches) confers the empowerment of the Word by the Holy Spirit. In the I AM tradition, the messenger is one through whom the Ascended Masters can speak. Mark Prophet was such a messenger, and after her training, Elizabeth Clare Prophet also became one.

In 1962, the Ascended Master Saint Germain established the Keepers of the Flame Fraternity, an order within the larger group of those receiving the *Pearls of Wisdom*, of men and women especially dedicated to the freedom and enlightenment of humanity. In 1966, the headquarters moved to Colorado Springs, Colorado, where the publishing of the teachings continued. Here a Montessorri preschool was established in 1970 to provide a spiritual and academic bilingual (English/Spanish) education for the children of the Keepers of the Flame. Over the years it has grown into a full elementary and high school program.

Summit University was founded in Santa Barbara, California, in 1971 to provide a more intensive and direct presentation of the teachings of the Ascended Masters to members of the Keepers of the Flame who have moved through the basic course of lessons. At an annual eight-week retreat each summer by Elizabeth Clare Prophet, students pursue the master's teachings on a wide variety of subjects including the study of world religions and their sacred texts, the "lost teachings" of Jesus as delivered by the Ascended Masters, as well as the masters' prophecy for the present age.

Mark Prophet died in 1973, and Elizabeth assumed full responsibility for the leadership and direction of the movement. During the remainder of the decade, as the work grew the organization added new departments and study groups were established across the United States and Canada, in Europe and Africa, and in Australia and the Philippines. In 1974, the Church Universal and Triumphant was incorporated. The church took on the liturgical functions of the Summit Lighthouse and expanded its original mission of publishing the teachings of the Ascended Masters.

Individuals may participate in the church at a variety of levels. The general public may take part in religious services and conferences. The teachings are made available in the many books and publications, such as the weekly *Pearls of Wisdom*, which contain messages from the Ascended Masters. Those who join the Keepers of the Flame pledge to keep the flame of Life and Liberty on behalf of earth's evolutions. They receive graded instruction dictated by Ascended Masters which are distributed monthly. At advanced levels of initiation and commitment, fraternity members may choose to become communicants (members) of the church and be formally baptized. Full church members must formally subscribe to the tenets of the church and tithe their income. The church has a number of teaching centers around the world with live-in facilities for church staff. These centers offer lectures and weekly services to the surrounding community.

In 1976, the headquarters of the church was moved temporarily to Pasadena, California, and two years later to the 200-acre campus in Malibu, California. The international headquarters moved in 1986 to a 28,000-acre Royal Teton Ranch just north of Yellowstone National Park in Montana. In addition to its publishing work and ongoing religious activities, the church is actively involved in organic farming, ranching, and in building a self-sufficient spiritual community.

Beliefs. The doctrines of the Church Universal and Triumphant are contained in the many books of messages of the Ascended Masters and the texts written by the Prophets, especially their basic text, *Climb the Highest Mountain*. The church describes the teachings as essentially Judeo-Christian but centered on the eternal truths of the Universal Christ wherever they are found in the religions of both East and West. The church teaches and builds upon the mystical paths at the heart of the world's major religions.

According to the church's teaching, the soul is the living potential of God. Souls were conceived in the mind of God in the first instance as a realization of God's unity. Then they were born as a manifestation of the duality of God, that is a being of both spirit and matter. The individual thus has two parts, the higher changeless self and the lower changing self. The whole of creation reflects the duality of unchanging spirit that is the fiery core and blueprint of creation, and the ever-changing material world.

The I AM Presence, or individualized presence of God, is a miniature replica of the Deity. It is the God-identity of each individual, the origin of the soul focused in the planes of spirit just above the physical form. Each individual is an extension of the presence into matter, time, and space.

The individual as spiritual being has an unlimited potential and dominion. As a material being, the individual is limited by boundaries set by the Deity. The power and authority of the I AM Presence are not to be transferred to the lesser aspect of the individual until it shall prove worthy by undergoing certain initiations and demonstrate a willingness to "affinitize" the soul with the Divine Nature—to be, in fact, the individualized manifestation of the God flame.

Eventually people can become an individualized manifestation of the God Flame. This flame is the divine spark which focuses the primary attributes of Power, Wisdom, and Love, a bestowal of God to every man and woman.

According to church teachings, the goal of life for the soul evolving through numerous incarnations is to purify him/herself and to become one with the Christ while in physical embodiment. The masters teach the science of the spoken word, i.e., the use of prayers, mantras, and decrees to call forth Light is the key whereby the soul can achieve this goal. The Ascended Master Saint Germain has given humankind the knowledge of how to use the violet flame. This violet flame of transmutation is the sacred fire of the Holy Spirit which, when invoked in conjunction with service to life, allows the soul to balance the karma of mistakes and errors that have been made in this and previous lifetimes. After the soul has become purified in the fullness of the Christ consciousness, it is called by God to return to the Divine Source through the ritual of the sacred fire known as the ascension, the ritual whereby the soul reunites with the I AM Presence. The ascension is the culmination of the soul's journey in time and space.

Organization. As the messenger of the Great White Brotherhood, Elizabeth Clare Prophet is the spiritual leader of the Church Universal and Triumphant. Administratively, the church is governed by a board of directors charged with managing its temporal affairs. The church sponsors a cable television program "Elizabeth

Clare Prophet/Prophetic Vision/Spiritual Solutions" which is seen on 206 stations nationwide. Summit University Press has published more than 50 books and an extensive library of audio- and videocassette recordings.

Membership: Not reported. It is against the policy of the church to report membership figures.

Educational Facilities: Summit University, Corwin Springs, Montana.

Periodicals: *Pearls of Wisdom.* • *Royal Teton Ranch News.*

Sources:

Morya, El. *The Chela and the Path.* Colorado Springs, CO: Summit University Press, 1976.

Prophet, Elizabeth Clare. *The Great White Brotherhood in the History, Culture, and Religion of America.* Los Angeles, CA: Summit University Press, 1976.

___. *The Lost Years of Jesus.* Livingston, MT: Summit University Press, 1984.

Prophet, Mark L., and Elizabeth Clare Prophet. *Climb the Highest Mountain.* Colorado Springs, CO: Summit Lighthouse, 1972.

___. *The Lost Teachings of Jesus.* 2 vols. Livingston, MT: Summit University Press, 1986, 1988.

___. *My Soul Doth Magnify the Lord.* Colorado Springs, CO: Summit Lighthouse, 1974.

___. *The Science of the Spoken Word.* Colorado Springs, CO: Summit Lighthouse, 1974.

★1630★
City of the Sun Foundation
Box 370
Columbus, NM 88029

The City of the Sun grew out of Christ's Truth Church and School of Wisdom, founded in 1968 by the Rev. Wayne Taylor as a New Age community under guidance and direction of the spiritual hierarchy, particularly Master Hilarion. The City of the Sun, as the growing community is known, is near Columbus, New Mexico, on the Mexican border. Taylor was for two years president of Sologa, Inc., and then helped edit *The Mentor*, published by the Sanctuary of the Master's Presence. During the time he was with Sologa, Inc. his wife, Grace Taylor, functioned as a channel. The move to New Mexico came as a result of messages received through that channeling. Preparation was made in the form of the acquisition of a tract of 159 acres near Columbus.

The basic teachings which led to the foundation are contained in Taylor's book, *Pillars of Light*. In it is told the story of man's fall, which has resulted in his being set back spiritually for missions of years. Taylor explains that through the "Light bearers of all ages the veil of spiritual darkness is being lifted. Man is about to enter the Golden Age, and the City of the Sun is one structure to prepare for transition."

Residents of the City of the Sun have set as their primary purpose the providing of a wholistic healing center, encompassing the mental, physical and spiritual aspects of each individual, but with special emphasis upon the spiritual. There are two distinctive features of their work. First, they use the Vortex of Light and the divine energies of the Central Sun for healing. Second, they allow each the freedom to follow his/her own Inner Christ guidance as long as it is in harmony with the Universal Truth. They believe in the Fatherhood of God and the brotherhood of man. The group is headed by a five-member board of trustees.

Membership: In 1988 there were 61 members of the foundation in the United States, most of whom reside at Columbus, New Mexico, and there were two Canadian members.

Periodicals: *The Golden Dawn.* Send orders to Box 356, Columbus, NM 88029.

Sources:

Taylor, Wayne H. *Pillars of Light.* Columbus, NM: The Author, 1965.

★1631★
The Foundation of Love
201 E. Callender St.
Livingston, MT 59047

The Foundation of Love is an independent "I AM" organization established in Livingston, Montana, in 1990 by Bill Guillot, its director. Based upon the teachings of the Ascended Masters who have spoken through the Messengers of the "I AM" Religious Activity and the Church Universal and Triumphant, the foundation emphasizes the one path, that is, the Path of Love, the only way to God. Sacrifice, service, surrender, and selflessness are the four essential "sure" ways to find true meaning and purpose in life.

The foundation's goals are to help people realize that they can be healthy, happy, and whole, to assist them toward a higher consciousness of divine love, and to work together in a cooperative Christ relationship.

Membership: The foundation is not a membership organization.

Sources:

The Master Book of Health, Happiness, and Higher Consciousness. Livingston, MT: The Foundation of Love, 1993. 50 pp.

★1632★
"I AM" Religious Activity
Saint Germain Foundation
1120 Stonehedge Dr.
Schaumburg, IL 60194

The "I AM" Religious Activity is the oldest branch of the Ascended Master thrust which was begun by Guy Ballard. It is also the most conservative branch, adhering strictly to the dictates of the Ascended Masters as brought forth through their only accredited Messengers, Guy and Edna Ballard. Through them was released a threefold truth not previously disclosed outside of the Ascended Masters' secret retreats: the knowledge of the "Mighty I AM Presence," the individualized presence of God; the use of the Violet Consuming Flame of Divine Love; and the use of God's Creative Name, "I AM."

The "I AM" Activity believes that the "I AM Presence" emanated from the heart of the cosmos and as it individualized, creation resulted. The "I AM Presence" is the essence of each individual. However, over the centuries, the misuse of God's energy has led to the present discord and evil present in the world. In spite of that discord and evil, a few individuals have risen above the world's situation and, by completely attuning themselves to their "I AM Presence" ascended into the light. Eventually, each person will follow them. In the meantime these Ascended Masters, also known as the Great White Brotherhood, work to lift humanity out of their present situation.

The central focus of the "I AM" Activity is contact and cooperation with the work of the Ascended Masters. The messengers left over 3,000 dictations from the Ascended Masters which present a total program for both individual and social life. The Saint Germain Foundation and Saint Germain Press work to publish and present this material to the public and its student body. The "I AM" Religious Activity considers itself a Christian religion. It adheres firmly to Jesus' teachings. His example of the Ascension, in particular, deeply influences its teachings, and members believe that the Ascension is possible for everyone.

Primary means of attuning oneself to the "I AM Presence" is quiet contemplation and the repetition of affirmations and decrees. Affirmations are sentences which both affirm the individual's attunement to God usually in relation to a specific aspect of life and recount the blessings due as a result of that attunement.

Decrees are fiats spoken from the perspective of the essential self, the "I AM Presence." They call forth the visible manifestation of a divine condition or the dissolution of an evil one. They are always given in the Name of God. Decrees are given daily.

Almost as definitive as decreeing, the patriotism of the "I AM" Activity is noteworthy. Freedom has been a persistent theme throughout the decrees dictated to the Ballards. America is seen as having a special role in the Ascended Masters' plans. Reflective of this emphasis are the prominent display of American flags at "I AM" centers and the special programs on patriotic holidays.

New students are introduced to the activity by their reading the first three books of the 15 volume Saint Germain series. The first two volumes, *Unveiled Mysteries* and *The Magic Presence*, tell the story of Guy W. Ballard's original contacts with the masters. Volume three, a series of dictations from Ascended Master Saint Germain, outlines the basic beliefs of the "I AM" Activity. After reading the books, they may attend an introductory class, held periodically in Chicago.

The Saint Germain Foundation is the parent organization of the "I AM" activity. It was led by Guy W. Ballard until his death in 1939. His wife Edna W. Ballard then led the work until her death in 1971. At that time the board of directors assumed collective leadership of both the foundation and the press. That board, orginally five members, was expanded to eighteen in 1982. The board charters the local centers and sanctuaries, which otherwise are independent and autonomous. It also oversees the work of appointed messengers and field workers. The foundation sponsors a variety of national and regional gatherings, several of which are held at Shasta Springs, the retreat center located at the base of Mt. Shasta in northern California. Annually at Mt. Shasta, the foundation sponsors a pageant on the Life of Christ, which in a spectacular finale emphasizes the importance of the Ascension of Christ.

Since 1978 headquarters of the activity have been in a new building complex in Schaumburg, Illinois, a Chicago suburb. The Press, previously located in Santa Fe, New Mexico, moved there in 1982, thus consolidating all the national offices. A radio show begun by Edna W. Ballard has been continued and is heard on over twenty-five stations. There is an independent "I AM" School in Mt. Shasta, California.

Membership: Not reported. In 1997 there were over 350 "I AM" sanctuaries and centers thoughout the world.

Periodicals: *The "Voice of the I AM".*

Remarks: Greatly affected by the court cases in the 1940s and the subsequent litigation to recover the foundation's tax-exempt status and the press' right to use the mails, the "I AM" Activity assumed a very low profile. Under Edna W. Ballard's leadership, it cut itself off from the media and refused contact with reporters and/or religious researchers. As a result, all of the material available about the activity was either written during the period of controversy or is heavily reflective of that period. That material is generally hostile and unreflective of the present status and beliefs of the activity.

Sources:

Germain, Saint, through Guy W. Ballard. *The "I AM" Discourses.* Chicago: Saint Germain Press, 1935.

"I AM" Fundamental Group Outline. Schaumburg, IL: Saint Germain Press, 1982.

King, Godfre Ray [Guy W. Ballard]. *Unveiled Mysteries.* Chicago: Saint Germain Press, 1934.

___. *The Magic Presence.* Chicago: Saint Germain Press, 1935.

★1633★
Joy Foundation, Inc.
418 E. Micheltorena, Ste. 5
Santa Barbara, CA 93101

The Joy Foundation, Inc. was founded in Santa Barbara, California, in 1977 by the Rev. Dr. Elizabeth Louise Huffer assisted by Richard Huffer and Donald Cyr. Dr. Huffer was raised a Roman Catholic but passed through a extensive and eclectic program of metaphysical/occult education after leaving the church. She studied astrology with renowned astrologer Carroll Righter and with the First Temple of Astrology in Los Angeles. She then studied with Dr. D. J. Bussell, founder of the Chirothesian Church of Faith; Dr. Fletcher Harding of the United Church of Religious Science in Tarzana, California; and Dr. Henry Cairns of the College of Divine Metaphysics, from which she received her doctorates in divinity and psychology. She was ordained in the Universal Church of the Master (UCM) in 1969 and in 1974 chartered the Joy Church as a congregation of the UCM. The Joy Foundation emerged as an independent body from the church in 1977.

The teachings and practice of the Joy Foundation reflect the eclectic background of the founder. Huffer draws upon the teachings of Alice Bailey, Ann Ree Colton, and Corinne Heline, but is also herself a channel for the Ascended Masters. She understands that planet earth is receiving the Rays of Light. Besides the seven rays commonly spoken of in "I AM" Religious Activity literature, Huffer describes 12 rays, five additional rays related to humanity's inherent possibilities of awareness and the entire 12 rays related to the signs of the zodiac. These rays are of particular colors and are related to the work of particular masters as are the first seven. The work of the foundation consists of being aware of the rays and qualifying (or directing them to particular tasks) by the process of decreeing and by meditation. (Decrees are invocations to the masters spoken in a forceful directive manner.) By using decrees and spending time in meditation, members are able to balance their physical and spiritual selves and thus become prepared to enter the New Age, the Age of Aquarius. Members daily use a variation of the Violent Flame Decree first popularized by the I AM Movement. A book of Invocations and Decrees offer decrees for all 12 rays to be used throughout the year.

Huffer describes a spiritual hierarchy consisting of chohans, elohim, archangels, and angels. The chohans (or lords) are individuals who have lived many lifetimes during which they have mastered the energies of the rays, but especially mastered the energy of one ray. They are known as Ascended Masters. The elohim are cosmic beings with a more depersonalized and planetary influence. Archangels preside over the seasons of the years. Angels assist all humanity and planetary life.

Centers of the foundation are found in Sedona, Arizona, and Santa Barbara, California. The three festivals popularized by Alice Bailey consisting of Easter, Wesak, and Goodwill are celebrated by foundation members, and additional celebrations are held to mark the solstice and equinox.

Membership: In 1992, the foundation reported 35 members in two centers led by two ministers.

Periodicals: *Prisms of Joy.* • *Waves of Joy.*

Remarks: Donald Cyr, co-founder of the foundation, operates a printing shop in Santa Barbara, California, and is the editor of *Stonehenge Viewpoint*, a popular magazine which attempts to discern the significance of Stonehenge and the other megalithic sites of Europe, North America, and elsewhere.

Sources:

Huffer, Elizabeth Louise. *Spiral to the Sun.* Santa Barbara, CA: Joy Foundation, 1976.

Invocations and Decrees. Santa Barbara, CA: Joy Foundation, 1982.

Law of Life Activity
8575 S. Crow Cutoff
Rye Star Rte.
Pueblo, CO 81004

A. D. K. Luk is an independent exponent of the I AM teachings who wrote and published the *Law of Life*, a popular variant treatment of I AM themes. It was also a comprehensive summary of the information scattered through the discourses given by the masters through Guy Ballard, founder of the "I AM" Religious Activity. During the 1960s a number of independent groups such as those advocated in the first volume of *Law of Life* formed to study, meditate, and decree. In 1971 Luk issued an instruction manual for group leaders to guide their efforts. Beliefs and practice follow those of the I AM Activity and the original Bridge to Freedom Activity. A. D. K. Publications issues a wide variety of materials for use by related groups. The books by Guy W. Ballard issued by the I AM Activity are also used, but there is no organizational affiliation. Besides the writings of Ballard, the Law of Life Activity also uses the works of Geraldine Innocente, who received messages for the Bridge to Freedom in the 1950s.

Membership: The Law of Life is not established formally as an organization and there is no accounting of members. The publications have been distributed to many countries of Western Europe, Africa, and to Australia and New Zealand.

Periodicals: *Law of Life Enlightener.*

Sources:

Luk, A. D. K. *Law of Life.* 2 vols. Oklahoma City, OK: A. D. K. Luk Publications, 1959-60.

___. *Law of Life Instruction for Group Directors.* Oklahoma City, OK: A. D. K. Luk Publications, 1983.

Morningland-Church of the Ascended Christ
2600 E. 7th St.
Long Beach, CA 90804

Morningland-Church of the Ascended Christ was founded by Daniel Mario Sperato (d. 1976), known within the church as "Donato," at Long Beach, California in 1973. During the 1960s Sperato, then in his forties, turned to metaphysics and initiated a spiritual search. On May 16, 1971, he experienced "avesha" (divine incarnation) of the Ascended Master Donato in his body. Sperato became the true personification of the Oneness. On May 30, 1973 he received a final initiation as the Christ avatar of the Aquarian Age. A few months later he incorporated Morningland. A second ashram (congregation) was begun in Escondido, and a retreat center opened in Crestline.

Morningland is seen as a church which assists its members in discovering a way to Oneness with themselves. Donato, having already achieved Oneness, served in a mediating position while on earth, opening communication through the planes of existence to the place of Oneness. In his death he created a permanent path through the planes. Donato is considered to be one of the Ascended Masters, and is currently at work with other Masters of the Great White Brotherhood for the betterment of the race and Morningland.

During the brief period between the founding of Morningland and his "ascension" (death), Donato trained a group of female minister-leaders who assumed authority under the leadership of Sri Patricia, Donato's widow.

Membership: In 1984 the church reported 5,000 members in two centers.

Periodicals: *As It Is.* Send orders to 2634 E. 7th St., Long Beach, CA 90804.

Sources:

Healing: A Thought Away from Donato. 2 vols. Long Beach, CA: Morningland Publications, 1981.

Jesus. 3 vols. Long Beach, CA: Morningland Publications, 1980.

Morningstaar. *A Thought Away from Donato.* Long Beach, CA: Morningland Publications, 1975.

Morningstaar. *The Way to Oneness.* Long Beach, CA: Morningland Publications, 1974.

Revelations. Long Beach, CA: Morningland Publications, 1979.

Ruby Focus of Magnificent Consummation
PO Drawer 1188
Sedona, AZ 86336

The Ruby Focus of Magnificent Consummation, Inc. was founded in the mid-1960s by Garman Van Polen and Evangeline Van Polen, both former students of the "I AM" Religious Activity and the Bridge to Freedom, now the New Age Church of Christ. Evangeline eventually became a channel of the ascended masters, and in the late 1950s began to issue discourses under the aegis of the New Age Clinic of Spiritual Therapy in Phoenix, Arizona. Influential in the emergence of the Magnificent Consummation were the writings of Dr. C. H. Yeang. Yeang agreed with the Bridge to Freedom that over the years a number of changes had occurred in the makeup of the spiritual hierarchy. Specifically, he noted that in 1955, Gautama Buddha replaced Sanat Kumara as Lord of this World, that Lord Maitreya, formerly the World Teacher, now held the office of Buddha, and that Jesus and Koot Hoomi, formerly Chohans (ascended masters) of the Sixth and Second Rays, respectively, jointly function as the World Teacher. Yeang also believed that Saint Germain had been elevated and that Godfre-Ray King and Lotus King (i.e., Guy Ballard and Edna Ballard) had replaced him as Chohan of the Seventh Ray. St. Germain, in 1965, proclaimed himself as Eolia, now radiating the Golden Liquid Snow of Eolian Consciousness, the Light of the Central Sun. From that position, he will continue to direct the Seventh Ray and its new Chohan.

The Magnificent Consummation is the particular child of the Ruby Light of the Sixth Ray. Sananda and Lady Nada, Chohans of the Sixth Ray, are the directors. (Sananda is so labeled on all the literature.) The special work is to aid the descent of the Ruby Light of freedom, justice, peace, confidence, balance, and magnificence into the physical world. Almost all of the literature of the Ruby Focus is on pink paper, usually with red ink.

In the early 1970s, new additions to the hierarchy were recognized in the persons of Ruby and Christos, two additional Rays of Light. Ruby's color is iridescent ruby and Christos' is iridescent mother of pearl. They represent the negative and positive electric polarities and, together, are said to be the perfect laser beam of light. They will bring in the Magnificent Consummation of all seven colors plus themselves as the Rainbow Ray Consciousness and thus usher in the Aquarian Age.

From its headquarters, the Ruby Focus issues a variety of books. An order of service is built around a call upon one of the Seven Rays (plus the Eighth and Ninth Rays daily), songs, a message from one of the masters, and the taking in and radiation of light into the country and the world. Decrees are used extensively. The channeled messages received each Sunday are printed in the *Open Letter.*

Membership: Ruby Focus is not a membership organization.

Periodicals: *Open Letter.*

Sources:

Van Polen, Garman and Evangeline Van Polen. *Catechism of Light.* 2 vols. Sedona, AZ: Magnificent Consummation, 1965.

Van Polen, Garman, and Theresa Martin. *A Treatise on Father-Mother Light as Golden Experiences.* The Author, 1966.

Yeang, C. H. *Who Am I? I Am That I Am.* Privately published, [1965].

★1637★
Sacred Society of the Eth, Inc.
Current address not obtained for this edition.

The Sacred Society of the Eth, Inc. is the creation of Walter W. Jecker, known by his celestial name, Jo'el of Arcadia. During the 1960s, he went into the Siskiyou Mountains (a range in California and Oregon) and for seven years compiled volumes of words regarding love, light, and life. The words were published in 1967. He also founded the Society. His particular contact was with Jesus the Christ, known as the Ascended Master Sananda.

According to Jo'el, man is an emanation (sun) of God. While living in a body, man must know that he is the God of his being. Basic to man is Breath. The intelligence, says Jo'el, is in the Breath. Breath is thought and breathing is mind. Through Breath is the constant flow of the water of life. The etheric body is the fallen Breath of life. The Breath is creational. Man's life is determined by the hate or love within his mind.

Membership: Literature is distributed to study groups and individuals around the country.

Sources:

Jecker, Walter W. *God in Man Alive.* Forks of Salmon, CA: Sacred Society of the Eth, 1972.

___. *God Speaks, I Hear His Voice.* Forks of Salmon, CA: Sacred Society of the Eth, 1967.

___. *The Words of Light.* Forks of Salmon, CA: Sacred Society of the Eth, 1967.

★1638★
Sanctuary of the Master's Presence
Current address not obtained for this edition.

Closely related to other I AM groups is the Sanctuary of the Master's Presence. The Sanctuary was formed in the 1960s, but the public manifestation was not made until 1966 with the appearance of *The Mentor,* a periodical which carried the messages from the ascended masters. The Mentor was one of the entities from the spirit world who spoke through Mary Myneta, the principal percipient and teacher.

According the Mentor, man is evolving to a greater awareness of his creator. The present age is a time of man's becoming aware of a truth and reality not known previously. This step is precipitated by the powerful radiations of spiritual light from ascended masters' spheres of activity. The masters are projecting a golden radiance into earth to stir up our awareness.

Originally, the Sanctuary was headquartered in New York City and its periodical, edited by the Rev. Wayne Taylor, was published from Melbourne, Florida. However, in 1968, both were moved to Scarsdale, New York. From 1965 to 1968 Taylor had been president of Sologa, Inc., for whom his wife Grace Taylor was a channel. However, in 1968 the Taylors moved to Columbus, New Mexico to found Christ's Truth Church and School of Wisdom. Besides the group in Scarsdale, there are a few classes and group meetings, though they are no longer as strong as they were in the 1960s.

Membership: Not reported. The Sanctuary peaked in support in the 1960s, and there remains only a group in Scarsdale and few students around the United States.

Periodicals: *The Mentor.* Send orders to 2 Larkin Rd., Scarsdale, NY 10583.

Sources:

The Order of the Service. New York: Sanctuary of the Masters' Presence, [1969].

★1639★
Shasta Student League Foundation
(Defunct)

The Shasta Student League Foundation, active in the 1930s from its headquarters in Long Beach, California, was a Christian theosophical group in the "I AM" tradition. According to the teachings of the foundation, creation was generated out of the Central Sun, the center of the universe, located beyond the Lyra section of the constellation Sagittarius. The Central Sun contains the Three-Fold Life-Flame and the Form Concept of Cosmic Creation, the pattern from which all forms were created. Creation began as the Three-Fold Life-Flame projected into expression. The Basic Elements of the Flame—Life (energy), Light (intelligence), and Substance—are incorporated in all individual creations. The first level of manifestation is the band of the Macrocosmic Forms and the second that of the White Light Forms of the Angels or Celestial Beings. The White Light Forms are the individual expressions of God that came into being when God said, "Let there be Light." Angels exist in interstellar space, outside the segment of space with stars and planets.

The White Light of the Central Sun travels into the realm of solar systems and planets. When it hits the atmosphere of a planet, such as Earth, it breaks into the seven bands of the light spectrum. The violet ray forms around the outermost atmosphere, the red band is closest to the planet. All manifestation in form occurs through the seven rays. Chief among the manifestations are human beings. Humans result from the projection of the Life Flame of the Cosmic Christ Beings (Angels) into the blue light band (the second band) in the planet's atmosphere. The projected flame became a human ego which then took its bodily substance from the blue light. This human then decided to experience life on the planet's (in this case Earth's) surface. It assumed a flesh body and became like an animal, with one important difference. The animal evolved as an expression of red ray, while humans were projections from the celestial realms into red ray existence.

The seven color bands form a ladder that the human must climb in order to return to its celestial origin. Through various lifetimes (reincarnations) humans search the various levels, and the dominant thoughts and feelings of a person at present indicate the levels explored in previous lives. As each level is explored and its vibrations absorbed, the individual enlivens the next body it inhabits. As the process nears completion, the rate of vibration of the body is so transformed that it is capable of transmutation into an etheric body and can rise to the higher realms of light never to incarnate again. Eventually each individual will ascend and return to the White Light Plane.

As with all "I AM" groups the members of the Foundation utilized decrees—the declaration of spiritual truth in the form of affirmative statements. Among the key decrees used was the Shasta Declaration of Being:

> I Am the Individualized Focus of God Mind, thinking my way back to my Source, the Great Central Sun, from which I was projected at the beginning of this Cosmic Day, and to which I must return at its end.

Sources:

Lyra (Lucy Simms Thompson). *The Shasta Cosmic Key Message.* Long Beach, CA: Shasta Student League Foundation, 1937. 37 pp.

★1640★
Sologa, Inc.
(Defunct)

Sologa, Inc., was established in 1959 by Dr. Ruth Scoles Lennox and included among its members Wayne Taylor, who succeeded to the presidency of the group upon Lennox's death in 1965, and Grace Taylor, his wife, a channel for the masters. In 1968, Taylor left Melbourne and Sologa for New Mexico, where he founded Christ's Truth Church and School of Wisdom and the City of the Sun Foundation.

Membership: In 1968 there were two Sologa groups, one in Miami and one in Melbourne, Florida.

University of the Christ Light with the Twelve Rays
3427 Denson Pl.
Charlotte, NC 28215

In the 1970s, Dr. Mary L. Myers, who has been trained for the previous 40 years by the Angelic Host, established a training center to pass on the material she was receiving to the world. The center has existed under various names, each reflective of the new rise in consciousness: Essene Teachings (1977), University of the Twelve Rays of the Great Central Sun (1982), and the Path of Light (1986). Most recently the center has taken the name, University of the Christ Light with the Twelve Rays. Beginning in 1982, intensive weekly lessons have been distributed that have allowed students to progress to ever higher states of consciousness and make direct contact with the Angelic Host and the Oneness of the Christ Light.

Myers' work has been directed toward the beginning of the New Age as Angelic Beings have entered the earth's atmosphere. The work has focused on pioneering new knowledge, raising the consciousness of members and leaders, and clearing them of their DNA and RNA genetic codes, thus enabling them to enter interdimensional levels through cleansing activities, as each individual established the advanced truth within themselves, their own spirits, and received into conscious awareness, their own souls.

According to Myers, Jesus the Christ is the World teacher who has become One with the Universal Light of the Creator, who created our earth. He represents three great Rays—the Rays of Truth, Wisdom, and Love. He is the perfect interpreter of every portion of the Bible. He is also Yahweh, who has mastered the 12 Rays of the Great Central Sun of our Universe. Yahweh, the Ancient of Days, is considered the administrator of the Path of Light. He is also known as Sanat Kumara. His divine complement is Lady Master Venus Kumara. Yahweh's body is considered so vast that it includes the entire earth and all of humankind.

As of the late 1980s, the organization of Myers' students has decentralized as the leaders she trained took her teachings around the world. Affiliated teachers can be found in Canada, England, France, Germany, Italy, Africa, Singapore, Malaysia, and Australia.

Membership: Not reported.

Sources:

Myers, Mary. *Here Comes the Sun!* N.p, n.d.

___. *My Truth.* Nurnberg, Germany: The Author, 1965.

Myers Kumara, Mary. *The Path of Light.* N.p., n.d.

Other Theosophical Groups

Agni Yoga Society
319 W. 107th St.
New York, NY 10025

The Agni Yoga Society was founded in the mid-1920s, beginning informally as a group of students who gathered to study a book *Leaves of M's Garden,* published in 1924. The Society was founded by Nicholas Roerich (1874-1947) and his wife, Helena Roerich. The Roerichs had left Russia at the time of the Revolution, he being an outstanding artist. They came to the United States in 1920 on the invitation of the Art Institute of Chicago. Very early in their new life in the West, the Roerichs had joined the Theosophical Society, and Helena translated Helena Petrovna Blavat-

sky's major work, *The Secret Doctrine,* into Russian. She also began to receive regular communications from one of the masters originally contacted by Blavatsky, the Master Morya. Her first book, received from him, was *The Leaves of M's Garden.* It and the subsequent volumes have become the prime teaching material of the Agni Yoga Society. Prior to founding the Society, Nicholas had founded several organizations to embody his ideal of art as a unifying force for humanity, the Master Institute of the United Arts and the Nicholas Roerich Museum.

The Roerichs settled permanently in the Punjab in 1929. Helena produced thirteen volumes of material from the Master Morya. Nicholas also wrote numerous books on his continuing concerns of art, peace, and spirituality. A building purchased for a museum to house a collection of his art, also houses the Agni Yoga Society. Membership in the Society is open after one to three years of study of the books. Study groups meet at various locations around the country.

Membership: In 1997 the society reported a membership of 500.

Sources:

Balyoz, Harold. *Three Remarkable Women.* Flagstaff, AZ: Altai Publishers, 1986.

Letters of Helena Roerich, 1929-1938. 2 vols. New York: Agni Yoga Society, 1954.

Nicolas Roerich. New York: Nicolas Roerich Museum, 1974.

Paelian, Garabed. *Nicolas Roerich.* Agoura, CA: Aquarian Educational Group, 1974.

Roerich, Nicolas. *Realm of Light.* New York: Roerich Museum Press, 1931.

Amica Temple of Radiance
Current address not obtained for this edition.

The Amica Temple of Radiance dates to the early 1930s and the experience of Ivah Bergh Whitten. As a young child stricken with an incurable disease, Ms. Whitten was cured through "colour awareness" and began to explore and teach on its potentials. The initial course was first published in 1932. Among Ms. Whitten's students were Roland Hunt and Dorothy Bailey, who structured the Amica Temple in Los Angeles in 1959. Roland Hunt, while in England in 1952, had described to him inwardly two strangers with whom he would become associated upon his return to the United States. The two, Paola Hugh and John Hugh, were, with Hunt, taken under the guidance of an elder brother of the inner wisdom schools. They joined in the formation of Amica. In 1971, an affiliate organization, the Fleur de Lys Foundation of East Sound, Washington, was founded. It is seen as a reflection of an inner order of illumined ones who are seeking the victory of man's higher self over his ego.

The Amica Temple is a continuation and expansion of the colour awareness teachings. As man has evolved, he has become aware of the various aspects of God-the Father principle, the Son, the Holy Ghost-and, in this new era, of the Spirit made manifest in seven colours. Each colour, or ray, as taught by the Theosophical Society, rules an aspect of existence and is in turn ruled by a master. By understanding which ray you were born under, you can discover your proper work and place in life. Each ray also has a healing potential. Overriding the seven rays is the white ray, which shines directly from the Logos. The Amica Temple continues as a structure to present Hunt's teachings to the world. Lessons are offered in color awareness to students around the country.

Membership: Not reported. Centers are located in California and Washington.

Sources:

Bailey, Dorothy A. *The Light of Ivah Bergh Whitten.* Southampton: A.M.I.C.A., n.d.

Hugh, Paola. *I Will Arise*. 2 vols. Tacoma, WA: Amica Temple of Radiance, 1972.

Hunt, Roland T. *Fragrant and Radiant Healing Symphony*. Ashingdon, Essex: C. W. Daniel Company, 1949.

___. *Man Made Clear for the Nu Clear Age*. Lakemont, GA: CSA Press, 1969.

___. *The Seven Rays to Colour Healing*. Ashingdon, Essex: C. W. Daniel Company, 1954.

Whitten, Ivah Bergh. *The Initial Course in Colour Awareness*. London: Amica, n.d.

★1644★
Anthroposophical Society
1923 Geddes Ave.
Ann Arbor, MI 48104-1797

Even before the death of Helena Petrovna Blavatsky, the Theosophical Society (which she had founded) had expanded from its strong center in England to other European countries. A branch of the Theosophical Society was established in Germany in the early 1890s and chartered in 1902. The same year of its chartering, the German Theosophical Society elected to its leadership Rudolf Steiner. Forty-one years old at the time, he had already distinguished himself as a scholar, having previously edited an issue of Goethe's scientific writings and having worked on the standard edition of Goethe's works. His writing, editing, and teaching increasingly led him into a mystic philosophy and experience, a decidedly Christian mysticism.

Invited to address an audience of Theosophists in the winter of 1901/02, he lectured on "Christianity as Mystical Fact," in which his thesis was that the ancient mystics had served to prepare the way for Christ on earth and that Christ was the focus of earth's evolution. Theosophists had generally been taught to regard Jesus as just another avatar. In spite of this disagreement, Steiner's intellectual and charismatic leadership was desired by the still small group. Steiner accepted a leadership role, while reserving his independence, because the Theosophists were the only ones with any interest in his work. In the next decade, he began to publish his ideas on the nature of man, the evolution of the earth and initiation. In 1909, he published *Spiritual Hierarchies*, which elucidated his teachings on the centrality of Christ. This work focused his growing dissatisfaction with Annie Besant, the recently elected president of the Theosophical Society.

Steiner's differences with Annie Besant and the Theosophical Society were fundamental. The society was becoming more and more involved in Eastern mystical occult practices. It practiced a system of withdrawal from the manifest material world and centered on meditative yogic disciplines. It regarded Christ as just another God-embodied teacher and Christianity as just another religion. Steiner approached the spiritual in a world-affirming scientific spirit, based upon his research in medieval forms, particularly those of the West. Eastern religion he saw as a way of the past, replaced by Christianity. For Steiner, Christ summed up the Eastern search and launched the new era of finding the spiritual in the material (science). The disagreements between Steiner and the Society climaxed after Annie Besant announced the return of Christ in Jiddu Krishnamurti. Steiner declared that no one could be a member of the German Theosophical Society and the Order of the Star of the East, an organization formed to prepare for the coming of a new Christ in Krishnamurti, then still a youth. Besant revoked the charter of the German Theosophical Society in 1912. Steiner took fifty-five of the sixty-five lodges and formed the Anthroposophical Society.

Anthroposophy hold that reality has a spiritual basis, i.e., matter is real, but it is derived from spirit. There is the belief in reincarnation and the possibility of initiatory experiences which expand consciousness of the spiritual realm. Steiner taught that humanity had originally shared the spiritual consciousness of the cosmos.

Humanity's present knowledge is only a vestige of primordial cognition. Human beings have, however, a latent capacity for horizonless vision and there are certain disciplines by which it can be recovered. Steiner did not limit the cover of vision to mere techniques, but held that initiatory openings might come throuh study, music, art, and the informed use of imagination. Steiner saw his work as the organization of a science of initiation. Jeasus Christ was viewed by Steiner as both the one fully initiated person in human history, the one with full sensory perception, as the Christ.

The headquarters of the society were established in Diornach, Switzerland, where a huge center was designed by Steiner. The architecturally unique, wooden building was built by volunteers from dozens of countries during World War I and was named the Goetheanum. It was burned by an arsonist in 1923, after which Steiner reformed the society and designed a new Goetheanum, one of the first large structures constructed from pre-formed concrete.

Steiner continued lecturing and writing until a few days before his death on March 30, 1925. His lifetime of work consisted of more than 400 published books and 6,000 lectures (collected into 300 volumes).

After World War I, Steiner's ideas on social reform, published in his book *The Threefold Commonwealth*, were given serious consideration in the restructuring of Germany, a prominence which led to the spread of his movement across Europe and England. It was brought to the United States in 1925. The society was legally established in the U.S. in 1938. It spread initially among German immigrants but soon was to found in urban centers throughout North America and Canada. After World War II, Steiner's books were translated into English; a publishing venture was then formed. The Anthroposophic Press, located in Hudson, New York, is part of a worldwide publishing effort to translate and distribute Steiner's work.

Work from Steiner's ideas continued to flourish in both the arts and sciences. In addition to his efforts to manifest the spiritual architecture, Steiner worked in other art forms. He wrote a series of modern mystery dramas. He developed Eurythmy, which translates the sounds, phrases, and rhythms of speech, or the dynamic elements of music into movement and gesture. It has been described as "visible speech," "visible sound," and the "movement language of the soul." The colors themselves are seen as opening the doors to an art that embodies the soul. He was also a sculptor who sought to influence this art form with "living forms."

In 1923 Steiner created Biodynamics, the first non-chemical or "organic" agricultural movement that related to the earth as a living organism (the Gaia hypothesis). Today, the Biodynamic gardeners launched the Community Supported Agriculture (CSA) movement. The Demeter Association certifies Biodynamic farms in the United States, Mexico, and the Dominican Republic. Since the 1950s, Soil scientists working with spiritual insight have successfully composted TNT and managed organic composting projects for the cities of New York and Los Angeles.

A Physicians Association for Anthroposophically Extended Medicine (PAAM) and the Artemesia Association of Therapies use Steiner's insights into health and healing. Companies such as Weleda in the United States and similar European pharmaceuticals and personal-care product corporations are based upon anthroposophical insights. In 1997, an anthroposophical cancer therapy based upon mistletoe extract was named to the National Institute of Health (NIH) shortlist of alternative therapies worthy of further study.

Other institutions that adhere to Steiner's insights are the Camphill Association, The Rudolf Steiner Foundation, and the Waldorf Schools.

The society is organized into branches throughout the country. Branches sponsor lectures, cultural events, and study groups discussing Steiner's writings. The Rudolf Steiner Library in New York houses a collection of more than 20,000 volumes including Steiner's works, additional anthroposophical titles, and books covering the whole of Western spirituality. They are indpendent national societies for Canada and Hawaii.

Membership: Not reported. There are 33 national Anthrophsophical Societies around the world.

Periodicals: *The Journal for Anthroposophy.*

Sources:

The Creed. London: Christian Community Press, 1962.

Derry, Evelyn. *Seven Sacraments in the Christian Community.* London: Christian Community Press, 1949.

Heidenreich, Alfred. *Growing Point.* London: Christian Community Press, 1965.

McKnight, Floyd. *Rudolf Steiner and Anthroposophy.* New York: Anthroposophical Society in America, 1967.

Richards, M.C. *Toward Wholeness: Rudolf Steiner Education in America.* Middletown, CT: Wesleyan University Press, 1980.

Rudolf Steiner, An Autobiography. Blauvelt, NY: Rudolf Steiner Publications, 1977.

Shepherd, A. P. *A Scientist of the Invisible.* New York: British Book Centre, 1959.

Wachsmuth, Guenther. *The Life and Work of Rudolf Steiner.* New York: Whittier Books, 1955.

★1645★
Bodha Society of America
(Defunct)

The Bodha Society of America was incorporated in 1936 by its president, Ms. Violet B. Reed. She described it as a movement fostering spiritual consciousness through self- realization and world service. Spiritual virility can be attained only through a better outlook on life and a deeper realization of the spiritual realm. According to the Society, the Bodha movement was begun in 1907 under the direction of the Sanctuaries of Tibet and Sikkim and assumed "the full responsibility which once rested in the Theosophical Society, this organization being no longer patronized by its founders, inspirers and real leaders: the masters." The Bodha Society was seen as the vehicle of the Great Brotherhood, the ascended masters who were once humans and who now as spirits teach people about spiritual realities.

The Society kept the three spiritual festivals associated with Buddhism, particularly Wesak. Associated centers were opened in France and Cuba; world headquarters were claimed to be in Tibet. National headquarters were in Long Beach, California. *Sun Rays*, a periodical was published.

★1646★
Christward Ministry
20560 Questhaven Rd.
Escondido, CA 92029

The Christward Ministry was founded by Flower A. Newhouse, a clairvoyant and teacher of Christian Mysticism since the 1920s. Current headquarters of the ministry are at Questhaven Retreat, founded in 1940—a 640-acre nature reserve and spiritual retreat near Escondido, California. The Christward Ministry utilizes the principles of Christian gospel, meditation, reincarnation, astrology, and Carl Jung's transformational psychology. The emphasis is on meditation's helpfulness with practical living, as well as awareness of angelic influence on spiritual development.

Man is considered an embodied soul evolving spiritually through a series of human incarnations, eventually rising to masterhood and beyond. The number of current masters is considered to be small, and incarnated Masters to anonymous, private individuals who avoid fame or worldly power. Newhouse has written a body of work describing angelic hosts and their hierarchies; angels are unrelated in evolution to humans, but certain hosts interact with humans and help in our spiritual guidance—guardian angels, nature angels, religious angels, and karmic angels are a few angelic orders that influence humankind.

Newhouse died in 1994. A staff of ordained ministers provides a program of weekly Sunday worship services, evening classes, and triannual weekend retreats. Most of Newhouse's books were published by The Christward Ministry and include titles on religion, prayer, meditation, and esoteric knowledge. Her works have been published in English, German, and Czechoslovakian and will also be available in French and Spanish during the next decade.

Membership: No membership policy. Freewill love offerings.

Educational Facilities: Questhaven Academy, Escondido, California.

Periodicals: *Life at Quest Haven.*

Sources:

The Christward Ministry. Vista, CA: Christward Ministry, 1947.

Isaac, Stephen. *The Way of Discipleship to Christ.* Escondido, CA: Christward Ministry, 1976.

Newhouse, Flower A. *The Christward Way.* 4 vols. (lessons 1-208). Vista, CA: Christward Publications, n.d.

___. *The Meaning and Value of the Sacraments.* Escondido, CA: Christward Ministry, 1971.

★1647★
Church of Cosmic Origin and School of Thought
Box 257
June Lake, CA 93529

The Church of Cosmic Origin was founded in 1963 at Independence, California, by Hope Troxell (b. 1906), who had for thirty years been lecturer on "expanded concepts." In her early life, she received three major healings from the angelic host, and during the 1950s, she received instructions from the masters and published several books of their material. *From Matter to Light* contains messages from several different masters, including Djual Khool, Alcyon, Univera of Jupiter, Melchizedek, and Nerfertiti. *The Mohada Teachings from the Galaxies* contains a series of messages from Mohada, a particularly significant master for Ms. Troxell.

The church teaches what is termed "cosmic Christianity." Man is considered an evolving being whose purpose is to become one with Light and escape the continual reincarnation and involvement in matter. Man originally fell from grace into matter after his creation by the Elohim, the family of God. Jesus came from the Elohim, is now a master and is due to return for judgment and to lift those who have followed the God-Way. In the coming age, America will lead the world in the spiritual plane of God's laws, according to the Church of Cosmic Origin.

The cosmic wisdom given by Jesus and the masters illumines the Bible. The Church of Cosmic Origin also use the writings from Qumran and models itself upon the resident community model of the Essenes. The symbol of the church is the Greek cross in a circle with a rose on it, symbolizing the risen Christ. The masters gave the format for the church services, which is, as in the original Christian church, the circle. The directors of the church are in the center, with members, students and visitors around them. Services include Scripture readings, readings from the masters, and a sermon as received by Ms. Troxell (without a trance-state). There are no ministers.

The church and school are headquartered at June Lake, California. Since the main work is the preparation of teachers, the number of residents at the school is very small. An adult community participates in daily classes for both advanced and beginning studies. Twice a day, prayer circles are held; church services are each Sunday. The bulk of students are those taking correspondence lessons across the United States and in several other English-speaking countries.

Membership: Not reported.

Periodicals: *Cosmic Frontiers.*

Sources:

Troxell, Hope. *From Matter to Light.* June Lake, CA: School of Thought, 1968.

___. *The Mohada Teachings.* Independence, CA: School of Thought, [1963].

___. *Through the Open Key.* El Monte, CA: Understanding Publishing Co., n.d.

★1648★
Ann Ree Colton Foundation of Niscience
336 W. Colorado
Glendale, CA 91209

The Ann Ree Colton Foundation of Niscience was formed in 1953 by Ann Ree Colton (1898-1984) and Jonathan Murro (d. 1991). Clairvoyant from childhood, Colton was in her twenties when she began to contact the Masters or Great Immortals. In 1932, she began her public ministry and became well-known as a prophet. A church was formed in 1936 in Florida and continued for nine years. In 1945, the church was closed, and Colton entered a transition period. In 1952, she met Jonathan Murro and together they established the foundation blending concerns of religion, philosophy, science, and the creative arts.

According to Colton, the Masters will no longer incarnate. 33 cosmos disciples scattered throughout the world are telepathically aligned to the higher worlds. They work with 13 telepathic disciples. (All of the disciples are advanced in the sciences or humanities, but their spiritual work is unknown to their colleagues.) When a cosmos disciple leaves the physical world, a telepathic disciple replaces him, and an advanced student becomes a telepathic disciple. Beyond the disciples, in the second heaven, in the spheres of light, dwell the masters. In the third heaven dwell the archangels, Jesus and his disciples, and the archetypes of God, the very blueprints for the creation of the earth. Through the archangels under the Christ, God initiates the archetypes and initiates the new in creation. The time when men are open to the third heaven of the archangels and the archetypes is a time of receiving the Holy Spirit.

Colton, when she was permanently united with the Niscience Archetype, was told that the "hum" of his archetype will bring a new spiritual impulse. It will unite people with the Jesus Ethic, thus bringing them closer to the Archetype of Niscience.

The foundation has found outward expression in the formation of chapels and research units, the main one located at the Glendale, California, headquarters. The foundation publishes and distributes books written by Ann Ree Colton and Jonathan Murro. Monthly White Paper Lessons are sent to all members. New members receive The Mediator series, a seven-month orientation course. Advanced students can qualify to become lay ministers through the Niscience Guild. Conclaves are held periodically around the country through the year for foundation members, or any interested individuals.

Membership: In 1995, the foundation reported 300 members in the United States, with foreign members in Canada, Holland, Barbados, and Australia.

Periodicals: *Agape Magazine.* Send orders to Box 2057, Glendale, CA 91209.

Sources:

Colton, Ann Ree. *Men in White Apparel.* Glendale, CA: ARC Publishing Company, 1961.

Colton, Ann Ree. *The Soul and the Ethic.* Glendale, CA: ARC Publishing Company, 1963.

Colton, Ann Ree. *Vision for the Future.* Glendale, CA: ARC Publishing Company, 1960.

Colton, Ann Ree, and Jonathan Murro. *Prophet for the Archangels.* Glendale, CA: ARC Publishing Company, 1964.

Murro, Jonathan. *God-Realization Journal.* Glendale, CA: ARC Publishing Company, 1975.

★1649★
Ecumenical Ministry of the Unity of All Religions
107 N. Ventura St.
Ojai, CA 93023

Philippine educator Benito F. Reyes, former president of the University of the City of Manila, migrated to the United States in the early 1970s with a vision for a new kind of university which, in its program, would be truly worldwide in its outlook. In 1974, he founded the World Institute of Avasthology which was soon renamed the World University of America. Reyes developed a philosophy which he called *avasthology*, or the science of total consciousness. Avasthology symbolized the joining of Eastern and Western civilization, and the integration of inner- and outer-consciousness. Avasthology became the main philosophy of the university which was opened in Ojai, California.

The university offers a degree program in philosophy, psychology, and religious studies, as well as vocational certificates in meditation, astrology, spiritual ministry, thanatology, and yoga. Its curriculum offers a full round of classes in transpersonal psychology and subjects related to altered states of consciousness (such as dreams and meditation). The philosophy of the school emphasizes the Allness of God and humanity's oneness with God; thanatology, the holistic approach to death; and altered states of consciousness experienced through meditation.

The Ecumenical Ministry of the Unity of All Religions is located adjacent to the university and connected to it through the leadership of Dr. Reyes and his wife Dominga L. Reyes. Its beliefs are consistent with the Avasthology philosophy of the school. Reyes believes that love is the essence of all religion. Love is defined as the primal urge to resume the state of Oneness with God and all of life. Weekly worship follows a liturgy with acknowledgement of the spiritual teachers of the ages. Among more recent teachers are Sathya Sai Baba of India, and Baha'u'llah of the Baha'i movement.

Membership: There is one congregation with 200 members. There are ten members in Canada.

Educational Facilities: World University of America, Ojai, California.

Parsophia Academy, Kobe, Japan.

Periodicals: *Avasthology.* • *Clear Light.* • *WWW.*

Sources:

Reyes, Benito F. *Christianizing Christians.* Ojai, CA: The Author, n.d.

___. *The Essence of All Religion.* Ojai, CA: The Author, 1983.

___. *On World Peace.* Ojai, CA: World University, 1977.

Reyes, Domingo L. *The Story of Two Souls.* Ojai, CA: The Author, 1984.

★1650★
Institute of Divine Metaphysical Research
℅ Dr. Kenneth Haverly, III
IDMR—Florida
PO Box 536156
Orlando, FL 32856-6156

The Institute for Divine Metaphysical Research grew out of a vision of Dr. Henry Clifford Kinley which occurred on June 6, 1931 in Springfield, Ohio. Kinley, a holiness church minister, was given a vision of Yahweh (who others mistakenly call God) and His plan for the ages. He began to give classes on the insight derived from the vision the following year and soon thereafter he founded the Kinley Institute. Among his first students was Carl F. Gross, who became his lifelong associate and president of the institute. In 1958, with approximately seventy of his students, Kinley moved to Los Angeles and incorporated the Institute for Divine Metaphysical Research. In 1961, Elohim the Archetype (Original Pattern of the Universe, the major exposition of the vision) appeared. Copies were immediately sent to a number of prominent world political and religious leaders. In 1971 twelve ministers of the institute were sent out on an Ecclesiastical Peace Mission to countries in Europe and the Middle East. A second such mission to countries on every continent was conducted in 1975.

The intent of the institute has been to spread the message of Kinley's vision as presented in his book. The teachings draw from a variety of sources including both the Sacred Name Movement and theosophy. In the vision he learned the real name of the Holy One of Israel (Yahweh) and of his nature and purposes. Yahweh is Spirit Substance, without form. As Elohim, Yahweh appears in His super incoporeal form and in that form was seen by Moses (Exodus 24), Isaiah (Isaiah 6:1-4), and the disciples at the Mount of Transfiguration (Matthew 17:1-2). Yahweh-Elohim has also taken physical form generally as the material creation (matter is condensed spirit) and specifically as Yahshua the Messiah (generally known as Jesus). After the death and resurrection of Yahshua, Yahweh continued in his physical form as the Comforter or Holy Spirit, and dwells in preachers of the true gospel.

Yahweh-Elohim, as was revealed to Kinley, is the archtypal pattern of the universe, a pattern revealed to Moses and embodied in the Hebrew tabernacle. It is, however, also repeated in numerous earthly structures, among which is the Kaballah, which Kinley terms "theosophy."

Yahweh's purpose is revealed through the ages (i.e., particular periods of history) and dispensations (i.e., the divinely appointed ordering of earthly affairs by Yahweh). The dispensations as recounted by Kinley generally follow that proposed by C. I. Scofield in his reference Bible, and adopt a traditional chronology. The first dispensation begins with Yahweh's covenant with Adam, the second with Noah, the third with Abraham, and the fourth with Noah. Kinley is insistent that the fifth dispensation, that of the "law of the Spirit" or New Testament, this present church age, began not at Jesus' birth but at his resurrection and Pentecost. Most importantly, the present dispensation is swiftly drawing to a close and the next dispensation, that of the Kingdom in Immortality, will begin around the year 2000. The revelation of Yahweh's purposes to Kinley and his work of spreading the information ushered in the last days of the church age.

Membership: In 1997, the Institute reported 137 groups in the United States and four in Canada. There were also a single group in Trinidad, two in Mexico, and one in Africa.

Remarks: The institute has published a statement of Aims which seems to draw directly upon the statement of objectives of the Theosophical Society. It reads, in part, that its aims include: "To form a nucleus of Universal Brotherhood of Humanity in Yahshua the Messiah without distinction of Race or Nationality, Creed, Sex, Caste or Color; To investigate the unexplained Spirit Law or so-called Law of Nature and the Powers latent in man; To encourage and promote the study of Scriptures, comparative Religions, Psychology, Philosophy and Modern (practical and occult) Science..."

Sources:

Kinley, Henry Clifford. *Elohim the Atchetype (Original) Pattern of the Universe.* Los Angeles, CA: Institute of Divine Metaphysical Research, 1969.

★1651★
Light of Christ Community Church
% Sparrow Hawk Village
11 Summit Ridge Dr.
Tahlaquah, OK 74464-9215

The Light of Christ Community Church grew out of the 1958 near-death experience of its founder, Carol E. Parrish-Harra (b. 1935). While giving birth to her sixth child, she was given sodium pentothal to ease her pain. She had an allergic reaction to the drug, her lung collapsed, and her consciousness slipped out of her body. As a result of the experience her life changed. She came to believe that she was an example of what in New Age circles came to be called a "walk-in." As defined by Ruth Montgomery, who originated the idea, a walk-in is an idealistic soul who, through progress in previous incarnations, has earned the privilege of taking over unwanted bodies. Parrish-Harra believes that the personality who inhabited her body left in 1958 and a new soul moved in.

Throughout the 1960s Parrish-Harra's life took a new direction. Toward the end of the decade she was led to a spiritualist church in St. Petersburg, Florida, where she met a teacher, Ann Manser. In 1971 she was ordained in the Christian Metaphysical Church and began a career as a pastor/teacher. In 1976 she founded the Villa Serena Spiritual Community in Sarasota, Florida, the core community of the Light of Christ Community Church.

In 1981 Parrish-Harra had a strong psychic message to found a new community, and in November of that year the trustees of the Light of Christ Community Church acquired 332 acres of land on Sparrowhawk Mountain near Tahlequah, Oklahoma. Sparrow Hawk Village became the new headquarters of the church and of its school, the Sancta Sophia Seminary. Sparrow Hawk was designed as a self-consciously New Age center that seeks to encourage the growth, freedom, and strength of its members. It is organized in clusters (tribes) in such a way that the community provides a balance between intimacy/community (smallness) and security (largeness). Each family owns its own home and shares a portion of the entire community's property.

The church's teachings are eclectic, drawing upon theosophical (especially the writings of Alice A. Bailey), Agni Yoga, the Kabbalah, and esoteric Christianity. It affirms the existence of One Almighty Power in the universe, the Cause of all creation, and the Great Ones (called Masters in the theosophy) who guide humanity and can be thought of as the Saviors of the world. Christ is seen as the vision of perfection, and his teachings are the path to perfection. The church believes that within each human is a spark of the Almighty Power, and each person is capable of unfolding his or her spiritual potential.

The Light of Christ Community Church is headed by a board of trustees, with Parrish-Harra serving as president. The Sancta Sophia Seminary offers a full program of ministerial training offering both master's and doctoral degrees. The church recognizes five forms of ministry: pastor, minister-scholar, minister-priest, theologian, and prophet-seer. The church affirms its allegiance to the Christian tradition and has affiliated with the International Council of Community Churches.

Membership: In 1997 the community reported 450 members.

Educational Facilities: Sancta Sophia Seminary, Tahlaquah, Oklahoma.

Periodicals: *Sparrow Hawk Villager.*

Sources:

Parrish-Harra, Carol W. *Aquarian Rosary: Reviving the Art of Mantra Yoga.* Tahlequah, OK: Sparrow Hawk Press, 1988.

___. *The Book of Rituals: Personal and Planetary Transformations.* Santa Monica, CA: IBS Press, 1990.

___. *Messengers of Hope.* Black Mountain, NC: New Age Press, 1983.

___. *A New Age Handbook on Death and Dying.* Marina del Rey, CA: De-Vorss & Co., 1982.

★1652★
Lighted Way
(Defunct)

The Lighted Way is described as a "New Age School for Discipleship Training." It was founded in 1966 by Muriel R. Tepper (known as Muriel Isis), under the direction of Master D.K. of the White Brotherhood. It is guided and inspired by the cosmic mother Isis. Muriel is the outer symbol of the mother principle-truth and inspiration. The mother as Isis reveals the cosmic laws and pure truths for the building of the immortal light body and the resurrection of the physical form. These laws include the laws of light radiation, magnetism, cause and effect, polarity, and correspondence.

The Lighted Way is the highway back to divinity. To help the members in their return, a variety of services is offered. Light Radiation Circles allow each person a chance to gain direct awareness of the Universal Mind. Individual counseling in Akashic records, in the aura and in personal soul evolvement is offered by Muriel, either in person or by mail on cassette tape. (Akashic records are the recordings on the "universal ethers" of all thoughts and actions; psychics can "tap into" these records. The auras are psychic emanations from the human body; psychics can see and interpret auras.) Full moon meditations are held monthly. Classes are offered in meditation, Yoga and the lessons of Isis on metaphysical truths. Healing services are held weekly.

Membership: In 1973 centers were functioning in Los Angeles, Pacific Palisades, Costa Mesa, and Hollywood, California.

Sources:

Tepper, Muriel R. *The Lighted Way Road to Freedom.* Los Angeles: Lighted Way Press, n.d.

___. *Mechanisms of the Personality through Personology.* Pacific Palisade, CA: Lighted Way Press, n.d.

★1653★
Oasis Fellowship
Current address not obtained for this edition.

The Oasis Fellowship began in the home of George White and his wife, Alice White. While meditating, they began to make contact with several spirit entities named Elawa, Malala and Yeban, believed to be teachers from a higher plane of evolvement. As messages began to come through, friends of the Whites began to attend the sessions. Healing prayer was a major concern. As time passed, the Whites disposed of their business and went in search of a place for a center to which those dedicated to the program could gravitate. After a year of searching, such a spot was located near Florence, Arizona, and the Oasis Fellowship began.

At Florence, on the 17.5 acres, members of the fellowship lead a communal-like existence in separate mobile homes and travel trailers. Many leave during the summer months. Soon after the establishment in Arizona, weekly "lessons in living" began to come through the channels. The lessons were taped, transcribed, and sent out, on request only, across the country. Early in the experiment, the teachers specified that no charge was ever to be made or money solicited. If ever there were insufficient voluntary "love gifts" to cover cost of production and mailing the lessons, they should be stopped, accepting the lack as "evidence that the power had gone out of them." From the beginning, adequate financial support has always been received.

Beliefs of the fellowship follow the teachings of Jesus and the lessons are frequently comments by the spirit teachers on a Bible passage. There is strong emphasis on the spiritual evolvement of the individual. Both psychic communication, if on a spiritual level, and reincarnation are accepted. God is seen as the center of life and a Spirit shining within.

Membership: Beside the small group residing at the Oasis in Florence, Arizona, between 120 and 150 regularly receive the lessons. Some of these in turn share them with others as the leaders of study groups. The lessons are sent out across the United States and Canada, as well as several foreign countries, most notably Nigeria.

★1654★
Open Way
Box 217
Celina, TN 38551

The Open Way is a New Age group centered in Celina, Tennessee, and headed by Lovie Webb Gasteiner. There is a close affinity with Mary L. Myers of the Essene Teachings. The Open Way teaches that God manifests as Father and Mother and lives in all. God is the source of life, love, peace, strength and abundant life. Man's goal is a return to God in self-realization. The law of life is giving and receiving, and the Open Way teaches exercises on giving and receiving divine energy. The secret is tensing and relaxing the muscles, nerves, and tissues of the body in combination with the human voice, used in speaking, chanting, humming, and singing.

Membership: Not reported.

★1655★
Order of the Cross
Current address not obtained for this edition.

The Order of the Cross was founded in 1904 in Great Britain by J. Todd Ferrier (1855-1943). Ferrier had been raised in Scotland and entered the Congregational Church ministry. He resigned from the ministry in 1903 and the following year began issuing a magazine, *The Herald of the Cross.* During the next decade he wrote his two most important books, *The Master: His Life and Teachings* (1913) and *The Logia,* or *Sayings of the Master,* were written. Following their publication, the order began to grow and in 1991 headquarters were established in London. Permanent headquarters were purchased in 1926.

Ferrier taught a form of Christian theosophy. The order believes that the earth has been subject to a gradual deterioration over many millennia. This deterioration is visible in the disorder in nature and society and is related to the fading of the divine Light in human life. It was to check the deterioration that Jesus came into the world and his Mission is now, in the twentieth century, beginning to bear fruit. The effects of His restoration of the Light has become visible and should become even more visible as more rapid changes occur. Individuals who participate in this restoration will recover a sense of purpose and the ability to communicate with the unseen.

Having perceived the nature of Jesus' work, to restore the resurrected spiritual life to humanity, Ferrier was able to clearly present in his many books the true message of Jesus apart from the distortion of the Christian church. In this light, the order has assumed an anti-institutional stance and teaches that Jesus did not intend the creation of an earthly institution but focused upon the restoration of souls to a spiritual state, which he termed "Jesushood" in which the oneness of life in realized. That state is followed by the state of "Christhood," or mystical illumination.

Ferrier's own awakening, as that of a number of his early followers, was through the animal rights movement. The order is vegetarian in practice and committed to anti-vivisection. It has called on the adoption of a "bloodless" diet. Members are also taught to seek after the Christ-life by following a path of self-denial, self-sacrifice, and self-abandonment to the Divine service and will.

The order is organized through a number of groups around the world. Where several groups are relatively close together, they are associated in councils made up of representatives of the groups. The order is guided by a self-perpetuating executive council and an advisory committee of representatives of the groups.

The order was brought to America through the circulation of Ferrier's many books. He made his first trip in 1939 and groups have been functioning around the country since that time. Among the early followers were J. F. Rowney, the owner of a metaphysical publishing house in Santa Barbara, California, who later published the only biographical work on Ferrier.

Membership: In 1990 the organization reported 96 members in six centers in the United States and one center with two members in Canada. There were 720 members worldwide in centers in the United Kingdom, France, Australia, and New Zealand.

Periodicals: *The Newsletter of the Order of the Cross.* Send orders to 10, De vere Gardens, Kensington, London Wb 5AE, United Kingdom.

Sources:

Ferrier, J. Todd. *The Divine Renaissance.* 2 vols. London: Order of the Cross, 1963.

___. *Life's Mysteries Unveiled.* London: Order of the Cross, 1953.

___. *The Logia* or *Sayings of the Master.* London: Percy Lund, Bradford and Co., 1916, 1926.

___. *The Master: His Life and Teachings.* London: Percy Lund, Humpries and Co., 1913, 1925.

Hymns for Worship with Tunes. London: Order of the Cross, 1965.

Kemmis, E. Mary Gordon. *Shepherd of Souls: Some Impressions of the Life and Ministry of John Todd Ferrier.* Santa Barbara, CA: J. F. Rowney Press, 1947.

Our Informal Fellowship: Some Foundational Statements. London: Order of the Cross, 1963.

★1656★
Philo-Polytechnic Center
(Defunct)

The Philo-Polytechnic Center of Los Angeles had aims similar to those of the Bodha Society of America. It was headed by Ronald Clifton and published *The Bodha Renaissance.*

★1657★
Sun Center
(Defunct)

The Sun Center was a theosophical group formed in Akron, Ohio, in the 1920s which developed a uniquely Christian emphasis. It took its name from the theosophical concept of God as the Great Central Sun. Much of the inspiration for the center came from Joseph S. Benner (d. 1941) author of the popular mystical/occult volume, *The Impersonal Life.* The small book, penned prior to World War I, was directed to what was considered to be the true self, the impersonal self, the spirit within, also identified with the "I AM," the Christ Self, and God's Holy Spirit. Beginning in the 1920s, Benner also developed a series of lessons to assist students to understand and progressively work with the ideas presented in *The Impersonal Life. The Way Out* and *The Way Beyond,* the first of these booklets, provided training for the development and discipline of the mind. *The Inner Life Course* dealt with the awakening of the soul. A final set of lessons led students to the unfolding of the spirit.

Through its magazine, *The Inner Life* begun in 1933, the Sun Center solicited support for its work as a group of followers of Christ to bring the Light of Christ to every soul ready to receive it. As a first step, those related to the center were asked to serve in the cause of brotherhood by entering into the silence each day at noon. During these silent moments, each person would see him/herself as a center of Love's Light and Power and would pour that Love out upon the world. Noon was chosen as the moment when the earth received the greatest downpouring of the light (wisdom), heat (love) and energy (power) of the sun (the visible expression of Father-God).

The Sun Center continued to operate through the 1930s, but eventually dissolved. There is no record of the size of the center's support, though in the mid-1930s there were more than 30 groups across the United States and in Australia, Canada, England, France, and New Zealand. After Brenner's death, the publishing rights of his books were eventually turned over to Willing Publishing Company which was in turn absorbed by DeVorss Publishing Company, which keeps *The Impersonal Life,* in print to this day.

Remarks: The Sun Publishing Company, intimately connected with the Sun Center, was publisher of the books of the Aquarian Foundation, a short-lived theosophical group in the 1920s.

Sources:

The Impersonal Life. San Gabriel, CA: Willing Publishing Co., 1971.

Morgan, Elise Nevins. *Your Own Path.* Akron, OH: Sun Publishing Co., 1928.

The Way Beyond Course. Akron, OH: Sun Publishing Co., n.d. [193-].

The Way Out. Akron, OH: Sun Publishing Co., 1930.

The Way Out Course. Akron, OH: Sun Publishing Co., [193-].

★1658★
Universal Great Brotherhood
Administrative Council of the U. S. A.
Box 9154
St. Louis, MO 63117

The Universal Great Brotherhood was formed by Serge Raynaud de la Ferriere (b. 1916), a Frenchman who had been involved in the esoteric from his childhood. As a young man, he traveled to Egypt, where, according to his biography, he was initiated as the "Sublime Crowned Cophto and Great Priest Khediviar." At the age of 22, in London, he received a degree of Doctor of Hermetic Science and the next year, in Amsterdam, Doctor of Universal Science. During World War II he became closely identified with the Theosophical Society in France and joined the Theosophical and Astrological Lodge in London. After the war, his occult work expanded and he became active in a Masonic body.

De la Ferriere's early esoteric work prepared him for an encounter with Master Sun W. K., described as the "Superior Power of Tibet," who gave de la Ferriere his mission to begin the exposition of initiatic principles to the general public. De la Ferriere founded the Universal Great Brotherhood and for the next three years traveled widely, establishing the brotherhood in centers around the world. Very early in his travels, he went to Venezuela where he met Jose Manuel Estrada, who was to become his leading student.

Estrada (b. 1900) had, for nine years, announced the arrival of an avatar (an incarnation of God) and had gathered a group waiting upon the avatar. After their meeting, Estrada accepted de la Ferriere, who spent eighteen months with Estrada and his group, and on March 21, 1948, reopened the Universal Great Brotherhood in a public manner.

In 1950, de la Ferriere turned over the management of the brotherhood to Estrada and retired to a quiet life of esoteric work and writing. Estrada assumed the title of director general. The work grew steadily in Latin America through the 1950s and 1960s. In 1969 Estrada sent Rev. Gagpa Anita Montero Campion to the United States. She settled in St. Louis and began to teach yoga classes. She shared the teachings of the brotherhood with her pupils and in 1970 organized the first brotherhood center. It soon spread to Ann Arbor, Michigan; Chicago; and New York City.

The brotherhood describes itself as an educational organization rather than a religion. It is an initiatic school designed to assist humanity in its transition to a new age, often spoken of as the transition from the Age of Pisces to the Age of Aquarius. The birthplace of this new age is the Americas, hence the reopening of the brotherhood of the West.

The Brotherhood is dedicated to the attainment of peace by raising the consciousness of humanity both individually and collectively. The brotherhood offers a number of services to pre-initiates. It sponsors health care programs with special emphasis on preventive medicine and natural cures. The organization strongly advocates vegetarianism. It also sponsors a variety of classes to promote personal growth, such as hatha yoga, martial arts, astrology, and meditation. In this regard it also promotes the Cosmic Ceremony, a Universal form of worship that allows each person to get in touch with his or her own highest concept of the divine.

Participants in brotherhood public programs, designated followers, may be invited to become initiates. Once initiated they become members of the Esoteric College and receive the title Gegnian, or Little Novice. Afterward they pass upward through several degrees: first degree, Getuls or Novice; second degree, Reverend Gag-pa, or affiliated; third degree, Right Reverend Gelong, or Adept; and the fourth degree, Respectable Guru, or Instructor. Currently held by only the international leaders, still higher degrees are, in principle, open to all. The fifth degree, Honorable Sat Chellah, or Disciple, is held by Domingo Dias Porta; and the sixth degree, Venerable Sat Arhat, or Missionry, is held by Estrada. Only one person can hold the seventh degree as Sat Guru, the Master, presently de la Ferriere. Administratively, the brotherhood is headed by the superior council, which operates under the Sat Guru and makes all the decisions concerning the activities of the brotherhood internationally. Under it are national and regional councils.

Membership: In 1988, the Brotherhood reported approximately 200 members in the United States. The Brotherhood has opened centers in seventeen countries. In the United States, centers can be found in St. Louis, Missouri; Chicago, Illinois; Ann Arbor, Michigan; Brooklyn, New York; Oklahoma City, Oklahoma; Los Angeles, California; and Jamaica Plains, Massachusetts. There is also a retreat facility, Shining Waters Ashram Community, near Fredericktown, Maryland.

Sources:

Biography, the Sublime Maestre, Sat Guru, Dr. Serge Raymaud de la Ferriere. St. Louis, MO: Educational Publications of the I. E. S., 1976.

Montero-Campion, Anita. *My Guru from South America: Sat Arhat Dr. Jose Manuel Estrada.* St. Louis: The Author, 1976.

★1659★
Universal Religious Fellowship
(Defunct)

The Universal Religious Fellowship was founded by Harriette Augusta Curtiss (1855-1932), also known by her religious name Rahmea, and Frank Homer Curtiss (1875-1946), also known by his religious name Pyrahmos. Homer Curtiss, a physician and graduate of the University of Pennsylvania, married Harriette in 1907. They began to head a study group which formally began its work on January 1, 1908. Originally known as the Order of The 15, a name derived by numerological reference, it soon took its more descriptive title, the Order of Christian Mystics, by which it was known through the 1920s. The Curtisses formed a corporation, the Universal Religious Fellowship in 1928, and that name gradually came to denominate their efforts through the 1930s. For a brief period in the 1920s, the name Church of the Wisdom Religion was also used. The Order was founded in Philadelphia, Pennsylvania, but moved its headquarters to California prior to World War I. Around 1925 it moved to Washington, D.C., where it remained until after Homer Curtiss' death in 1946, when it moved to Hollywood, California, where its remained duing its final years.

The Curtisses were former theosophists who originally established the Order of The 15 for the purpose of correlating advanced philosophical teachings (i.e., theosophy) with orthodox Christian teachings, and changed its original name to the Order of Christian Mystics so it could more easily approach members of Christian

churches. Its particular concern for expressing the universal principle in Christian terms and by using Christian scriptures (instead of eastern holy books) separated it from the main body of theosophists (the Liberal Catholic Church not having been created at the time of the order's founding). The order also saw itself as anti-organizational, and for many years did not incorporate.

Teachings of the order (and fellowship) were put forth in the numerous books (more than 20) written by the Curtisses, though their central teachings were summarized in *The Voice of Isis, The Message of Aquaria,* and *Letters from the Teacher.* In addition to their books, the Curtisses published a monthly lesson for order members, who were encouraged to form study groups and to use the "Prayer for World Harmony," printed in one of the textbooks. The order emphasized personal self-mastery and offered personal counsel via correspondence with the Curtisses.

The order followed theosophical teaching in general but developed its own special emphases. The Curtisses advocated a middle way on most issues within the occult community. It did not advocate vegetarianism or celibacy, though it strongly advocated reincarnation. It offered an occult interpretation of the Bible which the Curtisses believed had been lost due to emphases upon literal and historical interpretations. Psychic awakening, as a natural part of spiritual unfoldment, was emphasized and the use of special techniques for the development of psychic powers discouraged. Most importantly, the order was preparing for the advent of the Coming World Teacher, the Avatar. However, they sought to keep their pupils from being led astray by personality, i.e., from the Theosophical Society which was at that time promoting Jiddu Krishnamurti as the World Teacher. The order trained its pupils to recognize and respond to the teacher on the spiritual planes. Finally, the order emphasized the important theosophical teachings of the oneness of truth and univeral brotherhood.

The order survived only a few years after the death of the Curtisses, though several of their books were kept in print for many years.

Sources:

Curtiss, F. Homer. *Reincarnation.* Santa Barbara, CA: J. F. Rowney Press, 1949.

Curtiss, Harriette Augusta, and F. Homer Curtiss. *The Message of Aquaria.* San Francisco: Curtiss Philosophic Book Company, 1921.

___. *The Voice of Isis.* Los Angeles: Curtiss Philosophic Book Co., 1912.

Curtiss, Harriette Augusta, with F. Homer Curtiss. *Letters from the Teacher.* 2 vols. Hollywood, CA: Curtiss Philosophic Book Co., 1918.

The Fellowship of the Order of Christian Mystics. Washington, DC: Order of Christian Mystics, n.d.

★1660★
Universal White Brotherhood
Prosveta U. S. A.
Box 49614
Los Angeles, CA 90049

Alternate Address: International Headquarters: 2, rue du Belvedere de la Ronce, 92310 Sevres, France.

The Universal White Brotherhood reflects upon the material level what is believed to be an actual fraternity of highly evolved spiritual beings who exist on a higher plane. The earthly counterpart of the brotherhood was reestablished in its outer form in 1900 in Bulgaria by Peter Deunov (d. 1944). Sensing that political developments meant that his movement would have to go underground, Deunov sent Omraam Michael Aivanhov (1900-1986) to France in 1937 to carry on the teachings, known as initiatic science. Upon Deunov's death, Aivanhov succeeded him as leader.

The brotherhood is not seen as a new religious sect, but a new form or modern transmission of the eternal religion of Christ. It continues the tradition of the Church of St. John, considered by many to be the true embodiment of Christian Spirituality. For the members of the brotherhood, the Church of St. John follows the spirit rather than the letter of Christ's teachings. In contrast, the Church of St. Peter is the official and public religion. According to Aivanhov, the meaning of life is "to know oneself," to have one's human self unite with one's divine self. At that point, one becomes fully attuned to and capable of manifesting the great work of the brotherhood. The aim of the great masters is to bring the Kingdom of God on earth. As Aivanhov often remarked, quoting Hermes Mercurious Trismegistus, "As above, so below."

The teachings of the Universal White Brotherhood was brought to the United States after the appearance of the first English translations of Aivanhov's work in the early 1980s. Aivanhov himself visited the United States in 1983.

Two separate but related collections of Aivanhov's works are available. *The Complete Works* includes more than 35 volumes, with more due to appear. *The Izvor Collection* has 36 volumes with many more in the planning stages. Both collections are published by Editions Prosveta based in Frejus, France, or by branches and distributors worldwide. A new volume of *Daily Meditations* drawn from the work of Omraam Michael Aivahnov is published annually.

Membership: In 1998, the brotherhood reported members in 26 countries, most in Western Europe. There were 5,000 in France, 1,500 in Switzerland, 350 in Belgium, and 250 in Great Britain. There were 4,000 in Canada concentrated in French-speaking Quebec and several hundred in the United States.

Periodicals: *Circle of Light.* Send orders to Box 49614, Los Angeles, CA 90049.

Sources:

Aivanhov, Omraam Mikhael. *Life.* Frejus, France: Editions Prosveta, 1978.

Feuerstein, Georg. *The Mystery of Light: The Life and Teaching of Omraam Mikhael Aivanhov.* Salt Lake City, UT: Passage Press, 1992. 278pp.

___. *Love and Sexuality.* Frejus, France: Editions Prosveta, 1976.

___. *The Universal White Brotherhood is not a Sect.* Frus, France: Editions Prosveta, 1982.

Lejbowicz, Agnes. *Omraam Michael Aivanov, Master of the Great White Brotherhood.* Frejus, France: Editions Prosveta, 1982.

Renard, Pierre. *The Solar Revolution and the Prophet.* Frejus, France: Editions Prosveta, 1980.

Who Is the Master Omraam Michael Aivanhov? Frejus, France: Editions Prosveta, 1982.

★1661★
White Lodge
(Defunct)

Lady Elizabeth Carey was an agent of the White Eagle Lodge, a British New Age group, who was sent to the United States to open the work. In 1941 while in Los Angeles, she became aware that she was being guided by spirits, and, on Grouse Mountain near Vancouver, a group became aware through her of the imminent return of Christ. In 1943, a tract of land near Del Mar, California, was purchased as a site for a sacred shrine. The guidance was received from the Great White Brotherhood, a group of elder brothers identical to the Buddhist bodhisattvas or the Theosophical ascended masters. These brothers have often incarnated in the past and have existed as a group since the first godman walked the earth. Roselady, as Ms. Carey was known, was in contact with a Great White Brotherhood initiate, Azrael.

Through the shrine at Del Mar called the White Lodge, the message of Azrael began to be published through a monthly periodical, *Angelus.* Growing popularity led to the publication in the 1960s of four *Books of Azrael* containing collections of Azrael's messages. Advertising in such psychically oriented periodicals as *Chimes* made the shrine well known throughout the United States.

The teachings of Azrael are concerned with the work of the White Brotherhood and its role in bringing in the New Age of Aquarius. Azrael is helping to create a new humanity by raising the consciousness of those who receive the teachings. The content of Azrael's message is summed up in two words, "love" and "light." Love is the cohesive force of the universe, the principle by which God acts, judges and heals. Light is the symbol of man's path back to God. The Brotherhood dwells in the light and teaches the path to illumination through prayer and meditation. Reincarnation and karma were strongly held beliefs, and prayer for healing through the white light was a major practice. Healing prayer was accompanied by a "linking in," during which members scattered across the country joined in prayer at the same hour.

In the late 1960s, tension arose among the supporters of the shrine. On Easter Sunday, 1969, Eloise Mellor, the guardian of the shrine, asserted that she was the channel for Azrael and St. John the Beloved. According to the fourth Book of Azrael, a special work by St. John was directly to precede the coming of Jesus, the world teacher. Eloise also replaced members of the shrine's board of trustees. These changes were made with the claimed blessing of White Eagle, a guide from the spirit world, but without going through Roselady. Almost immediately, two factions arose and, in 1971, open schism appeared.

After Easter of 1969, Joseph E. Hall, deposed vice president of the shrine at Del Mar, California called the White Lodge, continued to receive the communications from Azrael and to circulate them among former supporters of the work. Then, in 1970, Philip Schraub of Corpus Christi, Texas, was confirmed by the aging Roselady as her successor as the channel of Azrael and the one to be used to carry forward the New Age teachings of John the Beloved. In the spring of 1971, public announcement of Philip's role, as well as a denoucement of Eloise, was made by Mr. Hall and nine other leading supporters of the Shrine in the first issue of a new monthly, *The New Angelus for the New Age.* A letter from the White Eagle Lodge denied support of Eloise. Through Philip, the Brotherhood announced its temporary withdrawal from the Shrine and the movement of the work to Corpus Christi.

Efforts began to recover the Shrine, at first through negotiation with Eloise, Mari Mae Napier and her husband, who at that time constituted the Shrine's board. In the midst of these negotiations, Eloise fell ill. During her convalescence, she repented of her activity and began to support Philip. She was also deposed as guardian of the Shrine, and five trustees appointed in her place. *Rays of Wisdom* replaced the *Angelus* as the periodical.

Upon her recovery, a court fight was initiated by Eloise to regain her guardianship, but she died in 1974, before the matter could be resolved. Several years later, the trustees turned the work and the property over to Elizabeth Clare Prophet and the Church Universal and Triumphant, into which it was completely absorbed.

Philip Schraub continued to publish *The New Angelus for the New Age* first in Corpus Christi and then in West Sedona, Arizona until 1983, after which the work was discontinued.

Sources:

Book of Azreal. 4 vols. Santa Barbara, CA: J. F. Rowny Press, 1965-67.

Eloise [Mellor]. *Youth: Open the Door.* Los Angeles: DeVorss & Co., 1969.

Section 20

Magick Family

Consult the Contents pages to locate the essay in Part II, Historical Essay Chapters,
that provides an historical discussion of this family

Intrafaith Organizations

★1662★
Alliance of the Phoenix
Current address not obtained for this edition.

The Alliance of the Phoenix is an umbrella organization of independent houses (centers/groups) dedicated to the Netjer (Egyptian gods). Alliance was formed in the mid-1990s to provide a supportive forum for all who worship the Netjer by promoting fellowship and encouraging ongoing education. It is closely associated with the House of the Open Eye, a San Francisco-based Egyptian Neopagan group.

Membership: Not reported.

Sources:

http://www.phoenix-alliance.crm/.

★1663★
American Council of Witches
(Defunct)

While several Pagan-wide ecumenical fellowships had formed in the early 1970s, there was a felt need by some NeoPagan witches for a similar group based in the Gardnerian witchcraft or Wiccan movement. Taking the lead in building such a structure was Carl Weschcke, owner of Llewellyn Publications and publisher of *Gnostica* magazine. In 1974 he called together a meeting of Wiccan leaders and members to be held in Minneapolis, Minnesota. At that meeting the council was formed and officers elected. Weschcke was chosen to head the council.

Possibly the most important work of the council was the issuing of a lengthy statement, the "Principles of Wiccan Beliefs," which summarized the consensus of belief of those groups that had emerged out of the Gardnerian Witchcraft revival. It affirmed witchcraft as a nature-oriented religion based in rites attuned to the natural rhythms of life exemplified in the phases of the moon and the seasonal movement of the sun. Wiccans seek to live in harmony with nature. They believe the Creative Power of the universe is manifested in polarity, male and female, and they value sex as pleasure, the symbol and embodiment of life, to be utilized as a source of energy in worship and magical practice. The statement went on to emphasize the non-hierarchial nature of the Wiccan movement and their non-belief in "absolute evil" or the concept of "Satan" or the "devil."

The council immediately ran into the fierce independency of Wiccans, many of whom saw any attempt to organize above the coven level as an attempt to control. While many gave tacit approval to the council, it was never able to function as it was designed. It survived into the early 1980s.

★1664★
American Vinland Association (AVA)
537 Jones, Ste. 2154
San Francisco, CA 94102

The American Vinland Association (AVA) is fellowship of Pagans following the traditions of northern and central Europe. A very similar Paganism, popularly termed Norse, was practiced from Iceland across Scandinavia to Poland, Russia, and Siberia. They are united in following the same deities, the old gods of the Aesir and Vanir, but have a wide range of beliefs and practices and use some very different terminology.

The association is headed by a board of directors, the Jafner. It functions as a licensing board for priests, priestesses, and elders. Regional coordinators have been appointed for Massachusetts, Wisconsin, Oregon, and New Mexico.

Membership: In 1998, the AVA reported some 100 members in 19 member groups in the United States and 20 members in two groups in Canada.

Periodicals: *Yarbok.* • *Yogdrasil.* • *Update.* Available from 1200 Madison, 657, Denver, CO 80206.

★1665★
Council of Themis
(Defunct)

The Council of Themis was an early attempt to form a cooperative ecumenical organization among the new Neo-Pagan groups which were emerging around the United States. It was founded by Fred Adams and Richard Stanewick of Fereferia in January 1969. They had previously received correspondence about such an organization from Tim Zell, the founder of the Church of All Worlds (CAW) and editor of possibly the most popular Pagan periodical at the time, *Green Egg*. Fereferia and CAW cojointly administered the council. Among the early members of the council were the Dancers of the Sacred Circle, The Ordo Templi Astarte, the Delphic Fellowship, the Psychedelic Venus Church, the Church of the Eternal Source, a variety of Wiccan covens, and the Hellenic Group, a member of the council in the United Kingdom.

The council, named for the Aegean goddess Themis, conceived of itself as a trans-sectarian council of Nature religions and had as its goal to serve as a forum for the exchange of information. It accepted as a common basis of association a belief in polytheism, worship of Nature focusing on the goddess and god as divine lovers, and reincarnation. It advocated freedom of worship, an openness to eroticism, non-violence, and a mythic approach to reality.

The council prospered for several years. Most of the member groups were located in Southern California, but its active leadership was offered by the St. Louis, Missouri-based Church of All Worlds, the largest Pagan group in terms of membership. Then in 1972, the council moved to expel two members, the Psychedelic Venus Church and the Hellenic Group. The former was accused of public advocation of the use of illegal drugs and the public exploitation of sexual practices. The Hellenic Group had advocated a public "bloody sacrifice" of a lamb. The actions provoked intense debate within the council, which led to its splitting; those members who left formed the Pagan Ecumenical Council. While the Council of Themis survived for several more years, it was an ineffective organization and for all practical purposes had ceased to exist.

An account of the Council of Themis, highly disputed as to its accuracy, appeared in *The New Pagans* by popular occult writer Hans Holzer (Doubleday, 1972). More accurate information can be found in the several official publications of the council and the pages of the *Green Egg*.

★1666★
Fellowship of Isis
% Clonegal Castle
Enniscorthy, Ireland

The Fellowship of Isis is an international association of goddess followers that operates both as an ecumenical fellowship and a primary religious home for individuals with pagan and other goddess worshipping beliefs. It was founded in 1976 by author and painter Olivia Robertson to revive worship and communion with the feminine principle in deity in the form of the goddess and to promote knowledge of the world's matriarchal religions. To this end, Robertson and her brother and coleader in the fellowship, Lawrence Durdin-Robertson (d. 1994), authored a number of books on goddess worship. Robertson also wrote a liturgy that is used by many Iseums, small groups referred to as Hearths of the Goddess.

The fellowship is organized on a democratic basis, and there are no vows of secrecy. It accepts religious toleration, as a wide variety of New Age thought coexists in the fellowship. Communication between members is maintained through literature and correspondence and its more than 600 centers worldwide. The fellowship includes the College of Isis, through which it offers a structured course in the fellowship's liturgy; the Order of Tara, an order of chivalry which works to save the environment; and the Druid Clan of Dana, whose primary work is the development of psychic gifts.

Membership: In 1997 the loosely organized fellowship had a total combined membership of approximately 14,032 individuals in groups located in 90 countries. In 1996 the College of Isis had 93 lyceums in 13 countries; the Druid Clan had 34 groves in 12 countries; and the Order of Tara had 22 priories in 9 countries.

Periodicals: *Isian News.*

Sources:

The College of Isis Manual. Enniscorthy, Erie: Cesara Publications, n.d.

Durdin-Robertson. *The Goddesses of Chaldea, Syria and Egypt.* Eniscorthy, Erie: Cesara Publications, 1975.

Durdin-Robertson and Lord Strathloch. *The Fellowship of Isis Directory for 1980.* Enniscorthy, Erie: Cesara Publications, 1979.

Robertson, Olivia. *The Call of Isis.* Enniscorthy, Erie: Cesare Publications, 1975.

___. *Dea: Rites and Mysteries of the Goddess.* Enniscorthy, Erie: Cesara Publications, 1996. 71 pp.

___. *The Handbook of the Fellowship of Isis.* Enniscorthy, Erie: Cesara Publications, 1996. 11pp.

★1667★
Frigga's Web Association for the Asatru Faith
PO Box 79592
Oklahoma City, OK 75147-0952

Frigga's Web, named for one of the Norse deities who is thought of as the spiritual mother of all Heathen people, is an ecumenical organization founded in 1995 and designed to further the cause of the Heathen society and promote Heathen solidarity. Founder Alissa Sorenson saw the Web as a fruitful space for pro-Heathen interaction by focusing upon the commonalities rather than differences. She emphasized the fact that most of the issues that divide the Asatru folk do not affect the great majority of Heathen existence.

Membership: In 1997, the Web reported 70 members in the United States, two in Canada, and 10 in other countries.

Periodicals: *Lina: The Quarterly Journal of Friga's Web*

★1668★
Order of Napunsakas in the West (O.N.)
PO Box 1219
Corpus Christi, TX 78403-1219

The Order of Napunsakas in the West (O.N.) was founded in 1996 as a special interest group (SIG) associated with the Servants of the Star and the Snake (S.S.S.). It was inspired by the writings of the late Alain Danielou (author of such books as *The Gods of India: Hindu Polytheism*; *Shiva and Dionysus*; and *While the Gods Play*). The Hindu word "napunsaka" designates some 16 categories of non-heterosexual, gender variant types mentioned in the Sanskrit dictionary of V. S. Apete. Members of the O.N. seek to reestablish the natural, divine order found in pre-Aryan Shaivism, but the emphasis is on gay, lesbian, bisexual, and transgendered Tantra. The Outer Order is open to all napunsakas; affiliates are considered as associate members. An Inner Order, the Cultus Skanda-Karttikeya (C.S.-K.), is open to gay males only, and only upon formal, in-person *diksha*, or initiation. The focus of the C.S.-K. is on gay Tantra with special emphasis on the *sadhana* (or worship or more properly, adoration) of the Hindu Deity Skanda as patron of gays, in His many forms (Kumara, Marugan, etc.).

The current head of the O.N./C.S.-K. is Sahajananda Skanda-Das.

Membership: Not reported.

Periodicals: *Zibaq.*

★1669★
Pagan Ecumenical Council
(Defunct)

The Pagan Ecumenical Council was an early, short-lived Pagan ecumenical association founded in 1972 following a split in the Council of Themis. The council, possibly the earliest of the Neo-Pagan efforts to build a cooperative body, expelled two members for un-Paganlike activities. Both the method and legality of the expulsion were questioned by various members of the Council of Themis, some of whom accused co-founder Fred Adams of Fereferia of assuming dictatorial powers. They left and founded the rival Pagan Ecumenical Council. Leading members of the new council included the Church of All Worlds, Church of the Eternal Source, the Rainbow Coven (a Wiccan group), the Dancers of the Sacred Circle, and popular writer Ed Fitch, associated with the Pagan Way. The new council was to be democratically organized and within the first year grew to include some five member groups.

The council continued to function for a few years but soon died as the Pagan movement, especially in Southern California, changed and developed.

★1670★
Pagan Federation/Federation paienne—Canada (PFFC)
Box 32, Stn. "B"
Ottawa, ON, Canada K1P 6C3

The Pagan Federation/Federation paienne—Canada (PFFC) was formed in 1994 based upon the model of the Pagan Federation (UK), founded in 1971 in the United Kingdom. Originally named the Pagan Front, the federation had functioned as an umbrella organization for the groups that emerged from the revival of pre-Christian Paganism initiated by Gerald B. Gardner in the 1950s. Some of those who resonated to the Gardnerian impulse called themselves Witches or Wiccans; others preferred the name Pagan. It functioned to provide communication between various British Pagan groups and new seekers; contact between British Pagans and those in other European countries; and information on Paganism, which was often parodied and defamed in the press, to the British public.

The need for a Pagan Federation in Canada emerged as many Canadian Witches and Pagans began to change their strategy of assuming a low profile in Canadian religious life to one of assuming a visible and recognizable place in the larger religious community. That change has been prompted in part by the open acknowledgement of Pagans by various government and religious authorities. In addition, some Pagan leaders have seen the need to provide religious services for Pagans in various institutional settings (prisons, hospitals, the armed services) and hence the need for chaplaincy services. Chaplains are usually appointed from recognized religious groups whose officials can interact with institutional authorities. Finally, there remains a need to fight for the religious rights and freedoms of Pagans and others in Canada's various new religions.

An opening for interaction with authorities was provided in 1994 when Lucie DuFresne of the Department of Religious Studies at the University of Ottawa was asked by the Canadian Association of Pastoral Education to lead a training session on Wicca and goddess worship. While at the meeting, she realized some of the major problems that would arise as chaplains attempted to relate to hospitalized Pagans.

Membership in the federation is open to anyone who accepts the Pagan minimal principles: Love for and kinship with Nature; the Pagan ethic: "That ye harm none, do what thou will"; and acceptance of deity as both male and female.

Membership: Not reported.

Periodicals: *Hecate's Loom*, Box 5206, Sta."B," Victoria, BC, Canada V8R 6N4.

Sources:

Du Fresne, Lucie, Adrienne Slater, and Dave Slater. "Pagan Federation/ Federation Paenne—Canada." *Hecate's Loom* 27 (Imbolc 1995): 9-10.

★1671★
Universal Federation of Pagans
Box 6006
Athens, GA 30604

The Universal Federation of Pagans (UFP) was founded in the mid-1990s as an international association of Pagans promoting the cause of Paganism in the world and the larger religious community and providing fellowship among Pagans of varying beliefs and practices. Inspiration for the federation came from the 1993 World's Parliament of Religions, which gathered in Chicago and at which Pagans were a highly visible presence. It accepts members from paths (equivalent to a denomination in Christianity), circles (equivalent to a congregation), or individuals. Affiliated paths (which must be legally incorporated and have at least five circles) are granted two seats on the UFP Council of Elders and in the UFP General Assembly, which guide the work of the federation. Member circles are granted one seat in the Council of Elders and representation in the General Assembly. Individual members (remembering that many Pagans operate as solitaires) are granted representation in the General Assembly.

Members of the federation are expected to be knowledgeable concerning Pagans, to conduct themselves in an ethical manner, and to promote actively the cause and ideals of Paganism in their daily life and in their relations with others. Members are generally expected to accept a basic consensus of Pagan belief and be in general agreement with the "Declaration of a Global Ethic" as for-

mulated and promulgated by the 1993 World's Parliament of Religions.

Membership: Among the original supporting members of the federation are the Church of All Worlds and the Avalon Isle Foundation.

Ritual Magick

★1672★
Abbey of Thelema
Box 666
Old Greenwich, CT 06870-0666

The Abbey of Thelema is an independently functioning initiatory magical group that provides a point of contact with The Order of the Silver Star (a.k.a. the A. A., *Astron Argon* (Greek) or *Argenteum Astrum* (Latin)), otherwise known as The Great White Brotherhood. The leader of the Abbey, Gregory von Seewald, has in turn been delegated to the Authority of the Triad, which originally was conferred upon George Cecil Jones (D.D.S.), Aleister Crowley (O.M.), and George Stansfeld Jones (O.I.V.I.V.I.O.). The Abbey provides for instruction in the A. A. following the magical practices and studies that were perfected by its foremost founder, Aleister Crowley. New members of the Order are expected to show their serious intentions by acquiring and reading a number of books in magick and mysticism, including the entire set of *The Equinox*, the magazine Crowley began in 1909 as the official organ of the A. A. Following an exam on his/her basic knowledge of magick, the student may become a Probationer and begin the path of magical training. There are 11 magical grades or degrees.

The secret, and secret practice (long ago publicly revealed), of the Ordo Templi Orientis (the other magical group Crowley headed) was sex magick. It was taught in stages as members attained the seventh through ninth degrees. However, in the A. A. system as taught by the Abbey, the Probationer who has reached the Zelator grade is invited to begin study in this practice. The sexual, magical practices constitute the essence of a second division of the Abbey, namely, the Sovereign Penetralia of the Gnosis, to which those who desire to follow the practice adhere.

A. A. members who have attained a level referred to as Zelatores are invited to membership within the Order of Thelemites (a.k.a. The Order of Thelema), which was conceived in the 1920s by Crowley. Various charters, in the form of constitutions, were conferred upon A. A. members of that era. These constitutions have recently been recognized and the Order of Thelemites has emerged from dormancy. The Order is not a mystical, magical, or occult order in the ordinary sense of these words. Its purpose is to enable its members to succeed in life by teaching them the correct attitudes toward life and how to avoid wasting time in lines of effort for which they are unsuited.

As the Abbey of Thelema is a secret Order, much of its teachings and practice are not revealed to outsiders. The leader of the Abbey, Gregory von Seewald, serves as Praemonstrator of the A. A., Outer Head of the Sovereign Penetralia of the Gnosis, and Abbot of Thelema for The Order of Thelemites. The Abbey of Thelema is affiliated with the Holy Order of RaHoorKhuit (H.O.O.R.), The Holy Gnostic Catholic Church (H.G.C.C.), The Qabalistic Alchemist Church (Q.B.L.H.), and The Company of Heaven.

Membership: There are fewer than 100 members of the Abbey, but it has members in Australia, Canada, England, France, Germany, Greece, and Spain.

Sources:

One Star in Sight. Old Greenwich, CT: Abbey of Thelema, n.d.

★1673★
American Gnostic Church
Box 1219
Corpus Christi, TX 78403

The Americn Gnostic Church was founded in 1985 by Rev. James M. Martin. It has served and continues to serve as an umbrella organization for several closely related spiritual movements, each claiming some form of illumination by stellar-gnosis. The church's ministry has a special concern for connections and cognate deities in both the Gnostic systems and the Oriental religions. The latest groups with which it maintains a relationship are the Servants of the Star and the Snake (S.S.S.), a tantric-thelemic "federation" of magicians, sorcerers, witches, pagans, shamans, and Natha yogis who network online and through several periodicals, and an S.S.S. SIG or special interest group, the Order of Napunsakas in the West (O.N.) which maintains an Outer Order for all non-heterosexual tantrikas and an Inner Order open only to males, known as the Cultus Skanda-Karttikeya (C.S.-K.). Both Tantra and Thelema (the system developed by Aleister Crowley) have sex magick as an essential component in their magical teachings.

Sources:

Crowley, Aleister. *The Law Is for All*. Phoenix, AZ: Falcon Press, 1985.

___. *Magick in Theory and Practice*. New York: Dover Publications, 1976.

King, Francis, and Stephen Skinner. *Techniques of High Magick*. New York: Destiny Books, 1976.

★1674★
Aurum Solis
Current address not obtained for this edition.

Aurum Solis, the Order of the Sacred Word, was founded in England in 1897 by Charles Kingold and George Stanton as a school of Western Kabbalistic magick. Like the Hermetic Order of the Golden Dawn, the Aurum Solis teaches a system of high magick, i.e., a disciplined approach to self-transformation. Its system, much of which has been published in the five-volume set *The Magical Philosophy* by Melita Denning and Osborne Phillips, centers upon the myth of the sacred king (i.e., the magician), who chooses of his own free will the path of sacrifice but subsequently rises again and passes into the light of attainment.

Melita Denning and Osborne Phillips are the pen names of Vivian Barcynski and Leonard R. Barcynski, who until recently served as grand master and administrator general of the order. Both had encountered the order while living in England and participated in its reconstitution in 1971. They brought the order to America in 1978 when they moved to St. Paul, Minnesota. Under their pen names they have authored numerous books on various occult topics.

Membership in the order is by invitation only, though inquiries are invited. In 1987 Carl Weschcke assumed the sole authority for the order as its Grand Master but has since resigned. The present status of the orfer is unknown. The teachings remain available mainly throught the earlier writings of the Bychinskis.

Membership: Not reported.

Sources:

Denning, Melita, and Osborne Phillips. *The Magical Philosophy*. 5 vols. St. Paul: Llewellyn Publications, 1974-81.

___. *The Magick of Sex*. St. Paul, MN: Llewellyn Publications, 1982.

___. *The Magick of the Tarot*. St. Paul, MN: Llewellyn Publications, 1983.

★1675★
Bavarian Illuminati
(Defunct)

The Bavarian Illuminati was founded in 1776 by the infamous Dr. Adam Weishaupt, a professor of canon law at the University of Ingoldstadt in Germany. The group associated with the Masons and gained a reputation as a secret revolutionary body. The group was present in England as the Hell-Fire Club headed by Sir Francis Dashwood. (This English group is supposedly the source of a flirtation with Masonry by the founding fathers of the United States, who allegedly placed the Illuminati pyramid and the Eye of Horus on the Great Seal of the United States.)

A modern version of the Order of the Illuminati was established during the 1970s with headquarters in San Francisco, California, and Nantes, France. It was one of a variety of half-serious/half-joking organizations created by magician-author Robert Anton Wilson, more recently a resident of Ireland. Wilson has authored a series of books on magick and occult philosophy using the Illuminatus metaphor, but drawing its content from the twentieth century Thelemic magick of Aleister Crowley and modern psychical and consciousness studies. Since Wilson's leaving the United States there are no formal representatives of the modern order, though it could be seen to have continued informally among Wilson's large reading audience. Even in the 1970s, the order existed only as a loose confederation of independent but like-minded magicians. It existed primarily to pursue Thelemic magick, as Wilson thought of Aleister Crowley as the twentieth-century inventor of the Illuminati tradition. Adherents were also devotees of Eris, the goddess of chaos and discord. The Order was a confederation of like-minded magicians who help each other over any times of problems in magical practice.

Sources:

Holmes, Donald. *The Sapiens System: The Illuminati Conspiracy*. Phoenix, AZ: Falcon Press, 1987.

Wilgus, Neal. *The Illuminoids*. New York: Pocket Books, 1978.

Wilson, Robert Anton. *Cosmic Trigger*. Berkeley, CA: And/Or Press, 1977.

___. *The Illuminati Papers*. Berkeley, CA: And/Or Press, 1980.

___. *Masks of the Illuminati*. New York: Pocket Books, 1981.

___. *Schroedinger's Cat*. 3 vols. New York: Pocket Books, 1980-81.

★1676★
Bennu Phoenix Temple of the Hermetic Order of the Golden Dawn
(Defunct)

A short-lived attempt to revive the Hermetic Order of the Golden Dawn emerged in the early 1970s, led by John Phillips Palmer. The Bennu Phoenix Temple continued the tradition of the H.O.G.D. prior to the revelations of its secrets by Aleister Crowley. Crowley was viewed as a former member "impervious to discipline. . .consequently degraded to the Paths of the Portal in the Vault of Adepti and expelled." The group also follows the tradition which rejected S. L. MacGregor Mathers' leadership. He is believed to have fallen to the dark powers of the left-hand path.

The Bennu Phoenix Temple followed the ten rituals of the Order of the Golden Dawn and used forms of the rituals published by Israel Regardie. Sex magick was allowed if practiced within the context of marriage. Sex magick outside of marriage with a homosexual partner or as a mystic masturbation was strictly condemned. Homosexual behavior was regarded as impure. Drugs and animal sacrifice were also forbidden.

Sources:

Regardie, Israel. *The Golden Dawn*. St. Paul, MN: Llewellyn Publications, 1969.

★1677★
Builders of the Adytum
5105 N. Figueroa
Los Angeles, CA 90042

Builders of the Adytum (B.O.T.A.) is a western mystery school whose teachings are based on the Holy Qabalah and Sacred Tarot.

According to B.O.T.A., the Holy Qabalah is the Mystical (occult) Wisdom Teaching of ancient Israel. The great prophets of the Old and New Testaments were versed in the Qabalah (including Jesus of Nazareth) and received their spiritual training therefrom. The Holy Qabalah is based on a diagrammatical and symbolic glyph called the *Tree of Life*. It is a pictorial-symbolic representation of the *One God* and man's relationship to God and creation. The Tarot is a pictorial textbook on Ageless Wisdom.

B.O.T.A. was founded in 1922 by Dr. Paul Foster Case, one of the American members of the Hermetic Order of the Golden Dawn, for the study of practical occultism. A recognized world authority on the Tarot and Qabalah, Dr. Case was given the task by the Inner School of re-interpreting the Ageless Wisdom into terms understandable to the modern western mind.

The primary purpose of B.O.T.A. is to teach and practice the doctrine of the Oneness of God, the brotherhood of man, and the kinship of all life patterned after the Ageless Wisdom mystery schools of spiritual training as particularly exemplified by the Holy Qabalah. Occult orders, such as B.O.T.A., have as their major objective "the promotion of the welfare of humanity." The great Masters of Wisdom, from whom flow the inspiration and spiritual impetus of this work, refuse to have anything to do with any Order which fails to recognize the primary importance of this great objective, for they devote all their energy and influence to that end. Their conception of the meaning of "the welfare of humanity" is embodied in the following seven-pointed program: 1. Universal Peace; 2. Universal Political Freedom; 3. Universal Religious Freedom; 4. Universal Education; 5. Universal Health; 6. Universal Prosperity; and 7. Universal Spiritual Unfoldment.

In order to promote the welfare of humanity, we need first to look to the units of which humanity is composed. Selfish personalities make their unhappy contribution to a selfish social structure. Chaotic thinking and immature emotions affect the mental and emotional levels of all humanity. We do not live unto ourselves alone. To the degree that the aspirant becomes a more effective unit in his personal environment, then to that degree does he bring spiritual powers into action for all humanity and prepares himself to serve Life in ever greater measure.

Dedicated work with the Tarot techniques as embodied in the B.O.T.A. curriculum has as its aim the transmutation of personality. A transformed personality will bring with it the ability to change its environment closer to the heart's desire. A fulfilled life becomes a positive radiating center, an effective channel through which the Higher Self can function, and a living example for others. The particular potency of the Western Mystery training system lies in its use of symbols which are a universal language that directly instructs subconsciousness with its pictorial wisdom.

B.O.T.A. is the outer school behind which stands an inner mystery school, offering instruction for students who wish to participate in the esoteric work. Qualified students may become members of a Pronaos, many of which are found in the United States and various other countries, and are referred to as Pronaons. After initiation in a Pronaos, members may participate in the group ritual work of B.O.T.A.

The external affairs of the order are managed by the Board of Stewards. The Proculator General is the primary link between the outer and inner schools. Prior to 1976, the only groups open to the general membership were in Los Angeles. However, during the next decade approximately 50 study groups and working groups (Pronaos) were formed in 19 states. Groups also appeared in Montreal and Toronto, Canada; Great Britain; the Netherlands; New Zealand; Columbia; and the island of Aruba, in the Caribbean.

Membership: Not reported.

Sources:

Case, Paul Foster. *The Book of Tokens*. Los Angeles: B.O.T.A., 1947.

___. *The Tarot*. Richmond, VA: Macoy Publishing Company, 1947.

___. *The True and Invisible Rosicrucian Order*. The Author, 1928.

Davies, Ann. *Inspirational Thoughts on the Tarot*. Burbank, CA: Candlelight Press, 1983.

___. *This Is the Truth about the Self*. Los Angeles: Builders of the Adytum, 1960.

Frazer, Felix J. *Parallel Paths to the Unseen Worlds*. Los Angeles: Builders of the Adytum, 1967.

★1678★
CIRCLES International
PO Box 279
Plainfield, IN 46168

CIRCLES International is the American (and English-language) affiliate of the Cercle International de Recherches Culturelles et Spirituelles (International Circle for Cultural and Spiritual Research). The International Circle was founded in France earlier in this century as a New Age initiatic association inspired by the Templar tradition. Integral to the understanding of the organization is the idea that each era is unique in the way the cosmos impacts the inner consciousness of humanity. New eras are defined by astrological ages. The previous age was keynoted by Jesus' admonition to "love one another." The keynote of the present Aquarian age is the desire for personal integration. In this age, the path formerly trod primarily by mystics and sages will become common to a large number of the human race. While many seek to bring peace to the warring factions of their mind, few have attained any positive results.

CIRCLES emphasizes two important truths regarding the discovery of a spiritual path that would lead to personal integration. First, each individual must find his/her own path, rather than slavishly follow a predetermined "true" path. Second, the discovery and treading of the path can be greatly enhanced by modern psychological insights. In this light, CIRCLES does not present doctrines and dogmas, but a variety of techniques that each member may use as they awaken to their own personal truth.

CIRCLES is open to all aspirants who are willing to live by the command, "love one another" and who are dedicated to the ideals of chivalry, world peace, and the reduction of human suffering. These goals are pursued by practice of the spiritual and psychological technologies. Members are encouraged to discover the way they can most effectively express the various spiritual values, including unconditional love, in daily life.

New members of Circles join the Outer Circle and participate in its work on three levels. In a (1) general research council, members pursue studies on a particular subject and attempt to apply results in a practical context. As part of a (2) commission, work of the research councils on related topics is synthesized. In the (3) Academy, which organizes all the work of the Outer Order, the member may pursue research in one of several colleges: the College of Arcane Sciences, the College of Mundane Sciences, or the College of Creative Sciences.

Members may also participate in the Inner Circle, where the traditional teaching of the Templars as understood by the Order are presented. Involvement begins with the Order of Sovereign Templar Initiates (OSTI). Since all instruction of the Inner Order is oral, attendance at the monthly gatherings of OSTI units is required of Inner Circle members. New members of the order may attend Inner Circle meetings but are not to participate verbally for the first year. Work in the Inner Circle progresses on a degree basis. There are two degrees in OSTI. It is followed by three degrees in the International Order of Pythagoreans. At the center of the order is the Universal Order of Melchisedech, into which some members may be invited.

CIRCLES International is headed by the Sovereign Grand Master, Fr. Raymond Bernard. Each country is organized as a Grand Commandery under a Grand Commander appointed by the Sovereign Grand Master. Regional divisions within a country are organized into Grand Preceptories headed by a Grand Preceptor. A Grand Preceptor can operate in the absence of the Grand Commander. Local groups are variously designated commanderies or templar research circles.

Membership: Not reported.

★1679★
Clan Invisible
Current address not obtained for this edition.

Clan Invisible is a small magical order which has emerged in the larger context of the spread of thelemic magic as revealed in *The Book of the Law*, revealed to Aleister Crowley in 1904. *The Book of the Law* is often summarized in the statements, "Do what thou will shall be the whole of the law," and "Love is the law, Love Under Will." Along with respect for the Law of Thelema or Will, the clan promotes fitness of the mind and body through the philosophies of Taoism and practice of the martial arts. It also practices a technique for gaining access to parallel dimensions utilizing dream walking, past-life regression, alchemy, and divination.

Unlike some thelemic groups, the clan does not use a grade structure; however, newer and more advanced aspirants are recognized and the former will be referred to the latter for assistance in the development process. The clan is administered by the Secretet.

Membership: Not reported.

Sources:

http://www.angelfire.com/ut/Invisible/.

★1680★
College/Temple of Thelema
PO Box 415
Oroville, CA 95965

The College and Temple of Thelema are two interrelated structures which focus on the thelemic teachings as passed to Phyllis Seckler (Soror Meral), an early American member of the Ordo Temple Orientis and student of the magical system of Aleister Crowley. The College of Thelema was opened in 1973 as a magical and spiritual education program offering instruction in the basic teaching of the Western esoteric tradition, especially in the thelemic mode as developed by Aleister Crowley. From 1976 to 1996, the college published *In the Continuum*, a journal featuring important (and rare) writings by Crowley, as well as other magical materials (copies of back issues are still available from the college). All teachers of the college are bound to the precepts and philosophy as revealed in *Liber AL vel Legis* (*The Book of the Law*) and Crowley's work as the Prophet of the current Aeon of Horus.

In 1904 Crowley claimed to have received the channeled dictation of *The Book of the Law* from a praeterhuman intelligence who declared its name to be Aiwass, and identified itself as "the minister of Hoor-paar-kraat," i.e., the instrument of the Egyptian God of Silence. *The Book of the Law* announced the dawning of a new spiritual era for humanity. The primary message of the book is contained in the Greek words thelema (will), or True Will inherent in each person, and in agape (love), referring to the passionate love of the Divine as a basis for authentic human love. For thelemites, the Great World is a matter of finding one's True Will and expressing loving within that context.

The curriculum of the College of Thelema is broken into four consecutive courses dealing with the practical application of psychology, thelemic philosophy, qabalah, astrology, and magick. Once enrolled, the student has two years to complete the course.

The Temple of Thelema was established upon the principles and methods of the College of Thelema, of which it is a part. The temple is an initiating order, a modern Mystery School, that focuses on the systematic teaching and training of its members in the spiritual disciplines of magick and mysticism. The old grade ceremonies of the legendary Hermetic Order of the Golden Dawn have been recast in conformity to thelemic symbols and principles. A "Three Ray" model of balanced development (Wisdom, Love, and Power) includes intellectual training, meditation, and magical ritual at every stage of progress. Initiation rituals, other ceremonies, and the ongoing group healing work are also a central aspect of the curriculum. While the actual content and ritual process taught is reserved for members of the order, a general understanding may be gained from reading Crowley's readily available magical writings.

Following a pattern set by the Hermetic Order of the Golden Dawn in the late nineteenth century, the work of the temple is divided into a series of steps based on a Qabalistic diagram called the Tree of Life. In each of these degrees of training, the member is given the opportunity and responsibility to explore himself/herself from a different point of view, climaxing in a stage of synthesis, or integration.

There are marked differences between Temple of Thelema and the original Golden Dawn order. For example, more practical instruction has been added in the early degrees that incorporate much that has been learned in the last century concerning personal transformation, and steps have been taken to remove the remnants of the previous era's sexist assumptions.

Membership: Not reported. In 1998, there were seven centers of the Temple of Thelema, all in the United States, and a branch of the college in Vancouver, British Columbia.

Periodicals: *Black Pearl.*

★1681★
Eglise Gnostique Catholique Apostolique
% The Diocese of the Midwest
5215 Randolph St. W.
Bellwood, IL 60104

The Eglise Gnostique Catholique Apostolique (the Gnostic Catholic and Apostolic Church) was brought to America in 1970 with the appointment of Roger Victor-Herard as the primate of the church for North America, but has its roots in the gnostic/mystical groups of eighteenth-century Europe. Through the centuries, Gnostic Christianity (a form of Christianity considered heretical by the Roman Catholic Church) disappeared from public view. However, in the wake of the Reformation in the sixteenth century a number of groups, such as the Rosicrucians, appeared that claimed to possess the teachings of the ancient wisdom (i.e., the gnosis). By the end of the eighteenth century (in the relative freedom created by the French Revolution) attempts were being made, initially among several French Roman Catholic clerics, to reestablish the Gnostic church, and as early as 1800, a Msgr. Mauviel was consecrated as a bishop and established the Johannine Church of Primitive Christians.

A short time later, a second gnostic thrust was initiated by Eugene Vintras (1807-1875), whose gnostic movement ran into trouble with a revived Roman Catholic Church. In 1848 he claimed that in a vision Christ had consecrated him to the Papal office and given him a new liturgy. After a brief period outside of France he returned to found, in 1865, the Sanctuary of the Interior of the Carmel of Elie in Lyon.

The Eglise Gnostique Catholique Apostolique, inspired by this growing gnostic milieu, can be traced to 1904 when Julius Houssaye (or Hussay) was consecrated by Paolo Miraglia-Gulotti, an Italian bishop who had been consecrated by Archbishop Joseph Rene Vilatte of the American Catholic Church. Houssaye was a gnostic, who under his ecclesiastical name of Abbe Julio published several occult texts. He passed the leadership of the Gnostic Church to Louis Francois Giraud, who he consecrated in 1911. Two years later, Giraud consecrated Jean Becaud, who took the ecclesiastical name Tau Jean II, and later as the first Patriarch of the church developed a considerable following in the city of Lyon. In 1918 he consecrated Victor Blanchard (Tau Targilius) who became head of the church in 1934. Blanchard, in part responding to pressures from the rise of Nazism, helped spread the Gnostic Church into Portugal, and on to Brazil. In 1945 Blanchard consecrated Roger Menard (Tau Eon II), who in 1946 consecrated Robert Ambelain (Tau Jean III). Ambelain consecrated Andre Mauer (Tau Andreas) who assumed the role of Patriarch of the church.

It was Tau Andreas who named Pedro Freire as Primate of South America. Then in 1970, Dom Antidio Vargas, a bishop of the Brazilian Catholic Church, consecrated Pedro Freire as Patriarch of the Eglise Gnostique Catholique Apostolique. As Mar Petrus-Johannes XIII, he succeeded Tau Andreas. Mar Petrus-Johannes XIII encouraged the spread of the church in the Americas and encouraged Roger Victor-Herard (d. 1989) to initiate work in the United States. In 1970 he named Herard (as Tau Charles) the Primate of the North American branch of the church. In 1977, Mar Petrus-Johannes XIII died. The synod decided against naming a new Patriarch. At that point in time the American branch became autocephalous (independent). The church is administered by the presiding bishop, Tau Charles Harmonius II who has been president of the board of directors since 1984.

The Gnostic Catholic Church perpetuates a gnostic interpretation of Christianity and has instituted a sacramental ministry to that end. In the gnostic view, the world is the end product of successive emanations from God. Humanity is trapped in this material world. Through the gnosis (or secret wisdom) we may receive initiation and a way back to God. Christ, the Logos, has been God's agent in salvation by his bringing the gnosis to us. The church is the custodian of the gnosis.

The church is divided into several dioceses, the one in the midwest serving as its national headquarters.

Membership: In 1995 the church reported approximately 3,000 members in the United States and 200 members in Canada.

Educational Facilities: Athenea Theologica, Bellwood, Illinois.

Periodicals: *Journal of the Athenea Theologica.*

★1682★
Fellowship of Ma-Ion
(Defunct)

In 1904, Aleister Crowley received *The Book of the Law*, which became the new revelation for Thelemic magicians. The revelation included the prediction of a "child" who would "discover the key of it all." In 1915 Crowley carried out a series of sex magic workings with Jane Foster. Nine months later Charles Stansfeld Jones (d. 1950), known within thelemic circles as Frater Achad, proclaimed his assumption of the magical grade of Master of the Temple. Crowley accepted Achad as a magical child, i.e., a product of his own magical workings. Over the next eighteen months, Achad worked out the kabbalistic formulas which allowed Crowley to interpret some of the obscure passages of *The Book of the Law.*

In spite of Crowley's acceptance of Achad as the child, in 1919 they broke relations, never to be associated again (though they periodically corresponded.) Achad wrote several books based upon his speculations on the kabbalah (qabala), but his interpretations never gained wide acceptance. Achad moved to London in the late 1920s. He initiated a period of intense selfreflection which issued forth in a new perspective which he termed the "arising of the Silver Star," artistically depicted as a silver pentagram in a blue circle. In 1932 he composed a set of magical rituals and in the spring opened the Immanual Lodge. The work of the lodge bore magical fruit sixteen years later when Achad proclaimed the arrival of the Aeon of Ma, the manifestation of Truth and Justice. (Maat was the ancient Egyptian goddess of Truth and Justice.) The Aeon of Ma superceded the Aeon of Horus proclaimed by Crowley in 1904. The Aeon was never announced publicly, but communicated to a few magicians in private letters.

According to some sources, a small following who responded to the proclamation of the Aeon of Ma and who followed Achad's unique interpretation of the kabbalah formed an informal Fellowship of Ma-Ion which had members in both England and America. No verification of the existence of this group has been located. In the 1970s, in the wake of the publication of much of Aleister Crowley's materials and material on the Aeon of Ma(at), several groups have arisen which have developed a Maatian perspective, but these have arisen without any connection with or even knowledge of a Fellowship of Ma-Ion. (See separate entry on Ordo Adeptorum Invisiblum.)

Sources:

Achad, Frater [Charles Stansfeld Jones]. *The Anatomy of the Body of God.* New York: Samuel Weiser, 1969.

Achad, Frater. *The Egyptian Revival.* New York: Samuel Weiser, 1969.

King, Francis. *Ritual Magic in England.* London: Neville Spearman, 1970.

★1683★
Foundation, A Hermetic Society
Current address not obtained for this edition.

The foundation was organized in 1971 by W. E. Stone, Jr., for the purpose of establishing a definite procedure for the study of ritual magick. Study was based upon the work of the Hermetic Order of the Golden Dawn, as updated and edited. Insights of such magicians as William E. Butler, W. G. Gray, Gareth Knight and Israel Regardie were utilized. Membership in the foundation was not solicited, but the leadership was quite open in sharing its findings with a wider audience through published articles and open lectures. In 1972, there were fewer than 20 members. The organization lasted only a few years.

The foundation offered students a method of ceremonial magick as a "determined effort to establish a working relationship through himself between his lower and higher selves." The form was modernized in line with what was viewed as the natural evolution of the art. Group work was stressed; several working together increase the power available. Beginning as a neophyte, the student passed through four degrees to the portal series. Along the way, he learned the basics of occultism, meditation, astrology, Tarot, Kabbalah, various forms of divination and psychic development. The portal series was training in pure magick. Headquarters were in Houston, Texas.

★1684★
Franz Bardon Foundation
Current address not obtained for this edition.

Franz Bardon (d. 1958) was an Austrian teacher of Hermetic initiatory magic. His important texts were published in the 1950s in Germany, shortly before his death, and translated into English in the 1970s. Bardon's three major books included a basic text on Hermetic magic, a commentary on the Kabbalah (which he spelled Quabbalah), and a system of spirit evocation. In spite of his absence, his books found an audience among English-speaking readers, and the foundation was begun in 1986 to propagate Bardon's teaching, provide a network among students of the books, and offer instruction in his system.

Membership: Not reported.

Periodicals: *The Franz Bardon News.*

Sources:

Bardon, Franz. *Initiation into Hermetics.* Wupperthal, Germany: Deiter Ruggeburg, 1970.

___. *Die Praxis der magischen Evokation.* Freiburg/Breisgau, Germany: Verlag Hermann Bauer, 1956. English ed. as *The Practice of Magical Evocation.* Wupperthal, Germany: Deiter Ruggeburg, 1970.

___. *Der Schkussel zur wahren Quabbalah.* Freiburg/Breisgau, Germany: Verlag Hermann Bauer, 1957. English ed. as *The Key to the True Quabbalah.* Wupperthal, Germany: Deiter Ruggeburg, 1971.

★1685★
Fraternitas L. V. X. Occulta
Box 5094
Covina, CA 91723

The Fraternitas L. V. X. Occulta, also known by its English name, the Fraternity of the Hidden Light, was founded in Covina, California in 1982 but traces its lineage to the American section of the Hermetic Order of the Golden Dawn (OGD). According to the present leadership of the fraternity, at one point in the early twentieth century, the head and three other officers of the OGD reorganized the order as a mystery school dedicated to being a transitional order to assist in bringing in the New Age or Age of Aquarius. The present heads of the fraternity have inherited this tradition, and have during the mid-1980s assumed a more public profile.

The fraternity has three main objectives: to act as a modern day repository of the ancient wisdom; to train members for selfless service to humanity through application of the ancient wisdom; and to promulgate the ancient wisdom. Teachings are drawn from the writings of Hermes Mercurious Trismegistus, the legendary Egyptian magus, and the Qabalah (or Kaballah). Instruction is also given in tarot, alchemy, astrology, and occult psychology.

The fraternity is organized in three levels. An outer level trains new initiates in the growth into wisdom, love, and power. The second order is composed of those initiates who have developed harmony and balance within themselves and received illumination and whose higher self is in control of their lives. The third level consists of the Great Adepts and Masters of the ages who guide the fraternity from the inner realms.

Members work through a curriculum of graded instruction in the occult, as well as through instruction in meditation and ritual. Rituals are used to invoke quantum changes in the consciousness (i.e., high magic). Probationers pass through a period of at least three months in which a basic knowledge of the occult must be acquired. They may then apply for full membership. Present head (steward) of the fraternity is Paul A. Clark.

Membership: In 1995 the fraternity reported five temples and members in 17 countries worldwide.

Periodicals: *The Hidden Light.* • *The Threshold.* • *The Path of Return.* • *The Halls of Thoth.* • *The Book of the Rose.*

Sources:

Clark, Paul A. *The Book of the Rose.* Covina, CA: Fraternity of the Hidden Light, 1985.

★1686★
Fraternity of Light
Current address not obtained for this edition.

The Fraternity of Light was formed in Philadelphia by a small group of Qabalistic magicians. It draws on the tradition of the Hermetic Order of the Golden Dawn, but has no organizational connection. The fraternity teaches that individuals are essentially a spark of divine consciousness which exists eternally and periodically cloths itself in a series of sheaths or bodies, the most dense of which is the physical. At death, the spark and its several bodies leave the physical and three days later the less dense bodies separate from the more dense. The spark may be attracted to a vortex created by two individuals during the sex act. If conditions are right and the woman's egg is fertilized, then the spark will begin to build a new set of bodies which enter the baby's physical body at the time of birth.

This evolutionary process which repeats itself many times is termed reincarnation. When the spark evolves enough, it no longer needs a physical body. Eventually everyone will complete the evolutionary process. The work of the fraternity is toward assisting people to speed the normal course of evolving. To this end the fraternity offers a set of lessons and involvement in ritual practice.

The lessons of the fraternity consist of a philosophy course in two levels. Probationers may, after completing the course, join the fraternity as neophytes and are accepted into either the Order of the Holy Grail or the Coven of Diana. The order offers course work in a Celtic approach to magic. The coven explores witchcraft, mysticism, and moon magic. Membership in both groups is prohibited. After completion of either the coven's or the order's study course, the initiate may become a full member of the fraternity through the Order of the Golden Sword. Membership begins with a 20-lesson series in ritual magic. Members at all levels must agree to refrain from the use of any illegal drugs.

The fraternity also schedules a regular series of rituals, both weekly and quarterly; additional rituals at the solstices and equinoxes; and individual initiations. As members become involved in the ritual life, they are introduced to the Scroll of Daath, the fraternity's holy book. Copies are available only to fraternity members who receive them on loan. Members leaving the fraternity are asked to return their copy.

The Fraternity of Light differs from many magical orders by its focus upon the All-Mother in its rituals. Integral to this focus is the importance of the high priestess as the chief spiritual guide and ritual leader of the group. Women participate fully at all levels of the fraternity.

The fraternity is headed by the Group Guide, the High Priest, and the High Priestess. Within the core of the fraternity are two secret circles. The Circle of the Pentacle is an elite group which manages the fraternity and does advanced work and study. The Brotherhood of the Cup is engaged in esoteric (magical) work under the direction of the Group Guide and the Inner Plane Adepti (i.e., those advanced sparks who have evolved beyond a need for a body and who guide the work of the fraternity from their present elevated state.)

Membership: Not reported. The fraternity has never been large, and has an estimated membership of less than 100.

Sources:

Gerber, Jack. "Paganism Is Where? In Philadelphia." *Gnostica* 4, no. 9 (July 1975).

The Path of Light. Philadelphia: Fraternity of Light, 1974.

★1687★
Hermetic Order of the Golden Dawn
PO Box 1757
Elfers, FL 34680

The Hermetic Order of the Golden Dawn (H.O.G.D.) is an organization dedicated to the continued preservation of that body of knowledge known as Hermeticism or the Western Esoteric Tradition. The order promotes the teachings of the original Hermetic Order of the Golden Dawn, the magical fraternity founded in London in 1888 by William Wynn Westcott and S. L. MacGregor Mathers. Although the Golden Dawn ceased to exist under that name in 1903, its teaching activity continued for a number of years under the names of two spin-off organizations, the Stella Matutina and the Alpha et Omega.

As originally designed by its founders, the Golden Dawn was to be an Hermetic Society dedicated to the philosophical, spiritual, and psychic evolution of humanity. It was supposed to be a school and a repository of knowledge concerning the principles of occult science and the various elements of Western philosophy and magic. Symbolism used within the H.O.G.D. came from a variety of religious sources and people from very diverse esoteric religious paths found themselves at home with the Golden Dawn.

The Golden Dawn system teaches students abstract esoteric concepts as well as the practical applications of ceremonial magic. The curriculum includes the study of Qabalah, astrology, divination, inner alchemy, Egyptian magic, skrying (clairvoyant reading), and Enochian magic.

Membership: Not reported.

★1688★

Hermetic Order of the Golden Dawn (Regardie)
270 N. Canon Dr., Ste. 1302
Beverly Hills, CA 90210

The Hermetic Order of the Golden Dawn and the Ordo Rosae Rubeae et Aureae Crucis (R. R. et A. C.) are two divisions of an initiatic and magical order which were founded by several high-ranking Freemasons in 1888 and 1892 respectively. The order has been credited with constructing a brilliant synthesis of mythical and magical material from varied sources of the Western magical tradition. When the order was discontinued early in the twentieth century, its work was carried on by organizations founded by several of its members, and most of its materials have been published. A most important event was the publication of its main rituals by Israel Regardie.

In the early 1980s, Regardie, then considered by many in the occult world the last contact point with the era of the Golden Dawn and its notorious child Aleister Crowley, and Cris Monnastre "magically" resurrected the Hermetic Order of the Golden Dawn and the R. R. et A. C. In 1982, under Regardie's guidance, Monnastre founded the Osiris Khenti Amenti Temple. Over the succeeding years other temples were opened.

As the twentieth century comes to a close, the Ordo Rosae Rubeae et Aureae Crucis operates temples of the Hermetic Order of the Golden Dawn around the world. The United Confederation of Independent and Autonomous Temples, officially known as the Confederatio Fraternitatis Rosae Crucis (C. F. R. C.), consists of temples from around the world, descending with initiatic and/or chartered lineage and affiliation from the Hermetic Order of the Golden Dawn, as reinstituted by Regardie and Monnastre. Within the confederation, it is believed, have been reunited initiatic and/or chartered lineages deriving from the Hermetic Order of the Golden Dawn, the Ordo Rosae Rubeae et Aureae Crucis, and the several groups formed from them early in the twentieth century, specifically the Stella Matutina, the Ordo Rosae Crucis, Alpha et Omega (Rosicrucian Order of Alpha et Omega), the Holy Order of the Golden Dawn (deriving from A. E. Waite), and the Order of the Sacred Word.

The order offers ritual initiation as well as instruction in the Rosicrucian system of ceremonial magic. It is claimed that this system facilitates personal as well as spiritual development through a systematic program of ritual initiation and the spiritual disciplines of ceremonial magic (a powerful tool for self-realization and transformation).

The order distinguishes itself from several other groups claiming roots in the Golden Dawn which engage in what the order views as dubious practices, in particular "initiation by proxy" or "astral initiation." All initiations marking the progress of the student are done while the student is physically in the presence of the initiator, during which time, it is believed, the actual transmission of magical energies occurs.

Membership: Not reported.

Remarks: In 1982, Cris Monnastre was given a number of Israel Regardie's personal magical accoutrements, among which were Regardie's Elemental Weapons, a complete Rosicrucian chess set, and a Rose Cross that he inherited from Elsa Barker (an important historical link in the Rosicrucian Order of Alpha et Omega between Mathers' Ahathor Mother Temple, No. 7, in Paris and the temples of the A. O. in the United States). She has donated these items to the R. R. et A. C.

Sources:

Regardie, Israel. *The Golden Dawn.* Chicago: Aries Press, 1937-40. 4 vols.

___. *The Middle Pillar.* Chicago: Aries Press, 1938. 154 pp.

___. *My Rosicrucian Adventure.* Chicago: Aries Press, 1936. Rept. St. Pau;. MN: Llewellyn Publications, 1971. 168 pp.

___. *What You Should Know about the Golden Dawn.* Phoenix, AZ: Falcon Press, 1983. 186 pp.

★1689★

Hermetic Order of the Morning Star International
4035 E. Guasti Rd., Ste. 306
Ontario, CA 91761

The Hermetic Order of the Morning Star International (founded in the 1980s as the Hermetic Order of the Golden Dawn International) is a worldwide fraternity dedicated to the "Great Work," the higher development of spiritual growth through the magical way of life. The order believes that magic is a powerful system of inner growth and spiritual development. As a Mystery school, it is designed to take the student step-by-step from where they are at present to the door of Adepthood. The Adept in the making learns the "secrets" of listening and hearing to what is thought of as one's inner voice of Light, often called the "Higher Genius" or "Holy Guardian Angel."

Students are taught through a series of graded lessons from the starting point of Neophyte. Each grade has a series of lessons, over 175 of which constitute the lessons for the Outer Order (neophyte to philosophus). Students receive the lesson for their grade, which they work on at their own speed. The student is tested on each grade before being passed into the next grade. The movement from grade to grade is marked with an initiation ceremony which is held in the Temple of Isis Mighty Mother in Southern California or in cases in which a person cannot come to the temple, initiations may take place through what is termed an "astral initiation."

The actual teachings of the order are given to members only, but flow from the now generally well-documented teachings of the Western Mystery tradition which have found a popular expression in the material produced by and written about the Hermetic Order of the Golden Dawn. Through the twentieth century, almost all of the rituals and teaching materials originally produced for the Golden Dawn early in this century have been published, and during the 1980s several groups have appeared that directly draw upon these materials. Lessons of the Morning Star include the study of Mystical Christianity, Qabalah Egyptian Mysteries, philosophy, Tarot, Greek Mysteries, alchemy, astrology, astral travel, clairvoyance, and ritual magic.

V.H. Frater T.D.L., the Imperator, and V.H. Soror R.D., the Praemonstratrix, are the current leaders of the order.

Membership: Not reported.

Periodicals: *Tablets of Thoth.*

★1690★

Holy Order of RaHoorKhuit
Box 24691
Tampa, FL 33623

The Holy Order of RaHoorKhuit (H.O.O.R), conceived in 1978 and founded in 1991, is an outer order of Thelema established to fulfill and teach the concepts and principles of the method of theurgy (magic) known as Thelema. The teachings of Thelema (from the Greek word for "will") derive from *Liber Al vel Legis* (a.k.a., *The Book of the Law*), a small volume dictated to the eminent magical theorist and practitioner Aleister Crowley (1875–1947) by a preter human intelligence known as Aiwass in 1904. The teachings of Thelema are generally summarized in several of the statements from *Liber Al*: "Do what thou wilt shall be the whole of the Law" and "Love is the law, Love under will."

In essence Thelema teaches that every human being is a complete, unique, and divine entity (a star). Each person has a unique purpose (destiny), which is the law. Each person's function is to follow one's destiny. Love serves as the agent, under the regency of will, which binds all things in their course. Thelemites see the law of Thelema as a law of freedom casting off the authority of priests and demanding that individuals learn to listen internally, by which method the will is discerned. The individual is thus empowered to decide upon the course of his/her own life—associations, movements, living arrangements, etc. "Do what thou wilt. . ." does not mean "do anything you want." Rather, it suggests that having discovered one's destiny/purpose, that destiny/purpose becomes the sole guide for action in the world. H.O.O.R. also teaches a method of theurgy which facilitates the discovery of the will and provides guidance for dealing with all aspects of life on planet earth.

The order is headed by Ray Eales (b. 1958), who took the lead in its formation. H.O.O.R. is organized in lodges, membership in which is open to all. Progress is through grades attained by study, accomplishment, and initiation. The lodges serve as instruments of fellowship, education, and the encouragement of society in the adoption of thelemic principles. The order is closely associated with the Abbey of Thelema, headed by Gregory von Seewald.

Membership: As of 1997 there were more than 100 members of H.O.O.R.

Periodicals: *Warriors LVX.*

Sources:

Preliminary Thoughts on H.O.O.R. Old Greenwich, CT: Holy Order of RaHoorKhuit, 1994.

★1691★
International Academy of Hermetic Knowledge
PO Box 4384
Charlottesville, VA 22905

The International Academy of Hermetic Knowledge was founded in 1991 as the outer court of an older magickal group, the Holy Order of the Winged Disk. The Holy Order was inspired by the predynastic teaching of ancient Egypt and its teachings are given only by oral instruction. Its teachings are secret and shared only with members.

The International Academy is the organization through which the teachings of the Holy Order are released to the public. The occasion of its formation was the observed development of a growing popular interest in alternative spirituality (Wicca, New Age, Eastern philosophy, and Magic). The Academy's curriculum concentrates on practical techniques for spiritual development.

Through the Academy, the esoteric knowledge of the Holy Order has been written down in a book, *The Practical Arcanum,* and a series of monographs that are distributed to the Academy's students. The monographs were written by Phaedron, the Hierophant of the Holy Order. People are invited to Academy membership initially for a year. They are tested on their mastery of the information in the monographs. Those who pass the tests and wish to continue, may pursue a second year and third year. Work in the Academy puts its students in contact with the Holy Order and opens the possibility for membership in that organization.

Membership: Not reported.

★1692★
Monastery of the Seven Rays
Box 1554
Chicago, IL 60690-1554

The Monastery of the Seven Rays is the organizational umbrella given to the various magical activities focused in the person of Michael Bertiaux, (b. 1935) a noted Chicago occultist-magician. Bertiaux is the inheritor of the French Martinist tradition which he received through his magical training in Haiti and by his ordination and consecration as bishop of the Neo-Pythagorean Church.

Louis Claude de Saint-Martin (1743-1803) was a Roman Catholic raised in France. As a soldier, he met Martines de Pasqually, a disciple of Emanuel Swedenborg and Rosicrucianism. De Pasqually founded an occult order, the Order of the Elect Cohens, which Saint-Martin joined in 1768. After de Pasqually's death in

1774, Saint-Martin became the focus of a group of occultists. He began to write books (published posthumously), and a movement, the history of which is still known only in fragments, was born.

By the end of the eighteenth century, a branch of the Martinist Order had been established in Haiti. This group continued to function after Haiti gained its independence. It tended to blend with voodoo. In the 1890s, there was a revival movement in the Martinist Order, emphasizing a purist strain of Gnostic philosophy. In the years between the world wars the Gnostic Church was established in Leogane, Haiti, and was brought to the United States after World War II. In general, the Gnostic philosophy emphasizes a secret knowledge that humans can attain, and denies the divinity of Christ.

The Monastery of the Seven Rays, which became widely known through its advertisments in *Fate Magazine* in the 1970s, is a magical order drawing upon modern thelemic magick (derived from the writings of Aleister Crowley), voodoo, and the nineteenth-century French gnostic-occult tradition. Bertiaux wrote the lessons which teach a basic magical system and lead the student into the higher levels of magical working.

The Neo-Pythagorean Gnostic Church is the ecclesiastical structure which, along with six other fraternal and psychically oriented structures with which it is interlocked, focus the Martinist occult/mystical tradition in North America. The tradition began in France, was brought to Haiti, and from there came to the United States in the mid-1950s. Bertiaux was consecrated by Bishop Hector Francois Jean-Maine, a Haitian who had received orders from the Spanish Albegensian Church which in turn had orders from the French gnostics. The famous French occultists Joseph-Antoine Boullan (1824-1893) and Eugene Vintras (1807-1875) are included in the lineage.

The Neo-Pythagorean Gnostic Church is a ritual theurgic body in which the eucharist is the center of initiation. Through it, the invocation of angels and planetary spirits is made, and spirit communication often takes place during the mass. Purity of ritual is emphasized, and no tallow (i.e. nothing that carries the suffering of animals) is used in the candles. All members of the clergy are clairvoyant and often have visions during mass. Also, during worship a mystical language is intuitively (i.e. clairvoyantly) perceived and mystically spoken.

A Gnostic hierarchical system is headed by the Absolute, similar to the Kabbalist Ein Soph. The Absolute emanates a Trinity, which in turn is the source of Lucifer and Sophia, the basic male/female polarity. Lucifer is the morning star, inferior to Christ but not to be confused with Satan. Sophia is paid homage in the cult of the Virgin, the archetypical divine being. She is often revered as Our Lady of Mt. Carmel. Satanism and black magick are strongly opposed.

The church is subject to a supreme heliophant (in 1984, Dr. Hector Francois Jean Maine, residing in Madrid). The American jurisdiction is under Bishop Pierre-Antoine Saint-Charles of Boston, who has direct authority over all Haitian-American members. Michael Bertiaux in Chicago is over the Caucasian-American members and Bishop Marc Lully of Chicago heads overseas development in South America and the West Indies. In 1979 Bertiaux exchanged consecrations with Bishop Forest Gregory Barber of the Catholic Apostolic Church in America.

Associated with the church are the Ancient Order of Oriental Templars, the Arithmosophical Society, Zotheria, and the Esoteric Traditions Research Society. The Ancient Order of Oriental Templars is a lodge with credentials derived from the pre-Crowleyite Ordo Templi Orientis in Germany. It teaches a 16-degree system of magick. The Arithmosophical Society concentrates on Saint-Martin's philosophy of numbers. Numbers form a key to Saint-Martin's system of magical correspondences and tie Saint-Martin to Pythagoras. Both Zotheria and the Esoteric Traditions Research Society are outer courts of the various esoteric structures.

Membership: Not reported.

Periodicals: *Esoteric Ontology Newsletter.*

Sources:

Baca, Docteur Bacalou [Michael Bertiaux.] *Lucky Hoodoo.* Chicago: Absolute Science Institute, 1977.

Grant, Kenneth. *Cults of the Shadow.* New York: Samuel Weiser, 1976.

McIntosh, Christopher. *Eliphas Levi and the French Occult Revival.* New York: Samuel Weiser, 1974.

★1693★
New England Institute of Metaphysical Studies
(Defunct)

The New England Institute of Metaphysical Studies was founded in the early 1970s by Ron Parshley and Mark Feldman as a correspondence school dedicated to the pursuit of occult knowledge. It was the Institute's perspective that Aleister Crowley placed magick in a system open to all. Through its own P-F Publications, it published the five-volume *Theorems of Occult Magick* by Feldman and Parshley as a study in Crowley's teachings. It also offered seventeen courses in occultism, divination, witchcraft and magick. A quarterly newsletter was sent to all students. Also associated was *Tamlacht*, published three times a year by Victor Boruta of Linden, New Jersey. Headquarters were in Methuen, Massachusetts.

Sources:

Feldman, Mark, and Ron Parshley. *Theorems of Occult Magick.* 10 vols. Methuen, MA: P-F Publications, 1971.

★1694★
Order of the Lily and the Eagle
PO Box 2919
Littleton, CO 80161-2919

The Order of the Lily and the Eagle was the "guardian" of the Eonian tradition cradled in India and Egypt and passed through Orpheus, Pythagoras, Plotinus, Christian Rosencreutz, Paracelsus, Thomas Vaughn and Louis Claude de Saint-Martin (among others). It was founded in 1915 when its two masters—Deon (d. 1924), the prototype of wisdom, and Dea (d. 1918), the prototype of Love—reestablished the order. Their goal was to work for the liberation of humanity and to announce the coming of the Holy Spirit as promised by our Savior.

The work of the order was to help individuals become initiates. The process begins in purification and continues through a knowledge of self and nature (the mysteries) to mastery of alchemy and theurgy (practical magick) and the initiatic sciences. The initiate struggles against evil, instructs others, and engages in healing of his fellow creatures. He is united with the invisible world and the masters (spirits who were once human and now teach humans about spiritual realities).

The Order of the Lily and the Eagle disseminated the teachings of the founders. They were structured in seven grades. The group also published *Eon/Justice and Truth*, a biennial periodical. Headquarters were in Englewood, Colorado.

★1695★
Order of the Thelemic Golden Dawn
1636 N. Wilcox Ave., Ste.418
Los Angeles, CA 90028

The Order of the Thelemic Golden Dawn was founded in 1990 as the Thelemic Temple and Order of the Golden Dawn in Los Angeles by David Cherubim, its Frater Superior Chief. It is a magical/religious/scientific order devoted to the teachings of Aleister Crowley, and exists to assist in the initiation of persons into the magical life of thelema. Thelema (or will) was the basic concept of Crowley's magical system. The order offers seven grades of initiation from neophyte to Ipsissimus, each level representing one of

the seven chakras of the human body in the Indian tantric system, one of the seven planets of traditional astrology, and one of the seven metals of alchemy.

The order has attempted to interpret *The Book of the Law*, the volume Crowley wrote in 1904 which became the basis of his proclamation of the new Aeon of Horus in which his followers now consider we are living. Regarding ritual, it believes that the injunction that "rituals shall be half-known and half-concealed," is to be understood that the initiation rituals should be developed in response to the nature of each initiate. Thus each initiation of a member becomes a unique event.

The members of the order together constitute a religious body of Free Warriors who are seeking to extend the Dominion of the Law of Thelema; that is, they are attempting to establish on earth the principles of *The Book of the Law* on earth. The methods for accomplishing this task are occult research, practical mysticism, ceremonial magick, and tantric alchemy. The order also offers members a system of self-initiation, based upon the Qabalah (Kabbalah) and the Tarot.

The order has been created in an environment in which the great majority of Crowley's writings (including the rituals of the Ordo Temple Orientis, which he headed) have been published and are readily available. It is assumed that members have or will gain a solid background in Crowley's thought.

Membership: In 1997, there were 200 members in the United States, 20 in Canada, and 100 in Brazil. There were temples for initiation in the United States and Brazil.

Sources:

http://www.tgd.org/.

★1696★
Order of Thelema
PO Box 511
Chula Vista, CA 91912

The Order of Thelema was a Thelemic magick group which rejected the attempt by various branches of the O.T.O. to establish their authority by reference to a line of succession from Aleister Crowley. It was structured as a Crowleyan study group. There was no system of rituals except those things which members interpreted from Crowley's revelatory bible, *Liber Al vel Legis* (*The Book of the Law*), each according to his own will. The group believed that Aleister Crowley still operated close to this plane of existence as a present and active force, and that it was possible for him to reach the order by psychic means. The written words of Crowley were the only source of Thelemic Law. Strong support was given the perspective of *The Book of the Law*. Headquarters of the Order of Thelema are in Chula Vista, California. The word "Thelema" means will.

★1697★
Ordo Adeptorum Invisiblum
Current address not obtained for this edition.

The Ordo Adeptorum Invisiblum (O.A.I.) is a British-based thelemicist order aligned to the Maatian magical "current." It has grown out of the proclamation of the magical Aeon of Ma (or Maat) proclaimed in 1948 by Frater Achad (Charles Stansfeld Jones). Maat is the ancient Egyptian goddess of Truth and Justice. The order looks toward a planetary manifestation of the presence of Maat. The coming of Maat has been heralded by the three twentieth-century trends: the great liberation movements leading to the recognition of human rights, the attempts to balance male-dominated Western magic and the non-elitist androgynous approach to magic practiced by Maatian groups. In recognition of their acceptance of feminist liberation concerns and the non-sexist nature of their magical workings, members of the O. A. I. have dropped the use of common designations of male and female members as "frater" and "soror" in favor of the single desination "persona."

The O.A.I. began in England in 1979 in the informal workings of three thelemic magicians (two women and one man). In 1980 they made a formal alignment to the Aeon of Maat and thus the O. A. I. came into existence. At the end of the year, the three original members separated. One went to Fez, Morocco, and the following year, one came to Chicago. The first members of the O.A.I were received in Chicago.

The order has developed as a very loose confederation of otherwise independent magicians pursuing their own magical experiments in alignment to the Maatian Aeon. Periodically, order members will gather for group rituals. New initiates are received after their successful performance of *Liber Samakh He*, a revised version of *Liber Samakh*, a thelemic ritual designed to promote conversation with one's Holy Guardian Angel (higher self). The order is non-hierarchial. Leadership can be exercised by any member and teaching is a matter of sharing the results of individual ritual workings with the larger membership. All members have access to all materials possessed by the order.

Membership: In 1985 members of the order could be found in England, the Chicago metropolitan area, and California. There are less than 100 members.

Sources:

Liber ANDANA. Chicago: Ordo Adeptorum, 1983.

Persona PVAD MASURUS 1043. *Liber Samakh He.* Chicago: Stellium Press, 1981.

Skia, Persona. *O.A.I. Manifesto: Origin, History, Organization.* Kenilworth, IL: Ordo Adeptorum Invisiblum, 1982.

★1698★
Ordo Lux Kethri
Current address not obtained for this edition.

The Ordo Lux Kethri (the Order of the Kethric Light) was formed in 1982 by April Schadler Bishop and Michael Albion Macdonald, both former initates of the Builders of the Adytum, through which they claim lineage from the Hermetic Order of the Golden Dawn. The order is similar in structure to the Rosicrucians and considers itself a fraternal order. Studies include Qabala (kabbalah), alchemy, hermetic meditation, and ritual magic. The initiatory grades, 10 in number, of the Golden Dawn system are followed. The hermetic teachings of Franz Bardon are used, especially his techniques of visualization and astral travel.

Membership: In 1987 the order had 14 members in one group. There was a second group, the Persephone Lodge in process of formation in London, England.

Sources:

Bardon, Franz. *The Key to the True Quabbalah.* Wuppertal, West Germany: Deiter Rueggeberg, 1971.

___. *The Practice of Magical Evocation.* Wuppertal, West Germany: Deiter Rueggeberg, 1970.

Macdonald, Michael-Albion. *The Secret of Secrets.* Berkeley Heights, NJ: Heptangle, 1986.

★1699★
Ordo-Temple Baphe-Metis
PO Box 1219
Corpus Christi, TX 78403-1219

The Ordo Temple Baphe-Metis (O.T.B.) was founded in January 1985. It is a Thelemic fraternal order "chartered" by fiat in Aleister Crowley's (1875-1947) *Khabs am Pekht*, though the O.T.B. is in no way connected to any of the branches of the O.T.O. either in America or Europe. In common with other Thelemic organizations, members of the O.T.B. must accept as a Holy Book, *Liber*

Al vel Legis (or *The Book of the Law*), given to the prophet Ankh-f-n-Khonsu (Crowley) by Aiwaz, his holy Guardian Angel, in Cairo in 1904. Additionally, Knights of the Order (which may be of either sex) promulgate the Law of Thelema, together with the Thelemic Bill of Rights, Liber 77 (Liber Oz). Current Grand Master Ekagratanath trance channeled the Order's own Holy Book, *Liber Ba Neb Tet* (or *Book of Baphomet*), available, with commentary, to members only. Members of the Order practice ritual and ceremonial magick. A study manual, *The Way of the Warrior-Magus*, is given to members.

The order operates the Invisible College, the designation of the home study course in ritual and ceremonial magick, alchemy, divination, and Hermeticism.

The order is closely related to the American Gnostic Church with which it shares an overlapping leadership and publishes a periodical, *Abrasax*.

Membership: Not reported.

Periodicals: *Abrasax.* • *The Philosopher's Stone.*

★1700★
Ordo Templi Astarte
Current address not obtained for this edition.

The Ordo Templi Astarte (Order of the Temple of Astarte-OTA), which also operates under the name Church of Hermetic Science, is a ritual magick group begun in 1970 to practice Kabbalistic Magick in the Western tradition. Based upon Jungian psychology, the OTA defined magick as a "system of ritual hypnotic induction (conjuration) that calls upon archetypal forms from the unconscious (evocation) and allows them to be visualized (manifestation) whereupon they can be used for numerous purposes ranging from the frankly psychotherapeutic to the more abstract system research and development."

The OTA traces its history to Aleister Crowley through Louis Culling. Culling claims to have a charter from Crowley for an autonomous lodge. This charter was given after Culling left C. F. Russell, who was deviating from Crowley's teachings. Culling turned the charter over to the OTA leadership before his recent death. The group also claims to possess the "secret rituals of the Ordo Templi Orientis in Crowley's original holographs." Though operating with a thelemic charter, the OTA does not consider itself fully thelemic. In describing the order, founder Carroll R. Runyon, Jr. has noted, " We operate a Collegium ad Spiritum Sanctum of the O.T.O. in our Philosophus Grade as a research and study program. In its own context, it is Thelemic; but we do not initiate or operate ceremonially under a Thelemic aegis. We have great respect for the works of Aleister Crowley, but we consider him a Master of the Art in much the same way that Sufis consider Jesus a Great Prophet—without calling themselves Christians."

The OTA is centered in a single lodge in Pasadena. During the 1970s there was for several years a second lodge in Pittsburgh. The lodge is headed by Carroll Runyon, also known as Frater Aleyin.

Membership: Not reported. There are less than 50 members.

Periodicals: *The Seventh Ray.* Send orders to Box 3341, Pasadena, CA 91103.

Sources:

Christensen, Cheryl JoAnne. *Magical Epistemic Communities: The Construction of Specialized Social Realities in Bunyoro, Uganda and Los Angeles, California.* Ph.D. diss., Massachusetts Institute of Technology, Cambridge, 1975.

Ellwood, Robert S., Jr. *Mysticism and Religion.* Englewood Cliffs, NJ: Prentice-Hall, 1980.

★1701★
Ordo Templi Orientis
International headquarters
JAF Box 7666
New York, NY 10116

The Ordo Templi Orientis, which had become disorganized following the death of Karl Germer (Frater Saturnus) (d. 1961) who had succeeded Aleister Crowley as Outer Head of the Order (OHO), was reborn in 1969 when Grady McMurtry (Hymenaeus Alpha) asserted his authority as the head of the O.T.O. McMurtry had been given two letters in 1946 from Crowley granting him authority to reform the order and act as Crowley's representative in the United States subject to the approval of Germer. Though these letters were originally intended to apply to the situation of the lodge in Pasadena, California which Crowley had specifically asked McMurtry to investigate, they literally gave McMurtry broad emergency powers. Crowley died in 1947, and the authorization was used with the cooperation of Crowley's successor, Karl Germer and was never withdrawn. Germer's death in 1962 left McMurtry the only person with power to act.

McMurtry also held that he was carrying out Crowley's wishes, that Crowley anticipated Germer's succession problems, and that he openly discussed same with McMurtry. It was Crowley, for example, who used the designation of "caliph" in discussing the continuing office of OHO. Crowley was tying the office to the religious tradition of Thelema, the name given to Crowley's particular magical teachings, assuming Crowley as prophet and his successors as a lineage of caliphs.

McMurtry had been initiated into the Agape Lodge of the O.T.O. in Pasadena in the early 1940s, and during World War II, while stationed in England, was the only American O.T.O. member to be with Crowley. McMurtry assumed the role of "caliph" (or acting OHO) in 1969 claiming that there was no OHO in a person, only a vacant international office. He rejected the claims of Kenneth Grant, the British leader of another O.T.O. group, noting that Grant had been expelled from the order in 1955. (More recently Grant dropped some of his claims to O.T.O. leadership.) He also rejected the claims of Hermann Metzger, head of a Swiss based O.T.O. organization, on the grounds of his "spurious" election without non-Swiss representation.

During the 16 years of McMurtry's leadership, the O.T.O. grew into a substantial body with chapters and lodges across the United States and Canada and ten countries overseas. Full membership in the O.T.O. requires physical participation in the ceremonies of initiation and the payment of subscription costs and dues. A correspondence-only associate membership is also available.

Several months after McMurtry's death in 1985, the IX degree members met and elected a middle-ranking member to replace him. He has chosen to remain anonymous except to members of the higher degrees of the order and has assumed the name-title of Hymenaeus Beta, caliph, frater superior, and acting Outer Head of the Order. After his election, the headquarters were moved from Berkeley, California, to New York City.

Integral to the O.T.O. is the Ecclesia Gnostica Catholica (Gnostic Catholic Church). As part of his magical work, Crowley had been consecrated a bishop in the French Gnostic lineage of Charles J. Doinel (1842-1902) and he in turn passed that lineage to others in the order. Hymanaeus Beta, in addition to holding a consecration in the Antiochean succession of Abp. Joseph Rene Vilatte, was consecrated in the Doinel line. He is designated as patriarch of the Ecclesia Gnostica Catholica. Integral to the work of the O.T.O. lodges is the regular perfomance of the Gnostic Mass composed by Crowley, and priests, priestesses, and bishops have corresponding rank in the O.T.O.

Membership: In 1992 the American order reported 1,000 members in 78 lodges, chapters, oases, and camps, and 50 clergy (priests and bishops of the Ecclesia Gnostica Catholica). There were 9 lodges, camps, and oases in Canada and 12 clergy. World-wide membership was 2,100 in 135 lodges, chapters, oases, and camps in 18 countries.

Periodicals: *The Magical Link.* • *The Equinox.* • *In the Continuum.* Send orders to Box 415, Oroville, CA 95965.

Remarks: During the 1980s the legitimacy of the O.T.O. as led by McMurtry and his successor was challenged in court by Marcelo Ramos Motta, head of the Society Ordo Templi Orientis in America. In rulings in 1985 and 1988 (from the United States Supreme Court), McMurtry was found to be the Outer Head of the Order of the O.T.O.

Sources:

Crowley, Aleister. *Equinox.* 10 vols. New York: Samuel Weiser, n.d.

___. *I.N.R.I. O.T.O. Introduction.* Berkeley, CA: Ordo Templi Orientis, 1981.

Crowley, Aleister, and Frater 137. *Source Book 93.* San Francisco, CA: Stellar Visions, 1981.

Heidrick, Bill. *Magick and Qabalah.* Berkeley, CA: Ordo Templi Orientis, 1980.

The Holy Books of Thelema. York Beach, ME: Samuel Weiser, 1988.

O.T.O. Systen Outline. San Francisco, CA: Stellar Visions, 1981.

Hymenaeus Beta, ed. *The Equinox* 3, no. 10. New York: Thelema Publications, 1986.

★1702★
Ordo Templi Orientis (Grant)
Current address not obtained for this edition.

Kenneth Grant emerged in the 1970s as the self-proclaimed leader of the British branch of the Ordo Templi Orientis. He had co-edited *The Confessions of Aleister Crowley* (1969), late head of the order, and had even earlier (in the 1950s) under the direction and charter of Crowley's successor, Karl Germer, established the New Isis Lodge in London. However, Germer's charter had given Grant the charter to work only the first three degrees. Grant began to work all eleven, writing his own materials where they were unavailable. Germer expelled him from the O.T.O. However, when Germer died, and with the O.T.O. almost extinct, they were few who could challenge Grant's leadership. In 1973 he published *Aleister Crowley and the Hidden God*, the first of six substantive books that began to explore the *Qliphoth*, the so-called backside of the Kabbalah, the mystical Tree of Life. His concentration on the magick of this shadowy realm of the consciousness both gave his brand of magick a unique quality and led other magicians, even Thelemites, to accuse him of tampering with black magick.

Except for the concentration on the Qliphoth in the experimental areas of magick, Grant's order follows much traditional O.T.O. tradition and practice, the secret material of the order having become public during the 1970s through the access given to the Crowley papers deposited at the Warburg Institute in London. Like the other thelemic groups, the O.T.O. (Grant) has as its aim the establishment of the law of Thelema. It does not undertake the training of novices and accepts for membership only those who have submitted a record of nine months' magical practice. They must also publish or disseminate *Liber LXXVII*, a brief statement by Aleister Crowley of some major Thelemic principles.

Organizationally, this branch of the O.T.O. has dropped the "quasi-masonic" structures typical of most magical groups, and its ten degrees are no longer conferred in secret, elaborate rituals. There is no set course to study. Advancement beyond the third degree is subject to the invitation of the governing body. Each applicant is aided to discover the great work which is her/his own true will.

The O.T.O. (Grant) came to the United States through individuals who contacted Grant after reading his several books. It grew and spread in the mid-1970s. For several years, a periodical,

Mezla, appeared. However, in the early 1980s, Soror Tanith (J. R. Ayers), head of the O.T.O. in North America, resigned and no successor has been named.

Membership: Not reported. At present, there are no known lodges and less than 100 members of the O.T.O. branch headed by Kenneth Grant in the United States.

Sources:

Grant, Kenneth. *Aleister Crowley and the Hidden God.* New York: Samuel Weiser, 1974.

___. *Nightside of Eden.* London: Frederick Muller, 1977.

___. *Outside the Circles of Time.* London: Frederick Muller, 1980.

★1703★
Ordo Templi Orientis (Roanoke, Virginia)
(Defunct)

The Ordo Templi Orientis headquartered in Roanoke, Virginia, had claimed to be the true O.T.O. It rejected the claims of the other groups which had emerged in the 1970s based on a charter or lineage dating to Aleister Crowley. Its head was Robert E. L. Shell who saw the mission of the OTO as preventing "hard-won knowledge from being lost in the upheavals and birth pangs of the Aeon Horus [the new era announced by Crowley in 1904]. . . ." One must validate claims by proving allegiance to the law of Thelema, or the Will, the primary principle guiding thought and action for Crowley's disciples. The goal is the Great Work, the ultimate lifting of all humanity to the status of gods. Shell claimed contact with the secret chiefs, the entities (much like the theosophical Great White Brotherhood), who guided the order from the inner planes of existence.

★1704★
Sacred Keltic Church of America
4 Favour Ct.
Stafford, VA 22554

The Sacred Keltic Church of America is a Neopagan group which worships the deities of the ancient Celtic lands, popularly referred to as the Norse gods. The church was founded as the American Church of Teutonic Life in 1992 at Carthage, New York. It is headed by a Senior Lord High Priest Eugene D. Kyle who is also the President of the National Council of Elders.

Membership: In 1998 the church reported 135 members and seven clergy in the United States. They also have five clergy members who are in the military and currently stationed overseas.

Periodicals: *Sacred Keltic Church of America.*

★1705★
Servants of the Light (SOL)
% Fran Keegan
PO Box 6563
Syracuse, NY 13217-6563

Alternate Address: International Headquarters: PO Box 215, St Helier, Jersey, Channel Islands, UK JE4 9SD.

Servants of the Light (SOL) is a contemporary Western Mystery school founded in 1965 by William E. Butler. Butler had begun his esoteric training in Dion Fortune's Fraternity of Inner Light, which in turn had developed from the Hermetic Order of the Golden Dawn (founded in the 1880s). He received further training from psychic Robert King, who later served as Director of Studies for the Servants of the Light until his death in 1978. Dolores Ashcroft-Nowicki succeeded King in 1978 and became head of the school following Butler's death.

The purpose of the SOL is to assist in spreading esoteric knowledge in an ethical manner to all who want to receive it. It has a loose structure which allows for a great degree of independence and free thinking among the students. The SOL teaches through correspondence, and each student is assigned a personal tutor to assist him/her. The First Degree Course consists of 50 lessons of one month each. Each lesson includes written teachings, exercises, and meditations. Students keep a journal which is periodically sent in for assessment.

Lesson material is centered upon the Western esoteric tradition, and the early lessons include discussions of Kabbalah (and the related Tarot) as a basic system leading to numerous other topics. The SOL also claims direct psychic contact with the Inner Planes where the true directors, members of the Inner Hierarchy, of the school are believed to reside.

Membership: In 1998, SOL reported 2,600 members in 23 countries.

Sources:

Ashcroft-Nowicki, Dolores. *First Steps in Ritual.* Wellingborough, Northamptonshire, UK: Aquarian Press, 1982. 96 pp.

___. *The Shining Paths: An Experimental Journey through the Tree of Life.* Wellingborough, Northamptonshire, UK: Aquarian Press, 1983. 240 pp.

Butler, William E. *Apprenticed to Magic and Magic of the Qabalah.* Wellingborough, Northamptonshire, UK: Aquarian Press, 1990.

___. *Magic: Its Ritual, Power and Purpose.* London: Aquarian Press, 1952. 76 pp.

___. *The Magician: His Training and Work.* London: Aquarian Press, 1959. 176 pp.

★1706★
Servants of the Star and the Snake (S.S.S.)
% Administrator-General
PO Box 642
Weslaco, TX 78599-0642

The Servants of the Star and the Snake (S.S.S.) is a federation of ceremonial magicians, shamans, witches, neopagans, sorcerers, and tantrikas founded in the spring of 1995 for the purpose of networking and mutual respect. A tantric-thelemic organization, it has no degree system, no grades, no official reading list, no attainments, no hierarchy, no pope, no head, no soteriology, no holy books, no gurus, and no formal initiation. All of these accoutrements are regarded by the S.S.S. as "Old Aeon" and more appropriate for masonic orders or religious sects. The S.S.S. evolved from the remnants of the Ordo Templi Baphemetis (O.T.B.), which dissolved in the early 1990s. It is based upon the teachings of the cofounder of AMOOKOS (the Arcane Magical Order of the Knights of Shambhala (AMOOKOS)), the late Sri Gurudeva Mahendrabath Paramahamsa "Dadaji" and the late Alain Danielou, but retains the thelemic character of the O.T.B. the federation is overseen by an administer-general, a revolving office. The current administrator-general is Frater Eeyore.

Associated with the S.S.S. is the Order of Napunsakas in the West.

Membership: Not Reported.

Periodicals: *Lila* (occasional).

★1707★
Shrine of Sothis
(Defunct)

The Shrine of Sothis made its appearance in 1973 by way of some ads in psychic/occult periodicals. It taught a system of practical theurgy (magick) as the highest and most efficient mode of communication between man and his inner self. A complete set of lessons, which could be obtained on a correspondence basis, took the student step-by-step through the magical disciplines. The student was taught about the pentagram (a disc-shaped talisman), the gods, initiation, reincarnation, black magick, divination, the construction of talismans and invocation. The goal of the lessons was to lift the student into the realization of the "great concealed one," God. Students practiced daily devotions and orations in their own homes. Members joined by paying an initiation fee. Headquarters were in San Francisco. After several years of operation, the order dropped out of sight.

★1708★
Society Ordo Templi Orientis in America
℅ David Bersson
PO Box 1131
Albuquerque, NM 87103

Among those who made claim to the lineage of the Ordo Templi Orientis following the death of Karl Germer (d. 1962), who had succeeded Aleister Crowley as Outer Head of the Order, was Marcelo Ramos Motta, a Brazilian member of the O.T.O. He claimed that on his death bed, Germer appointed him Outer Head of the Order. In the years following Germer's death, he completed his initiatic work and assumed the magical status needed to become the leader of the work. In 1975, through the Society of the Ordo Templi Orientis (S.O.T.O.), as his branch was known, he issued the first of four massive volumes of the *Equinox*, each issue of which contained writings by Crowley, Motta and others. These were seen as a revival of the semi-annual publication issued originally by Crowley (1909-1913). Other publications followed.

The S.O.T.O. immediately ran into a conflict with the Ordo Templi Orientis (see separate entry) over the copyright to the writings of Aleister Crowley that had been left to the O.T.O. in Crowley's will. The S.O.T.O. claimed to be that organization, and writers and organizations not associated with the S.O.T.O. who wrote about or published Crowley's writings were denounced in various issues of the *Equinox*. The tension between O.T.O., S.O.T.O., and Samuel Weiser , (the publisher of the first issue of the new *Equinox*) led to several law suits. In 1985 a libel suit filed by Grady McMurtry (caliph of the O.T.O.) and others, concerning remarks made in the *Equinox*, against Motta and the S.O.T.O. resulted in the awarding of all copyrights and trademarks to the O.T.O. and turned back all claims by Motta to be the Outer Head of the Order of the Ordo Templi Orientis. It is the belief of its members that the S.O.T.O. is the true O.T.O. and to reject Motta is to reject Crowley.

Membership: Not reported.

Periodicals: *Equinox*.

Sources:

Motta, Marcelo. *Letter to a Brazilian Mason*. Nashville, TN: Troll Publishing Company, 1980.

___. *Manifesto*. Nashville, TN: Society Ordo Templi Orientis in America, 1978.

___. *The Political Aims of the O. T. O.*. Nashville, TN: Ordo Templi Orientis in America, 1980.

___. *Thelemic Political Morality*. Nashville, TN: Society Ordo Templi Orientis in America, 1978.

★1709★
Temple of the Holy Grail (T.H.G.)
℅ Grailmaster
PO Box 777
Brookdale, CA 95077

Alternate Address: Bp. George Boyer, Bishop Templar, 53 College Rd., Colliers Wood, London, UK SW19 2BP.

The Temple of the Holy Grail (T.H.G.) is an initiatory mystery school for individuals wishing to undertake private advanced esoteric training in order to anonymously serve human and planetary evolution. Training is offered by invitation to people already ordained or otherwise advanced in recognized groups, or to individuals who, having prepared themselves apart from organizations,

manifest a devotion to the spiritual unfoldment of humanity and of the planet.

The T.H.G. teaches that the "Grail" mysteries existed in Western Europe long before the advent of Christianity as the "Graded Path of Initiation," comparable to the Lam Rim of Tibetan Buddhism. The mysteries evolved into an esoteric Christian school through the work of the legendary Graalmeister Treverezent in the ninth century and were later associated with chivalric orders, and the alchemical and Gnostic schools.

According to T.H.G. history, in the late 1800s a secret English Templar order in possession of an ancient Jewish terra cotta cup believed to be the true Eucharistic vessel of the Last Supper, now encased in gold, with two ancient silver auxiliary "grails," prepared to do the sacred Grail Rites that had been done once each century by the order and its predecessors in the year '88 (the mystical Christian Kabbalistic number). The purpose of the rite was to re-empower a channel for Divine Blessing upon the planet for the coming century and protect humanity from being overwhelmed by dark forces. The abbot of the order was an elderly man with great concern that the Grail chalices would be stolen by people who wished to use them for magical purposes.

The chalices were secretly transported to London, where the centennial rite (a theurgical Eucharist) was performed, but in spite of all precautions, all three chalices were stolen and used for black magical purposes. After the chalices were retrieved from the thieves, the gold of the True Chalice was melted down, and the pottery cup smashed into the earth. One of the auxiliary chalices turned up at an antiquities auction in Antioch and was purchased by the Metropolitan Museum in New York; it is now exhibited as the "Chalice of Antioch" with legends of it having been the "Holy Grail." The third chalice was never found.

In the 1980s, after two decades of spiritual training and progress, the unnamed person destined to become the present Grailmaster of the T.H.G., who knew nothing of these events, responded to interior guidance to construct a new chalice through white magical and theurgical preparations that required several years to complete. In August of 1988 he was inspired to travel without any knowledge of the final destination over 1,000 miles to a sacred site in Canada, where he used the chalice for a theurgical Eucharist to bless the planet and humanity. While returning home, he heard an interior voice naming him the "Grailmaster," a term unfamiliar to him. He then received teachings telepathically in lucid dreams from a Tibetan Lama which eventually became the First Empowerment of the First Order of T.H.G. Shortly after this, he discovered a written account of the Grail Blessing that had been done in 1888. He then began to understand what had been occurring: he had been instrumental in preparing a new vessel for the 1988 centennial Grail Blessing and the blessing had then occurred as scheduled.

Soon after these events, he was contacted by Bp. George Boyer of the Sanctuary of the Gnosis in London, who transmitted to the Grailmaster all of the charters, titles, and authorities necessary to preserve the esoteric European lineages deriving from the Grail traditions under the auspices of the Temple of the Holy Grail. Bishop Boyer also underwent the new initiations, and contributed to the teachings that the Grailmaster began to bring forth in the 1990s.

Part of the temple's authority resides in the apostolic authority of its leadership. Drawing on the community of independent bishops, all 18 historical apostolic and 22 European esoteric lineages flow by live transmission into temple orders. Additionally, the Grailmaster and temple are Keepers of the True Grail, which is the Divine Royal Blood (San Greal in Christian esoteric tradition, often confused with the Grail chalice itself). The T.H.G. believes that the Grail is the normally invisible and intangible divine sacrificial energy that nurtures evolutionary unfoldment in the physical universe and among beings developing in this level of existence. The power sanctifies matter. It is the philosopher's stone that transforms the lower into the higher, expands contracted heart-consciousness, and mediates inspiration, guidance, selfless service, and divine love.

In the Liturgy of the Chalice, the essences of the Holy Grail are poured out as a potent blessing and nurture for the spiritual evolution of all beings in all worlds.

Members of the order proceed through the mysteries it perpetuates in an ordered sequence.

Membership: Not reported.

★1710★
Temple of Truth
Current address not obtained for this edition.

One of the prime movers in the founding of the Ordo Templi Astarte was Nelson H. White, who served as its vice-president and, under his magical name, Frater Khedemel, served as its major apologist. In 1973, however, he left the Ordo Templi Astarte and he and his wife, Anne White (Soror Veritas) began the Temple of Truth (T.O.T.). The Temple differs from other occult orders in that it has no grades and no fixed curriculum. It has also dispensed with many of the ceremonial trappings of traditional ritual magick; emphasis is placed on individual independent study and spiritual development. Students adopt an individualized course after an initial series of classes. The teachings are basically Kabbalistic and follow the teachings in the Whites' books. As of 1988, the Whites had written and published more than 40 books on magick and the occult.

The T.O.T. is the magical order sponsored by the Light of Truth Church, a licensed corporation in California. The church is neither evangelistic nor fundamentalistic and recognizes the subjectivity of what most people call "Truth." Membership in both the church and the order is open to all persons, though periodically both will refrain from accepting new members if the White's teaching time is filled.

Headquarters of the church are in Pasadena, where the Whites operate a church-sponsored bookstore, The Magick Circle. *The White Light*, which began publication in the fall of 1974, has become one of the oldest continuously published magical magazines in the country.

Membership: Not reported, but in 1987 the newsletter reported a circulation of 200 copies. There is one center located in Pasadena, California. Individual students using the whites' material can be found in approximately 15 foreign countries, as well as Hawaii, Alaska, and Canada.

Periodicals: *The White Light*. Send orders to Box 93124, Pasadena, CA 91109-3124.

Sources:

White, Nelson, and Anne White. *Collected Rituals of the T.O.T.* Pasadena, CA: Technology Group, 1982.

___. *Secret Magick Revealed*. Pasadena, CA: Technology Group, 1979.

___. *The Wizard's Apprentice*. Pasadena, CA: Technology Group, 1982.

___. *Working High Magick*. Pasadena, CA: Technology Group, 1982.

★1711★
Temple ov Psychick Youth (TOPY)
℅ N A Station TOPY Dejavo
PO Box 4889 2A
Los Angeles, CA 90048

The Temple ov Psychick Youth (TOPY) is a loosely organized magical group that originated in 1981 out of the philosophical musings of musician Genesis P. Orridge. The beginning is marked by Orridge leaving a band, Throbbing Gristle, and starting the temple and a new musical group, Psychic TV. He wished to explore the nature of human limitations, conditioning, and potential and saw performance art as a tool for investigation. He soon concluded that he was doing magic. Early on, he reached the conclu-

sion that humans possessed an endless potential and came to resent any constraints on it, a belief echoing Aleister Crowley's *Book of the Law:* "The word of sin is restriction."

As TOPY developed, it ascribed the problem of society to the extreme narrowing of human choice to a few freedoms and the sleep state in which most people existed, unaware of their vast potential. In this sleep state, society reaches a crisis as more and more increasingly zombie-like individuals are required to produce less. Religion and politics are the primary forces putting people to sleep. Temple membership consists of people who are awake to their possibilities and are constantly fighting constraints even as they realize their potentials.

The first realization in the wakening process is the individual's acceptance of mortality and a coming to terms with physical transience. The acceptance of mortality liberates. Also, Temple members expect to come into a relationship with their True Will (in a Thelemic sense) and act in accordance with it. As Crowley expressed it, "Do what thou wilt shall be the whole of the Law." From such an approach to life, an intuitive way of action, acting as one believes rather than from any public moral code, emerges.

Essential to developing such an approach is attention to one's sexuality. Rather than conforming to accepted public sexual norms, one should express sexuality as one believes. Since sex is the basic and universal motivator of human action, it is the most appropriate tool for initially claiming self-control.

A logical extension of its belief about the power of sex, the Temple asserts that ritual sex magick is the best means of liberating energy needed to progress. As one grows and changes within the ever-changing environment, magical activity allows constant adaptiveness. As one discovers and moves toward realizing one's True Will, ritual magick allows its actualization. Ritual magick pushes the individual to test his/her own limitations and often moves him/her outside accepted behavioral patterns. Ritual magick includes the mastering of altered states of consciousness which in and of themselves produce a new view of reality.

TOPY is unusual in the magical community in that it is not organized in a hierarchical fashion. Members are seen as equals whose varying skills and interests complement each other. They are united in a visionary psychick alliance. TOPY also rejects the idea of secret rituals (a belief which grows out of and is made possible by the publication during the last generation of all of the secret Crowleyan magical rituals). While the rituals used and created by individual TOPY members vary considerably, the working of sigil magick, a practice especially associated with the late Austin Spare, is by far the most common practice. Sigils are symbolic representations of a magical goal that are created by writing out a sentence articulating one's goal and then reducing that sentence to a simple symbol. The symbol/sigil is then energized by an act of magick during which the sigil is anointed with a set of body fluids spittle, blood, and sexual secretions and the attachment of body hair. The visualization of a goal and the magical work on that goal causes its realization, the basic belief of the Temple.

Membership: Not reported. There are several centers of activity in the United States.

Sources:

Burton, Tina. *"Intuitive Magick"?: A Study of the Temple ov Psychic Youth, 1981-1989.* Unpublished paper, 1989. 46 pp.

An Introduction to the Temple ov Psychick Youth. Brighton, Sussex, UK: Temple Press Limited, 1989. 24 pp.

★1712★
Thelemic Order and Temple of the Golden Dawn
℅ New Falcon Publications
1739 E. Broadway Rd., Ste. I-277
Tempe, AZ 85282

The Thelemic Order and Temple of the Golden Dawn was established in 1989 by Christopher S. Hyatt and David Cherubim.

In the early 1980s, Hyatt, a student of the famous magician Israel Regardie (1907-1985) and founder of Falcon Press, conceived the idea of a new magical order inspired by the Hermetic Order of the Golden Dawn. The Golden Dawn was the original ceremonial magic organization founded in 1880 in England, and had become the fountainhead of modern magical teachings. Regardie made much of the teachings of the order available to the general public in 1937-40 when he published *The Golden Dawn*, a multi-volume reprint of the basic documents and rituals. Regardie also wrote a number of books that have become standard reading for anyone doing ceremonial magick. Falcon Press was also responsible for reprinting many of Regardie's books in the 1970s and early 1980s. David Cherubim, a ceremonial magician, met Hyatt shortly after Regardie's death in 1985. The first initiations for the order were made in March 1990. Since that time, initiation ceremonies have been held each equinox and solstice.

While inspired by the older Golden Dawn, the new order differs in several important aspects. The older Golden Dawn, for example, had a distinctly Christian cast. The new order is Thelemic. It accepts the revelation of the new aeon that began in 1904 with the giving of *The Book of the Law* to Aleister Crowley by the entity Aiwass. The new aeon is named for Horus, the son of Osiris and Isis, and is designated the Crowned and Conquering Church.

The Law of Thelema (or Will) as enunciated in *The Book of the Law* asserts the right of every person to be the god that they are rather than follow false gods and their outmoded commandments. There are no gods but man. Each individual has a duty to discover their true purpose in life, and to create and assert that purpose. The order initiates members into the truth of their godhood and supplies them with means (ceremonial magick, tantra, astrology, yoga, tarot, and the Qabalah) of realizing their true will. The goal of the order is to create a new race of free men and women who will in turn build a new civilization based upon the Law of Thelema.

Membership is limited to people over 18 years of age. The order has a correspondence course for members unable to attend lectures in either Phoenix or Los Angeles. Falcon Press publishes the writings of Hyatt, Regardie, and other writers in basic agreement with the Thelemic teachings. Associated with the order is the Israel Regardie Foundation in Los Angeles, originally established by Regardie's student Laura Jennings.

Membership: In 1993 there were approximately 200 members in the order.

Periodicals: *Newsletter.*

Sources:

Crowley, Aleister, Lon Milo DuQuette, and Christopher S. Hyatt. *Enochian World of Aleister Crowley: Enochian Sex Magick*. Phoenix, AZ: Falcon Press, 1991. 162 pp.

DuQuette, Lon Milo, and Christopher S. Hyatt. *Aleister Crowley's Illustrated Goetia: Sexual Evocation*. Phoenix, AZ: Falcon Press, 1992. 222 pp.

Hyatt, Christopher, ed. *An Interview with Israel Regardie: His Final Thoughts and Views*. Phoenix, AZ: Falcon Press, 1985. 144 pp.

New Golden Dawn: Flying Roll. Parts 1-15. Phoenix, AZ: Thelemic Order and Temple of the Golden Dawn, 1990-91.

Witchcraft and Neo-Paganism

★1713★
Alexandrian Wicca
Current address not obtained for this edition.

Most closely related to the older Gardnerian Wicca are the Alexandrians, followers of Alexander Sanders, termed by his biographer "The King of the Witches." According to Sanders, in 1933, as a seven-year old, he surprised his grandmother, who was nude and standing in a circle in the kitchen. She ordered Sanders into the circle and had him strip and bend over with his head between his thighs. She took a knife, nicked his scrotum and declared, "You are one of us now." Sanders realized that he was a witch. He was later initiated by her as third degree witch. In actual fact, all indications are that Sanders was an early member of one of the Gardnerian Wicca covens, and that he took the Gardnerian rituals, modified them slightly and began his own work independently. In any case, in 1967, after the failure of several marriages, Sanders settled in London with his third wife, Maxine Sanders.

In 1969, a sensationalized article on Sanders in a Sunday London newspaper led to a meteoric rise. Other papers and media turned him into a celebrity, and his biography was released during the year. He also made a film, "Legend of the Witches," which further boosted his popularity; he was a frequent guest on television talk shows. His text of the Witchcraft rituals were among the first to be published and become publically available. Sanders died in 1988.

The Alexandrians ritually resemble the Gardnerians, upon whom they base their practices. Like the Gardnerians, their rituals are skyclad (i.e., in the nude), and the coven in London became one of the most photographed in all the craft. Alexandrians have become noted for the culmination of the third-degree initiation in the Great Rite, i.e., sexual intercourse, also used at handfasting (marriage) ceremonies. Ideally, the rite is held for two people about to leave and form a new coven. The rite may be symbolic or actual.

The situation of Alexandrian witchcraft as a distinct tradition has been greatly altered by attacks within the Witchcraft community questioning Sanders's credentials and by the defection of a leading member, Stewart Farrar, who, with his wife Janet Farrar, began an independent coven. He has emerged as an important author and ritual innovator. Much of the attention that once came to Sanders now currently flows to the neo-Alexandrian system of Farrar. However, rather than creating a new lineage of covens, Farrar's work has tended to be absorbed into the larger Pagan-Witchcraft community as another source for eclectic covens to draw upon.

Membership: In America a few Alexandrian covens still exist, but their number has steadily decreased.

Sources:

Johns, June. *King of the Witches*. New York: Coward-McCann, 1970.

The Alex Sanders Lectures. New York: Magickal Childe, 1980.

Farrar, Stewart. *What Witches Do*. New York: Coward, McCann & Geoghegan, 1971.

Farrar, Janet, and Stewart Farrar. *Eight Sabbaths for Witches*. London: Robert Hale, 1981.

___. *The Witches' Way*. London: Robert Hale, 1984.

★1714★
Algard Wicca
Current address not obtained for this edition.

Algard (from "Alexandrian" and "Gardnerian") Wicca was formed in 1972 by Mary Nesnick, an Alexandrian Wicca high priestess, in New York City. Ms. Nesnick was initiated into the craft in 1964 by a college professor. She was a freshman at the time. The intent of Algard was to lead to a more independent sect of Wicca that would allow more latitude in ritual and action. As the name implies, both Alexandrian and Gardnerian rituals were sources for Algard practices (Alexandrian Wicca and Gardnerian Wicca are discussed in separate entries.) Combining the two was relatively easy, since they were similar and at many points even identical. Algard covens worship both skyclad and robed, at the coven's discretion. All initiation ceremonies are skyclad.

The Algard covens are governed by the grand high priestess (Ms. Nesnick) and a grand high priest, who oversee the covens and settle intercoven problems and who speak for the craft. Each coven is headed by a high priestess and high priest. Twenty elders assist the ten neophyte priestesses and priests in learning craft ways. A one-year waiting period is required before initiation. Homosexuality is grounds for rejection. Members must be eighteen years of age. Screening before initiation was a point at issue with Alexander Sanders, who felt that the first degree was the place for strict screening. Worship is centered on the eight festivals and thirteen full moon esbats. Only initiates attend.

The Algard Wiccans are one of the most highly organized bodies of covens. An *Algard Newsletter*, issued only to members, tied the leaders together. However, in the flux of the Wiccan community during the late 1970s, the tradition seems to have been largely dissipated.

Membership: Not reported. In 1973 there were a reported 48 covens with affiliated groups in England, Canada, and Greece. There was no verification of those claims, and there is good reason to doubt them. In the early 1980s, the tradition has been reduced to one or two covens in the New York area.

★1715★
American Order of the Brotherhood of Wicca
Current address not obtained for this edition.

The American Order of the Brotherhood of Wicca is an eclectic traditional Wiccan group headed by Lady Sheba (Jessie Wicker Bell). American Celtic is the name given the covens which combine Lady Sheba's Celtic heritage and American Indian magical tradition. Lady Sheba was initiated into the craft in the 1930s. She became the focus of controversy in the early 1970s for publishing her *Grimoire* and *Book of Shadows*, thus making public secret rituals and practices. These rituals turned out to be slightly revised versions of the Gardnerian rituals. She also referred to herself as a Witch Queen, a title used in Gardnerian Wicca for a priestess whose has raised coven members to the third degree and sent them out to form a new coven. The title was rejected by many of the more individualistic craft members.

Lady Sheba defines witch as "the wise one" and witchcraft as "magick," denying that it is nature worship or a fertility cult. To her, witchcraft is learning to manipulate and use the natural laws. Nature is the physical manifestation of the creator, who appears as Mother-Father. Astrology is also an important aspect of witchcraft. Lady Sheba's rituals adhere to the traditional Gardnerian Wiccan forms—the circle, the rituals, the three degrees, the eight festivals and covens of thirteen or fewer persons. They differ primarily in espousing a robed tradition (Gardnerian rituals are done in the nude). Couples and family relations are emphasized.

The American Order is organized into dependent covens tied together by their relationship to Lady Sheba, who is recognized as having come from a long line of witches. Covens are located across the country, and there are a few overseas.

During the 1970s, at the time Lady Sheba's books were being published, the American Order was among the most active groups in promoting interaction and cooperation among witches of various traditions. Much of the organizational leadership was assumed by Carl Weschcke, owner-publisher of Llewellyn Publications, who had been initiated by Lady Sheba. In 1973, the Twin Cities Area Council of the American Order of the Brotherhood of Wicca was formed as a council of coven leaders, and all traditions were invited to participate. In 1974, the Order was a strong force behind the formation of the short-lived ecumenical organization, the Council of American Witches. In more recent years the Order has assumed a much lower profile, and its current status is uncertain.

Membership: Not reported. There are only a few covens currently associated with the order.

Sources:

Sheba, Lady [Jessie Wicker Bell]. *Witch*. St. Paul, MN: Llewellyn Publications, 1973.

___. *The Grimoire of Lady Sheba*. St. Paul, MN: Llewellyn Publications, 1974.

★1716★
Ammonite Foundation
Current address not obtained for this edition.

The Ammonite Foundation is the modern expression of ancient Egyptian religion. Though recently becoming visible in Western Europe and North America, it traces its origin to the reign of Pharaoh Tutankhammun and the city of Thebes. The current head of the foundation is Her Grace Sekmet Montu. According to the foundation, the Ammonites were the original people of Egypt and their religion, now commonly treated as simply "mythology," was the Ammonite Faith. It is, according to the foundation, the oldest still-practiced religion in the world, religion being considered the whole range of codes of conduct (morality, diet, dress) and the psychological and philosophical aspects of living in the world. Its approach has both a monotheistic and polytheistic theological perspective, in that it affirms belief in one God as the root of faith which finds expression with a multitudinous or multi-faceted God face, i.e., a polytheistic expression of belief. It is comparable to modern systems in which the work of the one God is carried out through angels and/or saints. The Ammonite Faith has many obvious parallels to Hinduism and Native American faiths, but also to Christianity, as, it is believed, Jesus Christ borrowed many of his teachings from Egypt.

Individual believers are urged to work out a personal code of behavior based upon their acquisition of facts and the exercise of their free will. There are no commandments. The foundation also rejects the practice of tithing (or the payment of a designated amount of one's income to the religion's centers), but survives from the voluntary offerings of members.

A complete presentation of beliefs and practices is offered to prospective members through a correspondence course available from the foundation's headquarters. It is believed that after successfully restoring Ammun (the deity) to his temples, Pharaoh Tutankhammun decreed that the ancient religion of Egypt be preserved intact so the worship of Ammun could continue throughout the ages. Thus it was that Horemheb (the last pharaoh of the 18th dynasty) created the Ammonite Way to preserve the knowledge for future generations. The Ammonite Foundation claims to still possess the book commonly referred to as the *Book of Tehuti* or *Book of Thoth* in its complete form. The first half of that book, found on tomb walls and published as *The Book of the Dead*, is readily available to anyone. It deals with death and resurrection. The second half, that part not found in the tombs, deals with creation and life. It was kept secret to preserve the faith. The correspondence course prepares the believer for what is contained in the second part of the *Book of Tehuti*.

The foundation recommends a variety of books on Egyptian religion to those who wish to identify with the Ammonite Faith. The list includes the writings of E. A. Wallis Budge, Joan Grant's *Winged Pharaoh*, E. A. Schwaller de Lubicz's *Her-Bak*, and Elizabeth Haich's *Initiation*.

Membership: In 1995 the foundation reported 50 lay members and four clergy members in the United States but 270,000 lay members and 9,000 clergy worldwide. Members are found in Egypt, Iran, Nigeria, India, Germany, and Great Britain.

★1717★
Angelseaxisce Ealdriht
202 E. Mulbury
Huntsville, MO 65259

The Angelseaxisce Ealdriht (Anglo-Saxon Eldright) is a structured, closely knit society which seeks to understand and live the beliefs and values of Anglo-Saxon and other Germanic Heathens (or Pagans) in the context of modern life. Most of the group's deities, values, and beliefs are like those of other Norse Heathen/Asatru organizations and groups. Its deities are those termed the Aesir and the Vanir, including among others Woden (Odin), Frige (Frigg), Thunor (Thor), Tiw (Tyr), Ing Frea (Freyr), and Freo (Freya).

The word "Ealdriht" refers to the common-law rights, customs, and moral values that belong to people by ancient tradition and precedent, those rights and customs that have been earned, established, and held firm through many generations, the Magna Carta (1217 C.E.) being a worthy example. Building on the ancient Heathen ways, the modern Heathen seek to reestablish the enduring customs, values, and ways in the modern world. As modern Heathens, the Angelseaxisce Ealdriht value thoth (beliefs), which includes loyalty to the gods and goddesses, ancestors, and other Heathens. Thoth is strengthened through the swearing of holy oaths and vows.

The Angelseaxisce Ealdriht is organized on a Heathen Anglo-Saxon model. Social rankings are termed "arungs," and these are earned by demonstrating learning, skill, community service, and a level of acceptance of responsibility. The important decisions together are voted upon democratically during the quarterly maethelings (assemblies or Things). Ranks are conferred by democratic vote of the maethels (social units).

There are three categories of membership in the Eldright: the Folgere, an associate or a "friend of the Eldright" (without oath); the Laet, an apprentice preparing for full membership (requiring a provisional oath); and the full, oathed permanent members who have full voting rights and ranks. Members affiliate with "maethels," and each full member of the Eldright belongs to one and only one maethel. Incoming members must be accepted by a maethel which will sponsor and teach them, and promote their growth and well-being in the Eldright. The maethel leaders, either Maethelgerefa (with a temporary term of leadership, renewable by vote) or Maethel Ealdor (elected permanent leader), are elected from within each maethel, and serve on the Witangemot, the governing council of the Eldright. Maethel officers include the Heargweard (priest) if available, Hordere (hoarder/treasurer), and Stigeweard (steward).

Ideally, a maethel is comprised of people who live relatively close together, who can physically gather and get to know one another face to face. However, since Eldright members are scattered across the country, and it is often not possible to have enough members in one place to form a maethel locally, modern maethels often include members who are geographically distant from one another.

The governing body of the Eldright as a whole is the Witangemot, the Eldright council. It is comprised of the leaders of all the maethels, plus the Eldright's Thyle (the counsellor or rede-giver, who is also the educational coordinator) and the leader of Haligwaerstow, the Eldright's Priest Hall or Guild. The Witangemot and the whole voting body of the Eldright elects the leader of the Witangemot and the Eldright—the Eldright Ealdor. The Witangemot must approve the establishment of new maethels or guilds (independent social units, each focused on some defined area of skill, knowledge, and service).

Membership: Not reported.

Sources:

http://www.geocities.com/Aythens/Delphi/6909/.

★1718★
Aquarian Tabernacle Church
PO Box 409
Index, WA 98256

The Aquarian Tabernacle Church was founded by the Rev. Pete Davis and other Pagans in 1979. Davis had been a Pagan for several years when a decision was made to organize independently and incorporate the group as a church. The incorporation was completed in 1983. Since that time the church has emerged as an aggressive and assertive proponent of Neo-Paganism. In 1991 the church received its group tax exempt status from the Internal Revenue Service. Subsequently the church was granted a group exemption letter covering affiliated congregations. Davis and his wife Wende (nee Graebex) serve as the Archpriest and Archpriestess of the A.T.C. tradition.

Paganism is defined by the church as a set of common beliefs held by most Pagans. These include the following: the idea that divinity is both imminent and transcendent, and likely to manifest as both male and female; a multiplicity of gods and goddesses; a respect for nature; a distrust of monolithic religious organizations; life as joyful, loving, and pleasurable; ethics based on the avoidance of harm to others; magic; celebration of the solar and lunar cycles; eclecticism; faith in the ability of people to solve their own problems; commitment to growth, evolution and balance; human interdependence and the need for community cooperation; and the need for a consistency in lifestyle and professed belief.

The church operates church and retreat house in the Cascade Mountains. Its purpose is to re-treat the body, soul, and spirit. Near the church is the MoonStone Circle, a ring of menhirs used for worship and meditation. They also have a shrine dedicated to the Goddess Hecate located nearby. The church sponsors a Spring Mysteries Festival (Eostre), Hecate's Sickle Festival (Samhain), and the Pagan Church Conference, annually. The church operates a recorded-message phone service which features a two-to-three minute message on some aspect of Neo-Paganism. It is also affiliated with the Interfaith Council of Washington State. Davis was elected president of the Interfaith Council in March 1995, the first Wiccan priest ever to hold such a position in the United States. He served two terms. He also serves as a member of the Religious Advisory Commission of the Department of the Corrections in Washington.

Membership: In 1995 the church reported 1,894 members in 30 congregations in the United States, Canada, and Australia.

Educational Facilities: The Patricia Holmes Woolston Theological Seminary, Index, Washington.

Periodicals: *Panegyria*. • *Looking Upward*. • Hecate's Horn.

★1719★
Ar nDraiocht Fein: A Druid Fellowship, Inc.
PO Box 516
East Syracuse, NY 13057

Ar nDraiocht Fein: A Druid Fellowship, Inc. is a Neopagan Druid community founded in the mid-1980s by Isaac Bonewits. The attempt to reconstruct and revive a form of Druidism began at Carleton College during the 1962-1963 school year. It spread from there as the Reformed Druids of North America. Bonewits became a Druid in 1969. The following year he attained some degree of fame when he graduated from the University of California at Berkeley with a degree in Magic. He published his survey of the field, *Real Magic*, in 1971. Through the 1970s, Bonewits took a prominent role in Druid affairs. He published a newsletter and edited the *Druid Chronicles (Evolved)* (1976), but toward the end of the decade he withdrew from leadership and kept a low profile for several years.

Bonewits reasserted his position as an Archdruid in 1984 with the publication of the first issue of *The Druids' Progress* and the announcement of the founding of Ar nDraiocht Fein as a specifically Neopagan form of Druidism. The order maintains a contemporary faith based upon the latest academic research and assessment of ancient Druidism. While reviving the best aspects of the past, this approach advocates self-consciously living in a modern scientific, artistic, ecological, and holistic context. Like other Neopagan groups, it is a nature worshipping, polytheistic faith.

Bonewits also designed the new Druidism so it was not limited to Celtic traditions, but pan-Indo-European to allow a broad intercultural participation. Though Neopagan Druidism is seen as very close to Wicca, it is distinguished from Wicca by its emphasis upon polytheism rather than just two major Wiccan deities (the Sky God and the Earth Mother), its large group orientation as opposed to small covens, and its public inclusionary character.

Neopagan Druids are organized into groves that meet twice monthly and celebrate the common eight pagan festivals. Bonewits (with the assistance of other members) has written *The ADF Grove Organizers Handbook, The ADF Members' Guide, The ADF Study Manual*, and the *ADF Liturgical Manual*. Recently Bonewits retired and was named Archdruid Emeritus. Ian Corrigan has been named acting Archdruid in the interim before a New Archdruid is designated.

Membership: In 1992 there were approximately 375 members in the United States and approximately 15 in Canada. There were 12 chartered groves in the United States. Individual members could be found in Japan, Czechoslovakia, England, Australia, and Ireland.

Educational Facilities: The ADF study program provides college-level training for Druidic clergy and other leaders.

Periodicals: *The Druids' Progress.* • *News from the Mother-grove.* • *The ADF Membership Directory*

Remarks: It appears that most, if not all, of the various Druid groups that were functioning in the 1970s and 1980s have disbanded and that their work now survives through the ADF. However, at last report there was a former group of the Reformed Druids of North America still functioning in California.

Sources:

Adler, Margot. *Drawing Down the Moon.* Boston: Beacon Press, 1986.

Bonewits, Isaac. *Real Magic.* New York: Coward, McGann, and Goeghegan, 1971.

___. *What Do Neopagan Druids Believe?* Newark, DE: Mother Grove, 1991. Tract.

___. *What Is Ar nDraiocht Fein?* Newark, DE: Mother Grove, 1991. Tract.

★1720★
Artemisian Order
% Oriethyia
PO Box 7184, Capitol Station
Albany, NY 12224

One expression of the feminist emphasis in Neopaganism in the 1990s, the Artemisian Order, founded by Oriethyia, a feminist poet, is a clan of sisterhood, a society of women who protect one another while serving nature. Oriethyia was a Dianic Wiccan who decided to start a new Wiccan tradition with the goddess Artemis (the Greek equivalent of the Roman Diana) at the center. Artemisian faith affirmed the female image of god in opposition to the primary male image with which she had grown up, and, unlike most Wicca, Oriethyia saw no need to balance male-female energies by providing the goddess with a consort. The balancing of energies comes from asserting the feminine in a masculine-dominated culture.

Artemisians see themselves as Amazons, the moon women, the fierce fighters whom even the bravest of male warriors fear and respect. In describing their roots, they state, "We are proud, capable women who firmly worship the goddess Artemis. We bow to no man for any reason. If you believe we are war-like and man-haters, consider that men of strictly patriarchal cultures persecuted and killed us for our beliefs. We refuse to submit to the loss of our freedom and rights; therefore, many consider us to be dangerous and unnatural. One may find us running through the forests, hunting down and probably killing any men we find trespassing and spying on our activities. Only a few men survive and become slaves, known as the Gargareans and Philos of the Artemisians. Gargareans are the male companions of the Artemisians and trusted friends and devoted servants of the ideals of the clan. They are respected in the clan for their invaluable services and support. The Gargareans assist the female Artemisians with their duties to na-

ture and women. The Philos are the trusted friends who have fought many battles with us. Through hard work and courage, they have become a very important part of our Order. The Artemisians do not kill these men because they have come to respect them for their undying devotion to the Clan."

The modern Artemisian Order consists of the Sisterhood, Philos, and Gargareans. The Sisterhood maintains the workings of the order on a day-to-day basis. The Goddesses are seen as the order's patrons. The women form the Sophias, the council who lead with their wisdom, the High Priestesses who keep the rituals, the Amazons who defend the way of life, and the Maidens who assist with their strength of mind and spirit. The new Initiates learn from their elder sisters. The Gargareans and Philos, males, assist the Sisterhood by protecting their sacred ways. Present-day Gargareans and Philos are descendants of the men who once existed solely to serve the Amazon women as mates and slaves. Only females may become Initiates. Males may apply, but they will only be allowed to follow the ranks of Gargareans and Philos.

Membership: Not reported.

Sources:

Hopman, Ellen Evert, and Lawrence Bond. *People of the Earth: The New Pagans Speak Out.* Rochester, VT: Destiny Books, 1996. 402 pp.

★1721★
Asatru Alliance
PO Box 961
Payton, AZ 85547

One of the groups to emerge in the wake of the disbanding of the Asatru Free Assembly in 1987 was the Asatru Alliance, which followed the assembly in its basic teachings and a revived form of the ancient religion of the Northern European peoples. It formed as a free association of local Asatru groups called kindreds. The alliance promotes the growth of the faith on a national and regional level by sponsoring meetings and publishing materials. The alliance is headed by the Allthing, its representative legislative body to which all the kindred send a delegate.

Membership: Not reported.

Periodicals: *Vor Tru.*

Sources:

http://www.jcave.com/~eagle/.

★1722★
Asatru Free Assembly
(Defunct)

The Asatru Free Assembly was formed in 1972 from the Viking Brotherhood by Stephen A. McNallen, then a student at Midwestern University in Wichita Falls, Texas. McNallen had been a follower of the Norse deities for several years as an individual and he decided that the time had come for him to speak publically about them. He began to publish *The Runestone*, a quarterly periodical. Shortly after forming the brotherhood, McNallen went into the army and served as an officer with NATO in Europe. During this period *The Runestone* continued to appear, and other groups of Norse Pagans appeared. Upon returning to civilian life in 1976, McNallen began to refine the brotherhood's ritual and doctrine. This refinement led to the adoption of a new name, the Asatru Free Assembly. This change emphasized the great value placed on individualism, courage, integrity, and independence, and the general opposition to all collective ideologies (including fascism) within the assembly (which was home to a wide variety of belief and practice within its general framework). It also set itself apart from "Odinism" (the popular name for Norse Paganism) in that the assembly is looking to revive the "cults" of all the Norse deities, not just Odin.

Worship was viewed as a contradiction of the spirit of ego centrality in the Viking religion. However, basic rituals were devised to celebrate certain events and to recognize the gods, who epitomize certain values. New members were initiated, and name-givings and burials were also occasions for ritual. Adherents celebrated Yule (December 22); Ragnar's Day (March 28), in commemoration of Viking Ragnar Lodbrok, who sailed up the Seine River in 845 and sacked Paris, France; Lindisfarne Day (June 8); and Midsummer Day (summer solstice). *Runestone* regularly carried a calendar of ritual and remembrance days.

Local groups of the brotherhood were called "Skeppslags" or "ship's crews," and they consist of from two to 15 members. Each Skeppslag operated under the chieftain of the brotherhood. Also becoming active during the early 1980s were a variety of guilds, groups built around a particular interest. These vary from sewing guilds to warriors' and brewers' guilds. Some guilds published their own newsletters. In November 1987, McNallen announced the dissolution of the assembly in the wake of a failure to reorganize. Its periodical, *The Runestone*, was discontinued. At its height in the mid-1980s, the assembly had approximately 200 members.

Remarks: Within the larger Pagan community, the Norse groups have, as a whole, been condemned for their overt racism. The Asatru Free Assembly was largely free of racist expression and continued to be accepted by non-Norse Pagans.

Sources:

Hundingsbani, Heigi. *The Religion of Odin—A Handbook*. Red Wing, MN: Viking House, 1978.

McNallen, Stephen A. *Rituals of Asatru*. Breckenridge, TX: Asatru Free Assembly, 1985.

★1723★
Atlantion Wicca
(Defunct)

Atlantion Wicca, though originating in the 1960s, was based upon the teachings (and dedicated to the memory) of Elizabeth Sawyer, the witch of Edmonton, England. Ms. Sawyer was hung at Tyburn, England, on April 19, 1621, for supposedly killing by witchcraft a neighbor, Agnes Ratcleife. She had been known in the town as a healer and midwife and for helping farmers with their crops. The founding high priest was Don Sawyer, a descendant.

Rituals and teachings of Atlantion Wicca were found in its own *Book of Shadows*, which drew heavily upon Gardnerian Wicca practice. Esbats are held at both the full and new moons, and the sabbats were celebrated. Work was conducted within the circle. Reincarnation was a central belief. The group forbade the use of drugs, orgies, sacrifice, public nudity, and any behavior which might reflect poorly upon the craft.

The Atlantion witches were headquartered in Syracuse, New York and in 1977 they had three covens. For several years they engaged in vigorous activity to establish in the public's mind the image of Witchcraft as a serious religion and to destroy the negative images which connected Wicca to violence, black magic, and the worship of Satan. No sign of the survival of the covens into the mid-1980s has been manifest.

★1724★
Avalon Isle/Order of the Royal Oak
Current address not obtained for this edition.

Avalon Isle is the covenstead for the American branch of the Order of the Royal Oak, a chivalrous order established in 1660 by King Charles II to honor the men who had supported him during his exile from the throne. According to present members, Charles II was widely regarded as sympathetic to the ways of the wise (witches), and he created the Order of the Royal Oak as a defiant gesture against the Puritans who had run the now discarded Commonwealth. The original symbol of this order was a young oak growing from the cut stump of the old. It is the claim of present members that the old Pagan religion was kept alive for over 300

years, hidden from hostile eyes, and now a new modern version of the order is being revived.

Leading the new order is Lady Amythyst, a direct ancestor; and Sir George Carteritt, a knight of the Order of the Garter and an original member of the Order of the Royal Oak. Amythyst's family came to America in 1663 from the Isle of Jersey. She affirms that she has been a student of the Ancient Ways since her earliest childhood memories, and has taught the Craft of the Wise (Wicca) since 1976. Amythyst is the High Priestess of Avalon Isle and the leader of the Order of the Royal Oak. Lord Taliesin, the coleader, serves as the order's historian and bard.

Located in the hills of East Tennessee, on the edge of the Great Smoky Mountains, Avalon Isle provides a center for higher esoteric learning, and a gathering point for Wiccans of all traditions. Avalon Isle also sponsors an annual festival to honor the Elder Gods on the birth of the New Year on Samhain in the fall of every year. There is also a set of workshops and programs offered through the year.

Lady Amythyst and Lord Taliesin also operate one of the largest Wiccan-owned nonprofit charitable organizations in North America, a transitional home for men who are reentering the mainstream of life, and a shelter for battered women and children. These facilities admit residents regardless of race, creed, religion, or national origin.

Membership: Not reported.

Sources:

http://mindspring.com/~avalon/.

★1725★
Brothers of the Earth
% Church of the Earth
Box 13158
Dinkytown Sta.
Minneapolis, MN 55414

The Brothers of the Earth is a male-oriented neopagan fellowship composed of groups and individuals interested in exploring, creating, and celebrating a positive male, earth-centered, life-affirming spirituality that is nurturing, nonhomophobic, and nonsexist. It was founded in 1983 by Gary Lingen, (aka Earthkin), founding elder and priest of the Church of the Earth, a neopagan aquarian age church of nature in Minneapolis-St. Paul, Minnesota.

Lingen saw the emergence of men who had developed a new consciousness in response to the emergence of the feminist movement of the previous decade, but who had become isolated in a world of dominant patriarchal male values. Such men sought not only support, but participation in spiritual consciousness-raising for healing and empowerment, and in rituals which celebrated a new vision of manhood. Earlier attempts at male oriented groups had emerged in the neopagan community through the Radical Fairies (a gay group) and in all-male activities at pagan festivals. Brothers of the Earth differs in that it seeks to involve gay, heterosexual, and bisexual men of all ages and cultures.

As pagan men, the Brothers of the Earth affirms their link to the Earth, sun, moon, and all the elemental forces. The feminine principle in nature is worshiped as the Goddess, and the male principle as the Horned God (One). The Horned God is worshiped as an aspect of (Son, Lover, and Co-Creator) and equal to the Goddess (who tends to take precedence in most neopagan and witchcraft groups). The Horned God is neither effeminate nor a representation of machismo; he is the expression of positive male qualities of creativity and power within, rather than power over, and of natural regenerating potency inseparable from the Goddess, the prime and nurturing force.

Membership: In 1988 the fellowship reported 125 members in the United States, eight members in Canada, and 12 in other countries. Membership in the fellowship network comes from all parts of the United States and includes several Witchcraft and Neopagan groups.

Periodicals: *Brothersong.*

★1726★
Church and School of Wicca
Box 297
Hinton, WV 25951-0297

The Church and School of Wicca was founded in 1968 by Gavin Frost and his wife Yvonne Frost. It was one of the earliest of the organizations to develop in America out of the Neo-Pagan revival. In 1972, it received its IRS tax-exempt status, the first Wiccan organization so recognized. It became well-known because of the widely-advertised correspondence course it conducts. During the quarter of a century of its existence, the church has received more than a half-million inquiries and accepted more than 50,000 students.

The church has eclectic teachings which draw on a variety of religious and magical beliefs and practices. There is what is described as a Celtic flavor due to the personal history of the founders in that magical tradition. The current teachings of the church rest upon what are thought of as its five supports: 1. Old masters and new texts: The church members, many of whom possess specialized linguistic and scholarly skills, have examined and offered insights from many ancient and modern religious texts; 2. Experimental work: A continuous process of research on beliefs and practices. As a result, both undergo change and modification; 3. Research into modern remnants of pre-technological cultures: This area, especially as studies by social anthropologists continue, currently forms one of the expanding areas of new insight for the church; 4. Family traditions: The church began with the fragmentary family tradition passed to Gavin Frost. It has largely been discarded because if its patriarchal emphases; and 5. Students and other Wiccans and Pagans: As dialogue is had with Wiccans and Pagans outside the church, especially those who come to the church after years of practice elsewhere, new insights are brought into the church's teachings. The present philosophy of the church can be summarized in five basic tenets resting on a central affirmation of God, pictured as an impersonal reality. From this affirmation other ideas flow, including: 1. The Wiccan Rede: "If it harm none, do what you will;" 2. Reincarnation as an orderly system of learning. Reincarnation is not so much an accounting of sins and punishments, as it is a means of guiding learning; 3. The Law of Attraction: What I do to other living creatures, I will draw to myself; 4. Power through Knowledge. It is assumed that each living creature has power or energy within its body and that the skill to direct that power can be taught and learned; and 5. Harmony: It makes sense to live in harmony with the perceptible rhythms of the sun, moons, and seasons of the year.

Over the years, the church has chartered 28 subsidiary churches worldwide. All of these subsidiaries have completed their training period and have become independent entities. The church sponsors three national gathering every year.

The church continually fights for Wiccan rights and recognition in the public sphere. This has involved them in supporting religious freedom for incarcerated Wiccans and assisting the military in becoming informed about Wicca. The church also sponsors special interest groups for gay Wiccans, military Wiccans, solitary Witches, and other Wiccan groups founded around a particular interest or concern. The church runs a survival community called the Celtic Heritage Investigation Foundation, where land can be purchased by Wiccans and regular church services are held.

The school associated with the church teaches a full range of courses on occult topics. They are directed at serious students and require considerable independent study and reading. Approximately 250 students graduate from the school annually.

Membership: Not reported. At present, the church has limited the student body (enrolled in correspondence courses) to 5,000.

It currently sponsors three subsidiary churches (down from a peak of 28), the drop due in part to its insistence that each church attain its own credentials from the IRS.

Periodicals: *Survival.*

Sources:

Frost, Gavin, and Yvonne Frost. *The Magic Power of Witchcraft.* West Nyack, NY: Parker Publishing Company, 1976.

___. *Meta-Psychometry: Key to Power and Abundance.* West Nyack, NY: Parker Publishing Co., 1978.

___. *Power Secrets from a Sorcerer's Private Magnum Arcanum.* West Nyack, NY: Parker Publishing Co., 1980.

___. *Who Speaks for the Witch.* New Bern, NC: Godolphin House, 1991.

___. *The Witch's Bible.* New York: Berkley Publishing Company, 1975.

___. *A Witch's Guide to Life.* Cottonwood, AZ: Esoteric Publications, 1978.

★1727★
Church of All Worlds
Box 1542
Ukiah, CA 95482

Among the largest and most influential of all Neo-Pagan religious groups during the 1970s was the Church of All Worlds (CAW). The church traces its history back to April 7, 1962, when a "water-brotherhood," called "Atl," was formed by Tim Zell and Lance Christie at Westminster College in Fulton, Missouri. During the mid-1960s, the group was centered on the University of Oklahoma campus at Norman and operated under the name Atlan Foundation. A periodical, *The Atlan Torch* (later *The Atlan Annals*), was published, 1962-1968. In 1968, following a move to St. Louis, Missouri, the Church of All Worlds was legally incorporated. In March of that year, the *Green Egg* appeared. From its inauspicious beginnings as a one-page ditto sheet, it grew into a 60-page journal over 80 issues, becoming the most significant periodical in the Pagan movement during the 1970s and made Tim Zell, its editor, a major force in Neo-Paganism (a term which Zell coined). It was also the major instrument in the church's expansion.

The Church of All Worlds took much inspiration from the science fiction classic, *Stranger in a Strange Land* by Robert Heinlein. In the novel, the Stranger, Valentine Michael Smith, was an earthman born on Mars and raised by Martians. Among his other adventures upon being brought to earth was the formation of the "Church of All Worlds." The church was built around "nests," a combination of a congregation and an intentional community. A basic concept was "grokking," i.e., the ability to be fully empathic. CAW also emphasized the experience of non-possessive love and joyous expression of sexuality as divine union. The nests were places where this grokking and joyful sexual love could find expression. The common greeting was, "Thou art God," a recognition of immanent divinity in each person.

The non-fictional Church of All Worlds is organized around a Central Nest where master records are kept. Autonomous nests are composed of at least three members of *2nd Circle* or *inner* located in the same area. There are nine circles of advancement, named after the nine planets; each circle includes study, writings, magical training, sensitivity, and encounter-group experience, as well as active participation in the life of the church. The clergy, consisting of legally ordained priests and priestesses, begins at *7th Circle* and is made up of longtime members of the church who have worked through the other circles, undergone personal and leadership development, religious training, and completed the church's other ordination requirements. The Board of Directors includes representatives from all Circles attending quarterly board meetings with an annual General Meeting to elect officers and make periodic changes in the church's ever-evolving bylaws.

Incorporated in 1968, CAW was the first of the Neo-Pagan/Earth Religions to obtain full federal recognition. However, the church had some trouble being recognized as a legitimate religious body and was originally refused recognition by the Missouri Department of Revenue for purposes of state sales tax exemption. The rejection was on the basis of its lack of primary concern about the hereafter, God, the destiny of souls, heaven, hell, sin and its punishment, and other supernatural matters. The ruling was overturned as unconstitutional in 1971.

The basic theology of the CAW is a form of pantheism which focuses on immanent rather than transcendant divinity. The most important theological statement came in the form of a revelatory writings by Zell in 1970-73, on the theory which later came to be known as the *Gaia Thesis*. This concept is a biological validation of an ancient intuition: that the planet is a single living organism—Mother Earth (Gaia).

Pantheists hold as divine the living spirit of Nature. Thus, the CAW recognizes Mother Earth, the Horned God, and other spirits of animistic totemism as the Divine pantheon. In this manner, the Church of All Worlds became an early forerunner of the Deep Ecology movement. Through its focus on Mother Nature as a goddess, its recognition and ordination of women as priestesses, CAW can also rightly be held to be the first Eco-Feminist church. Its only creed states: "The Church of All Worlds is dedicated to the celebration of life, the maximal actualization of human potential and the realization of ultimate individual freedom and personal responsiblity in harmonious eco-psyhic relationship with the total Biosphere of Holy Mother Earth."

Worship in the Church involves weekly or monthly meetings which are held usually in the homes of nest members on a rotational basis. The basic liturgical form is based on a Circle where members take turns sharing their creativity. A chalice of water is always shared around the Circle either as the opening or closing of the ceremony. Other events are celebrated at the church sanctuary, a 55-acre parcel of sacred land called Annfwn, in northern California. Annwfn has a handbuilt two story temple, a garden, an orchard, and a small pond. It has solar electricity, propane hot water, and a cellular telephone. In addition to the eight Celtic seasonal festivals commonly associated with Witchcraft, the church holds handfastings (marriages), vision quests, initiations, workshops, retreats, workparties, and staff meetings on the land.

In 1974, the church reported nests located in Missouri, California, Illinois, Kansas, Wisconsin, Iowa, Wyoming, Minnesota, Pennsylvania, Tennessee, New Jersey, New York, and Ohio. It was publishing two periodicals, *Green Egg* and *The Pagan*. Two years later, Zell, having established the churched, moved from St. Louis to northern California with his new wife, Morning Glory, an ordained Priestess, for a rural life more centered upon writing, research in some areas of particular interest and the practice of the religion he had developed. They left the administration and the publication of the *Green Egg* in the hands of other church leaders. After only a few more issues, the magazine ceased to appear and many of the church nests dissolved in the wake of intense internal conflicts.

By the mid-1980s, CAW survived only in California, focalized around the sanctuary land bequeathed to the church by its bard, the late Gwydion Pendderwen. On and around this rural retreat, a pagan homesteading community grew up which included the Zells (Tim Zell had changed his first name to Otter in 1979 following a vision quest) and other long-time church members who moved to the community, as well as many new people. Two new clergy were ordained—Orion Stormcrow and Anodea Judith—who have since become significant leaders in the church (Anodea becoming the president for seven years).

In the late 1980s, following Otter and Morning Glory's emergence from eight years of living in the wilderness, the Church of All Worlds began a reorganization and revivification. The community on the land broke up as the other people moved back into civilization. The membership program was radically upgraded to include intensive training courses and new responsiblities, along with a new members-only newsletter, *The Scarlet Flame*.

The first issue of the revived *Green Egg (The Next Generation!)* appeared in May 1988 to commemorate the 20th anniversary of its original publication, and it has once again risen to a position of prominence among the 500 or so Pagan periodicals currently being published. In 1991, with 52 pages and a four-color glossy cover, *Green Egg* won the Silver Award from the Wiccan/Pagan Press Alliance for "Most Professionally Formatted Pagan Publication."

As of February 1992, the church has six chartered nests in California, with others in Florida, Illinois, Arizona, and Minnesota. A number of others are in the process of formation. Otter is presently engaged in the formation of the Universal Federation of Pagans, a worldwide association with which he hopes to unify the global Pagan community. A Grand Convocation is being planned for August of 1992 to mark the 30th anniversary of the church.

Over the years, the Church of All Worlds has chartered a number of subsidiary organizations through which it practices and teaches its religion. These subsidiaries have continued to function even while the main body of the church went dormant. These subsidiary orders and current (1992) addresses are as follows:

• Forever Forests: Box 212, Redwood Valley, CA 95470. Founded in 1977 by Gwydion Pendderwen. This is the ecology branch. Sponsors tree-planting events and rituals.

• Lifeways: 2140 Shattuck 2093, Berkeley, CA 94704. Founded in 1983 by Anodea Judith. The teaching branch. Offers workshops, classes, healing rituals, recovery programs, and training for the priesthood.

• Nemeton: Box 1542, Ukiah, CA 95482. Founded in 1972 by Gwydion Pennderwen and Alison Harlow. The marketing branch. Tapes, records, songbooks, T-Shirts, philosophical tracts, and books. Catalog available.

• Ecosophical Research Assn. (ERA): Box 982, Ukiah, CA 95482. Founded in 1977 by Morning Glory Zell. Branch devoted to research and exploration in the fields of history, mythology, and natural sciences. Produced the Living Unicorn project, the New Guinea Mermaid expedition and a Peruvian Pilgrimage, as well as a series of replicas of ancient God and Goddess votive figurines (sculpted by Otter).

• Holy Order of Mother Earth (HOME): 2140 Shattuck 2093, Berkeley, CA 94704. Founded in 1977 by the Zells and Alison Harlow. Magical and shamanic branch open only to trained initiates of this religious discipline. Creates and conducts the church's rituals and ceremonies.

• Peaceful Order of the Earth Mother (POEM): Box 212, Redwood Valley, CA 95470. Founded in 1988 by Willowoak Istarwood. This branch is dedicated to children and child nurturing. Provides enriching activities for children at gatherings, summer camps, and a quarterly magazine for Pagan youth, *How About Magic? (HAM)*, $7 per year.

Membership: No records are kept of 1st Circle members, but as of February 1992, 2nd Circle and inner members numbered 260.

Periodicals: *The Green Egg*. Send orders to Box 982, Ukiah, CA 95482. • *How About Magic?*

Remarks: The research initiated by Morning Glory and Otter Zell as part of the Ecosophical Research Assn. branch of CAW in the late 1970s lead to the production of the Living Unicorn, i.e., an animal with but a single horn growing from its forehead. These unicorns were produced by a simple operation on baby goats. The Zells claim that their research has shown that this is how the legendary creature was originally created by ancient pastoral people in the Middle East. The emergence of the first such animal, named Lancelot, was followed by a national publicity campaign, a shortlived periodical, *Unicornews* (1980-82) and the eventual lease of exhibition rights by the Ringling Bros./Barnum & Bailey Circus, which contract ended in 1988.

Sources:

Judith, Anodea. *Wheels of Life.* Illustrated by Otter Zell. St. Paul, Minn.: Llewellyn Publications, 1987.

Guiley, Rosemary. *Encyclopedia of Witches and Witchcraft.* New York: Facts on File, 1989.

The Living Unicorn. Los Gatos, CA: Living Unicorn, [1980].

Zell, Tim. *Cataclysm and Consciousness: From the Golden Age to the Age of Iron.* Redwood Valley, CA: The Author, 1977.

★1728★
Church of Aphrodite, Goddess of Love
(Defunct)

The Church of Aphrodite, Goddess of Love, was founded in 1939 on West Hemstead, Long Island, New York, by Gleb Botkin. Born and raised in Russia, the son of the czar's personal physician, he trained for the Russian Orthodox Church priesthood, but prior to ordination he had a change of heart. He decided that Aphrodite, the ancient Greek goddess of love, was a more appropriate object of his worship. Before Botkin was able to start a church in Russia, the 1917 revolution began. He fled to Japan and finally came to the United States in 1923. During the following years Botkin provided for his family by writing about his homeland. However, he never gave up his belief and he finally founded his church in his Long Island home. He acquired a life-sized statue of Venus de'Medici as a worship center.

By the time the church was formally chartered, it had some 50 members. Botkin was a monotheist of the feminine principle, and believed the "Eternal Feminine" was a truer personal symbol of the Divine than its masculine counterpart. The church's creedal statement affirmed a belief in Aphrodite, described as "the flower-faced, sweetly-smelling, laughter-loving Goddess of Love and Beauty." He was committed to the ideal of love as a primal virtue and advocated the concept of love both as ethical good will toward the neighbor and as an affinity with a beloved individual. He also favored greater freedom between the sexes as a means of reducing passion. Sex was seen as an ideal, divine and wonderful. Botkin believed in conditional immortality; one could gain immortal life by coming into a relationship with Aphrodite. Worship was held four times weekly on Sunday morning and afternoon, and Friday and Saturday evenings.

Botkin lived in New York for a number of years but at some point moved to Charlottesville, Virginia, where he died around 1970. The church ceased to exist at that time.

Sources:

"Church of Aphrodite." *Newsweek* (November 27, 1939): 32.

"Church of Aphrodite, Goddess of Love Is Chartered in New York." *Life* (December 4, 1939): 101.

★1729★
Church of Pan
114 Johnson Rd.
Foster, RI 02825

The Church of Pan was founded in 1970 by Kenneth Walker (d. 1987) and members of a nudist campground in rural Rhode Island. The organization of the church was occasioned by the request of two members to be married in the nude and the inability of the group to locate a minister to perform the ceremony. They decided to form a church and Walker became the minister.

The Church of Pan espouses naturalist principles. Reverence and devotion is directed toward the Creator, and actions follow patterns discerned to be in concert with the Creator's designs and purposes. While engaged in altruistic actions which attempt to modify the harshness of nature, in line with the destiny of creation, the church denounces human actions which have destroyed life-supporting systems and polluted nature. Humans have the task of

maintaining the balance of life on the planet. The church also opposes the distortions of human society in its treatment of sexuality. Forgetting the naturalness of sex, society tends to view it either as sinful or something to be marketed.

The church is headquartered at a nudist campground managed by Beulah A. Rathbun. Members are active in the promotion of environmental concerns. As might be expected from the nature of its beginning, the church has experienced difficulties over its status as a tax-exempt religious organization.

Membership: In 1988 the church reported 30 families, all members of the one "congregation" in Rhode Island.

★1730★
Church of Seven Arrows
PO Box 185
Wheat Ridge, CO 80034-0185

The Church of Seven Arrows was founded in 1975 by the Revs. George Dew and Linda Hillshafer, who serve as the shamans of the church. In 1977, the church was established in Wheatridge, Colorado, a Denver suburb, and began publishing the monthly periodical *Thunderbow*. While functioning within the larger Neo-Pagan Movement, the Church of Seven Arrows derives its system of belief and practice from a variety of sources, including contemporary western occultism, Hinduism, and, most prominently, the traditions of the Hopi and Plains Indians as expressed through the writings of Frank Waters and Hyemeyohsts Storm. The basic worldview and system of working is described in the two sets of books produced by the church, *Basics of Magic* and *Shaman's Notes*.

Beliefs of the church are expounded in terms of mythos, dogma, and doctrine. The church's mythos, its overall perspective on the nature of life and the universe, states that in the beginning, Creator existed as a State of Being. Creator acted, creating Nephew, who in turn created nine realms, one for Creator, Himself, and seven others. Spirits were created to populate the realms and the worlds. The world of humanity was given into the charge of "She Whom We Call Grandmother." She first created the body-forms of the animal and plant kingdoms and then the human species in which the spirit resides. The human spirit is special in that it is the only spirit that may choose whether or not to fulfill its place, and the only one that must learn it. Humanity's function is to lead all the beings of Earth in raising a harmonious sound to the Creator's realm.

Eventually, the original harmony was lost and the sound arising from earth became a cacophony. At this point, Nephew and Grandmother cleansed the world with fire, and the first world gave way to a second. The second world proceeded like the first, but added to the growing cacophony was a mistreatment of the earth for purposes never intended for it. A second cleansing by ice was followed by the third world, its disintegration, and a cleansing by means of water and geologic shift. We now live in the fourth world, which is progressing toward the time of another cleansing cycle. Those in touch with the harmony of Earth, Grandmother, and the original purpose and function of humankind will survive and pass through the cleansing activity.

The dogmas of the church include these: an affirmation that each being is a spirit and mirror of the Creator; a being cannot be destroyed; the universe exists in a state of patterned change; each being has a right to exist (but each form of existing may or may not be acceptable); bodies are masks of the spirit; no one path is proper for all people at all times; and the same basic principles manifest in both the spiritual and material realm.

Doctrine, the more ephemeral beliefs of the church, are summarized in nine statements as a "Guide for Daily Living on the Path of Seven Arrows." These statements call for members to know themselves, live in harmony, study the sciences (including the ancient science of magic), avoid self-destructive agreements, and live so that joyous sounds arise to the Creator's ear. The ancient sciences should be used so as to avoid harm to anyone. The church offers a set of rituals for both personal and group use.

The church is headed by a board of directors. A variety of classes on basic magic and shamanism are taught at regular intervals. Most members live in the Denver metropolitan area, but the periodical has a national audience. Rituals follow the solar and lunar cycles. *Thunderbow*, a popular Pagan periodical for a decade, was discontinued in 1987. Since 1990 the church has sponsored the Earth Home Society which networks among holistic healers in the Denver Metropolitan area.

Membership: As of 1997, approximately 50 participants attend church activities in the Denver area during any given period. Currently, approximately 500 "graduate-practitioners" of church training around the country kept in communication and retain some informal ties with it.

Periodicals: *Earth Home Society Resource Directory.*

Sources:

Basics of Magic. 2 vols. Wheatridge, CO: Church of Seven Arrows, 1980.

Shaman's Notes. 3 vols. Wheatridge, CO: Church of Seven Arrows, 1983-85.

Storm, Hyemeyohsts. *The Song of Heyoehkah.* San Francisco: Harper & Row, 1981.

Waters, Frank. *Book of the Hopi.* New York: Ballantine, 1963.

★1731★
Church of the Eternal Source
PO Box 44146
Tucson, AZ 85733

The Church of the Eternal Source, the most substantial of the several Egyptian Neo-Pagan bodies, was founded in 1970 by Donald D. Harrison and Harold Moss. Harrison, a former Roman Catholic, and Moss were converted to Paganism through the study of Greek and Roman religion and the attraction of the fine arts of ancient Egypt. In 1967, Harrison founded the *Julian Review*, which became the organ of the Delphic Fellowship, an early Pagan fellowship based upon Greek motifs. Moss organized a social group professing the Egyptian religion after seeing a movie, "The Egyptian," which focused on Akhenaten. In 1963, the group held an Egyptian costume party. The Church of the Eternal Source combines aspects of a number of Egyptian temples. Each priest and priestess acts autonomously in supervising ritual and initiation procedures for his or her temple.

The two basic principles of the Church of the Eternal Source are polytheism, the plurality of gods, and authentic Egyptianism. The church teaches that divinity is a balance of distinct divine vectors. The diversity of the gods, and their transactions, produce reality. Man's task is to achieve balance in his soul in the divine vectors. Authentic Egyptian religion relates to the early period when Egypt was relatively untainted by non-Egyptian ideas. This period becomes a source for all later religious insights. The mastery of Egyptian history is stressed. Many of the church leaders have made pilgrimages to Egypt.

Religious practices center on personal shrines, the study of theology, divination, the fine arts and personal worship with wide variations. Group worship is manifest in the festivals, which are dramatic reenactments of a holy myth. The Egyptian pantheon forms the basic content of faith. A typical myth is the story of the rebirth of Osiris. Osiris was killed by Set, the god of darkness. Isis, the wife of Osiris, sought him, her tears causing the Nile to overflow. She found the body and buried it, but not carefully. Set exhumed it, dismembered it and scattered the pieces through the land. Isis then carefully sought and assembled each piece. Osiris was then resurrected. Osiris and Isis are accompanied in the pantheon by Horus, their son; Bast, the beneficent solar goddess represented as a cat; Thoth, the god of wisdom; and Ra, the sun god often represented as Khepera, the beetle (believed to be self-generated). The myths are described in ancient literature, such as the *Egyptian Book of the Dead.*

Important festival days are held each full moon; on the birthdays of the deities, the latter occurring in July; and the equinoxes and the solstices. Ritual magick is performed, but no set ritual is prescribed. A typical Egyptian ritual is found in *Magic, An Occult Primer* by David Conway. The newsletter is for members only.

Membership: In 1992 the church reported four groups (located in the Boise, Idaho, and San Diego and Los Angeles, California areas), eight priests/priestesses, and approximately 100 members.

Periodicals: *Kephera.*

Remarks: Don Harrison, one of the Church' founders, is the author of several novels emphasizing both ancient religions and sexual themes.

Sources:

Conway, David. *Magic, An Occult Primer.* New York: E. P. Dutton, 1972.

Frankfort, Henri. *Ancient Egyptian Religion, An Interpretation.* New York: Harper & Row, 1961.

★1732★
Church of the Most High Goddess
Current address not obtained for this edition.

The Church of the Most High Goddess is a neo-pagan organization founded in 1986 by Mary Ellen Tracy and her husband, Wilbur Tracy. According to Wilbur Tracy, the church grew out of a 1984 revelation enabling him to discover the existence of a priestess with a lineage back to ancient Egypt. She could not publicly assume her religious functions, but ordained him. Mary Ellen Tracy soon had a similar revelation and was trained and ordained as a priestess by her husband.

The church teaches and practices a form of hedonism, a philosophy that sees the search for pleasure as the goal of life. It draws its inspiration from ancient Egypt, which it also sees as the originating point of Christianity. Thus, members consider themselves Christian but deny any relation to Judaism. They believe that Mary Magdalene was a priestess of Isis (or Eastar) and that it was to her that Jesus first appeared after his resurrection (also an old Egyptian belief). Jesus entrusted the church to Mary Magdalene, but the apostles later wrestled control away from her.

The essence of the church's practice is found in the rituals, the ordinances of the Goddess. The nature of these rituals is only hinted at in the church's few pieces of literature. Participation in the series of rituals is deemed necessary for individual progress. They begin with confession, a personal acknowledgement of one's spiritual state. Dedication (or commitment) is an act of devotion which leads to a higher order of hedonism. A sacrifice, or offering, is required as a sign of dedication. Immersion is the preparatory ritual for the communication through the Goddess, represented by the priestess.

In 1989 the Tracys were arrested for prostitution. The state of California charged that the church was merely a cover for their operating a house of prostitution, and that the rituals, which involve oral sex (dedication), the payment of a sum of money (sacrifice), and intercourse (immersion) constituted simple sex for money. The Tracys were convicted and have pursued an appeal. They claim interference with their right to freely practice their religion.

Membership: Not reported.

Sources:

Bush, G. M. "Priestess or Prostitute? Municipal Court to Consider Freedom-of-Religion Defense." *Los Angeles Daily Journal* (July 12, 1989).

"The Church of the Most High Goddess." N.p., 1987. Tract.

★1733★
Church of the Wyccan Rede
(Defunct)

The Church of the Wyccan Rede was a Celtic traditional Witchcraft group headed by Lady Cybele and headquartered in Madison, Wisconsin. The Goddess and Horned God were worshipped, the former taking slight precedence. The Goddess was thought to rule from Yule to Midsummer's Eve, and the God, the other half of the year. The eight sabbats were also celebrated. Midsummer's Eve is the most important. The sabbats were concluded with a shared meal. There are also regular esbats.

Worship was within the circle. Members took turns in being the coven leader and conducting the ceremonies. There were no overt sexual activities involved in the rituals. Oneness with nature was the prime goal. Members were pacifistic and charitable, and refused reward for their services. Black magic and Satanism were strongly condemned.

For several years, Lady Cybele managed The Cauldron, an occult supply store and center. It offered lectures on occult topics, psychic readings, books and health food. Lady Cybele is a herbalist and incorporated her knowledge of herbs into her teachings. Associated with the Church for the Wyccan Rede was a coven in Milwaukee headed by Frederic A. Buchholtz. Buchholtz was the operator of Sanctum Regnum, an occult supply and book shop.

★1734★
Church of Universal Forces
PO Box 93195
Columbus, OH 43203

The Church of Universal Forces is a Neo-Pagan nature-oriented religion founded in Columbus, Ohio, in 1980 by Lady Isis and Lord Adonis. It teaches a system of Pantheism that emphasizes freedom, joy, and self-worth. The church emphasizes the right and privilege of religious freedom and champions a "live and let live" philosophy. At the same time the church is opposed to those forms of religion that are preoccupied with sin and suffering to the extent that followers are not allowed to develop their own individuality.

The Church of Universal Forces is a pantheistic religion and acknowledges the Godhead of the Divine as the root of humanity. The Godhead, known under many names of gods and goddesses, is both male and female in equal portions. The Godhead is to be worshipped daily. Members are encouraged to have daily devotions in their home and to raise their children in the knowledge of the deities.

Ethically the church follows the Rede, "That ye harm none, do what you will." It also encourages members to develop a spirit of brotherly love toward one another and to watch over other members especially in times of illness. Members are admonished to be slow to take offense and quick to seek reconciliation with another member with whom there might have been differences.

The church has developed its own variation on the Neopagan rituals. It teaches development of psychic ability and affirms a belief in astrology. It offers a course on magick and magical religions whose graduates are ready to form their own group. The church also operates an occult supply house and offers a course to the general public on various occult and related topics.

Membership: In 1997 these approximately 50 members in a group served by three leaders.

★1735★
Circle
% Circle Sanctuary
Box 219
Mt. Horeb, WI 53572

Circle began in 1974 when Selena Fox, its founder, received the central concept, logo, and name in meditation. Shortly after this event, she and her partner Jim Alan began to host informal gatherings of people interested in magic and mysticism with a Wiccan focus in their home in Madison, Wisconsin. In June 1975, they moved to a farm near Sun Prairie, Wisconsin. This site, known as Circle Farm, was the meeting place for Circle's first coven and later for Circle's first community, which included several covens. Through their writings and music, Fox and Alan began to meet and correspond with Pagans around the United States and in the British Isles. In 1977, their first book, a songbook, was published, as well as a tape of their spiritual music. Fox also founded Circle Network that year. The following year Fox began to devote her full time to the expanding Circle ministry which was incorporated as the Church of Circle Wicca in October 1978. In May 1979, Fox compiled the first Circle resource guide, a networking directory and sourcebook, which contributed to the growth of the developing Pagan movement.

In November 1979, after being evicted from their first farm because of their religion, which had received national media attention, Circle moved first to a farm near Middleton, Wisconsin, and then to a farm outside of Black Earth. In 1983, a more permanent location, Circle Sanctuary Nature Preserve, was purchased near Barneveld, Wisconsin, and Circle changed its corporate name to Circle Sanctuary. The preserve includes a variety of ritual sites and meditation places, including a stone circle, outdoor shrines, and an indoor temple.

During this time, Circle became the focus of an ever-widening network of Neopagans and Witches throughout the United States and other countries. In 1980, Circle began publishing *Circle Network News*, in a quarterly newspaper format. Also that year, the Pagan Spirit Alliance was formed as an international and ecumenical Pagan friendship network. In 1981, the first of the annual week-long International Pagan Spirit Gatherings was held. In 1985, Circle expanded its Wiccan-Pagan religious freedom work through its leadership in a nationwide action, and in 1991, this form of ministry was further developed through the creation of the Lady Liberty League. In 1988, after a two-year legal battle, Circle Sanctuary land won local zoning as a church, and Circle began being listed alongside churches of other faiths in the worship directory of Madison area newspapers.

Circle has followed an evolving eclectic Pagan/Witchcraft faith, which Fox termed "Circle Wicca" in the 1970s and "Wiccan Shamanism" in the 1980s. This is a synthesis of Wiccan spirituality, nature mysticism, multicultural shamanism, and humanistic and transpersonal psychology. This path emphasizes communion with the Divine in nature and focuses upon honoring the Goddess as Mother Earth. Strong elements of ecofeminism, animism, shamanic healing, and Native American land spirit wisdom help to shape the ritual life. In the 1990s, Circle has increasingly used the term "Nature Spirituality" (a term coined by Fox in 1981) to describe its multifaceted networking and spiritual focus.

Circle has emerged as one of the most visible and public centers for Witchcraft and Neopaganism in the United States, and Fox is reguarly called upon by the media, the government, and other churches to speak for the broader Neopagan community. Through the variety of periodicals and festivals sponsored by Circle, it has built the largest network currently existing within the community. It has also been the seedbed for other Pagan groups, some of which have had their beginnings among those who have studied and worked at Circle's headquarters.

Currently the church is headed by Fox and her husband, Dennis Carpenter, who function as high priestess and high priest. Both are professionaly trained psychotherapists. Fox does counseling and spiritual healing, and Carpenter is involved in doing scholarly research and writing as part of their ministry. Fox heads the School for Priestesses, a ministerial training program for women in Goddess-oriented spirituality. In 1991, Circle begain its School for Ministers, an ecumenical leadership training program for women and men, which includes teaching by priestesses and priests from a variety of Pagan paths and groups affiliated with Circle Network.

The multifaceted local and global ministry of Circle is carried out by volunteers and full-time staff members. In 1992, Circle published its updated statement of purpose which identifies the thrust of its work as encouraging the growth and well-being of nature spirituality.

Membership: Not reported.

Educational Facilities: Circle Sanctuary, Barneveld, Wisconsin.

Periodicals: *Circle Network Bulletin.* • *Circle Network News.* • *Pagan Spirit Alliance Newsletter.* • *Sanctuary Circles.* • *Circle Guide to Pagan Arts.* • *Circle Guide of Pagan Groups.*

Remarks: Following the movement of the Church of Circle Wicca on the land that had been purchased as Circle Sanctuary, the church was forced into a still ongoing battle against elements in the county opposed to the existence of a pagan center in their community. An attempt was made to use zoning laws (in a heavily agricultural section of the state) to force the church from their land. After a lengthy fight to inform the public of the nature of their faith, in 1988 the Sanctuary finally received church zoning, though other issues remain to be resolved. In the midst of the debates with county officials, Fox founded the Pagan Strength Web, and broadened her efforts in defending religious rights of pagans in other parts of the country.

Sources:

Alan, Jim, and Selena Fox. *Circle Magick Songs.* Madison, WI: Circle Publications, 1977.

Blacksun. *The Elements of Beginning Ritual Construction.* Madison, WI: Circle, 1982.

Fox, Selena. *Circle Guide to Pagan Resources.* Mt. Horeb, WI: Circle, 1987.

★1736★
Congregation of Aten
(Defunct)

A growing split within the Pristine Egyptian Orthodox Church (discussed elsewhere in this chapter) led in 1974 to a schism and the withdrawal of Milton J. Neruda, who then formed the Congregation of Aten. At least one issue in the schism was the method of approaching the dominant American Christian faith. Neruda argued that Christianity was heavily reliant on Egyptian religion for such concepts as the Trinity, the virgin birth, Christmas and resurrection. He took a highly polemical stance with respect to the Christian faith. The Egyptian faith of the congregation of Aten offered answers "to one who is not blinded by prejudice and ignorance. Knowledge is the only path to true salvation!" The Pristine Egyptian Orthodox Church had taken a much milder stance. Neruda led the single congregation which existed for several years in Chicago.

★1737★
Congregationalist Witchcraft Association
PO Box 2205
Clearbrook, BC, Canada V2T 3X8

The Congregationalist Witchcraft Association was founded in the late 1980s by members of several Neo-Pagan Witchcraft covens across Canada after several years of discussion of its bases of agreement and constitution. When finally chartered in 1992 by the Canadian government as a non-profit corporation, the association began life as a confederation of self-governing groups (covens) in several Canadian provinces (Initially in Ontario, British Columbia, and Nova Scotia; it presently also has members in Alberta, Quebec, Manitoba, and Saskatchewan.). Groups share a common statement of belief and ethical principles, but whose members control their own administration and worship. The association was formed to accomplish tasks that no one of its members

(all of which tend to be small covens) can accomplish alone. It represents them to the government, promotes festivals and gatherings, and assists the growth of Wicca.

The association holds that divinity is multi-faceted and as such can be given a variety of names by which the many gods and goddesses are known. There are also levels of divinity; thus it is appropriate to speak of lesser deities such as guardian spirits. The divine is primarily immanent rather than transcendent, and thus ever-present and active in the world. Every woman and man is an embodiment of divinity, and all acts of love and pleasure are acts of praise of the Goddess. All forms of sexual expression that are non-coercive are considered legitimate by the association. Members also practice magic and believe that through petition, action, and ritual, the world may be changed according to their will.

Members of the association agree not to practice animal sacrifice, promote coercive activities, or charge fees either for teaching the Craft or initiation. Priests and priestesses are expected to keep pastoral confidences.

The association is headed by a national council of officers chosen by vote of the member covens.

Membership: In 1994 there were five full member congregations (one each in British Columbia, Alberta, Ontario, Quebec, and Nova Scotia) and seven associate members congregations (found in Alberta, Saskatchewan, Manitoba, and Nova Scotia). There were also 17 individual members.

Educational Facilities: The association was formed with the idea of creating a nondegree granting-college to train people for the priesthood.

Periodicals: The association publishes a newsletter, *Duck Tales,* for members only. Several of the member congregations also publish newsletters.

★1738★
Covenant of Gaia; Church of Alberta
PO Box 1742, Sta. M
Calgary, AB, Canada T2P 2L7

The Covenant of Gaia; Church of Alberta is a Neo-Pagan Wiccan church founded in Calgary, Alberta, in 1989. The church is congregational in structure, being composed of autonomous covens and solitary practitioners. It believes in a multiplicity of female and male deities, and follows the worship cycle of the eight common Pagan festivals by celebrating open circles on or near the dates of the festivals. Congregations also meet to celebrate the lunar cycles. The church offers many different clergy services to its community, such as weddings, funerals, and coming of age rites. It is also noted for the contract that is sanctioned between teachers of the Wiccan faith sponsored by the church, and the students that are taught. This contract calls upon teachers to refuse payment for teaching Wicca to anyone, to refrain from becoming sexually involved with their student, and to assist students in any way possible.

The church is headed by a board of directors and a president, who are elected annually.

Membership: In 1998, the church reported over 50 members.

Sources:

What Is the Covenant of Gaia? Calgary, AB: Covenant of Gaia, 1991. 5-page tract.

★1739★
Covenant of the Goddess
Box 1226
Berkeley, CA 94704

The Covenant of the Goddess (C.O.G.) was formed in 1975 by members of approximately ten covens in California as a confederation of autonomous covens to facilitate cooperation between covens and secure legal status and tax exemption for Witchcraft groups. Largely confined to California in its first years, by the end of the decade it had accepted covens in the East and during the early 1980s became a national organization which had shifted a significant amount of its activity to the Midwest. It now has covens in seven regional groupings across the country.

Membership is open to witches, both covens and individuals practicing as solitaries. New members must be recommended by two active C.O.G. members and follow the worship of the Goddess and/or the Old Goddess and the Gods. A code of ethics binds members to the Wiccan Rede, "An ye harm none, do as ye will." It also espouses guidelines on finances, the sovereignty of the individual covens, secrecy, and respect for diversity.

Annually members of the Covenant of the Goddess gather for the Merry Meet, an annual festival, during which the Grand Council meets and the officers are elected. Where three or more covens exist in close geographic proximity, they may organize a local council for the accomplishment of specific projects and general cooperative endeavor.

Membership: In 1992 there were 65 covens.

Periodicals: *The Covenant of the Goddess Newsletter.*

Sources:

Starhawk. *Dreaming the Dark.* Boston: Beacon Press, 1982.

___. *The Spiral Dance.* San Francisco: Harper & Row, 1979.

★1740★
Covenant of Unitarian Universalist Pagans (CUUPs)
Box 640
Cambridge, MA 02140

The Covenant of Unitarian Universalist Pagans (CUUPs) emerged in the mid-1980s among some Unitarian Universalists who had come into contact with the Neo-Pagan movement and had concluded that the two groups had much in common and much of value to share with each other. At the 1985 Assembly of the Unitarian Universalist Association (UUA) in Atlanta, Georgia, a spontaneous and spirited summer solstice ritual led to exploration of the possibility of an ongoing organization. A newsletter was begun, and Pagan scholar and writer Margot Adler was invited to address the 1987 assembly, at which time CUUPs was formally organized. The interim steering committee became the first board of directors. The possibility of such a group within the UUA is the result of its movement as primarily a liberal Christian body to one which acknowledges its life as a confluence of the world's religious traditions and insights. The association also places a great deal of emphasis upon individual freedom of belief and worship, intellectual inquiry, and toleration of differences. Religious pluralism has become an established way of life within the association.

CUUPs has developed a formal program of providing networking among Unitarian Universalists who identify themselves as Pagan, promoting dialogue among Pagans and those of the dominant western religious traditions, and serving as a liaison between Pagans and the larger UUA. In practice, CUUPs has provided the Pagan community with not only a means for Pagan clergy to gain a theological education and credentials, but also a spiritual home for many Pagans who otherwise have no relation to the UUA. Thus CUUPs operates as both a caucus within the association and as a growing and increasingly important Pagan grouping in its own right. In 1995 CUUPs experienced a major acknowledgement when the UUA Assembly voted to acknowledge "earth-centered spirituality" in the association by-laws as a major source of UUA beliefs. It was the first such recognition of the significance of Neo-Paganism by a major American religious body.

CUUPs is headed by a board of directors co-chaired by the Revs. Lesley Rebecca Phillips and Linda Sophia Pinti. It holds a national meeting in conjunction with the annual UUA Assembly, and numerous chapters have been formed around the United States and Canada.

Membership: Not reported. There are approximately 80 CUUPs chapters in North America.

Periodicals: *Pagan NUUS.*

★1741★
Cymry Wicca
PO Box 674884
Marietta, GA 30067

The Cymry Wicca is a Celtic traditional witchcraft group founded in 1967 in Washington, D.C., by William, or, as he is known in the craft, Rhuddlwm Gawr. The proper name is Cymry ab Prydian or Welsh Sons and Daughters of the Isle of Great Britain. The group was originally the Brotherhood of Wicca but changed the name, so as not to be confused with Lady Sheba's covens. William was initiated in England and afterwards spent four months studying in Wales. The Cymry received its laws and traditions from Great Britain through William. They are contained in eight volumes in manuscript form. The Cymry Wicca moved its headquarters to Georgia in 1973.

The Cymry has three deities: the Goddess, the Horned God, and their son, the Child of Light (corresponding to the Egyptian Isis, Osiris and Horus). Celtic names are employed by the Cymry. Worship is both skyclad (naked) and robed, and both inside and outside the circle, depending on the occasion. Reincarnation is stressed. Major focus of Cymry is on becoming attuned to nature and its forces. Drugs are forbidden.

The Cymry differs from other Wicca groups in that it is organized on seven levels. Each probationer is given a level name and a secret name, both in Welsh. Movement through the levels is occasioned by initiation ceremonies. The first level, the "naming," is coincidental with the members' identification with the coven. The Cymry is organized in autonomous covens. There is no witch king or queen, but there are elders who render binding decisions on questions put to them.

Cymry Wicca covens were most active in the mid-1970s. In 1974, there were approximately fifteen covens located in Georgia, Florida, Tennessee, North Carolina, Alabama, and Virginia. Rhuddlwm Gawr compiled two editions of the *Pagan/Occult/New Age Directory*, which included broad segments of the American wicca and neo-pagan community. In September 1978, in upstate Georgia, the Cymry hosted the first of several Gatherings of the Tribes, a conclave of Witches and Neo-Pagans from a wide variety of traditions and perspectives. During the 1980s the covens have been less active.

Membership: Not reported. In 1987, there were a reported 2457 subscribers to *The Sword of Dyrnwyn.*

Periodicals: *The Sword of Dyrnwyn.*

Sources:

Gawr, Rhuddlwn. *Pagan/Occult/New Age Directory.* Atlanta: Pagan Grove Press, 1980.

Gawr, Rhuddlwn, with Marcy Edwards, *The Quest.* Smyrna, GA: Pagan Grove Press, 1979

★1742★
Dancers of the Sacred Circle
(Defunct)

Closely related to Fereferia, an organization discussed elsewhere in this chapter, were the Dancers of the Sacred Circle, founded in the early 1970s by Richard Stanewick. Stanewick was one of the founders of Fereferia and served as its secretary until he moved to the San Francisco area and formed an autonomous group. Headquarters for the Dancers were near Redway, California, on a forty-acre nature sanctuary.

The Dancers attempted to build a total life based on the central figure of the Maiden divinity. Devotions were daily and seasonal, and had both aesthetic and erotic emphases. Included were wilderness mysteries, henge rites (a henge is an open air ring temple), and work in the maintenance and creation of gardens, orchards and wilderness shrines. The group was small, consisting of Richard, his wife, Phyllis Stanewick, and a few adherents. It disbanded in the early 1980s.

★1743★
Delphic Coven
(Defunct)

Among the early Goddess-worshipping groups in the United States was the Celtic traditional Delphic Coven founded by Bonnie Sherlock, who operated from a small town in Wyoming. According to Sherlock, the tradition had been handed down through the family, which migrated from Scotland in 1570, first to Ireland then to America. Ms. Sherlock was taught the craft by her great-grandmother, who imparted the first two initiations. The third was received from a Sioux medicine man.

The group claimed Celtic origins "in that we take our muse from the Cauldron of the Kerridwen, and will at length become as the radiant browed Taliesin." Egyptian and American Indian elements were added, though a basic dualistic cosmology remained. "The dragon of darkness is the great fetter of ignorance which we must overcome through educational enlightenment, communication, and involvement with others who are likeminded." Included in the group's belief were reincarnation and karma (the consequences of good and bad actions from former incarnations). Creative expression, primarily through arts, was a major theme; ecology and love of nature, especially as expressed in reverence of the mountain environment, were also emphasized. "The earth is a living, breathing thing to be reverenced and looked after, as are all the lesser creatures." Even the Horned God is visualized as a "Big Horned Sheep." Several issues of a periodical, *The Medicine Wheel*, were published. The coven dissolved following Sherlock's death in the late 1970s.

★1744★
Delphic Fellowship
(Defunct)

The Delphic Fellowship originated in 1967 when Michael Kinghorn and Donald D. Harrison began to publish the *Julian Review* as a forum of discussion of the Pagan religion. The Fellowship was formed the following year with the intent of restoring the heritage of Greece and rightful homage to the gods. A program was begun, to acquaint people of Christian, Jewish and agnostic/atheistic backgrounds with the Pagan option.

The Delphic Fellowship took its inspiration from the ancient oracle at Delphi. The Greek pantheon, headed by Zeus, was worshipped. The Delphian Affirmations asserted belief in the plurality of Gods; in the experience of the wholeness of nature; in the sacred character of the Cosmos (and the denial of its fall); in man as a child of Holy Earth; in moral freedom; in the beauty, purity, and holiness of man's sexuality; that the instinct to survive is natural and pleasing to the gods; that man's posture toward nature should be one of reverence and joyous participation, and in the Sacred Precepts of Elder Delphi, especially his admonition, "Know Thyself; Nothing in Excess."

The Delphic Fellowship was small and largely superceded by the Church of the Eternal Source, an Egyptian Pagan group which Harrison help found. The headquarters of the Delphic Fellowship was in Los Angeles.

★1745★
Dianic Wicca
% Susan B. Anthony Coven No. 1
Box 11363
Oakland, CA 94611

Dianic Wicca is a name given to those Witchcraft covens which have developed a strong emphasis upon feminism and the role of Witchcraft as the religion of females (wimmin). While most Wiccans recognize their origins in the work of Gerald B. Gardner and the new form of Witchcraft he developed in the 1940s, the Dianics claim a tradition independent of Gardner, in the worship of Diana, the ancient Greek Goddess, from Central Europe. It is the belief of Dianic witches that the worship of the Goddess in a primeval past co-existed with a period of peace on earth which was destroyed by the rise of men and patriarchal deities. In Dianic covens, worship is focused upon the mother Goddess as the Source of Life and as the Source of both sexes, and seen as including both sexes already. Individual covens vary from all-female separatist groups, to all female groups, to mixed male-female groups with a strong feminist emphasis.

Within the Dianic coven, the high priestess represents the Goddess and facilitates a ritual based upon the circle. She is assisted by a maiden, and occassionally (where men are allowed) by a high priest. They represent the consort and the child. Some all-female covens operate in the nude, weather and inclination permitting and some Dianic covens believe in parthenogenic birth, that is, birth not requiring male assistance.

Dianic Wicca began to emerge in the United States in 1971 when at least two different Dianic groups began. In southern California, Zsuzsanna Emese Budapest developed a coven associated with the Feminist Wicca, a "matriarchial spiritual center" in Venice, California. That original coven, known as the Susan B. Anthony Coven No. 1, survives today under the leadership of Ruth Barrett, a High Priestess trained by Budapest. It has been renamed the Circle of Aradia. In the early 1980s, Budapest moved to Oakland, California, and began a second coven which eventually took the name abandoned by the first one. In Oakland, Budapest has led in the formation of the Women's Spirituality Forum, an organization dedicated to bringing Goddess consciousness into the mainstream of feminist, earth conservationist, and peace and justice work in the United States. It has staged a number of conferences featuring leading feminists Wiccans such as Merlin Stone, Starhawk, Diana Paxton, Margot Adler, and, of course, Budapest.

At about the same time, in Dallas, Texas, a Dianic coven was founded by Morgan McFarland and Mark Roberts. High Priestess McFarland was a freelance photographer, writer, and feminist who began to explore the Craft in her early teens. She published a shortlived Neopagan periodical, *The Harp*, before going public in 1972. High Priest Roberts was also a freelance writer and photographer. Their group had originally been established as an occult group called the Seekers. In 1972, that group began to publish *The New Broom*. An article in *The New Broom* described the Dianic aspect as a blending of monotheism and pantheism. Dianic witches were monotheistic in that they worshipped the Goddess as the essential creative force. They were pantheists in their consideration of every creation in nature a child of the Goddess.

Withstanding attacks from those who complained that Dianic Witchcraft had lost the balance implied in the acknowledgement of the God and Goddess, the Dianics have become recognized as an important part of the Goddess tradition in North America. Beside the separate Dianic covens, Dianic Wicca has found strong advocates within otherwise non-Dianic groups. For example, Starhawk, popular feminist Wiccan writer, is the leader of the Compost Coven, a coven within the larger fellowship of the Covenant of the Goddess (see separate entry), as is the Susan B. Anthony Coven No. 1.

Membership: In 1995, the *Themosphoria* newsletter reported a circulation of 1,500 copies. Dianic is a designation describing a number of covens and Witchcraft groups. Their inclusion under that label does not imply any organizational connection or even mutual recognition. They are united only in their sharing and emphasizing a generally feminist perspective within the larger neopagan community. There are an estimated 20,000 Dranic Wiccans in the United States.

Periodicals: *Thesmophoria.* • *Of a Like Mind.* Send orders to Box 6021, Madison, WI 53704.

Sources:

Budapest, B. *The Feminist Book of Lights and Shadows.* Venice, CA: Luna Publications, 1976.

Budapest, Zsuzsanna. *The Rise of the Fates.* Los Angeles: Susan B. Anthony Coven No. 1, 1976. *The Holy Book of Women's Mysteries.* 2 vols. Los Angeles: Susan B. Anthony Coven No. 1, 1979-80.

Christ, Carol P. *Diving Deep and Surfacing.* Boston, MA: Beacon Press, 1980

Starhawk. *Dreaming the Dark.* Boston, MA: Beacon Press, 1982

___. *The Spiral Dance.* New York: Harper & Row, 1979

Stone, Merlin. *When God Was a Woman.* New York: Harcourt Brace Javonovich, 1976.

★1746★
Discordian Society
Current address not obtained for this edition.

There is one aspect of the Neo-Pagan movement in America which seems to be a complete put-on, the Discordian Society. As described in *Principia Discordia*, the "bible" of the group, Discordians worship Eris, the goddess of chaos. The Society was founded by someone named Malaclypse the Younger who, in 1958, upon evoking the Lady in the Erisian aspect, was told, "We Discordians must stick apart." Among the prominent Neo-Pagans who have identified themselves with the Society is Robert Anton Wilson, also known as Mordecai the Foul. Wilson is a popular writer and and advocate of the Illuminatus conspiracy. He coauthored with Robert Shea a three-volume fantasy novel *Illuminatus!*, describing the Discordian world, including its sister organization, the John Dillinger Died for You Society.

Members in the Discordian Society are initiated as popes. Being infallible, they have the power to excommunicate everyone. As pope, a member is in the Fifth House of Discordia, popularly known as the Out House. The member can then proceed to higher orders—bishop, knight, castle, priest, dupe and finally clown.

In fact the Discordian movement has not functioned as an organization but has been perpetuated as an inside joke and means of relieving tension within Pagan groups. Quite simply it is the Neo-Pagan version of "Murphy's Law." When things go wrong, the Goddess Eris is invoked with the phrase, "Hail, Eris!" Periodically, an individual will take it upon themselves to publish material in the name of the Society. The most well known literature, apart from *Principia Discordia* (which has been kept in print in ever newer editions) was a periodical, *St. John's Bread*, that enjoyed a brief life in the mid-1970s.

Sources:

Malacylpse the Younger. *Principia Discordia.* Mason, MI: Loompanics Unlimited, 1978.

★1747★
Divine Circle of the Sacred Grove
Box 1737
Fontana, CA 92334

The Divine Circle of the Sacred Grove was founded in 1985 by Janette Gordon, a priestess who has a long history of participation in Druidism as well as training in Wicca and a broad mastery of occultism in general. In 1965 she founded the Order of Druids, School and Church of Drunements, which was incorporated into the Divine Circle. The church holds weekly religious services and the school offers a full course of study on Wicca, magic, ritual, healing, occultism, and related topics. The school operates as a correspondence school under the tutelage of Janette and her husband, Norman Gordon. She has authored all of the curriculum lesson material.

The church teaches the balance of Nature affirmed in ritual activity, the polarity of Goddess and God, and a way of life based upon personal empowerment through magic. While operating out of a single center in Fontana, California, the church had extended its influence to Wiccans across the United States through its school, which offers master's and doctorate degrees to its graduates. It also offers special training for the priesthood and provides an opportunity for graduates to become initiates and priests of the church.

Membership: Not reported.

★1748★
Earthstar Temple
35 W. 19th St.
New York, NY 10011

The New York Coven of Welsh Traditionalist Witches was headed by Ed Buczynski, better known by his ritual name, Hermes, who had taken the "Celtic" rituals used by Gwen Thompson of the New England Welsh Traditionalist Coven and adapted them for use by a group in Brooklyn, New York. The form of Wicca followed was called "Gwyddoniaid" and is traced to the mixture of Celtic (male deity) and Pictish (female deity) religions in Wales. They worship the Earth Mother in her nine-fold aspects and the Horned God.

Covens are limited to thirteen male and female members, chosen alternately. Each coven is under the guidance of a high priest and high priestess. (Each coven is autonomous, but is tied to others by similar ritual and laws.) The high priestess is ascendent, in keeping with the matriarchal orientation. There are weekly and monthly (on the full moon) rituals as well as the eight sabbats. No magick is worked at the latter. Power usually raised for magick is "given directly to the god in loving sacrifice." Worship is done within a nine-foot circle. Identical red robes are worn, emphasizing the equality of individuals before the gods.

The New York Coven came into prominence in the early 1970s when Buczynski (recently deceased) and Herman Slater became public advocates for the craft. They have presented awards to the Inquisitional Bigot of the Year through Friends of the Craft, an affiliated organization. They also operated the Warlock Shop, an occult supplies store in Brooklyn, and, for several years published *Earth Religion News*. In the late 1970s, Slater, who had absorbed some elements of ritual magick in his practice, assumed leadership of the group and store. He moved both to Manhattan. The group was renamed Earthstar and the store is currently known as the Magickal Child. Slater has periodically sponsored large festive gatherings of Neo-Pagans, witches and magicians in New York City.

Membership: Not reported.

Sources:

Buczynski, Edmund M. *Witchcraft Fact Book.* New York: Magickal Childe, n.d.

Slater, Herman, ed. *The Magickal Formulary.* New York: Magickal Childe, 1981.

★1749★
Egyptian Temple of Fitness
Current address not obtained for this edition.

The Egyptian Temple of Fitness was founded in the mid-1980s by Master Gamal Selim as a center of the Egyptian religion, language, culture, and healing. It strives to teach the universal knowledge of the ancient Egyptians, which it believes can be of benefit to all. To reach its goal, it offers a weekly round of activities that begin with worship services each Sunday afternoon. Ongoing classes are held on the Egyptian sacred sciences, hieroglyphics, natural healing techniques, exercise, and oracle reading (with an Egyptian version of the tarot cards).

Membership: There is one center in Pasadena.

Periodicals: *TKA*.

★1750★
ESP Laboratory
Box 216
219 S. Ridge Dr.
Edgewood, TX 75117

The ESP Laboratory was founded in Los Angeles in 1966 by Al G. Manning. Manning was a certified public accountant who, during meditations, was contacted by a Prof. Reinhardt, his spirit teacher and guide. With Reinhardt's help, he wrote his first book and founded the ESP Laboratory, which functions as both psychic interest center and a church. Manning became a minister of Spiritual Science. He has since written several books. The keynote to Manning's approach to the psychic is results. An early program made use of color to aid attunement to the living light in its differing shades so as to attain personal goals of success, power, prosperity, and healing. Instruction in the mystic light was offered in a twenty-lesson correspondence course. Healing is a major emphasis.

Divination and the occult steadily became more important parts of the Laboratory's work. In 1970, a course on the "I Ching" was first offered. In 1971, a course on "White Magic and Witchcraft" was offered, and a new book, *Helping Yourself with White Witchcraft*, appeared the following year. Emphasis was placed not so much on the religion of Wicca but rather upon magick, control and the rituals to use for various purposes. One of the members of the Laboratory who completed the course has formed the Astral Coven.

The ESP Laboratory moved its headquarters from Hollywood to Texas in the early 1980s. Members, via correspondence, are found in all fifty states and some foreign countries. Ordination as a minister is offered after the passing of required courses. A monthly newsletter contains announcements, reports on research, a monthly light exercise and an astrology column.

Membership: Not reported. In 1997 there were ministers with credentials from the laboratory functioning in California, Ohio, Texas, and Virginia with members scattered around the United States and several foreign countries.

Periodicals: *E.S.P. Laboratory Newsletter*.

Sources:

Manning, Al G. *Helping Yourself with White Witchcraft*. West Nyack, NY: Parker Publishing Company, 1972

___. *Helping Yourself with the Power of Gnostic Magic*. West Nyack, NY: Parker Publishing Company, 1979.

★1751★
Fellowship of the Spiral Path
Box 5521
Berkeley, CA 94701

The Fellowship of the Spiral Path grew out of the early stages of the Goddess movement in the Bay Area of North California. In 1977 a small group of women, some of whom had a background in Neo-Paganism, gathered to perform a ritual for a friend who felt the need for a rite of passage into womanhood to complete the transition which had begun at puberty. That first ritual also proved to be a meaning-producing experience for the participants, who decided to continue meeting for the exploration of goddess-centered worship and as an expression of their own developing sense of community. They began to meet each new moon and called themselves the Dark Moon circle.

The group developed in stages but soon moved to a renovated carriage house in Berkeley, California, and developed rituals to celebrate various events in women's lives such as motherhood and the onset of menopause. In 1981 the Center for Non-traditional Religion was opened to host various groups and activities, including the Dark Moon Circle. That same year Diana Paxton authored the "Liturgy of the Lady," which began the focus of a monthly open ritual for the public. In 1982 the first priestesses were consecrated. At about that same time, the circle joined the Covenant of the Goddess. In 1986 the center transformed into the Fellowship of the Spiral Path.

The Fellowship of the Spiral Path sees itself as a center of the Old Religion. The Old Religion includes the indigenous religions of tribal cultures from Africa to Europe and North America, which bear a close relationship to Hinduism and Shinto in the East. The fellowship views European and American Old Religionists as engaging in a process of re-establishing themselves after a millennia of disruption by Christianity.

Old Religionists believe that the purpose of life is to live in harmony with nature and that creation is a continuum of consciousness from inanimate objects to the pantheons of gods and spiritual beings, all aspects of a single Divine principle. Since sacredness is in all things, no single form of deity can or should predominate. Old Religionists worship the Divine Energy as both male and female, Goddess and God. Life is essentially good, but evil results when natural processes are perverted or unbalanced. The moral life is based upon a reverence for all life, love and trust within the religious community, personal responsibility, respect for the free will of others, and an understanding that what is done to others will react upon the doer. Salvation is dependent upon one's own life-affirming decisions.

A respect for differences means that worship and leadership styles and forms will vary. Most traditions celebrate the rites of passage, and most acknowledge holidays marked by the astronomical/agricultural years, i.e., the solstices, the equinoxes, and the cross-quarter days halfway between.

In Berkeley, the fellowship sponsors several circles, a monthly celebration of the "Liturgy of the Lady," and various outreach activities. There is also a fellowship center in Sacramento, California. Among the leading members of the fellowship is popular fantasy novelist Marion Zimmer Bradley, many of whose novels reflect her own Neo-Pagan beliefs.

Membership: Not reported.

Periodicals: *Newsletter*.

Sources:

Bradley, Marion Zimmer. *The Best of Marion Zimmer Bradley*. Chicago: Academy Chicago, 1985.

★1752★
Fereferia
12318 Shady Ln.
Nevada City, CA 95959-3255

Fereferia, one of the oldest Pagan groups in North America, was founded in 1957 as the Fellowship of Hesperides by Fred Adams. As early as 1947 Adams had become involved in ritual magic and the practice of the Eleusinian mysteries, first at Stanford University and later at the University of Southern California. In 1956 he had a vision of the Goddess, and became a staunch believer in the worship of her. A short time later Adams met Robert Graves, the author of *The White Goddess*, and by 1958 had become fully paganized. He began to seek a purified paganism of the highly sacramental cultures of Crete and Minoa, and he believed that humankind could develop a utopian, paradisaic life on earth by basing culture on horticulture. In 1959 he established an open-air temple in the Sierra Madre. As the Pagan movement developed, Adams became a significant leader as a poet and artist. His stylized presentations of the Goddess circulated widely through the movement as did his calendars.

Fereferia is somewhat unique among Pagan groups in that it centers upon Kore, the Maiden (rather than the Great Mother). Kore is also identified with Persephone in the Eleusinian mysteries.

Fereferia's Maiden Way includes an emphasis on organic gardening; a reverence for all life especially trees; a vegetarian diet; outside living; the realization that health, vitality, and rejuvenation are basic to spiritual growth; handicraft technology; the dissolution of coercive structures and the elimination of artificial conditions; natural safeguards against overpopulation; a maximum of free, creative play and erotic development; the veneration of beauty, desire and creativity; and the affirmation of the divine mystery of sex as the central polarity of cosmic process.

After being headquartered for many years in Southern California, Adams moved to Nevada City in Northern California in the early 1990s. Here, with his wife Svetlana, he conducts Fereferia ceremonies nine times annually. For many years Adams published a newsletter but it has been discontinued.

Membership: Fereferia is a small group of less than ten members.

★1753★
First Occult Church
Current address not obtained for this edition.

The First Occult Church is an eclectic Pagan church formed in the early 1990s. It welcomes all who share an interest in occultism and magick from the range of possible perspectives including Wicca, ritual magick, voodoo, Norse Paganism, and other related systems. Members of the church condemn the idea that there is only one way to spiritual truth but also see patriarchal monotheism (which would include Judaism, Christianity, and Islam), as outside the realm of their belief—teachings that produce self-hatred, sexism, racism, and homophobia.

Distinct from most groups that operate in the Wiccan/Neo-Pagan context, the First Occult Church is open to Satanic religious expressions. "Manifesto 13," their statement of belief, notes that members are not to equate dark with "evil" and light with "good," and that Magick is neither black nor white, but varies with the intent of the practitioner.

Organizations within the church include the Coven of the Blue Candle, a traditional Wiccan group; the Temple of Aradia, a relatively new form of Witchcraft created by Lady Vgraine and based upon *Aradia: The Gospel of the Witches* by Charles Leland; and the Order of the Infernal Grotto, a satanic order headed by a former agent of the Church of Satan. The order has an inner circle called the Order of the Apocalypse. It follows what is termed "Infernal Paganism" that merges Satanic thought with pre-and post-Christian Pagan theories and practices.

Manifesto 13, whose first command is "Thou shalt not bore the gods," articulates the church's stance as a group of socially aware Pagans. They believe that magick should not become a means of escaping the world. Members should engage in activities that benefit the whole and avoid those activities that hurt it. Thus members are called upon to: support Pagan neighbors, avoid scapegoating, work to change unjust laws, and keep up a program of learning.

The church is headed by a board of directors called the Cauldron, which currently includes Rev. Lady Vgraine, president and high priestess; Rev. William Gidney, vice-president and high priest, and Lady Dymphna Reynard, Sabre Wilde, Vulcan Lupus, and the church guardian, Snow Eagle. Rev. Gidney and his wife, Lady Vgraine, have produced several occult documentaries including: *The War Against God: Occultism in Your Backyard.*

Membership: The church does not report membership statistics but has indicated that membership is found across the United States and in several foreign countries.

Periodicals: *A Taste from the Cauldron.*

★1754★
First Wiccan Church of Minnesota
(Defunct)

The First Wiccan Church of Minnesota grew out of the Camelot of the Star of the North Coven of the American Order of the Brotherhood of Wicca, a Wiccan group founded by Lady Sheba. The church was formed by Carl Weschcke (Gnosticus) and his wife Sandra Weschcke (Kashta) in 1973. Carl is head of Llewellyn Publications which during the 1970s published Lady Sheba's books and *Gnostica News*, which was a major voice within the Wicca/Pagan community. Though following much of the material of Lady Sheba, the First Wiccan Church also developed its own practices.

Three foci of coven activity were recognized. Worship occurred at the esbats held during the full moon and at the sabbats on the solstices and equinoxes. It was an effort to tune into the natural rhythms of the sun and moon. Magick is seen as the ceremonial work which brings people-integration. The ritual of the craft focuses on practical mundane success, the use of mind power to gain an object of desire. Like Lady Sheba, this group opposed the secrecy that has traditionally surrounded the craft. The church was dissloved in the late 1970s.

Sources:

Sheba, Lady. *The Grimoire of Lady Sheba.* St. Paul, MN: Llewellyn Publications, 1974.

Sheba, Lady [Jessie Wicker Bell]. *Witch.* St. Paul, MN: Llewellyn Publications, 1973

★1755★
Free Spirit Alliance
Box 25242
Baltimore, MD 21229

The Free Spirit Alliance is an association of Neo-Pagan and witchcraft groups that emphasize a shared belief in a pantheistic worldview. Groups with whom FSA members worship represent a wide variety of Pagan beliefs and practices including Traditional Wiccan traditions, non-Wiccan Pagans, and Druids. Those groups accept a basic belief in the many deities of Paganism who exist within the divine universe of nature. Most of the groups follow the eight festivals common to Paganism and many meet biweekly, on the new and full moon, or monthly.

The Alliance emphasizes the ethical standards for Pantheist groups and has published a code of honor to which its members must ascribe. It asserts a belief in human freedom, and the need to follow the Wiccan Rede, "an it harm none, do as ye will." Further, members are admonished to consider their pledged word sacred, to respect the rights and freedoms of others, to respect all life on the planet, to seek to undo any harm to another, and to value honesty. FSA sponsors an annual Free Spirit Gathering each summer which is attended by approximately 700 people.

Membership: In 1997 there were 29 covens, groups, and circles listed in the *Free Spirit Network Flyer* published by FSA. FSA has approximately 80 members and more than 1000 "friends" on its local mailing list.

Periodicals: *Free Spirit Rising,* Box 5358, Laurel, MD 20726.

★1756★
Gardnerian Wicca
% Lady Rhiannon
Box 6896, FDR Sta.
New York, NY 10150

Gerald B. Gardner (1884-1964) did more to revive modern Witchcraft than any single individual. He composed rituals with the assistance of a few others , including Doreen Valiente, which became the source of most rituals used by both Witches and Neo-Pagans. Several members of his British covens (for example, Alexander Sanders and Sybil Leek) took copies of his rituals and published their own edited versions of them as the basis for a new form of Wicca. However, the single largest group of Wiccans are those who continue to use the rituals as finally developed by Gardner in the 1960s.

Gardnerian Wicca was brought to America in the 1960s. It came through several individuals who traveled to Great Britain for initiation in one of Gardner's covens. Most of these revised and rewrote the rituals upon their return. Such was not the case with Raymond Buckland and his wife, Rosemary Buckland. Raymond (who claims a Ph.D. in anthropology) and Rosemary Buckland operated the Buckland Museum of Witchcraft and Magick on Long Island. Reared as good members of the Church of England, they began dabbling in occultism and were attracted to Gardner after settling in New York in the early 1960s. They corresponded with him and visited his home on the Isle of Man, where he operated a witchcraft museum. While there, the Bucklands went through a three-week crash program and were initiated in the second degree before they left. (The usual time between any of the three degrees of witchcraft is one year and a day.) Upon their return, they began to organize Gardnerian covens, which spread across the country. This growth was due in part to the widespread media coverage of the museum and the then unique religion espoused by the Bucklands.

Each Gardnerian coven is headed by a high priestess and a high priest. Without the former no ceremonies are held. Membership in the covens is primarily by couples, and the size of the coven is limited only by the space available in the nine-foot circle. New covens are usually formed by a witch's leaving a full-size coven and beginning a new one. The high priestess of the original coven becomes the "witch queen" of the new coven. Within Gardnerian covens there is a form of apostolic succession from Rosemary Buckland (who is no longer associated with the Gardnerian covens) through a lineage of witch queens to presently functioning priestesses.

Gardnerian witches worship in the nude, and by so doing have given to the craft a new word, "skyclad." The female witch does wear a necklace, a symbol of reincarnation. The high priest and priestess wear bracelets symbolic of rank, and the witch queen wears a crown and garter.

In 1973, the Bucklands, known in the craft as Robat and Lady Rowen, were divorced. They turned over the leadership of the Gardnerian covens to Judy Kneitel and her husband Tom Kneitel, known as Lady Theos and Phoenix. During 1973/74, they published Gardnerian Aspects as a magazine within the Green Egg, but discontinued it with issue No. 63 in favor of an intracoven letter. The Hidden Path, begun by Lady Dierdre of the Coven of the Silver Trine in Louisville, Kentucky, continues as a semi-public periodical. Buckland developed an alternative Wicca system called Seax Wica. On May 1, 1985, Judy Kneitel retired and turned over leadership to Roberta Faillace, known as Lady Rhiannon, and her partner Martin Fleischman, known as Theseus.

Membership: Membership is not available to the public, but it is estimated that several hundred people are involved in Gardnerian covens recognized by Theos and Phoenix. Many more consider themselves Gardnerian.

Periodicals: The Hidden Path. Send orders to Windwalker, Box 793 F, Wheeling, IL 60090.

Sources:

Bracelin, J. L. Gerald Gardner: Witch. London: Octagon Press, 1960.

Gardner, Gerald B. Witchcraft Today. London: Karrolds, 1968

Valiente, Doreen. Natural Magic. New York: St. Martin's Press, 1975.

___. Witchcraft for Tomorrow. London: Robert Hale Limited, 1978.

A Witch. The Devil's Prayerbook. London: Mayflower, 1975.

The Georgian Church
1908 Verde St.
Bakersfield, CA 93304

The Georgian Church, originally the Church of Wicca at Bakersfield, California, was formed by George E. Patterson (d. 1984). Patterson claimed a 1940 initiation from a Celtic group. After World War II, he settled in California and in the 1970s began to gather a coven. The group was eclectic, combining rituals from Gardnerian Wicca, Alexandrian Wicca, and other sources, and was termed Georgian. Eventually a charter came from the Universal Life Church, and Patterson obtained a doctor of divinity degree from the American Bible Institute. As with most witches, there is belief in the gods and goddesses, magick, the unity of life and reincarnation. The group does not accept Satanism, black magicians or groups organized only for sex. There are three degrees in Georgian Wicca. These degrees acknowledge attainment of knowledge and time devoted to the craft. The church publishes a periodical, noteworthy both for its size and quality as well as its longevity. Jean M. Davis succeeded Patterson as president of the church.

Membership: Not reported, but in 1987 the Georgian Newsletter reported a circulation of 250 copies. By 1973, there were four affiliated covens in Southern California. By 1978 there were associated covens in Missouri, New York, and New Jersey. As of the mid-1980s, there are loosely affiliated covens (many of them led by priests and/or priestesses trained by Patterson) across the United States and in several foreign countries.

Periodicals: Georgian Newsletter.

★1758★
Hawthorn Grove
Box 706
Monticello, NY 12701-0706

Hawthorn Grove is an independent congregation for Witches, Druids, shamans, deep ecologists, and Neo-Pagans founded in 1990 and incorporated two years later. It serves people in the Upper Delaware and MidHudson River Valleys. The grove is very eclectic in its beliefs and practices but is united in the acceptance of the basic Pagan ethical principle, the Wiccan Rede, "That ye harm none, do what thou will"; and the Charge to the Goddess, a passage of a modern sourcebook for Witchcraft, Aradia: The Gospel of the Witches, published in 1899 by Charles Leland. It reads:

Now when Aradia (the daughter of Diana) had been taught, taught to work all witchcraft, how to destroy the evil race (of oppressors), she (imparted to her pupils) and said unto him:

When I shall have departed from this world, Whenever you have need of anything, Once in the month, and when the moon is full, Ye shall assemble in some desert place Or in a forest all together join To adore the potent spirit of your Queen My mother, great Diana. She who fain Learn all sorcery yet has not won Its deepest secrets, then my mother will Teach her, in truth, all things as yet unknown. And ye shall all be freed from slavery, And so ye shall be free in everything; And as a sign that ye are truly free, Ye shall be naked in your rites, both men And women also; this shall last until The last of your oppressors shall be dead. . .

In order to encourage its diversity, the grove has remained organizationally independent of other Pagan groups. The grove is headed by a board of directors consisting of a Secretary, Pursewarden, and Summoner. There is no permanent designated High Priestess and/or Priest. Leadership in worship rotates among the members. There is a Council of Elders consisting of from three to 13 of the ordained clergy (elders). Elders are trained by the grove.

Membership: In 1995 the grove reported 50 members and three elders.

Periodicals: The Hawthorn Spinner.

Sources:

Leland, Charles G. *Aradia: The Gospel of the Witches*. 1899. Rept., New York: Samuel Weiser, 1974.

★1759★
Henge of Keltria
Minneapolis, MN 55448-0369

The Henge of Keltria was established in 1987 (incorporated in 1995) by cofounders Tony Taylor and Sable Taylor, both former members of the Ar nDraiocht Fein (ADF). The Taylors had some administrative difference with ADF and rejected its idea of multicultural Druidism. They work within a context of Celtic Druidism. The Henge of Keltria is a Neopagan group dedicated to protecting and preserving Mother Earth, honoring the ancestors, revering the spirits of nature, and worshipping the Celtic gods and goddesses. Special emphasis is placed on spiritual development fostered through study and practice of the Druidic arts and Celtic magick. Through training, networking, resource material, ritual participation, and meaningful communication, the group aims to provide a religious and spiritual framework through which people may reach their full potential.

Affiliated local groups are called groves. Each grove is free to compose and perform ritual and magick geared to its own particular focus, provided such work remains compatible with the beliefs, ethics, and ritual and structural framework of the Henge.

Members progress through three grades of initiation called rings, a symbolic name derived from the rings of a tree; the ring system measures the growth of its participants. The three rings are named for sacred trees: the Ring of the Birch, the Ring of the Yew, and the Ring of the Oak. Within the highest ring, the Oak, there are three tiers—Hawthorn, Rowan, and Mistletoe. Advancements are based on time, knowledge, and service to either a local grove or the Henge. Special provisions are made for those transferring from other Neopagan paths, so that those with several years of training and experience do not need to begin at the bottom.

Membership: Not reported. Groves are found in Minnesota, Wisconsin, and California.

Periodicals: *Kethria: A Journal of Druidism and Celtic Magic.* • *Serpent Stone: A Journal of Druidic Wisdoms.*

Sources:

Hopman, Ellen Evert, and Lawrence Bond. *People of the Earth: New Pagans Speak Out*. Rochester, VT: Destiny Books, 1996. 402 pp.

★1760★
Hollywood Coven
(Defunct)

The Hollywood Coven was formed as a Celtic traditional Wiccan group in 1967 by E. Tanssan of Hollywood, Florida. Tanssan had formerly been a member of a coven in Birmingham, Michigan. The Birmingham coven, headed by T. Milligan, had been established in the early part of the century. Tanssan had succeeded his teacher as leader in Birmingham shortly before the coven was disbanded because of police harassment. He and some of the members moved to Florida and established the new coven. Emerging as spokeswoman for the coven was Kitty Lessing, who edited its periodical, *The Black Lite*.

Worship was in the circle. No drugs were allowed. It was a robed tradition. Initiation was allowed only after a year of study of occultism and witchcraft. Initiates were eligible to become a coven lady or grand master. There were no priests or priestesses.

The basic deities were the Great One, the Horned God, and the Lady of Silver, the earth mother. The God was considered the father of all gods and guide to the afterlife. Nature was seen as the creation of the gods, hence sacred. Only four sabbaths—Halloween, Yule, Candlemas (February 2) and Lammas (August 1)—were celebrated. The solstices and equinoxes were not formally celebrated.

Esbats were held weekly or biweekly. In 1972 two covens were being operated in Hollywood, the main coven and a student coven. During the mid-1970s, Lessing moved to California, and shortly afterward the Hollywood Coven dropped out of sight. This may have been one of the few genuine pre-Gardnerian covens in the United States.

★1761★
Holy Order of Briget
(Defunct)

The Holy Order of Briget was a Wicca group formed in the late 1960s in Denver by Michael Myers. For several years, a co-op book store, Spell, Book and Candle, was operated in Denver, but it closed in November, 1973. Land was purchased in rural Colorado, and Craftcast Farm was begun as a "monastic" focus within American Wicca.

Craftcast was run during the brief period of its existence on a communal basis and set aside as a place where ritual would be continual. A deep love for the Mother was the motivating force. Witchcraft, viewed as seeking wisdom by changing knowledge into understanding, was practiced. The monastic ideal allows for "one spiritual goal" to become dominant. According to Myers, other covens in various locations throughout the West were affiliated with the Holy Order of Briget; however, since the dissolving of the farm in the late 1970s, considerable doubt has been cast upon Myers's claims.

★1762★
House of the Open Eye
Current address not obtained for this edition.

House of the Open Eye is a Neopagan group in the San Francisco Bay Area headed by Rev. Paula Ashton which draws its inspiration from ancient Egyptian religion and is intent upon revitalizing it. The group builds upon the knowledge of the Netjer (Egyptian pantheon) from history and archeology, and offers strong support to believers gaining all the knowledge of the past. However, members also understand that a significant period of time has passed and that just as culture has evolved, so should the Egyptian religious tradition and the practices associated with it. Thus, they propose a method of serving and honoring the Netjer in ways that are relevant to the modern psyche and environment.

The House of the Open Eye offers a course in Egyptian religion which includes a broad understanding of the Egyptian deities, ancient Egypt, the important concepts of theology and ritual, magick, divination, daily devotional disciplines, and the priesthood.

The group participates in the larger Neopagan community in the Bay Area, and maintains a web site on the Internet.

Membership: Not reported.

Sources:

http://www.phoenix-alliance.com/HoE.html/.

★1763★
IMBAS
PO Box 1215
Montague, NJ 07827-0215

IMBAS (an Irish word meaning "poetic inspiration," pronounced "im-bus") is a Druid Neopagan group founded in the mid 1990s. It promotes what it terms Celtic Reconstructionist Paganism and the cultural heritage of the Celtic peoples. Celtic Reconstructionist Paganism is grounded in folk tradition, mythological texts, and the archaeological and historical records of the Celtic people who include the modern peoples of Alba (Scotland), Breizh (Brittany), Cymru (Wales), ire (Ireland), Kernow (Cornwall), and Mannin (Isle of Man). It finds its focus in the home, the family, and the community/tribe in honoring the land, the ancestors, and the traditional Celtic gods and goddesses. Though Celtic in emphasis, IMBAS is open to people of all ethnic backgrounds.

In reconstructing the Celtic tradition, IMBAS members show a deep reverence for the pre-Christian Celtic deities. They attempt to make contact with both the ancestors and the land spirits, which in a modern context assumes a concern for family and a deep environmental awareness. Members are also students of history and strive to be as historically (and mythologically) accurate as the evidence allows. Gaps in the evidence often makes it necessary to create something new. New realities should nevertheless be as consistent as possible with what is known about the Iron Age Celts and their legacy. Thus IMBAS represents a balanced approach to understanding early Celtic religion, which relies on both sound scholarship and poetic inspiration without mistaking one for the other.

At the same time IMBAS has distanced itself from ceremonial magick (and modern traditions influenced by it, especially Wicca), romantic Revival Druidism (that is, anything inspired by Iolo Morganwg or the Druidic movements of the eighteenth and nineteenth centuries), and eclecticism (combining early Celtic religion with other cultural traditions).

IMBAS publishes a quarterly journal and other material, charters local IMBAS groups, provides a training program for prospective Seanch i (traditional lore keepers), and attempts to provide the public with accurate information about Celtic culture and Celtic Reconstructionist Paganism.

Membership: Not reported.

Periodicals: *An Trbhs Mhr: The IMBAS Journal of Celtic Reconstructionism.*

Sources:

http://www.morrigan.alabanza.com/imbas/.

★1764★
Irminsul Aettir
PO Box 423
Renton, WA 98057-0423

The Irminsul Aettir is an association of Asatruar (people who follow the Asatru or the old Pagan religion of Iceland and Scandinavia) formed in the mid-1990s. It consists of actual (and fictive) kin, family members, friends of the Irminsul Aett, and those affiliated with the Aett to practice and promote the religion of Asatru. The organization is headed by Susan Granquist, who assumed full administrative duties during Yule 1995 and was named Drottning. She is currently assisted by Andrew J. Cantrell, who was named Thule in 1997.

The basic organizational unit of the Aett is the family, followed by extended family type organizations and associations such as kindreds. Both exist to support the growth of individuals in their faith.

Members also believe that everyone should be free to choose their own godhi/gydhia (leader) as well as those with whom they wish to worship. Traditionally, a believer entered into a "Thing-agreement" (agreement of association) with the godhi or gydhia of choice. A godhi or gydhia is a person who serves the community and represents the people of his or her association at assemblies, holds meetings, and maintains meeting places and records, as well as performing other services. According to the ancient oath of office, holding the office of godhi involves perpetual dedication to the gods, folk, and other beings. Today, it is roughly equivalent to a community minister who sees to the needs of those associated with him/her. Given the nonhierarchical nature of the religion, the primary responsibility of the leader is to assist individuals to meet their own spiritual needs through example, providing resources and information and events where individuals can meet with others in their community.

In 1994, Irminsul Aettir organized its first godhordh, similar to a church. It is designed to be actively involved in outreach programs as is any other ministry. Members also sponsor Vinnuhoppurs and Felag groups, study groups, and fellowships, that provide focus on particular topics and more intimate contact between members.

Membership: Not reported.

Sources:

http://www.eskimo.com/~valkyrie/.

★1765★
Lady Sara's Coven
(Defunct)

Sara Cunningham was an Episcopalian who turned witch. During the late 1960s, she operated the Albion Training Coven and, in 1970, became one of the founders of the Church of the Eternal Source. She separated from that group in 1971 over eclecticism (which she expounded) versus a pure Egyptian religion. She founded the Temple of Tiphereth, which combined elements of Western ritual magick, Egyptian religion, and Wicca. The temple was located in Pasadena, where she also ran Stonehenge, an occult supply house. She also met Hans Holzer, who wrote about her psychic abilities in several of his books. In 1973, she moved to Wolf Creek, Oregon, where she formed Lady Sara's Coven, an eclectic Wicca group. She publishes a "Course in Wicca," a year-and-a-day study course which she offers to students around the country. Her coven has dropped out of sight in recent years.

Sources:

AUM, The Sacred Word. Glendale, OR: First Temple of Tipareth, 1975.

The Hermetic Art. Glendale, OR: First Temple of Tiphareth, 1975.

Sara [Cunningham]. *Candle Magic.* Hollywood, CA: Phoenix House, 1974.

Sara, Lady [Cunningham]. *Questions and Answers on Wicca Craft.* Wolf Creek, OR: Stonehenge Farm, 1974.

★1766★
Mental Science Institute
Current address not obtained for this edition.

Barney C. (Eli) Taylor, who is the grand master of what is termed druidic witchcraft, is a descendant of Thomas Hartley, who was burned at the stake for practicing witchcraft in England in the early 1550s. Hartley was a healer and herbalist. Because of persecution, others like him fled to America and settled in the mountain country of the Appalachians and the Ozarks. (Taylor grew up in the Ozarks.) The Mental Science Institute was organized in the late 1960s as a focus for Taylor's brand of herbal magick. He traces his particular kind of witchcraft to the druid, and it is thus termed druidic. It is also a robed tradition, in contrast to both the modern "naked ones" (i.e., the practitioners of Gardnerian Wicca), and the clothed ones who emphasize magick. The robed ones emphasize healing.

The membership of the Mental Science Institute is divided into covens of no more than twelve individuals, meeting under a wizard. Wizards in turn meet under a magi; the magis under a master magi; and the master magis under the grand master. Taylor is grand master for the United States. Apprentices are those studying in order to join the group. There are three degrees in the craft: a first degree, a basic member; a second degree, a wise leader; and a third degree, the wise doctor.

Worship is conducted in regular esbats and the four grand sabbats. The institute is the most male oriented of all the Wiccan groups and has a theology closely related to Christianity and to ritual magick. The universe is seen as a series of levels—celestial, terrestrial and telestial. The celestial is divided into sublevels at the top of which is God the Father, followed by the Lord of Lights, arch-angels and angels. Man, animals and plants are on the terrestrial level. At the lowest level, the telestial, are the mineral, chemical and electrical elements and creative thought. Just as there is a Father, there is a Mother of all people.

In a concept very close to Mormonism, the institute teaches that God the Father was at one time a child. The children will, in like measure, become gods. Reincarnation is part of that process. A complete cycle lasts for approximately 142 years: from birth to death, a year in purgatory, 70 years to integrate the life experience, and a year waiting for rebirth.

Membership: Not reported.

Sources:

Eli [Taylor]. *The First Book of Wisdom*. The Author, 1973.

___. *The Second Book of Wisdom*. N. p., n. d.

★1767★
Neo-Dianic Faith
(Defunct)

The late W. Holman Keith came to paganism early in the 1940s. He attended the Church of Aphrodite, an early pagan group founded in the 1920s by Gleb Botkin and, in the late 1960s, emerged as head of his own Neo-Dianic Faith. Keith described the revival of paganism as the recovery of the ancient spirituality embodied in the prehistoric nature religion and Mother Goddess worship. Though the Neo-Dianic Faith was confined to a small group in the Los Angeles area, as Paganism grew through the 1970s, Keith emerged as an elder brother for many just discovering Paganism.

Keith thought of the divine, the great mover, as eternal desire, ideally embodied in woman. Man's and woman's oneness with life and nature is expressed in a primal piety which includes an ethic of pleasure, beauty, subordination of the drive for power and its resulting machinations of control, and worship of the feminine. The Greco-Roman pantheon is favored, but not exclusively. The active participation in the experience of being alive, in worshipping the Goddess, brings its own assurance of immortality, the moment in time being identical with the eternal now.

After Keith's death in the late 1970s his small following dissolved.

★1768★
New England Coven of Welsh Traditionalist Witches
(Defunct)

The New England Coven of Welsh Traditionalist Witches was founded in the late 1960s by Gwen Thompson of North Haven, Connecticut. It was a Celtic traditionalist coven. Thompson had taken the Gardnerian rituals and rewritten them around a Welsh Celtic theme. Among the early covens, it was considered conservative in its form of worship, which was conducted only in a properly prepared circle or (for outside worship) grove. Members of the coven wore robes with cords and no footwear. Rituals were kept in a *Book of Shadows*. The basic belief in the Earth Mother, the Horned One and a family of pagan deities was set within a basic dualistic cosmology reminiscent of Manichaeism, which taught the release of the spirit from matter.

As Thompson stated, "Our doctrine involves the ancient battle between the hosts of Light and those of Darkness. . . in which Light lost. Light, in this case, may be referred to as Wisdom, or that force which sought to upgrade mankind from his primitive state into a being able to understand more fully his own nature, that of his planet, and the universe at large. It is our belief that our world is governed by the hosts of Darkness who are responsible for the 'three D's:' Death, Disease, and Disaster. We believe that mankind and his world were originally a perfect creation, but that both have been victimized for many thousands of years. We feel that Light will ultimately prevail."

In 1973 Thompson, the high priestess, moved to Gatlinburg, Tennessee. Lady Kerry and her high priest, Stock, succeeded Thompson as the leaders of the New England coven. Thompson began two covens in the Gatlinburg area. During the 1980s, none of the three covens has been located. They are presumed defunct.

★1769★
New, Reformed, Orthodox Order of the Golden Dawn
Current address not obtained for this edition.

The New, Reformed, Orthodox Order of the Golden Dawn (NROOGD) began in 1969 in the San Francisco, California, area when a group of friends assembled to help one of their number with a term project for a class on rituals. The original rituals were based on research in a variety of books by authors on witchcraft and magic such as Gerald B. Gardner and Margaret Murray and magical texts such as the *Greater Key of Solomon*. They decided to become a coven in late 1969, and by the early 1970s, other covens had emerged, all governed by a Red Cord Council. During these years, NROOGD published a magazine, *The Witch's Trine*.

NROOGD disbanded as a formal order in May 1976, when the Red Cord Council decided that henceforth NROOGD shall be a craft tradition rather than a general pagan religious society. In this form it continues to the present day, with covens in the San Francisco Bay area and along the West Coast. Since there is no longer any formal organization, no one really knows how many covens might be practicing in the NROOGD tradition nor where they all might be located. Over the years, a few thousand people have attended NROOGD events and many have incoorporated NROOGD elements in their rituals.

The Bay Area covens continue the tradition of holding rituals open to the neopagan and craft communities, with responsibility rotating informally among them. Most of the eight sabbats are celebrated, and there is an annual September ritual based on the Eleusinian mysteries. Attendance ranges from 50 to 300. The esbats (held at the new and full moons) are closed, celebrated privately by individual covens and their invited guests. The rituals used continue to evolve; sometimes old sabbat rituals are revised, sometimes completely new ones are written. The basic form of the esbat and many of the sabbat rituals are quite similar to the original ones written in 1968.

In February 1988, the NROOGD celebrated its 20th anniversary with a Brigid ritual in Berkeley, California, which brought together many of the past members, including most of the founders. NROOGD members (and former members) have been very active in the Covenant of the Goddess, both as founders and officers.

Membership: In 1988, NROOGD reported approximately 12 covens in the United States and Canada, most in the San Francisco Bay area. Attendance at major festivals has ranged up to 300 in recent years.

Sources:

Scott, Gini Graham. *Cult and Countercult*. Westport, CT: Greenwood Press, 1980.

★1770★
New Wiccan Church
Box 162046
Sacramento, CA 95816

The New Wiccan Church was originally founded as the Neo Celtic Church. Its present name was adopted in 1973, at which time it restricted itself to the practice of traditional English Witchcraft. Membership is open only to initiated witches of the following traditions: Gardnerian, Alexandrian, Algard, Kingstone, Majestic Covens, Majestic Order, Silver Cresent, Taran, and other similar traditions. (These traditions are three "degree" traditions of British origin and represent variations on Gardnerian Wicca.) While members do not perform same gender initiations, heterosexuals, lesbians, homosexuals, and bisexuals are represented in the membership. People from other traditions, or uninitiated individuals, are referred to other covens through a Coven Placement Service operated by the church. Persons under 18 years of age are not eligible for membership.

The "Dedication of the New Wiccan Church" affirms existence of the ultimate godhead, "Dryghtyn" (a Saxon term meaning

"Lord" or "God"). Dryghtyn is viewed as identical to the supreme being postulated in monotheistic religions. The NWC also affirms the primordial differentiation of this androgynous, all knowing, all pervading being into male and female, the "Lady of the Moon" and the "Lord of Death and Resurrection." Further differentiations or emanations from these two produce the innumerable subordinate deities to be found in world mythology. Members may worship, in addition to the Dryghtyn, Lord, and Lady, such of these subordinate gods as they please, provided the form of worship does not involve injury to people or animals. In addition to invoking deities, members respectfully "summon" the Mighty Ones of the Four Quarters, elemental guardian spirits who protect the places of worship. Reverence, but not worship, is directed to powerful ancestral spirits called "Mighty Dead." The church also circulates the Principles of Wiccan Belief adopted by the Council of American Witches in 1974. Actual rites are confidential, but published accounts of Gardnerian and Alexandrian ritual are typical. Traditions or orders (equivalent to "rites") vary in ceremonial dress from highly ornate robes, through street clothes, to sky clad (nude). Members are not allowed to solicit money for initiating anyone into witchcraft or performing acts of magic. Church membership was $20.00 in 1995; covens may have dues to cover costs. Members may retire or lapse membership without prejudice. Apostates must surrender confidential writings.

The church cooperates with a number of independent wiccan covens and with the Covenant of the Goddess. Its periodical carries a wide variety of announcements about Wiccan and Pagan events around the United States. The church has also been quite active in the struggle for public acceptance of the craft and its religious and civil rights.

Membership: In 1986 there were five church centers located in Pinole and Sacramento, California; Mt. Horeb, Wisconsin; Seattle, Washington; and Oregon. Membership figures are confidential, but most affiliated covens are in the Western United States.

Periodicals: *Red Garters.*

★1771★
Odin Brotherhood
Current address not obtained for this edition.

The Odin Brotherhood is a secret society which follows a polytheistic religion devoted to Odin, Thor, Sif, and the other deities of the Norse tradition. According to the brotherhood, Odinism is an ancient religion that acknowledges the gods by fostering thought, courage, honor, light, and beauty. It traces its existence to the fifteenth century, but now, having survived in the face of Christian attempts to annihilate it, it is making itself known. The brotherhood has no buildings (temples or churches) but attempts to honor the gods everywhere, as long as outsiders are excluded; all words are "whispered," and all "abominations" (promiscuity and assassination) are avoided.

The central rite of the brotherhood is called the "Glimpse-Of-Extraordinary-Beauty," during which the celebrants believe they are "enveloped and penetrated by the thoughts of a god." Members do not have faith so much as they are taught to seek knowledge. The brotherhood does, however, believe in life after death and that there are three "Other-Worlds," one of which is called Valhalla or the White-Kingdom. It is reserved for those heroes who die violent deaths. The existence of the Christian hell is denied.

The brotherhood glorifies strength, asserting that "it is only by becoming stronger that a man can realize his divinity." Initiates to the brotherhood must cut themselves three times with a dagger and "devote, hallow, and sanctify" their blood to "the gods who live."

The brotherhood has distanced itself from the racism that has infected Norse beliefs in the twentieth century and eschews the idea that there are either chosen peoples or master races.

Membership: Not reported.

Sources:

http://www.geocities.com/Athens/Acropolis/1043/.

★1772★
Odinic Rite Vinland
PO Box 2022
Sandusky, OH 44871-2022

Odinic Rite Vinland is the autonomous American branch of the Odinic Rite, an Odinist group based in Great Britain, which worships the deities of ancient northern Europe in a manner similar to that of the European branches. It recognizes the spiritual leadership provided by the Court of Gothar in Great Britain, the head of the Odinic Rite, and Heimgest, its director. (The American branch is led by the Witan ORV, a council of three, oathed in the realms of Gods and men to lead and advance the Holy Nation of Odin and the Odinic Rite Vinland). It consists of Osferth ORV, the High Wita; Heidrun ORV, the Witan Reeve; and Wulfgaest ORV, the Hofwarden.

The Odinic Rite Vinland has developed a gothi (clergy) training program for its members and publishes a range of Odinist materials including *The Book of Blotar of the Odinic Rite: Authentic Rituals of the Odinic Rite*, which contains the 12 major monthly rituals of the ORV, as well as rites of passage, a healing ritual, and a format for sword naming, land reclamation, banner consecration, and other short invocations.

Membership: Not reported.

Periodicals: *ORBriefing-Vinland.*

Sources:

http://wwwlrgbc.com/heathen/.

★1773★
Odinist Fellowship/Kirk of Odin
Vancouver Island, BC, Canada

The Odinist Fellowship is an international, Heathen organization intent on bringing back the pre-Christian beliefs and spirituality of northern Europe. The fellowship seeks to find those devotees of the Asatru faith who are isolated from others of a similar faith and provide a wider fellowship. The Odinist Fellowship is the functioning arm of the Kirk of Odin headquartered on Vancouver Island, British Columbia.

Any three members of the fellowship, living in reasonable proximity, may form a Kindred. A Kindred holds a minimum of four celebrations annually. The spokesperson for the Kindred has the title of Kirk Elder. The Kindred also appoints a Chronicler who keeps records of its activities.

Membership: Not reported.

Sources:

http://www.bcsupernet.com/users/wodan/odinist1.htm/.

★1774★
Omphalos
Current address not obtained for this edition.

While Greek Neopagan groups were among the first formed in the 1960s, Greek and Roman mythology have been a relatively minor theme in the developing Wiccan and Neopagan community, which has centered more on the ancient deities of Western and Northern Europe. Omphalos is a Neopagan organization established in the mid-1990s to bring together Pagans who find their inspiration and format in ancient Greek and/or Roman religion. It was formed by John Opsopaus, also known as Apollonius Omphalos. At present, Omphalos has its primary existence on the Internet, where it has established an information and networking presence. The web site includes information about publications, organizations, and festivals, as well as links to some relevant files on rituals, hymns, and other texts useful to Hellenic Neopagans. Omphalos has as a major goal of providing contact information of Pagans living in the same geographic area.

Membership: Not reported.

Sources:

http://www.cs.utk.edu/~mclennan/OM/BA/OM/.

★1775★
Open Goddess
(Defunct)

The Open Goddess was an eclectic Wicca group that drew on Alexandrian Wicca revised with insights from a broader perspective on Western occultism. The Kabbalistic symbolism of balance was predominant; both the Goddess (my Lady) and God (my Lord) are worshipped. The Goddess is identified with the sephirot Binah and the god with Chochman. These are the first emanations from Kether, the unseen Godhead. The God is the solar principle, the king to be enthroned. The Goddess is the lunar principle, veiled in the mysteries of nature and the universe. The name is derived from the belief that the various names of the Goddess are all equally valid.

At one point in the mid-1970s, the Open Goddess claimed over fifty affiliated covens scattered from New Hampshire to Florida. Headquarters were in Woodbridge, New Jersey, where High Priestess and Priest, Pennie Robbins and Kevin Robbins, resided.

★1776★
Order of Osirus
(Defunct)

The Order of Osirus dates from 1572, with Edward Wharton, a Cambridge graduate and schoolteacher who had early become interested in divination and the occult. During his last year at college, he became interested in witchcraft. He started his first coven in the 1510s, but it was disbanded. The first covens of the new order in 1572 had seven members (to avoid the accusation of being a parody on the twelve apostles). The order considers these the first "white covens," as opposed to popular "black" covens that were involved with Satanism and black magic. It was also Wharton's belief that the smaller, more intimate body could generate unlimited power.

The Osirian Order is said to have spread to Massachusetts in the seventeenth century. In 1676, Mary Austin and Anne Brintone arrived in Boston. They were apprehended by Richard Bellingham, who accused them of witchcraft. They were released, however, upon paying 10 pounds sterling and promising to leave Boston. To Simon Newell, who paid the money, credit is due for preservation of the rituals, spells and incantations. They moved to Salem and began the first Osirian coven. By 1692, there were thirty-seven covens in New England. The order then went underground for two hundred years.

Leading the order in the 1970s was Samuel R. Graves, who was introduced to witchcraft by Chris Newell of North Bristol, Massachusetts, a descendant of Simon Newell. Chris gave Simon's journals to Graves. Graves has led in a contemporary revival of the order and the publication of several books. For the order, witchcraft has to do with the mastering of the power of the mind, the strength of individual will and the power of suggestion. The group is primarily concerned with spells and incantations toward some positive goal. Work is done in a circle. Symbol of the Osirian Order is the goat skull, associated with the Horned God, Pan, and the love of nature.

Headquarters of the order were established in Kearney, Nebraska. Membership was open to all after payment of the five-dollar fee. A bimonthly newsletter was published. No recent evidence of the continuance of the order has been available.

Sources:

Graves, Samuel R. *Witchcraft: The Osirian Order*. San Francisco: JBT Marketing, 1971

Potions and Spells of Witchcraft. San Francisco: JBT Marketing, 1970.

★1777★
Ossirian Temple Assembly
Current address not obtained for this edition.

The Ossirian Temple Assembly/Order of Osirus was founded in 1979 by Kara Apu, the Guardian-Chief of the Ossirian Religion. The assembly is dedicated to the restoration of ancient Egyptian religion with the goal of creating a New Age of harmony between deity, entity, and humanity. The religion is based upon the sacred law of *Mayet* (or *Maat*) as carved upon the inner walls of the pyramids and on temple columns. The message of the religion has returned to the modern world through the instrument of the Rosetta Stone, which has allowed access to the ancient writings.

Ossirians believe in one eternally existing Creator God, *Ra*, who is identical to the same God recognized in all religions worldwide. Ra sent his message to humanity through the instrument of Lord Osiris, the same Son born in all ages to bring humanity back into fellowship with God. All who accept the Creator God become divine children of God, and all who seek to serve God receive his divine spirit, *Heru*. Through Heru, who lives in the inner mind, each person can work toward the state of *Ka-djed*, a state of stability of mind and spirit. One must enter that state before entering the ultimate state of union with the Creator. Reincarnation affords additional opportunities to enter that state.

All people who worship the Creator and seek to follow Mayet (justice, truth, and cosmic order) will be acceptable to Ra. However, the Egyptian rites open the way of understanding the mysteries of God and applying the divine power to energize the inner mind. All people can become Ossirians.

Ossirians find meaningful the story of Osiris, who with Lady Isis ruled in ancient Egypt via Mayet. Osiris was killed by Set out of envy, and his body was cut up into 14 pieces. At Isis' imploring, Ra restored Osiris and made him Judge of all souls. Meanwhile, Isis had lost her throne and bore her son Horus in the marshes of the Nile. She mothered Horus until he was an adult. Horus then fought and reclaimed the throne from Set and now rules with Isis at his side. Osiris, Isis, and Horus are a holy family serving as a contemporary model of harmony bringing in a new age of peace and prosperity for body, mind, and spirit.

Members of the Ossirian religion agree to maintain a daily adoration of the Creator, share the concept of living according to Mayet, sacrifice monthly a portion of gain to support the Temple, and observe the teachings and rituals of the temple. Individuals wishing to join first become *shenit* (seekers) and then *shemsu* (full members). Shemsu may become scribes of the temple or priests. The priesthood has three degrees, and there is also a high priesthood of four degrees. The temple/order is headed by a high council (consisting of scribes and priests) and a great council (consisting of some members, scribes, and priests).

Major festivals commemorate the death of Lord Osiris (November 13), his resurrection (December 26), the birth of Horus (December 25), the solstice of Ra (December 21), and Lady Isis' blessing of the sea (March 5). The temple also holds regular services at the full and new moons.

Membership: In 1985 there were 108 members.

Educational Facilities: Ossirian Theological College Seminary

Periodicals: *New Horizons*.

★1778★
Our Lady of Enchantment, Church of the Old Religion
Box 1366
Nashua, NH 03061

Our Lady of Enchantment, Church of the Old Religion was founded in 1978 in Danville, California, by Lady Sabrina. In 1980, the church and school moved to New Bern, North Carolina, and then moved again in 1982 to the New England area. Our Lady of Enchantment offers public classes, regular worship services, and degreed training programs for priesthood and ministerial credentials. Our Lady of Enhantment is recognized by both the state of New Hampshire and the federal government as a legally established church and educational institution with non-profit status.

Our Lady of Enchantment teaches various forms of Wicca, described as not exclusively a religion, but a teaching coming from a time when religion, art, science, and magic were part of an inclusive whole. Integral to Wicca is the practice of magic, a system of working with the powers of nature in order to bring about change and manifest desire.

The center of the church is a Wiccan Metaphysical Center located at 39 Amherst St., Nashua, New Hampshire, which houses the seminary, administrative offices, library, chapel, and a gift shop. Members as well as seekers gather for regular Friday night church services and campus classes. They also gather for a variety of other activities, mostly presided over by Lady Sabrina.

Membership: In 1997, Our Lady of Enchantment reported more than 25,000 students in more than 30 different countries and republics.

Periodicals: *Outer Court Communications.*

★1779★
Pristine Egyptian Orthodox Church
(Defunct)

The Pristine Egyptian Orthodox Church was founded in 1963 in Chicago by Milton J. Neruda and Charles Renslow. It grew out of a small group in suburban Chicago Heights, Illinois. The original name was the Egyptian Holy Church. Its tradition is traced to 1375 B.C. and Pharoah Amenhotep IV (Ikhnaton the Great). The church saw itself as the heir to the original (Pristine), authentic (Orthodox) Egyptian doctrines.

High priority was placed upon individuality and the right of the individual to reason toward belief. Salvation was equated with knowledge. All religions are man-made as outward expressions of God-given faith. The church believed in one creator (Khepera) but venerated the many gods as physical examples of the attributes of the creator. These found expression in the basic Egyptian pantheon. The church also taught living in harmony with nature, the equality of all humans and the spiritual (magical) powers. It sought not to judge individuals, but to leave questions of adultery, murder, homosexuality, etc., to civil authority. (Neruda was an activist in the Chicago homosexual community.) There were four major Holy Days: Easter (March, spring), the Unity of Hator (June 22), the Seb and Mut Festival (September 22) and the Festival of Lights (December 28). There was but a single congregation of the Egyptian Church, in Chicago. It was headed by the Rev. Charles Renslow, arkon of North and South America. There were three priests. *The Egyptian Bible*, composed of ancient Egyptian materials, formed the scriptures of the church. The church split following a disagreement between Renslow and Neruda over its stance in regard to Christianity. Neruda was more actively against the Christian faith and believed that the church should be vocal in its criticism. He left to found the Congregation of Aten. Neither group survived to the end of the decade.

★1780★
Psychedelic Venus Church
(Defunct)

The Psychedelic Venus was formed in 1969 partly as an outgrowth of a former body, the Shiva Fellowship. As its name implies, it combines elements of sexual freedom and psychedelic drugs. The Shiva Fellowship dates from November 1967, when Willie Minzey went to India and was dedicated and marked in the traditional way as a worshipper of Shiva. The practice of the religion includes the smoking of hashish. Minzey returned to the United States and established a temple to Shiva in his home in San Francisco. He also began to hold public services in Golden Gate Park. On April 16, 1969, Minzey was arrested and, in 1971, was sentenced to prison for a term lasting from ten years to life. The Shiva Fellowship disintegrated into other groups.

The Psychedelic Venus Church was founded by Jefferson Poland. As a pagan fellowship dedicated to the worship of the Hindu goddess Kali, who was equated with Venus, the church drew together elements implicit in the Sexual Freedom League, the Gay Liberation Front, emerging paganism, the Shiva Fellowship and various other radical activist groups in the Berkeley/San Francisco area. The Psychedelic Venus Church described itself as a "pantheistic nature religion, humanist hedonism, a religious pursuit of bodily pleasure through sex and marijuana."

Worship in the Psychedelic Venus Church focused upon its celebrations. Until the conviction of Minzey, these were held regularly and openly. Afterwards, they were held irregularly. Typical indoor celebrations would begin with the sacrament—smoking marijuana—during which time a liturgy would be held. After the liturgy, sensitivity sessions and partying in the nude would conclude the evening. Public celebrations would center upon the smoking of marijuana and participation in sexual activity. At one such ceremony, Jefferson Poland was arrested.

The church was governed by a board of directors (four females and three males) elected annually by the membership. The board appointed officers. The president through the late 1970s was Mother Boats. *Intercourse*, a magazine, and *Nelly Heathen*, appeared as occasional periodicals. At its height in 1971, there were 1,000 members, but the church steadily lost support through the 1970s. By 1974 the group reported only 250 members. By the end of the decade the group had disappeared.

★1781★
Reformed Druids of North America
℅ Live Oak Grove
616 Minor Rd.
Orinda, CA 94563

The Reformed Druids of North America was formed in 1963 by a group of students at Carleton College, Northfield, Minnesota, as a protest against a compulsory chapel attendance requirement. It began as the result of a conversation between David Fisher, Howard Cherniack and Norman Nelson. The idea emerged of forming a non-bloody, sacrificial Druidic group. If students were denied credit for attending its services, then they would claim religious persecution; if they received credit, the whole project would be revealed as a hoax, thus ridiculing the requirement. The requirement was dropped during the 1963-64 school year, but the group decided that, since it enjoyed the rituals so much, it would continue. At that time, the structure was completed and the major system of beliefs outlined.

Rituals had been constructed by the Reformed Druids from materials in anthropological literature, such as *The Golden Bough*, the classical text by Sir James Fraser. A henge (an open-air ring temple) was constructed on nearby Monument Hill, where the first Protestant service in Minnesota was held. Though frequently destroyed, the henge was constantly replaced. Ritual is directed toward nature and is held outdoors (in an oak grove) where possible. Robes of white are worn. The passing of the waters-of-life is a symbol of oneness with nature. Festival days are Samhain (Nov. 1), Mid-winter, Ormelc (Feb. 1), Beltane (May 1), Mid-summer, and Lugnasadh (Aug. 1). The Celtic/Druidic gods and goddesses are retained to help focus attention on nature. They include Donu, the mother of the gods and humanity, and Taranis, one of her children, the god of thunder and lightning.

The Reformed Druids are organized into autonomous groves. Each grove is headed by an arch-druid, a preceptor (for business matters) and a server (to assist the arch-druid). Three orders of the priesthood are recognized. Higher orders are honorary. *The Druid Chronicles*, consisting of the history, rules, and customs of the Reformed Druids of North America, serve as the scriptures. These were composed mainly by Jan Johnson and David Frangquist, who succeeded the first arch-druid.

Over the years, a continuity of organization was effected through a lineage of arch-druids. The original arch-druid entered the priesthood of the Episcopal Church. Others established groves in different parts of the country. In 1978, locally autonomous groves were functioning in Northfield and Minneapolis, Minnesota; Chicago and Evanston, Illinois; Ann Arbor, Michigan; Webster Groves, Missouri; New York City; and Palo Alto and Berkeley, California.

In the mid-1970s, leadership of the Druid movement passed to Isaac Bonewits, who had made national headlines when he graduated from the University of California at Berkeley with a degree in magick. Bonewits headed a Berkeley grove. More importantly, he compiled the Druid writings, adding material he had written on Druidism and in 1977 published the *Druid Chronicles (Evolved)*, which contain the history, rituals, laws, and customs for the Reformed Druids. In 1978 he began *Pentalpha* as a national Druid periodical. After several years of publishing the magazine and trying to promote Druidism, Bonewits withdrew from all leadership roles (though he continues to be active in Pagan affairs otherwise). Emmon Bodfish became preceptor of the Berkeley Grove, which was renamed the Live Oak Grove and moved to Orinda, California.

Membership: In 1997 there were two groves: Orinda, California and Keene, New Hampshire.

Periodicals: *Druid Missal-any.*

Sources:

Bonewits, P. E. Isaac. *Authentic Thaumaturgy.* Albany, CA: The CHAOSium, 1978.

___. *Real Magic.* New York: Coward, McCann & Geoghegan, 1971.

The Druid Chronicles (Evolved). Berkeley, CA: Berkeley Drunemetom Press, 1976.

★1782★
Ring of Thoth
PO Box 25637
Tempe, AZ 85285

The Ring of Thoth was founded shortly after the disbanding of the Asatru Free Assembly in 1987. It was established by Edred Thorsson and James Chisholm as an explicitly non-racist organization dedicated to the promotion of the religion of the Germanic peoples. (During the 1980s racism was a persistent charge leveled against groups promoting Norse Paganism.) It sees itself as taking a more liberal and scholarly approach than that taken by the other major group formed somewhat simultaneously, the Asatru Alliance. In other respects it continues the beliefs and practices of the former Asatru Free Assembly. Thorsson has authored a number of books on the Asatru traditions.

Membership: Not reported.

Periodicals: *Idunna.*

Sources:

Gundarsson, KveldulfR Hagan, ed. *Our Thoth.* N.p.: Ring of Thoth, 1992. 711 pp.

Thorsson, Edred. *A Book of Thoth.* St. Paul, MN: Llewellyn Publications, 1989.

★1783★
Runic Society
(Defunct)

The Runic Society was formed in 1974 by N. J. Templin. It advocated Wotanism, or Odinism, viewed as the oldest religion in the world and the religion of the Aryans since the late Stone Age. The Society believed that the Nordic Race is the "Chosen Race of Nature" and that only through Odinism can Nordics be true to nature. The Norse gods were worshipped and thought of as manifestations of nature. Since religion was considered a personal matter, there were no religious services. There were, however, religious festivals termed "blots," and priests, whose function it was to perform marriages and funerals. The family unit, self-respect, and loyalty to the ancestral heritage were promoted. The Odinist faith is opposed to Christianity. Odinism was seen as this-worldly; immortality is given through the improvement of the future generation. The Society sought to establish a true economic, racial and, spiritual community (not as a separate nation but within the nation).

The Runic Society was governed by the supreme council, made up of several Wotanist priests, a secretary, treasurer and advisory personnel. It published *Einherjar*, a quarterly. The associated House of Odin sold Odinist jewelry and articles. Headquarters were in Milwaukee, with a second group in Chicago. Around 1980 the group dissolved after a period of internal dissension.

During its years of existence, the Runic Society kept close association with Da-America (in Pittsburgh), which publishes the journal, *New America*, and with Die Artgemeinschaft (The Old Religion) in Germany. Also closely related to the Runic Society was the Odinist Movement headquartered in Toronto. It was formed in 1971 and published two periodicals, *The Sunwheel* and *The Odinist*.

★1784★
Sabaean Religious Order
3221 N. Sheffield
Chicago, IL 60657

The Sabaean Religious Order is a continuation of an Afro-Mediterranean religion that dates from prehistoric times to Ancient Sumer, Babylon, and Egypt. Frederic M. de Arechaga (now Odun) and his mother opened the Sabaean Center in Chicago with the Temple of Amn in the late 1960s. Its purpose is to study and research Sabaeanism as well as to celebrate its festivals and rites as a means of sparing it for posterity. This is the first Sabaean temple to be opened since the temple of the moon was closed in Harran in the sixth century by the then reigning Islam.

"Sabaeanism" means "from Saba". Saba is both the name of an ancient city and an ancient Egyptian word found in hieroglyphics and in Arabic. Sabaa (Arabic) means a star, rising or coming forth. The Egyptian hieroglyph means "star" or to emanate from a center point of light, like a star.

The Sabaeans believe in the concept of *Amn*, an idea that can be either plural or singular in number and implies the "hidden". Therefore "divinity" to a Sabaean is both genderless and awesome. The religion is described as "henotheistic" or rather "kathenotheistic", which is the belief in a "personal god without the exclusion of any other, sometimes emphasizing one supreme at a time without denying the rest."

In symbolic or poetic imagery Amn is referred to in the feminine and in four different colors. It is also associated with the four races of humanity, the seasonal stations, and the major colors of the spectrum. Thus in the winter it is the White goddess, the spring, the Blue goddess, in the summer, the Yellow goddess, and in the fall, the Red goddess. There are two "new year's days" acknowledged by Sabaeans, the autumnal equinox, which is the pontifical beginning, and the vernal equinox, the secular celebration. Following the influence of ancient Roman tradition, the common New Year (December 31-January 1) is also celebrated not as a New Year but rather as the ending of the Saturnalia that starts December 17 and continues through December 31 at midnight.

Beside the main body of "four" symbols there is also the image of the warriors, a trinity headed by the "trickster", the two-faced, Janus-like god that always begins the year and is the entity of the communication between gods and men. Its festival is usually around January 6, about the perihelion of the earth.

Astronomy and astrology are very important to the Sabaean system, not so much as divinatory tools but as relevant positions. Sabaean temples and shrines are usually sidereal-oriented, particularly with the rising and passing of the sun and the moon, but sometimes other stars as well. The precession of the equinoxes is observed and the zodiacal calculations are corrected to this phenomena with true sidereal composition.

Like some other ancient religions, Sabaeanism still observes the ritual of animal sacrifice that usually supplies food for the celebration for which the animals are slaughtered, making the food ritually pure. But other offerings of fruits, vegetables, and grains are made to the Amn as well as incense and flowers, which are more frequently given.

Marriages are called eclipses and are designed for a specific period of time at the end of which the couple can either re-eclipse or part their ways. The standard marriage contract is considered a partnership of possessions and it is imperative to sign at an eclipse. However, if the couple part at the end of their eclipse then this contract must be met with proper judicious courts of law, as the marrriage has no further link to the eclipse or the religion. Sabaeanism is inherently matriarchal. However, unlike its predecessors, it primarily identifies with the brothers and sisters as they are truly of the same blood. The mother is considered the matrix or source and is certainly honored for that function. It is obvious who the mother of an individual is, but it is very difficult to prove who the father is.

The Sabaean Religious Order headquarters is in Chicago, where its Temple of Amn is located. The group has run an occult store, El Sabarum, since 1968. For several years the group has also issued a periodical, Sabaean Chronicles, which has superseded previous periodicals titled Iris and Janus. The Sabaean Chronicles is usually printed on a quarterly basis relative to the passing of the seasons.

The Sabaean Religious Order occasionally writes and produces pagan mystery plays and trains a troupe of dancers called "hierodules" (temple servants) in different dances and pantomimes that use ancient Egyptian dance movements. It also has a small group of musicians that train on drums and bata for the festivals and supplement the electronic keyboard with original compositions.

Membership: Not reported. There is one group, in Chicago, Illinois.

Periodicals: Sabean Chronicles.

★1785★
Seax-Wica
Current address not obtained for this edition.

After his divorce in 1973, Raymond Buckland moved to New Hampshire, remarried, and emerged as a spokesperson (along with his second wife Joan Buckland) for a new tradition, Seax-Wica. Seax-Wica differs from other Wicca groups in that it claims no relation to previously existing covens. A Saxon background has been adopted as an alternative to the Gardnerian Wicca tradition. Buckland and his first wife, Rosemary Buckland, brought Gardnerian witchcraft to America in the early 1960s. Woden and Freya

are the names chosen for the male and female deities of Seax-Wica.

Seax-Wica covens are headed by a high priest and priestess chosen annually by a vote of the coven. Members, including priests, are termed "Gesith" after initiation and "Ceorl" before. Those outside the craft are termed "Theow". There is only one degree of initiation. The Tree is the name given the Book of Shadows, the traditional book of rituals.

Besides the matter of tradition, Seax-Wica differs from other groups in several ways. The male deity and the high priest are raised to equality with their female counterparts. Ritual scourging and binding have been dropped. Worship is either skyclad or in a short simple tunic. There is no sexual activity in the rituals.

Autonomous covens had, by 1974, been establsihed in New York, New Jersey, and Massachusetts. A decade later there were covens in most states and several foreign countries. Facilitating the rapid spread of Seax-Wica was a home study course in witchcraft written by Buckland. Seax-Wica Voys was published for several years as the official journal.

Membership: In 1992 Seax-Wica reported approximately 5,000 members in the United States and an additional 2,000 in foreign countries.

Educational Facilities: Seax-Wica Seminary, Charlottesville, Virginia.

Sources:

Buchland, Tara. Beauty Secrets of the Ancient Egyptians. Scottsville, VA: Taray Publications, 1982.

Buckland, Raymond. Practical Color Magick. St. Paul, MN: Llewellyn Publications, 1983.

___. The Tree. New York: Samuel Weiser, 1974.

★1786★
Skergard
20 E. Lakeview Dr., Ste. 250
PO Box 1755
Nederland, CO 80466

Skergard is a Pagan organization devoted to the deities of the old Norse religions generally referred to as Asatru and Vanatru. Included in this polytheistic faith is the worship of the gods/goddesses Odin, Thor, Freyr, Frigga, and Freyja, the gods of the old Norse sagas. Religious gatherings, blots, meet regularly and are given focus in the eight major blots held each year.

Membership: Not reported.

★1787★
SM Church
% Robin Stewart, Priestess
Box 1407
San Francisco, CA 94101

The SM Church emerged in the mid-1970s in Berkeley, California, among people who defined themselves as being into SM (i.e., sadism and masochism) and who had, in addition, come to believe in the ancient historical practices of Goddess worship (which had appeared in the previous decade throughout the San Francisco Bay area). The church began as discussions of the SM experience led to questions of spiritual meaning associated with intense SM fantasy, beyond simple sexual gratification. Early positive explorations led to the establishment of the "Temple of the Goddess" of the SM Church.

The SM Church opposes the male father image which has dominated Western religion and encourages members to focus upon the feminine aspects of God, which it seeks to uncover in ongoing research into periods and cultures which emphasized Goddess worship. The church differs from many other Neo-Pagan groups in that it believes in a powerful female deity, equivalent to the male monotheistic God. The church is feminist in orientation and from the beginning excluded male dominant-female submissive patterns from its organization. It allows both homosexual and heterosexual patterns of female dominance within the church's philosophy. Undergirding its approach is a belief in the great transition of Western culture. The church believes that society could collapse and, in that event, females would have to take control. The church is attempting to plan for that possibility.

Ritual life, initially adopted from other Neo-Pagan group patterns, includes a unique emphasis upon the use of controlled pain and mortification experiences as a sacrament of penance. On occasion, such rituals are designed to allow both males and females to experience the extremes of female dominance fantasies, though the church denies that female rule in the envisioned postmodern society would be vindictively harsh. Further, the sacramental atmosphere of the rituals attempts to separate them from any identification with commercialized exploitation of SM practices.

The church has published a set of purposes which includes the following: the purchase and/or erection of church facilities; the continuance of the seminary which trains women for the priesthood; the development of ordered communities as models of a matriarchial society; and assistance in improving the image of the SM community (through various charity projects). The church has initiated plans to build a monastery as a full-scale model of a female-dominated society.

The church is governed by a board of directors. Associated with it is the Essemian Society, a nonreligious social-educational group whose activities derive from SM Church perspectives.

Membership: Not reported. Membership in both the SM Church and Essemian Socity is limited to a single congregation in San Francisco. There are estimated to be less than 100 members.

Educational Facilities: The SM Seminary, San Francisco, California.

Sources:

Budd, Russell. "Interview: The SM Organizations of San Francisco." *Woman/Slave* no. 14 (October-December 1982): 30-37.

Green, Gerald, and Caroline Green. *SM, the Last Taboo.* New York: Ballantine Books, 1974.

Scott, Geni Graham. *Erotic Power: An Exploration of Dominance and Submissions.* Secaucus, NJ: Citadel Press, 1983.

★1788★
Temple of Bacchus
Current address not obtained for this edition.

The Temple of Bacchus was formed in 1978 by Bishop H. Carlisle Estes, the temple's pastor. Bacchus, also known as Dionysus, was the ancient Greek god of food and drink. Estes claimed in 1975 that Bacchus revealed to him the temple's teachings, which have been published in a pamphlet, *The Book of Bacchus.* The Temple believes that there is one God, known by many names, and that Bacchus is His disciple. Bacchus decreed that Estes should form a church to worship God and ordered that it be a place of joy and celebration. Bacchus taught that everything God created is good and humans should enjoy the pleasures of the body-food, wines, music, creative activity, and the arts. However, all should be enjoyed in moderation. Excess in any area leads to illness and pestilence and the disfiguring of bodily form.

According to the revelation, Bacchus has decreed daily worship with feasting and dancing. Six days of bacchanals are followed by a day of fasting and rest. Priests, bishops and cardinals of the church assist in the preparation of the daily feast with a primary responsibility of preventing the rituals from becoming repetitious and stereotyped.

Almost from its founding, the temple has been a subject of controversy. Critics charged Bishop Estes and his assistant, Cardinal Vincent Morino, with operating a restaurant under the guise of a temple in order to circumvent local zoning laws which had previ-

ously denied them permission to open a restaurant in the building occupied by the temple. They further charged that the nightly bacchanals (in which those in attendance are asked to contribute a stated donation and in return receive a full meal) are in fact not religious events at all. The controversy has led to several law suits which are, as of the time of this writing, still pending and which will determine the future of the temple.

The temple is one of several religious bodies chartered by the Universal Life Church of Modesto, California.

Membership: In 1979 the church reported 125 members of the single congregation in Maine, with new congregations beginning in Honolulu, Hawaii and in Wiltshire, England.

★1789★
Temple of Isis
% Crow Haven Corner
125 Essex St.
Salem, MA 01970

The Temple of Isis is the Wiccan center founded by Laurie Cabot (b. 1933), one of the more famous practitioners of witchcraft in America since then-Governor Michael Dukakis of Massachusetts named her the "Official Witch of Salem." She was introduced to witchcraft in high school in Boston by a teacher who revealed to her that she was a witch. According to her own story, she was initiated at the age of 16 in 1949, but it was not until 1965 that she decided to live totally as a witch. Since that time she has dressed in black and worn a pentacle (fivepointed star) and heavy black eye make-up. A short time later, following up on the suggestion of a friend, she moved to Salem.

In Salem she began to teach "Witchcraft as a Science" in local adult education programs and to work as a psychic and tarot card reader. She opened The Witch Shop, which was soon succeeded by Crow Haven Corner, a book and supply house and teaching center. This became her center of activity from the 1970s to the present. The "Witchcraft as a Science" classes are still being taught with an emphasis on psychic development and elementary magic. In the advanced class, students are introduced to ritual.

More recently she has added a class on "The Religion of Witchcraft" in which students are prepared for initiation into the Temple of Isis. Cabot was ordained and the temple chartered by the National Alliance of Pantheists. The temple centers its teaching upon an understanding of a basic creative force underlying and permeating the universe rather than the Goddess and God of the Gardnerian revival Wicca.

Cabot is also the founder of the Witches League for Public Awareness, an activist group which fights for the civil rights of Wiccans. The film version of *The Witches of Eastwick* became the occasion to call the league into existence.

Membership: Not reported.

Sources:

Cabot, Laurie, with Tom Cowan. *Power of the Witch.* New York: Delacorte Press, 1989.

★1790★
Temple of the Goddess Within
(Defunct)

The Temple of the Goddess Within was formed by Ann Forfreedom in the 1970s. Raised in the Jewish faith, Forfreedom rejected Judaism for being "too male-dominated." She was drawn into Witchcraft, or Wiccecraeft, through her activity in various feminist causes where she met other female Wiccans. Originally from Sacramento, she moved to Oakland in 1984. It was the teaching of the temple that the proper name for the religion of Witchcraft is Wiccecraeft or Wicce (Craft of the Wise). Wiccecraeft is the Old English feminine form of Witchcraft used by some feminist witches as the proper name of their religion.

As publisher/editor of *The Wise Woman*, Ann Forfreedom (a name assumed to accentuate her feminist concerns) became a leading spokesperson for Dianic Witchcraft, a term coined by Morgan McFarland and Mark Roberts to describe those traditions which focus mainly or totally on the Goddess. She does not believe, however, that the Dianic tradition is necessarily equated with either female separateness or anti-male attitudes. In the Dianic tradition worship is more Goddess- than God-oriented, but the male deities serve a complimentary role. The Goddess is seen as an expression of the life-force of the universe. Among the basic principles of the temple, it was said, "All Goddesses are one Goddess; all Gods are one God." Members were encouraged to act both collectively and individually upon their feminist goals.

Like other Wicce, the Dianics attend to lunar and solar cycles, gathering in the evenings for times of work (magic) and feasting (celebration). Wicce is a religion of love. Initiation into Wicce is an important step and should be preceded by a period of study. It should be entirely voluntary on the part of the initiate, and the initiator should perform his/her duties without monetary compensation. The temple was an autonomous coven. Unlike Gardnerian Wicca, Feminist Wicce does not have a single leader such as witch queen, nor a single sourcebook such as the Book of Shadows. Rituals are eclectic and variable.

In 1982 the temple sponsored a major conference, "Goddess Rising," which brought together many leading Goddess worshippers and feminists. As a result of the conference, a second organization, Goddess Rising, was founded and incorporated to educate men and women about Feminist Wiccecraeft and to explore Goddess lore. Goddess Rising has been discontinued as of 1992. Ann Forfreedom continues, as of 1992, as the California Director of the Witch's Anti-Discrimination Lobby, a coalition which seeks to educate the mass media and public about Witchcraft. The WADL was founded by Leo Louis Mortello.

Periodicals: *The Wise Woman*, the Temple's periodical, continues to be published as an independent periodical. Send orders to 2441 Cordova St., Oakland, CA 94602.

Sources:

Forfreedom, Ann. *Feminist Wicca Works*. Sacramento, CA: The Author, 1980.

___. *Mythology, Religion and Woman's Heritage*. Sacramento, CA: Sacramento City Unified School District, [1981].

Forfreedom, Ann, and Julie Ann, eds. *Book of the Goddess*. Sacramento, CA: Temple of the Goddess Within, 1980.

★1791★
Temple of the Pagan Way
Box 60151
Chicago, IL 60660

The Temple of the Pagan Way dates from 1966 and the formation of an occult study and worship group led by Herman Enderle and Virginia Brubaker. The group became associated with the British Pagan Front and began to use the rituals written by Donna Cole. However, divergences developed within the Temple over the ascendancy of the Mother Goddess, a prominent theme in the Pagan Way rituals. A system incorporating a balanced view of deity, both male and female, was adopted, with prominent elements from the Kabbalah. Enderle, who was a student of ritual magick, advocated a strong emphasis on magick in addition to "just worshipping the Goddess."

During the 1970s the Temple was the motivating force in the formation of a number of other Neo-Pagan bodies. Most of the currently existing Neo-Pagan and Wicca groups in the Chicago area derive from it. They include the Calumet Pagan Temple, Epiphanes, and the First Temple of the Craft of WICA (all now independent organizations). The Temple of the Sacred Stones, an eclectic witchcraft coven headed by Donna Cole, had a long association with the Temple, and it now meets in the building which formerly housed the Temple.

After several years as the Temple of the Pagan Way, the group adopted a new name in the spring of 1974, Uranus Temple. During this period, its emphasis upon ritual magick was at its height. Uranus was an initiatory temple with its basis in Western occultism and paganism. Members attended regular services associated with the full and new moon as well as the eight festivals. New members begin with a series of ethics classes which introduce them to the basic perspective of the temple. They are then prepared for a Ritual of Dedication where a public declaration of the acceptance of paganism is made. The next step is initiation. There are five degrees, each of which corresponds to the classical elements of the ancients and entails approximately one year of study.

The first degree is Earth, in which the student is taught to gain control over him/herself and is introduced to basic occult material and exercises. The second degree is Water, with emphasis on exploring the psychic and emotional self. The third degree is Fire, and deals directly with self-change through magick. The fourth degree is Air, and expresses the use of what has been learned and the ability to function easily as a magician and pagan. The fifth degree, Spirit, is the completed use of the first four degrees.

The Temple was headed by a high priest and high priestess elected annually from among the priests and priestesses. Members in the second degree can choose studies leading to the priesthood. A General Council consisting of all members is the highest authority, and there is a Council of Elders, composed of senior members of the community, to which the high priest and priestess are responsible.

In 1975 the high priest (Enderle) and high priestess (Brubaker) had sufficient irreconcilable differences that the group split. The majority (and hence the name) followed Brubaker. Enderle then formed the Earthstar Temple. After using the name Uranus for a short while, it was discarded for the original name. The group has since become a witchcraft coven, though retaining many of the unique ritual and magical emphases from the 1970s. The Temple has taken an active role in the Covenant of the Goddess.

Membership: Not reported. There is one group, located in Chicago, Illinois.

★1792★
Temple of the Pagan Way
(Defunct)

One of the most important groups spreading Neo-Paganism (as opposed to Witchcraft) was the Pagan Way, a loosely associated set of Neo-Pagan groves which emerged in the late 1960s. The group had several sources. Donna Cole, a witch in Chicago, had traveled to England in the 1960s and was initiated into Gardnerian Wicca. Upon her return to the United States, she made contact with Herman Enderle and Virginia Brubaker, who had formed an occult study group. Together they established a Pagan Temple. Cole also composed a set of Pagan rituals which were less magical and more celebratory than the Gardnerian ones. During this period, she met Ed Fitch, a California Pagan. Fitch later composed a second set of rituals similar in perspective to Cole's. During the early 1970s, Cole and Fitch circulated the Pagan Way rituals around the United States with the result that a number of Pagan Way Temples (groves) emerged.

One early grove was in Philadelphia and had among its leaders Penny Novak, Michael Novack, and Thomas (a pseudonym). Thomas became the editor in 1970 of the original pagan journal *Waxing Moon* (later the *Crystal Well*) when its founder, Joseph Wilson, moved to England. Wilson began a British *Waxing Moon*, thus precipitating the name change in America. *The Crystal Well* was never the official organ of the Pagan Way, but it had a close informal connection and functioned as a means whereby Pagan Way groups could stay in contact

The Pagan Way was a celebratory nature religion dedicated to the growth in understanding of the sacred quality of the seasonal rounds and the holy, mystic qualities of everyday life. Unlike most pagan groups, it was not a "magical" group and has no secret rituals. (The rituals were recently published in book form as *A Book of Pagan Rituals*.) While many individuals practiced magick, the group came together for celebration only. The Goddess was, of course, the central theme of the celebrations.

Pagan Way study centered on three basic steps: first, study of the myths and history of paganism; second, practice of rituals for both individuals and groups; and third, in-depth working in the craft (for those who desired it). In many areas the Pagan Way served as an outer portal to the more secretive craft.

In 1973, Pagan Way groves were functioning in Philadelphia, Pennsylvania; New York City; Wilmington, Delaware; Huron, South Dakota; Loiusville, Kentucky; San Bernadino, California; Passaic, New Jersey; and Chicago, Illinois. There were also numerous small Pagan Way groups scattered across the country. Ed Fitch headed the California Grove. In 1974, the Chicago Pagan Way became the Uranus Temple (now the Temple of the Pagan Way). There were between 30 and 60 members at Philadelphia. By 1980, the Pagan Way had largely died. Some groups had been destroyed by internal dissension. Most were were simply superceded by numerous Neo-Pagan and Witchcraft groups under the leadership of those trained in the groves, coupled with the retirement of many of the original leaders. The original rituals, which were not copyrighted, have been published in several editions and remain popular among Neo-Pagans in North America and England.

Sources:

A Book of Pagan Rituals. New York: Samuel Weiser, 1978.

Fitch, Ed. *Magical Rites from the Crystal Well*. St. Paul, MN: Llewellyn Publications, 1984

★1793★
Teutonic Temple
(Defunct)

In Dallas, Oregon, the Teutonic Temple functioned as a polytheistic religion derived from the folk customs and festivals of the English, German and Scandinavian peoples. Members believed in a supreme God and a pantheon of lesser deities including Tiw, the sky father; Wodan; Thunar; Fria; and Frua, goddess of fertility and magick. The eight pagan festivals were celebrated. Yule, the winter solstice, is the beginning of the Teutonic year. The Teutonic Temple was a conservative religion against free love, perversion, pornography, drugs, draft dodging and permissiveness. No evidence of its continuance into the 1980s had been located.

★1794★
Triskellion
Current address not obtained for this edition.

Triskellion is a traditionalist Wicca (in the Gardnerian and Alexandrian traditions) group which has incorporated elements of ritual magic which are placed in the service of Wiccan theology. The divine energy is mediated by three principles: the Masculine (god), the Feminine (the goddess) and the Collective (the community). Ultimately, all three principles merge into one and serve the growth of sentient beings. They operate as a team with ritual duties being passed through the group as different skills are needed. Triskellion rituals are based upon a cooperation between coven members, the gods and goddesses, and the particular energies raised in each ritual.

Triskellion sees itself as a second genesis fertility religion. First genesis fertility religions invoked divine energies for fecundity on the physical plane. Having no need of large families, Triskellion members leave the energies called forth on the astral plane and then draw upon them as needed for various creative activities.

Triskellion offers a 29-week course in basic Wicca training which may be followed by a 29-week course in ritual. The group is active in the Heartland Spiritual Alliance, a cooperative Wicca and Pagan fellowship in Kansas City, Missouri.

Membership: Not reported.

★1795★
Venusian Church
PO Box 905
Redmond, WA 98073-0905

The Venusian Church was formed in 1975 by Ron Peterson, a Seattle businessman, and chartered the following year by the Universal Life Church. During the 1960s and early 1970s, Peterson, a former member of the Seventh-Day Adventist Church, followed a spiritual pilgrimage which centered upon the release of sexual feelings repressed by the strict sexual code under which he was raised. He found assistance within the human potential movement and became an advocate of helping others who wished to confront their sexual feelings. Meanwhile, he had also become a professional pornographer.

Peterson gathered around him a group of interested people, including several sex therapists and human potential counselors, and began to explore the potential of sex and sexual experience in releasing human creativity and opening the realm of the spiritual. For a short while, the church operated a Temple of Venus in downtown Seattle which featured both pornographic films and sexually explicit presentations that attempted to communicate the church's attitude about open sexuality to the general public. In 1977 a retreat center, Camp Armac, was opened and became the focus of church activities. A variety of seminars, workshops, social events, and worship services were offered, all in an atmosphere in which clothes were optional and sexual experimentation was condoned and even encouraged.

The leaders of the church resisted any attempts to systematically build a belief system or pattern of worship, and the life of the group slowly emerged out of the spontaneous experiences of various gatherings of the members. First came the worship of nature in the form of the Goddess and the acknowledgment of Her at communal feasts and in the celebration of the solar equinox and solstice. Then in 1979 church members discovered the preexisting Neo-Pagan movement. Having found in Neo-Paganism a larger movement which already possessed a complete religious system toward which the Venusian Church seemed to be heading, the church began to absorb both thought and practices from their new acquaintances, especially from the Church of All Worlds.

In 1979 Camp Armac closed and for several years the church conducted its programs in the homes of members. In 1981 the church purchased a large tract of land near Redmond, Washington. A former warehouse was converted into a church center named the Longhouse, and a stonehenge was erected for outdoor rituals.

Because of its strong opinions that sex was divine, the church began to provide public events in Seattle's First Avenue pornography district. The programs, some of which featured nudity and even overt sex acts, placed the church in the center of a storm of controversy. Several members were arrested and a lengthy but futile battle with the Internal Revenue Service ensued. As a result, the facilities in Seattle were closed and all activity were restricted to members and their guests only. In more recent years, the church has sponsored workshops and seminars for its members and the public emphasizing personal growth and aspects of consciousness which expand the wholeness of humanity. These programs have also been offered to inmates in local penitentiaries and to several sex-offender programs.

The Venusian Church describes its theology as centered upon a unique sacred space technology, meaning it is a "spatial" system rather than a "conceptual" one. The church attempt to create sacred space to be experienced rather than sacred beliefs to which assent is given. Essential to the experience of this sacred space is both inner and outer freedom. The individual's divinity is experienced only in an environment where people have the freedom and opportunity to be whole and complete. The presence of such an environment would make the experience of a Venusian Paradise possible.

The church has as its immediate concern several steps that will allow for the emergence of the Venusian Paradise. It is attempting to realign members attitude toward their own sexuality so as to undo the damage that society and religion have done with its repressive opinions and rules. This realignment is accompanied with efforts aimed at healing the individual's damaged spirit. The church also works to remove any present outside interference from either church or state with the member's religious freedom.

To implement its goals, the church has launched one new program called "Paradise Now" through the resources of the Internet. Paradise Now presents a simulated version of a visit to the Isle of Eros and members are taken through the steps of preparation for entry into the Venusian Paradise under the leadership of a priest or priestess as a guide. The individual is led through several levels of purification, deconditioning and pleasuring as a prelude to their induction into the spiritual/erotic arts; introduced to Venusian technology; and given knowledge on maintaining legal rights and living the spiritual life free of government interference.

Through the 1980s into the mid-1990s, the church has kept a low profile and limited it activities primarily to its members. However, at present the church has developed a new outward thrust primarily through the opportunities supplied by the Internet. New "Sex Positive" religious training programs are in preparation and will appear over the next few years.

The church is formally led by a board of directors, but management of the church center and its programs has been placed in the hands of a loosely organized council of active members. Ministers are selected from among the members after demonstrating their leadership abilities and competence in dealing with people. Membership and involvement in church activities, at present, is limited to adults, however, the church is developing some programs for the children of members which would be both informative and age-appropriate.

Membership: Not reported. In 1988 the church reported approximately 80 members, all of whom reside in the greater Seattle, Washington, area.

Remarks: In the mid-1980s, the church failed to reclaim its tax-exempt status and members who had contributed had their deductions disavowed. The resulting financial reverses have greatly hindered the progress of the fragile group.

In January 1997, the Church of Ecstasy merged into the Venusian Church. The Church of Ecstasy had been founded by its high priest, Reve. Michael out of a vision he had experienced on June 27, 1992, on the beach in San Fracnisco. After having consumed a brownie laced and ganja (marijuana), he fell into a mystical oneness with the Earth and Universe and heard a voice within him say, "Canabis is the Sacrament, and your body is the Temple." He interpreted his vision as a spiritual directive to become an advocate of sensually-based spirituality through the sacraments of cannabis and nudism. He summarized the beliefs of the new Church of Ecstasy in five statements which affirm that nudity is a form of meditative yoga that assists in sensitizing people to their environment that Nature is the highest Power; and thus humans should live in harmony with it; that the right to expand spiritual consciousness is limited only by the violation of the rights of others; that the primary goal of the spiritual path is the development in sensitivity, kindness, and love toward others; and that members celebrate the vast diversity of human form, culture, and experience. The church existed as a network of like-minded individuals who accepted its basic spiritual perspective and were tied together by *Ekstasis,* the church's periodical.

After leading the church for several years, Rev. Michael concluded that he laced the resources to properly administer it and promote its vision. Having learned of the existence of the Venusian Church in who members he felt he had met some kindred souls, he took the lead in guiding the members of the Church of Ecstasy into the larger better-organized body. Rev. Michael has become an active leader in the Venusian Church.

★1796★
Wiccan Church of Canada
109 Vaughan Rd.
Toronto, ON, Canada M6C 2L9

The Wiccan Church of Canada is a Neo-Pagan Witchcraft group incorporated in 1979 by High Priestess Tamara James and High Priest Richard F. James. They had their first contacts with Neo-Paganism in 1977 in California. In 1979 they moved to Toronto and founded the Wiccan Church and opened an occult store catering to witches and pagans. With the expansion of their network, in 1983, they organized the area's first Pagan festival. The following year, the first of several covens formed within the church.

The church believes that the universe is selfaware and that portions of self-awareness within the universe have been differentiated and are properly designated gods, the number of which are unknowable, since self awareness is without gender, and deity may be personified as male or female. There are greater and lesser orders and thus one may speak of the gods and goddesses and also of angels, nymphs, fairies, and spirits.

The Wiccan Church espouses the idea that much about the universe is unknowable. We are ignorant ultimately of the origin of the universe, life after death, or the mechanics of miracles and prayer. In the face of such ignorance, the church asserts that religious expressions are purely subjective. Tolerance and nonjudgmental attitudes should hold sway when approaching another's religious life. Awareness is also amoral. Morality is a human creation, and society has the right to assert itself and legislate so as to be protected from violence and outside forces. Among the things that are knowable is that human life is interrelated and linked by karmic ties. Such ties may carry into the future.

The church follows the eight annual festivals common to witches and pagans and also normally gathers on the new and full moon every two weeks. It has developed a full set of rituals to mark the rites of passage from wiccaning (the naming and blessing of a child), to handfasting (marriage), and passing the veil (funeral). They also mark the coming of age (physical maturity) of men and women, bless pregnancies at each trimester, and hold handpartings for couples who are separating.

The church is led by its priesthood council, which includes all of the church's priests and priestesses. The council members lead ritual, train new members, and set qualifications for the priesthood.

Membership: Not reported. In the late 1980s the church reported approximately 100 full members and 300 constituency members who attend festivals. Affiliate branches are located in Toronto, Hamilton, and Ottawa.

Sources:

James, Richard. *The WIC-CAN Handbook.* Toronto: Wiccan Church of Canada, 1987. 21 pp.

Marron, Kevin. *Witches, Pagans, and Magic in the New Age.* Toronto: Seal Books, 1989. 230 pp.

Rabinovitch, Shelley TSivia. "The Institutionalization of the Wicca in Ontario via the Wiccan Church of Canada." Unpublished paper, 1991. 22 pp.

★1797★
Witches International Craft Associates (W.I.C.A.)
153 W. 80th St.
New York, NY 10024

Witches International Craft Associates (W.I.C.A.) is the public structure of the Sicilian Strege tradition headed in America by Dr. Leo Louis Martello. It was formed in 1970. Prior to that time Dr. Martello had been an active Spiritualist. In 1955 he was ordained and became the head of the International Guidance Temple of Bible Spiritual Independents, Mother Church & Seminary in New York City. He served the church for five years. He was also a national officer of the American Graphological Society, a hypnotist, and popular writer on occult subjects.

According to Martello, Witchcraft teaching and practice was passed through his family and was initiated in 1951. During the 1960s he returned to Sicily (from America where his parents had immigrated) and re-established contact with the Strege. In 1969 he published his first book on Witchcraft, and the following year he went public. He founded W.I.C.A.

Martello emerged as one of the earliest spokespersons of the new Witchcraft. His organization led in the formation of a number of necessary structures serving the emerging community in the early 1970s: Witches Encounter Bureau (to aid witches in contacting each other), the Witches Liberation Movement (which published the "Witch Manifesto"), and the Witches Antidefamation League. He also initiated two periodicals, *Witchcraft Digest* and the *W.I.C.A. Newsletter*.

According to Martello, the actualities of Strege Wicca have never been revealed, though Charles Leland's book *Aradia* comes close to revealing them. *Aradia* was meant to be a study of Strege. The basic deity is Diana, the first created before all creation. She divided into darkness and into light (Lucifer). Desiring the light, she tricked Lucifer into lying with her and thus became the mother of Herodias (Aradia). She also became the Queen of the Witches. The basic ritual is the conjuration of Diana and the invocation of Aradia. Cubes of meal, salt and honey in the shape of a crescent moon are consecrated and eaten. The climax of the ritual, performed at the full moon, is dancing and "love in the darkness." The ritual is skyclad (performed in the nude).

One point at which Sicilian Wicca differs from most traditions is its use of spells and incantations that threaten the deity. For example, Diana is addressed:

Or I may truly at another time So conjure thee that thou shalt have no peace Or happiness, for thou shalt ever be In suffering until thou grantest that Which I require in strictest faith from here!

Threats are a recognition of the essential divinity in each person, a sense of personal power which even the gods and goddesses cannot undermine.

Strege functions as an ethnic branch of the craft. Headed in the United States by Martello, who sees it as one with continuing Sicilian practices. In recent years Martello has discontinued the periodicals, but still circulates his many books though the publishing arm, Hero Press.

Membership: Not reported.

Sources:

Leland, Charles Godfrey. *The Mystic Will*. New York: Hero Press, 1980.

Martello, Leo Louis. *Curses in Verses*. New York: Hero Press, 1971.

___. *How to Prevent Psychic Blackmail*. New York: Samuel Weiser, 1975.

___. *Weird Ways of Witchcraft*. New York: HC Publishers, 1969.

___. *What It Means To Be a Witch*. New York: The Author, [1975]

___. *Witchcraft, The Old Religion*. Secaucus, NJ: University Books, 1973.

Voodoo

★1798★
African Theological Archministry
℅ Oyotunji African Yoruba Village
Box 51
Sheldon, SC 29941

In December 1973 a group of blacks from Harlem received national news coverage for their establishment of a "voodoo kingdom" in Beaufort County, South Carolina. The sacred village of Oyotunji is headed by King Oba Efuntola Oseijeman Adelabu Adefunmi I, born Walter Eugene King in 1928. King abandoned the Baptist Church of his family during his teens and began a search for the ancient gods of Africa. He traveled to Haiti in 1954 and discovered voodoo. Early in 1955, he travelled to Europe and North Africa and upon his return to the United States, he founded the Order of Damballah Hwedo Ancestor Priests. Then in 1959, he traveled to Cuba and was initiated in the Orisha-Vodu African priesthood by Afro-Cubans at Matanzas, Cuba. The Order of Damballah was superceded by the Shango Temple and in 1960 he incorporated the African Theological Archministry. The Shango Temple was renamed the Yoruba Temple.

In 1970 King Efuntola, as King became known, moved with most of the temple members to rural South Carolina where the Yoruba Village of Oyotunji was established. He began a complete reform of the Orisha-Vodu priesthood along Nigerian lines. In 1972 he traveled to Nigeria and was initiated into the Ifa priesthood. Upon his return he was proclaimed oba-king (Alashe) of Oyotunji. He opened the first Parliament of Oyotunji chiefs and landowners and founded the priests' council (Igbimolosha) in 1973. These two groups make the rules for the community. They attempt to adhere closely to African patterns.

Oyotunji has been modeled on a Nigerian village. A palace for the King and his wives (four in 1995) and children has been constructed. There are also several temples dedicated to the various deities. Only Yoruban is spoken before noon each day. He was invited to a convention of Orisha-Vodum priests at Ile-Ife, Nigeria, in 1981, and on June 5 was coronated by the King of Ife.

Yoruba Religion is considered to be the "rain forest version of the Ancient Egyptian Mystery System." It is the source for Afro-Cuban Santeria, but makes no attempt to equate its gods with Christian saints. The system is headed by Olorun, a universal energy without anthropomorphic characteristics. Olodumare, equated with Ifa, the god of destiny and divination, sets a destiny for everything in nature. It is Orishanla (Obatala)—the creator god who created the solid land mass and also the first earthlings. The pantheon also includes Eshu-Elegba, God of Luck, and the personification of the unpredictable element in life; Ogun, God of Iron—the violent element in life; Oshoun/osun/, Goddess of Sex and Beauty—the sensuous element in life; Shango, God of Lightening and Thunder—the political element in life. Practices of the Yoruba system include animal sacrifice, polygamy, ecstatic dancing, and the appeasement of the gods by various offerings. Worship centers upon the veneration of the deities. Worship is also directed toward ancestors, the closest level of spiritual forces to indviduals.

Membership: In 1995 there were 51 residents of Oyotunji. In 1995 there were 55 affiliated centers in the United States and a reported 10,000 members.

Educational Facilities: African Theological Archministry, Sheldon, South Carolina.
Yoruba Theological Archministry, Brooklyn, New York.

Remarks: King Efuntola had become a leader in the African Nationalist movement in the 1960s. Since moving to South Carolina, his village has become a pilgrimage site for many blacks, irrespective of their acceptance of his religious stance.

Sources:

Adefunmi, Baba Oseijeman. *Ancestors of the Afro-Americans.* Long Island City, NY: Aims of Modzawe, 1973.

Adefunmi I, Oba Efuntola Oseijeman Adelabu. *Olorisha, A Guidebook into Yoruba Religion.* Sheldon, SC: The Author, 1982

Canet, Carlos. *Oyotunji.* Miami, FL: Editorial AIP, n.d.

Hunt, Carl M. *Oyotunji Village.* Washington, DC: University Press of America, 1979.

Mason, John. *Ebo Eje (Blood Sacrifice).* New York: Yoruba Theological Archministry, 1981.

___. *Sin Egun (Ancestor Worship).* New York: Yoruba Theological Archministry, 1981.

___. *Usanyin.* New York: Yoruba Theological Archministry, 1983.

___. *Unje Fun Orisa (Food for the Gods).* New York: Yoruba Theological Archministry, 1981.

Odunfonda I Adaramila. *Obatala, The Yoruba God of Creation.* Sheldon, SC: Great Benin Books, n.d.

★1799★
Afro-American Vodoun
Current address not obtained for this edition.

Occasionally, a leader of a voodoo group will allow an outsider (such as a reporter) to gain limited access to their organization. Such a leader was High Priestess Madam Arboo of Afro-American Vodoun. Madam Arboo was active in Harlem in the 1960s as leader of an Afro-American Vodoun group. Born in Georgia, Madam Arboo was reared in voodoo and migrated to New York City. As described in a lengthy article which is the only source of information about her, she described vodoun as an Afro-Christian cult centered on Damballah (the chief voodoo deity), the god of wisdom, personified as a serpent. As high priestess, she is his messenger. Her group differs from Haitian voodoo groups in that it has reduced the remainder of the pantheon to the position of sub-deities or spirits. Damballah is equated with the serpent that Moses elevated in the wilderness (Numbers 21:9).

Healing is a high priority of Vodoun and includes both psychic and psychological counseling and (where permitted) the dispensing of folk remedies such as rattlesnake oil. Worship is held on the evening of the new moon and is centered on ecstatic dance accompanied by flute and drum and led by the papaloi (priest) and mammaloi (priestess). The members, as they dance, enter trance-like states which become occasions for revelations and messages from the spirits. Elements of Christianity survive in the use of spirituals. The threefold way of Vodoun teaches faith, love, and joy as virtues. The pentagram (for females) and the star of David (for males) are major symbols. Animals carry symbolic power: the goat, fertility; the eagle, majesty; the turtle, caution; and the vulture is Damballah's sanitation department.

Membership: No direct contact has been established with Madame Arboo and the current status of her group is uncertain. Vodoun groups exist along the East coast and are organized into gatherings of from 15 to 20 persons.

Sources:

Arboo, Madam, as told to Harold Preece. "What 'Voodoo' Really Is." *Exploring the Unknown* 4, no. 6 (April 1964): 6-19.

★1800★
Chamber of Holy Voodoo
Current address not obtained for this edition.

The Chamber of Holy Voodoo emerged in the 1970s as a semi-public voodoo organization which offers to teach voodoo to students via correspondence. While the specific teachings are revealed only to students, the Chamber offers to introduce those who join to the world of Holy Spirits and to teach them how to invoke them for various purposes. After a basic course, students may prepare themselves for the priesthood and learn the secrets of healing, exorcism and the process of spirit possession. The Chamber also has a special section devoted to dealing with the problems of its members, the Room of Blessing, in which voodoo is used to assist individuals in overcoming obstacles and reaching goals. Marriage counseling is a particular concern.

Membership: Not reported.

★1801★
Church of Lukumi Babalu Aye
℅ Ernesto and Fernando Pichardo
3720 SW 108th Ave.
Miami, FL 33165

The Church of Lukumi Babalu Aye was founded in the early 1970s, and incorporated in 1974 in Miami, Florida, by Ernesto Pichardo, its president, and his brother Fernando Pichardo in an effort to provide a public center for the largely secretive Santeria religion. Santeria has emerged as a significant practice in the Cuban-American community of southern Florida since the arrival of the first refugees from the Cuban Revolution under Fidel Castro. The church existed in relative quiet for many years with its main public appearance being in a class Pichardo conducted at Miami-Dade Community College and in a series of cases in the city courts in which the church defended its members. However, in the mid-1980s, a decision was made to open a Santeria church with public services in the Miami suburb of Hialeah.

Santeria is based upon the worship of the orishas, African deities from the present country of Nigeria, which was brought to the Americas by the many slaves transported to America from the seventeenth to the nineteenth centuries. In the Spanish colonies, such as Cuba, Nigerian religion took on a veneer of Roman Catholicism and many of the orishas identified with Catholic saints, and the resultant New World practice became known as the religion of the saints, i.e., Santeria. Worship in the religion is built around the possession of the priest/priestess and the believer by the orisha. During this time of possession the possessed person will take on the characteristic of the particular divinity. Integral to the worship of the deities, especially on special occasions such as a marriage ceremony, animals are sacrificed. This latter characteristic has made Santeria controversial in an otherwise very tolerant religious environment in Miami, New York, and Los Angeles, the three cities with the largest number of Santeria practitioners.

Shortly after announcing the opening of the church, the city of Hialeah passed four ordinances outlawing ritual animal sacrifice, ostensibly to protect residents from the spread of disease, to prevent cruelty to animals, and to prevent traumatizing any children who might witness the death of an animal. The case became the subject of a court battle that went to the U.S. Supreme Court. In 1993 the court struck down the ordinance.

Membership: Not reported.

Periodicals: *Newsletter.*

Sources:

Resnick, Rosalind. "To One City, It's Cruelty. To Cultists, It's Religion." *National Law Journal* (September 11, 1989).

★1802★
Church of the Seven African Powers
PO Box 453336
Miami, FL 33245

The Church of the Seven African Powers is one of several churches founded during the 1980s through which the largely secretive Santeria community could reach out to the public at large, especially those who had become curious about it and wanted to experience it first hand. The church promotes the worship of the orishas, the African deities whose actions form the heart of the

Santeria faith. The church offers a correspondence course for people wishing to become knowledgeable about the faith. Each lesson contains instructions for ebbos (spells) designed to aid the believer. The church also provides a means for seekers to come to Miami and to experience direct contact with the orishas through meetings with a Santeria priestess or priest.

Membership: Not reported.

★1803★
First Church of Voodoo
Current address not obtained for this edition.

Robert W. Pelton, a free-lance journalist, made an extensive study of voodoo in the early 1970s, traveling around the United States visiting magicians, conjure men and women and voodoo practitioners. His research led to a number of books surveying the topic. He also decided to organize a voodoo church which began meeting in the home of Francis Torrance and Candy Torrance, a voodoo priest and priestess in North Knoxville, who taught a course in voodoo magic at the University of Tennessee evening school. The church was incorporated in Tennessee in 1973. The Church teachings combined elements of voodoo, conjureman (hoodoo), and Christianity. Ordination is available by mail.

Membership: Not reported.

Sources:

Pelton, Robert W. *The Complete Book of Voodoo.* New York: G. P. Putnam's Sons, 1972.

___. *Voodoo Charms and Talismans.* New York: Drake Publishers, 1973.

___. *Voodoo Secrets from A to Z.* South Brunswick, NJ: A. S. Barnes and Company, 1973.

___. *Voodoo Signs and Omens.* South Brunswick, NJ: A. S. Barnes and Company, 1974.

★1804★
Religious Order of Witchcraft
(Defunct)

The Religious Order of Witchcraft was incorporated in 1972 in New Orleans, Louisiana, by Mary Oneida Toups, its high priestess. A housewife and mother, she began her magical career in 1969 in a Kabbalistic system. In 1970 she opened the Witches' Workshop (now the Witchcraft Shop), a magick/witchcraft/voodoo shop in the city. She continued her study in the ritual magick systems of Aleister Crowley and Israel Regardie and, in 1971, reached the point of mystical communion with her holy guardian angel. That communion led to the founding of the order. According to her textbook, *Magick, High and Low*, the order was focused in Kabbalistic magick with a strong emphasis on astrology, Egyptian mythology, and the Tarot. The members venerated the "God of the Witches" popularly known as the Goat of Mendes. They did not worship it, but rather what it symbolized: the magical light of universal intelligence always available to people when they learn how to use it, the belief that sacrifice must come before complete illumination, the balance between justice and mercy, eternal life, and the dual masculine-feminine nature of the body, among other things. Following her death, the Order disbanded. The Witchcraft Shop she operated in New Orleans continues under new management.

Sources:

Troups, Oneida. *Magick, High and Low.* Jefferson, LA: Hope Publications, 1975.

Satanism

★1805★
Brotherhood of the Ram
(Defunct)

Operating from the early 1960s into the 1970s, the Brotherhood of the Ram established a bookstore in Los Angeles. Satan was to this group a god of joy and pleasure. Some traditional aspects of Satanism, such as the "pact," were accepted. Members made a pact with Satan renouncing all other devotion and their Christian baptism, and then signed the pact with their own blood. Membership was confined to Southern California. As of the 1980s the store has been closed and the group reportedly disbanded.

★1806★
Church of Satan
Box 210666
San Francisco, CA 94121

One story repeated continually in the media through the 1970's was how Anton LaVey (1930-1997) shaved his head on Walpurgisnacht (April 30) in 1966, proclaimed the beginning of the Satanic era, and launched the Church of Satan. LaVey became a media event and the object of both features and front page newspaper articles. His early fame came from news coverage of such events as a Satanic funeral service for a Navy man killed in an accident at Treasure Island Navy Base, worship with a nude woman on the altar in his black house in San Francisco, the revelation of actress Jayne Mansfield's association with the church, and a bit part for LaVey in the movie "Rosemary's Baby" (as the Devil).

LaVey had been a former animal trainer and carnival organist. While with the carnival, he became intrigued by the psychic and gained a reputation as a ghosthunter. LaVey was the author of three books—*The Satanic Bible*, *The Satanic Rituals*, and *The Compleat Witch* released in 1989 as *The Satanic Witch*. Each contains the teachings of the Satanic Church.

The basic themes of LaVey's brand of Satanism are self-assertion, antiestablishmentarianism, and the gratification of man's physical or mental nature. Satan is a Promethean figure, representing indulgence, vital existence, undefiled wisdom, kindness to the deserving, vengeance, responsibility to the responsible, the notion that man is just another animal, and so-called sins which lead to physical or mental gratification. It is LaVey's opinion that Satan represents the source of these values. Rituals are conceived both as psychodramas and as magical acts that focus psychokinetic force, as in the ritual magick tradition.

Satanic philosophy is very close to the teachings of Aleister Crowley in *The Book of the Law*. Each person is seen as living according to his own set of rules. However, the Church of Satan opposes illegal acts at variance with laws established for the common good. Sex is viewed as the strongest instinct (next to self preservation) and natural. Drugs are viewed as escapist and contrary to the realistic view of life as preached by the church.

Ritually, the church celebrates three main holidays. For individuals, the most important day is their birthday. For the group, Walpurgisnacht and Halloween are the major days. Both have sexual implications as the spring rebirth of nature and the harvest festivals. Baptism is a ceremony of glorification of the one baptized. There are various rituals for different magical and celebratory purposes. The Enochian language, which first appeared in print in 1659 in a biography of John Dee (and was later used by the Hermetic Order of the Golden Dawn) is employed in rituals. The text used for the traditional Black Mass ritual, "Le Messe Noir," is found in *The Satanic Rituals* (published in 1972). As performed by the church, it is meant to be not simply a blasphemous pageant against the Catholic church, but a purging ritual, making full use of psychodrama to rid individuals of the influence of any sacred cow.

Operating from the San Francisco headquarters, the Satanic Church spread to urban centers across the United States, surfacing in Miami, Florida; New Orleans, Louisiana; New York City; and throughout the Midwest. By 1977, one spokesperson claimed more than 10,000 members for the church (lifetime membership is available for a $100.00 donation). In the mid-1970s, administratively centralized grottos were deemed counterproductive and were disbanded. A more cabalistic underground structure was instituted and continues today. Over the years, groups have emerged which use LaVeyan ritual and philosophy, but which may or may not give LaVey credit or be affiliated in any way with the Church of Satan.

Lavey died in 1997, Blanche Barton has succeeded him as the Church's administrative head.

Membership: Not reported. Church membership statistics are considered confidential. Church membership is granted for life to new members, and there is no count on active members (estimated to be several thousand). Internationally, the church reports concentrations of members in England, Holland, and Sweden. *The Satanic Bible* has recently been translated into Danish, Swedish, and Spanish.

Periodicals: *The Black Flame* (officially endorsed). Send orders to PO Box 499, Radio City Station, New York, NY 10101-0499. • *The Cloven Hoof*, Send orders to Box 210666, San Francisco, CA 94121.

Sources:

Alfred, Randall H. "The Church of Satan." In *The New Religious Consciousness*, Edited by Charles Y. Glock and Robert N. Bellah. Berkeley and Los Angeles: University of California Press, 1976.

Harrington, Walt. "The Devil in Anton LaVey." *The Washington Post Magazine* (February 23, 1986): 6-17.

LaVey, Anton Szandor. *The Compleat Witch*. New York: Lancer Books, 1971.

___. *The Satanic Bible*. New York: Avon, 1969.

___. *The Satanic Rituals*. Secaucus, NJ: University Books, 1972.

Wolff, Burton H. *The Devil's Avenger*. New York: Pyramid Books, 1974.

★1807★
Church of Satanic Brotherhood
(Defunct)

In the early 1970s, controversy began to develop among the Midwestern grottoes of the Church of Satan. Among those involved were Wayne West of Detroit and John de Haven of Dayton, Ohio. The dissolution of the Stygian Grotto of the Dayton area of the Church of Satan occurred on February 11, 1973. Anton LaVey had revoked the grotto's charter, accusing it of "having been acting in violation of the law." With members from Ohio, Indiana, and Michigan, the Church of Satanic Brotherhood was formed in March 1973 by John de Haven, Joseph Daniels, Ronald E. Lanting, and Harry L. Booth.

The church followed the practices of the Church of Satan with several exceptions that grew out of the controversy. Only those people who "can get along with others" were allowed in the Brotherhood. *The Satanic Rituals* by LaVey was viewed as a collection of butchered rites as used in their original form at the Central Grotto. An intense polemic against LaVey was launched.

After its founding, the Brotherhood spread rapidly. Grottoes were established in St. Petersburg, Florida; Dayton-Centerville, Ohio; Indianapolis, Indiana; Louisville, Kentucky; New York City; and Columbus, Ohio. A Council of the Churches was headed by the bishops (fourth degree). The priesthood made up its third degree. Each grotto was headed by a magister. A periodical, *The True Grimoire*, was published monthly.

The Church of Satanic Brotherhood lasted only a short period. In 1974 John de Haven publically renounced Satanism and pro-

claimed his conversion to Christianity. He made his announcement in the midst of a gathering of the Church in St. Petersburg during which he smashed many of the altar implements.

★1808★
Luciferian Light Group
PO Box 7207
Tampa, FL 33673

The Luciferian Light Group is an organization founded in the early 1990s that is dedicated to bringing forth the ancient teachings of Lucifer and hastening the establishment of the Satanic Empire. The order is organized as a secret society with an inner circle that is called the Church of Luciferian Light.

Membership: Not reported.

Periodicals: *Onslaught*.

★1809★
Order of Dionysus/Sabazios
Box 711
Lakewood, OH 44107

The Order of Dionysus/Sabazios was founded in 1990 as the Church of Satanic Youthfulness by Joseph E. Aufricht. Originally enjoying a good relationship with the Church of Satan, whose perspective inspired Aufricht to start his separate work, the two groups have pulled apart over various disagreements on specific teachings.

The order is essentially atheistic in belief but allows a belief in the existence of spiritual entities by members. Aufricht has argued that if a supreme creator exists, the creator would be responsible for both good and evil. God would have created Satan with the ability to rebel, and being all-knowing, would have known that Satan would rebel. Aufricht believes the basic philosophy of the Christian Bible to be mere myth written by very fallible human beings for the purpose of controlling the masses in one form or another. The order stands staunchly against forms of social control and for the destruction of Christianity and other forms of spirituality.

The order basically follows the teachings presented by Anton LaVey, the founder of the Church of Satan, in his various books and writings. It differs primarily in its advocacy of the rights of teenagers, who currently exist in a state of "slavery" from parents and other authorities, according to the order. The order believes that teens are essentially adults and should be so treated. Members of the order assert that teenagers should have the same freedom of choice, especially in matters of sexuality, as legal adults and fight for legal changes that will allow such freedom to become operative. Included in the freedoms the order advocates is the freedom of teenagers to engage in sexual relationships with adults.

Membership: Not reported.

Periodicals: *Rejuvenation*.

★1810★
Order of the Black Ram
Current address not obtained for this edition.

The Order of the Black Ram is a Satanic organization based on the belief in Aryan racial superiority and closely associated with the National Renaissance Party, a neo-Nazi organization. Adherents believe that each race is the embodiment of a racial soul which is expressed in its culture and philosophy. Individuality is stressed. The Order of the Black Ram is eclectic, drawing on the writings of Anton LaVey (founder of the Church of Satan); Robert Heinlein's novel, *Stranger in a Strange Land*; and Neo-Paganism. It was headquartered in suburban Detroit, Michigan, where its grand magister, the Reverend Seth-Klippoth, resided. *Liber Venifica* was an irregular periodical.

★1811★
Ordo Templi Satanas
(Defunct)

Closely associated with the Church of Satanic Brotherhood was the Ordo Templi Satanas (OTS). Some OTS members were former members of the Brotherhood. Practices, beliefs, and organization are similar. There were two temples of the OTS, one in Indianapolis, Indiana, and one in Louisville, Kentucky (headed by Clifford Amos). Leader of the OTS was Joseph Daniels, known as Apollonius, priest of Hermopolis. He was also one of the founders of the Brotherhood. This miniscule group disbanded after a few years.

★1812★
Our Lady of Endor Coven
(Defunct)

Existing for many years prior to the establishment of the Church of Satan was Our Lady of Endor Coven, the Ophite Cultus Satanas, founded by Herbert Arthur Sloane of Toledo, Ohio, in 1948. Satanas (the Horned God) appeared to him first when Sloane was a child. Later, Sloane saw him as the figure pictured on the dust jacket of Margaret Murray's *The God of the Witches*. (Murray is discussed in the introductory material to this volume.) The Lord Satanas appeared again when Sloane was twenty-five years old.

The system of Our Lady of Endor Coven was based heavily on Gnosticism; *The Gnostic Religion* by Hans Jonas was a highly recommended book. The Christian God, the creator, was identified with the Gnostic Demiurge. The Demiurge is the God beyond the creator God, an emanation of the transcendent God. Satanas is the messenger of the remote God who brought Eve the knowledge that there was a God beyond the God who created the cosmos. The God beyond takes no part of "this world," except as he is concerned with the return of his spirit, now entrapped in matter as the divine within humanity. The return of the divine within humanity to the God beyond is accomplished through Gnosis, occult knowledge which people can attain.

Satanism was believed to be the oldest religion, dating to the worship of the Horned God found in the prehistoric cave paintings in Europe. It differs from witchcraft in not turning the Horned God into a fertility god and thus retaining his spiritual significance. Organization followed a pattern similar to witchcraft, covens being the prime structure. The organization was headed by a priest but has no extra-coven structure.

There was but one coven led by Sloane. It dissolved after his death in the early 1980s.

Remarks: For a brief period of time Sloane was a member of the Church of Satan, but his membership did not visibly alter the coven he led.

★1813★
Temple of Set
PO Box 470307
San Francisco, CA 94147

The Temple of Set was founded in 1975 by members of the international priesthood of the Church of Satan who had resigned from that institution because of what they considered to be its over commercialism. A senior initiate, Michael A. Aquino, invoked the Prince of Darkness in quest of a new mandate to preserve and enhance the more noble concepts which the Church of Satan had conceived. The mandate was given in the form of *The Book of Coming Forth by Night*, a statement by that entity, in his most ancient semblance as Set. Set ordained the Temple of Set to succeed the Church of Satan. The temple describes itself as an initiatory institution dedicated to Set, an ancient Egyptian deity, the corrupted legends of whom became the basis for the Christian Satan.

Temple initiates do not consider Set an evil figure, nor do they consider the temple merely a refutation of conventional religion. According to temple philosophy, the universe is a nonconscious

environment possessed of mechanical consistency. In contrast to the universe, and occasionally violating its laws, is Set. Set has, over a period of millennia, altered the genetic makeup of humans in order to create a species possessing an enhanced, nonnatural intelligence. The techniques and teachings of the temple are designed to identify and develop this higher evolutionary potential in appropriate individuals.

The temple is governed by the Council of Nine, which appoints the high priest of Set and the executive director. There are six initiatory degrees: Setian, Adept, Priest(ess) of Set, Master of the Temple, Magus, and Ipsissimus. The program is designed principally for individuals, although there are local Pylons of the Temple in several parts of the United States. International conclaves for the entire temple are held annually. The temple provides an annotated reading list containing material on a wide range of occult, scientific, and religious subjects. Topics covered include ancient Egypt, historical and contemporary occultism, psychology, ethics, and experimental science.

Membership: In 1997 the temple had approximately 500 members.

Periodicals: *Scroll of Set*.

Remarks: Among those who joined in the founding of the Temple of Set was Lilith Sinclair, leader of what had been known as the Spottswood (New Jersey) Grotto of the Church of Satan, the largest group of its kind on the East Coast.

Sources:

Aquino, Michael A. *The Crystal Tablet of Set*. San Francisco, VA: Temple of Set, 1985.

———. *Temple of Set Reading List XIX*. San Francisco, CA: Temple of Set, 1984.

Scott, Gini Graham. *The Magicians*. New York: Irvington Publishers, 1983.

★1814★
Thee Satanic Church
(Defunct)

In 1974 Thee Satanic Church of the Nethilum Rite divided, and a second organization was established by Dr. Evelyn Paglini, one of the original cofounders. Its belief and structure were identical to those of the parent church. The Satanic Church opened a book and occult supply store in a Chicago suburb and Paglini began an occult periodical, *Psychic Standard*, which did not carry any Satanic material. Paglini's group slowly dropped their Satanic trappings. In one of their last public actions, they gathered at Comiskey Park prior to a Chicago White Sox baseball game to do a magical ritual to aid the faltering team.

The *Psychic Standard* ceased publication in 1980. Shortly after that time Paglini moved away from Chicago.

★1815★
Thee Satanic Orthodox Church of Nethilum Rite
(Defunct)

Centered in Chicago was Thee Satanic Orthodox Church of Nethilum Rite headed by High Priest Terry Taylor. Headquarters were at the Occult Book Shop in Chicago. The Church went public in 1971. It was opposed to the Satanism of Anton LaVey and the Church of Satan. Members believed in God as the creator of the universe and in Satan as the creature of God. Satan is the apex of creation who possesses all the power and knowledge of the universe. Members tried to acquire as much of Satan's knowledge and power as possible. This acquisition was to be achieved through magical rituals and psychic development and through the elders, described as an "international group of high ministers in the private end of Thee Satanic Church." The Church disappeared in the mid-1970s.

Only one center, in Chicago, was ever established. It claimed 538 members in 1973. Weekly Saturday night meetings were held including songs, prayers, a ritualistic mass, and introduction of new members. Recruitment was through evening public discussion sessions, the store, and classes given by Taylor.

Section 21

Middle Eastern Family, Part I: Judiaism

Consult the Contents pages to locate the essay in Part II, Historical Essay Chapters,
that provides an historical discussion of this family

Intrafaith Organizations

★1816★

American Association of Rabbis
350 Fifth Ave., Ste. 3304
New York, NY 10118

The American Association of Rabbis is a professional organization of rabbis who minister either in a congregation, an educational setting, or the chaplaincy.

Periodicals: *Quarterly Bulletin.*

★1817★

International Federation of Secular Humanistic Jews
28611 W. Twelve Mile Rd.
Farmington Hills, MI 48334

The International Federation of Secular Humanistic Jews is a worldwide organization that was established in 1986 in Detroit, Michigan, to offer a non-theistic approach to Jewish identity and culture. It exists as a distinct alternative to Orthodox, Conservative, Reform, and Reconstructionist Judaism. The organization exists through its regional structures (North America, Latin America, Europe, and Israel) and its national branches currently located in Argentina, Australia, Belgium, Canada, France, Great Britain, Israel, the United States, and Uruguay. The North American region consists of two organizations, the Society for Humanistic Judaism and the Congress of Secular Jewish Organizations.

The International Federation is headed by its president Yehuda Bauer, a historian and Holocaust scholar at the Hebrew University in Jerusalem. Serving as honorary president is Albert Memmi, a sociologist at the University of Paris. The federation supports the International Institute for Secular Humanistic Judaism, an intellectual and training center in Jerusalem.

The federation has affirmed its belief in the value of human reason, human existence and the power of human beings to solve their problems, Jewish identity and the survival of the Jewish people, and a secular humanistic democracy for Israel.

Membership: As of 1995 there were 9 national branches with a constituency of 30,000 people, approximately half of whom live in the United States.

★1818★

New York Board of Rabbis
10 E. 73rd St.
New York, NY 10021

The New York Board of Rabbis, founded in 1881, is the largest interdenominational rabbinic body in the world. The board consists of over 800 rabbis—Orthodox, Conservative, Reform, and Reconstructionist—who serve 1.5 million congregants. The Board furnishes chaplains for city, county, and state hospitals; nursing homes; and mental health and correctional institutions. It is involved in interfaith and interethnic dialogues with clergy of various faiths. It lobbies on behalf of Jewish religious interests on the city, county, and state levels. For example, it has called for kosher food to be served at public functions within the Jewish community; insisted on proper Jewish rites at funerals; enrolled rabbis to urge the issuance of a Get and the signing of a prenuptial agreement to obtain a Get; lobbied for Kashrut standards in public institutions and correctional facilities including the distribution of Passover food and religious articles for patients and inmates; moved to protect the rights of Sabbath observers; prevented the administering of exams in the public universities on the Sabbath and holidays; prevented the County Medical Examiner from forcing delays in burial. The Brith Milah Board, an affiliate of the New York Board of Rabbis, certifies Mohalim who satisfy halakic and medical requirements.

The board conducts television and radio programs and helps maintain the international synagogue at Kennedy Airport. In short, the New York Board of Rabbis is the voice of mainstream religious Jewry in the metropolitan area. For over 117 years, these accomplishments have come about by virtue of rabbis transcending their theological and religious differences and working together in mutual respect and understanding for the advancement of Jewish observance, education, and values.

Membership: In 1997, the board reported 810 members in the United states and 40 in Canada.

Periodicals: *Bulletin.*

Sources:

Rosenthal, Gilbert S. *Come Let Us Reason Together.* New York: New York Board of Rabbis, n.d. 27 pp.

Teplitz, Saul I. *The Rabbis Speak: A Quarter Century of Sermons for the High Holy Days.* New York: New York Board of Rabbis, 1986. 474 pp.

★1819★

Synagogue Council of America
327 Lexington Ave.
New York, NY 10016

The Synagogue Council of America was founded in 1926 for the purpose of providing the several branches of Judaism with a common voice and making the synagogue the center of Jewish spiritual influence. In recent years it has served as a coordinating body for several of the rabbinical and congregational associations, especially in speaking to the President of the United States and members of Congress.

Membership: Members of the council include the Central Conference of American Rabbis (Reform), Rabbinical Assembly (Conservative), Rabbinical Council of America (Orthodox), Union of American Hebrew Congregations (Reform), Union of Orthodox Jewish Congregations of America, and United Synagogues of America (Conservative).

Sources:

Rosenthal, Gilbert S. *Contemporary Judaism: Patterns of Survival.* 2nd ed. New York: Human Sciences Press, 1986.

Mainline Judaism

★1820★
American Sephardi Association
8 W. 40th St.
New York, NY 10018

The Jewish community is usually seen as divided into two main segments, the Ashkenazi and the Sephardi. The Ashkenazi refers to that branch of the community that derived from the Jewish communities of northern and eastern Europe, and in America, the Ashkenazi form, by far, the larger segment of the community at more than 90 percent. The Sephardi are those Jews who come, broadly speaking, from the lands of the Mediterranean and Western Asia. More narrowly the Sephardi are those Jews who derive from the prominent community of medieval Spain and Portugal. That community was disbursed in the 1490s and many left Iberia for the Americas and the eastern Mediterranean. The Sephardi differ form the Ashkenazi primarily on matters of culture. They have developed a distinctive culture in Spain, and have various differences in their Sabbath and high holydays liturgy.

Sephardi from Brazil were largely responsible for the founding of the Jewish community in what is now the United States. They had emerged at Recife during the period of the Dutch occupancy of that city, but were forced to flee when Portugal regained control. The initial group arrived in New York (then New Amsterdam) in 1654 and went on to establish the first synagogue, Shearith Israel. Shortly thereafter, other participants in the same migration founded the first Canadian synagogue, in Montreal. Subsequently, synagogues were opened in Philadelphia, Newport (Rhode Island), Savannah, and Charleston. At the time of the American Revolution (1775-83), the Sephardi constituted about half of the Jewish community, but were completely overwhelmed after the first wave of German Jews began to arrive following the fall of Napoleon. After the arrival of the massive numbers of Eastern European Jews in the 1880s, the Sephardi became an almost invisible minority.

Attempts to organize the Sephardic community in America began soon after the turn of the century; the earliest seem to have been in the New York area, a single urban area with several Sephardic synagogues. As early as 1912 the Federation of Oriental Jews was founded by the synagogues in New York, Montreal, and Philadelphia. It fell apart in 1918. Other attempts were made over the years, but it was not until 1972, with the founding of the American Sephardi Federation, that a permanent organization was effected. It drew strength from many immigrants of the Jewish communities of North Africa, Egypt, Lebanon, Iraq, and Iran, in particular. While many Sephardi have joined Ashkenazi congregations, many have formed their own congregations, a few nationally specific, and affiliated through the American Sephardi Federation.

Membership: As of the late 1980s, there were an estimated 150,000 Sephardic Jews in the United States, the largest percentage of which (60,000) live in the New York City area. There are organized Sephardic synagogues in 21 communities in all sections of the United States.

Periodicals: *Sephardic Connection.*

Sources:

Elazar, Daniel J. *The Other Jews: The Sephardim Today.* New York: Basic Books, 1989. 236 pp.

★1821★
Association of American Orthodox Hebrew Congregations
(Defunct)

The Association of American Hebrew Congregations was an early attempt to organize Orthodox Jewish synagogues. It was founded in 1887 by lay leaders in some 15 congregations. They advertised in Europe for a rabbi to come to America and serve as a Chief Rabbi. Jacob Joseph of Vilna came over the next year. His task was to supervise the congregations, establish a Beth Din (Jewish court), see to the proper observance of dietary regulations in the preparation of kosher food, and administer the religious schools.

Chief Rabbi Joseph met fierce opposition from other rabbis (none of whom were consulted by the association earlier) and people displaced by the attempt to establish kosher regulations. He died in 1902, by which time the association had been abandoned and new structures of a more permanent nature arose.

Sources:

Rosenthal, Gilbert S. *Contemporary Judaism: Patterns of Survival.* New York: Human Sciences Press, 1986.

★1822★
Congregation Bina
600 West End Ave., Ste. 1C
New York, NY 10024

Congregation Bina was founded in 1981 as a fellowship for Jews who had migrated to the United States from India. When Europeans began to invade India in numbers in the nineteenth century, they became aware of the existence of a small community, some 25,000 people who claimed that they were Jews, and who traced their existence to the 10 lost tribes of Israel and called themselves Bene Israel, Children of Israel. They traced their origin to the second century B.C.E. when they were shipwrecked off the coast of India near Bombay. Only seven families survived and they were cut off from their fellow religionists for many centuries. Another small group was discovered in southwest India centered upon the town of Cochin.

According to the accounts of Bene Israel historians, the survivors of the shipwreck lost their religious records and soon lost the Hebrew language which they replaced with Marathi, a west India language. However, they retained the Sabbath, the practice of the Holy Days, the dietary regulations, circumcision, and the Shema (the confession of the Jewish faith). Other historians have suggested that the Bene Israel arrived in India much later by way of Arabia or Yemen.

The Bene Israel seemed to have survived by becoming a separate caste within the complex caste system of India. They experienced a religious revival in the early 1800s when Christian missionaries, motivated by possible conversion of the Bene Israel to Christianity, translated the Bible into Marathi, created a Hebrew-Marathi grammar, and even hired members of the community to teach in their schools. However, few accepted Christianity and the missionary efforts contributed more to the establishment of contacts between the Indian Jews and their fellow believers in Europe. European and American publications began to flow into India.

The Bene Israel were scattered throughout India until the modern era and they did not erect a synagogue until 1796 in Bombay. However, there are no rabbis; worship is in the hands of the membership.

In the years since the independence of India and the emergence of the state of Israel, the community in India has been decimated by migration. While most have gone to Israel, during the 1970s a small number came to the United States. Thus in 1981 the Bene Israel in the United States came together and founded Congregation Bina. They seek to preserve the customs, liturgy, music, and folklore of the Indian Jewish community. The group is currently headed by Joseph Moses, its president.

Membership: In 1994 Congregation Bina reported 90 members in one synagogue in New York City.

Periodicals: *Kol Bina.*

Sources:

Strizower, Schifra. *The Bene Israel of Bombay.* New York: Schrocken Books, 1971. 176 pp.

★1823★
Conservative Judaism
% The United Synagogue of Conservative Judaism
155 Fifth Avenue
New York, NY 10010

Alternate Address: The Rabbinical Assembly, 3080 Broadway, New York, NY 10027.

As Reform and Orthodox polemics began to polarize the Jewish community, there arose a middle group that advocated an allegiance to traditional Judaism, but without strict attention to all the Orthodox ways. In 1887, drawn together by an affront to tradition accompanying the graduation of the first class at Hebrew Union College, the Reform college located in Cincinnati, Ohio, Rabbi Sabato Morais, Marcus Jastrow, and Henry Pereira Mendes formed a Jewish Theological Seminary Association to counteract the effects of the liberalizing Reform movement.

Not a strong movement at this time, Conservative Judaism nevertheless found champions in Cyrus Adler and Rabbi Solomon Schechter. The two revived the faltering Jewish Theological Seminary in the first decade of the twentieth century, and Schechter became the mainstay of a Judaism that respected tradition but was saturated with contemporary scholarship. The Conservative synagogue uses English as well as Hebrew, does not separate men and women, and emphasizes modern education. However, many Orthodox practices, such as covered heads during worship are retained.

The Jewish Theological Seminary in New York and Los Angeles remains the educational center of Conservatism. In 1913, Schechter pulled together the United Synagogue of America now the United Synagogue of Conservative Judaism which serves as the association of Conservative congregations in North America. The Rabbinical Assembly, a association of Conservative rabbis, was founded six years later.

The United Synagogue is an association of congregations that accepts the Standards for Congregational Practice. A delegated convention meets biennially and elects the national officers and a board of directors. Congregations are grouped into 20 regions each served by a regional office. National departments of education, youth activities, extension activities, and leadership development, among others, provide guidance and materials for the congregations. Internationally the Conservative movement finds expression through the World Council of Conservative/Masorti Congregations. The United Synagogue operates the Center for Conservative Judaism in Jerusalem.

During the twentieth century, the Conservative movement found favor in Canada among the older congregations just as massive waves of Russian and Eastern European migration (primarily Orthodox in makeup) were remaking the Jewish community. By 1960 more than 20 congregations had affiliated with the United Synagogue. That number almost doubled over the next two decades.

Membership: In 1995 there were approximately 800 Conservative congregations and 1,500,000 affiliated members in North America.

Educational Facilities: Jewish Theological Seminary, New York, New York and Los Angeles, California.

Periodicals: *United Synagogue Review,* c/o The United Synagogue, 155 Fifth Avenue, New York, NY 10010. • *Conservative Judaism.* Send orders to 3080 Broadway, New York, NY 10027.

Sources:

Davis, Moshe. *The Emergence of Conservative Judaism.* Philadelphia: Jewish Publication Society of America, 1963.

Karp, Abraham J. *A History of the United Synagogue of America, 1913-1963.* New York: United Synagogue of America, 1964.

Sklare, Marshall. *Conservative Judaism.* Glencoe, IL: Free Press, 1955.

★1824★
Jewish Reconstructionist Federation
Church Rd. & Greenwood Ave.
Wyncote, PA 19095

During the years following World War I, the Jewish community became prosperous and diffuse. In recognition of the not strictly religious nature of much of what was commonly labeled Judaism, conservative scholar Mordecai M. Kaplan proposed in the 1930s a new approach to Judaism, one which would take account of its diverse nature. In his *Judaism as a Civilization* (1934), he argued that Judaism was more than a religion, it was an evolving religious civilization. He called for a reconstruction of Judaism not around the synagogue but the community as a whole. Jewish civilization would unite Reform, Conservative and Orthodox religion, Zionism and various other Jewish interests.

The ideas of Kaplan appealed especially to nonorthodox Jews who were nonetheless attached to "Jewishness." Thus was founded the Reconstructionist movement, and in 1935 Kaplan began a periodical, *The Reconstructionist,* to propagate his ideas within Conservative Judaism. Kaplan's approach to tradition, his rejection of the divine origin of the Torah and his reevaluation of ritual in light of modern thought, however, proved a constant source of discord, and Kaplan and the Conservatives slowly drifted apart. The Orthodox were so annoyed with him that, in 1945 (after he published a revised prayer book), he was excommunicated. The excommunication was in turn attacked by the Conservative and Reform leadership.

The Reconstructionist Movement took organizational form in 1940 with the founding of the Jewish Reconstructionist Foundation. Reconstructionist congregations appeared, and in 1954 the Federation of Reconstructionist Congregations and Havurot was founded to coordinate the activities of the various centers. In 1968 a rabbinical college was established and more recently the Reconstructionist Rabbinical Association has formed. Formally known as the Federation of Reconstructionist Congregational and Harvurot, its current name was adopted in 1996.

Membership: In 1997 the federation reported 50,000 members, 90 congregations, and 220 rabbis in the United States, and 1,000 members, two congregations, and five rabbis in Canada.

Educational Facilities: Reconstructionist Rabbinical College, Wyncote, Pennsylvania.

Periodicals: *The Reconstructionist.* • *Raayonot.*

Sources:

Cohen, Jack J. *The Case for Religious Humanism.* New York: Reconstructionist Press, 1958.

Kaplan, Mordecai M. *Basic Values in Jewish Religion.* New York: Reconstructionist Press, 1948.

___. *The Future of the American Jew.* New York: Macmillan Company, 1949.

___. *The Meaning of God in Modern Jewish Religion.* New York: Reconstructionist Press, 1962.

Kohn, Eugene. *Religious Humanism.* New York: Reconstructionist Press, 1953.

★1825★
K'hal Adath Jeshurun
90 Bennett Ave.
New York, NY 10033

K'Hal Adath Jeshurun is an outpost of German Orthodox Judaism in the United States. In the 1880s, Solomon Breuer (1850–1926) had emerged as a staunch defender of Orthodoxy in Frankfort and in 1888 founded the Verbund orthodoxer Rabbiner (Association of Orthodox Rabbis) in Germany, frequently cited as an ultra-Orthodox group in that it refused membership to those Orthodox rabbis who cooperated with Reform Jewish rabbis on work for the Jewish community. Breuer was the son-in-law of S. R. Hirsh, a great Orthodox leader who had defined what was later called neo-Orthodoxy, a combination of extreme Orthodox Jewish belief combined with an openness to the modern world and culture on secular matters.

In 1926 Breuer was succeeded as head of the congregation in Frankfort by his son Joseph Breuer (1882–19??). In 1939, on the eve of World War II, Joseph Breuer migrated to the United States and became the spiritual leader of K'hal Adath Jeshurun. He saw himself as carrying on the work of his father in America. In 1944 he established a school, Yeshiva Rabbi Sampson Raphael Hirsh, named for a nineteenth-century German Orthodox leader, who also happened to be his maternal grandfather. The school followed the pattern he had learned in Germany.

Breuer emerged as a respected rabbi, if one seen as somewhat on the extreme side of the Orthodox community. He authored a number of books in both English and Hebrew. On his 80th birthday, he received a jubilee volume compiled in his honor.

Membership: Not reported.

★1826★
National Council of Young Israel
3 W. 16th St.
New York, NY 10011

The Young Israel movement began in 1912 at the Jewish Theological Seminary, the school serving Conservative Judaism. It was started by two professors, Israel Freidlander and Mordecai M. Kaplan (later to develop Reconstructionism), and Rabbi Judah Magnes. The movement attempted to unite Orthodox Jewish youth of Manhattan's lower east side. It developed an English language program and a supplementary program not generally available in other Orthodox centers. As the Conservative movement emerged and as the seminary became identified with it, in 1922 the Orthodox leadership of Young Israel repudiated conservatism, but found that this practice did not fit well with other Orthodox groups.

Young Israel emerged as a powerful adult movement over the next decade. The group incorporated in 1926. Within a few years it expanded through the Jewish community in America and entered Canada. In 1939 it reported 35 affiliated synagogues and by 1971 had reached 100. A variety of organizations have been created to carry out its program. The American Friends of Young Israel in Israel promotes the formation of Young Israel synagogues in Israel. An Armed Forces Bureau counsels Orthodox Jews in the armed forces in regard to sabbath and dietary behavior. The Mesilah Institute for Jewish Studies promotes Jewish education at all age levels. Young Israel Youth and Tong Israel Collegiates and Young Adults are age-specific programs for young people.

Beginning at the more liberal end of Orthodoxy, Young Israel has with age become more conservative. It calls for attention to Sabbath laws, separates men and women in worship services, and attacks non-Orthodox Jews. It has become staunchly pro-Zionist.

Membership: In 1994 there were more than 200 Young Israel congregations worldwide—United States, Canada, Netherlands, and several South American countries.

Periodicals: *Viewpoint.* • *Divrei Torah Bulletin.* • *CYIR Newsletter.*

Sources:

Rosenthal, Gilbert S. *Contemporary Judaism: Patterns of Survival.* New York: Human Sciences Press, 1986.

"Young Israel—Movement to Synagogue." In Ivan L. Tillem, ed. *The Jewish Directory and Almanac.* New York: Pacific Press, 1984.

★1827★
Neturei Karta of U.S.A.
Box 2143
Brooklyn, NY 11202

The Neturei Karta (Guardians of the City) emerged in 1935 as an ultra-Orthodox faction within the Agudat Israel, a movement that sought to focus Jewish attention on the Holy Land but was opposed to Zionism. Agudat Israel had also been a separatist movement in that it opposed cooperation with non-Orthodox Jews. In the early 1930s there had arisen among members of Agudat Israel residing in the Holy Land the demand for an independent Orthodox Jewish community separated from the "zionist" community. The larger membership of Agudat Israel opposed the demand, thus leading to the split. Those seeking the independent Orthodox community broke away and founded Hevrat ha-Hayyim, which eventually became Neturei Karta. Among the leaders of the breakaway group was Amram Blau (1895–1976).

After World War II, Neturei Karta members opposed the creation of the Jewish state of Israel and Israel's control of Jerusalem. They claimed that the Talmud prohibits cooperation with any state not created by revelation from the heavenly realms. They worked, unsuccessfully, for the internationalization of the city. Today, many among the Neturei Karta refuse to cooperate or even recognize the existence of Israel, which they manifest by refusing to vote, accept an Israeli identity card, or recognize the decisions of Israeli courts.

The Neturei Karta faced a severe test in 1966 when Blau married a convert, Ruth Ben-David, which led to a number of defections. In the meantime members they have established themselves in the United States and found an ally in the Satmar Hasidism, who share their anti-Zionist stance. The Satmar community contributes regularly to the support of the Neturei Karta.

Membership: Not reported.

Periodicals: *The Jewish Guardian.*

★1828★
Orthodox Judaism
Rabbinical Council of America
305 7th Ave.
New York, NY 10001

Alternate Address: Union of Orthodox Jewish Congregations of America, 333 7th Ave., New York, NY 10001.

The earliest divisions in American Judaism were linguistic. They came about as various national groups settled in America. While all professed a similar Old World form of faith, the groups were differentiated by peculiarities of the various national cultures. Orthodox Judaism remains one of the major facets of the American Jewish experience. Orthodox Jews are distinctive within the Jewish community in their Old World practices: strict keeping of the Sabbath, kosher food laws and special attention to tradition, the keeping of the exact forms of their elders. The learning and use of Hebrew is emphasized.

In the process of Americanization (and the demand for English in the service), and with the importation of German-based Reform Judaism, champions of Orthodoxy, such as Rabbi Isaac Leeser of the Mikveh Israel Congregation, arose. Orthodoxy is, in a real sense, an American product, arising as a tradition-affirming segment of Judaism in reaction to the Reform movement. Orthodoxy was also the poorest. The Orthodox scattered into urban centers around the country. Thus Orthodoxy, while continuing the much older traditions of European Judaism, only formalized an organization at the end of the nineteenth century.

Preliminary efforts at cooperative endeavor began among Orthodox adherents in the 1880s, in reaction to Reform activities. In 1898 the Union of Orthodox Jewish Congregations of America was formed. Only two years earlier, the first rabbinical school, the Rabbi Elchanan Theological Seminary (now Yeshiva University) had been established. In 1902, the Union of Orthodox Rabbis was formed by the Eastern European rabbis, who had come to control the congregational association. However, the English-speaking rabbis retained control of the seminary, which grew as the number of English-speaking Orthodox Jews grew, and in 1935, the English-speaking rabbis formed the Rabbinical Council of America.

The Rabbinical Council of America and the Union of Orthodox Jewish Congregations of America have emerged as the primary organizations serving Orthodox Jews in the United States. Following the basic congregation-based organizational life of American Judaism, both rabbis and congregations are free in their associations, and the Union serves congregations whose rabbis are orthodox but not members of the Rabbinical Council.

Prior to the 1880s, Canadian Jewry had been almost totally factions apparent in American Judaism. However, in Canada, the orthodox segment has remained the jamority due to the significant wave of immigration as the turn of the century supplemented by a second wave immediately after World War II, and in spite of the large advances of the conservative movement usually at the expense of Orthodoxy. Many of the Canadian Orthodox congregations are affiliated with the Union of Orthodox Congregations, though may remain independent and unaffiliated with any association.

The Union carries on a far-reaching educational program through numerous publications a Torach Tape Library, and materials for the deaf and developmentally disabled. It operates the National Orthodox Information Center and sponsors the National Conference of Synagogue Youth. Through it OU Kashruth Program it designates products which meet Orthdox standards and are free of items forbidden to Orthodox people. The Union and the rabbinical Council cooperate in support of the Institute of Public Affairs, an advocacy think tank created to represent the American Orthodox Jewish community.

Membership: Not reported. In 1980 there were an estimated 1,000,000 Orthodox Jews in the United States. In 1995, the Union of Orthodox Jewish Congregations reported about 1,000-member congregations.

Educational Facilities: Yeshiva University, New York, New York.
Hebrew Theological College, Chicago, Illinois.
Isaac Elchanan Theological Seminary, New York, New York.
Ner Israel Rabbinical College, Baltimore, Maryland.
Hayin Berlin, New York, New York.

Periodicals: *Jewish Action.* Send orders to 333 7th Ave., New York, NY 10001. • *Tradition.* Send orders to 1250 Broadway, Suite 802, New York, NY 10001.

Sources:

Hapgood, Hutchins. *The Spirit of the Ghetto.* New York: Schocken Books, 1966.

Mayer, Egon. *From Suburb to Shtetl.* Philadelphia: Temple University Press, 1979.

Schwartz, Elkanah. *American Life: Shtetl Style.* New York: Jonathan David, 1967.

★1829★
Reform Judaism
℅ Union of American Hebrew Congregations
838 5th Ave.
New York, NY 10021

Alternate Address: Central Conference of American Rabbis, 21 E. 40th St. New York, NY 10010.

One of the oldest congregations in America was the Sephardic congregation, Beth Elohim, in Charleston. In the 1820s, some of its younger members began to petition for reform. They wanted some English added for those who spoke no Hebrew. Rejected, they withdrew and in 1824 organized the Reform Society of Israelites, led by Isaac Harby. This effort was but the first of many that were to disturb Israel-in-America through the nineteenth century.

Reform was already a powerful movement in Germany, where educated Jews could reconcile their learning and religious heritage only by removing anachronisms and thoroughly modernizing Jewish thought and life. Among American reform congregations, ceremonial laws and many practices such as covering the head during worship were discarded as outdated cultural accretions. An openness to the general religious community was advocated.

The leader around whom the various reform efforts coalesced was Rabbi Isaac M. Wise. The Bohemian-born Wise came to America in 1846 and settled in Albany, New York. Eight years later, he moved to Cincinnati, where his career paralleled the growth in size and status of the German Jewish community. He immediately began to advocate reform. He founded a periodical, *The Israelite*, to oppose the Orthodox periodical *Occident* founded by Isaac Leeser. In 1857 he published his revised prayer book in both Hebrew and German. He began the *Deborah*, a German-language periodical. He traveled extensively around the country, spreading his ideas and organizing synagogues.

In 1875, Wise founded the Union of American Hebrew Congregations with headquarters in Cincinnati. Two years later its education center, Hebrew Union College, was established. In 1889 the rabbinical structure, the Central Conference of American Rabbis, with Wise as president, was formed.

During the nineteenth century, Cincinnati was a center for German Jews. In the twentieth century, New York has become the Jewish center of the United States. The extension of Judaism in New York beyond its meager German Jewish base was reflected in the founding in 1922 of the Jewish Institute of Religion (now the New York Campus of Hebrew Union College) and the movement in 1951 of the Union to headquarters on Fifth Avenue. Reform activities now largely originate out of the building popularly called the "House of Living Judaism."

The first Canadian Reform congregation, Temple Emanu-EL, was formed in Toronto, although in the absence of a community of the reform-minded Germans, it remained alone for many years. By 1950 there were only two Reform congregations in the entire country. A relatively rapid expansion occurred in the next 20 years during which time 10 were added. The Canadian Council of Reform Congregations is affiliated with the Union of American Hebrew Congregations.

Membership: Not reported. In 1980 there were approximately 715 congregations and 1,200,000 affiliated members. In 1980 there were 14 Reform congregations in Canada.

Educational Facilities: Hebrew Union College, Cincinnati, Ohio. (There are HUC campuses in New York, New York; Los Angeles, California; and Jerusalem, Israel.)

Periodicals: *Journal of Reform Judaism.* • *Reform Judaism.*

Sources:

Doppelt, Frederic A., and David Polish. *A Guide for Reform Jews.* The Authors, 1957.

An Intimate Portrait of the Union of American Hebrew Congregations—A Centennial Documentary. Cincinnati: American Jewish Archives, 1973.

Korn, Bertram Wallace. *Retrospect and Prospect.* New York: Central Conference of American Rabbis, 1965.

Marcus, Jacob R. *Israel Jacobson.* Cincinnati, OH: Hebrew Union College Press, 1972.

Plaut, W. Gunther. *The Rise of Reform Judaism.* New York: World Union for Progressive Judaism, 1963.

Reform Judaism. Cincinnati, OH: Hebrew Union College Press, 1949.

★1830★
Union of Orthodox Rabbis in the United States
235 E. Broadway
New York, NY 10002

The organization of Orthodox Judaism occurred very slowly in America as traditionalists came to terms with the strength and persistence of Reform Judaism at the close of the nineteenth century. Various efforts at the municipal level were attempted with more or less success. Finally in 1898 the union of Orthodox congregations was affected. Two years later the Rabbi Elchanan Theological Seminary (now Yeshiva University) was created. Finally, the Union of Orthodox Rabbis in the United States and Canada, the oldest Orthodox rabbinical organization in North America, was founded in 1902.

The union, also known as the Agudat Harabanin, called together Yiddish-speaking rabbis. It rejected the graduates of the Jewish Theological Seminary (the primary school of what was emerging as Conservative Judaism) and backed the Rabbi Isaac Elchanan Theological Seminary. It demanded of its members that they possess the traditional *semikhah*, ritual ordination.

The founders of the Agudat Harabanin were trained in Europe. The American graduates of Rabbi Isaac Elchanan Theological Seminary gradually americanized; that is, they began to lobby for more modern training and understood the need for proficiency in English more than Yiddish. Developing their strength through the school's alumni association in 1938 they organized the Rabbinical Council of America as a rival organization.

Since the founding of the council, the Union of Orthodox Rabbis has slowly declined in strength. It suffered greatly from internal dissension. It had only 600 rabbinical members in 1968, many serving very small synagogues. It opposes formal cooperation between Orthodox and non-Orthodox Jews, and in 1997 issued a declaration declaring that the Reform and Conservative movements were not Judaism but another religion. Orthodox rabbis affiliated with the Rabbinical Council denounced the Unions action.

Membership: Not reported.

Sources:

Rosenthal, Gilbert S. *Contemporary Judaism: Patterns of Survival.* New York: Human Sciences Press, 1986.

★1831★
Union of Sephardic Congregations
8 W. 70 St.
New York, NY 10023

The Sephardic Jews, those Jews who in the centuries of the Jewish diaspora settled in Greece, Spain, and Portugal, and were cast out of Spain and Portugal at the end of the fifteenth century, were among the first to come to the New World. They settled in Portuguese Brazil and from there came to what is now the United States and founded the first synagogues in New York City and Newport, Rhode Island. They were, however, eclipsed by the arrival of the German Jews in the nineteenth century and the Eastern European Jews beginning in the 1880s.

However, during the early years of the twentieth century, until the passing of the new immigration laws in 1924, thousands of Sephardic Jews immigrated to America. Through the centuries the Sephardic Jews had developed a number of cultural distinctives which tended to separate them from their Northern and Eastern European cousins. Thus, in 1928 the Union of Sephardic Congregations was formed for the "promotion of religious interests of Sephardic Jews."

The first major project of the union was the preparation of a prayer book with accurate Hebrew as well as an English translation. David de Sola Pool, rabbi from Shearith Israel, provided the necessary leadership and saw the publication of The *Daily and Sabbath Prayer Book* (1936), followed by books for the High Holy Days and festivals. These have found their way to Sephardic congregations throughout the U.S., Canada, Australia, and other locations around the world.

Membership: There are an estimated 300,000 Sephardic Jews in the United States, of which about 40 percent live in the greater New York City area.

Sources:

Cohen, Martin A., and Abraham J. Peck. *Sephardism in the Americas.* Tuscaloosa, AL: University of Alabama Press, 1993.

Hasidism

★1832★
Bluzhever Hasidism
Belzer Yeshiva
1779 51th
Brooklyn, NY 11213

Shapira is an outstanding Polish Hasidic family by which several dynasties were established in the nineteenth century. One was established at Bluzhever. The present Rebbe in Williamsburg is a descendant of Rabbi Elimelekh Shapira of Dinov. He survived the Holocaust; the American Army arrived at the concentration camp just before he was due to be executed.

Membership: Not reported.

★1833★
Bobov Hasidism
℅ Rabbi Solomon Halberstamm
Yeshiva Bnai Zion
4909 15th St.
Brooklyn, NY 11219

The Halberstamm family has contributed to the formation of several Hasidic groups. The Bobov dynasty was founded in the nineteenth century by Rabbi Benzion Halberstamm. He was a noted composer and his "niggun" (melody), "Yah-Ribbon" ("God of the world"), is still chanted on Sabbath evenings. The Bobov are known for their musical creativity. Under Rabbi Benzion's leadership, Hasidic education spread throughout Galicia in the Carpathian Mountain region of Southern Poland. Rabbi Benzion actively resisted the Nazis and was murdered for his efforts.

Though most of Rabbi Benzion, his family, and his following were wiped out in the Holocaust, Rebbi Sholomo Halberstamm (b. 1905) and his eldest son Naftali escaped and found their way to America. Here, Halberstamm began to gather a new following, many who had no Polish background, which grew steadily as Jewish families came to respect his mild-mannered pastoral approach. He founded a yeshivah which by 1985 had some 3,000 elementary students (many of whose families had no attachment to the Bobov organization) the largest religious school in the Boro Park area of Brooklyn. He also assisted displaced Jews in Europe and built a following in London and Antwerp, as well as gathering members in Canada and Israel. As Reb Sholomo has aged, his son and designated successor has begun to assume some of the responsibilities of maintaining the community he will soon lead.

Membership: By the end of the 1980s, the Bobov had approximately 2,000 families in Brooklyn; 100 families in Canada (Toronto); 400 families in London; more than 100 in Antwerp; and 1,000 families in Israel.

Sources:

Mintz, Jerome R. *Hassidic People: A Place in the New World.* Cambridge, MA: Harvard University Press, 1992. 434pp.

★1834★
Bostoner Hasidism
℅ New England Chasidic Center
1710 Beacon St.
Brookline, MA 02146

The Horowitz family has been a prominent Jewish family for many centuries, producing numerous rabbis. It was frequently divided between those supporting and those opposing Hasidism. Among the first Hasidic rebbes in the United States was Grand Rabbi Pinchas D. Horowitz, who settled in Boston around 1920. He came from that branch of the family which had settled in Jerusalem several generations earlier. The lineage is carried on by descendants, who have centers in Brookline, Massachusetts, and Brooklyn, New York. The Brookline center has become well known as a center for young Jews exploring their heritage through Hasidism. The center is led by Rabbis Meier Horowitz and Levi Horowitz.

Membership: Not reported. There are two centers.

Sources:

Shabbos, Zmiros, and Yon Tov. *From the Rebbe's Table.* Brookline, MA: New England Chasidic Center, 1983.

★1835★
Bratslav Hasidism
℅ Rabbi Loe Rosenfeld
864 44th St.
Brooklyn, NY 11219

Nachman of Bratslav (1772-1810) was a Ukrainian great-grandson of Baal Shem Tov. He became known, even as a child, for his asceticism. After he made a trip to the Holy Land, a group formed around him. He died at an early age, thirty-eight, and as he passed away he was heard to say, "My light will glow till the days of the Messiah." His followers interpreted his statement to mean that they would never need another rebbe. Unique in Hasidism without a living rebbe, the Bratslav are referred to by other Hasidic groups as the "dead Hasidim."

The main synagogue of the Bratslav is in Jerusalem and is headed by the Rosh Beth, who, though not a rebbe, is the spiritual leader. Emphasis in the movement is on utter simplicity and warmth of feeling. Prayer is a major activity. Teachings are found in the thirteen stories of Rebbe Nachman which emphasize that the trials of life are to be seen as preludes to new soarings of the spirit.

In Brooklyn, the Bratslav group is headed by Rabbis Leo Rosenfeld and Gedaliah Freer, who have gathered followers of the tradition primarily from young Orthodox Jews attracted to the Hasidic traditions. Through the Breslov Research Institute, attempts have been made to promote studies based on Rabbi Nachman's teachings and to translate his writings into English.

Membership: Not reported.

Sources:

Freer, Gedaliah. *Rabbi Nachman's Fire.* New York: Hermon Press, 1972.

___. *Rabbi Nachman's Foundation.* New York: OHR MiBRESLOV, 1976.

Green, Arthur. *Tormented Master.* New York: Schrocken Books, 1979.

Nachman, Rabbi. *Azamra!.* Brooklyn, NY: Breslov Research Institute, 1984.

★1836★
Chernobyl Hasidism
℅ Rabbi Israel Jacob Twersky
1520 49th St.
Brooklyn, NY 11232

The Twersky family has given the world of Hasidism several dynasties. The oldest began with Menaham Nahum ben Zevi (1730-1787) of Chernobyl in the Ukraine, a contemporary of the Baal Shem Tov. Never a zaddik himself, he helped the initial spread of Hasidism in the Ukraine and laid stress on purification of moral attributes to make one worthy of the Torah. His son, Mordecai Twersky (1770-1837), was the first zaddik and real founder of the Chernobyl dynasty. Mordecai had eight sons. Aaron Twersky, the eldest, continued the dynasty, and the rest founded their own dynasties, which dominated Russian Ukrainian Jewry in the nineteeth century. Members came to the United States after the Russian Revolution. Three Hasidic groups headed by members of the Twersky family currently function in the United States.

Chernobyl Hasidism is represented in the United States by Rebbe Israel Jacob Twersky.

Membership: Not reported.

★1837★
Congregation of New Square (Skver Chasidism)
N. Main St.
New Square, NY 10977

Isaac Twersky (1812-1895), seventh son of Mordecai Twersky, settled at Skver, southwest of Kiev, and began a new dynasty in the 1830s. Members of the Skver dynasty came to the United States after World War II. In 1963, they purchased more than one hundred and thirty acres in Spring Valley, Rockland County, New York, when they built the village of New Square (supposed to be New Skver, but erroneously recorded at the courthouse). Approximately 700 members live there; others remain in Williamsburg. The Rebbe Jacob Joseph Twersky lives at New Square. The building of the isolated village symbolizes the thrust of the Skver faith: the keeping of the law and no compromise with the modern world. Residents of New Square commute regularly to New York as a place of employment. Nonresident Skver Chasidism (Hassidism) is in a thirty-family, self-contained community at nearby Monsey, New York. Rebbe Twersky's son-in-law, Rabbi Mordecai Twersky, is head of the second group.

Membership: In 1988 the congregation reported 20,000 members in 15 centers in the United States and 2,000 members in one center in Canada. There were additionally 3,000 members in centers in England, Belgium, and Israel.

Educational Facilities: Rabbinical Seminary of New Square, New Square, New York.

Yeshiva of New Square, New Square, New York.

Sources:

Gould, Joan. "A Village of 'Slaves to the Torah.'" *The Jewish Digest* (October 1967): 49-52.

★1838★
Kabbalah Learning Centre
83-84 115th St.
Richmond Hill, NY 11418-9808

Alternate Address: International Headquarters: 25 Burgrashov St., Tel Aviv 63342, Israel.

The Kabbalah Learning Centre, also known as the Research Centre of Kabbalah, was founded in 1922 by Rabbi Yehuda Ashlag (1886-1955), a mystic and scholar who hoped to open the teaching of the Kabbalah, the Jewish mystical system, to anyone who desired to study it. Traditionally, the Kabbalah was considered the subject for a few elite scholars. To accomplish his goal, Ashlag translated the entire *Zohar*, the basic Kabbalistic text, from

Aramaic into modern Hebrew. He organized the text, breaking it into chapters and paragraphs. He also wrote an introductory text on the Zohar, which has been translated into English as *Ten Luminous Emanations*.

Ashlag was succeeded by his student, Rabbi Judah Brandwein, who continued translating the Aramaic Kabbalistic texts into Hebrew. Following his death in 1969, Brandwein was succeeded by Dr. Philip S. Gruberger, now known as Philip S. Berg. Berg, who is the present dean of the centre, was an orthodox rabbi who met Brandwein in 1962 and became his close disciple. In 1965, Berg opened the initial American office of the centre in New York City, New York. He moved to Israel in 1974 with his wife, Karen Berg, now the assistant director of the centre, who began teaching the Kabbalah in the early 1970s.

Under Berg's leadership the centre has expanded its program, opening offices across Israel, and in Europe, Canada, and Mexico. In 1981 Berg moved back to the United States. During his years leading the Research Centre, Berg has been a prolific author. His books written in English have provided a popular introduction to the Kabbalah and have attracted a wide following. The translation of his basic text, *Kabbalah for the Layman*, into Spanish, French, German, Russian, and Persian, led the way for the centre's spread in Europe and the Middle East. His texts on reincarnation and astrology have provided an introduction of the centre to Jews affected by the New Age Movement.

Membership: Not reported. There are two centers in the United States, in Los Angeles, California, and New York.

Periodicals: *Kabbalah Magazine*.

Sources:

Ashlag, Yehuda. *Kabbalah: A Gift of the Bible*. Jerusalem, Israel: Research Centre of Kabbalah, 1994.

Berg, Philip, ed. *An Entrance to the Zohar*. Jerusalem, Israel: Research Centre of Kabbalah, 1974.

___. *Kabbalah for the Layman*. 3 vols. Jerusalem, Israel: Research Centre of Kabbalah.

___. *The Wheel of the Soul*. Jerusalem, Israel: Research Centre of Kabbalah, 1984.

★1839★
Klausenburg Hasidism
Current address not obtained for this edition.

A branch of the Halberstamm family founded the dynasty at Klausenburg-Sandz in the nineteenth century. Rabbi Zevi Halberstamm was killed in the Holocaust. His son, Rabbi Yekutiel Jehudah Halberstamm settled in the United States, but in 1956 migrated to Israel and founded Shikun Kiryat Zanz near Nathania, which attained a population of 2,000. Kiryat Zanz has its own yeshiva, a school for girls, a kindergarten and a diamond factory. Only a remnant of the Klausenburg Hasidim remains in Williamsburg, a section of Brooklyn. In Montreal, there is a Metivta (Yeshiva) under the direction of Rabbi Samuel Undsorfer.

Membership: Not reported.

★1840★
Lubavitch Hasidism
770 Eastern Pkwy.
Brooklyn, NY 11213

By far the largest of the Hasidic bodies is the Lubavitch. The arrival of its rebbe, Rabbi Joseph Isaac Schneerson, (1902-1994)in New York in 1940 signaled the rebirth of Hasidism in the New World. Compared with most Hasidic groups, it is open and evangelistic toward its non-Hasidic Jewish neighbors, and has established Lubavitch Hasidism as a national body. Lubavitch Hasidism began in 1773 in Lithuania under the leadership of Rabbi Schneur Zalman (1745-1813), a child prodigy and student of Rabbi Dov

Baer, an outstanding Hasidic scholar. Upon Dov Baer's death in 1772, Rabbi Zalman was sent to Lithuania as a Hasidic missionary. He spent the rest of his life in Lithuania and Russia, teaching and writing. His works include the *Likutic Amarian*, better known as the *Tanya*, the essential text of the *Chabad*, as his teachings became known.

A second Rabbi Dov Baer (1773-1827), the Mittler Rebbe, the son of Rabbi Zalman, succeeded as leader of the Chabad. After his father's death, he settled in Lubavitch in White Russia, the town which gave the dynasty its name. Rabbi Dov Baer was succceeded in turn by Rabbi Menachem Mendel Schneerson (1789-1866), son of Rabbi Zalman's daughter; Rabbi Samuel Schneerson (1834-1882), Rabbi Mendel's son; Rabbi Sholom Dov Baer (1860-1920), Rabbi Samuel's son, and Rabbi Joseph Isaac Schneerson (1880-1950), the son and secretary of Rabbi Dov Baer, who brought the movement to America.

The Lubavitch work actually began in the mid-1920s when Rabbi Schneerson formed the Agudas Chassidas Chabad of the United States of America and Canada. He visited the United States in 1929, during which time he met with President Herbert Hoover. He had settled in Warsaw after World War 1. When his life was threatened by Hitler's legions, the Rebbe was finally persuaded to migrate to the United States.

Chabad is a combination of the initials of "Chochmah," "Binah," and "Daath," the highest virtues in the Kabbalistic system. Daath (knowledge), Chochmah (wisdom) and Binah (intelligence) are three sephirot on the Kabbalistic tree. Faith and belief in God share an insistence on intellectual study and understanding of religious truth. The emphasis on truth has made education basic to the Lubavitch program. The love of one's fellow Jew (Ahavas Yisroel) is a second emphasis of Lubavitch to an openness to the entire Jewish community, in contrast to most other Hasidim, who generally hold a low opinion of their lax, nonpracticing brethren.

Music and dancing are important to Lubavitcher life. Dancing is the bodily manifestation of inward joy. It is always done by males separately from females, as mixed dancing is prohibited by Jewish law. There are two varieties: circle dancing, in which the hand is placed on the shoulder of the brother in front, and rikkud, jumping and skipping up and down. Dancing is a vital part of the festivals, including Purim and the Hasidic historic anniversaries.

Headquarters of the Lubavitcher Rebbe, are in Brooklyn, where the Tomchoi T'mimim, the Lubavitcher Yeshiva, is located. A year after Rabbi Schneerson arrived in the United States in 1941, he was placed in charge of the Merkos L'Inyone Chinuch, the educational arm of the Lubavitch movement; more than 67 educational institutions have since been founded. He also guided the development of Merkos Publication Society, the major publisher of Hasidic literature in the United States, and the Ezrat Pleitim Vesidurom, a relief organization in 56 cities across the United States.

In the wake of the fall of Communism and the U.S. victory over Iraq in the Gulf War, Rabbi Schneerson suggested that a time of peace and tranquility, the time of Moshiach (messiah) was imminent. Many came to believe that he was the messiah. Following his death, no new leader has been designated, many awaiting his return. That position has been denounced by other non-Hassidic Jewish bodies.

Membership: There are more than 200,000 Lubavitchers worldwide.

Periodicals: *Talks and Tales.* • *The Uforatzto Journal.*

Sources:

Challenge. London: Lubavitch Foundation of Great Britain, 1970.

Ehrmann, Naftali Hertz. *The Rav*. New York: Feldheim Publishers, 1977.

Mindel, Nissan. *Rabbi Schneur Zalman of Ladi*. Brooklyn, NY: Chabad Research Center, Kehot Publication Society, 1973.

Schneerson, M. M. *Letters by the Lubavitcher Rebbe*. Brooklyn, NY: Kehot Publication Society, 1979.

Warshaw, Mal. *Tradition, Orthodox Jewish Life in America*. New York: Schrocken, 1976.

★1841★
Monastritsh Hasidism
Current address not obtained for this edition.

The Rabinowicz family has one of the most outstanding Hasidic lineages and is the source of several dynasties. The founder of the dynasty was Jacob Isaac Rabinowicz (1765-1814). As a wandering preacher, he was guided to Rabbi Jacob Isaac Horwitz, the father of Polish Hasidism, known for his psychic abilities and often referred to as the "sad-eyed Seer of Lubin." The Seer told Jacob Isaac that he was a reincarnation of Patriarch Jacob Mordecai and Rabbi Jacob ben Meir Tam (a twelfth-century scholar). He quickly became known as a Talmudic scholar and a seeker of justice. He gradually separated from the seer and established himself at Przysucha.

The emphasis of Jacob Isaac was introspection, aimed at making an individual a good Jew. He thought it essential that one neither lies to himself nor lives in superficiality. The highest pinnacle of the love of God could be acquired only by painstaking personal striving. He insisted on "Kavanah," concentration and devotion in prayer. Przysucha services were not always at the proper times; it was better to pray late than to pray without Kavanah. Action and service, charity and loving kindness were seen as the measures of sincerity.

The Biala dynasty was founded by Rabbi Isaac Jacob Rabinowicz (1847-1905), a direct descendant of Jacob Isaac. Rabinowicz became known for his devotion to the Sabbath, a topic that fills most of his writings. The Biala tradition was passed to Rabbi Yechiel Joshua Rabinowicz (b. 1895). He survived the Nazis by fleeing to Siberia, then in 1947 he settled in Israel. He was known as a miracle worker and he established a Yeshiva (a school for Talmudic study) at B'nai Brak. Rabbi Nathan David Rabinowicz heads the Biala in London.

The Monastritsh Hasidic tradition was brought to the United States in the early 1920s in the wave of Russian Jewish migration by Rebbe Joshua Hershal Rabinowicz (1860-1938). Monastyrshchina is a town west of Minsk in present-day Byelorussia.

Membership: Not reported.

★1842★
Novominsk Hasidism
℅ Rabbi Nahum M. Perlow
1569 47th St.
Brooklyn, NY 11220

The Novominsk dynasty was founded by Jacob Perlow (1847-1902) who as a young rabbi was advised to "go to Poland, raise a family and establish a dynasty." He settled at Minsk-Mazowiech, not far from Warsaw. His fame and following grew, and he built a Yeshiva and a large synagogue. Upon his death, his son, Alter Yisrael Shimon Perlow (1874-1933), succeeded him. Known for his intensity of prayer and passion while preaching, the young rabbi moved to Warsaw in 1917 and drew crowds to his Sunday discourses.

In 1925, Rabbi Yehuda Arye Perlow, brother of the Rebbe of Novominsk, arrived in New York and established the Novominsk dynasty. The current rebbe is Rabbi Nahum Perlow, son of A.Y.S. Perlow, who had accompanied his father from Poland.

Membership: Not reported.

★1843★
Satmar Hasidism
℅ Congregation Y L D'Satmar
152 Rodney
Brooklyn, NY 11220

The Satmar Hasidic tradition is one of the newest, having been founded by Rebbe Yoel Teitelbaum (b.1886) in the first decade of the twentieth century. Following the death of his father in 1904, Yoel, the second son, moved from Sighet, his birthplace, and founded his own group at Satmar in Northeast Hungary. Zionism was becoming a growing force in European Jewry in these formative years of Satmar, and from the yeshiva he had established at Orshovah, Yoel began actively to oppose Zionism. After the unexpected death of Rebbe Yoel's brother in 1926, the leadership of the dynasty passed to Yoel instead of the new Rebbe of Sighet. Yoel's prestige grew steadily until 1944, when the Holocaust hit Hungary. The Rebbe was saved, ironically, by his Zionist enemies, and he escaped to Switzerland.

In 1946 Rebbe Yoel settled in Williamsburg in Brooklyn with the few survivors of the Holocaust. The Congregation Yetev Lev D'Satmar, established in 1948, had 860 members by 1961. Many of these were converts. The anti-Zionist stand remains the distinctive feature of Satmar Hasidism. The Natorei Karta (Guardians of the City), an ultra-orthodox anti-Zionist group in Jerusalem, has placed itself under Satmar's care. Members believe that since only the Messiah can re-establish Israel, the attempt to set up a Jewish state is blasphemy. In 1965, Amram Blau, the leader of the Natorei Karta, was relieved of his position for marrying a divorced convert from Catholicism.

Headquarters of the Satmar movement are in Brooklyn, where there are a number of groups. They have purchased land at Monroe, New York, for the establishment of a Satmar Community. Satmar groups are also found in Jerusalem and B'nai Brak, Israel; Antwerp, Belgium; London, England; Montreal, Quebec, Canada; Montevideo, Uruguay; Sao Paulo, Brazil; and Buenos Aires, Argentina.

Rabbi Yoel had a stroke in 1968 and was somewhat hampered in the performance of his duties during the last decade of his life. He died in 1979. His nephew, Rabbi Moshe Teitelbaum, then the Rabbi of a small congregation in the Boro Park section of Brooklyn, was designated his successor and installed in office in 1980.

Membership: Not reported. In the early 1970s there were approximately 1,500 members of the group.

Sources:

Gersh, Harry M., and Sam Miller. "Satmar in Brooklyn." *Commentary* 28 (1959): 31-41.

Mintz, Jerome R. *Hassidic People: A Place in the New World*. Cambridge, MA: Harvard University Press, 1992. 434pp.

Rubin, Israel. *Satmar, An Island in the City*. Chicago: Quadrangle Books, 1972.

★1844★
Sighet Hasidism
152 Hewes St.
Brooklyn, NY 11211

Rebbe Moses Teitelbaum of Ughely, Hungary, was the founder of the Teitelbaum Hasidic dynasty. The third in the succession, Rebbe Zalmen Leib Teitelbaum, established the center of the work at Sighet (now in northern Rumania). Until 1926, Sighet was a prominent Hasidic center, but the sudden death of Rebbe Hayin Hersch Teitelbaum in that year left his fourteen-year-old son, Zalmen Leib Teitelbaum, as heir to the succession. Since Hasidism is built on the charisma of the rebbe, the Sighet center never regained its former authority. After the Holocaust, the Sighet Hasidic community was disrupted. Finally, it was re-established in Zenta, Yugoslavia by Rebbe Zalmen Leib's brother, Rebbe Moses Teitelbaum. Rebbe Moses moved to the United States and now leads the surviving members from Brooklyn.

Membership: Not reported.

★1845★
Stolin Hasidism
Stolin Bet Midrash
1818 54th St.
Brooklyn, NY 11211

Possibly the first zaddik to reach the United States was Rabbi Yaakov (Jacob) (d. 1946), the son of Rabbi Israel of Stolin. During his life there were four centers for prayer (stieblech) in Brooklyn and one in Detroit. By 1940, there were approximately 100 families under Reb Yaakov's leadership and holding the young adults was a major problem. In the meantime, the Stolin Hassidim in the Soviet Union suffered under the German onslought and three Reb Israel's other sons were killed by the Nazis. Only one, Reb. Yohanan survived the death camp and made his way to Israel. Following Reb. Yaakov's death, a delegation went to Israel and persuaded Reb. Yohanan (1955) to assume leadership of the American flock. Among his first efforts was the mobilizing of the community to create a yeshivah for the young men. Though not known for his public teachings, he was extolled for the miracles attributed to him.

Following Reb. Yohanan's death, the Stolin community was headed by two men designated by him, there being no family member ready to assume the task. In 1967, the properties were signed over to then 13-year-old grandson of Reb. Yohanan, and over the next decade, he gradually assumed his duties. Reb. Barukh Meir continues to lead the Stolin Hassidim in New York, though he has taken up residence in Israel. He has gained some notice for his efforts for Russian Jews and remains in contact with the small Stolin community that still exists in the Ukraine.

Membership: There are less than a hundred families associated with the Stolin Hassidim in the United States.

Sources:

Mintz, Jerome R. *Hassidic People: A Place in the New World.* Cambridge, MA: Harvard University Press, 1992. 434pp.

★1846★
Talnoye (Talner) Hasidism
Talner Beth David
64 Corey Rd.
Brookline, MA 02146

David Twersky (1808-1882), sixth son of Mordecai Twersky, established his dynasty at Talnoye, south of Kiev in Russia. It is said that he lived luxuriously and sat upon a silver throne with the words, "King David of Israel lives forever." In the United States, Rebbe Yitzhak Twersky carries on the tradition.

Membership: Not reported.

Sources:

Even, Issac. "Chasidism in the New World." *Communal Register* (New York) (1918): 341-46.

★1847★
Work of the Chariot
(Defunct)

The Work of the Chariot was a Jewish mystical group active during the 1970s which made its main objective the translation, publication, and distribution of Jewish, Christian, and Islamic mystical material, particularly Hasidic/Kabbalistic source materials. The work was centered in three groups which met to practice the principles of practical mysticsm. Two were in Los Angeles and one in Hollywood. Affiliate groups were located in England and Israel, and a number of distinguished scholars served as consultants in the translation work.

The Work of the Chariot published its own translation of Kabbalistic texts such as the *Book of Formation,* the *Book of Splendor* and the *Tree of Life* by Rabbi Yitzaq Luria, La'Ari. The Group was heavily Kabbalistic. The Chariot of God of Ezekiel is a major theme in Kabbalistic literature. Its authors attempted to know not the unknowable Ein Soph, but the Throne of God on its Chariot. Such knowledge is one of the "secrets" of God, to be obtained by theurgic (magical) means.

Sources:

Book of Formation (Sepher Yetzirah), The Letters of Our Father Abraham. Hollywood, CA: Work of the Chariot, 1971.

Book of Names. Hollywood, CA: Work of the Chariot, 1971.

Work of the Chariot, Ezekiel, Isaiah, II Kings. Hollywood, CA: Work of the Chariot, 1971.

Work of the Chariot, Introduction. Hollywood, CA: Work of the Chariot, 1971.

Black Judaism

★1848★
Church of God and Saints of Christ
% Bp. James R. Grant
10703 Wade Park Ave.
Cleveland, OH 44106

Elder William S. Crowdy, a black cook on the Sante Fe Railroad, claimed to have a vision from God calling him to lead his people to the true religion. He left his job and founded the Church of God and Saints of Christ in 1896 at Lawrence, Kansas. In 1900, he moved to Philadelphia, and the first annual assembly was held. Crowdy died in 1908, and Joseph N. Crowdy and William H. Plummer succeeded him as bishops. Joseph N. Crowdy died in 1917, the same year that the headquarters were moved to Bellville, Virginia, where the church had purchased a large farm. In 1931, Calvin S. Skinner, the last leader appointed by the founder, became bishop, but he lived only three months thereafter. He passed the leadership to Howard Z. Plummer, who held it for many years.

The doctrine of the Church of God is a complicated mixture of Judaism, Christianity and black nationalism. Members are accepted into the church by repentance, baptism by immersion, confession of faith in Christ Jesus, receiving communion of unleavened bread and water, having their feet washed by the elder, and agreeing to keep the Ten Commandments. They must also have been taught how to pray according to Matthew 6:9-13, and they must have been breathed upon with a holy kiss. They believe that black people are the descendants of the ten lost tribes of Israel. They believe in keeping the Ten Commandments and adhering literally to the teachings of both the Old and New Testaments as positive guides to salvation., The church observes the Jewish Sabbath and the use of corresponding Hebrew names. The church is a strong advocate of temperance.

The church is headed by its bishop and prophet who is divinely called to his office. He is believed to be in direct communion with God, to utter prophecies, and to perform miracles. When a prophet dies, the office remains vacant until a new call occurs. The prophet presides over the executive board of twelve ordained elders. The church is divided into district, annual, and general assemblies. There are four orders of the ministry: bishops, missionaries, ordained ministers, and nonordained ministers. Deacons care for the temporal affairs of the church. Each local church bears the denominational name and is numbered according to its appearance in the state. The church at Bellville is communalistic, but other churches are not. The Daughters of Jerusalem and Sisters of Mercy is a women's organization whose duty is to look for straying members, to help the sick and needy, and to care for visitors from other local churches.

Membership: Not reported. At last report (1959) there were 217 churches and 38,217 members. There are affiliated congregations in Jamaica.

Educational Facilities: Bellville Industrial Institute, Bellville, Virginia.

Sources:

Directory of Sabbath-Observing Groups. Fairview, OK: Bible Sabbath Association, 1986.

Fauset, Arthur Huff. *Black Gods of the Metropolis.* Philadelphia: University of Pennsylvania Press, 1944.

★1849★
Church of God (Black Jews)
Current address not obtained for this edition.

The Church of God (Black Jews) was founded in the early twentieth century by Prophet F. S. Cherry, who claimed to have had a vision calling him to his office as prophet. He was sent to America and began the church in Philadelphia. A self-educated man, Prophet Cherry became conversant in both Hebrew and Yiddish. He became famous for his homiletic abilities, colloquialisms, and biting slang.

The Church of God is open only to black people, who are identified with the Jews of the Bible. White Jews are viewed as frauds and interlopers. The church does not use the term synagogue, the place of worship of the white Jews (Rev. 3:9). The church teaches that Jesus was a black man. The first men were also black, the first white man being Gehazi, who received his whiteness as a curse (11 Kings 5: 27). The white man continued to mix with the black people, and the yellow race resulted. Esau was the first red man (Gen. 25:25). God is, of course, black. Black people sprang from Jacob.

The New Year begins with Passover in April. Saturday is the true Sabbath. Speaking in tongues is considered nonsense. Eating pork, divorce, taking photographs, and observing Christian holidays are forbidden. The end of the period that started with creation is approaching, and the Black Jews will return in 2000 A.D. to institute the millennium.

Membership: Not reported.

★1850★
Commandment Keepers Congregation of the Living God
1 W. 123rd St.
New York, NY 10027

The Commandment Keepers Congregation of the Living God emerged among West Indian blacks who migrated to Harlem. The group began with the Beth B'nai Abraham congregation founded in 1924 by Arnold Josiah Ford, an early black nationalist and leader in the Universal Negro Improvement Association founded by Marcus Garvey. Ford had repudiated Christianity, adopted Judaism, and learned Hebrew. During the years after the congregation began, Ford met Arthur Wentworth Matthew (1892- 1973). Matthew was born in Lagos, West Africa, in 1892. His family moved to St. Kitts in the British West Indies and then, in 1911, to New York. Matthew became a minister in the Church of the Living God, the Pillar and Ground of Truth, a black pentecostal church which had endorsed the U.N.I.A. Then in 1919, with eight other men, he organized his own group, the Commandment Keepers: Holy Church of the Living God, over which he became bishop. In Harlem, he had met white Jews for the first time and in the 1920s came to know A. J. Ford. Possibly from Ford, Matthew began to learn Orthodox Judaism and Hebrew and to acquire ritual materials.

Both also learned of the Falashas, the black Jews of Ethiopia, and began to identify with them. In 1930, Ford's congregation ran into financial trouble. Ford turned over the membership to Matthew's care and left for Ethiopia where he spent the rest of his life. The identification with Ethiopia merely increased through the

years. In 1935, when Haile Selassie was crowned emperor, Matthew declared himself the Falashas in America and claimed credentials from Haile Selassie.

The Commandment Keepers believe that the black men are really the Ethiopian Falashas and the Biblical Hebrews who had been stripped of the knowledge of their name and religion during the slavery era. It is impossible for a black man to conceive of himself as a "Negro" and retain anything but slave mentality. With other black Jews, adherents believe the biblical patriarchs to have been black. Christianity is rejected as the religion of the Gentiles or whites.

An attempt has been made to align the Commandment Keepers with Orthodox Jewish practice. Hebrew is taught and revered as a sacred language. The Jewish holidays are kept, and the Sabbath services are held on Friday evenings and Saturday mornings and afternoons. Kosher food laws are kept. An Ethiopian Hebrew Rabbinical college trains leaders in Jewish history, the Mishnah, Josephus, the Talmud, and legalism. Elements of Christianity are retained—footwashing, healing, and the gospel hymns. Services are free of what Matthew terms "niggeritions," the loud emotionalism of the holiness groups.

Matthew also taught Kabbalistic Science, a practice derived from conjuring, the folk magic of Southern blacks. By conjuring, Matthew believed that he could heal and create changes in situations. The conjuring is worked through four angels. In order to get results, one must call upon the right angel.

Matthew was succeeded by his grandson, David M. Dore, a graduate of Yeshiva University.

Membership: Not reported. In the early 1970s there were a reported 3,000 members in several congregations in the New York metropolitan area and the Northeast; 300 members attended the synagogue on East 123rd Street in New York City.

Sources:

Brotz, Howard M. *The Black Jews of Harlem.* New York: Schocken Books, 1970.

Ehrman, Albert. "The Commandment Keepers: A Negro Jewish Cult in America Today." *Judaism* 8, no. 3 (Summer 1959): 266-70.

★1851★
House of Judah
Current address not obtained for this edition.

The House of Judah is a small Black Israelite group founded in 1965 by Prophet William A. Lewis. Alabama-born Lewis was converted to his black Jewish beliefs (which are similar to those of the Church of God and Saints of Christ) from a street preacher in Chicago in the 1960s. Throughout the decade he gathered a small following out of a storefront on the southside and in 1971 moved the group to a twenty-two-acre tract near Grand Junction, Michigan. The group lived quietly and little noticed until 1983 when a young boy in the group was beaten to death. The incident focused attention on the group for its advocacy of corporal punishment. The mother of the boy was sentenced to prison for manslaughter. By 1985 the group had resettled in Alabama.

The House of Judah teaches that the Old Testament Jews were black, being derived from Jacob and his son Judah, who were black (Jeremiah 14:2). Both Solomon and Jesus were black. Jerusalem, not Africa, is the black man's land. The white Jew is the devil (Rev. 2:9); he occupies the black man's land but will soon be driven out. The House of Judah awaits a deliverer, whom God will send to take the black man from the U.S.A. to Jerusalem. He will be a second Moses to lead his people to the promised land. The group lives communally.

Membership: In 1985 there were approximately 80 members living on the farm in rural Alabama. There is only one center.

Sources:

De Smet, Kate. "Return to the House of Judah." *Michigan, the Magazine of the Detroit News* (July 21, 1985).

★1852★
Israeli Church of Universal Practical Knowledge
1 W. 125th St.
New York, NY 10027

The Israeli Church of Universal Practical Knowledge, founded in New York City in the early 1990s, is based in the identification of the biblical 12 tribes of Israel with the Black and Native people of North, Central, and South America. According to the church, Black Americans are of the tribe of Judah. The remaining tribes include the indigenous people of the various areas of the Americas: Benjamin (West Indians), Levi (Haiti), Simeon (Dominican Republic), Zebulon (Guatemala to Panama), Ephraim (Puerto Rico), Manassah (Cuba), Gad (North American Indians), Reuben (Seminole Indians), Napthali (Argentina and Chile), Asher (Columbia to Uruguay), and Issachar (Mexico).

According to the church, nine of the 12 tribes left Assyria in the eight century B.C.E. and sailed to the Americas. Three tribes—Judah, Benjamin, and Levi—were present in the Holy Land during the time of Christ. They were dispersed in 70 C.E. when Vespasian laid siege to Jerusalem. Some settled in West Africa. Here, Africans and Arabs sold them into slavery and eventually to the white men who brought them to America. The so-called American Blacks are not Africans, but Israelites. Since Africans and Arabs sold the members of the tribes of Israel into slavery, American Blacks should stay away from identification with Africans and those from Islam.

In America, the church asserts, all of the Israelites have suffered at the hands of European Americans. White people are Edomites, the descendants of the biblical Esau, the son of Isaac and Rebecca. The Edomites are the enemy of God's people, Israel, and their end is destruction. God's people should not integrate with the Edomites.

It is the goal of the Israeli Church to reunite the people of God now scattered across the Americas. According to the church, 1914 marked the beginning of the end of the Gentile Age, during which time the message of the Bible was sealed but is now being revealed to the people of God. The Israeli Church uses only the King James Version of the Bible.

Membership: Not reported.

Sources:

Chaa-Rask. *What You Need to Know about Islam and the Negroes.* New York: Israeli School of Universal Practical Knowledge, 1992.

Images of Israel in History. New York: Masha/Ahraya Iconographs, Inc., 1994.

Masha, Ahraya, and Yaiqah. *Change of World's!!!: About the Mystery Contained in the Bible.* New York: Israeli Church of U.P.K., n.d.

★1853★
Nation of Yahweh (Hebrew Israelites)
Current address not obtained for this edition.

History. The Nation of Yahweh, also known as the Hebrew Israelites or the Followers of Yahweh, is a movement founded by Yahweh ben (son of) Yahweh. Yahweh ben Yahweh was born Hulon Mitchell, Jr., considered a slave name, and no longer used. He was the son of a Pentecostal minister who at one point joined the Nation of Islam in which he became the leader of one of the mosques. He began to call together the Followers of Yahweh in the 1970s.

Beliefs. Yahweh ben Yahweh teaches that there is one God, whose name is Yahweh. God is black with woolly hair (Daniel 7:9; Revelation 1:13-15; Dueteronomy 7:21), and has sent His son, Yahweh ben Yahweh to the the Savior and Deliverer of His peo-

ple, the so-called black people of America. Those who believe in Yahweh ben Yahweh and His name are immortal. Black people are considered the true lost tribe of Judah. They have been chosen by Yahweh, but have yet to be put into their destined office of rulership. Members, upon joining, renounce their slave name and take the surname Israel. Many of then wear white robes as commanded in the Bible (Ecclesiastes 9:8). They believe that all people who oppose God are devils, regardless of race or color. The devil is one who is immoral and follows immoral teachings of wickedness and evilness. Many persons, regardless of their race or color are capable of being and actually are the devil.

While the Nation of Yahweh has a special place for the chosen black people of America, and see white people as especially used by Satan in exercising wicked rulership, in the end salvation is not a matter of color. Any person of any race or color can be saved by faith in Yahweh ben Yahweh.

Along with its particular religious beliefs, the Nation of Yahweh sees itself as establishing a united moral power to benefit the total community of America. It supports voter registration, education, self-help jobs, business opportunities, scholarships for children, health education, better housing, strong family ties, peace, love, and harmony among people regardless of race, creed, or color. Members are taught to practice charity and benevolence, to protect chastity, to respect the ties of blood and friendship, and revere the laws of Yahweh.

Organization. The Nation of Yahweh is headed by Yahweh ben Yahweh. In its work, the nation has purchased several hotels and apartment buildings. It owns, through its corporate entity, the Temple of Love, more than 42 (in 1988) businesses which are used to support the organization and its members.

Though the 1990s, the Nation of Yahweh was disrupted by accusations of violence and murder committed by leaders against both former members and nonmembers during the period 1981-1986. Concern about the group was heightened in 1986 when two residents of an apartment house were shot while members of the group were attempting an eviction. Then in 1988, a member of the group confessed to four murders and implicated the group's leadership in twelve more. Arrested in the early 1990's, Yahweh ben Yahweh and serveral of his leaders were convicted in federal court of conspiracy to murder in 1992 and received lengthy prison terms.

Membership: Not reported. In 1988, there were congregations in 37 cities and scattered followers in a number of others. The teachings had also spread to 16 countries.

Periodicals: *Yahweh Magazine.*

★1854★
Original Hebrew Israelite Nation
℅ Communications Press
PO Box 26063
Washington, DC 20001

The Black Israelites (members of the Original Hebrew Israelite Nation) emerged in Chicago in the 1960s around Ben Ammi Carter (born G. Parker), a black man who had studied Judaism with a rabbi, and Shaleah Ben-Israel. To the Black Jewish ideas (which were espoused by several groups in Chicago at this time) Carter and Ben-Israel added the concept of Black Zionism and held out the vision of a return to the Holy Land for their members. From headquarters at the A-Beta Cultural Center on Chicago's south side, they began to gather followers. The somewhat anonymous group came into prominence in the late 1960s as a result of their attempts to migrate to Africa and then to Israel. The group moved first to Liberia, seen as analogous to the Hebrew children's wandering in the desert for forty years to throw off the effects of slavery. Soon after their arrival, they approached the Israeli ambassador about a further move to Israel. They were unable to negotiate the move to Israel for members in Liberia. In 1968 Carter and 38 members from Chicago flew directly to Israel. Given temporary sanction and work permits, the group from Liberia joined them. By 1971, when strict immigration restrictions were imposed upon members of the group, over 300 had migrated. Other members of the group continued to arrive, however, using tourist visas which were destroyed upon moving into the colony (which had been established at Dimona). By 1980 between 1,500 and 2,000 had settled in Israel.

The Black Israelites feel they are descendants of the ten lost tribes of Israel and thus Jews by birth. They celebrate the Jewish rituals and keep the Sabbath. However, they are distinguished from traditional Jews by their practice of polygamy (a maximum of seven wives is allowed) and their abandonment of the synagogue structure.

The group is currently headed by Carter, the chief rabbi. He is assisted by a divine council of twelve princes (for each of the twelve ancient tribes of Israel). During the early 1980s, the American following was under the direction of Prince Asiel Ben Israel. Under the princes are seven ministers responsible for providing education, distribution of food, clothing and shelter, economics, transportation, sports, recreation and entertainment, life preservation, and sanitation.

In Israel, the group lives communally. According to most reports, the group (due to lack of legal status), lives under harsh conditions and the continual threat of mass deportation. They have been unable to obtain necessary additional housing (for those many members who immigrated illegally) and the children are not allowed to attend public schools. Within Israel, the group has asked for land to settle in order to create their own community.

Membership: Not reported. In 1980 there were an estimated 1,500 members in Israel (900 at Dimona, 400 at Arad, 100 at Mitzpe Ramon, and 100 at Eilat) and 3,000 living in the United States, scattered in black communities in urban centers such as Chicago, Atlanta, Georgia, and Washington, D.C.

Remarks: In the wake of continuous immigration problems with the State of Israel during the 1970s, the group gained new prominence in 1980 when members in the United States were charged with the systematic theft of money, credit cards, and blank airline tickets, all of which were being used to support the group and assist members in their movement to Israel.

Sources:

Carter, Ben Ammi. *God, the Black Man, and Truth.* Chicago: Communicators Press. 1982.

___. *Everlasting Life: from Thought to Reality.* Washington, D.C. Communicators Press, 1994. 190 pp.

Fish, H. Bashford. "Trouble Among the Children of the Prophets." *The Washington Post Magazine* (February 7, 1982).

Gerber, Israel J. *The Heritage Seekers.* Middle Village, NY: Jonathan David Publishers, 1977.

Whitfield, Thomas. *From Night to Sunlight.* Nashville, TN: Broadman Press, 1980.

Yehuda, Shaleak Ben. *Black Hebrew Israelites from America to the Promised Land.* New York: Vantage Press, 1975.

★1855★
Overcoming Saints of God
Current address not obtained for this edition.

The Overcoming Saints of God is a predominantly black Pentecostal church founded in 1959 by Anna Thompson Mobley. The original church, and still the lead congregation, is the Lethal Cathedral in Archer, Florida. Over the years other churches were founded along the Atlantic coast as far north as Massachusetts, and missions were opened in Africa, the Virgin Islands, Haiti, and the Bahamas. The doctrine is similar to that of the Church of God and Saints of Christ.

Membership: In 1990 there were 10 churches and close to 1,000 members.

Sources:

DuPree, Sherry Sherrod. *African American Holiness Pentecostal Charismatic: Annotated Bibliography.* New York: Garland Publishing, 1992.

★1856★
Pan African Orthodox Christian Church
13535 Livernois
Detroit, MI 48238

The Pan African Orthodox Christian Church dates to 1953 when 300 members of St. Mark's Presbyterian Church in Detroit walked out and formed Central Congregational Church. In 1957 they moved into facilities at 7625 Linwood in Detroit and over the next decade became intensely involved in community issues, especially those impinging upon the black community. In 1967, the church's pastor, Albert B. Cleage, Jr., preached what has become a famous sermon calling for a new black theology and a black church to articulate it. An 18-foot painting of a black Madonna was unveiled and the Black Christian Nationalist Movement was launched. The church building became known as the Shrine of the Black Madonna No. 1. In 1970 a book store and cultural center were opened. Cleage changed his name to Jaramogi Abebe Agyeman.

The Black Nationalist Creed, printed below, spells out a position which identifies the black man and the Hebrew Nation:

"I Believe that human society stands under the judgment of one God, revealed to all, and known by many names. His creative power is visible in the mysteries of the universe, in the revolutionary Holy Spirit which will not long permit men to endure injustice nor to wear the shackles of bondage, in the rage of the powerless when they struggle to be free, and in the violence and conflict which even now threaten to level the hills and the mountains."

"I Believe that Jesus, the Black Messiah, was a revolutionary leader, sent by God to rebuild the Black Nation Israel and to liberate Black People from powerlessness and from the oppression, brutality, and exploitation of the white gentile world."

"I Believe that the revolutionary spirit of God, embodied in the Black Messiah, is born anew in each generation and that Black Christian Nationalists constitute that living remnant of God's Chosen People in this day, and are charged by him with responsibility for the Liberation of Black People."

"I Believe that both my survival and my salvation depend upon my willingness to reject INDIVIDUALISM, and so I commit my life to the Liberation Struggle of Black people and accept the values, ethics, morals, and program of the Black Nation defined by that struggle and taught by the Black Christian Nationalist Movement."

During the 1970s the organization expanded significantly. Agyeman composed an ordination service and ordained eight ministers, who were given the title "Mwalimu," Swahili for "teacher." Agyemnan's own name means "liberator, blessed man, savior of the nation." Other congregations and centers were established in Detroit. In 1974 a shrine was opened in Atlanta, Georgia and in 1977 in Kalamazoo, Michigan. Also in 1974, a BGN training program to prepare leaders for the liberation struggle of black people was begun.

Membership: Not reported. In 1983 there were six congregations, four in Detroit, one in Kalamazoo, Michigan, and one in Atlanta, Georgia.

Sources:

Cleage, Albert B., Jr. *The Black Messiah.* New York: Sheed and Ward, 1968.

___. *Black Christian Nationalism: New Directions for the Black Church.* New York: William Morrow, 1972.

Ward, Hiley H. *Prophet of the Black Nation.* New York: Pilgrim Press, 1969.

★1857★
Rastafarians
Current address not obtained for this edition.

The Rastafarian Movement, a Jamaican black nationalist movement, grew out of a long history of fascination with Africa in general and Ethiopia in particular among the masses in Jamaica. The movement can be traced directly to the efforts of Marcus Garvey, founder of the Universal Negro Improvement Association, who, among other endeavors, promoted a steamship company that would provide transportation for blacks going back to Africa. In 1927 Garvey predicted the crowning of a black king in Africa as a sign that the redemption of black people from white oppression was near. The 1935 coronation of Haile Selassie as emperor of Ethiopia was seen as a fulfillment of Garvey's words.

Haile Selassie was born Ras Tafari Makonnen out of a lineage claimed to derive from the Queen of Sheba and King Solomon. He proclaimed his title as King of Kings, Lord of Lords, His Imperial Majesty the Conquering Lion of the Tribe of Judah. Elect of God. His name Haile Selassie means "Power of the Holy Trinity." Reading about the coronation, four ministers in Jamaica—Joseph Hibbert, Archibald Dunkley, Robert Hinds, and most prominently, Leonard Howell—saw the new emperor as not only the fulfillment of the Garveyite expectation, but also the completion of Biblical prophecies such as those in Revelation 5:2-5 and 19:16 which refer to the Lion of the Tribe of Judah and the King of Kings. The four, independently of each other, began to proclaim Haile Selassie the Messiah of the black people. Their first successes came in the slums of West Kingston, where they discovered each other and a movement began.

Howell began to proselytize around the island. He raised money by selling pictures of Haile Selassie and telling the buyers that they were passports back to Africa. He was arrested and sentenced to two years in jail for fraud. Upon his release he moved into the hill country of St. Catherine's parish and founded a commune, the Pinnacle, which, in spite of government attacks and several moves, became the center of the movement for the next two decades. At the Pinnacle, the smoking of ganga (marijuana) and the wearing of long hair curled to resemble a lion's mane (dread locks) became the marks of identification of the group.

As the Rastafarians matured, they adopted the perspectives of Black Judaism and identified the Hebrews of the Old Testament as black people. Their belief system was distinctly racial and they taught that the whites were inferior to the blacks. More extreme leaders saw whites as the enemies of blacks and believed that, in the near future, blacks will return to Africa and assume their rightful place in world leadership. Haile Selassie is believed to be the embodiment of God and, though no longer visible, he nevertheless still lives. Some Rastafarians believe Selassie is still secretly alive, though most see him as a disembodied spirit.

Relations with white culture have been tense, lived at the point of "dread," a term to describe the confrontation of a people struggling to regain a denied racial selfhood. Most Rastafarians are pacifists, though much support for the movement developed out of intense antiwhite feelings. Violence has been a part of the movement since the destruction of the Pinnacle, though it has been confined to individuals and loosely organized groups. One group, the Nyabingi Rastas, stand apart from most by their espousal of violence.

Rastafarians came to the United States in large numbers as part of the general migration of Jamaicans in the 1960s and 1970s. They have brought with them an image of violence, and frequent news reports have detailed murders committed by individuals identified as Rastafarians. Rastafarian spokespersons have only complained that many young Jamaican-Americans have adopted the outward appearance of Rastafarians (dread locks and ganga-smoking) without adopting Rastafarian beliefs and lifestyle.

A major aspect of Rastafarian life is the unique music developed as its expression. Reggae, a form of rock music, became popular far beyond Rastafarian circles, and exponents such as Bob Marley and Peter Tosh became international stars. Reggae has immensely helped in the legitimization of Rastafarian life and ideals.

In Jamaica the Rastafarian Movement is divided into a number of organizations and factions, many of which have been brought into the Jamaican community in America. Surveys of American Rastafarians have yet to define the organization in the United States though individual Rastafarians may be found in black communities across America, most noticably Brooklyn, New York, Miami, Florida, and Chicago, Illinois.

Membership: There are an estimated 3,000-5,000 Rastafarians in the United States, though the figures are somewhat distorted by the large number of people who have adopted the outward appearance of Rastafarian life.

Periodicals: *Arise.* Available from Creative Publishers, Ltd., 8 Waterloo Ave., Kingston, Jamaica, West Indies. • *Jahugliman.* Available from Carl Gayle, 19C Annette Cresent, Kingston 10, Jamaica, West Indies.

Sources:

Barrett, Leonard. *The Rastafarians.* Boston: Beacon Press, 1977.

Owens, Joseph. *Dread.* Kingston: Sangster, 1976.

Williams, K. M. *The Rastafarians.* London: Ward Lock Educational, 1981.

★1858★
United Hebrew Congregation
Current address not obtained for this edition.

The United Hebrew Congregation was the name of about a half dozen congregations of black Jews which during the mid-1970s were centered upon the Ethiopian Hebrew Culture Center in Chicago, which were headed by Rabbi Naphtali Ben Israel. It was this group's belief that Ham's sons were black. Included were the Hebrews of which one reads in the Bible. Abraham came from Chaldea, and the ancient Chaldeans were black. The congregation members believe Solomon was black (Song of Solomon 1:5). Sabbath services were held on Saturday. No sign of their continuance into the 1980s has been found.

Membership: Not reported

Other Jewish Groups

★1859★
Community of Micah (Fabrengen)
(Defunct)

The Community of Micah was one of several radical, left-oriented groups which emerged from the wave of social consciousness in the late 1960s. Members attempt to relate all action to the goal of human liberation. A major concern has been the survival of Judaism, and the group has been involved in Jewish consciousness-raising. An urban communal structure, the community in 1972 attempted to establish Kibbutz Micah as an experiment in Jewish rural communal living in central Pennsylvania, but it did not survive.

The Community developed an active study program which included Hasidic literature (especially the books of Martin Buber), mysticism, yoga and radical Jewish politics. The group was disowned by the Washington (D.C.) Jewish Community in 1971. The Community published the *Voice of Micah* and other Jewish and political action material.

Sources:

Waskow, Arthur I. *The Bush Is Burning.* New York: Macmillan Company, 1971.

★1860★
Congregation Kehillath Yaakov (Kehilat Jacob)
305 W. 79th St.
New York, NY 10024

Among the most charismatic leaders to arise in the 1960s outside of the normal synagogue structures was Shlomo Carlebach, (1925-1994) the "hippie" guitar-strumming rabbi. Born in Berlin and raised in a traditional Hassidic family, Carlebach combined the neo-Hassidim of Martin Buber, the havurat (small group) movement in Judaism, and the counter-culture lifestyle into a unique blend of traditional Judaism that has found a widespread audience among younger Jews.

Among the earliest structures which evolved out of Carlebach's work was the House of Love and Prayer, a Jewish community in San Francisco. It emerged in 1969 among Jews who had rediscovered their Jewishness in response to Carlebach's work in the drug culture. The emphasis of the House was placed on the shared life, Torah, and prayer. For several years Carlebach limited his travels to teach at the House's yeshivah. The San Francisco group published two periodicals, *Holy Beggers' Gazette* and *Tree*, and operated the Judaic Book Service. There were, in the mid-1970s, between 20 and 40 at the house, an optimum number for a havurat. Services were held on Friday evenings, Saturday mornings, and each day at 6:30 a.m. Open classes were conducted in Hebrew and the Talmud.

While the San Francisco group flourished, similar groups emerged in New York and Jerusalem. By the early 1980s the San Francisco group had disbanded, and Carlebach transferred his headquarters to New York. There, he took over the synagogue his father had founded. Carlebach was considered both rabbi and rebbe, the leader of a Hassidic group. He traveled widely and was a popular speaker, story-teller, and musician.

Membership: Carlebach's following is national and international (especially in Israel). His following has continued to grow, though the structure containing it has evolved through the years.

Sources:

Hoffman, Edward. "Judaism's New Renaissance." *Yoga Journal* 61 (March/April 1985).

Jacobs, Susan. "A New Age Jew Revisits Her Roots." *Yoga Journal* 61 (March/April 1985).

Skir, Leo. "Shlomo Carlebach and the House of Love and Prayer." *Midstream* (February 1970).

★1861★
Havurah Movement
Current address not obtained for this edition.

During the 1960s, as part of the larger wave of communalism which swept America, a variety of primarily young Jews began to combine their exploration of Jewish roots with experiments in communal living. Havurot Shalom was one of the first such experiments. It was established as a traditional Jewish community in Boston in 1968. It was conceived as a core community around which a larger constituency would be oriented. It offered adult education courses in Torah, Hasidism, traditional arts such as challah baking, and more contemporary subjects.

At about the same time and in the years following, other havurot communities emerged within Jewish communities in such widely scattered locations as New York City; Phoenix, Arizona; Madison, Wisconsin; Ithaca, New York; Philadelphia; Washington, DC; Rochester, New York; and Austin, Texas. Some were attached to congregations; many were completely independent enterprises. The movement has tried to draw from each of the three dominant Jewish traditions rather than identifying with any one of them. Full equality of women has been a major commitment of the movement. In 1979, 350 havurot members held a conference at Rutgers University and organized the National Havurot Coordinating Committee which immediately began planning programs to assist havurah communities survive by gaining a greater knowledge of their Jewish heritage.

Membership: Not reported. Recent estimates of the movement suggest that several hundred havurah communities have survived into the mid-1980s.

Sources:

Reisman, Bernard. "The Havurah: An Approach to Humanizing Jewish Organizational Life." *Journal of Jewish Communal Service* 52, no. 2 (Winter 1975): 202-209.

★1862★
New Synagogue
7 W. 96th St., Ste. 19-B
New York, NY 10025

Hungarian-born Rabbi Joseph H. Gelberman was a leader of a Conservative congregation who left it to found the Little Synagogue (Congregation Tel Aviv), a "modern Hasidic community" located just north of Greenwich Village in Manhattan in New York City. After more than 20 years with the Little Synagogue, he has continued his ministry with the New Synagogue. Gelberman's program combines elements of Hasidism, New Thought, and Eastern religious thought. Integral to the program is the Midway Counseling Center, specializing in psychological counseling and based upon the concept that learning to love is the key to growth on all levels of the self.

Rabbi Gelberman has become a popular figure in New Thought metaphysical circles and has often spoken at International New Thought Alliance (INTA) meetings and at the New York congregation of the Church of the Truth. Science of Mind lessons are a regular part of the weekly program. Over the years, Martin Buber's Hasidism has come more and more to the fore in Gelberman's thinking. The Synagogue seeks, through Hasidic thought and techniques, to find personal growth and the joy of worship. Sabbath services include chanting, silent meditation, and spontaneous verbalization leading to mystical and metaphysical encounter. Interpretation of the Zohar is a central feature of the educational program.

Although a single congregation, the New Synagogue has immense influence through media coverage and Gelberman's lecturing and leading workshops around the United States. Gelberman has also developed "Interfaith Seminars" as a means of interfaith dialogue between Jews, Christians, Muslims, and members of Eastern religions. Wisdom Press publishes Rabbi Gelberman's books and tapes, distributing them throughout the country.

Membership: Not reported. There is one center in Manhattan.
Educational Facilities: New Seminary, New York, New York.

Sources:

Gelberman, Joseph H. *Psychology and Metaphysics*. New York: Little Synagogue Press, n.d.

___. *Reaching a Mystical Experience: A Kabbalistic Encounter*. New York: Wisdom Press, 1970.

___. *To Be...Fully Alive*. Farmingdale, NY: Coleman Graphics, 1983.

"Kabbala for Moderns." *Hadassah Magazine* 54, no. 3 (November 1972).

★1863★
P'nai Or Religious Fellowship
6723 Emlen St.
Philadelphia, PA 19119

B'nai Or Religious Fellowship was founded in 1962 by Rabbi Zalman Schachter-Shalomi, one of the pioneers in the wave of Jewish spirituality which emerged among the youthful Jewish population in the 1970s. Schachter-Shalomi was born in Poland, but his family later moved to Belgium. There, he became associated with Lubavitch Hasidism. After arriving in New York during World

War II, Schachter-Shalomi trained for the rabbinate and was ordained in 1947. He served several Lubavitcher centers and took a master's degree in psychology of religion. Meanwhile, his personal mystical-religious quest led him to psychic and occult literature, non-Jewish forms of spirituality, and an early experimentation with psychedelic drugs. He found that his attachment to Judaism had deepened, but he also concluded that Judaism was not the only true religion. He believed truth expressed itself in all religions, especially in their mystical variations.

In the mid-1980s, the issue of the role of females within the fellowship was forcefully debated, and members committed themselves to make the fellowship more egalitarian, i.e., full participation at all levels for both men and women, and a welcome to gay and lesbian Jews. As part of this commitment, the name of the organization was changed from B'nai Or Religious Fellowship (sons of light) to P'nai Or (faces of light), a gender-free term derived from the Kabbalah.

P'nai Or is conceived of as a traditional Jewish center whose members pursue Judaism as a spiritual way of life. Its program centers upon traditional study of Torah, the mystical Kabbalah, and Hassidic writings, and the celebration of traditional Jewish practices of ritual and worship. However, the traditional practices are set within an atmosphere of acceptance of modern spiritual practice, meditation, and transpersonal psychologies, and the recognition of alternative spiritual paths, even for those born Jewish.

Activities in Philadelphia have centered around the fellowship's house of study and prayer. It houses a library, a study area, administrative offices, and a space for weekly and seasonal celebrations. Increasingly, the group has developed an outgoing perspective and a commitment to *tikkun olam*, by which is meant a commitment to improve the world, using spirituality to fuel this work personally and socially. A national and international network, the Chai Network, consists of individuals and groups that support the fellowship and its program of revival within the larger context of Judaism. Rabbi Schachter-Shalomi periodically travels around the United States to meet with members of the network.

Membership: P'nai Or is not a membership organization. There are approximately 50 people who gather regularly at the Philadelphia center. There are seven affiliated centers in the United States and two foreign countries, one each in Switzerland and the Netherlands.

Periodicals: *New Menorah.*

Sources:

Schachter-Shalomi, Zalman. *Fragments of a Future Scroll.* Germantown, PA: Leaves of Grass Press, 1975.

Schachter-Shalomi, Zalman, and Donald Gropman. *The First Step.* New York: Bantam Books, 1983.

Schachter, Zalman M., and Edward Hoffman. *Sparks of Light.* Boulder, CO: Shambhala, 1983.

Schwartz, Howard, and Zalman Schachter-Shalomi. *The Dream Assembly.* Warwick, NY: Amity House, 1987.

Weichselbaum, Lehman. "Reb Zalman Schachter-Shalomi, Rabbi to the Counterculture." *New Age* 7, no. 2 (September 1981).

★1864★
Sha'arei Orah
Current address not obtained for this edition.

Sha'arei Orah ("Gates of Light") is a neo-Hassidic congregation founded in 1982 by Rabbi David Din, a student of Rabbi Nachman of Bratslav (1772-1810). Following the death of Rabbi Nachman, his followers interpreted his words, "My light will glow till the days of the Messiah," as meaning that they would never need another rebbe, the traditional Hassidic leader. During the 1970s, Nachman's teachings have enjoyed a revival. New English editions of his writings and stories have appeared. Sha'arei Orah combines traditional Hassidic teachings with the newer move-

ment of younger Jews for a close community of intense spirituality. There is one center, located in New York City.

Membership: Not reported.

Sources:

Hoffman, Edward. "Judaism's New Renaissance." *Yoga Journal* 61 (March/April 1985).

Kramer, Mordechai, ed. *The Thirteen Stories of Rebbe Nachman of Breslev.* Jerusalem: Hillel Press, 1978.

★1865★
Society for Humanistic Judaism
28611 W. Twelve Mile Rd.
Farmington Hills, MI 48334

Within the American Jewish community, attempts have been made since the mid-nineteenth century to articulate a secular, humanistic, and even atheistic Judaism. Such efforts have resulted in structures such as the Ethical Culture Society (which while predominantly Jewish in membership did little to relate to the Jewish community) and a variety of Jewish agricultural communal experiments. Primarily, however, secular Jews were not related to synagogue life. In the 1960s there arose a group of rabbis who wished to combine the religious life and affirmation of their Jewishness within a humanist perspective. Rabbi Sherwin T. Wine led the way in the formation of the first humanist congregation, the Birmingham Temple (in suburban Detroit). He was joined by Rabbi Daniel Friedman who had led congregation Beth Or in Deerfield, Illinois, to adopt humanistic thought and practice. In 1969, they led in the formation of the Society for Humanistic Judaism and the Association for Humanistic Rabbis. Secular Humanistic Judaism has since grown into an international movement with supporters on five continents.

Humanist Judaism is a religion for Jews who value their Jewish identity but question the traditional view of Jewish history. It offers a non-theistic approach to the celebration of Jewish identity and Jewish culture. Humanistic Jews understand and appreciate the Jewish past and present in ways consistent with the best insights of modern enlightenment. Humanistic Judaism promotes certain important values in Jewish life that the traditional establishments have resisted. These values are rationality, personal autonomy, feminism, the celebration of human strength and power, and the development of a pluralistic world with mutual understanding and cooperation among all religions and philosophies of life.

Humanistic ethics assert that ethics and morality rest upon a human foundation, and that each person must be responsible for individual ethical decisions and their consequences. Humanistic ethics also assume that people must be treated noncoercively, with respect, and in such a way that their individuality and dignity are affirmed. Assisting others to assume responsibility for their own lives is a primary ethical activity.

The Society for Humanistic Judaism serves as a voice for Humanistic Jews. It publishes educational, philosophical, and celebrational materials, and helps to organize Secular Humanistic Jewish communities in North America. The society is affiliated with the International Federation of Secular Humanistic Jews led by noted Holocaust scholar Yehuda Bauer, and is served by the International Institute for Secular Judaism, based in Jerusalem, which functions as the intellectual center and leadership training structure for secular Judaism.

Membership: Not reported.

Educational Facilities: Institute for Secular Humanistic Judaism, Jerusalem, Israel; Farmington Hills, Michaign.

Periodicals: *Humanistic Judaism.• Humanorah.*

Sources:

Feldman, Ruth. "Beth Or Offers Alternative Form of Judaism, Maintains Low Profile, Earns Activists' Scorn." *North Shore* 2, no. 1 (January/February 1979): 56-59.

Goodman, Saul N. *The Faith of Secular Jews.* New York: KTAV Publishing House, 1976.

Weisman, Sidney M. "From Orthodox Judaism to Humanism." *The Humanist* 39, no. 3 (May/June 1979): 32-35.

Wine, Sherwin T. *The Humanist Haggadah.* Birmingham, MI: Society for Humanistic Judaism, 1979.

___. *Humanistic Judaism.* Buffalo, NY: Prometheus Books, 1978.

★1866★
Society of Jewish Science
109 E. 39th St.
New York, NY 10016

Jewish converts were mentioned in Christian Science literature in the 1890s. In the first decade of the twentieth century, substantial numbers in the still small Jewish community began to look to Mary Baker Eddy (who founded the Church of Christ, Scientist) for inspiration. In 1911, the California Grand Lodge of B'nai B'rith adopted a resolution denying membership to Jews adhering to Christian Science and, in 1912, the Central Conference of American Rabbis (Reformed) devoted a session at its annual meeting to a discussion of the issue. Of particular interest were those Jews who insisted that Christian Science only made them better Jews.

Out of this debate came Alfred Geiger Moses, a Reformed rabbi from Mobile, Alabama, who, in 1916, published his *Jewish Science.* Drawing upon Hasidic sources, he translated Chochmah (the Kabbalistic sephirot, generally translated as wisdom). He saw the Baal Shem Tov as the source of Eddy's thought and Christian Science as Hasidism with a veneer of Christology. He further emphasized "faith cure" as a genuinely Jewish tradition and recounted incidents of cures he had witnessed. Moses' position was actually nearer New Thought than Christian Science, inasmuch as he refused to deny the existence of matter. He emphasized thinking "right thoughts" and training the mind with affirmations (short statements "affirming" God and creation), following a proper diet, avoiding excesses, and refusing to become angered.

In 1922, the Lithuanian-born Rabbi Morris Lichtenstein gave organizational form to Moses' ideas, establishing the Society of Jewish Science in New York City. In 1925, he published *Jewish Science and Health* and, in subsequent years, several other books. From 1923 to the present, the Society of Jewish Science has published the *Jewish Science Interpreter* eight times a year. By 1938, there were 19 practitioners. Rival groups had begun to emerge almost immediately. Rabbi Clifton Harby Levy organized the Center of Jewish Science in 1923. Levy published a series of lessons, *The Helpful Manual* and a periodical, the *Jewish Life.* By 1929 he had six active groups in New York City and one each in Baltimore, Maryland; Rochester and Syracuse, New York; and Washington, D.C. The Center continued until the late 1950s.

Rabbi Lichtenstein died in 1938 and was succeeded by his wife, Tehilla Lichtenstein, who occupied his pulpit until his death in 1973. She was the first woman to fill such a role uninterruptedly and for so long (more than three decades). She wrote the basic introductory booklet, "What to Tell Your Friends about Jewish Science." Ms. Lichtenstein draws the distinction between Jewish Science and Christian Science by noting that within Judaism are all the spiritual goals any Jew needs. Jewish Science is a way of life which puts into application all the spiritual, ethical, and moral principles of the Jewish faith, and thus enables one to attain health and happiness. That the cure of physical and mental illnesses can be effected by restoring one's mental processes to their natural condition is a central postulate.

Membership: In 1995 the society reported 250 full members and 2,000 associate members. There are groups in New York City; Piscataway, New Jersey; Abuquerque, New Mexico; Los Angeles, California; and Netanya, Israel. Other adherents scattered across the country are affiliated through the society's literature.

Periodicals: *Jewish Science Interpreter.*

Sources:

Appel, John J. "Christian Science and the Jews." *Jewish Social Studies* 31 (April 1969): 100-121.

Levy, Charles Harby. *The Helpful Manual.* New York: Centre of Jewish Science, n.d.

Lichtenstein, Morris. *Jewish Science and Health.* New York: Jewish Science Publishing Company, 1925.

___. *Joy of Life.* New York: Jewish Science Publishing Society, 1938.

Lichtenstein, Tehilla. *What to Tell Your Friends About Jewish Science.* New York: Society of Jewish Science, 1951.

★1867★
Society of the Bible in the Hands of Its Creators, Inc.
Current address not obtained for this edition.

The Society of the Bible in the Hands of Its Creator, Inc., was formed in 1943. The inspiration for the Society was the work of Moses Guibbory, the Ukrainian-born international president and organizer of the group. He was assisted by British-born radio commentator and Jewish convert Boake Canter and by David Horowitz, founder of the United Israel World Union, who met Guibbory in Jerusalem. The object of the Society was to publish and spread the ideas of *The Bible in the Hands of Its Creators* by Guibbory and both a Hebrew and an English Bible as perfected by Guibbory's research, and to develop and maintain places of devotion and spiritual guidance for members of the Society.

The Bible in the Hands of Its Creators is a massive volume, the chief ideas of which center upon defining the nature of Jehovah, the one God, besides whom there is no other. Jehovah, while one, is also many. He is both male and female, the terrible God, the creator, the merciful and gracious God, the forgiving and long-suffering one. The prophetic day of Jehovah began in 1929 (5689 A.M.) and has since continued.

Guibbory, as the international president, controlled the Society, assisted by an executive board of from five to 13 members. Missionary work was begun in the Society but was stopped by Guibbory. In the late 1970s, the Society closed its New York office and no contact has been re-established. In the 1970s the only known gathering of members was at Guibbory's South Norwalk, Connecticut home for the major Jewish holidays. Gentile converts were included.

Sources:

Guibbory, Moses. *The Bible in the Hands of Its Creator.* New York: Society of the Bible in the Hands of Its Creator, 1943.

★1868★
United Israel World Union
1123 Broadway
New York, NY 10010

The United Israel World Union was formed in 1944 in Walerville, New York, by Swedish-born David Horowitz. The UIWU is based upon "the eternal monotheistic values contained in the Torah and the eternal precepts of Israel as emanating from Sinai under Moses." It accepts the Hebrew Bible as a blueprint not for Israel alone, but for all humanity. As such, a vigorous educational program to inform all people, particularly Christians, of its activities is being conducted. Among the leaders of the movement are a number of converts from various national, ethnic, religious, and racial backgrounds, including black Jewish rabbi Mosha Hailu Paris, and former Jehovah's witness, Olin Moyle. Horowitz has developed a special appreciation for Pastor Charles Taze Russell, first president of what is today known as the Jehovah's Witnesses, who was one of the earliest voices of Zionism, and in 1986 Horowitz authored a book about Russell's Zionist activities.

Underlying the UIWU credo is the recognition of untold numbers of Gentiles as the descendents of the 10 lost tribes of Israel.

A major goal of the organization is a reunion of Judah and Israel, and it sees itself as a meeting place for this reunion. Some acceptance of the union has been found among Reform Jews, who also seek to universalize the Jewish message. In America, groups were formed in New York, Michigan, Virginia, Illinois, and other states. In New York, the triannual *United Israel Bulletin* is published by the movement. Associated with the New York headquarters is the Brotherhood Synagogue in Manhattan.

Membership: In 1995 the union reported 21,100 members and 20 centers. Foreign members could be found in Israel, England, Germany, Ghana, Japan, Mexico, the Philippines, and Spain.

Periodicals: *United Israel Bulletin.*

Sources:

Horowitz, David. *Pastor Charles Taze Russell, An Early American Christian Zionist.* New York: Philosophical Library, 1986.

Section 22

Middle Eastern Family, Part II: Islam, Zoroastrianism, and Baha'i

Consult the Contents pages to locate the essay in Part II, Historical Essay Chapters,
that provides an historical discussion of this family

Intrafaith Organizations

★1869★

American Muslim Council
1212 New York Ave. NW
Washington, DC 20005

The American Muslim Council was founded in 1990 as a cooperative body serving the interests of the Muslim community in the United States. Its aims are to counter discrimination against Muslims, involve Muslims in the social and political life of the nation, develop consensus on issues of vital importance to the community, and serve as a resource center for Muslims of all ethnic backgrounds. The council has been active in preparing a demographic profile of the community, and preparing and distributing material on Muslim culture, especially about their holidays. It also holds an annual leadership conference.

★1870★

As-Sunnah Foundation of America (ASFA)
607A W. Dana St.
Mountain View, CA 94040

As-Sunnah Foundation of America (ASFA) was founded by a group of Muslims from various Islamic backgrounds who seek to promote the unity of Muslims. ASFA emphasizes a well-known Islamic principle that a believer may follow any School of Thought (fiqh), and as long as s/he accepts the Sunnah and the Shariah, s/he must be seen as living within the boundaries of the community (ummah) of the Prophet Muhammad. Experience has taught that the various schools of Islam have not been divisive but in fact have provided the basis of stability for the ummah.

ASFA has developed centers in the United States, Europe, the Middle East, the Subcontinent, Africa, and the Far East. These offices are centers for scholarship, Islamic leadership training, and the development of Islamic character. The foundation is also connected to a number of associate and affiliate organizations specializing in Islamic scholarship.

Membership: Among ASFA's affiliate organizations are Majlis Ugama Singapura (Islamic Council of Singapore); the Center for Islamic Thought & Research, University of Chicago; Human Rights Council, U.S.A.; School of Social and Islamic Sciences, Leesburg, Virginia; Muslim Forum International, London, UK; Idara Minhaj ul Quran, Lahore, Pakistan; Daar ul-Ehsaan, Faisalabad, Pakistan; and the Nur Institute of Islamic Studies, Baltimore, Maryland.

Sources:

Marcia K. Hermansen "Hybrid Identity Formations in Muslim America: The Case of American Sufism" Unpublished, undated paper in ISAR collection.

★1871★

Council of Islamic Organizations of America
5825 Kings Hwy.
Brooklyn, NY 10123

The Council of Islamic Organizations of America is a coordinating organization serving the many Muslim groups in the United States. It was founded in Saudi Arabia in 1973 by the representatives of different mosques who were in attendance at the Jeddah Unification meeting and was chartered in Washington, D.C., a short time later.

The council's main purpose is the propagation of Sunni Islam (as opposed to the Shi'a Islam which dominates in Iran and Iraq). It accepts the interpretation of Islam coming from Saudi Arabia. The council has a program of assistance for communities desiring to erect a mosque and financial assistance for activities that build and nurture the Muslim community as a whole (schools, summer camps, medical centers, etc.).

Membership: Members include a number of mosques across the United States and several cooperative associations such as the Muslim Students Association, the Federation of Islamic Associations, and the Islamic Society of North America.

★1872★

Council of Muslim Communities of Canada
Box 771, Station B
Willowdale, ON, Canada M2K 2R1

The Council of Muslim Communities of Canada was founded in 1962 to serve as a coordinating body among the numerous mosques which had been founded through and since the 1950s. It also works to improve relations between Muslims and their non-Muslim neighbors and to develop programs to pass Islam on to the second and third-generation children of the immigrants. The Council of Muslim Communities of Canada is affiliated with the Council of Islamic Organizations of America.

Periodicals: *Canada-Islam.*

★1873★

International Association of Sufism (IAS)
25 Mitchell Blvd., Ste. 2
San Rafael, CA 94903

The International Association of Sufism (IAS), founded in 1983, operates as a general advocacy organization for Sufism and seeks to provide a forum for a continuing dialogue between the different schools of Sufism. In furtherance of these goals, the association has developed an extensive publication program, which brings Sufi Masters together with writers, translators, editors, and other members of the English-speaking intellectual community. Association members have many articles, essays, and important Sufi works translated into English.

Among the more important IAS achievements is an annual Sufism Symposium. This international, multicultural festival brings prominent Sufi masters from around the world to the United States to share their wisdom with the largely English-speaking audience. Through the year, IAS also holds seminars, classes, gatherings, and conferences on such subjects as Sufism and psychology; Sufi poetry and literature; principles of Sufism; meditation; and Sufi music. IAS sponsors a Social Service and Awareness Program, the Sufism & Psychology Forum, the Sufi Women's Organization, and the Prison Social Service Project.

The association is closely associated with the School of Islamic Sufism, an Iranian Sufi order founded in the United States by Shah Maghsoud Angha. His daughter, Dr. Nahid Angha, is cofounder, along with Dr. Ali Kianfar, of the association.

Membership: Not reported.

Periodicals: *Sufism Journal.* • *Insight.* • *Sufism and Psychology.* • *Sufi Women.*

Sources:

Marcia K. Hermansen "Hybrid Identity Formations in Muslim America: The Case of American Sufism" Unpublished, undated paper in ISAR collection.

★1874★
Muslim World League
134 W. 26th St.
Box 1674
New York, NY 10001

Alternate Address: International headquarters: Box 537, Makkah al Mukarramah, Saudi Arabia.

The Muslim World League was founded in 1962 as a relief organization working in Muslim countries which also had the aim of advancing Islamic unity and solidarity. The league is supported by the government of Saudi Arabia and has distributed grants for the erection of mosques around the world (including the United States). It includes within its structure the World Council of Mosques and the World Assembly of Muslim Youth.

Islam

★1875★
His Highness Prince Aga Khan Shia Imani Ismaili Council for the United States of America
PO Box 77
Rego Park, NY 11374

The Shia Imami Ismaili Muslims, generally known as the Ismailis, belong to the Shia branch of Islam, one of the two major branches of Islam, the Sunni being the other. The Ismailis live in more than 25 different countries, mainly in Asia, Africa, and the Middle East, as well as in the West.

As Muslims, the Ismailis affirm the fundamental Islamic Testimony of Truth, the *Shahada*, that there is no god but Allah and that Muhammad is His Messenger. They believe that Muhammad was the last and final prophet of Allah, and that the Holy *Quran*, Allah's final message to mankind, was revealed through him.

In common with other Shia Muslims, the Ismailis affirm that after the Prophet's death, Hazrat Ali, the Prophet's cousin and son-in-law, became the first Imam—the spiritual leader—of the Muslim community and that this spiritual leadership (known as Imamat) continues thereafter by heredity through Ali and his wife Fatima, the Prophet's daughter. Sucession to Imamat, according to Shia doctrine and tradition, is by way of *Nass* (designation), it being the absolute prerogative of the Imam of the time to appoint his successor from amongst any of his male descendants whether they be sons or remoter issue.

His Highness Prince Karim Aga Khan is the 49th hereditary Imam of the Shia Imami Ismaili Muslims. He was born on December 13, 1936, in Geneva, son of Prince Aly Khan and Princess Tajuddawlah Aly Khan and spent his early childhood in Nairobi,

Kenya. He attended Le Rosey School in Switzerland for nine years and graduated from Harvard in 1959 with a B.A. in Islamic History. He succeeded his grandfather Sir Sultan Mahomed Shah Aga Khan on July 11, 1957, at the age of 20.

Among the major contributions to the growth of Islamic civilization made by the Ismailis are the University of al-Azhar and the Academy of Science, Dar al-Ilm, in Egypt. Indeed the city of Cairo itself is a testimony to their contribution. Among the renowned philosophers, jurists, physicians, mathematicians, astronomers, and scientists of the past who flourished under the patronage of Ismaili Imams are Qadi al-Numan, al-Kirmani, Ibn al Haytham (al-Hazen), Nasir-e-Khusraw, and Nasir al-Din Tusi. In more recent times, the 48th Imam, Sir Sultan Mahomed Shah Aga Khan, has been recognized for his contribution to the Muslim world and his efforts to promote international understanding, especially as the President of the League of Nations (1937-1938), the forerunner of the United Nations.

Spiritual allegiance to the Imam and adherence to the Shia Imami Ismaili tariqa (persuasion) of Islam according to the guidance of the Imam of the time, have engendered in the Ismaili community an ethos of self-reliance, unity, and a common identity. In a number of countries of their residence, the Ismailis have evolved a well-defined institutional framework through which they have, under the leadership and guidance of the Imam, made notable progress in the educational, health, housing and economic spheres, establishing schools, hospitals, health centers, housing societies, and a variety of social and economic development institutions for the common good of all citizens regardless of their race or religion. Programs and institutions established or expanded in recent years by the present Aga Khan, as Imam of the Ismailis, include the Aga Khan Foundation, the Aga Khan University, the Aga Khan Education Services, the Aga Khan Health Services, the Aga Khan Fund for Economic Development, and the Aga Khan Trust for Culture, all of which seek to contribute to the progress and development of the many nations where the Ismailis live, as well as the third world generally.

The Aga Khan Foundation is a noncommunal development agency committed to promoting sustainable and equitable social development. The foundation provides grants and technical assistance to people and institutions that are evolving innovative approaches to pressing social and environmental problems. Its particular emphasis is on health, education, and rural development in the low-income countries of Asia and Africa. The foundation, which has affiliates in Canada and the United States, collaborates with more than 30 other national and international organizations in financing development programs, including the Canadian International Development Agency (CIDA), the Commission for European Communities, the Overseas Development Administration in the United Kingdom, UNICEF, the U.S. Agency for International Development (AID), and the World Health Organization (WHO).

The Aga Khan University, chartered in 1983 as the first private university in Pakistan, dedicates itself to the establishment and maintenance of internationally accepted standards of education while addressing itself to problems of particular relevance to developing countries. The Aga Khan Unviersity's Faculty of Health Sciences, which includes a Medical College and a School of Nursing located in Karachi, seeks through strong academic, clinical, and community health training to graduate doctors and nurses who are better equipped to respond to the primary health care needs of the third world. Clinical training facilities for the Medical College and the School of Nursing are located at the 650-bed Aga Khan University teaching hospital in Karachi which opened in November 1985. Formal agreements for collaboration by the Medical College have been concluded with three major universities—Harvard, McGill, and McMaster—underlining the commitment of the University towards a high standard of endeaver. The Aga Khan University will establish additional faculties in other countries and is currently exploring alternatives for developing the University's international dimensions.

The Again Khan Education Services operates more than 300 institutions and programs from day care centers to unversity-level education, catering to some 50,000 students, the majority of whom are non-Ismaili. More than 5,000 students benefit from various Aga Khan scholarship programs.

The Aga Khan Health Services consists of more than 200 health care units and programs in the developing world, including maternity homes, primary care centers, diagnostic clinics, dispensaries, and five general hospitals. More than two million outpatients a year, the majority of whom are non-Ismaili, receive services through these institutions.

The Aga Khan Fund for Economic Development is committed to the support of economic development activities in the third world through the promotion of projects in the private sector, primarily through equity participation in third world enterprises, to increase productivitiy and raise standards of living. The fund also collaborates with national and international agencies in the promotion of development institutions. Since 1963, more than 100 new enterprises, ranging from building materials and textiles to mining and tourism which today employ some 10,000 people, have been established in East, West, and Central Africa, as well as in Asia.

The Aga Khan Trust for Culture focuses attention on contemporary expressions of the Islamic humanistic tradition, concentrating largely on the built environment. The triennial Aga Khan Award for Architecture and its associated program of seminars encourages architectural excellence in an effort to enrich the physical environment of the Islamic world, while the Aga Khan Program for Islamic Architecture at Harvard University and the Massachusetts Institute of Technology provide graduate education to a new generation of architects, planners, and researchers.

The Ismailis first arrived in the United States in the early 1960s. The majority were students from the developing world who in the post-independence years came to study at institutions of higher learning. In the 1970s, largely as a result of political instability in parts of Africa and Asia, the community's numbers in the United States increased significantly. Their education, linguistic, and professional skills have helped Ismailis to assimilate easily into the American social fabric. Today, Ismailis are settled throughout the country, and the community is administered by the Ismaili Council for the United States of America, based in New York. There are also local councils which operate under the direction of the national council in different regions of the country. Each council has portfolio members for community programs in such fields as education, health, youth and sports activities, economic development, and social welfare, who endeavor to secure continuing improvements in the quality of life of the community and assist it to make an effective contribution to the societies it lives amongst.

Membership: In 1987 there were an estimated 30,000 Nizari Ismaili Muslims and approximately 75 local centers in the United States, and 40,000 members in Canada.

Periodicals: *The American Ismaili.* Send orders to 3021 Margaret Mitchell Dr., No. 8, NW, Atlanta, GA 30327.

Sources:

Howell, Georgina. "The Story of K." *Vanity Fair* 51, no. 6 (June 1988): 100-108, 173-179.

Nanji, Azim. "The Nizari Ismaili Muslim Community in North America; Background and Development." In *The Muslim Community in North America*, Edited by Earle H. Waugh, Baha Abu-Laban, and Regula B. Qureshi. Edmonton, AB: University of Alberta Press, 1883.

Williams, Raymond Brady. *Religions of Immigrants from India and Pakistan: New Threads of the American Tapestry.* New York: Cambridge University Press, 1988.

★1876★
Shi'a Muslims
% Islamic Center of America
15571 Joy Rd.
Detroit, MI 48228

Alternate Address: Jaffari Islamic Centre, 7340 Bayview Ave., Thornhill, ON L3T 2R7.

Of the two orthodox branches of the Muslim Community the Shi'a is by far the smaller. It includes some Iranian-Americans though Shi'as of other nationalities (Lebanese, Pakistani, Yemeni) are also present in significant numbers. The oldest and among the most prominent Shi'a centers is the Islamic Center of America, a Lebanese center which emerged as the Detroit Islamic community split into the traditional Sunni and Shi'a factions early in the twentieth century. Growth in the Shi'as was marked by its 1949 invitation to Imam Mohamad Jawad Chirri to become the community's spiritual leader and the establishment of the center in the 1960s under his guidance.

More typical of the Shi'a centers established since 1965 is the Islamic Society of Georgia, a Pakistani-American center in Atlanta founded in 1970. It is a major distributor of Shi'a publications from around the world and publishes *Islamic Affairs*. It has made a major priority of its program the circulation of Shi'a literature to "willing readers" at little or no cost. The Midwest Association of Shi'a Organized Muslims is a similar center in Chicago.

A step forward in the organization of the Shi'a community was the 1970 formation of the Shi'a Association of North America by families in New York and New Jersey. Through its newsletter, *Islamic Review*, and other publications, it has led in the establishment of traditional standards of belief and practice in the Shi'a community nationally. The Iranian Revolution under the Ayatollah Khomeini has had a marked effect of uniting the American Shi'a community, which has responded with strong support. In like measure, the American-Lebanese Shi'as have identified with the Shi'as of Lebanon, though they are somewhat divided in their support of the various factions that emerged in the 1970s.

While the majority of English-language Shi'a literature still originates from foreign presses, several publishing ventures have emerged in the United States. The Detroit center has published a number of works by Imam Chirri, an eminent Islamic scholar. It is joined by Free Islamic Literature, Inc. of Houston, Texas and Mehfile Shahe Khorasan Charitable Trust of Englewood Cliffs, New Jersey.

Membership: Not reported. There are several dozen Shi'a centers scattered across the United States.

Educational Facilities: The Islamic Seminary, New York, New York.

Periodicals: *Islamic Affairs*. Available from the Islamic Society of Georgia, 172 Vine St., SW, Atlanta, GA 30314. • *The Islamic Review*. Available from the Shia Association of North America, 108 5363 62nd Dr., Forest Hills, New York, NY 11375. • *Husaini News*. Available from the Husaini Association of Greater Chicago, PO Box 6810, Chicago, IL 60645.

Sources:

Chirri, Mohammad Jawad. *The Brother of the Prophet Mohammad.* 2 vols. Detroit: Islamic Center of Detroit, 1979-82.

Chirri, Mohammad Jawad. *Inquiries About Islam.* Detroit: Islamic Center of Detroit, 1965.

Iman Khomeini, Pope and Christianity. Tehran, Iran: Islamic Propaganda Organization, 1983.

The Life of Iman Husain. Englewood Cliffs, NJ: Mehfile Shahe Khorasan Charitable Trust, n.d. Tract.

Shariati, Ali. *Islamic View of Man.* Houston, TX: Free Islamic Literature, 1979.

★1877★
Shiah Fatimi Ismaili Tayyibi Dawoodi Bohra (Daudi Bohras)
% Anjuman-e-Ezzi, Washington, DC
18720 New Hampshire Ave.
Ashton, MD 20806

Alternate Address: International Headquarters: Dawat-e-Hadiyah, Administration of the 52nd al-Dai al-Mutlaq, His Holiness Dr. Syedna Mohammed Burhanuddin, c/o Saifee Masjid, Burhani Park, Lagos Road, City Centre, Nairobi, Kenya. Canadian Headquarters: c/o Anjuman-e-Najmi, Toronto, 61 Queensmill Ct., Richmond Hill, ON L4B 1N2.

The Daudi Bohras constitute a worldwide religious group officially known as the Shiah Fatimi Ismaili Tayyibi Dawoodi Bohra, a community within the larger world of Orthodox Islam. This group follows a specific code of beliefs, doctrines, and tenets founded on the Qur'an and the Shariah, as taught and interpreted by their leader, the Dai al-Mutlaq. The Daudi Bohras traces its ancestry to the early conversions of Hindus in India in the eleventh century to the Ismaili branch of Shi'a Islam. These converts in turn gave their allegiance to the dai mutlaq in Yemen. They are named after their 27th dai, Daud ibn Qutubshah (d. 1612).

The Daudi Bohra community has largely been molded into its present form by the two dais who have led the community in the twentieth century. The 51st dai, Dr. Sayyidna Tahir Saifuddin (1915–1965), was an accomplished scholar and capable organizer who revitalized the community during his half century of leadership and guided it through the tumultuous period of world wars and independence of nations. The present dai, H. H. Dr. Sayyidna Mohammed Burhanuddin, has continued his predecessor's endeavors with particular emphasis on strengthening the community's Islamic practices.

The religious hierarchy of the Daudi Bohras is headed by the dai mutlaq who is appointed by his predecessor in office. The dai appoints two others to the subsidiary ranks of madhun (licentiate) and mukasir (executor). These positions are followed by the rank of shaykh and mullah, both of which are held by hundreds of Bohras. An Aamil (usually a graduate of the order's institution of higher learning, al-Jamiah al-Sayfiyah) leads the local congregation. The local organizations administer the activities of the local Bohras and report directly to the central administration of the dai, called al-Dawah al-Hadiyah.

At the age of puberty every Bohra believer takes the traditional oath of allegiance which requires the initiate to adhere to the shariah and accept the leadership of the imam and the dai. This oath is renewed annually. The Bohras follow the Fatimid school of jurisprudence that recognizes seven pillars of Islam, the first of which is *walayah* (love and devotion) for Allah, the Prophets, the imam, and the dai. The other six are *tahrah* (purity & cleanliness), *salah* (prayers), *zakah* (purifying religious dues), *sawm* (fasting), *hajj* (pilgrimage to Mecca) and *jihad* (holy war). Pilgrimages to the shrines of the saints are also an important part of the devotional life of Bohras.

Within their community, Daudi Bohras speak an arabicized form of Gujrati, called lisan al-dawah, which is permeated with Arabic words and written in Arabic script. They also follow a Fatimid lunar calendar which fixes the number of days in each month.

Dawat-e-Hadiyah, Allah's sovereignty over Heavens and Earth, is entrusted to the Imam (who in the Ismaili tradition is known as the Hidden or Secluded Imam). In his absence, the Dawat-e-Hadiyah is headed by the Dai al-Mutlaq, the Imam's representative and vicegerent, the supreme head of the Dawoodi Bohra Community. Today, al-Dai-al-Fatimi, His Holiness Dr. Syedna Mohammed Burhanuddin (TUS), is the 52nd Dai al-Mutlaq, the latest in a chain of succession that commenced in 1138 C.E. He succeeded to the throne of Dawat in 1965 as the successor to his father, H. H. Dr. Syedna Taher Saifuddin, the 51st Dai al-Mutlaq.

In the United States of America, the affairs of Dawat-e-Hadiyah are carried out in accordance with the wishes and direction of the Dai al-Mutlaq through the Dawat-e-Hadiyah (America). Members of the Daudi Bohra community migrated to the United States in the 1950s with the encouragement, permission, and blessings of the Dai al-Mutlaq. There are now a number of communities across the United States and Canada.

Membership: Not reported. Daudi Bohras number about a million and reside in India, Pakistan, the Middle East, East Africa (since the eighteenth century), and the West (since the 1950s).

Sources:

http://www.ececs.uc.edu/~imutaban/Islam/Shia/Bohra/.

★1878★
Sunni Muslims
% Islamic Center
2551 Massachusetts Ave. NW
Washington, DC 20008

Alternate Address: The Council of Muslim Communities of Canada, Box 771, Station B, Willowdale, ON, Canada M2K 2R1.

The Islamic world, though concentrated in the Arab nations of the Middle East, stretches from Yugoslavia to Indonesia and includes not only a large part of the U.S.S.R. but a growing community in Africa south of the Sahara. Since 1965, the Islamic community which had been concentrated in the Midwest and a few Eastern urban centers, has blossomed into a significant religious element of American life in every part of the United States. Literally millions of immigrants from Islamic Asia, Africa and Europe have settled in North America and begun the generation-long process of building ethnic community centers and facilities for worship (often the same building).

Unlike much of Christendom, Islam is organized into a number of autonomous centers. Each center (which may be called a community center, a mosque, a musjid) will tend to be dominated by one ethnic community, though outside the largest urban centers where a variety of mosques can be found, centers will have welcomed people of various nationalities into affiliation. Many of the major centers will have a periodical, which has both a primary local audience and a national circulation. The mosque, headed by the imam (minister-teacher) is the basic center of Islam.

Above the level of the local centers, a variety of national and continental organizations have been formed to mobilize the various local Islamic communities, provide the public (largely ignorant of Islam) with information, and coordinate the activities (particlarly the propagation of the faith) of the community at large. These organizations, whose membership will come from a variety of ethnic backgrounds, tend to be divided politically. Each of the different organization will be ideologically aligned to, for example, different factions in the Middle East, and/or atuned to a more-or-less activist role in support of various concerns of the land from which they immigrated. Political activism is particularly noticeable in those groups which serve the large Muslim community on the nation's campuses. Local centers will often affiliate with several of the competing national associations.

Symbolic of Sunni Muslim presence in America is the Islamic Center in Washington, D.C. Begun in 1949, it took seven years to complete. It was officially opened in 1957. While begun as a center for diplomatic personnel, with financial support from seventeen countries, with the growth of Islam in North America it has become a place to which all American Sunnis look as a visible point of unity in the otherwise decentralized Islamic community. The importance of the Center was dramatically underscored in the early 1980s when it was taken over by a group who supported the Iranian Revolution under the Ayatollah Khomeini and opposed the influence of the ambassadors from Saudi Arabia and other Islamic countries. The takeover disrupted the center for several years and led to the withdrawal of its prominent iman, Dr. Muhammad Abdul Rauf, a leading Islamic apologist in North America.

Among the oldest of the Canadian-United States organizations is the Federation of Islamic Organizations in the United States and Canada. It was founded in 1952, largely as a result of the efforts of Abdullah Ingram of Cedar Rapids, Iowa. He called a meeting attended primarily by Lebanese Muslims, representative of the older American Muslim centers, and formed the International Muslim Society, which two years later became the Federation. The Federation has as its goals the perpetuation of Islam and of Muslim culture and the dissemination of correct information about Muslim society worldwide. It publishes a periodical, *The Muslim Star*, and holds annual conventions, usually in the Midwest. The Federation accomplishments have been related to the fellowship of various Muslim centers across national and ethnic boundaries, and more activist groups, while acknowledging the contribution of the Federation, saw the need for further organizations.

The Islamic Society of North America emerged in the early 1980s out of the Muslim Students Association originally founded in 1952. It represents a broadening focus of concern by former students who moved into roles of leadership in the Muslim, academic and professional communities in America. The Society is headquartered at the Islamic Teaching Center, a large complex in suburban Indianapolis, from which it oversees the network of subsidiary organizations it has fostered and nurtured.

From its original goals, developed to assist graduate students temporarily in the United States for study to survive in a non-Muslim environment, the Society has since 1975 refocused its attention on building Islamic structures among a permanent and growing North American Islamic population and actively propagating the faith among the non-Muslim public. To these ends, the society has established the Islamic Medical Association, the Association of Muslim Social Scientists and the Association of Muslim Scientists and Engineers. It has published numerous books (including the proceedings of the many conferences its sponsors) and pamphlets (especially a set designed to introduce Islam to non-Muslims) and several periodicals, most prominently *Al-Ittihad* and *Islamic Horizons*. The Muslim Student Association continues as one department of the Society. The Islamic Teaching Center is the main structure engaged in *dawah*, the propagation of the faith.

Possibly the most inclusive Islamic organization for Sunni Muslims is the Council of Islamic Organizations of America (both the Federation of Islamic Associations and the Islamic Society of North America are affiliates). The idea of the Council emerged in 1973 at a meeting in Saudi Arabia. Then the Muslim World League, an international Muslim organization with offices in New York City, organized the first Islamic Conference of North America which met April 22-24, 1977 at Newark, New Jersey. The Council was organized at that gathering to meet primary needs for unity and co-ordination of the many Islamic centers in North America. In its lengthy list of goals, it set itself the task of fostering unity, establishing and propagating the faith in its fullness, the perpetuation of modest dress codes, assistance in building mosques and other facilities for Muslims, and the funding of various designated projects of broad Muslim interest.

Also formed in the 1970s, the Council of Imams in North America formed as a continent-wide professional organization for the leaders of the various mosques and Islamic centers.

The several organizations mentioned above are but a few of the many new structures being established in the Muslim Community. All of the organizations have been assisted by the development of Muslim publishing concerns, such as American Trust Publications, affiliated with the Islamic Society of North America; Kazi Publications in Chicago; and The Crescent Publications, Tacoma Park, Maryland. As of the mid-1980s, however, the majority of English-language literature produced for the American Muslim community is still published overseas.

Membership: Estimates vary on the size of the Sunni Muslim community. As many as 400 mosques and centers have been counted. Approximately 3,000,000 immigrants from predominantly Muslim countries have come to the United States. Together with converts, including large followings in American black communities, the total number of Muslims approaches the size of the Jewish community.

Educational Facilities: American Islamic College, Chicago, Illinois.

Periodicals: *Muslim Star*. Available from Federation of Islamic Associations in the U.S.A. and Canada, 25351 Five Mile Rd., Redford Twp., MI 48239. • *Islamic Horizons*. Send orders to Box 38, Plainfield, IN 46168. • *Al-Ittihad*, Box 38, Plainfield, IN 46168. • *The Minaret*. Both available from Islamic Center of Southern California, 434 S. Vermont Ave., Los Angeles, CA 90020. • *Path of Righteousness*. Available from Council of Imans in North America, 1214 Cambridge Crescent, Sarnia, ON, Canada N7S 3W4. • *Al' Nourl*. Send orders to 2551 Massachusettes Ave., Washington, D.C. 20008. • *Islam Canada*. Available from Council of Muslim Communities of Canada, Box 771, Station B, Willowdale, ON, Canada M2K 2R1.

Sources:

Abdalati, Hammudah. *Islam in Focus*. Indianapolis, IN: American Trust Publications, 1975.

Avdich, Kamal. *Outline of Islam*. Northbrook, IL: The Islamic Cultural Center, n.d.

Haneef, Suzanne. *What Everyone Should Know About Islam and Muslims*. Chicago: Kazi Publications, 1979.

Soddiqui, Moulana Mohammad Abdul-Aleem. *Elementary Teachings of Islam*. Tacoma Park, MD: Crescent Publications, n.d.

Rauf, Muhammad Abdul. *Islam, Creed and Worship*. Washington, DC: Islamic Center, 1974.

Hussain, S. Mazhar, ed. *Proceedings of the First Islamic Conference of North America*. New York: Muslim World League, 1977.

★1879★
United Submitters International
Box 43476
Tucson, AZ 85719

United Submitters International was founded by Rashad Khalifa (1935-1990), the imam (supreme leader) of a Muslim center in Tucson, Arizona. Born in Egypt, Khalifa was the son of a Sufi master in the Shadhili Order. He was trained in the natural sciences and moved to the United States in 1959 to study at the University of California at Riverside. He received a Ph.D. in biochemistry in the early 1960s. He married an American in 1963 and later became a citizen. While pursuing his career as an agricultural biochemist, he also conducted private research on the *Qur'an*, the Muslim bible. The results were first published in 1973 as *Miracle of the Quran: Significance of the Mysterious Alphabets*.

Khalifa was convinced of the miraculous nature of the *Qur'an* and his writing was a defense of this belief. His early writing was given broad coverage in the Islamic press because of his claims of scientific proof of the *Qur'an*'s miraculousness. Using a computer, he discovered what he believed was a complex mathematical coding within the book. He concluded that it was organized around the number 19, that the organization was so complex that no human being could have worked it out (the keystone for his argument of its divine element), and that only with the arrival of the computer could we now see the mathematical sophistication of it. He expanded upon this basic notion in a second and more popular book in 1981, *The Computer Speaks: God's Message to the World*.

While defending the *Qur'an*, Khalifa also began to attack some basic Islamic affirmations. He suggested that two verses of the *Qur'an* were Satanic insertions in the text. He attacked Muslims for their following the Hadith and the Sunna, both of which he saw as human inventions working against the *Qur'an*. He said it was idolatrous to venerate Muhammad and his writings. He also suggested that he was a messenger just as was Abraham or Muhammad. He claimed that on December 21, 1971, his soul was taken somewhere and introduced to all the prophets and they in turn designated him the "Apostle of the Covenant." His opinions concerning the Hadith and Sunna correlated with his notions of assimilation into Western society as he opposed the dress codes, the segregation of men and women, and other prohibitions they articulated. While many appreciated his work on the *Qur'an*, others denounced his ideas, questioning his authority and the unworthiness of the Hadith and Sunna. He was labeled a heretic and charlatan.

In the midst of the controversy, Khalifa found many supporters. Around 1979 he became the imam of a masjid (mosque) in Tucson, Arizona, and began a magazine, *Submitters Perspective*. He used his position to argue against the slavish adherence to what he saw as outdated Islamic practice. He was attacked by leading Muslim thinkers such as Ahmed Deedat of South Africa, Abu Ameenah Bilal Phillips, and Muzammil Saddiqi.

On January 31, 1990, Khalifa was murdered. James Williams, a member of an ultra-conservative muslim group, Al-Fuqra, was later arrested and convicted of Khalifa's murder. The center in Tucson has continued with a collective leadership and followers of its martyred imam can be found in Phoenix, Arizona, Southern California, and British Columbia.

Membership: Not reported.

Periodicals: *Submitters Perspective*.

Sources:

Haddad, Yvonne Yazbeck, and Jane Idleman Smith. *Mission to America: Five Islamic Sectarian Communities in North America*. Gainesville, FL: University Press of Florida, 1993. 226 pp.

Hosenball, Mark. "Another Holy War: Waged on American Soil." *Newsweek* 123, 9 (February 28, 1994): 30-31.

Khalifa, Rashid. *The Computer Speaks: God's Message to the World*. Tucson, AZ: Renaissance Productions International, 1981. 263 pp.

___. *Miracle of the Quran: Significance of the Mysterious Alphabets*. St. Louis, MO: Islamic Productions International, 1973.

Quran: The Final Scripture. Trans. by Rashid Khalifa. Tucson, AZ: Islamic Productions, 1981. 525 pp.

___. *Quran: The Final Testament*. Tucson, AZ: Islamic Productions International, 1989.

___. *Quran, Hadith, and Islam*. Tucson, AZ: Islamic Productions International, 1982.

Sufism

★1880★
Arica Institute
145 Palisades St.
Dobbs Ferry, NY 10522

The Arica Institute was founded by Oscar Ichazo in August 1971 in New York City. The name comes from Arica, a city near the northern border of Chile where, in 1970, 57 North Americans first received the teachings of Ichazo during a 10-month training.

Arica is described as a mystical school for the clarification of consciousness. It trains people in focused step-by-step work and in a daily routine which enables students naturally to accelerate the path to complete enlightenment. Utilizing the varied body of Arica's unique tools, each person is enabled to progress toward a state of happiness, health, and spiritual unity. It is Arica's belief that only a society composed of enlightened individuals operating in unity has the potential to solve the planetary problems now facing the human community.

To assist the student, Arica has published a number of books by Ichazo and derived from his teachings which carry through the several levels of the training from beginning texts to the advanced manual. The training program itself is divided into nine levels and

is designed to fit into the schedule of people who are also pursuing a career. They can generally be completed in three to four years.

While Ichazo's teachings are best known for their relationship to Georgei Gurdjieff's teachings, he has an eclectic background and had studied with a variety of spiritual masters prior to founding Arica. More recently, in 1991, he was given the Award of Excellence by the United Nations Society of Writers.

Membership: Not reported. In 1992 there were 300 certified teachers of Arica worldwide.

Periodicals: *Arica Institute Newsletter*.

Sources:

Ichazo, Oscar. *Arica Psycho-Calisthenics*. New York: Simon & Schuster, 1976.

___. *The Human Process for Enlightenment and Freedom*. New York: Arica Institute, 1976.

___. *The 9 Ways of Zhikr Ritual*. New York: Arica Institute, 1976.

Interviews with Oscar Ichazo. New York: Arica Institute Press, 1982.

★1881★
Bawa Muhaiyaddeen Fellowship
5820 Overbrook Ave.
Philadelphia, PA 19131

Bawa Muhaiyaddeen Fellowship was founded in 1971. Shaikh M.R. Bawa Muhaiyaddeen was a Sri Lankan Sufi teacher said to be over a hundred years old. In the 1930s he was discovered by pilgrims in the Kataragama Forest, and the Serendib Study Group was established in Colombo, the capial of Sri Lanka. He was first brought to Philadelphia in 1971 by a disciple, and as a group began to recognize him as their spiritual teacher, the Bawa Muhaiyaddeen Fellowship was organized. During the next years until his death in 1986 he traveled between Philadelphia and Sri Lanka.

Bawa saw himself not as the teacher of a new religion, but as dealing with the essence of all religion. He taught the unity of God and human unity in God. A Sufi is one who has lost the self in the Solitary Oneness that is God. It is the individual's sole duty to take the 3,000 qualities of God within him/herself. The soul is the point of divine wisdom at which the consciousness of individuals is known as being one with God. From this point the individual realizes God.

The conditions leading to God realizations are the following: 1) the constant affirmation that nothing but God exists; 2) the continual elimination of evil from one's life; and 3) the conscious effort to become God's qualities—patience, tolerance, peacefulness, compassion, and the assumption that all lives should be treated as one's own. The conditions lead naturally to the practice of *dhikr*, the remembrance of God.

Headquarters of the Bawa Muhaiyaddeen Fellowship is located in a large house in a residential section of Philadelphia where public meetings are held daily. Also on the grounds is the Mosque of Shaikh M.R. Bawa Muhaiyaddeen, where the traditional five times of prayer and the Friday congregational prayers are held regularly. In addition, one house west of the Philadelphia center is the *mazaar* (tomb) of M.R. Bawa Muhaiyaddeen that is open for visitation. Over the years more than 20 books about his teachings have been published by The Fellowship Press. Also available are numberous audio and video cassettes of Bawa Muhaiyaddeen's discourses.

Membership: Not reported. In 1982 there were nine fellowship groups in the United States and two in Canada, and 3,000 members worldwide. There were four branches in Sri Lanka and one in Great Britain.

Sources:

Muhaiyaddeen, M.R. Guru Bawa, Shaikh. *God, His Prophets and His Children*. Philadelphia: Fellowship Press, 1978.

___. *The Guidebook*. 2 vols. Philadelphia: Fellowship Press, 1976.

___. *Mata Veeram, or the Forces of Illusion.* York Beach, ME: Samuel Weiser, 1982.

___. *Truth and Light.* Guru Bawa Fellowship of Philadelphia, 1974.

___. *The Truth and Unity of Man.* Philadelphia: Fellowship Press, 1980.

★1882★
Bektashi Order
Current address not obtained for this edition.

The Bektashi Order of Sufis emerged in the Muslim community of Albania some 700 years ago, prior to the conquest of the country by the Ottoman Empire. Over the centuries it earned a reputation for its respect for other religions, for its allowance of participation by women, for the beauty of its spiritual poetry, and for its support of Albanian independence from the Turkish conquerors.

The Bektashi Order was brought to the United States by Baba Rexheb (1901–1995), an Albanian refugee who had left his homeland during World War II and finally settled on a farm near Detroit, Michigan, where he established a monastery in 1953. Rexheb was raised in Gjirokaster in southern Albania. He completed studies in Islamic theology, law, and literature and was fluent in a number of languages—Arabic, Turkish, Persian, Greek, and Italian—besides his native Albanian. At 21 he became a celibate Bektashi dervish. He was forced to flee in 1944 because of opposition to communism. When he finally made his way to the United States, he established the first Albanian-American Teqe Bektashiane Bektashi center. He built his primary following among Albanian Americans.

Membership: Not reported.

Sources:

Trix, Frances. *Spiritual Discourse: Learning with an Islamic Master.* Philadelphia: University of Pennsylvania Press, 1993.

★1883★
Beshara School of Intensive Esoteric Education
PO Box 2333
Mill Valley, CA 94942

The Beshara School of Intensive Esoteric Education (also known as the Beshara Foundation) was founded in 1971 at Swyre Farm in Gloucestershire, England. It is dedicated to the study of the writings of Muhyiddin Ibn'Arabi, a twelfth-century mystic born in Andalucia, Spain. Ibn'Arabi authored over 300 books, most growing out of his intense experience of God. He taught that there was only One Absolute Being, apart from which there is no other existence. He saw the unity of existence as the essence of all religion, a belief which causes many of his Islamic contemporaries and critics to judge him a pantheist.

The Beshara School has constructed a program which assists people in understanding their personal existence as an aspect of the One Reality. From the orginal center, other facilities were purchased throughout England. In the 1980s Sherborne House, which had served as the center of John Godolphin Bennett's work, was purchased and now serves as the international headquarters. Additional centers were opened in Canada, the Netherlands, and Australia. The Beshara School came to the United States when a center was opened in Berkeley, California in 1976. The American center has developed a study program, publishes the works of Ibn'Arabi, and holds a variety of workshops which apply his ideas to everyday life.

Membership: Not reported.

Sources:

al-'Arabi, Ibn. *The Bezels of Wisdom.* New York: Paulist Press, 1980.

___. *Sufis of Andalucia.* Berkeley and Los Angeles: University of California Press, 1971.

Landau, Ron. *The Philosophy of Ibn 'Arabi.* London: Allen and Unwin, 1959.

★1884★
Burhaniyya Sufi Order
Current address not obtained for this edition.

The Burhaniyya Sufi Order is a popular Sufi group in Egypt and the Sudan. In the 1980s members of this group moved to Canada and settled in Montreal. A center was formally organized in 1987 which now includes both first generation immigrants and some recent converts. Worship is held on Saturday evenings.

Membership: Not reported.

Sources:

McDonough, Sheila. "Muslims in Montreal." In *Muslim Communities in North America* by Yvonne Haddad and Jane Idleman Smith. Albany, NY: SUNY Press, 1994, pp. 321-22.

★1885★
Chishti Order of America
PO Box 7249
Endicott, NY 13761

The Chishti Order of America is one of several Sufi groups in the United States which traces its origins to the Chishti Order, one of the four main branches of Sufism. The Chishti Order was founded by Khwaja Abu Ishaq Chishti, who settled at Chishti in Khurasan in what is present-day Iran during the tenth century. The lineage of leaders of the Chishti Order stayed in Persia until the succession of Khwaja Muinuddin Chishti (1142-1236), the most renowned saint in the order's history. He took the order to India and is regarded as the true founder of the modern order.

Khwaja Muinuddin was born in Sistan, Persia, and raised as a Sufi. The constant warfare he witnessed during his early life reinforced the mystic tendencies he inherited through his family. He studied with Hazrat Khwara Usman Harvani, a teaching master of the Chishti Order, for twenty years and was, upon his departure, granted the khalifat, or succession, of his teacher. He traveled to Lahore and Delhi before settling in Ajmer, then the seat of an important Hindu state. He became a major force in establishing Islam in India. His tomb in Ajmer is sacred shrine as well as the location of the international headquarters of the order.

Over the centuries various leaders of the order have founded new branches. The two most important are the Nizami (founded by Nizamu'd-Din Mahbubiilahi) and the Sabiri (founded by Makhdum Ala'u'di-Din Ali Ahmad Sabiri). Both orders were started by students of Baba Farid Shakarganilj in the thirteenth century. The Chishti Order of America derives its lineage from the Sabiri branch of the Chishti Order. The Nizami branch is represented in America by the Sufi Order (see separate entry).

The Chishti Order of America was founded in 1972 by Hakim G. M. Chishti as the Chishti Sufi Mission, an affiliate of the Chishti Sufi Mission Society of India in Ajmer. Hakim was a student of Mirza Wahiduddin Begg who was the senior teacher at Ajmer during the 1970s. When Begg died in 1979, Hakim was granted his succession, a fact confirmed in a ceremony in Ajmer in 1980. At the same time, the Chishti Sufi mission was renamed the Chishti Order of America.

Khwaja Muinuddin stressed the essence of Sufism as the apprehension of Divine reality through spiritual means and the suppression of the lower self. He taught the need of devotion to one's spiritual master (Pir) as a necessity for salvation. He also stressed the obligation of humanitarian action in the face of the caste system

Membership: Not reported. In 1981 sheihks of the order were to be found in New York, Chicago, and Los Angeles.

Sources:

Begg, W. D. *The Holy Biography of Hazrat Khwaja Muinuddin Chishti.* Tucson, AZ: Chishti of Mission of America, 1977.

★1886★
Claymont Society for Continuous Education
Box 112
Charlestown, WV 25414

John Godolphin Bennett (1897-1974) met Georgei Gurdjieff in 1921 in Constantinople, where Bennett was serving in the British Army. He continued his off-and-on relationship with Gurdjieff until the latter's death in 1949. He subsequently authored a number of books which discussed his work with Gurdjieff and advocated his Fourth Way system. However, he was not bound by Gurdjieff, and in his mature years he also became enthusiastic about both Subud (discussed elsewhere in this chapter) and the yoga of Shivapuri Baba, an Indian teacher. He wrote an important book introducing each to the English-speaking world.

Bennett claimed that Gurdjieff had left him a commission as a teacher of the Gurdjieff system to the world. Bennett's interest in Sabud, for example, was prompted by his belief that Bapak Subuh, it founder, was identical with Ashiata Shiemash, a coming prophet of conscience, spoken of in Gurdjieff's book, *All and Everything*. Bennett also came to believe that humanity had reached the point in evolution that individuals could assume responsibility for its future course. Through spiritual training, individuals could become transformed and in the process begin to transform the world.

In 1971, to put his ideas into action, Bennett founded the International Academy for Continuous Education at Sherborne, Gloucestershire, near Oxford. The core of the program at Sherborne House consisted of a ten-month resident intensive based directly on Gurdjieff. Bennett died in 1974, and the following year the center was closed.

However, beginning with Bennett's American tour in 1971, and the subsequent circulation of his books in the United States, a cadre of American students arose. In 1975 some of those students picked up the thrust of Sherborne House and created the Claymont Society and School in West Virginia. Under the leadership of Pierre Elliot, who had worked with Gurdjieff's prime student Peter Demainovitch Ouspensky and then with Bennett for many years, the Claymont Society has established a community and continued the transformative thrust begun by Bennett. Beginning with Gurdjieff's and Bennett's teachings and methods, the group has incorporated a variety of techniques, especially those of the *Khwajagan*, Sufi teachers of Central Asia.

The Society is designed to function as a "Fourth Way" school, i.e., a community whose members are working together towards human transformation within the context of a task to be realized in the world. The particular task is the building of a community capable of surviving under harsh economic and social conditions and to educate others to do likewise. It is seeking to become self-sufficient economically and organizationally and is building an economic base in farming, cottage industry and in managing a school for interested outsiders to learn the life of the community and the transformative teachings which underly its existence.

The Claymont School provides the basic ten-month program developed for Sherborne House, plus a variety of more inclusive programs offered by other teachers from compatible Sufi, Hasidic, and Eastern perspectives. Coombe Springs Press continues from the Sherborne House establishment as publishers of Bennett's books and other literature of a related perspective. In the United States, Claymont Communications distributes Coombe Springs publications as well as Bennett's material published by others.

Membership: Not reported. The society has a potential for supporting 200 families on its present West Virginia acreage. Less than 100 currently reside there.

Sources:

Bennett, John G. *Creative Thinking.* Sherborne, England: Coombe Springs Press, 1964.

___. *Enneagram Studies.* York Beach, ME: Samuel Weiser, 1983.

___. *Gurdjieff, Making a New World.* New York: Harper & Row, 1973.

___. *Is There "Life" on Earth?* New York: Stonehill Publishing Company, 1973.

___. *Witness.* Tucson, AZ: Omen Press, 1974.

★1887★
Fellowship of Friends
PO Box 100
Oregon House, CA 95962

The Fellowship of Friends was founded in San Francisco in 1970 by Robert E. Burton as a school of spiritual development of the "Fourth Way" tradition that began with Georgei Gurdjieff and was developed and passed on through Peter Demainovitch Ouspensky and Rodney Collins. Central to the tradition as understood by Burton is the practice of self-remembering, a form of meditation in which students attempt to become more aware of themselves each moment of their lives. It is the school's understanding that human beings are as yet incomplete and are set to evolve further, to gain individuality, conscience, consciousness, and immortality, but that true change only occurs under pressure (like the pressure of an alchemical oven), and within the Fourth Way such pressure is provided by the disciplined psychological tools and work within a group.

Apollo, the main center of the Fellowship of Friends, is a 1,400 acre site in Yuba County, California, purchased in 1971. It is a community designed to assist the process of change in its members. Other members of the fellowship live in locations around the world and participate in nonresident groups.

At the community at Apollo, numerous events occur which provide opportunities to apply and verify the truth of the teachings. Such opportunities include concerts, lectures, classes, and work projects. Members are involved in the arts and come to understand how higher spiritual states can be created through beautiful and harmonious forms. The arts program gave birth in the early 1990s to the Apollo Opera, which draws most of its members from Apollo with additional assistance from guest singers and musicians drawn from across northern California.

As part of its program, the Apollo community created Renaissance Winery, one of the largest mountain wineries in North America. The members cleared the land (365 acres) and planted the vines by hand. The award-winning winery now produces approximately 23,000 cases per year.

Membership: As of 1998, the fellowship had approximately 2,000 members, approximately 650 of whom lived at Apollo. The remainder were scattered in seven centers across the United States, and additional centers in Toronto, Ontario; Paris; London; and Mexico City.

Sources:

Burton, Robert E. *Self-Remembering.* York Beach, ME: Samuel Weiser, 1991, 1995. 216 pp.

★1888★
Gurdjieff Foundation
85 St. Elmo Way
San Francisco, CA 94127

Georgei Gurdjieff (d. 1949) was a modern spiritual teacher greatly influenced by Sufism, but who blended it, with other spiritual teachings, into a unique philosophy which have in the several decades since his death become the springboard for a host of variations. Born in the 1870s in a small town on the Armenian-Turkish border, Gurdjieff studied the mysticism of Greek Orthodoxy and developed an interest in both science and the occult prior to leaving home as a young man. He began a period of wanderings that took him from Tibet to Ethiopia as a member of a legendary band, the Seekers of the Truth, in quest of esoteric wisdom. A significant period was spent among the Turkish Sufi masters.

In 1912 he surfaced in Moscow where he met his most important disciple, Pyotr Demainovitch Ouspensky. With his students, he left Russia as the revolution was beginning and settled in Paris, where in 1922 he founded the Institute for the Harmonious Development of Man. Here, the unknown and the famous gathered to study with Gurdjieff. Among his students were Alexander de Salzmann and his wife Jeanne de Salzmann, author Katherine Mansfield, writer/editor A. R. Orage, and Maurice Nicoll.

Gurdjieff taught that humans are asleep, that they are operated like puppets by forces of which they have no awareness. He looked for individuals who had awakened to their contact with the higher force that brought direct awareness (and hence some degree of control) of the other forces of their environment. Gurdjieff developed a variety of techniques to assist the awakening process. Possibly the most famous were the Gurdjieff movements, a series of dancelike exercises. He also generated considerable controversy for placing students in situations of tension and conflict designed to force self-conscious awareness. The system required an individual teacher-student relationship almost of necessity. It came to be known as the "fourth" way, the way of encounter with ordinary life, as opposed to the other ways of the yogi, monk or fakir. The way was symbolized by the enneagram, a nine-pointed design in a circle.

Two years after the opening of the Institute, Gurdjieff toured America with his students presenting demonstrations of the movements. He found a ready audience among people who had read Ouspensky's book, *Tertium Organum* (1920) and/or who had been influenced by Orage. The genesis of his American following dates from this trip. Gurdjieff closed the Institute in 1933, but continued to teach and to write for the rest of his life. Most of his writings were circulated privately to his students. Only one book, *The Herald of Coming God*, was published before his death. His writings include *Beelzebub's Tales to His Grandson* and *Meetings with Remarkable Men* (which was recently made into a film by Peter Brook).

During his last days, Gurdjieff spent much time with long-time pupil Jeanne de Salzmann, who following Gurdjieff's death founded the Gurdjieff Foundation in Paris. This became the model for similar structures around the world. Instrumental in the spreading of the work in the United States was John Pentland (1907-1984) who had studied with both P. D. Ouspensky and Madame Ouspensky in the 1930s and 1940s. He became the president of the Gurdjieff Foundation established in New York in 1953 and assisted in bringing forth the English-language editions of Gurdjieff's and Ouspensky's writings. He collaborated in establishing Gurdjieff societies in major metropolitan areas in the United States and in 1955 he founded the Gurdjieff Foundation of California of which he was president until his death.

Membership: Not reported. The foundation has centers in New York, San Francisco, Los Angeles, and most major cities.

Sources:

Driscoll, J. Walter. *Gurdjieff, An Annotated Bibliography.* New York: Garland Publishing, 1985.

Gurdjieff, Georges I. *Beelzebub's Tales to His Grandson.* 3 vols. New York: E.P. Dutton, 1978.

___. *Life is Only Then, When "I Am".* New York: E.P. Dutton, 1982.

___. *Meetings with Remarkable Men.* New York: E.P. Dutton, 1963.

Ouspensky, P. D. *The Fourth Way.* New York: Alfred A. Knopf, 1957.

___. *A New Model of the Universe* New York: Alfred A. Knopf, 1931.

Speeth, Kathleen Riordan. *The Gurdjieff Work.* Berkeley, CA: And/Or Press, 1976.

Speeth, Kathleen Riordan, and Ira Freidlander. *Gurdjieff, Seeker of Truth.* New York: Harper & Row, 1980.

Webb, James. *The Harmonious Circle.* New York: G. P. Putnam's Sons, 1980.

★1889★
Habibiyya-Shadhiliyya Sufic Order
Current address not obtained for this edition.

The Habibiyya-Shadhiliyya Sufic Order originated with Shaikh Muhammed Ibn Al-Habib, termed Perfect Shaikh and Gnostic of Allah. The Shadhiliyya Order originated in the thirteenth century with Shaikh Al Shadhili of Fez, Morocco, and subsequently divided into a number of sub-orders of which the Habibiyya is one. Al-Habib is designated the Qutb (head of the spiritual hierarchy of saints) and is venerated as the Light of the Messenger. Followers are urged to annihilate themselves in him. He is the author of the *Diwan*, a poetic presentation of his teachings.

Al-Habib speaks of God as the beloved; the goal of life is immersion in him. The way of the world is "Jahiliyya," pride and arrogance. Islam's way is submission and the recognition of our place in the harmonious whole. The main practice of the Habibiyya is Dhikr'Allah (or zhikr), the invocation, remembering and calling upon Allah.

The Habibiyya came to the United States in 1973 and opened a center in Berkeley, California. In 1977 the order claimed 5,000 American members. However, no work in the United States has been visible during the 1980s and its present status is unknown.

Membership: Not reported.

Sources:

The Sufic Path. Berkeley, CA: Privately printed, n.d.

★1890★
Institute for Religious Development
7 Chardavogne Rd.
Warwick, NY 19990

Dr. Willan A. Nyland, a Dutch chemist and founding trustee of the Gurdjieff Foundation, left the foundation in 1960 to found his own group, the Institute for Religious Development. He had studied with Georgei Gurdjieff from 1924 to 1949 and with Gurdjieffs disciple, A. C. Orage. The group is headquartered in Warwick, New York, where a sub-community manages a farm and several cottage industries. Dr. Nyland died in 1975, and his students now carry on his work. Emphasis is on the practical application of Gurdjieffs ideas. (For more information on the Gurdjieff Foundation please refer to the historical essay Middle Eastern Family, Part II.)

Membership: Not reported. Affiliated groups can be found in New York City; Santa Fe, New Mexico; Tucson, Arizona; Seattle, Washington; and Sebastopol, California. There are also groups in Australia, Canada, and the Netherlands.

Sources:

Nyland, Wilhem. *Firefly.* Warwick, NY: The Author, [1965].

Popoff, Irmis B. *Gurdjieff Group Work with Wilhem Nyland.* York Beach, ME: Samuel Weiser, 1983.

★1891★
Institute for the Development of the Harmonious Human Being
Box 370
Nevada City, CA 95959

In the early 1960s the Institute for the Development of the Harmonious Human Being emerged to present the teachings of E. J. Gold. The teachings and practices, whose theme is voluntary evolution as preparation for service to the Absolute, have been constantly refined and developed over the years through intensive research and work. Among the important, though by no means exclusive, sources which Gold drew upon have been the teachings of Georgei Gurdjieff. The hallmark of Gold's teachings, as presented in his numerous books, is the representation of the being or Essential Self as neither awake nor asleep, but identified, in ordinary life, with the body, emotions and psyche—collectively termed "the machine," which is asleep. In relation to the Essential self, the machine has a transformational function, but only if it is brought into an awakened state.

The awakened state can be brought about by practices and/or special living conditions within a lifestyle based upon the correct use of attention upon, and attitudes towards, the machine's psycho-physical activities. Long-term, gradual erosion—the wind-and-water method—are favored by Gold for achieving the awakening of the machine, activation of its transformational functions, and eventual transformation of the Essential Self in accordance with its true purpose. Gold has emphasized the discernment of the waking state, the use of indirect methods to overcome the fixed habits of the machine, and the individual's study of his/her "chronic," i.e. a defense mechanism against the waking state acquired by each person in early childhood. Over the years Gold's students have made a wide appplication of his teachings in such diverse field as architecture, psychotherapy, early childhood education, and computer programming.

Membership: In 1988 IDHHB reported 250 members, 20 centers, and 50 ministers in the United States and 30 members, five centers, and five ministers in Canada. Other members were to be found in Australia, Great Britain, West Germany, and Norway.

Periodicals: *Talk of the Month.*

Remarks: There has been much discussion concerning the relation of Gold and Gurdjieff. While there are obvious differences in their teachings, the inspiration of Gurdjieff is quite evident in Gold's choice of a name for his work, his use of the enneagram (a nine-pointed symbol used by Gurdjieff) in his Institute's logo, and his picturing a Gurdjieff look-alike on the cover of several books (such as his *Secret Talks with Mr. G*). Without detracting from the originality of Gold's work and thought, his reliance, especially in his early years, on Gurdjieff is undeniable. During the 1980s, those influences other than Gurdjieff upon which Gold has drawn for his own teachings have become more evident in his writing and other work. This broader base is visible in both the new publications and revised editions of older books issued by the institute since 1985, in the wake of which Gold's pre-1985 writings have been somewhat discounted.

Sources:

The Avatar's Handbook. Los Angeles: Institute for the Development of the Harmonious Human Being, n.d.

Christie, David, et al., eds. *The New American Book of the Dead.* Nevada City, CA: IDHHB Publishing, 1981.

The Gabriel Papers. Nevada City, CA: IDHHB, 1981.

Gold, E. J. *Autobiography of a Sufi.* Crestline, CA: IDHHB Publications, 1976.

___. *The Human Machine as a Transformational Apparatus.* Nevada City, CA: Gateways/IDHHB, Publishers, 1985.

___. *The Joy of Sacrifice.* Nevada City, CA: IDHHB, 1978.

___. *Shakti! The Spiritual Science of DNA.* Crestline, CA: Core Group Publications, 1973.

Practical Work on the Self. Nevada City, CA, IDHHB, Inc., 1983.

Secret Talks with Mr. G. Nevada City, CA: IDHHB Publishing, 1978.

★1892★
International Mevlevi Foundation
℅ Threshold Foundation
139 Main St.
Battleboro, VT 05301

In 1995 Dr. Celalettin Celebi (d. 1996), international head of the Mevlevi Order, requested that an international Mevlevi foundation be established to bring the Mevlevis of the world under one roof. The program of the foundation includes: an annual interna-

tional gathering of the heads of the various branches of the order in different parts of the world, the sponsoring of seminars in different parts of the world, and the publication of a journal. An initial international gathering was held in Bodrum, Turkey, in June 1996. Attendees included representatives from Turkey, the United States, England, Germany, Switzerland, Austria, Chile, and Iran.

The foundation also assumes responsibility to inform everyone about actions and applications that are inconsistent with the moral and spiritual values of the Mevlevi tradition which have been clarified in the last 700 years.

Following Dr. Celebi's death in April 1996, his son, Faruk Hemdem Celebi, succeeded him and now oversees the functioning of the International Mevlevi Foundation and other activities of the Mevlevi Order.

Membership: Not reported.

Sources:

Marcia K. Hermansen "Hybrid Identity Formations in Muslim America: The Case of American Sufism" Unpublished, undated paper in ISAR collection.

★1893★
Ja'far-Shadhiliyya Sufi Order
Current address not obtained for this edition.

The Ja'far-Shadhiliyya Sufi Order made a significant impact on the American Sufi community in the 1980s. The group was founded by Shaikh Fadhlalla Haeri, an Iranian formerly affiliated with the Habibiyya Sufis. In 1980, he and a group of followers established Zahra Trustand began to build a community, Bayt al-Deen (home of religion), at Bianco, Texas. The community had as its model the original Muslim community in Medina. Haeri published a number of books through the associated Zahra Publications.

The community survived through the 1980s, but toward the end of the decade, Haeri decided to relocate to England, and the present state of the American membership is unknown.

Membership: Not reported.

Periodicals: *Nuradeen: An Islamic Sufi Journal.*

Sources:

Haeri, Shaykh Fadhlalla. *Beginnings' End.* London/New York: KPI/Zahra Publications, 1987.

___. *The Elements of Sufism.* New York: Penguin, 1997.

___. *The Journey of the Self: A Sufi Guide to Personality.* San Francisco: Harper, 1991.

___. *Living Islam.* Dorset, UK: Element, 1989.

★1894★
Jerrahi Order of America
864 S. Main St.
Spring Valley, NY 10977

Alternate Address: International headquarters: 15 Nureddin Jerrahi Caddessi, Karaqumrek Duraqi, Istanbul, Turkey; Canadian headquarters: 120 Palomina Dr., Mississauga, ON Canada L42 3H7.

The Jerrahi Order of America is the North American affiliate of the Halveti-Jerrahi Sufi Order headquartered in Turkey. The Halveti (also spelled Khalwati) is regarded as one of the original source schools of Sufism, and members attribute its founding to several thirteenth-century Muslim ascetics. The Halveti developed many branches, one of which was founded in the seventeenth century by Hazreti Pir Nureddin Jerrahi (d. 1733). Born in a prominent Istanbul family, Jerrahi studied law and at the age of nineteen was appointed a judge for the Ottoman Empire's province of Egypt. Just as he was due to sail to his new post, he met Halveti Sheikh ali Alauddin and gave up his legal career to become a dervish. An accomplished student, he soon received *ijazat,* license to teach from his instructor.

The Halveti orders have been characterized by both a strict program of training and emphasis upon individualism (one cause of the continual branching). It has also invested great reverence in any of its leaders who could demonstrate power. Jerrahi is considered a *qutb,* a spiritual pole of the universe, and head of the hierarchy of saints. The order spread throughout the Ottoman Empire and beyond, from Yugoslavia to Indonesia.

The most distinctive practice of the Jerrahi Order is *dhikr* (or zhikr), literally the remembrance of God. Dhikr is the invocation of the unity of God and is performed by the dervishes within a circle headed by their sheikh.

The Jerrahi is currently headed by Sheikh Safer al-Jerrahi, who resides in Istanbul. The order was established within the American-Muslim community in the late 1970s. The The Mosque of the Jerrahi Order of America, its main center, is located in Chestnut Ridge, New York.

Membership: As of 1997, six centers were active in America, two in New York and one in California, Indiana, Illinois, and Washington State. There are also centers in Buenos Aire, Sao Paolo, Santiago, and Mexico City. The Canadian center is in Toronto. European centers are found in Belgium, Bosnia, Germany, Greece, Italy, and Spain.

Sources:

Al-Jerrahi, Muzaffer Ozak. *The Unveiling of Love.* New York: Inner Traditions International, 1981.

★1895★
Kebzeh Foundation
Box 1207-W
Vernon, BC, Canada V1T 6N6

Alternate Address: Essentialist Church of Christ, PO Box 1207-W, Vernon, BC Canada V1T 6N6.

Ahmusta Kebzeh is an ancient spiritual tradition from the Caucasus Mountains that embodies elements of Sufism and Christian mysticism. It describes itself as an applied science of processing the human being by awakening and developing latent human faculties under divine grace and guidance. It is an oral teaching which has been passed on through story, song, and the way of being of the people who carry it.

Ahmusta Kebzeh can be thought of as the science of processing human beings to the level of enabling them to activate and use their utmost human faculties without limit. The life in this universe came to existence as a reflection of a creative power which is the source of everything, and which exists without beginning and without end. This power is electromagnetic in nature with an intelligence and will of its own.

Ahmusta Kebzeh teaches that once an entity comes to existence with a vibration peculiar to potential manifestation of self it enters the World of Creation and starts its cycle of evolution. Every entity which came to existence in creation evolves until ultimately the end of its evolution comes to be one with the very thing it originated from. Evolution takes place in two areas of existence: 1) Material Area, and 2) Mental Area. This cycle of evolution is taking place in everything existing in the world. Humans completed their material evolution some one million years ago and for the last million years have been in the process of evolving in consciousness. The destination of the evolution of human consciousness is ultimately Cosmic consciousness (Christ consciousness), and to such consciousness there is no limit.

The manifestation of this potential is the job of the science of Ahmusta Kebzeh. The application of Ahmusta Kebzeh consists of a long series of physical and mental exercises, somewhat reminiscent of the spiritual exercises brought to the West by Georgei Gurdjieff.

In this generation, Ahmusta Kebzeh has been transmitted orally by Murat Yagan, a Circassian elder who is thought to be the last known living light-holder of this particular tradition. He received it directly from the elders of his people and for the past 20 years has been teaching it to a small group of students in western Canada. The North American group began to work with Murat Yagan in 1975. His teaching work has included lectures, seminars, workshops, evening classes, and casual conversations while working and socializing. Many of these talks were recorded and have been transcribed and now constitute over 4,000 typed pages of material, the first written form the tradition has taken.

The Kebzeh Foundation includes departments and committees, such as The Essentialist Church of Christ and Sunday School, Kebzeh Publications, Distance Education, Application of Kebzeh to the Business of Contemporary Life (AOK), Leaping Committee (includes workshops and proposed Kebzeh School), Newsletter Publication, and Transcription. Within the Kebzeh tradition it is not allowed to receive money for the teaching and the overwhelming percent of all the work done by volunteers.

The Essentialist Church of Christ was founded in 1988 for the purpose of meeting for worship, i.e., showing a loving respect for a higher spiritual power or for someone who represents such a power. The church is based fully on the principles of Ahmusta Kebzeh and on Jesus' teachings under the light of Kebzeh. The church is not interested in proselytizing.

The church takes as guidance the essence of Christ directly. Such guidance is an essential component of mysticism: a faculty peculiar to humans, relating to the direct communion with God, or Ultimate Reality that is neither apparent to the senses nor obvious to the intelligence, but which can be experienced through developing the finest receptivity down in the deepest realm of the subconscious mind; communion with God.

The church affirms a relationship to God and Cosmic Mind and Jesus as the highest example of completed man. Humans' birthright is Christhood. To claim their destiny, human beings must work to awaken their latent human faculties and come to know who they are by discovering God within. The second coming of Christ consists of the elevation of the consciousness of all the people on the planet to Christhood.

Membership: Not reported.

Periodicals: *Kebzeh Review Newsletter.*

Sources:

Yagan, Murat. *I Come from Behind Kaf Mountain: The Spiritual Autobiography of Murat Yagan.* Putney, VT: Thresholds Books, 1984.

___. "Sufism and the Source." *Gnosis* 30 (winter 1994): 40-47.

___. *The Teachings of Kabzeh: Essentials of Sufism from the Caucasus Mountains.* Vernon, BC: Kebzeh Publications, 1995.

★1896★
Khanegah Maleknia Naser Ali Shah
Current address not obtained for this edition.

Khanegah Maleknia Naser Ali Shah is a small Nimatullahis Sufi Order headed by Naser Ali Shah, who moved between centers in Istanbul, Turkey, and Paris, France. Shah's nephew, who resides in Rhode Island, had been designated his kahalifa, and leaders (murids) are found in New York City; Boulder, Colorado; and North Carolina.

Membership: Not reported.

Sources:

Marcia K. Hermansen "Hybrid Identity Formations in Muslim America: The Case of American Sufism" Unpublished, undated paper in ISAR collection.

★1897★
Khaniqahi-Nimatullahi
306 W. 11th St.
New York, NY 10014

Khaniqahi-Nimatullahi is the Western representative of the Ni-matullahi Order of Sufis, an Iranian Sufi order named after Nur ad-din M. Ni'matullah (1330-1431). Ni'matullah was born in Aleppo, in present-day Syria, the son of a Sufi master, and studied with several Sufi teachers before meeting his principal teacher, Abdullah al-Yafi-i, in Mecca. After Sheikh Yafi-i's death in 1367, Ni'matullah began a period of traveling, finally settling in Mahan, Persia (Iran), whence the order spread throughout Persia and India.

The present head of the order is Dr. Javad Nurbakhsh, former head of the Department of Psychiatry of the University of Teheran, Iran. Nurbakhsh brought the order to the West in the 1970s and by 1983 had established centers in London, England, and several United States cities. He also created Khaniqahi-Nimatullahi Publications as the publishing arm of the order, and it immediately began to generate English-language Sufi materials.

Nurbakhsh defines a Sufi as one who travels the path of love and devotion towards the Absolutely Real. Knowledge of the Real is accessible only to the Perfected Ones, the prime model being Ali, the son-in-law of Mohammad, to whom Iranian Shi'ite Muslims trace their authority. Ali traveled the path as a disciple of Mohammad and became not just a spiritual master, but the qutb, or spiritual axis, for his time. The head of the Nimatullahi Order continues in the succession of spiritual masters to whom disciples can look for knowledge.

Membership: In 1991 the order had nine centers in the United States: one each in New York City; Washington, D.C.; Boston, Massachusetts; Seattle, Washington; Chicago, Illinois; Santa Fe, New Mexico; and San Francisco, Santa Cruz, and Mission Hills, California. Several hundred people are involved in the order's work. Foriegn centers were located in Great Britain, Germany, France, the Netherlands, and the Ivory Coast (Africa).

Sources:

Nurbakhsh, Javad. *In the Paradise of the Sufis.* New York: Khaniqahi-Nimatullahi Publications, 1979.

___. *In the Tavern of Ruin.* New York: Khaniqahi-Nimatullahi Publications, 1978.

___. *Masters of the Path.* New York: Khaniqahi-Nimatullahi Publications, 1980.

___. *Traditions of the Prophet.* New York: Kahniqahi-Nimatullahi Publications, 1981.

___. *What the Sufis Say.* New York: Khaniqahi-Nimatullahi Publications, 1980.

★1898★
Mevlana Foundation
Current address not obtained for this edition.

The Mevlana Foundation was founded in 1976 by Reshad Feild, the first sheikh of the Mevlana school of Sufism to travel to the West. The Mevlana lineage was initiated by Mevlana Jelaluddin Rumi (1207-1272), the great thirteenth-century mystic poet. Raised as a Sufi, Rumi was an ecstatic and a visionary. He settled in Qonya, in present-day Turkey, and his tomb became the headquarters of his followers. They formally organized soon after his death.

Sufis share the basic beliefs of Islam but are organized around the leader, the sheikh, of the order who is considered the axis of the conscious universe. Rumi was especially devoted to music, and the Mevlana Order developed a musical emphasis. The order practices the *zhikr*, the remembrance of God, and became noted for its practice of the Turn, a dance in which individual Sufis attempted to establish a universal axis within themselves. For this practice the Mevlana became famous in popular folklore as the "whirling dervishes."

Reshad Feild was raised in London. He studied with a Gurdjieff/Ouspensky group as well as the Druids, and finally became a professional spiritual healer. In the early 1960s he met Pir Vilayat Khan, leader of the Sufi Order, and was initiated as a Sufi sheikh by him. In the fall of 1969, still on a spiritual pilgrimage, Feild encountered a man referred to as simply as Hamid. As a result of this encounter, he traveled to Turkey to study. While there he met Sheikh Suleyman Dede, the head of the Mevlana Order.

In 1976 Feild left Turkey and moved to Los Angeles, where he became a Sufi teacher and healer. Shortly after the move, he assisted Dede's visit to America. During this trip, Dede initiated Feild as the first sheikh in the West. Feild founded the Institute for Conscious Life which later became the Mevlana Foundation.

Membership: Not reported. Groups affiliated with the foundation can be found in the United States, Canada, and England.

Sources:

Feild, Reshad. *Cooperation in the Three Worlds.* Los Angeles: Institute for Conscious Life, 1974.

___. *The Invisible Way.* San Francisco: Harper & Row, 1979.

___. *The Last Barrier.* New York: Harper & Row, 1976.

___. *I Come from Behind Kaf Mountain.* Putney, VT: Threshold Books, 1984.

★1899★
Naqshbandi Sufi Order
% Haqqani Foundation
607 A W. Dana St.
Mountain View, CA 94041

The Naqshbandi Sufi Order is an Islamic school of thought and practice that arose in Central Asia and India, spread through China and the Soviet Union in the twentieth century, and came into Europe and North America in the past generation. The word "Naqshband" includes two ideas: naqsh or "engraving" the name of Allah in the heart, and band or "bond" designating the link between the individual and the Creator. Ideally, the Naqshbandi followers practice their prayers and obligations according to the Qur'an and the Sunnah of the Prophet (Muhammad) and keep the presence and love of Allah alive through the personal experience of the link between themselves and Allah. The Naqshbandi Way holds as an ideal continuous worship in every action, both external and internal. It includes the maintenance of the highest level of conduct, keeping an awareness of the Presence of God, Almighty and Exalted, and a complete experience of the Divine Presence.

The Naqshbandi traces its life to one of the Caliphs, Abu Bakr as-Siddiq, who succeeded the Prophet Muhammad in his role of guiding the Muslim community, and takes its foundations and principles from the teachings and example of him and six other outstanding followers of Islam, and Salman al-Farisi, Jacfar as-Sadiq, Bayazid Tayfur al-Bistami, Abdul Khaliq al-Ghujdawani, and Muhammad Baha'uddin Uwaysi al-Bukhari. Of these, Abdul Khaliq formulated worship in the *dhikr* (remembrance of God), and in his letters he set down the code of conduct (*adab*) that the students of the Naqshbandiyya were expected to follow.

Muhammad Baha'uddin Uwaysi al-Bukhari, known as Shah Naqshband, the Imam of the Naqshbandi Tariqat (path), was born in the year 1317 C.E. He adopted a silent method of remembering God which would become a distinguishing feature of the Naqshbandiyya within the larger Sufi community. Shah Naqshband made the Haj (pilgrimage to Mecca) on three occasions, after which he resided in Merv and Bukhara, and then toward the end of his life he settled in his native city of Qasr al-carifan. His school and mosque remain as the largest Islamic center of learning in Central Asia. Shah Naqshband was buried in his garden as he requested, and the succeeding kings of Bukhara care for his school and mosque. They were recently renovated and reopened after surviving 70 years of Communist rule.

The order is currently headed by Sheikh Muhammad Nazim al-Haqqani, the 40th in the chain of Naqshbandi Masters. He resides in Cyprus. His representative in the United States is Sheikh Hisham Kabbani, his son-in-law. Male followers of the group wear a distinctive dress that includes turbans and green robes.

Membership: Not reported. In 1998, there were 18 Naqshbandi centers in the United States and two in Canada. Additional centers could be found in Great Britain, Spain, Sweden, France, Germany, Holland, Italy, Turkey, Cyprus, Egypt, Lebanon, Kenya, Syria, Argentina, Guadeloupe, Indonesia, Japan, Malaysia, Singapore, Pakistan, Brunei, Brazil, South Africa, and Venezuela.

Remarks: Among the disciples of Sheikh Nazim is the sultan of Brunei, reportedly the richest man in the world.

Sources:

Kabbani, Sheikh Hisham. *The Naqshbandi Way: History and Guidebook of the Saints of the Golden Chain.* Chicago: Kazi Press, 1995.

★1900★
Naqshbandiyya-Mujaddidiyya Order of Sufism
% Golden Sufi Center
PO Box 428
Inverness, CA 94937

Naqshbandi Sufis, named after Bah ad-dn Naqshband (d. 1389), are known as the "silent Sufis" because they practice the silent meditation of the heart. They consider God to be the silent emptiness who is most easily accessed in silence. They also attach great importance to dreams, which they consider to be a form of guidance along the Path. Unlike other Sufis, they do not practice *samac*, i.e., sacred music or dance, nor do they adopt a different dress. Their meetings consist of a period of silent meditation followed by dream work.

Naqshbandi dream work utilizes both spiritual and psychological approaches, and attempts to assist individuals to understand inner guidance and the inner processes of the Path at which they are pictured in their dreams. Dream work assumes the role that the ancient Sufi teaching stories have in other groups. Participants in dream meetings are encouraged to share their dreams, particularly those deemed to have a spiritual dimension.

The Naqshbandi Sufi movement was brought to the West by Irina Tweedie, a Russian woman who had become a Theosophist. While staying at Theosophical Society headquarters in Adyar, India, she encountered a Naqshbandi teacher, Guru Bhai Sahib. After training her, he sent her to England as a teacher of the Great tradition. According to her guru, the teachings antedate Islam and are transmitted through the quickening power of the teacher.

Tweedie moved to England in 1963. Two years later her guru died and she assumed authority to teach and founded the Golden Sufi Center. She made her first visit to the United States in 1985. The center sees its task to be the presentation of the teachings of the Naqshbandiyya-Mujaddidiyya Order of Sufism to the public. Its central program is embodied in its meditation groups. Its center also sponsors retreats, lectures, and seminars. Tweedie retired in 1992, and has been succeeded by Llewellyn Vaughan-Lee.

Membership: Not reported. In 1998, the center reported North American meditation groups operating in northern California, New York City, Los Angeles, Seattle, Minnesota, Chicago, and Vancouver. There were also meditation groups in a variety of locations in Germany, Switzerland, England, Spain, and Australia.

Sources:

Bancroft, A. *Weavers of Wisdom: Women Mystics of the Twentieth Century.* London: Arkana, 1989.

Rawlinson, Andrew. *The Book of Enlightened Masters.* La Salle, IL: Open Court, 1997.

Tweedie, Irina. *Chasm of Fire: A Woman's Experience of Liberation through the Teachings of a Sufi Master.* Tisbury, UK: Element Books, 1979. Expanded version as: *Daughter of Fire.* Nevada City, CA: Blue Dolphin, 1986.

★1901★
Nimatullahi-Gunabadi Sufi Order
Current address not obtained for this edition.

The Nimatullahi-Gunabadi Sufi Order is a branch of the Nimatullahi Sufis headed by Sultan Husayn Tabandah, Rida al Sha (b. 1914), a resident of Iran. The majority of members in the United States are Iranian Americans. In 1960 he appointed his son as khalifa and successor.

Membership: Not reported. Centers are reported in Orange County, California; and Toronto, Canada.

Sources:

Marcia K. Hermansen "Hybrid Identity Formations in Muslim America: The Case of American Sufism" Unpublished, undated paper in ISAR collection.

★1902★
Prosperos
Current address not obtained for this edition.

Closely paralleling the Gurdjieff movement is the Prosperos, founded in 1956 in Florida by Phez Kahlil and Thane Walker, its present leader. Walker, described by all who have met him as an awe-inspiring, charismatic person, is a former Marine and student of Georgei Gurdjieff. He has modeled himself on Gurdjieff, but has broadened his sources with material from Jung, Freud, modern psychological techniques and the occult. The group was named after the magician in Shakespeare's *The Tempest*. It is described as a "Fourth Way" school.

The overarching reality for the Prosperos is the One Mind. Reality is experienced as one views from the perspectives of that One Mind. Both memory and the senses could be one vision, but via fourth way techniques, the self can be identified with the One. "Translation" is the name given that process. In Translation classes, the pupil is led through five steps: the statement of Being (What are the facts about reality?); Uncovering the Lie, the claims of the senses; Argument, or testing of the claims; Summing up Results; and Establishing the Absolute. Thane relies heavily on Gurdjieff's technique of disorientation of the pupil and the importance of the pupil-teacher relationship. He creates many kinds of experiences in various classes and intensive seminars. Pantomime, improvisation, body exercises and singing are all used as aids.

Headquarters of the Prosperos, termed the Inner Space Center, houses Publishing Programs, which produces the monthly *Newsletter*, instructional materials and Thane's book, *Not So Secret Doctrine*. Leadership is vested in Thane and the Mentors. The Mentors are drawn from the High Watch, an inner circle of advanced students who have completed three classes, submitted two theses and delivered an oral dissertation. There is an annual Prosperos assembly. In the Midwest, Thane operates through the Institute of Advanced Thinking, headquartered in Cleveland, Ohio.

Membership: In 1984, there were an estimated 3,000 members in groups in San Francisco; Hawaii; Oregon; New York; Ohio; New Orleans; and Seattle.

Educational Facilities: Prosperos Seminary, El Monte, California.

Periodicals: *Prosperos Newsletter.*

Sources:

Ritley, Mary. *Invitation to a Hungry Feast.* Santa Monica, CA: The Prosperos Inner Space Center, 1970.

★1903★
Qadiri Rifa'i Sufism
PO Box 2511
Napa, CA 94558

Qadiri Rifa'i Sufism began with Ahmed er Rifa'i (1118–1181) ,a descendant of the Prophet Muhammad who was born and grew up in what is now Iraq. As he matured he was sent to study Shaykh Vasiti. Among the stories related of Ahmed er Rifa'i concerns his visit to Medina to Muhammad's tomb. The guard didn't want to let him in because he was not wearing the special clothes that indicated he was a blood descendant of the Prophet. When the guard didn't let him in, he yelled towards the tomb and said, "Eselamu-aleyke ya jeddi" ("Peace be on you, my ancestor"), and then the Prophet answered, saying, "Aleykesselam ya veledi" ("And peace be on you, my son"), and the Prophet's hand came out of the tomb. Ahmed er Rifa'i then kissed the Prophet's hand. Upon witnessing this, the people went into a state of ecstasy and began cutting themselves with their swords and knives. When the ecstasy passed, the people were lying around wounded, so Ahmed er Rifa'i healed them all. After that, Ahmed er Rifa'i was known to have this gift, and his healing act was referred to as a Rifa'i miracle. Typical of Sufism, the Rifa'i Sufis have numerous stories of their founder.

Rifa'i Sufism is seen as a means to find peace and love in Allah's presence. The means is centered in practice designed to unfold the spiritual states in the individual. The shayhk assists individuals in establishing their own connection with Allah, Qadiri Rifa'i. Among the important spiritual practices are *zikr* (remembrance of Allah), which includes *verd* (spiritual reading) and practicing *tesbih* (repeating the names of God on a rosary); diet which for new followers begins with a 40-day period in which the person eats only rice and vegetables (no animal products except honey, no bread, and no other grains except rice); and isolation (during which one contemplates Allah for 10 days).

American Qadiri-Rifa'i Sufis are largely concentrated in the San Francisco Bay area. The American leader is Shaikh Taner Vergonen, who originally moved to the United States from his native Turkey in the 1970s in order to study at Western Michigan University. He returned to Turkey (1977–1992) before settling permanently in the United States.

Membership: Not reported. Main centers are in Berkeley, Marin County, and Los Angeles, California; and Santa Fe, New Mexico.

Sources:

Morreale, Don. The Complete Guide to Buddhist America. Boston: Shambhala, 1998.

★1904★
Rifa'i Marufi Sufi Fellowship
PO Box 202
Chapel Hill, NC 27514-0202

The Rifa'i Marufi Sufi Fellowship is an international Rifa'i Sufi group (a tradition that began with Ahmed er Rifa'i (1118–1181), a descendant of the Prophet Muhammad who was born and grew up in what is now Iraq). It has centers (*tekkes*) in Chapel Hill, North Carolina; New York City; Manisa, Turkey; and Baku, Azarbaijan. It is under the international leadership of Shaikh al-Hajj Sherif er-Rifa'i. American work began in 1992 when Shaikh Sherif Chatalkayacame to the United States following an invitation from the Jerrahi Order of America's center in New York City. He subsequently received an invitation to settle in North Carolina from a businessman who was a Sufi. The group's life is built around *dhikr* (remembrance of God), teaching sessions, and the performance of devotional songs.

Membership: Not reported. In 1995, there were 50 members in the United States.

Sources:

Hilaamn, Hugh Talat. "A Silk Road Runs in the U.S." Unpublished paper presented at the Islam in America Conference, Chicago, Illinois, 1995.

★1905★
School of Islamic Sufism (Oveyssi Sufi Order)
PO Box 5827
Washington, DC 20016

The School of Islamic Sufism (Maktab Tarighat Oveyssi Shahmaghsoudi) is the present manifestation of the Oveyssi Sufi Order. It traces its roots through a lineage of Sufi Masters to Amir-al Mo'menin Ali and Oveys Gharani, who lived in Yemen at the time of Muhammad. Amir al Mo'menin, also known as Hazrat Ali, represents the essence of the teachings of the School of Islamic Sufism. He was a close companion of Muhammad, and also received and cognized the teachings of the Holy Prophet inwardly. On the other hand, Hazrat Oveys received the teachings of Islam inwardly, and lived by the principles taught by him although he had never physically met Muhammad. According to the history of the school, the Prophet would speak of Hazrat Oveys whom he never met, "I feel the breath of the Merciful, coming to me from Yemen." Then, shortly before the Prophet passed from this life, he directed Omar (the second Caliph) and Hazrat Ali (the first Imam of the Shi'a) to take his Cloak to Hazrat Oveys. This act confirmed the method of heart-to-heart communication through which Hazrat Oveys had received the essence of Islam.

The method of the passing of the Cloak represents two significant elements in the teachings of the Holy Prophet which constitute the method of instruction of the School of Islamic Sufism — cognition (understanding) must take place inwardly, and cognition must be confirmed—as it was in the case of Hazrat Oveys, and Amir al-Mo'menin.

Since that time, the Cloak and the method of receiving knowledge through the heart, symbolizing Divine Illumination, and recognizing the recipient, has been handed down through an unbroken succession of Sufi Masters. This act creates the only hierarchy within the School of Islamic Sufism. The designated Sufi Master, called the Pir, represents the essence of the Sufi Way.

The present Master of the School is Molana-al-Moazam Hazrat Salaheddin Ali Nader Shah Angha (b. 1945), also known as Hazrat Pir. Hazrat Pir is the 42nd Master in lineage dating back 1,400 years. He was born in Tehran, Iran, and was tutored by his grandfather, who was the 40th Sufi Master of the Oveyssi Order, and father, Molana Shah Maghsoud Sadegh Angha, the 41st Sufi Master of the Oveyssi Order.

Hazrat Pir's duties have included the designing and supervision of the construction of the Sufi Center known as Sufi Abad in Karaj (close to Tehran). Following his move to the United States (with his father) in 1979, he took the lead in expanding the audience for the sacred teachings. He has authored more than 50 books.

Hazrat Pir's teaching includes the attempt to apply the knowledge of the sacred in tangible forms that become visible symbols of the creative power of the soul. One such symbol is a shrine near Novato, California, designed by Hazrat Pir as a memorial to his father. In accordance with the science of *jafr* (relation of letters and numbers), the dimensions of the building may be converted to letters that yield the name of his father. The shape of the roof structure represents Allah (in Arabic). All the sides of the roof join to form a summit representing the unification of the human being with God, signifying that God can be known in the heavens—the heart, the pure elevated state of the human being.

Membership: In 1998, the school included some 400,000 adherents in its global network of centers.

Sources:

Marcia K. Hermansen "Hybrid Identity Formations in Muslim America: The Case of American Sufism" Unpublished, undated paper in ISAR collection.

★1906★
Shadhiliyya-Miriamiyya

Current address not obtained for this edition.

Shadhiliyya-Miriamiyya is the name given to the group of students who have gathered around author Frithjof Schoun (1907–1998), who has studied with Shaikh Ahmad al-Awadiof the Shadhiliyya-AlawiyyaSufis in Algeria. Schoun was born in Basle, Switzerland, the son of a concert violinist. During his youth, he read the Upanishads and the *Bhagavad Gita*, and soon found the works of French esoteric philosopher Rene Guenon. As a young man he studied Arabic, and in 1932 made his first trip to Algeria where he met the celebrated Shaykh Ahmad al-Alawi, and six years later traveled to Egypt, where he met Guenon. He served in the French Army during World War II, became a prisoner of the Germans, and finally sought asylum in Switzerland. He lived there until moving to the United States in 1980.

Through his many books and articles Schoun became known as the leader of the traditionalist or perennialist movement, which centered on a mystical monist view of the cosmos. After emigrating to the United States, he settled in Bloomington, Indiana, where he continued to live until his death in 1998. Known to his students as Shaikh Isa Nur al-Din, he offered an eclectic Islamic Sufi *tariqa* (path) which, though based in Islam, included insights from Native American teachings, Hinduism, and various forms of mysticism. Additionally, at some point he had had some visionary experiences of the Virgin Mary (also a figure in Muslim teachings), and his teachings (Tariqa Miriamiyya) had a special place for her.

Membership: Not reported.

Sources:

Borella, Jean. "Rene Guenon and the Traditionalist School." In *Modern Esoteric Spirituality*. Edited by Antpoine Faivre and Jacob Needleman. New York: Crossroad, 1992, pp. 330-58.

Schoun, Frithjof. *The Essential Writings of Frithjof Schoun*. Edited by S. H. Nasr. World Wisdon Books, 1986.

___. *Islam and the Perennial Philosophy*. London: World of Islam Publications, 1976.

___. *Understanding Islam*. London: Allan and Unwin, 1963.

★1907★
Shadhiliyya Sufism

℅ Sidi Muhammad Press
Napa, CA 94558

The Shadhili Path of Sufism was founded in Egypt in the thirteenth century C.E. by as-Shaykh Ali Abu-l-Hasan as-Shadhili. Currently, leadership has passed to Shaykh al-Qutb al-Gawth, the Guide of the Shadhili Path. Since 1959, the shaikh has resided at the Mount of Olives in Jerusalem, and has been the Imam at the Masjid al-Aqsa (the Dome on the Rock) for many years. The Dome on the Rock is sacred to the Holy House in Mecca in the tradition of the Night Journey (al-Mi'raj) of the Prophet Muhammad from the Ka'ba in Mecca to the al-Aqsa Mosque and from there to the heavens. The shaikh is well known to many people both in Palestine and in other countries in the world. In 1993 he came to feel that he should travel to other countries, and at the same time an order came to him from Allah to give teachings to all those in every part of the world who were sincerely seeking for the truth of their existence. Up until then the teachings had been offered only in Jerusalem.

An American following began to be created in the mid-1990s. The Sidi Muhammad Press prints materials representative of the group.

Membership: Not reported. Centers are found in Philadelphia, Santa Fe, and the San Francisco Bay area.

★1908★
Society for Sufi Studies

℅ The Institute for the Study of Human Knowledge
Box 176
Los Altos, CA 94023

Alternate Address: Octagon Press, Box 227, London, UK N6 4EW.

Indries Shah (1924-1996) was a twentieth-century Sufi teacher who led a public career of note, but also became the focus of intense speculations about his true beliefs and affiliations. He was born in Simla, India, in 1924, to an Indian father and Scottish mother. Brought to England as a teenager, he would live most of his life in his adopted homeland. His father was a physician (who met his mother while studying in Edinburgh) from Afghanistan, and Shah claimed a lineage that went back to the Prophet Muhammad. Shah was tutored by his father and after finishing his secondary education in England attended the Edinburgh Medical School for a period, though he did not finish his course of study.

In his 30s, he became the Director of Studies for the Institute for Cultural Research and began a process of teaching on Sufism. His first book in Sufism, *The Sufis*, appeared in 1964. It was the first of 20 on the subject. He was considered by his followers as the greatest living exemplar of Sufism, but there was some debate over the source of his authority. Shah himself had to present a document to a prominent Western Sufi, John Godolphin Bennett, in support of a claim that he had been sent to the West by an esoteric school, possibly the same one that Georgei Gurdjieff represented. (Bennett was a student of Gurdjieff.) In his writings, Shah suggested that Gurdjieff was an amatuer who had stumbled on some true Sufi knowledge, and by implication suggested that he (Shah) was the true inheritor of the tradition.

Ja'far Hallaji suggested that Shah was a Naqshbandi Sufi who also had the authority to initiate people in the lineage of several Sufi orders, but no acknowledged Sufi teacher emerged to back that claim. In any case, a number of people emerged from Shah's vast writings who saw him as an authoritative teacher. Shah sees Sufism as only incidentally connected to Islam and more a more attractive set of teachings for a Western audience. Among his leading disciples in North America is psychologist Robert Ornstein.

As the actual content of the teachings is secret, details are somewhat difficult to substantiate, as is the very organization of followers of the society who operate in small groups across North America and Europe. In an early book, *The Diffusion of Sufi Ideas in the West*, a training program was laid out. The potential Sufi learns about Sufism and then makes contact with some Sufis. After an interview, the aspirant will be assigned some initial reading. The aspirant joins a study group or other low demand activity. The leader begins to guide the individual who eventually may be sent on a pilgrimage to further stimulate development. Members of study groups receive regular mailing of "Sufi stories" which form the content of their discussions.

In the United Kingdom, Octagon Press served as a publisher and distributor of Shah's books. In the United States, the Institute for the Study of Human Knowledge (ISHK) has been the principal distributor for Shah's materials. Since the mid-1970s, ISHK has also been sponsoring research and educational programs on the human mind, and the processes shaping one's beliefs, institutions, and experience.

In 1988 Shah suffered two heart attacks but continued to work and write until his death at the end of 1996.

Membership: Not reported.

Sources:

Lewis, L., ed. *The Diffusion of Sufi Ideas in the West*. Boulder, CO: Institute for Research on the Dissemination of Human Knowledge, 1972.

Shah, Indries. *Special Problems in the Study of Sufi Ideas*. Tunbridge Wells, UK: Society for the Understanding of the Foundation of Ideas, 1966.

___. *The Sufis*. New York: Jonathan Cape, 1964.

___. *The Way of the Sufis*. London: Octagon, 1968.

Williams, L. F. Rushbrook, ed. *Sufi Studies: East and West—A Symposium in Honour of Indries Shah's Services to Sufic Studies*. New York: Dutton, 1973.

★1909★
Subud

Current address not obtained for this edition.

In Georgei Gurdjieff's book, *All and Everything*, he speaks of Ashiata Shiemash, the Prophet of Conscious. Some of Gurdjieff's students claimed that the passages were prophetic and that the Ashiata Shiemash was yet to come. One of the students with Gurdjieff during the last years of his life claimed students were told that the Ashiata Shiemash was "already preparing himself a long way from here," (i.e., Paris) and that he would be associated with the Malay Archipelago. After Gurdjieff's death, many of his students awaited the coming of a teacher to pick up the master's mantle; many thought they had found him in the person of Bapak Subuh (b. 1901).

Muhammed Subuh was a local government official from Java. Acting on prophecy that he was to die in his twenty-fourth year, he began to search for spiritual guidance and turned to many teachers, including several Sufi shaikhs such as Shaikh Abdurrahman of the Nakshibendi Order of Dervishes. To a man, they told him that he was different, that they had nothing to teach him and that his enlightenment would come directly from God. However, no enlightenment came until 1925, when one evening a ball of light descended upon him, entered through the crown of his head and filled him with radiant light and vibrations. For the next three years, his body experienced spontaneous occurrences of the *latihans*, a cleansing and purifying process. After three years these stopped, and he entered a period of darkness and confusion. Finally in 1933, his true mission was revealed to him, and he was soon contacted by some Sufis whose teacher had requested the contact. Thus Subud became a movement.

Bapak (meaning father) Subud quit his job and devoted his life to the spread of the movement throughout Java. His work continued for twenty-three years. Some Europeans heard of his work and invited him to England in 1956. In England, Bapak soon gained a following, largely built upon former disciples of Gurdjieff. John Godolphin Bennett was particularly influential the author of the widely read *Concerning Subud*. Bennett, a well-known Gurdjieff disciple, had, in 1946, founded the Institute for the Comparative Study of History, Philosophy and the Sciences at Coome Springs, England, to further Gurdjieff's teachings. The Institute became the center for the spread of Subud in the English-speaking world.

Subud is a contraction of three Sanskrit words: "Sulisa," right living in accordance with the will of God; "Budhi," the inner force residing in the nature of man himself; and "Dharma," surrender and submission to the power of God. The key to Subud is the *latihan*, the process of surrendering to the power of god, and the only group occurrence (usually twice a week) in Subud. Beginners must go through several months of probation before entering the *latihan*. After establishing their sincerity, they are opened. Opening is accomplished through instrumentality of several experienced members (helpers) who are viewed as channels of the higher energies of God. It is believed by Subud that the power originally given directly to Bapak is transmitted by contact with a person in whom it is already established.

The *latihan* proper is a time of moving the consciousness beyond mind and desire and allowing the power to enter and do its work. During this time, males and females are in separate, darkened rooms. Often accompanying the spontaneous period are various body movements and vocal manifestations—cries, moans, laughter, and singing. These occur in the voluntary surrender of the self to the power. During this time, people report sensations of love and freedom and, often, healings. All reach a higher level of consciousness.

After coming to England, Subud spread rapidly. The healing of Eva Bartok in 1957 was a major event in its spread. In 1958, Bapak was invited to the United States by a John Cooke, and Subud found a home among Gurdjieff disciples in this country. It spread rapidly. A periodical, *Subud News* (later *Subud North American News*) was founded in 1959, and Dharma Book Company was established to publish the movement's literature. By 1972, Subud had more than seventy centers in North America.

Membership: Not reported.

Remarks: Some difficulty in studying Subud has been experienced because of the sharp distinction drawn between those who have experienced *latihan* and outsiders. Much literature is produced only for members and unavailable for researchers.

Sources:

Bartok, Eva. *Worth Living For*. New York: University Books, 1959.

Bennett, John G. *Concerning Subud*. New York: University Books, 1959.

Bright-Paul, Anthony. *Stairway to Subud*. New York: Dharma Book Company, 1965.

Muhammad-Subuh Sumohadiwidjojo. *Susila Budhi Dharma*. Subud Publications International, 1975.

Rofe, Husein. *The Path of Subud*. London: Rider & Company, 1959.

★1910★
Sufi Foundation of America

Box 75
Torreon, NM 87061

The Sufi Foundation of America was founded in the 1980s by Adnan Sardan, a Sufi master from Iraq who has studied and been recognized for his accomplishments in five Sufi Orders: the Qadri, Nashibandi, Rafai, Menlevi, and Malamari. He understands Sufism to have derived from the Arabic word *sufir*, to be clear. When the mind and body are pure, one can see the spirit within. Murky vision is caused by attachments to belief, family, traditions, and religion. The Sufi is free of such attachments and has nothing to do with the sense world of the physical, the ego, emotions, tension, and other problems.

The Sufi exercises, including music and dancing, chanting, drumming, and whirling, develop the person and teach selfreliance. The teacher merely assists the student on his or her own path to aloneness with god.

Sardan teaches at the center in New Mexico, the major program being a two-month camp each summer. Followers are found across North America and Europe.

Membership: Not reported.

Sources:

Sarhan, Adnan. *The Human Chicken*. Torreon, NM: Sufi Foundation of America, 1989.

___. "The Sufi Path: Making Life Lovable and Love Livable." *Tantra* 4 (1992): 33-47.

Way of the Spirit with Adnan Sardan: Remarkable Experiences Told by His Students. Torreon, NM: Sufi Foundation of America, 1989.

★1911★
Sufi Islamia Ruhaniat Society

410 Precita Ave.
San Francisco, CA 94110

Alternate Address: Center for the Dances of Universal Peace, 444 N.E. Ravenna Blvd., Seattle, WA 98115.

History. The Sufi Ismalia Ruhaniat Society (meaning the "way of peace through the breath") grew out of the work of Samuel L. Lewis (1896-1971), known by his religious name, Ahmed Murad Chisti, a Sufi teacher originally initiated by Pir Hazrat Inayat Khan in 1923. Following World War II, Lewis traveled to Africa and Asia where he received initiations from several Sufi orders as well as studying with a number of Buddhist and Hindu teachers. Returning to America in 1962 he began to teach and in 1966 initiated his first disciples. He found a responsive audience among the hippies of San Francisco, California, and he began to teach them the spiritual dances and walks he had developed. In 1968, he met Pir Vilayat Inayat Khan, son and successor to Hazrat Khan, and he and his disciple began to work with the Sufi Order.

After Lewis' death, his disciples continued to affiliate with the Sufi Order, but through the early 1970s issues emerged between them which led to their separation from Pir Vilayat and continuance as a separate movement

Beliefs. The teachings of the society draw upon the works of Pir Hazrat Inayat Khan and Murshid Samuel Lewis. It has developed a central focus upon the path of initiation and discipleship. The purpose of initiation is fulfilled in the realization of the One, within and without. The relationship between teacher and disciple is also stressed. It exists to provide the training that leads to realization of the Divine essence believed to be in each human and to lead to a life of service to God and humanity.

Lewis is most remembered for his introduction of spiritual dances and walks in the late 1960s. The dances use motion to facilitate a change the individual dancer's whole life, to make it whole. The dances usually combine simple dance motions with controlled breathing and a mantra (sacred words of power). They are usually done to simple rhythmic music and should lead to states of ecstasy and devotion to Allah. The first dances were derived from the dervish dances of the Middle East. The walks combined feeling, movement, and recitation of sacred phrases. Lewis also left a set of mystical writings that were published by the society. He is considered a true mystic.

Organization. The society is headed by a board of trustees. Centers have been established around the world to teach classes in various topics for the general public and the mureeds (those on the path of initiation), and to provide settings for the practice of the spiritual dances and walks. The Center for the Dances of Universal Peace has been created to facilitate the development of new dances and the training of dance leaders.

Membership: In 1997, the society reported approximately 800 mureeds in the United States, Canada, Russia, and Germany.

Periodicals: *Sufi Islamia Ruhaniat Society Newsletter.*

Sources:

Lewis, Samuel L. *In the Garden*. New York: Harmony Books, 1975.

___. *Introduction to Spiritual Brotherhood*. San Francisco: Sufi Ismalia, 1981.

___. *The Jerusalem Trilogy*. Novato, CA: Prophecy Pressworks, 1975.

___. *Sufi Vision and Initiation*. San Francisco: Sufi Ismalia, 1986.

★1912★
The Sufi Movement
Sufi Center of Washington
1613 Stoe Rd.
Reston, VA 27094-1600

Alternate Address: International Headquarters: 11 rue John Rehfous, 1208 Geneva, Switzerland. National Representative of Canada, 4432 John St. Vancouver, BC V5V 3X1.

The Sufi Movement emerged in 1927 following the death of Hazrat Inayat Khan (1892–1927), founder of the Sufi Order. Rabia Martin, a woman whom Khan had initiated and designated as his successor, was rejected by Khan's family and his European followers. Making use of an opening provided by Khan's not leaving a

written will, the European members reorganized as the Sufi Movement and selected Maheboob Khan (1887–1948), Inayat's brother, as its leader. He was succeeded in 1948 by a cousin, Mohammad Ali Khan (1881–1958). He was in turn succeeded by Musharaff Khan (1895–1967) and Fazal Inayat Khan (1942–1990), who resigned in 1982.

Following Fazal Khan's stepping down, a collective leadership was formed, but it fell apart in 1985 and the movement split. The core of the Sufi Movement continued under the joint leadership of Hidayat Inayat Khan (b. 1917) and Murshida Shahzadi. Hidayat, a son of Hazrat Inayat, became the sole leader of the movement in 1993.

Hidayat Inayat Khan was only 10 years old when his father passed away in 1927. He later studied music at L'Ecole Normale de Musique and eventually became a professor in the Music School of Dieulefit, Drome, France, and conducted an orchestra in Haarlem, Holland. He authored numerous compositions including both secular music and a collection of Sufi hymns. He is a founding member of the European Composers' Union.

The movement closely resembles the Sufi Order, headed by Vilayat Inayat Khan, and is organized in five divisions to focus on universal worship, community, healing, symbology, and esoteric activity. Internationally, the movement is based in Holland, but has spread across Europe to Canada and the United States. Members meet weekly for *dhikr* (worship) and classes.

Membership: Not reported.

Sources:

The Gathas. Katwijk, Neths.: Servire, 1982.

Khan, Fazal Inayat. *Old Thinking: New Thinking*. New York: Harper and Row, 1979.

Khan, Hidayat Inayat. *Sufi Teachings*. Canada: Ecstasis, 1994.

★1913★
Sufi Order
Sufi Order Secretariat
Box 574
Lebanon Springs, NY 12114

History. Sufism was brought to the United States in 1910 by Pir Hazrat Inayat Khan (1881-1927). An Indian-born musician, he was initiated into the Nizami branch of the Chishti Order, one of the main Sufi schools of India. (The other main branch, the Sabiri, is represented in the United States by the Chishti Order of America.) The Chishti School was brought to India from Persia, and in its new home it absorbed elements of Hindu Vedantic thought which gave it a distinctive position within the Sufi world. The idea in coming to the West was to westernize the Sufi path. By bringing together East and West, it was thought, a basis for unity in the religion of love and wisdom could be laid. Doctrinal bias would be replaced by the power of mysticism.

Khan brought the Sufi Order to America in 1910. His first initiate was Rabia Martin who developed a center in San Francisco prior to World War I, which included among its members Samuel L. Lewis. Pir Inayat died suddenly in 1927 and succession was passed to his then eleven-year old son Vilayat. In the United States, Martin claimed the succession as the first initiate and murshid (minister). The European members and the family refused to recognize her, partly because she was a female, and the American and European work separated. During the last years of her life, Martin (d. 1947) heard of and began to investigate a new Indian teacher, Meher Baba, but died before completing her evaluation. Martin was succeeded by Ivy Oneita Duce, who became a disciple of Meher Baba and led the Sufi following entrusted to her under his care.

The Sufi Order was reintroduced to the United States in the 1960s by Pir Hazrat Vilayat Khan (b. 1916). His work on the West Coast was boosted by the encounter with Samuel Lewis. Lewis, a former member of Martin's group, did not accept Meher Baba. After World War II he traveled to Asia and received several independent initiations and recognition as a Sufi murshid. he founded a Sufic group in San Francisco in 1966 which he brought into the Sufi Order in 1968. (Eventually, much of that work was lost when in 1977 some of Lewis's students rejected some of Khan's regulations for the Order and withdrew to form the Sufi Islamia Ruhaniat Society.) Khan succeeded in building a stable national organization during the 1970s, and has become one of the most respected and popular teachers within the loosely organized New Age Movement.

Beliefs. The teachings of Inayat Khan have been summarized in ten "Sufi Thoughts." The Thoughts affirm that there is but one God, Master, Holy Book (i.e., the sacred manuscript of nature), religion, law, brotherhood, moral principle, object of praise, truth and path. Meditation and dervish dancing are the main means to induce the mystic consciousness.

The activity headed by Khan has three aspects. The Sufi Order proper is an esoteric school into which individuals are admitted by initiation (*Bayat*) and accept Khan as their spiritual counsellor. Initiates follow a study program and follow a set of personal practices, including special breathing techniques and the repetition of a *wazifa* (or mantrum) usually delineated at the time of initiation. The more esoteric religious activity is called the Universal Worship of the Church of All. Universal Worship is built around a liturgy developed by Inayat Khan which attempts to emphasize what is perceived as the essence of religion within all religions. Inayat Khan initiated the building of the Universel, a temple of all religions, in France shortly before his death. The Healing Order is built around the group healing ritual developed by Inayat Khan. Under Vilayat, the healing work has pushed the Sufi Order into the middle of the holistic health movement which became a prominent part of the larger New Age movement during the 1970s.

Organization. The American work of the Sufi Order is headed by Pir Khan and the Board of Trustees, which control the property and assets of the Order. An Interstate Council, consisting of the Trustess and representatives of all the branches of the Order, oversees financial transactions and coordinates programs. Center and branch leaders are appointed by Pir Khan. The on-going administration of the Order is in the hands of Secretary General. Internationally the Sufi Order is headquartered in France with national branches in England, Holland, France, Germany, Austria, Italy, Switzerland, India, and Canada. Nationally, the order is headquartered at the Abode of the Message, a community near Lebanon Springs, New York on the site of a former Shaker Village.

Membership: Not reported. There are centers across the United States and Canada.

Periodicals: *The Message.* • *Under the Wings.* Both available from Sufi Order, Route 15, Box 270, Tucson, AZ 85715. • *Ziraat.* Send orders to 22 Pillow Road, Austin, TX 78745.

Sources:

de Jong-Keesing, Elisabeth. *Inayat Khan.* The Hague: East-West Publications Fonds B. V., 1974.

Initiation. Lebanon Springs, NY: Sufi Order, 1980.

The Sufi Order. New Lebanon, NY: Message, Sufi Order, 1977.

Toward the One. New York: Harper & Row, 1974.

Inayat Khan, Vilayat. *The Message in Our Time.* San Francisco: Harper & Row, 1978.

★1914★
Tayu Meditation Center
Box 11554
Santa Rosa, CA 95406

Tayu Meditation Center is a "Fourth Way" spiritual school founded in 1976 by Robert Daniel Ennis. The Fourth Way is the name given to the system of spiritual development expounded by

Georgei Gurdjieff, which is seen as an alternative to the three other major forms of spiritual life, those of the yogi, monk, and fakir. It also refers to its claim that, unlike other spiritual traditions that engage only one center of the human organism at a time, the Fourth Way addresses all three simultaneously. More intense in the beginning, it is seen as ultimately more efficient, and is often called the "sly Way."

The primary Tayu practice is a special form of meditation called "Self-observation," designed to accommodate those born in Western culture. It focuses the awareness in turn on each of the three major centers of the human organism—the motor/instinctive, the emotional, and the intellectual. According to Ennis, when sincerely engaged in, Self-observation reveals the true nature and inner workings of the human organism, and opens the way to full and continuous access to True Mind.

Ennis has been recognized as an accomplished spiritual teacher by contemporaries such as Lee Lozowick, E. J. Gold, and Robert DeRopp. He arrived at his level of adeptship on July 4, 1976, having attained the degree of "Reason of the sacred termoonald." His teaching style has been described as "powerful yet intense, disconcerting for those with preconceptions," and especially aimed at Westerners. The teaching center is located on a small farm in Sonoma County, California.

Membership: The center is a small group as Ennis has refused to work with more than a few select students who agree to work on a more intense level at their spiritual development.

Periodicals: *The Way Fourth - The Journal of Tayu.*

★1915★
The Threshold Society
139 Main St.
Battleboro, VT 05301

The Mevlevi Order emerged from the life and work traces of Mevlana Jelaluddin Rumi (d. 1273), one of the greatest mystic poets of all time, and possibly the most famous Sufi among non-Muslims. The late Dr. Celalettin Celebi (d. 1996) of Istanbul, Turkey, the international head of the Mevlevi Tariqa (order) and a direct descendant of Rumi, appointed Dr. Edmund Kabir Helminski as a representative of the order in North America. He is a Mevlevi shaikh, appointed to that position by Shaikh Suleyman Loras (d. 1985) of Konya, Turkey (whose son, Shaikh Jelaluddin Loras, was active in building a following for the order on the American West Coast). Helminski and his wife, Dr. Camille Helminski, have been working within the Mevlevi tradition for some two decades. They cofounded the Threshold Society, and the related Threshold Books, a publishing house focused upon Sufi and related contemporary spiritual writings. Kabir Helminski is the author/translator of three books of Sufi poetry, and he and Camille Helminski have edited two collections of Rumi's writings.

The most distinctive aspect of Mevlevi Sufis is the Sema Ritual, from which they have earned their popular designation as Whirling Dervishes. Just as the kirtan of the Hare Krishnas have often been the image people have of Hinduism, so the whirling ritual of the Mevlevi have set the image of Sufism for many. The ritual can be traced to Rumi, and Mevlevis understand that by revolving in harmony with all things in nature, the believer testifies to the existence and the majesty of the Creator, thinks of Him, gives thanks to Him, and prays to Him. It is their belief that revolving is the fundamental condition of our existence as all beings are comprised of revolving electrons, protons, and neutrons in atoms, and human beings live by means of a set of revolutions—of these particles, of the blood in one's body, and ultimately of the stages of one's life.

The ritual attempts to unite the three fundamental components of human nature: the mind (as knowledge and thought), the heart (through the expression of feelings, poetry, and music), and the body (by activating life, by the turning). It represents the human being's spiritual journey, an ascent by means of intelligence and love to Perfection (Kemal). Turning toward the truth, the believer grows through love, transcends the ego, meets the truth, and arrives at Perfection.

The Threshold Society, as an outpost of the Mevlevi Order, has set as its purpose the facilitating of the experience of Divine unity, love, and wisdom in the world. The society offers training programs, seminars, and retreats in North America and around the world. These are intended to provide a structure for practice and study within Sufism and spiritual psychology. The order is working to apply traditional Sufi principles to the conditions of contemporary life.

In May of 1994 at a conference in Konya, Turkey, on "Mevlana and Human Rights," a gathering of eminent cultural and spiritual figures declared the Threshold Mevlevi Center in Brattleboro, Vermont, "New Konya" in recognition of the work of the Threshold Society and Threshold Books in spreading Rumi's message of universal love. Following the death in 1996 of Dr. Celaleddin Celebi, Faruk Hemdem Celebi, his son, succeeded him as leader of the Mevlevi Order.

Membership: Not reported.

Sources:

Helminski, Kabir. *An Anthology of Translations & Versions of Jalaluddin Rumi*. Battleborro, VT: Threshold Books, 1998. 212 pp.

___. *Jewels of Remembrance: A Daybook of Spiritual Guidance: Containing 365 Selections from the Wisdom of Rumi by Jalal Al-Din Rumi*. Battleboro, VT: Threshold Books, 1996.

___. *Living Presence: A Sufi Way to Mindfulness and the Essential Self*. Los Angeles: Jeremy Tarcher, 1992.

___, and Camille Helminski, trans. *Rumi: Daylight: A Daybook of Spiritual Guidance*. Battleboro, VT: Threshold Books, 1995.

★1916★
Tijaniyya Sufi Path

Current address not obtained for this edition.

The Tijaniyya Sufi Path is based on the Qur'an and Hadith founded by Shaykh Ahmad al-Tijani (1737–1815). It began in a vision of the Prophet Muhammad and members champion the ability of believers to see the Prophet and receive communications from him. Shaykh Ahmad al-Tijani was 40 years old when he saw the Prophet in broad daylight and was told by the Prophet that he was his shaykh. The Prophet gave him the Tijani Wird, i.e., the form of the dhikr that is distinctive of the Tariqa Tijaniyya. The spiritual work that a Tijani is required to do in his or her journey to Allah is dhikr, i.e., remembrance of Allah. The specific dhikr of the Tariqa Tijaniyya consists of three basic activities: 1) Astaghfirullah (asking Allah for forgiveness); 2) celebrating the praises of Allah in the saying of "La Ilaha Illallah" (Muslims of the Tariqa Tijaniyya say "La Ilaha Illallah" at least 300 times a day); and 3) Salatal 'ala Nabi, the offering of prayers upon the Prophet.

In the years since Shaykh al-Tijani(RA) passed, the movement has been led by a worthy succession of leaders including Shaykh Umar Futi; Shaykh Muhammad al-Hafiz al-Tijani, a Mauritanian shaykh who brought the Tariqa to West Africa for the first time; Shaykh al-Hajj Abdullah Niasse, the father of Shaykh Ibrahim; Shaykh al-Hajj Malik Sy; and Shaykh Ibrahim Niasse (1990–1975).

The Tariqa Tijaniyya is currently led by Alhamdulillah Shaykh Hassan Cisse (b. 1945), the grandson and spiritual heir of Shaykh Ibrahim Niasse. He is Chief Imam of the Grand Mosque in Madina Kaolack, Senegal. Shaykh Hassan brought the tariqa to the United States in 1976. He is also the founder and chairman of the African American Islamic Institute, Inc., a tax-exempt, international humanitarian organization. He holds degrees in Islamic Studies and Arabic Literature from Ain Shams University in Cairo, Egypt, and a Master of Philosophy from the University of London. His pursuit of a Ph.D. in Islamic Studies at Northwestern University in Evanston, Illinois, was interrupted when his father, Sayyidi Ali Cisse,

passed away, and he was recalled to Senegal to assume his leadership of the Tariqa.

The Tijaniyya movement is quite widespread in West Africa, and the United States membership of the Tariqa Tijaniyya consists largely of immigrants from West Africa, though it also includes a number of African Americans. Centers are found in many of the major urban centers from New York to California. There is a large center in Chicago which meets at the Nigerian Mosque.

Membership: Not reported.

Sources:

Nasr, Jamil M. Abun. *The Tijaniyya*. London: Oxford, 1964.

Black Islam

★1917★
African Islamic Mission
1390 Bedford Ave.
Brooklyn, NY 11216

The African Islamic Mission emerged in the 1970s in Brooklyn, New York. It is an African American orthodox Muslim organization which is headquartered in the Al Masjid Al Jaaami'a under the leadership of Imam Alhaji Obaba Muhammadu. The mission is most noted for its development of a black history publication series, which includes reprints of many rare and hard to find books on the origins of the Africans.

Membership: Not reported.

Sources:

Introduction to Islam: The First and Final Religion. Brooklyn, NY: African Islamic Mission, n.d.

★1918★
Ahmadiyya Anjuman Ishaat Islam, Lahore, Inc.
1315 Kingsgate Rd.
Columbus, OH 43221-1504

Alternate Address: International Headquarters: ℅ Darus Salaam, 5 Usman Block, New Garden Town, Lahore-16, Pakistan; Canadian headquarters: Box 964, Postal Station A, Vancouver, BC, Canada.

Following the death of Hazrat Mirza Ghulam Ahmad (1835-1908), founder of the Ahmadiyya Movement in Islam, a disagreement arose among his followers concerning the founder's status. Those who followed Ahmad's family proclaimed him a prophet. However, others, led by Maulawi Muhammad Ali, considered Ahmad the Promised Messiah and the greatest *mujaddid*, i.e., renewer of Islam, but denied that Ahmad had ever claimed the special status of "prophet." Ali asserted that Ahmad's use of that term was entirely allegorical. The claim of prophethood for Ahmad has resulted in the assignment of Ahmadiyya Muslims to a status outside of the Muslim community and resulted in their persecution in several Muslim-dominated countries.

Members of the Ahmadiyya branch founded by Ali came to America in the 1970s and incorporated in California.

Membership: Not reported. There are four centers in the United States and two in Canada. There are an estimated 100,000 people affiliated with the movement worldwide. Centers are found in Indian communities around the world.

Periodicals: *The Islamic Review.*

Sources:

Ali, Muhammad. *The Founder of the Ahmadiyya Movement*. Newark, CA: Ahmadiyya Anjuman Ishaat Islam, Lahore, 1984.

Aziz, Zahid, comp. *The Ahmadiyya Case*. Newark, CA: Ahmadiyya Anjuman Ishaat Islam, Lahore, 1987.

Faruqui, N. A. *Ahmadiyyat in the Service of Islam*. Newark, CA: Ahmadiyya Anjuman Ishaat Islam, Lahore, 1983.

Faruqui, Mumtaz Ahmad. *Truth Triumphs.* Lahore, Pakistan: Ahmadiyya Anjuman Ishaat-I-Islam, 1965.

★1919★
Ahmadiyya Movement in Islam
2141 Leroy Pl., NW
Washington, DC 20008

The Ahmadiyya movement was not brought to the United States with the intention of its becoming a black man's religion. Ahmadiyya originated in India in 1889 as a Muslim reform movement. It differs from orthodox Islam in that it believes that Hazrat Mirza Ghulam Ahmad (1835-1908) was the promised Messiah, the coming one of all the major faiths of the world. It has, in the years since its founding, developed the most aggressive missionary program in Islam.

Ahmad had concluded, as a result of his studies, that Islam was in a decline and that he had been appointed by Allah to demonstrate its truth, which he began doing by authoring a massive book, *Barahin-i-Ahmaditah.* He assumed the title of *mujaddid,* the renewer of faith for the present age, and declared himself both Madhi, the expected returning savior of Muslims, and the Promised Messiah of Christians. He advocated the view that Jesus had not died on the cross, but had come to Kashmir in his later life and died a normal death there. The second coming is not of a resurrected Jesus, but the appearance of one who bore the power and spirit of Jesus.

Ahmadiyya came to the United States in 1921 and the first center was in Chicago. Its founder, Dr. Mufti Muhammad Sadiq began to publish a periodical, *Muslim Sunrise.* While recruiting some members from among immigrants, the overwhelming majority of converts consisted of blacks. Only since the repeal of the Asian Exclusion Act in 1965 and the resultant emigration of large numbers of Indian and Pakistani nationals has the movement developed a significant Asian constituency in the United States.

A vast missionary literature demonstrating Islam's superiority to Christianity has been produced. Jesus is widely discussed. He is viewed as a great prophet who only swooned on the cross. He then escaped from the tomb to India and continued many years of ministry. He is buried at Srinagar, India, where the legendary Tomb of Issa (Jesus) is a popular pilgrimage site. The denial of the divinity of Jesus is in line with the assertion of Allah as the one true God. Christianity is seen as tritheistic.

At present, the movement is small. Headquarters were moved to Washington, D.C., in 1950 after a quarter century in Chicago.

Membership: In 1992 the movement reported approximately 10,000 members. Active centers can be found in 37 cities of the United States and 18 in Canada. In addition, Ahmadiyya centers can now be found in most countries of the world.

Periodicals: *The Ahmadiyya Gazette.* • *The Muslim Sunrise.* • *Ayesha.*

Sources:

Dard, A. R. *Life of Ahmad.* Lahore, Pakistan: Tabshir Publications, 1948.

Ahmad, Hazrat Mirza Bashiruddin Mahmud. *Ahmadiyyat or the True Islam.* Washington, DC: American Fazl Mosque, 1951.

___. *Invitation.* Rabwah, Pakistan: Ahmadiyya Muslim Foreign Missions, 1968.

Khan, Muhammad Zafrulla. *Ahmadiyyat, The Renaissance of Islam.* London: Tabshir Publications, 1978.

Nadwi, S. Abul Hasan Ali. *Qadianism, A Critical Study.* Lucknow, India: Islamic Research and Publications, 1974.

★1920★
American Muslims
℅ Imam W. Deen Mohammed
Masjid Al-Faatir
1200 E. 47th St.
Chicago, IL 60615

Though there are a variety of Muslim groups functioning within the black community, when one reads in the media or hears mention of "Black Muslims," the most likely reference is to the Nation of Islam, founded by Master Wallace Fard Muhammad and headed for many years by its purported prophet, Elijah Muhammad (1897-1975). After Elijah Muhammad's death the organization's name was changed successively to the World Community of Islam in the West and in 1980 the American Muslim Mission. It is the most successful of the Black Muslim bodies, having spread across the nation in the 1960s during the period of the black revolution. Its success and that of one dissident member, Malcolm X, led to numerous books and articles about it.

Following the death of Noble Drew Ali, founder of the Moorish Science Temple of America, there appeared in Detroit, Michigan, one Wallace D. Fard, a mysterious figure claiming to be Noble Drew Ali reincarnated. He proclaimed that he had been sent from Mecca to secure freedom, justice, and equality for his uncle (the Negroes) living in the wilderness of North America, surrounded and robbed by the cave man. (The white man was also referred to as the "Caucasian devil" and "Satan.") He established a temple in 1930 in Detroit. Among his many converts was Elijah Poole.

The 1930s was a time of intense recruiting activity and dispute with the Nation of Islam. Within Fard's ranks discussion focused on his divinity, legitimacy, and role. In 1934, a second temple was founded in Chicago, and the following year Fard dropped from sight. By this time, Poole, known as Elijah Muhammad, had risen to leadership.

Under Elijah Muhammad's leadership, the Black Muslims emerged as a strong, cohesive unit. Growth was slow, due in part to Muhammad's imprisonment during World War II as a conscientious objector. As the new prophet, he composed the authoritative *Message to the Blackman in America,* a summary statement of the Nation of Islam's position.

The central teaching of the Nation of Islam can be seen as a more sophisticated version of the Moorish Science study of the black man's history. According to Muhammad, Yakub, a mad black scientist, created the white beast, who was then permitted by Allah to reign for six thousand years. That period was over in 1914. Thus the twentieth century is the time for the Nation of Islam to regroup and regain an ascendant position.

Education, economics, and political aspirations were major aspects of the Muslim program. The first University of Islam was opened in 1932, and parochial education (many of the schools being names for Clara Muhammad, Elijah Muhammad's wife) has been a growing and more effective part of the Nation ever since. Besides the common curriculum, Black Muslim history, Islam and Arabic have been stressed. Classes are offered through the twelfth grade. Economically, the Muslims have stressed a work ethic and business development. The weekly newspaper carries numerous ads by businesses owned by Muslims. Politically, Muslims looked to the establishment of a black nation to be owned and operated by blacks.

As Black Muslims, they excluded whites from the movement and imposed a strict discipline on members to accentuate their new religion and nationality. Food, dress, and behavior patterns are regulated; a ritual life based on, but varying from, Orthodox form, was prescribed.

Black Muslims instituted a far-reaching program in furtherance of their aspirations. An evangelizing effort to make the Muslim program known within the black community was sustained in a weekly newspaper, *Muhammad Speaks.* During the 1960 and into the 1970s, growth was spectacular. By the time of Elijah Muhammad's death there were approximately 70 temples across the nation, including the South, and over 100,000 members.

In 1975 Elijah Muhammad died and was succeeded by his son Wallace D. Muhammad. During the decade of Wallace's leadership, a move toward both Orthodox Islam and decentralization of the organization has occurred. These moves have been reflected in the name changes, the schism of conservatives who have left to found movements continuing the peculiar emphases of the Nation of Islam prior to 1975, and the beginning of acceptance of the American Muslim Mission by orthodox Muslims. *Muhammad Speaks* was renamed *Bilalian News*.

In 1985 Wallace Muhammad, with the approval of the Council of Imans (ministers), resigned his post as leader of the American Muslim Mission and disbanded the movement's national structure. That move represents the establishment of a fully congregational polity by the Muslims whose local centers are now under the guidance of the imans rather than the control of the Chicago headquarters. Wallace D. Muhammad, also known as Warith Deen Muhammad, now operates as an independent Muslim lecturer and a member of the World Council of Masajid which is headquartered in Mecca, Saudi Arabia. His emphasis is upon the proper image of Muslims worldwide.

Membership: Not reported. There were approximately 200 centers in the mission at the time of its disincorporation. Foreign centers were located in Barbados, Belize, Guyana, Bermuda, Jamaica, the Bahamas, Canada, St. Thomas Island, and Trinidad.

Periodicals: *Muslim Journal.* Send orders to 910 W. Van Buren, Chicago, IL 60607.

Sources:

Lincoln, C. Eric. *The Black Muslims in America.* Boston: Beacon Press, 1961.

Muhammad, Elijah. *Message to the Blackman in America.* Chicago: Muhammad Mosque of Islam, No. 2, 1965.

Muhammad, Wallace D. *Lectures of Elam Muhammad.* Chicago: Zakat Propagation Fund Publications, 1978.

Muhammad, Warith Deen. *As a Light Shineth from the East.* Chicago: WDM Publishing Co., 1980.

Muhammad, W. D. *Religion on the Line.* Chicago: W. D. Muhammad Publications, 1983.

★1921★
Ansaaru Allah Community
716 Bushwick Ave.
Brooklyn, NY 11221

Members of the Ansaaru Allah Community, also known as the Nubian Islaamic Hebrew Mission, believe that the nineteenth century Sudanese leader, Muhammed Ahmed Ibn Abdullah (1845-1885), was the True Mahdi, the predicted Khaliyfah (successor) to the Prophet Mustafa Muhammed Al Amin. After his death, Al Mahdi was buried in the Sudan, and the group he founded (the Ansaars) continued under his successors, mainly: 1) As Sayyid Abdur Rahman Muhammad Al Madhi (the first successor); 2) As Sayyid Al Haadi Abdur Muhammad Rahmaan Al Madhi (the second successor); 3) As Sayyid Al Imaan Isa Al Haadi Al Madhi (the third successor). Presently, the third successor, who is also Al Mahdi's great-grandson, leads the mission.

The Community teaches from the Old Testament (Tawrah), the Psalms of David (Zubuwr), the New Testament (Injiyl), and the *Holy Qur'aan.* The last testament, the *Holy Qur'aan,* was given to the last and seal of the Prophets of the line of Adam, Mustafa Muhammad Al Amin. The group teaches that Allah is Alone in His power, the All (which is Tawhiyd, "Oneness"), and does not use the term "God." They believe that Jesus is the Messiah and that Ali (599-661 C.E.) and Fatima (610-633 C.E.) are the succesors to Mustafa Muhammad Al Amin.

Adam and Hawwah (Eve) are believed to have been Nubians. After the flood, during the prophet Nuwh's (Noah) time, his son Ham desired to commit sodomy while looking at his father's nakedness. This act resulted in the curse of leprosy being put upon Ham's fourth son, Canaan, thus turning his skin pale. In such a manner did the pale races come into existence, including the Amorites, Hittites, Jebusites, Sidonites, all the sons of Canaan and their descendants. Mixing the blood with these "subraces" (so-called because they are no longer pure Nubians), is unlawful for Nubians.

From the seed of Ibrahiym (Abraham), two nations were produced, the nation of Isaac, whose descendants later became known as Israelites, through his son Jacob, and the nation of Ishmael, whose descendants are called the Ishmailites and the nation of Midian, whose descendents are known as Midianites from Ketura, Abraham's third wife. The Israelites were enslaved for 430 years in Egypt. The Ishmailites were predicted to be enslaved in a land not of their own for 400 years. The Nubians of the United States, the West Indies and various other places around the world are the seed of Ishmael (and hence Hebrews). Al Madhi taught that all with straight hair and pale skin were Turks; however, this does not include people of color such as the Latins, Japanese, Koreans, Cubans, Sicilians, etc.

Under As Siddid Al Imaan Isa Al Haahi Al Madhi's guidance, the Nubian Islaamic Hebrew Mission was begun in the late 1960s in New York. In 1970, the prophesies of the "Opening of the Seventh Seal" (Revelation 8:1) commenced with the opening of the Ansaaru Allah Community and the publishing of literature to help remove the veil of confusion from Nubians. In 1972, communities were established in Philadlephia, Pennsylvania; Connecticut; Texas; and Albany, New York. The following year centers were opened in Washington, DC; Baltimore, Maryland; North Carolina; South Carolina; Georgia; Michigan; Florida; and Virginia. In the Carribean, centers were opened in Trinidad, Jamaica, Puerto Rico, Guyana, and Tobago. During the next decade, the movement spread around the world and included South America, Ghana and Hawaii.

Symbol of the community is the six-pointed star (made from two triangles) in an inverted cresent. It is considered to be the seal of Allah.

Membership: Not reported. There are several hundred members in the United States.

Periodicals: *Ansar Village Bulletin.*

Sources:

Muhammad Al Madhi, Al Hajj Al Iman Isa Ibd'Allah, trans. *The Holy Qur'aan.* Brooklyn, NY: Ansaru Allah Community, 1977.

Warner, Philip. *Dervish, The Rise of An African Empire.* New York: Taplinger Publishing Company, 1975.

Dietary Laws of a Muslim. Brooklyn, NY: Ansaru Allah Community, 1979.

Muhammad Ahmad, The Only True Madhi!. Brooklyn, NY: Ansaru Allah Community, 1979.

Muslim Prayer Book. Brooklyn, Ansaru Allah Community, 1984.

What Is a Muslim?. Brooklyn, NY: Ansaru Allah Community, 1979.

★1922★
Calistran
(Defunct)

The Calistran was a short-lived splinter of the original Nation of Islam (now the American Muslim Mission) which came to public attention in the early 1970s, a period of heightened tension and internal violence within the black Muslim community generally. On October 7, 1973, two members of the Calistran who had reportedly "stepped out of line" were shot in Pasadena, California, by a "disciplinarian." No sign of the Calistran has been seen in the 1980s.

★1923★
Hanafi Madh-hab Center, Islam Faith
7700 16th St. NW
Washington, DC 20012

History. The Hanafi Madh-hab Center was first set up in the United States by Dr. Tasibur Uddein Rahman in the late 1920s. In 1947 Khalifa Hammas Abdul Khaalis (born Ernest Timothy McGee) met his teacher, Dr. Rahman, a Mussulman (or Muslim) from Pakistan, who gave him his new name and taught him the *sunnah* (the tradition and practice) of the Prophet Muhammad. In 1950, Dr. Rahman sent Khalifa Hamaas Abdul Khaalis into the Nation of Islam (now the American Muslim Mission) to guide the members into Sunni Islam (that faith and practice recognized by the great majority of Muslims). By 1956 Khalifa Hamaas Abdul Khaalis was the national secretary of the Nation of Islam. He left the Nation of Islam in 1958, after unsuccessfully trying to convince Elijah Muhammad, the leader of the Nation of Islam, to change the direction of the movement. He set-up the Hanafi Madh-hab Center in Washington, D.C.

Again at the beginning of 1973, Khalifa Hamaas Abdul Khaalis wrote letters to the members and leaders of the Nation of Islam asking them to change to Sunni Muslim belief and practice. On January 18, 1973, members of the Nation of Islam came into the center in Washington, D. C., (which also served as Khalifa Hamaas Abdul Khaalis' home) and murdered six of his children and his stepson. His wife was wounded. Subsequently, five members of the Philadelphia Nation of Islam group were convicted of the murders, only to receive relatively light sentences.

In 1977, Khalifa Hamaas Abdul Khaalis and other Al-Hanif Musselman took action against the showing of a motion picture, "Mohammad, Messenger of God," which they considered sacreligious, due to be released in theatres in America. They took over three buildings in Washington, D.C., and held people hostage for 38 hours. In the process, one man was killed. For this action Khalifa Hamaas Abdul Khaalis was sentenced to spend from 41 to 120 years in prison, and 11 of his followers were also convicted and sentenced. Since no believing Musselman was on the the the jury, Khalifa Hamaas Abdul Khaalis considers the jury to have lacked impartiality.

Beliefs. The Al-Hanif Hanafi Musselmans uphold the two standards of Islam, *Holy Qur'an* and the Hadiths, and are Sunni (obeying all things as laid down by Allah to the Prophet Muhammad) Muslims. Hanafi means unconditional and uncompromising. They also follow by way of the 124,000 Prophets major and minor, and believe in all holy books according to Allah's knowledge. The *Holy Qur'an* is the final Seal of All Prophets and Prophecy.

The Hanafi Mussulmans have taken a special interest in presenting Islam to African Americans and informing them that Islam is a religion that does not recognize distinctions of race or color.

Organization. Authority for Al-Hanif Hanafi Mussulmans is vested in the chief *Iman* (teacher), Khalifa Hammas Abdul Khaalis, and each mosque is headed by an iman appointed by him.

Membership: Not reported. There are estimated to be several hundred Hanafi Muslims in the United States. Mosques are located in Washington, D.C.; New York City; Chicago, Illinois; and Los Angeles, California.

Periodicals: *Look and See.*

Sources:

Khaalis, Hamaas Abdul. *Look and See.* Washington, DC: Hanafi Madh-hab Center Islam Faith, 1972.

★1924★
Lost-Found Nation of Islam
PO Box 57048
Atlanta, GA 30343

The Lost-Found Nation of Islam emerged in 1977 under the leadership of Silis Muhammad who had joined the original Nation of Islam in the 1960s. He developed a reputation for his promotion of the Nation's tabloid, *Muhammad Speaks*, and as a result was invited to the Nation's headquarters in Chicago to manage the national circulation of *Muhammad Speaks*. He became a close confidant of Elijah Muhammad and eventually assumed a role as his spiritual son (there was no biological relationship).

Following Elijah Muhammad's death in 1975, he rejected the changes instituted by the Nation's new leader, Warith Deen Muhammad, the son of Elijah Muhammad. In 1977 he charged Warith Muhammad with being a false prophet and demanded that he turn the property of the Nation back to his father's genuine followers. Soon afterward, he left to reorganize the Nation of Islam under his own leadership with headquarters in the South. In 1982 he started a new edition of *Muhammad Speaks*, the name of the original having been changed. In 1985 he published an expanded book-length version of his attack upon Warith Deen Muhammad and an alternative program for the reorganized Nation.

Soon after Silis attempted to resurrect the Nation of Islam, another prominent leader Louis Farrakhan also left and founded a rival Nation of Islam. Silis Muhammad and Farrakhan disagreed on the role of Elijah Muhammad in regards to Jesus. Farrakhan had interpreted some of Elijah Muhammad's statements as meaning that he had claimed to be the fulfillment of some of Jesus' prophecies. Silis Muhammad rejected the interpretation. In the wake of the disagreement the two have gone their separate ways.

The Lost-Found Nation of Islam headed by Silis Muhammad has established headquarters in Atlanta. The Nation has reaffirmed that Allah appeared in the person of Wallace Fard Muhammad in 1930 and that he spoke face to face with Elijah Muhammad from 1931 through 1933. Hence Elijah Muhammad is Moses, the biblical account (and the account in the *Qur'an*) being a prophetic and symbolic history of the African American of today.

Membership: In 1995 19 temples associated with Nation could be found across the United States.

Periodicals: *Muhammad Speaks.*

Sources:

Muhammad, Silis. *In the Wake of the Nation of Islam.* College Park, GA: The Author, 1985.

★1925★
Moorish Science Temple of America
Current address not obtained for this edition.

Timothy Drew (1886-1929), a black man from North Carolina, had concluded from his reading and travels that black people were not Ethiopians (as some early black nationalists were advocating) but Asiatics, specifically Moors. They were descendants of the ancient Moabites and their homeland was Morocco. He claimed that the Continental Congress had stripped American blacks of their nationality and that George Washington had cut down their bright red flag (the cherry tree) and hidden it in a safe in Independence Hall. Blacks were thus assigned to the role of slaves.

As Noble Drew Ali, Drew emerged in 1913 in Newark, New Jersey, to preach the message of Moorish identity. The movement spread slowly with early centers in Pittsburgh, Detroit, and several southern cities. In 1925, Ali moved to Chicago and the following year incorporated the Moorish Science Temple of America. In 1927 he published *The Holy Koran* (not to be confused with the *Koran* or *Qur'aan* used by all orthodox Moslem groups). Ali's *Koran* was a pamphlet-size compilation of Moorish beliefs which drew heavily upon *The Aquarian Gospel of Jesus Christ*, a volume received by automatic writing by Spiritualist Levi Dowling in the 1890s. The *Koran* delineates the creation and fall of the race, the origin of black people, the opposition of Christianity to God's people and the modern predicament of the Moors.

It was Noble Drew Ali's belief that only Islam could unite the black man. The black race is Asiatic, Moroccan, hence Moorrish. Jesus was a black man who tried to redeem the black Moabites and was executed by the white Romans. Moorish Americans must be united under Allah and his holy prophet. Marcus Garvey is seen as forerunner to Ali. Friday has been accepted as the holy day. Worship forms, particularly music, have been drawn from popular black culture and given Islamic content.

Ali died in 1919 and was succeeded by one of his young colleagues, R. German Ali, who still heads the movement. Shortly after Ali's death, one of the members appeared in Detroit as Wallace Fard Muhammad, the reincarnation of Noble Drew Ali, and began the Nation of Islam (now the American Muslim Mission). In spite of the competition from the Nation of Islam, the temple grew in the years after Ali's death, and during the 1940s temples could be found in Charleston, West Virginia; Hartford, Connecticut; Milwaukee; Richmond, Virginia; Cleveland; Flint, Michigan; Chattanooga, Tennessee; Indianapolis; Toledo and Steubenville, Ohio; Brooklyn; and Indiana Harbor, Indiana. In more recent years, the movement has declined. During the 1970s, the headquarters were moved to Baltimore.

Membership: Not reported.

Sources:

Fauset, Arthur Huff. *Black Gods of the Metropolis*. Philadelphia: University of Pennsylvania Press, 1971.

Ali, Noble Drew. *Moorish Literature*. The Author, 1928.

___. *Timothy Drew, The Holy Koran of the Moorish Science Temple of America*. [Baltimore: MD]: Moorish Science Temple of America, 1978.

★1926★

Moorish Science Temple, Prophet Ali Reincarnated, Founder
Current address not obtained for this edition.

In 1975, Richardson Dingle-El, a member of the Moorish Science Temple of America in Baltimore, proclaimed himself Noble Drew Ali 3d, the reincarnation of Noble Drew Ali (1886-1929), the founder of the Moorish Science Temple of America. As such he claimed succession to Noble Drew Ali 2d (d.1945), who had claimed succession in the 1930s. The followers of Noble Drew Ali 3d have established headquarters in Baltimore and have several temples around the United States. A periodical is published by the temple in Chicago. In most ways it follows the beliefs and practices of the Moorish Science Temple of America.

Membership: Not reported.

Periodicals: *Moorish Guide*. Send orders to 3810 S. Wabash, Chicago, IL 60653.

★1927★

Muslim Mosque, Inc.
(Defunct)

The Muslim Mosque, Inc., was founded in 1964 by Malcolm X (1925–1965), who at the time had just announced his departure from the Nation of Islam, then headed by Elijah Muhammad. Malcolm X had become the most prominent spokesperson of the Nation of Islam in the early 1960s, and in 1963 he was made the nation's first national minister. A short time after Malcolm X assumed his new position, news broke that Elijah Mohammed was the object of two paternity suits filed by former secretaries. Malcolm X received the news as a word of betrayal by the leader he so respected.

A major incident then occurred in November 1963, following the assassination of President John F. Kennedy. Elijah Mohammed had ordered a three-day period of silence on any comment on the

death. During this time, however, Malcolm X was approached by a group of reporters following a speech in New York. Pressed for a comment, he said simply that the assassination appeared to be a case of the ''chicken's coming home to roost.'' The comment was reported widely and in the wake of the negative publicity, Elijah Mohammed silenced Malcolm X for 90 days. Malcolm X soon found other Muslims shunning him and learned that a contract had been put out on his life.

In the heightened atmosphere, on March 1964, Malcolm X resigned from the Nation of Islam. The new Muslim Mosque was created to act as a spiritual force behind the social action to eliminate the oppression of Black Americans. As a first action, he decided to make the obligatory pilgrimage to Mecca, one of the basic requirements of a Muslim. While in the Middle East, he was impressed with the lack of racism among the pilgrims and among Muslims in general. The experience forced him away from the previously held belief that all white people were evil. He also became directly aware of the difference between the Nation of Islam's beliefs and the teachings of orthodox Islam.

Upon his return he began to build the program of the Muslim Mosque, but on February 21, 1965, he was shot and killed by several members of the Nation of Islam who were later tried and convicted for the murder. The Muslim Mosque did not survive Malcolm X's death for very long.

Sources:

Breitman, George. *The Last Year of Malcolm X: The Evolution of a Revolutionary*. New York: Schrocken Books, 1969.

Clark, John Henrik, ed. *Malcolm X: The Man and His Times*. New York: Macmillan, 1969.

Goldman, Peter Loomis. *The Death and Life of Malcolm X*. Urbana, IL: University of Illinois Press, 1979.

''Organizations and Leaders Campaigning for Negro Goals in the United States.'' *New York Times*, August 10, 1964.

★1928★

The Nation of Islam (Farrakhan)
4855 S. Woodlawn Ave.
Chicago, IL 60615

Of the several factions which broke away from the American Muslim Mission (formerly known as the Nation of Islam and then as the World Community of Islam in the West) and assumed the group's original name, the most successful has been the Nation of Islam headed by Abdul Haleem Farrakhan. Farrakhan was born Louis Eugene Wolcott. He was a nightclub singer in the mid-1950s when he joined the Nation of Islam headed by Elijah Muhammad. As was common among Muslims at that time, he dropped his last name, which was seen as a name imposed by slavery and white society, and became known as Minister Louis X. His oratorical and musical skills carried him to a leading position as minister in charge of the Boston Mosque and, after the defection and death of Malcolm X, to the leadership of the large Harlem center and designation as the official spokesperson for Elijah Muhammad.

In 1975 Elijah Muhammad died. Though many thought Louis X, by then known by his present name, might become the new leader of the nation, Elijah Muhammad's son, Wallace, was chosen instead. At Wallace Muhammad's request, Farrakhan moved to Chicago to assume a national post. During the next three years, the Nation of Islam moved away from many of its distinctive beliefs and programs and emerged as the American Muslim Mission. It dropped many of its racial policies and began to admit white people into membership. It also began to move away from its black nationalist demands and to accept integration as a proper goal of its programs.

Farrakhan emerged as a leading voice among ''purists'' who opposed any changes in the major beliefs and programs instituted by Elijah Muhammad. Long-standing disagreements with the new direction of the Black Muslim body led Farrakhan to leave the organization in 1978 and to form a new Nation of Islam. He reinstituted the beliefs and program of the pre-1975 Nation of Islam. He reformed the Fruit of Islam, the internal security force, and demanded a return to strict dress standards.

With several thousand followers, Farrakhan began to rebuild the Nation of Islam. He established mosques and developed an outreach to the black community on radio. He was only slightly noticed until 1984 when he aligned himself with the U.S. presidential campaign of Jesse Jackson, a black minister seeking the nomination of the Democratic Party. Jackson's acceptance of his support and Farrakhan's subsequent controversial statements (some claimed by critics to be anti-Semitic) on radio and at press conferences kept Farrakhan's name in the news during the period of Jackson's candidacy and in subsequent months.

Since the mid 1985, Farrakhan has been in the news continually as he has proposed and creating programs for the African American community and led followers in establishing business to build the economy for the community. He has also made a number of public statements which have included controversial sentences that critics charge evidence acontinuing anti-Semitism. Farrakhan has spoken on several occasions of European American's history of involvement in the African slave trade and has taken pains to note the ownership of slaves by Jews.

Most recently, Farrakhan called a mass day-long demonstration by African American males in Washington D.C. called the Million Man March. It attracted several hundred thousand men and a number of African American leaders who were included among the speakers. At the march he again asked the Jewish community to institute a dialogue with him to resolve their differences, an offer Jewish leaders have rejected until he publicly rejects his comments which they deem anti-Semitic.

Membership: Not reported. There are an estimated 10,000 members of the Nation of Islam. In 1995 Farrakhan was heard weekly over 85 televison stations and 43 radio stations.

Periodicals: *The Final Call.* 734 W. 79th St., Chicago, Il 60620.

Sources:

Lomax, Louis E. *When the Word Is Given.* Cleveland, OH: World Publishing Company, 1963.

Muhammad, Elijah. *Our Savior Has Arrived.* Chicago: Muhammad's Temple of Islam No. 2, 1974.

Muhammad, Tynnetta. *The Divine Light.* Phoenix, AZ: H.E.M.E.F, 1982.

Page, Clarence. "Deciphering Farrakhan." *Chicago* 33, no. 8 (August 1984): 130-35.

★1929★
Nation of Islam (John Muhammad)
14880 Wyoming
Detroit, MI 48238

John Muhammad, brother of Elijah Muhammad, founder of the Nation of Islam, was among those who rejected the changes in the Nation of Islam and the teachings of Elijah Muhammad which led to its change into the American Muslim Mission. In 1978 he left the mission and formed a continuing Nation of Islam designed to perpetuate the programs outlined in Elijah Muhammad's two books, *Message to the Blackman* and *Our Saviour Has Arrived.* According to John Muhammad, who uses the standard title of black Muslim leaders, "Minister" Elijah Muhammad was the last Messenger of Allah and was sent to teach the black man a New Islam.

Membership: Not reported. John Muhammad has support around the United States, but the only temple is in Detroit.

Periodicals: *Minister John Muhammad Speaks.* Available from Nation of Islam, Temple No. 1, 19220 Conant St., Detroit, MI 48234.

★1930★
The Nation of Islam (The Caliph)
Current address not obtained for this edition.

As significant changes within the Nation of Islam founded by Elijah Muhammad proceeded under his son and successor Wallace D. Muhammad, the Nation of Islam became a more orthodox Islamic organization. It was renamed the American Muslim Mission and dropped many of the distinctive features of its predecessor. Opposition among those committed to Elijah Muhammad's ideas and programs led to several schisms in the late 1970s. Among the "purist" leaders, Emmanuel Abdullah Muhammad asserted his role as the Caliph of Islam raised up to guide the people in the absence of Allah (in the person of Wallace Fard Muhammad) and his Messenger (Elijah Muhammad). One Islamic tradition insists that a caliph always follows a messenger.

The Nation of Islam under the caliph continues the beliefs and practices abandoned by the American Muslim Mission. A new school, the University of Islam, was begun and the Fruit of Islam, the disciplined order of Islamic men, reinstituted. A new effort aimed at economic self-sufficiency has been promoted, and businesses have been created to implement the program.

Membership: Not reported. As of 1982, the Nation of Islam under the caliph had only two mosques, one in Baltimore and one in Chicago.

Periodicals: *Muhammad Speaks.* Available from Muhammad's Temple of Islam No. 1, 1233 W. Baltimore St., Baltimore, MD 21223.

★1931★
Nation of the Five Percent
Current address not obtained for this edition.

The Nation of the Five Percent was founded in 1964 by Clarence 13X, a former member of the Nation of Islam. Clarence 13X was born Clarence Smith (1929–1969), and after joining the Nation in Islam in 1961 he took "X" as a last name, a practice within the nation that indicated that Black Americans' true names had been lost and they had been forced to take non-African "slave" names. Smith soon began to develop views divergent from those taught in the Harlem mosque. He believed that all Blacks were Allah and rejected the teaching that Allah had appeared in 1929 in the person of Wallace D. Fard. In 1964 he was expelled from the Nation of Islam.

The idea undergirding the Nation of Five Percent was Clarence 13X's belief that only five percent of Blacks understand the problem causing their condition and that these five percent are the only ones capable of leading the African-American community. He began to teach that all Black men were Allah, and that Black women were the Earth, a teaching that earned the group a popular designation as the Nation of Gods and Earths. Women were to raise a nation; their children were seen as the salvation of the nation.

From headquarters in New York, centers were soon established in neighboring Connecticut and New Jersey. In 1969 Clarence 13X was assassinated. The movement reorganized under a collective leadership and continued. In 1988 its Allah School of Mecca, its main outreach structure for Harlem, was burned to the ground. The organization has continued, however, though it still struggles to find its place in the African-American community as a whole.

Membership: Not reported.

Periodicals: *The Word; the Five Percenters.*

Sources:

As Sayyid Al Haadi Al Mahdi. *The Book of Five Percenters.* Montecello, NY: Original Tents of Kedar, 1991.

Prince-A-Cuba, ed. *Our Mecca Is Harlem: Clarence 13X and the Five Percent.* Hampton, VA: U.B. & U.S. Communications Systems, 1995.

Zoroastrianism

★1932★
Lovers of Meher Baba
% Meher Spiritual Center
10200 Hwy. 17 N.
Myrtle Beach, SC 29572

Meher Baba (1894-1969) was an Indian spiritual master born Merwan Sheriar Irani of Zoroastrian parents living in Poona, India. Baba is believed by his followers to be the Avatar of the age. As a young man, he met Hazrat Babajan, a Muslim woman considered by some to be "one of the five Perfect Masters of the Age." From her he received what he described as self-realization. According to Baba, the five Perfect Masters are always responsible for unveiling the Avatar when he comes. Thus, in 1921, the last Master, Upasani Maharaj, folded his hands and said, "Merwan, you are the Avatar. I salute you."

That same year he gathered his first disciples, who began to call him "Meher Baba," which means "Compassionate Father." In 1924 he opened a permanent colony near Ahmednagar, India, called Meherabad. There he established a free hospital and clinic for the poor, and a free school for students of all creeds and castes. In 1925, he began observing silence, which he maintained for the rest of his life. For many years he communicated by pointing to the letters of the alphabet painted on a wooden board. In the last period of his life, he relied on hand gestures alone. Baba asserted that he kept silent in order to speak the "Word" of God in every heart. He also said that enough words had been given and it was now time to live God's words.

Baba came to the West, including the United States, for the first time in 1931. Some of the westerners he met on this and subsequent trips became disciples and went to live and work with him in India. The number of followers in the West grew steadily, spurred by his occasional visits (he made a total of six trips during his lifetime).

Baba said that he had not come to establish a new religion or sect, but rather to awaken people to the love of God. He declared himself the *Avatar*, the same "Ancient One" who has come age after age as Zoroaster, Rama, Krishna, Buddha, Jesus, and Muhammad, to renew Divine Love in the world. He also indicated that his advent required that he shed blood in both the East and the West, which, it is claimed, occurred in two automobile accidents, one in the United States (1952) and one in India (1956). He stated that suffering was a necessary part of his mission as Avatar to bring about what he called a "new humanity." He spent much of his life in service to others, especially the poor, the lepers, and those he termed *masts* or God-intoxicated. He considered these activities to be outward manifestations of his real work of transforming consciousness by awakening humanity to the oneness of all life. According to Baba, God was within every living thing and the goal of all life was to become one with God through love.

Because Baba said that his only message was of Divine Love, people who follow him are often called "lovers of Meher Baba." Over the years many have been inspired to become Meher Baba lovers though there is no formal organization or membership. In the 1950s, many Americans came in contact with Meher Baba during his three visits to Meher Spiritual Center in Myrtle Beach, South Carolina, a place he called "my home in the West." Today, the center and his tomb shrine in Meherabad have become places of pilgrimage for thousands of Meher Baba lovers each year. Groups of followers gather informally throughout North America, India, Europe, and Australia. There are no set practices or creeds, and no formal organization to join. Meetings usually consist of sharing Meher Baba's love through film, music, discussion, and readings from his Discourses.

Membership: Since there is no formal membership, estimates of the number of Meher Baba's followers varies widely. The number of newsletters and centers suggest that there may be some 10,000 in the United States, Europe, and Australia, and hundreds of thousands in India.

Periodicals: *Glow International*. Send orders to Meher Baba Work, Box 10, New York, NY 10185.

Remarks: Within the larger body of Baba lovers, there is one special closeknit group called Sufism Reoriented. This group derives from the original Sufi groups organized early in the century by Hazrat Inayat Khan, founder of the Sufi Order. Khan appointed Rabia Martin of San Francisco his successor, an appointment not recognized by members in Europe, in large part because Martin was female. Toward the end of her life, Martin heard of Meher Baba and began to correspond with him. She became convinced that he was the *Qutb*, in Sufi understanding, the hub of the spiritual universe. Though Martin never met Baba, her successor, Ivy Oneita Duce, did. He confirmed her succession, but more importantly, in 1952 during a trip to Myrtle Beach, South Carolina, Meher Baba presented the group with a new plan contained in a document, "Chartered guidance from Meher Baba for the Reorientation of Sufism as the Highway to the Ultimate Universalized."

Within Sufism Reoriented, the Sufi path begins in submission and obedience to the murshid as the arm of Baba. For the student, there must be a need to know that God exists, to be able to discriminate between the real and the unreal, to be indifferent to externals, and to be ready to gain the six mental attitudes (control over thoughts, outward control, tolerance, endurance, faith, and balance).

Sources:

Baba, Meher. *Discourses*. Myrtle Beach, SC: Sheriar Press, 1987.

___. *God Speaks*. New York: Dodd, Mead and Company, 1973.

Davy, Kitty. *Love Alone Prevails*. Myrtle Beach, SC: Sheriar Press, 1981.

Duce, Ivy Oneita. *How a Master Works*. Walnut Creek, CA: Sufism Reoriented, 1971.

Hopkinson, Tom, and Dorothy Hopkinson. *Much Silence*. New York: Dodd, Mead and Company, 1975.

★1933★
Mazdaznan Movement
1701 Aryana Dr.
Encinitas, CA 92024

The first, and for many years the only, Zoroastrian group in the United States was the Mazdaznan Movement founded by the Rev. Dr. Otoman Zar-Adhusht Hanish (d. 1936). Dr. Hanish claimed to have been sent by the Inner Temple Community of El Khaman to bring Mazdaznan to the world. He began teaching around the turn of the century and formally inaugurated the movement in New York in 1902. Headquarters were established in Chicago where he began a periodical, *The Mazdaznan*, published by the Sun Worshippers Press (later the Mazdaznan Press). Headquarters were moved to Los Angeles in 1916, and to Encinitas, California in the 1980s.

Mazdaznan emphasizes the monotheistic faith in the Lord God Mazda, the creator. Man is in God and God in him. God is expressed as the Holy Family of Father (male creative principle), Mother (procreative female principle) and Child (destiny/salvation). Man is on earth to reclaim the earth and to turn it into a paradise suitable for God to dwell therein. The means to reclaim the material, the body, and make it as perfect as our spirit, is the power of breath. Mazdaznan teaches a discipline of breathing, rhythmic prayers and chants. These are supplemented by a recommended vegetarian diet and exercises.

Mazdaznan spread across America into Europe in its first decade. By the time Hanish died centers could be found in most urban centers. During the 1970s, centers were active in England (13), as well as Mexico, Belgium, Denmark, France, Germany, Holland, and Switzerland. In the mid-1980s, the longtime Los Angeles headquarters were abandoned for a new headquarters building which had been constructed in Encinitas, California. The movement is led by the international elector, Alfonso R. Calderon.

Membership: There is no formal membership. In 1985 there were six centers in the United States, one in Canada and others in 22 countries, including Belgium, Denmark, France, Germany, Holland, Switzerland, and Mexico. Approximately 1,000 people are affiliated with the movement.

Periodicals: *Mazdaznan—Master Thot.*

Sources:

Mazdaznan, What It Teaches. Los Angeles: Mazdaznan Press, 1969.

Hanish, O. Z. A. *The Power of Breath.* Los Angeles: Mazdaznan Press, 1970.

Hanish, O. Z., and O Rauth. *God and Man United.* Santa Fe Springs, CA: Stockton Trade Press, 1975.

Hanish, Otoman Zar-Adhusht. *Health and Breath Culture.* Chicago: Sun Worshipper Publishing Co., 1902.

___. *Inner Studies.* Mokelumne Hill, CA: Health Research, 1963.

___. *The Philosophy of Mazdaznan.* Los Angeles: Mazdaznan Press, 1960.

★1934★
Zoroastrian Associations in North America
5750 S. Jackson St.
Hinsdale, IL 60521

Followers of the Zoroastrian faith began to migrate to North America from their native Iran and India, where they had been prominent in the business community in the 1950s. As their numbers have grown, they have spread across the continent.

The Zoroastrian faith is monotheistic. Its founder, Zarathrustra, taught of Ahura Mazda, the one Supreme God. Ahura Mazda created an ideal existence but as the world progressed, conflict between the opposing forces of good and evil emerged. Ahura Mazda gave humans the opportunity to choose between good and the evil, as well as the responsibility to promote the good, vanquish evil, and move the world toward the final resurrection when all will be in a state of bliss and perfection.

Individual Zoroastrians are called to an ethical life based on good thoughts, words, and deeds. Humans should emulate the attributes of Ahura Mazda: *Vohu Manah* (Good Mind) is the freedom to choose the good. *Asha* (Divine Law) embodies truth, wisdom, justice, and progress. *Kshathra* (Divine Majesty) call humans to militantly promote good and fight evil. *Armaity* (Benevolent Spirit) elevates purity and devotion. The devout Zoroastrian can look forward to *Haurvatat* and *Ameratat* (perfection and immortality). The Zoroastrian is taught to lead an industrious active life characterized by honesty and charity. There is little room for asceticism. The generation of wealth is extolled as long as it is done honestly and used for charitable purposes. These teachings are contained in *The Avesta,* the ancient Zoroastrian texts, which include *The Gathas* (hymns) written by Zarathrustra.

The life of the Zoroastrian is marked by three important ceremonies. A child is initiated into the faith through the Navjote ceremony in which the child is given a *sudreh,* an undershirt made of white muslin with a pocket to remind the wearer to fill his/her life with good thoughts, words, and deeds, and a *kusti,* a cord by which the wearer girds himself or herself to practice the teachings of Zarathrustra. Wedding is a second blessed occasion. The death of a Zoroastrian is marked with extensive prayers that center upon the soul rather than the body. Each ceremony includes reading from *The Avesta.*

In the United States, Zoroastrians organized associations wherever a community of the faithful was located. In 1987, these associations created the Federation of Zoroastrian Associations of North America as an authorized body to represent Zoroastrians.

Membership: As of 1997, there were approximately 200,000 Zoroastrians in the world, 20,000 of them residing in North Ameri-

ca. There are 22 local Zoroastrian associations (in major cities) in the United States and four in Canada. There are approximately 72,000 Zoroastrians in India, 90,000 in Iran, and lesser numbers in Europe, Pakistan, Africa, and Australia.

Educational Facilities: Cama Oriental Institute, Bombay, India.

Periodicals: *Fezana Journal.* Send orders to, 1219 Elderberry Dr., Sunnyvale, CA 94087.

Remarks: The Center for Zoroastrian Research in Bloomington, Indiana, has been actively gathering information on the American Zoroastrian community as well as actively participating in its ongoing self-examination.

Baha'i

★1935★
Baha'i Faith
% National Spiritual Assembly of the Baha'is of the U.S.
536 Sheridan Rd.
Wilmette, IL 60091

In Persia (present-day Iran), a predominantly Muslim country, the expectation of the coming of the Mahdi, the successor to Muhammad promised in Islamic writings, was strong. In this environment was born Mirza Ali Muhammad (1819-1850), a Shi'a Muslim who declared himself the Bab or gate through whom people would know about the advent of another messenger of God. Many people accepted the messianic claims of the Bab after his declaration in 1844, and Babism was founded. The initial enthusiasm of the movement quickly encountered fierce opposition. Persecution followed. In 1850, the Bab was martyred.

Two years later, one of the Babis (followers of the Bab) attempted to kill the Shah, and persecution led to further imprisonments of Babis. Among those thrown in jail was Mirza Husayn-Ali (1817-1892), who, while languishing in prison, came to understand himself as the Holy One whom the Bab predicted; however, he kept the revelation to himself for several years. In 1853 he and his family were exiled and left Tehran to Baghdad. During the next years, leadership of the Babi movement was in the hands of Mirza Yahya, Husayn-Ali's half brother, but gradually it shifted to Husayn-Ali because of Mirza Yahya's incompetence. In 1863 Husayn-Ali revealed to a few close associates and members of his family that he was the messenger that the Bab had anticipated. From that time an increasing number of Babis accepted Baha'u'llah (as Husayn-Ali was called) and became Baha'is.

Baha'u'llah moved from Baghdad to Adrianople (now Edirne), to the penal colony at Akka (now Acco) in present-day Israel. Arriving in Akka in 1868, he spent the remainder of his life there. While still under house arrest by the Turkish authorities, he produced his most important works, considered scripture by his followers.

Baha'u'llah was succeeded by the third major figure in Baha'i history, Abbas Effendi (1844-1921), known to the world by his religious name, Abdu'l-Baha (meaning servant of Baha). Abdu'l-Baha, Baha'u'llah's son, is considered the exemplar of the Baha'i teachings. He served Baha'u'llah until his death and later found himself confined by the Turkish authorities until the Revolution of the Young Turks in 1908 brought a gradual easing of restrictions. Abdu'l-Baha then turned his attention to the spread of the Baha'i religion and traveled to Europe and North America in that effort. Upon his death in 1921, Abdu'l-Baha was succeeded by Shoghi Effendi (1897-1957), his grandson, as guardian of the faith.

The Baha'i Faith was brought to America in 1892 by Ibrahim Kheiralla, though he later left the movement and founded a rival organization. Kheirella founded a Baha'i group in Chicago in 1894 and several others sprang up as a result of his efforts. The first convert was Thornton Chase, who joined faith in 1894. The first United States Convention was held in 1907. In 1900, Agnes Baldwin Alexander encountered the Baha'i religion in Rome and took it to Hawaii. During 1912, Abdu'l-Baha spent eight months in the United States and laid the cornerstone of the Baha'i House of Worship in Wilmette, Illinois. The temple took forty years to complete and was dedicated in 1953. The temple's structure demonstrated the significance of the number nine. As the largest whole number, nine is for Baha'is a symbol of culmination and unity. The Wilmette temple, like all Baha'i temples, is nine sided and capped with a dome.

The Baha'i teachings are contained in the writings of the Bab, Baha'u'llah and Abdu'l-Baha, considered scriptures, and in the writings of Shoghi Effendi which are considered infallible guidance. They teach the essential oneness of all revealed faiths, which have been given at different stages and ages. The Baha'i Faith is the crown and summation of the previous world faiths to date. While Baha'u'llahs revelation is the most recent. Baha'is believe that God will continue to send messengers in the future.

The Baha'i Faith teaches that God is, in essence, unknowable, though his word is known through his chosen messenger. This word is often summarized in thirteen principles: the independent search for truth, the oneness of the human race, the unity of religion, the condemnation of prejudice, the harmony of science and religion, the equality of the sexes, compulsory education, the adoption of a universal language, the abolition of extremes of wealth and poverty, a world court, work in the spirit of service as worship, justice and universal peace. Baha'i scriptures also stress the immortality and continuous progress of the soul. While these principles form a popular enumeration of Baha'i emphases, the scriptures contain reflections on a variety of other topics and concerns, many of equal importance.

Work is held as a necessity for all and is considered a form of worship. However, regular weekly gatherings featuring prayer and the readings from the sacred writings are held. There are an annual fasting period and eight holy days commemorating various events in the lives of the founders. March 21 is also a holy day, celebrated as New Year's Day. Besides the Temple at Wilmette, six others have been built around the world.

After Shoghi Effendi's death, leadership of the faith passed to the Universal House of Justice, an international body headquartered in Haifa, Israel. The Universal House of Justice administers the affairs of the worldwide Baha'i community. It may enact laws and ordinances not expressly stated in the sacred Baha'i texts, but may not offer interpretation of scripture. Members of the Universal House of Justice are elected every five years at an international convention composed of the members of the National Spiritual Assemblies, which have been formed in most countries of the world. National Spiritual Assemblies are elected annually at the National Baha'i Convention. From its offices in Wilmette, Illinois, the National Spiritual Assembly of the Baha'is of the United States has charge of the national administrative affairs of the faith, including the management of the Baha'i Publishing Trust and the Baha'i Home for the Aged. Members elect local spiritual assemblies wherever there are at least nine Baha'is. There are no clergy.

The World Center of the Baha'i Faith is in Haifa, Israel, where the Bab's shrine is located and Abdu'l-Baha is buried. The National Assembly in England is one of the oldest, having been established in 1923. The British publishing house of George Ronald is a major publisher of English-language Baha'i books widely circulated in the United States.

Membership: In 1997 it was reported that approximately 133,000 Baha'is resided in the United States. There were approximately 1,300 local spiritual assemblies. Worldwide there are more than 5 million Baha'is in 15,000 spiritual assemblies in more than 230 countries of the world. There were 175 National Spiritual Assemblies as of April 1997.

Periodicals: *World Order.* • *Brilliant Star.*

Sources:

Balyuzi, H. M. *Abdu'l-Baha.* London: George Ronald, 1971.

___. *Baha'u'llah, The King of Glory.* Oxford: George Ronald, 1980.

Miller, William McElwee. *The Baha'i Faith.* South Pasadena, CA: William Carey Library, 1974.

Perkins, Mary, and Philip Hainsworth. *The Baha'i Faith.* London: Ward Lock Educational, 1980.

Whitehead, O. Z. *Some Early Baha'is of the West.* Oxford: George Ronald, 1976.

★1936★
Faith of God
(Defunct)

The Faith of God grew out of the work of Jamshid Maani, a Persian prophet known to the public as simply "The Man," a title used to signify the coming of maturity to humanity and that the real station of man is a spiritual station. The Man announced his mission in 1963 in Israel and then Iran. He began to gather followers in various nations around the world to the Faith of God. The Faith emerged following the death of Shoghi Effendi, the guardian of the Baha'i World Faith, and the failure of another guardian to emerge as his successor. Among the early converts to The Man's cause was John Carre, a lifelong Baha'i, who traveled extensively on his behalf and organized the House of Mankind, the administrative aspect of the Faith, in several countries.

The Man continued the Baha'i belief in progressive revelation to mankind through the various mediators or teachers from Zoroaster to Baha'u'llah, and sees himself as the latest in this series. Evolution is also a key notion. The universe and its various parts are in continuous evolution. The universe is alive. The culmination of material creation is man's moving toward spiritual man. This evolutionary process is part of a divine plan leading creation toward unity.

The overall evolution of humanity is toward perfection on all levels. This goal was the reason for all the prophets. Their teachings are one. All forms of worship are acceptable except those contrary to wisdom or detrimental to others. We must strive to give all persons the attributes of the saintly ones. The individual's progression is aided by thorough meditation and prayer but they must become effective in our thoughts and actions.

The House of Mankind was initially established in each of five areas of the world. Like the Baha'i Faith, there is no clergy. Pictured for the future was the development of the Universal Palace of Order, which will bring to realization the aspirations of mankind for the unity and oneness of government. The House of Mankind functioned for a period of approximately ten years in the United States from its headquarters in the residence of John Carre in Mariposa, California. However, during the 1970s, The Man lived with Carre for a number of months, during which time Carre came to know Maani personally and as a result withdrew his support. The movement, which had only several hundred members, ceased to exist in America soon after that action.

Sources:

Carre, John. *An Island of Hope.* Mariposa, CA: House of Light, 1975.

The Man [Jamshid Maani]. *"Heaven".* Mariposa, CA: John Carre, 1971.

___. *Universal Order.* Mariposa, CA: John Carre, 1971.

___. *The Sun of the Word of the Man.* Mariposa, CA: John Carre, 1971.

★1937★
Orthodox Baha'i Faith, Mother Baha'i Council of the United States
3111 Futura
Roswell, NM 88201

Members of the Orthodox Baha'i Faith, in contrast to most other Baha'is, believe that the Baha'i Administrative Order remains unchanged with all of its administrative institutions intact since the death of Shoghi Effendi (1897-1957), the first Guardian of the Faith. The Baha'i Administrative Order was dictated in the Will and Testament of Abdu'l-Baha (1844-1921), the son of Baha'u'llah (1817-1892), the author of the Baha'i Revelation. This document was characterized by Shoghi Effendi as divinely conceived, coequal in sacredness and immutability to Baha'u'llah's most holy book, *The Kitab-i-Agdas*, and the charter of his world order. In his will, Abdu'l-Baha appointed Shoghi Effendi the first Guardian of the Baha'i Faith and stipulated that each Guardian appoint his successor "in his own lifetime." Under the terms of this document, the Guardian is the head of the Faith, the sole interpreter of Baha'i Holy Writ, and the sacred head of the Universal House of Justice, the supreme legislative body of the Baha'i Administrative Order.

Shoghi Effendi became the Guardian in 1921 following the death of Abdu'l-Baha. For the next thirty years he painstakingly developed the Baha'i Administrative Order at the local and national levels. In 1951 he deemed that the time was ripe to establish the first embryonic international institution. Based upon the fact that there were then nine functioning national administrative institutions, he established the first International Baha'i Council, explaining that it was a temporary title given to what was to become the Universal House of Justice. Shoghi Effendi did not assume the presidency of the council. He appointed Charles Mason Remey, a leading American Baha'i who had been chosen by Abdu'l-Baha to design the Baha'i temple on Mount Carmel and who was the architect of other Baha'i temples. The council was never convened into a functioning body during Shoghi Effendi's lifetime, although he assigned tasks to individuals who had been appointed to it. Coincident to the passing of Shoghi Effendi in 1957, Remey became the functioning president of the council. It is the belief of the Orthodox Baha'is that president of the Universal House of Justice (i.e., the International Baha'i Council) and Guardian are synonymous terms, hence Remey became the second Guardian of the Faith. The majority of Baha'is refused to recognize the validity of the appointment and declared the office of Guardian terminated.

Members of the Mother Baha'i Council state that Mason Remey elected to appoint his successor in the same manner that Shoghi Effendi had employed. He established the second International Baha'i Council and appointed as its president Joel B. Marangella. However, he reinforced the appointment in a letter addressed to Marangella, telling him to advise the Baha'is that he was the third Guardian of the Faith.

As it was impracticable for the second International Baha'i Council to function as a body, due to lack of support from national Baha'i administrative bodies, and as a majority of supporters of the Guardian were to be found in the United States, Marangella established a National Baha'i Bureau in New York City. The Bureau, which moved to New Mexico in 1972, administered the affairs of the Faith in the United States on a provisional and limited basis.

In 1978, the Bureau's functions were assumed and expanded by the local Baha'i Council of Roswell, New Mexico, a body of nine believers designated by the third Guardian as the Mother Baha'i Council of the Orthodox Baha'is of the United States. The council was assigned national Baha'i administrative jurisdiction pending the formation of a national Baha'i council when circumstances permit.

The Mother Baha'i Council, in addition to propagating the Faith through various media such as newspapers and magazines, has inserted open letters and appeals by the Guardian in newspapers in the United States and foreign countries in order to convince Baha'is that Shoghi Effendi provided for the continuance of the Guardian's office. They aggressively declare that in terminating the Guardianship the other Baha'is have, in effect, negated the major provisions of *The Will and Testament* and hence are attempting to destroy the World Order of Baha'u'llah and have become violators of the Covenant.

Membership: Not reported.

Periodicals: *Herald of the Covenant.* • *Friends in Touch.* • *Star of the Covenant* (for Orthodox Baha'is only).

Remarks: The Mother Council is one of three groups which continue the Guardianship and recognize Mason Remey as the second guardian. Donald Harvey claims to have a letter from Remey appointing him to be the third guardian. In the United States, Harvey's followers are affiliated in the Remey Society. The third group, an offshoot of the Mother Council, is the Orthodox Baha'i Faith under the Regency.

Sources:

The Orthodox Baha'i Faith. Roswell, NM: Mother Baha'i Council of the United States, 1981.

★1938★
Orthodox Baha'i Faith under the Regency
% National House of Justice of the U.S. and Canada
Box 1424
Las Vegas, NM 87701

The Orthodox Baha'i Faith under the Regency is one of three organizations of former members of the Baha'i Faith who accepted the claims of Charles Mason Remey (see separate entry on Remey Society) to be the successor of Shoghi Effendi, the Guardian of the Baha'i Faith who died in 1957. Remey claimed to be the Second Guardian. After Remey's death in 1974, Joel B. Marangella was one of two men who claimed to have been appointed by Remey as the Third Guardian. Marangella organized his followers as the Orthodox Baha'i Faith.

Among those appointed to a leadership role by Remey, Reginald B. (Rex) King accepted Marangella as the Third Guardian but later came to the conclusion that both Remey and Marangella had taken actions which were contrary to Baha'i law. He concluded that Remey, rather than being the Second Guardian, was but a regent who assumed control until such time as the Second Guardian appeared and took his rightful place. Upon reaching that conclusion, King withdrew from Marangella and claimed to be the Second Regent.

King died in 1977. In his will he appointed four members of his family—Eugene K. King, Ruth L. King, Theodore Q. King, and Thomas King—as the Council of Regents to succeed him. In 1993 Ruth L. King resigned from the Council of Regents. Maeny Whitaker was appointed to take her place. The Orthodox Baha'is follow the teaching of the Baha'i Faith, differing only in their rejection of the authority of the Universal House of Justice in favor of the Regency.

Membership: Not reported. There are an estimated several hundred Orthodox Baha'is in the United States.

★1939★
Remey Society
% Jacques Soqhomonian
Boite Postal 593
F-13491 Marseille Cedex 04, France

The Remey Society is one of three organizations of former members of the Baha'i Faith who accept Charles Mason Remey (1874-1974) as the Second Guardian of the Faith. Remey was a prominent Baha'i for many years. He authored a number of books, designed several Baha'i temples, and served as president of the International Baha'i Council. In 1951 he was one of nine people named by Shoghi Effendi as a hand of the cause.

In 1957 Shoghi Effendi died without having fathered a child, leaving a will, or naming a successor. Remey then joined with the other hands of the cause in proclaiming the formation of a Baha'i World Centre made up of nine hands of the cause to assume temporarily the function of the guardian. Remey was one of the nine. However, during the next few years, Remey dissented from the position of the other hands. He argued that the guardianship was a necessary feature of the structure of the faith. He also asserted that, as the president of the International Baha'i Council (a position assigned Remey by Shoghi Effendi), he was the only one in a position to become the Second Guardian. He waited two years for the hands to accept his position. Then, in 1959, he left Haifa, Israel, where the Baha'i Faith has its international headquarters, and came to the United States. In 1960 he issued a proclamation to the Baha'is of the World and circulated it at the annual gathering of the American Baha'is that year. He also issued a pamphlet, "A Last Appeal to the Hands of the Faith," asking them to abandon plans to elect members of the International House of Justice in 1961. The hands continued to reject his claims and expelled him from the faith.

Throughout the 1960s Remey insisted upon his right to be designated the Second Guardian. Finally, in 1968 he appointed the first five Elders of the Baha'i Epoch and announced the organization of his followers under the name The Orthodox Abha World Faith. He retired to Florence, Italy, and lived out the last decade of his life in virtual retirement.

After Remey's death in 1974, two men, Donald Harvey and Joel B. Marangella, both claimed that he had appointed them as the Third Guardian of the Faith. The Remey Society unites the American followers of Donald Harvey. The society was organized by Francis C. Spataro. Following Harvey's death in 1991, Jacques Soqhomonian became the new Guardian of the Faith.

Membership: In 1995 the society reported 400 members in the United States, 150 in Canada, and 200 in two European centers in Italy and France.

Periodicals: *The Remey Letter.*

Sources:

Remey, Charles Mason. *The Baha'i Movement.* Washington, DC: J. D. Milans & Sons, 1912.

___. *Extracts from Daily Observations of the Baha'i Faith Made to the Hands of the Faith in the Holy Land.* Privately published, 1961.

___. *Observations of a Baha'i Traveller.* Washington, DC: J. D. Milans & Sons, 1914.

Spataro, Francis C. *Charles Mason Remey and the Baha'i Faith.* New York: Carlton Press, 1987.

___. *The Lion of God.* Bellerose, NY: Remey Society, 1981.

___. *The Rerum.* Bellerose, NY: The Author, 1980.

★1940★
World Union of Universal Religion and Universal Peace
Current address not obtained for this edition.

In the years after the death of Abdu'l-Baha and the elevation of his grandson, Shoghi Effendi, to the leadership of the Baha'i Faith as the Guardian of the Faith, an American Baha'i, Ruth White, began to question Shoghi Effendi's authority. In her first book, *Abdul Baha and the Promised Age* (1926), she voiced her opposition to his attempts to develop the Baha'i organization by quoting Abdu'l-Baha to the effect that, "The Baha'i Movement is not an organization. You can never organize the Baha'i Cause." More importantly, she began to voice opposition to Shoghi Effendi's role as guardian, and in her 1929 work, *The Bahai Religion and Its Enemy, the Bahai Organization*, she attacked the authenticity of the Will and Testament of Abdul-Baha, the document upon which Effendi's authority rested.

Though she lectured widely throughout the United States, her only success in recruiting supporters came in Germany where the Baha'i World Union was founded by Wilhelm Herrigel and other Baha'is, who were described as friends of Abdul-Baha. The Baha'i World Union continued until 1937 when the German government outlawed the Baha'i Faith.

Simultaneously with White's attack upon Effendi, though separate from it, Ahmad Sohrab, a close friend of Abdu'l-Baha who had accompanied him on his American tour in 1912, and an American Baha'i, Julie Chandler (Mrs. Lewis Stuyvesant Chandler), formed an independent Baha'i network in New York City. They felt that Effendi's increasing efforts to organize the faith were counterproductive. They established the New History Society which offered lectures by Sohrab and other prominent guests (Albert Einstein addressed it on one occasion) and opened the Baha'i Bookshop. Members of the New History Society considered themselves participants in the Baha'i movement but separate from the organization headed by Effendi. In response, the Baha'i Faith brought suit against Sohrab, Chandler, and the New History Society seeking to prevent their use of the name "Baha'i." The court ruled against them, however, stating that no group of followers of a religion could monopolize the name of that religion or prevent other groups of followers from practicing their faith.

Like the Baha'i World Union, the New History Society found support in Europe and opened offices in Paris in the 1930s, and Sohrab became the major spokesperson for the society. He spoke frequently and authored a number of books, including *Broken Silence*, a response to the 1941 court case.

Ruth White and Ahmad Sohrab both died in 1958 and Julie Chandler in 1961. Since their deaths, their work and thought have been carried on by Hermann Zimmer of Stuttgart, West Germany. Zimmer had returned to Germany in 1948 after being released from a POW camp. He picked up the remnants of Herrigel's organization and formed the World Union for Universal Religion and Universal Peace. In 1950 he published *Die Wiederkunft Christi* in which he equated Baha'u'llah with Christ returned in his Second Advent. Though never a large organization, the World Union remains a rallying point for "Free Baha'is" around the world.

Membership: Not reported. Estimates suggest that only a few hundred "Free Baha'is" reside in the United States.

Sources:

The Baha'i Case against Mrs. Lewis Stuyvesant Chandler and Mirza Ahmad Sohrab. Wilmette, IL: National Spiritual Assembly of the Baha'i of the United States and Canada, 1941.

Mirza Ahmad Sohrab. *Broken Silence.* New York: New History Foundation, 1942.

___. *The Will and Testament of Abdul Baha: An Analysis.* New York: New History Foundation, 1944.

White, Ruth. *Abdul Baha and the Promised Age.* New York, 1927.

___. *Baha'i Religion and Its Enemy, the Baha'i Organization.* Rutland, VT: Charles Tuttle, 1929.

Zimmer, Hermann. *A Fraudulent Testament Devalues the Baha'i Religion into Political Shoghism.* Stuttgart, Germany: World Union for Universal Religion and Universal Peace, 1973.

The Druze

★1941★
American Druze Society
755 W. Big Beaver, Ste. 2106
Troy, MI 48084

Alternate Address: American Druze Cultural Center 2239 Merton Ave. Eagle Rock, CA.

The Druze (or Duruz) community originated in Egypt in the eleventh century at a time when the Ismaili Shi'a Muslims had attained their greatest political success through the Fatimid dynasty. Some Ismailis began to view the caliph, al-Hakim, as a somewhat divine figure. He was considered the "imam" (leader) of the Ismaili movement. Among the leaders was al-Darazi. Following al-Darazi's death in 1020 C.E., leadership fell to Hamza b. Ali of Suzan in Persia (Iran). Hamza began to see himself as the imam and al-Hakim as the embodiment of the Godhead. He began to organize followers in expectation that al-Hakim would claim his position openly.

Al-Hakim disappeared in 1021. Hamza told the followers that he had merely gone underground for a while and would reappear in all power. The following year Hamza also disappeared. The movement faded in Egypt, although it survived and actually took on new life in an isolated area of Syria under the leadership of al-Muktana. Al-Muktana wrote many letters that, with a few surviving writings of al-Hakim and Hamza, would be compiled into the Druze scripture called Rasa'il al-Hikma, the *Book of Wisdom*.

The Druze survived in the mountainous terrain and for centuries lived a rather closed and isolated existence. It emerged as a distinct social group with its own unique customs and beliefs. Converts are not accepted, and intermarriage is not allowed. The community is divided into the *djuhhal*, the ordinary members of the community, and the *ukkal*, the initiated religious members. The ukkals wear a special white turban. Leaders, drawn from among the ukkals are termed *shaykhs*.

The religious life of the Druze is not wholly known to outsiders; even many of the faithful are not allowed to study the higher teachings of the faith. The Druze faith is a form of Islam with a mystical bent. There is a belief in reincarnation. However, Druze are most known for their strict moral code. The seven commandments include admonitions to: (1) speak truth within the community, (2) defend and assist the community, (3) renounce any former religion, (4) dissociate from nonbelievers, (5) recognize the unity of "Our Lord" in all ages, (6) be content with His actions, and (7) submit to His orders as conveyed through the community leadership.

Druze survival was frequently threatened over the centuries, because the Muslims treated them as heretics. During the twentieth century, as parcels of land changed hands, some Druze migrated to other parts of the Middle East and are now in Lebanon, Israel, and Saudi Arabia. Druze also moved to the United States in this century. By the end of World War II, enough had migrated to found the American Druze Society. In 1979 the society adopted a constitution that stated its purpose as the perpetuation of the Druze faith. Membership is open to any person of Druze descent.

The American Druze Society dates to a gathering in 1901 in Seattle, Washington by a small group of Druze immigrants, which led to the 1911 incorporation of Al Bakourat Alderziet. A second branch was opened in Cleveland, Ohio, in 1916. Additional branches were established across the United States, primarily in the Midwest. In 1947, at an convention in Charleston, West Virginia, a more formalized organization, the American Druze Society, was created.

Membership: There are more than 5,000 Druze in North America.

Periodicals: *Our Heritage.*

Sources:

Abu Izzedin, Nejla. *The Druze: A New Study of History, Faith and Society.* Leiden, Netherlands: E. J. Brill, 1984.

Makarim, Sami Nasib. *The Druze Faith.* Delmar, NY: Caravan Books, 1974.

Section 23

Eastern Family, Part I: Hinduism, Jainism, Sikhism

Consult the Contents pages to locate the essay in Part II, Historical Essay Chapters,
that provides an historical discussion of this family

Intrafaith Organizations

★1942★
Vishwa Hindu Parishad of America
217 Deerfield Dr.
Berlin, CT 06037

The idea of a cooperative world structure for Hindus was first proposed in 1964, and that proposal led to a gathering in India in 1966 at the time of the great Kumbha Mela festival. The First Hindu World Conference attracted some 25,000 attendees and included participants from the United States. An American branch of the Vishwa Hindu Parishad formed at that conference was established in New York in 1970.

In the United States, the organization has focused upon a number of programs aimed at providing fellowship for Hindus of different ethnic and religious groups, cultural programs for children, cooperative celebrations of Indian festivals, and the furthering of Hinduism both within the Indian American community and among the public at large. It has also developed several relief projects and sponsors medical facilities in India.

The Parishad holds an annual national conference. It has organized local chapters in different locations around the country which hold regular meetings.

Periodicals: *Hindu Vishwa.*

Hinduism

★1943★
Abhidhyan Yoga Institute
PO Box 1414
Nevada City, CA 95959-1414

The Abhidhyan Yoga Institute was founded in 1991 by Shri Acharya Abhidhyanananda Avahuta (Anatole Ruslanov) to prepare interested persons for what is termed Abhidhyan Yoga or All-Embracing Yoga, a form of tantric yoga which has survived through the centuries only in a few obscure Hindu and Buddhist tantric traditions.

Shri Acharya Abhidhyanananda Avahuta completed a period of monastic training in Varanasi, India, with Shri Shri Anandamurti (1921–1990), founder of the Ananda Marga Yoga Society. Following his monastic training he continued his study with Anandamurti and eventually became a spiritual teacher and a bearer of the lineage. Following his master's death, he founded his own teaching work. New students are expected to start a regular personal practice of meditation and *asanas* (postures), adhere to a set of moral principles, and find a competent trustworthy teacher to follow.

Membership: Not reported. There are members in seven countries.

Periodicals: *The Tantrik Path.*

Sources:

http://www.abhidhyan.org/contact.html/.

★1944★
Adidam
12040 N. Seigler Spring Rd.
Middletown, CA 95461

Adidam, formerly known as the Free Daist Communion, was founded in 1970 as the Dawn Horse Fellowship by Franklin Jones. In 1960, after a "crisis of despair," he began a period of introspection that led him to study with Swami Rudrananda (discussed elsewhere in this chapter), the American student of Swami Muktananda (also discussed elsewhere in this chapter). At Rudrananda's suggestion, he entered a Lutheran seminary. In 1968, he traveled to India to meet Muktananda. At Muktananda's ashram, he had his first adult experience of total absorption in the Transcendental Consciousness.

On September 10, 1970, he entered what he has termed the permanent state of Sahaj Samadhi, which is coessential with the Transcendental Being-Consciousness itself. This is the condition that he is believed to have surrendered at birth, and that he had tried to recover throughout his life. Soon after this experience, he began to teach in order to transmit the God-realization he had attained. In 1973, he undertook a pilgrimage to India. During this time he changed his name to Bubba Free John—"Bubba" denoting brother. Upon his return, he changed his method of teaching. He involved his students in the many experiences of life, including sexuality, the pursuits of money and material rewards, and spiritual and psychic encounters. Some experiences became quite intense, and all were aimed at showing their futility.

After three years of primary interaction with his students, Bubba Free John withdrew into seclusion. In 1979, he entered a new phase of work and adopted the name Da Free John—"Da" signifying "giver." This has been a phase of retirement from active teaching work and institutional involvement to concentrate on the transmission of the "transcendental condition." During the mid-1980s, he became known as Heart-Master Da Love-Ananda or more formally Avadhoota Da Love-Ananda Hridayam. He is now referred to as Avatar Adi Da Samraj. As Avatar's work has grown and changed, so has the name of the body of believers from Dawn Horse Fellowship to Free Primitive Church of Divine Communion to Johannine Daist Community to Free Daist Communion, and most recently as Adidam.

The teachings of Avatar have been termed the Way of Radical Understanding. It begins in the denial of the illusion of the separateness of our individual existence. We are the all-comprehensive Reality, Being-Consciousness-Bliss. This condition, which is native and natural to us, becomes obvious when all seeking is transcended, i.e., when radical understanding prevails. Enlightenment, thus, already exists; it cannot be attained. It is, however, to be realized. This realization can be measured through a process which Avatar has characterized as the seven stages of life. The seven stages provide a method of evaluating one's individual progress as well as the level of the mass of other spiritual teachings.

Stage one begins at birth and focuses upon adaptation to the world. Stage two, beginning around age seven, focuses upon the integration of the emotional self and the physical. The third stage is a period of development of the mind, will, and emotional-sexual functions. The fourth stage marks the beginning of spiritual awakening. The fifth stage relates to the mystical inner search capped with the experience of samahdi. The sixth stage is the profound state of "ego-death", or the transcendence of the separate self-sense, the awakening to Transcendental Consciousness. In the seventh stage, the individual recognizes everything as a modification of the Radiant Transcendental Being.

Membership: In 1998 there were approximately 1,066 members in the United States, 100 members in Canada, and several hundred overseas. Some members now live at the resident retreat center in the Fiji Islands. Foreign center are located in Great Britain, the Netherlands, Australia, and New Zealand.

Sources:

Avatar Ad. Da Samraj and the Firstg 25 years of His Divine Revelation Work. Middletown, CA: Dawn Horse Press, 1997.

Bubba Free John. [Franklin Jones]. *No Remedy.* Lower Lake, CA: Dawn Horse Press, 1976.

Da Free John. [Franklin Jones]. *The Dawn Horse Testament.* San Rafael, CA: Dawn Horse Press, 1985.

Da Love-Ananda. *The Holy Jumping-Off Place.* San Rafael, CA: Dawn Horse Press, 1986.

Feuerstein, Georg, ed. *Humor Suddenly Returns.* Clearlake, CA: Dawn Horse Press, 1984.

Jones, Franklin. *The Method of the Siddhas.* Los Angeles: Dawn Horse Press, 1973.

The Next Option. Clearlake, CA: Dawn Horse Press, 1984.

See the Brightness Face to Face: A Celebration of the Ruchira Buddha. Middletown, CA: Dawn Horse Press, 1997.

★1945★
Advaita Fellowship
221-B Indianapolis St.
Huntington Beach, CA 92648

The Advaita Fellowship was founded following Ramesh S. Balsekar's 1987 visit to the United States. Balsekar is a disciple of Sri Nisargadatta Maharaj (1897-1981). Nisargadatta was a guru in a lineage which began with Saint Jnaneshwara, who lived in Maharashtra, India, in the thirteenth century and passed on a practice of *jnana* yoga, the philosophical approach to spiritual enlightenment through *advaita vedanta* (the belief in nonduality). Sri Nisargadatta was a popular teacher known for his ability to speak about profound thought so all could understand. He rarely gave lectures, but generally taught by holding conversations with those around him.

Ramesh S. Balsekar was a graduate of London University who became a successful banker. He retired in 1970 and about the same time met Sri Nisargadatta. He became a close disciple and began to keep a record of his conversations, later the subject of several books. Meanwhile several Westerners came to know of Sri Nisargadatta and began to spread his teachings in Europe and America. Maurice Frydman transcribed and published the first book of his teachings, *I Am That: Talks with Sri Nisargadatta Maharaj* and in 1982 Peter Brent wrote of him in *Godmen of India.* Jean Dunn, noting the relationship between Nisargadatta's teachings and those of Ramana Maharshi, published articles about Nisargadatta in *The Mountain Path,* the magazine from Maharshi's *ashram* (religious community). Dunn later edited the first books on Maharaj published in America.

In the years since Maharaj's death, Balsekar has been active in spreading the teachings of advaita vedanta, and has traveled to the United States annually since his first visit in 1987. Advaita teaches

that suffering comes from the mistaken idea that we are separate entities. It emphasizes that, in fact, the human soul (Atman) and the universal soul (Brahman) are one and the same. In the realization of that simple truth ignorance and suffering are dispelled.

Membership: Not reported.

Sources:

Balsekar, Ramesh S. *Experiencing the Teachings.* Redondo Beach, CA: Advaita Press, 1988.

___. *From Consciousness to Consciousness.* Redondo Beach, CA: Advaita Press, 1989.

Brent, Peter. *The Godmen of India.* Chicago: Quadrangle Books, 1972.

"I Am That." *Hinduism Today* 11, no. 3 (March 1989): 1, 5.

Nisargadatta Maharaj, Sri. *The Blissful Life.* Comp. by Robert Powell. Durham, NC: Acorn Press, 1984. .

___. *I Am That.* Durham, NC: Acorn Press, 1983.

___. *Prior to Consciousness.* Edited by Jean Dunn. Durham, NC: Acorn Press, 1985.

___. *Seeds of Consciousness.* Edited by Jean Dunn. New York: Grove Press, 1982.

Sri Nisargadatta Maharaj Presentation Volume: 1980. Bombay, India: Sri Nisargadatta Adhyatma Kendra, 1980.

★1946★
Ajapa Yoga Foundation
℅ Shri Janardan Ajapa Yoga Ashram
Box 1731
Placerville, CA 95667

Ajapa yoga is a simple meditation and breathing technique believed by its practitioners to be the most ancient form of yoga, developed thousands of years ago by the *rishis* (seers) of India. Thus it is believed to be the original yoga, not a composite, abbreviation, or updated version of the forms of yoga. Ajapa yoga was rediscovered and given to the modern world by Guru Purnananda Paramahansa. He learned of the practice from Matang Rishi in a hidden monastery in Tibet. He created three ashrams in Bengal to spread the teachings which, while very old, had not been widely available until the last half of the nineteenth century. The work begun by Purnananda was continued by his disciple Guru Bhumananda Paramahansa who in turn passed the succession to Guru Janardan Paramahansa (b. 1888). Guru Janardan organized the World Conference on Scientific Yoga in New Delhi, which brought him into contact with many westerners. Following the conference he accepted an invitation to lecture in Czechoslovakia and expanded his western tour to include Germany, Canada, and the United States. After being in the West for over a year, he returned to India.

Some of the westerners he encountered upon his tour traveled to India in 1973. In 1974, upon their return to New York, they incorporated the Ajapa Yoga Foundation. Guru Janardan made visits in 1974, 1975, and 1976 establishing centers in Hamburg, Germany; Montreal, Quebec; Los Angeles; Baltimore; Atlanta; and Knoxville, Tennessee. A periodical was begun in 1976, and a book summarizing the teachings was published. From that modest beginning the foundation has steadily grown.

On January 6, 1966, Guru Janardan Paramahansa found a baby boy by the banks of the Ganges River, and named him Guru Prasad. He predicted that Guru Prasad would be a self-realized saint who would have a large role in helping suffering humanity. He trained him from birth for this purpose, and in 1980, Guru Prasad became the only living master of ajapa yoga. According to Guru Prasad, "A person has but to practice this technique and everything will be answered, naturally and automatically."

According to the foundation's teachings, humans have lost their true identities and are left in a world of pain, want, and illusion. True identity can be gained by the practice of ajapa yoga beginning with the meditation on the mantra given by the guru at the time of initiation, accompanied by specific breathing techniques.

Membership: In 1997 the foundation reported 500 members in three centers in the United States and 100 members in one center in Canada. Affiliated centers are also found in India, Germany, Poland, Czechoslovakia, and Japan. There were approximately 10,000 members worldwide.

Periodicals: *The Ajapa Journal.*

Sources:

Tattwa Katha: A Tale of Truth. New York: Ajapa Yoga Foundation, 1976.

★1947★
American Meditation Society
105 Lautner Ln.
Edwardsville, IL 62025

The American Meditation Society is the United States affiliate of the International Foundation for Spiritual Unfoldment founded in 1975 in Capetown, South Africa, by Purushottan Narshinhran (b.1932), whom his followers know by his spiritual name, Gururaj Ananda Yogi. As a child in his native Gujarat, he showed a distinct focus upon spiritual realities. When he was five years old he ran away from home to visit the temples in the neighborhood. When he was found, he explained to his parents that he had visited many temples, but had found to his frustration that "the Gods were lifeless and would not speak to me." His continued search for the Divine culminated when he discovered that what he sought lay within himself. Having found the inner reality and having fully and permanently entered the self-realized state, he set himself to the task of becoming a spiritual teacher in the West.

He moved to South Africa and became a successful businessman. In 1975, following a problem with his heart, he retired from business and turned to full-time work as a spiritual teacher. He founded the International Foundation for Spiritual Unfoldment. Within the first year it had spread to nine countries, in the British Commonwealth and throughout Europe. In 1977 it was organized in California as the American Meditation Society.

Gururaj Ananda Yogi teaches not a religion, but the basis which underlies all religions. His task is seen as merely to awaken the individual to the same reality that he discovered and to lead him or her along the path of unfoldment. Meditation is the individual's major tool in turning inward, and it works best if individualized. The society offers basic meditation courses which introduce the variety of ways to meditate. Gururaj assists in the process of individualizing sound which is intoned during meditation. Individuals send their pictures to Gururaj. He meditates upon the picture and hears the sound each person makes with the universe. He presents the distinct sound to each person as a unique personal mantrum.

Membership: In 1984 the society had approximately 2,000 members in 30 centers. Internationally, the foundation has centers in Canada, Australia, Zimbabwe, Spain, Denmark, Germany, Holland, Ireland, Great Britain, and South Africa.

Periodicals: *American Meditation Society Newsletter.*

Sources:

Ananda Yogi, Gururaj. *From Darkness to Light.* Farmingdale, NY: Coleman Publishing, 1987.

Partridge, Ted. *Jewels of Silence.* Farmborough, Hamps.: St. Michael's Abbey Press, 1981.

Taylor, Savita. *The Path to Unfoldment.* London: VSM Publications, 1979.

★1948★
American Vegan Society
56 Dinshah Ln.
PO Box H
Malaga, NJ 08328-0908

The American Vegan Society was founded in 1960 at Malaga, New Jersey, by H. Jay Dinshah. The basis of the Society is Ahimsa, defined as "Dynamic Harmlessness." The six pillars of Ahimsa (one for each letter) are Abstinence from all animal products, particularly for food or clothing; Harmlessness and Reverence for life; Integrity of thought, word, and deed; Mastery over oneself; Service to humanity, nature, and creation; and Advancement of understanding and truth. Veganism is conceived as an advanced and comprehensive program for living and draws its inspiration from Mahatma Gandhi, Albert Schweitzer, and other sages. Vegans are vegetarians and ecology-oriented.

Headquarters for the society are at Suncrest, run as a teaching center, at Malaga. An annual convention is held. The society is affiliated with the North American Vegetarian Society, headquartered at Dolgeville, New York, and the International Vegetarian Union, in England, and the Vegetarian Union of North America headquartered in Washington, D.C.

Membership: The society reported a membership of more than 1,000 in 1995.

Periodicals: *Ahimsa.*

Sources:

Dinshah, Freya. *The Vegan Kitchen.* Malaga, NJ: American Vegan Society, 1970.

Ghadiali, Dinshah P. *Gems in the Bible.* Malaga, NJ: Dinshah Publishing Company, 1952.

The Life of a Karma-Yogi. Malaga, NJ: American Vegan Society, 1973.

★1949★
American Yoga Society
513 S. Orange Ave.
Sarasota, FL 34236

The American Yoga Society was founded in 1971 as the Light of Yoga Society by Alice Christensen. Christensen began her spiritual quest in 1953 when she had a visionary experience in which she was engulfed with a white light. She subsequently learned of Swami Sivananda Sivananda (1887–1963), the head of the Divine Life Society in India, and corresponded with him for many years. In 1964, the year after Sivananda's death, she traveled to India and met Swami Rama of Hardwar, India (1900–1972) and became his student. Swami Rama (not to be confused with the person of the same name who founded the Himalayan International Institute of Yoga Science and Philosophy) had spent three years as a recluse in the Himalayas before settling in Hardwar as a teacher of yoga.

As Swami Rama's representative in the West, Christensen began to teach yoga in 1965 and six years later founded the Light of Yoga Society in Cleveland Heights, Ohio. At the time of Swami Rama's death in 1972, there were some eleven yoga centers in India, Australia and the United States that he guided. The name American Yoga Society was adopted in 1982. More recently headquarters were transferred to Florida.

Swami Rama developed a simplified form of the wisdom of the vedanta, and a form of hatha yoga especially for western practitioners. Members of the society practice both hatha and meditation daily. They also consume a vegetarian diet, practice ahimsa (nonviolence), avoid alcohol, tobacco, and drugs, and are restrained in their use of sex.

Membership: Not reported. There are two centers in the United States and two affiliated centers in India.

Sources:

Christensen, Alice, and David Rankin. *The Light of Yoga Society Beginner's Manual.* Cleveland Heights, OH: Om Ram Productions, 1972. Rev. ed.: Alice Christensen. *The American Yoga Association Beginner's Manual.* New York: Simon & Schuster, 1987.

★1950★
Amrita Foundation
Current address not obtained for this edition.

The Amrita Foundation is an independent organization founded in the 1970s and based upon the teachings of Swami Paramahansa Yogananda. The organization emphasizes the original nature of the material it uses, especially the original Praecepta Lessons (instructions by the teacher), the home study course through which the foundation presents Yogananda's teachings. The lessons detail the instructions for the practice of kriya yoga, including the practice of meditation, concentration, and physical exercises. It also includes teachings on diet and nutrition. Lessons are sent to students on a month-by-month basis. The Foundation has reprinted the first edition of many of Yogananda's books, such as *Whispers from Eternity, Songs of the Soul,* and *The Second Coming of Christ* (two volumes).

Membership: Not reported.

★1951★
Ananda
14618 Tyler Foote Rd.
Nevada City, CA 95959

Ananda Church of Self-Realization and Ananda World Brotherhood Village were founded by Kriyananda (J. Donald Walters). Both institutions are based on the spiritual principles set forth by yoga master, Paramhansa Yogananda, author of the spiritual book, *Autobiography of a Yogi.*

Born of American parents in Rumania in 1926, Kriyananda was educated in Rumania, Switzerland, England, and the United States. At the age of 22, he became a disciple of Paramhansa Yogananda and lived with him until the master's death in 1952. As a minister and director of center activities for the organization which Yogananda founded, Self-Realization Fellowship, and later as vice-president of SRF, he traveled and taught extensively in many countries. In 1962, he says God called him to serve his guru's mission in another capacity. He was separated from Self-Realization Fellowship to explore and expound through writing, teaching, and lecturing the implications of Yogananda's message for active yoga students and laypersons.

In 1968, Kriyananda founded Ananda Village near Nevada City, California, in response to inner guidance and to the "oft-uttered public plea" of Paramhansa Yogananda: "Cover the earth with world-brotherhood colonies, demonstrating that simplicity of living plus high thinking lead to the greatest happiness."

Kriyananda has published more than forty books, including *The Path: A Spiritual Autobiography; Rays of the Same Light;* and *The Essence of Self-Realization: The Wisdom of Paramhansa Yogananda.* He has also composed musical works including *Christ Lives,* an oratorio; *Shakespeare Quartet,* composed for two violins, viola, and cello; *Egyptian Suite,* written for harp, flute, and viola; and *The Divine Romance,* a piano sonata.

Ananda Village is situated at 2,600-foot elevation and on 750 acres of wooded and meadow land in the Sierra foothills of northern California. Members support themselves through a variety of businesses, some of which are privately owned and some owned and operated by the community. Children are educated, from preschool through junior high, at the Ananda Education-for-Life School located within the village. High school students attend public school in Nevada City. The community and its branches includes approximately 600 people from many cultural, ethnic, and racial backgrounds. About 25 nationalities are represented among the residents. A village council is elected annually by Ananda members. The Expanding Light is Ananda's guest facility, open year-round, offering personal retreats, week-long and four week-long training courses, and special events and holiday programs.

Ananda members practice regular daily meditation using the techniques of Kriya Yoga, as taught by Paramhansa Yogananda. Resident members are all disciples of Yogananda. The group is also directly involved in a worldwide outreach to those interested in the teachings of Paramhansa Yogananda and his line of gurus.

Ananda's church, established in 1990 in congregational form, has 2,000 members. The goal of the Ananda Church of Self-Realization is to provide fellowship and inspiration for those who want to find God through serving him in others, and through the practice of ancient Raja Yoga techniques for self-realization that were brought to the West by Paramhansa Yogananda. The church is open for membership for those who follow the teachings of Paramhansa Yogananda.

Membership: In 1997 there were 2,000 church members of Ananda worldwide; 350 people, including children, reside at the main community in Nevada City. Ananda Church has 150 ordained ministers, who serve in Ananda churches at home and abroad. Currently Ananda has five branch communities located in Seattle, Washington; Portland, Oregon; Sacramento and Palo Alto, California; and Assisi, Italy. In addition to these residential communties, there are 50 centers and meditation groups throughout the world.

Periodicals: *Clarity Newsletter.*

Sources:

Kriyananda, Swami [Donald Walters]. *Cooperative Communities, How to Start Them and Why.* Nevada City, CA: Ananda Publications, 1968.

___. *Crises in Modern Thought.* Nevada City, CA: Ananda Publications, 1972.

___. *The Path.* Nevada City, CA: Ananda Publications, 1977.

Nordquist, Ted A. *Ananda Cooperative Village.* Upsala, Sweden: Borgstroms Tryckeri Ab, 1978.

Walters, J. Donald. *Cities of Light.* Nevada City, CA: Crystal Clarity, Publishers, 1987.

★1952★
Ananda Marga Yoga Society
97-38 42nd Ave.
Corona, NY 11368

The Ananda Marga Yoga Society was founded in 1955 in Bihar, India by Prabhat Ranjan Sarkar (b.1921), known to his followers as Shri Anandamurti, which roughly translated means "one upon seeing Him falls into bliss." He was an accomplished yogi at four and began initiating devotees at age six. He is considered by his followers to be a miracle worker and Maha-Guru (or God incarnate), one of which appears every few thousand years. A former railway clerk, Sarkar took the vows of the renounced life at the time he founded Ananda Marga.

Anandamurti teaches a yogic philosophy, the practicing of which places one on the path of bliss. The path begins with initiation, in which the devotee is privately instructed in the method of initiation by a guru (teacher). He is then taught the requirements of yama and niyama (discussed in the introduction to this volume), and meditation (dharmacakra). The initiate is required to learn by heart the "supreme command," which instructs him/her to practice twice-daily meditation, observe yama and niyama, and the obligation to bring all into the path of perfection. Combined with the yogic philosophy was a strong movement toward social service.

Ananda Marga came to the United States in September, 1969, when Acharya Vimalananda was sent by Anandamurti (Dadaji) to establish the work in America. Under his leadership, Ananda Marga made rapid progress and, by 1973, had established more than 100 centers with approximately 3,000 members. A monthly newsletter, *Sadvipra*, was begun in 1973.

Ananda Marga appeared not just as a religious movement, but a political one as well. Sarkar's political ideals were articulated as the Progressive Utilization Theory (Prout), based upon which he began to organize the lower classes in opposition to both the Communists and the ruling government. The Proutist Bloc ran candidates for office in the 1967 and 1969 elections. In 1971, however, Sarkar was accused by a former follower of having conspired to murder some ex-members. Based upon his testimony Sarkar was arrested and jailed awaiting trial. His imprisonment lasted through the national emergency proclaimed by Indira Ghandi in 1975. Ananda Marga was one of the organization she banned nationally. Meanwhile Ananda Margis had been involved in a number of violent incidents, some aimed at protesting Sarkar's imprisonment. Sarkar was finally brought to trial, under the conditions of the emergency, and convicted. He was unable to call any witnesses in his behalf. He was finally retried in 1978 and found not guilty. Since that date the number of reported incidents has decreased markedly. While still a large movement, Ananda Marga has not recovered its former strength in India.

Ananda Marga brought its social idealism with it. In 1958 Sarkar had organized Renaissaince Universal to mobilize intellectuals and others for the improvement of humanity's condition. Renaissance Universal is organized in America and directly sponsored by Ananda Marga through Renaissance Universal Clubs on college campuses, ERAWS (Education, Relief and Welfare Section) working in development of various programs, the *Renaissance Universal* magazine, and RAWA (Renaissance Artists and Writers Association). Proutist Universal, which advocates Sankar's political ideals, is officially independent of Ananda Marga, but informally associated.

Membership: Not reported.

Periodicals: *Sadvipra*. Send orders to 854 Pearl Street, Denver, CO 80403. • *Delaware Valley Prout News*. Send orders to Proutist Universal, 228 S. 46th Street, Philadelphia, PA 19139.

Remarks: Acharya Vimalananda, who founded Ananda Marag in the United States, left the organization to found the Yoga House Ashram.

Sources:

Tadbhavananda Avadhuta, Acharya. *Glimpses of Prout Philosophy*. Copenhagen, Denmark: Central Proutist Publications, 1981.

Anandamurti, Shrii Shrii. *Baba's Grace*. Denver, CO: Amrit Publications, 1973.

___. *The Great Universe: Discourses on Society*. Los Altos Hills, CA: Ananda Marga Publications, 1973.

Nandita and Devadatta. *Path of Bliss, Ananda Marga Yoga*. Wichita, KS: Ananda Marga Publishers, 1971.

The Spiritual Philosophy of Shrii Shrii Anandamurti. Denver, CO: Ananda Marga Publications, 1981.

Sarkar, P. R. *Idea and Ideology*. Calcutta: Acarya Pranavananda Avadhuta, 1978.

★1953★
Anasuya Foundation
Current address not obtained for this edition.

Alternate Address: International headquarters: Sri Punitachariji, Girnar Sadhana Ashram, Bhavnath Taleti, Junagadh, Gujarat, India 362004.

The Anasuya Foundation dates to the 1975 experience of Indian teacher Swami Punitachariji (affectionately called "Bapu") with Lord Dattatreya. The encounter occurred at Mount Girnar, a place sacred to Dattatreya in the Himalayan Mountains. Lord Dattatreya, one of the Hindu deities, is described as the divine essence behind all wisdom, all aspects of god combined. He is Brahma,

Vishnu, and Shiva. He is usually pictured as a being with three heads and six arms with a minimal amount of clothing. He is satguru, and as such is capable of transmitting to others the power to understand life.

Prior to his encounter with Lord Dattatreya, Bapu had no physical guru, but had been a spiritual seeker wandering the forests and river banks for many years. He saw Lord Datta sitting on a rock being showered with flowers by saints and sages of past generations. He was chanting a mantra, "Hari Om Tatsat Jai Guru Datta." He gave this mantra to Bapu for the uplift of humankind.

It is the belief taught by Bapu that God created the world through sound. For every physical sound there is an equivalent sound on the subtle planes of creation. Thus by repeating certain charged sounds the creative plane is affected and those effects return to the physical plane and recreate it. Chanting the mantra of Lord Dattatreya brings his essence to the person doing the chanting and allows development without the need of an earthly guru.

Toward the end of the 1970s, the message of Bapu was brought to the West by Shantibaba, an early disciple. Centers were soon established in the United States, the United Kingdom, and Germany.

Membership: Not reported. Centers are located in California, New York, Colorado, New Jersey, Germany, and England.

Sources:

Matulay, Emily, and Shantibaba. *Spontaneous Meditation*. Basalt, CO: Anasuya Publications, 1983. 43 pp.

★1954★
Anoopam Mission
℅ Brahmajyoti
RR #8, Box 8066
Stroudsburg, PA 18360

Alternate Address: International Headquarters: Brahmajyoti, Yogiji Marg, Mogri-388 345 (Via Anand), Gujarat, India.

The Anoopam Mission was founded in 1965 as an independent branch of the Swaminarayan movement, a nineteenth-century Hindu movement most successful in the state of Gujarat. The Swaminarayan movement was founded by Shree Sahajanand Swami, popularly known as Swaminarayan (1781–1830). He championed the idea of theistic worship in opposition to the popular Vedanta idea of an impersonal divine reality. God manifests on earth through his incarnations and his saints. The proper response of the believer is devotional service (bhakti yoga). Swaminarayan declared himself to be the early manifestation of Lord Swami Narayan, the Supreme Being, and is so considered by his followers to this day. Swaminarayan was succeeded by a series of leaders who served as high priest. In the mid-twentieth century, the High Priest was His Supreme Divine Holiness Yogiji Maharaj (d. 1971), who first organized the followers of the movement in the United States in 1970.

The Anoopam Mission was founded by a young man named Jashbhai, born in Sokhada, Gujarat, in 1940. As a college student he met Yogiji Maharaj, who called him by a term of endearment, "Saheb," the name by which he has since been known. He began to hold meetings among his fellow students. He began to raise up a new order of dedicated young men who were commissioned to become holy men, *sadhus*, but without taking the traditional dress and vows of the *sanyassin*, the renounced life. They did not wear the saffron robe nor adopt a life of begging. Instead, they continued their education and afterwards worked at a job. They attempted to integrate their spiritual and secular life and to live a life of service.

Saheb's break with the larger movement came in 1965. Differences had arisen in the Swaminarayan movement over, among other issues, the place of women in the movement. The conservative leaders in the movement did not want to allow women to take the sannyas vows, and being in control, they excommunicated those who supported the women. Saheb and his followers were believed to be in the liberal camp and were asked to leave. Saheb reorganized with the sadhus of the order supplying the leadership. Saheb eventually settled at Mogri, Gujarat, and there the international headquarters of the movement, Brahmajyoti, has been constructed. Other centers were founded throughout Gujarat and adjacent states, and the movement supports a number of educational institutions and medical facilities.

Followers of the Anoopam Mission began to migrate to the United States in the late 1960s, and Saheb made his first visit to the West in 1973. He has regularly visited Europe and America since.

Membership: Not reported. As of the early 1990s there were three centers in the United States, one each in New York, New Jersey, and Maryland. The majority of members were recent immigrants from Gujarat. There is also one center in England.

Sources:

Saheb—Profile of a Guru and His Mission. Uxbridge, UK: Anoopam Mission, 1989.

★1955★
Arcane Magical Order of the Knights of Shambhala (AMOOKOS)
% Shri Shyamanath
PO Box 1425, Grand Central Station
New York, NY 10163

Alternate Address: Shambhala Nath, PO Box 661182, Los Angeles, CA 90066.

The Adinath Sampradaya is a tantric sect of yogis affiliated with the greater Natha tradition founded by Gorakhnath and Matsyendranath, two teachers credited with great magical powers. Matsyendranath (a.k.a. Macchagnanath) (c. 900 C.E.) is connected to the foundation of the Kaula school of tantra and the worship (puja) of the Goddess Kali. Gorakhnath (a.k.a. Gorakshanatha), the disciple of Matsyendranath, is credited with the foundation of laya or kundalini yoga and hatha yoga, and is revered by many of the Natha subsects as their founder.

Mahendranath (a.k.a. Dadaji) (1911–1992), the 23rd Adiguru (chief teacher) of the Adinathas, was born and grew up in London, where in his 20s he met magical teacher Aleister Crowley. After World War II, he traveled to his ancestral home and in Bombay he met his guru in the Natha tradition and initiated as a sadhu (holy man). For the next 30 years Dadaji wandered Southeast Asia as a penniless renunciate. In 1978 Dadaji initiated Lokanath Maharaj into the Adinath Sampradaya (sect), and he returned to England and initiated several people as Adinathas. He also founded AMOOKOS, or the Arcane Magical Order of the Knights of Shambhala, in 1982.

Dadaji had come to London in 1981, during which time he oversaw the writing of some papers by Lokanath for an organization that would act as a training ground for would-be magicians. These papers became the basis for AMOOKOS. Subsequently some of the papers were published, and over the next few years, international membership of AMOOKOS grew to over 200 individuals, several of whom started chartered lodges. One prominent member of AMOOKOS is Donald Michael Kraig, who ran a lodge in California in the 1980s.

The original material was presented to individuals for training purposes. Much of the material was and is tantric but presented in the English language for clarity and to avoid Indian words and jargon. Every individual who was initiated also became an initiate of the Adinath sect.

The Adinathas seek ultimate truth. They teach that a human being is already accomplished, a yogi or yogini. Conditioning and other factors prevent this yogic self from shining forth. In each individual, Shiva and Shakti coexist in equipoise. When they unite, the resulting bliss lights up the physio-psychological complex which is the Universe.

Much of the alchemy the Nathas used was based on the proposition that Breath is Time. According to the Nathas, a human being breathes 21,600 times during a 24-hour day. Half of these breaths are Sun (Shiva) breaths and half are Moon (Shakti) breaths. The out-breathing is Ha and the in-breathing, Sa. This is the so-called involuntary mantra Hamsah. One who has united the Solar and Lunar breaths is a Parama-hamsa (beyond Hamsa). The Natha aims to fight conditioning and to become free from Time.

A second aim is svecchacharya or acting according to one's own will; in other words, independently. The secret teachings of the Adinathas also included teachings from the left-hand path (in which symbolism is actualized in physical acts) and described in some detail the use of sexuality in the process of seeking truth.

AMOOKOS is in the process of publishing much of Dadaji's and Lokanath's writings through Azoth Publishing. Also, from 1977 to 1985, Mike Magee published *Azoth Magazine* on behalf of the group. There is also a vast literature now available on the history of the Adinathas and the related Indian tantric groups.

Membership: Not reported.

Sources:

Dadaji. *The Amoral Way of Wizardry.* Stockholm: Tryckt I Sverige, 1992.

MacGee, Mike. *Rituals of Kalika.* New York: Azoth Publishing, 1985.

___. *Tantrik Astrology.* Oxford: Mandrake, 1989.

★1956★
Arsha Vidya Pitham
PO Box 1059
Saylorsburg, PA 18353

Arsha Vidya Pitham was founded in the mid-1980s by Swami Dayananda Saraswati. Saraswati emerged in the 1970s as a leading disciple of Swami Chinmayananda and by the early 1980s was the heir apparent of the growing mission. Saraswati became the resident teacher at Sandeepany West, Chinmayananda's center in northern California. While associated with Chinmayananda, Saraswati taught several 30-month resident courses in Vedanta and Sanskrit. The graduates of these courses have gone on to become teachers themselves.

In 1982, however, after a long reappraisal of the direction of the growing work in America and his own likely future as head of it, Saraswati left Chinmaya Mission West to retain a more simple life as a teacher rather than an organizational director. Many of the people he had taught left the mission to keep their relationship with him.

Saraswati continued to teach and to write and, in 1986, purchased land in Pennsylvania for a new *ashram* (religious community). A temple to Lord Dakshinamurthi (a representation of the Hindu deity Shiva) was erected and a new 30-month resident course begun. Saraswati also continues his heavy schedule of travel and teaching around the United States and the world.

Membership: Not reported.

Sources:

Saraswati, Swami Dayananda. *Meditation at Dawn.* The Author, n.d.

___. *Purbamadah Purnamidam.* The Author, n.d.

___. *The Sadhana and the Sadhya (The Means and the End).* Rishikish, India: Sri Gangadhareswar Trust, 1984.

"Swami Dayananda Renounces Chinmaya Mission West: Changes and Challenges Ahead." *New Saivite World* (Fall 1983).

★1957★
Art of Living Foundation
PO Box 50003
Santa Barbara, CA 93150

The Art of Living Foundation is the vehicle for the teaching activity of Sri Sri Ravi Shankar, a Hindu spiritual teacher from Bangalore, India. A precocious child, he memorized the *Bhagavad Gita* when he was four, and began his studies of Indian literature at the age of eight. In the 1980s he began traveling the world teaching the Art of Living course which emphasizes the uses of the ancient sciences in modern life. A major emphasis of Sri Sri's teaching is *sudarsha kriya*, a technique to restore the natural rhythms of the mental, emotional, and physical life. In 1995, the President of India at the *World Conference on Yoga* gave him the title of "Yoga Shiromani" (Supreme Flowering of Enlightenment).

He established Ved Vignan Maha Vidya Peeth in Bangalore, India, to engage in community services and spreading Vedic knowledge. It established centers across India. In Canada, England, and the United States, work is carried forth under the name "Art of Living" and in Europe as the Association for Inner Growth.

Membership: Not reported. In 1990 there were centers in 23 countries in all parts of the world.

Sources:

Shankar, Ravi. *Bang on the Door: A Collection of Talks.* Santa Barbara, CA: Art of Living Foundation, 1990. 101 pp.

★1958★
Arunachala Ashrama
66-12 Clyde St.
Rego Park, NY 11374

Alternate Address: International headquarters: Sri Ramanasramam, Tiruvannamalai 606 603, Tamil Nadu, India.

Inspired by the life and teachings of Sri Ramana Maharshi (1879–1950), Arunachala Ashrama was founded in New York City on December 7, 1966. For five years prior to this, weekly meetings had been conducted by those interested in Maharshi and his teachings.

At the age of 16, Ramana Maharshi absorbed himself in a singular inner quest for truth that resulted in his total abidance in God, or the "Self," as he called it. He then left home and resided on the slopes of the Arunachala Mountain, a sacred place of pilgrimage in South India. Living an exceedingly pure life, never touching money, and wearing only a coupina, he remained there for the next 54 years.

His most potent teachings, as attested to by his followers, were imparted in the silence of his presence, which conferred to mature souls the peace of Self-realization. Orally he taught the path of Self-inquiry and Self-surrender. He asked seekers to inquire where from the "I-consciousness" springs, to return to that source, and to abide there. To inquire "Who am I?" is the method of Self-Knowledge he most often prescribed. He also taught seekers to throw all the burdens of life upon the Divine and to rest in perfect peace in the heart. He never interfered with outward religious practices or professions. Rather, he taught each person to seek his or her own source, as he believed there is only one source for all, the Supreme Self or God.

Arunachala Ashrama maintains facilities in New York City and a retreat in Nova Scotia, Canada. A routine of prayer and meditation is followed at both locations. Arunachala Ashrama maintains a loose affiliation with Ramana Maharshis ashrama in India, though there are no formal legal or financial ties.

Membership: The ashrama has 450 members. The ashrama is funded by unsolicited donations and the sale of literature on the life and teachings of Sri Ramana Maharshi.

Periodicals: *The Maharshi.*

Sources:

Brunton, Paul. *A Message from Arunchala.* New York: Samuel Weiser, 1971.

Mahadevan, T. M. P. *Ramana Maharshi, the Sage of Arunchala.* London: George Allen & Unwin, 1977.

Osborne, Arthur. *Ramana Maharshi and the Path of Self-Knowledge.* New York: Samuel Weiser, 1970.

_____, ed. *The Teachings of Ramana Maharshi.* New York: Samuel Weiser, 1962.

★1959★
Aurobindo, Disciples of Sri
℅ Sri Aurobindo Association
2288 Fulton St., Ste. 310
Berkeley, CA 94704

Alternate Address: Canadian Center: AUM Mother's Home, 50 Rang C, Wotton, Cte Richmond, PQ J0A 1N0; Other United States centers: East West Cultural Center, 12392 Marshall St., Culver City, CA 90230; Wilmot Center, Box 2, Wilmot , WI 53192; Matagiri, HCI Box 98, Mt. Tremper, NY 12457.

Of the many Hindu religious leaders who have arisen in the last century, none remains as enigmatic as Sri Aurobindo Ghose (1872-1950). He was given an English education and began to make his mark as a literary figure. When Bengal, his native state, was the center of the independence movement, Aurobindo became a political activist. Thrown in jail on sedition charges, he turned to the Hindu scriptures and began to practice yoga. He had a vision of Krishna which changed the course of his life. Released from jail, he soon fled to French-controlled Pondicherry as a refugee and continued his spiritual practice.

The next years were spent in writing, yoga, and the building of an ashram. Most of his famous books appeared in the sixteen years prior to what is referred to as "The Day of the Siddha," November 24, 1926. On that day he claimed that Krishna (the popular Hindu deity) descended into the physical, thus preparing for the descent of the Supermind (the Divine) and Ananda (Bliss). His spiritual collaborator was Mira Richards (1878-1973), a French divorcee who met Aurobindo prior to World War I. She built up the ashram and, after 1926, when Aurobindo ceased to see people, she became the contact between him and his disciples. The "Mother," as she is known, had seen Aurobindo in her dreams before she came to Pondicherry in 1914. From 1950 to her death in 1973, she sustained the work of transformation.

Aurobindo's thought has often been compared with that of Teilhard de Chardin, as it was an evolutionary philosophy based upon man's growth in consciousness both individually and collectively. God—pure existence, will force—draws man to himself. Creation is the result of his "descent" and the evolution is as much a divine work as man's progress. It is believed that the supermental consciousness and its manifestation in 1956 will eventually bring about the evolutionary change from "man" to "superman."

The means to achieve the life divine is yoga. Aurobindo taught what is termed "integral yoga," based in part on vedenta and tantra. It includes the traditional forms of yoga and psychology of the internal psychic self, but worked primarily by a descent of the shakti into the mind.

In India, the Sri Aurobindo Society has established an international section to service centers outside of the country. In the United States, a number of more-or-less independent centers have arisen. Among the important centers are Matagiri in Mt. Tremper, New York, and Lotus Light in Wilmot, Wisconsin. In California, three prominent centers have survived for years. These include the East-West Cultural Center, founded by Judith Tyberg in 1953; the Cultural Integration Fellowship, founded by Haridas Chaudhuri; and the Atmaniketan Ashram, a residence center in Pomona, California. There are numerous smaller centers.

International headquarters remain at the ashram in Pondicherry. In 1972, it published a 30-volume centenary edition of Aurobindo's works later superceded by a 20-volume set. More recently the Institute for Evolutionary Research in Mt. Vernon, Washington has released a 13-volume set of the *Mother's Agenda, 1951-1973.*

Membership: Not available.

Periodicals: *Collaboration.*

Sources:

Chaudhuri, Haridas. *The Evolution of Integral Consciousness.* Wheaton, IL: Theosophical Publishing House, 1977.

Donnelly, Morwenna. *Founding the Life Divine.* Lower Lake, CA: Dawn Horse Press, 1976.

McDermott, Robert, ed. *The Essential Aurobindo.* New York: Schrocken Books, 1973.

___. *Six Pillars.* Chambersburg, PA: Wilson Books, 1974.

Minor, Robert Neil. *Sri Aurobindo: The Perfect and the Good.* Columbia, MO: South Asia Books, 1978.

Prasad, Narayan. *Life in Sri Aurobindo Ashram.* Pondicherry, India: Sri Aurobindo Ashram, 1968.

★1960★
Badarikashrama
15602 Maubert Ave.
San Leandro, CA 94578

Badarikashrama is a spiritual and cultural center that promotes a life of dedicated service based upon Vedic wisdom. Established in 1983, the ashrama conducts three worship services daily, Sunday school, Hindu rites for family occasions, and festival celebrations. It also offers instruction in music, philosophy, literature, yoga, Sanskrit, meditation, and *puja* (techniques of worship). Ongoing activities include concerts, festivals, retreats, weekend programs and children's programs.

Badarikashrama's work is inspired by the teachings of Sri Ramakrishna and Swami Vivekananda. It was established by Swami Omkarananda, who as a young seeker in India came into contract with the teachings of Sri Ramakrishna. He came to the United States in 1970 and after several years of work returned to India where he took his final vows of sannyasa from Mandaleswara Sri Swami Vidyananda Giri at Kailashashrama in Rishikish. He returned to the United States and founded Badarikashrama. Swami Omkarananda combines the renounced life with a life of service. He makes himself available for spiritual counseling, satsanga, and guidance in spiritual and cultural issues. He offers home worship throughout California and promotes Vedic teachings throughout the United States.

In 1984, an associate branch of Badarikashrama was begun in Madihalli, Karnataka, India. Ongoing activities there include evening devotional singing (*kirtan*), weekly music and Sanskrit classes, and yoga training camps. There is also an ayurvedic herbal garden. Accomodations are provided for individuals and groups wishing to visit Madihalli ashrama for short and long-term spiritual retreats. At present, a variety of programs are being developed including local community training in health and sanitation, an English tutorial service, provisions of nutritional supplements, and the establishment of a resident school. It continues to serve as a place for the residence and training of women and men interested in leading a monastic life of service. Swami Mangalananda currently directs the program at Madihalli.

Membership: In 1997 the ashrama reported 900 adherents at its American center and an additonal 1,500 at its Indian center.

Periodicals: *Badarikashrama Sandesha • Sandesha.*

★1961★
Barry Long Foundation
Box 1001
Fairfax, CA 94978-1091

Alternate Address: International Headquarters: BCM Box 876, London, United Kingdom WC1.

Barry Long is a spiritual teacher who emerged in Australia in the 1970s but moved to England in the 1980s and has operated out of London since. Work began in the United States in the late 1980s. He introduced himself with the words, "I am Guru! Who are you?" He noted that there was only one guru, the power behind the person Barry Long, and that since time began that power has manifested through various enlightened beings. Barry Long is one aspect of guru's teachings, one of its manifold lives. Through Barry Long, guru demonstrates the living truth to people ready to hear. To be enlightened is to personify the truth of his presence. Through Long, guru speaks to the westernized world.

Long teaches that there is no duality between himself and the power. In his presence people change; they understand that they, too, are guru beneath the confused and anxious self usually designated "I." Long eschews most religious forms and emphasizes the living of truth. His teachings are introduced through what is termed the "Course in Being."

Membership: Not reported. There are centers of the foundation in England, Australia, and North America.

★1962★
Blue Mountain Center of Meditation
PO Box 256
Tomales, CA 94971

The Blue Mountain Center of Meditation, founded by Indian teacher Eknath Easwaran in 1961, offers programs and publications presenting an Eight-Point Program of meditation and allied living skills. The center considers its approach as nondenominational, nonsectarian, and free from dogma and ritual, and the organization is not affiliated with any religious group or movement. Easwaran was a Professor of English at the University of Nagpur, India, when he came to the United States on the Fulbright exchange program in 1959. He has been writing and offering instruction in meditation and world mysticism in the San Francisco Bay Area regularly since 1965. The interest in meditation he encountered while at the University of California-Berkeley prompted him to find the Blue Mountain Center of Meditation. His class at the university in 1967 is believed to be the first academic course on meditation taught for credit on a major American campus.

The basis of the Eight-Point Program is meditation while the other points integrate meditation with daily life. The program includes: 1) Meditation: Going slowly and silently, in the mind, through inspirational passages from the world's great religions, for half-an-hour each morning. (Because of its universality, everyone is encouraged to begin with the Prayer of St. Francis ("Lord, make me an instrument of the peace...")). 2) Mantram: Silent repetition in the mind of a holy name, mantram, or "prayer word" chosen from those hallowed by the world's great religions (the Jesus Prayer, Barukh attah Adonai, Allahu akbar, Om mani padme hum, Rama, Rama, etc.) whenever possible during the rest of the day. 3) Slowing Down: Simplifying activities and priorities so as to resist the pressure to hurry through the day. 4) One-Pointed Attention: Giving complete concentration to whatever one does. 5) Training the Senses: Undoing conditioned habits and learning to enjoy what is beneficial. 6) Putting Others First: Gaining freedom from self-centered thinking and behavior by focusing attention on the needs of the whole instead of dwelling on ourselves. 7) Spiritual Companionship: Spending time regularly with others who are following the same Eight-Point Program, for mutual inspiration and support. 8) Reading the Mystics: Filling the mind with inspiration from writings by and about the world's great spiritual figures and from the scriptures of all religions.

The Blue Mountain Center offers weekend and weeklong retreats in northern California near its headquarters in Tomales and one-day and weekend retreats at various sites around the country. Nilgiri Press, the center's publishing branch, publishes books and tapes on meditation and world mysticism. Eknath Easwaran has written 23 books which have been translated in 15 languages, in addition to translations of Indian scriptural classics (the Bhagavad Gita, the Upanishads, and the Dhammapada) and an anthology of passages for meditation from the worlds's major religions, *God Make the Rivers to Flow.*

Membership: The Blue Mountain Center is not a membership organization; however, some 25,000 people receive it newsletter.

Periodicals: *Blue Mountain.*

Sources:

Easwaran, Eknath. *The Bhagavad Gita for Daily Living.* Berkeley, CA: Blue Mountain Center of Meditation, 1975.

___. *Dialogue with Death.* Petaluma, CA: Nilgiri Press, 1981.

___. *Like a Thousand Suns.* Petaluma, CA: Nilgiri Press, 1979.

___. *A Man to Match His Mountains.* Petaluma, CA: Nilgiri Press, 1984.

___. *The Mantram Handbook.* Petaluma, CA: Nilgiri Press, 1977.

___. *The Supreme Ambition.* Petaluma, CA: Nilgiri Press, 1982.

★1963★
Brahma Kumaris World Spiritual University
Global Harmony House
46 S. Middle Neck Rd.
Great Neck, NY 11021

Alternate Address: International Headquarters: Post Office 3, Box 2, Mount Abu, Rajasthan, India 307501; Canadian headquarters: 897 College St., Toronto, ON, Canada M6H 1A1.

The Brahma Kumaris World Spiritual University was founded in Karachi, Sind (now part of Pakistan) in 1936. The founder, Dada Lekhraj, was a prosperous businessman who had experienced a number of spiritual awakenings, culminating with his experiencing a spiritual presence entering his body. The presence spoke, "I am the Blissful Self, I am Shiva, I am the Knowledgeable Self, I am Shiva, I am the Luminous Self, I am Shiva."

For fourteen years, until the partition of India and Pakistan, the founding group of 300 people lived as a self-sufficient community, spending their time in intense spiritual study, meditation, and self transformation. In 1951, the community moved to Mount Abu, Rajasthan, India, now the site of the university's international headquarters. In 1969, upon Lekhraj's death, two women from the founding group, Dadi Prakashmani and Didi Man Mohini, took responsibility for administration. The university continues to be administered by women to the present day.

The program of the Brahma Kumaris is centered upon the practice of Raja Yoga: a method of meditation focusing on the internal workings of the mind and intellect. No mantras or special postures are required. Students gradually gain experience in calming a busy mind, creating positive thoughts and forming a connection with God as the ultimate source of peace and power.

Membership: As of 1997, the Brahma Kumaris is located in 71 countries with 3,800 centers and approximately 400,000 regular members, or "students." The United States has centers in New York; Boston; Washington, DC; Chicago; Los Angeles; Miami; San Antonio; San Francisco; Seal Beach, California; Seattle; Tampa; and Honolulu. The centers in Canada are located in Toronto, Vancouver, Calgary, Alberta, Edmonton, Montreal, Quebec, and Winnipeg.

Periodicals: *The World Renewal.* • *Purity.* • *Retreat.*

Sources:

Brahma Baba—The Corporeal Medium of Shiva Baba. Mount Abu, India: Prajapita Brahma Kumaris Ishwariya Vishwa Vidyalaya, n.d.

Illustrations on Raja Yoga. Mount Abu, India: Prajapita Brahma Kumaris Ishwariya Vishwa Vidyalaya, 1975.

Living Values: A Guidebook. London: Brahma Kumaris World Spiritual University, 1995. 110pp.

Moral Values, Attitudes and Moods. Mount Abu, India: Prajapita Brahma Kumaris Ishwariya Vishwa Vidyalaya, 1975.

Visions of a Better World London. Brahma Kumars World Spiritual University, 1994. 205pp.

The Way and Goal of Raja Yoga. Mount Abu, India: Prajapita Brahma Kumaris Ishwariya Vishwa Vidyalaya, 1975.

★1964★
Center of Being
(Defunct)

The Center of Being was a short-lived movement founded in 1979 by Baba Prem Ananda, also known as "Anandaji" (b. 1949), and Her Holiness Sri Marashaam Devi, affectionately known as Mataji, an African American woman considered by her followers to be an avatar (a self-realized master of the highest order). Mataji was believed to have been born fully enlightened, and to have retained that state for the first twelve years of her life. At the age of 12 she began to regress in order to experience the separation from the divine and the path to reunion. During the twelve-year period of regression, she retained some communion with the divine and experienced many unusual powers, among them an ability to see Lord Shiva (considered a prominent Hindu deity) who functioned directly as her guru. At the age of 24, she regained the state of enlightenment and began to teach privately. One of her first disciples, Anandaji, assisted her in the formation of the Center of Being and in her public teaching activity. Anandaji also attained the enlightened state.

Mataji taught a path of Enlightenment, a spontaneous way of being beyond intellectual rules and answers. Mataji, as a divine personage, was able to bestow this grace, which leads to Enlightenment. She offered herself in weekly "darshans," sessions in which disciples sat in her presence, and in "grace intensives" (thrice annually). Darshan sessions included lectures by Mataji and question and answer sessions. Devotional worship services directed to the deities and to Mataji were held quarterly.

At the Center of Being's height in the mid 1980s, there was one center in Los Angeles and a journal, *Lila*, was published.

Membership: In 1986 there was only one center, in Los Angeles, and less than a hundred disciples.

Periodicals: *Lila.* Send orders to Box 3384, Los Angeles, CA 90078.

★1965★
Chinmaya Mission West
PO Box 129
Piercy, CA 95587

Alternate Address: International headquarters: Central Chinmaya Mission Trust, Powai Park Dr., Mumbai, 400072 India.

Swami Chinmayananda is an independent teacher of Vedanta who in 1949 was initiated into sannyas, the renounced life, by Swami Sivananda Saraswati at Rishikish, India. With Sivananda's blessing, Chinmayananda traveled into the Himalayan Mountains to Uttar Kasi to study with a learned teacher, Swami Tapovanam, known for his knowledge of the Hindu scriptures. He studied with Tapovanam for several years. In 1951 he began to share his knowledge with the public. As people responded the Chinmaya Mission evolved.

Chinmayananda first came to North America in the 1960s. As he periodically toured the country, groups of disciples came into existence. In 1975 Chinmaya Mission West was incorporated. Once formed, assisted by Chinmayananda's charismatic personality and drive, the Mission spread rapidly.

Chinmaya Mission has been distinguished both by its Vedantic teachings and its emphasis upon knowledge of the Upanishads and the *Bhagavad Gita*, the two main Hindu scriptures. Chinmayananda has authored numerous books, including commentaries on the *Gita* and Upanishads, and his discourses are available on video.

Membership: In 1997 the Mission reported 4,000 members in 200 centers in the United States and 1,000 members in seven centers in Canada. These are affiliated centers in India, Australia, Singapore, Hong Kong, and various locations across Europe.

Educational Facilities: Sandeepany Sadhanalaya, Mumbai, India.

Periodicals: *Mananam.* • *Mananam Quarterly Journal.* • *CMW Newsletter.*

Sources:

Chinmayananda, Swami. *Kindle Life.* Madras: Chinmaya Publications Trust, n.d.

___. *A Manual for Self-Unfoldment.* Napa, CA: Chinmaya Publication (West), 1975.

___. *Meditation (Hasten Slowly).* Napa, CA: Family Press, 1974.

___. *The Way to Self-Perfection.* Napa, CA: Chinmaya Publications (West), 1976.

The Holy Geeta with commentary by Swami Chinmayananda. Bombay: Central Chinmaya Mission Trust, n.d.

★1966★
Church of the Christian Spiritual Alliance (CSA)
Lake Rabun Rd.
Box 7
Lakemont, GA 30552

The Church of the Christian Spiritual Alliance (CSA) was founded in 1962 by H. Edwin O'Neal, a Baptist; his wife, Lois O'Neal, an advocate of Religious Science; and William Arnold Lapp, a Unitarian. Its stated purpose was "to teach the fatherhood of God and brotherhood of man as interpreted in the light of modern-day experience." It emerged as a highly eclectic organization which combined Christian, psychic and Eastern insights. It absorbed *Orion*, a popular independent occult monthly founded by Ural R. Murphy of Charlotte, North Carolina, and continues its publication, now as an annual.

In the late 1960s, the church was joined by Roy Eugene Davis, a former student of Swami Paramahansa Yogananda and leader of the Self-Realization Fellowship center in Phoenix, Arizona. Davis had left SRF and formed New Life Worldwide. He brought his organization and its periodical (which became *Truth Journal*) into CSA. Davis's traveling and speaking gave CSA a national audience.

CSA took a decisive turn in 1977 when O'Neal resigned as chairman of the board and president of the publishing complex and was replaced by Davis. The focus of CSA has in the ensuing years been that of Davis, who has established the church as part of the larger New Age movement with its concerns of astrology, holistic health, and meditation. The yoga teachings of Yogananda as presented through Davis have become the central core of the teachings. Davis keeps a year-round schedule of seminars around the United States. His ecumenical approach to religion is in keeping with the New Age emphases.

The educational arm of the church is the Center for Spiritual Awareness at Lakemont. Each summer a full retreat and workshop progam is held at CSA. Featured is a teacher training seminar designed to prepare CSA ministers. The Shrine of All Faiths and Sacred Initiation Temple are part of the headquarters complex. Initiation into kriya yoga is offered to members.

Membership: In 1991, the alliance reported 25 centers and meditation groups in the United States and five in foreign countries—Canada, Germany, Ghana, and South Africa.

Periodicals: *Truth Journal.* • *Orion.*

Sources:

Davis, Roy Eugene. *An Easy Guide to Meditation.* Lakemont, GA: CSA Press, 1978.

___. *God Has Given Us Every Good Thing.* Lakemont, GA: CSA Press, 1986.

___. *The Path of Soul Liberation.* Lakemont, GA: CSA Press, 1975.

___. *The Teachings of the Masters of Perfection.* Lakemont, GA: CSA Press, 1979.

___. *The Way of the Initiate.* St. Petersburg, FL: New Life World-Wide, 1968.

___. *Yoga-Darshana.* Lakemont, GA: CSA Press, 1976.

★1967★
Datta Yoga Center
RD 2, Box 2084
Moniteau Rd.
Sunbury, PA 16061

Alternate Address: International Headquarters: Sri Ganapathi Sachchidananda Ashrama, Datta Peetam, Mysore Ooty Rd., 570 004, India.

Datta Yoga Center is an outpost of the international movement built around His Holiness Sri Sri Ganapathi Sachchidananda Swamiji. Swamiji was born in Mekedati Village, Karnataka, in southern India. He became a postman, although as a youth he had been religiously inclined and a devoted practitioner of yoga. He became known for his healing powers and his ability to work miracles. During his early adulthood, Swamiji began to gather a following, and in the mid-1960s he founded a spiritual center that was located in Mysore, India, in 1966. He traveled widely around India and in the 1970s began to travel in Europe. He also traveled to the United States and the Caribbean, opening the first United States center in 1986 in Pennsylvania.

Swamiji is considered by followers to be an avadhuta (liberated one), in the tradition of Lord Dattatreya. His teachings are multifaceted and described as "universal and unconstrained by religious dogma." He teaches kriya yoga as a method to realize the One Reality as referred to in the teachings of advaita vedanta. The centers serve as temples at which *pujas* and *homas* (worship services) are performed. Always musically inclined, Swamiji has composed numerous *bhajans* (spiritual songs) and instrumental meditation music which are a major part of the gatherings of devotees. He is an advocate of ayurvedic medicine, and sponsors a hospital for the underprivileged in India.

Membership: The Center is not a membership organization. There are several hundred devotees (as of 1992) in the United States. Associated centers can also be found in Malaysia, Switzerland, Belgium, Germany, England, and Trinidad.

Periodicals: *Bhakti Mala.*

Sources:

Ganapati Sachchidananda, Swami. *Dattatreya the Absolute.* Trinidad: Dattatreya Yoga Centre, 1984.

___. *Forty-two Stories.* Trinidad: Dattatreya Gyana Bodha Sabha, 1984.

___. *Insight into Spiritual Music.* Mysore, India: The Author, n.d.

___. *Sri Dattatreya Laghu Puja Kalpa.* Mysore, India: The Author, 1986.

H. H. Sri Sri Ganapati Sachchidananda Swamiji: A Rare Jewel in the Spiritual Galaxy of Modern Times. Mysore, India: Sri Ganapathi Sachchidananda Trust, n.d.

Swamiji, Ganapati Sachchidananda. *Insight into Spiritual Music.* Mysore, India: The Author, n.d.

★1968★
Deva Foundation
336 S. Doheny Dr., No. 7
Beverly Hills, CA 90211

The Deva Foundation was founded in Sweden in the early 1980s by Dr. Deva Maharaj (1948), a high caste Hindu and doctor of ayurveda and homeopathic medicine. Before leaving India, he had studied yoga and meditation at the Yoga Research Hospital in New Delhi. He came to the United States in the mid-1980s and established headquarters in Beverly Hills, California. The stated aim of the foundation is to bridge the gap between Western psychology and Eastern philosophy. It offers members a wide variety of approaches drawn from both Eastern and Western techniques for personal growth, transformation, and enlightenment. These include various health classes, self-hypnosis, nutrition, acupressure, massage, and shaktipat, the awakening of the kundalini, the latent energy believed to rest at the base of the spine. Members may also participate in the activities of the Tantra House operated by the foundation, an educational center which teaches the esoteric secrets of sexuality and spirituality.

Deva travels widely and has become a radio and television personality because of his clairvoyant abilities.

Membership: In 1987, the foundation reported two centers in the United States and one in Canada. There were approximately 100 members in the United States and 1,000 members internationally.

Educational Facilities: Yoga Center, New Delhi, India.

★1969★
Devatma Shakti Society
Current address not obtained for this edition.

The Devatma Shakti Society was formed in 1976 by Swami Shivom Tirth (b. 1924) for the practice of the *shaktipat* system of yoga, a system revived by Swami Gangadhar Tirth Maharaj. Little is known of this swami; he lived in solitude and initiated only one disciple, Kali Kishore Gangopadhyay, who became known as Swami Narayan Tirth Dev Maharaj (1870-1935). He founded a meditation center in Madaripur, Faridpur, India and passed his succession to Shri Yoganandaji Maharaj (d.1959). Yoganandaji established an ashram in Rishikish. He initiated Swami Vishnu Tirth Maharaj (d.1969) who established the Narayan Kuti Sanyas Ashram at Dewas.

Swami Shivom Tirth was initiated by Vishnu Tirth in 1959 and took the vows of the sannyasin (the renounced life) in 1963. During the 1970s, Shivom Tirth began to propagate the shaktipat system outside of India, first in Europe and Southeast Asia and then in America. The first ashram in North America was established in central Texas. Shivom Tirth occasionally visits America on lecture tours, visiting his disciples across the United States.

Shaktipat is the descent of the power of the guru upon the disciple, thus activating the disciple's own latent kundalini shakti, often pictured as a serpent sleeping coiled at the base of the spine. The awakening of the energy and its movement up the spinal column to the top of the head produces enlightenment. This way to enlightenment is through the guru's grace and bypasses the years of effort and discipline necessary in other forms of yoga.

Membership: Not reported.

Sources:

Turth, Shivam. *A Guide to Shaktipat.* Paige, TX: Devatma Shakti Society, 1985.

★1970★
Devi Mandir
5950 Hwy. 128
Napa, CA 94558-9632

Devi Mandir, also called the Temple of the Divine Mother, is a Hindu center established in a town in the San Francisco Bay Area by two people known by their religious names, Shree Maa and Swami Satya Nanda. Nanda is an American who in the 1960s traveled to India as a seeker of spiritual enlightenment. He remained there, receiving spiritual nurture from various teachers and activities until meeting Maa in the 1980s. Shree Maa was born in Assam, India, and began to devote her life to spiritual practice as a teenager. She received many visions and became known throughout India as a spiritual teacher. She heads the Sanatan Dharma Societies in India with centers at Calcutta, Belur, and Gauhati. After their meeting, the pair became inseparable, and Nanda traveled with Maa as she held celebrations of worship. The two came to California in the mid 1980s and established the Devi Mandir as a center in Moraga (later relocated to Martinez and then to Napa) for the performance of the ancient Vedic fire worship.

The Devi Mandir is a traditional Hindu temple at which an annual round of Hindu festivals are celebrated. In the altar area, statues of many of the primary deities of Hinduism have been installed, including Shiva and Durga, Brahma and Saraswati, Vishnu and Lakshmi, Kali, and many others. Puja (worship) is offered daily. For three years at the end of the 1980s and into the 1990s, Shree Maa and Swami Satya Nanda devoted themselves to 1,000 days of continuous worship, during which neither left the temple. During this period they tended the fire inside the temple, making sure that it did not die out.

Maa promotes devotion to the deities through the performance of puja. Swami Satya Nanda has written and translated several books to assist attendees at the temple in their worship, including a beginner's guide to Sri Siva Puja. Shree Maa also promotes a behavior code that grows out of the devoted life. She advises attendees at the temple to be true, simple, and free. They should take refuge in God, cultivate wisdom, develop discrimination (or discernment), and allow their actions to manifest love. She notes that spirituality is very simple, noting the saying of a sage—that he is everywhere and thus if he hurts any form, he is hurting himself. In like measure, if he raises any form to a higher level, he elevates himself.

Membership: Not reported. The temple serves both Indian Americans and American converts to Hinduism.

Sources:

Johnsen, Linda. *Daughters of the Goddess: The Women Saints of India.* St. Paul, MN: Yes International Publishers, 1994. 128pp.

Satya Nanda, Swami, trans. *Kali Dhyanam: Meditation on MahaKali and the Adya Stotram.* Martinez, CA: Devi Mandir, 1990. 28 pp.

___. *Sri Siva Puja: Beginner.* Martinez, CA: Devi Mandir, 1990. 40 pp.

___. *Saty Narayan Katha: The Vow to Speak and Act in Truth.* Martinez, CA: Devi Mandir, 1990. 16 pp.

★1971★
Dhyanyoga Centers
Current address not obtained for this edition.

Indian yoga teacher Dhyanyogi Mahant Madhusudandasji Maharaj left home as a child of 13 to seek enlightenment. He spent the next 40 years as a wandering student, during which time he met and worked with his guru whom he discovered at Mt. Abu in Rajasthan State in northern India. From his guru he received shaktipat, a transmission of power believed to release the latent power of kundalini, pictured as residing at the base of the spine. The emergence of that power and the experience of its traveling up the spine to the crown of the head is considered by many Hindu groups to be the means of enlightenment.

In 1962 Dhyanyogi Madhusudandasji ceased his wanderings and began to teach. He established an ashram at Bandhvadi, Gujarat, the first of several in western India. He authored two books, *Message to Disciples* and *Light on Meditation*. During the 1970s followers moved to England and the United States. He made his first visit to his Western disciples in 1976 and began to build a following among American converts.

Dhyanyogi Madhusudandasji's teachings emphasize meditation (dhyan), or raja yoga, and kundalini yoga. He offers shaktipat to sadhuks (students). As the kundalini awakens the student is open to the guru's continuing influence and is able to shed past encumbrances and to move on the path of enlightenment.

Membership: Not reported.

Sources:

Madhusudandasji, Dhyanyogi. *Brahmanada: Sound, Mantra and Power.* Pasadena, CA: Dhyanyoga Centers, 1979.

___. *Death, Dying and Beyond.* Pasadena, CA: Dhyanyoga Centers, 1979.

___. *Light on Meditation.* Los Angeles, CA: 1978.

___. *Message to Disciples.* Bombay: Shri Dhyanyogi Mandal, 1968.

___. *Shakti, Hidden Treasure of Power.* Pasadena, CA: Dyanyoga Centers, 1979.

★1972★
Disciples of Ramma
Current address not obtained for this edition.

Rama Seminars was founded by Tantric Zen Master Rama (Frederick Lenz) in 1985 to carry on and supersede Lakshmi, an organization he had formed in the 1970s. Lenz is a former English professor and disciple of Sri Chinmoy, with whom he studied for eleven years. Under the name Atmananda, given him by Chinmoy, he taught yoga in New York and Europe. He left Chinmoy and, moving to California in 1979, founded Lakshmi. During the early years of his work in California, his students began to report a number of extraordinary experiences. According to the reports, Lenz would levitate, disappear completely, and/or radiate intense beams of light during group meditations. Soon after these reported experiences, at a gathering of approximately 100 students, Lenz announced that eternity had given him a new name, "Rama."

Rama teaches that humanity is at the end of a cycle. The present period, Kali Yuga, is a dark age. At the end of each cycle or age, Vishnu (a deity of the Hindus) is due to take incarnation. While Rama makes no claim to be the same conscious entity as the historic Rama, a previous incarnation of Vishnu, he does claim to be the embodiment of the "particular octave of celestial light which was once incarnated as Rama."

By 1985 there were approximately 800 full-time students in Lakshmi. Branches had been formed in Los Angeles, San Diego, San Francisco, and Boston. Lakshmi seemed inadequate to the growing task. Rama Seminars was formed to provide a "more sophisticated format. . .to aid persons seeking enlightenment." Rama describes the teaching of Rama Seminars as Tantric Zen. He claims to have been a Zen master in previous incarnations. Tantric Zen is described as a formless Zen, closely related to Chan (Chinese Zen), Tibetan Vajrayana Buddhism, Taoism, and jnana yoga.

During the 1990s, amid a controversy centered upon accusations of his misconduct by former members, Lenz relocated to New York and disbanded his organization. He taught computer science and founded a successful computer company, Advanced Systems, Inc., and authored two best-selling books entitled *Surfing the Himalayas* (1994) and *Snowboarding to Nirvana* (1997). In 1995 he was cited by *New York* magazine as one of the "100 Smartest New Yorkers". He died at the age of 48 in April 1998 in an accident at his home in Long Island. The exact circumstances of his death remain unclear. The death of Lenz makes the future of the circle of disciples uncertain.

Membership: Not reported. Rama regularly teaches seminars in Southern California.

Periodicals: *Self-Discovery.*

Sources:

The Last Incarnation. Malibu, CA: Lakshmi Publications, 1983.

Lenz, Frederick. *Life Times.* New York: Fawcett Crest, 1979.

Rama [Frederick Lenz]. *The Wheel of Dharma.* Malibu, CA: Lakshmi Publications, 1982.

★1973★
Divine Awareness Center
(Defunct)

The Divine Awareness Center was founded in 1989 by Yogi Kamal, an Indian teacher and disciple of Siddha Guru Swami Yogiraj Nanak an enlightened master, the founder of the Adhyatmic Sadhana Sangh in India. Yogiraj Nanak was the spiritual heir of the famous sixteenth-century saint and poet Malukdasji Maharaj, also looked upon as an enlightened master, who worked from his residence in Kara, Allahabad, India. The center taught the full range of yoga, but concentrated upon a new technique developed by Yogiraj Nanak, de-hypnotic meditation, a way of meditating that combined older yogic insights and metaphysics with new scientific discoveries.

According to Yogi Kamal, the modern world produced a peculiar heightened situation of tension, turmoil, unrest, and social destruction. The individual affected by the social disintegration manifested a variety of symptoms including shallow breathing, improper diet, degeneration of the nervous system, decreased energy, anxiety, and mental instability. Human problems were increased due to the intimate relationship of mind and body. What hurt one hurt the other, and curing one meant curing the other. The mind often retained the effects of illness and caused reoccurrences of illness when not cared for.

De-hypnotic meditation consisted of six steps: bodily relaxation, proper breathing, thought of the brilliant light, concentration on the organ of the sixth sense (pineal gland), concentration on the sound wave (symbolized in the word "om"), and quietness. It was believed that the practice of de-hypnotic meditation lead to the reduction of stress, self-healing, the harmonization of mind and body, the breaking of old habits, and the production of healthy vibrations. Those who practiced it learned how to keep negative thoughts away, to command the subconscious mind, to tap the divine power, and to develop the divine magnetic aura.

The initial Divine Awareness Center was opened in Los Angeles as a base for founding centers in other cities. In 1998 Yogi Kamal abandoned his work and closed the center.

Membership: The center is a non-membership organization.

★1974★
Fivefold Path Inc.
% Parama Dham
Rte. 8, Box 369
Madison, VA 22727

Fivefold Path Inc. was founded in Madison, Virginia, in 1973 by Vasant Paranjpe, who had received a divine command to come to the United States and teach kriya yoga, the Fivefold Path. From the Virginia headquarters, Paranjpe began to visit and teach in neighboring cities—Washington, D.C.; Baltimore, Maryland; Philadelphia, Pennsylvania; and Riverton, New Jersey. A semimonthly periodical was begun, and a fire temple consecrated at Param Dham, the name given the headquarters.

The Fivefold Path is a system of kriya yoga which begins with purification of the atmosphere as a step leading to the purification of the mind. Its steps include the following: 1. *Agnihotra*, a fire ceremony done at sunrise and sunset each day; 2. *Daan*, sharing one's assets in a spirit of humility; 3. *Tapa*, self-discipline; 4.

Karma, right action; and 5. *Swadhyaya*, self-study. The Fivefold Path, derived from the teachings of the Vedas, is also called the Satya Dharma (Eternal Religion). It respects all avatars and divine messengers and makes no distinction between them. Anyone of any religion may learn the teachings of the Fivefold Path. Vasant has stated that he has come to fulfill the biblical prophecy of Daniel 8:26: "This vision about the evening and moring sacrifices which has been explained to you (i.e., Agnihotra) will come true. But keep it secret now, because it will be a long time before it does come true" (*The Good News Bible* translation).

Membership: Fivefold Path Inc. is not a membership organization. As of 1995, the Fivefold Path had spread to all continents, and its literature has been translated into several languages.

Periodicals: *Satsang.*

Sources:

Paranjpe, Vasant V. *Grace Alone*. Madison, VA: Fivefold Path, 1971.

___. *Homa Farming, Our Last Hope*. Madison, VA: Fivefold Path, 1986.

___. *Homa Therapy: Our Last Chance*. Madison, VA: Fivefold Path 1989. 79 pp.

___. *Light Towards Divine Path*. N.p., n.d. 57 pp.

___. *Ten Commandments of Parama Sadguru*. Randallstown, MD: Agnihotra Press, 1976.

★1975★
Foundation of Revelation
59 Scott St.
San Francisco, CA 94117

The Foundation of Revelation was formed in 1970 in San Francisco by persons who recognized the existence of perfect knowledge and practical omnipotence in the form of a "beggar" then living in the village of Gorkhara near Calcutta, India. The man had been born of a ruling Brahmin family in 1913 and spent his early years as an avid student of various forms of modern knowledge. On the eve of June 14, 1966, he perceived that the illusions of these limited and disintegrating forms of modern knowledge were burned down by Agni, the fire of knowledge, and on September 19, 1966, the convergence of persisting cosmic existence, the luminous nature of consciousness, was concentrated in the person of this Yogi as Siva, the Destroyer. Thus 1966 is the first year of a new era of Siva Kalpa (meaning the period of time of Lord Siva's omnipotent imagination).

To the Foundation, Siva is the creator of conscious life and the destroyer of ignorance, whose pure love of knowledge moves the forms of ego into intensifying contradictions of their own divisive natures to the point of spontaneous recoil toward the synthesis of body, life and mind. He is considered the most accessible of powers. He never refused the request of a supplicant, perhaps his most dangerous attribute, and he surrounds himself with those from the extremes of the social spectrum whose natural penchant for truth, the power of self-expression, and the ability to manifest same, holds them apart from the world of mediocrity, always gravitating to the heights or depths of existence in the pull toward ultimate perfection.

The first Western contact with the holy man was in 1968 when he made an appearance at the Spiritual Summit Conference in Calcutta, India, sponsored by the Temple of Understanding of Washington, D.C. Several delegates followed him home and one, Charlotte P. Wallace, now president of the foundation, stayed to learn. Word spread of his work, and, in 1969, he was invited to the United States to take up residence in San Francisco, which became the world headquarters of the foundation. Those from countries around the world who witnessed his revelations firsthand returned to their respective countries to organize themselves within the spirit and corporate structure of the foundation to create bases for international communication and activity, with the single purpose of breaking down the barriers of nationality, religion, and race and foster the mutually beneficial and harmonious relationships of nations.

The foundation is led by a governing body consisting of the president and seven officers. Each country has a president directly responsible to the world president. Each local leader is responsible to the national president.

Membership: In 1997 the foundation reported 5,000 members in the United States and 25,000 members in the world. There were 21 centers worldwide in 10 countries.

★1976★
Gaudiya Vaishnava Society
Current address not obtained for this edition.

Alternate Address: International Headquarters: Sri Chaitanya Saraswati Math, Kolerganj, PO Nabadwip, Dist. Nadia, West Bengal, India.

The Gaudiya Vaishnava Society was founded in the mid-1980s by Tripurari Swami, formerly a leader in the International Society for Krishna Consciousness (ISKCON). Tripurari Swami had met A. C. Bhaktivedanta Swami Prabhupada in 1972, a year after he had joined ISKCON. Tripurari was initiated into *sannyas* (the renounced life) in 1975, two years prior to Prabhupada's death. In the years after Prabhupada's death, ISKCON was divided between reformists who denied the new initiating gurus (teachers) a status similar to that held by Prabhupada and the more conservative leaders who saw the new gurus carrying on a guru lineage that made it proper to receive veneration much as Prabhupada had. Tripurari was among the reformists who left the organization and turned to Bhakti Rakshak Sridhara Maharaj (1895-1988), Prabhupada's godbrother. (The godbrother relationship exists when two or more are initiated by the same guru.) Remaining in India when Prabhupada went to America, Sridhara Maharaj centered his work upon the Sri Chaitanya Saraswati Math in West Bengal. However, he had slowly acquired a worldwide network of centers that had placed themselves under his guidance.

Tripurari and a small group of like-minded ex-ISKCON devotees placed themselves under Sridhara Maharaj's direction. The Gaudiya Vaishnava Society emerged as the organizational expression of the group's work in the United States. Almost immediately the group ran into resistance from the city of San Francisco, California, which had passed an ordinance regulating the society's selling of their literature on the streets. In 1986 they took the city to court and won an injunction against the enforcement of the ordinance.

In 1988 the society released the first issue of its magazine, *The Clarion Call*, a high quality four-color quarterly in the tradition that had come to be expected from ISKCON. It has found a readership far beyond the Vaishnava community and has treated popular New Age topics such as reincarnation, animal rights, and vegetarianism, all regarded as issues of common concern.

The Gaudiya Vaishnava Society is as one with ISKCON in belief and practice. The issues that divided them have largely been resolved with the dominance of the reform party in ISKCON in the 1980s. However, the society now flows out of the lineage of Sridhara Maharaj, a lineage not found in ISKCON. The society emphasizes a theistic Vaishnava Hinduism, follows a path of devotional service and temple worship (bhakti yoga), and emphasizes as a primary spiritual practice the repetition of the Hare Krishna Mantra: "Hare Krishna, Hare Krishna

    Krishna Krishna, Hare Hare
    Hare Rama, Hare Rama
    Rama Rama, Hare Hare."

Membership: In 1989 there were approximately 100 families connected with the society. The society is part of the worldwide network of ashrams in the lineage of Sridhara Maharaj that can be found in Italy, England, Ireland, Venezuela, South Africa, Mexico, and Malaysia. The center of the network is in West Bengal, India.

There are two centers in the United States, one in San Francisco and one in New York City.

Periodicals: *The Clarion Call.*

Sources:

"*Clarion Call*, a Classy New Journal from S. F. Gaudiyas." *Hinduism Today* 10, 9 (September 1988): 1, 17.

Sridhara Deva Goswami, Srila Bhakti Raksaka. *The Golden Volcano of Divine Love.* San Jose, CA: Guardian of Devotion Press, 1984.

___. *The Hidden Treasure of the Absolute.* West Bengal, India: Sri Chaitanya Saraswati Math, 1985.

Thakur, Srila Bhaktivedanta. *Sri Chaitanya Mahaprabhu: His Life and Precepts.* Brooklyn, NY: Gaudiya Press, 1987.

★1977★
Grace Essence Fellowship
% Martin Lowenthal
53 Westchester Rd.
Newton, MA 02158

Grace Essence Fellowship was founded in the late 1970s by Lars Short, formerly a student of the late Swami Rudhrananda (1928–1973). Rudrananda, the founder of the Nityananda Institute, was among the first of the contemporary teachers of kundalini yoga in America. Lars Short trained with Rudrananda and in 1965 began his career as a yoga instructor. After Rudrananda's death, Green went on to study with His Holiness Dilgo Khyentse, a Tibetan master, and to absorb elements of Zen and Taoism into a synthesis which, he notes, Rudrananda had seen emerging as an all-encompassing Spiritual Work.

Short refers to his system as the Way of Radiance. The Way begins in the presupposition that it is possible to live life to the fullest rather than suffer, and to be an agent of grace rather than struggle. It proposes four principles: Life is a gift. All experience can nurture growth. We can live each moment so as to make our self-expression a celebration of life. If we commit ourselves to growth and freedom beyond any set agenda or identity, we can transcend present ways of relating to ourselves, others, and life itself. Short has adapted practices from his several teachers, including Tibetan mindfulness practices and tantric exercises.

Members of the fellowship have the opportunity to train to become practitioners and then seminarians, who take responsibility for passing on the Radiance teachings.

Membership: Not reported. There are eight study groups across the United States, two in Canada, and one in Venezuela.

Sources:

Lowenthal, Martin. "Grace Essence Fellowship: Supporting Growth and Freedom." *Tantra* 9 (1994): 64-65.

___. "A Spiritual Home in the Grace Essence Fellowship." *Tantra* 9 (1994): 65.

★1978★
Haidakhan Samaj
% Paul Gessler
104 Blue Jay
Placerville, CA 95667

Alternate Address: International headquarters: Haidakhan Ashram, P. O. Haidakhan, via Kathgodam. Dist. Nainital, Utter Predesh 263126, India.

The Haidakhan Samaj was founded in 1980 to coordinate the activities of followers of Haidakhan Baba, also known as Babaji and Mahavatar Babaji. Babaji is believed to be an *avatar*, a physical incarnation of divinity, who has a history of incarnation over a period of thousands of years. He is known as an incarnation of Lord Shiva, who, in the Hindu tradition, is considered to be the Master Teacher. Babaji incarnates in human form from time to time to demonstrate and teach ways that can lead people to harmony and unity with the Divine.

Present-day disciples of Babaji look to several ancient scriptural reference which may refer to him as well as several nineteenth and twentieth century accounts. The first, and still the major book in the West about Babaji is *Autobiography of a Yogi* (1946) by Swami Paramahansa Yogananda, founder of the Self-Realization Fellowship. Yogananda wrote of his master's teacher's first encounter with Babaji in the Indian Himalayas in 1863. There are many stories of people's miraculous encounters with Babaji in the last half of the nineteenth century.

There are several books in the Hindi language detailing the incarnation of an avatar-saint known as Haidakhan Baba, who lived in the Kumaon foothills of the Himalayas from about 1890 to 1922. He was recognized then as an incarnation of Lord Shiva and as a form of Mahavatar Babaji. Some of the stories about this incarnation of Babaji were collected and translated by Baba Hari Dass of the Sri Rama Foundation of Davis, California, in a book entitled, *Hariakhan Baba Known, Unknown.* When he left his body in 1922, Babaji is reported to have said that he would return to help humanity.

In 1949, an Indian saint named Mahendra Baba, who had seen Babaji several times in his childhood and youth, was blessed with a physical manifestation of Babaji in an ashram of Haidakhan Baba. From that time on, Mahendra Baba devoted his life to preparing for the return of Babaji. He wrote several books about Babaji, restored the old ashrams, and called upon people to be ready for his return. Mahendra died in 1969.

In June 1970 Babaji appeared again in Haidakhan Baba's ashram in the Kuaon village of Haidakhan. From then until his death on February 14, 1984, he traveled extensively in northern India and taught from several Babaji ashrams around the country, but spent the majority of his time in the remote village ashram in Haidakhan. Tens of thousands of Indians came to him, and hundreds came from Europe and America. Most of the time, he purposely avoided large crowds in order to perform the traditional guru's task of teaching and training people who were truly dedicated to the attainment of spiritual knowledge and growth. He taught them mostly by example, often on a mind-to-mind level rather than orally. He guided each devotee step by step through the experiences they needed for growth. Many people were brought to Babaji by miraculous experiences.

According to his own claim, Babaji came, in every incarnation, to restore the Sanatan Dharma—the eternal law of order under which the creation was manifested and operates in harmony with the Divine Will. He urged his followers to live in Truth, Simplicity, and Love, seeing all of creation as a manifestation of the Divine, and living in harmony with all. He respected all the established religions, and taught that each one can lead its devotees to unity and true devotion, renouncing the attachment to materialism which chains humankind to its lower nature. As an aid to keeping the Divine foremost in the followers' consciousness, he taught people to repeat the names of God at all times: the mantra which he taught to most people was "Om Namah Shivai," which may be translated as "I take refuge in God (Shiva)."

Babaji's followers worship him through a sung worship service called the *aarati*, morning and evening, and worship the formless Divine through an ancient fire ceremony, called the *yagya* or *hawan*. But the worship most advocated was that of selfless work, *karma yoga*, performed without ego for the benefit of all living beings, in harmony with the Divine Will.

There are Babaji ashrams and centers in Asia, Europe, Africa, Australia, and New Zealand. In the the United States, there are ashrams in Mountain View, Hawaii; Malmo, Nebraska; and at Consciousness Village near Sierraville, California, as well as centers in many cities. A major ashram is under construction in The Baca Grande, Crestone, Colorado.

Membership: In 1995 the ashram reported 90 members in the United States and 10 in Canada. There were 15 centers in the

United States and one in Canada. There were 8,000 members worldwide.

Periodicals: *American Haidakhan Samaj Newsletter.*

Sources:

Goodman, Shdema. *Babaji, Meeting with Truth at Hairakhan Vishwa Mahadham.* Farmingdale, NY: Coleman Publishing Co., 1986.

Hari, Dass Baba. *Hariakhan Baba Known, Unknown.* Davis, CA: Sri Rama Foundation, 1975.

Orr, Leonard [and Makhan Singh]. *Babaji.* San Francisco, CA: The Author, 1979.

Teachings of Babaji. Nainital, India: Haidakhan Ashram, 1983-84.

Yogananda, Paramahansa. *Autobiography of a Yogi.* Los Angeles, CA: Self-Realization Fellowship, 1946.

★1979★
Hanuman Foundation
Box 478
Santa Fe, NM 87501

The Hanuman Foundation, incorporated in 1974, is the focus of a number of activities that had their origin in the continuing career of Baba Ram Dass and were inspired by his guru, Neem Karoli Baba, popularly known as simply Baba. The Foundation's purposes have been to further the spiritual well being of society through education, service, and spiritual training. Its major project has been to support the spiritual teaching of Baba Ram Dass. Ram Dass is the name taken by Richard Alpert, the former professor of psychology at Harvard University who was fired along with Timothy Leary because of their LSD experiments. Within a short time he became discouraged with drugs as a means to attain higher states of consciousness and he turned to India. There he met Bhagwan Dass, a young American guru, and his teacher, Maharaji, who lived in the foothills of the Himalayas. From Maharaji he learned raja yoga, the path to God through meditation. Ram Dass also developed a devotion to Hanuman, the monkey-faced deity of popular Hinduism. Maharaj taught him to serve and worship Hanuman, a practice which he has continued over the years, though many of his fans are unaware of it.

Upon returning to the West, Baba Ram Dass wrote and published *Be Here Now,* which emphasized his ideal of living in the present, other than being tied to the past or contemplating the future. He sees all people on a journey to enlightenment. Each person needs and has a guru to help his progress. Some gurus are on the physical plane, but such is not necessary since the relationship is spiritual. Each person is at a different place on his journey, and, thus, differing exercises are needed by each individual. Some might need yoga, renunciation, mantras, sex, or even psychedelic drugs. For Baba Ram Dass, yoga was the path to enlightenment.

During his first years back in the United States, Ram Dass traveled and spoke from a base in his residence in New Hampshire. Gradually, several organizaitons emerged to dissiminate Ram Dass' teachings. The Orphalese Foundation controlled a tape library and the ZBS Foundation (also known as Amazing Grace) published several records. Ram Dass also found himself at the center of a network that included a variety of service projects. These included a prison-ashram library project and assistance to the Hanuman Foundation, an organization seen as perpetuating the spirit and teachings of Neem Karoli Baba. In the more than a decade of existence, several structures associated with the foundation have emerged as important aspects of the work.

The Hanuman Foundation Tape Library superceded the Orphalese Foundation. It currently distributes audio and video tapes of Ram Dass and several close associates such as Stephen Levine. The Prison Ashram project distributed spiritual literature to prison libraries and has created a manual specially designed for inmates who wished to learn to meditate and follow a spiritual path during their years of imprisonment. In recent years the project has ex-

panded to include residents of halfway houses, mental hospitals, and drug abuse programs.

The Neem Karoli Baba Hanuman Temple is located in a renovated adobe building at Taos, New Mexico. It houses a 1,500-pound marble statue of Hanuman carved to Ram Dass' specifications. It serves approximately 300 Hindu families in a strip from Albuquerque to Denver. There is an annual and a weekly cycle of devotional services anchored in the singing and chanting services each Tuesday (Hanuman day). Hanuman's birthday is celebrated in April and Neem Karoli Baba's Mahasamahdi (death) is celebrated in September.

Seva Foundation, founded by Larry Brillant, a devote of Baba, is an organization which began with a goal to end blindness in Nepal. Though independent of the Hanuman Foundation, Baba Ram Dass has given it his full support and the Hanuman Foundation Tape Library distributes recordings of Ram Dass' lectures promoting its work.

Membership: The Hanuman Foundation is not a membership organization.

Sources:

Dass, Baba Ram. *Grist for the Mill.* Santa Cruz, CA: Unity Press, 1977.

___. *Miracle of Love.* New York: E. P. Dutton, 1979.

___. *The Only Dance There Is.* New York: Jason Aaronson, 1976.

___. *Remember, Be Here Now.* San Christobal, NM: Lama Foundation, 1971.

Inside Out. Nederland, CO: Prison-Ashram Project, Hanuman Foundation, 1976.

★1980★
Hawaiian Goddess—Source School of Tantra Yoga
Box 69-12
Paia, Maui, HI 96779

Hawaiian Goddess—Source School of Tantra Yoga was founded in the mid-1980s by Charles and Caroline Muir. Charles Muir began to study yoga in 1965 and took his instructor training from Richard Hittleman. In 1974 he founded and directed the "Yoga for Health" Schools in California. In the meantime he became interested in tantra. Caroline Muir is a yoga instructor and massage instructor. The pair began working together in the early 1980s and now teach tantra as a means of physical, mental, and spiritual awakening.

The Muirs strive to facilitate their students to fully express themselves as both physical and spiritual beings and believe that sex and spirit are inextricably connected. Sexual activity thus becomes a means of profound meditation and sexuality a unifying, harmonizing, and spiritualizing force of the universe.

The school offers workshops and seminars in Hawaii, California, and Colorado, and the Muir's teachings are spread through several tapes and one book.

Membership: Not reported.

Sources:

Muir, Charles, and Caroline Muir. *Tantra: The Art of Conscious Loving.* San Francisco: Mercury House, 1989.

★1981★
Himalayan International Institute of Yoga Science and Philosophy
RR 1, Box 400
Honesdale, PA 18431

Swami Rama (1925–1996) was a learned philosopher and master yogi who came to the United States to teach. As a child, he was adopted by an accomplished yogi from Bengal and raised in the tradition of the cave monasteries of the Himalyas. In 1949 he attained the position of Shankaracharya, an honor he relinquished in 1952 to further his own teaching goals. He came to the United States in 1969 where he served as research consultant to Menninger Foundation Research Project on Voluntary Controls of External States. Working with psychologists Elmer Green and his wife Alyce Green, he demonstrated extraordinary physical feats of body-function control that offered significant material for the understanding of the mind/body connection. Swami Rama taught superconscious meditation, "a unique system to awaken the sleeping energy of consciousness, to raise its volume and intensity so that individual awareness becomes one with the Universal Self". It involves relaxation, posture, breathing, and mantras.

He founded the Himalayan International Institute of Yoga Science and Philosophy in 1971 in Illinois. The institute headquarters moved to Honesdale Pennsylvania, in 1977. Yoga, meditation, and holistic health are the main emphases of the institute. All levels of hatha yoga are taught, and raja yoga is emphasized as a means to balance body, mind, and spirit.

The Himalayan Institute publishes over 60 books on yoga science, meditation, health, psychology, and philosophy. It also publishes the bimonthly magazine *Yoga International*. Programs at the centers, especially at the headquarters campus, include a wide range of seminars, health programs, and residential programs.

Membership: In 1997 the institute reported 22 branch and affiliated centers in the United States and abroad. Foreign work is conducted in Canada, India, Germany, Italy, Great Britain, Trinidad, Curacao, and Malaysia. In 1997 there were 1,500 members in the United States.

Periodicals: *Yoga International*.

Sources:

Inspired Thoughts of Swami Rama. Honesdale, PA: Himalayan International Institute of Yoga Science and Philosophy, 1983.

Rama, Swami. *Lectures on Yoga.* Arlington Heights, IL: Himalayan International Institute of Yoga Science and Philosophy, 1972.

___. *Living with the Himalayan Masters.* Honesdale, PA: Himalayan International Institute of Yoga Science and Philosophy, 1978.

___. *Path of Fire and Light.* Honesdale, PA: Himalayan International Institute of Yoga Science and Philosophy, 1986.

___. *A Practical Guide to Holistic Health.* Honesdale, PA: Himalayan International Institute of Yoga Science and Philosophy, 1978.

Rama, Swami, Rudolph Ballentine, and Swami Ajaya [Allan Weinstock]. *Yoga and Psychotherapy.* Glenview, IL: Himalayan Institute, 1976.

★1982★
Hindu Yoga Society
(Defunct)

The Hindu Yoga Society was begun in the 1920s by Sri Deva Ram Sukul (d. 1965), an Indian residing in Chicago. In 1927 he started *Practical Yoga*, a quarterly journal, and issued a ten-part course in what he termed "Yoga Navajivan." From his Chicago base he toured the United States lecturing. He later settled in California, where he incorporated his work as the Yoga Institute of America. The institute continued to function until Sukul's death. Among his disciples was actress Mae West.

Sri Sukul taught the various forms of yoga (hatha, bhakti, jnana, karma, and raja), following the teachings presented in the classic work by Patanjali but with a distinct emphasis upon raja yoga, with additional insights gleaned from tantra. He also taught students the subtle anatomy of the chakra system and the means to raise the "kundalini," the power believed to reside in latency at the base of the spine. The rise of the kundalini along the spine to the crown chakra at the top of the head brings enlightenment. Integral to Sri Sukul's tantric teachings was the Gayatri Mantram, which was believed to contain the sevenfold planes of vibration of the soul's ascent (corresponding to the seven chakras).

Sources:

Sukul, Sri Deva Ran. *Yoga Navajivan.* New York: Yoga Institute of America, 1947.

___. *Yoga and Self-Culture.* New York: Yoga Institute of America, 1947.

Thomas, Wendell. *Hinduism Invades America.* New York: Beacon Press, 1930.

★1983★
Hohm Community
PO Box 4272
Prescott, AZ 86302

Hohm Community, known as Hohm Sahaj Mandir since 1996, was founded in 1975 by Lee Lozowick, a former meditation instructor and businessman who experienced a spontaneous spiritual awakening after some years of intense spiritual discipline. This event left him in what he has described as an abiding condition of God-realization that subsequently led to his teaching work and the establishment of the formal guru-disciple relationship with a small group of students. Shortly after that, while traveling extensively in India, Lozowick met his spiritual teacher, Sri Yogi Ramsuratkumar, to whom he attributes his own awakening and who he calls the "source" of his teaching work. Since 1976 Lozowick has maintained a close and uniquely intimate relationship with Yogi Ramsuratkumar as his own guru, and visits him annually at his ashram in Tiruvannamalai, India.

Lozowick adheres to an Eastern form within the lineage of Yogi Ramsuratkumar and his master Swami Papa Ramdas, but also has called his school the Western Baul Way because of the deep resonance which his teaching and the *sadhana* (spiritual life) of his students have with the Bauls of Bengal, an obscure sect of musicians and mystics who practice a form of tantric bhakti yoga called *kaya sadhana*, or realization through the body. The tenets of the Baul path are based on a blend Sahajiya Buddhism and a Vaishnava Hinduism; the Bauls encode their teaching in poems, song, and dance rather than in written texts or treatises and often travel about Bengali villages singing and chanting for alms.

The Western Bauls of the Hohm Community live a life of disciplined spiritual practice, with daily meditation, a vegetarian diet, exercise, and study of spiritual/classic literature and comparative religion recommended as foundation-level preparation in the school. Other recommended aspects of sadhana are: committed monogamous relationships, conscious (completely nonabusive and child-centered) child raising, and mutual respect between sexes. As Western Bauls the community has two bands—a rock & roll band called "liars, gods, and beggars", and an almost all-woman blues group called "Shri"—both of which perform almost all original music (lyrics by Lozowick) composed by his students on a professional basis.

Membership: The Holm Community maintains an ashram in Arizona and an ashram in central France. As of 1988 the Hohm Community includes about 150 members in the United States, Canada, and Europe. Lozowick travels extensively teaching and giving seminars and resides on the ashram in France four months out of the year and in Arizona the remainder of the year.

Periodicals: *Tawagoto*.

Sources:

A Basic Introduction of the Teachings and Practices of the Hohm Community. Prescott Valley, AZ: Hohm Community, n.d.

Lozowick, Lee. *Acting God.* Prescott Valley, AZ: Hohm Press, 1980.

___. *Beyond Release.* Tabor, NJ: Hohm Press, 1975.

___. *Book of Unenlightenment.* Prescott Valley, AZ: Hohm Press, 1980.

___. *The Cheating Buddah.* Tabor, NJ: Hohm Press, 1980.

___. *In the Fire.* Tabor, NJ: Hohm Press, 1978.

___. *Laughter of the Stones.* Tabor, NJ: Hohm Press, n.d.

The Only Grace is Loving God. Prescott Valley, AZ: Hohm Press, 1984.

★1984★
Holy Shankaracharya Order
Current address not obtained for this edition.

The Holy Shankaracharya Order had its beginning in 1968 when Swami Lakshmy Devyashram, a disciple of Swami Sivananda Saraswati, established the Sivananda Ashram of Yoga One Science. Through self-study and under Sivananda's spiritual inspiration, she found samadhi (a mystic state of altered consciousness) in 1963. In 1964, she had a vision of Swami Sivananda and was led by him to the Poconos. The guidance continued in the building of the retreat/camp. In 1969, she was ordained by Swami Swanandashram in the Holy Order of Sannyasa, Saraswati, the order in which Sivananda was ordained. In 1974, Swami Lakshmy was elected Mahamandaleshwari (Great Overlord) of the Holy Shankaracharya Order in the United States.

In 1974 property was purchased in Virginia and a second ashram-temple complex begun. It was dedicated in 1977. In 1978, from her superior in the Shankaracharya Order, Jagadguru Shankaracharya Abhinava Vidyateertha Maharaj, headquartered at Sringeri, the holy seat of the Order, she was requested to establish a shakti peetham (monastery), which was named Sri Rajarajeshwari Peetham. As the Swami gathered students around her, she ordained them, and they have become instructors in the various programs and activities. In the same year a Hindu Heritage Summer Camp was created. The response to this program led to the acceptance of the non-Indian, female swami by the Indian-American community.

In 1981, shortly before Swami Lakshmy died, Hindu priestly services were begun at the peetham. Swami Lakshmy was succeeded by Swami Saraswati Devyashram, one of her female students. Under her leadership the outreach to the Indian community has grown. A center has been opened in Tucson, Arizona, and a winter heritage camp initiated in 1982. Today, the Holy Shankaracharya Order is a major traditional Saivite Hindu center. In 1983 Swami Saraswati Devyashram was initiated by the Jagadguru Shankaracharya at Sringeri. In 1984 it joined the ecumenical Council of Hindu Temples. It now provides a full range of temple services at the peetham in the Poconos.

Membership: Not reported.

Periodicals: *Vedic Heritage Newsletter.*

★1985★
Indo-American Yoga-Vedanta Society
330 W. 58th St., Apt. 11-J
New York, NY 10019

The Indo-American Yoga-Vedanta Society was founded in New York City by His Holiness Sri Swami Satchidananda Bua Ji (b. 1896), popularly known as Swami Bua Ji. Swami Bua Ji had been crippled at birth and, the doctors being unable to treat him, he was not expected to survive into adulthood. However, he was turned over to Sri Yogeswar Ji Maharaj, a teacher who worked with him using yoga and herbal treatments. At the end of this period, the youthful Swami Bua Ji emerged as both healthy and an accomplished yogi. For many years he was associated with the Divine Life Society founded by Swami Sivananda Saraswati.

In the years after Indian independence (1948) he began to travel widely throughout Europe and North America giving popular demonstrations of yoga and allowing himself to become the subject of scientific investigations. In 1972 he settled in the United States and founded the Indo-American Vedanta Society.

Membership: Not reported. There is one center in the United States and several others in Europe and India.

★1986★
Integral Yoga International
% Satchidananda-Yogaville
Rte. 1, Box 1720
Buckingham, VA 23921

The Rev. Sri Swami Satchidananda, one of several disciples of Swami Sivananda Saraswati to carry his teaching around the world, founded the Integral Yoga Institute. Satchidananda, after years of spiritual seeking, met Swami Sivananda in 1947. In 1949, he was initiated as a sannyasin (monk) into a life of renunciation and selfless service, and was given his name, which means Existence-Knowledge-Bliss. Because of his mastery of all the branches of yoga he was given the title "Yogiraj," or master of yoga. After 17 years of work with Sivananda's Divine Life Society, he came to New York on an intended two-day visit, but was asked to stay to become the founder-director of the Integral Yoga Institute (IYI) and the spiritual head of Integral Yoga International.

The IYI teaches all aspects of Integral Yoga including Hatha Yoga, (to purify and strengthen the body and mind); Karma Yoga (selfless service): Bhakti Yoga (the path of love and devotion to God); Jnana Yoga (the path of wisdom); and Raja Yoga (the path of concentration and meditation).

Since 1975, Swami Satchidananda initiated disciples (both men and women) into the Holy Order of Sannyas. Sannyasins (monks) take the traditional vows to serve and to practice nonviolence toward all living beings. In 1980 the Integral Yoga Ministry was established. Integral Yoga ministers may be married or single; they take vows to live in the spirit of non-attachment, physical and mental purity, and obedience. In 1985, the headquarters of Integral Yoga International moved from the ashram in Connecticut to a new ashram in Virginia.

Sri Swami Satchidananda is known for his involvement in interfaith work. In 1986, at the Virginia ashram, the Light Of Truth Universal Shine (LOTUS) was dedicated to honor all the world religions. Here, people of all faiths can come to meditate and pray in the same place. A central column of light rises and divides into twelve rays to illuminate altars for individual faiths set within the petals of LOTUS. The LOTUS symbolizes the unity in diversity of all religions and reflects Satchidananda's teaching that "Truth is One—Paths are Many."

Membership: There is no formal membership in IYI. In 1997 it reported 23 centers in the United States and four in Canada headed by 60 monks and ministers worldwide. There were 11 affiliated centers in various foreign countries.

Periodicals: *Integral Yoga Magazine.* • *IYI News.* Send orders to 227 W. 13th St., New York, NY 10011.

Sources:

Bordow, Sita, et al. *Sri Swami Satchidananda: Apostle of Peace.* Yogaville, VA: Integral Yoga Publications, 1986.

Satchidananda, Sri Swami. *A Decade of Service.* Pomfret Center, CT: Satchidananda Ashram-Yogaville, 1976.

___. *The Healthy Vegetarian.* Yogaville, VA: Integral Yoga Publications, 1986.

Satchidananda, Swami. *Integral Hatha Yoga.* New York: Holt, Rinehart and Winston, 1970.

___. *The Glory of Sannyasa.* Pomfret, CT: Satchidananda Ashram-Yogaville, 1975.

Satchidananda, Swami, et al. *Living Yoga.* New York: An Interface Book, 1977.

Weiner, Sita. *Swami Satchidananda.* New York: Bantam Books, 1972.

★1987★
Intercosmic Center of Spiritual Awareness
℅ Ananda Ashram
RD 3, Box 141
Monroe, NY 10950

The Intercosmic Center of Spiritual Associations (ICSA), formerly the International Center for Self-Analysis, was founded by Dr. Rammurti Sriram Mishra, a student of Bhagavan Sri Ramana Maharshi. As a young yogi, Maharshi (discussed elsewhere in this chapter) was able to detach his consciousness from the transient world and experience transcendental reality. Upon returning to his physical body, he posed the question "Who am I?" The question was answered through a technique of self-analysis. ICSA seeks to help its adherents through a similar technique of analysis. Its stated goals are 1) to experience one's self as the cosmic center of vibrations; 2) to establish unity of all beings, especially all nations; 3) to promote global togetherness; 4) to promote a natural way of education, self-discipline and relations; 5) to promote the teaching of sanskrit; 6) to establish modern educational centers; 7) to promote natural, spiritual and psychological methods of healing; 8) to experience automatic and spontaneous psychosynthesis and psychoanalysis; and 9) to assist the individual in realizing the Godhood that always resides within.

The ICSA is the umbrella for a number of ashrams around the world under Mishra's direction. Dr. Mishra is a master of raja and kundalini yoga and a medical doctor with specialities in psychiatry and endocrinology. A significant part of the program centers on intensive self-analysis week-ends held at the Ashram Farm in Pulaski, New York. Srimarti Margaret Coble directs ICSA.

Membership: Not reported. In the United States the main centers are the Ananda Ashram in Monroe, New York; the Rochester Ashram; the I.C.S.A. of Syracuse; and the New York City yoga center (all sponsored by the Yoga Society of New York) and the Brahmananda Ashram, the teaching center of the Yoga Society of San Francisco in California.

Periodicals: *I Am News.*

Sources:

Coble, Margaret. *Self-Abidance.* Port Louis, Mauritius: Standard Printing Establishment, 1973.

Mishra, Rammurti. *Dynamics of Yoga Mudras and Five Suggestions for Meditation.* Pleasant Valley, NY: Kriya Press, 1967.

___. *Fundamentals of Yoga.* New York: Lancer Books, 1969.

___. *Self Analysis and Self Knowledge.* Lakemont, GA: CSA Press, 1978.

Mishra, Rammurti S. *Isha Upanishad.* Dayton, OH: Yoga Society of Dayton, 1962.

★1988★
Intergalactic Cultural Foundation
1569 Stonewood Ct.
San Pedro, CA 90732

Alternate Address: International headquarters: Sri Swami Prem's Ministry International, 138, Sector 23A, Chandigarh 160023, India.

The Intergalactic Cultural Foundation was founded in 1981 in Los Angeles by Sri Swami Prem Paramahansa Mahaprabho, an Indian spiritual teacher. Originally known as the Intergalactic Lovetrance Civilization Center, in 1986 the organization created four divisions, each of which assumed a Sanskrit name: Sarvam Kalvidam Brekmha Foundation, Aum Hrim Klim Chamudayai Vichche Foundation, Aum Namah Parvati Foundation, and Aum Namo Bhagavate Vasudevay Divided Foundation. Each of these divisions assisted aspirants from different intellectual and emotional backgrounds to attain the wisdom of Truth.

Sri Swami Prem and the foundation have published more than 100 titles, 60 *Lovetrance World* Journals, the *India Experience*

Newspaper, the *Journey Back in Time* Correspondence Course, and over 100 videos and 200 audio cassette tapes. Prem had made annual lecture tours across the United States and in 1998 plans the international Galactic Chronicles Lecture Tour.

Membership: Not reported.

Periodicals: *Hindu Digest.* • *Golden India.*

Sources:

Paramahansa, Swami Prem. *What Is ILCC?.* Hawthorne, CA: Intergalatic Lovetrance Civilization Center, [1983].

Prem, Sri Swami. *Galatic Chronicles Lecture Program.* Harbor City, CA: Aum Namo Bhagavate Vasudevay, 1995, 37 pp.

Swami Prem Paramahansa and His Message. Hawthorne, CA: Intergalatic Lovetrance Civilization Center, 1983.

Who Is Swami Prem Paramahansa Mahaprabho?. Hawthorne, CA: Intergalatic Lovetrance Civilization Center, [1982].

★1989★
International Babaji Kriya Yoga Sangam
595 W. Bedford Rd.
Imperial City, CA 92251

The International Babaji Yoga Sangam was founded in 1952 by Yogi S. A. A. Ramaiah. Yogi Ramaiah is the disciple of Kriya Babaji Nagaraj, the satguru of the order. Born and raised in Tamil, Nagaraj was initiated into Kriya Kundalini Pranayam by a sage named Agasthiya who resided at Kuttralam, India. He also traveled to Sri Lanka to study with another Siva Siddhanta teacher under whom he attained enlightenment. He eventually settled in the Himalayas, where he still lives. He has chosen to live quietly and allow his disciples to spread his teachings. The Babaji Yoga Sangam was founded under the guidance of Babaji Nagaraj. It is claimed that Nagaraj was born in 203 A.D. and lives on in defiance of the limitations of death.

Ramaiah became well-known in the early 1960s as a result of his submitting to a number of scientific tests in which he demonstrated his control over several body functions, including the ability to vary his body temperature over a fifteen-degree range. He brought the movement he had founded in India to America in the 1960s. By the early 1970s, fifteen centers had been opened across the country with headquarters in Norwalk, California. Sadhana centers, for more intense, live-in practice of kriya yoga, were established in several rural California locations. More recently the Yogi Ramaiah established the first shrine to Ayyappa Swami, a figure in the ancient Hindu holy books, the Puranas, in Imperial City, California. Each December, beginning in 1970, members of the sangam make a pilgrimage from the shrine, which also serves as the American headquarters of the group, to Mount Shasta, 800 miles away in the mountains of northern California.

Membership: Not reported.

Educational Facilities: KBYS Holistic Hospital and Colleges of Yoga Thearpy and Physiotherapy, Konapet Road, Athanor, Puddukotta, District, Tamil Nadu, India.

Sources:

Ramaiah, Yogi S. A. A. *Shasta Ayyappa Swami Yoga Pilgrimage.* Imperial City, CA: Pan American Babaji Yoga Sangam, n.d.

★1990★
International Divine Realization Society
℅ Devavand Yoga Cultural Center
2285 Sedgwick Ave., No. 102
Bronx, NY 10468

The International Divine Realization Society was founded by H. H. Swami Guru Devanand Saraswati Ji Maharaj, a spiritual teacher from India. Swami Devanand teaches a form of jnana yoga which is practiced by a form of meditation with the use of a mantra. It is Swami Devanand's claim that the use of Mantra Yoga Meditation will give the practitioner a growth of goodwill and stability, improve memory and concentration, bring an awareness of the supreme Being, and eliminate psychiatric disorders. The Center in New York hosts a complete round of activities including meditation sessions, Sunday puja, haitha yoga classes, and special activities in stress management and natural medicine. Most programs are held in both English and Spanish.

Membership: Not reported.

★1991★
International Meditation Institute
2542 Montclair Ave.
Montreal, PQ, Canada H4B 2J1

Alternate Address: International Headquarters: Kullu 175 101, Himalayas, India.

The International Meditation Institute grew out of the work of Swami Shyam (b. 1924). As a young man, he realized a state which he termed "Shyam Space" described as a state of pure existence and pure consciousness in which one drops one's identification with the world and identifies with the Pure self. This is a form of what is generally termed advaita vedanta. The future Swami Shyam was a government career worker when he began to teach out of his experience. In the 1970s he was discovered by two Canadian tourists who invited him to Toronto. His brief visit was extended to more than a year after his papers were stolen, and when he finally returned to India, he had a group of Canadians with him. They gave him the unofficial title of Swami.

From the original Western center in Montreal, other centers have been founded in Canada, the United States, Europe, New Zealand, Israel, Japan, and Taiwan.

Membership: Not reported.

Sources:

Cushman, Anne, and Jerry Jones. *From Here to Nirvana: The Yoga Journal Guide to Spiritual India.* New York: Riverhead Books, 1998. 399 pp.

★1992★
International Society for Krishna Consciousness (ISKCON)
% ISCKON International Ministry of Public Affairs
1030 Grand Ave.
San Diego, CA 92109

The International Society for Krishna Consciousness (ISKCON) is a major representative of that form of devotional Vaishnava Hinduism which grew out of the work of Chaitanya Mahaprabhu (1486-1534?), the famed Bengali saint. Chaitanya advocated a life of intense devotion centered upon the public chanting of the names of God, primarily through the chanting of the Hare Krishna mantra: Hare Krishna, Hare Krishna/Hare Hare, Krishna Krishna/Hare Rama, Hare Rama/Hare Hare, Rama Rama.

ISKCON developed out of the activity of A. C. Bhaktivedanta Swami Prabhupada (1896-1977). Prabhupada was a businessman. He was initiated into the revived Krishna Consciousness movement represented in the Guadiya Mission in 1932. In 1936 his guru told him to take Krishna worship to the West, but he was unable to fulfill his mission to spread the movement until the 1950s. In 1959 he took his vows for the renounced life in the sannyasin order. In 1965 he traveled to America where he established a movement to spread Krishna Consciousness. ISKCON was founded the following year in New York City. A magazine was begun and a San Francisco center opened in 1967. Besides leading the movement and serving as the initiating guru to the several thousands of adherents, Prabhupada was a prolific translator/author. He produced two series of translations and commentaries on the main scriptures of Krishna Consciousness, *The Srimad Bhagavatam* and the *Caitanya-caritamrita*. His primary work, the one that most new members first encounter, was his translation of and commentary on the Bhagavad-Gita, *The Bhagavad-Gita As It Is.*

The movement grew, though never in the great numbers that its media coverage often suggested. It was a frequent object of media coverage because of its colorful appearance and strange, exotic beliefs and practices. During the 1970s it became one of the major targets for the anti-cult movement.

The central thrust of ISKCON is bhakti yoga, which in this case takes the form of chanting the Hare Krishna mantra. The chanting is the process for receiving the pure consciousness of God (thought of in his prime incarnations of Krishna and Rama) and dispelling the maya or illusion in which the world is immersed. Devotion also includes the following: service to the deity statues found in all Krishna temples; *telok*, markings of the body with clay in twelve places, each representing a name of God; *kirtan*, the public chanting and dancing to Krishna; and eating and distribution of prasadam, food (vegetarian) offered to Krishna. Devotees also study much traditional Hindu lore (Vedic culture), the history of bhakti yoga, and the writings of the founder.

As the society has spread, it has gained fame for its festivals and feasts. Each summer one or more international festivals featuring a mass parade honoring Lord Jagannath are held, and everyone is fed a vegetarian meal. Weekly feasts (open to the public) are part of the normal activity of the local temple.

Prior to Prabhupada's death, he appointed a 22-member governing body commission (GBC) which had begun to function in the early 1970s and provided a smooth transition of power in 1977. Included in the GBC were the initiating gurus, i.e., those within the movement with the power of initiating new disciples. The initiating gurus are looked to for maintaining high spiritual standards and inspiring others to do so. The GBC provides overall coordination and administrative oversight to the movement which is divided into a number of zones. The various zones are further divided into different corporations, each independent and autonomous under the management of local teachers and the zonal GBC. There is no longer any central headquarters, although in the major cities and in Vrindavan, India, ISKCON temples are international centers for the movement as the destinations of mass annual pilgrimages. The decentralization has led to the formation of a variety of publishing programs in the several zones.

During the 1980s, ISKCON was hit with a serious controversy between the more conservative elements and those advocating reforms. Crucial to the disagreements were varying opinions on the *guru puja*, the veneration of the guru, which had been an integral part of the daily morning ISKCON ritual while Prabhupada lived. Reform-minded gurus began to question the legitimacy of the current initiating gurus receiving guru puja, and began to discontinue it in their zones. Some of the call for reform came as a response to several gurus who had been disciplined for not living according to their vows. Most vocal in the cause of reform was Satsvarupa dasa Goswami, who authored a number of books on the subject. Most persistent in defending the guru puja was Kirtananda Swami Bhaktipada, head of the New Vrindavan community in West Virginia. This was one major issue in the 1987 excommunication of Bhaktipada and the reorganization of the temples under him into a separate organization.

Membership: In 1984 the movement reported 3,000 core community members and 250,000 lay constituents. There were 50 centers in the United States. There are 8,000 members worldwide. Centers can be found in 60 countries.

Periodicals: *Back to Godhead.* Send orders to Box 18928, Philadelphia, PA 19119-0428. • *The ISKCON World Review.* Send orders to 3764 Watseka Avenue, Los Angeles, CA 90034.

Remarks: In Hawaii, ISKCON experienced a temporary schism when a rival group under Sai Young emerged. Young's followers, known as the Haiku Meditation Center and Krishna Yoga Community, followed Bhaktivedanta's teachings but did not don the saffron robes or shave their heads. The group disbanded in 1971 and ISKCON inherited its members.

In 1983 a former member of the movement, Robin George, was awarded $9,700,000 in a lawsuit against the movement. This judgment (now being appealed) could, if sustained, seriously damage the movement in California, New Orleans, New York, and Canada (the temples under direct attack by the suit). Much of the future of the movement is contingent upon the outcome of this litigation.

Sources:

Gelberg, Steven, ed. *Hare Krishna, Hare Krishna*. New York: Grove Press, 1983.

Goswami, Satsvarupa dasa. *Srila Prabhupada-lilamrta*. 6 vols. Los Angeles: Bhaktivedanta Book Trust, 1980-83.

Judah, J. Stillson. *Hare Krishna and the Counterculture*. New York: John Wiley & Sons, 1974.

Knott, Kim. *My Sweet Lord*. Wellingborough, Northamptonshire: Aquarian Press, 1986.

Prabhupada, Swami A. C. Bhaktivedanta. *Bhagavad-Gita As It Is*. New York: Bhaktivedanta Book Trust, 1972.

★1993★
International Society for Krishna Consciousness of West Virginia
RD 1, Box 318
Moundsville, WV 26041

During the 1980s the International Society for Krishna Consciousness (ISKCON), experienced a high level of internal tension caused in no small part by the inability of several of its initiating gurus to hold to the organization's standards particularly in the area of illicit sexual relations and the use of psychedelic drugs. Several gurus were expelled and others resigned. The tension led to demands for reform and the most intense debate centered upon the role of the guru in relation to A. C. Bhaktivedanta Swami Prabhupada (1896-1977), the founder of the society. Some members of the governing body commission (GBC) called for a more democratic structure, a lessening of the status of the guru vis-a-vis his disciples, and an end to the acceptance of guru puja (worship) by the current society leaders.

Among the most conservative gurus was Kirtananda Swami Bhaktipada, founder of New Vrindaban, the rural Krishna center in northern West Virginia. Kirtananda was among the earliest disciples of Prabhupada and in the 1960s was sent to West Virginia to build a rural community. Despite a variety of setbacks, the community prospered. During the 1970s, Kirtananda began work on a palacial mansion for Prabhupada, who died prior to its completion. The palace was continued and eventually completed as a monument to Prabhupada's life and work. Dubbed the "Palace of Gold," it has become one of West Virginia's top tourist attractions.

During the early 1980s the vision of New Vrindaban continued to grow even as the community began to swell. New support came from members of the society who moved from other centers to New Vrindaban, and substantial support was received from the ever-growing Indian-American community. Increasingly as the society decentralized, Rew Vrindaban was looked upon as the center of the movement in North America.

The debates on reform, largely confined within the GBC, became public in 1986 with the publication of the *Guru Reform Notebook* by Satsvarupa dasa Goswami, which demanded reform of the society's understanding of the guru, especially the elimination of any practices which tended to place current guru's on the same level as Prabhupada (as demonstrated in their receiving guru puja). Kirtananda quickly emerged as the major antagonist in the debate, arguing that organization and structure must remain as Prabhupada left them. The argument reached a culmination point on March 16, 1987, when the GBC expelled Kirtananda from the International Society for Krishna Consciousness. The GBC cited four major reasons for the expulsion by claiming that Kirtananda

(1) had minimized the position of Phadhupada; (2) had rejected the authority of the GBC (thus destroying the society's unity); (3) had established temples in areas assigned to other gurus; and (4) had, while acting independently of the society's authority, misrepresented the society to the public. Kirtananda answered the charges by noting that he had been merely following the pattern of life established by Prabhupada and the particular mission to which he had been assigned. Further he noted in his book, *On His Order*, an answer to Satsvarupa, that it was the GBC which was guilty of deviating from Prabhupada's teachings through their reform movement and the re-editing of Prabhupada's commentary on the Bhagavad-Gita.

While Bhaktipada was accusing ISKCON of deviating from the teachings and pattern of life established by Prabhupada, he was in turn accused of also deviating by his adoption of elements from the Rhristian tradition. He moved to have an organ installed in the temple at New Vrindaban and members of the community began to wear, at times, brown monk-like habits. ISKCON leaders have charged that these changes are far more drastic than those of which they have been accused of making.

Except for the issues mentioned above, including those which led to Kirtananda's expulsion from the society, New Vrindaban and its subsidiary temples follow the same pattern of worship and belief as for the temples and centers of the International Society of Krishna Consciousness. In the wake of the expulsion, New Vrindaban and its aligned centers (mostly in Ohio), having been founded originally as a separate corporation, merely reorganized as an independent entity under its corporate name, the International Society for Krishna Consciousness of West Virginia. Almost immediately, leaders from New Vrindaban were sent out to found new centers in such places as Philadelphia and New York City.

The year of Bhatipada's leadership of the independent ISKCON of West Virginia were one of intense controversy. He tried to exert leadership in the interfaith community and initially attracted a number of people to New Vrindaban from various religious communities. He also initiated plans for the creation of a large community on the ISKCON property. However, he was continually distracted by controversy. Shortly after his expulsion from ISKCON, authorities raided the community searching for evidence of supportive of allegations of fraudulent fund raising and information on the deaths of a former resident, Charles St. Dennis, killed in 1983, and in the 1986 murder of a vocal critic, Stephen Bryant. Earlier, in 1985, he was almost killed when a former devotee attacked him.

A variety of court actions followed including his being found not guilty in a trial for arson of a building to collect insurance, and a follower. Thomas Dreshner, being found guilty in connection with the murder of St. Dennis. Finally, on August 28, 1996, Bhaktipada pled guilty to a racketeering charge that included conspiracy to murder (Stephen Bryant). Dreshner, who had denied Bhaktipada's involvement in any illegal acts, eventually turned and offer testimony against him. Bhaktipada began serving a 20 year prison term in September 1996, a sentence more recently reduced to 12 years. In the wake of Bhaktipada's conviction, as well as revelation of his breaking his vows of sexual abstinence, there has been a move to integrate ISKCON of West Virginia back to the International Society of Krishna Consciousness. While many devotees have already switched their allegiance, the actual return of New Vrindaban awaits the clearing up of a number of legal encumbrances.

Membership: Not reported. Centers are located in West Virginia, Ohio, Pennsylvania, New York, and Boston, Massachusetts.

Periodicals: *Brijabasi Spirit.* • *New Vrindaban Worldwide.* Send orders to R.D. 1, Box 318A, Moundsville, WV 26041. • *Junior Brijabasi.* Send orders to R.D. 1, Box 319, Moundsville, WV 26041.

Remarks: Kirtanananda Swami and New Vrindaban have been the object of intense controversy which began in the early 1980s when charges of drug dealing and the stockpiling of weapons were published in newspapers and magazines across the United States. In October 1985, a fringe member of the society attempted to murder Kirtanananda with a lead bar. Then in 1986 a former member, Stephen Bryant, came to West Virginia and threatened Kirtanananda's life. In May, Bryant was murdered in Los Angeles. Following Bryant's murder, the local sheriff called for a federal probe of New Vrindaban. It was convened in September 1986, just a few weeks before two ex-members Daniel Reed and Thomas Dreshner, went on trial for the murder of a man who raped Reed's wife. Both ex-members were convicted. Reed was allowed to plead guilty to manslaughter and he received one to five years. Dreshner, an accessory after the fact (he assisted Reed in burying the body), was given a life sentence. Later Dreshner was accepted back as a full member by Kirtanananda who accepted him into the renounced or sanyassin order. Subsequently, Dreshner has frequently but incorrectly been cited in the press as a swami (teacher) and spokesperson for the group.

As a result of the federal investigation, Kirtanananda was indicted for setting fire to a building owned by the group in order to collect the insurance. At a trial in December 1987, he was acquitted of all charges. As this volume goes to press, the federal investigation continues. There is no word whether further indictments will be handed down concerning Kirtanananda or any leaders of the New Vrindaban community.

Embarrassed by the events at New Vrindaban, the GBC included the accusations and subsequent federal probe as a secondary reason for Kirtanananda's expulsion.

Sources:

Bhaktipada, Kirtanananda Swami. *Christ and Krishna*. Moundsville, WV: Bhaktipada Books, 1985.

___. *Eternal Love*. Moundsville, WV: Bhaktipada Books, 1985.

___. "A Community Struggles for Reinstatement." *Hare Krishna World* 5,5. (Jan/Feb.1997).

___. *On His Order*. Moundsville, WV: Bhakti Books, 1987.

___. *The Song of God*. Moundsville, WV: Bhaktipada Books, 1984.

Shinn, Larry D. *The Dark Lord*. Philadelphia: Westminister Press, 1987.

★1994★
International Society of Divine Love
% Barsana Dham
400 Barsana Rd.
Austin, TX 78737

The International Society of Divine Love was established in India in 1975 and America in 1981 by Swami H.D. Prakashanand Saraswati. Born in Ayodhya, India, he spent over 20 years in devotional seclusion in Braj, the birthplace of Krishn (who, according to the Hindu scriptures, the *Gita* and the *Bhagwatam* is the supreme personality of God). He is a Rasik Saint in the lineage of Chaitanya Mahaprabhu (1485–1533), the famous Saint of West Bengal who spread the *raganuga* (divine-love-consciousness or bhakti yoga) style of devotion associate with Radha Krishn.

Apart from the practice of yogic and psychic disciplines which are considered to be merely the exploration of the psychic powers of *maya* (illusion), Swami Prakashanand Saraswati teaches the path of god's love and the development of an affinity and personal feelings of love for the personal form of God, Radha Krishn. The devotional approach is explained in the Vedas, Upanishads, *Bhagvad Gita*, and the *Srimad Bhagwatam*. It is centered upon the remembrance of Radha Krishn and chanting His name while devotionally offering one's emotional feeling to Him.

During the 1990s, the society constructed a new temple and ashram complex in Austin, Texas, where the deity establishment of Shree Raseshwari Radha Rani was dedicated on October 8, 1995.

Membership: The society has some 3,000 names on its followers' mailing list in the United States. It also has members in England, Ireland, New Zealand, Australia, and Singapore.

Sources:

The Deity Establishment Ceremony of Shree Raseshwari Radha Rani of Barsana Dham, October 7-8, 1995. Austin, TX: International Society of Divine Love, 1995.

___. Prakashanand Saraswati, H.D. *The Path to God*. Austin, TX: International Society of Divine Love, 1995.

___. *The Philosophy of Diving Love*. Auckland, NZ: International Society of Divine Love, 1982.

___. *The Shikchashtek*. Philadelphia, PA: International Society of Divine Love, 1986.

★1995★
Kali Mandir
% Kali Mandir Puja Shop
PO Box 4700
Laguna Beach, CA 92652-4700

Kali Mandir was formed to facilitate worship of the Divine Mother in the form of Kali and to make worship available to all. The worship is modeled on the teachings and practice of Sri Ramakrishna and Sri Sarada Devi as established in the Dakshineswar Kali Temple in Calcutta, India. In adopting the Indian Hindu temple ideal, the leaders of the mandir are initially attempting to provide a place of worship for the seeker of God in the form of the Mother, especially in the form of Kali. Kali Mandir does not have a resident guru and is not based on any particular guru's teachings. Rather than seek to convert people away from previously held beliefs, the mandir simply welcomes all.

Future plans include the construction of a temple site in Laguna Beach, California. Each summer the mandir sponsors an annual Kali Puja in Laguna Beach, officiated by the priests from the Dakshineswar Kali Temple in India.

Membership: Not reported.

Sources:

http://www.kalimandie.org/.

★1996★
Kashi Church Foundation
11155 Roseland Rd., No. 10
Sebastian, FL 32958

The Kashi Church Foundation was founded by Ma Jaya Sati Bhagavati, a spiritual teacher who emerged as a result of an intense experience in the mid 1970s. She had been born Joyce Green into an orthodox Jewish family in Brooklyn where she grew to adulthood. She married into a Roman Catholic family and settled into life as a housewife. Then in December 1972 she had a vision of someone whom she recognized as Jesus Christ. He subsequently reappeared three more times. Hesitantly at first, she turned for guidance to residents of a nearby Catholic seminary. Then in the spring of 1973 she had a second set of apparitions, this time of a person who called himself Nityanada.

At the apparitions began, she no knowledge that such a person as Nityananda had actually lived. In fact, Swami Nyananda had been a prominent Hindu guru in India, had initiated a movement later headed by Swami Muktananda, and had an American disciple named Swami Rudrananda who initially brought his teachings to the United States. Nityananda, as he appeared to her, taught her about what he termed *chidakash*, the state in which love and awareness are one. He appeared to her almost daily for a year and taught her. He gave her a new name, *Jaya* (Sanskrit for "victory" or "glory"). Green, who began to call herself Joya Santanya, sought out Swami Rudrananda and shortly thereafter discovered

Hilda Charlton, an independent spiritual teacher in Manhattan who encouraged her to become a teacher.

The final events in her transformation began on Good Friday 1974, when she began to bleed in a manner similar to Jesus' crucifixion wounds. On Easter Sunday morning, much to the consternation of her Roman Catholic in-law, she bled profusely from both her hands and forehead. The stigmata presaged a third set of apparations, which began a few months later. An older man wrapped in a blanket appeared and introduced himself as her guru, and she was especially drawn to him as he seemed to share her devotion to Jesus. She would later see a picture of someone identified to her as Neem Karoli Baba (who had died the year before). This person had been a prominent Indian spiritual teacher who had deeply influenced Baba Ram Dass, who in turn had first introduced American audiences to his teachings.

Through the mid-1970s, thirteen small communities of people responded to Joya's teachings were founded. In July 1976 she moved to central Florida with a small group of disciples and founded Kashi Ashram. Over the next few years she regularly visited the several houses and expanded her teaching work to the West Coast. Then in 1978 she fell ill, and many thought she might die. Responding to her condition many of the people living in the cooperative houses moved to Florida. After she regained her health, the people decided to stay to what had become a greatly expanded ashram.

Teachings. Ma Jaya Sati Bhagavati teaches a form of Advaita Vendanta, the traditional monistic worldview derived from the Indian scriptures, the Vedas and the Upanisbads. Vendata sees the diversity of the visible world and human experience dissolves in the perception of the Oneness of ultimate reality. This insight is common to mysticism and may be found in esoteric forms of the major faiths, thus provides a meeting ground for people of other faiths.

Residents at Kashi come from very different backgrounds and are drawn more by their relationship to Ma as guru than the acceptance of any particular religious beliefs. They also bring varying attachments to the religions in which they were raised. No attempt is made to convert people; rather the individual's devotion to a particular religion is recognized and nurtured as one expression of the mystical unity. In this manner Kashi is following the tradition of Neem Karloi Baba who counted members of all the religions of India among his followers. Ma and members of the Ashram assumed a prominent role at the centennial Parliament of the World's Religions gathering in Chicago in 1933 and have been among those who arose to continue its work.

Through the 1990s Ma has developed an impressive ministry to people with AIDS and HIV-virus. Beginning with a small ministry in Los Angeles and southern Florida, the AIDS related work has become a dominant element of ashram life. Ma regularly invited terminal AIDS patients to spend the last weeks of their life at the hospice at the Ashram in Florida and enjoy the loving care it offers. The AIDS ministry, grew out of Anadana, the Ashram's community service organization which facilitates the participation of Kashi members in a variety of service projects in their community from delivering food for meals-on-wheels to manning the local crisis hot line. As the Ashram's ministries have grown and diversified, Ma established the River Fund to mobilize financial support. The community also has shown particular concern for ministering to children and has created a quality school to serve both the children of residents and the neighborhood.

Organizations. Kashi headed and tied together by Ma. The Florida Ashram is organized on a semi-communal basis with each adult resident responsible for an equal share of the community's needed support. Most of the members hold jobs outside of the Ashram. Residents follow a vegitarian diet supplemented with small quantities of fish and milk. Narcotics, alcohol, or tobacco are forbidden. Family life is encouraged and married couples live together though chastity is practiced except when couples are trying to have a child.

Members of the community gather daily for *puja* (worship ceremony) in the morning and for darshan (gathering with Ma) in the evening. Various different religious festivals are celebrated, especially Christmas and the Durga Puja (a major Hindu festival). Above community spiritual life, each individual is encouraged to follow personal devotional activities. Some are active in local churches.

Membership: From around 80 permanent residents in 1978 the community has grown to almost 200. There is a small core community in Los Angeles and several hundred members who regularly attend Ma's darshan sessions.

Sources:

Ma Jaya Sati Bhagavati. *Bones and Ash.* Sebastian, FL: Jaya Press, 1995.

___. *The River.* Roseland, FL: Ganga Press, 1994.

★1997★
Kirpalu Center for Yoga and Health
Box 793
Lenox, MA 01240

The Kirpalu Center for Yoga and Health was founded in 1966 as the Yoga Society of Pennsylvania by Amrit Desai who had learned yoga as a teenager in his native India. Desai came to the United States in 1960 and began teaching yoga while otherwise pursuing a secular career. In 1970, however, a significant moment in his developing work occurred as he was performing his daily yoga practices. He experienced a spontaneous flow of yoga postures in which the innate and autonomous intelligence of his body performed the postures without conscious or willful direction from his mind. Through repetition and study of his experience, he developed a technique by which others could experience the same spontaneous flow. He termed this new technique Kripalu yoga in honor of Swami Kripalvanandji, his yoga teacher in India.

In 1971 the first Kripalu residential community was established in Sumneytown, Pennsylvania, as a small retreat where Desai and his students could live the contemplative lifestyle. By 1974, the community had grown in number and became a non-profit organization known as the Kripalu Yoga Fellowship. In 1975 a retreat center was founded on a 370-acre plot near Summit Station, Pennsylvania, and approximately 170 residents moved into the new facilities. Then in 1983 the community moved to Shadowbrook, a former Jesuit novitiate in Lenox, Massachusetts. The ashram offered a full range of yoga and related programs and many teachers who trained there went forth to found affiliated yoga centers across the United States. By the mid 1990s there were some 2000 certified yoga teachers working in more than 130 affiliated support groups in North America and some 35 countries of Europe and Central America.

The work built around Yogi Desai was prospering. The 270 residents at the ashram in Lenox constituted the largest such yoga center in North America. Then in the fall of 1994 the center's board had to face the accusations of several women that Yogi Desai, who preached a celibate existence, had been forcing himself sexually upon them. In the face of the scandal, and following his admission of guilt, Desai was forced to resign as the spiritual director of the organization, which has since continued under the leadership of the centers board. The center's program continues in much the same format as in previous years, though life in the community is in a state of transition.

Membership: Not reported.

Periodicals: *The Kripalu Experience.*

Remarks: Among other disciples of Swami Kripalvanandaji in the United States is Shanti Desai, brother of Yogi Amrit Desai, head of the Shanti Yoga Institute and Yoga Retreat in New Jersey.

Sources:

Desai, Amrit. *Guru and Disciple.* Sumneytown, PA: Kripalu Yoga Ashram, 1975.

Gurudev, Sukanya Warren. *The Life of Yogi Amrit Desai.* Summit Station, PA: Kripalu Publications, 1982.

Kripalvanandji, Swami. *Science of Meditation.* Vadodara, Gujarat, India: Sri Dahyabhai Hirabhai Patel, 1977.

___. *Premyatra.* Summit Station, PA: Kripalu Yoga Fellowship, 1981.

MacDowell, Andie, and Isabella Rossellini. "Bad Karma." *Boston* 87, 12 (December 1995): 66—71, 78—92.

★1998★
Jean Klein Foundation
Box 2111
Santa Barbara, CA 93120

Jean Klein (d. 1998) was an Eastern European teacher of advaita, a teaching of nonduality. According to the advaita, our essential being or consciousness is beyond subject/object duality, beyond the thought process. In the year following the end of World War II, Klein, a musicologist and medical doctor, traveled to India on a spiritual quest. He had been stimulated to go to India by reading some of the writings of Rene Guenon. Within weeks he met a teacher who initiated him into the teachings of advaita vedanta, a teaching shared by such Indian teachers as Ramana Maharshi, Sri Nisargadatta Maharaj, and Atmananda Krishna Menon. He returned to France in 1960 and held dialogues and yoga seminars. His first book, *l'Ultimate Realite* was published in France in 1968. His first book in English, *Be Who Your Are,* appeared in London, England, in 1978.

During the 1980s, Klein visited the United States for seminars and in 1989 he formed the Jean Klein Foundation to spread the teachings of advaita vedanta as presented by Klein. The foundation carries on an active teaching program through seminars held throughout the United States. Third Millennium Publications of Santa Barbara, California, is closely associated with the foundation and publishes Klein's books.

Membership: Not reported.

Periodicals: *Listening, The Jean Klein Foundation Newsletter.*

Sources:

Klein, Jean. *Be Who Your Are.* London, England: Watkins, 1978.

___. *The Ease of Being.* Durham, NC: The Acorn Press, 1984.

___. *I Am.* Santa Barbara, CA: Third Millennium Publications, 1989.

★1999★
Krishna Samaj
(Defunct)

The Krishna Samaj was formed by Surendranath Mukerji (d. 1914), better known by his religious name, Baba Premanand Bharati. Baba Bharati was among the first Hindu teachers to come to America, arriving in the United States around 1902 from Bengal. He was a student of Swami Brahmanand Bharati and follower of the Krishna Consciousness movement which had been revived in Bengal in the nineteenth century (and which became well known in America and the West in the 1970s through the International Society for Krishna Consciousness (ISKCON), also known as the Hare Krishna movement). The Krishna Consciousness movement originated with Chaitanya Mahaprabhu (1486-1534?), a bhakti (devotional) yogi, who spread the practice of repeating the Hare Krisha mantrum as the way to enlightenment and release from the wheel of karma and reincarnation.

Bharati, the nephew of a prominent Bengali judge, formed the Krishma Samaj in New York City and lectured to popular audiences in other eastern cities. He eventually moved to Los Angeles, where a temple was constructed and he had his greatest following. In 1909 he returned to India where, with a few of his American disciples, he opened a mission in Calcutta. The mission failed for lack of financial support, and he and his followers returned to America. He died in Calcutta in 1914. The temple dissolved in America soon after Bharati's death.

In the years immediately after his death, Bharati was attacked by people opposed to the growth of Hinduism in America, such as Elizabeth A. Reed, whose study of Bharati and the other early gurus was a significant factor in building public support for the Asian Exclusion Act passed in 1917. The strength and devotion of Bharati's disciples, however, kept his memory alive over the years. In the 1930s, members of the Order of Loving Service, a California metaphysical group, dedicated the book *Square* as follows: "To Baba Premanand Bharati, who by his love, patience, and continued watchfulness has led me out of darkness into *Light*, out of weariness into *Rest*, out of confusion into *Understanding*, out of continuous striving into *Perfect Peace.*" In the 1970s, members of the AUM Temple of Universal Truth, founded in the 1920s, were reprinting Bharati's writings in their periodical and selling pictures of "Our Beloved Baba Bharati."

Sources:

Bharati, Baba Premanand. *Krishna.* New York: Krishna Samaj, 1904.

___. *American Lectures.* Calcutta: Indo-American Press, n.d.

Farquhar, J. N. *Modern Religious Movements in India.* New York: Macmillan, 1915.

Lalita [Maud Lalita Johnson]. *Square.* Laguna Beach, CA: Order of Loving Service, 1934.

Reed, Elizabeth A. *Hinduism in Europe and America.* New York: G. P. Putnam's Sons, 1914.

★2000★
Krishnamurti Foundation of America
Box 1560
Ojai, CA 93024-1560

The Krishnamurti Foundation of America was founded in 1969 to protect and disseminate the teachings of Jiddu Krishnamurti, a spiritual teacher who emerged into prominence early in the twentieth century, and carried on a unique independent teaching mission until his death in 1986.

Krishnamurti was born May 12, 1895 at Madanapalle, Andhra Pradesh, India into a Brahmin family. When he was fourteen years old he was designated by Annie Besant and Charles W. Leadbeater of the Theosophical Society as the vehicle for the coming world teacher whose appearance they had come to expect in their lifetime. Besant adopted Krishnamurti and took him to England where she saw to his education and groomed him for his messianic role. In 1911 he was made head of a newly formed organization, the Order of the Star of the East and through the 1920s he traveled around the world speaking on its behalf.

In 1929, after several years of questioning himself and his role, he dissolved the order, repudiated its claims, and returned all of the assets given to him for its furtherance. Setting the perspective that would dominate his future, he declared, "Truth is a pathless land and you cannot approach it by any path whatsoever, by any religion, by any sect. Truth, being limitless, unconditioned, unapproachable by any path whatsoever, cannot be organized; nor should any organization be formed to lead or to coerce people along any particular path. My only concern is to set humanity absolutely, unconditionally free."

Renouncing any allegiance to caste, nationality, particular religion, or tradition, he spent the rest of his life traveling he world and lecturing until shortly before his death. He suggested that individuals had to free themselves from all fear, conditioning, authority, and dogma through self-knowledge, and that the gaining of such selfknowledge would result in order and psychological mutation. Only this psychological mutation by enough individuals, brought about by self-observation, not by a guru or organized religion, could transform the world. No social engineering would bring a world of goodness, love, and compassion.

His assertion that humans have to be their own guru and his rejection of all authority, including his own, attracted many people. A number of intellectuals and religious leaders engaged him in dialogue and scientists discussed the bridging of science and mystical thought with him.

Krishnamurti was optimistic about the possibilities of education that emphasized the integral cultivation of the mind and heart and not just the intellect. Such education would allow students to discover the conditioning that distorts their thinking. To this end, he led in the founding of many schools in the United States, Great Britain, and India. The Foundation of America supports the Oak Grove School in Ojai, California.

Krishnamurti also established foundations in those countries where support for his work was manifest. During his lifetime, the foundations provided a focus for his teaching work and assisted in the publication and dissemination of his teachings. In the years since his death their role of protecting and continuing the process of making his material available has come to the fore. Krishnamurtis lectures and dialogues became the sources of numerous books and booklets, and during the last year of his life his lectures were taped on both audio and video.

The Krishnamurti Foundation of America works cooperatively with other foundations around the world including: Krishnamurti Educational Centre of Canada, 538 Swanwick Rd., R. R. 1, Victoria, BC, Canada V9B 5T7; the Krishnamurti Foundation Trust, Brockwood Park, Bramdean, Hants., UK SO24 0LQ; the Fundacion Krishnamurti Latinoamericana, c/o Juan Colell, Apartado 5351, Barcelona 08080, Spain; and the Krishnamurti Foundation of India, Vasnata Vihar, 64/65 Greensway Road, Madras 600 028, India. The Krishnamurti Foundation of America houses a library and archives of Krishnamurtis talks and related materials.

Membership: In 1995 there were approximately 1,000 friends of the foundation who contribute to its work.

Periodicals: *Newsletter.*

Remarks: Recently, Krishnamurti died. The Foundation has announced that it will continue to facilitate the distribution of Krishnamurti's tapes and books and to channel suppport to Oak Grove School.

Sources:

Alcyone [Jiddu Krishnamurti]. *At the Feet of the Master.* Adyar, India: Theosophical Publishing House, n.d.

Krishnamurti, Jiddu. *Commentaries on Living.* 3 vols. Wheaton, IL: Theosophical Publishing House, n.d.

Krishnamurti, Jiddu, and David Bohm. *The Ending of Time.* San Francisco, CA: Harper & Row, 1985.

Lutyens, Mary. *Krishnamurti, The Years of Awakening.* New York: Farrar, Straus & Giroux, 1975.

___. *Krishnamurti, The Years of Fulfillment.* London: J. Murray, 1983.

★2001★
Kriya Yoga Centers
Current address not obtained for this edition.
   Alternate Address: International Headquarters: Karar Ashram, Puri, Orissa, India.

The Kriya Yoga Centers were founded by Swami Hariharananda Giri, a teacher of kriya yoga from the same lineage as Swami Paramahansa Yogananda, founder of Self-Realization Fellowship. Swami Yogananda was a disciple of Sri Yukteswar who settled in Puri in the state of Orissa, India, in 1906, and built an *ashram* (religious community). Yogananda succeeded Yukteswar as president of the ashram. He was succeeded in 1936 by Sreemat Swami Satyananda. In 1970 Satyananda was succeeded by Swami Hariharananda Giri (b. 1911), who had been associated with the ashram for many years. Hariharananda spread the work of the ashram through India, and in 1974 made his first trip to the West, to Swit-

zerland. By the end of the decade he had several ashrams in Europe and in New York, New York. He continues to travel to the West periodically.

Kriya yoga is a technique imparted to disciples in initiation. It is based on breath control, which is believed to bring about God-realization by turning attention from the outward to the inner self. It transforms the life force into divine force by magnetizing the psychic centers believed to exist along the human spine.

Membership: Not reported. There are approximately 30 ashrams in India and centers in Europe. American centers are located in New York, New York; Washington, D.C.; and Santa Rosa, California.

Periodicals: *Soul Culture: A Journal of Kriya Yoga*, PO Box 9127, Santa Rosa, CA 95404.

Sources:

Hariharananda Giri, Swami. *Isa Upanishad.* Kriya Yoga Ashrams, 1985.

★2002★
Kriya Yoga Tantra Society
633 Post St., Ste. 647
San Francisco, CA 94109

Amid the larger movement of Hinduism to North America, tantric forms have also come and a noticeable tantric movement has emerged around a set of independent tantric teachers. Several have established organizations propagating tantra, among them the Kriya Yoga Tantra Society. The society was founded by Andre O. Rathel, better known by his spiritual name, Sunyata Saraswati. Sunyata was a student of martial arts, the occult, and tantra. He traveled to India, where he studied with Satyananda Saraswati, the most important of the modern tantric teachers at his Bihar School of Yoga in Bengal. In the early 1980s he founded Beyond Beyond in Los Angeles, California. The Kriya Yoga Tantra Society supersedes Beyond Beyond.

While he has studied with additional tantric teachers, as well as Chinese Taoist masters in Hong Kong, Sunyata believes the kriya tantra tradition to be the purest and most elevating. This tradition is ascribed to Babaji, the legendary Himalayan teacher who Swami Paramahansa Yogananda first introduced to the west in his kriya yoga teachings, though Yogananda did not emphasize the left-hand tantrism as has Sunyata.

According to the society, the goal of tantric practice is to generate intense sexual energy through tactile sensations and yogic practices. That energy (usually termed *kundalini*) is then transmitted to the brain and as the brain comes to life, the individual can perceive the Divine Order.

The society offers a wide variety of programs covering the range of tantric insight, and Sunyata travels the country giving workshops. Retreats are offered at a secluded center in Hawaii. He has also authored a basic text on the art of tantric union.

Membership: Not reported.

Periodicals: *Jyoti.*

Sources:

Rathel, Andre O., and Annette B. White. *Tantra Yoga: The Sexual Path of Inner Joy and Cosmic Fulfillment.* Hollywood, CA: Beyond Beyond, 1981.

Saraswati, Sunyata. *Activating the Five Cosmic Energies.* San Francisco: Kriya Jyoti Tantra Society, 1987.

___, and Bodhi Avinsha. *The Jewel in the Lotus: The Art of Tantric Union.* San Francisco: Kriya Jyoti Tantra Society, 1987.

★2003★
Kundalini Research Foundation
Box 2248
Darien, CT 06820

Alternate Address: International Headquarters: Gemsentra 7, 8006 Zurich, Switzerland.

Gopi Krishna (1903-84) was a Hindu master of kundalini yoga. After seventeen years of meditation, he experienced the kundalini at the age of thirty-four. He spent the years since exploring the nature of kundalini and has produced fourteen books on the subject. In 1970, American Gene Kietter organized the Kundalini Research Foundation to disseminate Gopi Krishna's books and writings and to continue his research.

Kundalini is the name given the divine energy believed to be lodged at the base of the spine. Often pictured as a coiled snake, the awakened energy travels up the spine and remolds the brain. It is identified with prana, the nerve energy which effects altered states of consciousness. The awakened energy is the biological basis of genius. Kundalini, according to Krishna, is concentrated in the sex energy. Awakening the kundalini redirects the prana from the sexual regions to the brain. In the awakening, a fine biological "essence" rises from the reproductive region to the brain through the spinal column. The flow can be felt behind the palate from the middle point of the tongue to the root, and can be objectively measured.

Membership: The foundation is not a membership organization. There are affilated groups in India, Switzerland, and Canada.

Sources:

Irving, Darrel. *Serpent of Fire: A Modern View of Kundalini.* York Beach, ME: Samuel Weiser, 19954. 229 pp.

Krishna, Gopi. *The Awakening of Kundalini.* New York: E. P. Dutton, 1975.

___. *The Biological Basis of Religion and Genius.* New York: Harper & Row, 1972.

—-. *The Goal of Consciousness Research.* Darien, CT: Friends of Gopi Krishna, 1998.

___. *The Riddle of Consciousness.* New York: Kundalini Research Foundation, 1976.

___. *The Secret of Yoga.* New York: Harper & Row, 1972.

___. *The Wonder of the Brain.* Noroton Heights, CT: Kundalini Research Foundation, 1987.

___. *Yoga, a Vision of Its Future.* New Delhi, India: Kundalini Research and Publication Trust, 1978.

★2004★
Light of Sivananda-Valentina, Ashram of
3475 Royal Palm Ave.
Miami Beach, FL 33140

The Ashram of the Light of Sivananda-Valentina was established in the early 1960s by Sivananda-Valentina, a guru whose name came from the experience of merging her consciousness with that of her teacher, Swami Sivanana Saraswati (1887-1963), the famous guru from Rishikish, India. Sivananda taught integral yoga, a combination of the several aspects of yoga with some attention to hatha yoga, the physical postures (or asanas) as preparation for the higher disciplines of yoga.

Sivananda-Valentina followed the integral yoga tradition, stressing particular aspects. For example, she emphasizes the mystical aspect of performing the yoga asanas which makes them more than a therapeutic exercise. She also concentrated on nada yoga, the yoga of sound, and the use of music, and the singing of bhajans (devotional songs) forms an important part of satsangs (student gatherings with their guru).

A weekly round of yoga and meditation classes, informal prayer classes, and Wednesday evening meditation were under-girded with periodic celebrations, many observed from those of the world's religions (Wesak, Christmas, Chanukah, etc.)

Membership: Not reported.

Sources:

The Heart and Wisdom of Sivananda-Valentina. 5 vols. Miami Beach, FL: Light of Sivananda-Valentina, 1970-73.

Sivananda-Valentina. *Meditations at Dawn.* Miami Beach, FL: Light of Sivanada-Valentina, 1977.

Wings of Sivananda-Valentina. Miami Beach, FL: Ashram of the Light of Sivananda-Valentina, 1976.

★2005★
Lokanath Divine Life Fellowship
℅ Mr. Paul Juneja
211 Gunther Ln.
Belle Chase, LA 70037

Alternate Address: Lokanath Divine Life Mission, P-591 Purna Das Rd., Calcutta 700 029, India.

The Lokanath Divine Life Mission was founded in 1987 by Swami Shuddhananda (b. 1949), a swami who has become famous for his social service work in Calcutta, India. Frequently compared to Mother Teresa, he has led in the founding of a variety of schools and medical services, and a number of economic ventures aimed at improving the life of city residents. As a young man, he had had a series of visions of the nineteenth-century saint Baba Lokanath. In the meantime he had become a professor of business at Hyderabad University. He eventually quit his job, wandered in the Himalayas for several years, and then opened the mission, in which he combines the spiritual teaching with social outreach in a manner reminiscent of Swami Sivanada Saraswati of Rishikish, the founder of the Divine Life Society.

In the 1990s, Swami Shuddhananda traveled to the United States to share his spirituality and information about his work in India. A small number of American disciples have begun to appear.

Membership: Not reported.

Sources:

Cushman, Anne, and Jerry Jones. *From here to Nirvana.* New York: Riverhead Books, 1998. 399pp.

★2006★
Ma Yoga Shakti International Mission
114-23 Lefferts Blvd.
South Ozone, NY 11420

The Ma Yoga Shakti International Mission was founded in 1979 by Ma Yoga Shakti Saraswati, an educator, reformer, philosopher, renunciate, and guru, and by her followers considered primarily as a loving mother. Saraswati has traveled internationally and established centers in India, England, and the United States and now spends her time traveling between them. In her teachings, presented in a number of books she has written, she emphasizes the unity of bhakti, gyaan, karma, and raja yoga for self-unfoldment and the adaptability of the ancient wisdom to modern life. Her centers offer regular devotional services, and yoga and meditation classes, workshops, and retreats.

Membership: In 1997 the mission reported 700 members in the two centers in South Ozone, New York, and Palm Bay, Florida. There were five centers in India and one in London.

Periodicals: *Yoga Shakti Mission Newsletter.*

Sources:

Chetanaschakti, Guru. *Guru Pushpanjali.* Calcutta: Yogashakti Mission Trust, 1977.

Yogashakti, Ma. *Yoog Vashishtha.* Gondia, India: Yogashakti Mission, [1970]

Yogashakti Saraswati, Ma. *Prayers & Poems from Mother's Heart*. Melbourne, FL: Yogashakti Mission, 1976

_____, trans. *Shree Satya Narayana Vrata Katha*. Melbourne, FL: Yogashakti Mission, n.d.

★2007★
Mahavidhya, Inc.
(Defunct)

Mahavidhya, Inc. was a small Hindu group which operated in the Midwest from the 1920s through the 1940s. Its leader was Mahasiddha Satchidananda, identified only as a master-teacher and a resident of Kansas City, Missouri. Little is known of the group, only a set of private lessons on *The Mahavidya Philosophy* having survived. The course consisted of 15 lessons on rejuvenation. In addition to a discussion of various points of Hindu philosophy, the lessons offered exercises for the student in breathing, nutrition, concentration, and psychic development.

Sources:

Satchidananda, Mahasiddha. *Private Class Lessons in the Mahavidya Philosophy*. 5 vols. Kansas City, MO: The Author, 1945.

★2008★
Mata Amritanandamayi Center
10200 Crow Canyon Rd.
Castro Valley, CA 94552

Alternate Address: International Headquarters: Mata Amritanandamayi Mission Trust, Vallickavu (Parayakadavu), (Via) Athinad, Quilon Dr., Kerala, India 690 542.

The Mata Amritanandamayi Center was established in 1987 as an outgrowth of the worldwide ministry of Mataji Amritanandamayi (b. 1953), an Indian spiritual teacher. A devoted worshipper of Krishna from childhood, at the age of seven she began to compose *bhajans* (devotional songs) to him. She so completely identified with God, that she was able to manifest any aspect or form of the Diety and would assume the mood of Krishna or Devi in order to facilitate devotion. Gradually during the 1970s, people began to recognize Amritanandamayi as a realized (enlightened) soul and her father gave her the family land upon which to build an *ashram* (religious community). Since 1988, she has built a number of temples, called Brahmastanams or the Abode of the Absolute, in which four dieties are installed as part of a single image representing the principle of the Unity of God.

Amritanandamayi teaches a form of *bhakti*, or devotional practice, built around her singing and meditation. She believes that all religions lead to the same goal; hence, meditation upon any of the prominent deity figures, including Jesus, is acceptable.

In 1987 Amritanandamayi made her first trip to the West, a trip prepared by a small number of Western devotees who had encountered her in India. Following a tour of the United States, she visited France and Switzerland. She makes a similar tour annually.

Membership: In 1997 there were 30 centers in the United States and more than 100 worldwide. Centers may be found across the United States. Additional centers are found in Australia, India, Singapore, Canada, England, France, Italy, Germany, Spain, Belgium, Switzerland, and the Middle East.

Periodicals: *Amritanandam*.

Sources:

Amritanandamayi, Mataji. *Awaken Children!* 2 vols. Vallickavu, Kerala, India: Mata Amritanandamayi Mission Trust, 1989-90.

___. *Bhajanamritam: Devotional Songs*. Vallickavu, Kerala, India: Mata Amritanandamayi Mission Trust, 1987.

Balagopal. *The Mother of Sweet Bliss*. Vallickavu, Kerala, India: Mata Amritanandamayi Mission Trust, 1985.

"Holy Woman Brings the Mother Spirit to the West." *Hinduism Today* 9, no. 4 (July 1987): 1, 15.

★2009★
Matri Satsang
Current address not obtained for this edition.

Matri Satsang is an organization of devotees of Sri Anandamayi Ma (1896-1982), one of the most prominent gurus in twentieth-century India. Born Nirmala Sundari in a Bengali Brahmin family, she had little schooling and was married at the age of 13. Five years later she went to live with her husband. Her husband recognized her as an unusual person; as her mystical nature clearly emerged he became her disciple. Her ecstatic state attracted others, and in 1929 her followers built an *ashram* (religious community) for her. She began to travel widely around India. A second ashram was built at Dehradun, India, in 1932. As the number of ashrams grew, Shree Shree Anandamayee Sangha was formed to administer them.

Anandamayi Ma did not lecture, but would answer questions put to her by seekers. Her writings consisted mainly of letters answering similar inquiries. Excerpts were later gathered into books. Anandamayi Ma supported traditional Hinduism and had no new message. Disciples seem to have been attracted to her because of the awakenings they had in her presence and the wisdom they attributed to her because of her answers to their questions.

Matri Satsang began in 1974 in Sacramento, California, as a point of focus for North American disciples of Anandamayi Ma. A small group, they see their task as supplying the world with materials, primarily those published in India by the Sangha, that communicate Anandamayi Ma's presence through her words and the books of those who knew her. Devotees of Anandamayi Ma are scattered around the world.

Sources:

Anandamayi Ma, Sri. *Matri Vani*. 2 vols. Varnasi, India; Shree Shree Anandamayee Charitable Society, 1977.

___. *Sad Vani*. Calcutta, India: Shree Shree Anandamayee Charitable Society, 1981.

Lipski, Alexander. *Life and Teachings of Sri Anandamayi Ma*. Delhi, India: Motilal Banaridass, 1977.

Matri Darshan: Ein Photo-Album Uber Shri Ananda Ma. Seegarten, Germany: Mangalam Verlag S. Schang, 1983.

Singh, Khushwant. *Gurus, Godmen, and Good People*. New Delhi, India: Orient Longman, 1975.

★2010★
Metamorphosis League for Monastic Studies
4130 SW 117th Ave., Ste. 171
Beaverton, OR 97005

The Metamorphosis League for Monastic Studies was founded in 1987 by Kailasa Chandra Das (birth name, Mark Goodwin), formerly a member of the International Society for Krishna Consciousness (ISKCON). The league was established at a time of intense controversy within ISKCON over the role of the leadership status of those individuals who had been appointed initiating gurus by founder A. C. Bhaktivedanta Swami Prabhupada. The league provides guidance for aspirants so they can come to a point of understanding about the nature of the guru (teacher, spiritual guide) and decide who might be a genuine guru. A bona fide guru must be a self-realized Vaishnava, i.e., a devotee of Vishnu, who has realized the Supreme Personality of Godhead, i.e., Krishna.

Members of the league are advised to avoid both the wild card guru, the charismatic figure whose own personality and personal attributes become the center of attention, and the institutional guru who derives authority from the group in which s/he functions and operates as an agent of the governing body of that institution. The genuine guru, of which Swami Prabhupada is the prime example, derives authority from God, and that authority is manifest in the purity of his/her life.

The league follows the beliefs and practices as transmitted by A. C. Bhaktivedanta Swami Prabhupada. Members must be vegetarians and do not use any intoxicating substances. They cannot be associated with ISKCON or gurus or groups that are considered bogus. Kailasa Chandra Das has published several booklets covering the major emphases of the league.

Membership: In 1995 the league reported nine members.

★2011★
Moksha Foundation
Current address not obtained for this edition.

The Moksha Foundation was founded in 1976 as the Self-Enlightenment Meditation Society by Bishwanath Singh, known by his religious name Tantracharya Nityananda. Nityananda began studying yoga at the age of seven. He became a student of Shrii Anandamurti and eventually served as a monk with the Ananda Marga Yoga Society. In 1969 he realized that he was a siddha yogi in his previous incarnation and that he had been reincarnated in this life to teach meditation and yoga. He left the Ananda Marga Yoga Society and began independent work, eventually establishing centers in India and England. He also renounced his vows as a monk and married.

In 1973 Nityananda moved to Boulder, Colorado, and established the Self-Enlightenment Meditation Society. The center served as a residence for several of his closest students. He taught meditation, tantric yoga philosophy, and lathi, a martial art, and offered personal instruction and initiation for his followers. From his Colorado headquarters, he regularly journeyed to meet with students in Chicago, Minneapolis, New York, and Los Angeles.

In 1981 Nityananda traveled to Europe on a speaking tour. While on the Continent, he was invited to lecture in Sweden. After leaving the plane in Stockholm, he disappeared. His body was found several months later; he had been murdered. Mira Sussman, a resident student at the Boulder center, succeeded to leadership of the foundation and has continued the program initiated by Nityananda.

Membership: Not reported. At the time of Nityananda's death, he had approximately 50 students in Boulder, with other groups in several U.S. cities. The centers previously founded in London and in Bihar, India, continued, and he regularly visited them.

Periodicals: *The Tantric Way.*

★2012★
Moksha Foundation (California)
39 Edison Ave.
Corte Madera, CA 94925

The Moksha Foundation (California) was founded in the late 1980s by Andrew Cohen (b. 1955). Cohen had been raised in a somewhat secular Jewish home. As a teenager, following the death of his father, he moved to Rome to live with his mother. There, at the age of 16, he experienced an extraordinary event of expanded consciousness that initiated a quest in search of someone who could explain the strange occurrence. His search led him to Swami Hariharananda Giri (a master of kriya yoga) and to the practice of martial arts and Zen meditation. Then in 1986, while in India, he met Harivansh Lal Poonja, a disciple of Sri Ramana Maharshi and his teachings of advaita vedanta. Poonja taught that human beings are in reality pure consciousness in the absolute, here and now, always free. Since human beings are already free, there is no need to search for spiritual freedom, merely realize it.

Cohen felt he immediately understood Poonja's message and after only a short time with him, he left his presence to begin teaching, first in Lucknow, India, and then in England. Early in 1987 he taught classes in Holland and Israel and the following year returned to the United States. His work was centered upon a group that began to form in Cambridge, Massachusetts.

In 1989 he moved his work to Marin County, California, where a group of his closest disciples established an intensive communal life that attempted to live out the implication of the freedom they have begun to realize. The group is informally known as the Sangha. The same year Cohen published his first book, *My Master is My Self*, a volume that includes his diary about meeting with and letters to his guru.

Meanwhile, some problems began to become apparent between himself and Poonjaji (the name used affectionately by Poonja's close followers). As Cohen began to teach, he had come to understand that the initial Enlightenment experience served to reveal the Absolute and gave the student a glimpse of his/her potential for liberation. The purpose of the community he formed was to learn to live in such a way that their lives express the Enlightenment. To the contrary, Poonjaji had taught that Oneness had nothing to do with anything manifested in human life. Cohen came to feel that he had surpassed his teacher, a realization he asserts in his second book, *Autobiography of an Awakening* (1992). He now teaches independently of Poonjaji.

Membership: Not reported.

Sources:

Cohen, Andrew. *Autobiography of an Awakening.* Corte Madera: Moksha Foundation, 1992.

___. *My Master is My Self.* Moksha Foundation, 1989.

★2013★
Mother Meera Society
% Meerama
26 Spruce Ln.
Ithaca, NY 14850

Alternate Address: International headquarters: Mother Meera, Oberdorf 4a, D-6255 Dornburg-Thalheim, Germany.

The Mother Meera Society was founded in Canada in the early 1980s by disciples of Mother Meera, an Indian spiritual leader believed by followers to be an incarnation of the Divine Mother, one of several currently present on earth. She was born Kamala Reedy in 1960 in a small village in Andhra Pradesh, in southern India. Her family were not religious people and she was given no religious training and had no guru. However, at the age of six she first entered that trance-like state called samadhi. When she was 14, her uncle and leading disciple, B. V. Reddy, noted her spiritual activities and took her to the ashram of Sri Aurobindo in Ponticherry. She told of receiving visionary guidance from Aurobindo and his colleague, the Mother. As might be expected, she was not accepted by many at the ashram and she left after a short stay and began holding *darshan* (sessions in which she met with her followers) throughout India.

In 1979 she left India with her uncle for Europe and a side trip to Canada, where the initial Mother Meera society was formed. In 1983, due to her uncle's illness, she settled in Thalheim, a small town near Frankfurt, Germany, where she has since resided. He uncle died in 1985. She made her first trip to the United States in May 1989 to attend a conference at Hobart and William Smith Colleges.

Mother Meera describes her work as that of the Cosmic Shakti, to bring down the light of Paramatma to prepare humanity for spiritual transformation. Not known for a specific body of teachings, disciples revere her for the transformations and healings they have experienced in her presence. She offers a simple discipline to people, "Remember the Divine in everything you do. If you have time, meditate. Offer everything to the Divine. Everything good or bad, pure or impure. This is the best and quickest way." Devotion to Mother Meera has especially spread through the writing of Andrew Harvey, a professor at Hobart and William Smith Colleges, who has written a book about his encounter with her in the late 1970s.

Membership: Not reported.

Sources:

Cox, Christine, and Jeff Cox. "Germany's Meera." *Hinduism Today* 11, 4 (April 1989): 1, 18.

Harvey, Andrew. *Hidden Journey*. New York: Henry Holy, 1991.

Mother Meera. *Answers*. Ithaca, NY: Meeramma, 1991. 120 pp.

★2014★
Narayanananda Universal Yoga Trust
% N .U. Yoga Ashram
W. 7041 Olmstead Rd.
Winter, WI 54869

Alternate Address: International Headquarters: N.U. Yoga Ashrama, Gylling, DK 8300 Odder, Denmark.

Narayanananda Universal Yoga Trust was founded by Sri Swami Narayanananda (1929–88) in 1967 in Rishikesh, India. In 1929 he renounced the world, became a monk, and then went to the Himalayas in search of God-realization. After a mental struggle, he attained Nirvikalpa Samadhi (Cosmic Consciousness) in 1933. After this struggle, he remained in seclusion until 1947 when he witnessed the bloodshed between the Hindus and Muslims during the partition of India. He then focused his energies on writing books about religion, philosophy, mind-control, and Kundalini Shakti. He began to work and guide spiritual seekers during the 1950s and 1960s. In 1971 he went to Europe to visit his international headquarters in Denmark.

Narayanananda uses the term "The Universal Religion" for his teachings. This religion is based on his perception of Ultimate Truth and contains both philosophy and practical spiritual advice. It states that there is only one God, which can be comparred to the center of a circle, while the many different religions of the world are like the radii of a circle—all ultimately reaching the same goal. With its motto: "Help a man from where he stands. Supplement but never supplant," it embraces all people irrespective of caste, creed, color, or sex.

The Universal Religion stresses the importance of a moral life, sex sublimation, and mind-control for spiritual growth. It also emphasizes the value of an education, which combines practical, intellectual and ethical training, and it works to promote understanding between the different religions and ideologies of the world.

The religion is of a monastic order as well as lay diciples. The monks and nuns living in the same ashramas (monasteries) follow the teachings of the founder—they combine meditation and mind-control with an active life in society, as well as, earn their own livelihood.

Membership: In 1998 the trust had approximately 30 centers in India, Denmark, Sweden, Norway, Germany, and the United States. There are approximately 5,000 members worldwide.

Periodicals: *Yoga—Magazine for the Universal Religion*.

Sources:

Narayanananda, Swami. *The Mysteries of Man, Mind and Mind Functions*. N.p., n.d.

___. *A Practical Guide to Samadhi*. Rishikish, India: Narayanananda Universal Yoga Trust, 1966.

___. *The Primal Power in Man*. Rishikish, India: Narayanananda Universal Yoga Trust, 1970.

___. *The Secrets of Mind-Control*. Rishikish, India: Narayanananda Universal Yoga Trust, 1970.

___. *The Secrets of Prana, Pranayana, and Yoga-Asana*. Gylling, Denmark: Narayanananda Universal Yoga Trust & Ashrama, 1979.

★2015★
Nityananda Institute, Inc.
PO Box 13310
Portland, OR 97213

Swami Rudrananda (1928-1973), born Albert Rudolph, was a spiritual seeker who had participated in groups following the methods of Georgei Gurdjieff and Subud, and later with the shankaracharya of Puri, prior to traveling to India. There, in 1958, he met Swami Nityananda (d. 1961) and his student Swami Muktananda (1908-1982). In these two swamis he found an end to his quest. He also arranged Muktananda's first visit to America in 1970 and helped launch his movement. However, after studying first with Nityananda and later with Muktananda for fifteen years, he broke with Muktananda in 1971 and founded the Shree Gurudev Rudrananda Yoga Ashram. The teachings followed essentially the Saivite teachings of Nityananda and Muktananda, both of whom emphasized the role of the guru who gave shaktipat to awaken the kundalini. Kundalini is the cosmic power believed to be resting dormant like a coiled snake at the base of the spine. Its awakening allows the power to travel up the spine to the crown of the head, thus producing enlightenment.

Rudrananda founded a string of ashrams across the United States and Europe and wrote one book, *Spiritual Cannibalism*, published within months of his death in an airplane accident. The largest and most substantial remnant of Rudrananda's following was organized under Swami Chetanananda, head of the ashram in Bloomington, Indiana in 1973. Several years later Chetanananda moved his headquarters to Cambridge, Masasachusetts, and in 1993 to Portland, Oregon.

The ashram is a community of disciples living the practical spiritual life under the direction of Swami Chetanandada. The Nityananda Institute is a meditation center whose aim is to make the spiritual life accessible to westerners. The Rudra Press is the publishing arm of the organization.

Membership: There are three centers. In 1997 there were approximately 1600 people involved with the Ashram in Oregon, the center in Massachusetts and in Santa Monica, California. There is also affiliated work in India.

Periodicals: *Rudra*. • Institute News.

Sources:

Chetanananda, Swami. *Songs from the Center of the Well*. Cambridge, MA: Rudra Press, 1983.

Hatengdi, M.U. *Nityananda, the Divine Presence*. Cambridge, MA: Rudra Press, 1984.

Hatengdi, M.U., and Swami Chetanananda. *Nitya Sutras*. Cambridge, MA: Rudra Press, 1985.

Nevai, Lucia. "Rudi, The Spiritual Legacy of an American Original." *Yoga Journal* no. 65 (July/August 1985): 36-38, 68-71.

Rudrananda, Swami. *Spiritual Cannibalism*. New York: Links, 1973.

★2016★
Para-Vidya Center
(Defunct)

The Para-Vidya Center was founded in Los Angeles, California, in the 1930s by Rishi Krishnananda who migrated to America around 1920, just prior to the United States ending immigration from India with Asian exclusion legislation. He taught small numbers of students for a number of years and opened a center in Los Angeles prior to World War II. The center was later relocated to New York City.

Krishnananda tried to adapt the Hindu teachings to a Western audience without losing their essence in the translation. While teaching hatha yoga postures, he also tried to communicate the complete system of yoga as contained in the Upanishads, the Hindu holy books. The goal of life is seen as self-realization, beginning with a consciousness awareness of the Universal Life Principle (i.e., God) which animates life and ending in an union with the Principle. A process of controlled breathing (*pranayana*) and a vegetarian diet was recommended.

There is no indication of how long the center lasted after its move to New York.

Sources:

Krishnananda, Rishi. *The Mystery of Breath*. New York: Para-Vidya Center, n.d.

___. *Yoga Science of Eating*. Los Angeles: Para-Vidya Center, 1941.

Nivenanda, Darha. *Strange Journey*. Los Angeles: Para-Vidya Center, 1941.

★2017★
Poonjaji, Disciples of Harivansh Lal
Satsang Foundation & Press
4855 Riverbend Rd.
Boulder, CO 80301

Harivansh Lal Poonja (1910-1998) (affectionately called Poonjaji by his students), is a teacher of advaita vedanta, the Indian philosophy of nonduality. He was born in 1910 in Gujranwala, India (Pakistan), and grew up in what is now Pakistan. His mother was the sister of Swami Rama Tirtha (d. 1906), an early twentieth-century vedanta teacher who was one of the first Hindu gurus in America. He married and joined the army, but his only interest was in the spiritual life. In 1944 he met Ramana Maharshi (1879-1950) and stayed with him until he was forced to return to his family at the time of the partition of Pakistan. He cared for his family until the last child left home, and then in 1966, he retired and began a period of his life as one who had discovered absolute oneness. He wandered for many years, but finally settled in Lucknow, India.

Poonjaji emphasizes a simple message. Human beings are pure consciousness and hence absolutely free. The spiritual life is not a matter of attaining freedom, but of realizing that one is already free.

Poonjaji met many of the Americans who came to India on spiritual quests beginning in the 1960s. During the 1980s he made several trips to America to teach, but established no permanent work. Then in 1988, Andrew Cohen, one of his students, began teaching in Cambridge, Massachusetts. More recently Cohen has separated from Poonjaji and now heads the Moksha Foundation (California).

In 1990, Antoinette Varner met Poonjaji. Confirming her Self-realization, Poonjaji gave her the name Gangaji and instructed her to carry this message of freedom to the west. Today, Gangaji travels throughout the world holding satsang, and has established Satsang Foundation & Press in Boulder, Colorado, to further the teachings of this lineage to all who are interested.

Membership: Not reported.

Sources:

Ingram, Catherine. "Plunge Into Eternity." *Yoga Journal* (September/October 1992): 56-63.

Poonja, H.W.L. *Wake Up and Roar*. Kula, Maui, HI: Pacific Center Press, 1992.

★2018★
Portal Enterprises
PO Box 1449
Columbia, MD 21044

Portal Enterprises is the teaching vehicle for Sri Akhenaton, a teacher of esoteric spiritual philosophy. Out of his mystical experience, he sees himself as transmitting the Divine Light Energy of the One Infinite Creator to facilitate the awakening of humankind to the God-Consciousness Being. It is also his belief that all things born of creation, not just humans, contain a Light/Life vibration of Divine Consciousness and should be treated accordingly.

Sri Akhenaton offers a series of classes, workshops and weekly spiritual gatherings where he teaches LoveLight Meditation and the practice of Trans-Cultural Consciousness. It is assumed that humans are on an evolutionary journey that includes various incarnations in the earthly realm. Sri Akhenaton seeks to assist people on that journey in such a way as to not interfere with the free will or promulgating eccentric exclusivist doctrines. Rather, he attempts to assist people in discovering their divine nature and their ability to cooperate with their own evolution.

Membership: Not reported.

Sources:

Akhenaton, Sri. *Crystal Communion*. Columbia, MD: Portal Press, 1994.

___. *Discussion of Spiritual Attunement & Soul Evolution*. 2 vols. Columbia, MD: Portal Press, 1992.

___. *Reflections from the Golden Mind*. Columbia, MD: Portal Press, 1994.

★2019★
Prana Yoga Ashram
℅ Swami Sivalingam
International Headquarters
1723 Alcatraz Ave.
Berkeley, CA 94703

The Prana Yoga Student Center was founded by Swami Sivalingam a former in hatha yoga at the Yoga Vedanta Forest Academy established at Rishikish on the Ganges River by Swami Sivananda Saraswati. Sivalingam began his stay at Sivananda's center in 1959. In 1962 he began his international work by bringing the yoga teachings first to Japan and then in Hong Kong, where he established several Sivananda Yoga Centers. He moved to the United States in 1973 and successively founded the Prana Yoga Foundation (1974), the Prana Yoga Ashram (1975), the Prana Yoga Center (1976), and the Ayaodhyanagar Retreat (1977). In 1975 he extended his work to Vancouver, British Columbia. As a result of this work and subsequent travels, he has established a string of centers which ring the globe from India to Japan, to North America to Denmark and Spain.

Sivalingam follows the yogic teachings and practices of Sivananda with an emphasis upon hatha yoga asanas (position) and the practice of pranayama (precise breath control). Through this practice, prana, or energy, is manifested and controlled and leads to purification of the nervous system and inner spiritual balance.

Membership: Not reported. In 1980 there were six centers in the United States and nine centers in other countries.

Periodicals: *Prana Yoga Life*. Send orders to Box 1037, Berkeley, CA 94701.

Sources:

Sivalingam, Swami. *Wings of Divine Wisdom*. Berkeley, CA: Prana Yoga Ashram, 1977.

★2020★
Raj-Yoga Math and Retreat
Current address not obtained for this edition.

The Raj-Yoga Math and Retreat is a small monastic community formed in 1974 by Fr. Satchakrananda Bodhisattvaguru. Satchakrananda began the practice when he experienced the raising of the kundalini, an internal energy pictured in Hindu thought as a snake coiled and resting at the base of the spine that, upon awakening, rises to the crown chakra (psychic center at the top of the head). That event produced an awareness of Satchakrananda's divine heritage. Following that event, he spent a short time in a Trappist monastery, attended Western Washington University, then became coordinator for the Northwest Free University, where he taught yoga. in the early 1970s.

In 1973 Satchakrananda was "mystically" initiated as a yogi by the late Swami Sivananda Saraswati (1887-1963), the founder of the Divine Life Society, through a trilogy of "female Matas" at a retreat he attended on the Olympic (Washington) Peninsula. The following year, with a small group of men and women, he founded the math (monastery). In 1977, he was ordained a priest by Archbishop Herman Adrian Spruit of the Church of Antioch (see separate entry) and has attempted to use both Hindu and Christian traditions at the math. Spiritual disciplines include the regular celebrations of the mass, though the major practice offered is the Jaya Yoga Sadhana, consisting of the sucessive practice of japa (mantra) yoga, meditation, kriyas (cleansings), mudras, asanas (hatha yoga postures), and pranayam (disciplined breathing). Jaya yoga allows practitioners to become aware of their divine nature.

The math is located in the foothills of Mt. Baker overlooking the Nooksuck River near Deming, Washington. It accepts resident students for individual instruction, but offers a variety of retreats/workshops for nonresidents. For those unable to travel to the math for instruction, Satchakrananda has put together a jaya yoga workshop packet.

Membership: The resident community at the math fluctuates between two and twelve. Several hundred individuals are associated with the math through an oblate order of men and women.

Sources:

Letters to Satchakrananda. Deming, WA: Raj-Yoga Math & Retreat, 1977.

Satchakrananda, Yogi. *Coming and Going, The Mother's Drama.* Deming, WA: Raj-Yoga Math & Retreat, 1975.

___. *Thomas Merton's Dharma.* Deming, WA: Raj-Yoga Math & Retreat, 1986.

___. *To Create No Freedom.* Deming, WA: Raj-Yoga Math & Retreat, 1983.

★2021★
Real Yoga Society
Current address not obtained for this edition.

The Real Yoga Society was founded in 1973 by Swami Shiva, a high-caste Hindu teacher from Calcutta, India. In India he had been the editor of a magazine, *Atma-Darshan* (Self-Realization) and a popular speaker on yoga. He was invited to the United States by Dr. J. M. Patel, an Indian-American resident of Chicago, and he began the society shortly after his arrival. A master of hatha yoga, Swami Shiva also taught all of the main forms of yoga—raja, karma, jnana, and bhakti. Yoga is seen as a means to self-realization and enlightenment.

The society florished in the late 1970s, and had centers in Chicago, Oak Park, and Wheaton, Illinois. The society has not been located in the 1980s and its current status is unknown.

Membership: Not reported.

Sources:

Shiva, Swami. *Dawn of Life Through Yoga.* Oak Park, IL: Real Yoga Society, 1975.

★2022★
S. A. I. Foundation
14849 Lull St.
Van Nuys, CA 91405

All religions have had their miracle workers, but Satya Sai Baba (b. 1926) is certainly the most outstanding in India today. The first miracle related to Sai Baba concerned a mysterious cobra found under his bed, proclaiming, say his followers, Sai Baba's role as Sheshiasa, Lord of Serpents. As a child he worked miracles for his classmates, producing objects out of nowhere, a favorite practice still continued.

In 1940, he fell into a coma which lasted for two months. Upon awakening suddenly, he announced, "I am Sai Baba of Shirdi." Sai Baba of Shirdi (1856?-1918) was an Indian holy man who had left behind a large following who still venerated him and observed his teachings. Satya Sai Baba, by his statement, claimed to be his reincarnation. Followers assert his ability to recall conversations between individuals who were disciples of the original Sai Baba.

The thrust of the Sai Baba movement is veneration of Sai Baba and recounting the miracle stories about him. Teachings are mainline Hinduism with emphasis on four aspects-Dharma Sthapana (establishing the faith on a firm foundation), Vidwathposhana (fostering scholarship), Vedasamrakshana (preservation of the Vedas) and Bhaktirakshana (protection of the devotees from secularism and materialism).

The Indian headquarters in Prasanthi Nilayam (Home of the Supreme Peace) are the focus of the Sai Baba movement. Here each Thursday devotees gather for a darshan or vision of Sai Baba. Special darshans are held during the Dasara holidays in October and his birthday celebration in November.

Interest in Sai Baba in America began with a set of lectures given in 1967 at the University of California at Santa Barbara. Movies of Prasanthi Nilayam were shown by Indra Devi, who had recently visited Sai Baba. The movement spread during the 1970s and groups have formed across the United States.

Membership: Not reported.

Periodicals: *Sathya Sai Newsletter.* Send orders to 1800 E. Garvey Ave., West Covina, CA 91791.

Sources:

Brooks, Tal. *Avatar of Night.* New Delhi, India: Tarang Paperbacks, 1984.

Hislop, John. *Conversations with Sathya Sai Baba.* San Diego: Birth Day Publishing Company, 1978.

Lessons for Study Circle. Prasanti Nilayam, India: World Council of Sri Sathya Sai Organizations, n.d.

Manual of Sri Sathya Sai Seva Dal and Guidelines for Activities. Bombay: World Council of Sri Sathya Sai Organizations, 1979.

McMartin, Grace T., ed. *A Recapitulation of Sathya Sai Baba's Divine Teachings.* Hyderabad, India: Avon Printing Works, 1982.

Murphet, Howard. *Sai Baba, Man of Miracles.* New York: Samuel Weiser, 1976.

Sandweiss, Samuel H. *Sai Baba, The Holy Man...and the Psychiatrist.* San Diego, CA: Birth Day Publishing Company, 1975.

★2023★
Saccha Dham Ashram
% Prem
1750 30th St., Ste. 223
Boulder, CO 80301

Alternate Address: International Center: c/o Swami Middha Ji, Tapovan Sari, Tehri-Garhwal 249 192, India.

Saccha Dham Ashram was founded by Maharajji Hans Raj Swami (b. 1924), an advaita vedanta teacher. As a guru, like Ramana Maharshi, he gives few verbal teachings, inviting devotees merely to sit in his presence instead. In the silence they can surrender to the unconditional love of the guru and contact the limitless love of Being itself. The reality of Maharaj, as he is usually referred to by his disciples, was brought to the West in the early 1990s by Shantimayi (b. 1950), an American woman who discovered him and sat at his feet for seven years. These sessions were usually accompanied with a period of chanting and the singing of *bhajans* (holy songs). She was sent to the West as Maharaj's spiritual ambassador, and as a result a number of Europeans and Americans began to find their way to the Indian ashram, and from their visits a community of disciples have begun to appear in the West. These remain small, as the essence of the devotion is sitting in the presence of the guru which can only be done at the ashram in India.

Membership: Not reported.

Sources:

Cushman, Anne, and Jerry Jones. *From Here to Nirvana: The Yoga Journal Guide to Spiritual India.* New York: Riverhead Books, 1998. 399 pp.

★2024★
Sadhana Ashram
Current address not obtained for this edition.

The Sadhana Ashram dates to 1981 and a vision of the Divine Mother to Shankar Das, an American yogi. Shankar Das spent several years in India as a seeker and many of the teachers he met encouraged him to establish an ashram. The Divine Mother told him, "Today I will reveal to you the ashram property." Later that day the farm upon which the ashram now rests was purchased.

Shankar Das teaches an eclectic spiritual perspective drawn from the variety of religious perspectives available in India. He acknowledges inspiration from Sai Baba, Swami Muktananda, Sri Ramakrishna, and Anandamayi Ma, and has concluded that "Many are the Ways," and that any aspect of God represents all aspects. Shankar Das operates as a Mahashakti yoga master and practices *shaktipat,* the stimulation of the kundalini energy believed to lie dormant at the base of the spine of his followers. When awakened, the kundalini travels upward along the spinal column and brings enlightenment.

Daily life at the ashram begins early in the morning with chanting, meditation, and shaktipat. Sunday is dedicated to the Divine Mother (often seen as synonymous with the kundalini energy), and often includes a fire ceremony (*yajna*) and feast. During weekdays, residents scatter to secular jobs in the area, but begin and end the day in spiritual activity. Food is vegetarian.

Membership: Not reported.

★2025★
Saeejis Temple of Peace
5627 Lexington Ave., No. 6
Los Angeles, CA 90038

Saeejis Temple of Peace is a small Hindu organization founded in Los Angeles in 1977 by Govindram T. Lathi. Lathi, an Indian-American teacher, is known by his followers as Gurudev Saeeji, or simply, Saeeji. It is the goal of Saeeji to address the need of modern individuals left without fulfillment in the fast moving technological social world. He offers prayer, meditation, and yoga as the solution to their need.

While a small organization, Saeeji has developed plans for a large retreat center in southern California that will offer the same spiritual atmosphere available at the sacred spots of India.

Membership: Not reported.

★2026★
Sahaja Yoga Center
13659 Victory Blvd., Ste. 684
Van Nuys, CA 91401

Alternate Address: 56 Cedars Ave., Walthamstow, London E17 7QN, England.

Among the fastest growing Eastern movements in the West is the Sahaja Yoga teachings as given by Shri Mataji Nirmala Devi. Born in 1923 into a Christian family in India, she is currently the wife of the retired secretary general of the International Maritime Organization of the United Nations.

Devi's career as a guru grew from her disappointment with some of the other gurus who had come to the West from India. She knew she was born a realized soul, but she sought a means to bring realization to masses of people. In her frustration, on the evening of May 5, 1970, she sat all evening under a bilva tree. During this time her *crown chakra* (believed to be at the top of the head) opened and the *kundalini* force (the cosmic power believed to be

resting like a coiled snake at the base of the spine) began to rise. She then felt ready to begin her work.

Nirmala Devi is believed to be connected with the power of the Life Source. She offers self-realization as the starting point of the spiritual life instead of as the end and goal of the practice of yoga or austerities. When one experiences self-realization, the kundalini energy rises. In her personal appearances Devi attempts to bring self-realization to her audiences. She also offers a meditation technique for those unable to be physically present. The meditation is done before one of her pictures.

From centers in Delhi, India, and London, England, Sahaja Yoga spread, especially in the 1980s. It came to North America in the mid-1980s. Centers have been opened across the United States, and in Toronto, Ontario, and Vancouver, British Columbia, in Canada. In 1989 Devi made her first trip to Russia and Eastern Europe.

Membership: Not reported.

Periodicals: *Nirmala Yoga.* Send orders to 43, Banglow Rd., Delhi 110007, India.

Sources:

Nirmala Devi, Shri Mataji. *Sahaja Yoga.* Delhi, India: Nirmala Yoga, 1982.

"The Russians' Love for Yoga: Nirmala Devi Shares Her Adventure." *Hinduism Today* 12, no. 10 (October 1990): 1, 7.

★2027★
Saiva Siddhanta Church
107 Kaholalele
Kapaa, HI 96746

The Saiva Siddhanta Church, originally known as the Subramuniya Yoga Order was founded by Master Subramuniya (b. 1927), a native of California who traveled to Sri Lanka and in 1949 was initiated by a guru Jnaniguru Yaganathan, more popularly known as Siva Yogaswami. He returned to the United States and spent some years in following his sadhana (spirtiual discipline). Then in 1957 he founded the Subramuniya Yoga Order and opened the Christian Yoga Church in San Francisco. He founded a periodical, *Christian Yoga World,* developed a radio program, the "Christian Yoga Hour," and wrote a correspondance course. Other Christian yoga centers were founded in Redwood City, California and Reno, Nevada and an ashram was opened in Virginia City, Nevada.

During the 1960s, all remnants of Christianity, which had earlier been woven into his teachings, were deleted as the Saivite Hinduism of Subramuniya's guru became dominant. The Subramuniya Yoga Order became first known as the Wailua University of the Contemplative Arts, in 1973 as the Saiva Siddhanta Yoga Order, and in the late 1970s as the Saiva Siddhanta Church.

Teachings of the church are derived from the ancient Saivite scriptures, the Vedas: the Rig, Sama, Yajur and Atharva. They also use the Saiva Agamas, the authoritative explanation of Saivism, and the Tirumantiram, written by Saint Tirumulkar approximately 2,000 years ago. The later volume is written in Tamil (not Sanskrit) and is a summary of Saivism. The teachings have been passed through a lineage of teachers (the Siva Yogaswami Guru Paramparai) to Yogaswami and Subramuniya.

The church is built around the worship of Siva, known as the only Absolute Reality, both immanent and transcendent. Siva is worshiped under the forms of the Siva Lingam, Ardhanarisava (as Siva/Sakti in whom all apparent opposites are reconciled), and Nataraja, the Divine Dancer. Siva created the other deities and the human soul, but not the essence of the soul, which is eternally one with God. This essence is the timeless, formless, spaceless Self—Parasivam. Realization of this self is the ultimate goal of existence. Dharma is Siva's divine law which governs creation.

The soul is immortal but veiled by the bonds of ignorance (anava), consequences of thoughts and deeds (karma), and illusions of matter (maya). In order to continue its spiritual evolution the soul periodically reincarnates in a physical body. It is the human task to follow the established dharma (pattern) in his/her personal and social life. Good conduct, as summarized in the yamas and niyamas of classical yoga, is also encouraged.

The communal life of Saivites is centered in the temples of Siva, considered the abode of the deity. Such a temple has been constructed in Hawaii on land adjacent to the church's headquarters. Here puja, the invocation of Siva and the other deities and an expression of love for Siva, is offered daily. Most homes also have a home shrine where the deity is invoked.

The church is headed by Subramuniya and the Saiva Swami Sangam, the ordained priesthood of swamis. Swamis train for 12 years before qualifying to join the order of sannyasin by taking lifetime vows of poverty, purity, renunciation confidence, obedience, and chastity.

In 1970 land was purchased in Hawaii on the island of Kauai for a temple and headquarters complex. It also houses the theological seminary. One education facility, the Himalayan Academy, attached to the church's San Francisco center, distributes the San Marga Master Course, a correspondance course for new and prospective members, as well as the church's periodical, *Hinduism Today*.

Membership: In 1988 the church reported 500 families as members and 5,000 people as students with various levels of commitment. There were 32 missions in eight countries: the United States, Canada, India, Sri Lanka, Mauritius, Malaysia, Singapore, and Germany.

Educational Facilities: Himalayan Academy, San Francisco, California.

Periodicals: *Hinduism Today*.

Sources:

Saiva Dharma Shastras. Kappa, HI: Siddhanta Press, 1986.

Siva's Cosmic Dance. San Francisco: Himalayan Academy, [1983].

Subramuniya, Master. *Beginning to Meditate.* Kapaa, HI: Wailua University of Contemplative Arts, 1972.

___. *Raja Yoga.* San Francisco: Comstock House, 1973.

___. *The Self God.* San Francisco: Tad Robert Gilmore and Company, 1971.

Subramuniya, Sr. *Gems of Cognition.* San Francisco: Christian Yoga Publications, 1958.

★2028★
Sarva Dharma Sambhava Kendra
Current address not obtained for this edition.

Sarva Dharma Sambhava Kendra was founded in the 1970s in India by Nemi Chand Gandhi (b. 1949), generally known by his religious name Chandra Swami Maharaj. His family moved from his birthplace in Rajasthan to Hyderbad where as a youth Chandra was involved in two popular social movements, one to save the language of Hindi and the other to save the cows, which led to the assassination of a prominent political figure, Gulzarilal Nanda. Shorthly afterwards, he began a spiritual search which took him to Kathmandu where he met and studied with a tantric master. During this time he absorbed the worship of the Indian goddess Durga into his inherited Jain faith. After three years, in 1972, he returned as Chandra Swami.

Soon after his return from Kathmandu, Chandra organized a *yagna* in Madhuban. The goddess Durga is conceived in Indian thought as one of the forms of the consort of Shiva (or Siva). Durga is pictured as the "delighter in blood," and is frequently worshipped with a fire ceremony, yagna, in which animals are sacrificed. (Prior to legal action by the British, the yagna often included a human sacrifice.) Since that first yagna, Chandra has annually organized Durga Puja (worship) at various locations around India. Many of these are attended by famous people and political figures.

In the 1980s Chandra expanded his activities to a number of locations around the world including Fiji, Canada, and the United States, where headquarters were established in Los Angeles, California.

Membership: Not reported.

Remarks: Chandra Swami Maharaj has become famous as the confidant and guru to the rich and powerful. In the United States he has had connections with tennis star John McEnroe, actress Elizabeth Taylor, actor George Hamilton, and U.S. House of Representatives majority leader James Wright. He is a frequent visitor with multimillionaire Arab arms dealer Adnan Khashoggi (one of the participants in the Iran-Contra arms deal in 1986-87), Prince Rainier of Monaco, and numerous political leaders in India.

★2029★
Sarvamangala Mission
% Srividya Center
366 Grapevine Dr.
Diamond Bar, CA 91765

Sarvamangala Mission is a Hindu organization built around the Hindu shakti tradition of Srividya. The mission is under the spiritual direction of Sri Rajagopala Anandanatha, a tantric saint and mystic. He is described by followers as a person who was born by divine dispensation, specially baptized by God at the age of eight, and who attained perfection at the age of 38. His arrival at a state of perfection followed a period of testing and temptations and a period of four years that he spent in prayer without food, drink, or sleep. Having traveled the higher levels of consciousness, he was commissioned by God to cure the sick and lead people to God.

Sri Rajagopala Anandanatha is a devotee of the Divine Mother and calls upon people to follow a path of realization through selfeffort, self-surrender, and worship of the Divine Mother. He teaches that it is possible, no matter how many lifetimes a person has lived, to reach self-realization in this life. Vegetarian food is considered helpful in achieving mental concentration.

The Sarvamangala Mission was established in Southern California during the 1980s.

Membership: In 1995, more than 50 families contributed to support the work of the mission.

Periodicals: *Shakti*.

★2030★
Satsang with Robert
Current address not obtained for this edition.

Robert Adams (b. 1928) is a disciple of the late-guru Ramana Maharshi (1879–1950). At the age of 14, while preparing for a math test, he had a profound mystical experience, a realization that the world was not real. There was only the Self, the immutable, all-penetrating, all-prevailing Source of existence. The visible world was merely a set of images superimposed by the Unchangeable Self on reality. Some time after this life-changing event, he discovered Ramana Maharshi's book, *Who Am I?* Upon seeing the picture of Maharshi, he recognized him as a little man he had seen standing at the end of his bed during his childhood years.

He soon became a disciple of Paramahansa Yogananda and became a monk at the monastery of the Self-Realization Fellowship in Encinatas, California. Yogananda advised him to go to Ramanashram, near Tiruvannamalai, India, and Adams remained with Ramana during the last three years of the guru's life.

For 17 years after Ramana's death, Adams traveled, met with other gurus, and discussed his enlightenment. He has since that time traveled and taught, never staying in one place for very long. In the mid1980s, Adams had a vision of many great teachers coming together and merging like a mountain. He understood the vision as a sign to cease his traveling and take a group of students. He settled in the Los Angeles, California, area and has been teaching since that time.

Membership: Not reported.

Sources:

Adams, Robert. *There Is No Suffering, There Is No Death: Satsang with Robert.* Canoga Park, CA: The Author, 1991.

★2031★
Satyananda Ashrams, U.S.A.
1157 Ramblewood Way
San Mateo, CA 94403

Swami Satyananda Saraswati (b. 1893), a former disciple of Swami Sivananda Saraswati (1887-1963), founder of the Divine Life Society, pioneered the modern opening of the yoga to all, both sannyasins and householders, regardless of sex, nationality, caste, or creed. After working with Sivananda for twelve years, he wandered India for nine more. In 1964, the year after his guru's death, Satyananda founded the Bihar School of Yoga. He built the Sivananda Ashram on the banks of the Ganges and the Ganta Darshan on a hill overlooking the river valley. Satyananda continued Sivananda's broad approach which integrated the various yogic techniques, but gave particular emphasis to tantra. Also, like Sivananda, he actively spread his teachings, first throughout India, and beginning with a world tour in 1968, to the West. During the 1970s he established ten ashrams and many centers in India and outside of India; followers could be found in Australia, Indonesia, Columbia, Greece, France, Sweden, England, and Ireland. As the movement spread, he organized the International Yoga Fellowship.

Satyananda's teachings came to the United States in two separate manners. First, in 1975 Llewellyn Publications, an occult publisher in St. Paul, Minnesota, released a major work by Swami Anandakapila (a.k.a. John Mumford), a leading disciple of Satyananda's in Australia. The publication of *Sexual Occultism* was followed by a United States tour in 1976 and feature articles in *Gnostica*, a major occult periodical. Concurrently with the publication of Anandakapila's book, a New York publisher released *Yoga, Tantra and Meditation* by Swami Janakananda Saraswati, a teacher for Satyananda in Scandinavia. Second, during the 1970s many students of Satyananda migrated to the United States from India, and as their numbers increased they formed small yoga groups. In 1980 Swami Niranjannan Saraswati (b. 1960), a leading teacher with Satyananda who had traveled extensively and organized ashrams for the International Yoga Fellowship, arrived in the United States. On October 28, 1980, he organized Satyananda Ashrams U.S.A., the American affiliate of the International Yoga Fellowship. Niranjananda remained in the United States teaching and organizing local centers. In the summer of 1982, Swami Amritananda, visited the United States. Her visit was followed immediately by Satyananda's first tour of North America.

While it is not the main emphasis of his teachings, Satyananda has become known as an exponent of the so-called left-hand path of tantric yoga. Tantra is built upon the blending and exchange of male and female sexual enengies and consciousness. In left-hand tantra, sexual intercourse is utilized as a means of reaching ananda (or bliss).

The International Yoga Fellowship is one of the largest yoga groups worldwide. Its extensive membership in the United States is somewhat hidden, being largely confined to the Indian-American community.

Membership: Not reported. Membership is estimated to be in the thousands as ashrams and centers may be found across the United States and Canada.

Periodicals: *Yoga.* Available from Bihar School of Yoga, Lal Darwaja, Monghyr 811201, Bihar, India.

Sources:

Janakananda Saraswati, Swami. *Yoga, Tantra & Meditation.* New York: Ballantine Books, 1975.

Mumford, John [Swami Anandakapila]. *Sexual Occultism.* St. Paul, MN: Llewellyn Publications, 1975.

Satyananda Saraswati, Swami. *Sure Ways to Self-Realization.* Munger, Bihar, India: Bihar School of Yoga, 1983.

___. *Taming the Kundalini.* Munger, Bihar, India: Bihar School of Yoga, 1982.

Teachings of Swami Satyananda Saraswati. Mongyar, Bihar, India: Bihar School of Yoga, 1981.

★2032★
Self-Realization Fellowship
3880 San Rafael Ave.
Los Angeles, CA 90065

The Self-Realization Fellowship (SRF) traces its beginning to 1861 and the work of Mahavatar Babaji, who revived and taught kriya yoga. He chose Swami Paramahansa Yogananda (1893-1952) to bring the teachings to the West. Yogananda was trained by Swami Sri Yukteswar (1855-1936) who left to Yogananda his succession and his ashram properties. Yogananda founded the Yogoda Satsanga Society of India in 1917. In 1920, Swami Yogananda came to the United States to attend the Pilgrim tercentenary anniversary of the International Congress of Religious Liberals. Impressed by what he found in America, he decided to stay (one of the last Indians to come into America before the change in immigration laws stopped Asian migration to America), and with those Americans who flocked around him, formed a small center of the Yogoda Satsang in Boston, Massachusetts. From that center he traveled throughout the eastern United States.

In 1924 he made his first transcontinental lecture tour which culminated in the founding of a headquarters for his work on Mt. Washington in Los Angeles, California in 1925. In the later 1920s, he toured the principal cities of the United States as a lecturer and concentrated upon compiling two volumes of inspirational writings: *Whispers of Eternity* (1929) and *Songs of the Soul* (1925). A magazine, *East-West* (now *Self-Realization*), and a course of printed lessons aided the rapid spread of the movement, but nothing was as effective as the personality of Yogananda. Born in India, Yogananda, after his graduation from college, joined the strict Swami Order and became the disciple of Sri Yukteswarji. In 1916, he discovered the techniques of Yogoda, a system of life-energy control for physical and spiritual development, which, combined with traditional yoga, became the central concern of his teachings.

The spread of the work in America led in 1935 to the incorporation of the Self-Realization Fellowship as an international society. In addition to the headquarters in Los Angeles, other centers were opened in Encinatas, San Diego, Hollywood, Long Beach, and Pacific Palisades, California, with smaller groups formed around the country. Yogananda in death was as impressive as in life. His demise was heralded by his disciples as an extraordinary event because of "the absence of any visual signs of decay in the dead body of Paramahansa Yogananda. . .even twenty days after his death," according to a notarized testimony from the Forest Lawn Mortuary in Glendale, California.

The emphasis of the Self-Realization Fellowship is teaching the way to bliss (ananda), or self-realization, or God-realization. The way to bliss is through "definite scientific techniques for attaining personal experience of God." The technique is kriya yoga, a system of awakening and energizing the psychic centers or chakras believed to be located along the spinal column. The basic practice is regular deep meditation which leads to a focusing of spiritual cosmic energies which leads to a direct perception of the Divine. By the practive of kriya yoga, blood is decarbonized and recharged with oxygen, the atoms of which are transmuted into "life current" to rejuvenate the brain and spinal centers.

The essential unity of Eastern and Western religious teachings is also stressed by SRF. To highlight this emphasis, lecture services include interpretations of parallel scriptural passages from the

New Testament and the *Bhagavad Gita*. Readings are also given from Paramahansa Yogananda's *Autobiography of a Yogi*, considered a modern spiritual classic, which has remained in print since its publication in 1946 and is widely used as a text book and reference work in colleges and universities around the world. Worship centers on the inner communion (meditation) practices of Yogananda. Followers can study his teachings in depth through the many books of his lectures and writings that have been published as well as through a series of lessons for home study.

Yogananda was succeeded by Swami Rajarsi Janakananda (James J. Lynn). Lynn died in 1955 and was succeeded by Sri Daya Mata, the present head of the fellowship.

Membership: In 1998 the fellowship reported nine temples and ashram centers: six in California and one each in Phoenix, Arizona; Front Royal, Virginia; and Nuremberg, Germany. There are also an additional 172 centers and meditation groups in the United States and 220 in 47 other countries. The Yogoda Satsang Society of India had 100 centers and operated a variety of charitable facilities.

Educational Facilities: There are four Yogoda Satsanga Society colleges in India: one each in Suraikhet and Palpara, and two in Ranchi.

Periodicals: *Self-Realization*.

Sources:

Mata, Sri Daya. *Only Love*. Los Angeles: Self-Realization Fellowship, 1976.

New Pilgrims of the Spirit. Boston: Beacon Press, 1921.

Self-Realization Fellowship Highlights. Los Angeles: Self-Realization Fellowship, 1980.

Self Realization Fellowship Manuel of Services. Los Angeles: Self-Realization Fellowship, 1965.

Yogananda, Paramahansa. *Autobiography of a Yogi*. Los Angeles: Self-Realization Fellowship, 1971.

___. *Descriptive Outlines of Yogoda*. Los Angeles: Yogoda Satsang Society, 1928.

★2033★
Self-Revelation Church of Absolute Monism
4748 Western Ave. NW
PO Box 9515
Washington, DC 20016

Several movements have grown out of the work of Swami Paramahansa Yogananda's disciples. The Self-Revelation Church of Absolute Monism is an independent church founded by Swami Premananda, who had been called from India by Yogananda in 1928. It now operates independently of the Self-Realization Fellowship. Besides the tradition of Kriya Yoga (self-realization) as taught by Premananda, the life and work of Gandhi are stressed, and the Mahatma Gandhi Memorial Foundation operates as an affiliate educational and cultural center. Swami Premananda established the Swami Order of Absolute Monism for those who wish to follow the ideals of advaita vedanta. The current leader of the church and the Ghandi Memorial Center is Srimata Kamala. She was ordained a minister in the Swami Order in 1973, and a swami in 1978.

Membership: No formal membership. In 1995, there was one center in Washington, D.C., two other centers in the United States, and a mission in Midnapur, West Bengal. There are four ministers.

Educational Facilities: The Gandhi Memorial Center administers a correspondence course on Mahatma Gandhi which is received as independent study credit at American colleges. The course leads to a certificate from the Gujarat Vidyapith, the university founded by Gandhi in 1920.

Periodicals: *The Mystic Cross*. • *The Gandhi Message*.

Sources:

Premananda, Swami. *Light on Kriya Yoga*. Washington, DC: Swami Premananda Foundation, 1969.

___. *The Path of the Eternal Law*. Washington, DC: Self-Realization Fellowship, 1942.

___. *Prayers of Self-Realization*. Washington, DC: Self-Realization Fellowship, 1943.

★2034★
Shanti Mandir
Box 1110
Pine Bush, NY 12566

Alternate Address: International Headquarters: c/o Greenfield School, A/Z Safdarjung Enclave, New Delhi 110029, India.

Before Swami Muktanandas death in 1982 he picked a brother/sister team, Swami Nityananda and Swami Chidvilasananda, to succeed him. For three years they coadministered the large global organization, Siddha Yoga Dham, that Muktananda had built. However, the apparent stability of the transition was soon disrupted by controversy and accusations, and in 1985 Swami Nityananda withdrew from Siddha Yoga Dham, renounced his vows as a sannyasin, and entered private life as a teacher of meditation in California.

On December 26, 1989, with a dip in the near freezing water of the Ganges River at Haridway, Nityananda reaffirmed his sannyas vow and his commitment to Muktananda and to do God's work. In July 1987, he founded Shanti Mandir (Temple of Peace) and began holding meditation retreats and other programs in America, Europe, Australia, and India. A lengthy period of conflict and harassment followed as members of Siddha Yoga Dham challenged his authority.

In May 1995 the Mahamandaleshwars in Haridwar, a network of spiritual leaders who act as advisors to the governing bodies of their respective regions, inducted him into their association in a ceremony at Suratgiri Bangla in Haridwar. Swami Nityananda, at the age of 32, became history's youngest Mahamandaleshwar.

Swami Nityananda continues the teachings of Swami Muktananda, offering Meditation Intensives designed for initiation, while emphasizing chanting as a powerful meditation practice and encouraging his followers to see all life as a manifestation of God's energy.

Membership: Not reported. Centers are found in India, Germany, and Australia.

Sources:

"Nityananda, One of Swami Muktananda's Successors, 'Retakes' Sannyasin Vows." *Hinduism Today* 12, 4 (April 1990).

★2035★
Shanti Temple
43 S. Main St.
Spring Valley, NY 10977

The Shanti Temple is a Hindu center founded in the 1980s by Swami Shantanand Saraswati. Swami Shantanand teaches a simple way centered upon regulation of the self, selfless service, and awareness. Awareness is attained through a seven-stage path of self-realization. The stages begin with *shubhechchha* (good desire), *suvicharana* (discrimination between the unreal and real), and *tanumansa* (steadfastness of mind). In the third stage, the practice of concentration begins the process of the development of detachment. In the fourth stage, *sattwapatti* (self-realization), one realizes the self as the Light of Pure Awareness, the non-judgmental observer of the mind. The fifth stage, *asansakti* (detachment) is a new level of detachment above ego, right and wrong, pride, and humility. The sixth stage, *padarthabjavni*, brings the ego into attunement with Spirit and leads to the final stage, *turyaga*, where the ego is completely immersed in Spirit.

The Shanti Temple operates out of a single center in Spring Valley, New York. Swami Shantanand is the author of several books.

Membership: Not reported.

Sources:

Shantanand Saraswati, Swami. *The Challenge of Wisdom.* Spring Valley, NY: Shanti Temple, 1987. 59 pp.

★2036★
Shanti Yoga Institute and Yoga Retreat
943 Central Ave.
Ocean City, NJ 08226

The Shanti Yoga Institute and Yoga Retreat was founded in 1974 by Shanti Desai. Yogi Desai became a disciple of Swami Kripalvanandji at a young age and was initiated at age 15. He came to the United States to pursue graduate studies in chemistry at Drexel University, earning his master's degree in 1964. In 1972 he left his job as a chemist to devote his life to teaching yoga. He returned to India and received shaktipat initiation from his guru. Upon his return to America he founded the Shanti Yoga Institute of New Jersey. In 1974 he opened the Yoga Retreat in Ocean City, New Jersey, and in 1981 he opened Prasad, a holistic health food store and restaurant. Shanti has published four books, an instructional yoga video, and a two-volume audio casette of *Healing Mantra Chants.* Shanti designed his instruction of yoga for a Western audience and has trained several thousand students and a number of yoga teachers.

Membership: In 1995, there was one center in New Jersey.

Remarks: Shanti Desai is the brother of Amrit Desai, founder of the Kirpalu Yoga Fellowship.

Sources:

Desai, Yogi Shanti. *The Complete Practice Manual of Yoga.* Ocean City, NJ: Shanti Yogi Institute, 1976.

★2037★
Shiva-Shakti Kashmir Shavite Ashram
Current address not obtained for this edition.

The Shiva-Shakti Kashmir Shavite Ashram is a small Hindu group that emerged around the leadership of Swami Savitripriya. Beginning in 1968, Swami Savitripriya had a series of mystical experiences that led her in the mid-1970s to proclaim herself a siddha guru of the highest level. She began to teach what she called Maha Siddha Yoga and to bring together a closely knit group of disciples who worked together as monks and nuns. During the 1980s they founded an ashram in Groveland, California.

The movement ran into some conflict in 1990 when the Siddha Yoga Dham challenged Swami Savitripriya's use of the term "Maha Siddha Yoga," as Siddha Yoga Dham had claimed ownership on the term "siddha yoga." The conflict was part of a larger conflict within Hindu circles over the trademarking of various terms common to Hinduism that had been pioneered in America by one particular organization. At last report the issue remains unresolved.

Membership: Not reported

Educational Facilities: Holy Mountain University, Groveland, California.

Sources:

"Privitizing Public Domain Yoga Terms." *Hinduism Today* 12, 11 (November 1990): 1, 23.

Savitripriya, Swami. *From Darkness to Light: My Autobiography.* Sunnyvale, CA: New Life Books, n.d.

___. *Psychology of Mystical Awakening.* Sunnyvale, CA: New Life Books, 1991.

★2038★
Shri Krishna Association of the U.S.A.
Current address not obtained for this edition.

The Shri Krishna Association of the U.S.A. is the American representative of the Pranami religion, a form of Hinduism that originated in India in the sixteenth century in the midst of the conflict between Hindus and Muslims. It was founded by Shri Prannath, a government official in the state of Jamnagar during the reign of Aurangzeb, a Muslim. In response to Aurangzeb's launching an evangelistic campaign that was disrupting the Hindu community, Prannath resigned his post and dedicated his life to saving Hinduism. He preached a monotheistic form of faith that rejected the many Hindu gods and goddesses in favor of Krishna, whom he believed to be the only god. Based upon his monotheism, he called for a reproachment between Hindus and Muslims.

The Pranamis have a holy book, *Tartam Sagar,* composed of some 18,000 verses written by Prannath. It draws on concepts from the *Bhagavad Gita,* the *Koran,* and other scriptures. The movement took hold in Jamnagar and eventually spread across India into Nepal.

The Pranami religion was initially brought to the United States in the 1970s by immigrants. Followers can now be found in most of the major urban areas with a significant Indian-American population, including Los Angeles, Houston, Chicago, Detroit, and Atlanta. There are also followers in Canada.

Membership: Not reported. The movement claims some four million followers and 400 temples in India and Nepal.

Sources:

Dongre, Archana. "Int'l Conference of Pranami Religion Held." *India-West* (July 3, 1992).

★2039★
Shri Ram Chandra Mission
Rte. 1, Box 122-5, Hwy. 109
Molena, GA 30258

Alternate Address: International Headquarters: c/o Gayathri, 19 North St., Sri Ram Nagar, Madras, 600 018, India.

Shri Ram Chandra Mission (India) was established in 1945 by His Holiness Shri Ram Chandraji Maharaj of Shahjahanpur, (U.P.), popularly known as "Babuji." The mission was founded in memory of Babuji's master, Samarth Guru Mahatma Shri Ram Chandraji Maharaj of Fatehgarh, (U.P.), who is affectionately known as "Lalaji." Its objectives are: To educate and propagate amongst the masses the art and science of yoga, made to suit present day conditions and needs; to promote the feelings of mutual love and universal brotherhood, irrespective of any distinction of caste, creed, color, etc.; to conduct research in the field of yoga and establish research institutes for that purpose; and to encourage research in yoga, including the granting of assistance to persons interested in carrying out this work.

Ram Chandra was born on April 30, 1899, at Shahjahanpur, to a Kayastha family, the son of a scholar. He was not an outstanding student but by his teen years had developed an interest in philosophy, literature, and geography. In his secular life, he joined the Court and retired after 30 years of service in 1954. He eventually found his way to Shri Ram Chandraji of Fategarh, (U.P.), who taught an old and forgotten method of "Pranahuti" (Divine Transmission) previously used by yogis in ancient times. He commenced his spiritual training of Abhyas under his guidance and gave up the practice of pranayama which he had been doing for the previous seven years.

When his guru died in 1931, Ram Chandra felt that his guru had transmitted to him everything he was. He had a sense of complete mergence of his guru into him. In 1932 he received further transmission from his guru master which he was not able to bear fully, and he was overfilled with Divine Energy. He gave the guru credit in 1944 when he had the vision of a light like that which

Moses saw and also Shri Krishna's Viratsvarupa. Shri Ram Chandra Mission was founded to carry out the mission of his master.

Shri Ram Chandraji Maharaj died on April 19, 1983. He was succeeded by his disciple, Shri Parthasarathi Rajagopalachari of Chennai, the current president of Shri Ram Chandra Mission. Affectionately known as "Chariji," Shri Parthasarathi Rajagopalachari was born in 1927 in a village called Vayalur near Madras. He graduated from Benaras Hindu University with a B.S. degree and found employment with Indian Plastics Limited in chemical engineering. He rose to an executive position with the T. T. Krishnamachari group of companies in Bombay, with whom he stayed until his retirement in 1985. In the meantime, his conscious spiritual aspirations were awakened at the age of 18 after hearing a lecture on the Bhagavad Gita. He discovered Shri Ram Chandraji Maharaj in 1964, and both he and his father accepted him as their new guru after hearing about this system of raja yoga. In recent years Chariji has traveled extensively worldwide. He regularly conducts public seminars, where he gives instruction on the Sahaj Marg system of meditation. During the past several years these seminars have been held in various cities around the world, including North America.

The way of Sahaj Marg is embodied in the "Ten Maxims" which lay out a daily schedule for the disciples. They rise before dawn to offer worship (*puja*) that begins with a prayer for spiritual elevation. Daily the disciple's goal is complete oneness with God. They strive to live a truthful, plain, and simple life and treat all people as their brothers and sisters. They eschew revenge and live out of gratitude so as to arouse feelings of love and piety in others. The day is ended in a feeling of the presence of God and the asking for forgiveness for any wrongs committed.

Membership: The mission has several hundred centers in India and numerous countries around the world. The training is imparted by the president of the mission and more than a thousand trainers, called preceptors, who are spread throughout the world.

Periodicals: *Sahag Marg Magazine*, SRCM Danmark, Vrads Sande, Vej4, 8654 Bryrup, Denmark.

Sources:

http://wwwsrcm.org/.

Ram Chandra. *Autobiography of Ram Chandra.* 2 vols. Shahjahanpur, India: Shri Ram Chandra Mission, 1974, 1986.

___. *Complete Works of Ram Chandra.* Vol 1. Pacific Grove, CA: North American Publishing Committee, 1989.

★2040★
Shri Shivabalayogi Maharaj Trust
℅ Sally Moburg
724 Fellowship Rd.
Santa Barbara, CA 93109

Alternate Address: Shri Shivabalayogi Maharaj Trust, J. P. Nagar, Bangalore 560 078, India

The Shri Shivabalayogi Maharaj Trust dates back to 1961 and completion of a period of austerity for Bala Yogi that led to his self-realization. Bala Yogi was born in 1935 in Adivarapupeta, a village in Andhra Pradesh, to a poverty-stricken family. As a child he went to work as a weaver of baskets. He also began a successful cigarette business. His commercial endeavors were blocked when, at the age of fourteen, he had an intense experience of the divine light, jyoti, and he heard the sound of Om, the basic creative sound of the universe. A person identified as Jangam Shiva, a Hindu deity, appeared before him and he went into a mystical state of consciousness, samadhi.

The experience changed the course of Bala Yogi's life. He began a period of intense meditation and austerity, which lasted for twelve years, and on August 7, 1961, he emerged as a sadhu (saint). He began a mission that consisted of holding darshan (vision of the realized person), giving consecrated Vibhuti (ash) for

healing of body and mind, and kirtan (singing). He offered no new teachings to his disciples but initiated them into dhyana diksha (concentrated meditation). In his presence, or the presence of his picture, disciples normally gather to sit in meditation, receive some holy ash, and move into a period of spontaneous singing and dancing while in an ecstatic prayerful state.

Bala Yogi founded two ashrams in Bangalore and others in additional Indian communities, including his home town. In the late 1980s he established his first Western center in London and moved to the United States, with early centers established in Portland, Oregon; Raleigh, North Carolina; and Santa Barbara, California.

Membership: Not reported.

Sources:

Bala Yogi Maharaj, Shri Shiva. *Life and Spiritual Ministration.* Bangalore, India: Shri Shivabalayogi Maharaj Trust, n.d. 128 pp.

___. *Spiritual Essence and Luminescence.* Bangalore, India: Shri Shivabalayogi Maharaj Trust, n.d. 18 pp.

"Shiva's Own Bala Yoga." *Hinduism Today.* 12, 8 (August 1990): 1, 25.

★2041★
Sivananda Yoga Vedanta Centers
673 8th Ave.
Val Morin, PQ, Canada J0T 2R0

Alternate Address: International affiliate: (unofficial) Divine Life Society, P.O. Shivanandanagar, Dist. Tehri-Garwal, Uttar Pradesh, India.

The Sivananda Yoga Vedanta Centers are the North American work founded by Swami Vishnu Devananda (b. 1927), the North American representative of the late Swami Sivananda Saraswati (1887-1963), who was sent to the West in 1957.

History. Swami Sivananda Saraswati (born Kuppuswami Iyer) was one of several renowned Hindu teachers to arise in this century and become revered as a saint and holy man. Reared by devout parents who encouraged his education, he began a medical course of study, cut short by the death of his father. He moved to Malaysia as a hospital administrator, but after ten years, in 1923, he returned to India to pursue a spiritual quest. He was initiated as a *sannyasin*, a follower of the renounced life, and settled at Swargashram, near Rishikish, where many sanyassins lived. He began to write, teach, and make pilgrimages around India. He advocated a life of devotion (bhakti yoga) and service (karma yoga).

Unwilling to forget the life of service upon which he had embarked as a youth, he moved to Rishikish and established an ashram. As part of the ashram facility, he opened a medical dispensary to serve the local community. By 1936 the work had grown considerably. He formed the Divine Life Trust and the Divine Life Society, an open membership auxiliary. The dispensary grew into a major medical facility and the ashram became a prime center for the propagation of yoga. It soon attracted many of the best teachers from throughout India.

Sivananda's teaching is summarized in the motto, "serve, love, give, meditate, purify, realize." He led his students upon a *sadhana* (path to enlightenment) which included bhakti (practicing love) and ahimsa (constant striving to do no harm and cause no pain). He developed a synthesis of yoga, which he call integral yoga and which included the four traditional forms of bhakti, jnana, karma, and raja, to which he added a fifth, japa (repetition of a mantra).

Sivananda never visited North America, but he sent several of his students. As early as 1959, Swami Chidananda, his succesor as leader of the ashram in India, visited the United States. Even before Sivananda's death his student began to establish work outside of India. Sivananda sent Swami Vishnu Devannada to work in Canada and the United States. While other students of Sivananda have also come to the United States, Vishnu Devananda is the teacher recognized by the Divine Life Society in India.

Swami Vishnu Devananda (1927-1993) was originally attracted to Swami Sivananda by reading his books and formally became his disciple in 1947. In 1949 at the Sivanandashram in Rishikish, Sivananda initiated him into the ancient sannyasin order of the renounced life, and Vishnu Devananda, through his studies and practice of the rigorous spiritual disciplines, went on to become one of Sivananda's most accomplished pupils. He came to the west in 1957 at Sivananda's direction. He founded several centers in the United States before settling permanently in Canada the following year. He established his North American headquarters in Montreal.

Beliefs. Swami Vishnu Devananda follows the teachings of Sivananda. He emphasizes the benefits of a rigorous spiritual discipline, and has focused upon raja and hatha yoga. He also shared the complete yoga teachings of his teacher.

Organization. The Sivananda Yoga Vedanta Ashrams are headed by Vishnu Devananda, and the various centers are headed by teachers trained by him. In 1962 he founded the Sivananda Ashram Yoga Camp in the Laurentian Mountains of Quebec and in 1967 the Sivananda Ashram Yoga Retreat in the Bahamas, both of which provide intensive yoga training in a vacation-like setting. He has established ashrams (sanctuaries for the systematic practice of yoga for residents) in Val Morin, Quebec; Woodburne, New York; Grass Valley, California; and Trivandrum, India. Other foreign work is located in Austria, France, Germany, Great Britain, Israel, Spain, Switzerland, and Uruguay.

The True World Order, Vishnu Devananda's continuing world peace and brotherhood mission, was founded in 1969. To demonstrate his concern for peace and the importance of the non-violent struggle for peace, he has flown around the world dropping leaflets and organizing peace demonstrations at designated trouble spots. He conducted one famous peace mission to Belfast, Northern Ireland, with the late actor Peter Sellers. He also has showered the Suez Canal and the Berlin Wall with leaflets and flowers.

Membership: Not reported. In 1992 there were 14 centers (including two ashrams) in the United States and four (including one ashram) in Canada. In addition, several thousand followers have been trained as yoga teachers and are now active in a wide variety of locations apart from the Sivananda Yoga Vedanta Centers. Vishnu Devananda's book, *The Complete Illustrated Book of Yoga*, has sold over three million copies.

Periodicals: *Yoga Life.* Available from Sivananda Yoga Vedanta Center, 243 W. 24th St., New York, NY 10011.

Remarks: Among the disciples of Sivananda was Swami Venkatesananda, who established work in Australia and South Africa. During the 1980s, the Chiltern Yoga Foundation was established in San Francisco, California for the sole purpose of publishing and distributing Swami Venkatesananda's books in the United States and Canada.

Sources:

Behera, Sarat Chandra. *The Holy Stream, The Inspiring Life of Swami Chidananda.* Sivanandanagar, India: Divine Life Society, 1981.

Devananda, Swami Vishnu. *The Complete Illustrated Book of Yoga.* New York: Julian Press, 1960.

___. *The Hatha Yoga Pradhipika.* N.p., n.d.

___. *Meditation and Mantras.* New York: OM Lotus Publishing Company, 1978.

___. *The Sivananda Upanishad.* New York: OM Lotus Publishing Company, 1987.

Krishna, Copala. *The Yogi: Portraits of Swami Vishnu-devananda.* St. Paul, MN: Yes International Publishers, 1995. 149 pp.

Sivananda, Swami. *Sadhana.* Sivanandanagar, India: Divine Life Society, 1967.

The Sivananda Yoga Center. *The Sivananda Companion to Yoga.* New York: Simon & Schuster, 1983.

Tawker, K. A. *Sivananda, One World Teacher.* Rishikish, India: Yoga-Vedanta Forest University, 1957.

Venkatesananda, Swami. *Gurudev Sivananda.* Durban, South Africa: Divine Life Society of South Africa, 1961.

★2042★
Society of Abidance in Truth
1834 Ocean St.
Santa Cruz, CA 95060

The Society of Abidance in Truth (SAT), founded in the mid-1970s is consecrated to the Teaching of Nonduality especially as revealed by Bhagavan Sri Ramana Maharshi, the great south Indian sage who flourished (1879–1950) at the holy mountain called Arunachala. SAT is under the spiritual guidance of Nome, with a background influence of Advaita Vedanta and Russell Smith with a background in non-dual Ch'an (Zen) Buddhism.

The Teaching of Non-Duality proclaims that the true nature of the Self, ones own Being or Consciousness, is that of the Absolute (ie., God, Brahman, Buddha nature, etc.) It proclaims that the Self, of the nature of undivided Being-Consciousness-Bliss, is infinite and eternal, verily the one reality, that both pervades and transcends all. This teaching places special emphasis on self-knowledge, attained by inquiring "Who am I?," which reveals the real Self, and which eliminates the illusion of a separate ego to reveal the homogeneous, infinite presence of Reality. The resultant experience is Self-realization, characterized by permanent peace and happiness.

The teaching has its roots in the *Upanisads*, the wisdom portion of the *Vedas*, the oldest and original scriptures of Hinduism (also called "Sanatana Dharma—the Way of Eternal Truth"). This teaching was also expounded by Sri Sankaracharya, the 8th-century Indian sage, as well as in numerous scriptures and sayings of many sages and saints of this tradition. It also has roots in non-dual Buddhism, as exemplified by the Ch'an Master of China during the T'ang Dynasty.

SAT endeavors to preserve and disseminate this supreme wisdom through its activities. These include maintaining a center in Santa Cruz, California, where seekers can imbibe the teaching, practice it, and realize self-knowledge. Other activities include the distribution of every book in English of or about Sri Ramana Maharshi; the distribution of Vedanta and Ch'an literature; and the translation and publication of books such as the *Ribbu Gita* (ancient treatise on nondual Truth), Sri Sankaras works, and teachings given by Nome and Russell Smith. SAT also conducts weekly Satsangs and other holy events, retreats, and a profusion of performances of sacred music from around the world, for which it has received international acclaim as well.

Membership: As of 1997, SATs membership was sprinkled worldwide, but is predominantly located in the Santa Cruz, California, area.

Periodicals: *Reflections.*

Sources:

The Journey Home. Santa Cruz, CA: Avadhut, 1986.

Maharshi's Gospel. Tiruvannamalai, India: T. N. Venkataraman, 1957.

Spiritual Instruction of Bhagavan Sri Raman Maharshi. Tiruvannamalai, India: T. N. Venkataraman, 1939.

★2043★
Sonorama Society
(Defunct)

The Sonorama Society was formed after the first trip at Maharishi Mahesh Yogi to the United States in 1959 and was devoted to the Maharishi's guru, the late Swami Brahmananda Saraswati Maharaj, the illustrious Jagad-Guru Bhagawan of Jyotir-Math, Bhadrikashraman, India. At the age of nine, Swami Saraswati Maharaj began a forty-year exploration of inner consciousness that allowed him to rediscover the mental technique (transcendental meditation) and become leader of the Shankaracharya Order. He is seen as the perfect master.

The Society was formed as an association of persons who are practicing transcendental meditation. Sonorama Society members were tied together by correspondence lessons and irregular contact with those who have mastered the techniques. Headquarters were established in Los Angeles under the leadership of R. Manley Whitman, the sponsor-director. The society lasted only a few years; its work was superceded by the growth of the TM movement, now organized by the World Plan Executive Council.

★2044★
Sri Chaitanya Saraswat Mandal
℅ Guardian of Devotion Press
2900 N. Rodeo Gulch Rd.
Soquel, CA 95073

Prior to the passing of A. C. Bhaktivedanta Swami Prabhupada (1896-1977), founder-acharya of the International Society for Krishna Consciousness (ISKCON) (the Hare Krishna movement in the west), he informed his senior disciples that in his absence, should the necessity arise, they should consult a higher authority. He instructed them to approach his trusted and revered godbrother Bhakti Raksaka Sridhara Deva Goswami. (By godbrother it is meant that they were both initiated by the same guru.) Both Prabhupada and Sridhara were initiated by Bhaktisiddanthanta Sarswati Thakur, the president-archarya of the Guadiya Math, which had been the main Krishna Consciousness organization in Bengal. In the wake of the disruption of the Guadiya Math in India, Sridhara was one of several disciples who had founded an independent organization, Sri Chaitanya Saraswati Math.

In the wake of Prabhupada's death, intense theological and organizational disputes emerged within the society and its governing board. Some of Prabhupada's disciples, following his instructions, turned to Sridhara for guidance and subsequently broke with the society and founded Sri Chaitanya Saraswat Mandal as an American branch of the Math.

Since its founding in the early 1980s, the Mandal has carried on an active publishing program through its Guardian of Devotion Press, which has issued many of Sridhara's books.

Membership: There is one temple affiliated with the mandal with approximately 100 members. Affiliated centers are also found in England, Mexico, Brazil, Venezuela, South Africa, Italy, Holland, Austria, Hungary, and Australia.

Sources:

Sridhara Deva Goswami, Bhakti Raksaka. *Parpanna Jivanamrta: Lifenectar of the Surrendered Souls.* Nabadwip Dham, West Bengal, India: Sri Chaitanya Saraswat Math, 1988.

___. *The Search for Sri Krsna, Reality the Beautiful.* San Jose, CA: Guardian of Devotion Press, 1983.

___. *Sri Guru and His Grace.* San Jose, CA: Guardian of Devotion Press, 1983.

___. *Subjective Evolution of Consciousness: Play of the Sweet Absolute.* San Jose, CA: Guardian of Devotion Press, 1988.

Thakura, Bhaktivinoda. *The Bhagavat: Its Philosophy, Its Ethics, and Its Theology.* San Jose, CA: Guardian of Devotion Press, 1985.

★2045★
Sri Chinmoy Centre
Box 32433
Jamaica, NY 11432

Sri Chinmoy Kumar Ghose, born in Bengal, India in 1931, entered the Sri Aurobindo Ashram at the age of 12. After two decades of intense spiritual discipline, he responded to an inner command and came to the West in 1964 to be of service to seekers in the West. He teaches a path of yoga that directs the practitioner to conscious union with God. He also encourages an active, dynamic life of service to the divine in humanity. His path calls for a disciplined life involving regular meditation, living and working in the world, vegetarianism, and celibacy.

As a spiritual teacher, Sri Chinmoy guides his students meditative discipline and spiritual growth. He never charges any fee for his service, and teaches that the path of love, devotion (bhakti) and surrender to God is the easiest way to God, but he accepts all religions and has the utmost devotion for Christ, Buddha, Krishna and the other great religious figures of the world. He encourages athletics as a means to the illumination of the physical consciousness, and his centres around the world have sponsored many running events. Among other activities, his students sponsor the Sri Chinmoy Oneness–Home Peace Run, a 70-nation relay run for the cause of world peace that has been held every other year since 1987.

Sri Chinmoy is a prolific author, composer and artist. He has written more than 1,300 books of poetry, essays and questions and answers and composed over 13,000 devotional songs in English and his native Bengali. He has also completed more than four million "soul-bird" drawings, depictions of the human spirit in the form of birds, which have been exhibited worldwide. Often described as an international ambassador of peace, he has offered hundreds of meditative concerts to the cause of world peace and has discussed peace with dozens of world leaders.

Inspired by his activities, authorities around the world have dedicated natural wonders or other sites to the cause of peace in his name. Among the worlds "Sri Chinmoy Peace-Blossoms," as these sites are collectively referred to, are the capital cities of Ottawa, Canada; Canberra, Australia; and Auckland, Australia; the Swiss Matterhorn mountain, Viet Nams Meklong Delta, Canadas Niagara Falls, Russias Lake Baikhal, and various locations in the United States.

Membership: In 1995 the centers reported 5,000 members worldwide; 1,500 in the United States, and 1,000 in Canada..

Periodicals: *Anahata Nada.*

Sources:

Chinmoy, Sri. *Arise! Awake!.* New York: Frederick Fell, 1972.

___. *Astrology, the Supernatural and the Beyond.* Hollis, NY: Vishma Press, 1973.

___. *My Lord's Secrets Revealed.* New York: Herder and Herder, 1971.

___. *A Sri Chinmoy Primer.* Forest Hills, NY: Vishma Press, 1974.

Madhuri [Nancy Elizabeth Sands]. *The Life of Sri Chinmoy.* Jamaica, NY: Sri Chinmoy Lighthouse, 1972.

★2046★
Sri Ram Ashrama
Current address not obtained for this edition.

The Sri Ram Ashrama was founded in 1967 at Millbrook, New York, as the Ananda Ashrama by Swami Abhayananda. Swani Abhayananda's guru was Rammurti Sriram Mishra, and the Ashrama was soon renamed in his honor. During the years in which Timothy Leary and his League for Spiritual Discovery was located at Millbrook, the two groups existed side by side on the Hitchcock Ranch. Later the Ashrama moved to Benson, Arizona. The Ashrama is a center for yoga in its practical, universal and scientific aspects. It is a universal and cosmic religion.

Members of the Ashrama are expected to manifest five resolutions: ahimsa, truthfulness, honesty, direction of all bodily and mental energies toward reality, and the renunciation of worldly goods. They study and follow eight principles: Yama, determination to live in the light of truth; Niyama, the five methods of cleanliness, contentment, critical examination of senses, study and complete self-surrender; Asana, the postures of yoga which leave the mind free for meditation; Pranayama, breath-energy control;

Pratyhora, sublimation of psychic energy to high purposes; Dharana, fixation of attention; Dhyana, continuous meditation and focusing attention, and Samadhi, transformation of all attention.

The Ashrama is run by its officers and board of trustees. Kriya Press is the publication arm.

Membership: Not reported. In 1970, the ashrama claimed 2,000 adherents in its greater family.

★2047★
Sri Rama Foundation
Box 2550
Santa Cruz, CA 95063

Sri Rama Foundation was formed in 1971 as the vehicle for the teachings of Baba Hari Dass and through the profits to support homeless children in India. Baba Hari Dass was born in Almora District, India, in the Himalayan foothills. He left home at the age of eight to join a renuciate group in the jungle. He became a mauni sadhu (a person who accepts a vow of silence), though he has led an active life managing ashrams and teaching yoga. He developed his own system of teaching the traditional ashtanga (eight-limbed) yoga. In 1971 some Western students persuaded him to come to the United States, and he began to hold regular satsang to a group of disciples who gathered around him.

Ashtanga yoga is the system the legendary figure Patanjali compiled from early teachings on yoga. Baba Hari Dass continues Patanjali's teachings of a process involving eight parts: yama (restraints); niyama (observances); asana (postures); pranayama (breathing); pratyahara (withdrawal of the mind from sense perception), dharana (concentration), dhyana (meditation) and samadhi (superconsciousness). In addition, a strong foundation of Samkhya philosophy, a spirit of devotion, and a deep understanding of nondualism (Vedanta) charaterizes the teachings of Babi Hari Das.

The major center of Baba Hari Dass's students is the Mount Madonna Center for the Creative Arts and Sciences in Watsonville, California. In Vancouver, British Columbia, in the mid-1970s a group of Babi Hari Dass's devotees began a series of publications, termed the Dharma Sara series, which resulted in several books and a magazine, *Dharma Sara*, since discontinued. Another group formed the Ashtanga Yoga Fellowship in Ontario and sponsor annual events with Baba Hari Dass. In 1980 Baba Hari Dass founded Shri Ram Orphanage in the Himalayan foothills of northern India. The orphanage is home to 30 children.

Membership: Not reported.

Sources:

Between Pleasure and Pain, The Way of Conscious Living. Sumas, WA: Dharma Sara Publications, 1976.

Dass, Baba Hari. *Ashtanga Yoga Primer*. Santa Cruz, CA: Sri Rama Publishing, 1981.

___. *Hariakhan Baba, Known, Unknown*. Davis, CA: Sri Rama Foundation, 1975.

___. *Silence Speaks*. Santa Cruz, CA: Sri Rama Foundation, 1977.

___. *Sweeper to Saint*. Santa Cruz, CA: Sri Rama Publishing, 1980.

★2048★
Swami Kuvalayananda Yoga Foundation
339 Fitzwater St.
Philadelphia, PA 19147

The Swami Kuvalayanananda Yoga (SKY) Foundation was founded by Dr. Vijayendra Pratap who earned a Ph.D. in applied psychology at the Bombay University. Dr. Pratap was the student of Swami Kuvalayanandaji, founder of Kaivalyadhama, the famous yoga center in Bombay, and served as its assistant director before coming to the United States. The SKY Foundation offers classes in hatha yoga at all levels, trains teachers, and holds classes on yogic philosophy based on Patanjali (the ancient writer who put into simple, cogent language the theory and techniques of yoga). One of the purposes of the Foundation is to research the older yogic traditions in the light of modern knowledge, and the foundation has sponsored several conferences on science and yoga. Headquarters are in Philadelphia above the Garland of Letters Bookstore, operated by the foundation. The foundation considers itself an educational organization rather than a religious or spiritual center.

Membership: Not reported. There is one center in Philadelphia.

Remarks: The SKY Foundation considers itself an educational and research organization, not a religious one. However, it falls under the broad definition of "religious" as used in this *Encyclopedia*, hence its listing is continued.

★2049★
SYDA Foundation
371 Brickman Rd.
South Fallsburg, NY 12779

Alternate Address: International headquarters: Gurudev Siddha Peeth, PO Ganeshpuri, Dist. Thoma, Maharastra, India.

Swami Muktananda Paramahansa (1908-1982) was the leading disciple of Bhagwan Nityananda (d. 1961), a siddha master who in his later years settled in Ganeshpuri, India. Muktananda, or Baba, as he was called by his followers, left home at the age of 15 to wander through India studying philosophy and mastering the different branches of yoga. In 1947, he sought out Bhagawan Nityananda, whom he had met in his youth, and received shaktipat initiation (for the awakening of the inner trnsformative energy, generally referred to as kundalini) from him. Nine years later, after intense spiritual practices under his guru's guidance, Muktananda attained self-realization. Before his death, Nityananda transferred the power of the siddha lineage to Muktananda. Following his guru's wishes, Muktananda established an ashram, Gurudev Siddha Peeth, in a small village called Gavdevi near the town of Ganeshpuri. It is considered the mother ashram of the movement.

In the 1960s, the first American seekers began to arrive. In 1970, some of these devotees requested Muktananda to undertake his first world tour which lasted three months and included stops in Europe, New York, Dallas, Los Angeles, and Australia. Baba Ram Dass accompanied Muktananda on much of this tour. After this initial visit, the first centers began to appear in America. Also as a result of this visit, Westerners came in even greater numbers to Ganeshpuri, among whom was Werner Erhart, the founder of Erhart Training Seminars (est). At Erhard's invitation, in 1974, Muktananda returned to the West, this time for two years. A final journey was made in 1978 which lasted for three years.

In 1974 the foundation was established to make the teachings of Siddha Yoga available to seekers around the world. Under its administration, SYDA oversees the Siddha yoga curriculum, the publication of books and magazines, the production of audiovisuals, and the administration of the several education/humanitarian projects including the Muktabodha Indological Research Institute (in India), the PRASDA Project, and the Prison Project sponsored by the practitioners. The foundation is headed by a board of directors.

The Muktabodha Indological Research Institute is dedicated to the preservation and dissemination of the scriptures and traditions of India and operates through a number of projects including scholarly publications, research and study programs, and archival projects. The Vedashala Project preserves the mantras and rituals of the Vedas. The institute is accredited by the University of Pune, India, for post graduate studies.

Before his death, Swami Muktananda designated Swami Chidvilasananda, known as Gurumayi, as his successor. He had trained her since childhood to succeed him. At that time he also appointed another successor, Swami Nityananda, Chidvilasananda's brother, but he retired from that position in 1985.

The path of siddha yoga is based upon shakipat initiation, or the awakening of the spiritual energy (kundalini) through the grace of the guru. The practice of the yoga includes meditation, chanting, selfless service, contemplation, and devotion to the guru.

Membership: There is no formal membership in Siddha yoga meditation. In 1997 there were more than 500 Siddha Yoga Meditation Centers throughout the world, and residential centers in Australia, England, Mexico, and the United States.

Educational Facilities: Muktabogha Indological Research Institute, South Fallsburg, New York.

Periodicals: *Darshan.* • *Transformation. Neeleswari.* • *Siddha Yoga.* Both available from Gurudev Siddha Peeth, PO Ganeshpuri, Dist. Thoma, Maharastra, India.

Remarks: During the 1980s, the Siddha Yoga Dham has had to weather two major scandals. Shortly after Swami Muktananda's death, several of his close associates left the movement and denounced him for taking sexual liberties with female disciples. The accusations became a occasion for widespread discussions of the nature and qualification of leadership in Indian-based movements in the West. Then in 1986, the *Illustrated Weekly of India* published two "expose" stories concerning charges made by Subash Shetty, until his retirement in 1985 known as Swami Nityananda, about his sister, Swami Chidvilasananda. A defamation case was filed against the magazine, and in 1987 they published a full retraction and apology. The movement has been able to put both incidents behind it.

Swami Nityananda, following his withdrawal from work with Swami Chidvalasananda, established a new organization, Shanti Mandir Seminars, and is continuing his work through it.

Sources:

Brook, Douglas Renfrew, et al. *Meditation Revolution: A History and Theology of the Siddha Yoga Lineage.* South Fallsburg, NY: Agama Press, 1997. 709 pp.

Muktananda, Swami. *Guru.* New York: Harper & Row, 1981.

___. *Play of Consciousness.* New York: Harper & Row, 1974.

___. *Reflections of the Self.* New York: SYDA Foundation, 1982.

Paramahansa, Muktananda. *Bhagawan Nityananda, His Life and Mission.* Ganespuri, India: Shree Gurudev Ashram, n.d.

Prajananda, Swami. *A Search for the Self.* Ganeshpuri, India: Durudev Siddha Peeth, 1979.

★2050★
Tantrik Order in America
(Defunct)

The Tantrik Order was one of the first Hindu groups founded in the United States, and possibly the first created by a Western student of the Eastern teachings. It was founded in New York City by Pierre Bernard (born 1875 as Peter Coons) (1875-1955), better known by members of the order as Oom the Omnipotent. The order had superceded the Bacchante Academy whose California operation had ceased in the San Francisco earthquake of 1906. Associated with the order was the New York Sanskrit College.

Bernard taught a form of Tantric Hinduism combined with hatha yoga. The sexual aspects of tantra were included as integral aspects of the instruction, and Bernard came under scrutiny during the early days of the order's operation as police began to suspect him of trying to seduce his pupils. He survived several early scandals, however, and in 1924 moved to an estate in Nyack, New York, on Long Island, and continued as leader of the order for the next three decades (closed only briefly during World War II when the estate was used as a center for refugees from Nazi Germany). His clientele included many wealthy people, including several members of the Vanderbilt family. Bernard became a wealthy and influential citizen. He donated a zoo to the community and eventually became president of the bank in nearby Pearl City.

As far as is known, the order died with its founder. There are reports of the existence of an offshoot, the New York Sacred Tantrics, which functioned during the 1960s. However, reports have not been confirmed and if the group existed, it had disbanded by the late 1970s.

Remarks: Pierre Bernard had several famous relatives. He was the cousin-by-marriage of Mary Baker Eddy, founder of the Church of Christ, Scientist. In the early years of his work in New York, he was the guardian of his half-sister, Ora Ray Baker, who became the wife of Hazrat Inayat Khan, founder of the Sufi Order. Bernard's nephew, Pierre Bernard, wrote what is a classic text on yoga as his thesis at Columbia University, *Hatha Yoga: The Report of a Personal Experience.*

Sources:

Boswell, Charles. "The Great Fume and Fuss over the Omnipotent Oom." *True* (January 1965): 31-33, 86-91.

"In Re Fifth Veda" in *International Journal of the Tantrik Order.* New York: Tantrik Order in America, n.d. [1909].

Sann, Paul. *Fads, Follies, and Delusions of the American People.* New York, 1967.

★2051★
Temple of Cosmic Religion
310 E. Lake St.
Mount Shasta, CA 96067

In 1966, while attending the Kumbha Mela (ritual bathing) Festival in the Ganges River, an independent Hindu teacher, later to be known as Satguru Sant Keshavadas, was told by a holy man named Lord Panduranga Vittala, to "Go to the West; spread the cosmic religion." When Keshavadas returned to Delhi, the advice was reinforced in a vision. The following year he began a tour of Europe and the Middle East and arrived in the United States in May. In 1968 he founded a center in Washington, D.C., as the American headquarters of the Dasashram International Center in India. In the mid-1970s the American headquarters moved to Southfield, Michigan, near Detroit, and adopted the name of the Temple of Cosmic Religion, a title long used in the movement.

In bringing Hinduism to the West, Keshavadas envisioned the beginning of a world cosmic religion, uniting all religious paths. This cosmic religion will propose that truth is one and that all paths lead to the realization of God. Keshavadas teaches yoga and meditation and devotion to God through chanting and singing (bhakti yoga, as discussed in the introductory material for this volume). He believes karma and reincarnation to be central to the beliefs of the religion.

From the world headquarters of the Temple of Cosmic Religion located in Bangalore, India, at the Panduranga Temple, temples have been established around India in five locations, and in England, Trinidad, and the United States. The U.S. temple is located in Mt. Shasta, California.

Membership: Not reported. In 1995 there was one temple and several study groups around the United States.

Sources:

Keshavadasasji, Sadguru. *The Doctrine of Reincarnation and Liberation.* Bangalore, India: Dasasharama Research Publications, 1970.

Keshavadasji, Sant. *This Is Wisdom.* Privately printed, 1975.

___. *The Purpose of Life,* New York: Vantage Press, 1978.

___. *Sadguru Speaks.* Washington, DC: Temple of Cosmic Religion, 1975.

Life and Teachings of Sadguru Sant Keshavadas, A Commemoration. Southfield, MI: Temple of Cosmic Religion, 1977.

Mukundadas [Michael Allen Makowsky]. *Minstrel of Love.* Nevada City, CA: Hansa Publications, 1980.

★2052★
Temple of Kriya Yoga
2414 N. Kedzie
Chicago, IL 60647

The Temple of Kriya Yoga was founded by Goswami Kriyananda (born Melvin Higgins), not to be confused with the Swami Kriyananda who founded the Ananda Ashrama. The temple is headquartered in a temple building on the northside of Chicago. Kriyananda had studied with a guru, spoken of only as Sri Sri Shelliji in the temple literature, who passed to him the kriya yoga tradition of Swami Paramahansa Yogananda, founder of the Self-Realization Fellowship. Kriyananda began teaching yoga in the 1940s and opened the temple in Chicago in the 1960s. Kriyananda, an accomplished astrologer, also opened the College of Occult Sciences which offered classes in a variety of esoteric subjects.

During the late 1970s, the temple abandoned its rented facilities in downtown Chicago for its new headquarters. Associated with the Chicago center is a retreat facility in South Haven, Michigan. In 1977 the Kriyananda Healing Center was established as a holistic health facility, adjacent to the temple. Traditional western medicine is supplemented by a program emphasizing yoga and meditation, fasting, biofeedback, and massage.

Kriyananda follows the yoga system of Yogananda, and over the years he has authored a variety of books delineating kriya yoga, meditation, and astrology. He sees religion as providing a deep personal understanding of the nature and purpose of God and the Universe. He teaches the oneness of law, spirit, and love and their identity with God. He affirms the meaningfulness of the universe and the possibility of attaining illumination and fulfillment (through the practice of kriya yoga) in this lifetime.

Membership: Not reported. There are several hundred temple members and many more individuals who receive the benefits of the temple through its classes, programs and astrology services.

Periodicals: *The Flame of Kriya.*

Sources:

Kriyananda, Goswami. *The Bhagavad Gita, The Song of God*. Chicago: Temple of Kriya Yoga, n.d.

___. *Pathway to God-Consciousness*. Chicago: Temple of Kriya Yoga, 1970.

___. *Yoga, Text for Teachers and Advanced Students*. Chicago: Temple of Kriya Yoga, 1976.

★2053★
Temple of Yoga (Acharya)
(Defunct)

The Temple of Yoga was founded by Besudeb Bhattacharya (d. 1949), an Indian poet, playwright, and yoga teacher, who came to America just prior to World War I. Under the name "Sree Besudeb" he authored several plays, but some time in the 1920s turned his attention to the teaching of yoga and Hinduism. He founded the Yoga Research School in New York City, but later moved to Long Island. Nyack became the center of his activities, which included Prana Press, Hope, Inc., and the Temple of Yoga. He wrote a number of books under his religious name, Pundit Acharya, though some of them were published posthumously by his students.

Integral to Pundit Acharya's approach to yoga was his attempt to reinterpret yoga in scientific terminology, in light of "neuro-bio electronics." He developed the Acharyan Method of yoga which resulted in a number of exercises to release the life force and bring relaxation. He believed that sleep was a great rejuvenator, as it was the time for recharging the brain from the energy reservoirs of the infinite universe.

Sources:

Acharya, Pundit. *Breath, Sleep, the Heart, and Life*. Clearlake, CA: Dawn Horse Press, 1976.

___. *Mukti*. Nyack, NY: Prana Press, 1967.

___. *The Saffron Veil*. New York: Prana Press, 1963.

___. *A Strange Language*. Nyack, NY: Yoga Research School, 1939.

★2054★
Transcendent Science Society
(Defunct)

The Transcendent-Science Society was founded in Chicago, Illinois, by Premel El Adaros, also known as Swami Brahmavidya, around 1920. The society is known by one book on its teachings written by its founder and several by Swami A. P. Mukerji, a prominent South Indian yogi. Brahmavidya claimed to be the United States representative of the same order, the South India Brotherhood, to which Mukerji belonged. Transcendent-science, the science of self-knowledge, was designed to lead to a knowledge of the self, union with the divine, and liberation or *mukti*. The practices of transcendent-science consisted of strict moral living, yoga postures, breathing exercises, concentration, and meditation.

Mukerji presented a course in yogi philosophy and practice based on concentration, meditation, and thought control. He included instructions on breath control (*pranayana*), hatha yoga exercises, diet (vegetarianism is advised), and various body cleansing techniques. He was among the earliest Hindus to introduce the concept of guru worship (reverence for the teacher who is a person of high spiritual attainment), a most controversial idea for Western audiences. Equally controversial was the concept of worshipping the terrible, i.e., becoming one with the negative, which he taught as a means of seeing its ultimate unreality.

The society survived only a brief time, however, the writings of A. P. Mukerji continue to be circulated, having been kept in print by the Yogi Publication Society.

Sources:

Brahmavidya, Swami. *Transcendent-Science or The Science of Self Knowledge*. Chicago: Transcendent-Science Society, 1922.

Mukerji, A. P. *The Doctrine and Practice of Yoga*. Chicago: Premel El Adaros, 1922.

___. *Spiritual Consciousness*. Chicago: Yogi Publication Society, 1911.

★2055★
Truth Consciousness
% Sacred Mountain Ashram
10668 Gold Hill Rd.
Boulder, CO 80302-9716

Truth Consciousness was founded by Swami Amar Jyoti in 1974 and is devoted to a vision of what it perceives as Truth and the freeing of human consciousness into Divine Consciousness. Prabhushri Swamiji, as he is called by his devotees, was born in northwest India in 1928. A few months prior to college graduation, he renounced his seemingly destined life of comfort and success to follow an inner dictum, "Know yourself and you shall know everything." After a decade of *sadhana* (spiritual practices) and meditation in the Himalayas, he achieved his goal. He then began traveling throughout India and in 1960, at the request of disciples, founded Jyoti Ashram in Pune (or Poona), Maharashtra State. In 1961 Prabhushri Swamiji visited the United States for the first time then returned to Pune, concentrating for a decade on his work in India.

Prabhushri Swamijis way is a classical path of spirituality, building a firm foundation with each soul based upon the principles of Dharma (living according to Divine Law). Principles such as truthfulness, humility, purity, and devotion are stressed. With compassion, patience, and wisdom, the Guru attempts carefully to guide each disciple toward a natural unfoldment unto the Divine.

Prabhushri Swamiji again visited the United States in 1973 and at that time founded his first ashram in the west, Sacred Mountain Ashram. Truth Consciousness is the non-profit corporation which ties together the American centers. There are currently two ashrams (for renunciates) and two community centers for individuals, couples, and families who wish to live a spiritually oriented life under the direct guidance of the Master.

The ashrams and community centers offer programs year round and sincere seekers are welcome. *Satsang* (Sanskrit for "communion with Truth") is held twice weekly and includes devotional music (chanting) and meditation. Other regular programs include *Guru Aarati* (morning prayers and worship), weekly group meditations, and weekend and extended retreats.

Membership: There is no formal membership. There are two Truth Consciousness ashrams in the United States: Sacred Mountain Ashram in Boulder, Colorado, and Desert Ashram in Tucson, Arizona. A community center is located adjacent or near each Ashram. An estimated several hundred individuals are affiliated with the organization. In India, Ananda Niketan, the trust founded by Swami Amar Jyoti, maintains Jyoti Ashram in Pune, four hours from Bombay. There is also a center in New Zealand.

Periodicals: *Light of Consciousness—Journal of Spiritual Awakening* (USA). • *Chinmaya Jeevan—Conscious Living* (India).

Sources:

Frey, Kessler. *Satsang Notes of Swami Amar Jyoti.* Boulder, CO: Truth Consciousness, 1977.

Jyoti, Swami Amar. *Dawning: Eternal Wisdom Heritage for Today.* Boulder, CO: Truth Consciousness, 1991.

___. *Spirit of Himalaya.* Boulder, CO: Truth Consciousness, 1985.

___. *Retreat Into Eternity,* Boulder, CO: Truth Consciousness, 1981.

★2056★
Universal Brotherhood Temple and School of Eastern Philosophy
(Defunct)

The Universal Brotherhood Temple and School of Eastern Philosophy was an early American Hindu organization founded by Yogi Sant Rama Mandal in San Francisco in the 1920s. During the 1930s it was headquartered in Santa Monica, California and is known today only through Mandal's surviving publications. Mandal taught a system of yoga for self-development and self-realization which included hatha yoga, meditation, the repetition of mantras, diet, and practical exercises. He also taught a method to awaken the "kundalini," the latent energy believed to be located at the base of the spine which, upon awakening, travels up the spinal column to bring enlightenment. No information on Mandal's early years or the eventual fate of the temple has been available.

Sources:

Mandal, Sant Rama. *Course of Instruction in Mystic Psychology.* Santa Monica, CA: Universal Brotherhood Temple and School of Eastern Philosophy, n.d.

___. *Gems of Aryan Wisdom.* San Francisco, CA: Universal Brotherhood Temple and School of Eastern Philosophy, 1931.

___. *The Self and the Not-Self.* San Francisco, CA: Universal Brotherhood Temple and School of Eastern Philosophy, 1927.

★2057★
Vedanta Centre and Ananda Ashrama
Box 8555
La Crescenta, CA 91224-0555

The Ananda Ashram of La Crescenta, California and the Vedanta Centre of Cohasset, Massachusetts, continue the work begun in the early twentieth century by Swami Paramananda, a disciple of Swami Vivekananda and a monk of the Vedanta Society. Paramananda was born Suresh Chandra Guha Thakurta (1884-1940). A pioneer swami of the Ramakrishna Order, he came to the United States in 1906 to assist Swami Abhedananda at the New York Vedanta Society. In 1909, he moved to Boston, to open a Vedanta center there. He also established a monastic community for American women. His first disciple was Laura Glenn, better known by her religious name, Sister Devamata. She became his platform assistant in 1910, but is best remembered for her literary work. She wrote many books, edited both Swami Vivekananda's and Swami Paramananda's lectures, and was the chief editor of the *Message of the East*, a monthly periodical published without interruption for 52 years.

During his 34-year ministry in the United States, Paramananda lectured all over the United States and Europe. He established the Ananda Ashrama in La Crescenta in 1923 and a second ashrama in Cohasset in 1929. In 1931, Sree Ramakrishna Ananda Ashrama was established in his name in Dacca, now in Bangladesh. This ashrama was moved to Calcutta after the partition of the nation. There are now two branches which serve destitute women, orphan children, and other students. During Paramananda's lifetime, all of these centers were part of the Ramakrishna Math (monastery) and Mission whose headquarters are at Belur Math, near Calcutta.

After Paramananda's death in 1940, his centers were excommunicated from the parent order because he left as his designated successor an Indian woman, Srimata Gayatri Devi (b. 1906). She had come to the United States in 1926 and had become the first Indian woman to teach Vedanta in the West. In 1952, she consolidated the eastern work by moving the Boston Vedanta Center to the ashrama in Cohasset, some 20 miles south of Boston.

Beliefs. The ashrama and center teach Vedanta. The essence of Vedanta's tenets are that Truth or God is One without a second; that an individual's real nature is divine; that all paths ultimately lead to the same goal; and that the purpose of human life is to realize God within one's own soul. It shares these beliefs with Ramakrishna Order, the break between the ashrama and the order being purely administrative.

Organization. For 55 years, until her death in 1995, Srimata Gavatro Devi was the spiritual mother of the several ashrams in the United States and India. She appointed an American woman, Srimata Sudha Puri Devi (Dr. Susan Schrager) as her successor. The ashramas are home to monastic men and women. Associated with them are number of householders who consider them their spiritual home. Many others attend the weekly services and classes. Vedanta Centre (Cohasset) publishes the books of Swami Paramananda and several of the female leaders: Sister Daya (Georgina Walton Jones), and Srimata Gayatri Devi, in addition to casettes and CDs of ashrama devotional music.

Membership: Neither the ashrama nor the center are membership organizations. There are approximately 60 residents of the four ashramas (two in India and two in America). In addition, an estimated 1,500 persons look to the ashramas for their spiritual nurture.

Sources:

Devamata, Sister. *Swami Paramananda and His Work.* 2 vols. La Crescenta, CA: Ananda Ashrama, 1926-41.

Devi, Srimata Gayatri. *One Life's Pilgrimage.* Cohasset, MA Vedanta Centre, 1977.

Hold Aloft the Light. La Crescenta, CA: Ananda Ashrama, 1973.

Levinsky, Sara Ann. *A Bridge of Dreams.* West Stockbridge, MA: Inner Traditions, 1984.

Paramananda, Swami. *The Path of Devotion.* Boston, MA: Vedanta Center, 1907.

___. *Vedanta in Practice.* Boston, MA: Vedanta Center, 1917.

★2058★
Vedanta Society
5423 S. Hyde Park Blvd.
Chicago, IL 60615

Alternate Address: International headquarters: Rama Kirshna Math and Mission, P.O. Belur Math, Dt. Howrah. W. Bengel 711 202 India.

Among Hindu groups, none has made as great an impact on America as the Vedanta Society, the only Hindu body established in America before 1900. The Society grew out of the vision of Sri Ramakrishna (1836-1886) and the work of his prime disciple, Swami Vivekananda (1863-1902).

Ramakrishna was a priest in a Calcutta temple of Kali, one of several forms in which God is worshipped as Universal Mother in popular Hinduism. Through long meditation and intense yearning for direct experience of the divine, he attained the state of samadhi or God-consciousness. Continuous samadhi became his goal, and he followed a number of sadhanas or paths to enlightenment, both within and outside the Hindu tradition. He became convinced that: 1. the Divine Mother wished him to remain on the threshold between the Absolute and the relative in order to serve as an instrument for the spiritual uplift of humanity, and 2. all religions (including Hinduism) were different paths to the same goal, and all gods were different aspects of the same Godhead.

A number of disciples, some of them college-trained intellectuals, gathered around Ramakrishna. Before his death some revered him as an avatar, or divine incarnation. Vivekananda, commissioned by Ramakrishna, forged the younger disciples into a monastic brotherhood and gradually convinced them that as Ramakrishna's followers they had a mission not only to seek enlightenment but also to work to alleviate the suffering of humanity through spiritual ministration and social service.

In 1893, Vivekananda came to America to teach the universal religion realized by Ramakrishna. He took the World Parliament of Religions by storm, and for two years he lectured throughout the United States, gathering followers. In November, 1894, the Vedanta Society of New York was formed, and in the next few years centers were added in San Francisco and Boston. Each is autonomous but works under the Ramakrishna Order. In 1897 Vivekananda returned to India and organized the Ramakrishna Mission, dedicated to serving humanity in a spirit of worship of the divine dwelling within each person.

The central ideas of Vedanta monistic philosophy can be summarized in three propositions:

1. Brahman or God is the underlying unity manifested in all. Each person in essence is divine, and the goal of human life is to realize this divinity within oneself and in all others. This realization is the true basis of unselfishness, as the divine unity is the basis of love.

2. Maya, the illusion of individual separateness, is an interpretation by the mind. We perceive variety rather than the underlying unity because of the condition of our mind, its prejudices, desires and fears. Absolute reality can be known even in this life through the purified mind; this has been verified by the great mystics of all religions.

3. The mind may be purified by a variety of means, and each person's spiritual life evolves according to his or her mental make-up. Four basic yogas or spiritual disciplines have been codified by Vivekanada: devotion, intellectual discrimination, unselfish work, and psychic control. These correspond to the four basic aspects of the human mind: the emotional, intellectual, active, and reflective. The predominance of one or more of these in an individual determines what path that person should follow.

Vedanta differs from most other Hindu movements in that it stresses principles over personalities. Vivekananda and his successors have emphasized the universal teachings of Vedanta rather than the personality of Ramakrishna. At the same time, freedom is given to the individual follower to worship Ramakrishna or any prophet of any religion as a means to enlightenment. Instruction by a qualified teacher is strongly recommended, although too much emphasis on the personality of the teacher is recognized as a danger.

Vedanta's intellectual approach to Hinduism has found expression in the publication of numerous books, including popular editions of the Upanishads, the Bhagavad-Gita, and the Yoga Aphorisms of Patanjali. Through these, it has stimulated interst in Hinduism among many thinking people. Gerald Heard, Aldous Huxley, and Christopher Isherwood all had a well-known interest in Vedanta.

Membership: In 1997 the society reported approximately 2,000 members in 12 centers led by 30 swamis. Centers are also found in Argentina, Bangladesh, France, Fiji, Great Britain, India, Japan, Mauritius, the Netherlands, Russia, Singapore, Sri Lanka, and Switzerland.

Periodicals: *Prabuddha Bharata or Awakened India.* Send orders to 5 Dehi Entally Rd., Calcutta, India 700 014. • *Vedanta in the West.* Published for many years by the Vedanta Press in Hollywood, California, was discontinued in the 1970s.

Sources:

Gambhrananda, Swami. *History of the Ramakrishna Math and Mission.* Calcutta: Advaita Ashrama, 1957.

Isherwood, Christopher. *Ramakrishna and His Disciples.* New York: Simon and Schuster, 1965.

_____, ed. *Vedanta for the Western World.* New York: Viking Press, 1945.

Johnson, Clive, ed. *Vedanta.* New York: Bantam Books, 1974.

Rolland, Romain. *The Life of Vivekananda and the Universal Gospel.* Calcutta: Advaita Ashrama, 1970.

★2059★
Vedantic Center
3528 N. Triunfo Canyon Rd.
Agoura, CA 91301

The Vedantic Center was founded in 1975 in Los Angeles by Alice Coltrane (b. 1937), an initiate of Swami Satchidananda, founder of the Integral Yoga International, with whom she journeyed in India and Sri Lanka. Raised in Detroit, Coltrane devoted her early life to music, as did her late husband, jazz musician John Coltrane, and like him attained a high level of success and fame. In 1968 at the age of 31, she entered a period described as a time of both spiritual isolation and re-awakening. Directly from the Supreme Lord, she also received an initiation into the renounced order of sannyas, but was instructed not to don the ochre robe, symbolic of the renounced life, until 1975. During the early 1970s she did a series of records expressing her spiritual pilgrimage and devotional life.

In 1975 Coltrane emerged as Swami Turiyasangitananda. A few months later, she organized the Vedantic Center. She authored several books, including *Monument Eternal* and *Endless Wisdom*, and began to build a following. In 1983 the center purchased 48 acres of land in rural southern California near the town of Agoura and established a community, Sai Anantam Ashram, for the center's members.

The Vedantic Center is unique in that it is one of the very few Hindu organizations drawing members predominantly from the American black community and led by a black person (though there are predominantly black centers within large and otherwise predominantly non-black Hindu groups). While beginning with the yoga system passed to her by Swami Satchidanand, Turiyasangitananda has developed an eclectic blend of Eastern philosophy which draws upon Western spiritual traditions as well. She teaches that the purpose of human life is to advance spiritually. The highest stage of life is devotional service (bhakti yoga), rendered unto the Supreme Lord (known in his three aspects as Brahma, Vishnu or Krishna, and Siva). In this light, devotional singing has attained an important role at the ashram, and Turiyasangitananda has composed new music with a decidedly Western flavor for the traditional bhajans (devotional songs).

The weekly schedule at Sai Anantam Ashram begins with Sunday school for children. There is worship, including chanting and satsang discourses by Swami Turiyasangitananda, on Sunday afternoons. A prayer service occurs on Wednesday evening. The center operates a bookstore at the entrance to the ashram grounds.

Membership: As of 1995 approximately 30 people live at Sai Anantam. A small number of non-residents also attend the ashram's worship services.

Periodicals: *Sai Anantam.*

Sources:

Turiyasangitananda, A. C. *Endless Wisdom.* Los Angeles: Avatar Book Institute, 1981.

___. *Monument Eternal.* Los Angeles: Vedantic Book Press, 1977.

★2060★
Vedantic Cultural Society
(Defunct)

The Vedantic Cultural Society was formed in 1983 by Hansadutta Swami (a.k.a. Hans Kary), a former initiating guru with the International Society for Krishna Consciousness (ISKCON). During the late 1970s, Hansadutta had been the subject of strong criticism by the other gurus in ISKCON because of his unorthodox fund raising, administrative, and recruiting activities. In the spring of 1980, he was arrested for possession of illegal firearms. While the charges were later dropped, his advocacy of survivalism and his possession of a number of weapons led to his being sent to India for a year. After consideration of the sacred nature of the relationship of initiating guru and his disciples (which constituted most of the Berkeley temple), the governing council reinstated him. However, his return to Berkeley did not ease the tension, and in 1983 ISKCON excommunicated Hansadutta. He left and took most of the Berkeley temple with him, forming the Vedantic Cultural Society. Hansadutta's troubles did not end with the break from ISKCON. In September of 1983, he was arrested and accused of shooting out several store windows in Berkeley. Several weapons and empty shells were found in his car. Following this incident, Hansadutta assumed a low profile. The Berkeley temple returned to ISKCON and the rural center was sold. Hansadutta has applied for reinstatement in ISKCON.

Membership: The Center has several hundred members, all in Berkeley and in one rural center.

Sources:

Hansadutta, Swami. *The Book, What the Black Sheep Said.* Berkeley, CA: Hansa Books, 1985.

___. *The Hammer for Smashing Illusion.* Berkeley, CA: Hansa Books, 1983.

___. *Kirtan.* Berkeley, CA: Hansa Books, 1984.

★2061★
Vimala Thakar, Friends of
Current address not obtained for this edition.

Alternate Address: International address: Vimala Thakar Foundation, Huizerweg 46, 1261 Az Balricum, Holland.

Vimala Thakar is a teacher in the tradition of Jiddu Krishnamurti. For several years she was a disciple of Vinoba Bhave. Bhave, a close associate of Mahatma Gandhi, initiated a voluntary land reform program in 1951. He traveled the length and breadth of India to solicit land from large landowners to give to the landless. The program failed, however, when it was recognized that the land actually transferred to new owners was almost worthless agriculturally. After graduating with a degree in philosophy from Nag

pur University, Thakar traveled the country as an exponent of the Land Gift Movement.

In 1956, a chance meeting with Krishnamurti began to change Thakar's life. She encountered him several times over the next five years and absorbed his message of the need for total inward revolution or transformation. She resigned from the Land Gift Movement and began to travel, teaching and lecturing about her experience and its implications. She advocated the meditative life, which begins in the observance and transcendence of mental processes. Meditation is seen not as an activity but as the state of total being where there is no movement; a dimension of full life.

Thakar's travels in Europe and America during the 1960s drew followers who organized the Vimala Thakar Foundation (much on the pattern of the Krishnamurti Foundation) in Holland and a group of Friends of Vimala Thakar formed in California. There organizations facilitate lecture tours, publish and distribute books and tapes of Thakar's lectures, and organize conferences. As with Krishnamurti, the structure is minimal, since Thakar wishes to speak as an individual teacher rather than the representative of an organization.

Membership: Not reported.

Periodicals: *Contact with Vimala Thakar.* Available from Vimala Thakar Foundation, Huizerweg 46, 1261 AZ Balricum, Holland.

Sources:

Thakar, Vimala. *On an Eternal Voyage.* Ahmedabad, India: New Order Book Co., 1972.

___. *Totality in Essence.* Delhi, India: Motilal Banarsidass, 1971.

___. *Towards Total Transformation.* Berkeley, CA: Friends of Vimala Thakar, 1970.

___. *Why Meditation?.* Delhi, India: Motilal Banarsidass, 1977.

''Vimala Thakar Speaks on Yoga.'' *Yoga Journal* (March/April 1977).

★2062★
World Community
Rte. 4, Box 265
Bedford, VA 24523

In 1970 Vasudevadas, a Western teacher of mystical and yogic disciplines, and his wife, Devaki-Ma founded Prema Dharmasala as a yoga ashram for dedicated lay-disciples and renunciates and the World Community as a community of householders and families who looked to Vasudevadas as their spiritual teacher. Throughout the 1970s Prema Dharmasala functioned as the main training center for those who had made a commitment to a life of renunciation and service to God and the human family. However, in the early 1980s, a shift of emphasis to the World Community occurred as a vision of a community to function as a symbol of the oneness of Truth and the transforming power of Prem (Divine Love) emerged. By 1984, Prema Dharmasala had been completely superceded by the Prema World Community.

As developed, the World Community will be located on the acreage previously occupied by the Prema Dharmasala. Centered upon a large Temple of All Religion will be a series of interrelated villages for various types of individuals, an educational center, a holistic health clinic, and a research and training center for the New Age. The outlines of the emerging plan has remained open to allow for new insight as members become more attuned to Truth.

Membership: Not reported. There are several hundred people associated with the community.

Sources:

Love Offerings at Thy Lotus Feet. Bedford, VA: Prema Dharmasala, 1975.

Vasudevadas. *Running Out of Time and Who Is Watching?* Bedford, VA: Prema Dharmasala Fellowship, 1979.

___. *A Time for Eternity*. Bedford, VA: Prema Dharmasala and Fellowship Association, 1976.

___. *Vasudevadas Speaks to Your Heart*. Bedford, VA: Prema Dharmasala and Fellowship Association, 1976.

★2063★
World Community Service
1021 E. Magnolia Blvd.
Burbank, CA 91501

World Community Service was founded in 1911 in Madras, India, by Yogiraj Vethathiri Maharaj, a successful businessman and teacher of kundalini yoga. Vethathiri was born in southern India into a family of weavers. While still a child he sought an education and also placed himself under a spiritual teacher. Very early in his development, he rejected the impersonal monism taught by many forms of Hinduism and became a devotee of Vinayaka, a Hindu deity. His own reflections upon his devotional activity led him to the conviction that God was without shape or form. At the age of eighteen he moved to Madras to continue his education and later to start his own business manufacturing cloth.

At some point after World War II, Vethathiri met Swami Paranjothi, a teacher of kundalini yoga and founder of the Temple of Universal Peace in Madras. The practice of kundalini yoga brought together the religious speculations which had held much of his attention throughout his life. He soon discovered that he could project the kundalini energy into others (shaktipat) and do good for others. In 1958, Vethathiri established the World Community Service in Madras. Three years later he moved the headquarters to his home town of Guduvancheri, from whence it spread throughout India.

Vethathiri teaches Simplified Kundalini Yoga (SKY), a process of arousing the latent kundalini force in each individual, generally pictured as resting like a coiled serpent as the base of the spine and bringing enlightenment. SKY is able to bypass the laborious techniques traditionally considered integral to kundalini yoga, and through shaktipat, Vethathiri is able to arouse the kundalini and teach the student how to control the working of the energy, a process called shanti yoga. Once having mastered shanti yoga, the aspirant can have the kundalini fully aroused by Vethathiri through a process called turiya yoga and experience a state of tranquility and blissfulness. Finally, the aspirant is led into a still higher state of consciousness, turiyateetha yoga, in which the individual consciousness is merged with the Infinite.

Vethathiri made his first visit to the United States in 1972 at the invitation of the younger brother of the leader of the New Delhi World Community Service Center. He resided in Bound Brook, New Jersey, where Vethathiri gave his first American lectures and organized the first American World Community Service Centre. The organization spread along the east coast primarily through the Indian-American community. Since the organization of the centre, Vethathiri has made annual visits to the United States and centres have been established across America.

Membership: Not reported.

Sources:

Vethathiri, Yogiraj. *Physical Transformation of Soul*. Madras, India: Vethathiri Publications, 1982.

___. *Sex and Spiritual Development*. Madras, India: Vethathiri Publications, 1982.

___. *The Story of My Life*. Madras, India: Vethathiri Publications, 1982.

★2064★
World Plan Executive Council-US
PO Box 370
Lake Shandelee Rd.
Livingston Manor, NY 12758

The World Plan Executive Council is one of several organizations in this *Encyclopedia* that claim they are not a religious group and hence should not be included in such a volume. Critics of the council and of the technique it teaches to those affiliated with Transcendental Meditation (TM), have argued forcefully that it is a religion, some going so far as to charge the council with hiding its religious nature in order to deceive the public and gain some benefits available only to nonreligious organizations in the West. Some of these critics took their case to court and in 1978, the U.S. District Court in Newark, New Jersey, ruled that the practice of TM was religious in nature and banned the teaching of TM in the public schools of New Jersey. Subsequently, the teaching of TM was dropped from other programs supported by public funds.

In response, the World Plan Executive Council has argued that the 1978 court decision was a mistake and draws attention to the specific nature of the practice of TM and the extensive scientific research on TM which has been completed and published in reputable journals. It also argues that its basic theoretical base, the Science of Creative Intelligence (SCI), was formulated as a scietific theory, not a religious teaching. Also, it notes the participation of people of many religions, even leaders of various religions, who not only practice TM, but are instructors for the council.

The argument between the council and its critics goes to the very heart of the ongoing discussion of the definition of religion in both the academic and the legal use of the term. Nor is it the task of this *Encyclopedia* to decide the issue, both sides of which have strong arguments. It has been decided to continue the entry on the council simply because the court has placed it on the religious agenda and inquiries concerning TM still emerge in the context of the growth of Eastern religious practice in the West. It is, in fact, impossible to tell the story of the rise of Hinduism in America without reference to TM, which participated in the initial wave of Indian teaching to come to America following World War II. However, the author is happy to acknowledge the contrary opinion of the council.

The founder of TM (or rather the modern rediscover) was Guru Dev, but its real exponent has been Maharishi Mahesh Yogi, who spent 13 years in seclusion with Guru Dev, and upon Guru Dev's death, came forth in 1958 to tell the world about TM. Prior to his life of meditation, he had obtained a B.S. in physics at Allahabad University. In 1959 he made his first world tour, which brought him to the United States. His movement grew slowly until the mid-1960s when some popular entertainers (the Beatles, Mia Farrow, Jane Fonda) identified with it.

In 1972 Maharishi announced the World Plan, the overall strategy which guides the movement and from which the council takes its name. The goal of the world plan is to share the Science of Creative Intelligence with the whole world. The immediate objective of the plan is to establish 3,600 World Plan centers (one for each million people on earth) and to staff each center with 1,000 teachers (one for each thousand people on earth.) The ultimate goal is to bring the Age of Enlightenment.

To carry out its agenda, the World Plan Executive Council has organized into five task-oriented structures. The International Meditation Society is the main structure for introducing the general public to TM. The Spiritual Regeneration Movement works with the "older" generation, i.e., people over thirty, while the Student International Meditation Society targets the campus population. Maharishi International University is a four-year university that offers both bachelor's and master's degrees, with instruction based on presenting traditional material with a TM perspective. The university is in Fairfield, Iowa. The American Foundation for the Science of Creative Intelligence is working within the business community.

In 1976 Maharishi created the World Government of the Age of Enlightenment, described as a nonpolitical global organization that "enjoys sovereignty in the domain of consciousness" and "activity in the eternally dynamic silence of the unified field of all of the forces of nature." The World Government became a momentary object of attention in 1983 when Maharishi offered its services to the world's governments to assist them in solving their problems.

The essence of TM is a form of japa yoga-meditation with a mantra, a sound constantly repeated silently during meditation and upon which the meditator concentrates. Each individual begins his process of meditation with initiation. At that time, he is given an individual mantra for his/her own use and which is not to be revealed to others. The mantra may be given by Maharishi, but most often today is given by a certified TM instructor. The initiation ceremony, during which members repeat a number of "prayers" to Hindu deities and offer veneration to a long line of gurus, became a foundation block in the case built by critics claiming TM was a religious practice.

The overall perspective of the council is spelled out in Maharishi's book, *The Science of Being and the Art of Living*, in which a complete cosmology is presented. According to Maharishi, underneath the universe is the absolute field of pure being—unmanifested and transcendental. Being is the ultimate reality of creation. The science of being teaches how to contact ultimate reality. TM is the tool. Once the meditation begins, one starts to "live the being" and the council offers instruction on correct thinking, speaking, acting, and health. The goal is God-realization. Maharishi's teaching is "the summation of the practical wisdom of the integrated life as advanced by the Vedic Rishis of ancient India." That is to say, the ultimate goal of TM is to "achieve the spiritual goals of mankind in this generation."

Currently, Maharishi has no legal affiliation to the World Plan Executive Council. He is looked upon as the founder of TM and the Science of Creative Intelligence. Through his books, taped lectures, and constant presence in picture and thought, he still dominates the organization.

Important to the establishment of TM as a popular practice have been the council's encouragement of widespread research and documentation of its effects. To date more than 500 research studies have been completeed at universities and colleges in more than 25 nations. Many of these have been published in academic journals and later reprinted and circulated by the movement. Such studies document the role of the practice of TM in (among other things) curbing alcohol and drug abuse, assisting in the rehabilitation of criminals and delinquents, increasing productivity on the job, producing a more healthy body, improving athletic performance, and raising intelligence quotients.

Growth of TM during the early 1970s was rapid and widespread media coverage helped provide openings in the business world, the Army, and the school system. Growth began to slow in the mid-1970s and decreased rapidly following the 1977 court decision. That same year TM announced its siddha program, a course in advanced techniques that allowed the student to gain various supernormal capacities including levitation, invisibility, mastery over nature, and fulfillment of all desires. The overall goal was the creation of the Age of Enlightenment. While many signed up for the course, it caused attacks from many who argued that it was impossible to produce the advertised results. In 1987 a former TM instructor sued the organization over the siddha claims and was granted a $138,000 judgement.

During the 1980s, the council has continued to extend its programs into broader areas of life. In the late 1980s, a major promotional program for Ayurvedic medicine was launched and the Maharishi Center for Ayur-Veda opened in Fairfield, Iowa (adjacent to the university). The center's directors have introduced "Maharishi Amrit Kalesh" as an herbal supplement. It is being marketed by Maharishi Ayurvedic Products International. Most recently, the council had sponsored the establishment of the Natural Law Party, a political party active in the United States and several European countries. The Natural Law Party offers the council's program to the electorate as an alternative to traditional political party platforms.

Membership: Not reported. By 1984 more than 1,000,000 people had taken basic TM courses in the United States; many of those, however, are not continuing to practice TM. In 1978, the organization had more than 7,000 authorized teachers and 400 teaching centers. Researchers have noted that TM peaked in 1976 when it initiated 292,273 people. By the end of that year, however, it had begun a radical decline. In 1977 it initiated only 50,000.

Educational Facilities: Maharishi International University, Fairfield, Iowa.

Periodicals: MIU World. Send orders to 1000 N. 4th St., DB 1155, Fairfield, IA 52557-1155. • Modern Science and Vedic Science.

Sources:

Bainbridge, William Sims, and Daniel H. Jackson. "The Rise and Decline of Transcendental Meditation." Edited by Rodney Stark and William Sims Bainbridge, *The Future of Religion*. Berkeley and Los Angeles: University of California Press, 1985.

Bloomfield, Harold H., Michael Peter Cain, and Dennis T. Jaffe. *TM, Discovering Inner Energy and Overcoming Stress*. New York: Delacorte Press, 1975.

Carrey, Normand J., and Lynn A. Suess. *TM and Cult Mania*. North Quincy, MA: Christopher Publishing House, 1980.

Ebon, Martin, ed. *Maharishi, the Guru*. New York: New American Library, 1968.

Goldhaber, Nat. *TM: An Alphabetical Guide to the Transcendental Meditation Program*. New York: Ballantine Books, 1976.

Lewis, Gordon R. *Transcendental Meditation*. Glendale, CA: G/L Regal Books, 1975.

Jefferson, William. *The Story of the Maharishi*. New York: Pocket Books, 1976.

Mahesh Yogi, Maharishi. *Life Supported by Natural Law*. Washington, DC: Age of Enlightenment Press, 1986.

___. *Love and God*. Age of Enlightenment Press, 1973.

___. *The Science of Being and Art of Living*. London: International SRM Publications, 1966.

Orme-Johnson, David W., and John T. Farrows, eds. *Scientific Research on the Tradscendental Meditation Program: Collected Papers, I*. Seelisberg, Switzerland: Maharishi European Research University Press, 1977.

Patton, John E. *The Case Against TM in the Schools*. Grand Rapids, MI: Baker Book House, 1976.

Scott, R. D. *Transcendental Misconceptions*. San Diego, CA: Beta Books, 1978.

White, John. *Everything You Want to Know About TM, Including How to Do It*. New York: Pocket Books, 1976.

★2065★

Yasodhara Ashram Society
Box 9
Kootenay Bay, BC, Canada V0B 1X0

Yasodhara Ashram Society was founded by Swami Sivananda (1911-1995) (Sylvia Hellman, a German-born Canadian citizen). In her forties, while meditating, she saw the face of Swami Sivananda Saraswati in a vision. She traveled to India, was initiated as a sanyasin (renuciate) by Sivananda into the Saraswati (monastic) Order in 1956. At Sivananda's direction, she returned to Canada to update the Eastern teachings for for the Western mind. From 1956 to 1963, the Ashram was in Vancouver, but then was moved to Kootenay Bay, in the mountains of southeastern British Columbia.

Swami Radha expanded the teachings of yoga to include Western psychology and symbolism in order to create a bridge of understanding between East and West. Unique to Swami Radha were numerous practical techniques that help to bring quality into daily living and to expand consciousness. She is one of the foremost authorities on Kundalini yoga. The ashram offers courses on many different aspects of yoga, retreat packages for groups and individuals, and a three-month personal growth intensive each winter. The Temple of Divine Light Dedicated to All Religions was completed in 1992. Connected with the ashram is the Association for the Development of Human Potential, also founded by Swami Radha and the ashram's publishing arm, Timeless Books, both located in Spokane, Washington.

Membership: In 1998 the Ashram reported 80 members. There are also affiliated centers, called Radha Houses, across Canada and the United States, as well as in Mexico, and England.

Educational Facilities: Yasodhara Ashram Society Centre, Kootenay Bay, British Columbia.

Periodicals: *Ascent.*

Sources:

Radha, Sivannada. *Gods Who Walk the Rainbow.* Porthill, ID: Timeless Books, 1981.

___. *Hatha Yoga, Hidden Language.* Port Hill, ID: Timeless Books, 1987.

___. *Kundalini, Yoga for the West.* Spokane, WA: Timeless Books, 1978.

___. *Mantras, Words of Power.* Porthill, ID: Timeless Books, 1980.

___. *Radha, Diary of a Woman's Search.* Porthill, ID: Timeless Books, 1981.

★2066★
Yoga House Ashram
Current address not obtained for this edition.

The Yoga House Ashram was founded in the mid-1970s by Vimalananda (b. 1942), a former leader of the Ananda Marga Yoga Society. Dadaji, as he is affectionately known, was born in Badwel, South India, of a Brahmin family. At the age of six he had an intense initiation experience of divine light filling his room and a voice instructing him on the path of enlightenment. He began to pursue the inner life, and at the age of sixteen became an instructor of meditation. In 1962 he met Shrii Anandamurti, founder of the Ananda Marga Yoga Society and was impressed with both his spirituality and his program of service to humanity, especially the sick, the elderly, and the poor. In like measure, Anandamurti was impressed with his young disciple and quickly elevated him to a teacher of yoga. In 1966 Dadaji left India to spread Ananda Marga. He was responsible for starting centers in Thailand, Singapore, Indonesia, Malasia, Hong Kong, and the Philippines. The government and the United Nations honored him for his efforts on behalf of the victims of the 1968 earthquake that struck Manila.

In 1969 Dadaji came to the United States and assisted in the spread of Ananda Marga. However, in the mid-1970s he left Ananda Marga and founded the Yoga House Ashram. Since that time he has spent his time creating his own following in the San Francisco Bay area of California. Dadaji came to the United States with a strong desire to bridge the gap between East and West. He teaches a traditional yoga but has retained the emphasis upon social action he found in Ananda Marga. He teaches his students to keep their role in society as they strive for God.

Membership: Not reported. The work of the Yoga House Ashram is confined to northern California where Dadaji Vimalananda teaches yoga at a variety of locations in the greater San Francisco Bay area.

Sources:

Vimalananda, Dadaji. *Yogamritam (The Nectar of Yoga).* San Rafael, CA: Yoga House Ashram, 1977.

★2067★
Yoga Research Foundation
6111 SW 74th Ave.
Miami, FL 33143

Alternate Address: Indian headquarters: International Yoga Society, Lal Bagh, Loni—201 102, Ghazlabad, U.P., India.

Swami Jyotirmayananda (b. 1931) is a learned teacher who began his religious pilgrimage in the ascetic life, emerged into teaching and editing, and became a leading figure at Swami Sivananda Saraswati's Yoga Vedanta Forest Academy. He came to America in 1962 and founded the Sanantan Dharma Mandir with headquarters in Puerto Rico. The headquarters were moved to Miami under the present name in 1969. Jyotirmayananda teaches integral yoga. He has developed a vast publishing program centered on his many books, cassettes, and monthly magazine.

Membership: In 1995 the foundation reported approximately 2,000 active members. There is one center in Miami and one near Delhi, India. The foundation considers the subscribers to the magazine and recipients of the *International Yoga Guide* to be members.

Periodicals: *International Yoga Guide.* • *Integral Light.*

Sources:

Jyotir Maya Nanda, Swami. *The Way to Liberation.* Miami, FL: Swami Lalitananda, 1976.

___. *Yoga Can Change Your Life.* Miami, FL: International Yoga Society, 1975.

___. *Yoga in Life.* Miami, FL: Swami Jyotir Maya Nanada, 1973.

___. *Yoga of Sex-Sublimation, Truth and Non-violence.* Miami, FL: Swami Lalitananda, 1974.

___. *Yoga Vasistha.* Miami, FL: Yoga Research Society, 1977.

★2068★
Yoganta Meditation Center
(Defunct)

The Yoganta Meditation Center was a small eclectic community based upon the concept of spiritual growth through a variety of meditative and yogic techniques. The center provided residential facilities where adherents could practice their own discipline for an extended time. There was no guru; the belief was that the exchange of personal experiences would benefit all.

Seminars were irregularly offered on such topics as mantras, hatha yoga, meditation and miscellaneous psychic topics. A quarterly journal, *The Yoganta Center Newsletter,* was published. During the 1970s there are approximately ten to fifteen residents at the center located at Nederland, Colorado.

★2069★
Yogi Gupta Association
Current address not obtained for this edition.

Yogi Gupta, born in Kanpur in North India, was a lawyer who left his profession to become a monk in the sannyasa order in Banaras. At that time, he was renamed Swami Kailashananda and became a major teacher of hatha and karma yoga. He also founded the Kailashananda Mission at Rishikesh. Basic to Yogi Gutpa's teaching is hatha yoga with its various postures (asanas). Hatha is the entrance into various other disciplines including psychic development, vegetarianism and yogic philosophy. Through yoga one can learn self-mastery and achieve the many goals of life-happiness, success and freedom. Yogi Gupta first came to the United States in 1954. He founded a center in New York City which is an outpost of the Indian centers.

Membership: Not reported.

Sources:

Gupta, Yogi. *Shradha and Heavenly Fathers.* New York: Yogi Gupta New York Center, n.d.

___. *Yoga and Long Life.* New York: Dodd, Mead, & Company, 1958.

___. *Yoga and Yogic Powers.* New York: Yogi Gupta New York Center, 1963.

★2070★
Yogiraj Sect
(Defunct)

Swami Swanandashram was born in Calcutta in 1921 and in his youth became a yogi. In college he was a student of philosophy, mathematics and sanskrit. In 1950, however, he renounced all possessions and for twenty years lived in a cave at Gangotri. He was initiated in the Shankaracharya Order and is now head of the Yogiraj Sect. In 1970, Swanandashram emerged from his cave and began a public ministry to teach a way of oneness with God through yoga. In his teaching, the essential reality of the unchangeable God is held up as that which is to be seen behind the transitory illusions of commonplace life. The erroneous identification of the body as the real self is the root of all evil, suffering and death. Yoga is the means to overcome the false identification. During the early 1970s there was one American center of Swanadashram's followers in Easton, Pennsylvania. It was absorbed into the Holy Shankaracharya Order.

Indian-American Hindu Temples

★2071★
Bharatiya Temple
6850 Adams Rd.
Troy, MI 48098

The Bharatiya Temple grew out of an informal meeting held by a group of first generation Inian-Americans in Detroit, Michigan, in January 1975. ("Bharata" is the ancient name for India.) An ad-hoc committee prepared a constitution which was adopted two months later. A board of trustees was elected, an organization to erect a temple was created, and land was purchased in Troy, a Detroit suburb. During the years of construction, bi-weekly religious meetings were held at the Unitarian Church in Southfield, Michigan. The temple was dedicated in July 1981. Swami Chinmayananda, head of the Chinmaya Mission West and Sant Keshavadas of the Temple of Cosmic Religion participated in the dedication ceremonies. The temple has become a gathering place for Detroit's Hindus and is used by many other Hindu organizations for public programs.

Membership: Not reported.

Periodicals: *Chetana.* Send orders to Box 61, Troy, MI 48099.

★2072★
Bochasanwasi Swaminarayan Sanstha
43-38 Bowne St.
Flushing, NY 11355

The Bochasanwasi Swaminarayan Sanstha, also known as Bochasanwasi Shri Akshar Purushottam Swaminarayan Sanstha, is the American branch of an international Hindu movement which originated in western India at the beginning of the nineteenth century. Its founder was Shree Sahajanand Swami, popularly known as Swaminarayan (1781-1830), and was born in Uttar Pradesh, India. He followed the teachings of Vaishnava leader Sri Ramanuja, who in the twelfth century advocated theistic worship, as opposed to the idea of an impersonal divine reality espoused by Shankaracharya and taught the necessity of devotional service (bhakti yoga) as a means to salvation. Swaminarayan emphasized Ramanuja's teaching that God manifests on earth through both his

incarnation and his fully realized saint. Swaminarayan was named the successor to his guru, Swami Ramanand. Shortly after assuming the mantle of his guru, he proclaimed that he was Lord Swami Narayan, the Supreme being, manifest on earth, and he is so considered to this day by members of the movement. Worship of Swaminarayan is central to the life of the movement. His work, concentrated in the Indian state of Gujarat, led to a revival of religious life and the establishment of centers throughout western India. Since his passing away, the movement has been led by a succession of High Priests, through whom Swami Narayan's presence continues to reside in the world. The movement remained small during the nineteenth century and into the twentieth, but has grown rapidly under the vigorous leadership of the present High Priest.

The Swami Narayan movement was brought to the United States by the immigration of devotees in the late 1960s. In 1970, the High Priest, His Supreme Divine Holiness Yogiji Maharaj, toured England, where a center had been created. While he was there, an American devotee traveled to England and requested that the movement be organized in America. In response, the High Priest sent four monks to America with a list of known devotees. Touring the country, they established centers wherever they found a small concentration of devotees. A correspondence network was established around the center in Flushing, Long Island, New York. In February 1972, the group in New York incorporated. The following year property was purchased, and in 1974 the High Priest His Supreme Divine Holiness Pramukh Swami Maharaj (on the first of his many tours to include the United States) visited America for the installation of deities. Fifteen hundred attended the ceremony. Since that time the movement has spread across the United States with major centers in Flushing, New York; Piscatway and Edison, New Jersey; Boston, Massachusetts; Erie, Pennsylvania; Chicago, Illinois; Dallas and Houston, Texas; Atlanta, Georgia; and San Francisco, San Jose, and Los Angeles, California. Deity statues were installed in the Chicago and Los Angeles temples during the 1984 visit of the High Priest; in Houston, Dallas, Atlanta, and Toronto, Canada, during the 1988 visit; and in Edison, New Jersey, and San Jose, California, during the 1991 visit. Internationally, major centers are found across India, Kenya, Tanzania, Uganda, South Africa, Australia, Belgium, Germany, England, Canada (Toronto and Kitchener, Ontario), Singapore, and Thailand. International headquarters are in Ahmedabad, India.

Membership: In 1991 there were an estimated 60,000 devotees in the United States organized around nine main temples and 43 other centers. The temples are in New York, Edison, Boston, Chicago, Los Angeles, San Jose, Houston, Dallas, Atlanta, and Toronto. Membership is largely confined to the Gujarat Indian-American community. B.S.S. has a worldwide following of millions of devotees with 450 saints and over 3000 centers.

Educational Facilities: Pramukh Swami Medical College, Karamsad, Gujarat State, India.

Pramukh Swami Institute of Electronics, Vidyanagar, Gujarat State, India.

School of Architecture, S. P. University, Vidyanagar, Gujarat State, India.

Pramukh Swami Science College, Kadi, Gurjarat State, India.

Akshardham-Centre for Applied Research in Social Harmony (AARSH), Gandhinagar, Gujarat State, India.

Remarks: The fellowship has recently encountered strong local opposition from residents of Independence Township, near Washington, New Jersey, where it had purchased land for a large religious-educational complex. Residents have been concerned about negative impact on the area by the development of the group's land.

Sources:

Dave, H. T. *Life and Philosophy of Shree Swaminarayan.* London: George Allen & Unwin, 1974.

Fisher, Maxine P. *The Indians of New York City.* Columbia, MO: South Asia Books, 1980.

Williams, Raymond Brady. *A New Face of Hinduism: The Swaminarayan Religion.* Cambridge: Cambridge University Press, 1984.

★2073★

Hindu Temple of Greater Chicago

% Ramalayam Hindu Temple
Box 99
Lemont, IL 60439

The Hindu Temple of Greater Chicago was founded in the 1970s. It is one of several such associations within the larger Indian-American community of Chicago. In 1980, it purchased 17 acres of land near Lemont, Illinois, and began construction of the Shri Rama Temple and Community Center. The ground breaking for the temple was held in the spring of 1981; the temple has recently been dedicated and opened for public worship.

Membership: Not reported.

Periodicals: *Newsletter.* Send orders to Box 697, Lombard, IL 60148.

★2074★

Hindu Temple Society of North America

45-57 Bowne St.
Flushing, NY 11355

The Hindu Temple Society of North America was founded in the early 1970s and has centered its activity upon the construction and maintenance of the first Indian-style temple built according to strict Vedic standards in the United States. It was dedicated on July 4, 1977, by His Holiness Sri La Sri Pandrimalai Swamigal of Madras, India. The central shrine of the temple is dedicated to Ganesha (Maha Ganapati), the deity known to be the remover of obstacles. Other shrines are dedicated to Siva (and his consort Parvati), Shanmukha (and his consorts Valli and Devayani), Vishnu-Venkateswara, and Lakshmi.

The temple was designed to serve all segments of the Indian-American community with shrines to Siva, Vishnu, and Devi. The temple supports a number of charities in India which include the Sri Venkateswara Balamandir Orphanage, a foster parents program, an artificial limb fitting center, and scholarships for Indian college students. In the United States, the temple supports a medical service center in Flushing, New York, and the distribution of secondhand clothing to the needy.

Membership: In 1992 the society reported 10,500 members.

Sources:

Ehrlicher, C. C. "The New Hindu Temple: India Comes to Flushing." *The New Sun* 1, no. 9 (September 1977).

★2075★

Hindu Temple Society of Southern California

1600 Las Virgenes Canyon Rd.
Calabasas, CA 91302

The Hindu Temple Society of Southern California was formed in July 1977 by a group of Indian-Americans to fulfill the religious needs of the Hindu Indian-Americans in the metropolitan Los Angeles area. As a focus for its concerns, it decided to construct a temple dedicated to Sri Venkateswara, the popular deity and incarnation of Vishnu. After a considerable search, a sight near Malibu, California, was purchased in December 1979. Construction of the temple began in 1980 and the initial shrine to Lord Genesh, the son of Shiva in Hindu thought and often worshipped as the remover of obstacles, was completed before the end of the year. Construction was immediately begun on the main shrine to Sri Venkateswara, and in May 1984, the shrine was completed to the point that the deity's statue could be installed with appropriate

ceremonies under the direction of Brahman priest Varadaraja Bhattar. Other shrines, including one to Krishna, another incarnation of Vishnu (installed October 1985), have also been added, and construction continues (as of 1986).

Though the Sri Venkateswara Temple is primarily a Vaishnava worship center, shrines have been constructed immediately adjacent to the main temple for Saivite worship in recognition of the temple's function within the larger Indian-American Hindu community. Ceremonies are scheduled daily at the temple, with special services, usually on weekends, to coincide with major Hindu holy days.

Membership: Not reported.

Periodicals: *Newsletter.*

★2076★

Hindu Temple Society of Texas

4533 Larch Ln.
Bellaire, TX 77401

In 1974 Hindus in Houston, Texas, formed the Hindu Temple Society of Texas. Land was purchased in suburban Bellaire, and construction of a temple begun. That same year, a monthly newsletter was begun by one of the members, Dr. Lal Sardana. Members of the temple follow traditional Hinduism which is interpreted as a monotheistic religion. "Om," the word chanted by many Hindus, is considered the symbol of the one Universal Monotheistic God, who is formless. That god is also symbolized in its three dimensions as creator (Brahma), sustainer (Vishnu), and changer (Siva), the main deities in the traditional Hindu pantheon.

Membership: In 1984 there were approximately 2,000 members of the temple, most residing in southeast Texas.

Periodicals: *Hindu Jyoti.*

★2077★

Sri Meenakshi Temple Society of Houston

Rte. 5, Box 5725
Pearland, TX 77584

The Sri Meenakshi Temple Society of Houston was initiated by a group of some 30 Indian-American families in Houston, Texas, who met together in October 1977. Over the next year they adopted a constitution, incorporated, and formed committees to pursue the construction of a traditional temple dedicated to the worship of Sri Meenakshi, a Shakti deity form. Land was purchased in suburban Pearland, and Phase I, the construction of the temple to Sri Ganesh (the popular elephant-headed deity considered to be the "remover of obstacles" by Hindus), was begun. That small temple was completed and the deity installed in 1979. Phase II, the building of the main temple to Sri Meenakshi, commenced immediately. Beside the main sanctum housing the statue of Sri Meenakshi are two other sanctums housing the prominent Hindu deity forms Lord Venkateswara (Vishnu) and Sri Sundareswara (Siva or Shiva, the consort of Shakti). Dedication of the temple and installation of the deity statues were completed in an elaborate week-long ceremony in June 1982. Further elements of the complete temple are still in process.

The goddess Sri Meenakshi is a form of shakti, the female form of divine energy. Integral to traditional shakti worship is the spreading of knowledge through mystic diagrams, called *yantras.* The installation of the yantras, inscribed on thin metal plates, was an important part of the dedication services at the temple. This temple was the first important temple for tantric worship established among Indian-Americans in the United States.

Membership: In 1992 the society had enrolled approximately 200 families.

Periodicals: *Temple News.*

Sources:

"Inaugural Ceremonies Held for Sri Meenakshi Temple in Houston, Texas." *The New Saivite World* 4, no. 2 (August 1, 1982): 1, 11.

★2078★
Sri Venkateswara Temple
S. McCully Rd.
Penn Hills
PO Box 17289
Pittsburgh, PA 15235

Among the first temples to be envisioned by the emerging Indian-American community in the 1970s was the Sri Venkateswara Temple in Pittsburgh, Pennsylvania. Planning for the temple began in January 1972, and construction was initiated four years later on a site in Penns Hills, east of Pittsburgh. The main deities were installed in November 1976.

The temple is modeled on the Tirupathi Shrine in South India. The main deity is Sri Venkateswara, an incarnation of Vishnu. Entrance to the temple is through a massive Rajagopuran (entrance tower). Besides Sri Venkateswara, statues to Padmavathi (an incarnation of Lakshmi, Vishnu's consort) and the mother earth goddess Andal (or Bhooma Devi) are also given a central place. Members of the temple, while following a full round of deity worship, view the idols (deities) as symbols of the one invisible spirit (God) to whom, in fact, the worship is offered. Manavala Iyengar is the current priest in charge of temple worship.

Membership: In 1985 the temple serviced approximately 5,000 families in western Pennsylvania and around the United States, almost all of which were first generation immigrants.

Periodicals: *Saptagiri Vana.* • *Indian Youth Review.* Both publications are available from Box 17280, Pittsburgh, PA 15235-0280.

★2079★
United Hindu Temple of New Jersey
% Dr. Raj P. Misra
1 CeCamp Ct.
West Caldwell, NJ 07006

The United Hindu Temple of New Jersey was formed in the mid-1970s by representatives of a variety of Indian-American organizations who wished to provide a place for traditional Hindu temple worship at a non-sectarian site. A coordinating council was selected and, by 1978, the first issue of a periodical, *Konarak,* appeared. Inspiration has been taken from Konarak, a town in Orissa, India, renowned for its beautiful temples.

Membership: Not reported.

Periodicals: *Konarak.*

Jainism

★2080★
International Nahavir Jain Mission
Acharya Sushil Jain Ashram
722 Tomkins Ave.
Staten Island, NY 10305

Since 1965, along with Hindus and Sikhs, Jains began to immigrate to the United States, though due to restrictions on travel over water, not in numbers as great as members of other Indian religious groups. Among the immigrants were individuals associated with the International Mahavir Mission. The Mission had been founded in India in 1970 by Guruji Muni Sushul Kumar (b. 1926). As a teenager, Guruji had entered the Sacred Order of Jain Munis, receiving from his guru two traditional symbols of nonviolence: the mukh-patti, a white mask worn over the face to keep the wearer from accidently swallowing an insect and thus killing a living soul, and an augha, a broom for sweeping surfaces before sitting lest a living entity be harmed. The Mission was brought to Europe and North America by its members. Guruji traveled to the United States in 1975 to visit the Jain communities.

The Mission emphasizes the Jain tenets of vegetarianism, *ahimsa* (nonviolence) and *anekantavada* (the many-faceted nature of truth). It teaches hatha yoga, *pranayama* (breath control), *japa yoga* (the use of mantric words of power), ayurvedic medicine, and chanting.

In the United States an urban ashram was opened in Staten Island and a rural center, Muni Sushil Yogville, in upstate New York. Centers have also been opened in England, France, Germany and Canada. International headquarters are in New Delhi, India. Guruji has been active in interreligious work (growing out of the Jain belief in anekantavada), and organized the World Fellowship of Religions which periodically sponsors international interreligious conferences. In 1977, Guruji also participated in the first North American Jain Conference held at Berkeley, California, in 1981.

Membership: Not reported.

Periodicals: *News from Jain Ashram.*

Sources:

Kumar, Acharya Sushil. *Song of the Soul.* Blairstown, NJ: Siddhachalam Publishers, 1987.

★2081★
Jain Meditation International Center
Current address not obtained for this edition.

Gurudev Shree Chitrabhanu had been a Jain muni (monk) for twenty-nine years. During that time he had become widely known and respected in his native India and had, in 1965, founded the Divine Knowledge Society in Bombay. Then in 1971 he gave up his monastic existence and rejected the millennia-long taboo on traveling over water and by means other than foot, to come to the United States at the invitation of the Temple of Understanding to lecture at a conference at Harvard University. Following that conference, he stayed in North America and lectured widely to both other Jains who, like him, had immigrated to America. In 1974, he founded New Life Now, an organization dedicated to the spiritual illumination of the West. New Life Now evolved into the Jain Meditation International Center. Chitrabhanu defines a Jain as one who "speaks of a personal responsibility for his own deeds, regards a person as a master of his own destiny, and refrains from violence."

The center is headquartered in New York City and teaches meditation, yoga, vegetarianism, and tai chi. While moving among Jains who have immigrated to the United States, Chitrabhanu has had great success among non-Indian-Americans. Groups have been established in Boston, Pittsburgh, Philadelphia, West Orange (New Jersey), and Toronto. He has also worked in Brazil. The associated Jain Peace Fellowship is headquartered in South Norwalk, Connecticut. Chitrabhanu participated in the first North American Jain conference held in Berkeley, California, in 1981.

Membership: Not reported.

Periodicals: *Newsletter.*

Sources:

Baakza, A. H. A. *Half-hours with a Jain Muni.* Bombay: Jaico Publishing House, 1962.

Chitrabhanu, Gurudev. *The Philosophy of Soul and Matter.* New York: Jain Meditation Center, 1977.

___. *The Psychology of Enlightenment.* New York: Dodd, Mead & Company, 1979.

___. *Realize What You Are.* New York: Dodd, Mead & Company, 1978.

___. *Twelve Facets of Reality.* New York: Dodd, Mead & Company, 1980.

★2082★
Osho Commune International
% Osho Viha Meditation Center
Box 352
Mill Valley, CA 94942

Alternate Address: International headquarters: Osho Commune International, 17 Koregoan Park, Poona, India 411001 or Osho International, 24 St. James St., London, United Kingdom SW1 1HA.

Osho, formerly known as Bhagwan Shree Rajneesh, was born Rajneesh Chandra Mohan in a small town in Madhya Pradesh, India, in 1931, and went on to become one of the most controversial spiritual mystics to travel to the West and establish his teachings. Born of Jain parents, Osho, even as a child, began to question the wide variety of traditional religious beliefs to which he was exposed as a young man—Hindu, Christian, Mohammedan, or Jain—and asserted that individual spiritual experience was the only true value and that such experience could not be organized into any belief system.

During his college days in 1953, at the age of 21, he had what he termed an experience of *samadhi*, or spiritual awakening. However, he decided to continue his academic studies, earning a masters degree in philosophy and sharpening his skills as a speaker by debating at universities all over India. In 1966, he resigned his post as Professor of Philosophy at the University of Jabalpur in order to share his understanding of religious experience and to conduct experimental "meditation camps" using his own unique methods.

In the early 1970s he began to initiate people into "neo-sannyas", a radical departure from the traditional Hindu form of sannyas in which the spiritual seeker renounces home, family, wealth, sex, and the material life. Instead, Osho taught that the real challenge for the Sannyasin is to remain in the world, enjoying life to the full, but not being attached to it—"to be in the market place but not of it." Initiates were asked to dress in orange, wear a *mala* (a necklace of 108 wooden beads containing a locket with Oshos picture), receive a new name, and meditate for at least one hour a day.

In 1972, the first westerners came to Osho while he was living in Bombay. Many of these newcomers were therapists from the Western humanistic psychology movement who were attracted by Oshos teachings that selfexpression and emotional release are useful preparations for meditation. In 1974, a group of disciples purchased property in Poona, near Bombay, and this quickly became an international ashram attracting thousands of visitors from around the world. Daily activities included a 90-minute discourse by Osho, a regular program of meditation, a wide variety of therapy groups, and working in the commune. The best known of Oshos meditation methods is Dynamic Meditation, which lasts one hour and has five stages: 1) deep, rapid, chaotic breathing through the nose; 2) emotional catharsis, allowing free expression to anger, sadness, joy, etc.; 3) jumping, with arms raised saying the mantra "hoo!"; 4) complete silence and stillness; and 5) celebration through dance.

In his daily discourses, Osho commented upon all of the major religious traditions and the sayings of many enlightened mystics, including Jesus, Gautam Buddha, Lao Tzu, Krishna, Mahavira, and Bodhidharma. Later, he explained this as his way of "gathering his people" who would otherwise have remained involved with other religious disciplines.

Osho came to the United States in 1981, and after a short stay in New Jersey moved to a 64,000 acre ranch in Central Oregon. Within a year, a city named Rajneeshpuram had been incorporated on the ranch, with a population that rose to 5,000 people.

Mounting opposition from local ranchers, Christian fundamentalists, and increasingly from the Oregon state government and the Reagan Administration soon created an embattled atmosphere, fueled by Oshos provocative fleet of 93 Rolls Royces and acts such as inviting thousands of Americas street people to live at the ranch and vote in local elections.

In 1985, Osho, who had been in silence from 1981 to 1984, publicly revealed that his secretary, Ma Anand Sheela, had been involved in a number of crimes against his disciples and people in Oregon, and invited the police to investigate. A few weeks later, Osho himself was arrested by federal agents, jailed, and charged with immigration fraud. Although insisting on his innocence, Osho agreed to a plea bargain with federal prosecutors and was deported from the United States. With Osho no longer in residence, the Oregon commune was no longer an economically viable proposition and the residents departed, turning Rajneeshpuram into a ghost town. Sheela, and a small group of close associates, arranged plea bargains with state and federal prosecutors and served jail sentences.

Osho returned to India, staying briefly in the Himalayas, then in 1986 embarked on a world tour during which, due in part to pressure from the Reagan Administration, he was refused entry by 21 countries. He went back to India once more and in January 1987 returned to his old ashram in Poona, which quickly revived as a large international commune. At about this same time, Osho advised his disciples to drop their distinctive clothing and the mala, since the Indian authorities were making it difficult for them to enter the country.

In 1988, he dropped the name Bhagwan Shree Rajneesh and assumed the name Osho, a Japanese term of reverence and endearment used by disciples to their spiritual masters.

During this time Oshos body became very weak and he suffered from a variety of puzzling symptoms, including severe bone pain, hair loss, and impaired vision, which led his disciples to believe that he had been poisoned while in the custody of the U.S. government. He died on January 19, 1990, and a sacred grave was made for his ashes inside the commune. Before his death, Osho had guided a group of 21 disciples into assuming control of the worldwide activities of his movement. This group is known as the Inner Circle.

In the United States, after Oshos departure, the movement decentralized and returned to its pre-1986 state, a loose association of meditation centers and small communes scattered around the country. A bi-monthly news magazine for sannyasins, titled *Viha Connection*, is produced by the Osho Viha Meditation Center in Marin County, California. An English-language edition of *Osho Times International* is available by direct mail from Poona. In 1995, about 500 sannyasins living in the United States gathered at an Osho center in Fairfax, California, to commemorate the tenth anniversary of Rajneeshpuram.

Meanwhile, legal actions growing out of events at Rajneeshpuram continue. In one direction, sannyasin attorneys continue against the U.S. Government under the Freedom of Information Act in the hope of gathering enough evidence to prove that the Reagan Administration acted illegally and unconstitutionally in destroying the Oregon commune. In the other, the U.S. Justice Department is also pursuing cases against Sheela and her associates. Most recently, in 1995, two former Osho disciples were extradited from England to Portland, Oregon, and convicted of conspiracy to murder former U.S. Attorney Charles Turner, who led the Reagan Administrations efforts to shut down Rajneeshpuram.

Through the 1990s, Osho Commune International in Poona has expanded greatly and has become one of the worlds largest centers for spiritual/personal growth activity; it offers a wide variety of classes, workshops, and trainings. Visitors still come from Europe and America, and increasingly from Japan, Korea, Taiwan, Russia, and Israel. Osho International has opened a headquarters in New York which oversees the publication of Oshos books, increasingly available through commercial publishing houses in England, Germany, and, most recently, in North America. Osho International also prepares videotapes of Oshos discourses for relay through a number of Asian commercial satellite television channels. In India, Oshos books and audiotapes can be found in stores nationwide.

Membership: Osho centers are found in over 60 countries. In the United States, as of 1997, there were 50 centers serving approximately 10,000 people and 20 centers serving some 4,000 peole in Canada. There are a reported 900,000 people related to the 750 centers worldwide.

Educational Facilities: Osho Multiversity, Poona, India.

Periodicals: *Viha Connection.* • *Osho Times International.*

Sources:

Belfrage, Sally. *Flowers of Emptiness.* New York: Dial Press, 1981.

Bharti, Ma Satya. *Death Comes Dancing.* London: Routledge & Kegan Paul, 1981.

Braun, Kirk. *The Unwelcome Society.* West Linn, OR: Scout Creek Press, 1984.

Gordon, James S. *The Golden Guru.* Lexington, MA: Stephen Greene Press, 1987.

Mehta, Gita. *Karma Cola.* New York: Simon & Schuster, 1979.

Milne, Hugh. *Bhagwan, The God That Failed.* New York: St. Martin's Press, 1986.

Prasad, Ram Chandra. *Rajneesh: The Mystic of Feeling.* Delhi: Motilal Banarsidass, 1978.

Rajneesh, Bhagwan Shree. *The Great Challenge, A Rajneesh Reader.* New York: Grove Press, 1982.

___. *I Am the Gate.* New York: Harper & Row, 1977.

___. *The Orange Book.* Rajneeshpuram, OR: Rajneesh Foundation International, 1983.

___. *Tantra, Spirituality & Sex.* San Francisco: Rainbow Bridge, 1977.

Rajneesh, the Most Dangerous Man Since Jesus Christ. Zurich, Switz.: Rebel Publishing House, 1987.

Rajneeshism. Rajneeshpuram, OR: Rajneesh Foundation International, 1983.

Strelley, Kate. *The Ultimate Game.* San Francisco: Harper & Row, 1987.

★2083★
Vedic Society of America
Current address not obtained for this edition.

The Vedic Society of America was founded by MahaGuruJi Dr. Pandit Bhek Pati Sinha, a Brahmin priest from Bihar, Bengal, India. He had studied at the Universities of Calcutta and Patna in India and eventually received his Ph.D. from Columbia University in New York City. Between 1948 and 1952 he lived in various parts of the world, and then settled in the United States. Through the 1960s he taught political science in several institutions of higher learning on the East Coast.

Sinha founded the Vedic Society of America in New York City in 1950 at a time when there were very few Hindu options available to religious seekers. It was designed to encourage spiritual disciplines, provide a sense of reverence for all life, promote brotherhood, and offer an awareness of the *Vedas*, the ancient scripture of India. A second center was opened in Pacific Palisades, California, in 1960. Sinha trained leaders who assumed ministerial duties at the two centers including the leading of the weekly worship services.

The society taught the ten Vedic moral commandments of nonviolence (*ahimsa*), truthfulness, honesty, inhering in the consciousness of God, detachment, purity of body, contentment, perseverance in the consciousness of truth, study of the scriptures, and devotion to God. It taught that Truth was God and true religion was the perception and realization of truth. Each individual is substantively divine and has the ability to realize that divinity. Humans are their own savior, and that growth in spiritual illumination and love and service to all is the only alternative in life.

The society operated a retreat center, Vedashram, and offered a correspondence course in its religious teachings. It published a periodical, *Lila.* Sinha authored several books, and the society members recorded two records of Vedic music and chants, which were distributed through the Vedic Book and Gift Shop in Pacific Palisades.

The society continued to exist through the 1970s, but in recent years attempts to contact it have not been successful. Its present status is uncertain.

Sources:

Jayne, Linda. *The Vedic Society of America: New York and California.* Pacific Palisades, Vedic Publishing House, 1968.

Sikhism

★2084★
Sikh Council of North America
95-30 118th St.
Richmond Hill, NY 11419

Alternate Address: International Sikh Organization, 2025 Eye St. NW, No. 109, Washington, D.C. 20006; International Sikh Organization, 238 Davenport Rd., Ste. 125, Toronto, ON Canada M2R 1J6.

The Sikh Council for North America is the major organization which attempts to provide communication and coordination for those Sikh congregations and temples located across the United States serving predominantly Indian-American Sikhs. Since 1965, the number of Sikhs has risen dramatically, doubling between 1975 and 1985.

The beginning of Sikh organization in America can be traced to the arrival of Jawala Singh and Wisakha Singh, two advocates of Indian independence, who came to California in 1908. They owned a ranch on the Holtville River near Sacramento where they practiced Gurbani Kirtan (singing the songs from *Sri Guru Granth Sahib*). Then in 1912 a lot was purchased at Stockton, California, and the *Sri Guru Granth Sahib* installed in a gurdwara (place of worship). The Pacific Coast Khalsa Diwan Society was organized to raise money for a temple. An original wooden temple was constructed in 1916, replaced with a brick structure in 1929. For several decades it was the only Sikh center in the United States and large gatherings were held there four times a year.

The temple in Stockton was closely associated with the Ghadar Party, an organization established in 1913 in San Francisco and financed in large part by Jawala Singh, which advocated Indian independence from British rule. Though largely destroyed during World War I due to its ties with German supporters, it continued into the 1940s and its building has been turned into a memorial to the struggle for Indian independence. In more recent years the Stockton temple has become identified with those Sikhs in the Punjab seeking independence from Indian rule which is largely Hindu.

After World War II and India's gaining of independence in 1948, there was further migration of Punjabis, enough so that a second temple was constructed at El Centro, California. In 1969 the largest Sikh temple in the world was erected in Yuba City, California. By 1974 there were close to 100,000 Sikhs from the Punjab in the United States. Centers can now be found in cities and towns across the United States.

In the 1970s the Sikh Foundation emerged as a public voice for East Indian Sikhs in the United States. From its headquarters in Redwood City, California, it published the quarterly, *Sikh Sandar*, and *Sikhs in the U.S.A. and Canada*, a directory. The Foundation was recently superceded by the Council.

Membership: As of the mid-1980s there are an estimated 250,000 Sikhs in the United States.

Sources:

Singh, Wadhawa. *Introduction to the Sikh Temple, Stockton, and the Ghadar Party*. Stockton, CA: Sikh Temple, 1983.

___. *Introduction to Sikhism and Its Holy Scripture: Sri Guru Granth Sahib*. Stockton, CA: Sikh Temple, 1981.

Sikhs in the U.S.A. & Canada. Redwood City, CA: Sikh Foundation, 1972.

★2085★
Sikh Dharma
Box 35330
Los Angeles, CA 90035

The chief religious and administrative authority for the Sikh Dharma in the United States, and the rest of the Western Hemisphere as well, is Yogi Bhajan, who arrived in the United States in 1969 and founded the Healthy, Happy, Holy Organization (better known as 3HO Foundation), the non-secular educational affiliate of the Sikh Dharma. Siri Singh Sahib Bhai Sahib Harbhajan Singh Khalsa Yogiji, popularly known as Yogi Bhajan, is a priest of the Sikh Dharma, which is headquartered in Amritsar, India. The teachings are based upon those of the Ten Sikh Gurus (the First being Guru Nanak, about whom the organization has published a book) and center on the praise of Gods name and the practice of kundalini yoga (a practice that has earned the Sikh Dharma some criticism from other orthodox Sikhs). (Although there are teachers of the Sikh Dharma, such as Yogi Bhajan, there will never be another Guru in human form.)

As Sikhs (literally "students of truth"), members follow the admonition of the Ten Sikh Gurus to rise before sunrise, bathe, and meditate upon Gods name. These individual practices are followed by gathering together with the congregation and singing the Gurus hymns (known as *Gurbani Kirtan*). Sikhs bow to the Word of God contained in *Siri Guru Granth Sahib*, the scriptures compiled from the original teachings of the Ten Gurus, that now serves as the "living" Guru. A copy of *Siri Guru Granth Sahib* is enthroned in every Sikh *gurudwara* (place of worship).

Members of the Sikh Dharma may be baptized and accept the 5 Ks of traditional Sikh practice. A baptized member is called an Amritdhari Sikh. Others affiliated with the group are called Sahajdhari. Members are vegetarian, and every Gurudwara has a free-kitchen. Several members have even opened vegetarian restaurants and grocery stores. Alcohol, tobacco, and intoxicating drugs are forbidden.

Leadership of the Sikh Dharma is vested in the Khalsa Council, which functions under Yogi Bhajan. It consists of the administrative and regional ministers, known as the Mukhia Singh Sahibs (men) and Mukhia Sardarni Sahibas (women), who oversee the local centers and local ministers.

Besides the center in Los Angeles, a second headquarters complex is located in Espanola, New Mexico, where Yogi Bhajan resides part of the time. It is also the site of the semiannual international gatherings on the summer solstice and of summer camps for women and children. There is also a womens auxiliary, the GGMWW (Grace of God Movement of the Women of the World), based on a body of teachings dealing with the evolving role of women. Women are "Shakti," or divine power in manifestation, and are accorded equal opportunities at all levels of leadership in the organization. In addition, the Kundalini Research Institute gathers data on the effectiveness of kundalini yoga, and publishes much of the movements literature.

Kundalini yoga, the yoga of awareness, is a particularly energetic form of yoga incorporating traditional hatha yoga postures and regulated breathing techniques. The practice of yoga has as its goal being able to remain centered and neutral in the face of lifes various challenges. It is also a method by which to help prepare and strengthen the nervous system to better be able to sit and meditate on Gods name.

Membership: In 1995 there were more than 139 ashrams and/or teaching centers in the United States, 11 in Canada, and 86 additional centers in 26 countries of the world. There are approximately 250,000 Sikhs in North America of which over 10,000 reside in or near Sikh Dharma ashrams and community centers.

Periodicals: *The Science of Keeping Up*. Order from 3H0 Foundation, 1620 Preuss Rd., Los Angeles, CA 90035.

Sources:

Kundalini Yoga/Sadhana Guidelines. Pomona, CA: KRI Publications, 1978.

Sahib Harbhajan Singh [Yogi Bhajan]. *The Experience of Consciousness*. Pomona, CA: KRI Publications, 1977.

___. *The Teachings of Yogi Bhajan*. New York: Hawthorn Books, 1977.

Kaur, Sardarni Premka. *Guru for the Aquarian Age*. San Rafael, CA: Spiritual Community, 1972.

Sant Mat

★2086★
Ancient Teachings of the Masters (ATOM)
PO Box 68290
Oak Grove, OR 97268

Darwin Gross, previously the leader of ECKANKAR, began teaching independently in 1983, Sounds of Soul (SOS Publishing), used by Gross to identify his writings, was phased out in 1989. He continued to characterize the teaching, as in earlier books and tapes, as the Ancient Teachings of the Masters (ATOM); that the individual soul is an atom. Gross had become active in ECKANKAR in 1968, quickly rising to a position of leadership in disseminating the teachings of Paul Twitchell, founder of ECKANKAR. Gross was selected as the new Eck Master when Twitchell died in 1971. The appointment was confirmed by a formal passing of "the rod of power" in October of that year. Gross married Twitchell's widow in 1973; they were divorced in 1977.

Gross nominated Harold Klemp to assist Gross in 1981 but continued to serve as president of ECKANKAR corporation. In 1983, Klemp took the position that Gross was no longer an Eck Master and terminated his membership in ECKANKAR and all agreements between him and the corporation. Gross responded by declaring that by these actions Klemp lost the "rod of power" nomination previously accorded to him. Gross emphasized he is not founding a separate path or teaching but maintaining the original teachings of Paul Twitchell. Retaining his own books and music copyrights previously published, he published these and others for those studying under his tutelage. Though Gross is known as the "972nd living master" in the line of masters described by Paul Twitchell, by agreement he has avoided specific terms trademarked by ECKANKAR corporation, including "ECK" and "ECKANKAR."

Membership: Not reported.

Sources:

Gross, Darwin. *Awakened Imagination* Oak Grove, OR: SOS Publishing, 1987.

___. *Be Good to Yourself*. Oak Grove, OR: The Author, 1988.

___. *The Golden Thread Discourses*. Oak Grove, OR: The Author, 1987.

___. *My Letter to You Discourses*. Oak Grove, OR: The Author, 1987.

___. *Treasures*. Oak Grove, OR: The Author, 1988.

★2087★
Church of the Movement of Spiritual Inner Awareness (MSIA)
3500 W. Adams Blvd.
Los Angeles, CA 90018

The Church of the Movement of Spiritual Inner Awareness (MSIA) was founded by John-Roger Hinkins and incorporated as a church in 1971. MSIA teaches Soul Transcendence, by which is meant a person's becoming aware of himself/herself as a soul and, more than that, as one with the Divine.

The focal point of MSIA is the consciousness of the Mystical Traveler, a spiritual consciousness that exists throughout all levels of creation, resides within each person, and is a guide into the higher levels of the Spirit. In December 1963, the MSIA believes that John-Roger received the spiritual mantle as the physical anchor point of the Mystical Traveler Consciousness, and in 1988, this passed to John Morton. John-Roger remains the spiritual wayshower for those he has initiated. The traveler can assist a person in working through karma (balancing past actions) on all the levels of consciousness, and the traveler's work with students is done inwardly, on the spiritual levels. John Morton currently serves as the Spiritual Director of MSIA, the administrative head being Church President Paul Kaye.

Students read a 12-year series of monthly Soul Awareness Discourses (after the series has been completed, study continues through the Soul Awareness Tape Series). Students are also encouraged to do spiritual exercises (silent meditation) for two hours each day. Nothing else is needed for a student in MSIA, although there are many videotapes, audiotapes, and books by John-Roger and John Morton that can support a person's study. Students may gather together to listen to or view a taped seminar by John-Roger, and he has a nationally syndicated television program, "That Which Is," that also shows his seminars. MSIA services are available, such as aura balancing, which helps to clear imbalances in the aura, the energy field around the body.

After two years of study, a person may apply for initiation, and levels of initiation in MSIA correspond to levels of consciousness both within and outside of each person: astral (imagination), causal (emotions), mental (mind), etheric (unconscious), and soul. The soul realm is considered our true home to which we seek to return. Through continued study and spiritual exercises, a person may be initiated to successive levels. After studying for two years in MSIA and receiving the first initiation, a person may apply for ordination. Ministers are ordained to minister to all, regardless of race, creed, color, situation, circumstance, or environment. The ministry is primarily spiritual, and the focus of the ministry is on service—to God, others, and self.

MSIA does not have rules and regulations governing behavior. Guidelines in MSIA are to take care of yourself so you can help take care of others, don't hurt yourself and don't hurt others, and use everything for your advancement and upliftment. Basic precepts include the following: Out of God come all things; God loves all of Its creations; not one soul will be lost; the kingdom of heaven is within; and each person is an heir to that kingdom.

Membership: MSIA has no formal membership. About 5,000 people currently study with the Church of MSIA (which means that they subscribe to Soul Awareness Discourses). About 2,700 are in the United States, and about 2,300 are in foreign countries, including approximately 30 students in Canada.

Educational Facilities: Peace Theological Seminary and College of Philosophy, Los Angeles, California.

Periodicals: *The New Day Herald.* Send orders to PO Box 513935, Los Angeles, CA 90051.

Remarks: Prior to the founding of MSIA, John-Roger was affiliated with several other groups including the Church of Jesus Christ of Latter-day Saints and ECKANKAR. Today MSIA has incorporated strong elements which resemble the sound current teachings of ECKANKAR along with a significant element of Christian piety.

Sources:

Beck, Sanderson, and Mark T. Holmes, eds. *Across the Golden Bridge.* Los Angeles: Golden Age Education Publications, 1974.

Hinkin, John-Roger. *The Christ Within & the Disciples of Christ with the Cosmic Christ Calendar.* Los Angeles: Mandeville Press, 1994.

___. *Psychic Protection.* Los Angeles: Mandeville Press, 1976. Revised 1997.

___. *Forgiveness—The Key to the Kingdom.* Los Angeles: Mandeville Press, 1994.

___. *The Sound Current.* New York: Baraka Press, 1976.

___. *The Spiritual Family.* Los Angeles: Mandeville Press, 1976. Revised 1997.

Lewis, James R. *Seeking the Light.* Los Angeles: Mandeville Press, 1997. 232 pp.

★2088★
Divine Knowledge Meditation Center
1434 Willow St.
Denver, CO 80220

The Divine Knowledge Meditation Center was founded by Mahatma Rama Nand, a disciple of Param Hansji Maharaj, the Indian Sant Mat teacher and founder of the Divine Light Mission. Following Sri Hans Ji's death, Rama Nand left the mission and, beginning in 1973, traveled through the United States teaching the way to divine knowledge he had learned. The Divine Knowledge Meditation Center is a direct outgrowth of his American work.

Rama Nand teaches the *surat shadba yoga* common to Sant Mat groups. The center offers a 10-week aspirant program designed to prepare people to learn the specific techniques for the practice. Preparatory practice includes simple hatha yoga, breathing, and meditation.

Rama Nand teaches that the purpose of existence is the realization of our spiritual nature and God, accomplished through surat shabda yoga. The immediate effect of meditation is a release of stress and the reduction of physical symptoms—reduced high blood pressure, hypertension, nervousness, and insomnia.

Membership: Not reported. Rama Nand's work is concentrated through a single center in Denver.

★2089★
Divine Light Mission
(Defunct)

The Divine Light Mission was founded in India in the 1920s by Shri Hans Ji Maharaj but became well known in the West in the 1970s after being brought to Europe and North America by his son Guru Maharaj Ji (b. 1957). Guru Maharaj Ji, then still a teenager, had assumed the leadership of the mission following the death of his father. The mission spread rapidly after its introduction into North America and by 1973 it had more than 40 centers and was publishing two periodicals, a magazine, *And It Is Divine,* and a tabloid, *The Divine Times.*

A former member of the eclectic Brahmo Samaj, Shri Hans Ji Maharaj had met a guru in the Sant Mat tradition, identified only as Dada Guru, who initiated him into *surat shabda yoga* (the yoga of the sound current) through four techniques, or *kriyas,* which were to become the trademark of the Divine Light Mission. In the 1920s, following the death of his guru, Shri Hans began to travel in north India and around 1930 first arrived in Delhi. His work grew informally for many years, spreading across the northern half of India from Bombay to Calcutta. In 1950 he commissioned the first mahatmas, assistants who had the authority to initiate as his representative, and a short time afterwards he issued the first copies of a monthly magazine, *Hansadesh.* His following was formally organized in 1960 as Divya Sandesh Parishad, i.e., the Divine Light Mission.

Shri Hans was considered a sat guru, or perfect master, by his followers. His death in 1965 was experienced as a great loss. However, at his funeral, in the midst of the mourning crowd, the youngest of Shri Hans four sons, then only eight years old, arose and addressed the crowd, "I feel that Maharaji is alive and will always remain." Afterwards, this eight-year-old was acknowledged by both his family and the followers of Shri Hans as his fathers successor and he became known as Maharaji.

Maharaj Ji had been an unusual child. He began meditating at the age of two and gave discourses when he was six. He entered his teen years with a blend of normal childhood urges and the meditative life of a sat guru. On November 8, 1970, at the India Gate in Delhi, he proclaimed the dawn of a new era, and his followers answered his call to mission. Early in 1971 he made his tour of the United States, mixing normal teenage activities (a visit to Disneyland) with meetings with prospective disciples. A second visit in the summer of 1972 centered upon a massive gathering of disciples at Montrose, Colorado. Each trip was accompanied by broad coverage in the media.

Following the Sant Mat tradition, Maharaj Ji was considered a perfect master and, as such, an embodiment of God. He offered initiation (termed the giving of knowledge) into the truth of life technique. Initiation involved instruction in the four yoga techniques taught to Shri Hans by his guru. They were taught to a *premie* (follower of the guru) by a mahatma (personal representative of the guru). These techniques were practiced daily by premies and were seen as allowing the premie to become attuned to the sound and light current emanating from the divine.

In the early 1970s the mission suffered greatly from its Millennium 73 program which proved unable of attracting enough people to fill (and pay for) the Houston Astrodome. This disaster was followed by an internal dissent within Maharaj Jis family. A month after the Houston event, Maharaj Ji turned 16 and took personal administrative control of the mission. A short time later he married without parental approval, and his mother reacted by asserting control of the Indian branch of the mission and declaring an older brother the new guru. A later agreement gave the family the older mission in India, while Maharaj Ji continued to lead his following internationally. All through this period, the mission was a major target of the anti-cult movement.

In the early 1980s, Maharaj Ji moved to disband the Divine Light Mission and he personally renounced the trappings of Indian culture and religion. After disbanding the mission, he founded Elan Vital, an organization to facilitate his future role as a teacher.

Membership: Not reported. In 1986 it was reported that several hundred people support the work monthly and approximately 4,000 periodically. Supporters are found on every continent and most European countries.

Remarks: Elan Vital is a nonprofit organization established by people who wanted to make available the teachings of Maharaji (the current spelling). Funded by voluntary contributions, Elan Vital holds events at which Maharaji is invited to speak and offers video and audio material of his talks to interested people.

Over the last decade Maharaji has emphasized a central premise that the source of contentment and happiness is within each individual. He continues to offer the set of four techniques as a means to access that inner experience which he calls Knowledge. Offered without charge, these techniques help individuals to focus their awareness inside of themselves. Kim Knott, who studied Elan Vital in the late 1980s, found that those now involved in Maharajis teaching process described the experience as one of being more in harmony with themselves. Maharaji had made every attempt to abandon the traditional Indian religious trappings in which the techniques originated and to make his presentation acceptable all the various cultural settings in which his followers live. He sees his teachings as independent of culture, religion, beliefs, or lifestyles, and regularly addresses audiences in places as culturally diverse as India, Japan, Taiwan, the Ivory Coast, Slovenia, Mauritius,

and Venezuela, as well as North America, Europe, and the South Pacific.

Elan Vital may be contacted at Box 6130, Malibu, CA 90264.

Sources:

Cameron, Charles, ed. *Who Is Guru Maharaj Ji?* New York: Bantam Books, 1973.

Collier, Sophia. *Soul Rush.* New York: William Morrow and Company, 1978.

Downton, James V., Jr. *Sacred Journeys.* New York: Columbia University Press, 1979.

An Introduction to the Divine Light Mission. London: Shri Hans Production, [1972].

Light Reading. Miami, FL: Divine Light Mission, 1980.

Maharaji. *Listen to the Cry of Your Own Heart. Something Wonderful Is Being Said.* Visions International, 1995.

Maharaj Ji, Guru. *The Living Master.* Denver, CO: Divine Light Mission, 1978.

Satgurudev Shri Hans Ji Maharaj. Delhi, India: Divine Light Mission, n.d.

★2090★
The Divine Science of Light and Sound
2554 Lincoln Blvd.
Box 620
Marina del Rey, CA 90291

The Divine Science of Light and Sound was formed in 1980 by Jerry Mulvin (b. 1936), formerly a leader in ECKANKAR. The Divine Science of Light and Sound is described as the study of the inner worlds via the movement of one's inner consciousness (attention/viewpoint) from the outer physical world into the Soul Body and then traveling into the inner world. It is considered the safe and natural way to travel into the inner worlds, beyond the known limits or boundaries of one's universe. In order to travel out-of-body, one must first learn the spiritual techniques that enables the individual to gather up the inner attention and shift it to the spiritual eye center.

By practicing the techniques of the Divine Science, Mulvin believes that one can rediscover their child-like innocence which is the attitude that will propel them out-of-body, into the direct experience of the inner realms. Truth derived from such direct experience supplies the opportunity to begin setting one free spiritually.

Mulvin has authored two books. The first describes his early life and his going through a process of raising the kundalini energy (believed to be residing at the base of the spine), and ultimately mastering it via out-of-body exploration. It also describes his past lives which played an important role in his spiritual unfoldment in this life; the disciplines, teachers and masters (such as Fubbi Quantz, a master first introduced in the writings of Paul Twitchell); and the spiritual techniques that led to his current state of spiritual mastership, beyond the raising of the kundalini energy.

In his more recent writings, Mulvin has stressed the goal of leaving one's body to travel beyond what humans call time and space. Through the techniques developed and taught by Mulvin, he claims that students can have direct experience of freedom and truth through contact with and traveling in the Soul Body. Use of these techniques will prove the existence of reincarnation and karma. The movement in the Soul Body is also sharply distinguished from what is commonly called astral or mental projection.

Mulvin teaches students physically by conducting weekly out-of-body workshops, and through Personal Discourses. He teaches them inwardly via the dream state, and while they are traveling outside their body.

Membership: Not reported. There is one center in Marina del Rey.

Sources:

Mulvin, Jerry. *The Annals of Time*. Manhattan Beach, CA: Divine Science of Light and Sound, 1982.

___. *Out-of-Body Exploration*. Marina del Rey, CA: Divine Science of Light and Sound, 1986.

★2091★
ECKANKAR
Box 27300
Minneapolis, MN 55427

ECKANKAR, Religion of the Light and Sound of God, was founded in 1965 by ECK Master Paul Twitchell (d. 1971). Twitchell, a former journalist, had been a student of various spiritual teachers, among them Sant Mat Master Kirpal Singh, founder of Ruhani Satsang and teacher of the Divine Science of the Soul. In 1964, Twitchell moved to San Francisco, California, and began to teach what was then considered an advanced form of surat shabda yoga, which emphasized attuning the "Soul to the Sound and Light emanating from God."

At that time, Twitchell also emphasized bilocation (later called "Soul Travel"), the ability of the conscious soul to leave the body and travel in the invisible realms. In 1965, Twitchell announced that he was the "Living ECK Master" and formed the first public ECKANKAR group. He is considered by members of ECKANKAR to be the 971st Mahanta and Living ECK Master of the Vairagi Order, taking his place in a line that began before recorded history. Twitchell is believed to have studied ECKANKAR under Sudar Singh in India and ECK Master Rebazar Tarzs in the Himalayas.

In many of its basic concepts, ECKANKAR appears to follow the Sant Mat teachings of Kirpal Singh and Western writer Julian Johnson, a disciple (like Kirpal Singh) of Sawan Singh, head of the Radha Soami Satsang, Beas. ECKANKAR, however, holds that the original teachings of the Light and Sound had been presented in various forms throughout history and that Paul Twitchell reunited them in a single, modern teaching. As presented by Twitchell and current Mahanta and Living ECK Master Sri Harold Klemp, ECKANKAR is distinguished from the Sant Mat tradition in significant ways. ECKANKAR, for example, teaches that the ultimate state for each individual is that of a co-worker with God, not oneness with God; inner techniques are more active spiritual exercises than yogic practices; and Eastern austerities (vegetarianism, extended meditation) are not espoused. Twitchell also presented a different vocabulary than that of Sant Mat teachings.

ECKANKAR considers the Shariyat-Ki-Sugmad to be its ancient scripture residing in the inner worlds. According to the ECK teachings, the original works are located in various Temples of Golden Wisdom, which can only be reached in the "soul body." Two volumes copied and translated by Twitchell have been published. The primary body of ECKANKAR writings has been authored by Sri Harold Klemp, the spiritual leader of ECKANKAR for the last 14 years.

ECKANKAR teaches that all life flows from God (Sugmad) downward to the physical universe. The divine life current (ECK) can be perceived as Light and Sound. This current may be identified with the Sanskrit Nam and the Christian Holy Spirit. A central ECK belief is that each individual is Soul, an eternal spark of God. Soul reaches higher spiritual states of wisdom and love through lessons learned via reincarnation over many lifetimes.

The spiritual exercises of ECKANKAR teach adherents, called ECKists or chelas, to expand their consciousness toward two successive states known as self-realization and God-realization. There are more than 100 spiritual exercises given by the Living ECK Master to aid ECKists in their spiritual unfoldment. Basic techniques involve singing sacred words such as HU, which is regarded as an ancient name for God. Others feature putting attention upon the Light and Sound or the spiritual form of the Mahanta, the Living ECK Master.

ECKANKAR considers itself a living religion rather than an orthodox religion, in that it follows a living spiritual teacher and guide, the Mahanta, the Living ECK Master. The Living ECK Master is respected but not worshipped. It is believed that the Living ECK Master links the chela with the ECK Current, thus leading Soul to total spiritual freedom. The Mahanta guides the chela personally through the lower astral and spiritual realms to the true God worlds and delivers Soul from the wheel of reincarnation. This guidance comes both outwardly through printed discourses, books, and talks, and inwardly via direct interaction. Spiritual travel of the soul body (Atma Sarup) through dreams, imagination, and direct projection is regularly reported by followers of ECKANKAR.

The international headquarters of ECKANKAR is in Minneapolis, Minnesota. It provides its members with study materials, local ECKANKAR classes, and international conferences that feature the Living ECK Master. After Paul Twitchell's death in 1971, he was succeeded by Darwin Gross. Gross married but later divorced Gail Twitchell, Paul Twitchell's widow. He passed on his position as Living ECK Master to Harold Klemp in 1981. Since 1984, Gross has not been associated with ECKANKAR, which no longer considers him an ECK Master.

Harold Klemp, as the present Mahanta, the Living ECK Master, is responsible for the continued evolution of the ECK teachings and ECKANKAR as a modern religion. For example, Klemp has emphasized that an individual cannot reach the highest spiritual realms without giving divine love and service to others in everyday life. In 1990 he oversaw the completion of a Temple of Golden Wisdom, the Temple of ECK in Chanhassen, Minnesota. The Temple is the spiritual home of the religion, and the building and its surrounding grounds are regarded as having special spiritual significance.

Klemp was raised on a Wisconsin farm and trained at a divinity school. He then enlisted in the U.S. Air Force, where he served as a language specialist. He first encountered ECKANKAR during his Air Force service.

Klemp has authored more than 30 books as well as ten year-long discourse series for members of ECKANKAR. ECKANKAR offers some 70 videocassettes and over 100 audiocassettes of his public talks. He speaks at ECKANKAR seminars in the United States, Europe, and the South Pacific. In July of 1991, he spoke to a group of over 10,000 at the ECK African Seminar in Lagos, Nigeria.

Membership: In 1995, there were 164 centers in the United States and 367 worldwide. Members are located in more than 130 countries. Major ECK seminars in the United States routinely draw two to six thousand attendees.

Periodicals: *The ECKANKAR Journal.*

Remarks: In the early 1980s, ECKANKAR became the center of a controversy when religious studies scholar David Christopher Lane made substantive charges that Paul Twitchell had plagiarized materials, especially the writings of Sant mat teacher Julian Johnson, in several of his books. He also charged that Twitchell had in essence fabricated a spiritual career out of his reading of and study with such teachers as L. Ron Hubbard, Kirpal Singh, and Swami Premananda. He presented evidence that articles that originally acknowledged his reliance upon these and other teachers were later republished with the names of former ECK masters substituted instead. The present ECK organization and current ECK Master Harold Klemp have acknowledged this problem in Twitchells writings but have continued the work he began believing that they do not distract from the eminent value of his larger work as an ECK Master.

Sources:

Klemp, Harold. *Ask the Master*. 2 vols. Minneapolis: ECKANKAR, 1993–94.

___. *Soul Travelers of the Far Country*. Minneapolis: ECKANKAR, 1987.

___. *The Temple of ECK*. Minneapolis: ECKANKAR, 1991. 149 pp.

___. *What Is Spiritual Freedom?* Minneapolis: ECKANKAR, 1995.

___. *The Wind of Change.* Menlo Park, CA: IWP Publishing, 1980.

Lane, David Christopher. *The Making of a Spiritual Movement.* Del Mar, CA: Del Mar Press, 1983.

Twitchell, Paul. *All About ECK.* Las Vegas, NV: Illuminated Way Press, 1969.

___. *ECKANKAR, the Key to Secret Worlds.* New York: Lancer Books, 1969.

___. *The Shariyat-Ki-Sugmad.* 2 vols. Menlo Park, CA: IWP Press, 1971-72.

___. *The Tiger's Fang.* New York: Lancer Books, 1969.

★2092★
Eureka Society/Elan Vital School of Meditation
Current address not obtained for this edition.

The Eureka Society and Elan Vital School of Meditation were founded in 1968 in Eureka, California, by Bruce K. Avenell. After a near fatal experience he was told, while sitting in meditation, that if he did not become a teacher, there was no reason to stay in his body. Since he was the father of five children, he decided to become a teacher. Having been a student of sant mat teachers Bhagat Singh Thind and Kirpal Singh, Avenell began to teach his own version of *surat shabda* yoga, the yoga of the sound current.

While Avenell acknowledges his roots in the sant mat tradition of India and the similarity of what he teaches with that school of practice, he states that the practices of Elan Vital also draw on advanced techniques from ancient Egypt and, as such, are unique. The basics of the Elan Vital system teach students to reach to the spiritual realms which are termed "heaven." One can reach these realms either by detaching from the physical body or by becoming attached to a spiritual master. Having attained this initial state, one is free to choose whether or not to pursue more advanced techniques.

Members are initiated by Avenell and practice the techniques he teaches through a series of correspondence lessons. There are semiannual gatherings in Texas and Mt. Shasta, California.

Membership: Not reported. There are an estimated several hundred students with the Eureka Society.

Sources:

Avenell, Bruce. *A Reason for Being.* La Grange, TX: Eureka Society, 1983.

★2093★
Kirpal Light Satsang
Merwin Lake Rd.
Kinderhook, NY 12106

Following the death of Kirpal Singh (b. 1929) in 1974 (see biographical sketch in separate entry on the Sawan Kirpal Ruhani Mission), Darshan Singh, Kirpal Singh's son, who most thought would succeed his father, was rejected by Madam Hardevi, who had been chosen the temporal chairman of the Sawan Ashram and the Ruhani Satsang in India. She supported Thakar Singh, a leading disciple who had, in the months following Kirpal Singh's death, developed a growing belief in his commission to serve as the movement's guru. Madam Haedevi died in 1979, and Thakar Singh took complete control of the ashram.

In the wake of the refusal of the directors of the American corporation, the Ruhani Satsang-Divine Science of the Soul, some American followers who recognized Thakar Singh reorganized as the Kirpal Light Ashram and established headquarters in the Bay Area of northern California. The small group has grown in the wake of several visits by Thakar Singh to America, but does not yet approach the size of the Sawan Kirpal Ruhani Mission.

Membership: Not reported. In 1994 there were 45 satsang and meditation groups.

Periodicals: *Kirpal Light Satsang International Newsletter.* • *Sat.*

Sources:

Singh, Thakur. *Gospel of Love.* Delhi, India: Ruhani Satsang, 1984.

★2094★
Master Ching Hai Meditation Association
Current address not obtained for this edition.

Alternate Address: Supreme Master Hai Meditation Association, PO Box 9, Hsi Hu, Miao Li Hsien, Taiwan, R.O.C.

: The Master Ching Hai Meditation Association is built around the teachings of Master Ching Hai Wu Shang Shih, a teacher of Shabd Yoga of the sound current, who has placed her teachings in a multi-religious context. Master Ching Hai was born in Vietnam, the daughter of Roman Catholic parents. She was introduced to Buddhism by her grandmother. When she was 18, she moved to England to study and then on to France and Germany. In Germany she married a physician, a Buddhist, and settled down to the rather mundane life as a housewife. However, during her married years, a long-time spiritual quest came to the fore and she sat at the feet of many teachers, both Buddhist and Hindu. Eventually, she left home in pursuit of spiritual enlightenment. She had reached the conclusion that the best way to assist others was to first attain total Realization herself.

In the Buddhist *Surangama Sutra,* she read of the Quan Yin method, the surest method to attain enlightenment, but it was not described and she could locate no one who understood of what the method consisted. Finally, her quest led her to northern India where she was initiated into the surat shabd yoga of the sound current by one of the masters of the Radha Soami tradition. This yoga, she concluded, was identical to the Quan Yin Method. Along with practicing the method, she moved to Taiwan and was ordained. In Taiwan, a group of devotees of Avalokitesvara (Quan Yin) sought her out and asked that she teach them her method.

Master Ching Hai taught in Taiwan through the 1980s and by the end of the decade was reaching out with her teachings worldwide, an initial network being established through Vietnamese refugee communities. Initiates are asked to follow the five precepts: to refrain from taking the life of sentient beings, speaking what is not true, taking what is not offered, sexual misconduct, and the use of intoxicants. Among the implications of the five precepts is the adoption of a vegan or lacto-vegetarian diet by initiates.

By the early 1990s, the movement had spread worldwide with followers in South Africa, Latin America (Argentina, Brazil, Chile, Costa Rica, Mexico, Panama, and Salvador), eleven countries of Europe, and around the Asian Pacific Rim from Korea and Japan to Australia and New Zealand. Writings by and about the teachings have been translated into a number of languages and are supplemented with both audio and video tapes.

Membership: Not reported. As of 1993 there were 35 centers in the United States and an additional 73 centers worldwide.

Periodicals: *The Supreme Master Ching Hai News,* The Supreme Master Ching Hai Meditation Association in China, No. 39, Dongsanhu, Sanhu Village, Hsihu Shiang, Miaoli Hsien, Taiwan, R.O.C.

Sources:

Ching Hai Wu Shang Shih. *The Key to Enlightenment.* 2 vols. Miaoli Hsien, Taiwan, R.O.C.: Meditation Association in China, 1991.

★2095★
MasterPath
1231 S. Bender
Glendora, CA 91740

MasterPath was founded in the mid-1980s by Gary Olsen. Olsen had been an associate of Darwin Gross, the former ECK master of ECKANKAR. Gross left ECKANKAR in 1983 to found Sounds of Soul (SOS). Olsen was associated with Sounds of Soul for a short while, but was appointed to leave to found MasterPath.

MasterPath teaches the way to truth through the reactivation of the sound current within. That reactivation is accomplished by the Living Master. The goal is to become a co-worker with Anami, a name for the deity. The first step on the path is self-realization, a realization of one's true self and place in the universe. The soul body, or true self, can travel the sound current to the higher spiritual worlds through the assistance of the Shabda Master, the inner teacher, who works through the Living Master.

Membership: Not reported.

Sources:

Olsen, Gary. *MasterPath*. Glendora, CA: MasterPath, 1988.

A Profile of the MasterPath. Glendora, CA: MasterPath, n.d.

★2096★
Nirankari Universal Brotherhood Mission
Current address not obtained for this edition.

The Nirankari Universal Brotherhood Mission is one of several Sant Mat groups which traces its lineage to Jaimal Singh, founder of the Radha Soami Satsang, Beas. It was founded by Boota Singh (1873-1943) a tatoo artist who in 1929 received a succession from Kahn Singh. Boota Singh became known for his opposition to the rigid conventions and rituals of the Sikhs; he opposed all taboos, castes, creeds, and divisions based upon external habits and appearances. He discarded all dictates concerning what one eats, drinks, or wears. Boota Singh was succeeded by Avtar Singh (1899-1969). After the partition of 1947 (which established Pakistan as a separate state), Avtar Singh moved the headquarters of the Nirankari Mission to Delhi and formally established the Sant Nirankari Mandal. He wrote a constitution and gave it its present organizational structure. He authored *Avtar Baani*, which functions as a holy book for the movement. Under Avtar Singh, the mission flourished and a colony was established on the Januma River in Delhi. In 1969 Avtar Singh was succeeded by Gurbachan Singh, who had the year previous traveled to Europe to establish the work there. By 1973 there were 354 branches with work outside of India in England, Hong Kong, Canada, and the United States.

The spread of the Nirankari Mission to the West began in 1955 when Bhag Mal, a member, moved to England. The mission was formally organized in 1962. Soon after becoming head of the mission, Gurbachan Singh, who had helped develop the work in the West, formed a foreign section to focus upon growth outside of India. In 1971 he made his first trip to North America. Beginning in Vancouver, he moved to San Francisco where he appointed Dr. Iqhaljeet Rai as president of the Nirankari Universal Mission in the United States. He continued his journey across the United States and visited Toronto and Montreal before returning home. In 1972 headquarters were moved to Madison, Wisconsin.

Internationally, the mission is headed by the Seven Stars, who are seven men picked by the guru to serve for life. The mission in India, after receiving persecution, organized the Sant Nirankari Seva Dal, a defense force to protect the group against acts of violence directed against it.

Essential to the life of the mission is *gian*, the giving of the knowledge by the guru to each member. This process, the exact nature of which is held confidential within the group, establishes the relationship of guru to disciple. As the mission has grown, specific disciples have been appointed to represent the guru in the giving of knowledge. Members of the mission agree to live by the five principles: 1) Nothing is ours. All possessions—physical, mental, material—are a divine loan which we must utilize only as trustees and not as masters. 2) No discrimination based upon caste, creed, color, religion, or worldly status. 3) No criticism of anyone's diet or dress, as this creates conflict and breeds hatred.

4) No renunciation of the world. One should continue performing one's normal vocations and functions of life and be always righteous. 5) No divulgence of the Divine Secret of the gian except with permission of the True Master.

Membership: In 1982, the mission reported 2,000 members in 20 centers in the United States. The mission claims more than 8,000,000 members worldwide in 26 countries.

Periodicals: *Sant Nirankari*. Send orders to Nirankari Colony, Delhi 1100009, India.

Sources:

Gargi, Balwany. *Nirankari Baba*. Delhi, India: Thomson Press, 1973.

★2097★
Order of the Blue Star
Current address not obtained for this edition.

The Order of the Blue Star was founded by Christopher Tims, a spiritual teacher who had experienced a broad range of spiritual training in yoga, reiki healing, and martial arts, but especially in the surat shabd yoga of the sound current. Members think of him as a spiritual traveler who resides on the inner planes. He accompanies his students as they make their journeys into spiritual realms, in a manner similar to that of the ECK master in ECKANKAR. New members are presented the work of the order in a workshop on light and soul healing. A second workshop introduces the idea of spiritual traveling in the inner planes. The inner teachings of the order are presented in a set of lessons called Discourses, on which one must pass a test in order to be admitted to the inner circle of the order.

Membership: Not reported.

★2098★
Radha Soami Satsang, Beas
10901 Mill Springs Dr.
Nevada City, CA 95959

Alternate Address: International headquarters: Dera Baba Jaimal Singh, Dist. Amritstar 143 204, Punjab, India; Canadian representative: Dr. J. Khanna, 5550 McMaster Rd., Vancouver, BC V6T 1J8.

History. Several groups presently operating in North America derive their existence from the spiritual movement begun in 1861 by Param Sant Soami Ji Maharaj, born Seth Shiv Dayal Singh (1818-1878), at Agra, India. It is reported that Soami Ji, as he is popularly called, began to expound on spiritual topics from an early age. The substance of his teaching were later gathered in his two books both with the same title, *Sar Bachan*, one written in prose and one in poetry. His teachings were not new, but continued the Bhakti Nam (devotion to the name of God) teachings previously expounded by such people as Kabir Singh, Guru Nanak (1469-1539), Tulsi Singh (1763-1843?), and Guru Ravi Das. But the unique element in Soami Ji's presentation was the simple and lucid manner of his teachings on the practice of Nam Bhakti, also known as surat shabd yoga or the yoga of the sound current. During his lifetime, he initiated more than 4,000 people into the path.

Soami Ji designated Rai Salig Ram (1829-1898) as his successor at Agra. Rai Salig Ram in turn appointed Pandit Brahmanand Shankar Misra as his successor. When Misra died, a controversy arose over the designation of the next leader. This resulted in a split in the Radha Soami Satsang headquartered at Agra into two groups. Neither has known representatives in North America. At the same time (1877) that Soami Ji designated Rai Salig Ram as his successor at Agra, he deputed Baba Jaimal Singh (1838-1903) to spread the teachings in the Pubjab. Baba Ji, as he is popularly called, was initiated by Soami Ji, who advised him to join the army rather than live a life as a recluse. During most of his army career, he was stationed at Agra and thus had frequent direct access to Soami Ji. He was still in the army when Soami Ji died and thus did not even begin to teach and initiate until 1884. In 1889, he retired from the army and settled near Beas on the river at a place known as Dera Baba Jaimal Singh. He remained there for the last years of his life giving satsang and meditating.

Baba Jaimal Singh, shortly before his death, appointed Maharaj Sawan Singh (1858-1948) as his successor. Like Baba Ji, he was a soldier, having served for 28 years. Initiated in 1894, he remained in the army until 1911 and then devoted the remainder of his life to teaching Sant Mat. He settled at the Dera and resided there the rest of his life. Sawan Singh built the Radha Soami Beas into the largest of the Radha Soami movements. During his period of leadership, the facilities at the dera greatly expanded. He traveled widely through the Punjab and India spreading the message to all parts of the land among people of all castes. During this period the number of initiates increased from 2,343 to 125,375.

It was also during the time of Sawan Singh that the teachings reached the United States. One of his disciples, Kehar Singh Sasmus passed them to Dr. H. M. Brock and his wife at Port Angelus, Washington, and initiated them in 1911. The Brocks in turn were authorized to initiate others. Julian Johnson was attracted to the movement in the 1920s and in 1931 was initiated. His book, *The Path of the Masters*, became a classic presentation of the teachings for English-speaking audiences. Brock was succeeded as the Master's representative by Harvey Myers and he by Roland de Vries. There are currently three additional representatives in the United States, H. F. Weekly, Roy E. Ricks, and Gene Ivash. There are two in Canada, J. Khanna and R. S. Davis.

Sawan Singh appointed Maharaj Jagat Singh (1884-1951) as his successor. Though only three years in the leadership post, he initiated more than 18,000 and gained a reputation as a practical mystic. The day before his death he designated Maharaj Charan Singh (b. 1916) as his successor. Charan Singh, the grandson of Sawan Singh, was largely raised at the Dera. Well educated, he became a lawyer in 1942 but gave up a florishing practice in 1951 to assume leadership of the movement. He developed the movement in areas far beyond those envisioned by his predecessors. Not only has he undertaken extensive tours of India but has traveled to many foreign lands. He has initiated 1.25 million individuals and under his leadership the Radha Soami Satsang, Beas has become larger than all the other Sant mat groups combined.

Beliefs. The Radha Soami philosophy is very much like the gnostic and Manichean beliefs of the ancient Mediterranean Basin. (These religions believed matter to be evil, and only spirit to be good.) The Radha Soami cosmology begins with Radha Soami Dayal, the Supreme Spiritual Being, from whom emanated all existence in His Mauj (literally, wave). It is the divine sound or "Shabd" or the "Word" from which emerged creation. As it descended into the lower realms of matter, maya and mind, it became imprisoned beyond any possibility of escape by itself. To teach individuals the way of escape is the purpose of the incarnations of the Supreme Being in the human form of living masters or sant satgurus.

Surat shabd yoga, it is believed, is the only way of return of the soul to its source. It consists of three parts: 1) *simram*, the repetition of the five holy names; 2) *dhyan*, contemplation of the form of the master; and 3) listening to the divine melody (shabd) which enables the student to become attuned to the sound and the light emanating from it. The practical guidance of a living master, who is believed to be the "Word made flesh," is deemed indispensable. The divine sound is like a radio wave that guides the soul back to its eternal home, where it merges and becomes liberated from the cycle of births and rebirths. Students on the path are required to be vegetarians, refrain from alcohol, and of a good moral character. Students are asked to devote two and a half hours a day to meditation, preferably in the morning.

Organization. International headquarters are in the Punjab. The movement internationally is headed by the living master, Charan Singh, also designated as Patron. The movement is organized as a trust society (similar in India to a non-profit corporation). The society consists of 11 members nominated by the Patron, from which is drawn a five-member governing body, the executive committee.

In North America the movement is very decentralized with four initiating representatives in various parts of the United States and two more in Canada. The periodical is published in Kansas and books centers are located in Washington, D.C., and Gardena, California.

Membership: Not reported. In 1986, there were more than 100 places of gathering for lectures and discussions of the Radha Soami teachings in the United States and seven such locations in Canada. There were more than 300 centers and sub-centers in India and more than 100 in various countries of the world.

Periodicals: *Radha Soami Greetings.* Send orders to 18 Countryside Dr., Hutchinson, KS 67501

Sources:

Fripp, Peter. *The Mystic Philosophy of Sant Mat.* London: Neville Spearman, 1964.

Radha Soami Satsang Beas and Its Teachings. Beas, India: Radha Soami Satsang, Beas, n.d.

Radha Soami Satsang Beas, Origin and Growth. Beas, Punjab, India: Radha Soami Satsang, 1981.

Singh, Huzur Maharaj Sawan. *Philosophy of the Masters.* 5 vols. Beas, India: Radhasoami Satsang, Beas, 1963-1967.

Singh, Maharaj Charan. *Light on Sant Mat.* Beas, India: Radha Soami Satsang, Beas, 1958.

___. *The Path.* Beas, India: Radhasoami Satsang, Beas, 1969.

★2099★
Sant Bani Ashram
Franklin, NH 03235

Among the early and more important centers of the followers of Kirpal Singh (see biographical material in item on Sawan Kirpal Ruhani Mission) was the Sant Bani Ashram in Franklin, New Hampshire. Headed by Russell Perkins, the center had handled much of the publishing for the movement over the decades. Among the significant titles are several volumes of Kirpal Singh's collected works. After the death of Kirpal Singh in 1974, Perkins refused to recognize Darshan Singh, the popularly supported candidate as Kirpal Singh's successor. Having heard of Ajaib Singh, he visited his ashram in the Rajasthan desert and eventually recognized him as Kirpal Singh's successor. Joining Perkins was Arran Stephens, Kirpal Singh's Canadian representative, and head of Kirpal Ashram in Vancouver. Stephens had been the first Westerner to hear of Ajaib Singh and had raised the possibility of his being Kirpal Singh's successor in an issue of the movement's magazine, *Sat Sandesh.*

Ajaib Singh was initiated in 1967 by Kirpal Singh. Ajaib Singh has his major following in North America and has visited his disciples in America on a several occasions. He adopted the name of the New Hamphire center as that of his own work in India.

Membership: Not reported.

Periodicals: *Sant Bani: The Voice of the Saints.* Available from Sant Bani Ashram, Franklin, NH 03235.

Remarks: After promoting Ajaib Singh for several years, Arran Stephens withdrew his support, claiming that Ajaib Singh contradicted many of Kirpal Singh's teachings and had on several occasions misrepresented both events which had occurred to him and his relationship to Kirpal Singh.

Sources:

Singh, Kirpal. *Morning Talks.* Franklin, NH: Sant Bani Ashram, 1974.

___. *The Way of the Saints.* Sanbornton, NH: Sant Bani Ashram, 1976.

Singh, Kirpal, Ajaib Singh, and Sawan Singh. *The Message of Love.* Sanbornton, NH: Sant Bani Ashram, n.d.

★2100★
Sawan Kirpal Ruhani Mission
8605 Villge Way, No. C
Alexandria, VA 22309-1605

Alternate Address: International headquarters: % Kirpal Ashram, 2 Canal Rd., Vijay Magar, Delhi, India 110009.

The Sawan Kirpal Ruhani Mission is one of three organizations which claims to continue the work of the Ruhani Satsang founded in 1951 by Kirpal Singh (1896-1974). In 1917 Kirpal Singh had a vision of a "Radiant Form" whom he took to be Guru Nanak (the founder of Sikhism). In 1924, however, he met Sawan Singh (head of the Radhasoami Satsang, Beas) and recognized him as the one in the vision. He stayed with Sawan Singh for the last twenty-four years of his life.

When Jagat Singh received the succession from Sawan Singh, Kirpal Singh left Beas and began the independent Sawan Ashram in Delhi. In 1951, at the time Charan Singh succeeded Jagat Singh, he formed the Ruhani Satsang. In 1949, T. S. Khanna, a disciple of Kirpal Singh, migrated to Canada and established the Ruhani Satsang in Toronto. Several years later he moved to the Washington, D.C. suburb of Alexandria, Virginia.

The growth of the work was accelerated by the two visits of Kirpal Singh in 1955 and 1963, during which time he toured cities in North America and initiated many individuals. As a result, a national association of members and centers was incorporated in California as the Divine Science of the Soul. Kirpal Singh, however, had initiated people without regard for their affiliations and religious background. Some preferred to create informal groups and became tied together very loosely under the Ruhani Satsang, incorporated by Khanna in Washington. In 1972 Kirpal Singh ordered the merger of the American work and the California corporation and the Washington corporation was dissolved. Khanna was elected chairman of the board of the merged body, Ruhani Satsang-Divine Science of the Soul.

Kirpal Singh died in 1974. The movement divided anew as various centers became aligned to the several claimants to Kirpal Singh's succession. In both India and the United States, the largest number of initiates and centers followed Darshan Singh (b. 1921), Kirpal Singh's son. Led by T. S. Khanna and other longtime disciples such as Olga Donenberg and Sunnie Cowen, these members reorganized as the Sawan Kirpal Ruhani Mission. (Meanwhile, the broad of the Ruhani Satsang-Divine Science, the continuing corporate structure, has refused to recognize any successor to Kirpal Singh.) Darshan Singh made his first visit to the United States in 1978. Having lost control of Sawan Ashram, due to his rejection by Madam Hardevi, who had been chosen temporal chairman of the Ruhani Satsang in India, he established a new center, Kirpal Ashram, also in Delhi. Following his 1978 tour, he also opened a free kitchen and medical dispensary at the ashram complex. Like his father, Darshan Singh has continued to promote interfaith work and has authored a number of books.

Outside of India, disciples of Darshan Singh could be found in over twenty-five countries of the world. Sawan Kirpal Publications is the publishing arm of the movement, and several structures have emerged to handle various audiovisual material.

Membership: Not reported. In the early 1980s, there were centers in over 100 towns and cities in the United States associated with the Sawan Kirpal Ruhani Mission. There were centers in 10 Canadian cities.

Periodicals: *Sat Sandesh.* • *Sawan Kirpal Ruhani Mission Newsletter.* Available from Rte. 1, Box 24, Bowling Green, VA 22427.

Sources:

A Brief Biography of Darshan Singh. Bowling Green, VA: Sawan Kirpal Publications, [1983].

Chadda, H. C., ed. *Seeing Is Above All.* Bowling Green, VA: Sawan Kirpal Productions, 1977.

Portrait of Perfection, a Pictorial Biography of Kirpal Singh. Bowling Green, VA: Sawan Kirpal Publications, 1981.

Sena, Bhadra. *The Beloved Master.* Delhi, India: Ruhani Satsang, 1963.

Singh, Darshan. *The Secret of Secrets.* Bowling Green, VA: Sawan Kirpal Productions, 1978.

Singh, Kirpal. *Godman.* Delhi, India: Ruhani Satsang Sawan Ashram, 1967.

___. *The Jap Ji.* Bowling Green, KY: Sawan Kirpal Productions, 1981.

★2101★
Sserulanda Foundation
PO Box 5578, Manhattanville Station
New York, NY 10027

Alternate Address: International headquarters: Sserulanda Nsulo Y'obulamu Spiritual Foundation, Sseesa-miremba, Uganda

The Sserulanda Foundation is the American affiliate of the Sserulanda Nsulo Y'obulamu Spiritual Foundation, founded in 1957 by Dr. Jozzewaffe Kaggwa Kaguwa Kaggalanda Mugonza, known by his followers as Bambi Baaba, a spiritual teacher from Uganda. Mugonza was born in Bugere village in Uganda, the son of Roman Catholic parents. Two serpents were said to have appeared at the moment of his birth; they symbolize his power and his mission of emancipating humanity from disease and the vicious cycle of birth and rebirth. He showed signs of a religious bent early in life. He would assume the role of a priest in playing with other children. He also had experiences of bi-location and had encounters with flying saucers, traveling in them to higher dimensional levels.

In 1969 he journeyed to India, where he apparently met a variety of spiritual teachers, including some in the Radha Soami lineages. While Bambi Baaba's teachings are largely identical to the Radha Soami Path of the Master, Bambi Baaba claims that he did not receive the teachings in India, but used his relationship with an Indian master to gain the acceptance of the people in Uganda with whom he initially worked. Upon his return, with his brothers he founded Kaliisoliiso Star, a company to study scientific and esoteric phenomena. He was arrested by the government on three occasions, the first time in 1972 when he was accused of bringing a new religion into Uganda which prevented members from eating meat and drinking alcohol. He was finally found innocent two years later. He was arrested again in 1974 and 1985, but again was released after a short while. In 1975 he discovered a location, a cave, which he had seen in a vision in 1949. There he established Sseesa-mirembe (Generator of Peace) and began building a future spiritual city for studying and practicing the path of the Masters.

The teachings of Bambi Baaba are quite similar to that of Radha Soami. Humans are seen as sparks of God who have for years associated with the alien nature of this life. To escape this life one needs a Perfect Living Saint and Master. The Master guides people through a process of initiation, termed *Okutendeka* (or training). The soul must travel from the lower body centers to the higher body centers to the various physical realms (astral, causal, and spiritual) to the fifth level, the natural home of souls. The true master initiates people into the Sound Current (shabd) which the soul will follow to the higher realms. He will also explain the colors that the soul will see at each level of development. The Master will meet the student as they travel the inner planes and assist them. Initiates are asked to eat a vegetarian diet and refrain from the consumption of alcohol, tobacco, and narcotics.

The Sserulanda Nsulo Y'obulamu spread to other locations in Uganda, and in 1985 a center was opened in Geneva, Switzerland. The first North American center opened in Montreal the next year. The New York community opened in 1987.

In 1992 Bambi Baaba released a petition to the world reflecting upon what he saw as the planetary dilemma of viceful behavior and worldwide discord that threatens human self-annihilation. He offered a message from the Ansenserenical adepts, those divine beings who had evolved and transcended to the higher planes of the spiritual world: It is now imperative that all of humanity institute a cooperative activity of sharing all knowledge and physical resources to accomplish planetary purification by means of an economic and cultural rejuvenation. The first step is the reconnection between the people of the world and the Ansenserenical beings.

Membership: Not reported.

Sources:

Bambi Baaba. *The Golden Advent of the Wisdom of the Ansenserenical of Planet Earth.* Unpublished paper, 1992. 42 pp.

Bijumiro-jjumiro, Bhuka B. M. *Bambi Baaba: Redeemer of the New Age.* Montreal, Sserulanda Spiritual Planetary Community, 1986. 102 pp.

Section 24

Eastern Family, Part II: Buddhism, Shintoism, Japanese New Religions

Intrafaith Organizations

★2102★
American Buddhist Congress
4267 W. Third St.
Los Angeles, CA 90020

The American Buddhist Congress grew out of an informal meeting of American Buddhist leaders in Boulder, Colorado, on August 24, 1986. They signed a declaration calling for the formation of such an organization and issued a call to all of the Buddhist organizations in the country to join them in its formation. They took as their common ground the essential teachings of Sakyamuni Buddha, especially the four Noble truths. The group formed an ad-hoc committee, which in turn appointed two chairpersons, the Ven. Dr. Havanpola Ratanasara and Rev. Karl Springer, to facilitate the holding of a convocation in 1987. At that convocation, hosted by the Kwan Um Sa Temple (Korean) in Los Angeles, the American Buddhist Congress was initiated and a constitution adopted.

The congress attempts to bring Buddhists together in projects for the common good, to promote understanding between the various Buddhist traditions, to educate the American public about Buddhism, and to carry out social, educational, cultural, and humanitarian projects.

The congress operates through a general council, which sets policy, and an executive council, which implements policy. There are several standing committees, including an education and promotion committee and a humanitarian committee. The congress is currently headed by its executive chairperson, Dr. Ratanasara, who is assisted by two co-chairpersons (the Ven. Do Ahn Kim and Karl Springer) and five vice-chairpersons (the Ven. Dr. Karuna Dharma, the Ven. Dr. Thich Thien Than, the Ven. Jomyo Tanaka, the Ven. K. Piyatissa, and William Baer).

Membership: In 1995 the congress reported 136 affiliated organizations.

Periodicals: *American Buddhist News.*

★2103★
Buddhist Council of the Midwest
2400 Prairie
Evanston, IL 60201

The Buddhist Council of the Midwest was founded in the 1970s as an ecumenical organization that now includes Dharma organizations in northeastern Illinois, southern Wisconsin, northern Indiana, and Southwestern Michigan. Among its major programs is an annual Visakha Day (Buddha's birthday) celebration near the full moon of the fifth lunar month. The council includes a spectrum of traditions and national ethnic groups.

Sources:

Directory of Midwest Dharma Centers. Evanston, IL: Buddhist Council of the Midwest, annual.

★2104★
Buddhist Sangha Council of Southern California
928 S. New Hampshire
Los Angeles, CA 90006

The Buddhist Sangha Council of Southern California emerged out of the experience of the thousands of Buddhists who migrated to America following the 1965 change in U.S. immigration laws relative to Asia. Buddhists from across Asia—Sri Lanka, Tibet, Burma, Kampuchea, Cambodia, Vietnam, China, Taiwan, and Korea—settled in the United States, the largest concentration of them in Los Angeles, Orange, and adjacent counties of Southern California. Many of these groups experienced the same problems in adjusting to a new land and new language. They also found an entrenched Buddhist establishment already thoroughly Americanized.

The Buddhist Sangha Council grew out of a need to give expression to Buddhist unity in a predominantly Christian country and to provide assistance to newly arriving immigrants, thousands of whom settled annually in Southern California. The council sponsors an annual community-wide celebration of Buddha's birthday each spring and has represented the Buddhist community to the government, in community activity, and in the media. In 1986 it became an official regional center of the World Fellowship of Buddhists.

Membership: Membership in the council is opened only to ordained clergy; it includes representatives of most of the ethnic Buddhist communities in Southern California. In 1997 the Council reported 50 members.

★2105★
Hawaii Buddhist Council
1128 Banyan St.
Honolulu, HI 96817

Buddhists of Hawaii, one of two places in the United States where a significant number of Buddhists have settled, first organized ecumenically in the 1930s through the International Buddhist Institute, which worked to spread a spirit of Buddhist unity in the face of its divisions into a variety of sectarian bodies. That effort was largely ended by the appearance in 1935 of a Buddhist leader with the Honpa Hongwanji, the largest of the Japanese groups, who rejected the ideals of the institute. The whole of organized Buddhism on the islands was disrupted following the bombing at Pearl Harbor until a number of years after World War II. However, in the 1950s a second effort at Buddhist cooperative activity was made in the formation of the Hawaii Buddhist Council, modeled on the councils of Christian churches which had been established across the United States.

The council has facilitated communication between the various Buddhist bodies and has provided the Buddhist community with a united voice to speak to the larger community of non-Buddhists. Among its first actions, the council in 1963 proposed that April 8 be designated Buddha's Day, a state holiday in Hawaii. The council argued that such a designation would exemplify American tolerance and acceptance of religious freedom and provide an opportunity for Japanese Americans to educate the general public about Buddhism. After a statewide debate, a compromise bill did pass the state senate naming April 8 as Buddha Day, but not in such a way as to make it a state holiday.

The council sponsors a variety of educational programs on Buddhism and Hawaiian Buddhist history and culture.

Membership: Members of the council include the Higashi Hongwanji Mission of Hawaii, Honpa Hongwanji Mission of Hawaii, Jodo Mission of Hawaii, Nichiren Mission of Hawaii, Shingon Mission of Hawaii, Soto Mission of Hawaii, and Tendai Mission of Hawaii.

★2106★
International Buddhist Institute
(Defunct)

The International Buddhist Institute (IBI) emerged in the late 1920s out of the realization of the spread of Buddhism around the world. In 1929, Abbot Tai Hsu of the Lin Yin Temple in Hangchow, China, made a world tour promoting the cause of a united Buddhism and the breaking down of sectarian barriers. Early branches of the institute were founded in New York, New York; Chicago, Illinois; and Honolulu, Hawaii. Soon other branches appeared in Los Angeles, San Francisco, and Oakland, California, and one appeared in Idaho.

The Honolulu branch, under the guidance of Bp. Yemyo Imamura and British convert Ernest Hunt, became the most active of the American branches of the movement. Hunt found it a perfect vehicle for reaching non-Japanese people with the message of Buddhism, for lessening tensions between the Japanese and white populations of the islands, and for slowing competition between the various branches of Buddhism operating in the Hawaiian Japanese community. Hunt believed that the practice of active goodwill was the surest way to Enlightenment, and he put his ideas into the institute's program, especially in its social service activities centered upon visitation to hospitals and prisons.

Hunt helped vitalize the Buddhist youth program, wrote books, and worked to spread understanding of Buddhism in the larger non-Buddhist community. He also published, beginning in 1930, four issues of and IBI *Annual* and a magazine, *Navayana*.

Unfortunately, much of what Hunt did was undone following the death of Bishop Imamura in 1932. Hunt succeeded Imamura as president of the IBI. He carried on under the brief leadership of his immediate successor, but in 1936 Gikyo Kuchiba was appointed the new bishop of the Hongwanji Buddhists in Hawaii (the group over which Imamura was bishop). He was the exact opposite of his predecessor. Imamura had been an able leader who operated with tact and goodwill in the difficult situation on the islands. He openly tried to build bridges between the Japanese Hawaiians and their neighbors. Bishop Kuchiba was a staunch Japanese nationalist who had little tolerance for other forms of Buddhism or making converts among non-Japanese people. He drove Hunt away and without the support of the Hongwanji, the largest of the Buddhist groups, the IBI quickly ceased to exist as a viable organization on the islands.

What little remained of the IBI nationally (and internationally) after the disruption of the Hawaiian branch was completely destroyed by World War II.

Sources:

Hunt, Ernest, ed. *Hawaii Buddhist Annual.* Honolulu: International Buddhist Institute, 1932.

Hunter, Louise. *Buddhism in Hawaii: Its Impact on a Yankee Community.* Honolulu: University of Hawaii Press, 1971.

★2107★
Korean Buddhist Sangha Association of Western Territory in U. S. A.
451 S. Serrano Ave.
Los Angeles, CA 90020

Korean Buddhism began to be established in the United States in the 1970s following the migration of a number of Buddhists following the change of the law regulating immigration from Asia in 1965. Members and priests of a number of different Korean Buddhist traditions settled across the United States, though the largest numbers were in California, New York, and Illinois. The Sangha Association emerged in the early 1980s and became known during its participation in the Korean Cultural Exhibition as part of Korea Expo 84. It has published a directory of all of the Korean Buddhist centers in the United States and Canada.

Sources:

Brief Introduction to Korean Buddhism. Los Angeles: Korean Buddhist Sangha Association of Western Territory in U.S.A., 1984.

★2108★
Los Angeles Buddhist Church Federation
123 S. Hewitt St.
Los Angeles, CA 90012

The Los Angeles Buddhist Church Federation is a Buddhist ecumenical group serving the large Japanese-American Buddhist community in Los Angeles, California. Until the waves of Southeast Asian immigration following the change in immigration laws in 1965, the Buddhist community was overwhelmingly Japanese in origin and Los Angeles the only city in which all of the major branches of Japanese Buddhism had established temples. Participating in the federation are the main temples of the Buddhist Churches of America (Honpa Hongwanji), the Higashi Hongwanji, the Shingon Mission, the Soto Zenshu, and the Nichiren-shu, most of which are located in that section of Los Angeles known as Little Tokyo.

In the early 1980s, the federation published a series of booklets collectively titled *Kokoro on Kate,* the name of the federation's bimonthly radio show of the same name. The essays were originally given as talks on the show.

Remarks: In the 1970s Buddhists from across Asia—Sri Lanka, Tibet, China, Kampuchea, Vietnam, Cambodia, Burma, Korea—arrived in California. They organized the Buddhist Sangha of Southern California and became the basis for the more recent organization of the American Buddhist Congress. As a whole, the Japanese, who represent a community of older immigrants to the United States, have remained cordial but organizationally aloof from the latest generation of Buddhists to settle in Southern California.

Sources:

Kokoro no Kate. 7 vols. Los Angeles: Los Angeles Buddhist Church Federation, 1981-88?

★2109★
White Plum Asanga
℅ Zen Mountain Monastery
PO Box 197
South Plank Rd.
Mt. Tremper, NY 12457

The White Plum Asanga is an association of the successors in the lineage of Soto Zen teacher Baian Hakujun Daiosho. The stated purpose of the Asanga is to promote and maintain harmony among the various Dharma successors in the lineage, many of whom are currently leaders of otherwise independent Zen centers. It provides a forum for conflict resolution, study and training, and the promotion of communication among its members as well as the leaders of other Buddhist schools/traditions.

Membership in White Plum Asanga is of several kinds. Voting members are those who are Shiho Dharma successors in the lineage of Taizan Maezumi Daiosho, best known as the founder of the Zen Center of Los Angeles and which most of the members were initially trained. Honorary membership is extended to the successors of Baian Hakujun Daiosho, and participating membership is drawn from shiho Dharma transmission, denkai, Dharma holders, or other senior students of the Dharma successors.

Membership: Current honorary members include Kojun Kuroda, Koshinji, Japan; Takeshi Kuroda, Zenkoji, Japan; and Junyu Kuroda, Kirigayaji, Japan. Officers are retired president Bernard Tetsugen Glassman (Zen Community of New York); president Dennis Genpo Merzel, Kanzeon 3Sangha; vice president John Daido Loori (Zen Mountain Monastery); secretary Susan Myoyu Andersen (Northwest Chicago Zen Group); and treasurer Gerry Shishin Wick (Great Mountain Zen Center).

Voting members include Jan Chozen Bays (Zen Community of Oregon); John Tesshin Sanderson, Mexico; Alfred Jitsudo Ancheta, California; Charles Tenshin Fletcher (Zen Mountain Center, Mexico); Nicolee Jikyo Miller-McMahon (Three Treasures Zen Community); William Nyogen Yeo, California; and Charlotte Joko Beck (Ordinary Mind Zen School).

Sources:

http://www.zen-ntn.org/zma/white-plum.shtml/.

★2110★
World Fellowship of Buddhists
℅ The Secretariat
33 Sukhumvit Rd.
Bangkok, Thailand

The World Fellowship of Buddhists was founded in 1950 in Colombo, Sri Lanka, by representatives of 27 countries of Asia, Europe, and North America as well as representatives of the major schools of Buddhism—Theravada, Mahayana, and Vajrajana. In the process of forming the fellowship, delegates accepted five objectives: 1. To promote among the members strict observance and practice of the teachings of the Buddha; 2. To secure unity, solidarity, and brotherhood amongst Buddhists; 3. To propagate the sublime doctrine of the Buddha; 4. To organize and carry on activities in the field of social, educational, cultural, and other humanitarian services; and 5. To work for happiness, harmony, and peace on earth and to collaborate with other organizations working for the same ends.

The fellowship is headed by a president and 12 vice-presidents who are elected at the biennial general conferences. The general conference also elects a chairman of the standing committees, an honorary secretarygeneral, two honorary assistant secretaries, and an honorary treasurer. There are seven standing committees which oversee finances, publishing, propagation of Buddhism, humanitarian services, unity, youth, and socio-economic development. All properties owned by the fellowship are vested in the general council, which is constituted by the representatives from each of the regional centers. Organizations may apply to the fellowship to become a regional center.

The standing committee on youth presented a report to the 1968 general conference that led to the formation of the World Fellowship of Buddhist Youth, an auxiliary organization.

Headquarters of the fellowship were in Colombo until 1958 and were then moved to Rangoon until permanent headquarters were established in Bangkok in 1963. The quadrennial general conference meets in a different locality for each session. In 1988 the conference met at the large Hsi Lai Temple complex in Hacienda Heights, California, the first time the meeting had been held in North America.

Membership: American regional centers include the American Young Buddhist Association, Buddha's Universal Church, Buddhist Churches of America, Buddhist Sangha Council of Southern California, Buddhist Temple of Chicago, Congregation of Vietnamese Buddhists of the U.S., Friends of Buddhism (Virginia), Kymer Buddhist Society of New England, Los Angeles Buddhist Church Federation, Sambosa Buddhist Temple of California, Tibetan Nyingmapa Meditation Center, Universal Buddhist Fellowship, Vajradatu, and WFB, Hawaii Regional Center. Some of these centers are headquarters of different Buddhist organizations, some local centers of a larger Buddhist fellowship, and some headquarters of ecumenical organizations.

Sources:

The 16th General Conference of the World Fellowship of Buddhists/The Grand Opening of Fo Kuang Shan Hsi Lai Temple, U.S.A., Souvenir Magazine. Hacienda Heights, CA: Fo Kuang Shan Hsi Lai Temple, 1988.

Theravada Buddhism

★2111★
Abhayagiri Buddhist Monastery
16201 Tomki Rd.
Redwood Valley, CA 95470

Alternate Address: International Headquarters: Amaratvati Buddhist Centre: Great Gaddesden, Hamel Hempstead, Hertfordshire HP1 2BZ, United Kingdom.

Abhayagiri Buddhist Monastery is a branch of the Amaravati Buddhist Monastery, a Thai Theravada Buddhist organization based in the United Kingdom which in turn is related to the Wat Pah Pong and Wat Pah Nanachat, two forest monastic communities in northeast Thailand. International leadership is provided by the Ven. Ajahn Sumedho (b. 1934), an American who studied with legendary Thai monk Ajaan Chaa.

Sumedho had originally encountered Buddhism while in the U.S. Army in Japan. After completing his college work, he went to Thailand as a teacher, where he became a student of Ajaan Chaa. In 1974 he founded Wat Paa Nanachat, which like the other wats influenced by Chaa emphasizes the whole lifestyle as practice above a special emphasis on meditation. In 1977 he visited England with Chaa and remained there. Two years later he founded the Chithurst Forest Monastery in rural Sussex, from which other similar centers have arisen.

The American monastery attempts to reproduce the beliefs and practice of the Thai forest monastic life in a Western setting.

While primarily a monastic community, visitors may stay for brief periods, especially if attending a retreat, if prior arrangements are made. Once a month, the monks go into San Francisco for public teaching sessions. There is also an affiliated sitting group in Berkeley.

Membership: Not reported.

Sources:

Cummings, Joe. *The Meditation Temples of Thailand: A Guide.* Bangkok: Wayfarer Books, 1990.

Kornfield, Jack. *A Still Forest Pool.* Wheaton, IL: Theosophical Publishing House, 1985.

Sumrdho, Ajahn. *The Path to the Deathless.* Hemel Hempstead, UK: Amaravati, n.d. 1985

___. *Teachings of a Buddhist Monk.* UK: Buddhist Publication Group, 1990.

★2112★
Ambedkar Mission
49 Templeton Ct.
Scarborough, ON, Canada M1E 2C3

The Ambedkar Mission, founded in Toronto in 1979, is an Indian based Buddhist mission which follows the ideology and social reform program enunciated by Indian reformer Dr. Brim Rao Ambedkar (1891–1956). Born into a family of Untouchables, the lowest caste of Indian society, he rose in 1947 to a prominent position in the government of the newly independent India. During his younger days he had suffered the humiliation and discrimination common to life as an Untouchable and campaigned against it. Following India's freedom, he was the country's first Minister for Law and chair of the committee to frame a new constitution, which he largely wrote, and defended once it was presented for adoption in 1948. One passage of the constitution wiped at Untouchability, at least in the eyes of the law.

Before leaving government service, he began in 1950 to consider Buddhism as a path that would help his people. He attended the Buddhist Conference in Ceylon (now Sri Lanka) in 1950 and shortly thereafter decided to become a Buddhist. In so doing he felt he was showing the way away from confusion while necessary changes were made in the economic and political life of the nation. Buddhism was an Indian faith. To deal with the problem of Untouchability, a way that did not harm Indian culture or history had to be selected (and hence his choice to stay away from Islam and Christianity). He formally embraced Buddhism at a ceremony on October 14, 1956. Unfortunately, he died two months later.

The centers of the mission host monks from India several times annually.

Membership: Not reported. There is an affiliated Ambedkar Memorial Association in Vancouver.

Sources:

Morreale, Don. *The Complete Guide to Buddhist America*. Boston: Shambhala, 1998.

★2113★
Bhavana Society
Rte. 1, Box 218-3
High View, WV 26808

The Bhavana Society is an independent Theravada Buddhist organization in the Sri Lankan tradition. The forest monastery was established by the Ven. Henepola Gunaratana with the intention of offering both the novice and advanced meditation students the opportunity to study with Gunaratana and his associate, Bhante Yogacacara Rahula. A variety of retreats are offered monthly and provisions are made for men and women who wish to eventually take monastic vows.

Gunaratana, the author of *Mindfulness in Plain English*, has become a popular Theravada teacher, and associated centers have arisen as a result of his travel and speaking.

Membership: Not reported. There is an associated center in Largo, Florida; and Fairfax, Virginia.

Periodicals: *Bhavana Society Newsletter*.

Sources:

Gunaratana, Henepola. *Mindfulness in Plain English*. N.p.: n.d.

★2114★
Cambodian Buddhism
℅ Ven. Maha Ghosananda
Khmer Buddhist Society of New England
178 Hanover St.
Providence, RI 02907

Significant numbers of Cambodians first arrived in the United States in the wake of the terrors of the Khmer Rouge regime of the mid-1970s during which Buddhism was systematically attacked. Reportedly, of 80,000 monks alive at the beginning of the decade, only 800 survived. More than 3,600 temples were destroyed and more than one-half million Cambodians fled the country. The immigration of Cambodian refugees to America peaked around 1982, but has continued through the decade.

Most instrumental in the formation of the American Cambodian Buddhist community has been the Ven. Maha Ghosananda (b.

1924), a disciple of the former head of the Cambodian Buddhist Sangha, the late Samdech Prah Sangha Raja Chuon Noth. Maha Ghosananda happen to be in Thailand when the worst of the troubles in his homeland began. He had completed his studies and adopted the life of a rural ascetic, when refugees began to flood the quiet area in which he had been living. In 1978, he began to work in the refugee camps establishing Buddhist temples. In 1981, he came to the United States to head the Cambodian Buddhist community in Rhode Island which became the center for establishing Buddhist temples in refugee communities around the world. A second office was established in Thailand to bring Buddhist monks to America. Between 1983 and 1986, more than 80 monks came to Providence, Rhode Island, and were sent to the 41 temples that were opened in the United States and Canada. Ghosananda personally started 30 of these temples. Some of the temples, such as the one serving the Washington, D.C. area, have prospered.

In Cambodia, Buddhism was the religion of the state prior to the advent of the Khmer Rouge, and the chief of state was the head of the Buddhist religious leadership. In the United States, the organization of the Buddhist community is undergoing transition as it attempts to reorganize without state support and the larger direct cultural support of the community.

Membership: As of 1986, there are an estimated 160,000 Cambodians in North America. There were 41 temples.

Sources:

Whitaker, Donald P., et al. *Area Handbook for the Khmer Republic (Cambodia)*. Washington, DC: U. S. Government Printing Office, 1973.

★2115★
Dhammakaya International Society of California
5950 Heliotrope Circle
Maywood, CA 90270

The Dhammakaya International Society of California is a single Theravada center connected with the Sister of Dhammakaya Foundation of Thailand. It is under the direction of Para Sudhamatanathera and Phra Vichak Suddhivaro, the resident teachers.

Periodicals: *The Light of Peace*.

Sources:

Morreale, Don. *The Complete Guide to Buddhist America*. Boston: Shambhala, 1998.

★2116★
Dharma Dena
℅ Desert Vipassana Center
HC-1, Box 250
Joshua Tree, CA 92252

Ruth Dennison emerged in the 1980s as one of the leading Buddhist teachers in North America, and one of the very few female Vipassana teachers. She learned meditation in the tradition of Burmese teacher Sayagyi U Ba Khin (1899–1971) and founded the Desert Vipassana Center, where she leads a regular schedule of retreats of varying length. The center is also open for individual retreats. As a result of her teaching, additional centers have been opened around the United States such as Rocky Mountain Insight in Colorado Springs, Colorado, whose leader Lucinda Green received Dharma transmission from Dennison.

Membership: Not reported.

★2117★
Dhiravamsa Foundation
Current address not obtained for this edition.

The Dhiravamsa Foundation, formerly the Vipassana Fellowship of America, was formed by Dhiravamsa, a Thai monk, who came to England in 1964 as chief incumbent monk of the Buddhapadipa Temple. He eventually gave up his monk's robe, finding it too confining in his work with Westerners. In 1969 he came to the United States and began to teach vipassana meditation, that form of meditation traditional to Thai Buddhism. An initial center was established in New England. Dhiravamsa now regularly tours the United States speaking, teaching meditation, and holding retreats. Dhiravamsa's students can also be found in Thailand, Canada, Sweden, Switzerland, Australia, and New Zealand.

Membership: Not reported.

Sources:

Dhirvamsa. *The Way of Non-Attachment.* New York: Schocken Books, 1977.

★2118★
Insight Meditation Society
Pleasant St.
Barre, MA 01005

The Insight Meditation Society was founded in 1976 by a group of people interested in creating a center for the teaching of Theravada Buddhism. The founding teachers were Jack Kornfield, Sharon Salzberg, and Joseph Goldstein, all of whom had spent many years in India and Southeast Asia studying and practicing Vipassana (insight) meditation under the guidance of such meditation masters as Ven. Achaan Chaa, Ven. Asabha Thera, Anagarika Munindra, Sri Satya Narayn Goenka, and most recently the Burmese master U Pandita Sayadaw. Upon their return to the United States in the 1970s, they began to teach insight meditation, the form of meditation that is central to Theravada Buddhism. The center in Barre, Massachusetts, offers teacher-led retreats throughout the year and is also available for individual retreats and long term meditation practice.

Since the formation of the society, other similar centers have opened around the United States and they frequently cooperate in programming, especially in the sponsoring of lecture tours by Asian Vispassana teachers.

Membership: The society is not a membership organization. In 1995 the society reported 13,000 adherents in the United States, 1,000 in Canada and an additional 1,000 worldwide.

Educational Facilities: Barre Center for Buddhist Studies, Barre, Massachusetts.

Periodicals: *Insight.*

Sources:

Goldstein, Joseph. *The Experience of Insight.* Boulder, CO: Shambhala, 1976.

Goldstein Joseph, and Jack Kornfield. *Seeking the Heart of Wisdom.* Boston, MA: Shambhala, 1987.

Kornfield, Jack. *Living Buddhist Masters.* Santa Cruz, CA: Unity Press, 1977.

Kornfield, Jack, and Paul Brieter. *A Still Forest Pool.* Wheaton, IL: Theosophical Publishing House, 1985.

★2119★
International Association of Burmese Buddhist Sanghas
% Burmese Buddhist Association
15 W. 110 Forest Ln.
Elmhurst, IL 60657

Throughout the 1970s, people from Myanmar (formerly known as Burma) began to arrive in the United States. The visit of the Ven. Taungpupa Kaba-Aye Sayadaw and several monks, who were on a goodwill tour in 1979, played an important role in the organization of these new American residents. U. Silananda, one of those monks, decided to remain in the United States to provide leadership for Burmese Buddhists. He founded the Dhammananda Vi-

hara in Daly City, California (serving primarily Burmese-Americans), and the Berkeley Vipassana Center (serving primarily non-Asian students). Throughout the 1980s, a number of teaching centers, such as the Burmese Buddhist Association in suburban Chicago, founded in 1987, emerged These centers have now associated with each other in the International Association of Burmese - Buddhist Sanghas.

Membership: Not reported.

★2120★
International Buddhist Meditation Center
928 S. New Hampshire
Los Angeles, CA 90006

The International Buddhist Meditation Center was founded in 1970 by Thich Thien-An (1926-1980), a Vietnamese monk and scholar who had come to the United States in 1966 as a visiting professor of languages and philosophy at UCLA. Intending to return to Vietnam in 1967, he stayed at the request of a group of students who wished him to become their teacher. In 1973, he started the College of Oriental Studies as a education enterprise adjacent to the center. Following the fall of Saigon and the end of the Vietnamese War, as one of the few Vietnamese scholars in the United States, Thien-An was called to serve a unique function. His energies began to be directed toward meeting the needs of the masses of war refugees, especially those being resettled in the United States. He provided, in part through bilingual monks he had trained, both secular and religious services for the new immigrants. He was especially noted for having founded most of the Vietnamese Buddhist temples established in the 1970s among the new arrivals in America, and was recognized during the last years of his life as the patriarch of Vietnamese Buddhism in America.

Thich Thien-An was of the Lieu-Quan Zen School, dating to its founder Thiet-Dieu Lein-Quan (d. 1743) in the eighteenth century. It is one of several popular Buddhist schools in Vietnam. However, in the United States, Thien-An began to emphasize a nonsectarian approach to Buddhism that slowly moved toward an indigenous American expression of Buddhist life and thought. As an expression of the nonsectarian approach, Buddhist leaders from a wide variety of national backgrounds and diverging lineages have been invited to teach at the center, and different Buddhist groups have been granted use of the center facilities for their own retreats and teachings sessions. The training of monks has followed a similar pattern with monks from various traditions servings as preceptors for those in training, and the ordination service borrowing from several traditions.

Worship has not been excluded from the changing patterns. The Sunday service reflects the syncratic nature of Buddhism practiced at the center. Chanting in English, along with the more common chants in Pali, Sanskrit, and Japanese are found in the daily service. Special chanting in Pali, Japanese, and Vietnamese are done in special ceremonies, but are then repeated in English. Wedding ceremonies are a blend of Eastern and Western elements.

The center was conceived as a place at which practice and education would integrate to produce the total practitioner. It strives to be one location that combines Sunday services, daily meditation, monthly retreats, and a full range of evening classes to provide both spiritual and educational experiences for the devotee.

As presently constituted, the center serves as a residence for 40 members and a training center for both males and females leading to full ordination in the Order of Bhiksus and Bhiksunis. In this regard, it has been the sight of a number of historic events in the Buddhist community. It became the sight of the first Grand Ordination Ceremony for Bhiksus in July 1974, the first Grand Ordination for Bhiksunis in August 1976, and the first traditional Grand Ordination in the English language in August 1981. It provided all of the monks to work as Buddhist chaplains in the three major American refugee camps, set up to process Southeast Asian refugees after the Vietnamese War. During the five years in which the American Vietnamese Buddhist community and the immigrant community functioned as one, the center itself housed 60 refugees and raised the funds to purchase and renovate property into two of the Buddhist temples in Los Angeles, California.

Thien-An trained and ordained seven monks who now hold leadership positions in Buddhist work around the world. Leadership of the center passed to Dr. Karuna Dharma who has by her own accomplishments during the 1980s emerged as one of the most important leaders in the American Buddhist community. She was one of the moving forces in the foundation and maintenance of the Buddhist Sangha Council of Southern California and a one of the major organizers of the American Buddhist Congress founded in 1987. She has served as a national president of the congress. She has been the spokesperson for Sakyadhita, the International Association of Buddhist Women, whose headquarters were originally at the center.

In 1994 the center held the first ordination where they ordained bhiksunis in both the Theravada and Tibetan forms of Buddhism.

Membership: In 1997, the center reported approximately 300 members in one center served by seven priests.

Educational Facilities: Thien-An Institute of Buddhist Studies, Los Angeles, California.

College of Buddhist Studies, Los Angeles, California.

Periodicals: *Monthly Guide.*

Sources:

Like a Lotus, Thich Thien-An. Los Angeles, CA: International Buddhist Meditation Center, [1981].

Thien-An, Thich. *Buddhism and Zen in Vietnam.* Rutland, VT: Charles E. Tuttle, 1975.

___. *Zen Philosophy, Zen Practice.* Berkeley, CA: Dharma Publishing, 1975.

★2121★
International Meditation Center-USA
538 Bankard Rd.
Westminster, MD 21158

The International Meditation Center-USA, founded in 1984, is the American representative of the International Meditation Centers, a worldwide Theravada Buddhist organization which has grown out of the teachings and practice of Burmese lay teacher Sayagyi U Ba Khin (1899–1971), who had started teaching while still working as an accountant. From 1948 to 1953 he was the Accountant General of Burma, and the year before his retirement, he founded the International Meditation Center in Rangoon. His teachings emphasized intense practice over theoretical understanding as the road to Enlightenment.

Membership: Not reported. There is one center in the United States and affiliated centers in Burma, Austria, Australia, and the United Kingdom.

★2122★
Lao Buddhist Sangha of the U.S.A.
Current address not obtained for this edition.

Like other southeast Asians, Laotians have come to the United States in significant numbers since 1965, and particularly since the end of the Viet Nam War. The number of new immigrants quadrupled during the period 1980-1985, and the religious scene is in great flux with new work only beginning to be stablized in each Laotian community. Temples have been established in Los Angeles, Chicago, and Washington, D.C.

Membership: Not reported. As of 1985 there are an estimated 220,000 Laotians in the United States.

★2123★
Mid-America Dharma Group
PO Box 414411
Kansas City, MO 64141-4411

The Mid-America Dharma Group is an umbrella organization uniting members of Vipassana sitting groups in Missouri, Kansas, and Iowa. Though independent, it has close relationships with the Insight Meditation Society from whom it borrows teachers.

Membership: In 1997, there were three groups in Missouri, four in Kansas, and one in Iowa.

Sources:

Morreale, Don. *The Complete Guide to Buddhist America.* Boston: Shambhala, 1998.

★2124★
Neo-Dharma
(Defunct)

Dr. Douglas Murray Burns is a psychiatrist born in Boston and raised in Oregon. As a high school student, he became interested in Buddhism. In 1960, he published his first work, *The Principles of Buddhist Philosophy.* He moved to California in 1961 and gathered around him a group interested, as he was, in a rational Theravada form of Buddhist faith, which he called Neo-Dharma. (Buddha's teachings outline the Dharma, the true way of life. Theravada Buddhism also called Hinayana, is a conservative, monastic Buddhism.) In 1965, Burns went to Thailand with the intent of entering a monastery, but was prevented by his induction into the Army. After his service in the Army, he continued to travel, write, and lecture. On one of his travels in 1976, he disappeared while in the jungle and has not been heard from since. He is presumed dead.

Burn's ideas can be summarized in a few statements, which obviously represent a neo-Buddhist or modernist approach: 1) The universe is regulated by impartial and unchanging laws. 2) Knowledge of these laws is acquired by insight and by unprejudiced reasoning in the light of one's experiences-not by faith in scriptures or mystical revelations. 3) Moral law, like physical law, is inherent in the workings of nature. Greed, hatred, and egotism result in proportionate amounts of unhappiness for one who is responsible for such motivations. 4) This three dimensional realm of space, time, and matter is not the only level of existence. The concrete world of sense perception is a reality, but it is not the only possible dimension of reality. His rational modern approach found an audience in Thailand, Ceylon, and the United States. For many years, the American membership, concentrated in California, published a newsletter, *Neo-Dharma Notes.*

Sources:

Burns, Douglas. *Nirvana.* Bangkok, Thailand: World Fellowship of Buddhists, 1967.

___. *Buddhism, Science and Atheism.* Bangkok, Thailand: World Fellowship of Buddhists, 1965.

★2125★
Order of Interbeing
% Community of Mindful Living
PO Box 7355
Berkeley, CA 94707

Among the more well-known figures to emerge during the Vietnam War was Thich Nhat Hanh (1926-), a Buddhist monk who traveled the world in his advocacy of peace. Nhat Hanh had been a Buddhist monk since his teenage years. He became a professor at Saigon University, where he was located as the Vietnam War developed. As the war heated up through the 1960s, he became the leader of a group of Buddhists committed to ending the conflict and bringing peace to their land. His efforts were recognized in 1967 when he was nominated for the Nobel Peace Prize.

In moving out of their isolation into the public sphere, Nhat Hanh and his monastic associates began to articulate what they termed "Engaged Buddhism." Engaged Buddhism is an attempt to bring Buddhism into contemporary issues—issues that range from helping the victims of war to critiquing government war policies. In this endeavor, at the beginning of 1964, Nhat Hanh founded the Tiep Hien Order and developed its guidelines. The first members were received on Wesak, the Buddha's birthday.

Nhat Hanh called for members of the order to loose their attachment to particular doctrines and views, to concentrate on realization drawn from direct experience, center themselves on appropriate teaching, and employ skillful means to guide people in their practice of Buddhism. The fourteen precepts of the order called upon members to find means of assisting those who suffer, to avoid the accumulation of wealth, and separate from anger, discord, and untruth. On the other hand, he encouraged them to remain centered and not allow the chaos of their environment to dissipate their efforts.

Immediately after the order was founded, Nhat Hanh began to travel the world on behalf of the peace process in Vietnam. He found a ready acceptance among anti-war activists in the United States, an early expression of which was his dialogue with Catholic priest Daniel Berrigan in 1975. He also attracted many people who wanted to begin practicing his form of Buddhism developed from traditional Vietnamese Buddhism that brought together Theravada and Zen in a complex mixture.

Through the 1980s especially, numerous groups have sprung up as a result of people being inspired by Nhat Hanh, and now exist as a loose network of Buddhist sitting groups and communities. Meanwhile, Nhat Hanh travels through the United States and Europe in a constant series of lectures and retreats that are directed at both English-speaking and Vietnamese audiences.

Membership: Groups are found across the United States and in various countries of Asia and Europe including Norway, France, and Switzerland. There is a core community of approximately 400 of which 250 live in the United States and 25 in Canada. The larger fellowship include some 10,000 persons of which 8,000 live in the United States and 1,000 in Canada.

Educational Facilities: Buddhist Institute at Plum Village, Loubes-Beancec, France.

Periodicals: *The Mindfulness Bell.*

Sources:

Berrigan, Daniel, and Thich Nhat Hanh. *The Raft Is Not the Shore.* Boston, MA: Beacon Press, 1975. 139 pp.

Nhat Hahn, Thich. *Interbeing: Commentaries on the Tiep Hien Precepts.* Berkeley, CA: Parallax Press, 1987. 77 pp.

___. *The Miracle of Mindfulness.* Boston, MA: Beacon Press, 1975. 108 pp.

___. *Zen Keys.* Garden City, NY: Doubleday & Company, 1974. 185 pp.

★2126★
Ordinary Dharma
℅ Manzanita Village
PO Box 67
Warner Springs, CA 92086

Ordinary Dharma, founded by Christopher Reed in 1982, is an independent organization which has grown out of the "Engaged Spirituality" generally associated with the Vietnamese teacher Thich Nhat Hanh, from whom Reed received Charmacarya transmission. Practice is in the Vietnamese tradition which combines Vipassana and Zen traditions. Practitioners are also called upon to engage in socially relevant activity, especially around issues of peace, deep ecology, and mindfulness in everyday life. Informal relations are maintained with the Spirit Rock Center and the larger Vipassana community. Ordinary Dharma, located in Santa Monica, California, maintains Manzanita Village, a rural retreat center.

The Santa Monica center regularly schedules monthly one-day retreats, classes, meditation sessions, study groups, and classes in Aikido. Manzanita is home to three annual 10-day retreats and a variety of retreats of lesser duration.

Membership: Not reported.

Periodicals: *Ordinary Dharma.*

Sources:

Morreale, Don. *The Complete Guide to Buddhist America.* Boston: Shambhala, 1998.

★2127★
Resources for Ecumenical Spirituality
PO Box 6
Mankato, MN 56002

Resources for Ecumenical Spirituality is a Theravada Buddhist group which began out of a desire to spread interfaith understanding through shared spiritual practice and dialogue. The group's life began to focus on a regular series of Vipassana retreats, some led by the resident teacher, Mary Jo Meadow, and various guest teachers. Once the program was established, the group moved to offer Vipassana events especially for Christians, with an emphasis upon their adopting the meditation procedures as a means of enriching their own Christian spirituality. Its meditation offerings have also moved into twelve-step programs.

Membership: Not reported. Resources for Ecumenical Spirituality also sponsors a forest monastery in Dunnegan, Missouri, and a sitting group in Chicago.

Sources:

Morreale, Don. *The Complete Guide to Buddhist America.* Boston: Shambhala, 1998.

★2128★
Saddhamma Foundation
5459 Shafter Ave.
Oakland, CA 94618

The Saddhamma Foundation was formed by students of Burmese meditation teacher U Pandita Sayadaw to provide for the holding of meditation events and the spread of his teachings in the West. The foundation has also been a major force in raising money to support Sayadaw's work in his homeland, including the building of a forest meditation center outside of Rangoon. The foundation also sponsors the Tathgatha Meditation Center in San Jose, California.

Membership: Not reported.

Sources:

Morreale, Don. *The Complete Guide to Buddhist America.* Boston: Shambhala, 1998.

★2129★
Sri Lankan Sangha Council of North America
No central address. For information:
American-Sri Lanka Buddhist Association, Inc.
84-32 126th St., Kew Gardens
New York, NY 11415

The Sri Lanka Sangha Council of North America was formed in 1987 by a group of Sri Lankan monks. It grew out of the needs of the burgeoning Sri Lankan Buddhist community which had developed so quickly in North America during the 1980s. The American-Sri Lankan community continues the tradition first introduced into America by Anagarika Dharmapala, a Ceylonese Buddhist who addressed the World's Parliament of Religion in 1893. Out of his visit an American chapter of the Maha Bodhi Society was organized, but no permanent Ceylonese Buddhism was established.

Then in 1964, while visiting the United States, the Most Ven. Madihe Panneseeha, Maha Nayake Thera of Ceylon, became aware of both an interest in Buddhism and the lack of a center for Theravada Buddhism in America. (At that time there was only one small Theravada Buddhist center in America, a Thai-inspired center in California headed by Douglas Murray Burns.) Acting upon his suggestion, the Sesana Sevaka Society of Maharagama, Ceylon (now Sri Lanka), sent the Ven. Thera Bope Vinita to Washington, D. C., in 1965. The Washington Buddhist Vihara Society was founded that year with assistance from the Ceylonese embassy. In 1967, Vinita was succeeded by the Ven. Pandita Mahathera Dickwela Piyananda who was in turn succeeded in 1968 by his assistant, the Ven. Mahathera Henepola Gunaratana, the present head of the vihara. For many years, it was the only Ceylonese Buddhist center in the United States.

Since 1965, and especially since the late-1970s, Buddhists from Sri Lanka have moved to the United States and settled along both coasts. Monks have arrived to provide leadership for the growing number of Buddhist temples which have emerged. Among the most prominent centers are the Dharma Vijaya Buddhist Vihara in Los Angeles, California, the California Buddhist Vihara Society in Berkeley, California, and the American-Sri Lanka Buddhist Association in New York City. Among the most prominent of the scholarly leaders of the American-Sri Lankan community is David J. Kalupahana, a professor of philosophy at the University of Hawaii. Sri Lankan Buddhism in North America remains primarily an ethnic religion though the number of non-Sri Lankans is growing. Assisting in that growth, which is common to Buddhist communities, has been the very popular writings of Walpola Rahula, especially his basic introductiory text to Ceylonese Buddhism, *What the Buddha Taught*.

Membership: Not available.

Periodicals: *Washington Buddhist*. Available from Washington Buddhist Vihara, 5017 16th St., Washington, DC 20011. • *New York Buddhist*. Available from New York Buddhist Vihara, 84-32 124th St., Kew Gardens, New York, NY 11415.

Remarks: During the twentieth century, the Ceylonese Buddhists have been among the most open to potential converts from Western countries and have placed considerable emphasis upon the publication of English-language books on Buddhism. Prominent in any collection of English language Buddhist literature are the Wheel Publications of the Buddhist Publication Society of Candy, Sri Lanka. Beginning in the 1950s, several hundred titles have appeared and have had a measurable effect in spreading Buddhism in North America.

Sources:

Buddha Vadana. Los Angeles: Dharma Vijava Buddhist Vihara, 1985.

Gunaratana, Henepola. *Come and See*. Washington, DC: Buddhist Vihara Society, n.d.

___. *The Path of Serenity and Insight*. Delhi, India: Banarsidass, Motilal. 1985.

Kalupahana, David J. *Buddhist Philosophy, A Historical Analysis*. Honolulu: University of Hawaii Press, 1976.

Maha Sthavira Sangharakshita. *Flame in Darkness, the Life and Sayings of Anagarika Dharmapala*. Pune, India: Triratna Grantha Mala, 1980.

Rahula, Walpola. *What the Buddha Taught*. New York: Grove Press, 1974.

★2130★
Stillpoint Institute
Current address not obtained for this edition.

The Stillpoint Institute was founded in 1971 as the Susana Yeiktha Meditation Center and Buddhist Society. The founder, an American now known by his Buddhist name, Anagarika Sujata, was a college dropout who went to Ceylon and took training as a monk in Theravada Buddhism. He was ordained in 1967, re-

turned to the United States and, in 1970, founded the Buddhist Society of Clearwater. In 1971, he moved to Denver. From there, Sujata developed his Theravada Buddhist perspective in lectures, in teaching meditation, and in leading retreats. Around him a small community developed.

The goal of the Institute is the "integration of body awareness techniques with the Satipatthana Vipassana Insight Meditation," in which the mind is trained to be more observant while refraining from comment on or judgment of what it views. In the mid-1970s the Institute moved to San Jose, California.

The emphasis of Sujata's teaching, as manifested in his book, *Beginning to See*, is on present-mindedness and detachment. Buddhist insight meditation is the key to the laying down of anger, attachment and selfishness, and to the attainment of loving kindness, compassion, sympathetic joy, and equanimity.

Membership: Not reported.

Sources:

Sayadaw, Mahasi. *The Satipatthana Vipassana Meditation*. Elgin, AZ: Unity Press, 1957.

Sujata, Anagarika. *Beginning to See*. Denver: Sasana Yeiktha Meditation Center, 1973.

★2131★
Taungpupu Kaba-Aye Dharma Center
18335 Basin Way
Boulder Creek, CA 95006

Alternate Address: Burma-America Buddhist Association, 1708 Powder Mill Rd., Silver Spring, MD 20903.

The Taungpupu Kaba-Aye Dharma Center is a center for the teaching of Burmese Buddhism; it was founded in 1981 by the Ven. Taungpupu Kaba-Aye Sayadaw, a Burmese monk then on a goodwill tour of the United States. Dr. Rina Sircar, a long-time student of Taungpupu Kaba-Aye Sayadaw and co-founder of the monastery, serves as the resident meditation teacher. The monastery offers periodic retreats for those already versed in vipasana meditation, the form of meditation most common to Theravada Buddhism. Dr. Sincar is also a member of the faculty in the Department of Philosophy and religion as the California Institute for Integral Studies in San Francisco. There is also a second center in San Francisco.

Membership: Not reported.

Educational Facilities: The center has a cooperative arrangement with Antioch College, Yellow Springs, Ohio, by which it accepts students on a quarterly or semester work study program.

Sources:

Sayadaw, Mahasi. *Purpose of Practising Kummatthana Meditation*. Silver Spring, MD: Burma-America Buddhist Association, n.d.

★2132★
Thai-American Buddhist Association
Wat Thai of Los Angeles
12909 Cantara St.
North Hollywood, CA 91506

The general unrest in Southeast Asia and the rescinding of the Oriental Exclusion Act in 1965 combined to increase immigration from Thailand to the United States in the late 1960s. Significant Thai-American communities emerged on the West Coast and in several urban areas further inland. Assisted by leadership from Thailand, the new immigrant communities began to organize their predominantly Buddhist religious life. In 1970, at the invitation of the American Thais, the Ven. Pharkhru Vajirathammasophon of Wat Vajirathamsathit toured the United States. During his visit, the Thai-American Buddhist Association was formally organized in Los Angeles, and plans were initiated to build the Wat Thai of Los Angeles, a temple complex which would serve the largest of the

Thai communities in the West. Later that year, three priests arrived to take up permanent residence.

The 1971 visit by the Ven. Phra Dhammakosacharn, a leading Thai Buddhist priest, was followed by the incorportion of the Wat Thai as the Theravada Buddhist Center and the beginning of a fund raising drive. In 1972 the United States government invited the supreme patriarch, Phra Wannarat of Wat Phra Jetuphon, and a group of Thai priests to make an official state visit. During this visit, the presentation of the land-title deed for the future site of the Wat Thai was held in the office of the Consul General in Los Angeles. The cornerstone was laid and construction commenced. It was finished in stages, and in 1980 the statue of Buddha in the main temple was consecrated.

While work on the complex in Los Angeles proceeded, other wats were being organized in other cities from San Francisco and Denver to Houston, Washington, D.C., and New York.

Theravada Buddhism has, as a major practice, insight meditation, described as the practice of mindfulness. Mindfulness is the observation point arrived at by the meditator from which he or she can truly understand mental and physical phenomena as they arise. In general, Theravada Buddhists are among the most conservative in their adherence to the oldest Buddhist traditions and they use the Pali-language texts of early Buddhism, as opposed to the Sanskrit texts used by the Mahayana Buddhists.

Membership: There are over 100,000 Thais in the United States and 40,000 in Los Angeles alone. As of 1991, wats had been established in 22 locations across the United States.

Periodicals: *Duangpratip.*

Sources:

Hamilton-Merritt, Jane. *A Meditator's Dairy.* New York: Harper & Row, 1976.

Jumsai, M. L. Manich. *Understanding Thai Buddhism.* Bangkok: Chalermit Press, 1973.

Narasapo, Phra Maha Singhathon. *Buddhism, An Introduction to a Happy Life.* Bangkok: Preacher's Association, Wat Phrajetubon, 1969.

★2133★
Tiep Hien Order
% Parallax Press
PO Box 7355
Berkeley, CA 94707

Alternate Address: International Network of Engaged Buddhists, PO Box 1, Ongkharak, Nakhorn Nayok, Thailand.

Among the more well-known figures to emerge during the Vietnam War was Thich Nhat Hanh (1926-), a Buddhist monk who traveled the world in his advocacy of peace. Nhat Hanh had been a Buddhist monk since his teenage years. He became a professor at Saigon University, where he was located as the Vietnam War developed. As the war heated up through the 1960s, he became the leader of a group of Buddhists committed to ending the conflict and bringing peace to their land. His efforts were recognized in 1967 when he was nominated for the Nobel Peace Prize.

In moving out of their isolation into the public sphere, Nhat Hanh and his monastic associates began to articulate what they termed "Engaged Buddhism." Engaged Buddhism is an attempt to bring Buddhism into contemporary issues—issues that range from helping the victims of war to critiquing government war policies. In this endeavor, at the beginning of 1964, Nhat Hanh founded the Tiep Hien Order and developed its guidelines. The first members were received on Wesak, the Buddha's birthday.

Nhat Hanh called for members of the order to loose their attachment to particular doctrines and views, to concentrate on realization drawn from direct experience, center themselves on appropriate teaching, and employ skillful means to guide people in their practice of Buddhism. The fourteen precepts of the order called upon members to find means of assisting those who suffer, to avoid the accumulation of wealth, and separate from anger, discord, and untruth. On the other hand, he encouraged them to remain centered and not allow the chaos of their environment to dissipate their efforts.

Immediately after the order was founded, Nhat Hanh began to travel the world on behalf of the peace process in Vietnam. He found a ready acceptance among anti-war activists in the United States, an early expression of which was his dialogue with Catholic priest Daniel Berrigan in 1975. He also attracted many people who wanted to begin practicing his form of Buddhism developed from traditional Vietnamese Buddhism that brought together Theravada and Zen in a complex mixture.

Through the 1980s especially, numerous groups have sprung up as a result of people being inspired by Nhat Hanh, and now exist as a loose network of Buddhist sitting groups and communities. Meanwhile, Nhat Hanh travels through the United States and Europe in a constant series of lectures and retreats that are directed at both English-speaking and Vietnamese audiences. World wide, work is carried on through the International Network of Engaged Buddhists headquartered in Thailand.

Membership: : Not reported: Groups are found across the United States and in various countries of Europe including Norway, France, and Switzerland.

Periodicals: *The Mindfulness Bell. Seeds of Peace,* International Network of Engaged Buddhists, PO Box 1, Ongkharak, Nakhorn Nayok, Thailand.

Sources:

Berrigan, Daniel, and Thich Nhat Hanh. *The Raft Is Not the Shore.* Boston, MA: Beacon Press, 1975. 139 pp.

Nhat Hahn, Thich. *Interbeing: Commentaries on the Tiep Hien Precepts.* Berkeley, CA: Parallax Press, 1987. 71 pp.

___. *The Miracle of Mindfulness.* Boston, MA: Beacon Press, 1975. 108 pp.

___. *Zen Keys.* Garden City, NY: Doubleday & Company, 1974. 185 pp.

★2134★
Viet Nam Buddhists
% Congregation of Vietnamese Buddhists in the U.S.
863 S. Berendo
Los Angeles, CA 90005

Because of the resettlement of the many Vietnamese Buddhists who entered the United States after the Viet Nam War, the number of Vietnamese temples far exceeds that of other Southeast Asians, and they may be found in all sections of the United States. The temples serve first generation Vietnamese-Americans and services are conducted in Vietnamese. Vietnamese Buddhism is distinctive in the way it has merged Theravada and Zen. Among the leading spokespersons for Vietnamese Buddhism is Thich Nhat Hanh, who became known to Americans during the Viet Nam War as a peace advocate. He works closely with the Fellowship of Reconciliation.

Membership: Not reported. There are an estimated 900,000 Vietnamese in the United States, concentrated in southern California. While a large percentage of them are Roman Catholics, the majority are Buddhists. Centers are found across the United States, including a number located in Los Angeles and Orange counties in California.

Sources:

Fields, Rick. *Taking Refuge in L.A.* New York: Aparture Foundation, 1987.

The Presence of Vietnamese Buddhists in America. Los Angeles: Vietnamese Buddhist Temple, 1981.

Hanh, Thich Nhat. *The Miracle of Mindfulness.* Boston: Beacon Press, 1976.

___. *Zen Keys.* Garden City, NY: Doubleday, 1974.

★2135★
Vipassana Meditation Centers
% Vipassana Meditation Center
PO Box 24
Sherburne Falls, MA 01370-2160

The Vipassana Meditation Centers have grown out of the teachings and practices offered by Satya Narayn Goenka (b. 1924), a prominent Burmese meditation teacher. A businessman, Goenka had turned to vipassana meditation as a means to cure migraine headaches. The meditation not only cured him but led him to drop his business career and become the student of Sayagi U Bba Khin (1899–1971), with whom he studied for 16 years. In 1969 he moved to India and held his first classes that same year. He established the Vipassana International Academy in India in 1976.

The first American center, in Sherburne Falls, Massachusetts, was founded in 1982 and subsequently other centers have been opened across North America. His work has spread through the Englishspeaking world.

Membership: Not reported. In 1997 there were 30 Vipassana Centers found across the United States and Canada.

Sources:

Morreale, Don. *The Complete Guide to Buddhist America.* Boston: Shambhala, 1998.

Japanese Buddhism

★2136★
Agon-shu
14518 S. Western Ave.
Gardena, CA 90247

Alternate Address: International Headquarters: Agon-shu Head Temple, 607 Kitakazan Omine-cho, Yamashina, Kyoto, Japan. Canadian Headquarters: Toronto Agon-shu Buddhist Association, 16 Burch Ave., 2nd Floor, Toronto, ON Canada M4V 1C8.

Agon-shu is a form of Japanese Buddhism founded in 1978 by Seiyu Kiriyama (b. 1921) who serves as its *Kancho* or leader. He had been a member of several different Buddhist groups and in 1954 founded Kannon Jijei-Kai, a small religious group superseded by Agon-shu. The great impetus for the founding of the new organization was the belief that emerged in the 1970s that the Agon (or Agama in Sanskrit) sutras contain the original teachings concerning the path to Buddhahood (enlightenment) and ultimate salvation as given by Buddha. The emergent organization incorporated insights from all three major schools of Buddhism, Mahayana, Hinayana, and the esoteric Buddhism of Tibet. The esoteric practices represent the final stage of development in Buddhist practice. There are also elements of Shinto incorporated in the rites.

While feeling that there is great value in all Buddhist groups, Agon-shu believes that it alone has the full teachings of true and genuine Buddhism. It teaches and practices Jobutsu-ho, the teachings and methods required to attain enlightenment and full salvation, which includes release from karma, the accumulated burden of cause and effect that has decisive influence on one's present life.

Even prior to his founding of Agon-shu, Kiriyama in 1970 held the first Dai-saito-goma Rite, an esoteric Buddhist ceremony centered on prayers offered up in a large outdoor bonfire. Today, the major ceremony of Agon-shu is the Hoshi Matsuri, literally the "Combined Shinto-Buddhist Fire Rites Festival" held near the group's main temple at Kyoto. It is concerned with the destiny of each individual and the reading of the future of each individual's birth star (esoteric astrology).

Agon-shu teachings are grounded in three principles, the Buddha, the dharma, and the sangha. The Buddha, or object of worship, is found in the Shinsei-busshari, a bone fragment from Shakyamuni Buddha that is preserved in a gold shrine. The dharma is the actual training members undergo. It consists of the Jobutsu-ho (Buddha's method for attaining enlightenment), the Nyoi Hoju-ho (the esoteric teachings) and the Gumonji Somei-ho (which incorporates elements of Taoism and Tantrism, including kundalini yoga).

Kiriyama has carried on a worldwide program in support of world peace and the spread of true Buddhism. He established centers in Cambodia, Mongolia, Sri Lanka, Brazil and eventually the United States (Hawaii and California). In 1989 he opened the Japanese American Agon Friendship Foundation in Washington, D.C.

Membership: Not reported. Agon-shu has a small following in the United States, as it was only established in California in the mid-1990s. It has offices in Japan and in 1990 became the first foreign-based religion to open an office in mainland China, in Beijing.

Remarks: The Agon-shu received some unwanted publicity when it was discovered that Soko Asahara, the founder of AUM Shinrikyo, and one of that group's leaders, Tomomitsu Niimi, had gotten their early training in Agon-shu. In fact, it appears that Asahara began AUM with an assertion that he had surpassed Kiriyama in enlightenment, a fact demonstrated by his levitating before several of the members. This fact accounts for the similarity of teachings between Agon-shu and AUM, but it should be noted that there is no hint of a connection between Agon-shu and the crime allegedly perpetrated by the leaders of AUM.

Sources:

Agon-shu and Its Activities. Tokyo: Agon-shu Public Information Division, 1990. 25 pp.

The Agon-shu: The Original Teachings of the Lord Buddha. Tokyo: Agon-shu, 1989 18 pp.

A Short Introduction to the Hoshi Matsuri. N.p.: Agon-shu, n.d. 15 pp.

★2137★
AUM Supreme Truth
Current address not obtained for this edition.

AUM Supreme Truth, also known by its Japanese name, AUM Shinrikyo, is a Japanese Buddhist group that became known internationally in 1995 after an incident in which nerve gas was released in a Tokyo subway station and was tied to members of the group. During the summer and fall of 1995, over 100 members of the group, including most of its leadership and its founding leader, Master Shoko Asahara, were arrested and a lengthy judicial process was begun. In the accompanying investigation, a variety of additional capitol crimes were tied to the groups officials as were other incidents of suspected gassings. In the wake of these events, the organization has been totally disrupted in Japan and its immediate future will be one of continued unstability.

AUM Supreme Truth was founded by Asahara (born Chizuo Matsumoto in 1955) in Japan in 1987, though it was rooted in another organization that published books and taught yoga. It brought together the teachings he had acquired from his study of tantric yoga, Buddhism, and Taoism, through which he developed a unique training method to bring students to their own enlightenment, a realization of Ones True Self. Asahara was most impressed by the Theravada and Tibetan Buddhist writings which he considered more authentic than those Buddhist scriptures most used by Japanese Buddhists; one of several opinions held by Asahara that contributed to his isolation from other Japanese Buddhist leaders.

According to Asahara, the world consists of the gross world of everyday experiences, the astral world of images that we experience in our dreams, and the causal world of ideas. Above these three is the world of truth, Maha-Nirvana. AUM practice leads to emancipation, the ability to move freely at will from one world to the next. Supreme bliss and freedom are experienced in Maha-Nirvana (death).

Asahara directed students to the spiritual path called *tantray-ana*, the goal being to become a buddha (enlightened one) in a single lifetime. The path demands total devotion to the guru and his initiations. New members were trained in yoga and meditation, and there was a stringent program of psychic development reminiscent of some of the austerities of Hindu sadhus.

Master Asahara offered three initiations. An earthly initiation included oral instructions on ethics, yoga, meditation, the use of mantras, and other matters leading to a purification of ones consciousness in regards to the gross world. The astral initiation via *shukufuku* (blessing) and *shaktipat* (awakening the kundalini energy) purifies one's consciousness, relative to the astral world. The causal initiation purifies ones superconsciousness and includes the transfer of energy from the master to the trainee. The causal initiation leads directly to emancipation and enlightenment. Ritual accompanying the initiations included the consumption of some of the bath water of the guru (a rite derived from an incident in Gautama Buddhas life in which followers consumed water from a pond in which he had washed), and some of his blood.

Those who passed through the three initiations were considered more spiritually advanced, and many were admitted into the ordered life. The monastic community, which included approximately ten to fifteen percent of the Japanese membership, lived at AUM facilities. The development of the ordered community, not a prominent part of Japanese Buddhist life, further separated AUM from the mainstream of Japanese Buddhism and also led to protests by many parents of AUM members who felt that AUM was disruptive of family units.

Organizationally, AUM was modeled after the Japanese government. It was divided into various departments each headed by a minister. Ministries included Health and Welfare, Science and Technology, Intelligence, Medical, Home Affairs, and Construction. AUM was headquartered at a rural center called Kaikuishiki, Yamanashi Prefecture near Mount Fuji. The organization operated a hospital in Tokyo and members formed many businesses aligned to the groups program.

Along with the Buddhist theology and psychic development program, Master Asahara had a fascination with prophecy and was a student of the Christian New Testament book of *Revelation* and the writings of Nostradamus. Through the early 1990s, he made a variety of predictions concerning the future of Japan including World War III/Armageddon in the later half of the 1990s. The public's awareness of these predictions was heightened following the unsuccessful bid by Asahara and the 24 other candidates who ran as members of AUM in the 1990 national elections. The various enterprises organized by AUM were in part designed to survive the apocalypse and emerge unscathed in the aftermath of the destruction of social order.

The first American branch of the AUM was opened in 1987 in New York City. While it survived for a period after the gas incident, it has subsequently disappeared.

Membership: Prior to the arrests in the summer of 1995, AUM reported some 50,000 members worldwide, of which 10,000 were in Japan and 40,000 in Russia. Several hundred members were found in New York City, Sri Lanka, and Germany.

Periodicals: *Truth Monthly.*

Remarks: The period of unstable existence that followed the gas incident and the subsequent arrest of Asahara and most of the group's leadership has continued as the time-consuming process of adjudicating the charges against the principles proceeds. As this edition goes to press, Asahara's trail continues, additional revelation of crimes committed by those in custody are being revealed, and the initial sentences are being pronounced. The government moved to disincorporate the group, its properties were seized, and it was forced into bankruptcy. In the wake of these actions, and the arrest of the last of the major leaders, Fumihiro Joyu, who had become the group's spokesperson in the months after the gassing, many predicted the group's disappearance. However, in 1996, the

court ruled that, with the accused in jail, the group (the overwhelming majority of members having no involvement or knowledge of the acts of its leadership) Aum Shinrikyo no longer posed a public threat and has allowed it to continue.

In wake of the courts ruling, the group which had been completely decimated by the governments's action against it, has begun to rebuild. As of early 1998, it appeared to have approximately 2,000 members in Japan (about twenty percent of its size in 1995). Its activities remain under close observation of the police, but activities have been centered on the previous religious practices. Asahara's sons, both still children, have been designated the official gurus of the group until such time as Asahara might be released (the prospect of which is highly unlikely).

The number of crimes, including the deaths of various people not connected to the gassing, have been revealed. Together, the crimes committed by AUM's leadership constitute most destructive serial crime wave ever in the country's history. The national trauma that the Japanese experienced has led to the passing of a new law that tightens government control of religious groups.

Sources:

Asahara, Shoko. *Supreme Initiation.* New York: AUM, U.S.A., 1988.

___. *Disaster Approaches the Land of the Rising.* Hitoana Fujuinimiya, Shizuyoko, Japan: AUM Shinrikyo Publishing Co., 1995.

___. *Tathagata Abhidhamma: The Ever-Winning Law of the True Victors.* 2 vols. Hitoana, Fujuinimiya, Shizuoka, Japan: AUM Shinrikyo Publishing Co., 1991–92.

___. *The Teaching of Truth.* 5 vols. Hitoana, Fujuinimiya, Shizuoka, Japan: AUM Shinrikyo Publishing Co. 1991–92.

Your Daily Practice. A Book of Esoteric Teachings: The Tantra Vajrayana System of Practice. Japan, AUM Shinrikyo, n.d.

Reader, Ian. *A Poisonous Cocktail? AUM Shinrikyo's Path to Violence.* Nordic Institute of Asian Studies, 1996. 116pp.

★2138★
Bodaiji Mission
1251 Elm
Honolulu, HI 96814

The Bodaiji Mission was founded in 1930 by Nisshyo Takao, the Holy Interpreter. It is continued by Roy S. Takakuwa as an independent congregation teaching "True Buddhism." Takakuwa is a baker in Honolulu, but he also serves as the sole teacher and priest. The bakery provides the total support for the mission, because no donations are allowed. The teaching of the mission is described as empirical, moving from fact to the source of facts.

The basic concept of Bodaiji teachings is Dai-O-Kyo, filial piety, the lack of which is a great cause of discord and trouble. Filial piety begins in Yojomanjo, the unconditional salvation of true motherhood. Just as motherhood was the source of our nurture, so cooperation, coexistence, and right living lead us to universal salvation. True Buddhism teaches how to live rightly.

An acceptence of the law of cause and effect underlies the teachings; where there is something wrong, one finds the cause and changes it. Thus, when one adopts a program of right living, salvation will come.

Healing is a concept basic to right living. Each person who comes for healing must stick to a rigid diet and must learn to breathe properly. Holy water is also used. Meditation is advised for all for fifteen minutes each day to replenish energy.

Membership: In 1982 there were approximately 100 members. There is but a single congregation, and no membership roll is kept.

★2139★
Dharma Sangha
Current address not obtained for this edition.

After leaving the Zen Center of San Francisco, California, Richard Baker, Roshi continued to teach independently for several years. He retained the loyalty of some of his students from earlier days and gained a new following. In early 1985 he announced the formation of a new group, Dharma Sangha. The group purchased a building in San Francisco as a center and also opened a graduate seminary in Santa Fe, New Mexico. The San Francisco center contains a lecture and meditation hall. The Santa Fe center will be for the training of senior students. Dharma Sangha is conceived as a lay-centered organization.

Membership: Not reported.

Sources:

"Baker Roshi Forms New Group." *Vajradhatu Sun* (March 1985): 4.

★2140★
Gedatsu Church of America
Current address not obtained for this edition.

The Gedatsu Church was formed by Gedatsu Kongpo (posthumous title of Shoken Okano), a priest in the Shugendo sect of Shingon Buddhism. Born in 1881, he rose to the rank of archbishop. In 1929, he founded the Gedatsu movement in his own town. A student of comparative religion, Gedatsu Konpgo borrowed freely from Shinto and Christianity to produce an eclectic Buddhist teaching.

According to Gedatsu, man desires wealth, fame, sex, food, and rest. Man runs into trouble whenever the search for these five, so necessary for survival, becomes directed solely to self-satisfaction. He then falls into the tragedies of life and suffers from ignorance of karmic law, hereditary problems, and selfish thoughts. The object of religion is to move from the problems and suffering of the present to the state of enlightenment—calm resignation and complete peace of mind. (By the law of karma, a person must experience the consequences of his or her actions.)

Gedatsu offers a method of attaining enlightenment through the development of wisdom, the purification of emotion, and the improvement of will power. Wisdom is developed by meditation on the symbol "AJI." The emotions are purified by service to the souls of ancestors and other spiritual entities. Will power is improved by the Way of the Holy Goho, a progressive method of disciplining the mind and spirit that can dissolve the bonds of karma.

Underlying the Gedatsu doctrine is the concept of universal law and universal truth. The universal law is the power of nature, absolutely unchangeable and indestructible. It is seen in the regular cycles of nature. This law also functions to bring to enlightenment those who follow the path.

Center of Gedatsu worship is the Goreichi Spiritual Sanctuary. This shrine is the resting place of all spirits and houses the Tenjinchigi, the spirit of the supreme creator, the source of the universal law. The shrine also contains a statue of Fudo Myo-Oh, who has the power to conquer all evil. Other bodhisattvas are also represented. A semiannual Thanksgiving Festival is observed in the spring and fall, and the Annual Roku Jizo Festival is observed in June. All are noteworthy for their ceremony. Central to all worship is Kuyo, the act of humbly repaying by absolute gratitude all the sources to which one is indebted. Kuyo is ritualized in the Nectar Service during which spirits in a state of unrest are brought to rest.

Gedatsu was brought to the United States in the late 1940s and incorporated in 1951. It has headquarters in San Francisco, and it maintains ten churches, including those in Sacramento, San Jose, Stockton, and Los Angeles, California. The Goreichi Shrine is in Mayhew, a Sacramento suburb. There is one temple in Honolulu.

Membership: Not reported.

Sources:

Gedatsu Ajikan Kongozen Meditation. San Francisco: Gedatsu Church of America, 1974.

Kishida, Eizan. *Dynamic Analysis of Illness through Gedatsu.* N.p., 1962.

Manual for Implementation of Gedatsu Practice. San Francisco: Gedatsu Church of America, 1965.

Yanagawa, Keiichi. *Japanese Religions in California.* Tokyo: Department of Religious Studies, University of Tokyo, 1983.

★2141★
Hawaii Council of Jodo Mission
% Jodo Mission of Hawaii
1429 Makiki St.
Honolulu, HI 96814

Alternate Address: International Headquarters: 400-8 Hayashishita Machi, Higashiyama-ku, Kyoto, Japan 605.

From the landing of the first 153 Japanese immigrants in 1868 until 1894, almost 30,000 Japanese arrived in Hawaii, most to work on the extensive plantation being developed there. They lived a demoralizing existence working (often at hard labor) 12-hour days and with no fixed days off. Gradually news of the living conditions made its way back to Japan and, given that most of the Japanese laborers were Buddhists, the major Buddhist denominations decided to respond. In 1894, Jodo Shu sent two clergymen, Revs. Matsuwo Taijyo and Okabe Gekuwo to comfort and reconstruct the lives of the demoralized workers.

For his efforts, Rev. Matsuwo caught tuberculosis and died a few years later while attempting to construct a temple at Kapaa on the island of Kauai. Rev. Okabe worked on the big island of Hawaii and succeeded in founding the first Jodo Mission at Hamakua in 1896. In subsequent years additional clergymen spread the work and built additional temples. Eventually 15 came to exist on Oahu, Maui, Kauai, and Hawaii. the Jodo movement celebrated its 100th anniversary, dated from the arrival of its initial two clergymen, in 1994. It is led by Chikai Shibamura.

In 1969 a nonprofit American religious entity was incorporated as the Hawaii Council of Jodo Missions. The council is an autonomous organization but cooperates with and receives guidance from Jodo Shu, headquartered in Japan. There is one Jodo Mission on continental North America, the Jodo Mission of Los Angeles, which operates an extension school of the Buddhist University of Kyoto, Japan.

Membership: In 1997 there were 15 temples in Hawaii and a membership 1,800. There was a single temple in Los Angeles.

Periodicals: *Jodo Mission of Hawai.* • *Hawaii Buddhism.*

Sources:

Light of Asia. Honolulu: Hawaii Jodo Mission, 1962.

Matsunami, Kodo. *Introducing Buddhism.* Honolulu: Hawaii Jodo Mission, 1965.

Tabrah, Ruth. *Buddhism, "A Modern Way of Life and Thought."* Honolulu: Hawaii Jodo Mission, 1969.

★2142★
Higashi Hongwanji Buddhist Church
505 E. Third St.
Los Angeles, CA 90013

Quickly following the Buddhist Churches of America, the largest of the Shin Buddhist groups, was the Higashi Hongwanji. However, since it has done little to Westernize, it has been slower to spread. In 1899, Shizuka Sazanami began to work on Kauai in Hawaii, where a temple was constructed in Waimea. It was 1916 before a temple appeared in Honolulu. On the mainland, the Higashi Honganji began with Rev. Junjyo Izumida who, in 1904, established the Los Angeles Buddhist Mission as an outpost of the Honpa Hongwanji. Two other churches were also formed in Los Angeles, and soon a rivalry developed between them. In 1917 a merger of the three congregations was ratified. Izumida, however, opposed the merger and, in a court suit, won the property of the congregation he had led. In 1921 he joined the Higashi Honganji and brought the congregation with him. Shortly after the establishment of the Higashi Honganji in Los Angeles, a second temple was opened in Berkeley, California. A third was added in Chicago after World War II. The Chicago temple, under the leadership of Gyomay Kubose also sponsors a Zen center. Kubose, who serves as both a Shin priest and Zen master, follows in the pattern of the late Daisetz Teitaro Suzuki, the most famous member of the Higashi Honganji (at least to Western audiences). The American branch of the Higashi Honganji is presided over by Gyoko Saito, the priest in Los Angeles.

Membership: In 1982 there were 1,800 members in six churches in Hawaii. There are three temples in the continental United States, though there are several branch churches attached to the Los Angeles temple.

Periodicals: *The Way.*

Sources:

Akegarasu, Haya. *The Fundamental Spirit of Buddhism.* Trans. by Gyomay M. Kubose. Chicago: Buddhist Temple of Chicago, 1977.

___. *Shout of Buddha.* Trans. by Gyoko Saito and Joan Sweany. Chicago: Orchid Press, 1977.

Higashi Hongwanji Dedication-1976. Los Angeles: Higashi Hongwanji Buddhist Church, 1976.

Jodo Shinshu. Tokyo: Otani University, 1961.

Kiyozuma, Manshi. *December Fan.* Trans. by Nobuo Haneda. Kyoto, Japan: Higashi Hongwanji, 1984.

Suzuki, Beatrice Lane. *Mahayana Buddhism.* New York: Macmillan, 1969.

Suzuki, D. T. *Shin Buddhism.* New York: Harper & Row, 1970.

★2143★
Honpa Hongwanji Buddhism
% Buddhist Churches of America
1710 Octavia St.
San Francisco, CA 94109

Alternate Address: Honpa Hongwanji Mission of Hawaii, 1727 Pali Hwy., HI 96813; Buddhist Churches of Canada, 220 Jackson, Vancouver, BC V6A 3B3.

The Honpa Hongwanji sect, one of the major representatives of Jodo Shinshu Buddhism in Japan, is represented in North America by three separate organizations, of which reports directly to the international headquarters in Kyoto. Shinshu Buddhists began to arrive in Hawaii, the mainland of the United States, and Canada in the 1880s, and through the twentieth century a Buddhist Mission spread through the Japanese community and has been a major bridge leading to the accommodation of that community to American ways. The Honpa Hongwanji is one of three prime groups teaching Pureland Shin Buddhism.

The Buddhist Churches of America has headquarters in San Francisco. Congregations in the United States are divided into seven administrative districts; four on the Pacific Coast, and one each for the Northwest, the Mountain States, and the Eastern States. Since 1996, Bp. Hakubum Watanabe has presided over the organization, assisted by a board of directors and a representative national council who oversees administrative functions.

The Honpa Hongwanji Mission of Hawaii, headquartered in Honolulu, is headed by Bp. Chikai Yosemori. Until World War II, the bishop was appointed from the international headquarters, but since then the Hawaiian members elect their bishop, who serves three-year terms. In 1967, Kanmo Imamura, the son of Bp. Yemyo Imamura, the long-time bishop who did so much for the Buddhist cause in Hawaii prior to World War II, began a term as bishop.

The Jikoen Hongwanji Temple in Honolulu was built in 1938 as a center for Okinawan Shinshu immigrants who had come to Hawaii during the 1920s and 1930s. It functions as a member of the Honpa Hongwanji.

In Canada, the first Shinshu church was organized in 1904. The work in Canada gradually separated from the American organization in a process culminating a short time after the end of World War II.

Membership: In 1997, the Buddhist Churches of America reported 16,000 members in 61 independent churches and six branches served by 60 ministers. There were 35 branches throughout the Hawaiian Islands. There were 10,000,000 members worldwide.

Educational Facilities: Institute for Buddhist Studies, Berkeley, California.
American Buddhist Academy, New York, New York.

Periodicals: *Horin* (in Japanese). • *Pacific World.* • *Wheel of Dharma* (in English).

Sources:

Buddhist Churches of America, 75 Year History, 1899-1974. 2 vols. Chicago: Norbet, 1974.

Buddhist Handbook for Shin-shu Followers. Tokyo: Hokuseido Press, 1969.

Shin Buddhist Handbook. Honolulu: Honpa Hongwanji Mission of Hawaii, 1972.

Traditions of Jodoshinshu Hongwanji-Ha. Los Angeles: Senshin Buddhist Temple, 1982.

★2144★
International Zen Institute of America
1760 Pomona Ave., No. 35
Costa Mesa, CA 92627

The International Zen Institute of America was founded by the Ven. Roshi Gesshin Prabhasa Dharma. Gesshin Roshi is an artist and poet. In 1967 she met the Japanese Zen Master Joshu Kyozan Sasaki Roshi with whom she studied for the next 15 years. In 1968 she was ordained in the Rinzai Zen lineage of Mayoshin-ji and among her duties was supervising the development of an affiliated center at Mt. Baldy, California. She was ordained a teacher in 1972 and spent the next year and a half in Japan studying Zen with Hirata Roshi at Tenryu-ji Monastery and learning Japanese and calligraphy.

Upon her return from Japan, Gesshin Roshi became head priest at Rinzai-ji Zen center. She began to travel and teach independently of the Rinzai-ji center. In 1983 she formally resigned from the lineage altogether. During this period Gesshin Roshi started to associate with the growing Vietnamese community centered in the International Buddhist Meditation Center in Los Angeles. In 1985 she received the Dharma Mind Seal Transmission from the Ven. Thich Man Giac of the United Vietnamese Buddhist Churches of America. She founded the International Zen Institute of America as an organizational umbrella for her work.

Though headquartered in Los Angeles, Gesshin Roshi has traveled widely and developed affiliated centers in France, Germany, the Netherlands, and Spain. affiliated centers in Florida, Germany, Holland, and Spain.

Membership: In 1998, the institute reported 600 members in one center in the United States and 600 additional members at the centers in Europe.

Periodicals: *Zen Today.* • *Zen Leben* (German). • *Zen* (Spanish).

Sources:

Friedman, Lenore. *Meetings with Remarkable Women: Buddhist Teacher in America.* Boston: Shambhala, 1987.

★2145★
Kailas Shugendo
Current address not obtained for this edition.

The Kailas Shugendo was founded by Dr. Neville G. Pemchekov-Warwick, known to his followers as Ajari. Shugendo is an old Buddhist tradition that borrows from pre-Buddhist Japanese shamanism and mountain religion. Ajari has been conducting Shugendo practices since 1940 and is termed Dai Sendatsu, which allows him to start his own movement. His background is Russian Buddhist, and he immigrated to America in the 1960s.

Central to the Shugendo is fire worship. Twice a day, members observe Goma, the fire ceremony. The ritual master conducts while the members chant. Once a week Hiwatari, fire purification, is performed. Members walk the sacred fire but are not burned. At intervals, members go to the mountains for ascetic practices—shugyo (climbing the mountain while chanting mantra), going under ice-cold waterfalls, and hanging people off rocks. Music is also a part of daily life. Headquarters of the ashram are in San Francisco, California, where it offers musical and cultural presentations to the Bay Area community and performs emergency community services.

Membership: Not reported.

★2146★
Karuna Tendai Dharma Center
1525 Rte. 295
East Chatham, NY 12060

The Karuna Tendai Dharma Center is a single outpost of the Japanese Tendai tradition, a significant element of Japanese Buddhism that has but few followers in North America. The temple was founded in 1994 by Monshin (Paul) Naamon and his wife Tamani Naamon, who had gone to Japan for study in 1988. Monshin returned as the Dharma son of Ichishima Shoshin, who occasionally travels from Japan to teach.

The temple is located on a former Shaker farmstead, the barn having been converted into a zendo. It was the desire of the Naamons to create a village-style temple in a rural area suggestive of the mountainous areas of Asia, and the intention to integrate the life of the temple into that of the larger community. There is no convent or monastery.

Tendai is a Vajrayana Buddhist school and one of the oldest introduced into Japan. As such it became a root school for many of the modern Japanese Buddhist groups. Tendai believers, however, treat the three vehicles (Mahayana, Hinayana, and Vajrayana) as one. Activities at the temple center on the Wednesday evening meditation service which includes a Dharma talk and potluck dinner. Order of Interbeing meditations (based on the teachings of Thich Nhat Hanh) are held twice monthly. Also, a wide range of classes, lectures, festivals, and retreats are sponsored. A vegetarian diet is preferred. The temple also operates the Bodhi Tree Inn, a bed & breakfast facility open to the public.

Membership: As of 1998, there were approximately 30 members affiliated with the temple.

Sources:

Morreale, Don. *The Complete Guide to Buddhist America.* Boston: Shambhala, 1998.

★2147★
Kongosatta-In Tendai Buddhist Temple
PO Box 212
Cape Girardeau, MO 63702-0212

Alternate Address: International Headquarters: Hieizan-Enryakuji, Sakamoto Honmachi, Otsu-Shi, Shiga-Ken, Japan.

The Tendai Sect of Japanese Buddhism originated in a monastery in China in the T'ien T'ai mountains. It was developed by Chih K'ai (538-597). Chih K'ai believed the Lotus Sutra to contain the essential embodiment of Buddhism. Buddhism had progressed through several periods leading up to the Lotus Sutra. The teachings flourished over the next few centuries and the T'ien T'ai movement became quite prominent in China. However, in the middle of the ninth century it came under heavy persecution and rapidly declined.

At the beginning of the ninth century, Dengyo Dhashi introduced T'ien T'ai Buddhism into Japan where it became known as the Tendai school. A center was established near Kyoto, Japan, on Mt. Hiei. Dengyo Dhashi taught that Buddha was the historical manifestation of a more primordial Buddha-nature, which may appear at any time. The appearance will assist in the universal attainment of Buddhahood. Gautama Buddha attained such Buddhahood in its fullness. Further, the goal of individual life is the attainment of Buddhahood; all other activity is ultimately in vain except for striving for such.

The Tendai is among the most recent of the Japanese schools to come to America. Its first center was opened in Missouri in the 1980s.

Membership: There are approximately 20 members of the single Tendai center. There are three million Tendai Buddhists worldwide, including a strong following in Brazil.

Sources:

A Dictionary of Buddhism. New York: Charles Scribner's Sons, 1972.

★2148★
Nichiren Mission
3058 Pali Hwy.
Honolulu, HI 96817

Alternate Address: International headquarters: Nichiren-shu, 1-31-15 Ikegami, Ota-ku, Tokyo, Japan; Mainland United States headquarters: Nicheren Order of North America, 3570 Mona Way, San Jose, CA 95130.

Nichiren (1222-1282) was a famous Buddhist reformer. In 1253 he began to preach a new doctrine—that salvation lay in the Lotus Sutra, the most famous Buddhist sanskrit text. The theme of the Lotus Sutra is the nature of Buddha's manifestations. Nichiren believed that the Lotus Sutra taught a combination of the methodologies of the other Buddhist groups—the ways of transformation, bliss and law. Rather than call upon the Amida Buddha, as in Shin Buddhist practice, one should call upon the Lotus Sutra. Daimoku, a repetitive chant of "Namu myoho renge kyo" (reverence to the wonderful law of the Lotus), became and remains the distinctive practice of the Nichiren Buddhists. Nichiren believed that the teachings known as the Lotus Sutra constituted pristine, true Buddhism and could unite the many Buddhist sects.

Nichiren divided history into the following three millennia: shobo, the period of the true law, which was the first millennium beginning at Buddha's death; zobo, or image law, the second millennium; and mappo, or end of the law, which is to last 10,000 years. During mappo, which began in 1052 C.E., the Lotus was the way of salvation. Since the Lotus was perfect, all Japanese should yield to it and allow it to spread. According to Chinese figuring, Buddha died in 949 B.C.E. (By Western figuring, he died in 486 B.C.E.) Nichiren followed the Chinese date. The first millenium was the period of Hinayana Buddhism; the second, of Provisional Mahayana Buddhism; the third, of the True Mahayana Buddhism treated in the Lotus Sutra.

The worship of the Nichiren Buddhist is centered upon the repetition of the Lotus chant. This act is performed in front of the gohonzon, a mandala upon which the chant is inscribed along with the names of Buddhas, bodhisattvas, and other Buddhist deities and personalities.

Nichiren was an ardent advocate of his new cause; so dogmatic were his polemics that he angered other Buddhists. He died seeking the union of his ideas with Japan's national policy. The

Nichiren Buddhists never reached their goal, but they have become one of the five largest Japanese Buddhist denominations.

Members of the Nichiren-shu (Nichiren religion) built a temple on the island of Hawaii at Pahala in 1902. This temple served the Japanese immigrants who had come to work on the plantations. In 1912 one more was added on Oahu, now the headquarters of the Nichiren Mission of Hawaii under the leadership of Bishop Senchu Murano.

An independent Nichiren congregation was established on Oahu in 1931 by a priest of the Kempon Hokke Sect (one of the Japanese Nichiren groups) under the name "Honolulu Myohoji." This temple joined the Nichiren Mission in 1979. It enshrines part of the relics of the Buddha. The Pahala Nichiren Temple ceased to exist in 1959 because of the evacuation of the Japanese people from the district, and it has recently been transferred to a Tibetan Buddhist group. Other temples have been added on the various islands. The Hawaiian temples are under the leadership of Bishop Senchu Murano.

Nichiren Buddhism came to California with the early Japanese immigrants. In 1914 the first temple was organized. It subsequently spread to Japanese communities across the United States. After World War II a national headquarters was established in Chicago, Illinois, which has more recently moved to San Jose, California. It is under the leadership of Bishop Ryusho Matsuda.

Membership: In 1988 there were 600 members and seven temples in Hawaii. The mainland membership was not reported. Affiliated temples were located in Japan, Korea, and Brazil with a reported worldwide membership of 8,000,000.

Educational Facilities: Rissho University, Tokyo, Japan. Minobusan Junior College, Minobu, Yamanashi-ken, Japan.

Periodicals: *The Newsletter.*

Sources:

Anesaki, Masaharu. *Nichiren, the Buddhist Prophet.* Cambridge: Harvard University Press, 1949.

Hasu No Oshie (The Teachings of the Lotus). Honolulu: Nichiren YBA of Honolulu, 1962.

A History of Nichiren Buddhism in Hawaii. Honolulu: Nichiren Mission of Hawaii, 1982.

Murano, Senchu. *An Outline of the Lotus Sutra.* Minobu-San, Japan: Kuonji Temple, 1969.

Nichiren-Buddhist Service Companion. Chicago: Headquarters of the Nichiren Buddhist Temple of North America, 1968.

★2149★
Nichiren Shoshu America
% Myohoji Temple
1401 N. Crescent Heights Blvd.
West Hollywood, CA 90046

In Japan the followers of Nichiren (1222-1282), the Buddhist reformer, divided into several factions. In 1290 one of the six main disciples of Nichiren, Nichiko (1246-1332), separated from the other five in a dispute which in part concerned the question of who had the responsibility for the upkeep of Nichiren's tomb. But the dispute also had a doctrinal element. Nichiko disagreed over the nature of the *Lotus Sutra*, the document upon which Nichiren had based his reforms and to which his followers looked as containing the teachings of true Buddhism. The *Lotus Sutra* contains twenty-eight chapters, divided into two sections of fourteen chapters each. Nichiko held that the first section, the Honmon, in which Buddha is revealed in his eternal aspect, was superior to the latter. The other five disciples saw the entire Lotus Sutra to be of equal value. Nichiko founded the Daisekiji temple at the foot of Mt. Fiji. His followers became the Nichiren Shoshu. Nichiren Shoshu was relatively small until after World War II. Then it began to grow rapidly because of the development of an affiliated lay or-

ganization whose efforts have made Nichiren Shoshu one of the largest Buddhist organizations in the world.

Nichiren Shoshu beliefs follow those of the Nichiren-Shu in most respects. Nichiren is regarded as the Buddha for this age. The *Lotus Sutra* is revered, and the reverence is reflected in the mantra whose repetition has become the central practice of believers, "namu myoho rengekyo" (adoration to the exquisite law of the *Lotus Sutra*). Also revered is the Dai-Gohonzon, the supreme object of worship (upon which the mantra is written in Japanese) housed at the head temple in Japan. Members of the Nichiren Shoshu generally have a model of the Dai-Gohonzon in their homes. Nichiren Shoshu teaches that those who embrace the same practice of chanting "namu myoho rengekyo" and reciting parts of the *Lotus Sutra*, as Nichiren did, can attain enlightenment just as he did. When enough people attain this enlightened state, a state of world peace and harmony can be achieved.

Nichiren Shoshu came to the United States through the immigration of its members to Hawaii and the West Coast after World War II. However, the origanization of work was largely the result of the arrival of leaders from Soka Kyoiku Gakkai (Creative Education Society), a Nichiren Shoshu lay movement founded in Japan in 1930. Repressed prior to World War II, it experienced growth in the decades after the war. In 1957, Soka Gakkai leader Masayasu Sadanaga moved to the United States and during the following year began holding meetings in Washington, D.C. The American chapter of Soka Gakkai was organized in 1960 following the visit of Soka Gakkai International's president Daisaku Ikeda.

In 1965, the group built the first Nichiren Shoshu temple that was constructed at Etiwanda, California. Over the next decade additional temples were opened in Chicago, San Francisco, Honolulu, and suburban New York City and Washington, D.C., each location being in an urban center with a large Japanese ethnic community. Each temple was headed by one or more priests sent from Japan. Through the 1980's the temples and the lay organization worked closely together, though Soka Gakkai had numerous centers across North America, most of which were not geographically close to one of the six temples and most members were not trained in temple worship.

During the late 1980's tension between the Soka Gakkai and the Nichiren Shoshu in Japan began to emerge and in 1990 became a public controversy. Then in 1991, Nichiren Shoshu excommunicated President Ikeda and cast the Soka Gakkai from the Nichiren Shoshu organization. As a result, the six temples in the United States and the Soka Gakkai went their separate ways. A polemic and legal war has continued between the two groups, and in 1997, the Nichiren Shoshu ordered all of its members to disassociate themselves from Soka Gakkai by November 30, 1997, or face losing their membership status.

Membership: Not reported. There are six temples in the United States.

Periodicals: *Soka Gakkai News.* Send orders to 32 Shinanomachi, Shinjuku-ku, Tokyo 160, Japan. • *World Tribune.* Send orders to 525 Wilshire Blvd., Santa Monica, CA 90406. • *Seikyo Times.* Send orders to 525 Wilshire Blvd., Box 1427, Santa Monica, CA 90406.

Remarks: Since World War II, as Soka Gakkai has grown in Japan, it has been strongly opposed by other Buddhist groups. First, Nichiren Shoshu articulated the doctrine of obutsu myogo, i.e., a government essentially aligned with Buddhism. It called for the unification of imperial authority and Buddhism as well as the designation of Buddhism as the state religion. To this end it entered the field of politics. By 1955, it had manifested a remarkable ability to have its candidates elected. In 1964, a political party, the Komei Kai, was organized and it soon became the third largest party in the Japanese Upper House. In 1965, the party elected 20 members. Secondly, in its evangelical efforts, it taught the practice of shaku-buku, literally "bend and flatten," the name given to the high pressure recruitment tactics used on potential converts. Such tactics were reported by the organization's opponents to include bullying and badgering, applying pressure to the vulnerable, and occasionally, physical assault. (Such practices have not been evident or reported in relation to the movement in the United States.) However, disturbed by Nichiren Shoshu's success, ninety-six Japanese religious bodies united in 1965 to fight it as a political entity. During the 1970s, its political influence waned considerably, though it remains a powerful force.

In 1979 Soka Gakkai International was briefly affected by a scandal which erupted when some members accused Ikeda of personal misconduct. When tried, those who had brought the accusations were found guilty of libel. Meanwhile, the organization lost the support of some members and a few Nichiren Shoshu priests resigned. The organization, however, quickly recovered.

Sources:

Ikeda, Daisaku. *Guidance Memo.* Tokyo: Seikyo Press, 1966.

Kirimura, Tasiji. *Fundamentals of Buddhism.* Tokyo: Nichiren Shoshu Center, 1977.

The Liturgy of Nichiren Shoshu. Etiwanda, CA: Nichiren Shoshu Temple, 1979.

Soka Gakkai. Tokyo: Soka Gakkai, 1983.

Williams, George M. *Freedom and Influence.* Santa Monica, CA: World Tribune Press, 1985.

★2150★
Palolo Kwannon Temple (Tendai Sect)
3326 Paalea St.
Honolulu, HI 96816

The Palolo Kwannon Temple in Honolulu is a small center of worship for Kwannon, the Japanese equivalent of Kwan Yin, the goddess of mercy. The temple was founded in 1935 as an outpost of a large Kwannon temple in southern Japan. Kwannon is thought of in much the same way that Amida is thought of in Shin Buddhism, that is, as a bodhisattva, one who appears spiritually to people to enlighten them. A statue of Juzo Busatsu, another popular bodhisattva and patron of fishermen, had been placed on the southern shore of Oahu. It was cast into the sea and broken during World War II. After the war, the statue was found and repaired, and it now rests in the dooryard of the temple.

Membership: Not reported.

★2151★
Reiyukai America
2741 Sunset Blvd.
Los Angeles, CA 90026

Alternate Address: International Headquarters: 1-7-8 Azabudai, Minato-ku, Tokyo, Japan; Reiyukai Canada Office, 8833 Selkirk Ave. Vancouver, BC V6P 4I6.

Reiyukai derives from the attempts of Kakutaro Kubo (1892-1944), a young Buddhist layman, to find an alternative to what he perceived as the dead, formal Buddhism of the 1920s in Japan. Born near the birthplace of Buddhist prophet-reformer Nichiren (1222-1282), Kubo developed an early interest in the *Lotus Sutra.* Nichiren had taught his followers to emphasize the teachings of the *Lotus Sutra,* one of a number of Buddhist texts. Moving to Tokyo at a still-youthful age, he was adopted by a childless family who encouraged his spiritual explorations. Kubo's study of the sutra led him to reject the Buddhism he saw practiced in the local temples and to emphasize the need to incorporate the practices and principles of the *Lotus Sutra* into daily life.

Following an admonition in the *Lotus Sutra,* he began to urge others to accept, read, recite, expound, and copy the *Lotus Sutra.* Following the teachings of an earlier Nichiren reformer, Mugaku Nishida (1850-1918), he advocated the lay practice of Buddhism

over control of Buddhist life to the priesthood, and followers were taught to practice in their home rather than at the temples.

In 1928, Kubo composed the *Blue Sutra,* bringing together materials mainly from the *Threefold Lotus Sutra.* Members were encouraged to recite the *Blue Sutra* daily in the morning and in the evening (approximately 30 minutes).

The first Reiyukai group, following Kubo's teachings, was formed in 1924 in Tokyo. A second Tokyo group formed in the mid-1920s, and yet another group formed in Fukushima City. The early years were plagued with schisms. The Fukushima group withdrew in 1930, and the leader of the original Tokyo group disagreed with Kubo's emphasis upon intense propagation of the *Lotus Sutra.*

In 1930, the remaining Reiyukai group formally installed officers and chose Baron Taketoshi Nagayama, a Japanese nobleman, as its president. Nagayama's presence in such a prominent position helped Reiyukai gain the social credibility and probably kept Reiyukai from some of the government persecution experienced by similar groups during World War II. Kubo was named chairman of the board, and Kimi Kotani (1901-1971), the sister-in-law of an original member and later Kubo's successor as the head of Reiyukai, was named honorary president. The work grew tremendously during the war, and by 1950 there were more than one million members. Kotani inaugurated the Youth Group Society in 1954. In 1964, she established Mirokusan, a center in Shizuoka Prefecture, dedicated to the practice of the teachings of Buddha and the realization of world peace.

Kotani was eventually succeeded by Dr. Tsugunari Kubo (b. 1936), Kubo's son and present head of the organization. Under his leadership, the organization began to expand abroad to Europe and America. He also inaugurated a political research center to provide information about political affairs to Reiyukai members. While Reiyukai has not entered directly into partisan politics, unlike the Soka Gakkai, another Nichiren-inspired lay-Buddhist group, it does encourage members to participate and to promote democratic ideals.

Reiyukai came to America in the 1970s and established headquarters in Los Angeles, California. While work was initially concentrated among Japanese-Americans, the practice has begun to attract the English-speaking public. To promote communication and understanding among young people, an international Youth Speech Festival, with national phases in each country, has been conducted each year. National contestants have been brought to Los Angeles, with the national winners traveling abroad to participate in special international festivals. In addition to Japan and the United States, Reiyukai can be found in Brazil, Canada, France, Great Britain, India, Italy, Korea, Mexico, Nepal, Paraguay, Peru, Philippines, Spain, Taiwan, and Thailand.

Beliefs. Reiyukai's teaching brings direct exposure to Buddhist practice and philosophy, through which one gains a personal understanding of how it can be applied to improve oneself and one's relationship with others. Reiyukai's fundamental concept is that people can open their own path to self development through the understanding and application of the basic Buddhist idea of the interconnection and interdependence of all things. Reiyukai's practice, which includes daily recitation of the *Blue Sutra* (English Meditation Text), can create awareness and appreciation of the vertical line of "past-time" interconnection extending from one's ancestors through one's parents to oneself. It can also create awareness and appreciation of the horizontal line of "current-time" interconnection extending throughout all of one's daily-life relationships. The culmination of practice is the sincere motivation to demonstrate to others, through one's own personal attitude, action, and example, effective ways of living together in harmony.

Membership: Not reported.

Periodicals: *Inner Quest.*

Sources:

The Development of Japanese Lay Buddhism. Tokyo: Reiyukai, 1986.

Offner, Clark B., and Henry Van Straelen. *Modern Japanese Religions.* New York: Twayne Publishers, 1963.

Thomsen, Harry. *The New Religions of Japan.* Rutland, VT: Charles E. Tuttle Company, 1963.

★2152★
Rissho Kosei Kai
% Rev. Kazuhiko K. Nagamoto
118 N. Mott
Los Angeles, CA 90033

Rissho Kosei Kai (the Society for the Establishment of Righteous and Friendly Intercourse) is one of the new Nichiren bodies that arose as World War II was beginning. The movement was founded by Nikkyo Niwano, a farmer's son, and Naganuma Myoko. Niwano (b. 1906), a self-taught man, was a member of Reiyukai, a Nichiren sect formed in 1922. Naganuma (1899-1957) was the wife of an iceman in Tokyo, and for many years suffered from a serious disease. On Niwano's advice, she joined Reiyukai and was healed. Together they left the organization and, in 1938, began Rissho Kosei Kai. The motivation seemed to be Niwano's desire for independence as well as a greater leadership role.

Rissho Kosei Kai follows Nichiren's interpretation of Buddhism. Attention is focused on the three Hokke Sutras (the Muryogi Sutra, the Lotus Sutra, and the Kanfugen Sutra). The Daimoku, the repetition of the mantra "Namu myoho renge kyo," is used. Unlike Nichiren Shoshu, Rissho Kosei Kai does not use the Daimoku for its power. It is an expression of gratitude and faith. Man is bound by the laws of reincarnation and cause and effect. The consequences of these laws can only be broken by repentance and perfect living. The goal of Rissho Kosei Kai is the attainment of perfect Buddhahood through faith and repentance.

Dharma worship takes place in instruction halls. It includes chanting of the Lotus Sutra and the Daimoku and a sermon. After the service, *hoza*, or group counseling, begins. The congregation divides into small groups for discussions of personal problems and of the deeper aspects of faith. Divinatory practices are often incorporated. There are three annual festivals: the Foundation Festival on March 5; the Flower Festival on Buddha's birthday, April 8; and the Grand Festival on October 13.

While Rissho Kosei Kai has grown strong in Japan, it has penetrated the United States slowly. It began in 1959 when Tomoko Ozaki opened her home in Kealakekua, Kona, Hawaii, for a gathering of members who had migrated from Japan. The occasion was the visit of Rev. Kazue Yukawe. During the 1960s the movement spread to Honolulu and then to California and Chicago. The group consists mainly of Japanese-Americans. Members are also located in Korea, Hong Kong, Thailand, and Brazil.

Membership: In 1984, the Rissho Kosei-Kai reported 10 centers, serving 1,200 families in the United States. There were four priests. It reported over 5,000,000 members worldwide.

Periodicals: *Dharma World.* Available from Kosei Publishing Co., 2-7-1 Wada, Suginami, Tokyo 166, Japan.

Sources:

Niwano, Nichiko. *My Father, My Teacher.* Tokyo: Kosei Publishing Co., 1982.

Niwano, Nikkyo. *Lifetime Beginner.* Tokyo: Kosei Publishing Co., 1978.

Rissho Kosei-Kai. Tokyo: Kosei Publishing Co., 1966.

★2153★
Shingon Mission
915 Sheridan St.
Honolulu, HI 96810

Shingon Buddhism is a Japanese esoteric right-hand tantric sect. It places great emphasis on ritual, imagery, and ceremony, as well as occultism. The central practice is the use of mantras as magical formulas. "Mantra" means "true word," and its use emphasizes the need for the correct formula to accomplish the end. The incorporation of popular magical practices is one secret of Shingon's success. The man who integrated the elements that became Shingon was a monk named Ku Kai or, as he is most popularly known, Kobo Daishi. A student of Chinese religion, he was initiated by the Chinese into esoteric studies. He returned to Japan and began Shingon in 808 C.E. In 816, he received a grant of land upon which to construct a monastery. The site was Koyasan, a mountain near Osaka, upon which a collection of temples and monasteries were built. It remains the international Shingon headquarters.

Shingon's right-hand tantrism specializes in the worship of masculine gods. The pantheon shows numerous Hindu deities. A central solar divinity is Vairochana, from whom emanates the world. Vairochana is represented by graphic forms—the mandala, a cosmological form which artistically represents the essence of the universe. Art is an important facet of Shingon; Ku Kai believed that only art could convey the inner meaning of the Buddha's teaching. Also to be seen on the mandalas are the Buddhas and bodhisattvas who personify the Godhead. They include Amida, Shakyamuni (Gautama Buddha), and Kannon (Kwan Yin). Practices of the Shingon include meditation (often with the mantra), mudras (symbolic gestures), postures, and handling of ritual instruments.

Shingon was brought to the United States in 1902 by Hogen Yujiri, an immigrant laborer who opened a preaching hall in Hawaii on the island of Maui. He claimed to have been cured of an eye ailment by the "limitless compassion of Kobo Daishi." In 1903, Kodo Yamamoto gathered a Shingon following and built on Kauai the "Eighty-eight Holy Places of Hawaii's Garden Isle," modeled on a Japanese shrine. Before the decade was out, temples had been founded in Honolulu and on the Big Island (Hawaii). The movement spread quickly through the plantations.

In 1914, Eikaku Seki came to Honolulu as an official representative from Koyasan. He considered deplorable the chaotic condition of the popularized manifestation of his faith. He set up headquarters and built a detached temple of the Kongobuji, the main temple on Koyasan. Shingon continued to grow and gradually came under Seki's control.

Shingon reached its peak in the years prior to World War II. Since then, it has declined. It had only thirteen temples in 1972, half of the number reported in 1926. Headquarters are in Honolulu where Bishop Tetsuei Katoda oversees twelve ministers.

Membership: Not reported. Beside the dozen temples in Hawaii, there is also a Shingon temple in Los Angeles, California.

Sources:

Light of Buddha. Los Angeles: Koyasan Buddhist Temple, 1968.

★2154★
Shinnyo-En
2220 Summit Dr.
Burlingame, CA 94010

Headquartered in Japan, Shinnyo-en is a lay Buddhist order founded in 1936 by Shinjo Ito (1906–1989) along with his spouse, Tomoji Ito (1912–1967). Ito mastered the esoteric Shingon tradition at Daigoji Temple in Japan, where he became a successor of the Buddhist Dharma stream. There, he was bestowed with the rank of great acharya ("great teacher"). Ito became a priest and studied traditional Buddhism believing his mission lay in making salvation available to a wide scope of human beings. Toward that end, he adopted the *Mahaparinirvana Sutra* (the final discourse of the Buddha Shakyamuni) as the main canonical scripture of Shinnyo-en.

Sesshin training, which plays a significant role in helping followers to apply the truth expounded in the *Mahaparinirvana Sutra*, is performed with the aid of the Shinnyo-en spiritual faculty. Spiritual mediums, who have mastered the faculty to correct training based on the Orders teachings, guide trainees in becoming aware of their innate Buddha-nature and how to apply the teachings of the Buddha and the *Mahaparinirvana Sutra*. Trainees are encouraged to put the spiritual insight they gain into daily practice within their family, workplace, school, and community.

Shinnyo-en urges its followers to become well-rounded members of society who show the way to others through their own example. Followers are taught to apply theoretical principles and recognize the inherent beauty and order of all things by becoming involved in their communities and engaging in harmonious and socially beneficial activities.

During the 1960s, Shinjo and Tomoji Ito made several trips to foster religious exchange and goodwill. In 1966 they traveled to Thailand to attend the eighth international conference of the World Fellowship of Buddhists; the following year they visited Europe and Israel to promote understanding between the worlds major religions. Included in this trip was an audience with Pope Paul VI at the Vatican. As a result of these travels, congregations have developed in various parts of Asia (Taiwan, Hong Kong, Singapore) and Europe (France, Italy, Belgium, the United Kingdom, Germany).

Ito first came to the United States in 1970 and the first Shinnyo-en temple was established in the state of Hawaii in 1973. Other congregations have since grown in San Francisco, Los Angeles, Seattle, White Plains, and Chicago. Shinnyo-en USA administers the temples in the continental United States and has its headquarters in Burlingame, California.

In 1991, two years after the death of Shinjo, Shinso Ito, his daughter, formally succeeded him as the new head of Shinnyo-en.

Membership: In 1995 Shinnyo-en reported 722,044 members worldwide, 6,209 in the United States, and 107 in Canada. Affiliated temples can also be found in France, Italy, Belgium, Germany, and the United Kingdom.

Educational Facilities: ITO Foundation.

The Universe Foundation.

Shinnyo-En Foundation.

Periodicals: *Kangi Sekai* (in Japanese). • *The Naigai Jiho* (in Japanese). • *The Nirvana* (in English).

Sources:

Ito Shinjo. *Tomoshibi Nen Nen: Buddha's Light Everlasting.* Tokyo: Shinnyo-En, 1976.

The Way to Nirvana. Tokyo: Shinnyo-En, 1977.

★2155★
Shinshu Kyokai Mission
Bentenshu Hawaii Kyokai
3871 Old Pali Rd.
Honolulu, HI 86817

The Shinshu Kyokai Mission is a Shinshu congregation in Honolulu which is independent of both the Honpa Hongwanji and the Higashi Hongwanji. As a congregational project, the group maintains a dormitory for students and working men.

Membership: In 1982 there were 800 members in one center.

★2156★
Soka Gakkai International (USA)
4603 Eastern Ave.
Mt. Rainier, MD 20712-2407

Alternate Address: International Headquarters: 15-3 Samoncho, Shinjuku-ku, Tokyo 160 Japan.

Soka Gakkai International dates to 1930 and the founding of Creative Education Society (Soka Kyoiku Gakkai) by Makiguchi Tsunesaburo, a layman associated with the Nichiren Shoshu Buddhism as an educational lay association of Nichiren Shoshhu be-

lievers in Japan. Makiguchi's beliefs and practices were at odds with Shintoism, the national religion of Japan from 1868 to 1945. When, during World War II, Makiguchi refused to worship the sun gooddess, the nominal head of the shinto pantheon, he was sent to prison, where he died. However, the Soka Gakkai, which numbered only 60 members, was reborn after World War II under the leadership of its new president, Josei Toda. His impact was clearly manifest in 1958 when more than 300,000 persons attended his funeral. Toda was succeeded by Daisaku Ikeda, the current international president. Soka Gakkai, which had spread internationally through the 1960s and 1970s,vwas superseded by Soka Gakkai International in 1975.

Soka Gakkai beliefs and practices follow those of the Nichiren Shoshu and the Nichiren-shu in most respects. Nichiren is regarded as the Buddha for this age. The Lotus Sutra is revered, and that reverence is reflected in the mantra whose repetition has become a central practice of believers, "namu myoho rengekyo" (adoration to the exquisite law of the lotus Sutra). Also revered is the Dai-Gohonzon, the supreme object of worship (upon which the mantra is written in Japanese) housed at the head temple in Japan. Member of the Nichiren Shoshu generally have a model of the Dai-Gohonzon in their homes. Nichiren Shoshu teaches that those who embrace the same practice of chanting "namu myoho rengekyo" and reciting parts of the Lotus Sutra, as Nichiren did, can attain enlightenment just as he did. When enough people attain this enlightenment state, a state of world peace and harmony can be achieved.

In the decades immediately after World War II, Nichiren Shoshu and Soka Gakkai worked closely together. In Japan, Nichiren-shu experienced a significant growth because of the vigorous proselytizing activity of Soka Gakkai, and in some foreign countries such as the United States and Canada, it was the overwhelming substance of the Nichiren Shoshu community. The great majority of followers in Nichiren's teachings were converted by Soka Gakkai and never had a relationship to the priests and temples around which the movement had traditionally centered. Nichiren Shoshu was organized in the United States after Masayasu Sadanaga moved to the United States and in 1958 began holding meetings in Washington, D.C. The American chapter of Soka Gakkai was formally organized following President Ikeda's visit in 1960.

Over the next several decades, Soka Gakkai grew significantly under the leadership of Sadanaga (who changed his name to George Williams), and under the name Nichiren Shoshu of America centers were opened across the United States. In 1965, the traditional temple structure began to appear with the first temple begun in Etiwanda, California. Eventually six temples would be opened.

While there had always been issues between the very successful Soka Gakkai and Nichiren Shoshu, tensions began to grow through the late 1980s and became a public controversy in 1990. Members of Soka Gakkai charged that the priesthood of Nichiren Shoshu had become corrupt and that High Priest Nikken had failed in his leadership. In November 1991 Nichiren Shoshu excommunicated Soka Gakkai. In the years since, a polemic and legal war has ensued. In 1997 Nichiren Shoshu told its members that they had to completely disassociate from Soka Gakkai or lose their status in the Nichiren Shoshu. Essentially, since 1991, the two organizations have gone their separate ways.

Soka Gakkai sponsors the work of the Pacific Basin Research Center, a joint research program conducted by Soka University (Japan) and Harvard University, to study public policy interactions in the Pacific Rim; the Boston Research Center, an international peace institute that fosters dialogue among scholars and activists on common values across cultures and religions aiming toward a global ethic for a peaceful twenty-first century; the Toda Institute for Global Peace and Policy Research, an independent, nonpartisan, nonprofit organization committed to the pursuit of peace through peaceful means and a complete abolition of war; and the

Institute of Oriental Philosophy to pursue research in the history, literature, and concepts of Buddhism and in the comparative study of Buddhism and other religions.

Membership: In 1998, Soka Gakkai reported 330,000 members and 60 centers in the United States. Internationally, Soka Gakkai was found in more than 128 countries.

Educational Facilities: Soka Gakkai University, Calabasas, California.

Periodicals: *World Tribune.* • *Living Buddhism.* • *Journal of Oriental Studies* (Institute of Oriental philosophy).

Sources:

Ikeda, Daisaku. *Guidance Memo.* Tokyo: Seikyo Press, 1966.

Voices of Protest: Priests Speak Out for the Reformation of Nichiren Shoshu. Tokyo: Soka Gakkai International, 1993. 204 pp.

Williams, George M. *Freedom and Influence.* Santa Monica, CA: World Tribune Press, 1985.

★2157★
Todaiji Hawaii Bekkaku Honzan
2426 Luakini St.
Honolulu, HI 96814

The Kegon sect was introduced into Japan from China in the eighth century and was one of the so-called Nara sects. Its basic text was the Avatamsakasutra. The sutra tells of the visit of Sudhana to some Buddhist worthies in order to realize the principle of dharmadhatu, the realization of the domain of Buddha's law. Basic is the idea of mutual interdependence and causation of all that exists. Symbolic of this interdependence is a figure known as Indra's Net, a huge net which bears a jewel at each point of intersection. Each jewel is seen to bear the image of all the others.

Nature is seen to exist in a set of polarities-universality/specialization, integration/differentiation, and similarity/diversity. Kegon is a traditional form of Buddhism. Ancestor worship is of prime importance and is coupled with the offering of food and drink in a gesture of belief in the non-dying of spiritual being. The mutual interaction of this life and the next is a strongly held belief.

There is only one Kegon center in the United States—the Todaiji Hawaii Bekkaku Honzan. The Todaiji was organized in Honolulu by Bishop Tatsusho Hirai, who claims to be the only female Buddhist bishop in the world. After an unsuccessful marriage to a second generation Japanese immigrant to Hawaii, she returned to Japan and entered the Todaiji Temple as a nun. After years of study, she returned to Hawaii as a missionary and, after the war, organized the Branch Temple (officially recognized in 1948). Construction of the present temple began in 1950 and was finished in 1958.

Bishop Hirai has faced opposition from the Buddhist clergy, who claim that she is incapable of expounding Kegon teaching. Nevertheless, she has persisted, aided by her adopted daughter, Kaeko Hirai, whom she trained and ordained.

Membership: In 1982 the center in Hawaii reported 30,000 adherents (i.e., the number who had received either a healing blessing and/or special amulet from the center).

Sources:

Hirai, Tatsusho. *Todaiji of Hawaii.* Honolulu: Todaiji Hawaii Bekkaku Honzan, n.d.

Zen Buddhism

★2158★
Association Zen Internationale (AZI)
℅ New Orleans Zen Temple
748 Camp St.
New Orleans, LA 70130

Alternate Address: International Headquarters: Association Zen Internationale, 175, rue de Tolbiac, 75013 Paris, France.

The Association Zen Internationale (AZI) was founded in 1970 by Taisen Deshimaru Roshi (1914–1982) in Paris, France, and brought to the United States in 1983 by Robert Livingston Roshi (b. 1933) who founded the American Zen Association, its American affiliate. Born in an old Samurai family, Taisen Deshimaru rejected both the Shinshu Buddhism of his mother and the Christianity which had captured his attention as a youth. He eventually found his way to Zen and to the Soto Master Kodo Sawaki.

Kodo Sawaki was a wandering monk. As a teenager he joined the army and after almost dying as a result of a wound, returned to Japan as a war casualty with neither family nor friends. He eventually found his way to Eiheiji monastery, where he stayed for several years. After leaving the monastery, he wandered the land and met Soto Master Koho Roshi, from whom he eventually received Dharma transmission. Over the years, a few disciples attached to him, including Taisen Deshimaru. They remained together until Deshimaru began his period of service in the Japanese Army during World War II. When the war was finally over, Deshimaru rejoined his Master and remained by his side until the latter's death. He received the monastic ordination shortly before the Master fell ill, and he received the Transmission (the Shiho) in 1965 while Kodo Sawaki was on his deathbed. The Master also commissioned Deshimaru to go to the West "so that Buddhism may again flourish."

Two years later Deshimaru entrusted the care of his family to his son, settled his business affairs, and took the Trans-Siberian to France, with no money nor knowledge of a single word of French. He was 53. He began sitting in the storage area of a diet food store. As the work grew he opened a dojo, founded other dojos throughout France, and eventually built the Gendronnire Temple, the biggest dojo in the West. In recognition of his accomplishment, he was recognized by the Soto authorities in Japan and named Kaikyosokan, responsible for Zen for all of Europe.

Deshimaru fell ill at the beginning of 1982, but continued teaching zazen each day. In the spring he left France for Japan, where he died on April 30th.

Deshimaru's lineage was brought to America by Robert Livingston Roshi, who had practiced with him in Europe for 10 years. Livingston had grown up in New York, California, and Texas, and graduated from Cornell University. He spent two years in Japan and Korea in the U.S. Army in the early 1950s, and became a businessman in Europe. He retired in the early 1970s and began practicing Zen with Master Deshimaru in Paris. Deshimaru authorized Livingston to teach and asked him to come to the United States to spread the teachings of true Zen. So in 1983 Livingston Roshi moved, opening the New Orleans Zen Temple.

The New Orleans Zen Temple continues the Soto Zen beliefs and practices earlier established in France. Members of the New Orleans community practice zazen and *samu* (work practice) together, and Livingston Roshi conducts *sesshin* (retreats) every month. From the initial efforts in New Orleans, centers have been opened in other cities.

AZI was brought to Canada by Philippe Duchesne, who opened work in Sutton, Quebec. Subsequently, centers have been opened at several locations in Quebec and one has opened in New Brunswick.

Membership: Not reported. Affiliated centers are now operating in New Orleans; Starkville and Jackson, Mississippi; Oklahoma City, Oklahoma; and Tiburon, California. AZI centers are found around the world in 36 countries.

Periodicals: *Zen magazine.*

Sources:

Morreale, Don. *The Complete Guide to Buddhist America.* Boston: Shambhala, 1998.

★2159★
Atlanta Soto Zen Center (ASZC)
1414 McLendon Ave. NE
Atlanta, GA 30307

The Atlanta Soto Zen Center (ASZC) was founded in the early 1970s with the leadership of Michael Zenkai Taiun Elliston-Roshi, who was a disciple of Rev. Dr. Soyu Matsuoka-Roshi (d. 1997) in Chicago during the 1960s. Elliston-Roshi remains the Zen Center's superintendent.

The ASZC provides a group, or Sangha, to sit with, a place to sit together with a full zazen schedule, as well as a lending library and experienced teachers to respond to any questions that arise. The Zen Center operates a prison outreach program and offers meditation instruction to prisoners throughout the state of Georgia.

Membership: Not reported. ASZC also has affiliate centers in Charleston, South Carolina; and Huntsville, Alabama.

Sources:

Morreale, Don. *The Complete Guide to Buddhist America.* Boston: Shambhala, 1998.

★2160★
Berkeley Zen Center
1931 Russell St.
Berkeley, CA 94703

The Berkeley Zen Center is one of several organizations which originated in the Zen Center of San Francisco during the years of its leadership by Shunryu Suzuki Roshi (1901–1971). The Berkeley center was founded in 1967 and was at one in belief and practice with its parent body. However, following Suzuki Roshi's death, and the issues raised concerning the conduct of his successor, the Berkeley center became independent under Suzuki Roshi's student, Sojun Mel Weitsman. Emphasis is on lay practice.

Membership: There is one center.

Periodicals: *Newsletter.*

★2161★
California Bosatsukai
5632 Green Oak Dr.
Los Angeles, CA 90068

The California Bosatsukai shares the tradition of both Soen Nakagawa, Roshi and Nyogen Senzaki (1876-1958), two Japanese Zen Buddhist pioneers in America. A Rinzai Zen monk, Senzaki came to California in 1905 and in 1928 established his own zendo in San Francisco. He started another in 1929 in Los Angeles. He was the Zen master of these two independent zendos until he died in 1958. The California Bosatsukai continues the tradition of Senzaki in Los Angeles.

In the early 1960s, Hakuun Yasutani, Roshi, who was a student of Soen Nakagawa Roshi and had been trained on both the Rinzai and Soto Zen traditions, came to the U.S. Hakuun Yasutani accepted the role of Zen master for the California Bosatsukai along with his duties at other centers. He continued working with the California Bosatsukai until his death in 1973. Besides the Los Angeles center, there are branches in Hollywood, Del Mar, Los Gatos, and San Diego, California.

Membership: Not reported. There are approximately 100 members.

Sources:

Nordstrom, Louis, ed. *Namu Dai Bosa.* New York: Theatre Arts Books, 1976.

Senzaki, Nyogen, and Ruth Stout McCandless, eds. *Buddhism and Zen.* New York: Philosophical Library, 1953.

Senzaki, Nyogen, and Salidin Reps, trans. *10 Bulls.* Los Angeles: DeVorss & Co, 1935.

★2162★
Cambridge Buddhist Association
75 Sparks St.
Cambridge, MA 02138

The Cambridge Buddhist Association, a nonsectarian center for lay Buddhist practice and studies, grew out of an interest in Zen Buddhism that developed in the 1950s at Harvard University. It first took shape during the 1957 visit to Cambridge, Massachusetts, of the noted Buddhist scholar Daisetz Teitaro Suzuki (1870-1966) and Dr. Shinichi Hisamatsu, professor emeritus of Kyoto University, the first scholar to give a series of lectures on Buddhism at the Harvard Divinity School. A group headed by Mr. and Mrs. John Mitchell persuaded the two scholars to remain in Cambridge for a while to establish a Western-style zendo (meditation center). Suzuki became the first president of the new association, a position he held until his death. For a period, Shunryu Suzuki Roshi, of the Zen Center of San Francisco, served as the spiritual advisor until the selection of a second president, the Rev. Chimyo Horioka, a Shingon Buddhist priest.

The current president and spiritual teacher of the association is Maurine Myo on Stuart, who received her permission to teach from the late Soen Nakagawa, Roshi of Kyoto, Japan. Stuart is also a musician, an instructor in Buddhism at Phillips Exeter Academy in New Hampshire, and a popular teacher at other Buddhist centers around the United States. Other directors and advisors of the association have included Dr. Masatoshi Nagatomi of Harvard University and the late Dr. Holmes Welch, author of a variety of books on Chinese Buddhism. Because the association was for many years the only Zen center in the Boston area, it served as a central locus for Buddhist-interfaith dialogue. Results of a particularly significant early Christian dialogue session were later published as *Conversations: Christian and Buddhist.*

The association's zendo is housed in an old house in a residential neighborhood of Cambridge. Though the association does not publish a periodical and/or handbooks, it does have an extensive library of books and periodicals on Buddhism and related topics that it makes available to members. Currently there is a daily (Thursdays excepted) meditation period open to the public, as well as monthly sesshin retreats, occasional lectures, and private interviews. There are no communal living facilities at the temple nor any shared Shanga dwellings nearby. A single resident, usually chosen from among the students, serves the temple for a short designated period. The emphasis of instruction at the temple is on zazen practice (sitting meditation). Local universities and other schools bring classes and groups to the center for instruction on Buddhism and zazen practice.

Membership: In 1988, the association reported approximately 150 members and include a group from the Vietnamese-American community.

Sources:

Cambridge Buddhist Association. Cambridge, MA: Cambridge Buddhist Association, 1960.

Fujimoto, Rindo. *The Way of Zazen.* Cambridge, MA: Cambridge Buddhist Association, 1969.

Graham, Aelred. *Conversations: Buddhist and Christian.* New York: Harcourt, Brace and World, 1968.

Renfrew, Sita Paulickpulle. *A Buddhist Guide for Laymen.* Cambridge, MA: Cambridge Buddhist Association, 1963.

Suzuki, Daisetz T. *The Chain of Compassion*. Cambridge, MA: Cambridge Buddhist Association, 1966.

★2163★
Dharma Rain Zen Center
2539 SE Madison
Portland, OR 97214

Dharma Rain Zen Center is a Soto Zen Temple established in 1973 for lay practice under the direction of Kyogen Carlson and Gyokuko Carlson, a married couple who are Zen priests formerly associated with the late Juyi Kennett Roshi (d. 1996) and the Order of Buddhist Contemplatives. Subsequently, additional satellite centers have been formed. The center in Eugene, Oregon, has created SAFE (Stop All Female Excision), a project aimed at educating African females. Meditation workshops are offered several times each month at no charge. One-day sittings and longer sesshins are held during the year.

Membership: Not reported. Four related groups are found in Portland, Eugene, Salem, and Pendleton, Oregon.

Periodicals: *Still Point Newsletter*.

Sources:

Morreale, Don. *The Complete Guide to Buddhist America*. Boston: Shambhala, 1998.

★2164★
Diamond Sangha
℅ Palolo Zen Center
2747 Waiomao Rd.
Honolulu, HI 96816

The Diamond Sangha is a Zen Buddhist society based in Hawaii and founded by Robert Aitken and his wife, Anne Aitken. It is part of the Sanbo Kyodan (Order of the Three Treasures), a lay stream of Soto Zen which includes aspects of Rinzai Zen (the two main schools of Japanese Zen). The Sanbo Kyodan, headquartered in Kamakura, Japan, is based on the teachings of Harada Dai'un, Roshi and was founded by Harada Roshi's successor, Hakuun Yasutani, Roshi (1885-1973) in the mid-1950s.

In 1962 Yasutani Roshi began periodic visits to Hawaii to guide the Diamond Sangha in Zen practice. The current abbot of the Sanbo Kyodan, Yamada Ko'un, Roshi, visited the Diamond Sangha annually during the 1970s and early 1980s.

Robert Aitken began his Zen practice in California with Nyogen Senzaki Sensei in 1947 and continued his training with Soen Nakagawa, Roshi and other teachers in Japan before establishing a bond with Sanbo Kyodan. In 1974 Yamada Roshi authorized him to teach and, in 1984, gave him full transmission with the name Chotan Gyo'un Ken, Roshi.

Robert Aiken Roshi retired in 1996 and was succeeded by Nelson Foster, who is also the teacher for the Ring of Bone community in Nevada City, California. Aitken now lives near his son on the island of Hawaii and continues to write and consult with other Buddhist leaders. He has published eight books on Buddhism. There are now 20 practice groups around the world officially affiliated with Diamond Sangha.

The Honolulu Diamond Sangha continues to meet the needs of lay practice at its two centers in Honolulu, a new zendo in the Palolo Valley of Honolulu and the Koko An residence near the University of Hawaii, which was the original zendo opened by Ann Hopkins Aitken and Robert Aitken in 1959. Several retreats (*sesshin*) are offered each year at the Palolo facility, and more extended residences are also available there. A journal, *Blind Donkey*, is published by the Diamond Sangha affiliate in Petaluma, California, and the Honolulu Diamond Sangha produces a monthly newsletter.

Membership: In 1995 the Sangha reported approximately 20 centers, including one in Argentina and two in Australia. Membership in each center is estimated at between 20 and 40 regular practioners.

Periodicals: *Blind Donkey*. • *California Diamond Sangha Newsletter*. Send orders to Box 2915, Petaluma, CA 94953.

Sources:

Aitken, Robert. *The Mind of Clover*. San Francisco, CA: North Point Press, 1984.

___. *A Zen Wave*. New York: Weatherhill, 1978.

Not Mixing Up Buddhism: Essays on Women and Buddhist Practice. Fredonia, NY: White Pine Press, 1986.

★2165★
First Zen Institute of America
113 E. 30th St.
New York, NY 10016

The First Zen Institute of America was founded in New York in 1930 by Sokei-an Sasaki, Roshi, who came to America in 1906 with a missionary group from Ryomo-Zen Institute of Tokyo. This effort to establish a center in San Francisco, California, was not successful, and all the members returned to Japan in 1910. Sokei-an settled in New York in 1916 and founded the institute there in 1930. It was incorporated the following year under the name The Buddhist Society of America, assuming its present name in 1944. Ever since its founding, regular meetings have been conducted. A periodical, *Cat's Yawn*, was published 1940-41, and later was published in book form. Sokei-an, interned for a period after the beginning of World War II, in 1944 married Ruth Fuller Everett (d. 1967), one of the most active members of the institute and former editor of *Cat's Yawn*. Sokei-an died the following year.

Sokei-an left no successor, but his students continued to meet and practice what he had taught them. Ruth Fuller moved to Daitoku-ji to continue her study. She became the first woman to become a Zen priest at that temple. She also organized the First Zen Institute of America in Japan to receive American students who wished to study abroad.

In 1954, the institute began a second periodical, *Zen Notes*, which included the writings of Sokei-an and other Zen Masters. In 1963, the institute moved into its present headquarters in Manhattan. A regular schedule of zazen meetings is held for members, and a weekly Wednesday evening session is open to newcomers. Still lay led, the institute periodically invites guest roshis to lead seshins and extended meditation retreats.

Governance of the institute is by its members through a council drawn from its senior members.

Membership: Not reported.

Periodicals: *Zen Notes*.

Sources:

Cat's Yawn. New York: First Zen Institute in America, 1947.

Sasaki, Ruth Fuller. *Zen, A Method for Religious Awakening*. Kyoto, Japan: First Zen Institute of America in Japan, 1959.

★2166★
Hazy Moon Zen Center
1651 S. Gramercy Pl.
Los Angeles, CA

Alternate Address: Centro Zen de Maezumi-Kuroda–Mexico City, Tlaxcaltitia 22, San Miguel Tecamachalco, Naucalpan, Edo De Mexico C.P. 53950.

The Hazy Moon Center is a Zen Buddhist congregation founded by william Nyogen Yeo, Sensei, a Dharma successor of Hakuyu Taizan Maezumi Roshi (1931–1995), the founder of the Zen Center of Los Angeles. The Sangha encompasses two practice centers, the Hazy Moon Zen Center (a.k.a. Koun-ji Soto Zen Temple) in Los Angeles and the Centro Zen de Maezumi-Kuroda in

Mexico City. Each center offers a variety of programs supporting seasoned practitioners as well as beginners.

The Sangha's spiritual heritage is grounded in the Soto Zen tradition, but also includes a thorough integration of koan practice (associated with Rinzai practice) introduced to the tradition by Maezumi, Roshi's teachers, Hakuun Yasutani, Roshi and Koryu Osaka Roshi.

Nyogen, Sensei, received Dharma transmission (authorization to teach) from Taizan Maezumi, Roshi, in 1995 after 26 years of intense practice and study. Following the Japanese Soto Zen way, in 1996 Sensei did his zuise ceremonies at the training monasteries of Eiheiji and Sojiji in Japan and thus completed the traditional Soto rites of recognition as a Zen Teacher (Sensei). Following Maezumi, Roshi's, death in 1995, Nyogen, Sensei, served for two years as the acting abbot of the Zen Center of Los Angeles before assuming his current role as the spiritual head of the Hazy Moon Sangha.

Membership: Not reported.

Sources:

Morreale, Don. *The Complete Guide to Buddhist America.* Boston: Shambhala, 1998.

★2167★
Kanzeon Zen Center
1274 E. South Temple
Salt Lake City, UT 84102

Kanzeon Zen Center is a training center for Zen meditation under the guidance of Genpo Merzel Roshi. Dennis Genpo Merzel Roshi (b. 1944) was born in Brooklyn, New York, and grew up in Long Beach, California. He attended California State University at Long Beach (B.A., 1966) and the University of Southern California (M.A., 1968). He taught school in Los Angeles and Long Beach from 1966 to 1971.

Genpo Roshi started formal Zen training under Taizan Maezumi Roshi at the Zen Center of Los Angeles in 1972. He was ordained by Maezumi Roshi in 1973 and given the title *Hoshi* (Dharma-Holder) after completing koan study in 1979. In 1980, Genpo Roshi received *Shiho* (Dharma transmission) from Maezumi Roshi, followed by *Zuisse* (another step toward full recognition as a teacher) in Japan in 1981. In the following year he began to conduct sesshins in several European countries, and in 1984, he left Los Angeles to devote himself completely to the international community of students he named the Kanzeon Sangha.

In 1988, Genpo Roshi completed *shinsanshiki* (installation as abbot) at Hosshinji Temple in Bar Harbor, Maine. In 1991 he moved to Oregon and in 1993, at the invitation of the Wasatch Zen Group, he relocated Hosshinji (Kanzeon Zen Center) to Salt Lake City, Utah. Genpo Roshi received the certificate of Dendokyoshi Kenshuso in 1995 at Green Gulch Farm in California. In October of 1996, he received *Inka* (formal recognition and authority to teach) from his elder Dharma brother, Tetsugen Glassman Roshi, in New York City. Tetsugen Roshi had received Inka from Maezumi Roshi shortly before the latter's death in May 1995.

To date, Genpo Roshi has given Dharma transmission to Catherine Genno Pages, the late John Shodo Flatt, and Anton Tenkei Coppens. Genno Sensei has recently set up a new Zen center in Paris, France, where she is the resident teacher.

The Kanzeon Center (named for the Buddhist goddess of compassion, also known as Kwan Yin) provides an extensive training program that emphasizes the traditional combination of sitting meditation (*zazen*) and frequent individual interviews with the teachers (*dokusan* and *daisan*). Besides a daily schedule, full-time training sessions (*sesshins*), lasting from three to nine days, are held regularly throughout the year. A three-month intensive (*ango*) takes place in winter, and includes a month-long sesshin.

At the center, various meditation methods are applied in order to respond to the needs of the individual student. These methods include breathing techniques, *shikantaza* (just sitting), and working with *koans* (questions to be resolved during sitting), but all aim at cutting through the delusion that obscures one's innate wisdom.

The center sponsors Kanzeon Jade Thread, which offers high-quality meditation cushions and custom-made meditation clothes for sale and provides service work for full-time Zen students.

Membership: As of 1998, this Sangha had over 1,000 members in the United States and Europe. American centers were located in Wahiawa, Hawaii; Champaign, Illinois; and Northampton, Massachusetts. European centers were found in France, England, Germany, Holland, and Poland.

Sources:

Merzel Roshi, Dennis Genpo. *Beyond Sanity and Madness—The Way of Zen Master Dogen.* Rutland, VT: Charles E. Tuttle Co., 1994.

___. *The Eye Never Sleeps—Striking to the Heart of Zen.* Boston: Shambhala, 1991.

★2168★
Kanzeonji Non-Sectarian Buddhist Temple
944 Terrrace 49
Los Angeles, CA 90042

The Kanzeonji Non-Sectarian Buddhist Temple was founded in the 1980s by the Rev. Ryugen Watanabe, also known as Swami Premananda. Born in Japan, Rev. Watanabe was inspired by Kanzeon Bosatsu (also known as Bodhisattva Kannon or Kwan Yin), the Buddha of compassion, to bring Buddhism to America. He is the 62nd Patriarch (counting from Bodhidharma) in his line of transmission in the Soto Zen tradition. He is the abbot of Kanzeonji and founder of the Siva Ashram Yoga Center, where he holds the additional title of Swami.

The temple offers daily zazen meditation and chanting. Classes in hatha yoga are taught, and Rev. Watanabe offers his services as a practitioner of Zen energy healing (popularly called acupressure or shiatsu). Rev. Watanabe practiced shiatsu in Japan and began his work in America as an alternative to drug-oriented medicine.

Watanabe understands Zen as the form of meditation practiced by Gautama Buddha. It has as its object the forcing of the practitioner beyond the sphere of words to an immediate encounter with ultimate truth.

Membership: There is a single center in Los Angeles, which in 1997 served approximately 1,500 participants.

Periodicals: *The Spiritual....*

Sources:

Guideline to Kanzeonji. Los Angeles: Zen Center of Kanzeonji Non-Sectarian Buddhist Temple, n.d.

★2169★
Living Dharma Centers
PO Box 513
Bolton, CT 06043

The Living Dharma Centers were founded by Richard Clarke (b. 1933), a psychotherapist who met Philip Kapleau in 1967 and became his student at the Zen Center of Rochester. In 1981, he dropped his relationship to Kapleau after 14 years of intensive Zen training. He founded a center in Bolton, Connecticut. The stated goal of the centers is the awakening of the True Self to be manifest in all of life. The teachings and practice of the centers, following the Rochester format, combine elements from both the Soto and Rinzai traditions.

Membership: Not reported. There is an affiliated center in Amherst, Massachusetts.

Periodicals: *Sangha News.*

Sources:

Clark, Richard. *Hsin Hsin Ming: Verse on the Faith-Mind by Sengtsan.* Buffalo, NY: White Pine Press, 1973, 1984.

Rawlinson, Andrew. *The Book of Enlightened Masters: Western Teachers in Eastern Traditions*. La Salle, IL: Open Court Press, 1997. 650 pp.

★2170★
Middlebar Monastery
2503 Del Rio Dr.
Stockton, CA 95204

One of the earliest Zen centers led by an American, the Middlebar Monastery was established in 1956 as the Beikukosan Sanzenji Soto Mission by Daino Doki MacDonough. MacDonough was a student of Tobase Roshi, the leader of the Sokoji Temple, the Soto Mission in San Francisco in the years prior to the arrival of his more famous successor Shunryu Suzuki Roshi. Rosen Takashina, an official with the Soto Zen community in Japan, named MacDonough the chief priest and then in 1963 gave him the title roshi. In that year, the monastery became independent of the Soto Mission. Middlebar's agenda has focused upon the training of Americans in traditional Zen practice adapted to American culture, values, and language. The program is built around morning zazen sessions for nonmonastic community residents.

Membership: Not reported.

Sources:

Rawlinson, Andrew. *The Book of Enlightened Masters: Western Teachers in Eastern Traditions*. La Salle, IL: Open Court Press, 1997. 650 pp.

★2171★
Minnesota Zen Meditation Center
3343 Calhoun Pkwy.
Minneapolis, MN 55408

The Minnesota Zen Meditation Center began in the 1960s with a group of people in Minneapolis, Minnesota, who began to practice zazen, Zen meditation. They developed an association with the San Francisco Zen Center and its assistant priest, Dainin Katagiri Roshi (1928-1990), who visited them on several occasions. In 1972, the group extended an invitation to Katagiri Roshi to become the leader of a new Zen center they were establishing. He accepted, and the Minnesota Zen Center was formed in January 1973.

Katagiri Roshi was born in Japan in 1928 and became a Zen monk in 1946. He trained at Eiheji Monastery, the original center of the Soto Shu Sect. He came to the United States in 1963 to work with the Japanese-American Soto Buddhists and was assigned to their Los Angeles, California, temple. After five months, however, he was sent to San Francisco, California, to assist Shunryu Suzuki Roshi in both the San Francisco temple (Sokoji) and the independent Zen Center of San Francisco. While there, he assisted in the opening of the Tassajara Zen Mountain Center.

After coming to Minneapolis, Katagiri Roshi attracted students throughout the Midwest, and affiliated centers emerged. In 1978, the center purchased 280 acres in southeastern Minnesota; it began construction of a year-round facility for intensive Zen practice.

The center is governed by a board of directors that is elected at the annual meeting of members. There are four categories of membership: supporting, general, associate, and participating. All receive the same benefits and have voting privileges.

Membership: In 1995, the center reported 220 members and five centers in the United States and 6 members in Canada. There is one head teacher, Shohaku Okumura, whose term ends in August 1996.

Educational Facilities: Hokyo-ji (Catching the Moon Zen Mountain Center), New Albin, Minnesota.

Periodicals: *MZMC Newsletter*.

★2172★
Mountain Moon Sangha
No. 10, 939 Avenue Rd.
Toronto, ON, Canada M5P 2K7

Mountain Moon Sangha is the name given to the students of Sei-un An Roselyn Stone, a teacher within the Sanbo Kyodan Buddhist lineage. In 1992 Stone established zendos in both Toronto, Ontario, and Brisbane, Australia, and now spends her time between the two centers.

New students are invited to attend a set of introductory lectures which include basic instruction in meditation and are then invited to join the regular meditation program. Stone also provides one-on-one contact with her students.

Membership: Not reported.

Sources:

Morreale, Don. *The Complete Guide to Buddhist America*. Boston: Shambhala, 1998.

★2173★
The Mountains and Rivers Order (MRO)
% Zen Mountain Monastery
PO Box 197
South Plank Rd.
Mt. Tremper, NY 12457

The Mountains and Rivers Order (MRO) is an organization of associated Zen Buddhist temples, practice centers, and sitting groups in the United States and abroad. Inspired by Zen Master Dogen's 13th Century Mountains and Rivers Sutra, MRO was founded by Abbot John Daido Loori, a Dharma heir of Hakuyu Taizan Maezumi Roshi, best known as the founder of the Zen Center of Los Angeles and abbot of Zen Mountain Monastery in Mt. Tremper, New York. Loori has received transmission in both the Rinzai and Soto lines of Zen Buddhism from which he has developed a distinctive style, involving both monastic and lay practitioners in a program of study that embraces every aspect of daily life. Loori is also president of Dharma Communications, a right-action enterprise devoted to making Buddhist teachings widely available through the production of videotapes, books, and meditation supplies.

MRO's function is maintaining the practice integrity of its member organizations. The main house of the order is Zen Mountain Monastery, a residential retreat center in the Catskills of New York state. The order also operates Dharma Communications, a media company supplying resources for home practice. Through the Society of Mountains and Rivers, groups of students around the world are joined in the MRO training program.

Zen Mountain Monastery is an American Zen Buddhist monastery and training center for monastics and lay practitioners. Each month an introductory weekend of Zen training is offered, as well as a week-long silent intensive meditation retreat (*sesshin*). Throughout the year, the regular daily schedule is supplemented with retreats in the Zen arts, martial arts, Buddhist studies, and other areas thought to be relevant and supportive to practitioners. Students can train in either full-time or part-time residency or as nonresidents whose practice at home is fueled by periodic visits to the monastery and the support of sitting together with others in one of the affiliate centers/groups of the Society of Mountains and Rivers Order.

Practice in Zen Mountain Monastery is based in what is termed the "Eight Gates". Loori observed that most Western practitioners come to Zen with virtually no background in Buddhism. Thus he felt it necessary to employ a broader spectrum of skillful means than just the traditional meditation and teacher-student relationship. As a result, he developed the "Eight Gates" of training, and each of these areas of training are pursued over 10 stages of spiritual development.

The first gate, *zazen* (meditation) is followed immediately with the development of a strong teacher-student relationship in the face-to-face teachings as the second gate. The third gate, academic study, explores, in addition to the particularly Zen Buddhist sutras, other schools of Buddhism, Buddhist history, philosophy, and psychology. The remaining five gates include liturgy, the Precepts, art practice, body practice, and work.

Membership: Not reported. The Mountains and Rivers Order includes the Zen Center of New York City; Providence Place Zendo, Albany, New York; Zen Affiliate of Vermont (ZAV), Burlington; and the Zen Institute of New Zealand (with sitting places at Temuka, Christchurch, Nelson, Wellington, and Auckland). The Lotus Flower Affiliate is located at Green Haven Correctional Facility, New York.

Periodicals: *Mountain Record.*

Sources:

Loori, John Daido. *The Eight Gates of Zen.* Mt. Tremper, NY: Dharma Communications, 1992.

___. *The Heart of Being.* Rutland, VT: Charles E. Tuttle Co., 1996.

___. *Liturgy Manual.* Mt. Tremper, NY: Dharma Communications, 1998.

___. *Mountain Record of Zen Talks.* Boston: Shambhala, 1988.

___. *Still Point.* Mt. Tremper, NY: Dharma Communications, 1995.

___. *Two Arrows Meeting in Mid-Air: The Zen Koan.* Rutland, VT: Charles E. Tuttle, 1994.

★2174★
One Drop Zendo
135 N. 75th St.
Seattle, WA 98103

One Drop Zendo was founded in 1989 in Seattle, Washington, by Shodo Harada Roshi, the Abbot of Sogenji, a Rinzai Zen monastery in Okayama, Japan. Since 1982 Sogenji has been one of those Japanese centers most open to study by students from the West. In the years following the zendo's founding, Harada Roshi has made annual trips to Seattle to lecture and lead retreats. In 1996, the zendo purchased a tract of land on Whidbey Island where a monastery is being constructed. When completed, Harada Roshi will move permanently to the United States.

The Zen Community of Oregon in Corbett, Oregon, is informally affiliated with One Drop Zendo.

Membership: Not reported.

Sources:

Morreale, Don. *The Complete Guide to Buddhist America.* Boston: Shambhala, 1998.

★2175★
Order of Buddhist Contemplatives
% Shasta Abbey
3724 Summit Dr.
Mount Shasta, CA 96067-9102

The Order of Buddhist Contemplatives was founded by the Rev. P.T.N.H. Jiyu-Kennett Roshi (1924-1996), a British-born Buddhist who spent most of her early years studying Theravada Buddhism. She was a member of the council of, and lectured at, the London Buddhist Society. She began her study of Buddhism with Ven. Saddhatissa. In 1962, she was ordained in Malaysia in the Chinese Rinzai Zen tradition before traveling to Japan to study at Dai Hon Zan Soji-ji, one of the two main temples of the Soto Zen Church. She became the personal disciple of the Very Rev. Chisan Koho Zenji, the temple's abbot, from whom she received her dharma transmission. After several years at the temple, she became head of its Foreign Guest Department and was placed in charge of instructing Westerners who came to Japan to learn Zen. She eventually became abbess of Unpuku-ji Temple in Mie Prefecture.

In 1969, after completing her studies and following the death of Zenji, she moved to San Francisco, California, and established the Zen Mission Society. In 1970, the society moved to Mt. Shasta, California, where a monastery and seminary were created. The society has more recently taken its present name, the Order of Buddhist Contemplatives.

Kennett Roshi had a commission to train and ordain others, and the prime thrust of the order has been to train both women and men for the Soto Zen priesthood. A Western environment is evident in the religious practice of the order. A complete course of study in Soto Zen Buddhism is offered, which includes religious music and temple administration skills. The order is among those Zen groups which place the most emphasis upon their Buddhist heritage. Along with *zazen* and the teachings of Soto Zen, a study is also undertaken in the teachings of the Buddha according to Theravada and Mahayana Buddhism. Priest-trainees live full-time at the Shasta monastery. Celibacy is required for all priests.

The publication of Kennett Roshi's several books, her lecture tours, and the development of trained teachers at Mt. Shasta have contributed to the growth of several affiliated centers. By 1998, there were priories established at Reading and Telford, England; Albany and Santa Barbara, California; Portland and Eugene, Oregon; McKenna, and Seattle, Washington; Vancouver, British Columbia. The order has a European monastery, Throssel Hole Buddhist Abbey, in Northumberland, England, which also trains priests. There are also numerous study-meditation groups in the United States, Canada, England, the Netherlands, and Germany. Following the death of Rev. Jiyu-Kennett in 1996, Rev. Daizui MacPhillamy was elected to succeed her as head of the order and Rev. Eko Little was elected to succeed her as Abbot of Shasta Abbey.

Membership: In 1998 the order reported approximately 80 active priests and 120 lay ministers at two monasteries and seven priories in the United States, Canada, and Europe. The order has many meditation groups in these places following its teachings, as well as several thousand of individual congregation members.

Educational Facilities: Shasta Abbey, Mt. Shasta, California. Throssel Hole Buddhist Avvey, Northumberland, England.

Periodicals: *The Journal of the Order of Buddhist Contemplatives.*

Sources:

Friedman, Lenore. *Meetings with Remarkable Women.* Boston, MA: Shambhala, 1987.

Kennett, Jiya. *How to Grow a Lotus Blossom.* Mt. Shasta, CA: Shasta Abbey, 1977.

___. *The Wild, White Goose.* 2 vols. Mt. Shasta, CA: Shasta Abbey, 1970-78.

___. *Zen is Eternal Life.* Emeryville, CA: Dharma Publishing, 1976.

Nearman, Hubert, trans. *The Monastic Offics.* Mount Shasta Abbey, 1993.

Nearman, Hubert, Rev. Master P. T. N. H. Jiyu-Kennett, and Daizui MacPhillamy, eds. *Buddhist Writings on Meditation and Daily Pracctice: The Serene Reflection Meditation Tradition.* Mount Shasta, CA: Shasta Abbey, 1994. 382 pp.

"Shasta Abbey, 1970—1995" Special issue of *The Journal of the Order of Buddhist Contemplatives* 10, 3/4 (Autum/Winter, 1995).

Zen Meditation. Mt. Shasta, CA: Shasta Abbey, 1980.

Zen Training. Mt. Shasta, CA: Shasta Abbey, 1982.

Zenji, Keizan. *The Denkoroku; or, The Record of the Transmission of the Light.* Mount Shasta, CA: Shasta Abbey, 1993. 303 pp.

★2176★
Ordinary Mind Zen School
% Zen Center of San Diego
2047 Felspar
San Diego, CA 92109

The Ordinary Mind Zen School was founded by Charlotte Joko Beck, who in the early 1980s had been named one of the four Dharma heirs of Zen Center of Los Angeles. Since her separation from the Los Angeles center, Beck has become recognized as an important Soto Zen teacher in her own right and the author of several widely read books.

The Ordinary Mind Zen School manifests and supports practice in what has come to be called the Awakened Way. It is composed of Charlotte Joko Beck, her Dharma successors, and the teachers and successors they, as individuals, have formally authorized. There is no affiliation between the Ordinary Mind centers and other Zen groups or religious denominations; however, individual membership does not preclude individual affiliation with other groups.

The Awakened Way is thought of as universal; the medium and methods of realization vary according to circumstances. Each Dharma successor in the school may apply diverse practice approaches and determine the structure of any organization that s/he may develop to facilitate practice. Within the school there is no hierarchy of Dharma successors. The successors acknowledge that they are ongoing students, and that the quality of their teaching derives from the quality of their practice. As ongoing students, teachers are committed to the openness and fluidity of practice, wherein the wisdom of the absolute may be manifested in /as our life. An important function of this school is the ongoing examination and development of effective teaching approaches to insure comprehensive practice in all aspects of living.

Dharma successors Elihu Genmyo Smith and Diane Eshin Rizzetto reside at the Prairie Zen Center in Champaign, Illinois, and the Bay Zen Center in Oakland, California, respectively. Beck is an active member of the White Plum Asanga.

Membership: Not reported. There are centers related to the school in San Diego and Oakland, California; Champaign, Illinois; and New York City.

Sources:

Beck, Charlotte Joko. *Everyday Zen: Love and Work.* San Francisco: Harper, 1989. 224 pp.

___. *Nothing Special: Living Zen.* Steve Smith, ed. San Francisco: Harper, 1994. 288 pp.

★2177★
Rinzai-Ji, Inc.
% Rinzai Zen Center
2505 S. Cimarron
Los Angeles, CA 90018

Rinzai-Ji, Inc. is an association of Zen centers in the Rinzai tradition which began in 1968 with the founding of the Cimarron Zen Center in Los Angeles by Joshu Kyozan Sasaki Roshi. Sasaki Roshi had received his Inka, acknowledg of his accomplishments as a student, by Joten Miura, later to become leader of the Myoshinji sect of Rinzai Zen in Japan. Sasaki Roshi left the monastery he headed in Japan to come to America in 1962. Rinzai-Ji began as a gathering of students who had responded to his several years of teaching in Southern California. In 1970 a second center began in Redondo Beach, California, and that same year, the main training center was opened on Mt. Baldy, east of Los Angeles. Sasaki Roshi continued an active schedule visiting centers, training students, and lecturing around the United States, and other centers developed in the East and in Puerto Rico (1983). A Canadian center in Vancouver can be traced to a group which formed in response to talks given by Sasaki Roshi in 1967. A set of lectures in Austria in 1979 led to the first European affiliated center being formed. Each

center of Rinzai-Ji offers an intensive program of zazen ("sitting with the master") and periodic sesshin ("extended sitting meditation"). All are headed by individuals trained by Sasaki Roshi.

Membership: Not reported. In 1997 there were 12 centers in the United States, four in Canada, and one each in Puerto Rico, and Austria.

Sources:

Sasaki, Joshu. *Buddha Is the Center of Gravity.* San Cristobal, NM: Lama Foundation, 1974.

★2178★
Sonoma Mountain Zen Center
6367 Sonoma Mountain Rd.
Santa Rosa, CA 95404

The Sonoma Mountain Zen Center was founded in 1973 by Jakusho Kwong Roshi (b. 1935), a student of Shunryu Suzuki Roshi. A former commercial artist, he began practicing at the Sokoji Temple, a Soto Zen temple serving the Japanese American community in San Francisco, and in 1970 was ordained by Suzuki Roshi(1904–1971). Kwong Roshi founded the Sonoma Center to honor his teacher and to perpetuate his Zen lineage. He also continued his study in Japan and in 1978 completed his Dharma transmission through Hoitsu Suzuki Roshi in Rinsoin, Japan. By this act he shared in a lineage that was traced back through 91 generations to Shakyamuni Buddha.

After relocating to Sonoma County, Kwong Roshi taught at Sonoma State University and laid plans for the development of a residential community for the practice of Zen. Within a short time, the center had a full program of *zazen* (meditation), *sesshin* (extended retreats), and one-day programs (seminars and sittings). Kwong Roshi has also extended his teachings internationally and now oversees two centers in Poland.

Membership: In 1997 there were 125 members in the single center in California and 75 members in the two centers in Warsaw, Poland.

Periodicals: *Mountain Wind.*

Sources:

Morreale, Don. *The Complete Guide to Buddhist America.* Boston: Shambhala, 1998.

★2179★
Soto Mission
Zenshuji Soto Mission
123 S. Hewitt St.
Los Angeles, CA 90012

The Soto Mission is the oldest presently existing Zen group in the United States and is the outgrowth of the work of the Rev. Hosen Isobe, bishop of the North American Mission. Of all the Zen bodies in America, this group has the closest connection with the parent body in Japan. In America, it operates primarily among the Japanese-American community. In comparison with other Zen groups, it is the least Americanized and still does much instruction and prints literature in the mother tongue.

Since its founding in Hawaii in 1915, it has spread throughout the Islands and in 1972 had 10 temples. In the continental United States, from the original Zenshuji Mission, centers have spread along the coast and have become the source for other Zen groups, most notably the Zen Center of San Francisco and the Minnesota Zen Meditation Center in Minneapolis.

Zen, like other religions imported from India and the Orient, carries with it a variety of cultural peculiarities, which can pose problems in an occidental environment, as, for instance, language barriers. Other cultural conflicts derive from the extreme authority system of the Japanese monasteries, a cultural form incompatible with individualism of a democratic society. Finally, there is the racial barrier between the Japanese-American community and its

Caucasian neighbors, a barrier accentuated by the conflict of World War II. Like other Buddhist groups, Zen bodies tend to be either all Japanese or all Caucasian.

Membership: In 1983 the Soto Mission in Hawaii reported 1,150 members attached to the single center in Honolulu. There are six other Soto temples in Hawaii. California has two Soto Missions, one in Los Angeles and one in San Francisco. In 1988 the Zenshuji Mission in Los Angeles reported 2,000 members in its single center.

Periodicals: *Soto Zen Journal.*

Sources:

Hunt, Ernest. *Gleanings from Soto-Zen.* Honolulu, HI: The Author, 1953.

A Short Manual of Soto Zen Buddhism. Tokyo: Evangelization Department of the Soto Zen Sect, 1962.

★2180★
Springwater Center for Meditative Inquiry and Retreats
7179 Mill St.
Springwater, NY 14560

Existing on the edge of the American Zen community and pioneering new expressions of what might become a new American Buddhism is Springwater Center led by Toni Packer (b. 1927). Packer was born in Germany of Jewish parents who survived the Holocaust, in part, by being baptized as Lutherans. After World War II she met and married an American and moved to the United States in 1951. In 1965, she discovered Zen through Philip Kapleau and from his book, *Three Pillars of Zen*, she learned of *zazen*, sitting meditation, and began practicing on her own. In 1967 she began practicing with him and became one of his most accomplished students.

Over the years, Packer began to question aspects of the Zen tradition such as the difficulty of getting at most Zen texts and the formalities and hierarchical nature of Zen life. In 1982, questioning whether to call herself a Buddhist any more, she left the Rochester center and established her own teaching center across town. Some 2,000 students followed her. Among the innovations she made was allowing students to choose their own *koans* (questions) upon which to ruminate. Two years later she established the Springwater Center.

In the years since, she has offered a form of what is termed meditative inquiry, an unpressurized attempt at listening and observing what is happening within and without, without judgment. It is her belief that the realization of emptiness, of no-self, allows the arising of a spontaneous compassion. As an instructor, Packer sees herself as a catalyst in communicating Truth, ultimately inexpressible in symbols, such as language, to others. Through her several books, Packer's new approach to Zen has found a large audience in the larger community.

Membership: Not reported.

Sources:

Packer, Toni. *Seeing Without Knowing: Writings on Zen Work.* New York: Genesee Valley Zen Center, 1983.

___. *What Is Meditative Inquiry?* Springwater, NY: Springwater Center, 1988.

___. *The Work of This Moment.* Boston: Shambhala, 1990.

Rawlinson, Andrew. *The Book of Enlightened Masters: Western Teachers in Eastern Traditions.* La Salle, IL: Open Court Press, 1997. 650 pp.

★2181★
Toronto Zen Centre
33 High Park Gardens
Toronto, ON, Canada M6R 1S8

The Toronto Zen Centre was founded in 1968 by Philip Kapleau, the founder of the Zen Center of Rochester and a number of affiliated centers. The Toronto center remained tied to the Rochester center for 18 years, but became autonomous in 1986. The center is led by Sensei Sunyana Graef, one of Kapleau's Dharma heirs. Though autonomous, the center follows the belief and practices of its parent body. The associated Vermont Zen Center in Sherburne was founded in 1988.

Membership: Not reported. Affiliated with the center is Casa Zen in Costa Rica.

Sources:

Morreale, Don. *The Complete Guide to Buddhist America.* Boston: Shambhala, 1998.

★2182★
Udumbara Zen Center
501 Sherman Ave.
Evanston, IL 60202

The Udumbara Zen Center was founded in the 1980s as an outpost of the Zen Center of San Francisco but has subsequently become independent even though a fraternal relation continues. The Udumbara center has remained a Soto center, but has incorporated elements of both Hinayana (Theravada) and Vajrayana (Tibetan) tradition in its life.

Membership: Not reported. Also affiliated with the Udumbara Zen Center are centers in Milwaukee, Wisconsin; Breaux Bridge and Lafayette, Indiana; Cleveland, Ohio; and Cupertino, California.

Periodicals: *Central Flower.*

Sources:

Morreale, Don. *The Complete Guide to Buddhist America.* Boston: Shambhala, 1998.

★2183★
Valley Zendo
Warner Hill Rd.
Claremont, MA 01330

The Valley Zendo was established in 1971 as an outpost of Antai-ji Temple, a Soto Zen center in Japan. From the beginning, Uchiyama Roshi has sent his students from the temple to serve as resident teachers at the zendo. They have established and maintained a strict schedule of sitting practice and retreats. A related zendo has been opened in Northampton, Massachusetts.

Membership: Not reported.

Sources:

Morreale, Don. *The Complete Guide to Buddhist America.* Boston: Shambhala, 1998.

★2184★
White Wind Zen Community (WWZC)
PO Box 203, Sta. A
Ottawa, ON, Canada K1N 8V2

The White Wind Zen Community (WWZC) is a Soto Zen organization founded by the Ven. Anzan Hoshin, a teacher who received his training at Hakukaze-ji monastery in Japan. During the early 1980s he gathered a group of students in the Ottawa area. In 1985 the original center was White Wind Zazenkai, after the name of the Soto Zen Lineage stream that he inherited. Zazenkai means "gathering together for zazen." Two years later the center was relocated into enlarged facilities and was able to provide morning and evening zazen along with regular classes and monthly sesshin and residential training for a few students. In 1988 Joan Shikai Woodward became the first student to receive postulant vows as a monastic.

In 1989, the Zazenkai was renamed White Wind Zen Community, and relocated to Ottawa's Chinatown area. In 1990 two branch centres were formed in Wolfville, Nova Scotia, and in Harrow, England. A sub-temple, Jomyo-in, was established in Ottawa in 1993, and allowed for residential training and an auxiliary practice space (Dojo).

In September 1996 the WWZC purchased a 9,700 square foot heritage mansion previously owned by the Brothers of the Sacred Heart (a Roman Catholic order) to serve as its permanent training monastery. It was given the temple name Honzan (meaning "root mountain" or "main center") Dainen-ji ("Great Mindfulness" or "Vast Mind Moment") in honor of Hoshin's late master Yasuda Joshu Dainen daiosho.

The White Wind Zen Community presents the transmission of the practice and teachings of Hakukaze Soto Zen, and provides a formal environment and intensive schedule for monastic and lay training.

Membership: Not reported. There are the centers in Canada and one in England.

Sources:

Lorie, Peter, and Julie Foakes. *The Buddhist Directory.* Rutland, VT: Chares E. Tuttle Co., 1997. 424 pp.

★2185★
Zen Buddhist Temple of Chicago
865 Bittersweet Dr.
Northbrook, IL 60062-3701

The largest Zen center in the Midwest is the Zen Buddhist Temple of Chicago, a Soto center established by Rev. Soyu Matsuoka in the late 1950s. The major activity of the group is the meditation service, which includes a lecture by one of the priests. Matsuoka was sent to the United States and served as a priest in California before coming to Chicago. The current head of the Chicago center is the Rev. Kongo Langlois. The Rev. Dale Ver-Kuilen is the instructor at the Long Beach Temple, and Matsuoka Roshi remains as spiritual leader of both. Small groups associated with the Chicago Temple can be found in the states surrounding Lake Michigan. Matsuoka opened a center in Detroit, Michigan in 1973.

Membership: Not reported.

Periodicals: *Diamond Sword.*

★2186★
Zen Center of Hawaii
PO Box 2066
Kamuela, HI 96743

The Zen Center of Hawaii was founded in 1993 by Robert Joshin Althouse with the blessings of his teacher, Taizan Maezumi Roshi, best known as the founder of the Zen Center of Los Angeles. He was ordained as a Soto Zen Buddhist priest by Maezumi Roshi in 1973 and spent 12 years working as an artist in Los Angeles. Besides Zen, he has also studied in the Tibetan tantric tradition with Trungpa Rinpoche and Gyaltrul Rinpoche.

He is a Dharma holder of his present teacher, Bernard Tetsugen Glassman Roshi. Althouse's wife, June Kaililani Tanoue, directs a program for Drug Addiction Services of Hawaii and is a master hula dancer and chanter.

The main center of the Zen Center of Hawaii is located on Hawaii in the small country town of Waimea (Kamuela) on the northern side of the island. The Zen Center offers weekly zazen schedules in all three of its zendo locations, as well as monthly sesshins at it s center in Waimea. The center also offers classes in anger management and working with conflict in relationships. The Zen Center has begun a community garden in North Hawaii on land belonging to Parker School in Waimea. The name of the garden is I Ka Pono, which means "cultivate the goodness". The garden site is located in the center of Waimea town, between Parker School and Paniolo Country Inn.

Membership: Not reported. Besides the zendo at Waimea, there are regular gatherings at Hilo, Kona, and Volcano.

Sources:

Morreale, Don. *The Complete Guide to Buddhist America.* Boston: Shambhala, 1998.

★2187★
Zen Center of Los Angeles
923 S. Normandie Ave.
Los Angeles, CA 90006

The Zen Center of Los Angeles was formed in 1967 by a group of students under the leadership of Hakuyu Taizan Maezumi Roshi (1931-1995), a Zen master formerly with the Zenshuji Soto Mission in Los Angeles. The inspiration for the center came from Hakuun Yasutani, Roshi's visits in the early 1960s. The Los Angeles center supports a variety of activities including daily zazen, weekly lectures by Maezumi Roshi or one of his associates, and beginning classes. Center members also attend *dokusan* (master/student interviews) and monthly sesshin (extended "sitting" meditation). A residence program allows a few students to live at the center.

During the 1970s, the center developed a vigorous publishing program and Maezumi Roshi developed a following across the United States. Groups affiliated with the Zen Center of Los Angeles developed in Arizona, Oregon, Utah, and New York. Two rural centers at Mt. Tremper, New York, and Mountain Center, California, provide accomodations for more intensive Zen practice. The Kuroda Institute develops programs aimed at the academic community. Internationally, affiliated centers have emerged in England, Mexico and the Netherlands.

Membership: In 1988, there were approximately 1,000 members in more than 20 centers in the United States. Affiliated centers are located in England, Holland, Poland, and Mexico with an additional 1,000 members. There are approximately 20 members in Canada, but no center has yet been organized.

Educational Facilities: Karoda Institute, Los Angeles, California.

Periodicals: *The Ten Directions.*

Remarks: In the early 1980s, the Zen Center of Los Angeles went through a crisis centered in part upon the alcoholism of Maezumi Roshi. After going through a treatment program, he remains at the head of the center. Meanwhile, he has named four dharma heirs: Bernard Tetsugen Glassman (1978); Dennis Genpo Merzelsensei, Jan Chozen Soule-sensei, and Charlotte Joko Beck.

Sources:

Buksbazen, John Daishin. *To Forget the Self.* Los Angeles: Zen Center of California, 1977.

Maezumi, Hakuyu Taizan, and Bernard Tetsugen Glassman, eds. *The Hazy Moon of Enlightenment.* Los Angeles: Zen Center of Los Angeles, 1977.

——. *On Zen Practice.* 2 vols. Los Angeles: Zen Center of Los Angeles, 1976.

★2188★
Zen Center of Rochester
Seven Arnold Park
Rochester, NY 14607

The Zen Center of Rochester grew out of the experience of Philip Kapleau. Kapleau had encountered Zen while in Japan as a war crimes trial court reporter. Further spurred by the lectures of lay scholar Daisetz Teitaro Suzuki at Columbia University, he returned to Japan and studied under Soen Nakagawa, Roshi, who assigned the "Mu" koan discussed elsewhere in this volume. Kapleau later trained for three years at the Soto monastery at Hosshinji. After five years, Kapleau experienced kensho, a deep mystic enlightenment, and followed it with eight more years of training under Hakuun Yasutani, Roshi, who in 1966, sanctioned him as a teacher of Zen.

At this same time, Kapleau published one of the most influential Zen books, *The Three Pillars of Zen*. There is strong emphasis on koan work, as well as the zazen meditation of his Rinzai training (with elements of Soto). Zazen means sitting still with a one-pointed, stabilized mind.

The Rochester Center was founded in 1966 and under Kapleau's leadership, grew steadily. In 1968, *Zen Bow* began as a quarterly publication. Affiliates of the Rochester Center are located in Chicago, Illinois, and Madison, Wisconsin. Foreign affiliates are located in Mexico City, Mexico; Stockholm, Sweden; and Berlin, Germany.

In 1987 Philip Kapleau went into semiretirement and sanctioned one of his senior disciples to succeed him as abbot of the Rochester Center. The new abbot, Bodhin Kjolhede, had trained under Kapleau for 16 years before being sanctioned by him to teach in 1986. Several of Kapleau's other senior students were sancitoned as teachers around the same time and presently direct independent Zen centers in Toronto and Montreal, Canada; Shelburne, Vermont; and Denver, Colorado.

Membership: In 1995 there were approximately 400 members in the United States and an additional 130 members worldwide. There are nine centers and six priests.

Periodicals: *Zen Bow*.

Sources:

Kapleau, Philip. *Three Pillars of Zen*. Garden City, NY: Doubleday, 1980.

___. *To Cherish All Life*. San Francisco: Harper & Row, 1982.

___. *Zen: Dawn in the West*. N.p., 1981.

Kapleau, Philip, ed. *The Wheel of Death*. New York: Harper & Row, 1971.

Low, Albert. *The Iron Cow of Zen*. Wheaton, IL: Theosophical Publishing House, 1985.

★2189★
Zen Center of San Francisco
300 Page St.
San Francisco, CA 94102

The Zen Center of San Francisco dates from 1959 when students began to gather around the newly arrived Shunryu Suzuki Roshi, head of the Sokoji Temple, the Soto Zen Mission in San Francisco, at that time primarily a temple for the Japanese-American community. After Suzuki Roshi arrived, American students began to sit and study with him. Eventually, this group emerged as a distinct organization.

In 1967, the group purchased Tassajara Hot Springs outside of Carmel Valley, California, as the site for a mountain center more accommodating to traditional monastic Zen practice. Since this time the Tassajara Center has offered monastic training period in the winter and a four month guest season as well as workshops and retreats in the summer. In 1969, a large building in San Francisco was purchased as a city temple and a residence which also provides guest accommodations. The third practice place, Green Gulch Farm, was founded in 1972. Those who live at the Farm follow the training schedule (as do residents at each of the other centers), as well as grow organic produce and care for the many guests and retreatants who visit yearly. Other affiliated centers have emerged in cities including Monterey, Berkeley, Los Altos, Santa Cruz, California; and Chapel Hill, North Carolina.

Suzuki Roshi was succeeded as Abbot of Zen Center by his student Richard Baker. During the next decade the center prospered, adding members as well as developing several businesses (a bakery, a restaurant, etc.) as means of self-support. In 1983, Richard Baker resigned. After a period of transition, Tenshin Reb Andersonl was installed as Abbot of Zen Center, to be joined two years later by Sojun Mel Weitsman as co-Abbot.

There are currently approximately 650 members of Zen Center, about half of whom are voting members. A voting member is one who has been a member for three years or more and is thus eligible to vote in the annual election for the Board of Directors, Zen Center's governing body. Many non-members also join the commuinity for meditation, workshops, classes, and retreats or in our Hospice Volunteer program and other forms of community out-reach. All programs are open to the public.

Membership: In the 1992 approximately 650 people were associated with the city center in San Francisco. Approximately 50 lived at Green Gulch.

Periodicals: *Wind Bell*.

Sources:

Brown, Edward Espe. *The Tassajara Bread Book*. Boulder, CO: Shambhala, 1970.

Butler, Katy. "Events are the Teacher." *COEvolution* 40 (Winter 1983): 112-123.

Suzuki, Shunryu. *Zen Mind, Beginner's Mind*, New York: Weatherhill, 1970.

★2190★
Zen Community of New York
14 Ashburton Pl.
Yonkers, NY 10703

The Zen Community of New York was founded in 1979 by Bernard Tetsugen Glassman, who had been named a Dharma heir of Taizan Maezumi Roshi (1931–1995), the founder of the Zen Center of Los Angeles. Over the years the community became independent of the work in California. It has also developed into one of the more unique Zen communities in America in that it has developed an outward-looking program that views its ministry primarily in terms of social work. For example, members hold retreats on the street with the local homeless community or in such locations in the local community as to bear witness to the social and economic problems of society. Glassman Roshi is currently working with his associate, Sensei Jishu Holmes, in building the Zen Peacemaker Order to promote initiatives for social change that are grounded in Buddhist teaching and practice. The zendo in New York holds weekly meditation at the Gay Men's Health Crisis center, provides scholarships for people with HIV/AIDS, and cares for those in need.

The outward-looking perspective of the community is also embodied in what is termed the Greyston Mandala. The Mandala consists of a number of "community-building" structures such as the Greyston Family Inn, the Greyston Bakery, Greyston Health Services, and Pamsula Patchwork and Sewing.

Several additional centers are associated with the community, and Glassman is an active leader in the White Plum Asanga.

Membership: Not reported. Affiliated centers are found in New York City, Brooklyn, East Hampton, and Sagaponack, New York; and Boca Raton, Florida.

Sources:

Morreale, Don. *The Complete Guide to Buddhist America*. Boston: Shambhala, 1998. http://www.zpo.org

★2191★
Zen Community of Oregon
PO Box 310
Corbett, OR 97019

The Zen Community of Oregon was founded by Sensei Jan Chozen Bays, who had been ordained in 1979 by Taizan Maezumi Roshi at the Zen Center of Los Angeles. Though she was married and continued to perform her duties as a mother, Maezumi Roshi allowed her to continue in her practice and in 1983 named her his fourth Dharma heir. However, shortly thereafter it became known that she and Maezumi were having an affair and in 1984 she left Los Angeles for Oregon.

She founded the Zen Community headquartered in suburban Portland and a rural retreat center, Larch Mountain Zen Center. She and her husband, also ordained by Maezumi Rioshi, serve as the only priests. Provision is made for classes, daily sittings, and monthly retreats. She is an active member of the White Plum Asanga, and the community is informally related to the One Drop Zendo in Seattle, Washington.

Membership: Not reported.

Periodicals: *Dharma Dust.*

Sources:

Rawlinson, Andrew. *The Book of Enlightened Masters: Western Teachers in Eastern Traditions.* La Salle, IL: Open Court Press, 1997. 650 pp.

Sidor, Ellen, ed. *A Gathering of Spirit: Women Teaching in American Buddhism.* Cumberland, RI: Primary Point Press, 1987.

★2192★

Zen Studies Society
⅟ Dai Bosatsu Zendo Kongo-ji
HCR 1 Box 171
Livingston Manor, NY 12758-9402

The Zen Studies Society was founded in 1956 to assist the work of Daisetz Teitaro Suzuki (1870–1966). Suzuki came to the United States in 1949 and settled at Columbia University in 1951. His lectures at Columbia lay behind much of the public interest in Zen, one visible result being the establishment of the Zen Studies Society. When Suzuki moved on to Harvard in 1957, the group continued its studies without the presence of a Zen Master. Then in 1965, Eido Tai Shimano, formerly a monk at the Ryutaku Ju (Dragon Temple) headed by Nakagawa Soen Roshi, moved to New York. He assumed leadership of the Zen Studies Society and shifted it from its more intellectual study to the practice of *zazen* (Zen meditation). He established the New York Zenbo Shobo Ji (Temple of True Dharma) in Manhattan in 1968, and then turned his attention toward the establishment of a rural Zen monastery. In 1971 land was purchased in the Catskill Mountains of upstate New York for the International Dai Bosatsu Zendo Kongo Ji (Diamond Temple), dedicated in 1976. In 1972 Eido Shimano Roshi received *inka*, Rinzai Zen Dharma transmission in the Hakuin/Torei lineage, from Soen Roshi. Roshi now served as abbot of the Zen Studies Society and the spiritual teacher at it two centers.

The New York Zendo Shobo Ji provides a place for Zen practice to residents of New York City. Beginners are invited to Thursday evening meetings. Otherwise the Zendo is open at various times each week for zazen. There are weekend sesshin (zazen intensives) five times annually, and periodic all-day zazen sessions. Monthly Dharma studies sessions are held. After a period of regular attendance and practice, one may apply for full membership.

Dai Bosatsu Zendo was dedicated on July 4, 1976, partially as act of commemoration of Americas Bicentennial. Here, twice annually in the spring and summer, a three-month traditional monastic training is held, which attracts students from around the world. Students follow a rigorous schedule which includes zazen, chanting, and physical labor. They also follow a vegetarian diet. A monthly session is also held during which time the population at the monastery swells.

Membership: In 1996 the society reported a constituency community of 5,000 though there are only several hundred members and students regularly engaged in zazen.

Periodicals: *The Newsletter of the Zen Studies Society.*

Sources:

Daily Sutras for Chanting and Recitation. New York: New York Zendo of the Zen Studies Society, n.d.

Shimano, Eido. *Golden Wind.* Tokyo: Japan Publications, 1979.

_____, ed. *Like a Dream, Like a Fantasy.* Tokyo: Japan Publications, 1978.

Shimano, Eido T. *Points of Departure: Zen Buddhism with a Rimzai View.* Livingston Manor, NY: Zen Studies Society Press, 1991. 194pp.

Shimano, Eido T., and Kosetsu Tani. *Zen Ward*, Zen Calligraphy. Boston: Shambhale, 1995. 154pp.

Chinese Buddhism

★2193★

Buddha's Universal Church
702 Washington St.
San Francisco, CA 94108

The largest of the Buddhist organizations centered upon the San Francisco, California, Chinese community is Buddha's Universal Church, founded in the late 1920s in Chinatown. The church is currently housed in a million-dollar temple begun during the 1950s and dedicated in 1963. It is one of the largest in the continental United States and contains a unique mosaic image of the Buddha.

Among the founders of Buddha's Universal Church was the late Dr. Paul F. Fung, a physician, a Doctor of the Dharma, and vice-president of the World Fellowship of Buddhists. Currently the church is led by Dr. Frederick Hong. Outstanding scholarly leadership has enabled the church to become an American Buddhist intellectual center that now houses a fine library and research facility. A project of translating Buddhist texts eventuated in the publication of *The Sutra of the Sixth Patriarch on the Pristine Orthodox Dharma* in 1964, the first of several projected volumes. *The Pristine Orthodox Dharma,* Volume I was published in 1977.

Public services are held every second and fourth Sunday at 11:30 a.m. and include a lecture and tour. On the roof is a garden with a Bodhi tree, grown from a cutting of the tree under which Buddha sat, and a lotus-shaped pool. A yearly bilingual (Chinese-English) costumed musical production depicting ancient China is presented by the young people of the church.

Membership: There are approximately 400 members of the church at the single center in San Francisco.

Sources:

Fung, Paul F., and George D. Fung, trans. *The Sutra of the Sixth Patriarch on the Pristine Orthodox Dharma.* San Francisco: Buddha's Universal Church, 1964.

Hong, Frederick, and George D. Fung, trans. *Pristine Orthodox Dharma.* San Francisco: Buddha's Universal Church, 1977.

★2194★

Buddha's Universal Church and Ch'an Buddhist Sangha
Current address not obtained for this edition.

Buddha's Universal Church was founded in the 1960s by the Rev. Dr. Calvin C. Vassallo, in Houston, Texas. The church was eclectic and drew upon all of the Buddhist traditions, though the Chinese was preferred. According to Vassallo, the church taught truth, the common denominator of all religion and philosophy. Truth is universal, and is to non-Buddhists equated with "God." Truth is your father; from truth you were born and from the truth you must go unto your savior, the Buddha. Great emphasis was placed on the four basic truths and the noble eightfold path, and a codified presentation of Buddha's teachings.

During the 1970s the Church was located in Houston, from which it carried on an active program. Worship was centered upon the daily family worship before the family shrine. Sunday services were adopted from the Buddhist Churches of America (Japanese Shin). Adjacent to the Houston headquarters was a nunnery headed by Mother Superior Samma Yasodhara. A Department of Buddhist Education offered courses in T'ai Chi Chuan (Chinese yoga), Buddhism, and Kung-Fu; in addition, there was an active social program reaching the needy in Houston through the city's welfare agencies.

Sources:

Truth: An Outline of the Buddhist Churches and Sangha. Houston, TX: Buddha's Universal Church, 1971.

★2195★
Buddhist Association of Colorado
8965 W. Dartmouth Pl.
Lakewood, CO 80227

The Buddhist Association of Colorado is a Chinese Pure Land organization (analogous to the Buddhist Churches of America, the Japanese Pure Land Buddhist organization) established in 1990 under the direction of the Rev. Pat Leong. The majority of members are of Chinese descent but all are welcomed. The primary gathering is a Sunday service at which the chanting of Buddha's name (Namo Amitabha) is a primary element.

Affiliated with the association is the Nan Hua Zen Buddhist Society of Las Vegas founded by two American teachers, Chaun Yuan Shakya and Chaun Chang Shakya, both of whom traveled to the People's Republic of China to be ordained at the monastery originally founded by Hui Neng, the Sixth Patriarch (of Zen Buddhism).

Membership: Not reported.

Sources:

Morreale, Don. *The Complete Guide to Buddhist America*. Boston: Shambhala, 1998.

★2196★
Buddhist Association of the United States
3070 Albany Cresent
New York, NY 10463

The largest of the Buddhist organizations centered in the old Chinese community of New York City is the Buddhist Association of the United States, formed in 1964. An active program presents a varied format attempting a synthesis of several Buddhist trends. The two most important are Ch'an, the Chinese form of Zen, and Pure Land Buddhism, which centers on the worship of Amida Buddha. A library is open to the public, and the Sunday schedule includes meditation, a lecture and discussion. The Association is led by President Log To and Vice President C. T. Shen. Shen is a popular author and has lectured widely in the East on Buddhism. There are approximately 150 adherents. A number of pamphlets have been produced.

Membership: Not reported. In the 1970s there were approximately 150 adherents.

Sources:

The Enlightenment Sutra with Annotations. Bronx, NY: Buddhist Association of the United States, 1955.

Hsu, T'an. *On Amidism*. Bronx, NY: Buddhist Association of the United States, 1973.

Shen, C. T. *A Glimpse of Buddhism*. Taipei, Taiwan: Torch of Wisdom, 1970.

___. *What We Can Learn from Buddhism*. Taipei, Taiwan: Torch of Wisdom, 1975.

Thera, Narada. *An Outline of Buddhism*. Bronx, NY: Buddhist Association of the United States, n.d.

★2197★
Chinese Buddhist Association of Hawaii - Hsu Yun Temple
42 Kawananakoa Pl.
Honolulu, HI 96817

The Chinese Buddhist Association of Hawaii - Hsu Yun Temple, established in 1955 at the suggestion of the Hong Kong Chi-

nese Buddhist Association, invited and received Abbot Sic Tse Ting (Abbot Sakya Jy-Din) the following year. The name of the temple was named in memory and honor of one of the greatest Buddhist monks in Mainland China in this century, Venerable Hsu Yun. There is a main temple for worship and two memorial halls for paying respect to ancestors. The temple has three ten-foot, gold-leaf statues of Buddha as the center of worship; the life of Buddha is depicted on its walls.

Membership: In 1992 there were about 1,500 members in one center, and about 500 are current members.

★2198★
Chung Fu Kuan (Taoist Sanctuary)
Current address not obtained for this edition.

The Chung Fu Kuan (Inner Truth Looking Place), popularly known as the Taoist Sanctuary, was formed in the 1960s by Dr. Khigh Alx Dhiegh, since 1935 a student of I Ching, the ancient art of Chinese divination. Dhiegh is known to television audiences as a popular character actor. The Sanctuary draws its inspiration from the philosophy of Lao-Tzu, an older contemporary of Confucius. A lower government official, he became discouraged and abandoned his post. According to tradition, as he was about to leave China, he was asked to write down his teachings. The result was the Tao Te Ching, the chief scripture of Taoism.

Tao (the Way of the universe) is harmony. When events and things are allowed to move naturally, harmony is the result. The chief aim of human existence is to attain fullness of life by attaining harmony with the Tao. The result of Taoist thinking is "Wu-wei," a quietistic, non-interfering style of life. Politically, Wu-wei finds its best expression in laissez-faire and the ideal self-contained village state. The balance of the two forces into yin and yang, encompassing the basic polarities of the universe, is also crucial. As Taoism developed, divination emerged as a major practice. The most popular form of divining the future was the I Ching.

The I Ching is built upon a series of trigrams, each a combination of two primary forms-the yang-hsiao, a straight line, the symbol of the male or positive principle, and the yin-hsiao, a broken line, the symbol of the female or negative principle. The two symbols can be arranged into eight different trigrams, and the trigrams can form sixty-four hexagrams. Each hexagram has been ascribed symbolic meanings, correlating with the eight fundamental elements or factors in the universe and sixty-four phenomena in the universe. Together, the hexagrams represent symbolically all the possible situations of creation. They may tell a person to do something or not to do it; to change or not to change, etc.

Associated with the Sanctuary is the International I Ching Studies Institute. Dr. Dhiegh has written a modern commentary on the I Ching, *The Eleventh Wing*. Ceremony-teaching services are regularly held on the first and third Sunday and gatherings on the first and third Friday. Taoist meditation occurs on Wednesday nights. The Institute offers Kung-fu, T'ai Chi Chuan (Chinese yoga), and courses in Chinese herbal practices.

Membership: In 1984 there were approximately 100 members in four centers: North Hollywood, San Diego, and Santa Barbara, California and Tempe, Arizona.

Sources:

Dhiegh, Khigh Alx. *The Eleventh Wing*. New York: Delta Books, 1973.

Meyers, Robert. "Khigh Dhiegh Digs I Ching." *TV Guide* (February 20, 1971): 45-48.

★2199★

Da Yuan Circle
℅ Frost Bell
Box 378
Fairfax, CA 98978

Da Yuan Circle is a modern Western group teaching the Orthodox Daoism of China. The teaching is generally ascribed to the ancient Daoist master Zhang Dao Ling, the eighth successor in the lineage of Zhang Liang, who lived in the second century B.C.E. Zhang Liang authored *The Classic of Auspicious Alliances*, a detailed text concerning the invocation of the unseen worlds. Zhang Dao Ling was a healer who fashioned talismans believed by patients to be a contact point with the unseen.

Orthodox Daoism differs somewhat with the philosophical Daoism (often spelled Taoism) introduced into the West in the nineteenth century and built around the *Dao De Ching* (or *I Ching*), a book of little importance in religious Daoism. All of Daoism shares a trust in Nature founded in a belief in the Truth of the Oneness (Dao). But religious Daoism is a compendium of cosmological ritual, alchemy, medical practices, macrobiotic diets, and yogic practices. These emerged out of, and eventually replaced, the older Chinese shamanistic systems. The early Dao Shem organized, systematized, and improved upon the trance practices of the shamans, which could be extreme and often brought physical harm to the shamans.

In trance, Master Zhang Dao Ling received the universal cosmology which in large part defined Orthodox Daoism. In his spirit journeys he also gathered the information for a new form of medicine. Trance activity was placed within a ritualized context and remains central to the Daoist worship experience. The ritual leader goes into trance and, it is believed, in a sense, takes the whole gathering on the shamanistic journey. As passed through the centuries, meditation and trance remain central to the tradition. Members practice meditation, the exploration of the internal environment, which begins in stilling the body and withdrawing attention to the internal world. Trance involves the journeying through a world populated with iconographical images set in place by ritual and story. Trance, the more complex spiritual practice, is done in the presence of a teacher who is able to understand what is occurring to the student.

The Da Yuan Circle is an Orthodox Daoist group founded in the 1980s by Lao Ge (Charles Belyea), who holds a lineage of Orthodox Daoism from Taiwan. Members are primarily Westerners. He also founded Five Branches Institute, a college of traditional Chinese medicine in Santa Cruz, California.

Membership: Not reported.

Educational Facilities: Five Branches Institute, Santa Cruz, California.

Periodicals: *Frost Bell.*

Sources:

Belyea, Charles. *Dragon's Play.* Berkeley, CA: Great Circle Lifeworks, 1991.

"The Shamanic Roots of Orthodox Daoism." *Tantra* 8 (1994): 54-57, 76.

★2200★

Dharma Realm Buddhist Association
City of Ten Thousand Buddhas
Talmage, CA 95481-0217

The Dharma Realm Buddhist Association was founded as the Sino-American Buddhist Association in 1959 by disciples of Tripitaka Master Hsuan Hua (d. 1995). In 1962, he moved from Hong Kong to San Francisco at their invitation. In 1968, the Buddhist Lecture Hall was established as a center for the study and practice of orthodox Buddhism in the West. Originally founded by Chinese-Americans, the center quickly attracted a large Caucasian membership. The organization expanded rapidly. The Gold Mountain Monastery in San Francisco was opened in 1970; the International Institute for the Translation of Buddhist Texts was founded in 1973; and the City of Ten Thousand Buddhas, an international study center for western Buddhists, opened in 1976. Gold Wheel Monastery was opened in Los Angeles (1976), Gold Summit Monastery in Seattle (1984), and Gold Buddha Monastery in Vancouver, British Columbia (1984).

Master Hsuan Hua had been a longtime student of Master Hsu Yun in China. He moved to Hong Kong after the Maoist Revolution in 1949. In accepting the invitation to come to the West, he did so with the intention of establishing Buddhism in its entirety. Among the young converts to Buddhism attracted to the lecture hall, he accepted some into monastic vows. In 1969, five disciples went to Taiwan to receive final ordination as bhikshus (monks) and bhikshunis (nuns), and by 1972 there were ten fully ordained monks and several novices preparing for ordination. The first full ordination of disciples in the United States occurred in 1976 at the City of Ten Thousand Buddhas. Since that time, the association has held such ordinations every three or four years.

The Dharma Realm Buddhist Association, though based in the Ch'an (Zen) school of Chinese Buddhism, teaches all five main varieties of Chinese Buddhism. New members accept Chinese Buddhist names. Lay members have "Kuo" as part of their name; those destined for the priesthood who received their novice vows from Master Hsuan Hua have "Heng" added to their name; and the fully ordained monks receive the surname "Shih," the first character of the Chinese word, Sakyamuni (Gautama Buddha). Each new member takes the Three Refuges (a ceremony similar to Christian confirmation, by which the new member promises to take refuge in the Buddha, the Dharma or teachings of Buddha, and the Sangha).

The association has emphasized the development of a Buddhist monastic community, an element of Buddhist life frequently missing in Western Buddhist organizations, and over 50 persons have entered the orders. Monastics lead a very disciplined life of practice and study. They are sexually celibate. They are strict vegetarians and do not eat after noon. The program emphasizes Sutra study (including language studies and translation, lectures, and chanting) and meditation.

The Dharma Realm Buddhist University was the first Buddhist university to be established in the Western World. It offers degreed courses in Buddhist studies, letters and science, and the creative and applied arts. It is located in the City of Ten Thousand Buddhas in Talmage, California. Through the Sangha Training and Laity Training Programs, the Buddhist equivalent of seminary education is offered for Buddhist leaders. Since its founding in 1973, the International Institute for the Translation of Buddhist Texts has become a major publisher of Buddhist literature. Managed by both Sangha (clergy) and lay scholars under the guidance of Hsuan Hua, it had by 1980 published translations of more than 100 volumes of Chinese Buddhist writings in various Western languages.

Membership: In 1992 the association reported 25,000 members in five centers served by 50 ministers in the United States and 5,000 members, two centers, and five ministers in Canada.

Educational Facilities: Dharma Realm Buddhist University, Talmage, California.

Periodicals: *Vajra Bodhi Sea.* Available from the Gold Mountain Monastery, 800 Sacramento St., San Francisco, CA 94108. • *The Proper Dharma Seal.* Send orders to City of Ten Thousand Buddhas, Box 217, Talmage, CA 95481.

Sources:

Hua, Hsuan. *Buddha Root Farm.* San Francisco: Buddhist Text Translation Society, 1976.

___. *The Ten Dharma-Realms Are Not Beyond a Single Thought.* San Francisco: Buddhist Text Translation Society, 1976.

World Peace Gathering. San Francisco: Sino-American Buddhist Association, 1975.

Yin, Heng, comp. *Records of the Life of the Venerable Master Hsuan Hua.* 2 vols. San Francisco: Committee for the Publication of the Biography of the Venerable Master Hsuan Hua, 1973-75.

★2201★
Eastern States Buddhist Association of America
64 Mott St.
New York, NY 10013

The Eastern States Buddhist Association of America was founded in 1963 as the first New York-area Chinese temple with a priest in attendance. Largely through the help of Mrs. James Ying, the program has grown and developed. In 1971 Dharma Master Bhikshu Hsi Ch'en, who had escaped China when the Communists took over, was brought to the United States to head the Temple Mahayana, an Association retreat center in the Catskill Mountains in New York.

The Eastern States Buddhist Association follows the T'ien-t'ai school founded by Chih-i (558-597), a monk at Mount T'ien-t'ai in China. The members emphasize the Lotus Sutra as inclusive of all Buddha's teachings. Meditation, the study of the Sutras, repeating the name of Amitabha Buddha, and living a disciplined life are emphasized.

Membership: Not reported.

★2202★
Fung Loy Kok Institute of Taoism
1310 N. Monroe St.
Tallahassee, FL 32303

Alternate Address: Fung Loy Kok Taoist Temple, Sam Tip Tem, Cheun Wan, New Territories, Hong Kong, China.

Fung Loy Kok Institute of Taoism was founded in Hong Kong in 1968 by the Taoist Priest Mui Ming-to, his wife, Mui Tang Yuan-may, and Taoist Master Moy Lin-shin. The particular Taoist tradition can be traced to the Earlier Heaven Wu-chi Sect founded by the Patriarch Tien-lung, who in turn had received the teaching of the Tao from Chen Hsi-I. Chaotic conditions in early twentieth-century China led Taoist teachers to bring the teachings out of the monastic context to a lay public. In 1981, Master Moy and Mr. Mui established an institute in Toronto, the first of several additional branches to be opened in Canada and the United States.

The institute is dedicated to the teaching and practice of Taoism through the Taoist arts such as chanting, meditation, chi-kung, book discussions, internal exercises, and the promotion of charity for others through community service. An associated Taoist Tai Chi Society also teaches the art of tai chi leading to an increase in humility, quietude, and compassion.

Membership: Not reported. Fung Loy Kok temples can be found in Toronto, Denver, Colorado, and St. Petersburg, Florida.

Sources:

Wong, Eva, trans. *Seven Taoist Masters: A Folk Novel of China.* Boston: Shambhala, 1990. 178 pp.

★2203★
Hawaii Chinese Buddhist Society
1614 Nuuanu Ave.
Honolulu, HI 96817

In 1953, a number of Chinese-American residents in Hawaii decided to take advantage of the movement of the many Buddhist monks into Hong Kong after the Maoist revolution and to establish work under their leadership. The initial Hawaiian group divided between those who wished to choose the monks from among their acquaintances and those who wished the Hong Kong Chinese Buddhist Association to select the most qualified.

The Hawaii Chinese Buddhist Society chose to make its own selection and brought the Rev. Chuen Wai from Hong Kong to head the temple in Honolulu. He was joined in 1957 by Dharma

Master Tsu Yin. They emphasize the Buddhist nature of the society, as opposed to the strong Taoist influence in some Chinese temples. All the statues are of traditional Buddhist bodhisattvas-Omito (Amida), Kwan Yin, Wei Ton (sometimes called General Wei Ton), who was asked by Buddha to protect Buddhist teachings, and Tay Chong Wong, the god of wisdom.

Membership: In 1982 there were 1,000 members in one center in Honolulu.

★2204★
Healing Tao Centers
% Taoist Esoteric Yoga Center & Foundation
PO Box 1194
Huntington, NY 11743

Alternate Address: International Headquarters: Tao Garden of Healing Tao, 274 Moo 7, Doi Sakep, Chiang Mai, Thailand 50220.

The Healing Tao Centers are a worldwide network of teachers and centers that have emerged around the work of Mantak Chia and his wife Maneewan Chia. Born and raised in Thailand, Mantak Chia studied Buddhism. Moving to Hong Kong as a young man, he studied the martial arts. More importantly, Chia met the Taoist Master White Cloud Hermit who presented an understanding of the human body as conceived by Taoism. This understanding pictures the body as the container of a variety of energies which, in health, flow freely through it. Chia combined his instruction from the Hermit with a Western education in anatomy. This led to his producing the healing Tao system, a synthesis of tradition Taoism with Western science.

Maneewan Chia, trained as a medical technician, brought to the Healing Taoist system an emphasis upon healthful nutrition and cooking from her native China. Moving to New York, in the early 1980s the Chias founded the Healing Tao Center and began to spread their Taoist perspective. Mantak Chia's first book, *Awaken Healing Energy through the Tao* appeared in 1983. Others soon followed. As he trained instructors, the movement spread across the United States and into Europe. In the mid-1980s they established the Taoist Esoteric Yoga Center and Foundation in Huntington, New York.

Membership: In 1995, the centers reported 40,000 members worldwide with 20,000 in the United States and 2,000 in Canada. Instructors and centers could be found in 18 states, three Canadian provinces, and seven European countries. There is also a center in India.

Educational Facilities: Santa Fe Acupuncture College, Santa Fe, New Mexico.

Periodicals: *The Healing Tao Journal.*

Sources:

Chia, Mantak. *Awaken Healing Energy through the Tao.* New York: Aurora Press, 1983.

___. *Taoist Ways to Transform Stress into Vitality: The Inner Smile/Six Healing Sounds.* New York: Aurora Press, 1985.

Chia, Mantak, and Maneewan Chia. *Healing Love through the Tao: Cultivating Female Sexual Energy.* Huntington, NY: Healing Tao Books, 1986.

Chia, Mantak, with Michael Winn. *Taoist Secrets of Love: Cultivating Male Sexual Energy.* New York: Aurora Press, 1984.

★2205★
Il Bung Zen Society
% Il Bung Zen Temple
Huntsville, AL

The Il Bung Zen Society was founded by Zen Master Don Gilbert, now known as Ta Hui, who in 1968 was initiated into the Chogye Order of Korean Zen Buddhism by Seo Kyung Bo, one of the first Korean Zen teachers who settled in the United States. In 1973, Gilbert was named Seo Kyung Bo's Dharma heir. Now known as Ta Hui, Gilbert holds services in three widely separated temples in Arcata and Carmel, California; and Huntsville, Alabama. He has authored two books, cartoon books on Zen that feature as characters a bloodhound and a canine Zen Master.

Membership: Not reported.

Sources:

Gilbert, Zen Master Don. *Jellyfish Bones*. Oakland, CA: Blue Dragon Press, 1980.

___. *The Upside Down Circle: Zen Laughter*. Nevada City, CA: Blue Dolphin Publishing, 1988.

★2206★
Institute of Chung-Hwa Buddhist Culture/Chan Meditation Center
90-56 Corona Ave.
Elmhurst, NY 11373

The Institute of Chung-Hwa Buddhist Culture/Chan Meditation Center was founded by Chan Master Sheng-yen, who came to the United States from Taiwan in 1975. Chan is the Chinese word for Zen. Master Sheng-yen was born in China and became a Buddhist monk at age 13. During his years of practice he became deeply committed to the propagation of Buddhism. In the late 1940s, as communism was spreading through China, he fled to Taiwan. He continued his practice in Taiwan, and spent six years in solitary retreat on a mountain. After the retreat, Sheng-yen saw the need to improve the quality of Buddhist education and felt that in this way the spread of Buddhism would be assured. He therefore went to Japan and received a doctorate in Buddhist Studies from Rissho University. He received Dharma transmission (affirmation of his enlightenment and the special qualification to guide others in Buddhist teaching) from both the Lin-chi (Rinzai) and Tsao-tung (Soto) Chan Buddhist lineage.

After moving to the United States, Sheng-yen settled in the Bronx, New York, where he became affiliated with the Buddhist Association of the United States, a predominantly Chinese Buddhist organization. He organized a Chan meditation class and began to hold meditation retreats that attracted many non-Chinese students. In 1977 he started the *Chan Magazine*, and two years later formally founded the Institute of Chung-Hwa Buddhist Culture/Chan Meditation Center. He has been active in spreading Buddhism in the United States ever since. He now divides his time between the Chan Centers in New York and Taipei, Taiwan.

Membership: In 1997 the institute reported approximately 200 members in the United States and 40 in Canada. There was one organized Chan center in North America, in Elmhurst, New York; two Chan monasteries and one Buddhist institute in Taipei, Taiwan; 10,000 members worldwide.

Educational Facilities: The Chung-Hwa Institute of Buddhist Studies, Taipei, Taiwan R.O.C.

Periodicals: *Chan Magazine*.

Sources:

Sheng-Yen, Ch'an Master. *Faith in Mind: A Guide to Ch'an Practice*. Elmhurst, NY: Dharma Drum Publications, 1987.

___. *Getting the Buddha Mind: On the Practice of Ch'an Retreat*. Elmhurst, NY: Ch'an Meditation Center, 1982.

___. *Ox Herding at Morgan's Bay*. Elmhurst, NY: Institute of Chung-Hwa Buddhist Culture, 1988.

★2207★
International Buddhist Progress Society
PO Box 5248
Hacienda Heights, CA 91745

Alternate Address: International Headquarters: Fo Kuang Shan, Tashu, Kaohsiung 84010, Taiwan.

The International Buddhist Progress Society is an organization adhering to Chinese Buddhism in America. It was originally founded in 1967 in Taiwan by the Ven. Master Hsing Yun. Hsing Yun was born in China in 1926. When he was 12 years old he became a monk and received a monastic education. He was ordained in 1941. In 1949, in the wake of the Communist emergence as the ruling force in the country, Hsing Yun left for Taiwan. It is there in 1967 that he established Fo Kuang Shan, a forest monastery, said to be the largest in the Republic of China.

During his life, Hsing Yun developed a great incentive to propagate Buddhism, and the society became the launching pad for evangelistic endeavors, not only throughout Taiwan, but in Hong Kong, Malaysia, Guam, and eventually the United States. Entering America in the early 1980s, the society began building Hsi Lai Temple, a temple/monastic complex in Hacienda Heights, California, the largest such complex in the West. Completed in 1988, it became the sight of the first meeting of the World Fellowship of Buddhists in North America.

This Buddhism is built around the teachings of the Ven. Master Hsing Yun, a form of Mahayana Buddhism that emphasizes the role of the monastic leadership of the Buddhist community and the presence of *bodhisattvas* (those who have attained enlightenment and have chosen to assist in the enlightenment of others) to assist Buddhists in their progress. The movement, especially in its American experience, is nonsectarian and offers programs and classes in a variety of Buddhist approaches from Japanese Zen to Tibetan. The Hacienda Heights temple/complex houses a large Buddhist cultural museum and sees itself as a focus for all of North American Buddhism.

Membership: In 1992 the society reported approximately 20,000 members in the United States and 5,000 members in Canada. There are temples in San Diego and San Francisco, California, Denver, Dallas, Austin, New York, Florida, Hawaii and in Guam. Canadian temples are found in Vancouver, Edmonton, and Toronto. Internationally there are 44 centers in Taiwan, one in Hong Kong, and three in Malaysia.

Educational Facilities: Chinese Buddhist Research Institute, Kaohsiung, Taiwan.
Eastern Buddhist College.
Taipei Women's Buddhist College, Kaohsiung, Taiwan.
Fu Shan Buddhist College, Kaohsiung, Taiwan.

Periodicals: *Hsi Lai News*. • *Buddha's Light Newsletter*. Send orders to 3456 S. Glenmark Dr., Hacienda Heights, CA 91745.

Sources:

The Buddhist Liturgy. Monterey Park, CA: International Buddhist Progress Society, n.d.

Hsing Yun, Ven. Master. *How to Be a Fo Kuang Buddhist*. Kaohsiung, Taiwan: Fo Kuang Publishers, 1987.

___. *Lectures on Three Buddhist Sutras*. Kaohsiung, Taiwan: Fo Kuang Publishers, 1987.

___. *Two Talks on Buddhism*. Kaohsiung, Taiwan: Fo Kuang Publishers, 1987.

Newton, Edmund. "East Settling into West." *Los Angeles Times* (January 10, 1988).

★2208★
Kuan Yin Temple
170 N. Vineyard St.
Honolulu, HI 96817

The oldest Chinese temple in America is the Kuan Yin Temple begun by Leong Dick Ying, a monk who in 1878 brought to Hawaii two gold-leaf statues—the Taoist Kwan Tai and the Buddhist Kuan Yin, the goddess of mercy. A temple was built in Chinatown in Honolulu and, after several moves, in 1921 found a permanent home on Vineland Blvd. in Honolulu. Along with the statue of Kuan Yin, there are many statues of Buddhas, bodhisattvas, and other deities.

The festival year which regulates the life of the various temples is followed at the Kuan Yin Temple. The Chinese New Year is the biggest festival, but throughout the year there are may festivals honoring the Buddhas, bodhisattvas, and deities, including the Chinese Moon Festival (August 15) and the winter solstice.

Membership: In 1982 the temple reported 850 members.

★2209★
Living Tao Foundation
PO Box 846
Urbana, IL 61801

The Living Tao Foundation was founded in the early 1980s by Chungliang Al Haing, a Chinese artist and Taoist teacher who migrated to the United States in the 1960s. Following a year in China as a Ford Foundation scholar (1966-1967), he spent four years in Urbana, Illinois, as a post-doctorate fellow with the Center for Advanced Study and as artist-in-residence at the Krannert Center for the Performing Arts. He headed the Oriental Institute at York University for two years (1972-1974) and spent three years as the director of the Lan T'ing Institute for the Alan Watts Society for Comparative Philosophy. While at the institute he worked on finishing Watts' last book, *Tao: The Watercourse Way*, published several years after Watts' death in 1975.

The Living Tao Foundation emphasizes a synthesis of Eastern and Western ways through Taoist principles and uses various inner growth techniques. Haing is best known as a master of Tai Ji (or Tai Chi), the Chinese form of body movements which are believed to develop the natural coordination of body and mind. The foundation jointly sponsors the Lan Ting Institute, a cross cultural study and conference center, with the government of the People's Republic of China. Haing is especially concerned with the recovery of Chinese culture, which suffered a severe blow from the Cultural Revolution in the 1970s; the institute sponsors trips to China to assist in that recovery.

Membership: Not reported.

Sources:

Haing, Chungliang Al. *Embrace Tiger, Return to Mountain.* Moab, UT: Real People Press, 1973.

___. *Living Tao: Still Visions and Dancing Brushes.* Millbrae, CA: Celestial Arts, 1976.

"Tai Ji: The Dance of Life. An interview with Chunglaing Al Huang." *The Empty Vessal: A Journal of Contemparary Taoism* (Spring 1994): 4-12.

Watts, Alan, with Chungliang Al Haing. *Tao: The Watercouse Way.* New York: Pantheon Books, 1975.

★2210★
George Ohsawa Macrobiotic Foundation
1999 Myers
Oroville, CA 95966

Closely related to Taoism is macrobiotics, a philosophy developed by George Ohsawa (Yukikazu Sahurazawa) (1893-1966) drawing on Zen, Taoism, and Chinese wisdom philosophy. Macrobiotics is based on the concept of yin and yang. All things are differentiated apparatus of one Infinity. Yin and yang are the poles of the Infinity's bifurcation. Everything changes. Yin is centrifugal and yang centripetal. By their attraction and repulsion, energy and all phenomena are produced. All things are made of unequal proportions of yin and yang. All physical forms are yang (male) at the center and yin (female) at the surface.

The object of macrobiotics, for the individual, is to balance the yin and yang as far as possible in one's life. As for diet, one ideally eats foods which are balanced; cereals and brown rice are good examples. One also learns to live in harmony with the environment.

Macrobiotics was introduced into the West in France by Ohsawa in the 1920s and it gradually spread through Europe. By the time of his death in 1966, macrobiotic centers in Europe could be found in Belgium, England, Germany, Italy, Spain, and Sweden. From the center in Japan, work had also spread to Brazil and Viet Nam. Macrobiotic teachings spread to America after World War II. During the 1950s, Herman Aihara, a student of Ohsawa from Japan, migrated to the United States. He founded the Ohsawa Foundation, since renamed the George Ohsawa Macrobiotic Foundation. It is the first Macrobiotic organization in North America, and in 1961 began a periodical, *Yin Yang.* The foundation, through its publications and sponsoring of lecturers, became the focus of the early spread of macrobiotic teachings, and continues as one of two national associations of people devoted to macrobiotic principles.

Membership: In 1997, the foundation reported 1,500 members in the United States, 60 members in Canada, and an additional 120 members worldwide. There is one center; it serves as a nexus of a network of independent macrobiotic centers around the United States and Canada.

Periodicals: *Macrobiotics Today.*

Sources:

Aihara, Herman. *Seven Macrobiotic Principles.* San Francisco: George Ohsawa Macrobiotic Foundation, 1973.

Ohsawa, George. *The Book of Judgment.* Los Angeles: Ohsawa Foundation, 1966.

___. *Guidebook for Living.* Los Angeles: Ohsawa Foundation, 1967.

___. *Practical Guide to Far Eastern Macrobiotic Medicine.* Oroville, CA: George Ohsawa Macrobiotic Foundation, 1976.

___. *Zen Macrobiotics.* Los Angeles: Ohsawa Foundation, 1965.

★2211★
One Peaceful World
Box 10
Becket, MA 01223

Michio Kushi (b. 1926), a student of George Ohsawa (1893-1966), the founder of Macrobiotics, came to the United States in 1949 and became active in the spread of its philosophy. Initially working through the Ohsawa Foundation (now the George Ohsawa Macrobiotic Foundation) headquartered in California, Kushi developed an independent following in New England. After Ohsawa's death, Kushi founded the Order of the Universe Publications and in 1967 began to issue a periodical, *The Order of the Universe.* In 1972 Kushi founded the East West Foundation (now the Kushi Foundation) to oversee the spread of the work of presenting macrobiotics to the public and nurturing the growing number of people who had accepted macrobiotic principles and practice. In 1979 the Kushi Institute was founded to train leaders in the movement.

Kushi's teachings are summarized in a set of theorems and principles which define the nature of yin and yang, the prime differentiation within the universe. All phenomena is composed of a complex of these two polar opposites and macrobiotics defines and assists individuals in relating to the yin-yang composition of the universe. While a major component of macrobiotic philosophy relates to developing a balanced diet, the philosophy encompasses every area of life, as spelled out in numerous publications by the Kushi and the Foundation.

Through the 1990s, Kushi has nurtured a network of people devoted to the twin issue, of macrobiotics and peace which he termed One Peaceful World. This group was formerly known as the East West Foundations.

Membership: Not reported. In 1998 functioned through national offices in 20 countries. A directory of the larger macrobiotic movement listed over 400 individuals, businesses, and centers promoting the teachings.

Educational Facilities: Kushi Institute, Beckett, Massachusetts.

Periodicals: *One Peaceful World.* Send orders to Box 10, Beckett, MA 01223.

Sources:

Kohler, Jean Charles, and Mary Alice Kohler. *Healing Miracles from Macrobiotics.* West Nyack, NY: Parker Publishing Co., 1979.

Kushi, Michio. *The Book of Macrobiotics.* Tokyo: Japan Publications, 1977.

___. *The Teachings of Michio Kushi.* 2 vols. Boston, MA: East West Foundation, 1971.

Kushi, Michio, with Stephen Blauer. *The Macrobiotic Way.* Wayne, NJ: Avery Publishing Group, 1985.

★2212★
Shaolin Buddhist Meditation Center
3165 Minnesota St.
Los Angeles, CA 90031

The Shaolin Buddhist Meditation Center is part of a complex of structures founded in the late 1980s by Jefferson Chan, a teacher in the Chinese Shaolin tradition (the tradition made famous by the television series "Kung Fu"). The center of the complex is the California Buddhist University, opened in 1988, which offers a full curriculum (for the doctoral level) in Buddhist studies. The university sponsors the Kewanee Mountain Zen Center, the Bodhi Book Store, and the California Buddhist University's Zen Garden.

Membership: Not reported.

Educational Facilities: California Buddhist University, Los Angeles, California.

Periodicals: *The Shaolin Monastery.*

Sources:

Morreale, Don. *The Complete Guide to Buddhist America.* Boston: Shambhala, 1998.

★2213★
Shrine of the Eternal Breath of Tao
1314 2nd St.
Santa Monica, CA 90401

The Shrine of the Eternal Breath of Tao was founded by Master Ni, Hua-Ching, who began his study of Taoism as a child in China. After the Chinese Revolution, he moved to Taiwan and continued his studies. Eventually he became a teacher of Taoism and its related martial and healing arts. During the 1970s he moved to the United States and began to teach in Los Angeles.

Master Ni teaches the universal law of subtle energy response. Everything in the universe is a manifestation of energy in either its grosser or its more subtle states. Understanding and developing the proper response to the energies of one's environment will bring harmony to one's life. The practice of Taoist meditation, martial arts (kung fu and t'ai chi ch'uan), and medical practices (acupuncture and herbs) assist in attaining a balanced relationship to life. The universal law of response is basic to all spiritual practices.

Membership: Not a membership organization. Affiliated with the Shrine is the Center for Taoist Arts in Alpharetta, Georgia.

Educational Facilities: College of Tao, Santa Monica, California.

Yo San University of Traditional Chinese Medicine, Santa Monica, California.

Sources:

Ni, Hua-Ching. *Tao, the Subtle Universal Law and the Integral Way of Life.* Malibu, CA: Shrine of the Eternal Breath of Tao, 1982.

★2214★
True Buddha School
℅ Ling Shen Ching Tze Temple
17012 NE 40th Ct.
Redmond, WA 98052

The True Buddha School was founded by the Master Sheng-Yen Lu, born in Taiwan in 1945. As a young man, he became a student of Buddhism and began the daily practice of yoga and meditation. He reached a stage of Enlightenment, and his students consider him a Living Buddha (Enlightened One). Throughout the 1980s he traveled widely, teaching and founding Buddhist societies. He eventually settled near Seattle, Washington. He offers initiation empowerment to those who wish to take refuge in him and the Buddhas, either in his personal presence or through "remote initiation empowerment" offered twice monthly.

Master Sheng-Yen Lu teaches a path of tantric enlightenment, which draws heavily upon Tibetan Buddhist teachings. After receiving personal empowerment, the student receives a picture of the Master and receives instruction in beginning practice. The Master advises students to set up a personal shrine as a place for daily practice and offerings to the Buddhas and Bodhisattvas. Students are instructed in the practice of meditation and the repetition of mantras, with the goal of ultimately achieving liberation for every human being.

Membership: Not reported. As of 1998 there were 16 centers of the True Buddha School in the United States, 20 in Canada, and one in Guam. These are an estimated 100,000 members in the United States and 100,000 members in Canada. A reported four million people have taken refuge in Master Sheng-Yen Lu worldwide.

Periodicals: *True Buddha News.*

Sources:

Sheng-Yen Lu, Master. *The Inner World of the Lake.* San Bruno, CA: Amitabha Enterprise, 1992.

Korean Buddhism

★2215★
American Buddhist Shim Gum Do Association
203 Chestnut Hill Ave.
Brighton, MA 02135

The American Buddhist Shim Gum Do Association was founded in 1978 by Korean Zen Master Chang Sik Kim. Shim Gum Do (Mind Sword Path) concerns the attainment of clear mind, thought, action, and enlightenment through a variety of techniques. The American center is also the international headquarters of the World Shim Gum Do Association.

Membership: Not reported.

Sources:

http://www.shimgumdo.org/.

★2216★
American Zen College
16815 Germantown Rd. (Rte. 18)
Germantown, MD 20767

The American Zen College was founded in 1976 by Zen Master Gosung Shin, Ph.D, for the purpose of studying and practicing religion and philosophy. Zen Master Gosung Shin was ordained a priest of the Chogye Sect of Korean Buddhism by Ven. Zen Master Sul-Bong in 1956. He arrived in the United States in May 1969 from South Korea where he had been the abbot of three Zen Buddhist temples. Since his arrival, he has established Zen schools and centers in Virginia, Pennsylvania, New York, and the District of Columbia.

In 1976, Zen Master Gosung Shin settled on the 12-acre farm near Germantown, Maryland. There, a 7,000 square foot zendo and dharma hall has been erected. The building houses a library, kitchen, dining room, offices, and guest quarters. Other buildings on the farm have been renovated for dorm and resident space and an art gallery. An azalea garden surrounds a 30-foot pagoda of carved Indian limestone which houses Buddha Sakyamuni's Saria, pearl-like remains of the historic Buddha Sakyamuni. The Saria were donated to the college by the national treasury of South Korea and are the only Saria in the United States.

Membership: Not reported. In 1984 the American Zen College reported 2,500 members in three centers.

Periodicals: *Buddha World.*

Sources:

Shin, Gosung. *Zen Teachings of Emptiness.* Washington, DC: American Zen College Press, 1982.

★2217★
Buddhist Society for Compassionate Wisdom
86 Vaughan Rd.
Toronto, ON, Canada M6C 2M1

Alternate Address: Zen Buddhist Temple, 1710 W. Cornelia Ave., Chicago, IL 60657-1219.

The Buddhist Society for Compassionate Wisdom, formerly known as the Zen Lotus Society, was officially founded in 1975 in Toronto, Ontario, but its roots date from the arrival in the United States in 1967 of an independent Korean Zen monk, Samu Sunim (Sam-Woo Kim). Born in 1941 and orphaned as a child, Sunim entered the monastery at the age of 17. After completing his three-year novice training and ordination, he began Zen meditation training under the guidance of Zen master Solbong. While in training, he was drafted into the army (as required of all Koren youth) and, after serving in the military for one year, he deserted to honor his pacifist beliefs. Sunim then resumed his Zen training under Master Solbong while hiding out form the army in the Pomo-Sa monastery in the mountains near Pusan. In the winter of 1966, he fled to Japan. In 1967, with the aid of friends, he emigrated to New York City and began to conduct meditation for the public.

In 1968, circumstances forced Sunim to move to Montreal, where he taught meditation while perfecting English and learning French. He was married for a short time and became a Canadian citizen. In 1972, he moved to Toronto, where a Korean community existed, but his plans to pursue an academic career or form a temple were frustrated by a serious illness. After a three-year solo retreat in his basement apartment, he resumed his religious duties in 1975.

By 1979, support had grown to the point where a building could be purchased, and the society was formally incorporated. The name was subsequently changed to the Buddhist Society for Compassionate Wisdom. A branch temple was founded in Ann Arbor Michigan, in 1981 and incorporated as the Zen Buddhist Temple—Ann Arbor. For more than 10 years, that temple has organized a Peace Camp for children aged 3-15; the camp emphasizes peace, cooperation, mindfulness, and fun. Inspired by children attending the camp, composer and camp teacher Dr. Nathaniel Needle has written and produced two audio tapes, "Dharma Moon" and "Bottom of the Ocean," collections of American Buddhist songs. The Michigan temple also sponsors a Right Livelihood Fund under the direction of Dharma teacher Dr. Gerri Larkin. The fund is a four-year, non-denominational pilot program to finance and assist businesses that embrace the five Buddhist precepts and support a strategy of gentle, sustainable development. Since 1983, the society has also maintained a growing community of members in Mexico City.

A third temple of the Buddhist Society for Compassionate Wisdom opened in Chicago, Illinois, in June 1992. The society purchased a building formerly used by a Pentecostal church on the north side of Chicago, and renovated it as a Buddhist temple. The top floor has been transformed into a year-round urban meditation retreat center. Sunim had the idea for that center years before, when he was spending a weekend in the society's Ann Arbor temple. A strange woman asked to stay the night. It turned out she lived a short distance away but needed to get away from the chaos of her family and household, with all its telephones and televisions and computers. She stayed two nights. Sunim resolved to have space for such a center if he ever started another temple. The urban meditation retreat center is designed for people who are effectively trapped by their living circumstances and need a place for peace and contemplation.

All three temples in the Buddhist Society for Compassionate Wisdom conduct daily Buddhist religious services and meditation sessions, instruct beginners in basic and advanced meditation, and hold regular weekend meditation retreats. The society also holds quarterly three-to-five day Yongmaeng Chongjin (intensive retreats) and a biennial precept-taking ceremony in which more than 100 people participated in 1997. Temple members are active in promoting social affairs, environmental awareness, and right livelihood.

In 1986, the society organized and hosted the first "Second Generation Zen Teachers Conference" at the Ann Arbor temple. The following year, the society hosted an eight-day "Conference on World Buddhism in North America." This conference was also the first of its kind and provided a special opportunity for encounters between ethnic and Western Buddhist teachers in both the Theravada and Mahayana traditions. Teachers from the United States, Canada, and England were represented. On that occasion, Sunim began the Buddhist Movement for Justice and Peace, an initiative to express a committed Buddhist concern for social injustice and human rights abuses.

The first national "Conference on World Buddhism in Canada" was held in Toronto in 1990 with monks, nuns, priests, and lay teachers from ethnic and Western Buddhist organizations across Canada. In July 1995, the society hosted an inaugural " Conference for Academics Drawn to Buddhism" in Toronto. These conferences represent a strong and ongoing commitment to the cause of pan-Buddhism and are seen as the first of many such activities.

In 1993, in Chicago, Sunim attended the Centennial Parliament of the World's Religions as a member of the assembly of religious and spiritual leaders. Since then, he has served as member of the board of trustees of the Council for a Parliament of the World's Religions.

Through the 1980s, the society published a journal, *Spring Wind: A Buddhist Cultural Forum* due to begin a new series in 1998. In 1985 Sunim inaugurated a priest training program that has now evolved into the Maitreya Buddhist Seminary run by the Buddhist Society for Compassionate Wisdom. The program offers a three-year training for Dharma teachers, junior priests, and monks. In 1998 a total of 32 students were enrolled.

Membership: In 1998 the society reported approximately 700 members in the United States, 350 in Canada, and 50 in Mexico.

Educational Facilities: Maitreya Buddhist Seminary, Toronto, Ontario.

Periodicals: *Spring Wind: A Buddhist Cultural Forum.* • *Temple News.* Send orders to Ann Arbor Zen Buddhist Temple, 1214 Packard Rd., Ann Arbor, MI 48104.

★2218★
Chokling Tersar Foundation USA (CTF)
PO Box 5162
Petaluma, CA 94955-5162

The Chokling Tersar Foundation (CTF) was established in 1996 as the American center of the Chokling Tersar, a lineage of Tibetan Buddhism within the Gelugpa school (the largest of the four main Tibetan schools of Buddhism). The tradition is presently embodied in the lineage holders, the four sons of Tulku Urgyen. They periodically come to the United States to lead events at the foundation. The foundation, presently the only center of the tradition in North America, is attempting to establish a rural retreat center. The foundation's material is published by Rangjung Yeshe Publications.

Chokling Tersar literally means the "new treasures of Chokgyur Lingpa" and owes its name to the nineteenth-century Tibetan Buddhist master, Chogyur Dechen Lingpa (1829–1870), whose teachings are widely practiced by both the Kagyu and Nyingma schools of Tibetan Buddhism. The collection of teachings from Chokgyur Lingpa are contained in the Chokling Tersar, a body of literature filling more than 40 large volumes. The connected teachings included in these 40 volumes were written over the last 150 years, chiefly by his contemporaries Jamyang Khyentse Wangpo and Jamgon Kongtrul the Great, as well as by the subsequent upholders of the lineage down until today.

The Chokling Tersar literature is meant to be studied and practiced as an addition to the traditional canonical scriptures of Tibetan Buddhism. These are found in the Kangyur and Tengyur, the written words of Buddha Shakyamuni and their commentaries by learned Indian Masters. These two collections occupy respectively 104 and 273 large volumes. In these scriptures are found detailed instructions on how to take full advantage of and imbue human life with its fullest meaning. These revealed scriptures were concealed by the ninth-century Buddhist saint Padmasambhava with the expressed wish to be uncovered at specific times in the future. Many of them contain predictions for those times and which particular spiritual practices would be most beneficial for the people of those times.

The independent American branch of the Chokling Tersar tradition is concerned with preserving, translating, and disseminating these teachings, in the most authentic and principled way possible. CTF aims at doing so by first inviting learned and authentic holders of the Chokling Tersar lineage to lecture and provide appropriate spiritual counsel corresponding to the current public demand in North America.

Membership: Not reported. The foundation is affiliated with Ka-Nying Shedrub Ling in Nepal and Rangjung Yeshe Gomde Retreat Land in Denmark.

Sources:

Morreale, Don. *The Complete Guide to Buddhist America.* Boston: Shambhala, 1998.

★2219★
Han-Ma-Um Zen Center
617 B Hale Ave.
Morgan Hill, CA 95037

Alternate Address: Han-Ma-Um Zen Center: 101-62, Sukso-Dong, An Yang, Kyung GiDo, 430-040, Korea

: The Han-Ma-Um Zen Center was founded in 1972 by Tae-heng Se Nim, an ordained Buddhist woman, in a small town south of Seoul, on the side of Kwanak-san Mountain. Tae-heng Se Nim draws inspiration from the Chogye Sect, the main group of Korean Buddhism, to which she has added material drawn from the Zen

teachings of Hui-neng (638-713 C.E.), the Sixth Patriarch of Chinese Zen, and her own original insights.

From the center in Korea, Tae-heng Se Nim leads the residents into the practice of Zen meditation in a schedule that begins at 4 a.m. each morning with chanting and meditation before breakfast. The goal of the meditation is enlightenment, which includes the attainment of Han-Ma-Um, or "One Mind," a realization of the interrelatedness of all things. Residents at the center are also vegetarians.

During the 1980s, centers were established around Korea and in the United States. In 1989 a first text containing teachings by Tae-heng Se Nim was translated into English.

Membership: : Not reported. In 1989 there were two centers in the United States, one in California and one in Anchorage, Alaska.

Sources:

Tae-heng Se Nim. *In Search of the Genuine "I."* Edited by Haewon. Seoul, Korea: Lotus Flower Publishing Company, 1989. 112 pp.

★2220★
Korean Buddhist Bo Moon Order
% Bup Choon
Bul Sim Sa Temple
5011 N. Damen
Chicago, IL 60625

The Bo Moon Order is one of the eighteen registered Buddhist Orders in Korea. It came to the United States in 1979 when the Bul Sil Sa Temple was organized in Chicago. A second temple was organized in the Los Angeles suburb of Garden Grove in 1980.

Membership: Not reported.

★2221★
Korean Buddhist Chogye Order
% Kwan Um Sa Temple
4265 W. Third St.
Los Angeles, CA 90020

Not until the 1970s did significant numbers of Korean Buddhists migrate to the United States. Most of these were affiliated with the Chogye Order, the largest in Korea. In February 1973 the Thalmahsa Buddhist Monastery and temple was established in Los Angeles. It was soon followed a second Los Angeles temple and others which followed in various California locations; Chicago; New York City; Tacoma, Washington; Detroit; and Honolulu. During the 1980s the number continues to grow. These temples are to be distinguished from those of the Kwan Um Zen School (from which they are organizationally separate) as they serve primarily first generation Korean-Americans.

Membership: Not reported. In 1984 there were 23 Chogye Order temples in the United States and three in Canada.

Periodicals: *Buddhist Times.* Send orders to 4267 W. Third St., Los Angeles, CA 90020.

Sources:

Har, Baba Moo, ed. *Brief Introduction to Korean Buddhism.* Los Angeles: Korean Buddhist Sangha Association of Western Territories in U.S.A., 1984.

Korea Buddhism. Seoul, Korea Buddhist Chogye Order, 1986.

★2222★
Kwan Um Zen School
K. B. C. Hong Poep Won
RFD No. 5
528 Pound Rd.
Cumberland, RI 02864

The Kwan Um Zen School was founded in 1983 to connect the various temples and centers previously founded by Seung Sahn.

Soen Sa Nim, as he is generally referred to by his students, is the Seventy-eighth Patriarch in the Chogye Order. As a young man in Korea, he became deeply involved in radical politics but turned to Buddhism during World War II. He became a student of Zen Master Ko Bong and eventually abbot of two temples. After the war, he became a leader in the effort to revive the Chogye sect which had suffered much damage in the final years of Japanese occupation. In 1965 he traveled to Japan and during his stay founded three temples. In 1972 he came to the United States and began a small temple in Providence, Rhode Island. That temple became the headquarters from which he traveled around New England and across the United States. Early branch centers were established in New Haven, Connecticut; Cambridge, Massachusetts; and New York City; followed by centers in Los Angeles and Berkeley.

Master Seung Sahn came to the United States with a missionary zeal to plant a new Buddhist tradition in the West. He emphasizes that the purposes of Zen are, first, to understand the True Self, i.e. attain Truth, and, then, to assist other people to attain the "Great Love, Great Compassion, Great Bodhisattva Way." Most people have a significant amount of karma which forms an obstacle to enlightenment, hence the necessity of masters and centers. Like the Japanese Rinzai masters, Seung Sahn uses the koan as a major teaching device. Besides the main practice of daily sitting meditation, each center associated with the school sponsors a silent three- or seven-day meditation retreat called Yong Maeng Jong Jin (to leap like a tiger while sitting), equivalent to the sesshin or extended meditation sessions at Japanese Zen centers.

The growth of the center in Providence led to its purchase of a tract of land in rural Rhode Island upon which it developed a residential community and to which it eventually moved its headquarters. Throughout the early 1980s, Soen Sa Nim extended his travels and developed centers in South America and Europe, with special success in Poland. By the early 1990's, major centers had been established in Spain, Russia, and most of the newly opened countries of Eastern Europe. There is also an additional center in South Africa.

Membership: In 1991 the school reported 11 centers and 14 affiliated groups in the United States and one center and one group in Canada. Internationally there are centers in Germany, Korea, Poland, South Africa, and Spain. There were approximately 500 members.

Periodicals: *Primary Point.*

Sources:

Sahn, Seung. *Bone of Space.* San Francisco: Four Season's Foundation, 1982.

___. *Dropping Ashes on the Buddha.* Edited by Stephen Mitchell. New York: Grove Press, 1976.

___. *Only Don't Know.* San Francisco: Four Season's Foundation, 1982.

___. *Ten Gates.* Cumberland, RI: Primary Point Press, 1987.

Sunim, Mu Soeng. *Thousand Peaks, Korean Zen—Tradition and Teachers.* Berkeley, CA: Parallex Press, 1987.

★2223★
Morgan Bay Zendo
PO Box 188
Surry, ME 04684

One of the oldest presently existing Zen centers in the United States, what is today known as Morgan Bay Zendo was founded in 1971 as the Moonspring Hermitage by Walter Nowick. A professional pianist, Nowick initially practiced Zen at the First Zen Institute of America in New York City. Then, shortly after World War II, he became one of the early Americans to go to Japan for further study with Zuigan Goto Roshi at Daitokuji (where Ruth Fuller Everett Sasaki has also traveled). Seventeen years of work led to his being named roshi, the first Westerner in the Rinzai lineage. He

returned to the United States with some Japanese disciples and founded the Hermitage. He retired in 1985.

Since Nowick's retirement, the Hermitage reincorporated and has continued as the leaderless and independent Morgan Bay Zendo. Nowick and the Hermitage were the subject of a book by Dutch disciple of Goto Roshi, Jan van der Wetering.

Membership: Not reported.

Periodicals: *Morgan Bay Zendo—Newsletter.*

Sources:

Rawlinson, Andrew. *The Book of Enlightened Masters: Western Teachers in Eastern Traditions.* La Salle, IL: Open Court Press, 1997. 650 pp.

Van der Wetering, Jan. *A Glimpse of Nothingness.* London: Routledge and Kegan paul, 1975. 184 pp.

★2224★
Sixth Patriarch Zen Center
2584 Martin Luther King Jr. Way
Berkeley, CA 94704-2630

The Sixth Patriarch Zen Center is an independent Korean center in the Chogye tradition founded in Vancouver, British Columbia, in 1986 by the Ven. Hyunoong Sunim, a Buddhist monk and herbalist. It moved to Berkeley, California, in 1991. It has a dual emphasis on traditional Zen practice and health care through the use of correct diet, herbs, and a form of Korean Taoist breath meditation called Sun-do. The center is unique in its offering along with a regular schedule of sittings and retreats, a full program of health counseling, and classes.

Membership: Not reported. There is one center in Berkeley and one in Seattle, Washington.

Sources:

Morreale, Don. *The Complete Guide to Buddhist America.* Boston: Shambhala, 1998.

★2225★
Zen Wind
PO Box 4176
Santa Rosa, CA 95402

Zen Wind is a radical lay Buddhist movement initiated by Tundra Wind, a former student of Korean Zen Master Seung Sahn, the head of the Kwan Um Zen School. Under his given name, Jim Wilson, he was given permission to teach by Seung Sahn but was having problems with his sexuality. According to his account, when questioning his Master about his problems with remaining celibate, Seung Sahn said that he should simply satisfy his sexual desire and forget about it. Wilson rejected the idea, which seemed to imply that sex was merely physical.

He broke with Seung Sahn and following a dream in which his new name, Tundra Wind, was bestowed on him, he began to teach and to reformulate what he had been taught in a manner he believed more culturally suitable for the West. Included in his reformulation was a transformation of the precept not to misuse sex to a more positive admonition, "Express the sacredness of sexuality." His reformulation also made provision for Tundra Wind's own gay sexuality.

Among his students he has eschewed temples, monasteries, professional clergy, and even centers. Meetings are held in members' homes. He regularly offers introductory lectures, invites those who respond into ongoing meditation groups, and provides individual instruction for any who wish it. He leads two retreats annually.

Membership: Not reported.

Sources:

Morreale, Don. *The Complete Guide to Buddhist America.* Boston: Shambhala, 1998.

Tibetan Buddhism

★2226★
American Buddhist Society and Fellowship, Inc.
Current address not obtained for this edition.

One of the oldest Tibetan Buddhist centers in the United States is the American Buddhist Society and Fellowship founded in 1945 (incorporated in 1947) by Robert Ernest Dickhoff. French-born Dickhoff migrated to the United States in 1927. He became involved in the occult and claims that, "Out of the Invisible Realm of the Spirit of Tibet" he was given recognition by several spiritual entities including Maha Chohan K. H. (i.e., the ascended master Koot Hoomi, first brought to the attention of the West by Theosophist Helena Petrovna Blavatsky). He was given the titles "Red Lama" and "Most Reverend" and instructed to gather the Buddhists in American into a society. In 1950, according to Dickhoff, he was given the title of Grand Lama of the White Lodge of Tibet, See of New York, by the Dalai Lama.

During the 1960s, Dickhoff became known in UFO circles for his advocacy of the theory that UFOs were hostile. He believes that the UFOs are winged garudas (a bird-like demon in Buddhist thought), capturing humans and killing them for food.

Membership: Not reported. The society consists of one center in New York City.

Sources:

Dickhoff, Robert E. *Agharta.* Mokelumne Hill, CA: Health Research, 1964.

___. *Behold...the Venus Garuda.* New York: The Author, 1968.

Dickhoff, Robert Ernest. *The Eternal Fountain.* Boston, MA: Bruce Humphries, 1947.

★2227★
Arya Maitrya Mandala
Current address not obtained for this edition.

German-born Lama Anagarika Govinda (b.1898) began to think of himself as a Buddhist while still a teenager. Working as an archeologist, he was able to travel freely in southern Asia and also worked for the promotion of an ecumenical Buddhism in Europe. In 1931 he traveled to Tibet and studied under Tomo Geshe Rinpoche. In 1933, in honor of his guru, he founded the Arya Maitreya Mandala as a Buddhist order. (Maitreya, it is noted, was the only bodhisattva (saint) acceptable to all Mahayana Buddhist groups.) Centers of the order were first established in Germany and throughout Europe.

The Home of the Dharma was founded in San Francisco 1967 by the Rev. Iru Price as the American branch of the Arya Maitreya Mandala. The order is held together by a common acceptance of the ideal of the awakening of our innermost spirit, the "Buddhanature" within us. This ideal is expressed by making Buddhism a way of life, assisting those wishing to understand the Buddha's teaching, and developing methods of religious practice suitable to Western psychology. Lama Govinda made his first visit to the United States in 1969. He lectured and exhibited his paintings at the Zen Center of San Francisco. Since that time, he has made several tours teaching meditation.

The Home of the Dharma holds regular meetings and conducts an annual Wesak celebration in the spring to honor Buddha. The Kwan Yin Free School for refugee children is supported in Hong Kong.

Membership: Not reported. There is one American center of the Arya Maitreya Mandala.

Sources:

Govinda, Anagarika. *Creative Meditation and Multi-Dimensional Consciousness.* Wheaton, IL: Theosophical Publishing House, 1976.

___. *Foundations of Tibetan Buddhism.* New York: Humanities Press, 1959.

___. *The Psychological Attitude of Early Buddhist Philosophy.* London: Rider & Company, 1961.

"Special Meditation Issue." *Human Dimensions* 1, no. 4 (1972).

★2228★
Centers for Dzogchen Studies
% Center for Dzogchen Studies in New Haven
847 Whalley Ave.
New Haven, CT 06515

The Centers for Dzogchen Studies constitute a worldwide community of practitioners dedicated to the teachings and practices of the Longchen Nyingthig lineage centered at Kalsang Monastery in Tibet. They teach what is known as the Heart Tradition of Tibetan Buddhism. These teachings are understood by the practitioner through direct experience of resting in awareness. Such awareness practice introduces the practitioner directly to his/her mind. The practices teach that the awakened state already exists within, and allows the rediscovery of our Great Completeness (Dzogchen).

Consistent awareness practice brings the individual into direct contact with the constant flux of thought patterns, and observing the insubstantial nature of self reveals the continuity of awareness within all manifestations. The experience of naked presence is a living example of the manner in which the Buddha's truths manifest within. The Heart Tradition calls attention to the conceptual processes as they are. The center's teachers also believe that one need not become Buddhist to learn Dzogchen practice; it can, by itself, be of great benefit to one's overall health and well-being, by promoting a sense of calmness and clarity in life.

The Center for Dzogchen Studies was established in New Haven in 1994 after three practitioners invited Lama Padma Karma Rinpoche (b. 1952) from Asia to act as the center's spiritual guide. Raised as a Christian in the Virgin Islands, Rinpoche had a diverse religious background that culminated in his initial study of Buddhism beginning in 1985 after settling in China as a teacher. He was given the titles of "Vajra Master" and "Rinpoche" in 1992 by Ksertok Padma Dorje Tulku with the authorization to teach under the auspices of the Nyingma and Kagyu schools of Tibetan Buddhism, and more specifically, within the Longchen Nyingthig Lineage of Kalsang Monastery, Tibet.

Since settling in New Haven, he has trained three teachers—Dorje Lobpon Padma Dondrub, Tamara Wolfson, and Lama Randolph Derby—within the lineage. Tamara Wolfson and Lama Randolph Derby teach at the New Haven, Connecticut, center. Dorje Lobpon Padma Dondrub has established her own center in Rio de Janeiro, Brazil. Lama Peme Dzogtril opened the Sante Fe, New Mexico, center in 1995, and two years later, Lama Padma Karma Rinpoche established a new center in Darjeeling, India.

Membership: Not reported.

Sources:

http://sover.net/~dogstar/dzogeds.html/.

★2229★
Chagdud Gonpa Foundation
Box 279
Junction City, CA 96048

Alternate Address: Chagdud Gonpa Canada, 10071 No. 2 Road, Richmond, BC V7E Canada.

Chagdud Gonpa Foundation was established in 1983 by Chagdud Tulku Rinpoche (b.1930), a meditation master, artist, and Tibetan physician, born in Eastern Tibet. As the Abbot of Chagdud Gonpa monastery, established in 1131, Rinpoche received extensive instructions in all aspects of Tibetan Buddhism. He then fled Tibet at the time of the Chinese occupation in 1959 and helped to establish and administer several refugee camps in both India and Nepal.

He was contacted by Americans who made pilgrimages to northern India, and at the request of several American students, he came to the United States in 1979. From his American headquarters he has concentrated on developing Padma Publishing for the translation and printing of sacred texts and teachings of Buddhist masters; the founding of centers for practicing and preserving Vajrayana teachings; and the training of students in the Vajrayana philosophy, practices, and rituals.

The foundation's headquarters, Rigdzin Ling, located in the mountains north of Redding, California, is home to Mahakaruna Foundation, a nonprofit organization devoted to supporting Tibetan practitioners in Nepal, India, and Bhutan; Padma Publishing; and Tibetan Treasures, which distributed videos and cassette tapes of Rinpoche's talks. Among the projects of Padma Publishing is the translating of Tibetan teacher Longchempa's *Seven Treasuries*. The Stupa Project at Rigdzin Ling has undertaken the construction of eight Tibetan chtens.

Membership: Not reported. There are 18 centers and practice groups in the United States, two in Canada, and additional centers in Brazil.

Sources:

Chagdud Tulku Rinpoche. *Gates to Buddhist Practice*. Junction City, CA: Padma Publishing, n.d.

___. *Life in Relation to Death*. Junction City, CA: Padma Publishing, n.d..

___. *The Lord of the Dance*. Junction City, CA: Padma Publishing, n.d..

★2230★
Chapori-Ling Foundation Sangha
766 8th Ave.
San Francisco, CA 94118

The Chapori-Ling Foundation is a Nyingmapa Tibetan Buddhist center founded in the 1970s by Dr. Norbu L. Chen, formerly physician of Dharma Chakra Monastery in Kathmandu, Nepal. He received his basic instruction in Buddhism and Buddhist healing practices from refugees who had fled Tibet to Nepal following the 1959 Chinese invasion. He subsequently came to the United States and established Chakpori-Ling, named for a famous healing center just outside Lhasa, the capital of Tibet.

The Foundation operates a college which offers courses in Buddhism for prospective monks and nuns and training in oriental medicine. There is also a clinic for those who wish to receive treatment from an oriental physician.

Membership: Not reported. There is one center in San Francisco, California.

Educational Facilities: College of Oriental Medicine, San Francisco, California.

★2231★
Chicago Rime Center
4026 N. Kenmore, Ste. 1
Chicago, IL 60613

The Rime (or "nonpartisan") tradition with Tibetan Buddhism began in the nineteenth century in eastern Tibet by some scholars who saw the need to overcome sectarian bias in the evaluation of the doctrinal traditions of the various schools and to accept each tradition on its own merits. The movement was initiated by the Sakyapa teacher Jamyang Khyentse Wangpo (1820–1892). Among his students, the most important were Chogyur Dechen Lingpa (1829–1870) and Jamgon Kongtrul the Great (1811–1899), who compiled the "Five Great Treasures," a compendium of teachings and practices of the various Tibetan traditions. The fundamental attitude of unbiasedness of the movement was most evident in the person and work of Jamgon Kongtrul's recent incarnation, Jamgon Kongtrul Rinpoche (1954–1992), a Karma Kagyu teacher who established the Rigpe Dorje Foundation.

The Rime teachers and their students restructured doctrinal and practical materials, based on the example of the Gelugpa school. The process within the Rime movement of reviving transmissions of teachings that had been thought lost and providing them with fresh commentary also embraced the traditions of the other schools. Works of the Kagyupa, Sakyapa, Kadampa (a.k.a. Gelugpa) and Chod lineages are also found in the Rime collection of texts. Additionally, the Rime teachers advocated revival of the Tibetan Bon teachings.

The Chicago Rime Center is a Western outpost of the Rime tradition which supports the development, practice, and integration of the various schools of Tibetan Buddhism. While exploring the richness unique to each lineage, Chicago Rime Center honors the unity inherent within the vast spectrum of Tibetan Buddhist teachings. The center offers activities including weekly practice sessions and dharma talks and works to provide access to traditional teachings by notable masters within the larger Tibetan Buddhist tradition.

Membership: Not reported.

Sources:

http://quietmountain.com/dharmacenter/chicago_rime/

★2232★
Diamond Way Buddhism
% Diamond Way Buddhist Center
1110 Merced Ave.
San Francisco, CA 94127

The Diamond Way Tibetan Buddhist tradition grew out of the efforts of Lama Ole Nydahl and his wife Hannah Nydahl, the first western students of the 16th Gyalwa Karmapa. He recognized them as protectors of his lineage and asked them to work for him. Beginning in 1969, he spent three years training in the Himalayas, and then initiated his teaching activity in the West, initially in Europe. His work spread to America in the 1980s and there are now centers across the United States. Teachings and practice are similar to those found in the centers of the Karma Triyana Dharma Chakra, but are administratively separate.

Diamond Way centers recognize the spiritual authority of the 17th Karmapa, Thaye Dorje, who now resides in New Delhi, India. They have a democratic structure and members share the responsibility for guiding meditations, answering questions, and giving teachings. In addition, Lama Ole has trained some 30 students who are now traveling and teaching internationally.

The Karma Kagyu school offers a variety of methods for people to develop the mind's inherent richness and clarity in one's daily activities through the three emphases of (1) verifiable nondogmatic teachings, (2) meditation, and (3) the means to solidify the levels of awareness which have been attained. The Diamond Way is considered the most "skillful" methods of the Buddha to the modern world. As a lineage of direct oral transmission, Karma Kagyu treasures meditation and interaction with a qualified teacher. The teaching is traced to the historical Buddha Shakyamuni and his closest students. They were later passed on through the Indian Mahasiddhas: Padmasambhava, Tilopa, Naropa, and Maitripa, and the famous Tibetan Yogis Marpa and Milarepa. In the twelfth century, the monk Gampopa gave the teachings to the first Gyalwa Karmapa, who is believed to have regularly reincarnated to the present.

Membership: In 1998, there were 184 Diamond Way centers around the world. In the United States, centers could be found in San Francisco, Los Angeles, and Friendswood, Texas.

Sources:

Nydahl, Ole. *Entering the Diamond Way: My Path Among the Lamas.* Grass Valley, CA: Blue Dolphin Press, 1990. 251 pp.

___. *Mahamudra: Boundless Joy and Freedom.* Grass Valley, CA: Blue Dolphin Press, 1991. 96 pp.

___. *Riding the Tiger: Twenty Years on the Road: Risks and Joys of Bringing Tibetan Buddhism to the West*. Grass Valley, CA: Blue Dolphin Press, 1992. 512 pp.

★2233★
Drikung Dharma Centers
Current address not obtained for this edition.

The Drikung Dharma Centers are the American branch of the Drikung Kagyu Order, one school within the Kagyupa Tibetan Buddhist sect (which dates to Milarepa, the famous teacher). The order is unusual in that the lineage is carried by two heads simultaneously. In the early 1960s, one of the heads, His Holiness Drikung Kyabgon Chetsang Rinpoche, left Tibet for India. Unable to leave Tibet, His Holiness Chung Tsang, the other head of the order, was separated from his colleague for over twenty-five years, their first meeting being in India in 1985. The first American Drikung Center was founded under the auspices of the Drikung Kyabgon in 1978.

The Drikung Order is noted for its teachings on meditation, particularly the Drikung Phowa Meditation, a meditation intimately connected with the experience of death. Traditionally the Phowa Benediction was given every twelve years.

Membership: In 1985, there were two drikung centers, one in Washington, D.C. and one in Los Angeles, California.

★2234★
Dzogchen Foundation
PO Box 734
Cambridge, MA 02140-0006

The Dzogchen Foundation was organized in March 1991 by Lama Surya Das and a small group of Dzogchen practitioners. Lama Surya Das was born Jeffrey Miller (b. 1950) in New York and graduated from SUNY Buffalo (1971). He traveled throughout India and Nepal studying with various spiritual teachers. He was given the name Surya Das by Indian Hindu teacher Maharajji (Neem Karoli Baba) and he lived and practiced in Tibetan monasteries under the guidance of Ven. Lama Thubten Yeshe, Ven. Kalu Rinpoche, and His Holiness Gyalwa Karmapa. During 1977–80 he lived in Woodstock, New York, establishing the Karmapa's monastery, Karma Triyana Dharma Chakra. In 1980, he joined the first Nyingmapa retreat center in Dordogne, France, where he completed two traditional three-and-a-half-year retreats under the guidance of Dudjom Rinpoche and Dilgo Khyentse Rinpoche, with Tulku Pema Wangyal and Nyoshul Khenpo Rinpoche. During this time, he became a lama in the Non-Sectarian Practice Lineage of Tibetan Buddhism. Surya Das is a member of the International Padmakara Translation Committee and the organizer of the Western Buddhist Teachers Network and its Teachers' Conferences with the Dalai Lama in Dharamsala, India.

The foundation has set as its mission the preservation of the teachings of Dzogchen and to transmit them to Westerners in an accessible form. It accomplishes this mission by offering opportunities to receive the guidance of Dzogchen teachers and by fostering the activities and emergence of Dharma teachers in both the East and the West. It also promotes non-sectarian dialogue, understanding, and cooperation between the various traditions of Buddhism.

The foundation believes that the Buddhism of Tibet represents the last extant wisdom culture to survive intact from ancient times. As an isolated cloister land, Tibet preserved all the teachings of the Buddha which included the Theravadin, Mahayana, and tantric Vajrayana traditions of Buddhadharma. Many Buddhist sutras and commentaries in the Sanskrit language, which were lost in India during the Moslem invasions of northern India, were later discovered intact in Tibetan monastery libraries.

Dzogchen, practiced mainly by the Nyingma Lineage, is seen as the consummate practice of Tibetan Buddhism. It is also considered an advanced and secret teaching.

The foundation conducts an annual month-long intensive meditation retreat; publishes a newsletter and schedule of the activities of Lama Surya Das and other lamas; engages in the translation and publication of texts and oral teachings; and brings venerable lamas to America to teach purposes.

Membership: Not reported. Centers related to Lama Surya Das are found in Cambridge and Northampton, Massachusetts; San Francisco; and New Jersey.

Sources:

Surya Das, Lama. *Awakening the Buddha Within: Eight Steps to Enlightenment*. New York: Broadway Books, June 1997. 320 pp.

★2235★
Ewam Choden
254 Cambridge St.
Kensington, CA 94707

Ewam Choden was the first center of the Sakyapa sect of Tibetan Buddhism founded in the United States. Its founder, Lama Kunga Thartse Rinpoche, came to the United States in the 1960s and settled in Kensington, California. He opened Ewam Choden in 1971. The Sakyapa sect was the last great reform movement in Tibetan Buddhism. It was founded in 1071 C.E.. by K'on-dkon-mch'og rgyal-po, who taught a "reformed" tantra that still retained parts of the older tantra practices (which contained significant magical and sexual aspects). Present head of the sect is Sakya Trizin, who paid his first visit to America, and Ewam Choden, in 1977.

Ewan Choden means the integration of method and wisdom, compassion and emptiness, and possessing the Dharma (the true way of life taught by the Buddha). The center was established to practice and study Tibetan religion and culture. Lama Kunga established a program of meditation, classes and ceremonial observation of holy days. The center administers the Tibetan Relief Fund and Tibetan Pen-Pal program. Public meditation services are held on Sunday evenings.

Membership: Not reported. There is one urban center in Kensington, California, overlooking San Francisco Bay, with a second rural center projected for Grass Valley, California.

Sources:

"His Holiness Sakya Trizin, An Interview." *Wings* 1, no. 1 (September/October 1987): 36-38, 51-53.

★2236★
Foundation for the Preservation of the Mahayana Tradition (FPMT)
PO Box 800
Soquel, CA 95073

The Foundation for the Preservation of the Mahayana Tradition (FPMT) is a worldwide association of Tibetan Buddhist centers founded by Lama Thubten Yeshe and Lama Thubten Zopa Rinpoche, both trained in the gelugpa tradition of Tibetan Buddhism (the tradition associated with His Holiness the Dalai Lama). They met in 1959 when, as refugees from Tibet, they both settled in Buxaduar, India. The young Zopa Rinpoche was sent to Thubten Yeshe for further instruction. In 1965 the pair met Zina Ruchevsky, a Russian-American who was ordained as a nun in 1967. The three established the Kopan Monastery near Kathmandu in 1969.

The center in Nepal began to attract Western students, and in 1973 the International Mahayana Institute, an organization of Western nuns and monks, was located at Kopan Monastery. The first Indian outpost, Tushita Retreat Center, was opened in Dharmasala in 1972. That same year the Mount Everest Center for Buddhist Studies opened at Lawudo, Nepal, to educate Nepalese children.

In 1974, the two Lamas were invited to tour the West by C. T. Shen of the Institute for the Advanced Study of World Religions in New York. They toured the United States and spoke at most of the

Tibetan Buddhist centers as well as several universities. An American publication and lectures given on this tour brought them more students and the eventual development of several centers. In 1977 students donated 30 acres of land near Boulder Creek, California, for the development of a retreat center called Vajrapani Institute, and in 1980 one student donated 270 acres in rural Vermont which became Milarepa Center.

In 1984, Lama Thubten Yeshe passed away at Cedars Sinai Hospital in Los Angeles and was cremated at Vajrapani Institute. One year later, on February 12, 1985, a boy was born in Spain who was later identified as Lama Yeshe's reincarnation. This boy, named Tenzin Osel Rinpoche, is now enrolled in Sara Je Monastery in India where he will be receiving both a traditional Tibetan education and a modern western education to prepare him for his future role as the spiritual head of the FPMT.

In the last two decades, FPMT has become a worldwide movement and recently moved its world headquarters to the United States from Europe. Wisdom Publication, now located in Boston, Massachusetts, distributes a wide array of books on Buddhism and related topics. A line of English-language books on Tibetan Buddhism have appeared as the Wisdom Basic Books (Orange Series), Intermediate Books (White Series), and Advanced Books (Blue Series).

Membership: In 1997 there were 18 centers affiliated with FPMT in the United States and 82 additional centers worldwide.

Periodicals: *Mandala.*

Sources:

Hopkins, Jeffrey. *The Tantric Distinction.* London: Wisdom Publications, 1984.

Amipa, Lama Sherab Gyaltsen. *The Opening of the Lotus.* London: Wisdom Publications, 1987.

MacKenzie, Vicki. *The Boy Lama.* San Francisco: Harper & Row, n.d.

Rabten, Geshe. *The Essential Nectar.* London: Wisdom Publications, 1984.

Rabten, Geshe, and Geshe Ngawang Dhargyey. *Advice from a Spiritual Friend.* New Delhi, India: Publications for Wisdom Culture, 1977.

Yeshe, Thubten, and Thubten Zopa. *Wisdom Energy.* Honolulu, HI: Conch Press, 1976.

★2237★
Ganden Tekchen Ling
Deer Park
4548 Schneider Dr.
Oregon, WI 53575

The Ganden Mahayana Center was formed in the mid-1970s by a group of students who had gathered around Geshe Lhundup Sopa, a professor in the Buddhist Studies Program at the University of Wisconsin at Madison. Sopa had been a teacher at the monastery at Sera until the Chinese invasion of Tibet. He fled to India but was sent to Labsum Shedrub Ling, the monastery in New Jersey in 1965 as a tutor for young monks. In 1968 he joined the faculty at the University of Wisconsin. Once formed, the center created Deer Park, a grove named after the place near Benares, India, where Buddha first taught, three miles from the university campus. A full program of both academic instruction in Buddhist, Tibetan and related subjects as well as facilities for the practice of traditional Tibetan Buddhism was offered.

The Center follows the branch of Tibetan Buddhism taught by the Dalai Lama and has, on several occasions, hosted the Dalai Lama, including his first American visit in 1979. In 1981, prior to the Dalai Lama's visit, the Center purchased acreage near Oregon, Wisconsin, and transferred its program to the new center. That new center was the site of the first performance in the West of the Kalachakra Initiation Ceremony by the Dalai Lama. The Kalachakra tantric path is one method of practicing Buddhist med-

itation which is considered for those who wish to progress speedily through intense meditational activity.

Membership: In 1981 the Center had 80 members.

Sources:

Gyatso, Tenzin. *The Buddhism of Tibet and the Key to the Middle Way.* New York: Harper & Row, 1975.

Gyatsho, Tenzin, the 14th Dalai Lama. *The Opening of the Wisdom-Eye.* Wheaton, IL: Theosophical Publishing House, 1972.

Kalachakra Initiation, Madison, 1981. Madison, WI: Deer Park, 1981.

Keegan, Marcia, ed. *The Dalai Lama's Historic Visit to North America.* New York: Clear Light Publications, 1981.

Sopa, Geshe Lhundub. *The Wheel of Time.* Madison, WI: Deer Park Books, 1985.

Sopa, Geshe Lhundup, and Jeffrey Hopkins. *Practice and Theory of Tibetan Buddhism.* New York: Grove Press, 1976.

★2238★
Jetsun Sakya Center
Current address not obtained for this edition.

Jetsun Sakya Center is a small Sakyapa center founded in 1977 by Dezhung Rinpoche. Like Ewam Choden, it is under the Sakya Trizin, the head of the Sakyapa Order who resides in India, but is organizationally separate.

Membership: Not reported.

★2239★
Kagyu Dharma
127 Sheafe Rd.
Wappingers Falls, NY 12590

Kagyu Dharma is the collective name given the several centers established by Kalu Rinpoche, a teacher of the Kargyupa sect of Tibetan Buddhism. Rinpoche studied at the Palpung Monastery in eastern Tibet. He left Tibet in 1957 to establish a monastery in Bhutan, at the request of the queen. He then settled at Sonada, Darjeeling, India, and established his own center, Samdup Tarjeyling Monastery. He trained a number of monks especially to head centers in the West, and during the 1970s he started centers in Europe and North America. Focus of the European work is in Belgium at the urban center in Antwerp and the rural retreat at Huy. Each center carries on a regular format of worship and meditation which follows a daily, weekly, and lunar month schedule.

Among the American centers, Kagyu Droden Choling in San Francisco is most active. It is headed by Lama Lodo, the author of several books, and administers a publishing arm, KDK Publications, which publishes books in both Tibetan and English. Khawachen Dharma Center in Anchorage, Alaska is an eclectic Buddhist center under the direction of N. Paljor, and it receives guidance from one of Rinpoche's students, Lama Karma Rinchen of Hawaii.

Rinpoche died in 1989. Several years later a young child born in 1990 was recognized by both the Dalai Lama and Tai Situ Rinpoche as the reincarnation of Rinpoche. The child is now being raised as Kalu returned and is traveling performing official ritual functions.

Membership: Not reported. North American centers can be found in New York, California, Oregon, Washington, Hawaii, and British Columbia, Canada.

Periodicals: *Dundrub Yong* (Song of Fulfillment). Available from Kagyu Droden Kunchab, 3476 21st St., San Francisco, CA 94110.

Sources:

Dorje, Kakhyab. *A Continuous Rain to Benefit Others.* Vancouver, BC: Kagyu Kunhyab Chuling, n.d.

Lodo, Lama. *Bardo Teachings.* San Francisco: KDK Publications, 1982.

Lodru, Lama. *Attaining Enlightenment*. San Francisco, CA: Kagyu Droden Kunchab Publications, 1979.

McLeod, Kenneth, trans. *The Total Flowering of Activity to Help Others*. Vancouver, BC: Kagyu Kunchab Chuling, 1975.

___. *The Chariot for Traveling the Path to Freedom*. San Francisco, CA: Kagyu Dharma, 1985.

Palzang, Rikzin, trans. *Prayers for Generating Guru Devotion*. San Francisco, CA: Kagyu Droden Kunchab Publications, 1979.

★2240★
Kampo Gangra Drubgyudling
200 Balsam Ave.
Toronto, ON, Canada M4E 3C3

The Kampo Gangra Drubgyudling was founded in 1973 as the Canadian center of Tibetan Buddhist teacher Vajra Archaya Lama Karma Thingley Rinpoche. Karma Thinley Rinpoche (b.1931) was born in Tibet and recognized at the age of two-and-a-half as the reincarnation of Beru Shaiyak Lama Kunrik, a Sakya master, by Sakya Trizin, the head of the Sakya School of Tibetan Buddhism. At a later date he was also recognized by H. H. the 16th Gyalwa Karmapa, head of the Kagyu tradition, as the fourth Karma Thinleypa, a highly realized bodhisattva of the Kagyu lineage. In addition to his position as a master of the Kagyu and Sakya schools, Rinpoche is also widely learned in the Nyingma and Gelug traditions. In 1974, His Holiness the Gyalwa Karmapa appointed him a Lord of Dharma of the Karma-Kagyu lineage. Karma Thinley Rinpoche resides in Toronto.

The Marpa Gompa Meditation Society (Tibetan: Marpa Gompa Changchub Ling) was founded in 1977 as the Alberta center of Thinley Rinpoche's work. It has as a resident dharma teacher Choge Susan Hutchison (Karma Khandro). Besides his centers in Canada, Karma Tingley Rinpoche has followers in England, whom he has placed under the care of Lama Jampa Thaye as his Dharma regent. Teaching is primarily from the Kagyu tradition.

Membership: Not reported. There is a center in Toronto; in Calgary, Alberta; and in England (Kagyu Dechen Dzong) at Harrowgate, Yorkshire.

Sources:

Morreale, Don. *The Complete Guide to Buddhist America*. Boston: Shambhala, 1998.

★2241★
Karma Triyana Dharmachakra
352 Meads Mountain Rd.
Woodstock, NY 12498

Karma Triyana Dharmachakra was begun in 1978 when Khenpo Karthar Rinpoche came to America to establish a monastery and retreat center at the direction of His Holiness, the Gyalwa Karmapa, head of the Karma Kagya branch of Tibetan Buddhism. The Gyalwa Karmapa had developed a vision of the center as a seat of the Kagya lineage in the Americas and a base from which the teachings of the lineage could spread in the Western hemisphere. Since 1982, a new monastery building has been under construction. Besides establishing the monastery, Rinpoche and his associates have traveled the United States teaching and organizing centers, each of which bear the name, "Karma Thegsum Choling."

Khenpo Kathar Rinpoche was born in 1922 in Eastern Tibet and entered the monastic community at the age of 12. He left Tibet in 1959, when the Chinese overran the land, and settled in Sikkim. He later served as abbot of the Tashi Choling Monastery in Bhutan and then the Tilokpur Nunnery in Northern India.

Internationally, the Karma Kagya lineage is headed by four coregents Sharmar Rinpoche, Tai Sita Rinpoche, Jamgon Kongtrul Rinpoche, and Gyaltsap Rinpoche. They have led since 1981 when the previous Karmapa (head to the lineage) died, the present

incornation, as of the beginning of 1988, had not yet been recognized.

Membership: In 1988 there were 22 centers in the United States, and two in South America.

Periodicals: *Densal*. Available from Karma Triyana Dharmachakra, 352 Meads Mountain Rd.; Woodstock, NY 12498.

Sources:

Karthar Rinpoche, Khenpo. *Dharma Paths*. Edited by Laura M. Roth. Ithaca, N.Y.: Snow Lion Publications, 1992.

★2242★
Kathok Shendrup Ling Center
5516 Vallejo St.
Oakland, CA 94608-2624

Kathok Shendrup Ling is the center established by Lama Kadag Choying Dorje (Lingtrul Rinpoche), a teacher of the Kathok lineage within the Nyingma School of Tibetan Buddhism. Lingtrul is the abbot of Draling Gompa, a monastery in Tibet with approximately 1,000 monks. He is also the lineage holder of what are termed the Great Perfection Teachings of the Ancients (Dzogchen), and believed by his followers to be a reincarnation of an emanation of the fourteenth-century Tibetan teacher Gwalwa Longchenpa, known as the author of a book published in the West as *Kindly Bent to Ease Us*.

Lingtrul Rinpoche was born in Amdo-Golok, Tibet, and recognized to be an incarnation of Ling Lama Dorje, a high lama of Eastern Tibet at the age of three. Ling Lama Dorje had earlier been recognized as the incarnation of the daughter of King Trisong Detsun, and of Longchenpa. However, due to the Chinese occupation of Tibet, the recognition and subsequent enthronement of Lingtrul Rinpoche occurred in secret, and as a young tulku, he was forced to work in labor camps and serve the needs of the Chinese government.

Lingtrul Rinpoche studied under his root teacher, the great Khenpo Munsel, Thubten Tsultrim Gyatso, who passed on the lineage of the Clear Light Great Perfection which began with Dharmakaya Buddha Kuntuzangpo and was passed to Longchenpa and eventually to Khenpo Munsel. Lingtrul Rinpoche received all the transmissions of Clear Light Great Perfection, Dzogchen, Ati-yoga, and over many years in retreat accomplished all the stages of development. He also received an extensive transmission of the Seven Treasures of Longchenpa, all other important Longchen Nyingthig transmissions, and a number of additional teachings from key Tibetan Buddhist masters.

Membership: Not reported.

Sources:

Morreale, Don. *The Complete Guide to Buddhist America*. Boston: Shambhala, 1998.

★2243★
Kunzang Odsal Palyul Changchub Choling
18400 River Rd.
Poolesville, MD 20837

Kunzang Odsal Palyul Changchub Choling (KOPCC) is a Tibetan Buddhist organization in the Nyingmapa tradition formed in 1982 as the World Prayer Center. It was founded by Jetsunma Ahkon Lhamo. KOPCC carries on a full program of teachings in Buddhism and practice sessions in Buddhist meditation. It conducts weekly classes and lectures and sponsors periodic retreats and workshops. Members are active in sponsoring Tibetan refugee children and youth. KOPCC owns a 65-acre wildlife refuge.

Membership: In 1993 there were approximately 150 members.

Educational Facilities: The Migyur Dorje Institute, Poolesville, Maryland.

Longchen Nyingthig Buddhist Society
Box 302
Harris, NY 12742

The Longchen Nyingthig Buddhist Society was founded in New York City by the Venerable Tsede Lhamo, Rhenock Chamkusho. The Longchen Nyingthig lineage extends unbroken to Padmasambhava, the famous teacher recognized as the founder of the Nyingmapa branch of Tibetan Buddhism. The teachings, which require intensive practice and close contact between student and teacher, offer the possibility of attaining permanent Buddhahood in a single lifetime. Its present leader, a female, Rhenock Chamkusko, was the daughter of Kyungtrul Pema Wangchen, a Nyingmapa rinpoche. Following the death of her father when she was only three years old, she was taken to study with another female guru, Jetsun Lochen Rinpoche. This guru's monastery was on White Brow Mountain where centuries earlier Nyingma Lama Gwalwa Longchenpa had founded the Longchen Nyingthig lineage.

In 1948 Chamkusko married Sonam Kazi, and in 1956 went with him to establish a monastery in Sikkim. Discovered by American pilgrims, they were invited to move to the United States, which they did in 1969. They established the Longchen Society. In 1972 the Dzogchen Pema Choling Meditation Center was opened in Philadelphia. The retreat center, which now serves as headquarters, was added in 1975.

Membership: Not reported. There are three centers and less than 200 members.

★2245★
Mahasiddha Nyingmapa Center
Box 87
Charlemont, MA 01339

The Mahasiddha Ningmapa Center is a small Nyingma center under the direction of Dodrup Chen Rinpoche. Students carry out a daily schedule of meditation and chanting.

Membership: In 1988, there were 25 members of the center.

Sources:

Thondup, Tulku. *Buddhist Civilization in Tibet.* Cambridge, MA: Maha Siddha Nyingmapa Center, 1982.

★2246★
Namo Buddha Seminar
1390 Kalmia Ave.
Boulder, CO 80304

Alternate Address: International Headquarters: Thrangu Tashi Choeling-Monastery, Namo Buddha Retreat Centre, PO Box 1287, Kathmandu, Nepal. Canadian Headquarters: Karma Tashi Ling, 10762 82nd Ave., Edmonton, AB T6E 2A8.

The Namo Buddha Seminar is a Kagyu Tibetan Buddhist group founded in 1988. Its spiritual leader is Khenpo Thrangu Rinpoche (b. 1933). In the fifteenth century, the seventh Gyalwa Karmapa Chodrak Gyatso (1454–1506) visited the region of Thrangu in Tibet, and he established Thrangu Monastery. He also enthroned Sherap Gyaltsen as the first Thrangu Rinpoche, and asserted that he was the re-established emanation of Shubu Palgyi Senge, one of the 25 great siddha disciples of Guru Padmasambhava, the eighth-century saint who brought Buddhism to Tibet.

The present, ninth incarnation of Thrangu Rinpoche is an eminent scholar. When he was four, H. H. the Gyalwa Karmapa and Palpung Situ Rinpoche recognized him as the incarnation of Thrangu Tulku by prophesying the names of his parents and the place of his birth. At the age of 23 he received ordination from H. H. Karmapa, along with Chogyam Trungpa Rinpoche (the founder of Vajradhatu International) and Surmang Garwang Rinpoche. He was introduced to the Absolute Nature by Lama Khenpo Gangshar

Wangpo. At the age of 27 he went to Rumtek Monastery in Sikkim at the direction of H. H. Karmapa. Today he is the holder of the zhentong lineage handed down by Jamgon Kongtrul the Great.

Upon his return to Rumtek he was named Khenpo (abbot) of Rumtek and the Kagyu sect. Since then he has been the personal tutor of the four main great Karma Kagyu tulkus. Thrangu Rinpoche, along with Khenpo Tsultrim Gyamtso Rinpoche (who succeeded Jamgon Kongtrul Rinpoche as head of the Rigpe Dorje Foundation), serves as the head Khenpo of the Nalanda Institute for Higher Buddhist Studies at Rumtek Monastery. In 1976 he founded the retreat center Namo Buddha in Nepal, and in 1981 he started to build his own *shedra* (college), Thrangu Tashi Choling, in Boudhanath, Kathmandu. In 1986 Thrangu Rinpoche accepted Chogyam Trungpa Rinpoche's invitation to be the Abbot of Gampo Abbey in Nova Scotia, Canada, Thrangu Rinpoche's first monastery in North America.

Membership: In 1998, the Namo Buddha Seminar reported 100 members in two centers in the United States, and a similar number in Canada. Additional centers are found in Nepal, India, Hong Kong, Malaysia, Taiwan, Tibet, Thailand, Great Britain, Germany, and Canada.

Educational Facilities: Thrangu Tashi Choling, Boudhanath, Kathmandu, Nepal.

Periodicals: *Namo Buddhist Seminar.*

★2247★
Nechung Drayang Ling
Box 250
Pahala, HI 96777

In 1972, the head of the Nyingmapa branch of Tibetan Buddhism visited Hawaii. Inspired by his visit, a group of students initiated efforts to bring a teacher to live on the islands permanently. One of their number consulted with the Dalai Lama concerning that possibility. The students had acquired the Woods Valley Temple, a Nichiren Buddhist temple at Pahala, Hawaii, which had been abandoned when Japanese workers moved out of the area. They found a teacher, Nechung Rinpoche in 1975. He was an accomplished master of both the Gelug and the older Nyingma branches of Tibetan Buddhism. Shortly after his arrival, a second center was opened in Honolulu, Hawaii, and periodically meetings are held on the other islands. Nechung Rinpoche attempts to integrate the practices and teachings of all the branches of Buddhism, and the center has been host to a wide variety of Tibetan Buddhist teachers who have come to Hawaii.

The center, five miles from Pahala, has a full schedule of lectures, daily meditation sessions, and ceremonies. A retreat center, formerly a Japanese Buddhist temple moved to the rural location from the town of Pahala, has become a retreat facility which can accomodate approximately 20 people. Contact is kept with the Nechung Dorje Drayang Ling Monastery in Dharmasala, India, considered the mother of the Hawaiian work. There is also a Nechung Monastery in Lhasa, Tibet, which has about 25 monks in residence.

Membership: In 1988, four people lived at the Woods Valley temple, though the population may swell to around 25 during retreats. Approximately 40 monks live at the monastery in Dharmasala.

Periodicals: *Newsletter.*

★2248★
New Kadampa Tradition (NKT)
℅ Mahakankala Buddhist Center
1B N. Alisos St.
Santa Barbara, CA 93103

Alternate Address: International Headquarters: Manjushri Mahayana Buddhist Centre, Conishead Priory, Ulverston, Cumbria, UK LA12 9QQ.

The New Kadampa Tradition of Tibetan Buddhism originated in the mid-1970s and the movement of the Ven. Geshe Kelsang Gyatso (b. 1931) to the West. He had been born in Tibet but left after the Chinese takeover. He trained for 19 years in the Tibetan monasteries of Jampaling and Sera-Je under his Spiritual Guide, the Ven. Trijang Rinpoche, before entering into a meditation retreat in the Himalayas for almost 20 years. In 1977 he was invited to England as the Resident Teacher at the Manjushri Mahayana Buddhist Centre in England, where he has remained ever since.

The Kadampa Tradition is traced to Atisha (982–1054 C.E.), who brought Buddhism to Western Tibet (1042) from India. He emphasized guru devotion and the need for a monastic disciple. His work was carried on by his disciple Dromton (1088–1164) who largely shaped the tradition. It was eventually passed to Je Tsong Khapa (1357–1419), who helped revive Buddhism across Tibet during a time it was at a low ebb. In more recent centuries the Kadampa tradition has become a branch of the Gelugpa Tibetan Buddhist School.

The New Kadampa Tradition has been created to present the old teaching in a manner which communicates with modern Westerners. To that end, Geshe Kelsang has published some 15 books ranging from volumes for beginners to detailed and lucid expositions of the profundities of Buddhist philosophy. He proposes the following of Atisha's instructions, called "Lamrim" or "Stages of the Path," which combines study and spiritual practice.

Membership: Not reported.

Periodicals: *Ocean of Nectar.*

Remarks: The New Kadampa tradition has become widely known for its involvement in a controversy internal to the Gelugpa School headed by the H. H. Dalai Lama. On July 13, 1978, in exile, the Dalai Lama gave a talk in which he attempted to discredit the worship of Dorje Shugden, a Tibetan Buddhist deity, who was enormously popular amongst the people of Gelugpa School. The worship of Dorje Shugden was also a practice of the Dalai Lama's own principal spiritual teacher, Kyabje Trijang Rinpoche.

The continued discrediting of Dorje Shugden led to the suppression of worship and some discrimination against those who continued the practice. The Dalai Lama raised the controversy to a new level in 1996 when in the main Thekchen Choeling Temple near Dharamsala, he publicly declared Dorje Shugden to be an evil Chinese spirit who was harmful to Tibetan independence and to the Dalai Lama's life. He then took the extraordinary step of banning the worship of Dorje Shugden and initiating its forcible suppression within the exile Tibetan communities. This action infuriated many who felt forced to choose between the Dalai Lama and their own traditional spiritual practice.

The New Kadampa Tradition has been the main supporter of Dorje Shugden among practitioners of Tibetan Buddhism in the West. The controversy, which pitched the Dalai Lama against the New Kadampa Tradition, was further escalated by a NKT campaign during the Dalai Lama's European visit in the summer of 1996. Then in February 1997 three of the Dalai Lama's close disciples were murdered near Dharamsala, India. Again, on May 3, 1998, followers of Dorje Shugden (including NKT members) demonstrated against the Dalai Lama in New York during his visit there, and no end of the controversy is in sight.

Sources:

Batchelor, Stephen. "Letting Daylight into Magic: The Life and Times of Dorje Shugden." *Tricycle: The Buddhist Review* 7, 3 (spring 1998): 60-66.

Kay, David. "The New Kadampa Tradition and the Continuity of Tibetan Buddhism in Transition." *Journal of Contemporary Religion* 12, 3 (October 1997): 277-93.

Lopez, Jr., Donald S. "Two Sides of the Same God" *Tricycle: The Buddhist Review* 7, 3 (spring 1998): 67–69.

★2249★
Padmasamblava Buddhist Centers
Box 1533, Old Chelsea Station
New York, NY 10011

The Padmasamblava Buddhist Centers (named for the eighth-century Tibetan saint) comprise a set of Nyingma Buddhist practice groups tied together by the teaching activity of Khenpo Tsewang Dongyal Rinpoche and Khenchen Palden Sherab Rinpoche, both students of H. H. Dudjom Rinpoche, head of the Nyingma lineage within Tibetan Buddhism. The members gather annually for a summer retreat at Padma Samye, a retreat center in upstate New York. The rest of the year the teachers travel between their centers, which are found across the United States, and in Puerto Rico and Russia.

Membership: Not reported. As of 1998 there were nine centers in the United States plus one in Puerto Rico.

Sources:

Morreale, Don. *The Complete Guide to Buddhist America.* Boston: Shambhala, 1998.

http://www.padmasambhava.org/info/.

★2250★
Palyul Changchub Dhaegye Ling
Box 1514
Mill Valley, CA 94941

Palyul Changchub Dhaegye Ling was established in 1996 by Khenpo Tsewang Gyatso Rinpoche, the American representative of the Palyul branch of the Nyingma tradition of Tibetan Buddhism. The Palyul Nyingma date to 1665 C.E. in Eastern Tibet. The supreme head of the Palyul Buddhists is H. H. Padma Nornu ("Penor") Rinpoche, the eleventh throne holder of Palyul. His seat is currently at the Namdroling Monastery of Byla-Kuppe, India.

In February 1997, H. H. Penor Rinpoche recognized actor Steven Seagal as a tulku, the reincarnation of Chungdrag Dorje of Palyul Monastery. Later that year he toured the United States to formally open his newly established centers.

Membership: Not reported. There is one center in California and one in Colorado.

Sources:

Morreale, Don. *The Complete Guide to Buddhist America.* Boston: Shambhala, 1998.

http://www.palyul.org/.

★2251★
Pansophic Institute
(Defunct)

The Pansophic Institute was founded in 1973 in Reno, Nevada, by Simon Grimes (Simon Theurgos, Choskyi Palden Konchog Chopel). One of its main goals was to bring the concepts of Tibetan Vajrayana (tantric) Buddhism into the mainstream of Western thought. The Pansophic Institute was most closely related to the Gelugpa sect of which the Dalai Lama is the head. In the eleventh century, Atisha Dipankara came from India and began a great reformation of the Tibetan practices. Atisha's work was followed up in the fifteenth century by Tsong Khapa. He introduced strict discipline and the practices of the mendicant monks. Vajradhara was the Buddha, and there was a strong belief in Maitreya, "the coming Buddha." The strong discipline was based on the authority of the Dalai Lama. By the seventeenth century, the Gelugpa sect became the established religion of Tibet.

One of the leading monasteries of the Gelugpa was Tashi Lhunpo Monastery near Shigatse. The successive reincarnations of its hierarch, beginning with the scholar Kas Grub-Je, were, according to tradition, installed as the Panchen Rinpoche. The sixth Panchen Rinpoche was Choskyi Nyima (1883-1937). It was prophesied that the line of the Panchen Rinpoche would disappear from Asia and reappear in the West with the mission of unifying Eastern and Western thought as the foundation of world culture. Many came to believe Simon Grimes, the founder of the Pansophic Institute who was born in North China, was the reincarnation of the sixth Panchen Lama.

According to the Pansophic Institute, the most important concept of Vajrayana Buddhism was "Mahamudra," total awareness of one's consciousness. It contained the seed of enlightenment and was the goal of meditation. A seven-point ethical code was adhered to: abstain from injury to other beings, taking what is not given, sexual obsessions, making false claims and slandering others; work to maintain conscious, clear awareness in oneself and others; cultivate this ethical code in oneself and in mankind.

The institute developed branch centers throughout the United States and in Canada, Australia, India, Nepal, and several countries in West Africa. It functioned through its School of Universal Wisdom and Church of Universal Light. The curriculum included Tibetan religion and culture, meditation, spiritual healing, parapsychology, comparative religion, esoteric (gnostic) cosmologies, and the four types of theurgy (tantra as adapted to the West). The institute also promotes planetary understanding, peace, and unity.

Membership: After two decades of activity, the institute ceased its operations in the early 1990s.

Educational Facilities: School of Universal Wisdom, Reno, Nevada.

Periodicals: *Clear Light.*

Sources:

The Graduated Path to Liberation. Reno, NV: Pansophic Institute, 1972.

Grimes, Simon. *The Flaming Diamond.* Reno, NV: Pansophic Institute, 1974.

★2252★
Rigpa Fellowship
℅ Orgyen Cho Lin
PO Box 607
Santa Cruz, CA 95061-0607

Alternate Address: International Headquarters 44 St. Paul's Crescent, London NW1 9TN, England.

Rigpa Fellowship is an association of Tibetan Buddhist meditation centers under the direction of Sogyal Rinpoche. Rinpoche is an incarnate lama of the Dzogchen lineage who studied first under Jamyang Khyentse Choekyi Lodroe, and then in the mid-1970s he accompanied the Dalai Lama on his first trip to the west, remaining behind in to attend Cambridge University. He founded Orgyen Choe Ling in London and attracted students in France and the United States and most recently in Australia. Rinpoche teaches dzoghen meditation, believed to be the final and ultimate teaching of Buddha, which brings the precise experience of the awakened state. Tapes and booklets by Rinpoche are circulated by Sound of Dharma in Santa Cruz, California. Radio shows consisting of interviews with Rinpoche are distributed to stations by New Dimensions Radio in San Francisco. Rinpoche resides in England but makes regular visits to the United States and conducts an annual weeklong retreat for students. In 1985 Rigpa hosted the first visit to the United States by the Dzogchen Rinpoche, Jugme Losel Wangpo.

Membership: In 1988 the fellowship reported 300 members in 11 centers in the United States. There were several thousand members in centers around the world including France, Ireland, Germany, the Netherlands, Switzerland, Australia, New Zealand, Japan, and India.

Sources:

Rinpoche, Sogyal. *Face to Face Meditation Experience.* London: Orgyen Choe Ling, 1978.

___. *View, Meditation and Action.* London: Dzogchen Orgyen Choe Ling, 1979.

★2253★
Rigpe Dorje Foundation
℅ Rigpa Dorje Center
PO Box 690995
San Antonio, TX 78269

The Rigpe Dorje Foundation was founded by His Eminence Jamgon Kongtrul Rinpoche (1954–1992), a Tibetan teacher believed by his followers to be the mind incarnation of Lodro Thaye, Jamgon Kongtrul the Great (1813–1899), pioneer of the nineteenth-century Rime Movement (an effort to overcome the difference among the major schools of Tibetan Buddhism). He also is believed to be the incarnation of Taranatha and Khyungpo Naljor, founders of the Jonangpa and Shangpa lineages. In 1948, when he was but six years old, the 16th Gyalwa Karmapa enthroned him and while growing up he lived and studied under the Karmapa's guidance at Rumtek Monastery in Sikkim.

Continuing the activity of the previous Kongtrul incarnations, he established retreat centers in Nepal and India. In his belief that Eastern wisdom and Western knowledge can combine to understand and resolve many contemporary problems, he initiated the Buddhism and Psychotherapy Conference in New York. He also funded Paramita Charitable Trust and the Rigpe Dorje Foundations in the United States, Canada, and Europe through which his followers have supported projects of educational, medical, social, and cultural development, mainly in India.

Jamgon Rinpoche was killed in Siliguri, India, in 1992 in a car accident. His work was assumed by Khenpo Tsultrim Gyamtso Rinpoche.

Membership: Not reported.

Sources:

Morreale, Don. *The Complete Guide to Buddhist America.* Boston: Shambhala, 1998.

★2254★
Sakya Monastery of Tibetan Buddhism
108 NW 83rd St.
Seattle, WA 98117

The Sakya Monastery of Tibetan Buddhism Seattle was founded in 1974 as Sakya Tegchen Choling by His Holiness Jigdal Dagchen Sakya, the head of the Sakya sect of Tibetan Buddhism. Dagchen Sakya Rinpoche studied and trained for many years with his father, Trichen Ngawang Thoptok Wangchug, who was the last throne holder of the Sakya sectum Tibet. He also studied with two esteemed lamas, H. E. Dzongsar Khyentse Rinpoche and H. E. Dingo Khyentse Rinpoche of the Sakya and Nyingma schools respectively.

Dagchen Sakya Rinpoche fled to India at the time of the Chinese invasion of Tibet in 1959. The following year he was invited to the University of Washington on a Rockefeller Foundation grant to participate in a study of Tibetan civilization. Subsequently, he founded Sakya Monastery in Seattle, and in 1981 a second center was opened in Olympia, Washington.

Sakya Monastery, Seattle was featured in Bernardo Bent. Lucci's 1993 film *Little Buddha.*

Membership: In 1995 the monastery reported approximately 300 members in the United States and 50 from Canada affiliated with the two centers. There are a number of affiliated Sakya centers around the world. There are over 1,000 members worldwide.

Educational Facilities: Sakya College, Rajpur, India.

Sources:

The Excellent Path Bestowing Bliss. Seattle, WA: Sakya Monastery of Tibetan Buddhism, 1987.

★2255★
Sang-Ngak-Cho-Dzong
% Aro Gar
PO Box 247 Chelsea Station
New York, NY 10113-0247

Alternate Address: % Aro Ter, 508 Eagle Ave., Alemeda, CA.

Sang-Ngak-Cho-Dzong is a Western representative of the Tibetan Aro gTer (or Morther Eesence) Nyingma lineage, a lineage that traces its origin to a succession of enlightened women culminating in the visionary Khyungchen Aro Lingma (1886–1923), and her son Aro Yeshe (1915–1951). Aro Lingma received transmission from Yeshe Tsogyel, an Enlightened female tantric. Sang-Ngak-Cho-Dzong is headed by Ngak'chang Cho-ying Gyamtso Ogyen Togden Rinpoche and Khandro Dechen Tsedrup Yeshe, the current holders of the Aro gTer lineage.

Rinpoche was born in Germany in 1952, the great grandnephew of Schubert the composer. Raised in England, he developed an interest in Tibetan Buddhism at the age of 13 and went on to become an art teacher, with a particular interest in thangka painting (tantric iconography). At the age of 19 he went to the Himalayas to study with some of the living tantric Buddhist teachers in a nonsectarian manner, though with particular attention to Nyingma teachers, and completed four years of solitary retreat in a cave. He was eventually recognized as the incarnation of Aro Yeshe, the son of Khyungchen Aro Lingma. In this life Ngak'chang Rinpoche, together with his wife Khandro Dchen, are the holders of the lineage of "treasure-teachings" given in vision to Aro Lingma by Yeshe Tsogyel, the enlightened consort of the tantric Buddha Padmasambhava.

Ngak'chang Rinpoche began to teach in the West in 1979. In 1989 he was awarded a doctorate from the University of West Bengal. He is the author of numerous books, including *Rainbow of Liberated Energy* (completely rewritten and to be republished as *Spectrum of Ecstasy*), *Journey into Vastness* (completely rewritten and to be republished as *Roaring Silence*), and *Wearing the Body of Visions*. He has been a lecturer at the Institute of Transpersonal Psychology in California and has contributed articles to several books, journals, and magazines on the subject of tantric psychology and its interface with therapy.

Khandro Dchen was born in 1960 and has been a committed vajrayana practitioner since the age of 21. She is the spiritual wife of Ngak'chang Rinpoche, who describes her as his most important teacher. She specializes in sKu-mNye, the Dzogchen Long-de psycho-physical practices which generate profound experiences of the inner elements. She is currently preparing a three-volume manual detailing the theory and practice of these exercises, which stem from the Dzogchen Long-de system. She teaches primarily through "personality-display" and is known for her Mirror-transmission; a powerful method of giving direct introduction to the nature of the mind. She is currently involved with writing a book with Ngak'chang Rinpoche on the path of romantic love and relationship in Tibetan Tantra, entitled *Entering the Heart of the Sun and Moon*.

The Aro gTer is a non-liturgical, non-monastic tradition which specializes in the teaching and practice of Dzogchen, a practice that offers direct experience of mind. It emphasizes the importance of everyday life as practice. It is unique because of the emphasis it places on integration with everyday working life; sexual equality; and the spiritual dimension of romantic relationships and artistic creativity.

Membership: Not reported. Practitioners in the Aro tradition reside in Great Britain, the United States, Canada, Austria, Germany, Switzerland, the Netherlands, Sweden, and Finland.

Sources:

Morreale, Don. *The Complete Guide to Buddhist America*. Boston: Shambhala, 1998.

★2256★
Tara Mandala
PO Box 3040
157 Hot Springs Blvd.
Pagosa Springs, CO 81147

Tara Mandala is a 500-acre Dzogchen Tibetan Buddhist center established in 1993 in the San Juan Mountains of southwestern Colorado. Dzogchen, the direct experience of the nature of mind, is acquired through a series of awareness practices taught by Chogyal Namkhai Norbu Rinpoche and the center's resident teacher, Tsultrim Allione, an outstanding female teacher. The center sponsors a full program throughout the year that includes group meditations, pilgrimages, Vajra dance practice, classes, and study groups. In addition, meditation instruction is promoted at locations around the United States and in other countries.

Membership: Not reported.

Periodicals: *Tara Mandala Newsletter*.

Sources:

Allione, Tsultrim. *Women of Wisdom*. New York: Penguin, 1988.

★2257★
Thubten Dargye Ling
2658 La Cienga Ave.
Los Angeles, CA 90034

Thubten Dhargye Ling Tibetan Center for Buddhist Studies was founded in 1979 by Geshe Tsultrim Gyeltsen, a teacher in the Gelugpa tradition of Tibetan Buddhism. The center's name, which means "Land of Increasing Buddha's Teachings," was given by the Dalai Lama. Geshe Gyeltsen was educated at Ganden Monastic University in Tibet. He completed a 23-year course of study and was awarded the title of Lharampa Geshe. Continuing his studies, he graduated from Gyuto Tantric College. In the 1960s, he was sent by His Holiness the Dalai Lama to Great Britain as the director of Tibet House in Sussex, England. In 1976, he came to America where he taught at the University of California—Santa Barbara and the University of Oriental Studies in Los Angeles, California.

In America, Geshe Gyeltsen has continued his close relationship with the Dalai Lama, and on several occasions has hosted his visits to Los Angeles. Besides the Los Angeles center, Geshe Gyeltsen has also founded two affiliated centers: Mahakaruna Tibetan Buddhist Meditation Center in Fairbanks, Alaska, and a small center near Paonia, Colorado. Activities at the center in Los Angeles include weekly services on Sunday mornings, special monthly ceremonies, meditation ocurses, and weekend seminars.

Membership: In 1988 Thubten Dhargye Ling reported approximately 50 active members in the Los Angeles area.

Periodicals: *TDL Newsletter*.

★2258★
Tibetan Buddhist Learning Center
93 Angen Rd.
Washington, NJ 07882-9767

The first Tibetan Buddhist group to arrive in America came in 1951 and settled near Howell, New Jersey. It included 200 members of the Kalmuck tribe of Mongolia who had fled Soviet authorities wishing to convert them to communism. In 1955, with the aid of Church World Service (a Christian ecumenical group), the Ven. Geshe Wangyal (d.1983), a Kalmuck-Mongolian lama who received his training at the Drepung Monastery near Lhasa, Tibet, came to America from Tibet. In 1958, he founded the Lamaist Buddhist Monastery of America (in Tibetan, Labsum Shedrub Ling) in Howell Township in central New Jersey, which he headed for the rest of his life. In 1968, the center was moved to its present location in Warren County. In 1984, the year after Geshe-la died, at the suggestion of His Holiness the Dalai Lama, the English name of the center was changed to Tibetan Buddhist Learning Center.

The center takes its name from its main task of teaching Tibetan Buddhism. Over the years, it has sponsored many Tibetan monk-scholars to stay. It has assisted in attending to the spiritual needs of both the original Kalmuck community as well as a new growing American Buddhist group attracted to the center by Wangyal. Among other services, the center nurtures the religious life of its students by providing the regular cycle of Tibetan Buddhist ceremonies and rituals. Monks now in residence include: Geshe Thupten Gyatso, Geshe Lobzang Tseten, and Ven. Thupten Tsephel Taikang.

The center attempts to convey to its students a basic knowledge of the many facets of Tibetan Buddhism. The study of the teachings is stressed as most important for the new Western Buddhists, and is followed by putting the principles learned into practice. Many of the students have deepened their appreciation of Buddhism by learning the Tibetan language. Instruction at the center is given in English by both the resident Tibetan monk-scholars and associated American scholars. This joint teaching, which makes the subject matter easier to assimilate, is seen as essential for the center to accomplish its main aim—to develop a Buddhism that is culturally American but, at its heart, not different from the Buddhism which travelled from India throughout Asia to Tibet, and from there arrived in twentieth century America.

Succeeding Wangyal as executive director of the center is Joshua W. C. Cutler, who trained with Geshe-la for 13 years, and his wife, Diana Cutler, who trained with Gesha-la for 11 years.

Membership: In 1997, the center reported that approximately 2,500 participate to some degree in center activities.

Sources:

Gonzalez, Arturo F., Jr. "New Jersey's Buddhist Shangri-La." *Coronet* (April 1950).

Wangyal, Geshe. *The Door of Liberation.* New York: Maurice Girodias Associates, 1973.

★2259★
Unfettered Mind
11600 Washington Place, Ste. 210
Los Angeles, CA 90066

Ken McLeod was senior student of Kalu Rinpoche, the Tibetan Kagyupa master who established a number of the Kagyu Dharma centers in the United States. McLeod also wanted to operate in a freer environment that that usually allowed in the more traditional centers. Unfettered Mind, founded in 1990, follows much of the Kagyu tradition (supplemented with practices drawn from Mahayana Buddhism), and emphasizes McLeod's making himself available for private consultations with his students.

The two centers, one in Los Angeles and one in Newport Beach, California, also offer opportunities to students for meditation, weekend retreats, and study groups.

Membership: Not reported.

Sources:

Morreale, Don. *The Complete Guide to Buddhist America.* Boston: Shambhala, 1998.

★2260★
Vajradhatu International
1084 Tower Rd.
Halifax, NS, Canada B3H 2Y8

Vajradhatu, the largest of the several Tibetan Buddhist groups in the United States, is a representative of the Kagyupa sect founded by Lama Marpa of Lhagyupa in the eleventh century. The Kagyupa tradition was brought to the United States by Rinpoche Chogyam Trungpa (1939-1987), the Vidyadhara. Trungpa is be-

lieved to be the incarnation of the Trungpa *tulkus* (emanation of a bodhisattva) and abbot of Surmang Monastery, a center of the Kagyupa tradition until the takeover of Tibet by the Chinese.

The Vidyadhara fled Tibet in 1959 and settled in England. While attending Oxford University, he established a small Buddhist center in Scotland which was named Samye-ling Mona. Two years later he left his center, dropped his monastic orders, and became a layperson. In 1970, he married and migrated to the United States as leader of Karme Choling, which had been formed by a group of his students in Vermont. He traveled, lectured, and established several centers over the next few years. Vajradhatu was created as an umbrella for the several activities in 1973. He had by this time moved to Colorado. In 1985 he moved to Nova Scotia to establish Vajradhatu International.

At and near Boulder, Colorado, a complex of interrelated organizations have been established. Under Vajradhatu proper are all the centers around the United States, called "dharmadatus." Karme Choling and the Rocky Mountain Dharma Center in Colorado are used primarily for retreats, study programs, and training sessions.

Trungpa created the Nalanda Foundation to direct several outreach programs. Of these, Naropa Institute, the educational arm, now a fully accredited college, is the most important. It has become an important center for Buddhist scholarship in the west through its varied and creative programs. Shambhala Training, a program of weekend intensives, provides a secular approach to the practice of meditation in everyday life.

Vajradhatu International is headed by the Sawang Osel Mukpowho, who has assumed the responsibility for administering the organization program.

Membership: In 1988, Vajradhatu reported 4,000 members worldwide in 90 dharmadatus, including the several major centers in Vermont, Colorado, Canada, and Europe. There were 2,000 members in the United States, 1,000 in Canada and 1,000 in Europe.

Educational Facilities: Naropa Institute, Boulder, Colorado.

Periodicals: *The Shambhala.*

Sources:

Clark, Tom. *The Great Naropa Poetry Wars.* Santa Barbara, CA: Cadmus Editions, 1980.

Guenther, Herbert V., and Choegyam Trungpa. *The Dawn of Tantra.* Berkeley, CA: Shambhala, 1975.

Tendzin, Osel. *Buddha in the Palm of Your Hand,* Boulder, CO: Shambhala, 1982.

Thinley, Karma. *The History of the Sixteen Karmapas of Tibet.* Boulder, CO: Prajna Press, 1980.

Trungpa, Chogyam. *Born in Tibet.* Boulder, CO: Shambhala, 1976.

___. *Cutting Through Spiritual Materialism.* Berkeley, CA: Shambhala, 1973.

___. *Shambhala: Sacred Path of the Warrior,* Boulder, CO: Shambhala, 1985.

★2261★
Vajrakilaya Centers of North America
% Dudul Nagpa Ling
7436 Sea View Pl.
El Cerrito, CA 94530

The Vajrakilaya Centers were established by H. H. Orgyen Kusum Lingpa, a Dzogchen meditation master and renowned doctor of Tibetan medicine. He is also the supreme abbot of Thupten Chorkor Ling, a monastery located in Golok, Eastern Tibet, and a Nyingma lineage holder with over 100,000 students worldwide.

It is believed by his followers that in a previous lifetime as Lhalung Palgyi Dorje, he was one of the 25 principal students of Padmasambhava, the eighth-century saint who brought Buddhism to Tibet, and that sealed in his mind are the teachings and transmissions received directly from Padmasambhava which are revealed today in the form of "mind treasures." Orgyen Menla or Medicine Buddha is one such treasure.

The centers are named for a Tibetan deity, Vajrakilaya, the supreme destroyer of obstacles to the attainment of enlightenment. His fierce form is looked upon as the embodiment of commitment to the development of wisdom, clarity, and compassion. Kusum Lingpa teaches meditation on this form by reciting the appropriate mantra with unwavering concentration. He has noted that the practice of Vajrakilaya is crucial now in order to overcome the many kinds of inner and outer upheavals which are prevalent in this age.

Centers in the West have been established beginning with Kusum Lingpa's initial visit in 1992.

Membership: In 1998, there were 10 centers in the United States.

Sources:

http://www.sirius.com~gomura/k_lingpa/.

★2262★
Vajrayana Foundation
% Peme Osel LiIng
2013 Eureka Canyon Rd.
Corralitos, CA 95076

The Vajrayana Foundation is a Nyingma Tibetan Buddhist organization founded in 1987 by Lama Tharchin Rinpoche and Tulku Thubten Rinpoche. Headquarters are at Peme Osel Ling, a 102-acre retreat center in the Santa Cruz Mountains south of San Francisco. Pema Osel Ling is the primary residence for Lama Tharchin Rinpoche, Tulku Thubten Rinpoche, Khenpo Orgyen Thinley Rinpoche, and Lama Gyaltsen, and serves as the administrative headquarters for Vajrayana Foundation.

Membership: Not reported. Vajrayana centers are located around the United States.

Periodicals: *Lotus Light.*

Sources:

Morreale, Don. *The Complete Guide to Buddhist America.* Boston, Shambhala, 1998.

★2263★
Yeshe Khorlo
1630 39th St., Box 356
Boulder, CO 80301

Yeshe Khorlo is the name assumed by the contemporary followers of the fourteenth-century Bhutanese Buddhist master Padma Lingpa, who constitute the Drugpa branch of the Kagyu School of Tibetan Buddhism. His lineage holders have held the throne of Gangteng Gonpa Monastery in Bhutan, and the ninth and present throne holder is Gangteng Rinpoche. The Yeshe Khorlo center in Denver was founded in 1991. The Yeshe Khorlo centers around the United States have established a retreat center in Crestone, Colorado.

Membership: Not reported.

Periodicals: *Yeshe Khorlo.*

Sources:

Morreale, Don. *The Complete Guide to Buddhist America.* Boston: Shambhala, 1998.

★2264★
Yeshe Nyingpo
19 W. 16th St.
New York, NY 10011

Yeshe Nyingpo was founded in 1976 by Dudjom Rinpoche, believed to be a reincarnation of one of Buddha's personal disciples and of Cheuchung Lotsawa, one of Padmasambhava's (who brought Buddhism to Tibet) disciples. Yeshe Nyingpo is envisioned as the instrument for the transmission of the pure Nyingmapa teachings and practice to the west. In 1980 land for an educational-retreat center, Orgyen Cho Dzong, was purchased in the Catskills. Construction on the projected complex is proceeding through the mid-1980s. Affiliated are centers across the United States and in Europe.

Membership: Not reported. In 1983 there were six centers in the United States: two in New York, one in California, and three in Oregon.

★2265★
Yun Lin Temple
2959 Russell St.
Berkeley, CA 94705

The Yun Lin Temple was founded in 1968 by Prof. Thomas Lin Yun. It is a center of Black Sect tantric Buddhism of Tibet (the various major forms of Buddhism being distinguished by association with a color). The Black Sect traces its origins to the ancient Bon religion, which was dominant in Tibet at the time Buddhism was introduced in the eighth century C.E. Of the several sects of Tibetan Buddhism, the Black Sect retains most of the older Bon practices and as it grows and spreads into China, incorporates elements of Chinese folk religion, healing practices, magic, and philosophy into its system. A very eclectic system, it has encountered modern scientific thinking and, within the Yun Lin Temple, attempts are made to reinterpret the tradition in modern forms.

Prof. Lin Yun was born and raised in Beijung and even as a child began to study Buddhism with Lama De De, a teacher in the Black sect tradition. He left mainland China as a teenager and relocated to Taiwan where he found other members of the Black Sect school. He became a recognized authority on Feng Shui, the art of placement, a valued part of Chinese philosophy concerning the proper placement of objects such as houses to make beneficial use of the spiritual forces of the environment. He came to the United States in 1980 and held teaching posts at the University of San Francisco, Stanford, and Seton Hall prior to his founding the temple, the first Black Sect center in the West.

Membership: Not reported.

Western Buddhism

★2266★
American Buddhist Movement
301 W. 45th St.
New York, NY 10036

The American Buddhist Movement, also known as the Association of American Buddhists, was founded in 1980 as an independent Buddhist order to promote Buddhism in America and ordain Buddhist monks. Rather than following any particular school of Buddhism, the movement respects all traditions as equal and encourages the unity of Buddhist thought and practice. Theravada, Mahayana, and Vajrayana Buddhists participated in the movement's founding. In defining its peculiar role, the movement asserts that an American form of Buddhism is possible and that Westerners do not have to adopt Asian cultural forms to be Buddhists.

The movement has established a variety of structures to perpetuate its program. Classes are offered on a variety of Buddhist concerns, including introduction to the several distinctive national traditions. Periodically, an *American Buddhist Directory* is published. Plans have been announced to build a permanent center in the New York City area to house a meditation hall, library, and lecture room.

Membership in the movement is open to all, and activities have been designed to serve those primarily affiliated with the movement as well as those affiliated with other groups. Leadership is invested in a four-person board of directors. Kevin R. O'Neil has served as its president since its inception.

Membership: In 1987 the movement reported 2000 members in 535 centers. Most of these centers have their primary affiliations with the other Buddhist organizations discusses in this volume.

Educational Facilities: Buddhist College, New York, New York.

Periodicals: *American Buddhist Newsletter.*

Sources:

The American Buddhist Directory. New York: American Buddhist Movement, 1985.

★2267★
Buddhist Fellowship of New York
331 Riverside Dr.
New York, NY 10025

The Rev. Boris Erwitt, an American ordained to the Buddhist priesthood in Japan, began the Buddhist Fellowship of New York in 1961. The original group consisted of eight friends of the Reverend Erwitt who banded together to practice, study and propagate Buddhism, and to provide a gathering for Buddhists of non-Buddhist background. The program is centered on bimonthly meetings with a service according to the Pure Land practice and a lengthy discussion in which all participate. A number of pamphlets have been published and distributed.

The membership is small and drawn largely from the intellectual and artistic community. Some were first interested in Buddhism through the "beat" generation's emphasis on Zen. Project Sujata (named after the girl who saved Buddha's life) practices the virtue of "Ooana" (giving) by sponsoring the education of an indigent American Indian child and scholarships for "untouchables" in India.

Membership: Not reported.

Periodicals: *Kantaka.*

★2268★
Buddhist World Philosophical Group
(Defunct)

The Buddhist World Philosophical Group was a small Buddhist fellowship headquartered in Three Rivers, Michigan. Its leader, Marie Harlow (b.1902), took over the longstanding Chicago-based occult periodical, *The Occult Digest,* in the 1940s and began almost immediately to emphasize Eastern religion, particularly Buddhism, over occult topics. In 1944 she renamed the magazine *World Philosophy,* and later moved its editorial office to Three Rivers, Michigan. In 1962 *World Philosophy* became *Buddhist World Philosophy,* and Harlow announced a set of four aims for the magazine: to promote universal brotherhood, to proclaim the sanctity of life, to destroy the "limitations of the negative Semitic religious God-concept," and to turn America toward Buddhism. A small group of people congregated around the ideals articulated by Harlow which continued to meet until her death in recent years.

★2269★
Center for Timeless Wisdom
555 Bryant St., No. 302
Palo Alto, CA 94301

The Center for Timeless Wisdom was established in 1992 to provide Westerners access to non-dualistic wisdom of Asia (pri-

marily Buddhism and Taoism). The center was founded by Peter Fenner and his wife Penny Fenner. Peter Fenner is a Buddhist scholar who has taught and written in Buddhist studies, Asian philosophy, and East-West psychology in Australia and the United States for more than two decades. Through the 1980s and 1990s he also developed a form of inquiry which he espouses as efficiently transmitting the liberating wisdom of Buddhism and other non-dualistic traditions in a pure and direct form. Penny Fenner is a psychologist who works with both individuals and groups and has studied with many leading Tibetan Buddhist masters.

The Fenners view the center's work as at the forefront of cross-cultural translation, and productive of a refined synthesis of Eastern and Western wisdom. The distance of the average Westerner both in space and time from the Ancient Eastern texts tends to communicate the impossibility of their attaining enlightenment. However, the Fenners attempt to combine perspectives found in Zen, Taoism, and the Buddhist Middle Path with an understanding of group dynamics in such a way that a simple and precise process for disclosing and releasing emotional and intellectual fixations emerges, and participants are meaningfully assisted in their spiritual progress.

The center's work is presented through dialogues, workshops, and retreats in Europe, the United States, and Australia. The Living Wisdom course is the core program offered by the center. The course presents the liberating essence of Asia's most profound wisdom traditions through an interactive process that opens up a way of being in which there is nothing more we need in order to be complete and fulfilled. The course offers participants an opportunity to cut through blockades to spiritual progress and experience a state of "natural meditation" that isn't disturbed by interpersonal activities and that dissolves the boundaries between practice and daily life. The participant is given skills for infusing all activities with peacefulness and clarity. In contrast to more traditional forms of spirituality, Living Wisdom isn't based on ritual or present beliefs and practices. Instead it offers a method that responds to the emotional and intellectual rhythm of each participant.

Membership: Not reported.

Sources:

Fenner, Peter. *The Ontology of the Middle Way.* Norwell, MA: Kluwer Academic Publishers, 1990.

___. *Reasoning into Reality: A System-Cybernetics Model and Therapeutic Interpretation of Buddhist Middle Path Analysis.* Sommerville, MA: Wisdom Publications, 1995.

___, and Penny Fenner. *Intrinsic Freedom: The Art of Stress-Free Living.* Agoura, CA: Millennium Books, 1994.

★2270★
Chan Nhu Buddhist Pagoda
7201 W. Bayaud Pl.
Lakewood, CO 80226

The Chan Nhu Buddhist Pagoda is a significant center seeking a new way for American Buddhists, especially females. It was founded in 1985 by Ayya Chan Nhu, a Vietnamese nun, now assisted as codirector by Dharmapali (Martha Sentnor). Though begun as a Vietnamese center, Chan Nhu came to believe that the temple would be of more use as an open Buddhist space. Thus it has come to house a Chinese Pure Land group, a Tibetan Vajrayana group, and a Vipassana meditation group. In addition, other groups may use the facilities for classes, retreats, or weekly meditation sessions.

Dharmapali began in Theravada Buddhism in the Sri Lankan community in Washington, D.C., but rejected what she saw as the inherent sexism in the rules regarding monastics. However, she went on to become a nun, taking her vows first with the Thai-based community led by Ajahn Sumedho in England and then with the Sri Lankan community in New York City. She has a goal of creating a nunnery which combines Thai and Sri Lankan practice with some elements of Mahayana Buddhism.

Membership: Not reported.

Periodicals: *Newsletter.*

Sources:

Bucher, Sandy. *Turning the Wheel: American Women Creating the New Buddhism.* San Francisco: Harper and Row, 1986.

Rawlinson, Andrew. *The Book of Enlightened Masters: Western Teachers in Eastern Traditions.* La Salle, IL: Open Court Press, 1997. 650 pp.

★2271★
Chowado Henjo Kyo
(Defunct)

Chowado Henjo Kyo was a Buddhist healing body founded by the Rev. Reisai Fujita, a former priest in the Shingi Shingon Chizan (a Shingon group without representatives in America). The worship and temple arrangement was typical of Shingon practice, and Kobo Daishi was worshipped. However, the healing experience and resultant teaching of the Reverend Fujita were the essential aspects of Chowado. Fujita, in spite of his success as a Shingon priest, was afflicted by chronic stomach and intestinal trouble that led to tuberculosis and paralysis. He tried unsuccessfully the method of Hakuin, the Zen priest, but soon discovered that he needed physical exercises as well as spiritual healing. Beginning with the practice of breathing, he developed a system which led to his cure. In 1906, he decided to devote his life to helping others as he had been helped.

Fujita's physical exercises, which were mastered by church members, included regulated breathing and harmony exercises of various parts of the body. The stomach, the most important part of the body, was singled out for special consideration; the correctly exercised abdomen was, according to Fujita, "gourd-shaped."

As part of his evangelistic endeavors, Fujita went to Hawaii in 1929 en route to California. In Hawaii he found both a need and an audience ready to listen. He sent his student companion on to California and ministered to the Japanese community in Hawaii, instead of going on to California. The mission flourished during the 1930's but was severely hurt by the war. After the war, Fujita moved to Honolulu and operated from a two-story church in Honolulu. The single congregation dissolved in 1990.

★2272★
Church of One Sermon
Current address not obtained for this edition.

The Church of One Sermon located in Lemon Grove, California, was formed in the 1970s to aid in "the Full Awakening in all people of that special Reality knowledge first testified to by Guatama Siddhartha, the Buddha." Its founder and director was Leonard Enos. An eclectic approach centered on Mahayana Buddhism, but including tantra and Zen and even some Sufism, was taught, with particular interest being given to current research in psychology on the meditative states of consciousness. The program consisted largely of meditation, exercise, and discussion sessions. One center was functioning in 1973, but in recent years no evidence of its continued existence had appeared.

★2273★
Davachan Temple
2 Dickey St.
Eureka Springs, AR 72632

Davachan Temple, established in 1980 in the health resort town of Eureka Springs, Arkansas, has pioneered the emerging American Buddhism. Over two decades, the temple's leader, Bhikkhuni Miao Keang Sudharma (Alexa Roy), studied, mastered, and was ordained in three distinct Buddhist traditions, Soto Zen (through Juyi Kennett Roshi, 1963), Sri Lankan Theravada (1973),

and Chinese Pure Land (1983). Her religious name indicates her varied background.

Devachan Temple has emerged as an eclectic center whose practices have been taken from Soto, Theravada, Ch'an (Chinese Zen), and Pure Land tradition, and chanting is done in both Pali and Chinese. The temple invites Buddhists from all traditions to use its facilities for personal retreats (for which there is no charge) and participate in its varied activities. The resulting practice constitutes a new unique Buddhism that is female friendly.

Membership: Not reported.

Sources:

Rawlinson, Andrew. *The Book of Enlightened Masters: Western Teachers in Eastern Traditions.* La Salle, IL: Open Court Press, 1997. 650 pp.

★2274★
Dharma Centre of Canada
RR #1, Galway Rd.
Kinmount, ON, Canada K0M2A0

The Dharma Centre of Canada was founded in 1966 by the renowned pioneering Canadian Buddhist leader, the Ven. Namgyal Rinpoche. Namgyal Rinpoche was born G. Leslie Dawson in Ontario, Canada, to Irish parents. In his mid-20s, he went to Bodh Gaya, India, the traditional site of the Buddha's enlightenment, and on October 28, 1958, took the vows of a novice monk. Two months later he was ordained a *bhikkhu*, or full Buddhist monk, in Rangoon. Following a period of intensive meditation, he was recognized by H. H. the Gyalwa Karmapa, head of the Kargyu School of Tibet, as the reincarnation of the famous Tibetan lama, Mipham Namgyal Rinpoche, one of the first Westerners so recognized. Returning to the West, he founded Johnstone House as a contemplative community in Scotland. Later through the auspices of Chogyam Trungpa Rinpoche, founder of Vajradhatu International, Johnstone House was converted into Samye Ling, one of the first Tibetan monasteries to be established in Europe.

The Dharma Centre of Canada and its associated centers across the country offer instruction and opportunity for the practice of meditation in order for individuals to develop awareness into the nature of mind and matter, and to develop compassion and wisdom. Instruction is also offered in comparative religion, philosophy, the arts and sciences. Both Western and Eastern spiritual insights are acknowledged.

Membership: Not reported. There are seven affiliated centers in Canada, two in the United States, and one each in England and New Zealand, and informal groups in France, Switzerland, Norway, Guatemala, Germany, and Japan.

Sources:

Morreale, Don. *The Complete Guide to Buddhist America.* Boston: Shambhala, 1998.

★2275★
Enlightened Heart Meditation Center
Current address not obtained for this edition.

Alternate Address: (For contact see the center's home page on the Internet.)

Enlightened Heart Meditation Center is a Dzogchen center and part of the network of centers under the spiritual guidance of Khyabje Palden Sherab Rinpoche. Dzogchen meditation is traced to an enlightened yogi-saint known as Sri Pramodavajra who came from the mountains of northern Pakistan (i.e., the Swat valley) and taught at Bodh Gaya, in India, in the seventh century C.E. His teachings, as transmitted through a line of male and female saints, are concerned with enabling individuals to discover their true nature, and the real meaning of life, through the direct experience of meditation.

Khyabje Palden Sherab Rinpoche was born in Tibet and lived as a yogi and wandering mystic in the highlands of Tibet, meditated in caves in the Himalayas, and dwelt in temples throughout India. He subsequently moved to the United States, where he guides a number of small meditation centers that have sprung up all across America. He also has students in Russia, Puerto Rico, Nepal, and India.

Khyabje Palden Sherab Rinpoche is helped in his spiritual work by his brother, Tulku Tsewang. Tulku Tsewang was the former head abbot of Gochen Monastery, and in 1987 he was invested with the title of Khenpo by H. H. Dudjom Rinpoche (the head of the Nyingma School of Tibetan Buddhism). Tulku Tsewang now lives in the United States.

The San Francisco center is headed by resident teacher and British-born lama, Ven. Kunzang Palden Rinpoche, who studied not only with Khyabje Palden Sherab Rinpoche, but with a number of other Buddhist teachers, especially the renowned Canadian lama, Tenzin Dorje Namgyal Rinpoche, founder of the Dharma Centre of Canada. He is concerned with the emergence of a distinctly American form of "Buddhism," which nevertheless is drawn from pure sources of Eastern wisdom. In particular, he extols Western culture (art, music, architecture, literature, medicine, science, and democratic principles) as an incomparable treasure that should not be rejected. Kunzang Palden Rinpoche also emphasizes an appreciation for the spiritual teachings of other religious traditions that manifests in an honoring of the world's great religious saints, and the revering of the universal truths taught through the ages by divine messengers such as Moses, Zarathustra, Lao-tse, Krishna, Jesus, Mani, and Mohammed. Kunzang Palden Rinpoche assumed leadership of the Enlightened Heart Meditation Center in the early 1990s.

Membership: Not reported.

Sources:

http://www.resonate.com/e_heart/.

★2276★
Friends of Buddhism-Washington D.C.
Current address not obtained for this edition.

Alabama-born Robert Stuart Clifton became interested in Buddhism as a student at Columbia University in the 1920s. He moved to San Francisco and lived in the Japanese community. In 1933, he was ordained as a priest in the Honpa Hongwanji Mission, now the Buddhist Churches of America, and began English language work along the West Coast. In 1934, he traveled to Japan and while there became a Higashi Hongwanji priest. Upon his return to America, he lectured widely and organized a number of "friends of Buddhism" societies, mostly in the East.

The Washington Friends of Buddhism was formed in the home of Mr. and Mrs. Lee Sirat at a gathering of persons Clifton had interested in Buddhism. There were 11 in the original group. The program has always centered on lectures and discussion of Buddhism, but meditation and worship have been included from the beginning. Wesak, the spring fesival honoring Gautama Buddha, is also celebrated.

The only one of the Friends of Buddhism groups, besides the Washington group, to survive through the 1960s was the Friends of Buddhism of New York, founded in the early 1950s. In the late 1960s, following the retirement of its leader, Frank E. Becker, the New York group merged with the Washington group. Kurt F. Leidecker, who succeeded Clifton as head of the Washington group, died in 1991, and the current status of the group is unknown.

Membership: Not reported.

Sources:

Leidecker, Kurt F. *History of the Washington Friends of Buddhism.* Washington, DC: United States Information Service, 1960.

★2277★
Friends of the Western Buddhist Order (FWBO)
% Aryaloka
14 Heartwood Circle
Newmarket, NH 03857

Alternate Address: International Heaquarters: c/o Sangharakshita, 329, Sauchiehall St., Glasgow, Scotland G2 3HW.

The Friends of the Western Buddhist Order (the FWBO) was founded by the Ven. Maha Sthavira Sangharakshita (b. 1925) as an instrument of a new Buddhist tradition for the West that would draw upon the whole Buddhist tradition while emphasizing its central principles in order to meet the spiritual needs of the modern world. Sangharakshita was born Denis Lingwood in South London, United Kingdom. Largely self-educated, he developed an interest in the Eastern teachings as a youth and at the age of 16 realized that he was a Buddhist.

He went to India during World War II and he stayed on to become the Buddhist monk Sangharakshita ("protected by the spiritual community"). He studied in various Buddhist traditions and became an accomplished teacher and the writer of more than 40 books. Sangharakshita worked for the revival of Buddhism in India, particularly through his work with the ex-Untouchables. He knew Dr. Bhim Rao Ambedkar (1891–1956), the Buddhist leader among the Untouchables, and after Ambedkar's death he continued to work for their conversion to Buddhism which Ambedkar had started.

The FWBO is committed to presenting Buddhism in a way felt to be relevant to the modern West. The modern environment of industry, technology, and communications is a world away from the conditions under which traditional Buddhism evolved and thrived. While some of the forms through which Buddhism has been expressed need change, the FWBO believes that the essence of Buddhism is universal and unchanging, and it is that essence that it is trying to communicate. As heirs to the whole of Buddhism, members of FWBO reject an attitude of eclecticism, though it attempts to make use of whatever is helpful for the actual spiritual needs of modern Westerners.

At the heart of the FWBO is the Western Buddhist Order, a body of men and women who have committed themselves to following the Buddhist path to Enlightenment, and made that commitment the central point of their lives. The order offers an alternative to the model found in some forms of Eastern Buddhism where everyone is either a monk or a lay person. It is open to any man or woman who is sincerely committed to the Buddhist path, not just to those who want to live a monastic lifestyle. Although order members try to lead a one hundred percent Buddhist life, they are not monks or nuns. The emphasis is not the lifestyle but the spiritual commitment.

Some order members live a monastic life in a retreat center while others live with their families and pursue a career. Others work full-time for a Right Livelihood business; others again are supported to work full-time at their local FWBO center. There are no rules, and as Buddhism does not recognize the existence of a creator god, there are no commandments to obey. However, at the time of their ordination, all order members undertake to practice a traditional set of ethical precepts applied to all actions of body, speech, and mind.

The FWBO has expanded worldwide. The aging Sangharakshita is, as the century draws to a close, completing the process of handing over responsibility to the members of the Western Buddhist Order.

Membership: As of 1996, there were approximately 70 FWBO urban centers and retreat centres, and activities in over 20 countries. The FWBO is one of the principal Buddhist movements in the United Kingdom, India, and Australasia and is increasingly well-established in Western Europe and the United States. In 1996 the order had 660 members in over 20 countries, and over 1,000 people have requested ordination and are working to prepare themselves to be ordained.

Sources:

Subhuti, Dharmachari (Alex Kennedy). *Buddhism for Today: A Portrait of a New Buddhist Movement.* Glasgow: Windhorse Publications, 1988. 234 pp.

★2278★
Harmony Buddhist Mission
Clarksville, AK 92830

The Harmony Buddhist Mission was founded in 1953 by Frank Newton. It is centered on Buddhist ethical and philosophical teachings. Self-responsibility and attunement to fact are stressed. Leaders in the mission (preceptors) are not allowed to receive any income for religious duties but must work at secular occupations. Frank Newton has gained a reputation as a writer and translator of Buddhist literature. Some 1,500 people have reportedly come into Buddhism through his efforts.

Membership: Not reported.

★2279★
Namgyal Monastery Institute of Buddhist Studies
PO Box 127
Ithaca, NY 14851

Namgyal Monastery Institute of Buddhist Studies is the American headquarters of the Dalai Lama in his role as head of the Gelugpa School of Buddhism and nominal head of the Tibetan Buddhist community. The Gelugpa Tradition is traced back to Lama Tsongkhapa (1357–1419), popularly known as Jetsun Tsongkhapa or Je Rinpoche in Tibet. He is thought to be a major reformer of Tibetan Buddhism. In his mature years, Je Rinpoche wrote a collection of texts on Buddhist doctrine and other related subjects, amongst them the Lam-Rim ChenMo, a study of the graduated path to enlightenment, which is considered by believers as the most authoritative volume on Buddhist teachings.

Je Rinpoche and his disciples founded the Gandan Monastery in 1409. His followers became known as the Gelugpas ("virtuous"), and his teachings spread throughout Tibet and further, to Mongolia, where almost the entire population became Gelugpa followers. The teachings also spread through China, influencing a succession of emperors who supported the spread of Buddhism.

The leader of this largest of Tibetan Schools is termed the Dalai Lama. The first Dalai Lama was Tsongkhapa's nephew. The Second Dalai Lama established the original Namgyal Monastery in the sixteenth century, and over the centuries it has served as the private monastery of each of the successive Dalai Lamas. In Tibet, this prestigious but relatively small monastery was located in the Potala in the capital city of Lhasa.

The present Dalai Lama, Gyalwa Tenzin Gyatso (b. 1935), was recognized as the new Dalai Lama at the age of two and in 1939 taken to Lhasa from his home in Eastern Tibet. Though only 16, in 1951 he assumed his responsibilities in order to deal with the perceived threat that the new Chinese government posed for the country. When the country was finally overrun in 1959, he fled and has since that time worked both to regain the autonomy of Tibet and to care for the 100,000 Tibetan refugees, including numerous religious leaders who fled with him. His worldwide travels on behalf of these two causes have given him status as a prominent world religious leader similar to the Ecumenical Patriarch (Eastern Orthodox Christianity) or the Pope. The Dalai Lama established his headquarters (both a government-in-exile and Tibetan Buddhist center) in Dharmasala, India, and recreated Namgyal Monastery in a building immediately adjacent to his residence. Today, a large community of monks are pursuing research and studies there.

In 1992, the monastery established a North American branch in Ithaca, New York, in conjunction with an innovative institute of study and practice for the benefit of lay as well as ordained Western women and men. With the approval of the Dalai Lama, the Administrative Committee of Namgyal Monastery in Dharmasala composed the charter for the Ithaca branch monastery and its institute and selected monks for its staff. Namgyal Institute has a program of bringing to the West both the program designed by the Dalai Lama and additional supplementary course work.

The Dalai Lama has written a number of books and overseen the translation of numerous Tibetan texts into Western languages. Snow Lion Publications was established in 1980 as an English-language publisher of books and other materials on Tibet, Tibetan culture, Tibetan Buddhism, and His Holiness the Dalai Lama. As a publishing house, it has been dedicated to the preservation of Tibetan culture and has become a major force in spreading Tibetan Buddhism in the West.

Remarks: During the 1990s, amid his broad work with the Tibetan Buddhist community, the Dalai Lama has become involved in two international controversies that have particular significance for Gelugpa Buddhists. The first concerns the Panchen Lama. The Panchen Lama is the second most important religious figure in Tibet. The Fifth Dalai Lama, who became the sovereign ruler of Tibet in 1642, gave Tashi Lhunpo Monastery to the 15th abbot of the monastery, Lobsang Choekyi Gyaltsen, and officially conferred the title Panchen ("great scholar") upon him. Since his death, Lobsang Choekyi Gyaltsen's reincarnations have been recognized and known as the Panchen Lama.

The Dalai Lama and the Panchen Lama have enjoyed a unique and supportive relationship. Over the centuries, adult Dalai Lamas have been the person to recognize the new incarnation of the Panchen Lama, and vice versa. And thus it came about that in May 1995 (in the wake of the death of the 10th Panchen Lama in 1989), the present Dalai Lama recognized a 6-year-old boy, Gedhun Choekyi Nyima, as the reincarnation of the Panchen Lama. However, shortly thereafter, the Chinese authorities detained Gedhun Choekyi Nyima and his parents and neither have been seen since. Then in November 1995, the Chinese government declared its recognition of another young boy, Gyslten Norbu, as the new Panchen Lama. The issue has become an important one in the ongoing relations between the Chinese government and the Dalai Lama, as the 10th Panchen had been severely treated in an effort to have him denounce the Dalai Lama, but he remained loyal.

The second issue has involved an internal struggle within the Gelugpa community. In 1978 H. H. the Dalai Lama gave a talk in which he spoke harshly of veneration ascribed to Dorje Shugden, a Tibetan Buddhist deity, who has enjoyed popular support among Tibetan Buddhists. His words led to the suppression of worship in the community in India and Nepal, and some discrimination against those who continued the practice. Largely an internal matter, little known outside of the inner circle of believers, the Dalai Lama heightened controversy in 1996, in the wake of his problems with the Chinese over the Panchen Lama when he publicly declared Dorje Shugden to be an evil Chinese spirit who was harmful to Tibetan independence and to the Dalai Lama's life. He then took the extraordinary step of banning the worship of Dorje Shugden and initiating its forcible suppression within the exile Tibetan communities. This action infuriated many who felt forced to choose between the Dalai Lama and their own traditional spiritual practice.

Among the major supporters of Dorje Shugden veneration were the leaders and members of a rival Gelugpa branch, the New Kadampa Tradition (NKT), which has its center in a monastery in England. Members of the NKT demonstrated against the Dalai Lama during his European visit in the summer of 1996. Then in February 1997, three of the Dalai Lama's close disciples were murdered near Dharmasala. Again, on May 3, 1998, followers of Dorje Shugden (including NKT members) demonstrated against the Dalai Lama in New York during his visit there.

Neither the Panchen Lama or Dorje Shugden controversy appear to be nearing a resolution. In each case, those opposed to the

Dalai Lama are out of his reach either in the controlled environment of Tibet or the free religious environment of the modern West. He has no power to locate and free his designated candidate as the Panchen Lama or to force the followers of Dorje Shugden in various branches of Tibetan Buddhism to discontinue their veneration. The Dalai Lama will probably have to live with both issues for a number of years in the future.

Sources:

Batchelor, Stephen. "Letting Daylight into Magic: The Life and Times of Dorje Shugden." *Tricycle: The Buddhist Review* 7, 3 (spring 1998): 60–66.

Dalai Lama. *Freedom in Exile: The Autobiography of the Dalai Lama.* San Francisco: Harper, 1991. 320 pp.

___. *My Land and My People.* Potala Corporation, 1983.

___. *Opening of the Wisdom Eye.* Wheaton, IL: Theosophical Publishing House, 1986.

___. *The Way to Freedom.* San Francisco: Harper, 1994. 192 pp.

Kay, David. "The New Kadampa Tradition and the Continuity of Tibetan Buddhism in Transition." *Journal of Contemporary Religion* 12, 3 (October 1997): 277–93.

Lopez, Jr., Donald S. "Two Sides of the Same God" *Tricycle: The Buddhist Review* 7, 3 (spring 1998): 67–69.

Snelling, John. *The Buddhist Handbook: A Complete Guide to Buddhist Schools, Teachings, Practice, and History.* Rochester, VT: Inner Traditions, 1991. 337 pp.

★2280★
Phoenix Buddhist Network
4701 N. 35th Way
Phoenix, AZ 85018

The Phoenix Buddhist Network includes a diverse set of Buddhist centers and activities among Buddhists in the greater Phoenix area and across Arizona. It includes the Center for Buddhist Development in Chandler, the Phoenix Vietnamese Zen Temple, the Buddhist Association of Arizona State University, and the Phoenix Buddhist Association. Dr. Terry Kinnard serves as the resident director for several of these groups. An emphasis is placed on both meditation and mindfulness and service in the community. Also associated with the centers in Arizona is the Rosemead Buddhist Monastery in Rosemead, California, and Bhante Chao Chu, the abbot who serves as the spiritual head of the network.

Membership: Not reported.

Periodicals: *Common Sense.* Available from 7833 Emerson Pl., Rosemead, CA 91770. • *Phoenix Buddhist Network Newsletter.* Available from the address given above.

Sources:

Morreale, Don. *The Complete Guide to Buddhist America.* Boston: Shambhala, 1998.

★2281★
Shivapuram
(Defunct)

Shivapuram was founded in 1963 by Radha Appu (also known as Rakshasi) in the Catskill Mountains of New York. While on a retreat and doing vigorous breathing and concentration exercises to raise the kundalini (creative energy), he became aware of the Master Vijaya Bhattacharya, who appeared to him. Over a period of time, the master gave instructions and told Radha Appu to "Go forward" and found Shivapuram. He remained as the sole contact with the master, though sporadic appearances were made to the shivas, the members of the Shivapuram. In 1967, Rakshasi was given instructions to found a worldwide Crusade of the Spirit to save humanity from self-destruction.

Though borrowing from Hinduism, the Shivapuram was basically Mahayana Buddhist with large portions of tantra. Adherents did not believe in escape into nirvana, but in accepting the world and using it as a means of liberation. They sought Buddhatva, the quality of being enlightened. They use chants and mantras and meditative yoga.

The Shivapuram members were largely drawn from California. There were in 1971 three priests, ten lecturers, and approximately 300 members. While committed to spreading the movement, the members were not openly evangelistic and were highly selective about who is invited to join or even attend meetings. There has been no evidence of a continuing movement in recent years.

★2282★
Universal Buddhist Fellowship
Current address not obtained for this edition.

The Universal Buddhist Fellowship was formed in 1951 by the Venerable H. H. (Tissa) Priebe of Ojai, California. It is described as autonomous and non-sectarian. Its purpose is dissemination of the Western Dharma (the true way of life taught by Buddha).

Membership: Not reported.

Periodicals: *Western Bodhi.*

Shintoism

★2283★
Church of World Messianity
960 S. Kenmore Ave.
Los Angeles, CA 90006

Sekai Kyusei Kyo, generally known by its English name, the Church of World Messianity, is also known as Johrei Fellowship. It was originally founded by Mokichi Okada (1882-1955), usually referred to by his honorific title, Meishu-sama. Raised in poverty and beset with illness and business failure, in the 1920s Okada turned to religion and joined Omoto, one of the newer religions of Japan. In 1926, however, he began to receive revelations, as a result of which, he began to see himself as a channel for the Light of God. He understood his mission as one of the transmission of *Johrei*, the Light of God for the purification of the spiritual body. Such purification would lead to the elimination of spiritual clouds, resulting in health, prosperity, and peace, ultimately creating an ideal world, a paradise on earth.

In 1934 Okada left Omoto and founded Dai Nihon Kannon Kai (Japan Kannon Society). As World War II approached, innovative religious groups were suppressed, and Okada had to give up the practice of *Johrei* until after the war, though the movement continued to grow. During the war, Okada moved to Hakone and constructed a "paradise," a model of a future paradise on earth. A second such model was built in Atami a few years later. After a series of name changes, the church assumed its present name Sekai Kyusei Kyo in 1957, two years after Okada's passing, which occurred on February 10, 1955. He was succeeded by his wife Yoshi, who served as Spiritual Leader until she passed away in 1962. Their daughter, Itsuki Fujieda, took over at that point and is still serving as the church's Spiritual Leader.

In the years after the war, members of the church immigrated to the United States. Okada sent Rev. Kiyoko Higuchi and Rev. Henry Ajiki to the United States to organize the church. The first center outside of Japan was incorporated in 1953 in Honolulu, Hawaii, followed by the second one in Los Angeles, California, in 1954.

Membership: During the past 40 years, more than a dozen centers have been established in many states, including the East coast. Internationally, the church has spread to nearly 40 countries, including Brazil, Korea, and Thailand.

Periodicals: *Johrei Newsletter.*

Sources:

Introductory Course of World Messianity and Joining the Church. Los Angeles: Church of World Messianity, 1976.

The Light from the East: Mokichi Okada. Atami, Japan: MOA Productions, 1983.

M. Okada, A Modern-Day Renaissance Man. New York: M. Okada Cultural Services Association, 1981.

Members' Handbook. Atami, Japan: Church of World Messianity, n.d.

Teachings of Meishu-Sama. 2 vols. Atami, Japan: Church of World Messianity, 1967-68.

★2284★
Honkyoku Shinto
Honkyoku-Daijingu Temple
61 Puiwa Rd.
Honolulu, HI 96817

In 1882 the Japanese designated thirteen shinto sects as approved but at the same time withdrew government financial support from them (as opposed to Buddhism which was not sanctioned by the government). Honkyoku Shinto was among the more traditionalist sects included on the government list. It bases its beliefs on the ancient Shinto text, the *Mojiki*, and sees itself as the Way of Nature, the spontaneous manifestation of the order of being taking form in human life. Worship is centered upon Ame-no-Minaka-Nushi-no-Kami (The Deity Who is Lord of the Center of Heaven), the primary source of all. On the altar of the Honkyoku shrine there is a mirror and a ball which symbolize God. This absolute deity gives rise to two other deities: Taka-Mimusibi-no-Kami and Kami-Musubi-no-Kami. The world arises from the interaction of these two very different deities. From them arise other deities, the Japanese Imperial family and the Japanese people. Through the ancestors of those now living, the people are tied to the divine as a great spiritual body. Shinto faith is best expressed in practice, reverence to the gods and one's ancestors, devotion to the Imperial family and patriotism.

Honkyoku Shinto prospered during the first half of the twentieth century. On the eve of World War II it could report over 3,300 centers and 1,200,000 members in Japan. It was also the earliest Shinto group to establish itself in Hawaii. The Daijingu Temple in Honolulu was founded around 1906 by Rev. Masasato Kawasaki. Because of its intense Japanese nationalism, it was closed, and the property confiscated, during World War II. A new temple was built after the war. In 1949 a statue of one of the Shinto goddesses confiscated and sent to Japan by the United States government was returned and enthroned at the Honolulu temple, then located on Buckle Street.

The Honkyoku temples in Hawaii hold monthly public services, but most worship is individual and private. There are annual festivals on New Year's Day and the second Sunday of September. Bishop Kazoe Kawasaki has succeeded his father as head of the Honkyoku in Hawaii.

Membership: Not reported. There are currently two temples, one in Honolulu and one in Hilo, Hawaii. In 1963 the Honolulu temple claimed to serve over 10,000 families.

★2285★
Inari Shinto
Current address not obtained for this edition.

In Hawaii the Inari have departed from the Inari deities common to the group in Japan. The Hawaiian Inari worship a main deity, Shoichii Shi Sha. The Wakamiya Shrine in Honolulu was founded in 1912 by the Rev. Yoshio Akizaki. Since his passing in 1951, his son, the Rev. Takeo Akizaki, has been in charge. He has begun to assume the role of pastor and the temple has regular worship services. A second temple is located on Molokai.

Membership: Not reported. There are two Inari shrines in Hawaii, one in Honolulu and one in Molokai.

★2286★
Jinga Shinto
Hawaii Ichizuchi Jinga
2020 S. King St.
Honolulu, HI 96817

The Rev. Shina Miyake founded the Hawaii Ichizuchi Jinga in Honolulu in 1913. In 1963, on the occasion of their fiftieth anniversary, a rebuilt shrine building was dedicated.

Membership: Not reported. There is one shrine in Honolulu, Hawaii.

★2287★
Konko Kyo
% Rev. Alfred Y. Tsyyuki
2924 E. 1st St.
Los Angeles, CA 90033

Konko Kyo was founded in 1859 by Bunjiro Kawate (1814-1883) (later given the title Konko Daijin), a Shinto farmer, who after years of misfortune and illness had a revelation of God as Tenchi Kane-no-Kami, the parent God of the universe. God revealed to him that the prosperity of men is the ultimate purpose of creation and that God without that purpose realized is morally imperfect. In 1882 Konko Kyo was recognized as one of the thirteen approved forms of sectarian Shinto in Japan.

The interrelation of God and man is the key to Konko Kyo teaching. Man cannot exist apart from God, and God's work can only be complete through man. Konko Daijin was the mediator who informed all men of this fellowship. Priests continue to function as mediators, just as Konko Daijin functioned. The process of mediation (*toritsugi*) is quite similar to Roman Catholic confessions.

Rites and ceremonies follow Shinto practice, but are demythologized. Konko Kyo is monotheistic and does not practice divination or magic. Much more emphasis is placed on the sermon, piety, and social concern. Belief in God with sincerity and a pious life are cardinal virtues. Social concerns have led to the founding of a hospital, a public library, museum, leper missions, and prison work.

Konko Kyo was established in the United States in 1919 by Mr. & Mrs. Bunjiro Hirayama who founded the Konko Kyo Association of Seattle, Washington. A second center was opened in Tacoma in 1925. The following year, the Rev. Kokichi Katashima, a Konko official from Japan, visited the Washington centers and, on his return route to Japan, organized believers who had recently migrated to Los Angeles and Honolulu. The work grew until the disruption of World War II and the internment of most of the leadership. The San Francisco headquarters were reestablished in the fall of 1945. The post-World War II freedom of religion in Japan has allowed Konko Kyo to grow and spread as a vigorous movement. Setsutane Konko, the present mediator and leader, has supported the work outside of Japan and has spurred the production of English-language materials. In 1965 a radio show was inaugurated by Konko minister Masaru Okazaki.

Membership: Not reported. In 1982 there were seven churches in the United States (apart from Hawaii) and two in Canada. The Hawaii Mission had an additional six churches.

Periodicals: *Konko Review.*

Sources:

Daily Service Book. San Francisco: Ministerial Staff of Konko Churches of America, 1971.

Fukuda, Yoshiaki. *Outline of Sacred Teaching of Konko Religion.* San Francisco: Konko Missions of North America, 1955.

Hombu, Konkokyo, ed. *The Sacred Scriptures of Konkokyo*. Konko-cho, Japan: Konkokyo Hombu, 1933.

Konko Daijin, A Biography. San Francisco: Konko Churches of America, 1981.

Konko Kyo's 50 Years in America. San Francisco: Konko Churches of America, 1976.

★2288★
Mahikari of America
3510 Torrance Blvd.
Torrance, CA 90503

Alternate Address: International headquarters: 1517-8, Yamada-oho, Takayama-city, Gifu, Japan.

Mahikari is the Japanese word for Divine True Light, believed to be a spiritual and purifying energy. Mahikari began in 1959 when Kotama Okada (1901-1974), at the time a member of the Church of World Messianity, received a revelation from God concerning how the use of the Divine Light of the Creator could produce health, harmony, and prosperity. Mahikari is viewed as a cleansing energy sent by SUSHIN, the Creator of Heaven and Earth, that both spiritually awakens and tunes the soul to its divine purpose. In 1960, he organized what became known as the Sekai Mahikari Bunmei Kyodan (Church of World True Light Children). Okada soon became known as *Sukuinushisama*, Saviour.

God also revealed to Okada the existence of a Divine Plan. According to his teachings, all of the phenomena of the universe have been controlled by the Plan of the Creator. Under this plan, human souls are dispatched to the earth for the specific purpose of learning to utilize its material resources in order to establish a highly evolved civilization governed by spiritual wisdom. These revelations and teachings are to be found in *Goseigen, The Holy Words*, the Mahikari scriptures, an English-language edition of which was published in 1982.

Okada dedicated his life to teaching the art of the Divine Light to anyone desiring to be of service to the Creator. Today it is taught in a three-day session at which attendees may learn to radiate the Light through the palm of the hand, a process known as *Mahikari no Waza*. At the time of initiation, new members receive an *Omitama*, a pendent used to focus the light.

In 1974, just prior to his death Okada passed the mission to his daughter, Seishu Okada, the present spiritual leader. Under her guidance, a new headquarters complex has been established at Suza, Takayama City, Japan.

Membership: Not reported. In 1988, there were 18 centers in the United States, one in Puerto Rico, and three in Canada. There are associatied centers in 14 countries.

Periodicals: *True Light*.

Remarks: It should be noted that the Church of World Messianity, of which Okada was a member prior to his revelations concerning Mahikari, has a similar teaching concerning what it calls *johrei*, God's healing light.

Also, after Okada's death, the leadership of his daughter was challenged by a prominent member, Sekiguchi Sakae. He filed a lawsuit and upon winning, took possession of the former headquarters of the group. He now leads a second Mahikari group in Japan.

Sources:

Davis, Winston. *Dojo*. Stanford, CA: Stanford University Press, 1980.

Goseigen, The Holy Words. Tujuna, CA: Sekai Mahikari Bunmei Kyodan, 1982.

Tebecis, A. K. *Mahikari, Thank God for the Answers at Last*. Tokyo: L. H. Yoko Shuppan, 1982.

★2289★
Ryugu, U.S.A.
11958 Hartsook St.
North Hollywood, CA 91607

Ryugu, U.S.A. is a Shinto organization headed by Himiko Fujita, known among her followers as Mother Otohime, and revered as a living Shinto goddess. She was born near Mt. Aso at Kumamoto, Japan. Her followers claim that her birth was heralded in the writings of Degichi Onisabuo (1871-1948), the founder of Omoto, and Yoshisane Tomokiyo, founder of Tenko-kyo Shinto, two Japanese new religions. As a child she had experiences of the ancient "holy spirits." Then in 1949 she was spiritually awakened and came to know the great love of Mother Deity.

In 1958 she felt led by Heaven to go to the Kansai district and began training herself for spiritual perfection at the sacred area on Ohmine Mountain. Her various spiritual experiences climaxed on October 7, 1973, as she stood before a great stone, Ama-no-Iwato (the Heavenly Gate of the Rock Cave), at Himuki, Kumamoto Province. As she looked at the stone, it suddenly opened and the Shinto deity Amaterasu-Oho-Mikami (the Sun Goddess) appeared to her in the form of a mermaid. Striking Himiko on the forehead, the goddess said, "I have lain hidden behind the Great Rock Gate for twelve thousand years, but I have now come back to life again in thy soul in order to prevent the world from extinction." These words gave Mother Otohime her mission in life.

In 1981 Mother Otohime had a dream. A snow white horse carried her on a flight over a Shinto shrine at the foot of a mountain. A short time later she was taken by a friend to the Izumo Great Shrine in Tampa Province. It was the shrine of her dream. She decided to remain and serve Amaterasu as a shrine maiden. As part of her duties, she left the shrine on a tour of 46 countries, including the United States, to bring to each a special stone with divine energy from Ryugu Kai (the Sea Goddesses). Ryugu, U.S.A. was formed as a result of her visit.

Ryugu is an expression of the maternal love of the goddess and comes as a blessing on the world. Mother Otohime offers the opportunity to each human being to have their inner Rock Gate opened, which will bring to consciousness old memories of the love of Amaterasu and a merger of God and Human into a state of oneness.

Membership: Not reported.

★2290★
Shinreikyo
% Kameo Kiyota
310C Uulani St.
Hilo, HI 96720

Shinreikyo is a post-World War II Japanese healing group based on Kami-no-michi, the Way of God. Shinreikyo was founded by Master Kanichi Otsuka, viewed by his followers as the great sage (who was to appear as Buddhism lost its power) and the messiah that Christians expected at the second coming. The message of Shinreikyo is that Kami-no-michi is the way to happiness and prosperity. It is identified with Nippon Seishin, the Japanese spirit, a way common to all since ancient times, based upon the laws of the universe. The intense nationalism is typical of much Shintoism.

The center of Shinreikyo is its healing miracles. Master Otsuka is said to attack disease in the three existences of past, present, and future. Accounts of healing of serious illnesses fill Shinreikyo literature. Shinreikyo came to the United States in 1963 when Mr. Kameo Kiyoto established a branch in Hilo, Hawaii. Literature in English is distributed by the Metaphysical Scientific Institute in Japan.

Membership: Not reported.

★2291★
Shinto
% Hawaii Kotohira Jinsha-Hawaii Dazaifu Tenmangu
1045 Kama Ln.
Honolulu, HI 96817-3349

Alternate Address: International headquarters: Dazaifu Tenmangu, 4-7-1 Zaifu-shi, Fukuoka Ken, Japan 818-01.

Representative of Japanese Shinto are two branch shrines, the Hawaii Kotohira Jinsha and Dazaifu Tenmangu in Honolulu.

Membership: In 1997, the Kotohira and Dazaifu Shrines reported 80,000 members worldwide and approximately 70 in Hawaii.

Periodicals: *Kotohira.* • *Tobiume.*

★2292★
Society of Johrei
Current address not obtained for this edition.

The Society of Johrei was formed in 1971 by former leaders of the Church of World Messianity who felt that it had departed from the teachings of founder Mokichi Okada. They began to work independently of the church and then organized the society. Their following included people in Korea and Brazil. An American office was opened in the 1980s and began to publicize the society through distribution of an edited volume of Okada's writings.

Membership: Not reported.

Sources:

Okada, Mokichi. *Johrei: Divine Light of Salvation.* Kyoto, Japan: Society of Johrei, 1984.

★2293★
Taishakyo Shinto
215 N. Kukui St.
Honolulu, HI 96817

Taishakyo Shinto, also known as the Oyashirokyo, was one of the original 13 religious Shinto sects (as distinguished from the Shrine Shinto) existing before World War II. It was founded in 1882 by Takatomi Senge at the ancient Grand Shrine of Izumo located at Taishamachi, Shimane, Japan. The God enshrined at the shrine is Okuninushi-no-Mikoto, the God of the spiritual and physical world, who settled the world and brought the foundation upon which mankind and the rest of the universe might exist. Some of the teachings, as set forth in the "Great Way," a catechism published in 1881, are as follows: the world was created by Three Creator Gods; God established the path for man—perform deeds in a sincere and trustworthy manner, to help make society perfect, to perform various virtues, and to maintain the proper relationships with his family, society, the leader of the country, God, and his environment. Man has a soul, born without sin, and upon death, the soul returns to the divine world.

The Hawaii Izumo Taisha was founded in 1906 by the Rev. Katsuyoshi Miyao as an affiliate of the Taishakyo sect. In 1923, a master shrine builder was brought from Japan to construct a shrine in Honolulu, Hawaii. In 1935, after his death, the Rev. Shigemaru Miyao succeeded him. During World War II, the property was gifted to the city to avoid confiscation due to the relocation of the Rev. Shigemaru Miyao, his family, and other leaders of the shrine organization. After release from the relocation camp, he again resumed church work at a temporary structure and reorganized and reincorporated the shrine organization in July, 1952. After gathering over 10,000 petitions in 1953 and lengthy hearings at the Board of Supervisors followed by court hearings, the shrine property was finally returned in 1962. The original shrine built in 1923 was soon thereafter moved to its present site due to redevelopment of the original site. The shrine was finally repaired and restored in 1969.

Membership: In 1997 there were approximately 200 members.

★2294★
Tenrikyo
Tenrikyo Mission Headquarters in America
2727 E. First St.
Los Angeles, CA 90033

Of the various groups termed "new religions," in Japan Tenrikyo is the largest, with more than 2 million members. It was founded by a Japanese woman, Miki Nakayama. In 1838, she began to go into trances and spoke as if God were speaking through her. Over a period of time, she gave away her possessions to attain ultimate poverty and began to practice spiritual healing. The rise of Tenrikyo coincided with a period of popular revolt, and its leaders were persecuted by the Japanese government. Finally in 1908 it was given recognition by the government as an approved Shinto sect.

According to Tenrikyo, God first revealed himself as Kami (the creator) and then as Tsuki-hi (the Moon/Sun God). The pantheon of Shinto is conceived as aspects of the one God. The center of Tenrikyo is Tenri-o-no-mikoto (Lord of divine wisdom), commonly referred to as Oya-gami (God the parent), who spoke through and dwelt in Nakayama. Nakayama is now believed to reside in spirit at her former home in Tenri, Japan.

Followers believe that humans are essentially good but have during their lives accumulated Hokori (dust). The various kinds of Hokori (greed, stinginess, partiality, hatred, animosity, anger, covetousness, and arrogance) stain our minds. As the dust is swept away, individuals will be opened to a joyous life (Yokigurashi), or salvation.

In the past there were a number of means to Yokigurashi, but today the main avenues are self-reflection, prayer, and "tsutome" or sacred service. An oft repeated prayer is "Ashiki o harote tasuke tamae, Tenri-o-no-mikoto" ("Sweep away all evils and save us, parent, Tenri-o-no-mikoto"). The prayer is accompanied by hand motions symbolic of dust being brushed away from the soul. Tsutome is a ceremony performed only at the international headquarters in Tenri. In the Jiba, the palace at Tenri, is the Kanodai (sacred stand) around which service and dancing are offered.

In order to manifest the parenthood of God and to realize Yokigurashi, a variety of social services and cultural institutions have been founded. They include orphanages, Tenri University, a library, museum, and churches.

Having spread to Korea and China in the first decades after receiving government recognition, Tenrikyo, as its 40th anniversary approached in 1926, gave attention to establishing the movement in America. In 1927, two missionaries, Yone Okazaki and Rinzo Torizawa were sent to Seattle and began work among members already living in Portland and Seattle. Within a few years churches were begun in Tacoma, Los Angeles, and Honolulu. By the beginning of World War II, the church had parishes along the West Coast from San Diego to Vancouver. By 1965, there were 15 congregations in Hawaii and by 1973, congregations had spread as far east as Chicago.

Membership: In 1987, the North American headquarters reported 54 churches and 68 fellowship groups in the United States, mostly in California. There also were four churches and seven fellowship groups in Canada. There were 850 yoboku (missionaries) and an estimated membership of over 3,000.

Periodicals: *Tenrikyo Newsletter.*

Sources:

The Life of Oyasama, Foundress of Tenrikyo. Tenri, Japan: Tenrikyo Church Headquarters, 1982.

Nishiyama, Teruo. *Introduction to the Teachings of Tenrikyo.* Tenri, Japan: Tenrikyo Overseas Mission Department, 1981.

A Short History of Tenrikyo. Nara, Japan: Tenrikyo Church, 1956.

Takano, Tomoji. *The Missionary.* Trans. by Mitsuru Yuge. Tenri, Japan: Tenrikyo Overseas Mission Department, 1981.

Tenrikyo, Its History and Teachings. Tenri, Japan: Tenrikyo Overseas Mission Department, 1966.

van Straelen, Henry. *The Religion of Divine Wisdom.* Kyoto: Veritas Shoin, 1957.

★2295★
Tensho-Kotai-Jingu-Kyo
Hawaii Dojo
888 N. King St.
Honolulu, HI 96817

Tensho-Kotai-Jingu-Kyo is a religion built around the remarkable charismatic figure, Sayo Kitamura (1900-1967), usually addressed as "Ogamisama" (The Great God) by her followers. A Japanese woman married to a farmer, Ogamisama had no particular religious convictions until 1943, when a series of divine revelations began. She reported that the Absolute God, Tensho-kotai-jin, descended into her body and told her to be the founder of the "Kingdom of God on Earth." The new religion spread rapidly and was registered with the government in 1947.

Tensho-kotai-jin is seen as the Absolute God of the universe, the heavenly Father (as in Christianity), and the eternal Buddha. The almighty God is a male-female pair, who by possessing Sayo Kitamura, formed a trinity. Both she and her followers describe her in deific terms. She is seen to have powers of prophecy and healing. She proclaimed 1946 as the first year of the New Era.

Ogamisama's sermons were sometimes "sung" while in a state of ecstasy and were always delivered without preparation. She taught her followers the prayer she received from God for the redemption of negative spirits and for world peace. As one way to express inner joy and gratitude, the followers perform a dance (ecstasy dance) in the state of non-ego.

Ogamisama's role is to establish the kingdom here and now by expanding God's teaching to humanity. For the individual, the process begins with purifying the world of the six roots of evil, which are regret, desire, hatred, fondness, love, and being loved excessively; the saving of evil spirits; severing personal karma; and continuing to polish the soul with sincerity and courage.

Ogamisama made her first trip to Hawaii in 1952. She advised her listeners to burn the relics of Shintoism and Buddhism, because they belonged to the past. The result of her trip was the establishment of eight branches of her religion. In October 1964, she began a nine-month worldwide tour which brought her to America for the last time. The movement had become worldwide by the time of her death in 1967. She was succeeded by her granddaughter, Kiyokazu Kitamura, revered as "Himegamisama."

An active evangelistic program of the Tensho-Kotai-Jigu-Kyo is supported by a number of publications. The central document is *Prophet of Tabuse*, introducing very briefly the life and teachings of Ogamisama. A periodical is published in Japanese, English, and Spanish, and other literature is available in ten different languages. In the United States, there is an annual gathering of members (doshi) for a conference in each of the three divisions of work—Hawaii, Northern California, and Southern California.

Membership: In 1992, there were 13 branches in Hawaii. Most of the mainland membership is located in several communities of California as well as Seattle, Washington; Chicago, Illinois; and Bound Brook, New Jersey. Worldwide, centers are found in 76 countries. Membership count is inexact, and no strict head-count is kept on registration. A member is called a *doshi* (comrade), which means a person sharing with another the same purposes, to attain world peace and the establishment of God's kingdom on earth. Anyone willing to work for those goals is welcomed.

Periodicals: *Voice from Heaven.* Available from Tensho-Kotai-Jingu-Kyo, Tabuse, Yamaguchi Pref., Japan.

Sources:

Lebra, Takie Sugiyama. "Logic of Salvation: The Case of a Japanese Sect in Hawaii." *The International Journal of Social Psychiatry* 16, no. 1 (Winter 1969/70): 45-53.

Ogamisama Says.... Tabuse, Japan: Tensho-Kotai-Jingu-Kyo, 1963.

The Prophet of Tabuse. Tabuse, Japan: Tensho-Kotai-Jingu-Kyo, 1954.

★2296★
Third Civilization
Current address not obtained for this edition.

The Third Civilization is one of the "new religions" of Japan and represents a twentieth-century form of Shintoism based upon the work of Sen-sei Koji Ogasawara. Ogasawara retranslated the *Kojiki* and *Nippon-Syoki* (*Nihongi*), the Shinto scriptures, in such a way as to lift the veil of symbolic mythology and to put the name of God into sound. The Third Civilization is involved in the study of the Kototama principle. "Kototama" is equated with the Biblical "Logos," the Chinese "Tao," and is the underlying life-principle which is the source of all.

According to the Third Civilization, history can be divided into three periods. Ten thousand years ago, our human ancestors perfected the Kototama principle and lived as one family in a peaceful society. This perfect society was the First Civilization and is equated with the Garden of Eden. About 5,000 years ago, the Kototama principle was hidden from society and a new principle guiding society toward the material-scientific or Second Civilization emerged. During this time, man divided into tribes and nations and became competitive. Basic to the Second Civilization is the division between physical and spiritual. The present time, in which the pollution of the planet is monumental, is the hellfire prophesied in prior ages. Our only hope is the "messiah," the capacity of the human soul which has been dormant, the Kototama principle. With this principle, the Third Civilization will emerge.

Membership: Not reported. European centers are located in Paris and Uppsala, Sweden.

Periodicals: *Third Civilization Monthly.*

Sources:

Nakazono, Masahilo. *Kototama.* Sante Fe, NM: Third Civilization, 1976.

___. *Messiah's Return, The Hidden Kototama Principle.* Santa Fe, NM: Third Civilization, 1972

___. *My Past Way of Budo.* Santa Fe: Kototama Institute, 1979.

Section 25
Unclassified Christian Churches

Unclassified Christian Churches

★2297★
Assembly of Christian Soldiers
Current address not obtained for this edition.

The upsurge of the Ku Klux Klan in the South in the 1960s led in 1971 to the formation of a Klan-based church, the Assembly of Christian Soldiers. Its founder and leader, Jessie L. Thrift, was a former Grand Wizard of the Original Knights of the Ku Klux Klan, one of several Klan schismatic groups. The assembly began a program of assisting the all-white segregated academies, which were established in reaction to the desegregation of public schools in the South. Money from the tax-exempt church funds was used to subsidize schools so that parents could transfer children from public schools without extra cost. There is an affiliated organization, "The Southerners", which organizes mass rallies.

Membership: In 1972 there were ten churches in Alabama, six in Georgia and Mississippi, and approximately 3,000 members.

★2298★
Body of Christ (Jim Roberts)
Current address not obtained for this edition.

The nomadic group called the Body of Christ was founded by Jimmie T. Roberts, a former marine. The group generated a number of news stories in the late 1970s as its presence became known and several members were deprogrammed. Roberts, the son of a part-time Pentecostal minister, grew up in the South in a religious family. But he had come to feel that the mainline churches had become too carnal. He wished to create a following similar to the disciples who moved around the countryside with Jesus, who traveled as he preached. He found support in Bible passages, calling believers to separate themselves from worldliness. He began to recruit members for his group around 1970 in Denver, Colorado, and in California. As the leader of the group, Roberts was generally known as Brother Evangelist.

As the group took shape, a hierarchical structure was formed and was headed by an elder (one of the oldest members). It was comprised of the older brothers and the middle brothers (the positions being related to their time in the group). Women basically cared for the children and assisted the male members. During the 1970s, the group wore a distinctive, monk-like garb which made them highly visible when they gathered as a group.

It was common practice for the Body of Christ to gather periodically, divide into groups of two or three, and travel by separate routes to the next designated gathering place. During gatherings members would listen to Brother Evangelist preach, sing, welcome new members, and fellowship with each other. The time on the road was for witnessing and preaching to any who would listen.

The existence of the group was first brought to the public's attention in 1975 when several members were involved in an accident in Fayetteville, Arkansas. The several members were kidnapped and deprogrammed. For the rest of the decade there was sporadic attention given to the group as parents of young adult members attempted to contact relatives in the group. In 1979, a book-length story of a former member, Rachel Martin, was published. Since then the group has dropped out of sight and little has been heard of its members, possibly a response to the growing amount of negative publicity. Its present whereabouts and status are unknown.

Among the activities of the group was its practice of raiding garbage bins behind restaurants and grocery stores to find free food. This practice earned them the label "Garbage Eaters". The group bathed infrequently and refused medical treatment.

Membership: At one time the group had as many as 100 members. The most recent reports, from the early 1980s, suggested membership was approximately 40.

Sources:

Martin, Rachel, as told to Bonnie Palmer Young. *Escape.* Denver, CO: Accent Books, 1979.

★2299★
Catholic Apostolic Church
Current address not obtained for this edition.

The outpouring of charismatic gifts in 1906 at the Azusa Street mission in Los Angeles, California, led to the modern Pentecostal movement. But prior sporadic charismatic events in the Western world figure in Pentecostal history as precursors of the twentieth century movement. One such outpouring in England led to the founding of the Catholic Apostolic Church. In 1828, the Rev. John McLeod Campbell, a Presbyterian who believed in the universal love of Christ and drew great crowds of people to hear of it, began to notice "supernatural" happenings in his parish. The first event was the death-bed conversion of James Grubber, remarkable for the change in his countenance from anxiety to peace, and for his words about Christ's imminent return. A Mr. Johnstone had a similar death the next year, and Isabella Campbell followed in the same fashion.

In 1830, Margaret MacDonald, weak and near death, began to experience visions of God's mercy and of heavenly hosts; two months later she was healed. In the excitement that followed the gathering at Margaret's house for prayer meetings, George, and then James MacDonald began to speak in tongues and to prophesy. A small group gathered around the MacDonalds and eventually a small chapel was rented to hold services. News spread to all corners of the British Isles.

One group that heard of the MacDonalds was composed of clergy and laymen gathered at the country estate of Henry Drummond to study the signs of the end of the world. Delegates were dispatched to investigate the occurrences associated with the MacDonalds and, upon their return, reported favorably. Greatly influenced by the report was the Rev. Edward Irving, a Presbyterian minister who had been impressed with John McLeod Campbell. Irving published the delegates' account, claiming that they had heard languages which were indeed unknown tongues. Irving became a prolific exponent of charismata. He was removed from the Presbyterian Church, and, from this split, the Catholic Apostolic Church dates.

As the new church took shape, a non-Presbyterian polity began to develop. Members believed that they were in community with the Biblical church and should possess a Biblical government. Apostles arose to lead the new church order, and other Biblical offices, such as the prophet, came into existence. The church grew and spread.

Members of the Catholic Apostolic Church came to America in the 1840s and organized a church at Potsdam, New York. In 1851, a society was organized in New York and a church was purchased three years later. Early congregations were established in Enfield and Hartford, Connecticut, and in Boston, Massachusetts. Members came largely from New England Congregationalism and Episcopalianism. The leader of the church was William Watson Andrews, a former Congregational minister.

The Catholic Apostolic Church is at variance with its parent Presbyterian, Congregational, and Episcopal bodies in its acceptance of and belief in the necessity of all the charismatic gifts and in its polity. Among the gifts it seeks are healing, speaking in tongues, and prophecy. However, at its formation, the church did not stress speaking in tongues as the sign of the Holy Spirit's indwelling. The church is not the first church within the Pentecostal movement because it did not initially describe the gift of tongues. The Catholic Apostolic Church accepts the Nicene Creed and closely follows the Church of England largely in its doctrine. It retains the sacramental view of baptism and the Lord's Supper. It has revived the sacrament of the laying-on-of-hands for the gift of the Holy Spirit. Sacraments of the second order include sealing and marriage. The church believes in the premillennial second coming of Jesus. One aim of the Catholic Apostolic Church was to reestablish the church in its apostolic order. In 1832, a new restoration of the college of "apostles" was begun in the call of John Bate Cardale. Also included among the 12 were Henry Drummond, Thomas Carlyle, and Henry Hilton. When these gentlemen died, the apostles' office was dissolved. Under the apostles were the servants (Luke 10:1). The three-fold ministry of angel (bishop), priest (or elder), and deacon functioned in the local church. Members of the ministry were exclusively called, appointed, and ordained by the apostles. The last of the 12 apostles died in 1901. Since that time there have been no ordinations.

The thrust of the Catholic Apostolic Church has been directed totally toward awakening other churches to its concerns. Such a program, often seen as a proselytizing endeavor, was successful in the nineteenth century. Soon after the death of the apostles, however, growth stopped. The 13 churches reported in 1916 had been reduced to seven in 1936 and at last report only one. It may have ceased to exist in the United States.

Sources:

Dallimore, Arnold. *Forerunner of the Charismatic Movement: The Life of Edward Irving.* Chicago: Moody Press, 1983.

Drummond, Andrew Landale. *Edward Drummond and His Circle.* London: James Clarke, 1934.

Shaw, P. E. *The Catholic Apostolic Church, Sometimes Called Irvingite: A Historical Survey.* New York: King's Crown Press, 1946.

★2300★
Christ Family
Current address not obtained for this edition.

The Christ Family was founded in the early 1960s by Charles Franklin Hughes, whose religious name is Lightning Amen. According to the group, Hughes went through a period of fasting for forty days in the Arizona desert before making a public appearance as Lightning Amen. He began gathering disciples who assumed new names, with "Christ" as their surname. The disciples

have adopted a nomadic lifestyle which keeps them moving around the United States preaching and accepting more converts. Members of the group generally dress in white, wear a headband, and, when not barefoot, wear shoes which are not made of leather or other animal products.

The Christ Family claims to follow the teachings of Jesus, and sees Lightning Amen as the Messiah returned to earth. Emphasized among members of the Family is living the Bible, whose central features include non-violence, abstinence from sex, and separation from materialism. Members are strict vegetarians and do not drink alcohol. They do, however, smoke tobacco and marijuana, natural weeds given by God.

The Family is organized very informally. A farm near Hemut, California, serves as the headquarters of the group, though most members travel throughout the United States the greater part of the year.

Membership: Not reported.

Remarks: Because of their nomadic nonconventional lifestyle, along with the difficulty of staying in contact with individual members of the group, families who have relatives in the Christ Family have added it to the list of contemporary groups called "cults." The group publishes little material, and the only substantive publication on the group is a booklet published by an anti-cult organization. The group has been the target of a number of deprogramming attempts.

Sources:

Long, Estelle. *The Christ Family Cult.* Redondo Beach, CA: Citizens Freedom Foundation, Information Services, 1981.

★2301★
Christian Catholic Church
Dowie Memorial Dr.
Zion, IL 60099

The Christian Catholic Church was founded by John Alexander Dowie (1847-1907). He was born in Scotland, but as a teenager migrated with his family to Australia. A short time later, he was healed of chronic dyspepsia. Dowie became a Congregationalist minister, but was dissatisfied with his life until he discovered the healing power of God during the plague of 1876 in Australia. In 1882 he founded the International Divine Healing Association and, as its president, was a champion of God's healing power and an avowed foe of liquor, tobacco, and drugs. In 1888 he left Australia to attend an International Healing Conference in England. However, he got only as far as the United States, where for several years he toured the country as an independent evangelist. In 1891 he settled in Chicago and launched a ministry in a mission to the city. Three years later he opened Zion Publishing House.

In 1896 Dowie founded the Christian Catholic Church in Chicago. Headquarters remained there until 1901, when 6,600 acres were purchased on Lake Michigan. The city of Zion was established and became a communal economic enterprise of church members for many years. Extensive industry and businesses were developed and controlled by an established theocratic order.

The flamboyant Dowie, recuperating from a stroke which partially paralyzed him, lost control of the church in 1906 to Wilbur Glenn Voliva, whom he had appointed to run the church in his absence. Voliva found the church near bankruptcy and led a revolt that saw Dowie deposed just a year before his death. Voliva was succeeded in 1942 by Michael J. Mintern, who, in 1959, was succeeded by Carl Q. Lee. In 1976, Roger W. Ottersen was installed as the fifth General Overseer of the Christian Catholic Church worldwide fellowship. He served through most of 1994 after which the office of General Overseer was discontinued. Also, as of 1995, the headquarters church in Zion was without a senior pastor.

The Christian Catholic Church is rooted in evangelical Protestantism, though it has borrowed from several traditions. The Bible is accepted as the rule of faith and practice. Other doctrine calls for belief in the necessity of repentance and personal trust in Christ for salvation, and other basic evangelical doctrines.

Each year, at the end of September, the annual convocation is held at the headquarters in Zion. Since 1935 the church has sponsored the presentation of the "Zion Passion Play," a live drama featuring a cast of over 200. During the years of Dowie's leadership, the church founded the Zion Conservatory of Music, currently enrolling over 190 pupils. Foreign work is sponsored in Canada, Guyana, Israel, Jamaica, Japan, the Philippines, Malawi, and South Africa with the Amazoni people. Domestic ministries include Camp Zion in Ellison Bay, Wisconsin; Zion Gospel Chapel, Michigan City, Indiana; Inscription House Navajo Mission, Tonalea, Arizona; and Liberty Community Church, Lindenhurst, Illinois. In 1975 the church joined the National Association of Evangelicals.

Membership: In 1997 the church reported 700 members in 3 congregations, served by 6 ministers in the United States. The most substantive foreign work is in the Philippines where there are 54 affiliated churches. There are 50 members in a single congregation in Canada. The church reports 6,000 members worldwide.

Sources:

Cook, Philip L. *Zion City, Illinois: John Alexander Dowie's Theocracy.* Zion, IL: Zion Historical Society, 1970.

Lindsay, Gordon. *John Alexander Dowie.* Dallas, TX: Christ for the Nations, 1980.

___. *The Sermons of Alexander Dowie, Champion of the Faith.* Dallas, TX: Voice of Healing Publishing Co., 1951.

Newcomb, Arthur. *Dowie, Anointed of the Lord.* New York: Century Company, 1930.

★2302★
Christian Survival Fellowship
(Defunct)

The Christian Survival Fellowship was formed as the Fellowship of Christian Men by its founder, Julius Rose. It was Rose's opinion that humanity was living in the last days and that atomic war was inevitable. He also believed that Christianity was essentially a white man's religion, given to the Western world and authoritarian in character. He proposed the establishment of several survival towns (hence the change of name in the 1970s), as the only effective civil defense strategy. Each town would be nominally populated at all times, have a vast supply of food and other necessities on hand, and be run on a semi-communal basis. These towns would then be able to offer hospitality to all in times of crises.

In the 1960s Rose moved to Richland, New Jersey, and began to clear land for a prototype survival town. He also created the General Development Company to manufacture and market low pollution, high gas mileage (over 100 m.p.h.) vehicles. In the center of the town, called Survival Town, was Fellowship Park, a place for Christians to meet and spend weekends together.

★2303★
Christian Union
% Christian Union Bible College
PO Box 27
Greenfield, OH 45123

The Christian Union was formed in 1984 in Columbus, Ohio by a group of like-minded men who had a "desire for a more perfect fellowship in Christ and a more satisfactory enjoyment of the means of religious edification and comfort." The theology is conservative and evangelical. There is no creed to which allegiance must be paid, but seven cardinal principles are considered essential: (1) the oneness of the church of Christ; (2) Christ, the only head; (3) The Bible, the only rule of faith; (4) good fruits, the only condition of fellowship; (5) the Christian Union without controversy; (6) each local church governing itself; and (7) the discountenance of partisan political preaching. These principles are set within a context of general Protestant affirmations.

The Christian Union, as can be implied from its principles, is congregational in government. Congregations are organized into state councils and a triennial General Council. Councils exist in the states of Oklahoma, Missouri, Iowa, Arkansas, Indiana, and Ohio. Missions are supported in Africa, Japan, and the Dominican Republic. Missionaries serve with various faith-mission organizations. The Macedonian Society raises money to support needy students preparing for a full-time Christian vocation. The Christian Union Extension Bible School offers training via correspondence to students around the United States.

Membership: In 1984 the union reported 114 congregations, 6,000 members, and 114 ministers.

Educational Facilities: Christian Union Bible College, Greenfield, Ohio.

Periodicals: *The Christian Union Witness.*

★2304★
Church for the Fellowship of All People
2041 Larkin St.
San Francisco, CA 94109

The Church for the Fellowship of All People is a single congregation founded in 1943 by a group under the leadership of Presbyterian clergyman, Dr. Albert G. Fisk, then chairman of the Department of Psychology and Philosophy of San Francisco State College. With a building and modest monthly stipend donated by the Presbyterian Church, the group began to meet for worship and in 1944 called Dr. Howard Thurman (1900-1981), the internationally known black minister and chaplain at Howard University, as its co-pastor. The original purpose of the group was the establishment of an interracial fellowship at all levels of the congregation's life. Under Thurman's leadership, the congregation expanded and eventually all ties to the Presbyterian Church dropped. Thurman remained pastor for nine years and has been succeeded by a series of pastors primarily from liberal Protestant backgrounds: Dr. Dryden Phelps (1953-1955), Francis Geddes, (1955-1963), John D. Magnum (1963-1967), and H. Don Guynes (1965-1967). After five years without a pastor, the church has been headed by Daniel Panger and Marvin Chandler, and more recently, its current pastor, Timothy T. Malone.

The church is interreligious with a commitment to see all people as children of God and to seek a vital experience of God as revealed in Jesus of Nazareth and other great religious spirits. The church members are also committed to an ethical awareness of and a bringing into fellowship people of varied national, cultural, racial, and creedal heritage.

The memory of Howard Thurman is kept alive in the church. His writings and tapes are available from the Howard Thurman Educational Trust.

During the summer, the church sponsors an intercultural workshop for children. It also owns Stonetree Ranch in the Valley of the Moon near San Francisco, a retreat center.

Membership: In 1992, the church reported 116 members.

Periodicals: *The Growing Edge.*

Sources:

Thurman, Howard. *Disciplines of the Spirit.* New York: Harper & Row, 1963.

___. *The First Footsteps.* San Francisco, 1975.

___. *Illuminous Darkness.* New York: Harper & Row, 1965.

___. *The Inward Journey.* New York: Harper & Row, 1961.

___. *With Heart and Head.* New York: Harcourt Brace Jovanovich, 1979.

Young, Henry James, ed. *God and Human Freedom*. Richmond, IN: Friends United Press, 1983.

★2305★
Church of Bible Understanding
Box 841
Radio City Sta.
New York, NY 10019-0841

The Church of Bible Understanding was founded in Allentown, Pennsylvania, in 1971 by Canadian-born Stewart Traill (b. 1936). An atheist at the time of his marriage in 1959, Traill turned to the study of religion after the birth of several children, and decided that Christianity was the true faith. He began attending an independent Pentecostal church in Allentown in 1970, held Bible meetings in the church's gymnasium, and frequented a coffeehouse sponsored by a Presbyterian congregation. Eventually, both the church and coffeehouse evicted Traill, citing his creation of doctrinal dissension. With a few followers, he began to hold meetings in several locations in Allentown. The group organized as the Forever Family. While never associating with the larger Jesus People Movement which had come to the East Coast from California, the Forever Family adopted many of his characteristics.

The Forever Family grew quickly throughout the East, Midwest, and even into Canada. At its peak it was reported to have as many as 10,000 adherents and 110 communal fellowships scattered as widely as Montreal, Charleston, and eastern Michigan. However, in the mid-1970s the group began to be attacked by the media as a cult, and several members were deprogrammed. At this time the church adopted its present name. Internal dissension grew when in the fall of 1976 Traill divorced and remarried within a few weeks.

Traill's teachings, which follow a conservative evangelical theology on most points, have two emphases which set it apart from other Christian bodies. First, Traill teaches that the Bible is a figurative book. He developed a simplified method of Bible interpretation called the "Colored Bible Method," as it breaks down the light of understanding into ten important subject areas. This method uses the Bible's own method of true interpretation, "the only real one!" Secondly, members of the group are aggressive in their evangelism and separatist in their lifestyle. The church is seen as a flock called together under Jesus the Good Shepherd. Members are His sheep. New members are generally referred to as lambs.

Organizationally, the church has adopted a communal lifestyle built around individual fellowships which live together in single residences. Each fellowship is headed by a male leader. All fellowships in a single area are grouped into "centers" over which a leader responsible to Traill is placed. The group has developed a number of businesses to support its fellowships and ministry.

Membership: It was estimated that by 1980 the church had approximately 700 members in 13 fellowships.

Periodicals: *Lamb Ledger*. Send orders to 607 W. 51 St., New York, NY 10019.

Sources:

Duffy, Joseph. "The Church of Bible Understanding, A Critical Expose." *Alternatives* (New York) 4, no. 6 (April/May 1977).

Traill, Stewart. *The Gospel of John in Colors*. Worcester, MA: Church of Bible Understanding, 1976.

★2306★
Church of the Christian Crusade
Box 977
Tulsa, OK 74102

Billy James Hargis was ordained as a minister in the Christian Church (Disciples of Christ). While pastoring a congregation at Supulpa, Oklahoma, in 1948, he founded the Christian Crusade, and by 1950 was devoting his fulltime efforts to the Crusade. The Crusade opposed modernism, liberal theology, and the social gospel. It advocated a fundamental Christian faith centered in Christ, premillennial eschatology, and the existence of Satan.

In 1955 the Crusade hired L. J. White, Jr., a public relations man who began to build the notoriety of Hargis and the Crusade. Anti-communism came to the forefront of the Crusade's program. A project to balloon copies of the Bible behind the Iron Curtain made Hargis a leader in the right-wing political movement that climaxed in Barry Goldwater's 1964 Presidential campaign. From that point on, the Crusade expanded and a variety of subsidiary structures emerged.

In 1966 the Church of the Christian Crusade became a single congregation in Tulsa, Oklahoma, and weekly services were held each Sunday. Some members of the Crusade, following Hargis' lead, withdrew from their "denominational churches" and transferred their membership to the new organization. As groups of members emerged in different locations, independent Bible churches affiliated with the Tulsa church were formed.

In the mid-1970s, Hargis suffered a nervous breakdown, and the ministry suffered during his absence of almost a year. Upon his return Hargis reassumed the reins of the church and began to revive and expand its ministries. Currently associated with the Church of the Christian Crusade are a variety of organizations conducting many specialized ministries. The David Livingstone Missionary Foundation and the Good Samaritan Children's Foundation conduct a large foreign missionary outreach program, the most developed in India. An anti-abortion crusade is conducted through Americans Against Abortion. Quarterly conferences are held at the church-owned Christian Crusade Log-School Cabin in the Ozark Mountains. The Christian Echoes National Ministry runs the Crusade, publishes the weekly periodical, and organizes conferences and rallies around the United States. Other associated ministries include the Billy James Hargis Evangelistic Association and Evangelism in Action.

Over 4,000 people belong to the Church by Mail, a ministry to homebound individuals. A monthly sermon and other tapes are sent to these individuals. The tape ministry also produces sets of teaching tapes on a variety of topics. A weekly television show "Pray for America" has recently been added to the longstanding radio ministry.

Membership: Over 200,000 people support the ministries of the Christian Crusade, though most are not members of the church. The monthly newspaper has a circulation in excess of 250,000.

Periodicals: *Christian Crusade*.

Remarks: In the mid-1970s, the Church of the Christian Crusade and its associated ministries suffered a severe setback when Hargis was charged with having had sexual relations with students of the American Christian College, a college founded by Hargis and affiliated with the church. Confronted with the testimony of the students in October 1974, the board of the college asked for Hargis' resignation as president and his retirement from the church and associated ministries. Six months after Hargis came out of retirement, he regained control of the church and all the allied ministries except the college. In 1976, when the charges became public, Hargis denied the accusations and attributed his split with David Noebel, who had succeeded him as president of American Christian College, to doctrinal differences.

Sources:

Hargis, Billy James. *Christ and His Gospel*. Tulsa, OK: Christian Crusade Publications, 1969.

___. *The Far Left*. Tulsa, OK: Christian Crusade, 1964.

___. *My Great Mistake*. Green Forest, AR: New Leaf Press, 1985.

Hargis, Billy James, and Bill Sampson. *The National News Media, America's Fifth Column*. Tulsa, OK: Crusader Books, 1980.

Hargis, Billy James, and Jose Hernandez. *Disaster File*. Tulsa, OK: Crusader Books, 1978.

★2307★
Church of the Living God
632 Mokauea
Honolulu, HI 96819

The Church of the Living God (known in Hawaiian as *Ka Makua Mau Loa Hoomana O Ke Akua Ola*) was formed shortly after the erection of the Honolulu branch of the Hoomana Naauoa O Hawaii. Twelve members of the Hoomana Naauoa O Hawaii left that church and founded an independent congregation, the first building of which was dedicated in 1911. Prominent members of the church are the Wise family. In 1937, long-time pastor Rev. John Wise, was succeeded by his daughter, Ella Wise Harrison.

The church is organized congregationally and generally follows the Reformed theology of its parent body, though it has added some distinctly Hawaiian ideas. For example, elements of kahuna healing practices have been taken into the church. The church conducts a prison ministry on Oahu.

Membership: In the late 1960s there were six congregations.

Sources:

Mulholland, John F. *Hawaii's Religions*. Rutland, VT: Charles T. Tuttle Company, 1970.

★2308★
Church of What's Happening Now
Current address not obtained for this edition.

Among the responses to the death of Martin Luther King, Jr., Imagene Stewart organized the Church of What's Happening Now in Dublin, Georgia. Her ministry includes a radical attack upon institutional religion and denominationalism. After a short time, headquarters of the church were moved to Washington, D.C., where a street ministry was begun and a weekly radio show developed. The ecumenical commitment of Stewart led her to seek ordination from an interfaith group of clergy and laity on Reformation Sunday, 1974. The act was considered an identification with King in his break with denominationalism, man-made doctrine, and educational requirements for ministers.

Membership: In the mid-1970s, the church had congregations in Washington, D.C.; Chicago; and Dublin, Wrightsville, and Atlanta, Georgia.

Remarks: The Rev. Stewart has encountered some tension with authorities because her church's name is the same as that of a fictitious church in a routine by popular black comedian Flip Wilson. In 1972 she was denied authorization to perform marriages in the District of Columbia.

★2309★
Disciples of the Lord Jesus Christ
% Rama Behera
Shawano, WI 54166

"Disciples of the Lord Jesus Christ" is the unofficial name of a small evangelical Christian group gathered around Rama Behera. The group has no name, has not incorporated, and has grown slowly over the few years of its existence. Behera came to the United States from India in 1962. He studied at Columbia and earned a master's degree in nuclear engineering. According to his account, Behera met God in 1966 and converted from Hinduism to Christianity. He became an evangelist and traveled throughout the United States and Jamaica. In 1974, with a few people who had been converted under his ministry, he settled in Shawano, Wisconsin, and established headquarters for his following.

The Disciples are a conservative, evangelical, non-Trinitarian Christian group. They affirm that Jesus Christ is the only true and living God and that sinful humans can only be saved by repenting and being born again by the "Spirit of the Living God, Jesus Christ our Lord." The Disciples are set against the compromises of the worldly church and have adopted a stringent moral code that centers upon becoming a servant of Jesus in all thoughts and desires, and with one's mind and heart. Discouraged activities include watching television, popular music, immodest dress, and attendance at motion pictures. The church is the body of believers established for worship and the comfort of the faithful.

Membership: Membership is scattered throughout Wisconsin and Minnesota. Gatherings are regularly held at Shawano, Wisconsin, and Rochester, Minnesota. In 1985 there were approximately 150 in regular attendance.

Remarks: The Disciples have been an object of controversy since their emergence in the 1970s. Families of people associated with the group complained of the rigid lifestyle they adopted, their unorthodox theology, and the control Behera seemed to have over their lives. At least three members have been kidnapped and deprogrammed and became the subjects of major lawsuits. As a result of the deprogrammings, media coverage, and what the group has considered undue harassment, it has developed a strong polemic against the Roman Catholic Church and the Lutheran Church, which are viewed as agents of persecution.

★2310★
Family of Love (Children of God)
Current address not obtained for this edition.

The Children of God, now known as the Family of Love, was one of the original groups to arise from the Jesus People Revival of the early 1970s. It was also the first to be separated from the mainstream of the movement, as it began to develop doctrinal deviations and come under attack from parents of youthful converts. The Children of God (COG) was formed by David Berg. Berg, a holiness preacher, came to Los Angeles in 1967 to do public relations work for Fred Jordan, head of the American Soul Clinic, a pentecostal missionary organization founded in 1944. In 1967 Berg moved to Huntington Beach, south of Los Angeles, to become leader of a Teen Challenge unit. Teen Challenge was the national organization established by Assemblies of God minister David Wilkerson to minister to youth. Under Berg, the work in Huntington Beach separated from Teen Challenge and was renamed the Light Club, the core of the future Children of God. In 1969 Berg received a revelation that California was threatened by an earthquake and that the members of the Light Club should leave. Berg and those that chose to follow him wandered through the Southwest for eight months, an event which has been compared to the Exodus of the Hebrew children from Egypt under Moses. During this period the group acquired the name Children of God.

In 1970 COG settled in Los Angeles, accepting the hospitality of the Soul Clinic's skid row mission. Jordan also offered the use of his ranches near Thurber, Texas and Coachella, California. The membership grew and a disciplined communal existence evolved. By 1971 the Children had become a national organization.

During the early 1970s, the life of the Children of God was changed by the organization of some of the parents of the youthful members. The parents opposed Berg, his practices, and his teachings, claiming the group was a destructive cult. In reaction to the activities of FREECOG (Free Our Children from the Children of God) and other anti-cult groups which grew out of it, Berg dispersed the Children in numerous colonies across the United States and then led them in a mass exodus from the United States. By the middle of the decade, only a small percentage of them remained in North America. It was also at this time that Berg introduced his most innovative and controversial practice, "flirty fishing." He ordered the female members of the group to use their feminine assets to become "hookers" for Jesus, a sexual variation on Jesus' admonition to become "fishers of men." This practice continued for several years until venereal disease spread through the group and forced its abandonment.

The Children of God began with the holiness perspective of the Christian and Missionary Alliance, to which it added views on the imminent end of the world, the need to abandon worldly structures (churches, governments, economic systems), communalism, and the coming Jesus revolution. Berg gradually assumed the role of a prophet much like Moses, and issued a number of directives and doctrinal treatises called "Mo Letters." He taught that the Children of God were the harbingers of God's New World. Berg has assumed the role of the end-time prophet whose message denounces the Old and ushers in the New World.

The Family of God is headed by David "Moses" Berg. At the time of its reorganization into the Family of Love, Berg requested the Family to refer to him as "Dad." Members were dispersed into numerous small family groups and the older hierarchial leadership of apostles and elders was dismissed.

Membership: By 1977 there were approximately 7,500 members, 7,000 of which lived in over 70 colonies throughout the world. There are still some members of the Family in the United States, but most remain in other countries.

Periodicals: *New Nation News.*

Remarks: The Family has been a matter of controversy since its earliest years. In 1974 the New York Attorney General issued a report accusing Berg and the leadership of the Children of God of a number of illegal and violent activities. Berg's former wife was among those who testified against him. More recently (1984) Berg's daughter, Deborah Davis, left the group and published a lengthy account of her life as a member of the group. The book included a lengthy attack upon Berg and the Family, Berg's sexual excesses, and the experience of "flirty fishing." While the Children of God issued a lengthy response to the earlier report of the New York Attorney General, only a short response which answered none of Davis' charges was published by the Family of God.

Sources:

David, Moses [David Berg]. *The Basic Mo Letters.* Gold Lion Publishers, 1976.

Davis, Deborah [Linda Berg]. *The Children of God.* Grand Rapids, MI: Zondervan Publishing House, 1984.

"Mo" [David Berg]. *The True Story of Moses and the Children of God.* Children of God, 1972.

Pritchett, W. Douglas. *The Children of God, Family of Love: An Annotated Bibliography.* New York: Garland Publishing, 1985.

★2311★
Followers of Christ
Current address not obtained for this edition.

The Followers of Christ is a small Bible-believing group founded by Mr. Riess. Riess came to Oklahoma when it opened to white settlers, and took up residence at Ringwood. He passed the leadership to Elder Morris by the laying-on-of-hands for imparting and consecrating in the Holy Spirit. Elder Morris is the father of Elder Marion Morris, the current leader. The group believes in the necessity of following Jesus, taking their lead from the biblical Gospel of Matthew 4:19. If a person is to be saved, he will repent, and God will grant time for following Christ. The King James Version of the Bible is used by the Followers.

The Followers believe in repentance, baptism, receiving the Spirit, and following Christ's commands. Baptism is for adults and by immersion. Children are sanctified by the faith of their parents. Footwashing and fasting are also practiced. No medicine is used; rather, members pray for the sick. For nonbelievers, deathbed repentence of sin is believed insufficient to assure salvation, for there must be a period of following Christ.

Membership: There is only one congregation, but members believe that there are followers of Christ scattered around the world.

★2312★
Free Church of Berkeley
Current address not obtained for this edition.

Factors which contributed to the formation of a free, or liberated, church included a renewed emphasis on social activism in the 1960s, the emergence of a counterculture with its "hippies" and flower children, and the reluctance of members of institutionalized churches to support ministries among people who wished to significantly alter worship patterns, associate with drug users, aid unchurched youth, and meet the needs of people outside the church. The liberated church was based upon liberal Protestant theology which defined the church as a mission, rather than the more traditional idea which conceived the church as having a mission to fulfill. According to this new perspective, the church is equated with those groups that do the work of the church— struggle against war, violence, racial injustice, male dominance, and pollution, to name but a few. The liberated church aligned itself with the late 1960s "movement," those involved in radical political activism.

One free liberated church developed in Berkeley, California, adjacent to a locus of much radical political thought, the University of California. The Free Church of Berkeley began in 1968 as the South Campus Community Ministry, sponsored by several Berkeley congregations. Dick York, a priest in the Protestant Episcopal Church, was appointed to an experimental youth ministry. His work expanded and additional space became necessary as did medical and psychiatric services, food, and clothing. People both outside and inside the church community organized to meet those needs, taking the name "Free Church." York's home became the center of their activity. After months of work, the Free Church began supplying people's needs for worship and opportunities to learn about Jesus. A radical liturgy developed and rap groups on the "Radical Jesus" emerged. The Free Church was transformed into a "radically involved ecumenical church made up of youth, street people, students, church dropouts, hippies, and activists." It followed the ideal of liberal Protestant social activism to its logical conclusion.

Illustrative of the Free Church lifestyle was the experimental liturgy. Baptism was seen as "going through the waters" in much the same way as Moses led the Hebrew children through the Red Sea. The Lord's Supper became the "Freedom Meal." Jesus was pictured as the Liberator of people, who though killed by his oppressors, led his people out of the house of exploitation.

The Free Church movement spread across the United States in the 1970s, though it was largely absorbed by the mainline churches in the 1980s. During the 1970s, the Berkeley Church published *A Directory of the Liberated Church in America, Win with Love.* The directory included "movement" groups as well as specifically Christian organizations which were theologically aligned. There was also a periodical, *Radical Religion,* published quarterly. Though the "movement" is defunct, the Free Church remains as a liberal Protestant congregation in Berkeley.

Membership: Recent attempts to contact the church have not been successful; its present status is unknown.

Sources:

Moody, Jess. *The Jesus Freaks.* Waco, TX: Word Books, 1971.

★2313★
Full Salvation Union
Current address not obtained for this edition.

The Full Salvation Union was formed in 1934 at Lansing, Michigan, by James F. Andrews, a former minister of the Free Methodist Church. Later that year he was joined by his father, E. A. Andrews, who was appointed general pastor. The first General Council meeting occurred the following year. The founding principles included a general protest against politics and human manipulation in the church, and a plea that "all of the Lord's children have a voice and that decisions be made through prayer and counsel."

The union developed at a number of points some distinctive doctrines. It adopted a dispensational view of Christian history, which it sees as divided into three dispensations: Father, Son, and Holy Ghost. The Son's dispensation occurred during Jesus' thirty years on earth. The union teaches that parts of the Bible are more relevant today than others. It is seen as a stream from the fountain; it is not the fountain, it is secondary, deriving its excellence from the Holy Spirit. Experimental religion, the witness of the Spirit, and the inward consciousness of God are stressed, but no absolute distinction between conversion and sanctification is made. The believer moves from conversion to the more abundant life, but holiness is not attained in a single experience only. The union also teaches that eventually everyone will have the opportunity to accept God.

It is the union's belief that during the dispensation of the Holy Ghost, no ceremonies, including the sacraments, should be observed. The Jewish practices were continued in the early church for a time, but only as a concession to custom. Baptism was considered a sign of the confession of faith, yet the union stresses Paul preached a baptism of the Spirit rather than of water. The union's main attribute is believed to be its unity of spirit, as manifested in the lack of artificial divisions by age and sex and in its making decisions without majority vote. The group believes in tithing and healing.

The union is governed by a general council and the elders. The general pastor is head of the union. Elders are those who have been recognized as eligible to govern. There are both ordained and unordained ministers.

Membership: Not reported.

★2314★
Harvest House Ministries
(Defunct)

Harvest House Ministries was one of the most successful and important of the Jesus People groups to emerge in the early 1970s. It grew out of David Abraham's conversion to Christianity in 1970. Abraham had been the editor of the *Oracle*, one of the prominent underground newspapers of the 1960s. From its San Francisco offices, the paper reached a circulation of over 100,000 with its coverage and promotion of the drug revolution, Eastern religion, and sexual freedom. It ceased publication in 1969 as the hippie community disintergrated. A short time later, Chris D'Alessandro met Alexander and became the force leading to his conversion. Abraham, a Jew, turned the rights of the *Oracle* to D'Alessandro, who became the new editor. *Oracle* was reborn in 1971 as the organ of Harvest House Ministries, then five communes in the Haight-Ashbury district of San Francisco.

Harvest House Ministries was started by Oliver Heath and his wife, Mary Louise Heath, who had moved to San Francisco from Alabama in 1970. Oliver was a Baptist who had experienced a charismatic renewal. He established Harvest House to offer a Pentecostal-charismatic alternative to the popular psychi-mystical-Eastern teachings of Stephen Gaskin, Edgar Cayce, Meher Baba, Swami Satchidananda, and groups such as the Self-Realization Fellowship and the Vedanta Society. D'Alessandro formerly a member of the International Society for Krishna Consciousness, led members of the Ministries to gatherings of the Eastern religion's group meeting to distribute literature and engage in evangelical activity.

Heath appointed an elder, assisted by one or more deacons, to supervise each house of 15 to 18 residents. Supervisors were supported by the income of the residents. While there was not a specific teaching program, each person was encouraged in Bible study and members met together for worship. No evidence of the

Ministries has been cited in recent years, and it is assumed that, like most of the Jesus People revival groups, Harvest House Ministries was absorbed into one of the larger Penetcostal churches.

★2315★
Hoomana Naauoa O Hawaii
910 Cooke St.
Honolulu, HI 96813

Hoomana Naauoa O Hawaii was formed in 1853 when the Rev. J. H. Poliwailehua and other Hawaiian members of the Kalahikiola Church, the Congregational Church congregation at Kohala, Hawaii, formed an independent congregation. The Kohala congregation was predominantly Hawaiian in membership. Friction had developed in these congregations because the nineteenth-century missionaries had been, to some degree, insensitive in their work with individuals; as they converted individuals the missionaries left them isolated from their larger family unit which in Hawaii included grandparents, aunts, uncles, and cousins.

Hoomana Naauoa O Hawaii spread through the islands as several large extended families affiliated with it. By the end of the century a group from the Kohala congregation relocated in Honolulu and built a parish. Other congregations were located in Hilo, Koae, and Lanai.

Membership: In the 1970s there were four congregations.

Sources:

Mulholland, John F. *Hawaii's Religions.* Rutland, VT: Charles T. Tuttle Company, 1970.

★2316★
Jesus People International/International Christian Ministries
(Defunct)

Jesus People International began in October 1969, when Duane Pederson, then an entertainer and Assemblies of God college dropout, noticed a *Los Angeles Free Press* hawker on Sunset Boulevard in Hollywood. He conceived the idea for a free Christian paper, and within three days had published the first issue of the *Hollywood Free Paper*. He distributed 10,000 copies, and circulation climbed with subsequent issues. As people were converted, a variety of ministries developed: coffee houses, emergency switchboards, Bible study groups, rock festivals, and drug counseling activities. In 1972 the first issue of the *Jesus People Magazine*, a Bible study monthly, was issued. At the same time Jesus People International was formally organized. A few years later, Jesus People International changed its name to International Christian Ministries.

The *Hollywood Free Paper* was distinctive in its use of cartoons with simple and direct Christian messages. A line of Jesus People posters and bumper stickers were also developed. In 1972, a record and a book telling Pederson's story were issued, and groups around the country began to look to Peterson for leadership. Affiliated groups were found in 11 California cities, as well as Tucson, Denver, Detroit, Minneapolis, St. Paul, Kansas City, Chicago, Cleveland, and Raleigh. Pederson ordained pastors to lead these groups. Over the years, as the Jesus People Revival was absorbed into the mainline evangelical and Pentecostal churches, the national ministry gave way to a set of ministries, primarily in the Los Angeles area. A focus on social projects assumed a place beside the evangelistic concern. The Ministries supplied housing, clothing, and other assistance to the poor, and developed two widely publicized programs for intercity children, "Christmas for Kids" and "Camp for Kids."

In the 1980s the headquarters of the Ministries was located in the Venice Community Church which Pederson pastored. He resigned that position in 1985 and returned to Hollywood. The name of the Ministries was changed to Duane Pederson Ministries (PO Box 1949, Hollywood, CA 80078). It is no longer a church-forming organization. Its program, in cooperation with a variety of pastors, congregations, and other ministries, continues its social service programs, but has placed a renewed emphasis upon cooperation with other street and prison ministries. Ex-prisoners and other converts are channeled into established congregations, many of which are now served by longtime associates of Pederson. Pederson released three issues of the *Hollywood Free Paper* in 1987 before ceasing the publication. In 1989 Pederson joined the Antiochean Orthodox Christian Archdiocese of North America and was ordained as a priest.

Periodicals: *Hollywood Free Paper.*

Sources:

Pederson, Duane. *Jesus People.* Pasadena, CA: Compass Press, 1971.

Streiker, Lowell D. *The Jesus Trip.* Nashville, TN: Abingdon Press, 1971.

Williams, Don. *Call to the Street.* Minneapolis, MN: Augsburg Publishing House, 1972.

★2317★
Ka Hale Hoano Hou O Ke Akua
1760 Nalani
Honolulu, HI 96819

Ka Hale Hoano Hou O Ke Akua (Hallowed House of God, King of Kings and Lord of Lords) is a 1948 schism of the Hoomana Naauoa O Hawaii. Lt. Com. W. H. Abbey was its early leader, and he was succeeded by Rev. Edward Ayau, pastor of the headquarters church on Molokai. A second congregation is at Kahili.

Membership: In the 1970s there were two congregations.

Sources:

Mulholland, John F. *Hawaii's Religions.* Rutland, VT: Charles T. Tuttle Company, 1970.

★2318★
Kealaokamalamalama
1207 Prospect
Honolulu, HI 96822

The Kealaokamalamalama (Way of the Light) was formed by former members of the Kawaiahao Church, a Congregational church parish and the oldest Christian church in Hawaii, in reaction to the death of Rev. Akaiko Akana. Akana served twenty-five years as pastor of the Kawaiahao Church. The new independent congregation was established in 1935 in his honor. Rev. Akana's brother, Rev. Francis K. Akana, was the first pastor of the new church. In 1970 he was succeeded by his son, Rev. Francis K. Akana, Jr. A second congregation is located in Honolulu.

Membership: There are two congregations.

Sources:

Mulholland, John F. *Hawaii's Religions.* Rutland, VT: Charles T. Tuttle Company, 1970.

★2319★
Megiddo Church
481 Thurston Rd.
Rochester, NY 14619

L. T. Nichols was an independent Bible student who became a minister, believing he had discovered religious truths obscured since the fourth century. The key truth was the responsibility of every man for his sins and the fact that "No man could be saved apart from knowing and keeping the Commandments of God." First in Oregon in 1880 and then in Minnesota in 1883, Nichols proclaimed this truth and gathered followers. He was spurred in his work by a belief, based on a study of Bible chronology, that the end time was near. In the 1890s he conceived the idea of building a mission boat which would bring the followers together in a common home. This boat, the "Megiddo," a Mississippi River steamer, was launched in 1901 and gave the movement its name.

The boat traveled the Mississippi and Ohio Rivers and their tributaries. It was sold in 1903 and the group moved to new mission fields. In 1903 a community was established in Rochester, New York. Nichols died in 1912. He was succeeded by Maud Hembree, a former Roman Catholic. She developed an active mission program with several boats on the Great Lakes and began its periodical, *The Megiddo Message,* in 1914, which is still published today.

The community in Rochester, previously known as the Megiddo Mission, currently worships in a building on the church's estate and carries on an active educational program. From their facilities a large literature ministry is carried on throughout the country. Through direct mail advertising of their monthly periodical and their set of eleven booklets on Bible teachings, they support a major evangelistic effort to encourage people to believe, study, and live by the Bible.

The crusade of the Megiddo Church is based upon the members' belief in the imminence of the second coming of Jesus. Its imminence is heralded, they say, by contemporary signs and political corruption, the craze for pleasure, universal fear, the armaments race, and the peace movement. Elijah the prophet will return to signal Christ's return as king. The judgment will lead to a revolt by all who will not acknowledge him. This revolt is the great Battle of Armageddon mentioned in the Bible. The millennium will follow the battle.

Members of the Megiddo Church deny the Trinity. Jesus is considered God's son and the Holy Spirit is seen as a Divine power not a person. Man is mortal; immortality comes only as God's reward for a life of righteous living. There is no eternal hell, only death for the wicked. Distinctive is their belief that man did not fall in Adam, but each person is responsible only for himself. If a person follows Christ's example, he will be saved.

Membership: In 1997 there were approximately 100 members worldwide. More than 16,000 receive the *Megiddo Message.*

Periodicals: *Megiddo Message.*

Sources:

Hembree, Maud. *The Known Bible and Its Defense.* 2 vols. Rochester, NY: The Author, 1933.

History of the Megiddo Mission. Rochester, NY: Megiddo Mission Church, 1979.

An Honest Man: The Life and Work of L. T. Nichols. Rochester, NY: Megiddo Press, 1987. 122 pp.

Millennium Superword. Rochester, NY: Megiddo Mission Church, 1980.

★2320★
New Apostolic Church
3753 N. Troy
Chicago, IL 60618

Alternate Address: International Headquarters: P.O. Box 532, CH 8044, Zurich, Switzerland.

The New Apostolic Church is a variant of the Catholic Apostolic Church, a movement which began in England in 1830. By the beginning of the 1860s, a crisis had developed within the Catholic Apostolic Church. The church was led by a group of "Apostles," and in the expectation that their generation was in its last days, they had established no system to appoint new Apostles as they were needed. In 1860, Heinrich Geyer, a member in Germany recognized by many as having the gift of prophecy, was moved to call two men to the Apostleship, though he knew the British leadership would disapprove. Immediate schism was averted by the appointment of the two men as "coadjutors" for Germany's Catholic Apostolic Church. However, Geyer then went on to appoint a third man as an Apostle, Elder Rosochacky of Knisberg. Although acknowledged as an Apostle by Angel (Bishop) F. W. Schwarz, Rosochacky later repented of accepting the office. In 1863, Schwarz and Geyer were excommunicated from the Catholic Apostolic Church. Geyer again called Schwarz to the Apostleship and a new structure, duplicating the Catholic Apostolic Church, was initiated.

The New Apostolic Church spread across Europe and, in the twentieth century, around the world, though it was hindered for some years when it fell victim to Nazi persecution. It believes itself to be the Church of Christ corresponding to the Apostolic churches in the days of the first Apostles; teaches the true doctrine of Christ and His Apostles; was set up following the revival of the Apostolate; and now addresses itself to one task, that is the care of souls and the preaching of the Gospel. In carrying out its task, the church refrains from all political activities, in compliance with Jesus' words, "My kingdom is not of this world." However, it expects its members to discharge their duties as citizens of the state, following Jesus' words, "Render unto Caesar the things which are Caesar's." A member of the New Apostolic Church can play an active part in public life, and the church takes it for granted that members of the church will discharge the duties incumbent upon them in public life, in their families, and in the profession they follow with all due efficiency and a sense of responsiblity.

Beliefs. Members of the New Apostolic Church believe in the omnipotent God, who created the world and rules in eternity; the immortality of the soul; that humans possess a free will which permits them to decide for and against God; that God has made the means of salvation available to all people; in the divine plan of redemption which aims at saving a fallen humanity; God's incarnation in Jesus; the sacrificial death of the son of God upon the cross, which enabled humans to be reconciled to God; Christ's resurrection and ascension, and the mission on which He sent His Apostles to preach the gospel to all nations; that it is necessary to be endowed with the Holy Spirit by an Apostle in order to have fellowship with God, the Father and Son; in the second coming of Christ at the First Resurrection when He will take unto Himself "all those who have accepted his teachings" (John 14:30); that Jesus will set up the Millennium, during which period the evil one will have no power over humankind, all human beings on earth and the beyond will be offered grace and redemption; in the Last Judgment, at which those who did not have a part in the First Resurrection, will be judged according to their works; and that the redeemed will enjoy everlasting fellowship with God.

Organization. The church consists of all the New Apostolic congregations worldwide, united to form one body. The head of the church is the Chief Apostle, who is the supreme authority in all church affairs. His official seat is in Zurich, Switzerland. The congregations in a district or region constitute an Apostolic District, over which a District Apostles serves. Apostles, Bishops, and District Rectors are appointed by the District Apostles to care for the congregations in their respective territories.

A rector in a priestly ministry is in charge of each congregation. The ministers discharging priestly functions are a Bishop, an Elder, a Shepherd, an Evangelist, and a Priest. They are assisted by Deacons and Subdeacons in pastoral work undertaken for the benefit of each member. Special attention is paid to the requirements of children and youth. As in the early church, the ministers are laymen. They come from all walks of life and have not been trained in theology. Nearly all of them serve in an honorary capacity.

Expenses incurred by churches (the building and maintenance of churches, missionary work, etc.) are covered by voluntary contributions made by church members. The church does not charge dues, ask for donations or pledges, nor requires members to sign church mortgages.

The church dispenses three sacraments, as was in the case of the first Apostles. They are: Holy Baptism, Holy Sealing, and Holy Communion. Holy Baptism is the first step towards fellowship with God. This sacrament is dispensed by a priestly ministry authorized by an Apostle. Holy Sealing is dispensed by the laying-on of hands and prayer by an Apostle. Holy Communion is celebrated every Sunday. It is preceded by the absolution pronounced in the name of Jesus by an Apostle.

In addition, the church solemnizes the following events with a special blessing: confirmation, engagement, marriage, and wedding anniversaries. These blessings are pronounced by priestly ministers authorized for that purpose. Funeral services are also conducted by such ministers. Moreover, a pre-natal blessing is pronounced at the parents request.

Membership: In 1994, the church reported congregations in 172 countries worldwide and a total membership of 8,280,679. In the United States, there were 404 congregations, 34,609 members, and 947 ministers.

Periodicals: *Our Family Magazine.* Available from Verlag Friedrich Bischoff, Gutleutstrasse 298, D-6000 Frankfurt a. Main, Germany.

Sources:

Guide for the Administration Brothers of the New Apostolic Church. Frankfurt a. Main, Germany: Apostles College of the New Apostolic Church, 1967.

Kraus, M. *Completion Work in the New Apostolic Church.* Waterloo, ON: New Apostolic Church, 1978.

Questions and Answers Concerning the New Apostolic Church. Frankfurt a. Main, Germany: J. G. Bischoff, 1978.

★2321★
United Christian Church of America
Current address not obtained for this edition.

The United Christian Church of America was begun in 1893, but was reorganized in the 1940s by Bishop Alexander A. Lowande, who is considered its founder. In 1944 Lowande was a partner in the promotion of a fraudulent "National Day of Prayer." After receiving the cooperation of numerous governors, congressmen, and even the White House, Lowande was exposed and the project fell through.

Upon Lowande's death, he was succeeded by the Rev. Herbert J. Elliott of Brooklyn, New York. For a short period of time in the 1940s, the church was a member of the American Council of Christian Churches.

Membership: Not reported.

Unclassified Christian Churches

★2322★
Bible Christians
(Defunct)

The Bible Christians, not to be confused with the Bible Christian Church (the Canadian body with Methodist roots), dates from the independent efforts of former Church of England minister William Cowherd, a popular preacher in Manchester, England. Feeling bound by unwanted sectarian pressures, he left the Church of England and eventually established an independent meeting house at Salford, England. He felt that all members should take their life patterns from the Bible. He refused to draw a salary and earned his living as a physician. Members called themselves simply Bible Christians.

The group held the Bible as its only creed and emphasized the doctrines of the Trinity, the incarnation of Christ, the revelation of God to the prophets and apostles, and the church. The Bible Christians also taught that the true church was composed of those who have responded to the truth, and that the order of the church centered on prayer, preaching, and worship. As the movement developed, Cowherd began to advocate and then impose upon his very large following the ideals of vegetarianism and abstinence from alcohol. He supplemented his biblical support for these ideas with the latest findings of the scientific study of the human body.

In 1817 two Bible Christian leaders, the Revs. James Freeman Clarke and William Metcalfe, migrated to Philadelphia, Pennsylvania. Clarke proceeded to the western United States and was lost to the movement, but Metcalfe established a congregation in Philadelphia, which by 1823 was strong enough to purchase land upon which a church building was erected. Under Metcalfe's leadership, the church survived for a number of decades. In 1847 it reported around 75 members in the single congregation.

Metcalfe is generally remembered as the first prominent vegetarian in the United States. He authored the first vegetarian tract published in America and in 1850 became the first corresponding secretary of the American Vegetarian Society. The Bible Christian Church was a center of the society during the years of Metcalfe's life.

Sources:

Metcalfe, William. "History of the Bible Christians." In *History of All the Religious Denominations in the United States.* Harrisburg, PA: John Winebrunner, 1848, pp. 123-29.

Numbers, Ronald L. *Prophetess of Health.* New York: Harper & Row, 1976.

Trall, Russell T. *The Scientific Basis of Vegetarianism.* St. Catherine's, ON: Provoker Press, 1970.

★2323★
Brotherhood of the Cross and the Star
Current address not obtained for this edition.

Alternate Address: International headquarters: c/o Leader Olumba Olumba Obu, The Sole Spiritual Head Brotherhood of the Cross and Star, 34 Ambo St., PO Box 49, Calabar, Cross River State, Nigeria.

The Brotherhood of the Cross and the Star is one of numerous new religions that have developed in post-World War II Africa. It was founded in Nigeria in 1954 by Leader Olumba Olumba Obu, designated as its Sole Spiritual Head. Obu was born in 1918 in Blakpan, Nigeria. Though not a part of any church, at the age of five he began to manifest extraordinary and mysterious spiritual behavior, and requested to be addressed as Teacher and Leader. Things he predicted soon came to pass. People began to bring their problems to him. By 1954 he already had a large following. In establishing the brotherhood, the kingdom of God has been established.

His followers believe that the appearance of Obu is the coming of the Holy Spirit, the Comforter, whom Jesus promised in John 14:16, and which is mentioned in the book of Revelation as the Word made flesh of the book (Rev. 12:5, 19:13-14). His message is one of repentance of, and refrain from, sin as the kingdom of God is now with humanity.

The brotherhood began to expand rapidly in 1981 when it sent out some 200 missionaries to various locations around the world, including the United States, but with special attention to the United Kingdom. The brotherhood's youth fellowship sponsored 40 missionaries to the UK and the next year 50 women, all ordained priests of the order, arrived in England and began to organize centers, especially among Africans who had previously migrated to the country. In August 1982 the youth fellowship sponsored a tour of 65 missionaries to the UK and America. They were joined by seven members of the Brotherhood's Christ Servants Fellowship in September, and organized meetings along the East Coast from Atlanta to New York City. Initial centers were established in New Jersey, New York, and Georgia.

Membership: Not reported.

Sources:

"The Brotherhood of the Cross and the Star: The Story of a New Kingdom." *New York Times* (September 5, 1983): 18. Full-page ad.

★2324★
Church of Ishtar
Current address not obtained for this edition.

The Church of Ishtar was founded in 1988 by Billy Rojas, the prophet, teacher, and leader of the church. The church was inspired by faith in the goddess Ishtar, who was worshipped in ancient Sumer. According to Rojas, Ishtar was a historic person, the wife of Dumuzi, the king of Sumer around 2500 B.C.E. She came to be worshipped as the goddess of love and war, and as the female principle of creation, the Creatrix.

The worship of Ishtar is a tolerant faith. It begins in a spiritual rebirth, a genuine change of heart by the individual member. Such rebirth means finding a new purpose in life, redirecting one's energies to become the best person you can be, and making no compromise with falsehood, especially that embedded in outdated religious traditions. It also means finding that path which is right for you as an individual. That path, while very individualized, should have a social/ethical dimension and not leave others (who choose different paths) out. The Ishtar faith also acknowledges that spirituality has a sexual dimension and that the fundamental religious sacrament is Hieros Gamos, the sacred sexual union of a king (male) and high priestess (representative of the Goddesss).

In announcing the formation of the Church of Ishtar in 1988, Rojos predicted the formation of a large national organization. The building blocks of that organization would be autonomous local church centers at which the worship of Ishtar would be celebrated. Among the functionaries at the local centers would be the "hierodules," sacred prostitutes who would offer counseling to church members and on occasion serve as sexual surrogates. The church recognizes two ancient covenants. First, Abraham's covenant with God (El Shaddai, not to be confused with the monotheistic God of later Judaism) as recorded in Genesis 17. Also valid for all time is the covenant between Ishtar and her husband Dumuzi. Ishtar covenanted to rescue her husband from death, i.e., she would recuse men from death-in-life, from loveless, sexless lives. The resurrected male, no longer lonely, would then restore the good life on Earth.

To become a follower of Ishtar it is essential to become a student of the teachings of the faith, to learn about the Goddess and the covenants, and to pledge oneself to Ishtar, El Shaddai, and the goal of becoming a better person. One should also pledge to help the church and other church members.

Membership: Not reported.

Sources:

Rojas, Billy. *The Church of Ishtar.* Eugene, OR: The Author, 1988. 11 pp.

★2325★
Dawn of Truth
(Defunct)

The Dawn of Truth was the name given to the teaching ministry of Mikkel Dahl, a Canadian who described himself as a nondenominational Christian. In his early life he pursued a spiritual pilgrimage that led him through a number of esoteric and metaphysical movements and finally culminated in his acceptance of Christianity. He then devoted his life to the "proving" of Christ to the masses. He often offered his teachings to those in the movements he had once investigated and frequently took out advertisements in metaphysically-oriented periodicals such as *Fate* Magazine. His literature and correspondence lessons were mailed out across North America and to many countries overseas.

In his autobiographical testimony, *The Land of Mist Illusion*, he stated, "But now is our Christ demonstrated, while the challenge is flung in the teeth; refute the proof! Believe nothing is my counsel, but receive that which defies refutation. Reject the God of those who preach tomorrow and the sweet by and by. God is today, while the arena of His power is Here in the Present World, and right now! That is the great joy I have to preach, teach and also demonstrate! A Christ who lives Now in the Here in jubilant defiance of lifes every storm; a Savior not for tomorrow, but for Now and for our Here.'' Such statements characterized his perspective and often led to his being described as a "doubting Thomas," or "one from Missouri."

Dahl retired in 1978 but several groups that saw themselves aligned with Dahls thinking have continued to publish and distribute his material, which covers a wide range of biblical, prophetic and current events topics. He also wrote in an attempt to explain Christianity to those who followed esoteric and metaphysical teachings.

Membership: Not reported.

Sources:

Dahl, Mikkel. *The Coming New Society.* Windsor, Ont.: Dawn of Truth, n.d.

___. *God's Master Plan of Love for Man.* Windsor, Ont.: Dawn of Truth, 1961.

___. *Have You Heard, the Great Pyramid Speaks.* Fulton, MO: Shepherdsfield, 1986.

★2326★
First Church of the Doors
Berkeley, CA

Social science observers have noted the likenesses between religious devotion and the veneration paid by fans to movie and music superstars. That observation was given some new support in early 1984 by the formation of the First Church of the Doors by Tony Spurlock. The church is built around the memory of rock musician Jim Morrison. Morrison, leader of a band, the Doors, died in 1971 at the age of 27 of a heart attack, but like Elvis Presley still has a large and faithful following. According to Spurlock, the church members "worship their potential to be as wise as Jim Morrison." Morrison is considered a symbol of anyone who wants to defy the laws of reality.

Members pay annual dues of $110.00. They gather annually to commemorate Morrison's death, to watch videos, and to sing Morrison's songs. The church is headed by Spurlock, the "high mojomaster" and editor of the church's semiannual newsletter. He has gathered a collection of Morrison artifacts that he keeps in trust for the unincorporated church.

Membership: In 1992 the church reported approximately 50 members.

Periodicals: *The Deadly Door Knell.*

Sources:

Slonaker, Larry. "First Church of the Doors Lights Some Fires Among Fans." *Wichita Eagle* (July 25, 1992).

★2327★
Osgoodites
(Defunct)

The Christian sectarian movement known as Osgoodites after its founder Jacob Osgood (1777-1844), was founded around 1818 in Warner, New Hampshire. Osgood, a farmer, was a member of the choir of the Congregational Church. However, he developed an aversion to both Calvinism and Universalism (the two theological perspectives that were warring for control of Congregationalism). Calvinism was trinitarian in faith with a strong emphasis on predestination. Unitarians denied the doctrine of the Trinity. Osgood's own individual approach led to a break with the Congregational Church. He joined the Free Will Baptists who preached an Arminian perspective (opposed to predestination) but, not feeling at home there, soon withdrew.

Osgood's own church began with the conversion of Thomas Hackett and soon developed a small congregation. Among Osgood's peculiar ideas was a belief in the laying on of hands for

healing of the sick. He also argued against the hiring of either lawyers or preachers. Most importantly, the group refused to vote, continually complained of taxes, and refused to train for the militia or to pay the fines coincidental with such refusal. The first members of the group were arrested and jailed in 1819. The following year Osgood was also arrested and incarcerated. During this time he began to write his autobiography, the major source of information about him and his group.

Through the 1820s, the movement spread. A second congregation was organized in Canterbury, New Hampshire, and disciples could be found in many of the nearby towns. They built no church buildings, content to meet in private homes. Dress was nonconforming, the men wearing out-of-style clothes and keeping their hair long and unkept. The women cut their dresses straight and plain, and wore a white kerchief around the neck with a bonnet on the head.

Following Osgood's death in 1944, he was succeeded in leadership by Nehemiah Ordway and Charles H. Colby. They did not have the enthusiasm and ability of the founder and the movement slowly died away. It entirely disappeared by 1890.

Sources:

Osgood, Jacob. *The Life and Christian Experience of Jacob Osgood with Hymns and Spiritual Songs.* Warner, NH: 1873.

Scott, Kenneth. "The Osgoodites of New Hampshire." *New England Quarterly* 16 (1943): 20-40.

★2328★
Shalom Ecumenical Church
Current address not obtained for this edition.

The Shalom Ecumenical Church was founded by Bishop Joergen Koch Larsen (1914-1989). Larsen was born in Denmark and raised in the Lutheran Church of Denmark, his father being a dean in the church. He was serving in the Danish Army when World War II erupted. After Hitler overran Denmark, he was arrested, escaped, and served in the Danish underground. He migrated to Canada after the war and served in the Royal Canadian Army Medical Corps in the Korean War.

Larsen claimed to have been in possession of a rare manuscript, a "fifth Gospel," possibly the book of Jesus' sayings that many scholars believe stood behind and was a source for the four gospels in the Christian Bible. His father had brought the manuscript to Denmark from the Holy Land around 1920. The original manuscript was destroyed by the Gestapo but not before Larsen made a copy of it. He claimed to have brought the copy with him to Canada.

Larsen was consecrated as a bishop by Peter Wayne Goodrich of the North American Episcopal Church. Shortly thereafter he founded the Shalom Ecumenical Church in Hamilton, Ontario. While possessing apostolic orders, the church differed considerably from the tradition from which he assumed his authority. Larsen articulated what he considered a scientific approach to Christianity. The church is non-Trinitarian. Jesus is accepted as Messiah, Son of Man, and Son of God, but all of God's children are also considered sons and daughters of God. One becomes a child of God by keeping the Ten Commandments and the strictures of the Sermon on the Mount (Matthew 6-8). The church disavows belief in purgatory, hell, or the devil. Evil exists, but not the Evil One. There are only two sacraments, baptism and the eucharist.

Church groups meet in private homes, there being no church buildings. Membership is limited to those with one or more college/university degree(s).

Membership: Not reported. In 1988 the church claimed approximately 200 members in Canada, the United States, and Scandinavia.

Sources:

Ward, Gary L. *Independent Bishops: An International Directory.* Detroit, MI: Apogee Books, 1990. 524 pp.

★2329★
Social Brethren
% Rev. Earl Vaughn, Moderator
R.R. 2
Flora, IL 62839

The Social Brethren emerged in Saline County, Illinois, in the wake of the Civil War. Some former members of the Methodist and Presbyterian churches, among them the Revs. Frank Wright and Hiram T. Brannon, were concerned with the reconciliation of Christians who had been split over the issue of slavery in the decades prior to the war. The members of the Social Brethren suggested that the biblical position was to have fellowship with all believers in Christ, regardless of their position on the slavery issue, a somewhat unpopular position in the northern states in the fervor created by the war.

The Social Brethren hold to the essential affirmations of Protestant Christianity including the sufficiency of the scriptures in matters of faith and salvation through Jesus Christ. They affirm the possibility of a believer falling into apostasy (in which they differed with the Presbyterians). They practice two ordinances (rather than sacraments): the Lord's Supper and baptism. Baptism may be by any mode: sprinkling (preferred by Methodists), pouring (preferred by Presbyterians), or immersion. They also believe, in keeping with their reconciling mission, that ministers should refrain from preaching on politics or any other subject outside of the central affirmations of the gospel.

The Social Brethren are organized as a loose congregational fellowship rather than following the presbyterial or episcopal polity of the Presbyterians and Methodists. Churches fellowship in three associations; each of the associations, the Midwestern, Illinois, and Union, meet annually. There is also an annual general assembly to elect a moderator. There is no general headquarters.

Membership: Not reported. In 1975 there were 40 churches, 1,784 members, and 47 ministers.

Sources:

Piepkorn, Arthur C. *Profiles in Belief: The Religious Bodies of the United States and Canada.* Vol. IV. San Francisco, Harper & Row, 1979.

★2330★
Summum
707 Genesee Ave.
Salt Lake City, UT 84104

Summum (Church) was founded in 1975 by Claude Rex Nowell, who claimed to have received direct instruction from advanced beings concerning the underlying principles (Natural Laws) that establish and maintain the universe. These principles were given as an eternal work and form the foundation for the teachings of the church. The church provides a forum for those searching for comprehension of creation that they might receive the keys to that understanding and use the keys in order to reconcile the many bits of religious, philosophical, and scientific knowledge that they have acquired, but that may not satisfy their understanding of the whole. These principles have always existed as an eternal work and were presented to Nowell, now known as Summum Bonum Amen Ra. The teachings of Summum cannot, thus, be accredited to any one person or human source for they are believed to represent the workings of creation itself. The church teaches that the understanding of the principles is the master key to the reconciliation of all religion and philosophy.

According to the church, the basic knowledge that it teaches forms the esoteric teachings of every race and religion. Despite the many diverse teachings that have evolved over the centuries, a certain basic resemblance and correspondence remains. These principles have been restored to their purity by the Summa Individuals, beings who untiringly work the pathways of spiritual evolution, and who have been referred to as the Neters in the ancient Egyptian hieroglyphs.

The Summum philosophy embodies what are considered the principles of creation itself, and is able to explain the Grand or First Cause. The principles are formulated through nature and are nature. They cannot be ascribed to gods or humans, but are the cause of gods, humans, and all that exists. Summum stresses the application of the Law of Knowledge to all the principles in order for one to assess real understanding as opposed to mere faith or belief.

The advanced beings instructed Nowell to build pyramids and produce Nectar Publications (wine especially created by fermentation and aging within a pyramid which the members transform through psychokinesis and imbue with knowledge) which is consumed in small amounts just before meditation. The church's early work centered around Summum Meditations, still an important aspect of the teachings. Meditation is seen as a means to ascend the consciousness and awaken the aspirant to their spirit.

One of Summum's key meditations is the Meditation of Sexual Ecstasy. Summum views the basis and foundation of all creation as a copulation between two subjective states referred to as the "Grand Opposites," and accordingly, maintains that everything is an effect of this grand copulation. As such, Summum holds sexuality as a divine and integral part of spiritual evolution and defines "ecstasy" as "the state of union with God." The teachings surrounding this meditation are that all progression and evolution is effected through sexual ecstasy. From the smallest subatomic particle to the highest forms of life, every element, at its level of consciousness, experiences sexual ecstasy in its bond-making and bond-breaking. This meditation, along with the other meditations Summum teaches, awakens the adherent to his/her spirit. Awakening to one's spirit is what Summum considers to be genuine religion.

During the mid-1980's, the church announced it was ready to reintroduce the art of mummification. The church states that mummification was practiced by early Jews, Christians, Buddhists, Egyptians, and other religions as a science that allows for permanent preservation of the body so that the spirit or the departed can be guided by means of the spiritual science known as transference. It is the church's teaching that the departed spirit can be assisted in its evolution by guidance from those still embodied and those spirit guides working the pathways of spiritual evolution.

The church provides mummification and transference for interested individuals from all religions. After the physical preparation, the body is placed in a mummiform that is positioned in a pyramid while the ceremonies of the transference are given. Afterward the mummiform is placed in a permanent sepulcher.

Membership: In 1997, the church reported 150,000 members in the United States (who are served by 400 ministers), and 5,000 members in Canada. Summum groups are also reported in 34 countries worldwide.

Sources:

Summum Bonum Amen Ra. *Allah: Sealed Except to the Open Mind.* Salt Lake City, UT: Summum, 1994.

★2331★
Three Treasures Zen Community
246 Santa Clara Dr.
Vista, CA 92083

The Three Treasures Zen Community consists of a set of centers founded by Nicolee Jikyo Miller-McMahon, Sensei, who had received her Dharma transmission from Taizan Maezumi Roshi (1931–1995) of the Zen Center in Los Angeles. The community strives to create an open and compassionate environment in which the Zen teaching can be transmitted to both lay and monastic students. A broad program includes both koan practice and sitting meditation, as well as art, sacred dance, the development of communication skills, and social concerns. There is a regular schedule of retreats.

Membership: Not reported. Affiliated centers are found throughout the Bay area.

Sources:

Morreale, Don. *The Complete Guide to Buddhist America*. Boston: Shambhala, 1998.

Homosexually Oriented Churches

★2332★
Ancient British Church in North America (The Autocephalous Glastonbury Rite in Diaspora)
9-47 Marion St.
Toronto, ON, Canada M6R 1E6

The Ancient British Church in North America is a small western rite Orthodox body founded by Bishop Jonathan V. Zotique (Mar Zotikos), its presiding bishop. Mar Zotikos was a Franciscan monk who received consecration through Old Catholic sources. The church's ministry, which is built around a small group of independent Franciscans, both priests and lay brothers, is directed to the sexual minorities of Toronto (homosexuals, transsexuals, transvestites, prostitutes) and others (drug addicts) who feel rejected by the Eastern Orthodox Communions and the Roman Catholic Church. As independent Franciscans, the group sees itself as being ''for, of, and by gay-Christians holding hope that in good faith we can touch the charity of the Church of Christ as a whole.''

The clergy of the church are self-employed, and ministers are worker-clerics. Both men and women are accepted for ordination to the priesthood. The church is headed by its presiding bishop and a governing synod. Those affiliated with the church in the ordered life are organized as the Celtic-Catholic Culdee Community of Orthodox Monks, Hermits, Missionaries, and Evangelists of the Old Church of the Blessed Virgin, St Mary of Glastonbury (Our Lady of Avalon), in Diaspora. Future plans call for the establishment of a rural retreat center (Avalon Abbey) for meditation-contemplation retreats.

Membership: Not reported.

★2333★
Brotherhood of Mithras
Box 94
Uniontown, OH 44685-0094

Alternate Address: International headquarters: 11 Ellswood Ct., Lovelace Rd., Surbiton, Surrey, London, KT6 6NQ, UK.

The Brotherhood of Mithras was founded in 1980 in Surrey, suburban London, by a group of men who wished to reconstruct and revive the ancient religion of Mithras. It is their belief that Mithras was a real person who lived some 3,500 years ago in Persia and that the Gods decided to make him a God like unto themselves. What is commonly known is that the religion of Mithras spread through the Roman Empire and competed for many centuries with Christianity. Statues of Mithras have been found throughout Roman ruins, many of which included Mithraic worship centers. The God is often pictured nude and entwined with a snake or in the act of plunging a knife into a bull. The latter statue, called a Tauroctonous, graces the intersanctum of Mithraic temples.

According to the story, Mithras was sent a task by the Gods to prove his worthiness. A respecter of nature and animals, he was sent a messenger in the form of a raven who told him to slay a bull. After meditating on the instructions, he herded a bull into a cave and there slew it with his knife. In this act Mithras became an object of worship for his bravery, virility, and manliness.

The brotherhood has attempted to reconstruct the worship of Mithras in the context of phallic worship and the contemporary revival of sex magic. Worship takes place in the nude in a temple which, like the original cave, is void of any natural source of light. It is believed that during the sex act, men create more energy than women. Thus it is felt that an all-male circle will create more energy than a mixed group. The energy thus raised is used for various worthy ends.

The brotherhood is open to all men over the age of 21. Initiation is an arduous ordeal which includes corporeal punishment and during which both humiliation and subjection are experienced. Individual limits are respected, but it is to be expected that they are to be extended and a new level of experience reached.

Membership: Not reported. There are centers in England and the United States.

Sources:

Speidel, M. P. *Mithras-Orion: Greek Hero and Roman Army God*. Leiden, Netherlands: Brill, 1984.

★2334★
Christianbrunn Brotherhood
Christianbrunn Kloster
RR 1, Box 149
Pitman, PA 17964

The Christianbrunn (Christianspring) Brotherhood is a gay spiritual community which draws its inspiration from the all-male ordered communities that existed in the eighteenth century in the Moravian Church. Most especially they look to Christian Renatus Graf von Zinzendorf (1727–1752), the homosexual son of Count Nicolas Ludwig von Zinzendorf, the Moravian leader whose efforts had led to the community's revival. As early as 1728, a group of 26 unmarried men moved into a common household. During the last eight years of his life, Christian Renatus had been in charge of the single Brother's Choirs of the Moravian Brethren.

In 1749 in the American colonies, the Moravians established Christianspring, a community west of Nazareth, Pennsylvania. It was occupied entirely by unmarried men for the next 50 years. However, by the end of the century it was caught up in the larger changes in the church and early in the nineteenth century merged into the community at Nazareth.

The attempt to reestablish Christianbrunn as an openly gay community was begun in 1987 with the founding of an ordered community. Bro. Johannes Renatus Zinzendorf is the chief councilman.

The reopening of Christianbrunn is viewed as a return to the Garden of Eden as guardian angels engaged in nurturing, protecting, and healing. The Garden is identified as mother earth, an incarnation of the Holy Spirit. The members of the brotherhood see themselves as the consciousness of the Holy Spirit, His eyes and hands. Members have separated themselves from the world in order to do their Holy Work of waiting upon the Holy Spirit.

The community follows a sixfold path by which members understand the Holy Spirit is coming to know itself through them. One step of the path is emphasized each day of the week— perception, recognition, acceptance, judgment, change, and reflection. Following this path leads to a lifestyle which emphasizes behaviors that are empathetic, patient, and nurturing.

The community has developed a self-sufficient economy centered on some small industries and the raising of rare breeds of animals, and members work at a level of technology that does not violate their decision to live in harmony with the earth. Thus, they use candles for light and carry needed water from the spring located on the property.

Membership: In 1995 the community had 70 members, including three clergy members.

Periodicals: *The Harmonist*.

Sources:

Hamilton, J. Taylor, and Kenneth G. Hamilton. *History of the Moravian Church.* Bethlehem, PA: Interprovincial Board of Christian Education, Moravian Church in America, 1967.

★2335★
Church of Universal Love (Washington)
PO Box 1620
Stanwood, WA 98292

The Church of Universal Love (Washington) was founded in the mid-1980s by Rev. Barbara Allen as a New Age fellowship. While open to all, it has a special mission within the homosexual community of the Pacific Northwest. The church considers itself omni-denominational. It has no creed and draws inspiration from all the master teachers, especially Jesus and Buddha. It sponsors workshops on metaphysics, parapsychology, world religions, and holistic healing techniques, as well as retreats on a variety of subjects. On most Sundays the church sponsors a circle of love meeting that includes guided meditation, group sharing at an intensive level, Sufi dancing, and a potluck supper.

The Church welcomes people from different spiritual paths and believes that each individual must develop his/her own individual way. The church attempts to assist the individual in their spiritual search and avoids proselytization to a particular view. Interaction between members is based upon the Golden Rule, nonjudgmental attitudes, and unconditional love.

Church activities are held throughout the Puget Sound area at various locations led by Allen and her associates. It sponsors an annual New Year's retreat.

Membership: Not reported.

Remarks: The Church of Universal Love is not connected with a church of the same name headquartered in El Paso, Texas.

★2336★
Church of Zeus and Ganymede (CZG)
Current address not obtained for this edition.

The Church of Zeus and Ganymede (CZG) takes its name from the ancient Greek tale of Ganymede, a prince of the house of Troy, who was so loved by Zeus that the mighty deity changed himself into a great eagle, took the youth away, and made him immortal. Ganymede became his cup bearer. While believing that there is only one religion, striving to come into greater harmony with the Almighty (Zeus, Yahweh, God, Allah, or any of the other names used by various groups over the centuries) and to achieve a greater knowledge of creation, the church particularly celebrates loving relationships in this model. That is to say, it sanctions and promotes man-boy sexual relationships.

The CZG describes itself as more of a disorganization than an organization, in that it has no hierarchy, no property, no bank accounts, and no schedule of meetings (as most of the activities it values are illegal in the countries of North America and Europe). Thus the church is somewhat diffuse and ephemeral. It exists to provide spiritual support for its members. Its basic principle and rule is love, which is defined as a deep caring for the happiness and well-being of someone else. The CZG also asserts that loving relationships (sexual or otherwise) between males, regardless of ages, are a gift of the Almighty.

Out of realization of the social disapproval shown the primary idea behind the church, the CZG has articulated a Boylove Code of Ethics drawing upon the nature of the practice in ancient Greece. Noting that the sexual aspect is a part of most man/boy relationships, it calls for participants to deal with the issue of sex "in a mature and responsible way." While attempting to take the exploitive and manipulative elements from such relationships, the code does not deal with the dominant cultural analysis that boylove relationships are by their very nature manipulative and exploitive of the younger party who because of his age cannot deal with the relationship in a mature manner.

Though the church has an Internet presence, it is unlikely that it will find a more visible and structured presence given the nature of its beliefs and practices.

Membership: Not reported.

Sources:

http://www.fortunecity.com/culdee/.

★2337★
Community of the Love of Christ (Evangelical Catholic)
Current address not obtained for this edition.

Among the oldest of the church organizations which have developed a specific ministry to the homosexual community and openly identified with its concerns is the Community of the Love of Christ (Evangelical Catholic), founded in 1959 as the Primitive Catholic Church (Evangelical Catholic) by Mikhail (Michael) Francis Itkin. Itkin began his work as a minister in the gay community in 1955 when he was licensed by George A. Hyde, later presiding bishop of the Orthodox Catholic Church in America. Hyde had founded the Eucharistic Catholic Church in the 1940s as a church for homosexuals. Itkin was ordained in 1957 and continued to work with Hyde and the Eucharistic Catholic Church for two more years. He left Hyde in 1959 (at the same time Hyde was moving his work into the American Holy Orthodox Catholic Apostolic Eastern Church). Itkin accused Hyde of backing away from an openly gay ministry and "moving back into the closet."

Itkin gathered those members who agreed with him and for more than a year led them as an episcopal administrator until he could be consecrated by Archbishop Christopher Maria Stanley in November 1960. Stanley had orders to consecrate Itkin from Hugh George de Willmott Newman of the Catholicate of the West, which carried a variety of lines of episcopal succession. Among those lines was that of the Syro-Chaldean succession of the Church of the East brought to the West by Ulric Vernon Herford (Mar Jacobus), founder of the Evangelical Catholic Communion.

The new church first chose the name Primitive Catholic Church (Evangelical Catholic), but the name was changed after Itkin's consecration to Gnostic Catholic Church (Evangelical Catholic). The new name led to confusion, as some thought the church emulated the gnostic heretics. Then the members called themselves "Free Catholics" but learned of a British Fascist group using that designation. Again the church adopted a new name—Western Orthodox Catholic (Anglican Orthodox). During this period, the church members became aware of Ulrich Vernon Herford and the Evangelical Catholic Communion. They began to see Herford's lineage as the primary line of the historical episcopate received from Stanley. Itkin began to correspond with some European bishops who were attempting to carry on Herford's work, and from them he received permission to reformulate the Evangelical Catholic Communion in the United States. In 1978, Mar Anthony (W. Martin Andrew), the British successor to Herford, recognized Itkin's work in America as "the sole jurisdiction actually carrying on the work of Mar Jacobus and the original Evangelical Catholic Communion."

A short time after the development of the Evangelical Catholic Communion, Itkin and Stanley broke communion due in large part to the strong social activism advocated by Itkin. Among Itkin's first actions as a bishop was the consecration of a woman to the priesthood. Stanley, while open to female deacons, was opposed to their admission to the priesthood. In 1963 the Communion underwent an internal reorganization, transforming itself into a religious order that originally called itself the Brotherhood of the Love of Christ: Evangelical Catholic Communion. That name was changed in 1970 to the Community of the Love of Christ (Evangelical Catholic), its present name, to eliminate the sexist connotations of the word "brotherhood."

During the 1960s the church attracted a number of able leaders such as John Perry-Hooker, a psychologist working with a youth ministry in Boston. It became deeply involved in civil rights and anti-war crusades. Itkin, heralding what would be termed liberation theology in the 1970s, articulated a revolutionary Christian theology which emphasized pacifism, freedom from oppression, and civil rights for minorities. He advocated gay liberation and the role of Christianity as a means for the creation of a universal androgynous community. The work, however, suffered a severe setback in 1968 when more conservative elements in the church, including those who rejected female priests, split the communion and took most of the property with them. They reorganized as the Evangelical Catholic Communion, the name under which they continue. Itkin and his followers have continued their efforts as the Community of the Love of Christ.

In the late 1980s, it became known that Itkin was suffering from AIDS. He passed away in 1991 and was succeeded by Bp. Marcia Herndon whom he had consecrated in 1985.

The Community has adopted a distinct position of those within the Syro-Chaldean tradition, as it also considers itself as part of the Mennonite-Radical Reformation heritage. From the Church of the East, it draws an apostolic liturgical heritage. It accepts only the first three Ecumenical Councils, which includes an acceptance of the Nicene Creed. However, because of its Radical reformation heritage, it takes a "low church" approach to the sacraments. Only three, not seven, are acknowledged. The church also accepts, for historical purposes only, the December 1903 Pastoral Letter to the Syro-Chaldean Christians in India authored by Herford.

Following its own statement of faith which acknowledges Christ as Sovereign and Liberator, the Community is fully committed to a liberation theological praxis that includes a struggle against sexism, heterosexism, racism, classism, imperialism, and violence. It strongly supports and works for Christian gay/lesbian liberation, feminism, racial integration, civil rights, economic mutuality, democracy, universal citizenship, and nonviolence. The community does not consider itself a gay or homosexual church, but rather "a Christian covenant-community for all people, preaching the inclusive love of God to everyone." "Everyone" includes, specifically, gay and lesbian individuals.

Membership: Not reported. As a matter of policy, the Community does not issue statistics on membership. The Community is estimated to be small and largely confined to the San Francisco Bay area.

Remarks: For a period of time beginning in the 1971, Itkin held joint membership in the Metropolitan Community Church. He saw MCC as committed to his own belief of "unity in diversity," but concluded by 1984 that such was not the case. He withdrew his affiliation with MCC as a member, though retaining status as a "friend."

In this author's *The Old Catholic Sourcebook*, co-authored with Karl Pruter, Bishop Itkin was confused with another bishop who had also taken the ecclesiastical title, Mar Mikhail and who resides in the San Francisco Bay area. The other Mar Mikhail is the leader of the Holy Apostolic-Catholic Church of the East (Syro-Chaldean).

Sources:

Faith and Practice of the Brotherhood of the Love of Christ. New York: Pax Christi Press, 1966.

Itkin, Michael Francis. *The Hymn of Jesus.* New York: Pax Christi Press, n.d.

Itkin, Michael Francis Augustine. *The Spiritual Heritage of Port-Royal.* New York: Pax Christi Press, 1966.

Itkin, Mikhail. *The Radical Jesus & Gay Consciousness.* Hollywood, CA: Communiversity West, 1972.

★2338★
Ecumenical Catholic Church
Box 32
Villa Grande, CA 95486-0032

The Ecumenical Catholic Church was founded by Mark Steven Shirilau. Shirilau was born in 1955 as Mark Steven Shirey. In 1984 he "married" Jeffery Michael Lau, and both assumed the last name Shirilau. The church is a liturgical body that draws upon Catholic, Episcopal, and Lutheran traditions, but is distinguished by its direct and open ministry to the gay and lesbian community as well as women; the divorced and others disentranchised by the mainline church. Shirilau was raised a Lutheran, but joined the Episcopal Church. He was consecrated to the episcopacy by Bishop Donald Lawrence Jolly of the Independent Catholic Church International on Pentecost in 1991. Shirilau is one of the more educated Independent Catholic leaders, having graduated from both the Episcopal Theological School at Claremont (Bloy House) and the School of Theology at Claremont and having earned his Ph.D. from the University of California at Irvine.

Membership: In 1995 the church reported 1,150 members in 10 churches in the United States and 50 members in one parish in Canada.

Educational Facilities: Holy Apostles Seminary, Forestville, California (correspondence seminary).

Periodicals: *The Tablet.*

Sources:

Shirilau, Mark Steven. *History and Overview of the Ecumenical Catholic Church: The First Ten Years: 1985—95.* Ville Grand, CA: Healing Spirit Press, 1995.

★2339★
Eucharistic Catholic Church
Current address not obtained for this edition.

The very first ministry to the homosexual community was begun in Atlanta, Georgia, in 1946 by the Rev. George A. Hyde. Eleven years later, Hyde was consecrated by Archbishop Cyril John Clement Sherwood and began to move his ministry into Sherwood's American Holy Orthodox Catholic Apostolic Eastern Church. As he worked under Sherwood, he moved to Washington, D.C., a prelude to his forming the Orthodox Catholic Church of America in 1960. He backed away from an identification of his new church with the homosexual community, but continued an interest in ministering to gay people.

One ministry authorized by Hyde was a new Eucharistic Catholic parish in New York City's Greenwich Village, begun in 1970 by Fr. Robert Clement. Clement stayed with Hyde for several years while seeing ordination in an apostolic liturgical church outside of independent Old Catholic circles. Unable to locate a bishop who would accept his gay congregation, he turned finally in 1974 to Archbishop Richard A. Marchenna (d. 1984), then head of the Old Roman Catholic Church (Marchenna), who consecrated him. Clement reorganized his work as a separate episcopal jurisdiction independent of the Orthodox Catholic Church of America.

Membership: There is one congregation of several hundred members.

★2340★
Gay and Lesbian Atheists (GALA)
Current address not obtained for this edition.

The Gay Atheist League of America (GALA) was formed in 1978 as the Gay Atheist League of America by Daniel Curzon and Tom Rolfsen, both former members of the Roman Catholic Church. Both had come to feel that there is a direct relationship between the doctrines of religion and social discrimination against homosexuals. The formation of GALA was occasioned by an exchange of letters between Rolfsen and John Raphael Quinn, the

Catholic archbishop in San Francisco. Rolfsen concluded that the church had developed a tradition of persecuting homosexuals. Curzon had come to feel that all religion was oppressive, especially Catholicism, born-again Protestantism, and Orthodox Judaism. The new organization also rejected the attempts of gay religious organizations to seek accomodation with the church.

Gay and Lesbian Atheists teach that each person must discover the moral basis of life, without reference to what it considers self-appointed religious experts. They also support separation of church and state and oppose attempts by religionists to impress their anti-gay moral codes on legislation. They also believe that churches should be taxed, i.e., treated as businesses. GALA has assumed an activist role, demonstrating in opposition to anti-gay legislation.

Membership: In 1988 there were over 700 members and chapters in San Francisco, New York, Chicago, Denver, Houston, Sacramento, and Los Angeles.

Periodicals: *Gala Review.*

Sources:

Curzon, David. *Something You Do in the Dark.* New York: Putnam, 1971.

★2341★
Gay Buddhist Fellowship
2261 Market St., Ste. 422
San Francisco, CA 94114

The Gay Buddhist Fellowship, like similar groups in other cities, exists to support Buddhist practice in the San Francisco gay community. Membership includes practitioners who identify with all of the various Buddhist traditions and a broad program is conducted to accommodate a spectrum of needs and desires. Offered on a regular basis are Dharma talks, classes, time for sitting meditation, retreats, and a variety of workshops and classes on topics of interest to the gay community from personal relationships to HIV to social action.

The fellowship, founded in 1990, a single center operating out of rented facilities in San Francisco, has analogous structures elsewhere, such as the Lesbian Buddhist Group and the Gay Zen Group, both of which are semiautonomous groups sponsored by the International Buddhist Meditation Center in Los Angeles. On the other hand, Buddhism has expressed no particular animus toward homosexuality similar to that found in many Christian and Jewish circles, and thus the actual number of explicitly gay and/or lesbian structures is relatively small.

Membership: Not reported.

Periodicals: *Gay Buddhist Fellowship Newsletter.*

Sources:

Morreale, Don. *The complete Guide to Buddhist America.* Boston: Shambhala, 1998.

★2342★
Hermetic Order of the Silver Sword
2483 Gerrard St. E.
Scarborough, ON, Canada M1N 1W7

The Hermetic Order of the Silver Sword was founded in 1982 in Toronto. It is a ceremonial magical order whose rituals are based upon those of the Hermetic Order of the Golden Dawn. The Silver Sword attempts to unify elements of Cabbalistic, Rosicrucian, and Pagan traditions into a workable magical system, a modern science of mental power and self-knowledge. The Order sees magic as utilizing ceremonial acts and images deeply rooted in the human consciousness. Ritual actions and the manipulation of symbols produce changes in the magician that affect the world.

The Order promotes communication among groups attempting to revive and explore Western spiritual and magical traditions and sees itself as working toward the healing of the Earth through en-

lightenment and friendship. The Order is currently headed by Ian Young and Sandy Busby. Membership is by invitation.

Membership: Not reported. As of 1997, there were two temples (Toronto and New York City), each of which may have as many as seven members. There are also additional members not currently affiliated with a temple. The New York temple sponsors public rituals through the Circle of the Free Spirit.

★2343★
The National Gay Pentecostal Alliance (NGPA)
PO Box 1391
Schenectady, NY 12301-1391

The National Gay Pentecostal Alliance (NGPA) is an Apostolic Pentecostal church with a special outreach to the gay/lesbian community. It was founded July 28, 1980, in the city of Schenectady, New York, by William H. Carey and Sister Schwarz. Carey, a 22-year-old ministerial student in the United Pentecostal Church International, was forced out when his homosexuality became public. A woman from the same congregation in which he worshipped in Schenectady, Sister Schwarz, left with him. Unable to locate a Pentecostal church that did not oppose gay and lesbian sexual orientations, they formed the Gay Pentecostal Alliance.

In the spring of 1981, a second similar congregation was founded in Omaha, Nebraska, occasioning the addition of the word "national" to the church's name. The first ordination occurred in August of 1981 in Omaha. Carey, E. Samuel Stafford, and Frances Cervantes were the first ordained ministers.

NGPA's belief is similar to that of the United Pentecostal Church. It believe's that the Bible in its original languages is the inspired word of God and affirms that there is only one God, the God of Israel, who took on human form and was born of the virgin Mary, to save sinful humanity. Salvation is available through repentance, water baptism by immersion in the name of Jesus for the forgiveness of sins, and receiving the Holy Ghost, evidenced by speaking in tongues. It extols the nine Gifts of the Spirit (I Cor. 12:8-10) and the living of a holy and moral life. It expects the imminent return of Jesus to claim His church. Thus, like the United Pentecostal Church, the alliance does not accept the doctrine of the Trinity as traditionally held within Christianity, and has a second significant divergence in its belief that homosexuality is not sinful. It accepts the view, common to all of the churches serving the homosexual community, that the scriptures fail to condemn homosexuality.

In 1990, a presbyterial form of church government was instituted. The church is now led by two presbyters, appointed by district elders. At present the two presbyters are Carey and Sister LaDonna C. Briggs. Lighthouse Ministries serves as the outreach and evangelism department of the alliance and is responsible for the printing and distribution of literature and cassette tapes. The Home Missions Department, operating out of Niagara Falls, New York, oversees the founding of new congregations in the United States, and the Foreign Missions Department performs the same function elsewhere. Home Missions also operates a Division of Prison Ministries, centered in West Monroe, Louisiana.

Membership: Not reported. In 1998, the alliance had affiliated congregations in New York, Arkansas, Georgia, Illinois, Louisiana, and Nevada. There were also churches in Russia and the Ukraine.

Educational Facilities: Pentecostal Bible Institute, Schenectady, New York.

Periodicals: *The Apostolic Voice.*

Sources:

http://www.cris.com/~Ngpa/.

★2344★
Orthodox Episcopal Church of God
Box 1528
San Francisco, CA 94101

The Rev. Ray Broshears (d. 1982), founder of the Orthodox Episcopal Church of God, was one of the most controversial of all gay ministers of the 1970s. Headquartered in that section of San Francisco popularly called the Tenderloin, the residence of the largest gay community in the United States, he became a national figure through his radical activism on behalf of civil rights for gay people. He opened and operated the Helping Hands Gay Community Service Center for political action on behalf of pro-gay politicians, legal counseling and assistance, drug rehabilitation, and other gay-oriented activities. He ran for Congress, unsuccessfully, on several occasions. Possibly his most controversial activity was starting the Lavender Panthers, a group he formed to prevent youth gangs from invading the Tenderloin and beating up gay people. The members were trained in judo and karate.

Broshears was reared in the Cumberland Presbyterian Church but became a Pentecostal at an early age. He attended school at the White Wing College (of the Church of God of Prophecy) at Cleveland, Tennessee. He left the Pentecostal movement and in 1966 founded the Orthodox Episcopal Church of God. It was not until 1969 that he and the church began involvement in the gay community.

The Orthodox Episcopal Church is eclectic, combining elements of traditional Catholicism with liberation theology and psychic/New Age thinking. Its program is mainly expressed in social activism. Congregations are centered in the gay communities of California (Los Angeles and San Jose) and El Paso, Texas. Broshears edited several Gay Alliance periodicals, including *Gay Pride Quarterly* and the *Gay Crusader*.

Membership: Not reported.

Periodicals: *The Light of Understanding.*

★2345★
Sarum Episcopal Church
161 W. Highland Ave.
San Bernardino, CA 92405-4015

The Sarum Episcopal Church was founded in 1989 in Riverside, California, by two priests ordained as independent Old Catholics. The church exists to provide a sacramental ministry to gay men and lesbians. The first parish, St. Aelred's, originated in a private home but soon moved to its present facilities in San Bernadino, California. There the church operates a coffee house (no alcoholic beverages served) and houses a number of services for the homosexual community in the area, and has a special ministry for people with AIDS.

The church took its name for Sarum, the old name of Salisbury, a city in England which, prior to the Reformation of the sixteenth century, served as an important center of English Catholicism. The liturgy used throughout England took its name from this city and was called the "Sarum Rite."

At present, the church is collectively headed by its priests, as the jurisdiction has not yet designated a bishop. The church has annually hosted a conference of independent Catholic bishops, priests, and laity for a day of discussions and worship.

Membership: As of 1995 there is one parish of 68 members.

Sources:

Breton, J. E. Paul. *Papers Presented at the First Annual Gathering of Independent Catholic Christians, September 15, 1990.* San Bernardino, CA: Sarum Episcopal Church, 1991.

Daily and Sunday Eucharist from the Book of Common Prayer of the Sarum Episcopal Church. San Bernadino, CA: Sarum Episcopal Church, 1990.

★2346★
Tayu Fellowship
Current address not obtained for this edition.

The Tayu Fellowship was organized in the 1970s by Daniel Inesse and others and is open to gay men and women who wish to follow and teach the Path of Truth, a spiritual life based upon the wisdom of the ancient Greeks. According to the fellowship, the gods of Greece began as the Guides to humanity. Each deity represents a basic personality facet of the universe and as such are keys to the inner life of humankind. A Tayu (true human) is one who has first understood an initial Guide, who symbolized the basic theme of his/her life, and moved on to integrate eleven other perspectives to a point that he/she becomes complete.

According to the fellowship, history evolves in cycles or aeons of 2120 years each. Each aeon is under one of the Guides. The last aeon was under Poseidon. The present aeon, begun in mid-1987, is under Athene, the Guide of Openness, symbolized astrologically by the constellation Aquarius, the water bearer. The name of the water bearer is Ganymede, the most beautiful of mortal youths, taken as a favorite lover by the god Zeus.

Members of the fellowship are expected to follow six precepts which admonish them, among other things, to seek understanding, create a fulfilling existence, harm nothing, and love themselves and others. Membership is concentrated in the San Francisco Bay area, with other members scattered along the Pacific coast. A correspondence program in Tayu Wisdom allows the fellowship a larger outreach. During the late 1970s, the fellowship operated a center in San Francisco, the Tayu Institute. A Grand Council meets in the summer at the time of the solstice. The solstices and the equinoxes are major days for gatherings and ceremonies. The fellowship, though organized in the 1970s, considers itself to possess "roots dating back thousands of years."

Membership: Not reported.

Periodicals: *Ganymede.*

Sources:

Wright, Ezekiel, and Daniel Inesse. *God Is Gay.* Santa Rosa, CA: Tayu Press, 1982.

★2347★
Temple of Priapus
PO Box 1164, Stn. H
Montreal, PQ, Canada H3G 2N1

Priapus was a Greek god of Dionysus and Aphrodite, guardian deity of gardens, vineyards, and herbs. Worship of Priapus spread to Greece during the time of Alexander. He personified male procreative power. Groups devoted to his worship, and similar groups in other cultures (including Southern Asia), have had a significant presence in the life of people, including those in such areas as northern Germany and the Slavic and Scandinavian lands. Evidence of groups involved in erotic worship practices, often times in the nude, in which ritual intercourse was part of the worship experience, survived throughout Europe, never having been completely suppressed nor dying out. The practice reappeared from time to time when a need presented itself.

Priapus worship reemerged in North America in the 1970s due to the efforts of a Reverend Jackson who had been ordained during a visit to Italy and subsequently in 1973 incorporated the church in California. The year before, a dentist in Calgary, Alberta, had incorporated the church in Canada. He remains as a high priest.

The affairs of the Temple of Priapus (also known as the Church of St. Priapus) are administered by the Governing Council, which meets every four years. In 1984, D. Francis Cassidy was elected the new Pontifex, a position he has held since. Membership in the temple consists primarily of gay and bisexual men though some temples have heterosexual gatherings. A greater variance can be found among temples in Europe, some of which (such as those in

Switzerland) include families. There are four levels of membership in the temple.

Members acknowledge the power and beauty of the phallus and see it as their path to truth and wisdom; a source of joy and pleasure whose power can destroy evil. Sex is a vital part of the services, which may also involve sex magick and other forms of magick (candle, ceremonial, etc.) Semen is regarded with reverence and is considered a Sacrament of the Most Holy Seed. High Priests are ordained following the rites of Mary Magdalen in the West and similar rites in the East.

The church has formed an alliance with the American Gnostic Church.

Membership: Not reported. In 1997 there were six temples in Canada and 11 in the United States.

Periodicals: *Cock.*

★2348★
United Order of the Family of Christ
Current address not obtained for this edition.

The United Order of the Family of Christ was founded in 1966 by David-Edward Desmond of Denver, Colorado, as a Mormon-inspired communal group whose membership was entirely gay men. All of the members had been raised in the Church of Jesus Christ of Latter-day Saints, known for its strong stand against homosexual practice. The order accepted the basic beliefs and practices of the Latter-day Saints, but rejects its leadership and their stance on self-affirming the gay life.

The Order was organized as a commune in which all the members' assets were held in common in an order savings and checking account. At the time of its founding, membership consisted of young males between the ages of 18 and 30. Officers, termed Keys, led the group. One of their number is designated the First Key, a position initially led by Desmond. The Keys obtain guidance from holding council with the Heavenly Father and attempt to direct the group, thought of as a family, in such a way that it will bring union and peace among the members and with the Father.

Desmond has performed a prophetic role within the group. It is believed that he has a special communion with God the Father and members report seeing a golden halo around his head as he teaches.

Membership: Not reported. Contact with the group has been lost in recent years and it may have dissolved.

Sources:

Shields, Steven L. *Divergent Paths of the Restoration.* Los Angeles: Restoration Press, 1990. 336 pp.

★2349★
Universal Fellowship of Metropolitan Community Churches
8704 Santa Monica Blvd., 2nd Fl.
Los Angeles, CA 90069

Alternate Address: MCC of Toronto, 115 Simpson Ave., Toronto, ON M4K 1A1

The largest of the several churches serving the homosexual community is the Universal Fellowship of Metropolitan Commu-

nity Churches, founded in 1968 in Los Angeles by Pentecostal minister Troy Perry. In his popular autobiography, *The Lord Is My Shepherd and He Knows I'm Gay,* Perry recounts the story of his early religious and sexual awakening. After discovering his homosexual tendencies, he repressed them and became a relatively happy married father, and the pastor of a Church of God of Prophecy congregation in Santa Ana, California. Certain events, however, led to the revelation of his homosexual life, and he left the ministry. He then began the Metropolitan Community Church with a few friends and an ad placed in *The Advocate,* a popular gay periodical.

Perry carried his Pentecostalism into the Metropolitan Community Church. But as the church grew, primarily by the addition of other ministers who acknowledged their homosexual orientation and subsequently joined the church, a wide variety of worship and belief emerged. The church has developed a theology of love in which the central affirmation is God's acceptance of all people, including homosexuals. The church's theology treats the Apostle Paul's statements about homosexuality in the Bible as cultural accretions much as his statements against women speaking in church. In line with this theology, Perry has blessed the union of gay couples living in a "married" relationship.

Growth has continued in spite of continued resistance to gay concerns in the general population, the burning of several congregational buildings (four in 1973 alone), and the death of several members. It is headed by a seven-person Board of Elders elected by the General Conference, which meets annually. In 1973 the first woman, Freda Smith, was elected to the board. In 1984 a majority of the board were women.

In 1985, as the AIDS crisis was beginning, the Metropolitan Community Churches began a programmed response that included a major education program and attempted to focus attention on the problem within the larger religious community. In 1987 they began a new newsletter, *Alert,* aimed at keeping the church informed on the ongoing crises and providing resources for those affected.

The Church is currently organized into 17 regions/districts, eight of which are located outside the United States and oversee churches in Africa, New Zealand, Australia, Great Britain, Denmark, Canada, Mexico, and the Philippines.

Membership: In 1987 the churches reported 86 chartered churches, 1707 commissioned churches (including study groups and missions), and 37 new and special works. Forty-five of these church and study groups are located in foreign countries: Nigeria, Denmark, France, England, Australia, Indonesia, Canada, Mexico, and Costa Rica.

Educational Facilities: Samaritan College, Los Angeles, California.

Periodicals: *Journey.* • *Alert.*

Sources:

Enroth, Ronald M., and Gerald E. Jamison. *The Gay Church.* Grand Rapids, MI: William B. Eerdmans, 1974.

Perry, Troy D. *The Lord Is My Shepherd and He Knows I'm Gay.* New York: Bantam Books, 1978.

Section 26
Unclassified Religious Groups

Unclassified Religious Groups

★2350★
All-One-God-Faith, Inc.
℅ Dr. E. H. Bonner
Box 28
Escondido, CA 92025

All-One-God-Faith, Inc. is not a church, it is a soap company. However, the products of the company have become the means of informing people of the religious vision of Rev. Henry Corey, a retired United States Marine, and Dr. E. H. Bonner, the soap maker. Their ideas are based upon the Dead Sea Scrolls, a group of Jewish religious writings from the first century B.C.E., discovered in 1948. The writings, which include texts of the Jewish Bible (the Old Testament) were found in a cave near the Dead Sea. Bonner termed their discovery the Second Coming of God's Law.

All-One-God-Faith, Inc. (originally called the All-One-Faith-in-One-God State)was founded in 1959. It unites all persons through the teachings of Confucius' absolutes, Hippocrates' ABCs of perfect health, Hillel's moral ABCs, Jesus' Manual of Discipline, Mohammad's love, and Thomas Paine's army of principles for the brotherhood of man. The teachings are printed in fine print on the labels of each of the products produced by the soap company.

Membership: In the 1970s there were four congregations in Cardiff-by-the-Sea, Modesto, and Oceanside, California, and Indianapolis, Indiana.

★2351★
Church of the Bride of Christ
(Defunct)

The Church of the Bride of Christ was founded in 1903 in Corvallis, Oregon by Edmund Franz Creffield. Born in Germany around 1867, Creffield studied for the priesthood. Before ordination, however, he migrated to Portland, Oregon, around 1902, then joined the Salvation Army and moved to Corvallis as an Army representative. In 1903 he had a sudden revelation from which he emerged with a new name, Joshua Elijah (the names of two prophets in the Hebrew Bible). He allowed his hair to grow freely.

Joshua Elijah founded the Church of the Bride of Christ and immediately began to recruit members from among the women in the town. The goal was to find the woman who would become the mother of a new Christ child. He began to hold meetings in which he and the female recruits would engage in some of the ecstatic practices associated with revival meetings, frequently in a state of nudity. As word circulated through the neighborhood of the activities, husbands and fathers began to pull their wives and daughters out of the church and in January 1904, they tarred and feathered Creffield. He remained in the neighborhood, was caught in bed with a married woman, and was eventually arrested for adultery. He was sentenced to two years in prison, and that seemed to end the church. However, following his release in December 1905, he began to correspond with his former members. He proposed the

founding of a community on the Oregon Coast, a protective haven against the curse he had placed on the cities of the west Coast, which included San Francisco. As members began to gather, in April 1906, San Francisco fell victim to and was largely destroyed by an earthquake and fire, prompting some to say Creffield's prophetic curse had come true.

The Prophet's vision of a new Garden of Eden came to an abrupt end a month later. He was assassinated in Seattle, Washington, on May 7, by the brother of Esther Mitchell, one of his devoted followers. Tried for murder, George Mitchell was found not guilty. Several days later he was shot by his sister at the Seattle rail station as he was journeying back to Corvallis. The small band of followers reportedly continued on for several years.

Sources:

Holbrook, Stewart H. "Oregon's Secret Love Cult." *American Mercury* (February 1941): 167-74.

Pintarich, Dick, and J. Kingston Pierce. "The Strange Saga of Oregon's Other Guru." *The Oregonian* (January 7, 1986).

★2352★
Church of the New Song
Current address not obtained for this edition.

The Church of the New Song emerged in 1970 as an expression of a new rights movement among residents of penitentiaries in the United States. It was begun by Bishop Harry W. Theriault, a convicted bank robber, in the federal prison at Atlanta, Georgia. The name of the church refers to the new song mentioned in Revelation 5:9 and 14:3, which church members believe is the sound of the new era, and also the new song being sung by the youth. Theriault, his co-founder Jerry M. Dorrough, and others began immediately to agitate for recognition within the prison system. In February 1972 a federal court recognized the church as a legitimate body, and ordered prison officials to permit it to meet and hold services. After that decision the church spread rapidly and became the focus of controversy. It was accused of causing a work strike at San Quentin, and its sincerity was questioned because of a claimed specification that porterhouse steak and Harvey's Bristol Cream were its communion elements. Theriault was soon transferred to the federal prison at La Tuna, Texas.

According to the church, "Eclat" is the "new name" of the divinity referred to in Revelation 3:2, thus the church is also termed the Eclatarian Movement. Eclatarianity is the highest fulfillment of Christian prophecy. The end of the Christian era, the era of grace, is the beginning of the Eclat era. The church considers the American governmental and bureaucratic system to be so corrupt that there is no more time for grace. The message of the Church of the New Song is the word of life. The Law of Nature is to act and have power. "Eclat is the Light and the deed is love; if you seek the Light, do the deed." Man's basic needs are said to be shelter, food, and someone to love. When these have been attained, men should busy themselves helping others attain their basic needs. The teachings of the church are summarized in *Holy Mizan,* termed a "para-testament." The paratestament is a third testament coming after the first, or Old, Testament and the second, or New, Testament.

The church is episcopal in polity, operating within the boundaries of prison existence. Theriault, the bishop of Tellus, is assisted by Dr. Stephen S. Fox, S.R.M. (sealed revelation minister), the international chancellor of information. Fox is also a professor of psychology at the University of Iowa. Other officers include Dr. Richard Tanner, S.R.M., prime coadjutor; Dr. Becky Hensley, envoy international; Robert Copeland, redactor international; and Jerry Dorrough, coadjutor of Tellus. Male Eclatarians are referred to as "Maverites," and females as "Sporades."

By 1972 the church had 27 chapters in state prisons and 16 in federal prisons. The church has grown in recent years both inside and outside the prison system, despite Theriault's isolation at La Tuna. A militant program concerning religious freedom in the prison system has been pursued. In 1972 Theriault took a Nazarite vow, which included a refusal to cut his hair (a primary requirement in most prisons). He also began to question the government's subsidy of religion through its salaries to prison chaplains.

Membership: Not reported.

Sources:

[Harry W. Theriault]. *Grass Roots of the New Song.* Millington, TN: Book University of the New Song, 1979.

Lightbringer Shiloh [Harry W. Theriault]. *Holy Mizan, Supreme Paratestament of the New Song.* Bend, OR: Sacred Text Press, 1982.

★2353★
Embassy of Heaven Church
8777 Basl Hill Rd., SE
Strayton, OR 97383-9630

The Embassy of Heaven Church was founded in 1987 by what it believed to be a revelation from Jesus Christ. The church considers itself a corporation of the kingdom of Heaven and thus refuses to incorporate under any government of the world. The members believe that all world governments are illegitimate. There is only one legitimate government, and it is known as the Kingdom of Heaven, established by Jesus Christ during the Lord's Supper (Luke 22:24-30). The church promotes separating from the systems of the world and giving allegiance to God's government with Jesus Christ as Head.

Drawing their authority from various biblical passages, members of the church promote the Kingdom of Heaven as a holy nation that exists outside of the jurisdictions of state and federal governments. Pastor Paul Revere and other church leaders see themselves as ambassadors for Christ, living under the laws of the Kingdom of Heaven. Out of that belief, the church issues Kingdom of Heaven passports, driver licenses, and vehicle plates for ambassadors using the Kingdom of Heaven highways.

The church provides sanctuary to anyone who repents and sins no more. In 1993 the church received broad publicity when it was raided by the federal government in search of a man who was receiving asylum.

The church came to public attention again on January 31, 1997, when its headquarters was raided military style by a swat team and tank. Members were locked out of their 34 acres and the property was sold at auction because the church did not pay property taxes. The church is continuing to function from mobile headquarters using buses, motor homes, and trailers. The church plans on peacefully taking back the land based on Truth and without court intervention.

The Embassy of Heaven Church has received much notoriety over the years through the media. Churches leaders have been guests on televisions and radio talk shows, and featured in newspaper and tabloid articles. It publishes numerous books and tapes and a bimonthly newsletter that follows the situation of the 400 ambassadors for Christ.

Membership: In 1997 there were some 400 ambassadors for Christ. The newsletter circulates approximately 1,000 copies per issue.

Periodicals: *Midnight Rider.*

Sources:

"Embassy of Heaven Says Its Above the Law". *The RegisterGuardian* (Eugene, Oregon) (August 6, 1993).

___. Revere, Paul. *What Is the Embassy of Heaven Church?* Sublimity, OR: Embassy of Heaven Church, 1991.

___. *Would Jesus Register with Caesar?* Sublimity, OR: Embassy of Heaven Church, 1991.

★2354★
Kennedy Worshippers
Current address not obtained for this edition.

Shortly after the death of the charismatic President John F. Kennedy, people began to claim contact with his spirit. They began ascribing healings of many serious diseases, some congenital and/or terminal, to that spirit. By 1970 more than 100 such reports were on file. Coincidental with these accounts of miracles was the emergence of a loosely organized movement in which John F. Kennedy was an object of worship. The first manifestations were home shrines centered upon pictures of Kennedy. In 1972 Farley McGivern organized a John F. Kennedy Memorial Temple in Los Angeles to provide headquarters for the movement. To believers, Kennedy is thought of as a god. McGivern believed that Kennedy gave his life for his people, to warn them of the evil around them.

The existence of this movement has been known only through the occasional encounters by reporters with people who claim to be a part of it. To most people involved in it, their belief is a very private matter which is rarely shared with others, even close friends. Hence, little information about it exists.

Membership: In the 1970s, 2,000 adherents around the United States were reported.

★2355★
Moral Re-Armament (MRA)
1156 15th St. NW
Washington, DC 20005

Dr. Frank N. Buchman (1878-1961) was an American Lutheran minister from Pennsylvania who, early in his ministerial career, had started a hostel in Philadelphia for underprivileged boys. A fight with his trustees led to his separation from the hostel, leaving him personally exhausted. In 1908, while traveling in Great Britain, he experienced a change of heart in a Keswick chapel. Buchman began to share his experience of release from resentment with others and became the center of an international fellowship, the First Century Christian Fellowship. The fellowship emerged in the early 1920s and included many students from both Cambridge University and Oxford University. The group was later dubbed the Oxford Group, by a South African reporter, a name by which it became popularly known.

Buchman taught that God could become real to anyone who was willing to believe in Him. Estrangement from God is man's fault, and is caused by moral compromise. People needed examine their lives against the standards of absolute purity, unselfishness, and love. The recovery of personal morality proceedes and leads to the recovery of social morality. Buchman emphasised the need for sharing and guidance. Sharing consists of the confession of one's sins and failures to another member of the group. Guidance could come directly from God during quiet moments when individuals record their inner thoughts. During the 1930s, the Oxford Group became known for its "house parties," group settings in which sharing was promoted. These house parties also became a source of controversy with critics charging that participants indulged in embarrassing confessions.

During the late 1920s, many Princeton University students became affiliated with the Oxford Group. However, because of opposition aroused due to the nature and content of the sharing sessions, the university kicked the movement off campus. An investigation by a university commission found the charges without weight and not only invited the group back on campus but gave it credit for the high moral standards enjoyed by the student body. The president of the school invited Buchman to conduct a chapel service with him.

In 1938, as Europe armed, Buchman reached the firm conviction that the next great world movement must be one for moral and spiritual rearmament. The Oxford Group's program for Moral Re-Armament (MRA), the name by which it then became known, was launched that year. Many of those trained by the program enlisted in the several armies or took part in resistance movements. In America, a group was deferred by the Selective Service that they might undertake a patriotic, morale building program, "You Can Defend America." General John J. Pershing lent strong support to the effort and wrote the foreword for the program's handbook.

After the war a group of Swiss acquired a large hotel, above Montreux, in the village of Caux, to offer Europe a platform for MRA's work of healing and reconciliation. Likening their efforts to an ideological equivalent of the Marshall Plan, MRA established a program which brought together those who had been on different sides of the war. The first group of Germans allowed to leave Germany by the Allied Occupation Forces came to Caux for meetings. In like measure the Japanese came. In 1986, Prime Minister Nakasone publically underlined the important role MRA played in building modern Japan.

After Buchman's death, MRA continued under an informal international leadership committed to the ideals of seeing the world governed by people who were governed by God. They also continued Buchman's emphasis on the discipline of spending time in quiet each morning to listen for God's guidance, and accepting the fact that change begins with oneself.

MRA functions under a number of independent national organizations, each organized as a charity in its own land. The large conference center at Caux, Switzerland, is unofficially seen as the world headquarters. A similar training center is located in Bombay, India, with smaller facilities in Australia, Brazil, Zimbabwe, Japan, and Great Britain. MRA offices are also located in 28 countries.

In the United States during the 1960s, Up With People, a program developed under MRA auspices, began to gain some fame because of a touring singing group made up of youth members. In 1968 the individuals associated with Up With People and the affiliated Pace Publications, severed all connection with MRA and incorporated independently.

Membership: MRA is not a membership organization. It has people at work throughout the world and seven offices in the United States which direct its program.

Periodicals: *Breakthroughs.* • *For a Change.* Send orders to The Good Road Ltd., 12 Palace St., London SW1E 5JF, England.

Remarks: Buchman was accused by his detractors of being sympathetic to Nazism. In the recent biography, *Frank Buchman—A Life,* author Garth Lean suggests that while he may have been naive about the prospect of "changing" Hitler, he was equally the victim of a smear campaign. Much of that campaign was spearheaded by journalist Tom Driberg, who has since been discovered to have been an agent of the KGB. On the other hand, several decades of observation of MRA has revealed no alignment either ideologically or in its policies and program to Nazism.

Sources:

Buchman, Frank N. *Remaking the World.* London: Blandford Press, 1961.

Driberg, Tom. *The Mystery of Moral-Re-Armament.* New York: Alfred A. Knopf, 1965.

Eister, Allen W. *Drawing-Room Conversion.* Durham, NC: Duke University Press, 1950.

Entwistle, Basil, and John McCook Roots. *Moral Re-Armament, What Is It?* Los Angeles: Pace Publications, 1967.

Howard, Peter. *The World Rebuilt.* London: Blandford Press, 1951.

Lean, Garth. *Frank Buchman: A Life.* London: Constable, 1985.

___. *On the Tail of a Comet.* Colorado Springs, CO: Helmes and Howard, IA.

Williamson, Geoffrey. *Inside Buchmanism.* New York: Philosophical Library, 1955.

★2356★
The New Church
(Defunct)

The New Church was founded by N. N. New in the first decade of the twentieth century, but grew out of the previous work of John Fair New, a nineteenth century religious lecturer who had previously founded a New Life Society and the New Life Church. John Fair New had become convinced early in life that Christianity was a life, that this life must begin at birth, and that a new birth initiated a new life. This new life is based upon the the understanding that Jesus is essentilly identical with God the Father, that the divinity and humanity of God are one, and hence God and man are the same being. Jesus is the highest example of the divine man. This discovery of the new life principle led to the further discovery of the power of prayer to heal all illnesses.

John Fair New passed along his teachings to his son N. N. New, who established headquarters in San Francisco, California, and London, England, and continued his father's work. He published his father's lectures in 1909 and shortly afterward issued his own version of the teachings as a booklet, *Newology, The New Bible*.

Essential to the movement was the emphasis upon healing. Newological medicine centered upon conscious cooperation with God, promised reconstruction of the human body, perpetual youth, and even physical immortality to the adherents. Adherents were discouraged from wearing black, the color of sin, poverty, despair, disease, and death. The use of alcoholic beverages was forbidden. New also believed that hair was the last remnant of horns and will disappear as Man evolves. All races will loose their hair as they grow white, intellectual, and spiritual. The New Church also advocated vegetarianism.

New's efforts met with some response within the larger metaphysical movement. Operating under the label of Newthot Science, New proposed the establishment of a NewThot Church (over which he would be the archbishop), printing plant and university. He began to enroll people in the university for $10 for which he was indicted for fraudulent use of the mails. Convicted in 1917, New was found by the court to be an imposter who regularly indulged in the very actions which he forbade to his followers. The conviction effectively ended the church.

Sources:

New, John Fair. *The New Life Theology.* New York: New Inc., Publishers, 1909.

New, N. N. *Newology, the New Bible.* San Francisco: Newthot Publishers, n.d.

Rubenstein, I. H. *Law on Cults.* Chicago: Ordain Press, 1981.

★2357★
New Enlightened Inspired Living
Current address not obtained for this edition.

New Enlightened Inspired Living is the designation given the movement inspired by and the program of Neil Howard Brandt (b. 1946), who has in recent years assumed the name David Neil and has announced that he is the Messiah, The King of Kings, and NEIL (the New Enlightened Inspired Leader).

According to Neil, he first came to know of his messiahship in 1973 when he was given a vision of the future. He saw himself surrounded by a group of reporters who were shouting "The Messiah! The Messiah!" Two years later he had a second vision in which he saw newspapers with dates from the future proclaiming him as the Messiah in bold headlines accompanied by his picture. An initial story on his claims ran in 1975 in *The Marin Independent Journal*. However, few were aware of Neil's claims until he published his autobiography and began a campaign to announce his mission.

Neil claims to at one time having been King David and Jesus Christ. However, he claims not to be a perfect person, rather an instrument of God. As he put it, "I co-habit my actual thinking mind with another consciousness." This God force now resides within him. The ability to access God's energy means he is able to influence major world events.

The messianic program is termed NEIL Deal. It includes a new government with a global rather than a national base and an international peacekeeping army, navy, and air force. Economically, it calls for a balanced national budget, new housing starts, and reduced federal income tax.

Having just announced his presence, it is yet to be seen whether he and his program will develop a following or be taken seriously.

Membership: Unknown.

Sources:

Neil, David. *I Am the Messiah!*. Novato, CA: The Author, 1992.

★2358★
The Nudist Christian Church of the Blessed Virgin Jesus
Current address not obtained for this edition.

The Nudist Christian Church of the Blessed Virgin Jesus grew out of a revelation received by the church's founder, Zeus Cosmos. During 1985, while a student at Iowa State University, he asked direction from God. The Spirit of Jesus Christ was sent to Zeus Cosmos, directing him to the West, where he would meet God. He journeyed to the Canaan Wilderness (which he renamed the Zeus Cosmos Nudist National Wilderness) near the Utah-Arizona border. God and the angel Ephygeneia, both naked, appeared to him, directing him to a cave on a nearby ridge. While engaged in a fast and living in a cave, Zeus Cosmos again met "God the Almighty the Triune God" and an angel. God gave him an additional revelation to be added to the Bible, called the *Book of Zeus*. It was to be placed next to the Book of Revelation.

The *Book of Zeus* begins with an admonishment for the Mormon polygamists to give up their adulterous pagan practices and their beliefs in the inferiority of the black race. Zeus Cosmos was told of the holy land of the Nudist Christian people northwest of the Grand Canyon where a city, Cosmos, would be built. Here men and women would have godly respect for each other, their nakedness, and the wholesome natural body.

It is the belief of the church that the human body is God's creation. Nudity means cleanliness, honesty, family atmosphere, modesty at its best, freedom, and goodliness. Life with nudity reduces sexual hang-ups, problems caused by undue expectations of one's body, pornography, and crime. The church actively seeks the establishment of clothes-optional public areas across the United States.

Membership: Not reported.

★2359★
Perfect Liberty Kyodan
700 S. Adams St.
Glendale, CA 91205

Perfect Liberty Kyodan was founded in Japan in 1946 by Tokuchika Miki, but its origin goes back to 1912 when Kanada

Tokumitsu, an Osaka cutlery dealer, founded the Shinto-Tokumitsu-Kyo (the divine way taught by Tokumitsu). The original group used elements of both Shingon Buddhism and Shintoism, drawing from them an emphasis on art and nature. Tokuchika's father, Tokuharu Miki, a Zen priest, joined Tokumitsu's group and brought into it an emphasis upon meditation. In 1919 Tokuharu inherited the leadership role. The group grew and changed its name several times before being suppressed during the 1930s. Tokuchika, who became the Oshieoya (Patriarch) in 1936, spent the final years of World War II in prison. Perfect Liberty was permanently established after his release from prison during the Allied occupancy. Perfect Liberty became the only one of the postwar Japanese religions to adopt an official English name. Tokuchika wanted the faith's cosmopolitan nature to be reflected in its name.

The teachings of Perfect Liberty are summarized in "Twenty-One Precepts." The first and most important is that "Life is Art," by which Tokuchika means that it is all important to see one's life as a total pattern, a single unified work of Art. Art is a striving to overcome limitation. It is a molding of what is outside of oneself into a form that is both true to itself and an expression of the artist. Life itself becomes a work of art by the artist's self. The remaining precepts provide guidelines for the artistic life.

The center of worship in Perfect Liberty is the asamairi, a daily morning service which starts before 5 A.M., and lasts about an hour. In the service each member pledges himself to lead an artistic life during the day. Leading the service is an appointed leader who is able to give mioshie, or divine instruction. Worship is directed toward Mioya-okami, the parent God.

The artistic nature of Perfect Liberty is expressed in worship and festivals. On August 1 of each year, a giant Founder's Day festival is held at the Perfect Liberty Seichi. Oshieoya's birthday is celebrated on April 8. These are times for massive displays of art, dance, fireworks, and music. The Perfect Liberty peace tower is a large modern sculpture on the grounds in Osaka. The headquarters are also the site of modern buildings, a golf course, a memorial garden, baseball grounds, and works of art.

Perfect Liberty came to the United States in 1960 when several immigrants began missionary work. A minister arrived in 1961. By 1972 the group had expanded, and a center, modeled on the one in Japan, was constructed in the Santa Monica Mountains above Los Angeles.

Membership: In 1974 Perfect Liberty had approximately 5,000 members in six churches and 15 missions in the United States, all on the West Coast. Approximately twenty-five percent of the membership is drawn from black and Spanish-speaking communities.

Sources:

Bach, Marcus. *The Power of Perfect Liberty*. Englewood Cliffs, NJ: Prentice-Hall, 1971.

Yashima, Jiro. *An Essay on the Way of Life*. N.p., 1950.

Unclassified Religious Groups

★2360★
Congregation de l'Aumisme
% Monastere de Ste-Lucie
Ste-Agathe, PQ, Canada J8C 2Z8

The Congregation de l'Aumisme is the Canadian center of the Aumist Religion, a new religion founded by Gilbert Bourdin, (1923-1998) better known by his religious name, Lord Hamsah Manarah. Bourdin was raised in France in a Catholic family but was attracted to mysticism as a young man and sought wisdom in various ancient wisdom and magical orders (Rosicrucians, Martinism, etc.) At one point he traveled to India to study with Swami Sivananda Saraswati, who in 1961 received him in the sannyasin order (the renounced life) and gave him the name Hamsananda

Saraswati. During his travels in Asia, Bourdin also explored and received initiations into Jainism, Sufism, and various forms of Buddhism. Several of the teachers he met bestowed titles upon him in recognition of his accomplishments.

Upon his return to the West, L. Hamash Manarah emerged as an accomplished master of both Eastern and Western initiatic traditions. In the winter of 1962-63 he resided in a cave in the mountains of southeastern France and subjected himself to the ascetic practices of the early Christian fathers. During this time an inner voice told him that he was destined to create an initiatic order teaching spiritual liberation while avoiding the mere search for psychic powers or passing satisfactions.

Manarah then created the Order of the Knights of the Golden Lotus and established a monastery in the Alps of Haute-Province, which grew into the Holy City of Mandarom, constructed by the members of the order. Since that time the order has spread through French-speaking Europe and during the 1980s to Quebec, Canada. In the late 1980s, plans were projected for the building of a Pyramid Temple of Unity. At about the same time, the order came under attack from the anti-cult movement represented in France by the Association pout la Defense de la Famille de l'Individu (ADFI). To date the building permit for the temple has not been obtained.

In 1967 Manarah established the Association of the Knights of the Golden Lotus (replaced in 1995 by the current Association of the Triumphant Vajra) and two years later founded the holy city of the Mandarom. Over the next years he revealed himself to be the Messiah: the Lord Hamsah Manarah, and in 1990 was publicly acknowledged as such in a ceremony. He also hoped to add to the existing temples at the Mandarom, representing all the great religions of the world and huge statues, a larger Temple-Pyramid.

However, an anti-cult campaign emerged against the group which became even more intense following the deaths associated with two other groups, the AUM Shinrikyo in Japan, and the Solar Temple in Switzerland and Canada. The campaign against the Mandarom has been largely orchestrated by the Association pout la Defense de la Famile de l'Individu (ADFI), the largest French anti-cult organization. The Mandarom was raided repeatedly between 1992 and 1995 by tax and police officers. Then in 1994 a former member filed a complaint against Bourdin, based upon a recovered memory, that she had been molested and raped. He and several members were arrested. He was released pending the trial, but in 1998, he died. While the case against him died with him, a new controversy immediately arose concerning his burial.

The Prefet of the French Alpes de Haute-Provence denied the permission needed under French law in order to bury Bourdin at the Mandarom as he had requested. The burial finally took place in Castillon on April 6, 1998, under the protests of both the Aumists and local residents (who did not want their town to become a pilgrimage site). Burial at the Mandarom is still being pursued by the Aumists.

It is not expected that the Aumists will designate a new leader. They believe that the Lord Hamsah Manarah will be reincarnated, and that they will be able to detect the male infant who will be the next leader as the reincarnated Lord (a procedure similar to the practice of Tibetan Buddhists in discovering a new lama). Once the boy is found, elder Aumists will guide him in assuming his duties as the reincarnated Lord. In the meantime a college of high priests will govern the movement.

Membership: Not reported.

★2361★
Daheshism
% Dahesh Heritage
304 W. 58th St.
New York, NY 10019-1107

Daheshism is the name given to the teachings of Dr. Dahesh (1909–1983), a twentiethcentury Lebanese religious teacher and miracle worker. Dahesh was born in Jerusalem but grew up in Lebanon. He received little formal education but became known as a healer. In his teen years he began to speak of the return of Christ and the need of people to prepare for his appearance and to purify themselves. In 1930 Dahesh was granted an honorary doctorate in psychic research by the Sage Institute in Paris.

On March 23, 1942, Dahesh believed that he had received the Divine Command proclaiming his mission to the people of the world. Over the previous decade, a group of followers had already begun to form around him. His activity increased, and proportionately, opposition emerged. In 1944 Dahesh and several of his closest followers were arrested, and a short time later, without a trial, he was expelled from the country. He secretly returned to Lebanon and began to publish a series of controversial booklets attacking his accusers. Then occurred one of the more famous events in the Daheshian story. In 1947 Dahesh was stripped of his citizenship and expelled from Lebanon again. On June 28 he entered Azerbaidjan and on July 1, 1947, was reportedly executed and buried. The Iranian government, then in control of Azerbaidjan, issued a formal statement of his death, and his picture appeared in the newspapers in Beirut. On that same day, however, his followers attest that Dahesh reappeared in Beirut. In any case, he later surfaced publicly and continued his work. His citizenship was returned in 1953, following a change of government in 1952.

Over the succeeding years, Daheshists began to migrate to the United States. Dahesh first came to the United States in 1976. During his two-year stay he organized the work in North America through the Daheshist Publishing Co., though it was not until the 1990s that his books began to be translated into English. The majority of his followers are still found in the Arabic-speaking Lebanese-American community.

Daheshists believe that Dahesh fulfills the yearning in all religions for a redeeming Messenger, most prominently symbolized as the returning Jesus Christ or the Mahdi spoken of by Muslims. They believe that Dahesh was the Coming Christ who in his person unites the personalities of all of the promised Messengers of the world's faiths.

Dahesh taught belief in God as the Creator and compassionate father. Creation began with the world of Spirits, the Heavens inhabited by the Holy Spirits. Humans, in essence a Holy Spirit, need to strive for purity and freedom from attraction to materialism so they can return to the Heavenly Worlds. Dahesh performed his miracles to instill belief in God and the heavenly realms.

Dahesh taught belief in the Christ, the Spiritual Divine Force constituting the highest degree of Heaven. Union with this force is the only way of return to God. This force extends itself into the material world in the form of spiritual fluids. These fluids are incarnated in certain people known as the prophets (Moses, Jesus of Nazareth, Muhammad) and guides (Lao Tsu, Confucius, Buddha, Socrates, Ghandi). Various spirits also extend their life into the visible world, some of their fluids condensing into matter.

In 1995 the Daheshists in New York opened the Dahesh Museum, an art museum specializing in the art of the French Salon and Academy of the nineteenth and early twentieth centuries and including art works from the personal collection of Dr. Dahesh.

Membership: Not reported. Members are found in Lebanon, France, Germany, and Italy.

Periodicals: *Dahesh Voice.*

Sources:

Brax, Ghazi. *Lights upon Dr. Dahesh and Daheshism.* New York: Daheshist Publishing Co., 1986.

Onbargi, Salim. *Born Again with Doctor Dahesh.* New York: Daheshist Publishing Co., 1993.

★2362★
Humanity Benefactor Foundation
University of Lawsonomy
4529 Highway 41
Sturtevant, WI 53177

The Humanity Benefactor Foundation and the University of Lawsonomy are the two institutions that grew out of the thinking of Alfred William Lawson (1869–1954), whose thoughts include a system of philosophy and theology, as well as extensive writings on science, health, and economics. Lawson, one of the more creative thinkers in American history, was simultaneously hailed by some as a genius and reviled by critics as a crackpot.

Lawson was born in London, England, but his parents moved to Canada when he was three weeks old, and then to Detroit, Michigan, in 1874. He attended public school, but dropped out and in 1888 began a career in baseball as a pitcher and a manager. He is credited with introducing night baseball in 1901 with a portable electric light system that he carried from city to city. He was both a right and left hand pitcher. He organized more clubs, leagues, and mergers than any other man. A 1908 newspaper wrote: "As an organizer, Lawson perhaps stands without a peer, as history records that he was the father of the Central League and Interstate League, which are now in existence and which are two of the strongest circuits in organized baseball. . . .When Lawson floated the Atlantic League last winter the matter was looked upon as a joke, but Lawson showed his master hand by steering the organization through the season. He managed the Reading (Pennsylvania) club, and in addition to winning the pennant for that city he successfully bucked the invasion of the Tri-State League and cleared up $12,000 profit on the season."

In 1908 he entered the world of aviation and began the first aeronautic magazine, *Fly* (1908–1909), succeeded by *Aircraft* (1910–1914). He began flying in 1910. At the beginning of World War I, he became the general manager of a small aircraft company and designed several training planes for the government. As early as 1909 he had conceived of the idea of a passenger airliner, and after the war he found backing to build such a plane. He became president of the Lawson Airplane Company. During 1919 he built and demonstrated the practicality of a passenger plane. While his work on the passenger plane was probably his most lasting contribution, he continued to work in aviation and transportation through the 1920s.

During his years in aviation, Lawson had begun to think about economics and the injustices of the capitalist system. The Great Depression of 1929 became the occasion of his pulling his thoughts together and developing the direct credits alternative system, the outlines of which first appeared in a book, *Direct Credits for Everyone*, in 1931. In essence, Lawson saw three players in the economic system: labor, capital, and the financiers. He saw the latter as the problem and called upon labor and capital to make common cause against them. He also proposed a new understanding of money, as nothing of value in itself, but as a measure of wealth and of ones ability to facilitate trade. He proposed doing away with interest and placing control of money in the hands of the government. The government would then make available credits to people in the form of grants and interestfree loans to nurture wealth-producing activities.

Lawson gave organizational form to his new economic system through the Direct Credits Society and through the 1930 he gained a large following. Popular support for the direct credits idea waned during the years of World War II and never regained its prewar following. Lawson also continued to expand his thought into other areas and gradually created a whole system of knowledge that came to be known as Lawsonomy, the basic ideas of which were summarized in a three-volume book entitled *Lawsonomy* (1935–39). In 1943 he purchased the campus of the former Des Moines University and renamed it the Des Moines University of Lawsonomy.

The volumes on Lawsonomy treated some of Lawsons theological ideas. Further elucidation of his religious thought led in 1948 to the establishment of Lawsonian Religion, the basic principles of which were laid down more definitively in a 1949 work, *Lawsonian Religion*. Lawsonian religion builds upon Lawsonomy, the knowledge of life and the basic laws that govern physical, mental, moral, and spiritual manifestations. It includes the highest understanding of God, the Omniparent who created humanity and is its Benefactor. It espouses a pure birth, clean life, honest dealings, kind treatment to all people (especially to people of different religions), provable education, and perpetual improvement. It is the ultimate goal to bring all humans together for the worship of the one God.

Lawson died in 1954. At a later date the university moved to rural Wisconsin, south of Milwaukee. The Humanity Benefactor Foundation was founded as the publishing arm of the Lawsonomy movement. Students of Lawsonomy may participate by reading Lawsons many books and taking correspondence courses offered by the school. Resident students engage in a self-guided reading and study of Lawsons writings, punctuated by a monthly gathering of the students. Worship services are held at noon on the last Sunday of each month, and include the singing of songs specially geared to the movement.

Membership: Membership is not counted but is national and international. People acquire the Lawson literature and become voluntary students without legal requirements. Associated centers include the Humanity Benefactor Foundation Inc., Box 3243, Melvindale, MI 48122; the Direct Credits Society, Inc., Box 3243, Melvindale, MI 48122; Lawsonian Religion Inc., Box 3243, Melvindale, MI 48122; the Chapel at the of University of Lawsonomy, 4529 Highway 41, Sturtevant, WI 53177; and the Lawsonian Religion churches in Detroit; Wichita, KS; and Murrieta, CA.

Periodicals: *Benefactor.*

Sources:

Farrell, V. L. A. *Lawson: From Bootblack to Emancipator.* Detroit, MI: Humanity Benefactor Foundation, 1934. 79 pp.

Henry, Lyell, Jr. *Zig-Zag-and-Swirl: Alfred W. Lawson's Quest for Greatness.* Iowa City, IA: University of Iowa Press, 1991. 336 pp.

Lawson, Alfred W. *Direct Credits for Everybody.* Detroit, MI: Humanity Benefactor Association, 1931. 80 pp.

___. *Lawsonian Religion.* Detroit, MI: Humanity Benefactor Foundation, 1949. 255 pp.

___. *Lawsonomy.* 3 vols. Detroit, MI: Humanity Benefactor Association, 1935-39.

Taylor, Margaret C., and Arlene Osmun. *Songs of Lawsonomy.* Detroit, MI: Humanity Benefactor Foundation, 1961. 247 pp.

★2363★
Ligmincha Institute
PO Box 1892
Charlottesville, VA 22903

Ligmincha Institute is a contemporary Western center of the ancient B'n (pre-Buddhist) religion of Tibet. It was founded in the early 1990s by Tenzin Wangyal Rinpoche. The transmission of the B'n religion to the West began in 1961 when Tenzin Namdak (b. 1926), the head of the B'n religious community, moved to London, England. Namdak became Lopon (head) of the group in 1953 but had to flee Tibet in 1959 following the Chinese invasion. He moved to London two years later and cooperated with David Snellgrove in the translation and publication of *The Nine Ways of Bon*, a basic text on the B'n tradition. Upon his return to India in 1964, he founded New Menri as a center for the B'n community in exile. He made his first trip to the United States in 1989 and on that occasion founded the Tibetan B'n Temple Foundation in Signal Hill, California.

The B'n religion was founded by Tonpe Shenrab Miwache, and as the teachings were passed and developed, they emerged into what is termed the Dzogchen teachings. The master practitioner is termed a Shen. Shenrab's teachings are classified in the nine ways, or vehicles, to relieve sufferings. The initial four are termed the causal ways: *Chashen* (the Way of the Shen of Prediction), *Nangshen* (the Way of the Shen of the Visible World), *Trulshen* (the Way of the Shen of Magical Illusion), and *Sichen* (the Way of the Shen of Existence). These include various healing, divinatory, and astrological practices; purification rituals; practices to subdue spirits; and work with the soul of the living and dead. All of these practices the B'n practitioners share with Tibetan shamanism.

B'n is unique in its practice of the five resultant vehicles, which are built upon a universal compassion and deal most directly with the life beyond death. These teachings comprise the oral teaching of the B'n religion and are generally passed on orally from teacher to student. The founder passed the teaching on to the first nine masters, most of whom were from Zhang Zhung, a country west of Tibet near Mt. Kailash. The next masters, 24 in number, taught what is known as the oral transmissions of Zhang Zhung, which are contained in the *Zhang Zhung Nyn Gyud*, a multivolume text of Dzogchen teachings. Other teachings of the Dzogchen are contained in the *A-khrid*.

Dzogchen is described as a path of self-liberation. Human problems are located in the five poisons—attachment, anger, ignorance, pride, and jealousy. They are the creation of the mind and do not exist in the true condition of the mind. The goal is to return to the true condition of the mind. Rather than attempt to either renounce the five poisons or somehow transform them, Dzogchen suggests that we examine our problems, and in the process we discover that they have no roots; they vanish. We are freed into a state where there are no passions.

Tenzin Wangyal Namdak Rinpoche received his transmission directly from Lopon Tenzin Namdak Rinpoche. Through the institute, he offers the B'n tradition in a manner he feels can communicate with Western audiences, as well as provide a spiritual home for Tibetan residents in the United States. The institute's library houses a number of rare Tibetan texts, and work has begun on translations. Of special interest is Tibetan medicine. Students may enter a seven-year program, focused in three-week summer retreats, through which they can be trained in the B'n religion and the spiritual exercises it perpetuates.

Membership: The institute is not a membership organization.

Periodicals: *The Voice of Clear Light.*

Sources:

Wangyal Rinpoche, Tenzin. *The Essence of Dzogchen in the Native B'n Tradition of Tibet.*

___. "Shamanism in the Native B'n Tradition of Tibet." *Tantra* 8 (1994): 50-53.

___. "The Way of Dzogchen: The Great Perfection." *Tantra* 5 (1992): 76-79.

★2364★
The Truth
(Defunct)

The Truth was an organization founded by Peter Crames (b. 1957) in September 1983 in Cambridge, Massachusetts. Crames, born into the Jewish faith, had a deep spiritual crisis that precipitated a spiritual quest. The quest climaxed in November 1982 when Crames realized he was a machine controlled by God. During the next year he composed an essay that explained this basic truth and published it as a booklet entitled *The Truth That Will Make You Free.* While writing the essay, Crames claimed that God informed him that he was the messiah, the one who was to fulfill Christs mission of establishing Gods kingdom on earth. Crames has circulated the essay locally and nationally through magazine advertisements.

The essence of "The Truth" revealed that "the universe is one large mechanical machine whose movements, including Human thoughts and actions, are planned and caused by one God." The universe began with Gods first cause, the Big Bang. Everything was determined from that initial thrust. God does have a plan for the universe, though it is as yet unknown to humankind. The state of sin was equated with our ignorance of the Truth, and the state of salvation with our knowledge of it. At the time of salvation, individuals would be born again with Gods personality.

For many years Crames circulated some 2,500 copies of his essay, but by the mid-1990s had made no converts. In the meantime, he had concluded that the essay was not as accurate as the Bible. He abandoned the essay and became a Bible student.

Sources:

Crames, Peter. *The Truth That Will Make You Free.* Cambridge, MA: The Author, 1984.

Geographic Index

Arranges organizations included in the directory listings sections according to the countries in which they are located. The United States appears first, with entries arranged alphabetically by state and subarranged by city. Canadian entries are listed next, and are arranged alphabetically by province and subarranged by city. International entries follow alphabetically by country, with entries subarranged by city within country. Citations include organization name and address, followed by the book entry number in parentheses.

UNITED STATES

Alabama

Apostolic Faith Mission Church of God (598)
3344 Pearl Ave. N
Birmingham, AL 36101

Apostolic Overcoming Holy Church of God (600)
1120 N. 24th St.
Birmingham, AL 35234

Liberty Fellowship of Churches and Ministers (743)
2732 Old Rocky Ridge Rd.
Birmingham, AL 35216

Universal Church of Scientific Truth (1340)
1250 Indiana St.
Birmingham, AL 35224

Traditional Protestant Episcopal Church (156)
6 Derby Ln.
Fairhope, AL 36532

Bible Methodist Connection of Churches (487)
1216 Taylor Rd.
Glencoe, AL 35905

Church of God (World Headquarters) (518)
1270 Willow Brook SE, Apt. 2
Huntsville, AL 35802

Cumberland Presbyterian Church in America (357)
226 Church St.
Huntsville, AL 35801

Il Bung Zen Society (2205)
% Il Bung Zen Temple
Huntsville, AL

Integrity Communications (and related ministries) (734)
Box Z
Mobile, AL 36616

House of God Which Is the Church of the Living God, the Pillar and Ground of Truth Without Controversy (Keith Dominion) (666)
% J. W. Jenkins, Chief Overseer
Box 9113
Montgomery, AL 36108

Ecumenical Orthodox Christian Church (217)
308 Bear Creek Cut-Off Rd.
Tuscaloosa, AL 35405

Assembly of Yahvah (1042)
Box 89
Winfield, AL 35594

Alaska

Music Square Church (565)
PO Box 398
Alma, AK 72921

Harmony Buddhist Mission (2278)
Clarksville, AK 92830

Central Alaskan Mission (931)
Glennallen, AK 99588

Christian Identity Church (1071)
Box 1779
Harrison, AK 72601

Kingdom Identity Ministries (1077)
PO Box 1021
Harrison, AK 72602

United Orthodox Church (274)
202 International Ave.
Hyder, AK 99923

Alaska Yearly Meeting (803)
% Walter E. Outwater
Box 687
Kotzebue, AK 99752

Arizona

Suns Ahman Israel-I:A:O: (1172)
Chevrah B'Qor Community
HC 65, Box 535
Canebeds, AZ 86022

United Order Effort (1173)
Colorado City, AZ 86021

Blue Rose Ministry (1460)
Blue Rose Starlight Spiritual Center
Box 332
Cornville, AZ 86325

Old Holy Catholic Church, Province of North America (1621)
% Mt. Rev. Alvin Lee Baker
3600 E. 7th Ave., No. 34
Flagstaff, AZ 86804

Anglican Churches of America (120)
2402 Usery Pass Rd.
Mesa, AZ 85207

International New Thought Alliance (1287)
5003 E. Broadway Rd.
Mesa, AZ 85206

Asatru Alliance (1721)
PO Box 961
Payton, AZ 85547

Infinite Way (1290)
Box 2089
Peoria, AZ 85380-2089

Bethany Bible Church and Related Independent Bible Churches of the Phoenix, Arizona, Area (930)
6060 N. 7th Ave.
Phoenix, AZ 85013-1498

Church of Essential Science (1352)
Box 62284
Phoenix, AZ 85082

Evangelical Catholic Church (58)
PO Box 6821
Phoenix, AZ 85005-6821

Hall Deliverance Foundation (583)
Box 9910
Phoenix, AZ 85068

Independent Episcopal Church (Anglican Rite, Old Catholic Church) (145)
5414 W. Pierson St.
Phoenix, AZ 85031

Miracle Life Fellowship International (588)
11052 N. 24th Ave.
Phoenix, AZ 85029

Miracle Life Revival, Inc.   (589)
Box 20707
Phoenix, AZ 85036

New Age Community Church   (1541)
6418 S. 39th Ave.
Phoenix, AZ 85041

Phoenix Buddhist Network   (2280)
4701 N. 35th Way
Phoenix, AZ 85018

University of Life Church   (1400)
% Richard Ireland
5600 Sixth St.
Phoenix, AZ 85040

Hohm Community   (1983)
PO Box 4272
Prescott, AZ 86302

Teleos Institute   (1554)
PO Box 12009-418
Scottsdale, AZ 85267

Aquarian Educational Group   (1593)
Box 267
Sedona, AZ 86336

Ruby Focus of Magnificent
    Consummation   (1636)
PO Drawer 1188
Sedona, AZ 86336

Ring of Thoth   (1782)
PO Box 25637
Tempe, AZ 85285

Thelemic Order and Temple of the
    Golden Dawn   (1712)
% New Falcon Publications
1739 E. Broadway Rd., Ste. I-277
Tempe, AZ 85282

Church of the Eternal Source   (1731)
PO Box 44146
Tucson, AZ 85733

United Episcopal Church (1945)
    Anglican/Celtic   (158)
PO Box 1931
Tucson, AZ 85702

United Submitters International   (1879)
Box 43476
Tucson, AZ 85719

Peyote Way Church of God   (1487)
Star Rte. 1, Box 7X
Willcox, AZ 85643

Arkansas

Christian Research   (1072)
% Dan Gentry, Dir.
PO Box 385
Eureka Springs, AR 72632

Davachan Temple   (2273)
2 Dickey St.
Eureka Springs, AR 72632

Associated Brotherhood of
    Christians   (602)
PO Box 3256
Hot Springs, AR 71914-3256

Baptist Missionary Association of
    America   (844)
716 Main St.
Little Rock, AR 72201

International Convention of Faith
    Ministries   (584)
10801 Executive Center Dr., Ste. 502
Little Rock, AR 72211

New Testament Church of God   (452)
Box 611
Mountain Home, AR 72653

Holy Eastern Orthodox Catholic and
    Apostolic Church in North
    America   (232)
HC74, Box 419-2
Mountain View, AR 72560

Free Christian Zion Church of
    Christ   (411)
1315 Hutchingson
Nashville, AR 71852

Sovereign Grace Baptist Churches   (870)
Calvary Grace Baptist Church
Box 7464
Pine Bluff, AR 71611-7464

Christian Catholic Church (Old Catholic)
    in the United States of America   (51)
1205 Thomas Blvd.
Springdale, AR 72762

Shiloh Trust   (1250)
% James Janisch
Sulfur Springs, AR 72763

California

Vedantic Center   (2059)
3528 N. Triunfo Canyon Rd.
Agoura, CA 91301

Home of Truth   (1317)
1300 Grand St.
Alameda, CA 94501

Triumph Prophetic Ministries (Church of
    God)   (1017)
Box 292
Altadena, CA 91003

Association of Vineyard Churches   (543)
Box 18329
Anaheim, CA 92817

The (Local) Church   (967)
% Living Stream Ministry
1853 W. Ball Rd.
Anaheim, CA 92804

Apostolic Episcopal Church—Order of
    Corporate Reunion   (37)
PO Box 2401
Apple Valley, CA 92307

Holy Celtic Church   (144)
% Most Rev. Donald E. Hugh, Presiding
    Bishop
PO Box 2401
Apple Valley, CA 92307

Esoteric Fraternity   (1231)
Box 37
Applegate, CA 95703

Believers' Circle   (1349)
% Rev. Estel Merrill
7437 Bear Mt. Blvd.
Bakersfield, CA 93313

The Georgian Church   (1757)
1908 Verde St.
Bakersfield, CA 93304

Lectorium Rosicrucianum   (1566)
Western North American Headquarters
Box 9246
Bakersfield, CA 93389

Anglican Province of Christ the
    King   (125)
% Robert S. Morse
Box 40020
Berkeley, CA 94704

Aurobindo, Disciples of Sri   (1959)
% Sri Aurobindo Association
2288 Fulton St., Ste. 310
Berkeley, CA 94704

Berkeley Area Interfaith Council   (1)
2340 Durant Ave.
Berkeley, CA 94704-1607

Berkeley Zen Center   (2160)
1931 Russell St.
Berkeley, CA 94703

Church of Divine Man   (1499)
% Berkeley Psychic Institute
2018 Allston Way
Berkeley, CA 94704

Covenant of the Goddess   (1739)
Box 1226
Berkeley, CA 94704

Fellowship of the Spiral Path   (1751)
Box 5521
Berkeley, CA 94701

First Church of the Doors   (2326)
Berkeley, CA

Order of Interbeing   (2125)
% Community of Mindful Living
PO Box 7355
Berkeley, CA 94707

Pacific Yearly Meeting of Friends   (816)
% Eric Moon
2151 Vine St
Berkeley, CA 94709

Prana Yoga Ashram   (2019)
% Swami Sivalingam
International Headquarters
1723 Alcatraz Ave.
Berkeley, CA 94703

Sixth Patriarch Zen Center   (2224)
2584 Martin Luther King Jr. Way
Berkeley, CA 94704-2630

Tiep Hien Order   (2133)
% Parallax Press
PO Box 7355
Berkeley, CA 94707

Yun Lin Temple   (2265)
2959 Russell St.
Berkeley, CA 94705

Deva Foundation   (1968)
336 S. Doheny Dr., No. 7
Beverly Hills, CA 90211

Hermetic Order of the Golden Dawn
   (Regardie)   (1688)
270 N. Canon Dr., Ste. 1302
Beverly Hills, CA 90210

Universal Pantheist Society   (1123)
PO Box 265
Big Pine, CA 93513

Independent Church of Antioch   (1613)
% The New Church Center
350 Santa Cruz St.
Boulder Creek, CA 95006

Religious School of Natural
   Hygiene   (1550)
PO Box 1011
Boulder Creek, CA 95006

Taungpupu Kaba-Aye Dharma
   Center   (2131)
18335 Basin Way
Boulder Creek, CA 95006

Temple of the Holy Grail   (1709)
% Grailmaster
PO Box 777
Brookdale, CA 95077

Solar Logos Foundation   (1282)
PO Box 2008
Buellton, CA 84110

Missionary Dispensary Bible
   Research   (1048)
Box 5296
Buena Park, CA 90622

World Community Service   (2063)
1021 E. Magnolia Blvd.
Burbank, CA 91501

Shinnyo-En   (2154)
2220 Summit Dr.
Burlingame, CA 94010

The Colony   (1228)
Burnt Ranch, CA 95527

Hindu Temple Society of Southern
   California   (2075)
1600 Las Virgenes Canyon Rd.
Calabasas, CA 91302

Christian Nations—Eagle Warriors   (1056)
% Rev. St. Michael Doc Balzarini
Box 5002
Caliptris, CA 92233-5002

Universal Shrine of Divine
   Guidance   (275)
% Most Rev. Mark Athanasios Constantine
   Karras
PO Box 1771
Camarillo, CA 93011

Society of Novus Spiritus   (1552)
35 Dillon Ave.
Campbell, CA 95008-3001

Interplanetary Connections   (1467)
% Bashar Tapes, Inc.
7210 Jordan Ave., Ste. B53
Canoga Park, CA 91301

Pre-Nicene Church (de Palatine)   (1625)
% Most Rev. Seiji Yamauchi
23301 Mobile St.
Canoga Park, CA 91307-3322

American Fellowship Church   (1125)
225 Crossroads Blvd., No. 345
Carmel, CA 93923

Mata Amritanandamayi Center   (2008)
10200 Crow Canyon Rd.
Castro Valley, CA 94552

Order of Thelema   (1696)
PO Box 511
Chula Vista, CA 91912

Church of God's Truth   (1001)
Box 2109
Corona, CA 91718-2109

Vajrayana Foundation   (2262)
% Peme Osel Lilng
2013 Eureka Canyon Rd.
Corralitos, CA 95076

Moksha Foundation (California)   (2012)
39 Edison Ave.
Corte Madera, CA 94925

International Zen Institute of
   America   (2144)
1760 Pomona Ave., No. 35
Costa Mesa, CA 92627

Fraternitas L. V. X. Occulta   (1685)
Box 5094
Covina, CA 91723

Holy Apostolic-Catholic Church of the
   East (Chaldean-Syrian)   (291)
% Metropolitan Mar Mikhael OSJ, Ph.D
PO Box 3337
Daly City, CA 94015

Orthodox Catholic Synod of the Syro-
   Chaldean Rite   (295)
% Bashir Ahmed
100 Los Banos Ave.
Daly City, CA 94014

Catholic Apostolic Church at Davis   (284)
% Gates of Praise Center
921 W. 8th St.
Davis, CA 95616

Filipino Assemblies of the First
   Born   (554)
1229 Glenwood
Delano, CA 93215

Sarvamangala Mission   (2029)
% Srividya Center
366 Grapevine Dr.
Diamond Bar, CA 91765

Synod of Independent Sacramental
   Churches   (1561)
% Abp. Julian Gillmon
Box 227
Dulzura, CA 92107

Mexican National Catholic Church   (74)
4011 E. Brooklyn Ave.
East Los Angeles, CA 90022

Unarius-Science of Life   (1474)
143 S. Magnolia
El Cajon, CA 92022

Vajrakilaya Centers of North
   America   (2261)
% Dudul Nagpa Ling
7436 Sea View Pl.
El Cerrito, CA 94530

Mazdaznan Movement   (1933)
1701 Aryana Dr.
Encinitas, CA 92024

All-One-God-Faith, Inc.   (2350)
% Dr. E. H. Bonner
Box 28
Escondido, CA 92025

Christward Ministry   (1646)
20560 Questhaven Rd.
Escondido, CA 92029

American Exarchate of the True (Old
   Calendar) Orthodox Church of
   Greece   (179)
% St. Gregory Palamas Monastery
Box 398
Etna, CA 96027

Barry Long Foundation   (1961)
Box 1001
Fairfax, CA 94978-1091

Da Yuan Circle   (2199)
% Frost Bell
Box 378
Fairfax, CA 98978

Divine Circle of the Sacred Grove   (1747)
Box 1737
Fontana, CA 92334

World Christianship Ministries   (1143)
PO Box 8041
Fresno, CA 93947

Miracle Distribution Center   (1324)
1141 East Ash Ave.
Fullerton, CA 92831

True Jesus Church   (633)
11236 Dale St.
Garden Grove, CA 92841

Agon-shu   (2136)
14518 S. Western Ave.
Gardena, CA 90247

Korean American Presbyterian
   Church   (360)
1901 W. 166th St.
Gardena, CA 90296

Seicho-No-Ie   (1334)
North American Missionary Headquarters
14527 S. Vermont Ave.
Gardena, CA 90247

United Spiritualist Church   (1392)
813 W. 165th Pl.
Gardena, CA 90247

Ann Ree Colton Foundation of
   Niscience   (1648)
336 W. Colorado
Glendale, CA 91209

Community Churches of America   (934)
% United Community Church
Box 90
Glendale, CA 91209

Independent Catholic Clergy
   Association   (21)
Box 6903
Glendale, CA 91205

Perfect Liberty Kyodan   (2359)
700 S. Adams St.
Glendale, CA 91205

Philippine Independent Catholic Church
   in the Americas   (149)
PO Box 6
Glendale, CA 91209

Apostolic Orthodox Catholic
   Church   (195)
PO Box 1834
Glendora, CA 91740

MasterPath   (2095)
1231 S. Bender
Glendora, CA 91740

International Buddhist Progress
   Society   (2207)
PO Box 5248
Hacienda Heights, CA 91745

Temple of the People   (1586)
Box 7095
Halcyon, CA 93420

Aetherius Society   (1457)
6202 Afton Pl.
Hollywood, CA 90028

The Association of Love and Light   (1404)
3399 Bennett, No. 28
Hollywood, CA 90068

Ancient Church of the East   (279)
% Mar Emannuel
St. Mary's Church
PO Box 1191
Hughson, CA 95326

Advaita Fellowship   (1945)
221-B Indianapolis St.
Huntington Beach, CA 92648

International Babaji Kriya Yoga
   Sangam   (1989)
595 W. Bedford Rd.
Imperial City, CA 92251

Naqshbandiyya-Mujaddidiyya Order of
   Sufism   (1900)
% Golden Sufi Center
PO Box 428
Inverness, CA 94937

Dharma Dena   (2116)
% Desert Vipassana Center
HC-1, Box 250
Joshua Tree, CA 92252

Institute of Mentalphysics   (1531)
59700 29 Palms Hwy.
Joshua Tree, CA 92252

White Star   (1478)
Box 307
Joshua Tree, CA 92252

Chagdud Gonpa Foundation   (2229)
Box 279
Junction City, CA 96048

Church of Cosmic Origin and School of
   Thought   (1647)
Box 257
June Lake, CA 93529

Ewam Choden   (2235)
254 Cambridge St.
Kensington, CA 94707

Vedanta Centre and Ananda
   Ashrama   (2057)
Box 8555
La Crescenta, CA 91224-0555

American Catholic Church   (1601)
% Most Rev. Simon Eugene Talarczyk
430 Park Ave.
Laguna Beach, CA 92651

Kali Mandir   (1995)
% Kali Mandir Puja Shop
PO Box 4700
Laguna Beach, CA 92652-4700

Old Catholic Church (Anglican Rite)   (79)
489 Jasmine St.
Laguna Beach, CA 92651

Independent Assemblies of God,
   International   (704)
24411 Ridge Rte. Dr.
Laguna Hills, CA 92653

Johannine Catholic Church   (1616)
Rancho Vista Mobile Home Estates
13490 Highway 8 Business, Space 143
Lakeside, CA 92040

American Catholic Church—Old
   Catholic   (27)
Church of the Good Shepherd
5420 Clark Ave.
Lakewood, CA 90712

Christ's Apostolic Church of North
   America   (932)
% Most Rev. Ronald D. Nowlan, D.D.
Chancery Office
316 Hullett St.
Long Beach, CA 90805-3424

Community of James the Just   (214)
% R. Rev. Clyde Ramon Allee
936 Cedar Ave., No. 15
Long Beach, CA 90813-4231

Missionary Christian and Soul Winning
   Fellowship   (448)
350 E. Market St.
Long Beach, CA 90805

Morningland-Church of the Ascended
   Christ   (1635)
2600 E. 7th St.
Long Beach, CA 90804

Harmony of Life Fellowship   (1011)
1434 Fremont Ave.
Los Altos, CA 94022

Society for Sufi Studies   (1908)
% The Institute for the Study of Human
   Knowledge
Box 176
Los Altos, CA 94023

American Buddhist Congress   (2102)
4267 W. Third St.
Los Angeles, CA 90020

Apostolic Old Catholic Church   (38)
% Rt. Rev. Hans B. Kroneberg
1157 N. Bronson Ave.
Los Angeles, CA 90038

Aspects of Light   (1402)
12540 Braddock Dr., Ste. 218B
Los Angeles, CA 90066

Associated Churches of Christ
   (Holiness)   (472)
1302 E. Adams Blvd.
Los Angeles, CA 90011

Buddhist Sangha Council of Southern
   California   (2104)
928 S. New Hampshire
Los Angeles, CA 90006

Builders of the Adytum   (1677)
5105 N. Figueroa
Los Angeles, CA 90042

Byzantine Catholic Church   (205)
PO Box 3682
Los Angeles, CA 90078

California Bosatsukai   (2161)
5632 Green Oak Dr.
Los Angeles, CA 90068

Christ Faith Mission   (718)
6026 Echo St.
Los Angeles, CA 90042

Church of Light   (1575)
2341 Coral St.
Los Angeles, CA 90031

Church of Scientology   (1504)
% Church of Scientology International
6331 Hollywood Blvd., Ste. 1200
Los Angeles, CA 90028-6329

Church of the Movement of Spiritual Inner
   Awareness   (2087)
3500 W. Adams Blvd.
Los Angeles, CA 90018

Church of Utrecht in America   (54)
% Mt. Rev. Derek Lang
2103 S. Portland St.
Los Angeles, CA 90007

Church of World Messianity   (2283)
960 S. Kenmore Ave.
Los Angeles, CA 90006

Concilio Olazabal de Iglesias Latino
   Americano   (688)
1925 E. 1st St.
Los Angeles, CA 90033

Ecclesia Gnostica   (1606)
4516 Hollywood Blvd.
Los Angeles, CA 90027

Fellowship of Inner-City Word of Faith
   Ministries   (580)
% Crenshaw Christian Center
7901 S. Vermont Ave.
Los Angeles, CA 90044

General Assembly of the Korean
   Presbyterian Church   (359)
1251 Crenshaw Blvd.
Los Angeles, CA 90019

Gnostic Association of Cultural and
   Anthropological Studies   (1576)
Box 291488
Los Angeles, CA 90029

Hazy Moon Zen Center   (2166)
1651 S. Gramercy Pl.
Los Angeles, CA

Higashi Hongwanji Buddhist
   Church   (2142)
505 E. Third St.
Los Angeles, CA 90013

International Buddhist Meditation
   Center   (2120)
928 S. New Hampshire
Los Angeles, CA 90006

International Church of the Foursquare
   Gospel   (561)
1100 Glendale Blvd.
Los Angeles, CA 90026

International Churches of Christ   (909)
3530 Wilshire Blvd., Ste. 1750
Los Angeles, CA 90010

Kanzeonji Non-Sectarian Buddhist
   Temple   (2168)
944 Terrrace 49
Los Angeles, CA 90042

Kingdom of God on Earth Within
   Man   (1058)
% Kingdom of God Headquarters
PO Box 77659
Los Angeles, CA 90007

Konko Kyo   (2287)
% Rev. Alfred Y. Tsyyuki
2924 E. 1st St.
Los Angeles, CA 90033

Korean Buddhist Chogye Order   (2221)
% Kwan Um Sa Temple
4265 W. Third St.
Los Angeles, CA 90020

Korean Buddhist Sangha Association of
   Western Territory in U. S. A.   (2107)
451 S. Serrano Ave.
Los Angeles, CA 90020

Los Angeles Buddhist Church
   Federation   (2108)
123 S. Hewitt St.
Los Angeles, CA 90012

Order of the Thelemic Golden
   Dawn   (1695)
1636 N. Wilcox Ave., Ste.418
Los Angeles, CA 90028

Oriental Missionary Society Holiness
   Church of North America   (952)
3660 S. Gramercy Pl.
Los Angeles, CA 90018

Philosophical Research Society   (1579)
3910 Los Feliz Blvd.
Los Angeles, CA 90027

Reiyukai America   (2151)
2741 Sunset Blvd.
Los Angeles, CA 90026

Rinzai-Ji, Inc.   (2177)
% Rinzai Zen Center
2505 S. Cimarron
Los Angeles, CA 90018

Rissho Kosei Kai   (2152)
% Rev. Kazuhiko K. Nagamoto
118 N. Mott
Los Angeles, CA 90033

Saeejis Temple of Peace   (2025)
5627 Lexington Ave., No. 6
Los Angeles, CA 90038

Self-Realization Fellowship   (2032)
3880 San Rafael Ave.
Los Angeles, CA 90065

Shaolin Buddhist Meditation
   Center   (2212)
3165 Minnesota St.
Los Angeles, CA 90031

Sikh Dharma   (2085)
Box 35330
Los Angeles, CA 90035

Soto Mission   (2179)
Zenshuji Soto Mission
123 S. Hewitt St.
Los Angeles, CA 90012

Superet Light Doctrine Church   (1389)
2516 W. Third St.
Los Angeles, CA 90057

Temple ov Psychick Youth   (1711)
% N A Station TOPY Dejavo
PO Box 4889 2A
Los Angeles, CA 90048

Tenrikyo   (2294)
Tenrikyo Mission Headquarters in America
2727 E. First St.
Los Angeles, CA 90033

Thubten Dargye Ling   (2257)
2658 La Cienga Ave.
Los Angeles, CA 90034

Traditional Anglican Communion   (112)
% Rev. Gregory Wilcox
4510 Finley Ave.
Los Angeles, CA 90027

Unfettered Mind   (2259)
11600 Washington Place, Ste. 210
Los Angeles, CA 90066

United Church of Religious
   Science   (1338)
3251 W. 6th St.
Box 75127
Los Angeles, CA 90075

United Church of the Living God, The
   Pillar and Ground of Truth   (678)
Los Angeles, CA

United Lodge of Theosophists   (1590)
245 W. 33rd St.
Los Angeles, CA 90007

Universal Fellowship of Metropolitan
   Community Churches   (2349)
8704 Santa Monica Blvd., 2nd Fl.
Los Angeles, CA 90069

Universal White Brotherhood   (1660)
Prosveta U. S. A.
Box 49614
Los Angeles, CA 90049

Universal World Church   (753)
123 N. Lake St.
Los Angeles, CA 90026

Viet Nam Buddhists   (2134)
% Congregation of Vietnamese Buddhists
   in the U.S.
863 S. Berendo
Los Angeles, CA 90005

Zen Center of Los Angeles   (2187)
923 S. Normandie Ave.
Los Angeles, CA 90006

Kingdom and World Mission of Our Lord
   Jesus Christ (741)
5039 Franklin Ave.
Los Feliz, CA 90027

Church of Revelation (Hawaii) (1355)
21475 Summit Rd.
Los Gatos, CA 95030

School of Natural Science (1442)
25355 Spanish Ranch Rd.
Los Gatos, CA 95030

Arcana Workshops (1594)
Box 605
Manhattan Beach, CA 90266

The Divine Science of Light and
   Sound (2090)
2554 Lincoln Blvd.
Box 620
Marina del Rey, CA 90291

Dhammakaya International Society of
   California (2115)
5950 Heliotrope Circle
Maywood, CA 90270

Adidam (1944)
12040 N. Seigler Spring Rd.
Middletown, CA 95461

Heart Consciousness Church and New
   Age Church of Being (1523)
PO Box 82
Middletown, CA 95461

Beshara School of Intensive Esoteric
   Education (1883)
PO Box 2333
Mill Valley, CA 94942

Osho Commune International (2082)
% Osho Viha Meditation Center
Box 352
Mill Valley, CA 94942

Palyul Changchub Dhaegye Ling (2250)
Box 1514
Mill Valley, CA 94941

Universal Life Church (1141)
601 Third St.
Modesto, CA 95351

Han-Ma-Um Zen Center (2219)
617 B Hale Ave.
Morgan Hill, CA 95037

Ascended Master Teaching
   Foundation (1627)
Box 466
Mount Shasta, CA 96067

Association of Sananda and Sanat
   Kumara (1459)
Box 35
Mount Shasta, CA 96067

Order of Buddhist Contemplatives (2175)
% Shasta Abbey
3724 Summit Dr.
Mount Shasta, CA 96067-9102

Temple of Cosmic Religion (2051)
310 E. Lake St.
Mount Shasta, CA 96067

As-Sunnah Foundation of
   America (1870)
607A W. Dana St.
Mountain View, CA 94040

Naqshbandi Sufi Order (1899)
% Haqqani Foundation
607 A W. Dana St.
Mountain View, CA 94041

Devi Mandir (1970)
5950 Hwy. 128
Napa, CA 94558-9632

Qadiri Rifa'i Sufism (1903)
PO Box 2511
Napa, CA 94558

Shadhiliyya Sufism (1907)
% Sidi Muhammad Press
Napa, CA 94558

Abhidhyan Yoga Institute (1943)
PO Box 1414
Nevada City, CA 95959-1414

Ananda (1951)
14618 Tyler Foote Rd.
Nevada City, CA 95959

Fereferia (1752)
12318 Shady Ln.
Nevada City, CA 95959-3255

Institute for the Development of the
   Harmonious Human Being (1891)
Box 370
Nevada City, CA 95959

Radha Soami Satsang, Beas (2098)
10901 Mill Springs Dr.
Nevada City, CA 95959

Chirothesian Church of Faith (1495)
% Chirothesian Way Chapel
23548 Lyons Ave., Unit E
Newhall, CA 91321

Church of the Living Word (701)
Box 858
North Hollywood, CA 91603

Ryugu, U.S.A. (2289)
11958 Hartsook St.
North Hollywood, CA 91607

Tara Center (1599)
Box 6001
North Hollywood, CA 91603

Thai-American Buddhist
   Association (2132)
Wat Thai of Los Angeles
12909 Cantara St.
North Hollywood, CA 91506

Apostolic Episcopal Church, Diocese of
   California/Nevada (36)
1933 73rd Ave.
Oakland, CA 94621

Dianic Wicca (1745)
% Susan B. Anthony Coven No. 1
Box 11363
Oakland, CA 94611

Kathok Shendrup Ling Center (2242)
5516 Vallejo St.
Oakland, CA 94608-2624

Saddhamma Foundation (2128)
5459 Shafter Ave.
Oakland, CA 94618

Universal Association of Faithists (1453)
% Pahspe Publishingq
6115 LaSalle Ave., Ste. 215
Oakland, CA 94611

Rosicrucian Fellowship (1569)
2222 Mission Avenue
Oceanside, CA 92054

Ecumenical Ministry of the Unity of All
   Religions (1649)
107 N. Ventura St.
Ojai, CA 93023

Krishnamurti Foundation of
   America (2000)
Box 1560
Ojai, CA 93024-1560

Meditation Groups, Inc. (1596)
Box 566
Ojai, CA 93023

William Samuel Foundation (1293)
307 N. Montgomery St.
Ojai, CA 93023

Truth Center (1294)
566 Crestview Dr.
Ojai, CA 93023

Hermetic Order of the Morning Star
   International (1689)
4035 E. Guasti Rd., Ste. 306
Ontario, CA 91761

Fellowship of Friends (1887)
PO Box 100
Oregon House, CA 95962

Michael Educational Foundation (1431)
10 Muth Dr.
Orinda, CA 94563

Reformed Druids of North
   America (1781)
% Live Oak Grove
616 Minor Rd.
Orinda, CA 94563

College/Temple of Thelema (1680)
PO Box 415
Oroville, CA 95965

George Ohsawa Macrobiotic
   Foundation (2210)
1999 Myers
Oroville, CA 95966

Pastoral Bible Institute (1035)
1425 Lachman Ln.
Pacific Palisades, CA 90272

Anglican Episcopal Church of North
America   (122)
% Walter Hollis Adams
789 Allen Ct.
Palo Alto, CA 94303

Center for Timeless Wisdom   (2269)
555 Bryant St., No. 302
Palo Alto, CA 94301

The Church of Gnosis (Ecclesia Gnostica
Mysteriorum)   (1605)
3437 Alma, No. 23
Palo Alto, CA 94306

American Orthodox Catholic Church
(Kochones)   (186)
810 E. Walnut St.
Pasadena, CA 91101

Church of God, Philadelphia Era   (997)
Box 371
Pasadena, CA 91102

International Alliance of Churches of the
Truth   (1322)
690 E. Orange Grove Blvd.
Pasadena, CA 91104

Theosophical Society   (1587)
PO Box C
Pasadena, CA 91109-7107

Worldwide Church of God   (1024)
300 W. Green St.
Pasadena, CA 91129

Chokling Tersar Foundation USA   (2218)
PO Box 5162
Petaluma, CA 94955-5162

Inner Light Foundation   (1528)
Box 750265
Petaluma, CA 94975

Chinmaya Mission West   (1965)
PO Box 129
Piercy, CA 95587

Ajapa Yoga Foundation   (1946)
% Shri Janardan Ajapa Yoga Ashram
Box 1731
Placerville, CA 95667

Haidakhan Samaj   (1978)
% Paul Gessler
104 Blue Jay
Placerville, CA 95667

Lemurian Fellowship   (1577)
Box 397
Ramona, CA 92065

Evangelical Anglican Church in
America   (138)
2401 Artesia Blvd., Ste. 106-213
Redondo Beach, CA 90278

Abhayagiri Buddhist Monastery   (2111)
16201 Tomki Rd.
Redwood Valley, CA 95470

New Wiccan Church   (1770)
Box 162046
Sacramento, CA 95816

American National Catholic Church
(Bridges)   (182)
Box 472
San Bernardino, CA 92402

Sarum Episcopal Church   (2345)
161 W. Highland Ave.
San Bernardino, CA 92405-4015

Charismatic Episcopal Church   (130)
St. Michael's Pro-Cathedral
107 W. Marquita
San Clemente, CA 92672

Affiliated New Thought Network   (1286)
% New Thought Center, San Diego
5520 Ruffin Rd., Ste. 101
San Diego, CA 92123

American Association for the
Advancement of Atheism   (1090)
Box 2832
San Diego, CA 92112

Assemblies of God International
Fellowship (Independent/Not
Affiliated)   (697)
8604 Commerce Ave.
San Diego, CA 92121

EarthStar Alliance   (1414)
3416 Waco St., Apt. 4
San Diego, CA 92117-6350

Essene Foundation   (1514)
2536 Collier Ave.
San Diego, CA 92116

Free Catholic Church   (62)
% St. Thomas the Doubter Free Catholic
Church
1010 University Ave., No. 158
San Diego, CA 92103

Global Church of God   (1010)
Box 501111
San Diego, CA 92150-1111

Inner Circle Kethra E'Da Foundation,
Inc.   (1426)
Box 1722
San Diego, CA 92112

International Society for Krishna
Consciousness   (1992)
% ISCKON International Ministry of Public
Affairs
1030 Grand Ave.
San Diego, CA 92109

Liberal Catholic Church
International   (1617)
741 Cerro Gordo Ave.
San Diego, CA 92102

National Missionary Baptist Convention of
America   (887)
719 Crosby St.
San Diego, CA 92113

New Psychiana   (1543)
% Psychiana Study Group
4069 Stephens St.
San Diego, CA 92103

Ordinary Mind Zen School   (2176)
% Zen Center of San Diego
2047 Felspar
San Diego, CA 92109

Reformed Orthodox Catholic
Church   (259)
1674 Palm Ave.
San Diego, CA 92154

Teaching of the Inner Christ, Inc.   (1553)
% International Center
4444 Zion Ave., Ste. A
San Diego, CA 91220-2328

Western Orthodox Catholic Church of
California   (276)
% Most Rev. Martin J. Hill
4109 Louisiana St.
San Diego, CA 92104-1691

American Vinland Association   (1664)
537 Jones, Ste. 2154
San Francisco, CA 94102

Buddha's Universal Church   (2193)
702 Washington St.
San Francisco, CA 94108

Chapori-Ling Foundation Sangha   (2230)
766 8th Ave.
San Francisco, CA 94118

Christian Orthodox Catholic Church   (52)
United States Chancery Office
795 La Playa St., No. 1
San Francisco, CA 94121-3258

Church for the Fellowship of All
People   (2304)
2041 Larkin St.
San Francisco, CA 94109

Church of Amron   (1405)
2254 Van Ness
San Francisco, CA 94109

Church of Satan   (1806)
Box 210666
San Francisco, CA 94121

Diamond Way Buddhism   (2232)
% Diamond Way Buddhist Center
1110 Merced Ave.
San Francisco, CA 94127

Ecclesia Catholica Traditionalis
"Conservare et Praedicare"   (56)
Box 26414
San Francisco, CA 94126-6414

Foundation of Revelation   (1975)
59 Scott St.
San Francisco, CA 94117

Gay Buddhist Fellowship   (2341)
2261 Market St., Ste. 422
San Francisco, CA 94114

Gurdjieff Foundation   (1888)
85 St. Elmo Way
San Francisco, CA 94127

Honpa Hongwanji Buddhism   (2143)
% Buddhist Churches of America
1710 Octavia St.
San Francisco, CA 94109

Kerista Commune   (1268)
PO Box 410068
San Francisco, CA 94141-0068

Kriya Yoga Tantra Society   (2002)
633 Post St., Ste. 647
San Francisco, CA 94109

Molokan Spiritual Christians
   (Postojannye)   (828)
841 Carolina St.
San Francisco, CA 94107

Orthodox Catholic Church   (249)
% Most Rev. Carlos A. Florido, Presiding
   Bishop
544 Oak St.
San Francisco, CA 94127

Orthodox Episcopal Church of
   God   (2344)
Box 1528
San Francisco, CA 94101

SM Church   (1787)
% Robin Stewart, Priestess
Box 1407
San Francisco, CA 94101

Sufi Islamia Ruhaniat Society   (1911)
410 Precita Ave.
San Francisco, CA 94110

Temple of Set   (1813)
PO Box 470307
San Francisco, CA 94147

Traditional Catholic Church—Conservare
   et Praedicare   (100)
1760 Bush, Ste. 507
San Francisco, CA 94107

West Coast Communities   (1285)
% Church of the Sojourners
866 Potero
San Francisco, CA 94110

White Robed Monks of St.
   Benedict   (110)
% Most Rev. Robert M. Dittler, OSB
Box 27536
San Francisco, CA 94127

Zen Center of San Francisco   (2189)
300 Page St.
San Francisco, CA 94102

Ancient and Mystical Order of the Rosae
   Crucis   (1562)
San Jose, CA 95191

Christian Assembly   (1303)
PO Box 6120
San Jose, CA 95150

Congregation of God (Biblical Church of
   God)   (1003)
Box 612440
San Jose, CA 95161

Badarikashrama   (1960)
15602 Maubert Ave.
San Leandro, CA 94578

Satyananda Ashrams, U.S.A.   (2031)
1157 Ramblewood Way
San Mateo, CA 94403

Intergalactic Cultural Foundation   (1988)
1569 Stonewood Ct.
San Pedro, CA 90732

Norwegian Seaman's Church
   (Mission)   (335)
1035 Beacon St.
San Pedro, CA 90731

International Association of
   Sufism   (1873)
25 Mitchell Blvd., Ste. 2
San Rafael, CA 94903

Calvary Chapel   (547)
3800 S. Fairview Rd.
Santa Ana, CA 92704

Art of Living Foundation   (1957)
PO Box 50003
Santa Barbara, CA 93150

Joy Foundation, Inc.   (1633)
418 E. Micheltorena, Ste. 5
Santa Barbara, CA 93101

Jean Klein Foundation   (1998)
Box 2111
Santa Barbara, CA 93120

New Kadampa Tradition   (2248)
% Mahakankala Buddhist Center
1B N. Alisos St.
Santa Barbara, CA 93103

Shri Shivabalayogi Maharaj Trust   (2040)
% Sally Moburg
724 Fellowship Rd.
Santa Barbara, CA 93109

Spiritual Education Endeavors—The Share
   Foundation   (1448)
1556 Halford Ave., No. 288
Santa Clara, CA 95051

Universal Church of the Master   (1395)
National Headquarters
501 Washington St.
Santa Clara, CA 95050

Concordant Publishing Concern   (959)
15570 Knochaven
Santa Clarita, CA 91330

Biblical Church of God   (989)
Box 1234
Santa Cruz, CA 95061

Federation of St. Thomas Christian
   Churches   (1608)
% Joseph Vredenburgh
134 Dakota, No. 308
Santa Cruz, CA 95060

Rigpa Fellowship   (2252)
% Orgyen Cho Lin
PO Box 607
Santa Cruz, CA 95061-0607

Society of Abidance in Truth   (2042)
1834 Ocean St.
Santa Cruz, CA 95060

Sri Rama Foundation   (2047)
Box 2550
Santa Cruz, CA 95063

New Age Bible and Philosophy
   Center   (1567)
1139 Lincoln Blvd.
Santa Monica, CA 90403

Old Catholic Church in North America
   (Catholicate of the West)   (81)
2118 Wilshire Blvd., Ste. 582
Santa Monica, CA 90403

Shrine of the Eternal Breath of
   Tao   (2213)
1314 2nd St.
Santa Monica, CA 90401

Christian International Network of
   Prophetic Ministries   (700)
PO Box 9000
Santa Rosa, CA 32459

Sonoma Mountain Zen Center   (2178)
6367 Sonoma Mountain Rd.
Santa Rosa, CA 95404

Tayu Meditation Center   (1914)
Box 11554
Santa Rosa, CA 95406

Western Orthodox Church in
   America   (277)
% Mt. Rev. Nickolas Carone
200 Fifth St.
Santa Rosa, CA 95401

Zen Wind   (2225)
PO Box 4176
Santa Rosa, CA 95402

Atheists United   (1098)
14542 Ventura Blvd., Ste. 211
Sherman Oaks, CA 91403

Foundation for the Preservation of the
   Mahayana Tradition   (2236)
PO Box 800
Soquel, CA 95073

Sri Chaitanya Saraswat Mandal   (2044)
% Guardian of Devotion Press
2900 N. Rodeo Gulch Rd.
Soquel, CA 95073

Middlebar Monastery   (2170)
2503 Del Rio Dr.
Stockton, CA 95204

Dharma Realm Buddhist
   Association   (2200)
City of Ten Thousand Buddhas
Talmage, CA 95481-0217

Blue Mountain Center of
    Meditation (1962)
PO Box 256
Tomales, CA 94971

Mahikari of America (2288)
3510 Torrance Blvd.
Torrance, CA 90503

Church of All Worlds (1727)
Box 1542
Ukiah, CA 95482

Astara (1572)
792 W. Arrow Hwy.
Box 5003
Upland, CA 91785

American Traditional Catholic
    Church (32)
Valencia, CA

Independent Catholic Church
    International (1611)
% Mt. Rev. R. V. Bernard Dawe
1260 American Canyon Rd., No. 148
Vallejo, CA 94589

International Evangelism Crusades (737)
14617 Victory Blvd.
Van Nuys, CA 91411

S. A. I. Foundation (2022)
14849 Lull St.
Van Nuys, CA 91405

Sahaja Yoga Center (2026)
13659 Victory Blvd., Ste. 684
Van Nuys, CA 91401

Ecumenical Catholic Church (2338)
Box 32
Villa Grande, CA 95486-0032

GAF International/Adamski
    Foundation (1466)
Box 1722
Vista, CA 92085

Interdenominational Ministries
    International (735)
PO Box 2107
Vista, CA 92085-2107

Three Treasures Zen Community (2331)
246 Santa Clara Dr.
Vista, CA 92083

Ordinary Dharma (2126)
% Manzanita Village
PO Box 67
Warner Springs, CA 92086

Nichiren Shoshu America (2149)
% Myohoji Temple
1401 N. Crescent Heights Blvd.
West Hollywood, CA 90046

The Family (1263)
14118 Whittier Blvd., Ste. 116
Whittier, CA 90605

Christ's Church of the Golden
    Rule (1223)
Ridgewood Ranch
16100 N. Hwy. 101
Willits, CA 95490

Universal Industrial Church of the New
    World Comforter (1284)
PO Box 1447
Windsor, CA 95492

Colorado

American Synod: Holy Orthodox Catholic
    Church (191)
% Abp.
12245 E. 14th Ave., No. 110
Aurora, CO 80011

Evangelical Friends International (806)
3823A S. Genoa Circle
Aurora, CO 80013

Assembly of YHWHHOSHUA (1043)
% Pastor Laycher Gonzales
1998 - 58th Ln.
Boone, CO 81025

Intermountain Yearly Meeting (809)
% Martin Cobin
1720 Linden Ave.
Boulder, CO 80304

Namo Buddha Seminar (2246)
1390 Kalmia Ave.
Boulder, CO 80304

Poonjaji, Disciples of Harivansh Lal -
    Satsang Foundation & Press (2017)
4855 Riverbend Rd.
Boulder, CO 80301

Saccha Dham Ashram (2023)
% Prem
1750 30th St., Ste. 223
Boulder, CO 80301

Truth Consciousness (2055)
% Sacred Mountain Ashram
10668 Gold Hill Rd.
Boulder, CO 80302-9716

Yeshe Khorlo (2263)
1630 39th St., Box 356
Boulder, CO 80301

Brotherhood of the White Temple (1573)
PO Box 966
Castle Rock, CO 80104

The Christian and Missionary
    Alliance (430)
8595 Explorer Dr.
Colorado Springs, CO 80920

Emmanuel Association (441)
% Peoples Bible College
2713 W. Cucharas
Colorado Springs, CO 80904

Evangelical Episcopal Church
    (Owen) (140)
17275 E. Goshawk Rd.
Colorado Springs, CO 80908

American Orthodox Catholic Church
    (Irene) (185)
851 Leyden St.
Denver, CO 80220

Bible Missionary Church (489)
822 S. Simms
Denver, CO 80211

Colorado Reform Baptist Church (890)
% Bishop William T. Conklin
Box 12514
Denver, CO 80212

Divine Knowledge Meditation
    Center (2088)
1434 Willow St.
Denver, CO 80220

Divine Science Federation
    International (1313)
1819 E. 14th Ave.
Denver, CO 80218

General Conference of the Church of God
    (Seventh-Day) (1008)
% General Conference Offices
Box 33677
Denver, CO 80233

House of Prayer for All People (1076)
Box 837
Denver, CO 80201

Universalia (1456)
Box 6243
Denver, CO 80206

Buddhist Association of Colorado (2195)
8965 W. Dartmouth Pl.
Lakewood, CO 80227

Chan Nhu Buddhist Pagoda (2270)
7201 W. Bayaud Pl.
Lakewood, CO 80226

The Continuing Episcopal Church (134)
% Rt. Rev. Colin James III
2080 Kipling
Lakewood, CO 80215

Evangelistic Missionary Fellowship (938)
5405 W. 1st Ave.
Lakewood, CO 80226

LaPorte Church of Christ (1078)
3206 E. Country Rd. 52
LaPorte, CO

Order of the Lily and the Eagle (1694)
PO Box 2919
Littleton, CO 80161-2919

Emissaries of Divine Light (1511)
5569 N. Country Rd. 29
Loveland, CO 80537

Skergard   (1786)
20 E. Lakeview Dr., Ste. 250
PO Box 1755
Nederland, CO 80466

Tara Mandala   (2256)
PO Box 3040
157 Hot Springs Blvd.
Pagosa Springs, CO 81147

Law of Life Activity   (1634)
8575 S. Crow Cutoff
Rye Star Rte.
Pueblo, CO 81004

Church of Seven Arrows   (1730)
PO Box 185
Wheat Ridge, CO 80034-0185

Rocky Mountain Yearly Meeting   (817)
3350 Reed St.
Wheat Ridge, CO 80033

New Order of Glastonbury   (1619)
Box 285
Yellow Jacket, CO 81335

Connecticut

Vishwa Hindu Parishad of
   America   (1942)
217 Deerfield Dr.
Berlin, CT 06037

Living Dharma Centers   (2169)
PO Box 513
Bolton, CT 06043

Kundalini Research Foundation   (2003)
Box 2248
Darien, CT 06820

Christian Millennial Fellowship   (1028)
307 White St.
Hartford, CT 06106

Community of Catholic Churches   (55)
% Thomas Sargent
3 Columbia St.
Hartford, CT 06106

American Apostolic Catholic Church   (26)
% Mt. Rev. Richard Cardarelli
547C Hilliard St.
Manchester, CT 06040

Orthodox Roman Catholic
   Movement   (90)
% Our Lady of Rosary Chapel
PO Box 283
Monroe, CT 06468

Centers for Dzogchen Studies   (2228)
% Center for Dzogchen Studies in New
   Haven
847 Whalley Ave.
New Haven, CT 06515

Life Study Fellowship Foundation,
   Inc.   (1323)
Noroton, CT 06820

Abbey of Thelema   (1672)
Box 666
Old Greenwich, CT 06870-0666

Northeast Atheist Association   (1117)
Box 63
Simsbury, CT 06070

Independent Old Roman Catholic
   Hungarian Orthodox Church of
   America   (70)
% Edward C. Payne, Catholicos-
   Metropolitan
Box 290261
Weatherfield, CT 06129-0261

Universal Life: The Inner Religion   (1454)
PO Box 3549
Woodbridge, CT 06525

Delaware

African Union First Colored Methodist
   Protestant Church   (408)
2611 N. Claymont St.
Wilmington, DE 19802

District of Columbia

African-American Catholic
   Congregation   (25)
1015 I St. NE
Washington, DC 20002

Ahmadiyya Movement in Islam   (1919)
2141 Leroy Pl., NW
Washington, DC 20008

American Muslim Council   (1869)
1212 New York Ave. NW
Washington, DC 20005

Bible Way Church of Our Lord Jesus
   Christ World Wide   (604)
1130 New Jersey Ave., NW
Washington, DC 20001

Church of the Saviour   (1227)
2025 Massachusetts Ave., NW
Washington, DC 20036

Foundation Church of Divine
   Truth   (1420)
Box 66003
Washington, DC 20035-6003

Foundation Church of the New
   Birth   (1421)
Box 996, Benjamin Franklin Sta.
Washington, DC 20044

Gospel Spreading Church   (480)
2030 Georgia Ave., NW
Washington, DC 20003

Hanafi Madh-hab Center, Islam
   Faith   (1923)
7700 16th St. NW
Washington, DC 20012

Highway Christian Church of
   Christ   (620)
436 W St. NW
Washington, DC 20001

Independent African American Catholic
   Rite   (65)
Church of Martin de Porres
PO Box 41449
Washington, DC 20018

Inner Peace Movement   (1529)
Box 4897
Washington, DC 20008

Moral Re-Armament   (2355)
1156 15th St. NW
Washington, DC 20005

National Spiritual Science Center   (1377)
409 Butternut St., NW, Ste. 1
Washington, DC 20012

Original Hebrew Israelite Nation   (1854)
% Communications Press
PO Box 26063
Washington, DC 20001

Progressive National Baptist Convention,
   Inc.   (888)
601 50th St., NE
Washington, DC 20019

Roman Catholic Church   (24)
National Conference of Catholic Bishops
1312 Massachusetts Ave. NW
Washington, DC 20005

School of Islamic Sufism (Oveyssi Sufi
   Order)   (1905)
PO Box 5827
Washington, DC 20016

Self-Revelation Church of Absolute
   Monism   (2033)
4748 Western Ave. NW
PO Box 9515
Washington, DC 20016

Seventh-Day Pentecostal Church of the
   Living God   (574)
1443 S. Euclid
Washington, DC 20009

Sunni Muslims   (1878)
% Islamic Center
2551 Massachusetts Ave. NW
Washington, DC 20008

True Grace Memorial House of
   Prayer   (676)
205 V St., NW
Washington, DC 20001

The United House of Prayer for All People
   of the Church on the Rock of the
   Apostolic Faith   (681)
1721 1/2 7th St. NW
Washington, DC 20001

Florida

Rex Humbard Ministry   (942)
Box 3063
Boca Raton, FL 33431

Gospel Crusade Ministerial
  Fellowship   (731)
1200 Glory Way Blvd.
Bradenton, FL 34202

International Free Catholic
  Communion   (1614)
PO Box 3454
Clearwater, FL 34630

Mount Zion Overcoming Body of Christ—
  The True Bride   (1243)
Rte. 1
Crescent City, FL 32012

United Biblical Church of God   (1020)
Box 547
Crystal River, FL 32623

Holy Temple of God   (531)
Big Apple Rd.
East Palatka, FL 32077

Hermetic Order of the Golden
  Dawn   (1687)
PO Box 1757
Elfers, FL 34680

Independent Catholic Churches   (68)
3460 Powerline Rd.
Fort Lauderdale, FL 33309

Mark-Age, Inc.   (1469)
Box 290368
Fort Lauderdale, FL 33329

Reformed (Slavonic) Orthodox
  Church   (260)
808 W. Sunrise Blvd.
Fort Lauderdale, FL 33311

Triumph the Church in
  Righteousness   (484)
PO Box 1572
Fort Lauderdale, FL 33302

Laodicean Home Missionary
  Movement   (1033)
Rte. 38
9021 Temple Rd., W.
Fort Myers, FL 33912

Maranatha Christian Churches   (708)
Box 1799
Gainesville, FL 32602

African Universal Church, Inc.   (644)
2336 SW 48th Ave.
Hollywood, FL 33023

Essenes of Arkashea   (1515)
21450 SW 240th St.
Homestead, FL 33031

Primitive Church of Jesus Christ   (629)
% Bethel Church of Jesus Christ
Hwy. 19 N.
Inglis, FL 34449

The Afro-American Social Research
  Association   (1488)
Box 2150
Jacksonville, FL 32203

Church of God by Faith   (719)
3220 Haines St.
Jacksonville, FL 32206

New Congregational Methodist
  Church   (401)
% Bishop Joe E. Kelley
354 E. 9th St.
Jacksonville, FL 32206

American Evangelistic Association   (715)
PO Box 1954
Lake City, FL 32056-1954

United Catholic Church   (106)
5115 S. A1A Hwy.
Melbourne Beach, FL 32951

Universal Religion of America   (1398)
% Christ Universal Church
295 N. Tropical Trail
Merritt Island, FL 32952

African Orthodox Church   (170)
% Rt. Rev. Donald A. Smalls
3010 NW 211th St.
Miami, FL 33169

Church of Lukumi Babalu Aye   (1801)
% Ernesto and Fernando Pichardo
3720 SW 108th Ave.
Miami, FL 33165

Church of the Seven African
  Powers   (1802)
PO Box 453336
Miami, FL 33245

Church of Transition   (1131)
210 NE 48th Terr.
Miami, FL 33137

Endtime Body-Christian Ministries,
  Inc.   (703)
Miami, FL

St. Anne's African Orthodox
  Church   (265)
2485 NW 65th
Miami, FL 33054

Soldiers of the Cross of Christ, Evangelical
  International Church   (694)
636 NW 2nd St.
Miami, FL 33128

Yoga Research Foundation   (2067)
6111 SW 74th Ave.
Miami, FL 33143

Light of Sivananda-Valentina, Ashram
  of   (2004)
3475 Royal Palm Ave.
Miami Beach, FL 33140

Ethiopian Zion Coptic Church   (1484)
PO Box 1161
Minneola, FL 34755-1161

Epiphany Bible Students
  Association   (1031)
Box 97
Mount Dora, FL 32757

United States Raelian Movement   (1475)
Box 611793
North Miami, FL 33261

The Catholic Church of the Antiochean
  Rite   (1603)
% Archbishop Primate
2008 Chesapeake Dr.
Odessa, FL 33556

Institute of Divine Metaphysical
  Research   (1650)
% Dr. Kenneth Haverly, III
IDMR—Florida
PO Box 536156
Orlando, FL 32856-6156

Anglican Province of America   (124)
% Saint Alban's Anglican Cathedral
3348 W. State Rd. 426
Oviedo, FL 32765

Traditional Episcopal Church   (155)
% Most Rev. Richard G. Melli
Rte. 4, Box 1235, Hwy. 19 S.
Palatka, FL 32177

United Episcopal Church of North
  America   (160)
% John Gramley
PO Box 9374
Pensacola, FL 32513

American Evangelical Christian
  Churches   (922)
Waterfront Dr.
Pineland, FL 33945

Old Roman Catholic Church
  (Shelley/Humphreys)   (88)
5501 62nd Ave.
Pinellas Park, FL 33565

American Anglican Church   (113)
10120 Oak Hill Dr.
Port Richey, FL 34666

Lotus Ashram   (1370)
% Rev. Noel Street
264 Mainsail
Port St. Lucie, FL 33452

American Yoga Society   (1949)
513 S. Orange Ave.
Sarasota, FL 34236

Church of Metaphysical
  Christianity   (1353)
2717 Browning St.
Sarasota, FL 34237

Kashi Church Foundation   (1996)
11155 Roseland Rd., No. 10
Sebastian, FL 32958

Universal Harmony Foundation   (1397)
5903 Seminole Blvd.
Seminole, FL 33542

The United Spiritual Church of the
   Spiritual Advisory Council   (1557)
14345 SE 103rd Terr.
Summerfield, FL 34491

Fung Loy Kok Institute of Taoism   (2202)
1310 N. Monroe St.
Tallahassee, FL 32303

Churches of Christ (Non-Instrumental,
   Conservative)   (904)
℅ Florida College
119 Glen Arven Ave.
Tampa, FL 33617

Holy Order of RaHoorKhuit   (1690)
Box 24691
Tampa, FL 33623

Luciferian Light Group   (1808)
PO Box 7207
Tampa, FL 33673

Georgia

Universal Federation of Pagans   (1671)
Box 6006
Athens, GA 30604

Anglican Church, Inc.   (118)
℅ Rt. Rev. Frank H. Benning
Box 52702
Atlanta, GA 30355

Anglican Church of North America   (119)
℅ Rt. Rev. Robert T. Shepherd
Chapel of St. Augustine of Canterbury
1906 Forest Green Dr., NE
Atlanta, GA 30329

Atlanta Soto Zen Center   (2159)
1414 McLendon Ave. NE
Atlanta, GA 30307

Churches of God, Holiness   (478)
170 Ashby St., NW
Atlanta, GA 30314

First Interdenominational Christian
   Association   (524)
Calvary Temple Holiness Church
1061 Memorial Dr., SE
Atlanta, GA 30315

Karin Society   (1535)
2531 Braircliff Rd. NE, Ste. 217
Atlanta, GA 30329

Lost-Found Nation of Islam   (1924)
PO Box 57048
Atlanta, GA 30343

Presbyterian Church in America   (362)
℅ Stated Clerk
1852 Century Plaza, Ste. 190
Atlanta, GA 30345

Pure Holiness Church of God   (630)
St. Timothy's Pure Holiness Church
408 McDonough Blvd., SE
Atlanta, GA 30315

Triumph the Church and Kingdom of God
   in Christ   (483)
℅ Rt. Rev. A. Scott, Chief Bishop
213 Farrington Ave., SE
Atlanta, GA 30315

Holy Orthodox Catholic Church   (236)
℅ The Order of the Servants of Jesus
PO Box 350
Clarkdale, GA 30020

Primitive Baptists-Progressive   (881)
℅ Pat McCoy
PO Box 69
Culloden, GA 31016

Church of God of the Union
   Assembly   (517)
Box 1323
Dalton, GA 30720

Network of Kingdom Churches   (709)
4650 Flat Shoals Rd.
Decatur, GA 30034-5095

Asbury Bible Churches   (388)
℅ Rev. Jack Tondee
Box 1021
Dublin, GA 31021

Congregational Holiness Church   (519)
3888 Fayetteville Hwy.
Griffin, GA 30223

Congregation of God, Seventh
   Day   (1004)
Box 2345
Kennesaw, GA 30144

Church of the Christian Spiritual
   Alliance   (1966)
Lake Rabun Rd.
Box 7
Lakemont, GA 30552

Healing Temple Church   (662)
660 Williams St.
Macon, GA 31201

Cymry Wicca   (1741)
PO Box 674884
Marietta, GA 30067

Shri Ram Chandra Mission   (2039)
Rte. 1, Box 122-5, Hwy. 109
Molena, GA 30258

Church of God General Conference
   (Abrahamic Faith)   (972)
5823 Trammell Rd.
PO Box 100000
Morrow, GA 30260

Christ's Sanctified Holy Church
   (Georgia)   (432)
Box 1376
CSHC Campgrounds and Home for the
   Aged
Perry, GA 31068

Church of Jesus Christ of Georgia   (611)
℅ Elder Wilbur Childres
Rte. 1
Ranger, GA 30734

Church of Christ Holiness unto the
   Lord   (509)
1650 Smart St.
PO Box 1642
Savannah, GA 31401

Holy Church of God   (530)
PO Box 6455
115 W. 49th St.
Savannah, GA 31405

Hawaii

Shinreikyo   (2290)
℅ Kameo Kiyota
310C Uulani St.
Hilo, HI 96720

Apostolic Faith (Hawaii)   (597)
1043 Middle St.
Honolulu, HI 96819

Bodaiji Mission   (2138)
1251 Elm
Honolulu, HI 96814

Celtic Evangelical Church   (129)
PO Box 90880
Honolulu, HI 96835-0880

Chinese Buddhist Association of Hawaii -
   Hsu Yun Temple   (2197)
42 Kawananakoa Pl.
Honolulu, HI 96817

Church of the Living God   (2307)
632 Mokauea
Honolulu, HI 96819

Diamond Sangha   (2164)
℅ Palolo Zen Center
2747 Waiomao Rd.
Honolulu, HI 96816

Door of Faith Church and Bible
   School   (520)
1161 Young St.
Honolulu, HI 96814

Hawaii Buddhist Council   (2105)
1128 Banyan St.
Honolulu, HI 96817

Hawaii Chinese Buddhist Society   (2203)
1614 Nuuanu Ave.
Honolulu, HI 96817

Hawaii Council of Jodo Mission   (2141)
℅ Jodo Mission of Hawaii
1429 Makiki St.
Honolulu, HI 96814

Honkyoku Shinto   (2284)
Honkyoku-Daijingu Temple
61 Puiwa Rd.
Honolulu, HI 96817

Hoomana Naauoa O Hawaii   (2315)
910 Cooke St.
Honolulu, HI 96813

International Christian Churches   (736)
2322-22 Kanealii Ave.
Honolulu, HI 96813

Jinga Shinto   (2286)
Hawaii Ichizuchi Jinga
2020 S. King St.
Honolulu, HI 96817

Ka Hale Hoano Hou O Ke Akua   (2317)
1760 Nalani
Honolulu, HI 96819

Kealaokamalamalama   (2318)
1207 Prospect
Honolulu, HI 96822

Korean Christian Missions of
   Hawaii   (376)
1832 Liliha St.
Honolulu, HI 96817

Kuan Yin Temple   (2208)
170 N. Vineyard St.
Honolulu, HI 96817

Lamb of God Church   (563)
612 Isenburg St.
Honolulu, HI 96817

New Catholic Communion   (75)
1750 Kalakaua Ave., No. 3-183
Honolulu, HI 96826-3785

Nichiren Mission   (2148)
3058 Pali Hwy.
Honolulu, HI 96817

Palolo Kwannon Temple (Tendai
   Sect)   (2150)
3326 Paalea St.
Honolulu, HI 96816

Philippine Independent Church   (150)
% St. Andrew's Episcopal Cathedral
Queen Emma Sq.
Honolulu, HI 96813

Shingon Mission   (2153)
915 Sheridan St.
Honolulu, HI 96810

Shinshu Kyokai Mission   (2155)
Bentenshu Hawaii Kyokai
3871 Old Pali Rd.
Honolulu, HI 86817

Shinto   (2291)
% Hawaii Kotohira Jinsha-Hawaii Dazaifu
   Tenmangu
1045 Kama Ln.
Honolulu, HI 96817-3349

Taishakyo Shinto   (2293)
215 N. Kukui St.
Honolulu, HI 96817

Tensho-Kotai-Jingu-Kyo   (2295)
Hawaii Dojo
888 N. King St.
Honolulu, HI 96817

Todaiji Hawaii Bekkaku Honzan   (2157)
2426 Luakini St.
Honolulu, HI 96814

Zen Center of Hawaii   (2186)
PO Box 2066
Kamuela, HI 96743

Saiva Siddhanta Church   (2027)
107 Kaholalele
Kapaa, HI 96746

Extraterrestrial Earth Mission   (1465)
PO Box 959, No. 0432
Kihei, HI 96753

Huna International   (1526)
PO Box 663
Kilauea, HI 96754

Nechung Drayang Ling   (2247)
Box 250
Pahala, HI 96777

Hawaiian Goddess—Source School of
   Tantra Yoga   (1980)
Box 69-12
Paia, Maui, HI 96779

Alpha and Omega Christian
   Church   (714)
96-171 Kamahamaha Hwy.
Pearl City, HI 96782

Idaho

Seventh-Day Church of God   (1016)
Box 804
Caldwell, ID 83606-0804

Church of Jesus Christ Christian, Aryan
   Nations   (1074)
Box 362
Hayden Lake, ID 83835

General Council of the Churches of
   God   (1009)
1827 W. 3rd St.
Meridian, ID 83642-1653

Illinois

Plymouth Brethren (Tunbridge Wells
   Brethren)   (919)
No central headquarters. For Information:
% Bible Truth Publishers
59 Industrial Rd.
PO Box 649
Addison, IL 60101

Baptist General Conference   (889)
2002 S. Arlington Heights Rd.
Arlington Heights, IL 60005

Church of Christian Liberty   (933)
502 W. Euclid Ave.
Arlington Heights, IL 60004

Eglise Gnostique Catholique
   Apostolique   (1681)
% The Diocese of the Midwest
5215 Randolph St. W.
Bellwood, IL 60104

Ukrainian Evangelical Baptist
   Convention   (872)
% Olexa R. Barbuiziuk
6751 Riverside Dr.
Berwyn, IL 60402

Evangelical Church Alliance   (935)
% Dr. George Miller, President/CEO
205 W. Broadway, PO Box 9
Bradley, IL 60915

Mennonite World Conference   (757)
465 Gundersen Dr., Ste. 200
Carol Stream, IL 60188

African Orthodox Church of the
   West   (172)
% G. Duncan Hinkson
St. Augustine's African Orthodox Church
5831 S. Indiana St.
Chicago, IL 60637

American Muslims   (1920)
% Imam W. Deen Mohammed
Masjid Al-Faatir
1200 E. 47th St.
Chicago, IL 60615

Apostolic Orthodox Old Catholic
   Church   (39)
PO Box 879
Chicago, IL 60690

Chicago Rime Center   (2231)
4026 N. Kenmore, Ste. 1
Chicago, IL 60613

Cosmic Circle of Fellowship   (1462)
4857 N. Melvina Ave.
Chicago, IL 60630

Ecumenical Institute   (1230)
4750 N. Sheridan Rd.
Chicago, IL 60640

Evangelical Covenant Church   (382)
5101 N. Francisco Ave.
Chicago, IL 60625

Evangelical Lutheran Church in America
   (1988)   (322)
8765 W. Higgins Rd.
Chicago, IL 60631

Fifth Epochal Fellowship   (1517)
529 Wrightwood Ave.
Chicago, IL 60614

Jesus People USA   (1266)
4707 N. Malden
Chicago, IL 60640

Korean Buddhist Bo Moon Order   (2220)
% Bup Choon
Bul Sim Sa Temple
5011 N. Damen
Chicago, IL 60625

Lutheran World Federation   (303)
% Office of Ecumenical Affairs
Evangelical Lutheran Church
8765 W. Higgins Rd.
Chicago, IL 60631

Monastery of the Seven Rays   (1692)
Box 1554
Chicago, IL 60690-1554

Moody Church   (950)
1630 N. Clark
Chicago, IL 60614

The Nation of Islam (Farrakhan)   (1928)
4855 S. Woodlawn Ave.
Chicago, IL 60615

New Apostolic Church   (2320)
3753 N. Troy
Chicago, IL 60618

North American Old Roman Catholic
  Church (Schweikert)   (77)
4200 N. Kedvale
Chicago, IL 60641

Pentecostal Churches of Apostolic
  Faith   (628)
14 S. Ashland
Chicago, IL 60607

REMAR International   (1275)
% Angel Jimenez
917 S. Western Ave.
Chicago, IL 60612

Sabaean Religious Order   (1784)
3221 N. Sheffield
Chicago, IL 60657

Temple of Kriya Yoga   (2052)
2414 N. Kedzie
Chicago, IL 60647

Temple of the Pagan Way   (1791)
Box 60151
Chicago, IL 60660

Temple of Universal Law   (1391)
5030 N. Drake
Chicago, IL 60625

Thee Orthodox Old Roman Catholic
  Church   (99)
Box 49314
Chicago, IL 60649

U.S. National Committee for the Lutheran
  World Federation   (305)
% Office of Ecumenical Affairs
Evangelical Lutheran Church
8785 W. Higgins Rd.
Chicago, IL 60631

Universal Foundation for Better
  Living   (1341)
11901 Ashland Ave.
Chicago, IL 60643

URANTIA Foundation   (1559)
533 Diversey Pkwy.
Chicago, IL 60614

Vedanta Society   (2058)
5423 S. Hyde Park Blvd.
Chicago, IL 60615

Christian Believers Conference   (1026)
% Berean Bible Students Church
5930 W. 29th St.
Cicero, IL 60650

Church of St. Joseph   (53)
2307 S. Laramie
Cicero, IL 60650

Independent Spiritualist Association of the
  United States of America   (1366)
% Rev. Harry M. Hilborn
5130 W. 25th St.
Cicero, IL 60650

Berean Bible Fellowship (Illinois)   (957)
PO Box 6
Collinsville, IL 62234

Plymouth Brethren (Reunited
  Brethren)   (918)
No central headquarters. For information:
Grace and Truth
210 Chestnut St.
Danville, IL 61832

Church of God in Christ,
  Congregational   (652)
1905 Bond Ave.
East St. Louis, IL 62201

American Meditation Society   (1947)
105 Lautner Ln.
Edwardsville, IL 62025

Church of the Brethren   (792)
1451 Dundee Ave.
Elgin, IL 60120

International Association of Burmese -
  Buddhist Sanghas   (2119)
% Burmese Buddhist Association
15 W. 110 Forest Ln.
Elmhurst,, IL 60657

Old Roman Catholic Church (English
  Rite)   (85)
% Most Rev. Floyd A. Kortenhof
1722 N. 79th Ave.
Elmwood Park, IL 60635-3505

Buddhist Council of the Midwest   (2103)
2400 Prairie
Evanston, IL 60201

Reba Place Church and Associated
  Communities   (1274)
727 Reba Pl.
Evanston, IL 60602

Udumbara Zen Center   (2182)
501 Sherman Ave.
Evanston, IL 60202

Liberal Catholic Church, Province of the
  United States   (1618)
9740 S. Avers
Evergreen Park, IL 60642

Christian Conservative Churches of
  America   (1070)
Box 575
Flora, IL 62839

Social Brethren   (2329)
% Rev. Earl Vaughn, Moderator
R.R. 2
Flora, IL 62839

Christian Apostolic Church (Forest,
  Illinois)   (824)
Forrest, IL 61741

Serbian Orthodox Metropolitanate of New
  Gracanica—Diocese for America and
  Canada   (267)
% Metropolitan Iriney Kovachevich
Box 371
Grayslake, IL 60030

Zoroastrian Associations in North
  America   (1934)
5750 S. Jackson St.
Hinsdale, IL 60521

Hindu Temple of Greater Chicago   (2073)
% Ramalayam Hindu Temple
Box 99
Lemont, IL 60439

Serbian Eastern Orthodox Church for the
  U.S.A. and Canada   (266)
% Rt. Rev. Mitrofan, Vicar Bishop of
  Toplica
St. Sava Monastery
Box 519
Libertyville, IL 60048

Apostolic Catholic Assyrian Church of the
  East, North American Diocese   (281)
% Mar Aprim Khamis
North American Diocese
8908 Birch Ave.
Morton Grove, IL 60053

Zen Buddhist Temple of Chicago   (2185)
865 Bittersweet Dr.
Northbrook, IL 60062-3701

Fellowship of Lutheran
  Congregations   (326)
% Rev. Robert J. Lietz, President
320 Erie St.
Oak Park, IL 60302

North American Baptist
  Conference   (861)
1 S. 210 Summit Ave.
Oakbrook Terrace, IL 60181

International Council of Community
  Churches   (375)
% Rev. J. Ralph Shotwell, Executive
  Director
7808 College Dr., No. 25E
Palos Heights, IL 60463

New Testament Association of
  Independent Baptist Churches   (860)
1079 Westview Dr.
Rochelle, IL 61068

Salem Acres   (1277)
7419 E. Brick School Rd.
Rock City, IL 61070

General Association of Regular Baptist
  Churches   (853)
1300 N. Meacham Rd.
Schaumburg, IL 60173

''I AM'' Religious Activity   (1632)
Saint Germain Foundation
1120 Stonehedge Dr.
Schaumburg, IL 60194

Stelle Group   (1582)
127 Sun St.
Stelle, IL 60919

Living Tao Foundation   (2209)
PO Box 846
Urbana, IL 61801

Christian Brethren (Open or Plymouth
   Brethren)   (913)
Interest Ministries
218 W. Willow
Wheaton, IL 60187

Conservative Baptist Association   (849)
25W560 Geneva Rd.
Box 66
Wheaton, IL 60189-0066

National Association of Evangelicals   (14)
Box 28
Wheaton, IL 60187

Theosophical Society in America   (1589)
Box 270
Wheaton, IL 60189-0270

World Evangelical Fellowship   (19)
Box WEF
Wheaton, IL 60189

Baha'i Faith   (1935)
% National Spiritual Assembly of the
   Baha'is of the U.S.
536 Sheridan Rd.
Wilmette, IL 60091

Christian Catholic Church   (2301)
Dowie Memorial Dr.
Zion, IL 60099

Indiana

Central Yearly Meeting of Friends   (804)
% Ollie McCune, Supt.
Rte. 1, Box 226
Alexandria, IN 46001

Church of God (Anderson, Indiana)   (434)
Box 2420
Anderson, IN 46018

Calvary Ministries, Inc.,
   International   (548)
Box 365
4450 N 50W
Angola, IN 46703

Faith Mission Church   (444)
1817 26th St.
Bedford, IN 47421

Old German Baptist Brethren   (801)
% Elder Clement Skiles
Rte. 1, Box 140
Bringhurst, IN 46913

Mennonite Church   (763)
421 S. 2nd St., Ste. 600
Elkhart, IN 46516

Bethel Ministerial Association   (603)
4350 Lincoln Ave.
Evansville, IN 47715

Evangelical Mennonite Church   (785)
1420 Kerrway Ct.
Fort Wayne, IN 46805

Lutheran Churches of the
   Reformation   (334)
4014 Wenonah Ln.
Fort Wayne, IN 46809

Missionary Church, Inc. (U.S.)   (449)
3901 S. Wayne Ave.
Fort Wayne, IN 46807

Pentecostal Church of Zion   (571)
% Zion College of Theology
Box 110
French Lick, IN 47432

National Association of Holiness
   Churches   (494)
351 S. Park Dr.
Griffith, IN 46319

Church of the United Brethren in
   Christ   (415)
% Bishop C. Ray Miller
302 Lake St.
Huntington, IN 46750

Byzantine Orthodox Catholic Church (St.
   Peters)   (207)
6329 E. 55th Pl.
Indianapolis, IN 46226-1647

Christian Church (Disciples of
   Christ)   (900)
222 S. Downey Ave.
Box 1986
Indianapolis, IN 46206

Evangelical Methodist Church   (393)
68385 Gray Rd.
Indianapolis, IN 46237

Free Methodist Church of North
   America   (445)
PO Box 535002
Indianapolis, IN 46253

Orthodox Catholic Church of
   America   (252)
% Alfred Louis Lankenau
PO Box 1222
Indianapolis, IN 46206

Universal Christian Church   (682)
2140 Martindale Ave.
Indianapolis, IN 46202

Wesleyan Church   (458)
Box 50434
Indianapolis, IN 46250-0434

Branham Tabernacle and Related
   Assemblies   (578)
% The William Branham Evangelistic
   Association
and The Branham Tabernacle
Box 325
Jeffersonville, IN 47130

Truth for Today Bible Fellowship   (963)
Box 6358
Lafayette, IN 47903

Anglican Rite Synod in the
   Americas   (128)
% Rt. Rev. Larry Lee Shaver
195 E. 68th Pl.
Merrillville, IN 46410

Universal Spiritualist Association   (1399)
4905 W. University Ave.
Muncie, IN 47304-3460

Soulcraft   (1581)
Box 192
Noblesville, IN 46060

CIRCLES International   (1678)
PO Box 279
Plainfield, IN 46168

Friends United Meeting   (808)
101 Quaker Hill Dr.
Richmond, IN 47374

Pilgrim Holiness Church of the
   Midwest   (496)
% Union Bible Seminary
434 S. Union St.
Westfield, IN 46074

Padanaram Settlement   (1272)
R.R. 1, Box 478
Williams, IN 47470

Fellowship of Grace Brethren
   Churches   (796)
Winona Lake, IN 46590

Iowa

Gospel Assemblies
   (Sowders/Goodwin)   (730)
Gospel Assembly Church
7135 Meredith Dr.
Des Moines, IA 50322

Kingsway Fellowship International   (742)
3707 S.W. 9th St.
Des Moines, IA 50315-3047

Open Bible Standard Churches,
   Inc.   (566)
2020 Bell Ave.
Des Moines, IA 50315-1096

Amana Church Society (Community of
   True Inspiration)   (1214)
% Kirk Setzer, President
PO Box 103
Middle Amana, IA 52307

Iowa Yearly Meeting of Friends   (810)
% Del Coppinger, Gen. Supt.
Box 657
Oskaloosa, IA 52577

Anglican Church in America   (117)
% Mt. Rev. Louis W. Falk
4807 Aspen Dr.
West Des Moines, IA 50265

Kansas

Apostolic Faith (Kansas)   (542)
1009 Lincoln Ave.
Baxter Springs, KS 66713

Catholic Church (Pope Michael I)   (45)
4137 102nd Rd.
Delia, KS 66418

Mennonite Brethren Church of North
   America (Bruedergemeinde)   (779)
3155 Lincoln
PO Box V
Hillsboro, KS 67063-0155

Congregational Bible Churches
   International   (551)
PO Box 165
Hutchinson, KS 67501

Bible Holiness Church (1995)   (427)
600 College Ave.
Independence, KS 67301

Church of God in Christ,
   Mennonite   (759)
420 N. Wedel
Moundridge, KS 67107

General Conference Mennonite
   Church   (778)
722 Main St.
Newton, KS 67114

Church of God (Holiness)   (436)
7415 Metcalf
Overland Park, KS 66204

Dunkard Brethren Church   (794)
% Dale E. Jamison, Chairman
Board of Trustees
Quinter, KS 67752

Christian Apostolic Church (Sabetha,
   Kansas)   (825)
Sabetha, KS 66534

Kentucky

Antiochian Catholic Church in
   America   (280)
Box 1061
Campton, KY 41301

Archdiocese of the Antiochean Catholic
   Church in America   (40)
% Most. Rev. Gordon Mar Peter
PO Box 1061
Campton, KY 41301

House of God, Holy Church of the Living
   God, The Pillar and Ground of Truth,
   the House of Prayer for All
   People   (663)
548 Georgetown St.
Lexington, KY 40508

Independent Catholic Church of
   America   (66)
% Bp. Maurice McCormick
8701 Brittany Dr.
Louisville, KY 40220

Old Roman Catholic Church in North
   America   (86)
1207 Potomac Pl.
Louisville, KY 40214

Presbyterian Church (U.S.A.)   (366)
100 Witherspoon St.
Louisville, KY 40202

Separate Baptists in Christ   (866)
% Rev. Roger Popplewell, Moderator
Rte. 5
Russell Springs, KY 42642

Kentucky Mountain Holiness
   Association   (466)
PO Box 2
Vancleve, KY 41385

Christian Holiness Partnership   (422)
% CHP Center
Box 100
Wilmore, KY 40390

Louisiana

Church of Mercavah   (1503)
Box 66703
Baton Rouge, LA 70896

National Baptist Convention of the U.S.A.,
   Inc.   (885)
% Dr. T. G. Jemison, President
915 Spain St.
Baton Rouge, LA 70802

Lokanath Divine Life Fellowship   (2005)
% Mr. Paul Juneja
211 Gunther Ln.
Belle Chase, LA 70037

Independent Church of Jesus Christ of
   Latter Day Saints   (1195)
% Mark Cortez, Pres.
22 Homas Pl., Apt. C
Destrehan, LA 70047

Christ's Sanctified Holy Church
   (Louisiana)   (433)
S. Cutting Ave. at E. Spencer St.
Jennings, LA 70546

Anglican Catholic Church   (115)
3841 Veterans Memorial Blvd., Ste. 202
Metairie, LA 70002-5624

New Christian Crusade Church   (1082)
Box 426
Metairie, LA 70004

Volunteers of America   (457)
3939 N. Causeway Blvd.
Metairie, LA 70002

AEGA (Association of Evangelical Gospel
   Assemblies) International   (695)
2152 Hwy. 139
Monroe, LA 71203

Association Zen Internationale   (2158)
% New Orleans Zen Temple
748 Camp St.
New Orleans, LA 70130

Full Gospel Baptist Church
   Fellowship   (660)
3030 Canal St.
New Orleans, LA 70119-6306

Voodoo Spiritual Temple   (1591)
828 N. Rampart St.
New Orleans, LA 70116

Congregational Church of Practical
   Theology   (1508)
31916 University Circle
Springfield, LA 70462

Maine

United Society of Believers in Christ's
   Second Appearing   (1255)
Sabbathday Lake, ME 04274

Morgan Bay Zendo   (2223)
PO Box 188
Surry, ME 04684

Maryland

New Covenant Churches of
   Maryland   (710)
804 Windsor Rd.
Arnold, MD 21012

Shiah Fatimi Ismaili Tayyibi Dawoodi
   Bohra (Daudi Bohras)   (1877)
% Anjuman-e-Ezzi, Washington, DC
18720 New Hampshire Ave.
Ashton, MD 20806

Church of God in Christ Jesus
   (Apostolic)   (607)
Baltimore, MD

Evangelical Bible Church   (723)
2436-44 Washington Blvd.
PO Box 7476
Baltimore, MD 21227

Free Spirit Alliance   (1755)
Box 25242
Baltimore, MD 21229

Grace and Hope Mission   (465)
4 S. Gay St.
Baltimore, MD 21202

Greater Gospel World Outreach   (941)
6025 Moravia Park Dr.
Baltimore, MD 21206

Pentecostal Full Gospel Church   (746)
212 East 25th St.
Baltimore, MD 21211

Reformed Episcopal Church   (152)
2001 Frederick Rd.
Baltimore, MD 21228-5599

Savitria   (1551)
2405 Ruscombe
Baltimore, MD 21209

True Fellowship Pentecostal Church of
    God of America   (675)
4238 Pimlico Rd.
Baltimore, MD 21215

United Church of Jesus Christ
    Apostolic   (636)
2226 Park Ave.
Baltimore, MD 21217

Way of the Cross Church of Christ   (642)
% Bishop Leroy H. Cannady Sr.
600 E. 43rd St.
Baltimore, MD 21212

Association of Torah-Observant
    Messianics   (927)
% Rabbi Yeshayahu Heiliczer
PO Box 578
Bowie, MD 20715

Scripture Research Association   (1050)
14410 S. Springfield Rd.
Brandywine, MD 20613

United Holy Church of America   (680)
825 Fairoak Ave.
Chillum, MD 20783

Portal Enterprises   (2018)
PO Box 1449
Columbia, MD 21044

People of Destiny International   (711)
7881-B Beechcraft Ave.
Gaithersburg, MD 20879

American Zen College   (2216)
16815 Germantown Rd. (Rte. 18)
Germantown, MD 20767

Conservative Mennonite
    Conference   (784)
% Ivan J. Miller
Grantsville, MD 21536

American Rescue Workers   (424)
% Robert N. Coles
National Field Office
1209 Hamilton Blvd.
Hagerstown, MD 21742-3340

American Orthodox Church   (189)
% Saint Christopher Paris
PO Box 321
Monkton, MD 21111-0321

Orthodox Catholic Church in North
    America   (166)
PO Box 321
Monkton, MD 21111-0321

Soka Gakkai International (USA)   (2156)
4603 Eastern Ave.
Mt. Rainier, MD 20712-2407

Kunzang Odsal Palyul Changchub
    Choling   (2243)
18400 River Rd.
Poolesville, MD 20837

Body of Christ Movement   (698)
% Foundational Teachings
Box 6598
Silver Spring, MD 20906

Seventh-Day Adventist Church   (981)
12501 Old Columbia Pike
Silver Spring, MD 20904

International Evangelical Church   (706)
13901 Central Ave.
Upper Marlboro, MD 20772-8636

International Evangelical Church and
    Missionary Association   (707)
% Evangel Temple
13901 Centural Ave.
Upper Marlboro, MD 20772

International Meditation Center-
    USA   (2121)
538 Bankard Rd.
Westminster, MD 21158

Massachusetts

Insight Meditation Society   (2118)
Pleasant St.
Barre, MA 01005

One Peaceful World   (2211)
Box 10
Becket, MA 01223

Albanian Orthodox Archdiocese in
    America   (173)
% Metropolitan Theodosius
529 E. Broadway
Boston, MA 02127

Church of Christ, Scientist   (1288)
Christian Science Center
Boston, MA 02115

Unitarian Universalist Association   (1119)
25 Beacon St.
Boston, MA 02108

American Buddhist Shim Gum Do
    Association   (2215)
203 Chestnut Hill Ave.
Brighton, MA 02135

Bostoner Hasidism   (1834)
% New England Chasidic Center
1710 Beacon St.
Brookline, MA 02146

Church of Greece   (212)
% Metropolitan Demetrios
Holy Cross Church
50 Goddard Ave.
Brookline, MA 02140

Talnoye (Talner) Hasidism   (1846)
Talner Beth David
64 Corey Rd.
Brookline, MA 02146

Cambridge Buddhist Association   (2162)
75 Sparks St.
Cambridge, MA 02138

Covenant of Unitarian Universalist
    Pagans   (1740)
Box 640
Cambridge, MA 02140

Dzogchen Foundation   (2234)
PO Box 734
Cambridge, MA 02140-0006

Mahasiddha Nyingmapa Center   (2245)
Box 87
Charlemont, MA 01339

Valley Zendo   (2183)
Warner Hill Rd.
Claremont, MA 01330

The Eloists, Inc.   (1415)
Drawer O
Duxbury, MA 02331

National Spiritual Alliance of the
    U.S.A.   (1376)
RFD 1
Lake Pleasant, MA 01347

Kirpalu Center for Yoga and
    Health   (1997)
Box 793
Lenox, MA 01240

Old Roman Catholic Church-Utrecht
    Succession   (89)
% Roy G. Bauer
21 Aaron St.
Melrose, MA 02176

Anglo-Saxon Federation of
    America   (1067)
Box 177
Merrimac, MA 01860

General Convention of the New Jerusalem
    in the United States of
    America   (1344)
48 Sargent St.
Newton, MA 02158

Grace Essence Fellowship   (1977)
% Martin Lowenthal
53 Westchester Rd.
Newton, MA 02158

New England Evangelical Baptist
    Fellowship   (859)
% Dr. John Viall
40 Bridge St.
Newton, MA 02158

Holy Orthodox Church in North
    America   (240)
850 South St.
Box 129
Roslindale, MA 02131

Temple of Isis (1789)
% Crow Haven Corner
125 Essex St.
Salem, MA 01970

Vipassana Meditation Centers (2135)
% Vipassana Meditation Center
PO Box 24
Sherburne Falls, MA 01370-2160

Sirius (1281)
Baker Rd.
Shutesbury, MA 01072

Slaves of the Immaculate Heart of
Mary (96)
Box 22
Still River, MA 01467

Michigan

American Eastern Orthodox Catholic
Church (177)
5330 Oakhill Dr.
Alger, MI 48610

Anthroposophical Society (1644)
1923 Geddes Ave.
Ann Arbor, MI 48104-1797

Lower Lights Church (493)
Ann Arbor, MI

Church of Daniel's Band (390)
% Rev. Wesley James Haggard, President
Croll Rd.
Beaverton, MI 48612

Apostolic Assemblies of Christ, Inc. (592)
26798 Sumter Rd.
Belleville, MI 48111-9629

Israelite House of David (1053)
Box 1967
Benton Harbor, MI 49023

Israelite House of David as Reorganized
by Mary Purnell (1054)
Box 187
Benton Harbor, MI 49023-0187

Assembly of Free Spirit Baptist
Churches (882)
3627 Mt. Elliott
Detroit, MI 48207

Church of Universal Triumph/The
Dominion of God (477)
% Rev. James Shaffer
8317 LaSalle Blvd.
Detroit, MI 48206

Nation of Islam (John
Muhammad) (1929)
14880 Wyoming
Detroit, MI 48238

National Baptist Evangelical Life and Soul
Saving Assembly of the U.S.A. (886)
441-61 Monroe Ave.
Detroit, MI 48226

Pan African Orthodox Christian
Church (1856)
13535 Livernois
Detroit, MI 48238

Pentecostal Church of God (627)
9244 Delmar
Detroit, MI 48211

Romanian Orthodox Church of
America (261)
% Most Rev. Abp. Victorin Ursache
19959 Riopelle
Detroit, MI 48203

Shi'a Muslims (1876)
% Islamic Center of America
15571 Joy Rd.
Detroit, MI 48228

Full Gospel Truth, Inc. (557)
304 3rd St.
PO Box 886
East Jordan, MI 49727

International Federation of Secular
Humanistic Jews (1817)
28611 W. Twelve Mile Rd.
Farmington Hills, MI 48334

North American Committee for
Humanism (1089)
28611 W. 12 Mile Rd.
Farmington Hills, MI 48018

Society for Humanistic Judaism (1865)
28611 W. Twelve Mile Rd.
Farmington Hills, MI 48334

Christian Reformed Church in North
America (344)
2850 Kalamazoo Ave. SE
Grand Rapids, MI 49560

Free Reformed Church of North
America (347)
% Rev. P. VanderMeyden
950 Ball Ave. NE
Grand Rapids, MI 49503

Grace Gospel Fellowship (960)
2125 Martindale SW
PO Box 9432
Grand Rapids, MI 49509

Netherlands Reformed
Congregations (349)
% J. R. Beeke
2115 Romence, NE
Grand Rapids, MI 49503

Reformed Ecumenical Council (341)
2050 Breton Rd. SE, Ste. 102
Grand Rapids, MI 49546-5547

Robin's Return (1441)
1008 Lamberton St., NE
Grand Rapids, MI 49505

Strict Baptists (871)
% Zion Strict Baptist Church
1710 Richmond NW
Grand Rapids, MI 49504

Independent Fundamental Churches of
America (946)
Box 810
Grandville, MI 49468

Protestant Reformed Churches in
America (351)
4949 Ivanrest Ave.
Grandville, MI 49418

Assemblies of Yahweh (Eaton Rapids,
Michigan) (1041)
Box 102
Holt, MI 48842

Romanian Orthodox Episcopate of
America (262)
% Rt. Rev. Nathaniel, Bishop
2522 Grey Tower Rd.
Jackson, MI 49201-9120

Amended Christadelphians (899)
% Christadelphian Book Supply
14651 Auburndale
Livonia, MI 48154

Evangelical Presbyterian Church (358)
% Office of the Evangelical Assembly
29140 Buckingham Ave., Ste. 5
Livonia, MI 48154

Anchor Bay Evangelistic
Association (539)
Box 188
New Baltimore, MI 48047

International Congregational
Fellowship (340)
% Richard Kurrasch
1314 Northwood Blvd.
Royal Oak, MI 48073

American Druze Society (1941)
755 W. Big Beaver, Ste. 2106
Troy, MI 48084

Bharatiya Temple (2071)
6850 Adams Rd.
Troy, MI 48098

Mariavite Old Catholic Church, Province
of North America (73)
% Robert R. Zaborowski
2803 10th St.
Wyandotte, MI 48192-4994

Coptic Fellowship of America (1509)
1735 Pinnacle, SW
Wyoming, MI 49509-1339

Minnesota

Plymouth Brethren (Ames Brethren) (915)
% Christian Literature, Inc.
Box 1052
Anoka, MN 55303-1052

Fellowship of Christian Assemblies (553)
% Henry Jauhiainen, Chairman
Heritage Committee
520 N. 34th Ave., E.
Duluth, MN 55804

Church of the Lutheran Brethren of
America   (314)
1007 Westside Dr.
Box 655
Fergus Falls, MN 56537

International Ministerial Fellowship   (738)
PO Box 32366
Fridley, MN 55432-0366

Latvian Evangelical Lutheran Church in
America   (331)
2140 Orkla Dr.
Golden Valley, MN 55427-3432

National Association of Kingdom
Evangelicals   (1080)
% Gospel Temple
PO Box 72
Hopkins, MN 55343

Evangelical Lutheran Church in
America   (321)
% Rev. Truman Larson
Rte. 1
Jackson, MN 56143

Evangelical Lutheran Synod   (324)
% George Orvick, President
6 Browns Ct.
Mankato, MN 56001

Resources for Ecumenical
Spirituality   (2127)
PO Box 6
Mankato, MN 56002

American Association of Lutheran
Churches   (306)
PO Box 17097
Minneapolis, MN 55417

Association of Free Lutheran
Congregations   (313)
3110 E. Medicine Lake Blvd.
Minneapolis, MN 55441

Atheist Alliance Inc.   (1097)
PO Box 6261
Minneapolis, MN 55406

Brothers of the Earth   (1725)
% Church of the Earth
Box 13158
Dinkytown Sta.
Minneapolis, MN 55414

Church of the Lutheran Confession   (315)
460 75th Ave. NE
Minneapolis, MN 55432

ECKANKAR   (2091)
Box 27300
Minneapolis, MN 55427

Evangelical Free Church of
America   (383)
1551 E. 66th St.
Minneapolis, MN 55423

Henge of Keltria   (1759)
Minneapolis, MN 55448-0369

Minnesota Baptist Association   (858)
% Richard L. Paige Jr., Executive Secretary
5000 Golden Valley Rd.
Minneapolis, MN 55422

Minnesota Zen Meditation Center   (2171)
3343 Calhoun Pkwy.
Minneapolis, MN 55408

Apostolic Lutheran Church of
America   (307)
% Rev. George Wilson, President
New York Mills, MN 56567

Laestadian Lutheran Church   (330)
10911 Hwy. 55, Ste. 203
Plymouth, MN 55441-6114

Christ's Household of Faith   (1260)
355 Marshall Ave.
St. Paul, MN 55102-1898

Conservative Congregational Christian
Conference   (374)
7582 Currell Blvd., Ste. 108
St. Paul, MN 55125

Mississippi

National Anglican Church   (146)
401 S. Nacaise Ave.
Bay St. Louis, MS 39520-4429

Congregational Methodist Church   (391)
Box 9
Florence, MS 39073

Association of Independent
Methodists   (389)
Box 4274
Jackson, MS 39216

Church of Christ (Holiness) U.S.A.   (474)
329 E. Monument St.
Jackson, MS 39202

Methodist Protestant Church   (400)
% Rev. F. E. Sellers
Monticello, MS 39654

Missouri

Huna Research, Inc.   (1527)
1760 Anna St.
Cape Girardeau, MO 63701-4504

Kongosatta-In Tendai Buddhist
Temple   (2147)
PO Box 212
Cape Girardeau, MO 63702-0212

United American Orthodox Catholic
Church   (273)
Rte. 3, Box 31
Excelsior Springs, MO 64024

Davidian Seventh-Day Adventist
Association   (977)
Bashan Hill
Exeter, MO 65647

Shepherdsfield Community   (1278)
777 Shepherdsfield Rd.
Fulton, MO 65251-9473

United Pentecostal Church
International   (639)
8855 Dunn Rd.
Hazelwood, MO 63042

Christ Catholic Church   (48)
% Most Rev. Karl Pruter
Box 98
Highlandsville, MO 65669

Angelseaxisce Ealdriht   (1717)
202 E. Mulbury
Huntsville, MO 65259

Center Branch of the Lord's
Remnant   (1175)
709 W. Maple
Independence, MO 64050

Church of Christ (Fetting/Bronson)   (1178)
1138 E. Gudgell
Independence, MO 64055

Church of Christ (Temple Lot)   (1185)
Temple Lot
Independence, MO 65051

The Church of Christ "With the Elijah
Message," Established Anew in
1929   (1186)
608 Lacy Rd.
Independence, MO 64050

Church of Jesus Christ (Cutlerite)   (1202)
807 S. Cottage St.
Independence, MO 64050

Church of Jesus Christ (Zion's
Branch)   (1193)
108 S. Pleasant
Independence, MO

Reorganized Church of Jesus Christ of
Latter Day Saints   (1198)
The Auditorium
Box 1059
Independence, MO 64051

Restoration Branches Movement   (1199)
No central address. For information:
Price Publishing Co.
915 E. 23rd St.
Independence, MO 64055

Restoration Church of Jesus Christ of
Latter-day Saints   (1200)
801 W. 23rd St.
Independence, MO 64055

The Restored Church of Jesus Christ
(Walton)   (1210)
Box 1851
Independence, MO 64055

Pentecostal Church of God   (569)
4901 Pennsylvania
Joplin, MO 64802

Church of the Nazarene   (439)
6401 The Paseo
Kansas City, MO 64131

Mid-America Dharma Group   (2123)
PO Box 414411
Kansas City, MO 64141-4411

Society of St. Pius X   (98)
% Regina Coclihouse
2918 Tracy Ave.
Kansas City, MO 64109

Yahweh's New Covenant
   Assembly   (1055)
PO Box 50
Kingdom City, MO 65262

Church of Christ (Restored)   (1183)
% Uel Sisk
609 C Lilac Pl.
John Knox Village
Lee's Summit, MO 64063

Zion's Order, Inc.   (1161)
Rte. 2, Box 104-7
Mansfield, MO 65704

Church of Christ (David Clark)   (1177)
PO Box 126
Oak Grove, MO 64075

General Association of General
   Baptists   (891)
100 Stinson Dr.
Poplar Bluff, MO 63901

Yahweh's Assembly in Messiah   (1052)
Rte. 1, Box 364
Rocheport, MO 65279

International Ministerial
   Association   (622)
9455 Lackland Rd.
St. Louis, MO 63114

Lutheran Church-Missouri Synod   (333)
International Center
1333 S. Kirkwood Rd.
St. Louis, MO 63122

Universal Great Brotherhood   (1658)
Administrative Council of the U. S. A.
Box 9154
St. Louis, MO 63117

Church of Christ at Halley's Bluff   (1176)
Schell City, MO 64783

Church of Israel   (1073)
Box 62 B3
Schell City, MO 64783

Baptist Bible Fellowship   (843)
Box 191
Springfield, MO 65801

Churches of Christ (Non-Instrumental,
   Non-Class, One Cup)   (905)
% Old Paths Advocate
Box 10811
Springfield, MO 65808

Fundamental Methodist Church   (398)
1034 N. Broadway
Springfield, MO 65802

General Council of the Assemblies of
   God   (560)
1445 Boonville Ave.
Springfield, MO 65802

Unity School of Christianity   (1339)
1901 NW Blue Pkwy.
Unity Village, MO 64065-0001

Interfaith Church of Metaphysics   (1532)
Windyville, MO 65783

Montana

Church Universal and Triumphant   (1629)
Box 5000
Livingston, MT 59047

The Foundation of Love   (1631)
201 E. Callender St.
Livingston, MT 59047

Hutterian Brethren-Dariusleut   (1236)
% Rev. Elias Walter
Surprise Creek Colony
Stanford, MT 59479

Hutterian Brethren-Lehreleut   (1237)
% Rev. Joseph Kleinsasser
Milford Colony
Wolf Creek, MT 59648

Nebraska

Gnostic Orthodox Church of Christ in
   America   (1610)
Box 75, Rte. 1
Geneva, NE 68361

Berean Fundamental Churches   (929)
Box 6103
Lincoln, NE 68506

Free Orthodox Church
   International   (222)
353 S. 46th St.
Lincoln, NE 68510

Reformed Church in the United
   States   (353)
% Rev. Vernon Polleme, President
3930 Masin Dr.
Lincoln, NE 68521

Fellowship of Evangelical Bible
   Churches   (777)
5800 S. 14th St.
Omaha, NE 68107

Nevada

Albanian Orthodox Diocese of
   America   (174)
% Rev. Ik. Ilia Katre, Vicar General
6455 Silver Dawn Ln.
Las Vegas, NV 89118

Institute of Cosmic Wisdom   (1530)
3528 Franciscan Ln.
Las Vegas, NV 89121

New Hampshire

Church of the Living God
   (Sandford)   (438)
Amherst, NH 03031

Sant Bani Ashram   (2099)
Franklin, NH 03235

Our Lady of Enchantment, Church of the
   Old Religion   (1778)
Box 1366
Nashua, NH 03061

Friends of the Western Buddhist
   Order   (2277)
% Aryaloka
14 Heartwood Circle
Newmarket, NH 03857

New Jersey

World Fellowship of Religions   (7)
% Siddhachalam
RD 4, Box 374, Mud Pond Rd.
Blairstown, NJ 07825

Holy United Catholic and Apostolic
   Church   (242)
PO Box 703
Browns Mills, NJ 08015

Bible Presbyterian Church   (355)
Haddon and Cuthbert Blvd. S.
Collingswood, NJ 08108

International Association of Reformed and
   Presbyterian Churches   (339)
756 Haddon Ave.
Collingswood, NJ 08108

International Council of Christian
   Churches   (13)
% Suzanne L. Deacon, Sec.
756 Haddon Ave.
Collingswood, NJ 08108

Dawn Bible Students Association   (1030)
199 Railroad Ave.
East Rutherford, NJ 07073

Mt. Zion Sanctuary   (564)
21 Dayton St.
Elizabeth, NJ 07202

Antiochean Orthodox Christian
   Archdiocese of North America   (193)
358 Mountain Rd.
Englewood, NJ 07631

Fellowship of Fundamental Bible
   Churches   (395)
Box 43
Glassboro, NJ 08028

Gospel Mission Corps of the American
   Rescue Workers   (464)
Box 175
Hightstown, NJ 08520

Coptic Orthodox Church (285)
% Gabriel Abdelsayed
427 W. Side Ave.
Jersey City, NJ 07304

Association of Reformed Baptist
  Churches (841)
28 Meadows Rd.
Lafayette, NJ 07848

American Vegan Society (1948)
56 Dinshah Ln.
PO Box H
Malaga, NJ 08328-0908

IMBAS (1763)
PO Box 1215
Montague, NJ 07827-0215

Deliverance Evangelistic Centers (656)
505 Central Ave.
Newark, NJ 07107

Shanti Yoga Institute and Yoga
  Retreat (2036)
943 Central Ave.
Ocean City, NJ 08226

Universal Church of Christ (684)
19-23 Park St.
PO Box 146
Orange, NJ 07050

World Alliance of Reformed Churches
  (Presbyterian and
  Congregational) (342)
% Rev. James Dempsey Douglas
Princeton Theological Seminary
Princeton, NJ 80542

Ukrainian Orthodox Church of the
  U.S.A. (272)
Box 495
South Bound Brook, NJ 08880

Byelorussian Orthodox Church (204)
190 Turnpike Rd.
South River, NJ 08882

Syrian Orthodox Church of Antioch
  (Patriarchal Vicariates of the United
  States and Canada) (Jacobite) (297)
% Eastern U.S. Vicariate
260 Elm Ave.
Teaneck, NJ 07666

Anglican Rite Catholic and Orthodox
  Church in America (126)
% Most Rev. James N. Meola
9 Abaco St.
Toms River, NJ 08757-3736

Old Orthodox Catholic Patriarchate of
  America (247)
66 N. Brookfield St.
Vineland, NJ 08360

Orthodox Catholic Patriarchate of
  America (167)
66 N. Brookfield St.
Vineland, NJ 08360

Tibetan Buddhist Learning Center (2258)
93 Angen Rd.
Washington, NJ 07882-9767

United Hindu Temple of New
  Jersey (2079)
% Dr. Raj P. Misra
1 CeCamp Ct.
West Caldwell, NJ 07006

Pillar of Fire (469)
Zarephath, NJ 08890

New Mexico

Society Ordo Templi Orientis in
  America (1708)
% David Bersson
PO Box 1131
Albuquerque, NM 87103

Trinity Foundation (1452)
7410 Montgomery Blvd. NE, Ste. 206
Albuquerque, NM 87109-1574

Church of Jesus Christ of Latter Day Saints
  (Strangite) (1204)
% Vernon Swift
Box 522
Artesia, NM 88210

T.O.M. Religious Foundation (1390)
Box 52
Chimayo, NM 87522

City of the Sun Foundation (1630)
Box 370
Columbus, NM 88029

Light Institute (1536)
HC-75, Box 50
Galisteo, NM 87540

Orthodox Baha'i Faith under the
  Regency (1938)
% National House of Justice of the U.S.
  and Canada
Box 1424
Las Vegas, NM 87701

Orthodox Baha'i Faith, Mother Baha'i
  Council of the United States (1937)
3111 Futura
Roswell, NM 88201

Lama Foundation (1269)
Box 44
San Cristobal, NM 87564

Dispensable Church (1312)
Box 8444
Santa Fe, NM 87504-8444

Hanuman Foundation (1979)
Box 478
Santa Fe, NM 87501

Sufi Foundation of America (1910)
Box 75
Torreon, NM 87061

New York

Artemisian Order (1720)
% Oriethyia
PO Box 7184, Capitol Station
Albany, NY 12224

Pilgrim Holiness Church of New
  York (495)
32 Cadillac Ave.
Albany, NY 12205

American Humanist Association (1093)
7 Harwood Dr.
Box 8188
Amherst, NY 14226-7188

Council for Secular Humanism (1109)
Box 664
Amherst, NY 14226-0664

Church of the True Orthodox Christians of
  Greece (Synod of Archbishop
  Andreas) (213)
% Holy Trinity Church
38-10 20th St.
Astoria, NY 11105

Hellenic Orthodox Church in
  America (229)
22-68 26th St.
Astoria, NY 11105

Our Lady of the Roses, Mary Help of
  Mothers Shrine (91)
Box 52
Bayside, NY 11361

Grail Movement of America (1424)
2081 Partridge Ln.
Binghamton, NY 13903

Bible Church of Christ (545)
1358 Morris Ave.
Bronx, NY 10456

Damascus Christian Church (689)
% Rev. Enrique Melendez
170 Mt. Eden Pkwy.
Bronx, NY 10473

Ethiopian Orthodox Church in the United
  States of America (289)
% His Eminence Abuna Yeshaq,
  Archbishop
Holy Trinity Ethiopian Orthodox Church
140-142 W. 176th St.
Bronx, NY 10453

Holy Temple Church of the Lord Jesus
  Christ of the Apostolic Faith (621)
2075 Clinton Ave.
Bronx, NY 10457

International Divine Realization
  Society (1990)
% Devavand Yoga Cultural Center
2285 Sedgwick Ave., No. 102
Bronx, NY 10468

African Islamic Mission (1917)
1390 Bedford Ave.
Brooklyn, NY 11216

Ansaaru Allah Community   (1921)
716 Bushwick Ave.
Brooklyn, NY 11221

Ausar Auset Society   (1563)
% Kamit Publications
140 Buckingham Rd.
Brooklyn, NY 11226

Bluzhever Hasidism   (1832)
Belzer Yeshiva
1779 51th
Brooklyn, NY 11213

Bobov Hasidism   (1833)
% Rabbi Solomon Halberstamm
Yeshiva Bnai Zion
4909 15th St.
Brooklyn, NY 11219

Bratslav Hasidism   (1835)
% Rabbi Loe Rosenfeld
864 44th St.
Brooklyn, NY 11219

Chernobyl Hasidism   (1836)
% Rabbi Israel Jacob Twersky
1520 49th St.
Brooklyn, NY 11232

Church of God in Christ,
   International   (653)
% Rt. Rev. Carl E. Williams, Presiding
   Bishop
170 Adelphi St.
Brooklyn, NY 11205-3302

Council of Islamic Organizations of
   America   (1871)
5825 Kings Hwy.
Brooklyn, NY 10123

Hispanic-Brasilian Confraternity of
   Christian Doctrine, Saint Pius X   (63)
% Most Rev. Msgr. Hector Gonzales
10 Stagg St.
Brooklyn, NY 11206

Jehovah's Witnesses   (1032)
25 Columbia Heights
Brooklyn, NY 11201

Lubavitch Hasidism   (1840)
770 Eastern Pkwy.
Brooklyn, NY 11213

Neturei Karta of U.S.A.   (1827)
Box 2143
Brooklyn, NY 11202

Novominsk Hasidism   (1842)
% Rabbi Nahum M. Perlow
1569 47th St.
Brooklyn, NY 11220

Satmar Hasidism   (1843)
% Congregation Y L D'Satmar
152 Rodney
Brooklyn, NY 11220

Sighet Hasidism   (1844)
152 Hewes St.
Brooklyn, NY 11211

Stolin Hasidism   (1845)
Stolin Bet Midrash
1818 54th St.
Brooklyn, NY 11211

Tridentine Catholic Church-Traditional
   Catholic Archdiocese in
   America   (104)
1740 W. 7th St.
Brooklyn, NY 11223-1301

International Federation of Orthodox
   Catholics United Sacramentally   (165)
% Mt. Rev. Seraphim MacLennan
R.R. 1, Box 185
Brushton, NY 12916

Malankara Orthodox (Syrian)
   Church   (294)
% His Grace, Dr. Thomas Makarios
Episcopal Diocesan House
1114 Delaware Ave.
Buffalo, NY 14209

True Church of Christ,
   International   (1556)
Box 2, Sta. G
Buffalo, NY 14213

Servant Catholic Church   (95)
50 Coventry Ln.
Central Islip, NY 11722

Tioga River Christian Conference   (911)
% Rev. Calvin Duvall
RD 1, Box 134
Cherry Valley, NY 13320

Ananda Marga Yoga Society   (1952)
97-38 42nd Ave.
Corona, NY 11368

Arica Institute   (1880)
145 Palisades St.
Dobbs Ferry, NY 10522

Karuna Tendai Dharma Center   (2146)
1525 Rte. 295
East Chatham, NY 12060

Ar nDraiocht Fein: A Druid Fellowship,
   Inc.   (1719)
PO Box 516
East Syracuse, NY 13057

Institute of Chung-Hwa Buddhist
   Culture/Chan Meditation
   Center   (2206)
90-56 Corona Ave.
Elmhurst, NY 11373

Chishti Order of America   (1885)
PO Box 7249
Endicott, NY 13761

Bochasanwasi Swaminarayan
   Sanstha   (2072)
43-38 Bowne St.
Flushing, NY 11355

Hindu Temple Society of North
   America   (2074)
45-57 Bowne St.
Flushing, NY 11355

Brahma Kumaris World Spiritual
   University   (1963)
Global Harmony House
46 S. Middle Neck Rd.
Great Neck, NY 11021

Longchen Nyingthig Buddhist
   Society   (2244)
Box 302
Harris, NY 12742

Hungarian Reformed Church in
   America   (348)
% Rt. Rev. Dr. Andrew Harsanyi
PO Box D
Hopatcong, NY 07843

Healing Tao Centers   (2204)
% Taoist Esoteric Yoga Center &
   Foundation
PO Box 1194
Huntington, NY 11743

Mother Meera Society   (2013)
% Meerama
26 Spruce Ln.
Ithaca, NY 14850

Namgyal Monastery Institute of Buddhist
   Studies   (2279)
PO Box 127
Ithaca, NY 14851

Sri Chinmoy Centre   (2045)
Box 32433
Jamaica, NY 11432

Tabernacle of Prayer for All People   (674)
Jamaica, NY

Ukrainian Orthodox Church in America
   (Ecumenical Patriarchate)   (270)
St. Andrew's Ukrainian Orthodox Diocese
90-34 139th St.
Jamaica, NY 11435

Kirpal Light Satsang   (2093)
Merwin Lake Rd.
Kinderhook, NY 12106

The Bridge to Spiritual Freedom,
   Inc.   (1628)
Box 333
Kings Park, NY 11754

Sufi Order   (1913)
Sufi Order Secretariat
Box 574
Lebanon Springs, NY 12114

Elim Fellowship   (552)
7245 College St.
Lima, NY 14485

World Plan Executive Council-US   (2064)
PO Box 370
Lake Shandelee Rd.
Livingston Manor, NY 12758

Zen Studies Society   (2192)
% Dai Bosatsu Zendo Kongo-ji
HCR 1 Box 171
Livingston Manor, NY 12758-9402

Embassy of the Gheez-Americans (1510)
Mt. Helion Sanctuary
Rock Valley Rd., Box 53
Long Eddy, NY 12760

American Orthodox Catholic Church—
Western Rite Mission, Diocese of New
York (31)
℅ Most Rev. Joseph J. Raffaele
318 Expressway Dr. S.
Medford, NY 11763

Intercosmic Center of Spiritual
Awareness (1987)
℅ Ananda Ashram
RD 3, Box 141
Monroe, NY 10950

Interfaith Fellowship (1321)
459 Carol Dr.
Monroe, NY 10950

Hawthorn Grove (1758)
Box 706
Monticello, NY 12701-0706

The Mountains and Rivers Order (2173)
℅ Zen Mountain Monastery
PO Box 197
South Plank Rd.
Mt. Tremper, NY 12457

White Plum Asanga (2109)
℅ Zen Mountain Monastery
PO Box 197
South Plank Rd.
Mt. Tremper, NY 12457

Congregation of New Square (Skver
Chasidism) (1837)
N. Main St.
New Square, NY 10977

Agni Yoga Society (1642)
319 W. 107th St.
New York, NY 10025

American Association of Rabbis (1816)
350 Fifth Ave., Ste. 3304
New York, NY 10118

American Buddhist Movement (2266)
301 W. 45th St.
New York, NY 10036

American Ethical Union (1092)
2 W. 64th St.
New York, NY 10023

American Sephardi Association (1820)
8 W. 40th St.
New York, NY 10018

Arcane Magical Order of the Knights of
Shambhala (1955)
℅ Shri Shyamanath
PO Box 1425, Grand Central Station
New York, NY 10163

Arcane School (1595)
113 University Pl., 11th Fl.
Box 722, Cooper Sta.
New York, NY 10276

Armenian Apostolic Church of
America (283)
℅ Mesrob Ashjian
138 E. 39th St.
New York, NY 10016

The Assembly of Christian Churches,
Inc. (687)
℅ Bethel Christian Temple
7 West 110th St.
New York, NY 10026

Autocephalous Slavonic Orthodox
Catholic Church (in Exile) (199)
2237 Hunter Ave.
New York, NY 10475

Buddhist Association of the United
States (2196)
3070 Albany Cresent
New York, NY 10463

Buddhist Fellowship of New York (2267)
331 Riverside Dr.
New York, NY 10025

Bulgarian Eastern Orthodox Diocese of the
USA, Canada, and Australia (202)
℅ Metropolitan Joseph
550 A, W. 50th St.
New York, NY 10019

Church of Bible Understanding (2305)
Box 841
Radio City Sta.
New York, NY 10019-0841

Church of Our Lord Jesus Christ of the
Apostolic Faith (612)
2081 Adam Clayton Powell Blvd.
New York, NY 10027

Commandment Keepers Congregation of
the Living God (1850)
1 W. 123rd St.
New York, NY 10027

Congregation Bina (1822)
600 West End Ave., Ste. 1C
New York, NY 10024

Congregation Kehillath Yaakov (Kehilat
Jacob) (1860)
305 W. 79th St.
New York, NY 10024

Conservative Judaism (1823)
℅ The United Synagogue of Conservative
Judaism
155 Fifth Avenue
New York, NY 10010

Daheshism (2361)
℅ Dahesh Heritage
304 W. 58th St.
New York, NY 10019-1107

Diocese of the Armenian Church of
America (288)
℅ Khajag Barsamian
630 2nd Ave.
New York, NY 10016

Earthstar Temple (1748)
35 W. 19th St.
New York, NY 10011

Eastern States Buddhist Association of
America (2201)
64 Mott St.
New York, NY 10013

Eclesia Catolica Cristina (1360)
2123 Grand Ave.
New York, NY 10453

Episcopal Church (136)
815 2nd Ave.
New York, NY 10017

Evangelical Episcopal Church (139)
℅ Rt. Rev. Edward H. Marshall
600 W. 113th St.
New York, NY 10025

First Zen Institute of America (2165)
113 E. 30th St.
New York, NY 10016

Gardnerian Wicca (1756)
℅ Lady Rhiannon
Box 6896, FDR Sta.
New York, NY 10150

Greek Orthodox Archdiocese of North
and South America (223)
℅ Archbishop Iakovos, Primate
8-10 E. 79th St.
New York, NY 10021

Holy Spirit Association for the Unification
of World Christianity (1525)
4 W. 43rd St.
New York, NY 10036

Indo-American Yoga-Vedanta
Society (1985)
330 W. 58th St., Apt. 11-J
New York, NY 10019

Inter-Religions Federation for World
Peace (3)
℅ Frank Kaufmann
4 West 43rd St.
New York, NY 10036

International Association for Religious
Freedom (1086)
North American Office
576 Fifth Ave.
New York, NY 10036

Israeli Church of Universal Practical
Knowledge (1852)
1 W. 125th St.
New York, NY 10027

K'hal Adath Jeshurun (1825)
90 Bennett Ave.
New York, NY 10033

Khaniqahi-Nimatullahi (1897)
306 W. 11th St.
New York, NY 10014

Latin-American Council of the Pentecostal
Church of God of New York   (693)
115 E. 125th St.
New York, NY 10035

Muslim World League   (1874)
134 W. 26th St.
Box 1674
New York, NY 10001

The National Conference for Community
and Justice   (4)
71 First Ave., 11th Floor
New York, NY 10003

National Council of the Churches of Christ
in the U.S.A.   (16)
475 Riverside Dr.
New York, NY 10027

National Council of Young Israel   (1826)
3 W. 16th St.
New York, NY 10011

New Synagogue   (1862)
7 W. 96th St., Ste. 19-B
New York, NY 10025

New York Board of Rabbis   (1818)
10 E. 73rd St.
New York, NY 10021

Ordo Templi Orientis   (1701)
International headquarters
JAF Box 7666
New York, NY 10116

Orthodox Catholic Church in America
(Verra)   (251)
% Michael Edward Verra
238 Mott St.
New York, NY 10012

Orthodox Judaism   (1828)
Rabbinical Council of America
305 7th Ave.
New York, NY 10001

Padmasamblava Buddhist Centers   (2249)
Box 1533, Old Chelsea Station
New York, NY 10011

Patriarchial Parishes of the Russian
Orthodox Church in the U.S.A.   (258)
% St. Nicholas Patriarchal Cathedral
15 E. 97th St.
New York, NY 10029

Reform Judaism   (1829)
% Union of American Hebrew
Congregations
838 5th Ave.
New York, NY 10021

Reformed Church in America   (352)
475 Riverside Dr.
New York, NY 10115

Russian Orthodox Church Outside of
Russia   (263)
% His Eminence Vitaly, Metropolitan
75 E. 93rd St.
New York, NY 10028

Salvation and Deliverance Church   (591)
37 W. 116 St.
New York, NY 10026

Sang-Ngak-Cho-Dzong   (2255)
% Aro Gar
PO Box 247 Chelsea Station
New York, NY 10113-0247

Seventh-Day Christian Conference   (984)
246 W. 138th St.
New York, NY 10030

Society of Jewish Science   (1866)
109 E. 39th St.
New York, NY 10016

Sri Lankan Sangha Council of North
America   (2129)
No central address. For information:
American-Sri Lanka Buddhist Association,
Inc.
84-32 126th St., Kew Gardens
New York, NY 11415

Sserulanda Foundation   (2101)
PO Box 5578, Manhattanville Station
New York, NY 10027

Standing Conference of Canonical
Orthodox Bishops in the
Americas   (168)
8-10 E. 79th St.
New York, NY 10021

Synagogue Council of America   (1819)
327 Lexington Ave.
New York, NY 10016

Syrian Orthodox Church of
Malabar   (298)
% Dr. K. M. Simon
Union Theological Seminary
Broadway and 120th St.
New York, NY 10027

Temple of Understanding   (5)
% Cathedral Church of St. John the Divine
1047 Amsterdam Ave. (at 112th St.)
New York, NY 10025

Unification Association of Christian
Sabbath Keepers   (985)
255 W. 131st St.
New York, NY 10027

Union of Orthodox Rabbis in the United
States   (1830)
235 E. Broadway
New York, NY 10002

Union of Sephardic
Congregations   (1831)
8 W. 70 St.
New York, NY 10023

United Church and Science of Living
Institute   (1337)
4140 Broadway
New York, NY 10033

United Israel World Union   (1868)
1123 Broadway
New York, NY 10010

United Wesleyan Methodist Church of
America   (421)
% David S. Bruno
270 W. 126th St.
New York, NY 10027

Witches International Craft
Associates   (1797)
153 W. 80th St.
New York, NY 10024

World Conference on Religion and
Peace   (6)
% Secretary-General
777 United Nations Plaza, 12th Floor
New York, NY 10017

World Council of Churches   (18)
425 Riverside Dr.
New York, NY 10115

Yeshe Nyingpo   (2264)
19 W. 16th St.
New York, NY 10011

American Mission for Opening
Churches   (923)
6419 E. Lake Rd.
Olcott, NY 14126

American World Patriarchs   (192)
% Most Rev. Emigidius J. Ryzy
19 Aqueduct St.
Ossining, NY 10562

Society of St. Pius V   (97)
8 Pond Pl.
Oyster Bay Cove, NY 11771

Shanti Mandir   (2034)
Box 1110
Pine Bush, NY 12566

Holy Orthodox Church in America   (239)
PO Box 192-B
Preston Hollow, NY 12469

Societas Rosicruciana in America   (1570)
Box 192-3
Preston Hollow, NY 12469

Apostolic Episcopal Church   (35)
80-46 234th St.
Queens, NY 11427

Arunachala Ashrama   (1958)
66-12 Clyde St.
Rego Park, NY 11374

His Highness Prince Aga Khan Shia Imani
Ismaili Council for the United States of
America   (1875)
PO Box 77
Rego Park, NY 11374

Kabbalah Learning Centre   (1838)
83-84 115th St.
Richmond Hill, NY 11418-9808

Sikh Council of North America   (2084)
95-30 118th St.
Richmond Hill, NY 11419

Bruderhof Communities in New York,
    Inc.   (1219)
PO Woodcrest, Rte. 213
Rifton, NY 12471

General Assembly of Spiritualists   (1362)
27 Appleton St.
Rochester, NY 14611

Latin-Rite Catholic Church   (72)
Box 16194
Rochester, NY 14616

Megiddo Church   (2319)
481 Thurston Rd.
Rochester, NY 14619

Zen Center of Rochester   (2188)
Seven Arnold Park
Rochester, NY 14607

Charismatic Catholic Church: Independent
    Rite of America   (47)
% Mt. Rev. Daniel C. Braun
102 Freay Rd.
Rocky Point, NY 11128

Foundation for *A Course in
    Miracles*   (1316)
1275 Tennanah Lake Rd.
Roscoe, NY 12776-5905

North American Old Roman Catholic
    Church (Rogers)   (76)
% James H. Rogers
118-09 Farmers Blvd.
St. Albans, NY 11412

The National Gay Pentecostal
    Alliance   (2343)
PO Box 1391
Schenectady, NY 12301-1391

SYDA Foundation   (2049)
371 Brickman Rd.
South Fallsburg, NY 12779

Ma Yoga Shakti International
    Mission   (2006)
114-23 Lefferts Blvd.
South Ozone, NY 11420

Jerrahi Order of America   (1894)
864 S. Main St.
Spring Valley, NY 10977

Shanti Temple   (2035)
43 S. Main St.
Spring Valley, NY 10977

Springwater Center for Meditative Inquiry
    and Retreats   (2180)
7179 Mill St.
Springwater, NY 14560

International Nahavir Jain Mission   (2080)
Acharya Sushil Jain Ashram
722 Tomkins Ave.
Staten Island, NY 10305

Greek Orthodox Missionary Archdiocese
    of Vasiloupolis   (227)
44-02 48th Ave.
Sunnyside/Woodside, NY 11377

Orthodox Church in America   (255)
% Very Rev. Robert Kondratick, Chancellor
Box 675
Syosset, NY 11791

Servants of the Light   (1705)
% Fran Keegan
PO Box 6563
Syracuse, NY 13217-6563

Kagyu Dharma   (2239)
127 Sheafe Rd.
Wappingers Falls, NY 12590

Institute for Religious
    Development   (1890)
7 Chardavogne Rd.
Warwick, NY 19990

Zion Fellowship   (755)
PO Box 79
Waverly, NY 14892

Holy Ukrainian Autocephalic Orthodox
    Church in Exile   (241)
% Rt. Rev. Sirhij K. Pastukhiv
103 Evergreen S.
West Babylon, NY 11704

Ecumenical Catholic Diocese of
    America   (57)
151 Regent Pl.
West Hemstead, NY 11552

Karma Triyana Dharmachakra   (2241)
352 Meads Mountain Rd.
Woodstock, NY 12498

Mount Hebron Apostolic Temple of Our
    Lord Jesus of the Apostolic Faith   (623)
Mt. Hebron Apostolic Temple
27 Vineyard Ave.
Yonkers, NY 10703

Zen Community of New York   (2190)
14 Ashburton Pl.
Yonkers, NY 10703

North Carolina

School for Esoteric Studies   (1597)
58 Oak Terrace
Arden, NC 28708-2820

Original Free Will Baptists, North Carolina
    State Convention   (894)
Box 39
Ayden, NC 28513

Emmanuel Holiness Church   (521)
Box 818
Bladenboro, NC 28320

Rifa'i Marufi Sufi Fellowship   (1904)
PO Box 202
Chapel Hill, NC 27514-0202

Advent Christian Church   (971)
Box 23152
Charlotte, NC 28212

African Methodist Episcopal Zion
    Church   (407)
Box 23843
Charlotte, NC 28232

American Orthodox Catholic and
    Apostolic Church   (183)
PO Box 8041
Charlotte, NC 29202-8041

Carolina Evangelistic Association   (508)
Garr Memorial Church
7700 Wallace Rd.
Charlotte, NC 28212

Church of the Great God   (1002)
Box 471846
Charlotte, NC 28247-1846

National Primitive Baptist Convention of
    the U.S.A.   (878)
6433 Hidden Forest Dr.
Charlotte, NC 28213

University of the Christ Light with the
    Twelve Rays   (1641)
3427 Denson Pl.
Charlotte, NC 28215

Pentecostal Free Will Baptist
    Church   (536)
Box 1568
Dunn, NC 28334

Black Primitive Baptists   (876)
% Primitive Baptist Library
Rte. 2
Elon College, NC 27244

Christian Spirit Center   (1350)
Box 114
Elon College, NC 27244

Primitive Baptists-Absolute
    Predestinarians   (879)
% Primitive Baptist Library
Rte. 2
Elon College, NC 27244

Primitive Baptists-Moderates   (880)
% Primitive Baptist Library
Rte. 2
Elon College, NC 27244

Apostolic Faith Church of America   (646)
Fremont, NC 27830

General Conference of the Evangelical
    Baptist Church   (527)
Kavetter Bldg.
3400 E. Ash St.
Goldsboro, NC 27530

Holiness Church of God   (529)
% Bishop B. McKinney
602 E. Elm St.
Graham, NC 27253

Shiloh True Light Church of
    Christ   (1063)
Rte. 1, Box 426
Indian Trail, NC 28079

World Methodist Council (381)
Box 518
Lake Junaluska, NC 28745

Church of God, Body of Christ (992)
Rte. 1
Mocksville, NC 27028

Lumber River Annual Conference of the
Holiness Methodist Church (467)
% Bishop C. N. Lowry
Rowland, NC 28383

Anglican Orthodox Church (123)
323 Walnut St.
Box 128
Statesville, NC 28687

Christian Unity Baptist Association (848)
% Elder Thomas T. Reynolds
Thomasville, NC 27360

Apostolic Faith Church of God Giving
Grace (504)
Rte. 3, Box 111G
Warrenton, NC 27589

New Beginnings (1081)
Box 228
Waynesville, NC 28786

Apostolic Church of Christ (593)
2044 Martin Luther King, Jr. Dr.
Winston-Salem, NC 27107

Apostolic Church of Christ in God (594)
% Bethlehem Apostolic Church
1217 E. 15th St.
Winston-Salem, NC 27105

Church of God (Apostolic) (606)
3683 Old Lexington Rd.
Winston-Salem, NC 27107-5262

North Dakota

International Lutheran Fellowship (328)
% President
% Rev. E. Edward Tornow
387 E. Brandon Dr.
Bismarck, ND 58501

Ohio

Celtic Orthodox Christian Church in North
America (211)
Box 72102
Akron, OH 44372

Orthodox Catholic Church of North and
South America (253)
Box 1213
Akron, OH 44309

Synod of Autonomous Canonical
Orthodox Churches in North
America (169)
Box 72102
Akron, OH 44372

Brethren Church (Ashland, Ohio) (789)
524 College Ave.
Ashland, OH 44805

Ohio Yearly Meeting of the Society of
Friends (815)
61830 Sandy Ridge Rd.
Barnesville, OH 43712

Association of Fundamental Gospel
Churches (787)
9189 Grubb Ct.
Canton, OH 44721

Evangelical Friends Church, Eastern
Division (805)
5350 Broadmoor Circle, NW
Canton, OH 44709

Christian Churches and Churches of
Christ (901)
No central address. For information:
North American Christian Convention
4210 Bridgetown Rd.
Cincinnati, OH 45811

Church of the Living God (Christian
Workers for Fellowship) (654)
% Bishop W. E. Crumes
434 Forest Ave.
Cincinnati, OH 45229

Pentecostal Assemblies of the
World (626)
% Paul A. Bowers, Bishop
1150 W. Galbraith Rd.
Cincinnati, OH 45231

Churches of Christ in Christian
Union (462)
1426 Lancaster Pike
Circleville, OH 43113

Church of God and Saints of
Christ (1848)
% Bp. James R. Grant
10703 Wade Park Ave.
Cleveland, OH 44106

Church of God (Jesus Christ the
Head) (995)
% Pastor M. L. Bartholomew
Box 02026
Cleveland, OH 44102

Church of God (O'Beirn) (996)
Box 81224
Cleveland, OH 44181

Church of the Blessed Hope (973)
7450 Wilson Mills Rd.
Cleveland, OH 44143

United Church of Christ (380)
700 Prospect Ave. E.
Cleveland, OH 44115-1100

Old Order (Reidenbach)
Mennonites (764)
% Henry W. Riehl
Rte. 1
Columbiana, OH 44408

Old Order (Wenger) Mennonites (765)
% Henry W. Riehl
Rte. 1
Columbiana, OH 44408

Old Order (Wisler) Mennonite
Church (766)
% Henry W. Riehl
Rte. 1
Columbiana, OH 44408

Ahmadiyya Anjuman Ishaat Islam, Lahore,
Inc. (1918)
1315 Kingsgate Rd.
Columbus, OH 43221-1504

Church of Universal Forces (1734)
PO Box 93195
Columbus, OH 43203

Emmanuel Tabernacle Baptist Church
Apostolic Faith (522)
329 N. Garfield Ave.
Columbus, OH 43203

International Ministers Forum (739)
PO Box 1717
433 Oak St.
Dayton, OH 45401-1717

United Methodist Church (386)
% Council on Ministries
601 W. Riverside Ave.
Dayton, OH 45406

Apostolic Christian Churches of
America (823)
% Bill Schlatter
14834 Campbell Rd.
Defiance, OH 43512

Original Glorious Church of God in Christ
Apostolic Faith (625)
995 Foster Ave.
Elyria, OH 44035

Christ Catholic Orthodox Church (50)
PO Box 17600
Euclid, OH 44117-0006

Churches of God, General
Conference (346)
700 E. Melrose Ave.
Box 926
Findlay, OH 45839

Christian Union (2303)
% Christian Union Bible College
PO Box 27
Greenfield, OH 45123

Conservative Mennonite Fellowship (Non-
Conference) (761)
Box 36
Hartville, OH 44632

Apostolic Faith Church of God and True
Holiness (503)
825 Gregg Rd.
Jefferson, OH 44047

Assembly of God in Christ Jesus (986)
Box 770537
Lakewood, OH 44107

Order of Dionysus/Sabazios (1809)
Box 711
Lakewood, OH 44107

International Pentecostal Church of
   Christ   (532)
PO Box 439
2245 U.S. 42, SW
London, OH 43140

Eastern Orthodox Christian Church in
   America   (216)
℅ His Eminence, Archbishop Michael
Box 687
New Albany, OH 43054

The Way International   (964)
PO Box 328
New Knoxville, OH 45871

SOL Association for Research   (1447)
Box 2276
North Canton, OH 44720

Bulgarian Eastern Orthodox Church
   (Diocese of North and South
   America)   (201)
519 Brynhaven Dr.
Oregon, OH

Beachy Amish Mennonite
   Churches   (783)
9650 Iams Rd.
Plain City, OH 43064

Autocephalous Traditional Orthodox
   Catholic Church   (200)
Box 17105
St. Bernard, OH 45217

Allegheny Wesleyan Methodist
   Connection   (485)
1827 Allen Dr.
Salem, OH 44460

Interdenominational Holiness
   Convention   (423)
Salem, OH

Odinic Rite Vinland   (1772)
PO Box 2022
Sandusky, OH 44871-2022

Brotherhood of Mithras   (2333)
Box 94
Uniontown, OH 44685-0094

American Orthodox Exarchate:
   Archdiocese of North America   (190)
1829 Coronada Ave.
Youngstown, OH 44504

Oklahoma

Church of God (Anadarko)   (991)
900 W. Alabama St.
Anadarko, OK 73005

Philadelphia Church of God   (1013)
PO Box 3700
Edmond, OK 73083

Bible Sabbath Association   (970)
RD 1, Box 22
Fairview, OK 73737

Church of God (Guthrie,
   Oklahoma)   (435)
℅ Faith Publishing House
7415 W. Monsur Ave.
Guthrie, OK 73044

Universal Church of God   (1022)
Rte. 1, Box 52
Manna, OK 74845

Anglican Episcopal Church   (121)
℅ Rt. Rev. R. H. Hawn
7804 Lyrewood Ln., Ste. 157
Oklahoma City, OK 73132

Bible Churches (Classics Expositor)   (958)
℅ Dr. C. E. McLain
1429 NW 100th St.
Oklahoma City, OK 73114

Church of God (Which He Purchased with
   His Own Blood)   (476)
1628 NE 50th
Oklahoma City, OK 73111

Communion of Evangelical Episcopal
   Churches   (133)
℅ Rt. Rev. Michael D. Owen
6825 W. Wilshire Blvd.
Oklahoma City, OK 74137

Ecumenical Communion of Catholic and
   Apostolic Churches   (20)
℅ Rt. Rev. Michael D. Owen
6825 W. Wilshire Blvd.
Oklahoma City, OK 74137

Frigga's Web Association for the Asatru
   Faith   (1667)
PO Box 79592
Oklahoma City, OK 75147-0952

International Pentecostal Holiness
   Church   (533)
PO Box 12609
Oklahoma City, OK 73157-2609

Light of Christ Community
   Church   (1651)
℅ Sparrow Hawk Village
11 Summit Ridge Dr.
Tahlaquah, OK 74464-9215

Azusa Interdenominational Fellowship of
   Christian Churches   (649)
8621 S. Memorial Dr.
Tulsa, OK 74133-4312

Church of the Christian Crusade   (2306)
Box 977
Tulsa, OK 74102

Victory Fellowship of Ministries   (754)
7700 S. Lewis
Tulsa, OK 74136-7700

Oregon

Metamorphosis League for Monastic
   Studies   (2010)
4130 SW 117th Ave., Ste. 171
Beaverton, OR 97005

Bride of Christ Church   (1259)
330 SE Sabbath Way
PO Box 885
Canyonville, OR 97417

Zen Community of Oregon   (2191)
PO Box 310
Corbett, OR 97019

North Pacific Yearly Meeting of the
   Religious Society of Friends   (813)
3311 NW Polk
Corvallis, OR 97330

Church of Antioch   (1604)
℅ Mt. Rev. Meri Louise Spruit
32378 Lynx Hollow Rd.
Creswell, OR 97426

Federation of Independent Catholic and
   Orthodox Bishops   (162)
32378 Lynx Hollow Rd.
Creswell, OR 97426

Bible Study Association   (1044)
28877 Summerville Rd.
Eugene, OR 97405

Church of God (Reinertsen)   (1057)
℅ Olaf Egge
33738 McKenzie Vw. Dr.
Eugene, OR 97401

Church of God, the Eternal   (1000)
Box 755
Eugene, OR 97440

Seth Network International   (1445)
Box 1620
Eugene, OR 97440

Foundation of Human
   Understanding   (1520)
Box 811
Grants Pass, OR 97526

Aggressive Christianity Missions Training
   Corps   (920)
Klamath Falls, OR 97601

Northwest Yearly Meeting of Friends
   Church   (814)
200 N. Maridian St.
Newberg, OR 97132-2714

Ancient Teachings of the Masters   (2086)
PO Box 68290
Oak Grove, OR 97268

The Apostolic Faith Mission of Portland,
   Oregon, Inc.   (506)
6615 SE 52nd Ave.
Portland, OR 97206

Associates for Scriptural
   Knowledge   (988)
PO Box 25000
Portland, OR

Dharma Rain Zen Center   (2163)
2539 SE Madison
Portland, OR 97214

Faith Tabernacle Council of Churches,
International   (657)
7015 NE 23rd Ave.
Portland, OR 97211

Full Gospel Pentecostal
Association   (661)
1032 N. Sumner
Portland, OR 97217

National Black Evangelistic
Association   (15)
5736 N. Albina Ave.
Portland, OR 97217

Nityananda Institute, Inc.   (2015)
PO Box 13310
Portland, OR 97213

Church of the New Covenant in
Christ   (1168)
Box 3910
Salem, OR 97302

Church of the Trinity (Invisible
Ministry)   (1309)
Box 4608
Salem, OR 97302-8608

Evangelical Church of North
America   (463)
3000 Market St. NE, Ste. 528
Salem, OR 97301

Union of Independent Catholic Churches
of the North American Old Catholic
Church   (23)
% The Rt. Rev. Bill Peckenpaugh, OSFL
135 Fiske St.
Silverton, OR 97381-2012

Church of the Culdees   (132)
% Most Rev. Ivan B. D. G. MacKillop,
OCC
2665 "C" St.
Springfield, OR 97477

Embassy of Heaven Church   (2353)
8777 Basl Hill Rd., SE
Strayton, OR 97383-9630

Foundation for the Realization of Inner
Divinity   (1422)
PO Box 458
White City, OR 97524

Solar Light Retreat   (1472)
7700 Avenue of the Sun
White City, OR 97503

Pennsylvania

Assemblies of Yahweh   (1040)
Bethel, PA 19507

American Council of Christian
Churches   (8)
625 E. 4th St.
PO Box 5455
Bethlehem, PA 18015

Council of Bible Believing Churches
International   (10)
625 E. 4th St.
PO Box 5455
Bethlehem, PA 18015

Moravian Church in America   (384)
Northern Province
1021 Center St.
Box 1245
Bethlehem, PA 18016-1245

Evangelical Christian Church
(Wesleyan)   (442)
Box 277
Birdsboro, PA 19508

General Church of the New
Jerusalem   (1343)
% Rt. Rev. L. B. King, Executive Bishop
Bryn Athyn, PA 19009

The Lords New Church   (1345)
1725 Huntingdon Rd.
Box 7
Bryn Athyn, PA 19009

Celtic Christian Communion   (210)
% Rt. Rev. Joseph A. Grenier
PO Box 299
Canadensis, PA 18325-0299

St. Ciaran's Fellowship of Celtic Christian
Communities   (153)
% Rt. Rev. Dr. Joseph A. Grenier
PO Box 299
Canadensis, PA 18325-0299

Layman's Home Missionary
Movement   (1034)
Chester Springs, PA 19425

United Christian Church   (417)
% Elder John Ludwig Jr.
523 W. Walnut St.
Cleona, PA 17042

Full Gospel Assemblies
International   (725)
% Dr. Anna Mae Strauser
PO Box 1230
Coatesville, PA 19320-1230

Stauffer Mennonite Church   (769)
% Bishop Jacob S. Stauffer
Rte. 3
Ephrata, PA 17522

United Zion Church   (770)
% Bishop Luke Showalter
181 Hurst Dr.
Ephrata, PA 17522

Parkville Bible Church   (468)
800 Whisler Rd.
Etters, PA 17319

Free Gospel Church, Inc.   (555)
% Rev. Chester H. Heath
Box 477
Export, PA 15632

The Peace Mission Movement   (1247)
% The Woodmont Estate
1622 Spring Mill Rd.
Gladwyne, PA 19035

Brethren in Christ   (758)
PO Box 290
Grantham, PA 17027-0290

Apostolic Orthodox Church   (282)
% Rt. Rev. James H. Hess
2410 Derry St.
Harrisburg, PA 17111-1141

Himalayan International Institute of Yoga
Science and Philosophy   (1981)
RR 1, Box 400
Honesdale, PA 18431

Delval UFO, Inc.   (1464)
948 Almshouse Rd.
Ivyland, PA 18974

American Carpatho-Russian Orthodox
Greek Catholic Church   (176)
% Metropolitan Nicholas Smisko
312 Garfield St.
Johnstown, PA 15906

Reformed Mennonite Church   (768)
% Bishop Glenn M. Gross
602 Strasburg Pike
Lancaster, PA 17602

Independent Churches Affiliated   (945)
% Dr. Robert E. Mayer
810 E. Canal St.
Lebanon, PA 17042

Congregational Bible Church   (760)
% Congregational Bible Church
Marietta, PA 17547

Church of God House of Prayer   (511)
% Rev. Charles Mackenin
Markleysburg, PA 15459

Church of Jesus Christ
(Bickertonite)   (1201)
6th & Lincoln Sts.
Monongahela, PA 15063

Evangelical Congregational Church   (416)
100 W. Park Ave.
Box 186
Myerstown, PA 17067

Twentieth Century Church of God
(Pennsylvania)   (1019)
Box 25
Ninevah, PA 15344

Schwenkfelder Church in America   (830)
Pennsburg, PA 18073

Apostolic Church   (540)
142 N. 17th St.
Philadelphia, PA 19103

Aquarian Research Foundation   (1258)
5620 Morton St.
Philadelphia, PA 19144

Bawa Muhaiyaddeen Fellowship   (1881)
5820 Overbrook Ave.
Philadelphia, PA 19131

Calvary Holiness Church   (459)
3415-19 N. Second St.
Philadelphia, PA 19140

Church of the Lord Jesus Christ of the
    Apostolic Faith (Philadelphia)   (613)
22nd & Bainbridge Sts.
Philadelphia, PA 19146

Deliverance Evangelistic Church   (579)
2001 W. Lehigh Ave.
Philadelphia, PA 19132

Friends General Conference   (807)
1216 Arch St., 2B
Philadelphia, PA 19107

Friends World Committee for
    Consultation   (756)
% Office of the Executive Secretary
Section of the Americas
1506 Race St.
Philadelphia, PA 19102

House of God Which Is the Church of the
    Living God, the Pillar and Ground of
    Truth, Inc.   (665)
6107 Cobbs Creek Pkwy.
Philadelphia, PA 19143

Mount Sinai Holy Church   (670)
1469 N. Broad St.
Philadelphia, PA 19122-3327

P'nai Or Religious Fellowship   (1863)
6723 Emlen St.
Philadelphia, PA 19119

Shiloh Apostolic Temple   (632)
1516 W. Master
Philadelphia, PA 19121

Swami Kuvalayananda Yoga
    Foundation   (2048)
339 Fitzwater St.
Philadelphia, PA 19147

Christianbrunn Brotherhood   (2334)
Christianbrunn Kloster
RR 1, Box 149
Pitman, PA 17964

Associated Gospel Churches   (925)
1919 Beach St.
Pittsburgh, PA 15221

Kodesh Church of Emmanuel   (481)
% Kenneth O. Barbour
2601 Centre Ave.
Pittsburgh, PA 15219

Reformed Presbyterian Church of North
    America   (367)
% Louis D. Hutmire, Stated Clerk
7408 Penn Ave.
Pittsburgh, PA 15208

Sri Venkateswara Temple   (2078)
S. McCully Rd.
Penn Hills
PO Box 17289
Pittsburgh, PA 15235

Fraternitas Rosae Crucis   (1564)
Beverly Hall
Quakertown, PA 18951

Arsha Vidya Pitham   (1956)
PO Box 1059
Saylorsburg, PA 18353

Polish National Catholic Church   (93)
% Mt. Rev. John F. Swantek
1002 Pittston Ave.
Scranton, PA 18505

Autocephalous Orthodox Catholic
    Apostolic Church   (198)
Smock, PA

Anoopam Mission   (1954)
% Brahmajyoti
RR 8, Box 8066
Stroudsburg, PA 18360

Datta Yoga Center   (1967)
RD 2, Box 2084
Moniteau Rd.
Sunbury, PA 16061

Bible Fellowship Church   (426)
% Pastor W. B. Hottel
404 W. Main St.
Terre Hill, PA 17581

General Council of Christian Church of
    North America   (559)
Rte. 18 & Rutledge Rd.
Box 141-A, R.D. 1
Transfer, PA 16154

Association of Evangelicals for Italian
    Missions   (840)
314 Richfield Rd.
Upper Darby, PA 19082

American Baptist Churches in the
    U.S.A.   (839)
Valley Forge, PA 19481

Primitive Methodist Church   (420)
1045 Laurel Run Rd.
Wilkes-Barre, PA 18702

Orthodox Presbyterian Church   (361)
607 N. Eastern Rd.
Bldg. E, Box P
Willow Grove, PA 19090-0920

International Church of Ageless
    Wisdom   (1367)
Box 280
Wyalusing, PA 18853

Jewish Reconstructionist
    Federation   (1824)
Church Rd. & Greenwood Ave.
Wyncote, PA 19095

International Alliance of Messianic
    Congregations and Synagogues   (948)
Box 417
Wynnewood, PA 19096

(Original) Church of God   (534)
PO Box 592
Wytheville, PA 24382

Puerto Rico

Defenders of the Faith   (690)
PO Box 2816
Bayamon, PR 00621-0816

Mita's Congregation   (590)
Calle Duarte 235
Hata Rey, PR 60919

Iglesia Evangelica Congregacional, Inc., de
    Puerto Rico   (691)
Box 396
Humacao, PR 00792

Rhode Island

Kwan Um Zen School   (2222)
K. B. C. Hong Poep Won
RFD No. 5
528 Pound Rd.
Cumberland, RI 02864

Church of Pan   (1729)
114 Johnson Rd.
Foster, RI 02825

General Six-Principle Baptists   (892)
Rhode Island Conference
350 Davisville Rd.
North Kingstown, RI 02852

Cambodian Buddhism   (2114)
% Ven. Maha Ghosananda
Khmer Buddhist Society of New England
178 Hanover St.
Providence, RI 02907

South Carolina

Episcopal Missionary Church   (137)
Box 1294
Aiken, SC 29802

Reformed Methodist Union Episcopal
    Church   (412)
% Rt. Rev. Leroy Gethers
1136 Brody Ave.
Charleston, SC 20407

Apostolic Christian Churches,
    International   (696)
Box 3966
Florence, SC 29502

Associate Reformed Presbyterian
    Church   (354)
% Associate Reformed Presbyterian Center
1 Cleveland St.
Greenville, SC 29601

South Carolina Baptist Fellowship   (867)
% Dr. Richard Hughes
Tabernacle Baptist Church
3931 Whitehorse Rd.
Greenville, SC 29611

Southwide Baptist Fellowship   (869)
% John R. Waters
Faith Baptist Church
1607 Greenwood Rd.
Laurens, SC 39360

Lovers of Meher Baba   (1932)
% Meher Spiritual Center
10200 Hwy. 17 N.
Myrtle Beach, SC 29572

Southern Methodist Church   (405)
% Richard G. Blank
PO Drawer A
Orangeburg, SC 29116-0039

General Association of Davidian Seventh-
   Day Adventists   (978)
Box 450
Salem, SC 29676

African Theological Archministry   (1798)
% Oyotunji African Yoruba Village
Box 51
Sheldon, SC 29941

South Dakota

Hutterian Brethren-Schmiedeleut   (1238)
% David D. Decker
Tachetter Colony
Olivet, SD 57052

Tennessee

Holy Orthodox Church, American
   Jurisdiction   (237)
238 Overby Dr.
PO Box 415
Antioch, TN 37011-0414

National Association of Free Will Baptists,
   Inc.   (893)
PO Box 5002
Antioch, TN 37011-5002

Open Way   (1654)
Box 217
Celina, TN 38551

Southern Appalachian Yearly Meeting and
   Association   (820)
% Peggy Bonnington, Clerk
408 Coy Circle
Clarksville, TN 37043

Church of God (Cleveland,
   Tennessee)   (510)
Keith St. at 25th St., NW
Cleveland, TN 37311

Church of God (Jerusalem Acres)   (512)
% Chief Bishop John A. Looper
Box 1207
1826 Dalton Pike (Jerusalem Acres)
Cleveland, TN 37364-1207

Church of God of Prophecy   (515)
PO Box 2910
Cleveland, TN 37320-2910

Evangelistic Messengers'
   Association   (937)
PO Box 4018
Cleveland, TN 37320

Full Gospel Evangelistic
   Association   (556)
PO Box 1122
Cleveland, TN 77327-0122

Pentecostal World Conference   (501)
% Dr. Ray H. Hughes
Box 2430
Cleveland, TN 37320

United Christian Church and Ministerial
   Association   (749)
Box 700
Cleveland, TN 37311

Church of God/Mountain Assembly   (513)
110 S. Florence Ave.
PO Box 157
Jellico, TN 37762

Central Baptist Association   (847)
309 Lebanon Rd.
Kingsport, TN 37663

Church of Jesus Christ (Kingsport)   (609)
5836 Orebank Rd.
Kingsport, TN 37664

Evangelical Methodist Church of
   America   (394)
Box 751
Kingsport, TN 37662

Christian Congregation   (902)
% Ora Wilbert Eads, General Supt.
804 W. Hemlock St.
La Follette, TN 37766

Duck River (and Kindred) Association of
   Baptists   (850)
% Elder Wayne L. Smith, Moderator
Duck River Association
Rte. 1, Box 429
Lynchburg, TN 37352

People of the Living God   (1248)
Rte. 2, Box 423-46
McMinnville, TN 37110-9512

Assemblies of the Lord Jesus Christ,
   Inc.   (601)
875 N. White Station Rd.
Memphis, TN 38122

Christian Methodist Episcopal
   Church   (410)
564 Frank Ave.
Memphis, TN 38101

Church of God in Christ   (651)
272 S. Main St.
Memphis, TN 38103

Cumberland Presbyterian Church   (356)
Cumberland Presbyterian Center
1978 Union Ave.
Memphis, TN 38104

African Methodist Episcopal
   Church   (406)
500 8th Ave. S
Nashville, TN 37203

Church of God (Sanctified Church)   (475)
1037 Jefferson St.
Nashville, TN 37208

Church of the Living God, the Pillar and
   Ground of the Truth, Inc.   (655)
4520 Hydes Ferry Pike
Box 80735
Nashville, TN 37208

Churches of Christ (Non-
   Instrumental)   (903)
No central headquarters
For information:
% Gospel Advocate
Box 150
Nashville, TN 37202

National Baptist Convention of
   America   (884)
% National Baptist Publishing Board
7145 Centennial Blvd.
Nashville, TN 37209

Southern Baptist Convention   (868)
% Executive Committee
901 Commerce St., Ste. 750
Nashville, TN 37203

Southern Episcopal Church   (154)
% Most Rev. Huron C. Manning Jr.
234 Willow Ln.
Nashville, TN 37211

The Farm   (1264)
100 The Farm
Summertown, TN 38483

First Church of Jesus Christ   (616)
1100 E. Lincoln St.
Tullahoma, TN 37388

Texas

House of Yahweh (Abilene,
   Texas)   (1046)
Box 2498
Abilene, TX 79604

Full Gospel Church Association   (526)
Box 265
Amarillo, TX 79105

World Baptist Fellowship   (875)
3001 W. Division
Arlington, TX 76012

American Atheists, Inc.   (1091)
Box 2117
Austin, TX 78767

International Society of Divine
Love   (1994)
% Barsana Dham
400 Barsana Rd.
Austin, TX 78737

Old Catholic Church in America
(Brothers)   (80)
% Metropolitan Hilarion
1905 S. Third St.
Austin, TX 78704

The Original Kleptonian Neo-American
Church   (1486)
Box 3473
Austin, TX 78764

Hindu Temple Society of Texas   (2076)
4533 Larch Ln.
Bellaire, TX 77401

Quartus Foundation for Spiritual
Research   (1548)
PO Box 1768
Boerne, TX 78006

American Gnostic Church   (1673)
Box 1219
Corpus Christi, TX 78403

Order of Napunsakas in the West   (1668)
PO Box 1219
Corpus Christi, TX 78403-1219

Ordo-Temple Baphe-Metis   (1699)
PO Box 1219
Corpus Christi, TX 78403-1219

Apostolic Catholic Church of the
Americas   (194)
421 Fairmont
Dallas, TX 75219

Full Gospel Fellowship of Churches and
Ministers International   (582)
4325 W. Leadbetter Dr.
Dallas, TX 75233

Holy Orthodox Catholic Church   (235)
% Paul Gilbert Russell
5831 Tremont
Dallas, TX 75214

International Deliverance Churches   (585)
Box 353
Dallas, TX 75221

Today Church   (1336)
504 Business Pkwy.
Dallas, TX 75081

Union of Messianic Jewish
Congregations   (955)
6304 Beltline Rd.
Dallas, TX 75240

The Word Foundation, Inc.   (1592)
Box 180340
Dallas, TX 75218

ESP Laboratory   (1750)
Box 216
219 S. Ridge Dr.
Edgewood, TX 75117

All Faiths Ecumenical Diocese of the
South and Southwest   (175)
% Mt. Rev. Leo E. Rondeau
1204-1206 House St.
El Paso, TX 79903

Church of the First Born of the Fullness of
Times   (1166)
5854 Mira Serana
El Paso, TX 79912

Christ Holy Sanctified Church of
America   (429)
5204 Willie St.
Fort Worth, TX 76105

Christ Truth League   (1302)
2409 Canton Dr.
Fort Worth, TX 76112

Christ's Holy Sanctified Church of
America   (473)
5201 Willie St.
Fort Worth, TX 76105

Timely Messenger Fellowship   (962)
% Pastor Charles Wages
Grace Bible Church
1450 Oak Hill Rd.
Fort Worth, TX 76112

Churches of Christ (Non-Instrumental,
Non-Sunday School)   (906)
% Gospel Tidings
500 E. Henry
Hamilton, TX 76531

The Pure Truth   (1014)
Lock Box 126
Hamilton, TX 76531

Anglican Rite Old Catholic Church   (127)
PO Box 451006
Houston, TX 77245-1006

Apostolic Catholic Orthodox Church   (34)
% Most Rev. Diana C. Dale
2650 Fountainview, Ste. 444
Houston, TX 77057

Berachah Church   (928)
2815 Sage Rd.
Houston, TX 77056

Churches of Christ (Pentecostal)   (908)
Conference on Spiritual Renewal
Box 457
Missouri City, TX 77459

Church of the White Eagle   (1406)
% Rev. Jean Le Fevre
% Star Center for the Americas
St. John's Retreat Center
9 St. Beulah Rd.
Montgomery, TX 77356

House of Yahweh (Odessa, Texas)   (1047)
% Jacob Hawkins
Box 4938
Odessa, TX 79760

Unity of the Brethren   (385)
% Marvin Chlapek
2513 Revere Dr.
Pasadena, TX 77502

Sri Meenakshi Temple Society of
Houston   (2077)
Rte. 5, Box 5725
Pearland, TX 77584

Family of Abraham   (1416)
Box 690070
San Antonio, TX 78269

Free Liberal Catholic Church   (1609)
107-111 E. Locust
San Antonio, TX 78212

Infant Jesus of Prague Catholic
Church   (71)
3442 W. Woodlawn St.
San Antonio, TX 78228

Mayan Order   (1578)
Box 2710
San Antonio, TX 78299

Rigpe Dorje Foundation   (2253)
% Rigpa Dorje Center
PO Box 690995
San Antonio, TX 78269

American Baptist Association   (838)
4605 N. State Line Ave.
Texarkana, TX 75501

Church of God, International   (994)
Box 2525
Tyler, TX 75710

Intercontinental Church of God   (1012)
PO Box 1117
Tyler, TX 75710

Servants of the Star and the Snake   (1706)
% Administrator-General
PO Box 642
Weslaco, TX 78599-0642

Anamchara Celtic Church   (114)
432 W. High St.
Wills Point, TX 75169

Utah

Confederate Nations of Israel   (1169)
% Alexander Joseph, Presiding King
Long Haul, Box 151
Big Water, UT 84741

Apostolic United Brethren   (1162)
3139 W. 14700 S., No. A
Bluffsdale, UT 84065

Aaronic Order   (1144)
Box 57095
Murray, UT 84157-0095

School of the Prophets   (1158)
PO Box 396
Salem, UT 84653

Church of Jesus Christ of Latter-day
    Saints   (1149)
50 E. North Temple
Salt Lake City, UT 84150

HomeWords   (1425)
Box 57396
Salt Lake City, UT 84157

Kanzeon Zen Center   (2167)
1274 E. South Temple
Salt Lake City, UT 84102

Summum   (2330)
707 Genesee Ave.
Salt Lake City, UT 84104

Vermont

International Mevlevi Foundation   (1892)
% Threshold Foundation
139 Main St.
Battleboro, VT 05301

The Threshold Society   (1915)
139 Main St.
Battleboro, VT 05301

Messianic Communities of New
    England   (1270)
Box 443
Island Pond, VT 05846

Society of Pragmatic Mysticism   (1335)
R.R. 1
Box 800
Pawlet, VT 05761

Virginia

Salvation Army   (454)
615 Slaters Ln.
Alexandria, VA 22313

Sawan Kirpal Ruhani Mission   (2100)
8605 Villge Way, No. C
Alexandria, VA 22309-1605

World Community   (2062)
Rte. 4, Box 265
Bedford, VA 24523

Integral Yoga International   (1986)
% Satchidananda-Yogaville
Rte. 1, Box 1720
Buckingham, VA 23921

International Academy of Hermetic
    Knowledge   (1691)
PO Box 4384
Charlottesville, VA 22905

Ligmincha Institute   (2363)
PO Box 1892
Charlottesville, VA 22903

Apostolic Faith Churches of God   (648)
700 Charles St.
Franklin, VA 23851

Apostolic Faith Church of God Live
    On   (647)
2300 Trenton St.
Hopewell, VA 23860

Liberty Baptist Fellowship   (857)
Candler's Mountain Rd.
Lynchburg, VA 24502

Fivefold Path Inc.   (1974)
% Parama Dham
Rte. 8, Box 369
Madison, VA 22727

Old Holy Catholic Church of the
    Netherlands   (83)
4 Briarcliff Ln.
Madison Heights, VA 24572

True Vine Pentecostal Holiness
    Church   (677)
929 Bethel Ln.
Martinsville, VA 24112

United Church of Jesus Christ
    (Apostolic)   (637)
% Bishop J. R. Ziglar
606 2nd St.
Martinsville, VA 24112

Anglican Consultative Council   (111)
6733 Curran St.
McLean, VA 22101

Baptist World Alliance   (836)
6733 Curran St.
McLean, VA 22101

North American Baptist Fellowship   (837)
6733 Curran St.
McLean, VA 22101

The Sufi Movement   (1912)
Sufi Center of Washington
1613 Stoe Rd.
Reston, VA 27094-1600

Redeemed Assembly of Jesus Christ,
    Apostolic   (631)
% Bishop James F. Harris
7556 Hudgins Rd.
Richmond, VA 23228

Seventh-Day Adventist Reform
    Movement   (983)
Box 7239
Roanoke, VA 24019

Reformed Zion Union Apostolic
    Church   (413)
% James C. Feggins
416 S. Hill Ave.
South Hill, VA 23970

Sacred Keltic Church of America   (1704)
4 Favour Ct.
Stafford, VA 22554

Association for Research and
    Enlightenment   (1491)
Atlantic Ave. at 67th St.
Box 595
Virginia Beach, VA 23451

Fellowship of the Inner Light   (1418)
% The Fellowship Center
620 14th St.
Virginia Beach, VA 23451

North Carolina Yearly Meeting of Friends
    (Conservative)   (812)
% Lloyd Lee Wilson, Clerk
536 Carnaby Ct.
Virginia Beach, VA 23454

The Rock Church   (748)
640 Kempsville Rd.
Virginia Beach, VA 23464

Washington

Church of Jesus Christ at
    Armageddon   (1261)
14724 184th NE
Arlington, WA 98223

Aquarian Tabernacle Church   (1718)
PO Box 409
Index, WA 98256

Cosmic Awareness
    Communications   (1411)
Box 115
Olympia, WA 98507

Remnant of Israel   (1084)
11303 E. 7th
Opportunity, WA 99206

Calvary Fellowship, Inc.   (1069)
Box 128
Rainier, WA 98576

True Buddha School   (2214)
% Ling Shen Ching Tze Temple
17012 NE 40th Ct.
Redmond, WA 98052

Venusian Church   (1795)
PO Box 905
Redmond, WA 98073-0905

Irminsul Aettir   (1764)
PO Box 423
Renton, WA 98057-0423

Associated Churches, Inc.   (987)
Box 4455
Rolling Bay, WA 98061

Apostolic Catholic Church in
    America   (33)
5311 13th Ave. S.
Seattle, WA 98108

Aquarian Foundation   (1348)
315 - 15th Ave. E.
Seattle, WA 98112

Bethel Temple   (544)
2033 Second Ave.
Seattle, WA 98121

Community Chapel and Bible Training
    Center   (702)
18635 8th Ave. S.
Seattle, WA 98148

One Drop Zendo   (2174)
135 N. 75th St.
Seattle, WA 98103

Sakya Monastery of Tibetan
    Buddhism   (2254)
108 NW 83rd St.
Seattle, WA 98117

SHEM Ministries International   (713)
13232 Ambaum Blvd. SW, Ste. 102
Seattle, WA 98146

Religious Science International   (1331)
W. 1636 1st Ave.
Spokane, WA 99204

Church of Universal Love
    (Washington)   (2335)
PO Box 1620
Stanwood, WA 98292

Sabian Assembly   (1580)
% Sabian Publishing Society
PO Box 7
Stanwood, WA 98292

Conservative Lutheran Association   (318)
3504 N. Pearl St.
PO Box 7186
Tacoma, WA 98407

Conservative Lutheran Association   (319)
PO Box 7186
Tacoma, WA 98407

Church of Christ (Restored)   (1184)
4717 NE 15th Ave.
Vancouver, WA 98663

Pentecostal 7th Day Assemblies   (747)
% Elder Garver C. Gray, Chairman
4700 NE 119th St.
Vancouver, WA 98686

Orthodox Church of the East   (296)
12504 SW 232nd St.
Vashon, WA 98070

Ramtha's School of Enlightenment   (1440)
Box 519
Yelm, WA 98587

West Virginia

Claymont Society for Continuous
    Education   (1886)
Box 112
Charlestown, WV 25414

Bhavana Society   (2113)
Rte. 1, Box 218-3
High View, WV 26808

Church and School of Wicca   (1726)
Box 297
Hinton, WV 25951-0297

International Society for Krishna
    Consciousness of West
    Virginia   (1993)
RD 1, Box 318
Moundsville, WV 26041

Church of God (Seventh-Day, Salem, West
    Virginia)   (999)
79 Water St.
Salem, WV 26426

Primitive Advent Christian Church   (974)
% Donald Young
1640 Clay Ave.
South Charleston, WV 25312

Wisconsin

Church of Jesus Christ (Drew)   (1203)
35315 Chestnut
Burlington, WI 53105

Seventh Day Baptist General Conference
    USA and Canada   (897)
Seventh Day Baptist Center
3120 Kennedy Rd.
PO Box 1678
Janesville, WI 53547

Metropolitan Church Association   (447)
323 Broad St.
Lake Geneva, WI 53147

Freedom from Religion
    Foundation   (1112)
Box 750
Madison, WI 53701

National Spiritualist Association of
    Churches   (1378)
% Morris Pratt Institute
11811 Watertown Plank Rd.
Milwaukee, WI 53226

Wisconsin Evangelical Lutheran
    Synod   (338)
2929 N. Mayfair Rd.
Milwaukee, WI 53222

Circle   (1735)
% Circle Sanctuary
Box 219
Mt. Horeb, WI 53572

For My God and My Country   (61)
W5703 Shrine Rd.
Neceda, WI 54646-7916

National Association of Congregational
    Christian Churches   (378)
8473 S. Howell Ave.
PO Box 1620
Oak Creek, WI 53154-0620

Orthodox Catholic Church in
    America   (250)
% Walter X. Brown
W 1207 W. River Dr.
Oconomowoc, WI 53066

Ganden Tekchen Ling   (2237)
Deer Park
4548 Schneider Dr.
Oregon, WI 53575

Native American Church   (1485)
% Douglas Long, President
Rte. 1, Box 67
Osseo, WI 59758

The Protes'tant Conference   (336)
1033 Colan Blvd.
Rice Lake, WI 54868

Disciples of the Lord Jesus Christ   (2309)
% Rama Behera
Shawano, WI 54166

Humanity Benefactor Foundation   (2362)
University of Lawsonomy
4529 Highway 41
Sturtevant, WI 53177

Narayanananda Universal Yoga
    Trust   (2014)
% N .U. Yoga Ashram
W. 7041 Olmstead Rd.
Winter, WI 54869

CANADA

Alberta

Apostolic Church of Pentecost of
    Canada   (541)
200—809 Manning Rd. NE
Calgary, AB, Canada T2E 7M9

Covenant of Gaia; Church of
    Alberta   (1738)
PO Box 1742, Sta. M
Calgary, AB, Canada T2P 2L7

Evangelical Missionary Church of
    Canada   (443)
550 1212 - 31st Ave., NE
Calgary, AB, Canada T2E 7S8

Canadian Convention of Southern
    Baptists   (846)
% Rev. Allen E. Schmidt, Executive Dir.-
    Treasurer
Postal Bag 300
Cochrane, AB, Canada T0L 0W0

British Columbia

Congregationalist Witchcraft
    Association   (1737)
PO Box 2205
Clearbrook, BC, Canada V2T 3X8

Christian Community and Brotherhood of
    Reformed Doukhobors (Sons of
    Freedom)   (826)
Site 8, Comp. 42
Cresent Valley, BC, Canada V0G 1HO

Union of Spiritual Communities of Christ
    (Orthodox Doukhobors in
    Canada)   (835)
% USCC Central Office
Box 760
Grand Forks, BC, Canada V0H 1H0

Yasodhara Ashram Society   (2065)
Box 9
Kootenay Bay, BC, Canada V0B 1X0

Sons of Freedom (Doukhobors)   (833)
Krestova, BC, Canada

Canadian Atheist Society   (1100)
PO Box 41613
923 12th St.
New Westminster, BC, Canada V3M 6L1

Christian Episcopal Church of
   Canada   (131)
4300 Corless Rd.
Richmond, BC, Canada V7C 1N2

Bold Bible Living   (699)
International Headquarters
5774-132 A St.
Surrey, BC, Canada 98230

Bible Holiness Movement   (428)
Box 223
Postal Sta. A
Vancouver, BC, Canada V6C 2M3

Glad Tidings Missionary Society   (728)
3456 Fraser St.
Vancouver, BC, Canada

Kabalarian Philosophy   (1534)
5912 Oak St.
Vancouver, BC, Canada V6M 2W2

Lutheran Church-Canada   (332)
3022 E. 49th Ave.
Vancouver, BC, Canada V5S 1K9

Old Catholic Church of British
   Columbia   (1620)
715 E. 51st Ave.
Vancouver, BC, Canada V5X 1E2

Traditional Roman Catholic Church in the
   Americas   (103)
% Mt. Rev. Walter Allard
425 E. 11th Ave., Apt. 215
Vancouver, BC, Canada V5T 4K8

Odinist Fellowship/Kirk of Odin   (1773)
Vancouver Island, BC, Canada

Kebzeh Foundation   (1895)
Box 1207-W
Vernon, BC, Canada V1T 6N6

Manitoba

Reinland Mennonite Church   (781)
PO Box 96
Rosenfeld, MB, Canada R0G 1X0

Chortitzer Mennonite Conference   (773)
Box 968
Steinbach, MB, Canada R0A 2A0

Evangelical Mennonite Conference (Kleine
   Gemeinde)   (775)
Box 1268
440 Main St.
Steinbach, MB, Canada R0A 2A0

Old Colony Mennonite Church   (780)
% John P. Wiebe, Bishop
Box 601
Winkler, MB, Canada R6W 4A8

Evangelical Lutheran Church in
   Canada   (323)
1512 St. James St.
Winnipeg, MB, Canada R3H 0L2

Evangelical Mennonite Mission
   Conference   (776)
526 McMillan
Winnipeg, MB, Canada R3C 2G1

Lutheran Council in Canada   (301)
1512 S. James St.
Winnipeg, MB, Canada R3H 0l2

Smith Venner   (831)
% Lothar Dreger
470 Ediron Ave.
Winnipeg, MB, Canada R2G 0M4

Ukrainian Orthodox Church of
   Canada   (271)
9 St. John's Ave.
Winnipeg, MB, Canada R2W 1G8

Newfoundland

Pentecostal Assemblies of
   Newfoundland   (568)
57 Thorburn Rd.
PO Box 8895, Sta. "A"
St. John's, NF, Canada A1B 3T2

Nova Scotia

Vajradhatu International   (2260)
1084 Tower Rd.
Halifax, NS, Canada B3H 2Y8

Ontario

Old Order Amish Mennonite
   Church   (786)
Pathway Publishers
Rte. 4
Aylmer, ON, Canada N5H 2R3

Standard Church of America   (455)
Box 488
Brockville, ON, Canada K6V 5V7

Associated Gospel Churches
   (Canada)   (926)
3430 S. Service Rd.
Burlington, ON, Canada L7N 3T9

Canadian and American Reformed
   Churches   (343)
PO Box 62053
Burlington, ON, Canada L7R 4K2

Presbyterian Church in Canada   (363)
50 Wynford Dr.
Don Mills, ON, Canada M3C 1J7

Markham-Waterloo Conference
   (Mennonite)   (762)
% Clare Frey
Rte. 2
Elmira, ON, Canada N3B 2Z2

United Church of Canada   (379)
The United Church House
3250 Bloor St. W.
Etobicoke, ON, Canada M8X 2Y4

Old Catholic Churches   (22)
1307 Bethany Ln.
Gloucester, ON, Canada K1J 8P3

Unamended Christadelphians   (912)
% Edward W. Farrar
4 Mountain Park Ave.
Hamilton, ON, Canada L9A 1A2

Dharma Centre of Canada   (2274)
RR 1, Galway Rd.
Kinmount, ON, Canada K0M2A0

Free Protestant Episcopal Church   (142)
% Mt. Rev. Benjamin C. Eckardt
430 Elizabeth St.
London, ON, Canada N5W 3R7

Orthodox Church of Canada   (257)
901-580 Dundas St.
London, ON, Canada N6B 1W9

Evangelical Fellowship of Canada   (11)
175 Riviera Dr.
Markham, ON, Canada L3R 5J6

Old Catholic Church of Canada   (82)
R.R. 1, Inverary Farm
Midland, ON, Canada L4R 4K3

Canadian Baptist Ministries   (845)
7185 Millcreek Dr.
Mississauga, ON, Canada L5N 5R4

Pentecostal Assemblies of Canada   (567)
6745 Century Ave.
Mississauga, ON, Canada L5N 6P7

Federation of Orthodox Catholic
   Churches   (163)
Christ Catholic Church International
6160 Barker St.
Niagara, ON, Canada L2G 1Y4

Christ Catholic Church International   (49)
% St. Lukes Cathedral
5165 Palmer Ave.
Niagara Falls, ON, Canada L2G 1Y4

Independent Catholic Church of
   Canada   (1612)
% Mt. Rev. William Hains-Howard
4520 Huron St., Apt. 602
Niagara Falls, ON, Canada l2E 6Y0

Missionary Church of Canada   (450)
% Dr. Alfred Rees, Pres.
89 Centre Ave.
North York, ON, Canada M2M 2L7

Anglican Catholic Church of
   Canada   (116)
% Bp. Alfred Woolcock
709 Attersley Dr.
Oshawa, ON, Canada L1K 1P9

Humanist Association of Canada   (1115)
Box 3726, Station C
Ottawa, ON, Canada K1Y 4J8

Pagan Federation/Federation paienne—
Canada   (1670)
Box 32, Stn. "B"
Ottawa, ON, Canada K1P 6C3

White Wind Zen Community   (2184)
PO Box 203, Sta. A
Ottawa, ON, Canada K1N 8V2

Ambedkar Mission   (2112)
49 Templeton Ct.
Scarborough, ON, Canada M1E 2C3

Hermetic Order of the Silver
Sword   (2342)
2483 Gerrard St. E.
Scarborough, ON, Canada M1N 1W7

United Apostolic Faith Church   (575)
2 Delbert Dr.
Scarborough, ON, Canada M1P 1X1

Independent Holiness Church   (446)
% Rev. R. E. Votary, Gen. Supt.
Box 194
Sydenham, ON, Canada K0H 2T0

Ancient British Church in North America
(The Autocephalous Glastonbury Rite
in Diaspora)   (2332)
9-47 Marion St.
Toronto, ON, Canada M6R 1E6

Armenian Evangelical Union of North
America   (924)
% Rev. Yessayo Sarmaziam
42 Glenforest Rd.
Toronto, ON, Canada M4N 1Z8

Association of Regular Baptist Churches
(Canada)   (842)
130 Gerrard St., E
Toronto, ON, Canada M5A 3T4

British-Israel-World Federation (Canada)
Inc.   (1068)
313 Sherbourne St.
Toronto, ON, Canada M5A 2S3

British Methodist Episcopal Church of
Canada   (409)
460 Shaw St.
Toronto, ON, Canada M6G 3L3

Buddhist Society for Compassionate
Wisdom   (2217)
86 Vaughan Rd.
Toronto, ON, Canada M6C 2M1

Byelorussian Autocephalic Orthodox
Church in the U.S.A.   (203)
% Archbishop Mikalay, Primate
Church of St. Cyril of Turau
524 St. Clarens Ave.
Toronto, ON, Canada

Canadian Council of Churches   (9)
40 St. Clair St.
Toronto, ON, Canada M4T 1M9

Estonian Evangelical Lutheran Church in
Exile   (320)
% Abp. Udo Petersoo
383 Jarvis St.
Toronto, ON, Canada M5B 2C7

Kampo Gangra Drubgyudling   (2240)
200 Balsam Ave.
Toronto, ON, Canada M4E 3C3

Mountain Moon Sangha   (2172)
No. 10, 939 Avenue Rd.
Toronto, ON, Canada M5P 2K7

Pentecostal Fellowship of North
America   (500)
% Rev. James M. McKnight, Chairperson
10 Overlea Bvd.
Toronto, ON, Canada M4H 1A5

The Peoples Church   (953)
374 Sheppard Ave. E
Toronto, ON, Canada M2N 3B6

Toronto Zen Centre   (2181)
33 High Park Gardens
Toronto, ON, Canada M6R 1S8

Wiccan Church of Canada   (1796)
109 Vaughan Rd.
Toronto, ON, Canada M6C 2L9

Council of Muslim Communities of
Canada   (1872)
Box 771, Station B
Willowdale, ON, Canada M2K 2R1

Prince Edward Island

Free Church of Scotland on Prince Edward
Island   (141)
% Rev. William R. Underhay
Box 977
Montague, PE, Canada C0A 1R0

Quebec

Catholic Charismatic Church of
Canada   (42)
La Cite de Marie
11,141 Rte. 148, RR 1
Ste. Scholastique
Mirabel, PQ, Canada J0N 1S0

International Meditation Institute   (1991)
2542 Montclair Ave.
Montreal, PQ, Canada H4B 2J1

Italian Pentecostal Church of
Canada   (562)
6724 Fabre St.
Montreal, PQ, Canada H2G 2Z6

Temple of Priapus   (2347)
PO Box 1164, Stn. H
Montreal, PQ, Canada H3G 2N1

Catholic Church of the Apostles of the
Latter Times   (44)
% Monastery of the Magnificat
Box 308
St. Jovite, PQ, Canada J0T 2H0

Congregation de l'Aumisme   (2360)
% Monastere de Ste-Lucie
Ste-Agathe, PQ, Canada J8C 2Z8

Sivananda Yoga Vedanta Centers   (2041)
673 8th Ave.
Val Morin, PQ, Canada J0T 2R0

INTERNATIONAL

Australia

Temple Society   (1254)
% Dr. Richard Hoffman
152 Tucker
Bentleigh, Australia

England

International Humanist and Ethical
Union   (1087)
% IHEU Secretariat
47 Theobald's Rd.
London WC1X 8SF, England

Universal Link   (1455)
1, St. Georges Sq.
St. Annes, Lancs., England

France

Remey Society   (1939)
% Jacques Soqhomonian
Boite Postal 593
F-13491 **Marseille** Cedex 04, France

Ireland

Fellowship of Isis   (1666)
% Clonegal Castle
Enniscorthy, Ireland

Israel

Church of God (Jerusalem)   (1045)
Box 10184
91101 **Jerusalem**, Israel

Workers Together with Elohim   (1051)
Box 14411
Jerusalem, Israel

Netherlands

Theosophical Society (Hartley)   (1588)
% Blavatskyhius
de Ruyterstratt 74
NL-2518 AV **Gravenhage**, Netherlands

Philippines

American Orthodox Church   (188)
% Archbishop Aftimios Harold J. Donovan,
Exarch
San Antonio, Los Vanos
Laguna 3732, Philippines

Republic of South Africa

School of Truth   (1333)
Box 5582
Johannesburg, Republic of South Africa

Thailand

World Fellowship of Buddhists   (2110)
℅ The Secretariat
33 Sukhumvit Rd.
Bangkok, Thailand

Subject Index

Provides access to the material in the directory listings sections through a selected list of subject terms. The index also includes *see* and *see also* references. References include the full organization name and book entry number.

Garuda

American Buddhist Society and Fellowship, Inc. 2226

Gifts of the Spirit

Apostolic Church 540
Assemblies of the Called Out Ones of Yah 1038
Assembly of Yahvah 1042
Association of Vineyard Churches 543
Calvary Chapel 547
Catholic Apostolic Church at Davis 284
Church of Christ with the Elijah Message (Rogers) 1187
Church of God, Body of Christ 992
Community Chapel and Bible Training Center 702
Elim Fellowship 552
Fountain of Life Fellowship 1007
General Conference of the Evangelical Baptist Church 527
General Six-Principle Baptists 892
Holy Apostolic-Catholic Church of the East (Chaldean-Syrian) 291
Independent Churches of the Latter-Rain Revival 705
Jesus People USA 1266
Kingdom and World Mission of Our Lord Jesus Christ 741
Liberty Fellowship of Churches and Ministers 743
Messianic Communities of New England 1270
Mt. Zion Sanctuary 564
New Beginnings 1081
New Covenant Churches of Maryland 710
New Life Fellowship 1049
Reorganized Church of Jesus Christ of Latter Day Saints 1198
Seventh-Day Adventist Church 981
Temple Society 1254
United Apostolic Faith Church 575
United Christian Church and Ministerial Association 749
World Insight International 1023

Glossolalia See: Speaking-in-tongues

Gnosticism

The Aquarian Academy 1490
Aurobindo, Disciples of Sri 1959
Brotherhood of the White Temple 1573
The Church of Gnosis (Ecclesia Gnostica Mysteriorum) 1605
Ecclesia Gnostica 1606
Edta Ha Thoma 1607
Federation of St. Thomas Christian Churches 1608
Gnostic Orthodox Church of Christ in America 1610
Hermetic Society for World Service 1584
Lectorium Rosicrucianum 1566
Michael Teachings 1432
Monastery of the Seven Rays 1692

Old Holy Catholic Church, Province of North America 1621
Our Lady of Endor Coven 1812
Plymouth Brethren (Raven-Taylor Brethren) 917
Pre-Nicene Church (de Palatine) 1625
Ramtha's School of Enlightenment 1440
Roman Catholic Church 24
Suns Ahman Israel-I:A:O: 1172

Grace—Prevenient

Southern Methodist Church 405

Great Pyramid

Brotherhood of the White Temple 1573
Lemurian Fellowship 1577

Great White Brotherhood

The Aquarian Academy 1490
Church Universal and Triumphant 1629
Harmony of Life Fellowship 1011
Trinity Foundation 1452
Universe Society Church 1477

Guru

AUM Supreme Truth 2137
Barry Long Foundation 1961
International Society for Krishna Consciousness of West Virginia 1993
Metamorphosis League for Monastic Studies 2010
Transcendent Science Society 2054

Handfasting

Alexandrian Wicca 1713

Healing

Afro-American Vodoun 1799
Altrurian Society 1296
The Apostolic Faith Mission of Portland, Oregon, Inc. 506
The Aquarian Ministry 1300
Association for Research and Enlightenment 1491
AUM Temple of Universal Truth 1493
Believers' Circle 1349
Calvary Pentecostal Church 549
Chamber of Holy Voodoo 1800
Chapori-Ling Foundation Sangha 2230
Chirothesian Church of Faith 1495
Chowado Henjo Kyo 2271
Christ Ministry Foundation 1496
Christian Institute of Spiritual Science 1497
Church of Basic Truth 1498
Church of Divine Man 1499
Church of the Gift of God 1506
Church of the Lord Jesus Christ (Ishi Temple) 1507
Church of the New Civilization 1307
Church of the White Eagle 1406
Church of Universal Triumph/The Dominion of God 477
Circle of Inner Truth 1408
College/Temple of Thelema 1680
Comforter League of Light 1310

Commandment Keepers Congregation of the Living God 1850
Cosmic Star Temple 1463
Da Yuan Circle 2199
Datta Yoga Center 1967
Divine Circle of the Sacred Grove 1747
Egyptian Temple of Fitness 1749
The Eloists, Inc. 1415
Emissaries of Divine Light 1511
ESP Laboratory 1750
Etherian Religious Society of Universal Brotherhood 1516
Foundation Faith of God 1519
Full Salvation Union 2313
Future Foundation 1521
Heart Consciousness Church and New Age Church of Being 1523
Holy Order of Ezekiel 1524
Independent Churches of the Latter-Rain Revival 705
Intercosmic Center of Spiritual Awareness 1987
International Alliance of Churches of the Truth 1322
International Church of Spiritual Vision, Inc. (Western Prayer Warriors) 1533
Kanzeonji Non-Sectarian Buddhist Temple 2168
Kennedy Worshippers 2354
Last Day Messengers 1468
Ligmincha Institute 2363
Meditation Groups, Inc. 1596
Mental Science Institute 1766
Mt. Zion Sanctuary 564
New Age Church of Truth 1540
New Psychiana 1543
"Now" Folk 1327
Open Bible Standard Churches, Inc. 566
Order of the White Rose 1379
Pentecostal Full Gospel Church 746
People's Temple Christian (Disciples) Church 1545
Quimby Center 1549
Rosicrucian Fellowship 1569
Shinreikyo 2290
Shrine of the Eternal Breath of Tao 2213
The Sufi Movement 1912
Tensho-Kotai-Jingu-Kyo 2295
Unarius-Science of Life 1474
Vajrakilaya Centers of North America 2261
Voodoo Spiritual Temple 1591
Yasodhara Ashram Society 2065

Healing—Divine

Apostolic Church of Pentecost of Canada 541
Apostolic Faith (Hawaii) 597
Apostolic Faith (Kansas) 542
Apostolic Faith Mission Church of God 598
Apostolic Gospel Church of Jesus Christ 599
Apostolic Overcoming Holy Church of God 600

Love feast
Christ's Assembly 791
Church of the Brethren 792
Church of the Brotherhood 1225
Moravian Church in America 384
Reformed Methodist Union Episcopal
Church 412

Macrobiotics
George Ohsawa Macrobiotic
Foundation 2210
One Peaceful World 2211
Shrine of the Eternal Breath of
Tao 2213

Magic(k)
Abbey of Thelema 1672
American Gnostic Church 1673
American Order of the Brotherhood of
Wicca 1715
American School of
Mentalvivology 1297
Arcane Magical Order of the Knights of
Shambhala 1955
Aurum Solis 1674
Bavarian Illuminati 1675
Bennu Phoenix Temple of the Hermetic
Order of the Golden Dawn 1676
Builders of the Adytum 1677
Church and School of Wicca 1726
Church of Satan 1806
Church of Satanic Brotherhood 1807
Church of Universal Forces 1734
Circle 1735
Clan Invisible 1679
College/Temple of Thelema 1680
Congregationalist Witchcraft
Association 1737
Divine Circle of the Sacred
Grove 1747
Earthstar Temple 1748
ESP Laboratory 1750
Ewam Choden 2235
Fellowship of Ma-Ion 1682
First Occult Church 1753
First Wiccan Church of
Minnesota 1754
Foundation, A Hermetic Society 1683
Franz Bardon Foundation 1684
Fraternity of Light 1686
The Georgian Church 1757
Henge of Keltria 1759
Hermetic Order of the Golden
Dawn 1687
Hermetic Order of the Golden Dawn
(Regardie) 1688
Hermetic Order of the Morning Star
International 1689
Hermetic Order of the Silver
Sword 2342
Holy Order of RaHoorKhuit 1690
Huna Research, Inc. 1527
Lady Sara's Coven 1765
Mental Science Institute 1766
Monastery of the Seven Rays 1692
New England Institute of Metaphysical
Studies 1693
New, Reformed, Orthodox Order of the
Golden Dawn 1769

Order of the Lily and the Eagle 1694
Order of the Thelemic Golden
Dawn 1695
Order of Thelema 1696
Ordo Adeptorum Invisiblum 1697
Ordo Lux Kethri 1698
Ordo Templi Astarte 1700
Ordo Templi Orientis 1701
Ordo Templi Orientis (Grant) 1702
Ordo Templi Orientis (Roanoke,
Virginia) 1703
Reformed Druids of North
America 1781
Religious Order of Witchcraft 1804
Servants of the Light 1705
Servants of the Star and the
Snake 1706
Shrine of Sothis 1707
Society Ordo Templi Orientis in
America 1708
Temple of the Holy Grail 1709
Temple of the Pagan Way 1791
Temple of Truth 1710
Thelemic Order and Temple of the
Golden Dawn 1712
Triskellion 1794
Universal Spiritualist
Association 1399
Work of the Chariot 1847
Yun Lin Temple 2265

Mahatmas/masters
AUM Temple of Universal Truth 1493
Chapter of Perfection 1221
Church Universal and
Triumphant 1629
Holy Order of Ezekiel 1524
Light of Christ Community
Church 1651
Universe Society Church 1477

Mail, ordination by
American Fellowship Church 1125
Brotherhood of Peace and
Tranquility 1126
Calvary Grace Christian Church of
Faith 1127
Calvary Grace Churches of
Faith 1128
The Church of Holy Light 1129
Church of the Holy Monarch 1130
Church of Universal
Brotherhood 1132
Crown of Life Fellowship 1133
Foundation Church of Divine
Truth 1420
Hilltop House Church 1134
Life Science Church 1136
Missionaries of the New Truth 1137
Omniune Church 1138
Shingon Mission 2153
United Church of the Apostles 1139
Universal Free Life Church 1140
Universal Life Church 1141
Universal Life Mission Church 1142

Manichaeism
New England Coven of Welsh
Traditionalist Witches 1768

Manisis
Fraternitas Rosae Crucis 1564

Mantras
American Meditation Society 1947
Anasuya Foundation 1953
Haidakhan Samaj 1978
Himalayan International Institute of
Yoga Science and
Philosophy 1981
Hindu Yoga Society 1982
International Divine Realization
Society 1990
International Society for Krishna
Consciousness 1992
Krishna Samaj 1999
Raj-Yoga Math and Retreat 2020
Shingon Mission 2153
Sufi Islamia Ruhaniat Society 1911
Sufi Order 1913
True Buddha School 2214
Universal Brotherhood Temple and
School of Eastern Philosophy 2056
Vajrakilaya Centers of North
America 2261
World Plan Executive Council-
US 2064
Yasodhara Ashram Society 2065
Yoganta Meditation Center 2068

Marriage
Roman Catholic Church 24
Servant Catholic Church 95

Marriage—With nonmembers
Christian Nation Church, U.S.A. 431

Martial arts
Buddha's Universal Church and Ch'an
Buddhist Sangha 2194
Chung Fu Kuan (Taoist
Sanctuary) 2198
Clan Invisible 1679
Embassy of the Gheez-
Americans 1510
Healing Tao Centers 2204
Hohm Community 1983
Jain Meditation International
Center 2081
Living Tao Foundation 2209
Moksha Foundation 2011
Ordinary Dharma 2126
Shrine of the Eternal Breath of
Tao 2213

Massage
Church of Loving Hands 1502
Deva Foundation 1968

Meditation
Abhayagiri Buddhist Monastery 2111
Abhidhyan Yoga Institute 1943
Altrurian Society 1296
American Buddhist Movement 2266
American Meditation Society 1947
American Yoga Society 1949
American Zen College 2216
Amrita Foundation 1950
Ananda 1951
Ananda Marga Yoga Society 1952
Anthroposophical Society 1644

Missions and Foreign Affiliates—Greece

Missions and Foreign Affiliates—Guam

Missions and Foreign Affiliates—Guatemala

Datta Yoga Center 1967
Dawn Bible Students
    Association 1030
Deliverance Evangelistic Church 579
Deva Foundation 1968
Dhyanyoga Centers 1971
Divine Light Mission 2089
Ecumenical Institute 1230
Evangelical Churches of
    Pentecost 615
Evangelical Congregational
    Church 416
Evangelical Friends Church, Eastern
    Division 805
Fellowship of Christian
    Assemblies 553
Fellowship of Evangelical Baptist
    Churches in Canada 851
Free Church of Scotland on Prince
    Edward Island 141
Free Gospel Church, Inc. 555
Friends of the Western Buddhist
    Order 2277
Gaudiya Vaishnava Society 1976
General Conference Mennonite
    Church 778
Gospel Assemblies
    (Sowders/Goodwin) 730
Gospel Harvesters Evangelistic
    Association (Buffalo) 732
Grace Gospel Evangelistic Association
    International Inc. 733
Haidakhan Samaj 1978
Hall Deliverance Foundation 583
Himalayan International Institute of
    Yoga Science and
    Philosophy 1981
Hindu Temple Society of North
    America 2074
Holy Shankaracharya Order 1984
House of Yahweh (Abilene,
    Texas) 1046
Indo-American Yoga-Vedanta
    Society 1985
Integral Yoga International 1986
Intergalactic Cultural
    Foundation 1988
International Babaji Kriya Yoga
    Sangam 1989
International Meditation
    Institute 1991
International Ministers Forum 739
International Pentecostal Church of
    Christ 532
International Society for Krishna
    Consciousness 1992
International Society of Divine
    Love 1994
Jain Meditation International
    Center 2081
Kagyu Dharma 2239
Kali Mandir 1995
Kirpal Light Satsang 2093
Krishna Samaj 1999
Krishnamurti Foundation of
    America 2000
Kriya Yoga Centers 2001
Margaret Laird Foundation 1292

Lokanath Divine Life Fellowship 2005
Lutheran Church-Missouri Synod 333
Ma Yoga Shakti International
    Mission 2006
Malankara Orthodox (Syrian)
    Church 294
Mata Amritanandamayi Center 2008
Metropolitan Church Association 447
Moksha Foundation 2011
Moral Re-Armament 2355
Namo Buddha Seminar 2246
Narayanananda Universal Yoga
    Trust 2014
National Association of Congregational
    Christian Churches 378
National Association of Free Will
    Baptists, Inc. 893
National Association of Holiness
    Churches 494
Nechung Drayang Ling 2247
Nirankari Universal Brotherhood
    Mission 2096
Original Free Will Baptists, North
    Carolina State Convention 894
Original Glorious Church of God in
    Christ Apostolic Faith 625
Orthodox Reformed Church 350
Palyul Changchub Dhaegye
    Ling 2250
Pansophic Institute 2251
Pentecostal Evangelical Church 572
Pillar of Fire 469
Radha Soami Satsang, Beas 2098
Reformed Church in America 352
Reiyukai America 2151
Reorganized Church of Jesus Christ of
    Latter Day Saints 1198
Restoration Church of Jesus Christ of
    Latter-day Saints 1200
Rigpa Fellowship 2252
Rigpe Dorje Foundation 2253
S. A. I. Foundation 2022
Saccha Dham Ashram 2023
Saiva Siddhanta Church 2027
Salvation and Deliverance
    Church 591
Sant Bani Ashram 2099
Sarva Dharma Sambhava
    Kendra 2028
Sarvamangala Mission 2029
Satyananda Ashrams, U.S.A. 2031
Sawan Kirpal Ruhani Mission 2100
Self-Realization Fellowship 2032
Self-Revelation Church of Absolute
    Monism 2033
Seventh-Day Adventist Reform
    Movement 983
Seventh-Day Church of God 1016
Shanti Mandir 2034
Shanti Yoga Institute and Yoga
    Retreat 2036
Shivalila 1280
Shri Krishna Association of the
    U.S.A. 2038
Shri Shivabalayogi Maharaj
    Trust 2040
Sikh Council of North America 2084

Sivananda Yoga Vedanta
    Centers 2041
Society of Abidance in Truth 2042
Sri Chaitanya Saraswat Mandal 2044
Sufi Order 1913
SYDA Foundation 2049
Theosophical Society in
    America 1589
Tioga River Christian Conference 911
Transcendent Science Society 2054
Truth Consciousness 2055
Undenominational Church of the
    Lord 456
United Church of Christ 380
United Church of Religious
    Science 1338
United Evangelical Churches 750
United Full Gospel Ministers and
    Churches 576
The United Network of Christian
    Ministries and Churches 751
Vedanta Society 2058
Vimala Thakar, Friends of 2061
Wisconsin Evangelical Lutheran
    Synod 338
World Community Service 2063
Yogi Gupta Association 2069
Yogiraj Sect 2070
Zoroastrian Associations in North
    America 1934

Missions and Foreign Affiliates—Indonesia
Anchor Bay Evangelistic
    Association 539
Baptist General Conference 889
Bethel Temple 544
Christ Faith Mission 718
Christian Reformed Church in North
    America 344
Door of Faith Church and Bible
    School 520
Evangelical Congregational
    Church 416
Foundation for the Preservation of the
    Mahayana Tradition 2236
Naqshbandi Sufi Order 1899
Netherlands Reformed
    Congregations 349
Subud 1909
Wisconsin Evangelical Lutheran
    Synod 338

Missions and Foreign Affiliates—Iran
Ammonite Foundation 1716
Baha'i Faith 1935
Evangelistic Missionary
    Fellowship 938
International Mevlevi
    Foundation 1892
Nimatullahi-Gunabadi Sufi
    Order 1901
United Evangelical Churches 750
Zoroastrian Associations in North
    America 1934

Missions and Foreign Affiliates—Ireland
American Meditation Society 1947
Anglican Church in America 117
Ar nDraiocht Fein: A Druid Fellowship,
    Inc. 1719

Churches of Christ (Non-Instrumental-Premillennial) 907
Churches of God (Independent Holiness People) 440
Cumberland Presbyterian Church 356
Delval UFO, Inc. 1464
Dharma Centre of Canada 2274
Diamond Sangha 2164
Divine Light Mission 2089
Evangelical Congregational Church 416
Evangelical Covenant Church 382
Evangelical Free Church of America 383
Evangelical Mennonite Mission Conference 776
Fellowship of Christian Assemblies 553
Fellowship of Evangelical Baptist Churches in Canada 851
Fellowship of Evangelical Bible Churches 777
First Zen Institute of America 2165
Gedatsu Church of America 2140
General Association of General Baptists 891
General Church of the New Jerusalem 1343
General Conference Mennonite Church 778
General Convention of the New Jerusalem in the United States of America 1344
Gnostic Association of Cultural and Anthropological Studies 1576
Grace Gospel Evangelistic Association International Inc. 733
Hawaii Council of Jodo Mission 2141
Higashi Hongwanji Buddhist Church 2142
Holy Spirit Association for the Unification of World Christianity 1525
Honkyoku Shinto 2284
Honpa Hongwanji Buddhism 2143
Inari Shinto 2285
International Meditation Institute 1991
Jinga Shinto 2286
Kongosatta-In Tendai Buddhist Temple 2147
Konko Kyo 2287
The Lords New Church 1345
Lutheran Church-Missouri Synod 333
Master Ching Hai Meditation Association 2094
Minnesota Zen Meditation Center 2171
Naqshbandi Sufi Order 1899
National Association of Free Will Baptists, Inc. 893
Nichiren Mission 2148
Nichiren Shoshu America 2149
North American Baptist Conference 861
One Drop Zendo 2174
Oriental Missionary Society Holiness Church of North America 952

Orthodox Presbyterian Church 361
Palolo Kwannon Temple (Tendai Sect) 2150
Perfect Liberty Kyodan 2359
Prana Yoga Ashram 2019
Reformed Church in America 352
Reformed Presbyterian Church of North America 367
Reorganized Church of Jesus Christ of Latter Day Saints 1198
Rigpa Fellowship 2252
Rinzai-Ji, Inc. 2177
Rissho Kosei Kai 2152
Seicho-No-Ie 1334
Shingon Mission 2153
Shinreikyo 2290
Shinshu Kyokai Mission 2155
Shinto 2291
Society of Johrei 2292
Soka Gakkai International (USA) 2156
Soto Mission 2179
Southwide Baptist Fellowship 869
Taishakyo Shinto 2293
Tara Center 1599
Tenrikyo 2294
Tensho-Kotai-Jingu-Kyo 2295
Third Civilization 2296
Todaiji Hawaii Bekkaku Honzan 2157
United Christian Church 417
United Evangelical Churches 750
United Israel World Union 1868
Vedanta Society 2058
Wisconsin Evangelical Lutheran Synod 338
Zen Buddhist Temple of Chicago 2185
Zen Center of Los Angeles 2187

Missions and Foreign Affiliates—Jordan
Apostolic Church of Pentecost of Canada 541
Church of the Lord Jesus Christ of the Apostolic Faith (Philadelphia) 613
Friends United Meeting 808

Missions and Foreign Affiliates—Kenya
American Exarchate of the True (Old Calendar) Orthodox Church of Greece 179
Associated Gospel Churches 925
Bible Fellowship Church 426
Bible Holiness Movement 428
Bochasanwasi Swaminarayan Sanstha 2072
The Church of Christ "With the Elijah Message," Established Anew in 1929 1186
Church of Christian Liberty 933
Church of God (Anderson, Indiana) 434
Church of God in Christ, Mennonite 759
Church of God (World Headquarters) 518
Evangelical Congregational Church 416
Evangelical Episcopal Church (Owen) 140

Friends United Meeting 808
Greater Gospel World Outreach 941
Hall Deliverance Foundation 583
International Pentecostal Church of Christ 532
Moral Re-Armament 2355
Naqshbandi Sufi Order 1899
Orthodox Presbyterian Church 361
Shiah Fatimi Ismaili Tayyibi Dawoodi Bohra (Daudi Bohras) 1877

Missions and Foreign Affiliates—Korea
American Evangelistic Association 715
American Zen College 2216
Brethren in Christ 758
Buddhist Society for Compassionate Wisdom 2217
Christ Faith Mission 718
Christian Reformed Church in North America 344
Church of Christian Liberty 933
Church of God (Anderson, Indiana) 434
Church of World Messianity 2283
Evangelical Ministers and Churches, International, Inc. 936
General Church of the New Jerusalem 1343
Han-Ma-Um Zen Center 2219
Korean American Presbyterian Church 360
Korean Buddhist Bo Moon Order 2220
Korean Buddhist Chogye Order 2221
Kwan Um Zen School 2222
Lutheran Church-Missouri Synod 333
Master Ching Hai Meditation Association 2094
Orthodox Presbyterian Church 361
Reorganized Church of Jesus Christ of Latter Day Saints 1198
Rissho Kosei Kai 2152
Shinnyo-En 2154
Society of Johrei 2292
Tenrikyo 2294
Undenominational Church of the Lord 456
United Church of Christ 380
United Evangelical Churches 750

Missions and Foreign Affiliates—Kuwait
Reformed Church in America 352

Missions and Foreign Affiliates—Laos
Evangelical Covenant Church 382

Missions and Foreign Affiliates—Lebanon
American Druze Society 1941
Church of God (Anderson, Indiana) 434
Holy Gospel Church IV, Inc. 1135
Kingdom and World Mission of Our Lord Jesus Christ 741
Lutheran Church-Missouri Synod 333
Naqshbandi Sufi Order 1899

Missions and Foreign Affiliates—Lesotho
Evangelical Mennonite Church 785
The Farm 1264

Missions and Foreign Affiliates—South Africa

American Meditation Society   1947
Anglican Church in America   117
Anglican Orthodox Church   123
Aquarian Foundation   1348
Associated Gospel Churches   925
Association of Vineyard
   Churches   543
Bochasanwasi Swaminarayan
   Sanstha   2072
Brethren in Christ   758
Calvary Ministries, Inc.,
   International   548
Christian Catholic Church   2301
Church of God, International   994
Church of the Creator   1106
Church of the Living Word   701
Divine Science Federation
   International   1313
Faith Tabernacle Council of Churches,
   International   657
Free Church of Scotland on Prince
   Edward Island   141
Gaudiya Vaishnava Society   1976
General Church of the New
   Jerusalem   1343
Hall Deliverance Foundation   583
International Churches of Christ   909
International New Thought
   Alliance   1287
Jehovah's Witnesses   1032
Jesus People Church   740
The Lords New Church   1345
Metropolitan Church Association   447
Moral Re-Armament   2355
Netherlands Reformed
   Congregations   349
Philadelphia Church of God   1013
Religious Science International   1331
School of Truth   1333
Seventh-Day Adventist Reform
   Movement   983
Sri Chaitanya Saraswat Mandal   2044
Theosophical Society   1587
United Apostolic Faith Church   575
Wesleyan Church   458
White Robed Monks of St.
   Benedict   110
Worldwide Church of God   1024

Missions and Foreign Affiliates—Spain

Abbey of Thelema   1672
Association of Occidental Orthodox
   Parishes   196
Association of Regular Baptist Churches
   (Canada)   842
Brethren in Christ   758
Congregational Holiness Church   519
Evangelical Congregational
   Church   416
Evangelical Covenant Church   382
Evangelical Ministers and Churches,
   International, Inc.   936
The Family   1263
Gnostic Association of Cultural and
   Anthropological Studies   1576
Holy Gospel Church IV, Inc.   1135
Holy Palmarian Church   64

International Zen Institute of
   America   2144
Jerrahi Order of America   1894
Krishnamurti Foundation of
   America   2000
Mata Amritanandamayi Center   2008
Monastery of the Seven Rays   1692
Naqshbandi Sufi Order   1899
Naqshbandiyya-Mujaddidiyya Order of
   Sufism   1900
National Association of Free Will
   Baptists, Inc.   893
George Ohsawa Macrobiotic
   Foundation   2210
Philanthropic Assembly   1036
Pillar of Fire   469
Prana Yoga Ashram   2019
Reiyukai America   2151
Sivananda Yoga Vedanta
   Centers   2041
Soldiers of the Cross of Christ,
   Evangelical International
   Church   694
Southwide Baptist Fellowship   869
Tara Center   1599
United Israel World Union   1868

Missions and Foreign Affiliates—Sri Lanka (Ceylon)

Agon-shu   2136
Associated Gospel Churches   925
AUM Supreme Truth   2137
Bawa Muhaiyaddeen
   Fellowship   1881
Christian Reformed Church in North
   America   344
Integral Yoga International   1986
Lutheran Church-Missouri Synod   333
Moral Re-Armament   2355
Saiva Siddhanta Church   2027
Seventh-Day Adventist Reform
   Movement   983
Shinnyo-En   2154
Southern Methodist Church   405
Sri Lankan Sangha Council of North
   America   2129
Vedanta Society   2058

Missions and Foreign Affiliates—Surinam

African Methodist Episcopal
   Church   406
Church of Christian Liberty   933
Evangelical Congregational
   Church   416
Orthodox Presbyterian Church   361

Missions and Foreign Affiliates—Sweden

American Exarchate of the True (Old
   Calendar) Orthodox Church of
   Greece   179
Ancient and Mystical Order of the
   Rosae Crucis   1562
Association for Research and
   Enlightenment   1491
Bible Fellowship Church   426
Calvary Ministries, Inc.,
   International   548
Community Chapel and Bible Training
   Center   702
Dhiravamsa Foundation   2117

Estonian Evangelical Lutheran Church
   in Exile   320
General Church of the New
   Jerusalem   1343
Hall Deliverance Foundation   583
The Lords New Church   1345
Michael Educational Foundation   1431
Moral Re-Armament   2355
Naqshbandi Sufi Order   1899
Narayanananda Universal Yoga
   Trust   2014
George Ohsawa Macrobiotic
   Foundation   2210
Satyananda Ashrams, U.S.A.   2031
Tara Center   1599
Theosophical Society   1587
United Church of Religious
   Science   1338
Zen Center of Rochester   2188

Missions and Foreign Affiliates—Switzerland

Ancient and Mystical Order of the
   Rosae Crucis   1562
Association of Occidental Orthodox
   Parishes   196
Association of Regular Baptist Churches
   (Canada)   842
Church of God, the Eternal   1000
Church of the Christian Spiritual
   Alliance   1966
Community Chapel and Bible Training
   Center   702
Datta Yoga Center   1967
Dharma Centre of Canada   2274
Dhiravamsa Foundation   2117
Faith Assembly   724
Holy Orthodox Church in North
   America   240
International Mevlevi
   Foundation   1892
Italian Pentecostal Church of
   Canada   562
Mata Amritanandamayi Center   2008
Mazdaznan Movement   1933
Moral Re-Armament   2355
Naqshbandiyya-Mujaddidiyya Order of
   Sufism   1900
New Beginnings   1081
Order of Interbeing   2125
The Peace Mission Movement   1247
Philanthropic Assembly   1036
Rigpa Fellowship   2252
Semjase Silver Star Center   1471
Sivananda Yoga Vedanta
   Centers   2041
Sserulanda Foundation   2101
Sufi Order   1913
Tiep Hien Order   2133
United Church of Religious
   Science   1338
Vedanta Society   2058
White Robed Monks of St.
   Benedict   110

Missions and Foreign Affiliates—Syria

Naqshbandi Sufi Order   1899
Reformed Presbyterian Church of North
   America   367

Women—Rights of...

Women—Superiority/inferiority

World teacher

Yoga

Master Index

Provides a single alphabetic arrangement of all organizations, acronyms, individuals, and other significant details mentioned within the introductory and historical essays and the directory listings sections. The index also includes inversions on significant keywords appearing in the names of organizations and other entities. Because of the difference between the essays and directory listings sections, citations referring to pages in the essays are designated with a "p." and are separated from the directory citations with a semicolon. A boldface number following an organization name indicates that organization's main entry in the directory section.

A

3HO Foundation 2085 1985 2111
A. A. Allen Revivals, Inc. 588
A.C.R.Y. Annual 176
A-Lan 1479
A.M.E. Christian Recorder 406
A.M.E. Review 406
A.R.E. Library Newletter 1491
The A.S.K. Exposition 988
AAI (Atheist Alliance Inc.) **1097**
Aaron, Teofilo Vargas Sein 590
Aaronic Order **1144**, 1161
Aaron's Star 1144
(AARSH); Akshardham-Centre for Applied Research in Social Harmony 2072
Aba Mexican Baptist Institute 838
Abbenhouse, Dorothy 1589
Abbey of Thelema **1672**, 1690
Abbey, W. H. 2317
Abbot, Francis Ellingwood 1095, 1111
Abd-ru-shin 1424
Abdel-Messiah, Marcos 285
Abdelsayed, Gabriel 285
Abdu'l-Baha p.180; 1935, 1937, 1940
Abdurrahman, Shaikh 1909
A'Becket, Thomas p.41
Abell, Theodore Curtis 1093
Abernathy, Donald 599
Abha World Faith; Orthodox 1939
Abhayagiri Buddhist Monastery **2111**
Abhayananda, Swami 2046
Abhedananda, Swami p.185; 2057
Abhidhyan Yoga Institute **1943**
Abhidhyanananda Avahuta, Shri Acharya 1943
Abilene Christian University 903
Abingdon Press 386
Abode of the Message 1913
Abraham 1416
Abraham, David 2314
(Abrahamic Faith); Church of God General Conference **972**
Abrasax 1699
Absolute Predestinarians; Primitive Baptists- **879**
Academy for Scriptural Knowledge 988
Academy of Christian Theatre Sciences 740
Academy of Creative Living 1514
Academy of Humanism 1093, 1109
Academy of Mind Dynamics 1336

Academy of Science, Dar al-Ilm 1875
Academy of the Brotherhood 1126
Academy of the New Church College 1343
Academy of the New Church Theological School 1343
Acadia Divinity College 845
(ACD); Association for Christian Development 987
ACD Newsletter 987
Achad, Frater p.166; 1682, 1697
Acharya, Pundit p.186; 2053
Acharya Sushil Jain Ashram 2080
Acker, Richard C. 156, 157, 158, 159
(ACLU); American Civil Liberties Union 1092
Action 1337
Activity Bulletin 1005
Acts 1009
Adair, Don 978
Adams, A. P. p.117; 1076
Adams Apple 548
Adams, Barry 1273
Adams, Fred 1665, 1669, 1752
Adams, George J. 1205
Adams, John Quincy 721
Adams, Joseph p.140; 640
Adams, Judy Carolyn 62
Adams, Raphael John 86
Adams, Robert 2030
Adams, Ruth 1560
Adams, Walter Hollis 118, 122, 155
Adamski Foundation; GAF International/ **1466**
Adamski, George p.150; 1461, 1466
Adaros, Premel El 2054
Addai, Mar 279
Addams, Jane p.31
Addie, Jack 454
Addyman, John 419
Adelphi Organization 1582
The ADF Membership Directory 1719
Adhani p.179
Adhyatmic Sadhana Sangh 1973
Adidam **1944**
Adirondack Bible College 491
Adler, Cyrus 1823
Adler, Felix 1092, 1111
Adler, Margot 1740, 1745
Adler, Randolph 130
Adonai-Shomo **1212**
Adonis, Lord 1734

Adrian College 386
Advaita Fellowship **1945**
Advance 1504
The Advancer 844
Advent Christian Church p.116; 14, 461, 546, **971**, 972, 974
Advent Christian Church; Primitive **974**
Advent Christian News 971
Advent Christian Village 971
Advent Christian Witness 971
Adventist Association; Davidian Seventh-Day 976, **977**
Adventist Church; Evangelical 971
Adventist Church in Europe; Seventh-day 983
Adventist Church; Seventh-Day 975, 976, 977, 978, 979, **981**, 985, 1008, 1061, 1795
Adventist Reform Church (Rowenite); Seventh-Day **982**
Adventist Reform Movement; Seventh-Day **983**
Adventist Review 981
(Adventist) Unattached Congregations; Church of God 1008, 1084
Adventists; General Association of Davidian Seventh-Day **978**
Adventists; General Association of the Shepards Rod Seventh-Day 978
Adventists; The Shepherd's Rod Seventh-day 977
Advocate 903
The Advocate 2349
The Advocate of Truth 999
Adytum; Builders of the **1677**, 1698
AEGA (Association of Evangelical Gospel Assemblies) International **695**
Aenon Bible School 626
Aerial Phenomena Research Organization p.150
Aetherius of Venus, Master 1457
Aetherius Society **1457**
AEU Reports 1092
Affiliated New Thought Network (ANTN) **1286**
African-American Catholic Congregation **25**, 65, 182
African American Catholic Rite; Independent **65**
African American Islamic Institute, Inc. 1916
African Association 845

Master Index

David, Samuel 193
David Spiritual Temple of Christ Church Union (Inc.) U.S.A., St. Paul's Spiritual Church Convocation; National 683
Davidian Seventh-Day Adventist Association 976, **977**, 978
Davidian Seventh-Day Adventists; General Association of **978**
The Davidic-Levitical Institute 977
David's Spiritual Temple of Truth Association; King 683
Davidson College 366
Davidson, Gordon 1281
Davidson, Peter 1575
Davies, A. Donald 131, 137
Davies, William W. 1155
Davis & Elkins College 366
Davis, Andrew Jackson p.148; 1347, 1378
Davis, Barry 1273
Davis, C. Truman 120
Davis, Deborah 1263
Davis, Dorothy 1441
Davis, George 77, 82
Davis, Jean M. 1757
Davis, John 1509
Davis, John Shelton 1609
Davis, Pete 1718
Davis, R. S. 2098
Davis, Ray 1441
Davis, Roy Eugene 1966
Davison, Ira 674
Davison, Samuel 1008
Daw, William H. 49, 119, 1609, 1612, 1617
Dawat-e-Hadiyah (America) 1877
Dawe, R. V. Bernard 1611
Dawkin, Reynolds Edward 716
The Dawn 1030
Dawn Bible Students Association 1027, **1030**, 1034
Dawn Bible Students; Millennial 1026
Dawn Horse Fellowship 1944
Dawn of Truth **2325**
Dawn, Rose 1578
Dawson, G. Leslie 2274
Daya Mata, Sri 2032
Dayspring Christian Fellowship 575
Dayton Theological Seminary p.119; 1069
Dazaifu Tenmangu 2291
de Arechaga, Frederic M. 1784
de Brebeuf, Jean p.5, p.20
de Champlain, Samuel p.20
de Chardin, Pierre Teilhard 1116
de Chardin, Teilhard 1959
de Charms, Richard 1343
de Cock, Theodore p.42
de Graca, Marcelino Manoel 676
de Grimston, Robert 1519, 1547
de Haven, John 1807
De Hemelsche Leer 1345
de la Ferriere, Serge Raynaud 1658
de Leon, Moses p.164
de Montmorency Laval, Francious p.20
de Oliveira, Josivaldo Pereira 195
de Ortega Maxey, Wallace D. 37
de Padilla, Juan p.4

(de Palatine); Pre-Nicene Church **1625**
de Palatine, Richard, Duc 1606, 1625
de Payens, Hugh p.164
de Petri, Catherose 1566
de Porres, Martin 177
de Purucker, Gottfried 1587
de Saint-Omer, Geoffrey p.164
de Salzmann, Alexander 1888
de Salzmann, Jeanne 1888
de Voe, Walter 1415
de Vries, Roland 2098
De Wachter 344
de Waters, Lillian p.141
de Zirkoff, Boris Mihailovich 1585
Dea 1694
Deaconess College of Nursing 380
Dead Sea Scrolls 297
Dean, Elizabeth 1558
Deborah Coleman Ministries 1322
deCatanzaro, Carmino J. 116
Dechen Tsedrup Yeshe, Khandro 2255
Decker, David D. 1238
DeCock, Hendrik 344
Dede, Suleyman 1898
Dederich, Charles E. 1283
Dederich School of Law; Charles E. 1283
Dee, John p.163; 1806
Dees, James Parker 118, 269
The Defender 690
Defenders of the Faith **690**
Defenders Seminary 690
Defenseless Mennonite Brethren of Christ in North America 777
Defenseless Mennonite Church 785
Defiance College 380
Defries, Garland p.84
Degiovanni, Stephen 227
Deism p.121, p.146
Deistical Society p.123
Deistical Society of New York **1110**, 1124
Deists, Inc.; Confraternity of **1108**
Deja Vu Publishing Company 1499
Delaware Valley Prout News 1952
Deliverance Church of Atlanta; First **581**
Deliverance Church; Salvation and **591**
Deliverance Churches; International **585**
Deliverance Evangelistic Bible Institute 579
Deliverance Evangelistic Centers **656**
Deliverance Evangelistic Church **579**
Deliverance Voice 656
Delphic Coven **1743**
Delphic Fellowship 1665, 1731, **1744**
Delval UFO, Inc. **1464**
Demers, Modeste p.25
Demetrios I 177
Demoret, Fred 1071
DeMoulin, David 1438
Dena Foundation 1455
Denck, Hans p.87
Dengyo Dhashi 2147
Denning, Melita 1624, 1674
Dennis, Dean 908
Dennis, James A. 1607
Dennison, Ruth 2116
Densal 2241

Denton, D. P. 488
Denver Bible Institute 929
Denver Conservative Baptist Seminary 852
Denver Seminary 849
Deon 1694
DePauw, Gommar A. 53
DePauw University 386
DePauw, Washington C. p.76
dePugh, Robert 1070
Der Bote 778
Der deutsche evangelische Kirchenverein des Westens 380
Derby, Lama Randolph 2228
Derderian, Hovnan 288
Derek Prince Ministries 734
DeRopp, Robert 1914
Derstine, Gerald G. 731
Dervishes; Nakshibendi Order of 1909
des Lauriers, Gerard 72, 90
Des Moines University of Lawsonomy 2362
Desai, Amrit 1997, 2036
Desai, Shanti 1997, 2036
Descalona, Luis p.4
Deseret News 1149
Desert Vipassana Center 2116
Deshimaru Roshi, Taisen 2158
Desmond, David-Edward 2348
Destiny of America Foundation p.119
Deunov, Peter 1660
deutsche evangelische Kirchenverein des Westens; Der 380
Dev, Guru 2064
Deva Foundation **1968**
Devaki-Ma 2062
Devamata, Sister 2057
Devan, Anthony 178
Devanand Saraswati Ji Maharaj, H. H. Swami Guru 1990
Devananda, Swami Vishnu 2041
Devatma Shakti Society **1969**
Devi, Indra 2022
Devi Mandir **1970**
Devi, Shri Mataji Nirmala 2026
Devi, Sri Marashaam 1964
Devi, Sri Sarada 1995
Devi, Srimata Gavatro 2057
Devi, Srimata Gayatri 2057
Devi, Srimata Sudha Puri 2057
DeVorss Publishing Company 1657
Dew, George 1730
Dewey, John p.31; 1093
Dewhirst, H. T. 1054
DeWitow, Mrs. G. E. S. 239
DeWitow, Theodotus Stanislaus 239
DeWold, A. C. 1183
DeWolfe, Minnie 845
Dhammakaya International Society of California **2115**
Dhammakosacharn, Phra 2132
Dhammananda Vihara 2119
Dharma Centre of Canada **2274**, 2275
Dharma Chakra Monastery 2230
Dharma Communications 2173
Dharma Dena **2116**
Dharma Dust 2191
Dharma, Karuna 2102, 2120

F

Johnson, William Monroe   634, 677
Johnson, Win   957
Johnston-Cantrell, Andrew   84, 86
Johnstone House   2274
Johrei Fellowship   2283
Johrei Newsletter   2283
Johrei; Society of   **2292**
Jolly, Donald Lawrence   2338
(Jolly); Gospel Assemblies   **729**
Jolly, Raymond   1031, 1033, 1034
Jolly, Tom M.   729, 730
Jomyo-in   2184
Jonas, Eugen   1258
Jonas, Hans   1812
Jones, A. D.   p.117
Jones, Abner   p.103; 380
Jones, Bryn   711
Jones, C. C.   p.178
Jones, C. P.   472, 474, 480, 651
Jones, Charles Stansfeld   p.166; 1682, 1697
Jones, Christopher William   247
Jones, Clifton   1304
Jones, Curtis P.   605
Jones, David L.   273
Jones, Franklin   1944
Jones, George Cecil   1672
Jones, George Stansfeld   1672
Jones, Jack Alwin   105
Jones, Jacque A.   105
Jones, James Francis Marion   477
Jones, Jenken Lloyd   p.30; 1085
Jones, Jim   1545
Jones, Jr., O. T.   651
Jones, Marc Edmund   1580
Jones, Margot   1560
Jones, Peter   p.24
Jones, Prophet   477
(Jones); Tridentine Old Roman Community Catholic Church   **105**
Jones University; Bob   399, 867
Jones, Vendyl   867
Jones, Wayne   942
Joques, Issac   p.5
Jordan College   497
Jordan, Fred   1263, 1368, 2310
Jordan, Jr., Fred   1368
Jordan, Lewis G.   885
Jordan, Orvis F.   375
Jordan, Theodore   564
Joseph, Alexander   1169
Joseph, Elizabeth   1169
Joseph, Jacob   1821
Joseph L. Vredenburgh   1608
Joseph, Metropolitan   202
Joshua Elijah   2351
Josiah Royce   p.146
Journal Apostolica   209
The Journal for Anthroposophy   1644
A Journal from the Radical Reformation   972
Journal of Instrumented UFO Research   1403
Journal of Oriental Studies   2156
Journal of Reform Judaism   1829
Journal of the Association for the Understanding of Man   1403
Journal of the Athenea Theologica   1681

The Journal of the Order of Buddhist Contemplatives   2175
Journal of Theology   315
Journey   2349
Joy Church   1633
Joy Foundation, Inc.   **1633**
Joy, Vincent J.   931
Joyful   **1240**
Joyous Light   262
Joyu, Fumihiro   2137
Juby, Marcus   1200
Jud, Brother   1268
Judaic Book Service   1860
Judaism; Conservative   **1823**
Judaism; Orthodox   **1828**
Judaism; Reform   **1829**
Judaism; Society for Humanistic   1089, **1865**
Judge, Bishop   429, 473
Judge, William Q.   p.159; 1586, 1587, 1589, 1590, 1592
Judith, Anodea   1727
Judson, Adoniram   p.100; 839
Judson, Ann   839
Judson College   839, 868
Judson Press   839
Julian Review   1731, 1744
Julio, Abbe   1681
Julius I   246
Jung, C. F.   317
Juniata College   792
Junior Brijabasi   1993
Jurcsek, George   1262
Juren, H.   385
Justin Martyr   p.114
Jyotirmayananda, Swami   2067

K

Ka Hale Hoano Hou O Ke Akua   **2317**
Ka-Nying Shedrub Ling   2218
Kabalarian Courier   1534
Kabalarian Philosophy   p.27; **1534**
Kabbalah   p.157, p.164, p.168, p.173; 1684
Kabbalah for the Layman   1838
Kabbalah Learning Centre   **1838**
Kadag Choying Dorje, Lama   2242
Kadam School   p.192
Kagahi, Soryu   p.194
Kagyu Dharma   **2239**, 2259
Kagyu School   p.193
Kahl, Gordon   p.119
Kahlil, Phez   1902
Kai, Ku   2153
Kaichen, Troy A.   122
Kailas Shugendo   **2145**
Kailasa Chandra Das   2010
Kailashananda Mission   2069
Kailashananda, Swami   2069
Kaiser, Elsworth Thomas   1061
Kaivalyadhama   2048
Kalamazoo College   839
Kaleidoscope   138
Kali Mandir   **1995**
Kaliisoliiso Star   2101
Kalu Rinpoche   2234, 2259
Kalupahana, David J.   2129
Kalweit, Martin   821

Kamal, Yogi   1973
Kamala, Srimata   2033
Kaminski, Stephen   92, 93, 247
Kamp, Beata   1560
Kampo Gangra Drubgyudling   **2240**
Kankakee; Diocese of   250
Kannon Jijei-Kai   2136
Kansas City College and Bible School   436
Kansas Wesleyan   386
Kanski, Francis   1601
Kantaka   2267
Kanzeon 3Sangha   2109
Kanzeon Jade Thread   2167
Kanzeon Sangha   2167
Kanzeon Zen Center   **2167**
Kanzeonji Non-Sectarian Buddhist Temple   **2168**
Kaplan, Mordecai M.   1824, 1826
Kapleau, Philip   2169, 2180, 2181, 2188
Kappeler, Max   1291
Kapustin, Sabellius   p.93; 835
Kara Apu   1777
Karahissaridis, Paul Eftymios   268
Karahissaridis, Socrates Ermis   268
Kardec, Allen   1350, 1360
Karezza   p.133, p.166
Karin Society   **1535**
Karish, Bella   1419
Karma Tashi Ling   2246
Karma Triyana Dharma Chakra   2232, 2234
Karma Triyana Dharmachakra   **2241**
Karmapa, Gyalwa   2240, 2241, 2274
Karme Choling   2260
Karoda Institute   2187
Karoli Baba, Neem   1979, 1996, 2234
Karras, Mark   164, 259, 260, 275
Karsleigh, Daisy   1476
Karsleigh, Zelrun   1476
Karthar Rinpoche, Khenpo   2241
Karuna Tendai Dharma Center   **2146**
Kary, Hans   2060
Kashi Church Foundation   **1996**
Kashta   1754
Kashyapa   p.189
Katagiri Roshi, Dainin   2171
Katashima, Kokichi   2287
Katharsis   **1267**
Kathok Shendrup Ling Center   **2242**
Katoda, Tetsuei   2153
Katre, Rev. Ik. Ilia   174
Kaufman, Ishi   p.174
Kaufmann, Frank   3
Kawahara, Senyei   p.194
Kawartha Lakes Bible School   913
Kawasaki, Kazoe   2284
Kawasaki, Masasato   2284
Kawate, Bunjiro   2287
Kaye, Paul   2087
Kazi, Sonam   2244
KBYS Holistic Hospital and Colleges of Yoga Thearpy and Physiotherapy   1989
KDK Publications   2239
Kealaokamalamala   **2318**
Kebzeh Foundation   1895
Kebzeh Publications   1895
Kebzeh Review Newsletter   1895

M

Niranjannan Saraswati, Swami   2031
Nirankari Universal Brotherhood
 Mission   **2096**
Nirmala Yoga   2026
Nisargadatta Maharaj, Sri   1945
Nisbet, James   p.24
Nishida, Mugaku   2151
Nishijimi, Kakuryo   p.194
Nitschman, David   p.70
Nityananda, Bhagwan   2049
Nityananda Institute   1977
Nityananda Institute, Inc.   **2015**
Nityananda, Swami   2015, 2034, 2049
Nityananda, Tantracharya   2011
Niwano, Nikkyo   2152
Nizami   p.179
Nizhoni School for Global
 Consciousness   1536
Nizza, Alexis   199
NKT (New Kadampa Tradition)   **2248**
(NKT); New Kadampa Tradition   2279
No Longer Children   1263
Noble, Abel   p.102
Noble, Kerry   1075
Nobunaga, Oda   p.191
Noebel, David   2306
Nolan, David James   1295
Noli, Fan Stylin   p.54; 173, 247
Noli, Theophan   191, 273
Nome   2042
(Non-Instrumental); Churches of
 Christ   901, **903**, 904, 909
(Non-Instrumental, Conservative);
 Churches of Christ   **904**
(Non-Instrumental, Non-Class, One Cup);
 Churches of Christ   **905**
(Non-Instrumental, Non-Sunday School);
 Churches of Christ   **906**
(Non-Instrumental-Premillennial);
 Churches of Christ   **907**
(Non-Papal Catholic); Evangelical
 Orthodox (Catholic) Church in
 America   60, 122, 128
Noohra Foundation   **1326**
Noohra-Light   1326
Noonan, Allen Michael   p.134; 1284
Norbu, Gyslten   2279
Norbu Rinpoche, Chogyal
 Namkhai   2256
Norman, Ernest L.   1474
Norman, Ruth   1474
Norris, J. Frank   843, 875
North American Baptist Association   844
North American Baptist College   861
North American Baptist Conference   836,
 861
North American Baptist Fellowship   **837**,
 897
North American Baptist General
 Conference   837
North American Baptist Seminary   861
North American Christian
 Convention   901
North American Committee for
 Humanism   1087, **1089**
North American Episcopal Church   119,
 1612, 2328

North American Old Catholic Church,
 Ultrajectine Tradition   61, 69
North American Old Roman Catholic
 Church   22, 54, 73, 76, 77, 78, 80, 81,
 82, 86, 109, 139, 250, 272, 1612
North American Old Roman Catholic
 Church (Rogers)   60, 70, 74, **76**, 92
North American Old Roman Catholic
 Church (Schweikert)   **77**, 83
North American Old Roman Catholic
 Church-Utrecht Succession   52, **78**,
 105, 161, 208, 1610, 1616
North American Orthodox Catholic
 Church   205, 293
North American Pentecostal
 Fellowship   500
North American Presbyterian and
 Reformed Council   361
North American Renewal Service
 Committee   552
North American Synod of the Holy Eastern
 Orthodox Catholic and Apostolic
 Church   188
North American Theological
 Seminary   844
North American Vegetarian Society   1948
North Carolina Wesleyan College   386
North Carolina Yearly Meeting of Friends
 (Conservative)   **812**
North Central Bible College   560
North Central College   386
North Greenville College   868
North, Lucy   1432
North Pacific Yearly Meeting   816
North Pacific Yearly Meeting of the
 Religious Society of Friends   **813**
North Park College and Theological
 Seminary   382
The North Star Baptist   858
Northeast Atheist Association
 (NAA)   **1117**
Northeastern Christian College   903
Northern Baptist Convention   p.100; 839,
 840, 853, 858, 893
Northern Baptist Theological
 Seminary   839
Northern Baptists   849
Northland College   380
Northnagel, Sr., Davis B.   1044
Northwest Baptist Institute   838
Northwest Baptist Seminary   853
Northwest Bible and Music
 Academy   510
Northwest Bible College   567
Northwest Chicago Zen Group   2109
Northwest Christian College   900, 901
Northwest College of the Assemblies of
 God   560
Northwest College of the Bible   901
Northwest Free University   2020
Northwest Indian Bible School   485
Northwest Nazarene College   439
Northwest Yearly Meeting of Friends   806
Northwest Yearly Meeting of Friends
 Church   **814**
Northwestern Bible Training
 School   p.110
Northwestern College   338, 352

Northwestern Holiness Association   463
The Northwestern Lutheran   338
Norton, Joseph   845
Norwegian-Danish Evangelical Free
 Church Association   383
Norwegian Evangelical Lutheran Synod;
 Hauge's   321
Norwegian Lutheran Church in
 America   300
Norwegian Seaman's Church
 (Mission)   **335**
Norwegian Seaman's Mission   158
Norwegian Synod of the American
 Evangelical Lutheran Church   324
Nostradamus   2137
Notes from Lollygog   1293
Notes from Woodsong   1293
Noth, Samdech Prah Sangha Raja
 Chuon   2114
Nova Scotia Baptist Association   845
Novack, Michael   1792
Novak, Penny   1792
Novominsk Hasidism   **1842**
Now   1327
"Now" Folk   **1327**
Nowell, Claude Rex   2330
Nowick, Walter   2223
Nowlan, Ronald D.   932
Noyes, John Humphrey   p.133; 1246
NRCEA   349
Nubian Islaamic Hebrew Mission   1921
The Nudist Christian Church of the
 Blessed Virgin Jesus   **2358**
Numerology   p.145
Nur Institute of Islamic Studies   1870
Nuradeen: An Islamic Sufi Journal   1893
Nurbakhsh, Javad   1897
Nurbakhshi   p.179
Nurse, Gladstone St. Clair   170, 230, 265
Nyabingi Rastas   1857
Nyack College and Alliance Theological
 Seminary   430
"Nyah"   1484
Nyananda, Swami   1996
Nybladh, Carl A.   265
Nydahl, Hannah   2232
Nydahl, Lama Ole   2232
Nyima, Choskyi   2251
Nyima, Gedhun Choekyi   2279
Nyland, Willan A.   1890
Nyombolo, E. B.   644

O

O.N. (Order of Napunsakas in the
 West)   **1668**
Oahspe   1415
Oak Grove School   2000
Oakland City College   891
Oakwood College   981
Oasis Fellowship   **1653**
Oates, Virgil   592
Oba Efuntola Oseijeman Adelabu
 Adefunmi I, King   1798
Obadiah School of the Bible   1040
O'Beirn, Carl   996
Oberholtzer, John H.   778
Oblates of St. Martin of Tours   87
Oblates of the Blessed Sacrament   31

S

St. Germain, Ecclesia Catholica Liberalis; Order of   1621, **1622**

Saint Germain Foundation   p.161; 1632

St. Germain; Order of   1622

Saint Germain Press   p.161; 1632

St. Gregory Palamas Monastery   179

Saint Gregory Seminary   242, 274

St. Gregory's Church   31

St. Herman of Alaska; Orthodox Brotherhood of   227

St. Herman Seminary   256

Saint Hilarion's Monastery   80

St. Ignatius School of Theology   52

St. James House in Philadelphia   253

Saint John Bernadone; Order of   1616

St. John Chrysostom Theological Seminary   209

St. John the Divine, Bishop   1247

St. John the Divine; Cathedral Church of   5

St. John the Evangelist; Diocese of   143

St. John's Bread   1746

St. John's Theological Seminary   205

St. John's University   713, 1294, 1508

St. Joseph; Church of   44, **53**

Saint Joseph of Arimathea Anglican Theological College   125

St. Joseph's Seminary   98

Saint Jude Abbey   69

St. Jude; Missionaries of   84

Saint Jude the Apostle; Missionary Order of   30

St. Louis Christian College   901

St. Luke; Diocese of   143

St. Luke Magazine   49

St. Luke the Physician; Order of   p.80

St. Mark; Diocese of   143

Saint-Martin, Louis Claude de   p.163; 1692, 1694

St. Martin of Tours; Oblates of   87

St. Martin's Seminary   54

St. Mary Magdalen Old Catholic Church   85

St. Mary Mystical Rose; Church of   103

St. Mary's College and Academy   98

St. Mary's Seminary   49

St. Mary's Theological College   117

Saint Matthew American Catholic Church   20

St. Matthew; Diocese of   143

St. Matthew's Cathedral Seminary   119

St. Matthew's Church   p.20

Saint Methodius   199

Saint Michael; Order of   91

Saint Michael; Religious Order of   254

St. Michael; Third Order of   249

St. Nersess Seminary   288

St. Nicholas Seminary   253

St. Olaf College   322

St. Paul Polish Catholic Church; St. Peter and   92

Saint Paul School of Theology   386

St. Paul the Apostle; Diocese of   20

St. Paul's Bible Institute   591

St. Paul's Church   p.20

St. Paul's Church of Aquarian Science   **1383**

St. Paul's College   136

St. Paul's Guild   64

St. Paul's Monastery Old Catholic Church   246

St. Paul's Spiritual Church Convocation; National David Spiritual Temple of Christ Church Union (Inc.) U.S.A.,   683

St. Paul's United College   379

St. Peter and St. Paul Polish Catholic Church   92

St. Peters, Donald   207

St. Pius V; Society of   **97**

Saint Pius X; Fraternite Sacerdotale de   98

St. Pius X; Society of   97, **98**

St. Primordia's Guild   1604

St. Raphael's Old Catholic Church   1620

St. Sava Seminary   267

St. Seraphim's Center for Theological Studies   50

Saint-Simon, Claude Henri   p.132

St. Sincletike Convent   229

St. Sophia Orthodox Theological Seminary   272

St. Sophia Press   272

St. Stephens Baptist Church   660

St. Stephen's College   379

St. Therese of Lisieux   91

St. Thomas Aquinas Seminary   98

St. Thomas Christian Churches; Federation of   148, 222, 1561, 1607, **1608**, 1614, 1623

St. Thomas Institute   1607

St. Thomas the Apostle   178

St. Tikhon's Orthodox Theological Seminary   255

St. Timothy, Ecclesia Catholica Liberalis; Order of   1621

St. Vladimir's Orthodox Theological Seminary   255

St. Willibrords Press   48

Saints Herald   1198

Saito, Gyoko   2142

Saiva Siddhanta Church   **2027**

Saiva Siddhanta Yoga Order   2027

Sakae, Sekiguchi   2288

Sakuma, Henry T.   952

Sakya College   2254

Sakya Jy-Din   2197

Sakya Monastery of Tibetan Buddhism   **2254**

Sakya School   p.192

Sakya Tegchen Choling   2254

Sakyadhita   2120

Salem Academy and College   384

Salem Acres   **1277**

Saliba, Philip   193

Salisbury, W. L.   1394

Saltonstall, Gordon   818

Salvat, Geary   1346

Salvation and Deliverance Church   **591**

Salvation Army   p.76; 14, 422, 424, 428, 447, **454**, 457, 561, 920

Salvation Army-Canada and Bermuda   9

Salvation Army College/Schools for Officer Training   454

Salvation Army in Canada   422

Salvationist   454

Salve Regina   72

Salves Exchange for Refugee Rehabilitation Vocations   792

Salzberg, Sharon   2118

Sam-Woo Kim   2217

Samarin, William   p.79

Samaritan Church; New Age   **1542**

Samaritan College   2349

Sambosa Buddhist Temple of California   2110

Samdup Tarjeyling Monastery   2239

Samford University   868

Sams, Clarence Francis   878

Samuel, Bishop   285

Samuel Foundation; William   **1293**

Samuel, Mar Athanasius Y.   297

Samuel, William   1293

Samye Ling   2274

Samye-ling Mona   2260

San Diego Bible College and Seminary   946

San Francisco Theological Seminary   79, 366

San Jose Christian College   901

Sananda   1458, 1459, 1636, 1637

Sananda and Sanat Kumara; Association of   **1459**

Sananda (Jesus)   1469

Sanantan Dharma Mandir   2067

Sanat Kumara   1636

Sanbo Kyodan (Order of the Three Treasures)   2164

Sanborn, Donald J.   97, 98

Sanches, Antonio   595

Sanches, George   595

Sancta Sophia Seminary   1651

Sanctification   p.75

(Sanctified Church); Church of God   **475**

Sanctified Church of America; Christ Holy   **429**

Sanctified Church of America; Christ's Holy   **473**

Sanctified Church of Christ   **470**

Sanctified Holy Church Colored; Christ's   433

Sanctified Holy Church (Georgia); Christ's   **432**

Sanctified Holy Church (Louisiana); Christ's   **433**

Sanctified Holy Church (South Carolina); Christ's   433

Sanctified School; Christ's Holy   473

Sanctuary Circles   1735

Sanctuary of the Gnosis   1709

Sanctuary of the Interior of the Carmel of Elie   1681

Sanctuary of the Master's Presence   1630, **1638**

Sande, Gene   1567

Sandeepany Sadhanalaya   1965

Sandeepany West   1956

Sandeman, Robert   p.103

Sander, J. A.   403

Sanders, Alexander   p.168; 1713, 1714, 1756

Sanders, Maxine   1713

Sanderson, John Tesshin   2109

Sandesha   1960

Sandford, Frank Weston   438

T

Master Index

Master Index

X

Y